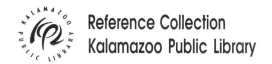

THE
NAVAL HISTORY
OF THE
CIVIL WAR

THE
NAVAL HISTORY
OF THE
CIVIL WAR

ADMIRAL DAVID D. PORTER

DOVER PUBLICATIONS, INC.
Mineola, New York

Published in Canada by General Publishing Company, Ltd., 30 Lesmill Road, Don Mills, Toronto, Ontario.

Published in the United Kingdom by Constable and Company, Ltd., 3 The Lanchesters, 162–164 Fulham Palace Road, London W6 9ER.

Bibliographical Note

This Dover edition, first published in 1998, is an unaltered and unabridged republication of the work first published by the Sherman Publishing Company, New York, in 1886. The errata notice bound into the original book is reproduced in this edition on page 844.

Library of Congress Cataloging-in-Publication Data

Porter, David D. (David Dixon), 1813–1891.
   The naval history of the Civil War / David D. Porter.
      p.   cm.
   Originally published: New York: Sherman Pub. Co., 1886.
   ISBN 0-486-40176-6 (pbk.)
   1.   United States—History—Civil War, 1861–1865—Naval operations.
2. United States. Navy—History—Civil War, 1861–1865.   I. Title.
E591.P84   1998
973.7'5—dc21   98–13377
                                                                                                              CIP

Manufactured in the United States of America
Dover Publications, Inc., 31 East 2nd Street, Mineola, N.Y. 11501

To the Regular Officers, the Patriotic Volunteers and the Brave Sailors
and Marines of the Navy

THIS BOOK IS RESPECTFULLY INSCRIBED, WITH THE HOPE THAT IT WILL REMIND THOSE

STILL LIVING OF THE MANY THRILLING SCENES THROUGH WHICH THEY PASSED FROM

1861 TO 1865, AND ALSO ASSURE THEM THAT THE AUTHOR IS STILL ALIVE TO

THE GREAT SERVICES THEY ALL PERFORMED, THE SACRIFICES THEY MADE,

AND THE SMALL REWARDS THAT WERE RECEIVED BY THOSE WHO SO

STEADFASTLY FOUGHT AN INTELLIGENT FOE THAT THIS UNION

MIGHT BE PRESERVED TO MILLIONS YET UNBORN.

PREFACE.

THE Naval incidents of the War of 1812 with Great Britain are better understood to-day by the great mass of American readers than are the naval incidents of the Civil War between the northern and seceding States, which lasted from 1861 to 1865. In the War of 1812 half a dozen frigates and a dozen sloops of war on the ocean, and three small squadrons on the lakes, made up about the sum total of our Navy afloat when the war commenced, and those vessels performed such marvelous exploits, considering the great superiority in ships of Great Britain, that the events, comparatively few in number, have impressed themselves indelibly on the mind of every schoolboy who read of them in books that were put in their hands at an early age : events that were taught them as part of the history of a nation which, previous to that time, had not paid much attention to the Navy, or even calculated that it would become so famed.

Since that era the Navy of the United States has been making history for the country on a scale almost bewildering, and could the old pioneer captains of 1812 have been permitted to look on from their present abode (wherever that may be), we doubt not but that they would have been astonished at the large fleets we were putting afloat with such wonderful rapidity; and they would also have acknowledged that their descendants had nobly borne themselves in the war for the salvation of this Union, which was as dear to our forefathers as it is to us at the present time.

A man who undertakes to write a history of the naval events of such a war as we were forced into, has a great responsibility resting upon him. He has to be careful of his statements and the sources from which he obtains them; as a person has a right to know before he purchases a book, whether the facts stated for his perusal are taken from substantial authority, or from the common traditions which have been passed down from decade to decade, and have been finally accepted as truth.

History could not be properly written after such a fashion as the latter; it must be taken from the official naval records of the times, which, with but rare exceptions, have been found to be remarkably correct. Many of them—indeed nearly all—have been written by persons holding the most prominent positions in command, who have left the stories of their achievements written in that truthful language which carries conviction with it. No naval officer during the war would have dared to write any thing in his official reports that was not strictly correct, for there were too many witnesses (and interested ones) who would not have hesitated to impeach the veracity of any officer who made anything but a proper report.

As far as it goes this history is made up from the official record of the Navy, and the author has endeavored as far as possible to confine himself strictly to naval matters, except in cases where the Army and Navy co-operated.

Several books claiming to be naval histories were written directly after the war, but as a rule these were of a partisan character, not written particularly to do justice to the Navy but to give credit to particular individuals who had a good deal to do in the matter of ensuring success, and who no doubt deserved much of the praise that was bestowed upon them; but in all cases the authors lost sight of the main object of the history, and that is to do justice to all, and not allow themselves to be diverted from the true facts because they may have had official relations with those they took care to applaud. There was too much of this in some histories which dwelt so much on the virtues of the heads of departments that they forgot to do justice to those who fought the battles. In all the histories the author has read there have been serious misrepresentations, *purposely* printed and written with the intention to do harm to the reputation of some who deserved not only the highest praise from the government but the truth from impartial historians.

While our Army has been written of by a thousand ready pens, the Navy has not, as a rule, been a popular theme for the historian, and now and then only do we meet with some well drawn story of the Navy and the benefits it conferred upon the country. Our Army was full of writers who could delineate in the most happy manner all the events that were transpiring around them—they were also ready with the pencil; the photographer, while he traveled with the army, would spend his days in photographing every noted scene, reprints of which were scattered broadcast over the Union, keeping the movements of our armies as clearly before the millions of people in the North as if the battles had been reflected in a mirror. The camp, the march, the bivouac, the battle-field were almost as familiar to the friends and relations of those in the field as if they had been on the spot, but there were no such means of bringing the Navy before the public. Naval ships did not travel with reporters, photographers or sketchers, there was no room for these on board ship, and if perchance some stray reporter should get on board, the discomfort of a man of war, the exacting discipline, and the freer life in camp sent him back to shore, where in most cases he only remembered his associations with the Navy as a trip without any satisfaction, and with no desire to do justice to the work of the naval service.

The author is quite aware that he may not possess all the requisites for a historian, but he thinks he can put the records in plain shape and write them down in plain English, which on the whole is quite as much as has been done by others. The object will be to show how little the work of the Navy was appreciated by the people of this country, while they lavished all their attention on the Army. It is true our Armies were entitled to all that could be showered on them by a grateful people; yet the part performed by the Navy when placed in its true light before the world, will show to advantage compare it as you may with any other branch of public service. Time with unsparing hand has swept away nearly all the men who led our fleets to battle during the war. But one or two remain, while those who were in the flower of manhood when the war was at its worst, have reached the highest honors the country had to bestow, and with no more naval duty afloat to perform, except in time of war, when they can offer their services, none the less efficient for a green old age, are waiting calmly (enjoying the rest from the hardships of the past) to reap those higher rewards for duties well performed on earth, where the sounds of battle will no more be heard, and where the laurels they have gained will never wither—these officers must not be forgotten, and wish to be remembered.

If this work does not satisfy public expectations, it may point out the way for some future historian, some patient, plodding man, who will delve into old closets and bureaux until he finds the missing links which may escape the heedless writer of this fast age.

History is better written after the lapse of years, when those who have taken part in it have all passed away, when prejudices have all been laid aside, and when the historian knows nothing of the actors' deeds besides what is told in the records. But the present age is an impatient one, and the young American who was not on the scene of action when civil discord plunged the country into the most bloody war the world ever saw, is anxious now to know all that occurred at the time that tried men's souls; they particularly desire to see how their forefathers deported themselves on fields of battle or in ships of war, and to become familiar with all the thrilling scenes which, though pleasant reading now, brought sorrow and desolation to thousands of homes, homes where to this day they worship the memory of the loved one who left them in the vigor of manhood, and on whom they never looked again.   THE AUTHOR.

CONTENTS.

NOTE.—At the commencement of each Chapter will be found a detailed syllabus of the matter therein contained. The following embraces only the principal subjects of each Chapter. See General Index for List of Vessels and Officers of Squadrons.

INDEX TO ILLUSTRATIONS.

GENERAL INDEX.

NOTE.—Persons, Vessels, Places, Rivers, etc., casually mentioned in this History, are not noted in this Index.

CHAPTER I.

ORGANIZATION OF THE NAVY DEPARTMENT.—THE WRETCHED CONDITION OF THE NAVY
AT THE OUTBREAK OF THE CIVIL WAR.—WHAT COULD HAVE BEEN DONE.—BLOCKADE
RUNNERS.—LOSS TO THE CONFEDERACY.—PRIZES.—NAVAL TRIUMPHS.—FAITHFUL
OFFICERS.—GIDEON WELLS.—GUSTAVUS V. FOX.—LAVISH PRAISE OF THE ARMY.—
UNPREPARED FOR WAR.—PREMEDITATED SECESSION.—SEPARATE GOVERNMENT —THE
NAVY AND THE HAPPY CONDITION OF AFFAIRS NOW EXISTING, &C.

AT the outbreak of the great rebellion our Navy was not in a condition to render that assistance which the occasion demanded; the larger portion of it was employed on foreign stations, and the Government had not at its disposal a class of vessels that could enter Southern ports and act offensively.

Had a proper naval force existed at the time the Southern people first proposed to throw off their allegiance to the Union, there would have been less difficulty in suppressing the efforts of the Secessionists, for every Southern harbor could have been taken possession of—our ports would have remained in charge of the Federal officers, and if the South did obtain supplies from Europe, they would have been obliged to land them on the open coast.

If two monitors like the "Miantonomoh" and the "Monadnock" could have entered Charleston harbor when Sumter was first threatened, they would have prevented the erection of works for the bombardment of that fort, and would have held it throughout the war, as would have been the case with all the ports on the Southern coast.

The first policy of our Government should have been to get possession of all the ports in the South, and no doubt the Administration would gladly have done so, but for their inability to carry out such designs if entertained, owing to the fact that we had no Navy of any account to commence with. Many of our vessels of war were, as a rule, too large, and drew too much water to enter the shoal Southern harbors, and a majority of them were sailing frigates and sloops of war not at all suited to the work required of them.

Therefore, the Navy Department had to resort to a system of blockade which was called for by all European nations with which the South had held commercial relations. The Southern people once recognized as belligerents, it was necessary to close their ports, and the system of blockade resorted to is unparalleled in the naval records of the world—reaching, as it did, along the entire sweep of our Atlantic and Gulf coasts, from the Chesapeake to the mouth of the Rio Grande.

So efficiently was the blockade maintained, and so greatly was it strengthened from time to time, that foreign statesmen, who at the beginning of the war, did not hesitate to pronounce the blockade of nearly three thousand miles of coast a moral impossibility, twelve months after its establishment were forced to admit that the proofs of its efficiency were so comprehensive and conclusive that no objections to it could be made.

It is true they would point to the number of blockade runners that eluded the vigilance of our vessels, but they were fairly startled with the numbers of fast steamers which were constantly falling into our hands, and which the Government often bought and equipped for employment in capturing blockade runners These latter were built in large numbers in England with much profit to the ship-yards of that country, but generally, as fast as they were built, they were picked up by the improvised cruisers under command of some energetic naval officers, and their loss was so greatly felt by the Southern people that they were at times very much hampered, if not crippled.

What the loss to the Confederacy was, and how severely injured they were in their resources from abroad, by the activity and energy of the Navy, will appear from the mention of the fact that during the war 1,119 prizes were brought in, of which number 210 were fast steamers.

"There were also 355 vessels burned, sunk, driven on shore, or otherwise destroyed— a total of 1,504. The value of these vessels and their cargoes, according to a low estimate, was equal to thirty millions of dollars." They were condemned for an amount equal to twenty-eight millions of dollars.

Many may consider that keeping up a blockade was a pleasant pastime, and that officers were rewarded handsomely with prize money; but that did not obviate the hardships of the duty, nor remove the many obstacles which the officers encountered at every point.

The blockade was a military measure of vital importance, and it depended upon the manner in which it was conducted, whether the Confederacy would be deprived of arms and munitions of war, provisions, clothing, and, in fact, everything that goes toward maintaining a great military establishment.

Without the supplies which the Confederates procured from abroad, they could not have maintained their position for many months, for they were very destitute, as compared with the North, of all the appliances for making weapons of war, or for furnishing clothing and other material necessary to armies.

Hence, it might be well said that without the close blockade which was kept up by the Navy, the war might have been carried on indefinitely, while the battles would have been far more bitter and bloo ly than they were.

The naval battles that were fought were more exciting to the public than that close, dreary blockade, but we doubt very much if they were of any more value to the Union cause.

As long as the Confederacy could be furnished with provisions, clothing, arms and the munitions of war they could fight on, even in a desperate cause, but when the sinews of war were taken from them they collapsed.

With the capture of the last of the enemy's seaports, from which they had been drawing all their supplies, the rebellion was virtually ended. Taking into consideration the extent of coast that had to be blockaded, and the short time in which it was all accomplished, the work can scarcely be comprehended by the ordinary mind,

but it is not yet forgotten by those who managed the industrial necessities in Europe, and whose cupidity led them to embark in what was then considered a wide field for accumulating large profits, supposing at the time that our crippled Navy was incompetent to comply with the obligations imposed upon the Government in completing a *bona fide* blockade of the whole coast.

Of all the naval triumphs of the war, this was one of the greatest. There were questions raised, it is true, with regard to the competence of the blockade in certain localities, but they were seldom sustained by the courts, and foreign Governments were obliged to admit, notwithstanding the great commercial interests they had at stake, that the blockade was the most complete of any that had ever been undertaken.

At the breaking out of the rebellion, our serviceable Navy consisted of two sailing frigates, eleven sailing sloops, one screw frigate, five screw sloops of the first class, three side-wheel steamers, eight screw sloops of the second class, and five screw sloops of the third class.

Eighteen sailing vessels of various classes, five screw frigates, one screw sloop and three or four side-wheel steamers were what is called available, that is, they were laid up at the different yards; but of all these, and those in commission, there were only eight vessels that the Government could use immediately—those of the Home Squadron—and only four were steamers

That was a poor showing for the Navy Department to commence with. Twenty-eight of the vessels in commission were on foreign stations, and by the time the Navy could be assembled the Confederates had ample time to prepare to meet them with offensive weapons, and keep them out of Southern ports.

When Mr. Toucey handed over the Navy Department to Mr. Welles, it was in a rather demoralized condition—Southern officers were resigning right and left, officers of the bureaux, even, were talking of going with their States, and there was a want of confidence in all quarters. When men who had held the highest and most influential positions in the Navy came forward and offered their resignations, there was apparently no one upon whom the Secretary could rely; distrust seemed to pervade every branch of the naval service. No commander could be sure who would be faithful to the flag, and the Secretary of the Navy could not be certain of any Southern officers being true to the Government. It was a bad state of affairs for a Secretary to commence his administration with, but the eventful year, 1861-62, will show that the operations and achievements of the Navy were such, that great credit was reflected not only upon the Secretary but upon the personnel of the service, which so signally aided the Department in carrying out the measures tending so greatly to cripple the Confederate cause.

rebellion—or, to use the language of the present day, in persuading our Southern brethren to come back into the Union. It is but justice to the Navy Department to explain to the reader the difficulties under which that branch of the Government la-

HON. GIDEON WELLES, SECRETARY OF THE NAVY, 1861-69.

It is only intended, in this narrative, to give a comprehensive history of the naval events of the war, so that the general reader can form a rapid idea as to the conduct of naval affairs, and understand how much the Navy had to do with putting down the

bored to carry out a system of offense, on which hung the whole problem of bringing the contest to a happy conclusion.

The Navy Department is different in its organization from any other department under the Government. Its relations to the central Government, it is true, are the same as the others, yet its operations and wants are not understood except by experts who have had a long training in the Department; a politician who takes charge of the office for the first time will find himself quite at sea, and entirely in the hands of those who run the different branches of the department.

The Secretary, then, should be considered as surrounded by his Cabinet officers, on whom he must depend at all times for such advice and council as he may need.

His chiefs of bureaux are not clerks. They are, or ought to be his advisers, and should hold to the Secretary the same relations as the heads of departments hold to the President. It depends upon the fitness of bureau chiefs whether the Secretary can conduct his department with success or not.

The Navy Department combines in itself so many branches, that it would be an impossibility for any one man to comprehend them all, much less direct them.

We have had a number of secretaries who have attempted to "run the machine on their own account," and make themselves independent of the chiefs of bureaux, but those who have made the effort have always scored a dead failure, and have left no record behind them that would innure to their benefit, publicly or privately.

It is quite clear that the head of the Navy Department should be a statesman, thoroughly acquainted with the policy of the country; he should be a constitutional lawyer, should have a thorough knowledge of international law, and of the obligations we are under to all foreign Governments; he should be familiar with all the mercantile interests of the country, and understand the relations the Navy holds to our commerce afloat. He should be a man of sound judgment in all business matters, and should possess executive ability of the highest order. Above all, he should be a man of liberal ideas; not considering that he is placed at the head of the Department to do nothing but find fault with the officers under him, but to aid them with all his power to build up a Navy, and keep it in a proper condition to defend the country. In fact, the Secretary of the Navy should be the political, judicial and financial head of the Navy Department.

When the war broke out it was very apparent that the organization of the Navy Department was very defective, and that the system of bureaux which worked fairly well in time of peace, did not work at all in time of war. It was like a balky team; it required a professional hand to guide the several bureaux which seemed to be trying to run their departments, each without regard to the other, with no unanimity of opinion, and it was soon found necessary to add a professional man to the department with the title of Assistant Secretary, who should supervise all the operations of the different bureaux, and take charge, under the Secretary, of all professional matters.

The vast operations of the Department during the war were divided into two great branches, one belonging to matters pertaining particularly to the Navy, the other embracing civil transactions, together with the whole business machinery and operations of the Department.

Mr. G. V. Fox, who had formerly been an officer of the Navy, was placed at the head of the first named branch of the Department; while the Chief Clerk, Mr. Faxon, was placed at the head of the Civil Corps; he was really the representative of the Secretary of the Navy, Mr. Gideon Welles.

This organization was found necessary, owing to the defective system then existing, which exists now, and which will be found defective again if we should ever be involved in a war of any magnitude.

It was rather remarkable that the Government, after the war, should have fallen back upon the old bureau system without any professional head, when its defects were so glaring just after the commencement of hostilities.

Mr. Fox, on entering upon the duties of Assistant Secretary of the Navy, brought with him into the Department a knowledge of naval matters which could not by any possibility have been attained by a pure civilian, and though he did not, perhaps, have the prestige that would have been held by a Board of Admirals or the Board of Naval Commissioners, the success of the Navy during the war, its rapid increase in numbers and efficiency, showed that he was alive to all the requirements of the service, and was always ready to meet the demands made upon the Navy Department by the exigencies of the moment.

Congress, at all times, has been slow to recognize the importance of a Navy commensurate with the interests of this great country, and has doled out ships and sailors, even in times of great need, with a parsimony that has, on several occasions, placed the country in great straits.

It was even so in the outset of the great rebellion, and it was some time after the commencement of hostilities before our legislators could be made to understand the necessity for a large number of vessels to blockade the Southern ports, and put down the privateers and vessels of war which the Confederates were putting afloat, and which were destroying our commercial marine in all parts of the world.

Almost from the beginning, the Navy Department had proper appreciation of what the struggle was to be, and how necessary it was for the Secretary of the Navy to be provided with the means of purchasing ships, guns and supplies of all kinds, and it would be idle to say, in the light of results, that the Department did not put forth all the energy required on such an occasion—first, by gaining the confidence of Congress, and, by using the large amounts intrusted to its charge with a fair degree of economy, considering the vastness of the field of operations.

The administration of the Department was conducted with ability, which is the most convincing proof of the fitness of its officers for the important duties they were called upon to perform. It would be untrue to say that such results as happened could have been achieved by persons of ordinary capacity, or that the head of such a combination of officers was deficient in the qualities necessary to control so many grave matters as came within his jurisdiction.

The communications that were addressed to Congress from time to time, by the Navy Department, show conclusively that the officers who filled the different positions, from the Secretary down, had a very clear comprehension of the situation in all its details, and that at no time was Congress without information of all that was going on in the Navy, or of what was required to keep it in efficient condition.

It was seen very early in the struggle that the policy of England and France was unfriendly to the Union side, which was fully evinced in the case of the "Trent"

later on, and all the influence and argument of the Navy Department was brought to bear upon Congress to place our Navy in a position to meet every attempt on the part of foreign governments to meddle in our affairs. Hence it was that we finally commenced building a class of vessels that set at defiance those who seemed disposed to interfere with us, and left us, at the end of the civil war, mistress of the situation at home and abroad.

With these preliminary remarks, which do not by any means convey what is due to those who had charge of naval matters at the Department, we will proceed to give as near as we can a short, but comprehensive, account of the various events which occurred during the war, and endeavor to show the bearing they had, not only on particular movements of the army, but the influence they exerted in the quelling of the rebellion in general.

We do not desire to take one atom of praise from our gallant soldiers, who, throughout the war, showed courage and energy unsurpassed; but we feel with many others, that while the country has been lavish of its praise to the Army, it has not always rendered that justice to the Navy which it actually deserved.

The writer does not hesitate to say, that but for the exertions put forth by the naval branch of the government, the rebellion would not have been brought to a close so rapidly as it was.

No nation was ever more unprepared for war than were the United States when the rebellion of eleven States was thrust upon them, and when the people of the South committed their first hostile acts by seizing

GUSTAVUS V. FOX, ASS'T SECRETARY OF THE NAVY, 1861-66.

upon the forts and arsenals that were built for their protection, without the expectation that they would be used against the government. No pen could adequately express the utter impotence of the general government for attack or defence when it was called upon to perform the imperative duty of rescuing the federal fortifications from the hands of the rebels, or of yielding up all authority over them, and thereby sacrificing the life and honor of the nation.

The Navy, in particular, on which alone the government seemed disposed to depend at the first outbreak, was unquestionably in a bad condition to undertake all that was required of it.

Some there were who—rebels at heart and purpose—after holding for several years previous to the war high positions in the administration preceding that of Mr. Lincoln, had done all they could to dispose of the Navy, so that it could not be used in the event of trouble between the North and the South. The object was to destroy all its resources, to cripple the navy yards, dismantle the ships or have them on distant stations, so as to render it impossible for the Navy to strike an effective blow; or, if possible, to throw the ships and Southern yards into the hands of the Secessionists. How well they succeeded the history of the war will tell.

It may be supposed by those unfamiliar with the events of the times, that the rebellion was the result of measures forced upon the South just previous to the election of Abraham Lincoln, and that in his election they saw the death blow to the hopes they had cherished for extending slavery into new states and territories. If any one supposes that the rebellion was an impulsive measure, let him dismiss such an idea, for the writer was told by a Southern Senator in 1860, that, as far back as 1855, when the "Colorado" class of ships were built, he and others had voted to have them and all other vessels constructed of such a size and such a draft of water, that they could not enter any Southern ports; so it seems that the thought of secession had been maturing for years, and while Southern statesmen were apparently urging the building of large vessels instead of small ones, on the ground that the dignity of the Nation called for these cumbersome structures, it was really for the purpose of crippling the Government in case the Southern States should secede. In this they succeeded admirably, so much so, in fact, that these large ships were of little use in the beginning of the war, as they could enter no Southern ports, and their guns, without so doing, could not reach the opposing forts.

Young men of the present day who will want to make themselves informed of the events of our Civil War, will scarcely believe that it was the settled purpose of the South to organize a separate government, or that they would resort to such means to carry out their plans, especially when, after a careful investigation of affairs at that time, it will be clearly perceived that they had no actual ground for complaint. On the contrary, the South for years had enjoyed more than their share of honors and emoluments, and had gained from the North compliance with urgent demands, which often passed the bounds of proper concession.

From the time Mr. Lincoln became President, all the Southern ports were in the possession of Secessionists: they were sealed against our large ships, and open to blockade runners, which immediately began to supply the South with munitions of war, thus giving that section a start, from which they were benefited for a year to come.

Had our Navy at that time consisted of some thirty small gun-boats, or a dozen monitors, the rebellion would have been unable to raise its head. Yet, with all the experience we have had before us, we are at the present time in a worse condition than we were on the breaking out of the rebellion. If to-day events occurred similar to those of 1861, we would be in a worse condition to prevent them. Why does this settled purpose to keep the Navy down exist, when it was shown so conclusively during the Civil War, that without the aid of the Navy the South would have succeeded in its attempt to dismember the Union? Does it not look as if that good service had been forgotten, and that it is determined that only a ghost of a Navy shall remain—a shadow that can be of no actual use in war, and fit to serve only as an idle pageant in time of peace?

If the Navy in the first outburst of the war did not perform any act that would show its importance in putting down the rebellion at once, it was because it was in such a crippled condition regarding its ships, while over two hundred of its officers were throwing up their commissions and hastening South to try their fortunes with the seceding States.

A retrospective view of the history of the times will show how opposed the country was to commence a war, the end of which no man could see. So much was this the case that the North humiliated itself with concessions, and it was not until violent resistance had begun on the part of the South, and the honored flag of the Republic had been fired upon, that the North awoke to the indignity, and never rested until its Army and Navy had wiped out the foul blow that had been struck, and the Union was once again restored in all its entirety.

The Navy Department was beset with difficulties at the very beginning; the friends of the South in Congress did all they could to withhold supplies of money. Our merchant marine did not then, as now, hold out the same facilities for improvising a naval force. Six hundred vessels were demanded at once for the purposes of blockade and for putting afloat a force that could keep down the Southern privateers, and when it is considered what the Department did under all the adverse circumstances attending the execution of these requirements, the highest praise cannot be withheld from those who managed its operations.

Every man who held position of honor and trust in the Navy Department in those trying times is dead and gone, and the multiplying events of a quarter of a century have crowded out for a time the great works which emanated from their conjoint exertions; but those who will take the trouble to hunt up and read over the documentary history of the times, will find ample evidence that to the Navy Department and the Navy is the present generation largely indebted for the happy condition of affairs now existing in a united country —a prosperity never exceeded in the history of the land—and the most substantial proofs that the Navy will always be found foremost to support this union of States, no matter what may be the sacrifices made by its officers and other personnel.

CUMMINGS POINT.　　FORT SUMTER.　　CHARLESTON.　　FORT MOULTRIE.　　FLOATING BATTERY.

ATTACK ON FORT SUMTER BY THE SECESSIONISTS, APRIL 12, 1861—FORT MOULTRIE IN THE FOREGROUND.

CHAPTER II.

BOMBARDMENT AND FALL OF FORT SUMTER.—DESTRUCTION OF THE NORFOLK NAVY YARD BY THE FEDERAL OFFICERS.

First Gun of the Civil War Fired.—Batteries at Cummings Point.—Capt. McCready's Battery.—Capt. Hamilton's Floating Battery.—Major Anderson.—Sumter Returns the Fire.—Unequal Contest.—Tardy Attempts to Relieve Sumter.—Indignant People.—Anderson's Gallant Fight, and Surrender to the Secessionists.—Effect of the Surrender of Sumter.—Lincoln's Position Toward Virginia.—Gen. Scott and the Virginians.—Commodore McCauley.—Secrets of the Navy Department Made Known by Disloyal Officers.—Conspirators at Work.—A Plot to Seize Norfolk Navy Yard.—The Navy Department Powerless.—Commodore Paulding Summoned.—Hostile Attitude of the People of Norfolk and Portsmouth.—Vessels at the Norfolk Navy Yard.—Ships that were Historic.—Aggressive Movements of the Confederates.—Commander James Alden.—Chief Engineer Isherwood.—Indecision of Commodore McCauley.—The Torch Applied to the Navy Yard and Vessels by the Federal Authorities.—Vessels that were Saved.—The Greatest Misfortune to the Union Cause.—The Merrimac, etc., etc.

A T thirty minutes past 4 o'clock, on April 12, 1861, the first gun of civil war was fired, the battery on James Island discharging the first howitzer shell, which fell inside Fort Sumter, blowing up a building; this was almost immediately followed by another shell, which scattered destruction all around.

Fort Moultrie then took up the assault, and in another moment the guns from the gun battery on Cummings Point, from Captain McCready's battery, from Captain James Hamilton's floating battery, the enfilading battery, and every other point where a gun could be brought to bear on Sumter, opened in succession; and the guns poured forth their wrath as if the fort standing out in the bay had been some vengeful foe on which they desired to wreak their vengeance, instead of considering that it had been placed there for their protection against all foreign enemies.

It was well understood by all those in that beleagured fort what would be the result of building all those earth-works, and that it was only a matter of a few days or perhaps

hours, ere the South Carolinians would proceed to extremities—had they waited until the 15th of April the garrison would have been starved out, and obliged to surrender for want of provisions. But that would not have suited them; they wanted to strike a blow that would make separation inevitable, and one that would unite the whole South in the measures then pending to form a Southern Confederacy, or whatever kind of government they might finally drift into.

Major Anderson, the Commander of Sumter, received the first shot and shell in silence; the batteries at regular intervals continued to belch forth their deadly missiles, and still no answer was returned by the besieged, until about an hour after the firing commenced, then two shots were fired from Sumter and glanced harmlessly from the face of Fort Moultrie. Sumter fired no more until between six and seven o'clock when, as if enraged at the onslaught made upon it and kept up with increasing vigor, it then opened from casemate and parapet a hail of shot and shell on Moultrie, steam iron battery, and the floating battery, that fairly made them shake. This was returned with great vigor by the South Carolina gunners. There were good soldiers on both sides, men trained to arms and neither to be daunted by a few shot and shell. The story of that day is known to all who read history, and it is not necessary to further refer to it, excepting in connection with the naval expedition which was fitted out in the earlier part of April to go to the relief of Sumter, the history of which will appear further on in this narrative.

Secretary Welles, with a decision worthy of the occasion, did fit out an expedition for the relief of Sumter, the last vessel of which sailed from New York on the 9th of April, but owing to various reasons did not reach Charleston harbor in time to be of any use, and the attack on the fort commenced soon after the leading vessels showed themselves off the bar. A number of the smaller vessels never arrived at all, and under the circumstances could have been of no use had they arrived twenty-four hours before the attack. The expedition arrived only to see the declaration of war between the North and the South, which was promulgated by the thunder of cannon and the hissing of the shot and shell, as they carried death and destruction to those who had been united by the strongest bonds of love and friendship. Those who from the ships witnessed the fiery shells as they crossed each other in the night, knew that this was war that would never cease until one or the other of the contending parties were deprived of the resources to carry it on; war that would oblige the Government to call forth large armies to put down rebellion on the field of battle, and to build and equip large fleets to blockade the insurgent's ports, and bombard the heavy forts the enemy had snatched from the hands of their lawful owners. The men in that fleet of succour to the besieged Sumter knew then that ten times the number of vessels could not have rendered aid to the fort in face of that terrible fire, and that their missions might better have never been undertaken. They started homeward to carry the news to the startled North, but the telegrams far out-traveled them, and as its messages on the wires were announced to an indignant people, there was but one general feeling, namely, to resist the audacity of the insurgents and bring them back to reason, if it took every man in the country to do it. The rebellion was a dreadful thing to inaugurate, to be sure, and those who undertook to bring it about must have been imbued with some other ambition than was apparent, or the desire to escape from a form of government which had so far proved the best yet known to man : there must have been greater inducements to break up this most

beneficent union than has ever appeared on the face of events.

The South was a great oligarchy, holding their millions of slaves, and they aimed to be recognized by the world as a power above the gift of the people. Perhaps the best thing that ever happened to this great country was the firing on Fort Sumter with the guns of Moultrie and other forts. Who can say that we are not a greater nation to-day, with freedom throughout the land, than we were in the days of the errors and follies of the South, and the anger and prejudices of the North, which embittered one against the other, and made the great Council Hall of the nation a place of violence and discord? All that has been swept away with the fall of slavery, and instead of it has come a union of all the States, more earnest and fraternal than before, with the Southern section of the country growing more prosperous and more happy under free labor and equal rights for all those who live in the South. In another generation people will likely bless the day when James Island and Moultrie opened their guns on Sumter, and caused to be wiped out that dark blotch on our escutcheon, which the whole world were pointing at and asking us how we could call ourselves a free country while four millions of people were held in bondage. Who knows what we might have been but for that long war, which brought so much sorrow and desolation to so many homes? Slavery, with its seductive influences, might have led us all away, and in the course of a century our country might have become a land of slaves.

Let this country not forget, then, the men who so nobly risked their lives in the cause of freedom, and let them erect monuments to those who died that this union of States might live to be an asylum for all time to come for those who love not despotism, and love liberty.

The Navy had a large share in bringing about the happy results which grew from the war, and many on both sides do not hesitate to say that, but for the Navy the South never would have been brought back into the Union—and yet, who is there that has taken the trouble to erect a monument to the sailors?

As this narrative continues people will learn with surprise that the Navy did so much towards putting down the rebellion; yet the author will scarcely find time or space to give a fair account of all the Navy did do, and must leave untold many events to be related hereafter by some more graphic historian. As years pass on, people who have been born long after the great War of the Rebellion, will long to know of the great battles by land and sea, which took place from 1861 to 1865, and it is to be hoped that by each one contributing his mite, in the course of time a true history will be written. The best of efforts will be made in this history to make it a true if not an interesting one.

When President Lincoln entered upon the duties of his office, his position towards Virginia differed somewhat from that which he assumed towards the States farther South. It was deemed desirable that the Administration should do nothing to wound the sensitive feelings of the Virginians, and General Scott, the General-in-Chief of our Army, was particularly solicitous that the Government should give the State of Virginia no excuse to secede.

There were several reasons for this extra tenderness towards Virginia—one of the principal navy yards, filled with Southern officers, was within the limits of the State. The commanding officer, Commander McCauley, was considered loyal, and had in his day stood high in the service; but he was now old, and at a time when he should have maintained his self-possession he appears to have completely lost his head.

The Secretary of the Navy, Mr. Welles, had not yet made himself familiar with the conditions of affairs in his department. His position was a difficult one for a man advanced in years, for the duties were complicated, and such as only an expert could be expected to fathom in so short a time.

Mr. Welles was surrounded with officers and clerks, some of whose loyalty was doubted, and one bureau of the Department in particular, presided over by an officer of Southern birth and of national reputation, was the headquarters of naval officers who were plotting the downfall of the country to which they owed their position and whatever importance they possessed.

It was bad enough for officers to openly desert their flag, but far worse treachery to continue holding positions in order to hamper the Government and betray its secrets. Every official act in the Navy Department was known at once to these plotters, and immediate steps taken to render it abortive. Officers with pleasant faces, but with treason in their hearts, assembled in conclave in the Department to devise plans for the overthrow of the Government.

A short time before Fort Sumter was fired upon, the commandant of the Washington Navy Yard gave a large party at his quarters, on the occasion of the marriage of his daughter, to which the President and his cabinet were invited. A number of disloyal naval officers were present, and the house was everywhere festooned with the American flag, even to the bridal bed; yet just after Sumter was fired on, the Commandant, with most of those under his command, including his new son-in-law, resigned their commissions and left the Washington Navy Yard to take care of itself.

At that very time the secession of Virginia had been resolved upon, which was known to these disloyal officers, although not to the Government; for the action of the Secessionists had been delayed and kept secret, so that the blow would be more decisive and enable the conspirators to seize the public property at Norfolk and elsewhere, to help them carry out their designs.

At one time it was even thought doubtful if Washington could be held, as the people at the North, unprepared for such an emergency, were slow in getting troops to the Capitol.

Those who had been plotting against the Government in the Navy Department, felt sure that the Norfolk Yard must fall into the hands of the Secessionists, as everything possible had been prepared for that event. They lost no opportunity to impress upon the mind of the Secretary of the Navy the importance of doing nothing to offend the State of Virginia and give it an excuse for seceding from the Union on the ground of invasion of "State rights;" which meant that the Government should exercise no authority over its own property within the limits of a seceding State. The Naval Department at that moment seemed powerless to preserve the public property at Norfolk against the rebel troops then assembling in Virginia. General Scott threw cold water on every attempt to hold the Norfolk Yard, on the ground that he had no troops to spare, as he could not deplete Fortress Monroe, which must be held at all hazards.

It seems a pity that the Secretary should not have selected some loyal and energetic officer, placed him in command of a few gunboats and armed tug-boats and sent him to Norfolk with orders to bring all the vessels away, and even put the Commandant under arrest if he should interpose any obstacles. A guard of fifty marines would have been sufficient to overawe all malcontents. These proceedings would not have influenced the secession of Virginia, which was already decided upon.

The Secretary of the Navy, finding himself unable to cope with the difficulties of the situation, summoned to the Navy Department Commodore Hiram Paulding, a loyal officer, but who was now declining in years and not equal to a position which required not only energy of mind but great bodily vigor. Commodore Paulding broke up the conclave which was in the habit of meeting in the Bureau of Ordnance, for he felt that these officers were inimical to the government, and he recommended the Secretary of the Navy to change the suspected Chief of Bureaux for another known to be loyal.

Frequent accounts reached Washington of the hostile attitude of the people in Norfolk and Portsmouth towards the government, and their determination that the Navy Department should not remove a ship or a gun from the station. Large bodies of troops were reported moving towards Norfolk to enforce this decision. In fact, Norfolk, which had for many years lived on the bounty of the government and flourished by the appropriations for the support of the Navy Yard, was now the very hot-bed of secession.

COMMODORE HIRAM PAULDING.

The Southern officers could hardly restrain their impatience until the State of Virginia should secede, so anxious were they to show their gratitude to the United States Government, which had conferred upon them whatever importance they possessed, by pulling it to pieces, and endeavoring to dim the glory of the flag under which they had served from boyhood.

Most of the officers of the Navy Yard were Southern men whose honor had heretofore been unquestioned, but their heads were now so turned that they were as wild as the *sans culottes* of the French Revolution.

Commodore McCauley, who commanded the Navy Yard, had long and faithfully served the government, but was now advanced in years and no match for the wily secessionists about him, who so hampered and bewildered him, that he for a time rested under the suspicion of being luke-warm in his allegiance.

At this time there were lying at the Navy Yard the following named vessels:

The steam frigate "Merrimac," of 40 guns, the same vessel which, after being converted into an ironclad by the rebels, made such havoc among our ships at Hampton Roads; the sloop of war, "Germantown," 22 guns; sloop of war, "Plymouth," 22 guns; brig, "Dolphin," 4 guns. All these could have been prepared for sea in a short time.

There were also the following named old ships which were of no great use, but they had been associated with the history of the Navy and were dear to the country. These were the "Pennsylvania," "United States," "Columbus," "Delaware," "Raritan," and "Columbia."

There was also an unfinished ship-of-the-line, the "New York," in one of the ship houses.

The sloop-of-war "Cumberland," was moored at the Navy Yard. These vessels were valued at about two millions of dollars.

Any one to see these ships lying quietly at their moorings, the officers and men going to and fro about their duties, the sentries pacing up and down guarding public property and preserving order, would have supposed that the interests of the United States Government were being well taken care of; but this was merely the calm which precedes the storm—the fearful storm which was soon to burst upon the country, when "Hope for a season bade the world farewell," and truth and honor hung their heads with shame.

Early in April the Navy Department began to get very uneasy for the safety of the Navy Yard, for it was by this time well understood that the Secessionists would make an aggressive movement on the first favorable opportunity.

The Department was most anxious to get the "Merrimac" away from the yard to a place of safety, but was informed by Commodore McCauley that it would take a month to put her machinery in working order.

The department did not seem to reflect that a few armed tow-boats with marines on board, could have been sent from New York to tow all the vessels under the guns of Fortress Monroe. One tug with a twenty four pound howitzer on board, properly handled, would have been master of the situation, and if the Navy Department had displayed a little forethought in this emergency, the government would have been saved deep humiliation and a loss in ships, guns and stores not easy to repair.

On the 31st of March 250 seamen and landsmen were ordered to be transferred from the New York Navy Yard to Norfolk, and fifty seamen were transferred to the revenue steamer "Harriet Lane," which vessel was ordered to proceed at once to Norfolk. It shows the miserable condition of the Navy when the department had nothing but a revenue cutter to depend upon.

Days went by before anything else was attempted. On the 11th of April Commodore James Alden was ordered to report to Commodore McCauley to take command of the "Merrimac," and Chief Engineer Isherwood was sent to Norfolk to get the ship's engines in working order as soon as possible.

On the 14th the work was commenced, and on the 17th the engines were in working order—so much for the Commandant's assertion that it would take a month to get the ship ready to move, as he was made to believe.

It is no wonder, under these circumstances

The work was all done with the consent of Commodore McCauley; but when he was informed that everything was ready to fire up, he replied that next morning would be time enough. At midnight the fires were started and the engines worked at the dock, and were found to be in good order.

Next morning the Commandant was again informed that everything was ready, but he replied that he had not decided to send the "Merrimac" out. It was in vain that he was reminded of the peremptory character of the order which Mr. Isherwood had brought from the Secretary of the Navy to get the "Merrimac" out at the earliest possible moment. He only replied that he would let his decision be known in the course of the day. He gave as a reason the obstructions that had been placed in the channel, but when assured that they could

THE STEAMER "HARRIET LANE."

that the loyalty of the Commandant should have been questioned, yet he was simply influenced by officers whom he trusted and who were desirous that the "Merrimac" should be retained for the future navy of the Southern Confederacy.

In a majority of instances when Southern officers had determined "to go with their States," they turned over their commands or trusts to the government and went away with clean skirts, but in the case of navy yards this rule did not seem to hold good, as was shown at Pensacola and Norfolk; and every impediment was thrown in Commodore McCauley's way by his own subordinates to prevent his carrying out the orders of the department.

The disloyalty which existed to such an extent among the officers did not at that time extend to the mechanics, for they worked night and day until the "Merrimac's" machinery was repaired.

Then forty-four firemen and coal-heavers volunteered for the service of taking the "Merrimac" out.

be easily passed, and that every moment increased the danger, he gave orders to haul the fires, and thus the noble "Merrimac" was finally lost to us.

It is difficult at this late date to tell all the motives that influenced the Navy Department and the Commandant at Norfolk. Indecision seemed everywhere to exist, and some of the best officers in the Navy were apparently quite dazed at the course which events were taking. Commodore McCauley at one time was master of the situation, and with promptness and decision might have saved all the ships, guns, and stores, even if he judged it advisable to abandon the Navy Yard.

The Commodore probably thought that by retaining the "Merrimac" and her battery he would have a strong force to repel any attack that might be made from the outside. The old Commodore, who had fought gallantly for his country in former days, was completely acquitted of anything like disloyalty by the officers who were sent down to take the "Merrimac" away from

Norfolk, but it is unfortunate that he did not show more decision of character when the crisis came upon him.

Every officer connected with the destruction of the Norfolk Navy Yard came in for a share of censure, which is not to be wondered at when it is now known that every ship and gun could have been saved. The broadside of the "Germantown," which was all ready for sea and only waiting a crew, or the "Plymouth," in the same condition, would, with a few men on board, have saved the Navy Yard against attack, overawed Norfolk and Portsmouth, and prevented the channel from being obstructed by the Confederates.

Even when the yard was abandoned and the buildings set fire to, the work was done in a panic in which the coolest persons seem to have lost their heads. The destruction took place when the yard had been re-enforced by a regiment of Massachusetts Volunteers under Colonel Wadsworth, while the "Pawnee" of fifteen guns had brought Commodore Paulding from Washington with instructions "to save what he could and act as he thought proper."

When Commodore Paulding arrived at the Navy Yard he found that all the Southern officers had sent in their resignations and abandoned their posts. The mechanics, following their example, had left the yard in a body, and persons had even come in from outside and possessed themselves of the Government arms. It was reported that several thousand men were organizing for the purpose of seizing the yard. The powder had been taken from the Government magazine near Norfolk, and batteries were being erected along the approaches to the Navy Yard, and hulks sunk in the channel near Craney Island and Sewell's Point, three light boats having been used for the purpose; and this was done, notwithstanding the Commandant of the yard had ample force to have prevented it. Actual war existed between the Government and the inhabitants of Norfolk, who were doing all in their power to destroy public property and obstruct the public highway. Worse than all, the "Merrimac," "Germantown" and "Plymouth" had been scuttled by orders.

All the guns in the Navy Yard had been spiked, with the exception of some two hundred, as well as those on shipboard, except five heavy guns on a side on board the "Pennsylvania," which sturdy old castle commanded the whole yard; and fifty good seamen on board could have bid defiance to 5,000 Confederates in arms, and held Norfolk and Portsmouth under her guns until every ship was hauled out of harm's way.

After the arrival of the "Pawnee" had made the yard doubly secure, the shells were drawn from the "Pennsylvania's" guns and the guns spiked!

The whole thing looked so hopeless to Commodore Paulding that, in view of the orders he had received from the Department not to let anything fall into the hands of the Confederates, he determined to destroy everything.

It must have been a painful alternative to that faithful old officer, Commodore Paulding, who abhorred everything in the shape of rebellion, to be obliged to apply the torch to the historic ships of the Navy, and destroy the other valuable property the Government had been so many years accumulating; especially since he was aware that most of the destruction might easily have been prevented, had not so many days been lost in deciding what to do.

But the fiat had gone forth, the mania for destruction had seized upon every one, as we see boys go mad over the burning of a hay-rick, which they have set fire to in wanton sport.

All the ships, except the "Cumberland," were well filled with combustibles, and the whole saturated with oil and turpentine. The ship-houses and other buildings were prepared in the same manner, and nothing left to chance so that the rebels could derive any benefit from what was left behind. The fine dry-dock that had cost millions to build was undermined, and a hundred men ran to and fro with heavy hammers trying to knock off the trunnions of the heavy guns, but with a few exceptions these attempts were failures.

It was a beautiful starlight night, April 20, when all the preparations were completed. The people of Norfolk and Portsmouth were wrapped in slumber, little dreaming that in a few hours the ships and public works which were so essential to the prosperity of the community would be a mass of ruins, and hundreds of people would be without employment and without food for their families.

The "Pawnee" had towed the "Cumberland" out of the reach of the fire, and laid at anchor to receive on board those who were to fire the public property. Commodore McCauley had gone to bed that night worn out with excitement and anxiety, under the impression that the force that had arrived at Norfolk was for the purpose of holding the yard and relieving him of responsibility, and when he was called at midnight and informed that the torch would be applied to everything, he could hardly

THE BURNING OF THE NORFOLK NAVY YARD, THE FRIGATE "MERRIMAC," AND OTHER VESSELS, APRIL 24, 1861.

realize the situation, and was chagrined and mortified at the idea of abandoning his post without any attempt to defend it.

At 2:30 A. M., April 21st, a rocket from the "Pawnee" gave the signal; the work of destruction commenced with the "Merrimac," and in ten minutes she was one vast sheet of flame. In quick succession the trains to the other ships and buildings were ignited and the surrounding country brilliantly illuminated.

The inhabitants of Norfolk and Portsmouth, roused from their slumber, looked with awe at the work of destruction, and mothers clasping their children to their breasts bewailed the fate that cut them and their offspring off from their support. Yet this was but a just retribution for the treason which the inhabitants had shown towards the best government on earth. They had killed the goose that laid the golden egg.

As the boats containing the firing party moved off down the river to the "Pawnee" and "Cumberland," the rebels from Norfolk and Portsmouth rushed into the Yard to save what they could from the flames, and were more fortunate than they expected to be. The dry-dock was not materially injured, some of the work-shops and officers' quarters were preserved, and the frigate "United States" was not much damaged. Even the "Merrimac," though burned to the water's edge and sunk, was afterwards raised and converted into the powerful ironclad which wrought such havoc in Hampton Roads and carried consternation through the North.

The loss of the Navy Yard at Norfolk was felt all through the North to be a great calamity. Misfortunes seemed accumulating, and people began to doubt whether the administration had sufficient vigor to meet the emergencies that were continually arising. The destruction of the Navy Yard seems now to have been the result of a panic which was not justified by the facts of the case, but the actors in that scene believed they were consulting the best interests of the Government. No one can doubt the loyalty of those gallant old seamen, McCauley and Paulding, for undoubtedly they had the best interests of the country at heart, and acted with good intent.

In the midst of our other misfortunes the loss of the Navy Yard was soon forgotten. It was abandoned by the Confederates after the defeat of the "Merrimac" by the "Monitor" in a panic quite as causeless as our own, and has not yet risen like the Phœnix from its ashes, its reconstruction progressing very slowly.

Congress has apparently viewed with distrust appropriations made for this yard, scarcely yet realizing that the people employed there are worthy of confidence in consequence of their past acts of rebellion, which caused the destruction of the most important naval station in the United States.

The greatest misfortune to the Union caused by the destruction of the Navy Yard, was the loss of at least twelve hundred fine guns, most of which were uninjured. A number of them were quickly mounted at Sewell's Point to keep our ships from approaching Norfolk; others were sent to Hatteras Inlet, Ocracocke, Roanoke Island and other points in the sounds of North Carolina. Fifty-three of them were mounted at Port Royal, others at Fernandina and at the defences of New Orleans. They were met with at Fort Henry, Fort Donelson, Island No. 10, Memphis, Vicksburg, Grand Gulf and Port Hudson. We found them up the Red River as far as the gunboats penetrated, and took possession of some of them on the cars at Duvall's Bluff, on White River, bound for Little Rock. They gave us a three hours' hard fight at Arkansas Post, but in the end they all returned to their rightful owners, many of them indented with Union shot and not a few permanently disabled.

Had it not been for the guns captured at Norfolk and Pensacola, the Confederates would have found it a difficult matter to arm their fortifications for at least a year after the breaking out of hostilities, at the expiration of which time they began to manufacture their own ordnance, and import it from abroad. Great as was, therefore, the loss of our ships, it was much less than the loss of our guns.

CHAPTER III.

CLOSING OF THE SOUTHERN PORTS.—OPERATIONS AGAINST THE FEDERAL COMMERCE BY PRIVATEERS.—TRIPLE TASK OF THE NAVY DEPARTMENT.—INCREASE OF THE NAVY.—PURCHASES UNWISELY MADE.—BRITISH VESSELS AND THE BLOCKADE.—SUFFERERS BY THE BLOCKADE.—FLAG OFFICERS APPOINTED TO COMMANDS.—DIFFICULTIES OF THE BLOCKADING FORCES.—ENERGY AND WATCHFULNESS OF NAVAL OFFICERS.—REMARKABLE ACTIVITY OF THE CONFEDERATES.—INADEQUATE APPROPRIATIONS BY CONGRESS.—CONDITION OF THE NAVY.—LIST OF VESSELS AND THEIR STATIONS —AVAILABLE VESSELS.—THE HOME SQUADRON.—OLD NAVY.—PURCHASED VESSELS.—VESSELS CONSTRUCTING.—REORGANIZATION OF THE SERVICE.—PROMOTIONS.—THREE GRADES ADDED.—SCHOOLS OF GUNNERY AND NAVAL TRAINING ESTABLISHED.—PATRIOTIC VOLUNTEER OFFICERS.—THE COMMERCIAL MARINE.—HIGH TRIBUTE TO THE SECRETARY OF THE NAVY.

THE Navy Department, with its limited resources, had a weighty task imposed upon it from the very outbreak of the civil war. In a very brief period the rebellion assumed such formidable proportions, and naval operations had to be maintained on such an extensive scale to include over three thousand miles of coast line, that the energy and ability of the naval authorities were put to the severest tests.

First. There was the closing of all the ports along our Southern coast under the most exacting regulations of an international blockade, including the occupation of the Potomac River from its mouth to the Federal Capitol.

Had the Potomac been blocked by the enemy's guns at any time during the war, it would have rendered the position of our armies in Virginia and around the Capitol very embarrassing.

Second. The necessity of establishing an effective organization of combined naval and military expeditions against various points on our Southern coast, including also all needful naval aid to the Army in cutting off communication with the rebels. Besides this it was seen at an early date that a large naval force would be required on the Mississippi River and its tributaries.

Third. There had to be provided a suitable number of swift vessels for the active pursuit of the Confederate cruisers, which might elude the vigilance of our blockading forces and proceed to prey upon our commerce in every part of the world. Immediately on the breaking out of the rebellion the Confederates prepared to operate against Federal commerce, and after the escape of their first privateer the destruction of our vessels became very common.

This was the triple task the Navy Department was called upon to perform, and it is but fair to say that, considering the disadvantages under which the Department labored, never were duties better performed.

When the proclamation was issued declaring all the Southern ports under blockade, it found the Navy Department totally unprepared for such a contingency. Congress had adjourned without providing for it, and it devolved on the Secretary of the Navy to meet the difficulties of the situation in the best way he could.

There were but few vessels in the Navy which could be relied on for blockading service, and none suitable for the pursuit of Confederate cruisers, which would naturally be very swift steamers. The only thing to be done was to put into commission every vessel in the Navy that was fit to go to sea, and to purchase from the mercantile marine such as would answer for temporary service; but so few vessels in the merchant service were fit even for blockade duty, much less for ships of war, that it was with difficulty that a sufficient number could be obtained to make such a blockade as was called for by the law of nations.

Purchases were unwisely made, and some unfit vessels were thus added to the Navy—through that spirit of grasping cupidity which is sure to come to the surface in time of war.

Some men who had always been considered honest and patriotic, did not hesitate to take advantage of the necessities of their country, and deplete the Federal treasury without adding to the efficiency of the Navy, thus hampering the naval authorities at the very outset of hostilities.

Purchases and contracts were made to meet the exigencies of the times. Orders were issued to equip vessels that under ordinary circumstances would not have been considered safe to go to sea in.

The force thus hastily gathered and stationed along our coast would scarcely have been considered an "efficient blockade" if a European power had thought fit to institute close inquiries into our proceedings. Now and then a British vessel of war made her appearance for the purpose of observing that the blockade was effectual, but as far as the writer's observations are concerned, this duty was always performed in the most delicate manner, and the British commanders were satisfied with the appearance of a blockade that was far from satisfying to the Federal Government.

A great deal has been said by Boynton, the naval historian, about the exacting character of the British Government in relation to the blockade of our coasts, but we rather think his style of writing was adapted to the public sentiment of the time, which was prepared to find fault with any nation that did not sympathize with the Union cause.

The English people were the great sufferers in our war by the loss of a commerce that was absolutely necessary for them to keep their manufactories going, and they exercised no greater surveillance than the Federal Government would have done had there been a blockade of the Irish coast established.

Flag Officers were appointed to the command of the different stations, and vessels were sent to each according to the necessity of the case as fast as they could be purchased and fitted out. Under the supervision of these flag officers the coasts and harbors of the Confederates were subjected to as close a blockade as the limited force of vessels would admit.

The difficulties of the blockading forces were much increased owing to the number of great bays, sounds and rivers of the South, but in spite of all drawbacks the duties of the blockade were remarkably well performed.

What was lacking in vessels was more than compensated for by the energy and watchfulness of the naval officers on the different stations.

The expectation of prize-money was doubtless a stimulus to both officers and men, yet there was a higher motive governing their conduct, a determination to do all in their power to put down the rebellion by cutting off foreign supplies, without which they felt the Confederate resistance would soon terminate.

One of the most remarkable features of the war was the manner in which at an early date the Confederates had seized upon and fortified so many important points on the Southern coast, actually cutting Federal vessels off from any port of shelter in stormy weather, and compelling supply vessels of the different squadrons to keep out to sea. Our ships were compelled oftentimes to anchor in heavy gales on the open coast, where in case of accident to machinery or cables a steamer would be liable to drift on shore into the heavy breakers which lined the coast, and where a sailing vessel under like circumstances would have great difficulty in clawing off a lee shore.

The Confederates doubtless considered all these circumstances when they undertook the task of freeing themselves from what they were pleased to consider the thraldom of the North. With all ports of shelter closed against the Federal Navy, and storms continually raging along the coast, they laughed at the idea of a blockade.

They did not know the energy which animated the Federal Navy when circumstances should arise to call it forth. The officers themselves did not know until called upon to act what zeal and energy they could evince, and the present generation can hardly realize the hardships and dangers of the work then performed.

To many of the survivors of those scenes it may seem like the dreams of early childhood, shadows of which flit through the mind, dim and shapeless as reflected images from misty waterfalls.

The necessity of seizing some of the Southern ports soon became apparent; for though our officers had shown great ability in taking care of their ships on the blockade in the most tempestuous weather, and at the same time had rendered it difficult for blockade runners to enter Southern ports, yet it was found that harbors of refuge were indispensable to properly carry on such extensive operations.

Great demands were made upon the Navy, notwithstanding Congress had adjourned in 1861 without making adequate appropriations, considering the condition of affairs.

WATERWITCH. MISSISSIPPI. POWHATAN. SUSQUEHANNA. FREEBORN. MACEDONIAN. CUMBERLAND. BROOKLYN. POCAHONTAS. SABINE. SUPPLY.

ST. LOUIS.

HOME SQUADRON OF THE UNION NAVY.

It is true that the measures adopted by Mr. Secretary Welles in advance of the session, and which had been rendered necessary in consequence of events that had been precipitated upon the country, had been approved by Congress, but that, after all, only provided for a comparatively small force of vessels and men, not even enough for ordinary police operations along the Atlantic coast, much less a strict blockade.

In order that the condition of the Navy may be understood, the list of vessels and their stations is herewith inserted. In the eyes of one not familiar with naval affairs it appears like a large show of available vessels, but not half of them were really fit for the service required of them.

The Home Squadron consisted of twelve vessels, and of these only four were in Northern ports and available for service, viz.:

NAME.	CLASS.	NO. OF GUNS.	WHERE STATIONED.
Pawnee	Screw Sloop....	8	Washington.
Crusader..	Steamer.........	8	New York.
Mohawk	Steamer........	5	"
Supply ...	Storeship.......	4	"
4 vessels........		25	

The remaining vessels of the Squadron were stationed as follows:

NAME.	CLASS.	NO. OF GUNS.	WHERE STATIONED.
Sabine.	Frigate	50	Pensacola.
St. Louis...	Sloop	20	"
Brooklyn.	Steamer	25	"
Wyandotte. ..	Steamer........	5	"
Macedonian ...	Sloop....	22	Vera Cruz.
Cumberland....	Sloop	24	Returning from
Pocahontas. ..	Steamer........	5	Vera Cruz.
Powhatan.. ...	Steamer........	11	
8 vessels.......		162	

The Powhatan arrived at New York March 12, 1861, and sailed early in April for Fort Pickens.

The Pocahontas reached Hampton Roads on the 12th of March, and the Cumberland on the 23d of the same month.

Of vessels on foreign stations the following had returned in obedience to orders from the Department.

FROM MEDITERRANEAN:

NAME.	CLASS.	NO. OF GUNS.	DATE OF ARRIVAL.
Richmond... ...	Steam Sloop....	16	July 3.
Susquehanna...	Steam Sloop....	15	June 6.
Iroquois.	Steam Sloop....	6	June 15.

FROM COAST OF AFRICA:

NAME.	CLASS.	NO. OF GUNS.	DATE OF ARRIVAL.
Constellation....	Sloop	22	Sept. 28.
Portsmouth. ...	Sloop....	22	Sept. 23.
Mohican........	Steam Sloop....	6	Sept. 27.
Mystic.........	Steamer........	5	Oct. 7.
Sumter........	Steamer ...	5	Sept. 15.
San Jacinto....	Steam Sloop....	13	Nov. 15.
Relief.........	Storeship.	2	Oct. 12.

FROM COAST OF BRAZIL:

Name.	CLASS.	NO. OF GUNS.	DATE OF ARRIVAL.
Congress.......	Frigate	50	August 12.
Seminole.......	Steam Sloop....	•5	July 6.

The following had not arrived, Dec., 1861.
FROM EAST INDIES:

NAME.	CLASS.	NO. OF GUNS.	
John Adams...	Sloop	20	
Hartford.	Steam Sloop...	16	
Dacotah... ..	Steam Sloop....	6	

The following were to remain abroad:

NAME.	CLASS.	NO. OF GUNS.	WHERE STATIONED.
Saratoga..	Sloop	18	Coast of Africa.
Pulaski.... ..	Steamer.......	1	Coast of Brazil.
Saginaw ., ...	Steamer	3	East Indies.

Add to these the vessels on the Pacific coast, the steam frigate Niagara, returning from Japan, and four tenders and store-ships, and there was a total of 42 vessels, carrying 555 guns and about 7,600 men, in commission on the 4th of March, 1861.

Without awaiting the arrival of vessels from our foreign squadrons, the department early directed such as were dismantled and in ordinary at the different yards, and which could be made available, to be repaired and put in commission. They are exclusive of those lost at Norfolk Navy Yard, embraced in the following table:

NAMES.	WHERE.	ORDERED TO BE PREPARED FOR SEA SERVICE WITH DISPATCH.	PUT IN COMMISSION, OR READY FOR OFFICERS AND CREW.	SAILED.
		1861.	1861.	1861.
Frigates—				
Potomac..	New York.........	April 27	July 30	Sept. 10
St. Lawrence...	Philadelphia.......	April 20	Late in May.	June 29
Santee.........·	Portsmouth, N. H.	April 17	May 27	June 20
Sloops—				
Savannah	New York	April 1	June 1	July 10
Jamestown.....	Philadelphia..... ..	April 9	May 18	June 8
Vincennes......	Boston	April 9	June 24	July 12
Marion...... ...	Portsmouth	April 20	June 30	July 14
Dale	"	April 20	June 30	July 17
Preble. ...	Boston..........	April 20	June 22	July 11
Brigs—				
Bainbridge	Boston..........	April 20	May 1	May 21
Perry....	New York.........	April 20	May 1	May 14
Steamers—				
Roanoke	New York	April 20	June 20	June 25
Colorado	Boston...........	April 20	June 3	June 18
Minnesota.	"	April 3	May 2	May 8
Wabash	New York	April 9	April 29	May 30
Pensacola.....	Washington	......	......	......
Mississippi. ...	Boston...........	April 6	May 18	May 23
Water Witch....	Philadelphia.......	Feb. 14	April 10	April 17

When the vessels then building and purchased of every class, were armed, equipped, and ready for service, the condition of the Navy would be as follows:

OLD NAVY.

NUMBER OF VESSELS.	GUNS.	TONNAGE.
6 Ships of the Line (useless)	504	16,094
7 Frigates (useless)........................	350	12,104
17 Sloops (useless)........................	342	16,031
2 Brigs (useless)........................	12	539
3 Storeships		7	342
6 Receiving Ships, &c	106	6,340
6 Screw Frigates	222	21,460
6 First-class Screw Sloops....	109	11,953
4 First-class Sidewheel Steam Sloops......	46	8,003
8 Second-class Screw Sloops.............	45	7,593
5 Third-class Screw Sloops...........	28	2,405
4 Third-class Sidewheel Steamers	8	1,808
2 Steam Tenders.......	4	599
76	1,783	105,271

PURCHASED VESSELS.

	GUNS.	TONS.
36 Sidewheel Steamers.	160	26,680
43 Screw Steamers.........	175	20,403
13 Ships	52	9,998
24 Schooners.....	49	5,324
18 Barks............................	78	8,432
2 Brigs	4	469
136	518	71,297

VESSELS CONSTRUCTING.

	GUNS.	TONS.
14 Screw Sloops.........................	98	16,787
23 Gunboats..	92	11,661
12 Sidewheel Steamers.............	48	8,400
3 Ironclad Steamers	18	4,600
52	256	41,448

Making a total of 264 vessels, 2,557 guns, and 218,016 tons. The aggregate number of seamen in the service on the 4th of March, 1861, was 7,600. The number in December, 1861, was not less than 22,000.

This was a very good exhibit for the Navy in less than a year after the commencement of the war, but it must be remembered that of these vessels 6 were ships-of-the-line, on the stocks, 7 sailing frigates, 17 sailing sloops-of-war, 2 brigs, 3 storeships, 6 receiving ships, 13 sailing merchant ships, 24 schooners, 18 barks and 2 brigs. All these may be said to have been of little use as blockading vessels, as a swift blockade runner would have little difficulty in eluding them.

Yet our vessels were the best the Federal government could procure, and they were used to the best advantage.

Just before the breaking out of the rebellion the Navy was in a stagnant condition for want of those inducements which infuse life into a military service.

There was little hope of promotion, and the navy list was encumbered with the names of a lot of elderly gentlemen who had long since bade farewell to any hope of advancement. Some of the younger officers had sought temporary service in the mercantile marine, many had outlived their usefulness, and lieutenants on the verge of fifty years of age, with large families of children, had to employ all their faculties to feed them.

One of the acts of the new Secretary of the Navy was to recommend a reorganization of the service to increase its efficiency.

In December, 1861, Mr. Secretary Welles recommended that the permanent organization of the line officers of the Navy should be as follows, adding three grades to the number then in existence :

Flag Officers to command Squadrons,
Commodores,
Captains,   to command
Commanders,   single vessels.
Lieutenants-Commanding,

Lieutenants, Masters, Passed Midshipmen, Midshipmen, Cadets.

At the same time were established the sensible rules for promotion for gallant conduct in time of war, which did so much to elevate the service, and also to retire those who from age or other disability were no longer fit for active duty.

For all this the Navy was indebted to Mr. G. V. Fox, the Assistant Secretary, whose ideas were promptly adopted by Mr. Secretary Welles. It was the first gleam of sunshine that had illuminated the Navy for half a century, and the first time that the sanction of Congress had been given to the President to appoint to the highest grades, officers on the list of Commanders who had shown themselves gallant or efficient in the performance of their duties.

The efficiency of the service was further promoted by a provision which enacted that officers should be retired from service on three-fourths of their sea pay after being forty-five years in the Navy, or on attaining the age of sixty-two years.

Towards the close of the year 1861, many important measures were recommended by the Secretary of the Navy for the improvement of the personnel of the service, which showed that he appreciated the claims of officers upon the country to which they were devoting their lives and energies.

Many officers of ability had left the Navy to cast their fortunes with the seceding States, and the result was a scarcity of officers for the vessels in service or about to go into commission. A law, therefore, passed Congress, authorizing the Secretary of the Navy to appoint from the mercantile marine for service during the war, persons who could pass satisfactory examinations and show that they possessed necessary qualifications.

In order to prepare the different classes of officers introduced into the Navy for " temporary service," schools of gunnery and naval-training were established at the different Navy Yards, where the appointees were kept busily employed under competent naval instructors learning the duties peculiar to the service.

It is with the greatest pleasure we state that the volunteer officers were, with very few exceptions, capable and patriotic; they offered their lives as freely for the preservation of the Union as did their comrades who had been brought up in the service. Composed as they were of the best material of the finest commercial marine in the world, the spirit and zeal with which they surrendered peaceful pursuits to undergo the severe discipline of the Navy, was honorable alike to themselves and to their country.

Should it ever be our good fortune once

more to build up a commercial marine such as we possessed at the outbreak of the Civil War, its officers will be our dependence in time of need to fill up the complement required by the addition of ships, that will then have to be made, to the Navy, and if they exhibit the same qualities evinced by the volunteer officers of the late war, the honor of our country will be safe in their hands.

The trained officers who are at present in the Navy would be a mere handful in case of a foreign war. They would serve as a nucleus and as instructors to those taken from the commercial marine. The cry of demagogues that the Navy is overburdened with officers, is as shallow as it is false, and should be treated with the contempt such misrepresentations deserve.

There was comparatively little opportunity during the year 1861, except at Hatteras and Port Royal, for the Navy to exhibit the zeal, courage and ability which it manifested at a later period. Yet in his report for that year, Mr. Secretary Welles pays the highest tribute of praise to the officers and men of the service.

The Honorable Secretary says:—" To the patriotic officers of the Navy and the brave men who in various scenes of naval action have served under them, the Department and the Government justly owe an acknowledgement even more earnest and emphatic. Courage, ability, unfaltering fidelity and devotion to the cause of their country, have been the general and noble characteristics of their conduct in the arduous and important service with which they have been intrusted. We state in all confidence, that in their hands the historic renown of the American Navy has been elevated and augmented."

This is not too much to say about the Navy, which even in the beginning of the civil war showed its determination to wrench from the grasp of the insurgents the property seized by them from the Government, and it is but just to the Secretary of the Navy, who paid its officers and men so high a tribute, to assert that he showed a spirit of loyalty and devotion to duty which was worthy of his high position, and that he met the very heavy responsibilities with which he was burdened with entire honesty of purpose, laboring faithfully to the end.

Mr. Welles made mistakes during the war, as any man in such a perplexing condition of affairs must have done, and was sometimes unjust, owing to intriguers who made representations against certain officers, by which the Secretary allowed himself to be influenced; but when left unbiased to the exercise of his own judgment he was as impartial as any man who would likely have been selected for his position.

CHAPTER IV.

DEATH OF ELLSWORTH. — CAPTURE OF ALEXANDRIA, VA. — POTOMAC FLOTILLA.

CONJECTURES AND UNCERTAINTIES. — SECESSIONISTS AND THE POTOMAC. — SECESSIONISTS ERECT BATTERIES IN SIGHT OF THE CAPITAL. — THE POTOMAC FLOTILLA ESTABLISHED. — LANDING OF ELLSWORTH ZOUAVES AT ALEXANDRIA. — DEATH OF ELLSWORTH. — COMMANDER ROWAN DEMANDS THE EVACUATION OF ALEXANDRIA. — ALEXANDRIA EVACUATED BY THE SECESSIONISTS. — BATTERIES AT AQUIA CREEK. — ARDUOUS DUTIES OF THE POTOMAC FLOTILLA. — ENGAGING THE BATTERIES AT AQUIA CREEK. — THE BATTERIES SILENCED. — THE "FREEBORN," "ANACOSTIA" AND "RESOLUTE." — RENEWAL OF THE ATTACK AGAINST THE AQUIA CREEK BATTERIES. — THE "FREEBORN" DAMAGED. — THE "BALL OPENED" ALONG THE POTOMAC. — ATTACK ON THE BATTERIES AT MATTHIAS POINT. — REPULSE OF THE FLOTILLA. — DEATH OF COMMANDER WARD. — SECESSIONISTS AND THEIR SUPPLIES. — LIEUT. HARREL DESTROYS A SCHOONER IN QUANTICO CREEK. — UNDESERVED CRITICISM OF THE FLOTILLA. — THE PUBLIC OBLIGED TO ACKNOWLEDGE THE VALUE OF THE FLOTILLA. — VESSELS ARRIVING FROM FOREIGN STATIONS. — OFFICERS RESIGNING, CASHIERED, ETC., ETC.

A T the commencement of the war, many wild conjectures were made as to its duration, and many of those who had hitherto stood high in the nation's opinion, were listened to anxiously, as if on their views depended the life and safety of the country, but as the war went on it was seen that the wisest statesmen and the ablest soldiers were at fault. Indeed, as events multiplied, the question of the Republic's future baffled all human ingenuity. That which all men predicted did not come to pass, and that which all declared impossible, was constantly being done, and our leaders were compelled to adopt measures they had before rejected, not only as unsound, but impossible.

It is not our province to write about matters concerning our Army, or about the immense line of insurrection which early in the war stretched across our country in chains of military posts within supporting distance of one another, but as these increased and Rebellion continued to raise its hydra head from Chesapeake Bay to Southwestern Missouri, it was found to be neces-

sary to increase the Navy, not only for the protection of our long line of sea-coast, but to guard our great lines of river transportation which the enemy was rapidly seizing upon for the purpose of strengthening their great lines of defence, the speedy maturing of their plans enabling them to get possession.

One of the first ideas of the Confederates was to get possession of the Potomac River, fortify its banks, and thereby cut off all communication between Washington and the sea. Their object was to prevent the transportation of troops from the North to the seat of government by sea, for as there was but one line of railroad between Baltimore and Washington, the Confederates were of the opinion that the North could not supply troops in sufficient numbers by that route; besides, at any moment, it might pass into the hands of the enemy. So satisfied were the rebels of this fact that they considered the fall of Washington as certain. The authorities of Maryland forbade the passage of troops across that State, heavy batteries were rapidly thrown up by the Confederates along the banks of the Potomac, and parties of rebel soldiers, with their colors flying, were in sight of the Capitol on the west bank of the river.

The first thing the Navy Department effected amidst all the difficulties of the situation, was the establishment of a flotilla of small steamers, armed with light guns, upon the Potomac.

It could hardly be supposed that the Navy would attempt, with these fragile vessels, to contend with the guns in battery on shore, or that they would be of any other service than that of patrolling the river, watching every movement of the enemy along the banks, and their operations; but those who are left to remember those days, will not forget the daily watchfulness, the sleepless nights, the sickly toil, and the hazardous character of the expeditions upon which the officers and crews of those vessels were engaged.

COMMANDER JAMES H. WARD.

The first landing of Northern troops upon the Virginian shore was under cover of these improvised gun-boats, when the gallant Ellsworth landed with his Zouave regiment at Alexandria, and went to almost instant death at the hands of an assassin— an event which, unimportant as it was compared with others at the time, so fired the Northern heart that it added thousands of soldiers to our armies.

In this case Alexandria was evacuated by the Confederates upon demand of a naval officer—Commander S. C. Rowan— commanding the "Pawnee," carrying a battery of fifteen guns, and when Ellsworth's troops were landed the American flag was hoisted on the Custom House and other prominent places by the officer in charge of a landing party of sailors—Lieutenant R. B. Lowry.

This, though not a very important achievement, gave indication of the feelings of the Navy, and how ready was the service to put down secession on the first opportunity offered.

The death of Ellsworth created a great impression upon the minds of the naval officers and sailors from its brutal accompaniments, and showed them forcibly that treason would only carry in its train rapine and murder, with all the horrors attending vindicative warfare.

As early as the last of May, 1861, the Confederates had completed three batteries on the Potomac, at Aquia Creek—railroad terminus—and others above and about the landing. The guns mounted in these works were mostly rifles, giving the Confederates an advantage over our vessels, which mounted only smooth-bore thirty-two-pounders.

As the Government had already, on several occasions, shown great decision, it is remarkable that it did not at once proceed to put down this work of the Confederates in fortifying the commanding points of the Potomac, but there seemed to have been an indisposition on its part at that moment to take any hostile action; and amidst the daily increasing confusion of affairs which startled the Nation, even the Navy Department did not exhibit an unusual activity.

The Potomac flotilla was chiefly engaged in moving up and down the river, gaining information of the enemy's movements, convoying transports to and from Washington, often fired upon, and only able to return the fire without much effect, and with no power to land and capture the batteries for want of a proper landing force— which had been declined by General Scott whenever application had been made to him. It was a national disgrace, and bespoke the weakness of a country when, at the very outset of the war, a great highway—the Potomac—could be closed, and our own people slaughtered in transit by these rebel batteries, which seemed to increase in numbers with a rapidity never conceived of, while it appeared as if they had all the military depots of the country to draw from.

It was at last determined by the Department that the Potomac flotilla should take the initiative, and make an effort to clear the river banks of the rebel batteries.

Commander James H. Ward, an energetic officer, had been placed in command of the flotilla, and on the 20th of May, 1861, he started to engage the batteries at Aquia Creek, with no expectation, we imagine, of any great success against them with the small and fragile vessels under his command. These consisted of the "Freeborn," a paddle-wheel steamer of two hundred and fifty tons, and carrying three guns; the "Anacostia," a small screw steamer of two hundred tons, and the "Resolute," a small craft of ninety tons and two guns.

The largest gun on board this little squadron was a thirty-two pounder, most of the others being small howitzers. The impoverished condition of the Navy may be imagined when it had to depend upon such craft as these to crush a rebellion, while two or three thousand rebel troops were in the field with batteries against them.

No one who knew anything about such matters would form any favorable idea of succeeding against land batteries with this small flotilla, but notwithstanding the disparity of force, the batteries were silenced altogether in two hours, and the Secessionists driven to their earthworks on the hills overlooking the landing. These hills proved too high for the elevation to be obtained from the guns of the vessels, and the enemy's shot falling all around them without chance of return, the flotilla was withdrawn out of range. Little damage was done to the vessels, the enemy not proving to be very good marksmen.

keeping up an incessant fire for five hours, only ceasing upon the over-fatigue of his men. The enemy were again driven out of their works, but carried their artillery away with them. Some damage was done the flotilla, and the "Freeborn" was obliged in consequence to go to Washington for repairs ; there was no loss of life, nor were there any wounded on this occasion.

The flotilla had been increased by the "Pawnee," Commander Rowan, who had reported on the previous evening. More than a thousand shot were fired by the enemy, but though a number struck the hulls of the vessels, there was no irreparable damage done. This little affair may be said to have "opened the ball" along the banks of the Potomac, and it gave the Secessionists some idea of what they might expect in the future under the energetic management of Commander Ward; but unfortunately the career of that officer was cut short soon

ATTACK ON THE AQUAIA CREEK BATTERIES BY THE U. S. STEAMERS "FREEBORN," "ANACOSTIA" AND "RESOLUTE."

This was, I believe, the first battle of the war where the enemy's batteries were engaged by the Navy, and though not an important affair, it marks an era in the struggle which shows how remiss our Government had been up to that time in not having in the Navy a class of vessels suitable for just such occasions as this, and how poor indeed was our merchant marine when it could provide nothing better than the "Freeborn," "Anacostia" and the "Resolute"— three high-sounding names, which seem now so insignificant beside the "Miantonomoh," "Puritan," etc., vessels that eventually revolutionized the navies of the world, and made us, at one time, as regards the defence of our coast, equal if not superior to England and France.

On the following day Commander Ward resumed the engagement at Aquia Creek,

after in the attack on Matthias Point, when he attempted to disperse some batteries, having also made preparations to land; but in the heat of the action, and while sighting a gun, he was shot in the abdomen and soon after died. The Navy lost a gallant officer, whose example would have inspired his men to deeds of daring if any example was needed, for it was a noticeable fact that the blue-jackets of the Navy were up with the foremost in their devotion to the flag, and viewed these hostile movements on the Potomac against the government with something akin to horror. Let us remark here, that, during the war, we do not remember an instance where a sailor was found untrue to the flag of the Union, or where one ever hesitated to volunteer for an expedition, no matter how dangerous it was.

In the affair at Matthias Point our party was overwhelmed by numbers, and Lieutenant Chaplin of the "Pawnee," who had charge of a landing party, only succeeded in bringing off his men by his coolness and intrepidity under a perfect shower of bullets. In those days, when the war was in its infancy, the soldiers of both sides lacked that precision of fire which they acquired later in the contest, and which made the battles so bloody. But for this our repulse at Matthias Point would have been a bloody one, indeed.

Criticism of this expedition is disarmed when we reflect that the gallant officer who planned it sacrificed his own life in the performance of a duty he considered necessary to clear the Potomac of the bushwhackers that lined the banks of the stream all along, and were firing on unarmed merchant vessels and transports as they pursued their course up or down.

small affairs which took place on the river rose to importance from the fact that there was then no other field of naval enterprize.

So great were the facilities of communication between the shores of Virginia and Maryland that the Secessionists could hold intercourse with their friends in the latter State by means of small boats, and obtain not only information, but supplies of all kinds, including munitions of war which the Marylanders were too willing to provide them with. Hence it became a necessity not only to guard every salient point on the river, but to capture all boats that were secreted in the numerous creeks and nooks with which the river abounded.

This duty, apparently insignificant, was

SKIRMISH BETWEEN THE "FREEBORN" AND "RESOLUTE" AND A SECESSION FORCE, AT MATTHIAS POINT.—DEATH OF CAPTAIN WARD.—JUNE 27, 1861.

Had Commander Ward lived, he would have made as high a mark as any officer in the Navy; no one ever entered the contest with more zeal and activity than he, and to this day the shock of his death has not been forgotten, though thousands died afterwards on more important occasions.

It was only when these deaths of gallant officers occurred that the country began to realize the Secessionists were animated with a fell purpose which would not be appeased until the whole land was saturated with blood and sorrow walked over the battle-fields where friends and foes lay mingled together in the arms of death.

The Potomac naturally became the first theatre of war as regards the Navy, for the Department at that moment had no ships with which to operate elsewhere, and some

in fact most important, for the mischief carried on by these small boats, which performed postal service and transported spies back and forth, was so constant that it was necessary to repress it if possible.

On the 11th of October, Lieutenant A. D. Harrel was informed that a large schooner was lying in Quantico Creek, and that a body of troops had assembled there for the purpose of crossing the Potomac, and he determined to make an attempt to destroy her.

He manned three boats, and under cover of darkness, started up the creek, boarded the schooner and set her on fire, then pulled away under a heavy volley of musketry from the rebel soldiers. The vessel was totally destroyed, and the crossing of the Secessionists put a stop to.

In all this river service performed by officers of the Navy there was great peril, and no hope of reward held out as remuneration for the risk of life. Every covert on the banks of the river held men in ambush, and many unerring riflemen, who would wait until our people atttempted to land, or came near their place of concealment, when they would pull trigger on them with as much malignity as if firing upon the bloodiest pirates instead of conservators of the peace. They seemed to forget altogether that the men they were slaying not long before may have met them in amity at the festive board.

Such was the strife already begun, and it could not be hoped that it would diminish as the war progressed.

In this river work, as in all other where the Navy was called upon to act, it performed its duty with unflinching courage. The public did not know what the service had to contend with, or how much good work they were actually doing; with all their discomforts, toil and suffering they received but little commendation; the country was too busy watching the black clouds gathering in the South and West to note the ordinary events that were taking place on the Potomac, yet they formed the small links in the chain which, in the end, shackled the arms of the great rebellion.

A steamer captain coming up the river would be fired upon from some point where there were none of the flotilla in sight, and though he might receive no damage whatever, he would make complaints of what he called the useless Potomac Flotilla, which complaints would find their way to the papers, with the usual result of abuse; but in the end the public were obliged to acknowledge the value of the service, for though the intercourse between the opposite banks of the river could not be altogether prevented, it was made so harrassing and dangerous to those who followed it that its effectiveness was destroyed.

The Secessionists, finding they could neither close the river against the Government transports, nor keep it open for their friends, abandoned the plan of erecting batteries, and in 1862 withdrew from the line of the Potomac River. The patrol of the Potomac was, however, carried on by the Navy during nearly all the war, and though the river had been freed of the hostile batteries, the duties of the officers and men still remained more or less hazardous.

The public, as a general rule, are not attracted by events which have not some brilliancy in them ; they read only of battles by land and sea ; they never then stopped to consider the importance of such tedious work as occurred on the great highway from Washington to the sea, nor did they ever seem to reflect that if the river was once closed the very life of the Union would be imperilled. It was only in reading over the accounts of a successful battle that they became really interested in the subject, and their minds rested simply on the central figure of the successful chief, who monopolized for the moment all the glory.

Few ever thought of all the toil and hardships officers and men had to undergo to win one of these battles, or cared what became of the workers and sufferers in the conflict. Nor, while carried away with the glamour of a great contest, did they ever reflect upon the dead and wounded, who, to secure victory, had given up their life's blood that their country might live, and the time-honored flag under which they received their first inspirations of glory might float proudly at the peak, without a stain to dim its stripes and stars.

While these apparently unimportant matters were carried on along the Potomac, the Navy Department was putting forth all its energy to get every ship to sea ; vessels were beginning to arrive from foreign stations, many of the officers tinctured with secession sentiments, and handing in their resignations, some departing without, and being cashiered : about two hundred and fifty in all leaving the Navy. The ships, after undergoing hasty repairs, were put into commission as soon as possible, and from this time commenced that series of brilliant actions which gave the Navy a name it will never lose, and which ought to make it dear to the heart of every true American.

CHAPTER V.

CAPTURE OF THE WORKS AT HATTERAS INLET BY FLAG OFFICER STRINGHAM.—DESTRUCTION OF THE PRIVATEER "JUDAH."

DETERMINATION OF LINCOLN TO REGAIN POSSESSION OF THE SOUTHERN PORTS AND HARBORS.—A BOARD OF EMINENT CIVILIANS AND NAVAL OFFICERS CONVENED.—THE SOUNDS OF NORTH CAROLINA, THEIR DEFENCES, ETC.—HATTERAS INLET.—A SQUADRON FITTED OUT TO CAPTURE HATTERAS INLET.—VESSELS COMPOSING THE SQUADRON AND THEIR COMMANDERS.—COMMODORE STRINGHAM.—THE SQUADRON LEAVES HAMPTON ROADS.—THE SQUADRON ANCHORS AT HATTERAS ISLAND.—BOMBARDMENT AND CAPTURE OF FORTS HATTERAS AND CLARK.—THE GARRISON SURRENDER TO GENERAL BUTLER AND COMMODORE STRINGHAM.—EFFECT OF THE CAPTURE OF FORTS HATTERAS AND CLARK ON THE CONFEDERATES.—DESTRUCTION OF FORT OCRACOKE.—THE PAMLICO AND ALBEMARLE SOUNDS.—COLONEL HAWKINS SENDS A REGIMENT TO TAKE POSSESSION OF CHICACOMICO.—CAPTURE OF THE TRANSPORT "FANNY" BY CONFEDERATE STEAMERS.—PLANS OF THE CONFEDERATES FRUSTRATED.—COLONEL BROWN AND COLONEL HAWKINS JOIN HANDS.—THE "MONTICELLO" RENDERS GOOD SERVICE.—DISASTROUS RETREAT OF THE CONFEDERATES.—CUTTING OUT OF THE CONFEDERATE PRIVATEER "JUDAH."

IT was evident to any one who had studied the subject, that the United States Government could make no headway against the Confederates while the seaports and their defences remained in the hands of the latter. From the beginning President Lincoln had boldly avowed his purpose to regain possession of all the Southern ports and harbors.

A board of eminent civilians and naval officers had been convened by the Navy Department to consider the whole subject, and report upon the best means of approaching and attacking the ports then in the possession of the Secessionists; and the result of their labors, when placed in the hands of the Secretary of the Navy, was of great service in enabling the Department promptly to take proper measures for the recapture of the ports along the Southern coast.

From the beginning the Secessionists had appreciated the necessity of securing possession of the Sounds of North Carolina and defending their approaches against our gunboats. There is in this region a network of channels communicating with the Chowan, Neuse and Roanoke Rivers by which any amount of stores and munitions of war could be sent by blockade runners to supply the South.

The numerous inlets are navigable for light draft vessels, but owing to their shallow water our vessels of war could not penetrate them.

The main channel for entering the Sounds was Hatteras Inlet, and here the enemy had thrown up heavy earthworks to protect the most important smuggling route then in operation; for, although Charleston and Mobile were considered important ports for smuggling supplies to the South, Hatteras Inlet was none the less so.

For the purpose of capturing the defences of Hatteras Inlet a squadron under command of Commodore Stringham was fitted out. It consisted of the "Minnesota," Captain Van Brunt, "Wabash," Captain Mercer, "Monticello," Commander J. P. Gillis, "Susquehanna," Captain Chauncey, "Pawnee," Commander Rowan, "Cumberland," Captain Marston, and the Revenue Steamer "Harriet Lane," Captain Faunce.

Three transports accompanied the squadron. The "Adelaide," Commander Stell-wagen, "George Peabody," Lieut.-Com-manding Lowry, and the "Fanny," Lieut.-Commanding Crosby. They carried about 900 troops under command of Major-General B. F. Butler.

On the 27th of August, 1861, the day after leaving Hampton Roads, the squad-

five on shipboard, but even this allowance made the squadron superior to the forts, without considering the heavier guns and better equipments of the frigates.

Part of the troops landed on the island under cover of the guns of the squadron, and at 8:45 on the morning of the 28th, the battle commenced. The "Wabash," of fifty

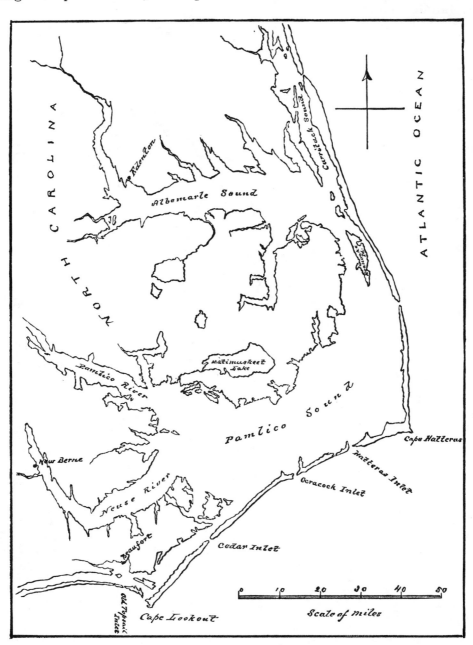

THE SOUNDS OF NORTH CAROLINA.

ron anchored off Hatteras Island, on the extreme southwestern point of which were Forts Hatteras and Clark, separated by a shallow bay, half a mile wide. Of these works Fort Hatteras was the larger, and together they mounted twenty-five guns.

In those days of wooden ships one gun mounted on shore was considered equal to

guns, with the "Cumberland" in tow and followed by the "Minnesota," stood in to-wards Fort Clark and opened fire, and were soon joined by the "Susquehanna."

The plan of attack, although afterwards followed in several cases during the Civil War, was not the best calculated to bring an engagement to a speedy conclusion. The vessels were kept in motion in a circle or ellipse, passing and repassing the enemy's works.

The plan has the advantage of bothering the enemy's gunners, as the ships are constantly changing their range, but it detracts from the accuracy of the fire on board the vessels and it tends to lengthen out an engagement. At Hatteras what should have been finished in six hours required twenty-four to accomplish.

In our opinion had all the larger vessels anchored in line abreast of the forts, with the smaller vessels on their flanks, the enemy's batteries would have been quickly silenced. As it was the people in the forts were almost smothered by the fire from the frigates, and their aim made so uncertain, that little damage was done to the ships. Shortly after noon the Confederate flags had disappeared from both forts, and the enemy were evidently abandoning Fort Clark, on which our troops moved up the beach and hoisted the Union flag on that work.

Fort Hatteras still kept up the fire, and at night the squadron hauled off.

At 7:30, on the morning of the 29th, the ships again opened on Fort Hatteras, and continued the fire with vigor until 11:10, when a white flag was displayed by the enemy.

Although the reduction of these works was not a very great achievement for a squadron mounting 158 guns, yet the work was well done, and little damage was received from the enemy.

As soon as the white flag was shown from Fort Hatteras, some of the light draft vessels entered the inlet and drove off the reinforcements that were evidently endeavoring to reach the forts.

At 2:30 P. M. General Butler went on board Com. Stringham's flagship, taking with him Flag Officer Samuel Barron, C. S. N., commanding naval defences of Virginia

COMMODORE SILAS H. STRINGHAM, U. S. N.

(AFTERWARDS REAR ADMIRAL.)

and N. Carolina, Col. Martin, 7th Reg., N. C. Infantry, and Col. Andrews, commanding Forts Hatteras and Clark, who had surrendered unconditionally with their commands.

Soon after the Commodore proceeded in the "Minnesota" to New York, where all the prisoners were transferred to Governor's Island.

This was our first naval victory, indeed our first victory of any kind, and should not be forgotten. The Union cause was then in a depressed condition, owing to the reverses it had experienced. The moral effect of this affair was very great, as it gave us a foothold on Southern soil and possession of the Sounds of North Carolina, if we chose to occupy them. It was a death-blow to blockade running in that vicinity, and ultimately proved one of the

"Pawnee," who rendered useless twenty-two guns and a quantity of munitions of war.

The closing of these inlets to the Sounds of North Carolina sent the blockade runners elsewhere to find entrance to Southern markets, but as channel after channel was closed the smugglers' chances diminished and the labors of the blockading vessels were much reduced.

The great value of the Albemarle and Pamlico Sounds may be judged by reference to subsequent events, when they formed a base of operations for the enemy which we found it extremely difficult to

PAWNEE. MINNESOTA. CUMBERLAND. SUSQUEHANNA.   FORT CLARK.

HARRIET LANE. WABASH.

CAPTURE OF THE FORTS AT HATTERAS INLET.—FLEET OPENING FIRE AND BOATS LANDING THROUGH THE SURF.

AUGUST 28, 1861.

most important events of the war; and if we recall the pertinacity with which the Confederates fought for these Sounds, even to the end of the war, we can appreciate the value they placed upon them.

To prevent Hatteras Inlet from again falling into the hands of the Confederates, the forts were garrisoned, although difficult to hold owing to unforeseen circumstances.

Fort Ocracoke, on the inlet of that name, twenty miles south of Hatteras, was abandoned by the enemy soon after the fall of Forts Hatteras and Clark, and was destroyed by a party from the U. S. S.

break up, and it was not until the Navy had been largely increased by the addition of the proper kind of vessels, that the United States Government was able to get possession of all the important points in the Sounds.

"The subsequent operations upon Pamlico and Albemarle Sounds and their rivers show how important a base these formed for the Confederates, and how difficult it would have been to crush the rebellion had they remained in their possession."

Colonel Hawkins, who had been left in command of Fort Hatteras after its capture, found his position to be an uncomfortable and dangerous one.

The troops were subjected to annoying privations and dangerous exposure, and on one occasion narrowly escaped capture by the Confederates.

On September 29th, 1861, Colonel Hawkins sent the 20th Indiana Regiment to take possession of and fortify Chicamacomico, the northern point of Hatteras Island.

As soon as the Confederates learned the true condition of affairs, they conceived the bold design not only of capturing the six hundred men of the Indiana regiment, but of retaking the forts at Hatteras. Their plan was to land a large body of men above the Union regiment and another below, between them and Hatteras, and thus render

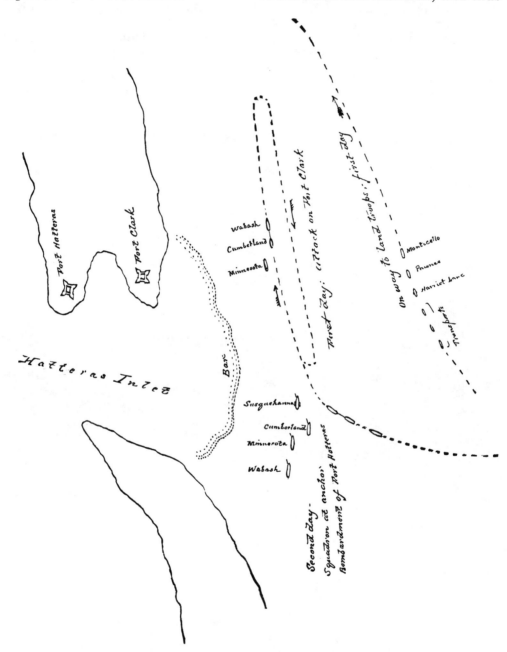

PLAN OF THE ATTACK ON FORTS HATTERAS AND CLARK, AUGUST 28TH AND 29TH, 1861.

These troops were but partially equipped and scantily provisioned, their supplies being sent the next day in the army transport "Fanny." Just as this vessel arrived she was met by three Confederate steamers, but their true character was not known until they opened fire, and but few of the "Fanny's" crew escaped.

retreat impossible and their capture certain. At the same time a fleet of light steamers was to pass quickly down the Sound and make a sudden attack upon the forts at the inlet.

But for unforeseen events they might perhaps have succeeded.

The Confederates having collected ten

transports, six steamers, one cotton-barge and two flat boats, carrying in all about 3,000 men, commenced their movement on the 4th of October, intending to land a part above and a part below the Indiana encampment.

Colonel Brown, commanding the Union troops, divided his forces also, intending to fight the enemy at the two points threatened, but at this juncture he received peremptory orders to retreat, and as he was now some distance from his camp and there was no time to lose, he was obliged to start on a march of forty miles without supplies of any kind.

had been re-enforced, the Confederates began a retreat up the island which proved far more disastrous to them than that of the Union troops had been, for they were at once pursued, not by marching troops, but by a gun-boat, following them on the outside of the island.

This steamer was the "Monticello," commanded by Lieutenant D. L. Braine, and she rendered good service on this occasion by inflicting heavy loss upon the enemy, and driving him on board his vessels in a thoroughly demoralized condition.

The Confederates, when first seen from the "Monticello," were marching along the

INTERIOR OF FORT HATTERAS AFTER THE BOMBARDMENT.

The Confederate steamers attempted to cut off his retreat by landing troops about eighteen miles below, and it now seemed to be reduced to a question of speed between steamers, and men wading through the loose and scorching sand.

The Confederate flotilla, however, was delayed by some of the boats getting aground, and their troops were not landed until after dark. Captain Brown, passing the fleet without being perceived, reached Hatteras light-house after a day of intense suffering and fatigue, and was soon re-enforced by Colonel Hawkins' regiment sent up from the forts to his relief.

Upon learning that the Indiana regiment

narrow strip of sand in close order, and being entirely without cover offered an excellent mark for the Union gunners.

The "Monticello's" fire was very well directed, and the bursting shells caused great havoc in the ranks of the enemy.

They soon broke and ran, many of them taking refuge in a clump of woods abreast of their steamers.

The Confederate vessels at once sent boats to bring off the troops, and as they neared the shore the soldiers rushed wildly into the water, having lost all idea of order or discipline in their great eagerness to escape.

Two of the boats loaded with men were

struck by shells and sent to the bottom, several officers were killed, and the shore for a distance of four miles was strewn with killed or wounded.

The Confederate steamers fired several times across the island at the "Monticello," but their projectiles fell short and they soon desisted. Lieutenant Braine continued his attack until 5:25 P. M., when, as he was running short of ammunition and the enemy were completely scattered and disorganized, he decided to withdraw.

DESTRUCTION OF THE PRIVATEER SCHOONER "JUDAH."

There is always an excitement in a cutting-out expedition that does not exist in any circumstances, have been successful without any serious loss to the boarding party; but under whatever circumstances it may be undertaken, a "cutting-out" party is always attended with the greatest peril.

When Fort Pickens was fully manned and all the guns mounted necessary to give it a superiority over the batteries of General Bragg on the navy yard side, it was supposed that Pensacola was hermetically sealed, not only against the entrance of blockade runners, but that Pickens would prevent the exit of any hostile vessel intended to prey upon American commerce.

But this was not the case—notwithstanding that the guns of Fort Pickens commanded all the works under General Bragg,

DESTRUCTION OF FORT OCRACOKE, ON BEACON ISLAND, BY A PARTY FROM THE U. S. S. "PAWNEE.

other service during war, and many events of that kind which happened in the American and British navies hold a larger place in the memory of old sailors than some more important achievements.

One of these cutting-out expeditions took place in the harbor of Pensacola, and is worthy to be chronicled in history, for from all accounts it was a gallant affair, and most creditable to those who commanded and executed it.

There is no act in naval science requiring more skill, courage, dash and judgment than the cutting out of an armed vessel in an open roadstead. or under the guns of a ship or fort. Some of these have been at times connected with scenes of terrible slaughter; others, by taking advantage of favorable and could have knocked them to pieces in the course of a few hours. The Confederates did not seem to attach much importance to the Union fort or its auxilliary works, and it was reported to Commodore Mervin, the commander of the naval forces off Pensacola, that the schooner "Judah" was fitting out at the Pensacola Navy Yard as a privateer to prey upon our commerce. This vessel had been seen from day to day lying in a small basin formed by the Navy Yard on one side, and a dock on the other. She could be seen from the fort and her daily progress noted, as her rigging was being fitted and other preparations being made towards sending her to sea—but not a protest was made by the guns of Fort Pickens against this cool proceeeding of fitting out a privateer right in the sight of the fort, and in reach of its shot and shell.

This vessel had been watched for some time by the officers of the squadron lying four miles outside, and Commodore Mervin determined to make an effort to destroy her, knowing the damage she would commit if once permitted to get out to sea.

The schooner was secured in such a position that it was very difficult for an attacking party to get at her without great exposure to themselves. The Confederates concluded that they had made her so safe that no naval force would undertake to cut her out, and General Bragg evidently attached little importance to the guns of Fort Pickens—a 10-inch Columbiad and a 12-pound field-piece, were mounted so as to command the schooner's deck and also the wharf, to which she was secured by chains—and it was reported that there were a thousand soldiers stationed in and about the yard ready to repel any number of boats that might attempt to approach the wharves. To attack the schooner under such circumstances was a perilous undertaking, but Commodore Mervin considered the destruction of this privateer of so much importance as to warrant the risk of a failure and the loss of men.

On the night of the 13th September a boat expedition was fitted out from the frigate " Colorado," consisting of the following boats : first launch, Lieut. J. H. Russell, commanding the expedition, 39 men ; first cutter, Lieut. J. G. Sproston, 18 men ; second cutter, F. B. Blake, 26 men ; third cutter, Midshipman J. Steece, 17 men ; in all the expedition there were 100 officers, sailors and marines.

The plan was for Lieut. Sproston and Midshipman Steece to land with their boats' crews and (if possible) spike the two guns mounted in the yard, while at the same time Lieuts. Russell and Blake were to attack and carry the schooner.

The attack was made on the morning of the 14th September, 1861, at 3 o'clock A. M. The schooner was found moored to the wharf, one pivot gun and two in broadside mounted, with all her crew on board ready to repel boarders.

The boats were discovered and hailed. When about one hundred yards from the wharf the sentry gave the alarm by firing his gun, and immediately after followed a volley from the schooner's deck. The sailors sprang to their oars, and in less time than one could think Lieuts. Sproston and Steece from their respective boats sprung upon the wharf, followed by their men, and made a rush to find the guns—the other boats boarding the schooner. Only one man was found guarding the guns, and he was shot down by gunner Bireton as he was in the act of firing on Lieut. Sproston, both weapons going off at the same time. In the darkness the party became separated, and Lieut. Sproston and the gunner succeeded in finding the guns, which they immediately spiked.

Then came the contest for the schooner, which was a severe one while it lasted. In addition to the crew on deck some of the Confederates had gotten into the fore-top, from whence they poured a destructive fire upon the boats, while a hand-to-hand fight took place on the deck; but the sailors soon drove the crew of the schooner to the wharf, where they rallied, and being joined by the guard on shore (which had marched to the rescue) they kept up a continuous fire on the boarding party.

While this fight was going on, parties of the expedition were engaged in setting fire to the schooner, as it was found to be impossible to move her. An effectual fire was kindled in the cabin by Assistant-Engineer White and a coal-heaver named Patrick Driscoll. The "Judah" was soon in flames, and as there was no prospect of doing anything more, the boarding party shoved off.

By this time a large force of the enemy began to collect in the Navy Yard, and opened fire on the boats, but the officers and men, nothing daunted, returned the fire on the disorganized crowd with two howitzers loaded with grape and canister, firing six rounds before they were out of range of the enemy's sharpshooters. All this time the schooner was burning rapidly, with a great blaze, by the light of which the sailors could see where the enemy had posted themselves on shore, and they were soon scattered. The schooner blazed up so rapidly that she soon broke from her moorings and, having burnt to the water's edge, floated off and sank opposite to Fort Barrancas. The boats remained near the place until it was certain that the " Judah " would never be of any more service to the Confederates, and then returned to the " Colorado " which they reached at daylight. Here they were welcomed with that heartiness which belongs to the sailors, who were on the alert to greet their chums and look after wounded messmates.

To show the dangerous character of this expedition and the severity of the encounter, nearly one fifth of the boarding party were either killed or wounded; but the regrets that were felt for the loss of the gallant fellows who fell were somewhat compensated for (in the minds of the sailors) by the fact that their comrades had met the death of brave men fighting for the country they loved better than their lives.

This was without doubt the most gallant cutting-out affair that occurred during the war. The boarding party had not only the crew of the schooner to contend with, but there was a force of over a thousand troops stationed a short distance off, that could be called upon at a moment's notice to drive away intruders. There was every prospect of a failure when the party started out, and no certainty whatever of success. It was one of those cases where men carried their lives in their hands, and no one there had a right to hope that he would return scatheless from such a daring adventure. The young officers who went out on this expedition have since that time been engaged in some momentous battles, but in none of them did they run such risks or require more nerve than on the night of the 13th of September, 1861, when they boarded and set fire to the schooner "Judah" and sent her, in flames, drifting down the harbor, as a proof of what American officers and seamen were willing to undertake to put down rebellion and uphold the majesty of the law. Those officers and men may think that their brave act has been forgotten amid the grander events that dazzled the imagination; but its completeness has given it a place in history it should never lose, and in after years when millions yet unborn realize what they owe to the Navy for the work performed during an intestine war to save this galaxy of States from disruption, the burning of the "Judah," with all its attendant gallantry, will be read with as much avidity as any action of the kind that took place during the war.

CHAPTER VI.

NAVAL EXPEDITION AGAINST PORT ROYAL AND CAPTURE OF THAT PLACE.

COMMANDER RODGERS.—RIVER STEAMERS FITTED AND ARMED AS GUN-BOATS.—COMMENCE-
MENT OF THE MISSISSIPPI SQUADRON.—CAPTAIN A. H. FOOTE ORDERED TO COMMAND
THE WESTERN FLOTILLA.—JAMES B. EADS.—COMMODORE STRINGHAM RELIEVED.—COM-
MANDS GIVEN TO FLAG OFFICERS DUPONT AND MCKEAN.—THE PORT ROYAL EXPEDITION
FITTED OUT.—ASSEMBLING OF THE SHIPS OF WAR AND TRANSPORTS AT HAMPTON
ROADS.—FRAIL SHIPS.—THE EXPEDITION REACHES PORT ROYAL HARBOR.—GREAT
SUFFERINGS OF OFFICERS AND MEN.—RECONNOISSANCE BY COMMANDER RODGERS AND
BRIGADIER-GENERAL WRIGHT—BATTLE OF PORT ROYAL.—THE BATTERIES AT HILTON
HEAD OPEN FIRE.—FORTS WALKER AND BEAUREGARD.—ORDER OF BATTLE.—LIST OF
VESSELS COMPRISING THE FIGHTING SQUADRON.—COMMODORE TATNALL WITHDRAWS.—
LOYALTY OF COMMANDER PERCIVAL DRAYTON.—EVACUATION OF FORT WALKER BY THE
CONFEDERATES.—TREACHEROUS FOES.—EXPLOSION OF A TORPEDO LEFT BEHIND BY THE
CONFEDERATES.—CAPTURE OF FORT BEAUREGARD.—PRISONERS TURNED OVER TO GEN-
ERAL T. W. SHERMAN.—NAVAL BATTLES CONTRASTED.—SHERMAN'S LEGIONS.—DUPONT'S
EMINENCE AS A COMMANDER.—ATTEMPTS TO DESPOIL DUPONT OF HIS HONORS.—DU-
PONT'S HIGH COMMENDATION OF HIS OFFICERS.—GENERAL SHERMAN'S HEADQUARTERS
SECURELY ESTABLISHED AT HILTON HEAD.—TATNALL ESCAPES.—COLONEL GILMORE'S
RECONNOISSANCE.—RESULTS OF THE LOSS OF THE NORFOLK NAVY YARD.

OWING to the increase of the Confederate forces in the States of Tennessee, Kentucky and Missouri, it became necessary to fit out armed vessels on the Western rivers. In May, 1861, Commander John Rodgers, U. S. N., was directed to report to the War Department, which in the early stages of the conflict practically assumed the control of the Western flotilla, although the vessels were under command of naval officers.

Commander Rodgers proceeded at once to the West and purchased a number of river steamers, which were fitted and armed as gunboats; and this was the commencement of the Mississippi Squadron which afterwards performed such efficient service for the Union.

Captain Andrew H. Foote was afterwards ordered to the command of the flotilla, which under him swelled to the proportions of a fleet, all his talents and energies being devoted to the task of making it a formidable force such as the necessities

of the case demanded. In this work Captain Foote was assisted by that distinguished engineer, James B. Eads, who planned and built that class of ironclads known on the Mississippi as "turtle backs," which gave such a good account of themselves during the war, and fought their way through many a bloody encounter, from Fort Henry to Grand Gulf, Port Hudson and the Red River.

After the capture of Fort Hatteras, Commodore Stringham was relieved of the command at his own request. Two squadrons were organized on the Atlantic coast, one to guard the shores of Virginia and North Carolina under Flag Officer L. M. Goldsborough; the Southern Squadron, extending from South Carolina to the Capes of Florida, was assigned to Flag Officer S. F. Dupont, and the Gulf Squadron to Flag Officer W. W. McKean.

Although the capture of the ports at Hatteras Inlet was an important achievement, yet it did not accomplish all the Navy Department aimed at.

There was no entrance to the Sounds except for vessels of very light draft of water, and there was no harbor in the vicinity where a depot could be established for large vessels to carry on operations along the Southern coast.

A depot was required for supplying coal, provisions and stores at a point where our ships could find safe anchorage at all times, and where machine shops and docks could be constructed for refitting vessels.

The work of supplying vessels was one of vital importance, and a harbor was also

and so well aware were the Confederates of its importance that one of their first acts was to fortify it against the entrance of our ships.

It was determined by the Government to fit out a naval expedition against Port Royal under command of Flag Officer Dupont, reinforced by an Army corps under General T. W. Sherman.

Notwithstanding that the greatest precautions were taken to keep the proposed expedition a secret, the Confederates ascertained that a movement against Port Royal was on

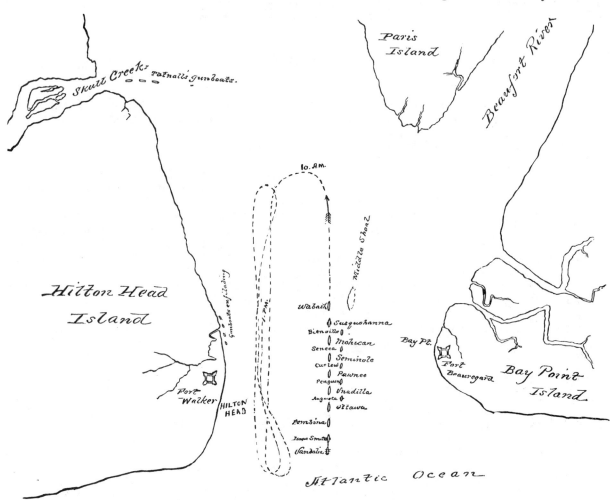

PLAN OF THE ATTACK ON FORTS WALKER AND BEAUREGARD, NOVEMBER 7, 1861.

needed as a base of operations against the whole Southern States.

The choice of harbors lay between Bull's Bay, Port Royal, Brunswick and Fernandina. The latter, for some reasons, was considered an available place, but finally the Department concurred in the opinion of Flag Officer Dupont that Port Royal contained all the required advantages.

Port Royal is one of the finest harbors in the United States, with water sufficient for the largest vessels. It is about equidistant between Charleston and Savannah,

foot, and with their accustomed energy prepared to receive it by mounting all the guns they could collect, with a proper force to man them.

By the 27th October, 1861, all the ships of war, transports for troops, and supply vessels had assembled at Hampton Roads, presenting a formidable appearance. They numbered fifty sail, not including twenty-five coal vessels which had sailed the day previous.

Never before in our history had any officer command of so large a fleet.

The weather had been unpleasant for some time, but now gave promise of a change for the better; and when on the 29th the signal went up from the flag-ship "Wabash"—"underway to get"—the sounds all through the fleet showed that sailors and soldiers were equally glad to move towards the scenes of glory that opened before them.

By the time the expedition reached Fort Hatteras it came on to blow a gale, which increased to a hurricane, scattering the fleet in every direction. On the fourth day out there was but one vessel to be seen from the deck of the flag-ship.

What were the feelings of Flag-officer Dupont on that occasion can be imagined. Many of the naval vessels were far from staunch. The transports, of course, were still weaker, and it was doubtful if half of them would ever be seen again.

The sufferings of the men on board the transports, the decks of which were swept by the heavy seas, were extreme and but little appreciated by those on shore who afterwards read the vivid accounts of these hardships.

Such sufferings are part of the unwritten history of the war, which because they are not surrounded by the glamor of battle have but little interest for the public.

Who is there that in reading an account of these scenes of suffering and disaster which often overtake naval and military expeditions, ever realize the sufferings of officers and men battling for their lives against the stormy ocean?

Certainly the soldiers in these transports would have dared a dozen battles on shore, rather than experience one such night of storm as raged around their vessels.

A better seaman than Dupont never trod a ship's deck, but he could do nothing for that scattered fleet; he could only trust to his subordinates, whom he knew would do all that was possible to avert disaster.

All things have an end, and the gale which had so jeopardized the expedition at length abated with less damage to the fleet than might have been expected. On the morning of the 4th of November, 1861, twenty-five vessels in company with the flag-ship "Wabash," came to anchor off the bar of Port Royal, while the remainder of the squadron were continually heaving in sight.

Although the gale was over, the safety of the expedition was by no means assured. The bar or shoalest water at the entrance of Port Royal extended ten miles out to sea. All buoys and other guides to the navigator had been removed.

As soon as the flag-ship came to anchor Captain C. H. Davis, Chief of Staff, and Assistant Boutelle of the Coast Survey, pro-ceeded in search of the channel, which by three P. M. was sounded out and buoyed, and before dark the smaller naval vessels and the transports were anchored in Port Royal Roads. Some small Confederate steamers, under Commodore Tatnall, formerly of the U. S. Navy, were chased and took refuge under the Confederate batteries.

Next morning the "Wabash," "Susque-hanna," "Vanderbilt," and "Atlantic" were piloted into deep water inside the bar, and a reconnoissance in force was made of the harbor by Commander John Rodgers and Brigadier-General Wright, with four gun-boats. These drew the fire of the batteries on Hilton Head and Bay Point, which were shown to be strongly built and fortified.

When the fleet was safely anchored within this spacious roadstead, the Flag-Officer had cause to congratulate himself on his selection of Port Royal in preference to any other point on the Southern coast for the establishment of a naval depot; and having perfected all his arrangements made preparations for battle.

The Confederates, attaching great importance to Port Royal as a strong military position, had built two large forts, Fort Walker on Hilton Head, and Fort Beauregard on Bay Point, opposite; and it seems strange that the Navy Department did not send a couple of gun-boats early in the war and prevent the enemy from erecting these works.

Of the two earthworks defending the entrance, Fort Walker was considered the stronger, and the Flag-Officer therefore determined to direct the weight of his fire upon this work, and after reducing it to make the final attack on Fort Beauregard.

The order of battle comprised a main squadron ranged in line ahead, and a flanking squadron to engage the gun-boats under Tatnall, which might prove troublesome and therefore required attention.

The following is a list of vessels which comprised the fighting squadron of Flag Officer Dupont, which operated in line ahead, steaming in an ellipse from the commencement to the close of the action.

Steam frigate "Wabash" (flagship), Commander C. R. P. Rodgers; steam frigate "Susquehanna," Captain I. L. Lardner; steam sloop "Mohican," Commander S. W. Godon; steam sloop "Seminole," Commander J. P. Gillis; steam sloop "Pawnee," Lieut.-Commanding R. H. Wyman; steam gunboat "Unadilla," Lieut.-Commanding N. Collins; steam gunboat "Ottawa," Lieut.-Commanding T. H Stevens; steam gunboat "Paulina," Lieut.-Commanding J. P. Bankhead; sailing sloop "Vandalia," Commander F. S. Haggerty, towed by steamer "Isaac Smith."

FORT WALKER.　　OTTAWA.　　PEMBINA.　　　　PENGUIN.　　AUGUSTA.　　FORT BEAUREGARD.
　　　　　　　UNADILLA.　SENECA.　SEMINOLE.　SUSQUEHANNA.　　　　PAWNEE.
　　　　　　　　　BIENVILLE.　WABASH.　MOHICAN.
　　　　　　　　　CURLEW.

BOMBARDMENT AND CAPTURE OF FORTS WALKER AND BEAUREGARD AT PORT ROYAL ENTRANCE BY THE NAVAL EXPEDITION
UNDER FLAG OFFICER S. F. DUPONT.

The flanking squadron consisted of the steam gunboat "Bienville," Commander Charles Steedman, leading ship; steam gunboat, "Seneca," Lieut.-Commanding Daniel Ammen; steam gunboat "Curlew," Lieut.-Commanding P. G. Watmough; steam gunboat "Penguin," Lieut.-Commanding T. A. Budd; and the steam gunboat "Augusta," Commander E. G. Parrott.

The plan of attack was to pass up midway between Forts Walker and Beauregard, which were distant from each other about two and one-third miles, receiving and returning the fire of both. When about two and a half miles north of Beauregard the line was to turn southward, round by the west, and close in with Fort Walker, encountering that work in its weakest flank, and enfilading in nearly a direct line its two water faces.

When abreast of Fort Walker the engines were to be slowed and the movements of the fleet reduced to a speed just sufficient to preserve the order of battle. On reaching the extremity of the shoal ground making off from Hilton Head the line was to turn north by the east and passing to the northward engage Fort Walker with the port battery nearer than when they passed it on the same course before. These evolutions were to be repeated as often as necessary.

The two forts had been constructed with great skill and were sufficiently armed, one would have thought, to have beaten off a squadron of the size of Dupont's, which was indeed scarcely large enough for so important a service.

The attack on the Hatteras forts had given a very fair idea of what our guns and shells could effect against earthworks, but those works were small affairs in comparison with the defences of Port Royal, and Commodore Stringham's force was comparatively much more powerful than that of Dupont, to say nothing of a clear sea in which Stringham had plenty of room to perform his elliptical movements.

The forts at Hatteras had inflicted little injury on the Union ships, but here it looked as if the case would be different, and that our squadron would have as much as it could attend to.

FORT WALKER.

Upon the sea front were mounted upon the best improved modern barbette carriages and circular railways, the following guns :

1 6-inch rifle.
6 32-pdrs. of 62 cwt., 1845, navy pattern.
1 10-inch Columbiad, of 13,220 lbs. weight.
1 8-inch Columbiad, 9,018 lbs.
3 sea-coast howitzers, 7-inch, 1,600 lbs. weight.

1 rifled, 6 inch.
In the left wing were:
1 32 pdr., same class as others before mentioned.
1 sea-coast howitzer, 42 pdr., not mounted.
Outer work in rear commanding land approach :
2 32-pdrs.
1 8-inch heavy howitzer, mounted on navy carriage, commanding approach to angle of outer work, the only gun in embrasure.
1 English siege gun, 12 pdr., behind embankment at right of right wing.
1 English siege gun, mounted to the right of the magazine to command the ditch of the main work.
In the right wing were mounted :
3 32-pdrs., same class as others before mentioned.
Making a total of 23 guns.

FORT BEAUREGARD.

The fort had four faces upon which guns were mounted, each face looking on the water, and each gun so mounted as to command the water approach to Broad and Beaufort Rivers. The guns were 13 in number, of the following sizes :
5 32's, navy pattern, 1845.
1 rifled, 6-inch, new.
5 sea-coast guns, 42 pdrs., long and very heavy.
1 ten-inch Columbiad, weight 13,226 lbs.
1 8-inch Columbiad.
Upon the outer works on the left flank were mounted
2 24-pdrs.
Upon outer works on right flank:
3 32-pdrs. of 63 cwt., navy pattern, 1845.
Within the fort were also two field pieces, 6-pounders, old Spanish pattern, making in all 20 pieces of ordnance.

Several circumstances prevented Dupont from moving against the enemy until the 9th of November, when early in the morning the signal was made to get under way, form line of battle and prepare for action. The sailors had previously had their breakfast, for Dupont knew the necessity of looking after their comfort and not to take them into a fight on empty stomachs.

By 9 o'clock the squadron was in line ahead in close order, the flanking column in position. The vessels passed within 800 yards of Fort Walker, on which work the main line poured in its fire, while the flanking line opened on Beauregard as soon as it came within range.

It was soon evident that the accuracy of the naval fire would be too much for the Confederates. Our shells burst with great regularity inside Fort Walker, throwing sand into the guns and into the eyes of the gunners.

Commodore Tatnall, who was watching the operations from his flotilla of fragile river steamers, which were entirely unfit to go into action against our vessels, wisely withdrew into Skull Creek, a convenient waterway just north of Hilton Head.

The Confederate gunners, when they found our ships seemingly unaffected by their fire, were very much surprised, as they had expected to destroy them all. They had no idea how strong were those old wooden hulls that had so long braved the storms of ocean, or what dreadful blows those shell guns could deal out under the management of skillful officers and men.

When the ships again swept by Fort

to pieces, scattering the gun-carriages to fragments, and killing the gunners, they could bear it no longer, but turned and fled. These deluded people had believed their position impregnable and their force sufficient to sink or scatter all the ships that could be sent against them. But when they saw the fleet pass and repass with automatic regularity, the hulls and spars of the vessels showing no signs of injury, and the ponderous cannon each time firing with more rapidity and accuracy, they became panic-stricken.

What hope could they have? Their guns were shattered to pieces, and whole guns' crews swept away, while they could inflict no injury upon the wooden ships. It was

EXTERIOR OF FORT WALKER AT HILTON HEAD, MARINES LANDING.

Walker from the north, passing within five hundred yards, the fire from their batteries was withering. Again the vessels turned into the harbor, delivering their broadsides as coolly and dexterously as if they were engaged in exercising.

This was too much for the enemy's gunners, who had never formed any idea of what the effect of a fifty-gun frigate's broadside would be, firing shrapnell and shell aimed by the steady eye of American sailors, with whom the idea of rebellion was simply mutiny against the highest authority.

The Confederates stood three or four broadsides as well as could be expected, but as the ships got their range, and shells fell right in their midst, tearing everything

evident to the Confederates that the Union fleet was having its own way, and that it was only a matter of time when every gun in the forts would be destroyed and every gunner killed who remained at his post.

In addition to the broadside firing in front, the enemy's works were enfiladed by gunboats stationed on either flank. This fire distressed the garrison of Fort Walker very much, for there were no guns on either flank of the bastion to reply with. On the right flank a long 32-pounder had been shattered by a shot from the ships, and there was no gun mounted on the other. After the fourth fire a ten-inch Columbiad and a twenty-four pounder rifle gun in the fort became useless.

The whole affair on the part of Dupont's

squadron had been conducted in a masterly manner. Hardly a shot was sent from the ships that did not reach its mark. What shots did not strike the guns and kill the gunners, rebounded and fell among the troops encamped outside Fort Walker.

When the Confederates commenced to run they went in a body, officers and all, for no one cared to leave his bones in the sacred soil of Hilton Head; yet these men were doubtless as gallant soldiers as were to be found in the South. They had reckoned without their host, and had certainly forgotten the history of the Navy, and the sea fights where our ships had been made slaughter-pens ere they would strike their flag to the foe.

The Navy had come with a determination to wipe the mutineers off the face of the earth if necessary, and no one in the fleet had any idea of failure; all were as certain of victory when the first gun was fired, as if the horoscopes of the Confederates had been cast beforehand.

At a little past one o'clock P. M., the Confederates were reported as leaving Fort Walker. At this time the enfilading vessels were within 600 yards of the fort, having everything their own way, throwing in eleven-inch shells, twenty-pounder rifle shots and even shots from twenty-four-pound howitzers.

Before the close of the bombardment the steam gunboat "Pocahontas," Commander Percival Drayton, came into port and joined in the attack.

Her commanding officer was brother to General Drayton, the Confederate commander of the forts.

Commander Drayton, although attached to the South by the strongest ties of consanguinity and friendship, chose to sever them all rather than prove faithless to the Government to which he had sworn allegiance, and to which he considered himself bound by every honorable sentiment. He condemned the action of the South from the beginning, and now he had an opportunity to strike a blow for his country before the Confederate flag was hauled down, and his brother with the forces under his command had retreated from the well beaten fort.

As soon as the flag officer learned that Fort Walker was being evacuated he sent Commander John Rodgers on shore with a flag of truce, and at half past two this officer hoisted the flag over the deserted post, and three hearty cheers went up from the fleet.

The enemy had left behind them the greater portion of their effects, their main idea being evidently to get out of the reach of our shells, but they were treacherous to the last. Honorable men when defeated accept the situation and bide their time, in the hope of getting even with their foes in a legitimate way, but on this occasion an unworthy attempt at revenge was made by the defeated foe.

Commander Rodgers went into the house which had been used as headquarters, and over which he had hoisted the American flag. A sailor moving about the premises caught his foot in a wire which was attached to some kind of torpedo. There was an explosion, a cloud of smoke, and the frame building was demolished. The sailor was knocked senseless but soon recovered, so that no loss of life occurred.

Fort Beauregard had not been considered by Dupont as an important point of attack, although fired upon at long range as the vessels wheeled into the ellipse. At sunset it was seen that the work had been abandoned, and next morning the Union flag was hoisted over that fort, and thus a permanent lodgment was gained on the Southern coast that proved of great advantage to the Union cause.

The victory had been gained entirely by the Navy, for although there were troops at hand yet they took no part in the engagement, nor was it necessary that they should. They went along simply to hold the place after the Navy had captured it, and after the works had been occupied a short time by the marines of the squadron the Flag officer turned them over to General T. W. Sherman.

Fort Beauregard made but little resistance, and hauled down its flag when it ascertained that Fort Walker was evacuated, the commanding officer remarking to his subordinates: "This work is evidently not suited for the purpose for which it was intended, and we had better leave it." Although very little firing was concentrated on Fort Beauregard, yet it had thirteen men wounded.

General Drayton, commanding the Confederate forces, reported that in Fort Walker there were ten killed and twenty wounded. In De Saussier's Regiment, one killed, four wounded severely and twenty missing—a small number, considering the severe fire to which the enemy were subjected. On board the ships eight were killed, six severely wounded and seventeen slightly wounded.

The small number of casualities on board the ships is due to the furious and destructive fire kept up on Fort Walker, which from the first rendered the Confederate gunners' aim very uncertain.

The attack on the defences of Port Royal was ably planned and skilfully executed. No time was lost by vacillating movements, and although this cannot be considered a great naval engagement, yet it was undoubtedly one of the best exhibitions of naval tactics that occurred during the Civil War, and has stood the test of criticism both at home and abroad. It was not so momentous an affair as the battles of New Orleans, Mobile or Fort Fisher; but it was of greater importance to the country, for it was a gleam of sunshine bursting through the dark clouds which enveloped the Union horizon.

The Union forces had met with little save misfortune from the day when the Confederates fired on Fort Sumter, and the battle of Bull Run had humiliated us before the world and incited France and England to meddle in our affairs. The victory at Port Royal put new life into Union hearts.

The North had seen arsenals and fort all

short time when he would be compelled to submit.

The battle of Port Royal gave the powers of Europe (who were longing for and expecting the success of the South) notice that we could and would win back the forts that had been filched from us, and that our hearts of oak in wooden ships could bid defiance to well-constructed earthworks and solid masonry.

This affair showed conclusively that the time-honored theory that one gun on shore was equal to five on shipboard no longer held good, when applied to the heavy artillery carried by modern ships and served with skill and precision.

Dupont demonstrated that ships under steam were much more powerful factors

INTERIOR OF FORT BEAUREGARD AT BAY POINT, S. C., CAPTURED BY THE NAVAL FORCES UNDER CAPTAIN DUPONT.

along the Southern coast fall into Confederate hands with scarcely an effort made to prevent it, and now, when least expected, the Union people were exalted in their own estimation. The Navy had come to the rescue and gained a complete victory in the immediate vicinity of Charleston and Savannah, the hotbeds of secession, establishing a permanent foothold, and affording an opportunity of throwing into the heart of the South a great army, had we of the North been wise enough to force the fighting in a quarter where it would have eventually brought matters to a speedy conclusion.

This happened in the end when Sherman's legions swept through the South, and the Army and Navy closed up the last outlet of the enemy, leaving it only a matter of a

against forts than when they had only sails to propel them, and that to make success certain all that was required was skill in their management, and a determination to attempt anything within the bounds of reason.

All the qualities of a great commander were possessed in an eminent degree by Dupont.

He was well informed in everything relating to naval matters, had great influence in naval circles, and at the first sign of obtaining a command, he gathered around him a fine corps of officers, whose zeal and intelligence greatly lightened the labors by which he was oppressed, during his service on the Southern coast.

Dupont was a man of fine presence, and

there was something so winning in his manner to all with whom he came in contact, that no man in the Navy had more friends and admirers.

The battle of Port Royal was important

There might be more difficult places to conquer than Port Royal, but no man could hereafter decline to attack an enemy's works with a squadron of war vessels. From the experience gained at Port Royal there could

FLAG OFFICER S. F. DUPONT, U. S. N.
(AFTERWARDS REAR ADMIRAL.)

in more ways than we have enumerated. Its moral effect counted prodigiously. It opened the way for the more important operations with wooden ships against the enemy's forts at a later period of the war.

be no difficulty in estimating hereafter what number of ships and guns would be necessary for a certain service. So no matter in what aspect we view this victory, its importance cannot be overestimated.

Later in the war it was attempted to take from Dupont some of the laurels he had won, and to mention with faint praise the work he had accomplished; but this scheme of detraction did not affect his reputation, for he lived honored and died regretted by all who knew him.

The good he did lives after him in the hearts of those in whom he implanted the seeds of discipline, and encouraged that chivalrous conduct which was once paramount in the Navy.

Dupont gave all his officers full credit for their gallantry in the affair of Port Royal; but for these particulars we must refer the reader to the official reports of the day, since this is intended to be a general review of naval events and cannot enter into all the particulars.

Flag Officer Dupont highly commends the services of Fleet-Captain C. H. Davis, Commander C. R. P. Rodgers, and some of the subordinate officers of the flag-ship; but leaves it to the commanding officers of vessels to mention the personnel of their own ships.

The first thing to be done after the capture of the forts was to establish the Army under General T. W. Sherman securely on Hilton Head Island. This Island is bordered on the north by "Skull Creek," a fair waterway of from two and one half to four fathoms, through which Tatnall escaped with his steamers, and where it was thought he should have been followed by our gunboats, though from some unexplained reason they failed to do so. A few heavy guns at Seabrook Landing, midway in Skull Creek, would have commanded a long stretch of the waterway and completely closed it against ordinary gunboats; but, as it happened, there were no defences of the kind, and our forces lost the opportunity of capturing General Drayton and all his command, who escaped either in Tatnall's steamers or in army transports.

Colonel Gilmore, of the Engineers, made a thorough survey of the vicinity, and his plans for defence were adopted, making the island of Hilton Head secure against any attack from the enemy.

Thus our forces were established in South Carolina, a constant menace to the enemy; the hostile movements from Hilton Head keeping Georgia and South Carolina in constant alarm.

Hilton Head Island became in course of time a place of refuge for hundreds of slaves, fleeing from their masters, who had forced them to throw up intrenchments against their friends, who offered them liberty and protection.

Colonel Gilmore's reconnoissance after the battle showed the demoralized condition of the retreating enemy. The road from Fort Walker to Seabrook Landing was strewn with accoutrements thrown away by the soldiers in their flight, and at the landing a quantity of commissary stores had been abandoned.

It may seem surprising that the Secessionists were enabled in so short a time after the breaking out of the hostilities, to erect so many formidable earth-works armed with heavy guns. This was owing to the United States Government allowing Norfolk Navy Yard, with its abundant supply of guns and munitions of war, to fall into the hands of the insurgents. From Norfolk the guns were sent all along the Southern coast, by way of the Dismal Swamp Canal, and through the inland channels with which our coast is supplied, as far as Florida. The number of guns captured at Norfolk is variously estimated from 1,400 to 1,500, but at all events the number was amply sufficient to provide a barrier against the entrance of such small vessels as we could get into commission on the first breaking out of the war.

But for the misfortune of losing, or we may say throwing away, the Norfolk Navy Yard, all the unarmed ports of the South would have easily fallen into our hands, and thus enabled us to break up blockade running at a much earlier date than we were able to accomplish it.

CHAPTER VII.

THE "TRENT" AFFAIR.

DETENTION OF THE BRITISH STEAMER "TRENT," AND CAPTURE OF MASON AND SLIDELL.

ONE of the first orders issued to naval officers in command afloat, should have been one instructing them particularly with regard to neutral obligations.

But this was not done; the Navy Department taking it for granted that every commander would be well posted in International Law, and would not fail to ask instructions on such matters when doubts were involved.

This want of a proper precaution came very near precipitating the United States into a war with Great Britain, at a time when it was most desirable to have no complications of any kind with foreign powers. We were likely to have enough trouble in the adjudication of liable blockade runners; but those cases would come before legally authorized Admiralty courts, and it was not likely that any injustice would be done to innocent parties, except detention, for which the parties detained could have recourse to law for damages.

In cases of non-condemnation, compensation was always allowed by the courts, and sometimes to a large amount.

There is no nation so particular in the care of its commerce as Great Britain. She keeps large fleets in all parts of the world solely for its protection, and wherever the British flag flies on a merchant vessel you will find a ship of war not far off, ready to protect it with her guns; and to this protection from their Navy do the British people owe that prosperity of their commerce which it enjoys in every part of the world.

It could readily be imagined that in a war which would so seriously affect so many branches of British trade, that the English government would observe with a jealous eye every step taken by our government for the purpose of preventing the Confederates from receiving supplies, contraband of war, from all foreign countries; but it is only fair to say, that although there were at times English ships-of-war sent along the coast to see that the blockade was closely kept, yet there were but few instances where British officers made any protest against our method of arresting the vessels engaged in the contraband trade.

The English government itself seemed disposed to take no action in regard to the seizure of English vessels, beyond having agents in this country to be present at the proceedings of the Admiralty courts, and to report the results to their Government.

Our Admiralty courts and the British being founded pretty much on the same principles, there was not much misunderstanding between the two Governments, considering the large number of vessels that came before the prize courts. On the whole, matters went on quite pleasantly between the two countries, notwithstanding that many Americans indulged in the idea that the whole English nation was hostile to the North, and only held this feeling in check until a favorable opportunity should occur, when, with some show of reason, it could assume an offensive attitude.

With such opinions existing it would have been wiser for our Government in its then weak condition to have avoided anything that could in any way be considered unjustifiable, and to have endeavored as much as possible to prevent collisions of any kind with foreign powers, unless it was positively clear that we were in the right.

On the 8th of November, 1861, an event occurred which created the wildest excitement throughout all parts of the United States and Great Britain; in fact, all Europe looked on with anxiety, anticipating a war between England and the Northern States of the Union.

This excitement grew out of the arrest of the British mail steamer "Trent" on the high seas, by Captain Charles Wilkes, of the

Eustis and McFarland, attachés to the commissioners.

The "Trent" was one of a line of British steamers which ran regularly between Vera Cruz and Havana, thence to St. Thomas, and from there to England.

The company had a contract with the British Government to carry the mails, and

CAPTAIN CHARLES WILKES.

United States frigate "San Jacinto," and taking from her four male passengers who claimed the protection of the British flag.

Two of these gentlemen were Messrs. Mason and Slidell, formerly members of the U. S. Senate, who were now bound to Europe as commissioners from the Confederate Government to the Courts of England and France; the other two were Messrs.

its steamers had ample accommodations for the passenger travel between England and the West Indies.

The "Trent" left the port of Havana on the morning of the 7th of November, under the command of Captain Moir.

Nothing of interest occurred until about noon of the 8th, when, in the narrow passage of the Old Bahama Channel, opposite the Panador Grande light, from the "Trent" was seen a steamer ahead, apparently waiting and showing no colors.

The "Trent" at this time was on her legitimate voyage; she had touched at no port in the Southern Confederacy, and had held no communication with vessels coming from or going to the insurrectionary States; neither was she bound herself to any Southern port, but was pursuing the route usually traveled by the company's mail steamers.

Her captain had taken on board as passengers the four gentlemen above named, as he had a right to do, for the British company had no authority to question the right of these persons to travel on their steamers, as long as they paid their passage money and conformed to the rules and regulations of the vessel.

The story of this affair is best told by an officer belonging to the "San Jacinto," who states as follows:

"At about 10.40 A. M. the look-out at the masthead reported a smoke from a steamer from the westward, and at 11 A. M. she was visible from the deck. We were all ready for her; beat to quarters, and as soon as she was in reach of our battery, every gun was trained on her from the starboard side. A shot from the pivot gun was fired across her bow; she hoisted English colors, but showed no disposition to slacken her speed or heave-to; we hoisted the star-spangled banner, and as soon as she was close upon us, fired a shell across her bow, which brought her to. Our captain hailed her and said he would send a boat on board, and gave an order to Lieut. Fairfax to board her. Fairfax went in the second cutter. At the same time Lieut. Greer was all ready in the third cutter to shove off from the port side, in case his services should be needed.

"On coming alongside of the packet, Lieut. Fairfax ordered the other officers to remain in the boat with the crew until it should become necessary to use force, and he went on board the 'Trent' alone. The captain of the mail steamer refused to show his papers and passenger list, knowing very well the object of our visit and the character and mission of the Commissioners; but Mr. Mason being recognized, a part of the armed crew was ordered from the boat and went on board. Messrs. Mason and Slidell were then requested to go on board the 'San Jacinto,' but declined, and said that they would only yield to force, Mr. Slidell remarking that it would require considerable force to take him on board the 'San Jacinto.' Lieut. Fairfax then ordered Mr. Houston to return to the 'San Jacinto' and report that the Confederate Commissioners were on board the 'Trent' (mail steamer) and refused to go on board the 'San Jacinto' by other means than force.

"Lieut. Greer then shoved off and went alongside of the 'Trent,' sent his armed crew and marines on board and stationed them at both gangways. After a gentle application of force the four gentlemen were taken in the second cutter and conveyed on board the American frigate, where they were received by Captain Wilkes at the gangway, and shown into the cabin which they afterwards occupied.

"Two other boats were sent on board the 'Trent' to remove the luggage; and the ladies belonging to the Commissioners' party having declined the hospitalities offered them by Captain Wilkes on board the 'San Jacinto,' at 3.30 the 'Trent' and 'San Jacinto' parted company."

This is a condensed account of this affair, but it fully explains the manner in which the Commissioners were taken out of the "Trent."

The whole matter on board the "Trent" was conducted by Lieut. Fairfax with the utmost courtesy. He had a very unpleasant duty to perform, especially as he was much embarrassed by the presence of the ladies belonging to the party, who expressed themselves without restraint regarding the outrage which they asserted had been committed; but the lieutenant bore their reproaches with great equanimity, and performed his duty as gently as possible.

The Commissioners themselves appeared to be very much outraged by the proceedings of Captain Wilkes in taking them out of the "Trent," though he did all he could while they were on board his ship to make them forget their troubles in the comforts of a fine cabin; but nothing could have pleased these Commissioners more than the fact that they *were arrested* on the high seas on board of a British ship, with the British flag flying at the peak, and *forcibly* taken from her to an American frigate.

This was just what would suit the Confederacy and the Commissioners at the same time, for it would bring about a collision, or at least a dispute, between England and the Federal Government, and very much increase the importance of the Commissioners on their landing in England, where they expected to be received (when released) with the wildest enthusiasm.

They both were too well posted not to know the tenacity with which the British people hold on to an idea, particularly the idea that when a man or a number of men seek the protection of the English flag, he or they cannot be taken from under its folds by force of arms on the high seas without a swift demand from the British Government for ample reparation. It is an idea that does honor to the British nation, and is one that her descendants in America have cherished since 1812, when the United States went to war with England, determined to resist the right of search which the English ships-of-war claimed the right to exercise over American vessels upon the high seas.

Thoughtful people saw in the act of Captain Wilkes nothing to approve of. On the contrary, they could only see trouble ahead, unless the Federal Government should at once disavow the act of that officer, and restore Messrs. Mason and Slidell and the attachés to their liberty.

The Commissioners themselves made a protest almost immediately after getting on board the "San Jacinto," against the seizure of their persons, and laid it before Captain Wilkes, not with the expectation that it would have any effect on their detainer, but it would add to the effect of what they considered their false imprisonment, and create an extra amount of sympathy for them throughout Europe.

The following is a pretty fair statement of the Commissioners, and as it is a part of the history of the times at a very important point, it is herewith inserted :

"U. S. Ship 'San Jacinto,'
"At Sea, Nov. 9, 1861.

"*Sir:*—We desire to communicate to you by this memorandum the facts attending our arrest yesterday on board the British mail steamer 'Trent,' by your order, and our transfer to this ship.

"We, the undersigned, embarked at Havana on the 7th inst. as passengers on board the 'Trent,' Captain Moir, bound to the Island of St. Thomas, in one of the regular passenger lines of the British Royal Mail Steamship Company, running from Vera Cruz, via Havana, to St. Thomas, and thence to Southampton, England. We paid our passage money for the whole route from Havana to Southampton to the British consul at Havana, who acts as the agent or representative of the said company; Mr. Slidell being accompanied by his family, consisting of his wife, four children and a servant, and Mr. Eustis by his wife and servants.

"The 'Trent' left Havana about 8 o'clock, a. m., on the morning of the 7th inst., and pursued her voyage uninterruptedly until intercepted by the United States steamer 'San Jacinto,' under your command, on the following day (the 8th) in the manner now to be related :

"When the 'San Jacinto' was first observed, several miles distant, the 'Trent' was pursuing the usual course of her journey along the Old Bahama or Nicholas channel, was about 240 miles from Havana, and in sight of the light-house Panador Grande ; the 'San Jacinto' being stationary, or nearly so, about the middle of the channel, and where it was some fifteen miles wide, as since shown on the chart,

"The nationality of the ship being then unknown, when the 'Trent' had approached near enough for her flag to be distinguished, it was hoisted at the peak and at the main, and so remained for a time. No flag was shown by the 'San Jacinto.' When the 'Trent' had approached within a mile of the 'San Jacinto,' (still pursuing the due course of her voyage) a shotted gun was fired from the latter ship across the course of the 'Trent,' and the flag of the United States displayed at the same time at her peak.

"The British flag was again hoisted as before, and so remained.

"When the 'Trent' had approached, still on her course, within from two to three hundred yards of the 'San Jacinto,' a second shotted gun was fired from your ship again across the course of the 'Trent.'

"When the 'Trent' got within hailing distance, her captain enquired what was wanted; the reply was understood that you would send a boat. Both ships being then stationary, with steam shut off, a boat very soon put off from your ship, followed immediately by two other boats with full crews armed with muskets and side-arms.

"A lieutenant in the naval uniform of the United States Navy, and with side-arms, boarded the 'Trent,' and in presence of most of the passengers assembled on the upper deck, said to Captain Moir that he came to demand his passenger list.

"The captain refused to produce it, and formally protested against any right to visit his ship for the purpose indicated.

"After some conversation importing renewed protests on the part of the captain against the alleged object of the visit, and on the part of the officer from the 'San Jacinto' that he had only to execute his orders, the latter said that two gentlemen, Mr. Slidell and Mr. Mason, were known to be on board, as also two other gentlemen (naming Mr. Eustis and Mr. McFarland), and that the orders were to take and carry them on board the U. S. Frigate 'San Jacinto.'

"It should have been noted that on first addressing the captain the officer announced himself as a lieutenant of the United States Steamer 'San Jacinto.'

"The four gentlemen thus mentioned being present, the lieutenant addressing Mr. Slidell, and afterward Mr. Mason, repeated that his orders were to take them, together with Mr. Eustis and McFarland, and carry them on board his ship, which orders he must execute.

"Mr. Slidell and Mr. Mason, in reply, protested, in the presence of the captain of the 'Trent,' his officers and passengers, against such threatened violation of their persons and their rights, and informed the lieutenant that they would not leave the ship they were in, unless compelled by the employment of actual force greater than they could resist; and Mr. Eustis and Mr. McFarland united with them in expressing a like purpose.

"The officer stated he hoped he would not be compelled to resort to the use of force, but if it should become necessary to employ it in order to execute his orders he was prepared to do so. He was answered by the undersigned that they would submit to such force alone.

"The lieutenant then went to the gangway, where his boats were, the undersigned going at the same time to their staterooms on the deck next below, followed by Captain Moir and the other passengers. The lieutenant returned with a party of his men, a portion of which were armed with side-arms, and others appeared to be a squad of marines, having muskets and bayonets.

"Mr Slidell was at this time in his stateroom, immediately by, and in full view.

"The lieutenant then said to Mr. Mason that, having his force now present, he hoped to be relieved of the necessity of calling it into actual use. That gentleman again answered that he would only submit to actual force greater than he could overcome, when the lieutenant and several of his men, by his order, took hold of him in a manner and in numbers sufficient to make resistance fruitless, and Mr. Slidell joining the group, two or more of the armed party took hold of him, and these gentlemen at once went into the boat.

"During this scene many of the passengers became highly excited, and gave vent to the strongest expressions of indignation, seeming to indicate a purpose of resistance on their part, when the squad, armed with bayonets fixed, made a sensible advance of one or two paces with their arms at the charge.

"It must be added here (omitted in the course of the narrative) that before the party left the upper deck, an officer of the 'Trent,' named Williams, in the naval uniform of Great Britain, and known to the passengers as having charge of the mails and accompanying them to England, said to the lieutenant that, as the only person present directly representing his Government, he felt called upon in language as strong and emphatic as he could express to denounce the whole proceeding as a piratical act.

"Mr. Slidell and Mr. Mason, together with Mr. McFarland, against whom force in like manner was used, were taken to the 'San Jacinto' as soon as they entered the boat. When they reached your ship you received them near the gangway, announcing yourself as Captain Wilkes, the commander of the ship, and conducted them to your cabin, which you placed at their disposal.

"When the undersigned came on board they found the men at quarters, and the guns bearing on the 'Trent.'

"After some time occupied bringing on board our luggage and effects, the 'San Jacinto' proceeded to the northward through the Santilla channel, the 'Trent' having been detained from three to four hours.

"The foregoing is believed to be a correct narrative, in substance, of the facts and circumstances attending our arrest and transfer from the British mail steamer to the ship under your command, and which we doubt not will be corroborated by the lieutenant present, as well as by all who witnessed it.

"The incidents here given may not have been witnessed by each one of the undersigned individually, but they were by one or more of them.

"As for the most part they did not pass under your notice, we have deemed it proper to present them in the form before you, expressing the wish that if considered incorrect in any part the inaccuracies may be pointed out.

"With a respectful request that you will transmit a copy of this paper to the Government of the United States, together with your report of the transaction, to facilitate which a copy is herewith enclosed,

"We have the honor to be,
"Very respectfully,
"Your obedient servants,
"JOHN SLIDELL,   GEORGE EUSTIS,
J. M. MASON,   J. E. McFARLAND.
"To CAPTAIN WILKES, U. S. N.,
"Commanding 'San Jacinto.'"

This is no doubt a strict version of the affair, and is corroborated by Captain Wilkes' report.

Captain Wilkes, when he parted company with the 'Trent,' made the best of his way to Boston. Why he did not go into New York or Hampton Roads, where he could have communicated at once with the Government, is unexplained, but the information of the capture was kept from the Department four days longer than it should have been.

When it was announced in the Boston papers that Captain Wilkes had seized upon the persons of two Confederate Commissioners, the excitement and joy were unbounded; though why it should have been so no one could tell.

What use two Commissioners from the Confederate States could be to the Federal Government, when their places could easily be filled by the first outgoing blockade runner, was a question no one stopped to inquire about. It was sufficient that the "San Jacinto" had important State prisoners on board, and that they had been taken from under the protecting folds of the British flag.

The conservative Bostonians completely lost their heads, and made Captain Wilkes lose his, for they gave him ovations in such quick succession that it was quite enough to make his brain whirl.

In the meantime the wires under the sea were flashing the news to England about the outrage to the British flag.

The exultation of the Confederates knew no bounds when they heard the news, and saw their cherished hope about to be realized in a difficulty—perhaps war—between England and the Northern States; in which event the success of the Confederate cause would in the estimation of the Confederacy be consummated.

In fact, everyone seemed for the moment to have lost their judgment in the joy of the capture of Mason and Slidell. Even the wisest men in the Cabinet, including Mr. Seward, did not at first realize the situation.

The President alone kept his mind clear, and did not commit himself in any way that could prejudice the case. Yet it was very plain to able jurists that the position we held on account of the capture of Mason and Slidell was not a defensible one, and the first act of the Government should have been to disavow the act of Captain Wilkes, and order him to proceed to the nearest British port and land the party he had arrested.

It no doubt would have been very humiliating to Captain Wilkes, but that was not to be considered.

A national vessel belonging to the Navy had, without any instructions whatever, stopped a British mail steamer upon the high seas, which was engaged in her usual business of carrying passengers from the West Indian ports to England, four of whom were taken from under the English flag—these persons charged with no offense.

If the Captain of the "Trent" had been guilty of any infraction of international law—had sailed from any Southern port, or had taken his passengers from any vessel at sea—then he was liable to arrest; but to prove him to be so Captain Wilkes should have taken the "Trent" into a Federal port (the nearest), and brought the case before a court of Admiralty, giving the owners of the vessel so detained an opportunity to sue for damages if she had committed no unlawful act.

But instead of that, Captain Wilkes instituted a court of Admiralty on the high seas, and undertook to condemn the persons arrested without trial, and let the vessel carrying them proceed on her voyage, on the ground that her detention by taking her into port for trial and adjudication would put the passengers to great inconvenience.

When we look back after the lapse of so many years, when the passions of men have cooled down, we can hardly realize that a nation which had gone to war with Great

Britain on the subject of this right of search, should for a moment have hesitated to do the proper thing, by at once redressing the wrong committed by its officers, instead of waiting until a demand was made for a return of the prisoners with a sufficient apology. But if there were no mistakes made in the world there would be no work done.

As soon as Captain Wilkes made his report to the Department, the Hon. Secretary of the Navy wrote him the following letter, which showed that Mr. Welles, if not sound in an international point of view, was sound in his dislike for the Confederates and all that savored of disloyalty. He no doubt touched the national heart, which at that moment did not beat with the most friendly feelings towards Great Britain. It was hard to make our people believe that England did not sympathize with the South, and that, while she was full of friendly professions towards the North, she was not ready at the first opportunity to throw her weight in the scale against us.

"NAVY DEPARTMENT,
"November 30, 1861.

"SIR: I congratulate you on your safe arrival, and especially do I congratulate you on the great public service you have rendered the Union in the capture of the rebel commissioners.

"Messrs. Mason and Slidell have been conspicuous in the conspiracy to dissolve the Union, and it is well known that when seized by you they were on a mission hostile to the Government and the country.

"Your conduct in seizing these public enemies was marked by intelligence, ability, decision and firmness, and has the emphatic approval of this department.

"It is not necessary that I should in this communication (which is intended to be one of congratulation to yourself, officers and crew) express an opinion on the course pursued in omitting to capture the vessel which had these public enemies on board, further than to say that the forbearance exercised in this instance must not be permitted to constitute a precedent hereafter for infractions of neutral obligations.

"I am respectfully yours,
"GIDEON WELLES,
"Secretary of the Navy.
"CAPTAIN CHARLES WILKES,
"Commanding U. S. S. 'San Jacinto,'
"Boston, Mass."

The news of the arrest of Mason and Slidell was received by Congress with great enthusiasm, and that body passed the following resolution by a decided vote:

"*Resolved*, That the President of the United States be requested to present to Captain Charles Wilkes a gold medal with suitable emblems and devices, in testimony of the high sense entertained by Congress of his good conduct in promptly arresting the rebel commissioners, J. M. Mason and John Slidell."

But this resolution was indefinitely postponed, and after Congress had time to examine coolly into the merits of the case, it was never resurrected. But there is no doubt it expressed the sentiments of the loyal people of the country, who never stopped to think what the consequences might be; nor did they reflect that we were not in a condition to go to war with Great Britain on a point of this kind, where we could find no exact precedents by which to justify ourselves; and when in like cases on the part of England we had placed her in the wrong in the war of 1812, and retaliated on her so severely that she was glad to invoke peace.

In the mean time Messrs. Mason and Slidell were confined in Fort Warren (in Boston harbor), as close prisoners.

The excitement in England was intense, and all those who entertained ill-feelings against the United States and her institutions were not slow in manifesting them.

The British Government took the matter in hand at once, and preparations for war were commenced on a large scale. Troops were sent to Canada without the English Government making inquiries into the matter, or waiting to see if the United States had not some explanation to make in relation to the action of Captain Wilkes.

This was not generous conduct in a great nation towards another with which its government professed to be at amity, and which at that time (before the United States had fairly collected her armies), was struggling with many disadvantages to hold her own against the most powerful rebellion ever yet known.

Common justice should have led the English Government to extend to us the courtesy that would have been extended to France or Russia under like circumstances.

It all looked very much as if the British people were (as report stated) sympathetic with the South, and were anxious to take advantage of the opportunity and seek a quarrel with the United States, and thus secure a separation of the two sections, which would weaken both, and give to England a powerful ally that would enable her to dictate such terms to the Federal Government as would best suit her purposes.

The first step taken by the British Ministry was a demand for the surrender of the Commissioners, with an apology by the United States government for the act committed by Captain Wilkes.

It would have been so much easier for the United States to have anticipated at once the action of the British government; but diplomatists have their methods, and they sometimes lead nations to the verge of war rather than admit a defect in their system.

On the 30th of November, 1861, Mr. Seward wrote to Mr. Adams, our minister to

England, informing him that Captain Wilkes had boarded a British colonial mail steamer and taken from her deck two insurgents, who were proceeding to England and France on an errand of treason against their own country. He says:

" We have done nothing on the subject to anticipate the discussion, and we have not furnished you with any explanations. We adhere to that course now because we think it more prudent that the ground taken by the British government should be first made known to us here, and that the discussion (if there must be one) shall be made here.

" It is proper, however, that you should know one fact in the case, without indicating that we attach much importance to it, namely, that in the case of the capture of Messrs. Mason and Slidell on board a British vessel, Captain Wilkes having acted without any instructions from the government, the subject is therefore free from the embarrassments which might have resulted if the act had been specially directed by us."

On the same day Lord Russell wrote to Lord Lyons, the British minister in Washington, relating the facts of the case as he had received them from the commander of the colonial steamer "Trent," and thus states the demands of his government in relation to the matter:

" Her Majesty's government, bearing in mind the friendly relations which have long subsisted between Great Britain and the United States, are willing to believe that the United States naval officer who committed the aggression was not acting in compliance with any authority from his government; or that, if he considered himself so authorized, he greatly misunderstood the instructions which he had received.

" For the government of the United States must be fully aware that the British government would not allow such an affront to the national honor to pass without full reparation, and her Majesty's government are unwilling to believe that it could be the deliberate intention of the government of the United States unnecessarily to force into discussion between the two governments a question of so grave a character, and with regard to which the whole British nation would be sure to entertain such unanimity of feeling.

" Her Majesty's government, therefore, trusts that when this matter is brought under the consideration of the government of the United States, that government will, of its own accord, offer such redress as could alone satisfy the British nation, namely, the liberation of the four gentlemen and their delivery to your lordship, in order that they may again be placed under British protection, and a suitable apology for the aggression which has been committed.

" Should these terms not be offered by Mr. Seward, you will propose them to him."

This demand seemed reasonable enough. It is what the United States would have done under like circumstances.

The official document placed Lord John Russell in a more forbearing light than the people of the United States expected of him, for he had the reputation of being not only a sympathizer with the Confederates,

but of being strongly hostile to the Federal government, which was somewhat remarkable, inasmuch as the United States of the North had proclaimed themselves as antislavery, both in theory and practice; it was, therefore, natural to suppose that the English, who stood before the world as the champion emancipators, should altogether sympathize with the Northern States.

If, however, there was any doubt regarding Lord Russell's sympathies, it was dissipated by a private letter which he wrote to Lord Lyons at the same time he wrote his official one.

He says in his private letter:

" In my previous dispatch of this date I have instructed you, by command of her Majesty, to make certain demands of the Government of the United States.

" Should Mr. Seward ask for delay in order that this grave and public matter should be deliberately considered, you will consent to a delay not exceeding seven days.

" If at the end of that time no answer is given, or any answer is given except that of a compliance with the demands of her Majesty's Government, your lordship is instructed to leave Washington with all the members of the legation, and to repair immediately to London.

" If, however, you should be of the opinion that the requirements of her Majesty's Government are substantially complied with, you may report the facts to her Majesty's Government and remain at your post till you receive further orders."

A copy of the first dispatch from Lord John Russell was handed to the Secretary of State, Mr. Seward, by Lord Lyons.

Our wily diplomatist and statesman was not in the least flurried or taken aback by the implied threat of the British Government. He believed in the oft-told story that the pen was mightier than the sword, and was satisfied that if the correspondence could be confined to this side of the water, he would make some points on the British Premier, if he did not get the best of the argument and prove that Captain Wilkes was altogether in the right.

Mr. Seward, in reply to Lord Russell's first dispatch, carefully states all the facts and then reviews them with a cleverness quite enough to upset the English equanimity, and if the latter were not convinced, they could not help but admire his dexterity in handling this very delicate matter.

He states to Lord Lyons as follows:

" Your Lordship will now perceive that the case before us, instead of presenting a merely flagrant act of violence on the part of Captain Wilkes, as might well be inferred from the incomplete statements of it that went up to the British Government, was undertaken as a simple, legal and customary belligerent proceeding by Captain Wilkes, to arrest and capture a neutral vessel engaged in carrying contraband of war, for the use and benefit of the insurgents.

" The question between us is, whether this proceeding was authorized by, and conducted according to the law of nations.

"It involves the following inquiries :

"First—Were the persons named and their supposed dispatches contraband of war ?

"Second—Might Captain Wilkes lawfully stop and search the 'Trent' for these contraband persons and dispatches ?

"Third—Did he exercise that right in a lawful and proper manner ?

"Fourth—Having found the contraband persons on board, and in presumed possession of the contraband dispatches, had he a right to capture the persons ?

"Fifth—Did he exercise that right of capture in the manner allowed and recognized by the law of nations ?

"If all these inquiries shall be resolved in the affirmative, the British Government will have no claim for reparation.

"The first four questions are briefly answered by himself in the affirmative, and only the fifth remains for consideration."

But admitting that Mr. Seward's inquiries are correct, he does not refer to the fact that Captain Wilkes constituted himself a Court of Admiralty upon the high seas, and undertook to make a seizure of the persons contraband of war, and omitted to seize the vessel.

If the persons seized were contraband, the vessel knowingly carrying them as passengers was contraband also, and should have been taken into a United States port and the case tried before an Admiralty Court; which would most likely have decided in favor of the "Trent" and awarded damages.

This course would have saved the United States the humiliation of making a forced apology.

England was not the only nation that took exceptions to the seizure of the persons of Mason and Slidell, for, on the 10th of December, the Minister of Foreign Affairs in France wrote to the representative of that court at Washington :

"The arrest had produced in France, if not the same emotion as in England, at least extreme astonishment and sensation. Public sentiment was at once engrossed with the unlawfulness and consequence of such an act.

"The desire to contribute to prevent a conflict perhaps imminent between two powers for which the French Government is associated by sentiments equally friendly, and the duty to uphold (for the purpose of placing the right of its own flag under shelter from any attack) certain principles essential to the security of neutrals, have, after mature reflection, convinced the French Government that it could not, under the circumstances, remain entirely silent.

*   *   *   *   *   *   *   *

"There remains therefore to invoke in explanation of the capture of Mason and Slidell only the protest that they were the bearers of official dispatches from the enemy; but this is a moment to recall a circumstance which governs all this affair and which renders the conduct of the American cruiser unjustifiable.

"The 'Trent' was not destined to a point belonging to one of the belligerents; she was carrying to a neutral country her cargo and passengers, and, moreover, it was in a neutral port that the passengers were taken on board.

"The cabinet at Washington could not, without striking a blow at the principles which all neutral nations are alike interested in holding in respect, nor without taking the attitude of contradiction of its own course up to this time, give its approbation to the proceedings of the commander of the 'San Jacinto.'

"In this state of things it evidently should not (according to our view of the case) hesitate about the determination to be taken."

In view of the pressure brought to bear upon the government and the attitude taken by France, wise counsels finally prevailed; and it was determined by the Federal Government to give up Messrs. Mason and Slidell to the representatives of the British Government authorized to receive them, and instructions were sent to the commanding officer at Fort Warren to place them on a small steamer and have them delivered on board a British war steamer then lying at Provincetown.

The Commissioners and their suite were conveyed in this steamer to the island of St. Thomas, and thence by the colonial steam line which took passengers to Southampton, England, where they arrived safely. But notwithstanding the excitement in England. they were received with no official distinction.

The exultation of the Confederates at what they chose to call the humiliation of the United States was excessive. though it would have pleased them better if the Federal government had adhered to the first impulse, and refused to give up the Commissioners. This, of course, would have brought about a war between England and the United States, which would most likely have insured the temporary independence of the insurgent States ; for with England's navy to back the South we could not have maintained the blockade, and all our available force would have been required to defend the Northern coast, and to commence a raid upon the English commerce in every sea.

The English may not have calculated all the damages the United States cruisers could have inflicted upon English commerce in every part of the world ; a proof of which may be seen in the performances of the "Alabama," and one or two other Confederate cruisers, which caused so much havoc to our commerce that it was almost driven from the ocean.

The United States government found itself placed in a very unpleasant dilemma, having to satisfy the demands of the British government and at the same time quiet the public feeling at home, which was intense; for the idea of surrendering Mason and Slidell was scouted by thousands of people, who, having no responsibility in the matter, gave vent to their feelings in the most unmeasured terms, not only against the British government for what was considered its arrogant demands, but against the administration for tamely submitting to them.

Unreasonable people could not be made to believe that the three hundred improvised gunboats, and the long array of frigates which ornamented our navy list, were not sufficient to set the whole British Navy at defiance. But the government had to admit its weakness as an excuse to satisfy the people at large, who were clamoring so loudly to go to war with the English at a time when we could scarcely comply with the demands made on us to perform the proper blockade duty.

The government had not only to allay the excitement existing throughout the country, but it had to defend itself against the opposition party ; which was ever ready to seize upon any weak point in Mr. Lincoln's administration, bring it before the people, and endeavor to weaken the government by their cries of incapacity.

It was finally decided by the administration that the long settled policy of this country was to resist the right of search

U. S. FRIGATE "SAN JACINTO," CAPTAIN CHARLES WILKES, OVERHAULING THE BRITISH STEAMER "TRENT," HAVING ON BOARD THE CONFEDERATE COMMISSIONERS, MASON AND SLIDELL.

upon the high seas; and by way of being consistent we had but one course to pursue, and that was to repudiate the acts of Captain Wilkes, which would have been the better policy to pursue from the beginning.

To Mr. Seward more than any one else were the people indebted for not having the country involved in a war of great magnitude, at a time when it would have been ruin to us for three years at least; for it would have taken us that length of time to prepare for a definite resistance against England, which we were quite capable of

making at the close of the war, when we were launching our invulnerable iron-clads as fast as our machine shops and ship-yards could turn them out.

It is not improbable that neither France nor England would have taken so fierce a stand if the "Trent" affair had happened in the latter part of 1864.

Whatever may have been Mr. Seward's opinions on the subject of the "Trent" matter, and though he made a faint attempt at making an argument, yet, with that astuteness that characterized him in all his foreign intercourse during the war, he thought it better to conform to the established principles which had always governed this nation, and avoid a foreign war in addition to what we already had on our hands.

An attempt was made to show that Mr Seward had pursued a timid policy in opposition to the broad principles laid down by the representatives of the people, that we could claim our insurgents wherever we might find them on the high seas— on which principle we might claim the right to take them out of the packet boat running between Calais and Dover.

Laws of nations are but conventional rules for the safe guidance of governments in time of war, but are only so far binding when they do not infringe upon a settled policy of some government, whose best interests would be jeopardized by adhering to the opinion of any international code, which the policy of a powerful government might change at any moment.

When ministers and ambassadors were of more importance than they have become since the introduction of steam and the telegraph, it might have been allowable to arrest them in transit from their own country to one where they were accredited, for the purpose of preventing them from laying an important treaty of alliance before an enemy's government.

Vattel says that "the *ambassador* of an enemy may be stopped in transit." An ambassador represents a person clothed with full powers to contract with some foreign government matters of high importance, and is carefully instructed by a well established government in all he has to do.

Messrs. Mason and Slidell *were not ambassadors;* they were simply commissioners from an unrecognized country of insurgents, and it was uncertain whether they would be received or not by France or by England

It was necessary that the administration should place itself in the right before the people, and for this purpose Senator Sumner was selected to defend the government on the floor of the Senate; which he did in the most able manner, and in a way satisfactory to the public mind.

The British government confined itself to a single point of complaint, in that it appeared "that the present objections were not founded on the assumption by the American vessel-of-war of the belligerent right of search, nor on the ground that this right was exercised on board a neutral vessel between two neutral ports, nor that it was exercised on board a mail steamer sustained by a subvention from the Crown and officered in part from the Royal Navy, nor that it was exercised in a case where the penalties of contraband could not attach, but it was founded simply and precisely on the idea "that other than officers in the military or naval service cannot be taken out of a neutral vessel at the mere will of the officer who exercises the right of search, and without *any form of trial.*"

As far as the English Government was concerned, it was not illiberal in confining the question at issue to·one single point, and it was thought that if time had been allowed our government, it could have triumphantly met the argument advanced by the British minister.

But the British people were impatient, and clamoring for immediate redress or else demanding war. The United States was too weak at that moment to enter into a war with Great Britain on a matter where it was not certain that we were in the right, and discretion being in this instance "the better part of valor," our government, after a small show of argument, disavowed the act of their officer.

This was the wisest thing that could have been done under the circumstances, for it was better that an officer should suffer for his great mistake, than that we should have been involved in a war with so powerful a nation, on a question in which all the powers of Europe would be sure to agree with our antagonist.

The aggressive position taken by the British Government on the first important question that had arisen between it and the United States, and the evident desire of Lord John Russell to humble us "in our hour of need" before the whole world, did not leave a friendly feeling in the minds of the American people towards the English; and while there was no immediate redress for us in regard to the departure of England from principles which had governed her for over a century, and the adoption of new ones to meet the occasion, there was but one thing to be done, namely, to bide our time until we could repay in a measure the arrogance the British Government had displayed towards us.

It was not that England had claimed redress for an assumption of power on our part which we had no right to exercise, but it was the haste which Lord John Russell was in to push us to the wall, that made the English action so offensive.

On the whole this action of Captain Wilkes had a good effect in the end. It rendered our officers more circumspect in their dealings with neutral questions, and prevented them from going out of their legitimate course to pick up foreign mail steamers with Confederate emissaries on board.

It also opened the eyes of the Government and Congress to the fact that, although we might use the coasting steamers to make blockading ships-of-war, we had no vessels that could be used to contend with any arrogant nation that might feel disposed to try and humiliate us.

It was but a short time after the event of the arrest of the "Trent," that the government gave its attention to building a class of vessels that could bid defiance to the heaviest ships in the British Navy; and it is safe to say here, that those vessels were not so much intended for the purpose of putting down the rebellion, as they were to put a check on the interference of the English and French in our affairs, which we considered that no foreign power had a right to meddle with.

Notwithstanding that the United States came near being mortified before the whole world because we were not prepared to encounter a great adversary like England, and were made partially to eat "humble pie," yet the people have forgotten that we were ever forced into making a submissive explanation in a matter where at most a mistake had been made.

We might be placed in the same position to-morrow by some insignificant power, because the knowledge of those who call themselves statesmen does not extend far enough to show them that if we want to hold any prestige amongst foreign powers, we must have a naval force adequate not only to protect our own coast but to carry war into the enemy's country.

We are more deficient to-day in naval ships, than we were in 1861. If called upon to-morrow to redress an insult, we would be no better prepared to do it than we were at the time when the English threatened us with her army and navy for "pursuing a course which is common enough in English practice."

When it suits arbitrary nations to alter established principles for others which are more in keeping with their own policy, they have no difficulty in changing.

It is said by a naval writer "this is the last haughty and unreasonable demand that Great Britain will ever make upon the United States. She has abdicated the dominion of the seas and she can never again ascend her ocean throne. Her insolent officers have for the last time lorded it with impunity over an American deck, and the threat which was made of sending the 'Warrior' to Washington, will not in any form be repeated." How little that man knew of the American people or of naval matters! He judged from the rapid manner we were putting afloat the clever creations of Ericssen's brains, that we were a progressive nation, and that having been taught one lesson of humiliation we would not let it happen again. That we would go on building up a navy (after the war) commensurate with the needs of our great country, and that the war, if it had no other good effect, would open the eyes of men in power to the fact that it is to the Navy alone we must look in all wars to protect our people, and to vindicate the honor of our flag.

But what assurance have we that we will benefit by past lessons? The exigencies of the war taught us nothing, and, like the Bourbons, we cannot learn. Our famous iron-clads, which once gave us considerable prestige, are lying about in rotten rows, and politicians are quareling over their bones. The "Warrior" with which we were once threatened, is without doubt somewhat impaired by age, but there is not to-day a single vessel or number of vessels in our entire Navy that could prevent her from being sent to Washington if the British Government thought proper to send her there.

If we have not the naval power, then, to assert any proper principle of International Law, let us not undertake to do so, until we have on hand a force that will in a measure arrest the first movement of *any* nation that may attempt to threaten us. The "Trent" affair was very humiliating.

Let us see to it that something like it does not happen again.

At the time of the "Trent" affair it would not have been wise in anyone to put himself in opposition to the public feeling which was then paramount. Men refuse to be convinced, no matter how logical and persuasive the argument, when it runs counter to their opinion. There was not at that time one man in ten who believed in the doctrine that we had no right to arrest bearers of treasonable dispatches when under the protection of the British flag; but now that a quarter of a century has passed away, and the passions of men have cooled down, and they are governed by reason, we can discuss those matters with a chance of being patiently listened to. It may be interesting also to read the arguments made on our side of the case, to ascertain how far right we were in demanding to hold Mason and Slidell; and though that will not help the case now, after such a lapse of years, it may be a satisfaction to the American reader to know that we made a good fight on paper, though we could not make it on the water.

In order to place ourselves right, our statesmen made diligent search through the records of the past for the lengthy discussions which arose between the United States and Great Britain, on the subject of the "right of search," when that power was truly mistress of the seas, and when, in accordance with a long-settled policy, she claimed the right to take British seamen out of any neutral vessel. Whenever the necessities of the British Navy called upon her to do so her heavy hand was laid upon American ships unsparingly; and having no navy at that time with which to assert our rights against so powerful an adversary, we had to resort to argument, in an extreme defense of the rights of neutrals, which covered much ground.

These arguments were now brought up against us in the "Trent" case, and it was shown that our statesmen in their arguments, in 1812, had specified the only classes that could be lawfully stopped in transit, namely, persons apparently in the naval or military service of an enemy. We had no answer to make to our own arguments, and had almost to resort to the same special pleading practiced by Great Britain in regard to the right of searching neutrals in 1812. Our statesmen in 1861 tried to prove that the two Commissioners, Messrs. Mason and Slidell, were far more dangerous to the United States, if let loose in Europe to work against us, than a dozen military men would be; and it was considered absurd to contend for the privilege of stopping at pleasure any man wearing an enemy's uniform, and prevent the most treasonable characters to go unquestioned because they have not the insignia of a soldier or of a sailor. The English view was considered, on our own side, a very narrow interpretation of phrases, to say nothing of a departure from a principle which the English had always claimed to protect.

There was one thing which did not strike our statesmen—that Messrs. Mason and Slidell had committed no overt act. There was no proof that they had ever shown their dispatches, or that they had said to any one that they were bound on a mission to a foreign government—that was all mere surmise.

Some argued that it was not necessary to take the vessel into court for adjudication, as there was no question with regard to the identity of these men, or as to the official capacity in which they were acting; that it needed no military insignia to show that they were distinguished public agents, in the service of the Confederate government.

If the Captain of the "Trent" knew all these facts and was aiding and abetting Mason and Slidell in any treasonable acts against the United States, then his vessel became liable, and Captain Wilkes, in assuming the authority to let the ship and passengers pass free, was guilty of a violation of a grave principle of international law; he could as well open a neutral ship's hatches, and take from her hold what *he might consider* contraband of war, and transferring it to his own vessel to be taken before an Admiralty Court and condemned without evidence, let the ship go. Contraband of war makes the vessel liable, be it in carrying a regiment of soldiers or munitions of war. This is the view of the case taken by the President (Lincoln), and with that wisdom which never failed him he decided to give up the prisoners, and save the nation from a war in which it was not at that time in a condition to embark. The President did not want to go back on the principles for which the United States had so strongly contended in 1812; and he was right, as all unprejudiced minds must see.

CHAPTER VIII.

CAPTURE OF FERNANDINA AND THE COAST SOUTH OF GEORGIA.

Reconnoitering Along the Coast.—Confederates Evacuate Their Defences on Tybee and Warsaw Islands.—A General Stampede.—The Effect of Dupont's Victory.—Lost Opportunities.—"Sea Islands."—Congregation of Slaves at Hilton Head.—Entrenchments Erected at Hilton Head.—General Stevens.—Beaufort Occupied.—Reconnoissance up the Tybee River to Fort Pulaski.—Expedition to Fernandina.—Commanders of and Vessels Composing the Expedition.—Capture of the Works on Cumberland and Amelia Islands.—Fort Clinch Occupied.—Capture of Fernandina.—Capture of the Steamer "Darlington."—General Lee and Fernandina.—Fine Harbors for Blockade Runners.—Good Service of the Navy.—The Forts and Town of St. Augustine Surrender to the Union Forces.—Dupont Establishes Government Authority in the Harbor of St. Johns.—Retreating Confederates Burn Saw-Mills and Other Property.—Dupont Returns to Port Royal.—Planting Batteries on Tybee Island.—The Navy Take Part in the Bombardment and Capture of Fort Pulaski.—Cordiality Between the Army and Navy Officers.—The Officers Under Dupont.—High Rank Reached by Some of Dupont's Officers.

A S soon as Flag-officer Dupont could find the time, he sent the smaller gunboats in different directions to reconnoitre the enemy's positions up the river and along the coast. The larger vessels were sent to perform blockade duty, which at that moment, owing to the paucity of vessels, was very arduous.

Commander John Rodgers was sent with the "Seneca" and "Paulina" to examine the enemy's defences on Tybee Island, in the Savannah River, and ascertained that all the works in that quarter had been abandoned, except those at Stono Inlet.

Commander Drayton, in the "Pawnee," accompanied by one or two gunboats, entered St. Helena Sound and found on the point of Otter island some heavy fortifications; but the magazine had been blown up and the armament removed.

At the same time Commander C. R. P. Rodgers made a reconnoissance of Warsaw Sound, and found the fort on Warsaw Island dismantled and the magazine destroyed. An examination of Wilmington River showed heavy works still occupied by the enemy. On the Ogeechee and Vernon rivers heavy earth-works were being erected by the Confederates.

Commander Drayton crossed the North Edisto Bar, and found an abandoned earth-work, intended to mount ten guns. In fact, there had been a stampede all along the coast, which indicated the moral effect of Dupont's victory on the Southern people. Had a suitable body of troops been landed on the coast at the time, Charleston and Savannah would have fallen into our possession, and have been held throughout the war, to the great detriment of the Confederates, who depended on these ports as bases of supplies. The government, however, failed at that period to take in the situation, and our statesmen were quite paralyzed with the difficulties which threatened the Union cause. The superannuated army officers, called by the administration to its councils, were altogether unequal to the emergency, and they led the government into many difficulties.

When General W. T. Sherman declared that an army of two hundred thousand men was required to put down the rebellion, he was thought to be crazy; but the President's advisers discovered, ere the war had lasted a year, that Sherman had in no way exaggerated the difficulties of the situation.

Whatever may have been the reason of the failure to send a larger army to occupy the Southern coast as soon as the necessary gunboats could be improvised to penetrate the inlets of that region, it is certain the movement was not made until too late, and the principal theatre of war had been transferred to other points, around which the contending forces gathered, leaving the coast to be taken care of by the Navy; a duty which, we think it will be admitted, the Navy performed with great credit to themselves and to the satisfaction of the country.

From the first the Navy had to contend with the indisposition of the War Department to co-operate with it in getting up combined expeditions against the enemy. Until the battle of Cape Hatteras and Port Royal occurred, it was not supposed that the Navy would take such a prominent part in the war. It was supposed our gunboats would be barred out of the Southern ports, which the large ships could not enter, owing to their great draft of water; and, apparently, no one considered the great advance which the Navy had made in ordnance, having at that time the most powerful shells and shell guns that had ever been known. These guns, as they were used at Port Royal, gave an example of the manner in which our heavily-armed gunboats could deal with earth-works; for it was here proven that the defenders of a fortification would all be killed if they attempted to stand to their guns in the face of such a fire as could be poured into them from naval vessels.

It was conclusively shown that our wooden steamers, armed with nine and eleven-inch Dahlgren guns, could engage the most formidable batteries on shore, with a good prospect of success.

In those days gunboats were improvised by the hundred, and if the government had been so minded, all the smaller earth-works along the Southern coast could have been easily made to yield to the Dahlgren guns.

One result of the victory at Port Royal was our obtaining possession of the famous "sea islands," which, through slave labor, had so enriched their proprietors; and it was upon these planters that the greatest injury was inflicted, as our gunboats penetrated the network of inlets along the coast, and the rich cotton harvests lay at their mercy.

The slaves took advantage of the panic, and fled with their families to seek the protection of the Union flag. A large number of them congregated at Hilton Head, and about a thousand picked up by the vessels of war were located on the southeast end of Edisto Island, where a gunboat was stationed for their maintenance and protection. Most of these negroes were given employment and served the Union during the remainder of the war. Others found homes on the "sea islands," within Union protection, where they raised corn and sweet potatoes sufficient to satisfy their simple needs; and if they sometimes suffered from the want of clothing, food and shelter, yet they exhibited a striking example of how dear is liberty to man in whatever position of life, and how much he will undergo to secure it.

The officers of the Navy may be said to have first erected the Freedman's Bureau, and given an asylum to those poor creatures who, with all their ignorance, had still sufficient manhood to appreciate the boon of freedom, which perhaps some of them had once enjoyed on the wild shores of their native Africa.

While the Navy had been busy in penetrating the numerous inlets of the vicinity, General T. W. Sherman had constructed large and strong entrenchments on Hilton Head, outside of Fort Walker. The Army had also occupied Beaufort, a pleasant village near Port Royal, where many wealthy land-holders resided during the hot season. Posts were also established on Tybee and other islands.

The enemy gradually recovered from the panic which had seized them at the battle of Port Royal, and seemed disposed to commence offensive operations against our forces, and re-occupy the works they had so precipitately abandoned. Upon this an expedition was fitted out under General Stevens and Commander C. R. P. Rodgers, which resulted in the abandonment of any attempt of the enemy to plant batteries within range of the gunboats, whose far-reaching shells committed some havoc among them on this occasion; nor did they ever attempt to obtain a lodgment on Port Royal Island, which remained in possession of the government during the war.

A reconnoissance up the Tybee River was made by Captain C. H. Davis and Commander C. R. P. Rodgers with the "Ottawa," "Seneca," "Ellen," "Western World," and the armed launches of the "Wabash," accompanied by three transports, having on board 2,400 troops, commanded by Brigadier General H. G. Wright. The expedition crossed the bar, and reached a point nearest Fort Pulaski on its land side. No shots were fired at the vessels, as the enemy had no rifle guns mounted in that quarter, so that the expedition was enabled to accomplish its object without difficulty, and return unmolested.

Several similar expeditions were sent out under Commander John Rodgers and others, which served to keep the enemy in a continual state of uneasiness and made our officers acquainted with all the surrounding land and water.

Having done all that was necessary in the vicinity of Port Royal, Flag Officer Dupont turned his attention towards Fernandina in Florida, twenty-five miles north of the St. John's River. On the second of March, 1862, the "Wabash," and what other vessels could be spared from blockading duty, anchored off St. Andrew's Island, twenty miles north of the entrance to Fernandina.

Hoisting his flag temporarily on board the "Mohican," Commander S. W. Godon, Dupont's squadron entered Fernandina in the following order: "Ottawa," "Mohican," "Ellen," "Seminole," "Pawnee," "Pocahontas," "James Adger," "Bienville," "Alabama," "Keystone State," "Seneca," "Huron," "Paulina," "Isaac Smith," "Penguin," "Potomska," armed cutter; "McClellan," armed transport, with a battalion of marines under Major Reynolds, and six transports containing a brigade under command of Brigadier General Wright.

The vessels anchored at 10:30 A.M. on the second of March, to examine the channel and wait for the tide. Here the Flag-officer learned from residents of Cumberland Island, that the Confederates had hastily abandoned the defences of Fernandina, and were at that moment in full retreat, carrying with them such of their munitions of war as their precipitated flight would allow.

Such was the moral effect of the Port Royal victory, that there seemed to be a stampede all along the coast as soon as our naval vessels made their appearance.

The object of taking the vessels through Cumberland Sound was to turn the heavy works on Cumberland and Amelia Islands; but on receiving intelligence that the enemy had abandoned their works, Dupont detached the light gun-boats and light draft steamers from the main line under Commander Drayton, and ordered that officer to push through the Sound with the utmost dispatch to try and save the public and private property from destruction, and to prevent those outrages, by the perpetration of which the leaders of the rebellion hoped to exasperate their deluded followers.

While this expedition was on its way through the narrow inlets, Flag-officer Dupont proceeded by sea to the main entrance of the harbor.

On entering Fernandina Harbor, Commander Drayton sent an officer to hoist a white flag on Fort Clinch, the first of the national forts on which the ensign of the Union had resumed its proper place since the first proclamation of President Lincoln was issued.

A few scattering musket shots were fired by the enemy and that was all the defence made by them. A railway train left the town as the gun-boat arrived. Commander Drayton in the "Ottawa" gave chase to it along the river and fired several shells at the locomotive, it is said, with some damage to the train.

Commander C. R. P. Rodgers pushed ahead with the steam launches and captured the steamer "Darlington" containing military stores, and fortunately secured and held the draw-bridge of the railroad.

The same night Commander C. R. P. Rodgers ascended the St. Mary's River in the "Ottawa," and driving away the enemy's pickets, took possession of the town of St. Mary's, while a force of seamen and marines, under Lieut. Miller, was sent to hold Fort Clinch.

The whole number of guns captured amounted to thirteen, among them one eighty-pounder and one one-hundred-and-twenty-pounder rifle.

Fort Clinch and the earthworks thrown up by the enemy were found to be in condition for a most vigorous defence, and it is surprising that after making such formidable preparations, the Confederates should have left without attempting any resistance.

All the batteries were as perfect as art could make them—six of them were protected by sand hills, and were so covered by the growth of the country and so isolated from each other that striking them from the sea would have been almost a matter of chance.

These earthworks and the heavy guns of Fort Clinch commanded the main ship channel so as to rake an approaching foe. Besides these was a battery of four guns on the south end of Cumberland Island, the fire of which crossed the channel inside the bar. The crookedness of the channel and shoalness of the bar gave the Confederates a great advantage, for even after vessels had passed the outer defences they would have to encounter a well-constructed masked battery at the town, which commanded the anchorage.

General Lee had pronounced Fernandina perfectly defensible against a naval attack, but he did not appreciate the brave spirits that manned our ships or the power of 11-inch guns.

It was fortunate for the Union cause that Fort Clinch and its outlying batteries fell into our hands without resistance, as the Confederates might have made it warm work for the Navy; though the latter would doubtless have prevailed in the end, owing to good discipline and accurate gunnery.

Thus, Flag Officer Dupont accomplished an important part of the plan he orginally proposed, viz.: to take and hold the whole line of the sea coast of Georgia, believing that the power controlling the sea coast controls the State, a proof of which was that the heavy works at St. Simms, armed with Columbiads, had been abandoned on hearing the news from Fort Royal, and on the approach of the fleet.

Thus was virtually placed in the hands of the government the fine harbor of Brunswick, the harbor and inlets of Fernandina, the town and river of St. Mary's, and the coast and inland waters from St. Simons northward. All these places, if left undisturbed, would have afforded a fine refuge for blockade runners, which must have supplied the Confederacy with any quantity of munitions of war, and much prolonged the conflict.

From what we have narrated it will be seen that while the North was not always successful in military operations, the Navy was doing good service by drawing tighter the coil around the Confederacy and depriving them of the means of carrying on the war. Even during the short time which had elapsed since our Navy had been placed upon a respectable footing, it held all the important approaches to the Southern States, from Cape Hatteras to Florida, with the exception of Charleston, Savannah and Wilmington, which places we were not yet quite in condition to assail, and which, for the want of a sufficient Navy on the part of the North at the commencement of the war, remained in possession of the enemy till nearly the close of hostilities.

Every effort was made by the Navy to capture these places, and much gallantry was displayed, which, though often without result, still showed the indomitable spirit of the service while contending against odds greater than they were able to overcome. History has not done justice to the hard work performed at Charleston, and slurs have been cast on gallant officers who deserved all the commendation a grateful country could bestow.

The Army remained in charge of the fortifications at Fernandina, and Flag Officer Dupont proceeded in the "Wabash," accompanied by several gun-boats, and on the evening of March 8 anchored off St. Augustine, where the town and fort were quietly surrendered to the Union forces; Dupont assuring the inhabitants of kind treatment as long as they respected the government authority and acted in good faith, and that municipal authority would be left in the hands of the citizens.

Thus Dupont not only displayed the gallantry and energy of an able commander, but also the tact which he possessed in an eminent degree; for while he was determined to restore to the government the property which belonged to it, he felt it due to the deluded people to undeceive them, by kind treatment, of the numerous misrepresentations of the Southern leaders in relation to the designs of the Federal authorities.

The places that had so far been captured could be easily held by a few gun-boats; and although the Confederate Government realized the importance of attempting to recover what they had lost, they finally gave up the idea of holding these harbors and inlets and confined their operations to the interior, where the Navy could not follow them.

The harbor of St. John's was next visited by Dupont and the government authority established. The inhabitants were assured protection while they abstained from acts of hostility, and they more readily accepted these assurances as at night the whole heavens were illuminated by the burning saw mills, set on fire by the retreating enemy, in order to prevent them from falling into the hands of the Navy, forgetting that Dupont had promised at Fernandina to respect private property.

There were many interesting incidents connected with this naval campaign which the limits of this work will not allow us to narrate. Suffice it to say, Dupont's labors were entirely successful and quite up to the expectations of the Navy Department— not always profuse in praise of its officers.

Leaving a sufficient force of gun-boats to guard the harbors and inlets. Dupont returned to Port Royal in the "Wabash."

Dupont found that during his absence from Port Royal, the Army had planted batteries of rifled guns and Columbiads on Tybee Island for the purpose of reducing Fort Pulaski: but as this was purely a military operation, the Flag Officer did not claim to interfere, although General Hunter permitted the Navy to take part in the bombardment, allowing a detachment of officers and seamen from the "Wabash" to serve one of the breaching batteries.

The detachment under Commander C. R. P. Rodgers reached Tybee Island on the 10th of April, just before the firing commenced, but too late to take part in it that day.

On the following morning the firing continued with excellent effect, the rifled shots boring through the brick work, while the shots from the Columbiads broke off great masses of masonry from the walls.

Four rifled guns in battery, about 1,600 yards distant from the fort, had been assigned to the detachment from the "Wabash," and no doubt the most skillful gunners in the ship were assigned to the management of the guns.

The Union batteries kept up a steady fire until the Confederate flag was hauled down.

Before the fort surrendered many of the barbette guns were dismounted and the fort breached in two places, so as to be quite practicable for a storming party. The garrison were convinced that it was useless to contend against the Federal batteries, as the rifled shots passed through the walls and threatened to destroy the magazine.

When General Totten, the chief of Engineers, built Fort Pulaski, it was deemed impregnable to the assault of a naval force armed with the heaviest guns then in use, 32-pounders, and he would have been astonished if he had been told that in a few years a rifled projectile would be invented that would bore through his walls and crumble them to pieces.

The guns used by the naval detachment were three 30-pounder Parrots and one 24-pounder James. Commander Rodgers speaks in high terms of the officers and men. Lieut. Irwin, Acting-Master Robinson and Midshipmen Johnson and Pearson, Lewis Brown, Captain of the Forecastle, and George H. Wood, Quartermaster.

There were many gallant affairs constantly occurring, in which reconnoitering parties from the Navy were concerned, and they gave the enemy no rest. In these affairs the Army participated whenever an opportunity offered; and here we would remark, that at no period during the war was there a more cordial co-operation between the Army and Navy than while Flag Officer Dupont commanded on the Southern coast. His courtesy to every one with whom he came in contact gained him hosts of friends, and his example was followed by his subordinates in their intercourse with the army officers; so that whatever combined enterprise was undertaken, it was vigorously executed with perfect accord on both sides.

Among the galaxy of bright spirits who served under Dupont in the early part of his campaign, there were many who have since passed away; but their names should not be forgotten. They were among the first to set the example of attacking heavy fortifications with light-built vessels; a departure from former usage that was first made in our civil war, and is now an established rule the world over.

A commander-in-chief, no matter how clever, does not stand much chance of success against the enemy unless he is well supported by his officers; and as Dupont up to this time had been everywhere successful, we must give a portion of the credit to those who served under his command.

That Dupont was fortunate in his selection, the names of Captain C. H. Davis, Commanders John Rodgers, Drayton, C. R. P. Rodgers, Godon, Parrott, Steedman, Gillis, Prentiss, Lieutenants-Commanding Balch, Stevens, Ammen, Nicholson, Truxton, Rhind, Bankhead, Conroy, Watmough, Budd, Semmes and Phœnix, in command of vessels, will show, besides the junior officers mentioned favorably by their commanding officers.

Nearly all the commanding officers reached high rank, and the youngest of them are now well up on the list of commodores and captains.

Eleven of them attained the rank of rear-admiral; and of these six are still living, have retired from active duty, and are reaping the reward of faithful service.

They will figure again in the course of this narrative, as their service continued throughout the war.

CHAPTER IX.

OPERATIONS OF ADMIRAL DUPONT'S SQUADRON IN THE SOUNDS OF SOUTH CAROLINA.

ARDUOUS DUTIES PERFORMED BY DUPONT'S OFFICERS.—VARIOUS EXPEDITIONS.—VALUABLE SERVICES OF CAPT. BOUTELLE AND OFFICERS OF COAST SURVEY.—COM. C. R. P. RODGERS MAKES RECONNOISSANCE OF WARSAW INLET.—LIEUTENANT BARNES INVADES FORTS.—COMMANDER DRAYTON GOES UP THE NORTH EDISTO RIVER.—OBJECT OF THE EXPEDITIONS.—DIFFICULTIES IN THE WAY OF GUNBOATS.—OGEECHEE SOUND AND THE GREAT OGEECHEE RIVER EXAMINED.—A SECOND RECONNOISSANCE TO SAINT HELENA SOUND.—GUNBOATS ANNOYING CONFEDERATE TROOPS.—THE TORCH PLAYS A PROMINENT PART.—DESOLATION.—FRIENDSHIP OF THE BLACKS FOR THE UNION CAUSE.—EXPEDITIONS TO VARIOUS POINTS—ADMIRAL DUPONT CONSULTS WITH GEN. THOMAS W. SHERMAN.—A JOINT EXPEDITION.—ENGAGEMENT AT PORT ROYAL AND SEABROOK FERRY.—CONFEDERATES DISPERSED.—EFFECT OF CO-OPERATION OF THE ARMY AND NAVY.—REPORTS OF OFFICERS OF THE FLEET.—EXPEDITION OF FLEET-CAPTAIN C. H. DAVIS TO WARSAW SOUND.—REGIMENTS ACCOMPANYING EXPEDITION.—TATNALL'S GUNBOATS OPEN FIRE ON UNION FLEET AND GET WORSTED.—EXCITEMENT IN SAVANNAH.—OFFICERS WHO WERE CONSPICUOUS.—PATRIOTISM OF COLORED PEOPLE.—COURAGEOUS AND HEROIC ACT OF ROBERT SMALLS, A COLORED MAN.—CAPTURING THE STEAMER "PLANTER."—GREAT SERVICES OF DUPONT ALONG COASTS OF SOUTH CAROLINA, GEORGIA AND FLORIDA.

SHORT references have been made to the various duties performed by Admiral Dupont's officers on the coast and in the Sounds of South Carolina, the writer not deeming that the limits of this work would permit of a more extended account of the operations of the South Atlantic Squadron.

These operations show not only a desire to meet the enemy on all occasions, but a wise forethought on the part of Admiral Dupont regarding the ultimate use which the possession of certain points would be to the government in the future. He saw that the enemy was daily exhibiting more energy and an astonishing amount of resources, with a fixed determination to carry on the war as long as they could muster a regiment or obtain powder to fire a gun.

The accounts of the various expeditions fitted out cannot be narrated in order, as the reports came in irregularly; but they will be sufficiently so to enable the reader to judge of the important services rendered from time to time.

The enemy were continually erecting batteries, and they moved about from point to point with a rapidity that was marvelous, and embarrassing enough to test the highest qualities of a commander-in-chief to meet the various movements of so active an adversary.

The soldiers of South Carolina seemed determined that the Northerners should not plant their feet on Southern soil, if they could keep them out by earnest watching and fighting; and it is safe to say that this untiring energy was met by equal energy and perseverance on the Union side; and if the latter did not actually occupy all the points held by the Confederates, they rendered them so ineffectual to do harm that they might just as well have been taken possession of.

The coast of South Carolina is indented with many sounds, bays and inlets, most of them accessible to small light-draft blockade runners. It required some time to become acquainted with the topography and hydrography of these places, as no charts gave an exactly fair representation of many of them; and it was to close up all these gaps in the line of blockade that the smaller vessels were employed in constant reconnoissances and skirmishes, some of which were full of danger and required nerve and daring to execute.

It must have been surprising at times to the people residing along these narrow inlets, to see good-sized gun-boats ploughing their way at full speed through their tortuous and shallow channels, where the keel of a war vessel had never before passed. It was gall and wormwood to them to witness these excursions of floating batteries, against which they soon found that their flying artillery was of no mortal use.

Admiral Dupont had in his squadron a corps of officers belonging to the coast survey, under the immediate direction of Captain Boutelle, First Assistant. The Coast Survey office had abandoned its legitimate duties at the commencement of the war, and now furnished most valuable aid by sending its officers to any squadron requiring them. Captain Boutelle was invaluable to Admiral Dupont, and frequent mention is made of the honorable service he performed in piloting vessels through these intricate inlets.

The reconnoissance in St. Helena Sound, by Commander Drayton, has been already referred to. This bay was considered invaluable for a harbor, owing to its proximity to Charleston. By its occupation the Federals would be drawing the net close

REAR-ADMIRAL C. R. P. RODGERS,

(FROM PHOTOGRAPH TAKEN IN 1885.)

around that pugnacious fort; and by cutting off all communication with the interior of the State, through the large rivers that communicated with it, with a few gunboats would remain masters of the situation.

Commander C. R. P. Rodgers was employed to make a reconnoissance of Warsaw Inlet, in order to ascertain the position and force of the enemy's battery there, which information was desired by the Commanding-General of our military forces, in anticipation of landing troops on Tybee Island.

On approaching within a mile of the fort, and seeing neither men nor guns, Lieutenant Barnes was sent up with a flag of truce to examine the place, and found it evacuated.

It was a heavy work, with platforms for eight guns. But the guns had been removed, the platforms cut and the magazine blown up.

The expedition (consisting of the gun-boats the "Ottawa," "Seneca," and "Pembina") then pushed on to Cabbage Island, where another battery was expected to be found. The vessels went to the mouth of the creek, through the Romilly marsh, and to the mouth of Wilmington River—a bewildering cruise among a network of shoals, inlets and marshes, enough to test the patience of officers of the most energetic type. But these men's minds were bent on fathoming the intricacies of southern navigation, and they succeeded in obtaining their object, and before they had been three months on the southern coast every sound and inlet was as familiar to our officers as to the Southern pilots.

This expedition brought back valuable information, ascertaining the position of forts, making reconnoissances on shore with the marines of the "Savannah," until their progress was stopped by an unfordable stream and nothing more could be accomplished.

On the 16th of December, 1861, Commander Percival Drayton was sent on a reconnoissance of the North Edisto river, in the steamer "Pawnee," accompanied by the "Seneca," Lieutenant-Commanding Ammen, and the Coast Survey steamer "Vixen," Captain Boutelle, who was generally the pioneer in these expeditions and whose knowledge of the hydrography of the country gave much valuable assistance.

While Captain Drayton was examining into the condition of some works (which proved to be deserted), Lieutenant Ammen proceeded with the "Seneca" five miles up the river and burned some cotton houses and out-buildings.

A landing was made at the small town of Rockville in hopes of surprising a large body of the enemy's infantry, but they decamped in a great hurry, leaving in Commander Drayton's hands a sloop, loaded with cotton and provisions, large quantities of commissary stores, consisting of rice, sugar, bacon, corn, etc., which were removed to the "Vixen."

An encampment a mile from the water was visited and broken up, all the tents and stores being removed to the boats.

The smaller gunboats pushed on until they ran aground and could go no further. They burnt one sloop, which had been run on shore by the enemy and which could not be gotten off.

A large number of the negroes in that section greatly feared that the whites would retaliate upon them for the pleasure they had shown when the Union gunboats arrived, and now most of them claimed and obtained the protection of the Union flag.

The sentiment which pervaded the minds of naval officers in the early part of the rebellion, that the negroes were the sacred property of the Southern planters, not to be touched under any circumstances, evaporated a short time after operations had begun, and when the Southern soldiers compelled the negroes to throw up their earthworks, dig their ditches and haul their loads, while they enjoyed what comfort they could get from camp life. The Federal officers determined to remove as far as they possibly could this important factor of war from their masters, and give them that liberty to which all men are entitled. Hundreds of these negroes were removed in the gunboats and finally located on Hilton Head Island.

This expedition found the fortifications on Edisto Island entirely deserted and partially destroyed, though on these occasions the rebels always managed to carry off the guns. Having obtained all the necessary information the vessels returned to Port Royal.

Another expedition, under Commander C. R. P. Rodgers, left Tybee Roads on the 11th of December, 1861, with the "Ottawa," "Pembina," "Seneca" and "Henry Andrew."

Entering and passing up Vernon River, they discovered a fort on the eastern end of Green Island, mounting eight guns, apparently of heavy calibre, and near it an encampment of 75 tents.

The fort was advantageously placed, and its approaches landward were well protected by marshes. It commanded not only Vernon River, but the Little Ogeechee, and Hell Gate, the passage from Vernon River into the Great Ogeechee.

The reader should have a good map of the coasts of South Carolina and Georgia by him, in order to obtain some idea of the immense net of natural defences on which the Southern engineers had erected fortifications with great skill and judgment.

These expeditions may appear to some readers to be of very little importance, but if they will carefully examine the map they will see for themselves how difficult it was for our gunboats to reach these places, which were important military points and convenient refuges for light-draft blockade runners.

It was to obtain possession of all the prominent positions held by the enemy that Admiral Dupont sent out these expeditions, and he desired to accomplish the work with as little loss as possible.

It may be asked why this last expedition did not attempt to capture the enemy's works.

In the first place, the expedition was simply a reconnoissance, and he is an unwise officer who goes to fighting and risks the object in view. In the second place, the vessels could not approach the fort nearer than two miles, which was beyond the reach of their guns.

The enemy fired at the "Pembina" with a heavy smooth-bore gun, but the shot fell far short, and the commander of the expedition did not think it well, under the circumstances, to return the fire, and give the enemy the opportunity of reporting an engagement with and the repulse of Yankee gun-boats.

Ogeechee Sound and the Great Ogeechee River were examined and no batteries found. A full reconnoissance was accomplished, by which the Commander-in chief was placed in possession of information that would much facilitate any operations of the Army and Navy which might be decided on in the future.

On December 5th Commander Drayton again proceeded on a reconnoissance to Saint Helena Sound in the "Pawnee," accompanied by the gunboats "Unadilla," Commander N. Collins, "Isaac Smith," Lieut. Commander J. W. Nicholson, and Coast Survey steamer "Vixen," Captain Boutelle.

He reached the anchorage off the fort on Otter Island at mid-day; pushed on up Mosquito Creek (no doubt appropriately named), but found no traces of white people, except some burning buildings on Hutchison's Island. Very little was effected to repay this expedition, yet what fine harbors were found for blockade runners, what places of safety for our fleets to lie in during winter storms, and what vigilance would be required to keep these retreats from being made useful by an enemy so quick to take advantage as were the soldiers of the South!

Whenever the enemy's troops appeared they were reminded by a bursting shell that the annoying gunboat was at their heels, and would follow and harass them until they retreated from the coast.

On landing at Hutchison's Island, they found that two days before all the negroes' houses, overseer's house, and out-buildings, together with the picked cotton, had been burned.

Thus early in the war did the torch begin to play that prominent part by which hundreds were driven from their homes, and by which the Southern soldiers in their folly thought to defeat the Federals in their cherished object of securing plunder.

This system led to retaliation, which in the end impoverished the Southern people from Cape Hatteras to Florida.

An attempt had been made on the approach of the gunboats to drive off the negroes and prevent their escaping, A great many did escape, however, though some of the number were shot in the back in the attempt.

The scene of complete desolation which on this occasion met the eyes of our officers beggars description; the negroes cowering amid the smoking ruins of their homes would have touched the hardest heart. These poor creatures still clung in despair to the spot where their houses once stood, but where they could no longer find shelter, and here they bewailed in piteous accents the loss of what was once the only Paradise they had on earth. In one moment they had seen all that was most precious to them reduced to ashes; but they preferred to remain near the place where their homes once stood, in the hope of obtaining comparative liberty, rather than to follow the fortunes of their masters and remain in bondage.

The most painful spectacle of all was that of old and decrepit men and women wandering about in search of the places where they were wont to dwell, and searching with bleared eyes in the hot ashes for any little memento of by-gone days that might cheer them in the few years they had yet to live.

Little children crawled around at the risk of falling into the burning embers, while their heart-broken mothers sat alone and gazed with despair at the wreck of all they once owned—though they had only owned it at the will and pleasure of their masters.

Much sympathy was felt for these poor creatures; but it was not entirely deserved, for the gunboats had hardly dropped down the creek for the night (which they did as a matter of precaution) before signal lights were made at the very spot they had left, to inform the enemy of their departure. It could only have been done by the negroes, for there was not a white man within a mile of the plantation. This might appear like treachery on the part of the blacks, but it was only for fear of further punishment that they pretended an interest in the cause of their masters.

That strange infatuation which possessed some of the cabinet of Mr. Lincoln, that by the Constitution the negroes were the goods and chattels of the South and could not be liberated until that clause in the Constitution was annulled, did much towards bringing desolation upon these poor people, who having formed some indefinite idea of freedom, would escape to the Union lines, in the hope of receiving protection; but they were often disappointed, for though they were kindly treated they were not protected in the full sense of the word. They were allowed to hang around the camps and naval stations, and live upon the debris of the soldiers' and sailors' rations, but it cannot be said that they were actually taken care of. They were allowed to till the land around them, put up cottages of brush and straw, and eke out an existence scarcely superior to that of an animal, and that was called philanthropy.

At first the officers of the Navy were afraid to take the responsibility of openly liberating the slaves, being held back by the old idea of the right of the white man to property in human flesh which was guaranteed to him by the Constitution.

The Cabinet would not for a time approach this subject, for some of its members still adhered to the delusion that the South would never come back into the Union if the subject of slavery was tampered with in any way.

If Abraham Lincoln's emancipation act had been promulgated the day Sumter was fired upon, the liberated slaves would have flocked to the North, and thus have deprived the Southerners of that factor in the war (the slave labor) which built their forts, hauled their loads, worked their plantations, and furnished them with food while fighting. They even attended their masters on the battle-field, carried off the wounded, drove teams, etc., and every negro thus employed saved a soldier to the Confederacy.

Instead of depriving the Confederates of their services, we avoided the expense of providing for them, and left them to take care of themselves. Hundreds died from neglect: they were a shiftless, lazy people and could not take care of themselves. Many in despair wandered back to their masters, who in fact treated them better than we did, hoping some day to make use of them again, when their cause was gained, and the negro once more regarded as a chattel.

Is it any wonder that they made signal lights to inform their masters that the gunboats had departed?

The slaves seemed on the whole to be embued with more liberal sentiments towards the white man of the North, than the latter held for them.

It is true that they had been removed from points where they were suffering to places of shelter, but not beyond the reach of the Southern fanatics, who shot at them as they would at dogs or cats.

This was done by men who would blow up light-houses, burn villages and destroy springs, so that those favorable to the Union cause might not enjoy a glass of fresh water.

In spite of our neglectful treatment of the blacks, they were always more than friendly to us. They would assist in destroying a fort, though it might bring them lashes or death; they would give information with regard to the movements of the enemy, and would hurrah when a Union shell burst in the midst of Confederate troops. But they did not receive that aid which would have kept them from starving, and so have prevented their old masters using them to build up forts to drive the Union people away.

On the above-mentioned occasion, Commander Drayton's policy was a generous one. A large number of the negroes had left Hutchison Island after they had been burned out, and now crowded upon the beach with what was left of their goods and chattels, and prayed to be removed to another island.

They were taken away by the gunboats, and if the expedition had accomplished nothing else, the Commander would have deserved credit for thus relieving suffering humanity.

Otter Island Fort and the adjacent waters were, on this occasion, placed in charge of Lieut.-Commanding Nicholson, who was directed to supply the negroes with food and do what he could for their comfort.

The attention of Admiral Dupont had, in January, been drawn to the fact that the enemy designed to shut up the troops on Port Royal Island, by placing obstructions in the Coosaw River and Whale Branch, by erecting batteries at Port Royal Ferry, at Seabrook, and at or near Boyd's Neck, and by accumulating troops in the vicinity in such a manner as to be able to throw a force of three thousand men upon any of these points at short notice.

On a consultation with General T. W. Sherman, it was determined to arrest the designs of the enemy and to do it in such a manner as to prevent any more attempts of the kind. A joint expedition was agreed upon, and a plan of conduct settled upon by the commanders of the Army and Navy. The first day of the year was selected for the attack.

Commander C. R. P. Rodgers was appointed to the command of the naval forces, consisting of the "Ottawa," Lieut.-Commanding Stevens, "Pembina," Lieut.-Commanding Bankhead, and four armed boats from the "Wabash," carrying howitzers, under charge of Lieutenants Upshur, Luce and Irwin, and Acting Master Kempff, all of which were to enter the Coosaw by Beaufort river; the gun-boat "Seneca," Lieut.-Com. Ammen, and the tug-boat "Ellen," Acting-Master Budd, to participate, both of which were to move up Beaufort River and approach the batteries at Seabrook and Port Royal Ferry, by Whale Branch. The armed Tug "Hale," Acting-Master Foster, was also ordered to report to the commander of the expedition.

The gun-boats reached Beaufort on the 31st December, 1862, and in order not to give the enemy notice of their approach, they remained there until after dark, when they ascended the river to within two miles of the Coosaw. At 4 o'clock the next morning the gun-boats moved up and joined General Stevens at the appointed rendezvous. Here the troops embarked, crossed the Coosaw, and landed at Haywood's plantation, and with them went the two howitzers of the "Wabash," to serve as a section of light artillery, under Lieutenant Irwin.

The troops and gun-boats engaged the enemy (who was on the alert) at Port Royal and Seabrook Ferries. The Confederates also appeared in force, in line of battle, on the right of the Federal troops, but were dispersed with some loss by the fire of the gun-boats, which was very galling.

At sunset the enemy sent in a flag of truce, asking permission to carry off their dead and wounded; just then the gun-boats opened fire, and before General Stevens could send a messenger to stop it, the officer who brought the flag of truce galloped off.

The enemy again showed themselves in force the next morning, but the gunboats opened such a fire on them that they soon retired to a point where they could not be followed and made no more demonstrations.

The military portion of the expedition recrossed the Coosaw and started on their return march, while the gunboats, watching the tide and their opportunity, passed down the channel, leaving the enemy to understand that they would be chased up whenever they attempted to plant batteries on sounds, inlets or rivers.

The co-operation of the Army and Navy was very complete on this occasion. The services of the officers are highly spoken of by Commander Rodgers, particularly the work of Lieut.-Commander Ammen with the "Seneca" and "Ellen" at Seabrook.

The work was performed in very narrow and crooked rivers, but with care and skillful handling the gunboats (though often aground) were brought out with but little damage.

The reports of Lieuts.-Commanding Truxton and Nicholson, though not containing an account of severe service, are instructive as showing how each officer of the fleet was kept employed in chasing up the enemy, and how the latter kept on the move.

Admiral Dupont made it a rule (and it was a very good one) to give his staff officers an opportunity to distinguish themselves where opportunity offered, without taking away from others what they might consider theirs of right, namely, to do all the fighting while the staff were attending to what might be considered their legitimate duties.

Hence we find the Fleet-Captain, Charles H. Davis, getting underway on January 26, 1862, for an expedition into Warsaw Sound. He had under his command the gunboats "Ottawa," Lieut.-Commanding Stevens; "Seneca," Lieut.-Commanding Ammen, and the armed steamer, "Isaac Smith," Lieut.-Commanding Nicholson; the "Potomska," Lieut.-Commanding Watmough; the "Ellen," Master Budd; "Western World," "Gregory," and the two armed launches of the "Wabash," and having in company the transports "Cosmopolitan," "Delaware" and "Boston," on board of which were the 6th Connecticut, the 4th New Hampshire and the 97th Pennsylvania regiments, in all 2,400 men, commanded by Brig.-General H. G. Wright. Commander C. R. P. Rodgers accompanied the expedition.

The object of this move was to cut off the communication between Fort Pulaski and Savannah.

The vessels entered Little Tybee River, or Freeborn Cut, and passed Fort Pulaski, but were not fired into, as the fort was not prepared for an enemy on this side. Preparations were at once made, however, to receive the expedition warmly on its return. The distance was that of long-range guns.

The vessels were brought to a stop, after passing Wilmington Island, by heavy piles driven in a double row across the channel; they were anchored and a reconnoissance made, in boats, of the numerous creeks with which this country was intersected.

At 5 P. M. five Confederate steamers, one of them carrying a square flag at the fore (probably Commodore Tatnall's), anchored at the mouth of the creek. They had it in their power to choose their distance, and this led to an expectation of an attack, but the night passed quietly.

At 11:15 the five steamers composing Commodore Tatnall's squadron attempted to pass down the river with some scows in tow. Commander John Rodgers, who lay at anchor in Wright River, and Captain Davis opened fire upon them, which they returned with spirit. The result of the engagement, which lasted less than half an hour, was that Commodore Tatnall and one of his squadron were driven back; the other three vessels made good their passage down to Fort Pulaski, and afterwards passed up the river again to Savannah, where one of them sunk at the dock.

As a demonstration the appearance of the gun-boats was a success, as Savannah was thrown into a great state of excitement, and all the energies of the people were put forth to increase the military defences.

The information required by this expedition was gained without loss of life or injury to the gun-boats.

Surveys and examinations were made up Wright and Mud Rivers by Commander John Rodgers, and a great amount of good service done. The officers and boats' crews were in continual danger from the fire of bush-whacking Confederates, who were always ready for a fight.

The names of Commanders John Rodgers, Drayton, C. R. P. Rodgers, Godon, Rhind, Stevens, Balch, Ammen, Truxton, Watmough, and Semmes, were conspicuous wherever a Confederate shot was heard, or wherever there was a chance to gain a point on the enemy.

Heavy knocks were received by our gunboats from Confederate flying batteries, which would often make desperate stands behind earthworks thrown up for the occasion. The long steel shot from their Whitworth guns would pass easily through the sides of our vessels and inflict death or injury on all around. These attacks were, in most instances, followed by summary punishment from the heavy guns of the Federal vessels. Our officers and men had a most persistent enemy to deal with, but they never flinched from any kind of duty until the whole coast was under Federal control.

All along the coast and up the rivers, where gun-boats could reach, heavy earthworks were found abandoned, their magazines blown up, and their guns removed, evidently showing that the Confederates did not care to dispute with our gun-boats the occupancy of the soil. They would scarcely have finished many of their batteries before they would abandon them, and erect new works again at some other point.

A remarkable instance of patriotism on the part of the colored people was evinced in the bringing out of the armed steamer "Planter" from Charleston, and delivering her over to the naval officer blockading that port. Robert Small, who performed this courageous act, was employed on board the "Planter," which was used as a dispatch and transportation steamer attached to the Engineer Department in Charleston, under Brigadier-General Ripley.

The taking out of the "Planter" would have done credit to anyone, but the cleverness with which the whole affair was conducted deserves more than a passing notice. Small was a very clever light mulatto who had been running this steamer for some time, and he had gained the confidence of his employers to that extent that, on the 13th of May, the Captain went on shore for the night and left Small in charge. He had made all his arrangements to carry off his family, and at 4 o'clock in the morning, left the wharf with the Palmetto and Confederate flags flying, passed the forts and saluted them as he went by, by blowing his steam whistle. After getting out of reach of the Confederate guns, he hauled down the flags and hoisted a white one at the fore. All this required the greatest heroism, for had he been caught while leaving the wharf, or stopped by the forts, he would have paid the penalty with his life.

The "Planter" mounted two guns of her own, and had lying upon her deck four guns intended for the forts, one a 7-inch rifle.

Small was the pilot of the boat, and had no difficulty in making his way through the obstructions placed in the channels. Besides the vessel and guns which he brought out, he gave much valuable information which only a man of his intelligence could impart. When he left Charleston he brought away with him eight men and five women.

Robert Small was an object of great interest in Dupont's fleet, not only for his courageous act, but for being the most intelligent slave that had yet been met with. He was one of the first, if not the first, colored man who was elected to Congress from Brunswick, S. C., and he held his own with white men who were far better educated than himself. It was not often that a negro was met with of such intelligence, from the fact that the system of slavery so tended to degrade the colored race that few, if any, could ever rise to superiority.

When Admiral Dupont gave up the command of the South Atlantic Squadron there was not much left for his successor to do in the way of gaining information along the coasts of South Carolina, Georgia and Florida. The officers under Dupont's command had made themselves so well acquainted with the hydrography and topography of the country that they needed no pilots to point the way for them through any bay or inlet.

All the sounds or inlets where a blockade runner could get in or out were so closely watched, or hermetically sealed, that few vessels attempted to communicate with the Confederacy in that direction. As a rule they had abandoned their beats, and either kept to running into Charleston or Wilmington, or went to the coasts of Alabama and Texas, where their chances were better than in the South Atlantic.

The South Atlantic coast was throughout the war the favorite ground for blockade runners, and the hardest blockading duty was performed in that quarter. Rich prizes were sometimes taken, and watchful commanders often reaped uncommon rewards; but with it all there was a monotonous watchfulness that wore men out, and many officers after the war fell into bad health, if they did not altogether succumb to the influence of a climate which in winter or summer was not conducive to longevity.

CHAPTER X.

NAVAL ENGAGEMENT AT SOUTH-WEST PASS.—THE GULF BLOCKADING SQUADRON IN NOVEMBER, 1861.

ATTEMPT TO BLOCKADE THE PASSES OF THE MISSISSIPPI.—ESCAPE OF THE "SUMTER."—THE "MANASSAS" RAMS THE "RICHMOND."—THE BATTLE AT THE PASS.—ATTEMPT TO DESTROY THE "VINCENNES."—FINAL RESULTS OF THE ENGAGEMENTS.—CAPTURE OF THE "ROYAL YACHT" IN GALVESTON HARBOR BY LIEUT. JAMES E. JOUETT.—ATTACK ON FORT McRAE AND FORT PICKENS BY THE "NIAGARA" AND "RICHMOND," NOVEMBER 22, 1861.—CORRECT ACCOUNT OF ATTEMPT TO RELIEVE FORT SUMTER, APRIL 12, 1861, AND OF RELIEF OF FORT PICKENS, APRIL 17, 1861.—LIST OF SHIPS AND OFFICERS OF WEST GULF BLOCKADING SQUADRON, 1861.

IT would be a pleasant task to be able to record nothing but successes and have no defeats checked against us; but that could not very well be unless we admitted that our enemy was deficient in all the qualities which distinguish the American soldier and sailor, and that we gained our victories easily because we had no one of any courage, energy or ability to contend with.

On the contrary, we had all these to meet us at every step; and our enemies, although men of the same stamp as ourselves, had their energies quickened by an amount of rancor which the Federals could never be made to feel, as they were fighting simply to preserve the Union, while the Confederates were fighting with a cherished object, to gain something new and beyond their reach, which they thought would conduce to their happiness, and of which they thought the North was trying to deprive them.

We could not expect impunity from losses and defeats upon the water any more than the soldiers could on the land; for though the Confederates had nothing like the resources of the North in naval matters, yet they put forth so much more energy and converted so many ordinary vessels into powerful rams and gunboats, that they made up in that way for what they lacked originally.

The reader must not therefore be surprised if the Union Navy was now and then caught tripping; nor must they take it for granted that every officer in the Navy was a perfect man, patterned after some rare type, who never made mistakes or knew defeat.

In so great a field of operations as that through which our Army and Navy labored for so long a time, it would be strange indeed if a great many mistakes were not committed.

New Orleans was the Queen City of the South; the great emporium through which the Confederates at one time hoped to inflict great injury upon the North by fitting out vessels-of-war or privateers to prey upon the Northern merchant ships, and by converting the factories of this place into shops for casting guns and making small arms.

The Confederates considered that it would be a difficult matter for the Union forces to blockade the different mouths of the Mississippi, the bayous and sounds, and flattered themselves that New Orleans would become the rendezvous for all the blockade runners that had early in the war commenced to swarm upon the coast like bees about the honey flowers. But they were disappointed in their expectations, for as early as June, 1861, Commodore McKean sent the "Powhatan," Lieut. D. D. Porter, to close up the Southwest Pass of the Mississippi, and Com-

U. S. SLOOP OF WAR "BROOKLYN," OFF PENSACOLA.

mander Charles Poor, in the " Brooklyn," to blockade Pass à l'Outre.

It was through the latter channel that the " Sumter," Captain Semmes, escaped to sea, while the " Brooklyn " was off in chase of a strange sail, and she was thus enabled to commence her career of havoc on American commerce.

This drew the attention of the Navy Department particularly to the mouths of the Mississippi, and a small squadron of vessels (quite inadequate for the purpose) was appointed to blockade the different passes.

The river Mississippi divides into several channels before reaching the Gulf of Mexico, and this division takes place at a point simply known as " the head of the passes," about fifteen miles above the mouths of the river. It was supposed that if a squadron could occupy this point it would be able to intercept anything going up or down.

It was not until the 12th of October, 1861, that this squadron reached " the head of the passes."

It was composed of the following vessels: " Richmond," screw steamer, Capt John Pope, twenty-two 9 inch guns; " Vincennes," sloop-of-war, ten guns; " Preble," sloop, eleven guns: " Water Witch," small screw steamer, four guns.

This squadron, mounting in all forty-seven guns, seemed to be quite able to defend " the head of the passes " and not only prevent anything going up or down, but to drive off any force the Confederates could collect at that moment.

But the Confederates had already fitted out a ram (the " Manassas"), armed with one gun in the bow, covered with iron and considered of sufficient power to sink a heavy ship with one of her blows.

The Commander of the Union squadron did not seem to be aware that the enemy had a vessel of this kind on the river, or if he did, he attached but little importance to the fact, having the impression that she was nothing more than a small converted tug.

The rule that a man should never despise his enemy was never more thoroughly illustrated than on this occasion.

The " Richmond " was coaling from a schooner which lay alongside of her, not keeping any particular lookout, her crew being employed in getting the coal on board. It was 3:45 in the morning, the " Water Witch " was *not* in the advance, keeping a lookout, and the ships of war were all anchored in the stream, when the " Richmond " discovered a strange craft approaching, which immediately afterwards struck her a heavy blow abreast the port fore-channels, tearing the schooner from her fastenings, crushing in three planks of the ship's side and making a small hole two feet below the water line.

That was the only blow the ram struck, for, as we now know, she was somewhat disabled by the shock, and she moved off slowly up the river, glad to get away so easily.

This vessel proved to be the ram " Manassas," at that time one of the improvised squadron of Commodore Hollins, late of the U. S. Navy.

The " Richmond's " crew flew to their quarters as soon as she was struck, and, as soon as they could they fired a random broadside, for there was not much chance of seeing anything in the darkness which then prevailed.

The ram. it is reported, remained under the quarter of the " Richmond " for some time, apparently trying to give another blow (but in fact partly disabled), and then drifted away.

COMMODORE J. S. HOLLINS, C. S. N.

Had the " Richmond " stood up the river until daylight the " Manassas " would have fallen into her power. The " Preble " opened her port battery on the ram as it passed slowly up the river, but without any effect.

After a time the " Richmond " got underway and went a short distance above the passes, but Acting-Master Wilcox reported that she was getting too close to the starboard shore (where there was water enough to float a three-decker), and the helm was put hard a starboard (instead of proceeding on up, as could easily have been done) and the vessel sheared off into the stream with her broadside bearing up the river; she then drifted down with the current until she neared the " head of the passes," when "ineffectual attempts were made to get her head up stream" (which could easily have been done by letting go an anchor).

The vain efforts continued until the steamships had drifted a mile and a half down the Southwest Pass, when they were discontinued, the helm put up, and the vessel headed towards Pilottown, where her commander thought he would be able to turn round !

When she arrived at Pilottown she still drifted on, and strange to say, she drifted toward the exit from the river. All this time the other vessels were doing all they could to drift after the "Richmond!" In other words, having been sent to the passes to defend them, on the first appearance of an enemy they deserted their posts and made a most shameful retreat—a retreat from a few river boats that a broadside of either ship would have sent to the bottom in five minutes. In fact, it was a perfect stampede if there ever was one, and there seems to have been a desire to get into deep water, which was entirely unwarranted by the circumstances.

The "Richmond" and "Vincennes" both drifted broadside on until near the bar, when they grounded in that position (the most favorable one to receive an attack from the enemy.)

The day before Captain Pope had mounted on the "Richmond's" forecastle one of his 9-inch guns, in order to be ready for any emergency, and it served him a good turn when the time came for using it.

As soon as the enemy saw that the two ships had grounded near the bar, they came down below Pilottown and opened fire on them with some light Whitworth guns of good range, which could reach the Federal ships while the heaviest guns on the Richmond could not reach them.

The enemy kept up this fire for about two hours without doing any particular damage, the bolts from their rifles being quite small. One of them lodged in a drawer of the bureau containing Captain Pope's clothes, and there seemed to have spent itself, without doing any harm whatever.

There is no account of any injury being inflicted on the vessels, or of any one being killed or wounded. It was very much like the celebrated " battle of the kegs " which once set a whole fleet in motion.

While the firing was going on, the enemy's shot flying over and the shot from our ships falling short, it was reported to Captain Pope that several boats filled with men were leaving the "Vincennes."

Some went on board the steamer "Water Witch," others went to the "Richmond," and Captain Handy (the Commander of the "Vincennes"), in company with several of the officers, presented himself on the quarter-deck before Captain Pope, with the American flag wrapped around his waist in large folds [!], and on being asked the object of his coming in that guise, stated

that he had abandoned his ship in obedience to signal, and on being informed that no such signal had been made, he insisted that Captain Winslow of the "Water Witch" had so read it.

When Captain Winslow was asked regarding the matter, he said that he saw no such signal. It was, in fact, simply the power of imagination acting on Capt. Handy's nerves.

He did send to Capt. Winslow asking if that was not the meaning of a signal that was made by the flagship, but the answer he received was "No; it is impossible that any such signal can have been made. Get your guns out of your stern ports and defend your ship."

It appears that on leaving his ship Capt. Handy determined that nothing of her should fall into the hands of Commodore Hollins, and he therefore ordered that a slow match should be placed near the magazine, and a train of powder laid, so that by the time he reached the "Richmond" the old "Vincennes," that had performed many a useful cruise, should go up in a blaze of glory. He never reflected that his small 32-pounders might be whisked about in the air and fall upon the decks of the stranded "Richmond."

Capt. Handy's reception on board the flagship by Capt. Pope was not a flattering one. He was immediately ordered back to his vessel when it was seen that she did not blow up, and the quarter-gunner who had been directed to light the match informed them that he had cut the lighted part off and thrown it overboard.

In the mean time the steamer "McClellan" came in with stores for the squadron and some rifled-guns of large calibre, and this put the Commander of the squadron at his ease. He could now drive the Hollins flotilla off if it should reappear.

The "McClellan" was then set to work to get the grounded vessels afloat, which she finally succeeded in doing, and they crossed the bar and anchored *safely* in deep water.

Capt. Pope in his report of this unhappy affair says : "My retreat down the pass, though painful to me, was to save the ships and prevent them from being sunk and falling into the hands of the enemy [!] as it is evident to me that they had us in their power by means of the ram and fire-rafts. If I have erred in all this matter it is an error of judgment. The whole affair came upon me so suddenly that there was no time left me for reflection, but called for immediate action and decision. The ram having made her appearance next day at the mouth of the river [!] the impression is she sustained no injury from our shot, only waiting an opportunity to destroy our ships.

"It having been rumored that there was a panic on board this ship at the time she was engaged with the enemy, I state it to be false. Both officers and men maintained their coolness and determination to do their duty. My orders and those of the officers were carried out with as much coolness as if it had been an every-day affair, and their whole conduct merits high commendation.

"They would be gratified to prove their bravery by being permitted to take part in the contemplated attack on Pensacola, as requested in notes from me to you on the subject.

"In both engagements with the enemy the fire appeared to be directed to the destruction of this ship, most of the shot being apparently directed to the quarter of this vessel, presumed for the purpose of disabling our rudder and propeller."

This relation would not be complete if Capt. Handy had not had the opportunity to place himself on record, on the eve of his ship getting aground, as follows:

"SIR: We are aground. We have only two guns that will bear in the direction of the enemy.

"Shall I remain on board after the moon goes down with my crippled ship and nearly worn-out men?

"Will you send me word what countersign my boats shall use if we pass near your ship?

"While we have moonlight would it not be better to leave the ship? Shall I burn her when I leave her?

"Respectfully,
"ROBERT HANDY."

Capt. Pope seemed quite aware of the ludicrousness of this proposition, and wrote Handy as follows:

"U. S. Str. 'RICHMOND,'
"SOUTH WEST PASS.
"October 12, 1861.

"SIR: You say your ship is aground. It will be your duty to defend your ship up to the last moment, and not to fire her unless it be to prevent her falling into the hands of the enemy.

"I do not think the enemy will be down to-night, but if they do come, fight them to the last.

"You have boats enough to save all your men. I do not approve of your leaving your ship until every effort is made to defend her from falling into their hands. Respectfully, etc.,
"JOHN POPE,
"Captain, U. S. N.
"COM. ROBERT HANDY, U. S. N.,
"Commanding 'Vincennes.'"

There is not much more to tell of this painful business—it would have been better to have left out the telling of it, but history cannot be written fairly if that alone is told which is creditable, and if that which smacks of the disgraceful is omitted.

There is no excuse for anything that happened in this squadron, and the mistakes made were not redeemed by any after-acts of gallantry.

To say that this stampede happened be-cause these ships were taken by surprise, and because the most extravagant reports had been spread by Hollins about the force he had in rams and fire-rafts, was all folly.

Suppose the rebels had invented the most destructive methods, which lively imaginations had invested with supernatural power, there was no reason why 47 heavy guns and 700 men should run away from such goblins.

A badly-constructed ram ran her snout into the "Richmond" and ripped off three pieces of her planking; there were no fire-rafts, and Hollins' squadron was all a sham. His gunboats were nothing more than frail river craft with small rifled guns—like those which Bailey's division sent to the bottom after a fifteen minutes' engagement at the battle of Forts Jackson and St. Philip.

Put this matter in any light you may, it is the most ridiculous affair that ever took place in the American Navy. There is no instance during the war like it. To think that we should have to write of such a retreat is mortifying, but it stands on record, described in language that almost claims merit for the flight of the "Richmond" and her consorts, chased by a ram that was going in an opposite direction as fast as her disabled machinery would take her,— her officers thanking their stars that they got away so easily!

There is nothing that can equal the comicality of Capt. Handy's performance—laying a train with a slow match to his magazine, and then hastening away in his boats with the American flag wound around him, and his remarkable antics when he found that his ship would not blow up. This presents an example unmatched in any navy in the world.

After the ships had safely passed the bar, it was a subject of great congratulation to them that they were out of reach of Hollins, his rams and his fire-rafts; the very enemies they had been sent into the river to subdue.

New Orleans was illuminated on this occasion, and Hollins was fêted as if he had won a great victory.

Perhaps this fiasco had a good effect by causing the Confederates to underrate the Northern Navy; if so, they dearly paid for it, for only a few months afterwards all their rams, ironclads, fire-rafts, and gunboats were swept away by a squadron bravely commanded, notwithstanding the heavy forts prepared with every skill for the enemy's protection, and with all the devices human ingenuity could conceive of.

Such events as we have related are not without their benefit in time of war. They make officers more careful in their plans, and teach them that good commanders and brave men should never be taken by surprise; they also warn a government to be careful whom it places in command of its ships at a time when it is required that only the bravest and best should be selected for all occasions where success is demanded or where the honor of the flag is at stake.

A small detachment of vessels. under the command of Captain Henry Eagle, was at this time blockading the coast of Texas. His particular command was the frigate "Santee." She was not a suitable vessel for this purpose (being a sailing ship), and her crew of 500 men might have performed more effective service by being divided up amongst five or six small steamers, armed with howitzers.

A good deal of force was expended in this way during the war, which might have been exerted to better purpose; but the object of the Navy Department was to have a large number of guns afloat in view of European complications, and these large sailing ships, though perfectly useless for blockading purposes, carried a large number of men who could at times be used with good effect in landing on the enemy's coast.

Among the privateers which the Confederates were fitting out was one called the "Royal Yacht," which was being prepared in Galveston harbor to be let loose on the Federal commerce. This fact was known to Captain Eagle, and he made preparations to destroy her before she could get to sea.

On the 7th of November, 1861, an expedition was fitted out and placed under the command of Lieutenant James E. Jouett, with Lieutenant John J. Mitchell, Gunner William Carter and Master's Mate Chas. W. Adams in the first and second launches, each carrying a howitzer and a picked crew of men.

At 11:40 P. M. the two boats entered the harbor unperceived, intending, if they could pass the armed schooner guarding the entrance and the Bolivar and Point forts, to try to surprise and burn the man-of-war steamer "General Rusk," lying under Pelican Island fort.

The boats succeeded in passing the schooner and two forts, but in attempting to avoid the sentinels on Pelican fort they grounded on Pelican Spit and were discovered by the enemy. It was then too late to attempt the capture of the "General Rusk" (a heavily armed vessel) as the alarm was given at once, therefore that part of the expedition was abandoned.

The boats then turned about and pulled for the schooner "Royal Yacht," which they boarded and carried after a short but sharp conflict. By this time the people in the forts were aroused and opened fire in the direction of the boarding party. Lieut.

Jouett proceeded to secure his prisoners, 13 in number. and leave the vessel; before doing which, he spiked the only gun the schooner carried and set fire to her, as she had a shot through her at the water line, and the pilot on whom Jouett had depended to take the vessel out was shot down.

Lieutenant Jouett himself was severely wounded by a boarding pike in the hands of an enemy; Mr. William Carter, gunner, was wounded, one man killed of the boat's crew and six wounded, one of whom afterwards died.

REAR-ADMIRAL JAMES E. JOUETT.

(FROM A PHOTOGRAPH TAKEN IN 1885.)

This was a gallant and well-executed affair, and no doubt the "General Rusk" would have been captured but for the discovery of the boats. A boarding party against an enemy well armed and prepared for such an event is always a dangerous affair. The odds are always in favor of those on board the vessel, but in this case the schooner was carried by one boat only, because the other one did not get alongside in time to be of much assistance.

Captain McKean, who commanded the Gulf blockading squadron, issued a public order, thanking Lieut. Jouett and his officers and men for their gallantry and coolness on this occasion, with a hope that "their names might be enrolled by a grateful country with those which in former years shed so much lustre on the American flag."

On November 22d, 1861, Commodore McKean, after consultation with General Harvey Brown at Fort Pickens, determined to make an attack on Fort McRae and its defences with the "Niagara" and "Richmond," while Fort Pickens was to open on the Confederate batteries with its guns.

It was time something should be attempted in this quarter, for from April 16th up to this time (Nov. 22d) nothing had been

fathoms and the "Richmond" in 20 feet of water, Fort McRae bearing from the "Niagara" north, distant two miles.

The vessels opened fire, but finding that the "Niagara's" shells fell short, boats were sent out and a buoy placed in 23 feet of water near the edge of the shoal—distant one and three-quarters miles from the fort. Here the "Niagara" finally anchored and again opened fire, "this time with marked effect, many of her shells falling into the sand battery and others passing through the wall of the fort [?]. The barbette guns were silenced immediately after the firing began, and the casemates visibly slackened until 5 P. M., when it ceased entirely." The vessels fired no more after sundown, but again attacked the fort in the morning, as did also Fort Pickens.

CAPTURE OF THE PRIVATEER "ROYAL YACHT" BY A VOLUNTEER CREW FROM THE FRIGATE "SANTEE," UNDER COMMAND OF LIEUT. JAMES E. JOUETT.

done to show that there was any hostile feeling between the Federal and Confederate forces at Pensacola.

Both the "Niagara" and "Richmond" were vessels of heavy draft; the former could not enter the harbor, and the latter, to co-operate with her, would have to lie a long way outside of the fort and earthworks. The "Niagara" was lightened as much as possible and her draught reduced to 21 feet.

During the night of the 21st, a position had been selected and a buoy placed to mark the spot where the ships were to anchor. On the following morning at 10 o'clock, Fort Pickens fired the signal gun and the "Niagara" stood in, followed by the "Richmond" (Captain F. B. Ellison); both ships came to an anchor with springs on their cables, the "Niagara" in four

It was thought by those on board the ships that Fort McRae and its defenses were considerably damaged by the bombardment, but that remains doubtful. There was no return of the fire from the ships during the second day of the attack, as the Confederates saw that the naval commanders had no intention of entering the harbor, and that they were unnecessarily exposing themselves to the fire of Fort Pickens. So they withdrew from their works and let the fort and ships expend their ammunition at their own pleasure. (There was a cross-fire from the ships and Fort Pickens on the enemy's sand works which it was not possible to withstand.)

The "Richmond," owing to her lighter draught of water, was able to take a position closer to the northern shore than the "Niagara," and so far in the rear of both

fort and battery that their guns could not
be brought to bear upon her. For *several
hours* she escaped being struck, but on the
afternoon of the second day "ε masked
battery among the sand hills on t le main
land back of the lagoon opened fire upon
her." Finding that the enemy were getting
her range and fearing that she would be
struck, she changed her position, and finally, as her shells were falling short, she was
signalled to retire out of the line of fire. It
was thought that the guns in the masked
battery were rifled and of very heavy calibre [?] as their projectiles were thrown beyond the "Richmond."

At the end of the first day's bombardment the ships retired, uninjured. On the
second day they took up about the same
positions, but their shells failed to reach the
forts, while the Commander says, "the
enemy's shells fell thick about us, some
passing over the ships, and far beyond
them." "Therefore," says the Flag Officer,
"I deemed it my duty to withdraw the ship,
as to have retained our position would have
been to expose both her and the crew to serious injury with no possible advantage.
Our not being able to get within range was
owing to the fact that the northerly wind
had lowered the water and was directly *in
face* of our fire."

In this bombardment of two days two
shot struck the "Niagara," one abaft the
fore chains, lodging in the woodwork, the
other near the mizzen chains, also lodging
in the woodwork, the injuries being trifling.
The "Richmond" was also struck twice. A
shot struck the rail and hammock nettings
forward, another (a shell) exploded four
feet under water, "breaking and pressing
inboard several of her planks and causing
a serious leak." The loss during this engagement was one man killed and seven
slightly wounded by splinters.

Our object in mentioning this affair is not
for the purpose of claiming any brilliant
victory for the Navy, but to show the futility of ships engaging forts (especially
sand forts) at such long ranges that their
shell will not reach, and where they burst
five seconds before the proper time! Nor
is the bombardment mentioned as a naval
exploit of any great importance, for there
were no results from it which could benefit
the Government in any way, beyond showing the enemy that they would not be allowed to rest quietly while they were building their sand forts and preparing to make
Pensacola Harbor impregnable against
Fort Pickens and the Union fleet.

Had this action on the part of Flag Officer McKean and General Harvey Brown
been concerted earlier in the year it might
have had the good effect of driving the Confederates out of their works some time

sooner; but from April 17, 1861, when Fort
Pickens was reinforced with men and guns
and made strong enough to resist any attack from the Pensacola side, up to November 22d of the same year, not a movement
had been made by our Army or Navy to
check the work of the Confederates in building earthworks and mounting guns.

It is more than possible that this work
could have been arrested if proper steps had
been taken in the first place to send in a
strong naval force well backed by the
Army. The Confederates would have evacuated Pensacola a month after troops had
been sent to its relief, on April 17th, 1861.

There does not seem to have been any
particular object in the bombardment of
Fort McRae, beyond at the same time destroying the navy yard and its contents,
which, it is true, was in the hands of the
Confederates; but the latter did not seem
at all disposed to injure anything, and why
our own forces should want to destroy
what the enemy were taking care of cannot be understood.

There was nothing in the yard but machinery which the enemy could not use,
and guns which they had already mounted
and which could not have been of a very
dangerous character, as our ships were
only struck twice each in a two days' bombardment.

The history of the manner in which Pensacola was held by the Confederates from
April 1st, 1861 to May 9th, 1862, offers one
of the most curious commentaries on the
conduct of the war in this quarter. It had
the best harbor in the Gulf of Mexico, belonging to the United States. It had a good
navy yard, with the ordinary facilities for
fitting out and repairing ships, and water
enough on the bar to admit of the passage
of all but five or six of the heaviest ships of
the Navy. It was just the point wanted by
our naval commanders from which to carry
on operations against New Orleans and the
coast of Louisiana and Texas, and from
which to intercept blockade runners bound
for Southern ports from Havana and Nassau.

Before even Fort Sumter was fired on
President Lincoln saw the importance of
our holding Fort Pickens, and at the same
time that Secretary Welles sent his expedition to reinforce Sumter, the President and
Secretary Seward sent one to reinforce Fort
Pickens and prevent it from falling into the
hands of the insurgents.

This is an important part of the history
of the war, and as it had an important bearing on naval matters in the Gulf of Mexico,
and exhibited a great want of decision or
forgetfulness on the part of those who were
charged with the duty of recovering the
Government property, it may not be unin-

FORT PICKENS.　　FORT McRAE.　　NAVY YARD.

PANORAMIC VIEW OF PENSACOLA BAY, THE NAVY YARD AND FORTS.

teresting to restate some events connected with this place during the time of its occupation by the Confederates.

In the early part of the difficulties between the North and South, and before the Confederates had taken the bold step of firing upon Fort Sumter, and when the Government was anxious to ascertain the true condition of affairs at Charleston, Mr. G. V. Fox, formerly a Lieutenant in the Navy and later the Assistant Secretary, offered his services to go to Charleston, communicate with Colonel Anderson, and return with the required information.

The late administration of Mr. Buchanan, with a policy as feeble as it was unwise, had done nothing towards asserting the authority of the government over Fort Sumter, nor taken any energetic steps for its relief, even when it became known that the insurgents were waiting only for an opportunity to seize upon it, and turn its guns against any force which the National Government might send against Charleston.

The commander at Sumter, if he was not ordered to remain supine under all provocations, was at least given to understand that it would not be agreeable to the administration if he should attempt to prevent the Southerners from erecting such earthworks as they might think proper within reasonable bounds : but that he might hold on to the government property in Fort Sumter as long as he could do so without precipitating hostilities. That was the *spirit* of the understanding between Major Anderson and the Government, if not the actual one.

Though it was known to the late administration that the insurrectionists in Charleston were openly constructing strong earthworks opposite Sumter, avowedly with the intention of forcing its surrender, yet no steps were taken to relieve Major Anderson by sending reinforcements or supplies; nor did they protest against the action of the Southern forces who were making every preparation to attack him.

The Southern leaders had been prepared for the contingency of secession before Mr. Buchanan gave up the reins of office. All their plans were well matured and all precautions taken to insure their success. Thus, when President Lincoln came into office he found himself face to face with the most perplexing state of affairs that ever beset a statesman. The little garrison at Sumter was surrounded by guns, and the indignant people of the North were demanding that it should be relieved at all hazards.

The steamer "Star-of-the-West," under Captain McGowan, of the Revenue Marine, was chartered during President Buchanan's administration, and ordered to carry provisions to the beleaguered fort; but on entering the harbor and getting within range of the guns on Morris Island, she was fired upon, and finding that he would be sunk if he persevered in going on, Captain McGowan turned his vessel about and left the harbor.

Mr. Fox presented certain plans for the relief of Sumter to the Buchanan administration, but for various reasons they were not accepted, although at first deemed feasible, even by General Scott. But on the next day (Febuary 5th, 1861) news was received of the election of Jefferson Davis to the Presidency of the Southern Confederacy, and then General Scott intimated to Mr. Fox that probably no efforts would be made to relieve Fort Sumter.

On the 12th of March, Mr. Fox received a telegram from Postmaster-General Montgomery Blair to proceed to Washington; and when he arrived there he was induced by this gentleman to lay the same plans before President Lincoln that had been offered to President Buchanan, Mr. Blair informing Mr. Fox at the same time that General Scott had advised the President that Fort Sumter could not be relieved and would have to be given up. Having been introduced to the President by Mr. Blair, Fox unfolded his plans and was directed to call upon General Scott and discuss the matter with him.

The General did not approve Mr. Fox's plans, and informed Mr. Lincoln that it might have been practicable in February, but owing to the increased number of Confederate forts and guns it was not possible then.

These difficulties in carrying out his plans for the relief of Sumter, induced Mr. Fox to go in person to Charleston to see if he could not ascertain by the visit something that would strengthen his argument. He also wished if possible to visit Major Anderson.

In consequence, with the consent of the President, Secretary of War and General Scott, he proceeded by way of Richmond and Wilmington to Charleston and arrived there on the 25th of March. At that time there was a general feeling in Charleston and thereabout that the Government had concluded to give up Fort Sumter without an attempt to retain it.

On Mr. Fox's arrival in Charleston he sought an interview with Lieut. Hartstene, formerly of the U. S. Navy, and stated to him his desire to visit Major Anderson, and Hartstene in consequence introduced him to Governor Pickens, to whom he showed the orders under which he acted.

Governor Pickens directed Lieut. Hartstene to take Mr. Fox to Fort Sumter, where they arrived after dark and remained two hours.

Major Anderson seemed to think it was too late then to undertake to relieve Sumter by any other means than by landing an army on Morris Island. He thought an entrance from the sea impracticable, but while discussing the matter on the parapet Mr. Fox heard the sound of oars, and though the boat was very near she could not be seen through the haze and darkness of the night until she had actually reached the landing. This gave Mr. Fox the idea of supplying the fort by means of boats. He found the garrison very short of supplies, and it was decided by him and Major Anderson that he could report to the government that the fort could not hold out after the 15th of April unless supplies were furnished.

Mr. Fox made no arrangements with Major Anderson for reinforcing or supplying the fort, and very wisely did not inform him of his plans. On his return to Washington he was frequently called before the Cabinet to discuss his propositions and answer the objections of General Scott and other military authorities.

His plan was a naval one altogether, and he intended that it should be carried out by naval officers. It was simply running past batteries over 1,300 yards distant, at right angles with the enemy's fire, and there were many examples where such things had been done in perfect safety. Steamships had even been known to pass within 100 yards of a fort on a dark night without being seen.

The President inquired if there was at that time any officer of high rank in Washington who would sustain Mr. Fox in his project, directing that if one could be found he should be brought to the executive mansion.

Mr. Fox took Commodore Stringham to the President, who that morning had held a long conference with Commodore Stewart, and both declared that Sumter could be relieved on the plan Mr. Fox proposed.

On the 10th of March the President sent Mr. Fox to New York to make inquiries about obtaining vessels for the voyage, and he there consulted Messrs. George W. Blunt, Wm. H. Aspinwall and Charles H. Maxwell with regard to the necessary preparations. There were many delays in getting off the expedition, caused principally by everybody's desire to avoid a war. As late as the 4th of April the President informed Mr. Fox that he would allow the expedition to start for Charleston, but that he would in the meantime write a letter to the authorities of that place and promise that no attempt would be made to land troops if vessels were allowed to supply Sumter with provisions. There were but nine days left between the time Mr. Fox

would arrive in New York and the time when Major Anderson would be out of provisions, when he would be at liberty to surrender. In these few days Mr. Fox had to charter steamers, provide men and boats, and employ tugs, and then to pass over 632 miles before he could reach his destination.

The Secretary of the Navy had in the waters of the United States the steamers "Powhatan," "Pocahontas" and "Pawnee," which he placed at Mr. Fox's disposal. On the "Powhatan," which had gone out of commission, Mr. Fox depended for his boats and men. He arrived in New York on the 5th of April, 1861, engaged the steamer "Baltic" of Mr. Aspinwall, and delivered confidential orders to Colonel H. L. Scott, aide to the General-in-Chief, and Colonel D. D. Tompkins, Quartermaster, to supply all the needed stores.

Colonel Scott ridiculed the idea of any attempt to relieve Sumter, and by his indifference and delay half a day was lost. The recruits that he finally furnished were "entirely unfit to be thrown into a fort likely to be attacked by the Confederates."

Mr. Fox had applied to the Secretary of the Navy before leaving Washington, to have Commodore Stringham take command of the expedition; but that officer declined, as he considered it too late to be successful and likely to ruin the reputation of the officer who undertook it !

The hiring of three tugs was intrusted to Russell Sturgis, who obtained them with great difficulty on account of the danger of going to sea, and the Government had to pay the most exorbitant prices for them. These tugs were the "Yankee," the "Uncle Ben," and the "Freeborn." The "Yankee" being fitted to throw hot water. Mr. Fox received all the aid he desired in the mercantile line, and supposed that the naval vessels were all hurrying to the appointed place of meeting off Charleston.

Now on March 13th, 1861, the "Powhatan" came from sea into New York harbor. She was surveyed and found unfit for further service. Orders came from the Navy Department to put her out of commission, give the officers leave of absence, and send her crew to the receiving ship. On April 1st the stores were all landed, the ship stripped, officers granted leave of absence, crew sent to the receiving ship, and the vessel put out of commission.

To read the account of the naval historian (Boynton), the Navy Department depended on the "Powhatan" for the success of this expedition, yet on the 2d of April she was lying at the Navy Yard a "sheer hulk," preparing to go into dock !

Mr. Fox states that the "Powhatan," Captain Mercer, sailed on the 6th of April ; the "Pawnee," Commodore Rowan, on the

9th; the "Pocahontas," Captain Gillis, on the 10th, the "Harriet Lane," Captain Faunce, on the 8th, the tug "Uncle Ben," on the 7th, the tug "Yankee" on the 8th, and the "Baltic," Captain Fletcher, on the 8th; rather an unusual way for an expedition to start out, and calculated to cause a failure even if there were no other obstacles in the way. Three army officers accompanied the troops.

Soon after leaving Sandy Hook a heavy gale set in, and continued during most of the passage to Charleston, and the "Baltic," the fastest and staunchest vessel, only arrived off Charleston harbor on the 12th of April, and communicated with the "Harriet Lane," the only vessel that had arrived before her. At 6 A. M. the "Pawnee" arrived, and Mr. Fox went on board of her and informed Commander Rowan of his orders to send in provisions, asking him to stand in towards the bar.

Commander Rowan replied "that his orders required him to remain ten miles east of the light and await the arrival of the 'Powhatan,' and that he was not going into the harbor to inaugurate a civil war." Mr. Fox then stood in towards the bar with the "Baltic" and the "Harriet Lane." As these vessels showed themselves, heavy guns were heard up Charleston harbor and the smoke from the batteries which had opened upon Sumter was distinctly visible. Fox then turned and stood towards the "Pawnee," intending to inform Commander Rowan of the state of affairs, and met him coming in. Rowan hailed and asked for a pilot, declaring his intention of standing in and sharing the fate of his brethren of the Army. Fox went on board the "Pawnee" and informed the Commander that the Government did not expect such gallant sacrifice, having settled naturally upon the policy indicated in the instructions to Captain Mercer and himself.

No other naval vessels arrived that day except the "Pocahontas," but the steamer "Nashville" and a number of merchant vessels arrived off the bar and awaited the result of the bombardment, thus leading the people of Charleston to suppose that there was a large naval fleet lying off the bar.

Meanwhile the weather continued very bad, with a heavy sea. Neither the "Pawnee" nor the "Harriet Lane" had the necessary boats to land men or provisions, and it is very clear to the writer that any attempt to have done so would have been madness in the face of that sea and the enemy's fire. In fact, the expedition was useless from the time the first gun was fired at Sumter. It could only have been successful provided the water had been smooth, and the boats could have reached the fort late at night.

The moment the Confederates knew of the arrival of vessels off the bar, the bombardment commenced, and there was no stopping it then in the excited condition of the Southerners. They had been looking for the opportunity for weeks, and having found it they made the most of it, and did what they so longed to do—fired on the fort and flag which had stood there so many years to protect them.

All this time Mr. Fox was awaiting the arrival of the "Powhatan." Finding that she did not appear he went in the offing and made signals all night, so that she might find the "Baltic" in case she should arrive. The morning of the 13th was thick and foggy with a very heavy ground swell on, and the "Baltic," feeling her way in, ran aground on Rattlesnake Shoal, but got off without damage, and was obliged by the heavy swell to anchor in deep water, several miles outside of the "Pawnee" and "Harriet Lane."

One gallant army officer (R. O. Tyler), though suffering from seasickness, as were most of the troops, organized a boat's crew and exercised them for the purpose of having at least one boat (in the absence of the "Powhatan") that could go to the relief of Fort Sumter—as if one boat pulled by raw recruits could ever even cross the bar, much less reach the fort under such a fire. But fortunately the adventure ended where it began, and no boat was sent.

In the morning a great volume of black smoke burst forth from Fort Sumter, through which the flash of Major Anderson's guns could be seen replying to the Confederates. The quarters in the fort were on fire, but most of the officers thought it to proceed from an attempt to smoke out the garrison with fire-rafts," as if the buildings of the officers inside the fort with all their inflammable material would not make smoke enough without the addition of fire-rafts!

It was the opinion of the naval officers that no loaded boats could reach Sumter in that heavy sea. The tug-boats, like everything else in this expedition, had gone astray, and it was determined to seize a schooner lying at the bar with a load of ice, fill her with stores and men and send her on the following night to the relief of Sumter. The records do not say who proposed this scheme—for what chance could this slow-moving vessel have had under a fire which eventually caused the surrender of the fort itself? Fortunately this plan was also abandoned, and on the 14th Major Anderson evacuated, and with his troops was taken north on the steamer "Baltic."

This ended the Sumter expedition.

It is no more than justice to Mr. Fox to state what his plan really was, and we will give his own words :

"My plan for supplying Sumter required 300 sailors, a full supply of armed launches and three tugs. The 'Powhatan' carried the sailors and launches, and when this vessel was about to leave in obedience to an order from the Secretary of the Navy, two officers, Lieut. D. D. Porter, U. S. N., and Captain M. C. Meigs, U. S. Engineers, presented themselves on board with an order from the President of the United States authorizing the former to take any vessel whatever in commission, and proceed immediately to the Gulf of Mexico.

"This order did not pass through the Navy Department, and was unknown to the Secretary of the Navy, and when signed by the President he was not conscious that his signature would deprive me of the means to accomplish an object which he held to be of such vital importance."

To tell the rest of this history we must further quote Mr. Fox's report :

"The tug 'Freeborn' was not permitted to leave New York ; the tug Uncle Ben' was driven into Wilmington by the violence of the gale and eventually captured by the Confederates ; the tug 'Yankee' reached Charlestown a few hours after the 'Baltic' left for New York with Major Anderson's command on board."

Mr. Fox from his statement seems to have relied on the " Powhatan " to assist him, and considers her absence to be the cause of failure.

On the 2d of April he had not even received the written authority to undertake this expedition, and no decision had been come to by the President until April the 4th, and it was not until the morning of April 6th that a telegraphic dispatch was received by Captain Foote (commanding New York Navy Yard) as follows : " Prepare the 'Powhatan' for sea with all dispatch. (signed) Gideon Welles." On April 1st President Lincoln wrote an order to put the " Powhatan " in commission. On April 2d the work commenced on her.

On April 5th she went into commission, and on April 6th sailed for the relief of Fort Pickens, under the command of Lieut D. D. Porter.

On the day (April 6th) when a telegram came for Mr. Welles to prepare the " Powhatan " for sea with all dispatch, that vessel was about to sail on another mission. On the 7th, came orders for Captain Mercer to take command of the expedition to Charleston.

Supposing that the " Powhatan " had been taken in hand from her " sheer-hulk " condition on the 6th, and working on the best time, she could not have more than been ready by the 11th. She could only at the best make eight knots an hour. Charleston being 630 miles distant would require 79 hours, or three days and seven hours, to make the passage. This would

have brought them to Charleston only on the evening of the 14th, when Sumter was past all help.

Mr. Fox says he depended on her splendid launches and 300 sailors. The "Powhatan " had two wheel-house launches in the shape of a half watermelon, which were perfectly useless for want of repair, and sank when they were put in the water off Fort Pickens. She had two large quarter boats that would carry 35 men each, and two smaller boats that would carry about 25 men each in smooth water. Then where could Mr. Fox find the launches and men on the " Powhatan ?" Mr. Fox was not at all responsible for the failure, in fact no one connected with the Navy was to blame. The absence of the " Powhatan " had nothing to do with it. It was mostly due to the inaction of the Government, the disagreement between Army and Navy officers as to the feasibility of the plan, and the length of time elapsing between the period when Mr. Fox first proposed to relieve Fort Sumter and the time when he was allowed to get off. No one seemed desirous of helping him, and most of those whose business it was to get off the expedition threw obstacles in its way.

Whether it would have succeeded under the most favorable circumstances is doubtful, for an enemy that could (and did during the next four years) hold all approaches to Charleston against our heaviest iron-clads would not have been likely to fail in keeping out a few heavily-laden boats and tugs, with their high-pressure steam announcing their presence. We know now that boats and tugs would have been sacrificed in any attempt to relieve Sumter.

Mr. Fox, himself, manifested great courage in volunteering for such desperate service, which finally brought him into connection with the Navy Department, where his services were at that time much required. Mr. Welles showed a loyal spirit in this attempt to succour those whom the country thought should be relieved at all hazards, and he needed no defense.

The cause of the contretemps which directed the " Powhatan " from the Sumter expedition was in the organization of the Navy Department, which, with the bureau system existing then as it exists to-day, was unfit to carry on a great war. The Secretary wanted at his side an Advisory Board, or what was afterwards established, a clever man as Assistant Secretary.

The fact of sending a civilian down to Charleston to direct the movements of a naval commander, without any authority of law, was all wrong, no matter if the person had once been in the Navy. This produced complications from the very first; for no naval officer who was acquainted with the forms and precedents of the Navy would submit quietly to what he might well consider a reflection on his corps.

There are plenty of reasons why such an expedition should fail without referring to such as did not exist, and as a large portion of history (which should have been devoted to important duties performed by naval officers) has been taken up in showing that the preparations of the Navy Department for the succor of Fort Sumter were interfered with, it is time the matter was made plain. The quotations from Mr. Fox's report explain it all.

It was fortunate that nothing was attempted after the few vessels of the expedition met at the bar, and the fact that the Confederates opened fire on Sumter the moment the vessels did appear off Charleston was proof positive that they were prepared, not only to use up Sumter, but any number of vessels that should attempt to enter the harbor.

As the "Powhatan" has so constantly been quoted by a naval historian (Boynton), and he has stated certain matters in a way not altogether historical (though no doubt with a most sincere desire to write the truth), it may not be amiss to give a little sketch of *how* the "Powhatan" was spirited away and sent on another mission.

It is part of the history of the war, has been only incidentally alluded to by the writer, and will not in the least detract from the Fort Sumter relief expedition.

Mr. Lincoln had been installed in the Presidential office, and almost immediately after the question of relieving Fort Sumter was proposed to him (on the 12th of March), as will appear from Mr. Fox's letter, which has been quoted.

Captain Montgomery Meigs, of the Engineer Corps, had been thinking of a plan by which the Government might vindicate its authority over its own forts; and as Fort Pickens was very weakly manned by Capt. Slemmer and 25 men, and was in danger every hour of falling into the hands of the Confederates, he proposed an expedition for its relief by throwing in troops and mounting heavy guns.

Neither Mr. Seward nor Captain Meigs believed in the plan to succor Fort Sumter. In their opinion the opportunity had passed. This seemed to be the opinion of leading naval and military men and the surrender of Sumter was already looked for at an early day; many thinking it better that it should be evacuated to prevent bloodshed, and others not dreaming any plan of relief feasible.

Mr. Seward was anxious that the Administration should show its determination to maintain its authority over its forts, no matter where situated.

The Sumter expedition had been settled on by the Cabinet in council, and to Secretary Welles was left the selection of the ships and the manner of conducting the whole matter.

Captain Meig's plan, as proposed to Secretary Seward, was to charter a large steam transport that would carry 600 troops and stores, also artillery of all kinds, and with a naval vessel to protect the landing. Mr. Seward was new to all this kind of business, and was slow to act, though precious time was flying. Captain Meigs conferred with Lieut. D. D. Porter, who conceived the plan perfectly feasible, and showed a desire to go on the expedition : all of which was reported to the Secretary of State. Lieut. Porter was at that time under orders for California, and was to have left for New York to meet the California steamer on April 1st. In two or three hours he would have taken the train. A note was sent him at 2 P. M., notifying him that the Secretary of State wished to see him at his office immediately. On his arrival at the office the Secretary asked him if he knew how the Administration could prevent Fort Pickens from falling into the hands of the Confederates.

He answered promptly that he did know, and then suggested the plan proposed by Captain Meigs. "You are the very man I want," said the Secretary. "Come with me to the President." At that moment Captain Meigs came in and accompanied the party.

Those familiar with the early events of the Rebellion will remember that Fort Pickens was under the command of Captain Slemmer, of the Army, who held it with a handful of men, and was preparing to defend it against a large force of Confederates on the Pensacola side, who were daily augmenting their numbers, and making preparations to bombard the fort, as had been done at Sumter.

Pensacola, with its well-equipped Navy Yard, was too tempting a bait for the Confederates to leave, and no doubt the General commanding was ordered to put forth all the energy and science known in the art of war to encompass the destruction or capture of the formidable fort.

Lieut. Porter told the Secretary of State that if the government would give him command of the "Powhatan" (then lying in New York) and supply the troops, he would guarantee the safety of the fort. It was not known then to any of the party that the "Powhatan" was lying at the Navy Yard "stripped to a gantline," and that on or about that day she had gone out of commission preparatory to being repaired, and would be in the dry-dock in a day or two. It was thought that she was in commission and all ready for service, which should have been the case.

When the party reached the executive mansion, the President was evidently prepared to receive it, and was well acquainted with all the plans that had been proposed. He had talked with Mr. Seward and Captain Meigs, and was so heartily interested in the scheme, that he agreed to all that was proposed.

There was none of that indecision or "apparent inaction" (which is spoken of in Boynton's Naval History of the War) from March 4th to April, 1861. Mr. Lincoln was either belied when that expression was used, or he had learned better. He had for his advisers old men who moved and thought slowly, and his military and naval advisers were evidently more cautious than there was any justification for.

When the President was told that the "Powhatan" would have to get ready very quickly, the Commander (Mercer) changed for Lieutenant Porter, and all the orders written without the knowledge of the Navy Department (for the reason that everything would be carried on in that department in the usual red-tape style, and the whole matter would be known to the Confederates by being flashed across the wires an hour after Secretary Welles got an order to prepare the ship for sea), he merely remarked "it seems to me like a very irregular proceeding, but, Mr. Secretary, do not let me burn my fingers. I want that fort saved at all hazards."

Then Mr. Seward explained to him how, as President and Commander-in-Chief of the Army and Navy, he could issue orders from the executive mansion, without passing them through an intermediary, and that he (the Secretary of State) would satisfy Mr. Welles of the necessity of the present way of proceeding.

The President at that time had not the faintest idea that the Secretary of the Navy intended to use the "Powhatan," nor did he know the name of any vessel intended for the Sumter expedition, neither did the Secretary of State or any of the party.

It is a well-known fact now that all the orders issued by the Navy Department for the relief of Sumter were telegraphed to Charleston an hour after they were press-copied; for it was assumed at that time, when treachery was rampant in every branch of the Government, and when the insurrectionists had their spies and emissaries everywhere about the Government offices, that every man who did not openly declare his hostility to the Government was sound on the question of loyalty. It is now known that some of the meekest-looking supporters of the Government were its greatest enemies.

Secretary Seward evidently understood the situation, and determined that *his* expedition should not come to grief for want of proper secrecy. There was no wavering then on Mr. Seward's part, there was not a particle of hesitation on the part of the President, there was no long talk to prove the practicability of the expedition. The success of the affair was all taken for granted, and in half an hour everything was settled. How was it then that the President has been represented as hesitating, and Mr. Fox had to work so hard and travel to and fro until his patience was almost exhausted?

He was twenty-five days in accomplishing what was done in this instance in half an hour. The vacillation in the Sumter case did not rest with the President, but with those who tried to shift their want of success to the President's shoulders. It was, in fact, owing to circumstances which none could foresee.

After the President had decided that there was nothing to be done but write the necessary orders, Lieut. Porter wrote out and Capt. Meigs transcribed them.

They were as follows:

"EXECUTIVE MANSION,
April 1st, 1861.

"LIEUT. D. D. PORTER will take command of the steamer 'Powhatan,' or any other United States steamer ready for sea, which he may deem most fit for the service to which he has been assigned by confidential instructions of this date.

"All officers are commanded to afford him all such facilities as he may deem necessary for getting to sea as soon as possible. He will select the officers who are to accompany him.
ABRAHAM LINCOLN."
"Recommended,
"WM. H. SEWARD."

"EXECUTIVE MANSION,
April 1st, 1861.

"LIEUT. D. D. PORTER, U. S. NAVY:
"SIR: You will proceed to New York and with the least possible delay assume command of any naval steamer available. Proceed to Pensacola Harbor, and at any cost or risk prevent any expedition from the mainland reaching Fort Pickens or Santa Rosa.

"You will exhibit this order to any naval officer at Pensacola if you deem it necessary after you have established yourself within the harbor, and will request co-operation by the entrance of at least one other vessel.

"This order, its object, and your destination will be communicated to no person whatever until you reach the Harbor of Pensacola.
ABRAHAM LINCOLN."
"Recommended,
"WM. H. SEWARD."

"WASHINGTON CITY,
April 1st, 1861.

"SIR: Circumstances render it necessary to place in command of your ship, and for a special purpose, an officer who is duly informed and instructed in relation to the wishes of the Government, and you will therefore consider yourself detached; but in taking this step the Government does not intend in the least to reflect upon your efficiency or patriotism; on the contrary, have the fullest confidence in your ability to perform any duty required of you. Hoping soon to be able to give you a better command than the one you now enjoy, and trusting that you will have full confidence in the disposition of the Government towards you,

        "I remain,   ABRAHAM LINCOLN.'
" CAPTAIN SAMUEL MERCER, U. S. N.
    " A true copy.
" M. C. MEIGS, Chief Engineer of expedition under Col. Brown."

                "EXECUTIVE MANSION,
                      April 1st, 1861.
"TO THE COMMANDANT OF THE NAVY YARD, NEW
    YORK :
    " SIR : You will fit out the 'Powhatan' without delay. Lieut. Porter will relieve Capt. Mercer in command of her ; she is bound on secret service, and you will under no circumstances communicate to the Navy Department the fact that she is fitting out.   ABRAHAM LINCOLN."

        "WASHINGTON, EXECUTIVE MANSION,
                      April 1st, 1861.
    " All officers in the Army and Navy to whom this order may be exhibited, will aid by every means in their power the expedition under Colonel Harvey Brown, supplying him with men and material, and co-operating with him as he may desire.
                        ABRAHAM LINCOLN."
    "A true copy.
" M. C. MEIGS,
    "Chief Engineer of the expedition."

Similar orders were issued to Major-General Scott and the Adjutant-General of the Army, directing that everything should be done to make the expedition a success.

Then Capt. Meigs and Lieut. Porter called on Gen. Scott, and after a very short time he issued the necessary order for the troops to go in a chartered steamer, and there was nothing more wanted.

That night Lieut. Porter left for New York, and at 10 o'clock A. M., on April 2d, presented himself to Capt. Foote (who was acting Commandant of the Navy Yard at that time), and gave him the order to fit out the " Powhatan ;" which order Foote received with much surprise at this unusual way of doing business. It required three hours to convince Capt. Foote that he must obey the President's order, and that he was not to telegraph to Secretary Welles for instructions in this embarrassing position. He at last consented to take Capt. Mercer into the conference, give him the letter for himself, and be guided by his answer. Capt. Mercer considered it absolutely necessary for Foote to carry out the President's orders to the letter. He was rather pleased with the idea of getting rid of an old, worn-out ship, and offered to stay by the vessel as her Captain, fit her out, and take her down the harbor as far as Staten Island, in order the better to conceal the intended movement. Capt. Meigs also urged Foote to obey the President's order, and he finally decided to do so, and commenced the work

of fitting out the " Powhatan" with all possible dispatch.

The "Powhatan's" engines were all apart, and they were preparing to hoist out her guns and take her into dry-dock, at 2 o'clock P. M. of that day (April 2d), when the order was issued to employ a double force of men and work them day and night until she was ready for sea. The officers who had been granted leave were telegraphed for, and on the fourth the crew was put on board. No repairs had been put on the vessel—not a pound of paint, not a new rope rove, nor a sail mended. She was in a shocking condition for any service; there was no time even to repair her boats, which were leaky (those fine boats depended upon to land the troops and provisions at Fort Sumter). On the 6th of April, four days after the "Powhatan" was taken in hand, steam was up, everything in place, the pilot on board, and the lines ready to cast off. Then a telegram came to Capt. Foote from the Navy Department: " Prepare the 'Powhatan' for sea with all dispatch." Here was a dilemma ! Again Foote wanted to telegraph the state of affairs to the Secretary of the Navy, and stop the ship until he could hear from the Department. But his attention was again and again drawn to the President's order, and at last he succumbed.

Lieut. Porter stepped on board the "Powhatan" in citizen's dress, and was unobserved among the crowd of people who were bidding their friends good-by. He went into the cabin and locked himself in the Captain's state-room. The ship steamed away from the dock at one o'clock, P. M. on the 6th of April, going as far as Staten Island before Captain Mercer left her.

The moment the ship had left the yard, Foote could contain himself no longer, and he at once telegraphed to Secretary Welles that the " Powhatan " had sailed in command of Lieut. Porter under orders from the President.

The moment this telegram was received, Secretary Welles went straight to the President to request an explanation, at the same time informing him that he had depended upon the " Powhatan " to carry out his orders concerning the relief of Fort Sumter. The President was astonished, as he did not even know that the " Powhatan " had been connected with that expedition. Mr. Welles was much excited at what he considered Mr. Seward's interference with his affairs, and demanded the ship restored to him. Secretary Seward was sent for in haste, and when he came into the President's presence he found Secretary Welles in as great a state of excitement as his placid temperament would admit of.

"Give up the ship, Seward," said Mr. Lincoln, "we will get another." And Mr. Seward consenting to do so, a telegram was sent to Lieut. Porter as follows:

"Give the 'Powhatan' up to Capt. Mercer.
"April 6, 1861.   SEWARD."

While the ship was lying off Tompkinsville, Staten Island, waiting for the boat to return that had carried Capt. Mercer on shore, a swift little steamer came alongside, and Lieut. Roe of the Navy delivered Mr. Seward's telegram.

Lieut. Porter read it, and decided that there was only one thing for him to do, and that was to disobey it. The artillery for the troops was on board the "Powhatan," the steamer "Atlantic," with the troops on board, he supposed had sailed at 12 o'clock, and was ten miles ahead of him. His stopping to restore the ship would make the expedition fail, his orders were from the President and he determined to obey them. He telegraphed back:

"I received my orders from the President, and shall proceed and execute them.
"April, 6, 1861.   D. D. PORTER."

The boat was hoisted up, the ship's head put seaward, and the "Powhatan" proceeded on her voyage.

The weather was dreadful, but on the 17th of April the "Powhatan" arrived off Fort Pickens and found that the chartered steamer "Atlantic," with the Army contingent, had arrived the day before. Lieut. Porter stood in towards the bar and had crossed it and was standing for Fort McRea, with his crew at their guns, when Capt. Meigs in a large Government vessel laid right in the track of the "Powhatan" and signalled that he wanted to communicate. The ship was stopped and Capt Meigs came on board, handing to Lieut. Porter a protest against his going inside the harbor, on the ground that Fort Pickens was unprepared for an attack from the enemy's batteries, and if the "Powhatan" entered it would draw their fire upon the fort! Capt. Meigs had obtained, before he left Washington, authority from the President to take this course of action in case the officer commanding the troops objected to the ship going in.

There was nothing to be done but listen to Col. Harvey Brown's plea, and obey the implied order of the President; and thus the opportunity was lost of reasserting the authority of the Government to have its vessels go in and out of any port as it pleased their commanders to do. As it happened there was no actual necessity for the ship to go inside, but that was not the question: it was whether the Government had any right to its own forts, ships and har-

bors; and in starting to enter the harbor, Lieut. Porter wished to test how far the Government rights would be respected, and if not respected to cause them to be so by the power of his guns.

The President and the Secretary of State had shown great decision in fitting out this expedition, and, for the times, great moral courage in permitting it to go on, with the certainty that the guns of the "Powhatan" would be liberally used in dealing with the insurgents. But the timid policy of Col. Brown and his authority to prevent the commander of the "Powhatan" from entering Pensacola harbor, took all that was exciting out of this expedition, and turned what would have been a handsome dash into simply convoy duty.

After Lieut. Porter had discussed Col. Brown's protest with Capt. Meigs, and carefully considered the matter, he reluctantly turned the "Powhatan's" head toward the steamer "Atlantic," and anchored within 20 fathoms of the beach, with hawsers to keep her broadside bearing on the Navy Yard. The work of unloading the "Atlantic" went on in safety under the guns of the "Powhatan," and that night 600 soldiers were lodged in the fort, with provisions, artillery and other munitions of war sufficient to withstand a seige. Fort Pickens could now bid defiance to the Confederate soldiers, who stood in groups on the opposite shore watching the proceedings, but with no apparent intention of interfering for the present. This indifference arose from the fact that they had no ammunition to use in the guns which they had found in the Navy Yard—but they were biding their time and would no doubt be heard from when the opportunity offered.

On the second day after the arrival of the "Powhatan," a flotilla, composed of steam tugs, schooners and large launches, filled with soldiers, was seen to be coming from the direction of Pensacola, and heading for the two ships lying outside of Santa Rosa Island. There were about twenty-five of these small vessels, but the number of troops was not known.

This flotilla approached to within a mile and a half of the beach on Santa Rosa Island, and as they were either going to land there, or reinforce the insurrectionary army, it was time to stop their approach. The 11-inch gun on board the "Powhatan" was cast loose, and a shell fired, which burst directly over the middle of the flotilla. The consequence was a rapid retreat of the expedition towards Pensacola. No doubt they had taken the "Powhatan" and "Atlantic" for two store-ships which they expected to capture. Perhaps it was intended to attack Fort Pickens, for the troops from the "Atlantic" had been landed at night, and had not been seen by the enemy.

The "Powhatan's" 11-inch gun was reloaded and pointed in the direction of the Navy Yard, where groups of idle soldiers were watching the operations. It was fired, and the shrapnel shell exploded in the midst of the yard, and at once cleared it of all occupants.

If the Confederates wanted an excuse to commence hostilities the opportunity had been given them ; but the fact was, they were not at all prepared for such a contingency, as the troops in Charleston were, and after a year's occupation of Pensacola never advanced sufficiently with their fortifications to keep three steam frigates out of their harbor.

By the 20th of April Fort Pickens was so well protected that it could bid defiance to all the Confederate forces in that quarter, and so it remained until the end of the war.

Pensacola was evacuated by the Confederates about a year afterwards, on a scare —they thinking that Farragut's fleet was on the way to take it. The Confederates knew that they could not hold out twenty minutes against a close naval attack, and therefore wisely decamped in time. Thus the harbor of Pensacola again fell into the hands of the Government, and was of great use to the Gulf blockading squadron as a base for its operations.

The above is a strict account of the relief of Fort Pickens ; there were no mistakes made, nor any hitches anywhere. In seventeen days after the matter was first broached to the President Fort Pickens was reinforced with troops enough to hold it, and armed with heavy guns which could far outmatch any possessed by the enemy. With the exception of the attack of the "Niagara," "Richmond" and Fort Pickens on Fort McRae and other forts, Nov. 22, 1861, there were no attempts made to disturb the enemy, who, as long as he remained unmolested, followed a do-nothing course, which in the end was quite as effective as if he had built a thousand-gun fort.

Mr. Boynton, a very clever and pleasant historian, and who has written the only book that has in any way done justice to the Navy, gives a different version of this affair. But Mr. Boynton was not altogether fair when anything regarding the claims of the Navy Department was concerned; he received his information from that source and naturally followed it as that to be put in his history, whereas a historian should leave nothing undone to obtain a true statement of affairs. Mr. Boynton while writing his history held an appointment under the Navy Department, which he could only hold as long as his writings were acceptable to its chief ; not that we mean to say that he surrendered the right of an historian to be impartial, but that in his close connection with the Navy Department, where articles were prepared for his book, he could not very well reject or revise them without severing his relations with a party who had given him an easy office, in order that he might have time to devote himself solely to writing his Naval History. Many officers of the Navy say it is simply a history of the Navy Department, but in this we do not altogether agree, for it has given the most vivid accounts of naval battles yet written, and has in *most* cases done full justice to those who made themselves prominent in the war.

It was only in cases where Mr. Boynton felt called upon to adopt the views of the Navy Department, and not follow the records, that he failed in his history.

In the case of Fort Pickens he followed the information he received from Secretary Welles, who really believed that what he asserted was a fact, viz.: that the expedition to relieve Fort Pickens was all useless, as he had provided against any contingency by instructing the Commander of the Gulf Squadron to hold himself in readiness to assist Fort Pickens in case it was threatened. He, however, did not provide for one thing—the indifference of an officer whose sympathies were with the South; who, in undertaking to carry out the Secretary's order, did it with a reservation, not to do anything to offend his friends on the other side.

Mr. Welles' orders were never carried out. The commander of the squadron laid four miles away from the fort, where he could scarce see a signal by day or by night, and with a strong wind against the boats, he could not have reached the fort to relieve it under two hours after the attack could have been made, even if he desired to do so.

As far back as January, 1861, the question of "State sovereignty" and "no coercion" was discussed in Mr. Buchanan's cabinet, and as the "no coercion" party was in the majority he was influenced by this policy, and it was owing to it and to outside sympathizers that the President refused to re-enforce Sumter. These Southern sympathizers around the President left nothing undone to delude him with the idea of the impolicy of attempting to retain any of the Southern forts by force, and it was in consequence of these representations that the following telegram was sent on January 29, 1861:

"To CAPTAIN JAMES GLYNN, *commanding the* '*Macedonian*'; CAPT. W. S. WALKER, *commanding the* '*Brooklyn*,' *or other naval officers in command; and* LIEUT. A. J. SLEMMER, 1*st Regt. Artillery, U. S. A., commanding Fort Pickens:*

"In consequence of the assurances received from Mr. Mallory in a telegram of yesterday to Messrs.

Bigler, Hunter and Slidell, with a request that it should be laid before the President, that Fort Pickens would not be assaulted, and the offer of such an assurance to the same effect from Col. Chase, for the purpose of avoiding a hostile collision, upon receiving satisfactory assurances from Mr. Mallory and Col. Chase that Fort Pickens will not be attacked, you are instructed not to land the company on board the 'Brooklyn' unless said fort shall be attacked or preparations shall be made to attack it. The provisions necessary for the supply of the fort you will land. The 'Brooklyn' and other vessels of war on the station will remain, and you will exercise the utmost vigilance and be prepared at a moment's warning to land the company at Fort Pickens, and you and they will instantly repel any attack on the fort.

"The President yesterday sent a special message to Congress, communicating the Virginia resolutions of compromise. The commissioners of the different States are to meet here on Monday, February 4th, and it is important that during their session a collision of arms should be avoided, unless an attack should be made or there should be preparations for an attack. In either event the 'Brooklyn' and the other vessels will act promptly. Your right and that of other officers in command at Pensacola freely to communicate with the Government by special messenger, and its right in the same manner to communicate with yourselves and them, will remain intact as the basis of the present instructions.

"J. HOLT, Secretary of War.
"J. TOUCEY, Secretary of the Navy."

There was no mistaking the purport of this telegram. The Confederates could assemble any number of troops they pleased at Pensacola, erect batteries, and prepare for any contingency, without the commanders of our naval vessels being able to interfere with them; at least, so these instructions were construed by Capt. Adams, the commanding naval officer, and when Gen. Scott (subsequent to Mr. Lincoln's inauguration) sent an order to land the company of troops that was on board the "Brooklyn" and place them in Fort Pickens, Capt. Adams refused to obey the order, and tried to justify himself on the ground that it would be violating the armistice which had been entered into with the Confederate leaders.

How could the government hope to put down a rebellion in the South when there was such rebellion against its orders by a captain in the Navy? The order directing the landing of these troops was dated March 12, 1861.

On April 1, 1861, Captain Adams, in a letter addressed to the Secretary of the Navy, says:

"I declined to land the men as it would be in direct violation of the orders of the Navy Department, on which I was acting; the orders to land the troops may have been given without a full knowledge of the condition of affairs—there would be no justification in taking such a step without the clearest orders from the proper authority—it would be regarded as a hostile act, and could be resisted to the utmost. It would be considered by Gen. Bragg and his officers not only a debarkation, but an act of war; it would be a serious thing to

bring on, by any precipitation, a collision which may be against the wishes of the Department. Both sides are faithfully observing the agreement entered into by the U. S. government with Mr. Mallory and Col. Chase. This agreement binds us not to reinforce Fort Pickens unless it shall be attacked or threatened; it binds them not to attack it unless we should attempt to reinforce it.

"I saw Gen. Bragg on the 30th ultimo, who reassured me that the conditions on their part should not be violated. While I cannot take on myself, under such insufficient authority as Gen. Scott's order, the fearful responsibility of an act which seems to render civil war inevitable, I am ready at all times to carry out whatever orders I may receive from the Hon. Secretary of the Navy.

"In conclusion, I beg you will please to send me instructions as soon as possible, that I may be relieved from a painful embarrassment.

"Very respectfully,
"Your obedient servant,
"H. A. ADAMS, Captain,
"Senior officer present."

This officer's motto should have been "Festina lente." He was pursuing just the course that would soonest throw Fort Pickens into the hands of the Confederates. And the date of writing (April 1, 1861), was the very day President Lincoln started on foot the Fort Pickens expedition. There were only twenty-five men in the fort under Capt. Slemmer, and at that time Naval Historian Boynton states that Mr. Welles had taken all the necessary precautions to secure Fort Pickens against an attack from the enemy.

It was not until April 6, 1861, the day on which the "Powhatan" and "Atlantic" left New York for Pensacola, that Mr. Secretary Welles answered the letter of Capt. Adams as follows:

"NAVY DEPARTMENT, April 6, 1861.
"To CAPT. H. A. ADAMS, *Commanding Naval Force off Pensacola.*

"SIR—Your dispatch of April 1st is received. The department regrets that you did not comply with the request of Capt. Vodges to carry into effect the orders of General Scott, sent out by the 'Crusader' under the orders of this department.

"You will immediately, on the first favorable opportunity after the receipt of this order, afford every facility to Capt. Vodges by boats and other means to enable him to land the troops under his command, it being the wish and intention of the Navy Department to co-operate with the War Department in that object."

"I am, respectfully yours,
"GIDEON WELLES.
"Secretary of the Navy."

These orders were sent to Capt. Adams by a special messenger (Lieut. John L. Worden), who crossed the rebellious States to deliver them. He committed the orders to memory, in case the papers should be lost or he be arrested, but he arrived in safety, and delivered the document to Capt. Adams on the 12th of April. Capt. Vodges' company was immediately landed at Fort Pickens.

Thus from the time Capt. Vodges arrived

and was placed on board the "Brooklyn," and from the time of General Scott's orders to land the troops, dated March 12, 1861, twenty-four days elapsed before any thing was done to relieve Fort Pickens, Capt. Slemmer remaining in command of the fort all that time with only twenty-five men. Where, then, is the protection that was granted by the Navy Department?

Three days after Mr. Welles issued his instructions to have General Scott's orders obeyed, the steamer "Atlantic," chartered by Capt. Meigs, arrived and threw 600 men into the fort, with all that was necessary to resist a seige, and the next day the "Powhatan" was there to protect the fort with her batteries.

The military relief that was placed in the fort from the "Brooklyn" (75 men) was not at all adequate to its defence against Gen. Bragg's forces; not one man was ordered by the Navy Department to be landed from the ships at that time anchored off Pensacola, and this help never would have been afforded, for on or about the 20th, when a concerted signal was said to have been made for succor, the "Powhatan's" boats with marines were the only ones that responded to it. One of these boats got alongside the flagship by mistake and was detained there until daylight, with the remark that they knew nothing about concerted signals!

The historian Boynton rather sneers at the manner in which Pickens was relieved by the "Powhatan" and "Atlantic," and reflects on the brilliancy of the exploit. Certainly there was nothing brilliant about it, but it was successful, and it must have reassured the Northern people when they heard that there was some decision still left in President Lincoln's Cabinet, when they saw that a merchant steamer had thrown 600 men into Fort Pickens and that a frigate was protecting them with her guns; best of all, that the President had asserted his right to man and use the Government forts as he pleased.

If there was any compact between the Confederates and the Government, it was broken on the arrival of the "Powhatan" —for she fired upon them the moment they attempted a water expedition towards Santa Rosa Island.

All the claims for saving Fort Pickens from the enemy, put forward by anyone in favor of the Navy Department, are null and void.

Capt. Meigs puts the matter truthfully and squarely, when in answer to questions concerning the expedition, he stated:

"An order was issued on the recommendation of Secretary Seward, detaching the 'Powhatan' from the Sumter expedition, and sending her to Fort Pickens.

"In conclusion permit me to remark that this, the first successful military expedition of the war, originated with Mr. Seward; until it sailed the United States had declined every where."

The above account, in relation to the steps taken to relieve Sumter and Pickens, is perfectly correct, and the attempt of any one to detract from the credit of the Fort Pickens expedition is unworthy of consideration.

Several attempts were made to credit the Navy Department with the merit of saving Fort Pickens to the Union, and the same authority attempted to show that the Fort Pickens expedition caused the failure at Sumter. There was no necessity for making an excuse for the Secretary of the Navy, Mr. Fox, or anybody else who was concerned in the attempt to rescue Sumter. War was a foregone conclusion with the leaders at Charleston, but they still retained sufficient right feeling to wish to have some valid excuse for striking the first blow. Mr. Secretary Welles gave them the opportunity by sending down the relief vessels: the first blow had to come and the sooner it came the better.

No one can cast any reflection on Secretary Welles or Mr. Fox for the failure (if it may be so called) at Charleston. It was a matter beyond their control; they were both loyal men and did all they could to bring about the relief of the men in Fort Sumter, and their loyalty and determination to put down the rebellion was unceasing during a four years' war, which required the most eminent ability to conduct the Department in which each of them exercised that control best suited to his capacity.

If Mr. Secretary Welles does not deserve the credit of succoring Pickens in time, it is because he had not an officer in command of the squadron at Pensacola who would anticipate orders, or who was enough interested in the Union cause to take the responsibility of using active measures without instructions. Secretary Welles also labored under the disadvantage of having the general of the army sending down orders to the captain of the company on board the "Brooklyn" to land, without properly passing his orders through the Navy Department, so that there might be perfect concert of action between the commander of the troops and the commander of the vessel.

When Mr. Welles was called on to act he did act promptly, and if late in doing so it mattered very little, for the expedition inaugurated by Mr. Seward arrived a day or two after, and made the place so secure that no Confederate force could have any effect upon it.

These two places, Sumter and Pickens, on which at one time so much depended (whether war or peace would rule the day), are too prominent subjects to pass over lightly, and if the writer has dwelt on the matter longer than the reader may think justifiable, it is because he desired to give a true account of the whole affair.

The operations of the Gulf and East Gulf blockading squadrons were mostly confined to blockading duty, with an occasional smart skirmish with the enemy. The names of the following officers are spoken of as active in the performance of all the duties which fell to their lot in this limited sphere of action : Lieut.-Commander Francis Winslow, Commander Geo. F. Emmons, Lieuts. J. C. Howell and A. F. Crossman, Commander H. S. Stellwagen, Lieut. Abbot, Capt. Cicero Price and Act.-Master Elnathan Lewis.

These officers all did good service, and gave evidence of loyalty and zeal which promised greater usefulness when employed in a wider sphere of action.

The duty in the Gulf was harrassing, and at the same time tedious and monotonous; and if not as brilliant as that performed by the Navy in other localities, it performed its share of the work of putting down the rebellion by maintaining the blockade of the Southern Coast, the most severe duty performed by any officers during the war.

GULF SQUADRON, 1861, VESSELS AND OFFICERS.

FLAGSHIP "NIAGARA." Captain Wm. W. McKean, Flag Officer; Lieuts., John Guest, Wm. F. Spicer, J. C. P. De Krafft, Robt. L. May and Edw. E. Potter ; Fleet Surg., G. R. B. Horner; Surgeon, J. Foltz; Asst. Surg., James McAllister; Chaplain, C. S. Stewart; Paymaster, G. B. Barry; Masters, J. D. Marvin, James O'Kane, T. L. Swan, H. B. Robeson and Silas Casey, Jr.; Capt. Marines, Josiah Watson; First Lieut., Geo. Butler; Chief Engineer, Robt. H. Long ; Asst.-Engineers, D. B. Macomb, C. B. Kidd, E. A. C. DuPlaine, L. R. Green, R. H. Grinnell, A. H. Fisher and Robt. Potts; Boatswain, A. M. Pomeroy ; Gunner, R. J. Hill ; Carpenter, John Rainbow ; Sailmaker, Stephen Seaman.

FRIGATE "SANTEE." Captain, Henry Eagle; Surgeon, T. M. Potter ; Lieuts., James E. Jouett, J. J. Mitchell, B. N. Wescott, James H. Spotts; Act.-Master's Mate, Charles W. Adams; Asst.-Surg., C. H. Burbank ; Paymaster, L. Warrington; Midshipmen, Frederick Rodgers, George M. Brown, S. H. Hunt ; Boatswain, William Black; Carpenter, Wm. H. Edgar; Gunner, William Carter ; First Lieut. of Marines, C. D. Hebb.

STEAMER "RICHMOND." Capt., F. B. Ellison ; Lieuts., N. C. Bryant, A. B. Cummings, Robert Boyd, Jr., Edward Terry, Byron Wilson ; Surgeon, A. A. Henderson; Asst.-Surgeon, William Howell ; Paymaster, Geo. F. Cutter; Boatswain, I. T. Choate; Sailmaker, H. T. Stocker ; Carpenter, H. L. Dixon ; Gunner, James Thayer ; Act.-Master's Mate, H. W. Grinnell ; First Lieut. Marines, Alan Ramsey ; Chief Engineer, John W. Moore ; Asst.-Engineers, Eben Hoyt, J. L. Butler, Wm. Pollard, A. W. Morley, G. W. W. Dove, R. B. Plotts, C. E. Emery.

SLOOP-OF-WAR "VINCENNES." Commander, Robert Handy ; Lieut., John E. Hart ; Surgeon, S. A. Engles ; Paymaster, R. C. Spalding ; Asst. Surgeon, Somerset Robinson ; Midshipmen, O. A. Batcheller, B. F. Haskin, M. W. Sanders and E. M. Shepard; Boatswain, Jos. Shankland ; Gunner, William Wilson ; Sailmaker, Nicholas Lynch ; Second Lieut. Marines, J. H. Higbee.

SLOOP-OF-WAR "PREBLE." Commander, Henry French ; Lieut., William E. Hopkins ; Surgeon, Stewart Kennedy ; Paymaster, C. P. Wallach ; Boatswain, John Bates ; Gunner, E. J. Waugh ; Carpenter, James Kinnear ; Sailmaker, G. A. Wightman.

STEAMER "WATER WITCH." Commander, Wm. Ronckendorff (in August) ; Lieut., Francis Winslow (in October) ; Lieuts., J. L. Davis, James Stillwell, C. H. Cushman and Allan V. Reed ; P. Asst.-Surgeon, P. S. Wales ; Asst.-Engineers, Wm. C. Selden, Reynolds Driver, Edw. Scattergood, A. H. Able.

FRIGATE "POTOMAC." Capt., L. M. Powell, Lieuts., Samuel Marcy, Lewis A. Kimberly; Geo. E. Law; Master, W. S. Schley; Surgeon, J. D. Miller; Asst.-Surgeon, A. O. Leavitt; Paymaster, James D. Murray; Midshipmen, Wm. T. Sampson, C. H. Humphrey, Merrill Miller, John H. Reed, D. D. Wemple; Boatswain, C. E. Bragdon; Gunner, W. H. French; Carpenter, O. T. Stimson; Sailmaker, Geo. Thomas.

STEAMER "HUNTSVILLE." Com. Cicero Price; Lieut., Henry Erben; Midshipmen, E. C. V. Blake, Louis Kempff.

STEAMER "R. R. CUYLER." Lieut. Francis Winslow; Act.-Lieut., J. Van Ness Philip; Act.-Master, Henry K. Lapham; Midshipmen, L. R. P. Adams, A. C. Alexander, Wm. R. Bridgman.

STEAMER "HATTERAS." Com., Geo. F. Emmons; Act.-Master, Hoffman; Master's Mates, McGrath and Hazlett.

STEAMER "MASSACHUSETTS." Com., Melancton Smith.

STEAMER "NEW LONDON." Com., James Alden.

NOTE.—Names of officers obtained mostly from Navy Register of August 31, 1861.

CHAPTER XI.

GOLDSBOROUGH'S EXPEDITION TO THE SOUNDS OF NORTH CAROLINA.

EXPEDITION TO ROANOKE ISLAND.—REAR-ADMIRAL GOLDSBOROUGH IN COMMAND OF NAVAL FORCES.—ARMY FORCES UNDER COMMAND OF GENERAL BURNSIDE.—VESSELS AND OFFICERS IN COMMAND.—A NONDESCRIPT SQUADRON.—COMMANDER ROWAN GIVEN COMMAND.—DESCRIPTION OF ROANOKE ISLAND.—THE DEFENSES.—ATTACK ON WORKS AND VESSELS.—BARRACKS AT FORT BARTOW ON FIRE.—LANDING OF TROOPS AT ASHLEY'S HARBOR.—CAPTURE OF FORT BARTOW.—DESTRUCTION OF STEAMER "CURLEW" AND BATTERIES AT REDSTONE POINT.—"HEARTS OF OAK" IN WOODEN SHIPS.—CONFEDERATES SURRENDER TO GENERALS FOSTER AND RENO.—LOSSES OF ARMY.—ADVANTAGES OF CAPTURE OF ROANOKE ISLAND.—ESCAPE OF CONFEDERATE FLEET.—CASUALTIES AMONG NAVAL FORCES —COMMANDER ROWAN PURSUES CONFEDERATE FLEET.—DESTRUCTION OF CONFEDERATE FLEET AND FORTS ON PASQUOTANK RIVER.—ATTEMPT TO BURN ELIZABETH CITY.—EXPEDITIONS UP RIVERS LEADING INTO SOUNDS.—BRAVERY OF LIEUT. FLUSSER.

OWING to the fact that the commanding officer of the Hatteras expedition did not push the advantages he had gained by the capture of Forts Hatteras and Clark, in August, 1861, the victory was almost a barren one, with the exception of its moral effect and the recapture of many of the guns which had fallen into the hands of the Confederates.

The principal entrances into the sounds of North Carolina were secured, but the Confederates had still the means not only of annoying the coast-wise commerce passing daily before these inlets, but also of supplying their armies through the intricate and numerous channels belonging to the several sounds, and known only to themselves.

In January, 1862, it was determined by the Navy Department to fit out an expedition for the purpose of capturing Roanoke Island, and getting possession of Pamlico and Albemarle Sounds.

This had become a necessity, as the Confederates had facilities for fitting out light armed and swift vessels, which could get in and out at their pleasure and attack our commerce whenever it suited their convenience. It was also known that the Confed-erates were fitting out some powerful iron-clads in the western waters of the sounds, and it was absolutely necessary for the Federal government to obtain a foothold there before these vessels were completed. There were many other reasons why so large and important a body of water should be secured, and it was a case where the Navy only could take the initiative, and where success could only be obtained by the use of well-armed vessels-of-war.

Rear-Admiral Louis M. Goldsborough was selected to command the naval expedition, and General A. E. Burnside was directed to co-operate with him : the latter to have under his command some 17,000 troops.

The following is a list of the vessels which composed the naval part of the expedition, with the names of their commanders :

"Stars and Stripes," Lieut.-Comdg. Reed Werden; "Louisiana," Lieut.-Comdg A. Murray; "Hetzel," Lieut.-Comdg. H. K. Davenport; "Underwriter," Lieut.-Comdg. W. N. Jeffers; "Delaware," Lieut.-Comdg. S. P. Quackenbush; "Commodore Perry," Lieut.-Comdg. C. W. Flusser ; "Valley City," Lieut -Comdg. J. C. Chaplin; "Com. Barney," Act.-Lieut.-Comdg R. T. Renshaw; "Hunchback," Act.-Vol.-Lt.-Comdg. E. R. Colhoun; "Southfield," Act.-Vol.-Lt.-

Comdg. C. F. W. Behm; "Morse," Acting-Master Peter Hayes; "Whitehead," Acting-Master Charles French; "Lockwood," Acting-Master G. W. Graves; "Brincker," Acting-Master John E. Giddings; "I. N. Seymour," Acting-Master F. S. Wells; "Ceres," Acting-Master John McDiarmid; "Putnam," Acting-Master W. J. Hotchkiss; "Shawsheen," Acting-Master T. G. Wood-

ring his flag temporarily to the steamer "Southfield."

Hatteras Inlet, through which our vessels had to pass to get into Pamlico Sound, was not the most desirable channel in the world; on the contrary it was beset with difficulties, and only those who went on that expedition will ever know of the perilous adventures in which the officers and men were engaged.

REAR-ADMIRAL LOUIS M. GOLDSBOROUGH.

ward; "Granite," Acting-Master's Mate E. Boomer.

These vessels were placed by Admiral Goldsborough under the "general command" of Commander S. C. Rowan, who carried his divisional flag on the steamer "Delaware."

The flagship "Philadelphia" being "unfit for the purpose" took no part in the engagement; the Commander-in-Chief transfer-

At the time when this expedition was undertaken, the Navy Department had great difficulty in obtaining suitable vessels for its purpose. If the vessels were of light draft, they were naturally slightly built, and not calculated to contend with the winter gales which rage in the vicinity of Cape Hatteras. It will be seen by a look at the list of naval vessels employed in this expedition that the squadron was a nondescript affair. It was made up of river steamers, ferry-boats, tug-boats and almost anything that would turn a wheel or screw. It was a great change for our naval officers to come down from the staunch old ships of live oak (in which they had been accustomed to sail about the world) to these frail craft loaded to the water's edge with guns of heavy calibre, not knowing whether they would ever reach the place for which they were destined, much less hoping to get home safe and sound to their anxious relatives. It was a mere matter of luck with them, as their success depended on whether they should meet a gale of wind or not, while off the coast. Our government was not always careful as to what kind of vessels it purchased, and if the people of the country could have seen the craft in which our sailors went to sea and fought their country's battles they would have given them more sympathy.

But there were hearts of oak in that non-descript squadron, and they never stopped to inquire whether there was danger in the enterprise or not, or whether their vessels would sink or swim; all they cared for was to reach the post of danger, well knowing that when once in the smooth water of the sounds they would be amply repaid for any risks they might run in getting there.

The reason why such vessels had been selected for this important work was that the Navy Department had no others. Gun-boats were built as fast as possible, but all of them were of such draft of water that they could only with great difficulty cross the bars at the southern inlets. The Army transports were worse even than the so-called naval gun-boats, for the War Department had been even more unfortunate than the naval authorities in selecting vessels. They had no skill in such matters, and were easily deceived by the harpies who are always ready to take advantage of their country's need, without regard to any sacrifice of life which might result from their avarice: and yet some of these men were considered to be loyal citizens, working for the Government. They took good care to make close contracts, securing themselves from loss in case of damage to their chartered steamers.

This heterogeneous crowd of naval vessels and transports arrived at Hatteras Inlet on the morning of the 13th of January, 1862, and were all taken across the bar, where there was barely seven and one-half feet of water. They arrived at the beginning of a northeast gale which lasted two days, during which time many of the vessels were severely battered ere they could reach safe quarters.

On the 20th seventeen naval armed steamers were over the bar and safely anchored inside, under the command of Com.

S. C. Rowan. This in effect gave the Federal forces full control of Pamlico Sound, but the military command could only be retained by the capture of Roanoke Island. It was not until the 22d that Gen. Burnside was able to get all his transports over the bar and into still water.

Had the enemy been on the alert with what gun-boats they had, they would have caused great disturbance to our fleet while it was beset with dangers on the bar, where the naval vessels would have found it difficult to use their guns, and where great havoc might have been made among the closely packed troops on board the transports. The enemy's gun-boats did not take advantage of their opportunity, however, but kept close to their fortifications, merely amusing themselves by throwing an occasional shell from their long range guns at the vessels in the harbor, but never reaching the danger point.

On the 21st, Rear-Admiral Goldsborough sent a steamer out to examine a certain buoy, to see whether it was in the right place. While engaged upon this service two steamers were descried in the distance. On the fact being signalled to Com. Rowan he gave chase to them with several of his vessels, but the enemy escaped.

It must have been very evident to the Confederates, when they beheld the comparatively large force that was sent against them, that they would have a hard tussle to keep possession of the sounds; but they had a strong position, and seemed determined to maintain it.

When everything was in readiness for the movement to commence, the naval vessels were all placed under the command of Commander Rowan, who was to take the lead and open the way for the transports.

Before giving any account of the operations it will be necessary to give the readers some idea of the defenses of Roanoke Island.

This island is about ten miles long and three wide, running in a northwesterly and southeasterly direction.

By the capture of Hatteras Inlet forts the Federal Government gained possession only of Pamlico Sound, and therefore the first object of this expedition was to gain possession of Albemarle Sound and the connecting waters, through which the Confederates were carrying on an active trade. Roanoke Island barred the way between these two sounds, and the Confederates had made it a formidable barrier by the erection of heavy fortifications

The channel connecting Pamlico and Albemarle Sounds in which Roanoke Island lies is very shallow, and could therefore be easily obstructed by sunken vessels or piles. The sheet of water on the west side of the island is called Croatan Sound, and that on the east side Roanoke Sound. All of these waters are navigable to a certain extent, but large vessels can only pass through the western channel. (See the plan, which will more fully explain the situation than any description.)

It is quite clear that Roanoke Island in the hands of the Confederates was the key to that great chain of sounds and passages

If the Northern Government had established a formidable army in North Carolina in the neighborhood of Plymouth, Greenville and Newbern, connected by lines of communication and supported near these places by a fleet of gun-boats with powerful guns, the Wilmington Railroad, Raleigh and Welden would have been within striking distance of our army, and the Confederates would have been obliged to use more

VICE-ADMIRAL S. C. ROWAN.

running from Hatteras Inlet to the Dismal Swamp canal, and that in order to retain control of these highways it was necessary for the Unionists to capture this position at all hazards.

It was a great strategic point which enabled the Confederates to cover Norfolk in the rear, Welden and the Northeast railroads, and keep open their communications with Lee's army at Richmond.

northern railroads to obtain their supplies, even if they did not have to evacuate Richmond. The final movement of our army under Sherman in his "March to the Sea," was directed towards some of these points in North Carolina, and it was not long after this that Lee surrendered and General Joe Johnston laid down his arms.

When the Confederates found that the Hatteras forts were incapable of keeping the

Federal gun-boats out of the sounds, and that the Neuse and Pamlico Rivers must fall into our hands, they determined to fortify Roanoke Island and prevent our getting into Albemarle Sound; so that they could hold communication with Norfolk through the Currituck Inlet and save Plymouth and the Roanoke River. They were building some heavy iron-clads up that river, and all the material, machinery and guns had to be transported from Norfolk and Richmond.

The defences of Roanoke Island consisted of six separate works. Five of these guarded the water approaches and the sixth was a masked battery intended to prevent troops from landing and attacking the main works in the rear.

This last battery was armed with three guns and was flanked on either side by a dense cedar swamp, so that an army landing at this point was only supposed to be able to advance by the roadway, towards the water defence at Pork Point, where their principal work, Fort Bartow, was situated. The swamp was considered impassable, and to render further protection a barrier of fallen trees was formed on each side of the road.

The following is a list of the defences, taken from Rear-Admiral Goldsborough's report: "They consisted of two elaborately constructed works, mounting altogether twenty guns, three of them being 100-pounder rifles; four other batteries, mounting together twenty guns, a large proportion of them being of larger calibre and some of them rifled; eight steamers, mounting two guns each, and each having a rifled gun with the diameter of a 32-pounder; a prolonged obstruction of sunken vessels and piles to thwart our advance, and, altogether, a body of men numbering scarcely less than 5,000. . . ."

This was a strong position, and a large number of guns (56 in all) to meet the attack of 48 guns on our frail steamers without any protection to hull or machinery.

The naval vessels, under the lead of Com. Rowan, made the attack on the works and vessels at Roanoke Island, on February 7th, at nine o'clock in the morning.

The plan of battle was for the naval force to lead up to the attack, and engage the batteries at Pork and Sandy Points and the Confederate vessels. While this was going on the Army was to advance and land under cover of the naval fire. A naval brigade of artillery was also detailed to land from six launches, at Ashby Harbor, or, if possible, at Sandy Point, half a mile above.

The naval division under Com. Rowan was arranged in three columns, commanded respectively by Lieuts. Worden, Murray and Davenport, these to be followed by the Army transports, also in divisions.

Two days were occupied by our fleet in threading its way through the intricate channels of the marshes, owing to fogs and foul weather. These channels were so narrow that only two vessels could proceed abreast, and in this order they continued until reaching the wider and deeper waters of Croatan Sound.

The naval division, composed and commanded as stated above, was accompanied, as predetermined, by the "Picket," Capt. T. P. Ives; "Huzzar," Capt. Frederick Crocker; "Pioneer," Capt. Charles E. Baker; "Vidette," Capt. John L. Foster; "Ranger," Capt. Samuel Emerson; "Lancer," Capt. M. B. Morley, and "Chasseur," Capt. John West, of the army division. Keeping in close order it approached the enemy near enough to begin the attack, and to devote most of its firing against the fort on Pork Point (not neglecting the enemy's vessels), a battery between Pork and Weir's Points, and another on Redstone Point (see plan), all of which returned the fire of the Federal fleet, but without much effect.

The Federal vessels having obtained position the action became general between them and the enemy, the army transports also joining in with the rifle guns they had mounted.

At 1:30 the shells from our fleet set fire to the barracks behind Pork Point, and in a short time they were in full blaze and beyond control, as at this time the Federal vessels, having got their range, were throwing in a very destructive fire.

At 3 P. M. the troops shifted to light-draft steamers and boats and started to land at Ashby's Harbor. This place was guarded by a large body of the enemy with a field battery, but Commander Rowan in the "Delaware," taking up a flanking position to the southward of Pork Point, turned his 9-inch guns towards the harbor and compelled the enemy to retreat, thus clearing the way for a landing.

At 4.30 Pork Point Battery and the one next to the northward of it ceased firing; five of the Confederate steamers went behind Weir's Point disabled, and the first landing of our troops took place.

At 5 P. M. these batteries re-opened, and the enemy's steamers having repaired damages put forth again and opened fire. In a short time, however, the steamers were again obliged to retire, and one of them, the "Curlew," in a disabled condition, took refuge under the battery at Redstone Point. As evening came on, the Rear Admiral commanding made signal to cease firing—not wishing to waste ammunition.

In the course of the afternoon, six launches, under the command of Midshipman B. H. Porter, had landed their howitzers and a body of men, which were employed during the night in guarding the main road and its two forks. On the following morning they assisted in the active operations of the Army. By midnight some ten thousand of our troops had been landed safely at Ashby's Harbor.

On February 8th it was arranged by General Burnside that his forces should move at an early hour in the morning, and begin their attack upon the enemy; and as the direction they were obliged to take would bring them in the line of fire occupied by the Navy it was agreed between the two commanders, that the naval fire should cease until the General gave notice that it would *not* interfere with his operations.

to hear from Gen. Burnside. The fleet continued its fire upon the forts until the firing in the interior of the island sensibly slackened, when it was taken for granted that our troops were approaching the batteries, and carrying everything before them. Then came the order to clear the channel of obstructions, to enable the squadron to pass up and destroy the battery on Redstone Point, which had only one gun left to fire, and also the "Curlew," which lay disabled under the enemy's batteries. In two hours and a half this service was per-

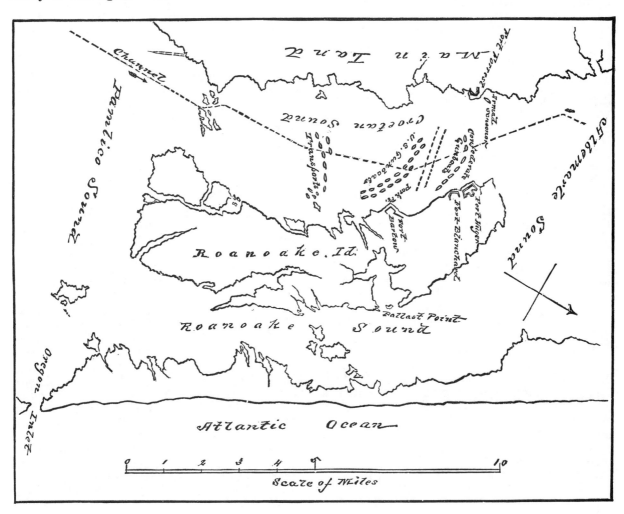

MAP AND PLAN OF THE ATTACK ON ROANOKE ISLAND.

At daylight none of the enemy's vessels, except the "Curlew," could be discovered. At 9 A. M. a continuous firing in the interior of the island showed that the Army was hotly engaged with the enemy between Ashby's Harbor and Pork Point. The Admiral being thus informed of the position of our troops, and seeing that they were now beyond his line of fire, at once moved up and engaged the forts, without waiting

formed by the "Underwriter," "Valley City," "Seymour," "Lockwood," "Ceres," "Shawsheen," "Putnam," "Whitehead" and "Brincker," and these vessels passed through.

Just at this moment our troops hoisted the American flag on the battery at Pork Point, and in a few minutes afterwards the enemy himself fired the works at Redstone Point and the Confederate steamer "Curlew:" both blew up early in the evening.

Thus ended the attack on the forts of Roanoke Island, the Confederate works being now completely in the hands of the Army and Navy.

To discriminate between the two branches of the service on this occasion would be making an invidious distinction; both performed their duties in the most admirable manner, and worked together most harmoniously.

The casualties among the naval vessels were few in number, which is considered strange when the light character of these steamers is taken into account and the number of guns (56) which were brought to bear upon them by the enemy; but the fire from the eight and nine-inch shell guns and rifles of the fleet was so vigorously kept up and accurately aimed that it was the same old story of Port Royal—hearts of oak in wooden ships.

The military forces had some hard fighting on shore, and the attack was conducted with great skill. The entire force of the enemy stationed in the batteries and as sharpshooters was 4,000. Governor H. A. Wise had a force in reserve at Nag's Head, but retreated when he heard of the fate of the two forts.

The enemy's troops were well posted and their batteries well masked, so that the Federal forces were really fighting an unseen foe.

Over 150 officers and 2,500 men surrendered to Generals Foster and Reno. The losses of the Confederates are unknown, but they did not exceed 150 killed and wounded. Our Army lost 15 officers and 32 men killed, 10 officers and 264 men wounded, and 13 men missing.

Thus was a very important capture made, with but little loss of life, when it is considered that the enemy held a strong position and was completely concealed in bushes and masked batteries. The advantages which resulted from the capture of this island cannot be over-estimated. A large quantity of military stores of all kinds fell into the hands of the Federal Army which the enemy could not well spare, and altogether it was a very happy ending of what promised at first to be a very difficult undertaking.

The only regret was that the enemy's fleet escaped. These vessels mounted 16 or 17 heavy guns, and had taken a secure position behind the barricades, prepared to defend the way against the Federal fleet. Commodore Lynch (the commander of this naval force) and many, if not all, of his officers, had once served in the United States Navy ; but they could not stand the attack of their old comrades and were obliged to retreat. Strange to say, all of these steamers, except the "Curlew," made good their escape. As regards vulnerability these vessels were as defective as those of the Federal fleet, and

their commanders saw from the first what the result would be, and took advantage of the darkness to move away to a safer position.

Great praise was given to General Burnside for the manner in which he conducted his part of the affair. There was no instance during the war where the Army and Navy worked together more harmoniously. It was a case where each was necessary to the other and where neither could have won alone.

History will show that, throughout the war, whenever the Army and Navy co-operated harmoniously success followed; but when difficulties occurred between the military and naval commanders the results were unsatisfactory.

By the capture of these works and their garrisons, all the sounds of North Carolina came under Federal jurisdiction, as the naval vessels and military transports were now able to reach all parts of these waters and soon swept from them all traces of the Confederate power: a great loss to the enemy and one that he deeply mourned.

The casualties in the Union fleet were 6 killed, 17 wounded, 2 missing.

Admiral Goldsborough lost no time after the surrender of the forts on Roanoke Island in chasing up the Confederate Navy, which had disappeared entirely; and on the 9th of February he directed Com. Rowan to pursue them with the following vessels: "Louisiana," Lieut.-Com. Murray; "Hetzel," Lieut.-Com. Davenport; "Underwriter," Lieut.-Com. Jeffers; "Delaware," Lieut.-Com. Quackenbush; "Commodore Perry," Lieut.-Com. Flusser; "Valley City," Lieut.-Com. Chaplin; "Morse," Acting-Master French; "Lockwood," Acting-Master Graves; "Ceres," Acting-Master McDiarmid; "Shawsheen," Acting-Master Woodward; "Brincker," Acting-Master Geddings; "Putnam," Acting-Master Hotchkiss.

This was not a very formidable squadron, but it was equal to the occasion. Late in the afternoon of the 9th this fleet of vessels entered Albemarle Sound in search of the enemy, and soon after sighted the smoke of two steamers, which were seen to be heading for Pasquotank River. Chase was given and an attempt made to cut them off, but without success, and the Confederates escaped over the bar and then up the river. The Union fleet was then anchored for the night, ten miles distant from Fort Cobb.

Commander Rowan knew very little about the condition of affairs up the river, whether there were any batteries, torpedoes or obstructions, but he well knew that if there *were* any forts the Confederate gun-boats would naturally seek their protection and rely on their aid in any encounter that might follow with the Federal forces. The

ATTACK ON ROANOKE ISLAND BY COMMODORE GOLDSBOROUGH'S GUN-BOATS, AND LANDING OF TROOPS UNDER COMMAND OF GENERALS

FOSTER, RENO AND PARKS. FEBRUARY 8, 1862.

enemy could select their point of attack or defence, and the Union commander was obliged to advance against them without having the slightest idea of the strength of their position.

The little steamers under Rowan's command were certainly the frailest vessels that had ever been improvised for meeting the stern hazards of war. They carried heavy guns, however, and the gallant spirits who manned them were determined to win, no matter what the risks.

Commander Rowan's plan was to avoid a protracted combat, and to bring the enemy to close quarters as soon as possible, for the reason that his ammunition was reduced to 20 rounds for each gun in the fleet (owing to the battle of Roanoke Island). He made signal for the commanders of vessels to come on board the flagship, and after conferring with them in regard to the proper measures to be adopted he gave them their final orders.

It was naturally expected that the Confederate fleet would take position behind the battery at Cobb's Point, and there await the attack; but the result was not feared, as it had been shown in the battle of Roanoke Island that the Confederate vessels could not hold their own, even when supported by heavy forts.

The plan of attack was that the gun-boats should approach in close order and proceed up the river without firing a shot until ordered to do so, dash through the enemy's lines, crushing and sinking him if possible, or engage in hand-to-hand conflict; after capturing or destroying the steamers to take the forts in reverse and act according to signal.

The little fleet weighed anchor at daylight on the 10th of February, and proceeded up the river in the prescribed order: the "Underwriter," "Perry," "Morse" and "Delaware" keeping in advance as pickets, the little "Ceres" nearer shore on the right flank, and the "Louisiana" and "Hetzel" leading up the remainder of the flotilla. The "Valley City" and "Whitehead" were ordered to leave the line as soon as the fort was passed and attack it in reverse.

The Confederate steamers were soon discovered drawn up in order of battle behind the fort, which mounted four heavy 32-pounders. Opposite the fort on the other side of the river a large schooner was moored, mounting two heavy 32-pounders, and the enemy's line of vessels, under Commodore Lynch, was anchored diagonally across the channel between these two defences.

Thus they may be said to have held a very powerful position, and it looked almost like rashness for the Federal commander to attack an enemy so situated. But there

was no hesitation on the part of Com. Rowan or his officers. As soon as the Federal vessels got within fair range, the Confederates opened upon them from their 32-pounders from the fort and the schooner "Black Warrior," followed by the 80-pounder rifles of their gun-boats.

Though shot and shell passed thick and heavy over the foremost vessels and fell in the midst of the main column, not a shot was fired by the Federal vessels in return until they got within short range, when the signal was made "Dash at the enemy." Throttle valves were opened and the steamers put at full speed, at the same time opening fire all along the line.

Sweeping forward as rapidly as their engines could drive them they were quickly in the midst of the enemy, who were completely panic-stricken by this bold and unexpected attack and offered but a feeble resistance to the officers and men, who jumped on board their vessels with sword and pistol in hand. Those in the batteries seeing what had happened to their gun-boats immediately deserted and fled. Those on board the "Black Warrior" set fire to her and got to the shore.

Some of the steamers endeavored, unsuccessfully, to save themselves by flight, among others the flagship "Seabird," but she was run into and sunk by the "Commodore Perry" (Lieut.-Com. Flusser), and nearly all of her officers and crew made prisoners.

In fifteen minutes the whole affair was ended, all the Confederate gun-boats having been either run ashore and set fire to, or captured by hand-to-hand conflicts; and thus the fleet on which they had depended to defend the sounds against any force that could be sent there, was entirely annihilated, and there was no one left to dispute the control of the interior waters of North Carolina.

Although this was comparatively a small affair, it was one of the best conceived and best executed battles of the war, in which just as much skill and dash were displayed as in the grander achievements which took place at a later date. In fact, greater credit is due the commander of this expedition when one takes into consideration the character of the vessels which he had at his disposal and the strong position of his enemy. The attack of the Union vessels was like the spring of a pack of greyhounds upon a brood of foxes—it was just such a scene as naval officers delight in.

No one who has read an account of this dashing adventure has failed to give to the brave spirits who took part in it all the credit they deserved for the skill and daring which they exhibited throughout the affair.

After the battle was over, Com. Rowan

sent some of the steamers up to Elizabeth City. At their approach the enemy made a hasty retreat through the town, having set it on fire before their departure.

It being evident to Com. Rowan that it was the design of the enemy to throw the blame of burning the city upon the Union forces, he sent his men on shore to extinguish the flames. Having accomplished this object, and taken prisoner one of the officers belonging to the "Wise Legion," who was caught in the act of setting fire to the houses of the inhabitants, they returned immediately to their ships.

A great deal of Confederate property was destroyed at this place. The steamer "Forest," one gun-boat and a small vessel on the stocks were burned at the ship-yard, and all the machinery, boilers, railways, etc., destroyed. Also the machinery of the steamers "Seabird" and "Fanny," which had been sunk.

After this a number of expeditions were started all through the Sounds of North Carolina for the purpose of destroying the enemy's property and blocking up the canals, so that no communication could be held with Norfolk. But we cannot refer to these operations at this time, as events of far greater importance were now taking place at Hampton Roads, which require us to transfer our history to that quarter.

Before leaving the Sounds of North Carolina, we cannot but express our unqualified admiration at the happy manner in which the Army and Navy co-operated, and the brilliant results which followed from the skill and energy displayed by both branches of the service.

The Federal forces had not yet gained entire possession of the interior waters of the Sound, but that came a few months later, and will all be narrated in its proper place.

On the 9th of July, 1862, an expedition was fitted out from Goldsborough's fleet for the examination of certain rivers leading into the Sounds of North Carolina, in order to ascertain whether the enemy was fortifying the river banks or building men-of-war at the small towns in the interior.

The expedition consisted of the "Commodore Perry," Lieut. C. W. Flusser; the "Ceres," Lieut. John McDiarmid; and the "Shawsheen," Acting-Master T. T. Woodward, with a detachment of about forty soldiers in addition to their regular crews.

The first of the places to be examined was the town of Hamilton on the Roanoke River. The banks of this river were high in places and afforded many commanding positions from which an enemy upon the water could be attacked with little danger to the attacking party.

The Confederates did not fail to make the most of their opportunities, and the gun-boats had not proceeded far on their way before they were fired upon by concealed riflemen, and although the men returned the fire promptly it was with little apparent effect. The river banks seemed lined with sharpshooters, and for ten hours the vessels, being obliged to run slowly, were kept under a galling fire.

The men were struck down by an invisible foe, who lurked in the bushes or fired from over the edge of the bluffs without any danger of being struck from the vessels.

Flusser had been ordered to go to Hamilton, and he was determined to get there, no matter what might be the consequence. This gallant officer was now placed in a most trying position, but he stood unflinchingly at his post and continued on his way. The only thing to be done was to keep the men under cover as much as possible and return the enemy's fire when opportunity offered. In spite of all precautions, however, the fleet had one man killed and ten wounded.

The Confederates deserted their forts as the steamers approached, and Hamilton was reached. Having taken possession of the Confederate steamer "Nelson" at this place, the expedition returned in safety to the Sound.

In the latter part of October, 1862, another expedition, a combined military and naval force, was started for Hamilton, and proved successful beyond all expectations. Great risks were run, some valuable lives lost, and great skill shown in the management of the gun-boats. Thus the Navy, when co-operating with the Army, always made its usefulness felt. Without the presence of the Navy to capture and destroy the enemy's improvised gun-boats, to destroy their steam transports and cut off their means of rapidly moving an army, not a single point on the Southern coast could have been wrested from the enemy, or, if captured at great expense and labor, could not have been retained without the continual watchfulness of the Navy.

This co-operation on the part of the Navy seldom failed of success, and this support to the Army was of more value to it than large numbers of men or hundreds of cannon. The Army had with them in the gun-boats a train of field-pieces no enemy could resist.

The American people as a rule, knew nothing during the war of the continuous, exhaustive and perilous labor to which the officers and men of the Navy were subjected, and in a victory sometimes made sure by the presence of the gun-boats, the Navy was nowhere mentioned. This was not the fault of the gallant soldiers who received the support of the Navy, but rather the fault of the military historians, who in almost all cases ignored the Navy altogether.

Did the limits of this paper permit, and could the numerous cases of support to the Army be specially noted, it would readily be seen that in the Sounds of North Carolina, under Goldsborough, in the rivers, bayous and inlets along the Southern coast under Dupont, on the coast of Louisiana and Texas and the whole length of the Mississippi, Tennessee, Cumberland, White, Arkansas and Red Rivers, a distance of over 3,000 miles, the Navy more or less contributed towards success; and if defeat overtook our Armies at any time while the Navy was at hand, the enemy gained no important or lasting advantage. Our Army always had a line of defense (the naval gun-boats) on which they could fall back, regain its formation and send the enemy retreating in his turn.

For the present we must leave the sounds and inlets and follow other adventures. All the sounds of North Carolina and the rivers emptying into them as far up as the gun-boats could reach were virtually in the hands of the Federal Government.

North Carolina was no longer a base of supplies for the Confederates The sounds and inlets of Georgia, South Carolina and Florida were nearly all closed up by the Navy, and Wilmington and Charleston were really the only two places by which the Confederacy could obtain supplies or munitions of war from abroad.

All of this work had been done within a year of the commencement of the war, in spite of delays which enabled the enemy to erect earthworks and sink obstructions that required herculean labors to remove.

Inadequate as were the vessels supplied to the Navy, the officers seldom failed to accomplish what they attempted, and it was a well-deserved compliment when an old soldier said, "every man should carry a gun-boat in his pocket, and then he could accomplish wonders."

CHAPTER XII.

FIGHT BETWEEN THE "MERRIMAC" AND "MONITOR," MARCH 8, 1862.

APPEARANCE OF THE "MERRIMAC."—DESTRUCTION OF THE "CONGRESS" AND "CUMBERLAND."—ARRIVAL OF THE "MONITOR."—THE FIGHT.

WHILE the Federal arms were so successful in the sounds of North Carolina, a great disaster overtook the Federal cause in Hampton Roads, filling the country with dismay, and even bringing many of the Union people to doubt the success of the cause for which they had labored so hard.

When the Union naval officers set fire to the buildings of the Norfolk Navy Yard, they supposed they had taken such precautions that everything of value would be destroyed, but as soon as the Federals had departed a detachment of Virginia volunteers rushed in to extinguish the flames. The "Merrimac" had been sunk, but the lower part of her hull and her engines and boilers were substantially uninjured.

Lieutenant John M. Brooke, one of the most accomplished officers among those who had left our Navy and joined the Confederate cause, visited the scene of the conflagration, and it at once occurred to him that the "Merrimac" could be rebuilt as an iron-clad; and his plans being accepted by Mr. Mallory, the Secretary of the Confederate Navy, orders were issued to have them carried out at once.

The vessel was raised and cut down to the old berth deck, both ends for a distance of seventy feet were covered over, and when the ship was in fighting trim were just awash. On the midship section, a length of one hundred and seventy feet was built over, the sides being at an angle of fifty-five degrees, a roof of oak and pitch pine extending from the water line to a height of seven feet above the gun-deck. Both ends of this structure were rounded, so that the pivot guns could be used as bow and stern chasers, or quartering; over the gun-deck was a light grating, making a promenade twenty feet wide.

The wood backing was covered with iron plates rolled at the Tredagar Works in Richmond. These plates were eight inches wide and two inches thick. The first covering was put on horizontally, the second up and down, making a total thickness of iron of four inches, strongly bolted to the woodwork and clinched inside.

The ram, or prow, was of cast-iron, projecting four feet, and, as was found subsequently, was badly secured. The rudder and propeller were entirely unprotected. The pilot-house was forward of the smoke-stack and covered with the same thickness of iron as the sides.

The motive power was the same as had been in the ship before; both boilers and engines were very defective, and the vessel was not capable of making more than five knots an hour.

Another able officer, formerly of the United States Navy, Lieut. Catesby ap R. Jones, had charge of the preparation of the "Merrimac's" armament, and to his skill was due the efficiency of her battery. It consisted of two seven-inch rifles, re-enforced with three-inch steel bands shrunk around the breech; these were the bow and stern pivots. There were in broadside two six-inch rifles similar to the above, and six nine-inch smooth-bores—in all ten heavy guns.

When this formidable vessel was completed the name of the "Virginia" was bestowed upon her, and she was placed under the command of Flag Officer Franklin Buchanan, who had resigned from the United States Navy, where he had reaped the highest rewards that could be bestowed in time of peace. He was a man of undoubted courage, and his professional ability was of the first order. Buchanan was fortunate in surrounding himself with excellent officers, men capable of performing any naval duty, and no commander was ever better seconded by his subordinates.

The crew of the iron-clad were not all seamen, but that was comparatively unimportant as there were no sails to handle. Gunners were selected from the army at Richmond,

Lindsay; Clerk, Arthur Sinclair, Jr.; Volunteer Aid, Lieut. Douglas Forrest; Captain, Kevil, commanding detachment of Norfolk United Infantry.

Thus equipped, officered and manned, the iron-clad represented at the moment the most powerful fighting ship in the world, and the Federal Government might well feel uneasy at the tidings they received of this monster which threatened to carry destruction all along the Northern coast.

The government was not, however, aware

COMMODORE FRANKLIN BUCHANAN, COMMANDER OF THE "MERRIMAC."

and they proved to be excellent men for the duty required of them.

The officers of this historic vessel were as follows:

Lieutenants, Catesby ap R. Jones (Executive and ordnance officer), Lieutenants Charles C. Simms, Robert D. Minor (Flag), Hunter Davidson, John Taylor Wood, J. R. Eggleston, Walter Butt; Midshipmen, Fonte, Marmaduke, Littlepage, Craig, Long and Rootes; Paymaster, Semple; Surgeon, Phillips; Assistant Surgeon, Algernon S. Garnett; Captain of Marines, Reuben Thorn; Engineer, Ramsay; Assistants, Tynan, Campbell, Herring, Jack and White; Boatswain, Hasker; Gunner, Oliver; Carpenter,

of the rapidity and energy with which the Confederates had conducted their work; in fact, in this instance the Navy Department was rather taken by surprise, and was not quite up to the mark, for as a general rule it had shown great energy in improvising a Navy.

There were several large steam frigates at that time which might have been cut down and covered with iron in much better fashion than was done in the case of the "Merrimac." The Department, it is true, had contracted for iron-clad vessels, but two of them were far behind time in building, and the other was a "little nondescript" that no one in the Navy Department, with the exception of Commodore Joseph Smith, had any confidence in. This vessel, designed by John Ericsson, was to be paid for only in case she proved successful against the enemy's batteries; but had the steam frigates been cut down and plated we need have given little anxiety to the appearance of the "Merrimac" or any other vessel, and would have been first in the field with this new factor in war which was to revolutionize naval warfare.

But there are many things we cannot account for—we received humiliation at first to teach us not to underrate an enemy. Providence came to our assistance in our emergency with "Ericsson's nondescript," to show what skill and enterprise could do in behalf of the Union.

As the "Monitor" of Ericsson approached completion the Navy Department hurried the work on learning that the "Merrimac" was further advanced than they had supposed.

This was in consequence of the fact that Commander D. D. Porter had been sent to New York to examine the vessel, and report his opinion as to her capacity to deal with an enemy. After a thorough examination of all the details of the vessel, Commander Porter telegraphed to the Navy Department: "This is the strongest fighting vessel in the world, and can whip anything afloat." But when he returned to Washington a few days after he was laughed at by a high official, and a clever one at that: "Why, man," he said, "John Lenthall predicts that Ericsson's vessel will sink as soon as she is launched."

Mr. Lenthall was unquestionably high authority, but he was certainly mistaken on this occasion. Like most others he looked upon the nondescript as a clever scheme to obtain money from the government, but he subsequently did ample justice to Ericsson and built many vessels after the distinguished inventor's models, which for a time placed the United States Government ahead of all other naval powers. We did not long maintain this position however, for our statesmen do not appreciate the necessity of a navy sufficient to protect our extensive coasts and sixty millions of people, so we have fallen back into our original condition, without a single iron-clad that would command the respect of the weakest nations; yet Ericsson still lives, with vigor unimpaired and intellect as bright as when his "Monitor" saved the honor of the country nearly a quarter of a century ago.

A month before the "Monitor" was launched the Confederates, through their spies, had learned the exact condition of the vessel and the day on which she would probably be put into the water; in consequence of which information the number of workmen on the "Merrimac" was doubled and the work carried on by day and by night. This extra energy made all the difference in the world, and doubtless gained the one day which enabled the Confederate vessel to commit such havoc without any effectual opposition.

Lieut. John L. Worden, who had been assigned to the command of the "Monitor," watched her building for several months, urging on the work by every means in his power, in which he was heartily supported by the inventor. When the vessel was launched and equipped, Lieut. Worden started at once for Hampton Roads, without a trial trip, and with no means of judging how the vessel was going to behave. At one time on his passage to Hampton Roads, he was doubtful if the little "Monitor"

LIEUT. CATESBY AP R. JONES,

(EXECUTIVE OFFICER OF THE "MERRIMAC.")

would live through the rough seas and arrive in time to be of any assistance to our fleet; or, even if she did arrive, whether she could accomplish what her inventor claimed for her. In fact Worden was somewhat doubtful whether he should ever again set foot on land, for his vessel was almost inundated and leaking apparently enough to sink her.

In the meantime the "Merrimac," alias "Virginia," was all ready to leave the Norfolk Navy Yard on what was said to be her trial trip, and up to the last moment she was filled with mechanics working to complete her.

On the 8th of March, 1862, the iron-clad got under way and proceeded down Elizabeth River, cheered by hundreds of people who crowded the banks, and as she passed

MAP SHOWING FORTRESS MONROE, NEWPORT NEWS, CHESAPEAKE BAY, JAMES RIVER, AND SURROUNDING COUNTRY.

Craney Island and through the obstructions, the ramparts of the fort were lined with soldiers who shouted success to her until their throats were hoarse. Thus the "Merrimac" started off with all the glamor of success, for there was no one on board who doubted that she could destroy the fleet then lying in the roads.

Buchanan and his officers knew the weak points of every vessel in the Federal fleet, and the number and calibre of their guns. He knew that none of their shot could pierce the "Merrimac" and that he could choose his distance and fire with his rifled guns at the ships as if at a target, should

a. Prow of Steel.
b. Wooden Bulwark.
h. Pilot House.   THE "MERRIMAC."
dd. Iron under water.
c. Propeller.

(FROM A SKETCH MADE THE DAY BEFORE THE FIGHT.)

he think proper to do so. Instead of making it a "trial trip," as first intended, Buchanan determined to make it a day of triumph for the Confederate Navy.

At this time there was at anchor in Hampton Roads, off Fortress Monroe, the "Minnesota," of forty guns, Capt. Van Brunt; "Roanoke," of forty guns, Capt. Marston; "St. Lawrence," fifty guns, Capt. Purviance; and several army transports. Seven miles above, off Newport News, lay the "Congress," fifty guns, and the "Cumberland," thirty guns. Newport News was well fortified and garrisoned by a large Union force.

It was a beautiful day, following a storm. The water was smooth and the vessels in the Roads swung lazily at their anchors. Boats hung to the swinging booms, washed clothes on the lines, nothing indicated that an enemy was expected, and no one had, apparently, the least idea that the "Merrimac" was ready for service. The utmost ignorance seems to have prevailed in our squadron with regard to her capacity to do harm.

The writer was in Hampton Roads a short time previous to the appearance of the "Merrimac," and while standing on the wharf a decent looking mechanic landed from a small boat. He told the writer that he had escaped from Norfolk, where he had been employed on the "Merrimac," which vessel he said was very formidable and nearly completed. His account of affairs was correct as has since been proved, but

when the man was taken to Captain Van Brunt, that officer questioned him fiercely and then roughly dismissed him, as if he considered him an impostor. The writer was of a different opinion and wrote at once to Mr. Fox, Assistant Secretary of the Navy, urging him to hurry up the "Monitor;" but no one in the squadron seemed to anticipate any danger.

Rear Admiral Goldsborough was in the sounds of North Carolina and could easily have left what was there to be done to the skill of the gallant Rowan, but he evidently apprehended no danger from the "Merrimac" or he would have returned at once to Hampton Roads. One would have thought that the Federals could have learned through spies how near the "Merrimac" was ready for service, and all the particulars regarding her. Many things which ought to have been done were left undone, but of this it is useless to repine.

As the squadron lay quiet, little dreaming of the danger that was so near, "three small steamers" were reported to the senior officer at 12:45 P. M. coming around Sewell's Point. It was soon ascertained by her large smoke stack that one of these vessels was the "Merrimac," and great excitement prevailed. Signal was made to the "Minnesota" to slip her cables, get underway and pursue the enemy; but when within a mile and a half of Newport News the frigate grounded and remained fast during the events which took place that day and the one following.

The "Merrimac" stood straight for the "Congress" and "Cumberland," and when she was within three-quarters of a mile the latter vessel opened on her with heavy pivot guns, closely followed by the "Congress." Paymaster McKean Buchanan, a brother of the Confederate commander, was an officer of the "Congress," and the "Merrimac" passing that vessel steered direct for the "Cumberland," the Confederate Flag Offi-

THE "MONITOR" IN BATTLE TRIM.

cer hoping that the "Congress" would surrender on seeing the fate of her consort, and that his brother would thus escape. In passing the "Congress" the "Merrimac" delivered her starboard broadside, which was quickly returned, and a rapid fire from both vessels was maintained on the iron-clad. The "Merrimac" continuing her course, struck the "Cumberland" at right angles, under the fore channels on the starboard side, and the blow, though hardly perceptible on board the iron-clad, seemed to those on board the "Cumberland" as if the whole ship's side had been smashed in. Backing out, the "Merrimac" put her helm hard-a-starboard, and turned slowly, while the two Union ships poured in a continual fire, which apparently fell harmless on the iron plating of the enemy. On the other hand, as the iron-clad swung round from the "Cumberland," the "Congress" lay with her stern to the enemy, which raked her three times, fore and aft. In fact, the "Congress" was a mere target for the enemy's shot and shell, with little danger of the latter being injured in return.

In the meantime the "Cumberland" was settling in the water from the effects of the great opening in her side, and although it was evident to all on board that the day was lost, and that the ship must inevitably go to the bottom, these brave fellows kept

pearing beneath the waves, and his gallant crew fighting to the last.

Of course as long as the "Cumberland" kept up her fire the enemy returned it, their shells inflicting death on all sides. Those who had escaped from below were decimated by the merciless shot and shell poured into them by the enemy as they stood crowded together on the spar deck. There is little generosity or sentimentality in war: the object is to kill and wound, and this was too favorable an opportunity to be neglected. In the absence of Com. Radford, Lieut. George N. Morris was in command of the "Cumberland," and his heroism inspired his crew to the deeds which they performed on that eventful day. Of the "Cumberland's" crew one hundred and twenty-

THE CONFEDERATE RAM "MERRIMAC" SINKING THE "CUMBERLAND."

up a rapid fire until driven by the water from the lower deck guns, when they retreated to the upper deck and continued to fight the pivot guns till the "Cumberland" went down with her colors still flying.

During the whole war there was no finer incident than this, and the bravery of the officers and men of the "Cumberland" even won the applause of the enemy.

Commander William Radford, of the "Cumberland," was engaged that day on a Court of Inquiry, which was sitting on board one of the vessels in Hampton Roads. When the "Merrimac" was reported as coming down, all else was lost sight of, and procuring a horse, Radford started at full speed for Newport News; but he only reached there in time to see his ship disap-

one were either killed outright or drowned, while of those saved a large portion were wounded.

When the commanding officer of the "Congress" saw the fate of the "Cumberland," and realized how little chance there was for him, he slipped his cable, set his foretopsail and endeavored to get closer in shore so as to have the assistance of the land batteries, but the ship ran ashore, where she continued the unequal contest for more than an hour after the sinking of her consort, the "Merrimac" lying at a safe distance and boring her through and through with her shells, and finally setting her on fire.

While this unequal contest was progressing between the "Merrimac" and the "Congress," the two Confederate gun-boats accompanying the iron-clad joined in the fray. They were both armed with rifle guns. In a few minutes they dismounted one of the stern guns of the "Congress" and knocked off the muzzle of another, so that, not being able to bring any of her broadside guns to bear, she lay perfectly helpless. Her gallant commanding officer, Lieut. Joseph B. Smith, was killed, her decks were strewn with killed and wounded, and further resistance was hopeless. The colors were accordingly hauled down and a white flag hoisted. A Confederate tug ran alongside the "Congress," and the officer in charge ordered the crew out of the ship, saying he intended to set fire to her.

The garrison at Newport News, not comprehending the state of affairs, opened on the Confederate vessel with artillery and musketry, so that she was obliged to leave the side of the "Congress" with only thirty-nine prisoners.

Although the white flag was still flying, the "Merrimac" again opened fire on the "Congress." This was certainly most inhuman, since the crew of the "Congress" were not responsible for the act of the troops on shore. The Confederates claim that two of their officers were killed on board the tug while assisting the Union wounded out of the "Congress," and that many of our own men were killed and wounded by the fire of the shore batteries.

The "Congress" having been set on fire, Lieut. Pendergrast and most of the crew undertook to escape to the shore in small boats, or by swimming, leaving the ship with the white flag still flying at her mainmast head.

Flag-Officer Buchanan claimed that he was unable to take possession of his prize owing to the fire from the shore, for which reason he ordered hot shot to be fired into the "Congress" until she was set on fire. Buchanan and his flag-lieutenant, Lieut. Minor, personally directed this matter, and while doing so both were severely wounded. The command of the "Merrimac" then devolved on Lieut. Jones.

Notwithstanding the heavy armor of the "Merrimac," her loss in killed and wounded was twenty-one, showing the good use of their artillery made by the Union ships. The armor was, however, but little damaged by the Federal shot, although the Confederates asserted that at one time they were under the fire of one hundred heavy guns afloat and ashore!

Everything on the outside of the "Merrimac" seems to have been badly injured. The muzzles of two of the guns were shot off, the anchors, smoke-stack and steam pipes were shot away, railing, stanchions, boat davits, every thing was swept clean. The flagstaff was repeatedly shot away, and finally a boarding pike was substituted.

During the engagement the "Roanoke" and "St. Lawrence," in tow of tugs, made every effort to join in the combat, but like the "Minnesota," they ran on shore some two miles above Fortress Monroe.

While the above incidents were taking place, the day had passed, and the commanding officer of the "Merrimac," finding he could not take possession of the "Congress," abandoned her to the flames. How glorious it must have seemed to this officer, who served nearly half a century under the stars and stripes, to see that flag hauled down by rebel hands, and those gallant men, who had once served under and admired him, ruthlessly slaughtered at his

CAPTAIN JOHN ERICSSON, INVENTOR OF THE "MONITOR."

cool command! He may have thought it glory then, but in after years, we believe, regret possessed him, and contributed to shorten his life.

At five o'clock P. M. the "Merrimac" turned towards the "Minnesota," which ship lay aground apparently at her mercy, but the pilots would not attempt the middle channel with the ebb tide, and night was fast approaching. So the "Merrimac" returned to Sewell's Point and anchored. In passing the "Minnesota" the iron-clad opened fire, but only a single shot struck the frigate; the gun-boats, however, accompanying the "Merrimac" did much greater damage with their rifled guns, though they were finally driven off by the heavy guns which the "Minnesota" carried forward.

The ten-inch pivot gun of the "Minnesota" produced no effect on the iron-clad, the shot glancing like pebbles from her sides, and it was plain that the "Minnesota," as soon as the tide would allow the Confederate vessel to come to close quarters, would be as helpless before the "Merrimac" as the "Congress" and the "Cumberland" had been. The commanding officer of the Union frigate therefore made all preparations to abandon his ship and set her on fire, anticipating an attack early next morning.

Thus closed one of the most memorable days of the civil war, a day which carried gloom and sorrow to the hearts of all loyal citizens. The authorities at Washington were dismayed, and it appeared to those most familiar with the circumstances that this was the crisis of the Union cause.

All through the South there were scenes of rejoicing; bonfires blazed on the hill tops, and everywhere the Confederates ex-

sons had confidence, and which had not yet reached the scene of action. What hope could there be for the "Minnesota," hard and fast aground, or for the frigate "Roanoke," with her disabled machinery, or the "St. Lawrence" with no machinery at all! The commanding officers must either destroy their vessels and escape into Fortress Monroe or let them fall into the hands of the enemy.

But the avenger was at hand, and at nine o'clock that night Ericsson's little "Monitor," under the command of Lieut. John L. Worden, arrived from New York, after experiencing trials and difficulties sufficient to have appalled an ordinary officer.

REAR-ADMIRAL JOHN L. WORDEN, COMMANDER OF THE "MONITOR."

pected that the next news would be the total destruction of the Federal fleet at Hampton Roads, and the advance of the "Merrimac" to Washington.

As a result of their victory the Southern people saw an abandonment of the advance on Richmond, the capture of Washington, the laying of the seaboard cities under contribution, the raising of the blockade of the Southern coast, and the recognition of the Confederate Government by the powers of Europe.

There was apparently nothing between them and success, for the Federal Government had no means of arresting the disaster which threatened it, except a diminutive, experimental war vessel in which few per-

It was a great relief to the officers and men of the squadron to know that an iron-clad of any kind was at hand to assist them, but when they saw the little "nondescript," her decks level with the water, and appearing above it only her pilot-house and a small turret, in which latter were two eleven-inch guns, and compared her with the apparently invulnerable iron-clad of the enemy, they could not feel very sanguine of the result of the coming conflict.

Lieutenant Worden was ordered to proceed at two o'clock A. M. and take position alongside the "Minnesota" to be ready to receive the "Merrimac."

The morning dawned clear and bright, and everything looked so calm and peaceful that it was hard to realize that two hundred and fifty men had the previous day given up their lives in defence of their flag in a contest hopeless from the beginning.

The flag still floated from the "Cumberland," whose light masts appeared above the surface of the water, marking the spot where the dead slept their last sleep in the shattered wreck, while the smoke from the burning "Congress" ascended to heaven, a funeral pyre over the corpses which strewed the decks of that ill-fated ship.

The "Minnesota," badly cut up, still lay hard and fast aground, and it was evident to all that should the "Monitor" fail them there was nothing but destruction to look forward to.

As the "Merrimac" approached the frigate the crew of the latter went to quarters, the drum sounding more like a funeral knell than a summons to triumphant battle, but, contrary to expectation, the "Merrimac" passed the frigate and "Monitor" and headed towards Fortress Monroe. At the "Rip Raps" she turned into the main channel by which the "Minnesota" had gone up and again rapidly approached the latter.

When the "Merrimac" was within the distance of a mile, the "Minnesota" opened fire with her stern guns and at the same time the "Monitor" was signalled to attack.

Worden showed his confidence in the "Monitor" and her eleven-inch guns by

NEWPORT NEWS.   MONITOR.   MINNESOTA.   MERRIMAC.   FORTRESS MONROE.

THE "MONITOR" AND "MERRIMAC."—THE FIGHT AT SHORT RANGE.

The crew of the "Merrimac" were astir at early daylight preparing for the conflict, and as soon as it was fairly light the iron-clad was under way and heading towards the "Minnesota." On approaching their expected prey the Confederates discovered a strange-looking craft which they knew at once to be Ericsson's "Monitor," of which they had received a description from their spies at the North. The "Monitor" was but a pigmy in appearance alongside the lofty frigate which she guarded, and the enemy anticipated little difficulty in overcoming her. Still, her arrival was inopportune for the Confederates, causing a change in their plans, which were to destroy the "Minnesota" and then the remainder of the squadron.*

* Confederate account.

steering directly for the Confederate iron-clad. The latter slowed her engines and paused as if to survey her little adversary and ascertain her character; but if there was any doubt on board the "Merrimac" there was none on board the "Monitor," which kept straight on her course, and the Confederates saw that in a few moments she would be directly alongside of them.

The "Merrimac" opened fire from her forward gun upon what seemed more like a large floating buoy than a man-of-war, but not having a frigate's broadside to aim at the shot passed harmlessly over. The "Monitor's" answering guns were better aimed The solid eleven-inch shots struck the "Merrimac" fairly, with a blow that resounded through the vessel. This was returned by a broadside from the "Merrimac," but those shots that struck the turret glanced harmlessly off.

Both vessels then turned and approached each other still closer, the "Monitor" firing about every seven minutes, each shot striking the "Merrimac." The latter vessel, having lost part of her smoke-stack the day before, was not working so well, the chief engineer reporting that the draft was so poor that it was with great difficulty he could keep up steam. The "Merrimac" drew twenty-three feet of water, and was thus confined to a narrow channel, while the "Monitor" drawing but twelve feet could take any position and always keep within range of her antagonist's guns, and though the enemy had many more guns, the "Monitor" stuck so close to her adversary that the latter could use but a small proportion of them. Worden's plan was to keep near to his enemy and endeavor to break in her sides with his solid shot.

The "Merrimac" kept up as rapid a fire as possible upon what was visible of the "Monitor," pausing now and then when the smoke cleared off to see whether the little vessel had been demolished, but always finding her apparently unharmed and active as ever, pouring in her solid shot and shaking the great iron-clad's huge frame in a manner which her officers feared might in the long run cripple their ship, unless they could manage in some way to cripple their antagonist.* The "Merrimac's" fire was then concentrated upon the "Monitor's" pilot-house, as the turret seemed impervious to their shot.

More than two hours had passed in this apparently unequal duel, the Confederates had made no impression on the "Monitor" and their own wounds were *apparently* slight, since the "Monitor" had not yet succeeded in penetrating the "Merrimac's" heavy armor.

The "Monitor" had on board some forty steel shot which it was intended to fire with heavy charges in case of an encounter with the "Merrimac," but previous to leaving New York, Lieut. Worden received orders from the Bureau of Ordnance not to use those shot with the increased charges, as fifteen pounds of powder was as much as the eleven-inch guns would bear. Worden felt obliged to conform to these instructions, as the responsibility of bursting the guns would have fallen upon him. It was subsequently proved by experiment that the eleven-inch Dahlgrens would easily bear twenty-five pounds of powder, and this difference in the charge of the guns, as is now known, would have made all the difference in the world in the final result. The "Merrimac's" armor would have been

broken, and she would have laid at the mercy of the "Monitor," as her speed was not sufficient to have enabled her to escape.

Lieut. Jones having occasion to visit the "Merrimac's" gun-deck saw a division standing at ease, and inquiring of the officer in command why he was not firing, that individual replied, "After firing for two hours I find I can do the enemy about as much damage by snapping my fingers at him every two minutes and a half."*

As Lieut. Jones found he could make no impression on the "Monitor" with his shot, he determined to run her down or board her, and for nearly an hour he maneuvered for position, but his ship was too unwieldy for that kind of work. The "Monitor"

LIEUT. SAMUEL DANA GREENE.

(EXECUTIVE OFFICER OF THE "MONITOR.")

danced around her like a yacht around a three-decker, pouring in her shot and endeavoring to find a vulnerable point.

At last Jones thought he saw a chance of ramming the "Monitor," and gave the order to go ahead at full speed, but before the great vessel could gather headway the agile "Monitor" turned, and the disabled prow of the "Merrimac" gave a glancing blow which did no harm whatever.

Again the "Monitor" came upon the "Merrimac's" quarter, her bow actually against the ship's side, and at this distance fired twice. Both shots struck about half way up the "Merrimac's" armor, abreast of the after pivot, and so severe was the blow that the side was forced in several inches. The crew of the after guns were knocked over by the concussion,

* Confederate account.

* Confederate account.

bleeding from the nose and ears. A few more shots in the same place would have made an opening, and had Worden known this at the time, he would doubtless have taken the responsibility of using double charges of powder and the steel shot, and thereby secured a complete victory.

While the vessels were together on this occasion, boarders were called away on board the "Merrimac," and started to get on "the little cheese-box on a shingle," as the enemy called her, but the "Monitor" slipped quickly astern and opened her batteries upon the quarter ports. So for hours this struggle was continued with apparently little results.

Thousand of spectators with beating hearts watched the conflict from Fort Monroe, and from the ships. It seemed to them as if the battle would never end, but at length the Confederate commander, thinking it useless to try his broadsides on the "Monitor" any longer, steered off towards the "Minnesota," which opened on the "Merrimac" with all her broadside guns and the ten-inch pivot. The "Merrimac" returned the fire with her rifled bow gun, and a shell passed through the frigate, tearing four rooms into one, and exploding a couple of charges of powder, which set fire to the ship, but the flames were promptly extinguished. Another shell passed through the boiler of the tug "Dragon," causing an explosion.

Then the "Minnesota" concentrated her broadside upon the "Merrimac," and kept up an incessant fire; and, although it is said fifty shots struck the slanting roof of the iron-clad, they did no apparent damage.

By the time the "Merrimac" fired her third shell the little "Monitor" had come up with her again, and placed herself between the "Minnesota" and the enemy, compelling the latter to change her position. While doing this the "Merrimac" grounded and the "Minnesota" poured into her the fire of all the guns she could bring to bear. As soon as the "Merrimac" got off the bottom, she proceeded down the bay, then suddenly turned and attempted to run the "Monitor" down, but failing in the attempt she concentrated all her broadside guns on the little vessel, which was keeping up a rapid fire.

Suddenly the "Monitor" was seen to move away from the "Merrimac" in rather an erratic manner, and it was at this instant that Lieut. Worden was so disabled that he could no longer direct the movements of his vessel. He was looking through one of the slits in the pilot house, when a shell exploded in front of the opening, driving the powder into his face and eyes, rendering him blind and helpless. He turned over the command of the vessel to

the executive officer, Lieut. S. D. Greene, who was in the turret, with instructions to continue the action, and the vessel was again headed towards the enemy and her fire recommenced.

During the time between the fall of Lieut. Worden and the arrival of Lieut. Greene in the pilot house, the "Monitor" was entirely under control of the man at the wheel, who having no one to direct him, and doubtless being excited by the fall of his commanding officer, steered off on another course without any particular aim or object. This is substantially the view given of the occurrence by Prof. Soley in his work, "The Blockade and the Cruisers," and he obtained his information from the late Commander Greene.

LIEUT. GEORGE U. MORRIS.

(ACTING COMMANDER OF THE "CUMBERLAND.")

Prof. Soley further says: "Seeing the 'Monitor' draw off, Van Brunt, under the supposition that his protector was disabled and had left him, prepared for the worst, and made ready to destroy his ship; but at this point the 'Merrimac' withdrew to Norfolk. Greene fired at her twice, or at most three times. He then returned to the 'Minnesota,' and remained by her until she got afloat." This is no doubt a correct version of the affair. The "Merrimac" moved off (those on board of her glad to do so in an apparently creditable manner), knowing that if the battle lasted much longer the "Monitor" would be successful.

When the Confederates saw the "Monitor" moving away, they naturally concluded she was disabled, or had run short of ammunition, and their first idea was to proceed again to the attack of the "Minnesota."

By Capt. Van Brunt's account, the "Merrimac" and the two Confederate gun-boats did head towards his ship, and realizing his helpless condition he made every preparation to destroy the "Minnesota," determined that she should not fall into the hands of the enemy. Capt. Van Brunt goes on to say: "A short time after the 'Merrimac' and her consorts had changed their course, and were heading for Craney Island."

In writing history it is no more than fair that both sides should have a hearing. Lieut. Greene, in his report to the Secretary of the Navy, dated March 12, 1862, says:

"At 8 A. M. perceived the 'Merrimac' underway and standing towards the 'Minnesota;' hove up anchor and went to quarters

"At 8:45 A. M. we opened fire on the 'Merrimac,' and continued the action until 11:30 A. M., when Capt. Worden was injured. Capt. Worden then sent for me to take charge of the vessel. We continued the action until 12:15 P. M., when the 'Merrimac retreated to Sewell's Point, and we went to the 'Minnesota' and lay by her."

LIEUT. JOSEPH B. SMITH.

(ACTING COMMANDER OF THE "CONGRESS.")

This is rather a meagre report of so important a transaction, but no one else in the squadron at Hampton Roads, so far as known, says anything about the matter except Capt. Van Brunt, who writes: "For some time after this the Confederates concentrated their whole battery upon the turret and pilot-house of the 'Monitor,' and soon after the latter stood down for Fortress Monroe."

A Confederate officer on board the "Merrimac" says: "At length the 'Monitor' withdrew over the middle ground where we could not follow, but always maintaining a position to protect the 'Minnesota.' To have run our ship ashore on a falling tide would have been ruin. We awaited her

return for an hour and at two P. M. steamed for Sewell's Point and thence to the dock-yard at Norfolk. Our crew were thoroughly worn out from the two days' fight. Although there is no doubt that the 'Monitor' first retired, the battle was a drawn one as far as the two vessels engaged were concerned, but in its general results the advantage was with the 'Monitor.'"

This seems to be a fair statement and its author pays a high tribute to the "Monitor." He says: "The 'Monitor' was well handled and saved the 'Minnesota' and remainder of the fleet at Fortress Monroe," which seems evident enough, for had the "Monitor" failed to appear every vessel in the roads must have been captured or destroyed.

There is glory enough in this fact for the little "Monitor" without claiming more for her. She saved not only the squadron, but the honor of the nation, and her gallant commander is fully entitled to all the honors he received. Had he not been disabled at such an inopportune moment he would, in our opinion, have compelled the "Merrimac" to surrender; for the tide was ebbing and in another hour the "Merrimac" could not have maneuvered and would have grounded; the "Monitor" then could have taken position under the iron-clad's stern and knocked her frame in.

Thus ended this remarkable engagement, which, in the bravery and ability displayed on both sides, has never been excelled; and the foreign officers who witnessed the conflict, could judge from it how desperately we could meet a foe attempting to invade our shores.

It is stated by the Confederate authority, to whom we referred, that "the 'Merrimac' was not penetrated by any of the shot fired by the 'Monitor.' Had the fire been concentrated on one spot the shield could have been forced; or had larger charges been used the iron on the 'Merrimac' could not have withstood them. Most of the 'Monitor's' shot struck obliquely, in most cases breaking both courses of iron, but not injuring the vessel's backing. When struck at right angles the wood backing would be broken but not penetrated." These are matters of interest, since it has been a mooted point as to the amount of damage the "Merrimac" received. The "Monitor," we know, received none, except to her pilot-house, and could have fought all day without danger of vital injury to her hull or machinery, but the "Merrimac" was obliged to go into dry-dock to be very thoroughly repaired.

The joy of the Confederates at the news of the first day's fight in Hampton Roads, was much dampened when the information came that the "Merrimac" was obliged to leave the fighting-ground on the second day without effecting anything. It was a severe disappointment, since they had reckoned on the capture of the whole Union fleet in the Roads, and an advance of the "Merrimac" upon Washington.

As soon as the "Merrimac" was again ready for service, on the 29th of March, 1862, Commodore Josiah Tatnall was ordered to command her instead of the cool and judicious Catesby Jones. who had conducted the engagement with the "Monitor" with so much skill and bravery. Commodore Tatnall had a high reputation in the old Navy as a brave and chivalric officer. The writer served as his executive officer in some desperate encounters with the enemy during the Mexican War, and knew him as

supplied with steel-pointed solid shot, and one hundred tons of ballast were put on board to increase the vessel's draught and bring her weak point under water, though this decreased her speed. The "Merrimac" was greatly improved, when a month later, on the 11th of April, she left the Navy Yard, and steamed down towards Hampton Roads accompanied by six gun-boats.

Commodore Tatnall fully expected the "Monitor" to be ready to meet him as soon as he had passed Sewell's Point, but the Federal authorities had grown wary. The fleet had been re-enforced by the "Vanderbilt," fitted as a powerful ram, and she lay ready to attack the "Merrimac" in conjunction with the "Monitor." Could the

COMMODORE JOSIAH TATNALL.

well as one man can know another. Tatnall was ready for any desperate service, but he lacked Catesby Jones' coolness and judgment.

Up to the time Tatnall took command the iron-clad had been in dock undergoing repairs, and it would seem from this circumstance that she had been more roughly handled by the "Monitor" than the Confederates chose to admit. At all events they were convinced that she was not fit to cope with the "Monitor" in her original condition. The hull for four feet below the water line was covered with two-inch iron, a new and heavier ram was strongly secured to the bow, the damage to the armor was repaired, and wrought-iron port shutters were fitted. The rifled guns were

"Vanderbilt" have but struck the "Merrimac," going at half speed, she would have penetrated her as easily as a knife opens a watermelon.

To Tatnall's surprise no one seemed to notice his appearance, the "Monitor" and her consorts lying quietly at anchor below Fortress Monroe. The "Monitor" was just as we left her after the fight; she needed but trifling repairs, while the "Merrimac" had been long enough in dock to make her doubly strong. The "Monitor" had been kept in readiness in case the "Merrimac" attempted to pass the fleet and make towards Washington, although the Confederate vessel could hardly have passed the Kettle Bottom shoals in the channel of the Potomac.

The officers of the "Merrimac," knowing Tatnall's reputation, expected a desperate engagement at the outset, but he showed more than ordinary judgment when he found how matters stood. He had requested permission from the Confederate government to act on his own discretion and to pass Fortress Monroe if he thought proper; but this was denied him for prudential reasons. While the "Merrimac" remained intact it was supposed that Norfolk would be secure against attack, and the way for an army to Richmond would be barred by the iron-clad; all of which was in a measure true. For equally prudent reasons the "Monitor" was kept out of battle for the present, and lay off Fortress Monroe under command of Lieut. Jeffers. There were no Federal war vessels above Fortress Monroe, but there were three merchant sailing vessels within the bar off Hampton.

Tatnall ordered Lieut. Barney, in the "Jamestown," to go in and bring them out. This was accomplished, although the gunboat was fired on by the forts. Two of the vessels contained supplies for the Federal Army.

This was a humiliation and should not have been suffered, but prevented at all hazards, especially as the crew of an English corvette cheered the Confederates as they towed their prizes away.

"That night the 'Merrimac' lay at anchor above Sewell's Point, and a few days later she went within gunshot of the fort at the Rip Raps, with which she exchanged a few rounds. It is said that the 'Merrimac' opened fire, hoping that the 'Monitor' would go out and meet her, when by numerous devices it was intended to board the little vessel, smother the officers and crew, put out the fires and tow her into Norfolk! The 'Monitor,' however, lay quietly at anchor biding her time, and the 'Merrimac's' engines breaking down, she was obliged to return to Norfolk.

"On the 8th of May the 'Merrimac' again appeared and found the 'Monitor,' 'Galena,' 'Nantucket' and a number of heavy ships shelling the works at Sewell's Point; but on the appearance of the iron-clad they all returned below Fortress Monroe. Tatnall stood direct for the 'Monitor,' which retreated with the other vessels, the 'Merrimac' and consorts following close down to the Rip Raps, where shot passed over the ship and a mile beyond. Tatnall remained for some hours in the Roads until finally in disgust he gave an order to Lieut. Jones to fire a gun to windward and take the ship back to her buoy."

The above Confederate account does not agree with the report of Rear Admiral Goldsborough, who says:

"By direction of the President our vessels shelled Sewell's Point yesterday, mainly with a view to see the practicability of landing a body of troops thereabouts. The 'Merrimac' came out but was even more cautious than ever. The 'Monitor' was kept well in advance and so that the 'Merrimac' could have engaged her without difficulty had she been so disposed, but she declined to do so, and soon returned and anchored under Sewell's Point."

This disposes of the statement that the Federal Squadron retired before the "Merrimac" and consorts, for the writer can find nothing on record to substantiate the Confederate account. There is every reason to believe the commander of the "Merrimac" was willing to let the "Monitor" alone, for he was too clever a man to risk his vessel against all the ships awaiting his attack.

The Federals were evidently desirous to draw him as far as possible from his base and then overwhelm him with the "Monitor," heavy frigates and powerful rams that were prepared to attack him.

That was the last appearance of the "Merrimac." According to a Confederate account: "On the 9th of May, while at anchor off Sewell's Point, it was noticed at

LIEUT. JOHN TAYLOR WOOD, OF THE "MERRIMAC."

(AFTERWARDS COMMANDER OF THE PRIVATEER "TALLAHASSEE.")

sundown that the Confederate flag was not flying over the batteries. A boat was sent on shore and found them abandoned. Lieut. Pembroke Jones was then dispatched to Norfolk, and returned with the news that Norfolk was evacuated, and the Navy Yard on fire."

That determined the fate of the "Merrimac." Her occupation was gone, and to prevent her from falling into the hands of the Federal Government, she was blown up and entirely destroyed.

Several plans had been proposed to save the vessel for further use, such as lightening her and getting her up the James River as a protection to Richmond, but they were found impracticable.

It was just as well that the Merrimac's career ended thus, for she would never have been of any more use in Confederate hands, and her officers and crew would have fallen victims to the temerity of any commander who ventured to attack the " Monitor," backed as she was by an overwhelming force. The Federal government had made a great mistake in not being prepared for the " Merrimac" on her first appearance; they were not going to be caught again, and in their precautions to this effect they rather overdid the matter. The lesson was not lost on the Government during the war. The experience we gained by the loss of the " Congress " and " Cumberland " was worth a dozen frigates, although we mourned the brave fellows who fell gloriously fighting for their country.

Had there been no " Merrimac" we should never have built those magnificent iron-clads, which for a time placed our Navy in the front rank of the navies of the world, and enabled us to bid defiance to England and France, who were too much inclined to meddle with our affairs.

The " Merrimac" taught our legislators the necessity of being more liberal in our naval expenditures, and to build armored vessels such as would not only be able to stand the heaviest seas, but to batter down the strongest forts, or destroy any enemy's vessel that came upon our coast.

After the war was over the lesson was unfortunately soon forgotten, and in a few years the Navy, which was so powerful at the close of the rebellion, relapsed into an insignificance from which it will take long to recover; while other nations, taking advantage of our experience, have gone on building iron-clads which astonish the world with their power.

To this day the principle of the " Monitor " is recognized in every navy in the world, and the fame of Ericsson promises to endure for centuries to come.

The " Monitor " did not long outlast her huge antagonist. She was lost a few months afterwards in a gale off Cape Hatteras in attempting the impossible, for it was never intended she should be used as a cruiser. She was not intended to ride out heavy gales, and of this the government had had proof in her first voyage to Hampton Roads, when she was very near going to the bottom. When she foundered she carried down with her some brave fellows who stood by her to the last. May they rest in peace !

After reading all the accounts which have been published in regard to this engagement, we come to the conclusion that the " Monitor " was too much for the " Merrimac." The latter was damaged so much that she had to remain some time in dock for repairs. For a short time after Lieut. Worden was wounded, the " Monitor " headed away from her antagonist until Lieut. Greene could get into the pilot-house, and the commanding officer of the " Merrimac " took advantage of this circumstance to return to Norfolk.

Catesby Jones was too clever an officer not to know that if he should get aground in the narrow channel the " Monitor " would certainly capture him. Had Worden not been wounded the " Merrimac " would have been captured as it was.

After the " Merrimac " retreated Worden was removed to Washington, where he received every attention his condition required, and all the honors the government could bestow for his skill and bravery, which had averted a terrible catastrophe and humilation. To Worden belongs the credit of having performed one of the most important achievements of the war.

CHAPTER XIII.

BUILDING A NAVY ON THE WESTERN RIVERS.—BATTLE OF BELMONT.

James B. Eads Engaged to Build Gun-boats.—Depot Established at Cairo.—Navy Yard at Mound City.—Flag-officer Foote in Command of Mississippi Squadron. —Captain Pennock and Assistants.—The "Taylor," "Lexington" and "Conestoga."—Grant Seizes Paducah.—Commander Walke Attacks the Batteries near Columbus.—Battle of Belmont.—Grant gains two Victories in one day.— Efficient Services Rendered by Gun-boats.—The Western Flotilla, etc., etc.

TO enable us to keep pace with the progress of events we must now turn our attention in another direction, and see what the Navy was doing in the western rivers.

Early in 1862 the attention of the Navy Department was directed towards the West. The necessity of building gun-boats there to assist the Army in its operations had become evident to the dullest comprehension.

There were more than four thousand miles of navigable rivers, the control of which was absolutely necessary to the Federal Government to enable it to crush out rebellion, and the only way to obtain this control was to build a fleet peculiarly adapted to smooth and shallow waters, while carrying the heaviest smooth-bore and rifled ordnance.

Strange as it may at this day appear, some of the Army officers argued that gun-boats would be useless to co-operate with the Army in the West, as the Confederates would establish heavy forts all along the rivers, and knock the vessels to pieces; in April, 1862, after the war had progressed for a year, General Leonidas Polk seized upon the heights near Belmont, Ky., and mounting heavy guns there blocked the way for Army transports from Cairo to the sea. Then the Army began to talk of improvising a Navy of their own, and the Navy Department sent Commander John Rodgers to St. Louis to superintend the construction of an army flotilla.

While the North had its Ericsson, the West was fortunate in possessing, in the person of Mr. James B. Eads, the very man for the occasion. Mr. Eads undertook to build seven large gun-boats, heavily plated on the bow and lighter on the sides, which were calculated to carry very heavy ordnance.

It is strange how slowly even the cleverest of men receive new ideas. These gun-boats, intended for service in the smooth waters of the western rivers, could have been plated with iron sufficient to have turned the heaviest shot, instead of which they were only partially covered, and owing to this defect met with many mishaps. In three months three of the vessels were ready to receive their armament.

As the Army were now making great demands for gun-boats, Com. Rodgers was authorized to purchase three river steamers and convert them into war-vessels without plating. These were the first gun-boats that fired a shot in support of the Union, and became well known for their many encounters with the enemy, and for valuable services throughout the war.

Flag-officer Andrew H. Foote was ordered to command the Mississippi Squadron on the 6th of September, 1862, and he took with him to the West a number of officers whose names will appear from time to time in our pages—a more gallant set of men never trod the deck of a vessel-of-war.

Foote, Rodgers, Eads and their assistants put forth all their energies to get the squadron ready for service, as the enemy were fortifying the banks of the rivers in Tennessee, and Polk's heavy batteries at

Columbus barred the way against vessels from above. The civilians who had charge of the building of the gun-boats were not skilled in the construction of war-vessels, and the time of the naval officers was therefore completely occupied in supervising the work of construction; but with their aid Mr. Eads soon completed an efficient flotilla, which obtained a fame in the annals of the war surpassed by no other vessels.

One of Flag-officer Foote's first acts was to establish a depot at Cairo, Illinois, where his vessels could be repaired and could replenish their stores; and those who remember the Navy Yard at Mound City, near Cairo, and the large fleet which grew from the small squadron first put afloat, will wonder why we should require so many navy yards at the present time when we hardly fit out a dozen vessels in a year.

Com'r A. M. Pennock was placed in command of the depot at Cairo, the navy yard being literally afloat in wharf boats, old steamers, tugs, flat-boats, or even rafts, as the government owned no land at that point; but when the station was subsequently established at Mound City, just above Cairo, the Union exulted in the possession of a real navy-yard of some ten acres, which, although sometimes under water from freshets, soon grew to a respect-

able size, although its machine shops, carpenter shops, etc., were all afloat in steamers. Capt. Pennock had charge of the naval station until the close of the war, and his services called forth the unqualified commendation of the several commanders-in-chief of the Mississippi Squadron under whom he served. Capt. Pennock's first assistants at the naval station were Lieutenants I. P. Sanford and O. H. Perry, Chief Engineer, Capt. Geo. D. Wise, U. S. A., Quartermaster, and Acting Naval Constructor Romeo Friganza, the latter sent from New York navy yard to fill this important position.

This, then, was all the establishment the Navy Department at that time considered necessary to keep in repair the Mississippi Squadron, that was expected to successfully control an active enemy occupying thousands of miles of navigable rivers, where the nature of the country offered every advantage to an enterprising foe.

The difficulties with which the Navy had to contend on the Atlantic coast were many, and their duty was harrassing, but at least they had generally sea-room and intervals of rest. An officer could retire to repose without the expectation of having a volley of musketry crash through his state-room window, or, when walking on deck, did

REAR-ADMIRAL A. H. FOOTE.

not risk being knocked over by some cowardly bushwhacker, who would watch all day for the chance of picking off somebody on board a gun-boat—just as in peaceful times he had laid in wait for a coon or a wild turkey. In the West a man carried his life in his hands, yet few took pains to avoid the danger, although always in readiness to meet and repel attacks upon their vessels. Coolness and courage were at all times required, and a readiness for duty that interfered with the natural rest, so essential a preservative of vitality.

The three wooden gun-boats which formed the advance guard of the Western Flotilla, were the "Taylor," "Lexington" and "Conestoga," which had been so altered from river steamers that they became efficient vessels of war. The "Taylor" mounted six sixty-four-pounder guns in broadside and one thirty-two-pounder in the stern; the "Lexington" mounted four sixty-four-pounders in broadside and one thirty-two-pounder astern, and the "Conestoga" carried two thirty-two-pounders in broadside and one light gun in the stern—not a very formidable flotilla to encounter strong earthworks, many of them mounting rifle guns of great range.

The Confederates had not at first attempted to extemporize a river navy, although they were not long in following the Federal example ; and the Navy Yard at Memphis, turned over to the State of Tennessee with all its appliances, by act of Congress, was soon in full blast preparing vessels to attack anything we might put upon the rivers. But our light gun-boats showed themselves not only fit for picket duty and for clearing the banks of bushwhackers, but even to take a hand in shelling heavy batteries.

At this period of the war General Grant had been transferred to the command of the District of Southeast Missouri, and on the 4th of September, 1861, he established his head-quarters at Cairo, Illinois. His district included Southern Illinois and so much of Western Kentucky and Tennessee as might fall into possession of the national forces. It comprised the junction of the Mississippi, Ohio, Tennessee and Cumberland Rivers, and was at the time the most important point of operations in the West.

Kentucky, in the early part of the war, endeavored to preserve a neutral position between the contending sections, but the Confederate General Polk soon violated this neutrality, seizing Columbus, some twenty miles below Cairo, and threatening Paducah; whereupon Grant seized this latter place and garrisoned it. Thus the two armies were near each other. Grant had nothing but ordinary transports to operate with, and these were liable to be cut to pieces

from the banks of the river by the Confederate light artillery.

On the 14th of September Commander Henry Walke, in command of the "Taylor," under orders from Flag-officer Foote, proceeded down the river towards Columbus to make reconnoissance, accompanied by officers of General Grant's staff. At Norfolk, six miles below Cairo, the "Taylor" took on board a hundred men of the Ninth Illinois Regiment, and then approached Columbus to ascertain the strength of the batteries. "These batteries were built upon what was called the Iron Banks, at the first Chickasaw Bluff, which rose from two to three hundred feet above the river, overlooking its course for a distance of twenty miles north and south. The Confederate batteries were placed on the spurs of the bluff, one of them, fifty feet above the water, mounting two heavy guns, with a floating battery of sixteen heavy guns moored at Columbus landing. Their heaviest rifled guns were planted and pivoted on the summit of the river banks, where they commanded a long range up the river and towards their rear."

When Com. Walke arrived off these works, he fired eight or ten eight-inch shells into them, killing and wounding several of the enemy, and the reconnoissance having been completed the vessel returned to Cairo.

The "Taylor" and "Lexington" were constantly employed on such service, and their value soon became apparent to the army officers, who had at first thought they would be of little use.

Soon after the above mentioned reconnoissance, General Grant wrote to Commander Walke, requesting the services of the gun-boats to accompany him to Belmont landing, and on the 16th of November, 1861, the General started down the river with 3,100 men in transports, convoyed by the "Taylor," Com. Walke, and the "Lexington," Com. R. N. Stembel.

Grant landed his troops at Hunter's Point, on the Missouri side, out of range of the Columbus batteries, and marched direct on Belmont, three miles distant, where the Confederates had posted their camp in an open space protected by fallen timber. By nine o'clock Grant's entire command was hotly engaged, except one battalion left at the landing as a reserve, and to protect the transports.

General Grant had requested Com. Walke, with the two gun-boats, to attack the batteries at Columbus as a diversion, which was done. As the gun-boats were under fire of some twenty heavy guns having a plunging fire, it was necessary to manage them with great skill to prevent their being disabled, and they moved around in short circles, loading and firing as rapidly as possible. When their object was accomplished the gun-boats withdrew, as it would have been madness to have continued longer under the fire of such heavy guns.

In the mean time Grant had been fighting four hours and his horse had been shot under him. The officers' example stimulated the men, who though novices in war fought like veterans, driving the enemy to the river, capturing all his artillery and several hundred prisoners, and breaking up the camp.

Instead of pursuing the enemy as they huddled together under the river bank, the Federal soldiers began to plunder the camp. Meanwhile, Confederate transports, crowded with men, were discovered coming up the river from Columbus, and Grant

have whipped them once and can do it again." As soon as the men found that Grant meant to fight, not to surrender, they charged the enemy, who disappeared in the woods.

Grant pushed on to the landing and most of his men went on board the transports. A detachment was sent back to gather up the wounded, and it was, for a time, undisturbed. Then Grant in person went to withdraw his reserve force, which he found had already returned to the transports, thus leaving the General completely outside his army. Ascending a knoll he discovered the enemy advancing in line of battle in greatly increased force, with the evident intention of getting above the transports and cutting them off. The General

BATTLE OF BELMONT.

endeavored to reform his men in order to get back to his own steamers before these troops could land, but it was not until he had ordered the camp to be set on fire that his men would cease plundering. The fire drew the attention of the artillerists at Columbus, who opened on the Federal troops.

The march back to the transports then began, but the defeated enemy, finding no notice was being taken of them, reformed in the woods just above Belmont, where three regiments from Columbus joined them, and this combined force was interposed between Grant and his transports. Some of the troops cried out " we are surrounded." "Well," said Grant, "in that case, we must cut our way out as we cut our way in; we

saw that it was impossible to save the party who were out in search of the wounded, so he turned and rode slowly back towards the transports to avoid attracting attention.

The enemy's fire was opened on the transports, which were about getting under way, leaving Grant behind, but a plank was hastily run out from one of the vessels and he rode on board. At that moment the "Taylor" and "Lexington" opened upon the enemy in a corn-field about fifty yards distant with grape and canister, mowing them down " in swaths," as General Badeau expresses it, and causing them to retreat in great confusion. By five o'clock the last of our transports was out of range of the enemy's batteries, officers and men equally pleased with having gained a victory, which but for the gun-boats would have been a bloody defeat. It is true the soldiers in the transports kept up a constant fire on the enemy, but being raw troops they no doubt aimed too high, as did the Confederates, and there was very little execution done; but in the case of the gun-boats there was no mistake, their guns were handled by trained men directed by experienced officers, and such was the rapidity and accuracy of their fire that the enemy fled in all directions.

Thus Grant gained two victories in one day, and against double his own force, for the Confederates admit having 7,000 men in action. Grant lost 485 in killed, wounded and missing; 125 of the wounded fell into the enemy's hands, but in lieu of these Grant captured 175 prisoners and two guns. The Confederate loss was 685 killed and wounded, mostly by the gun-boats.

Soon after the defeat of the enemy and the departure of the transports, General McClernand discovered that some of his soldiers had been left behind, and at his request Capt. Walke returned and succeeded in recovering most if not all these, together with forty of the enemy's wounded, who had been left on the field, proof positive that the Confederates had retreated in a panic.

The assistance given the army by the gun-boats disposed of the question " as to the utility and practicability of gun-boats carrying on hostilities on the rivers, where it was believed the batteries on the banks could prevent their passage." It is strange how an opposite idea could have been entertained by those who ought to have known better.

In Gen. Grant's official report he says: " The gun-boats convoyed the expedition and rendered most efficient service. Immediately upon our landing they engaged the enemy's batteries on the heights above Columbus, and protected our transports throughout. For a detailed account of the part taken by the gun-boats I refer with pleasure to the accompanying report of Capt. Walke, senior officer."

This was warm commendation from Gen. Grant, who was moderate in his praise of men, but it scarcely gave an idea of the service performed by the gun-boats that day. The Confederates had to land their troops that crossed from Columbus three miles below, giving the men a long march. The gun-boats " Taylor " and " Lexington " attacked the batteries three times during the day, and kept up a fire on the enemy all along the banks. When our soldiers retreated to the transports the gun-boats covered them so with their fire that they received little injury.

This battle was claimed by both sides, which is apt to be the case with raw troops; but the list of killed and wounded was in favor of the Federals, although they had less than one-half the enemy's force.

The gallant conduct of Commanders Walke and Stembel does not appear to have secured even a passing notice from the Secretary of the Navy, which was certainly a great injustice to two officers who had demonstrated so plainly the efficiency of gun-boats on the Western rivers.

It was a part of the Confederate plan early in the civil war to seize and hold Missouri and Kansas, thus threatening the free States in the Northwest, to hold Kentucky and Tennessee, cross the Ohio, and make the Northern States the theatre of war, thus punishing the Northern people for their obstinacy in declining to yield to the demands of the secessionists. This plan, which had been discussed long before the Southern States seceded, would doubtless have been carried out had it not been for the multitude of men in the North who sprang to arms and frustrated the Confederate plans. Lee had to retreat from Pennsylvania, where it was determined that the Confederates should endure all the hardships of war to teach them the folly of rebellion.

To circumvent the grand schemes of the enemy in the West, it was necessary that we should have a naval force on all the rivers, and Attorney General Bates seems to have been the first person in the government to point out the necessity of such a force to get possession of all the tributaries of the Mississippi, and finally of the great river itself to the sea. Mr. Bates' ideas were not at first considered practicable; even the veteran Secretary of the Navy, Mr. Welles, who is credited with a vast knowledge of naval matters, seemed to doubt, and stated that " there was with many great incredulity as to the utility and practicability of the use of gun-boats on the Western waters, where it was believed batteries on the banks could prevent their passage." The Secretary might have observed that the enemy's batteries on the Potomac did not stop even ordinary transports.

At first the naval forces on the Western rivers were put under the direction of the War Department, as it was supposed the armed vessels would be a mere appendage of the land forces; and there does not seem to have been a man in the Cabinet at that time who knew the difference between a gun-boat and a transport.

In July, 1861, Quartermaster General Meigs contracted with Mr. Eads to build a number of iron-clad gun-boats for the Western waters, and from the fact that Gen. Meigs contracted for them it is presumed the War Department paid for them, and that the Navy Department had not then risen to the height of the occasion. Seven of these gun-boats were each to be about 600 tons, to draw six feet of water, to be plated with two and a half inch iron, and steam nine knots. They were to be each 175 feet long and 51½ wide, their sides at an angle of 35 degrees from the water line, their gun decks being but a foot above the surface of the water. The bow and stern were at an angle of 45 degrees, and the wheel for propelling the vessels was placed in the stern. Of course these vessels had many imperfections, as we were new in the business of building iron-clads, and seem to have had very little idea what thickness of iron plating was necessary to turn the heavy shot of the enemy.

The iron-clads carried four thirty-two pounders on each side, three nine or ten-inch guns in their bow ports, and two lighter

with the others to the Navy Department, her name was changed to "Baron de Kalb," as there was already a "St. Louis" in the Navy. In the course of the succeeding twenty days the "Carondelet," "Cincinnati," "Louisville," "Mound City," "Cairo" and "Pittsburg" followed in rapid succession. An eighth vessel, the "Benton," superior in every respect to the above, was undertaken. She was originally a wrecking boat, purchased by General Fremont and sent to Mr. Eads, whose ideas developing as he went on building, he produced from this wrecking boat an iron-clad of remarkable strength.

Thus in one hundred days this energetic man constructed a squadron of iron-clad gun-boats, aggregating five thousand tons,

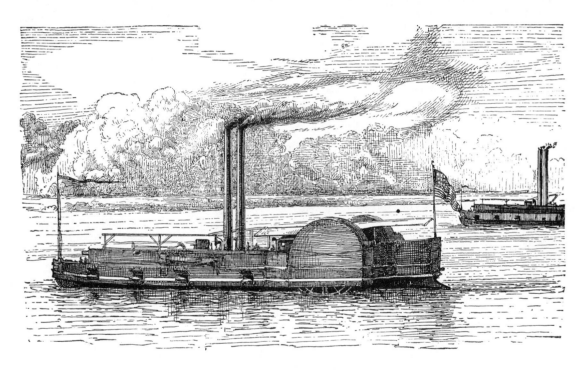

U. S. GUN-BOATS "TAYLOR" AND "LEXINGTON."

guns in the stern. A casemate enclosed the wheel at the stern, and there was a conical pilot-house forward covered with iron. The writer is particular in describing these vessels, as they performed such remarkable service all through the war, and notwithstanding their defects and the vicissitudes they experienced, no vessels in the Navy engaged in so many successful battles or made such a record for their commanding officers.

Within two weeks after the contract with Eads was signed, four thousand men were busily engaged in constructing the vessels. The work was pushed night and day, and on the 12th of October, 1861, the "St. Louis" was launched at Carondelet, Missouri, forty-five days after her keel was laid. When this vessel was transferred

ready for their armament of one hundred and seven heavy guns. Such a performance needs no eulogy, and even had Mr. Eads done no more in the cause of the Union, he would have been entitled to the thanks of the nation. Since then he has gone on executing great works, and his reputation as a civil engineer is world-wide.

A ninth powerful vessel, the "Essex," was afterward added to this formidable flotilla. She carried nine heavy guns, and though built in later fashion was not equal to the "Benton."

When Flag-officer Andrew H. Foote took command of the Western Flotilla in September, 1862, it consisted of these nine "iron-clads" (so-called), three wooden gun boats, the "Taylor" "Lexington" and

"Conestoga," which had been purchased and equipped by Commander John Rodgers, and thirty-eight mortars mounted on rafts.

This service was of a somewhat anomalous character, since the gun-boats were under control of the army, and their accounts were under the supervision of the Quartermaster General. There was no navy yard at first where the vessels could be refitted or repaired, but Flag-officer Foote, with his energetic assistants, overcame the impediments that retarded his operations, and displayed the highest qualities as a naval commander by establishing an efficient force on the Western rivers, and by leading it to victory in subsequent engagements with the enemy.

Previous to the time when Foote took command of the squadron, the "Taylor," "Lexington" and "Conestoga" were constantly employed by General Grant, with the commanders mentioned, in making reconnoissances, during which they came frequently under fire of the enemy's batteries, which even at that early day infested the banks of the rivers. In one of these affairs the "Conestoga" particularly distinguished herself.

The Commander-in-Chief of a squadron may be very energetic himself and possess all the qualities necessary for his position, but he cannot succeed unless he is assisted by brave and efficient officers. The mention of subordinate officers has been too much neglected by naval historians, a fault which in this account the writer would wish to avoid. Nothing is more pleasing to an officer than to see himself credited with faithful service, though there are some officers so avaricious in this regard that they would fain monopolize all the glory to themselves. Such men should write their own histories.

CHAPTER XIV.

BATTLE AND CAPTURE OF FORT HENRY BY THE NAVY.

COMMANDING POSITIONS OF FORTS HENRY AND DONELSON.—GRANT GIVEN PERMISSION TO ATTEMPT THE CAPTURE OF THE FORTS.—FOOTE'S GUN-BOATS AND THE ARMY UNDER GRANT LEAVE CAIRO.—LANDING OF THE ARMY AT BAILEY'S FERRY.—DEFENSES OF FORT HENRY.—FORT HIEMAN EVACUATED.—THE GUN-BOATS OPEN FIRE ON FORT HENRY.—DESCRIPTION OF THE BATTLE BY A CONFEDERATE HISTORIAN.—THE "ESSEX" DISABLED.—COMMODORE WILLIAM D. PORTER WOUNDED.—FORT HENRY SURRENDERS. —CAPTAIN WALKE TAKES POSSESSION OF THE FORT.—LOSSES.—GALLANT FOOTE.— DREADFUL SCENES OF THE ENGAGEMENT DESCRIBED BY AN OFFICER OF THE "ESSEX." —VESSELS ENGAGED IN ATTACK ON FORT HENRY.

SHORTLY after the battle of Belmont the Confederates established a strong line of operations reaching to the centre of Kentucky. On their left was Columbus, where they had collected a strong force and 140 guns. One of their largest armies was at the junction of the Louisville and Nashville, and Memphis and Ohio Railroads (the northernmost point then held by the Confederates west of the Alleghany Mountains). These armies threatened Northern Kentucky and protected Nashville and Middle Tennessee.

At the centre of this strategic line the Tennessee and Cumberland Rivers formed the natural avenues into all the disputed territory north of the cotton States. These two streams approach within twelve miles of each other, at a point near the boundary between Kentucky and Tennessee. Here, at a bend in each river, the Confederates had erected two batteries, Fort Henry, on the Tennessee, and Fort Donelson, on the Cumberland. These forts completely commanded the navigation of the two rivers, and by forbidding any advance of the Union gun-boats or transports, prevented the transportation of our army by water, either into Kentucky or Tennessee.

The reader may think it strange that the Confederates, with nothing like the Federal resources, should be able to throw up so many formidable fortifications on coast and river, and mount them with heavy guns, and will naturally ask where the guns came from.

The answer to this question is that, by our terrible blunder in surrendering the Norfolk Navy Yard at the commencement of the war, we put into the hands of the Confederates 1,400 guns of all calibres. Our Navy had already recaptured 211 of these Norfolk guns, and it remains to be seen what account it will render of those which now confront it at Columbus, Fort Henry and Fort Donelson.

Grant knew the nature of these works better than any other officer, and saw that Bowling Green and Columbus could both be turned as soon as Henry and Donelson fell. Halleck and others were making great strategic movements, which amounted to nothing, but Grant kept his mind steadily fixed on these two forts, knowing the effect their fall would have.

On the 23d of January Grant visited Halleck at St. Louis, and urgently requested permission to make the attempt to take Forts Henry and Donelson; both of which General C. F. Smith, who had made a reconnoissance, reported could easily be done.

The gun-boats at that time were subject to General Halleck's orders, and Flag-officer Foote, who commanded them, had recommended a united movement of Army and Navy against the forts. The desired permission was finally granted to these officers, but the gallant commander of the Army contingent was greatly hampered by detailed instructions furnished by the Commander-in-Chief.

Grant started from Cairo on the 2d of February, 1862, with 17,000 men in transports, and Foote accompanied him with seven gun-boats. After reconnoitering the forts the Army landed at Bailey's Ferry, just out of reach of the enemy's fire.

The Confederates had erected their works at Fort Henry on both sides of the river, with a garrison of 2,800 men, under Brigadier General Tighlman. The main fortification was on the eastern bank. It was a strong field-work with a bastioned front, defended by seventeen heavy guns, twelve of which bore on the river. Embrasures had also been formed by placing sand-bags on the parapets between the guns. On the land side there was an entrenched camp, and beyond this an extended line of rifle-pits, located on commanding ground. The earthworks covered the Dover road, by which alone communication could be held with Fort Donelson. The heights on the west commanded Fort Henry, but the works at this point were unfinished.

Grant's plan was to land and attack the enemy in the rear, while Foote was to attack their batteries in front with the gun-boats.

When the Confederates discovered this plan they prepared for a determined resistance. New lines of infantry cover were established and additions were made to the fortifications on both sides of the river. Tighlman at once ordered up re-enforcements from Danville and the mouth of Sandy River, as well as from Fort Donelson.

The country around Fort Henry was all under water from the overflow of the Tennessee River, which impeded the movements of the troops on both sides. The rain fell in torrents on the night of the 5th of February, and Grant having an insufficiency of transports was obliged to send some of his steamers back to Cairo to bring up part of his command. He did not therefore succeed in getting all his men on shore until 11 P. M.

The original plan was to invest Fort Hieman on the west bank simultaneously with Fort Henry, in order to prevent re-enforcements, and also the escape of the garrisons. The Confederates perceiving the impossibility of holding both works against such a force, evacuated Fort Hieman, and gave all their attention to defending Fort Henry.

Grant was ignorant of this withdrawal, and that night ordered General C. F. Smith to seize the heights on the west with two brigades. The rest of Grant's force, under Gen. McClernand, was to move at 11 A. M. on the 6th to the rear of Fort Henry, and take position on the road leading to Fort Donelson and Dover, where they could intercept fugitives and hold themselves in readiness to take the works by storm promptly on the receipt of orders.

COMMODORE FOOTE'S IRON-CLAD GUN-BOATS AT CAIRO.

The fleet got under way at two o'clock on the day of the battle in the following order : The "Essex," 9 guns, Com. Wm. D. Porter, on the right; "Cincinnati" (flag ship), 13 guns, Com. Stembel, on the left of the "Essex;" "Carondelet," 13 guns, Com. Walke, on the left of the "Cincinnati;" and the "St. Louis," 13 guns, Lieut. Paulding, on the left of all. The "Conestoga" (wooden), 3 guns, Lieut. Phelps; "Taylor" (wooden), 9 guns, Lieut. Gwin; "Lexington" (wooden), 9 guns, Lieut. Shirk. These vessels all told mounted 76 guns; but as they were obliged to fight "bow on" and could therefore only use their bow guns, there were only twelve guns brought into action by the iron-clads and five or six by the wooden vessels, which were well in the rear.

The position of Fort Henry had been selected with great care. It stood at the end

the naval discipline and accuracy of fire soon told on the troops in the fort.

The battle is described as follows by a Confederate historian :

"A few moments before the surrender, the scene in and around the fort exhibited a spectacle of fierce grandeur ; many of the cabins and tents in and around the fort were in flames (from the Federal shells)—added to the scene were the smoke from the burning timber, and the curling of the dense wreaths of smoke from the guns, the constantly recurring spatter and whizzing of fragments of bursting shells, the deafening roar of artillery, the black sides of five or six gun-boats, belching fire at every port-hole, and the army of General Grant, 10,000 strong, deploying around our small army, attempting to cut off its retreat. The gallant Tighlman, exhausted and begrimed with powder and smoke, stood erect at the middle battery and pointed gun after gun, and remarked, 'It is vain to fight longer, our gunners are disabled, our guns dismounted— we can't hold out five minutes longer,' and finally he ordered the white flag to be hoisted."

When the gun-boats had obtained a sta-

ATTACK ON FORT HENRY.

of a straight reach in the river, which its guns commanded for two miles. Two 64-pounders were planted on an elevation above the fort, which might, however, have been stormed and taken by our own troops, and turned against the enemy.

The gun-boats moved on up to within a mile of the fort, firing an occasional shot, and finally moved to within a third of a mile of the batteries, when the firing commenced in earnest from both sides.

General Grant and Flag-officer Foote had intended to have the Army and Navy make a simultaneous attack, but it is a pretty difficult matter to time such events. In combined movements something always happens to delay one party or the other; in this instance the roads were dreadful, and the Army was so delayed that it did not reach the fort until some time after its surrender to the Navy. For over an hour the guns on both sides kept up a deafening roar, but

tionary position and were able to get their range, almost every shot and shell went to its mark, and the destruction caused was marvelous; but with all the damage our fire was doing to the enemy they fought like devils, and only gave in when it was no longer possible to hold out.

The gun-boats did not get off "scot free" in this attack; they had their share of damage as well as the fort, and a fair share of killed and wounded. About twenty minutes before the Confederates surrendered, the gun-boat "Essex" was pierced through the boilers by a shot, which resulted in wounding and scalding 29 officers and men, including her gallant commander, William D. Porter. She drifted out of the fight totally disabled, and took no further part in it.

After the "Essex" dropped out, the firing from the fort continued with undiminished rapidity upon the three iron-clads which remained in position, and was continued without intermission until the flag was hauled down, after a hotly-contested action of one hour and fifteen minutes.

At the end of the battle a boat containing the Adjutant General and Captain of Engineers went alongside the flagship and reported that Brig. Gen. Lloyd Tighlman, the commander of the fort, wished to communicate with the naval commanding officer. Lieuts. Stembel and Phelps were then sent on shore to hoist the American flag on Fort Henry, and a request was sent to Gen. Tighlman that he visit the flagship, which he did, and surrendered himself a prisoner.

All the prisoners were received on board the fleet, and thus ended the battle of Fort Henry.

Besides the General and his staff there were 60 or 70 prisoners, and a hospital ship containing 60 invalids, all of whom were treated with that kindness which naval officers always extend to an enemy in distress. Captain Walke of the "Carondelet" was directed to go on shore and take charge of the fort and all within it until the arrival of the Army, which took place an hour afterward, when everything was handed over to Gen. Grant.

This was a well-fought battle on both sides, and the gun-boats were skillfully handled by the naval commanders. The gallant Foote might well feel proud to be the first to remove that absurd idea that "gun-boats would not prove serviceable in Western waters as they could not resist the fire of heavy guns in earthworks."

On taking possession of the fort Commander Walke beheld a perfect scene of destruction. Everything in and about the works was either knocked to pieces or set on fire; and it is remarkable that with such evident effects of the naval fire so few of the enemy were disabled (six killed and seventeen wounded).

Twenty heavy guns fell into our hands as well as a large amount of military stores. The "Essex" was the only gun-boat that suffered any severe damage from the enemy's fire. But the Confederate practice was excellent, and the iron-clads were frequently struck. According to Flag-officer Foote's report the "Cincinnati" was struck thirty-one times, the "Essex" fifteen times, the "St. Louis" seven times and the "Carondelet" six times, though Commander Walke claims to have been struck much oftener.

The "Essex" lost 29 men killed and wounded by scalding steam, and also nine soldiers who were serving on board of her. The casualties on the other vessels were few and unimportant, as their iron plating (though only two and a half inches thick), had done them good service.

This is the result of the first action between gun-boats and shore batteries in Western waters. It was an unequal contest against a fort that mounted 20 heavy guns, but it was so quickly settled that it gave the Confederates a great dread of the iron-clads; and in building forts thereafter, they were more careful not to have them in accessible places.

Where all did their duty so well it would be hard to discriminate. Each one received his full meed of praise from Foote, and their conduct on this occasion was long remembered by the people of the country, for it was now clearly demonstrated that the naval vessels on the Western rivers could sustain the fire of the heaviest batteries, notwithstanding the high authority to the contrary.

To give an idea of some of the dreadful scenes to which our gun-boats were liable, we insert an interesting letter written after the battle of Fort Henry, by James Laning, the Second Master of the "Essex," in which he thus describes the engagement:

"On February 1st, 1862, the iron-clad gun-boat 'Essex,' whilst lying off Fort Holt, received orders from Flag-officer A. H. Foote, commanding the Western flotilla, to proceed up the Tennessee River, and anchor some five miles below Fort Henry, blockading the river at that point. The iron-clads 'Carondelet,' Commander Henry Walke; the 'Cincinnati,' Commander Stembel, and the 'St. Louis,' Lieutenant Commanding Leonard Paulding, were completed and put into commission a few days previous, making, with the 'Essex,' four iron-clads, besides the wooden gun-boats 'Taylor,' 'Lexington' and 'Conestoga,' now ready for offensive operations.

"On the 5th of February, after reconnoitering up the Tennessee to Fort Henry, we fired a few shots at the fort and returned towards our anchorage. The enemy made no reply, and apparently took no notice of our shots, until we were well on our way back. When about two, or two and a half miles distant, the fort fired a rifle shot, which passed over our boat to the right and cut down a number of saplings on shore. In a few moments another shot, fired with more precision, passed over the spar-deck amongst the officers; through the officers' quarters, visiting in its flight the steerage, commander's pantry and cabin, passing through the stern; doing, however, no damage except breaking some of the captain's dishes, and cutting the feet from a pair of his socks, which happened to be hanging over the back of a chair in his cabin. These shots reaching us at so great a distance, rather astonished us, as the enemy intended they should.

"After this reconnoissance it was decided to remove the torpedoes from the island chute, and instead of going up the main channel, to steam up the chute, and forming line of battle under cover of the timber on the island, advance towards the fort and open fire as we reached the head of the island at the distance of a mile to a mile and a half, and continue advancing. The wooden gun-boats, 'Taylor' and 'Lexington,' were, therefore, ordered to remove the torpedoes, which they did without much difficulty. The army, which was encamped on both sides of the river, was to move at daylight on the morning of the 6th, so as to make a land attack, and prevent the escape of the garrison, whilst the gun-boats were to attack as before mentioned.

"On the afternoon of the 5th, Flag-officer Foote came on board the 'Essex,' and our crew were called to quarters for drill and inspection. After putting them through the evolutions he addressed the crew and admonished them to be brave and courageous, and above all to place their trust in Divine Providence. The writer, who was in command of the battery, was especially charged with the importance of wasting no shots. 'Remember,' said he, 'that your greatest efforts should be to disable the enemy's guns, and be sure you do not throw any ammunition away. Every charge you fire from one of those guns cost the government about eight dollars. If your shots fall short you encourage the enemy. If they reach home you demoralize him, and get the worth of your money.' After commending all to the care of Divine Providence he left us, and repaired on board the 'Cincinnati,' which was his flag ship at that time.

"During the night of the 5th, or morning of the

it was conceded that one gun on land was about equal to three on water.

"Upon arriving at the head of the island, the flagship 'Cincinnati' opened fire, which was the signal to commence the general engagement. The writer had, however, received orders from Capt. Porter not to fire until he had particularly noted the effect of the 'Cincinnati' shots, so as to profit by their mistakes, if they made any, in elevation. The first three shots from the flagship fell short, so there was $24 worth of ammunition expended. A lesson, however, had been learned on board the 'Essex,' and orders were at once given to increase elevation. At that moment the captain's aide appeared on the gun-deck with orders to fire high, and blaze away ; and before I could repeat the order, the No. 2 port-bow gun belched forth her fiery flame, and sent a nine-inch shell plump into the breastworks, which, exploding handsomely, caused a considerable scattering of earth, and called forth

REAR-ADMIRAL R. N. STEMBEL, COMMANDER OF THE "CINCINNATI."

(FROM A PORTRAIT TAKEN IN 1883.)

6th, a heavy rain fell, which very much retarded the movements of the army, and made the roads so heavy that they did not succeed in reaching the scene of action until after the fort had surrendered. The naval forces, after waiting until 11 o'clock A. M., got under way and steamed up the river. Arriving at the island chute, the line of battle was formed, the 'Essex' on the extreme right, the 'Cincinnati,' with Flag-officer Foote on board, on our left, the 'Carondelet' on her left, and the 'St. Louis' on the extreme left—the wooden boats taking position in our rear under cover of the island, and firing over us at long range.

"As we could only use the bow batteries on each boat, we could only bring, on the four iron-clads, 11 guns to bear. The fort, although mounting 17 guns, could only bring 11 of them to bear on the island chute, so it was a fair and square fight, and the problem was about to be solved whether iron-clad gun-boats could compete with mud fortifications. Under the old system of warfare, I believe,

a cheer from the fleet, whilst it produced great consternation in the fort. The 'Essex' had therefore won the honor of putting the first shot into the enemy's breastworks.

"And here I must record the fact, in justice to the memory of a brave man, who lost his life in that engagement, that the honor of that shot belonged to Jack Matthews, captain of the No. 2 gun. Jack was an 'old tar,' who had seen much service on men-of-war in both the English and American navies, and was always restive under the command of a volunteer officer. Jack, ever on the alert to put in the first licks, and feeling, no doubt, jealous and insubordinate, had increased the elevation of his gun, and just as I was in the act of repeating the captain's order, pulled his lockstring and blazed away.

"The fort seemed a blaze of fire, whilst the boom of the cannon's roar was almost deafening. The wind was blowing across our bows, carrying the smoke away so rapidly as to prevent any obstruction to the view. Our fleet kept slowly approaching the fort, and gradually shortening the distance. Our shells, which were fused at 15 seconds, were reduced to 10, and then to five seconds. The elevation of the guns was depressed from seven degrees to six, five and four, and then three degrees, and every shot went straight home, none from the 'Essex' falling short.

"Twenty or thirty minutes after the action had begun, some one of the officers ventured to call the attention of Capt. Porter to the fact that the officers on the other vessels were leaving the spar-decks and going below. 'Oh, yes,' says Porter. 'I see; we will go too, directly.' Just then a shot struck the pilot-house, making the splinters fly terribly, as no plating had as yet been put on it. At this the order was given for all to go below, and soon all joined us on the gun deck. Capt. Porter, on coming below, addressed the officers and crew, and complimented the first division for their splendid execution, asking us if we did not want to rest, and give three cheers, and they were given with a will.

"By orders I turned over the command of the battery to the third master, and ordered the first division to give way to the second. Capt. Porter then ordered the first division to the stern battery. This was a precautionary measure, the importance of which could scarcely be estimated at that time, but became dreadfully apparent a few moments after. A few of my men, however, reluctant to quit the scene of action, lingered by their guns on the forward gun deck; amongst the number was Jack Matthews. In the twinkling of an eye the scene was changed from a blaze of glory to a carnival of death and destruction. A shot from the enemy pierced the casemate just above the port-hole on the port side, then through the middle boiler, killing Acting Master's Mate S. B. Brittan, Jr., in its flight, and opening a chasm for the escape of the scalding steam and water. The scene which followed was almost indescribable. The writer, who had gone aft in obedience to orders only a few moments before (thus providentially saved), was met by Fourth Master Walker, followed by a crowd of men rushing aft. Walker called to me to go back; that a shot from the enemy had carried away the steam pipe. I at once ran to the stern of the vessel, and looking out of the stern port saw a number of our brave fellows struggling in the water. The steam and hot water in the forward gun deck had driven all who were able to get out of the ports overboard, except a few who were fortunate enough to cling to the casemate outside. On seeing the men in the water, I ordered Mr. Walker to man the boats and pick them up; Capt. Porter, who was badly scalded, being assisted through the port from outside the casemate by the surgeon, Dr. Thomas Rice, and one of the men.

"When the explosion took place Captain Porter was standing directly in front of the boilers, with his aide, Mr. Brittan, at his side. He at once rushed for the port-hole on the starboard side, and threw himself out, expecting to go into the river. A seaman (John Walker) seeing his danger, caught him around the waist, and supporting him with one hand, clung to the vessel with the other, until, with the assistance of another seaman, who came to the rescue, they succeeded in getting the captain on to a narrow guard or projection, which ran around the vessel, and thus enabled him to make his way outside, to the after port, where I met him. Upon speaking to him, he told me that he was badly hurt; and that I must hunt for Mr. Riley, and if he was disabled I must take command of the vessel, and man the battery again. Mr. Riley was unharmed, and already in the discharge of his duties as Captain Porter's successor. He had been saved by a sailor (John W. Eagle) from going overboard in much the same manner that Captain Porter had

been. This man Eagle was Captain of No. 1 gun, and like Jack Matthews, would not leave his gun, and although badly wounded, with his right hand in a sling, he begged me, with tears in his eyes, not to remove him, but to let him fight his gun. I reported the case to Captain Porter, who decided to let him remain; and this brave fellow fought his gun most admirably through the action, and then 'capped the climax' of his bravery and heroism by grasping the casemate with his wounded hand, and clasping Executive Officer Riley with the other one as he was falling overboard, sustaining him until both regained a footing on the projection before mentioned.

"In a very few minutes after the explosion our gallant ship (which had, in the language of Flag-officer Foote, fought most effectually through two-thirds of the engagement) was drifting slowly away from the field of glory; her commander badly wounded, a number of her officers and crew dead at their posts, whilst many others were writhing in their last agony. As soon as the scalding steam would admit, the forward gun-deck was explored. The pilots, who were both in the pilot-house, were scalded to death. Marshall Ford, who was steering when the explosion took place, was found at his post at the wheel, standing erect, his left hand holding the spoke, and his right hand grasping the signal bell-rope. Pilot James McBride had fallen through the open hatchway to the deck below; he was still living, but died soon after. The captain's aide, Mr. S. B. Brittan, Jr., had fallen by the shot as it passed through the gun-deck before entering the boiler. A seaman named James Coffey, who was shot-man to the No. 2 gun, was on his knees in the act of taking a shell from the box to be passed to the loader. The escaping steam and hot water had struck him square in the face, and he met death in that position. Jack Matthews had gone overboard badly scalded. He was picked up by the boats. Third Master Theo. P. Terry was severely scalded, and died in a few days. He was a brave officer.

"Our loss in killed, wounded and missing amounted to 32. Of these three were killed instantly, four died that night, several were drowned (the number not definitely known), and about one-half the wounded recovered.

"The Flag-officer continued approaching nearer and nearer to the fort, pouring shot and shell from the boats at still shorter range . . . until they showed the white flag to surrender.

"When I told Captain Porter that we were victorious, he immediately rallied, and raising himself on his elbow, called for three cheers, and gave two himself, falling exhausted on the mattress in his effort to make a third. A seaman named Jasper P. Breas, who was badly scalded, sprang to his feet, naked to the waist, his jacket and shirt having been removed to dress his wounds, exclaiming: 'Surrendered! I must see that with my own eyes before I die.' Before any one could interfere, he clambered up two short flights of stairs to the spar-deck, where he was gladdened with the sight of his own flag proudly and victoriously floating in the breeze. He shouted, 'Glory to God!' and sank exhausted on the deck. Poor Jasper died that night, that his country might live.

"The 'Essex' fired seventy-two shots from two 9-inch guns during the battle. In obedience to battle orders, I had instructed the powder boys to keep count of the number of charges served to each gun. Job Phillips, a boy fourteen years old, was powder-boy of No. 1 gun. After the action, I asked Job how many shots his gun had fired. He referred me to a memorandum on the whitewashed casemate; where with a rusty nail he had carefully and accurately marked every shot his gun had fired; and his account was corroborated by the gunner in the magazine. This may be considered as a striking example of coolness and bravery in a boy of fourteen, who had never before been under fire."

SECRETARY WELLES TO FLAG-OFFICER FOOTE.

"NAVY DEPARTMENT,
February 13, 1862.

"SIR : Your letter of the 7th inst., communicating the details of your great success in the capture of Fort Henry, is just received. I had previously informed you of the reception of your telegraphic dispatch, announcing the event, which gave the highest satisfaction to the country.

"We have to-day the report of Lieutenant Commanding Phelps, with the gratifying results of his successful pursuit and capture and destruction of the Confederate steamers, and the disposition of the hostile camps as far up the Tennessee as Florence. I most cordially and sincerely congratulate you, and the officers and men under your command, on these heroic achievements, accomplished under extraordinary circumstances, and after surmounting great and almost insuperable difficulties. The labor you have performed, and the services you have rendered in creating the armed flotilla of gunboats on the Western waters, and in bringing together for effective operation the force which has earned such renown, can never be overestimated. The Department has observed, with no ordinary solicitude, the armament that has so suddenly been called into existence, and which under your well-directed management has been so gloriously effective.

"I am, respectfully,
"Your ob't servant,
[Signed] "GIDEON WELLES.
"Flag-officer A. H. FOOTE, U. S. N.,
"Commanding Gun-boat Flotilla, &c., Cairo, Ill."

OFFICIAL THANKS TO THE ARMY AND NAVY.

The State of Ohio deemed this battle sufficiently important to merit a vote of thanks, as appears from the following:

"Relative to a vote of thanks to General Grant, Flag Officer Foote and others, for their courage and gallantry exhibited in the bombardment of Fort Henry. Resolved by the General Assembly of the State of Ohio, That the thanks of the people of Ohio be, and through their representatives are, hereby tendered to General Grant and Flag-officer Foote, and the brave men under their command, for the courage, gallantry and enterprise exhibited in the bombardment and capture of Fort Henry, a victory no less brilliant in itself than glorious in its results, giving our Army a foothold in Tennessee, and opening the way for early advance to the capital of the State.

"Resolved, That the Governor transmit copies of these resolutions to said officers, with the request that the same be read to the men under their command. "JAMES L. HUBBELL,
"Speaker of the House of Representatives.
"B. STANTON, President of the Senate.
"Passed, February 14, 1862."

The following is a list of the vessels and officers engaged in attack on Fort Henry:

GUN-BOAT "CINCINNATI."—R.N. Stembel, U. S. N., Commander; William R. Hoel, First Master; Oscar H. Pratt, Second Master; Charles G. Perkins, Third Master; John Pearce, Fourth Master; R. H. Attenborough, Pilot; Isaac D. Gaugh, Pilot; John Ludlow, Surgeon; Baron Proctor, Paymaster; William D. McFarland, Chief Engineer; Samuel H. Lovejoy, First Assistant Engineer; James Armstrong, Second Assistant Engineer; William J. Shannon, Third Assistant Engineer; James McB. Stembel, Master's Mate; Philip Shell, Master's Mate; John R. Hall, U. S. N., Acting Gunner; Thomas B. Gregory, Carpenter; Jacob Vitinger, Armorer.

GUN-BOAT "CONESTOGA."—S. L. Phelps, U. S. N., Lieutenant Commanding; John A. Duble, First Master; Charles P. Noble, Second Master; Benjamin Sebastian, Third Master; Richard H. Cutter, Fourth Master; Aaron M. Jordan, Pilot; William Attenborough, Pilot; William H. Wilson, Assistant Surgeon; Alfred Phelps, Acting Paymaster; Thomas Cook, Chief Engineer; Alexander Magee, First Assistant Engineer; Charles Marshall, Second Assistant Engineer; Michael Norton, Third Assistant Engineer; James Kearney, Master's Mate; Henry Hamilton, U. S. N., Acting Gunner; Andrew Woodlock, Carpenter; James O'Neil, Armorer.

GUN-BOAT "ESSEX"—William D. Porter,

IRON-CLAD GUN-BOATS "ST. LOUIS," "CARONDELET" AND "ESSEX."

U. S. N., Commander; Robert K. Riley, First Master; James Laning, Second Master; Theodore P. Ferry, Third Master; George W. Walker, Fourth Master; James McBride, Pilot; Marshall H. Ford, Pilot; Thomas Rice, Surgeon; Joseph H. Lewis, Paymaster; Charles M Blasdell, Chief Engineer; R. J. Stearns, First Assistant Engineer; George D. Simms, Second Assistant Engineer; Jeremiah Wetzel, Third Assistant Engineer; S. B. Brittan, Master's Mate; Matthias B. Snyder, Gunner; Thomas Steel, Carpenter; ——Fletcher, Armorer.

GUN-BOAT "LEXINGTON."—James W. Shirk, U. S. N., Lieutenant Commanding ; Jacob S. Hurd, First Master ; Martin Dunn, Second Master ; James Fitzpatrick, Third Master ; Sylvester Poole, Fourth Master ; James McCamant, Pilot ; William Ford, Pilot ; George W. Garver, Assistant Surgeon ; Augustus F. Taylor, Acting Paymaster ; Samuel Vroon, Gunner ; Richard Carroll, Carpenter ; Reuben Story, Armorer.

GUN-BOAT "TAYLOR."—William Gwin, U. S. N., Lieutenant Commanding; Edwin Shaw, First Master; Jason Goudy, Second Master; James Martin, Third Master; Patrick McCarty, Fourth Master; John Sebastian, Pilot; David Hiner, Pilot; Thomas H. Kearney, Assistant Surgeon; William B. Coleman, Acting Paymaster; Samuel Goble, Chief Engineer; D. Edward Weaver, First Assistant Engineer; Edward W. Goble, Second Assistant Engineer; Oscar S. Davis, Third Assistant Engineer; Ferdinand T. Coleman, Master's Mate; Herman Peters, U. S. N., Acting Gunner; Thomas Russell, Carpenter; Elihu Stevens, Armorer.

GUN-BOAT "ST. LOUIS."—Leonard Paulding, U. S. N., Lieutenant Commanding; John V. Johnson, First Master; James Y. Clemson, Second Master; Charles S. Kendrick, Third Master; Alexander Fraser, Fourth Master; John B. McDill, Assistant Surgeon; Llewellyn Curry, Acting Paymaster; Frank A. Riley, Pilot; Robert G. Baldwin, Pilot; William Carswell, Chief Engineer; T. F. Ackerman, First Assistant Engineer; James L. Smith, Second Assistant Engineer; John Wilcoxsen, Third Assistant Engineer; Sydney H. McAdam, Master's Mate; James P. Paulding, Master's Mate; John A. McDonald, U. S. N., Acting Gunner; Robert H. Medill, Carpenter; —— Sypher, Armorer.

GUN-BOAT "CARONDELET."—Henry Walke, U. S. N., Commander; Richard M. Wade, First Master; John Doherty, Second Master; Charles C. Gray, Third Master; Henry A. Walke, Fourth Master; William Hinton, Pilot; Daniel Weaver, Pilot; James S. McNeely, Assistant Surgeon; George J. W. Nixsin, Acting Paymaster; William H. Faulkner, Chief Engineer; Charles H. Caven, First Assistant Engineer; Samuel S. Brooks, Second Assistant Engineer; Augustus F. Crowell, Third Assistant Engineer; Theodore L. Gilmore, Master's Mate; Edward E. Brennand, Master's Mate; Richard Adams, Gunner; Oliver Donaldson, Carpenter; H. H. Rhodes, Armorer.

By referring to the public or official dispatches of the war, the names of the commanders and officers above mentioned will be found constantly referred to in battles with the enemy, and were very frequently distinguished by acts of bravery and heroism creditable alike to themselves and the naval service. The position of the Navy in the West at that time was an anomalous one, belonging as they did neither to one or the other branches of the service; and the hands of the naval commander were so tied down by the orders of General Halleck, that he could make no move without his permission. The same may, however, be said of General Grant, who was completely handicapped by his own superior.

There was only one killed and eleven wounded on the iron-clads in this battle at Fort Henry, a small number for so long a fight, but this is accounted for by the fact that the accuracy of the gun-boats' fire was so great, and the discharges so rapid, that the enemy were constantly driven from their batteries—even the great bravery of their Commander (General Loyd Tighlman), and the example he set in firing the guns himself, could not induce the Confederates to stand up to their work under such a fire, especially after seven of the fort's guns had been dismounted.

CHAPTER XV.

CAPTURE OF FORT DONELSON AND BATTLE OF SHILOH.

GRANT'S MESSAGE TO HALLECK.—THE ARMY IN FRONT OF DONELSON.—THE GUN-BOATS PUSH UP THE TENNESSEE RIVER.—BURNING OF THE CONFEDERATE TRANSPORTS.—FORT DONELSON AND ITS STRATEGIC POSITION.—THE GUN-BOATS OPEN FIRE ON THE FORT.— THE GUN-BOATS ARE CRIPPLED AND WITHDRAW.—FLAG-OFFICER FOOTE WOUNDED.— GALLANTRY OF CAPTAIN WALKE.—LOSSES.—GENERAL GRANT'S VICTORY.—RESULTS.— GUN-BOATS REPAIR TO CAIRO.—GRANT PREPARES TO ADVANCE TOWARDS SHILOH.—BATTLE AT PITTSBURG LANDING (SHILOH).—SERVICES RENDERED BY THE GUN-BOATS "LEXINGTON" AND "TAYLOR."—CAPTAIN GWIN'S REPORT.—THE NAVY AIDS MATERIALLY IN SAVING THE ARMY FROM DESTRUCTION.—A TERRIBLE BATTLE AND GREAT LOSS OF LIFE.—THE CONFEDERATES AS FIGHTERS.—EXTRACTS FROM RECORDS OF THE TIMES.— CONGRATULATORY ORDERS, &C.

ON the 8th of February, 1862, Gen. Grant telegraphed to Gen. Halleck: "Fort Henry is ours; the gunboats silenced the batteries before the investment was completed. I shall take and destroy Fort Donelson on the 8th, and return to Fort Henry."

The same reasons which had induced Grant to undertake the capture of Fort Henry still urged him to take Fort Donelson; that is, to get the control of the Tennessee and Cumberland Rivers and be able to penetrate into the heart of Tennessee with his troops and Foote's gun-boats.

On the 7th of February his cavalry penetrated to within a mile of Fort Donelson, but they could obtain no information as to the strength of the place or the number of troops.

Foote was notified of Grant's intentions, and was requested to have what gun-boats he could muster ready to attack the batteries before the army made its assault. But the great rise in the Tennessee River prevented Grant from completing his proposed movement. The water overflowed the river banks, and gave the army as much as it could do to save its stores and tents from the flood.

In the meantime three gun-boats, under Lieut. Phelps, had pushed on up the Tennessee as far as Florence, Alabama, greatly alarming the inhabitants, but carrying comfort to the loyal citizens, who were glad to see the old flag floating over their waters.

When about twenty-five miles above the fort, Phelps found the draw at the railroad-crossing closed, and the machinery for working it disabled, but men were landed, in an hour the draw was opened, and the following gun-boats passed through: "Taylor," Lieut.-Com. Gwin; "Lexington," Lieut.-Com. Shirk, and the "Conestoga," "Lieut.-Com. Phelps.

In a short time this flotilla caused the enemy to abandon and burn three steam transports, filled with military stores, submarine batteries, powder, cannon and projectiles. These vessels exploded with such force as to endanger the Union gun-boats. Skylights were broken, doors forced open and the light upper decks raised bodily. This did not stop the progress of the latter, however, and they proceeded up the river, doing good work in breaking up railroads and destroying camp equipage wherever they could find it. At a place called Cerro Gordo, they came across the steamer "Eastport," which was being converted into a gunboat—a strong, powerful vessel, afterwards used as a gun-boat and ram by the Federal Government. She had been abandoned and scuttled, and her suction-pipes broken, but the leaks were stopped, and the vessel raised and taken back to Fort Henry.

On the 8th of February the flotilla arrived

at Chickasaw, near the state line, and seized two steamers. They then proceeded up to Florence, Alabama, near the mussel shoals, where three steamers had been set on fire by the Confederates. A force was landed and a large amount of stores, marked "Fort Henry," were saved from the burning vessels; also a quantity that had been landed and stored.

The results of this expedition were three steamers and one gun-boat seized, six steamers burned by the enemy to prevent their falling into our hands, all the timber and saw-mills in the neighborhood destroyed, and a large quantity of stores captured. From the 6th to the 10th of the month the labors of this little flotilla were immense, and its gallant commander inflicted damage upon the enemy which was irreparable.

In the course of this raid our officers met the most gratifying proofs of loyalty wherever they went. Across Tennessee, and in those portions of Alabama and Mississippi which they visited, men, women and children came in crowds and shouted their welcome to the old flag under which they had been born. A reign of terror had existed all along the river, and loyal people did not dare to express their thoughts openly. They intimated to our officers, however, that if arms were placed in their hands they would not hesitate to espouse the Union cause and put down rebellion in their midst.

This shows exactly what kind of a government the secession leaders intended to substitute for the one under which these people had lived so contentedly, in the enjoyment of freedom of speech and all the other rights which belong to every free American.

This expedition had an excellent effect wherever it appeared, and it showed the necessity of further increasing our naval force on the Western waters, in order to have a sufficient number of gun-boats on all the rivers to keep them open, to drive the guerrilla army away from their banks, and also to give confidence to the Union people, who only needed some such support to induce them to proclaim their sentiments openly.

Grant lost no time in getting together a force which he deemed sufficient for the attack on Fort Donelson. Reinforcements were rapidly coming in from various quarters, and Halleck, who up to this time had thrown every objection in the way of the expedition, now seemed anxious to take the credit of the movement to himself, and was doing all he could to hurry troops, stores and siege implements to the scene of action. On the 10th he informed Grant that large re-enforcements would be sent to him.

Grant did not, however, wait for these re-enforcements, but while Halleck was writing about picks and shovels he informed

Foote that he was only waiting for the return of the gun-boats to attack Fort Donelson.

This fortification was the strongest military work in the entire theatre of war. It was situated on the west bank of the Cumberland River, north of the town of Dover, on a peculiarly rugged and inaccessible series of hills which rose abruptly to the height of one hundred feet. Every advantage had been taken of the character of the ground. The country was densely wooded, but the timber had been felled far out in advance of the breastworks, and the limbs, cleaned and sharpened, were formed into an almost impenetrable abbatis.

Two streams which emptied into the Cumberland formed the right and left defenses of the Confederate breastworks, which extended nearly three miles, and were strongly entrenched with secondary lines of rifle pits and detached batteries posted on commanding heights.

It was a marvelous work and evidently a difficult place to take, provided the enemy had a sufficiently strong garrison to hold all points of his line of defense.

The main fort was built on a precipitous height, close by a deep gorge open to the South. It was three-quarters of a mile from the breastworks, and overlooked both the river and the interior. It covered a hundred acres of ground and was defended by fifteen heavy guns and two carronades.

There were heavy water-batteries placed to control the river navigation, and the whole armament of the batteries, including the light artillery, was sixty-five pieces.

The garrison numbered (as well as could be ascertained) 21,000 men, a great part of whom had recently been thrown into the works by the Confederates, who appreciated the importance of the position as fully as Grant did, and were now straining every nerve to hold it.

While Grant was making his movements in the rear of the fort, so as to completely surround it and prevent the escape of any of the garrison, the gun-boats on the water side were preparing for the attack.

Foote, according to his own report, did not consider himself properly prepared for such an adventure, as his force was not sufficiently strong to make an attack on the fort; but at the earnest request of Halleck and Grant, he felt called upon to do what he could, and at 3 P.M. on the 14th, he moved up with his fleet in the following order: iron-clads, "St. Louis," (flag-ship), Lieut. Paulding; "Carondelet," Com. Walke; "Louisville," Com. Dove; "Pittsburg," Lieut. E. Thompson; gun-boats: "Taylor," Lieut.-Com. Gwin; "Conestoga," Lieut.-Com. Phelps, the two latter in the rear.

After a severe fight of an hour and a half,

during part of which time the iron-clads were within 400 yards of the fort, the flag-ship "St. Louis," and the iron-clad "Louis-ville," had their wheels disabled and drifted out of action.

The fire of the fort, which had during the greater part of the engagement been very rapid and accurate, was now concentrated on the remaining vessels of the fleet, and soon proved too hot for them. The iron-clads "Pittsburg" and "Carondelet" were much cut up between wind and water, and with the wooden gun-boats were finally compelled to drop out of action. The flag-ship "St. Louis" had received fifty-nine shots, four of which were between wind and water, and one in the pilot-house which killed the pilot and wounded the flag-officer himself.

Foote says in his report: "Notwithstanding our disadvantages, we have every reason to believe that in fifteen minutes more, could the action have been continued, it would have resulted in the capture of the forts. The enemy's fire had slackened, and he was running from his batteries when the two gun-boats, 'St. Louis' and 'Louisville,' dropped out of action owing to their crippled condition, seeing which, the enemy returned to his guns and again opened fire from the river batteries, which had been silenced."

This was evidently not a success on the part of the Navy, as the gun-boats were compelled to retire; the "St. Louis" and "Louisville," in consequence of having their rudders crippled, and the "Caronde-let" and "Pittsburg" because they were not able to withstand the concentrated fire of the enemy.

It has been asked, "If the enemy was deserting his batteries and it was thought that in fifteen minutes more the gun-boats would have been victorious, why were not the drifting vessels lashed alongside of the "Carondelet and "Pittsburg" and thus brought back into action, where they could have taken part with the Army in obtaining the victory, and have obtained more than a passing notice by army historians?" As it was, the only notice they obtained was the statement that "the gun-boats were so disabled as to be unfit to take any part of importance in the succeeding operations." This mention of the Navy was disingenuous, to say the least, and is not history. The "Carondelet" and "Pittsburg," though struck pretty often, were still intact and fit for any service, and their two commanders would have been glad to have availed themselves of the opportunity to run past the batteries and enfilade them on the side where they were least protected.

There are two ways of fighting batteries on river heights; one is to engage them at close quarters with grape and canister, and the other, to remain at long range, where the enemy's fire would be uncertain, especially if the vessels were kept well apart.

All these things will be considered after a fight is over, but no one knows what he would do unless placed in like circumstances. In this case the flag-officer had received a serious wound in the foot, and in addition to the physical pain which he suffered, he was no doubt taken by surprise at meeting with such a reception at Fort Donelson after having made such short work with Fort Henry.

Nothing is said in official reports or general orders about the gallant attack made by Captain Walke in the "Carondelet."

On the morning of the 13th (before Foote had arrived), General Grant requested Captain Walke to take a position and throw shells into the fort in order to create a diversion, which he hoped to be able to take advantage of.

Captain Walke immediately complied with this request, and threw 139 15-second and 10-second shells into the enemy's works, receiving in return a fire from all the batteries. The "Carondelet" was only struck twice, however, as most of the projectiles passed over her. One 128-lb. solid shot passed through the front casemate, and glancing over the barricades which protected the boiler, struck and burst a steam-heater and then fell into the fireroom. No other damage was done, and it is thus shown how much more difficult it is to strike one vessel moving about than a number of vessels in groups.

Foote's vessels were struck about fifty times each by 128 and 32-lb. shot, and had fifty-four officers and men killed and wounded.

We regret that we cannot chronicle a victory for the gun-boats, but it was a fair stand-up fight while it lasted, and Foote did not hesitate to take the bull by the horns and engage the enemy at 600 yards, the best distance for the forts and the worst for the vessels; and, although the gun-boats were forced to drop out of action, they lost no credit in so doing.

There was one omission in this naval attack, which is due to the history of the times, and should be mentioned. Had the flag-officer sent his remaining gun-boats past the batteries at night, when the darkness would have prevented the enemy from estimating his distance, these vessels would have been ready on the following day to en-filade the works in their weakest point; and what is more important still, they would have cut off all hope of escape of the garrison. The transports in which Floyd and Pillow with 5,000 men escaped across and up the river, would all have fallen into our hands.

Having looked into all the details of this

interesting affair we feel obliged to say that all the credit for the capture of Fort Donelson belongs to the Army, as there was no truth in the statement that the enemy were so demoralized by the attack of the gun-boats, that they could not be brought into effective use on the following day in the actions which resulted in their defeat and the surrender of 16,000 men, sixty-five guns and 17,600 small-arms to General Grant. (Twenty-five hundred of the Confederates were killed and wounded during the siege.)

This victory belonged exclusively to General Grant and no one can take from him one iota of the credit of that great military feat, in which he showed his fitness to lead the armies of the Union. The results of this victory were that "the whole of Kentucky and Tennessee at once fell into the hands of the national forces—the Tennessee and Cumberland rivers were opened to national vessels for hundreds of miles. Nashville, the capital of Tennessee and a place of great strategic importance, fell. Bowling Green had become untenable as soon as Donelson was attacked, and was abandoned on the 14th of February, the day before the Confederate works on the Cumberland were carried, while Columbus and the other end of the strategic line were evacuated early in March, thus leaving the Mississippi river free from the Confederate flag from St. Louis to Arkansas.

The news of this victory was very encouraging to the Union people, especially when they beheld its results. When city after city fell and stronghold after stronghold was abandoned, and they saw that it was all in consequence of the capture of Fort Donelson, it is not strange that the national amazement and gratification knew no bounds, and it is only to be regretted that the Navy should not have had a greater share in the honors.

Grant was made a Major-General, and we only regret that the opportunity did not serve to make Foote a Rear-Admiral and give some promotion to his gallant officers.

It is always difficult to procure reliable information with regard to the force of the enemy, either of men or guns. In this case the report of Flag-officer Foote was very indefinite, and he only gives a general idea of what he had to contend against.

He says, "the enemy must have brought over twenty heavy guns to bear upon our vessels from the water-batteries and the main fort on the side of the hill, while we could only return the fire with twelve bow guns from the four boats.

It is not the intention of the writer to mention all the small affairs in which the gun-boats performed splendid service, such as making reconnoissances up and down the rivers or skirmishing with the enemy's forts

and light batteries, unless some definite object was gained or some serious injury inflicted on the enemy, as the limits of this book forbid it. It is his intention, however, to fully describe the work of the Navy in Western waters, and when it is possible to give every officer due credit for what he accomplished, without, as a rule, going beyond official reports.

After the battle of Fort Donelson, Foote's gun-boats had to go to Cairo for repairs, which they sorely needed, and to replenish their crews, for they were all very much in want of men.

As fast as the vessels were made ready for service they were kept moving in the work of reconnoitering down towards Columbus, or else they were employed on the Cumberland and Tennessee rivers to deter the enemy from erecting batteries along the banks; also to assure the inhabitants that they would be protected by the Federal government, and that the Confederates would soon be driven out of the State.

These, however, are mere details of duty which cannot be brought out in a history of this kind. The fall of Forts Henry and Donelson compelled the Confederates to change their plans almost immediately. Their line of defense was moved farther South and was now established on the following points: Island No. 10, Fort Pillow and Memphis on the Mississippi, a point in Tennessee near Pittsburg, and the town of Chattanooga. All of these points were strongly fortified and defended by large armies, thus closing up East Tennessee, and preventing our armies from marching southward.

On the 15th of February, Gen. Grant was assigned to the new military district of West Tennessee, with limits undefined, and Gen. W. T. Sherman to the command of the district of Cairo.

Grant commenced at once to concentrate his forces and make his dispositions to meet the new order of defense established by the Confederates. His first step was to send Gens. Wright and McClernand up to Pittsburg, while he remained himself at Savannah, superintending the organization of the new troops which were arriving from Missouri, and making preparations to advance towards Pittsburg Landing (Shiloh).

The account of the famous battle which soon occurred at this place must be left to military writers, but the battle of Shiloh with its changes of fortune from hour to hour, its keen anxieties, splendid fighting on both sides, and the splendid victory which was finally wrenched from the enemy after he had driven our troops back upon the river, will always be remembered by those who have read the history of that day.

We will only refer to the moment when

our troops, having been driven by the enemy from point to point and ridge to ridge, had reached the river bank and were brought to bay. Here the gun-boats "Lexington" and "Taylor" rendered good service, and the national troops, rallying under the cover of their guns, made a superb resistance, and although the enemy flung himself fiercely upon the Union lines he was again and again driven back.

The military historians have not done justice to the work of the gun-boats at this important juncture. Croly disposes of the subject by saying: "the gun-boats were of some importance as they had been for some time previous engaged in checking the advance of the enemy on the extreme left." Badeau, the historian, also speaks of the gun-boats "being employed during the night in throwing shells amongst the enemy's troops, which annoyed them greatly and set fire to the woods, which were ablaze all around them."

It is not likely that the two gun-boats would be idle at Pittsburg Landing while our Army was being driven back by the enemy, and it is the belief of many officers that without the aid of these vessels the Federal army would have been annihilated. But there are no reliable Army accounts of the matter and we must be satisfied with the statement that "the Federal troops with their backs to the river, and no cover but the gun-boats, there made an unconquerable stand."

The following account, taken in substance from Boynton's Naval History, seems to be the most correct version of the part taken by the gun-boats "Taylor" and "Lexington," in the battle of Shiloh:

"From the beginning of the fight until after one o'clock P. M., the wooden gun-boats 'Lexington' and 'Taylor' had been moving up and down the stream, anxious to render some assistance, but received no orders to do so. At that time Lieut.-Com. Gwin, of the 'Taylor,' having as yet received no instructions from any quarter, and growing impatient as shot and shell fell around the vessels, sent an officer to communicate with Gen. Hurlburt and requested permission to open on the Confederates. Gen. Hurlburt expressed his thanks for this offer of support, saying that without aid he could not hold his position for an hour, and indicated the proper line of fire. At 10 o'clock the 'Taylor' opened fire on the enemy, and with such effect that in a short time the Confederate batteries at that point were silenced.

"About 4 o'clock the 'Taylor' dropped down to Pittsburg Landing to communicate with Gen. Grant. His reply was that Lieut. Gwin must use his own judgment in the case.

"Directly after the 'Taylor' and 'Lexington' went up in company and took up a position only three-quarters of a mile above the landing.

"In thirty-five minutes the enemy's batteries on the right were again silenced, thus relieving the national troops on the left, but at half-past 5 p. m. our lines had been so forced in towards the river that the enemy gained a position on our left only an eighth of a mile from the landing and massed their troops for a final charge, with which they ex-

pected, and not without cause, to crush what remained of the organization of the national army. Between our position and where the enemy had prepared for this last rush, was a ravine which they must cross in the assault, and here the two gunboats took up a position. At the same time Col. Webster, of Gen. Grant's staff, hastily collected some scattered guns and placed them where they would play on the left flank of the enemy's line when they should advance.

"This was the decisive point in the battle. The next half hour would settle the question whether or not a victorious Confederate army should occupy and lay under contribution the States north of the Ohio.

"There was a brief lull in the firing while the Confederate host was making its final preparations, and our troops were being collected in a semi-circular mass with the centre not half a mile from the river. Our men (with the exception of the shameless skulkers) had fought bravely, but were now in a disorganized condition, and it seemed as if their main dependence must now be upon the guns which Col. Webster had collected to check the advance of the enemy.

"The delay was for a few moments only, and they came preceded by a storm of shot from their batteries which swept over all the intervening space and up to the very banks of the river.

"As stated by Gen. Grant, their troops were massed so as to strike the main blow at our left, so that by turning it they could seize the transports and stores. It did not occur to the enemy that this would bring their column under the guns of the gun-boats at point-blank range.

"The 'Lexington' and 'Taylor' had rounded to opposite the ravine, so that their batteries could be brought to bear upon the dense mass swarming in across the line of fire."

So far Mr. Boynton: Capt. Gwin will tell the rest:

"* * * Both vessels opened a heavy and well-directed fire on them, and in a short time, in conjunction with our artillery on shore, succeeded in silencing their artillery, and driving them back in confusion.

"At 6 P. M. the 'Taylor' opened deliberate fire in the direction of the enemy's right wing, throwing 5 and 10-second shell. * * * *

"At 9 P. M. the 'Taylor' again opened fire, * * * * throwing 5, 10 and 15-second shell, and an occasional shrapnel from the howitzer at intervals of ten minutes, in the direction of the enemy's right wing, until 1 A. M., when the 'Lexington' relieved us, and continued the fire at intervals of fifteen minutes until 5 A. M., when, our land forces having attacked the enemy, forcing them gradually back, it made it dangerous for the gun-boats to fire."

In this engagement the "Taylor" fired 188 shell, and the "Lexington" about the same number, and it can be imagined what gaps were made in the enemy's ranks by our expert gunners, when they were massed at the ravine for a rush upon our disorganized troops, already driven nearly to the river.

The military historian says, "the gunboats gave mutual support at this moment." Boynton says, "thus, on the same day, the Navy on the Western rivers received the surrender of one of the Confederate fortifications on the Mississippi, and aided very materially in saving from destruction our Army at Pittsburg Landing by repelling the last attack of the Confederates, demoralizing their army by the destructive broadsides of the steamers' heavy guns, and holding them back during the night until Nelson and Buel were ready to attack."

The reader can take either version of the story that suits him best.

There is a tradition in the Navy which will go down to posterity, that the "Taylor" and "Lexington" prevented part of our Army on that day from being driven into the river, and turned the enemy back when he considered that victory was in his hands.

Lieut. Gwin in writing to Foote, puts it

by both parties, but the Federals remained masters of the field.

It broke up the delusion of many in the North who, up to this time, had believed that after a few heavy defeats the Southern people would return to their allegiance. For here it was seen that after the victories of Donelson and Shiloh, and the capture of Columbus, Nashville and Bowling Green, no perceptible effect was made upon the resolution of the Confederates. Their energy was not in the least diminished.

Gen. Grant himself believed that the contest was to be prolonged and desperate, and

REAR-ADMIRAL HENRY WALKE, (COMMANDER OF THE "CARONDELET.")

modestly thus: "Your 'old wooden boats,' I feel confident, rendered invaluable service on the 6th instant to the land forces." And so will think the reader.

Why Gen. Grant did not have a large number of gun-boats at Pittsburg Landing is not understood, as it was a most favorable position for their use, and the 60,000 Confederates spread over a large area of ground would have offered many opportunities for them to throw in an effective fire.

The battle of Shiloh was a terrible one, and the losses on both sides were very great (12,000 each). The victory was claimed

as we go on with the history of events it will be seen that his view was the correct one. The more the Confederates were beaten the harder they fought, and even when they had "robbed the cradle and the grave" to fill up their ranks, and when many of them were satisfied that their cause was hopeless, they fought on as if engaged in some pastime in which they took great delight.

In conclusion we would call attention to the fact that the victories which perched upon the banners of the Federal army were frequently due in a great measure to the aid rendered by the heavy guns of the Navy, which were easily transported from place to place, and could deliver a fire which no army could return or withstand.

BATTLE OF FORT DONELSON.

The following extracts from the records of the times are interesting, as throwing light on the history of those affairs :

It is now stated by one of our most brilliant writers of history and biography that Foote sent the " Carondelet " to Fort Donelson upon a reconnoissance, and other friends of the Admiral are evidently led into the same error; but on the contrary, to our knowledge, he never approved or disapproved of Commander Walke's co-operation with General Grant, nor did he reply or allude to the following letters upon that subject. And it is evident that no other officer would have taken the responsibility of revoking the orders for the " Taylor," " Lexington " and " Conestoga " to join the " Carondelet " upon the reconnoissance at Fort Donelson, but the flag-officer himself. And as he was previously informed of all the circumstances, by the letters of Commander Walke, there was no explanation asked for, or made, when they met on the night of the 13th. The flag-officer, however, seemed to be satisfied when Commander Walke. informed him that the " Carondelet " would be ready for battle again as soon as she had replenished her ammunition, early on the following morning. We may, however, be assured by the remarks in Pollard's *Southern History of the War,* that if four or five steamers, instead of one, had menaced Fort Donelson on the 11th of February, a day or two before the enemy's re-enforcements had arrived, the effect would have been much more discouraging to the enemy. General Grant, being under the impression at least that Foote's flotilla could not assist him immediately, instructed Commander Walke to proceed without delay to commence the attack on Fort Donelson in connection with our Army before the enemy could receive re-enforcements or could strengthen his position.

The following is the letter referred to, preceding the battle of Fort Donelson.

FROM COMMANDER WALKE TO FLAG-OFFICER FOOTE.

" U. S. GUN-BOAT 'CARONDELET,'
" *Paducah, Feb 10th,* 1862.

" SIR:—I received instructions from General Grant this evening, to proceed with this vessel to Fort Donelson, on the Cumberland river, to co-operate with our Army in that vicinity. I expect to meet you before I reach there. The 'Alps' will take me in tow. I will call at this place. General Grant will send the 'Taylor,' 'Lexington,' and 'Conestoga' after me.

" We heard that you were on your way to Fort Donelson, but I hear no tidings of you here to-night.

" The ' Taylor ' has just returned from up the Tennessee River, as far as navigable. She, with the ' Lexington ' and ' Conestoga,' destroyed or captured all the enemy's boats, broke up their camps, and made a prize of their fine new gun-boat.

" I write this in anticipation of not seeing you before I leave here, as I am (or the ' Carondelet ' is) very slow, and General Grant desires that I should be at Fort Donelson as soon as I can get there. But I hope you will overtake me, or send me your orders upon this occasion, as I am now acting upon your general instructions repeated at Fort Henry. I expected to send this letter from here to-night, but am disappointed in this also.

" Most respectfully and truly,
" Your ob't servant,
" H. WALKE,
" *Commander U. S. N.*

" To Flag-officer A. H. FOOTE, U. S. N.,
" *Commander U. S. Naval Forces, Western Waters.*"

This letter explains the part taken by the " Carondelet " in the battle of Fort Donelson. After the capture of Fort Henry, Flag-officer Foote was requested by Generals Halleck and Grant to co-operate with the latter in an attack on Fort Donelson, situated on the west bank of the Cumberland river, near the town of Dover. The fort was stronger, both in natural position and artificial defenses, than Fort Henry, and a land attack was more difficult, as there were heights above, below, and all around the works. The " Carondelet " had the honor of commencing the attack on Fort Donelson; having arrived before the fort two days in advance of the other gun-boats, she fired upon the enemy's works on the morning of February 12th; and also, at the request of General Grant, made a diversion in his favor on February 13th, as narrated in the following report of Commander Walke to Admiral Foote.

" U. S. GUN-BOAT 'CARONDELET,'
" *Near Fort Donelson, Cumberland River, Feb.15th.*

" SIR :—I arrived here (towed by the ' Alps ') on the 12th instant, about 11:20 A. M., and seeing or hearing nothing of our Army, I threw a few shell into Fort Donelson, to announce my arrival to General Grant, as he had previously requested. I then dropped down the river a few miles, and anchored for the night, awaiting General Grant's arrival.

" On the morning of the thirteenth, I weighed anchor, and came again to this place, where I received a dispatch from General Grant, informing me that he had arrived the day before, and had succeeded in getting in position, almost entirely investing the enemy's works.

" 'Most of our batteries' (he writes) 'are established, and the remainder soon will be. If you will advance with your gun-boat at 10 o'clock in the morning, we will be ready to take advantage of any diversion in our favor.'

" I immediately complied with these instructions by throwing some 139 15-second and 10-second shell into the fort; receiving in return the enemy's fire from all their batteries ; most of their shot passing over us, and but two striking us, one of which was a 128-pounder solid shot. It passed through our port casement forward, and glancing over our barricade at the boilers, and again over the steam-drum, struck, and burst the steam-heater ; and fell into the engine room without striking any person, although the splinters wounded slightly some half-dozen of our crew. I then dropped down to this anchorage, but the sound of distant firing being heard we again attacked the fort, throwing in some forty-five shell, and receiving little damage.

"I returned to this place to await further orders, when I received a second dispatch from General Grant, stating that you were expected on the following morning. I am, sir, most respectfully,

"Your ob't servant,
"H. WALKE.
"*Commander U. S. Navy.*

"Flag-officer A. H. FOOTE,
"*Commanding U. S. N. Forces in Western Waters.*"

In this engagement the "Carondelet" commenced firing on the fort at a distance of a mile and a quarter, the enemy replying immediately as the vessel advanced, the attack lasting from ten o'clock in the morn-

ble naval authorities. A few particulars are called for from those who were present on that occasion to dispel the idea that Fort Donelson was captured by our fleet, under Admiral Foote, for in reality it was taken by General Grant, with the Army.

The following are a few quotations from reliable correspondence on the reconnoissance. A reliable correspondent of the Army on this occasion writes: "According to the admission of the rebel officers the casualties from the attacks by the 'Carondelet' were greater than those which resulted from the combined attack of the whole fleet the next day. The attack of the next day on the water batteries was neither the most brilliant nor the most suc-

UPPER BATTERY.   WATER BATTERY.   GEN. GRANT'S ARMY ATTACKING THE ENEMY, IN THE DISTANCE.   U. S. GUNBOATS.

BATTLE OF FORT DONELSON.

ing to meridian, and being renewed in the afternoon. Three of the enemy's guns were reported to be disabled.

Our naval history is silent on some important facts in its version of this event, viz.: that four gun-boats were to have participated therein to make it more effective, and that three of them failed to obey the orders of General Grant and Commander Walke to accompany the "Carondelet" on this reconnoissance; but it gives an unfavorable view of the "Carondelet" alone on this occasion, especially in comparison with the brilliant action, or "what was *expected* to be the decisive battle, the next day;" which is represented as having resulted in the surrender of Fort Donelson, by our highest possi-

cessful effort of the siege. About the only result was that a single gun of the enemy was dismounted and the unequaled fighting qualities of the fleet demonstrated. The gunnery was generally of a different character."

Query: Is it at all improbable that the deliberate firing of one gun-boat by experienced gunners, with heavy rifled guns of long ranges, should do as much execution in six hours, upon a battery of twelve or fifteen guns of much less range, than the firing of four such gun-boats with less experienced crews, upon these batteries at close quarters for one hour and a half, at various distances, and much less deliberation?

In reference to the reconnoissance and the bombardment on the following day, Captain Morgan made the same statement to the officers on board the "Carondelet" on Sunday, the morning of the surrender.

NEWSPAPER CORRESPONDENTS ON THE ACTION.

The *Missouri Republican* of February 28th, 1862, has this report in its correspondence of the day before the battle: "During the day much uneasiness was felt as to the gun-boat fleet. It was therefore with no little gratification that information was at last received about noon on Thursday, that the *avant courier* of the fleet, the 'Carondelet,' Commander Walke, had arrived below the fort. In the afternoon the report of her guns was received with cheer upon cheer by the troops encircling the beleaguered fort.

"Commander Walke's operations this afternoon, although partaking more of the nature of a reconnoissance, were considered by the rebel officers, as I have since ascertained, as one of the most formidable attacks they have had to encounter. Hidden behind a jutting promontory of the river bank, the 'Carondelet,' herself secure from all heavy shot of the columbiads of the fort, hurled shell upon shell into the water batteries of the fortifications. The commander of these batteries has recently informed me that the fire of the 'Carondelet' did more actual damage to his guns than the heavy bombardment of the following day."

Another reliable army correspondent writes: "The rebel officers commanding the river batteries also assure me that the practice of our gunners, in the excitement of the *bombardment*, was much inferior to that displayed in *reconnoissance*, when matters were conducted with more deliberation." And this is corroborated by the official reports in the Southern press.

The *Chicago Times'* correspondent reports: "The 'Carondelet's' movements led to several skirmishes, though of no serious nature. They were covered by a gallant cannonade of the gun-boat 'Carondelet,' the only one that arrived. Thus single-handed one hundred and thirty-eight rounds were thrown into the enemy's works, and she was finally compelled to withdraw, having received a shot from the enemy's 128-pounder gun in her bow, crippling her severely, and wounding seven men. She fell back but a short time, to repair damages and put her wounded on board the transport 'Alps.' At 1:15 P. M., she commenced firing again upon the fort, and kept up a brisk fire until she had expended all or nearly all of her long-range

shell, when at dusk she retired from the contest, having annoyed the enemy and encouraged our Army."

The "Carondelet" anchored about three miles below the fort, at about 4 in the afternoon. Admiral Foote arrived at 11:30 P.M., with the partially iron-clad "St. Louis" (flag steamer, Lieut. Paulding), "Louisville" (Commander Dove), and "Pittsburg" (Lieut. Egbt. Thompson); also the wooden gun-boats "Conestoga" (Lieut. Phelps), and "Taylor" (Lieut. Gwin), and several transports with re-enforcements for General Grant of 8,000 men. About midnight Captain Walke reported in person to the flag-officer.

AFTER THE BATTLE OF FORT DONELSON.

Three gun boats remained until after the surrender of Fort Donelson, which took place on Sunday, February 16th, when they steamed up the river above the fort to Dover. There our officers and men met in good cheer. Our usual "divine service" was then performed on board the "Carondelet," as the most appropriate way of giving thanks to God, "the only Giver of victory," and under such circumstances it makes a very happy impression on all sincere hearts.

The "Carondelet" had had two 32 or 42-pounder shot in her bow "between wind and water," and leaked badly; her hull and her crew being more cut up and disabled than any other gun-boat of the squadron. As General Grant could then dispense with her services, she returned to Cairo for repairs. Arriving there on the morning of the 17th, Commander Walke reported to the flag-officer the success of our arms, and the surrender of Fort Donelson to General Grant. Flag-officer Foote immediately issued the following

CONGRATULATORY ORDER

"*February* 17th, 1862.

"Flag-officer Foote, the Commander-in-chief of the Naval Forces on the Western waters, while he congratulates the survivors of the distinguished gun-boat, 'Carondelet' in the several actions so bravely fought, sympathizes with the wounded who have gloriously periled their lives in honor of the Union and the dear old flag. He also sympathizes with the friends of those gallant dead, who could not have died in a more glorious cause. Let us thank God from the heart, and say, 'Not unto us alone, but unto Thy Name, O Lord, belongs the glory of the triumph of our arms.'

"[Signed]   "A. H. FOOTE,
                              "Flag-officer."

The above order was read to the officers and crew assembled on board the "Carondelet," and then returned to the flag-officer by the bearer, in compliance with his verbal order.

CHAPTER XVI.

OPERATIONS ON THE MISSISSIPPI.

Operations Against Fort Columbus and Island No. 10.—Running of the Batteries by the Gun-boats "Carondelet" and "Pittsburg."—Evacuation of Batteries Along the Tennessee Shore and Surrender of Island No. 10.—Advance on Fort Pillow by the Army and Navy.—Attack on Fort Pillow.—Evacuation of Fort Pillow by the Confederates.—Battle Between the Enemy's Rams and the Union Gun-boats, &c., &c.

WHEN the gun-boats were obliged to drop down before the fire of the works at Fort Donelson, Flag-officer Foote proceeded to Cairo to repair some of his vessels, leaving behind him the iron-clads "Louisville," Commander B. M. Dove, "Carondelet," Commander Henry Walke, and the "St. Louis."

From all accounts the "Carondelet" seems to have suffered more than any other vessel in the fleet, both in killed and wounded and damage to her hull. Commander Dove, the senior officer present, reports on the 16th of February that the condition of the "Carondelet's" wounded would not admit of their being moved, or the guns to be used, and it is difficult to understand why a vessel in such a condition should not have been sent to a dock-yard and her wounded placed in the hospital; but the "Carondelet" was a sturdy craft and was always found in the front of battle.

Commander Dove, as senior officer, had the satisfaction of receiving the surrender of Fort Donelson. He says: "On approaching near enough two white flags were seen flying from the upper fort. * * * I proceeded in a tug, with a white flag flying, and landed at the foot of the hill below the fort. I was met by a Major who handed me his sword, which I declined to receive, thinking it proper to consult with General Grant. I took the Major on board the tug and proceeded up to General Buckner's headquarters, where I found General Wallace. General Grant arrived about half an hour after the fort had surrendered." * * * Commander Dove seemed to have the proper idea on this occasion in declining to claim anything, as the fort properly fell to the Army.

As soon as Flag-officer Foote was able he proceeded with the "Conestoga," Lieut.-Com. Phelps, and the "Cairo," Lieut.-Com. Bryant, on an armed reconnoissance up the river, taking with him Colonel Webster, Chief of General Grant's staff, who, with Lieut.-Com. Phelps, took possession of the principal works and hoisted the Union flag.

Foote had applied to General Halleck for permission to advance up the Cumberland on Nashville, and just as he was about moving for that point Halleck telegraphed to Grant: "Don't let the gun-boats proceed higher than Clarksville," an order in keeping with the "conservative policy" that seemed to influence General Halleck on all occasions. The latter seemed to wish to direct all the battles himself by telegraph, and to give as little authority as possible to General Grant, who being on the ground knew the exact situation of affairs. This was certainly not the way to conquer such an indomitable enemy as that with which the national government had to contend; but the gun-boats did finally move up to Nashville, with an army force in company, and took peaceful possession of the capital of Tennessee.

Foote finding there was nothing further to be done on the Tennessee and Cumberland Rivers, turned his attention to Fort Columbus, which still held out, though by all the rules of Jomini it ought to have surrendered when Donelson fell, the great strategic line of the enemy having been broken and most of Tennessee lying at the mercy of the Federal Army. As Columbus still declined to yield, Flag-officer Foote, in company with General Cullom of Halleck's staff, started with four iron-clads, ten mortar-boats and three transports, containing a thousand soldiers, to make a reconnoissance in force. As the expedition neared Fort Columbus it was met by a flag of truce, with a message from General Polk to the effect that he hoped the courtesies he had extended to the captured Union officers would be reciprocated should an opportunity occur.

Having accomplished the object of the reconnoissance, Foote returned to Cairo, February 23, with a view to complete all the gun-boats and mortar-rafts and make the necessary preparations for the work required of him.

In the meantime the gun-boats in condition for service were busy assisting the Army to move where it desired, and patroling the river and clearing the flying artillery from the banks.

On the 1st of March Lieut.-Com. Gwin learned that the enemy were fortifying Pittsburg Landing, and proceeded up the river in the "Taylor," followed by the "Lexington," Lieut.-Com. James W. Shirk. When within 1,200 yards of the landing the gun-boats were fired on by the Confederate batteries, consisting of six or eight field-pieces, some of them rifled, but did not notice the attack till they were within a thousand yards, when they opened fire and soon silenced the enemy.

The gun-boats then continued on till abreast of where the enemy had posted his heaviest batteries, and under cover of a fire of grape and canister, a force was landed in two boats from each of the vessels, including a portion of Co. C, Capt. Phillips, and Co. K, Lieut. Rider, of the 32d Illinois Volunteers (sharpshooters). The boats of the "Taylor" were commanded by Master J. Goudy, and those of the "Lexington" by Master Martin Dunn.

It was found on landing that besides the artillerists, the enemy had two regiments of infantry and one of cavalry, and this little landing party held them in check until their object was accomplished, viz.: to ascertain the enemy's force and purpose, and to destroy a building in the vicinity of which the batteries had been placed.

This little affair was well conducted, and much information was gathered in regard to fortifications being erected by the enemy. Lieut.-Com. Gwin, the leader of the expedition, was one of the most gallant officers in the Western Flotilla, and delighted in such service, where the usefulness of the gun-boats could be demonstrated.

On board the "Taylor" there was one killed and six wounded, including Capt. Phillips, of the Army; on board the "Lexington" there were two killed and two missing, small casualties considering the heavy force opposed to the gun-boats. The enemy's loss was said to be nine killed and upwards of one hundred wounded.

On the same day that the above affair took place, Flag-officer Foote sent Lieut.-Com. Phelps to Columbus with a flag of truce. As he drew near the fort he saw that the Confederates were burning their winter quarters and removing their heavy guns from the bluff. Of the latter two were cast in Richmond, and named respectively, "Lady Davis" and "Lady Polk."

In their hurry to get away the Confederates had left the water batteries intact. A large force of cavalry was drawn up ostentatiously on the bluff, but these were the only troops in sight; while the fires burning in the town of Columbus and along the river showed that the enemy were determined to destroy everything they could not carry away.

The Confederates often made a Moscow of a town when forced to abandon it, which certainly did not convince the wretched inhabitants that the Confederates were their best friends. Indeed, there was often an inhumanity in their proceedings which added unnecessarily to the horrors of war. The writer knew General (formerly Bishop) Polk before the war. He was a fine specimen of a man, a kind master to his numerous slaves, in short, a Christian gentleman. His case shows how the influence of war will demoralize the best of men.

From March 4th to the 16th, the wooden gun-boats, "Taylor" and "Lexington," were actively employed on the Tennessee and Cumberland conveying troops—for without such assistance the Army could not have moved—and obtaining information of the enemy's movements.

This information was to the following effect: At Corinth, Mississippi, eighteen miles from the Tennessee River, the junction of the Mobile and Ohio, and Memphis and Charleston railroads, there were from fifteen to twenty thousand Confederate troops; at Henderson Station, eighteen miles from the Tennessee River and thirty-five miles by rail from Corinth, there were some ten or twelve thousand more, with daily accessions from Columbus and the South; at Bear Creek Bridge, seven miles back of Eastport, Mississippi, eight or ten thousand men were throwing up fortifications; and at Chickasaw, Alabama, there were being erected heavy batteries, supplied, no doubt, with the guns taken from the Norfolk Navy Yard.

It was learned from a reliable source that General Joseph E. Johnson was falling back from Murfreesboro on Decatur, Alabama, the point where the Memphis and Charleston Railroad crosses the Tennessee River and joins the railroad leading to Nashville; showing that the Confederates were making every exertion to hold on to Tennessee, which was to them the most important of all the States, except, perhaps, Virginia; since it was wedged in between five secession States: and the Confederates, while they held it, could keep the Federal troops from advancing South. Should the latter obtain possession they would control Northern Mississippi, Alabama and Georgia, with parts of North Carolina and Virginia. With the Cumberland and the Tennessee Rivers, and all the railroads in the Union possession, the rebellion would have been

COMMANDER JAMES W. SHIRK.

confined to the other States, and the resources of Tennessee would have been lost to the Confederate cause. It would have been better to have thrown three hundred thousand men at once into Tennessee and crushed the rebellion there, instead of losing a greater number in the end and prolonging the war for four years.

On the 4th of March Flag-officer Foote got under way from Cairo, and proceeded down the river towards Columbus. Besides the flag-ship "Benton," there were the "Mound City," Commander A. H. Kilty; "Louisville," Commander B. M. Dove; "Carondelet," Commander H. Walke; "Cincinnati," Commander R. N. Stembel; "St. Louis," Lieut.-Commanding L. Paulding; "Pittsburgh," Lieut.-Commanding E. Thompson; "Lexington," Lieut.-Command-

ing J. W. Shirk, with four transports, each having five mortar-boats in tow; also a magazine boat and a provision boat. The squadron was accompanied by troops under General Buford, in four steamers, half a dozen tugs, and a large number of barges and lighters in tow.

As this expedition approached Columbus the Union flag was seen floating from the ramparts. It had been taken possession of two days before by a company of cavalry scouts from Paducah, under Col. Haas.

The enemy had already fortified certain positions further South on the Mississippi, and had also re-inforced Island No. 10. Gen. Pope, with an army of ten thousand men, hastened to occupy New Madrid, on the west bank of the Mississippi, below Island No. 10, and he at once detected the weakness of the enemy's position. Pope established a line of batteries from New Madrid to a point fifteen miles below Island No. 10, thus shutting the enemy off from his only source of supply along the river; for everywhere, on both sides of the river for sixty miles, nothing but swamps existed, through which provisions could not be transported.

Having established his batteries, it was Gen. Pope's intention to cross the river with his army and attack the enemy's position from below, and to do this the aid of gunboats was necessary. In anticipation of this, the enemy had erected batteries at every point where they would be likely to do harm to the Federal squadron.

Gen. Pope, seeing that a floating force was indispensable to the success of his operations, requested Flag-officer Foote to send down a gun-boat past the enemy's batteries at night; but as the gun-boats were slow-moving machines and difficult to manage in the strong current of the Mississippi, the Flag-officer informed the General that he would send him two tugs through a bayou, and would endeavor to get two gun-boats down to him in time.

On the 20th of March the squadron, with the mortar vessels, were lying above Island No. 10, throwing shells into the enemy's batteries, occasionally dismounting a gun, but doing no material damage; but so urgent was Gen. Pope's appeal for a gun-boat that Flag-officer Foote, for the first time, summoned a council of his commanding officers. To use Foote's own words, "The officers, with one exception, were decidedly opposed to running the blockade, believing it would be certain destruction to all the vessels that should attempt it." There were six forts, with over fifty guns bearing on the vessels. Foote does not mention who was the exception, and who in this instance was certainly a wiser man than his brother officers. Running the enemy's batteries had not at that time been much practiced, but as the war progressed it was found not to be a very dangerous thing by night, and often practicable even in the daytime.

Foote on this occasion remarked: "When the object of running the blockade is adequate to the risk, I shall not hesitate to do it." He had a difficult task before him in assisting Gen. Pope to drive the enemy from Island No. 10 and the adjacent heights along the Mississippi, where they altogether are stated to have mounted seventy heavy guns, in addition to a "floating battery" of sixteen guns; but making every allowance for exaggeration, there certainly were mounted not less than seventy-five guns in the immediate vicinity. If the Union gun-boats could hold the river above, and New Madrid be occupied by a large force of troops, with batteries placed along the river below the enemy's works and to the edge of the great swamp surrounding them, the Confederate garrison would be hemmed in, and must yield when its supplies gave out.

The Confederate fortifications were placed at such a height above the river that the fire of the gun-boats had little effect on them. Foote therefore determined to open on the enemy with his 13-inch mortars, from which he expected much better results. There is, however, a great difference in using mortars against forts constructed of masonry, and earth-works on high hills. Now and then a gun would be dismounted, but it was immediately replaced, and the garrison were well protected against bursting shells. To attack the enemy from above was a matter of great difficulty and responsibility. The current of the river was not less than four miles an hour, and the iron-clads were not able, under the most favorable circumstances, to do much more than stem it. In case of accident to machinery they would drift helplessly under the enemy's guns. To fight bow on, and depend upon the stern wheel to back up stream while fighting would have been absurd, so that in this case the commander-in-chief of the squadron was in a dilemma. While much was expected of him he was obliged by circumstances to observe a caution which was not agreeable to his enterprising spirit.

On the morning of the 16th of March the mortar-boats were placed in the best possible position and opened fire on the enemy's batteries, driving several regiments out of the works. The mortars were under charge of Capt. Maynardier, U. S. Army, and Lieut. J. P. Sanford, U. S. Navy.

On the morning of the 17th the gun-boats commenced an attack. The "Benton," "Cincinnati" and "St. Louis" were lashed together, on account of the deficient steam power of the "Benton," which was otherwise the most formidable vessel in the

squadron. The fire of the gun-boats was not very effective; they were at a distance of nearly two miles and the enemy's batteries, separated from each other, presented but small targets to fire at. The fire was kept up from mid-day until night-fall. The "Benton" was struck four times, but the most serious disaster was the bursting of a rifled gun on board the "St. Louis," by which fifteen men were killed and wounded.

In the official records only three gun-boats are mentioned as taking part in the engagement of March 17th, whereas the "Carondelet" and "Mound City" were actively engaged on the west side of the river.

Until the 26th of March these attacks with gun-boats and mortars were maintained without important results, as the enemy kept but few men exposed to the fire.

At this time the squadron at Island No. 10 comprised six iron-clads, one wooden gun-boat and sixteen mortar-rafts, while, according to Flag-officer Foote, the Confederates had thirteen gun-boats, besides five below New Madrid.

Foote soon saw that it was a positive necessity that Gen. Pope should transport his troops to the opposite side of the river in order to turn the enemy's flank; and the idea of running the blockade having been abandoned, it was proposed to open a way through a bayou which traversed the swamp on the west side of the Mississippi, and came out to the river again at New Madrid.

In this labor the Army and Navy co-operated, and for nineteen days and nights the work of cutting a canal through the swamp was prosecuted, the men undergoing every hardship with the utmost cheerfulness. Soldiers and sailors stood in mud and water up to their waists, cutting away trees, and hauling along the tugs and transports on which Pope depended to cross his troops over the Mississippi.

When these vessels reached New Madrid, the soldiers there received them with great enthusiasm. "Now," they said, "we shall cross over and drive the Confederates out." But the work was not yet finished These unarmed steamers could not be used for the purpose of transporting troops in the face of the enemy and the gun-boats he had improvised, and the question was again asked: "Is it possible for any of our iron-clads to run the gauntlet of the batteries?" But Flag-officer Foote still hesitated for reasons already given, and, furthermore, General Halleck had notified him that measures had already been taken which would compel the enemy to evacuate his works. If the gun-boats were to run the batteries, Foote thought it advisable to diminish the risk as much as possible, and therefore an expedition was organized to seize upon the upper fort on Island No. 10, on which was mounted one ten-inch Columbiad and other guns. The boats from the "Benton," "St. Louis," "Cincinnati" and "Pittsburg" carried, beside their crews, fifty soldiers of Co. A., 42d Regiment, Illinois Volunteers, making in all one hundred men, exclusive of officers, all under command of Col. George W. Roberts of the above named regiment.

The boats surprised the sentinels, who fired their muskets and fled. The garrison and the crew of the Confederate gun-boat "Grampus" were at once aroused, but Col. Roberts lost no time in landing his men and spiking the battery; after which the party re-embarked and returned to the squadron. On this battery of eleven heavy guns the enemy had depended to sink any of our vessels that might attempt to run by their works.

There was also a floating battery moored way. She might have drifted down the river without a shot being fired at her, yet there was danger that she might run ashore and be found at daylight a fair mark for the enemy, or the pilot, in the intense darkness, might mistake the channel, or the plunging fire from the enemy's batteries might penetrate the boilers, in which case a horrible fate awaited many of her crew. It was the first venture in running batteries, and therefore more creditable to all concerned, for even in after times, when such feats became more common, there was always an element of uncertainty in the enterprise.

The "Carondelet" passed the first battery unobserved, but at the second a sheet of flame issued from the heavy guns, and the huge shot ricocheted along the water, but did no harm to the Union vessel. The

THE GUN-BOAT "CARONDELET" RUNNING THE BATTERIES AT ISLAND No. 10.

at the head of the island which it was important to remove; so on the following day the guns of the squadron were concentrated on this latter obstruction with such effect, that the crew of the battery cut the lashings and drifted from under fire of the gun-boats to take new position some distance below.

After these two impediments had been removed the passage of the enemy's batteries was considered practicable, and Com. Walke, of the "Carondelet," volunteered to perform this perilous duty. His ingenuity and that of his officers was taxed to the utmost to prepare the "Carondelet" to resist the enemy's shot. First-Master Hoel of the "Cincinnati," one of the best pilots on the Mississippi, whose gallantry finally placed him in command of an iron-clad, volunteered to pilot the vessel.

On the night of the 4th of April, in storm and darkness, the "Carondelet" got under- "Carondelet" steamed steadily on without noticing these attentions, while fort after fort took up the fire, until seventy powerful guns joined in the melee; doing no harm, but adding to the grandeur of the storm. Now and then the "Carondelet" became visible to the enemy through the vivid flashes of lightning. In half an hour the vessel was below Island No. 10 and soon passed beyond the reach of the Confederate batteries.

Then the sound of minute guns coming faintly from below assured those who were waiting anxiously in the squadron that the "Carondelet" was safe, and that General Pope could now bid defiance to the enemy's gun-boats and cross his troops to the other side of the Mississippi. Upon this, cheer after cheer went up from the gun-boats, and made the Confederates aware that the time had arrived when their position was no longer tenable.

That night the "Carondelet" lay un-scathed just below New Madrid, and early next morning steamed up to the landing, where she was warmly welcomed by the soldiers who had so long looked for aid of this kind, without which they were hopeless of turning the enemy's position.

The enemy's gun-boats, armed with long-range rifles, had been harrassing Pope's command from below, and from their position could do a great deal of havoc to the light transports on which Pope depended to pass his troops over the river. The enemy had thirteen gun-boats, improvised from river steamers, but as soon as the "Caron-delet" appeared they departed for Memphis.

Flag-officer Foote, finding that the risk of running the batteries was less than he had supposed, and urged by General Pope to send him another iron-clad, dispatched the "Pittsburg," Lieut.-Com. Egbert Thompson, which vessel ran the batteries on a stormy night under pretty much the same circumstances as the "Carondelet," and like her received no injury.

As soon as the "Pittsburgh" arrived be-low Island No. 10 she was sent with the "Carondelet" to drive away some field bat-teries which the enemy had placed to pre-vent the Union troops crossing the river. This was accomplished, and the enemy see-ing they could no longer hold their works began to evacuate them, leaving all their guns and munitions of war in the hands of the victors.

Island No. 10 surrendered on the 7th of April to Flag-officer Foote just as he was preparing to attack with the gun-boats above, in conjunction with the forces under General Buford. Seventeen officers, three hundred and sixty-eight privates, one hun-dred sick, and one hundred men employed on the enemy's transports, surrendered to the Navy from steamers afloat. Two wharf boats loaded with provisions were also cap-tured. The floating battery of sixteen guns and most of the gun-boats were sunk, but were easily raised again.

The Confederate works consisted of eleven forts mounting seventy guns, from 32 to 100-pounders. The magazines were well supplied, and there were also large quantities of provisions. The works were very strong, and built with great skill. Six thousand prisoners fell into General Pope's hands.

Commander Walke in the "Carondelet," supported by the "Pittsburgh," silenced the heaviest battery below Island No. 10 and spiked the guns, picking up a number of fine sixty-four pounders left behind by the Confederates in their flight.

The precipitancy with which the enemy re-treated when the gun-boats appeared below Island No. 10, was astonishing. It was the turning point in the siege, and to this Gen-eral Pope had looked forward from the time he moved his army to New Madrid.

Foote would no doubt have sent the iron-clads down past the batteries sooner than he did, had not General Halleck notified him of a plan which he had in view to capture Island No. 10 and all the batteries on the Tennessee shore. The credit, however, fell where it was due, to Pope and Foote, for their harmonious co-operation, and to Com-mander Walke and Lieut.-Com. Thompson, who so gallantly passed the enemy's bat-teries.

The victory at Island No. 10, although a bloodless one, was as important as the bat-tle of Shiloh. It opened a long stretch of the Mississippi River, down which our forces were continually working their way toward the sea. By this victory and the great battle at Shiloh, was broken up the second line of defences which the Confeder-ates had established from the Mississippi to Chattanooga, and all their attempts to pene-trate the Northern States in this direction were foiled. It does not in the least detract from the gallantry of our Army to say that neither of these victories would have been won without the aid of the Navy. Though the latter was but an auxiliary to the Army yet it was a most valuable one, and should receive the credit to which it is entitled.

In concluding our account of the capture of Island No. 10, we avail ourselves of the opportunity to make a few remarks relative to those who worked so faithfully to bring about the result. We have already stated that General Pope considered it essential to the success of his plans that at least two of the gun-boats should run the blockade and join him below Island No. 10, and that Com-mander Walke volunteered to perform what was considered a very hazardous duty, and performed it unflinchingly.

It occurs to the writer that such a service was worthy a much warmer eulogium than Commander Walke received for his success-ful conduct of a perilous undertaking; for these "iron-clad" gun-boats were really a very vulnerable class of vessels, and utterly inadequate to resist the plunging shot from the enemy's elevated batteries. A single shot going in above and coming out through the bottom would have com-pletely crippled a vessel. It could hardly be anticipated that any boat could pass so many heavy works, even at night with rain and storm to help her, and yet receive no damage, and it was the merest accident that the "Carondelet" was not struck by the enemy's shot. As to the passage of the "Pittsburg," she was sent down after it was ascertained that the "Carondelet" had re-ceived no damage whatever, and hence her commanding officer was not entitled to the same amount of credit as Commander Walke.

When the "Carondelet" did arrive below the enemies batteries, her performances redounded greatly to the credit of her commander and his officers. At the request of General Pope, Walke attacked and silenced every battery below the point where the Federal troops were to be landed, and spiked the guns so that the enemy could not return and use them.

It would seem in regard to these transactions that the accuracy of official reports may be called in question, and that we must rely on other sources than the published histories of the war. The intention of the writer is to make as few digressions in his account of affairs as possible, but justice demands that corrections shall be made, especially when due credit has been heretofore withheld.

Due credit in regard to services on the Western rivers has often been withheld from both Army and Navy, and this injustice is nowhere more distinctly manifested than in the capture of Island No. 10, and the heavy batteries which lined the Tennessee shore. The work of the Army was a master-piece of strategy, and the part played by the Navy was scarcely inferior. The work performed was indeed creditable to all concerned.

Farragut maintained that whatever errors are made by contemporary historians, posterity will always give honor to whom honor is due; and sincerely hoping that such is the case, the writer will endeavor to do justice in these pages.

The surrender of Island No. 10 and the adjacent works opened the Mississippi all the way to Fort Pillow, another stronghold which could only be conquered by a combined army and navy force.

Gen. Pope, with twenty thousand men in transports protected by gun-boats, now moved towards Fort Pillow, and prepared to attack the enemy's works. Five Confederate gun-boats were descried down the river, but their size and strength could not be ascertained. The Confederates had improvised a river flotilla, but nothing could be learned concerning it.

Pope's first idea was to reach the enemy's works by landing five miles above them, while the gun-boats and mortars attacked them from the river; but finding this plan impracticable, it was proposed to cut a canal, as was done at Island No. 10, through the Arkansas shore to a point opposite Fort Pillow, and thus pass some of the gun-boats below the fortifications.

At this time Flag-officer Foote was suffering from the effects of his wound, so that it was impossible for him to attend to his manifold duties, and a few days after he relinquished active service, never again to resume it, and the command of the squadron devolved upon Capt. Charles H. Davis,

a gallant officer, well qualified for this important duty.

The sudden withdrawal of Gen. Pope with nearly all his force from before Fort Pillow, to proceed to Pittsburg Landing by order of Gen. Halleck, had quite disappointed Foote. He saw no immediate prospect of taking Fort Pillow and did not care to remain, while suffering so much from his wound, merely to keep up a blockade. Only two regiments of soldiers under Col. Fisk remained of all Pope's army.

Fort Pillow mounted forty guns and there were nine gun-boats below the fort and at Memphis. In addition, at this time the enemy were building a number of heavy gun-boats along the Mississippi; among them, at New Orleans, the iron-plated "Louisiana," of sixteen guns (which vessel figured so prominently in Farragut's attack on Forts Jackson and St. Philip), and the ram, "Arkansas."

The following letter will throw some light on the siege of Island No. 10, and give credit where it is justly due:

SECRETARY WELLES TO FLAG-OFFICER FOOTE.

"By telegraph from NAVY YARD, WASHINGTON, }
                                          April 10, 1862. }
"*To Flag-officer Foote, Commanding Gun-boat Flotilla:*

"A nation's thanks are due to you, and the brave officers and men of the flotilla on the Mississippi, whose labor and gallantry at Island 10, which surrendered to you yesterday, has been watched with intense interest. Your triumph is not the less appreciated because it was protracted and finally bloodless. To that Being who has protected you through so many perils, and carried you onward to successive victories, be praise, for His continued goodness to our country; and especially for this last great success of our arms. Let the congratulations of yourself and your command be also extended to the officers and soldiers who co-operated with you.   [Signed]

"GIDEON WELLES, *Secretary of the Navy.*"

The following is the general order issued immediately after the receipt of the telegram from the Secretary of the Navy, in answer to that of Flag-officer Foote:

[General Order, No. 7.]

"U. S. FLAG-STEAMER 'BENTON,' }
ISLAND NO. 10, *April* 11, 1862. }

"It is with the highest gratification that the Commander-in-Chief promulgates to the officers and men under his command, comprising the gun and mortar-boats, ordnance-boats, tugs, transports, and others, as well as to General Buford, and officers and soldiers of the Army, who so effectually co-operated in the reduction of Island No. 10, the following telegram received from the Secretary of the Navy; and he trusts that the future will be crowned with the same success to our arms as the past has been; and may we all, in letter and spirit, as suggested by the Honorable Secretary, render our hearty thanks to God for His goodness in giving us the victory.

"A. H. FOOTE, *Flag-officer.*"

SECRETARY WELLES TO FLAG-OFFICER FOOTE.

'NAVY DEPARTMENT, *April* 12, 1862.

"SIR:—The Department desires you to convey to Commander Henry Walke, and the officers and men of the 'Carondelet,' also to Acting First Master Hoel, of the 'Cincinnati,' who volunteered for the occasion, its thanks for the gallant and successful services rendered in running the 'Carondelet' past the rebel batteries on the night of the 4th inst. It was a daring and heroic act, well executed and deserving a special recognition. Commendation is also to be extended to the officers and crew of the 'Pittsburg,' who in like manner on the night of the 7th inst. performed a similar service. These fearless acts dismayed the enemy, enabled the army under General Pope to cross the Mississippi, and eventuated in the surrender to yourself of Island 10, and finally, to the capture by General Pope, of the forts on the Tennessee shore, and the retreating rebels under General Mackall. I would also, in this connection, render the acknowledgements which are justly due the officers and crew of the several boats, who, in conjunction with a detachment of the Forty-second Illinois regiment, under Colonel Roberts, captured the first rebel battery and spiked the guns on Island No. 10, on the night of the 1st inst.; such services are duly appreciated by the Department, which extends its thanks to all who participated in the achievement.

"I am respectfully, your obedient servant,

"GIDEON WELLES.

"Flag-officer A. H. FOOTE,
"*Commanding Gun-boat Flotilla.*"

"Forwarded with the order that this paper, which the commander-in-chief is most happy in transmitting to the brave and gallant officers and men to whom it refers, shall be publicly read on board the 'Carondelet' and 'Pittsburg,' and afterwards retained by Commander Walke, who commanded with so much ability and gallantry (assisted by First-Master Hoel, of the gun-boat 'Cincinnati'), below New Madrid, which enabled the Army to cross the Mississippi at that point, and to secure, with the aid of the flotilla above, the possession of Island No. 10, and the adjacent batteries on the Tennessee shore.

"A. H. FOOTE, *Flag-officer.*
Commanding Naval Forces, Western Waters
"OFF FORT PILLOW, *April* 22, 1862."

ENGAGEMENT OF THE "CARONDELET" AND "PITTSBURG" WITH THE ENEMY IN THE VICINITY OF NEW MADRID, APRIL 6TH, 1862.

"U. S. Flag Steamer 'BENTON,'
ISLAND No. 10, *April* 11, 1862.

"SIR:—I have the honor to enclose a report from Commander Walke, of the gun-boat 'Carondelet,' detailing the services rendered by him, and the 'Pittsburg,' Lieutenant-Commander Thompson, in the vicinity of New Madrid; from which it will be seen that the boats opened upon, and effectually silenced and captured several heavy batteries on the Tennessee side of the river, on the 6th and 7th instants, without which destruction it would have been impossible for General Pope to have crossed over the river, for the purpose of attacking the Confederates in the rear at No. 10, while the gun and mortar-boats would make the attack in front.

"There has been an effective and harmonious co-operation between the land and naval forces, which has, under Providence, led to the glorious result of the fall of this stronghold, No. 10, with the garrison and munitions of war, and I regret to see in the dispatches of Major-General Halleck, from St. Louis, no reference is made to the capture of the forts, and the continuous shelling of the gun and mortar-boats, and the Navy's receiving the surrender of No. 10, when, in reality, it should be recorded as a historical fact that both services equally contributed to the victory—a bloodless victory—more creditable to humanity than if thousands had been slain.

"I also enclose reports from Lieutenants-Commanding Gwin and Shirk, of the gun-boats 'Taylor' and Lexington,' on the Tennessee, giving a graphic account of that great battle, and the assistance rendered by these boats near Pittsburg; stating that 'when the left wing of our Army was being driven into the river, at short range, they opened fire upon and silenced the enemy, and, as I hear from many army officers on the field, totally demoralizing his forces, and driving them from their position in a perfect rout, *in the space of ten minutes.*'

"These officers and men, as well as those of Commander Walke, and the officers and men of the 'Carondelet' and 'Pittsburg,' behaved with a degree of gallantry highly creditable to themselves and the Navy.

"I proceed to-day with the entire flotilla to New Madrid, and leave to-morrow for Fort Pillow, or the next point down the river which may attempt to resist the raising the blockade.

"I have the honor to be, very respectfully, your obedient servant,

[Signed] "A. H. FOOTE, *Flag-officer.*

"Hon. GIDEON WELLES, *Secretary of the Navy, Washington, D. C.*"

Flag-officer Davis assumed command of the squadron on the 9th of May, 1862, and had little time for reflection before he became engaged in active operations. The heights of Fort Pillow had been repeatedly shelled by the gun-boats and bombarded by the mortars, with little perceptible effect on the works. The Confederate gun-boats occasionally showed themselves around the bend in the river, but on the first movement of the squadron they would scud away. Exaggerated reports were rife about the formidable rams that were at Memphis ready to attack our fleet, among them the monster "Louisiana," which the Confederates boasted could alone clear out all the Union vessels. It was impossible to tell how much truth there was in these reports, but the gun-boats had orders to keep up steam and be prepared at all times for battle.

On the 10th of May, the Union squadron lay in two divisions: the first division of these iron-clads, with the flag-ship "Benton," moored on the Tennessee shore; the second, of four gun-boats, moored on the Arkansas shore, with bows down stream. At a little past seven o'clock A. M., eight Confederate gun-boats, four of them fitted as rams, came around the point above Fort Pillow and steamed up the river, evidently prepared for battle. The enemy's leading vessel made directly for mortar-boat No. 16, which for the moment was unprotected. Acting-Master Gregory and his crew behaved with great spirit, and during the action fired the mortar eleven times nearly point blank at the enemy. The morning being hazy signals could not be distinctly made out, nor could the enemy's vessels approaching be seen as well as was desired. The "Cincinnati,"

Com. Stembel, the leading vessel in the line of iron-clads, hastened to the support of the mortar-boat, followed immediately by the "Mound City," Com. Kilty; and both were repeatedly struck by the Confederate rams before the latter were disabled and driven away. The boiler or steam-pipe of one of the leading vessels of the enemy was exploded by a shot from the flag-ship "Benton," Lieut.-Com. Phelps, and three of the enemy's vessels, including the one encountered by the "Cincinnati," were disabled and drifted down the river. A fifty-pound rifle shot from the "Carondelet" passed through the boilers of another of the enemy's vessels, rendering her helpless

ate vessels made great holes in the "Mound City" and the "Cincinnati," and were considerably damaged themselves, they all succeeded in escaping. The "Cincinnati," after proceeding some distance up the river, sunk near the Tennessee side. The "Cairo" assisted the "Mound City" to the first island above the scene of action, where she also sunk.

The incidents of this engagement are so lightly passed over by Flag-officer Davis, that it is difficult to get much information from the official reports. The enemy's side of the affair can best be learned by the following dispatch of the Confederate Commander-in-chief :

MOUND CITY.　CARONDELET.　　　　　CINCINNATI.　　VAN DORN.　　　　SUMTER.
　　　　　　MORTAR.　　　　　　　　　　　　　GEN. PRICE.　　BRAGG.　LITTLE REBEL.

BATTLE OF FORT PILLOW.　FIRST POSITION.

for the time being. All these disabled vessels might have been captured had there been any means at hand of towing them up stream, but the motive power of the gunboats was so limited that they could scarcely make any headway against the current, and they had to be continually on the watch to avoid drifting under the enemy's batteries.

This was the first naval engagement of the war, pure and simple, where the squadrons of both sides were pitted against each other. Our iron-clads showed themselves unsuited in respect to steam power, to cope with swift river vessels that could ram them and then escape. Although the Confeder-

"FLAG-BOAT 'LITTLE REBEL,'
FORT PILLOW, May 12, 1862.

"SIR:—I have the honor to report an engagement with the Federal gun-boats at Plum Point Bend, four miles above this place. Having previously arranged with my officers the order of attack, our boats left their moorings at 6 A. M., and proceeding up the river passed around a sharp point, which soon brought us in full view of the enemy's fleet, numbering eight gun-boats and twelve mortars. The Federal gun-boat 'Carondelet' ['Cincinnati'] was lying nearest us, guarding a mortar-boat that was shelling the fort. The 'General Bragg,' Captain Leonard, dashed at her, she firing her heavy guns and retreating towards a bar where the depth of water would not be sufficient for our boats to follow. The 'Bragg' continued boldly on under fire of nearly their whole fleet, and struck her a blow that stopped her further flight. The 'Bragg' rounded to down the river under a broadside fire, and drifted until her tiller rope, that had got out of order, could be re-adjusted.

"A few moments after the 'Bragg' struck her blow, the 'General Sterling Price,' First-officer J. E. Harthorne, ran into the same boat aft, a little starboard of her amidships, carrying away her rudder, sternpost and a large piece of her stern. This threw the 'Cincinnati's' stern towards the 'Sumter,' Captain M. W. Lamb, which struck her running at the utmost speed of his boat.

"The 'General Earl Van Dorn,' Capt. Folkerson, running according to orders in the rear of the 'Price' and 'Sumter,' directed his attention to the 'Mound City,' at the time throwing broadsides into the 'Price' and 'Sumter'; and, as she proceeded, by skilful shots from her 32-pounder silenced a mortar-boat that was filling the air with its terrible missiles; the 'Van Dorn' still holding on to the 'Mound City.' In the act of striking, the 'Mound City' sheered and the 'Van Dorn' struck her a glancing blow, making a hole four feet deep in her starboard forward quarter, evidenced by the splinters left on the iron bow of the 'Van Dorn.'

"At this juncture, the 'Van Dorn' was above four of the Federal boats, as the remaining boats, 'General Jeff Thompson' and 'Colonel Lovell,' Capt. Hart, were entering boldly into the contest in the prescribed order. I perceived from the flag-boat that the Federal vessels were taking positions where the water was too shallow for our boats to get at them, and as our cannon were far inferior both in number and size, I signalled our boats to fall back, which was accomplished with a coolness which deserves the highest commendation.

"I am happy to inform you that while exposed at close quarters to a most terrible fire for thirty minutes, our boats, though struck repeatedly, sustained no serious injuries.

"General Jeff Thompson was on board the 'General Bragg,' his officers and men were divided among the boats. They were all at their posts ready to do good service should the occasion offer.

"To my officers and men I am highly indebted for their courage and promptness in executing all orders.

"On the 11th instant, I went in the 'Little Rebel' in full view of the enemy's fleet, and saw the 'Carondelet' ['Cincinnati'] sunk near the shore, and the 'Mound City' sunk on the bar.

"The position occupied by the enemy's gun-boats above Fort Pillow, offers more obstacles to our mode of attack than any between Cairo and New Orleans, but of this you may rest assured that they will never penetrate further down the Mississippi River.

"Our casualties were two killed and one wounded.

"[Signed.]   J. E. MONTGOMERY,
"Senior Captain Commanding,
"River Defence Fleet."

On the Federal side there were only four wounded, Commander Stembel seriously, Fourth-Master Reynolds and two seamen slightly. This was a small list of casualties for such a desperate brush, and would seem to indicate rather indifferent gunnery practice on the part of the Federals, who, with their heavy ordnance, ought to have swept the enemy from the face of the water, as his vessels were of wood and lightly built.

The attack on the Federal vessels was, however, by a new method; for this was the first time ramming had been practiced on this river during the war, and the "Cincinnati" and "Mound City" had been put *hors de combat* almost at the beginning of the action.

The Confederate Commander-in-chief was not accustomed to command vessels *en masse* and does not seem to have understood the necessity of concert of action. Each Confederate vessel seems to have been fighting on her "own hook." There is no doubt they received more damage than they were willing to admit.

All their damages were, however, quickly repaired at Memphis, where they had a good navy yard with all the necessary appliances.

It appears evident that our gun-boats did not altogether act in concert, probably owing to their want of speed, In the case of the flag-ship, her deficiency in speed kept her behind the rest, but when she did join the battle, her heavy guns told on the enemy and everything gave way before her.

It is exceedingly difficult to give a correct account of this engagement, owing to the many conflicting versions which were published in the West at the time, but we know enough to be satisfied that victory remained with the Federal squadron.

The report of Flag-officer Davis was of course intended to represent the true position of the vessels, but he was new to the command, and the iron-clads smaller than the "Benton" were so much alike, that any one was liable to mistake one for the other at the distance of a mile, and give another vessel credit for work done by her consort. On this occasion if reports were made to the Commander-in-chief, they were not published in the annual report of the Secretary of the Navy; but notwithstanding the conflicting statements, it appears certain that every officer and man on board the Union gun-boats did their duty, and drove off a fearless and enterprising enemy, who had a flotilla well equipped for the purpose intended.

Flag-officer Davis had the satisfaction of winning the first naval squadron fight, and certainly deserved the thanks of the Navy Department for himself, his gallant officers and crew; especially since all in the squadron had shown such courage and energy, ever since the day when Foote first left Cairo with the gun-boats and mortars.

CHAPTER XVII.

EVACUATION OF FORT PILLOW AND BATTLE OF MEMPHIS.

BOMBARDMENT AND EVACUATION OF FORT PILLOW.—COL. ELLET'S RAM FLOTILLA.—
CAPTURE OF A CONFEDERATE TRANSPORT.—THE VESSELS COMPOSING THE CONFEDERATE
FLEET.—BATTLE OF MEMPHIS.—CAPTURE OF THE CITY.—DESTRUCTION OF THE CONFED-
ERATE FLEET.—A BRILLIANT VICTORY.—NOBLE ACTION OF THE COMMANDER OF THE
"MONARCH."—CAPTURE OF FORTS UP THE WHITE RIVER.—EXPLOSION OF THE STEAM
CHEST OF THE "MOUND CITY."—VALUABLE LIVES LOST.—SAVING THE CREWS OF THE
CONFEDERATE VESSELS.—CONFEDERATE ACCOUNTS.

AFTER this river battle, Flag-officer Davis commenced a heavy and continuous bombardment of Fort Pillow, which lasted up to the 4th of June, and gave the enemy great annoyance, although he continued to reply with a constant and well-directed fire. But the Confederate guns were defective, and their shell often exploded before reaching the point intended to be struck.

Davis determined to have no more surprises, and two of the gun-boats were detailed to guard the mortar-rafts until evening, when they were towed to a position where they would be under the protection of the fleet until morning.

The constant explosion of the bombs in the fort or in the air, by which numbers of the garrison were killed, had its effect at last. The enemy saw that it was now only a matter of time, and that the Union forces must win in the end. The Confederate troops at Iuka, Corinth and other places in West Tennessee, were being gradually driven back, and once more the base of operations was to undergo a change in obedience to the law of strategy.

Fort Pillow had to be evacuated, and when the Confederates did evacuate a position they generally did so with an unaccountable haste. In this case they may have heard that an army was marching on them from the rear, or that Pope was returning with a great force from Pittsburg Landing. Whatever it was, something had a very demoralizing effect upon the garri-

son, and the guns of the fort were no longer well aimed or rapidly fired.

On the night of June 4th, a great many explosions were heard in the fort, which indicated to the officers of the fleet that the enemy was preparing to evacuate. The Flag-officer on receiving this intelligence, gave orders for the gun-boats to get under way at 4 o'clock on the morning of June 5th, and to move down the river in the following order: "Benton," "Mound City," "Louisville," "Carondelet," "Cairo," and "St. Louis." (The "Mound City" had been fished up out of the river and repaired, but the "Cincinnati" was still at Cairo.)

Since the battle with the Confederate rams a new organization had been added to the Union fleet in the shape of a ram flotilla, commanded by a very gallant man, Col. Charles Ellet, of the U. S. Army. These vessels were simply ordinary river steamers converted into rams, though not in a very effective manner. They had been strengthened with timber and had the boilers partially protected from shot, but they were not nearly so well designed as the Confederate rams. They were named the "Monarch," "Queen of the West," "Switzerland" and "Lancaster," all commanded by an Ellet, brother, son, or nephew, all gallant men, and ready for any enterprise.

The Flag-officer assigned a proper position to Col. Ellet, and the combined fleet proceeded down the river to Fort Pillow, which they found to be abandoned.

Capt. Davis sent for Col. Fitch U. S. A.

and turned over the fort to him. This officer brought a detachment of his troops over in a transport without delay, and the American flag was soon floating over this stronghold, which at one time seemed able to defy all the gun-boats and armies of the Republic.

Large army spoils were captured, and many heavy guns (40 at least); for although the Confederates had set fire to the works, they had neglected to make the destruction

At 8 P. M. the fleet anchored at the lower end of Island No. 45, a mile and a half above the City of Memphis. The mortar-boats, tow-boats, ordnance and commissary vessels, anchored for the night at Island 44.

At daylight the enemy's fleet of rams and gun-boats, now numbering eight vessels, was discovered lying at the levee at Memphis. They dropped below Railroad Point, and returning again arranged themselves below the city.

REAR-ADMIRAL CHAS. H. DAVIS.

complete and retired with their usual precipitancy.

At noon the fleet again steamed down the river, leaving the "Pittsburg" and "Mound City" to co-operate with the Army.

At a bend in the river on the way down, a Confederate transport came in sight of the fleet, but turned and attempted to escape. She was captured by a fast tug, with a body of armed men, under the command of Lieut. Joshua Bishop: she proved to be a valuable prize.

At 4.20 the Union flotilla got under way in the following order: Flagship "Benton," Lieut.-Com. Phelps; "Louisville," Com. B. M. Dove; "Carondelet," Com. H. Walke; "Cairo," Lieut.-Com. N. E. Bryant; "St. Louis," Lieut.-Com. Nelson McGunnegle.

They dropped down the river according to signal, and prepared for battle. The Confederate gun-boats opened fire upon our fleet as it moved down, with the seeming intention of having the city injured by the return fire; but due care was taken in re-

ACTION OF THE GUN-BOATS AT MEMPHIS, JUNE 6 1862.

gard to this matter, and shot and shell were sent among the Confederates with good effect.

At this moment the ram fleet was several miles up the river, though coming down rapidly, and it was necessary for our gun-boats to maneuver so as to enable it to overtake them.

The Confederate vessels (still under the command of Montgomery) were the rams "General Van Dorn," "General Price," "General Lovell," "General Beauregard" and "General Jeff Thompson," mounting each four heavy guns; the "General Bragg" and "General Sumter," mounting three guns, and the "Little Rebel," mounting two guns.

When the battle had fairly commenced, two of the army rams, the "Queen of the West," Col. Charles Ellet, and the "Monarch," Lieut.-Col. Ellet (a younger brother), dashed fearlessly ahead of the gunboats and ran for the enemy's fleet. At the first encounter they sank one and disabled another of the Confederates, who were taken greatly by surprise, as they did not know that we had any rams, but took them for transports.

The rams were closely followed by the Union gun-boats in order of battle, under the lead of Flag-officer Davis, and opened a vigorous fire which was kept up until the end of the battle.

Up to the time of the attack by the Union rams, the enemy had kept up a spirited and rapid fire, but as the vessels closed it became necessary for the gunners on both sides to exercise more care.

The "Queen of the West" being in advance of the "Monarch," was now badly rammed by the "Beauregard," which vessel, in company with the "General Price," then made a dash at the "Monarch" as she approached them, but missed their mark and crashed together, the "Beauregard" cutting the "Price" down to the water line and tearing off her port wheel. The "Monarch" then rammed the "Beauregard," and she quickly sank in the river opposite Memphis, being struck at the same time in the boilers by a shell from an iron-clad.

The "General Lovell" having been struck by the "Queen of the West," or the "Monarch" (as the latter claims), went to the bottom so suddenly as to take a number of her officers and crew down with her. The "General Price," "Queen of the West" and "Little Rebel" being disabled (the latter by a shot through her steam-chest), were run ashore on the Arkansas side of the river to prevent their sinking. By this time the best part of the Confederate rams and gun-boats had been disabled and the fight now became a running one. The ram "Van Dorn" escaped down the river and was pursued by the "Switzerland" and "Monarch," but not overtaken. The "Jeff

Thompson" was set on fire by the shells from the iron-clads, and ran into the right bank of the river, where she burnt to the water's edge, and finally blew up. The "Sumter" and 'Bragg" were somewhat cut up, but did not sink, and thus of all the Confederate fleet, the "Van Dorn" alone escaped.

The commander of the "Monarch," after disabling the "Beauregard" and putting her in a sinking condition, towed her into shoal water and saved her crew. This was a noble action, as enemies in combat do not often stop to save sinking ships that have been firing into them. But this was not the only instance where humanity was shown during this battle: when it was known in the fleet that some of the enemy's vessels were sinking, and a cry came up for help, the flagship "Benton" lowered her boats and sent her officers and men to the rescue of their bitter foes. So eager was the rush to undertake this duty that the first boat was swamped.

How glorious was this conduct when compared with the treatment which the sailors of the "Cumberland" and "Congress" received at Hampton Roads, when they were struggling in the water and subjected to a murderous fire from the guns of the victorious "Merrimac." At Hampton Roads the cry was "Death to the Federals!" At Memphis it was "Help for the drowning Confederates!"

The battle had carried most of the Union vessels ten miles below Memphis, and they now found themselves to have been successful beyond all hopes. The enemy was completely swept away, as if his vessels had been made of paper—a result which our officers had hardly expected since the gallant action at Plum Point, in which these same vessels, under Montgomery, proved such formidable foes.

Rear-Admiral Davis had no military authority over the ram fleet. He could only request co-operation, which the Commander, Col. Ellet, was eager to give. The latter fought well, but unfortunately his vessels did not keep together and therefore did not accomplish as much as they would have done by a combined attack. Three of the rams did not get into action until after the "Queen of the West" and "Monarch" had made their charge upon the enemy. Had they made a rush at the same time, it is probable that five of the enemy's vessels would have been sunk, and not even the "Van Dorn" would have escaped. However, as matters turned out, it was a brilliant victory, and the Union commander had every reason to be satisfied with it.

The Confederates fought with a coolness and energy that entitled them to the greatest credit, and although the "Van Dorn" escaped, it was only after the commander saw that he could be of no further use to his friends.

Capt. Maynardier, who commanded the mortar batteries, accompanied the fleet in a tug and rendered good service. When the "Beauregard" was disabled he steamed alongside of her and made her crew prisoners—he also received many persons of the Confederate fleet, who returned and delivered themselves up after their vessels had been deserted. Rear-Admiral Davis says: "It is with pleasure that I call the attention of the Department to his personal zeal and activity, the more conspicuous because displayed while the mortar-boats under his command could take no part in the action."

Two of the enemy's rams, the "Price"

slow moving and awkward iron-clads off the face of the river. Who can tell what they felt when they saw the Confederate fleet sunk, blown up, or burnt—for it was an awful sight to see a ship going down in an instant with all on board, not even her masts appearing above the deep waters of the Mississippi. Can any one who witnessed the battle ever forget the heart-rending shrieks of drowning men as the waters closed over their heads, or the sounds of woe that went up from relatives and friends upon the river bank who witnessed the appalling scene !

The "Lovell" was the first vessel that went to the bottom, giving the spectators a fair idea of what would be the fate of all

QUEEN. MONARCH.   LOUISVILLE. CAIRO. ST. LOUIS. BENTON. CARONDELET.
PRICE.   LITTLE REBEL.   BRAGG.   SUMTER.   BEAUREGARD.   LOVELL.
    VAN DORN.   JEFF. THOMPSON.

BATTLE OF MEMPHIS, ENEMY RETREATING.—(DRAWN BY REAR-ADMIRAL WALKE.)

and the "Bragg," were sea-going vessels, strongly built and heavily armed, each of them being superior to any in Ellet's fleet. No doubt the enemy calculated a great deal on them. They were saved and refitted, and afterwards formed part of the Union fleet in Western waters. The "Sumter" and "Little Rebel" were also saved and made use of, but all the rest were destroyed by sinking or blowing up.

To those who stood on the river bank at Memphis, this battle must have appeared like a horrid dream, so different was the result from what they had anticipated. Here were assembled the relatives of those who manned the powerful and swift vessels, which were fully expected to wipe the

the rest. Many human beings were buffeting the waves while the battle was going on, and the cry for help arose above the sounds of conflict. No aid could reach them from the shore, and their friends clasped their hands over their faces to shut out the agonizing sight.

But even in the excitement of battle, humanity was uppermost in the hearts of our brave western sailors ; boats were lowered with that rapidity which can only be seen on board a vessel-of-war, and the sinking wretches, who a moment before had given up all hope, were rescued and taken to a place of safety.

The "Monarch," even before the battle was ended, towed the "Beauregard" on to a shoal, while Capt. Pike, of the Ordnance department, went along-side and helped the wounded into his tug. Bright, amid all the horrors of that day, will shine these deeds of humanity, and our sailors may feel a more glorious pride in having saved their helpless enemies than in having conquered them.

The capture of Memphis was a terrible blow to the South, for this city had been of great use to the Confederacy as a base of supplies for their armies in Tennessee, which supplies we had not up to this time been able to intercept. This naval success opened the river all the way down to Vicksburg, and three other depots of supplies were soon to fall into our hands, when our fleet penetrated the Yazoo River in the heart of the enemy's country.

For the second time Rear Admiral Davis won a strictly naval victory, and won it without a single mistake. He was no doubt much assisted by the two rams, "Queen of the West" and "Monarch," which by their gallant and unexpected attack did so much to demoralize the enemy.

The Confederate account of this battle differs very little from the Union one, the only exception being in the case of the "General Lovell," which vessel, they say, was sunk by a shot from the fleet, and not by being rammed by the "Queen of the West." The Confederates ought to know which is the correct version.

Rear-Admiral Davis, in his report, makes no distinction among his officers. He simply says, "the officers and men of the flotilla performed their duty." The proof of the manner in which it was performed was the total annihilation of the enemy's forces.

Take the battle, together with its results, it was one of the handsomest achievements of the war, but it did not receive that general notice which it deserved.

If Mr. Secretary Welles, who was liberal with his eulogistic letters to those whom he approved of, ever congratulated Rear-Admiral Davis and his officers for their brilliant success, it nowhere appears in the Secretary's Report for 1862. But history will eventually give due credit to all the brave men who served their country faithfully in the time of her greatest need. The prejudices and jealousies of the times will have passed away, and the truthful historian who takes time to examine the records carefully, will give to each his proper place, and render justice to those who have not yet received it. The writer of this work regrets that his space is so limited that he can only do partial justice to the scenes enacted in the war.

In the battle just described, there were only three men wounded and one killed in the Union fleet, and only one vessel was struck by the enemy's shot—which looks like a cheap victory; yet it was none the less important. The city of Memphis was surrendered that day to the Army and Navy, and garrisoned at once by the Indiana Brigade under Colonel Fitch.

A great deal of property fell into the hands of the Federal troops, who kept possession of the place until the end of the war, and soon converted it into a loyal city.

The Confederates had now to seek a new strategic line of defence : they established their fifth Gibraltar at Vicksburg, where the gunboats will catch up with them after a while.

EXPEDITION AGAINST ST. CHARLES, ON THE WHITE RIVER.

On June 16th, 1862, Rear-Admiral Davis sent an expedition up the White River to destroy some batteries located at St. Charles. The expedition was under the charge of Com. Kilty, and was composed of the gun-boats "Mound City," "St. Louis," "Lexington," and "Conestoga," and several transports with troops under Col. Fitch, U. S. A.

The Confederates had mounted batteries at this point and had obstructed the river with piles and sunken vessels.

On June 17th, Com. Kilty reconnoitered the place in a tug, and having gained the desired information, at six o'clock next morning the gun boats got under way in the following order: "Mound City," "St. Louis," "Lexington," "Conestoga," and opened fire on the enemy's works.

The "Mound City" had advanced to within 600 yards of the forts, when a well-directed shell penetrated her port casemate, killing three men and exploding in the steam-chest. The ship was instantly filled with scalding steam, and many of the crew jumped overboard in their agony. All boats were manned and sent to pick up these men, and as the ship was disabled she was towed out of action by the "Conestoga."

The "St. Louis," Lieut.-Com. McGunnegle, moved close up to the forts and continued to pour in shot and shell, while the enemy kept firing on the "St. Louis" and also on the men who were struggling in the water. A more dastardly thing never was done in the history of the war, and was very different from the conduct of the Federals at Memphis, where, as stated above, boats were lowered in the heat of battle to pick up the drowning enemy.

At this moment Col. Fitch made signal for the gun-boats to cease firing, and having gained a position he immediately charged the enemy's works and carried them without the loss of a single man. Eight of the enemy were killed and twenty-nine were taken prisoners, including Capt.

Fry (formerly a Lieutenant in the U. S. Navy), Commander of the post. All their guns and ammunition fell into the hands of the Federals. The batteries consisted of two 12-pounder brass pieces, two 9-pounder parrot guns (rifled) and two 42-pounder sea-coast howitzers.

The victory was a complete one, but the loss of life on board the "Mound City" was frightful. To describe the scene after the explosion is beyond the power of any pen. Among the scalded and suffering was Com. Kilty, who, a moment before the accident, was seen coolly walking the deck and fighting his ship most gallantly. All honor to his name.

Out of the entire crew of the "Mound City" (175 officers and men), only three officers and twenty-two men escaped uninjured; eighty-two died from wounds or scalding, and forty-three were either drowned or killed in the water. The wounded men received the greatest care and consideration, and were finally sent to Memphis on board the "Conestoga" and an army transport.

To Lieuts. McGunnegle, Shirk and Blodgett is due the highest honor, not only for their bravery during the action, but for their humanity in providing for the comfort of the poor fellows who were so badly scalded. Dr. George W. Garber, of the "Lexington," and Dr. William H. Nelson, of the "Carondelet," also deserve great credit for their judicious care of the wounded.

With regard to Col. Fitch, who stormed and carried the fort with his soldiers, we have only to say that he exhibited that cool courage and judgment which he had always displayed since co-operating with the Navy at Island No. 10.

This victory, though a small one, was very important, as it opened the White River to our gun-boats and transports, and showed the enemy the futility of attempting to bar the way against our vessels with Confederate batteries. It also showed what could be done by a small force of the Army and Navy when working together harmoniously.

Although the Confederates congratulated themselves on the great death-roll of the "Mound City," they had to bear the ignominy of having fired upon drowning men, which almost debarred them from the clemency of their victors.

CHAPTER XVIII.

CAPTURE OF FORTS JACKSON AND ST. PHILIP, AND THE SURRENDER OF NEW ORLEANS.

NAVAL EXPEDITION FITTED OUT.—FARRAGUT COMMANDS EXPEDITION.—FARRAGUT'S AND PORTER'S FLEETS.—THEIR APPEARANCE IN THE MISSISSIPPI.—FORTS JACKSON AND ST. PHILIP.—CONFIDENCE OF CONFEDERATES IN THE DEFENSE OF NEW ORLEANS.—OBSTRUCTIONS.—CONFEDERATE FLEET.—PORTER'S MORTAR FLEET.—BOMBARDMENT OF FORTS JACKSON AND ST. PHILIP.—TERRIBLE WORK OF MORTAR FLEET.—THE CHAINS CUT. —PASSAGE OF FORTS BY WAR VESSELS.—ORDER OF VESSELS IN PASSING.—DESPERATE NAVAL BATTLE.—THE VARUNA SUNK AFTER A GALLANT FIGHT.—THE "HARTFORD" ATTACKED BY FIRE RAFTS.—BRAVE WORDS OF FARRAGUT.—THE RAM "MANASSAS" ATTACKS THE "HARTFORD" AND "BROOKLYN."—THE LITTLE "ITASCA."—GRAPHIC SCENES. —FARRAGUT ON HIS WAY TO NEW ORLEANS.—THE RAM "MANASSAS" DESTROYED.—THE CHALMETTE BATTERIES.—FORTS JACKSON AND ST. PHILIP CAPITULATE.—FLAG OF TRUCE VIOLATED.—EXPLOSION OF THE "LOUISIANA."—MISCELLANEOUS INCIDENTS.— FARRAGUT BEFORE NEW ORLEANS.—CONGRATULATORY LETTERS OF HON. GIDEON WELLES.

ON the 12th of November, 1861, President Lincoln ordered that a naval expedition should be fitted out for the capture of New Orleans.

Captain David G. Farragut was detailed for the command of this expedition, with the title of Flag-officer, and an efficient mortar flotilla was fitted out under Com. David D. Porter, and attached to the force. Besides the mortar vessels, there were in the flotilla seven steamers to manage the former in the swift current of the Mississippi, and to aid them with their fire in case of necessity.

Farragut sailed on the 20th of January, 1862, with the following orders from the Secretary of the Navy:

"There will be attached to your squadron a fleet of bomb-vessels, and armed steamers enough to manage them, all under command of Com. D. D. Porter, who will be directed to report to you. As fast as these vessels are got ready they will be sent to Key West to await the arrival of all, and the commanding officers will be permitted to organize and practice with them at that point.

"When these formidable mortars arrive, and you are completely ready, you will collect such vessels as can be spared from the blockade and proceed up the Mississippi River and reduce the defences which guard the approaches to New Orleans, when you will appear off that city and take possession of it under the guns of your squadron, and hoist the American flag therein, keeping possession until troops can be sent to you.

"If the Mississippi expedition from Cairo shall not have descended the river, you will take advantage of the panic to push a strong force up the river to take all their defences in the rear."

Farragut, as soon as possible, proceeded to his station, and assumed command of the West Gulf Blockading Squadron.

While the foregoing plans were developing at the North, the Confederates had not remained inactive. Acquainted, almost from its incipiency, with the object of the expedition, they had exerted themselves to the utmost in strengthening the river defenses at Forts Jackson and St. Philip; which included obstructions on the river itself, besides the preparation of what might well be considered a formidable naval force.

Of the latter, the ram "Manassas," was improved and commissioned, while the "Louisiana," iron-clad, of sixteen heavy guns, was rapidly nearing completion. Two other powerful iron-clads, intended to clear the southern coast of blockaders, were under construction at New Orleans, while further inland, at Yazoo City, the iron-clad ram "Arkansas" was almost ready for service. Several other iron-clad vessels were, at the same time, building at various points on the tributaries.

time of Nelson. Not only had the North failed to avail itself of its great resources for the construction of powerful armorclad vessels in sufficient numbers to strike at once a heavy blow, but up to the departure of this expedition, a commencement

ADMIRAL DAVID G. FARRAGUT.

A comparison of the work done by the North and the South, up to the advance on New Orleans, is largely in favor of the latter; for not one among all the vessels sent to Farragut possessed any power of resistance, save what had been shown from the

only had been made, by the construction of the "Monitor," one small iron-clad, and the new "Ironsides." The subsequent encounter of the former vessel with the "Merrimac" seemed to show for the first time the great utility of such craft. The action of the Federal Government in this matter seems inexcusable.

By the middle of March, the following ships, assigned to Farragut's command, had assembled at Key West, the rendezvous: "Hartford," 25 guns, Com. Richard Wainwright; "Brooklyn," 24 guns, Capt. T. T. Craven; "Richmond," 26 guns, Com. James Alden; "Mississippi," 12 guns, Com. Melancton Smith; "Pensacola," 24 guns, Capt. H. W. Morris; "Cayuga," 6 guns, Lieut. Com. N. B. Harrison; "Oneida," 9 guns, Com. S. P. Lee; "Varuna," 10 guns, Com. Charles S. Boggs; "Katahdin," 4 guns, Lieut. Com. George H. Preble; "Kineo," 4 guns, Lieut. Com. George M. Ransom; "Wissahickon," 4 guns, Lieut. Com. A. N. Smith; "Winona," 4 guns, Lieut. Com. E. T. Nichols; "Itasca," 4 guns, Lieut. Com. C. H. B. Caldwell; "Pinola," 4 guns, Lieut. Com. Pierce Crosby; "Kennebec," 4 guns, Lieut. Com. John H. Russell; "Iroquois," 9 guns, Com. John De Camp; "Sciota," 4 guns, Lieut. Com. Edward Donaldson. Total guns, 177.

Also the following steamers belonging to the mortar flotilla: "Harriet Lane," "Owasco," "Clifton," "Westfield," "Miami," "Jackson;" besides the mortar schooners, which will be named hereafter.

The frigate "Colorado," of fifty guns, is not enumerated, for though present, both Flag-officer Farragut and Capt. Bailey, his second in command, concluded that it was impossible to lighten her sufficiently to cross the bar at Southwest Pass.

Towed by the "Harriet Lane," "Owasco," "Westfield," and "Clifton," all the mortar schooners crossed the bar at Pass à l'Outre on March 18th, and were ordered by Farragut to proceed *via* the junction to the Southwest Pass.

At this time the only vessels that had crossed the bar at the Southwest Pass, after an unsuccessful attempt with the "Brooklyn" at Pass à l'Outre, were the "Hartford" and the "Brooklyn." The Navy Department had been mistaken in sending vessels of such draught as the "Colorado," "Pensacola," and "Mississippi," for though the two latter ships were finally with great difficulty worked over, the time lost amounted to at least twelve days, with a corresponding delay of the fleet.

Farragut's first act upon reaching the Mississippi was to despatch his Chief of Staff, Capt. Henry H. Bell, with the gunboats "Kennebec" and "Wissahickon" up the river on a reconnoissance. After returning from the neighborhood of the forts, Capt. Bell reported that "the obstructions seemed formidable. Eight hulks were moored in line across the river, with heavy chains extending from one to the other.

Rafts of logs were also used, and the passage between the forts was thus entirely closed."

Forts Jackson and St. Philip had been much strengthened since the expedition was started. Situated in a most commanding position, at a turn in the river, the former on the west bank and the latter on the east, they commanded the stream above and below; Fort St. Philip being particularly well placed to rake the lower approach.

The works themselves were of masonry. Fort Jackson was of pentagonal form, with bastions, its river front being about one hundred yards from the levee, above which its casemates just appeared. The armaments consisted of a total of seventy-five guns, distributed as follows: Two ten-inch columbiads, one six-inch rifle, and thirty-three thirty-two pounders on the main parapet; two ten-inch columbiads and one nine-inch mortar in the second bastion; one columbiad and two eight-inch mortars in the third bastion; eight thirty-two pounders in the northwest casemate, six thirty-two pounders in the northeast casemate, and ten short guns and two brass field-pieces in the bastion casemates. The water battery of this fort, having the command of the lower approach, was a powerful work, mounting seven guns, as follows: One ten and one nine-inch columbiad, two heavy rifle guns and three thirty-two pounders.

Fort Jackson was altogether in a good condition; its citadel, in the centre of the works, contained large amounts of war stores and provisions, while the bombproofs had been made more secure by sand bags piled upon them to a depth of some six feet, and all vulnerable parts protected in like manner.

The guns of Fort St. Philip were all in barbette, and numbered a total of fifty-three pieces of ordnance, as follows: Forty-three guns, chiefly thirty-two pounders, one thirteen-inch mortar, one six-inch rifle, four ten-inch sea-coast mortars, one ten-inch siege mortar, one eight-inch siege mortar, and three pieces of light artillery.

Each of the forts was garrisoned by some seven hundred men, and both, with their adjuncts, were under command of Brigadier General Johnson K. Duncan, whose gallantry and ability were conspicuous.

Less current and fewer eddies existed close under the west bank, near Fort Jackson; consequently the best passage up river was in that channel. The Confederates had obstructed this way by means of a heavy raft of logs, which closed the only part of the river not blockaded by the hulks and their chain connections, anchored across, below the forts, almost from bank to bank. The raft was fitted to act as a gate, opening or closing at the pleasure of the defenders.

Besides the land defenses, a fleet of war vessels, of more or less power, had been organized by the Confederates, from such material as they could procure; heavy tugs and merchant vessels were converted with some success, until a fleet of eighteen vessels, including the ram "Manassas," and the iron-clad "Louisiana," was gathered under the command of Com. John K. Mitchell, of the Confederate Navy.

This fleet was composed of two divisions, one belonging to the regularly organized Navy and the other forming what was called the River Defense, under the immediate command of a merchant captain named Stephenson.

Of the regular Navy were the following: The iron-clad "Louisiana," sixteen heavy guns, crew two hundred men, a powerful vessel, with armor sufficient to turn the projectiles of any gun in the Union fleet. Upon the roof of the casemate was a gallery for sharp-shooters, running around the entire space. The machinery, consisting of twin screw engines and central paddles, was unfinished, and her inactivity at the time of the fight was due to that fact. The "Louisiana" was commanded by Com. Charles F. McIntosh, formerly of the U. S. Navy.

The "McRae," commanded by Lieut. Thomas B. Huger, was a sea-going steamer, mounting six thirty-two pounders and one nine-inch shell gun.

The steamer "Jackson," Lieut. F. B. Renshaw, commanding, mounted two thirty-two pounders.

The ram "Manassas," Lieut. A. F. Warley commanding, mounted one thirty-two pounder in bow.

The foregoing, with two launches armed with one howitzer each, constituted the regular Navy command.

Included in this division there were also the following sea-steamers converted into State gun-boats belonging to Louisiana. These vessels were lightly protected with pine and cotton barricades over the machinery and boilers.

The "General Quitman," commanded by Capt. Grant, mounting two thirty-two pounders; The "Governor Moore," Commander Beverly Kennon, mounting two thirty-two pounder rifled guns. According to Commander Mitchell the above, "being converted vessels, were too slightly built for war purposes."

Attached to his command were the following unarmed steamers: The "Phœnix," "W. Burton," and the "Landis."

Subject to his orders, but chartered by the Army, were the small tugs "Mosher," "Belle Algerine," "Star," and "Music."

The second division, the River Defense, commanded as before stated, consisted of the following converted tow-boats: The "Warrior," "Stonewall Jackson," "Resolute," "General Lovell," "Defiance," and the "R. I. Breckenridge."

These vessels mounted from one to two thirty-two pounder pivots each, some of the guns being rifled. By means of iron casing their bows, they had been fitted for use as rams.

Little assistance to the fleet resulted from the employment of these boats, on account of the insubordination of their division commander.

As a whole, the Confederate fleet mounted thirty-nine guns, all, with the exception of two, being thirty-two pounders, some nine of which were rifled.

From the foregoing enumeration it will be seen that strongly-built works, mounting one hundred and twenty-eight guns, assisted by a partially armored fleet carrying thirty-nine guns, opposed the passage of Farragut's wooden vessels carrying one hundred and seventy-seven guns.

Much assistance was expected by the Confederates from numerous fire-rafts that were placed at Commander Mitchell's disposal for the purpose of lighting the passage, and confusing the order of the Union fleet.

Assuming, upon the general concession of military men, that one gun in a fort was equal to about three afloat, and considering the disadvantage of a contrary three-and-a-half knot current to the Federal vessels (with the additional channel obstructions of fire-rafts and chains), the odds were greatly in favor of the Confederate defenses. This was thoroughly realized by the Confederates, who were rather impatient than otherwise for Farragut's advance, believing him certain to meet with disaster. Like vigilant foes, however, they fully improved the time afforded by the delay of the fleet at the bar, and materially increased the strength of their position in the interim preceding the attack.

With this understanding of the defense, we will return to the attacking force.

The position selected for the first and third divisions of the mortar fleet, during the bombardment, was on the west bank of the river, at a point thoroughly screened from the forts by a thick growth of wood. The mast-heads of the schooners rose above the trees, and afforded a capital outlook from which to direct the fire, but being ingeniously covered with brush, they were rendered indistinguishable to the Confederate gunners.

The mortar vessels were organized as follows:

First division, Lieut. Com. Watson Smith,

consisted of the following vessels: "Norfolk Packet," Lieut. Smith; "O. H. Lee," Act. Mast. Godfrey; "Para," Act. Mast. Furber; "C. P. Williams," Act. Mast. Langthorne; "Arletta," Act. Mast. Smith; "Bacon," Act. Mast. Rogers; "Sophronia," Act. Mast. Bartholomew.

Second division, under Lieut. W. W. Queen: "T. A. Ward," Lieut. Queen; "M. J. Carlton," Act. Mast. Jack; "Matthew Vassar," Act. Mast. Savage; "George Mangham," Act. Mast. Collins; "Orvetta," Act. Mast. Blanchard; "Sidney C. Jones," Act. Mast. Graham; " Adolph Hugel," Act. Mast. Van Buskirk.

Third division.—Lieut. K. R. Breese: "John Griffiths," Act. Mast. Henry Brown; "Sarah Bruen," Act. Mast. Christian; "Racer," Act. Mast. Phinney; "Sea Foam," Act. Mast. Williams; "Henry James," Act. Mast. Pennington; " * Dan Smith," Act. Mast. George W. Brown.

The leading vessels of the first division were moored at a distance of 2,850 yards from Fort Jackson, and 3,680 yards from Fort St. Philip, the others occupying positions close under the bank and below the first—this same order being preserved by the third division. The second division was placed at the opposite bank of the river, with its head 3,680 yards from Fort Jackson.

The bombardment commenced on the morning of April 16th, each vessel firing at the rate of one shell every ten minutes.

Forts Jackson and St. Philip returned the mortar fire immediately, though not at once effectually, owing to the secure position of the vessels behind the natural rampart afforded by the bank. The Confederate fire becoming better upon obtaining the range, Lieut. Com. Guest with the "Octorara," was sent to the head of the line to open fire with his eleven-inch gun. This position was occupied for an hour and fifty minutes, and only abandoned for more ammunition.

The second division of mortar-boats, on the east bank, did excellent work during this day, but being exposed, suffered much from the fire of the forts. The position was retained until the cessation of the evening's fire at sunset, when the division was removed to the west bank with the others, under cover.

About 5 P. M. of the first day, fire was seen to break out in Fort Jackson, and the garrison soon left the guns to fight the flames. Some in the Federal fleet were inclined to believe the fire to be from a raft, but this was disproved by Com. Porter, who pulled up the river in a boat and ascertained

that the fort itself was burning, a fact at once reported to the flag-officer,

The heavy work exhausted the men at the mortars by nightfall, but the evidences of accurate practice, as shown in the condition of the fort, increased their activity until shells were thrown at the rate of one in five minutes from each vessel, or, in all, two hundred and forty shells an hour. To admit of rest, the fire was limited to one shell each half hour during the night. In the light of subsequent events this first day's fire was shown to have been the most effective of any during the bombardment, and had the fleet been ready to move at once, the passage could have been effected without serious difficulty.

The bombardment was opened afresh on the following day, and continued without intermission until the final attack of the fleet on April 24th.

The effects of this fire are best described by Colonel Edward Higgins (the commander at Fort Jackson), dated April 4, 1872.

"Your mortar-boats were placed in position on the afternoon of the 17th of April, 1862, and opened fire at once upon Fort Jackson, where my headquarters were established. The practice was excellent from the commencement of the fire to the end, and continued, without intermission, until the morning of the 24th of April, when the fleet passed at about four o'clock.

Nearly every shell of the many thousand fired at the fort lodged inside of the works.

On the first night of the attack, the citadel and all buildings in rear of the fort were fired by bursting shell, and also the sand-bag walls that had been thrown around the magazine doors.

The fire, as you are aware, raged with great fury, and no effort of ours could subdue it. At this time, and nearly all this night, Fort Jackson was helpless; its magazines were inaccessible, and we could have offered no resistance to a passing fleet.

The next morning a terrible scene of destruction presented itself. The wood-work of the citadel being all destroyed, and the crumbling walls being knocked about the fort by the bursting shells, made matters still worse for the garrison. The work of destruction from now until the morning of the 24th, when the fleet passed, was incessant.

I was obliged to confine the men most rigidly to the casemates, or we should have lost the best part of the garrison. A shell, striking the parapet over one of the magazines, the wall of which was seven feet thick, penetrated five feet and failed to burst. If that shell had exploded, your work would have ended.

Another burst near the magazine door, opening the earth and burying the sentinel and another man five feet in the same grave.

The parapet and interior of the fort were completely honey-combed, and the large number of sand bags with which we were supplied, alone saved us from being blown to pieces a hundred times, our magazine doors being much exposed.

On the morning of the 24th, when the fleet passed, the terrible precision with which your formidable vessels hailed down their tons of bursting shell upon the devoted fort made it impossible for us to obtain either rapidity or accuracy of fire, and thus rendered the passage comparatively easy.

There was not very considerable damage done to

---

* The names of the vessels were those under which they were known in the merchant service, and were unchanged after purchase by the Government.

our batteries, but few of the guns being dismounted by your fire; everything else in and around the fort was destroyed."

A deserter from the forts presented himself at the Union position on the third day, and excited much incredulity by the statements he made concerning the condition of affairs at Fort Jackson. He represented the garrison as in a desperate and demoralized condition from the effects of the bombs, hundreds of which had struck the works, crushing the bomb-proofs, cutting the levees by which the fort was flooded, and firing the citadel.

Farragut, to whom the deserter was taken to relate his story, was prevented from taking advantage of the state of affairs as represented, by the supposition that the obstructions in the channel were as yet insurmountable, and time was required for a further examination.

Lieut. Crosby with the "Pinola," and Lieut. Caldwell with the "Itasca," were detailed on April 20th for a night expedition to break the chain which was supposed to extend from shore to shore below the forts.

U. S. FLAG-SHIP "HARTFORD."

The charge of this expedition was given to Captain Bell, Chief of Staff. The Confederates, however, detected the manœuvre, and the fire of Fort Jackson was concentrated upon the gun-boats, but with little or no effect, on account of the tremendous fire from the mortar flotilla. The cables were parted, and a passage-way on the left bank of the river opened.

For nearly six days and nights the mortars continued their fire—sending in about 2,800 shells every twenty-four hours, or a total of nearly 16,800. At the end of this time the men were giving out, ammunition was exhausted, one schooner—the "Carlton" —sunk, and the others severely racked by the repeated concussion upon their decks.

By the 23d instant, Farragut concluded that the condition of affairs warranted an attempt to pass the forts. A council of the commanding officers decided upon an advance to be made on the early morning of the 24th.

Meantime the iron-clad "Louisiana" had

been brought to the forts, and an effort was made by the fort Commander, General Duncan, to have her take up a position below the works, from which her heavy guns would reach the fleet. The following communication from General Duncan to Commander Mitchell was written on April 22d:

"It is of vital importance that the present fire of the enemy should be withdrawn from us, which you alone can do. This can be done in the manner suggested this morning, under the cover of our guns, while your work on the boat can be carried on in safety and security.

Our position is a critical one, dependent entirely on the powers of endurance of our casemates, many of which have been completely shattered, and are crumbling away by repeated shocks; and, therefore, I respectfully, but earnestly, again urge my suggestion of this morning on your notice. Our magazines are also in danger."

General Duncan's suggestion was unheeded, however, and the really formidable obstruction to the Union fleet remained inactive at the river's bank during the subsequent action.

Various other efforts were made to dislodge the mortar flotilla, and a body of riflemen were sent against them as sharpshooters, but all without success.

Having previously issued detailed orders to the commanders of vessels, concerning their preparation for the approaching operations, such as slinging chains over vital part of the hulls, sending down light spars, painting hulls mud color, tricing up whiskers, etc., Farragut issued the following general order:

"UNITED STATES FLAG-SHIP, 'HARTFORD,' ⎱
MISSISSIPPI RIVER, April 20, 1862. ⎰

"The Flag-officer, having heard all the opinions expressed by the different commanders, is of the opinion that whatever is to be done will have to be done quickly, or we shall be again reduced to a blockading squadron, without the means of carrying on the bombardment, as we have nearly expended all the shells and fuses, and material for making cartridges. He has always entertained the same opinions which are expressed by Com. Porter; that is, there are three modes of attack, and the question is, which is the one to be adopted?

"His own opinion is, that a combination of two should be made, viz.: the forts should be run, and, when a force is once above the forts, to protect the troops, they should be landed at quarantine from the gulf side by bringing them through the bayou, and then our forces should move up the river, mutually aiding each other as it can be done to advantage.

"When, in the opinion of the Flag-officer, the propitious time has arrived, the signal will be made to weigh and advance to the conflict. If, in his opinion, at the time of arriving at the respective positions of the different divisions of the fleet, we have the advantage, he will make the signal for close action, No. 8, and abide the result, conquer or to be conquered, drop anchor or keep under way, as in his opinion is best.

"Unless the signal above mentioned is made, it will be understood that the first order of sailing will be formed after leaving Fort St. Philip, and we will proceed up the river in accordance with the original opinion expressed.

"The programme of the order of sailing accompanies this general order, and the commanders will hold themselves in readiness for the service as indicated.

"Very respectfully, your obedient servant,
"D. G. FARRAGUT,
"Flag-officer West Gulf Blockading Squadron."

The original and best plan of Farragut was that the heavier vessels of the squadron should lead the attack, as they would more easily overcome any obstruction to be met afloat. According to this plan he was to lead in the "Hartford," being followed immediately by the "Brooklyn," "Richmond," "Pensacola," and "Mississippi." The senior commanders interposed the objection to this that wisdom would not permit the Commander-in-chief to receive the greatest shock of the battle; and he was finally induced, very reluctantly, to consent to an arrangement whereby the fleet would be separated into three divisions, with his immediate position in the centre of the line. Thus formed the vessels were in the following order :

First Division. CAPT. BAILEY.	*Centre Division.* FLAG-OFFICER FARRAGUT.	*Third Division.* CAPT. H. H. BELL.
Cayuga, Pensacola, Mississippi, Oneida, Varuna, Katahdin, Kineo, Wissahickon,	Hartford, Brooklyn, Richmond,	Sciota, Iroquois, Kennebec, Pinola, Itasca, Winona.

Besides this arrangement of the fleet, the mortar-steamers were directed to move forward and be ready to engage the water-battery of Fort Jackson, while the former were passing the forts. The Confederates placed much dependence upon this battery on account of its heavy armament and wide range down the river.

According to signal, on the morning of April 24th, at two o'clock, the Federal fleet commenced to get under way. The Confederates, ever alert, detected the movement, probably from the noise of capstans and cables.

Before following the fleet in its movements, a word in relation to the advantages and disadvantages of each side will not be amiss. One fact was strongly in favor of the fleet, the division of the Confederate defenses into three branches, viz.: the land forces, the regular naval forces, and the river defense—thus preventing concert of action. The odds were against Farragut in all other respects.

The impressions of the French Admiral, and Captain Preedy, of the British Navy, —obtained during a visit to the forts before capture—that it would be an impossibility for the fleet to pass the defenses, did not tend to augment hopes of capture; but the washing away of the obstructions and rafts by the strong current restored confidence, and the advance was made with ardor.

It was half-past two o'clock before the fleet was fully under way. The strong current impeded their progress to such an extent that it lacked but a quarter of three o'clock before the leading vessel, the "Cay-

COMMANDER (NOW REAR-ADMIRAL) CHARLES F. BOGGS,
OF THE "VARUNA."

uga," was under fire. This commenced from both forts simultaneously.

As the fleet advanced, the five mortar-steamers opened fire from their position, two hundred yards from the water-battery of Fort Jackson, quelling its fire by pouring in canister, shrapnel, and grape, while the mortars threw in their bombs with great fury.

Captain Bailey's division, led by the "Cayuga," passed the line of obstructions in close order, but from this point the vessels were somewhat damaged by the heavy fire of St. Philip before it was possible for them to reply. Captain Bailey kept on steadily in the "Cayuga" and ran the

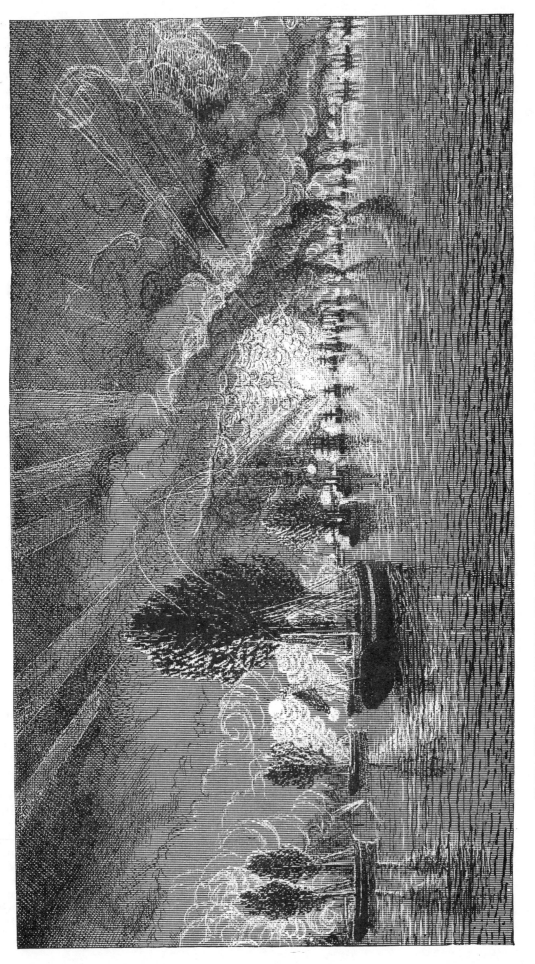

FARRAGUT'S FLEET PROCEEDING UP THE MISSISSIPPI RIVER PAST FORTS JACKSON AND ST. PHILIP.

PORTER'S MORTAR FLOTILLA IN THE FOREGROUND (DRESSED WITH TREES) BOMBARDING FORT JACKSON.

(FROM A SKETCH BY REAR-ADMIRAL WALKE, U. S. NAVY.)

gauntlet safely, pouring in a destructive fire of grape and canister as his guns could be brought to bear.

Above the forts the enemy's gun-boats were congregated, and several of them made a dash at the "Cayuga" at once, but were driven off, the "Oneida" and "Varuna" coming to her assistance, and, by their rapid and heavy fire, dispersing the opposing vessels. The coolness and discipline of the Union vessels here showed to great advantage, while this work was more congenial than that of battling with forts.

The leading division continued on up the river, engaging everything that was met, most of the enemy's vessels being disabled by the time the centre division had passed the forts, and the action decided in favor of the Federal fleet.

Colonel Higgins, of Fort Jackson, admitted this when he saw the large ships of the Flag-officer's division pass, exclaiming: "Better go to cover, boys; our cake is all dough! the old Navy has won!"

The "Varuna," Com. Boggs, of the first division, being a fast vessel, had out-stripped all her consorts, and chased the enemy alone until she found herself surrounded by them. Supposing her to be one of their own vessels, in the darkness, the Confederates did not attack the "Varuna" until Com. Boggs apprised them of his identity by a rapid fire from both sides. Three of the enemy were driven ashore in flames, and one large steamer with troops on board drifted ashore with an exploded boiler from this encounter. At daylight the "Varuna" suffered a double attack from the "Governor Moore" and the "Stonewall Jackson."

The former, a powerful vessel, fitted as a ram, was commanded by Lieut. Beverly Kennon, formerly of the U. S. Navy. This vessel ranged up on the quarter of the "Varuna" and raked her along the port gangway with her bow-gun, killing some five or six men; also ramming her. Engaging this enemy, the "Varuna" was exposed to a blow from the ram "Stonewall Jackson," which penetrated her starboard side below water. A second blow was planted in the same place, but the enemy was exposed to a destructive fire of grape and canister from the "Varuna's" eight-inch guns, and finally hauled off, disabled and on fire. But the "Varuna" had received her death wound, was filling rapidly, and to save life her gallant commander headed her for shoal water where she soon sank; the officers and crew being rescued by the "Oneida" and "Pensacola."

Both the attacking vessels in this spirited engagement were fired by the crews, and abandoned.

The conflict of vessels above the forts was mainly between the small vessels of both sides, and great skill and gallantry were exhibited on either side.

Bailey's division may be said to have swept the way. The gunners of Fort St. Philip were driven to shelter by the heavy batteries of the "Pensacola" and "Mississippi," and the difficulties of the rear ships diminished.

Most of the injuries inflicted upon the fleet were from St. Philip, which had not been exposed to the bombardment as had Fort Jackson.

The Flag-officer, in the centre division, came abreast the forts as Bailey's division reached the turn in the river above. The "Hartford" and "Brooklyn" kept the line, but the "Richmond" had fallen out, and passed up on the west or right bank. Before this time the Fort Jackson garrison had been nearly all driven from their guns by the fire of the mortar-steamers at the water-battery, and the bombs from the schooners, while the river had been illuminated by two fire-rafts, and the brightness as of day revealed everything distinctly.

The difficulty of keeping a line of seventeen vessels of various degrees of speed in close order, against a three-and-a-half knot current in an irregular channel, can be readily appreciated, and it is not singular that some of Farragut's fleet "broke line" under the trying circumstances of the hour. The "Iroquois," under Com. De Camp, a very gallant officer, diverged from the line, and being very swift, passed ahead of the vessels of her division. Above Fort Jackson, from which she did not receive a single shot, though passing its levee within fifty yards, the "Iroquois" was attacked by a ram and the gun-boat "McRea," both of which were driven off, and the commander of the latter (Lieut. Huger), mortally wounded.

The "Iroquois" suffered much loss and was considerably cut up in her actions with the gun-boats and Fort St. Philip.

As Farragut engaged Fort St. Philip at close quarters, the Confederate gunners were again driven to shelter by the fire of his heavy ships, but an attack of another kind was now made upon the "Hartford," his flag-ship. The Confederate tug "Mosher," commanded by a brave fellow named Sherman, pushed a burning raft alongside the Union vessel, which vainly tried to avoid the contact by porting her helm. This brought her upon a shoal, and to a standstill. The fire-raft was shoved against the port side, while the flames threatened the entire destruction of the ship. But there was no confusion, the starboard battery continued to engage Fort St. Philip, while the firemen fought the blaze that had caught upon the side and rigging. The

"Hartford" succeeded in backing off the shoal, the raft was turned adrift, the flames extinguished, and the advance taken up as before. The situation had been one of great peril, but Farragut was the great commander throughout. Walking the poop coolly, he allowed the fire to be fought by Commander Wainwright and his men. The fire was a sharp one; and, at times, rushing through the ports would drive the men back from the guns. Seeing this, Farragut called out, "Don't flinch from that fire, boys; there's a hotter fire than that for those who don't do their duty! Give that rascally little tug a shot, and don't let her get off with a whole coat!"

The tug did escape from the "Hartford," though by Confederate accounts she was destroyed during the fight.

The loss to the "Hartford" in the passage

Much of this engagement, it must be remembered, was fought in darkness, except for the light emitted by the flashes of the guns through the smoke-clouded air, and the ships groped their way by these uncertain guides.

Passing the forts the "Brooklyn" was attacked by a large steamer at a distance of not more than fifty or sixty yards. A single broadside from the sloop's heavy battery, drove her out of action in flames.

The "Brooklyn" received but seventeen hits in the hull, during the heavy fire to which she was subjected, but these did much execution, nine men being killed and twenty-six wounded.

The fleet's success was virtually decided when the large ships had passed the forts, and the head of the third division under Captain Bell found but comparatively slight

CAPTAIN BAILEY'S DIVISION MEETING THE ENEMY'S FLOTILLA ABOVE THE FORTS.

of the forts was three killed and ten wounded, with thirty-two shot in hull and rigging.

The "Hartford" was followed as closely as possible by the "Brooklyn," Captain Thomas T. Craven; the smoke from rafts and guns rendered this very difficult, but the sweeping fire of the "Hartford" was supplemented by hers, and she passed the forts in safety, to be attacked, however, immediately after, by the little ram, "Manassas," the most troublesome vessel in the Confederate service, not excepting the "Louisiana"—as she behaved in the action.

Commanded by Lieutenant Warley, a gallant young officer, formerly of the U. S. Navy, this craft made directly for the "Brooklyn's" starboard-side, but inflicted only slight damage. A second attack gave the same result, for the chain protection to the machinery saved the "Brooklyn," and the ram glanced off into the darkness.

resistance to the passage of his leading vessel, the "Sciota."

Farragut's first intention, to place the heavy ships in the van, would probably have resulted in the immediate crushing of the enemy, and the rear of his line would have followed a *beaten* path.

With the exception of the "Itasca," Lieutenant Caldwell; the "Winona," Lieutenant Nichols; and the "Kennebec," Lieutenant Russell, the fleet succeeded in passing the forts

The "Itasca" was much cut up, and having a shot through her boiler, was compelled to drop down the river, out of action, after which she was run ashore to prevent sinking. Fourteen shot and shell had passed through her hull, but the list of casualties was small.

The "Kennebec" and "Winona," being at the end of the line, had been left below the forts at daylight, and were there exposed to the fire of both works, with small ability to reply. Being slow vessels, with a rapid current against them, they were long exposed to the deliberate practice of the enemy and were obliged to haul out of action below. The demoralization of the enemy was evident, however, from their escape.

No grander or more beautiful sight could have been realized than the scenes of that night. From silence, disturbed now and then only by the slow fire of the mortars, —the phantom-like movements of the vessels giving no sound—an increased roar of heavy guns began, while the mortars burst forth into rapid bombardment, as the fleet drew near the enemy's works. Vessel after vessel added her guns to those already at work, until the very earth seemed to shake

LIEUT. (NOW COMMODORE) W. W. QUEEN.

(COMMANDING A DIVISION OF MORTAR FLOTILLA.)

from their reverberations. A burning raft adding its lurid glare to the scene, and the fiery tracks of the mortar-shells as they passed through the darkness aloft, and sometimes burst in mid-air, gave the impression that heaven itself had joined in the general strife. The succeeding silence was almost as sudden. From the weighing of the anchors, one hour and ten minutes saw the vessels by the forts, and Farragut on his way to New Orleans, the prize staked upon the fierce game of war just ended.

As the fleet was approaching quarantine, some distance above the forts, the "Manassas," the most active and troublesome of the Confederate fleet, was seen, in the early daylight, coming up river in chase. The Flag-officer directed Commander Smith to leave the line with the "Mississippi," and run the ram down.

The "Mississippi" turned instantly and started for the enemy at full speed. The "Manassas" had evidently practiced her parts before, for, shifting her helm quickly when but a short distance from the big vessel's bow, she dodged the blow, but in so doing ran ashore, where she was deserted by her crew.

Commander Smith wished to preserve the "Manassas," but was obliged to recall the boats sent to secure her, on account of a burning wreck approaching him. The ram was therefore set on fire, and riddled with shot, after which she drifted away from the bank, and finally blew up below the forts.

This ended the irregular fighting with the Confederate vessels; ten of them had been sunk or destroyed, while the "Varuna," with her two adversaries, lay at the bottom of the river near the bank, evidence of the gallantry of Boggs.

After the fleet had passed the forts, there remained no necessity for the presence of the mortar-flotilla steamers off the water-battery. They accordingly dropped down the river to the position of the mortar-schooners, and the signal made the latter to cease firing.

The situation of the vessels left below the forts seemed far from secure. The ironclad, "Louisiana," was still at her moorings, uninjured, and three other vessels of war could be seen moving from one side of the river to the other. Their character could not be ascertained, but presuming they were gun-boats, with the assistance of their huge consort they were more than a match for the Union vessels if properly handled.

Commander Porter took immediate steps to meet contingencies. The failure of the "Itasca," "Kennebec" and "Winona" to pass the batteries had added the two latter to his force (the "Itasca" being disabled), which now amounted to seven effective gun-boats; these he at once prepared for emergencies. His plan, in case of attack, was to place as many as possible of the vessels alongside the "Louisiana," have each one make fast to her, let go two anchors, and then "fight it out on that line."

No attack was made, however, and the iron-clad lost an opportunity to strike a final blow, which she could have inflicted even with her machinery in a defective condition.

Meanwhile Farragut had passed on up the river, leaving one or two gun-boats to guard the lazaretto. The right-of-way was disputed at Jackson's old battle ground of January 8, 1815, by the Chalmette batteries.

These works—on both sides of the river—mounted twenty heavy guns, and were prepared to receive the approaching vessels, coming up in two columns at their best speed. The vessels that had passed the forts below, gave short account of these batteries, though the work was very sharp while it lasted, especially on account of the time during which the slow ships were held under a raking fire.

From this point resistance ceased, and about noon on the 25th of April, the fleet anchored off New Orleans, which the retreat of General Lovell left defenseless and in the hands of the civil authorities.

Lieut. Com. John Guest was sent at noon of the 25th to Fort Jackson under a flag of truce, to call upon the Confederate commander, in view of the uselessness of further bloodshed, to surrender the forts and the remnants of the Confederate Navy at the place, as Farragut had passed up the river with little loss, and was probably then in New Orleans.

General Duncan replied very civilly, but declined to surrender before hearing from the city. Immediately upon the receipt of this reply by Commander Porter, a very rapid mortar-fire was opened upon Fort Jackson.

The effect was such as to cause a mutiny among the garrison, who refused to longer undergo the probability of useless slaughter, and many deserted from the works and retreated up river out of range. The remainder refused to fight the guns, and reasoned that as they had unflinchingly borne the terrible six days' bombardment, and had exposed themselves to the night ordeal of the fire of the passing fleet, it was time the fort should be surrendered without further loss of life.

The bombardment was continued during the afternoon until the shells were exhausted, and on the following day (the 26th) the schooners were got under way and sent to Pilotstown to replenish their ammunition. Six were ordered thereafter to cross the bar at Southwest Pass and proceed to the rear of Fort Jackson, holding themselves in readiness for any service.

At midnight of the 28th, General Duncan sent an officer on board the "Harriet Lane" to inform Commander Porter of his willingness to capitulate.

On the following day Commander Porter with nine gun-boats, proceeded up river to Fort Jackson, under a flag of truce, and upon his arrival a boat was sent for the commanding officer of the river defenses, and such other officers as he might desire to have accompany him. These officers were received on board with all the respect due to brave men, and they bore themselves accordingly, though there must have been a mortification in surrendering to what was, in many respects, an inferior force. At the time of the capitulation, however, the Federal officers knew nothing of the internal troubles which had immediately

induced the surrender—the mutiny and desertion of the men, and the final strokes of the fleet above. In any case, whether Farragut had succeeded or failed in his operations above, it was important to obtain possession of the forts as early as possible, and to that end terms of capitulation had been already prepared, and these were accepted by General Duncan and Lieut. Col. Higgins.

As the terms were being signed, Porter found, to his surprise, that the capitulation of the defenses was not to include those afloat, General Duncan asserting that he had no authority whatever over the naval branch. The commander of the regular

COMMANDER (NOW ADMIRAL) DAVID D. PORTER.

naval forces (Commander Mitchell) had, in fact, set the military at defiance. Porter waived the point, however, being determined upon the course to pursue when possession of the forts was secured.

All connected with the capitulation were seated at the table on board the "Harriet Lane," with the articles before them. Porter had signed them, as had Commander Renshaw, of the "Westfield." Lieut. Com. Wainwright, of the "Harriet Lane," was about to follow with his signature, when one of his officers requested him urgently to come on deck. He returned at once with the report that the "Louisiana" was drifting down river on fire, coming toward the Union vessels which were anchored about thirty yards apart. Being broadside to the current the iron-clad would not have room to pass.

"This is sharp practice," Porter remarked to the Confederate officers, "but if *you* can stand the explosion when it comes, we can. We will go on, and finish the capitulation.' He then gave Lieutenant Wainwright orders to pass the word to each of the other vessels to veer to the end of their chains, and to use steam in sheering clear of the burning wreck if necessary, but not to leave the anchorage. The pen was then handed to General Duncan and to Colonel Higgins, the boldness of whose signatures gave no evidence of the proximity of a possibly fatal explosion.

COMMANDER JOHN K. MITCHELL.

(COMMANDER OF THE CONFEDERATE NAVAL FORCES IN THE MISSISSIPPI.)

The signatures being duly attached, all awaited quietly the result, which was not long delayed, the explosion taking place with a shock that fairly unseated the expectant officers, and threw the "Harriet Lane" well over to port. The capitulation was regularly finished, despite the interruption.

The "Louisiana" had fortunately exploded before reaching the line of vessels, and injured nothing but Fort St. Philip, at which one man was killed.

The action of the Confederate naval officers in destroying the "Louisiana" was severely censured by those of the army. The latter assured the Federal officers that they felt in no way responsible, as the vessel was entirely under Commander Mitchell's control.

The Federal commander was much disappointed in the loss of the "Louisiana," as he had calculated upon her usefulness against her former owners in operations further up the river.

Within ten minutes after the departure of the Confederate officers, the colors of the forts were hauled down, and both works delivered over to the officers appointed to receive them. The enemy's flag was still shown on the river, however, for Commander Mitchell, after setting fire to the "Louisiana," transferred his crew to a river steamer, and made for the opposite bank, a mile or so above the forts.

As soon as General Duncan had left the "Harriet Lane," Commander Porter, to whom Mitchell's movements had been reported, ordered Lieutenant Wainwright to get under way and beat to quarters Steering directly for the vessel carrying Mitchell's flag, the "Harriet Lane" sent a shot at the flag-pole, but the hint was taken and the colors hauled down at once. Lieutenant Wainwright was sent aboard the steamer to take possession. He was met by Commander Mitchell, and requested to extend the same terms as had been granted the officers and men of the forts. Mitchell was given to understand that no terms would be extended him or his officers, that they would be held close prisoners to answer for a violation of a flag of truce, and that all would be sent to the North.

In a communication made to Commander Porter, Mitchell at once removed the responsibility for the act from all but three or four officers. The prisoners were sent up river to Flag-officer Farragut for his disposition, but though afterward sent to the North, and held in confinement for some time, nothing was done to the guilty actors, and the matter finally dropped.

After all the defenses were in Union hands Commander Porter dispatched a steamer to the bar, and brought up a vessel of General Butler's expedition, having on board General Phelps with a number of infantry, to whom the forts were turned over.

The total loss in the fleet during these engagements was 35 killed, and 128 wounded. The chief sufferers were the "Pensacola," 37; "Brooklyn," 35; and the "Iroquois," 28.

The rising sun, the morning after the fight, shone on smiling faces, even among the wounded. Farragut received the congratulations of his officers, as he had conducted the great fight, with imperturbility. He wasted no time in vain regrets over the saddening features of his victory, but making the signal "Push on to New Orleans," seemed to forget the imperishable fame he had won, while in thought he was following up his great victory to the end.

The two following letters were issued by

the Hon. Gideon Welles on receiving the announcement of the important victory at New Orleans, and he expressed his feelings and those of the Union people in terms not only felicitous, but worthy to be engraved in letters of gold. This victory was the first great blow the enemy had received; it was the step towards dividing the slave territory and separating the two parts by a great river, on the bosom of which the Navy could advance with its gun-boats, and with their heavy guns bring the people along the banks of the Mississippi to a sense of their obligations to the Government. It was the wedge that had been driven into the vitals of the rebellion that would finally tear it asunder, and it was a blow that had been dealt by the Navy alone. It fact, it was a blow that shortened the war one-half, and which rung through Europe in unmistakable language, giving the world to understand that we were determined to hold the legitimate property of the Government in defiance of English threats or French intrigues, and that the Navy, even with its paucity of ships and guns, would again assert its power, energy and devotion to the flag which had always characterised it since we first became a nation.

The praise bestowed on the officers and sailors of the fleet by the Secretary of the Navy was nothing more than their due, and the votes of thanks which were sent from the halls of Congress would have been more acceptable if that body had not hesitated for so many years to do justice to the fleet by voting them the prize-money they were legally entitled to, and which they had won by a valor never surpassed—those to whom this would have been a boon died before the money was appropriated, and even Farragut did not live to receive all that was due him.

"Navy Department,
  May 10, 1862.

" Sir—Captain Bailey, your second in command, has brought to the department the official despatches from your squadron, with the trophies forwarded to the national capital.

" Our Navy, fruitful with victories, presents no more signal achievements than this, nor is there an exploit surpassing it recorded in the annals of naval warfare. In passing, and eventually overcoming Forts Jackson and St. Philip, the batteries above and below New Orleans, destroying the barriers of chains, steam-rams, fire-rafts, iron-clad vessels, and other obstructions, capturing from the Confederate forces the great southern metropolis, and obtaining possession and control of the Lower Mississippi, yourself, your officers, and our brave sailors and marines, whose courage and daring bear historic renown, have won a nation's gratitude and applause. I congratulate you and your command on your great success in having contributed so largely towards destroying the unity of the rebellion, and in restoring again to the protection of the national government and the national flag the important city of the Mississippi valley, and so large a portion of its immediate dependencies.

" Your example and its successful results, though attended with some sacrifice of life and loss of ships, inculcate the fact that the first duty of a commander in war is to take great risks for the accomplishment of great ends.

" One and all, officers and men, composing your command, deserve well of their country.

" I am, respectfully, your obedient servant,
     " (Signed)   " Gideon Welles.
" Flag-officer D. G. Farragut,
     " Commanding Western Gulf Blockading
        " Squadron, New Orleans."

                              " Navy Department,
                                 May 10, 1862.

" Sir—Your dispatch of April 30, inclosing the articles of capitulation of Forts Jackson and St. Philip, which surrendered on the 28th, after a bombardment of one hundred and forty-four consecutive hours by the mortar flotilla, has been received. I have also to acknowledge the receipt of the flags taken in the two forts on that occasion, including the original one hoisted on Fort St. Philip when the Confederate forces declared the State of Louisiana to have seceded from the Union, which have been sent forward to the Department.

" The important part which you have borne in the organization of the mortar flotilla, and the movement on New Orleans, had identified your name with one of the most brilliant naval achievements on record ; and to your able assistance with the flotilla is Flag-officer Farragut much indebted for the successful results he has accomplished. To yourself and the officers and seamen of the mortar flotilla the Department extends its congratulations.   " I am, respectfully,
                              " Gideon Welles.
" Commander David D. Porter,
     " Commanding U. S. Mortar Flotilla, etc., etc.'

CHAPTER XIX.

BATTLE OF THE FORTS AND CAPTURE OF NEW ORLEANS.

INTERESTING REPORTS OF FLAG-OFFICER FARRAGUT; CAPTAINS BAILEY, BELL, MORRIS, CRAVEN; COMMANDERS WAINWRIGHT, LEE, SMITH, BOGGS, DE CAMP, ALDEN, NICHOLS, CALDWELL, PORTER, MITCHELL, AND OTHERS. OFFICIAL LETTERS OF GIDEON WELLES, MAYOR MONROE, AND THE CITY COUNCIL OF NEW ORLEANS, ETC.

IT is desirable in *some* respects to make this a book of reference, especially in regard to official letters, which seldom or ever are seen by the public, the several reports of Admiral Farragut, also those of his officers, contain details of the battle at the forts, and of the capture of New Orleans, which can best be told by those who were participators in those stirring scenes, and they are appended to the general account of the battle. In the course of a few years these letters will become inaccessible, except from the files of the Navy Department, and they should be treasured as the ground-work of the history of the most important naval battle of modern times,—we do not think any excuse is needed for inserting them here.

COMMENCEMENT AND PROGRESS OF THE BOMBARDMENT OF FORT JACKSON.

UNITED STATES FLAG-SHIP "HARTFORD,"
MISSISSIPPI RIVER, April 2, 1862.

SIR—We commenced the bombardment of Fort Jackson on the 16th, which was the earliest day possible after the arrival of coal. On the first day the citadel was set on fire, and burnt until two o'clock the next morning. On the 17th we made but little apparent impression on the fort.

On the 18th we dismounted one of their heavy Columbiads and otherwise appeared to damage them, and drove the men from the parapet guns, so that they only appeared occasionally when the gun-boats took part in the bombardment to draw the fire from the bomb vessels. On the 19th a

deserter came to us from the fort, and gave the information that I have stated above, and much other information in relation to the armament of the forts and their general condition.

The wind was blowing from the northwest, and chilly, the current running with great strength, so that the ships, when under way, could scarcely stem it, so that I shall await a change of wind and a consequent less violent current before I attack the forts, as I find great difficulty in avoiding collisions among the vessels. Two of the gun-boats, "Katahdin" and "Sciota," have been seriously damaged by getting across-hawse of the ships and running into each other. We lose a great many anchors and cables, and those articles are very much wanted in the squadron. The "Hartford" is almost the only ship that has not lost both.

On the first day's fire of the enemy they put a shot through one of the mortar vessels and killed one man but did not destroy her efficiency. The second day they sunk one with a rifle shot, but hurt no one materially. They have sent down five fire-rafts; none produced any effect on the fleet except the last, which only caused the collision of the "Sciota" and "Kineo," both of which vessels dragged across the bows of the "Mississippi," and carried away the mainmast of the first, and damaged them both very much otherwise; the raft was turned clear of all the vessels of the fleet, but as the wind and strong current were peculiarly favorable, it gave us more trouble than on any former occasion.

I sent up Commander Bell last evening to destroy the chain and raft across the river, but the current was so strong that he could accomplish but little, in consequence of one of his gun-boats getting on shore, and she was only saved by great exertion, as the enemy was firing on them all the time.

Commander Porter, however, kept up such a tremendous fire on them from the mortars that the enemy's shot did the gun-boats no injury, and the cable was separated and their connection broken sufficiently to pass through on the left bank of the river. The petard operator failed to fire his petards, owing to the breaking of his wires, which prevented the full destruction of the chain and the vessels; but great allowance is to be made for the violence of the current, which exceeds anything we have had to contend with since our arival in the river.

In conclusion, I regret to say that the fleet is in want of all the essentials to carry on our work—shells, fuses (15" and 20",) serge and yarn, to make cartridge-bags, grape and canister shot—for all of which I made large requisitions, and the articles may be on their way out.

The medical department is miserably supplied for the care of the wounded. General Butler has offered to share with us, in fact, everything he has, which will supply many of our wants; but justice to myself requires me to say that I required all these supplies some time before I left Hampton Roads, and others immediately on my arrival at Key West or Ship Island, and I suppose accidental causes have stopped them on their way out here.*

My coal arrived just in time.

All of which is respectfully submitted by your obedient servant,

D. G. FARRAGUT, *Flag-officer,*
Western Gulf Blockading Squadron.

Hon. GIDEON WELLES,
Secretary of the Navy, Washington, D. C.

ATTACK ON FORTS JACKSON AND ST. PHILIP.

UNITED STATES FLAG-SHIP "HARTFORD,"
AT ANCHOR OFF NEW ORLEANS,
April 25, 1862.

SIR—I have the honor to inform the department that on the 24th instant, at about half-past 3 A. M., I attacked Fort St. Philip and Fort Jackson with my little fleet, while Commander Porter most gallantly bombarded them, and, besides, took them in the flank with his steamers, aided by the

"Portsmouth." Such a fire I imagine, the world has rarely seen, but, thank God, we got past the forts with a loss of only twenty-four killed and eighty-six wounded; but as I have not heard what became of the three gun-boats, "Kennebec," "Itasca," and "Winona," I fear they were lost in passing, and the "Varuna" was run into by two of the Confederate steamers, and finally sunk: I took (and burnt) eleven steam gun-boats, and two hundred troops or upwards. I then pushed up for the city of New Orleans, leaving two gun-boats to aid General Butler in landing at the quarantine, and sent him a communication by Commander Boggs, requesting him to come up at once. I came up to within six or seven miles of the city, when two forts opened on us, but we silenced them in fifteen or twenty minutes, although it was warm work while it lasted. I have not yet heard of the killed and wounded. We only lost one man and none wounded, although Captain Bailey, in the "Cayuga," with Lieut. Com. Harrison, and this ship, stood the first brunt of the action, before the other vessels could get up. We drove them from their guns, and passed up to the city in fine style, and I now send this notice of our having taken possession of the city at meridian or a few minutes P. M.

But I must say I never witnessed such vandalism in my life as the destruction of property; all the shipping, steamboats, etc., were set on fire and consumed. The new iron-clad ram, just finished, but without her machinery, went floating by us. While I am finishing this report, Captain Bailey has been sent to demand the surrender of the city to me in the name of the United States.

I shall now send down with this letter Commander Smith, in the "Mississippi," to look after General Butler, and a ram, which it appears we left behind at Fort Jackson, as it might be more than a match for the two gun-boats I left behind.

In conclusion, I hope I have done all I proposed to do, which was, to take the city of New Orleans; and I will now, in conjunction with the Army, General Butler, reduce the forts, and take care of the outlet from the west, and purpose immediately to ascend to meet Flag-officer Foote.

The conduct of the officers and men has been such as to command my highest admiration, and shall hereafter be a subject of more special commendation.

I am, very respectfully, your obedient servant,

D. G. FARRAGUT, *Flag-officer,*
Western Gulf Blockading Squadron.

Hon. GIDEON WELLES,
Secretary of the Navy, Washington, D. C.

---

* The ordnance and hospital stores were shipped on the United States steamer "Kensington," which was prevented by bad weather, breaking of machinery, and other causes, from reaching her destination as early as designed. She arrived, however, in season.

ANNOUNCEMENT OF THE CAPTURE OF FORTS JACKSON AND ST. PHILIP AND SURRENDER OF NEW ORLEANS.

UNITED STATES FLAG-SHIP "HARTFORD,"
AT ANCHOR OFF NEW ORLEANS,
April 29, 1862.

SIR—I am happy to announce to you that our flag waves over both Forts Jackson and St. Philip, and at New Orleans over the custom-house. I am taking every means to secure the occupation by General Butler of all the forts along the coast. Berwick's Bay and Fort Pike have been abandoned; in fact, there is a general stampede, and I shall endeavor to follow it up. * *

I am bringing up the troops as fast as possible. We have destroyed all the forts above the city, four in number; which are understood to be all the impediments between this and Memphis.

I am, very respectfully, your obedient servant,

D. G. FARRAGUT, *Flag-officer,*
Western Gulf Blockading Squadron.
Hon. GIDEON WELLES,
Secretary of the Navy, Washington, D. C.

———

FLAG-OFFICER FARRAGUT'S DETAILED REPORT OF THE BATTLES OF THE MISSISSIPPI.

UNITED STATES FLAG-SHIP "HARTFORD,"
AT ANCHOR OFF NEW ORLEANS,
May 6, 1862.

SIR—I have the honor herewith to forward my report, in detail, of the battle of New Orleans. On the 23d of March I made all my arrangements for the attack on, and passage of, Forts Jackson and St. Philip.

Every vessel was as well prepared as the ingenuity of her commander and officers could suggest, both for the preservation of life and of the vessel, and, perhaps, there is not on record such a display of ingenuity as has been evinced in this little squadron. The first was by the engineer of the "Richmond," Mr. Moore, by suggesting that the sheet cables be stopped up and down on the sides in the line of the engines, which was immediately adopted by all the vessels. Then each commander made his own arrangements for stopping the shot from penetrating the boilers and machinery that might come in forward or abaft, by hammocks, coal, bags of ashes, bags of sand, clothes bags, and, in fact, every device imaginable. The bulwarks were lined with hammocks by some, by splinter nettings made with ropes by others. Some rubbed their vessels over with mud to make their ships less visible, and some whitewashed their decks, to make things more visible by night during the fight, all of which you will find mentioned in the reports of the commanders. In the afternoon I visited

each ship, in order to know positively that each commander understood my orders for the attack, and see that all was in readiness. I had looked to their efficiency before. Every one appeared to understand their orders well, and looked forward to the conflict with firmness, but with anxiety, as it was to be in the night, or at 2 o'clock A. M.

I had previously sent Capt. Bell, with the petard man, with Lieut. Com. Crosby, in the "Pinola," and Lieut. Com. Caldwell, in the "Itasca," to break the chain which crossed the river, and was supported by eight hulks, which were strongly moored. This duty was not thoroughly performed, in consequence of the failure to ignite the petards with the galvanic battery and the great strength of the current. Still, it was a success, and under the circumstances, a highly meritorious one.

The vessel boarded by Lieut. Com. Caldwell appears to have had her chains so secured that they could be cast loose, which was done by that officer, and thereby making an opening sufficiently large for the ships to pass through. It was all done under a heavy fire and at a great hazard to the vessel, for the particulars of which I refer you to Captain Bell's report (marked A). Upon the night preceding the attack, however, I despatched Lieut. Com. Caldwell to make an examination, and to see that the passage was still clear, and to make me a signal to that effect, which he did at an early hour. The enemy commenced sending down fire-rafts and lighting their fires on the shore opposite the chain about the same time, which drew their fire on Lieut. Com. Caldwell, but without injury. At about five minutes to two o'clock A. M., April 24, signal was made to get under way (two ordinary red lights, so as not to attract the attention of the enemy), but owing to the great difficulty in purchasing their anchors, the "Pensacola" and some of the other vessels were not under way until half-past three. We then advanced in two columns, Captain Bailey leading the right in the gun-boat "Cayuga," Lieut. Com. Harrison, he having been assigned to the first division of gun-boats, which was to attack Fort St. Philip in conjunction with the second division of ships, and the "Hartford," the left; Fleet Captain Bell leading the second division of gun-boats in the "Sciota;" Lieut. Com. Donaldson to assist the first division of ships to attack Fort Jackson, as will be shown by the general order and diagram sent herewith. The enemy's lights, while they discovered us to them, were, at the same time, guides to us. We soon passed the barrier chains, the right column taking Fort St. Philip, and the left Fort Jackson. The fire became general, the smoke dense, and we had nothing to aim at but the flash of their guns; it was very difficult to distinguish friends from foes. Captain Porter had, by arrangement, moved up to a certain point on the Fort Jackson side with his gun-boats, and I had assigned the same post to Captain Swartwout, in the "Portsmouth," to engage the water batteries to the southward and eastward of Fort Jackson, while his mortar-vessels poured a terrific fire of shells into it. I discovered a fire-raft coming down upon us, and in attempting to avoid it ran the ship on shore, and the ram "Manassas," which I had not seen, lay on the opposite of it, and pushed it down upon us. Our ship was soon on fire half-way up to her tops, but we backed off, and through the good organization of our fire department, and the great exertions of Captain Wainwright and his first lieutenant, officers and crew, the fire was extinguished. In the meantime our battery was never silent, but poured in its missiles of death into Fort St. Philip, opposite to which he had got by this time, and it was silenced, with the exception of a gun now and then. By this time the enemy's gun-boats, some thirteen in number, besides two iron-clad rams, the "Manassas" and "Louisiana," had become more visible. We took them in hand, and, in the course of time destroyed eleven of them. We were now fairly past the forts and the victory was ours, but still here and there a gun-boat making resistance. Two of them had attacked the "Varuna," which vessel, by her greater speed, was much in advance of us; they ran into her and caused her to sink, but not before she had destroyed her adversaries, and their wrecks now lie side by side, a monument to the gallantry of Captain Boggs, his officers and crew. It was a kind of guerrilla warfare; they were fighting in all directions. Captains Bailey and Bell, who were in command of the first and second divisions of gun-boats, were as active in rendering assistance in every direction as lay in their power. Just as the scene appeared to be closing, the ram "Manassas" was seen coming up under full speed to attack us. I directed Captain Smith, in the "Mississippi," to turn and run her down; the order was instantly obeyed by the "Mississippi" turning and going at her at full speed. Just as we expected to see the ram annihilated, when within fifty yards of each other, she put her helm hard a-port, dodged the "Mississippi," and ran ashore. The "Mississippi" poured two broadsides into her, and sent her drifting down the river a total wreck. This closed our morning's fight.

The department will perceive that after the organization and arrangements had been made, and we had fairly entered into the fight, the density of the smoke from guns and fire-rafts, the scenes passing on board our own ship and around us (for it was as if the artillery of heaven were playing upon the earth), that it was impossible for the Flag-officer to see how each vessel was conducting itself, and can only judge by the final results and their special reports, which are herewith enclosed; but I feel that I can say with truth that it has rarely been the lot of a commander to be supported by officers of more indomitable courage or higher professional merit.

Captain Bailey, who had preceded me up the quarantine station, had captured the Chalmette regiment, Colonel Szymanski; and not knowing what to do with them, as every moment was a great loss to me, I paroled both officers and men, and took away all their arms, munitions of war and public property, and ordered them to remain where they were until the next day. I sent some of the gun-boats to precede me up the river, to cut the telegraph wires in different places.

It now became me to look around for my little fleet, and to my regret I found that three were missing—the "Itasca," "Winona," and "Kennebec." Various were the speculations as to their fate, whether they had been sunk on the passage or had put back. I therefore determined immediately to send Captain Boggs, whose vessel was now sunk, through the quarantine bayou, around to Commander Porter, telling him of our safe arrival, and to demand the surrender of the forts, and to endeavor to get some tidings of the missing vessels. I also sent a despatch by him to General Butler, informing him that the way was clear for him to land his forces through the quarantine bayou, in accordance with previous arrangements, and that I should leave gun-boats there to protect him against the enemy, who I now perceived had three or four gun-boats left at the forts—the "Louisiana," an iron-clad battery of 16 guns; the "McCrea," very similar in appearance to one of our gunboats, and armed very much in the same way; the "Defiance," and a river steamer transport.

We then proceeded up to New Orleans, leaving the "Wissahicon" and "Kineo" to protect the landing of the General's troops. Owing to the slowness of some of the vessels, and our want of knowledge of the river, we did not reach the English Turn until about 10:30 A. M. on the 25th; but all the morning I had seen abundant evidence of the panic which had seized the people in New Orleans. Cotton-loaded ships on fire came floating down, and working implements of every kind, such as are used in ship-yards. The destruction of property was awful. We soon descried the new earthwork forts on the old lines on both shores.

We now formed and advanced in the same order, two lines, each line taking its respective work. Captain Bailey was still far in advance, not having noticed my signal for close order, which was to enable the slow vessels to come up. They opened on him a galling fire, which caused us to run up to his rescue; this gave them the advantage of a raking fire on us for upwards of a mile, with some twenty guns, while we had but two 9-inch guns on our forecastle to reply to them. It was not long, however, before we were enabled to bear away and give the forts a broadside of shell, shrapnel and grape, the "Pensacola" at the same time passing up and giving a tremendous broadside of the same kind to the starboard fort; and by the time we could reload, the "Brooklyn," Captain Craven, passed handsomely between us and the battery and delivered her broadside and shut us out. By this time the other vessels had gotten up, and ranged in one after another, delivering their broadsides in spiteful revenge for the ill-treatment of the little "Cayuga." The forts were silenced, and those who could run were running in every direction. We now passed up to the city and anchored immediately in front of it, and I sent Captain Bailey on shore to demand the surrender of it from the authorities, to which the Mayor replied that the city was under martial law, and that he had no authority. General Lovell, who was present, stated that he should deliver up nothing, but in order to free the city from embarrassment he would restore the city authorities, and retire with his troops, which he did. The correspondence with the city authorities and myself is herewith annexed. I then seized all the steamboats and sent them down to quarantine for General Butler's forces. Among the number of these boats is the famous "Tennessee," which our blockaders have been so long watching, but which, you will perceive, never got out.

The levee of New Orleans was one scene of desolation. Ships, steamers, cotton, coal, etc., were all in one common blaze, and our ingenuity was much taxed to avoid the floating conflagration.

I neglected to mention my having good information respecting the iron-clad rams which they were building. I sent Captain Lee up to seize the principal one, the "Mississippi," which was to be the terror of these seas, and no doubt would have been to a great extent; but she came floating by us all in flames, and passed down the river. Another was sunk immediately in front of the custom house; others were building in Algiers, just begun.

I next went above the city eight miles, to Carrolton, where I learned there were two other forts, but the panic had gone before me. I found the guns spiked, and the gun-carriages in flames. The first work, on the right reaches from the Mississippi nearly over to Pontchartrain, and has 29 guns; the one on the left had six guns, from which Commander Lee took some fifty barrels of powder, and completed the destruction of the gun-carriages, etc. A mile higher up there were two other earthworks, but not yet armed.

We discovered here, fastened to the right bank of the river, one of the most herculean labors I have ever seen—a raft and chain to extend across the river to prevent Foote's gun-boats from descending. It is formed by placing three immense logs of not less than three or four feet in diameter and some thirty feet long; to the centre one a two-inch chain is attached, running lengthwise the raft, and the three logs and chain are then frapped together by chains from one-half to one inch, three or four layers, and there are 96 of these lengths composing the raft; it is at least three-quarters of a mile long.

On the evening of the 29th Captain Bailey arrived from below, with the gratifying intelligence that the forts had surrendered to Commander Porter, and had delivered up all public property, and were being paroled, and that the Navy had been made to surrender unconditionally, as they had conducted themselves with bad faith, burning and sinking their vessels while a flag of truce was flying, and the forts negotiating for their surrender, and the "Louisiana," their great iron-clad battery, blown up almost alongside of the vessel where they were negotiating; hence their officers were not paroled, but sent home to be treated according to the judgment of the Government.

General Butler came up the same day, and arrangements were made for bringing up his troops.

I sent on shore and hoisted the American flag on the custom-house, and hauled down the Louisiana State flag from the city hall, as the mayor had avowed that there was no man in New Orleans who dared to haul it down; and my own convictions are that if such an individual could have been found he would have been assassinated.

Thus, sir, I have endeavored to give you an account of my attack upon New Orleans from our first movement to the surrender of the city to General Butler, whose troops are now in full occupation, protected, however, by the "Pensacola," "Portsmouth," and one gunboat, while I have sent a force of seven vessels, under command of Captain Craven, up the river, to keep up the panic as far as possible. The large ships, I fear, will not be able to go higher than Baton Rouge, while I have sent the smaller vessels, under Commander Lee, as high as

Vicksburg, in the rear of Jackson, to cut off their supplies from the west.

I trust, therefore, that it will be found by the government that I have carried out my instructions to the letter and to the best of my abilities, so far as this city is concerned, which is respectfully submitted.

I am, sir, very respectfully, your obedient servant, D. G. FARRAGUT, *Flag-officer,*
Western Gulf Blockading Squadron.
HON. GIDEON WELLES,
Secretary of the Navy, Washington, D. C.

FLEET-SURGEON J. W. FOLTZ.

CORRESPONDENCE RELATING TO THE SUR-
RENDER OF NEW ORLEANS.

No. 1.

UNITED STATES FLAG-SHIP "HARTFORD."
AT ANCHOR OFF NEW ORLEANS,
April 26, 1862.

SIR : Upon my arrival before your city I had the honor to send to your honor, Captain Bailey, United States navy, second in command of the expedition, to demand of you the surrender of New Orleans to me, as the representative of the government of the United States. Captain Bailey reported to me the result of an interview with yourself and the military authorities. It must oc-

cur to your honor that it is not within the province of a naval officer to assume the duties of a military commandant. I came here to reduce New Orleans to obedience to the laws of, and to vindicate the offended majesty of the United States. The rights of persons and property shall be secure. I therefore demand of you, as its representative, the unqualified surrender of the city, and that the emblem of sovereignty of the United States be hoisted over the city hall, mint, and custom-house by meridian this day, and that all flags and other emblems of sovereignty other than those of the United States shall be removed from all the public buildings by that hour. I particularly request that you shall exercise your authority to quell disturbances, restore order, and call upon all the good people of New Orleans to return at once to their vocations ; and I particularly demand that no person shall be molested in person or property for professing sentiments of loyalty to their government. I shall speedily and severely punish any person or persons who shall commit such outrages as were witnessed yesterday, armed men firing upon helpless women and children for giving expression to their pleasure at witnessing the old flag.

I am, very respectfully, your obedient servant, D. G. FARRAGUT, *Flag-officer,*
Western Gulf Blockading Squadron.
HIS EXCELLENCY THE MAYOR *of the City of New Orleans*

No. 2.

UNITED STATES FLAG-SHIP "HARTFORD,"
AT ANCHOR OFF THE CITY OF NEW OR-
LEANS, April 26, 1862.

Your honor will please give directions that no flag but that of the United States will be permitted to fly in the presence of this fleet so long as it has the power to prevent it ; and as all displays of that kind may be the cause of bloodshed, I have to request that you will give this communication as general a circulation as possible.

I have the honor to be, very respectfully, your obedient servant,

D. G. FARRAGUT, *Flag-officer,*
Western Gulf Blockading Squadron.
HIS HONOR THE MAYOR *of New Orleans.*

No. 3.

General Order.

UNITED STATES FLAG-SHIP "HARTFORD,"
OFF THE CITY OF NEW ORLEANS,
April 26, 1862.

Eleven o'clock this morning is the hour appointed for all the officers and crews of the fleet to return thanks to Almighty God for His great goodness and mercy in permitting us to pass through the events of the last two days with so little loss of life and blood.

At that hour the church pennant will be hoisted on every vessel of the fleet, and their crews assembled will, in humiliation and prayer, make their acknowledgments therefor to the Great Dispenser of all human events.

D. G. FARRAGUT, *Flag-officer,*
Western Gulf Blockading Squadron.

MAYORALTY OF NEW ORLEANS, ⁆
City Hall, April 26, 1862. ⁆

SIR : In pursuance of the resolution which he thought proper to take, out of regard for the lives of the women and children who still crowd this great metropolis, General Lovell has evacuated it with his troops, and restored back to me the administration of its government and the custody of its honor.

I have, in concert with the city fathers, considered the demand you made of me on yesterday of an unconditional surrender of the city, coupled with a requisition to hoist up the flag of the United States on the public edifices, and to haul down that which still floated to the breeze from the dome of this hall ; and it becomes my duty to transmit to you the answer which the universal sentiment of my constituency, no less than the promptings of my own heart, dictate to me on this sad and solemn occasion.

The city is without means of defence, and utterly destitute of the force and material that might enable it to resist the overpowering armament displayed in sight of it.

I am no military man, and possess no authority beyond that of executing the municipal laws of the city of New Orleans. It would be presumptuous in me to attempt to lead an army to the field, if I had one at my command, and I know still less how to surrender an undefended place, held as this is at the mercy of your gunners and mouths of your mortars. To surrender such a place were an idle and unmeaning ceremony. The city is yours by the power of brutal force, and not by any choice or consent of its inhabitants. It is for you to determine what shall be the fate that awaits her.

As to the hoisting of any flag than the flag of our adoption and allegiance, let me say to you, sir, that the man lives not in our midst whose hand and heart would not be palsied at the mere thought of such an act, nor could I find in my entire constituency so wretched and desperate a renegade as would dare to profane with his hand the sacred emblem of our aspirations.

Sir, you have manifested sentiments which would become one engaged in a better cause than that to which you have devoted your sword. I doubt not but that they spring from a noble though deluded

nature, and I know how to appreciate the emotions which inspire them: You will have a gallant people to administer during your occupation of this city ; a people sensitive of all that can in the least affect its dignity and self-respect. Pray, sir, do not allow them to be insulted by the interference of such as have rendered themselves odious and contemptible by the dastardly desertion of the mighty struggle in which we are engaged, nor of such as might remind them too painfully that they are the conquered and you the conquerors. Peace and order may be preserved without a resort to measures which could not fail to wound their susceptibilities and fire up their passions.

The obligations which I shall assume in their name shall be religiously complied with. You may trust their honor, though you might not count on their submission to unmerited wrong.

In conclusion, I beg you to understand that the people of New Orleans, while unable at this moment to prevent you from occupying this city, do not transfer their allegiance from the government of their choice to one which they have deliberately repudiated, and that they yield simply that obedience which the conqueror is enabled to extort from the conquered.

Since writing the above, which is an answer to your verbal communication of yesterday, I have received a written communication, to which I shall reply before 12 o'clock M., if possible to prepare an answer in that time.   Respectfully,

JOHN T. MONROE, Mayor.
Flag-officer D. G. FARRAGUT,
United States Flag-Ship "Hartford."

CITY HALL, April 25, 1862.
Honorable Common Council:

GENTLEMEN : At half-past one o'clock to-day I was waited upon by Captain Bailey, second in command of the Federal fleet now lying in front of the city, bearing a demand from Flag officer Farragut for the unconditional surrender of the city of New Orleans and hoisting of the United States flag on the custom-house, post-office, and mint. He also demanded that the Louisiana flag should be hauled down from the city hall. I replied that General Lovell was in command here, and that I was without authority to act in military matters. General Lovell was then sent for, and to him, after stating that his mission was to the mayor and council, Captain Bailey addressed his demands.

General Lovell refused to surrender the city or his forces, or any portion of them but accompanied his refusal with the statement that he should evacuate the city, withdraw his troops, and then leave the civil authorities to act as they might deem proper.

It is proper here to state that, in reply to the demand to haul down the flag from the city hall, I returned an unqualified refusal.

I am now in momentary expectation of receiving a second peremptory demand for the surrender of the city. I solicit your advice in the emergency. My own opinion is, that, as a civil magistrate, possessed of no military power, I am incompetent to perform a military act such as the surrender of the city to a hostile force; that it would be proper to say, in reply to a demand of that character, that we are without military protection; that the troops have withdrawn from the city; that we are consequently incapable of making any resistance, and therefore we can offer no obstruction to the occupation of the place by the enemy; that the custom-house, post-office, and mint are the property of the Confederate Government, and that we have no control over them; and that all acts involving a transfer of authority be performed by the invading forces themselves; that we yield to physical force alone, and that we maintain our allegiance to the Government of the Confederate States. Beyond this a due respect for our dignity, our rights, and the flag of our country does not, I think, permit us to go.

Respectfully,

JOHN T. MONROE, *Mayor.*

The above message, which want of time prevented me from having copied, I enclose for information.   Respectfully,

JOHN T. MONROE, *Mayor.*

Per MARION N. BAKER, *Secretary.*

MAYORALTY OF NEW ORLEANS, }
CITY HALL, April 26, 1862. }

COMMON COUNCIL OF THE CITY OF NEW ORLEANS—NO. 6002.

The common council of the city of New Orleans, having been advised by the military authorities that the city is indefensible, declare that no resistance will be made to the forces of the United States.

Resolved, That the sentiments expressed in the message of his honor the Mayor of the common council are in perfect accordance with the sentiments entertained by these councils and by the entire population of this metropolis, and that the Mayor be respectfully requested to act in the spirit manifested by the message.

S. P. DE LABARRE,
Pres. pro tem of Board of Aldermen.

J. MAGIONI,
Pres. of Board of Assistant Aldermen.

Approved, April 26, 1862.

JOHN T. MONROE, *Mayor.*

A true copy,   MARION N. BAKER,
Secretary to Mayor.

UNITED STATES FLAG-SHIP "HARTFORD," }
AT ANCHOR OFF THE CITY OF NEW }
ORLEANS, April 28, 1862. }

SIR—Your communication of the 26th instant has been received, together with that of the city councils.

I deeply regret to see, both by their contents and the continued display of the flag of Louisiana on the court-house, a determination on the part of the city authorities not to haul it down. Moreover, when my officers and men were sent on shore to communicate with the authorities and to hoist the United States flag on the custom-house, with the strictest orders not to use their arms unless assailed, they were insulted in the grossest manner, and the flag which had been hoisted by my orders on the mint was pulled down and dragged through the streets. All of which go to show that the fire of this fleet may be drawn upon the city at any moment, and in such an event the levee would, in all probability, be cut by the shells, and an amount of distress ensue to the innocent population which I have heretofore endeavored to assure you that I desired by all means to avoid. The election is therefore with you; but it becomes my duty to notify you to remove the women and children from the city within forty-eight hours, if I have rightly understood your determination.

Very respectfully, your obedient servant,

D. G. FARRAGUT, *Flag-officer,*
Western Gulf Blockading Squadron.

His Honor the MAYOR AND CITY COUNCIL
of the City of New Orleans.

MAYORALTY OF NEW ORLEANS, }
CITY HALL, April 28, 1862. }

To the Common Council:

GENTLEMEN—I herewith transmit to you a communication from Flag-officer Farragut, commanding the United States fleet now lying in front of the city. I have informed the officer bearing the communication that I would lay it before you, and return such answer as the city authorities might think proper to be made.

In the meantime permit me to suggest that Flag-officer Farragut appears to have misunderstood the position of the city of New Orleans. He had been distinctly informed that at this moment the city has no power to impede the exercise of such acts of forcible authority as the commander of the United States naval forces may choose to exercise, and that therefore no resistance would be offered to the occupation of the city by the United States forces.

If it is deemed necessary to remove the flag now floating from this building, or to raise United States flags on others, the power which threatened the destruction of our city is certainly capable of performing those acts. New Orleans is not now a military post; there is no military commander within its limits; it is like an unoccupied fortress, of which an assailant may at any moment take possession. But I do not believe that the constituency represented by you or by me embraces one loyal citizen who would be willing to incur the odium of tearing down the symbol representing the State authority to which New Orleans owes her municipal existence. I am deeply sensible of the distress which would be brought upon our community by a consummation of the inhuman threat of the United States commander; but I cannot conceive that those who so recently declared themselves to be animated by a Christian spirit, and by a regard for the rights of private property, would venture to incur for themselves and the government they represent the universal execration of the civilized world by attempting to achieve, through a wanton destruction of life and property, that which they can accomplish without bloodshed, and without a resort to those hostile measures which the law of nations condemns and execrates, when employed upon the defenceless women and children of an unresisting city.

Respectfully,

JOHN T. MONROE, *Mayor.*

———

MAYORALTY OF NEW ORLEANS, }
City Hall, April 28, 1862. }

SIR—Your communication of this morning is the first intimation I ever had that it was by "*your strict orders*" that the United States flag was attempted to be hoisted upon certain of our public edifices by officers sent on shore to communicate with the authorities. The officers who approached me in your name disclosed no such orders, and intimated no such designs on your part; nor could I have for a moment entertained the remotest suspicion that they could have been invested with powers to enter on such an errand while the negotiations for a surrender between you and the city authorities were still pending. The interference of any force under your command, as long as these negotiations were not brought to a close, could not be viewed by me otherwise than as a flagrant violation of those courtesies, if not of the absolute rights, which prevail between belligerents under such circumstances. My views and my sentiments in reference to such conduct remain unchanged.

You now renew the demands made in your last communication, and you insist on their being complied with, unconditionally, under a threat of bombardment within forty-eight hours; and you notify me to remove the women and children from the city, that they may be protected from your shells.

Sir, you cannot but know that there is no possible exit from this city for a population which still exceeds in number 140,000, and you must therefore be aware of the utter inanity of such a notification. Our women and children cannot escape from your shells, if it be your pleasure to murder them on a question of mere etiquette. But if they could, there are but few among them who would consent to desert their families and their homes, and the graves of their relatives, in so awful a moment. They will bravely stand the sight of your shells rolling over the bones of those who were once dear to them, and would deem that they died not ingloriously by the side of the tombs erected by their piety to the memory of departed relatives.

You are not satisfied with the peaceable possession of an undefended city, opposing no resistance to your guns, because of its bearing its doom with something of manliness and dignity, and you wish to humble and disgrace us by the performance of an act against which our nature rebels. This satisfaction you cannot expect to obtain at our hands.

We will stand your bombardment, unarmed and undefended as we are. The civilized world will consign to indelible infamy the heart that will conceive the deed and the hand that will dare to consummate it. Respectfully,

JOHN T. MONROE, *Mayor.*

MR. FARRAGUT,
Flag-officer of the United States fleet in front of the City of New Orleans.

———

UNITED STATES FLAG-SHIP "HARTFORD." }
AT ANCHOR OFF THE CITY OF NEW OR- }
LEANS, April 28, 1862. }

SIR—Hereafter, when I desire to communicate with the authorities, I will hoist a square flag with a diagonal red cross, when, if your honor will send your secretary, or any other person, to receive my communication to the shore opposite to the ship bearing that flag, a boat will be sent with an officer to deliver the document.

When the city authorities desire to communicate with me, by the messenger holding his handkerchief by two corners opposite the ship, a boat will be sent for him or his communication.

As my duties call me away from before the city for a short time, I request that you will send your reply to any other vessel that may be present.

Very respectfully, your obedient servant,

D. G. FARRAGUT, *Flag-officer,*
Western Gulf Blockading Squadron.

HIS HONOR THE MAYOR of New Orleans.

UNITED STATES FLAG-SHIP "HARTFORD," AT ANCHOR OFF THE CITY OF NEW ORLEANS, April 29, 1862.

SIR—The forts St. Philip and Jackson having surrendered, and all the military defences of the city being captured or abandoned, you are required, as the sole representative of any supposed authority in the city, to haul down and suppress every ensign and symbol of government, whether State or Confederate, except that of the United States. I am now about to raise the flag of the United States upon the custom-house, and you will see that it is respected with all the civil power of the city.

I have the honor to be, very respectfully, your obedient servant,

D. G. FARRAGUT, *Flag-officer,*
Western Gulf Blockading Squadron.

HIS HONOR THE MAYOR of the City of New Orleans.

UNITED STATES FLAG-SHIP "HARTFORD," AT ANCHOR OFF THE CITY OF NEW ORLEANS, April 30, 1862.

GENTLEMEN—I informed you, in my communication of the 28th of April, that your determination, as I understood it, was not to haul down the flag of Louisiana on the city hall, and that my officers and men were treated with insult and rudeness when they landed, even with a flag of truce, to communicate with the authorities, etc., and if such was to be the determined course of the people, the fire of the vessel might at any moment be drawn upon the city. This you have thought proper to construe into a determination on my part to murder your women and children, and made your letter so offensive that it will terminate our intercourse; and so soon as General Butler arrives with his forces, I shall turn over the charge of the city to him and assume my naval duties.

Very respectfully, etc.,

D. G. FARRAGUT, *Flag-officer,*
Western Gulf Blockading Squadron.

HIS HONOR THE MAYOR AND CITY COUNCIL of New Orleans.

REPORTS OF CAPTAIN T. BAILEY, SECOND IN COMMAND.

UNITED STATES GUN-BOAT "CAYUGA," AT SEA, May 7, 1862.

SIR—Having found it impossible to get the "Colorado" over the bars of the Mississippi, I sent a large portion of her guns and crew, filling up deficiencies of both in the different vessels, and, with my aid, Act. Midshipman Higginson, steward, and boat's crew, followed up myself, hoisting, by authority of the flag-officer, my red, distinguishing flag as second in command,

first on the "Oneida," Commander Lee, and afterwards on the "Cayuga."

That brave, resolute, and indefatigable officer, Commander D. D. Porter, was at work with his mortar fleet, throwing shells at and into Fort Jackson, while General Butler, with a division of his army, in transports, was waiting a favorable moment to land. After the mortar-fleet had been playing upon the forts for six days and nights (without perceptibly diminishing their fire), and one or two changes of programme, Flag-officer Farragut formed the ships into two columns, "line ahead;" the column of the red, under my orders, being formed on the right, and consisting of the "Cayuga," Lieut. Com. Harrison, bearing flag, and leading the "Pensacola," Capt. Morris; the "Mississippi," Com. M. Smith; "Oneida," Com. S. P. Lee; "Varuna," Com. C. S. Boggs; "Katahdin," Lieut. Com. Preble; "Kineo," Lieut. Com. Ransom; and the "Wissahickon," Lieut. Com. A. N. Smith. The column of the blue was formed on the left, heading up the river, and consisted of the flag-ship "Hartford," Com. R. Wainwright and bearing the flag of the Commander-in-chief, Farragut; the "Brooklyn," Capt. T. T. Craven; the "Richmond," Com. Alden; the "Sciota," bearing the divisional flag of Fleet-Capt. H. H. Bell; followed by the "Iroquois," "Itasca," "Winona," and "Kennebec."

At 2 A. M. on the morning of the 24th, the signal "to advance" was thrown out from the flag-ship. The "Cayuga" immediately weighed anchor and led on the column. We were discovered at the boom, and, a little beyond, both forts opened their fire. When close up with St. Philip we opened with grape and canister, still steering on. After passing this line of fire, we encountered the "Montgomery flotilla," consisting of eighteen gun-boats, including the ram "Manassas" and iron battery "Louisiana," of twenty guns.

This was a moment of anxiety, as no supporting ship was in sight. By skillful steering, however, we avoided their attempts to butt and board, and had succeeded in forcing the surrender of three, when the "Varuna," Capt. Boggs, and "Oneida," Capt. Lee, were discovered near at hand. The gallant exploits of these ships will be made known by their commanders. At early dawn discovered a Confederate camp on the right bank of the river. Ordering Lieut. Com. N. B. Harrison to anchor close alongside, I hailed and ordered the colonel to pile up his arms on the river bank and come on board. This proved to be the Chalmette regiment, commanded by Colonel Szymanski. The regimental flags, tents, and camp equipage were captured.

On the morning of the 25th, still leading, and considerably ahead of the line, the Chalmette batteries, situated three miles below the city, opened a cross fire on the "Cayuga." To this we responded with our two guns. At the end of twenty minutes the flag-ship ranged up ahead and silenced the enemy's guns.

From this point no other obstacles were encountered, except burning steamers, cotton ships, fire-rafts, and the like. Immediately after anchoring in front of the city I was ordered on shore by the flag-officer to demand the surrender of the city, and that the flag should be hoisted on the post-office, custom-house, and mint. What passed at this interview will be better stated in the flag-officer's report.

On the 26th I went with the flag-officer some seven miles above the city, where we found the defences abandoned, the guns spiked, and gun carriages burning These defences were erected to prevent the downward passage of Captain Foote. On the 27th a large boom, situated above these defences, was destroyed by Captain S. Philip Lee. On the 28th General Butler landed above Fort St. Philip, under the guns of the "Mississippi" and "Kineo." This landing of the army above, together with the passage of the fleet, appears to have put the finishing touch to the demoralization of their garrisons (300 having mutinied in Fort Jackson). Both forts surrendered to Commander Porter, who was near at hand with the vessels of his flotilla.

As I left the river General Butler had garrisoned Forts Jackson and St. Philip, and his transports, with troops, were on their way to occupy New Orleans.

I cannot too strongly express my admiration of the cool and able management of all the vessels of my line by their respective captains. After we passed the forts it was a contest between iron hearts in wooden vessels and iron-clads with iron beaks, and the " iron hearts " won.

On the 29th the " Cayuga," Lieut.-Com. Harrison, was selected to bring me home a bearer of despatches to the government.

I have the honor to be, very respectfully, your obedient servant,

THEODORUS BAILEY,
Captain.

Hon. GIDEON WELLES,
Secretary of the Navy.

UNITED STATES GUN-BOAT, " CAYUGA,"
OFF NEW ORLEANS, April 25, 1862.

FLAG-OFFICER—Your boldly-conceived and splendidly-executed plan of battle having resulted in complete success, leaves me time to make up the report of my division.

You will find in Lieut.-Com. Harrison's report an accurate outline of the noble part taken by the "Cayuga," under his command, and bearing my divisional flag. We led off at 2 A. M., in accordance with your signal, and steered directly up stream, edging a little to starboard, in order to give room for your division.

I was followed by the "Pensacola" in fine style, the remainder of my division following in regular and compact order. We were scarcely above the boom when we were discovered, and Jackson and St. Philip opened upon us. We could bring no gun to bear, but steered directly on. We were struck from stem to stern. At length we were close up with St. Philip, when we opened with grape and canister. Scarcely were we above the line of fire when we found ourselves attacked by the Confederate fleet of gun-boats. This was *hot* but more congenial work. Two large steamers now attempted to board, one on our starboard bow, the other astern; a third on our starboard beam. The 11-inch Dahlgren being trained on this fellow, we fired at a range of thirty yards. The effect was very destructive; he immediately steered in shore, ran aground and burnt himself up.

The Parrott gun on the forecastle drove off one on the bow, while we prepared to repel boarders, so close was our remaining enemy. About this time Boggs and Lee came dashing in, and made a finish of the Confederate boats—eleven in all.

In the gray of the morning discovered a camp with Confederate flags flying; opened with canister, and at 5 A. M. received the sword and flag of Colonel Szymanski and his command of five companies, arms and camp equipage. While engaged at this point, observed the " Varuna " in conflict with a number of gun-boats. She had been butted by one of them and sunk; but, with his forward guns still above water, her commander was bravely maintaining the fight, driving off his enemies and saving his crew. Informing Captain Lee, of the " Oneida," who had also been engaged with the enemy, of the " Varuna's " situation, he instantly steamed up and made a finish of the Confederate boats. The remainder of the fleet now came up. The " Mississippi " had been detained below with the " Manassas " and another iron-clad. After this everything passed under your observation.

The pleasant duty now remains of speaking of the " Cayuga " and her brave officers and crew. From first to last, Lieut. Com. N. B. Harrison displayed a masterly ability in steering his vessel past the forts under a hurricane of shot and shell, and afterwards in maneuvering and fighting her among the gun-boats. I cannot say too much for him. He was gallantly sustained by Lieutenant George H. Perkins and Acting Master Thomas H. Morton. These officers have my unbounded admiration

I must, in conclusion, express the pleasure which I experienced in witnessing the seamanlike manner in which all the ships were handled. The reports of the divisional captains will inform you of the particular part borne by each ship.

Respectfully, your obedient servant,

T. BAILEY,
Captain Commanding Division of the Red.
Flag-officer D. G FARRAGUT.
Commander-in-Chief, etc., New Orleans.

REPORT OF FLEET-CAPTAIN H. H. BELL.

UNITED STATES FLAG-SHIP "HARTFORD,"
      OFF THE CITY OF NEW ORLEANS,
            April 26, 1862.

SIR—On the night of the 23d instant, I went on board of the United States gunboat "Sciota," Lieutenant-Commanding E. Donaldson, the leading vessel of the second division of gun-boats, which you did me the honor to assign to my command for the ascent of the river. At 4 A. M. of the 24th instant, the "Sciota," accompanied by the division, followed in the wake of the "Richmond," for passing Forts Jackson and St. Philip.

Having run safely through the batteries of the forts and rebel steamers, Captain Donaldson set fire to and burned two steamboats (one loaded with gun-carriages, the other with rosin and combustible materials). He also sent a boat's crew to take possession of an armed steamer which surrendered to him, to bring her up the river; but finding her hard and fast ashore, and under the guns of the fort, the boat returned without her. This delayed the movements of the "Sciota," and brought her within half a mile of the ram "Manassas," whence I witnessed the decided manner in which the noble old steamship "Mississippi," Commander Melancton Smith, met that pigmy monster. The "Mississippi" made at her, but the "Manassas" sheered off to avoid the collision, and landed on the shore, when her crew escaped over her roof into the swamp. The "Mississippi" pelted her meanwhile with her heavy guns. After a while she slipped off the bank, and was last seen by some of the officers floating down the stream, passing the "Mississippi" without smoke-stack. I counted nine of the enemy's steamers of all kinds destroyed; all but two being well armed on the bow and stern.

Upon the assembling of the fleet at quarantine, I observed, for the first time, that the gun-boats "Itasca," Lieutenant-Commanding C. H. B. Caldwell; "Winona," Lieutenant-Commanding Ed. T. Nichols, and "Kennebec," Lieutenant-Commanding John Russell, belonging to the second gun-boat division, were missing. As they were the three rearmost vessels of the fleet, it was apprehended that the fire of the forts and of the enemy's steamers had been concentrated upon them after the passage of the larger vessels, which had attracted and divided the fire of the enemy while they were in sight. I am happy to report none killed and only two slightly wounded in this brilliant dash of the fleet.

The "Sciota," next preceded the fleet up to English Turn, and was the fourth vessel ahead in the attack on and capture of the forts at the city of New Orleans, on the 25th, and the third in passing up in front of the city. She has shared in all the active operations of the fleet to this date.

The immediate object of this expedition having been gained, I hauled down my pennant at one P. M. to-day, to resume my duties as fleet-captain on board the "Hartford," having no further casualties to report.

Throughout the trying scenes of this dashing exhibition, which is second to none on record, Captain Donaldson, his officers and crew, were conspicuous for their coolness, intrepidity and good conduct. Her guns were well and skillfully handled by their crews, under the direction and careful instruction of Lieutenant H. A. Adams; Midshipman Woodward gallantly working the rifle on the top-gallant forecastle, and Act.-Master Foster the 11-inch pivot gun. Act.-Master McFarland was always at the *con*, and acquitted himself zealously and handsomely in the discharge of that duty.

I am, very respectfully, your obedient servant,   H. H. BELL,
            Captain of the Fleet,
      Western Gulf Blockading Squadron.
Flag-officer D. G. FARRAGUT,
      Western Gulf Blockading Squadron,
            off the City of New Orleans.

REPORT OF COMMANDER RICHARD WAINWRIGHT, UNITED STATES FLAG-SHIP "HARTFORD."

UNITED STATES FLAG-SHIP "HARTFORD,"
      OFF CITY OF NEW ORLEANS,
            April 30, 1862.

SIR—I have the honor to submit the following report of the part taken by this ship in the actions of the mornings of April 24th and 25th instant, off Forts Jackson and St.

Philip, and below the city of New Orleans.

At 3:30 A. M., on the morning of the 24th, got under way, and at 3:55 the "Hartford" opened fire from bow guns, engaging Fort Jackson, and receiving a galling fire from both forts. At 4.15 grounded on shoal near Fort St. Philip in the endeavor to clear a fire raft, which was propelled by a ram on our port quarter, setting fire to the ship, the flames bursting through the ports and running up the rigging, endangering the ship as much from fire, if not more, than from the guns of the enemy. Went to "fire quarters," extinguished flames, and backed off—a heavy fire being kept up by both forts upon us all the time, and we continuing to fire in return upon them until out of

COMMANDER RICHARD WAINWRIGHT, OF THE "HARTFORD."

range. Passed and fired into several Confederate steamers on our way up the river.

On the 25th instant, steaming up the river, cleared ship for action at 9:30 A. M., at 11:30 discovered two batteries, one on each bank of the river. which commenced firing. We then opened fire with bow guns, and shortly were in position to use both batteries, and at first fire of the port battery drove the enemy on the right bank from his guns. After passing were fired on by riflemen, but without injury. The ship was much riddled, having received 32 shots, some of them of a serious nature. There were also two guns disabled by the enemy's fire.

I herewith enclose the reports of the heads of the different departments. We have to mourn the loss of three of our brave crew, and also had ten wounded. The guns were well worked and served, and when officers

and men behave with such courage and coolness, I consider it a credit to the ship to say that it is impossible for me to individualize.

On April 26th, at 3.25 p. m., proceeded up the river to attack some batteries ; at 5 went to quarters, and at 5.35 discovered two batteries, both of which, however, had been evacuated, and gun-carriages set on fire. Sent a boat to battery on left bank and spiked twenty-nine guns.

Respectfully yours,
R. WAINWRIGHT,
Commander United States Ship "Hartford."

Flag-officer FARRAGUT,
Commanding Western Gulf Blockading Squadron.

REPORT OF CAPTAIN HENRY W. MORRIS, UNITED STATES STEAM-SLOOP "PENSACOLA."

UNITED STATES SLOOP "PENSACOLA," AT ANCHOR OFF NEW ORLEANS, April 28, 1862.

SIR—I have the honor to report the following incidents and occurrences of the conflict of the 24th and 25th of April in passing Forts Jackson and St. Philip and their adjacent batteries ; also the engagement with the rebel gun-boats and the "ram," which were stationed above those forts; also, the action with the batteries located a few miles below this city, and which latter took place on the 25th instant.

Your order to me was that this ship should, after passing the barricade below the forts, proceed to the attack of Fort St. Philip, in order to divert its fire from your division, so that you should not be exposed to the fire of both of these forts at the same time. On our arrival at the opening of the barricade the enemy opened his fire on us. We proceeded slowly through it, firing only our bow guns, until we reached a position where our broadside guns could be used; we then continued slowly on, frequently stopping and returning his fire, and sustaining that of the rebel gun-boats at the same time, until we had reached a point above that fort where its fire could no longer reach us. The ram, after having struck the "Varuna" gun-boat, and forced her to run on shore to prevent sinking, advanced to attack this ship, coming down on us right ahead. She was perceived by Lieutenant F. A. Roe just in time to avoid her by sheering the ship, and she passed close on our starboard side, receiving, as she went by, a broadside from us. The gun-boats of the enemy now fled up the river, and some of them were run on shore and set fire to by their own crews. We were under the fire of the enemy about two hours. We then steamed up the river to render assistance to the "Varuna." We sent our boats to her to assist in taking off her officers and crew, and have seven of the former and about sixty of the latter now on board.

The conduct of the officers and crew of this ship was in every respect praiseworthy, evincing coolness and courage of the highest order. The fire of the guns was kept up with all the rapidity which the circumstances of the action demanded, to insure injury to the enemy without the wasting of ammunition. The amount of damage inflicted by us on him cannot be ascertained, but I believe that it must have been very considerable. It is impossible in a night attack to do justice to each officer's merits by specifying his particular conduct in the battle, but the result of the conflict is the best evidence of the great good behaviour of them all.

I *must speak* of the coolness and ability displayed by Lieutenant F. A. Roe, the executive officer of this ship. His station being on the bridge next to me enabled me to witness it. My eyesight is quite defective, especially at night, and I am compelled to rely on that of others. I was, therefore, obliged to give to Lieutenant Roe the duty of directing the ship's course through the opening of the barricade, as well as the ascending of the river during the whole action. The judgment and skill shown by him in the performance of this duty cannot be surpassed. We had no pilot on board, and he performed that duty with the most remarkable ability and success. I recommend and most strongly urge upon the Navy Department the propriety and justice of promoting him to the rank of commander, as a reward for the highly important services which he has rendered in this battle. In my opinion he has fairly earned it and ought to receive it.

In the action of the 25th instant with the batteries just below the city the ship received but little injury in her hull or rigging, and none of the officers or crew were killed or wounded, I enclose herewith a report of the surgeon of the killed and wounded; also, one of the injury sustained by the ship in hull and rigging.

I am, very respectfully,
HENRY W. MORRIS, *Captain.*
Flag-officer D. G. FARRAGUT,
Commanding Western Gulf Blockading Squadron.

REPORT OF CAPTAIN T. T. CRAVEN, UNITED STEAM-SLOOP "BROOKLYN.

UNITED STATES STEAM-SLOOP "BROOKLYN,"
MISSISSIPPI RIVER, OFF NEW ORLEANS,
April 26, 1862.

SIR—Herewith I have the honor to enclose reports from the executive officer, surgeon, gunner, carpenter and boatswain, relative to the occurrences, casualties, expenditure of ammunition, and damages on board this ship on the mornings of the 24th and 25th instant.

It becomes my duty to add that, on the morning of the 24th, soon after the action between our fleet and the forts, St. Philip and Jackson, commenced, in consequence of the darkness of the night and the blinding smoke, I lost sight of your ship, and when following in the line of what I supposed to be your fire, I suddenly found the "Brooklyn" running over one of the hulks and rafts which sustained the chain barricade of the river. For a few moments I was entangled and fell athwart the stream, our bow grazing the shore on the left bank of the river. While in this situation I received a pretty severe fire from Fort St. Philip. Immediately after extricating my ship from the rafts, her head was turned up stream, and a few minutes thereafter she was feebly butted by the celebrated ram "Manassas." She came butting into our starboard gangway, first firing from her trap-door, when within about ten feet of the ship, directly toward our smoke-stack, her shot entering about five feet above the water-line and lodging in the sand-bags which protected our steam-drum. I had discovered this queer looking gentleman, while forcing my way over the barricade, lying close into the bank, and when he made his appearance the second time I was so close to him that he had not an opportunity to get up his full speed, and his efforts to damage me were completely frustrated, our chain armor proving a perfect protection to our sides. He soon slid off and disappeared in the darkness. A few moments thereafter, being all the time under a raking fire from Fort Jackson, I was attacked by a large Confederate steamer. Our port broadside, at the short distance of only fifty or sixty yards, completely finished him, setting him on fire almost instantaneously.

Still groping my way in the dark, or *under the black cloud* of smoke from the fire-raft, I suddenly found myself abreast of St. Philip, and so close that the leadsman in the starboard chains gave the soundings, "thirteen feet, sir." As we could bring all our guns to bear, for a few brief moments we poured in grape and canister, and I had the satisfaction of completely silencing that work before I left it—my men in the tops witnessing, in the flashes of their bursting shrapnels, the enemy running like sheep for more comfortable quarters.

After passing the forts we engaged several of the enemy's gun-boats; and being at short range—generally from sixty to a hundred yards—the effects of our broadsides must have been terrific. This ship was under fire about one hour and a half.

We lost eight men killed, and had twenty-six wounded, and our damages from the enemy's shot and shell are severe. I should not have been so particular, sir, in recording so many of the incidents of the morning of the 24th, had I not been out of my proper station; but justice to my officers and crew demand that I should show that the "Brooklyn" was neither idle nor useless on that never-to-be-forgotten occasion.

In conclusion, I must here beg leave to add that my officers and crew, all, without a *single* exception, behaved in a most heroic manner; indeed, I was surprised to witness their perfect coolness and self-possession, as they stood at their guns while the rebels were hailing shot and shell upon us for nearly half an hour before I gave the order to "open fire." I have to congratulate myself on being so ably assisted by my executive officer, Lieutenant R. B. Lowry. He was everywhere, inspiring both officers and crew with his own zeal and gallantry in the performance of their duty. Lieutenant James O'Kane, who had charge of the 1st division, was severely wounded soon after we commenced the action; but not until he had himself primed, sighted and fired two guns, and from loss of blood fallen to the deck, would he consent to be carried below. Lieutenant James Forney, commanding the marines, had two guns assigned him, and, with his men, fought most gallantly.

I was early deprived of the services of my signal officer and aid, Acting Midshipman John Anderson, by a shot, which cut him and the signal quartermaster, Barney Sands, nearly in two. Young Anderson was a most promising and gallant young gentleman, and had, only a few days previously, volunteered from another vessel, which had been detailed for other duty, to join this ship; he was knocked overboard and killed instantly. Immediately afterward, my young clerk, Mr. J. G. Swift, (who had been meanwhile taking notes,) asked me to let him act as my aid; and the prompt, self-possessed manner in which he performed his duty in conveying my orders elicited my highest admiration.

The conduct of Quartermaster James Buck, stationed at the wheel, merits particular mention. Early in the fight he received a severe and painful contusion by a heavy splinter; but for seven hours afterwards he stood bravely at his post and performed his duty, refusing to go below until positively ordered to do so; and on the morning of the 25th, without my knowledge, he again stole to his station and steered the ship from early daylight until 1.30 P. M., over eight hours. I beg particularly that you will bring this man's conduct to the especial notice of the Navy Department.

On the morning of the 25th of April, as the fleet was proceeding up the river, at about a quarter-past 11 o'clock, two batteries were discovered, one on our starboard bow, and the other almost directly ahead. Signal was made from your ship to prepare for action. At this time the flag-ship was the leading vessel, the "Brooklyn" was the second in the line, and the "Iroquois" third; the others were astern, and somewhat scattered. A few minutes after your signal the "Cayuga" passed the "Brooklyn," and so close as to compel me to hail and request her commander not to force me out of my station. She pushed on, and even passed the flag-ship.

About noon, being then one and a quarter miles distant from them, the batteries opened a raking fire upon us. The fire of starboard battery was immediately responded to by this ship, then about half a cable's length astern of the "Hartford," and twenty-one shots from our 80-pounder rifled gun were rapidly, and with remarkable precision, thrown into it, only two of these shots failing to take effect. A few minutes afterward the "Brooklyn," then steaming at the rate of ten knots, by the sudden sheering off and slowing down of the "Hartford," for the purpose of engaging the enemy, necessarily sheered in shore, which brought her up within one hundred and fifty or two hundred yards of the port-hand battery, and so as to obstruct the fire of the "Hartford." The "Brooklyn" then opened fire with grape and canister, stopped her engines, and, lying within less than one hundred yards of the river bank, delivered two other broadsides, which completely drove the enemy pell-mell from their guns and from the field.

In conclusion, sir, permit me to congratulate you upon this most brilliant success. The attack by our squadron upon two strong and garrisoned forts, steaming within grape and canister range, and partially silencing them, and the pursuit and destruction of almost their entire fleet of gun-boats, have not been surpassed, if equaled, by any navy in the world. Under the providence of Almighty God we have achieved a most glorious victory.

Very respectfully, your obedient servant,
THOS. T. CRAVEN, *Captain.*

Flag-officer D. G. FARRAGUT,
Commanding Western Gulf Blockading Squadron.

REPORT OF COMMANDER S. PHILLIPS LEE, COMMANDING UNITED STATES STEAM-SLOOP "ONEIDA."

UNITED STATES STEAM-SLOOP "ONEIDA,"
NEW ORLEANS, April 26, 1862.

I report the part born by the "Oneida" during the actions on the morning of the 24th, between 3 and 6 A. M., with Fort Jackson and Fort St. Philip and the Confederate gun-boats, and in the battle of New Orleans, at noon on the 25th.

ACTION WITH FORTS JACKSON AND ST. PHILIP.

The "Oneida" was, under your order, the fourth in line in the leading division, which was instructed by you to pass on the Fort St. Philip side and not to fire the port battery. Hence the port 32s were shifted to, and our pivot guns trained on the starboard side.

The enemy's fire was very heavy, and began from both forts as soon as we got within long range of their guns, which was on opening the point a mile and a half below Fort Jackson.

I found it necessary, until past the forts, to pilot and to direct all operations from the forecastle after nearing the opening in the barrier, where the "Mississippi" (our next ahead) seemed at a stand as if aground, on the Fort St. Philip side, when she commenced firing her port battery.

This obstruction to our passage was removed, as, caught by the current on the starboard bow, the "Mississippi" shot over to and rather down on the Fort Jackson side. Then the "Varuna" (our next astern) appeared on our port side and showed black smoke. The "Oneida" was steered in for the Fort St. Philip side, passed up quickly in the strong eddy, and close under the guns of that fort, (so that the sparks from its immense battery seemed to reach us,) fired rapidly bolts from two rifled guns, (we had no shell for them,) grape and canister from the forward 32s, and shrapnel from the two 11-inch pivot guns, whilst passing this long line of works. (It was, perhaps, the burning of the sulphur in our 11-inch shrapnel which occasioned the officers in Fort St. Philip to inquire after the surrender, if our shells were not filled with Greek fire.

The terrific fire from the heavy batteries of Fort St. Philip passed over us, their guns seeming to be too much elevated for our close position.

ACTION WITH THE GUN-BOATS.

When just above the forts we encountered the gun-boats and transports of the enemy. The former, it seems from the subsequent reports of our prisoners, were tied to trees along the steep bank above Fort St. Philip; thence passing over to the Fort Jackson side, these gun-boats came down to meet us. It was very thick from darkness and smoke. We had now got on the Fort Jackson side. A flash revealed the ram "Manassas," gliding down our port side below our guns, and passing too close and swiftly aided by steam and the current, to enable us to bring our heavy guns to bear on her. Next came a gun-boat quite near, and passing from the Fort Jackson to Fort St. Philip side, across our bow. Ran into it with a full head of steam, and cut it down with a loud crash on its starboard quarter. Clear of our guns in a moment, it drifted down stream in the darkness. We now slowed down, and afterwards used the steam as necessary to get or keep position in fighting the gunboats, firing right and left into them as we could ascertain (from other indications than black smoke, on account of the "Varuna") that we were not firing into one of our own steamers; forbore to fire into those steamers that appeared to be river transports, and ceased firing into others when they made no return.

In this manner we fired into and passed several Confederate boats on the right bank, leaving it for those who came after to pick up the prizes. A black gun-boat with two masts—a converted sea steamer—ran ahead after a brief contest. At or near daybreak we found the "Cayuga" on our port side. After consultation with Captain Bailey, we concluded to wait for the fleet to come up and form in order. Captain Bailey afterwards hailed that the "Varuna" might be ahead. Looked for her but could not make her out, and received reports from the first lieutenant and the officer on the forecastle that she was not in sight. We had steamed a mile or more ahead of the "Cayuga," saw her general signal No. 80, but as there was nothing in sight of us needing assistance, supposed the signal to refer to some vessel astern of the "Cayuga." Moving ahead, reconnoitering, came up with what in the gray of the morning appeared to be a fort, but which, on nearer approach, proved to be a Confederate camp on the right bank, with a large Confederate flag flying over it. Fired into it, but no reply was made, no one was seen moving, and the camp seemed deserted. Passed on, leaving the trophy flag flying, and soon received a report that the "Varuna" was ahead, and that the enemy was trying to board her. Went ahead with all speed to her assistance. Approaching rapidly, saw the "Varuna" ashore on the left bank of the river, where she had been driven by two rebel gun-boats. At 5.30 A. M., fired on one of them, the black gun-boat, our previous acquaintance, with the forcastle rifle gun. He had hoisted his jib (his wheel-ropes being gone) and was trying to escape up river, but both rebel gun-boats, finding they could not get away, ran on shore—the black one, which proved to be the "Governor Moore," Commander Kennon, on the left bank, above the "Varuna," and the ———, (name yet unknown,) on the right bank, opposite the "Varuna," with her head up stream. After we had driven them ashore their crews deserted, but not before setting fire to their vessels.

With our boats captured Commander Kennon, (formerly of our navy,) one first lieutenant of artillery, one chief engineer, and fourteen of the crew of the "Governor Moore"; also, a rebel signal-book and some official papers, showing that the rebel gunboats were ordered to ram our vessels and to distinguish themselves by showing lights, which they must soon have found prudent to haul down. Seeing that the "Varuna" was sinking, sent our boats and went to her assistance. Brought on board "Oneida" the first lieutenant, two acting masters, two mates, and forty petty officers and seamen of the "Varuna," and sent ten others, seven of whom were wounded, to the "Pensacola."

The "Varuna" had been rammed and badly stove by both of these rebel gun-boats, which had kept with or after her up river, and she was filling, with her magazine flooded, when the "Oneida" drove off her assailants, prevented her officers and crew from being captured, and was received by them with loud and hearty cheers.

The "Cayuga," (Captain Bailey's flag,) also cheered the "Oneida" heartily for opportunely coming to his support that morning.

BATTLE OF NEW ORLEANS.

In the action of the 25th, the "Oneida," being next to the "Pensacola," shared in the actual engagement with Fort Chalmette, on the famous old battle-ground. The entire action lasted but 10 minutes.

The enclosed report of the surgeon shows the extent of our loss to be but three persons slightly wounded in these three actions.

Fort Jackson sent a heavy shell through our port side and coal bunker, (which was full of coal) the shell falling, and fortunately without exploding, on our berth-deck.

The gun-boats gave us one glancing shot on the starboard bow and a quantity of grape, mostly on the starboard side.

The officers and men of my command displayed courage, coolness and skill.

I have the honor to be, sir, very respectfully yours,

S. PHILLIPS LEE, *Commanding.*

Flag-officer D. G. FARRAGUT, U. S. N.,

Commanding Western Blockading Squadron.

REPORT OF COMMANDER SAMUEL SWARTWOUT, UNITED STATES SLOOP-OF-WAR "PORTSMOUTH."

UNITED STATES SLOOP-OF-WAR "PORTSMOUTH," OFF PILOT TOWN, MISSISSIPPI RIVER, April 28, 1862.

SIR—In compliance with your orders, I got under way at 3.30 A. M. on the 24th instant, and proceeded toward Fort Jackson, in tow of the steamer "Jackson," for the purpose of enfilading that fort, to draw their fire from your squadron whilst passing by. Upon arriving at the position designated by you in your directions to Lieutenant Johnson, I ordered the ship to be anchored, and had a spring run out, to breast her broadside to. I had scarcely accomplished this when a very brisk and galling fire, with shell and solid shot, was opened upon the ship from a masked water battery only a few hundred yards distant, and so completely concealed from our view that we could only judge of its location by the flashes from the Confederate guns. We returned their fire with as much precision as we could under the circumstances, but with what effect I have been unable to ascertain. After firing one round from my port battery and four rounds from my Parrot gun, the spring was shot away, and the ship swung around, so that I was unable to bring any of my guns to bear upon Fort Jackson or the water battery. By this time the rebels had got their range, and were dropping their shell and shot with great rapidity all around and close to the ship, many of them cutting away the rigging just above our heads. A 68-pounder solid shot was thrown on board, falling upon the spar deck, just under the top-gallant forecastle, tearing away the plank about ten feet, splitting one of the beams, and in its passage striking John Hancock, seaman, in the left leg, shattering it so much as to render amputation necessary. He has since died of his wound. Finding that the ship was a target for the enemy's batteries, without being able to bring my guns to bear, and, as the squadron had passed the forts, the object of my visit was accomplished, I reluctantly gave the order to slip the cable, and was soon drifted out of range of the rebel guns by the wind and tide. I cannot speak in too high praise of the bravery, coolness, and subordination of the officers and crew upon this trying occasion.

Commander Porter called to see me on the afternoon of the 24th instant, and, upon consultation, we decided that the most judicious course would be for all the vessels, with the exception of a few of his most powerful steamers, to drop down to this anchorage, under my protection, so that in case any of the rams and fire-rafts should escape his steamers this ship could arrest their progress here.

Having received the glorious tidings today that Forts Jackson and Philip have surrendered to Commander Porter, I have concluded to proceed up the river again, in order to recover, if possible, the cable and anchor which I slipped on the 24th instant, and also to render all the assistance in my power. I have just received intelligence from Ship island that Lieutenant-Commanding Abner Read, of the steamer "New London," is in a critical situation, as there are five rebel steamers preparing to attack him. I will therefore order one of our gun-boats to proceed with all dispatch to his assistance.

Very respectfully, your obedient servant,
S. SWARTWOUT, *Commander.*
Flag-officer D. G. FARRAGUT,
Commanding United States Naval Forces, Western Gulf of Mexico.

COMMANDER (NOW REAR-ADMIRAL) MELANCTON SMITH,
OF THE "MISSISSIPPI."

UNITED STATES STEAMER "MISSISSIPPI,"}
MISSISSIPPI RIVER, April 26, 1862.}

SIR—I have to report that the injuries sustained by this ship in the engagements of the 24th and 25th instant, with Forts Jackson and St. Philip, the rebel gun-boats, the ram "Manassas," and the batteries below the city of New Orleans, are not of a very serious nature.

Ten shots were received, eight of which passed entirely through the ship. The ram "Manassas" likewise inflicted an extensive wound on the port quarters, below the water line. All these injuries can be temporarily remedied, with the exception of the latter, and the severe damage done to the outer shaft-bearing and mizzen-mast. I regret exceedingly that my disabled machin-

ery, and a burning steamer that was drifting down upon us, did not allow me to take the "Manassas" in tow after her surrender, thereby preserving her intact for our own use, as the engines were still in operation when my boats, with an engineer and crew, boarded her. At this time it became necessary to recall my boats, when I directed her to be set on fire, and then so riddled her with shot that she was dislodged from the bank and drifted below the forts, when she blew up and sank.

I respectfully refer you to the accompanying report of Surgeon R. F. Maccoun for the casualties that occurred among the crew, and to the enclosed statements of the carpenter and gunner of the damages done to the vessels and the expenditure of ammunition.

I have much pleasure in mentioning the efficient service rendered by Executive Officer Geo. Dewey, who kept the vessel in her station during the engagement, a task exceedingly difficult from the darkness and thick smoke that enveloped us from the fire of our vessel and the burning gun-boats.

I would also refer, in terms of praise, to the conduct of all the officers and men under my command. As I consider that all the vessels under fire did their utmost to subdue the enemy and destroy his defences, I deem it unnecessary to enter into any further detail of the exploits performed by the "Mississippi," as we all must share alike in the honor of your victory.

Very respectfully, your obedient servant,

MELANCTON SMITH,
Commander United States Navy.
Flag-officer D. G. FARRAGUT,
Commanding Western Division Gulf Blockading Squadron.

REPORT OF COMMANDER CHARLES S. BOGGS,
UNITED STATES STEAMER "VARUNA."

UNITED STATES STEAM GUN-BOAT "CAY-}
UGA," AT SEA, May 8, 1862.}

SIR—I have the honor to enclose herewith a duplicate of the report of Commander Boggs, late of the "Varuna," and attached to my division of the attacking force. This gallant officer came up to my support when I had more of the enemy's steamers attacking me than I could well attend to. I afterwards saw him in conflict with three of the enemy's steamers, and directed Commander Lee, of the "Oneida," to go to his support, which he did in the most dashing manner.

Commander Bogg's description of the loss of his vessel I believe to be accurate. I saw him bravely fighting, his guns level with the water, as his vessel gradually sank underneath, leaving her bow resting on the shore and above water.

I have the honor to be your obedient servant, T. BAILEY, *Captain.*

Hon. GIDEON WELLES,
Secretary of the Navy, Washington.

UNITED STATES GUN-BOAT "CAYUGA," }
May 5, 1862. }

SIR—I have the honor to enclose a copy (with slight verbal alteration) of the very hasty report drawn up at the last moment and sent to the flag-officer. My absence on special duty immediately after the action, and the necessity of forwarding it immediately, before the sailing of this vessel, must be my excuse for not forwarding it through you, my immediate commander, who so gallantly led the van of the division to which the "Varuna" was attached.

Very respectfully,
CHARLES S. BOGGS,
Commander United States Navy.

Captain T. BAILEY.
Commanding First Division of Gun-boats.

UNITED STATES STEAMER "BROOKLYN," }
OFF NEW ORLEANS, April 29, 1862. }

SIR—I have the honor to report that, after passing the batteries with the steamer "Varuna," under my command, on the morning of the 24th, finding my vessel amid a nest of rebel steamers, I started ahead, delivering her fire, both starboard and port, at every one that she passed. The first on her starboard beam that received her fire appeared to be crowded with troops. Her boiler was exploded, and she drifted to the shore. In like manner three other vessels, one of them a gun-boat, were driven ashore in flames, and afterwards blew up.

At 6 A. M. the "Varuna" was attacked by the "Morgan," iron-clad about the bow, commanded by Beverly Kennon, an ex-naval officer. This vessel raked us along the port gangway, killing four and wounding nine of the crew, butting the "Varuna" on the quarter and again on the starboard side. I managed to get three eight-inch shells into her abaft her armor, as also several shots from the after rifled gun, when she dropped out of action partially disabled.

While still engaged with her, another rebel steamer, iron-clad, with a prow under water, struck us in the port gangway, doing considerable damage. Our shot glanced from her bow. She backed off for another blow, and struck again in the same place, crushing in the side ; but by going ahead fast, the concussion drew her bow around, and I was able, with the port guns, to give her, while close alongside, five eight-inch shells abaft her armor. This settled her,

and drove her ashore in flames. Finding the "Varuna" sinking, I ran her into the bank, let go the anchor, and tied up to the trees.

During all this time the guns were actively at work crippling the "Morgan," which was making feeble efforts to get up steam. The fire was kept up until the water was over the gun-trucks, when I turned my attention to getting the wounded and crew out of the vessel. The "Oneida," Captain Lee, seeing the condition of the "Varuna," had rushed to her assistance, but I waived her on, and the "Morgan" surrendered to her, the vessel in flames. I have since learned that over fifty of her crew were killed and wounded, and she was set on fire by her commander, who burned his wounded with his vessel.

I cannot award too much praise to the officers and crew of the "Varuna" for the noble manner in which they supported me and their coolness under such exciting circumstances, particularly when extinguishing fire, having been set on fire twice during the action by shells.

In fifteen minutes from the time the "Varuna" was struck she was on the bottom, with only her top-gallant forecastle out of water. The officers and crew lost everything they possessed, no one thinking of leaving his station until driven thence by the water. I trust the attention of the department will be called to their loss, and compensation made to those who have lost their all.

The crew were taken off by the different vessels of the fleet as fast as they arrived, and are now distributed through the squadron. The wounded have been sent to the "Pensacola."

I would particularly commend to the notice of the department Oscar Peck, second class boy, and powder boy of the after rifle, whose coolness and intrepidity attracted the attention of all hands. A fit reward for such services would be an appointment at the naval school.

The marines, although new recruits, more than maintained the reputation of that corps. Their galling fire cleared the "Morgan's" rifled gun, and prevented a repetition of her murderous fire. Four of the marines were wounded, one I fear mortally.

So soon as the crew were saved I reported to you in person, and within an hour left in the only remaining boat belonging to the "Varuna," with your despatches for General Butler, returning with him yesterday afternoon. Very respectfully,

CHARLES S. BOGGS,
Commander United States Navy.

Flag-officer D. G. FARRAGUT,
Commanding Western Gulf Blockading Squadron.

REPORT OF COMMANDER JOHN DE CAMP, UNITED STATES STEAMER "IROQUOIS."

UNITED STATES STEAMER "IROQUOIS," }
OFF NEW ORLEANS, May 3, 1862. }

SIR—I beg to submit the following report respecting our engagement with Forts Jackson and St. Philip, and a fleet of Confederate steamers and rams in this river, April 24th and 25th.

The "Iroquois," being on picket duty during the night of the 24th, and being about one mile in advance of the squadron, we observed the signal for action made on board the flagship at about 3 A. M. Soon after, the ship of the first division having passed ahead, we fell into our place, astern of the "Sciota," and stood towards the forts. At 4 A. M. we were hotly engaged with the forts, and shortly after a ram and the Confederate gun-boat " McCrea" came upon our quarter and astern of us and poured into the " Iroquois" a most destructive fire of grape-shot and langrage, part of which was copper slugs; a great many of them were found on our decks after the action. We succeeded in getting one 11-inch shell into the "McCrea," and one stand of canister, which drove her away from us. We suffered severely from the raking cross-fire of Fort St. Philip, but Fort Jackson inflicted no injury, although we passed within fifty yards of its guns.

Passing the forts, we were beset by five or six Confederate steamers. We gave each a broadside of shell as we passed, and the most of them were entirely destroyed. Four miles above the forts we captured the enemy's gun-boat " No. 3," armed with one 24-pound brass howitzer, and well supplied with small arms, fixed ammunition, sails, etc. At this point we also captured about forty soldiers, including Lieutenant Henderson, of the Confederate army. These men were paroled and landed at New Orleans. Some of them were so badly wounded that I sent them to the hospital without parole; they will not trouble us again very soon, I think. Anchoring, by order, at 9 P. M., we were again under way at daylight on the 25th, and, in company with the squadron, stood up the river. At Chalmette we encountered two Confederate batteries, but their attempt to annoy us scarcely deserves the name of a battle. Some people on shore fired a few musket shots at us, but our marines soon dispersed them, and thus ended the battle of New Orleans.

The greatest praise I can bestow upon the officers of the "Iroquois" is to say that they all did their duty, and each one of them always expressed his determination to conquer. The crew and marines behaved with spirit and gallantry, which we may always expect in well drilled Americans.

Our loss in killed and wounded, I am sorry to say, is large. One master's mate and five seamen and two marines are killed, and twenty-four wounded. Mr. George W. Cole, master's mate, was killed by a cannon shot, and he died bravely, shouting to the men not to mind him, but go on with their guns.

The "Iroquois" is badly injured in her hull, but her masts and spars are sound, except the bowsprit and jibboom. These are hit with large shot; all our boats are smashed, and most of them are not worth repairs.

I am, most respectfully, your obedient servant,

JOHN DE CAMP,
Commander United States Navy.
Flag-officer D. G. FARRAGUT,
Commanding Western Gulf Blockading Squadron, New Orleans, La.

REPORT OF COMMANDER JAMES ALDEN, UNITED STATES STEAMER "RICHMOND."

UNITED STATES STEAMER "RICHMOND," }
OFF NEW ORLEANS, April 27, 1862. }

SIR—In accordance with your instructions, I herewith enclose copies of the boatswain's and carpenter's reports of the damage done to this vessel by the enemy's shot during the engagement of Forts Jackson and St. Philip on the morning of the 24th instant. The list of casualties I have already forwarded to you; it is very small, there being but two killed and four wounded. Much injury to the men, I am sure, was saved by a carefully prepared " splinter netting." At one point between the guns the netting was forced out to its utmost tension; indeed, large pieces of plank were thus prevented from sweeping the deck, and perhaps destroying the men at the guns. I would therefore recommend that in our future operations, these simple "pain-savers" or "life-preservers" be adopted in the other ships of the fleet.

I must beg leave to call your attention to another simple and very effective expedient which was resorted to on board this vessel to obtain *light*—an element so essential in a night attack on board ship. The *deck* and *gun-carriages* were *whitewashed* fore and aft, and it was truly wonderful to note the difference; where before all was darkness, now side-tackle, falls, handspikes, ammunition, and indeed everything of the kind about our decks, was plainly visible by the contrast. The idea being so novel, and, at the same time, effective, I trust it will receive, through you, the notice it deserves, so that when others are driven to the *dire necessity of a night attack* they may have all the advantages the discovery insures.

We had much difficulty in groping our way through that "fiery channel," our ship being so slow, and the enemy was met in the "worst form for our profession," but the hand of a kind Providence gave us the victory. No men could behave better throughout that terrible ordeal than the crew of this vessel did. My thanks for support are due to them and the officers generally. I am especially indebted to Mr. Terry, our second lieutenant, for his ready and intelligent aid in the management of the ship during the action; but to Mr. Cummings, our first lieutenant, are mainly due, as far as this ship is concerned, the handsome results of that morning. By his cool and intrepid conduct the batteries were made to do their whole duty, and not a gun was pointed nor a shot sent without its mark. My thanks are due to Mr. Bogart, my clerk, who took the place of Mr. John B. Bradley, master's mate, who was shot down at my side while gallantly performing his duty as my aid.

I am, sir, respectfully, etc.,

JAMES ALDEN, *Commander.*

Flag-officer D. G. FARRAGUT,

Commanding Western Gulf Blockading Squadron.

REPORT OF LIEUTENANT-COMMANDING ED-
WARD T. NICHOLS, UNITED STATES
GUN-BOAT "WINONA."

UNITED STATES GUN-BOAT "WINONA," }
NEW ORLEANS, April 30, 1862. }

SIR—I beg leave respectfully to present the following report of the operations of this vessel in the engagement with Forts Jackson and St. Philip on the morning of the 24th inst.

After getting under way, I took my station as soon as possible in the line, astern of the "Itasca," and followed her red light, but suddenly found myself involved in a mass of logs and drift stuff, held by the chain and moorings of the hulks. Whilst trying to back clear the "Itasca" backed and fouled me on the starboard bow. After a delay of from twenty minutes to half an hour, I proceeded on my way, though I felt pretty sure that the bulk of the fleet had passed. Day was breaking fast, and my vessel was brought out in bold relief against the bright sky, presenting a fair mark for the gunners of the fort. Fort Jackson fired at me as I approached, and the first gun killed one man and wounded another; the third or fourth gun killed or wounded every man at the rifle gun except one. Judging that the burning raft was on the Fort Jackson side, I steered to pass it on the port hand, and did not discover my error until the whole lower battery of Fort St. Philip opened on me at less than point blank range. Steering off with starboard helm, I shot across to

the Fort Jackson side, but, owing to the obscurity caused by the smoke, got so close to the shore that I had no room to turn head up stream, and was forced to head down. At this time both forts were firing nearly their entire batteries at me. It would have been madness to attempt turning again in such a fire; three of my men were killed, four severely wounded, and one slightly so, the vessel hulled several times, and the deck wet fore and aft from the spray of falling shot.

It was with reluctance that I gave the order to head down stream and run out of the fire, first ordering the officers and crew to lie down on deck. I cannot, sir, speak too highly of the conduct of all on board. My orders were obeyed with alacrity, and (considering the suddenness of the fire opened on us, from Fort St. Philip, and the naturally depressing effect produced by the fatality of the first few shots,) with but little confusion. Mr. Walker, the first lieutenant, was very active and vigilant, and gave his personal attention in every part of the vessel—he was slightly wounded in the ear. Permit me, sir, to call your attention to the conduct of acting-master's mate William F. Hunt, in charge of the rifle gun —it was admirable. He assisted in working his gun, as his crew was weakened, and remained at it after none were left, until ordered from the forecastle by me. Four of my wounded men are in the hospital at Pilot Town; the dead I buried on the left bank of the river, a short distance below our late anchorage.

Since the 24th I have been acting under the orders of Commander Porter, and on the 28th I had the satisfaction of receiving the surrender of Fort St. Philip and hoisting in its proper place once more the flag of our country. I was unfortunate, sir, in not passing the forts, but, I trust, not censurable.

I am, sir, very respectfully, etc.,

EDWARD T. NICHOLS,

Lieutenant-Commanding.

Flag-officer D. G. FARRAGUT,

Commanding Western Blockading Squadron, New Orleans.

REPORT OF LIEUTENANT-COMMANDING GEO.
H. PREBLE, UNITED STATES GUN-
BOAT "KATAHDIN."

UNITED STATES GUN-BOAT "KATAHDIN," }
AT ANCHOR OFF NEW ORLEANS, }
April 30, 1862. }

SIR—It gives me pleasure to report that, in the passage of the forts on the morning of the 24th. and the engagement with the defences of New Orleans on the 25th, as well as on previous occasions when on advanced guard duty, and exposed to the deliberate fire from the rifled cannon of the enemy, the officers and crew of this vessel have shown a bravery and cool determination worthy of all praise. While exposed to the iron hail rained over us from both forts, and the simultaneous fire of the enemy's gun-boats on the 24th, not a man flinched from his gun or hesitated in the cool performance of his duty. Where all performed so well it is, perhaps, invidious to particularize. I may mention, however, as coming under my immediate notice, the deliberate way in which the First Lieutenant, Mr. Green, gave his general superintendence to the serving and supplying the guns, and the other duties assigned him, and the cool, collected manner in which Acting Master W. H. Polleys conned the ship between the forts and throughout, giving his orders to the helm as promptly, decidedly, and coolly as when piloting the vessel to a usual anchorage. Acting Master George Harris, in charge of the pivot gun, and Acting Master's mate, J. H. Hartshorn, in charge of the Parrott rifle gun, did their best to annoy the enemy.

At the most critical moment of the passage, and when exposed to the fire of both forts, the fire of our pivot gun was embarrassed and delayed by the shells jamming in the gun, their sabots being too large to fit the bore. As many as five shells were passed up before one could be found to fit the gun. Two became so jammed that the shells were torn from the sabots before they could be extracted, and the sabot of one had to be blown out and the gun reloaded. Mr. Harris, the master in charge of the pivot-gun, attributes this serious fault, first, to the swelling of the light wood of the too nicely fitted sabot in the damp climate of this Gulf; and, second, to the shells being packed in bags instead of boxes, which allowed of the sabots getting bruised, even with the most careful handling.

The station assigned this vessel, close under the stern of the "Varuna," I maintained until the dense canopy of smoke from the cannonade, aided by the night, hid everything from our view. I ordered full speed, however, to maintain my station; and seeing, by the flash from her broadside, that we were passing the "Mississippi," I gave orders to cease firing for a time until we had passed her, when I became engaged with the enemy's gun-boats. Above the forts we passed along the broadside and within fifty yards of the iron-plated battery "Louisiana," lying at anchor. To our surprise she did not fire at us, though she could have blown us out of water. After passing her, I directed to keep the vessel off, and give her a shot from the 11-inch pivot and Parrott, which was done, and, as I have since learned from one on board of

her, with good effect, tearing a hole the size of the shell through and through the iron plating of her bow.

Until beyond the fire of the forts, acting-assistant paymaster Ladd attended in the wardroom to give his assistance to the surgeon, but later volunteered his services in boats, and brought off to the ship refugees from the burning gun-boats and the shore; he assisted, also, in disarming that portion of the Chalmette regiment which surrendered, and was encamped opposite the quarantine.

I am happy to have no casualties to report, and that the surgeon, though ready, had no opportunity to testify his skill on board. Several of the men had their clothing torn by shot or fragments of shell, but not a man was even scratched. At the request of Captain Bailey, Dr. Robinson went on board the "Cayuga" after the action, where he rendered efficient service to her wounded. The vessel, also, escaped without serious injury. One shell passed through the smokestack and steam escape-pipe and burst, making a dozen small holes from the inside outward, and another has cut about four to six inches into the foremast, while the same, or another, cut the foresail and some of the running rigging about the foremast, which is all the damage sustained. I attribute our escaping with so little injury to our being near the head of the line, to the rapid manner in which we passed the forts, and to our passing so close under the forts that all their shot went over our heads. I believe, also, that for a time the fire of Fort St. Philip was silenced. The two shots we received, however, were from that fort.

On the arrival of the fleet at New Orleans, seeing the schooner "John Gilpin" lying at the levee on the Algiers side, loaded with cotton and surrounded by burning vessels and sunken docks, and fearing she might be fired, I boarded her and hoisted the American flag at her masthead, and brought her captain, Archibald Forsaith, (whom you afterwards released on parole,) on board as a hostage for her safety and future delivery, not deeming it prudent or safe to put a small prize crew in possession. Captain Forsaith claimed that his vessel was British property, and that his papers were in the English consulate, but acknowledged that she was intended to run the blockade. In passing down the river since, I have noticed that a portion, if not all, of her deck load of cotton, and perhaps her remaining cargo, has been removed. Captain F. stated to me that she had 265 bales of cotton on board.

In conclusion, flag-officer, allow me to congratulate you upon the success which has attended this "running of the forts," beyond a doubt the most brilliant and daring achievement of the war.

Very respectfully, your obedient servant,

GEO. HENRY PREBLE,

Lieutenant-Commanding.

Flag-officer D. G. FARRAGUT,

Commanding Western Gulf Blockading Squadron.

REPORT OF LIEUTENANT-COMMANDING C. H. B. CALDWELL, UNITED STATES GUN-BOAT "ITASCA."

UNITED STATES STEAM GUN-BOAT "ITASCA," PILOT TOWN, MISSISSIPPI RIVER, April 24, 1862.

SIR—Agreeably to your instructions, I proceeded up the river, in the boat furnished from the "Hartford," to make a final reconnoissance of the schoon-

LIEUTENANT-COMMANDING (AFTERWARDS COMMODORE) CHAS. H. B. CALDWELL, OF THE "ITASCA."

ers on the west bank of the river, and a careful examination as to the chains that were originally stretched from them to the schooners on the starboard side, one of which we ran on shore on the night of the 20th. I succeeded in reaching them after a long, fatiguing pull against the current, without opposition or discovery, although we were directly in range between the forts and a fire lighted on the opposite shore to illuminate the reach across the river, and I could distinctly hear the voices of the rebels at Fort Jackson as they were busily engaged in some outside work. I found two of the three schooners on shore, and the outside one riding head to the current, with a number of chains hanging from her bow. I passed ahead, leaving her fifty yards on the port hand, and dropped over a deep-sea lead, veering to twelve fathoms of line. We then lay on our oars, and drifted down the stream, without feeling any obstructions. We found all the booms attached to the in-shore schooners, and a number of rafts in-shore

of them, aground; the outside schooner was entirely clear. Returning, I stopped alongside of the east bank, and dropped the lead over, with fifteen fathoms of line, floating by within twenty yards of her.

Having satisfied myself fully, by these and other observations, that no obstructions whatever existed, and that the chains we slipped on the night of the 20th had disarranged and almost destroyed the whole apparatus for preventing our passage up the river, and that the condition of things was precisely as I had previously reported, and that the whole fleet could safely pass, I made with confidence and inexpressible satisfaction, on my return, our pre-concerted signal that the channel was clear and everything propitious for the advance of the fleet.

I regret to be obliged to state that my progress afterwards with the fleet was attended with serious misfortune and disappointment. On arriving abreast of Fort Jackson a storm of iron hail fell over and around us from both forts, which was continued without intermission while we were under their guns. A number of shots took effect, several passing through us. One, a 42-pound shot, passed through the port side, a coal-bunker full of coal, iron-plate bulkhead, and entered the boiler, making a large hole, and breaking the dry-pipe therein; from this hole the steam rushed in a dense cloud, filling the fire and engine room, and driving every one from below, and almost suffocating those on the quarter-deck.

The loss of our motive power having destroyed our efficiency and left us almost helpless, I ordered every man to throw himself flat on the deck, the helm put hard a-starboard, and, turning, floated down the river. When out of range of the forts, I ordered the pumps manned fore and aft, and our deck was soon several inches deep with water, which was pouring also out of every scupper. Supposing the ship to be in a sinking condition, I ran her on shore below the mortar fleet, where I remained until I satisfied myself that the leak was not as bad as I had at first supposed, and then hauled off and anchored.

I am happy to state that but three men were injured during the engagement—two firemen, scalded by the steam, and the captain of the hold, wounded in the head by a splinter. I have received fourteen hits, as follows: three shot holes through the vessel below the deck, the plank-shear badly shattered, and four slight hits on the port side; one through the vessel below decks, and one through the bulwarks on the starboard side; one through the cutwater, grazing the bowsprit; one cutting away a davit span and shivering the jury mainmast (the main gaff), and one 8-inch shell exploded over the quarter-deck, driving a large piece through the port signal locker and bulwarks. One shot took out of the port side a piece of plank three feet long, shivered five feet of the next plank, crushed all of the timbers in its passage, and split one knee; another shot hole in the starboard side is nearly as bad.

Allow me, flag-officer, respectfully and sincerely, to congratulate you upon the glorious passage of the fleet, and to express to you the heartfelt sorrow and disappointment I felt that my disabled condition prevented my being a participant in its complete success; and to assure you it was owing to circumstances that Providence alone could control.

Very respectfully, your obedient servant,

C. H. B. CALDWELL,

Lieutenant-Commanding.

Flag-officer DAVID G. FARRAGUT,

Commander-in-Chief of Western Gulf Blockading Squadron.

REPORT OF LIEUTENANT-COMMANDING N. B. HAR-
RISON, UNITED STATES GUN-BOAT "CAYUGA."

UNITED STATES GUN-BOAT, "CAYUGA," MIS-
SISSIPPI RIVER,
April 24, 1862.

SIR—The following extract from the log will present to you, in the briefest form, the part borne by
this ship in the conflict of this morning with Forts
Jackson and St. Philip, and the rebel gun-boats:

"At 2 A. M., in obedience to the flag-officer's signal, weighed anchor, and led the advance column
toward the barrier, and stood up stream close to
Fort St. Philip. At 3.45 both forts opened their fire.
At 3.50 opened on Fort St. Philip with grape and
canister. At 4 passed the line of fire of Fort St.
Philip, and encountered some eleven gun-boats, no
supporting ships in sight. At 4.25 one steamer
surrendered, and two more were driven on shore.
At this moment discovered the 'Varuna' and
'Oneida' dash gallantly into the fight. At 5
anchored in front of Camp Lovell, and received the
submission of Colonel Szymanski and his command."

We were struck forty-two times. Both masts are
so badly hurt as to be unfit for further service.
Our 11-inch Dahlgren carriage struck, but still fit
for duty; the smokestack perforated, but not materially injured; all other damages have been repaired.
I regret to add that six of our crew have been
wounded, but so far the surgeon has made but one
amputation.

It is needless for me to inform you, who had us
under your eye, that all did their duty fearlessly
and well; but I must commend to your special
notice my executive officer, Lieutenant George R.
Perkins. The remarkable coolness and precision of
this young officer, while aiding me in steering the
vessel through the barrier and past the forts, under
their long and heavy fire, must have attracted your
attention. Of volunteer Acting-master Thomas H.
Morton I must speak in terms of high praise. He
fought the Parrott gun, and his daring example had
a most happy effect on the crew.

I am indebted to Assistant Surgeon Edward S.
Bogert, not only for his rapid and skillful attention
to the wounded, but for his general officer-like bearing. My clerk, Mr. Charles M. Burns, Jr., was of
material assistance in communicating my orders.
Our engines, although generally unreliable, were,
on this occasion, worked successfully by Second-
assistant George W. Rogers and his assistants. In
conclusion, I must mention with praise the conduct
of the following men: Charles Florence, captain
of 11-inch gun; William Young, captain of Parrott
gun; William Parker, at the wheel; Edward Wright,
at the lead.

April 25.—I continue this report through the battles of to-day. At 11 A. M., being at that moment
some half a mile in advance of the flag-ship, the
batteries on either hand opened on us at short
range. Being pivoted to port, I edged off with the
port helm and responded with our 11-inch and Parrott, slowly but with great precision of aim. This
unequal contest lasted just fifteen minutes, when
the flag-ship ranged up in splendid style, diverting
their fire and silencing the battery on the right bank.

We were again repeatedly hulled, and much cut
up in spars and rigging, and the iron stock of the
port anchor cut away. I lost no men; this I attribute to an order which I gave for the men to lie
down flat during the time we could bring no gun to
bear. To speak again of the constancy and devotion of my brave officers and crew would be to repeat an old story. Respectfully,
N. B. HARRISON,
Lieutenant-Commanding.
Capt. T. BAILEY,
*Commanding the Leading Division of Gun-
boats, off New Orleans, Louisiana.*

REPORT OF LIEUTENANT PIERCE CROSBY, COM-
MANDING UNITED STATES GUN-BOAT "PINOLA."

UNITED STATES STEAM GUN-BOAT "PINOLA,"
OFF NEW ORLEANS, April 26, 1862,

SIR—I have the honor to report that, in obedience to your signal on the morning of the 24th instant, after having passed your orders to the "Pensacola" and other vessels of the squadron, I took
my position at 3.30 A. M. in line of battle next after
the "Iroquois," thinking the vessel which was to
have preceded me had taken her's in advance, which
I could not ascertain at that time, and followed on
in line, passing so close to one of the enemy's hulks
which had been used to hold the chain-rafts, that
one starboard quarter-boat was crushed against her
sides; continued on our course, and as soon as Fort
Jackson bore abeam of us, about four hundred
yards distant, commenced firing with the 11-inch
Dahlgren pivot and Parrott rifles at the flashes of
the enemy's guns, that being the only guide by
which to distinguish their position, which the fort
answered promptly and rapidly, but, owing to our
proximity, their shot passed over, with the exception
of two, one of which killed Thomas Kelly, captain
of the forecastle, slightly wounding Acting-master
J. G. Lloyd, the other cutting away the launch's
after-davit. I then ran over within one hundred
and fifty yards of Fort St. Philip, from which we
received a terrific volley of shot, canister, grape,
and musketry, nearly all of which passed over us.
The fire-rafts, which were burning very brightly,
exposed us to the full view of the enemy, and enabled them to fire at us with great precision, while
we were only able to answer their forty guns with
the twenty-pound rifles, the 11-inch pivot being engaged with Fort Jackson. Of those shot that
struck us from Fort St. Philip, one entered our starboard quarter, cut away part of the wheel, and severely wounded William Acworth, quartermaster,
who returned to his station as soon as his wounds
were dressed. Acting-master's mate William H.
Thompson, promptly took the wheel at the time of
the disaster. The second entered the hull at the
water-line on the starboard side, eight inches forward of the boilers, passed through the coal bunker,
and lodged in the pump-well and cut the sounding-
well in two. The third cut away the top of the
steam escape pipe. The fourth cut away the starboard chain cable from the anchor, passed through
the bow and yeomans' storeroom, and lodged in the
port side, starting off the outside planking. The
fifth struck the topgallant forecastle and carried
away part of the rail. The sixth passed through
the plankshear, abreast of the 11-inch pivot gun.
The seventh struck a barricade of hammocks forward of the forehatch. The eighth cut away one
of the dead-eyes of the starboard fore rigging. The
ninth cut a bucket from the hands of Acting-
master William P. Gibbs, in charge of the pivot-
gun. The Tenth knocked the rammer from the
hands of Harrington, loader, who soon, with the
assistance of the gun's crew, made a temporary one,
the spare rammer having been lost overboard at the
commencement of the action. The eleventh passed
entirely through the hull, immediately over the
magazine, demolishing completely in its course the
dispensary and its contents. The twelfth passed
through the starboard and lodged in the port side
of the berth-deck. These two last mentioned shot
killed John Nolta and Robert H. Johnson, landsmen, and dangerously wounded Thomas Jones,
wardroom steward; Thomas Ford, landsman; Henry
Stokely, wardroom cook, and Thomas L. Smith,
coalheaver, slightly; also, Thomas Foster, captain
of the hold, who received dangerous and painful
wounds from splinters while zealously performing
his duty, completely disabling the powder division,
there being but one man left to pass ammunition,
with the exception of Acting-master's mate C. V.

Rummell, in charge of his division, who immediately gave his personal assistance, although he had been knocked down a few moments previous by splinters; and James A. Bashford, was slightly wounded by splinters. A number of other missiles grazed our sides, doing, however, but slight damage. Immediately following the disaster on the berth-deck, it was reported to be on fire, whereupon the Gunner's-mate, S. B. Frisbee, instantly closed the magazine, he remaining inside. All traces of fire having been quickly extinguished by the fireman, re-enforcements to the powder division were quickly supplied, and the guns continued their fire.

After passing the forts, and out of range of their heavy cross fire, we came suddenly in view of our squadron, which had been hidden from us by the dense smoke, and noticed at the same time a steamer on the starboard hand, which at first sight I supposed to be the "Iroquois," but as day dawned and we approached nearer I soon discovered my mistake and gave her a shot from the 11-inch and Parrott rifles, both of which took effect in her hull near the water-line. At this moment the iron ram "Manassas" was seen following close astern of us, and being in range of our howitzers we opened fire on her with them, aiming at her smokestack. The "Mississippi" being near, now turned upon her and soon succeeded in driving her ashore and destroying her. In obedience to signal, I then ran up and anchored with the squadron off Quarantine Landing and sent ashore to destroy the telegraph wire, which I afterwards learned was on the opposite bank. At 9 A. M. got under way and steamed up the river, in obedience to order, in company with the "Sciota." At 3 P. M. sent the dead on shore and buried them; then continued on our course in company with the squadron and anchored at ———. At 3.30 we got under way and steamed up the river in company with the squadron, At 4 P. M. we opened fire with the squadron on the batteries below New Orleans, and as soon as the batteries were silenced we proceeded with the squadron up to the city, and, in obedience to orders, ran up the river to look after the iron floating-battery, which I discovered off the upper part of the city, in flames, floating down with the current. Returned to the flag-ship and received orders to destroy the batteries below the city; ran down in company with the "Oneida," Captain S. P. Lee commanding, and by his directions I destroyed the battery on the port hand while he took charge of that on the opposite side. Found a large supply of ammunition, together with twelve 32 and 24-pound guns, also a 10-inch mortar, all of which we spiked, burned the carriages, threw the shot into the river, and destroyed everything belonging to the fort. After accomplishing this work, set fire to and burned a schooner loaded with combustible material lying alongside the battery, and then returned to the anchorage off New Orleans at 9.30, thus ending our operations of the 24th and 25th of April.

Our total loss was three killed and eight wounded. It gives me great pleasure and gratification to be able to bear testimony to the zeal and intrepid conduct of the officers and crew of this vessel, during the desperate conflict and terrific fire through which they passed on the morning of the 24th instant. Amid that storm of iron hail perfect order reigned ; officers and men did their duty faithfully, and nobly sustained the well-earned reputation of the Navy and our glorious old flag, for which they fought so manfully.

The conduct of Thomas Gehegan, boatswain's mate and captain of the 11-inch gun, is worthy of mention, as well for the brave example he set his crew as by the faithful manner with which he served his gun, bringing up his own ammunition as soon as the men composing the powder division had been nearly all killed or wounded.

Acting-paymaster C. Stewart Warren acted as signal officer. William H. Byrn, captain's clerk, attended to passing my orders.

Dr. L. M. Lyon, assistant surgeon, displayed great zeal and promptness in his attentions to the wounded during the heat of the battle.

Senior-assistant engineer John Johnson, with his junior assistants, managed his department with skill and ability.

To A. P. Cook, first lieutenant and executive officer, I was greatly indebted for his able assistance. Throughout the entire action he was ready and prompt in the performance of his duties, displaying a coolness and gallantry which won the admiration of all.

With my earnest congratulations upon the brilliant success which has crowned your efforts and attended the forces under your command, I remain, very respectfully, your obedient servant,

PIERCE CROSBY,
Lieutenant-Commanding.

Flag-Officer D. G. FARRAGUT, *U. S. Navy,*
Commanding United States Western Gulf Squadron, Gulf of Mexico.

REPORT OF LIEUTENANT-COMMANDING GEORGE M. RANSOM, UNITED STATES GUN-BOAT "KINEO."

UNITED STATES GUN-BOAT "KINEO," MISSISSIPPI RIVER, ABOVE THE FORTS,
April 25, 1862.

SIR—I have the honor to report that, on arriving close under the guns of Fort St. Philip, on the morning of the 24th instant, the firing was commenced from this vessel, and kept up briskly and effectively until we had passed entirely beyond the range of the enemy's guns from either forts or gun-boats.

Soon after the signal of the flag-ship to discontinue action, I was hailed by Commander Smith of the "Mississippi," who invited me to accompany him in the pursuit of the ram. It turned immediately on the shore and was abandoned, its people escaping under a brisk fire of musketry from both vessels. I made preparations for taking it in tow by a hawser, when, the "Mississippi" coming between the "Kineo" and the ram, Commander Smith hailed, and informing me that two vessels under a point below had struck, requested me to take possession of them. I was met there by the rebel gun-boat "McRea," which opened a sharp fire, backed by two other gun-boats, all within range of the guns of either fort. The "Kineo" returned the fire of the "McRae," but was obliged to *put her head up stream.* Having had the slide of the pivot carriage shattered by a shot from Fort St. Philip, the gun was temporarily disabled; and not being able, with her head up stream, to bring anything to bear effectually, I was obliged, very reluctantly, to withdraw.

I have the pleasure to state, sir, that the conduct of officers and men of this vessel throughout the action was specially admirable for its steadiness, without an exception. I enclose herewith a report of Assistant-surgeon A. S. Oberly, of killed and wounded.

I have the honor to be, &c.,
GEORGE M. RANSOM,
Lieutenant-Commanding

Flag-officer D. G. FARRAGUT,
Commanding Western Gulf Blockading Squadron.

REPORT OF LIEUTENANT-COMMANDING A. N. SMITH UNITED STATES GUN-BOAT "WISSAHICKON."

UNITED STATES GUN-BOAT "WISSAHICKON," OFF QUARANTINE STATION, MISSISSIPPI RIVER,
April 26, 1862.

SIR—I have to report that at 2 A. M. on the 24th instant, in obedience to general signal, got under way and proceeded up the river, keeping our position in the prescribed order of sailing till a detention, by running on shore and the dense smoke of the battle, already some time commenced, rendered it impossible to keep it longer. Using our battery vigorously and to the best advantage possible, we succeeded in passing the forts and water batteries under a storm of shot, shell and volleys of musketry, without loss of life or serious damage to the gunboat, which can only be attributed to the lowness of the vessel on the water.

At daylight, above the forts, we were unavoidably crowded on the west bank of the river, the ram "Manassas" being a short distance astern and heading for us, but unable to make much progress against the current. Before it reached us, we had fortunately gotten off, and witnessed, with great satisfaction, shortly after, its destruction by the United States steamer "Mississippi."

I have to report but two of the crew slightly wounded; four round shot through the hull of the vessel, and one through the mainmast. Officers and men performed their duty nobly, and with admirable coolness. In this feeble tribute to their worth and services I desire to include Third-assistant-engineer G. M. White, a volunteer from the United States steamer "Colorado."

Very respectfully, your obedient servant,
A. N. SMITH.
Lieutenant-Commanding.
Flag-officer D. G. FARRAGUT,
Commanding Western Gulf Blockading Squadron.

REPORT OF LIEUTENANT-COMMANDING JOHN H. RUSSELL, UNITED STATES GUN-BOAT "KENNEBEC."

UNITED STATES GUN-BOAT "KENNEBEC,"
MISSISSIPPI RIVER, April 29, 1862.

SIR—On the morning of the 24th instant, during the engagement, this vessel became entangled with the rafts, and struck one of the schooners (which afterwards sunk), at the same time parting the chain. I then made several attempts, in the midst of a heavy fire, to pass the batteries; but, it being daylight, and the squadron having passed above the forts, I deemed it prudent to withdraw, and reported to the senior officer, Commander Porter, who attached me temporarily to his fleet, and placed me on picket duty.

Yesterday morning, by order of Commander Porter, I proceeded up the river, in company with the United States steamers "Harriet Lane" and "Westfield," and gun-boat "Winona," to witness the surrender of the forts, after which, by order of Commander Porter, I received on board this vessel the prisoners from Fort Jackson—29 officers and 90 men.

Very respectfully, your obedient servant
JOHN H. RUSSELL,
Lieutenant-Commanding.
Flag-officer D. G. FARRAGUT,
Commanding Western Gulf Blockading Squadron

PAPERS RELATING TO THE SURRENDER OF FORTS JACKSON AND ST. PHILIP.
No. 69.]
UNITED STATES FLAG-SHIP "HARTFORD, OFF
THE CITY OF NEW ORLEANS,
May 1, 1862.

SIR—I have the honor to forward herewith to the department all the papers relating to the surrender of Forts Jackson and St. Philip to the forces under my command.

I am, very respectfully, your obedient servant,
D. G. FARRAGUT,
Flag-officer, Western Gulf Blockading Squadron.
Hon. GIDEON WELLES,
Secretary of the Navy, Washington, D. C.

UNITED STATES STEAMER "HARRIET LANE,"
April 29, 1862.

SIR—The morning after the ships passed the forts I sent a demand to Colonel Higgins for a surrender of the forts, which was declined. On the 27th I sent Lieutenant-Colonel Higgins a communication, herewith enclosed, asking again for the surrender. His answer is enclosed.

On the 28th I received a communication from him, stating that he would surrender the forts, and I came up and took possession, drew up articles of capitulation, and hoisted the American flag over the forts. These men have defended these forts with a bravery worthy of a better cause. I treated them with all the consideration that circumstances would admit of.

The three steamers remaining were under the command of Commander J. K. Mitchell. The officer of the fort acknowledged no connection with them, and wished in no way to be considered responsible for their acts. While I had a flag of truce up they were employed in towing the iron floating battery of sixteen guns (a most formidable affair) to a place above the forts, and, while drawing up the articles of recapitulation in the cabin of the "Harriet Lane," it was reported to me that they had set fire to the battery and turned it adrift upon us. I asked the general if it had powder on board, or guns loaded. He replied that he would not undertake to say what the navy officers would do. He seemed to have a great contempt for them. I told him "we could stand the fire and blow up if he could," and went on with the conference, after directing the officers to look out for their ships. While drifting down on us, the guns, getting heated, exploded with a terrific noise, throwing the shot about the river. A few moments after the battery exploded with a terrific noise throwing fragments all over the river, and wounding one of their own men in Fort St. Philip, and immediately disappeared under water. Had she blown up near the vessels, she would have destroyed the whole of them.

When I had finished taking possession of the forts, I got under way in the "Harriet Lane," and started for the steamers, one of which was still flying the Confederate flag. I fired a shot over her, and they surrendered. There were on board of them a number of naval officers and two companies of marine artillery. I made them surrender unconditionally, and, for trying to blow us up while under a flag of truce, I conveyed them to close confinement as prisoners of war, and think they should be sent to the North, and kept in close confinement there until the war is over, or they should be tried for their infamous conduct. I have a great deal to do here, and will send you all papers when I am able to arrange them.

I turned over the forces to General Phelps. Fort Jackson is a perfect ruin. I am told that over 1,800 shells fell in and burst over the centre of the fort. The practice was beautiful. The next fort we go at we will settle sooner, as this has been hard to get at. The naval officers sank one gun-boat while the capitulation was going on, but I have one of the other steamers at work, and hope soon to have the other. I find that we are to be the hewers of wood and drawers of water; but as the soldiers have nothing here in the shape of motive power, we will do all we can.

I should have demanded an unconditional surrender, but with such a force in your rear it was desirable to get possession of these forts as soon as possible. The officers turned over everything in good order, except the walls and buildings, which are terribly shattered by the mortars.

Very respectfully,
D. D. PORTER,
Commanding Flotilla.
Flag-officer D. G. FARRAGUT.

HEADQUARTERS FORTS JACKSON AND ST. }
PHILIP, April 27, 1862. }

SIR—Your letter of the 26th instant, demanding the surrender of these forts, has been received. In reply thereto, I have to state that no official information has been received by me from our own authorities that New Orleans has been surrendered to the forces of Flag-officer Farragut, and until such information is received no proposition for a surrender can be for a moment entertained here.

Respectfully, your obedient servant,
EDWARD HIGGINS,
Lieutenant-Colonel-Commanding.

Commodore DAVID D. PORTER,
United States Navy, Commanding Mortar Fleet.

———

UNITED STATES STEAMER "HARRIET LANE," }
MISSISSIPPI RIVER, April 27, 1862. }

SIR—When I last demanded the surrender of Forts Jackson and St. Philip, I had no positive assurance of the success of our vessels in passing safely the batteries on the river; since then I have received communications from Flag-officer Farragut, who is now in possession of New Orleans. Our troops are, or will be, in possession of the prominent points on the river, and a sufficient force has been posted on the ouside of the bayous to cut off all communication and prevent supplies.

No man could consider it dishonorable to surrender under these circumstances, especially when no advantage can arise by longer holding out, and by yielding gracefully he can save the further effusion of blood.

You have defended the forts gallantly, and no more can be asked of you. I feel authorized to offer you terms sufficiently honorable to relieve you from any feeling of humiliation.

The officers will be permitted to retire on parole with their side arms, not to serve again until regularly exchanged. All private property will be respected, only the arms and munitions of war will be surrendered to the United States government, and the vessels lying at or near the forts. No damage must be done to the defences. The soldiers will also be paroled and be permitted to return to their homes, giving up their arms. I am aware that you can hold out some little time longer, and am also aware of your exact condition as reported to us by a deserter, which convinces me that you will only be inflicting on yourself and those under your command unnecessary discomforts without any good results arising from so doing.

Your port has long been closed to the world, by which serious injury has been experienced by many loyal citizens. I trust that you will not lend yourself to the further injury of their interests, when it can only entail calamity and bloodshed without any possible hope of success or relief to your forts. Your surrender is a mere question of time, which you know is not of any extent, and I therefore urge you to meet my present proposition. By doing so you can put an end to a state of affairs which will only inflict injury upon all those under you, who have strong claims upon your consideration.

I remain, very respectfully,
Your obedient servant,
D. D. PORTER,
Commanding Mortar Fleet.

Colonel EDWARD HIGGINS,
Commanding Confederate forces in Forts Jackson and St. Philip.

———

UNITED STATES STEAMER "HARRIET LANE," }
MISSISSIPPI RIVER, April 30, 1862. }

SIR—I enclose herewith the capitulation of Forts Jackson and St. Philip, which surrendered to the mortar flotilla on the 28th day of April, 1862. I also enclose in a box (forwarded on this occasion) all the flags taken in the two forts, with the original flag hoisted on Fort St. Philip when the State of Louisiana seceded. Fort Jackson is a perfect wreck; everything in the shape of a building in and about it was burned up by the mortar shells, and over 1,800 shells fell in the work proper, to say nothing of those which burst over and around. I devoted but little attention to Fort St. Philip, knowing that when Jackson fell, Fort St. Philip would follow.

The mortar flotilla is still fresh and ready for service. Truly, the backbone of the rebellion is broken.

On the 26th of the month I sent six of the mortar schooners to the back of Fort Jackson, to look up the bayous and prevent supplies getting in. Three of them drifted over to Fort Livingston, and when they anchored the fort hung out a white flag and surrendered. The "Kittatinny," which had been blockading these for some time, sent a boat in advance of the mortar vessels, and reaching the shore first, deprived them of the pleasure of hoisting our flag over what had surrendered to the mortar flotilla. Still, the fort is ours, and we are satisfied. I am happy to state that officers and crew are all well and full of spirits.

I have the honor to remain,
Your obedient servant,
DAVID D. PORTER.

Hon. GIDEON WELLES.

———

UNITED STATES STEAMER "HARRIET LANE," }
FORTS JACKSON AND ST. PHILIP, MISSIS- }
SIPPI RIVER, April 28, 1862. }

By articles of capitulation entered into this twenty-eighth day of April, one thousand eight hundred and sixty-two, between David D. Porter, commander United States Navy, commanding the United States mortar flotilla, of the one part, and Brigadier-General J. K. Duncan, commanding the coast defences, and Lieutenant-Colonel Higgins, commanding Forts Jackson and St. Philip, of the other part, it is mutually agreed :

1st. That Brigadier-General Duncan and Lieutenant-Colonel Higgins shall surrender to the mortar flotilla Forts Jackson and St. Philip, the arms, munitions of war, and all the appurtenances hereunto belonging, together with all public property that may be under their charge.

2d. It is agreed by Commander David D. Porter, commanding the mortar flotilla, that Brigadier-General Duncan and Lieutenant-Colonel Higgins, together with the officers under their command, shall be permitted to retain their side arms, and that all private property shall be respected; furthermore, that they shall give their parole of honor not to serve in arms against the government of the United States until they are regularly exchanged.

3d. It is furthermore agreed by Commander David D. Porter, commanding the mortar flotilla, on the part of the United States Government, that the non-commissioned officers, privates, and musicians shall be permitted to retire on parole, their commanding and other officers becoming responsible for them; and that they shall deliver up their arms and accoutrements in their present condition, provided that no expenses of the transportation of the men shall be defrayed by the government of the United States.

4th. On the signing of these articles by the contracting parties, the forts shall be formally taken possession of by the United States naval forces composing the mortar flotilla; the Confederate flag shall be lowered, and the flag of the United States hoisted on the flagstaffs of Forts Jackson and St. Philip.

In agreement of the above, we, the undersigned, do hereunto set our hands and seals.

DAVID D. PORTER,
Commanding Mortar Flotilla.

W. B. RENSHAW,
Commander United States Navy.

J. M. WAINWRIGHT,
Lieutenant-Commanding " Harriet Lane."

J. K. DUNCAN,
Brigadier-General, Commanding Coast Defences.

EDWARD HIGGINS,
*Lieutenant-Colonel C. S. A., Commanding Forts
Jackson and St. Philip.*

Witnessed by—

EDWARD T. NICHOLS,
Lieutenant-Commanding " Winona."

J. H. RUSSELL,
Lieutenant-Commanding " Kanawha."

LIST OF OFFICERS AT FORT JACKSON, LOUISIANA.

HEADQUARTERS FORTS JACKSON AND ST.
PHILIP, April 28, 1862.

Brigadier-General J. K. Duncan, P.C.S.A.

Lieutenant Wm. M. Bridge, aid and inspector general.

Captain W. J. Seymour, aide-de-camp, volunteers.

Captain J. R. Smith, volunteer aide-de-camp.

Somerville Burke, assistant-surgeon, P.C.S.A.

Dr. Bradbury, volunteer-surgeon.

Lieutenant-Colonel Edward Higgins, P.C.S.A., commanding Forts Jackson and St. Philip.

Charles N. Morse, lieutenant Louisiana artillery regiment, and post-adjutant.

Wm. B. Robertson, captain Louisiana regiment artillery.

J. B. Anderson, captain Louisiana regiment artillery.

R. J. Bruce, first-lieutenant Louisiana regiment artillery, commanding company D.

E. W. Baylor, first-lieutenant Louisiana regiment artillery, commanding company H.

T. Peters, captain company I, twenty-second regiment Louisiana volunteers.

James Ryan, captain company H, twenty-second regiment Louisiana volunteers.

S. Jones, captain company I, twenty-third regiment Louisiana volunteers.

F. C. Comars, captain company St. Mary's cannoniers.

Beverly C. Kennedy, first-lieutenant Louisiana regiment artillery.

Abner N. Ogden, first-lieutenant Louisiana regiment artillery.

James W. Gaines, first-lieutenant Louisiana regiment artillery.

D. Simon, first-lieutenant twenty-second Louisiana volunteers.

George Nongesser, first-lieutenant twenty-second Louisiana volunteers.

George O. Foote, first-lieutenant St. Mary's cannoniers.

Wm. T. Mumford, first-lieutenant Louisiana regiment artillery.

Edw. D. Woodlief, second-lieutenant Louisiana regiment artillery.

Charles Dermers, second-lieutenant twenty-second Louisiana volunteers.

Christian Jacobs, second-lieutenant twenty-second Louisiana volunteers.

George Menn, second-lieutenant twenty-second Louisiana volunteers.

Thomas J. Royster, second-lieutenant twenty-second Louisiana volunteers.

Walter S. Jones, second-lieutenant twenty-third Louisiana volunteers.

Robert Maurer, second lieutenant twenty-third Louisiana volunteers.

Minor T. Gardy, second-lieutenant St. Mary's cannoniers.

Official list :

CHARLES N. MORSE,
Lieutenant and Post-Adjutant.

APRIL 28, 1862.

The company of St. Mary's cannoniers eighty-eight strong, also came up on the United States gunboat " Kennebec."

Corporal Murray, of company E, Louisiana regiment artillery.

One private from company D, Louisiana regiment artillery.

Official :

CHARLES N. MORSE,
Lieutenant and Post Adjutant.

LIST OF OFFICERS AT FORT ST. PHILIP, LOUISIANA, INCLUDED IN CAPITULATION OF FORTS JACKSON AND ST. PHILIP, APRIL 28, 1862.

M. T. Squires, captain Louisiana regiment artillery, senior officer.

Richard C. Bond, captain Louisiana regiment artillery.

J. H. Lamon, captain Louisiana regiment artillery.

Charles Assenheimer, captain Louisiana volunteers.

Armand Laityell (absent at date of capitulation), captain Bienville Guards, recruited in the parish.

J. K. Dixon, second-lieutenant C. S. A., commanding company.

Charles D. Lewis, assistant-surgeon, P. C. S. A.

Charlton Hunt, first-lieutenant Louisiana regiment artillery.

Henry W. Fowler, first lieutenant Louisiana regiment artillery.

Lewis B. Taylor, first-lieutenant Louisiana regiment artillery, and acting-assistant quartermaster.

W. C. Ellis, first-lieutenant regiment Louisiana artillery.

P. Ruhl, first-lieutenant Louisiana volunteers.

Andrew J. Quigly, second-lieutenant Louisiana regiment artillery.

Wm. B. Jones, second lieutenant Louisiana regiment artillery,

H. L. Blow, second-lieutenant C. S. A.

George House, acting-second-lieutenant C. S. A.

J. Dressell, second-lieutenant Louisiana volunteers.

J. A. Guershet, second-lieutenant Louisiana volunteers.

S. Martin, second-lieutenant Bienville Guards, recruited in the parish.

A. Chaussier, second-lieutenant Bienville Guards, recruited in the parish.

Official:

CHARLES N. MORSE,
Lieutenant and Post-Adjutant.

DISPOSITION OF PRISONERS CAPTURED.

No. 70.]

UNITED STATES FLAG-SHIP " HARTFORD," AT
ANCHOR OFF THE CITY OF NEW ORLEANS,
May 1, 1862.

SIR—I have to inform the department that in consequence of my not having any suitable place to put the crews of the rebel gun-boats captured by this fleet, I have released them on parole. But having been informed by Commander Porter and others that the conduct of the officers has been such as to deprive them of any claim for indulgence on our part—they having sunk two of the vessels while under a flag of truce—I have determined to send them to the North as prisoners of war, to be dealt with as the department may think proper. They will be sent in the "Rhode Island."

I am, very respectfully,
Your obedient servant,

D. G. FARRAGUT,
Flag-officer, Western Gulf Blockading Squadron.

Hon. GIDEON WELLES,
Secretary of the Navy, Washington, D. C.

PAYMASTER GEO. F. CUTTER (NOW PAY DIRECTOR), U. S. N.

COMMANDER PORTER'S DETAILED REPORT.

UNITED STATES STEAMER "HARRIET LANE,"
FORTS JACKSON AND ST. PHILIP,
April 30, 1862.

SIR—I have the honor to lay before you a report of the proceedings of the mortar flotilla under my command since the day the vessels entered the Mississippi River.

On the 18th of March, all the mortar fleet crossed "Pass à l'Outre" bar, towed by the "Harriet Lane," "Owasco," "Westfield," and "Clifton," the two latter having arrived that morning. I was ordered by Flag-officer Farragut to proceed to Southwest Pass, which I accordingly did; there we awaited orders, being at any moment ready to go to work on the forts.

As yet only the "Brooklyn" and "Hartford" had crossed the bar, a short time after the "Richmond" passed over, and the "Mississippi" and the "Pensacola" came from Ship Island to try their hand at getting through; there was not at the time a great depth of water, and their pilots were not at all skillful or acquainted with the bar. I volunteered my services with the steamers belonging to the mortar flotilla, and, after eight days' laborious work, succeeded in getting the ships through and anchored them at Pilot Town. I do not hesitate to say, but for the exertions of Commander Renshaw, Lieutenant-Commanding Baldwin, and Lieutenant-Commanding Wainwright, that the two latter ships would never have got inside; the "Miami," Lieuten-

ant-Commanding Harrell, also rendered assistance, but as his vessel was an unmanageable one, he could do no more than act as a steam anchor to heave the ships ahead by.

Too much praise cannot be awarded to the commanders of the "Westfield" and "Clifton" (Renshaw and Baldwin), for the exertions they displayed on this occasion; they knew that the success of the expedition depended on getting these ships over. and they never once faltered in their duty, working against adverse circumstances, and impeded by a fog of eight days' duration, which obscured a vessel at the distance of fifty yards; the "Harriet Lane" also did all she could with her small power, and in the end the united power of these vessels succeeded in getting over the bar the heaviest vessels that ever entered the Mississippi River.

When the ships were all ready to move up, I directed Mr. Gerdes (assistant in the Coast Survey) to proceed in the "Sachem" and make a minute survey from Wiley's Jump up to the forts. He detached Mr. Oltmanns and Mr. Harris, the first an assistant in the Coast Survey, the latter sent out by the superintendent (Mr. Archibald Campbell) of the northwestern boundary, to perform what might be required of him; the work was performed by boats; Lieutenant-Commanding Guest, in the "Owasco," being detailed by me for the purpose of protecting them. These two gentlemen, Messrs. Harris and Oltmanns, performed their duty most admirably: in three days they had surveyed and triangulated over seven miles of the river, their observations taking in Forts Jackson and St. Philip; much of this time they were under fire from shot and shell at a distance of 2,600 yards, and were exposed to concealed riflemen in the bushes. On one occasion Mr. Oltmanns was fired upon from the bushes while surveying in one of the "Owasco's" boats, one of the balls striking an oar, but the boat's crew drove the enemy off with their rifles, and Mr. Oltmanns proceeded with his work, establishing the positions the mortar vessels were to occupy with great coolness and precision. I deem it due to these gentlemen to mention their names honorably, as a tribute to the Coast Survey—the utility of which is not properly appreciated—and as a mark of high satisfaction with them for their invaluable services.

The survey being completed, and marked positions being assigned to the vessels where their distance from the fort could be known to a yard, I brought up three of the schooners to try their range and durability at a distance of three thousand yards. I found the range satisfactory, and had no reason to doubt the durability of the mortar beds and foundation. I received but little encouragement from any one about the success of the mortars, it having been confidently predicted that "the bottoms of the schooners would drop out at the tenth fire." I had no doubts myself about the matter, having perfect confidence in the schooners. Lieutenant-Commanding John Guest guarded the Coast Survey party while they were employed, returning the enemy's fire whenever he thought he could do so with effect.

On the 16th, Flag-officer Farragut moved up the fleet, and I was told to commence operations as soon as I was ready. The schooners sailed up partly or were towed by the steamers, and on the morning of the 18th, they had all reached their positions ready to open fire. Previous to taking their places I had directed the masts to be dressed off with bushes, to make them invisible to the enemy and intermingle with the thick forest of trees and matted vines behind which they were placed; this arrangement proved to be an admirable one, for never once during the bombardment was one of the vessels seen from the forts, though their *approximate* position was known. As the bushes were blown away during the bombardment they were renewed, and the masts and ropes kept covered from view. The place I selected for the mortar vessels was under the lee of a thick wood closely interwoven with vines, and presenting in the direction of Forts Jackson and St. Philip an impenetrable mass for three hundred yards, through which shot could scarcely pass. From our mast-heads the forts could be plainly seen, though observers there could not see us in return. The head vessel of the first division, Lieutenant-Commanding Watson Smith, was placed at this point, 2,850 yards from Fort Jackson, 3,680 from St. Philip; the vessels were then dropped in a line close to each other, their positions having been marked by the Coast Survey party, and Messrs. Oltmanns and Harris superintending personally that each one was acquainted with proper distance. Next to Lieutenant-Commanding Smith's division of seven vessels ("Norfolk Packet," Lieutenant-Commanding Watson Smith; "Oliver H. Lee," Acting-Master Washington Godfrey; "Para," Acting-Master Edward G. Furber; "C. P. Williams," Acting-Master Amos R. Langthorne; "Arletta," Acting-Master Thomas E. Smith; "William Bacon," Acting-Master William P. Rogers; "Sophronia," Acting-Master Lyman Bartholomew) was placed the six vessels of the third divison, under Lieutenant-Commanding K. R. Breese ("John Griffith," Acting-Master Henry Brown; "Sarah Bruen," Acting-Master Abraham Christian; "Racer," Acting-Master Alvin Phinney; "Sea Foam," Acting-Master Henry E. Williams; "Henry James," Acting-Master Lewis W. Pennington; "Dan Smith," Acting-Master George W. Brown), and one vessel, the "Orvetta," Acting-Master Blanchard, all lying in line close together.

All the vessels mentioned were anchored and secured to spring their broadsides, as occasion might require. In the meantime, Lieutenant-Commanding John Guest was sent ahead in the "Owasco" to clear the bushes of riflemen which had been found to lurk there, and cover the vessels from the fire of the forts, when it should open; the "Westfield," "Clifton," and "Miami" being engaged in towing the vessels to their posts.

I placed six vessels of the second division, under command of Lieutenant W. W. Queen, on the northeast shore of the river, the headmost one 3,680 yards from Fort Jackson, to which the division was directed to turn its attention. The following vessels composed this division:

"T. A. Ward," W. W. Queen, commanding second division.

"M. J. Carlton," Charles E. Jack, acting-master.

"Matthew Vasser," Hugh H. Savage, acting-master.

"George Mangham," John Collins, acting-master.

"Orvetta," Francis E. Blanchard, acting-master.

"Sydney C. Jones," J. D. Graham, acting-master.

When the divisions were all placed, signal was made to "commence action," and they opened in order, each one firing every ten minutes. The moment the mortars opened, Forts Jackson and St. Philip responded with all their guns that could bear, but for some time did not appear to get the right range; the hulls of the vessels on the northeast shore, being covered with reeds and willows, deceived them somewhat, though their shot and shell went over. The fire of the enemy was rapid, and, as the shell and shot began to grow rather hot, I sent to the flag-officer, asking that some of the gun-boats should be sent to draw their fire. For one hour and fifty minutes Lieutenant-Commanding Guest had, at the head of the mortar fleet, borne the fire of the forts uninjured, and only left there to get a supply of ammunition. After I went on board his vessel and ordered him to retire, the mortar vessels having been re-enforced by the gun-boats sent up by the flag-officer, by midday the fire on the vessels on the northeast shore (Lieutenant-Commanding Queen's division) became so rapid, and the shot and shell fell so close, that I went on

board to remove them. One large 120-pound shell had passed through the cabin and damaged the magazine of Lieutenant-Commanding Queen's vessel, the "T. A. Ward," coming out near the waterline, her rigging was cut, and shot flying over her fast. The "George Mangham," Acting-Master John Collins, had received a 10-inch shot near her waterline, so I moved them both (contrary to the wishes of the officers) two hundred yards further astern, throwing the enemy out of his range, which he did not discover for two or three hours. At five o'clock in the evening the fort was discovered to be in flames, and the firing from the enemy ceased. We afterwards learned that the citadel had been fired by our bombshells, and all the clothing of the troops and commissary stores had been burnt up, while great distress was experienced by the enemy, owing to the heat and danger to the magazine. Had I known the extent of the fire, I should have proceeded all night with the bombardment; but the crew had had nothing to eat or drink since daylight. I knew not how much the mortar beds and vessels might have suffered. Night firing was uncertain, as the wind had set in fresh, and not knowing how long a bombardment I might have to go through with, I deemed it best to be prudent. A little after sunset I ordered the firing to cease, and made the only mistake that occurred during the bombardment. The fire in the fort blazed up again at night, but I thought it one of the fire-rafts they lighted up every night at the fort.

The first and third divisions, under Lieutenants-Commanding Smith and Breese, acquitted themselves manfully that day, and though the shot and shell fell thick about them, behaved like veterans. We fired on this day over 1,400 shells, many of which were lost in the air, owing to bad fuses. No accident of any kind occurred from careless firing, and after a careful examination the vessels and mortar-beds were found to be uninjured. On that night, at two o'clock, I ordered Lieutenant-Commanding Queen to drop out of the line of fire, and I placed him on the south shore in a safer and closer position, though not one where he could work to such good advantage, the fort being plainly visible from his late position, and the effect of the shells could be more plainly noted. On the south shore, the pointing of the mortars could only be done from sights fixed to the mastheads, and many curious expedients were resorted to to obtain correct firing, expedients very creditable to the intelligence of the commanders of the vessels. We heard afterwards that our first day's firing had been more accurate than that of any other day, though it was all good.

On the morning of the 19th, we opened fire on the enemy again, when he tried his best to dislodge us from behind our forest protection, without effect; our fire was kept up as rapidly as the men could carefully and properly load, the enemy returning it with what heavy guns he could bring to bear on us, most of his shot going over us amongst the shipping and gun-boats, which were on guard and employed drawing the fire away from us. About nine o'clock on the second morning the schooner "Maria J. Carleton," Charles Jack, master, was sunk by a rifle-shell passing down through her deck, magazine, and bottom. I happened to be alongside at the time and had nearly all her stores saved, also the arms. As she went down, the mortar was fired at the enemy for the last time, and that was the last of the "Carleton." We hauled her on to the bank when we found that she was sinking, and were thus enabled to save many of her stores; but she finally slipped off the bank into deeper water, and nothing was left visible but her upper rail. Two men were wounded in the "Carleton." Acting-Master Charles Jack came out in this vessel from New York; he lost his mainmast in a gale off Cape Hatteras, but persevered until he arrived at Key West, and sailed with the flotilla to Ship Island

He went through another gale, but got into port safe. He was almost always up with the rest in working up the river under sail with his one mast; and when his vessel sunk he volunteered his services on board the vessel of Lieutenant-Commanding Queen, to whose division he belonged. On the second day the firing from the forts was rather severe on the masts and rigging of the first division. I wanted to remove them a little further down, but was prevented from doing so at the request of Lieutenant-Commanding Smith, who seemed determined not to withdraw until something was sunk. He had one man killed in the "Arletta," Acting-Master Smith, by a ten-inch shot striking between the stop of the mortar bed and the mortar, which disabled it for a time only; it was repaired in two or three hours, the men meanwhile under fire, without any occupation to keep up their interest. One or two men were wounded this day. We had another conflagration in the fort, the shells having set fire to some quarters put up for officers on the northwest angle of the works; they were all consumed. The firing seemed to be good this day, though some said the shells went over, and others said they fell short. The proof of accuracy was that the batteries were silenced every time the shells were concentrated on any one point. The fuses being so bad, I gave up the plan of timing them, and put in *full-length fuses*, to burst after they had entered the ground. In some respects this was disadvantageous, but we lost but few by bursting before time in the air. The ground being wet and soft, the shells descended 18 or 20 feet into the ground, exploding after some time, lifted the earth up, and let it fall back into its place again, not doing a great deal of harm, but demoralizing the men, who knew not what the consequences might be. The effect, I am told, was like that of an earthquake. When the shells hit the ramparts they did their work effectually, knocking off large pieces of the parapet and shattering the casemates. On the third and fourth day the ammunition on board began to grow short, and the steamers had to be sent down to bring it up, the boats of the squadron also assisting all they could, in the strong current, to supply the vessels. The steamers lay close to the mortar vessels while the shot and shell were flying all about; but strange to say, not a vessel was struck, though I expected to see some of them injured. The employment of them in that way could not be avoided. Everything was conducted with the greatest coolness, and the officers and men sat down to their meals as if nothing was going on—shells bursting in the air and falling alongside, and shot and rifle-shell crashing through the woods and tearing up trees by the roots. On the fifth day, the fire from the forts on the head of the first division was very rapid and troublesome. One hundred and twenty-five shots fell close to the vessels in one hour and thirty minutes, without, however, doing them any damage beyond hitting the "Para," the headmost vessel, and cutting up the rigging and masts. The fire of the enemy had been attracted to the mastheads of one of the large ships which had been moved up, and which they could see over the woods. I deemed it prudent to move three of them two or three lengths, much to the annoyance of the officers, who seemed indisposed to yield an inch. Still, my duty was to look out for the vessels and not have them destroyed. The "Norfolk Packet" got a piece of a shell through her decks, and had her rigging and crosstrees cut away, and one man wounded. For three days and nights the officers and men had had but little repose and but few comfortable meals, so I divided the division into three watches of four hours each, firing from one division about 168 times a watch, or altogether, during 24 hours, 1,500 shells. This I found rested the crews and produced more accurate firing. Overcome with fatigue, I had seen the commanders and

crews lying fast asleep on deck, with a mortar on board the vessel next to them, thundering away and shaking everything around them like an earthquake. The windows were broken at the Balise, thirty miles distant. It would be an interminable undertaking, sir, if I were to attempt to give a minute account of all the hard work performed in the flotilla, or mention separately all the meritorious acts and patient endurance of the commanders and crews of the mortar vessels. *All* stuck to their duty like men and Americans; and though some may have exhibited more ingenuity and intelligence than others, yet the performance of all commanded my highest admiration. I cannot say too much in favor of the three commanders of divisions, Lieutenants Watson Smith, W. W. Queen, and K. R. Breese. I can only say I would like always to have them at my side in times of danger and difficulty. They were untiring in their devotion to their duties, directing their officers, who could not be supposed to know as much about their duties as they did. I left the entire control of these divisions to themselves, trusting implicitly that they would faithfully carry out the orders which I had given them previous to the bombardment, and knowing that no powder or shell would be thrown away if they could help it. The end justified my confidence in them. During a bombardment of six days they were constantly exposed to a sharp fire from heavy guns. If they sustained no serious damage to their vessels it was no fault of the enemy, who tried his best to destroy them, and who, after I had withdrawn the vessels of Lieutenant-Commanding Queen from a very exposed position, reported that he had sunk them.

After bombarding the fort for three days, I began to despair of taking it, and, indeed, began to lose my confidence in mortars, but a deserter presented himself from Fort Jackson, and gave me such an account of the havoc made by our mortar practice that I had many doubts at first of his truth; he represented hundreds of shells falling into the fort, casemates broken in, citadel and out-buildings burnt, men demoralized and dispirited, magazine endangered, and the levee cut; we went to work with renewed vigor, and never flagged to the last.

On the night of the 20th, an expedition was fitted out, under Commander Bell, for the purpose of breaking the chain; it was composed of the gunboats "Pinola" and "Itasca"; it was arranged that *all* the mortars should play upon the fort while the operation was going on, which they did as fast as they could safely load and fire, nine shells being in the air frequently at one time. The vessels were discovered, and the forts opened fire on them at a distance of three and eight hundred yards. Lieutenant Crosby informed me that but for the rapid and accurate fire of the mortars the gun-boats would have been destroyed. The mortars silenced the batteries effectually, and Colonel Higgins ordered the men into the casemates, where they were in no way loath to go. These facts have been obtained from prisoners. The "Itasca," Lieutenant Caldwell, slipped the chain of one vessel, and was swept ashore by the current, when the "Pinola," Lieutenant-Commanding Crosby, got her off, both remaining in that position over thirty minutes, though seen by the enemy and seldom fired at.

On the 23d, I urged Flag-officer Farragut to commence the attack with the ships at night, as I feared the mortars would not hold out, the men were almost overcome with fatigue, and our supply ships laid a good way off. The enemy had brought over two heavy rifle guns to bear on the head of our line, and I was aware that he was daily adding to his defenses and strengthening his naval forces with ironclad batteries. The 23d was appointed, but the attack did not come off. I had fortunately dismounted with a shell, on that day, the heaviest rifle gun they had on St. Philip, breaking it in two, and it annoyed us no more. I did not know it at the time, but thought the ammunition had given out. On the 23d, the order was given to move at 2 o'clock, in the order which the flag officer will mention in his report. The steamers belonging to the mortar flotilla were assigned the duty of enfilading a heavy water battery of six guns and the barbette of guns which commanded the approach to the forts; and the mortars having obtained good range during the day, were to try and drive the men from the guns by their rapid fire, and bursting shell over the parapets. The flotilla steamers, composed of the "Harriet Lane," Lieutenant-Commanding Wainwright, leading; "Westfield," Commander Renshaw; "Owasco," Lieutenant-Commanding Guest; "Clifton," Lieutenant-Commanding Baldwin, and "Miami," Lieutenant-Commanding Harrell, moved up (when the flag-officer lifted his anchor), 70 fathoms apart, and took position under the batteries; the leading vessel 500 yards off, the others closing up as the fire commenced. Then, as soon as the "Hartford," "Brooklyn" and "Richmond" passed, they opened with shrapnel on the forts, having received the fire ten or fifteen minutes before replying to it. As the fire was high, and they were close in shore, nearer the forts than the enemy supposed, they occupied, as it turned out, a safer position than the vessels further out, there being only one killed and one wounded on board the "Harriet Lane," while the other steamers remained untouched. The commanders of all the vessels on this occasion did their duty, coolly kept their vessels close up, fired rapidly and accurately, and the signal was not made to retire until the last vessel of our gallant squadron passed through the flames, which seemed to be literally eating them up; every man, spar or rope was plainly seen amid the light, and every movement of the ships noted; that last vessel, the gallant "Iroquois," would provokingly linger and slow her engines opposite the forts to give the rebels a taste of her formidable battery. When she also disappeared in the smoke, our signal was hung out to retire, our duty having been accomplished, and the fort turning its entire attention to our little force. It could not, however, do us much harm, as the rain of mortar shells almost completely silenced them; never in my life did I witness such a scene, and never did rebels get such a castigation. Colonel Higgins ordered the men from the batteries into the casemates to avoid the mortar shells, which fell with particular effect on that night, while grapeshot and shrapnel from the ships gave them but few opportunities to fire from their casemates. The ships had gone by, the backbone of the rebellion was broken, the mortars ceased their fire, and nothing was heard for a time but the booming of guns as our fleet went flying up the river, scattering the enemy's gun-boats and sinking them as they passed. We all sat down to rest and speculate on the chances of seeing our old friends and brother officers again.

I was very hopeful myself, for I knew that the enemy had been too much demoralized during the last week by mortar practice to be able to stand against the fire of our ships. I gave the ships, when they started, forty-five minutes to pass the forts: they were only seventy from the time they lifted their anchors. I lost the services of a well armed and useful vessel, the "Jackson," for the attack on the batteries. Her commander, Lieutenant-Commanding Woodworth, during the affair was appointed to tow the "Portsmouth" ahead of the mortar steamers, but was carried down the stream. He persisted, however, in taking her into her berth after the battle was over and the steamers had retired, and anchored her, I believe, within nine hundred yards of the fort. His reception and that of the "Portsmouth" was a warm one, for the east batteries opened fire upon them; and, after escaping miraculously, the "Portsmouth," with some shots in

her hull and rigging, and one or two killed and wounded, coolly drifted out from under the guns and took her old position. Had the rebels not been overcome with despair she would have fared badly.

Immediately on the passage of the ships I sent Lieutenant-Commanding Guest up with a flag of truce, demanding the surrender of the forts. The flag of truce was fired on, but apologized for afterwards. The answer was, "The demand is inadmissible." Giving the men that day to rest, I prepared to fill up the vessels with ammunition and commence the bombardment again. Having in the meantime heard from Flag-officer Farragut that he had safely passed the batteries, I determined to make another attempt on these deluded people in the forts to make them surrender, and save the fur-

CAPTAIN J. L. BROOME (NOW LIEUT. COL.), MARINE CORPS.

ther effusion of blood. Flag-officer Farragut had unknowingly left a troublesome force in his rear, consisting of four steamers and a powerful steam battery of four thousand tons and sixteen guns, all protected by the forts. I did not know in what condition the battery was, only we had learned that she had come down the night before, ready prepared to wipe out our whole fleet. If the enemy counted so surely on destroying our whole fleet with her, it behooved me to be prudent, and not let the mortar vessels be sacrificed like the vessels at Norfolk. I commenced, then, a bombardment on the ironclad battery, supposing it lay close under Fort Jackson, and also set the vessels to work throwing shells into Fort Jackson again, to let them know that we were still taking care of them; but there was no response: the fight had all been taken out of them.

I sent the mortar vessels below to refit and prepare for sea, as also to prevent them from being driven from their position in case the iron battery came out to attack them. I felt sure that the steamers alone could manage the battery. Six of the schooners I ordered to proceed immediately to the rear of Fort Jackson and blockade all the bayous, so that the garrison could not escape or obtain supplies. I sent the "Miami" and "Sachem" to the rear of Fort St. Philip, to assist in landing troops. These vessels all appeared at their destination at the same time, and, when morning broke, the enemy found himself hemmed in on all sides. It was a military necessity that we should have the forts. Our squadron was cut off from coal, provisions, and ammunition ; our soldiers had but little chance to get to New Orleans through shallow bayous ; the enemy in the city would hesitate to surrender while the forts held out ; communication was cut off between them, and neither party knew what the other was willing to do. So I demanded a surrender again, through Lieutenant-Commanding Guest, offering to let them retain their side-arms and engage not to serve against the United States during the rebellion until regularly exchanged, provided they would honorably deliver up, *undamaged*, the forts, guns, muskets, provisions, and all munitions of war, the vessels under the guns of the fort, and all other public property. The answer was civil, and hopes were held out that, after being instructed by the authorities of New Orleans, they would surrender. In the meantime their men became dissatisfied at being so surrounded ; they had no hope of longer holding out with any chance of success, and gave signs of insubordination. On the 28th, a flag of truce came on board the "Harriet Lane," proposing to surrender Jackson and St. Philip on the terms proposed, and I immediately proceeded to the forts, with the steamers "Westfield," "Winona," and "Kennebec" in company, and sent a boat for General Duncan and Lieutenant-Colonel Higgins, and such persons as they might see fit to bring with them. These persons came on board, and, proceeding to the cabin of the "Harriet Lane," the capitulation was drawn up and signed, the original of which I have had the honor of forwarding to the department by Captain Bailey, no opportunity occurring to send it through Flag-officer Farragut, without loss of time. The officers late commanding the forts informed me that the vessels would not be included in the capitulation, as they (the military) had nothing to do with the naval officers, and were in no way responsible for their acts. There was evidently a want of unanimity between the different branches of the rebel service. I afterwards found out that great ill feeling existed, the naval commander having failed, in the opinion of the military, to co-operate with the forts ; the true state of the case being that they were both sadly beaten, and each laid the blame on the other. While engaged in the capitulation, an officer came below and informed me that the iron floating battery (the "Louisiana") had been set on fire by two steamers which had been lying alongside of her. This was a magnificent iron steam floating battery of four thousand tons and mounting sixteen heavy guns, and perfectly shot-proof. She had been brought down from New Orleans the day before, and on it the hopes of their salvation seemed to depend, as will appear by the following letter from General Duncan, taken in the fort :

FORT JACKSON, LOUISIANA, }
April 22, 1862. }

CAPTAIN—Your note of this date relative to the steamer "Louisiana," the forwardness of her preparations for attack, the disposition to be made of her, etc., has been received.

It is of vital importance that the present fire of the enemy should be withdrawn from us, which you alone can do. This can be done in the manner suggested this morning, under the cover of our guns, while your work on the boat can still be carried on in safety and security. Our position is a critical one, dependent entirely on the powers of endurance of our casemates, many of which have been completely shattered, and are crumbling away by repeated shocks, and therefore I respectfully, but earnestly, again urge my suggestions of this morning upon your notice. Our magazines are also in danger.

Very respectfully, your obedient servant,
J. K. DUNCAN,
Brigadier-General.

Captain J. K. MITCHELL,
Commanding Naval Forces, Lower Mississippi River.

I was in hopes of saving this vessel as a prize, for she would have been so materially useful to us in all future operations on the coast, her batteries and strength being sufficient to silence any fort here, aided by the other vessels. Seeing her lying so quiet, with colors down and the two steamers under our guns, I never dreamed for a moment that they had not surrendered. The forts and ourselves had flags of truce flying, and I could not make any movement without violating the honor of the United States and interrupting the capitulation which was being drawn up. The burning of the vessels was done so quietly that no one suspected it until the battery was in a blaze. I merely remarked to the commanders of the forts that the act was in no way creditable to the rebel commander. The reply was, "We are not responsible for the acts of these naval officers." We proceeded with the conference, and while so engaged an officer came to inform me that the ironclad battery was all in flames and drifting down on us, having burnt the ropes that had fastened her to the bank. I inquired of the late commanders of the forts if they knew if the guns were loaded, or if she had much powder on board. The answer was, "I presume so, but we know nothing about the naval matters here." At this moment the guns, being heated, commenced going off, with a probability of throwing shot and shell amidst friend and foe. I did not deign to notice it further than to say to the military officers, "If you don't mind the effects of the explosion which is soon to come, we can stand it." If the ever memorable Commander Mitchell calculated to make a stampede in the United States vessels by his infamous act, he was mistaken ; none of them moved or intended to move, and the conference was carried on as calmly as if nothing else was going on, though proper precautions were taken to keep them clear of the burning battery. A good Providence, which directs the most unimportant events, sent the battery off towards Fort St. Philip, and as it got abreast of that formidable fort it blew up with a force which scattered the fragments in all directions, killing one of their own men in Fort St. Philip, and when the smoke cleared off it was nowhere to be seen, having sunk immediately in the deep water of the Mississippi. The explosion was terrific, and was seen and heard for many miles up and down the river. Had it occurred near the vessels it would have destroyed every one of them. This, no doubt, was the object of the arch-traitor who was the instigator of the act. He failed to co-operate, like a man, with his military confederates, who looked to the means he had at his disposal to save them from destruction, and who scorned alike his want of courage in not assisting them, as well as the unheard of and perfidious act which might, in a measure, have reflected on them.

How different was the course of the military commanders, who, though engaged in so bad a cause, behaved honorably to the end. Every article in the fort was delivered up undamaged. Nothing was destroyed, either before the capitulation or while the capitulation was going on, or afterwards. The most scrupulous regard was paid to their promises. They defended their works like men, and had they been fighting for the flag under which they were born instead of against it, it would have been honor enough for any man to have said he had fought by their side.

After the capitulation was signed, I sent Commander W. B. Renshaw to Fort Jackson, and Lieutenant-Commanding Ed. Nichols to Fort St. Philip to receive the surrender of the forts. The rebel flag was hauled down and the stars and stripes once more floated over the property of the United States. The sun never shone on a more contented and happy looking set of faces than those of the prisoners in and about the forts. Many of them had not seen their families for months, and a large portion had been pressed into a service distasteful to them, subject to the rigor of a discipline severe beyond measure. They were frequently exposed to punishments, for slight causes, which the human frame could scarcely endure, and the men who underwent some of the tortures mentioned on a list of punishments I have in my possession, must have been unable afterwards to do any duty for months to come. Instead of the downcast countenances of conquered people, they emerged from the fort (going home on their parole) like a parcel of happy school-boys in holiday times, and no doubt they felt like them also.

When the flags had been exchanged, I devoted my attention to Commander Mitchell, who was lying a half mile above us with three steamers, one of which he had scuttled. Approaching him in the "Harriet Lane," I directed Lieutenant-Command- ign Wainwright to fire a gun over him, when he lowered his flag. I then sent Lieutenant-Com- manding Wainwright on board to take possession and receive the unconditional surrender of the party, consisting of fourteen naval officers and seven engineers, temporarily appointed; the crew of the ironclad battery consisted of three hundred men and two companies of marine artillery, nearly all from civil life, and serving much against their will, so they said. Commander Mitchell and the other naval officers were transferred to the "West- field" as prisoners of war, and as soon as time would allow, the marines and sailors were sent in one of the captured vessels to Flag-officer Farragut, at New Orleans. The captured military officers were sent up to New Orleans on their parole, and thus ended the day on which the great Mississippi rejoiced once more in having its portals opened to the commerce of the world. From the appearance and talk of the soldiers, we might soon hope to see the people united again under the folds of the flag of the Union. While the capitulation was going on I sent the steamer "Clifton" down to bring up troops, and when General Phelps came up I turned the forts, guns, and munitions of war over to his keeping. My next step was to visit Forts Jackson and St. Philip. Never in my life did I witness such a scene of desolation and wreck as the former pre- sented. It was plowed up by the thirteen-inch mortars, the bombs had set fire to and burnt out all the buildings in and around the forts; casemates were crushed and were crumbling in, and the only thing that saved them were the sandbags that had been sent from New Orleans during the bombard- ment, and when they began to feel the effects of the mortars. When the communication was cut off between them and the city, this resource of sand- bags could avail them no longer. It was useless for them to hold out; a day's bombardment would have finished them; they had no means of repair- ing damages; the levee had been cut by the thir- teen-inch bombs in over a hundred places; and the water had entered the casemates, making it very uncomfortable, if not impossible to live there any

longer. It was the only place the men had to fly to out of reach of the bombs. The drawbridge over the moat had been broken all to pieces, and all the causeways leading from the fort were cut and blown up with bombshells, so that it must have been impossible to walk there or carry on any oper- ations with any degree of safety. The magazine seems to have been much endangered, explosions having taken place at the door itself, all the cotton bags and protections having been blown away from before the magazine door. Eleven guns were dismounted during the bombardment, some of which were remounted again and used upon us. The walls were cracked and broken in many places, and we could scarcely step without treading into a hole made by a bomb-shell; the accuracy of the fire is, perhaps, the best ever seen in mortar practice; it seems to have entirely demoralized the men and astonished the officers. A water battery, contain- ing six very heavy guns, and which annoyed us at times very much, was filled with the marks of the bombs, no less than 170 having fallen into it, smash- ing in the magazine, and driving the people out of it. On the night of the passage of the ships this battery was completely silenced, so many bombs fell into it and burst over it. It had one gun in it, the largest I have ever seen, made at the Tredegar works. I would not pretend to say how many bombs fell in the ditches around the works, but soldiers in the forts say about three thousand; many burst over the works, scattering the pieces of shell all around. The enemy admit but fourteen killed and thirty- nine wounded by the bombardment, which is likely the case, as we found but fourteen fresh graves, and the men mostly staid in the casemates, which were three inches deep with water and very un- comfortable. Many remarkable escapes and inci- dents were related to us as having happened dur- ing the bombardment. Colonel Higgins stated an instance where a man was buried deep in the earth by a bomb striking him between the shoulders, and directly afterwards another bomb exploded in the same place, and threw the corpse high in the air. All the boats and scows around the ditches and near the landing were sunk by bombs; and when we took possession the only way they had to get in and out of the fort to the landing was by one small boat to ferry them across. All the lumber, shingles, and bricks used in building or repairs were scat- tered about in confusion and burnt up, and every amount of discomfort that men could bear seemed to have been showered upon those poor deluded wretches.

I was so much struck with the deserted appear- ance of what was once a most beautiful spot, that I ordered Mr. Gerdes and his assistants on the Coast Survey to make me an accurate plan of all the works, denoting every bomb that fell, and (as near as possible) the injury the fort had sustained, every distance being accurately measured by tape-line and compass, and the comparative size of fractures noted. The work has been executed with great zeal and accuracy, though it will only give a faint idea of the bombs that fell about the fort; many are lost sight of in the water which has been let in by the cut levees; many burst over the fort; but enough have been marked to indicate the wonder ful precision of fire and the endurance of the forts. Had the ground been hard instead of being soft mud, the first day's bombardment would have blown Fort Jackson into atoms; as it is, it is very much injured, and will require thorough repair be- fore it can be made habitable.

Fort St. Philip received very little damage from our bombs, having fired at it with only one mortar, and that for the purpose of silencing a heavy rifled gun which annoyed us very much; we were fortun- ate enough to strike it in the middle, and break it in two, and had not much more annoyance from that fort; two guns were capsized by a bomb at one time, but without injuring them; they were soon replaced; some trifling damage was done to the works, though nothing to affect the efficiency of the batteries; it was from Fort St. Philip that our ships suffered most, the men and officers there, having had, comparatively, an easy time of it. I felt sure that St. Philip would surrender the moment Jackson hauled down the secession flag, and consequently directed all the attention of the mortar schooners to the latter fort. The final result justified me in coming to this conclusion.

I trust that you will excuse me, sir, for dwelling so minutely on matters relating to this important victory, though I have endeavored to make my report as short as possible.

Every little incident in this ever to be remembered drama will be interesting to the true lovers of our Union, who will rejoice over the fact that the great river which is the main artery of our country is once more in our possession, and that we may soon hope to see the stars and stripes floating over every hut and hamlet along its banks. It only remains for me, sir, to do justice to the officers who have been under my command during this arduous and sometimes unpleasant service. Commander Renshaw, Lieutenant-Commanding Guest, Lieutenant-Commanding Wainwright, Lieutenant-Commanding Harrell, Lieutenant-Commanding Baldwin, Lieutenant-Commanding Woodworth, are the officers commanding steamers connected with the flotilla. Their duties were various and arduous—towing, supplying, and getting under the guns of the fort when opportunities offered, or they were permitted to expose their vessels. In the attack on the water batteries Lieutenant-Commanding Wainwright commanded the "Harriet Lane" (as I noticed) coolly and bravely; and his officers and crew did their duty, all the vessels lying quietly under the heavy fire for fifteen minutes, until it was time to open their batteries, which they did with effect, until the time came to retire. Commander Renshaw made his rifle gun tell with effect, keeping his vessel in close order. Lieutenant-Commanding Guest, with his zealous crew, who had fired over 200 shell at the forts at different times, kept his shell flying as fast as usual, bursting (as I witnessed) with good effect in the midst of the batteries. Lieutenant-Commanding Baldwin, whom I have always found ready for any duty, no matter how arduous or thankless, was in no way behind any one; his heavy battery of nine-inch and thirty-two-pounders rattled through the outer works of the fort, helping to keep Jackson quiet while our heavy ships were forcing their way through logs chained together, fire-rafts, rams, to say nothing of the enemy's gun-boats, iron batteries, and forts built to dispute the passage of any fleet which might be sent against them. The steamer "Jackson," Lieutenant-Commanding Woodworth, towed the "Portsmouth" gallantly into fire, though his position was more gallantly than wisely taken; he was fortunate that his vessel and the "Portsmouth" were not cut to pieces. I have been so struck with the energy and zeal of Lieutenants-Commanding Woodworth and Baldwin, that I hope the Navy Department will reward them by re-appointing them as permanent officers in the service (if they will accept it), for while the Navy is composed of such men it will never be defeated in equal contests. Lieutenant-Commanding Harrell, of the "Miami," has had under his command a most wretched and unmanageable vessel, and has not had an opportunity to do himself full justice; he was always ready to do any service required of him, and on the night of the attack, with the rest, worked his battery with effect. As soon as the forts had been passed, on account of his light draught, I sent him to co-operate with General Butler in landing troops outside, which duty he performed to my entire satisfaction.

If the efforts of the mortar flotilla have not met your expectations in reducing the forts in a shorter time, it must be remembered that great difficulties existed, first in the soil, which allowed the bombs to sink at least twenty feet, by measurement, before exploding, the difficulty of seeing the fort, as it is not much above the surrounding bushes, and the endurance of the casemates, which were deeply covered with earth, and better constructed than supposed; but I am firmly of opinion that the moral effect of this bombardment will go far towards clearing all forts of rebels, and I draw attention to the case of Fort Livingston, which held out a flag of truce the moment three mortar vessels appeared before it. Flag-officer Farragut has ordered me to repair to Ship Island to await the arrival of the larger vessels, but not to commence any operations until he arrives.

I herewith enclose the reports of the commanders of steamers in relation to the conduct of those under their command.

I have the honor to remain,
Very respectfully,
Your obedient servant,
DAVID D. PORTER,
Commanding Flotilla.

Hon. GIDEON WELLES,
Secretary of the Navy.

REPORT OF COMMANDER W. B. RENSHAW, UNITED STATES STEAMER "WESTFIELD."

UNITED STATES STEAMER "WESTFIELD," }
MISSISSIPPI RIVER, May 5, 1862. }

SIR—Agreeably to your order, I have the honor to submit the following report of the operations of the United States steamer "Westfield," under my command, since her arrival in the Mississippi River.

Upon our reaching Pass à l'Outre, on the morning of the 18th of March, I had the honor of reporting my arrival to you in person, and by your order at once proceeded to tow the mortar schooners inside the bar. From that date until the 13th day of April, we were constantly engaged towing and assisting in getting the United States ships "Mississippi" and "Pensacola" over the bar at Southwest Pass.

On the 13th, while engaged covering the Coast Survey party, who were triangulating the river, you joined us with the "Harriet Lane" and other vessels of the squadron, and ordered me to start ahead and endeavor to reach with our rifle-shot two of the rebel gun-boats that were below the point watching our motions. Two discharges of the rifle caused them to retire and join some six or eight of their squadron lying under the guns at Fort Jackson. We continued our advance, and soon brought the whole squadron within range of our 100-pounder rifle, when we again opened fire, and so successfully that (as I have since learned from prisoners) we broke the shaft of the gun-boat "Defiance," and otherwise so much crippled her that she was subsequently sunk by her crew. The forts having opened upon us, our signal of recall was made, and we returned to our station.

On the morning of the 17th, our boats, together with those of the mortar flotilla, extinguished the fire, and towed on shore a large fire-raft; and on the night of the 17th, we ran alongside to windward of another large fire-raft. We threw water from our force-pumps upon it, and materially assisted in subduing the flames.

On the afternoon of the 18th, after assisting in towing the mortar schooners to their positions, I was directed by you to proceed up the river and drive off a steamer that menaced the head of our line of mortar vessels. The steamer fled upon our approach, but having reached a position that brought the forts in easy range of our rifle, we fired deliberately ten shots with that gun, many of which, I have reason to believe, took effect upon Fort St. Philip, the enemy at the same time throwing their rifle and 10 inch shot and shell thickly around us.

At 3.30 A. M., on the morning of the 21st, we discovered another large fire-raft, which we ran alongside of and assisted in extinguishing. From the 19th to the 24th instant, we were engaged with the rest of the flotilla steamers in supplying the mortar schooners with ammunition.

On the morning of the 24th, we got under way, in company with the flotilla steamers, led by yourself in the "Harriet Lane," together with all the vessels of the squadron, for the attack on Forts Jackson and St. Philip. At 3.45 we opened fire with all our guns upon Fort Jackson at an estimated distance of 600 yards, and remained in this position until your signal was made to cease firing and retire from action.

I am happy to inform you that during this heavy cannonade this ship was not injured or a man hurt on board, owing to the fire of the enemy, from the face of the fort we engaged, having passed over us.

It also affords me the highest gratification to express my unqualified approbation and high appreciation of the bravery and zealous attention to duty of the officers and crew of the ship, whether engaged in our unremitting duties or when under fire of the enemy's guns.

During our operations against the forts we have expended thirty-five rifle-shot and shell, eleven 9-inch shell, and seventeen 8-inch shell. Here let me state, sir, that upon the several occasions this ship has been under the fire of the forts, I have been constrained from using my very efficient rifled gun as frequently as I could have desired, in consequence of there being no more projectiles (than those we had on board) upon the station. I will also state that it was in accordance with your wishes that I was thus careful of the few shot and shell we had.

Permit me, in conclusion, to call your attention to the fact, in explanation of the seemingly small amount of ammunition we have expended, that upon all the occasions this ship has been engaged (save the action of the 24th ultimo) it was advantageous to fight her "head on," which prevented the use of all the guns except the rifle.

Respectfully submitted,

W. B. RENSHAW,
Commander United States Navy.

Commander D. D. PORTER,
Commanding Mortar Flotilla, Mississippi River.

REPORT OF LIEUTENANT-COMMANDING A. D. HAR-RELL, UNITED STATES STEAMER "MIAMI."

UNITED STATES STEAMER "MIAMI," }
MISSISSIPPI RIVER, April 24, 1862. }

SIR—I have the honor to report that, in obedience to your order, I weighed anchor at half-past two o'clock on the morning of the 24th instant, and took my assigned position in the line. At the proper time opened and continued fire upon Fort Jackson until ordered to discontinue.

I have pleasure in adding that officers and men did their whole duty, and although shot and shell passed over and fell thickly around us, we sustained no injury.

Very respectfully,
Your obedient servant,
A. D. HARRELL,
Lieutenant-Commanding.

Commander D. D. PORTER,
Commanding Mortar Flotilla, Mississippi River.

UNITED STATES STEAMER "MIAMI," }
MISSISSIPPI RIVER, May 3, 1862. }

SIR—I have the honor to report that, in obedience to your order of the 24th ultimo, which I received immediately after the action of that morning, I received General Butler and staff on board, and proceeded to Pilot Town for the boats which I was ordered to procure.

After obtaining them, I immediately started to Isle au Breton Bay, and there received on board one regiment of troops, which I landed at Quarantine Station, above and in the rear of Fort St. Philip. I continued conveying and landing troops until the forts surrendered. I then proceeded and landed seven hundred and fifty troops at New Orleans on the first instant.

Very respectfully,
Your obedient servant,
A. D. HARRELL,
Lieutenant-Commanding.

Commander D. D. PORTER,
Commanding Mortar Flotilla, Mississippi River.

REPORT OF LIEUTENANT J. M WAINWRIGHT. COMMANDING UNITED STATES STEAMER "HAR-RIET LANE."

UNITED STATES STEAMER "HARRIET LANE." }
MISSISSIPPI RIVER, April 25, 1862. }

SIR—In obedience to your order, I beg leave to submit the following report of the part taken by this vessel in the action on the morning of the 24th instant, between the United States naval forces and the batteries of Forts Jackson and St. Philip.

At 1.30 A. M., all hands were called, in anticipation of the signal from the flag-ship to prepare to get under way, which was made at two A. M. Every preparation for a move being completed, we impatiently waited the moment when our turn would come.

In the meantime the vessels of the fleet were getting under way, and forming in their respective lines, the starboard under Captain Bailey, in the gun-boat "Cayuga," leading. At 3.28 A. M., the fleet being all under way, and steaming up the river, signal was made to the steamers of the mortar flotilla to weigh anchor, and we stood up towards the forts, our duty being to take an enfilading position below the water battery of Fort Jackson.

At 3.45 A. M., the forts opened on the leading ships, and immediately thereafter the mortar vessels commenced, and at 3.50, were raining a rapid and continuous fire on the enemy such as has rarely before been witnessed.

The crew were now called to quarters, and we steamed rapidly up the river to take our appointed position. Shortly after we passed the head of the line of mortar vessels, we found ourselves under the fire of the enemy, which was very hot, but most fortunately, too high. It was not till 4.20 A. M., that our guns could be brought to bear, when we opened on them with shell and shrapnel.

At 4.30 A. M., a shot carried away one of the stanchions and a portion of the railing of the bridge between the wheel-houses, the fragments of which killed one man, and seriously wounded another stationed at the 9-inch gun on the quarterdeck.

We retained our position within five hundred yards of Fort Jackson, firing as rapidly as possible, till 4.50 A. M., when the last vessel was seen to pass between the forts. The signal was then made to retire from action, and we stood down the river to our former anchorage, followed by the steamers of the mortar flotilla. At 4.55 A. M., four rockets were sent up, as a signal to the mortar vessels to cease firing, and shortly after we came to an anchor astern of them.

It gives me great pleasure to say that one and all

the officers and crew of this vessel did their duty like men, and displayed commendable coolness under a heavy fire, which they were obliged to endure for some minutes before it could be returned. My especial thanks are due to the executive officer, Lieutenant Edward Lea, who had the general superintendence of the battery ; Acting-Masters Willis F. Munroe and Charles H. Hamilton, commanding the gun divisions, and Acting-Master J. A. Hannum, in charge of the powder division, which was well and rapidly served ; also to Acting-Master George W. Sumner, an *eleve* of the Naval Academy attached to the "Horace Beales," who volunteered for service, and gave me his valuable assistance in superintending the cutting of shrapnel, etc.

In conclusion, you must permit me to render the humble tribute of my admiration to the coolness, ability, and untiring zeal you have displayed during the arduous and perilous duty so gallantly performed for the last six days by the mortar flotilla. Such an example could not fail to inspire the confidence of those under your command in the glorious success which has attended their exertions, and which the result has proved to be so well founded.

I herewith enclose the report of the medical officer of the casualties which occurred on board this vessel.

I am, very respectfully,
Your most obedient servant,
J. M. WAINWRIGHT,
Lieutenant-Commanding.
Commander DAVID D. PORTER,
Commanding Mortar Flotilla.

REPORT OF LIEUTENANT-COMMANDING JOHN GUEST, UNITED STATES GUN-BOAT "OWASCO."

UNITED STATES STEAM GUN-BOAT "OWASCO,"
MISSISSIPPI RIVER, April 28, 1862.

SIR—In obedience to your instructions I submit this report :

At meridian on the 12th of April, the "Owasco" being at the head of the passes, by your order I got under way to protect the steamer "Sachem," having on board the Coast Survey party, under Mr. F. H. Gerdes, while making a reconnoissance of the river. On reaching our advanced squadron of gun-boats, Commander S. P. Lee, senior officer, I reported to him that I was about to pass ahead for the purpose above indicated.

Captain Lee said the enemy were in large force, and that he would follow with all the gun-boats. As it was too late, when the "Sachem" got up to us, to work, we deferred proceeding till morning. In the meantime I advised you, sir, of the state of affairs, and next morning, shortly after I commenced work, I had the satisfaction to see you pass me with all the steamers of the mortar flotilla, which doubtless prevented much annoyance from the enemy.

Clearing the bushes with canister from our howitzers, the surveyors, Messrs. Oltmanns and Bowie, landed in one of our boats and prosecuted their work without molestation.

On the 14th, we resumed the work, and carried the triangulation well up to the forts on the right bank of the river, supported by the "Westfield," Commander Renshaw. The surveyors were landed at the point desired, in the "Owasco's" gig, under charge of Master's Mate Thomas D. Babb. As the boat shoved off I observed three of the rebel steamers within gunshot, and fearing they might fire upon our boat, I opened upon them. After firing four shells from the 11-inch gun and three from the rifled gun, the steamers moved up to the forts. At this moment some riflemen in the bushes fired at the gig-boat, without hurting any one, although an oar was struck. Mr. Babb, with perfect composure, returned the fire from his boat. The surveying party, with equal coolness, put up their signals and

took three angles, one hundred yards from the spot where they were fired at.

On the 15th, as the work had not been carried sufficiently high up on the left bank of the river, by your order I took the party up that side, followed by the "Miami" as a support.

After the surveyors had finished, finding myself within easy range of the forts, just before leaving I fired an 11-inch shell into Fort Jackson, to try their range. They fired twice in return, one of the shots passing over us and falling a quarter of a mile astern, the other just ahead of us.

Too much praise cannot be awarded Messrs. Oltmanns and Bowie for the intrepid and skillful manner in which they performed this service.

On the 16th, the "Owasco" accompanied you in your experimental trial with three of the mortar schooners in trying the ranges on the forts from the left bank of the river. This day the enemy fired about twenty shots, but without effect.

On the 17th, our boats, in charge of Mr. Babb, were employed in towing fire ships clear of the fleet.

On the 18th, at 6 A. M., we got under way, and soon received orders from you to proceed ahead of the bomb schooners, on the right bank, to clear the bushes of riflemen near the designated position of the mortar schooners. In obedience thereto, we steamed close along the bank of the river until we arrived at a smoke pipe of a sunken steamer, when the forts, at five minutes past nine, fired two shots at us, which I immediately returned from my 11-inch gun. This was followed by sharp firing from both forts.

Being within easy range of Fort Jackson, I directed my fire upon it and continued the action ; twenty minutes after that the first mortar schooner opened, and after that at intervals, as fast as they could be got into position.

At 10 o'clock, I was glad to see the "Iroquois," Captain De Camp, come to my support, and after her the gun-boats, one by one. The fire of the forts was dispersed among them, and was not so severe around us, although still quite sharp.

Previous to the appearance of the "Iroquois," in the thickest of the firing, all on board the "Owasco" were much gratified at a visit from you, sir, when you came to tell us that you had asked that the gun-boats of the fleet might be sent to our support.

We maintained our position for two hours and three-quarters, until we had expended our last shell, when we retired from action by your order, having fired one hundred 11-inch shells and thirty-seven shells from our rifled gun.

We went down immediately to the ordnance ship "Sportsman"; filled up with ammunition ; found there were no cartridges made ; but my men cheerfully worked all night, cutting out and sewing up cylinders, and by next morning (the 19th) we were ready for action again.

Coming up with the bomb fleet, and hearing you were on board the flag-ship, steamed up to our old position, and opened fire again on Fort Jackson. Fired fifty-five 11-inch shells, and twelve from the rifled gun.

The firing from the forts was very sharp. At this time I had another welcome visit from you, and retired, at your order, as it was thought 11-inch ammunition was running short, and it was desirable to keep it for closer distance.

By your permission I crossed the river to look for an anchor I had slipped the night before ; but not finding it, I returned to my old position, near the smoke pipe of the sunken steamer, and finding the three leading mortar schooners in great danger of being sunk by the enemy's fire, I delivered ten 11-inch shells to Fort Jackson, and then sought you to inform you of the fact. Having received orders to withdraw them for a time, I returned and delivered your order to Lieutenant-Commanding Watson Smith, who executed it.

15

On the 20th, 21st, 22d, and 23d, we were engaged in supplying the mortar schooners with ammunition—very often under fire.

On the 24th, at 3.15 A. M., in the general attack, the "Owasco" took her position—the third in your line, by order—and followed your motions.

Opened with shrapnel at 4 A. M., and continued a deliberate fire until 4.45, taking care not to fire in the direction of our ships which were passing the forts.

At 4.45, observed your signal "Retire from action," which we did.

Very respectfully, your obedient servant,
JOHN GUEST,
Lieutenant-Commanding.

Flag-officer D. G. FARRAGUT,
Commanding Flotilla.

REPORT OF ACTING LIEUTENANT-COMMANDING C.H. BALDWIN, UNITED STATES STEAMER "CLIFTON."

UNITED STATES STEAMER, "CLIFTON," }
NEW ORLEANS, May 1, 1862. }

SIR—I have the honor to report that, since my arrival at Pass à l'Outre, on the 18th of March, I have been employed, with little intermission, as follows : Towing the mortar vessels attached to the flotilla to the Southwest Pass, and for the succeeding two weeks was constantly engaged in assisting the larger vessels belonging to the flag-officer's squadron, viz : the "Pensacola," and "Mississippi," over the bar on which they had grounded, and in aiding the gun-boats attached to same squadron when aground in the river.

After this we were employed in making reconnoissances of Forts Jackson and St. Philip, and in protecting the officers of the Coast Survey service while they were engaged in obtaining their distances, and in driving back the enemy's gun-boats, which occasionally made their appearance outside the chain.

On the 17th of April, we were assisting in towing mortar schooners into their positions, and, during the six days of the bombardment by these vessels, we were unremittingly employed in supplying them with powder and shell and in guard duty—our nights being passed in looking after the fire-rafts which the enemy sent down against the fleet, and in towing them ashore. In this duty, I believe I may say, we were quite successful.

These various duties during the six days of the bombardment carried our vessels pretty constantly under the fire of the enemy. We have, however, been so fortunate as to escape any injury from their shot.

On the morning of the 24th, in obedience to your order, we got under way, taking our appointed station in the line of steamers under your personal command, and proceeded to within short range of the guns of Fort Jackson, and opened fire on the enemy from our two forward nine-inch guns, aided at times by our nine-inch after-pivot gun and 32-pounder forward broadside gun, using five-second shell and shrapnel. This we continued until the flag-officer's squadron had passed both forts, when, in obedience to your signal, we drifted out of range. I am happy to state that we escaped without injury.

The duties now entailed upon us were to keep a strict lookout upon the gun-boats and floating battery of the enemy, which were lying close under the guns of Fort Jackson. Until the morning of the 28th, when Forts Jackson and St. Philip having surrendered to you, we were dispatched some sixteen miles down the river to bring up a portion of the force under General Butler's command, then lying there. On the afternoon of that day this was accomplished, and we arrived in sight of the forts just as our own flags were hoisted in place of the rebel ensigns.

I towed up a large transport ship with 1,300 troops on board, under Brigadier-General Phelps, and taking five companies of them on board the "Clifton," landed them at both forts—they receiving their possession of them from the naval officers of your squadron, then in charge of the work.

I also, under your order, placed crews aboard the two rebel steamers, then in your possession, and transferred some 250 prisoners taken from the rebel gun-boats and floating battery to the officer in charge at Fort St. Philip.

We have just arrived here, having towed a transport up the river with a large number of General Butler's troops on board, intended to garrison the city of New Orleans, now held by our squadron.

Permit me here respectfully to state that officers and crew, whether employed in the harassing duties which so constantly devolved upon us of towing and getting large vessels over the bar, or while engaged with the enemy, have behaved so uniformly well that I hesitate to particularize any one individual. During the time above referred to, neither the ship, engines, nor boilers have been for a moment out of order in any respect.

I have the honor to be, sir,
Respectfully, your obedient servant,
C. H. BALDWIN,
Acting Lieutenant-Commanding.

Commander D. D. PORTER,
Commanding Flotilla

REPORT OF LIEUTENANT-COMMANDING WATSON SMITH, FIRST DIVISION MORTAR FLOTILLA.

UNITED STATES MORTAR SCHOONER "NOR- }
FOLK PACKET," MISSISSIPPI RIVER, }
May 3, 1862. }

SIR—On the 18th ultimo, in obedience to your order, the first division of the flotilla moved up the right bank of the river to the flag indicated by you as distant from Fort Jackson 2,950 yards, and from Fort St. Philip 4,260 yards ; the head vessel securing at that point with an anchor a little off shore, and light lines from the port bow and quarter to trees. The other vessels of the division, extending in close order to the distance of 3,620 yards from Fort Jackson, were secured in the same manner.

At 10 A. M., commenced firing upon Fort Jackson, discharging each mortar at intervals of ten minutes. The forts responded, their shot and shell falling around the vessels, and one, a 68-pound shot, killing a man on board the "Arletta," and lodging under the mortar, but not disabling it. At 6.30 P. M., ceased firing, by signal from "Harriet Lane."

April 19, at 7.30 A. M., the "Harriet Lane" made signal to commence firing. Discharged each mortar, at intervals of twenty minutes, upon Fort Jackson, until 8.45 A. M., when the interval was shortened to ten minutes. A shell bursting near the main masthead disabled one man who was aloft, destroyed a halliard block, and cut two main shrouds. At 4 P. M., ceased firing, the bombardment being continued by the divisions in watches.

On the 20th, 21st, 22d, and 23d, the firing was continued by the divisions in watches, excepting during the watch from 8 to midnight of the 20th, when the whole flotilla fired rapidly, while an expedition from the squadron cut the barrier chain near the forts.

No further injuries were sustained by persons in the first division, and but little damage to hulls, rigging, or spars, besides the occasional cutting by fragments of shells.

From the 21st, the firing from Fort St. Philip

was at times annoying, and by your direction two vessels at the head of the line directed their fire upon it. On the 23d, the enemy did not reply.

April 24, at 3.30 A. M., the firing commencing between the forts and the squadron passing up the river, the whole flotilla commenced firing rapidly upon Fort Jackson. At 4.45 A. M., the squadron, with few exceptions, had passed the forts. Ceased firing by signal from "Harriet Lane." During this one hour and fifteen minutes this vessel fired twenty-eight shells, being at the rate of one in two and two-thirds minutes. The other vessels fired as rapidly. After the bombardment, on examining the vessels, all were found in condition to continue the fire or perform other service.

The heaviest charges used were twenty-three pounds, to reach Fort St. Philip, distant 4,710 yards, against a fresh wind.

Slight damage was done to the light bulwarks by the shock from the mortars but the mortar supports and the hulls below the plank sheer were unaffected.

On the same afternoon, six of the mortar vessels were sent to sea upon blockading service, and three of them, the "Arletta," "C. P. Williams," and "O. H. Lee," belonged to this division. Their quick departure and continued absence prevents my giving you the aggregate number of shells fired by the first division during the bombardment. The four remaining vessels fired 1,512 shells, using 30,994 pounds of powder.

It was not always possible to mark and register the course of each shell, because of our not having a distinct view of the enemy and the mingling of so many shells as they converged in the direction of the forts. The accompanying reports of the acting-masters commanding the mortar vessels are in a comprehensive form furnished by them, and are as full as accuracy will permit.

The following is from the surgeon's report:

Killed: James Laver, ordinary seaman, on board the "Arletta," native of Isle of Jersey; struck by an eight-inch solid shot on April 18.

Slightly wounded, disabled: Michael Brady, carpenter's mate of this vessel, aged 32, native of New York; struck by a fragment of a shell on April 19.

Although the enemy's fire was so well directed at times as to threaten the destruction of the vessels, the duties at quarters were performed, and the intervals of rest between watches enjoyed, with commendable coolness and composure throughout the division. Respectfully yours,

WATSON SMITH,
Lieutenant Commanding First Division.

Commander D. D. PORTER,
Commanding U. S. Mortar Flotilla,
Mississippi River.

REPORT OF LIEUTENANT-COMMANDING WALTER W. QUEEN, SECOND DIVISION MORTAR FLOTILLA.

UNITED STATES SCHOONER "T. A. WARD,"
MISSISSIPPI RIVER, May 3, 1862.

SIR—I beg leave to submit to you the following report of the second division of the mortar flotilla:

On the morning of the 18th of April, 1862, my vessel was towed into position by the United States steamer "Miami" at 8.30 A. M. I anchored 3,900 yards below Fort Jackson, on the eastern bank of the river. The schooners of my division anchored astern of me in the following order, viz: "Matthew Vassar," "George Mangham," "Adolph Hugel," "Maria J. Carlton," and "Sydney C. Jones," the "Orvetta" having previously taken a position on the western bank of the river, and thus being separated from the division.

Both forts immediately opened on us, firing very

rapidly. At 8.45, we commenced firing on Fort Jackson, the shot from the fort falling in every direction around us, one of which struck so close to our quarter as to throw down some barrels of powder in the magazine by the concussion, but doing no damage. Shortly afterwards, another struck us, cutting away the forward shroud of port main rigging, passing through the wardroom, bulkhead pantry, stateroom, deck, storeroom, and extra magazine, escaping through the starboard quarter six inches above water line, doing considerable damage. I at once directed Mr. Hatch to drop the vessel down some 300 yards, which he did, followed by the three vessels lying immediately astern of me. I then went to the "Sydney C. Jones." After taking their new positions the vessels which had dropped astern recommenced firing. While lying in her former position, the "Mangham" received a shot in her port bow, which passed through her galley and lodged in the mortar bed, doing no further injury.

The vessels were now actively engaged in throwing shells into the forts, and as no intervening object obstructed our sight, we could see the effect of our shells as each one lodged in or near the forts. We continued firing all day, not even ceasing for the men to eat their meals. About 5.30 P. M., we could see heavy smoke rising from a building outside the fort, caused by the bursting of a shell, and soon after the fort was seen to be on fire in three separate places, which soon formed into one mass of flames, since discovered to have been the citadel. At 6 P. M., we ceased firing, in obedience to signal from the "Harriet Lane." At this time, we could distinguish men upon the ramparts trying to extinguish the flames.

At 9 o'clock, I received an order from you to drop down 800 yards and be in readiness to move across the river early in the morning, as you thought it likely the enemy would move his guns down the river and open on us in the morning. This we did, and nothing more of any importance occurred during the night. It is strange to say that, although the shot came around us in immense numbers, yet not one man was even wounded during the first day's engagement.

On the morning of the 19th instant, we were taken in tow by the "Clifton," and took our position in line with the rest of the flotilla, on the west bank of the river, and at 8.30 A. M., were all engaged in throwing shells into the fort. The "Hartford" moved up and anchored off her beam, but finding she was drawing the enemy's fire on the flotilla (as they fell short of her,) she moved down again. The shot and shells from the forts fell thick around us, but did not do us any injury, with one exception, viz: about 10 o'clock A. M., the "Maria J. Carlton," of this division, was struck by a shot which passed through her magazine floor and out at her bottom. She immediately began to sink, and the crew, with the assistance of others, soon got most of the moveables out of her. The mortar and shells they left, as they could not remove them.

We ceased firing at 12 M., and from this time continued firing by watches, each division taking a watch. Nothing particularly important occurred during the next day, until 10.35 P. M., when the gun-boats "Pinola" and "Itasca" went up the river to cut the chain. As soon as they started, the mortar flotilla commenced firing very rapidly, and continued until 12.35 A. M., when the gun-boats returned. We continued, as usual, firing by watches until the morning of the 24th of April, when we commenced at 2.30 A. M. to fire as rapidly as possible, while the steamers passed up the river to attack the forts. We did not cease until signaled to do so by you at 5.30 A. M.

Both officers and men behaved gallantly; and where everyone did his duty so well, it is almost impossible to award praise to any single individual. As our galley was rendered almost useless during the bombardment, the men suffered some inconvenience in getting cooked the rations that were served out to them, and their sleep was also much interrupted; but I am glad to say that not a murmur of dissatisfaction was to be heard among them. I may also mention that Acting-Master J. Duncan Graham, my executive officer, was in command of the United States schooner "Sydney C. Jones" during the whole of the bombardment, and acted to my entire satisfaction. The conduct of William Hatch and John Richards, masters' mates, during the bombardment, has also met my warmest approval—the former having sighted the mortar every time it was fired during the action; the latter having charge of the powder division, and making himself generally useful about the vessel. The only wounded in this division were two of the crew of the "Carlton," one severely, the other slightly.

Very respectfully your obedient servant,

W. W. QUEEN,
*Lieut.-Com'd'g, in Command of
2d Div. Mortar Flotilla.*

Commander D. D. PORTER,
Commanding Mortar Flotilla.

REPORT OF LIEUTENANT-COMMANDING K. RANDOLPH BREESE, THIRD DIVISION MORTAR FLOTILLA.

U. S. BARKANTINE, "HORACE BEALES,"
MISSISSIPPI RIVER, April 30, 1862.

SIR—I have the honor to submit the following report of the part taken by the third division mortar flotilla, under my command, in the bombardment of Fort Jackson. At 9.30 A. M., of the 18th instant, the "John Griffiths," (on board of which vessel I hoisted my divisional flag,) "Racer," and "Sarah Bruen," were taken in tow by the "Clifton," and towed into position assigned, astern of the first division, on the right bank of the river, at the following distances from the centre of Fort Jackson: "John Griffiths," 3,900 yards; "Racer," 3,940 yards, and the "Sarah Bruen," 3,980 yards. About 10 A. M., the "John Griffiths" opened fire from her mortar, and was soon followed by the "Racer" and "Sarah Bruen." At 2 P. M., the rear vessels of the first division having been advanced, the "Henry James," "Dan Smith," and "Sea Foam" came up under sail and took their positions ahead of the "Griffiths," at the following distances from the fort: "Henry James," 3,630 yards; the "Dan Smith," 3,730 yards; and the "Sea Foam," 3,850 yards. At about 2.15 P. M., they opened fire from their mortars. A constant fire was kept up by each vessel from the time of taking position until 6.37 P. M., when signal to "cease firing" was made. During the day the "John Griffiths" threw 69 shells; the "Racer," 50; the "Sarah Bruen," 61; the "Henry James," 24; the "Dan Smith," 31; and the "Sea Foam," 43.

Second day.—At 6.25 A. M., April 19, recommenced fire upon Fort Jackson from the whole division, which was kept up, each vessel firing at intervals of about ten minutes, until 8 P. M., when ceased firing. During the day, the "Griffiths" threw 92 shells; the "Racer," 88; the "Sarah Bruen," 88; the "James," 97; the "Dan Smith," 92; and the "Sea Foam," 88.

Third day.—At 4 A. M., April 20, opened fire upon the fort from the division, each vessel firing at intervals of about ten minutes. At 8 A. M., ceased firing, and at 10.13 A. M., reopened from the whole division as before. From 4 P. M. to 10.10 P. M., each vessel firing at intervals of twenty minutes. From 10.10 P. M. to 3.03 A. M., (21st,) as rapidly as possible, supporting the gun-boats cutting the chain. From 3.03 A. M. to 4 A. M., at intervals of fifteen minutes. During the day, ending at 4 A. M., the "Griffiths" threw 119 shells; the "Racer," 117; the "Sarah

Bruen," 117; the "Henry James," 113; the "Dan Smith," 119; the "Seam Foam," 111.

Fourth day.—At noon the division again commenced fire, each vessel firing at intervals of about ten minutes, ceasing at 4 P. M. At 8 P. M. reopened as before, keeping up the fire until midnight. During this day the "Griffiths" threw 50 shells; the "Racer," 50; the "Sarah Bruen," 56; the "Henry James," 55; the "Dan Smith," 55; the "Sea Foam," 47.

Fifth day.—At 8 A. M., April 22, each vessel of the division commenced fire, firing at intervals of about ten minutes. Ceased fire at noon; reopened at 6 P. M. and fired until 8 P. M., firing as before. During the day the "Griffiths" threw 56 shells; the "Racer," 46; the "Sarah Bruen," 49; the "Henry James," 40; the "Dan Smith," 67; and the "Sea Foam," 52.

Sixth day.—At 4 A. M., April 23, the division reopened fire, each vessel firing at intervals of about ten minutes, ceasing at 8 A. M. At 4 P. M., again opened fire from each vessel of the division at intervals of about twelve minutes, keeping it up until 6 P. M. During the day the "Griffiths" threw 38 shells; the "Racer," 28; the "Sarah Bruen," 36; the "Henry James," 34; the "Dan Smith," 63; the "Sea Foam," 51.

Seventh day.—At midnight, April 24, the division opened fire, each vessel firing at intervals of ten minutes. At 3.40 A. M., the guns of the fort having opened on the fleet passing up the river, the division commenced firing as rapidly as possible, ceasing at 4.52 A. M., by signal, the fleet having passed the fort. At 5.30 A. M., opened fire upon the enemy's steamers near the fort; ceased at 5.48 A. M. At 3.55 P. M., commenced again upon the fort; ceasing at 5.04 P. M. At 5.20 P. M., the division got under way and dropped down the river. During the day the "Griffiths" threw 54 shells; the "Racer," 81; the "Sarah Bruen," 67; the "Henry James," 52; the "Dan Smith," 66; and "Sea Foam," 60. The "Horace Beales," with ordnance stores, temporarily under the command of Acting-Master George W. Sumner, executive officer, was towed up to within 600 yards of the rear of the mortar vessels, and discharged her ordnance stores, as was required, with great promptness. During the bombardment she received many of the articles saved from the "Maria J. Carlton," and a ten-inch gun carriage and ammunition from the "Jackson." She also received the sick and wounded of the flotilla and several of the wounded of the squadron. Ten of the men of the "Beales," with Acting-Master Sumner, served on board the "Harriet Lane" during the engagement with the forts. The enemy's shot and fragments of shell, at times, flew about the division in all directions. Several pieces of the latter, of the size of an egg, and many smaller pieces, were picked up on board of the different vessels, but, through God's mercy, not a person was struck, nor have I a casualty of any kind to report during the whole bombardment. The "Sarah Bruen" has a hole through her foremast, which I am at a loss to account for, unless a fragment of the enemy's shell, which struck the face of the mortar at the edge of the bore, as it was about to be fired, fell into the mortar, and, being discharged, went through the mast. A little rigging cut here and there is all the damage I have to report done by the enemy.

The general effect of firing the mortars upon the vessels was to knock out the round houses forward and the light pine board bulwarks in the line of fire. The "John Griffiths" leaked more than usual during the bombardment, but has since tightened up; she has always been considered a weak vessel. The "Racer's" deck, on port side abreast of fore hatch, started from the carlines giving way, they not having been (originally) properly strengthened. The mortars show no kind of injury. The mortar carriages worked remarkably well. The only damage being (in some instances) the loss

OF THE CIVIL WAR.

of the feather to the eccentric axle, and the breaking of the screws that confine the socket to eccentric. These very slight injuries did not hinder the working of the mortar in the least. The screws were promptly replaced, a number of spare ones having been made. The turn-table on some of the vessels was found to have recoiled in the line of fire from an inch to an inch and a half; it was easily pressed into position and kept so by breeching. Twenty-two and a half pounds of powder were fired from the "Griffiths" at the rebel iron-clad gunboat with no visible strain in vessel or carriage beyond that already experienced. The mortars were served equally well by the mortar crew and gun's crew, watch and watch, during the bombardment. Not a mistake or an accident occurred in loading the mortars or in filling and fuzing the shell, evincing the care and pains taken by the officers of the division in training their crews, as well as the attention, in time of action, by the latter to their duties. Notwithstanding the loss of sleep and regular meals and cooked food, the officers and men were ever ready to volunteer for any expedition or service against the enemy. And I must remark upon the cheerfulness and alacrity with which, when much exhausted, they manned their boats to keep up a proper supply of powder and shell. The acting-masters commanding the different vessels of the division gave the direction of fire from the mainmast head (from which place only was Fort Jackson to be seen) regulating the charges used as required. They kept their posts while engaged with scarce any relief, subject not only to the shock of their own mortars, but also from the one in the rear.

The conduct of the officers and the men during the bombardment is worthy of all praise. The different missiles of the enemy, flying about the division in all directions, did not distract them in the least in the discharge of their duties, nor, I may say, from their well-earned rest at the close of their watch.

Accompanying me to the "John Griffiths" from the "Horace Beales" was Assistant-Surgeon Edes, Mr. Bacon, (my clerk,) and my boat's crew. Dr. Edes had every preparation made for the care of wounded men, he remaining on board the "Griffiths" during the bombardment, ready to give his services wherever needed. Mr. Bacon acted as signal officer, and was engaged in taking notes.

I visited each vessel of the division frequently, night and day, while in action, finding the same good order in each. The minute directions given by you were strictly carried out.

I have only to add that, as the vessels and mortars are now fitted, the preparations for action and the service of the mortars made beforehand were ample, and did not require to be altered in the least during the bombardment, nor has any suggestion from the seven days' actual service been made in the way of improvement, except as a precaution, the breeching around the turn-table.

Very respectfully, your obedient servant,

K. R. BREESE,
Lieutenant-Commanding Third Division Mortar Flotilla.

Commander DAVID D. PORTER,
Commanding Mortar Flotilla.

REPORT RELATIVE TO PRISONERS IN THE CONFEDERATE NAVAL SERVICE CAPTURED AFTER THE SURRENDER OF THE FORTS.

UNITED STATES STEAMER "HARRIET LANE," }
FORTS JACKSON AND ST. PHILIP, May 2, 1862. }

SIR—Enclosed is a list of prisoners of war captured by me, after the capitulation of the forts, on board of the steamers "Burton," "Landes," and "Defiance," the latter of which was sunk by order of John K. Mitchell, late commander in the United States Navy. By order of Flag-officer Farragut I

send them home in the "Rhode Island," subject to the order of the department, on account of their infamous and perfidious conduct in setting fire to and blowing up the floating battery "Louisiana" and sending her adrift upon the vessels of ours that were at anchor, while they had a flag of truce flying and were engaged in drawing up the capitulation of the fort, the vessels under the command of J. K. Mitchell, with the exception of one, having no colors up at the time. These prisoners have forfeited all claim to any consideration, having committed an infamous act, unknown in any transaction of this kind. Had the "Louisiana" blown up in the midst of our vessels she would have destroyed every one of them. As it was, good fortune directed her towards Fort St. Philip, where she exploded with great force, scattering fragments all over the work, killing one of their own men in the fort, and landing a large beam close to the tent of Commander McIntosh, who was lying with one arm blown off and another broken, his knee-cap shot away and a leg broken. The surgeon in attendance pronounced it the most perfidious act he had ever heard of. The explosion was seen and heard for many miles, and it was supposed that the forts were blown up.

Enclosed is a letter from J. K. Mitchell stating that the persons mentioned therein had nothing to do with the transaction. I shall, however, carry out the orders of the flag-officer, and send them home in the "Rhode Island," subject to the consideration of the department.

I have the honor to remain, very respectfully,

DAVID D. PORTER,
Commanding Flotilla.

Hon. GIDEON WELLES,
Secretary of the Navy.

LIST OF CONFEDERATE OFFICERS:

Captain J. K. Mitchell, 1st-Lieutenant J. N. Wilkinson, 2d-Lieutenant W. H. Ward, 3d-Lieutenant W. C. Whittle, jr., Lieutenant A. F. Warley, Surgeon John D. Grafton, Lieutenant F. M. Harris, ex-naval officers of the United States; Purser L. E. Brooks, Gunner Wilson, Boatswain Jones, Carpenter Cherry, Captain's Clerk George Taylor, Captain's Clerk W. Clark, Chief Engineer W. Youngblood, 2d Assistant Engineer James Harris, 2d Assistant Engineer M. Parsons, 3d Assistant Engineer Theo. Hart, 3d Assistant Engineer James Elliott, 3d Assistant Engineer James Waters.

Engineers from the "Manassas."—Menzis, 3d assistant engineer; Weaver, 2d assistant engineer; Culver, 2d assistant engineer; Newman, 3d assistant engineer.

UNITED STATES STEAMER "CLIFTON." }
NEAR FORT ST. PHILIP, May 2, 1862. }

SIR—The following officers of the Confederate States navy now held on board this vessel as prisoners of war, had no voice in the council which determined upon the destruction of the Confederate States steamer "Louisiana," on the 28th ultimo, viz: Surgeon James D. Grafton, Assistant Paymaster L. E. Brooks, Captain's Clerk George Taylor, Captain's Clerk William Clark, 1st Engineer W. Youngblood, 2d Assistant Engineer James Harris, 2d Assistant Engineer M. Parsons, 3d Assistant Engineer Theo. Hart, 3d Assistant Engineer James Elliott, 3d Assistant Engineer James Waters, 2d Assistant Engineer Orvel Culver, 2d Assistant Engineer George W. Weaver, 3d Assistant Engineer T. A. Menzis, 3d Assistant Engineer William Newman, Engineer Henry Fagin, Engineer J. H. Toombs, Engineer J. H. Dent, Gunner James Wilson, Boatswain Samuel Jones, Carpenter Virginius Cherry, Paymaster's Steward D. Porter.

I make the above statement in consequence of having learned informally that all such officers would be paroled on a representation of the fact to you.

I have the honor to be, very respectfully, your obedient servant,

JOHN K. MITCHELL, *Commander,*
Late in command of the C. States Naval Forces near Fort Jackson.

Com. DAVID D. PORTER,
Commanding United States Naval Forces near Fort St. Philip.

———

SPECIAL REPORT OF COMMANDER PORTER, COMMENDING THE CONDUCT OF THE OFFICERS OF THE MORTAR FLOTILLA.

UNITED STATES STEAMER "HARRIET LANE," }
SOUTHWEST PASS, May 3, 1862. }

SIR—In my general report to the department, I made honorable mention of the officers commanding vessels and divisions in this flotilla, but I think there is something more due to these officers than a general notice, in which manner most every officer comes in for a share of approval, without its being specified what particular qualities entitle them to it.

To the commanders of divisions of mortar flotilla, the country is mainly indebted to the fall of Forts Jackson and St. Philip, for the latter is consequent on that of the former. I cannot express to you in sufficient terms the zeal and ability displayed by Lieutenants-Commanding Watson Smith, W. W. Queen, and K. R. Breese. They have been indefatigable in drilling their men, infusing a proper spirit into them, and carrying out my orders during the bombardment, which lasted without intermission for six days and nights. They gave themselves but little rest. I could draw no distinction between them. Neither flagged for a moment in their duty, and though they lost but few men in killed and wounded, they have been exposed to as hot a fire as the enemy were capable of showering upon them. They are the kind of men to lead our ships into battle, and I hope that the department will take such notice of their conduct as this great occasion merits.

To Commander Renshaw, Lieutenants-Commanding Guest, Baldwin, Wainwright, and Woodworth, my thanks are particularly due for the zeal they manifested on all occasions to serve, no matter in what capacity, and the condition of their vessel for service. If I have not detailed in my general report the various acts of these officers, it is not because I did not appreciate them, but because it would lengthen my report, already voluminous, intending to do them full justice on this occasion. Lieutenant-Commanding Harrell has not had the opportunity to give the same evidence of ability, though I have ever found him ready to carry out my wishes, as he says his vessel is unmanageable. He has, however, done good service, and is a zealous officer.

I have to remain, very respectfully,
Your obedient servant,
DAVID D. PORTER,
Commanding Flotilla.

Hon. GIDEON WELLES.
Secretary of the Navy.

———

LETTER OF COMMANDER D. D. PORTER, ENCLOSING PAROLES OF OFFICERS TAKEN AT FORTS JACKSON AND ST. PHILIP.

UNITED STATES STEAMER "HARRIET LANE," }
SHIP ISLAND, May 15, 1862. }

SIR—I have the honor to enclose the paroles of the officers captured in Fort Jackson, with the list of men remaining at the time of the surrender. The list of officers and men in Fort St. Philip must have been sent to the flag-officer, together with the list of persons captured by the "Harriet Lane" in the steamers "Burton," "Landes," and "Defiance," under late Commander J. K. Mitchell, consisting of two hundred and fifty of the crew of the iron steam battery "Louisiana," and the Crescent artillery, composed of over a hundred officers and men. The number of men in the two forts during the bombardment was eleven hundred, but about two hundred left before the flag of truce was sent down. The rolls of the fort were handed in to the officers taking charge, but our troops taking possession a short time after everything was thrown into disorder, and it was not possible to obtain them.

Very respectfully, your obedient servant,
DAVID D. PORTER,
Commanding Flotilla.

Hon. GIDEON WELLES,
Secretary of the Navy.

[Parole omitted.]

———

CONGRATULATORY LETTER OF THE SECRETARY OF THE NAVY.

NAVY DEPARTMENT, May 10, 1862.

SIR—Your dispatch of April 30, enclosing the articles of capitulation of Forts Jackson and St. Philip, which surrendered on the 28th ultimo, after a bombardment of 144 consecutive hours by the mortar flotilla, has been received. I have also to acknowledge the receipt of the flags taken in the two forts on that occasion, including the original one hoisted on Fort St. Philip when the rebel forces declared the State of Louisiana to have seceded from the Union, which have been sent forward to the Department.

The important part which you have borne in the organization of the mortar flotilla, and the movement on New Orleans, has identified your name with one of the most brilliant naval achievements on record, and to your able assistance with the flotilla is Flag-officer Farragut much indebted for the successful results he has accomplished.

To yourself and the officers and seamen of the mortar flotilla, the department extends its congratulations.

I am, respectfully, &c.,
GIDEON WELLES.

Commander DAVID D. PORTER,
Commanding United States Mortar Flotilla, Gulf of Mexico.

———

COAST SURVEY REPORTS.

TREASURY DEPARTMENT, May 22, 1862.

SIR—At the instance of the Superintendent of the Coast Survey, I have the honor to transmit herewith a copy of the journal of Assistant F. H. Gerdes, United States Coast Survey, showing the services rendered to the fleet under command of Flag-officer Farragut, United States Navy, and to the mortar fleet under command of Captain D. D. Porter, United States Navy.

I am, very respectfully,
S. P. CHASE,
Secretary of the Treasury.

Hon. GIDEON WELLES.
Secretary of the Navy.

———

EXTRACTS FROM A REPORT OF ASSISTANT F. H. GERDES, COMMANDING SURVEYING STEAMER "SACHEM," TO PROFESSOR A. D. BACHE, SUPERINTENDENT OF THE COAST SURVEY.

April 13.—At daylight of the 13th of April, I again got under way and took the lead, the gun-boats of the flotilla and the naval vessels in the vicinity following the "Sachem."

The following disposition was made of my party:

1. Sub-Assistant J. G. Oltmanns and Mr. T. C. Bowie repaired on board the "Owasco," and used during the day a boat and armed crew from that vessel; they ascended the river on the west bank.

2. Myself and Assistant Jos. Harris, after leaving the "Sachem" off the Salt Works at anchor, took our own boat, with an armed crew, and ascended the river on the east bank.

3. Sub-Assistant R. E. Halter went with another of our boats and an armed crew to the Salt Works, to occupy with a theodolite the top of the chimney of the old engine building, which had been trigonometrically determined by the Coast Survey.

We succeeded in the operations, and came within three miles of the fort before night set in. The last lines of this day were observed on Fort St. Philip flagstaff.

On our return on board the "Sachem," we mapped the work and brought it up as far as we had progressed during the day.

April 14.—On the 14th of April, at sunrise, I consulted with Captain Porter, and we concluded to continue the work and to ascend the river until the positions of the hulks, which support the chain across the Mississippi could be properly determined.

A large portion of the fleet went up to the conspicuous point (which I have named Porter's Point), just two miles below Fort Jackson, and engaged the enemy to draw their attention from our boats. This, however, was only partially effected; they had probably found out the day previous that engineering operations were in progress, and now undertook to stop them. When Mr. Oltmanns passed Porter's Point, he was fired on with eight or nine rifled shot, but fortunately the whole damage consisted in breaking the blade of an oar. The fire was promptly returned, and the operations were continued. The observations were successfully continued during this day, and the mapping was completed during the evening and part of the night.

April 15.—In the morning, Captain Porter came on board, and we consulted as to the continuance. I sent Mr. Oltmanns and Mr. Bowie again up the river in the "Owasco." They ascended within one mile and a half of the lower fort, and were quite successful in getting intersections on the hulks and on the two flagstaffs of the fortifications.

They found that during the previous night all the signals which we had put up during the day before had been removed; besides, it was ascertained that a number of men were hidden in the bushes. There was hardly anywhere on the shore a footing to be got, and we had to resort to all kinds of observations, instruments and positions, some stations consisting of flags in overhanging branches, and the angles were measured below the same with a sextant, in a boat; others were chimney-tops of deserted houses, on which we mounted small theodolites, having to work our way through the roof. A few only were on *terra firma*.

April 17.—I saw and consulted with Captain Porter and the flag-officer. To the latter, I gave a copy of the map and a memorandum of distances, for which he expressed much gratification. He spoke with the highest regard of the Coast Survey, and said many kind things of the intrepidity, determination, system and dispatch of the party under my charge, and considered our services of great value to the fleet.

Captain Porter desired me to furnish him with points along the shore every 100 or 150 metres apart, on both banks of the river, for the purpose of placing the mortar vessels at given distances from the forts. This was accomplished to-day, Mr. Oltmanns and Mr. Bowie taking the west side, and Mr. Harris the east side of the river. Meantime, three more copies of the map and memorandum were finished on board and distributed to the fleet.

Several of the enemy's gun-boats came out, and both our boats were fired at repeatedly.

April 18.—Before daylight on the 18th of April, Mr. Oltmanns went on board the "Harriet Lane," and Mr. Harris on some other gun-boat, both with directions to assist in placing the mortar vessels exactly in such positions as were marked out by Captain Porter the day before, and which had been determined by the same gentlemen. Tow after tow, consisting of one of the former ferry-boats, "Westfield" and "Clifton," each with three or four mortar boats, came up, and the latter were in a short time stationed at given distances from the forts. As soon as all were in position the enemy commenced firing, and from our side the bombardment fairly commenced.

Mr. Oltmanns and Mr. Harris both carried out my instructions to the letter, and placed the mortars in the exact spot as designated by Captain Porter, at accurately known distances. They were during the whole day under fire. General Butler made his appearance in the river with 7,000 men, which he offered to the flag-officer.

April 19.—Early in the morning, I had a conference with the commander, who desired me again to send two officers to the flotilla for the purpose of moving some of the mortars to other places, and furnish them with the distances and bearings. This was done accordingly. One of the vessels on which Mr. Harris was engaged was struck by a round shot, and another vessel where Mr. Oltmanns was in a boat alongside was sunk while he was speaking with the captain. During the day, we furnished also two more charts for the fleet. In the evening, Captain Porter sent me word again to dispatch early next morning two officers for giving data. You see they kept us pretty busy.

April 20.—Early in the morning, Messrs. Oltmanns and Halter made the rounds of the mortar vessels at the request of the commander of the flotilla, and changed the position of a few, giving them again bearings and distances.

I went on board the "Harriet Lane" in the forenoon, but did not see Captain Porter, who was in his gig among the fleet. The mortar firing during the day was kept up vigorously, and I presume that 1,500 shots were sent towards the forts.

In the evening, an officer from the "Pensacola" came on board to get some information about the depth of the river in the immediate locality of the forts, and Mr. Oltmanns and myself gave him all the details that had come under our observation.

April 22.—At daylight, Captain Porter sent me a note requesting me to drop down to the Jump, and to wait for a boat which had been sent on an expedition in the rear of Fort Jackson, and to bring her up the river directly on her arrival in the Mississippi. I went down with the steamer and anchored off the upper point of the Jump, and took the opportunity to reconnoitre that passage more specially. At sundown, I sent Mr. Halter to the commander of the flotilla to report that we did not see anything of his boat, but that I would wait during the night. I received a letter from him in return, stating his fears that the boat's crew would be lost, and begging me to go in search of them, as he had his hands full of the attack that in all probability was to come off during the night. This, of course, was resolved on, and to-morrow, by sunrise, a boat will be sent for the purpose.

April 23.—At daylight, I dispatched Mr. Oltmanns, the first mate, and a crew of six men, all doubly armed and well provisioned with food and water, in the second cutter in search of the missing boat expedition, directing him to leave written notices at the mouth of the multifarious bayous, naming the route to be pursued, to hoist in his boat the American ensign, and to do anything in his power to find out the crew which must have lost their way in the labyrinth of marsh streams. Mr. Harris returned from the fleet and brought me a message from Capt. Porter to come up and run alongside. I fired two 32-pounders as a signal for Mr. Oltmanns to return, and set also a blue signal at the fore. Calling on the flag-officer, he said he had no vessel to spare from the engagement, and would consider it a favor if I would carry some of his wounded men in the "Sachem" to the hospital at the mouth of the Southwest Pass. He further added that, as he was preparing a severe night attack with the fleet, it would seem too hard to carry those poor crippled fellows with him in the fight.

Of course I at once consented very cheerfully, and repeated that, whenever he could make use of me, I would be at his service. Meanwhile, Mr. Oltmanns had not returned from his search for the boat expedition, but I had to let him shift for himself, knowing that he would bring up somewhere safely.

At four in the afternoon, the wounded men were sent on board, two of whom had suffered amputation, and all of them in a dangerous state. At a quarter to 5, I was steaming down, having made the poor men as comfortable as I could. Mr. Harris brought the hospital physician on board, who took charge of the patients, and we sent them in our double-bunked boat on shore.

April 24.—The gun-boat "Miami" anchored alongside the "Sachem," bringing me a verbal request from Captain Porter to accompany General Butler's expedition to the rear of Fort St. Philip. I had previously sent Mr. Harris up to the fleet to see the commander and report the derangement of our engine. At 5 P. M., General Butler arrived in the "Saxon" and called on me in person, bringing me a letter at the same time from Captain Porter. I arranged with him to meet him as soon as my repairs had been made at Isle au Breton, and to send an officer with him in the "Saxon" to pilot his vessel through Pass à l'Outre. Mr. Oltmanns also came back from his boat expedition in the rear of Fort Jackson, having been within one mile and a half of the fort.

April 26.—In the morning, Captain Boggs, of the "Varuna" steam gun-boat, came on board to go with me to General Butler's ship; he had lost his vessel during the passage of the fleet past the forts on the 24th, being run into from two different quarters by iron-clad steamers of the enemy. This was a most brilliant exploit. His ship sunk with her colors flying, but not before she had crippled, burned and sunk six of the opposing steamers.

In the afternoon, I got under way, the machinery working well forward. We dropped anchor alongside the "Harriet Lane," and I had a conference with the commander. He sent his and other engineers to examine the "Sachem's" machinery, when all appeared right.

April 27.—We got under way after sunrise and stood off Pass à l'Outre, and brought over the bar 15 feet. At noon, we arrived off Sable Island, where we found General Butler in the steam transport "Mississippi." I called on him and had a long conversation respecting the coast. At 2 o'clock, he came on board the "Sachem" and I took him to the rear of Fort Jackson; from thence he took a boat up to the Quarantine, using one of the smaller bayous for his passage. I dispatched Mr. Harris at once to stake out a four-foot line along the coast, as the general intends to make an experiment with his rifled guns on the forts from here. We also ascertained the distance by bearings on Forts St. Philip and Jackson. Mr. Halter reported again to me, and was sent out at 8 o'clock in the evening to stake out the boat channel to the Quarantine with lamps, so that troops might be conveyed there during the night. He returned at 2 o'clock, having successfully performed the task. Four hundred men were sent in safety during the night, and the garrison at the camp of the Quarantine now consists of one full regiment. In the morning, the captain

of the gun-boat "Miami," which was aground close by the "Sachem," sent on board requesting assistance. I ran ahead of him, sent him a nine-inch hawser, and got him afloat by 8 o'clock in the morning. In the afternoon, I sent Messrs. Oltmanns and Harris to Fort Bayou to put up a signal—Mr. Halter having found out in the morning that both signals at this place and at Raccoon Point were lost. While the boat was away, at 2.30 P. M., both secession flags at Forts Jackson and St. Philip were hauled down. The most intense excitement followed. I saw the "Harriet Lane" and three other steamers, with a flag of truce on the fore, steaming up to the forts, and directly afterwards saw a large steamer of the enemy enveloped in flames. This proved to be the new iron-clad battery "Louisiana;" she burned entirely down. At about quarter before 3, her magazine exploded with a crash and shock the like of which I never witnessed. The cloud of smoke rose to an estimated height of at least six hundred feet, and pieces of the wreck could be seen flying in the air very distinctly. At 3 o'clock, the "Harriet Lane" came up, and, after the firing of one gun, I had the inexpressible delight of seeing the stars and stripes waving once more over Forts Jackson and St. Philip. I fired a salute directly, and gave the information to other vessels near. I sent a recall for my party, there being no further use to prosecute the work here, and Captain Porter had expressed a desire that I should join him at the forts as soon as they were ours. In the evening, General Williams came in the "Miami," and when I communicated the news, the cheering, "Yankee Doodle" and "Hail Columbia" it seemed would never end. At 11 o'clock P.M., we got under way and steamed towards Pass à l'Outre.

April 29.—We crossed the bar at 6 A. M. with fifteen feet, half-tide, running the north side of the "middle ground" again as before. We passed the forts early in the afternoon. At 4 o'clock, I took the commander of the flotilla over to Fort Jackson, my officers having also arrived in a separate boat. We inspected closely for a couple of hours the damage done by the mortars, and I cannot understand to this minute how the garrison could have possibly lived so long in the enclosures. The destruction goes beyond all description; the ground is torn by the shells as if a thousand antediluvian hogs had rooted it up; the holes are from three to eight feet deep, and are very close together, sometimes within a couple of feet; all that was wood in the fort is completely consumed by fire; the brick-work is knocked down; the arches stove; guns are dismounted; gun carriages broken, and the whole presents a dreadful scene of destruction.

April 30.—Early in the morning I received a communication from the commander requesting me to await here his return from New Orleans, where he goes to-day in the "Harriet Lane."

I also hear that a gun-boat is going north, and I conclude therefore this report, to send by the same.

Allow me to add a few words to express the high gratification which the gallant and able deportment of my officers has given, not only to myself, but, I have reason to believe, to everybody in the fleet, and to the general of the land forces. I hope you will say that we have done our duty.

Very respectfully, your obedient servant,

F. H. GERDES,
Assistant United States Coast Survey.

REPORT OF JOSEPH HARRIS, UNITED STATES COAST SURVEY, OF SOME OF THE INCIDENTS THAT CAME UNDER HIS NOTICE AND OF HIS OBSERVATIONS AT THE FORTS, ETC.

SOUTHWEST PASS, MISSISSIPPI }
RIVER, May 4, 1862. }

SIR—While engaged in the survey of the injuries received by Fort Jackson during the bombardment and the passage of the fleet, several incidents came under my notice, which, at your request, I have now the honor to submit to you in writing.

While waiting for the boat to take us off, on the last day on which we were engaged on the survey, Mr. Oltmanns and I fell into conversation with some men who had been in the fort as part of the garrison. One of them, who said he was a New Yorker, particularly informed us—a reliable, intelligent man, from the moderation of his statements—and I think his information well worthy of note.

I shall merely record his statements, as the conversation on our part, which drew forth information on the points where we especially desired, is not necessary to the understanding of them, and this communication is likely to be very long without the introduction of any irrelevant matter.

General J. K. Duncan had command of both forts, and Colonel Higgins, who some years ago was an officer of the United States navy, had the immediate command of Fort Jackson. Colonel Higgins has the credit of being a most brave and vigilant officer.

For forty-eight hours my informant thought Colonel Higgins had not left the ramparts, and never seemed in the least disconcerted when the bombs were falling thickest around him.

A large proportion of the forces inside the fort were northern men; and there were also many foreigners. The party that seized the fort early in 1861, was a company of German Yagers, and there were a number of Irish also. In all there were some 600 or 700 men in the fort at the time of the bombardment. The northern men were mostly sent down at an early stage of the proceedings, and I imagine most of them volunteered, hoping in that way to avoid suspicion, and perhaps not have to fight against the government after all.

(Colonel Higgins had no expectation of being attacked; that is, he thought no fleet could be brought against him sufficiently strong to risk an attack.)

There was a company of sharpshooters attached to the forces, under the command of Captain Mullen. They numbered about two hundred, and were largely recruited from the "riffraff" of New Orleans. They scouted so far down as eight or nine miles below the forts, and brought nightly reports to Fort Jackson, traveling by the bayous or passes on the southwest side of the river. The main body, however, lay in the edge of the woods below Fort Jackson, about a mile and a half from it. From here they fired on the boat that pulled up under that shore on the 14th. The grape and canister shot that the "Owasco" threw into the bushes made their berth uncomfortable, and they broke up their camp, came into the fort all wet and draggled, having thrown many of their arms away, and swore that they would go to New Orleans; and they went.

My informant voluntarily gave the credit of reducing the fort to the "bomb fleet." The fort was so much shaken by this firing that it was feared the casemates would come down about their ears. The loss of life by the bombs was not great, as they could see them coming plainly and get out of the way; but the effect of their fall and explosion no skill could avert.

About one shell in twenty failed to explode, even those that fell in the water going off as well as the others. It is well worth noting that the bombs that fell in the ditch close to the walls of the fort, and exploded there, shook the fort much more severely than any of those that buried themselves in the solid ground.

The firing was most destructive the first day, and the vessels lying on the northeast side of the river, which were in plain view of the forts, made much the most effective shots. The bomb vessels lying on the other side of the river were at all times

totally invisible, the best glasses failing to distinguish their bush tops from the trees around them.

During the bombardment the only guns that were much used were the rifled guns, of which there were three, and the four 10-inch columbiads and Dahlgren 8-inch guns, eight in number. The mortars (in the fort) fired occasionally. One of the rifled guns, mounted on the fort proper before the bombardment, was sent two days before the fire opened to Island No. 10.

One of the rifles in the water battery was originally one of the barbette guns, a 32-pounder. It was sent to New Orleans to be rifled, and a week after the second one was sent; but the first, on trial, proving a failure, the second was not changed.

The large columbiad in the water battery was made somewhere in Secessia, but exactly where my informant did not know.

The fort was in perfect order when the bombardment commenced, it having always been very strictly policed, and the dirt, which now disfigures everything, is the accumulation of a few days.

The water did not enter the fort until the levee had been broken with bombs, and during the summer of 1861, when the Mississippi was even higher, the parade ground was entirely dry. There was very little sickness in the fort, the water probably not having stood long enough to create miasma.

The discipline in the fort was very strict; but what seemed to be felt more than the strictness was the bringing in of very young and entirely inexperienced officers, who were placed in command of others much their superiors in knowledge.

Suspected men were closely watched, and the punishment for improper talk among them was to tie a rope around the offenders and let them float in the stinking ditch.

The impression we derived from this part of the conversation, however, was that the fort was very well governed, and that the man who was speaking had not often come under the displeasure of the authorities, for he was not eloquent on the subject of his wrongs.

The chain, as first stretched across the river, was quite a formidable obstacle. The chain was brought from Pensacola, and was a very heavy one. It was supported by heavy logs, 30 feet long, only a few feet apart, to the under side of each of which the chain was pinned near the up stream end. The chain was kept from sagging down too far by seven heavy anchors, from which small chains ran to the main chain.

These anchors were buoyed with can-buoys taken from Pilot Town. In a few months a raft formed on the upper side of this chain which reached up to the forts, and its weight swept away the whole obstruction, and went to sea, carrying the buoys with it.

It was then replaced by the lighter chain, buoyed by hulks there, three weeks ago. Two of the large can-buoys were placed in the magazine in the water battery. The night that Flag-officer Farragut's fleet passed up, Colonel Higgins was so sure of destroying it that he allowed the first vessel to come up with the fort before opening fire, fearing that they would be driven back prematurely and escape him. When they succeeded in passing, he remarked: "Our cake is all dough; we may as well give it up."

During this engagement a Captain Jones, from the back country, had charge of those casemate guns which were firing hot shot. He depressed the muzzles of his guns very considerably, fearing to fire too high, and being desirous of working his guns vigorously had them run out with a jerk, the consequence of which was that the balls rolled harmlessly into the moat, and the guns blazed away powder and hay-wads at a most destructive rate. This continued until some of the officers on the ramparts, observing how much his shot fell short, told him of it. He then commenced operations on one *particular vessel*, which he kept at until some one informed him that he was devoting himself to one of their own chain hulks.

The enemy's gun-boats did not come up to the expectations that were formed of them. The "Louisiana" especially, was very much relied on, but her crew of 200 men were drunk at the time that they should have done their duty best. I could not find out anything about her from this man, as he had never been aboard of her, and did not believe the exaggerated stories that were told here about her.

The small loss of life in the fort is due, to a great extent, to the fact that the men have been carefully kept below, only the guns' crew being allowed out of shelter. The "New Yorker" was a powder-passer for the battery in which the rifled gun and the large columbiads of the main fort were, and, therefore, had a good opportunity of seeing what went on, they being in pretty constant use.

One bomb broke into the officers' mess-room while they were at dinner, and rolled on the floor; as it lay between them and the door they could not escape, but all gathered in a corner and remained there in terrible suspense until it became evident that the fuse had gone out, and they were safe.

On the first night of the firing, when the citadel and outhouses were all in flames, the magazine was in very great danger for some time, and a profuse supply of wet blankets was all that saved it; there was great consternation that night, but afterwards the garrison got used to it, and were very cool. A bomb broke into the secret passage cut in the fort. One of the soldiers went into it some distance when he was discovered by General Duncan and ordered out. The passage was then filled up and a guard placed over the entrance to keep every one away from it. This was told me by Major Santelle, commandant of the fort.

Fort Jackson mounted 33 32-pounders on main parapet, 2 columbiads on main parapet, 1 rifle gun on main parapet, 2 columbiads in 2d bastion, 1 9-inch mortar in 2d bastion, 1 columbiad in 3d bastion, 2 8-inch mortars in 3d bastion, 8 32-pounders in northwest casemates, 6 32-pounder guns in northeast casemates, 10 short guns in bastion casemates, 2 brass field pieces, 2 rifled guns in water battery, 1 10-inch columbiad in water battery, 1 9-inch columbiad in water battery, 3 32-pounder guns on outer curtain—75 guns in all.

I am not positive about the calibre of the guns. Those that I called 32-pounders had a calibre of 6.4 inches, and I am not quite positive that there are 10 short 32-pounder guns in the bastion casemates, though such is my recollection. Of these guns four were dismounted, but I could not see that the gun proper was injured in any case; of the gun

carriages eleven were struck, several of them being entirely destroyed; and of the traverses no less than thirty were injured. A large proportion of the last injured were on the western side of the outer curtain (where only these guns were mounted), twenty out of thirty-nine being more or less injured.

The ramparts of the fort proper were very severely damaged on every side; but particularly on the two northern ones ; there has been great patching with sand bags needed; several of the entrances from the parade ground under the ramparts are masses of ruins, some of them being one-third choked up with debris.

The casemates are cracked from end to end ; one of the bastion casemates has the roof broken through in three places; another in one place, and its walls are so badly cracked that daylight shines through very plainly, the cracks being about four inches wide.

The entrances to the casemates are nearly all damaged, the roofs cracked and masses of brick thrown down or loosened. All the buildings were destroyed by fire or bomb-shells, the two western bastions and the citadel being completely burned out. The walls of the citadel are cracked in many places very badly.

Eighty-six shot and splinters of shell struck its faces. The amount of damage here reported would hardly be credited by any one who had taken a casual survey of the premises, and I myself should have considered it exaggerated if I had read it after passing through hastily the first time. After careful examination, however, the impression left on my mind is of a place far gone on the road to ruin, which will stand but little more before it will come down about its defenders' ears. Everything about the fort appears to have started from its place, some hardly preceptible, others so much that it would be hard to find where the proper place is.

I do not profess an acquaintance with such matters, but it looks to me as if the whole structure would have to be demolished and rebuilt, if the government ever intend to fortify the site again.

I have thus, sir, hastily thrown together the more important part of the information I was able to collect; had my time been more extended I might have been able to gather more of the incidents of the siege; and had I supposed it desirable to reduce it to writing I might have obtained a fuller account from those I did question; but my conversation was merely to gratify my own curiosity and pass away an unoccupied hour. Hoping that you may find this communication of some value, I remain,

Very respectfully, your obedient servant,
JOSEPH HARRIS.

F. H. GERDES, ESQ.,
Assistant United States Coast Survey.

CHAPTER XX.

A Brave Officer's Mortification.—History Set Right.

ADMIRAL FARRAGUT says in a communication made in April, 1869: "Historians are not always correct; for my own part, I maintain the conviction that whatever errors may be made by the hands of historians and others, posterity will always give justice to whom justice is due."

This is true, and in no case has it been more clearly demonstrated than in that of Admiral Farragut himself, who reaped the highest honors that could be won in the Navy, without a dissenting voice; and who, as time passes, will only gather more laurels to surround his monument and be handed down to posterity as the most famous Admiral of the American Navy.

Farragut received so many honors himself that he could well afford to spare to those who served under him, any that may have been withheld from them by accidental omission or otherwise. He leaves it to posterity to do justice where justice has not been awarded, and therefore we give a piece of history not generally known, and which should be published in authentic form.

There was no braver officer in Farragut's fleet than Captain Theodorus Bailey, who led the first division at the passage of Forts Jackson and St. Philip. Bailey had that dashing courage which ought to delight the eye of any commander-in-chief, and no man was ever more pleased with the conduct of a subordinate than was Farragut with Bailey all through the several battles, even up to the levee of New Orleans. There, again, Bailey showed the great courage he possessed by volunteering to face a howling mob, and carry Farragut's demands to the mayor of the city for its unconditional surrender. This was more than brave conduct, it was sublime, for he and his companion, Lieutenant Perkins, had to force their way, unarmed and unguarded, through a fierce crowd that might at any moment tear them to pieces.

Farragut had been so much pleased with Bailey's coolness and daring during the rapid and successful events that had taken place within a few days, that he determined to make him the bearer of dispatches to the seat of government, and when the reports were all ready Bailey embarked in the "Cayuga," (the vessel he had so gallantly led through heavy fire and smoke), and started on his way down the Mississippi bound for Washington City. Stopping to communicate with the fleet at Forts Jackson and St. Philip, he received the rebel flags that had flown over those works and took them on with him as trophies.

Farragut had written his report of the affairs at the forts in full at New Orleans, and this Bailey aimed to deliver as soon as possible.

He went on his way home perfectly posted, as he supposed, in all that had occurred, and ready to give the Department a clear outline of the battles before the Secretary could have time to wade through the mass of reports that were sent on together.

On Bailey's arrival at the Navy Department he was received with great enthusiasm by the Secretary of the Navy and every officer and man connected with the service, all of whom listened with bated breath to his vivid recital of scenes fraught with danger and romance, until nothing more was left to tell.

While he was stating the history of events, Senator James W. Grimes (the eminent statesman, and friend of the Navy), entered the Secretary's room, and listened with the others. When Bailey had finished, the Senator said "Come with me, and some one bring the trophies," pointing to the Confederate flags. "The account of this great battle must be told on the floor of the Senate," and they started for the Senate Chamber, the Secretary of the Navy being left to overhaul the despatches.

On the arrival of Senator Grimes with Captain Bailey, on the floor of the Senate, the latter was received by Senators with the wildest enthusiasm. Members of the House rushed into the Senate Chamber as soon as they heard the news, and the floor was packed. Bailey was the hero of the hour, and was congratulated by all who could get near him. He told the story of the capture of the forts and city in his own simple way, and it carried conviction to every listener.

occurred it is impossible to conceive, and it can only be surmised that Farragut, in the excitement and hurry of the moment, sent the first order of battle to the Secretary of the Navy, instead of the one which was last issued to the fleet.

Secretary Welles and those about him at once detected the difference between Farragut's report and Bailey's recital of the passage of the fleet, and the impression was left on the minds of all, that Bailey was disposed to obtain more credit than was due him. They could not have known him well, for he was truthful as he was brave,

CAPTAIN THEODORUS BAILEY (AFTERWARDS REAR-ADMIRAL).

Congress is an impulsive body, and some of the members of the House of Representatives went back to the House to prepare a resolution giving Farragut and Bailey a vote of thanks on the spot, while the Senate, in the enthusiasm of the moment, was about to do the same thing. An hour or more had passed away while the Senators were listening to Bailey's account, during which time Secretary Welles was employed in reading Farragut's report. It was not a long one, but did not clearly mention the fact that Bailey had led the fleet, or at least show it on the plan. Why the omission

and although naturally somewhat exalted at the important position he filled at the passage of the forts, nevertheless he related it all in the simplest and most unpretending language.

Secretary Welles, on reading Farragut's report, lost no time in writing a note to Senator Grimes, and sending it off with all dispatch. It read, " Don't take any steps resulting from Captain Bailey's account of the passage of the fleet by the forts. There is a discrepancy between his report of the affair and that of Flag-officer Farragut, which must be inquired into."

Senator Grimes had just taken the floor, and was eulogizing the brilliant victory that had been reported, when Secretary Welles' note was put into his hand. He was taken all aback on reading it, and after finishing its perusal, he held up his hand. "Stop," he said, "we are going too fast," and he handed the note around the Senate. Senators, after reading it, returned to their seats and took up some matter quite foreign to the one before them, and the proposed resolutions were so completely killed that nothing on earth could have resurrected them; no one in that Senate seemed to take the least interest in the New Orleans matter, and Bailey sat on a reserved seat in the rear of the Chamber, wondering what it all meant.

In ten minutes more he would have been the recipient of a vote of thanks in connection with the flag-officer—the highest honor he could have hoped for—and he likely would have been made the next Rear-Admiral on the list.

Senator Grimes, in the kindness of his heart, went to him and showed him Mr. Welles' letter, and told him that he had better go to the Department at once and set the matter right, that it was useless to remain in the Senate, that nothing more would be done, and Bailey went out crushed to the earth with mortification. How he ever got to his lodgings he never knew; he was a proud man, and his heart almost broke at the idea that he was suspected of making a false report.

The truth came to the Department a month or two afterwards, but Bailey only benefitted by it so far that his story was believed.

Farragut received a vote of thanks, but Bailey was left out except on the general vote which included all the officers and men.

This event was not generally known in the service; or, if known, not fully understood, and it was not until 1869, seven years after the action, that the whole matter was rectified.

Then the correspondence which took place between Farragut and Bailey became part of the records of the Navy Department, and as it is due to both those officers that this correspondence should be fully known, and as it is a part of the history of the war, it should appear in this narrative. The reader will see at a glance that Captain Bailey was a clear-headed writer as he was a clear-headed fighter, and places himself clear on the record. Why he should have remained silent so many years under an injustice he should have corrected at once, no one can tell, but likely it arose from a disappointment which led him to believe there was no disposition on the part of the Secretary to do him justice. It was not until he was im-

portuned by his friends to have the matter set right, that he consented to draw Admiral Farragut's attention to the subject.

Farragut himself had most likely forgotten all about his report, and as Bailey had failed to notice the discrepancy therein just after the affair occurred, he regarded it as out of place to open up a discussion at so late a date, and when his first report had become a matter of history. As soon, however, as convinced by Bailey of his mistake, Farragut rectified it, and placed the (then) Rear-Admiral's request on the records of the Navy. This every officer is justified in claiming when he has performed a gallant act without recognition.

It is not only due to history that this should be done, but also to the family and friends of those who served so faithfully through the war of the rebellion. Bailey's misfortune in this mistake was that the error stood recorded so long without correction. He should have had it rectified at once, for his position in the Navy was materially affected by it.

HISTORY SET RIGHT.

The following correspondence is reproduced from the files of the Navy Department. We publish it in justice both to the truth of history and to the reputation of those gallant officers whom it most concerns.

REAR-ADMIRAL BAILEY TO ADMIRAL FARRAGUT.

WASHINGTON, D. C., April 1, 1869.

MY DEAR ADMIRAL—I feel compelled to call your attention to an oversight of which I spoke to you some time since, and which has afforded me and other officers the keenest annoyance, by historical statements growing out of the omission to make the desired correction.

You recollect that when the "Colorado," under my command, was found (after lightening her) to draw too much water to be got over the bar into the Mississippi River, I applied to you for the command of a division of gun-boats, and coveted the honor of leading, under your orders, the attack on New Orleans and its defences. Having been assigned by you to the command of a division of your fleet, with your concurrence, and at the request of Commander S. P. Lee, I hoisted my divisional flag on board the steam sloop-of-war "Oneida," commanded by him. On the 20th of April, 1862, you issued a General Order, with a programme directing the fleet to pass the forts and ascend the river in two columns abreast. You, in your flag-ship, the "Hartford," at the head of one column, and I at the head of the other. About this time Commander Lee expressed a regret that he had invited me to lead my division in his vessel, the "Oneida," alleging as a reason that I would get the credit for what might be achieved by his vessel. Lieutenant-Commanding Harrison immediately begged me to hoist my divisional flag on board of his little gun-boat the "Cayuga," and give him a chance to lead the division, which, on going on board of your flag-ship and stating the facts, you kindly consented to my doing; and on giving the gallant Harrison the opportunity he sought, the "Oneida," Commander Lee, was assigned a position further astern. After the chain and booms, constituting the enemy's obstructions, were cut by Captain Bell and Lieutenant Caldwell, it became apparent that if the fleet went up in two columns abreast, according to your written order and programme of the 20th of April, the parallel columns of vessels would likely get foul of the obstructions on either side, and the whole fleet be thrown into confusion under the fire of the enemy's forts, especially as you had determined to make a night attack (two o'clock in the morning). Therefore, with your proverbial foresight and sagacity. you ordered me to get my division of eight vessels under way as soon as the dusk of the evening should obscure the movement from the enemy, and anchor them, line ahead, near the east bank, and gave me a further verbal order, directing me that when the signal should be made (two red lights) from the "Hartford," to lead up with my division and to receive but not answer the fire of Fort Jackson (which I was directed to leave for you to take care of when you should come up, as you expressed it, "I will take care of Fort Jackson"). I was then to open on Fort St. Philip and pass it; but you directed that in case at any time you should come up in the "Hartford," we should leave room for you on the port or west side. I accordingly passed up at the head of my division (in the "Cayuga" receiving but not returning the fire of Fort Jackson. After passing the obstructions I ordered the helm put a-port and led close to the levee, and under the guns of Fort St. Philip, thinking that the guns of that fort would be trained and sighted for mid-river, and that they would consequently overshoot me (which they did), their shot and shell riddling our masts, spars, sails and rigging, with comparatively little damage to the hulls). At this time something occurred to the "Pensacola's" machinery, which caused a detention of the vessels of my division astern of her. Losing sight of them, we in the "Cayuga," alone encountered the rebel iron-clads "Louisiana" and "Manassas" and their flotilla of gun-boats, and maintained unaided a conflict with them, until Boggs in the "Varuna" came up, and after delivering a broadside, which came into the "Cayuga" as well as into the enemy in conflict with us, he passed up the river out of sight. The "Oneida," Commander Lee, came up soon after and fired into a steamer that had already surrendered to the "Cayuga" (being her third prize). I then ordered Lee to go to the assistance of Boggs of the "Varuna," then engaged with two of the enemy's steamers up the river, which had been drawn off from their attack on us of the "Cayuga," to follow and head off Boggs in the "Varuna." After seeing our ("Cayuga's") third prize in flames, we steamed up the river and captured the Chalmette regiment, encamped on the west bank of the river opposite the quarantine hospital. This rebel regiment of infantry I had the honor to hand over to you for your disposition when you came up the river after your severe contest with the forts and fire-ships below.

To give a history of all the incidents of the battle within my observation or the part of which each vessel of my division took, would make this communication too long.

The great object of this letter is to call your attention to the fact that in the hurry of making up your dispatches after the battle, you sent home the written order of the 20th of April, which has been published and has passed into history, instead of your verbal order of the 23d, which was the one in accordance with which the fleet passed up the river, and the battle was fought.

This error has resulted in an inextricable historical muddle, as the history of the battle has been written on the basis of the published programme of April 20th, never carried out; the formation and position of the attacking force being therefore en-

tirely misunderstood by the historians. One (Rev. Mr. Boynton's) history not even mentioning me, although it did those of officers commanding vessels under me. My name was merely inserted (as commanding a division) at the instance of a friend, who discovered the omission too late to make a further correction. The resolution of the United States Senate of June 6, 1862, and accompanying documents, of which two thousand were printed, perpetuates the error of our passing the forts in two columns abreast. Mr. Greeley in his "American Conflict," and other authors, are led into the same misstatements. "Lossing's Pictorial History" erroneously describes the "Cayuga" as retiring from the fight on account of her damages, whereas she was continually in action notwithstanding she was much cut up with forty-two shot holes. The "Varuna," which had passed us while heavily engaged, went up the river and drew off three of the "Cayuga's" assailants. The fight of the "Varuna" with two of which is treated as the great event of the battle, while the leading up and heavy single-hand fighting of the "Cayuga" (Harrison's gun-boat), her taking the surrender of three enemy's steamers, the Chalmette regiment of infantry, and cutting the telegraphic communication between the forts and New Orleans, and other circumstances are not mentioned. Now, as I do not wish to be compelled, even in justice to myself, or the officers of my division, to go into the mode of correcting history by pamphleteering or newspaper articles, now so common, I must ask of you to correct this error, which I know you will not hesitate to do, seeing how much annoyance it is giving your friends and followers; or, if you still have any delicacy in doing this as you appeared to have when I spoke to you before, in consequence of a regulation of the Department that you seemed to consider in the way, may I ask if you see any impropriety in my requesting a Board of Inquiry, in order to get the facts on record, since the truth of history, my duty to my officers, and to my family, requires that I should see it done while I am here to do it.

I have the honor to be, respectfully, your obedient servant,

THEODORUS BAILEY,
Rear-Admiral U. S. Navy.
To Admiral D. G. FARRAGUT, *U. S. Navy.*

ADMIRAL FARRAGUT'S REPLY.

NEW YORK, April 3, 1869.

MY DEAR ADMIRAL—I have received your letter of the 1st, and am really at a loss to understand how you, or even historians can take the views you express in relation to the part in the memorable fight in the Mississippi in 1862.

I have just re-read my report of May 6th, and your two reports following, and cannot conceive how you could be more prominently mentioned to the Department.

In the former, you are reported as "leading the right column in the gun-boat "Cayuga," as having "preceded me up to the quarantine station," and as having "captured the Chalmette regiment," and every possible credit is given you for the manner in which you conducted your line, and preceding us to attack the Chalmette forts.

As to historians, I can, of course, do nothing. I have read but one account to which you allude (Dr. Boynton's), and that in reference to Mobile Bay, in which several mistakes occur, going to prove that historians are not always correct.

I do not see how it is possible for me to give you greater credit for your services than is embodied in that report where your name is always prominent; but if you think that full credit has not been done you, which I confess, I regret to learn, you have, of course, a perfect right to make your appeal to the Department; for my own part, I always maintain the conviction that whatever errors may be made in the records of historians and others, posterity will always give justice to whom justice is due.

Very truly, yours,
D. G. FARRAGUT, *Admiral.*
Rear-Admiral T. BAILEY, *U. S. Navy.*

P. S.—By referring to pages 334 and 335--337, of Draper's history, you will find that he gives you all the credit claimed by your own report, as well as that given you by mine. D. G. F.

RESPONSE OF REAR-ADMIRAL BAILEY.

WASHINGTON, D. C., April 27, 1869.

MY DEAR ADMIRAL—I have received and carefully read your letter of the 3rd, in reply to mine of the 1st instant, and admit all you say about prominently mentioning my name to the Department. But your remark: "As to historians, I can do nothing." This is so; but the difficulty is, that the historians derived their erroneous account of the battle from your report of the 6th of May, 1862, and from the diagram which you sent to the Department, as the true order of sailing into the battle with the forts. Those who have written on the subject are not to be blamed for using the official reports of the occurrences; but in seeking for the correction of that report, I hope to prevent similar error and confusion in the future. I do so with the greatest reluctance, as a duty to the officers under my immediate command, and to myself, and I appeal to your sense of justice whether I could do less.

You state, "I have just re-read my (your) report of May 6th, and your (my) two reports following, and cannot conceive how you could be more prominently mentioned to the Department." In the former, you are reported as leading the right column in the gun-boat "Cayuga," and as having preceded me to the quarantine station."

How could there have been a "right" and left column practically, when I led my division to the attack and passage of the forts an hour before you lifted anchors in the "Hartford," and your center division? What I did was done by your orders and inspiration, and to you the world has given the credit of the attack and its success, as fully as it gave to Lord Nelson the credit of the battle of the Nile; but did it detract from his glory that the report of the battle *described how it was fought,* and the exact position of his own vessel, and those of his subordinates?

This matter has been the subject of much discussion among officers then commanding vessels *in my division*; all say that no vessel of your center division came up abreast of, or lapped their vessels. Practically, the effect of your verbal order was, to divide the fleet into four divisions, viz:

1st. The mortar fleet, Commander Porter.
2d. The first division of the gun-boats, under my command, to which was added the two sloops-of-war, "Pensacola" and "Mississippi," of which the gun-boat "Cayuga" (with my division flag) was the leading vessel.
3d. The center division, with your flag on the "Hartford," and
4th. The rear division, bearing the flag of Captain H. H. Bell.

The first, center, and rear divisions went up to the attack in single file, or line ahead. I went up at the head of my division at 2 P. M., or as soon thereafter as it took the "Pensacola" (the next vessel astern of the "Cayuga"), to purchase her anchors —supposed to be about twenty minutes. You followed without lapping the sternmost vessel of my

division, and the division of gun-boats commanded by Captain Bell followed in the wake of your division. The fact practically was that the first division, the mortar fleet, covered the advance, the second was the vanguard, the third the main body of the fleet, and the fourth the rear, and that the advance being made up a river and line ahead, the diagram does not give any idea of the action other than to produce confusion and error. How could it be otherwise when no vessel of the third division lapped any one of the second?

I enclose a copy of this (to us) unfortunate diagram, as attached to your report of the battle, which you will notice places the "Cayuga" (my flag gun-boat) third in line of my division, whereas, according to your own statement (of two columns abreast), that gun-boat should have been recorded as first in line, leading. I would ask of your friendship and your fairness whether this diagram gives the faintest idea of the action, and whether if the names of the vessels were altered, it would not apply equally well or better to many other battles.

As an evidence how far the "Cayuga" was ahead of the rest of the fleet the first news received at the North is announced in the New York *Times* of Sunday, April 27, 1862, thus: "An important report from the rebels.—One of our gun-boats above Fort Jackson and San Philip. Washington, Saturday April 26th. The Richmond *Examiner* of the 25th, announces that one of our gun-boats passed Fort San Philip, sixty miles below New Orleans on the 24th. The report was telegraphed to Norfolk, and brought to Fortress Monroe under a flag of truce, and received from there to-day by the Navy Department."

The next rebel telegram announced the arrival of the fleet before the city. The "Cayuga" in the interval had captured the Chalmette regiment, five miles above the forts, and cut the telegraphic communication, so that the fleet were not again reported until they arrived opposite the city.

Now, my dear admiral, you have entirely misconceived the object of my addressing you. It is not to complain that you have not mentioned me prominently in your dispatch, but it is because in your report of the battle, dated May 6th, and the accompanying diagram, you do not give the circumstances of the fight as they occurred, but those which would apply to your former plan which was abandoned. From that report, the reader would infer that the fleet went to the attack of the forts in two columns abreast, when it was done in single column (line ahead)—that the "Hartford" was the leading vessel, when in reality it was ninth in line astern of the "Cayuga," in a single line or line ahead, and there was no left or right of line, but single file.

That you should for a moment leave so erroneous a report or record uncorrected, is a matter of surprise to your officers, and that you should not have made the correction as soon as your attention was called to it is still more embarrassing to us.

They know that under your orders, I led the vanguard of your fleet, not as represented on the diagram you have filed, but in an entirely different order, and received forty-two certificates in the way of rebel shots striking my vessel, in corroboration of what is known to every one of our gallant companions in that engagement.

I have delayed my reply, both because I have been occupied, and since have heard you were ill, which I deeply regretted, and because I wished to be certain that I said nothing in haste that would be annoying to you, or improper in me to say, and I hope you will now see the matter as I and others do, and make the correction so necessary to justice in your report dated May 6, 1862, and substitute a diagram of the actual positions your vessels and officers occupied in the line of attack, in

BATTLE OF NEW ORLEANS.

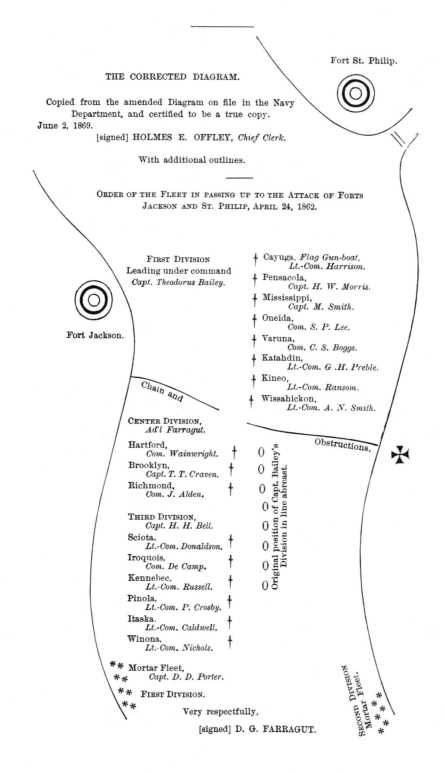

Fort St. Philip.

THE CORRECTED DIAGRAM.

Copied from the amended Diagram on file in the Navy Department, and certified to be a true copy. June 2, 1869.

[signed] HOLMES E. OFFLEY, *Chief Clerk.*

With additional outlines.

ORDER OF THE FLEET IN PASSING UP TO THE ATTACK OF FORTS JACKSON AND ST. PHILIP, APRIL 24, 1862.

FIRST DIVISION
Leading under command
Capt. Theodorus Bailey.

Fort Jackson.

† Cayuga, *Flag Gun-boat,*
    Lt.-Com. Harrison.
† Pensacola,
    Capt. H. W. Morris.
† Mississippi,
    Capt. M. Smith.
† Oneida,
    Com. S. P. Lee.
† Varuna,
    Com. C. S. Boggs.
† Katahdin,
    Lt.-Com. G .H. Preble.
† Kineo,
    Lt.-Com. Ransom.
† Wissahickon,
    Lt.-Com. A. N. Smith.

Chain and

CENTER DIVISION,
    Ad'l Farragut.

Hartford,
    Com. Wainwright. †
Brooklyn,
    Capt. T. T. Craven. †
Richmond,
    Com. J. Alden. †

THIRD DIVISION,
    Capt. H. H. Bell.
Sciota,
    Lt.-Com. Donaldson. †
Iroquois,
    Com. De Camp. †
Kennebec,
    Lt.-Com. Russell. †
Pinola,
    Lt.-Com. P. Crosby. †
Itaska,
    Lt.-Com. Caldwell. †
Winona,
    Lt.-Com. Nichols. †

Obstructions.

Original position of Capt. Bailey's Division in line abreast.

0
0
0
0
0
0
0
0

** Mortar Fleet,
    Capt. D. D. Porter.
** FIRST DIVISION.

SECOND DIVISION Mortar Fleet.

Very respectfully,

[signed] D. G. FARRAGUT.

place of those now on the files of the Navy Department.

I have the honor to be, respectfully, your obedient servant,

THEODORUS BAILEY,
Rear-Admiral.

Admiral D. G. FARRAGUT, *U. S. Navy.*

CORRECTION BY ADMIRAL FARRAGUT.

NEW YORK, May 19, 1869.

MY DEAR ADMIRAL—I have received your two letters, the first one of which was not given to me until to-day, as my physician has advised a total suspension of business until I should become fully convalescent, which I am happy to say, is now the case. It affords me pleasure to make the correction you desire, in the diagram of the Mississippi battle, as I now fully comprehend what you wish in this matter. In fact, I cannot understand how this sketch of the first proposed order of battle—wherein you are placed *third* instead of at the head of the column—should have been attached to the report in lieu of the one which was afterwards adopted.

By referring to this report, you will observe that the diagram accompanies a general order, issued four days before the action, as a preparatory plan of attack, which was subsequently changed. But, still, I cannot understand why, even in this sketch, you should not have been placed at the head of the starboard column.

This diagram, as you are aware, was the original plan, to be changed, as a matter of course, as circumstances might justify, and the vessels were placed according to the rank of the officers respectively commanding them ; but should not have been made part of the report of the final action, as, on reflection, I decided that when the chains were parted the plan of "line ahead" should be adopted, as the best calculated for the preservation of the vessels and for avoiding all chances of fouling. Therefore, when the time arrived, and the signal given, the order of sailing was changed to line of battle, the verbal instructions to which you allude carried out, and you led at the head of your division, and it has always afforded me the greatest pleasure to say that you performed your duties most fearlessly and gallantly.

For this reason I was, at the outset, a little surprised that you should have apparently complained of my report, but my examination of the printed diagram has fully satisfied me of the justice of your appeal.

I shall, therefore, forward to the Department a correct sketch of the final attack as we passed up the river.

I am, very truly, your friend and obedient servant,

D. G. FARRAGUT,
Admiral U. S. N.

Rear-Admiral T. BAILEY, *Washington.*

LETTERS TO THE SECRETARY OF THE NAVY.

NEW YORK, May 24, 1869.

SIR—My attention having been called by Rear-Admiral Bailey to an incorrect sketch which accompanied my report of May 6, 1862, upon the passage of Forts Jackson and St. Philip, I have the honor to forward herewith a corrected diagram, showing the position of the vessels at the time they passed through the obstructions after the chains had been separated. This will demonstrate that Rear-Admiral (then Captain) Bailey led the fleet in the "Cayuga," up to the attack on the forts, as had been previously ordered, he taking St. Philip with his division, while I reserved Jackson for the remainder of the squadron under my command.

The skeleton lines show how the vessels moved up from their original position of two lines into the line ahead.

This correction has not been made before, because I was not aware of the existence of the mistake—the diagram being evidently a clerical error—and in opposition to the text, in which I distinctly state that Rear-Admiral Bailey not only led, but performed his duty with great gallantry, to which I call the attention of the Department.

Very respectfully, your obedient servant,

D. G. FARRAGUT,
Admiral U. S. N.

Hon. A. E. BORIE,
Secretary of the Navy, Washington.

WASHINGTON, D. C. May 25, 1869.

Hon. A. E. BORIE, *Secretary of the Navy.*

SIR—I have the honor to enclose herewith, original and certified copies of a correspondence which I have had with Admiral D. G. Farragut, relating to the battle below New Orleans, and to request that the letters marked from A to E, be placed on the files of the Navy Department, as furnishing a correction of that officer's report, with an accompanying diagram heretofore made to the Department.

The object of my addressing Admiral Farragut is now gained by the admission on his part of the correctness of my statements, that the fleet under his command went up the Mississippi River to attack and pass Forts Jackson and St. Philip, in order of battle, "line ahead," or single file; that I led the fleet into the battle at the head of, and in command of the vanguard division; and that the "Hartford," flag-ship, with Admiral Farragut on board, followed my division, he being thus ninth in line, and at the head of the rest of the fleet in the order represented by the list of vessels which I hereto annex. After this frank admission by my distinguished commander, I have only the regret remaining, that the error into which he was led was not discovered and corrected at an earlier date, thereby possibly affecting my position in the service.

I have the honor to be, respectfully, your obedient servant,

THEODORUS BAILEY,
Rear-Admiral, U. S. Navy.

VESSELS AND OFFICERS ENGAGED IN THE CAPTURE OF NEW ORLEANS.

FLAG-OFFICER DAVID G. FARRAGUT, COMMANDER-IN-CHIEF.

CAPTAIN T. BAILEY, COMMANDING FIRST DIVISION.

CAPTAIN H. H. BELL, COMMANDING SECOND DIVISION.

COMMANDER DAVID D. PORTER, COMMANDING MORTAR FLOTILLA.

STEAMER "BROOKLYN."

Captain, Thomas T. Craven; Lieutenants, R. B. Lowry and James O'Kane; Acting-Masters, George Dewhurst, W. C. Gibbs, J. C. Spofford and Lyman Wells; Midshipmen, John R. Bartlett and H. T. Grafton; Surgeon, Samuel Jackson; Assistant Surgeon, J. S. Knight; Paymaster, C. W. Abbott; First-Lieutenant, James Forney, U. S. M. C.; First-Assistant Engineer, Benj. E. Chassaing; Second-Assistant-Engineers, James Atkins and A. V. Fraser, Jr.; Third-Assistant Engineers, C. F. Mayer, B. D. Clemens, J. L. Bright and Jos. Morgan; Acting-Masters' Mates, R. Beardsley, H. Bartlett, James Buck and H. C. Leslie; Boatswain, J. A. Selmer; Gunner, William Yates; Carpenter, W. D. Toy; Sailmaker, J. Stevens.

STEAMER "CAYUGA."

Lieutenant-Commanding, N. B. Harrison; Lieutenant, George H. Perkins; Acting-Masters, John Hanson and E. D. Percy; Assistant Surgeon, Edw. S. Bogert; Acting-Assistant Paymaster, G. W. Whiffin; Second-Assistant Engineer, J. M. Harris; Third-Assistant Engineers, J. W. Sydney, J. C. Chaffee and Ralph Aston; Acting-Masters' Mate, W. W. Patten.

STEAMER "CLIFTON."

Acting-Lieutenant, C. H. Baldwin; Acting-Masters, E. A. Howell, Robert Rhodes and P. S. Weeks; Midshipmen, H. T. French and H. B. Rumsey; Acting-Assistant Surgeon, D. D. T. Nestell; Acting-Assistant Paymaster, J. H. Carels; Acting-Second-Assistant Engineer, James A. Fox; Acting-Third Assistant Engineer, Samuel Vallum; Acting-Masters' Mate, Charles Albert, L. Cannon, David Harvey and W. W. Wells.

STEAMER "HARTFORD" (FLAG-SHIP).

Commander, Richard Wainwright; Lieutenants, J. S. Thornton, Albert Kautz, J. C. Watson and D. S. Murphy; Acting-Master, T. L. Petersen; Acting-Ensign, E. J. Allen; Midshipmen, H. B. Tyson, J. H. Read, E. C. Hazeltine and H. J. Blake; Fleet Surgeon, J. M. Foltz; Assistant Surgeon, Joseph Hugg; Paymaster, George Plunkett; Captain of Marines, J. L. Broome; Chief Engineer, J. B. Kimball; Second-Assistant Engineers, E. B. Latch, W. W. Hopper and F. A. Wilson; Third-Assistant

Engineers, Isaac De Graff, C. M. Burchard, A. K. Fulton, H. H. Pilkington and W. H. Gamble; Acting-Master's Mates, H. H. Judson, C. H. Loundsberry, T. Mason and J. M. Smalley; Boatswain, James Walker; Gunner, John Duncan; Carpenter, J. H. Conley; Sailmaker, J. A. Holbrook.

STEAMER "HARRIET LANE."

Commander, J. M. Wainwright; Lieutenant, Edward Lea; Acting-Masters, J. A. Hannum, C. H. Hamilton and W. F. Monroe; Assistant Surgeon, T. N. Penrose; Assistant Paymaster, J. J. Richardson; Second-Assistant Engineers, W. H. Plunkett and C. H. Stone; Third-Assistant Engineers, J. E. Cooper, R. N. Ellis and A. T. E. Mullen; Acting-Masters' Mate, C. M. Davis.

STEAMER "IROQUOIS."

Commander, John De Camp; Lieutenants, D. B. Harmony and Fred. V. McNair, Acting-Ensign, C. F. Willard; Midshipman, John McFarland; Surgeon, Benj. Vreeland; Paymaster, R. H. Clark; First-Assistant Engineers, John H. Long and B. C. Bampton; Second-Assistant Engineers, E. S. Boynton and F. K. Haine; Third-Assistant Engineer, J. H. Hunt; Gunner, J. L. Staples; Carpenter, John A. Dixon.

STEAMER "ITASCA."

Lieutenant-Commanding, C. H. B. Caldwell; Acting-Masters, Edward Jones, Amos Johnson and S. Nickerson; Assistant Surgeon, Heber Smith; Assistant Paymaster, A. J. Pritchard; Second-Assistant Engineer, J. H. Morrison; Third-Assistant Engineers, T. M. Jones, John Borthwick and E. A. Magee; Acting-Masters' Mates, N. Alexander and W. E. Bridges.

STEAMER "JOHN P. JACKSON."

Acting-Lieutenant-Commanding, S. E. Woodworth; Acting-Masters, M. B. Crowell, J. F. Dearborn, Wm. Hedger and James Scannell; Acting-Assistant Surgeon, T. S. Yard; Acting-Second-Assistant Engineer, J. B. Morgan; Acting-Third-Assistant Engineers, James Barnes, J. D. Caldwell and Samuel Strade; Acting-Masters' Mates, W. H. Howard, W. J. B. Lawrence and J. Murphy.

STEAMER "KENNEBEC."

Lieutenant-Commanding, John H. Russell; Lieutenant, F. B. Blake; Acting-Masters, Wm. Brooks and H. C. Wade; Assistant-Surgeon, C. H. Perry; Acting-Assistant Paymaster, C. L. Burnett; Second-Assistant Engineer, H. W. Fitch; Third-Assistant Engineers, B. G. Gowing, E. E. Roberts and L. W. Robinson; Acting-Masters' Mates, J. D. Ellis, J. W. Merriman, J. W. Page and H. E. Tinkham.

STEAMER "KINEO."

Lieutenant-Commanding, Geo. M. Ransom; Acting-Masters, Oliver Colbourn and John Whitmore; Assistant Surgeon, O. S. Oberly; Second-Assistant Engineer, S. W. Cragg; Third-Assistant Engineers, C. F. Hollingsworth, C. J. McConnell and James Manghlin; Acting-Masters' Mates, John Bartol, W. H. Davis, G. A. Faunce and W. S. Keen.

STEAMER "KATAHDIN."

Commander, George H. Preble; Lieutenant, Nathaniel Green; Acting-Masters, George Harris and W. H. Pollup; Assistant Surgeon, S. Robinson; Second-Assistant Engineer, T. M. Dukehart; Third-Assistant Engineers, Wm. J. Reid, W. W. Heaton and John McIntyre; Acting-Masters' Mates, A. Hartshorn, Geo. Leonard, J. W. Thode and A. Whiting.

STEAMER "MISSISSIPPI."

Commander, Melancton Smith; Lieutenants, Thos. McK. Buchanan and George Dewey; Acting-Masters, C. T. Chase, F. E. Ellis, F. T. King and George Munday; Midshipmen, Albert S. Barker and E. T. Woodward; Surgeon, R. T. Maccoun; Assistant Surgeon, J. W. Shively; Paymaster, T. M. Taylor; Chief Engineer, E. Lawton; Captain of Marines, P. H. W. Fontane; First-Assistant Engineer, Wm. H. Hunt; Second-Assistant Engineer, J. Cox Hull; Third-Assistant Engineer, F. G. McKean; Acting-Masters' Mates, R. C. Bostwick, H. B. Francis and M. Porter; Boatswain, Jos. Lewis; Gunner, Wm. Cope; Carpenter, John Green.

STEAMER "MIAMI."

Lieutenant-Commanding, A. D. Harrell; Acting-Masters, John Lear, M. Rodgers and W. N. Wells; Assistant Surgeon, Wm. B. Mann; Chief Engineer, J. F. Lambdin; Acting-Assistant Paymaster, W. H. Sells; Acting-Second-Assistant Engineer, L. W. Simmonds; Third-Assistant Engineers, H. D. Heiser, C. C. Davis and Guy Sampson; Acting-Masters' Mates, Robert Roundtree and R. E. Stevens.

STEAMER "ONEIDA."

Commander, S. P. Lee; Lieutenant, S. F. Brown; Acting-Masters, Thomas Edwards, Pierre Giraud and Elijah Ross; Midshipmen, G. W. Wood and F. J. Naile; Surgeon, John Y. Taylor; Paymaster, C. W. Hassler; Chief Engineer, F. C. Dade; Second-Assistant Engineers, H. McMurtrie and R. H. Fitch; Third-Assistant Engineers, W. D. McIlvaine, A. S. Brower, G. W. Stivers and R. M. Hodgson; Acting-Masters' Mates, Edw. Bird and Daniel Clark; Boatswain, James Herold; Gunner, Wm. Parker.

STEAMER "OWASCO."

Lieutenant-Commanding, John Guest; Lieutenant, Chester Hatfield; Acting-Masters, T. D. Dabb and D. P. Heath; Assistant Surgeon, W. M. Leavitt; Acting-Assistant Paymaster, Richard Beardsley; Second-Assistant Engineer, W. K. Purse; Third-Assistant Engineers, J. A. Scott, C. H. Greenleaf and D. B. Egbert; Acting-Masters' Mates, W. M. Tomlinson and John Utter.

STEAMER "PENSACOLA."

Captain, Henry W. Morris; Lieutenants, F. A. Roe, Jas. Stillwell and C. E. McKay; Acting-Masters, Edw. Herrick, G. C. Shultze and E. C. Weeks; Acting-Ensign, A. H. Reynolds; Surgeon, J. W. Taylor; Assistant-Surgeon, W. B. Dick; Paymaster, G. L. Davis; Chief Engineer, S. D. Hibbert; Second-Assistant Engineers, S. L. P. Ayres and C. H. Ball; Third-Assistant Engineers, J. L. Vanclain, G. W. Magee, J. T. Hawkins, F. G. Smith, Jr., and J.C. Huntly; First-Lieutenant of Marines, J. C. Harris; Acting-Masters' Mates, Chas. Gainsford, Jos. Kent, L. Richards and G. A. Storm; Boatswain, N. Goodrich; Gunner, D. A. Roe; Carpenter, J. E. Cox; Sailmaker, Charles Lawrence.

SLOOP-OF-WAR "PORTSMOUTH."

Commander, Samuel Swartwout; Lieutenant, F. O. Davenport; Acting-Masters, W. G. Mitchell, E. A. Terrill and A. A. Ward; Midshipman, Walter Abbott; Surgeon, J. S. Dungan; Assistant Surgeon, H. M. Wells; Assistant Paymaster, Casper Schenck; First-Lieutenant of Marines, Wm. H. Hale; Gunner, T. S. Cassidy; Carpenter, John Shannon; Sailmaker, N. J. Hayden; Acting-Masters' Mate, S. S. Beck.

STEAMER "PINOLA."

Lieutenant-Commanding, Pierce Crosby; Lieutenant, A. P. Cooke; Acting-Masters, W. P. Gibbs and J. G. Lloyd; Assistant Surgeon, L. M. Lyon; Acting-Assistant Paymaster, C. S. Warren; First-Assistant Engineer, John Johnson; Third-Assistant Engineers, P. A. Sassæ, Wm. F. Law and J. Everding; Acting-Masters' Mates, C. V. Rummell and W. E. White.

STEAMER "RICHMOND."

Commander, James Alden; Lieutenants, A. B. Cummings and Edward Terry; Acting-Volunteer-Lieutenant, T. F. Wade; Acting-Masters, C. J. Gibbs and F. S. Hill; Acting-Ensign, H. F. Moffatt; Surgeon, A. A. Henderson; Assistant Surgeon, J. D. Murphy; Paymaster, George F. Cutter; Captain of Marines, Alan Ramsey; Chief Engineer, J. W. Moore; First-Assistant Engineer, Eben Hoyt; Second-Assistant Engineer, J. L. Butler; Third-Assistant Engineers, A. W. Morley, G. W. W. Dove, R. B. Plotts and C. E. Emery; Acting-Master's Mate, J. R. Howell; Boatswain, J. L. Choate; Gunner, James Thayer; Carpenter, H. L. Dixon; Sailmaker, H. T. Stocker.

STEAMER "SCIOTA."

Lieutenant Commanding, Edw. Donaldson; Acting-Masters, G. P. Foster and A. McFarland; Assistant Surgeon, G. H. E. Baumgarten; Second-Assistant Engineer, C. E. De Valin; Third-Assistant Engineers, H. M. Quig, A. H. Price and Edward Curtis; Acting-Masters' Mates, John Staples and G. O. Taylor.

STEAMER "SACHEM."

Acting-Masters, L. G. Crane and Robert Tarr; Acting-Assistant Surgeon, G. H. Van Deusen; Acting-Third-Assistant Engineer, P. P. Staat; Acting-Masters' Mate, W. L. Pavy.

STEAMER "VARUNA."

Commander, Chas. S. Boggs; Lieutenant, C. H. Swasey; Acting-Masters, J. D. Childs and Ezra Leonard; Acting-Masters' Mates, S. H. Bevins and H. D. Foster; Gunner, T. H. Fortune.

STEAMER "WINONA."

Commander, Edward T. Nichols; Lieutenant, John G. Walker; Acting-Masters, Chas. Hallett and Felix McCurley; Acting-Ensign, Wm. F. Hunt; Assistant Surgeon, A. Mathewson; Paymaster, H. M. Denniston; Second-Assistant Engineers, John Purdy, Jr., and Joseph Watters; Third-Assistant Engineers, Edward Gay and R. L. Wamaling; Acting-Masters' Mates, F. H. Beers and H. T. Burdett.

STEAMER "WESTFIELD."

Commander, Wm. B. Renshaw; Acting-Masters, W. L. Babcock, F. C. Miller, L. D. Smalley and Gustav Vasallo; Midshipman, C. W. Zimmerman; Acting-Assistant Surgeon, E. H. Allis; Acting-Assistant Paymaster, C. C. Walden; Acting-Second-Assistant Engineer, Wm. R. Green; Acting-Third-Assistant Engineers, G. S. Baker, Chas. W. Smith and John Van Hogan; Acting-Masters' Mate, J. P. Arnett.

STEAMER "WISSAHICKON."

Lieutenant Commanding, A. N. Smith.

MORTAR FLOTILLA.

First Division.

LIEUTENANT WATSON SMITH, Commanding Division.

Schooner "Norfolk Packet."—Lieutenant Watson Smith.
Schooner "Oliver H. Lee."—Acting-Master Wash. Godfrey.

Schooner "Para."—Acting-Master Edward G. Furber.
Schooner "C. P. Williams."—Acting-Master A. R. Langthorne.
Schooner "Arletta."—Acting-Master Thomas E. Smith.
Schooner "William Bacon."—Acting-Master Wm. R. Rogers.
Schooner "Sophronia."—Acting-Master Lyman Bartholomew.

Second Division.

LIEUTENANT W. W. QUEEN, Commanding Division.

Schooner "T. A. Ward."—Lieutenant W. W. Queen.
Schooner "M. T. Carlton."—Acting-Master Chas. E. Jack.
Schooner "Matthew Vassar."—Acting-Master Hugh H. Savage.
Schooner "George Mangham."—Acting-Master John Collins.
Schooner "Orvetta."—Acting-Master Francis E. Blanchard.
Schooner "Sydney C. Jones."—Acting-Master J. D. Graham.
Schooner "Adolph Hugel."—Acting-Master J. Van Buskirk.

Third Division.

LIEUTENANT K. R. BREESE, Commanding Division.

Barkentine "Horace Beals."—Lieutenant K. R. Breese.
Schooner "John Griffith."—Acting-Master Henry Brown.
Schooner "Sarah Bruen."—Acting-Master Abraham Christian.
Schooner "Racer."—Acting-Master Alvin Phinney.
Brig "Sea Foam."—Acting-Master Henry E. Williams.
Schooner "Henry James."—Acting-Master L. W. Pennington.
Schooner "Dan Smith."—Acting-Master George W. Brown.

LIST OF OFFICERS ATTACHED TO THE MORTAR FLOTILLA AND WEST GULF SQUADRON, THE NAMES OF WHOSE VESSELS DO NOT APPEAR IN THE NAVY REGISTER.

MORTAR FLOTILLA.

Acting-Master, A. M. Gould.
" " Newell Graham.
" " J. H. Johnstone.
" " H. B. Jenks.
" " E. C. Merriman.
Midshipman, N. W. Thomas.
" George W. Sumner.
Assistant Surgeon, A. B. Judson.
" " Robert T. Edes.
" " A. A. Hoehling.
Assistant Paymaster, Clifton Hellen.
" " H. M. Hanna.
Acting-Master's Mate, August Adler.
" " " E. O. Adams.
" " " T. H. Baker.
" " " James Baker.
" " " J. H. Butler.
" " " John Bath.
" " " J. W. Cortelyou.
" " " R. M. Clark.

Acting-Master's Mate, D. B. Corey.
" " " Wm. Collins.
" " " J. A. Chadwick.
" " " G. R. Clifton.
" " " J. W. Comer.
" " " William Dade.
" " " Peter Decker.
" " " George Drain.
" " " L. E. Daggett.
" " " A. Felix.
" " " E. Gabrielson.
" " " D. H. Griswold.
" " " William Hatch.
" " " J. S. Hyde.
" " " T. G. Hall.
" " " J. B. Johnson.
" " " G. W. Lane.
" " " Anthony Loper.
" " " Thomas Levindsell.
" " " Thomas McEllmell.

WEST GULF SQUADRON.

Acting-Master, L. A. Brown.
  " " W. H. Churchill.
  " " D. H. Hayden.
  " " R. L. Kelley.
  " " W. M. Stannard.
  " " George Wiggin.
  " " O B. Warren.
Assistant Surgeon, John H. Clark.
  " " Wm. B. Gibson.
  " " W. F. Terry.
  " " C. J. S. Wells.

Assistant Surgeon, C. S. Giberson.
Third-Assistant Engineer, John D. Ford.
  " " " J. E. Speights.
  " " " J. F. Walton.
Acting-First-Assistant Engineer, David Fraser.
Acting-Second-Assistant Engineer, George L. Harris.
Acting-Third-Assistant Engineer, Samuel Robinson.
Acting-Master's Mate, F. G. Lowe.
  " " " S. H. Johnson.
  " " " Oscar Peck.
  " " " George Taylor.

CHAPTER XXI.

CAPTURE OF NEW ORLEANS.—FIRST ATTACK ON VICKSBURG BY FARRA-
GUT'S FLEET AND MORTAR FLOTILLA.—JUNCTION OF FLAG-OFFICERS
FARRAGUT AND DAVIS ABOVE VICKSBURG.—RAM "ARKANSAS."

FARRAGUT APPROACHES NEW ORLEANS.—DEFENCES OF NEW ORLEANS.—TWO BRAVE MEN
(CAPT. BAILEY AND LIEUT. PERKINS) FACE A MOB.—THE ARMY UNDER GENERAL
BUTLER PLACED IN POSSESSION OF NEW ORLEANS.—FARRAGUT'S SHIPS PUSH UP THE
MISSISSIPPI AND PASS VICKSBURG.—SHELLING THE BATTERIES.—FARRAGUT AND DAVIS
JOIN HANDS.—THE RAM "ARKANSAS" MAKES HER APPEARANCE.—A VIGOROUS PURSUIT.
—ENGAGEMENT BETWEEN THE "ARKANSAS" AND "CARONDELET."—THE "CARONDE-
LET" DRIFTS ASHORE.—THE "ARKANSAS" SLIPS BY THE FLEET, TO VICKSBURG.—THE
ATTACK ON VICKSBURG ABANDONED.—FLAG-OFFICER DAVIS RELIEVED.—REPORTS
OF FLAG-OFFICER FARRAGUT, CAPTAIN CRAVEN, COMMANDERS ALDEN, WAINWRIGHT,
PALMER, DE CAMP, PORTER, AND FLEET SURGEON FOLTZ, LIEUT.-COMMANDERS BALD-
WIN, PREBLE, RUSSELL, LEE, DONALDSON, NICHOLS, CROSBY, WOODWORTH AND LOWRY.
—COMMODORE W. D. PORTER'S REPORT OF ENGAGEMENT AT PORT HUDSON.—REPORT
OF COMMANDER RILEY.

WHEN Farragut passed the Chalmette batteries, and the vessel approached New Orleans, the city levee presented a scene of desolation. Ships, cotton, steamers and coal, were in a blaze and it looked as if the whole city was on fire.

It required all the ingenuity of the commanding officers to avoid coming in contact with the floating conflagration, and when the ships dropped anchor before the conquered city, thousands of people crowded the shore, shouting and bidding defiance to the victorious invaders.

There was no insulting epithet these maniacs did not heap upon the heads of those on board the ships; it was as if bedlam had broken loose and all its inmates were assembled on the levee at New Orleans.

Farragut at once ordered the seizure of a large ram which was intended to be a very formidable vessel, but was still unfinished. Before the officer who had been sent to take possession could reach the ram she came floating down the river enveloped in flames. Another was sunk right opposite the Custom House. Others, which were just begun

at Algiers, on the opposite side of the river from New Orleans, were burning.

Truly, the Queen city of the South was doing her share in building rams to annihilate our Navy and Commerce, but where were our rams that should have been built by the North which boasted of its great skill and resources? These should have been ready to sally out within three months after the war began, to drive the "Louisiana," "Manassas," "Mississippi," "Tennessee," "Arkansas," "Albemarle," and others, back to their holes or crush them like so many egg shells. Our formidable vessels were not even begun—the little "Monitor" even was due to the energy and public spirit of a private citizen, John Ericsson, who furnished his vessel just in time to save the honor of the nation.

The nondescript, wooden Navy, with scarcely a rifled gun, was called upon to attack these monster iron-clad rams sheltered by forts and floating obstructions and protected by torpedoes and fire-rafts; and was expected in all cases to win, notwithstanding the difficulties to be encountered.

The American people do not know, and

probably never will appreciate, the value of the capture of New Orleans. Had the city been left three months longer, to perfect its defences and finish its works of offence, our wooden fleet would have been driven North and the entire Southern coast would have been sealed against us. The blockade would have been raised, and the independence of the South recognized by the powers of Europe. All this was prevented by the Navy without the assistance of the Army —that same Navy which is to-day a mere shadow owing to the neglect of Congress to foster and uphold it.

What were the intentions of the Confederates at New Orleans can be easily understood by reading Flag-officer Farragut's report. When he went up the river to Baton Rouge, he found the banks bristling with cannon, including many of the guns the government had so ignominiously deserted at Norfolk. These were intended to bar the way against any invading squadron approaching New Orleans from the North; but the panic had spread even to that point, and all the guns were spiked and their carriages destroyed.

One work eight miles above New Orleans, reached from the Mississippi nearly across to Lake Ponchartrain, and was partly mounted with twenty-six heavy guns, intended to bid defiance to our Navy and Army. A mile above this were two other works waiting only for more of the Norfolk guns, or for some of the heavy Brooke rifles which the Tredegar works in Richmond were turning out by wholesale.

Still further up the river the Confederates had constructed one of the most herculean works of the kind ever beheld. It was an immense raft of logs bolted and chained together with much ingenuity; and was intended to be thrown across the Mississippi on the approach of the Federal iron-clads should they descend the river so far.

Had New Orleans not been attacked from the sea at the time it was the Confederates would have laughed at our old "turtles," and would have had rams and iron-clads enough to have easily crushed them. They would not have needed the great raft to keep out the Federal gun-boats. Nay, more, these great iron-clads would have made their way up the river and our towns on the Mississippi and its tributaries would have been at their mercy. All this disgrace and mortification was saved the country by the energy, zeal, and bravery of the Navy, in wooden ships armed with smooth-bore guns. St. Vincent, the Nile, Trafalgar, were all great victories, but they were no more important to England than was Farragut's achievement to the United States.

One of Farragut's first acts on reaching New Orleans was to send Captain Bailey on shore, accompanied by Lieutenant George H. Perkins, to demand from the mayor the surrender of the city. These two officers went on their perilous service without an escort and passed right through the crowd of maniacs who were making all sorts of threats from the levee at any one who should dare come on shore from the ships. At this time the whole city was in an uproar, such as was perhaps never before seen in this country. All the vagabonds of the town, thieves, ragpickers, abandoned women, the inhabitants of the slums, all were abroad. their faces distorted by passion, the riffraff, hobnobbing with the well-to-do, and all animated by a common hatred of the detested Yankees.

LIEUTENANT (NOW CAPTAIN) GEORGE H. PERKINS.
(FROM A PORTRAIT TAKEN 1884.)

It looked as if law and order could never be re-established. The steamers that had been left unburned were lying at the levee, with crowds of maniacs rushing over their decks, the men smashing in the rice tierces, the women scraping up all that could be gathered. Such portions as could not be carried off were thrown into the river— "the damned Yankees shan't have it!" they cried. There was no way of testifying their rage to which the mob did not resort.

All at once a boat was seen pulling for the shore with two officers sitting in the stern-sheets. These officers landed, faced the crowd, and walked as steadily as if they had a thousand men at their backs.

" I want to see the mayor," said Captain Bailey, " show me where he lives "; and now the crowd woke again from the brief silence that had fallen upon it. Again they roared and shouted, "Down with the Yankees!" "shoot them!" "hang them to a lamp post!" and they crowded around the two officers who walked fearlessly on. In a few moments the officers were lost sight of in the crowd, and no one in the squadron knew what might be their fate, but Bailey and Perkins walked coolly on in defiance of the rabble until their determined courage won respect even from that howling mob.

The guns of the "Hartford" were loaded with grape and canister, and as Bailey and Perkins were shut in by the crowd, the men stood to their guns ready for the first sign from the tops, that harm had come to the officers, to open the battery on the mob.

However, no harm came to those two brave men. It would seem that, in an American mob, there is always some little spark of chivalry, especially where men show pluck. So it was in this case; the two officers reached the mayor's house, and were shown into the presence of the mayor, Mr. Monroe, a cool, brave gentleman, to be sure, but one ruled by the rabble, which has always had undue influence in New Orleans.

"We have come," said Captain Bailey to the mayor, "to demand the surrender of New Orleans, and that the State flag be hauled down from the public buildings, and that only the United States flag be hoisted there."

"You have the power in your own hands," replied the mayor, "and can do as you please, but I doubt if there is a man in New Orleans who would haul down that flag without being assassinated on the spot."

The officers having performed their mission, took their leave. The crowd had received some intimation of their demand, and on their appearance again howled, if possible, louder than before, but Bailey and Perkins waved them aside, and strode back to the levee. It was a brave action, and should not be forgotten by those who have lived to read the events of the civil war.

Soon after the return of Captain Bailey and Lieutenant Perkins, Captain Charles H. Bell landed with a guard of marines and two boat howitzers loaded with grape and canister. The same howling mob met Captain Bell at the levee, but gave way before the marines, who marched steadily towards the State House. Arriving there the marines were drawn up in line, with the howitzers pointed at the mob, ready to mow them down if it became necessary to do so. Bell ascended to the roof of the building, down came the Confederate flag and up went the stars and stripes. The crowd was hushed into silence, they realized that the howitzers would decimate their ranks if the order was given to fire, and that was something they did not fancy.

At the Custom House the same scene was enacted while cheer after cheer came from the ships, the signal that the majesty of the law had been upheld and the integrity of the Union vindicated.

A few days afterwards the steamers of the mortar flotilla towed the transports containing Major-General Butler's army to New Orleans, and under the guns of Farragut's squadron the troops landed, and order was re-established in the city.

Then Flag-officer Farragut pushed on towards Vicksburg, whose heights had been heavily fortified. The flag-officer did not feel justified in attacking the stronghold without the mortar flotilla, which he "deemed indispensable to shell out the heights," but the mortars were then at Pensacola and it took them some twenty days to reach the scene of action.

Sixteen mortars being then placed in position they proceeded to shell the batteries on the hills, with such good effect that Farragut's ships passed Vicksburg with very little loss. But the soldiers in the hill forts refused to stay shelled out, and when the mortars stopped playing on them they would come back from the fields and again open fire. It was not here as at Fort Jackson, where the beseiged were cooped up in casemates with bricks and mortar all around, where a shell in falling would displace huge masses of masonry, dealing death and destruction to the garrison. The fortifications of Vicksburg were scattered over the hills in groups, the guns fifty yards apart, and concealed from view. The heavy shells would whistle over the ships, throwing up the water in spouts and occasionally crashing through the vessels' timbers, to let the invaders know how well Vicksburg was fortified, and what improvements had taken place in this respect within a month.

The whole power of the Confederacy had been set to work to save this Gibraltar of the Mississippi, the railroads poured in troops and guns without stint, enabling it to bid defiance to Farragut's ships and the mortar flotilla.

There was an area of twenty-eight square miles within which the Federals might throw all the shot and shells they pleased. The Confederates did not mind it much, even when the shots fell in the city. This was their last ditch, so far as the Mississippi was concerned, and here they were determined to make a final stand.

Farragut could only obey his orders and effect a junction with Flag-officer Davis above the city, and they pummelled away to their hearts' content with shells and mortars for many days, with little effect.

Our combined fleet lay there and gazed in wonder at the new forts that were constantly springing up on the hill tops, two hundred and fifty feet above the river, and a mile and a half back from the shore, while water batteries seemed to grow on every salient point It was evident enough that Vicksburg could only be taken after a long siege by the combined operations of a large military and naval force.

Flag-officers Farragut and Davis here learned that a large ram was building at Yazoo City, but they did not believe the Confederates had sufficient resources to build a powerful vessel in such an out-of-the-way place, so they let their vessels' steam go down to save coal, which was very hard to get at Vicksburg, and contented themselves with sending the "Carondelet" and "Taylor" up the Yazoo River in company with the Ellet ram, "Queen of the West."

On their way up the Yazoo River, and six miles above its mouth, the two gun-boats met the iron-clad ram "Arkansas" advancing boldly to attack them. She was commanded by Lieutenant Brown, late of the U. S. Navy, whose name will go down in history as one who performed a most gallant and desperate undertaking.

The iron plating of the "Arkansas" rendered her impervious to the shot and shells of our fleet, her formidable iron prow could pierce any ship's side, and she had a formidable battery of rifled guns.

The two gun-boats and the "Queen of the West," turned to retreat down the river firing upon the "Arkansas" as they did so. The Confederate ram pursued the three vessels, keeping up a vigorous fire with her bow guns, and had greatly the advantage, being thoroughly protected from their shot, and having a much heavier battery.

This running fight went on for an hour until the "Arkansas" came up with the "Carondelet," the slowest of the three vessels, and tried to run her down. The "Carondelet" avoided her prow, and as the "Arkansas" came abreast, exchanged broadsides with the enemy. The "Arkansas" then passed ahead, and the "Carondelet" opened on her with the bow guns, the shot from which seemed to glance harmlessly from her stern.

At this moment, the "Carondelet's" wheel ropes were shot away for the third time, and she sheered into the shore, while two shot holes were observed in the "Arkansas," and her crew were seen pumping and bailing.

The "Carondelet" was much damaged in hull and machinery, and had thirteen shot holes in her hull, steam gauge, three escape pipes and two water pipes cut away. Nineteen beams and thirty timbers were cut away, three boats destroyed, deck pumps shot away and many other injuries. Thirty men were killed, wounded and missing. All through the fight, the "Taylor," Lieut.-Com. Gwinn, gallantly sustained Commander Walke in the "Carondelet."

There can be no comparison drawn between the "Arkansas" and her antagonists, for with but one gun she would have been superior to all the "Carondelet" class of gun-boats put together and would have been more than a match for the "Benton;" yet, notwithstanding her inferiority, the "Carondelet" hung on to the last, inflicting all the damage on the ram that she possibly could until her wheel ropes were shot away and she drifted ashore.

It was the object of the commanding officer of the "Arkansas" to reach Vicksburg undiscovered, and she would have done so but for the three vessels she encountered in the Yazoo. When the "Carondelet" parted her wheel ropes the "Arkansas" never stopped, but made the best of her way in pursuit of the "Taylor" and "Queen of the West," both of which were carrying on all steam to notify the squadron that the "Arkansas" was coming.

The sound of the guns was heard in the fleet but it was taken as an indication of some conflict with "bushwhackers." The ram "General Bragg," was the only vessel that had steam up and her captain unfortunately waited for orders instead of slipping her chain and attacking the "Arkansas," when she came up with the fleet. Had the "Bragg" done this she would doubtless have disabled the "Arkansas" by ramming her as the latter vessel was already damaged in her motive power.

Flag-officer Farragut says : "We were all lying with low fires—none of us had steam up or could get it up in time to pursue her (the 'Arkansas') but she took the broadsides of the whole fleet. It was a bold thing, and she was only saved by our feeling of security. She was very much injured, and was only able to drift down at the lowest speed and with the current she got down to the forts at Vicksburg before any of us had steam up."

The "Arkansas" was undoubtedly much damaged by the fire of the fleet ; her smokestack was riddled, and although she was built to be invulnerable, several eleven-inch shots penetrated her, cutting her up inside and killing and wounding twenty of her crew. Among the killed was the first pilot, and among the wounded were the commanding officer, Lieutenant Isaac N. Brown, and another pilot.

The vessels of the fleet suffered from the "Arkansas" as she passed down, each of the wooden ships receiving one or two shots. Commander William D. Porter, of the gun-boat "Essex," volunteered to go down with his vessel and destroy the ram, but his gallant attempt was unsuccessful, and the "Essex" was much cut up by the batteries.

The morning after this affair, Farragut got under way with his ships and proceeded down the river to protect the mortars and transports below, each vessel firing into the "Arkansas" as they passed her under the guns of Vicksburg. The morning was misty and the forts were firing into the ships, so that the "Arkansas" was not materially damaged.

Flag-officers Farragut and Davis, finding it a loss of time to attempt the reduction of Vicksburg without the co-operation of a large Army, determined to abandon the idea for the present and return to their stations—Davis up river and Farragut to New Orleans, where he could inaugurate fresh expeditions against the enemy. So Vicksburg was left alone in her glory to strengthen her fortifications and for a time bid defiance to the Federal Government.

The original plan of sending an Army of ten thousand men to take possession of Vicksburg, under cover of Farragut's squadron, was never carried out. Three thousand troops only (under command of General Williams) were landed opposite Vicksburg, but, as they attempted nothing important, their presence was perfectly useless. The ten thousand men who should have been sent to Vicksburg were retained by General Butler at New Orleans. Had this Army been pushed up the river directly after the fall of New Orleans, Vicksburg would have fallen into the hands of the Federal forces. This failure to act promptly cost the Government many lives and millions of money.

Flag-officer Davis at first determined to occupy the Yazoo River, and from thence carry on operations against the enemy, but he found that nothing could be done in the Yazoo at low water, and besides, the enemy had constructed formidable barricades, well defended by heavy batteries, at Haines' Bluff, some miles above the mouth of the river ; and with these he had not sufficient force to contend.

His line of operations was entirely too extended for the force he had in hand, and all his vessels needed repairs. Flag-officer Davis, therefore, returned to Cairo, where, in October, 1862, he was relieved from the command of the Mississippi Squadron by Acting-Rear-Admiral David D. Porter.

The following reports will give a pretty full account of what was done in the first naval attack on Vicksburg.

FLAG-OFFICER FARRAGUT REPORTS THE NECESSITY OF 12,000 TO 15,000 ARMY FORCES TO COOPERATE IN THE TAKING OF VICKSBURG.

FLAG-SHIP "HARTFORD," }
ABOVE VICKSBURG, June 28, 1862. }

SIR—I passed up the river this morning, but to no purpose ; the enemy leave their guns for the mo-

ment, but return to them as soon as we have passed, and rake us. Our loss, as far as ascertained, is not very great. Commander Porter shelled them two days to get his ranges, and all his vessels entered into the attack with great spirit, and did excellent service. The fire of the ships was tremendous. The "Brooklyn," "Kennebec," and "Katahdin" did not get past the batteries. I do not know why.

I am satisfied it is not possible for us to take Vicksburg without an army force of 12,000 or 15,000 men. General Van Dorn's division is here, and lies safely behind the hills. The water is too low for me to go over twelve or fifteen miles above Vicksburg.

Very respectfully, your obedient servant,
D. G. FARRAGUT,
Commanding Western Gulf Squadron.
Hon. GIDEON WELLES,
Secretary of the Navy, Washington, D. C.

———

FLAG-OFFICER FARRAGUT'S REPORT OF THE ACTION OF JUNE 28, 1862, AT VICKSBURG.

UNITED STATES FLAG-SHIP "HARTFORD," }
ABOVE VICKSBURG, MISSISSIPPI, }
July 2, 1862. }

SIR—In obedience to the orders of the department and the command of the President, I proceeded back to Vicksburg with the "Brooklyn," "Richmond," and "Hartford," with the determination to carry out my instructions to the best of my ability.

My difficulties and expenses in getting coal and provisions up the river have been very great, and it has only been accomplished by great exertions on the part of Captain H. W. Morris, aided by the Army. Captain D. D. Porter's mortar flotilla, which was deemed indispensable to shell out the heights, had also to be towed up. All this caused great delay, but by the steady exertions of that officer, and the assistance of all in whose power it was to help, we succeeded in getting up sixteen mortar vessels, and arrangements were soon made to bombard the forts on the heights of Vicksburg. Owing, however, to some imperfection in the fuzes (which Captain Porter will explain), he was two days getting his ranges. On the evening of the 27th, he reported to me that he was ready, and I issued my general order (a copy of which is hereto appended) for the attack on the 28th, at 4 A. M.

At 2 A. M., on the 28th June, the signal was made to weigh, and we proceeded up to the attack in the order of steaming prescribed in the diagram accompanying the general order. At 4 o'clock precisely, the mortars opened fire, and at almost the same moment the enemy fired his first gun, which was returned by the leading vessels – "Iroquois," Commander J. S. Palmer ; "Oneida," Commander S. P. Lee ; and the "Richmond," Commander James Alden. The other vessels—"Wissahickon," Commander John DeCamp ; "Sciota," Lieutenant-Commanding Edward Donaldson ; (this ship, Commander R. Wainwright ;) "Winona," Lieutenant-Commanding E. T. Nichols ; and "Pinola," Lieutenant-Commanding Pierce Crosby—next came up, and poured in their fire successively. At almost the same instant, Commander D. D. Porter came up on our starboard quarter with the "Octorora," "Westfield," "Clifton," "Jackson," "Harriet Lane," and "Owasco," and opened in fine style upon the enemy. The "Hartford" fired slowly and deliberately and with fine effect—far surpassing my expectations in reaching the summit batteries. The rebels were soon silenced by the combined efforts of the fleet and of the flotilla, and at times did not reply at all for several minutes, and then again at times replied with but a single gun.

I passed up at the lowest speed (we had but eight pounds of steam), and even stopped once, in order that the "Brooklyn" and sternmost vessels might close up.

The "Hartford" received but very little injury from the batteries in or below the town, but several raking shots from the battery above the town did us considerable damage ; they were 50-pounder rifle and 8-inch solid shot. The first passed through the shell-room in the starboard forward passage, and lodged in the hold, but did no other harm. The 8-inch struck the break of the poop and passed through the cabin, but hurt no one ; the rigging was much cut, and the port main-topsail yard was cut in two.

If the ships had kept in close order, in all probability they would have suffered less, as the fire of the whole fleet would have kept the enemy from his guns a longer space of time, and, when at his guns, his fire would have been more distracted.

When we reached the upper battery we soon silenced it, and it was reported to me that its flag was struck. We therefore gave three cheers ; but when we had passed about three-quarters of a mile above they reopened fire with two heavy guns. I was unable to reply to this raking fire, being out of range. Although their shots were well directed, they either had too much or too little elevation, and only cut our rigging to pieces,.without injuring any one seriously, which was strange, as the "Iroquois," "Winona," and "Pinola" were on our quarter.

At 6 A. M., meeting with Lieutenant-Colonel Ellet, of the ram fleet, who offered to forward my communications to Flag-officer Davis and General Halleck, at Memphis, I anchored the fleet and went to breakfast, while I prepared my hasty dispatch (No. 120) and telegram for the department. I also sent across the peninsula to see what was the cause of Captain Craven and the vessels astern of him in the line not passing up. I also desired a list of the casualties, which appears by their letters to have been "*none.*" The casualties in the fleet, as far as heard from, in the passing vessels, were seven killed and thirty wounded. Commander Porter reports eight killed and ten or twelve wounded ; but that was not his official report, probably, but referred more particularly to the two steamers, "Clifton" and "Jackson," each of which had an accidental shot—the "Jackson" in .the wheel-house, killing the helmsman, and the "Clifton" a shot through her boiler, killing (by scalding) the men in her magazine, six in number, and one man was drowned by jumping overboard. I herewith forward the report of Acting Lieutenant-Commanding C. H. Baldwin, of the "Clifton."

The department will perceive from this (my) report, that the forts can be *passed*, and *we have done it*, and can *do it again as often as may be required* of us. It will not, however, be an easy matter for us to do more than silence the batteries for a time, as long as the enemy has a large force behind the hills to prevent our landing and holding the place.

General Williams has with him about three thousand men, and, on the occasion of our attack and passing, placed a battery of artillery nearly opposite the upper forts, for the purpose of distracting the raking fire from us while running up ; but the fort, having a plunging fire upon them, dismounted one of the guns, and killed a man and a horse.

It gives me great pleasure to say that General Williams, Colonel Ellet, and the army officers of this division generally, have uniformly shown a great anxiety to do everything in their power to assist us ; but their force is too small to attack the town, or for any other purpose than a momentary assault to spike guns, should such an opportunity offer.

It gives me great pleasure also to report that the officers and men of the ships which accompanied me up the river behaved with the same ability and steadiness on this occasion as in passing Forts Jackson and St. Philip. No one behaved better than

Commander J. S. Palmer, of the "Iroquois," who was not with me on the former occasion. It pains me much to limit my praise, but I cannot speak of those who did not come up. It was their duty to have followed me, with or without signal, particularly as it was too early and too smoky to distinguish signals. I enclose their explanations herewith.

As to Commander R. Wainwright and the officers and crew of this ship, I cannot speak too highly of their steadiness and coolness, and the energy with which they performed their duties. This ship was conducted as coolly and quietly as at an ordinary drill at general quarters. There was no confusion of any kind throughout the whole action, and, as far as I could observe the other vessels, the same feeling actuated all the officers and crews engaged.

The captain of the fleet, Commander H. H. Bell, was on the poop by my side, and, not being able, as I before stated, to do much in the management of the fleet, owing to the darkness and the smoke. gave his attention to looking up the batteries and pointing them out to the officers in charge of the guns, and assisting them with his judgment on all occasions.

My secretary, Mr. E. C. Gabaudan, noted the time of passing events, and acted as my aid when required, which duty he performed with coolness and steadiness.

I must not fail to mention the coolness of our pilot, John J. Lane, who, although this was the first time he had ever been under fire, did not for a moment quit his post, but steadily guided the ship in her course. He is not a *professional* pilot, as *they* can only be obtained by force in New Orleans.

All of which is respectfully submitted by your obedient servant,

D. G. FARRAGUT,
Flag-officer Commanding Western Gulf Blockading Squadron.
Hon. GIDEON WELLES,
Secretary of the Navy, Washington, D. C.

OFFICIAL LIST OF KILLED AND WOUNDED IN THE AFFAIR OF JUNE 28, AT VICKSBURG.

FLAG-SHIP "HARTFORD," ABOVE }
VICKSBURG, MISSISSIPPI, June 28, 1862. }
SIR—I have the honor to report the following list of killed and wounded in that portion of the fleet which passed above Vicksburg in the engagement of this morning, viz :

KILLED—15.

Flag-ship "Hartford."—Edward E. Jennings, seaman, from Massachusetts.

"Richmond."—George Allstrum, ordinary seaman ; Thomas Flarity, seaman.

"Oneida."—Stephen H. Randall, seaman.

"Pinola."—William H. Thomas, quarter-gunner ; Thomas Graham, landsman.

"Sciota,"—Augustine Ellsworth, ordinary seaman.

Mortar flotilla.—6 scalded, 1 killed, 1 drowned.

WOUNDED—30.

Flag-ship "Hartford."—Charles Allen, seaman, slightly ; Alexander Capron, landsman, slightly ; Lawrence Fay, boy, slightly ; Patrick Roach, coal-heaver, head ; Philip Roberts, seaman, severely ; Sylvester Becket, landsman, slightly ; Alfred Stone, landsman, slightly ; John H. Knowles, quarter-master, slightly ; John Hardgan, landsman, slightly ; Joseph ———, ordinary seaman, slightly ; Nathan Salter, ordinary seaman, contusion ; Captain John L. Broome, marine corps, contusion ; Flag-officer D. G. Farragut, slight contusion.

"Richmond."—Howard F. Moffat, master's mate, amputated arm ; James Noonan, ordinary seaman, contusion ; Thomas Nolan, marine, contusion ; George W. Harris, marine, contusion; James Reddy, seaman, severely ; James Mohegan, landsman, severely ; George Millard, seaman, severely ; William Nicholas, landsman, slightly ; Charles Howard, ordinary seaman, severely.

"Oneida."—Richard M. Hodgson, assistant engineer, severely ; William Cowell, seaman, severely ; Henry Clark, boatswain's mate, slightly.

"Pinola."—John Brown, ordinary seaman, severely ; William H. Shucks, landsman, slightly.

"Sciota."—Edward Hathaway, seaman, amputated arm ; William Orne, landsman, slightly ; Clarence Miller, ship steward, severely.

Returns have not yet been received from Captain Porter's mortar flotilla, and that portion of the fleet below Vicksburg.

I am, very respectfully, your obedient servant,
J. M. FOLTZ,
Fleet Surgeon.

Flag-officer D. G. FARRAGUT,
Commanding Western Gulf Blockading Squadron.

GENERAL ORDERS.

UNITED STATES FLAG-SHIP, "HARTFORD,"}
BELOW VICKSBURG, June 25, 1862.   }

The mortar boats and gun-boats of the mortar flotilla having been placed by Commander D. D. Porter, according to his judgment, to the best advantage to act upon the batteries on the heights and the fort below the hospital : at 4 A. M., to-morrow they will open fire upon the same and on the city of Vicksburg.

At the display of the signal for the ships and gunboats to weigh, they will form in a double line of sailing, the "Richmond," Commander James Alden commanding, leading ; the ships "Hartford," Commander R. Wainwright commanding, next ; "Brooklyn," Captain T. T. Craven, third. The gun-boats will form another line, so as to fire between the ships, in the following order : "Iroquois," Commander James S. Palmer, and "Oneida," Commander S. Phillips Lee commanding, ahead, but on the port bow of the "Richmond," so as to fire into the forts at the upper end of the town, without interfering with the fire of the "Richmond ;" next in order, the "Wissahickon," Commander Jno. DeCamp, and the "Sciota," Lieutenant-Commanding Ed. Donaldson, in the line with the "Iroquois" and "Oneida," but on the port bow of the flag-ship, so as to fire between the "Richmond" and flag-ship ; next the "Winona," Lieutenant-Commanding Ed. T. Nichols, and "Pinola," Lieutenant-Commanding Pierce Crosby, on the port bow of the "Brooklyn."

The "Hartford" will, as often as occasion offers, fire her bow guns on the forts at the upper end of the town ; but the broadside batteries of all the ships will be particularly directed to the guns in the forts below and on the heights. The free use of the shrapnel is considered the best projectile, but care must be taken in cutting the fuzes, so as always to be sure that they burst short of their destination. When close enough give them grape. The enclosed diagram will show the position of the respective vessels in the order of attack.—[For diagram see original.]

When the vessels reach the bend in the river, the "Wissahickon," "Sciota," "Winona," and "Pinola," will continue on ; but, should the enemy continue the action, the ships and "Iroquois" and "Oneida" will stop their engines and drop down the river again, keeping up their fire until directed otherwise.

D. G. FARRAGUT,
Flag-officer Commanding Western Gulf Blockading Squadron.

The "Kennebec," Lieutenant-Commanding Jno. Russell, will take position in the rear of, and in a line with, the "Pinola," so as to fire astern of the "Brooklyn."

D. G. FARRAGUT,
Flag-officer.

UNITED STATES STEAMER "CLIFTON,"}
TWO MILES BELOW VICKSBURG, June 28, 1862.}

SIR—I have the honor to report that this morning, at 3.45 A. M., in obedience to orders, we got under way and proceeded in our station just astern of the "Westfield," in the line headed by your own ship, to engage the batteries on the heights around Vicksburg. When within range, we opened our fire on the upper batteries on the hill from our rifled gun, and forward 9-inch and forward 32-pounder, using 15-second shells. On receiving your orders, we directed our fire at the battery known as the "water battery," advancing to within about 1,200 yards, where we kept our station, using shrapnel from the 9-inch guns. At times, as opportunity offered, we used

ACTING LIEUT. (NOW REAR ADMIRAL) CHARLES H. BALDWIN.

our after 9-inch guns. This we continued for some half to three-quarters of an hour, with, I think, good effect, until we were hailed by the "Jackson," asking our assistance to tow them out of fire, that ship being temporarily disabled.

While in the act of taking her line, we received a shot under the guard, just forward of the wheel, which, going through the ship's side, made its way into the end of the starboard boiler, and, partially coming out on the other side, caused such a rush of steam as to blow off at once the cover to the forward hatch, filling the forward berth deck (under which is the forward magazine) with steam, and killing instantly Thomas Collins, gunner's mate ; Robert Sargent, ship's cook ; Wm. Morris, captain's cook ; John Burke, ordinary seaman ; John B. Carter, landsman, and Peter Hall, landsman, of the forward powder division ; and severely scalding George B. Derwent (colored), wardroom steward, who died a few hours afterwards of the effects of his injuries, and John Hudson, master at arms, who is doing well, his wounds, though severe, not being thought dangerous. But one man from this division escaped, he being at the head of the ladder at the time. Some eight men from the forward pivot gun jumped overboard to escape the steam. With the aid of the "Jackson's" boats we were fortunate enough to recover all these, except John Connor, second-class fireman, who was drowned.

This shot, which proved to be a fifty-pound rifled shot, prevented any further movement of our wheels for the time. We, however, continued our fire from the forward and after thirty-twos, and after nine-inch guns, until you noticed our mishap, and came alongside to tow us out of action. At this period the signal to retire was given.

I have great satisfaction in stating that officers and crew generally behaved well. Mr. Weld, acting-master's mate, in charge of the nine-inch and rifled Parrott gun forward, is entitled to credit for the admirable manner in which those guns were served, and his coolness and self-possession at the time of the accident.

On examination of the injured boiler by the chief engineer of this ship, it is his opinion that the repairs to it will require at least ten days to complete and will need the aid of a shop and experienced workmen. In the meantime, the ship is ready for such service as she may be called upon to perform, which will not entail a greater speed than six knots an hour. This rate, I think, we shall be able to maintain.

I have the honor to be, respectfully, your obedient servant,

CHAS. H. BALDWIN,
Acting Lieutenant-Commanding.

Commander D. D. PORTER,
Commanding Bomb Flotilla.

UNITED STATES STEAM-SLOOP "BROOKLYN,"
BELOW VICKSBURG, June 30, 1862.

SIR—In compliance with your order of yesterday's date, to make my official report of my attack on Vicksburg, on the 28th instant, and to give my reason for not following the flag-ship up the river, etc., I submit the following :

At 3.15 A. M., June 28, got under way, took position in the prescribed line of battle, and followed the flag-ship ; at 4.05 A. M., the enemy opened fire upon the advanced vessels. When this ship arrived abreast of the lower batteries the steamers of the mortar flotilla, which seemed to be without any form of order, obstructed our passage in such a manner as to oblige us to stop our engines, and thus delayed our progress. At 4.45 A. M., as the 80-pounder rifle was the only gun bearing upon the hill, and able to reach, we opened with that vigorously, keeping well inside their line of fire. At 5.15, the gun-boats, and a few minutes after, the bomb vessels of the mortar flotilla, having ceased firing, all the batteries which had previously been partially silenced, immediately renewed the action, hailing a cross fire on this ship and the two gun-boats. At this time the smoke cleared away ahead of us, and, to my surprise, I could see nothing of the flag or other ships in the line. Whilst we were hotly engaged, trying with our two rifles to silence their most annoying battery, fire was opened upon us by a battery of five pieces of flying artillery, from a position about two-thirds of the way down the hill, and in front of the southernmost battery. Being within easy range, we opened our starboard broadside with shells and shrapnel, and drove them from their position. Finding myself entirely unsupported, except by the "Kennebec" and "Katahdin," which two vessels gallantly performed their part in the engagement, and knowing that it was impossible to reduce a single one of those hill-top batteries, at 7.25 A. M., after sustaining their fire

for two hours and forty minutes, I discontinued the action, and at 8.25 A. M., came to anchor about two and a half miles below Vicksburg.

My reason for not following the flag-ship up the river, that is, *above* and *beyond* the fire of the forts, is simply because, in your general order of the 25th instant, you say "Should the action be continued by the enemy, the ships and the 'Iroquois' and 'Oneida' will stop their engines and drop down the river again ;" and, on the evening of the 27th, twice (when in the cabin and on the quarter-deck of your flag-ship) I asked you if it was your wish or desire for me to leave any batteries behind me that had not been silenced, you answered "No, sir ; not on any account."

It affords me great pleasure to bear witness to the excellent deportment of my officers and men ; a more cool, or a braver set of men, was never on board of any vessel.

We were hulled but twice, one shot taking effect below water, on our starboard bow ; and we received some damage to our rigging. We have no casualties on board. We expended, in the action, 28 nine-inch shells, 41 nine-inch shrapnel, 62 Hotchkiss eighty-pound rifle shells, 3 Dahlgren eighty-pound rifle shells, 14 Parrott thirty-pound rifle shells.

Very respectfully, your obedient servant,

THOS. T. CRAVEN,
Captain.

Flag-officer D. G. FARRAGUT,
Commanding Western Gulf Blockading Squadron,
United States Ship "Hartford," above Vicksburg.

UNITED STATES GUN-BOAT "KATAHDIN,"
BELOW VICKSBURG, MISSISSIPPI RIVER,
June 29, 1862.

SIR—Agreeably to your order of this date, I have to report that I received no orders "to follow the flag-ship up the river," nor any written order whatever, and was entirely ignorant of your plan of attack.

Agreeably to your verbal instructions, which were "to take the rear of the line, and to follow the 'Kennebec,' and fire at anything and everything I saw fit, or could see," I got this vessel under way at 3.30, yesterday morning, took position as the rearmost vessel, and followed the "Kennebec" to attack the batteries at Vicksburg. After the squadron, with the exception of the "Brooklyn," "Kennebec," and "Katahdin," had passed the batteries, the mortar flotilla ceased firing, and the enemy opened their batteries anew. We continued under their fire until 8 A. M., when we dropped down, in company with the "Brooklyn" and "Kennebec" and at 8.20 came to anchor out of range. I have no casualties to report, and the vessel was not hit, though the enemy's shot flew around and over us. The officers and men behaved with their usual cool and determined bravery under fire. We expended in the action eleven shells from the eleven-inch pivot gun, and thirteen from the Parrott rifle on the forecastle. Every shot was deliberately aimed at one or the other of the batteries. In consequence of the position assigned us, and the number of vessels engaged, it was impossible to fire rapidly without firing into or over, and endangering other vessels of the squadron and the steamers and schooners of the mortar flotilla. The vessel had to be manœuvred to fire every shot. We were three hours under the fire of the batteries.

Very respectfully, your obedient servant,

GEO. H. PREBLE,
Lieutenant-Commanding.

Flag-officer D. G. FARRAGUT,
Commanding Western Gulf Blockading Squadron,
United States Flag-ship "Hartford," above Vicksburg.

UNITED STATES GUN-BOAT, " KENNEBEC,"
BELOW VICKSBURG, MISSISSIPPI,
June 29, 1862.

SIR—In obedience to your order of the 29th, I have the honor to make my report of the attack on Vicksburg and my reason for not following you up the river; also the casualties that have occurred on board this vessel.

My position was in the rear of the " Pinola " and on the port quarter of the " Brooklyn," which I held. On the batteries opening fire, I found, from the position of the steamers under the command of Commander Porter, that I could not bring my guns to bear on the batteries without serious injury to them. Immediately on their dropping astern I opened fire on the bluff battery, which had not yet been silenced. When the dense smoke which previously obscured the vessels had passed away, I found that you, with the rest of the fleet, with the exception of the " Brooklyn," " Katahdin," and this vessel, had passed up, and that the mortar vessels had discontinued their fire. Placed in this position, I again referred to your orders, which were: " But if the action should be continued, the ships and the " Iroquois " and the " Oneida " will stop their engines and drop down the river again, keeping up their fire until directed otherwise." Retaining my position astern of the " Brooklyn," I continued firing upon the batteries until my supply of ammunition was so reduced that I deemed it advisable to desist. The hospital and other batteries, which had been silenced for a while, had at this time opened again. The battery on the bluff was firing with vigor, and was assisted by some artillery in the woods. With shot and shell falling around us, I am happy to report no casualties or injury to this vessel. The officers and men performed their duty with the greatest alacrity and coolness. I cannot refrain from mentioning my executive officer, Lieutenant F. B. Blake, who personally attended to the firing of every gun. The following is the expenditure of ammunition, viz : 14 eleven-inch shells, 10m. fuze ; 2 eleven-inch shells, 15m. fuze ; 16 Parrott shells, percussion ; 5 Parrott shells, time fuze, 5m.; 5 Parrott shells, time fuze, 10m.

Very respectfully your obedient servant,
JOHN H. RUSSELL,
Lieutenant-Commanding.
Flag-officer D. G. FARRAGUT,
Commanding Western Gulf Blockading Squadron.

UNITED STATES STEAM-SLOOP " ONEIDA,"
ABOVE VICKSBURG, JUNE 28, 1862.

SIR—I have the honor to report the part borne by the " Oneida " in the engagement with the rebel batteries at Vicksburg this morning.

At 2.10 A.M., the flag-ship made private signal to the fleet to get under way. Stopped coaling, cast off from the coal bark, called all hands and got under way, lashed the hammocks along the starboard side to hold splinters, beat to quarters and cleared ship for action, and stood up the river, the " Iroquois " in line ahead, the " Richmond " astern of us, and the rest of the fleet following. At 3.55, the enemy opened fire on us from his numerous batteries below, over, and above the town. At 4.15, opened on the enemy's batteries in succession, firing for fifteen minutes or more at the flash or smoke of the batteries below and over the town, viz.: the marine hospital battery and the batteries on the ridge over that hospital, it being too dark to see distinctly the batteries on the shady side of the hills.

As it grew light, orders were given to fire as soon as the smoke cleared off, and with good aim. We used shells 5m. fuzes', shrapnel and grape, according to distance, steaming so as to keep between the " Iroquois " and " Richmond," and going ahead when the enemy got our range well.

Having reached the bend in the river (the " Iro-

quois " ahead and the " Richmond " astern of us), and none of our starboard guns now bearing on the batteries, pivoted guns and lashed hammocks on the port side, and prepared for enfilading the batteries above the town, when the flag-ship came up in the proposed line of fire. At 6.30 the " Oneida," anchored near the " Hartford."

This ship was struck four times. One 6-inch rifle shell came through the starboard after-pivot port, killing S. H. Randall, seaman, at the after-pivot gun; severely wounding Richard Hodgson, third assistant engineer, at the engine bell, and passing through the combings of the engine-room hatch, picked up three loaded muskets (each lying flat on the deck, on the port side of that hatch), and burst in the bulwarks, over the first cutter, which was lowered to near the water's edge, drove the muskets through the open port there, and severely wounded William Cowell, seaman, who was in the boat sounding, and slightly wounding Henry Clark, chief boatswain's mate. One 8-inch solid shot struck on our starboard quarter, near the copper, and cut the mizzen mast half in two between decks. One 32-pounder shot passed through the rail. A second 8-inch solid shot carried away, amidships, the keel of the launch which was partly lowered, and, entering on the starboard side, struck the steam drum, and, glancing, fell into the fire-room.

We expended 19 eleven-inch shells, 5m. fuzes; 16 eleven-inch shrapnel; 3 eleven-inch grape, from the two pivot guns; 12 six-inch shells; 6 32-pounder grape, from the two thirty-twos; and 28 thirty-pounder bolts, from two rifle guns—most of these from the forecastle pivot-gun.

The officers and men did their duty well. The enemy's fire was heavy. I enclose the surgeon's report. We have no carpenter.

Respectfully yours, S. PHILLIPS LEE,
Commander.
Flag-officer D. G. FARRAGUT,
Commanding Western Gulf Blockading Squadron.

UNITED STATES STEAMER " RICHMOND,"
ABOVE VICKSBURG, MISSISSIPPI, June, 28, 1862.

SIR—In accordance with your instructions, I have the honor to enclose herewith the surgeon's report of the casualties on board this vessel during the engagement with the batteries at Vicksburg this morning. I also send, for your information, the reports of the carpenter and boatswain, showing the injury done to the " Richmond " by the enemy's shot.

Where all behaved so well I find it impossible to designate any particular individual, either among the officers or men, as meriting especial notice for gallantry and good conduct during the spirited fight which lasted nearly an hour, and was, for the most part, at short range. Still, I feel that I should be doing great injustice to the officer to whom the careful training and consequent steadiness of the crew is due, if I were to fail to give him the credit he has so fairly won ; I refer to Lieutenant Cummings, the executive officer of this ship, and I trust that a grateful country will soon reward him in some way for his untiring zeal and devotion to his profession and her cause.

With great respect, I am, sir, your obedient servant,   JAMES ALDEN,
Commander.
Flag-officer D. G. FARRAGUT,
Commanding Western Gulf Blockading Squadron.

UNITED STATES FLAG-SHIP "HARTFORD,"
ABOVE VICKSBURG, June 29, 1862.

SIR—I have the honor to report the part taken by this ship in the battle of yesterday, in passing the forts at Vicksburg.

We were under way before daylight, and reached the scene of action as day was breaking, when the enemy opened fire upon us from his scattered batteries on shore. We returned it as they came in range, going at slow speed, our guns being worked with admirable coolness and deliberation, which was absolutely requisite, as we labored under the great disadvantage of not knowing the situation of the batteries, which were only discovered by the flash and the smoke of their guns; some, also, were on high bluffs, rendering it difficult to elevate our guns to reach them.

We were under fire about one hour and a half, receiving it on the broadside, and being raked ahead and astern. The enemy fired with great precision, and, although we silenced some of their batteries, they returned to them when we had passed and our guns would no longer bear, and recommenced firing. We stopped opposite one of the lower batteries more effectually to silence it. It would have been easy to have passed by the batteries under full steam and speed, with much less risk from the enemy's fire; but then our object would not have been gained in driving them away from their guns.

We are much cut up, both in hull and rigging, which the enclosed reports of boatswain and carpenter will show. The rigging was soon temporarily secured, under the direction of our indefatigable boatswain, James Walker. The enemy used—as was shown by our finding them on board after the action—80-pounder rifle, 32-pounders and 8-inch shot; also, rifle and musket balls—one of our men being wounded by the latter while working a howitzer in the top.

The executive officer, James S. Thornton, deserves much credit for his excellent distribution of the crew, at the gun and other divisions, and his efficient distribution of them during the action. The commanding officers of divisions also deserve mention—doing their duty with spirit and ability. They were: Lieutenant Albert Kautz, first division; Master John C. Watson, second division; Acting-Master Daniel C. Murphy, third division; Acting-Master Ezra L. Goodwin, powder division.

The marine guard, under charge of Captain John L. Broome, had charge of two broadside guns, and fought them well, thus sustaining the reputation of that distinguished corps. In making this report it gives me an opportunity to supply an omission inadvertently made in my last report of the battle of the 24th and 25th of April; it is in speaking of the medical department, which, under its head, Fleet Surgeon Foltz, was administered admirably, both in this and the former battles. The engineer department, under Chief Engineer James B. Kimball, won much praise for his prompt and efficient working, both in passing the forts and batteries at New Orleans and also in this fight; a failure promptly to obey the bells or the giving out of the engines might have led to much disaster. Acting-Midshipman Herbert B. Tyson, doing the duty of acting-master, besides carrying on those duties with credit, also had charge of a broadside gun manned by his division. In fact, all—officers and men—were a credit to the ship and to the country for which they have so gallantly fought.

We have much to be thankful for, in only having to mourn the loss of one man—Edward E. Jennings, seaman—and having a few only slightly wounded, under such a heavy fire. I enclose the fleet surgeon's report. Very respectfully, your obedient servant,

R. WAINWRIGHT,
Commander United States Navy.
Flag-officer D. G. FARRAGUT,
Commanding Western Gulf Blockading Squadron.

FLAG-SHIP "HARTFORD,"
ABOVE VICKSBURG, June 28, 1862.
SIR—I have the honor to report the following list of killed and wounded on board this ship during the engagement with the batteries at Vicksburg, viz:

Killed.—Edward E. Jennings, seaman.

Wounded.—Charles Allen, seaman, head; Alex'r Capron, landsman, head; Lawrence Fay, boy; Patrick Roach, coal-heaver; Sylvester Becket, Alfred Stone and John Hardigan, landsmen; Jno. H. Knowles, quartermaster and Nathan J. Salter, ordinary seaman; all slightly. Philip Roberts, seaman, severely; Joseph Guido, ordinary seaman, thigh; Flag-officer D. G. Farragut and Jno. L. Broome, captain of marines, slight contusions.

I am, very respectfully, your obedient servant,
J. M. FOLTZ,
Fleet Surgeon.
Commander RICHARD WAINWRIGHT,
Commanding United States Flag-ship "Hartford."

UNITED STATES GUN-BOAT "SCIOTA,"
ABOVE VICKSBURG, June 28, 1862.
SIR—I have to report that, in passing the batteries this A. M., Aug. Ellsworth, ordinary seaman, was killed; E. W. Hathaway, seaman, lost his left arm above the elbow; Wm. Orme, landsman, was slightly wounded; and Clarence Miller, landsman, slightly wounded in the head. The vessel was struck on the starboard quarter, demolishing the quarter-boat and driving in the spirketing. Another shot came through the starboard bulwarks, under the top-gallant forecastle, shattering and carrying away one of the knees and round houses; another shot went through the centre of the foremast, half way up.

Herewith, I beg leave to enclose the surgeon's report of the casualties.

I am, respectfully, your obedient servant,
EDW'D DONALDSON,
Lieutenant-Commanding.
Flag-officer D. G. FARRAGUT,
Commanding Western Gulf Blockading Squadron.

UNITED STATES GUN-BOAT "WINONA,"
ABOVE VICKSBURG, June 28, 1862.
SIR—I am happy to be able to report no casualties to life or limb in the action of this morning with the batteries in or about the city of Vicksburg. Two small shots, either grape or small field-piece, passed through our forward starboard bulwark, cutting away one stanchion and slightly splitting the spirketing. The damage is easily repaired. The vessels of the fleet, while passing the city, were first exposed to a heavy plunging fire from the batteries on the top of the bluffs, cross-fires from batteries (five in number, I think), in various places, then to raking fires above and below; and, while passing the last battery at the upper end of the city, to heavy fire of musketry from concealed marksmen, and, lastly, to the raking fire of heavy guns for nearly two miles above the last battery.

When I came abreast of the upper battery it was entirely clear of men, having been cleared by the guns of the flag-ship; but, as soon as I passed, they returned and opened a very spiteful fire upon the flag-ship, "Iroquois," "Pinola," and this ship, until beyond range. Taking all things into consideration, it seems miraculous that no more damage was sustained by the fleet.

From the experience of this morning I am satisfied that ships *can* clear batteries when placed on a level with them, or nearly so, though the men return to them as soon as the ships' guns cease to bear; but as to batteries placed on hills and bluffs, ships are almost useless against them.

I conclude, sir, by commending to your notice the good conduct of all on board. Where all were alike conspicuous it would be unjust to particularize.

Mr. Sanborn, acting as pilot, remained in the

gangway during the whole action, and assisted in conning the ship. Mr. Sanborn is not a regular river pilot, but a raftsman, partly pressed into the service, and I think a good Union man. Some notice from you, sir, I think would be appreciated by him, and others like him in the fleet.

Herewith I transmit the return of ammunition expended in the engagement of this morning.

I am, sir, very respectfully, your obedient servant,
ED. T. NICHOLS,
Lieutenant-Commanding.

Flag-officer D. G. FARRAGUT,
Commanding Western Gulf Blockading Squadron.

UNITED STATES STEAMER "IROQUOIS,"
ABOVE VICKSBURG, June 30, 1862.

SIR—Agreeably to your order, I submit the following report:

At two in the morning of the 28th, the signal being made from the flag-ship, I got under way and steamed slowly up (the programme being that the "Iroquois" was to lead the attack upon Vicksburg), and was up close into the lower battery before we were discovered, when they opened fire, which was immediately returned. We so fought our way up, running close into the town, having a raking fire from the fort above and a plunging fire from the batteries on the hill, together with broadsides from the cannon planted in the streets, and, what is most strange, through all this heavy concentrated fire, with the exception of cutting away both our mainstays, and some other immaterial damage to the rigging, we escaped without injury. One shell burst on board of us, scattering its fragments around, and yet no casualty occurred.

We remained off the upper battery until joined by the flag-ship, when, following your motions, we anchored out of range. My men and officers behaved with the same coolness which I learn so distinguished them in the attack on the forts below New Orleans.

I have the honor to be, sir, very respectfully, your obedient servant,
J. S. PALMER,
Commander.

Flag-officer D. G. FARRAGUT,
Commanding Western Gulf Blockading Squadron.

UNITED STATES GUN-BOAT "WISSAHICKON,"
OFF THE YAZOO RIVER, June 29, 1862.

SIR—I have the honor to submit the following report of our engagement with the rebel batteries on the heights of Vicksburg. Yesterday morning, at about two o'clock, observing the signal from the flag-ship for the fleet to weigh anchor and proceed to the attack, as arranged by general order, we were soon under way and steaming slowly up the river. By four o'clock we were in our station, astern of the "Iroquois," and on the port quarter of the "Richmond," the "Oneida" ahead and close to us, the remainder of the vessels of the squadron not in sight.

At 4.15, the batteries opened a heavy fire upon us, which we immediately returned with our Parrott rifle and eleven-inch gun. Arriving opposite the city, and within four hundred yards of the lower batteries, our two 24-pounder howitzers, charged with shrapnel, were brought into operation, and did good service in clearing the batteries of their crews. The action continued for one hour, during which the "Wissahickon" received four shots. Our port main rigging was shot away, and an eight-inch shell struck the vessel at the water line, entering the berth-deck, where it killed one man and wounded all the men stationed to pass shot and powder on that deck. Our loss in the battle, though not heavy, is still severe. Master's Mate Charles M. Bird, received a compound fracture of the left arm; ward-room cook killed, and five of the crew

wounded. A severe attack of fever had confined me to bed for several days previous to the action, and I could do but little during its continuance except to encourage, by my presence on deck, the crew to do their duty faithfully.

To Lieutenant E. E. Potter, the executive officer, belongs the credit of our success, and it affords me pleasure to inform you that the officers and crew of the "Wissahickon" did their duty faithfully, and to my entire satisfaction.

After passing the batteries, I proceeded, according to my orders, to the mouth of the Yazoo River, but the gun-boats named in your order, which were to join me, not having come up, I deemed it imprudent to attempt the ascent of the river alone. I shall, therefore, await your further orders.

I am, most respectfully, your obedient servant,
JOHN DeCAMP,
Commanding.

Flag-officer D. G. FARRAGUT, U. S. N.
Commanding Western Gulf Squadron, near Vicksburg, Miss.

FLAG-OFFICER FARRAGUT'S REPORT OF AFFAIRS ABOVE VICKSBURG, JULY 6, 1862.

UNITED STATES FLAG-SHIP, "HARTFORD,"
ABOVE VICKSBURG, July 6, 1862.

SIR—I have to inform you that we are still at this place, bombarding it by the mortars from both sides of the peninsula. Flag-officer Davis has four mortars, and Commander Porter sixteen. Commander Porter has hard work to keep them from attacking him with riflemen; thus far, however, he has always got the best of them, and forced them to retreat. He reported yesterday that he had found five dead bodies in the swamp near him, and large quantities of shoes, knapsacks, muskets, etc., showing that he had driven them precipitately from the woods.

I received a telegram yesterday from General Halleck, a copy of it is herewith enclosed, by which it appears that he will not be able to co-operate with us for some weeks yet.

Flag-officer Davis received a letter from General Grant at the same time, at Memphis, stating that it was reported that Richmond was taken. Should this be true, no doubt but what Vicksburg will soon fall, but it must be by troops coming down in the rear. The city is sacrificed by the soldiers; it has been abandoned by the inhabitants. The ditch across the peninsula will soon be deep enough for the water to run through, unless the river should fall very fast. We are now in hopes of a little rise, a foot or so will accomplish the object.

I have the gun-boats looking to the bluffs below, and giving convoy to our supply vessels.

I hear nothing of the "Cayuga" or "Kearsage."

I hope the department will not supersede Commander Bell in the command of the "Brooklyn," for you may depend upon it the Navy has not a braver man or better officer. * * * * * * *

I hear by a deserter to General Williams that General Breckinridge is in command at Vicksburg, and they are seizing every one for the army.

Very respectfully, your obd't serv't.
D. G. FARRAGUT,
Flag-officer.

Hon. GIDEON WELLES,
Secretary of Navy, Washington.

UNITED STATES MILITARY TELEGRAPH,
MEMPHIS, July 3, 1862.

The scattered and weakened condition of my forces renders it impossible for me, at the present, to detach any troops to co-operate with you on Vicksburg. Probably I shall be able to do so as soon as I can get my troops more concentrated;

this may delay the clearing of the river, but its accomplishment will be certain in a few weeks.

Allow me to congratulate you on your great success.

H. W. HALLECK,
Major General.

Flag-officer FARRAGUT,
Commanding United States flotilla in the Mississippi.

COMMANDER D. D. PORTER'S REPORT OF THE OPERATIONS OF THE MORTAR FLEET AT VICKSBURG.

UNITED STATES FLAG-SHIP "HARTFORD,"
ABOVE VICKSBURG, MISSISSIPPI,
July 7, 1862.

SIR—I herewith forward the report of Commander D. D. Porter of his operations since the receipt of his orders to join me at Vicksburg up to date, and it gives me great pleasure to say that nothing could exceed that officer's perseverance in getting to the scene of his labors, or the steadiness with which his officers and men have carried on his work of demolition and annoyance to the enemy, while I deeply regret the chance shots which caused the death of his brave men. But, as I stated in my last communication, Commander Porter's service has been hard upon his officers and crew, though they have performed it well, willingly and unflinchingly.

We hope soon to have the pleasure of recording the combined attack by Army and Navy, for which we all so ardently long.

Very respectfully, your obedient servant,

D. G. FARRAGUT,
Commanding Western Gulf Blockading Squadron.

Hon. GIDEON WELLES,
Secretary of the Navy.

UNITED STATES STEAMER "OCTORORA,"
VICKSBURG, July 3, 1862.

SIR—Agreeably to the orders received from you I sailed from Pensacola on the 3d of June, and on the 9th had all the mortar vessels in New Orleans. On the 13th, sixteen vessels, in tow of the steamers, had left for Vicksburg, on half rations, the officers and men being desirous to arrive at the scene of action in good time. On the 20th, we were before Vicksburg, ready for service, having met with no delay or accidents on the passage. On one occasion the flotilla was attacked with field-pieces at Ellis Bluffs, but the rebels were handsomely repulsed by the "Owasco" and "Jackson," Lieutenants Commanding Guest and Woodworth. The mortar schooners "George Mangham" and "Arletta," Acting-Masters John Collins and Thomas E. Smith, and the "Horace Beales" and "Sarah Bruin," Lieutenant-Commanding Breese and Acting-Master A. Christian, were also attacked at different times, but they whipped off the rebels, and pursued their voyage in peace. The latter schooner had two men seriously hurt, having each lost an arm by a 12-pound shot. Lieutenant-Commanding Breese gives his officers full credit for behaving handsomely under a troublesome fire from field-pieces and concealed riflemen.

On the 21st, with a mortar schooner alongside, I proceeded up toward the city of Vicksburg, to obtain ranges and draw the fire of the enemy's forts, about which we had no information. The rebels allowed us to get within good range, when they opened on us with all their batteries, without, however, doing any harm, and enabled us to get the desired information. I gave them four bombs, to let them see they were in range, and some 100-pound rifle shots, and returned to the anchorage, after satisfying myself about the proper position to place the mortar vessels in.

On June 26, I was employed all night getting the mortars in position. Nine on the right-hand side going up, under command of Lieutenant-Commanding Smith, and eight on the left side, under command of Lieutenant-Commanding Queen. Lieutenant-Commanding Breese was left at New Orleans to bring up the last vessels. He was detained, also, getting the "Sea Foam" afloat, which vessel had grounded badly on a sand-bar, where she will most likely remain for the rest of the season. The position selected here for the mortars was a beautiful one on the starboard side of the river, at 2,500 yards from the main battery, and 2,200 from the water battery. The vessels on the port side about 700 yards, further off, were rather exposed to the enemy's fire, but were so covered up with bushes that it was not easy to see them at that distance, much less to fire accurately at them.

When the mortars were all in position they opened their fire deliberately for the purpose mainly of getting ranges, which they succeeded in doing after a few fires. The enemy opened on them from all their batteries in range, but, though they fired all around and over them, none were struck. A kind Providence seems to look out for this little fleet. They soon silenced the batteries, and were enabled to pursue their experiments unmolested.

On June 27, the mortars opened again on the forts at 5.45 A. M., firing rapidly. The rebels attempted to respond, but were driven away from their guns, after we had fired a little less than an hour. The steamers were also employed, throwing in an effective fire with their rifle-guns. The practice was kept up during the day with good effect, many of the bomb shells going into the forts or bursting over them. Only one vessel, the "C. P. Williams," was struck on this day, a 7-inch shell lodging in her bow and sticking there, showing that the enemy's powder was bad. At sunset we ceased firing, and at 8 o'clock opened again with all the mortars, on the town, doing much damage. At 8.30, I sent the "Owasco," Lieutenant-Commanding Guest, up abreast of the town to throw some incendiary shells, which proved to be failures, as they did not explode.

June 28, at 3 o'clock A. M., the squadron made a move to pass the batteries, and the flotilla steamers got under way to take their position, which was to enfilade the water batteries as the ships passed. The headmost vessels of the squadron passed along a little before time, unsupported, and our vessels could not get near enough to them to be of any service. Five of the above mentioned vessels went gallantly on, despite the fire of the batteries, throwing in their grape and canister, favored much by the heavy atmosphere and early morning light. At 4 o'clock, the flag-ship came along, with two gunboats. By that time the mortar steamers had got nearly into position, and moved up toward the batteries, throwing in a quick fire. Nearly all the mortars had commenced as the "Richmond" passed, and the shells were falling very well and rapidly, the "Hartford" and gun-boats opening their batteries with grape, canister and shrapnel. The air seemed to be filled with projectiles. The lower batteries were silenced for the time, though I saw that the rebels would manage to get a shot or so at the ships after they had passed along. The batteries out of range of the mortars were very severe, and I am sorry to say that some ships lost, in killed and wounded, as many as they did at Forts Jackson and St. Philip. I regret that the mortars were not able to reach these batteries.

About the time the "Hartford" passed, the "Octorora's" wheel-ropes got jammed below, and there was a fair prospect of drifting out of action, or into some of the vessels astern. As I went drifting by the "Miami," I hailed her commander, and ordered him up within six hundred yards of the battery. Also hailed the "Jackson," and ordered the "Westfield" and "Clifton" to go ahead of me until I could relieve myself from my unpleasant position. The "Owasco," Lieutenant-Commanding Guest, and "Harriet Lane," Lieutenant-Commanding Wainwright, had been ordered to act at discretion, and throw on their fire to the best advantage, which they did effectually. The river being narrow, and the current very strong, it was impossible to manœuvre so many vessels to advantage, and leave room for the squadron of ships to pass.

I had cleared my wheel-ropes, and succeeded in getting again to my place ahead, and was in fine position (with all the steamers firing very rapidly and effectually) to cover the "Brooklyn," "Katahdin," and "Kennebec" as they came along, presuming that they were going to follow the "Hartford." That vessel was now two miles ahead, and appeared to be under a heavy fire from a battery of six guns at the upper end of the city, out of mortar range. The "Brooklyn" came up a little ahead of the mortar vessels and opened fire, as did the gun-boats astern of her, but did not pass through.

Not a shot had, up to this time, struck one of the mortar steamers; when, finding it necessary to slow the engines, to get out of the line of the "Brooklyn's" fire, the vessel became stationary, and a fair target for what guns the enemy were able to fire. The "Jackson," Lieutenant-Commanding Woodworth, was struck badly with rifle shells, one of which exploded in her wheel-house, disabling the man at the wheel by cutting off his leg, and knocking her steering apparatus to pieces which disabled her. The other struck the pillar block support, almost cutting it in two. This steamer being disabled, the "Clifton," Lieutenant-Commanding Baldwin, went to her assistance (by signal), and, while in the act of taking her in tow, a 7-inch shot passed in on the "Clifton's" port bow, going through her boiler. By this catastrophe, six of the men in and about the magazine were scalded to death, and others were scalded severely. The steam drove eight or ten men overboard, one of whom was drowned. The "Jackson," Lieutenant-Commanding Woodworth, now became the helping ship, and picked up out of the water the "Clifton's" men, that steamer being completely disabled. The "Westfield," on approaching to assist her, was struck on the frame of her engine by a heavy rifle shot, which, fortunately, did not go through, having struck butt-end foremost, and consequently caused but short delay. In the meantime, the "Octorora" dropped out of fire, took the "Clifton" in tow, and removed her to a place of safety. The "Jackson" drifted out clear. No further necessity existing for the flotilla steamers remaining under fire (the "Brooklyn" and those astern of her having slowed their engines, and proceeding no further), the signal was made to retire under cover of the woods, having been sixty-five minutes under fire. Although the steamers disabled were in a strong current, and narrow, crowded river, they were handled and taken out of action without confusion of any kind, beyond that occasioned by the escaping steam on board the "Clifton." Such a calamity is always appalling to those unused to the effects of such a terrible enemy on board their own vessel. The conduct of the officers and men on board the "Clifton" was creditable in the highest degree, and I regret to say that those scalded to death were some of the leading men of the vessel.

No further casualties occurred of any consequence. The "Jackson" and "Clifton" are temporarily repaired, the latter working under one boiler. All the steamers took good positions, and their commanders did their duty properly. It is to be regretted that a combined attack of Army and Navy had not been made, by which something more substantial might have been accomplished. Such an attack, I think, would have resulted in the capture of the city. Ships and mortar vessels can keep full possession of the river, and places near the water's edge, but they cannot crawl up hills three hundred feet high, and it is that part of Vicksburg which must be taken by the Army. If it was intended merely to pass the batteries at Vicksburg, and make a junction with the fleet of Flag-officer Davis, the Navy did it most gallantly and fearlessly.

It was as handsome a thing as had been done during the war; for the batteries to be passed extended full three miles, with a three-knot current, against ships that could not make eight knots under the most favorable circumstances. Again, sir, I have to mention favorably the divisional officers, and the acting-masters commanding mortar vessels. Anchored at all times in a position selected by myself, more with regard to the object to be accomplished than to any one's comfort or safety; knowing that they will have to stay there without a chance of getting away till I think proper to remove them (no matter how thick the shot and shells may fly), there has always existed a rivalry as to who shall have the post of honor (the leading vessel), almost certain to be struck, if not destroyed.

They know no weariness, and they really seem to take a delight in mortar firing, which is painful even to those accustomed to it. It requires more than ordinary zeal to stand the ordeal. Though I may have at times been exacting and fault-finding with them for not conforming with the rules of the service (which requires the education of a life-time to learn), yet I cannot withhold my applause when I see these men working with such earnest and untiring devotion to their duties while under fire.

The officers and crew of the "Octorora" behaved like veterans; and I am much indebted to that excellent officer, Lieutenant George Brown, for the drill of the crew, and the perfect arrangements made for going into action. On the day the squadron passed up, the mortars were engaged in divisions in firing on the enemy and keeping his guns quiet, and so on up to the 1st of July.

Two or three deserters came in, one of them asserting a marvelous story that the ships and mortars had killed and wounded seven hundred persons. No doubt some were killed, but very likely fewer than stated, and only in and about the forts. Only two schooners were struck. One, the "C. P. Williams," Acting-Master Amos R. Langthorne, in the bow; the other, the "Orvetta," Acting-Master Blanchard, through the foremast. Nobody has been hurt, so far, in the mortar vessels.

On the first of July, our pickets (which were thrown out about a hundred yards) were surprised by a large body of rebels close to them, evidently intending to surprise the mortar schooners. They immediately came in to report, the enemy firing on them as they retreated. In a moment all the guns of the mortar vessels and flotilla steamers opened on the woods with grape, shrapnel, canister, shells, and round shot (the mortars throwing in bombs with small charges), and we knew if an enemy was there he could not face a fire like ours, from fifty guns, spread out along the levee for about a mile. After the woods were well shelled, the pickets went in and captured three rebel soldiers, who were helplessly stuck in the mud, from which they had much difficulty in extricating themselves, and cried out lustily that they had surrendered. They were brought in, with their arms and accoutrements. These men state that two regiments, one from Tennessee, the other from Mississippi, were put under arms, and made to believe that they were going to attack some United States troops. Finding the head of our schooners guarded, the rebels attempted to pass through the middle of the wood and enfilade us, but got helplessly stuck in the middle of the swamp, or the thick mud which exists here. While in this condition, our guns commenced shelling the woods, and the two regiments were panic stricken.

They threw away their knapsacks, cartridge boxes, and everything that would impede their progress. In going over the ground afterwards, our men found evidences of a general stampede throughout the woods; amongst other things they picked up from the mud the heavy boots of a general officer, with silver spurs on. There was evidence in the marks that the enemy had been completely "bogged," or sunk in the mud, and our prisoners informed us that, had we gone into the woods at that moment with two hundred men, we could have captured the two regiments, as they were for a time perfectly helpless, having thrown away many of their arms, etc. It was on this marsh I depended for safety when I placed the schooners in position; for, without such a natural defence, we should have been at the mercy of the concealed riflemen.

Not wishing to have any mishaps, I landed five howitzers, threw up works, posted fifty marines as pickets, and had a large bell slung up in the woods with lines leading to it from different points, so that the pickets might give immediate alarm. After which the mortar flotilla went to their repose with great confidence. We have held the position we first took. We have advanced, indeed, 300 yards with the mortars. We are within 2,100 yards of the enemy's batteries, and in short distance of an Army (which they say consists) of thirty thousand men—a very doubtful estimate, as it will not amount to a half or a third of that number. From what I can learn from pretty reliable sources, the regiments are small, and do not average 500 men each. I do not think there are 6,000 men in this town and the surrounding country, and many of them are sick.

I respectfully submit a list of the killed and wounded on board the steamers "Clifton" and "J. P. Jackson." On the "Clifton" there were eight killed and one wounded : Thomas Collins, gunner's mate ; Robert Sargeant, ship's cook ; John Burke, ordinary seaman ; William Morris, captain's cook ; John B. Carlton, landsman, and George B. Derwent (colored), wardroom steward, killed ; and John Hudson, master-at-arms, severely wounded ; John Connor, 2d-class fireman, was drowned. On the "Jackson," Alexander Greenwall, seaman, was severely, if not mortally, wounded.

On the 2d of July the enemy made another attack on our pickets and drove them in, wounding two of them, and succeeded in getting so close as to fire on our decks ; but they soon met with the fire of five field-pieces which I had placed near the edge of the woods, and which must have inflicted severe punishment. Five dead bodies have since been found and evidences of some wounded, from the muskets and other arms thrown away, I suppose, in the retreat. Since then we have fortified ourselves so that they cannot annoy us without getting the worst of it. They have shelled our position, fired hot shot and rifled shot in abundance ; and though they have made some holes in the mortar vessels, we have held our own, and shell them out whenever we open on them with mortars.

Very respectfully, your obedient servant,
DAVID D. PORTER,
Commanding Mortar Flotilla.
Flag-officer D. G. FARRAGUT,
Commanding Western Gulf Squadron.

REPORTS OF LIEUTENANT-COMMANDING CROSBY, OF THE "PINOLA," AND LIEUTENANT-COMMANDING WOODWORTH, OF THE "J. P. JACKSON," OF THE ATTACK ON VICKSBURG, JUNE 28, 1862.

UNITED STATES FLAG-SHIP "HARTFORD," ?
ABOVE VICKSBURG, July 8, 1862.)

SIR—I have the honor to forward the report of Lieutenant-Commanding P. Crosby, of the attack on Vicksburg, June 28, 1862 ; also the report of Lieutenant-Commanding Selim E. Woodworth,

commanding the gun-boat "J. P. Jackson," of the same affair.

Very respectfully, your obedient servant,
D. G. FARRAGUT,
Flag-officer, Commanding Western Gulf Blockading Squadron.
Hon. GIDEON WELLES,
Secretary of the Navy, Washington, D. C.

UNITED STATES GUN-BOAT "PINOLA," ?
ABOVE VICKSBURG, June 30, 1862.)

SIR—I have the honor to report that I took my position in line of battle on the 28th instant at 3.10 A. M., in obedience to signals, and stood up the river in company with the squadron. At 4 A. M., opened fire on the enemy's batteries, which we continued until 6.10 A. M., when we had passed Vicksburg and were beyond the range of our stern guns (24-pound howitzers), but within range of the enemy's heavy rifled guns for some twenty minutes after we had ceased firing. At 6.40 A. M., anchored above Vicksburg ; fired from the 11-inch gun 20 shells, 3 grape and 1 shrapnel ; from the Parrott rifle 29 shells, from the howitzers 13 shells, and 20 shrapnel—total 86. Owing to the smoke and remarkably scattered positon of the enemy's guns, we labored under great disadvantage in

LIEUT.-COMMANDING (NOW REAR-ADMIRAL) PIERCE CROSBY.

aiming, which hindered us from firing more rapidly. The fire from the enemy upon us was very severe, owing in a great measure, I think, to our being the last vessel that passed their batteries. But, I am thankful to say, only a few shots struck us, one of which, a heavy shot, struck John Brown, ordinary seaman, at the 11-inch gun, seriously wounding him ; another, a 50 pound rifle shot, cut away the timber-head of the starboard after port : struck the howitzer and carriage, slightly defacing the former and slightly injuring the latter ; it also struck the cabin hatch, destroyed the barometer and thermometer, and landed in the port water-ways ; and, I regret to say, it killed William H. Thomas, quarter-gunner and captain of the gun, while sighting the piece, and mortally wounded Thomas Graham, landsman, who died in a few minutes after ; it also slightly wounded William H. Shucks, landsman. Daniel Colleran, landsman, was wounded by a musket ball, volleys of which were fired at us from hills and bushes. We received some four or five large grape shot in the hull just below the water-ways. I am happy to say that neither the vessel nor guns were disabled. The howitzer continued firing after the accident, under the direction of Acting-Master's Mate William H.

Thompson, who, by his brave example, restored confidence to his crew, and did great service in the action.

I have again the pleasant duty of bearing testimony to the gallant conduct of the officers and crew of this vessel, and the spirit and zeal exhibited in the performance of their duties on this occasion. John R. Tennant, quartermaster, gave the soundings with as much coolness as though he had been making an ordinary survey. Mr. John McHugh, our pilot, behaved in a remarkably cool and self-possessed manner, and gave me great assistance. Great credit is due Lieutenant A. P. Cooke for the efficient manner in which the guns were worked, and for the good training of the ship's company. Accompanying this report I send Assistant-Surgeon L. M. Lyon's report of casualties.

I am, sir, very respectfully, your obedient servant,
PIERCE CROSBY,
Lieutenant-Commanding.
Flag-officer D. G. FARRAGUT,
U. S. N., Commanding Western Division of United States Blockading Squadron.

UNITED STATES STEAMER "J. P. JACKSON,"
OFF VICKSBURG, July 30, 1862.

SIR—I have the honor to report the following casualties on board the United States steamer "J. P. Jackson" during the engagement on the morning of the 28th ultimo, before Vicksburg. In endeavoring to obtain the position assigned me, by your order, in front of the lower "water battery," my vessel was struck by a 7-inch rifle projectile, which, entering on the starboard side of the forward bulkhead, passed obliquely through the forward wheel-house, destroying the wheel, and passed out through the hurricane deck, taking off the right foot of one of the steersmen, and wounding the left foot.

The vessel was for awhile rendered unmanageable, but, by the aid of a jury tiller, we were enabled to steer down the river out of the action, when the signal to retire was made. We received another 7-inch rifle projectile in our starboard wheel, cutting away one-half of the bridge piece supporting the other end of the shaft immediately under the pillar block. We were struck slightly by two grape, or other shot, doing no damage. We fired from our guns during the engagement 117 shot, shells, grape and shrapnel. I take pleasure in stating that the gallant conduct of my men and officers during the action met with my highest commendations.

Enclosed I send you the report of Surgeon Thomas Yard, containing list of wounded.

I have the honor to be, very respectfully, your obedient servant,
SELIM E. WOODWORTH,
Lieutenant-Commanding, United States Navy.
Commander D. D. PORTER,
Commanding Mortar Flotilla.

ENGAGEMENT WITH THE RAM "ARKANSAS,"
JULY 15, 1862.
UNITED STATES FLAG-SHIP "HARTFORD,"
BELOW VICKSBURG, July 17, 1862.

SIR—It is with deep mortification that I announce to the department that, notwithstanding my prediction to the contrary, the iron-clad ram "Arkansas" has at length made her appearance and taken us all by surprise. We had heard that she was up at Liverpool, in the Yazoo River, and Lieutenant-Colonel Ellet informed me that the river was too narrow for our gun-boats to turn, and was also shallow in places, but suggested that Flag-officer Davis might send up some of his iron-clad boats, which draw only six or seven feet of water.

When this was proposed to Flag-officer Davis he consented immediately, and General Williams of-fered to send up a few sharpshooters. The next morning they went off at daylight, and by six in the morning we heard firing up the river, but supposed it to be the gun-boats firing at the flying artillery, said to be lining the river. In a short time, however, the gun-boats appeared, and the ram in pursuit. Although we were lying with low fires, none of us had steam, or could we get it up in time to pursue her; but she took the broadside of the whole fleet. It was a bold thing, and she was only saved by our feeling of security. She was very much injured, and was only able to drift or go at the slowest speed—say, one knot, and with the current she got down to the forts of Vicksburg before any of us had steam up.

I had a consultation with Flag-officer Davis, and we thought it best to take the evening, when he dropped down to take the fire of the upper battery, and my squadron passed down with the determination of destroying the ram, if possible; but, by delays of getting into position, etc., it was so dark by the time we reached the town that nothing could be seen except the flashes of the guns, so that, to my great mortification, I was obliged to go down and anchor, with the rest of my fleet, to protect the transports, mortar boats, etc.

The ram is now repairing damages—for we put many holes through her—though we do not know the extent of damage done to her. Be assured, sir, however, that I shall leave no stone unturned to destroy her. I regret to report that the loss from this vessel was one officer and two men killed, and five wounded. The total loss in the fleet was five killed and sixteen wounded. I enclose herewith the fleet surgeon's report of casualties.

Very respectfully, your obedient servant,
D. G. FARRAGUT,
Flag-officer, Commanding Western Gulf Blockading Squadron.
Hon. GIDEON WELLES,
Secretary of the Navy, Washington, D. C.

FLAG-SHIP "HARTFORD,"
BELOW VICKSBURG, July 16, 1862.

SIR—I respectfully report the following list of killed and wounded in the fleet during the engagements on the 15th instant, viz:

FLAG-SHIP "HARTFORD."
Killed.—George H. Loundsberry, master's mate; Charles Jackson, officers' cook, and John Cameron, seaman, by cannon shot.

Wounded.—Captain John L. Broome, marine corps, and Thomas Hoffman, paymaster's steward, severe contusions; John D. Barnes, fireman, and Michael Martin, landsman, contusions; George Royer, marine, and Henry Downs, boy, slightly.

"WISSAHICKON."
Killed.—John Garrett, ordinary seaman, by a cannon shot.

Wounded.—Edward York, fireman, and Daniel Hayes, ordinary seaman, and Joseph Ranahan, landsman, severely; James Revell, ordinary seaman, slightly.

"WINONA."
Killed.—John H. Harway, landsman, by a shell.

Wounded.—John Jones, captain afterguard, severely; William Malley, landsman, slightly.

"SCIOTA."
Wounded.—James H. Mathist, landsman, and Peter Lasher, ordinary seaman, severely.

"RICHMOND."
Wounded.—William Somes and William Nelson, seamen, slightly.

Total—5 killed; 16 wounded.

I am, very respectfully, your obedient servant,
J. M. FOLTZ,
Fleet Surgeon.
Flag-officer D. G. FARRAGUT,
Commanding Western Division Gulf Blockading Squadron.

UNITED STATES STEAM-SLOOP "ONEIDA," }
BELOW VICKSBURG, July 16, 1862. }
SIR—I make the following report of the action with the batteries and with the rebel iron-clad ram "Arkansas," last evening, in passing Vicksburg.

At 6.40 P. M., flag-ship made general signal 1,218; got under way, steaming as necessary, whilst the fleet was formed according to the plan for the morning of the 28th ultimo. Renshaw's mortars were now firing at the batteries. At 6.55, the army mortars commenced firing; at 7, the "Benton" opened fire on the new upper battery; at 7.20, passed two of the army gun-boats—now holding their fire to allow us to pass—our fleet having formed and closed up; at 7.30, we opened fire on the new upper battery; fired, in passing, at the upper batteries and rifle-pits with our battery and small arms, whilst under like fire from the rebels.

We passed near the left (east) bank, stopped the engine, and drifted by the town; saw the wharf boat; fired bolts from two rifled guns and solid shot from the two 11-inch pivot guns at the "Arkansas," which lying under the bank, exposed her position by firing. Stopped firing at 7.50, having expended the following projectiles: 6 shells, 11-inch, 5m. fuze; 9 grape, 11-inch; 2 solid shot, 11-inch (at the ram); 10 shells, 32-pounders, 5m. fuze; 1 stand 32-pounder grape; 2 solid 32-pounder shot; 16 bolts and 1 shell from the 30-pounder Dahlgren rifle gun. No casualties occurred on board. The officers and men on the sick list who were able to go to their guns did so. Anchored with the fleet.

Respectfully yours,
S. PHILLIPS LEE,
Commander.

Flag-officer D. G. FARRAGUT,
Commanding, etc., etc.

———

FLAG-SHIP "HARTFORD," }
BELOW VICKSBURG, July 22, 1862. }
SIR—I herewith enclose the reports of these vessels, the "Iroquois," "Richmond," "Sciota," and "Winona," of their passage down the river from above this place, and the encounter with the ram "Arkansas."

I am, sir, respectfully, your obedient servant,
D. G. FARRAGUT,
Commanding Western Gulf Blockading Squadron.
Hon. GIDEON WELLES,
Secretary of the Navy, Washington, D. C.

———

FLAG SHIP "HARTFORD," }
BELOW VICKSBURG, July 16, 1862. }
SIR—The following officers and crew of this ship were killed and wounded in the engagement last night, viz:

Killed.—George H. Loundsberry, master's mate, killed by a cannon ball; Charles Jackson, officers' cook, killed by a cannon ball; John Cameron, seaman, killed by a cannon ball.

Wounded.—Thomas Hoffman, paymaster's steward, struck in head and chest with splinters; John D. Barnes, fireman, contusion of shoulder; Michael Martin, landsman, contusion of arm, slightly; George Royer, marine, contusion of arm, slightly; Henry Downs, boy (colored), contusion of arm, slightly; Captain John Broome, marine, contusion of head and shoulder.

Total.—Killed, 3; wounded, 6.

I am, very respectfully, your obedient servant,
J. M. FOLTZ,
Fleet Surgeon.
Commander R. WAINWRIGHT,
Commanding United States Steamer "Hartford."

———

UNITED STATES STEAMER "IROQUOIS," }
BELOW VICKSBURG, July 17, 1862. }
SIR—At twenty minutes after six in the afternoon of the 15th, signal being made from the flag-ship to weigh and form the line ahead (the "Iroquois" being ordered to lead), I was immediately under way, and stood down the river toward the newly erected battery, having been preceded about half an hour by Flag-officer Davis and the "Benton," with two other iron-clad gun-boats, whose instructions were to keep in play the upper battery, whilst we passed on to the attack.

At seven we passed the head of their line, and were immediately under fire, which we returned at once; and very soon after the hill battery, in the upper part of the town, commenced its raking fire, the shot and shells flying over us, their guns not being sufficiently depressed. In a short time we were abreast of the town, from which we received volleys of musketry and artillery, which we returned with shrapnel and grape. Now the lower hill batteries commenced their plunging fire and at this critical moment our worn-out engines suddenly stopped, and we drifted for twenty minutes under fire which, as night was now setting in, was ill-directed, and very soon gave me no concern.

As we dropped down, the lower water battery, and what I supposed might be the iron-clad ram, opened upon us. This we returned with solid shot. But with all this fire of heavy shot and shells from the batteries, of musketry and field-pieces with which the town was crowded, with the exception of a 6-pound shell, fired from a field-piece, left sticking in our side between wind and water, we escaped without damage.

By the indefatigable exertions of our chief engineer the engine was set going again, and when below their line of fire, I turned and stood up again for the batteries, thinking the flag-ship was still above. But afterwards, finding that in the darkness she had passed below unobserved by us, I dropped down and anchored beside her.

I have the honor to be, sir, very respectfully, your obedient servant,
JAMES S. PALMER,
Commander.

Flag-officer DAVID G. FARRAGUT,
Commanding Western Gulf Squadron.

———

UNITED STATES STEAMER "RICHMOND," }
NEAR VICKSBURG, July 16, 1862. }
SIR—I have the honor herewith to enclose the surgeon's report of casualties, and also those of the boatswain and carpenter, showing the injury done to this vessel by the enemy's shot during the action of last evening. Every one on board behaved well. A careful lookout was kept for the ram as we passed, but owing to the obscurity of the night we could not make her out.

Respectfully, sir, your obedient servant,
JAMES ALDEN,
Commander.

Flag-officer D. G. FARRAGUT,
Commanding Western Gulf Blockading Squadron.

———

UNITED STATES GUN BOAT "SCIOTA," }
ABOVE VICKSBURG, July 15, 1862. }
SIR—This morning, about 6.10 o'clock, heavy firing was heard on board this vessel apparently from the direction of the Yazoo River, the cause of which soon manifested itself in the appearance of the gun-boat "Taylor," Lieutenant-Commanding Gwinn, running before, and closely followed by an iron-clad rebel ram—since ascertained to be the "Arkansas"—escaped out of the Yazoo River. This vessel—of a similar construction to the "Louisiana" and "Mississippi" destroyed at New Orleans; that is, with a screw propeller and inclined iron sides, armed with nine guns—seemed, from her movements, to trust entirely to her invulnerability for a safe run to the cover of the Vicksburg batteries. The "Taylor" made a running fight until within our lines, when the vessels opened as their guns bore, the rebel's speed diminishing very visibly. This gun-boat was anchored fourth

in line from up river, without steam, and engines under repairs; but as soon as I heard the firing I ordered fire started and steam to be raised with all dispatch. My eleven-inch gun being loaded with a ten-second shell, which I had endeavored in vain to draw, as the rebel came within my train I fired, striking him fair, but the shell glanced off almost perpendicularly into the air and exploded. At the same time I opened a brisk fire with all my small arms against his ports, which, I am confident, prevented them from manning her port guns till after she had passed us. I observed one man in the act of sponging, tumble out of the port, sponge and all, evidently shot by a rifle ball.

I found my officers and men ready, but such was the suddenness of the appearance and passing of this formidable vessel of the enemy that but little time was afforded for any continued attack upon her with the unwieldy gun carried by this vessel. After passing down stream out of my line of fire, which he did in from four to six minutes, I was unfortunately only a spectator of the final result of this event.

I am, very respectfully, your obedient servant,
R. B. LOWRY,
Lieutenant-Commanding, U. S. Gun-boat "Sciota."
Flag-officer D. G. FARRAGUT,
Commanding Western Gulf Blockading Squadron.

UNITED STATES GUN-BOAT "SCIOTA," }
BELOW VICKSBURG, July 16, 1862. }

SIR—I have the honor to report that, in obedience to general signal, made yesterday at 7 P. M., I got under way and took position fifth in line and steamed down the river. On nearing the point opposite the city, found an active bombardment kept up from the iron-clad vessels of Flag-officer Davis's fleet, while the rebels were replying with great spirit from all the hill and water batteries, strengthened by large bodies of sharpshooters posted in rifle-pits and in the woods. As we turned the point the bullets began to fly over us very thickly. We opened on the riflemen with small arms, in the hands of our sick and disabled officers and men, who, too feeble to work the heavy guns, still zealously used their little strength to annoy the enemy by a return fire of musketry. Our two 24-pounder howitzers were worked rapidly and efficiently, throwing shrapnel into the enemy's troops, which were seen to burst with good range and effect. I proceeded under this fire and the cross fire of the batteries till beyond range, when I rounded to and anchored at 8.10 P. M.

On passing Vicksburg could see nothing distinctly of the ram, though I received a fire, as from a battery, at or near the level with the water. A shell from this battery passed horizontally through this vessel, tearing the metallic boat, cutting bulwarks on port side, starting wood-ends and bolts on deck, and finally bursting in the starboard spirketing, tearing water-ways, covering-board, futtock ends and timbers, and breaking boat davit on starboard side. Several grape and other shots passed through the ship, and one heavy shot struck under port bow—a plunging, grazing shot from the hill forts.

I have to report, and thankfully so, but two casualties—two men wounded, as per surgeon's report. My officers and men behaved well and bravely.

* * * * * * *

Very respectfully, your obedient servant,
R. B. LOWRY,
Lieutenant-Commanding "Sciota."
Flag-officer D. G. FARRAGUT,
Commanding Western Gulf Blockading Squadron.

UNITED STATES GUN-BOAT "WINONA," }
BELOW VICKSBURG, July 16, 1862. }

SIR—I have the honor to report that this vessel got under way last evening, and passed, in company with the rest of your fleet, from the anchorage above

Vicksburg to that below. All the vessels were subjected to a heavy fire from the numerous batteries, as also to a heavy fire of musketry. We were enabled to fire our 11-inch gun but three times, owing to having received a shot on our port side, which started a heavy leak. Started our deck pumps immediately, but finding the water gaining, ran in and pivoted the 11-inch gun to starboard to raise the leak out of water; water still gaining, pivoted rifle gun to starboard; shifted port howitzer over, and shifted shot and shells to starboard. My orders being to anchor at the old anchorage below Vicksburg, I ran down to the lower end of the island and rounded to, with the intention of anchoring, but finding the leak still gaining fast on the pumps, the water up to the top of the ash-pit doors, and being ignorant of the position and nature of the damage causing the leak, I deemed it the safest plan to run the vessel on shore, which was done at the foot of the island, her bow in eight and stern in eleven feet water. Upon examination, we found that a shot had entered, just above water line, and close to opening of outboard delivery, breaking valve and cast iron valve-chest. I enclose herewith the report of Mr. Purdy, senior engineer in charge. Our other shot struck the spirketing in wake of long port, but did not penetrate. One shell burst among the crew of 11-inch gun, killing one man and very slightly wounding two others. The fragments of this shell tore up the deck water-ways, hatch-combings, and gun-carriage, but the injuries are not serious. In the engagement with the iron-clad gun-boat our side was perforated in several places by fragments of a shell which exploded near the vessel, wounding two men.

I cannot speak too highly of the conduct of all on board. I enclose herewith reports of Assistant Surgeon Matthewson, of the casualties of yesterday; also report of ammunition expended,

Very respectfully, your obedient servant,
ED. T. NICHOLS,
Lieutenant-Commanding.
Flag-officer D. G. FARRAGUT,
Commanding Western Division Gulf Blockading Squadron.

COMMODORE W. D. PORTER'S REPORT OF RECONNOISSANCE, WITH ACCOUNT OF ENGAGEMENT OF THE "ANGLO-AMERICAN," ON THE 28TH OF AUGUST, AT PORT HUDSON, LA.

UNITED STATES GUN-BOAT "ESSEX," }
OFF NEW ORLEANS, Sept. 9, 1862. }

SIR—I have the honor to report that, on the 23d ultimo, having remained off the city of Baton Rouge two days after its evacuation by our troops, I proceeded up the river to reconnoitre reported batteries in progress at Port Hudson, Louisiana, and also coal my vessel at Bayou Sara, the only place I could obtain any, save New Orleans. Arriving there, I found the town entirely deserted, and the coal burning. Sending a boat's crew on shore, they were fired at by guerillas from the houses in heavy force. My men drove them out, and burnt the buildings in the lower part of the town to prevent such being used to protect the enemy. These guerillas had a few days previously fired at and wounded several of the crew of the United States gun-boat "Sumter." On the 24th, I was necessitated to send the wooden gun-boat "Anglo-American," which I had fitted out and armed, to New Orleans for coal, and I again dropped down the river and awaited her return off Port Hudson. I could discover no guns at this place, but earthworks were in progress, and whilst destroying these I had the misfortune to burst my heavy 10-inch gun. The "Anglo-American" not arriving, I returned to Bayou Sara, where we were again fired at from buildings left, on which I ordered those remaining to be destroyed.

The "Anglo-American" joined me on the 29th,

and reported three batteries as having opened on her whilst passing Port Hudson. She received seventy-three shots in her *en passant.* I had received information that the rebel gun-boat "Webb" was at Natchez, to which city she had convoyed transports with supplies from Red River. I followed to that city, but found they had sought the protection of the Vicksburg guns. At Natchez, a boat's crew from the "Essex" were sent on shore to procure some ice for my sick, when they were wantonly attacked by over two hundred armed citizens, wounding the officer in command, and killing one and wounding five seamen. I immediately opened fire on the lower town, and set a considerable number of the houses from whence they were firing on us on fire. After bombarding the place for an hour, the mayor unconditionally surrendered the city.

I followed the rebel gun-boat "Webb" to the batteries at Vicksburg, under the guns of which she, with two transports, lay. Heavy ordnance batteries, extending three miles further down the river than during the siege in July, prevented my nearer approach to these boats. Having exchanged some shots, and ascertained that the upper fleet was not in the vicinity of the town, being short of provisions, my battery weakened by the loss of two guns burst, and also short of ammunition, I determined to steam down the river to New Orleans for supplies, and, if possible ascertain the strength of Port Hudson batteries. On the 7th instant, at 4.15, A. M., we were off that place, and, on coming within range, the enemy opened on us a vigorous fire with heavy siege guns. The "Essex" was struck with heavy shot fourteen times. As nearly as I can judge, the enemy had in position from thirty-five to forty guns of 10-inch, 9-inch, and 8-inch calibre, in three batteries commanding the river to the extent of five miles. A 68-pound, 32-pound, and also a 10-inch shot, lodged in the "Essex," but without material damage. We were under fire an hour and three-quarters, during which time the guns were worked well and incessantly, and I have reason to believe the enemy was considerably damaged. Mr. J. Harry Wyatt, acting fourth master, and my secretary, had command of the forward battery, and his conduct met my entire approbation.

A land force will be necessary to complete the destruction of this fort, which, if allowed to again be restored, would seriously interrupt the free navigation of the Lower Mississippi.

Very respectfully, your obedient servant,

W. D. PORTER,
Commodore, United States Navy.

Hon. GIDEON WELLES,
Secretary of the Navy, Washington, D. C.

P. S.—In the various encounters I have had since leaving St. Louis on the last cruise (July 6), the "Essex" has been struck by heavy shot perceptibly one hundred and twenty-eight times—glancing shot have left no record; three have broken the iron, and but one through, and that at a distance of a few feet from the battery delivering it. W. D. P.

UNITED STATES GUN-BOAT "ANGLO-AMERICAN,"
OFF BAYOU SARA, LOUISIANA, Aug. 29, 1862.
SIR—In pursuance of your order, I proceeded down stream on the 24th instant, for New Orleans, arriving there on the morning of the 25th. We loaded up with coal, and left that city at 3.15 P. M., on Thursday, the 28th instant. Nothing of importance occurred until I reached Port Hudson. I noticed earthworks had been thrown up on the bluffs as well as the water line, but no guns being in sight, I kept on for about a mile, when another line of earthworks was discovered, as well as indications of rifle-pits. I immediately ordered my rifle 50-pounder to be fired. At this moment the enemy opened on the boat. My rifle gun unfortunately could not be used, as the cartridge had been made wet by a just passed heavy rain. Our howitzer was useless, as no ammunition could be obtained for it at New Orleans. We were now just abreast of the last mentioned earthworks, the enemy's guns playing on us with great rapidity. I could see two 32-pounder cannons and eighteen field-pieces, 6 and 12-pounders. The fire was so heavy on my frail wooden boat, that had it not been a matter of urgent necessity to reach you, I should have dropped back, as I had no protection for the machinery, and the fire was so heavy that the firemen were driven from their post. I determined, from the importance of the case, to push on and rejoin you, if possible. I am happy to report we succeeded.

The following casualties occurred: Mr. Parker, pilot, severely wounded in the back from a bursting shell, and James Banes, seaman, slightly wounded by splinter over the eye. We received seventy-three shots—fifteen heavy shots, the balance 12-pounder and grape. One 32-pounder struck the upright brace of the walking beam, breaking it in two.

It is with pleasure, I here state the gallant conduct of Mr. H. Glasford, executive officer, and Mr. B. S. Williams, pilot, who never left their post of danger, and, by their energy and coolness, contributed to the saving of the boat. Mr. Miller, chief engineer, Mr. Parker, third master, and Mr. Jacobi, of the "Essex," all did their duty nobly.

I have the honor to be, very respectfully, your obedient servant,

R. K. RILEY,
Commanding Gun-boat "Anglo-American."
Commodore W. D. PORTER,
Commanding Naval Forces below Vicksburg.

DESTRUCTION OF THE RAM "ARKANSAS."

FLAG-SHIP "HARTFORD,"
BATON ROUGE, Aug. 7, 1862.
SIR—It is one of the happiest moments of my life that I am enabled to inform the department of the destruction of the ram "Arkansas;" not because I held the iron-clad in such terror, but because the community did.

On the 4th instant I sent the "Tennessee" up to Baton Rouge with provisions for Commander Porter and the gun-boats stationed at that place. On the night of the 5th, she returned with the information that the enemy had made a combined attack upon Baton Rouge by the ram and two gun-boats, the "Webb" and "Music," and calling for assistance. At daylight, the "Hartford" was under way for this place, with orders for the other vessels to follow me as fast as ready.

I arrived here to-day at 12 M., in company with the "Brooklyn," "Westfield," "Clifton," "Jackson," and "Sciota." I had sent the "Cayuga" up before me, agreeably to a request of General Butler, in consequence of some of the guerillas firing into some of his transports. On my arrival I was informed by Commodore W. D. Porter that yesterday morning at 2 o'clock the enemy's forces, under General Breckinridge, attacked General Williams, drove in his pickets, etc. General Williams, having had ample warning, we all prepared for him. The fight was continued with great energy on both sides until 10 A. M., by which time the enemy had been driven back two or three miles, but, unfortunately, the gallant General Williams, while cheering on his men, received a Minie ball through his heart.

General Williams had informed Lieutenant-Commanding Ransom the evening before of his plans, and requested him not to fire a gun until he notified him; and when he did so, our gun-boats—the "Kineo" and "Katahdin"—opened with fine effect, throwing their shells directly in the midst of the enemy, producing great dismay and confusion among them. Lieutenant Ransom had an officer on the State house, which overlooks the adjacent country, and could direct the fire of every shell.

As soon as the enemy was repulsed, Commander Porter, with the gun-boats, went up stream after the ram "Arkansas," which was lying about five miles above, apparently afraid to take her share in the conflict, according to the preconcerted plan. As he came within gunshot he opened on her, and probably soon disabled some of her machinery or steering apparatus for she became unmanageable, continuing, however, to fire her guns at the "Essex."

Commander Porter says he took advantage of her presenting a weak point towards him, and loaded with incendiary shells. After his first discharge of this projectile, a gush of fire came out of her side, and from that moment it was discovered that she was on fire, which he continued his exertions to prevent from being extinguished. They backed her ashore and made a line fast, which soon burnt, and she swung off into the river, where she continued to burn until she blew up with a tremendous explosion, thus ending the career of the last iron-clad ram of the Mississippi. There were many persons on the banks of the river witnessing the fight, in which they anticipated a triumph for Secessia; but on the return of the "Essex" not a soul was to be seen.

I will leave a sufficient force of gun-boats here to support the Army, and will return to-morrow to New Orleans, and depart immediately for Ship Island, with a light heart that I have left no bug-

bear to torment the communities of the Mississippi in my absence.

Very respectfully, your obedient servant,
D. G. FARRAGUT,
Flag-officer, Commanding Western Gulf Blockading Squadron.
Hon. GIDEON WELLES,
Secretary of the Navy, Washington, D. C.

ON GUN-BOAT "ESSEX,"
OFF BATON ROUGE, August 6, 1862.

SIR—This morning at 8 o'clock, I steamed up the river, and at 10 o'clock attacked the rebel ram "Arkansas," and blew her up. There is not now a fragment of her left.

Very respectfully, your obedient servant,
W. D. PORTER,
Commanding Division of Flotilla in Western Waters.
Rear-admiral D. G. FARRAGUT.

When New Orleans fell, the towns all along the river were ablaze with defiance, and did all they could to delay Union vessels by firing on them on their way up river; all of which will be better understood by reading the dispatches of the times. Thus ended the first attack on Vicksburg. It failed from the fact that the combined forces of the Army and Navy delayed too long in New Orleans. The opportunity slipped away, and one of the best planned expeditions of the war was not fully carried out.

CHAPTER XXII.

THE POTOMAC FLOTILLA.—NAVAL OPERATIONS IN THE POTOMAC.—DESTRUCTION OF
CONFEDERATE BATTERIES.—CONFEDERATE RAMS.—CONDITION OF THE NAVY, AND
LIST OF VESSELS IN DECEMBER, 1862.—LOSSES BY SHIPWRECK, IN BATTLE, ETC., ETC.

ON the Potomac, the flotilla seems to have been actively employed from December, 1861, to May 2d, 1862.

Although no important event occurred on this water highway to Washington, early in the war the Confederates left nothing undone to stop the passage of transports, and even men-of-war, but they were not very successful. Cockpit Point was one of the places made quite strong by the enemy, and for a time it was considered quite a dangerous place to pass.

No persistent attack was made upon it until March, 1862, and as our Army was advancing into Virginia at the same time, the Confederates were now compelled to abandon this troublesome battery and blow up the magazine.

Before retreating, they destroyed all the guns and carriages, munitions of war, stores and provisions, having no means of transportation by which they could be taken away. The guns were of heavy calibre, having been mostly obtained from the Norfolk Navy Yard, where they had been abandoned by our forces early in the war. But for that affair, we would not have encountered so many forts in the South and West, and would have escaped the disgrace of having the public river way to Washington obstructed for so long a time.

An expedition under Lieutenant Wyman penetrated the Rappahannock as far as Fredericksburg after this place had surrendered to the Army, and captured twenty small vessels and a quantity of stores.

Some of his command also penetrated the Severn, Pianketank and North Rivers, and captured some small vessels that had, no doubt, been used in transporting goods and information from the Maryland shore.

The Union vessels were frequently attacked by field-pieces and riflemen, but they always managed to give a good account of themselves, while they demoralized the enemy by their persistent pursuit of him —but these adventures were not very exciting.

The Potomac may be said to have been opened with the fall of the forts at Cockpit Point, for though the flotilla was maintained, and there were skirmishes with the enemy from time to time, there was nothing to hinder the passage of vessels up and down the river.

About the end of the year 1861, the United States Government began to realize the necessity of building vessels that would be able to contend with the heavy iron-clads which had been constructed by the Confederates.

By May, 1862, the latter had finished the powerful "Merrimac," together with the "Louisiana" and "Arkansas," both equally powerful with the "Merrimac," and had nearly completed the "Mississippi" at New Orleans, the "Albemarle," the "Atlanta," the "Tennessee," at Mobile, and several other iron-clads on the tributaries of the Mississippi.

Up to this time the United States Government had only Ericsson's little "Monitor" to show, but the success of that famous vessel stirred the Navy Department up to building iron-clads able to cope with anything in the way of ships or forts that the Confederates could devise. Previous to the memorable encounter between the "Monitor" and the "Merrimac" the Department had exhibited neither zeal nor intelligence in dealing with this important problem.

The following is a list of vessels of our Navy, published by the Navy Department in December, 1862; an enumeration which is calculated to mislead, for if any one supposes that the vessels therein described as "iron-clads" bore any comparison to those built by the Confederates, he is mistaken. The Northern States, with all their resources, all their vessels which could have been cut down and made impervious to shot and shells, had not an iron-clad stronger than those hastily built on the Mississippi River. Naval commanders had to take whatever would carry a gun, no matter how frail or vulnerable, and attempt impossible things with, at times, deplorable consequences to themselves, their officers and crews, from bursting steam pipes and boilers, which added new horrors to the ordinary havoc of war.

The work performed by Foote and Davis and their officers and men on the Western rivers, with the so-called "iron-clads," was herculean from the time the first gun-boats got afloat in January, until July 1862. They had captured, or assisted to capture, seven heavy forts armed with one hundred and ninety-eight guns, and manned or supported by over fifty thousand men, besides destroying thirteen or more of the enemy's vessels armed with forty guns and a floating battery of sixteen guns; and all this without the enemy's capturing a single vessel.

In the Navy Department list, the Western "iron-clads" are put down as twenty-six armed vessels, a formidable force on paper, but in this number are included at least fifteen "tin-clads"—small stern wheel merchant steamers, covered with quarter-inch iron to turn musket balls, but easily penetrated by a twelve pound shot or shell.

The list may be interesting as showing the "historical account" of our naval forces in December, 1862, but it conveys no idea of the frail barks in which the officers and men of the Navy had to fight the heaviest kind of earthworks, often perched at a great height above the water where their plunging fire could perforate the vessels' decks and boilers, or even pass down through their bottoms.

NAVAL FORCE AT DATE OF THE LAST ANNUAL REPORT.

DESCRIPTION.	NUMBER.	GUNS.	TONS.
Old Navy	76	1,783	105,271
Purchased vessels	136	518	71,297
New vessels, completed and under construction	52	256	41,448
Total	264	2,557	218,016

PRESENT NAVAL FORCE.

DESCRIPTION.	NUMBER.	GUNS.	TONS.
Old Navy	74	1,691	100,008
Purchased vessels	180	688	86,910
Transferred from War and Treasury Departments	50	230	32,828
New vessels, completed and under construction	123	659	120,290
Total	427	3,268	340,036
Increase since last reported	163	711	122,020

LOSSES BY SHIPWRECK AND IN BATTLE.

NAME.	CLASS.	GUNS.	TONNAGE	REMARKS.
R. B. Forbes	Steamer.	3	329	Wrecked Feb., 1862, coast of North Carolina.
Congress	Frigate.	50	1,867	In action with Merrimac, March 8, 1862.
Cumberland	Sloop.	24	1,726	do.
Whitehall	Steamer.	4	323	At Old Point, March 9, 1862, by fire.
M. J. Carlton	Mortar schooner	3	178	Attack on Forts Jackson and St. Philip, April 19, 1862.
Varuna	Steamer.	9	1,300	In action with confederate gun-boats below New Orleans, April 24, 1862.
Sidney C. Jones.	Mortar schooner	3	245	Grounded below Vicksburg and burned to prevent falling into the hands of the enemy.
Island Belle	Steamer.	2	123	Grounded in Appomattox river June, 1862, and burned to prevent falling into the hands of the enemy.
Adirondack	Screw sloop.	9	1,240	Wrecked near Abaco, Aug. 23, 1862.
Henry Andrew	Steamer.	3	177	Wrecked in a gale near Cape Henry Aug. 24, 1862.
Sumter	Steam Ram.	2	400	Grounded in Mississippi river and abandoned.
		112	7,908	

VESSELS ADDED SINCE FOURTH OF MARCH, EIGHTEEN HUNDRED AND SIXTY-ONE. (EXCLUSIVE OF THOSE LOST.)

	NO. OF VESSELS.	GUNS.	TONS.
By purchase	180	688	86,910
By transfer	50	230	32,828
By construction	123	659	120,290
	353	1,577	240,028

ADDED BY CONSTRUCTION.

DESCRIPTION.	NO. OF VESSELS.	GUNS.	TONS.
Second-class screw sloops-of-war	13	116	16,396
Screw gun-boats	27	108	14,033
Side wheel gun-boats	39	296	36,337
Armored wooden vessels	12	65	20,893
Armored iron vessels	32	74	32,631
	123	659	120,290

IRON-CLAD NAVY.

DESCRIPTION.	NO. OF VESSELS.	GUNS.	TONS.
Seaboard.			
Armored wooden vessels	8	56	19,005
Armored iron vessels	20	42	22,611
Western Rivers.			
Armored wooden vessels	4	9	1,883
Armored wooden vessels (transferred from War Department)	10	122	6,284
Armored iron vessels	12	32	10,020
	54	261	59,808

NAVY ON WESTERN WATERS.

DESCRIPTION.	NO. OF VESSELS.	GUNS.	TONS.
Armored vessels	26	261	59,808
Wooden gun-boats	18	79	6,380
Transports and ordnance steamers	10	2	9,000
Rams	5	24	11,200
Armed tugs	13	13	650
	72	379	87,038

When the vessels now under construction are completed, the Navy will consist of

SAILING VESSELS.

DESCRIPTION.	NUMBER.	GUNS.	TONS.
Ships-of-the-line	6	504	16,094
Frigates	6	300	10,237
Sloops-of-war	16	289	14,305
Brigs	4	20	999
Ships, including store and receiving vessels	23	139	18,087
Schooners	29	69	5,821
Barks	18	92	8,432
Yachts	2	2	200
Total	104	1,415	74,175

STEAM VESSELS.

DESCRIPTION.	NUMBER.	GUNS.	TONS.
Screw frigates	5	228	18,272
Screw sloops, 1st class	6	133	11,955
Screw sloops, 2d class	21	167	23,992
Screw gun-boats (new)	27	108	14,033
Iron-clad vessels	54	261	59,803
Side wheel frigates	4	49	8,003
Side wheel gun-boats (new)	39	296	36,367
Side wheel gun-boats (old Navy)	5	11	2,190
Screw steamers (purchased)	53	215	23,490
Side wheel steamers (purchased)	63	250	38,617
Screw steamers (old Navy)	6	27	2,590
Gun-boats, transports, etc., transferred from other departments	40	108	26,544
Total	323	1,853	265,861

RECAPITULATION.

DESCRIPTION.	NUMBER.	GUNS.	TONS.
Sailing vessels	104	1,415	74,175
Steam vessels	323	1,853	265,861
Total	427	3,268	340,036

CHAPTER XXIII.

Remarks on letting the Mississippi River below Vicksburg fall into the hands of the Confederates again.—Destruction of the Ram "Arkansas."—Capture of Galveston by a portion of Farragut's Squadron.—Recapture of Galveston by the Confederates.—Destruction of the "Westfield."—Commander Renshaw and a Portion of his Crew blown up.—The Steamer "Harriet Lane" Captured by the Confederates.—The Blockade Abandoned.—Appearance of the "Alabama."—Sinking of the "Hatteras" by the "Alabama."—Hardships Endured by Officers and Crew of the "Hatteras"—Attempt to Pass Port Hudson by Farragut's Squadron and Loss of the Frigate "Mississippi."—Casualties.—The effect of the return of Farragut's Fleet before Vicksburg.—Capture of Baton Rouge, La.—Effect of the Destruction of the Ram "Arkansas."—Confederates Attack Baton Rouge and are Repulsed.—Honor to whom Honor is due.—Attack on Donaldsonville.—Fight with the Confederate Iron-clad "Cotton."—Capture of the "A. B. Seger."—Ascending the Louisiana Bayous.—Miscellaneous Engagements of the Gun-boats.—Death of Commander Buchanan.—Vessels and Officers of the West Gulf Squadron, January 1, 1863.

U P to the time of the escapade of the ram "Arkansas," a general idea has been given of the performances of Farragut's fleet.

After leaving Rear - Admiral Davis and running the Vicksburg batteries, he proceeded down the river to New Orleans with the "Hartford," "Richmond," "Brooklyn," "Pinola" and "Kennebec." The old mortar fleet, which under Commander Porter had done such good service at Forts Jackson and St. Philip, and at Vicksburg, had been divided up and withdrawn from the upper Mississippi, and the river from Baton Rouge to Vicksburg was now virtually left to the Confederates, who deliberately went to work and lined the banks with guns, making, besides Vicksburg, another Gibraltar at Port Hudson, which caused much trouble to the Union commanders before they were able to retake it.

The Mississippi had been so easily opened, all the way from New Orleans to Vicksburg, that it ought never to have been closed again, even if it required the whole power of the Federal government to keep it open. The importance of this river to the Confederates was too great for them not to strain every nerve to keep possession of its banks; but the reader will naturally wonder that the Federal government should have allowed such important positions to fall back into their hands.

It is certain that great ignorance or indifference was shown with regard to the importance of Vicksburg and the part it was to play in the war, and this ignorance or indifference, or whatever it may be called, cost the United States many millions of dollars to remedy.

The several historians of the war have managed to glide by this subject with only a passing notice, but it is worthy of careful investigation.

The great importance of the Mississippi to both parties had been manifest from the beginning, but its importance was much greater to the Confederates than to the Federals. It washed the shores of ten different states, northern and southern, and received the waters of fifty or sixty navigable rivers. It was the great connecting link between the two sections, and was in fact the backbone of the rebellion. We had provided the Confederates with guns enough at Norfolk to fortify it in all its length, and they had not failed to make the most of all their means of defence.

The possession of the great river was equally sought by both parties; for it was evident from the first that whichever side obtained control of it and its tributaries would possess an immense advantage.

If the Confederates lost it they would be cut off from their great source of supplies and be compelled to obtain everything from

Europe through blockade runners. This consideration alone would have been sufficient to account for all the blood and treasure which was expended in its defence, and the strength of the fortifications upon its banks show that the importance of the Mississippi had been well estimated by the Confederate generals at the very beginning of the war.

All of the strongholds to the north of Vicksburg had fallen into the hands of the Federals as early as the spring of 1862, and they were now brought face to face with the great Gibraltar of the West, which still barred the way down the river, although all that portion below it had been opened after the capture of New Orleans. But it now seems that we were about to give up all the advantages we had gained, and allow the Confederates to obtain fresh strength by again yielding to them the most important part of the river, after we had so firmly secured it.

While the river was held by our gunboats, the Confederates were prevented from obtaining cattle and supplies from Texas. A report of Lieut.-Commanding Ransom, U.S.N., shows that at one blow he captured 1500 head of cattle which the Confederates were trying to pass across the river, and succeeded in getting them down to New Orleans, where they became the property of the Federal Army.

DESTRUCTION OF THE RAM "ARKANSAS" BY THE U. S. GUN-BOAT "ESSEX,"
COMMANDER WM. D. PORTER.
(FROM A SKETCH BY REAR-ADMIRAL WALKE.)

Had the original plan been carried out (to push on to Vicksburg after the fall of New Orleans, and hold it with ten thousand men) the Mississippi would never again have been closed against us. We sent a few soldiers up to Vicksburg, it is true, but scarcely enough to form a corporal's guard, and instead of landing at Vicksburg they took the opposite bank of the river and commenced digging a ditch, but soon they all became sick and returned to Baton Rouge.

The building of the forts at Port Hudson had so far emboldened the Confederates that they refitted the "Arkansas" and sent her down to Baton Rouge to co-operate with their Army against that port; but both the ram and the Army came to grief.

The fire of the Union gun-boats "Keneo" and "Katahdin" repulsed the Confederates when they attacked our Army with a superior force, and the ram "Arkansas" was engaged by the "Essex," Captain W. D. Porter, accompanied by the "Cayuga" and "Sumter." She was soon set on fire and totally destroyed—whether from the shells of the "Essex" or by the Confederates to escape capture is not known. The Confederates claim that one of her engines was disabled, and that she was destroyed by them ; but, be that as it may, her destruction was due to the presence of the "Essex" and her two consorts.

It was a great relief to Farragut and his officers to get rid of the ram "Arkansas," as she had been a regular *bête noir* to them, and no one could sleep comfortably while she was about. Farragut could now go to the Gulf and arrange for blockading the coast off Galveston.

The mortar flotilla steamers were, in October 1862, placed under the command of Commander W. B. Renshaw. These vessels were the "Harriet Lane," Commander Wainwright, "Owasco," Commander Guest, "Clifton," Lieut.-Commander Richard L. Law and the schooner "Henry Janes." The mortar vessels which had been left at New Orleans were afterwards employed at the siege of Port Hudson with good effect.

On October 6th, Commander Renshaw reported to Rear-Admiral Farragut that with the above named vessels he had captured the city of Galveston after a feeble resistance, and now held it ready for a garrison. This was an important capture as it closed up effectually one of the favorite resorts of blockade runners. It was at once garrisoned by the Army, and Renshaw's vessels took positions in the several entrances of the harbor to prevent the exit or entrance of the enemy.

We did not hold this place long. On January 1st, 1863, General Magruder attacked our vessels with three steamers, fitted with cotton-bale defences, and manned by sharpshooters. At 11.30 A. M., these steamers were discovered coming down the bay towards our fleet. The "Harriet Lane" was above the city and she was first attacked. At 4 A. M., two of the enemy's steamers ran alongside of her and swept her decks with a fire from hundreds of rifles. Commander Wainwright was killed while gallantly leading his men; Lieutenant-Commander Lea, the Executive, fell mortally wounded, the next officer was severely wounded and half the people on deck shot down. It was a case of complete slaughter, and in ten minutes the "Harriet Lane" was in the enemy's possession. The other Union vessels opened their batteries but were not able to do much execution while the enemy's steamers were alongside the "Harriet Lane."

At the same time that he attacked the

would be allowed to take any one vessel, put his people on board of her, and leave the harbor. This proposition was indignantly rejected by the Union commander, who seeing that his steamer was immoveable, resolved to destroy her and transfer his crew to the Army steamer "Saxon," at the same time giving orders to Lieutenant-Commander Richard L. Law to go outside of the harbor with all the vessels that could move.

In the meantime the Confederates had posted their steamers and batteries for a renewed attack. Commander Renshaw got all his men into the boats and sent them

CAPTURE OF THE U. S. STEAMER "HARRIET LANE" BY THE CONFEDERATES, UNDER GEN'L MAGRUDER, IN GALVESTON HARBOR ON THE NIGHT OF JANUARY 1st, 1863.

Union fleet, General Magruder filled the streets of Galveston with a superior force of troops, captured all our soldiers and stationed heavy batteries of artillery at prominent points to prevent our other vessels (which were mostly aground at low tide) from escaping.

It was a well conceived plan and carried out with great gallantry.

The "Westfield" was at this moment hard and fast aground, and could not be moved. The Confederates seeing her helpless condition sent a flag of truce to Commander Renshaw, to inform him that if he would surrender his command he

off, remaining with his own boat and a few officers to set the "Westfield" on fire. This they did, but the flames spread so rapidly that they reached the magazine just as Renshaw entered his boat, and he, with Lieutenant Zimmerman, Chief Engineer Green, and a dozen men, were blown up.

A flag of truce had been flying during the negotiations but it was soon hauled down on our side and our remaining vessels succeeded in leaving the harbor, after some of them had made a gallant resistance.

Lieutenant-Commander Law, (now senior officer), seeing that he had only one vessel, (the "Owasco"), that was in any condition to meet the "Harriet Lane" in case she was refitted by the enemy, decided to *abandon the blockade,* and return to New Orleans! This he did, and reported to Admiral Farragut the sad disaster.

The "Harriet Lane" and two coal vessels were left in the hands of the Confederates, and they naturally exulted a great deal over their victory. They had good reason to do so for the force opposed to them was greatly superior, and many officers consider the retreat from before the harbor a disgraceful affair. Had the gallant Renshaw lived, it would have been different.

In January, 1863, another disaster befell Farragut's fleet. As soon as he heard of the capture of Galveston, he sent Captain Bell with the "Brooklyn" and six gun-boats to retake the place. They had not all arrived on the 11th of January, 1863, when in the evening of that day a sail, which afterwards proved to be the Confederate steamer "Alabama," appeared in the offing and Captain Bell sent the "Hatteras" in pursuit of her. On approaching the stranger, Captain Blake of the "Hatteras" hailed her and asked for her name. The reply was, "Her majesty's steamer 'Vixen.'" The Union commander then said that he would send a boat, and one was immediately lowered and shoved off from the ship's side. At this moment the stranger opened his broadside upon the "Hatteras" from a distance of only one hundred yards with terrible effect. The "Hatteras," though taken by surprise, returned the fire with spirit, and both vessels steamed ahead leaving the boat behind. The action was a short one and ended disastrously for the Federal vessel, as her inferior guns were no match for the armament of the "Alabama," (six rifles in broadside and two pivot guns), and the "Hatteras" soon went to the bottom; her crew was picked up by the enemy, and the latter steamed away.

The appearance of the "Alabama" on the coast created much excitement. No doubt she came with the intention of capturing the small blockading force on the Southern coast, where no very large vessels were maintained.

As soon as the flashes of the guns were seen from the "Brooklyn" she got underway and steamed in that direction, but did not discover anything until the next morning when the masts of the "Hatteras" were seen above the water with the pennant gaily flying. She had gone down in nine fathoms of water, twenty miles south of Galveston light.

This action offers a good moral, "never send a boy on a man's errand." Had Commodore Bell sent two gun-boats instead of one, the "No. 290" or "Alabama," would probably have fallen into our hands, and

her wild career would have ended then and there. As it was she gained great prestige abroad by sinking a United States vessel of war, for people never stopped to inquire whether the conquered vessel had one gun or twenty.

"When put on shore the condition of officers and men was pitiable, no one saved an article of extra clothing, and many had not sufficient to protect their bodies from the inclemency of the weather—landed on an *unfriendly* shore in a state of abject destitution that should have commanded the sympathy of even avowed enemies. The officers and men of the "Hatteras" were made to feel keenly the unkind criticisms of those who professed no unkind feeling towards the United States or its people."

From January, 1863, Farragut was employed in conjunction with General Banks

COMMANDER WILLIAM D. PORTER,
(AFTERWARDS COMMODORE U. S. NAVY.)

in forcing his way into the interior of Louisiana, and bringing all of the country that could be secured under subjection. This was a difficult task, for the Confederates opposed our forces at every step, with a courage and determination very difficult to overcome. The lives of some valuable officers were sacrificed, among them that of Lieutenant-Commander Thomas McKean Buchanan, who had been, while living, the leading spirit of the fleet.

In the enterprises which were undertaken to possess the enemy's inlets and harbors some reverses were met with and some small vessels lost. These were mostly sailing vessels which were captured pretty much as the "Harriet Lane" had been, by river steamers protected by cotton-bales and manned by large numbers of sharp-shooters.

The fact of our government using sailing vessels for blockade duty was simply absurd. Only steamers make a blockade effective, and they should have speed enough to escape from a superior foe or capture an inferior one.

On the 14th of March, 1863, it was decided by Rear-Admiral Farragut and General Banks that the former should move with his fleet past Port Hudson, which was at that time well fortified with nineteen heavy guns bearing on the water approaches. General Banks was to make a diversion with his Army against the forts, and what was left of the mortar flotilla was to open on the batteries prior to and during the passage of the fleet.

Farragut seldom undertook to make a passage by a fort unless he had the mortar boats stationed where they could back him, notwithstanding would-be historians have stated that he did not desire their services. On every occasion he spoke of them in the highest terms, and the statements which have been made in a "Life of Farragut," written after his death, and in an article on the subject by a *quasi*-statesman, which pretend to give his opinions, are fabrications and unworthy of any one who undertakes to write history.

It would be difficult to find out why General Banks allowed these formidable works to be built within striking distance of his Army, and at a place which effectually blocked the way against our forces and secured the Red River to the Confederates as a great highway for their supplies. They had for the time being completely turned the tables on us, and although it was their last stand in this part of the country, it was a stubborn one and a great expenditure of force was necessary to overcome it.

When General Banks reported his Army ready to move on the enemy's works, and the mortar boats were in position, Farragut made his final preparations and at about 11 P. M. got underway with the following vessels: "Hartford," "Mississippi," "Richmond," "Genesee," "Kineo" and "Albatross." Each of the larger vessels, except the "Mississippi," had a gun-boat lashed to her port quarter.

The "Hartford" attended by the "Albatross" led the attack, and was well fought and skillfully handled by her commander Captain James S. Palmer, who passed close to the enemy's works and delivered an effective fire. The Confederates were at first taken by surprise, but soon rushed to their guns and opened a rapid fire upon the fleet, which was passing within one hundred yards of the muzzles of their guns.

The "Richmond," Captain James Alden, came next to the "Hartford," with the "Genesee" as her consort. These vessels were admirably handled, but their commanders and pilots were greatly bothered by the smoke from the "Hartford's" guns which hung over the river obscuring their view of the enemy's works and the other vessels in line. It required great vigilance to prevent getting out of line or running ashore, but the "Richmond" had reached the turn of the river in safety and was about passing the last battery when a plunging shot carried away the safety valves of her boilers and allowed so much steam to escape into her fire-room, that the pressure was reduced to nine pounds. The "Richmond" being thus deprived of her motive force, it was found that the "Genesee" was not able to drag both vessels up against the strong current then running, and under these circumstances there was nothing left to do but to drop down the stream again and anchor below the forts.

The "Monongahela" and "Kineo" came next in line, and these vessels also met with bad luck. The firing from the "Hartford" and "Richmond" had by this time so filled the air with smoke that it was found impossible to distinguish objects near by, and the pilots were completely at sea. At 11.30, the "Monongahela" grounded on the west shore and the "Kineo," not touching, broke away from her, and ranging ahead a short distance grounded also. The enemy soon got the range of these vessels and disabled their principal guns. A heavy shot carried away the supports of the bridge on which Commander McKinstry was standing and precipitated him to the deck, by which he was seriously injured and incapacitated for further duty. The command of the "Monongahela" then devolved upon Lieut.-Commander N. W. Thomas, the executive officer, who with great coolness and judgment backed the vessel off and continued on his way up the river. As he was nearing the bend, however, the engines suddenly ceased to move, owing to a hot crank-pin, and the ship being unmanageable, she drifted down and was obliged to anchor below the batteries.

The steamship "Mississippi," Captain Melancton Smith, followed up in the wake of the "Monongahela," firing whenever her guns could be brought to bear. At 11.30, she had reached the turn which seemed to give our vessels so much trouble, and Captain Smith was congratulating himself on the prospect of soon catching up with the flag-officer, when his ship grounded and heeled over three streaks to port. The engine was instantly reversed and the port guns run in in order to bring her on an even keel, while the fire from her starboard battery was reopened upon the forts. The engines were backed with all the steam that could be put upon them and the backing was continued for thirty minutes but without avail : it was now seen that it would be impossible to get the ship afloat. Captain Smith gave the order to spike the port battery and throw the guns overboard, but it was not done, for the enemy's fire was becoming so rapid and severe that the Captain deemed it judicious to abandon the ship at once in order to save the lives of his men. While preparations were being made to destroy the ship, the sick and wounded were lowered into the boats and conveyed ashore, while the men at the starboard battery continued to fight in splendid style, firing at every flash of the enemy's guns. The small arms were thrown overboard, and all possible damage was done to the engines and everything else that might prove of use to the enemy, The ship was first set on fire in the foreward storeroom, but three shots came through below the water line and the water rushed in and put out the flames. She was then set fire to in four places aft, between decks, and when the flames were well underway so as to make her destruction certain, Captain Smith and his first-lieutenant left the ship, (all the officers and crew having been landed).

The "Mississippi" was soon in a blaze, fore-and-aft, and as she was now relieved of a great deal of weight, (by the removal of her crew and the destruction of her upper works) she floated off the bank, and drifted down the river much to the danger of the Union vessels below; but she passed without doing them any injury and at 5.30, blew up and went to the bottom. The detonation was heard for miles around, and exceedingly rejoiced the hearts of the Confederates along the river banks.

Thus ended the career of this old ship, which had been dear to many a naval officer and sailor. Many pleasant memories clustered about her, and no ship ever performed more faithful service, or came to a more glorious end. Her commander, officers and men lost no credit by the manner in which they performed their duty on this occasion; on the contrary everyone who knows anything about the matter is aware that every possible exertion was made to get the ship afloat, and that when she was finally abandoned it was done in a cool and orderly manner. It is in such trying moments that men show of what metal they are made, and in this instance the metal was of the very best.

Farragut in the "Hartford," with the "Albatross" alongside, reached the mouth of Red River, and Port Hudson was as completely cut off from supplies as if fifty gunboats had been there. But this affair was a great triumph to the enemy and equally depressing to the Federals for the time being. It was soon seen however that the object aimed at had been gained—the works at Port Hudson were cut off from supplies and the fate of the garrison sealed.

Farragut was much disappointed at the loss of the "Mississippi" and the failure of the other vessels to get up, but he bore it with his usual equanimity and looked upon it as the fortune of war.

He was satisfied that his commanders had all done their duty and was well aware of the fact that the "Hartford" had fewer difficulties to contend with than the vessels in her rear. Her pilot could see everything ahead, while those astern were blinded by the smoke of her guns.

The list of killed and wounded is as follows :

"Hartford," 2 killed, 6 wounded; "Richmond," 3 killed, 12 wounded; Mississippi," 64 missing, of which 25 were believed to have been killed ; "Monongahela," 6 killed, 21 wounded:—Total 114 killed, wounded and missing, nearly as heavy a loss as was sustained by the whole fleet at the passage of Forts Jackson and St. Philip.

Rear-Admiral Farragut steamed on up to the mouth of the Red River which he closely blockaded, and remained there until relieved by Rear-Admiral Porter in the "Benton" on May 2d, 1863, when he returned overland to his fleet below Port Hudson.

The effect of the return of Farragut's squadron from before Vicksburg was bad for the people living along the river. The population of the towns that had abstained from hostile acts, and in fact had assumed a very humble attitude, now became quite defiant—the mayors of the little municipalities putting on the airs of autocrats, their importance being doubtless stimulated by the fact that Farragut and his officers did not seem disposed to molest them or even question their loyalty to the United States.

When the news of Farragut's victory was carried up the river by escaping steamers, there was a panic all through the region, and for the moment every one seemed disposed to submit to the Federal authority. Many persons were in their hearts glad to see the Union flag once more triumphant, and looked forward with pleasure at the idea that the old order of things would soon be restored. But when the mayor of Vicksburg at first mildly then defiantly treated Farragut's demand for the surrender of the city, and the other towns learned of the unsuccessful attempt of the fleet to obtain possession of Vicksburg, either by persuasion or force, their ardor in the Confederate cause was suddenly stimulated. Each little hamlet determined to share in the glory that enveloped Vicksburg and not only to forswear allegiance to the United States but fire upon the Union flag whenever it appeared in their neighborhood.

This may have been heroic, but it was far from wise, as the Confederates had at that period few troops along the river and no guns except field-pieces, which although they might annoy would hardly arrest the progress of vessels of war. Baton Rouge, Natchez, and in fact every town along the river, seemed to have entered into a league against the Federal vessels, putting it out of the power of the Union officers to exercise that forbearance they desired to show both from motives of policy and humanity.

It was desirable to satisfy the people living along the Mississippi, that the mission of the Navy was simply to restore the authority of the Federal government, not to destroy property or do harm to non-combatants; but this course, instead of con-

vessels, well knowing that they could inflict no serious damage on their hulls although they might kill or wound some of their crews. Such acts were bound to lead to retaliation, and create a bitter feeling on the Federal side. Military and naval men do not stop long to think when a battery is opened upon them and the shot are falling in their midst. They naturally fire back without much considering whom they may hurt. This is one of the results of war. It is not intended to excuse the retaliatory measures of the Federal officers but merely to give their reasons.

Baton Rouge was one of those defiant towns, notwithstanding its proximity to New Orleans and the large Federal Army stationed at the latter place. When summoned to surrender by Captain Palmer of the "Iroquois," the mayor replied that "Baton Rouge will not be voluntarily surrendered to any power on earth!" Upon

BATON ROUGE, THE CAPITAL OF LOUISIANA, CAPTURED BY CAPTAIN PALMER OF THE "IROQUOIS," AND AFTERWARDS OCCUPIED BY GENERAL WILLIAMS.

ciliating the populace, only inflamed their dislike to the "invaders," as they were pleased to call the Union forces. The mild propositions of the naval commander were considered as proof of the weakness of the Federal government, and finally the military, which had but little to lose in the way of property, became so harassing that retaliation had to be resorted to in self-defence and the innocent often suffered in consequence.

Never in the course of any war was there so great a desire on the part of the Navy to abstain from harsh measures, and if the Confederate troops had confined themselves to firing upon naval vessels at places away from towns, our officers would have been satisfied to try consequences with them on their own terms. Such, however, was not the case, the Confederate artillery generally selected points in the immediate vicinity of towns and sometimes in the towns themselves to fire upon the passing

receiving this reply Captain Palmer informed the mayor that he would stand no nonsense and forthwith landed his men, hoisted the Union flag, and took possession of the public property. Fortunately this capture was accomplished without bloodshed, although that might easily have followed owing to the contumacy of the municipal authorities.

In this case the rights and property of all citizens were respected, and only the property claimed by the Confederate government was taken possession of. These were easy terms for people who had sturdily defied the Federal authority and refused to listen to any terms.

Natchez offered fewer impediments to the Union commander. The mayor was a sensible man, compared with the one at Baton Rouge, and on receiving a communication from Captain Palmer to the effect that the city must surrender, he replied: "Coming as a conquerer, you will need not the interposition of the city authorities to possess the place. An unfortified city, an entirely defenceless people, have no alternative but to yield to an irresistible force, or uselessly to imperil innocent blood. Formalities are absurd in the face of such reality. So far as the authorities are concerned there will be no opposition to your possession of the city. They cannot however guarantee that your flag shall be unmolested in the sight of an excited people," etc., etc. As if the people who for a lifetime had existed under the protection of that flag were now unable to endure the sight of it.

The mayors of these little cities used high sounding words, which seemed rather ridiculous coming from people who had neither guns nor soldiers. It would have been more to their credit to have accepted the situation without trying to delude the more ignorant part of the population with the idea that the Union fleet sought the destruction of their lives and property. The course taken by these municipal authorities led to very bad results and its evil influence was felt by the inhabitants all along the river.

The same summons was given at Vicksburg, where the mayor in the first instance bade defiance to the Army and Navy under Butler and Farragut. The result of the negotiations with the authorities of Vicksburg is best told in the account of the attack by Farragut's squadron, where, owing to the long drawn out negotiations, all the energies of the Confederates had time to concentrate on the defences of the city, which in a month was rendered impregnable against a purely naval attack.

Grand Gulf, at that moment a place of no importance, following in the footsteps of its illustrious neighbor Vicksburg, set to work to erect batteries and opened fire on the gun-boats. In consequence of this, Captain Palmer, in the "Iroquois," with the other vessels under his command, dropped down the river and shelled the town, the first instance of such a proceeding on the part of our Navy. The little town was set on fire and destroyed. This was considered a great outrage by the Confederates, and was taken advantage of to inflame the minds of the people against the Union forces.

From this time forth the Confederate artillery began to assemble at commanding positions along the river banks, and the once peaceful scene was marred by burning plantations, from whence the enemy attacked the gun-boats. There was no longer a hope of peace for the inhabitants of the river region.

It was a great relief to Admiral Farragut to know that the ram "Arkansas"

was disposed of, and that thus terminated the existence of one of the most troublesome vessels the Confederates had built. She was at that time the last Confederate ram on the Mississippi River. At the moment of her destruction there was considerable excitement along the river on hearing of her approach towards Baton Rouge, where General Williams was in command of the Federal military forces, and expecting an attack from the Confederate troops under General Breckenridge, to be supported by the ram "Arkansas" and the gun-boats "Webb" and "Music."

The Union vessels that were on the spot to meet the enemy and co-operate with the Army, were the "Katahdin," Lieut.-Commander Roe, and the "Kineo," Lieut.-Commander Ransom. The report that the enemy were approaching Baton Rouge for the purpose of attacking that place, was not an idle one, for on the morning of the 5th of April, at one o'clock, General Breckenridge attacked General Williams' position with great vigor. The Union troops withstood the attack bravely, while the "Kineo" and "Katahdin" poured in a heavy fire on the enemy's lines. This battle was kept up fiercely until one o'clock, A. M., and the enemy would no doubt have succeeded but for the accurate firing of the gun-boats, which threw their shells right into the midst of the Confederate lines, causing great dismay.

Lieut.-Commander Ransom, commanding the "Kineo," had an officer stationed on the State-house, who directed the firing by signal so successfully that the enemy was obliged to retreat.

Unfortunately the gallant General Williams fell in this engagement, and the Government lost the services of a most valuable officer.

The ram "Arkansas" and her consorts did not appear upon the scene of battle, or it might have been still more hotly contested, or even ended disastrously for the Federal cause, for if the attention of the gun-boats could have been diverted by the Confederate vessels, the Army would not have received that aid which contributed so much toward the repulse of the enemy; and there is no knowing how deplorable a defeat the Federal forces would have met with or what the consequences might have been.

Soon after this affair was ended the smoke of a steamer (supposed to be the "Arkansas") was seen coming down the river with rapidity, to act apparently in concert with the land forces. She stopped about a mile above the bend of the river, moving up and down as if uncertain how to act. Later, she was passed by her two consorts, the "Webb" and "Music."

The "Essex," Commander Porter, accompanied by the "Cayuga" and "Sumter," then moved up towards the bend to meet the Confederate squadron, which was apparently afraid to take its share in the conflict according to the preconcerted plan; a general signal was made for the "Katahdin" and "Kineo" to follow the other vessels.

As the "Essex" came within gunshot of the "Arkansas," Commander Porter opened fire on her, and in a short time the ram appeared to be disabled, though she still continued her fire on the "Essex." Some incendiary shells were now fired from the latter; directly after, there was seen a gush of flame from the "Arkansas'" side, and she was soon enveloped in fire. Her crew attempted to make her fast to the bank with a hawser, and then escaped to the shore, the "Essex" still keeping up her fire to prevent the flames from being extinguished. The lines which had held the "Arkansas" to the bank soon burned away, and the Confederate ram swung off into the river, where she blew up with a terrible explosion, and went to the bottom. Thus ended the career of one of the most formidable rams the Confederates had ever built.

Up to the time the "Essex" attacked the "Arkansas," the machinery of the latter was in perfect order, and she went into action, no doubt, certain of vanquishing her clumsy foe, which could not do much more than stem the current of the river. But the "Arkansas" was driven ashore and destroyed after a short engagement.

An attempt was made to take from Commander W. D. Porter, his officers and crew, the credit of destroying this vessel, because some of her crew that were picked up, stated that one of the engines was out of order, and that the captain tied up to the shore to keep his vessel from drifting down the river, and that the Confederates set fire to her themselves. This is a very unlikely story. It is not credible that a vessel, which had run the gauntlet of the two fleets, under Farragut and Davis, at Vicksburg, inflicting great injury upon them and receiving no vital injury in return, would avoid a conflict with the "Essex" (a vessel of weaker hull and very much less speed), unless she had been first so crippled by the "Essex's" guns that her commander saw no hope of success. Certain it is that the commander of the "Essex" did not hesitate to attack a Confederate ram that had defied the whole Union fleet, and she sunk while under his fire.

The two Confederate gun-boats escaped up the river when they witnessed the fate of their powerful companion which was to have driven all the Union naval forces from before Baton Rouge.

There is no doubt but what the enemy depended on the ram "Arkansas" and her two consorts for his success at Baton Rouge, as General Williams depended upon the Union gun-boats for success over any force that could be brought against him. It shows what important factors in war the so-called gun-boats were (on either side). They could move about with their heavy guns, take positions which the enemy could not outflank and pour in a destructive fire, directed by the best drilled gunners in the world, dealing death and destruction on any enemy that might venture to face them.

The result of this battle was a complete victory for the Union forces by land and by water, and there would have been cause for great rejoicing on the Federal side but for the untimely fate of the gallant General Williams, who fell with a Minie-ball through his heart while cheering on his men, who chased the Confederates three or four miles away from the scene of battle and then returned to their entrenchments.

When Admiral Farragut, who was at New Orleans, heard of the attack on Baton Rouge, he proceeded to that point without delay with the "Hartford," and on learning of the happy result, and the destruction of the Confederate ram, he was delighted; for although the admiral, on the whole, "did not attach much importance to Confederate rams," he had seen enough of the performances of the "Arkansas" to know, that if properly managed, she was the most formidable vessel on the Mississippi River, and that there would be no security against her while she floated.

To render everything secure at Baton Rouge, Farragut left a sufficient force there to guard against all contingencies, and returned to New Orleans, satisfied that for the present he would hear no more of Confederate rams. He was not aware at the time, that the enemy had been so well satisfied with the performances of the "Arkansas" that they had commenced to build at Yazoo City two more rams, more powerful than any they had yet planned.

Great credit was due the officers and men of the little flotilla, which co-operated so handsomely with General Williams in defeating General Breckenridge, particularly to Lieutenant Roe of the "Katahdin" and Lieutenant Ransom of the "Kineo," who threw the enemy's ranks into confusion by the remarkable accuracy of their fire.

The commander of the "Arkansas," on this occasion, was Lieutenant H. K. Stevens of the Confederate Navy, her former fearless commander, Lieutenant Brown, having been taken sick at Vicksburg. The events that took place on board the ram, except through vague reports, have never come to light.

Notwithstanding the want of success of the Confederates in their attacks on the approaches or outposts to New Orleans, they still kept up a guerilla warfare on the vessels moving up and down the river—a mode of warfare of no avail whatever, and calculated only to bring distress upon the small towns where these roving bands held their headquarters.

For a long time this practice of firing on armed and unarmed vessels had been practiced with impunity, and Farragut determined to repress it if possible. He had sent messengers several times to the town of Donaldsonville, to inform the authorities that, unless steps were taken to stop this useless and inhuman practice, the town would be held responsible.

When passing up the river to the support of Baton Rouge, he anchored the "Hartford" two miles above Donaldsonville and heard them firing on vessels ascending the river (the transport, "Sallie Robinson" and the steamer "Brooklyn"), in the latter case, the enemy getting more than they bargained for and being driven to cover. The next night they fired upon the transport "St. Charles."

Farragut, in consequence of these wanton and useless attacks, notified the authorities to send their women and children out of the town as he intended to destroy it on his way down the river, and he fulfilled his threat to a certain extent. He burned the hotels and wharf buildings, also all buildings belonging to one Phillippe Landry, who was said to be a captain of the guerilla band. Landry attacked the firing party but the sailors gave chase to him and he fled. Some twenty negroes were taken from this place and a number of cattle and sheep for the use of the squadron.

Thus Farragut, while inflicting necessary punishment, endeavored to make it fall as lightly as possible on the innocent, and only those suffered who invited it by setting at defiance their conquerors, who were disposed to extend the greatest liberality to all those residing within reach of the Federal guns—all that was required of them being to abstain from hostile proceedings against Federal vessels.

This punishment of towns may smack somewhat of barbarity, and should not, in fact, be practiced but for very grave offenses, as an indiscriminate burning inflicts severe punishment upon innocent people. But in this instance the punishment fell on the guilty ones, who took advantage of the security the town gave them to commit their hostile acts against Federal vessels, supposing that the Federal authorities would respect the towns where these acts were committed.

They did so until forbearance ceased to be a virtue.

One of the most gallant officers under the command of Rear-Admiral Farragut, was Lieutenant-Commander Thomas McKean Buchanan, commanding the steamer "Calhoun." He had been employed on Lake Pontchartrain, where he performed good service, and on October 25th, he proceeded to Southwest Pass, expecting to be met by the gun-boats "Estrella" and "St. Mary's," and intending to co-operate with General Weitzel in the waters of Atchafalaya. He had on board the 21st Indiana regiment. With a great deal of difficulty he succeeded in getting the "Estrella," "St. Mary's," "Kinsman" and "Calhoun" into Atchafalaya Bay, from the channels of which the enemy had removed all the stakes and buoys. Entering the Atchafalaya River the little flotilla met the Confederate iron-clad "Cotton," which after a sharp engagement made her escape up the river. (The guns of this vessel were in iron casemates and she was very fast.) That same night, Lieutenant-Commander Buchanan captured the steamer "A. B. Seger," belonging to the Confederate Navy.

Notwithstanding the shoals and low tides, Buchanan brought up the "St. Mary's" and anchored her off Brashear city, showing the enemy that there was no point when the Union gun-boats would not reach when commanded by an energetic officer. No one who had not tried it could estimate the difficulties of ascending these Louisiana bayous and rivers. It was on these occasions (where men held their lives in their hands), that the most daring deeds of the war were performed.

It cannot be said that these expeditions were always of advantage to the Union cause, for a great deal of energy was often wasted, and frequently valuable lives were lost. But at Army headquarters these operations were called for under the pretext that they were important strategic movements, and our naval officers were too glad of the opportunity to face danger and aid the cause, to interpose any objections to them.

Buchanan's expedition having forced its way through the narrow and shallow channels with great difficulty, reached Brashear City only to find that a large force of the enemy had crossed over and was making its way up to Franklin. They were immediately followed by the flotilla up the Atchafalaya River, through Bayou Teche to a point five miles above Pattersonville, and three from the mouth of the Teche—where the enemy was found posted in force. The gun-boats opened fire, and the enemy retreated to a point two miles further up the river, where they had obstructed the approaches with piles, and where they were also supported by the gun-boat "Cotton," which vessel was posted above a bridge.

The "Calhoun's" Parrott gun became disabled almost at the first fire, and Lieutenant-Commander Cooke was sent ahead with the other two vessels to open the way. The second shot from the Confederate gun-boat struck the "Estrella" in her port bow, killing two soldiers and wounding another, and also carrying away the vessel's wheel-ropes, which caused her to run into the bank. The "Diana," having her gun mounted on an iron carriage, got it disarranged and had to stop, while the "Kinsman" (Acting-Master George Wiggins) pushed on right up to the batteries (which contained eleven field-pieces), and to within 1,000 yards of the iron-clad "Cotton," as close as he could get.

This courageous attack seemed to demoralize the enemy on shore, for they retreated immediately with their field-pieces. The "Kinsman" then opened her guns on the "Cotton," and kept up the unequal contest until relieved by the "Calhoun," which vessel backed up to the bridge and brought her guns to bear upon the enemy. After enduring a hot fire for about twenty minutes, the "Cotton" escaped up the river.

While the "Kinsman" was under fire of the enemy's guns she received fifty-four shot through her hull and upper works, and three through the flag, which still waved. One round shot passed through the magazine and shell-room, demolishing shell-boxes but doing no other damage. One man was killed and five wounded—among the latter being the pilot, who died next day.

By the time the "Cotton" withdrew, the "Estrella" and "Diana" succeeded in getting up, and Buchanan landed his men and tried to remove the obstructions and haul the "Diana" over the shoals to pursue the enemy, but without effect Not deeming it prudent to lie in the Teche all night (where the enemy could surround him and open fire from concealed places), he dropped down to Brashear City to repair damages and bury the dead.

The Confederate gun-boat "Cotton" was no trifling enemy; she was heavily armed and gallantly fought, and besides the fifty-four shot she put in the "Kinsman" she put eight into the "Calhoun," three into the "Diana," and three into the "Estrella." Fortunately their machinery was not touched.

The enemy had exhibited a great deal of intelligence in blocking the river. The obstructions consisted of the steamer "Flycatcher," thrown across the river and sunk, backed by a schooner, with heavy oak logs thrown in between and around the two vessels in such quantities that it was found impossible to remove them without the aid of a stronger land force than Buchanan had at his command; for the men of the expedition could not have worked under such a fire as the enemy would have brought to bear upon them from the rifles and field artillery, to say nothing of the guns of the iron-clad which were still intact.

The Confederate force was under the command of General Monson, and numbered from three to four thousand men. They were badly cut up, and finally moved their camp to Centreville, three miles above the obstructions, keeping only their cavalry and artillery below.

All that day the gun-boats were busy repairing damages. Buchanan, no way disheartened at the superiority of the enemy's force, started up the river, on the 5th, with the "Estrella," leaving the other vessels to continue their repairs. The enemy was driven off as before, but the vessel did not fare so well as formerly, a shot from the indomitable "Cotton" disabled the Parrott gun, killing two men instantly, and finding that he could do no more, Lieutenant-Commander Buchanan withdrew down the river.

The encounter with this heavy work, and the greatly superior force defending it, showed the character of this brave officer who had forced a well-equipped and well-posted enemy from a strong position, and only ceased his exertions when the Confederates had reached a defence from which it was impossible to dislodge them without the assistance of a large body of troops.

Buchanan was ably seconded by his officers and men, and although he was unsuccessful in forcing the barricades and capturing the Confederate gun-boat, yet he compelled her to retreat up the river to a point where she was unable to do any damage.

The next day, the gallant Acting-Master Wiggins, commanding the "Kinsman," started with that vessel and the captured steamer "Seger," in pursuit of two steamers said to to be concealed in some of the bayous. The latter were eventually captured in Bayou Cheval, nine miles from Grand Lake. As the vessels were aground and it was impossible to move them, they were set on fire and destroyed. The result of this expedition was the evacuation of the district by the enemy for the time, but before leaving they burned over a hundred railroad cars and destroyed many plantations, which compelled the planters to desert their homes, carrying their negroes off with them. These constant attacks resulted in driving the enemy from that part of the country, and gave our officers a knowledge of the topography and hydrography of the region, which was of much benefit later in the war.

In the management of these small expeditions our younger officers showed the metal of which they were made, and Lieutenant-Commander Buchanan became particularly conspicuous. This gallant officer lost his life January 14, 1863, being killed by a Minie-ball fired from a rifle-pit. He died regretted by all who knew him, and by none more sincerely than Admiral Farragut.

Buchanan had long been operating in the waters of the Atchafalaya. In October, 1862, he attacked the enemy as before mentioned, in the Teche, drove him from a strongly fortified position and blockaded the Confederate iron-clad above the obstructions near Pattersonville. In January, 1863, he was again on the Teche chasing the Confederate forces and was this time accompanied by a brigade of infantry and cavalry under General Weitzel. The enemy were strongly posted and covered by the Confederate iron-clad "Cotton." Buchanan was advancing on the river, side by side with the troops who were marching along the banks, when they came in sight of the enemy's position.

The "Cotton" at once opened fire while the Federal troops were deployed as skirmishers to pick off the gunners of the Confederate vessel, a task they speedily accomplished. At the same time the enemy's field-pieces were driven back and the only part of his forces remaining were the rifle-men, who from their pits kept up a galling fire. Buchanan was not the man to let any one get ahead of him, especially the soldiers whom it was his duty to cover with his guns; he pushed on in the "Calhoun" to the attack and was soon in advance of the troops, but he paid with his life the penalty of his gallantry and was shot through the head by a concealed rifleman while standing on deck directing affairs. A number of his men fell, killed or wounded at the same time. Had Buchanan lived five minutes longer he would have had the satisfaction of seeing the enemy fleeing in every direction.

At the same time the gallant Acting-Master Wiggins was severely wounded by a Minie-ball through the shoulder, and Acting-Ensign Foster through the cheek. On board the "Calhoun" on this occasion three were killed and six wounded, and on board the "Kinsman" one was wounded.

Lieutenant-Commander Buchanan was a great loss to the Union cause, but the object for which he had labored many months, —the opening of the Teche—had been accomplished. This would have happened earlier if a sufficient number of troops had been sent to accompany the gun-boats in the first instance, but it seems seldom to have been realized that these expeditions would be comparatively fruitless unless conducted as combined military and naval operations, when they were generally successful.

WEST GULF SQUADRON, JANUARY 1ST, 1863

REAR-ADMIRAL DAVID G. FARRAGUT, COMMANDER-IN-CHIEF.

STEAMER "HARTFORD," FLAG-SHIP.

Captain, James S. Palmer, commanding; Fleet Captain, Thornton A. Jenkins; Lieutenant-Commander, Lewis A. Kimberly; Lieutenants, J. C. Watson and H. B. Tyson; Fleet Surgeon, J. M. Foltz; Surgeon, W. M. King; Assistant Surgeon, Joseph Hugg; Paymaster, W. T. Meredith; Chief Engineer, J. B. Kimball; Marine Officers: Captain, J. L. Broome; 1st Lieutenant, J. H. Higbee; Ensigns, J. H. Read, J. J. Read, D. D. Wemple and C. D. Jones; Midshipman, H. J. Blake; Assistant Engineers, E. B. Latch, F. A. Wilson, Isaac de Graaf, C. M. Burchard, A. K. Fulton, H. H. Pilkington and J. E. Speights; Boatswain, James Walker; Acting-Gunner, J. L. Staples; Carpenter, O. T. Stimson; Sailmaker, J. A. Holbrook; Acting-Master, T. L. Peterson; Acting-Master's Mates, H. H. Judson and Henry Western, Jr.

STEAMER "PENSACOLA."

Commodore, Henry W. Morris; Lieutenants, Geo. H. Perkins and C. E. McKay; Surgeon, J. W. Taylor; Assistant Surgeons, W. B. Dick and Chas. Giberson; Paymaster, G. L. Davis; Chief Engineer, D. D. Hibbert; 2d Lieutenant Marines, J. C. Harris; Assistant Engineers, S. L. P. Ayres, C. H. Ball, F. G. Smith, J. L. Vauclain, J. T. Hawkins, J. C. Huntley and E. A. Magee; Boatswain, Nelson Goodrich; Gunner, D. A. Roe; Carpenter, J. E. Cox; Sailmaker, Charles Lawrence; Acting-Masters, G. C. Schulze, F. H. Grove and Edw. Herrick; Acting-

Masters' Mates, G. A. Storm, Joseph Kent and Chas. Gainsford.

STEAMER "BROOKLYN."

Commodore, H. H. Bell; Lieutenant-Commander, Chester Hatfield; Lieutenant, A. N. Mitchell; Surgeon, Samuel Jackson; Assistant Surgeon, C. J. S. Wells; Paymaster, C. W. Abbot; Chief Engineer, W. B. Brooks; 1st Lieutenant Marines, James Forney; Ensign, M. W. Saunders; Midshipmen, John R. Bartlett and H. T. Grafton; Assistant Engineers, B. E. Chassaing, James Atkins, A. V. Fraser, Jr., C. F. Mayer, Jr., J. L. Bright, James Morgan and J. F. Walton; Boatswain, J. A. Selmer; Gunner, T. H. Fortune; Carpenter, W. T. Toy; Sailmaker, Jacob Stevens; Acting-Masters, T. L. Pickering, J. C. Stafford, Lyman Wells and W. C. Gibbs; Acting-Masters' Mates, E. S. Lowe, H. C. Leslie, Robert Beardsley, H. S. Bolles and James Buck.

STEAMER "SUSQUEHANNA."

Commodore, R. B. Hitchcock; Lieutenant-Commander, Montgomery Sicard; Lieutenant, Louis Kempff; Surgeon, Joseph Beals; Assistant Surgeon, H. C. Nelson; Chief Engineer, George Sewell; Captain of Marines, P. R. Fendall, Jr.; Ensign, Walter Abbott; Assistant Engineers, J. M. Hobby, James Butterworth, E. R. Arnold, Nelson Ross, R. H. Buel and F. T. H. Ramsden; Boatswain, Charles Miller; Gunner, E. J. Waugh; Carpenter, G. M. Doughty; Sailmaker, J. C. Herbert; Acting-Masters, G. B. Livingstone, A. L. B. Zerega and W. L.

Churchill; Acting-Masters' Mates, F. G. Adams and E. B. Pratt.

STEAMER "ONEIDA."

Captain, Samuel F. Hazard; Lieutenants, W. N. Allen and F. S. Brown; Surgeon, John Y. Taylor; Paymaster, C. W. Hassler; Chief Engineer, F. C. Dade; Assistant Engineers, Horace McMurtrie, J. H. Morrison, R. H. Fitch, W. D. McIlvaine and A. S. Brower; Boatswain, James Herold; Gunner, Wm. Parker; Acting-Masters, F. M. Green, Thos. Edwards and Elijah Ross; Acting-Masters' Mates, Edward Bird and D. H. Clark.

STEAMER "MONONGAHELA."

Captain, James P. McKinstry; Lieutenant-Commander, Jos. Watters; Lieutenant, N. W. Thomas; Surgeon, David Kindleberger; Assistant Paymaster, Forbes Parker; Acting-Ensigns, C. R. Pomeroy, H. W. Grinnell and Robert Barlow; Acting-Masters' Mates, H. B. Rowe, W. S. Arnaud, Frederick Beldon and C. H. Blount; Engineers: Chief, Geo. F. Kutz; Joseph Frilley, N. B. Clark, P. G. Eastwick, Edw. Cheney, G. J. Bissett and P. J. Langer; Boatswain, William Green; Gunner, J. D. Fletcher.

STEAMER "MISSISSIPPI."

Captain, Melancton Smith; Lieutenant, George Dewey; Surgeon, R. T. Maccoun; Assistant Surgeon, J. W. Shively; Paymaster, T. M. Taylor; Chief Engineer, W. H. Rutherford; Captain of Marines, P. H. W. Fontane; Ensigns, A. S. Barker, O. A. Batcheller and E. M. Shepard; Assistant Engineers, G. B. N. Tower, J. Cox Hull, F. G. McKean, S. R. Brooks, J. J. Noble and H. W. Phillips; Boatswain, Joseph Lewis; Gunner, Wm. Cope; Carpenter, John Green; Acting-Masters, F. T. King, George Munday, C. F. Chase, B. L. Kelly and F. E. Ellis; Acting-Masters' Mate, H. B. Francis.

STEAMER "COLORADO."

Captain, John R. Goldsborough; Lieutenant-Commander, Edw. W. Henry; Lieutenant, H. W. Miller; Assistant Surgeons, T. H. Whitney and Matthew Chalmers; Paymasters, J. O. Bradford and W. H. H. Williams; Chaplain, D. X. Junkin; Marine officers: Captain, George R. Graham; 1st Lieutenant, S. C. Adams; Acting-Masters, Thomas Hanrahan and C. G. Folsom; Ensign, G. K. Haswell; Acting-Ensigns, Henry Arey and J. J. Butler; Acting-Masters' Mates, J. S. Russ, A. O. Child, C H Littlefield, W. G. Perry and J. L. Vennard; Engineers: Chief, Richard M. Bartleman; Acting-Assistants, C. W. Pennington, G. L. Perkins, C. G. Stevens, T. J. Lavery, A. E. McConnell, Robert Wallace and H. B. Green; Boatswain, A. W. Pomeroy; Gunner, Robert H. Cross; Carpenter, John A. Dixon; Sailmaker, William Maull.

SLOOP-OF-WAR "PORTSMOUTH."

Commander, Samuel Swartwout; Surgeon, J. S. Dungan; Assistant Surgeon, G. Baumgarten; Assistant Paymaster, Caspar Schenck; 1st Lieutenant Marines, Wm. H. Hale; Boatswain, John Ross; Gunner, T S. Cassidy; Carpenter, John Shannon; Sailmaker, H. T. Hayden; Acting-Masters, Gilbert Redmond, W. G. Mitchell and E. A. Terrell; Acting Masters' Mates, T. P. Jones and T. B. Gannon.

FRIGATE "POTOMAC"—STORESHIP.

Commander, Alex. Gibson; Lieutenant, A. V. Reed; Surgeon, J. D. Miller; Assistant Surgeon, N. H. Adams and G. R. Brush; 1st Lieutenant Marines, Geo. W. Collier; Boatswain, C. A. Bragdon; Gunner, Wm. H. French; Carpenter, J. C. Hoffman; Acting-Masters, W. H. Wood and G. D. Upham; Acting-Masters' Mates, S. H. Johnson and Wm. Baker; Acting-Assistant-Paymaster, W. W. Bassett.

STEAMER "RICHMOND."

Commander, James Alden; Lieut.-Commander, A. B. Cummings; Lieutenant, Edward Terry; Surgeon, A. A. Henderson; Assistant Surgeon, J. D. Murphy; Paymaster, Edwin Stewart; Chief Engineer, John W. Moore; Captain of Marines, Alan Ramsay; Ensign, Benj. F. Haskin; Assistant Engineers, Eben Hoyt, Jr., A. W. Morley, G. W. W. Dove, R. B. Plotts, C. E. Emery, John D. Ford and Robert Weir; Boatswain, Isaac T. Choate; Gunner, James Thayer; Carpenter, H. L. Dixon; Sailmaker, H. T. Stocker; Acting-Volunteer-Lieutenant, Fredk. S. Hill; Acting-Master, Chas. Gibbs; Acting-Ensign, R. P. Swan; Acting-Master's Mates, W. R. Cox, J. R Howell and T. S. Russell.

STEAMER "R. R. CUYLER."

Commander, Geo. F. Emmons; Lieutenant, James O'Kane; Acting-Masters, P. C. Gibbs and J. F. Alcorn; Acting-Ensigns, W. Collins, C. C. Gill and J. O. Morse; Acting-Assistant-Surgeon, Henry Shaw; Acting-Assistant-Paymaster, Emory Wright; Acting-Masters' Mates, N. M. Dyer and N. R. Davis; Acting-Engineers Henry Waite, W. D. Adair, Wm. Morris, T. D. Hulse and T. W. Bolman.

STEAMER "WESTFIELD."

Commander, W. B. Renshaw; Lieutenant, C. W. Zimmerman; Acting-Masters, F. C. Miller, L. D. Smalley and J. H. Warren; Acting-Masters' Mates, J. P. Arnett and J. B. Johnson; Acting-Assistant-Surgeon, E. H. Allis; Acting-Assistant-Paymaster, C. C. Walden; Acting-Engineers, Wm. R. Greene, G. S. Baker and C. W. Smith.

STEAMER "HARRIET LANE."

Commander, J. M. Wainwright; Lieutenant-Commander, Edward Lea; Paymaster, J. J. Richardson; Assistant Surgeon T. N. Penrose.

IRON-CLAD STEAMER "ESSEX."

Commander, C. H. B. Caldwell; Assistant Surgeon, Wm. F. Terry; Acting-Vol.-Lieutenant, H. A. Glassford; Acting-Masters, J. C. Parker and M. B. Snyder; Acting-Masters' Mate, J. H. Mammen; Acting-Gunner, R. M. Long; Acting-Assistant-Paymaster, C. W. Slamm; Acting-Engineers, J. K. Heap and W. H. Manning.

STEAMER "MONTGOMERY."

Commander, Charles Hunter; Acting-Masters, Geo. H. Pendleton and C. G. Arthur; Acting-Ensigns, Robert Wiley and W. O. Putnam; Acting-Masters' Mates, H. M. Mather, C. H. Walker and Henry Hamre; Acting-Assistant-Surgeon, D. F. Lincoln; Acting-Assistant-Paymaster, Joseph Watson; Acting-Engineers, G. H. Wade, James Pollard, John Mulholland, F. W. H. Whitaker and John McEwan.

STEAMER "KANAWHA."

Commander, John C. Febiger; Assistant Surgeon, J. H. Tinkham; Assistant Engineers, Edward Farmer, F. S. Barlow, Hiram Parker and W. S. Cherry; Acting-Master, T. C. Dunn; Acting-Master's Mates, E. L. Hubbell, R. P. Boss and R. B. Smith; Acting-Assistant-Paymaster, L. L. Penniman.

STEAMER "NEW LONDON."

Lieutenant-Commander, Abner Read; Lieutenant, Benj. F. Day; Acting-Master, W. D. Roath; Acting-Master's Mate, Peter Faunce; Acting-Assistant-Surgeon, L. H. Kindall; Acting-Assistant-Paymaster, F. H. Thompson; Acting-Engineers, H. P. Powers, D. M. Howell, John Brooks and Henry Farmer.

GUN-BOAT "KINEO."

Lieutenant-Commander, George M. Ransom; Lieutenant, Frederick Rodgers; Assistant Surgeon, A. S. Oberly; Assistant Engineers, S. W. Cragg, James Maughlin, C. F. Hollingsworth and C. J. McConnell; Acting-Masters, Oliver Colburn and L. A. Brown; Acting-Masters' Mates, W. S. Keen, John Bartol, Jr., W. H. Davis and G. A. Faunce; Acting-Assistant-Paymaster, S. P. N. Warner.

GUN-BOAT "PEMBINA."

Lieutenant-Commander, Wm. G. Temple; Lieutenant, Roderick Prentiss; Assistant Surgeon, A. W. H. Hawkins; Assistant Paymaster, H. L. Wait; Assistant Engineers, Jefferson Young, John Van Vovenberg, Absalom Kirby and J. F. Bingham; Acting-Masters, Wm. Rogers and J. A. Jackaway; Acting-Ensigns, Wm. Sydden and B. M. Chester; Acting-Masters' Mate, H. C. Cochrane.

SLOOP-OF-WAR "VINCENNES."

Lieutenant-Commander, John Madigan, Jr.; Assistant Surgeon, D. M. Skinner; Second-Lieutenant Marines, N. L. Nokes; Acting-Boatswain, John Smith; Acting-Gunner, Wm. Wilson; Acting-Carpenter, A. O. Goodsoe; Acting-Sailmaker, Nicholas Lynch; Acting-Masters, W. H. Churchill, J. T. Seaver, J. R. Hamilton and O. B. Warren; Acting-Assistant Paymaster, J. J. A. Kissam.

STEAMER "HATTERAS."

Lieutenant-Commander, Homer C. Blake; Assistant Surgeon, E. S. Matthews; Acting-Masters, H. O. Porter, Enoch Brooks and G. D. Hoffner; Acting-Masters' Mates, J. W. Hazlitt, A. H. Berry and T. G. McGrath; Acting-Assistant Paymaster, F. A. Conkling; Acting-Engineers, A. M. Covert, J. C. Cree, Jacob Colp and B. C. Bourne.

GUN-BOAT "SCIOTA."

Lieutenant-Commander, Reigart B. Lowry; Lieutenant F. O. Davenport; Assistant Surgeon, J. H. Clark; Assistant Engineers, C. E. De Valin, H. M. Quig, A. H. Price and Edw. Curtis; Acting-Master, A. McFarlane; Acting-Ensigns, J. H. Field and S. S. Beck; Acting-Master's Mate, S. H. Bemis; Acting-Assistant Paymaster, C. H. Lockwood.

GUN-BOAT "CAYUGA."

Lieutenant-Commander, D. A. McDermot; Assistant Surgeon, Edw. Bogart; Assistant Engineers, J. M. Harris, W. W. Sydney, J. C. Chaffee and Ralph Aston; Acting-Masters, E. D. Percy and John Hanson; Acting-Masters' Mates, James Gillin, W. W. Patten, F. P. Stevens, and R. O. Lanfere; Acting-Assistant Paymaster, J. W. Whiffen.

STEAMER "CLIFTON."

Lieutenant-Commander Richard L. Law; Midshipman, H. T. French; Acting-Masters, Robert Rhodes and B. S. Weeks; Acting Ensign, W. W. Weld; Acting-Masters' Mate, Loring Cannon; Acting-Assistant Surgeon, D. D. T. Nestell; Acting-Assistant Paymaster, J. S. Carels; Acting-Engineers, James A. Fox, S. S. Vollum, F. J. Bradley and G. W. Spies.

GUN-BOAT "AROOSTOOK."

Lieutenant-Commander, Samuel R. Franklin; Lieutenant, T. S. Spencer; Assistant Surgeon, C. J. Cleborne; Assistant Engineers, W. J. Buehler, George R. Holt, James Entwistle and Samuel Gragg; Acting-Masters, Eben Hoyt and W. A. Maine; Acting-Masters' Mates, Louis R. Hammersly, C. F. Palmer, Edw. Culbert and J. C. Henry; Acting-Assistant Paymaster, W. L. Pynchon.

GUN-BOAT "KATAHDIN."

Lieutenant-Commander, Francis A. Roe; Lieutenant, Nathaniel Green; Assistant Surgeon, Somerset Robinson; Assistant Engineers, T. M. Dukehart, W. J. Reid, W. W. Heaton and John McIntyre; Acting-Ensigns, J. H. Hartshorn and J. G. Green; Acting-Masters' Mates, Geo. Leonard, John Leeds and Frank Kemble; Acting-Assistant Paymaster, H. LeRoy Jones.

GUN-BOAT "ALBATROSS."

Lieutenant-Commander, John E. Hart; 2d Assistant Engineer, C. H. Ball; Acting-Masters, T. B. Dubois and C. S. Washburne; Acting-Ensign, J. H. Harris; Acting-Masters' Mate, Wm. Harcourt; Acting-Assistant Surgeon, W. J. Burge; Acting-Assistant Paymaster, G. R. Martin, Acting Engineers, J. W. Smyth, L. J. M. Boyd and C. H. Slack.

STEAMER "POCAHONTAS."

Lieutenant-Commander, W. M. Gamble; Lieutenant, J. F. McGlensey; Assistant Surgeon, A. C. Rhoades; Assistant Engineers, Caleb E. Lee, W. F. Fort and G. C. Julan; Acting-Masters, Edw. Baker and Thomas Symmes; Acting-Masters' Mates, J. M. Braisted, O. S. Willey and Caleb Fellowes; Acting-Assistant Paymaster, Theo. Kitchen; Acting-Engineer, John Jordan.

GUN-BOAT "KENNEBECK."

Lieutenant-Commander, John H. Russell; Assistant Surgeon, Chas. H. Perry; Assistant Engineers, Henry W. Fitch, B. C. Gowing, E. E. Roberts and L. W. Robinson; Acting-Masters, H. C. Wade and Wm. Brooks; Acting-Masters' Mates, J. W. Merryman, H. E. Tinkham and J. D. Ellis; Acting-Assistant Paymaster, C. L. Burnett.

GUN-BOAT "ITASCA."

Lieutenant-Commander, R. F. R. Lewis; Assistant Surgeon, Heber Smith; Assistant Paymaster, A. J. Pritchard; Assistant Engineers, T. Jones and John Borthwick; Acting-Masters, Edmund Jones and Sylvanus Nickerson; Acting-Masters' Mates, J. B. Crane, W. E. Bridges, George Spencer and Henry Miron; Acting-Engineers, David Frazier, H. C. Henshaw and M. Gerry.

STEAMER "TENNESSEE."

Lieutenant-Commander, P. C. Johnson; Assistant Surgeon, H. M. Wells; Acting-Masters, J. D. Childs, Ezra Leonard, G. E. Nelson and S. V. Bennis; Acting-Masters' Mates, M. W. McEntee, A. P. Sampson and Oscar Peck; Acting-Gunner, Nathaniel Hobbs; Acting-Assistant Paymaster, B. F. D. Fitch; Acting-Engineers, J. E. Schultz, G. L. Harris, Samuel Robinson, E. C. Mayloy and Thomas Fitzgerald.

GUN-BOAT "OWASCO."

Lietenant-Commander, Henry Wilson; Assistant Surgeon, W. W. Leavitt; Assistant Engineers. W. K. Purse. J. A. Scott, C. H. Greenleaf and D. M. Egbert; Acting-Masters, S. A. Swimmerton and T. D. Babb; Acting-Masters' Mates, John Ulter and J. G. Arbona; Acting-Assistant Paymaster, Richard Beardsley.

GUN-BOAT "WINONA."

Lieutenant-Commander, Aaron W. Weaver; Lieutenant, W. S. Schley; Assistant Surgeon, Arthur Mathewson; Assistant Engineers, E. S. Boynton, Edward Gay and R. L. Wamaling; Acting-Master, Charles Hallet; Acting Ensign, F. H. Beers; Acting-Master's Mates, H. D. Burdett and Alfred Staigg; Acting-Assistant Paymaster, S. F. Train; Acting-Assistant Engineer, J. W. Milestead.

GUN-BOAT "PINOLA."

Lieutenant-Commander, James Stillwell; Lieutenant, G. Watson Sumner; Assistant Surgeon, L. M. Lyon; Assistant Engineers, John Johnson, B. B. Clemens, W. F. Law, John Everding and W. F. Pratt; Acting-Masters, W. P. Gibbs and J. G. Loyd; Acting-Masters' Mates, W. H. Thompson, C. V. Rummell and J. G. Rosling; Acting-Assistant Paymaster, C. Stewart Warren.

STEAMER "J. P. JACKSON."

Lieutenant-Commander, Henry A. Adams; Acting-Masters, M. B. Crowell, J. F. Dearborn and Wm. Hedger; Acting-Masters' Mates, Wm. H. Howard, Jeremiah Murphy and W. J. B. Laurence; Acting-Assistant Surgeon, T. S. Yard; Assistant Paymaster, H. Melville Hanna; Acting-Engineers, J. B. Morgan and J. D. Caldwell.

STEAMER "CALHOUN."

Lieutenant-Commander, T. McK. Buchanan; Acting-Master, M. Jordan; Acting-Ensign, H. D. Foster; Acting-Master's Mates, R. C. Bostwick and J. L. Blauvelt; Acting-Assistant Surgeon, Ira C. Whitehead; Acting-Assistant Paymaster, W. M. Watmough; Acting-Engineers, W. D. Brown, R. W. Mars, G. W. Baird and P. H. Fales.

STEAMER "ESTRELLA."

Lieutenant-Commander, A. P. Cooke; Acting-Master's Mate, L. Richards; Acting-Assistant Surgeon, B. F. Wilson; Acting-Engineer, Robert Stott.

STORE-SHIP "RELIEF."

Acting-Volunteer-Lieutenant, B. D. Manton; Acting-Master, N. S. Morgan; Acting-Master's Mates, Wm. Jenney and M. J. Nicholson; Acting-Assistant Surgeon, Celso Pierucci; Acting-Assistant Paymaster, E. K. Gibson.

STEAMER "KINSMAN."

Acting-Volunteer-Lieutenant, Geo. Wiggins; Acting-Master, A. S. Wiggins.

STEAMER "KENSINGTON."

Acting-Volunteer-Lieutenant, Fred. Crocker; Acting-Volunteer-Lieutenant, N. W. Hammond; Acting-Masters, Geo. Taylor, C. M. Tinker and C. W. Wilson; Acting-Masters' Mates, Robert Finney and F. A. Leach; Acting-Assistant Surgeon, John E. Cobb; Acting-Assistant Paymaster, John F. Tarbell; Acting-Engineers, Alex. Auchinbeck, T. W. O. Conner, W. S. Harden, S. B. Runnels, A. B. Besse and J. C. Mockabee.

BARK "ARTHUR."

Acting-Volunteer Lieutenant, Thomas F. Wade; Acting-Masters, W. O. Lunt and Albert Cook; Acting Masters' Mates, Wm. Barker, J. C. Constant and C. S. Bellows; Acting-Assistant Surgeon, O. D. Root; Acting-Assistant Paymaster, M. B. Osborn.

SCHOONER "RACHEL SEAMAN."

Acting-Volunteer-Lieutenant, Quincy A. Hooper; Acting-Ensign, Edwin Janorin; Acting-Master's Mate, Wm. H. Metz.

SCHOONER "HENRY JANES."

Acting-Volunteer-Lieutenant, Lewis W. Pennington.

SCHOONER "ORVETTA." (BOMB.)

Acting-Master, F. E. Blanchard; Acting-Master's Mates, E. O. Adams and W. H. Monroe.

BRIG "BOHIO."

Acting-Masters, Geo. W. Browne and W. M. Stannard; Acting-Masters' Mates, James Sheppard and S. C. Heath; Acting-Assistant Paymaster, J. M. Skillman.

SCHOONER "JOHN GRIFFITHS." (BOMB.)

Acting-Master, Henry Brown; Acting-Master's Mates, Asa Hawes and John McAllister.

SCHOONER "CHARLOTTE."

Acting-Master, E. D. Bruner.

SCHOONER "SARAH BRUEN." (BOMB.)

Acting-Master, A. Christian; Acting-Master's Mates, Sylvester Rowland, B. G. Cahoon and J. M. Chadwick.

SCHOONER "MARIA A. WOOD."

Acting-Master, Samuel C. Cruse; Acting-Master's Mates, F. C. Way and Charles Fort.

SHIP "MORNING LIGHT."

Acting-Masters, John Dillingham, H. W. Washburn, W. W. Fowler and L. H. Partridge; Acting-Masters' Mates, Geo. H. Rice and J. L. Chambers; Acting-Assistant Surgeon, John W. Shrify; Assistant Paymaster, W. S. Blunt.

BARK "W. G. ANDERSON."

Acting-Masters, N. D'Oyly and Wm. Bailey; Acting-Masters' Mates, Roswell Davis and R. H. Carey; Acting-Assistant Surgeon, Winthrop Butler; Acting-Assistant Paymaster, Louis L. Scovel.

STEAMER "DIANA."

Acting-Master, Ezra S. Goodwin; Acting-Master's Mate, John D. Trott.

BARK "HORACE BEALES."

Acting-Master, D. P. Heath; Assistant Surgeon, R. T. Edes; Acting-Ensign, J. F. Perkins; Acting-Master's Mates, James West and Eugene Biondi.

STORE-SHIP "NIGHTINGALE."

Acting-Masters, D. B. Horne and Edwin E. Drake; Acting-Masters' Mates, Thomas Stevens and Alonzo Gowdy; Acting-Assistant Surgeon, Arthur Ricketson; Acting-Assistant Paymaster, H. D. Kimberly.

COAL-SHIP "PAMPERO."

Acting-Master, Charles Huggins; Acting-Master's Mate, Charles Bostwick; Acting-Assistant Surgeon, J. H. Langsley; Acting-Assistant Paymaster, A. A. Pancoast.

STEAMER "SACHEM."

Acting-Master, Amos Johnson; Acting-Ensign, A. H. Reynolds; Acting-Master's Mates, G. C. Dolliver and L. C. Grainger; Acting-Engineers, John Fraser, J. R. Wall and G. C M. Wolfe.

SCHOONER "KITTATINNY."

Acting-Masters, G. W. Lamson and A. H. Atkinson; Acting-Masters' Mate, J. G. Crocker; Acting-Assistant Paymaster, E. C. Bowman.

BARK "KUHN."

Acting-Masters, R. G. Lee, J. T. Harden and W. F. Hunt; Acting-Masters' Mate, Wm. Edgar; Acting-Assistant Paymaster, J B. Hazelton.

STORE-SHIP "FEARNOT."

Acting-Masters, Daniel S. Murphy and T. W. Williams; Acting-Masters' Mates, Fred. Furbish and G. H. Benson; Acting-Assistant Paymaster, Augustus Esenwein.

SLOOP-OF-WAR "PREBLE."

Acting-Master, Wm. F. Shankland; Acting-Ensigns, B. B. Knowlton, L. B. King and J. S. Clark; Assistant Surgeon, J. S. Knight; Acting-Master's Mate, F. P. Parks; Acting-Assistant Paymaster, W. J. Hoodless; Boatswain, John Bates; Acting-Gunner, J. A. Cummins; Carpenter, J. McFarlane; Sailmaker, G. W. Giet.

YACHT "CORYPHEUS."

Acting-Master, A. T. Spear.

SCHOONER "OLIVER H. LEE." (BOMB.)

Acting-Master, Washington Godfrey; Acting-Master's Mates, A. T. Parsons, J. A. Chadwick and T. G. Hall.

SCHOONER "SAM HOUSTON."

Acting-Master, Geo. W. Ward; Acting-Ensign, J. J. Kane.

BRIG "SEA FOAM."

Acting-Ensign, Thomas H. Baker; Acting-Master's Mates, D. F. O'Brien and Joseph Moss.

CHAPTER XXIV.

SECOND ATTACK ON VICKSBURG, ETC.

REAR-ADMIRAL PORTER TAKES COMMAND OF THE MISSISSIPPI SQUADRON.—GUERILLA WAR-
FARE.—GENERAL GRANT'S PLANS.—THE ARMY AND NAVY CO-OPERATE.—EXPEDITION
UP THE YAZOO.—THE "CAIRO" SUNK BY TORPEDOES.—DIFFICULTIES SURMOUNTED BY
THE ARMY.—OPERATIONS OF EARL VAN DORN AND FORREST.—REPULSE OF GENERAL
SHERMAN NEAR CHICKASAW BAYOU.—ATTACK ON HAINES' BLUFF BY THE UNITED STATES
STEAMER "BENTON," ETC., AND DEATH OF LIEUT.-COM. GWINN.—ARRIVAL OF GENERAL
MCCLERNAND TO RELIEVE SHERMAN.—EXPEDITION TO ARKANSAS POST.—LAST ACT OF
THE NAVY IN THE YAZOO.—VESSELS THAT TOOK PART IN THE YAZOO EXPEDITION.

REAR-ADMIRAL PORTER took command of the Mississippi Squadron in October, 1862. Rear-Admiral Davis had ordered all the vessels except the "Benton" and the "Carondelet" up to Cairo for repairs, for what with being rammed and shaken up by constant firing of the guns, they required a thorough overhauling.

There being at this moment no actual operations in progress, Rear-Admiral Porter devoted his attention to putting the vessels in thorough order, changing their batteries to Dahlgren guns, and adding a number of small stern-wheel vessels, covered with light iron (called "tin-clads"), to the squadron.

Up to this time the gun-boats had, strictly speaking, been under the control of the Army, but now all this was changed, and the Mississippi Squadron, like all the other naval forces, was brought directly under the supervision of the Secretary of the Navy. The Commander-in-Chief of the squadron had no longer to receive orders from General Halleck or Army headquarters, but was left to manage his command to the best of his ability, and to co-operate with the Army whenever he could do so. This was a much better arrangement, as it allowed the naval commander-in-chief to exercise his judgment, instead of being handicapped, as Foote and Davis were.

It may be remembered when Donelson fell, and Foote suggested to Halleck the importance of pushing on with the gun-boats to Nashville, General Halleck forbade his doing so. The new arrangement left the commander of the squadron at liberty to undertake any expedition he thought proper, and he was not in the least hampered by any instructions from the Navy Department regarding his movements; so that when the Army was operating in the interior of Tennessee, which seemed at that time the great battle-ground, the Navy could take advantage of the opportunity and make raids on the enemy along the Mississippi and its tributaries, keeping down guerillas, and enabling army transports to go and come without hindrance.

In October, 1862, the guerillas were exceedingly troublesome all along the rivers, firing at every unarmed steamer which passed. Large quantities of goods were shipped from St. Louis to points along the river professedly Union, which ultimately reached the Confederates. All this was stopped, and the guerillas, when captured, were summarily dealt with, and the houses where they were harbored laid in ashes. No commerce was allowed on the Mississippi except with Memphis, and the river looked almost as deserted as in the early days of its discovery, its silence being seldom disturbed except by gun-boats and army transports, and the sharp report of the howitzers as they sent the shrapnel shells into the dense woods or over the high banks where it might be supposed guerillas were lying in wait to fire on the transports.

This was slow work compared to the active warfare the iron-clads had been engaged in under Foote and Davis, but they were merely getting ready for the hard work before them and will be heard from ere long again.

Before Admiral Porter left Washington he was informed by the President that General McClernand had been ordered to raise an Army at Springfield, Ill., to prosecute the siege of Vicksburg. The President expressed the hope that the rear-admiral would co-operate heartily with General McClernand in the operations to be carried on. But as Vicksburg never would have been taken if it had depended on General McClernand's raising an Army sufficient for the purpose, the admiral, immediately on his arrival at Cairo, sent a message to General Grant, at Holly Springs, Miss., informing him of McClernand's intention, that he, Porter, had assumed command of the Mississippi Squadron, and was ready to co-operate with the Army on every occasion where the services of the Navy could be useful.

A few days afterwards General Grant arrived at Cairo and proposed an expedition against Vicksburg, and asking the rear-admiral if he could furnish a sufficient force of gun-boats to accompany it. Grant's plan was to embark Sherman from Memphis, where he then was, with thirty thousand soldiers, to be joined at Helena, Arkansas, by ten thousand more. Grant himself would march from Holly Springs with some sixty thousand men upon Granada. General Pemberton would naturally march from Vicksburg to stop Grant at Granada until reinforcements could be thrown into Vicksburg from the south, and while Pemberton was thus absent with the greater part of his Army Sherman and Porter could get possession of the defences of Vicksburg.

General Grant having been informed that the gun-boats would be ready to move at short notice, and having sent orders to Sherman to put his troops aboard the transports as soon as the gun-boats arrived in Memphis, returned immediately to Holly Springs to carry out his part of the programme.

This interview between Grant and Porter lasted just half an hour, and thus was started the expedition against Vicksburg, which, after a long and arduous siege and a great expenditure of men and money, resulted in the capture of the strongest point of defence occupied by the enemy during the war.

The expedition from Memphis got away early in December, 1862, Commander Walke, in the "Carondelet," being sent ahead with the "Cairo," "Baron DeKalb," and "Pittsburg," (iron-clads,) and the "Signal" and "Marmora" ("tin-clads"), to clear the Yazoo River of torpedoes and cover the landing of Sherman's Army when it should arrive. This arduous and perilous service was well performed. On the 11th of December, Commander Walke dispatched the two "tin-clads" on a reconnoisance up the Yazoo. They ascended some twenty miles, when they were apprized of the presence of torpedoes by a great number of small boats along the channel of the river and an explosion near the "Signal." Another torpedo was exploded from the "Marmora" by firing into it with a musket as it appeared just below the surface. The commanding

LIEUT.-COMMANDER T. O. SELFRIDGE,
(NOW CAPTAIN U. S. NAVY.)

officers of these two vessels reported that with the assistance of two iron-clads to keep down the sharpshooters, they could clear the river of torpedoes, but not otherwise, as there were rifle-pits all along the left bank of the Yazoo, and the enemy were supplied with light artillery. At Lieutenant-Commander Selfridge's request he was sent on this duty in the "Cairo," with the "Pittsburg," Lieut.-Commanding Hoel, and the ram "Queen of the West," Colonel Charles Ellet, Jr., commanding. These officers were cautioned to be particularly careful and run no risks.

On the 12th of December the vessels proceeded on the duty assigned them under a shower of bullets from the rifle-pits, which was only checked by the gun-boats dropping close into the left bank and enfilading the rifle-pits with shrapnel. This cleared the enemy out, and the boats from the vessels were enabled to drag for the infernal machines and haul them to the shore, where they were destroyed by firing volleys of musketry into them.

After this work had been prosecuted for some time Lieut.-Comr. Selfridge proceeded ahead in the "Cairo" to cover the "Marmora," which was thought to be sorely beset by the enemy's sharpshooters. The "Cairo" encountered a floating torpedo. Two explosions in quick succession occurred, which seemed almost to lift the vessel out of the water. Everything was done to keep the "Cairo" afloat, but without avail, and she sank in twelve minutes after the explosion, in six fathoms of water, with nothing but the tops of her chimneys showing above the surface. All the crew were saved. No fault was imputed to the commanding officer of the "Cairo." It was an accident liable to occur to any gallant officer whose zeal carries him to the post of danger, and who is loath to let others do what he thinks he ought to do himself.

This was a bad day's work for a beginning, but the admiral looked upon it simply as an accident of war, and Selfridge was immediately given command of the "Conestoga." The loss of the "Cairo" was the more regretted as she had lately been made "shot proof," by covering her weakest points with railroad iron. It appeared on examination of the river banks that the torpedo wires were connected with galvanic batteries, and that the enemy was prepared with a system of torpedo defence that would require the utmost caution in ascending the Yazoo and seizing a point at which to land an Army.

Rear-Admiral Porter arrived in the Yazoo a day or two after the loss of the "Cairo," and the whole squadron was set to work to clear the river of torpedoes. The gun-boats ascended to within range of the forts on Haines' Bluff and brought on an engagement with the enemy's batteries, during which the boats of the squadron pushed ahead, and succeeded in destroying numbers of torpedoes.

General Sherman moved his transports to a point on the river called Chickasaw Bayou

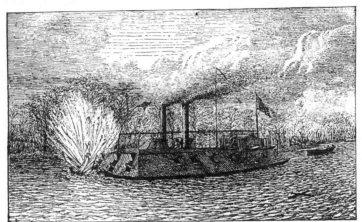

U. S. IRON-CLAD "CAIRO" SUNK BY A TORPEDO.
(FROM A SKETCH BY REAR-ADMIRAL WALKE.)

without the loss of a man from torpedoes or sharpshooters, his landing being covered in every direction by the gun-boats.

Sherman first made a feint on Haines' Bluff as if to attack the works and then landed at Chickasaw Bayou. Owing to the late heavy rains he found the roads to Vicksburg heights almost impassable, and when he attempted to advance with his Army he was headed off by innumerable bayous, which had to be bridged or corduroy roads built around them. It was killing work.

Even at this time Vicksburg had been fortified at every point, and its only approaches by land led through dense swamps or over boggy open ground, where heavy guns were placed, so as to mow down an advancing Army. A general has seldom had so difficult a task assigned him, and there was little chance of Sherman's succeeding unless Pemberton had drawn off nearly all his forces to oppose Grant's advance on Granada, thus leaving Vicksburg without a garrison; for even a small force could hold the place against a vastly superior attacking one.

There was only one point where the Confederates had possibly left a loophole open for an enemy to get in; if they neglected that point it would be because they never supposed any one would attempt to penetrate swamps where men had to wade up to their middle in mud and water, and the passage of artillery was almost an impossibility.

At the time of which we are writing the rain had fallen in such torrents that the low lands in the vicinity of Vicksburg were submerged, the water extending nearly to the base of the frowning hills covered with earthworks and rifle-pits, against which an Army would have made little impression. There was, then, no other course but to attack the enemy's works by the road leading from Chickasaw Bayou and attempt to reach the landing at the foot of the high hills overlooking river and plain, where nature had placed obstacles nearly as formidable as the enemy's guns at other places.

Sherman gained that point and established himself under the high hills it was necessary to assault before he could see the inside of Vicksburg; but what was encountered in reaching that point no one but the brave officers and men of that Army will ever know. An Army of thirty thousand men can accomplish a great deal when well directed but it cannot convert swamps into dry land.

But the enemy had not neglected the swamps around Chickasaw Bayou or the approaches to Vicksburg on that side. On the contrary they seemed to have exercised their ingenuity to make that route impassable. Acres of wood had been felled, the trees overlapping one another and forming a *chevaux de frise* which extended through the swamp for several miles.

The difficulties seem great enough in the description, but this falls far short of the reality. However Sherman and his Army overcame everything and at last reached *terra firma.*

In the meanwhile the Navy was doing what it could to help the Army, but its work was necessarily confined to the water, shelling the edges of the woods all around the peninsula where Sherman and his Army were struggling, and keeping the enemy from bringing their artillery to bear.

Sherman was of course aware of the perilous character of his undertaking, and the probability of his being driven back, but he had one strong motive to induce him to extra exertions and that was his loyalty to General Grant. The latter had run considerable risk in leaving his base at Holly Springs to draw Pemberton from Vicksburg. Time was precious and Sherman had to act with promptness, and he felt that it was due to his chief that he should leave nothing untried that would help Grant to carry out his plans. Those plans were well conceived but the best calculations in the world were liable to be upset in the face of such elements as prevailed at Chickasaw Bayou, when Sherman found himself in the swamp beneath the heights of Vicksburg.

Grant had left Holly Springs with a large Army at the time he had appointed, merely with the design of drawing Pemberton from Vicksburg and thus helping Sherman in his attack on that place. This was all Grant proposed to do, although it was suggested that in case Pemberton retreated before him, Grant would follow him up.

Grant moved towards Granada and everything looked well, but the Confederate general, Earl Van Dorn, dashed into Holly Springs twenty-eight miles in the rear of the Union Army, capturing the garrison and all their stores. At the same time General Forrest pushed his cavalry into West Tennessee, cutting the railroad to Columbus at several points between that place and Jackson. This completely cut Grant off from his only line of communication with the North and also from his several commands. Due precautions had been taken to prevent

this mishap by leaving a strong force behind at Holly Springs, but the commanding officer was not on the alert and his capture was a complete surprise. In this raid of the Confederates a million dollars' worth of stores were destroyed.

Under the circumstances it was impossible for Grant to continue his march on Granada, which Pemberton perceiving, the latter returned to Vicksburg in time to assist in Sherman's repulse.

Had Grant been satisfied that he could subsist his Army in the enemy's country, he would have doubtless pushed on to Vicksburg at all hazards and the place would have fallen at that time, but such was not to be. "There's a divinity that shapes our ends, rough hew them as we may." Had Vicksburg been taken at that moment, one of the best opportunities of displaying the strength and resources of the North would have been lost.

Sherman made all his arrangements to attack the enemy's works on the 29th of December, 1862, and the assault took place early on that day. One division succeeded in occupying the batteries on the heights and hoped shortly to reach those commanding the city of Vicksburg, but the division that was to follow the advance was behind time and the opportunity was lost. A portion of Pemberton's Army had returned from Granada, just in time to overwhelm and drive back the small force that had gained the hills. The latter were outnumbered four to one and were driven back. The enemy did not follow, being satisfied with driving our troops from the heights and there was nothing left for Sherman to do but to get his Army safely back to the transports.

Throughout these operations the Navy did everything that could be done to ensure the success of General Sherman's movement. As the soldiers pushed their way through the swamps the "Benton" and two other iron-clads with the "Marmora" and ram "Queen of the West," moved up to within easy range of Haines' Bluff. The "Benton" opened on the Confederate batteries and also shelled the road leading to Vicksburg to prevent the enemy from sending reinforcements to Vicksburg and also to make them believe that Haines' Bluff was the intended point of attack.

Boats were sent towards the forts to drag for torpedoes with the intention if the latter could be removed to advance the gun-boats to close quarters. When the small boats approached the enemy's works a rapid fire was opened on them, but they did not retire until it was supposed that the torpedoes were removed and the way was clear. Then the "Benton" advanced to the point where the boats had ceased work, some twelve hundred yards from the fort, or as near as the boats could operate against such a fire.

At this point the Yazoo River was very narrow and only one iron-clad could pass up at a time. There was no room for two vessels to fight abreast, consequently the "Benton" had to bear the brunt of the battle, which lasted two hours. During this time the "Benton" received many heavy blows from the enemy's shot and shells, while her consorts had to lie idle, for if they threw shells over the "Benton" they might endanger those on board. Although the "Benton" was much cut up her efficiency was not impaired. She was hit on her bow casemates, which were "shot-proof," thirty times without damage, but plunging shots passed through her decks. Lieut.-Commanding Gwinn, stood on the upper deck

LIEUT.-COMMANDER WILLIAM GWINN, U. S. NAVY.

during the whole action, as he was of opinion that a pilot-house or casemate was no place for the commander of a ship of war in battle. This idea cost him his life, for he was struck with a fifty-pound rifle shell which tore away the muscles of his right arm and breast. His executive officer, Acting Lieutenant George P. Lord, was severely wounded, and ten of the crew were killed and wounded.

It was impossible for gun-boats alone to capture the works at Haines' Bluff, as but one vessel at a time could operate against them. Their reduction required a combined Army and Navy attack. The Confederates proved themselves good artillerists but had two of their guns dismounted by the "Benton's" fire. The gallant commander of the "Benton" notwithstanding his dreadful wounds, lingered two days and died in the admiral's cabin deeply regretted by every

officer and man in the squadron. The gunboats withdrew from before Haines' Bluff for it appeared evident that Vicksburg could not be taken from that direction.

General Sherman came to the same conclusion with regard to attacking it from the Chickasaw Bayou. He met with no loss in withdrawing his troops to the transports, but in the assault he lost in killed, wounded, and missing, seventeen hundred men, a large number considering the short time his Army was actually engaged. The soldiers had to work their way back to the Yazoo through heavy rains, and the hardships they encountered in the march can hardly be realized by those who did not share them. That evening the sun came out again as if to let the soldiers dry themselves and all the signs promised fair weather.

Rear-Admiral Porter being still hopeful, proposed to run the iron-clads at night close up under the forts and attack at close quarters with grape and canister, while a division of the Army disembarked and assaulted Haines' Bluff in the rear. General Sherman approved the plan and General Steele and his division were assigned to co-operate with the Navy on the following night, but the good weather indications proved a delusion and a snare, and on the afternoon of the day when the attack was to have been made on Haines' Bluff, a fog set in that shut out all objects at a distance of fifty feet, and this continued until the next day.

The proposed expedition could do nothing on such a foggy night. At noon the following day it began to rain again heavier than ever and the land almost disappeared from sight. There was no longer any chance for a successful attack on Haines' Bluff and nothing was left but for the Army and Navy to retire from the scene where they had been so unsuccessful.

General Sherman, on visiting the rear-admiral on board his flag-ship, opposed further operations and at once proposed that Vicksburg should be given up for the present, and as his troops were somewhat demoralized he must go with them to attack Arkansas Post and secure a success which would impart new confidence to them. He desired the admiral to go along with the gun-boats, and this being agreed to, preparations were made to start next day on the new expedition.

The following morning General Sherman learned that Major-General McClernand had arrived at the mouth of the Yazoo to take command of Sherman's Army. This was a surprise to every one, for although it was known that McClernand had received orders to proceed to Illinois and raise troops for the purpose of undertaking the siege of Vicksburg, yet it never was supposed that he would take command of forty thousand men of Grant's Army, without even paying the latter, his superior officer, the compliment of informing him of his intention. However, General McClernand came with such orders from Washington that Sherman unhesitatingly agreed to turn over the command to him.

As Admiral Porter did not come under Army rule and knew exactly the terms on which General McClernand had received his orders, he declined to have anything to do with the proposed expedition to Arkansas Post, unless General Sherman should go in command of the troops. To this McClernand agreed, only stipulating that he should accompany the expedition. So the matter was arranged, and the expedition started.

The last act of the Navy in the Yazoo was one to be remembered by the Confederates who, finding that our troops were re-embarked and ready to depart, determined to pounce on the rear transports and give them a parting remembrance.

Two regiments made an attack with field-pieces which were hauled along the road made by Sherman's soldiers, but unfortunately for the enemy they mistook the " Lexington," " Marmora," " Queen of the West " and " Monarch "—the two latter Colonel Ellet's rams—for transports. Before the Confederates could fire a second round, these vessels opened on them with shrapnel, grape and canister, cutting them up and sending them flying in all directions without the loss of a man on our side.

In the meantime the transports steamed down the river in good order leaving nothing behind that could be of any use to the enemy.

The following named vessels took part in the Yazoo expedition : " Black Hawk,"(flagship) Lieutenant-Commander K. R. Breese, " Benton," Lieutenant-Commander Wm. Gwinn, " Baron DeKalb," Lieutenant-Commander Jno. G. Walker, " Carondelet," Commander Henry Walke, " Louisville," Lieutenant-Commander E. K. Owen, " Cincinnati," Lieutenant-Commanding G. M. Bache, " Lexington," Lieutenant-Commander James W. Shirk, " Signal," Acting-Volunteer-Lieutenant John Scott, " Romeo," Acting-Ensign R. B. Smith, " Juliet," Acting-Volunteer-Lieutenant Edward Shaw, " Forest Rose," Acting-Master Geo. W. Brown, " Rattler," Lieutenant-Commander Watson Smith, " Marmora," Acting-Volunteer-Lieutenant Robert Getty, " Monarch," (ram) " Queen of the West," (ram) Colonel Chas. Ellet, Jr.

The second attack on Vicksburg terminated quite as unsatisfactorily as the first, and every one came to the conclusion that Vicksburg could only be conquered by a long and troublesome siege which would severely test the endurance of both parties.

CHAPTER XXV.

CAPTURE OF FORT HINDMAN OR ARKANSAS POST.

ARRIVAL OF THE EXPEDITION.—THE ARMY IN THE REAR OF ARKANSAS POST.—PLAN OF
THE FORT.—THE GUN-BOATS IN POSITION.—THE FORT OPENS FIRE.—THE GUNS OF THE
FORT SILENCED BY THE GUN-BOATS.—SAD HAVOC.—THE "RATTLER'S" HOT RECEPTION.
—THE BATTLE RENEWED AT DAYLIGHT.—THE GUNS OF THE FORT AGAIN SILENCED.—
SHERMAN STORMS THE FORT IN THE REAR.—THE ARMY MEETS WITH AN UNEXPECTED
RECEPTION.—THE FORT SURRENDERS.—THE HONOR OF THE DEFENDERS OF THE FORT
DIMMED.—HARROWING SCENES.—TERRIBLE LOSS OF LIFE.—McCLERNAND ON HAND.—
EXPEDITION UP THE WHITE RIVER.—ST. CHARLES DESERTED.—MUNITIONS OF WAR
CAPTURED.—GRANT ASSUMES COMMAND OF ALL THE FORCES.

THE expedition against Arkansas Post arrived at a point four miles below the enemy's works, January 10th, 1863.

The Army landed without delay at 10 A. M., and proceeded on their march to get in the rear of the enemy's works; but they had bad roads on which to travel and thick undergrowth to make their way through. Fifteen miles had to be marched over before the back of Arkansas Post could be reached, and the major part of the night was occupied in achieving their purpose. There were some extensive rifle-pits and works thrown up from which to operate with field pieces. These, as the Army started on their march, were manned and prepared to contest the advance, but the flag-ship "Black Hawk," Lieutenant-Commander Breese, and the "Rattler," Lieutenant-Commander Watson Smith, closed up on the enemy's works and drove them into the woods, so that the Army had no impediment in its way.

General McClernand had accompanied the expedition, it was supposed merely as a spectator, but about 3 o'clock, he rode up to the bank near which the gun-boats laid and informed Admiral Porter that Sherman was in position in the rear of the work, and waiting for the gun-boats to begin the attack on the fort. This could not very well be the case, but the gun-boats "Louisville," Lieutenant-Commander Owen, the "De

Kalb," Lieutenant-Commander Walker, and the "Cincinnati," Lieutenant-Commanding George Bache, were ordered to go up within 400 yards, while the smaller vessels were to follow and use their howitzers as circumstances would admit.

Arkansas Post was a large, well constructed fort built with the best engineering skill. It mounted thirteen guns: two ten-inch Columbiads, one nine-inch Dahlgren, and ten rifled guns of various calibres. The Columbiads were mounted in casemates covered in with four layers of heavy railroad iron, neatly fitted together to offer a smooth surface, and slanting iron roof to make the shot glance off. These were simply after the plan of the iron-clads afloat and were formidable structures.

The nine-inch gun was mounted in an embrasure protected by sand-bags, as were the ten rifled guns. All the guns except one bore down the river and on the vessels coming abreast of the forts. The fort itself was built close to the river; the front not being more than twenty yards from the bank.

There was nothing known to the military art that had been neglected in constructing these works, and to look at them one would suppose they could defy a naval force three times as strong as that now about to be brought against them.

As was afterwards learned, the Confederates supposed the gun-boats would attack

the works from a distance of 1200 yards, and
range buoys had been placed at that distance by which to regulate the enemy's fire,
and they had been practicing at that distance on targets so that the gunners would
become expert. But all these calculations
were upset by the "DeKalb" leading, and
the "Cincinnati" and Louisville" close
behind her, running up and taking position
close to the fort where the current was slack

LIEUT.-COMMANDER JOHN G. WALKER (NOW CAPTAIN)
U. S. NAVY.

and the vessels could maintain their places
without any difficulty; while the other vessels could take such positions in the river
as best suited and throw in shrapnel from
their small shell guns.

The fort opened on the iron-clads as soon
as they reached the range buoys—made
some good shots, and then lost their range,
during which time the gun-boats were
within 150 yards of them and firing accurately and steadily through their iron casemates, and committing sad havoc in the
rear amongst the soldiers. It was evident
from the first that this fort was doomed to
fall, under the fire of the gun-boats. The
superiority of their fire over that of the
guns in the fort was such that the latter
were silenced in the space of an hour, and
the gun-boats ceased firing. As darkness
was coming on and the smoke hung densely
over the river, the gun-boats dropped down
and tied up to the bank.

Just before the gun-boats dropped down
the tin-clad "Rattler" was ordered to run
past the fort and try to reach a point seven
miles up the river, and cut off the enemy's
troops in case they should attempt to es-

cape by that way, the only road open to
retreat by.

Lieutenant-Commander Smith performed
this duty handsomely as far as he could, but
after passing the fort he became entangled in
some piles the enemy had driven down, and
which were just awash, the enemy opened on
him while in this condition, and raked him
very effectually fore and aft, knocking his
cabins to pieces and doing a good deal of
damage to his hull, but as the iron-clads
opened their batteries again the firing from
the forts ceased, and the "Rattler" drifted
back out of the enemy's range.

In this attack, all the gun-boats were beautifully handled and not much injured; the
success of the afternoon gave good promise
for the morrow. The "Lexington," Lieutenant Commander Shirk, held a position
400 yards below the forts, and although
pretty well cut up had no casualties.

General McClernand's report that General
Sherman had arrived in the rear of the
works with his troops, might have led to ill
results, for the enemy might have escaped
that night with all his forces across the
ferry; but fortunately General Churchill,
the Confederate commander-in-chief, was

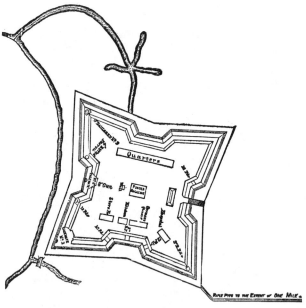

PLAN OF FORT HINDMAN OR ARKANSAS POST.

five miles away from the fort, waiting to
anticipate Sherman and attack him at a
disadvantage, and knew not how roughly
the forts were being handled by the gun-
boats; and Colonel Dunnington, the commander of the fort, (who had formerly been
a lieutenant in the U. S. Navy) being a brave
man and having a brave set of naval officers with him, did not consider himself as
worsted by a great deal.

For many hours the garrison worked with
great zeal to repair damages, and the heavy

strokes of their hammers on the iron covering could be heard all through the night.

At daylight, the enemy seemed prepared for action again, and this time General Sherman having sent a messenger to inform the admiral that he was in position and was gradually encircling the Confederate Army, the gun-boats were ordered to take position again not further than 50 yards from the fort and begin to fire as soon as they pleased.

The battle commenced and soon became very hot; when the tin-clads "Glide," Lieutenant-Commanding Woodworth, and "Rattler," Lieutenant-Commander Smith, and the ram "Monarch," Colonel Ellet, were ordered by the admiral to force their way through the obstructions above the forts, reach the ferry and cut off the enemy's retreat.

In a short time all the guns in the works were silenced and the flag-ship "Black Hawk" was run to the bank alongside the fort to board it with her crew; at the same

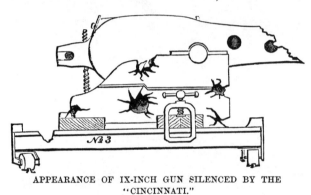

APPEARANCE OF IX-INCH GUN SILENCED BY THE "CINCINNATI."

time a messenger was sent to General Sherman informing him of the condition of affairs, and that if he would send a storming party from the rear, the Navy would board from the water side.

While waiting for Sherman's troops the "Black Hawk" laid alongside the fort, her high upper works on a level with the embrasures, while three boat-guns on wheels, on the upper deck, completely commanded the inside of the works, which presented a dreadful scene of killed and wounded. A large number of artillery horses had been kept in the fort for some reason, and the shells and shrapnel had made sad havoc with the dead and dying men, mixed up with the killed and wounded animals. It was a scene ever to be remembered.

In the meantime, while waiting for Sherman's assaulting party, all firing had ceased on both sides and the victorious sailors were quietly looking on at the dreadful havoc that had been made inside the works, not anticipating that the enemy would make any more resistance. Their

colors had been shot away and had not been hoisted again.

At one time the admiral determined to assault without waiting for the Army, but courtesy to the general required that the Navy should wait until the Army assaulting party should appear, which they did in a few minutes, then there was a simultaneous movement from all parts of the fort by the Confederates (who had been concealed behind or underneath the buildings that had been knocked down), and with muskets in their hands they rushed to the rear parapet and crouched down behind the works.

It was not known what this movement signified, the boat-guns on the flag-ship's upper deck (the flag-ship was a large river steamer unaltered), could have cut them to pieces, but there had been so much slaughter, the admiral would not fire on them, thinking they would throw down their arms as soon as Sherman's men got within twenty yards of them; but not so, for when our troops got within thirty or forty yards the Confederates rose together and poured in a withering volley from about 450 muskets, and nearly every bullet told.

Our soldiers staggered at this unexpected reception, stopped, and then retreated, while at the same moment there appeared a white handkerchief or white cloth held up by every one of the Confederate shooters.

The officers and men from the "Black Hawk" boarded the fort as the enemy fired their volley, when the latter all laid down their arms and surrendered; the commander and officers handing their swords to the admiral.

It was an embarrassing moment when the Federal troops were moving to the assault, and the enemy were waiting to receive them with bullets. The Navy could not fire without hitting the Federal troops, and the whole thing was so sudden and unexpected that the guns were not fired from the "Black Hawk."

It seems that the garrison of the fort belonged to the Confederate Navy and determined to surrender only to the U. S. Navy; yet they wanted to have a last blow at the soldiers, which they did; but it dimmed the honor they had won in so gallantly defending the fort; for there could be nothing gained by this act, their capture was too certain. They could not run away from the forts, for Sherman's army surrounded the entire Confederate force on the outside, including General Churchill and 6,000 troops, and the ferry was blockaded by the light gun-boats above—but these were some of the things the Confederates did which might properly have prevented them from receiving any quarter.

Besides the 6,000 men that surrendered to General Sherman, there were 500 left alive in the forts, and it was curious in looking over the list of prisoners to see added to the names, "Seaman," "Ordinary Seaman," "Coal-heaver," "Fireman," etc. These men were part of the crew and officers of the Confederate ram "Ponchartrain," built at Little Rock, Ark., and the guns in the fort had been intended to form the battery of that vessel, which was destroyed by the enemy on hearing of the capture of Fort Hindman (Arkansas Post).

General McClernand assumed all the direction of affairs on the surrender of the fort and the Confederate troops, and wrote the report of this affair, in which he gave fair credit to the Navy ; but he actually

at Little Rock, which could have caused the Federal Navy in the West a great deal of trouble, was ensured.

In the battle, everything went on so smoothly, there were no mistakes made, and the officers and seamen gained confidence in the gun-boats which they lacked before. But these had been much strengthened and improved since the battles of Forts Donelson and Henry, and had entire new guns on them instead of the inferior batteries they started out with ; moreover, the officers had learned that the way to fight these batteries was at close quarters.

Lieutenant-Commanders Walker, Owen, Bache, Shirk, Watson, Smith, Woodworth, Breese, and the commander of the "Monarch" were all handsomely mentioned by

CASEMATE NO. 1 DESTROYED BY THE U. S. GUN-BOAT "BARON DE KALB."

CASEMATE NO. 2 DESTROYED BY THE U. S. GUN-BOAT "LOUISVILLE."

APPEARANCE OF CASEMATES BEFORE THE ATTACK (COVERED WITH RAILROAD IRON).

REAR VIEW OF CASEMATE NO. 2.

had nothing to do with the management of the Army, and was down four miles below the forts during all the operations. Sherman was virtually the military commander. But from this time the Army was under McClernand's command, and after the prisoners were received and sent off in transports and the forts and guns demolished as far as could be done by the Army, the fleet and transports retraced their steps towards Vicksburg, and landed at Milliken's Bend or Young's Point about seven miles above Vicksburg.

The fight at Fort Hindman was one of the prettiest little affairs of the war, not so little either, for a very important post fell into our hands with 6,500 prisoners, and the destruction of a powerful ram

the admiral in his report to the Navy Department.

This battle gave general satisfaction to the public. It was unexpected and few knew where Fort Hindman was situated.

Directly after the capture of Fort Hindman, Lieutenant-Commander Walker in the "De Kalb," and Lieutenant-Commander George Bache in the "Cincinnati," were sent up the White River to capture the forts erected there by the Confederates, and General Gorman, U. S. A., accompanied the expedition with troops in the transports.

On the arrival of the expedition at St. Charles, the fort under construction was evacuated and the guns carried off in the steamer "Blue Wing," but these were recaptured at Duvall's Bluff, shipped in cars ready to be transported to Little Rock, the Confederates deserting the place. The railroad depot was destroyed by fire, all the rolling stock burned, and all the munitions of war placed on board the transports.

This was the last expedition necessary to send up the White River for some time. It remained open during the war excepting on several occasions when guerillas infested its banks. The Arkansas River also remained open; its difficult navigation offered no inducement for any one to seek adventures in its treacherous waters.

To show how carelessly the history of the war of the Rebellion has been written as regards the Navy, the following quotation from a military historian is inserted here:

"McClernand immediately acquiesced in Sherman's proposition and moved his force up the Arkansas, the fleet under Porter accompanying. A naval bombardment lasting several days occurred, and on the 11th the troops assaulted the works, when the Post surrendered after a fight of three hours, in which the squadron bore a conspicious part. McClernand [Sherman it should be] lost about 1,000 men in killed, wounded and missing. The guns of the fort were silenced by the fleet, and Admiral Porter received the sword of its commander.

General Grant did not approve of this movement on Arkansas Post when he first heard of it, as he thought it improper to divert the army from the original design to capture Vicksburg. He supposed the idea originated with General McClernand; but when he knew all the circumstances connected with the movement, and that the Army left Vicksburg because no longer able to operate owing to the floods, and that the troops wanted a success after their late discouraging defeat, he became reconciled to the attack on Arkansas Post, though it was a side movement and could in no way contribute to the final overthrow of Vicksburg.

Certain it is, the success at Arkansas Post had a most exhilarating effect on the troops, and they were a different set of men when they arrived at Milliken's Bend than they were when they left the Yazoo River.

After the troops were settled in their tents opposite Vicksburg, it became apparent that there could be no harmonious co-operation while McClernand remained in command of all the military forces. His peculiarities unfitted him for such a command, and these peculiarities became so offensive to Generals Sherman and McPherson, and to Admiral Porter, that they urged General Grant to take command himself as the only chance for the success of the enterprise, and in consequence, the latter hastened to Milliken's Bend or Young's Point and assumed the command of all the forces, which he was entitled to do, being military commander of the department.

MISSISSIPPI SQUADRON, JANUARY 1, 1863.

(Excepting some of the vessels engaged at Vicksburg.)

ACTING REAR-ADMIRAL DAVID D. PORTER, COMMANDER-IN-CHIEF.

RECEIVING-SHIP "CLARA DOLSON." (CAIRO.)

Lieutenant-Commander, Thomas Pattison, Acting-Assistant Surgeon, Emile Gavarret; Paymaster, Edward May; Acting-Master, John C. Bunner; Acting-Ensigns, E. C. Van Pelt and D. W. Tainter; Acting-Master's Mates, H. G. Masters and John D. Holmes; Acting-Engineer, Geo. W. Fulton; Acting-Carpenter, G. W. Armstrong.

STEAMER "EASTPORT."

Lieutenant-Commander, S. L. Phelps; Assistant Surgeon, Adrian Hudson; Acting-Assistant Paymaster, W. H. Gilman; Acting-Master, J. L. Avery; Acting-Ensign, R. M. Williams; Acting-Master's Mates, J. W. Litherbury and E. A. Decamp; Engineers: Acting-Chief, Henry Hartwig; Acting-Assistants, T. F. Ackerman, James Vanzant, G. W. Heisel and G. W. Aiken; Acting-Gunner, Reuben Applegate; Acting-Carpenter, James Kirkland.

STEAMER "LEXINGTON."

Lieutenant-Commander, James W. Shirk; Acting-Volunteer-Lieutenant, Martin Dunn; Acting-Assistant Surgeon, L. M. Reese; Assistant Paymaster, Geo. A. Lyon; Acting-Master, James Fitzpatrick; Acting-Ensigns, Sylvester Pool and James Marshall; Acting-Master's Mates, J. G. Magler, W. E. Anderson, F. O. Blake and S. S. Willett; Engineers: Acting-Chief, Wm. H. Meredith; Acting-Assistants, Michael Kelly, J. H. Hilliard, Wm. Bishop and Job Cummins.

IRON-CLAD STEAMER "BARON-DE-KALB."

Lieutenant-Commander, John G. Walker; Acting-Volunteer-Lieutenant, J. V. Johnston; Acting-Assistant Surgeon, John Wise; Acting-Assistant Paymaster, Wm. A. Mann; Acting-Masters, Chas. Kendrick and R. H. Medill; Acting-Ensign, Charles Hunter; Acting-Masters' Mates, H. H. Gorringe, E. D. Breed, F. E. Davis and J. M. Meacham; Engineers: Acting-Chief, Thomas Hebron; Acting-Assistants, J. L. Smith, J. S. Wilcoxen and Geo. Britton.

STEAMER "CONESTOGA."

Lieutenant-Commander, Thomas O. Selfridge; Assistant-Surgeon, J. Otis Burt; Acting-Assistant Paymaster, E. D. Ellsley; Acting-Master, George Hentig; Acting-Ensigns, Benj. Sebastian, James Kearney, Charles Pease and John Swaney; Acting-Master's Mates, S. J. Dwight, Henry Haskins, Thomas Devine and J. C. Petterson; Engineers: Acting-Chief, Thomas Cook, Alex. McGee, Michael Norton, James O'Neil and Andrew Lusk; Acting-Gunner, Gilbert Morton; Acting-Carpenter, J. J. Hays.

STEAMER "FAIRPLAY."

Lieutenant-Commander, Le Roy Fitch; Acting-Assistant Surgeon, S. D. Bolton; Acting-Master, Geo. J. Groves; Acting-Ensigns, J. C. Coyle and Thad. Conant; Acting-Master's Mates, W. C. Coulson, John Reville and Isaac Summons; Acting-Engineers, Robert Mahatha, G. S. Collins, Chas. Egster and Wm. Bell; Acting-Carpenter, Thomas Manning.

STEAMER "TAYLOR."

Lieutenant, James M. Prichett; Acting-Assistant Surgeon, G. W. Ballentine; Acting-Assistant Paymaster, C. A. Gardiner; Acting-Master, W. H. Minor; Acting-Ensigns, Eliphalet Loring, C. T. Stanton, J. F. Holmes and S. E. Brown; Acting-Master's Mates, Charles Ackley, H. S. Wetmore and Ira Athearn; Engineers: Acting-Chief, James Fleming; Acting Assistants, J. R. Ramsey, Wm. Furch and E. M. Bumpus; Acting-Carpenter, A. B. Chapman.

STEAMER "ROBB."

Acting-Volunteer-Lieutenant, Jason Goudy; Acting-Ensigns, Rob't Wilkinson, W. Stoneall and E. C. Roe; Acting-Master's Mates, Lloyd Thomas and E. F. Rowe; Acting-Engineers, Benj. Emerson and John Miller.

STEAMER "ST. CLAIR."

Acting-Volunteer-Lieutenant, J. S. Hurd; Acting-Assistant Surgeon, D. D. Winslow; Acting-Master, G. W. Fontly; Acting-Ensign, Jos. Watson; Acting-Master's Mates, H. A. Proctor, Jos. Hurd and E. C. Williams; Acting-Engineers, Wm. McLain, Edward Lozier and C. C. Hamilton.

STEAMER "BRILLIANT."

Acting-Volunteer-Lieutenant, Chas. G. Perkins; Acting Assistant Surgeon, W. W. Howard; Acting-Assistant Paymaster, Horace Talcott; Acting-Ensigns, J. B. Dales, George Munday and G. D. Little; Acting-Master's Mate, J. J. Perkins; Acting-Engineers, W. A. Willey, Samuel Ecoff and James Cutter.

RAM "LITTLE REBEL."

Acting-Volunteer-Lieutenant, Thomas B. Gregory; Acting-Ensign, N. T. Rennell; Acting-Master's Mate, J. S. Flint; Acting-Engineers, A. E. Giles, A. M. Smith and Robert Russell.

STEAMER "GREAT WESTERN."

Acting-Volunteer-Lieutenant, Wm. F. Hamilton; Acting-Assistant Paymaster, J. S. Harvey; Acting Master, J. C. Little; Acting-Ensign, Richard Ellis; Acting-Master's Mates, L. F. Knapp and Richard Mitchell; Acting-Chief Engineer, Chas. Christopher; Engineers, Jos. Goodwin, B. A. Farmer and G. S. Baker; Acting-Gunner, Robert Sherman; Acting-Carpenter, Jos. Morton.

STEAMER "JUDGE TORRENCE."

Acting-Volunteer-Lieutenant, J. F. Richardson; Acting-Ensign, Jeremiah Irwin; Acting-Master's Mate, James Ross; Acting-Chief Engineer, P. R. Hartwig; Engineers, J. Stough, J. C. Barr and W. Y. Sedman.

STEAMER "NEW ERA."

Acting-Master, F. W. Flammer; Acting-Assistant Paymaster, Wm. B. Purdy; Acting-Ensigns, Wm. C. Hanford and Geo. L. Smith; Acting-Master's Mates, G. E. Cheever, W. C. Renner, W. B. Shillits and Wm. Wharry; Acting-Engineers, Israel Marsh, John Darragh and Richard Fengler; Acting-Gunner, Louis Fredericks.

RECEIVING SHIP "NEW NATIONAL."

Acting-Masters, Alex. M. Grant and O. H. Pratt; Acting-Ensign, John Hill; Acting-Master's Mate, Wm. C. Herron; Acting-Engineers, W. H. Price, James Wilkins and C. C. Rensford.

STORESHIP "SOVEREIGN."

Acting-Master, Thomas Baldwin; Acting-Assistant Paymaster, Geo. L. Meade; Acting-Ensign, A. M. Rowland; Acting-Master's Mates, C. H. Gulick, T. J. Sheets and G. V. Meade; Acting-Engineers, T. W. Blair, A. L. Mann, Patrick Scanlon and Benj. Cainda.

MEDICAL STAFF.

Fleet Surgeon, Ninian Pinkney; Acting-Assistant Surgeons, G. H. Bixby and Geo. Hopkins.

STEAMER "GENERAL PILLOW."

Acting-Ensign, Joseph Moyer; Acting-Master's Mates, J. H. Rives and E. M. Woods; Acting-Engineers, Peter Wagner and Jos. J. Wagner.

INSPECTION SHIP "ABRAHAM."

Acting-Ensign Wm. Wagner; 1st Assistant-Engineer, E. Hozier,

STEAM-TUG "PANSY."

Acting-Ensign, Amos Bolander; Acting-Master's Mate, Anthony McCarthy: Acting-Engineers, John Gilliss and A. F. Gardiner.

STEAM-TUG "FERN."

Acting-Ensign Alpheus Semms; Acting-Master's Mate, John M. Kelly; Acting-Engineer, John Reed.

STEAM-TUG "MISTLETOE."

Acting-Ensign, W. H. H. Ford; Acting-Master's Mate, Hamilton Bateman; Acting-Engineers, W. F. Sandford and Silas Hasky.

STEAM-TUG "SAMSON."

Acting-Ensign, James D. Buckley; Acting-Master's Mate, Wilmot Duley; Acting-Engineers, Geo. Kimber and C. F. Yager.

STEAM-TUG "LILLY."

Acting-Ensign, Richard H. Smith; Acting Engineers, James Miller and J. C. Jones.

STEAM-TUG "MYRTLE."

Acting-Engineer, Thomas Guernsey.

NAVAL STATION AT CAIRO, ILL.

Commander, Alex. M. Pennock, Fleet-Captain; Paymaster, A. E. Watson, Inspector-in-charge; W. Brenton Boggs, Purchasing Paymaster and Navy Agent; E. W. Dunn, Paymaster attached to Squadron; A. H. Gilman, Paymaster attached to Station; Acting-Lieutenant, J. P. Sandford, Ordnance Officer; Acting-Chief-Engineer, W. D. Faulkner, Superintendent; Acting-Chief-Engineer, Samuel Bickerstaff, Superintendent of light draughts; Acting-Master John W. Atkinson, Superintendent of tugs; Acting-Ensign, Peter O'Kell, Executive-Officer; Acting-Ensign, A. H. Edson, and Gunner, John T. Ritter on Ordnance Duty.

MARINE OFFICERS.

Captain, Mathew R. Kintzing; 1st Lieutenants, Frank Munroe and S. H. Mathews; 2nd Lieutenant, Frank L. Church.

OFFICER AT NAVAL RENDEZVOUS, CINCINNATI.

Acting-Master, A. S. Brown.

OFFICERS AT NAVAL STATION, MEMPHIS.

Acting-Master, John R. Neild; Acting-Assistant Surgeon, Wm. P. Baird; Acting-Assistant Paymaster, J. H. Benton

CHAPTER XXVI.

SIEGE OF VICKSBURG.

Loss of the "Queen of the West," after Running the Vicksburg Batteries and Destroying a Great Deal of the Enemy's Property.—Running of the Batteries by the Iron-clad "Indianola."—Combat between the "Indianola" and Confederate Flotilla, consisting of the "Webb," "Queen of the West" and two Armed Transports.—Capture of the "Indianola" by the Confederates.—An Account Written by her Commanding Officer Lieut.-Commander George Brown.—Attempt to cut a Canal to Lake Providence.—Yazoo Pass Expedition by Gunboats and Transports.—Engagement with Fort Pemberton on the Tallahatchie River, etc.

THE siege of Vicksburg may be said to have commenced January 26th, 1862, on which day the Army was landed at Young's Point, seven miles above Vickburg, and at Milliken's Bend, two or three miles above Young's Point.

This was rather a desperate movement, but there was no other alternative. When Sherman first came down with the gunboats in company, he did not start out with the idea that he was to undertake a siege, but that Vicksburg was to be taken by an unexpected attack. Time was an important factor in this expedition, and that could not be lost by delaying for the purpose of collecting siege tools, etc. Therefore, when the Union Army landed above Vicksburg, it was deficient in all the many appliances for undertaking a siege. They had but four siege guns, and three were supplied by the Navy.

Their position opposite Vicksburg was such a poor one that a sudden rise of water would have drowned them out; and, worst of all, they had a leader in whom not an officer of the expedition could put any confidence. McClernand had come to supersede Sherman in the Yazoo River just after the troops had fallen back to the transports, and he had accompanied the Army to Arkansas Post, but with the express understanding with Admiral Porter that he would not interfere with General Sherman. This

he refrained from doing until the enemy was beaten, and at that moment he assumed command and made all the reports himself.

There were splendid generals in that Army, all men of the highest military acquirements, such as Sherman, McPherson, Steele and Smith, who now saw placed at their head an officer who had not only no qualifications for managing an Army of such a size, but had not the necessary knowledge to be the leader of anything more than a division under another general. These and many other considerations induced General Grant to take the command of the Army at Vicksburg himself. He had become convinced that the siege would be a long one, and made his preparations accordingly. He arrived in person at Young's Point on the 29th of January, 1863, and assumed command of the Army on the 30th. McClernand at once protested against this arrangement, but in vain, and thereafter was simply a divisional commander.

At this time the naval force at Vicksburg consisted of the following vessels : "Benton," "Cincinnati," "De Kalb," "Louisville," "Mound City," "Carondelet," "Pittsburg," and "Chillicothe," iron-clads; "Rattler," "Glide," "Linden," "Signal," "Romeo," "Juliet," "Forest Rose," and "Marmora," light-draughts; the "Taylor" and "Black Hawk," wooden armed steamers; "Queen of the West," "Monarch,"

"Switzerland," and "Lioness," rams; During the following month the "Lafayette" and "Indianola," iron-clads, joined the fleet. The carpenter shops, machine shops, provision boats, ordnance department, hospital, etc., (all on large steamers) were ordered to the mouth of the Yazoo; also ten of the mortar boats which had been used by Foote and Davis at Island No. 10 and Fort Pillow.

Besides these, there were a number of "tin-clads" with light batteries stationed all along the river from Cairo to Vicksburg, each vessel having its beat.

In this manner the Army transports were conveyed from one station to another, and the gun-boats performed this duty so efficiently that during the whole siege of seven months, the transportation of troops and stores was not interrupted. The guerillas along the bank were so handled by these small vessels, and so summarily dealt with, that they soon withdrew to other parts.

General Grant soon saw that Vicksburg could not be taken by the Army sitting down and looking at it from Young's Point. The wide and swift running Mississippi was between them. No force could land in front of the city with its long line of heavy batteries on the hills and at the water front, with 42,000 men in garrison under a very clever general (Pemberton), and Gen. J. E. Johnston with 40,000 more troops at Jackson (the capital of Mississippi), within easy distance of the besieged—if those may be so called who had ten times as much freedom and a hundred times more dry land to travel about on, than the besiegers.

There was no use attempting to attack the place on either flank. The attempt had been made by Sherman at Chickasaw Bayou without effect, and since then that point had been made doubly secure against invasion. The Federal Army could not cross the river below the town, for there were no transports on that side of the batteries, and it was then thought impossible to pass them.

General Banks at one time received orders to march up to Vicksburg and assist Grant, and so envelop the city, but for some reason this movement was delayed from time to time, and the latter had to depend upon his own resources.

Vicksburg and Port Hudson were both receiving large supplies *via* the Red River, and the first step necessary to be taken was to send a vessel (or vessels) to establish a blockade. This, it was thought, would hasten the evacuation of Port Hudson, and thus leave Banks at liberty to ascend the Mississippi in steamers.

On the 3d of February, 1863, the ram, "Queen of the West," Colonel Charles R.

Ellet, was selected to perform the perilous duty of running the batteries and carrying out Admiral Porter's orders. Ellet was a gallant young fellow, full of dash and enterprise, and was delighted with this opportunity to distinguish himself; and, although his vessel was a very frail one for such an enterprise, he did not hesitate to accept the risk when this duty was proposed to him.

The admiral depended a great deal on the darkness of the night to shield the vessel during the passage, and gave his orders accordingly. The "Queen of the West" started on her mission after midnight, but owing to the bad position of the wheel for manoeuvering, Ellet stopped on his way to shift it to a point from which he thought he could manoeuvre his vessel better, and lost so much time by the operation that the advantages of the darkness were lost. It was nearly daylight when he reached the first

ELLET'S STERN WHEEL "RAM."

battery, which he passed at full speed. The alarm gun was fired from the fort and in an instant the gunners of the lower batteries were at their posts, and when the "Queen" arrived abreast of the city battery after battery opened upon her. As it was supposed that Colonel Ellet would pass during the night-time, he had been ordered to ram a large steamer (the "Vicksburg") lying at the levee, and also to throw lighted tow balls on board of her to set her on fire. This could have been easily done at night, but it was almost certain destruction to attempt it in the day-time, but the gallant young fellow determined to carry out his orders at all hazards, rammed the vessel as directed and endeavored to set her on fire, but by this time the enemy's shot were rattling about him, and the current carrying him past the steamer, he was obliged to speed on.

This being the first vessel to run their batteries the Confederate gunners were nervous and did not at first get the proper range and many a screaming rifle shell went over Ellet's head, and passed harmlessly by. The steamer at the levee burst into flames but they were afterwards extinguished by the Confederates.

The "Queen of the West" had been well packed with cotton-bales to make her shot proof, but it did not make her shell proof, for at the moment she struck the "Vicksburg" and became stationary a shell from the enemy exploded in a cotton bale and in a moment the vessel was all ablaze. The flames spread rapidly and the dense smoke suffocated the engineers in the engine-room—so all attempts to ram the Vicksburg again were given up and the "Queen" turned her head down stream. Every one was set to work to extinguish the fire, which was done by cutting away the barricades and throwing the cotton overboard. The enemy of course were not idle but continued to pour their shot and shells into the Missis-

"THE QUEEN OF THE WEST."

(FROM A DRAWING BY REAR-ADMIRAL WALKE, MAY 15, 1862.)

sippi River without stint. The "Queen" was struck twelve times, twice just above the water line.

Ellet reached Red River and committed great havoc along the shore. He had been ordered to sink or destroy all steamers he might capture, and to blockade the river so closely that no provisions could get to Port Hudson or Vicksburg. Almost immediately on his arrival he captured and burned three large steamers loaded with army stores for Port Hudson. Five army officers were also captured.

Ellet then proceeded ten miles up the Red River where the enemy were known to have had a number of fine steamers engaged as army transports—but they all fled on hearing that a Federal gun-boat was approaching. Ellet got out of coal and took advantage of this panic to run up to Warrenton just below Vicksburg, to obtain a fresh supply and report progress.

He was again sent off to burn, sink and destroy or capture, and did good execution. He captured two steamers loaded with army stores for Port Hudson, and destroyed a wagon train returning from Shreveport: then the "Queen of the West" started up Red River but a treacherous pilot grounded her under the guns of a fort; the enemy opened upon her with four 32 pounders, every shot from which, struck her and killed or wounded many of the crew. At length a shot cut the steam pipe and the scalding steam amidst the wounded and dying made a never-to-be-forgotten scene. Every one who was able to do so jumped overboard to escape being scalded, and Ellet with what was left of his crew floated down the river on cotton-bales until he fell in with one of his prizes, the "New Era," when all got on board and made their escape up to the Federal landing below Vicksburg.

The Confederates soon repaired the "Queen of the West," manned her with a good crew of sharpshooters, and sent her in company with the "Webb," (another powerful ram) in pursuit of the "New Era."

The "Queen of the West" had been so successful it was determined (to make matters doubly sure) to send down an ironclad, and the "Indianola," with a bow battery of two 11-inch guns, was prepared to pass the batteries at night. She was commanded by Lieutenant-Commander George Brown, an officer whose gallantry and prudence had been well established. She carried a coal-barge on each side of her with orders to cut them adrift if she should meet the "Webb," and every precaution was taken to prevent her being captured in case she got into an action.

She passed the batteries in safety, but a few days after her departure two of her crew appeared and stated that she had fallen in with the rams "Queen of the West" and "Webb," in company; that she had been rammed six times and being in a sinking condition had surrendered. This was a great disappointment to the admiral and General Grant, but she was blown up next night by a Yankee ruse, and the Confederates did not benefit by her capture.

In justice to Lieutenant-Commander Brown, his account of this affair is inserted. It will show the kind of fighting that took place on the Mississippi, and the desperate character of the foe the Federals had to contend with.

WASHINGTON, D. C., May 28, 1863.

SIR—At this my earliest opportunity, I respectfully submit to the department a report of the operations of the U. S. steamer "Indianola," while below Vicksburg, Mississippi; also the particulars of the engagement with the rebel armed rams "Queen of the West" and "William H. Webb," and armed cotton-clad steamers "Dr. Batey" and "Grand Era," in which the "Indianola" was sunk and her officers and crew made prisoners.

In obedience to an order from Acting-Rear-Admiral Porter, commanding Mississippi squadron, I passed the batteries at Vicksburg and Warrenton on the night of the 13th of February last, having in tow two barges containing about 7,000 bushels of coal each, without being once struck, although eighteen shots were fired, all of which passed over us.

I kept on down the river, but owing to dense fogs made but slow progress until the morning of the 16th, when, about ten miles below Natchez, I met the steamboat "Era No. 5," having on board Colonel Ellet, of the ram fleet, and a portion of the officers and crew of the steamer "Queen of the West." I then learned for the first time of the loss of that boat, and after consulting with Colonel Ellet, I concluded to continue on down as far as the mouth of the Red River. On the afternoon of the same day I got under way, the "Era No. 5," leading. On nearing Ellis's Cliffs the "Era" made the pre-arranged signal of danger ahead, soon after which. I made out the rebel steamer "Webb."

Before I got within range of the "Webb" she had turned and was standing down stream with great speed. I fired two shots from the 11-inch guns but both fell short of her. She soon ran out

THE IRON CLAD "INDIANOLA."

of sight, and in consequence of a thick fog setting in I could not continue the chase but was obliged to anchor.

I reached the mouth of the Red River on the 17th of February, from which time until the 21st of the same month I maintained a strict blockade at that point.

I could procure no Red River pilots and therefore did not enter that river. The "Era No. 5," being unarmed, and having several prisoners on board, Colonel Ellet decided to go up the river and communicate with the squadron, and sailed at noon on the 18th of the same month for that purpose.

On learning that the "Queen of the West" had been repaired by the rebels, and was nearly ready for service, also that the "William H. Webb" and four cotton-clads, with boarding parties on board, were fitting out to attack the "Indianola," I left the Red River for the purpose of getting cotton to fill up the space between the casemate and wheel-houses so as to be better able to repel the boarding parties.

By the afternoon of the 22d of the same month, I had procured as much cotton as I required, and concluded to keep on up the river, thinking that I would certainly meet another boat the morning following, but I was disappointed.

I then concluded to communicate with the squadron as soon as possible, thinking that Colonel Ellet had not reached the squadron, or that Admiral Porter would expect me to return when I found that no other boat was sent below.

I kept the bunkers of the "Indianola" full of coal, and would have sunk what remained in the barges; but knowing that if another boat was sent below Vicksburg, I would be expected to supply her with coal, I concluded to hold on to the barges as long as possible.

In consequence of having the barges alongside we could make but slow progress against the current, the result of which was, that I did not reach Grand Gulf until the morning of the 24th, at which point and at others above we were fired on by parties on shore.

As I knew that it would be as much as I could do to get by the Warrenton batteries before daylight the next morning, I returned the fire of but one party.

At about 9.30 P. M. on the 24th, the night being very dark, four boats were discovered in chase of us. I immediately cleared for action, and as soon as all preparations had been completed I turned and stood down the river to meet them. At this time the leading vessel was about three miles below, the others following in close order. As we neared them I made them out to be the rams "Queen of the West" and "William H. Webb," and two other steamers, cotton-clad and filled with men.

The "Queen of the West" was the first to strike us, which she did after passing through the coal barge lashed to our port side, doing us no serious damage.

Next came the "Webb." I stood for her at full speed; both vessels came together bows on, with a tremendous crash, which knocked nearly every one down on board both vessels, doing no damage to us, while the "Webb's" bow was cut in at least eight feet, extending from about two feet above the water line to the keelson.

At this time the engagement became general and at very close quarters.

I devoted but little attention to the cotton-clad steamers, although they kept up a heavy fire with field-pieces and small arms as I knew that everything depended on my disabling the ram. The third blow crushed the starboard barge, leaving parts hanging by the lashings, which were speedily cut. The crew of the "Indianola," not numbering enough men to man both batteries, I kept the forward guns manned all the time, and fired them whenever I could get a shot at the rams. The night being very dark, our aim was very uncertain, and our fire proved less effective than I thought it at the time. The peep-holes in the pilot-house were so small that it would have been a difficult matter to have worked the vessel from that place in daylight, so that during the whole engagement the pilots were unable to aid me by their knowledge of the river as they were unable to see anything. Consequently they could do no more than obey such orders as they received from me in regard to working the engines and the helm. No misunderstanding occurred in the performance of that duty, and I was enabled to receive the first five blows from the rams forward of the wheels, and at such angles that they did no more damage than to start the plating where they struck.

The sixth blow we received was from the "Webb," which crushed in the starboard wheel, disabled the starboard rudder and started a number of leaks abaft the shaft. Being unable to work the starboard engine, placed us in an almost powerless condition; but I continued the fight until after we received the seventh blow, which was given us by the "Webb."

She struck us fair in the stern and started the timbers and starboard rudder-box so that the water poured in in large volumes. At this time I knew that the "Indianola" could be of no more service to us, and my desire was to render her useless to the enemy, which I did by keeping her in deep water, until there was two and a half feet of water over the floor, and the leaks were increasing rapidly as she settled, so as to bring the opening made by the "Webb" under water.

Knowing that if either of the rams struck us again in the stern, which they then had excellent opportunites of doing on account of our disabled condition, we would sink so suddenly that few if any lives would be saved, I succeeded in running her bows on shore by starting the screw engines. As further resistance could only result in a great loss of life on our part, without a corresponding result on the part of the enemy, I surrendered the "Indianola," a partially sunken vessel, fast filling with water, to a force of four vessels, mounting ten guns and manned by over one thousand men.

The engagement lasted one hour and twenty-seven minutes. I lost but one killed, one wounded and seven missing, while the enemy lost two officers and thirty-three men killed and many wounded.

Before the enemy could make any preparations for endeavoring to save the "Indianola," her stern was under water. Both rams were so very much crippled that I doubt whether they would have tried to ram again had not their last blow proved so fatal to us.

Both signal books were thrown into the river by me a few minutes before the surrender.

In conclusion, I would state that the 9-inch guns of the "Indianola" were thrown overboard, and the 11-inch guns damaged by being loaded with heavy charges and solid shot, placed muzzle to muzzle and fired by a slow match, so that they were rendered useless.

This was done in consequence of the sham monitor, sent from above, having grounded about two miles above the wreck of the "Indianola."

I have the honor to be, etc.,
GEORGE BROWN,
Lieut.-Commander U. S. Navy.
Hon. GIDEON WELLES.
Secretary of the Navy.

Other means had now to be invented to get into the rear of the enemy or down the river in order to stop his supplies.

The importance of this late move cannot be estimated. The communications between Texas and Vicksburg had been cut off, and the capture of so many steamers loaded with army stores for Port Hudson had sealed the fate of that place; they could not hold out, and Bank's Army would soon be free to march upon Vicksburg by the left shore of the river.

At this time Vicksburg mounted seventy-five heavy guns, and possessed a number of heavy rifled field-pieces, which, being able to move about, were quite as annoying to vessels running the blockade.

The guns at Vicksburg were so scattered about and so cunningly concealed that it was almost impossible to detect them. A clever plan was adopted by a naval photographer to bring all the guns to light. A large photograph of the city was taken, and that again enlarged, when by means of magnifying glasses, every gun was revealed. They were situated in many queer places; some inside the railroad depot, one in an engine house, others screened by carts tipped up, etc., etc.; but from

that time forth the Federal mortars and rifled guns sent their missiles to the right place.

Eight mortars on rafts were kept playing on the town and enemy's works day and night, and three heavy rifled guns that could reach any part of Vicksburg, were placed on scows to protect the mortars.

Vicksburg was by nature the strongest point on the river, but art had rendered it almost impregnable. It was very certain even in the early part of February, that this was to be a long and tiresome siege, and so General Grant viewed it.

A naval contingent could not do more than give protection to the Army, which was very important; but as to the vessels alone possessing the power to knock down these inaccessible forts, it was not to be thought of. If batteries should be placed on the right bank of the river, they would soon be driven out by the plunging shot and shells from the enemy.

The military engineers in Vicksburg had employed many expedients to render the Federal fire ineffectual. For a distance of six miles all their heavy guns were scattered except at two points where water batteries were placed to concentrate their fire upon passing vessels. One of these batteries mounted thirteen guns and the other eleven.

The fire of the Navy upon Vicksburg might in time have destroyed the city and its fine public buildings, but that would have brought the Army no nearer the desired object: the possession of this stronghold and the opening of the Mississippi.

When General Williams ascended the river in company with Farragut, with 3,000 men, he announced that this force was not sufficient to hold Vicksburg, even if he could capture it. In which opinion he was right. He set his troops to work to cut a canal across the isthmus, hoping to direct the waters of the Mississippi into this cut and make the river take a new direction, by which the city would have been left out in the cold; but the plan did not work as it had done in many other cases, and when General Williams departed he left only a dry ditch.

General Grant being anxious to get transports past Vicksburg, determined to try the ditch again, and had dredges brought down to work on it. It was hoped that when the river rose it would cut its way through, but that wished for event did not come to pass until after the fall of Vicksburg. The enemy mounted heavy guns opposite the mouth of the canal, and prevented any work upon it.

General Grant now hit upon a new expedient—which was to deepen Lake Providence. This Lake communicated with the

Tensas River (a deep stream), and the Tensas emptied into the Washita, and this latter into the Red River—thus forming a beautiful system of inland navigation which if properly opened and intelligently directed would have been of great service to the country bordering on the rivers mentioned. But it was not to be, the engineers were not successful. Several transports were taken in, but there were miles of forest to work through and trees to be cut down. The swift current drove the steamers against the trees and injured them so much that this plan had to be abandoned.

Then some one proposed to cut away the levee at a place called Delta near Helena and open Yazoo Pass. This used to be the main way to Yazoo City and to the Talla-hatchie and Yallabusha Rivers, before the Southern railroad was built, and it had been closed up to reclaim some millions of acres of land. It led into the Tallahatchie, and if our Navy could succeed in getting through it, a way would be opened for the Army to get into the rear of Vicksburg.

The levee was cut and the Mississippi being on the rise the water rushed through the opening with great force, sweeping everything before it and cutting a channel 200 yards wide at the mouth. It took several days for the water to reach its level, as it had at first a fall of nine feet.

In the mean time gun-boats were detailed and prepared for the expedition. These vessels were the "Chillicothe," Lieutenant-Commander Foster, the "Baron DeKalb," Lieutenant-Commander Walker, the tin-clad "Rattler," "Lioness" (ram) and two other light draft vessels. All were under the command of Lieutenant-Commander Watson Smith, who had instructions to open the way to the Yazoo River and destroy all of the enemy's means that could not be carried away. General Grant sent an Army contingent along with the gun-boats to assist in forcing the way through the obstructions. This force was com-manded by Brigadier-General Ross.

To describe the difficulties which attended this expedition would be impossible and they could only be realized by those who saw them. The pass had been closed for many years and trees had grown up in the middle of the channel which had become dry after the levee was built across its mouth. Great rafts were left in this dry channel as the water ran off and bushes and vines now grew thickly around them and tied them together as with withes. Overhanging trees joined together over the channel—and their branches were so low that steamers could not pass without having their smoke-pipes knocked down and all their boats and upper-works swept away.

The current was running swiftly, for the vessels entered the cut before the water had reached its level. On the first day, not more than six miles was made, and this was only accomplished by all hands going to work and sawing or cutting away the obstructions.

Colonel Wilson, an Army engineer, who directed all this kind of work, was a thoughtful, energetic man, and he con-ducted the operations in an intelligent man-ner, and though the vessels did not make very rapid headway, they did wonderfully well considering the difficulties. They all had to be carefully handled with hawsers around the bends, for the Yazoo Pass, fol-lowing the example of the mother Missis-sippi, was as crooked as a ram's horn.

On the second day, the vessels were so torn to pieces that no more harm could be done to them—they had hulls and engines left and that had to suffice. The officers and men performed a great deal of manual

U. S. NAVAL HOSPITAL BOAT "RED ROVER" PASSING

RANDOLPH NEAR FULTON, TENN.

(FROM A SKETCH BY REAR-ADMIRAL WALKE.)

labor, but no one found fault, and their jolly songs echoed turough the woods as they worked, frightening the birds out of their quiet retreats, where they had rested undisturbed for a quarter of a century.

The men were rewarded after four days' of terrible labor by getting forty miles on their journey through such obstructions as they had never dreamed of. At last they arrived at the Tallahatchie (a clear and swift running river), and the vessels form-ing in some kind of order, with the gun-boats leading, hastened on. Much time had been lost at Helena in getting the troops on board the transports, and the pass was not entered until the 8th of March, and not passed until the 11th; then, when every-one thought the way clear before them, they suddenly came upon a formidable fort, with a large steamer sunk in the mid-dle of the channel to obstruct the passage of the Federal fleet. Here was a surprise to all parties. The Confederates did not expect to see iron-clads in these waters, nor the Federals to find forts where the contrabands had reported the way clear before them.

Fortunately the people in the fort had not yet removed the powder from the steamer, and the transports had time to back up the stream and take position behind the woods in a bend, and there make their preparations for attack. The "Chillicothe," Lieutenant-Commander Foster, and the "DeKalb," Lieutenant-Commander Walker, took position, side by side, tied up to the bank with bows down, and began the action with a mortar boat that had accompanied the expedition, in the rear.

At this time, unfortunately, Lieutenant-Commander Watson Smith gave evidence of aberration of mind, and much hampered Foster and Walker by contradictory orders which they felt bound to obey.

The "Chillicothe" was temporarily disabled by having her port shutter closed by a shot from the fort, which returned the fire of the gun-boats as soon as the Confederates got their powder from the steamer; and when they did get to work they kept up a rapid and well directed fire. In obedience to the order of Lieutenant-Commander Smith, the two iron-clads had to withdraw from action, and this was put down as a reconnaissance.

In the afternoon of the same day, the "Chillicothe" went down and attacked the fort at close quarters, but got the worst of it. She proved herself to be a poor vessel for resisting shot. During the afternoon fight she lost four men killed and fifteen wounded.

On the 13th, the two iron-clads again went into action, lying alongside of each other as before. The "Chillicothe" remained in action one hour and thirty-eight minutes, and then had to withdraw for want of ammunition, besides being much cut up by the enemy. The "DeKalb" remained in position and finally silenced the Confederate battery, after losing but three killed and three wounded.

The only way this fort could be taken was by siege guns brought up close to the works; but this was not done. The general commanding the military contingent did not consider himself strong enough to attempt anything of consequence, and after a delay of thirteen days, in which neither side did anything, the Federal forces withdrew.

The Navy did all that was required of it on this occasion, but there was no hearty co-operation on the part of the Army. Fort Pemberton, though well fortified and in a strong position, ought to have been taken. This would have given the Federals command of the Tallahatchie, Yallabusha and Yazoo Rivers, and of course a clear way to the rear of Vicksburg.

On the 18th of March, Lieutenant-Commander Watson Smith, owing to aberration of mind, gave up the command of the Naval force to Lieutenant-Commander Foster, who after trying all that could be thought of, followed the Army which had been ordered to retire from before Fort Pemberton.

A great deal of cotton was taken by this expedition, but the result was a failure in the main object. The enemy burned two large steamers loaded with cotton, or they were set on fire by the shells of the gunboats.

The Confederates had a narrow escape here, and had it not been for the delay in embarking the troops at Helena the Federals would have been successful. As soon as the Confederates discovered the object of this movement (which they did as soon as the levee was cut at Delta) they went to work and built the two formidable forts, Pemberton and Greenwood on the Tallahatchie and Yallabusha, and blocked the way effectually.

General Pemberton showed a great deal of ability in his defense of Vicksburg, all through, and won the respect of his opponents by his zeal and fidelity to his cause, to say nothing of his spirit of endurance. But in nothing did he show more energy than in watching the Federal tactics, and guarding against all attempts made to turn his flanks, especially by way of the streams which would have commanded the approaches to Vicksburg if held by an enemy.

Pemberton took care that these passes should never be left unguarded in the future. These attempts to turn his flanks sharpened his wits and set them to work in other directions to make Vicksburg stronger than ever.

The vessels which composed the expedition through Yazoo Pass, worked their way back by the route they had entered. The zeal they exhibited in getting in had all left them, their vessels were much injured and their labors seemed interminable. It was a happy day to all when they found themselves on the wide Mississippi, which seemed to the explorers like an ocean in comparison with the small and tortuous streams over which they had been fighting their way.

The shot and shell of the enemy were nothing compared to the manual labor of soldiers and sailors in removing obstructions which to many seemed insurmountable. Yet all alike were these difficulties to be overcome in getting into Vicksburg, and this was only one in a number of cases where the energy and courage of our Army and Navy were taxed to the utmost.

In reading over some of the Western

papers of those days one would suppose that the two branches of the service were sitting down quietly before Vicksburg, watching the daily performances of the besieged without making any efforts to get inside the city, while, in fact, from the general down, there was but one feeling,—a total disregard of personal comfort and a stern determination to capture Vicksburg at any cost.

Disappointment after disappointment was met with a stern philosophy which showed that the word "fail" was not understood in that Army and Navy. Whenever our soldiers and sailors laid aside their work for a short time to rest, it was the signal for renewed libelous newspaper attacks upon their commanders, but these articles were read by our men with the same feeling of contempt which has been felt in later times by those who have wasted life and health in saving the unity of this great country for millions yet unborn, whom, it is hoped, will feel more grateful than their forefathers.

CHAPTER XXVII.

EXPEDITION THROUGH STEELE'S BAYOU AND DEER CREEK.

THE NAVAL EXPEDITION THROUGH THE WOODS.—SCENES AND INCIDENTS.—THROUGH BLACK AND STEELE'S BAYOU.—A HAZARDOUS JOURNEY.—DESTRUCTION OF COTTON AND OTHER PROPERTY BY THE CONFEDERATES.—A SKIRMISH WITH TREE CUTTERS.—SHERMAN MARCHING TO THE RELIEF OF THE GUN-BOATS.—DREADFUL WORK OF THE SHARP-SHOOTERS.—THE CONFEDERATES ATTEMPT TO CAPTURE THE FLEET.—SHERMAN ARRIVES.—REPULSE OF THE CONFEDERATES.—RETREAT OF THE ARMY AND NAVY.—REPAIRING DAMAGES.—GOOD EFFECT OF THE EXPEDITION.—LOSS TO THE CONFEDERATES.—GRAND GULF FORTIFIED.—A COUNCIL OF WAR.—GRANT'S DECISION.—THE RAMS RUN THE BATTERIES —THE "LANCASTER" SUNK.—THE "SWITZERLAND" JOINS FARRAGUT.—BRAVE VOLUNTEERS, ETC., ETC.

ABOUT the time of the Yazoo Pass expedition, Lieutenant McLeod Murphy, U. S. N., discovered a pass through the woods some ten miles above the mouth of the Yazoo, by which it was thought the gun-boats could reach the valley of Deer Creek, and, perhaps get into the Yazoo River by the Sunflower and Yallabusha, thereby reaching the rear of Vicksburg. The water in the Mississippi had risen remarkably, so much so that land usually dry for miles in the interior, now had seventeen feet of water over it. The question was, could the gun-boats get through the woods and thick underbrush which abounded in that locality. The route was examined by General Grant and Admiral Porter, and being found apparently practicable for the purpose intended, it was determined between the Army and Naval leaders that an attempt should be made to get to the rear of Vicksburg in this way.

So important was this route considered that Admiral Porter determined to go himself in charge of the naval part of the expedition, while General Sherman was to lead an army contingent of 8,000 or 10,000 men. A man who knew all about the country, and who gave his opinion that this was a favorable opportunity to get into the desired position in rear of the beleagured city, was employed to accompany the expedi-

tion as pilot; and at the start everything promised well.

On the 14th of March, Admiral Porter started with the following vessels: "Cincinnati," Lieutenant-Commanding Bache; "Louisville," Lieutenant - Commander Owens; "Carondelet," Lieutenant-Commanding Murphy; "Mound City," Lieutenant-Commanding Byron Wilson; "Pittsburgh," Lieutenant-Commanding Hoel; two mortar floats and four tugs.

When the fleet came to the pass into which it was to turn, after having ascended the Yazoo, the entrance could scarcely be made out, so dense was the growth of the overhanging bushes and trees, but these the men cut away with cutlasses and axes, and a pass wide enough for three vessels abreast, showed itself, lined out by heavy trees, and through this the gun-boats followed one another in line, their leadsmen singing out in melodious song, "quarter less three." There was no more channel here than elsewhere, as the water overflowed every place alike, but there was a long, straight pass opening through the forest, about 170 feet wide, which was, no doubt, a road cut through the woods for hauling cotton to some landing.

It was a novel scene. Thousands of crows flew from their perches, and broke the silence of the forest with their discordant notes, no doubt wondering what could have caused those great "mud-turtles" to invade their hitherto inaccessible abode, where for centuries they had reared their young and digested their plunder without interruption.

On went the gun-boats, officers and sailors alike, delighted with the romantic scenery, which baffled description; every heart was cheered with the hope that the long sought for road to Vicksburg had been found, and that the great prize would soon be in their hands. Now and then, a stray tree as much as three feet in diameter would be found standing in the middle of the channel as if to dispute the way. The vessels might have passed on either side, but the desire to try the strength of these outlying sentinels proved so great that the flagship "Cincinnati" would run into them with her strong, broad bow, and topple them over, a feat rendered possible by the softening action of the water upon the earth about their roots. The vessels in the rear were told to haul them out of the way. This was good practice, and came into play before the expedition had proceeded many miles. It was all fair sailing at first, but became rough work in the end.

After some ten miles of easy progress through the woods, the fleet arrived at Black Bayou, a place about four miles long, leading into Deer Creek—and here the plain sailing ended. The gun-boats, being too wide to pass between the trees, had to go to work and knock them down, and pull them up by the roots. The line of vessels was broken, and each went to work to make her way through the tangle as best she could. Saws and axes now came into use, and every means was resorted to for clearing the way. The narrow tugs and the mortar floats had no difficulty in getting along, but the wider iron-clads were, for a time, brought to a stand. The open roadway had vanished, and the pilot confessed his ignorance of this locality. There was plenty of water, and the stentorian voice of the leadsman was still heard singing out "quarter less three!"

There is nothing that will daunt the American sailor but a lee shore and no sea room. There was plenty of sea room here, but no room to pass between the tangle. The obstruction was passed, after working twenty-four hours consecutively, and that four miles overcome, leaving a good road for those coming after, but a number of trees were moved away, Titans of the forest that had reigned there for a century or more.

Sherman had arrived at Black Bayou with part of his force, another part had started to march over from a point twenty miles above the Yazoo River, on the Mississippi, following a ridge of land not inundated. The part of the Army embarked had been transported in small stern-wheel steamers, which being very narrow, succeeded in passing between the trees with only the loss of a few smoke-stacks. From Black Bayou, the gun-boats turned again into Steele's Bayou, a channel just one foot wider than the vessels, and here came the tug of war, such as no vessels ever encountered before. The keel of the skiff was the largest thing that had ever floated in waters now bearing vessels of 600 tons burthen. These had to break through bridges spanning this muddy ditch, pass through the smoke and fire of burning cotton-bales (which the enemy set in a blaze as soon as the fleet was discovered), and work on, at the rate of half a mile an hour, through lithe willows growing in the middle of the stream, which at intervals was choked up with rafts that had been there for years. The pilot proved to be a fraud, he had never seen the place before.

This bayou was bordered on both sides with overhanging trees, whose Briarean arms would cling around the passing vessels and sweep away boats and smoke-stacks, while the limbs of decayed trees would fall upon the decks, smashing skylights to pieces, and injuring the people.

It was dreadful to witness the infatuation of the Confederate Government agents, who, riding about on horseback, were setting fire to the cotton far and near. They must have imagined the expedition sent to gather cotton—a purpose never thought of.

Houses were often consumed with the cotton piles, and everything betokened a Moscow affair. It was the cotton of the Confederate government, and they were allowed to burn it. It was the Confederate sinews of war they were destroying; they were burning up their cash with which they had expected to carry on the struggle.

The leaders of the expedition soon saw they were discovered; the move was certainly known in Vicksburg, and the whole Confederacy would be at work to defeat this measure, as they had at Fort Pemberton. The expedition hurried on to get into the Rolling Fork, and thence into the Sunflower, whence it could reach the Yazoo above Haines' Bluff. It seemed insane to proceed, there were so many dreadful obstacles in the way, yet no one apparently minded them. The work was hard on the sailors, nevertheless they only made a lark of it.

Vicksburg was never so aroused as on hearing of the raid right into the heart of her preserves. The expedition had struck that city's store-house: here were the flesh-pots that would make any people glad; cattle, corn, "hog and hominy" enough to subsist a great Army.

The government agents assembled in

numbers, they seemed to spring from the earth: the cattle, pigs and poultry were all driven to the woods. Corn ricks were set on fire that the Federals might not have a grain. The latter were not thinking of the flesh-pots, they were too intent upon getting to the rear of Vicksburg, too intent upon clearing out the obstructions in the muddy Bayou to think of "hog and hominy."

In the first twenty-four hours of this work, the fleet made four miles! At dark it tied up for the night that the hard worked men might rest, but there was no rest for any one there. At ten o'clock that night, lights were flitting about in the woods, and the sounds of wood chopping fell upon the ears of the watchers in the fleet, and the falling of trees satisfied them that the enemy was on the alert, cutting down trees across their path to pen in the gun-boats.

Armed landing parties were made up from each vessel, and put ashore; a tug, with a boat howitzer mounted on board, was sent up the bayou, and found two trees, two and a half feet in diameter each, cut down and lying across the stream, completely obstructing it. The tug fired after the tree cutters, and the landing party of 300 men, under Lieutenant McLeod Murphy, worked all night with axes and tackles to remove the fallen timber. The fleet moved on at night, the banks being lighted by lanterns. They were determined not to be detained by tree cutters. The tug went ahead for twelve miles, firing her gun wherever a white man and an axe could be heard of.

Twenty-five trees had been commenced upon by the cutters, but the latter were driven off by the howitzer. It was found that a large gang of negroes had been pressed into service by the Confederate agents who, with pistols at their heads, compelled them to cut the trees; but when the shrapnel from the howitzer began to rattle through the woods, government agents, woodcutters and all, left in a panic.

Slowly as the naval vessels moved, they made greater progress than the troops, and got ahead of them some twenty miles; the troops met difficulties they were not prepared for, and the fleet moved on in advance. After four days of the greatest labor one can imagine, the fleet arrived at or near the entrance to the Rolling Fork, where it was supposed all difficulties would be at an end. Here, for a distance of 600 yards, a bed of willows blocked the way. The flag-ship "Cincinnati," ran into it under a full head of steam, and there she stuck; the willow wythes caught in the rough iron of her overhang, and held her as if in a vise. All the arts of seamanship could not displace this obstacle, it would have taken weeks to remove the willows.

After working a whole day and night with saws, chisels and cutlasses, the men stopped for a breathing spell, during which a steamer landed at the bank, four miles off on the Rolling Fork. Another soon came higher up, and both landed artillery, which, in two hours, opened a cross fire on the fleet with about twenty shells a minute, driving the men on the banks to seek the shelter of the iron-clads. The mortars were brought to bear on the enemy, and for a time, checked the fire. Spy-glasses, used from the top of an Indian mound—disclosed the fact that the enemy were landing a large force of infantry—the guns of the iron-clads were so far below the banks of the bayou that they were not a particle of use, the vessels themselves were so jammed up against the bank on either side that there was danger of their crews being kept prisoners on board by sharpshooters. Sherman's troops were not in sight and it became necessary to send back a messenger to the general urging him to hurry up to the assistance of the gun-boats, which were very helpless at one time.

The united efforts of the steamers astern of the "Cincinnati" pulled her out of the willows, but not without great trouble, the people on deck and on the banks being exposed to the artillery which kept up a sharp fire.

There was but one thing to be done under the circumstances, and that was to fall back and meet the Army, which the admiral received assurances was moving on as fast as possible. As soon as Sherman received the dispatch announcing the condition of the gun-boats, he started off his troops, though it was night, and made his way along the tortuous route by the light of pine knots. He got into swamps and cane brakes, and made but slow progress. This did not prove to any one the fair road to Vicksburg. The soldiers were as severely tried as the sailors.

As night came on, the gun-boats were ordered to unship their rudders, and drop down with the current; and, the water now running rapidly into the bayou, owing to the cut at Delta—which was overflowing the whole country—the vessels bumped along at double the rate they had ascended, bounding from tree to tree, and bringing down the dead branches on the decks, to the destruction of everything around— boats were smashed, and more or less injury done to everything.

As the gun-boats departed, the enemy appeared upon the Indian mound, and owing to the tortuous windings of the stream, kept the fleet under fire without the latter being able to fire more than an occasional gun until nightfall, when it was found necessary to tie up. A watch of armed men and all the howitzers were put ashore in preparation for emergencies.

In the night the patrolling parties captured two of the enemy's officers and some men, who stated that two batteries had been landed, and three thousand sharpshooters, and that they were quite satisfied they would capture the gun-boats in twenty-four hours. They were not aware that an army was with the fleet; they took this for a raid of gun-boats only, and, as one of them remarked, "a crazy one at that."

At daylight the fleet started down stream again, stern foremost, hoping to meet the army by noon, but at 8 A. M., they were surrounded by sharpshooters, who kept up such a fire that it was almost impossible for any one to show himself on deck. The riflemen on board, lying behind defences, kept up a brisk fire whenever they saw a curl of smoke. The howitzers were kept at work from behind the deck-houses, and the mortars, which were fired with small charges, landed their shells in amongst the enemy, and kept them at a distance. Now and then a mortar shell, landing at the foot of a tree behind which was a sharpshooter, would overthrow the tree as it exploded—making trees unsafe as a protection. Still, the sharpshooters increased in numbers, when, suddenly, the fleet had to come to a stand. Eight or ten large trees, some three feet in diameter, had been felled right across their track, from either side of the bayou, thus completely blocking the way, and the loud cheers of the Confederates as they rang through the woods showed they thought their prey entrapped.

The officers and men of the fleet, undaunted by this state of things, went to work to surmount the difficulty and remove the trees. Five hundred armed men were put on shore, and took to the trees to meet the enemy's sharpshooters, while howitzers and mortars kept up a rapid fire which was more than the enemy cared to face.

The working party from the vessels commenced operations below the banks, out of reach of the enemy's fire, and by using hawsers, tackles, and that powerful adjunct, steam, in six hours the trees were all removed, and the fleet went on its way down rejoicing.

Sherman had heard the firing, and had pushed on to get to the aid of the gun-boats. In the meantime, the enemy had landed more infantry—there were about four thousand in all. Pemberton, at Vicksburg, was well posted in all that was going on, and was determined to leave nothing undone to capture the venturesome fleet.

Again the fleet came to a stand-still, but this time only two large trees had been felled. The crews of the vessels commenced the work of removal, when a large body of Confederate troops were seen advancing directly through the woods upon the steamers. while the sharpshooters in redoubled numbers opened fire on the fleet from behind trees not more than fifty yards distant.

The working parties were called on board to defend the vessels, but before they could get to their arms, there was a rattle of musketry in the woods, a cheering of the crews, and a rapid retreat by the Confederates. They had fallen in with the head of Sherman's column, which was a great surprise to them, and after one or two volleys, they broke and fled back to their steamers. Sherman arrived just in the nick of time. Whether the gun-boats could have held their own under the circumstances is impossible to say. They were well prepared for a brave fight, and from behind the banks they could have mown down the enemy as they rushed on, but it was better as it was, and they were not subjected to the trial.

The broadside guns of the vessels had been given their greatest elevation, and loaded with grape and cannister. The iron sides of the vessels had all been well greased, and nothing was left for assailants to hold on by. Fourteen hundred good men, with breech-loaders and howitzers, were ready to repel boarders, but there is no knowing what a desperate set of men under good leaders might have accomplished, with such a prize in view as the best vessels of the Mississippi squadron. No set of people were ever so glad to see the soldiers as the men of that fleet were to see Sherman and his Army; and, as the gallant general rode up to the gun-boats, he was received with the warmest cheers he ever had in his life.

That was the end of the Steele's Bayou expedition; the impossibility of going on again in the face of all the difficulties was conceded by all parties, and it was decided to get the fleet out of that ditch before the enemy blocked up the entrance in the rear and left it in the mud.

The impracticability of the campaign had been fully demonstrated. So much time had been consumed by the numerous obstacles the Army and Navy had to contend with that the enemy had the opportunity to produce the means of checkmating the expedition.

The point where the gun-boats would have to leave Steele's Bayou to get into the Rolling Fork was so blocked up that it would take many days to remove the obstacles, and the Confederates could throw in such a force as would prevent their opponents from working at it.

The enemy had clear, open rivers to work in; and, in two days, could transport any number of troops and guns they desired. The country would not answer for a base of operations, so the Union forces returned to the woods and deep water, having gained a great deal of experience, and the knowledge that Vicksburg could not be taken in that direction.

This expedition greatly alarmed the Vicksburg people: the Army and Navy had thereby found the way right into the store-house from which the besieged had been fed, and upon which they depended in the future.

This greatly changed their system of defence; guns were removed from prominent points along the Mississippi, while the rivers Tallahatchie, Sunflower and Yazoo were strongly fortified, and were guarded against any attack in the future. Every precaution was likewise taken to protect the flanks of the city, but the soldiers and sailors reveled in all the good things which abounded in this district, and thinking there was vastly more food there than the Confederates could possibly want, the gun-boats and transports carried off an astonishing amount of loot, which reconciled them in a measure for their disappointment in not fully succeeding in their attempt to reach the rear of Vicksburg.

The Navy carried away over a hundred thousand dollars' worth of cotton, marked "C. S. A.," which the Confederates had collected for the use of their government, only waiting for the opportunity to carry it to the sea-board. Over three hundred thousand dollars' worth of cotton was destroyed by fire, by command of Confederate agents, who determined that it should not fall into the hands of the Federals. This was all a great loss to the enemy, but unimportant in comparison with what the combined forces had hoped to attain.

When it was decided that no more could be done on this expedition, the Army returned to their transports, and the Navy led the way out of the woods, the men at the leads singing out "quarter less three," in cheery tones, as if everything had gone on smoothly with them, and the gun-boats had not been almost smashed to pieces while rebounding from tree to tree in Steele's Bayou.

On the 26th of March, the fleet arrived at its old anchorage on the Yazoo. All the machinists, carpenters, boatbuilders, etc., from the shops afloat were set to work to repair damages, and in a week, with the finishing touch of a new coat of paint, they looked as good as new.

This expedition, though in a measure unsuccessful, still had a good effect on the Army and Navy. While the men were kept so employed on what were really very exciting expeditions, they had no time to become disheartened by only looking at the frowning hills of Vicksburg, which they, as well as the officers, could see were not to be taken in front. It inured both services to hard work which would the better enable them to overcome like obstacles in the future ; the constant employment hardened their bodies, while it benefited their minds, and kept them in good spirits. They gained a thorough knowledge of the difficulties they had to encounter, and all this prepared them to battle with others of the same kind.

These persistent attempts of the Army and Navy to overcome all the obstacles in the way of getting into Vicksburg, kept the enemy continually on the alert, and obliged them to be moving through a country filled with all kinds of obstacles, and made them doubtful where the blow would fall. On this account, Pemberton had to reduce his Army in the city, and keep a larger portion of it at points remote from the real objective point at which the Union general aimed.

The Confederate soldiers were worn out and dispirited by the numerous marches and countermarches they were obliged to make. They were compelled to live upon the country when they went to expel the invaders, and this soon exhausted the stores in the invaded district on which the people in Vicksburg depended when the hardest time should come. Besides the Confederates were raiders even among their own people. The Union soldiers did pay a little respect to private property, but the former paid no such compliment to anything that could add to their comfort, or fill their commissariat ; and, on the whole, the Federal invaders were more acceptable to the people on the estates than were the Confederates.

In this invasion, the Army and Navy both inflicted serious losses on the owners of slaves, and large numbers of the latter went off either in the transports or on the gun-boats. The negroes stated that they had been employed in working on the fortifications at Vicksburg, Haines' Bluff, etc., and the fact that they had been employed to cut down the trees on Steele's Bayou, thereby to hem in the gun-boats, was a good reason for taking them away. The last and best reason was that the undeniable right of freedom was theirs, and it was the duty of every Christian officer and man to help them escape from the most miserable slavery that ever existed in any part of the world.

General Grant, though disappointed in the result of this last expedition, was not discouraged He saw that this was the last attempt that could be made in this direction, and turned his attention to other ways, believing, with the Duke of Marlborough, that though all trials might fail, there was always one way left to get into a fortified city.

So evident was it to the Confederates that in both the Yazoo Pass and the Steele's Bayou expedition they had left the northern flank of Vicksburg unprotected, that they removed the depot at once. Not only that, though there was no apparent necessity for it, they went to work to strengthen their left flank also, as far down the river as Grand Gulf, thinking, perhaps, that the gun-boats might pass the batteries at Vicksburg, pass up the Black River, and gain the rear of the besieged city by arriving at Jackson, the capital of Mississippi—a thing much more easily done than getting through Steele's Bayou.

Whether they were influenced by these ideas or not, they proceeded at once to fortify Grand Gulf in such a manner that no vessel could pass up Black River, and with hope that the forts would be strong enough to prevent vessels of war from passing up and down the Mississippi itself. While the Confederates were considering these matters, Admiral Farragut arrived in the "Hartford," just below Warrenton, in pursuit of coal and provisions. This was after his passage of the Port Hudson batteries. From him Grant obtained information of affairs at the latter place, and the little probability there was of General Banks making the Confederates evacuate it.

On hearing this, General Grant thought of sending an army corps to co-operate with Banks, get possession of the works at Port Hudson, and then bring all Banks' forces to operate against Vicksburg. But this idea did not exist long, the general coming to this opinion through the fact that the water had overflowed everything about the upper part of Vicksburg, and dry land could only be found on the heights. There was no foot-hold for an army, and Grant thought a better chance of turning Vicksburg might be found below, between Warrenton and Grand Gulf.

Having consulted with Admiral Porter regarding the possibility of passing the batteries at Vicksburg with a sufficient force —a point on which his mind was made easy —he called a council of war, at which all the divisional commanders, except Sherman and McClernand, were present.

The plan proposed to the council was to send the gun-boats below Vicksburg with a sufficient number of transports, well packed with cotton—to protect their boilers and machinery—to march the Army over to Carthage, and thence transport it to the Vicksburg side, as circumstances warranted.

This proposition was respectfully but strongly opposed by all the generals present. Sherman sent his objections—which

were good ones—in writing; and McClernand, to whom Grant had spoken on the subject, wrote a letter, and proposed the plan of going below, as originating with himself, which was a habit this general had when anything of importance was about to be undertaken.

This plan of Grant's seemed to those around him to be full of danger, and they left no eloquence untried to persuade him not to undertake a move threatening so much peril to his Army. They urged that to move his Army below Vicksburg was to cut himself off from his base of supplies at the North, to cut his own communications, and do exactly what his enemies most desired him to do: to place himself in a position, where, if defeated, the defeat would be overwhelming. The inundated state of the country was pointed out to him, and the difficulty of moving an Army and supplies over such roads as there were. Some of the most accomplished soldiers in his Army, men who had won their way to fame, urged him, with all the power of eloquence, not to undertake the rash movement. Grant listened to them respectfully, and when the last had spoken, he said: "I am sorry to differ with you all, but my mind is made up; the Army will move to-morrow at ten o'clock."

When Grant was asked how he would get the transports past the batteries, he replied: "That is the Admiral's affair. Where the 'Queen of the West' and 'Switzerland' can go in broad daylight, the transports can pass at night."

A few days before this council, Admiral Farragut, who had come up from Red River, as before mentioned, requested Colonel Alfred Ellet to let him have two of the Ram fleet (to run the batteries at night) for the purpose of returning with him to the blockade of the Red River—saying he would make it all right with Admiral Porter, etc. To this Colonel Ellet at once agreed. Accordingly the rams "Lancaster" and "Switzerland" were prepared to run the batteries, the former commanded by Lieutenant-Colonel John A. Ellet, the latter by Charles Rivers Ellet. These Ellets were all brave fellows, and were full of the spirit of adventure. Instead of going past the batteries with comparative ease at night, they chose a time near daylight, and by the time they got abreast of the city all the batteries opened on them. The "Lancaster's" boilers were exploded by a shell, and being a frail vessel, she went to pieces and sunk immediately. The "Switzerland" had her boilers perforated by a plunging shot, and received a number of hits, but otherwise the damage done to her was not material, and she joined Farragut, and afterward performed good service down river.

If such frail boats as these could pass in open daylight, there was no reason why transports could not pass at night, under the lee of the iron-clads. A number of transports were prepared by packing them well with cotton-bales. Their crews in most cases declining to serve, their places were filled by volunteers from the Army. The pilots, as a rule, determined to stay by their vessels, and put them through, if possible. It was a hazardous task, but the pilots, a brave set of officers, got used to it after awhile, and running the batteries came to be considered by them as not much more dangerous than racing with another steamer, with the captain sitting on the safety-valve. This seemed to be the spirit which animated soldier volunteers who were, in many cases, sailors.

With these preparations the expedition was ready to move at the appointed time—the night of April 16th.

CHAPTER XXVIII.

PASSAGE OF THE FLEET BY VICKSBURG AND CAPTURE OF GRAND GULF. —CAPTURE OF ALEXANDRIA, ETC.

PLANS FOR RUNNING THE BATTERIES.—THE FLEET UNDERWAY.—THE BATTERIES OPEN FIRE. —THE TRANSPORT "HENRY CLAY" SUNK.—A GRAND SCENE.—THE BATTERIES RUN.— THE FLEET ANCHORS BELOW THE CITY.—MCCLERNAND CONFRONTED WITH "QUAKER GUNS."—GRANT PUSHES ON TO GRAND GULF.—THE "PRICE" IN FRONT OF THE BATTERIES.—INSUBORDINATION OF MCCLERNAND.—GRAND GULF DESCRIBED.—THE GUNBOATS COMMENCE THE ATTACK.—THE FIGHT FIERCELY CONTESTED.—THE "BENTON'S" WHEEL DISABLED.—DAMAGES TO THE VESSELS.—THE GUN-BOATS TIE UP AT HARD TIMES.—BURYING THE DEAD.—THE ATTACK RENEWED.—THE CONFEDERATES STAND TO THEIR GUNS.—SO-CALLED "HISTORY."—GRANT'S BRIGHTEST CHAPTER.—ATTACK ON HAINES' BLUFF.—CAPTAIN WALKE CAPTURES SHARPSHOOTERS.—GRAND GULF CAPTURED.—PORTER CONFERS WITH FARRAGUT.—UP THE RED RIVER.—FORT DERUSSY PARTIALLY DESTROYED.—CAPTURE OF ALEXANDRIA.—GENERAL BANKS TAKES POSSESSION —UP THE BLACK RIVER.—HARRISONBURG SHELLED.—OPERATIONS OF THE MISSISSIPPI SQUADRON SUMMARIZED.

THE Army had already moved on the 15th of April, 1863, and that night was selected for the naval vessels to pass the batteries of Vicksburg.

Orders had been given that the coal in the furnaces should be well ignited, so as to show no smoke, that low steam should be carried, that not a wheel was to turn except to keep the vessel's bow down river, and to drift past the enemy's works fifty yards apart.

Most of the vessels had a coal barge lashed to them on the side away from the enemy, and the wooden gun-boat "General Price," was lashed to the off side of the iron-clad "Lafayette."

When all was ready the signal was made to get under way and the squadron started in the following order: "Benton" (flagship) Lieutenant-Commander James A. Greer ; "Lafayette," Commander Henry Walke ; "General Price," Lieutenant-Commander Selim Woodworth ; "Louisville," Lieutenant - Commander E. K. Owen ; "Mound City," Lieutenant - Commander Byron Wilson ; "Pittsburg," Volunteer-Lieutenant Hoel ; "Carondelet," Lieuten-

ant - Commander J. McL. Murphy, and "Tuscumbia." Lieutenant-Commander J. W. Shirk. The tug "Ivy" was lashed to the "Benton," three army transports were in the rear and the "Tuscumbia" was at the end of the line to take care of them.

The "Benton," passed the first battery without receiving a shot, but as she came up with the second, the railroad station on the right bank of the river was set on fire, and tar barrels were lighted all along the Vicksburg shore, illuminating the river and showing every object as plainly as if it was daylight. Then the enemy opened his batteries all along the line, and the sharpshooters in rifle-pits along the levee commenced operations at the same instant. The fire was returned with spirit by the vessels as they drifted on. and the sound of falling buildings as the shells burst within them attested the efficiency of the gun-boats' fire.

The vessels had drifted perhaps a mile when a shell exploded in the cotton barricades of the transport "Henry Clay," and almost immediately the vessel was in a blaze ; another shell soon after bursting in her hull, the transport went to pieces and sank. The "Forest Queen," another transport, was also disabled by the enemy, but she was taken in tow by the "Tuscumbia" and conveyed safely through.

The scene while the fleet was passing the batteries was grand in the extreme, but the danger to the vessels was more apparent than real. Their weak points on the sides were mostly protected by heavy logs which prevented many shot and shells going through the iron. Some rents were made but the vessels stood the ordeal bravely and received no damage calculated to impair their efficiency.

Texas would be cut off and they would have to depend on what they could receive from Richmond.

General Steele had been sent up to the Steele's Bayou region to destroy all the provisions in that quarter, and Pemberton knew that if Grant's Army once got below Vicksburg it would eat up everything in the way of food between Warrenton and Bruensburg.

Although the squadron was under fire from the time of passing the first battery until the last vessel got by, a period of two hours and thirty minutes, the vessels were

THE MISSISSIPPI SQUADRON, UNDER ADMIRAL PORTER, PASSING THE BATTERIES AT VICKSBURG ON THE NIGHT OF APRIL 15, 1863.

The management of the vessels on this occasion was virtually in the hands of the pilots, who handled them beautifully and kept them in line at the distance apart ordered.

The enemy's shot was not well aimed; owing to the rapid fire of shells, shrapnel, grape and canister from the gun-boats, the sharpshooters were glad to lay low, and the men at the great guns gave up in disgust when they saw the fleet drift on apparently unscathed.

They must have known that Vicksburg was doomed, for if the fleet got safely below the batteries their supplies of provisions from

struck in their hulls but sixty-eight times by shot and shells, and only fifteen men were wounded. At 2.30 A. M., all the vessels were safely anchored at Carthage, ten miles below Vicksburg, where was encamped the advanced division of the Army under General McClernand.

The plantation at this place was owned by an ultra Confederate who exulted over the expected loss of all the gun-boats when he heard that they were to attempt the passage of the batteries, but when at two o'clock he saw them one after another heave in sight their night numbers up and signaling to the flag-ship, "all's well," he went off in despair, got drunk, set fire to his house and all the negro cabins, and departed to parts unknown. The negroes had already joined the Union Army, having no attachment to their brutal master, who had become so debased that he scarcely bore resemblance to a man.

When the day broke after the arrival of the squadron at Carthage, some four hundred men, the advance guard of McClernand's division, were found behind intrenchments hastily thrown up with a log on a pair of cart-wheels, to represent a field piece, while less than a thousand yards in front of them was a formidable looking set of earth-works with four large guns in position; and Generals McClernand and Osterhaus were momentarily expecting an attack.

LIEUT.-COMMANDER (NOW CAPTAIN) JAMES A. GREER,
COMMANDING FLAG-SHIP "BENTON."

The enemy's works appeared to be full of men, and as the Union troops had been under arms all night, the arrival of the gunboats was a great relief to them. The "Tuscumbia" was sent down to shell the enemy out, but the latter scampered off as soon as they saw the gun-boat coming. The Confederates had been playing a "bluff game" with McClernand, and held him in check until part of their force could get away with some light field-pieces. The frowning guns on the parapet proved on examination to be nothing but logs—such are the devices in war!

The advance of General Grant's Army moved but slowly on its way to Carthage. The roads were in wretched condition, and the artillery and wagons were continu-

ally stalled. The soldiers had therefore to "corduroy" the roads so that those coming after could get along faster, but it was terrible marching at the best.

From the little damage that had been inflicted on the gun-boats, General Grant felt satisfied he could send transports by the batteries of Vicksburg, and shortly afterwards six of these, on a dark night, passed down in charge of their pilots—a daring set of men who never shrunk from any dangerous service,—only one steamer was sunk by the enemy's shot.

A sufficient number of gun boats had been left at the mouth of the Yazoo River to take care of the upper Mississippi, and to look out for two formidable rams that were building at Yazoo City, forty miles from the mouth of the river.

Sherman remained with his division at Young's Point, ready to make another attack from the Yazoo if opportunity offered, and also to protect the supplies at Milliken's Bend from General Sterling Price, who with a large Confederate force was encamped some thirty miles away on the west bank of the Mississippi.

The Mississippi Marine Brigade, consisting of two thousand men, under Brigadier-General Alfred Ellet, in six or seven large steamers, was left there. These flying troops were attached to the Navy. Every precaution had been taken to prevent a surprise from the Confederates, or any attempt on their part to fortify the river banks again in the absence of the Army.

General McClernand had been ordered by Grant to push forward with his division, and with the help of the Navy, to seize upon Grand Gulf. Had it not been for the great overflow at that time, the Union Army might have landed on the east side of the river, but Vicksburg was now almost surrounded by water, which obliterated all roads except those on the high lands, which could only be reached by going further down the Mississippi. Hence it was that after a careful examination of the left bank of the river, Grant decided to push on to Grand Gulf, a long and tedious march.

General McClernand had been given the advance to satisfy his ambition, but he was not equal to the occasion, and this desire of General Grant to show McClernand that he was anxious to give him an opportunity for distinction, might have hazarded the success of the campaign. Had McClernand pushed on at once with the Navy to back him Grand Gulf and its batteries would have easily fallen into Federal hands; Big Black River, which led up to the rear of Jackson, would have been kept open by the gunboats; and the main Army instead of having to land at Bruensburg, eight or ten miles below Grand Gulf, could have disembarked at the latter point and marched to the rear of Vicksburg by favorable roads. Instead of carrying out his instructions, McClernand advanced only to Perkins' Landing, where he pitched his tents (although he had been directed to leave these behind on account of the difficulties of transportation), and called upon General McPherson for rations, of which he had failed to provide himself a sufficient supply. Perkins' Landing seemed to have such a fascination for McClernand that he remained there until Grant ordered him to move on.

Admiral Porter proceeded in the wooden gun-boat "General Price" to reconnoitre Grand Gulf, and ascertained that large numbers of troops were engaged in constructing extensive fortifications. Some guns were already mounted and others lying on the ground.

The "Price" had but two guns and with these Lieutenant-Commanding Woodworth was ordered to proceed within twelve hundred yards of the upper battery, and open fire. The shells exploded in the battery, and the workers sought the shelter of the hills. The "Price" kept up a fire for over an hour, the Confederates firing only two shots from a Whitworth field-piece; for, as was afterwards ascertained, they had at that time received no ammunition for the great guns.

The Admiral having satisfied himself that the works could be easily carried by assault under cover of the fire of the gun-boats, hastened back to Perkins' Landing, and stated the case to General McClernand, urging the co-operation of two thousand soldiers to enable him to occupy Grand Gulf, but no heed was given to the application; for McClernand, wrapped in his dignity, scorned all advice.

Failing in that direction, the Admiral wrote to General Sherman, detailing the state of affairs and begged him to induce General Grant to come to the front and take charge in person, before the favorable opportunity should pass away.

Grant was then at Milliken's Bend, forty miles distant. It took Sherman twenty hours to get the dispatch to him, and twenty-four hours more for Grant to reach Perkins' Landing, where he assumed command of the advance in spite of McClernand's objections, which were manifested in such an insubordinate way that most commanding generals would have at once relieved him from duty.

Three or four days had passed since the reconnoissance of Grand Gulf by the Admiral and time was lost which could never be regained. The Confederates concluded from the reconnoissance that measures were on foot to attack Grand Gulf, and they worked incessantly to strengthen the defences. Men and munitions of war were poured in from Vicksburg, and the enemy were prepared to make a strong resistance to the gun-boats or to any assault from the land forces.

Grand Gulf was by nature as strong as Vicksburg, the Confederates in their pride called it "the Little Gibraltar." The principal work called Bald Head, was on a bold bluff promontory at a bend in the river commanding a view for miles up and down the Mississippi. The current of the river, which ran here five miles an hour with innumerable eddies, had cut away the shore until beneath the fort was a perpendicular wall more than eighty feet in height, while in the rear hills rising three hundred and fifty feet above the river were dotted with field works to protect the flanks of Bald Head, which fort mounted four heavy guns, Brooke rifles and 8-inch Columbiads. In front of this the river formed a large circular bay or gulf from which the place took its name. Black River emptied into the gulf and the approach to it was commanded by two 8-inch Columbiads.

The lower forts were half a mile below Bald Head, and were connected with the latter by intrenchments by which troops could pass under cover from one fort to another. The lower batteries mounted nine heavy guns situated on the brow of a hill eight hundred yards from the river and one hundred and fifty feet above it. The guns were mostly long 32-pounders and 8-inch. There were some smaller batteries in which were rifled field pieces. All these batteries were more formidable from the fact that they were in very elevated positions, giving them a plunging fire, while it was difficult to elevate the guns afloat so that their shot would reach the enemy.

After Grant had got his Army in motion part of McClernand's division was embarked on transports, the rest of the troops being obliged to march to Hard Times, twenty-two miles from Perkins' Landing.

Five barges and a steamer were sunk by the batteries at Vicksburg when the last six transports ran the blockade, which made transportation by water for all of the troops out of the question.

When the troops arrived at the point abreast of Bald Head, and the soldiers on the transports were ready to land as soon as the batteries should be silenced, Admiral Porter got under way with the squadron and commenced the attack at 8 A. M., on the 29th of April, 1863.

The "Pittsburg" "Louisville," "Mound City," and "Carondelet" attacked the lower batteries, while the "Benton," "Tuscumbia," and "Lafayette" attacked Bald Head battery, the two former as close as they could get, and the "Lafayette" lying in an eddy four hundred yards above the fort where she could enfilade it.

As the vessels approached the works the enemy opened fire and in ten minutes the battle was raging all along the line. The fight was severely contested, and it was not until three hours after the first gun was fired, that the enemy deserted his guns at the lower batteries, and then only after the "Lafayette" had been ordered from her first position to reinforce the gun-boats below.

In the meantime the flag-ship "Benton," and the "Tuscumbia" were doing their best to silence the upper battery, getting close *under* the guns and endeavoring to knock

minutes—the "Pittsburg" lost six killed and had twelve wounded.

After all the vessels concentrated their fire on Bald Head, there was less resistance, although the Confederates still stood to their guns. When the battle had lasted more than five hours, General Grant, who from a tug up the river, was looking on, made signal to the Admiral that he wished to communicate, and the "Benton" joined him two miles above the forts. The Confederates had now ceased firing, but the gun-boats maintained their position around Bald Head, occasionally firing a shell to keep the enemy out of the works.

When General Grant went on board the

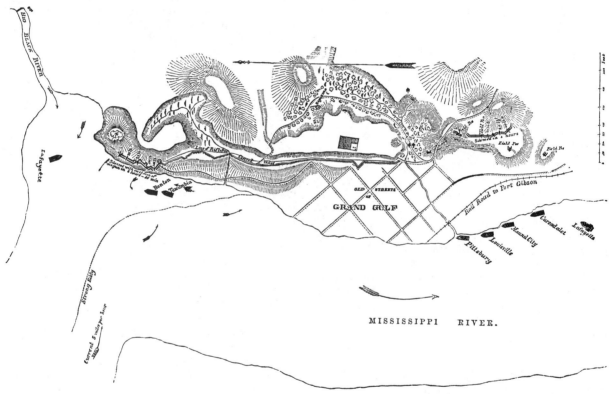

BATTERIES AT "GRAND GULF" CAPTURED BY THE U. S. MISSISSIPPI SQUADRON, MAY 3, 1863.

off their muzzles, when they were run out to fire. The current was so strong, however, that it was impossible to keep the two vessels in position and they sheered about very much. In one of these sheers, a shot entered the "Benton's" pilot house, disabled the wheel and cut Pilot Williams' foot nearly off. Though the brave pilot never left his post it was impossible to manage the vessel and she was accordingly run into the bank to repair damages.

The gun-boats at the lower batteries had been signalled to double up on Bald Head, the "Lafayette" to resume her old position, and the "Pittsburg," Volunteer - Lieutenant Hoel, arrived opportunely to take the "Benton's" place. During the time the latter vessel was out of action—twenty-five

flag-ship, he decided that it would be too hazardous to attempt to land troops, as it did not appear that the guns in the enemy's works were dismounted and the gunners would therefore jump to their batteries again, open on the unprotected transports and destroy many of the troops. For the same reason the general concluded not to send the transports past the batteries with the soldiers on board but to march the latter around by land. In this he was quite right, as afterwards appeared.

As there was no longer any object in keeping the gun-boats under the batteries, all but the "Lafayette" were recalled, and the latter was left in her old position to keep the enemy from reoccupying the works and repairing damages. This duty Commander Walke effectually performed, firing a shell every five minutes into the works until darkness set in.

The engagement was fought under great disadvantages; the current around the pro montory of Bald Head ran with great rapidity, and it was as much as the gun-boats could do to stem it. Clumsy vessels at best, the iron-clads would frequently be turned completely round, presenting their weak points to the enemy, of which the expert Confederate gunners were not slow to take advantage, and seldom missed their mark so close were the vessels to the forts. The light armor plates of most of the vessels offered but an imperfect resistance to the heavy missiles of the enemy, and, in consequence, the list of killed and wounded in the squadron was large.

The "Tuscumbia," on which vessel great reliance was placed to resist heavy shot, proved herself the weakest vessel in the squadron, although Lieutenant-Commander Shirk stood up to his work manfully. In the beginning of the engagement, a rifle shell struck the outer edge of the shutter of the midship port—she fought three 11-inch guns in the bow—opened the port and entered the casemate, killing six men and wounding several others.

Another shell jammed the shutters of the same port so tightly, that the gun could not be used for the remainder of the action. A shell from the lower battery entered the stern port, disabling every man at the 9-inch gun, and yet this vessel was supposed to be shot proof! Some of the armor on the forward casemate fell overboard from repeated blows, and all of it was started from its seat.

The "Tuscumbia" was struck eighty-one times by shot and shells, and was completely riddled; one engine was disabled, six men killed and twenty-four wounded, some of them mortally.

The flag-ship "Benton," although the strongest of the gun-boats, was badly cut up. A shell passed through her armor on the starboard quarter and exploded in a stateroom, setting fire to the vessel.

The "Benton" was struck forty-seven times in the casemates, and seventy times in all by heavy shot, the three-quarter inch iron was perforated twelve times, the two and-a-half inch, four times. A hundred pound shot passed through the pilot-house, smashing the wheel and severely wounding the pilot, nine men were killed and nineteen wounded.

The "Lafayette," Commander Walke, proved herself an excellent fighting vessel. She was struck by cannon shot forty-five times, but only five shots did any serious damage. She had only one officer wounded.

The "Pittsburg," Volunteer-Lieutenant-Commanding Hoel, was struck in the hull thirty-five times, and had six killed and thirteen wounded.

The other vessels, although considerably cut up, were not materially damaged, and all reported "ready for service" half an hour after the action, when the gun-boats tied up to the bank at Hard Times.

Then came the melancholy duty of burying the dead, who were followed mournfully to their graves by their messmates and friends.

Three hours afterwards the squadron got underway and again attacked the batteries, while the transports all passed in safety below Hard Times. Some of the Confederate gunners fired at the gun-boats but did no damage. During the whole engagement the Confederates stood to their guns manfully, and certainly pointed them to some purpose. Colonel Wade, the commanding officer at Bald Head, was killed; his chief-of-staff also, and eleven men were reported killed by the Confederates, although more graves than that were counted. The enemy had many wounded, but the number was not mentioned in the returns.

Rear-Admiral Porter, in his report, speaks in the highest terms of Commander Walke, Lieutenant-Commanding Murphy, Lieutenant-Commanders Shirk and Owen, Lieutenants-Commanding Hoel and Wilson, some of whom had already distinguished themselves on the upper Mississippi.

The remarks on this battle of Grand Gulf by military historians show how reluctant they are to give the Navy credit. The following quotation from a well known writer, is an instance in point. Speaking of Grand Gulf he says:

"The vessels were handled with skill and boldness, but the rebel batteries were too elevated for Porter to accomplish anything. He was not able to dismount a solitary piece and it would have been madness to attempt a landing under unsilenced guns like these. No serious injury was sustained by any of the fleet. [!] The Admiral withdrew after the utter futility of his effort had been amply demonstrated. The enemy also suspended fire."

Such are the statements that have for years passed for "history," one "historian" repeating another only changing a little the language of his predecessor to make it pass for his own. The above quotation reads like an excuse for the Army not landing, although no excuse was needed. It was General Grant's opinion that it would be wiser to land the Army lower down, in which opinion the naval commanding officer concurred. Grant had too few men with him to run the risk of losing any of them, and there was no particular advantage to be gained by landing immediately at Grand Gulf, as was afterwards proven.

The military historian whom we have

quoted has not stated the case truthfully, but his statements are in keeping with those of many other writers who seem to fear that by giving credit to the Navy, they may detract from that which is due the other arm of the service. An intelligent reader will readily understand that a campaign such as is here described must have been a failure without the assistance of the Navy. In default of credit from the "military historians," the officers and men of the Navy must rely on the reports of their own chiefs to do them justice.

The night following the attack on Grand Gulf information was obtained from a negro, that there was a good landing at Bruensburg, six miles below Grand Gulf, and that from Bruensburg an excellent road led to Port Gibson, twelve miles in the interior. In consequence of this information the gunboats and transports were next morning crowded with troops, and steamed down the river. About noon, Grant disembarked thirty-two thousand men with four days' rations, and without transportation determined to live upon the enemy, as he was satisfied the supply of provisions in the district was ample to meet all his requirements.

Here Grant started on that remarkable march against an enemy who outnumbered his forces two to one; he outgeneraled the Confederates, fought battle after battle and finally reached the rear of Vicksburg, shutting General Pemberton inside the fortifications and causing General Joseph E. Johnston to evacuate Jackson and retreat.

Grant's conduct of this campaign forms the brightest chapter in his military record and can only be appreciated by those who know the difficulties with which he had to contend, and particularly the nature of the country through which he had to march his Army.

General Grant had made arrangements for Sherman's division to make a feint up Yazoo River the same day the gun-boats attacked Grand Gulf. Accordingly, on that day Sherman moved up the Yazoo in transports preceeded by "the gun-boats," as the military historian puts it. Most of these gunboats were what were called "workshops," i. e., the machine vessel, carpenter shop, store vessel, powder vessel and hospital vessel. These were simply river steamers painted black. The naval forces were led by Lieutenant-Commander K. R. Breese in the "Black Hawk" and comprised the "Baron DeKalb," Lieutenant-Commander John G. Walker, "Choctaw," Lieutenant-Commander F. M. Ramsay, "Taylor," Lieutenant-Commander Prichett, "Signal," "Romeo," "Linden" and "Petrel" with three 13-inch mortars.

The naval demonstration was really a fine one, calculated to impress the Confederates, who had seen so many nondescripts pass Vicksburg that they hardly knew a gunboat from a transport.

While Pemberton was making his preparations to meet Grant's Army on Big Black River, he received a dispatch informing him that Haines' Bluff was the real point of attack and that a large Army supported by numerous gun-boats was moving against that place. It was desirable that the Confederates should be encouraged in the belief that Haines' Bluff was the real point of attack, and the "DeKalb," "Choctaw" and "Taylor," approaching as near as they could get, opened a heavy fire on the works while Sherman disembarked his troops.

There was but one narrow road which led along the levee, and this was wide enough for but four men to march abreast. As Sherman advanced along this road towards Haines' Bluff the three gun-boats maintained their incessant fire and confirmed the Confederates in their belief that this was really the point of attack, although the condition of the country ought to have assured them that no Army would be likely to attack a place so strongly fortified, under the circumstances.

The fire of the gun-boats was kept up as long as possible, and videttes and skirmishers were thrown out by the Army on the road leading to the Bluff; upon this road the enemy opened with heavy guns and apparently could have swept away any force approaching from that direction. At dark, General Sherman re-embarked his men, having accomplished the object of his movement, which was simply to deceive the Confederates.

Notwithstanding the movement was but a feint, the three gun-boats, "Choctaw," "DeKalb," and "Taylor," together with the "Black Hawk," kept up a hot fire for three hours as well as they could—wedged in a stream which was here not over forty yards wide; as, since the demonstration was considered of such importance by General Sherman, it was necessary to do everything that would make the attack appear a real one. The morning after these transactions, it was discovered that new works had been thrown up by the Confederates during the night, that the old ones had been extended, and several additional heavy guns had been placed in position.

This feint against Haines' Bluff continued for several days, and Pemberton was obliged, in answer to solicitations, to send re-inforcements, thus weakening his Army below. Ox teams were observed hauling heavy guns to mount at Haines' Bluff, to check the advance of the Federal forces, showing that the enemy was exerting all his energy to strengthen the threatened position.

During this movement, the "DeKalb," while temporarily dropping out of action was attacked by sharpshooters from some buildings on the eastern bank. Lieutenant-Commander Walker immediately ran the vessel into the bank and landed twenty-five men under command of Acting-Master C. S. Kendrick, who dislodged the enemy and chased them into the swamp, killing one officer and three privates, and taking a lieutenant of the Third Louisiana Infantry prisoner. This officer was captured in a hand-to-hand fight by Mr. Kendrick, who knocked him down with a pistol. In two days firing, the "DeKalb" expended two hundred rounds of shot and shells, did not suffer materially in her hull, and had only one casualty.

The "Choctaw," Lieutenant-Commander Ramsay, had an opportunity of showing her fighting qualities. She was a sister ship to the "Lafayette," and had lately joined the squadron. She was struck forty-seven times in her hull, and had thirteen shots through her smoke-stack. The turret was struck six times. A ten-inch shot penetrated the crown, and a six-inch rifle shot buried itself in the iron plating. Two shots struck below the water line on the starboard side forward of the turret. With the exception that the good order of the vessel was rather marred, no great injury was done, and, fortunately, no one was killed.

The "Taylor," being a wooden vessel, could only take an occasional part in the bombardment. She was struck below the water line with a rifle shot, and made to leak so badly that she had to withdraw from action to repair damages.

At one time the fire of the gun-boats was so effective that the enemy's fire almost ceased, and but for a raft which blocked the further advance of the vessels, the latter would have endeavored to get close enough to use grape and canister, which might have made quite a difference in the state of affairs. As it was, everything turned out to General Sherman's satisfaction, and returning to Young's Point, he started with his division to join General Grant, crossing the river at Grand Gulf and overtaking the main body of the Army in time to be present during the important events which laid Vicksburg at the mercy of the Federal Army.

After General Grant and his troops landed at Bruensburg, Admiral Porter returned the same night to Grand Gulf with the intention of trying to get possession of the enemy's works. As seven o'clock, on the following morning, the "Lafayette" was sent up to draw the fire of the forts. As she approached, the magazine in the lower battery blew up, throwing a vast cloud of dust into the air. Several other magazines in the smaller forts followed, and the Confederate troops evacuated all the works.

The fort at Bald Head, on Point of Rocks, was left intact, and a tiny Confederate flag was left sticking in a flower-pot to show that the enemy did not surrender.

There is no other instance during the war of a fort holding out so determinedly as this one at Bald Head. The destruction wrought inside the work was marvellous— one would suppose that no living thing could have continued there under such a fire. The military historian whom we have quoted was wrong, for every gun in the fort was rendered useless by the shot and shells from the gun-boats; only one gun could be fired and that could not be trained, owing to the destruction of its carriage.

Some of the guns in the lower batteries were still intact, and these opened on the fleet. In the evening, the guns were all dismounted by the sailors and laid along the levee, where they could be shipped to Cairo.

The following is a copy of a report made by T. M. Farrell, U. S. N., May, 1863:

"These batteries mounted one 100-pounder, two 64-pounders, two 7-inch rifles, one 30-pounder Parrott, two 30-pounder Parrotts in battery, two 20-pounder Parrotts in main magazine, three 10-pounder Parrotts on the hills.

"Batteries engaged by the gun-boats for five hours and thirty-five minutes, the lower battery silenced in three hours, the upper battery silenced with the exception of one gun. The "Lafayette" laid opposite this battery and kept the people from working until dark, when it was partially repaired. The defences were all earthworks.

"In addition to the above, four or five small field-pieces were used by the rebels and shifted about from place to place."

Admiral Farragut was still at the mouth of Red River in the flag-ship "Hartford," where he had remained ever since he had made the passage by Port Hudson, and Admiral Porter having left Lieutenant-Commander Owen in charge at Grand Gulf with the "Louisville" and "Tuscumbia," proceeded down the river to meet Farragut and relieve him of the command of that part of the river.

On the 3d of May, 1863, Admiral Porter reached the mouth of Red River and after conferring with Admiral Farragut, proceeded up that stream with the "Benton," "Lafayette," "Pittsburg," "General Price," tug "Ivy" and ram "Switzerland." Meeting two of Admiral Farragut's vessels, the "Arizona" and the "Estella," they were turned back and accompanied Admiral Porter's squadron which arrived next morning at Fort DeRussy,

This work was a casemated battery built in the most substantial manner and plated after the style of the rams with railroad iron. On the rumored approach of the gun-boats the Confederates hastily dismounted and carried off all the guns except one 64-pounder.

There were at Fort DeRussy, three case-mates intended for two guns each, and a flanking battery at right angles to the case-mates calculated to mount seven guns more. There was also a large square earth-work eight hundred yards inland not yet ready for guns.

These works would have been very formidable had they been finished, and it was as well they were not completed and manned. They were a monument of the energy and determination of the enemy, which seemed to be without limit.

After partially destroying the works at Fort DeRussy, the squadron proceeded up to Alexandria which place submitted with-out a dissenting voice, many of the inhabi-tants professing themselves Unionists. The day after the arrival of the gun-boats Major-General Banks marched into Alexandria and the town was turned over to him by the Navy. The following day the squad-ron returned down the Red River with the exception of the "Lafayette," "Estella" and "Arizona," and the ram "Switzer-land" which were left to co-operate with General Banks in case he should require the assistance of the Navy.

While in Red River, Lieutenant-Com-manding Woodworth was sent up Black River, a branch of the former stream, to make a reconnaissance with the "General Price," "Pittsburg," "Estella," and "Ari-zona." These vessels ascended as far as Harrisonburg which was found to be strongly fortified. The works were shelled for some time with little apparent effect and after destroying a large amount of Con-federate Army stores, amounting to three hundred thousand dollars in value, the gun-boats returned to Red River, and the "Ben-ton" and consorts proceeded to Grand Gulf to co-operate with General Grant in any of his plans where the Navy could be useful.

Thus within ten days the flag-ship and her consorts, after dismantling the fortifica-tions at Grand Gulf, had ascended Red River, had destroyed the works at Fort DeRussy, broken up an immense raft intended to obstruct Red River, captured Alexandria, destroyed a large amount of the enemy's stores on Black River, and returned to Grand Gulf, where it was found that General Grant had moved his Army to-wards Vicksburg.

The whole squadron then ascended the river to a point two miles below Vicksburg, and the admiral again hoisted his flag on board the "Black Hawk," at Young's Point, ready to communicate with General Grant the moment his Army should arrive in the rear of the besieged city.

In less than a month, the Mississippi squadron had passed through a sharp and exciting campaign, had failed in nothing it had undertaken, and had given the Army the assistance necessary to enable it to reach a position which ensured the fall of Vicksburg.

CHAPTER XXIX.

SIEGE OF VICKSBURG—Continued.

The Army marches from Bruensburg towards Vicksburg.—Destruction of the last works built by the Confederates on the Mississippi.—Admiral Porter opens Communication with General Grant in the rear of Vicksburg, and occupies Haines' Bluff.—Midnight attack on Vicksburg by the Army and Navy.—Attack on Yazoo City by the Gun-boats and Destruction of three Iron-clad Rams.—Attack on the Vicksburg Works, May 22, by the Army and Navy.—Loss of the "Cincinnati" before Vicksburg.—Her Guns transferred to the rear of the City.—Destruction of Nine Confederate Steamers up the Yazoo, by Lieutenant-Commander Walker.—Attack on Vicksburg, June 19, by the Army and Navy.—All the Enemy's Guns Silenced.—General Price's Army repulsed by General Mower and the Marine Brigade.—Energy shown by the Confederates in Vicksburg.—Short Summary of the Work Accomplished before Vicksburg by the Navy.—Surrender of Vicksburg, July 4, 1863.—Meeting of the Officers of the Army and Navy on Board the Flag-ship "Black Hawk."—Letters from General Sherman to Admiral Porter.—Generous Terms granted the Besieged after the Capture of Vicksburg.—True History.—Harmony in Army and Navy Co-operation.—Last words of Grant.—Detailed Report of Rear-Admiral Porter.—Congratulatory Letter of Secretary Welles.

AS THE Army had marched from Bruensburg, and was well on the way to Vicksburg, Admiral Porter changed his station from Grand Gulf to the flag-ship "Black Hawk" at the mouth of the Yazoo River, ready to co-operate with the Army the moment it should make its appearance in the rear of Vicksburg.

Two iron-clads were left at the mouth of the Red River, blocking it up closely, which sealed the fate of Port Hudson. No more supplies would get to the Confederates from that quarter.

One iron-clad was left at Carthage, three at Warrenton, (where the enemy aimed at building heavy works), and two or three in the Yazoo.

Notwithstanding the Confederates were so hardly pressed, they still clung to the idea that they would beat the Federal Army back from its hard-won positions, and they were not even willing that the gun-boats should have the satisfaction of going to the landing opposite Warrenton to obtain provisions and coal. They proceeded to erect a heavy work there that would command the river both ways, and particularly the opposite landing.

The enemy had labored hard on these works, night and day, in hopes of having them ready by the time the vessels of the fleet returned. It was intended to mount eight 10-inch guns and some 100-pound rifles. The work was built of cotton-bales covered with logs—the logs to be covered with several layers of railroad iron and the whole to be covered with bags of earth—a fort, in fact, impervious to shot or shells.

Lieutenant-Commanding Wilson, in the "Mound City," appeared below Warrenton about the 12th of May, and seeing these works and no persons about, sent a party on shore to reconnoitre. These mounted the parapets and discovered a number of artillerists inside the fort, who, to make themselves secure from observation, were crouching under the parapets.

The Federal party emptied their revolvers into the enemy and then, jumping down, hailed the "Mound City" and told those on board to open fire on the works, which was done. A stray shell found its way into a cotton-bale—in ten minutes this formidable work was in a blaze, and in less than an hour the whole fabric was consumed.

This was the last work built by the Confederates on the Mississippi River. All the appliances of a fort and a quantity of stores were in the houses at Warrenton, which the Confederates set fire to and destroyed. And what houses were left in the town were destroyed by the "Mound City's" men. Warrenton had been a troublesome place and merited its fate.

On the 15th of May, the admiral joined the fleet in the Yazoo, and on the 16th firing was heard in the rear of Vicksburg—a sign that General Grant's Army was not far off, and that he was driving Pemberton into the

LIEUT.-COMMANDING (NOW CAPTAIN) BYRON WILSON, U. S. N.

city. The flag-ship pushed up the river as near as she could get to the combatants, and it was soon discovered by the aid of glasses that General Sherman's division was coming in on the left of Snyder's Bluff, cutting off the enemy at that place from joining the troops in the city.

The "DeKalb," Lieutenant-Commander Walker, the "Choctaw," Lieutenant-Commander Ramsay, the "Linden," "Romeo," and "Forest Rose," all under the command of Lieutenant-Commander Breese, were now sent up the Yazoo to open communication with the Army. In three hours, letters were received by the Admiral from Generals Grant, Sherman and Steele, informing him of their complete success in driving General J. E. Johnston away with his Army of 40,000 men, and forcing Pemberton into

Vicksburg with about the same number of troops.

In the meantime the "DeKalb" pushed on to Haines' Bluff, which had been the great obstacle to our advance in that direction, and which the enemy had commenced evacuating the day before. A part of the garrison had remained behind in hopes of carrying off a quantity of stores, but they were driven away by the "DeKalb" and were cut off by some of Sherman's command who had marched in that direction.

The Confederates had been so completely surprised by the sudden appearance of our gun-boats and Army that they had not time to destroy anything—guns, tents, equipage and all kinds of stores were left in good order and fell into the hands of the Federals.

As soon as the Army appeared, driving the Confederates into Vicksburg, all the gun-boats below the city were ordered up to attack the batteries, which fire was kept up for three hours. At midnight the fire was reopened and directed to all points where it might be possible to harass the enemy's troops, and it was continued all night. The Confederates must have had an uncomfortable time of it, after marching and fighting all day with little hope of rest within their trenches. Shot and shells were whistling about them and every now and then a fire broke out in the city, threatening destruction to their stores and munitions of war.

The Admiral ordered up the army transports with stores and provisions, which the Union forces were glad to get that day before sunset.

The works at Haines' Bluff were found to be very formidable—far too much so to have been taken by our Army; or from the water side; there were eighteen of the heaviest guns (8-inch and 10-inch columbiads, and 7½-inch rifles) with ammunition enough to last a long siege, and much of it suited for the guns of the naval vessels. The works and encampment (which consisted of permanent houses), covered many acres of ground, and the fortifications and rifle-pits extended over one mile and a quarter. Wide ditches, chevaux-de-frise, and net works (obstructions that would delight any military engineer,) formed part of their defenses; and these were but a counterpart of miles of the same kind of work, in and around Vicksburg. Most of these works were destroyed as not conducing in any way to the requirements of the Federal Army, and to prevent their being used to check the advance of the gun-boats, in case the enemy by superior force caused the siege to be raised.

As soon as the Confederates had evacuated Haines' Bluff, and all the rafts which blocked the river above had been removed,

Lieutenant - Commander Walker, in the "DeKalb," was sent up the Yazoo River with a sufficient force to destroy all the works at Yazoo City, which had been used in the construction of their rams.

As this naval force approached Yazoo City, the Confederate property was set on fire by Lieutenant Brown, late commander of the "Arkansas," and our men had only to add fuel to the flames which were well under way. Three powerful rams were burned: the "Mobile," a screw steamer ready for her plating; the "Republic," already plated with railroad iron, and a monster steamer on the stocks (310 feet long and 70 beam), intended to be the most powerful vessel of the kind ever built. She was to have had six engines, four side wheels and two propellers, with a speed of sixteen knots.

The Confederates were unfortunate in their rams—they built them only to lose them. But the amount of energy they exhibited in endeavoring to obtain vessels of this class was remarkable, and what they accomplished, in this line, was more astonishing still. Every ram which they built was either destroyed by our Navy, or by themselves to prevent the Navy from capturing them. Naval officers knew how much damage one of these vessels would commit, if she could ever get fairly afloat, and when one was heard of as building at any point, no effort was left untried to reach the place and destroy her.

Yazoo City fared badly for its misfortune in being selected as a site for a Navy Yard. The expedition which had been directed to do its work with all dispatch and return as quickly as possible to headquarters, set fire to everything of a public character. The Navy Yard contained five saw-mills, besides planing-mills, machine shops, carpenter and blacksmith shops, in fact all the appliances for building a Navy. Saw-mills above the city were also destroyed and the Federal forces left nothing that could be used towards building a boat even.

Yazoo never built another ram; the people were quite satisfied to have their houses left standing.

The expedition returned down the river, having fully accomplished all they went for.

They were attacked at Liverpool Landing, at a very sharp bend in the narrow river, by three field-pieces and 200 rifle-men concealed in the bushes; but these were soon made to retreat. The vessels only lost one man killed and eight wounded—but the amount of destruction which they caused can hardly be realized.

The Confederates now lost all hope of being able to build rams or any other vessels on the tributaries of the Mississippi, and though Yazoo City was for some time after the rendevous of the cowardly guerillas, yet it no longer formed a source of anxiety to the Union forces.

On the evening of the 21st of May, Admiral Porter received a communication from General Grant to the effect that he intended to make a general attack upon the Confederate works at Vicksburg at 10 A. M. the next day. He had closely invested the enemy's works and was so near that he thought he could get inside. The Admiral was requested to attack on the water side, and shell all the batteries from 9.30 to 10.30 A. M., to annoy the garrison and draw off as many as possible from the trenches.

In the meantime the Admiral with the "Benton," "Tuscumbia," "Carondelet," and "Mound City" opened on the hill batteries and silenced them one after another, and the "Mound City" had the honor of disabling the heaviest gun the enemy had mounted, called "Whistling Dick," a gun that had hitherto defied the best marksmen.

"WHISTLING DICK."

(SKETCHED BY REAR-ADMIRAL WALKE FROM A PHOTOGRAPH BY PAYMASTER BENTON.)

The Confederates did not stand to their guns this day as they had been accustomed to do. They were receiving a heavy fire in the rear as well as in front, and the shriek of the shells from the army field-pieces, as they fell by the hundred in the Confederate works, could be heard down on the water amid the roar of the heavy cannon. The batteries one after another were silenced, as the gun-boats, firing bow and broadside guns, moved upon them until they came to the 13-gun battery in front of the city.

This battery was commanded by Colonel Higgins (formerly a lieutenant in the U. S. Navy), who had so gallantly defended Fort Jackson. He felt called upon to show his old naval friends that he would not flinch from his post no matter what force was brought against him. But the water was high (nearly level with the banks), and the gun-boats were *above* the enemy's water batteries; the first time they had ever enjoyed this advantage. They had nothing but this one battery to engage their attention, as all the others had been silenced. This was the hottest fire the gun-boats had yet been under, as Col. Higgins clung to his works with the greatest tenacity and placed a number of shot (fortunately they were not shells) below the water-line. This went on for two hours and a quarter when it was quite time, according to rule, that the enemy should abandon his post, but he still held on.

The "Tuscumbia" was brought up with her 11-inch guns, but Higgins soon made her turret untenable, and she was finally completely disabled and had to drop out of action.

The gun-boats had started down the river with a large amount of ammunition, but they had been under fire a good deal and up to this time had had no opportunity of replenishing their supply. Reports came up from below that the ammunition was running short and would be out in a few minutes. This was provoking. Colonel Higgins' fire had begun to slacken and in half an hour more he would have been silenced; but no; one after another the gun-boats got out of ammunition, and were obliged to drop down, and finally the last one was obliged to retire and Colonel Higgins was left master of the field. It is not likely that he enjoyed the sport however, as he afterwards confessed to losing a great many of his men.

The gun-boats had done what was required of them by General Grant, and more. He asked an hour's attack to annoy the garrison, while his Army assaulted in the rear; they fought the batteries for two hours and a half, more than twice as long as was required, and with what success will be seen from the following letter of General McArthur.

HEADQUARTERS, 6TH DIVISION, 17TH ARMY CORPS, IN FIELD NEAR VICKSBURG, MISS., May 23, 1863.

ADMIRAL—I received your communication with regard to silencing the two batteries below Vicksburg, and in reply would say that I witnessed with intense interest the firing on that day, it being the finest I have yet seen.

I would have taken advantage of the results thus gained by your vessels, and had given the necessary orders to do so, when I received peremptory orders from Major-General McClernand to move my command around to the right of my position, to support a portion of his troops who had gained a lodgment in the enemy's works.

I arrived, however, too late, and have now been ordered back to my former position and to follow up any advantage your vessels may gain.

I have made a request to have some rifle guns sent me, which I require, and on receipt of which I expect to enfilade "Whistling Dick's" position; at any rate I will try. . . . .

I am, your obedient servant,
I. McARTHUR,
Brig.-Gen. Com'ding 6th Division, 17th Corps.

Had Gen. McArthur been let alone, and not been prevented from occupying the works from which the Navy had driven the Confederates, he would have kept possession of every fort on the ridge of hills which overlooked Vicksburg, and decided the fate of the city.

To show that these attacks of the gun-boats were not child's play, the reports of some of the injuries received by them are herewith mentioned :

"'MOUND CITY,' May 22d, 1863.

"A shot struck and lodged in starboard bow near the stern, and five feet under water. . . . .

"A shot went through the forecastle on port side into the coal bunkers; a shot on starboard side went through the hammock netting and starboard chimney at the lower band, tearing the chimney half off, then through the galley and overboard. A shot in front passed through two heavy thicknesses of boiler iron, the iron of the the pilot-house near the deck, and through the deck, cutting away carlines, and lodged in a mess-chest.

"A shot on starboard side passed through half of the hog-chain stanchion, passed through wheel-house, cutting away iron wheel and brace; then through the steerage, tearing up eight feet of the planks and breaking carlines and woodwork in ward-room. A shell burst close to No. 6 gun, knocking off part of the muzzle. A shot on starboard side struck the iron near the top, cutting half through and bending one of the plates, knocking out a stanchion and starting the bolts on the inside. A shot on starboard side struck the muzzle of No. 7 gun, wrecking the gun, then glanced, went through the hammock netting and fell into the pitman. A shot struck the iron on starboard side, over shell-room, knocking off the plate and driving a piece of it through the iron plating of the casemate. A shot on starboard side cut away an awning stanchion, and passed through cabin skylight tearing up the plank.

"A shot struck front chimney twenty feet from deck. A shot through brace of forward stanchion and skylight. A shot on starboard side struck iron plating between guns Nos. 4 and 5, three feet above the water, and glanced off bending the plates and starting the bolts. A shot on starboard side at shell room two feet below water; a shot struck binacle on port quarter, and glanced knocking hole in the plating of casemate. A shot struck boat davit and bent it, etc."

Half the number of these shots striking a wooden vessel would have destroyed her.

The "Benton" was struck in her hull thirteen times; four times at the water line, etc.

While this was going on, the Army assaulted in the rear of Vicksburg, but did not succeed in getting in. Pemberton had at this time 42,000 men to man his ramparts.

The gun-boats kept up their attack until the 27th when there was a lull for a time.

On the 29th, General W. T. Sherman signalled to the flag-ship, requesting that two gun-boats be sent down to clear out a battery of two guns that prevented him from extending his right flank. It being a rule with the Navy never to refuse a request from the Army, the "Cincinnati" was prepared for the adventure.

Sherman was under the impression that the enemy had moved a battery of eleven heavy guns from a bluff commanding the Mississippi to the land side, but the guns had only been lowered from their carriages to avoid the naval fire, and Colonel Higgins (who had made out all the signals passing between our Army and Navy), quickly remounted them under cover of the night and screened them with bushes.

Next morning the "Cincinnati," Lieutenant George M. Bache, started down the river to attack the small battery mentioned by Sherman, but as the vessel rounded to and opened her broadside, the battery on the bluff opened on her stern with its heaviest guns.

The first shot from the enemy passed through the magazine and then through the bottom, causing the "Cincinnati" to fill rapidly. Then the starboard tiller was shot away, the enemy firing rapidly and with great accuracy; 8-inch and 10-inch shot went clear through the bulwarks of hay and logs, and plunging shots from the heights went through the deck and did much damage.

The vessel could not return this fire and putting on steam crept along the shore, up river, making against the current not more than three miles an hour.

The "Cincinnati" was soon in a sinking condition, and her gallant commander ran her into the bank and got out a plank to save his crew before the vessel went down. A hawser was taken on shore and made fast to a tree, but, unfortunately, it was not properly secured, and giving way allowed the vessel to slide off into deep water. All this time the enemy continued to pour in a destructive fire. Bache would not haul down his flag, but nailed it to the stump of his flag-pole which had been shot away.

As the vessel was now sinking the order was given for all who could to swim to the shore, which was not far off; the boats had all been shot to pieces and were of no use. There were but three fathoms of water where the "Cincinnati" went down, and her colors and smoke-pipes remained in sight. Fifteen men were drowned in at-

tempting to reach the bank and twenty more were killed or wounded.

This was an unfortunate affair, but the calamity was somewhat deprived of its sting by the cool and courageous conduct of the commander, officers and crew, who withstood the Confederate fire unflinchingly and preferred to sink rather than haul down their colors. The Confederates kept up their fire on the flag, and many of the plunging shot found their way through the vessel's hull.

As soon as General Sherman saw what had happened he sent a company of the 76th Ohio to the relief of our officers and men.

Sherman wrote to the Admiral, deploring the loss of the vessel, but said: "the importance of the object desired to be accomplished fully warranted the attempt. It has proved successful and will stimulate us to further efforts to break the line which terminates on the Mississippi in such formidable batteries."

In a few days the water in the river fell sufficiently for the guns to be removed from the "Cincinnati." This was done by the Army at night when the enemy could not see what was going on. Some of the guns were mounted in front of Sherman's division, and were under the command of Lieutenant-Commander T. O. Selfridge, with blue-jackets to work them; and this battery finally accomplished what the "Cincinnati" had not time to do; viz., clear out the batteries which threatened Sherman's right flank. These guns were also employed in firing upon such points as Sherman pointed out, where he thought it advantageous to clear a way for the Army in case of another assault.

The "Cincinnati's" 9-inch guns were temporarily mounted in the rear of the city, and worked by a party of blue-jackets under Lieut.-Commander Walker. Both of these batteries did good service during the siege.

The Secretary of the Navy wrote a handsome letter to Lieutenant Bache, concluding as follows:

LIEUTENANT GEORGE M. BACHE, NOW COMMANDER U. S. N.

"Amid an incessant fire of shot and shells, even when the fate of the vessel had been sealed, and destruction both from the elements and the enemy was threatened, the officers and men appear to have stood bravely at their posts, and it is a proud record of the "Cincinnati" that when her last moments came, she went down with her colors nailed to the mast.

"It is with no ordinary pleasure that I express to you and the surviving officers and crew of the "Cincinnati" the department's appreciation of your brave conduct."

There was still work for the Navy to do in the Yazoo, while General Grant was starving the Confederates out in Vicksburg. There was no use in wasting life in assaulting a place with such defences, and the Army continued to make their approaches and mount their batteries until they were within fifty feet of the enemy's works. The surrender was but a matter of time, and a short time at that. Every opening was stopped up, no one inside could get out, nor those outside get in. The enemy now had to subsist on what provisions they had on hand, which was not much, and unless relieved by a superior force a month more or less would bring about a surrender. It was not likely that the siege would be raised, for if the Federal Army, with all the disadvantages under which it labored, could manage to dispose of an enemy 80,000 strong in a country where the latter occupied all the strong positions, it could prevent the escape of that portion of them which had been driven into the city.

It is not the province of the writer to give an account of the military operations of the siege of Vicksburg; this book is mostly confined to the naval operations, and he is not sufficiently informed on the subject to do full justice to the movements of the Army. He knows enough, however, to be satisfied that everything was done by the generals of our Army in a masterly manner, and that they had posted themselves so securely around Vicksburg that all the power of the Confederacy could not affect them in any way, and that while our soldiers were fed by a commissariat that had no equal in any part of the world, Pemberton and his troops inside the city were living on short rations. The Con-

federates were now acknowledging one to another that Pemberton (clever as he was) had more than met his match in the leader of the Federal Army, and that the Union soldiers, when well commanded, could meet a larger number of the enemy and defeat them with ease.

There were still a number of steamers on the Yazoo that might in some way be serviceable to the enemy and an expedition under Lieutenant-Commander Walker of the "DeKalb" was sent up that river to capture or destroy them.

The "Forest Rose," "Linden," "Signal" and "Petrel" (vessels whose names have appeared frequently in this history) accompanied the expedition. The "Signal" knocked down her chimney among the trees the first night, and had to return. Walker pushed on with the smaller vessels (leaving the "DeKalb" to follow after) to within fifteen miles of Fort Pemberton, where the steamers "John Walsh," "Lockwood," "Golden Age" and "Scotland" were found sunk on a bar, completely blocking the way. Failing in his efforts to make a passage through the boats, he set fire to them and they were all destroyed.

The expedition was attacked at this point by

U. S. GUN-BOAT "CINCINNATI" SUNK BY THE UPPER WATER BATTERY
AT VICKSBURG, MAY 27, 1863.
(FROM A PEN-AND-INK SKETCH BY REAR-ADMIRAL WALKE.)

artillery and sharp-shooters in force, but they were driven off with loss. Saw-mills were burned, the corn on which an enemy could subsist was destroyed, and at Yazoo City the crews landed and brought away all the bar, round and flat iron intended to be used in the building of their ironclads.

Armed boats were sent through the Rolling Fork and into bayous which were inaccessible at that moment to the gun-boats. Four other steamers were found hidden away in snug retreats and burned—almost rivalling the mischief done by the "Alabama," who had taught us how to retaliate upon an enemy.

This was a terrible raid and involved a loss to the enemy of more than two millions of dollars. The performance showed how easily the Delta expedition could have obtained possession of the Yazoo River and district as far as the rear of Vicksburg but for the delay at Helena. It also assured the success of the Steele's Bayou expedition, which was undertaken soon after the expedition to Yazoo Pass.

On the 19th of June, Admiral Porter received a notification from General Grant that he intended to open a general bombardment on the city at 4 A. M. and continue it until 10 o'clock. At the appointed time the bombardment commenced all along the army line and was joined on the water side by every gun-boat, the guns on scows and the mortars, until the earth fairly shook with the thundering noise. The gun-boats spread themselves all along in front of the city—cross firing on everything in the shape of a battery—but there was no response whatever—the works were all deserted; even the indefatigable Colonel Higgins, who loved to give his old shipmates a reminder of his gallantry, failed to fire a shot from his spiteful water-battery which had so often defied them.

After the fire was all over on the Union side, the city of Vicksburg was as quiet as the grave—not a soul could be seen. The women had all taken refuge in the shelters built in the hillsides, and every man that could hold a musket or point a bayonet was in the trenches. There they would stay for days and nights, lying in the mud and having what food they could get served out to them there.

The trials and privations which the Confederates suffered at this time can only be described by those who took part in the defence. The day on which they surrendered was a day of jubilee to them, for the Federal commanders served out full rations to everybody, which were eaten with an enjoyment that can only be realized by people who have been on quarter rations for a month.

Every effort was made to bring relief to the Confederates through Louisiana. General Price had been moving about some twelve miles from Young's Point among the swamps and bayous, and it was reported that he intended to seize Young's Point with some ten thousand men and try to provision Vicksburg by the front.

There was only a small force of Federal troops at Young's Point and Milliken's Bend at this time, and Price might have gained a partial success, but nothing substantial.

One attempt was made on Milliken's Bend, and quite a number of the garrison killed, but the gun-boats "Choctaw" and "Lexington" went immediately to the relief of our troops and the Confederates were driven off with loss

The Marine Brigade under Brigadier-General Alfred Ellet had joined the squadron and reported to Admiral Porter. This organization consisted of about two thousand men, well equipped and fairly disciplined. General Mower, a very brave officer, had about 8,000 men at Young's Point, and uniting the marine brigade with his troops he marched out to hunt up General Price's army,—found it and scattered it after a short and decisive battle. Price's army now left this district and troubled it no more. This was the last hope of the besieged, if they had ever hoped anything from so forlorn a scheme, and they sat in their trenches waiting for the time when the last ration should be served out.

On the 26th of June, this was the condition of affairs in the city. The gun-boats were by turns throwing shells day and night; the mortars kept up an incessant bombardment, which if it damaged no works demoralized the enemy's troops; a constant fire from the Army and Navy guns in the rear was kept up, day and night, and a 6-inch rifle battery taken from the gun-boats was served with great skill by General McArthur on the left flank. General McPherson had blown up what was called the citadel of the Confederate works, and mounted on the *debris* four 9-inch guns from the squadron, and some rifled 30-pounders.

These guns now commanded a large portion of the enemy's works, and when they opened fire the requiem of Vicksburg was sung by the shrieking shell, as they flew through the air carrying death and destruction all over the city.

On the 4th of July, 1863, that historic day was rendered more memorable by the surrender of Vicksburg to the Federal forces after a desperate but vain resistance, in which the Confederates had won the respect of their conquerors by the bravery and endurance displayed during a siege of seven months.

Southern historians have eulogized them for their faithful adherence to a cause which received its death-blow when they surrendered, but as this history is more particularly connected with the boys in blue than with the boys in gray we must leave the latter to the *future* military historian, who, when the excitements and prejudices of the time have worn away, will no doubt do them justice.

It was from no want of ability on the part of our military leaders that this surrender was not brought about sooner, but owing to the magnitude of the Confederate defences, which were intended to keep at bay any force the Federal Government could bring against them, and calculating that even were the city to be enveloped by troops the Confederacy could always send a sufficient number from the South to raise the siege. No doubt the will and energy were with the

Confederates to do as they thought could be done, but the great oak that has been torn and twisted by the winds for centuries must succumb at last to a tornado: the Confederacy had now received many telling blows, and its strength had begun to fail.

Many could see the end of the rebellion, and no one knew how near it was, better than the Confederates themselves. If doubts still remained with any of them, the fall of Vicksburg, the opening of the Mississippi from the Northern States to the sea, and the complete severance of the three most important States (as regarded supplies from others) would have removed their delusion. But they still fought on, though it was only with the spirit of the game-cock which strikes at random while the life-blood is flowing from its veins

History has seldom had an opportunity of recording so desperate a defence on one side, with so much ability, courage, perseverance and endurance on the other. The Army of the Tennessee covered itself with honor of which no one can ever deprive it.

Though the Navy performed naturally a less conspicuous part than the Army, yet it did its duty in a manner which not even the most exacting could find fault with. Less zeal on the part of its officers and men would doubtless have extended the siege to some indefinite time.

A short summary of the work done by the Navy during the last forty days of the siege, may not be amiss. It will assure those who served at this critical period in the Navy, that they are not forgotten, and that their names will go down to history, honored as they deserve to be.

The mortar boats were kept at work for forty days, night and day, throwing shells into every part of Vicksburg and its works, some of them even reaching the trenches in the rear of the city. Three heavy guns placed on scows, one 9-inch, one 10-inch, and a 100-pounder rifle were placed in position a mile from the town, and commanded all the important water batteries. They kept up an incessant and accurate fire for fourteen days, while the path of the missiles was filled with destruction.

Five 8-inch, four 9-inch, two 42-pounder rifled guns and four 32-pounder shell guns were landed from the gun-boats at different points during the siege at the request of the officers commanding divisions, or of General Grant, and whenever officers and men could be spared from the fleet they were sent on shore to work the guns. As no dissatisfaction was expressed by the officers in command, it was presumed that the sailors performed their duty well.

The banks of the Mississippi were so watchfully guarded from Vicksburg to Cairo that the Army transports went through with troops and stores, for a distance of about 450 miles, without molestation. The marine brigade, under Brigadier-General Ellet, was constantly landing along the river to break up guerilla warfare. Without a watchful eye on the Mississippi, on the part of the Navy, the operations of the Army would have been often interrupted. Only one Army steamer was disabled during the siege operations, and six or seven men killed on board of her.

When the whole of our Army was in the rear of Vicksburg, with the exception of a small force at Young's Point under General Mower, and that place was attacked by Major-General Price with 12,000 men, the marine brigade and the gun-boats united with General Mower's force to put the Confederates down, which was effectually done; and General Grant was satisfied that Young's Point would be taken care of by the Navy, while he was engaged in reducing the monster on the east bank of the Mississippi.

When the Army and Navy started out to capture Vicksburg the Mississippi was closed against the Federal forces from Helena to Port Hudson. This latter place fell shortly after the surrender of Vicksburg and the river was thus open to the sea.

There was no longer a doubt that the rebellious states were divided, and that the uninterrupted navigation of the "father of waters" and its tributaries was soon to be restored to the Union. So satisfied were the Confederate leaders that Vicksburg was the key to this great network of water which enriched the vast domain through which it found its way to the sea, that they staked their cause upon its retention. When they failed in this effort they were almost in their last throes, though their vitality enabled them to prolong the struggle (that was impoverishing and ruining their country,) for some time longer.

But there could be no hope of success for the Southern cause, when the great slave power which had controlled so many miles of the banks of the Mississippi no longer existed. The chain which held slavery together was broken, and the commerce of the nation went rejoicing on its way to the great ocean, once more to barter with the people of the outside world.

That 4th of July was a happy day to all those who had joined in the herculean efforts to bring about the desired end. At a certain hour the American flag was to be hoisted on the court-house where the Confederate emblem had so long flaunted in the face of the Union forces. At the moment the flag went up every vessel in the river, gun-boats and transports, decked with flags, started from above and below to reach the levee in front of the city, sounding their steam whistles and firing a national salute that seemed like a renewed attack.

The flagship "Black Hawk" had scarcely reached the levee when General Grant and many of his officers rode up, and dismounting, went on board, where they were received with that warmth of feeling and hospitality that delights the heart of a sailor. The leader, who with his Army had achieved the greatest victory of the war, now received the congratulations of the officers of both Army and Navy, and although no one would judge from his manner that anything remarkable had happened yet he must have felt that this was the triumph of his life.

Sherman was one of those whose absence was regretted by all, but he was off with a division of the Army in pursuit of General Johnston, who had been lingering in the vicinity of Jackson in hopes of rendering aid to the besieged. He was too formidable an enemy to be allowed to remain near the prize which had been so hardly won, and Sherman had gone to show him that he must move his headquarters somewhere else.

But even while engaged on so important a duty, Sherman did not forget those of the Navy with whom he had co-operated for so many months, and he wrote a letter to the Admiral in which he expressed his satisfaction at the final result of the siege. This letter is so like the warm-hearted and gallant soldier, that no one can help feeling pleasure when he reads it, and it is here inserted.

HEADQUARTERS EXPEDITIONARY ARMY, }
BLACK RIVER, July 4, 1863. }

DEAR ADMIRAL—No event in my life could have given me more personal pride or pleasure than to have met you to-day on the wharf at Vicksburg—a Fourth of July so eloquent in events as to need no words or stimulants to elevate its importance.

I can appreciate the intense satisfaction you must feel at lying before the very monster which has defied us with such deep and malignant hate, and seeing your once disunited fleet again a unit, and better still, the chain that made an enclosed sea of a link in the great river broken forever.

In so magnificent a result I stop not to count who did it. It is done and the day of our nation's birth is consecrated and baptized anew in a victory won by the united Navy and Army of our country.

God grant that the harmony and mutual respect that exist between our respective commanders, and shared by all the true men of the joint service, may continue forever, and serve to elevate our national character, threatened with shipwreck.

Thus I muse as I sit in my solitary camp out in the woods, far from the point for which we have jointly striven and so well, and though personal curiosity would tempt me to go and see the frowning batteries and sunken pits that have defied us so long, and sent to their silent graves so many of our early comrades in the enterprise, I feel that other tasks lie before me, and time must not be lost.

Without casting anchor, and despite the heat and the dust, and the drought, I must again into the bowels of the land, to make the conquest of Vicks-

burg fulfill all the conditions it should in the progress of this war.

Whether success attend my efforts or not, I know that Admiral Porter will ever accord to me the exhibition of a pure and unselfish zeal in the service of our country.

It does seem to me that Port Hudson, without facilities for supplies or interior communication, must soon follow the fate of Vicksburg and leave the river free; and to you the task of preventing any more Vicksburgs or Port Hudsons on the bank of the great inland sea.

Though further apart, the Navy and Army will still act in concert, and I assure you I shall never reach the banks of the river or see a gun-boat but I will think of Admiral Porter, Captain Breese, and the many elegant and accomplished gentlemen it has been my good fortune to meet on armed or unarmed decks of the Mississippi Squadron.

Congratulating you and the officers and men of your command at the great result in which you have borne so conspicuous a part,

I remain, your friend and servant,
W. T. SHERMAN,
Major-General.

Admiral D. D. PORTER,
Commanding Fleet.

Army and Navy vied with each other in their efforts to alleviate the discomforts of those who had spent so many months under a merciless fire and suffered all the miseries attending a siege. The commanding General set the example by giving all the provisions, stores and transportation General Pemberton required for the officers and men of his Army, who had been paroled and allowed to return to their homes. The naval officers opened their stores for those officers who had families, and though they did not leave Vicksburg in much style, they were comparatively comfortable after suffering so many evils.

It was curious to see, an hour after the surrender, the soldiers of the two armies fraternizing as if they belonged to the same party; there was not, in fact, much difference between them, only one party had gone off on the wrong track, and, owing to bad leaders, had drifted considerably out of their course. Confederate officers on horseback would join naval officers, who, mounted on the sorry-looking steeds which had been loaned them, were riding about the city, and chat with them as pleasantly as if they were honored guests. Groups of officers in blue and gray mingled together in the most friendly manner.

Officers who visited houses where there were ladies, were received courteously if not warmly, and it was difficult to realize that the people of this battered city had been within a few days doing all they could to harm those with whom they now seemed to be on such pleasant terms. The people of Vicksburg were thoroughly subdued, they had gone through so much misery and endured so many privations that any change was acceptable.

Besides, their conquerors had been generous far beyond their expectations, and had furnished them the means to depart and meet again their absent friends, with whom they had not communicated for many days.

The regret of being conquered was mitigated by the promised pleasure of seeing their loved homes, and getting away from scenes which continually reminded them of the horrors which they had undergone for so many months. Over 5,000 had died in hospital or been killed in the trenches since the close siege had commenced, and many must have left there with deep regrets for the loss of loved ones, who were buried in the soldier's cemetery without a stone to mark their resting places.

As time moves on and the military and naval history of the war are being chronicled by impartial authors, the facts connected with the most important events are being brought to light.

The war has been mostly written up through the reporters, who accompanied the Armies of the Republic, and although they have described the scenes in a most graphic manner, yet their accounts were given a coloring that detracted from, rather than embellished, the picture.

There was no scene of action during the war where more misrepresentations were made, or where less desire seemed to be manifested by the newspaper correspondents to do justice to both the naval and military movements, than at Vicksburg, and to read the numberless accounts that were transmitted from these to the various newspapers, one would form an altogether erroneous opinion of what took place.

Some of these descriptions of events were written with only a desire to please the public, and they were of a sensational character—pleasant reading over a breakfast table, but far from being history.

Many of the correspondents wrote from hearsay, and were not near the scene of action which they so graphically described, and the people at the North, greedy to drink in the news from distant battlefields, were satisfied to believe the wanton mistakes which were sent abroad without revision, and adopted them as the true version of affairs.

It was not, and is not now, generally understood, that the operations against Vicksburg were a combination of Army and Navy, in which each commander acted on his own responsibility, neither having received any instructions from their several Departments.

The plans for the capture of Vicksburg from the first to the last were arranged by General Grant and Admiral Porter, and carried out to the end with that unanimity of purpose which always leads to success.

General Grant never undertook any movement without consulting the commander of the Mississippi Squadron, while the latter never did anything without consulting General Grant, and thus a harmony of action prevailed which probably never was obtained in any other military and naval co-operation.

Grant and Porter were of assimilated rank, and neither could give an order to the other; therefore it was only through that high courtesy bred in a purely military school, that so perfect an understanding could be arrived at, or that the wishes of either military or naval commander could be anticipated.

Some naval officers, after the reduction of Vicksburg, were disposed to find fault with General Grant for not being more demonstrative in his remarks concerning the work the Navy had performed ; but Grant was never a demonstrative man; he left it to the Commander-in-chief of the Mississippi Squadron to mention the services of his own officers and vessels, and would, no doubt, have thought it peculiar if the naval commander had undertaken to go into an elaborate eulogy on the performances of the Army. But Grant, in his last days, did not forget the great help he received from the naval part of the expedition to capture Vicksburg. In his reminiscences of the war, he says :

"The Navy under Porter was all it could be during the entire campaign. Without its assistance the campaign could not have been successfully made with twice the number of men engaged. It could not have been made at all in the way it was, with any number of men without such assistance. The most perfect harmony reigned between the two arms of the service. There never was a request made, that I am aware of, either of the Flag-officer or any of his subordinates, that was not promptly complied with."

This should afford satisfaction to those naval officers who for a time doubted General Grant's generosity. Words of ordinary praise coming from him were of more import, than words from a man who was too lavish of his commendations. Those last words of Grant's were grains of gold, and will go down in history, never to be erased from the book of fame.

The commander of the Mississippi Squadron was contented with General Grant's reticence in regard to naval movements before Vicksburg. He felt satisfied that he alone could do full justice to the brave officers and men who served under him, as will appear from the following letter written after the surrender of Vicksburg.

[DETAILED REPORT OF ACTING-REAR-ADMIRAL PORTER.]

U. S. MISSISSIPPI SQUADRON, FLAG-SHIP }
"BLACK HAWK," OFF VICKSBURG, }
July 13, 1863. }

SIR—I have made reports to the Department of the different actions that have occurred on this river since the investment of Vicksburg; and it now remains for me to give credit to the different officers who have participated in the events transpiring here.

When I took command of this squadron this river was virtually closed against our steamers from Helena to Vicksburg. It was only necessary to impress the officers and men with the importance of opening communication with New Orleans, and every one, with few exceptions, have embarked in the enterprise with a zeal that is highly creditable to them, and with a determination that the river should be opened if their aid could effect it.

With such officers and the able general who commanded the Army I have not feared for the result, though it has been postponed longer than I thought it would be.

First and foremost, allow me to speak of Captain Pennock, fleet captain and commandant of station at Cairo. To him I am much indebted for the promptness with which he has kept the squadron supplied with all that was required or could be procured.

His duty has been no sinecure, and he has performed it with an ability that could not have been surpassed by any officer of the Navy. He has materially assisted me in the management of the Tennessee and Cumberland squadrons, keeping me promptly informed of all the movements of the enemy, and enabling me to make the proper disposi- tions to check him, exercising a most discreet judgment in moving the vessels to meet the rebels when there was no time to hear from me.

The war on the banks of the Tennessee and Cumberland has been carried on most actively. There has been incessant skirmishing between the guerrillas and gun-boats, in which the rebels have been defeated in every instance. So constant are these attacks that we cease to think of them as of any importance, though there has been much gallantry displayed on many occasions.

Lieutenant-Commanders Phelps and Fitch have each had command of the Cumberland and Tennessee Rivers, and have shown themselves to be most able officers. I feel no apprehension at any time with regard to movements in that quarter. Had it not been for the activity and energy displayed by Lieutenant-Commander Fitch, Captain Pennock and Lieutenant-Commander Phelps, General Rosecrans would have been left without provisions.

To Captain Walke, Commander Woodworth, Lieutenant-Commanders Breese, Foster, Greer, Shirk, Owen, Wilson, Walker, Bache, Murphy, Selfridge, Prichett, Ramsay and Acting - Volunteer-Lieutenant Hoel, I feel much indebted for their active and energetic attention to all my orders, and their ready co-operation with the Army corps commanders, at all times, which enabled them to carry out their plans successfully.

The "Benton," Lieutenant-Commander Greer, "Mound City," Lieutenant Byron Wilson, "Tuscumbia," Lieutenant - Commander Shirk, "Carondelet," Acting Lieutenant Murphy, and the "Sterling Price," Commander Woodworth, have been almost constantly under fire of the batteries at Vicksburg since the forty-five days' siege commenced.

The attack of the 22d of May, by the "Benton," "Mound City," "Carondelet" and "Tuscumbia" on all the water batteries, in which *three* were silenced and four guns injured or dismounted, was one of the best contested engagements of the kind during the war.

On the next attack of the same gun-boats, when General Grant opened all his batteries for six hours, the river batteries were *all* silenced and deserted, and the gun boats moved up and down the river without having a shot fired at them, showing the moral effect of the first attack.

The attack of the "Cincinnati" (Lieutenant-Commanding Bache), on the outer water battery

will long be ranked among the most gallant events of this war; and though Lieutenant Bache had the misfortune to have his vessel sunk under him, he well deserves the handsome commendations bestowed upon him by the Department.

To Lieutenant - Commander Ramsey, of the "Choctaw," was assigned the management of three heavy guns placed on scows and anchored in a position to command the town and water batteries. Every gun the enemy could bring to bear on these boats was fired incessantly at them, but without one moment's cessation of fire on the part of our seamen, though the enemy's shots and shells fell like hail among them. This floating battery completely enfiladed the enemy's batteries and rifle-pits in front of General Sherman, and made them untenable.

The mortar-boats were under charge of gunner Eugene Mack, who for thirty days stood at his post, the firing continuing night and day.

He performed his duty well and merits approval. The labor was extremely hard, and every man at the mortars was laid up with sickness, owing to excessive labor. After Mr. Mack was taken ill, Ensign Miller took charge and conducted the firing with marked ability. We know that nothing conduced more to the end of the siege than the mortar firing, which demoralized the rebels, killed and wounded a number of persons, killed the cattle, destroyed property of all kinds, and set the city on fire. On the last two days we were enabled to reach the outer works of the enemy by firing heavy charges of twenty-six pounds of powder; the distance was nearly three miles, and the falling of shells was very annoying to the rebels, to use the words of a rebel officer, "your shells intruded everywhere."

Lieutenant - Commander Breese has been very efficient in relieving me of a vast amount of duty, superintending personally all the requirements made on the Navy, and facilitating the operations of the Army in every way that laid in his power. In every instance where it was at all possible to bring the "Black Hawk" into action against the enemy's batteries, he has not hesitated to do so, though she is not fortified exactly for such a purpose. His long range guns have done most excellent service at different times.

I beg leave to mention the different commanders of the light draughts who have carried out my orders promptly, aided in keeping guerillas from the river, convoyed transports safely, and kept their vessels in good condition for service, viz: Acting-Volunteer-Lieutenant George W. Brown, commanding "Forest Rose"; Acting-Volunteer-Lieutenant C. Dominey, commanding "Signal"; Acting-Volunteer Lieutenant J. H. Hurd, commanding "Covington"; Ensign Wm. C. Hanford, commanding "Robb"; Acting-Master J. C. Bunner, commanding "New Era"; Acting-Volunteer-Lieutenant John Pierce, commanding "Petrel"; Acting-Volunteer-Lieutenant J. V. Johnstone, commanding "Romeo"; Acting-Master W. E. Fentress, commanding "Rattler"; Acting-Volunteer-Lieutenant T. E. Smith, commanding "Linden"; Acting-Volunteer-Lieutenant E. C. Brennan, commanding "Prairie Bird"; Acting-Volunteer-Lieutenant J. Goudy, commanding "Queen City." There are others who deserve commendation, but these seem to be the most prominent.

The action of the 4th of July, at Helena, wherein the "Taylor" participated so largely, has already been reported to the Department.

There is no doubt left in the minds of any, but that the "Taylor" saved Helena, for, though General Prentiss fought with a skill and daring not excelled in this war, his little force of thirty-five hundred men were fast being overpowered by the enemy with eighteen thousand men, when the "Taylor" took a position and changed the fortunes of the day.

I must not omit to mention Acting-Volunteer-

Lieutenants Hamilton and Richardson of the powder vessels "Great Western" and "Judge Torrence." They were unremitting in their attention to their duties during the siege, supplying without delay every requisition made on them by the Army and Navy, and volunteering for any service.

When the Army called on the Navy for siege guns, I detailed what officers and men I could spare to man and work the batteries.

Lieutenant-Commander Selfridge had command of the naval battery on the right wing in General Sherman's corps. This battery was worked with marked ability, and elicited the warmest praises from the commanding general. One thousand shells were fired into the enemy's works from Lieutenant-Commander Selfridge's guns. His services being required up the river, I relieved him a few days before the surrender, and Lieutenant-Commander Walker supplied his place and conducted the firing with the same ability.

Acting-Master Charles B. Dahlgren was ordered to report to General McPherson for duty, and was assigned the management of the 9-inch guns, which were admirably served.

Acting-Master Reed, of the "Benton," had charge of the batteries at Fort Benton—so named by General Herron in honor of the occasion. General Herron generously acknowledged the services of those I sent him, which communication I enclose with this report.

I have endeavored to do justice to all who were immediately engaged in the struggle for the mastery of the Mississippi. To the Army do we owe immediate thanks for the capture of Vicksburg; but the Army was much facilitated by the Navy, which was ready at all times to co-operate. This has been no small undertaking. The late investment and capture of Vicksburg will be characterized as one of the greatest military achievements ever known. The conception of the siege originated with General Grant, who adopted a course in which great labor was performed, great battles were fought and great risks were run. A single mistake would have involved us all in difficulty, but so well were all the plans matured, so well were all the movements timed, and so rapid were the evolutions performed, that not a mistake has occurred from the passage of the fleet by Vicksburg and the passage of the Army across the river, up to the present time. So confident was I of the ability of General Grant to carry out his plans when he explained them to me, that I never hesitated to change my position from above to below Vicksburg. The work was hard, the fighting severe, but the blows struck were incessant.

In forty-five days after our Army was landed, a rebel Army of 40,000 men had been captured, killed and wounded, or scattered to their homes perfectly demoralized, while our loss has been only about 5,000 killed, wounded and prisoners, and the temporary loss of one gun-boat.

The fortifications and defences of the city exceed anything that has been built in modern times, and are doubly unassailable from their immense height above the bed of the river.

The fall of Vicksburg insured the fall of Port Hudson and the opening of the Mississippi River, which, I am happy to say, can be traversed from its source to its mouth, without apparent impediment, the first time during the war.

I take this opportunity to give to Mr. Fendall and Mr. Straus, assistants in the Coast Survey, the full credit they deserve for their indefatigable industry.

Since they have been attached to the Squadron, they have been connected with almost every expedition that has been undertaken; they have kept both Army and Navy supplied with charts, when they could not otherwise be obtained; they were found ready at all times to go anywhere or do anything required of them, whether it was on a gunboat expedition or in the trenches before Vicksburg, engineering, when the general-commanding asked for volunteers from the Navy.

They have added to our collection of maps many geographical corrections which are valuable, and they have proved to me that no squadron can operate effectively without a good corps of surveyors.

I have the honor to be, very respectfully, your obedient servant,

DAVID D. PORTER,
Acting-Rear-Admiral, Commanding Mississippi Squadron.
Hon. GIDEON WELLES,
Secretary of the Navy, Washington, D. C.

CONGRATULATORY LETTER TO REAR-ADMIRAL PORTER ON THE SURRENDER OF VICKSBURG.

NAVY DEPARTMENT, July 13, 1863.

SIR—Your dispatch of the 4th instant announcing the surrender of Vicksburg on the anniversary of the great historic day in our national annals, has been received.

The fall of that place insures a severance of the rebel territory, and must give to the country the speedy uninterrupted navigation of the rivers which water and furnish the ocean outlet to the great central valley of the Union.

For the past year the key to the Mississippi has been Vicksburg, and so satisfied of this was the rebel chief who pioneered the rebellion and first gave the order to open the fires of civil strife, that he staked his cause upon its retention.

By the herculean efforts of the Army under the admirable leadership of General Grant, and the persistent and powerful co-operation of the Navy, commanded by yourself, this great result, under the providence of Almighty God, has been achieved.

A slave empire, divided by this river into equal parts, with liberty in possession of its banks, and freedom upon its waters, cannot exist.

The work of rescuing and setting free this noble artery, whose unrestricted vital current is essential to our nationality, commenced with such ability by the veteran Farragut and the lamented Foote, and continued by Davis, is near its consummation.

You have only to proceed onward and meet that veteran chief whose first act was to dash through the gates by which the rebels assumed to bar the entrance to the Mississippi, whose free communication to and above New Orleans he has ever since proudly maintained.

When the squadrons of the Upper and Lower Mississippi shall combine, and the noble river be again free to a united people, the nation will feel its integrity restored, and the names of the heroic champions who signalized themselves in this invaluable service, will be cherished and honored.

Present and future millions on the shores of those magnificent rivers which patriotism and valor shall have emancipated, will remember with unceasing gratitude, the naval heroes who so well performed their part in these eventful times.

To yourself, your officers, and the brave and gallant sailors who have been so fertile in resources, so persistent and enduring through many months of trial and hardship, and so daring under all circumstances, I tender, in the name of the President, the thanks and congratulations of the whole country, on the fall of Vicksburg.

Very respectfully, etc.,

GIDEON WELLES,
Secretary of the Navy.
REAR-ADMIRAL DAVID D. PORTER,
Commanding Mississippi Squadron, Vicksburg, Miss.

CHAPTER XXX.

Naval and Military Expedition to Yazoo City.—Capture of the Enemy's Works.—The "Baron-de-Kalb" blown up by Torpedoes.—Expedition up the Red, Black and Tensas Rivers, under Lieutenant-Commander Selfridge.—Destruction of Enemy's Vessels and Stores.—The Marine Brigade, its Important Services.—Operations of Lieutenant-Commander Le Roy Fitch on the Tennessee River.—Attack on Colored Troops at Milliken's Bend.—Attack on Helena, Arkansas, by General Price.—Defeat of the Enemy owing to the fire of the Gun-boat "Lexington."—The Raid of General John Morgan into Ohio and Indiana, and the Capture of his Forces owing to the energy of Lieutenant-Commander Le Roy Fitch with his Gun-boats.—Gallant Conduct of Engineer Doughty in Capturing two of the Enemy's Steamers.—Eulogy upon the Pilots and Engineers of the Mississippi Squadron.—Important Services of Lieutenant-Commander Phelps in the Tennessee River.—Vessels employed at Vicksburg during the Siege, with List of Officers.—Vessels employed at other points on the Mississippi River, 1863-65.

AFTER the surrender of Vicksburg, there was still much to be done in the vicinity, particularly in driving off the Confederates, who lingered on the banks of the Yazoo and fired on our small gun-boats as they patrolled that river.

A report reached Vicksburg that General Joseph E. Johnston was fortifying Yazoo City, with the apparent intention of occupying that neighborhood with his Army. For this the region was well adapted, being rich in cattle and grain, "hog and hominy."

It was also reported that a number of large river-steamers that had been employed by the enemy, and had been hiding in the Tallahatchie, were at Yazoo City and employed in supplying Johnston's troops.

A military and naval expedition was therefore arranged to go after these steamers and break up the enemy's resort at Yazoo City.

The "Baron de Kalb," "New National," "Kenwood" and "Signal" composed the naval part of the expedition under Lieutenant-Commander John G. Walker, while General Herron, with five thousand troops in transports, composed the military part.

On approaching Yazoo City the enemy appeared in force, and the "DeKalb," being the heaviest vessel, pushed ahead and opened her batteries to ascertain the number and position of the enemy's guns. Finding the defences formidable, Walker dropped back and notified General Herron, who at once landed his troops and the Army and Navy made a combined attack. After a sharp conflict the enemy fled, previously setting fire to the four large steamers in their possession, which before the war had been considered the finest passenger vessels on the Mississippi River. General Herron captured the enemy's rear-guard of two hundred and fifty men and pressed on after the retreating foe, taking prisoners every minute.

There were six heavy guns mounted in the enemy's works and one vessel was captured which had formerly been a gun-boat. Unfortunately, while the "De Kalb" was moving slowly along and firing on the enemy she ran foul of a floating torpedo, which exploded, and the vessel sank almost immediately, a second torpedo exploding under her stern as she went down.

The squadron had pushed ahead with too much enthusiasm to bring the enemy to close quarters where grape-shot and canister would tell. It seems that Lieutenant Isaac N. Brown, of the Confederate Navy, had on a former occasion been prevented by the citizens from placing torpedoes in front of

Yazoo City, and it was supposed that it would not be permitted on this occasion for fear of the consequences in the destruction of the property of the inhabitants, should the Union forces get possession of Yazoo City. Lieutenant-Commander Walker therefore felt confident that he could proceed without encountering any of these destructive machines.

The loss of the "DeKalb" was a serious one—four of the armored gun-boats lay at the bottom of the rivers—the "Cincinnati" before Vicksburg, and the "Cairo" and "De-Kalb" in the Yazoo, while the "Indianola" was sunk below Vicksburg. But this is the fortune of war—to achieve anything risks must be run, and while a Confederate flag floated in the breeze the officers and men of the Mississippi squadron never stopped to count the cost in pursuit of it.

With the exception of the loss of the "De-Kalb," whose officers and men were all saved, the expedition was a complete success. The enemy's rendezvous was broken up, and a large amount of cotton, beef and pork captured, the enemy's forces driven away and many of them captured by General Herron. Yazoo City was never again troubled by the Confederates planting batteries there.

It had been an important place for the Confederates, and but for the constant attention it received from the Navy and the destruction of all the vessels hiding there, they would probably have sent down a force that would have destroyed our iron-clad gun-boats, and perhaps have made a material change in the final result of the campaign.

The Confederate government relied a great deal on the completion of the three iron-clad rams building at Yazoo City, and with their assistance hoped to drive off the Federal squadron from below Vicksburg and thereby cause the siege to be raised—while Haines' Bluff could block the way with its guns and the huge raft which filled up the Yazoo River for half a mile. The Confederates worked on their iron-clads without molestation, and even when General Grant had gained the rear of Vicksburg they relied on General J. E. Johnston's army to protect them while they completed the work on the rams.

If the "Arkansas," which ran the gauntlet of Farragut and Davis' squadrons, was a specimen of the iron-clad that could be built at Yazoo City, the Federals had cause to congratulate themselves that the Yazoo was open by the evacuation of Haines' Bluff, and the last attempt of the Confederates to carry on naval operations in that quarter abandoned.

At the same time that the expedition was sent up the Yazoo another was dispatched up the Red River, ascending the Black and Tensas Rivers. Lieutenant-Commander Selfridge penetrated to the head of navigation on the latter stream, at Tensas Lake and Bayou Macon, thirty miles above Vicksburg, and within five or six miles of the Mississippi River.

Parties of the enemy's riflemen were in the habit of crossing this narrow strip of land and firing upon transports passing up and down the Mississippi, sometimes killing women and children who happened to be on board. Quite a large force of Confederates were assembled in that quarter, considering themselves secure from the attacks of the gun-boats, the distance by water from Vicksburg being so great: the route being first to the mouth of the Red River, then up the Black and Tensas, both narrow streams, to Tensas Lake and Bayou Macon. The guerillas fancied they could carry on their raids with impunity. So when Selfridge appeared with his little flotilla on the 12th of July, they were taken by surprise. As soon as the gun-boats hove in sight the enemy's transports, of which there were here quite a number, made their escape among the intricate water-ways with which that region abounds, and where for want of pilots they could not be immediately followed.

Selfridge now divided his forces, sending the "Manitou" and "Rattler" up the Little Red River, a small tributary of the Black, and the "Forest Rose" and "Petrel" up the Tensas. The night was dark and rainy and the vessels had to grope their way carefully along, keeping a good lookout ahead. Suddenly the "Manitou" and "Rattler" came upon a very large steamer, the finest of those now remaining afloat, which had been the pride of the Mississippi River before the war. This was the "Louisville," afterwards converted into a war-vessel carrying fifty guns.

Selfridge's other two vessels about the same time captured the steamer "Elmira," loaded with stores for the Confederate army under General Walker, who on hearing of the arrival of the Federal gun-boats embarked his army and disappeared up some of the tortuous channels known only to pilots. Selfridge started in pursuit and soon overtook two of the transports, but the Confederates immediately abandoned the vessels after setting them on fire, and they were totally destroyed.

One steamer loaded with ammunition escaped above the fort at Harrisonburg, a strong work impregnable to wooden gun-boats with light batteries. The expedition could proceed no further in this direction.

Lieutenant-Commander Selfridge fortunately learned of a large amount of ammunition that had been sent up from Natchez, whence large quantities of provisions, stores and ammunition were often transported. Natchez took no part in the war beyond making money by supplying the Confederate armies.

Selfridge captured at one place fifteen thousand rounds of smooth-bore ammunition, one thousand rounds of Enfield rifle and two hundred and twenty four rounds of fixed ammunition for guns, a rifled thirty-pounder Parrott gun-carriage, fifty-two hogsheads of sugar, ten puncheons of rum, nine barrels of flour and fifty barrels of salt; and General Walker's army being left without a supply of ammunition, he moved his forces into the interior and troubled the Mississippi no more. Thus these constant raids of the gun-boats harassed and weakened the enemy, broke up the steamboat transportation so necessary for their movements, and deprived them of ammunition and provisions, without which they could not fight.

One portion of Admiral Porter's command—the Marine Brigade—is entitled to special mention. When he assumed command of the Mississippi Squadron, the Admiral applied for a force of marines to be carried in suitable vessels accompanying the gun-boats and to be landed at points where parties of guerillas were wont to assemble. The gun-boats alone could not break these parties up, and it was therefore necessary to have trained soldiers at hand to chase and annihilate them.

The Navy Department could not furnish the marines asked for, but the War Department undertook to organize a Marine Brigade, and also to furnish the necessary vessels to carry these soldiers about. The command was given to Brigadier General Alfred Ellet, and as the members of this family had before proved themselves brave and enterprising men several of them were given appointments in the Marine Brigade.

As soon as this organization was fully equipped General Ellet was ordered by the Commander-in-chief of the Mississippi squadron to proceed to the Tennessee River before reporting at Vicksburg, and help put down the numerous guerilla bands that infested the banks of that stream. These guerillas, although enlisted by the Confederates in the usual way as soldiers, were in fact made up of men too cowardly to join the regular Army and worthless fellows who would rather hang around home, pretending to save the Confederacy, than go where bullets were flying thick and fast on the field of battle. During the whole war bitterness and treachery flourished in Tennessee owing to this guerilla system. In some parts of the State almost every family had one or more of these quasi-soldiers belonging to a gang whose occupation was firing on unarmed steamers, and seldom or ever, even when supported by artillery, making a successful stand against the light gun-boats called "tin-clads." Now and then they would receive severe punishment and some of them get killed; occasionally when overtaken they were summarily dealt with.

In April, 1863, Lieutenant-Commander LeRoy Fitch was patrolling the Tennessee River with the gun-boats "Lexington," "Robert," and "Silver Lake." This active officer made matters so uncomfortable for the guerillas that they did not often come within range of his guns. One of his first acts was to take on board his vessels one hundred and fifty soldiers from Fort Hindman, under command of Colonel Craig, and visit the landings infested by guerillas. At Savannah, where Lieutenant-Commander Fitch landed two hundred soldiers and sailors, he burned a mill which was used in making cloth to clothe the guerillas; a quantity of horses, mules, and wagons belonging to the Confederate cavalry were also made prize of war.

The plantations of those persons who were known to have aided and abetted the outrages of the guerillas were destroyed, as an example to others. The war had been carried on by these worthless marauders in such a way that this course was found to be necessary to put a check on operations which had the effect of embittering both parties without in any way benefitting the Confederate cause.

On the bodies of some of the guerillas who were killed in one of the attacks was found an oath of allegiance to the United States Government. A certain class of persons would take the oath of allegiance to the United States one day, to secure protection, and the next would be found firing upon unarmed vessels.

The command of Lieutenant-Commander Fitch was increased as fast as the small stern-wheel merchant-steamers could be altered into gun-boats, the Navy Department having authorized Admiral Porter to purchase as many of these as he deemed requisite to put down the guerillas and protect loyal citizens, and a large number of naval vessels were soon in commission on the western waters. One requisition alone for seven hundred pieces of ordnance will show how this tin-clad service was increased. Many engagements occurred when Lieutenant-Commander Fitch had a sufficient number of vessels to effectually patrol the Tennessee, where by night and day he was indefatigable in trying to put down the marauders. The gun-boats never remained at a bank for fear of a surprise, and when anchored in the stream men were always at the guns, and at night all lights were kept covered.

Such was the condition of affairs when Brigadier-General Alfred Ellet, with the marine brigade, entered the Tennessee in five steamers, admirably equipped for the accommodation of the men, and united with Lieutenant-Commander Fitch to suppress the guerillas. These combined forces penetrated to the furthest part of the river when the water would permit, and when the river was very low Lieutenant-Commander Fitch was provided with a class of gun-boats drawing only sixteen inches of water, which could almost always make their way to any desired point. The remarkable energy and perseverance of Fitch won the approbation of the Union men in Tennessee, and gained the entire confidence of his Commander-in-chief. His officers were all volunteers, but with his example and training they were quite equal to any in the regular service for the duty in which they were engaged.

The Confederates were much surprised at the advent of the Marine Brigade, who were gun-boat men and soldiers at the same time, and could land fifteen hundred troops with field artillery at a moment's notice to pursue the enemy. In fact, when Fitch and Ellet co-operated, they made short work of the Confederates, who had really been a scourge to both parties in Tennessee.

General Ellet's command included cavalry, with which he made night marches to pounce on the camps of the guerillas and destroy the stores on which these marauders relied for subsistence. The Marine Brigade also co-operated with the Army under General Dodge and afforded material assistance in breaking up the command of the Confederate general, Cox, some eighteen miles above Savannah on the Tennessee.

General Ellet's command was not popular with the Confederate inhabitants, as the former did not trouble themselves much about the "amenities of war." They saw so many "irregularities" committed by the enemy that they retaliated in many instances by destroying the property of disloyal persons, and often returned from an expedition with sufficient stores captured from the enemy to last the command a month.

On the morning of April 25, 1863, the Marine Brigade was attacked at a place called Duck River by a Confederate force of seven hundred men and two field-pieces under Colonel Woodward. It seems the enemy mistook the Marine Brigade vessels for transports and were quite unprepared for the reception they encountered. As soon as possible a landing was effected and the enemy pursued for twelve miles. Major

White, of the 6th Texas Rangers, was found mortally wounded in a house four miles from the field of battle where eight of the Confederates were killed.

The water in the Tennessee River becoming too low for the Marine Brigade steamers to operate, they left the river on the 7th of May, having destroyed great numbers of boats and scows and all the ferry-boats they could find. Tennessee became not only a battle-ground for the contending armies, but her vindictive home-guards brought upon her more misery than can be compensated for by fifty years of prosperity.

On his way down to Vicksburg General Ellet heard of some Confederate troops at a place called Austin and dispatched a cavalry force of two hundred men, commanded by Major Holland, in pursuit, followed by infantry. The cavalry encountered the main body of the Confederates, one thousand strong, with two pieces of artillery. Holland found his retreat cut off, but by getting a good position and dismounting his men he managed to hold his ground until the infantry came up, when the enemy retreated leaving five of their number dead on the field. The Union loss was two killed and nineteen wounded. A wagon train and a quantity of arms were captured, together with three prisoners, and the town of Austin was set on fire and destroyed with a large amount of provisions, thus breaking up a nest of guerillas who were making preparations to commence a system of firing on vessels as they had done on the Tennessee.

While the town was on fire numerous explosions showed where arms and ammunition had been secreted.

On the 29th of May the Marine Brigade reached the Yazoo River, after having performed much valuable service.

After the Brigade left the Tennessee River the guerillas re-commenced their operations, but the commanding officers of the small gun-boats exerted themselves to the utmost to make up for the loss of the landing parties. On the 19th of June Acting-Master W. C. Hanford, commanding the U. S. S. "Little Rebel," heard that a party of guerillas under Colonel Bissell were lying in wait for gun-boats, proposing to give them one round from their battery and then make off. Hanford mounted two howitzers as field-pieces, manned them with sixteen of his best men, and started them in search of the marauders.

On the following morning, June 19th, on hearing the firing of guns the "Robb" and the "Silver Cloud" got underway and ran down to the point where the battery had been placed. Here Hanford found that Bissell had attacked his battery with four hundred men, but as the Confederates advanced, four abreast, the Union guns opened on them, making large gaps in their ranks and firing so rapidly that they at length turned and fled, having lost about fifty in killed and wounded, while Hanford had but one killed and two wounded.

On this occasion the gun-boats fired with grape and canister at close quarters, and the enemy's column was enfiladed on both sides as it advanced. The Confederates had dismounted from their horses to charge the battery.

In June, 1863, a great sensation was created throughout the country by a thrilling account of an attack made on a body of colored troops stationed at Milliken's Bend, by a portion of the Confederate army under General Price. Milliken's Bend is but two or three miles above Young's Point and was in daily communication with that place.

It was a mooted question whether the blacks enlisted as soldiers would be reliable in battle and they were mostly employed, as at Milliken's Bend, in guarding stores or in other duty, where they could relieve white soldiers sent to the front. As far as appearances went, the colored troops were good soldiers and many enthusiasts declared that they would stand the shock of arms as well as the whites.

At Milliken's Bend was also a portion of a white regiment which was looked upon by those who were not enthusiasts as by far the most reliable part of the garrison.

On the 6th of June, the Admiral, who had general charge of matters in that quarter, hearing that some of the enemy's troops had been seen hovering around Milliken's Bend, sent the "Choctaw," Lieutenant-Commander F. M. Ramsay, up to that place with orders to be ready for an emergency. At 2.15 A. M., on the 7th instant, an Army officer hailed the "Choctaw" and reported that his pickets had been attacked and driven in by the enemy. A few minutes later firing was heard in the main camp. The "Choctaw" immediately opened in direction of the enemy with a hundred - pounder rifle and a nine-inch shell-gun, the Federal troops, with the exception of the 23d Iowa, retreating at the first attack of the enemy.

It was impossible for the "Choctaw" to fire except by signs from those on shore, who pointed out the direction of the enemy; but the practice turned out to be good, and at 8.30 the Confederates retreated much cut up. The "Lexington," Lieutenant Commanding George M. Bache, reached the scene of action as the enemy were making off and opened on the retreating columns with eight-inch shells.

Had it not been for the presence of a gun-boat, the enemy would have captured everything at Milliken's Bend, for they were in strong force and charged right over the colored troops, who fled to the trenches and thence fired at random. The enemy then swarmed over the parapets and shot right down among the crouching blacks, filling the trenches with killed and wounded. A majority of the slain had bullet-holes in the top of their heads, showing that the brilliant defence made by the black troops was altogether imaginary, the only resistance being made by the white soldiers.

Such statements were often made by sensational correspondents during the war. In the present instance the black troops were given credit for bravery which they did not display and the 23d Iowa regiment and the Navy were completely ignored.

In justice to the colored troops it may be said that their white officers were the first to run away, and that with better leaders the soldiers might have stood their ground.

On the 3d of July, General Ellet, with the Marine Brigade, was ordered to proceed to Goodrich Landing, where some Confederate raiders had attacked a detachment of United States troops there stationed. When the brigade reached Goodrich Landing the troops were found under arms, and the presence of the enemy was indicated by the burning mansions, cotton-gins and negro quarters in the vicinity—one of those acts of wanton destruction for which the class of Confederate soldiers along the river banks were famous. If they could not find an enemy to harass they would often destroy the property of their own people.

The entire Marine Brigade, artillery, infantry and cavalry, was immediately landed and started in pursuit of the Confederate forces; Colonel Wood, who commanded the colored troops at this point, accompanying the brigade. The cavalry overtook the enemy at Bayou Tensas, and detained him until the main body of the Union forces arrived. The enemy had a strong force of cavalry and several pieces of artillery, and endeavored to recross the Bayou and turn the right flank of the brigade. In this movement he met with a severe repulse. The brigade then advanced on the enemy, who rapidly retreated, throwing away all the plunder taken from the houses that had been burned, including a fine piano! These were some of the men enlisted to "protect" the Southern people, who, finding the latter already well treated and cared for by the Union forces, turned their vengeance against the inhabitants of their own section, and overcoming the small garrison at Goodrich Landing destroyed and carried off everything on which they could lay hands.

But this is the kind of war one must expect to be waged by a government without power to maintain the position it has assumed and liable at any moment to collapse. As the cause of rebellion became more hopeless. the rancor of the guerillas increased, and there were frequent occurrences which curdled the blood in the veins of loyal people. Yet some of the people, while well satisfied to receive protection from the Union forces, would give information to these predatory bands and secrete them when in danger.

General Ellet gave the party at Goodrich Landing a lesson they did not soon forget, and having completely routed the enemy re-embarked his command and returned to the mouth of the Yazoo River.

We have dwelt on these events to show the character of the war as waged by the Confederates in that section of the country, and the energy and enterprise of the officers and men of the Mississippi squadron.

The Army under General Price, or his subordinate. General Holmes, which hung about the swampy region to the west of Vicksburg, found, on the surrender of that place, their occupation gone. All the Federal stores and munitions of war were transferred from Young's Point and Milliken's Bend to Vicksburg, and the Confederates could no longer hope to replenish their stock by raids on these points. General Price therefore determined to change his base and carry on operations elsewhere. He was an active, enterprising officer, and had under his command some twelve or fourteen thousand men who were inured to hardships and capable of long and rapid marches.

In the latter part of June, Admiral Porter received information from deserters that General Price was moving with a large force from Arkansas towards the Mississippi, intending to unite with other troops near Vicksburg to operate along the river. The Admiral immediately made arrangements to meet this force by sending gunboats to such points as it would be most likely to attack. The "Taylor," Lieutenant-Commander Prichett, "Bragg," Lieutenant-Commanding Bishop, and the "Hastings," were sent to Helena, where Major-General B. M. Prentiss was in command of the U. S. forces.

That officer was rather astonished when the gun-boats arrived and he was informed that he might soon expect an attack. He had expected nothing of the kind and felt sure he could defend his post without the aid of gun-boats, although he was glad to welcome them. The "Bragg" came to anchor off Helena, and the "Taylor" and "Hastings" cruised up and down the river in search of guerillas, Lieutenant Commander Prichett quite neglecting the instructions he had received—under no circumstances to leave Helena without positive orders from the Admiral.

However, on one of his expeditions, Prichett happened to read his orders over again,

and seeing how positively they were worded, hastened back to Helena, where he learned that General Prentiss was expecting an attack from Price with twelve to fourteen thousand troops, to oppose which the Union commander had about three thousand five hundred men. Prentiss made the best disposition possible of his small force, determined to hold the works as long as he could. This was on the 4th of July, the very day of the surrender of Vicksburg.

Prichett had hardly got into the position he deemed most desirable to render the fire of the gun-boats effective, when the enemy appeared in sight and attacked the centre defences in overwhelming force. These were soon carried, as also a battery on the hills in the rear which commanded Helena and all the other defences.

The enemy then pushed his forces down the slope of the ridge into the gorges, and his sharpshooters under cover commenced driving the artillerists from their guns in the main fort. The Confederates had planted their artillery above and below the turn in the most commanding positions and opened fire on the line of defensive works across the river bottom, about one thousand yards in width, and large bodies of troops were massed near to secure the advantages the capture of the forts on the heights would offer for closing upon the town of Helena.

The "Taylor" at once covered the approach to Helena by what was called the "old farm road;" but discovering the enemy pouring down the hills, after capturing the works in the Federal centre, Lieutenant-Commander Prichett took up a new position where his broadside guns enfiladed the ravines which were filled with Confederates, and bow-guns at the same time played upon the enemy's batteries above, and his stern guns upon those below.

This was a reception General Price had never dreamed of. He had attacked Helena with the expectation of "walking over the course," and his first success in capturing the most commanding position in the defences confirmed him in his idea of an easy victory, but the broadsides of the gun-boat soon put a new face on affairs. The slaughter caused by the "Taylor's" guns was terrible, the shells falling in the thickly massed troops of the enemy and tearing them to pieces. A panic seized the enemy and he was soon in full retreat, pursued by the fire of the gun-boat, until the road was strewed with the killed and wounded.

Those of the Confederates who had gained the inside of the Union works, seeing the slaughter and retreat of their comrades, lost no time in moving to the rear, urged on by the Federal garrison, who, encouraged by the success of the "Taylor," added the fire of their batteries to that of the gun-boat.

The victory was complete, and it took little more time than we have occupied in telling the story. The whole affair was one continuous roar of cannon and bursting of shells, the latter thrown with an accuracy the crew of the "Taylor" had acquired by long experience. Three hundred and eighty of the Confederates were left dead on the field near the forts and in the ravines, eleven hundred were wounded and as many more taken prisoners. For several days the Federal cavalry were constantly discovering killed and wounded, and steamboats on the river were hailed by deserters from Price's army, asking to be taken on board. No troops were ever worse beaten or more demoralized.

Although the Union troops had stood manfully against the attack of Price's apparently overwhelming force, the slaughter in the enemy's ranks was due to the judgment shown by Lieutenant-Commander Prichett in taking such an admirable position, where he could use his guns effectively. On two previous occasions—at Belmont and at Pittsburg Landing—the "Taylor" had saved the day to the Union cause, yet we doubt if a vast majority of the American people are aware that such a vessel ever existed, and we deem it only fair to say that the garrison of Helena, although they fought with a courage unsurpassed during the war, owed their victory over an enemy which so greatly outnumbered them entirely to the batteries of the sturdy wooden gunboat. General Prentiss, like a brave soldier as he was, grows eloquent in his praise of Lieutenant-Commander Prichett and his officers and men for the service they had performed. In his report to the Admiral he says: "I attribute not a little of our success in the late battle to his (Lieutenant-Commander Prichett's) full knowledge of the situation and his skill in adapting the means within his command to the end to be attained. . . . . Permit me to add, sir, that I can conceive of no case wherein promotion would be more worthily bestowed than in that of Lieutenant-Commander Prichett, and it will give me great pleasure to learn that his services have received a proper reward." Prichett never received any "reward" save an eloquent letter from Mr. Secretary Welles, which that gentleman knew so well how to indite, but he had the satisfaction of not having dimmed the lustre of that 4th of July made so glorious by the capture of Vicksburg and the victory of Gettysburg.

On the 9th of August the "Mound City," Lieutenant-Commanding Byron Wilson, while at Lake Providence, gave the enemy a severe lesson. Captain John McNeil,

C. S. A., notorious raider, made a descent on Lake Providence with some seventy men, for the purpose of carrying off some mules, horses and wagons, a number of the latter having congregated there during the occupation of the place by a part of the Federal army.

As McNeil's men entered the town the "Mound City" opened on them with her port battery and the enemy fled to the woods, leaving seven dead on the field and carrying off many wounded. The enemy never expected to see an ironclad at Lake Providence and never troubled the place again.

It was exceedingly difficult to suppress this system of guerilla warfare, but it was finally put an end to by the Navy when the surrender of Vicksburg relieved a large number of gun-boats from imperative duties which could not be neglected for minor matters.

One of the most remarkable incidents of the civil war was the raid of General John Morgan, one of the daring partisan leaders of the Confederate Army, and the manner in which the raid was averted from Indiana—the point aimed at by the audacious Morgan—by three or four so-called "tin-clads," armed with boat-howitzers.

Hearing that Morgan was moving in force up the left bank of the Ohio River, pursued by the Union forces under General Judah, Lieutenant-Commander Fitch determined, if possible, to cut him off. The water in the river was very low and the five light draft gun-boats which Fitch had with him worked night and day to intercept the raiders, who were seeking for a place to ford the Ohio.

To get the gun-boats over the shoal places it was often necessary to "jump them" by placing two heavy spars, carried for the purpose, forward of the bow at an angle and set taut, a heavy tackle leading from the head of the spars to the deck. Steam was then put on, and as the vessel pushed ahead her bow was raised and she was forced forward eight or ten feet; this operation was repeated until the shoal was passed, and this was the way the officers and men on the Ohio had to work to prevent Morgan from reaching Indiana, whose people were wholly unprepared for a movement which, had it succeeded, must have been most disastrous to the State.

Morgan's object after devastating Indiana was to march into Ohio with the hope of capturing Cincinnati and plundering it. This, to say nothing of the loss to the citizens of their property, would have been an indelible disgrace to the Federal cause.

Morgan pushed his way leisurely along the bank of the Ohio, calculating that he could cross from one side to the other as circumstances might require in order to elude any pursuing force, although he knew of none in the vicinity that he need fear, and he intended that his followers should enjoy themselves among the flesh-pots of the North, and leave the marks of their trail so wide that the Union people would remember John Morgan's raid for a century to come. Indeed he marched so leisurely and committed so many depredations that the people began to rise and arm themselves in the interior on his left, which induced him to cling to the river bank, little dreaming of the danger threatened him from the gun-boats. General Judah's forces pushing after him, Morgan determined to cross the river, but here he was confronted by Fitch and his "tinclads," which were spread out for the space of two miles ready to prevent his passage. As the river was fordable in many places, Morgan could easily have crossed with all his forces but for the presence of the gunboats.

As soon as the Confederate column appeared in sight, they received a volley that staggered them so they gave up the idea of crossing at that point and continued up the river, while the gun-boats kept ahead shelling the enemy whenever they showed themselves. It was a novel sight, a flotilla of gunboats (very "gallinippers") in pursuit of a land force. It was in every respect a new feature of the war.

When Morgan found himself hemmed in on the left, on the right, and in the rear, he saw that his best course was to push on up the Ohio to a point where the water was too low to float the gun-boats, probably not dreaming that the vessels had been selected for just such an emergency and drew barely sixteen inches. With all he could do, Morgan could find no place to cross, for the gun-boats pressed close to him night and day, firing upon his men whenever they approached the river.

This odd march of the Confederates and the pursuit of the gun-boats continued up the river for five hundred miles. On the morning of the 19th of July, Fitch attacked Morgan's troops just above Buffington Island. The enemy made a desperate resistance with artillery and musketry for over an hour, at the end of which time they broke and fled, leaving behind two pieces of artillery, wagons, horses, arms, etc. A portion of them rallied and moved rapidly up along the river bank; but Fitch followed them so closely that they soon scattered among the hills out of the reach of the shells.

The road along the bank was strewed with plunder left by the Confederates—cloth, boots, shoes, and dainties of every description. Among the articles abandoned were some carriages, one of which was said to have been used by Morgan when weary of

horseback exercise. The gunboats pushed on up river to look after the remnant of Morgan's band, leaving it to General Judah to pick up the stragglers in the rear.

About fifteen miles above the scene of his last conflict, Fitch encountered another portion of Morgan's command who were fording the river. The current was here so swift and the channel so narrow and crooked, that it was sometime before the gun-boat could get within range. At length Fitch opened on the enemy, emptying a number of saddles and driving most of them back to the bank, whence they started off up the river again; a few got across the river and escaped; and twenty horses, whose riders had perhaps been drowned or shot, were left standing on the bank. On went Fitch till no more enemies were to be seen and he was brought to a stand by shoals he could not pass.

This was the end of Morgan's raid, one of the most remarkable events of the civil war, and the very boldness of which almost insured its success. It could not have been intended to benefit the Confederate cause, and must be regarded as an insane military frolic. The rude partisan who had conceived the plan which he carried out with such bravery and zeal, meeting at first with no opposition, seems to have fancied himself master of the situation. He lost his head, and when he took to riding in a carriage his followers began to lose faith in him, which may account for the numerous desertions and for the rapidity with which the raiders fled from the gun-boats.

But for the energy of Lieutenant-Commander Fitch, Morgan's enterprise would doubtless have been disastrous to the people of Indiana and Ohio and disgraceful to the United States Government, which had taken so little pains to guard against such incursions.

Morgan and most of his men were captured, and although he had committed no greater infractions of the laws of war than many others, he and his officers were sent to the Ohio penitentiary. To have shot him as he stood at bay, like a wild boar in the forest, would have been kinder and more in keeping with the romantic nature of his enterprise.

The Secretary of the Navy wrote to Lieutenant-Commander Fitch, eulogizing his conduct in the highest terms. Maj.-Gen. Burnside and Brig.-Gen. Cox also wrote the warmest acknowledgements to Admiral Porter for the part Fitch had taken in the capture of Morgan. Fitch certainly demonstrated the importance of the little "tinclads," which seemed from their appearance to have been gotten up more for pleasure-boats than for war purposes, where a strong shot was liable to send them to the bottom.

After the loss of the "Cincinnati," on which occasion Lieutenant Bache and his officers and men exhibited so much coolness and bravery, Bache was ordered to Command the "Lexington," sister-ship to the "Taylor," and one of the gun-boats that had braved the storm of battle at Belmont, Shiloh, Fort Henry, Donelson and Arkansas Post.

The Confederates were again assembling in White River, where it was easy for them to get from Little Rock, Arkansas, and escape back again if attacked. Lieutenant-Commanding Bache was ordered up White River to suppress these raiders, whose zeal and persistency seemed without limit. The great Confederate armies of the West appeared to have been divided into small bodies, which could move with greater celerity. The "Lexington," "Cricket" and "Marmora" were the vessels comprising Lieutenant Bache's command.

On the arrival of the expedition at Des Arc, it burned a large warehouse filled with Confederate stores, which the thoughtless enemy had supposed was safe from the attack of gun-boats. On the second morning, on arriving off the mouth of Little Red River, a narrow and tortuous tributary of the White, the "Cricket" was sent up that stream in pursuit of two Confederate steamers, while the "Lexington" went twenty-five miles further up the White to Augusta. At that place Lieutenant-Commanding Bache was informed that the indefatigable General Price was assembling an army at Brownsville, and that two kindred spirits, Generals Kirby Smith and Marmaduke, were with him.

Lieutenant Bache immediately proceeded up the Little Red River and met the "Cricket" returning with her two prizes, after having destroyed a pontoon bridge constructed by General Marmaduke. As the two captured steamers were the only ones relied on for transportation in this river, the schemes of the Confederates were thwarted for the time being, and the fact that gun-boats had penetrated their lines and were destroying their pontoons and stores quite dampened the ardor of the three chiefs.

Although no blood was spilled, this incursion of the little flotilla was equal to a victory over General Price, whom it would have required an army of twenty thousand men to drive back. By these movements of the gun-boats the Confederate transportation on the rivers was broken up—they had not a steamer left in this vicinity except one on the White River.

A little later, Volunteer-Lieutenant J. P. Couthouy, commanding the "Osage," who had been sent to cruise in Red River, receiving information of a Confederate steamer tied to the bank in his neighborhood, fitted out an expedition of twenty men under command of Chief Engineer Thomas Doughty. The party, after incredible labor, forcing their way through the thick undergrowth and vines, surprised the steamer lying at the bank and captured her. A few moments later Mr. Doughty caught sight of another steamer, which he also captured in a similar manner, and besides her crew found himself in possession of nine Confederate soldiers, commanded by an aide to General ("Dick") Taylor. The aide had been sent up for the "Fulton," a remarkably fine vessel, to transport some troops across Atchafalia Bay. The other steamer was filled with military stores.

There was an impassable shoal across the Red River at that time, and as Chief Engineer Doughty could not take the steamers out of the river he burned them with all their stores, and returned safely to his vessel. These steamers were a great loss to the Confederates in that quarter as their means of transporting troops and supplies by water was greatly impaired, growing smaller by degrees and beautifully less, and confining the raiders within narrower limits than ever.

After the capture of Vicksburg the gun-boats were stationed all along the Mississippi from Cairo to Red River, and on the Ohio, Tennessee and Cumberland Rivers. The gun-boats were in divisions extending between specified points, each under command of an officer in the regular Navy. Strict discipline was maintained and all the spare time was devoted to exercising the men with the great guns and small arms. Most of the officers in the squadron were volunteers, natives of the West, who had never had any naval experience previous to the war, but it was wonderful to see how quickly they accommodated themselves to circumstances and what excellent officers they became. Their energy and zeal was equal to their courage, and many of them made fine records before the war ended. The commanding officers of the divisions were well qualified as instructors as well as leaders, and the exploits of many of the vessels, if properly set forth, would adorn the pages of history.

Some of the boldest and most enterprising officers in the fleet were pilots and engineers, who, leaving the steering-wheel or the engine, and buckling on sword and pistols, would start out on the most hazardous expeditions. These officers would go into action as if it were pastime, the engineers well knowing that a single shot striking the boiler—which in many cases stood unprotected on the deck—would scald every one near it to death, and the pilots feeling that they were special targets for the enemy to shoot at. To kill a pilot or an engineer at his post of duty would excite as much glee among the Confederates as if they had gained an important victory.

The men who served in the Mississippi squadron as pilots and engineers are to this day ostracized by Confederate sympathizers for their devotion to the cause of their country. The pilots received neither prize-money nor pension, and there are some of them who now suffer from the wounds and exposure to which they were subjected. Comparatively few of them remain to read this tribute to their fidelity to the cause of the Union, but those who still live well know the estimation in which they are held by their Commander-in-chief, who has never failed to press their claims on the gratitude of their country whenever an opportunity occurred.

Lieutenant-Commander S. L. Phelps performed important service in the Tennessee River, his command extending from Fort Henry as far up stream as his vessels could ascend. He chose command of this district to enable him to attend to the reconstruction of the "Eastport," a vessel captured by him in the Tennessee after the fall of Fort Henry. At the time of her capture the Confederates were transforming the vessel into an iron-clad ram. This was the "Eastport," hitherto mentioned in our narrative.

Phelps was very active in harassing the enemy, and gave them no rest. His first act after assuming command on the Tennessee was to proceed from Paducah, Ky., with the "Covington," "Queen City," "Argosy," "Silver Cloud" and "Champion," up the river, destroying everything on the way that could be of any use to the enemy. All boats and scows were destroyed, so that communication from one bank to another was pretty effectually cut off. The "Covington" ascended as far as Eastport, the highest point attainable at that stage of the river, offering protection to Unionists and bringing out of the country those desiring to escape conscription; for at that time the enemy had strong parties going through Tennessee seizing upon all the able-bodied men they could find to recruit the Confederate army. Among these were many who would not willingly have served against the Union. Thus the Confederate government, after dragging Tennessee out of the Union, making it the theatre of war, destroying its resources and reducing its people to penury, gave the final stroke in the shape of conscription. The conscripts were seized and bundled off pretty much as slaves were transported in former days.

This was the "liberty" promised the Southern people by their leaders when they started on their wild crusade against the Union. Had they succeeded, there would have been such a depotism established in this country as was never dreamed of.

Lieutenant-Commander Phelps determined to try and break up these conscription raids if possible, and as he could not land parties of sufficient force to cope with the enemy, he made an arrangement with Lieutenant-Colonel Breckenridge at Fort Henry to supply a body of cavalry for the purpose.

There was a conscription party at Linden, Tennessee, which had made itself particularly odious, and it was arranged that Colonel Breckenridge should be landed with his men at a certain point, and the gun-boats should be spread along the river, so that the troops could retreat to them in case the enemy was too strong to be resisted.

The gun-boats being placed at night in the positions assigned them, Phelps dropped

LIEUTENANT-COMMANDER S. LEDYARD PHELPS.

down to Decatursville, where he took on board Colonel Breckenridge and fifty mounted men and landed them on the opposite side of the river.

At daybreak Colonel Breckenridge reached Linden, twelve miles from the river-bank, and completely surprised the enemy. The latter made little resistance, and only three of their number were killed. These men were evidently not anxious to fight themselves, but were looking for others to fight in their places.

The small Union force returned to the gun-boats with one lieutenant-colonel, one captain, four lieutenants, and forty privates as prisoners, besides fifty horses and equipments, two transportation wagons, arms, etc. The Court House, which was the rendezvous of the conscriptors, was burned with a quantity of arms and stores. The

Union party lost only a horse killed. This was the end of the conscription business in that quarter.

In the latter part of June, 1863, Lieutenant-Commander Phelps crossed fifteen hundred cavalry under Colonel Conger, of the 10th Missouri Volunteers, over the river. Colonel Conger made a forced march on Florence, Alabama, and captured the place after a sharp engagement. The expedition destroyed an immense amount of property of various kinds, valued at two millions of dollars, among which were three large cotton mills and magazines of corn; they also captured sixty-five prisoners.

Meanwhile one hundred and fifty cavalry had landed at Savannah, under cover of the guns of the "Covington," intending to operate in that neighborhood and keep open communication between Colonel Conger and the gun-boats. The "Forest Rose" and "Robb" covered the landing opposite Hamburg. The force at Savannah had captured some stock and brought it in; but on one occasion, while returning from an expedition, the commanding officer of the party, being pressed by a superior force of the enemy, abandoned his captured stock and barely succeeded in reaching Savannah, where Lieutenant-Commander Phelps found his troops covered by the "Covington."

Colonel Bissel, the Confederate commander, had invested the town, and given one hour for the removal of the women and children before proceeding to the attack. The answer of the two Union commanders to this summons was, "Come and take it."

That night Colonel Conger arrived, and the Confederates raised the siege and departed. The same night the gun-boats crossed Colonel Conger's force safely over the river, during which brisk skirmishing was going on, and a number of Union families were taken away by the gun-boats to escape the vengeance of the Confederate raiders.

Large quantities of hides were carried off by the gun-boats to keep them from falling into the enemy's hands, for the Confederates maintained quite a large body of men in the State, whose business it was to collect such material as would be useful to their army.

Thus the war was carried on in the region of the Tennessee with much bitterness, the Federal authorities being obliged in self-defence to resort to extreme measures, and to follow a system which they naturally abhorred It was found that by practicing the amenities of war we only gave encouragement to the bands of guerillas and conscriptors to pursue their work of bloodshed and rapine, so the Union forces gradually became almost as indifferent to suffering as their opponents. Unfortunately, this reacted in many cases on those citizens who claimed to be Unionists and to be willing to acknowledge the government if they could only receive protection.

This protection, however, could not always be given, as we had only a certain number of soldiers in the Western army, which with its extended lines was taxed to its utmost. It was slowly but certainly making its way South, and although its rear was not unprotected, yet it was not always strong enough to follow up the roving bands of irregulars who to avoid conscription had perhaps become conscriptors themselves.

Sympathizers with the Southern cause may affirm that every Southerner had a right to fight for life and liberty, and that all combatants were entitled to be treated alike, but if they could not secure what they wanted by the weight of their numbers or appeals to reason, they should not have attempted to bring on civil war; and those who were fighting to preserve law and order, though themselves justified in pursuing extreme measures to put an end to a struggle which by all the rules of warfare should have terminated when Vicksburg fell; for the Federal government was daily increasing its strength, and the Confederates were fighting from foolish pride or pure vindictiveness to inflict all the injury possible on the North.

Although the strength of our army along the Tennessee and other rivers was not great, it had powerful coadjutors in those little gun-boats which the enemy at first professed to despise, but which they were anxious to avoid when circumstances brought them near together. On many occasions a few gun-boats were of more advantage than a division of soldiers would have been.

MISSISSIPPI SQUADRON.

VESSELS EMPLOYED AT VICKSBURG DURING THE SIEGE, WITH LIST OF OFFICERS.

Names of vessels, officers, etc., are obtained from the Navy Register of January, 1863, unless some other date is appended thus (1864), (1865). Officers who received favorable notice in Admiral Porter's official report, dated July 13, 1863 (concerning the fall of Vicksburg and operations on the river), are marked thus ⁎.

FLAG-SHIP "BLACK-HAWK" (3D RATE).

⁎Lieutenant-Commander, K. R. Breese; Fleet-Surgeon, Ninian Pinkney; Assistant Surgeon, J. C. Bertolette; Acting-Assistant Paymaster, W. H. Sells; Ensigns, W. B. Bridgeman, Merrill Miller, S. H. Hunt and G. M. Brown; Acting Ensigns, G. D. Gove, W. Wardrop, E. W. Clark, R. R. Hubbell and D. P. Rosenmiller; Acting-Master's Mates, F. J. Turner, P. H. Brown, James DeCamp, C. H. Porter and F. D. Campbell; Engineers. G. W. Walker, O. G. Ritchie, A. P. Sutherland and Frandford Shepard.

IRON-CLAD STEAMER "LOUISVILLE" (4TH RATE).

⁎Lieutenant-Commander, E. K. Owen; Acting-Assistant Surgeon, W. D. Hoffman; Acting-Assistant Paymaster, D. L. Ruth; Acting-Ensigns, F. Bates; J. T. Blackford, J. G. Waters and S. M. B. Servos; Acting-Master's Mate, H. D. Coffenberry; Engineers, J. B. Fulton, A. W. Hardy. C. W. Reynolds and C. W. Degelman; Acting-Gunner, Wm. Shields, Acting-Carpenter, D. H. Curry. (Jan., 1864.)

IRON-CLAD STEAMER "CHOCTAW" (3D RATE).

⁎Lieutenant-Commander, F. M. Ramsay; Acting-Assistant Paymaster, Wm. N. Whitehouse; Acting-Master, W. A. Griswold; Acting-Ensigns, E. Beaman, W. C. Bennett, A. S. Palmer and L. R. Hamersly; Acting-Master's Mates, T. Hopkins and H. Marsh; Engineers, N. P. Baldwin, C. E. Arbuthnot, Joseph Blake, S. C. Babbitt and E. H. Austin; Acting-Gunner, Reuben Applegate; Acting-Carpenter, J. A. Stewart.

IRON-CLAD STEAMER "LAFAYETTE" (4TH RATE.

⁎Captain, Henry Walke; Acting-Volunteer-Lieutenant, James Laning; Acting-Assistant Surgeon, Collins D. White; Acting-Assistant Paymaster, James P. Kelly; Acting-Ensigns, J. L. Moran, Elias Smith and W. C. Bennet; Acting-Master's Mates, H. G. Warren, C. H. Slocum, H. C. Marsh, S. O. Lovell, S. R. Winram, W. P. Higbee, Thomas Twitchell and Paul Morgan; Engineers, Robert Tate, A. M. Rowe, E. B. Hill and J. W. Paull; Acting-Gunner, G. W. Price; Acting-Carpenter, C. M. Underwood.

IRON-CLAD STEAMER "CARONDELET" (4TH RATE).

⁎Lieutenant, J. McLeod Murphy; Acting-Volunteer-Lieutenant, E. E. Brennard; Assistant Surgeon, D. R. Brannan; Acting-Assistant Surgeon. S. B. Harriman; Acting-Assistant Paymaster, F. M. Hawley; Acting Ensigns, W. E. H. Fentress, O. Donaldson, J. C. Gipson, M. F. Benjamin and R. P. Petty; Acting-Master's Mates, J. Bath, and C. W. Miller; Engineers, C. H. Cavin, John Huff and L. Fulton; Acting-Gunner, F. Beaufort.

IRON-CLAD STEAMER "CHILLICOTHE" (4TH RATE.

Lieutenant-Commander, J. P. Foster; Acting-Assistant Surgeon, J. C. Foster; Acting-Assistant Paymaster, J. H. Hathway; Acting Ensigns. W. J. Power and Walter Muir; Acting-Master's Mates, Henry Baker, H. A. Hannon and Joseph Brown; Engineers, A. W. Hardy, J. G. Briggs, G. L. Kingsley, Charles Trotter and W. B. Fleming; Acting-Carpenter, James C. Hall.

IRON-CLAD STEAMER "PITTSBURG" (4TH RATE.

Acting-Volunteer-Lieutenants, ⁎William R. Hoel and J. C. Bentley; Acting-Assistant Surgeon, H. M. Miner; Acting-Assistant Paymaster, C. H. Gould; Acting-Master, Charles Germain; Acting-Ensigns, G. W. Paulding and G. W. Rogers; Acting-Master's Mates, G. W. Garlick, F. Vincent and James Ovett; Engineers, S. B. Goble, G. H. Atkinson, J. L. Auble, Wm. Mills and W. H. Mitchell; Acting-Gunner, Jos. Simons.

STEAM GUN-BOAT "TAYLOR" (4TH RATE).

⁎Lieutenant, Jas. M. Prichett; Acting-Assistant Surgeon, G. W. Ballentine; Acting-Assistant Paymaster, C. A. Gardner; Acting-Master, Wm. H. Minor; Acting-Ensigns, E. Loring, C. T. Stanton, J. F. Holmes and S. E. Brown; Acting-Master's Mates, Charles Ackley, H. S. Wetmore and Ira Athearn; Engineers, James Fleming, J. R. Ramsey; Wm. Finch and E. M. Bumpus; Acting-Carpenter, A. B. Chapman.

STEAMER "HASTINGS" (4TH RATE.

Acting-Volunteer Lieutenant, A. R. Langthorne; Acting-Assistant Surgeon, J. M. Flint; Acting-Assistant Paymaster, P. J. Stone; Acting-Master, J. W. Morehead; Acting-Ensigns, W. C. Turner and C. H. Reed; Acting Master's Mates, E. C. Urner, Frank Seymour and F. M. Clark; Engineers, J. H. Scott, Edwin Senior, Samuel Weaver, A. M. Wasson and G. W. Amsden.

STEAMER "FOREST ROSE" (4TH RATE).

⁎Acting-Master, Geo. M. Brown; Acting-Ensigns, James Kearney and F. F. Smith; Acting-Master's Mates, Jacob Rutherford, J. Robinson, C. W. Johnson and W. B. Anderson; Engineers, Francis Marsh, Edw. H. Goble and J. Lozier.

IRON-CLAD STEAMER "CINCINNATI" (4TH RATE.

⁎Lieutenant, George M. Bache; Acting-Assistant Surgeon, R. R. Hall; Acting-Assistant Paymaster, S. R. Hinsdale; Acting-Masters, J. Pearce and C. Germaine; Acting-Ensigns, A. F. O'Neil, G. L. Coleman and P. R. Starr; Acting-Masters' Mates, Henry Booby, Daniel Winget and D. W. Stebbins; Engineers, W. O. McFarland, Simon Shultice, Reuben Storey and F. Hense; Acting-Gunner, J. F. Ribbitt; Acting Carpenter, G. H. Stevens.

STEAMER "JULIET" (4TH RATE).

Acting-Volunteer-Lieutenant, Edward Shaw; Acting-Assistant Paymaster, Geo. W. Winans; Acting-Ensigns, W. L. Holcomb, W. C. Turner and M. K. Haines; Acting-Master's Mates, Hugh Kuhl, D. F. Davids and Raymond Wigand; Engineers, P. M. Strickland, Joseph Bolejack and Julius Gale.

IRON-CLAD STEAMER "INDIANOLA" (4TH RATE.

⁎Lieutenant-Commander, George Brown; Acting-Ensigns, J. A. Yates, W. S. Pease and Thomas McElevell; Acting-Assistant Paymaster, Thomas Carstairs; Acting-Master's Mates, P. W. Frost, W. S. Ward, James Williams, Gardner Phipps and L. Kenney; Engineers, Thomas Doughty, David Hawksworth, W. B. Hovey, G. W. Voice, George Wadell and Josephus Blake; Acting-Carpenter, James E. Green.

STEAM GUN-BOAT "GENERAL BRAGG" 4TH RATE).

Lieutenant, Joshua Bishop; Acting-Assistant Surgeon, W. A. Collins; Acting-Assistant Paymaster, J. H. Jenkins; Acting-Ensigns, T. J. McLaughlin and Edw. F. Phelps; Acting-Master's Mates, Alex. Lee, John Lawson and John Ackley; Engineers, Oliver Titcomb, E. W. Andrews and Joseph Anderson; Acting-Gunner, Lewis Dawson; Acting-Carpenter, L. D. Johnston.

IRON-CLAD STEAMER "MOUND CITY" (4TH RATE).

⁎Lieutenant, Byron Wilson; Acting-Assistant Surgeon, R. Cadwallader; Acting-Assistant Paymaster,

B. J. Donohue; Acting Ensigns, James Martin, F. T. Coleman, S. B. Coleman and DeWayne Stebbins; Acting-Master's Mate, R. V. Lamport; Engineers, Edw. Merriman, R. M. Gardiner, A. N. Derby, Elihu Stephens and J. N. Hartnett; Gunner, Herman Peters.

STEAMER "GENERAL PRICE" (4TH RATE).

*Acting-Lieutenant, S. E. Woodworth (1863); Acting-Assistant Surgeon, George Harvey; Acting-Assistant Paymaster, J. W. McLellan; Acting-Ensigns, G. W. Pratt, J. H. Seever and D. P. Boseworth; Acting-Master's Mates, D. McKay and Peter Barclay; Engineers, D. E. Weaver, W. H. Coulter, Alex. Campbell, J. B. Baldwin and R. A. Kyle.

STEAMER "MARMORA" (4TH RATE).

Acting-Volunteer-Lieutenant, Robert Getty; Acting-Assistant Surgeon, Fayette Clapp; Acting-Assistant Paymaster, G. S. Sproston; Acting-Master, Elias Reese; Acting-Ensigns, Edw. Alford, H. H. Walker, Elliot Callender and Edward Morgan; Acting-Master's Mates, J. W. Foster, D. B. Lawrence and D. C. Bond; Engineer, G. W. Smith, W. C. Armstrong and J. S. Armstrong.

STEAMER "CRICKET" (4TH RATE).

Acting-Master, A. R. Langthorne; Acting-Assistant Surgeon, H. A. Bodman; Acting Assistant Paymaster, S. T. Savage; Acting-Ensign, J. W. Morehead; Acting-Master's Mates, E. C. Hubbell, Wm. Gregg and W. O. Stephenson; Engineers, B. Hand, David Chillas and George Shipley.

STEAMER "ROMEO" (4TH RATE).

*Acting-Volunteer-Lieutenant, J. V. Johnston; (Admiral's Report, '86) Acting-Assistant Surgeon, J. S. McNeely; Acting-Assistant Paymaster, E. R. Maffat; Acting-Ensigns, J. B. Dwyer, Pat. Murphy, Robert P. Smith and Eugene Zimmerman; Acting-Master's Mates, J. E. Ernest, R. P. Shaw and G. C. Cox; Engineers, J. McCurdy, Joseph Grippen and J. P. Williams.

STEAMER "RATTLER" (4TH RATE).

*Acting Master, W. E. Fentress; Acting-Assistant Surgeon, W. H. Wilson; Acting-Master, W. E. H. Fentriss; Acting-Ensigns, G. S. West, Wm. Ferguson and John Bath; Acting-Master's Mates, H. E. Church, Daniel Welsh and S. H. Strunk; Engineers, James Whitaker, Jefferson Bell and A. J. Bashloe; Acting-Gunner, T. Carpenter.

MAIL-BOAT "NEW NATIONAL" (4TH RATE).

Acting-Masters, Alexander M. Grant and Oscar H. Pratt; Acting-Ensign, J. Hill; Acting-Masters' Mate, W. C. Herron; Engineers, W. H. Price, James Wilkins and E. C. Rensford.

IRON-CLAD STEAMER "BENTON" (4TH RATE).

*Lieutenant-Commander, James A. Greer; Acting-Master, G. P. Lord; *Ensign, J. F. Reed; Acting-Ensigns, C. A. Wright, J. M. Walker, W. J. Lees and Frank Reed; Acting-Assistant Paymaster, C. G. Lowndes; Acting-Master's Mates, E. C. Brennan and W. H. Lemassena; Engineers, J. V. Starr, C. W. Fairfowl, R. Hoffman, C. W. Ridgely, Robert Long and Oliver Bragg; Gunner, N. B. Willetts; Carpenter, R. Blackford.

HOSPITAL-SHIP "RED ROVER."

Acting-Master, W. R. Welles; Acting-Assistant Paymaster, A. N. Pearson; Acting-Ensign, Wm. Harris; Acting-Master's Mates, C. King and F. Lowe; Engineers, W. J. Buffington, G. W. Gimbeo, W. O. Logne, Julius Eliter and J. A. Goodloe; Acting-Carpenter, H. Kenney; Acting-Assistant Surgeons, George H. Bixby and George Hopkins (Jan. 1864).

IRON-CLAD STEAMER "TUSCUMBIA."

*Lieutenant-Commander, James W. Shirk; Assistant Paymaster, George A. Lyon; Acting-Ensigns, Lewis Kenny and E. M. Clark; Engineers, John W. Hartupee, Perry South and William J. Milligan.

TUG "IVY."

Acting-Ensign, E. C. Boss; Acting-Master's Mate, S. H. Carson; Engineers, A. Miller and E. Callahan.

STEAMER "W. H. BROWN" (4TH RATE).

Acting-Volunteer-Lieutenant, J. A. French; Acting-Ensign, J. B. Hawthorne; Acting-Master's Mates, Jacob Shinn and William Cassidy; Engineers, G. L. Scott and Geo. W. Taylor.

TUG "LAUREL."

Engineers, Acting-Second-Assistant, N. Mierstang, and Acting-Third Assistant O. Rosebush.

TUG "DAHLIA."

Acting-Ensign, Thomas Wright; Acting-Master's Mate, W. H. Strope; Engineers, B. Nannah and H. Sullivan.

TUG "PANSY."

Acting-Ensign, D. C. Bowers; Acting-Master's Mate, S. Johnson; Acting-Second-Assistant Engineers, J. W. Lindsey and F. H. Majors.

STEAMER "GREAT WESTERN" (POWDER VESSEL.)

*Acting-Volunteer-Lieutenant, Wm. F. Hamilton; Acting-Assistant Paymaster, Jos. S. Harvey; Acting-Master, J. C. Little; Acting-Ensign, Richard Ellis; Acting-Master's Mates, L. F. Knapp and R. Mitchell; Engineers, Chas. Christopher, Joseph Goodwin, B. A. Farmer and G. S. Baker; Acting-Gunner, Robert Sherman; Acting-Carpenter, Joseph Morton.

STEAMER "JUDGE TORRENCE" (POWDER VESSEL).

* Acting-Volunteer-Lieutenant J. F. Richardson; Acting-Ensign, Jeremiah Irwin; Acting-Master's Mate, James Ross; Engineers, P. R. Hartwig, J. Stough, John C. Barr and W. Y. Sedman.

MORTAR BOATS.

Commanded by Gunner * Eugene Mack, afterwards by *Ensign Miller.

VESSELS EMPLOYED AT OTHER POINTS ON THE RIVER (1863-5).

Steamer "Peosta" (4th rate).—Acting-Volunteer-Lieutenant, T. E. Smith (1864.

Steamer "Kenwood" (4th rate).—Acting-Master John Swaney (1864).

Steamer "Paw-Paw" (4th rate).—Acting-Master A. F. Thompson (1864).

Steamer "Conestoga" (4th rate).—Lieutenant-Commander * T. O. Selfridge.

Steamer "Argosy" (4th rate).—Acting-Ensign J. C. Morong (1864).

Steamer "Alexandria" (4th rate).—Acting-Master D. P. Rosenmiller (1864.

Steamer "Fairplay" (4th rate).—Lieutenant-Commander Le Roy Fitch (1863); Acting-Master Geo. G. Groves (1864).

Steamer "Fawn" (4th rate).—Acting-Master J. R. Grove (1863.

Steamer "Silver Cloud" (4th rate).—Acting-Volunteer-Lieutenant A. F. O'Neil (1864).

Steamer "Silver Lake" (4th rate).—Acting-Master J. C. Coyle (1864-5).

Steamer "Springfield" (4th rate).—Acting-Master Joseph Watson (1864; Acting-Master Edward Morgan (1865.

Steamer "Victory" (4th rate).—Ensign Frederick Read (1864-5.

Steamer "Champion" (4th rate).—Acting-Master Alfred Phelps (1864).

Steamer "Curlew" (4th rate.)—Acting-Ensign H. A. B. O'Neil (1864).

Steamer "Little Rebel," (4th rate).—Acting-Volunteer-Lieutenant T. B. Gregory; Acting Ensign J. B. Petts (1865.

Steamer " Signal".—*Acting-Volunteer-Lieutenant, C. Dominey (1863) ; Acting-Ensign W. P. Lee (1864).

Steamer " Covington."—Acting-Volunteer-Lieutenant."—* J. S. Hurd (1863); Acting-Volunteer-Lieutenant George P. Lord (1864). ·

Steamer " Robb."—* Ensign W. C. Handford; Acting-Ensign Lloyd Thomas (1864).

Steamer " New Era."—* Acting-Master J. C. Brenner; Acting-Master John Marshall (1864).

Steamer " Romeo.'—Acting-Volunteer-Lieutenant J. V. Johnstone ; Acting-Master Thomas Baldwin (1864 .

Steamer " Petrel."—Acting-Volunteer-Lieutenant * John Pierce; Acting-Master Thomas McElroy (1864).

Steamer " Linden."—Acting-Volunteer-Lieutenant *T. E. Smith; Acting-Master T. M. Farrell (1864).

Steamer " Prairie Bird."—Acting-Volunteer-Lieutenant *E. C. Brennard (1863); Acting-Ensign J. W. Chambers (1864).

Steamer " Queen City."—Acting-Volunteer-Lieutenant *J. Goudy (1863 ; Acting-Volunteer-Lieutenant G. W. Brown (1864).

Steamer " Sybil.'—Lieutenant-Commander J. G. Mitchell (1865).

Steamer " Neosho."—Acting-Volunteer-Lieutenant Samuel Howard (1864).

Steamer " Moose."—Lieutenant-Commander LeRoy Fitch (1864).

Steamer ' Ouichita."—Acting-Ensign E. Zimmerman (1864).

Steamer " Osage."—Acting-Master Thomas Wright (1864).

Steamer "Reindeer."—Acting-Volunteer-Lieutenant H. A. Glassford (1864).

Steamer "St. Clair."—Acting-Volunteer-Lieutenant J. S. Hurd; Acting-Volunteer-Lieutenant T. B. Gregory (1864).

Steamer "Lexington."—Lieutenant G. M. Bache (1864).

Steamer "Naumkeag."—Acting-Master John Rogers (1864).

Steamer "Fort Hindman."—Acting-Volunteer-Lieutenant J. Pearce (1864).

Steamer " Winnebago."—Building at St. Louis (1864).

Steamer "Tensas" (4th rate). —Acting-Ensign E. C. Van Pelt (1864-5).

Steamer " Gen. Pillow " (4th rate).—Acting-Ensign Joseph Moyer.

Tug " Fern."—Acting-Ensign Alpheus Semmes; Acting-Ensign J. M. Kelly (1864).

Tug " Mistletoe."—Acting-Ensign W. H. H. Ford (1863); Jas. M. Quigley (1864).

Tug " Mignonette."—Acting-Ensign E. S. Hamlin (1863); Acting-Ensign H. D. Green (1864).

Tug "Myrtle."—Second Assistant-Engineer Thomas Guernsey (1863); Acting-Ensign J. N. Goldsmith (1864).

Tug " Hyacinth."—Acting-Ensign J. B. Heizerman (1863-4).

Tug " Thistle."—Acting-Ensign P. H. Timmons; Acting-Ensign R. E. Ettingham (1864).

Tug " Daisy."—Acting-Ensign D. C. Bowers (1863-4).

Despatch Steamer " Gen. Lyon."—Pilot R. E. Birch.

Steamer " Brilliant."—Acting-Volunteer-Lieutenant C. G. Perkins (1864).

Tug " Lilly."—Acting-Ensign R. H. Smith.

Steamer " Vindicator."—Acting-Volunteer-Lieutenant H. H. Gorringe (1865).

Iron-clad " Essex."—Commander Robert Townsend (1864); Commander Andrew Bryson (1865 .

Steamer " Ozark."—Acting-Volunteer-Lieutenant G. W. Brown (1865).

Steamer " Chickasaw.' — Building at St. Louis (1864).

Steamer " Kickapoo."—Building at St. Louis 1864 .

Steamer " Milwaukee." — Building at St. Louis (1864).

Steamer " Tawah."—Acting-Volunteer-Lieutenant Jason Goudy (1864).

Steamer "Keywest."—Acting-Volunteer Lieutenant E. M. King (1864).

Steamer "Exchange."— While commanding " Covington." See page 18.) *Acting-Volunteer-Lieutenant J. S. Hurd (1864); Acting-Volunteer-Lieutenant J. C. Gipson (1865).

Steamer " Gazelle."—Acting-Ensign A. S. Palmer (1865).

Steamer " Avenger."—Acting-Volunteer-Lieutenant C. A. Wright (1865).

Steamer " Elfin."

Steamer " Naiad."—Acting-Master Henry T. Keene (1865).

Steamer " Nymph."—Acting-Master Patrick Donnelly.

Steamer " Undine."

Steamer "Siren."—Acting-Master James Fitzpatrick (1865).

Steamer " Huntress."—Acting-Master John L. Dennis (1865).

Steamer " Peri."— Acting-Master T. M. Farrell (1865).

Store-ship " Sovereign."—Acting-Master Thomas Baldwin.

Steamer " Glide."—Acting-Lieutenant S. E. Woodworth.

Iron-clad " Eastport."—Lieutenant-Commander S. L. Phelps (1864).

Steamer " Tennessee."—Lieutenant-Commander E. P. Lull (1865).

Steamer " Gen. Burnside."—Lieutenant Moreau Forest (1865).

Steamer " Gen. Thomas."—Acting-Master Gilbert Morton (1865).

Steamer "General Sherman."—Acting-Master J. W. Morehead (1865).

Steamer "General Grant."—Acting-Master Joseph Watson (1865).

Steamer "Volunteer."—Acting-Ensign M. K. Haines (1865).

Iron-clad " Baron-de-Kalb."—* Lieutenant-Commander J. G. Walker.

VESSELS STATIONED AT CAIRO.

Inspection-ship " Abraham."—Acting-Ensign Wm. Wagner.

Tug " Sampson."—Acting Ensign J. D. Buckley.

Receiving-ship " Clara Dolson."—Lieutenant-Commander Thomas Pattison.

Receiving-ship " Grampus."—Acting-Master Elijah Sells (1864).

CHAPTER XXXI.

Bounds of Farragut's Command up to 1863.—Operations of Farragut's Vessels on the Coast of Texas.—Gallant attack on Corpus Christi by Volunteer-Lieutenant Kittredge.—Galveston, Sabine Pass and Corpus Christi fall into the Federal hands.—An Expedition of the Army and Navy defeated at Sabine Pass.—Farragut blockades Red River in the "Hartford."—Capture of the "Diana" by the Confederates.—Loss of the Union Gun-boat "Barrataria."—Destruction of the "Queen-of-the-West" by Lieutenant-Commander A. P. Cooke.—Farragut relieved from Command in the Mississippi, May 7th, 1863. — Expedition up Red River under Lieutenant-Commander Hart.—Farragut arrives below Port Hudson, and Commences Active Operations against that Place.—Attack on Donaldsonville by Confederate General Green.—His Retreat under the fire of the Gun boat "Princess Royal."—Attack of Confederate Artillery on the Gun-boat "New London."—Gallant Conduct of Lieutenant-Commander Geo. H. Perkins.—Death of Commander Abner Reed.—Rejoicing of the Army and Navy at New Orleans on hearing of the Fall of Vicksburg and Port Hudson.—General Remarks.

WHILE Flag-officer Farragut was engaged in the operations before Vicksburg, down to the time when he passed the batteries at Port Hudson, many events occurred in the fleet which have not been mentioned heretofore, as it could not have been done without interrupting the narrative of current events.

Farragut's command up to May, 1863, included the Mississippi River as far as Vicksburg, and all its tributaries below; also the coasts of Louisiana, Florida and Texas, extending from Pensacola on the east to the mouth of the Rio Grande, including that network of bays, streams, inlets, bayous, sounds, and island groups which extends from the mouth of the Mississippi as far west as Sabine Pass, and the difficult bars and channels leading to Galveston, Matagorda and Corpus Christi, where none but the smallest vessels could enter, and which afforded safe refuges for blockade-runners during the entire war.

This coast, with its indentations, is over 600 miles in length, and had to be guarded with great care to prevent supplies reaching the Confederates through the numerous gates leading into Louisiana and Texas.

The Federal officers had to exercise great watchfulness in guarding against the people they had to contend with, for they were a brave, hardy set of men, regardless of danger, and amply supplied with small-arms and field-artillery to withstand any attack that could be made upon them by the combined forces of our Army and Navy.

The blockade of this part of the Southern coast had been indifferently carried on while Farragut was confined to his operations in the Mississippi, for it took every vessel he had to control that part of the river which was under his command; and it was not until after the fall of Port Hudson, when the navigation of the river was once more free, that the smaller vessels could be spared.

All this time the Confederates on the coasts of Louisiana and Texas kept up active operations with their blockade-runners, which had nothing to interfere with them until August, 1862, when Farragut sent down a small force of sailing-vessels and one small steamer (the "Sachem") to try and close some of the Texan ports.

Acting-Volunteer-Lieutenant J. W. Kittredge, with the bark "Arthur," the above-mentioned steamer, and an armed launch, proceeded on this duty. He captured Corpus

Christi and the adjacent waters, from whence so many small craft had been running to Havana.

Lieutenant Kittredge showed not only great cleverness in the performance of this duty but cool courage. He had under his command a small yacht (the "Corypheus") and with the aid of her crew he removed some obstructions which the Confederates had placed in Corpus Christi "dug-out" to protect several small schooners which they had collected at that point. Lieutenant Kittredge ran his vessel through the gut and attacking one of the schooners, she was soon driven ashore and burned. Another one was also set on fire by the enemy. He then ran across the bay to Corpus Christi, with his little flotilla following him, and called upon the authorities to surrender and for the military forces to evacuate the town.

The Confederates set fire to a sloop on his approach and asked for a truce of forty-eight hours. At the end of that time they refused to evacuate the place, and on August 16th opened fire on Kittredge's vessel from a battery planted behind the levee. This was replied to with spirit by the Union vessels, which kept up such an incessant and accurate fire on the enemy, that they were three times driven from their guns on that day. At night-fall the Union forces withdrew out of range. The next day the Confederates set fire to a steamer that had run aground and could not be moved.

On August 20th, Lieutenant Kittredge went to work again on the enemy. He landed a 12-pounder howitzer under command of Master's Mate A. H. Reynolds, placed the schooner "Reindeer," Master's Mate William Barker, in position to cover the landing party, and proceeded to enfilade the enemy's battery and pour shrapnel and canister into his flank.

Master's Mate Reynolds moved up his howitzer to within musket range, and mowed the enemy down, the latter deployed 100 infantry to the right of the land party with the intention of flanking it, but they were soon scattered and driven off by the fire of the "Reindeer" and her consorts. The Confederates then charged the 12-pound howitzer with 250 men, and for a time its capture seemed certain. But Lieutenant Kittredge moved the "Corypheus" and "Sachem" close in shore, and met the enemy with so heavy a fire of canister that they wavered and retreated with considerable loss. The engagement continued all day, the enemy's battery was silenced and the vessels shelled the town.

This was a very gallant affair, conducted entirely by volunteer officers, who, although they had not received a regular naval training, displayed as much ability as if they had.

Not having the force to hold the town, the flotilla laid out in the bay and blockaded it. Unfortunately the gallant Kittredge was surprised and with his boat's crew captured while reconnoitering.

Galveston, Sabine Pass and Corpus Christi fell into the Federal hands a short time afterwards; the former place being captured by Commander Renshaw without the loss of a man. This for a time put a stop to blockade-running on the Texas coast. Its unfortunate recapture, the loss of the "Harriet Lane" and the blowing up of the "Westfield," have been already related, and Galveston once more became a shelter to blockade-runners, which much rejoiced the hearts of our enemies in Texas. Their success at this point fired the hearts of the Texan soldiers and they assembled in large numbers along the coast, making it very dangerous to attempt any landing operations without the assistance of the army, which it seems was not prepared for such a purpose.

Several unimportant affairs occurred along the coast, but nothing of a very satisfactory nature.

Maj.-Gen. Banks, who had relieved General Butler at New Orleans, wishing to commemorate his appointment by a signal victory over the enemy, proposed a combined expedition against Sabine Pass, which had been retaken and fortified by the enemy. The defences on shore, it was supposed, consisted only of two 32-pounders, while on the water the Confederates had two steamboats converted into rams.

The Army organization consisted of 4,000 men under General Franklin; and Commodore H. H. Bell, who commanded the naval force at New Orleans in the absence of the Flag-officer, detailed Volunteer-Lieutenant Frederick Crocker to command the naval part of the expedition, consisting of the steamer "Clifton," the steamer "Sachem," Volunteer-Lieutenant Amos Johnson; steamer "Arizona," Acting-Master H. Tibbetts, and steamer "Granite City," Acting-Master C. W. Lamson. This force was considered quite sufficient for the purpose intended.

It was concerted with General Franklin that the gun-boats should make the first attack alone, led by Lieutenant Crocker, assisted by 180 sharp-shooters divided amongst the vessels, and after driving the enemy from his defences and destroying or driving off the rams, the transports were to advance and land the troops. In all, these vessels carried twenty-seven guns, which one would suppose was enough to dispose of the few guns the enemy had mounted.

The attack, which was to have been a surprise at early dawn, was not made until

3 P. M. on the 8th of September, 1863, twenty-eight hours after the expedition had appeared off the Sabine.

A reconnaissance had been made in the morning by Generals Franklin and Weitzel and Lieutenant Crocker, when they decided on a plan of attack. Commodore Bell had sent two good pilots down in the "Granite City." At 3 P. M. the transports were over the bar, the "Granite City" leading them in, for the purpose of covering the landing of the troops

The "Clifton," "Sachem" and "Arizona" engaged a battery of seven guns. A shot struck the boiler of the "Sachem" and she was soon enveloped in steam. The "Clifton" ran directly under the fort and for twenty minutes fired rapidly grape, canister and shell, receiving a heavy fire in return. She soon afterwards got on shore, and not being able to back off, hauled down her colors—as did also the "Sachem."

The "Arizona" stood down the channel and took her station ahead of the transports. *She* got ashore also; several of the transports were aground and the "Granite City" went to the support of the "Arizona," which it was necessary to do, for a Confederate steamer (probably one of the rams) was coming down the river. This steamer, whatever she was, got the "Clifton" and "Sachem" afloat and towed them up the river.

The "Arizona," "Granite City" and transports got over the bar and made the best of their way to South West Pass, the army having made no attempt to land. The "Granite City" and "Arizona" do not appear to have received any injuries, but they made no attempt to rescue the two steamers that had surrendered.

This was rather a melancholy expedition and badly managed   It resulted in the loss of some twenty men killed and many wounded on board the "Clifton" and "Sachem," and was somewhat injurious to the prestige of the Navy. It did not, however, reflect any discredit upon the officers of the "Clifton" or "Sachem," as both of these vessels were gallantly fought.

This affair, with some minor matters, ended the operations of the West Gulf blockading squadron on the coast up to September, 1863. The latter year had not been as successful as the one previous, yet the squadron did a great deal of hard work and its officers were engaged in scenes where they gained reputation, and the Union flag was in no ways dimmed.

After Farragut had passed Port Hudson with the "Hartford" and "Arizona," he was quite isolated from the rest of his squadron, but was finally re-enforced by the gunboat "Estrella," which worked its way up through the Atchafalaya into the Red River and joined the other vessels at its mouth, at the same time running the risk of being mistaken for a Confederate ram and getting a broadside from her consorts.

Farragut might have run past Port Hudson with his vessels in the night without firing a gun or receiving a shot, but he was doing more good where he was. Port Hudson was completely cut off from supplies *via* Red River, and the two gun-boats could patrol it perfectly fifty or more miles up, and prevent any supplies from being sent overland to the side of the river opposite Port Hudson.

It was now simply a case of starving out the garrison, for there seemed no prospect of the place being taken by the Army, for as late as May 8th, 1863, General Banks marched a large portion of his army to Alexandria, La., at the very time he should have been closely besieging Port Hudson. For what purpose he marched no one could ever discern, for the gun-boats under Admiral Porter had arrived there before him, taken possession of and destroyed the defences along the river, and opened it so thoroughly that there was no danger of its being closed against the Federal vessels.

While Farragut was away up the Mississippi, after the passage of Port Hudson, Commodore Morris was left in charge at New Orleans with directions to co-operate with the military commander at that place, and perform all the duties which would have devolved upon the Flag-officer had he been present in person.

Some of the expeditions fitted out by Commodore Morris, and later by Commodore Bell, properly belong to this history, as showing the numerous duties performed by the Navy, and also that, notwithstanding Farragut was not at New Orleans himself to conduct matters, his orders were carried out, and there was the heartiest co-operation between the Army and Navy.

On the 28th of March the "Diana," Acting-Master Thos. L. Peterson, was sent into Grand Lake on a reconnaissance, with Lieutenant Allen, U. S. A., of General Weitzel's staff, and two companies of infantry on board. She was ordered to proceed down the Atchafalaya River as far as the mouth of the Teche and return by the lake.

Disobeying this order, Acting-Master Peterson attempted to return to Berwick Bay by the way of Atchafalaya. After passing the mouth of the Teche he was attacked from shore by field-pieces and sharp-shooters. The men fought well, and the action lasted two hours and three-quarters. The captain of the "Diana" was killed early in the action, and his executive officer, Acting-Master's Mate Thomas G. Hall, was mortally wounded; also Master's Mate Geo. C.

Dolliver and Engineer Jas. McNally, leaving only one officer (Master's Mate Charles P. Weston), who carried on the fight and behaved most admirably. The tiller-ropes were shot away and the engine disabled so that the "Diana" became unmanageable and drifted ashore, when it was impossible to longer defend her.

As soon as the firing was heard at the bay, the "Calhoun," Acting-Master M. Jordan, was sent into the lake to ascertain the cause of it. She arrived at the mouth of the Atchafalaya, where she grounded and remained until midnight.

Several of the crew of the "Diana" had escaped, and they informed the commanding officer of the "Calhoun" that the "Diana" had been captured near Petersonville. Acting-Master Jordan threw overboard part of his ballast, his coal, provisions, and even ammunition, and finally reached the bay at 2 A. M.; but the "Diana" was a prize to the enemy.

Another of the United States vessels was lost a short time after, the "Barrataria," Acting-Ensign Jas. T. Perkins, at the mouth of the Amite River, on Lake Mariposa She was on a reconnaissance with some army officers in Lake Mariposa, intending to examine the mouth of the Amite River. The pilot stated that there was always five feet of water there, but the vessel struck on a sunken snag and stuck fast. Everything possible was being done to relieve the vessel and get her off, when they were attacked by a force of concealed riflemen and a brisk engagement took place, in which the "Barrataria" used her guns and also musketry with good effect.

There were on board the "Barrataria" Colonel Clarke, Captain Gordon, Lieutenant Ellis, and ten privates of the 6th Michigan Volunteers; the latter did good service with their rifles. The engagement lasted over half an hour, when the enemy ceased firing.

Efforts were still made to get the "Barrataria" off, but without avail. The bow gun was spiked and thrown overboard and the water blown out of the boilers; the "Barrataria" still stuck fast.

Fearing that the vessel might fall into the hands of the enemy, Acting Ensign Perkins got his crew and passengers into boats, and after spiking all the guns, shoved off under a fire of musketry from the concealed enemy. Mr. Gregory, Acting-Master's Mate, who was left behind to set fire to the vessel, then ignited the inflammable matter and shoved off in a small boat. The vessel was soon in flames and shortly afterwards blew up. After being assured of the vessel's destruction, the party made the best of its way back and arrived at South Pass in safety.

In the case of the "Diana" there were six killed and three wounded; in the case of the "Barrataria" there was only one wounded. Affairs of this kind were very provoking and harassing to a Commander-in-chief, but the officers seem to have performed their duty faithfully. Some of them died at their posts—there could be no fault found with them.

The navigation through all these lakes, bayous and so-called rivers was full of snags and shoal places, and was of the most perplexing kind. Most of the officers in the above-mentioned vessels were volunteers, full of zeal and courage and anxious not to have it said of them that the case would have been better managed if a regular line-officer had been present. Acting-Ensign Perkins may have lacked a little in judgment in pushing ahead, but when it came to the point about letting his vessel fall into the enemy's hands, there was nothing wanting, and he abandoned his command in open boats at the risk of the lives of his crew, conscious that the enemy could derive no benefit from anything left behind.

A short time afterwards an expedition was fitted out in Berwick Bay under Lieutenant-Commander A. P. Cooke, who, with the "Estrella" and other vessels, engaged the "Queen-of-the-West" (formerly captured from Colonel C. R. Ellet), and after a fight of twenty minutes destroyed her. He also, a short time after, destroyed two other steamers, the "Diana" and "Hart."

Farragut was relieved by Acting-Rear-Admiral Porter at the mouth of the Red River, May 7th, 1863, and crossing overland, joined his squadron below Port Hudson. He might have run by the batteries at night, but the old "Hartford" he thought had been subjected to enough of that kind of work, and it was scarcely worth while to expose her officers and crew to any more such trials, especially as it was expected that Port Hudson would soon be evacuated by the enemy. So Captain Palmer remained with the "Hartford at the mouth of Red River until after the fall of Port Hudson, it having been left discretionary with him to pass the batteries or not.

Before Farragut's departure overland he had sent an expedition up the Red River to co-operate with General Banks, who was expected at Alexandria with a large military force (he being under the impression that there were military stores at this point and that it was heavily fortified on the water side, or would be in a short time).

There were also some other military movements under consideration to disconcert General Kirby Smith (Confederate), who had gone to Alexandria, so it was said, to provide troops with which to reinforce General Dick Taylor. Neither of these generals had any idea of operating below

Alexandria, which was their natural base; for the gun-boats might get up that far very easily, but would find it a difficult matter to proceed further, as was proved in the end.

The expedition sent by Farragut was composed of the wooden gun-boats "Albatross," "Estrella," Lieutenant-Commander A. P. Cooke, and "Arizona," Volunteer-Lieutenant-Commanding D. P. Upton, all under Lieutenant-Commander John E. Hart. It arrived off Fort de Russy on May 3d, and found the enemy in the act of abandoning the works and removing their guns. Two steamers were engaged in this duty, and two others were moored to the bank alongside the earthworks, with their bows down stream. Lieutenant-Commander Hart at once attacked them with

LIEUTENANT COMMANDER (NOW CAPTAIN) AUGUSTUS P. COOKE, U. S. N.

his broadside guns and a regular battle commenced, the Confederate steamers returning the fire promptly, and it was kept up on both sides until a dense smoke enveloped the river.

Lieutenant-Commander Hart states that the enemy had the most guns and fired shot and shell with great rapidity, and certainly with accuracy. The "Albatross" went into action alone, but the enemy had too many guns for her and she was considerably cut up, and finally obliged to retire, having got aground on the very spot where the "Queen-of-the-West" had been disabled and captured. Hart claims that the other two vessels did not assist him; but the probability is that the pilots did not think

there was room for three vessels to get into action at one time, as this was the worst point on the river to manage a vessel in—the current ran rapidly and the eddies were very annoying to the best pilots; besides, that class of vessel was not at all suited for this work.

The "Albatross" lost two killed, one being the pilot, Mr. J. B. Hamilton, and four wounded—a small number, considering that her commander reported such a severe engagement.

The Confederate steamers carried off the guns, but left a large raft across the river to obstruct the passage. The Confederate commanders had already heard of the arrival at the mouth of the river of a large force of iron-clads, and of the advance of Bank's Army, and their object now was to get the guns to Shreveport. All idea of fortifying Alexandria was abandoned and two or three days afterwards the place surrendered to Rear-Admiral Porter without any resistance.

On Farragut's arrival below Port Hudson he again commenced operations against that place, in conjunction with General Banks, who, as he reported, had the forts closely invested.

Farragut furnished a breaching-battery of four 9-inch guns, under Lieutenant Terry, and the army mounted four 24-pounders. These guns were kept firing day and night to harass the enemy, and also when the Confederates opened fire upon the Federal troops. The mortar schooners also kept up a continuous fire upon the interior of the works, to distress the enemy as much as possible.

It was expected that Port Hudson would hold out as long as Vicksburg did, for the officers of the fort declared that they would never surrender as long as that stronghold remained to them.

In the meantime the enemy were assembling quite a large force from Texas, under a very clever leader (General Green). Demonstrations had been made by this party against Donaldsonville, but they were driven off by the fire of the gun-boats, and finally settled down in Brashear City to await the arrival of their main body of troops from Texas. The object of this raid was no doubt to raise the siege of Port Hudson, or draw off enough of General Banks' troops to enable the garrison to evacuate that place.

As soon as Admiral Farragut heard of these Confederate movements he went down the river to attend to affairs personally, and placed the gun-boats where they would do the most good. Unfortunately, there was only one vessel (the "Princess Royal," Commander M. B. Woolsey) stationed at Donaldsonville, the place the enemy was marching to attack, but this officer was equal to the emergency.

About noon on the 27th of June, hearing the long roll beaten in the fort where the Federal troops were assembled, he sent to inquire the cause, and was informed that General Green had written a letter to the commander of the post to notify the women and children of the town to remove three miles outside of it, as it was his intention to attack the place. A reply was sent back by the flag's truce notifying the Confederate general that the inhabitants would be duly warned. Commander Woolsey got under way early in the evening—his vessel cleared for action—ready to take any position that might be required of him. At midnight a red light was burned in the fort (the pre-arranged signal denoting that the enemy was in motion), and at a little past 1 A.M. the Confederates attacked the Federal post with musketry, which the latter returned with great guns. At the same moment the " Princess Royal " opened on the enemy, in a wood to the right of the fort, with shells, and also fired shells over the fort up the bayou for the purpose of disturbing troops that were in the rear.

Finding that the enemy was pressing upon the water-side of the fort for the purpose of assaulting it, the " Princess Royal " sheered close in to the levee and kept up a rapid fire of shrapnel and canister from all her guns until 2 A. M., when the smoke became so dense that it was impossible to see the fort from the steamer. Commander Woolsey then stood up the river two hundred yards and continued his fire upon the enemy, who were in a wood north of and at a distance of four hundred yards from the Federal fort. Their position was indicated by their yelling, as the flashes of their guns could not be seen for the smoke.

The " Princess Royal " then stood up river for an opening in the levee which her commander remembered, and when abreast of it, he poured in upon the enemy grape and canister at point-blank range and enfiladed them.

The enemy then attacked the steamer with rifles and she turned down river and presented her other broadside. The enemy opened on her from the town, when Commander Woolsey fired one broadside up the main street and another one up the north side of the bayou. He then stood up stream again and took position to enfilade the north side of the fort. In fact this flying battery of heavy guns seemed to be everywhere at the same time, disconcerting all the plans of the Confederate general, who had evidently placed his men expecting to have an easy victory.

This fire was kept up until 3.30 A. M., while the Confederate riflemen returned it so steadily that the men of the " Princess Royal " had several times to lie flat on the deck until the line of fire was passed.

At about 4 A. M., the yelling of the Confederates ceased and their fire slackened, and shortly afterwards cheers went up from the Federal ramparts.

At this moment the gun-boat " Winona," Lieutenant-Commander A. W. Weaver, joined in the engagement, and continued in it until the end.

At daylight the American flag floated gaily over the fort—none of its stars dimmed. General Green and his army retreated and left Donaldsonville in peace. One hundred and twenty of the Confederates got inside of the fort, and were captured and distributed among the different vessels for safe-keeping.

Take it altogether, this was a handsome affair. There is no knowing what might have happened had it not been for the skill with which the naval steamer was handled and the bravery of her commander, officers and crew, who at times fought their guns lying on the deck, which they were obliged to do to escape the riflemen's unerring aim.

What vessels remained of the mortar flotilla had been for three months in front of Port Hudson bombarding that place, and the vessels, with their commanders, officers and crews were spoken of by those who witnessed their work in the most enthusiastic manner. Not only naval officers, but officers of the Army who witnessed the practice, acknowledged the efficiency of the mortar-shells when managed by intelligent officers and men. And yet a high official, whose duty it was to perform a fair and impartial part towards every officer and man in the Navy, attempted to depreciate the services of this gallant little flotilla that had more than once helped Army and Navy on to victory.

Admiral Farragut on June 3d, 1863, recommended for promotion a young Ensign (Adams) who had commanded one of the mortar vessels (the " Orvieto ") at Port Hudson, at the same time calling the attention of the department to his heroism, endurance and obstinate determination to hold his ground until compelled by his commander to fall back, when his vessel was being cut to pieces.

The last affair of any importance that took place in the river before July 10th, 1863, was the attack of some Confederate field batteries upon the U. S. steamer " New London," Lieutenant-Commander G. H. Perkins.

The " New London " was on her way from Port Hudson, having on board a bearer of dispatches from General Banks, announcing the unconditional surrender of that place.

On his arrival at Donaldsonville, Lieutenant-Commander Perkins was directed to proceed to New Orleans, the "Winona" to accompany him past some batteries at Whitehall Point.

At 1 o'clock, A. M., as the "New London" was passing this point, the enemy opened on her with artillery and musketry. The third shell entered one of the boilers, and exploding, made seven holes in a line with the upward flues, scalding six persons severely. Another perforated the steamdrum, and the vessel was disabled and enveloped in steam. The Captain put the vessel's head toward the eastern shore, but the steam escaped so rapidly that the men could not stay at the wheel and the "New London" grounded under the battery. A rocket was sent up to call the attention of the "Winona" that she might come to the assistance of her consort, but she was not in sight. The port battery was manned and commenced playing on the opposite shore where the Confederates were posted. The fire of the enemy's batteries was very severe, and though it was night their range was improving all the time.

Lieutenant-Commander Perkins lowered all his boats and got kedges out astern to haul his vessel off the bottom, which he succeeded in doing, and drifted down the river until out of range of the upper batteries. The principal battery being below, Lieutenant-Commander Perkins towed the "New London" with his boats to the east bank and made her fast. During this operation, a continuous fire was kept up by the enemy's infantry upon the boats and also on the vessel. It was nearly daylight and the Union commander, expecting a renewed attack by the enemy, sent his men on shore under cover of the levee to guard against it. Pickets were stationed up and down the river and messengers sent to Donaldsonville to state the condition of affairs, and also down the river to obtain the assistance of the iron-clad "Essex" and steam-sloop "Monongahela."

The messengers returned from Donaldsonville, stating that no assistance could be rendered, and the two couriers from below returned with the unsatisfactory news that the "Essex" and "Monongahela" could not be found.

This was not the kind of an answer the Army would have received from the Navy if the general in command had made a requisition for gun-boats when attacked by the Confederates. It was not the kind of message Commander Woolsey sent from the "Princess Royal" when the post at Donaldsonville was attacked by General Green, who with his large force would have carried the works but for the tremendous enfilading fire of the Federal gun-boat.

But General Weitzel was in command at Donaldsonville and he did not seem to think a gun-boat of much importance. or perhaps did not think it prudent to weaken his garrison while there were Confederate field-pieces in the neighborhood.

But Lieutenant-Commander Perkins, knowing that the Confederates would attack him at night with a force he could not resist, determined to go and convince General Weitzel of the necessity there was for sending troops to the assistance of his vessel, and succeeded in doing so; but on returning to the place where he had left the "New London," he found her gone. During his absence, which was only of two hours' duration, the "Essex" and "Monongahela" had come up the river and towed the "New London" down !

The Confederates did not easily relinquish what no doubt they considered a certain prize. They contested the passage of the "Essex" and "Monongahela" with much determination, and the infantry even stood up for some time against the fire of the heavy guns of three vessels; but they were scattered by grape, canister and shrapnel, which proved too much for them.

This affair was well managed by Lieutenant-Commander Perkins, who did all that lay in his power to prevent his vessel falling into the enemy's hands; displaying cool judgment and bravery through all. Some officers under the circumstances might have abandoned the gun-boat in the night, and escaped in the boats after setting fire to her; but Perkins preferred to use his boats to tow her out of range of the enemy's guns until he could obtain assistance, which by his perseverance he succeeded in doing. Farragut blamed him for leaving his ship to go after assistance himself. No doubt the principle that every commanding officer should be the last man to leave his vessel, is the right one, but here there was no danger of capture in his absence, as the enemy was on the opposite shore and could not reach his vessel in the short time that he was away from her.

The last of the reports from Admiral Farragut to the Navy Department, published in the year 1863, conveyed the melancholy news of the death of Commander Abner Reed of the "Monongahela." He was mortally wounded by a rifle-shell while passing the batteries, twelve miles below Donaldsonville, and Farragut says of him: "Commander Reed was one of the most enterprising and gallant officers in my squadron, and the very mention of his name was a source of terror to the Confederates—the country could well have spared a better man." No higher eulogium was ever passed upon any officer, and it should be recorded in history.

Captain T. A. Jenkins, who was on board, was severely wounded.

This brings the narrative of events up to July 28th, 1863.

The news of the surrender of Vicksburg had been received in New Orleans, and that of Port Hudson immediately followed.

The Father of Waters flowed peacefully to the sea, free and untrammelled. The great chain of slavery was broken, never to be again united. The work of setting free the great artery of the North and South, so essential to our nationality, had been accomplished. and the foul blot of human slavery had disappeared forever from our escutcheon. The squadrons of the Upper and Lower Mississippi had shaken

COMMANDER ABNER REED

hands in New Orleans, and the great highway between Cincinnati and the Queen City of the South was once more open to commerce with the North and with foreign countries. The power of the United States Government had been restored and its authority vindicated in more than half the territory claimed by the insurgents.

It is to be hoped that the future millions who will dwell along the banks of these mighty waters, which were emancipated by the valor of the Army and Navy, will not withhold a due share of credit to the officers and men of the Navy, who performed their important part in those eventful times with such an unflinching devotion to the Union.

A quarter of a century has passed away since the events took place which are here narrated. Many of the men who figured in those scenes have been overtaken by age, and Time, the great destroyer, has somewhat impaired their faculties, but they are the same in spirit as in 1861, and still entitled to the gratitude of their country

The men in civil life who read the stirring incidents of the war by their cosy firesides should not forget that they have reaped the benefits arising from the incessant toil of the Navy, and should therefore forbear to speak unkindly of a profession whose officers and men would tomorrow—if war should again arise—exhibit the same zeal, energy and courage as was shown by those who so well performed their parts in the late conflict.

On the receipt of the news of the fall of Vicksburg and Fort Hudson at New Orleans, on the 10th of July, there was great rejoicing on the part of our Army and Navy. The commanding officers of both branches of the service ordered salutes of one hundred guns to be fired—the sound of which carried joy to the hearts of those who sympathized with the Union cause, and dismay to the hearts of the Confederates. The latter element predominated very largely, yet on the whole the people of New Orleans were pleased with the hope of seeing the commerce of the North and West return to their once flourishing city and again crowd its levees with the splendid steamers that formerly kept their storehouses supplied with the products of the Upper Mississippi. But war had made sad ravages in this class of vessels; hundreds of them had been sunk or burned in the Red, Yazoo, Arkansas and White Rivers, and the few that now came creeping out of the bayous and small streams where they had been laid away, were in so dilapidated a condition that on their appearance at the levee, the very sight of these vessels called to mind the decayed condition of this once flourishing city and brought tears of sorrow to many an eye. These people were only repaid for their faithlessness to a form of government under which they had reaped so much prosperity and from which, even in their wildest enthusiasm for the Confederacy, they received protection.

Few of the seceders would believe that Vicksburg and Port Hudson had surrendered, for they were so infatuated with the Confederacy that they could not but believe that it was the strongest government on the face of the earth, and that its resources were illimitable; forgetting that it only derived its present strength from coming into possession of the forts, navy-yards and arsenals which had been taken from the true government by the very persons for whose protection they had been built.

New Orleans, after it had been conquered by Farragut's fleet, became a model city as regards its police and sanitary departments, for the first time in its history. No city in the world ever possessed a more turbulent mob—and in no city were the municipal laws less respected (before its capture)—at the end of 1862 its streets were as well kept as those of the cleanest village at the North and the citizens had never enjoyed such safety as they did under the Butler regime, when General Shipley was the military governor of the city.

With the fall of Vicksburg and Port Hudson the flying detachments of Confederates that lingered along the Mississippi and in the bayous and inland rivers drew back into the western part of Louisiana, or into Texas, where most of them came from. They were a fearless set of men (unlike the home-guards of Tennessee), who seem to have been drawn to the banks of the Mississippi for the purpose of aiding their besieged friends in Vicksburg and Port Hudson; and although they were sufficiently active in annoying gun-boats and transports going up or down the river, they did not resort to the vile measures of the Tennessee home-guards or commit depredations upon inoffensive citizens. They were soldiers in every sense of the word, and risked their lives fearlessly in making attacks on the Union fortifications; fighting in what they considered the defence of their own soil, until the last Confederate stronghold on the Mississippi had fallen.

The surrender of the two great fortifications relieved a large force of the Army and Navy from close confinement around the enemy, and allowed them to be used all along the river and coast. This, too, in a measure helped to get rid of the artillery and mounted rangers, who, though not numerous enough to make a stand against the Federal troops, had been very annoying. The Federals had frequently to acknowledge that the Texas and Louisiana troops were more than a match for them; and if they had not been so strongly backed by the naval force, it is doubtful whether Butler or Banks could have held their positions for a month.

After the fall of Vicksburg, Rear-Admiral Porter descended the Mississippi as far as New Orleans, where the command of the entire river and all its tributaries was turned over to him by Farragut, who could now give his whole attention to the coast and its inlets, which were still in the hands of the enemy.

Farragut had calculated on capturing some of the enemy's strongholds on the coast as early as 1862, but the latter held out defiantly—very much strengthened, doubly armed and trebly manned—their commanders arrogantly flying the Confederate flag and bidding our wooden vessels to come to the sacrifice that awaited them.

After Farragut had turned over his part of the command in the Mississippi, it belonged to his successor to see that the enemy built no more forts along the banks of the great river; to guarantee a safe passage to army transports and commercial steamers, and to see that no provisions or troops reached the Confederates from Arkansas, Louisiana or Texas.

These duties were faithfully performed. The tin-clads and gun-boats, now amounting to about 112, were spread along the whole length of the river (below Vicksburg) and at or near the mouth of all tributaries. The vessels were divided into squadrons under young and competent officers, who vied with each other in carrying out the orders that were issued from time to time "to keep open the free navigation of the rivers."

It cannot be said that peace was actually established, but the transit from Cairo to New Orleans was not at all hazardous for the travelling community; the little towns began to exhibit a desire to trade, and the people on the plantations soon found that they received more protection from the gun-boats than they did from the half-starved Confederates, who had been accustomed to make frequent raids upon the coast (as they called the river-banks) in search of food and plunder.

CHAPTER XXXII.

Condition of the Navy Department at the Breaking out of the Rebellion.—Secretary Welles, his Character and Ability.—Commodores Stringham and Paulding connected with the Navy Department to assist Secretary Welles.—Paulding drives the Secessionists out of the Department.—President Lincoln selects Mr. G. V. Fox as Assistant to Secretary Welles.—Preparations of the Confederate Leaders.—Confederate Iron-clads.—Policy of the United States Government in Building Ships and Mounting Guns.—Slowness of the Government in taking in the Situation.—Apparent Supineness of the Navy Department.—Department Overwhelmed with Plans and Contractors, but Rises to the Occasion and Puts forth its Energy.—Difficulties in the way of Adopting the Right kind of Iron-clad.—The Department at first doubtful of the Plans of Ericsson's " Monitor."—Boards Appointed to Discuss the matter of Iron-clads.—Mistake in not Cutting down some of our Heavy Steamships and Converting them into Iron-clads.—Mr. Fox bends all his Energies towards Introducing Iron-clads into the Navy.—Mr. Lenthall Chief-Constructor.—Mr. Isherwood Chief of Bureau of Engineering.—Rear-Admiral Dahlgren and his Guns.—Mr. Fox Introduces the 15-inch Gun into the Navy.—Ericsson's claim as an Inventor.—Congress wakes up in Regard to the Requirements of the Navy.—Citizens to whom Credit was Due.—Twenty Single and Four Double Turreted Monitors Contracted for.—Preparations to attack Charleston.

WHEN the civil war broke out, the Navy Department, like every other branch of the government, was totally unprepared for the event.

The right of secession had been openly declared in the Senate and House of Representatives, and Southern members were daily leaving their seats; yet the Administration held back, and, deluded by Confederate sympathizers, sat still and looked on with dismay at the dismemberment of the country without seeming to take any steps to prevent it.

No department of the government seemed to rise to the occasion, and the Navy Department was no exception to the rule. The Secretary of the Navy, Mr. Gideon Welles, was not a naval man in any sense of the word. His life had been passed amid civil pursuits, and the only connection he had ever had with the Navy was for a short time when he was Chief of the Bureau of Provisions and Clothing—a purely political appointment. He had spent many years of his life as editor of a newspaper, and during his administration of affairs in the Navy Department gave evidence of ability in the use of his pen. The numerous dispatches and reports which he wrote during the war showed that as a literary man he had few superiors.

But Mr. Welles was far advanced in years when he took charge of the Navy, and had reached a period when men generally desire to retire to the shades of private life, and follow pursuits more congenial to their tastes. He was not a rapid thinker—was cautious by nature and extremely methodical in all he did. Having been at the head of a bureau where he constantly came in contact with contractors, he naturally surrounded himself with guards of all kinds, and introduced so much red tape into the Department, that it must have been a bold man who would have attempted to break through it all with the hope of overreaching the chief or his assistants.

Some of the bureau officers were inoculated with secession sentiments, and their rooms were daily filled with officers who exchanged opinions hostile to the government, meanwhile leaving the Secretary to assume that they were loyal. The Secretary, as a matter of course, received no aid from these men; on the contrary, they held him back and delayed his doing what good he attempted.

Mr. Welles began to find out gradually that he was not surrounded by the kind of men it was desirable to have about him under the circumstances, and he called to his aid in the department Commodore Stringham, the best dock-yard officer in the Navy and a thorough seaman, loyal to the last degree and of a most honorable character. But he possessed no administrative abilities, disliked an office life, and soon sought relief from it by applying for active duty afloat. He was therefore appointed to the command of a small squadron, to attempt the capture of the forts at Hatteras Inlet, which he succeeded in doing.

To show how slowly secretaries or officers had risen to the occasion, and how little all concerned could form any estimate of what was actually necessary to be done at the breaking out of the civil war (though the coming events cast their shadows plainly before them), the Hatteras expedition was looked upon as a great event, and it was thought that the success of it was likely to carry such terror into the hearts of the Confederates that it would break up any further attempt to fortify the Southern coast!

Commodore Paulding relieved Commodore Stringham in the Navy Department. He was a faithful officer, who looked upon the flag of his country as the emblem of all that was great and glorious. He regarded secession as the worm at the root of the flower, sure to destroy it unless speedily removed, and he was in favor of exterminating every man in the Navy of whose loyalty there was even a doubt. He had served many years of his life in active duty at sea, but he now began to show the advance of age, and did not at once realize the gravity of the situation. Running in a groove, as he had done for so many years, he was not able to change his nature suddenly and adopt new methods.

He soon found that he did not suit the place, nor the place him, and as his ideas of naval discipline were so dissimilar to the system which governed a civil department that he had at times to defer to the opinions of the chief clerk, and the associations were not pleasant, he soon tired of the position, especially when he found that he would have to bear responsibilities which he did not care to shoulder.

In fact, Commodore Paulding disliked the atmosphere of the Navy Department as much as Commodore Stringham had done, and soon obtained duty at the New York Navy Yard, where he thought he could be of more service to his country. But before he left the Department he not only rooted out the disloyal officers who were attached to the different bureaus, but forbade any man who uttered disloyal sentiments, or who hesitated to espouse the Union cause, from entering the building.

It never struck these loyal old officers, when they heard that the Confederates were building iron-clads, that something might be done in that direction by the North. They had fought their battles on the open decks of ships and they thought that was a good-enough way for any one to fight. They did not believe in men who would resort to a shelter of iron for protection against shot or shell, and rather had a contempt for any one who would suggest such a mode of fighting. Consequently, their thoughts did not run in the direction of iron-clads.

It was absolutely necessary that Mr. Welles should have an adviser in his department who could take charge of the practical part of naval affairs, and who by his knowledge of the wants of the Navy could assist him to meet the difficulties which were daily accumulating, and almost overpowering him. It would not have been looked upon favorably had he selected a naval officer below the highest grades, no matter what his abilities were, for such a thing had never occurred in the Navy! That was argument enough, without mentioning that it would have been a reflection upon the older officers. It was for this reason that Mr. G. V. Fox, late a lieutenant in the Navy, was selected by President Lincoln as naval adviser, and finally appointed Assistant Secretary of the Navy. It was not until Mr. Fox was appointed that due attention was paid to the building of iron-clads and other vessels appropriate for coast and river service, and it was to Mr. Fox that we were indebted during the war for the life and energy that pervaded the naval administration, and his ready compliance with the requisitions of officers, which enabled them to carry on naval operations with vigor.

Secretary Welles was not an eminent statesman, yet he had qualities of a high order. He was loyal to his government, held no intercourse with men of disloyal sentiments, and drove out of the service all those officers who wavered in their allegiance. He was a man of good judgment in many matters relating to the business that came before him, and he never showed more wisdom than when he acquiesced in the President's appointment of Mr. Fox as his naval adviser.

The civil war had now assumed such large proportions, and so rapidly, that even the wisest men were at fault as to what should be done to meet the style of warfare which the Confederates were inaugurating all over the South. With the assumed resources of the North, every step the Confederates made in military or naval warfare should have been more than met by a corresponding move on the Federal side; but this was not done. It was known early in the war that the Confederates were building iron-clads of a peculiar character, but no one seemed to know *exactly* what their character was.

There is no doubt of *one* thing, viz., that long before the prominent secession leaders had signified their intention of leaving their seats in Congress, every move had been determined. It was known exactly how many small arms were wanted, and how many great guns and pieces of artillery; and it was known that for a beginning there were enough of these arms stowed away in the Government arsenals scattered through the Southern States, to say nothing of the great armament that had been supplied from time to time to the States for the use of their militia. It is thus seen that in respect to arms the Confederates had no right to complain of deficiencies. At the battle of Bull Run they were as well supplied with all the appliances of war as were the government troops, who were forced to retreat on that day before the fire of this first army of the insurgents.

For some time all these matters had been considered by the southern leaders; and when the time came to act, eleven States rose as one man, and the government had not only to put down the State of South Carolina, with a small number of insurrectionists, but millions of people from Kentucky to Maryland, all armed and equipped and formed into battalions, as if they had been the great reserve of the nation, ready to jump to their arms at the call of the general government. This system of preparation extended to the Navy as well as to the Army. The Confederate leaders knew, two years before the war, what officers of the Navy would unite with them in humiliating the old flag, and though these officers made no pledges, and doubtless hoped that the event would never take place that would disturb their position under the United States Government, yet they had made up their minds what to do in case the struggle ensued.

It is not likely that the Southern leaders would lose any opportunity of gaining information from Southern officers that would enable them to carry out their plans, and it is free to presume, from what we now know, that a full discussion of all matters was carried on between the promoters of secession and officers of the Army and Navy up to the last moment; many of the latter may have entered into these discussions and given all the desired information without realizing that they were unfaithful to the trusts confided to them by their lawful government.

We believe that all the iron-clads that finally got afloat or were burned on the stocks were calculated for before the war, the places of building them decided upon, the difficulties the Federal Government would have to contend with to get at them, the material required for their construction, the time required to build them, and the officers and artisans who were to be employed in the work selected. This may seem doubtful, but the Confederates could never, with all their energy and determination to win, have achieved such work as they performed in the building of an iron-clad navy without having had preconceived plans.

It is a compliment to their energy and ingenuity to say that they could build anything at all at the South beyond their light river-steamers. They had so long depended upon the Northern machine-shops for all heavy work needed in the South, that they had no great factories of their own. Even the Tredegar Works at Richmond, which supplied a large number of the Brooke rifles for the Confederacy, owed its existence to the fact that it was sustained by the United States Government in the first instance, and by large contracts given it for naval ordnance up to 1861, some of which was on the lathe when Sumter fired the first gun.

If the Southerners did not make their plans before the war actually broke out, they deserve unbounded credit for the energy displayed in getting into existence such formidable vessels as they did before the North had done anything but build the little "Monitor," which was ready nearly on the same day that the "Merrimac" created such consternation at Hampton Roads.

It is true, that through the enterprise and energy of a western man, Mr. James B. Eads, we got some iron-clads afloat on the Mississippi, but it was not until the 17th of June, 1861, that the Quartermaster-general of the Army issued proposals for building the vessels. Great progress was made upon these *quasi* iron-clads when the work was once under full headway; but with all the remarkable services they performed, what were they when compared with the "Virginia," the "Louisiana," the "Albemarle," "Atlanta," "Mobile," and three large vessels built or building at Yazoo City —the "Mississippi," burnt at New Orleans —the "Tennessee," that fought a whole squadron (including three iron-clads) in Mobile Bay—and the " Arkansas," that passed through a fleet of vessels (carrying 150 guns), without receiving more serious injury than the wounding of some fifteen men and the slight derangement of part of her armor and machinery?

Previous to the civil war it had been the aim of the United States Government to excel all other nations in the quality and size of its vessels-of-war. If a steam-frigate was built in Europe of large size and heavily armed, the U. S. Government at once laid down the lines of a larger vessel carrying many more guns, and these guns of a calibre hitherto unknown in naval warfare. We had, in fact, reached the point of excellence in our ships some years previous to the breaking out of the Rebellion, and the great steam-frigates which figured during the war in attacks on heavy earth-works were sample vessels of our Navy. They had all steamed to different parts of the world, and their appearance and power called forth the applause of all foreign officers who visited them. There were no vessels in Europe of this class that could compare with them; yet, with all these triumphs over foreigners, we had only one vessel at the time of the " Merrimac's " appearance that was able to compete with her. The only vessels we had building were the " New Ironsides " (a splendid ship of her class) and the " Galena," a perfect failure as an iron-clad, as proved by her weakness on the James River, where she attacked the Confederate batteries.

It required some time for the Department to take in the true situation of affairs, and it was not until after the battle between the " Monitor " and " Merrimac " that they saw how nearly the nation escaped a great calamity, which had been averted by the invention of John Ericsson, and the gallant officer who fought the Union iron-clad with so much skill and bravery. Then the Navy Department rose to the occasion, and putting forth all its energy, more than redeemed itself for the *apparent* supineness of the past.

At first neither the constructors nor the Navy Department had a fair conception of what was needed in the Navy to meet the new order of vessels that were being built in the South. The Department was overwhelmed with a multiplicity of plans that were presented by outside parties, who were backed by strong political friends in Congress whom it was advisable the Secretary should conciliate. Some of these plans were so wild and impracticable that they could not be considered for a moment. The attention required by these claimants and their political backers hampered the Department greatly; and they were not so much indebted to John Ericsson for driving

the " Merrimac " into port, as for getting rid of the pack of inventors and advisers who had been hanging about the doors of the Secretary of the Navy, until none but a person of Mr. Welles' placid temper or Mr. Fox's inflexible will could have been able to stand the strain. The little " Monitor " settled all these inventors at the same time that she settled the " Merrimac," and Ericsson not only rose at once in the estimation of the public, but his standing with the Government became assured.

From that time forth the Navy Department may be said to have assumed new life and vigor, and the most hypercritical historian can scarcely find fault with it for want of energy displayed in building vessels of the new type, which, when finished, could bid defiance to the heaviest ships of any foreign navy.

There was at one time in England a large number of British naval officers who would not listen to the idea of having an iron-clad navy. The French were trying to introduce iron-clads into their service, but on a small scale; and their want of success did not encourage Englishmen to copy their traditional enemies. They still clung to their idols, the staunch old wooden three-deckers, seventy-fours and frigates, and scouted the idea of laying aside these noble structures for a class of vessel that had never been tested at sea, and which, in the opinion of many, would go to the bottom in the first gale of wind they encountered. They had in some cases partially protected the wood-work abreast of the guns, but not to any extent.

There was no master-mind to take hold of the subject, and to evoke a system that would at once show up the weakness of the British navy, and convince the authorities that the days of the wooden monarchs of the sea were numbered.

The Federal Navy Department long before had its eyes on the great English navy that made no move in the direction of changing the character of its vessels—a navy full of clever and scientific men, who should have been ever alive to any theory that makes one navy superior to another, but who now refused to listen to the talk about iron-clad ships and scouted the idea of adopting them.

It would have been a bold man, indeed, who, as Secretary of the Navy, would have taken the responsibility of building any number of untried " Monitors " without something to justify him in doing so. The Secretary of the Navy himself and those about him had no positive belief at first in the success of Ericsson's " Monitor." The plan was so contrary to all preconceived ideas of a fighting-ship that they could not believe it would do what Ericsson predicted for it.

The chief constructor of the navy, Mr. John Lenthall, at first condemned the "Monitor" *in toto*, and he was at that time the ablest naval architect in any country, having built some of the most effective ships afloat.

All these things were enough to have deterred Secretary Welles from embarking in the iron-clad business; but he did take hold of the Ericsson plan, and in view of the fact that it was necessary to have something with which to meet the "Merrimac," he made a contract with this inventor which in the end led to much larger vessels. As soon as the invulnerability of the "Monitor" was established by her encounter with the most powerful iron-clad afloat, Secretary Welles was no longer backward in advocating this class of vessel.

To show how little was known about iron-clads in the U. S. Navy and how little support the Department received from that direction: A Board, established by Act of Congress, "to consist of three skillful line officers of the Navy," was appointed to look into the subject of iron-clads; and, if their report was favorable, the Secretary of the Navy was to be authorized to build one or more armored or iron-clad, or steel-clad, steamships or floating batteries, etc., etc. This law was passed in September, 1861. The Board of Officers appointed to decide upon this matter approached the subject very carefully, saying: "Distrustful of our own ability to discharge this duty, which the law requires should be performed by three skillful naval officers, we approach the subject with diffidence, having no experience and but scanty knowledge in this branch of naval architecture."

This Board was governed very much in their reports by the information and opinions which they could obtain from English authorities. They recommended three out of seventeen plans that had been submitted (one of them John Ericsson's), but with reservations and a proviso (which was enough to frighten off any constructor) that the vessels must be a success in all respects, or else be thrown back on the hands of the contractors!"

The Board on their own account recommended that armor and heavy guns be placed on one of our *river craft;* "or, if none will bear it, to construct a scow that will answer, to plate and shield the guns for river service on the Potomac; to be constructed or prepared at the Washington Navy Yard for immediate use!" The Board did not say how this iron-clad warrior was to be propelled.

When three of the most skillful officers of the Navy could give the Secretary no better information than this, it is no wonder that he was doubtful of his own ability to decide in such a case; but he did decide, and in favor of Ericsson, who proposed not only the most reasonable price for

JOHN LENTHALL, CHIEF OF BUREAU OF CONSTRUCTION.

his vessels, but the unity of the design seemed to strike the Board as something likely to succeed. The "New Ironsides" was also contracted for with Cramp & Sons in Philadelphia, and the "Galena," to be armored with three-inch iron, to be built by Bushnell & Co., New Haven, Connecticut. These three vessels, it is said, were to represent the three types of the American idea of iron-clads—though, with the exception of the "New Ironsides," very few persons had any faith in them.

This was the first attempt at building an iron-clad navy for operations on the coast, and the "Monitor" was the only one of them that was ready to meet the enemy's greatest fighting-machine, "just in the nick of time."

There was one thing which the Navy Department lost sight of altogether, and that was that the "Merrimac" was simply a large frigate being metamorphosed into an iron-clad. We had five vessels similar to the "Merrimac," and any two of them could have been cut down and armored much more effectively than the "Merrimac" was. The work could have been done at our northern navy yards in half of the time it could be done by the Confederates, and we would have had two heavy iron-clads ready to meet the Confederate monster if ever she should get out of Norfolk.

What matters it? some will say. The "Monitor" drove the "Merrimac" back, and demonstrated the superiority of the American type of iron-clad over the most powerful war-ship ever until that time built in any navy, placed us on an equality with England and France, and gave our government a sure plan they could follow with safety.

Yes, but we would have been saved the disgrace and disaster of seeing two of our finest frigates sunk or destroyed at Newport News, 250 gallant officers and men slain almost in cold blood, three frigates run on shore and at the mercy of the "Merrimac," and every ship at Hampton Roads thrown into a state of panic, which unfortunately was witnessed by a foreign man-of-war lying at anchor off Fortress Monroe. It would have saved the government a shock which it did not recover from for some time, and the Northern people from the mortification of knowing that our entire fleet at Hampton Roads had been beaten by one Confederate vessel in the first naval encounter of the war.

With all this, the lesson learned was a useful one. It opened the eyes of Congress to the necessity of making more liberal appropriations for the Navy, and made them listen at last to the appeals of the Secretary of the Navy to strengthen this branch of the service.

The Board above referred to recommended that the Department should ask Congress, at the next session, to appropriate $10,000 for experiments on iron plates of different kinds! As if the Department could wait while the enemy was thundering at its doors! But it is due to the Navy Department to state that it was not at all influenced by such a procrastinating policy. Mr. Welles while Secretary of the Navy received his share of abuse, and on no point was he more severely criticised than on his selection of the "Monitor" as the type of American iron-clads, for the princi-

ple did not meet with favor among that class of officers who were expected to serve in them. Mr. Welles could not expect to be exempt from criticism, or be excused from the responsibility of any failure that might attend his experiments with the Navy. He was in the position of the commander of a fleet, being alone responsible for success or failure. Though his subordinates may do a great deal of the work, and make a great many suggestions, yet the Commander-in-chief is entitled to all the honors in case of success, and must also bear the blame of failure. Such has been the history of war since wars began. This rule also applies to heads of departments. They may have the ablest subordinates and be relieved of many of the cares of office, yet they must shoulder all responsibility and take the odium of every case of failure.

In writing history, one must be careful not to let his predilections in favor of one man lead him to do injustice to another, especially if this other is the head of a department and the responsible party.

No matter what the abilities of the subordinates are, or how much their services have conduced to the desired end, one must look only to the head of his department for reward, as a lieutenant does to his captain.

It is not always that men receive in their life-time the amount of credit due for their work; it oftener happens that they receive more honor after death. In the course of years history will do them justice. The patient, plodding historian will come along, and taking no account of time, will delve into the mass of records which lie at his disposal, when every word is carefully scanned, and the truth is sure to be evolved. Then men are weighed according to their merits, and assigned to their rightful positions.

All the sensational histories written during the war, or directly after it, have long since been consigned to that bourne from which sensational history never returns. He who now undertakes to write of the war must prepare himself for severe criticism if he tries to deprive any one of credit.

Time is a great promoter of good feeling and softener-down of asperities, enabling a writer of the present day to view things in a different light from what he did twenty years ago. It would be better, nevertheless, that a century should pass before the history of a war is written, when all the participators in it are dead; for history can be better told from the written or printed records of the day than from the recollections of any one who lived among the scenes he attempts to describe; but, if men will write, they must lay aside all personal feeling, and keeping the records before their eyes, do their duty " tho' the heavens should fall."

Thus, in this history, in speaking of the work done by the Navy Department to bring to an end the terrible rebellion that was devastating the country, the writer can only recognize Mr. Welles, the Secretary of the Navy, as the one who controlled the great machine that was turning out ships, gun-boats, iron-clads, etc., with a rapidity that astonished the powers of Europe, who were looking on with amazement at the Federal Government while the latter was building a Navy capable of setting at defiance even France or England.

While Mr. Fox, the Assistant Secretary, was bending all *his* energies to devise the class of vessels best suited for the purposes of our war, and to meet the necessities of the occasion, and Mr. Faxon, the chief clerk, was giving his undivided attention to the civil branch of the Department, Mr. Welles was presiding over all and giving to each his moral support.

Mr. Welles was the responsible head; it was his judgment that decided almost all matters; it was his coolness and placidity of temper that controlled those around him and smoothed over the little asperities and jealousies which would spring up among his subordinates—with a smooth word he brought back to his proper position anyone who attempted to assume more than his rightful authority—in this way making a unit of the department. Mr. Fox was the able assistant, in charge of the general naval duties that had in years gone by pertained to the Board of Naval Commissioners, while Mr. Faxon was the chief clerk in charge of the Civil Department and the records.

Secretary Welles was the judicial, financial, and political head, under whose direction everything was done; all plans were submitted to him, and no movement was made without his consent, and he weighed every matter before coming to a conclusion. He knew everything that was going on in the Navy; and as a proof that he understood and appreciated all that was taking place, and that he was observing the proper steps to provide for the future, it is only necessary for one to read the numerous able reports he wrote from time to time on the condition of the Navy and its requirements, or his descriptions of the operations of the different squadrons. These documents will convince any one that Secretary Welles had abilities of no ordinary kind, and that, with few omissions, he did everything that could be done to put the Navy in a creditable condition.

That he could have accomplished all he did without Mr. Fox's assistance no one pretends to claim; but he showed his judgment in listening to this gentleman's recommendations, and by placing confidence in one who had the best interests of the service at heart. Hereafter, then, when speaking of the Navy Department, we shall regard Secretary Welles as the responsible head to whom all under him owed proper obedience and their best efforts to aid in the difficult task he had before him.

In all that regarded the general increase of the Navy, the Department had made good use of the means at its disposal. The Navy Yards and private establishments were full of work to overflowing. Mr. John Lenthall, a constructor of the highest order, was always ready, with his practical skill and science, for any emergency. He had planned the great frigates, " Colorado," " Wabash," " Minnesota," " Merrimac," and " Franklin," which had elicited the applause of the world. He planned the " 90-day gun-boats" immediately after the breaking out of the war (a small class of vessel carrying one 11-inch gun forward and two light 32-pounders aft, drawing only eight or ten feet of water, and therefore able to enter any of the Southern ports). These vessels were of the greatest use during the war, and their value could not be overestimated.

On a requisition from Mr. Fox, Mr. Lenthall designed the double-enders, with their heavy batteries of 9 and 11-inch guns and ten feet draft of water, that could follow the " 90-day gun-boats" through the most narrow and tortuous streams, where, not having room to turn, they could go out again stern foremost, like a New York ferry-boat going from slip to slip.

And when Mr. Lenthall was notified that the Confederates were having built in England fast clippers armed with English guns, manned by English seamen, and commanded by Confederate officers, he at once designed a score of swift and beautiful corvettes, that were able to overtake any of the Confederate cruisers and capture them when they got them under their guns. One of these did actually destroy the " Alabama."

Mr. Lenthall also designed those large ships-of-war of over 3,000 tons (on Mr. Fox's suggestion), the first of which made seventeen and one-half knots per hour for twenty-four consecutive hours, the greatest speed that had been attained at that time by any naval power. In this case the ability of Mr. Isherwood, chief of Bureau of Steam Engineering, was brought into play. He designed the engines and boilers of these ships, as he did the machinery of all others planned by Mr. Lenthall.

Mr. Lenthall could not at first be made to admit that a vessel of the " Monitor's" build could be made efficacious for war purposes, or live in a sea-way, and he did not hesitate to say, while she was building, that she would go down as soon as she was launched. It was not until after the battle of the "Monitor" and "Merrimac" that he had any confidence in the former. Then Mr. Lenthall's ideas underwent a radical change, and while he sighed over what he knew would be the end of all his beautiful wooden vessels, with whose fine models he had spent so many hours of his life, his practical mind at once grasped the subject, with new ideas engrafted on the first project, and in the end he produced vessels of the Monitor type that had not their equals at that time in any European navy.

Whatever alterations may have been made in the Monitor system, the original idea was that of John Ericsson; any change

B. F. ISHERWOOD, U. S. NAVY, CHIEF OF BUREAU OF
STEAM-ENGINEERING.

or improvement that left the hull submerged, or nearly so, and retained the revolving turret, was his by right. The criticisms on his first invention led him to consider the importance of somewhat changing his plans, and out of this came the "Miantonomah," "Monadnock," etc., double-turreted monitors, which, with their four 15-inch guns, were more than a match for any three-decker.

Though there were some objections to the first Monitor, there was nothing to call for the bitter criticisms with which the vessel was assailed. Theoretically, the original plan had advantages over the later ideas: for instance, the armor projected over the sides, stern and bow on what was called the overhang, which carried out the idea

Ericsson first conceived of building a raft that could not sink; which could not be struck by shot below the water line; which could not be rammed; where the rudder and propeller were entirely secure from shot or ramming; and where raising the anchor and all other operations could be performed without a single person appearing on deck.

If the "Monitor" was not as efficient a vessel as some of those that came after her, it is no reason why any of her arrangements should be condemned. She performed a more important part in the history of the war than any of her successors, and her name will go down in history when the names of other vessels of her class will have been forgotten. Had the original design been received by the government as it ought to have been, and money spent without stint to produce at the first such vessels as the "Miantonomah" and "Monadnock," either of them would have destroyed the "Merrimac" in twenty minutes.

We prided ourselves in those days on the character of our ordnance, which was the best of its kind in the world—we refer to the 11-inch and 9-inch smooth-bore—rifled cannon had not at that time made such an advance as to satisfy us that it would be the gun of the future. Admiral Dahlgren, who had brought our naval ordnance to a state of perfection, considered the 11-inch the most powerful gun in the world; and having accomplished what he considered the grandest feat of gun-making in modern times, he was contented to rest upon his laurels.

There was a diversity of opinion at that time between the ordnance authorities of the Army and Navy in regard to the kind of guns that were required, which engendered some ill-feeling between the heads of the two branches of the service, the result of which was that there was no interchange of ideas. The Naval Chief of Bureau was satisfied that he had found in the 11-inch gun all that was desirable for naval purposes, never considering the great change that might occur at any moment in the shape and character of war ships that would involve the necessity of using larger guns. The result was that the new era came and found us with only the 11-inch gun on hand in the Navy.

It is not certain that the original Monitor would have carried two guns of larger size, but her dimensions and steam power might easily have been increased at small additional expense, and she could have been provided with 15-inch guns.

The ordnance department of the Army had gone to work very quietly and cast some guns of that size, somewhat on the Dahlgren pattern. Whether the Naval Ordnance Department knew of the casting of this 15-inch gun we are not prepared to say, but it is certain neither Secretary Welles nor Mr. Fox knew anything about it until after the battle of the "Monitor" and "Merrimac."

The account of the destruction of the "Cumberland" and "Congress" had been flashed over the wires to the Secretary of the Navy, and Mr. Fox started at once for Hampton Roads to see if he could be of any service, and to report on the condition of affairs.

Mr. Fox was on the dock at Fortress Monroe, where he could witness the fight between the iron-clads. He noticed that the shot from the "Monitor's" guns glanced off from the sloping sides of the "Merrimac," while the rifled shot of the "Merrimac" seemed to have no effect on the turret of the "Monitor." "I wonder," he said, mentally, "why no one has ever thought of casting larger guns with heavier shot, that would knock in that fellow's sides at the first broadside." As this idea struck him, he cast his eyes on a monster gun that was lying on the dock under the lifting-crane, and on examining it he found it to be a 15-inch gun, army pattern, intended to be mounted at Fortress Monroe. This was a revelation to the Assistant Secretary, and he returned to Washington with his ideas much enlarged, and said to the Secretary, "We must have Monitors that will carry turrets large enough for 15-inch guns;" and Mr. Welles, on hearing his story, agreed with him in his conclusions.

When an invention which has been doubted and decried shows its superiority over all its competitors, and its detractors are set at naught, it immediately rises to the extreme of popularity; and so it was with the Monitor system, though some officers, who thought more of their personal comfort than they did of results to be achieved, greatly preferred the "New Ironsides," with her sixteen 11-inch guns, to a Monitor with two, or even four, 15-inch guns.

The "New Ironsides" was without doubt a splendid vessel, and we ought to have built more of the same kind; but although she was better suited for attacking fortifications under certain conditions than the Monitors were (owing to the number of her guns and the consequent rapidity of her fire), she would have stood no chance in a contest with one of the single-turreted class—much less with the "Monadnock" or "Miantonomah."

The "New Ironsides" did not represent an idea that could be carried out in all future naval ships; no vessels built on her plans have maintained their positions, while the Monitor system has been combined in all the grand fighting-ships of the line in England. The Monitor turret has even been used for land fortifications, and it will no doubt in the future be extensively applied to the defence of bays and harbors.

That Ericsson deserves the credit for the original idea of the Monitor system, no one will deny; but, next to Mr. Ericsson, the Assistant Secretary of the Navy did more than any one else to improve on this idea, and apply it to naval warfare. It was a matter which the Navy Department had to handle cautiously; for though the "Monitor" had demonstrated her superiority over the "Merrimac," yet the plan was not altogether acceptable to the majority of naval officers; their objections were taken up by members of Congress, particularly those belonging to the "opposition," who were averse to giving liberal appropriations to "oppress the Southern people;" and it was only when anxiety was felt lest we might be involved in a war with France or England that patriotic feelings got the upper hand of sectional tendencies, and Congress came forward and voted the necessary money to build as many vessels of the Monitor type as the Navy Department asked for.

To go further into an explanation of all the merits of the Monitor class of vessels would take the writer beyond the limits assigned to this history. The reader must judge of their merits from what has been done with them by intelligent officers.

To the uninitiated the history of the difficulties attending the introduction of this new type of vessel into the Navy will be very much less interesting than the battles in which they engaged and the hard service they performed on the Atlantic coast, in shelling forts and riding out heavy gales, while anchored out at sea—defying the elements in their most disastrous forms.

It is not only in regard to the men who fought the battles of the war that the public should be interested, but they should also be glad to understand the work done by those in official positions at headquarters in overcoming tiresome details, in fighting against ignorance and prejudice, or in providing for the thousand wants of fleets and ships, which, without proper forethought on their part, might have been paralyzed, perhaps in a time of great danger to the nation.

When the United States was drawn into the dreadful contest, which brought sorrow and desolation to so many homes, the country was in no condition to go into a war of any kind. Had we become involved at that time with a fifth-rate naval power, we should have been humiliated beyond anything one can conceive; our cities would have been bombarded and laid waste, our commerce would have been driven from the ocean to seek shelter under some neutral flag, and our Navy, instead of being in condition to take the sea against our enemies, would have been laid up to prevent its being captured.

That is not exactly the kind of Navy a great country like this should possess, fit only to cruise in peaceful times and over summer seas. But such has been the policy of our statesmen from decade to decade, and the Navy has never received proper attention. Even the great civil war did not seem to stir up Congress to remedy the evils that had fallen upon it during the long peace.

The cry was in the halls of Congress, "We want no Navy," and the Secretaries of the Navy, up to 1861, echoed the oft-told tale that we only wanted a "small but efficient Navy!" As if a small Navy could be at all efficient, when it would have been obliged to retire under the guns of our forts in case of a foreign war, or else be towed up some inaccessible river and stowed away until peace was restored.

We at times almost think that the rebellion was a blessing in disguise, if only to show how unprepared we were for hostilities with a foreign foe, by whom we would to a certainty have been humiliated and no doubt have been mulcted in damages to an amount that would have crippled the country for years to come. Though we might incur great losses by a civil war, yet there would be no humiliation in it. What chagrin may have been felt on both sides, we could share it alike; and having set fire to our estates and burned up each other's houses, it would be *our* free fight and not the business of any one else. We could put our shoulders to the wheel after the fight was over, and with the energy possessed by no other people we could gather the fragments of our greatness together again, and become stronger than ever. There would be no humiliation to the nation in such a strife, and we would show the world at large how impossible it would be for any foreign army to land on our shores without being exterminated. The naval officers who gained success in the war of the rebellion ought not to forget, amidst the honors and rewards they won, how much they were indebted to the herculean efforts of those in the Navy Department for the support they received under the most trying circumstances—how, after the first surprise of being forced into a great war, and the slow process of realizing the situation had been passed, ships and guns were furnished as if by magic; when at the beginning of the war, few officers counted on obtaining commands, and there was little prospect of our acquiring a class of vessels that would be impregnable against the heavy shot and shell which the enemy seemed to possess in abundance, even a year after the war

began. Yet all this was provided for in less than a year.

Though the Navy Department has been at times severely criticised by those in opposition to it, yet the naval officers, as a whole, can but acknowledge that, with the exception of not keeping pace in the early part of the war with the Confederates in the building of heavy iron-clads, there was a remarkable degree of efficiency in all the civil branches of the Navy as well as in the Navy afloat.

It would occupy a large space to enumerate all that was done by the Department: the difficulties overcome, the resources created almost out of nothing, the opposition of partisans, the strife that had to be conciliated and the enemies that had to be op-

CAPTAIN H. A. WISE, U. S. NAVY, CHIEF OF BUREAU OF ORDNANCE.

posed, out of all which grew up a Navy that at one time bade defiance to France and England, who, in consequence, let us alone to work out our own destiny.

Among others who were in favor of building up an iron-clad navy were citizens whose names should ever be remembered. At the time when the greatest opposition was being manifested against Ericsson's invention, and the government would only authorize the construction of the first "Monitor" on a guarantee that she should prove a success *in battle*, John A. Griswold, Bushnell and Winslow, and Erastus Corning, came forward to the inventor's assistance, and it was mainly due to the capital furnished by these gentlemen that the

"Monitor" was ready in time to meet the "Merrimac." It is thus seen that, although there was a want of liberality in Congress, our private citizens were more generous, and would not let an invention which common-sense told them was invaluable, be lost for want of money, even though they ran the risk of losing all that they ventured.

Men frequently occupy subordinate positions where their lives are expended in carrying on important work which without their services would result in failure. To such men great credit is due, although they generally receive but little.

Captain Henry A. Wise, Chief of the Bureau of Ordnance in the Navy Department, was one of those steady workers who labored from the beginning to the end of the

HORATIO BRIDGE, PAY DIRECTOR, U. S. NAVY, (CHIEF OF
BUREAU OF PROVISIONS AND CLOTHING.)

war. Of him it may be truly said that the right man was in the right place while he occupied his important post.

Everything in Captain Wise's bureau moved like clockwork, and ships and squadrons lost no valuable time in waiting for guns and ammunition. The occasions were many in which commanding officers paid the highest eulogiums to Captain Wise's energy and ability, and he was thoroughly appreciated by the head of the Department and by Assistant Secretary Fox.

The Board of Admirals convened at the close of the civil war paid Captain Wise the high compliment of recommending his promotion to the grade of commodore, but owing to the wording of the law Mr. Secre-

tary Welles did not feel himself authorized to recommend to the President to send Captain Wise's name to the Senate.

Paymaster Horatio Bridge, Chief of the Bureau of Provisions and Clothing, also made his mark in the Navy Department under the administration of Mr. Welles. He was Paymaster-General and Commissary-General of the Navy, and had over six hundred vessels-of-war of all classes to keep supplied. This important duty he performed in a most satisfactory manner, and his exertions contributed much to the success of naval operations.

Surgeon P. J. Horintz, Chief of the Bureau of Medicine and Surgery, displayed marked ability in the Management of the Bureau over which he presided. Of the importance of the duties of Surgeon-General, particularly in time of war, it is not necessary to speak, and we can only say that Dr. Horintz did his duty in a most satisfactory manner.

To Rear-Admiral Joseph Smith, Chief of the Bureau of Yards and Docks, the country was largely indebted for the practical advice which he gave the Department, the fruit of his long and varied experience.

Rear-Admiral Smith, with the other officers whom Mr. Secretary Welles had to assist him, formed a fine combination, and although the former was advanced in years at the breaking out of the war, and not very robust, yet he was ever punctual in the performance of his duties.

Such men as we have mentioned assisted greatly in lightening the labors of the venerable Secretary of the Navy, and enabled him to carry the Navy successfully through a great crisis.

It was sometime in April, 1862, that the Department determined to build up an iron-clad navy on the Ericsson idea, and by December of that year twenty single-turreted Monitors were contracted for, or under construction, all their plans having been made ready for the assembling of Congress. These vessels were to be of about 614 tons displacement, excepting a few of 844 tons. They were very much larger than the original "Monitor" and were designed to carry two 15-inch guns in a revolving turret. The idea of the first "Monitor" was carried out in these vessels to a great extent, but with such modifications as experience warranted. The side-armor was five inches thick, fastened to a three-foot oak backing, and the turrets of eleven 1-inch plates, bolted together with all the skill and ingenuity American mechanics were capable of.

There were also contracted for, or under construction, four double-turreted Monitors, to be armed with four 15-inch guns, the object of the government in building these vessels being to provide a turreted ocean-cruiser. They were large vessels of 1,564 tons displacement, 257 feet in length, and 56 feet in breadth, and drawing about 18 feet of water. The side-armor was equal to 11 inches of solid iron, not counting the wood backing; the turrets were 12 inches thick, of laminated plates. Weight of broadside 1,800 pounds, more than equalling the broadsides of the heaviest French or English frigate.

This was a wonderful step for the Navy Department to take after hesitating so long over the contract for the first "Monitor," but that little vessel had so effectually demonstrated her capability of coping with the great leviathan of the Confederacy that there was no longer, as regarded the Monitor system, a pin to hang a doubt on. It was evident that the principle could be carried out to any extent, and that vessels-of-war of this construction could be built to cross the ocean and withstand the heaviest weather.

Nine of the single-turreted Monitors were pushed to completion for the purpose of taking Charleston, and for such other work as could not be accomplished by wooden ships.

From the time Rear-Admiral Dupont took command of the squadron, Charleston had been closely watched from outside the bar, and the whole southern coast blockaded to the satisfaction of the Department.

This was good work to accomplish from November, 1861, to October, 1862, for it included, in addition to keeping up a vigorous blockade, a great many expeditions against the enemy in the numerous sounds and inlets; and these expeditions had often to be undertaken at the risk of neglecting the blockade for a day or two.

The Navy Department had not yet been supplied with a sufficient number of vessels to comply with all the demands made upon it. There was a large amount of coast under blockade from the capes of Virginia to the Rio Grande in Texas, and every commander of a squadron was applying for more vessels to enable him to carry out his instructions.

The great desire of Secretary Welles had been for the Navy to capture Charleston, the original seat of insurrection and disunion. Preparations were made for the occupation of the harbor and the reduction of the defences of this city. The completion of the iron-clad vessels was pushed with all the power of the Department, though it was found a difficult matter to urge the contractors to move faster than their limited means would permit. It was a new work on which they were engaged, and it was necessary to feel the way for fear of making mistakes; besides, in almost all cases, it was necessary to get up a new plant.

In order to enable Rear-Admiral Dupont to carry out the wishes of the Department, his squadron was now re-inforced by the following iron-clads: "New Ironsides," "Weehawken," "Montauk," "Keokuk," "Patapsco," "Nahant," "Nantucket" and "Catskill." This was a powerful fleet, and the Secretary of the Navy depended upon it to close the port of Charleston so effectively that nothing in the shape of an enemy could get in or out; and finally, if opportunity offered, to make an attack on the batteries, remove the obstructions, and go on up to the city.

The "New Ironsides" carried sixteen 11-inch guns and one heavy rifle; the Monitors each carried one 15-inch and one 11-inch gun (except one that carried a heavy rifle instead of the 11-inch).

This was the force that would be called into play in case Dupont determined to attack the batteries, and with which he was expected to be victorious. For after the fight of the "Monitor" with the "Merrimac," and her success, the turreted vessels had grown in favor with all classes of people, and many ran to the other extreme of supposing that the Monitors were invulnerable, that all they had to do was to haul up alongside the Confederate fortifications and drive the gunners away.

Some of these vessels arrived at Charleston bar as early as January, 1863, and Dupont, who was a sagacious and prudent officer, considered it his duty, before commencing any important operations, to have them tested to see what their turrets and hull would bear, and to ascertain whether anything could be done to improve their defensive power.

The turret principle had only been tried once in battle, and then only against guns the largest of which were the 7-inch rifles in the bow and stern of the "Merrimac," neither of which, it is clear, ever struck the "Monitor" in hull or turret. To determine this point, Commander John L. Worden was sent down to Ossabaw Sound to operate up the Great Ogeechee River and capture, if he could, a fort at Genesee Point, under cover of which the steamer "Nashville" was lying, fitted out as a privateer, and only waiting an opportunity to get to sea and prey upon Federal commerce. He was also instructed to destroy the railroad at that point, if successful in taking the fort and destroying the "Nashville."

Commander Worden arrived off the bar at Ossabaw Sound on January 24th, 1863, but a thick fog prevailed at the time, and the "Montauk" did not get under-way and stand up the river until the next morning. When just outside of the range of Fort McAllister's guns Worden again anchored, and was there joined by the gun-boats "Seneca," "Wissahickon," and "Dawn."

The enemy had range-stakes or buoys planted in the river, and a boat expedition under the command of Lieutenant-Commander Davis was sent up to destroy them, and any obstructions or torpedoes that he might find in the way.

At 7 A. M., on the 27th, Commander Worden got underway with the "Montauk" (the gun-boats following), moved up to 150 yards below the obstructions—anchored—and opened fire on the fort. The enemy returned the "Montauk's" fire very briskly at first, no doubt wondering what kind of a nondescript they were firing at. After about an hour's practice the "Montauk" had the enemy's range so well that his fire began to slacken. At 11.15, A. M., all the shells of the "Montauk" had been expended and solid shot had to be used in their stead—but as they did not seem to have the same effect upon the enemy as the shells, Commander Worden, considering that he was throwing away ammunition, got underway and stood down the river, accompanied by his consorts.

The practice of the Confederates during this battle was very fine, striking the "Montauk" a number of times but doing no damage, and towards the end only firing at intervals. The report does not say what weight of shot or shell the enemy fired, whether smooth-bore or rifle, or how many times, or in what part of the vessel, the "Montauk" was struck; but we presume that Commander Worden was satisfied with the result of his experiment, and so reported to Rear-Admiral Dupont.

Worden, whose experience in the lighter "Monitor" at Hampton Roads ought to have made him a good judge of the strength of the "Montauk" on this occasion, seemed to treat the matter lightly, and it is probable that he thought his vessel would give a good account of herself when she was brought into action against the Charleston defenses.

As no battle of the war has been so closely criticised as the one between our iron-clads and the forts at Charleston, we will give a separate chapter to the operations of Rear-Admiral Dupont while he commanded at that point.

In the next chapter we will also give an account of such events as occurred prior to this attack, which cannot help but be interesting to the reader.

CHAPTER XXXIII.

OPERATIONS commenced in January, 1863, by some of the vessels of Rear-Admiral Dupont's squadron capturing a large blockade-running steamer, which proved to be one of the most valuable prizes of the war.

To show the nature of the blockading service, it may not be uninteresting to give an account of the capture of the above-mentioned vessel.

On the morning of the 29th of January a blue light was observed from the U. S. S. "Unadilla," Lieutenant-Commander S. P. Quackenbush, in an easterly direction, supposed to be from the U. S. S. "Blunt." The "Unadilla" slipped her cable and stood in shore in a north-west direction, guided by a rocket thrown up apparently by the "Blunt," and indicating the course of a vessel attempting to run the blockade. After proceeding inshore a mile and a half, a steamer was observed from the "Unadilla" standing along close to the shore, and heading for Charleston. Two shots were fired at her by the "Unadilla," when the strange steamer changed her course and ran upon the beach, where she was immediately taken possession of. The prize proved to be the iron steam-propeller "Princess Royal," four days out from Bermuda—one of the principal depots of the blockade-runners —loaded with rifle-guns, small-arms, ammunition, steam-engines for iron-clads, etc., etc.

Thus was the Confederacy kept afloat by our cousins across the water, not so much from sympathy with the Southern people as from a desire to obtain cotton, which was so necessary for them to have to keep their mills going and prevent a revolt of the factory operatives. The English Government did nothing to prevent blockade-running, and doubtless considered it a fair business enterprise. If a vessel got safely in past the blockaders, her cargo sold at a large profit, and she loaded with cotton, worth three times as much as the ingoing cargo. There was great excitement as well

blockade-running continued, the task of putting down the Rebellion was greatly increased, and it could only be prevented by the untiring energy and watchfulness of the Navy, incited somewhat by the hope of prize-money, which is a great incentive to extra exertions in time of war both to officers and men. Blockade-runners were captured in large numbers, and the vessels and cargoes condemned by our Admiralty Courts, without protest from the British Government.

There was plenty of timber in the South, and the Southerners could build vessels as fast as Perry did on Lake Erie, but they could not build engines of the kind they required.

SURRENDER OF THE U. S. STEAMER "MERCEDITA" TO THE CONFEDERATE RAM, "PALMETTO STATE," OFF CHARLESTON HARBOR, JAN. 31, 1863.

as profit to the hardy Britons who engaged in this trade.

In some respects the Confederates had advantages superior to our own. The markets of Europe were glutted with rifled guns and engines, and almost all the blockade-runners carried rifled field-guns for the Confederates, while the conservative Army and Navy Departments of the North felt it due to the people that all the implements of war should be made at home. The result was that the Confederates at an early stage of the war had their forts partly armed with heavy rifled guns, while in our vessels-of-war a rifled gun was an exception.

It was plainly to be seen that, as long as

The British merchants who went into blockade-running with such alacrity probably never dreamed of the facility with which the United States Government could equip a large number of vessels exactly calculated to run down and capture their own. There was another factor that these traders had not taken into account—the watchfulness and energy of the American naval officers, who were ever on the alert, and would either run the blockade-runners off the coast or upon the beach, where they would fall into Federal hands, often with their cargoes in perfect order. This was the case with the "Princess Royal," which was floated off without sustaining the least injury, and was fitted up by the Navy Department as a gun-boat, and performed good service, under Commander M. B. Woolsey, at the capture of the forts at Donaldsonville, La.

During January, 1863, the harbor of Charleston was not occupied by the Federal squadron, but the vessels lay outside the bar, keeping a bright look-out. Towards the end of the month two of the heaviest ships, the "Powhatan" and "Canandaigua," had to proceed to Port Royal for coal, leaving some lighter vessels to continue the blockade. The Confederates had two iron-clad rams, the "Chicora" and "Palmetto State," under Commodore D. N. Ingraham, in Charleston Harbor, and on the 31st of January, about 4 A. M., they succeeded in crossing the bar unperceived in the darkness and attacked the "Mercedita," Captain H. S. Stellwagen, which had just returned from the chase of a strange vessel.

The captain was below, and Lieutenant-Commander Abbott in charge of the deck, when the faint appearance of a vessel showing black smoke was seen through the gloom. All the Federal vessels burned anthracite, while the Confederates and blockade-runners burned bituminous coal, the smoke from which can be seen even in the darkness of night.

All hands were called to quarters, the captain appeared on deck, and saw what, for all he knew, might be a tug belonging to the squadron. The guns were trained on the approaching stranger, who was then hailed and ordered to heave-to. The answer to the first hail from the "Mercedita" was "Hello!" The other replies were purposely indistinct, and the stranger crashed into the Federal vessels, with the reply, "This is the Confederate States' steam-ram, 'Palmetto State.'"

The order was given to fire, but no gun could be brought to bear on the enemy as she approached. At the moment of striking, the "Palmetto State" fired a rifle-shell diagonally through the Federal steamer, which penetrated the condenser, the steam-drum of the port-boiler, and exploded against the port-side of the vessel, making a hole four or five feet square in its exit. The "Mercedita" was instantly enveloped in vapor, while cries came from below: "Shot through the boiler! Fires put out—gunner and one man killed and a number fatally scalded—water over fire-room floor—vessel sinking fast! The ram has cut us through at and below water line, and the shell has burst at the water line on the other side!"

This was appalling information, and it must be a well-trained crew that would not feel nervous at such intelligence. Captain Stellwagen could do nothing, for the enemy's ram was under his counter. He had made a mistake in not firing on the stranger as soon as she appeared, for none but an enemy would have approached so stealthily.

He should have had steam up and chain ready to slip at a moment's notice. No one expected that the enemy's rams would dare cross the bar, but the same love of adventure existed in the Confederate navy as in the Federal, and this affair was another illustration of the importance of never underrating a foe.

After the "Palmetto State" struck the "Mercedita" she swung round under the latter's counter, and the Confederate commander called out, "Surrender, or I will sink you!" Captain Stellwagen replied, "I can make no resistance, my boiler is destroyed." "Then, do you surrender?" inquired the other. "I do," replied Stellwagen.

The Confederate commander hailed several times for a boat to be sent him, threatening to fire in case of further delay. Lieutenant-Commander Abbott then proceeded on board the ram, where the parole of the officers and crew of the "Mercedita" was demanded; after receiving which, the ram started in the direction of the "Keystone State," which vessel and three other blockaders Captain Stellwagen had tried to alarm by burning signal-lights.

Soon after the ram left the "Mercedita" the people on board that vessel saw a shell from the "Keystone State" explode against her armor, and several shells from the ram hit the "Keystone State," followed by smoke and vapor, which poured from the latter. The firing then receded to the north and east and finally died away, and it was supposed the ram had engaged all the blockading vessels in turn.

The commanding officer of the "Mercedita" now set to work to save his vessel, about which nothing had been said on board the ram. The enemy supposed the vessel was sinking, and probably thought those on board could take care of themselves. In two hours repairs were made, and with the assistance of the "Stettin" and "Flag" the "Mercedita" reached Port Royal.

When the "Keystone State" was attacked, Commander Le Roy gallantly returned the enemy's fire, but the ram lodged a shell in the fore-hold of his vessel, which set the "Keystone State" on fire and obliged her to shear off till it could be extinguished. By this time the ram "Chicora," Commander John R. Tucker, had attacked the "Keystone State" and Le Roy turned upon the enemy, and putting on full steam ran right for one of the rams at the rate of twelve knots an hour, when a shell from the enemy penetrating both steam-chests rendered the "Keystone State" powerless. Two rifle-shells burst on the quarter-deck, but most of them struck the hull, and there were two feet of water in the hold; but some of the other vessels of the blockading squadron now came to the assistance of the "Keystone State" and took her in tow. These vessels were the "Augusta," Commander E. G. Parrott, the "Quaker City," Commander J. M. Frailey, and the "Memphis," Acting-Lieutenant P. G. Watmough.

All these steamers kept up a brisk fire on the enemy's rams while the "Keystone State" was towed out of their reach. The "Augusta" and "Quaker City" were both struck in their hulls, but the "Memphis" only in her rigging.

As daylight approached, the rams hauled off to the north-west, chased by the U. S. S. "Juniata," and anchored inside the shoals of the swash-channel, their commanders doubtless thinking they had done enough for one night and that they must reserve their strength for a future occasion.

On board the "Mercedita" there were twenty killed and as many wounded, a number being scalded to death, among whom was Assistant Surgeon Jacob H. Gotwold and his steward. It was a heavy list of killed and wounded for so short an engagement, but the Confederates wasted very few shots, and the striking of the boilers of two of the Federal vessels was no doubt a matter of calculation and not mere accident.

The attack of the Confederate rams on the Union squadron was a gallant affair, and the one that encountered the "Mercedita" might have sunk that vessel while the commanding officer was hesitating to answer the hails. After disabling the "Mercedita" and encountering four other vessels, finding doubtless that the Federal ships were too numerous to be agreeable, the rams moved off uninjured and sought the safety of well-known channels. Admiral Dupont was much chagrined when he received the news of this engagement; but a nation cannot expect to carry on a war with a skillful and energetic enemy without mishaps, especially under circumstances like the above, where the Confederates could slip out in the darkness, make a dash at the blockading vessels and retire when necessary to do so.

The Confederate authorities endeavored to make great capital out of this affair, and General Beauregard, who commanded the defences, proclaimed officially that the blockade had been raised, as the United States Navy was powerless to maintain it. However, next morning, the blockading vessels were at their posts as usual, ready to prevent the ingress or egress of any vessel.

The claim of the Confederates that the blockade had been raised by the raid of their two rams was, of course, absurd. To raise a blockade, it would be necessary to drive away the blockading vessels altogether and hold the positions they occupied, yet, strange to say, the foreign consuls at Charleston, and an officer commanding one of Her Britannic Majesty's ships-of-war, united in a statement that the blockade of Charleston had been raised!

The "New Ironsides," "Powhatan," and "Canandaigua" were immediately added to the force off Charleston, which, without further argument, settled the question. The port of Charleston remained blockaded more closely than ever, and it was generally accepted by the world that the gentlemen who had put their names to a paper stating the blockade had been raised had prostituted their offices, by giving currency to a statement which could not have been forced upon their conviction as truth.

CAPTAIN PERCIVAL DRAYTON, U. S. N.

On the 1st of February Admiral Dupont received notice of the capture of a gunboat. It seems that the "Isaac Smith," Acting-Lieutenant-Commanding F. S. Conover, was sent up Stone River to make a reconnaissance. No enemy was seen; but when the vessel was on her way back three concealed batteries opened a concentrated fire on her from heavy rifle-guns. The gun-boat "McDonough," Lieutenant-Commander Bacon, was at anchor down the river, and on hearing the firing got underway, and went to the assistance of the "Isaac Smith;" but owing to the number, position and weight of the enemy's guns could render no aid without the certainty of losing his own vessel. The "Isaac Smith" was aground and enveloped in a cloud of vapor, and the "McDonough" was soon driven off by the superior range of the enemy's fire.

The commanding officer of the "Isaac Smith" endeavored to get out of the trap in which he found himself by dropping below the batteries; but for upwards of a mile, on account of a bend in the river, the vessel was subjected to a raking fire of 30 guns, and was only able now and then to answer with her pivot-gun. To add to the difficulty, a large number of concealed riflemen were firing upon the vessel. Eight of the gunboat's crew were killed and 17 wounded. But for the latter, the commanding officer would have set fire to his vessel and escaped with his officers and men; but to escape with the vessel was impossible, and she was therefore surrendered.

It may have been observed by the reader that many cases occurred during the civil war where vessels were entrapped as the "Isaac Smith" was; but, as a rule, the defence of these vessels was characterized by great courage. In such cases it was not possible to ascertain the loss of the enemy, and we abstain from unreliable conjectures.

It was impossible to circumvent the enemy without running such risks as were encountered by the "Isaac Smith." "Nothing venture, nothing have," is a maxim which all should profit by who go to war. Though now and then the Federals met with losses of vessels, yet the experience gained was beneficial and stimulated the younger officers to deeds of daring, while teaching them at the same time the necessity of prudence.

On the 1st of February the "Montauk," Commander John L. Worden, was ordered to engage the forts at Ogeechee River, a duty which was well performed; but the Confederates shifted their guns from point to point, as the range of the "Montauk" improved, and finally the vessel withdrew from action after expending a large amount of ammunition and being struck thirty-nine times without apparent injury.

The Confederate steamer "Nashville" had been closely watched for eight months by the blockading steamers "Wissahickon," Lieutenant-Commander John L. Davis, the "Dawn," Lieutenant John S. Barnes, and the "Seneca," Lieutenant-Commander William Gibson. The "Nashville" lay under Fort McAllister loaded with cotton, and although a swift and well-appointed steamer, never ventured to run out. After several months she withdrew up the Ogeechee River and returned in the guise of a privateer, presenting a formidable appearance.

Fort McAllister was strengthened and the river lined with torpedoes to prevent the ascent of vessels to attack the "Nashville."

The vessel frequently came near the forts, watching an opportunity to run out and perform the part of the "Alabama" or "Florida." The "Nashville" was armed with a heavy pivot-gun, and, being fast, would no doubt have rivalled the other Confederate cruisers that had done so much injury to our commerce. For this reason she was closely watched, and it was as great a triumph to dispose of such a craft as it would have been to win a considerable victory.

On the 27th of February, Commander Worden, on making a reconnaissance, observed that the "Nashville" had grounded in that portion of the river known as "Seven Mile Reach," and on the 28th at daylight the

COMMANDER (NOW REAR-ADMIRAL) DANIEL AMMEN.

"Montauk" "Seneca" and "Dawn" moved up the river. Worden was able to approach within twelve hundred yards of the "Nashville," though under a heavy fire from the fort. The "Montauk" opened on the privateer, while the gun-boats enfiladed the fort at long range.

In a short time Commander Worden had the satisfaction of seeing the "Nashville" in flames from the shells exploding in different parts of her. The "Nashville's" pivot-gun was soon exploded by the heat, and in a short time the vessel blew up with a terrific crash. The fort continued a brisk fire on the "Montauk," but only struck her five times, and inflicted on her no damage whatever, which indicated that she was impervious to shot and shell. A torpedo exploded near the vessel as she dropped down the river out of range of the enemy's guns, but did no harm, and that night Commander Worden had the satisfaction of reporting to Rear-Admiral Dupont the destruction of a vessel that might have proved as troublesome as the "Alabama."

It was deemed advisable to try the iron-clads of the squadron in action with some fort, so as to be certain of their impenetrability, and fully test the working of the turrets. Captain Percival Drayton, commanding the "Passaic," was directed to proceed with the "Patapsco," Commander Daniel Ammen, and the "Nahant," Commander John Downes, up the Ogeechee River, and make an attack on Fort McAllister.

The fort had been subjected to three previous attacks from the "Montauk;" but damages to earth-works are easily repaired, and the work made stronger than ever, unless the guns have been dismounted, as during a bombardment the weak points are discovered and strengthened.

Fort McAllister was 20 feet above the river, solidly built, with high traverses between the guns, protecting them from anything but a direct fire. It contained one 10-inch columbiad, a 100-pounder rifle, four 32-pounders, and one Whitworth rifle, throwing bolts.

The three vessels anchored 1,200 yards below the fort, at 8 A. M., March 3, 1863, opened fire, and, as Captain Drayton reported, the parapets were much cut up and large holes made by the bursting shell, but no damage was done that could not be repaired in a few hours.

Captain Drayton did not consider the fort nearly as great an obstacle to his advance as the piles which were driven in the channel of the river, and which rendered it impassable till they could be removed.

The iron-clads were subjected to the fire of Fort McAllister for eight hours without receiving any serious injury, but the same thing was true of the fort.

Captain Drayton expressed some mortification at what he called his want of success in this attack; but experience has proved that iron-clads, although so valuable against ships, or fortifications built of masonry, are not so serviceable against earth-works as vessels carrying a greater number of lighter guns.

The power of the 15-inch gun as a breaching force against masonry is considerable, but against a work constructed of sand-bags it has not the value of a 11-inch gun, and nothing like the power of a 100-pounder rifle for boring through the sand. The 15-inch gun in a turret is slow firing, not being able to discharge oftener than once in five minutes, while the breech-loading rifle can

be pointed and fired once a minute, which in an hour would give 60 shots from the rifled-gun to 12 from the 15-inch.

While the iron-clads were turning their turrets, the enemy would wait until the port-holes appeared, would fire, knowing the exact range, hide in their bomb-proofs until the iron-clads had fired, then stand to their guns again, until the port-holes once more came round.

In attacking forts, in conjunction with other vessels carrying many guns, iron-clads are valuable for distances not exceeding 600 yards; but the initial velocity of the 15-inch shot is only about 1,500 feet per second, which is much reduced even at the distance of 1,200 yards. At 800 yards a 15-inch shot would not, with the charges assigned to the gun, penetrate a 4-inch iron plate.

More was expected from our iron-clads during the war than they had power to accomplish. Any one of them armed with 15-inch guns could have destroyed a vessel like the "Merrimac" in half an hour, but against earth works, sand especially, none of the monitor class were equal to the "New Ironsides," with her quick-firing batteries of 11-inch guns.

All these matters were fully discussed during the siege of Charleston. Admiral Dupont had a great responsibility on his shoulders, as he was the first officer to whom these iron-clads had been assigned. He was determined to leave nothing undone to give these vessels a full trial to determine their capabilities. It cannot be doubted that the experience to which the iron-clads had been subjected in the attack on Fort McAllister afforded valuable information in relation to their qualities, and several imperfections were detected which could be remedied in other vessels of their class.

The capture of Fort McAllister, in itself, was of no special importance, except, perhaps, to prevent its protecting some other privateer or blockade-runner.

Captain Drayton's opinion was that the fire of the iron-clads was not effective, and that the fort fired more rapidly towards the end than it did at the beginning of the action.

In the demonstration against Fort McAllister it was discovered that the fuses for the shells were not good, and the shells exploded at irregular intervals—a very important matter to ascertain before the grand engagement with the forts at Charleston took place. The "Patapsco" carried one 15-inch gun, and one 150-pounder rifle. She fired fourteen 15-inch shells and 46 shells from the one 150-pounder rifle—over three to one in favor of the rifle.

The "Nahant" was not struck by the shells from Fort McAllister, the enemy seeming to concentrate his fire on the "Passaic."

Up to the 10th of March was a busy and successful time with the blockaders of Admiral Dupont's squadron. Two large steamers, the "Queen-of-the-Wave" and the "Georgian," loaded with munitions of war for the Confederates, were destroyed, which served to indicate that the blockade was still effective.

As Charleston had taken the lead in the movement for a division of the Union, the government naturally desired that the laws should be vindicated there at as early a date as practicable, and the Navy Department wished to have the honor of bringing about so desirable an end. Therefore, Assistant Secretary Fox, with the approbation of the Secretary of the Navy, directed all his energies towards getting as large a number of iron-clads as possible to Charleston to

COMMANDER (NOW REAR-ADMIRAL) WILLIAM E. LE ROY.

enable Admiral Dupont to force his way up to the city.

The harbor of Charleston had been closely guarded and many blockade-runners captured, but the Confederates calculated to strengthen their fortifications and add new ones, so as to hold the hot-bed of secession against all the forces that could be brought to bear.

Besides establishing a close blockade, an attempt had been made by the Federals to obstruct the passage across the bar with sunken vessels, which proved unsuccessful, as the vessels soon disappeared in the quicksands, or the currents washed out new channels. So the blockade-runners, though closely watched, continued to run into Charleston and supply the Confederacy with munitions of war.

Several plans for the reduction of the

Confederate stronghold were proposed, but none were thought advisable, and in the absence of a large land force it seemed that the duty must devolve entirely upon the Navy.

This was a most serious task for the Navy to undertake without any support from the Army; but even at that stage of the war the Government had not learned the importance of using large land and naval forces in conjunction when attacking heavily fortified places—attacks which, when conducted with good judgment, seldom or ever failed. The Navy Department was, doubtless, very willing to have the co-operation of the Army, but they were frequently unable to obtain it, and the War Department did not attach the same importance to the capture of Charleston as did the Navy.

Much was expected of the iron vessels by the Navy Department, and their hopes were confirmed by the attacks on Fort McAllister, where none of the vessels were seriously injured, and none of their crew killed. The Department had been abused for expending so much money on these vessels, which their detractors affirmed would perform no effective service, and would founder, as the "Monitor" had done; not taking into consideration the fact that they were superior to the original "Monitor," and that the defects of the latter had been eliminated in these later structures. The Department naturally wanted to show that it had made no mistakes in this instance, and they pushed on the work of preparation regardless of the criticism of those who were in favor of a different class of vessel carrying more guns. Some of these detractors were persons whose plans had been rejected, and who thought there was no other mode but their own of bringing the contumacious city under subjection.

On the other hand, the Department had rather too much faith in these vessels, and was inclined to expect from them more than they could perform, and was, therefore, disinclined to listen to the advice of officers who, by their standing and length of service, were entitled to consideration. Almost everybody admitted the value of the turret-vessels as harbor defences, but many doubted their efficiency against the earthworks of Charleston.

Admiral Dupont was pressed by the Navy Department to attack the batteries, and on the 7th of April, 1863, he determined to attempt what he was far from certain would be a success, in order to carry out the wishes of the government, and meet, if possible, the public expectations.

To understand the harbor of Charleston, with its intricate shoals and channels, requires the study of a chart. In some respects it resembles the harbor of New York, although it is on a much smaller scale. The city of Charleston stands on a neck of land, bounded by two rivers, and projecting into a narrow bay. The bay was protected by Fort Pinkney, Fort Ripley, Fort Moultrie, Fort Beauregard, Fort Sumter, Battery Bee, Battery Gregg, Battery Wagner, etc. These defences were so placed that a vessel attempting to pass Sumter would be under a cross-fire from them all, every fort being armed with the heaviest and most destructive ordnance then known.

After crossing the bar, there were several channels leading into Charleston harbor— the "Main-Ship Channel," "North Channel" and "Swash Channel." In taking either of these, a vessel would be under a raking and cross fire. Should she get by Sumter, she would still be subjected to a raking fire from that work and the works on the upper part of Sullivan's Island—from Battery Gregg, Fort Johnson, Fort Ripley and Castle Pinkney, and some smaller batteries. To run past these defences, if there were no obstructions in the channel, would be much easier with a small squadron than to stop and give the forts battle with iron-clads. This fact was established during the civil war, and the subject has been ably treated in a work published in 1868 by Lieutenant-Colonel Von Sheliha.

Before proceeding to attack the defences of Charleston, Rear-Admiral Dupont issued the following order:

The bar will be buoyed by the "Keokuk," Commander Rhind, assisted by C. O. Boutelle, Assistant United States Coast Survey, commanding the "Bibb," by Acting-Ensign Platt, and by the pilots of the fleet.

The commanding officers will, previous to crossing, make themselves acquainted with the value of the buoys.

The vessels, on signal being made, will form in the prescribed order ahead at intervals of one cable's length.

The squadron will pass up the Main Ship Channel without returning the fire of the batteries on Morris Island, unless signal should be made to commence action.

The ships will open fire on Fort Sumter when within easy range, and will take up a position to the northward and westward of that fortification, engaging its left or north-west face at a distance of from 600 to 800 yards, firing low, and aiming at the centre embrasure.

The commanding officers will instruct their officers and men to carefully avoid wasting a shot, and will enjoin upon them the necessity of precision rather than rapidity of fire.

Each ship will be ready to render assistance to any vessel that may require it.

The special code of signals prepared for the iron-clads will be used in action.

After the reduction of Fort Sumter, it is probable that the next point of attack will be the batteries on Morris Island.

The line of battle will be in line ahead, as follows:

1. "Weehawken,"   Captain John Rodgers.
2. "Passaic,"   Captain Percival Drayton.
3. "Montauk,"   Captain John L. Worden.
4. "Patapsco,"   Commander Daniel Ammen.
5. "New Ironsides," Captain T. Turner.
6. "Catskill,"   Commander G. W. Rodgers.
7. "Nantucket,"   Commander D. M Fairfax.
8. "Nahant,"   Commander John Downes.
9. "Keokuk,"   Commander A. C. Rhind.

A squadron of vessels, of which Captain J. F. Green will be the senior officer, will be formed outside the bar, near to the entrance buoy, consisting of the following vessels: "Canandaigua," "Housatonic," "Huron," "Unadilla," "Wissahickon," and will be held in readiness to support the iron-clads when they attack the batteries on Morris Island.

S. F. DUPONT,

Rear-Admiral commanding South-Atlantic Blockading Squadron.

When Admiral Dupont hoisted his flag on board the "New Ironsides," he took with him his personal staff, who remained with him during the operations at Charleston. To the officers of the staff he pays the highest encomiums for the assistance they rendered him in the battle and otherwise. They were as follows:

Commander C. R. P. Rodgers, Fleet Captain; Lieutenant S. W. Preston, Flag Lieutenant; Lieutenant A. S. Mackenzie, Ordnance Officer; Ensign M. L. Johnson, Aide and Signal Officer. All these gentlemen are mentioned with that warmth of feeling which distinguished Dupont in cases where officers under him performed their duty faithfully.

On the 7th of April the vessels moved to the attack, the "Weehawken" leading with a torpedo raft in front. On the way up the Main Ship Channel, the leading vessel passed a number of buoys indicating torpedoes, one of which exploded near the "Weehawken," without, however, doing any harm.

At 2 P. M., the squadron approached the obstructions extending across the harbor from Fort Moultrie to Fort Sumter. These were indicated by several lines of casks, beyond which piles were seen extending "from James Island to the Middle Ground."

At 2.50 P. M., the guns of Fort Moultrie opened upon the "Weehawken," followed shortly after by Fort Sumter, and all the batteries on Sullivan's Island.

Being unable to pass the obstructions, the iron-clads were obliged to turn, which threw the line into confusion. The flagship became entangled with the Monitors, and could not bring her batteries to bear on the enemy without danger of firing into them. The "New Ironsides" was compelled to anchor twice to prevent going ashore, —on one of these occasions the Monitors and the "Keokuk" were able to get within easy range of Fort Sumter—at distances varying from 550 to 800 yards—in which position they were subjected to a fire from the batteries on Sullivan's Island, Morris Island and Sumter.

The effect of the concentrated fire of the

forts on the Monitors would have been bewildering to officers and men whose nerves were not of the strongest kind. The enemy had been anxiously looking forward to the time when they could get the Federal iron-clads in just such a position, and their only apprehension was that the opportunity would not be offered them. The Confederate engineers felt that it would be impossible for any force of vessels such as the Federals possessed to pass the forts and obstructions to Charleston. Owing to repeated practice at targets, the Confederate officers felt certain of planting two out of three of their heaviest shots on the Monitors' turrets at the rate of sixty shots a minute.

The trial of the Monitors before Fort McAllister afforded no real test of their endurance, for there could be no comparison between such a work as McAllister and the defences of Charleston. The fire on the iron-clads was such as an equal number of the heaviest European ships-of-war could not have withstood many minutes.

The severity of the fire was shown by the effect on the Monitors and the sinking of one of their number, and yet the vessels retired from the conflict without confusion.

That attack will always stand the severest criticism from those disposed to be hypercritical; and those capable of judging will admit that it was conducted with skill and judgment. It was very well in those who could sit in their cosy arm-chairs and direct great naval and military movements, who seldom reflect that while undertaking to direct battles from a distance they are meddling with that which properly should be managed by the professional leader, and uselessly sacrificing the lives of officers and men.

Admiral Dupont found it impossible, owing to currents and an unmanageable ship, to place the " New Ironsides " where he desired, although he was within one thousand yards of Fort Sumter; night was coming on, and the squadron in some disarray. He therefore signalled the vessels to withdraw from action, intending to renew the engagement.

That evening the commanding officers of the iron-clads visited the flag-ship to report the condition of affairs on board their respective vessels, which caused Admiral Dupont to change his mind about renewing the attack next morning, for he was now satisfied that it was impossible to take Charleston with the force under his command.

And here arises the question—Was it wise to undertake so great a task as the capture of Charleston at one blow? It would have been a good beginning to have taken Fort Wagner. To have attacked that place eight hundred yards to the southward would have placed the squadron two and a half miles

from the forts on Sullivan's Island and a mile and three-quarters from Sumter. Of course, if the iron-clads could not reduce Wagner, it would be useless to attempt to go up to the city. There was a great desire, on the part of the Northern people, that Charleston should be taken, and the officer who could at that moment have captured the place would have won unbounded popularity. It was certainly the hardest task undertaken by the Navy during the war. In fact, without the co-operation of an army, the taking of Charleston was an impossibility.

Charleston was approached by tortuous channels filled with obstructions, that even without the fortifications would have been formidable to the squadron that went to at-

COMMANDER (NOW REAR-ADMIRAL) A. C. RHIND.

tack it. It is difficult to manœuvre a squadron in a narrow space with strong currents running; how much more difficult must it be, then, when crooked channels are filled with obstructions?

In such a case a Commander-in-chief is entitled to use his own discretion, and not undertake a movement against a place unless he is confident the obstructions are not of a character to impede the progress of his fleet. Had Dupont persevered and entangled his vessels in the contrivances placed in the channels for that purpose, those who urged him on would have put the blame of the necessary failure upon his shoulders. He discontinued the attack in good time, and let us see the result:

No ships had been exposed to the severest

fire of the enemy more than forty minutes, yet in that brief period five iron-clads were wholly or partially disabled.

Commander Rhind, in the "Keokuk," had been able to fire only three times during the period he was exposed to the guns of the enemy, when he was obliged to withdraw from action to prevent his vessel from sinking, which event did happen on the following morning. The "Nahant," Commander Downes, was seriously damaged, her turret so jammed as to prevent its turning, many of the bolts of both turret and pilot house broken, and the latter rendered nearly untenable by flying bolts and nuts. Captain Drayton, in the "Passaic," after the fourth fire from her 11-inch gun, found himself unable to use it again during the action. His turret, also, became jammed, although he

COMMANDER (NOW REAR-ADMIRAL) D. Mc. N. FAIRFAX.

was finally enabled to get it in motion again. Commander Ammen, of the "Patapsco," lost the use of his rifled-gun after the fifth fire, owing to the carrying away of the bolts of the forward cap-square. Commander Fairfax, of the "Nantucket," reports that after the third shot from the 15-inch gun, the port-stopper became jammed, several shot striking near the port, driving in the plates and preventing the further use of the gun during the action.

The other iron-clads, although struck many times, were still able to use their guns, but it seems probable that in a short time they would have been placed *hors-de-combat.*

The position of the squadron was simply that of being in a trap, and having to bear the cross-fire of all the forts within a circle

of two miles. Only one hundred and thirty shot and shell were fired by the iron-clads during the action, while many hundred were fired by the enemy, the character of which is well described by a contemporary writer, who remarks :

In order to more fully understand the terrible severity of the fire to which these vessels were to be exposed, it is necessary to consider some statements in the circular of the Confederate General Ripley. He mentions three circles of fire which had been prepared for the reception of the fleet. He meant that there were three points beyond each other in passing up the harbor upon which circles the batteries on shore would concentrate their fire as upon a focus, and to these points the range of the guns had been actually adjusted by experimental firing, and the points were marked by guides, buoys and obstructions, so that no shot could miss its mark.

The first focus of fire into which the fleet would come was formed between Sumter and Moultrie. Three obstructions of various kinds were placed in and across the channel, through which it was thought the fleet could not pass, and where the leading vessels being stopped the line would be thrown into confusion, and the Monitors would be huddled together and could be crushed by the concentrating fire of the circle of forts and batteries.

According to the Confederate accounts seventy-six guns bore on this single point, while our own officers placed the number at a hundred. If now it is considered that bearing on this spot were 7-inch, 8-inch, Brooke and Blakely rifles, 10-inch columbiads, for which had been prepared square-head bolts, with chilled ends, much heavier than the ordinary shot, and guns for hot shot and shells containing moulten iron, an idea may be formed of what these iron-clads were to meet. The enemy's guns, moreover, had been so tried that there could be no random shooting. The Confederate plan of defence lacked nothing which skill, experience and science could suggest.

So far the writer whom we quote pictures in glowing terms the difficulties with which the Monitors would have to contend in an attack on Charleston; but after stating the damages received by the Federal vessels, and quoting the opinions of all the principal officers that a continuation of the attack would have resulted in the destruction of the squadron, the chronicler suddenly changes his course, as if impressed by a new idea, and attempts to show that a prolongation of the struggle would have led to a Union victory, and that the opinions of ten brave and experienced officers were of no account whatever!

There was no officer in the Navy whose reputation stood higher than that of Dupont. He had gallantly won the first naval battle of any importance in the war, and had shown so much ability at Port Royal as to entitle him to the full confidence of the Government, and his opinions should have been preferred in all matters relating to his command to those of any other person. The belief was general at the time that Dupont was not well treated by the Navy Department—a belief which prevails in the Navy to this day.

When the Department commenced build_

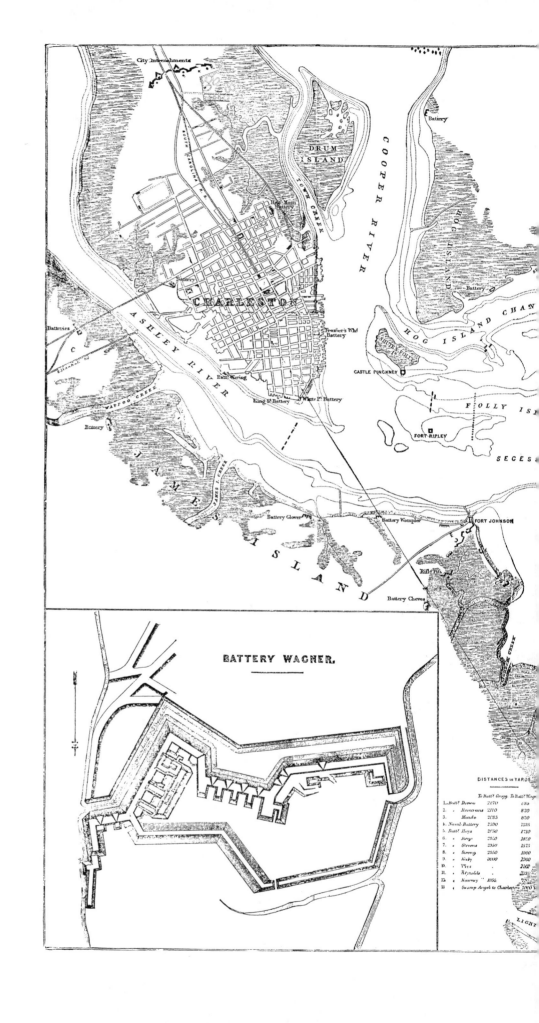

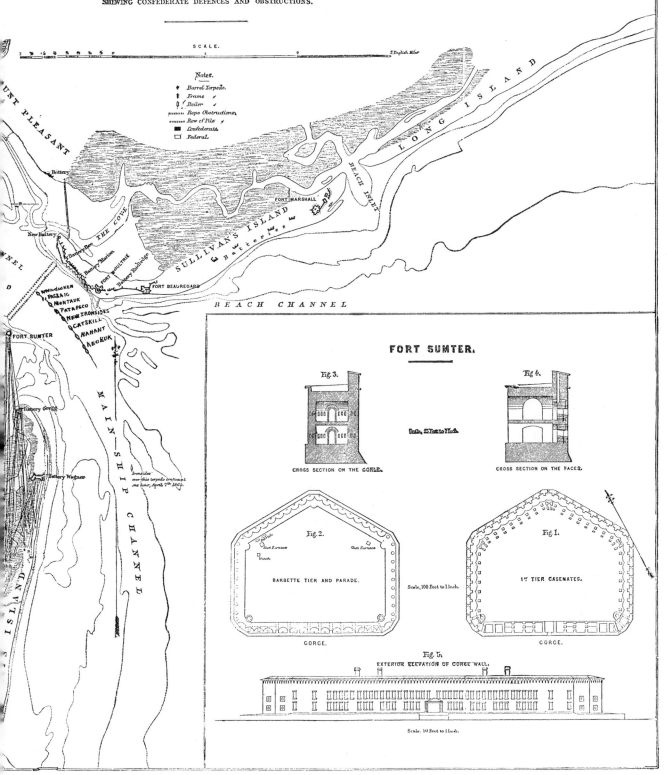

ing small Monitor-shaped vessels with great rapidity, the Secretary and Assistant Secretary of the Navy were unjustly assailed from various quarters for adopting the Monitor system in preference to all others.

In this matter, Mr. Secretary Welles and Mr. Fox showed good judgment, for the "Keokuk," which was not a Monitor-built vessel, was shattered so by the enemy's fire at Charleston that in a few minutes she withdrew from action to avoid sinking, and did sink some hours afterwards from the effects of the enemy's shot.

Having prepared these Monitors, the Navy Department were naturally anxious to prove to their detractors that this was the right form of vessel to carry out the ideas of the government; but the Department did not take into consideration that seven Monitors, each with two slow-firing guns, were no match for seventy-six pieces of ordnance of the heaviest calibre then in use. If we further consider that half of the guns in the Monitors were 11-inch, there remained but seven 15-inch guns with which to breach the masonry of Fort Sumter and the thick earth-works of the numerous other fortifications.

The Confederate accounts disagree in the number of their guns, but it is probable that in the aggregate they fell not much short of a hundred.

In their anxiety to triumph over those who had attacked them so unjustly, the Navy Department required of Dupont more than could be accomplished with his small force, and did not pay that deference to his opinion to which his reputation and position entitled him. On Dupont alone would have rested the responsibility of defeat had he entangled his vessels in the meshes prepared to receive them, and rendered them targets for the enemy to destroy at their leisure. In that event there would have been such an outcry at the North against the Monitor system that the Navy Department could not have withstood it. All the blame would have been thrown upon Dupont in the same way that the blame of failing to continue his attack was ascribed to him.

But the Navy did not look upon the action of the 7th of April as a defeat, by any means. It was a prudent withdrawal from engagement with a force more than six times its superior. It must not be forgotten that the Monitors had to take position and get their range under a most terrific fire; and although none were so disabled that they could not have resumed the action next day, they were enough so to be obliged to retire temporarily.

The difficulty lay in having too few vessels to accomplish so great a work — an

opinion which was generally acquiesced in by those cognizant of the facts of the case.

It is now an axiom that, no matter how strong you may build an iron-clad, guns can be made that will knock her to pieces in a given space of time. In the case of the Monitors, the enemy had in forty minutes weakened some of them, and an hour longer would perhaps have made it necessary for them to go to the machine-shop.

We do not consider the official report of Chief Engineer A. C. Stimers to the Navy Department as carrying any weight with it, particularly in view of the terrible mistakes made by that officer in the building of a number of light-draft Monitors which were consigned to the scrap-heap as worthless. In his communication to the Navy Department Mr. Stimers says: "In consideration of the vast importance to our country that this stronghold of the rebellion should be reduced, I take the liberty to express to the Department my firm opinion that the obstructions could be readily passed with the means already provided, and our entire fleet of iron-clads pass up successfully to the wharves at Charleston, and that the Monitors will retain sufficient enduring power to enable them to pass all the forts and batteries which may reasonably be expected."

Mr. Stimers also expressed great confidence in the efficiency of the torpedo rafts designed by Mr. Ericsson, for the purpose of removing torpedoes and blowing up obstructions, which the historian of the Navy says "naval officers were unwilling to use "

Mr. Stimers—or any other person in like circumstances—could express what opinion he pleased, as he had no responsibility in the matter and was not likely to have any. The intelligent reader will doubtless attach more importance to the opinion of the Commander-in-chief and his well-tried officers, who always did their duty faithfully in whatever situation they were placed.

To show that the commanding officers of the Monitors did not lose their coolness, and that they were not deficient in courage during the time they were under the fire of so many guns, it is only necessary to state the accuracy of the fire of those vessels. One hundred and twenty-four shots were fired at Sumter, and during the engagement the Monitors had to be kept in position to preserve their range under the storm of shot that was showered upon them.

The Confederate accounts state that fifty-five of the Monitors' shot struck the walls of Sumter, and others struck inside the works, which was excellent practice considering the situation. The firing also showed that the 15-inch shot had a breaking force against masonry that it did not possess against earth-works.

The distance at which the vessels were from the fort is differently stated by the Federal and Confederate officers, the former placing it at 600, the latter at 1,000, yards. As both were liable to error, we will take the mean of the two, or 800 yards, as correct, at which distance both the 15-inch and the 11-inch guns must have great breaching power. Only two of the 15-inch shot passed through the walls of Fort Sumter and exploded—one in a casemate, the other in the parade-ground. Other 15-inch shells exploded against the walls, making deep craters, but not essentially injuring the fort; " embrasures were destroyed, and one shot cracked the masonry for twenty-four feet in length;" "one large shell went over the parapet, demolished the officers' quarters, and damaged several walls." "Other 15-inch shells and shot and fragments of shells were picked up in and about the fort." These facts we glean from the Confederate official account.

We quote the historian of the Navy, who is anxious to show that Admiral Dupont and his officers had no idea of the damage they were doing to the fort, otherwise they would have continued the attack. The fact is, if the Monitors had been filled with shot and shell and every one had struck Fort Sumter, they would not materially have injured its powers of resistance unless they could have disabled the guns.

The naval historian says: "That nothing was more certain, in view of what was actually done, than that Sumter could not long have resisted even such a fire as the Monitors delivered that day. The result would have been not such a gradual crumbling of the walls as took place under the long-range firing of the heavy rifles afterwards from the land batteries, but they would have come down with a crash, and the whole interior of the fort would have been torn in pieces by the enormous shells." In giving such opinions, it is very plain the Naval historian, whom we quote, had never seen a fort after a bombardment, where the ground was strewn with shells and *débris*, yet remaining in fair fighting condition. He seems not to consider that while the fort is getting battered the iron-clads are at the same time receiving a severe hammering, and that, when the bombardment is continued for a length of time, the iron turrets will be likely to yield to repeated blows, on the same principle that the trunnions of a heavy gun can be broken off by repeated strokes from an ordinary hammer.

There was another argument urged in favor of the Monitors maintaining the fight with Sumter, viz.: "That, in judging of the actual power of these large guns, one very important point must be considered. These guns were novel weapons, and there

was an apprehension that they would burst in firing, and consequently were used with a caution which in the light of subsequent experience appears like timidity. The charge of powder was limited to thirty-five pounds. They have since been fired repeatedly and safely with double that amount—with seventy pounds of powder, or one hundred of mammoth powder, which is equal to seventy or seventy-five of common powder. From the results that were actually reached with only thirty-five pounds of powder, it is rendered certain that, if the charges had been suitably increased, every shot and shell striking fairly would have gone through the walls and the fort would have been destroyed, or, at the very least, it would have been so shattered that none would have doubted the propriety of a second attack, for it could be seen that it could easily be destroyed by a second attack."

CAPTAIN (AFTERWARDS REAR-ADMIRAL) THOMAS TURNER.

This kind of "argument" will not stand against the statement of the facts. Its purpose was to throw on Dupont the odium of failure in the attack on Charleston.

All the talk of increasing the charges of the guns to obtain more breaching power was sheer folly, for the charges for the guns were established by the Bureau of Ordnance in the Navy Department, and no officer could take the responsibility of doubling the charges of the guns during an action, for should they burst and kill his own men he would be held blamable.

The Naval historian labors in all this to show that there was wanting the energy in the attack on Sumter which characterized subsequent proceedings; but it must be remembered that Rear-Admiral Dahlgren, who relieved Dupont, with the light of the latter's experience to guide him, accomplished no more than his predecessor. In fact, the historian admits as much, and acknowledges that nothing was effected until Fort Wagner, the key to the situation, was attacked by the Army and Navy at the same time, when, to use his words: "The Monitors and 'New Ironsides' played a most conspicuous part." In fact, he says, "it does not appear how Wagner could have been taken without their assistance." The north end of the island was in possession of the Confederates, and, of course, in communication with Charleston and the other forts, and Wagner could at any time be re-inforced, and it would have been just as easy for the Confederates to have advanced by sap towards Gilmore's batteries as for him to approach them, had it not been for the presence of the iron-clads; but the latter

LIEUTENANT-COMMANDER (NOW REAR-ADMIRAL) S. B. LUCE.

effectually prevented any operations outside the walls of the fort, nor were the enemy even able to make a sortie to check the working-parties of Gilmore, nor use their batteries with effect upon the position, for the men could not stand to their guns under the fire of the Monitors or "New Ironsides."

Day by day, and even by night, it was the business of the Monitors to go up and attack the forts, gradually weakening their defence till, on the day when Gilmore expected to make the final assault, Rear-Admiral Dahlgren, the successor of Dupont, reported that he had knocked the fort into sand-heaps under the fire of the land and naval batteries; it was no longer tenable, and that night Morris Island was evacuated.

No one will pretend that Fort Wagner

compared in strength to Fort Sumter, which it was expected six Monitors would knock down; the Commander-in-chief of the squadron, indeed, being blamed for not settling it in the first attack; and when we consider all the events at Charleston, from Dupont's first attack until the evacuation of the place on the advance of General Sherman's army, we are confirmed in our idea that Rear-Admiral Dupont was right in saying that "the place can only be taken by a combined attack of the Army and Navy; and attacking the forts with the Monitors and iron-clads alone would never end in any favorable results."

It was not until after the fall of Morris Island, when General Gilmore could erect batteries armed with heavy rifled-guns, that Fort Sumter began to crumble, day by day, until it became a mere heap of rubbish to outward seeming, although still powerful, even in its crippled condition, and protecting the obstructions from the Monitors and "New Ironsides," so that no one could tell any more of their character than was known to Dupont when he relinquished his command.

To show the Confederate determination to hold Charleston at all hazards, we here insert the circular of General Ripley. It shows that the Confederates were alive to everything necessary to circumvent an enemy.

[CIRCULAR.]

HEADQUARTERS FIRST MILITARY DISTRICT,
SOUTH CAROLINA, GEORGIA AND FLORIDA.
CHARLESTON, December 26, 1862.

In case the proposed attack on this harbor is known beforehand, special directions will be given for the service of the different batteries. As, however, it may happen that a surprise may be attempted, or that the intervening time between the knowledge of the intention and the event may be too short, the instructions hereinafter contained will be carefully attended to.

Each commanding officer of a fort or battery will give his attention immediately to the strengthening of his carriages and the complete preparation of his material. Besides making the proper requisitions on the staff departments, let him endeavor to do as much as possible from his own resources. While staff departments are to a great extent crippled for want of material and workmen, much can be accomplished by ready expedients without their aid. Every carriage must be kept carefully screwed up, and, if any defects, made at least temporarily efficient. All the elevating screws, eccentric wheels, and traversing gear must be put in order and kept so, and especial care must be taken to see that a full supply of small implements is constantly on hand.

Ammunition should be examined, and immediately apportioned to the several guns, reference being had to the orders heretofore given on that subject; but where the quantity is not sufficient, the greater portion should be given to the heavier guns, as on them principally the success of the defence must depend.

Officers and men of each command must be kept on the alert, and instructions given to go to each battery at once, upon an alarm; and especial care must be taken that each battery is in readiness for instant action as the men arrive at their guns.

It is hoped and believed that most of these things

are habitually attended to; but, as constant vigilance is our only security, they cannot be too forcibly insisted upon.

Upon observing a disposition to attack on the part of the enemy, the nearest fort or battery will give the alarm. By day a shotted gun and dipping the flag will communicate the danger to the other fortifications and head-quarters. All commands will go at once to battery, and the circumstances of the alarm communicated to the head-quarters by telegraph or signal.

By night a shotted gun and a rocket will give the intelligence.

In whatever way the attack is made by the enemy, he is to be engaged as soon as possible, to do so effectually, with a few long-range guns from every fort that will bear. The number of guns must be left to the discretion of the commanding officer, who must see that the fire is as accurate as possible. They must not engage too great a number, and be careful not unduly to excite their men, or strain their guns and carriages. While the long-range fire is valuable, if accurate, to annoy the enemy and force him to develop his attack, it is not to be depended on for more. Other things being equal, it will be well that the guns to leeward are first engaged. The remaining guns of the batteries will be trained by battery on different points where the enemy must pass, care being taken to have the fire of each battery concentrated.

As the enemy approaches, let the distance he will be in passing be accurately estimated by the distance-buoys, and the elevation made to correspond, making it too little rather than too great for direct fire. If the vessels are passing rapidly the guns should be discharged by battery, just as the prows of the vessels come across the line of sight.

In the case of wooden vessels, the object will be to hit them near the water line, just abaft the smoke-stack. In the case of iron-clad vessels, to hit the deck or turrets at the intersection with the deck, and especially to let all the shots strike at once.

The first fire will be concentrated upon the leading vessels, and will be continued upon them as long as the guns by battery will bear well, and especially if they become entangled in obstructions, even if certain vessels engage to draw off the attention of the outermost batteries and remain behind.

Should some of the vessels succeed in passing, the action must then pass into the hands of commanding officers of batteries. They will pour in their fire as far as practicable by battery, and as fast as it can be done with accuracy, on whatever vessels of the enemy may be nearest them.

The guns of Beauregard Battery, Fort Moultrie, Battery Bee, and the eastern, north-eastern, and north-western faces of Fort Sumter, will be used to form the first circle of fire to which the enemy must be subjected, the centre being a little to the eastward of a line between the forts and midway. Every effort must be made to crush his vessels and repel his attack within this circle, and especially while he is entangled in the obstructions.

All the mortars of Fort Sumter and Fort Moultrie will be trained on the centre above indicated. The fuses will be of the full length, and the shells have large bursting charges, it being better to have the fuses fail than the shells to burst in the air, and the full effect of the explosions being desirable if successful. The mortar batteries will be fired by battery when the enemy's vessels are about two ships' length from the point on which they are trained.

If the fleet is large, the mortars will be kept trained on the same point and fired by battery as rapidly as possible while the fleet is passing. If small, and a portion has passed the first circle of fire, the mortars of Fort Sumter will be trained to operate on the second circle, the centre of which will be at a point

about midway between Forts Sumter and Ripley, and to the southward of the middle-ground shoal. It will be formed by the heavy guns of Fort Johnston, Fort Ripley, Castle Pinckney, Battery Bee, the north-western and western faces of Fort Sumter.

The guns of Forts Johnston and Ripley and Castle Pinckney will open on the leading vessels as they come within easy range, care being taken that every shot finds its mark. Those of Fort Sumter and Battery Bee will continue upon the leading vessels as long as they are close; but, if they elongate their distance, the fire will concentrate on the vessels nearest them.

Should any vessel succeed in passing the second circle of fire, the third will be formed and put into action by the guns of White Point Battery and Battery Glover, with such guns of Forts Johnston and Ripley and Castle Pinckney as will bear. Concentration on the leading vessels will be the object, as before.

During the action care will be taken, as far as possible, to prevent the chances of shot from the batteries taking the direction of our own works. The best way of doing this will be to let none miss the enemy, and when he is between the works most especial accuracy will be striven for.

The vessels of the Confederate navy will engage during the action, and they may often pass our batteries. In this case officers and gunners cannot be too careful to avoid hitting them. The fire by battery, as a general thing, will be discontinued at those vessels of the enemy which our ships engage closely; but, if occasion offers, endeavors will be made to hit the ports of the revolving turrets on the enemy's vessels when turned from our ships, to disarrange and throw out of gear the machinery for closing the ports.

Accurate fire by single guns will be concentrated on the enemy's vessels, if two or more attack one of ours; and should the distance admit, then it will be advisable to pour upon one of them a heavy fire by battery.

The plunging fire from Fort Sumter is expected to be particularly effective, and when single-rifled guns are fired from the barbettes of that fort, it will be well to hit the grated roofs of the turrets with square-headed bolts, followed by shells filled with molten iron.

The square-headed bolts for the 10-inch columbiads and the heavier guns will be fired by battery when the enemy is within close range. Solid shot and bolts will be used generally against iron-clads during the action.

The furnaces for melting iron and heating shot will be kept in heat, and heated projectiles will be used whenever occasion offers advantage.

Should it happen that any of the enemy's vessels become disabled and endeavor to get out of fire, the outermost batteries must pay particular attention to prevent them; and in case other of the enemy's ships come to the assistance of the disabled, let every gun and mortar which will bear be turned upon them by battery.

The great object of the enemy will probably be to run by, and every effort must be made to crush him in each successive circle of fire which he encounters.

Hog Island Channel will be obstructed, and the obstructions must be guarded by the long-range guns of Fort Sumter and the columbiads of Battery Bee nearest it.

It is doubtful whether the enemy will attempt to pass by Folly Channel. If he does, a circle of fire will be formed by the guns of Fort Ripley, Castle Pinckney and White Point Battery.

The position of torpedoes will be communicated to commanding officers, and the effort made to drive the enemy's vessels upon them if he is taking other courses.

The obstructions will also be designated, and

under no circumstances will the enemy be permitted to reconnoitre them.

The headquarters of the undersigned will be at Fort Sumter, and directions will be sent by telegraph and signal to different posts, should anything require special directions.

Batteries Marshall and Wagner will be worked to the extent of their capacity for injuring the enemy, by their commanding officers, without unduly exposing their commands.

The directions given above relate, generally, to the defeat of an attack by the enemy's fleet alone Should a combined attack be made by land and water, other orders can be issued, as nothing of that kind can be done by surprise.

The present circular will be studied and reflected upon by all officers who will be engaged in this honorable duty of the coming defence. With careful attention, coolness and skillful gunnery, success is far more than possible.

R. S. RIPLEY,
Brigadier-General Commanding.

Official :

WM. F. NANEE, *Acting-Assistant Adjutant-General.*

COMMANDER (NOW REAR-ADMIRAL) JOHN H. UPSHUR.

We think we have established that Admiral Dupont was right in the conclusions which he submitted to the Navy Department immediately after the engagement of the 7th of April. The public, knowing that he retired from his command directly after this affair, might suppose that some blame was attached to him.

Dupont was too popular an officer to be treated with injustice, and in the course of a month it was seen by the Secretary of the Navy that his views were correct, and that the siege of Charleston by the Navy still continued with no better results than before.

Overtures were then made to the Admiral

and he could have had any command he desired, but Dupont was a proud man and would not listen to terms from those whom he thought had censured him for doing his duty and forced him from his command at Charleston. To accept another command, Dupont thought, would imply that he concurred in the views of the Department.

The following letters will explain in a measure the reasons for the misunderstanding between the Secretary of the Navy and Rear-Admiral Dupont. The Secretary's letter is an implied order for Dupont to succeed at all hazards, while the Admiral's undertakes to show the Department how little prospect there was of meeting its expectations:

SECRETARY WELLES TO REAR-ADMIRAL DUPONT.

NAVY DEPARTMENT, }
April 11, 1863. }

SIR—It has been suggested to the Department by the President, in view of operations elsewhere, and especially by the Army of the Potomac, that you should retain a strong force off Charleston, even should you find it impossible to carry the place. You will continue to menace the rebels, keeping them in apprehension of a renewed attack, in order that they may be occupied; and not come North or go West to the aid of the rebels, with whom our forces will soon be in conflict. Should you be successful, as we trust and believe you will be, it is expected that General Hunter will continue to keep the rebels employed and in constant apprehension, so that they shall not leave the vicinity of Charleston. This detention of the iron-clads, should it be necessary, in consequence of a repulse, can be but for a few days.

I trust your success will be such that the iron-clads can be, or will have been, dispatched to the Gulf when this reaches you. There is intense anxiety in regard to your operations.

This day is the anniversary of the assault on Sumter, and God grant that its recurrence may witness the destruction of that fortress by our naval forces under your command.

I am very respectfully,
Your obedient servant,
GIDEON WELLES,
Secretary of the Navy.

Rear-Admiral S. F. DUPONT,
Commanding S. A. B. Squadron, Port Royal, S. C.

President Lincoln was greatly disturbed at the want of success at Charleston, and sent the following communications to Admiral Dupont:

EXECUTIVE MANSION, }
(TELEGRAM.) WASHINGTON, April 13, 1863. }

Hold your position inside the bar near Charleston; or, if you shall have left it, return to it and hold it till further orders.

Do not allow the enemy to erect new batteries or defences on Morris Island. If he has begun it, drive him out. I do not herein order you to renew the general attack. That is to depend upon your own discretion or a further order.

A. LINCOLN.

Admiral DUPONT.

———

EXECUTIVE MANSION, }
WASHINGTON, April 14, 1863. }

This is intended to clear up an apparent inconsistency between the recent order to continue operations before Charleston, and the former one to remove to another point in a certain contingency. No censure upon you or either of you is intended ; we still hope that by cordial and judicious co-operation you can take the batteries on Morris Island and Sullivan's Island and Fort Sumter. But whether you can or not, we wish the demonstration kept up for a time for a collateral and very important object ; we wish the attempt to be a real one (though not a desperate one , if it affords any considerable chance of success. But if prosecuted as a *demonstration* only, this must not become public, or the whole effect will be lost. Once again before Charleston, do not leave till further orders from here ; of course, this is not intended to force you to leave unduly exposed Hilton Head, or other near points in your charge.   Yours truly,

                                    A. LINCOLN.
General HUNTER and Admiral DUPONT.

P. S.—Whoever receives this first, please send a copy to the other immediately.   A. L.

COMMANDER (NOW REAR-ADMIRAL) CHARLES STEEDMAN,

COMMANDING FLANKING DIVISION, BATTLE OF PORT ROYAL.

REAR-ADMIRAL DUPONT TO SECRETARY WELLES.
                    FLAG-SHIP "WABASH,"
PORT ROYAL HARBOR, S. C., April 16, 1863.

SIR—I have the honor to acknowledge the receipt this morning, by the "Freeborn," of your communication of the 11th instant, directing the maintaining of a large force off Charleston to menace the rebels and keep them in apprehension of a renewed attack in the event of our repulse.

I have also to acknowledge the receipt of a copy of a telegraphic despatch of the 13th instant, from the President of the United States, sent from Fortress Monroe.

The Department will probably have known, on the 12th instant, the result of the attack.   In my dispatch of the 11th instant, dated off Charleston, the department was made aware of my withdrawal, with the iron-clads, from the very insecure anchorage inside the bar, and just in time to save the Monitors from an easterly gale, in which, in my

opinion and that of their commanders, they would have been in great peril of being lost on Morris Island Beach.   Their ground-tackling has been found to be insufficient, and from time to time they have dragged even in close harbors.

I have since been doing all in my power to push forward their repairs in order to send them to the Gulf as directed; but I presume that your dispatch of the 11th instant, and the telegraphic message from the President, revoke your previous order.

I shall spare no exertions in repairing, as soon as possible, the serious injuries sustained by the Monitors in the late attack, and shall get them inside Charleston bar with all dispatch, in accordance with the order of the President.   I think it my duty, however, to state to the Department that this will be attended with great risk to these vessels from the gales which prevail at this season, and from the continuous fire of the enemy's batteries, which they can neither silence nor prevent the erection of new ones.

The "New Ironsides" can only cross the bar with certainty at spring-tides, which are twice a month. She is more vulnerable than the Monitors, and at the distance she must necessarily anchor could not elevate her guns sufficiently to reach any batteries of the enemy, while at the same time she would be liable to injury, particularly in her wooden ends, from a fire which she could not return.   If this vessel is withdrawn from the blockade and placed inside, the blockade may be raised by the rebel rams coming out of Charleston harbor at night by Maffit's Channel, in which case she could give no assistance to the fleet outside.   But for the "New Ironsides," the raid of the 31st of January would have been repeated with more serious effect.

The lower and greater part of Morris Island exhibits a ridge or row of sand-hills, affording to the enemy a natural parapet against the fire of shipping and facilities for erecting batteries in very strong position.   The upper part of the island is crossed by Fort Wagner, a work of great strength, and covered by the guns of Fort Sumter.   The island is in full communication with Charleston, and can, in spite of us, draw fresh re-inforcements as rapidly as they may be required.   Shoals extend from the island, which prevent the near approach of the Monitors, and our experience at Fort McAllister does not encourage me to expect that they will reduce well-defended sand batteries, where the damage inflicted by day is readily repaired by the unstinted labor of the night.   The ships, therefore, can neither cover the landing nor afterwards protect the advance of the small force of the army available for operations in this quarter, which will meet fresh troops at every sand-hill, and may look also for a reverse fire from the batteries on James Island.

As it is considered necessary to menace Charleston by a demonstration of land and naval forces, North Edisto will afford a better point from which to threaten an advance, and a concentration of troops and ships in that quarter would accomplish the purpose of the Government mentioned in your dispatch of the 11th instant, as it is a military point from which Charleston could be attacked now, James Island being fully occupied by the enemy's batteries.

I have deemed it proper and due to myself to make these statements, but I trust I need not add that I will obey all orders with the utmost fidelity, even when my judgment is entirely at variance with them, such as the order to re-occupy the unsafe anchorage for the iron-clads off Morris Island, and an intimation that the renewal of the attack on Charleston may be ordered, which, in my judgment, would be attended with disastrous results, involving the loss of this coast.

For eighteen months in these waters I have given whatever of professional knowledge, energy and zeal I possess to the discharge of my duties, and to the close study of our military and naval position in the tenure of the sea-coasts within the limits of my command, and I claim to know what best pertains to the disposition of my fleet in carrying out the instructions of the Department.

I know not yet whether the confidence of the Department so often expressed to me has been shaken by the want of success in a single measure which I never advised, though intensely desirous to carry out the Department's orders and justify expectations in which I could not share.

I am, however, painfully struck by the tenor and tone of the President's order, which seems to imply a censure, and I have to request that the Department will not hesitate to relieve me by an officer, who, in its opinion, is more able to execute that service in which I have had the misfortune to fail—the capture of Charleston. No consideration for an individual officer, whatever his loyalty and length of service, should weigh an instant if the cause of his country can be advanced by his removal.

Very respectfully, your obedient servant,
S. F. DUPONT,
Rear-Admiral, Commanding S. A. B. Squadron.
Hon. GIDEON WELLES,
Secretary of the Navy, Washington.

CAPTAIN (NOW REAR-ADMIRAL) WM. ROGERS TAYLOR.

After the attack on Charleston, Rear-Admiral Dupont returned to Fort Royal and the blockade continued as before with the wooden gun-boats.

In the latter part of April, Major-General Hunter applied for a gun-boat to assist a land force in an expedition against Buffington, on May River, which town had been the head-quarters of Confederate marauders for some time.

The army force numbering one thousand men, under Colonel Barton, embarked on board the gun-boat "Mayflower" and a transport, and were landed near Buffington under cover of the guns of the "Commodore McDonough," and took possession of the town from which the Confederates had retreated. By order of Colonel Barton the

town was destroyed by fire, the church alone being spared. The enemy returned and made several charges on the Federal troops, but were driven back by the shells of the "McDonough," which burst in their ranks.

The burning of the town seems to have been an unnecessary act of severity, but such is the tendency of civil war. The inhabitants of a town are held responsible for the acts of lawless guerillas, and punished for aiding and abetting the enemy, when perhaps they may not have been to blame.

While the blockade of Charleston still continued, the Confederates, with the persistent energy by which they were distinguished, were constructing iron-clads at Savannah. They had been for some time past engaged in altering the blockade-runner "Fingal" into a casemated vessel of the same type as the "Merrimac" and others so popular in the South.

The fancy for this description of iron-clad arose doubtless more from necessity than from anything else. The Confederates had few machine-shops, and it was hardly practicable to roll out a sufficiency of wide plates, but they had a plenty of railroad iron, and of this they made liberal use. The Southern iron-clads were very formidable vessels when brought into conflict with wooden ships-of-war of the old type. It is only necessary to recall to the reader's memory the two small iron-clads which slipped out of Charleston and did such damage to the Federal gun-boats, not to mention other instances, to show the value of the Confederate war machines.

The slanting roof was the Southern idea pitted against the Monitor plan, which was that of the North. These represented the two most powerful types of fighting-ships in existence, and, if the "Merrimac" had destroyed the "Monitor," the former would no doubt have been the type of vessel used for coast and harbor defence the world over.

The Confederates never conceded the Northern claim that the "Monitor" drove the "Merrimac" back to Norfolk. The Confederate naval authorities knew how the Federal Navy Department was abused and criticised throughout the North for adopting the Ericsson principle instead of some of the numerous other devices that were offered, and the South took the view of the question which coincided with their own preconceived ideas. They believed in their plan of vessel with rifled guns, and rather derided the Monitors with their slow-moving turrets and short-range guns.

The want of success of the Monitors at Charleston also lowered their prestige, though this was unjust to the vessels, for they certainly showed their endurance at that place sufficiently to prove that they could stand the attack of the "Atlanta."

The "Atlanta," then called the "Fingal," had succeeded in running the blockade and getting into Savannah soon after the capture of Port Royal. She had since been closely watched, and finding it would be almost impossible to get out of port again as a blockade-runner, she was sold to the Confederate Government and converted into an iron-clad, supposed to be one of the best that had been built in the South.

The "Weehawken," Captain John Rodgers, and the "Nahant," Commander John Downes, were employed blockading the "Atlanta" at the mouth of Wilmington River.

Early in the morning of June 17th, 1863,

the "Nahant." At this time the "Atlanta" lay across the channel waiting the attack of the Monitors. Commander William A. Webb, her commanding officer, showed more courage than judgment, as he was not called upon to await the attack of two vessels which together were superior in force.

The "Weehawken" approached within three hundred yards of the enemy and at 5.15 A. M. opened fire. In fifteen minutes the "Atlanta's" colors were hauled down and a white flag was hoisted. The "Weehawken" fired but five shots altogether, but that number was quite sufficient.

As soon as the Confederate steamer struck her colors, Captain Rodgers steamed close to her and ordered a boat to be sent on board the "Weehawken." Lieutenant

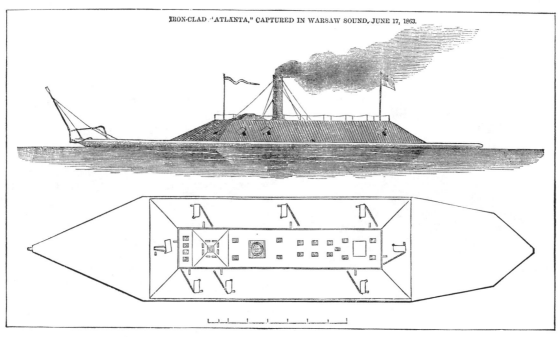

IRON-CLAD "ATLANTA," CAPTURED IN WARSAW SOUND, JUNE 17, 1863.

CONFEDERATE IRON-CLAD "ATLANTA," CAPTURED IN WARSAW SOUND.

it was reported to Captain Rodgers that a Confederate iron-clad was coming down the river. The "Weehawken" was immediately cleared for action, the cable slipped, and the Monitor steamed slowly towards the northeast end of Warsaw Island, then turned and stood up the Sound, heading for the enemy, who came on with confidence, as if sure of victory. Two steamers followed the Confederate iron-clad, filled with people who had come down to see the Union vessels captured or driven away. The "Nahant," having no pilot, followed in the wake of the "Weehawken."

When the "Atlanta" was about a mile and a half from the "Weehawken" she fired a rifled shot which passed across the stern of the later vessel and struck near

Alexander, of the Confederate Navy, went on board to surrender the "Atlanta," which he informed Captain Rodgers was aground on a sand-spit. Soon after, Commander Webb of the "Atlanta" repaired on board the "Weehawken" to deliver up his sword, and a prize-crew, under Lieutenant-Commander D. B. Harmony, was sent to take charge of the prize.

The "Weehawken" received no damage from the "Atlanta's" shot, the only injury she received was from her consort running foul of her. The "Nahant" took no part in the battle, which was ended before she could obtain a position to use her guns.

The "Atlanta" was struck four times by the "Weehawken's" shot, first on the inclined side by a 15-inch cored shot, which broke through the armor and wood-backing, strewing the deck with splinters, prostrating about forty men by the force of the concussion, and wounding several by splinters and fragments of armor. The second shot—11-inch solid—struck the "knuckle" or edge of the overhang, and did no damage except breaking a couple of plates. The third shot —15-inch—struck the top of the "Atlanta's" pilot-house, knocking it off, wounding the pilots and stunning the man at the wheel. The fourth shot — 11-inch — struck a port-stopper in the centre, breaking it in two and driving the fragments through the port.

The "Atlanta" had sixteen wounded, one of whom died from the effects of his

we have before stated, viz., that the 15-inch shot could not penetrate four inches of iron with the ordinary backing at a distance of 800 yards.

The "Atlanta" was considered by the Confederates the best iron-clad they had built, and in the capture was verified the statement we have made, that either of the Monitor-built vessels, armed with 15-inch guns, could have destroyed the "Merrimac" in half an hour. The "Weehawken" defeated a better ship than the "Merrimac" in half the time mentioned.

It was probably the intention of the commanding officer of the "Atlanta" to get out where he could have plenty of sea-room and choose his distance—which the

CAPTURE OF THE CONFEDERATE RAM "ATLANTA" BY THE MONITOR "WEEHAWKEN."

wounds, but there is no mention of any one being killed outright.

The armament of the Confederate vessel was two 6-inch rifles in broadside, and two 7-inch rifles working on pivots, either as broadside or bow and stern guns. The "Atlanta" had a complement of 145 officers and men, including marines.

The fact that the vessel was aground when she struck her colors does not account for the feeble defence she made after running down so defiantly and engaging two Monitors, whose strength must have been well known to the Confederates. Only two of the shots which struck the "Atlanta" did any great damage, and the armor and backing, though much shattered, were not penetrated. This confirms what

great speed of the "Atlanta" would have enabled him to do—and attack the Monitors at long range, which would only have ended in the expenditure of a large amount of ammunition without any result, except that the "Atlanta" might have escaped to do harm elsewhere.

It seemed to be the fate of all the Confederate iron-clads to be either captured, or destroyed by their officers to prevent them from falling into the hands of the Federals, and the "Merrimac" was about the only one of them which effected much previous to her destruction.

The "Atlanta" had a speed of ten knots, and her officers had confidently counted on capturing both the Monitors. From the nautical instruments on board the Confederate vessel, her commanding officer evidently intended to go to sea or cruise along the coast, and her excellent engines and equipments and good model would have justified such an attempt. The 15-inch shot which struck the "Atlanta" dispelled all these illusions and demoralized the crew, and, although the vessel fired some shots, they all went wide of the mark.

When it was determined to fit the "Atlanta" as an iron-clad, she was cut down so as to have the deck two feet above the water. Upon this deck was built a casemate with inclined sides similar to the "Merrimac," with ports in which to mount four heavy rifle-guns of the Brooke pattern. Her armor was four inches thick, composed of two layers of plates seven inches wide placed horizontally and vertically to each other.

The vessel was two hundred and four feet

CAPTAIN (NOW REAR-ADMIRAL) J. F. GREEN.

long, forty-one feet breadth of beam, and about sixteen feet draft of water. The bow terminated in an iron beak for ramming, and the vessel carried a torpedo apparatus on the bow, to be used when opportunity offered. The "Atlanta" was, in fact, an improved "Merrimac."

This is a general description of a vessel from which so much was expected and so little realized, and which instead of capturing two Monitors, was captured by one of them in fifteen minutes.

There was a good deal of ingenuity displayed in the construction of the "Atlanta," but the question of the superiority of the Monitor type over the flat or angular type of vessel may be considered set at rest by her capture.

Notwithstanding the battle of the original "Monitor" with the "Merrimac," many people declined to believe in the superiority of the turret system. The English, even after the news reached them, commenced building armed ships with plated sides like the "Warrior" class, judging from the effect of the "Monitor's" shot on the "Merrimac," that they could build vessels with teak or oak backing and four inches of iron that would resist the most powerful American gun. But here was a new and more powerful gun, of which they had taken no account, and which, exceeding in size anything in the ordnance line heretofore manufactured, might smash in the sides of the "Warrior" class, even if the shot did not pass clear through them.

This fight with the "Atlanta," therefore, set Europe to thinking, and convinced the Navy Department it had taken a step in the right direction. If their little floating batteries could not demolish the heaviest fortifications, they could break up and send to the bottom the heaviest ships.

The battle between the "Weehawken" and the "Atlanta" satisfied the United States Government that it could safely intimate to the governments of Europe that we would submit to no interference in our domestic concerns so long as we complied with the law of nations. There was established a more hopeful feeling for the speedy suppression of the rebellion, now that we had demonstrated that we could build vessels that were more than a match for the war-ships of Europe.

The news of this engagement was received in Europe with great interest. It was a contest between English and American ideas. The American idea was the Monitor-built vessel with the 15-inch gun; the English idea was the "Atlanta" with her plated sides and rifled guns. No persons were more interested in the result of the conflict than the Lords of the British Admiralty, ever alive to what might exercise an influence upon their navy. They had commenced the plating system and seemed to cling to the idea, but the success of the "Weehawken" shattered their faith. The Monitor system remained master of the field and has so continued to this day.

On this occasion the Secretary of the Navy was eloquent in his praise of Captain Rodgers, recognizing in the handsomest manner his services not only on the present occasion, but also on the Mississippi at the commencement of the war and at Drury's Bluff on the James, where Rodgers attacked the enemy's fortifications in the so-called iron-clad "Galena." The Secretary also dwelt on the moral courage exhibited by Captain Rodgers in putting to sea in the face of a violent storm to test the sea-going qualities of the "Weehawken"—one of a class of vessels so unjustly decried by many persons.

For his important services, the Secretary informed Captain Rodgers that he had presented his name to Congress for a vote of thanks, and certainly the distinction was well deserved, for John Rodgers was one of the most gallant officers in the Navy. He had that cool courage which would flinch from no danger, and his capacious mind was ever ready to meet emergencies which might have unnerved many clever officers. All of Rodgers' friends and associates in the Navy felt that his honors were fairly earned, and they were worn with the modesty which distinguished him.

The capture of the "Atlanta" was the last important event that occurred while the South Atlantic squadron was under the command of Dupont, and he was well pleased to terminate his official communications to the Navy Department with such gratifying intelligence; and on the 4th of July, 1863, at his own request, he was relieved from the command of the squadron by Rear-Admiral John A. Dahlgren.

In the later communications which passed between Rear-Admiral Dupont and the Secretary of the Navy, some asperity may be observed on both sides; but the capture of the "Atlanta" seemed to have smoothed all this away, and Admiral Dupont's friends hoped on his arrival in Washington he would be appointed to some important command where he could give the country the benefit of his talents and experience. On his retirement from the command of the squadron, Mr. Secretary Welles wrote the Admiral the following letter, which would seem to indicate that if he had ever had any feeling against Dupont he had outgrown it:

NAVY DEPARTMENT, }
June 26, 1863. }

SIR—The Department has received your several dispatches announcing the capture of the rebel iron-clad steamer "Fingal," *alias* "Atlanta," and enclosing the detailed reports of Captain John Rodgers and Commander John Downes of the affair.

I take occasion to express the Department's appreciation of your prompt measures to prepare for the expected appearance of the rebel iron-clad by sending off Savannah two of our own ably commanded ships, and congratulate you on the acquisition of so powerful a vessel, which promises to be of important service on the station.

To your ceaseless vigilance and that of the officers under your command were we indebted some months since for the destruction of the steamer "Nashville," which the enemy had armed and fruitlessly endeavored to send out to destroy our commerce, and now to your timely measures and to the efficient means provided do we owe the capture of one of the most powerful iron-clads afloat, a vessel prepared after several months of toil and great expenditure of money, and sent forth with confidence to disperse our blockading fleet and overcome our Monitors.

You may well regard this, and we may with pleasure look upon it, as a brilliant termination of a command gallantly commenced and conducted for nearly two years with industry, energy and ability.

The Department desires you to recommend to it an officer of the South Atlantic Blockading Squadron to command the "Atlanta."

Very respectfully,
GIDEON WELLES,
Secretary of the Navy.

Rear-Admiral S. F. DUPONT,
Commanding S. A. B. Squadron, Port Royal, S. C.

SOUTH ATLANTIC SQUADRON, JANUARY, 1863.

LIST OF VESSELS AND OFFICERS UNDER REAR-ADMIRAL SAMUEL F. DUPONT.

CAPTAIN C. R. P. RODGERS, CAPTAIN OF THE FLEET.

STEAM-FRIGATE "WABASH," FLAG-SHIP.

Commander, Thomas G. Corbin; Lieutenant-Commander, John Irwin; Lieutenant Alexander S. Mackenzie, Ordnance-Officer; Lieutenant Samuel W. Preston, Flag-Lieutenant; Lieutenants, Lloyd Phenix, John H. Rowland and James P. Robertson; Fleet Surgeon, George Clymer; Assistant Surgeons, Henry F. McSherry and Theoron Woolverton; Paymaster, John S. Cunningham; Chaplain, George W. Dorrance; Acting-Master, Townsend Stiles; Marine Officers: Captain, James Lewis; First-Lieutenant, H. B. Lowry; Ensigns, James Wallace, M. L. Johnson, Philip W. Lowry, La Rue P. Adams and Frederick Pearson; Acting-Master's Mates, Wm. A. Duer, W. F. Horton and Joel R. Hinman; Engineers: Chief, Robert W. McCleery, Acting-Second-Assistant, J. B. Hathaway; Third-Assistants, J. S. Green, Thomas Crummey; Acting-Third-Assistants, J. L. Marshall, J. B. Place and J. T. Dennett; Boatswain, Zachariah Whitmarsh; Gunner, Thomas Stewart; Carpenter, Charles Bordman; Sailmaker, G. T. Lozier

IRON-CLAD STEAMER "NEW IRONSIDES."

Captain, Thomas Turner; Lieutenant-Commander, Geo. E. Belknap; Lieutenant, H. B. Robeson; Surgeon, Marius Duvall; Assistant Surgeons, W. T. Plant and Edward Kershner; Paymaster, Alex. W. Russell; Marine Officers: First-Lieutenant, H. A. Bartlett; Second-Lieutenant, J. B. Young; Acting-Masters, G. W. Domett, J. M. Skillings and J. M. Butler; Acting-Master's Mates, C. W. Howard, G. H. Bradley, S. S. Hand, T. E. Harvey, B. F. Morris and Robert Shepherd; Engineers: Chief, Harmon Newell; First-Assistant, N. B. Littig; Second-Assistants, O. H. Lackey, R. L. Harris; Third-Assistants, Edward Battelle, H. C. Beckwith and W. S. Wells; Boatswain, Thomas Bennett; Gunners, Charles Stuart and R. J. Hill; Carpenter, Theodore Bishop; Sailmaker, J. B. Birdsall.

IRON-CLAD STEAMER "NANTUCKET." [JAN. 1864.]

Lieutenant-Commander, S. B. Luce; Lieutenant, H. L. Howison; Assistant Surgeon, A. B. Judson; Acting-Assistant Paymaster, L. L. Brigham; Acting-Master, W. H. Maies; Acting-Ensigns, J. T. Otis, C. C. Starr and John Meyers; Engineers: Second-Assistants, Geo. H. White, Isaac McNary; Third-Assistants, W. W. Buckhout, J. K. Smedley and Acting-Third-Assistant A. L. Grow. [Commander Donald McN. Fairfax commanded the "Nantucket" at Charleston.]

IRON-CLAD STEAMER "CATSKILL." [JAN. 1864.]

Lieutenant-Commander, F. M. Bunce; Assistant-Surgeon, Robert Willard; Acting-Assistant Paymaster, G. F. Barker; Acting-Master, G. W. Parker; Acting-Ensigns, C. P. Walters and George M. Prindle; Engineers: Second-Assistant, G. D. Emmons; Third-Assistant, J. F. Booth; Acting-Third-Assistants, Frank Marsh and James Plunkett; Acting-Master's Mate, Peter Trescott. [Commander George W. Rodgers commanded the "Catskill" at Charleston.]

STEAM-SLOOP "POWHATAN."

Captain, S. W. Godon; Lieutenant-Commander, E. P. Williams; Lieutenants, A. R. McNair and F. J. Higginson; Surgeon, Henry O. Mayo; Assistant Surgeon, Edw. D. Payne; Paymaster, L. J. Brown; First-Lieutenant of Marines, P. C. Pope; Acting-Masters, Jas. Ogilvie, Lothrop Baker, C. R. Wilkins and E. L. Haines; Acting-Ensign, C. P. Walters; Acting-Masters' Mates, W. S. Curtis, Wm. Frost and C. H. Howland; Engineers: Chief, John A. Grier; First Assistant, H. B. Nones; Second-Assistant. Henry Brown; Third-Assistants, W. H. Glading, R. A. Wright, G. W. Carrick, John Franklin and M. Cuthbert; Boatswain, Wm. Long; Gunner, G. W. Omensetter; Carpenter, Amos Chick; Sailmaker, W. S. L. Brayton.

IRON-CLAD STEAMER "PASSAIC."

Captain, Percival Drayton; Lieutenant-Commander, Joseph N. Miller; Assistant Surgeon, Edgar Holden; Assistant Paymaster, J. P. Woodbury; Acting-Ensigns, H. B. Baker and L. G. Emerson; Engineers: First-Assistant, G. S. Bright; Second-Assistant, H. W. Robie; Third-Assistants, W. A. Dripps and Joseph Hoops.

STEAM SLOOP "CANANDAIGUA."

Captain, Joseph F. Green; Lieutenant-Commander, J. J. Cornwell; Lieutenant, H. De H. Manley; Surgeon, James Suddards; Paymaster, C. H. Eldredge; Acting-Master, Samuel Hall; Ensign, Benjamin H. Porter; Acting-Ensign, John L. Gifford; Acting-Master's Mates, A. S. Eldridge, J. N. Pease, W. T. Vincent and C. S. McCarty; Engineers: Chief, Wm. S. Stamm; First-Assistant, H. C. Victor; Second-Assistant, G. W. Rogers; Third-Assistants, Albert Jackson, Alfred Hedrick, Philip Miller and E. S. Phillippi; Boatswain, Thomas Smith; Gunner, John Gaskins; Carpenter, S. N. Whitehouse; Sailmaker, David Bruce.

IRON-CLAD STEAMER "WEEHAWKEN."

Captain, John Rodgers; Lieutenant-Commander, L. H. Newman; Assistant Surgeon, E. M. Stein, Acting-Assistant Paymaster, J. H. Pynchon; Acting-Master, B. W. Loring; Acting-Ensigns, J. C. Cox and Stephen Balles; Engineers: Second-Assistants, J. H. Bailey and David Hardie; Third-Assistants, H. W. Merian and Augustus Mitchell.

STEAM-SLOOP "HOUSATONIC."

Captain, Wm. Rogers Taylor; Lieutenants, M. S. Stuyvesant and E. T. Brower; Surgeon, S. F. Coues; Assistant Paymaster, J. S. Woolson, Acting-Masters, J. W. Congdon and J. K. Crosby; Acting Ensign, Weston Gregory, Acting-Master's Mates, C. D. Bordman, E. A. Butler, G. A. Harriman and B. F. Jacobs; Engineers: Chief, John S. Albert; Second-Assistant, P. A. Rearick; Third-Assistants, I. R. McNary, F. L. Cooper, G. W. Geddes and J. H. Harmany; Boatswain, H. P. Grace; Gunner, Benjamin Roberts.

STEAMER "MERCEDITA."

Captain, Henry S. Stellwagen; Lieutenant-Commander, Trevot Abbott; Acting-Assistant Surgeon, C. H. Mason; Acting-Assistant Paymaster, T. C. Stellwagen; Acting-Masters, C. B. Wilder, F. J. Gover and T. J. Dwyer; Master's Mates, Edward Rogers and G. A. Steins; Engineers: Acting-First-Assistant, Alexander Doig; Acting-Third-Assistants,

Simon Rockefellow, E. F. Martin and J. A. Munger; Gunner, Jacob Amee.

STEAM GUN-BOAT "PAUL JONES."

Commander, Charles Steedman, Lieutenant, Edward A. Walker; Acting-Masters, Wm. Buckholdt; C. H. Boutelle and J. O. Ormond; Assistant Surgeon, J. H. Hazleton; Acting-Assistant Paymaster, J. A. Berry; Acting-Master's Mates, C. V. Kelly, Jeremiah Potts and Charles Weidenbine; Engineers: First-Assistant, Alexander Greer; Second-Assistant, James Sheriden; Third-Assistants, J. H. Chassmar, W. H. G. West and E. D. Weems; Acting-Gunner, O. B. Holden.

STEAMER "SOUTH CAROLINA."

Commander, John J. Almy; Acting-Assistant Surgeon, G. A. Bright; Assistant Paymaster, A. S. Kenny; Acting Masters, J. W. Magune, G. A. Crabb, W. H. Garfield and F. W. Baury; Acting-Ensign, C. T. Taylor; Acting-Master's Mates, Eliphalet Holbrook, Wm. C. Nye, A. S. Hitch and S. S. Withington; Engineers: Acting-Second-Assistants, B. B. Carney, B. D. Mulligan and J. H. Rowe; Acting Third-Assistants, Henry Gormley and James Jamison.

STEAMER "FLAG."

Commander, James H. Strong; Acting-Assistant Surgeon, C. W. Sartori; Acting-Assistant Paymaster, Lynford Lardner; Acting-Master, Wm. H. Latham; Acting-Master's Mates, E. G. Welles, G. W. Veacock and C. S. Lawrence; Engineers: Acting-First-Assistant, L. H. Flowry; Acting-Second-Assistants, John Harris, W. W. Tunis and M. Dandreau; Acting-Third-Assistants, J. S. Johnson and Edw. Alin; Acting-Gunner, B. F. Ritter.

STEAMER "QUAKER CITY."

Commander, James M. Frailey; Lieutenant-Commander, S. Livingston Breese; Acting-Assistant Surgeon, J. J. Brownlee; Acting-Assistant Paymaster, H. J. Bullay; Acting Master, H. S. Blanchard; Acting-Ensigns, T. F. DeLuce, A. Delano, Jr., and J. H. Bennett; Acting-Master's Mates, E. H. Dewey and E. W. Hale; Engineers; Acting-First-Assistant, G. W. Farrer; Acting-Third-Assistants, James Barnes, E. F. McGinniss, Henry Wauklin, J. F. King and John Proshero; Gunner, Daniel Dunsmore.

STORE-SHIP "VERMONT."

Commander, William Reynolds; Surgeon, Charles Eversfield; Assistant-Surgeon, I. H. Hazleton; Acting-Assistant Paymaster, J. S. Isaacs; Second-Lieutenant Marines, Alfred Devereaux; Acting-Masters, Howard Tibbatts and C. C. Kingsbury; Acting Ensigns, C. A. Pettit and R. T. Westcott; Acting-Master's Mates, W. Van Wyck, O. F. Wixen, J. G. Rose, Sidney Gray, Arthur Taffe and J. S. Griscom; Boatswain, William Winchester; Acting-Gunners, G. W. Allen and J. G. Bills; Carpenter, C. W. Babbitt; Sailmaker, John Joins.

STEAMER "KEYSTONE STATE."

Commander, Wm. E. Le Roy; Lieutenant Commander, T. H. Eastman, Assistant Surgeon, J. H. Gotwold; Acting-Assistant Paymaster, J. S. Stimson; Acting-Masters, C. H. Corser, Curtis Redman and L. E. Degn; Acting-Ensign, C. M. Bird; Acting-Master's Mates, J. C. Murphy, J. E. Jones and J. T. Ridgeway; Engineers: Acting-First-Assistant, A. K. Eddowes; Acting-Second-Assistant, James Doran; Acting-Third-Assistants, Wm. F. Warburton, John Smith and Pearson L. Fry; Acting-Gunner, David L. Briggs.

STEAMER "CIMMERONE."

Commander, Maxwell Woodhull; Lieutenant-Commander, B. B. Taylor; Acting-Masters, G. E. Thurston, Edward D. March and Samuel A. Waterbury; Assistant Surgeon, Eugene S. Olcott; Acting-Assistant Paymaster, D. W. Hale; Acting-Master's Mates, John F. Miller, Peter J. Marcoe, Wm. H.

Herring and Augustus Lippitt; Engineers: First-Assistant, E. A. C. Du Plaine; Second-Assistant, Reynold Driver; Third-Assistants, G. J. Burnap, George W. Beard and David Jones; Gunner, John Caulk.

STEAMER "BIENVILLE."

NOTE.—List of officers not given in the Navy Register.

IRON-CLAD STEAMER "MONTAUK."

Commander, John L. Worden; Lieutenant-Commander, C. H. Cushman; Assistant Surgeon, S. N. Brayton; Acting-Assistant Paymaster, S. T. Browne; Acting-Master, Pierre Giraud; Acting-Ensigns, I. J. McKinley and Geo. A. Almy; Engineers: Second-Assistants, Robert Potts and T. A. Stephens; Third-Assistants, D. P. McCartney and Geo. M. Greene.

STEAM GUN-BOAT "CONEMAUGH."

Commander, Reed Werden, Lieutenant, B. J. Cromwell; Assistant Surgeon, J. J. Allingham; Paymaster, George Lawrence; Acting-Masters, J. W. Stapleford and J. L. Lee; Acting-Ensigns, W. F. Reading and G. F. Morse; Acting-Master's Mates, J. H. Wainwright, A. R. Bashford, John Brown and G. H. French; Engineers: Second-Assistant, L. J. Allen; Third-Assistants, C. P. Gardner, P. H. Hendrickson, John Lloyd and J. W. Boynton.

STEAMER "JAMES ADGER."

Commander, Thomas H. Patterson; Acting-Assistant Surgeon, R. N. Atwood; Acting-Assistant Paymaster, W. W. T. Greenway; Acting-Master, R. O. Patterson; Acting-Ensigns, C. F. Keith and J. T. Chadwell; Acting-Master's Mates, W.W. Reed, George Couch and Wm. B. Dyer, Jr.; Engineers: Acting-First-Assistant, E. A. Whipple; Acting-Second-Assistant, John Carren; Acting-Third-Assistants, Andrew McTurk, Wm. Moran and W. R. Nutz; Acting-Gunner, J. H. Pennington.

IRON-CLAD STEAMER "PATAPSCO."

Commander, Daniel Ammen; Lieutenant, Henry Erben, Jr.; Assistant Surgeon, W. L. Wheeler; Acting-Assistant Paymaster, Daniel Leach, Jr.; Acting-Master, William Hamilton; Acting-Ensigns, J. T. Ross and Henry Kloeppel; Engineers: First-Assistant, B. B. H. Wharton; Second-Assistant, John B. Carpenter; Third-Assistants, J. W. Huxley and G. C. Cook.

STEAM-SLOOP "PAWNEE."

Commander, G. B. Balch; Lieutenant, F. M. Bunce; Surgeon, W. T. Hord; Assistant-Paymaster, F. R. Curtis; Acting-Masters, J. C. Champion and J. P. Lindsay; Acting-Ensign, Thomas Moore; Acting-Master's Mates, C. J. Rogers, J. G. Bache and A. A. Franzen; Engineers: Second-Assistant, Alfred Adamson; Third-Assistants, H. D. Sellman, Benjamin Bunce, W. J. Clark, Jr., John G. Brosnahan and Arthur Price; Boatswain, James Brown.

IRON-CLAD STEAMER "NAHANT."

Commander, John Downes; Lieutenant-Commander, D. B. Harmony; Assistant Surgeon, C. E. Stedman; Assistant Paymaster, Edwin Putnam; Acting-Master, Wm. W. Carter; Acting-Ensigns, C. C. Ricker and C. E. Clark; Engineers: First-Assistant, F. J. Lovering; Second-Assistant, T. H. Bordley; Third-Assistants, Abram Michener and W. S. Neal.

STEAMER "NORWICH."

Commander, James M. Duncan; Ensign, A. H. McCormick; Acting-Assistant Surgeon, G. E. McPherson; Acting-Assistant Paymaster, G. C. Boardman; Acting-Masters, C. F. Mitchell and R. B. Arrants; Acting-Master's Mates, Peter Mookler, A. J. L. Baker and G. M. Smith; Engineers: Acting-Second-Assistant, Nicholas Coyle; Acting-Third-Assistants, A. A. Odell, Benjamin Cobb, Jr., and W. W. Thain.

STEAM GUN-BOAT "SEBAGO."

Commander, John C. Beaumont; Lieutenant, H. M. Blue; Assistant Surgeon, John P. Quinn; Acting-Assistant Paymaster, S. G. Thorn; Acting-Masters, Thomas M. Gardner, Wm. C. Mallard and J. F. Anderson; Acting-Ensign, C. B. Dorrance; Acting-Master's Mate, E. D. Martin; Engineers: First-Assistant, S. F. Savage; Third-Assistants, G. E. Tower, W. H. De Hart, O. W. Allison and J. A. Bullard.

STEAMER "MOHAWK."

Lieutenant-Commander, Aaron K. Hughes; Assistant Surgeon, Geo. W. Woods; Acting-Assistant Paymaster, G. H. Andrews; Acting-Masters, G. R. Durand, Anthony Smally and Alex. Tillinghast; Acting-Master's Mates, T. Holland and T. J. Speights; Engineers: Acting-First-Assistant, Alfred Lapoint; Acting-Third-Assistants, William King, Geo. E. Whitney and R. K. Morrison.

STEAM GUN-BOAT "HURON."

Lieutenant-Commander, Geo. A. Stevens; Assistant Surgeon, C. H. White; Acting-Assistant Paymaster, Charles Stewart; Acting-Masters, J. W. Gill, W. H. Baldwin and Wm. A. Mills; Acting-Master's Mates, Peter O'Conner, Sam'l Delano, J. M. Blake and Wm. Henderson; Engineers: Acting-First-Assistant, Wm. Craig; Third-Assistants, Sylvanus McIntyre, J. P. Kelley, John Lowe and F. C. Russell.

STEAM GUN-BOAT "UNADILLA."

Lieutenant-Commander, S. P. Quackenbush; Assistant Surgeon, C. T. Hubbard; Acting-Assistant Paymaster, Geo. B. Tripp; Acting-Masters, Edw. Van Sice, W. L. Tuttle and P. N. Cruse; Acting-Ensign, R. M. Cornell; Acting-Master's Mates, Geo. E. Thomas, C. N. Hall and Wm. Field; Engineers: Second-Assistant, R. S. Talbot; Third-Assistants, R. H. Thurston, Fred'k Bull, Jr., and M. N. Knowlton.

STEAMER "FLAMBEAU."

Lieutenant-Commander, John H. Upshur; Lieutenant, Fred'k R. Smith; Acting-Assistant Surgeon, J. R. Layton; Acting-Assistant Paymaster, F. V. D. Horton; Acting-Masters, W. B. Sheldon, A. C. Megathlin and Wm. L. Kempton; Acting-Ensign, Gardner Cottrell; Acting-Master's Mate, J. F. Burrows; Engineers: Acting-First-Assistant, A. G. Pemble; Acting-Second-Assistant; Alex. Gillanders; Acting-Third-Assistant, William Richardson.

STEAM GUN-BOAT "OTTAWA."

Lieutenant-Commander, Wm. D. Whiting; Lieutenant, Geo. B. White; Assistant Surgeon, C. O. Carpenter; Acting-Assistant Paymaster, C. H. Noyes; Acting-Master, Samuel Hanes; Acting-Ensigns, J. L. Gamble and B. Mitchell; Acting-Master's Mates, E. M. Dimon, A. W. Tripp and David McKewan; Engineers: Second-Assistant, J. P. Sprague; Third-Assistants, E. W. Koehl, F. C. Prindle and R. B. Hine.

STEAM GUN-BOAT "SENECA."

Lieutenant-Commander, William Gibson; Lieutenant, Thomas C. Bowen; Assistant Surgeon, J. H. Macomber; Assistant Paymaster, G. W. Beaman; Acting-Masters, J. H. Rodgers, Henry Vaughan and G. W. Ewen; Acting-Master's Mates, E. W. Fiske, J. W. Paine and C. E. Culver; Engineers: Second-Assistant, J. W. De Krafft; Third-Assistants, H. H. Burritt, Thomas Lynch and R. T. Bennett.

STEAM GUN-BOAT "WISSAHICKON."

Lieutenant-Commander, John L. Davis; Lieutenant, Silas Casey; Assistant Surgeon, Henry Ackley; Acting-Assistant Paymaster, A. W. Kelsey; Acting-Masters, Geo. W. Parker and T. S. Steel; Acting-Ensign, J. W. Hathorn; Acting-Master's Mates, R. B. Crapo, G. E. Senter and A. L. Pendleton; Engineers: Acting-First-Assistant, J. F. Riley; Acting-

Third-Assistants, J. J. Newton, C. A. Stuart and H. J. Tarr.

STEAM GUN BOAT "MARBLEHEAD."

Lieutenant-Commander, R. W. Scott; Lieutenant, Geo. C. Remey; Assistant Surgeon, R. H. Kidder; Acting-Assistant Paymaster, J. H. Mulford; Acting-Masters, Geo. Martin and B. Allen; Acting-Master's Mates, D. S. Gross, B. O. Low, G. F. Winslow and Harry West; Engineers: Second-Assistant, Clark Fisher; Third-Assistants, W. L. Nicoll, James Long and H. W. Bulkley.

STEAMER "WATER WITCH."

Lieutenant - Commander, Austin Pendergrast; Acting-Assistant Surgeon, W. H. Pierson; Acting-Assistant Paymaster, L. G. Billings; Acting-Masters. C. W. Buck and H. S. Kimball; Acting-Ensign, J. M. Forsyth; Acting-Masters' Mates, J. J. Bigley and E. D. Parsons; Engineers: Acting-First-Assistant Samuel Genther; Acting-Third-Assistants, J. P. Cooper, John Hawkins and John Overn.

STEAMER "COMMODORE M'DONOUGH."

Lieutenant-Commander, George Bacon; Acting-Assistant Surgeon, J. W. Gibson; Acting-Assistant Paymaster, J. F. Quintard; Acting-Ensigns, Wm. Knapp and A. Buxton; Acting-Master's Mates, J. K. Winn, J. W. Goodwin and D. B. Hallett; Engineers: Acting-Third-Assistants, T. O. Reynolds, J. T. Booth and S. S. Hetrick.

STEAMER "ISAAC SMITH."

Acting-Lieutenant, F. S. Conover; Acting-Assistant Surgeon, G. H. Marvin; Acting-Assistant-Paymaster, F. C. Hills; Acting-Masters, J. W. Dicks and Robert Tarr; Acting-Ensigns, Whitman Chase, F. J. Brenton and H. S. Borden; Engineers: Acting-First-Assistant, Jacob Tucker; Acting-Second-Assistant, J. S. Turner; Acting-Third-Assistants, Wm. Ross and Erastus Barry.

STEAMER "DAWN."

Acting-Lieutenant, John S. Barnes; Acting-Assistant Surgeon, A. R. Holmes; Acting-Assistant Paymaster, R. C. Pierce; Acting-Masters, James Brown and J. W. Saunders; Acting-Master's Mates, A. Hartshorn, P. W. Morgan and Charles Myers; Engineers: Acting-First-Assistant, N. D. Bates; Acting-Third-Assistants, Sam'l Tomlinson, M. V. B. Darling and W. P. Ayres.

STEAMER "WHITEHEAD."

Acting-Volunteer-Lieutenant, Chas. A. French; Acting-Ensigns, J. M. Holmes and J. R. Dickinson; Acting-Master's Mates, T. E. Quayle and T. M. Nelson; Engineers: Acting-Second-Assistant, Moses Petersen; Acting-Third-Assistants, R. H. Ryan and G. B. McDermott.

BARK "GEM-OF-THE-SEA."

Acting-Volunteer-Lieutenant, J. B. Baxter; Acting-Assistant Surgeon, B. G. Walton; Acting-Assistant Paymaster, H. A. Strong; Acting-Masters, P. F. Coffin and H. B. Carter; Acting-Ensign, Samuel Bliss.

STEAMER "POTOMSKA."

Acting-Volunteer-Lieutenant, William Budd; Acting-Assistant Surgeon, S. C. Smith; Acting-Assistant Paymaster, F. H. Swan; Acting-Masters, R. P. Walter, B. W. Leary and Abner West; Acting-Master's Mates, J. D. Wells and Woodward Carter; Engineers: Acting-Second-Assistant, G. H. Guyer; Acting-Third-Assistants, C. A. Martine, Edwin Vaughan and W. L. McKay.

STEAMER "MEMPHIS."

Acting-Lieutenant, P. G. Watmough; Acting-Assistant Surgeon, S. H. Brown; Acting-Assistant Paymaster, W. E. Foster; Acting-Master, C. A. Curtis; Acting-Ensigns, E. A. Magone and J. B. Childs; Acting-Master's Mates, N. P. Dickinson, Silas Owens and J. M. Moore; Engineers: Acting-First-Assistant, J. L. Peake; Acting-Second-Assist-

ant, C. H. McCarty; Acting-Third-Assistants, H. L. Churchill, Chas. Hardwick and J. H. Vaile.

STEAMER "STETTIN."

Acting-Master, C. J. Van Alstine; Acting-Assistant Surgeon, J. S. Cohen; Acting-Assistant Paymaster, E. P. Heberton; Acting-Master, G. P. Lee; Acting-Ensigns, G. R. Bailey and Joseph Frost; Acting-Master's Mates, G. E. Short, Marcus Baird and G. N. Ryder; Engineers: Acting-Second-Assistant, J. B. Edwards; Acting-Third-Assistants, P. B. Robinson, Thomas Slater and S. B. Cornell.

BARK "RESTLESS."

Acting-Master, Wm. R. Brown; Acting-Assistant Surgeon, J. B. Calkins; Acting-Assistant Paymaster, W. S. Cushman; Acting-Masters, Maurice Digard and J. B. Rogers; Acting-Ensigns, Henry Eason, J. J. Russell and C. N. Hicks; Acting-Master's Mates, J. W. Mackie and Henry Oakley.

STEAMER "MADGIE."

Acting-Master, F. B. Meriam; Acting-Assistant Surgeon, Louis Michel; Acting-Assistant Paymaster, B. Huscull; Acting-Ensign, W. C. Underhill; Acting-Master's Mates, E. H. Vail, E. P. Blague and Jason Ryan; Engineers: Acting-Second-Assistant, G. L. Palmer; Acting-Third-Assistants, A. F. Rockfeller, Maurice McCarty and C. M. Goodwin.

BARK "MIDNIGHT."

Acting-Master, Nicholas Kirby; Acting-Assistant Surgeon, J. G. Bacon; Acting-Assistant Paymaster, F. Miller; Acting-Masters, S. D. Joy and Edwin Coffin; Acting-Ensign, Zera L. Tanner; Acting-Master's Mates, A. K. Noyes, Nicholas Pratt and Thos. Hollins.

SHIP "VALPARAISO."

Acting-Master, A. S. Gardner; Acting-Assistant Surgeon, A. B. C. Sawyer; Acting-Assistant Paymaster, Tracy Coit; Acting-Masters, J. W. Godfrey and Wm. Haffords; Acting-Master's Mates, John Blitz and Charles Cooke.

STEAMER "UNCAS."

Acting-Master, William Watson; Acting-Assistant Surgeon, G. H. Van Deusen; Acting-Assistant Paymaster, C. E. Taylor; Acting-Ensigns, Wm. L. Pavy; Acting-Master's Mate, Geo. Newlin; Engineers: Acting-Second-Assistant, C. Dandreau; Acting-Third-Assistant, Paul Dandreau.

STEAMER "WAMSUTTA."

Acting-Master, S. C. Gray; Acting-Assistant Surgeon, S. F. Quimby; Acting-Assistant Paymaster, Sam. Jorden; Acting-Master's Mates, G. F. Goodrich, Chas. Crayton and Thomas Kennedy; Engineers: Acting-Third-Assistants, Wm. A. Andress, John Seaman and W. J. Carman.

SHIP "COURIER."

Acting-Master, W. K. Cressy; Acting-Assistant Surgeon, W. R. Bonsall, Acting-Assistant Paymaster, M. W. Blake; Acting-Master, W. B. Stoddard; Acting-Ensigns, W. P. O'Brien and Wm. McDermott; Acting-Master's Mates, C. J. Hill and E. H. Shee.

BARK "FERNANDINA."

Acting-Master, Edward Moses; Acting-Assistant Surgeon, S. P. Boyer; Acting-Assistant Paymaster, T. N. Murray; Acting-Masters, R. B. Hines and C. C. Childs; Acting-Ensigns, Wm. H. Thomas; Acting-Master's Mates, J. B. Henderson, W. C. Gibson and Alonzo Townsend.

BARK "KINGFISHER."

Acting-Master, J. C. Dutch; Acting-Assistant Surgeon, W. H. Westcott; Acting-Assistant Paymaster, A. N. Blakeman; Acting-Ensigns, S. W. Rhodes and T. E. Chapin; Acting-Master's Mates, Tom. Nelson, H. G. Seaman and Frank Jordan.

BARK "BRAZILIERA."

Acting-Master, W. T. Gillespie; Acting-Assistant

Surgeon, S. N. Fisk; Acting-Assistant Paymaster, C. H. Longstreet; Acting-Masters, J. J. N. Webber and Jeremiah Chadwick; Acting-Master's Mates, W. N. Smith, J. B. F. Smith and W. H. Roberts.

STEAMER "COLUMBINE."

Acting-Master, J. S. Dennis; Acting-Ensign, C. S. Flood; Acting-Master's Mates, Edwin Daly and F. W. Sanborn; Engineers: Acting-Second-Assistant, W. H. Ogden; Acting-Third-Assistants, E. H. Lawrence and S. C. Clark.

TUG "DAFFODIL."

Acting-Master, E. M. Baldwin; Acting-Master's Mates, Francis Such and S. C. Bishop; Acting-Second-Assistant Engineer, J. P. Rossman; Acting-Third-Assistant Engineer, Geo. Cunningham.

TUG "DANDELION."

Acting-Master, A. S. Gardner; Acting-Master's Mate, John Brittingham; Engineers: Acting-Second-Assistant, J. M. Case; Acting-Third-Assistant, E. F. Hedden.

SCHOONER "C. P. WILLIAMS."

Acting-Master, S. N. Freeman; Acting-Master's Mates, F. W. Towne, John Gunn and F. E. Daggett.

SCHOONER "NORFOLK PACKET."

Acting-Ensign, G. W. Wood; Assistant-Surgeon, A. B. Judson; Acting-Assistant Paymaster, T. Merritt; Acting-Master's Mates, Leaken Barnes, Jackson Kingsley and Tim. Ryan.

SCHOONER "HOPE."

Acting-Master, J. E. Rockwell; Acting-Master's Mates, J. B. Williamson, J. C. Sanborn and Jacob Cochrane.

SCHOONER "PARA."

Acting-Master, E. C. Furber; Acting-Master's Mates, Edward Ryan, John McDonough and W. H. Morse.

YACHT "AMERICA."

Acting-Master, Jonathan Baker; Acting-Master's Mates, G. H. Wood, August Adler and W. H. Thompson.

SCHOONER "G. W. BLUNT."

Acting-Master, J. R. Beers; Acting-Master's Mates, B. D. Reed, A. H. Comstock and G. W. Cleaves.

STEAMER "RESCUE."

Acting-Ensign, C. A. Blanchard; Acting-Master's Mate, E. D. Smith; Engineers: Acting-Third-Assistants, M. C. Heath and G. W. Howe.

TUG "O. M. PETTIT."

Acting-Ensign, T. E. Baldwin; Engineers: Acting-Second-Assistant, Reuben McClenahan; Acting-Third-Assistant, Augustus Wandell.

IRON-CLAD "KEOKUK."

Lieutenant-Commander, A. C. Rhind; Lieutenant, Moreau Forrest; Acting-Master, James Taylor; Acting-Ensigns, W. H. Bullis, Ira T. Halstead and Alex McIntosh; Acting-Assistant Surgeon, Geo. D. Slocum; Acting-Assistant Paymaster, John Read; First-Assistant Engineer, Wm. H. King; Second-Assistant Engineer, J. H. Hunt; Third-Assistant Engineers, J. M. Emanuel and H. A. Smith.

LETTERS RELATING TO THE BATTLE OF PORT ROYAL AND OCCUPATION OF THE CONFEDERATE FORTS.

FROM FLAG-OFFICER DUPONT, COMMANDER STEEDMAN, AND LIEUTENANTS-COMMANDING C. R. P. RODGERS, AMMEN, STEVENS AND WATMOUGH—MAJOR JOHN G. REYNOLDS, U. S. M. C. —COMMENDATORY LETTERS OF SECRETARY WELLES—GENERAL ORDERS, ETC

REPORT OF FLAG-OFFICER DUPONT:

FLAG-SHIP "WABASH," OFF HILTON HEAD, }
PORT ROYAL HARBOR, Nov. 8, 1861. }

SIR—I have the honor to inform you that yesterday I attacked the enemy's batteries on Bay Point and Hilton Head (Forts Beauregard and Walker), and succeeded in silencing them after an engagement of four hours' duration, and driving away the squadron of rebel steamers under Commodore Tatnall. The reconnoissance of yesterday made us acquainted with the superiority of Fort Walker, and to that I directed my especial efforts, engaging it at a distance of, first, eight, and afterwards six, hundred yards. But the plan of attack brought the squadron sufficiently near Fort Beauregard to receive its fire, and the ships were frequently fighting the batteries on both sides at the same time.

The action was begun on my part at twenty-six minutes after 9, and at half-past 2 the American ensign was hoisted on the flag-staff of Fort Walker, and this morning at sunrise on that of Fort Beauregard.

The defeat of the enemy terminated in utter rout and confusion. Their quarters and encampments were abandoned without an attempt to carry away either public or private property. The ground over which they fled was strewn with the arms of private soldiers, and officers retired in too much haste to submit to the encumbrance of their swords.

Landing my marines and a company of seamen, I took possession of the deserted ground, and held the forts on Hilton Head till the arrival of General Sherman, to whom I had the honor to transfer its occupation.

We have captured forty-three pieces of cannon, most of them of the heaviest calibre and of the most improved description.

The bearer of these dispatches will have the honor to carry with him the captured flags and two small brass field-pieces, lately belonging to the State of South Carolina, which are sent home as suitable trophies of the day. I enclose herewith a copy of the general order, which is to be read in the fleet to-morrow morning at muster. A detailed account of this battle will be submitted hereafter.

I have the honor to be, very respectfully,
Your most obedient servant,
S. F. DUPONT,
Flag-Officer, Commanding
South Atlantic Blockading Squadron.
Hon. GIDEON WELLES,
Secretary of the Navy,
Washington, D. C.

P. S.—Bearer of dispatches will also carry with him the first American ensign raised upon the soil of South Carolina since the rebellion broke out.
S. F. D.

GENERAL ORDER NO. 2.

FLAG-SHIP "WABASH," HILTON HEAD, }
PORT ROYAL BAY, Nov. 8, 1861. }

It is the grateful duty of the Commander-in-chief to make a public acknowledgment of his entire commendation of the coolness, discipline, skill and gallantry displayed by the officers and men under his command in the capture of the batteries on Hilton Head and Bay Point, after an action of four hours' duration.

The flag-officer fully sympathizes with the officers and men of the squadron in the satisfaction they must feel at seeing the ensign of the Union flying once more in the State of South Carolina, which has been the chief promoter of the wicked and unprovoked rebellion they have been called upon to suppress.　　　　S. F. DuPont,
Flag-Officer, Commanding
South Atlantic Blockading Squadron.

REPORT OF FLAG-OFFICER DUPONT.

United States Flag-ship "Wabash," }
Port Royal Harbor, S. C., Nov. 11, 1861. }

Sir—I have the honor to submit the following detailed account of the action of the 7th of November:

From the reconnoissance of the 5th we were led to believe that the forts on Bay Point and Hilton Head were armed with more than twenty guns each, of the heaviest calibre and longest range, and were well constructed and well manned, but that the one on Hilton Head was the strongest. The distance between them is two and two-tenths nautical miles—too great to admit of their being advantageously engaged at the same time, except at long shot. I resolved, therefore, to undertake the reduction of Hilton Head (or, as I shall hereafter call it, Fort Walker) first, and afterwards to turn my attention to Fort Beauregard—the fort on Bay Point. The greater part of the guns of Fort Walker were presented upon two water-fronts, and the flanks were but slightly guarded, especially on the north, on which side the approach of an enemy had not been looked for.

A fleet of the enemy—consisting of seven steamers, armed, but to what extent I was not informed further than that they carried rifle-guns—occupied the northern portion of the harbor, and stretched along from the mouth of Beaufort River to Scull Creek.

It was high water on the 7th instant at 11h. 35m. A. M. by the tables of the Coast Survey.

These circumstances—the superiority of Fort Walker and its weakness on the northern flank, the presence of the rebel fleet, and the flood-tide of the morning—decided the plan of attack and the order of battle.

The order of battle comprised a main squadron ranged in line ahead, and a flanking squadron, which was to be thrown off on the northern section of the harbor, to engage the enemy's flotilla and prevent them taking the rear ships of the main line when it turned to the southward, or cutting off a disabled vessel.

The main squadron consisted of the frigate "Wabash," Commander C. R. P. Rodgers, the leading ship; the frigate "Susquehanna," Captain J. L. Lardner; the sloop "Mohican," Commander S. W. Godon; the sloop "Seminole," Commander J. P. Gillis; the sloop "Pawnee," Lieutenant-Commanding R. H. Wyman; the gun-boat "Unadilla," Lieutenant-Commanding N. Collins; the gun-boat "Ottawa," Lieutenant-Commanding T. H. Stevens; the gun-boat "Pembina," Lieutenant-Commanding J. P. Bankhead; and the sailing sloop "Vandalia," Commander F. S. Haggerty, towed by the "Isaac Smith," Lieutenant-Commanding J. W. A. Nicholson.

The flanking squadron consisted of the gun-boat "Bienville," Commander Charles Steedman, the leading ship; the gun-boat "Seneca," Lieutenant-Commanding Daniel Ammen; the gun-boat "Curlew," Lieutenant-Commanding P. G. Watmough; the gun-boat "Penguin," Lieutenant-Commanding T. A. Budd; and the gun-boat "Augusta," Commander E. G. Parrott, the closing ship of that line.

The plan of attack was to pass up mid-way between Forts Walker and Beauregard (receiving and returning the fire of both) to a certain distance, about two and a half miles north of the latter. At that point the line was to turn to the south around by the west, and close in with Fort Walker, encountering it on its weakest flank, and at the same time enfilading, in nearly a direct line, its two waterfaces. While standing to the southward the vessels were head to tide, which kept them under command, whilst the rate of going was diminished.

When abreast of the fort, the engine was to be slowed and the movement reduced to only as much as would be just sufficient to overcome the tide, to preserve the order of battle by passing the batteries in slow succession, and to avoid becoming a fixed mark for the enemy's fire. On reaching the extremity of Hilton Head and the shoal ground making off from it, the line was to turn to the north by the east, and, passing to the northward, to engage Fort Walker with the port battery nearer than when first on the same course. These evolutions were to be repeated. The accompanying plan will explain the preceding description.

The captains of the ships had been called on board and instructed as to the general formation of the lines and their own respective places.

At 8 o'clock the signal was made to get under way. At 8h. 10m. the ship, riding to the flood, tripped her anchor; and at 8h. 30m. the ship turned, and was headed in for the forts. At 9 the signal was made for close order. At 9h. 26m. the action was commenced by a gun from Fort Walker, immediately followed by another from Fort Beauregard. This was answered at once from this ship, and immediately after from the "Susquehanna." At 10 o'clock the leading ship of the line turned to the southward, and made signal to the "Vandalia" (which ship, in tow of the "Isaac Smith," was dropping astern, and was exposed, without support, to the fire of Fort Beauregard) to join company. At 10h. 15m. the signal was made for closer action, the "Wabash" slowly passing Fort Walker at a distance, when abreast, of eight hundred yards. At 11 the signal was made to get into and preserve stations, and at 11h. 15m. to follow the motions of the Commander-in-chief.

Standing to the northward, nearly in the line shown in the diagram, the ship's head was again turned to the southward, and she passed the guns of Fort Walker at a distance less than six hundred yards (the sights were adjusted to five hundred and fifty yards). At 11h. 30m. the enemy's flag was shot away.

The second fire with the starboard guns of the "Wabash," and Captain Lardner, in the "Susquehanna," my second in command, who always kept so near as to give me the entire support of his formidable battery, seems at this short distance to have discomfited the enemy. Its effect was increased by the shells thrown from the smaller vessels at the enfilading point. It was evident that the enemy's fire was becoming much less frequent, and finally it was kept up at such long intervals and with so few guns as to be of little consequence.

After the "Wabash" and "Susquehanna" had passed to the northward, and given the fort the fire of their port battery the third time, the enemy had entirely ceased to reply and the battle was ended.

At 1h. 15m. the "Ottawa" signalled that the works at Hilton Head were abandoned. This information was, a few minutes later, repeated by the "Pembina." As soon as the starboard guns of this ship and the "Susquehanna" had been brought to bear a third time on Fort Walker, I sent Commander John Rodgers on shore with a flag of truce. The hasty flight of the enemy was visible, and was reported from the tops. At twenty minutes after two Captain Rodgers hoisted the flag of the Union over the deserted post. At forty-five minutes after two I anchored and sent Commander C. R. P. Rodgers on shore with the marines and a party of seamen to take possession and prevent, if necessary, the destruction of public property.

The transports now got underway, and came rapidly up, and by nightfall Brigadier-General Wright's brigade had landed and entered upon the occupation of the ground.

I have said, in the beginning of this report, that the plan of attack designed making the reduction of Fort Walker the business of the day. In passing to the northward, however, we had improved every opportunity of firing at long range on Fort Beauregard. As soon as the fate of Fort Walker was decided, I dispatched a small squadron to Fort Beauregard to reconnoitre and ascertain its condition, and to prevent the rebel steamers returning to carry away either persons or property.

Near sunset it was discovered that the flag upon this fort was hauled down, and that the fort was apparently abandoned.

At sunrise the next day the American ensign was hoisted on the flag-staff at Fort Beauregard by Lieutenant-Commanding Ammen.

The "Pocahontas," Commander Percival Drayton, had suffered from the gale of Friday night so badly as not to be able to enter Port Royal until the morning of the 7th. He reached the scene of action about 12 o'clock, and rendered gallant service by engaging the batteries on both sides in succession.

Lieutenant-Commanding H. L. Newcomb, of the "R. B. Forbes," which vessel had been employed in towing in the "Great Republic," arrived in time to take good part in the action.

And, finally, the tug "Mercury," Acting-Master Martin commanding, employed his single Parrott gun with skill and effect.

After congratulating you upon the success thus far of our expedition, which had its origin in the counsels of the Department, and which the Department has fostered and labored to render efficient, the gratifying duty remains to be performed of according to each and all their due share of praise for good conduct in their encounter with the enemy. This duty, though most welcome, is still delicate.

I am well aware that each one did his part in his place, and when I discriminate it is in cases that necessarily fell under my own immediate observation. I have no doubt that all would have embraced and improved the same opportunities of distinction; and in noticing those who were made prominent by their stations, or who were near me during the action, I am showing no invidious preference.

The General Order No. 2, already forwarded to the Department, expressed in general terms my commendation of the gallantry and skill of the officers and men.

The reports of the commanding officers of the several ships, herewith enclosed, do justice to those under them; while the results speak for the commanding officers themselves. The names of the latter are mentioned in the beginning of this dispatch. I refer with pleasure to them again. They did their duty to my satisfaction, and I am most happy to bear testimony to their zeal and ability.

The officers of this ship, to whom I am deeply indebted, will be mentioned by her commander, C. R. P. Rodgers, in his special report.

It affords me the highest gratification to speak of the manner in which this ship was handled during the engagement, owing, in a great measure, to the professional skill, the calm and rapid judgment and the excellent management of Commander C. R. P. Rodgers. His attention was divided between this duty and the effective service of the guns, which involved the estimation of distances, the regulation of fuses and the general supervision of the divisions. His conduct and judicious control of everything within the sphere of his duty, though no more than

was to be expected from his established reputation, impressed me with a higher estimation than ever of his attainments and character.

I had also an opportunity to remark the admirable coolness and discrimination of the first-lieutenant, T. G. Corbin. The good order, discipline and efficiency, in every respect, of this ship are, to a great extent, the results of his labors as executive officer, and they were conspicuous on this occasion. Acting-Master Stiles, acting as pilot, was devoted and intelligent in the performance of his duties; and the third-assistant engineer, Missieveer, who attended the bell, was prompt and always correct.

Acting-Master S. W. Preston, acting as my flag-lieutenant, displayed throughout the day an undisturbed intelligence and a quick and general observation, which proved very useful. His duties as signal-officer were performed without mistake. This gentleman and the young officers—Mr. R. H. Lamson, Mr. J. P. Robertson and Mr. J. H. Rowland, who were also under my eye, in immediate command of the pivot-guns and spar-deck divisions—sustained the reputation and exhibited the benefits of the Naval Academy, the training of which only could make such valuable officers of such young men.

Commander John Rodgers, a passenger in this ship, going to take command of the steamer "Flag," volunteered to act upon my staff. It would be difficult for me to enumerate the duties he performed, they were so numerous and varied, and he brought to them all an invincible energy and the highest order of professional knowledge and merit. I was glad to show my appreciation of his great services by allowing him the honor to hoist the first American flag on the rebellious soil of South Carolina.

My secretary, Mr. Alexander McKinley, was by my side throughout the engagement, making memoranda under my direction. He evinced the same cool bravery which he once before had an opportunity of showing under fire in a foreign land. It gives me pleasure to mention him here as a gentleman of intelligence, of great worth, and of heartfelt devotion to his country.

I have yet to speak of the chief of my staff and fleet-captain, Commander Charles H. Davis. In the organization of our large fleet before sailing, and in the preparation and systematic arrangement of the duties of our contemplated work—in short, in all the duties pertaining to the flag-officer—I have received his most valuable assistance. He possesses the rare quality of being a man of science and a practical officer, keeping the love of science subordinate to the regular duties of his profession. During the action he watched over the movements of the fleet, kept the official minutes, and evinced that calmness in danger, which, to my knowledge, for thirty years has been a conspicuous trait in his character.

I have the honor to be, sir, respectfully,
Your most obedient servant,

S. F. DuPont,
Flag-Officer, Commanding
South Atlantic Blockading Squadron.

Hon. Gideon Welles,
Secretary of the Navy,
Washington.

REPORT OF LIEUTENANT-COMMANDING C. R. P. RODGERS.

United States Steamer "Wabash," }
Port Royal, Nov. 10, 1861. }

Sir—Although I know that the conduct of the officers and crew of the "Wabash" are warmly commended by you in the action of the 7th instant, yet, in obedience to your demand for a special report, I respectfully submit the following:

The men did their duty, as became American

seamen, with calmness, precision and resolute earnestness. They fought their guns with energy, and pointed them with admirable coolness.

The three gun-deck divisions of 9-inch guns, under Lieutenants Luce, Upshur and Barnes, were commanded by those officers in a manner which illustrated the highest power of both men and guns, and exhibited the greatest effect of manhood and training. I beg leave to commend these officers in terms of the warmest praise, both for skill and conduct; and also Lieutenant Irwin, who, in command of the powder division, did everything that a brave and earnest man could do to make his ship efficient.

Acting-Masters Lamson, Rowland and Robertson, in command of the spar-deck guns, followed the example of their seniors on the gun-deck, and did honor to the Naval School, which had, at their early age, trained them to do such efficient service in battle.

Acting-Masters W. H. West, Rockwell, Gregory and Palmer, stationed at the various divisions, evinced patriotic zeal and courage.

Mr. Coghlan, the boatswain, not only did his duty in the sixth division, but also skillfully served the rifled boat-guns, with which he did good service.

The gunner, Mr. Stewart, in the magazine, and the carpenter, Mr. Boardman, with his shot-plugs, did their duty manfully.

The engine and steam, during the whole action, were managed with consummate skill, which did great credit to Chief Engineer King and his assistants. Third-Assistant Engineer Missieveer, who stood upon the bridge by my side during the action, impressed me very favorably by his cool intelligence and promptness.

All the other officers, in their various departments, did their whole duty faithfully.

Acting-Master Stiles rendered most valuable service by his careful attention to the steerage and soundings of the vessel, and by his skill and vigilance in keeping the ship clear of the shoals. I desire to commend him especially to your notice.

My clerk, Mr. Blydenburgh, acted as my aide, and did prompt and good service.

The two oldest seamen in the ship, John Dennis and Henry L. Coons, both quartermasters—the one at the wheel and the other at the signals—well represented the gallantry of their class and generation.

The marines were used as a reserve, and, whenever called upon, rendered prompt assistance at the guns, with the good conduct that has always characterized their corps.

It only remains for me to speak of the executive officer, Lieutenant Corbin, who has filled that post since the "Wabash" was commissioned. The admirable training of the crew may, in a high degree, be attributed to his professional merit; and his gallant bearing and conspicuous conduct throughout the whole action were good illustrations of the best type of a sea-officer.

At the close of the action the "Wabash" was engaged with Fort Walker at a distance of six hundred yards or less, and her officers and men may well feel satisfied with the precision of their aim and the overwhelming power of their rapid fire. Eight hundred and eighty shells were fired from her guns, chiefly with 5-second fuses. Some grape was fired with good effect from the 10-inch gun, in the latter part of the action.

I have to thank that most brave and distinguished officer, Captain C. H. Davis, the captain of the fleet, for the aid he gave me when not engrossed by the important duties of his special station; and I desire to pay the same tribute to Commander John Rodgers, who, being a passenger on board, had volunteered to serve on your staff, and never failed to give me most valuable assistance. Nor must I fail to bear witness to the gallant bearing and striking coolness of your young flag-lieutenant, Mr.

Preston. I thank you, sir, in the name of the officers and men of your flag-ship, for the example you gave us.

I have the honor to be, very respectfully,
Your obedient servant,
C. R. P. RODGERS,
Lieutenant-Commanding U. S. Steamer "Wabash."
Flag-Officer S. F. DuPont,
Commanding South Atlantic Blockading Squadron.

REPORT OF COMMANDER CHARLES STEEDMAN.

UNITED STATES STEAMER "BIENVILLE," }
PORT ROYAL HARBOR, Nov. 8, 1861. }

SIR—I have the honor to report that in the action of yesterday with the forts this vessel was struck several times, one shot passing through and through her, another striking bulwarks, forward, unfortunately mortally wounding two men, Patrick McGuigan and Alexander Chambers (since dead), and slightly wounding three others, Peter Murphy, Alexander Finey and William Gilchrist, while gallantly fighting at their guns.

The other shots did but little damage. It affords me the utmost gratification to bring to your notice the excellent conduct of the officers and men. It would be impossible to particularize the bearing of any one officer or man, such was their gallant conduct.

During the engagement, we fired from this vessel eighty-four 32 solid shots, thirty-nine 32-pound shell, and sixty-two rifle-shell.

I am, sir, very respectfully, your obedient servant,
CHARLES STEEDMAN,
Commander.

Flag-Officer S. F. DuPont,
Commander-in-Chief of Naval Forces, etc., etc.

REPORT OF LIEUTENANT-COMMANDING DANIEL AMMEN.

UNITED STATES GUN-BOAT "SENECA," }
PORT ROYAL, S. C., Nov. 15, 1861. }

SIR—In obedience to your order of this date, I have the honor to make the following report:

On Monday, the 4th, this vessel entered Port Royal, and sounded the channel until within three miles of Bay Point, when we were signalled from the "Ottawa" to return and anchor, which we did at 4 P. M., near her, about a mile further out and a cable's length nearer the batteries. The fleet generally, at this time, was standing in and anchoring. An hour later, three rebel steamers approached us and opened fire with rifled guns, but at a distance which proved ineffective. The "Ottawa," "Pembina" and this vessel got underway, and, standing in at an angle, allowing our heavy guns to bear, drove them before us. At sunset we returned, and anchored as before.

At daylight on Tuesday several rebel steamers again attacked us. We got underway, and, obeying signals from the "Ottawa," accompanied her, with the "Pembina," "Curlew," "Isaac Smith," and afterwards the "Pawnee," drove them until we were within a cross-fire of the batteries of Hilton Head and Bay Point, both opening upon us. No material damage was sustained. A heavy shell—or shot, probably—struck the vessel on the port-side, but I have been unable to find it, and probably will not until we get in a sea-way. Our rigging was struck three times. The object being effected—that of ascertaining the strength of the rebel batteries—we returned and anchored, as before, about half-past 8.

Two or three hours after, the rebel steamers again approached us, and, finding that they were within range, I had the satisfaction of firing an 11-inch shell at the flag-ship, which was seen from aloft, as well as by several persons on deck, to strike just abaft the starboard wheel-house. The vessel put into Bay Point, and on returning, or rather showing herself, in the afternoon, had a large white plank forward of the port wheel-house, probably where the shell went out. On the morning of the 7th, obeying signal, we took position assigned us in the line, and, passing up, delivered our fire at Bay Point, and on arriving out of fire of the batteries, made chase—as directed by instructions—to the rebel steamers. They, being river boats, soon left us, and I had the chagrin of having wasted several shells at them at ineffective distance.

Returning to the attack on Hilton Head, we passed so near to the shore as to be fired upon by riflemen, who kept quiet on being fired on by our Parrott 20-pounder. From an enfilading position we began with 10-second fuses, and, closing up, found ourselves within effective 5-second range. As to the latter part of the action, we were within howitzer range, and were using both howitzers effectively, as well as 11-inch gun and Parrott 20-pounder.

During the engagement we fired sixty-three 11-inch shells, 9 with 15-second fuses, 28 with 10-second fuses and 26 with 5-second fuses. Thirty-three projectiles from the Parrott-gun were also fired, and twelve 24-pounder shrapnel.

I am sorry to say that the Parrott shell appears defective; its flight was wild and range short. As I fired once myself, I know they were not to be depended on, and the captain of the gun was much disappointed at his results.

During the engagement an officer was kept at the mast-head, whose duty it was to report our firing, by which we were governed. I have, therefore, reason to believe that our fire was effective.

Few of our crew have served before in a vessel-of-war, and as we went into commission only three weeks before the engagement, Mr. Sproston, the first-lieutenant of the vessel, fired nearly all the 11-inch shells with his own hands. Of him, as well as of the officers and crew generally, I have to express my warmest commendations, and my surprise that amidst such a shower of shot and shells we received no damage.

I am, very respectfully,

Your obedient servant,

DANIEL AMMEN,
Lieutenant-Commanding " Seneca."

Flag-Officer SAMUEL F. DuPONT,
*Commanding South Atlantic Blockading
Squadron.*

REPORT OF LIEUTENANT-COMMANDING T. H. STEVENS.

UNITED STATES GUN-BOAT " OTTAWA," }
OFF HILTON HEAD, Nov. 8, 1861. }

SIR—I have the honor to report that, as soon as the "Ottawa," under my command, could take up her position in the order of battle, I weighed anchor, following in the wake of our leading vessel. When abreast of Bay Point battery, finding that our 11-inch gun was doing good execution, I stopped the engine to engage it, and threw about a dozen shells in and about the fortifications. Discovering, however, that we were under a cross-fire, I steamed up to take distance, in the order assigned. About this time a 32-pound shot struck the "Ottawa" in the port-waist, just abaft the pivot-gun (11-inch), wounding severely Mr. Kerne, one of the acting-masters (who subsequently lost his leg by amputation), one other man seriously, and four others slightly, and doing considerable damage to the deck of the vessel, the coamings of the forward coal-bunker hatch, and splitting two of the upperdeck beams.

Discovering, as we ranged up with the fort on Hilton Head, that we occupied an enfilading position, I continued to occupy it until the enemy deserted their batteries, when, being nearest to them, I signalized the same to the flag-ship and

stopped firing, about 500 yards from the fort. While engaging at a distance of about 1,000 yards, and when within 300 yards of the beach of Hilton Head, some of the riflemen of the enemy commenced firing upon us, when we opened with the howitzers charged with shrapnels, and quickly dispersed them.

It only remains for me to notice the good conduct, coolness and gallantry of both officers and men upon the occasion, who behaved with the steadiness of veterans, and to commend them to your favorable notice, and the notice of the Department, as worthy supporters of the cause we have espoused.

Very respectfully,

T. H. STEVENS,
Lieutenant-Commanding, U. S. N.

Flag-Officer S. F. DuPONT,
*Commanding South Atlantic Blockading
Squadron.*

ORDER FOR "UNADILLA" AND OTHER SHIPS TO TAKE POSSESSION OF BEAUFORT, S. C.

FLAG-SHIP, "WABASH," }
PORT ROYAL HARBOR, Nov. 10, 1861. }

SIR—It has been reported to me by Lieutenant-Commanding Ammen that, on taking possession of the town of Beaufort, under my orders of the 8th instant, he found that most of the white inhabitants had abandoned the town, and that the negroes were committing excesses and destroying private property.

You will proceed with the most convenient dispatch in the gun-boat "Unadilla," under your command, to Beaufort, where you will find the gun-boat "Pembina" (Lieutenant-Commanding Bankhead), and the gun-boat "Curlew" (Lieutenant-Commanding Watmough), and assume command of the station.

You will employ your forces in suppressing any excesses on the part of the negroes; and you will take pains to assure the white inhabitants that there is no intention to disturb them in the exercise of their private rights, or in the enjoyment of their private property.

Acting on this principle of conduct, you will pursue any other measures that may tend to create confidence, to bring back the people to their houses and to re-establish order.

You will please send Lieutenant-Commanding Watmough to report to me to-morrow morning in person upon the actual state of things, and upon the steps you may have found it expedient to take.

Any information you may have it in your power to collect, concerning the state of the surrounding country, will be valuable.

S. F. DuPONT,
*Flag-Officer, Commanding South Atlantic
Blockading Squadron.*

Lieutenant NAPOLEON COLLINS, U. S. N.,
*United States Gun-boat " Unadilla," Port
Royal Harbor.*

LETTER COMMENDING THE OFFICERS OF THE "CURLEW" BY ACTING-LIEUTENANT-COMMANDING WATMOUGH.

UNITED STATES GUNBOAT " CURLEW, }
PORT ROYAL, S. C., Nov. 17, 1861. }

SIR—It affords me great pleasure to speak with praise of the general gallantry, coolness, and cheerfulness of the officers and men under my command during the several actions with the rebel squadron and batteries on the 4th, 5th, and 7th instants. Master H. E. Mullan, acting executive officer, rendered efficient service by his readiness and zeal. Acting-Master C. A. Curtis, in charge of the battery of 32s, is deserving of all praise for the spirit he instilled the men with, and effectualness and accuracy of the divisional firing. Acting-Master Spavin's steadiness at the wheel merits commendation. Acting-Master H. N. Parish, who had charge of the Parrott pivot-gun, disabled early in the action of the 7th by the enemy's shot, afterwards assisted with his crew at the broadside battery.

The paymaster, Wm. A. A. Kerr, acting as signal-officer, by his coolness and watchfulness was of material assistance; he also kept a careful record of the incidents of the several actions. Messrs. Emory, Swasey, McConnell and Lloyds, engineers of the vessel, with great difficulties to contend against, in the general unfitness of the engine, boilers and condensing apparatus for such rough service, managed to carry us through the action, for which I was thankful.

Fortunately, the readiness of our medical officer, Mr. Perucer, was not called upon. Master's Mate Duncan, acting as gunner, provided a bountiful supply of ammunition for the battery.

I have the honor to be, sir, your obedient servant,

PEN. G. WATMOUGH,
Acting-Lieutenant-Commanding.

Flag-Officer S. F. DuPONT,
Commanding South Atlantic Squadron.

Respectfully forwarded,   S. F. DuPONT,
Flag-Officer.

COMMENDATORY LETTER TO FLAG-OFFICER DUPONT.

NAVY DEPARTMENT,
November 16, 1861.

SIR—It is with no ordinary emotion that I tender to you and your command the heartfelt congratulations and thanks of the Government and the country for the brilliant success achieved at Port Royal. In the war now raging against the Government in this most causeless and unnatural rebellion that ever afflicted a country, high hopes have been indulged in the Navy, and great confidence reposed in its efforts.

The results of the skill and bravery of yourself and others have equalled and surpassed our highest expectations. To you and your associates, under the providence of God, we are indebted for this great achievement by the largest squadron ever fitted out under that flag, which you have so gallantly vindicated, and which you will bear onward to continued success. On the receipt of your dispatches announcing the victory at Port Royal, the Department issued the enclosed general order, which, with this letter, you will cause to be read to your command.

I am, respectfully, etc.,

GIDEON WELLES.

Flag-Officer SAMUEL F. DUPONT,
Commanding South Atlantic Blockading Squadron.

GENERAL ORDER.

NAVY DEPARTMENT,
November 13, 1861.

The Department announces to the Navy and to the country its high gratification at the brilliant success of the combined Navy and Army forces, respectively commanded by Flag-officer S. F. Du-Pont and Brigadier-General W. T. Sherman, in the capture of Forts Walker and Beauregard, commanding the entrance of Port Royal harbor, South Carolina.

To commemorate this signal victory. it is ordered that a national salute be fired from each Navy Yard at meridian on the day after the receipt of this order.

GIDEON WELLES,
Secretary of the Navy.

FLAG-OFFICER DUPONT'S REPORT CONCERNING THE MARINE BATTALION, NOV. 15.

FLAG-SHIP "WABASH,"
PORT ROYAL HARBOR, S. C., Nov. 15, 1861.

SIR—I avail myself of the first moment of leisure to transmit to you the report of Major John George Reynolds, commanding the battalion of marines attached to my squadron, in which he relates all the circumstances attending the loss of the chartered steamer "Governor," and the rescue of himself and his command by the frigate "Sabine," Captain Ringgold.

The Department will find this report exceedingly interesting, and will be gratified to learn that the conduct of the officers and of nearly all the men of the battalion was such as to command Major Reynolds' approval, as it will, I doubt not, receive the favorable notice of the Department. The established reputation and high standing of Major Reynolds might almost dispense with any observations of my own upon the bravery and high sense of honor which he displayed in disputing with Mr. Weidman (though not a seaman) the privilege of being the last to leave the wreck.

I have the honor to be, sir, respectfully, your obedient servant,

S. F. DuPONT,
Flag-Officer, Commanding South Atlantic Blockading Squadron.

Hon. GIDEON WELLES,
Secretary of the Navy, Washington.

REPORT OF MAJOR JOHN GEO. REYNOLDS, U. S. M. C.

UNITED STATES SHIP "SABINE,"
AT SEA, November 8, 1861.

SIR—I have the honor to report that the marine battalion under my command left Hampton Roads on transport steamboat "Governor," on the morning of Tuesday, the 29th of October, with the other vessels of the fleet, and continued with them, near the flag-ship "Wabash," until Friday, the 1st of November.

On Friday morning, about 10 o'clock, the wind began to freshen, and by 12 or 1 blew so violently that we were obliged to keep her head directly to the wind, and thereby leave the squadron, which apparently stood its course. Throughout the afternoon the gale continued to increase, though the "Governor" stood it well till about 4 o'clock. About this time we were struck by two or three heavy seas, which broke the port hog-brace in two places, the brace tending inward. This was immediately followed by the breaking of the hog-brace on the starboard side. By great exertions on the part of the officers and men of the battalion, these braces were so well stayed and supported that no immediate danger was apprehended from them. Up to this time the engine worked well. Soon after, the brace-chains, which supported the smoke-stack, parted, and it went overboard. Some three feet of it above the hurricane-deck remained, which enabled us to keep up the fires. Soon after the loss of the smoke-stack, the steam-pipe burst. After this occurrence we were unable to make more than fourteen pounds of steam, which was reduced, as soon as the engine commenced working, from three to five pounds. The consequence was, we had to stop the engine frequently in order to increase the head of steam. At this period the steamer was making water freely, but was easily kept clear by the pump of the engine, whenever it could be worked. About 5 o'clock we discovered a steamer with a ship in tow, which we supposed to be the "Ocean Queen." To attract attention, we sent up rockets, which signals she answered. When our rockets, six in all, were gone, we kept up a fire of musketry for a long time, but the sea running high and the wind being violent, she could render us no assistance. She continued on her course, in sight the greater part of the night. About 3 o'clock Saturday morning the packing around the cylinder-head blew out, rendering the engine totally useless for some time. The engine was finally put in running order, although it went very slowly. The rudder-chain was carried away during the night, the water gaining constantly on us, and the boat laboring violently. At every lurch we apprehended the hog-braces would be carried away, the effect of which would have been to tear out the whole starboard-side of the boat, collapse the boiler, and carry away the wheel-house. Early in the morning the rudder-head broke, the engine was of very little use—the water still gaining on us rapidly—and we entirely at the mercy of the wind. It was only by the un-tiring exertions of our men that we were kept afloat. Nearly one hundred of them were kept constantly pumping and bailing, and the rest were holding fast to the ropes which supported the hog-braces. Towards morning, the weather, which during the night had been dark and rainy, seemed to brighten and the wind to lull. At daybreak two vessels were seen on our starboard-bow, one of which proved to be the United States steamer "Isaac P. Smith," commanded by Lieutenant J. W. A. Nicholson, of the Navy. She descried our signal of distress—which was ensign half-mast, union down—and stood for us. About 10 o'clock we were hailed by the "Smith," and given to understand that, if possible, we would all be taken on board. A boat was lowered from her, and we were enabled to take a hawser. This, through the carelessness of Captain Litchfield, of the "Governor," was soon cut off or unavoidably let go. The water was still gaining on us. The engine could be worked but little, and it appeared our only hope of safety was gone. The "Smith" now stood off, but soon returned, and by 1 o'clock we had another hawser from her, and were again in tow. A sail (the propeller-bark "Young Rover", which had been discovered on our starboard-bow during the morning, was soon within hailing-distance. The captain proffered all the assistance he could give, though at the time he could do nothing, owing to the severity of the weather. The hawser from the "Smith" again parted, and we were once more adrift. The "Young Rover" now stood for us again, and the captain said he would stand by us to the last, for which he received a heartfelt cheer from the men. He also informed us a large frigate was ahead, standing for us. He then stood for the frigate, made signals of distress, and returned. The frigate soon came into view, and hope once more cheered the hearts of all on board the transport. Between 2 and 3 o'clock the United States frigate "Sabine" (Captain Ringgold) was within hail, and the assurance given that all hands would be taken on board. After a little delay, the "Sabine" came to anchor. We followed her example, and a hawser was passed to us. It was now late in the day, and there were no signs of an abatement of the gale. It was evident that whatever was to be done for our safety must be done without delay. About 8 or 9 o'clock the "Sabine" had payed out enough chain to bring her stern close to our bow. Spars were rigged out over the stern of the frigate, and every arrangement made for whipping our men on board, and some thirty men were rescued by this means. Three or four hawsers and an iron stream-cable were parted by the plunging of the vessels. The "Governor," at this time, had three feet of water, which was rapidly increasing. It was evidently intended by the commanding officer of the "Sabine" to get the "Governor" alongside, and let our men jump from the boat to the frigate. In our condition this appeared extremely hazardous. It seemed impossible for us to strike the frigate without instantly going to pieces. We were, however, brought alongside, and some forty men succeeded in getting on board the frigate ; one was crushed to death between the

frigate and the steamer in attempting to gain a foot-hold on the frigate.

Shortly after being brought alongside the frigate, the starboard quarter of the "Sabine" struck the port-bow of the "Governor," and carried away about twenty feet of the hurricane-deck from the stem to the wheel-house. The sea was running so high, and we were being tossed so violently, it was deemed prudent to slack up the hawser and let the "Governor" fall astern of the frigate with the faint hope of weathering the gale till morning. All our provisions and other stores—indeed, every movable article—were thrown overboard, and the water-casks started, to lighten the vessel. From half-past 3 till daylight the "Governor" floated in comparative safety, notwithstanding the water was gaining rapidly on her. At daybreak, preparations were made for sending boats to our relief, although the sea was running high, and it being exceedingly dangerous for a boat to approach the guards of the steamer; in consequence, the boats laid off, and the men obliged to jump into the sea and then hauled into the boats. All hands were thus providentially rescued from the wreck, with the exception, I am pained to say, of one corporal and six privates, who were drowned or killed by the crush or contact of the vessels.

Those drowned were lost through their disobedience of orders in leaving the ranks or abandoning their posts. After the troops were safely re-embarked, every exertion was directed to securing the arms, accoutrements, ammunition and other property which might have been saved after lightening the wreck. I am gratified in being able to say nearly all the arms were saved and about half the accoutrements. The knapsacks, haversacks and canteens were nearly all lost. About ten thousand rounds of cartridges were, fortunately, saved, and nine thousand lost. Since being on board this ship every attention has been bestowed by Captain Ringgold and his officers towards recruiting the strength of our men, and restoring them to such condition as will enable us to take the field at the earliest possible moment. Too much praise cannot be bestowed upon the officers and men under my command—all did nobly. The firmness with which they performed their duty is beyond all praise. For forty-eight hours they stood at ropes and passed water to keep the ship afloat. Refreshments in both eating and drinking were passed to them at their posts by non-commissioned officers. It is impossible for troops to have conducted themselves better under such trying circumstances. The transport continued to float some hours after she was abandoned, carrying with her when she sunk, I am grieved to say, company books and staff returns. In order to complete the *personnel* of the battalion, I have requested Captain Ringgold to meet a requisition for seven privates, to which he readily assented. I considered this requisition in order, as I have been informed by Captain Ringgold it is his intention, or orders were given, for his ship to repair to a Northern post, in which event he can be easily supplied, and my command, by the accommodation, rendered complete, in order to meet any demand you may make for our services.

Under God, we owe our preservation to Captain Ringgold and the officers of the "Sabine," to whom we tender our heartfelt thanks for their untiring labors while we were in danger, and their unceasing kindness since we have been on board the frigate.

This report is respectfully submitted.

I am, Commodore, very respectfully, your obedient servant, JOHN GEO. REYNOLDS,
Commanding Battalion Marines, Southern Division.

Flag-Officer SAMUEL F. DUPONT,
Commanding United States Naval Expedition, Southern Coast, U. S. N. America.

THE CAPTURE OF TYBEE ISLAND, GEORGIA.

FLAG-SHIP "WABASH," }
PORT ROYAL HARBOR, Nov. 25, 1861. }

SIR—I have the honor to inform the Department that the flag of the United States is flying over the territory of the State of Georgia.

As soon as the serious injury to the boilers of the "Flag" had been repaired, I dispatched Commander John Rodgers to Tybee entrance, the mouth of Savannah River, to report to Commander Missroon, the senior officer, for a preliminary examination of the bars, and for the determination of the most suitable place for sinking the proposed obstructions to the navigation of the river.

Captain Rodgers was instructed to push his reconnoissance so far as to "form an approximate estimate of the force on Tybee Island, and of the possibility of gaining access to the inner bar;" and further, "if the information acquired by this reconnoissance should be important, to return and communicate it to me immediately."

I was not surprised when he came back and reported that the defences on Tybee Island had probably been abandoned. Deeming it proper, however, to add the "Seneca," Lieutenant Commanding Ammen, and "Pocahontas," Lieutenant-Commanding Balch, to his force, I directed him to renew his approaches with caution, and, if no opposition was met with, to occupy the channel.

I am happy now to have it in my power to inform the Department that the "Flag," the "Augusta," and the "Pocahontas," are at anchor in the harbor abreast of Tybee beacon and light, and that the "Savannah" has been ordered to take the same position.

The abandonment of Tybee Island, on which there is a strong Martello tower, with a battery at its base, is due to the terror inspired by the bombardment of Forts Beauregard and Walker, and is a direct fruit of the victory of the 7th inst.

By the fall of Tybee Island, the reduction of Fort Pulaski, which is within easy mortar distance, becomes only a question of time.

The rebels have themselves placed sufficient obstructions in the river at Fort Pulaski, and thus by the co-operation of their own fears with our efforts, the harbor of Savannah is effectually closed.

I have the honor to be, sir, very respectfully, your most obedient servant,

S. F. DUPONT, *Flag-Officer,*
Commanding South Atlantic Blockading Squadron.

Hon. GIDEON WELLES,
Secretary of the Navy,

NOTE.—The reports of the other commanding officers do not contain any statements of historical interest, being general in their character, and are therefore omitted.

CHAPTER XXXIV.

Further Operations of Flag-Officer Goldsborough in the Sounds of North Carolina.—Importance of Gun-boats in Co-operating Expeditions of the Army and Navy.—Commander S. C. Rowan's General Order to the Officers and Men under his Command.—Operations in the Blackwater River under Lieutenant Flusser. —The Gun-boats Extricate Themselves from a Dilemma.—Notice of Lieutenant Cushing, his Attack on the Town of Jacksonville and his Gallant Defence of the "Ellis."—Capture of Fort Macon by the Army and Navy.—Surrender of Yorktown, May 5, 1862.—Co-operation of the Navy.—Attack on Sewell's Point by Flag-Officer Goldsborough.—Evacuation of Sewell's Point and Craney Island.—"Merrimac" blown up by the Confederates, June 11.—"Susquehanna," "Seminole" and "Dakota" anchor before Norfolk.—The Retreating Enemy set Fire to the Navy Yard.—Attack on Drury's Bluff by Commander John Rodgers with the "Galena," the "Monitor," and other Vessels. — Remarks on the Services of the North Atlantic Squadron.—Flag-Officer Goldsborough and Commander Rowan receive the Thanks of Congress.—Attack on Hamilton by Lieutenant Flusser.—Attack on Confederate Troops at Washington, N. C., by Lieutenant R. T. Renshaw.—Blowing up of the Army Gun-boat "Picket."— Exhibit of the Work done by the North Atlantic Squadron under Flag-Officer Goldsborough.

A S soon as Flag-officer Goldsborough received the news of the battle of the "Monitor" and "Merrimac," he returned to Hampton Roads to superintend matters in that quarter, leaving Commander S. C. Rowan in charge of the sounds of North Carolina.

The gallant service performed by Commander Rowan, in the capture of Newburn and Elizabeth City, has already been related, though complete justice has not been done to the officers and men who embarked in frail vessels never intended to go under the fire of a battery, and who exhibited as much courage as if they were fighting behind the bulwarks of stout frigates. The manner in which the little flotilla in the sounds of North Carolina operated is worthy of all praise, and confers the highest honors on the able commander and his officers, who, scorning all the dangers of an intricate navigation, concealed riflemen, and masked batteries, pushed on up the sounds and rivers wherever a Confederate flag could be heard of or a Confederate gun was mounted, and who never failed to achieve

victory when there was an enemy to engage.

There was a large army force in the sounds, commanded by brave and energetic officers, but it is no disparagement to them to say that, without the hearty co-operation of the gun-boats, they would not have achieved half the success they did. It became evident, at a very early period of the war, that no army operations along rivers or sounds could be successful unless aided by gun-boats. Most of these vessels carried guns of heavy calibre which could not have been dragged along by an army, and these guns always proved to be more than a match for the lines of defence thrown up by the Confederates all along the rivers and sounds. The Federal Army could not have held these works unless the gun-boats were at hand to drive off or capture the improvised vessels-of-war, which it has been seen were equally as well armed as the Union vessels, and for a time made a sturdy opposition to the advance of the Navy.

It must not be supposed that the Federal officers and men conquered the enemy without a struggle, or that their victories were easy ones; if they were, it was because the enemy were not prepared for the bold dashes that were made upon them, and did not suppose that any officer would lead a weakly built flotilla right up to the mouths of heavy batteries, around which the enemy's gun-boats had assembled for safety and protection.

The good account his officers and men gave of themselves in their various encounters with the enemy drew from Commander Rowan the following General Order, which is as remarkable for the handsome compliments it pays to all who served under him, as for its brevity and truthfulness; he could have said no more had he used a folio of words:

[ORDER.]
UNITED STATES STEAMER "DELAWARE,"}
OFF ELIZABETH CITY.   }
FEBRUARY 11th, 1862. }

The commander of the flotilla in Albemarle Sound avails himself of the earliest moment to make a public acknowledgment of the coolness, gallantry and skill displayed by the officers and men under his command in the capture and destruction of the enemy's batteries and squadron at Cobb's Point.

The strict observance of the plan of attack and the steady but onward course of the ships, without returning a shot until within three-fourths of a mile of the fort, excited the admiration of our enemies.

The undersigned is particularly gratified at the evidence of the high discipline of the crews in refraining from trespassing in the slightest degree upon the private property of defenceless people in a defenceless town; the generous offer to go on shore to extinguish the flames applied by the hands of a vandal soldiery to the houses of their own defenceless women and children, is a striking evidence of the justice of our cause, and must have its effect in teaching our deluded countrymen a lesson in humanity and civilization.

S. C. ROWAN,
Commanding Flotilla, Albemarle Sound,

For the present we must discontinue the narrative of operations in the sounds of North Carolina.

As has been seen, there was scarcely a large gun left in the hands of the enemy, of the many that were mounted when the little naval flotilla entered the sounds through Hatteras Inlet, January 19, 1862, and the preparations which were made by the Navy Department for carrying on the war in this important section of the Confederate strongholds had been carried out with a judgment and success which entitled all concerned to the highest praise.

In the latter part of September, 1862, a joint expedition of the Army and Navy was prepared to operate against Franklin, a small town on the Blackwater River. It was agreed between the military commander, General Dix, and the commander of the gun-boats, that the attack should be made on the 3d of October.

The expedition was under the command of Lieutenant C. W. Flusser, on board the steamer "Commodore Perry." Acting-Lieutenant Edmund R. Colhoun commanded the "Hunchback," and Acting-Master Charles A. French the "Whitehead."

On the morning of October 3d, 1862, the three above-mentioned steamers got under-way and proceeded up the river, which was so crooked and narrow in some places that these vessels, small as they were, could not turn the bends without the aid of hawsers. At 7 o'clock the "Perry," being ahead, came to one of three short turns, and, while engaged in running out a line, a heavy fire was opened upon her from a steep bluff, almost overhead, by a body of the enemy's concealed riflemen.

The guns of the steamer could not be brought to bear, and the only way to escape the fire of the riflemen was to work by the point and obtain a position where the great guns could be brought into play. This was attempted, but the vessel ran ashore. At this moment, a daring color-bearer of the enemy started towards the gun-boat, trying to get his companions to follow him and board her. But he was instantly shot down and the enemy were driven back to their cover.

In a few moments the gun-boat was off the bottom, and pushed ahead until she could bring her guns to bear, and from this position cover the passage of the other two steamers. Having passed the turn in safety, these vessels joined the "Commodore Perry" above, where they were still fired upon from the bluff, without being able to make any effective return.

To make their position more critical, they now came upon a barricade which they found it impossible to pass. The enemy soon noticed the dilemma of the gun-boats, and began to flatter themselves that they were about to have an easy victory. A large body of men collected below the Federal vessels and commenced felling trees across the narrow stream to cut off their retreat, after which they calculated to capture them all by driving the men from the decks with their rifles.

In his anxiety to get ahead, Lieutenant Flusser had not waited for the troops, and he now found himself caught in a trap. He had got into the difficulty through an error of judgment, and the only way to get out of it seemed to be to fight until the troops came up.

It was most difficult to work the guns under such a terrific fire from concealed riflemen without a great loss of life, but there was no alternative. Flusser threw 11-inch shells towards the town of Franklin, while with the forward 32-pounder he poured grape and canister into the woods on his left. With the after 32-pounder and a field-gun he fought the enemy on the right and with his 9-inch gun aft he shelled the bluff, from whence the weight of the enemy's fire proceeded. Thus he fought on like a lion at bay, scattering shell, grape and canister on all sides, while his men were exposed to a deadly fire from marksmen no one could see.

The other steamers were not idle, but followed the tactics of their leader, and their rapid fire disconcerted the aim of the riflemen.

When a lull occurred, the steamers made a dash down the river, and although their decks were still swept by the enemy's fire, they succeeded in passing the bluffs. During this movement the Union commanders kept their men under cover, and thus saved many lives. When they came to the fallen timber they put on a full head of steam and pierced their way through and over it. It was "neck or nothing" with them, and it was only through great exertions that they succeeded in getting beyond the range of the enemy's fire by nightfall.

The "Commodore Perry" lost two killed and eleven wounded (a severe loss for so small a vessel). The "Hunchback" had two killed and one wounded.

This was not a great battle, but it was more trying than some great battles have been, and was accompanied by much more danger. It shows that the gun-boat commanders were of good metal, determined to sell their lives as dearly as possible. There is nothing in the world so harassing as to be caught in a narrow river under such circumstances, and there is scarcely anything to justify it, unless the vessels are supported by a land force. In the above case the land force unfortunately did not come up.

Flusser was a cool and daring officer, and his name has already been mentioned several times in the course of this narrative. He was always to be found where fighting was going on.

There was another young officer in the North Atlantic squadron at this time, Lieutenant William B. Cushing, who made a name for himself by his total disregard of danger.

He would undertake the most desperate adventures, where it seemed impossible for him to escape death or capture, yet he almost always managed to get off with credit to himself and with loss to the enemy. He commanded the small gun-boat "Ellis," and in November, 1862, it struck him that he would enter New River Inlet, push up the river, sweep it clear of vessels, capture the town of Jacksonville or Onslow Court-house, take the Wilmington mail and destroy any salt-works he could find on the banks. He expected to surprise the enemy on going up, and then fight his way out.

Five miles from the mouth of the inlet he came in sight of a vessel bound out with a load of cotton and turpentine. The enemy set fire to her in order to prevent her falling into Cushing's hands ; but this officer did not waste time over her. After assuring himself that she was thoroughly ignited, and that the owner could not return and extinguish the flames, he proceeded on his way up the river. He reached the town of Jacksonville, landed, threw out pickets and placed guards over the public buildings.

Jacksonville was the county-seat of Onslow County, and quite an important place. Here he captured 25 stand of arms in the Court-house, and a large mail in the post-office. He also took two schooners and confiscated the negroes of the Confederate postmaster.

Jacksonville being situated on the main road to Wilmington, it was not long before the news of Cushing's performances reached the latter place, and the Confederates at once took measures to prevent his escape.

As soon as he had finished with the town, Cushing dropped down with his two prizes until he came in sight of a camp on the river-bank, which he shelled very thoroughly. The enemy opened fire on the "Ellis" with rifles, but they were soon dispersed. Night coming on, the pilots declined to take the vessels out of the river until daylight next morning. In consequence, Lieutenant Cushing anchored five miles from the outer bar, took his prizes alongside and prepared for an attack. All night the signal fires of the enemy could be seen on the banks, and the Union commander had very little doubt that he would be attacked at daylight.

As soon as possible next morning Cushing got underway, and had nearly reached the most dangerous place in the river when the enemy opened upon him with two field-pieces. He placed his vessels in position, hoisted the battle-flag at the fore, his crew gave three cheers and he went into action. In one hour he had driven the enemy from his guns and from the bluff, and he passed on within a hundred yards of their position without being fired at.

Up to this time the fortune of the Federal party had been in the ascendant, but they were destined to meet with an accident which changed the fortunes of the day, and resulted in the destruction of the "Ellis." About 500 yards from the bluff, the pilots, making a mistake in the channel, ran the steamer hard and fast aground. All hands set to work at once to lighten her and every effort was made to get her afloat, but without avail. When the tide fell, Cushing sent a party on shore to take possession of the artillery which had been abandoned by the enemy, but found it gone. There was nothing now left but for Cushing to save his crew from the overwhelming force which he knew would soon be brought to bear upon the gun-boat. So, "all hands" were "called to muster" and told that they could go on board the schooners and get off down the river and over the bar. He called for six volunteers to stay with him and defend the steamer until the last. The volunteers came forward at once; also two Master's Mates, Valentine and Barton.

The schooners were ordered to drop down the channel out of range of any guns the enemy might mount on the bluff, and there to wait the termination of the action, and if the "Ellis" was destroyed to proceed to sea.

Early in the morning the enemy opened fire upon the steamer with three heavy guns and one Whitworth. It was a cross-fire and very destructive. Cushing replied as well as he could, but in a short time the engine was disabled and the vessel so much cut up that the only alternative was surrender or a pull of a mile and a half in an open boat under the enemy's fire.

The last expedient was adopted. The "Ellis" was set on fire in five places, and leaving the battle-flag flying, Cushing trained his guns upon the enemy so that the vessel could fight to the last, started down the river, reached the schooners and put to sea. A party of Confederates attempted to cut off his retreat, but they were unsuccessful, and the sailors gave three cheers and hoisted the Union flag as they sailed out over the bar.

Cushing brought away all his men, his rifled howitzer and ammunition, the ship's stores and clothing, the men's bags and hammocks, and most of the small-arms. As he crossed the bar the "Ellis" blew up and the enemy were disappointed in getting her.

Cushing was famous for this kind of adventure, and he will be heard of frequently here-

ATTACK ON FORT MACON BY THE NAVAL FLOTILLA.

after. He was what might be called a "Free-lance," who was always ready to perform any act of daring; and although he was not always successful, the honor of the flag never suffered at his hands.

There were plenty of young officers in the Navy who were equally brave, and with more judgment, but Cushing was of a peculiar temperament, always doing something to astonish his commanders, and whether fortunate or not in his undertakings, he was sure to create a sensation.

The account of the loss of the "Ellis" is given as an illustration of this young officer's character and his fancy for seeking adventures. There was nothing particularly to be gained by his trip up New Inlet River, and there was a chance of losing his vessel. He lost her, but, in doing so, showed his spirit of adventure, risking his life and the lives of his men, and then escaping with his crew, arms, provisions and clothing, setting fire to his vessel and training her guns upon the enemy so that she might give them a broadside as she went out of existence.

Among the captures made by co-operating vessels of the North Atlantic squadron was that of Fort Macon, Beaufort Harbor, N C. A combined expedition of the Army and Navy attacked this place on April 25, 1862, and after a bombardment of some hours, by land and sea, the American flag was hoisted over the fort.

The naval part of the expedition consisted of the following vessels under the command of Commander Samuel Lockwood:

Steamer "Daylight" (flag-ship).

Steamer "State of Georgia." — Commander J. F. Armstrong.

Steamer "Chippewa."—Lieutenant-Commanding A Bryson.

Bark "Gemsbok." — Acting - Volunteer-Lieutenant Edward Cavendy.

Steamer "Ellis."—Lieutenant-Commanding C. L. Franklin.

The gun-boats attacked the fort by passing it in an ellipse and firing when abreast of it.

Major-General Burnside commanded the land forces, and to him the fort surrendered.

The losses were small on both sides, which was rather remarkable, as Commander Lockwood states that the interior of the fort was literally covered with fragments of bombs and shells, and many of the guns disabled.

Beaufort was a valuable acquisition to the North Atlantic squadron, and a fine rendezvous for the smaller vessels engaged in blockading the coast.

With regard to the bombardment, the reports of both Army and Navy are somewhat obscure, but it appears that a good deal of

damage was inflicted upon the fort in spite of a heavy sea, which rendered the firing from the vessels somewhat uncertain. The gun-boats themselves suffered little damage.

On May 5, 1862, Yorktown was evacuated by the Confederates, and General McClellan telegraphed to Captain Wm. Smith of the "Wachusett" to assist in communicating with Gloucester and to send some of the gun-boats up York River to reconnoitre.

The flotilla was immediately underway, and proceeded to Gloucester Point, where the American flag was hoisted. The "Corwin," Lieutenant T. S. Phelps, and the "Currituck," Acting-Master W. F. Shankland, pushed on some twelve miles further up. Commander T. H. Patterson, in the "Chocura," proceeded up the river as far as

LIEUTENANT-COMMANDER (NOW REAR-ADMIRAL) T. S. PHELPS.

West Point, which had been deserted by the enemy. White flags were flying all along the river. A few small vessels were captured, but the enemy had fled from that quarter.

About the 7th of June, Flag-officer Goldsborough was ordered by the President to make an attack on Sewell's Point and to ascertain the possibility of landing a body of troops thereabouts. The wooden vessels were to enfilade the works, while the "Monitor," accompanied by the "Stevens," went up as far as the wrecks to engage the "Merrimac" in case she made her appearance.

The "Monitor" had orders to fall back into fair channel-way and only to engage the "Merrimac" seriously in such a position that the "Minnesota," together with the merchant-ships prepared for the occasion, could run her down if an opportunity presented itself. The ramming-vessels were directed to run at the "Merrimac" at all hazards, and the "Baltimore," an unarmed steamer with a curved bow of light draft and high speed, was kept in the direction of the "Monitor," to throw herself at the "Merrimac" forward or aft, as circumstances might require.

The demonstration was made, and the ships shelled Sewell's Point, and ascertained the fact that the number of the enemy's guns had been materially reduced and did not amount to over seventeen.

Whether it was this demonstration, or the fact that the Confederates found that they could not hold their works at Sewell's Point in the face of even a small number of troops, or that they did not care to stand a shelling from the Federal ships, is not

COMMANDER (NOW REAR-ADMIRAL) A. L. CASE, U. S. N.

REAR-ADMIRAL GOLDSBOROUGH'S FLEET CAPTAIN.

known, but on the 10th of May, 1862, Norfolk surrendered to a Federal force under General Wool, who had landed at Willoughby's Point. All the works on Sewell's Point were evacuated, and also those at Craney Island, and early in the morning of the 11th the "Merrimac" was blown up.

Thus ended the farce of the Confederate occupation of Norfolk. It should never have fallen into their hands, and could have been retaken at any time by a force of ten thousand men and the vessels at Hampton Roads.

Flag-officer Goldsborough, supposing that Sewell's Point and Craney Island might not have surrendered, ordered all the fleet to get underway and proceed to the attack of those places, but remembering that when the army had got into their rear that the enemy would no longer stay there, he sent

Lieutenant Selfridge in a tug to Sewell's Point, and Commander Case in another to Craney Island, to ascertain the position of affairs.

Selfridge landed at Sewell's Point and found that the enemy had departed, on which he hoisted the American flag on the ramparts. When Commander Case arrived at Craney Island he also found the forts deserted. Two Confederate flags were still flying over the works, which he hauled down and replaced with the American colors.

The "Susquehanna," "Seminole," "Dakota" and "San Jacinto" proceeded up to Norfolk without difficulty, and cast their anchors before the town. The deserting Confederates played the same part that had been played by the Federal forces when they gave up the Navy Yard. They set fire to all the useful buildings, and most of them were destroyed; the commandant's and the officers' quarters being left intact, in hopes that the Confederate officers might have a chance some day to live in them again.

Thus Norfolk became the head quarters of the Navy, as it ought to have been from the beginning of the war to the end. There had been no good reason for deserting the place, for there were as many ships in front of the town at the time when the Navy Yard was burned, as on May 9, 1862, while the Confederates were much weaker. The retreat from Norfolk was caused by a panic which sometimes seizes upon people, and leads them to do things at the moment for which they rebuke themselves when they come to their senses.

The re-occupation of Norfolk Navy Yard was a great convenience to the North Atlantic squadron, which had been obliged to send most of its vessels to Philadelphia and New York for repairs, and now the operations up the James River could be carried on more effectively.

On May 18, 1862, Flag-officer Goldsborough reports to the Department an engagement which took place on the James River between some gun-boats under Commander John Rodgers and a heavy battery on Drury's Bluff (a high point commanding a long reach of the river).

The vessels which attacked this stronghold were the iron-clad (so-called) "Galena," Commander John Rodgers, the "Monitor," Lieutenant W. N. Jeffers, and the unarmored steamers "Aroostook," "Port Royal" and "Naugatuck."

These vessels moved up the James River on the 15th of May and encountered no artificial impediments until they reached Drury's Bluff, eight miles below Richmond, where the Confederates had erected batteries and placed two separate obstructions in the river. These barriers were made by driving piles, and sinking vessels loaded with stone. It was said that the enemy's gun-boats, "Jamestown" and "York-town," were among the vessels sunk.

It cannot be doubted that these obstacles were too formidable for the gun-boats to pass, unless they could succeed in dis-mounting the guns on Drury's Bluff, which was not easily done. Any attempt to re-move these obstructions (even if the fort was silenced) without the aid of a large land force would have been unavailing, for the banks of the river all along, up to and past the bluff, were lined with rifle-pits filled with marksmen, who made it almost impossible for the Federals to stand at their guns.

The "Galena," leading, ran within 600 yards of the batteries, and as near to the obstructions as it was deemed prudent to go. She let go her anchor, and swinging with a spring across the channel, not more than twice the length of the ship, opened fire on the enemy at Drury's Bluff. The wooden vessels anchored about 1,300 yards below, and the "Monitor" anchored just above the "Galena," but finding that her guns could not be elevated sufficiently to reach the forts, she dropped to a position to enable her to do so.

After an action of three hours and fifteen minutes, the "Galena" had expended nearly all her ammunition, having but six charges left for the rifled Parrott gun and not a 9-inch shell filled. Thirteen men had been killed and eleven wounded on board. Sig-nal was made to discontinue the action, and the vessels dropped out of fire.

The "Monitor" was unhurt, though struck once squarely on the turret by an 8-inch shot, and twice on her side armor. The rifled 100-pounder burst on board the "Nau-gatuck," and disabled her.

Commander Rodgers reported that the "Galena" was not shot-proof, exactly what was predicted of her when she was on the stocks. The vessel was so much cut up that it was reported she would have to be thor-oughly repaired before she could go to sea.

It was intended to ascertain by this ac-tion whether the "Monitor" or "Galena" was the best vessel for fighting forts. It was settled in favor of the "Monitor," which was not damaged seriously.

It was a one-sided battle altogether, for the forts on Drury's Bluff could not be taken by a naval force alone. They could only be taken by a combined attack of the Army and Navy.

If it was intended to show the enemy that the courage of naval officers would under-take anything, this was amply demon-strated by the cool manner in which the vessels anchored and went at what they must have known was hopeless work. There was not an officer there who did not know

that, no matter how often they might drive the enemy away from their guns by an overwhelming fire, that they would just step inside their bomb-proofs until a good opportunity offered to return to their guns.

The Confederates knew that no naval force would attempt to land and scale the bluff, 200 feet high. In fact, it was simply good practice for the enemy; and whatever defects their works showed were remedied in twenty-four hours.

That Commander Rodgers and his officers showed the greatest courage, in attacking works so far superior to them in every way, every one will admit. The "Galena" was simply a slaughter-house, and the other vessels, except the "Monitor," would have fared worse than the "Galena" had not the enemy been intent upon destroying the vessel which carried the divisional flag at her main.

Commander Rodgers still thought that the "Galena" and "Monitor" could reduce the works if they had plenty of ammunition; but experience had by this time taught most of our commanders that very few expedi-tions of this kind were successful unless the Army and Navy acted together, and it was only the desire of a brave man to try and get even with the enemy.

This expedition convinced Commander Rodgers "that an army could be landed on the James River within ten miles of Richmond, on either bank, and that this land force with naval co-operation could march into Petersburg; that such a move would cause the evacuation of Drury's Bluff in its then condition, and other forts along the James River; that obstructions could then be removed, and perhaps the gun-boats might work their way on to Richmond."

This was the hardest fight that had oc-curred on the James. The duties on that river were, as a rule, monotonous in the ex-treme, and the officers of the Navy were de-lighted with this opportunity to show that the same spirit existed at this point as else-where to perform the most hazardous un-dertakings.

The work of the North Atlantic squadron in the James and York rivers was deficient in those dashing strokes which had been made in other squadrons, and which so at-tracted the attention of the Northern peo-ple. With the single exception of the affair of the "Merrimac," nothing had been done by the northern portion of this squadron to attract much notice, yet it was in some re-spects the most important squadron afloat. The security of Washington greatly de-pended on its efficiency, for, in the event of a move of the Confederates upon the Cap-ital, a large force of gun-boats could be sent up the Potomac and prevent the enemy from marching directly upon the city, and give time to assemble troops enough to meet him in the field. Washington City would have been cut off entirely in its river communications with the North, in the earlier part of the war, but for the presence of this squadron at Hampton Roads, where it was within easy reach. Without it, the Grand Army of the Potomac could not have been moved so successfully to the Peninsular; and it is scarcely yet forgotten how, in the most trying times, when that army

its great discipline, the energy of the officers and the skill of its commanders, it not only often arrested defeat, but sometimes changed defeat into victory.

It might appear to some people that there was a larger number of vessels lying idle in Hampton Roads than was necessary, and that these might in the earlier part of the war have pushed on up the James and kept that river free of batteries until the Federals could mount guns enough afloat to

COMMANDER (AFTERWARDS REAR-ADMIRAL) JOHN RODGERS.

seemed to be in danger of annihilation, the Navy was at hand to give shelter under its guns to our retiring and weary troops, and drive back the excited and victorious foe, who would have driven our soldiers into the river, or made them lay down their arms.

These things are mentioned not for the purpose of claiming undue credit for the Navy, but to show that it was always on hand to perform its part of the duty in putting down the rebellion, and that, through

push on up to Richmond. But war cannot be carried on without mistakes, and these occurred in the Navy as well as in the Army; but we will venture to say that there were not near so many in the Navy. The sins of the Navy were more those of omission than commission. The situation was a new one to *all* concerned, and the stern reality could only be learned by wading through battle-fields, or in the slaughter-pens of gun-boats when under the fire of heavy artillery.

Owing to the change of the head-quarters of the North Atlantic squadron, reports of naval occurrences were not always received at the Navy Department in regular order, and being quickly recorded as they were received, it happens that many of the events of the war are narrated out of their proper order, and the earlier performances are behind the later ones. This cannot well be helped, and it would probably make confusion if the writer attempted to remedy the evil.

When General McClellan had captured Yorktown he almost immediately moved part of his army up the river in transports in the direction of West Point.

On the 7th of May, 1862, Lieutenant T. H. Stevens reported that, hearing the firing of heavy cannon, he proceeded on board the

LIEUTENANT LEONARD PAULDING.

"Wachusett," for the purpose of joining his command, which he had passed on the way up; when General Franklin telegraphed him that he was attacked by a superior force and desired the assistance of the gun-boats — "that he wanted immediate support," etc.

At this moment the gun-boat "Maratanza" was engaged, two miles below, in endeavoring to haul the gun-boat "Marblehead" off a shoal. Receiving Captain William Smith's orders to go on board the "Maratanza" and bring her into action, Stevens took a boat from the "Wachusett" and joined his vessel.

The "Wachusett" and "Sebago" went into action with some batteries that had been posted on hills to prevent the advance of the Union Army. The gun-boats shelled the Confederate artillery for nearly an hour

with their heavy rifled guns, when the enemy retired. It was the opinion of General Franklin's officers that the rapid and accurate fire of the gun-boats "was greatly instrumental in saving the Army from severe disaster, if not defeat."

The gun-boats followed along on the flanks of the Army, ready to aid it in every way, until the river became so narrow and crooked that they could go no farther, and in returning had to drop stern foremost.

General Franklin's object in advancing on West Point was to cut off the retreat of the Confederates from Yorktown. But he encountered a much larger force than he had expected, and but for the gun-boats would have been roughly handled.

Acting-Rear-Admiral S. P. Lee assumed command of the North Atlantic squadron on July 16, 1862, taking the place of Flag-officer Goldsborough, who was promoted to the rank of Rear-Admiral, and relieved at his own request. Though the services of the latter officer had not been brilliant, yet his duties had been well performed and his record is that of a faithful, zealous officer, who, if he had been employed in a wider field of operations, would no doubt have made his name more conspicuous. The President considered that his services in the sounds of North Carolina entitled him to a vote of thanks from Congress and sent in his name, and afterwards that of Commander Rowan.

Goldsborough was a Southerner by birth, and although no officer deserves particular credit for standing by the Government that had taken care of him for fifty years, yet he showed an example of live patriotism which entitled him to respect and to any honors his country had to bestow.

From July 11th up to November 30th, 1862, there was little done by the North Atlantic squadron except in the sounds of North Carolina, which for a time were under the control of Commander Rowan.

The operations in the sounds, after the time mentioned, were not of a very important nature, but as they form part of the history of the war we will give a brief sketch of them. There was great danger in some of the expeditions, and good judgment and gallantry shown in all.

Lieutenant C. W. Flusser, who has already figured as a brave and energetic officer, was a leading spirit in every enterprise set on foot. He seemed to delight in making explorations where little was to be gained except hard knocks, and it is remarkable that in the severe river-fighting to which he was exposed he did not sooner lose his life.

On the 9th of July, 1862, he left Plymouth for Hamilton in the steamer "Commodore Perry," having taken on board Captain W.

W. Hammell, Company F., 9th New York Volunteers, and twenty of his men, with the steamers "Shawsheen" and "Ceres" in company; the latter vessel having on board Second-Lieutenant Joseph A. Green and ten men.

While ascending the river, at 1 o'clock P. M., the flotilla was fired upon from the south bank by riflemen. Flusser returned the fire and pushed on, expecting to meet the enemy at Hamilton in force. The vessels were under fire from the banks and rifle-pits for two hours, during which time they had to run very slowly, looking out for batteries. When they reached Hamilton, the enemy, who had been firing from concealed places, retreated, being afraid to meet Flusser's little force of 100 sailors and soldiers in the open field.

The only reward which they received for all their exposure was the capture of an unimportant town and a small schooner.

The loss on board the vessels, fortunately, was small (two killed and ten wounded), but these casualties often repeated ran up in time to a large number. In this warfare not much was to be gained except gunshot wounds. There was no prize-money, but the officers and men of this expedition were spoken of in the highest terms of praise, which cheered them on in the absence of other rewards.

Acting-Volunteer-Lieutenant John Macdearmid and Acting-Master Thomas J. Woodward, who commanded the steamers "Ceres" and "Shawsheen" on this expedition, were highly spoken of.

Acting-Lieutenant R. T. Renshaw, commanding U. S. steamer "Louisana," reports that while at Washington, N. C., on the 6th of September, 1862, the enemy attacked that place in force and opened on his vessel "with volleys of musketry." "That he returned the fire with grape and shell, killing a number and finally driving them back."

He also followed them up with shell and killed a number in their retreat.

During this action the Army gun-boat "Picket" blew up, killing the captain and 18 men, and wounding others, who were taken on board the "Louisiana" and properly cared for.

Acting-Master Edward Hooker is well spoken of for the manner in which he managed the guns of the "Louisiana." The action must have lasted some time, as 137 shot, shell, stands of grape, and howitzer shell were fired from the "Louisiana;" and, if less justice is done the occasion than it deserves, it is because the accounts of the commanding officer are so obscure.

This closes the account of the operations of the Navy in the sounds of North Carolina up to November 10th, 1862, at which time these waters were in charge of Commander H. K. Davenport. The sounds at this time were virtually in possession of the Federal Army and Navy, though the enemy would make useless raids along the banks of the rivers for the purpose of firing on the gun-boats.

During the command of Flag-officer Goldsborough all the sounds had been taken possession of under the admirable management of Commander Rowan, Lieutenant Flusser and others. Newbern, Plymouth, Elizabeth City, and every important place, was in charge of a gun-boat or was garrisoned by soldiers, and most of the Confederate troops that had been sent to resist the Union forces had returned to Richmond, where at that time an attack was expected.

The harbor of Beaufort was in the hands of the Federals and part of the coast of North Carolina was under blockade.

All of which, when closely examined, exhibits as much gallantry, energy and hard work, in proportion to the means at hand and the objects in view, as appears elsewhere.

LIST OF VESSELS AND OFFICERS IN THE NORTH ATLANTIC BLOCKADING SQUADRON, UNDER REAR-ADMIRAL L. M. GOLDSBOROUGH.

COMMANDER A. LUDLOW CASE, CAPTAIN OF THE FLEET.

OBTAINED FROM THE SECRETARY'S REPORT OF 1862, AND NAVY REGISTER OF SEPT. 1862.

STEAM-FRIGATE "MINNESOTA"—FLAG-SHIP.

Commander, A. L. Case; Lieutenant-Commanders, E. C. Grafton and John Watters; Lieutenant, Adolphus Dexter; Midshipman, R. S. Chew; Fleet Surgeon, W. M. Wood; Surgeon, J. S. Kitchen; Assistant Surgeons, S. J. Jones, Edgar Holden and E. R. Dodge; Paymaster, Robert Pettit; Chaplain, T. G. Salter; Captain of Marines, W. L. Shuttleworth; First-Lieutenant of Marines, W. H. Cartter; Chief Engineer, C H. Loring; Assistant Engineers, J. H. Bailey, E. J. Whittaker, Alfred Colin, L. A. Haverly, T. W. Rae and G. W. Thorn; Acting-Masters, D. A. Campbell, W. G. Saltonstall and Wm. Wright; Boatswain, Paul Atkinson; Gunner, C. W. Homer; Carpenter, Ebenezer Thompson; Sailmaker, A. A. Warren.

STEAMER "MARATANZA."

Commander, G. H. Scott; Lieutenant-Commander, Wm. P. McCann; Assistant Surgeon, Job Corbin; Acting-Assistant Paymaster, C. S. Perley; Acting-Masters, Charles Cortney, Jacob Kimball and J. B. Wood, Jr.; Acting-Engineers, Edward Scattergood, Wm. H. Kilpatrick, L. H. Harvey and R. L. Webb; Acting-Master's Mates, J. Creighton and E. W. Flowers.

STEAMER "MORSE."

Acting-Masters, Peter Hayes and G. W. Caswell;

Acting-Assistant Paymaster, Henry Russell, Acting-Assistant Engineers, Thomas Divine, Tim. Flanders and George West; Acting-Master's Mates, William Dunne and C. E. Rich.

IRON-CLAD "MONITOR."

Commanders, John L. Worden, Wm. N. Jeffers and T. H. Stevens [commanding at different times]; Lieutenant, S. Dana Greene; Acting-Volunteer-Lieutenant, Wm. Flye; Acting-Assistant Surgeon, D. C. Logue; Acting-Assistant Paymaster, W. F. Keeler; Acting-Master, L. M. Stodder; Assistant Engineers, A. B. Campbell, Geo. H. White, R. W. Hands and M. T. Sunstrom; Acting-Master's Mates, Geo. Frederickson and Peter Williams.

STEAMER "JACOB BELL."

Lieutenant-Commander, E. P. McCrea; Acting-Assistant Surgeon, O. J. Bissell; Acting-Assistant Paymaster, Samuel Anderson; Acting-Assistant Engineers, Arthur Clements, Nelson Ross and R. H. Buel; Acting-Master's Mate, E. McConnell.

STEAMER "PORT ROYAL."

Lieutenant-Commander, George U. Morris, Acting-Volunteer-Lieutenant, Wm. P. Randall [commanding at different times]; Lieutenant, H. D. Todd; Assistant Surgeon, W. S. Fort; Assistant Paymaster, J. A. Bates, Jr.; Assistant Engineers, W. C. Selden, G. W. Sensner, O. C. Lewis, F. B. Allen and E. M. Breese; Acting-Master's Mates, W. F. Reynolds, Jr., E. V. Tyson and Benj. Woods.

STEAMER "SUSQUEHANNA."

Captain, R. B. Hitchcock; Lieutenant-Commander, J. H. Gillis; Surgeon, Joseph Beale; Paymaster, W. H. Thompson; Assistant Surgeon, H. C. Nelson; Captain of Marines, P. R. Fendall; Chief Engineer, George Sewell; Assistant Engineers, J. M. Hobby, James Renshaw, James Butterworth and E. R. Arnold; Acting-Masters, W. L. Churchill and G. B. Livingston; Boatswain, Chas. Miller; Gunner, Wm. Summers; Carpenter, G. M. Doughty; Sailmaker, J. C. Herbert.

STEAMER "AROOSTOOK."

Lieutenant-Commander, S. R. Franklin; Lieutenant, T. S. Spencer; Acting-Masters, Eben Hoyt and W. A. Maine; Acting-Assistant Paymaster, W. L. Pynchon; Assistant Engineers, W. G. Buehler, Geo. R. Holt, James Entwistle and Samuel Gragg; Acting-Master's Mates, C. F. Palmer, Louis Hammersley and Edw. Culbert.

STEAMER "DACOTAH."

Captain, J. P. McKinstry; Lieutenant, G. C. Wiltse; Surgeon, Delavan Bloodgood; Acting-Masters, Wm. Earle and W. Moslander; Assistant Paymaster, Richard Washington; Chief Engineer, P. G. Peltz; Assistant Engineers, Elijah Laws, G. P. Hunt, Geo. W. Melville and Jas. H. Perry; Acting-Master's Mates, Charles Trathen, Paul Borner, C. H. Chase and C. H. Davidson; Boatswain, G. C. Abbott; Gunner, Geo. Edmond.

STEAM-FRIGATE "SAN JACINTO."

Commander, Wm. Rockendorff; Lieutenant-Commander, Ralph Chandler; Lieutenant, B. P. Smith; Assistant Surgeon, I. W. Bragg; Assistant Paymaster, T. C. Masten; Acting-Masters, John Baker, H. J. Coop and D. G. McRitchie; Captain of Marines, L. L. Dawson; First-Lieutenant of Marines, Robert Kidd; Chief Engineer, M. Kellogg; Assistant Engineers, G. W. Hall, H. S. Davids, H. C. McIlvaine, Edwin Wells, H. W. Scott, Edm. Lincoln and N. P. Towne; Boatswain, John Marley; Carpenters, J. W. North and R. A. Williams; Gunner, C. A. Stephenson; Acting-Master's Mates, J. D. Weed, H. T. Keen and A. H. Fuller.

TUG "DRAGON."

Acting-Assistant Engineer, John Jordan.

IRON-CLAD. "GALENA."

Captain, John Rodgers; Lieutenant-Commander, L. H. Newman; Assistant Surgeon, R. E. Van Giesen; Acting-Assistant Paymaster, J. H. Sellman; Acting-Masters, S. B. Washburn and B. W. Loring; Assistant Engineers, J. W. Thompson, T. T. Millholland, F. A. Breman, James Dodd and A. S. Chipman; Acting-Master's Mates, J. H. Jenks, Andrew McCleary, Alex. Meldrum and E. A. Galindo; Gunner, J. D. Boorom; Boatswain, Rob't Dixon.

STEAMER "STEVENS."

Lieutenant, D. C. Constable.

STEAMER "DAYLIGHT."

Commander, Samuel Lockwood; Acting-Master, J. D. Warren, [commanding at different times]; Acting-Masters, J. R. Dickinson and J. H. Gleason; Acting-Assistant Surgeon, F. M. Dearborne; Acting-Assistant Paymaster, A. J. Clark; Acting-Assistant Engineers, C. D. Kiersted, Wm. Emmons and T. McIntosh; Acting-Master's Mates, Chas. Attmore and James Corlace.

STEAMER "GENESEE."

Commander, Wm. H. Macomb; Lieutenant-Commander, Wm. H. Dana; Assistant Surgeon, G. B. Slough; Acting-Masters, Wm. Hanson, C. M. Merchant and R. T. Wyatt; Acting-Engineers, W. H. Green, C. H. Harrab, G. H. Griggs, M. McLoughlin and C. Moulton; Acting-Master's Mates, W. J. Crosby, John Connor, G. M. Fludder and E. W. Halcro.

STEAMER. "ELLIS."

Lieutenant, C. L. Franklin; Acting-Master's Mate, Omar Smith; Midshipman, B. H. Porter; Acting-Assistant Engineer, F. A. Whitfield.

STEAMER "HUNCHBACK."

Acting-Lieutenant, E. R. Colhoun; Acting-Master, Ric'd Pasquell; Acting-Assistant Paymaster, Henry Cushing; Acting-Assistant Engineers, Henry Armstrong and John Wall; Acting-Master's Mates, Wm. Weaver and Chas. Weaver.

STEAMER "HENRY BRINKER."

Acting-Master, John E. Giddings; Acting-Master's Mate, W. B. Miles; Acting-Engineers, J. W. Kelsey, Robt. Ross and W. H. Yates.

SLOOP "GRANITE."

Acting-Master, E. Boomer.

STEAMER "HETZEL."

Commander, H. K. Davenport; Lieutenant, C. L. Franklin; Acting-Assistant Surgeon, N. L. Campbell; Acting-Assistant Paymaster, G. W. Morton; Acting-Assistant Engineers, Joshua Eddowes, J. B. Dick, T. B. Cole, J. H. Paget and W. H. Tower; Acting-Master's Mates, John Rudrow and Benj. Walker.

STEAMER "I. N. SEYMOUR."

Acting-Master, F. S. Wells; Acting-Assistant Engineers, N. Eggleston, Stephen Mealeus, Philip Hublitz and J. A. Whittaker.

STEAMER "MONTICELLO."

Lieutenant-Commander, Daniel L. Braine; Acting-Masters, L. A. Brown and Richard Hustace; Acting-Ensign, A. G. Stebbins; Acting-Assistant Engineers, W. S. Montgomery, John Pick, C. O. Morgan, Thomas McGough, J. Thomas and H. Webster; Acting-Master's Mate, E. A. Nassau.

STEAMER "MYSTIC."

Lieutenant-Commander, H. N. T. Arnold; Acting-Masters, R. S. Coffin, B. W. Loring and S. B. Meaders; Acting-Assistant Surgeon, W. F. Browne; Acting-Assistant Paymaster, T. E. Smith; Acting-Assistant Engineers, J. B. Lovell, J. B. Allen, H. F. Loveaire, S. Rockefeller and G. W. Shank; Acting-Master's Mates, G. R. Durand, J. M. C, Reville and J. B. Swett.

STEAMER "LOUISIANA."

Lieutenant-Commander, Alex. Murray, and Acting-Lieutenant, R. T. Renshaw [commanding at different times] ; Lieutenant-Commander, Alfred Hopkins; Acting-Master Edward Hooker; Assistant Surgeon, Michael Bradley; Assistant Paymaster, W. W. Williams; Assistant Engineers, J. M. Lay, D. P. McCartney, J. H. Huxley and T. J. McK. Daniels.

STEAMER "MT. VERNON."

Commanders, O. S. Glisson and A. G. Clary [commanding at different times] · Acting-Masters, J. W. Simmons and E. W. White; Acting-Assistant Surgeons, S. B. Hoppin and Joseph McKnight; Acting-Ensign, O. L. S. Roberts; Acting Assistant Engineers, J. H. Hosford and John Lardner; Acting-Master's Mates, G. C. Kellogg and Lloyd Rogers.

STEAMER "MAHASKA."

Lieutenant, N. H. Farquhar ; Acting-Master, C. L. Moses; Assistant Surgeon, J. C. Spear ; Acting-Assistant Paymaster, Chas. Fairchild; Midshipman, E. C. V. Blake; Engineers, B. B. H. Wharton, Elisha Harsen, Thos. Le Blanche, J. C. Stevens and E. L. Hewitt; Acting Master's Mates, N. W. Black, G. E. French, Thomas Smith and B. F. Trask.

STEAMER "SABAGO."

Commander, Daniel Ammen ; Lieutenant-Commander, E. W. Henry; Acting-Masters, Benj. Dyer, J. F. Anderson, T. M. Gardner and W. H. Mallard ; Assistant Surgeon, J. P. Quinn ; Assistant Engineers, G. F. Savage, G. E. Tower, W. H. De Hart, O. W. Allison and J. A. Bullard; Acting-Master's Mates, Wm. Manning and E. D. Martin.

STEAMER "OCTORARA."

Lieutenant-Commander, George Brown; Acting-Master, L. G. Cook; Surgeon, James Laws; Assistant Paymaster W. S. Higbee; Midshipman, Chas. W. Tracy; Acting-Ensign, G. F. Hollis; Assistant Engineers, Jackson McElwell, E. J. Brooks, C. R. Morgan, J. G. Cooper and E. W. Clark.

STEAMER "WHITEHEAD."

Acting-Master, Charles A. French; Acting-Assistant Engineers, Morris Petersen and W. W. Baker.

STORE-SHIP "WILLIAM BADGER."

Acting-Master's Mate, Reuben Rich ; Acting-Assistant Paymaster, W. M. Whittemore.

MORTAR SCHOONERS, "ARLETTA" AND "PARA."

FRIGATE "ST. LAWRENCE."

Captain, H. Y. Purviance, and Commander J. F. Schenck [at different times in command] ; Lieutenant, H. F. Picking; Acting-Masters, G. L. Allyn, G. J. Murray and Wm. H. Smith ; Second-Lieutenant of Marines, R. S. Collum; Acting-Master's Mates, John Fisher, V. W. Jones and T. W. Jones ; Boatswain, J. A. Briscoe; Gunner, C. De Bevoise; Carpenter, J. A. Krim; Sailmaker, L. Rogers.

STEAMER "DELAWARE."

Lieutenant-Commander, S. P. Quackenbush; Assistant Surgeon, Lorenzo Traver; Assistant Paymaster, F. R. Curtis ; Acting-Ensign, J. H. Kerens; Acting-Engineers, J. D. Williamson, T. J. Brown, A. Dunbar and James Mellen ; Acting-Master's Mate, J. H. Springman.

SLOOP-OF-WAR "CUMBERLAND."

Commander, William Radford ; Lieutenants, George U. Morris, T. O. Selfridge, and M. S. Stuyvesant; Chaplain, J. H. Lenhart; Acting-Masters, W. P. Randall and W. W. Kennison ; Surgeon, Charles Martin; Assistant Surgeon, Edward Kershner; Lieutenant of Marines, Charles Haywood; Acting-Master's Mates, Henry Wyman, E. V. Tyson, Chas. O'Neil and J. M. Harrington; Boatswain, E. B. Bell; Gunner, Eugene Mack; Carpenter, W. M. Leighton; Sailmaker, David Bruce.

STEAMER "JOHN L. LOCKWOOD."

Acting-Masters, G. W. Graves and W. F. North ; Acting-Assistant Engineers, J. T. Newton, W. W. Whiting and J. T. Miller; Acting-Master's Mate, Samuel Horton.

STEAMER "WACHUSETT."

Commander, Wm. Smith and Capt. T. A. Jenkins [commanding at different times]; Lieutenant-Commanders, C. A. Babcock and C. E. Fleming ; Surgeon, J. H. Otis; Assistant Paymaster, F. K. Moore; Lieutenant Wm. Whitehead; Acting-Masters, Edm. Kimble, S. P. Lathrop and P. Leach; Midshipman, H. C. Tallman ; Chief Engineer, W. C. Wheeler ; Assistant Engineers, W. D. Pendleton, W. H. Messinger, C. J. Coney, H. Holmes and M. H. Knapp; Acting-Master's Mates, A. Ellwell, Wm. McCreary and C. A. Stewart ; Boatswain, John Burrows; Gunner, Samuel Cross.

FRIGATE "CONGRESS."

Lieutenants, Joseph B. Smith and Austin Pendergrast ; Acting-Master, Thomas Moore ; Master's Mate, Peter J. Hargous; Pilot, Wm. Rhodes.

BARK "GEMSBOK."

Acting-Volunteer-Lieutenant, Edward Cavendy ; Acting-Masters, J. E. Giddings, O. Thatcher. T. Werthoff and Samuel Very; Acting-Assistant Surgeon, Thomas Welch; Acting-Assistant Paymaster, E. H. Roberts.

SHIP "SUPPLY."

Commander, Geo. Colvocoresses ; Assistant Surgeon, W. L. Wheeler ; Paymaster, Edw. Foster; Acting-Masters, Zac. Kempton and J. D. Wood ; Acting-Ensign, A. B. Axtell; Acting-Master's Mate, Peter Faunce.

STEAMER "STARS AND STRIPES."

Lieutenant-Commander, Reed Werden and Lieutenant, R. S. McCook [commanding at different times].

STEAMER "STATE OF GEORGIA."

Commander, J. F. Armstrong ; Acting-Masters, A. D. Littlefield and J. J. Rogers; Acting-Assistant Surgeon, J. W. Hamilton ; Acting-Assistant Paymaster, T. H. Haskell ; Acting-Engineers, James Wilkinson, David Pyke, Wm. H. Miller, Thomas Nesbitt and J. D. Rogers ; Acting-Master's Mates, J. T. Hughes and Isaac Halleck.

STEAMER "SOUTHFIELD."

Acting-Volunteer-Lieutenant, C. F. W. Behm ; Acting-Master, W. F. Pratt; Acting-Assistant Engineers, George Ashby and James Kennedy.

STEAMER "SHAWSHEEN."

Acting-Volunteer Lieutenant, T. C. Woodward; Acting-Master's Mates, G. W. Barrett and G. C. Williams; Acting-Assistant Engineers, Richard Anderson and M. Smith.

STEAMER "PENOBSCOT."

Commander, J. M. B. Clitz ; Lieutenant, F. M. Bunce; Assistant Surgeon, E. C. Ver Meulen; Assistant Engineers, T. J. Jones, Thos. Petherick, G. P. Wilkinson, G. W. Hall; Acting-Master's Mates, G. H. Smith, J. P. Semple, S. H. Daman, H. P. Edwards and S. K. Luce; Acting-Assistant Paymaster, Addison Pool.

STEAMER "PHILADELPHIA."

Commander, S. C. Rowan, Flag-officer ; Acting-Master, Silas Reynolds, Commanding ; Assistant Surgeon, Sam'l J. Jones; Carpenter, H. M. Griffith.

STEAMER "RESCUE."

Acting-Assistant Engineers, W. H. Capen and B. D. Mulligan.

STEAMER "UNDERWRITER."

Lieutenant, Alfred Hopkins and Lieutenant-Commander, Wm. N. Jeffers [commanding at different times]; Acting-Assistant Paymaster, Dan'l Harman;

Acting-Assistant Engineers, John Cohill, John Morse and John Whittaker; Acting-Master's Mates, Wm. K. Engell and Daniel Ward.

STEAMER "VALLEY CITY."

Lieutenant-Commander, J. C. Chaplin and Acting-Volunteer-Lieutenant, H. K. Furniss [commanding at different times]; Acting-Assistant Surgeon, F. E. Martindale; Acting-Assistant Paymaster, G. W. Moore; Acting-Assistant Engineers, Perry Short, James Hitchcock and B. Hildebrand; Acting-Master's Mates, C. W. Campbell, John Cullaton, H. Dickenson and T. Langton; Gunner, John Davis.

STEAMER "VICTORIA."

Lieutenant Commander, G. A. Stevens; Acting-Masters, Alfred Everson and H. A. Phelan; Acting-Ensign, W. H. Mayer; Acting-Assistant Surgeon, J. G. Parke; Acting-Assistant Paymaster, H. S. Bradford; Acting-Assistant Engineers, J. M. Barron, E. A. Hurd and T. D. Webster; Acting-Master's Mate, G. B. Howard.

STEAMER "CAMBRIDGE."

Commander, Wm. A. Parker; Acting-Masters, J. A. J. Brooks; W. H. Maies, F. W. Strong; Acting-Assistant Surgeon, Ezra Pray; Acting-Assistant Paymaster, J. C. Canning; Midshipman, C. L. Huntington; Acting-Engineers, G. B. Orswell, C. C. Pennington, S. B. Ellis, H. F. Hayden and James Powers; Acting-Master's Mate, W. F. Durgin; Gunner, W. Ferguson; Carpenter, T. D. Wilson.

STEAMER "CHOCURA."

Commander, T. H. Patterson; Lieutenant-Commander, R. F. Bradford; Assistant Surgeon, Charles Carter; Acting-Masters, P. S. Borden and T. B. Sears; Acting-Assistant Paymaster, E. L. Turner; Assistant Engineers, Z. Talbot, W. H. Harrison, Theo. Cooper and Andrew Blythe; Acting-Master's Mate, A. P. Atwood.

STEAMER "CURRITUCK."

Acting-Master, W. F. Shankland; Acting-Assistant Surgeon, Henry Johnson; Acting-Assistant Paymaster, L. S. Yorke; Acting-Assistant Engineers, Alfred Clum, W. H. Borcum and Wm. Godard; Acting-Master's Mate, T. H. Strong.

STEAMER "COMMODORE PERRY."

Lieutenant-Commander, Charles W. Flusser; Acting-Masters, F. J. Thomas and W. B. Cushing; Acting-Assistant Paymaster, Henry Anderson; Acting-Assistant Engineers, J. W. Cross, J. L. Bowers and G. W. Richards; Acting-Master's Mates, R. Dolly, John Lynch and H. C. Webster.

STEAMER "CORWIN."

Lieutenant Commander, T. S. Phelps.

STEAMER "COMMODORE BARNEY."

Acting-Lieutenant, R. T. Renshaw; Acting-Master, J. R. Grace; Acting-Assistant Surgeon, G. R. Mann; Acting-Assistant Paymaster, Benj. Page; Acting-Assistant Engineers, Strong Conklin and Lemuel Albert; Acting-Master's Mates, J. Aspinwall, Jr., Wm. Betts, John Hill and C. Washburn.

STEAMER "COHASSET."

[Commander not found]; Acting-Master's Mates, Wm. P. Burke and Jacob Daggett; Acting-Assistant Engineers, Sidney Smith and Chas Robinson.

STEAMER "CERES."

Acting-Volunteer Lieutenant, John Macdearmid; Acting-Master, G. B. Thompson.

STEAMER "A. C. POWELL."

Acting-Master's Mate, A. P. Matthews; Acting-Engineer Wm. Mahan.

STEAMER "W. G. PUTNAM."

Acting-Master, W. J. Hotchkiss; Acting-Assistant Engineers, James Osborne and John Henry.

STEAMER "YOUNG AMERICA."

Acting-Master, G. W. Graves; Acting-Assistant Engineers, James Hamilton, C. E. Rainer and W. B. Whitmore.

STEAMER "ZOUAVE."

Acting-Assistant Engineers, John Badgely and Isaac Buck.

NOTE.—The above list of officers is necessarily incomplete and not strictly correct, from the fact that the Navy Register for September, 1862, does not furnish the information usually given.

CHAPTER XXXV.

OPERATIONS OF THE NORTH ATLANTIC SQUADRON, 1863.

SUCCESSFUL EXPEDITION OFF YORKTOWN AND UP NEUSE RIVER. — LOSS OF "MONITOR."
—GALLANT RESCUE OF GREATER PORTION OF "MONITOR'S" CREW BY THE "RHODE
ISLAND."—SERIOUS LOSS TO THE GOVERNMENT.—OPERATIONS OF LIEUTENANT FLUSSER
ON THE CHOWAN RIVER.—ATTACK ON PLYMOUTH, N. C.—THE "SOUTHFIELD" DIS-
ABLED.—ACHIEVEMENTS OF GENERAL J. G. FOSTER.—ARMY AND NAVY CO-OPERATE
IN EXPEDITION AGAINST GOLDSBOROUGH, N. C.—LIEUTENANT CUSHING'S EXPEDITION
AGAINST WILMINGTON PILOTS. — CUSHING CAPTURES A FORT AND PUTS ENEMY TO
FLIGHT.—OTHER ADVENTURES.—LIEUTENANT FLUSSER'S EXPEDITION TO HERTFORD,
N. C.—CONFEDERATES ATTACK FORT ANDERSON.—ASSISTANCE RENDERED BY GUN-BOATS.
— ENEMY WITHDRAWS.— LETTER OF COL. BELKNAP.— GREAT HAVOC COMMITTED BY
STEAMER "HETZEL."—VESSELS DISPATCHED TO OCCUPY NANSEMOND RIVER.—GUN-
BOATS IN DEMAND.—LIEUTENANT LAMSON DISTINGUISHES HIMSELF AT HILL'S POINT.—
CUSHING PREVENTS LONGSTREET AND FORCES FROM CROSSING RIVER. — REPULSE OF
CONFEDERATES AT SUFFOLK.—GENERAL GETTY ACKNOWLEDGES MERIT.—THE "MOUNT
WASHINGTON" FIGHTS HER WAY OUT OF MUD.—THE "BARNEY" ENGAGES ENEMY.
—BRAVERY OF OFFICERS AND MEN.—NOBLE ACTS.—LIEUTENANT LAMSON RUNS HIS VES-
SELS UNDER ENEMY'S GUNS.—CAPTURE OF CONFEDERATE ARTILLERY.—COMMENDATION
OF LAMSON AND CUSHING BY SECRETARY WELLES.—CAPTURE AND DESTRUCTION OF
BLOCKADE-RUNNERS.— OPERATIONS IN SOUNDS OF NORTH CAROLINA.— CONFEDERATES
INVEST WASHINGTON, N. C., BUT COMPELLED TO RETIRE. — GUN-BOATS ENGAGE AND
SILENCE MANY BATTERIES ON PAMLICO RIVER.—NAMES OF OFFICERS AND MEN WHO
RECEIVED COMMENDATIONS. — GENERAL SPINOLA'S TESTIMONY IN REGARD TO GAL-
LANT CONDUCT OF NAVY. — LIEUTENANT FRENCH'S EXPEDITION. — IMPORTANT CAP-
TURES. — GENERAL DIX EVACUATES WEST POINT, COVERED BY GUN-BOATS. — EXPE-
DITIONS UP NORTH, YORK, AND MATTAPONY RIVERS.—CUTTING OUT OF CONFEDERATE
STEAMER "KATE" FROM UNDER GUNS OF FORT FISHER. — ACTS OF BRAVERY DIS-
PLAYED. — ATTEMPT TO DESTROY STEAMER "HEBE." — LIEUTENANT CUSHING "CUTS"
OUT AND DESTROYS BLOCKADE-RUNNER "ALEXANDER COOPER." — DESTRUCTION OF
THE "VENUS."—MISCELLANEOUS.

WHEN Acting-Rear-Admiral S. P. Lee succeeded Rear-Admiral Goldsborough in the command of the North Atlantic squadron there was not much left to be done except keeping up a strict blockade of the coast and keeping the Albemarle and Pamlico Sounds under subjection.

All the naval force of the enemy between Norfolk and Howlet batteries had either been destroyed or made its escape to Richmond, enabling the Navy Department to decrease the large force kept in and about Hampton Roads.

From September 1st up to January there was but little of moment to report in the North Atlantic squadron, beyond the operations in the sounds of North Carolina and the naval expedition under Commander Foxhall A. Parker, off Yorktown, which proved successful, the Navy being of much service to the Army contingent under General Negley; also a successful military expedition up the Neuse River under General Foster, in which the Navy participated, with much credit to its commander, Commander Alexander Murray.

On December 31st, 1862, the Government

met with a serious loss by the sinking at sea of the famous little "Monitor," which had set the huge "Merrimac" at defiance and driven her back to Norfolk. This was not only the great actual loss of a fighting vessel, but in addition there were associations connected with this little craft which made her name dear to every Union-loving man, and it was hoped by all those who had faith in her that she might be long permitted to float the flag of the Union at her staff and become a terror to its enemies. But it seems that she was only permitted to perform the great service for which she was built, an event that made her name as famous as that of the old "Constitution," and then she sank from sight in the depth of ocean, leaving behind her not as much of her hull as would serve to make a small memento of the past.

The "Monitor" left Hampton Roads in tow of the U. S. steamer "Rhode Island," on the 29th of December, 1862, at 2.30 P. M., with a light southwest wind, and clear, pleasant weather, with a prospect of its continuance. At 5 A. M., the next morning, a swell set in from the southward with an increase of wind from the southwest, the sea breaking over the pilot-house forward and striking the base of the turret, but not with sufficient force to break over it. But it was found that the packing of oakum under and around the base of the turret had worked out, as the "Monitor" pitched and rolled, and water made its way into the vessel, though for some time the bilge pumps kept her free.

The wind hauled to the south, increasing all the time, the vessel towing badly and yawing about very much. By 8 P. M., the wind began to blow heavily, causing the "Monitor" to plunge deeply, the sea washing over and *into* the turret, and at times into the hawse-pipes. Commander J. P. Bankhead, of the "Monitor," signalled several times to the "Rhode Island" to stop towing, in order to see whether that would prevent the influx of water into his vessel, but she only fell off into the trough of the sea and made matters worse, the water coming on board so rapidly that it became necessary to start the centrifugal pumps.

It was quite evident to many on board that the last days of the "Monitor" had come unless the wind should abate and the sea go down, which did not seem at all likely; but the enthusiasm of the commander, officers and men kept them at their posts until it became necessary to signal to the "Rhode Island" for assistance, which was promptly given. The officers and men of the "Rhode Island" (Commander Stephen D. Trenchard) did not hesitate to jump into their boats in that tempestuous weather and go to the relief of their comrades. The Commander

of the "Monitor," in order to keep his vessel afloat as long as possible, cut the large cable by which she was towed and ran down to the "Rhode Island," which enabled him to use all the pumps.

Two boats reached the "Monitor" from the "Rhode Island," and the Commander ordered Lieutenant S. Dana Green (who had been first-lieutenant during the fight with the "Merrimac") to put as many of the crew in them as they would safely carry. This was a very dangerous operation, and it brought into play that cool courage which is more admirable than that shown in battle. A heavy sea was breaking entirely over the deck and there was great danger of the boats being crushed by the overhang, if not pierced by the sharp prow which was first high above the waves, then completely submerged by the crushing billows. The "Rhode Island" herself was in great danger, as she was lying close by and liable at any moment to be struck by the "Monitor's" bow.

THE "MONITOR" LOST IN A GALE.

The first two boat-loads safely reached the "Rhode Island" amid the storm and darkness, and again returned on their mission of mercy to rescue the remaining persons, the vessel being most difficult to find in the gale. In the meantime the captain and the remnant of his crew retired to the turret and there held on, though several of the men were washed overboard and lost. Fortunately the vessel was on soundings, and the captain gave the order to let go an anchor in hopes it would bring the "Monitor's" head to wind, and that the chain would hold her there long enough to get the crew out. At this moment the water was over the ash-pans and increasing rapidly, and the engine-room had to be abandoned.

Fortunately the "Monitor" came head to wind, when the cable brought her up. By this time the vessel was filling rapidly, the deck was on a line with the water, and all the men left on the turret were ordered by the captain to gain the deck and endeavor to reach the two boats that were again approaching. At that time there were twenty-five or thirty men left on board.

The boats had to approach the "Monitor" very carefully. She was as dangerous as a reef of rocks just above the water over which the sea was breaking furiously. Several men were washed overboard in their attempt to reach the boats, and only one of them was picked up. With great difficulty one of the boats succeeded in getting into a position where a number of the crew could get into her, but there were several persons still on the turret who would not come down, either being unmanned, or not supposing the vessel would sink so soon. These went down in her.

The captain had done all a good officer could do to save his vessel and his crew. He had stood at his post like a hero, helping the men into the boats, and now finding that he could be of no more use he jumped into the already deeply laden boat and shoved off, the heavy, sluggish motion of the "Monitor" giving evidence that she would soon go down.

The boats had scarcely reached the "Rhode Island" when the gallant little craft that had done so much to save the honor of the nation, and had by her one battle destroyed the prestige of the best fighting ships in Europe, sank to the bottom, the wild winds howling a requiem over her resting-place!

While regrets remain that not all her crew were saved (many of whom had served in the fight with the "Merrimac"), it is wonderful, considering the dangerous condition of the "Monitor," that so many were rescued.

In mustering the crew of the "Monitor," on the deck of the "Rhode Island," two officers and twelve men were found to be missing. All honor to their memories! Two great battles had they fought in a short time, one with the Confederate monster, the other with the wrath of the ocean, and in both cases had they shown that indomitable courage and skill which are among the highest attributes of the American sailor.

There was no instance during the war where greater courage, skill and coolness were exhibited than on this ever-to-be-remembered occasion, and it is due to the officers and men of the ill-fated "Monitor" that this small tribute should be paid them for standing so manfully by the historic vessel which had added some of the greenest laurels to the fame of the American Navy.

The position of the vessel on that dark and tempestuous night was enough to appall the stoutest heart, but neither officers nor men quailed before the danger which seemed to cut off all hope of rescue. Lieutenant S.

Dana Greene and Acting-Master L. N. Stodder stood by Commander Bankhead to the last, and Acting-Master's Mate Peter Williams, and Richard Anjier, Quartermaster, showed conduct entitling them to all praise. The quartermaster remained at his post until the vessel was sinking, and when ordered by the captain to get into the boat, said, "No, sir, not until you do so."

This may seem to be a long and tedious description of an event the like of which happens so often in peace or war, and frequently without grave comment; but the "Monitor" was an historic vessel whose name and fame should be handed down to posterity, and as the memorable event of her great battle is known to almost every school-boy, it is but fitting that the story of her tragical end should be told also.

One of the boats of the "Rhode Island," which had been successful in taking off a load from the "Monitor," was driven off by the storm and supposed to be lost. Search was made for her all the following day, but without success, and she was given up. But, fortunately, after many perils, she was picked up by the schooner "Colby," of Buckport, Maine, and restored to the steamer "Rhode Island." The poor fellows in this boat suffered great hardships, and their adventures would form by themselves an interesting chapter of incidents.

Lieutenant-Commander Flusser, so prominent under the command of Rear-Admiral Goldsborough, continued to hold his reputation under Rear-Admiral Lee. He was a terror to the marauding troops of the enemy, who made a note of all his movements.

On December 9th, 1862, he left Plymouth to operate on the Chowan River, leaving the "Southfield," Acting-Volunteer-Lieutenant C. F. W. Behm, to protect the place. He had not much more than started when the enemy appeared and commenced a heavy musketry fire from the shore. Lieutenant Behm immediately beat to quarters and trained his guns so as to command the Plymouth shore. The river-bank was lined with people flying before the Confederates, who were firing alike on friend and foe, and it was difficult for the "Southfield" to open fire, for fear of harming those citizens who had proved themselves friendly and favorable to the Union cause. The steamer immediately got underway and stood up the river where her guns could be brought to bear upon the enemy, who now opened upon her with their artillery, and succeeded in putting a shell through her steam-chest and filling the gangways and hold so full of hot steam that the powder-passers could not get to the magazines. Of course, the "Southfield" could no longer use her guns, and the boats had to be lowered to tow her down the river. In the meantime the enemy committed all the mischief possible and then decamped.

Lieutenant-Commander Flusser hove in sight a short time after, and taking the "Southfield" in tow returned to Plymouth, where his presence restored confidence and quiet.

Thus the Confederate marauding parties continued, on every favorable opportunity, to molest the citizens in the sounds of North Carolina, determined that no loyal feeling should exist among them, or, if it did, that the citizens should pay the penalty for their allegiance to the North. The mistake of the Navy Department at that moment was that it did not keep a larger force of vessels in the sounds to gain the confidence of the inhabitants and secure them against the raids of the Confederate troops.

COMMANDER (AFTERWARDS CAPTAIN) J. P. BANKHEAD.

One of the most energetic of the military commanders in this neighborhood was General J. G. Foster, who was always on the alert to circumvent the enemy in his movements.

The war in North Carolina was not prosecuted on a scale that could accomplish any decisive results. The military force in that region was only sufficient to keep down the Confederate raids, which were made with forces consisting of five or six hundred men. These seldom accomplished anything beyond oppressing the inhabitants of towns along the rivers where Federal troops were stationed, covered by the gun-boats. Notwithstanding the apparent insignificance of these small bands, if they could have united they would have driven the Federal troops out of the country. The difficulty of the Confederates was that the naval vessels

were always at hand, and they had received so many proofs of the effectiveness of their "batteries" that they seldom attacked the military posts except in the absence of the gun-boats.

General Foster was fully alive to the value of the naval branch of the forces, and availed himself on all occasions of its services. In December, 1862, he planned an attack upon the Confederate fortifications of Kinston and the railroad at or near Goldsborough, and asked the co-operation of the naval flotilla, at that time commanded by Commander A. Murray.

The following gun-boats were assigned to this expedition: "Delaware," Acting-Volunteer-Lieutenant A. P. Foster; "Shawsheen," Acting-Volunteer-Lieutenant T. C. Woodward; "Lockwood," Acting-Master G. W. Graves; "Seymour," Acting-Master F. S. Wells, and the Army transports, "Ocean Wave," Major Uliam; "Allison," Gunner, E. A. McDonald, U. S. N.; "Port Royal," Acting-Master G. B. Thompson, U. S. N.; "Wilson," Captain Rodgers, and "North State," Captain Berry.

This flotilla left Newbern on the evening of the 12th of December. The "Allison," "Port Royal," "Ocean Wave" and "Wilson" were in the advance, under Colonel Manchester of the "Marine Artillery," with orders to push ahead and reconnoitre, and in case of an attack, or the discovery of the enemy's batteries, to fall back on the heavier vessels.

Colonel Manchester, in charge of the military expedition, anchored his steamers for the night and made preparations to ascend the Neuse River. At daylight next morning he got underway and with great difficulty forced his way up to within two miles of Kinston, meeting with but slight opposition from the guerilla bands which infested that neighborhood, and only losing one man.

About two miles from Kinston the officers of the vessels, on turning a bend, suddenly found themselves faced by a 10-gun battery, while they were penned within the river with a space of only a hundred feet in which to move their boats. The "Port Royal," Ocean Wave" and "Wilson" were ordered to back out, and the "Allison" was interposed between them and the battery, which now opened a rapid fire. It took some minutes to back the vessels down the river, it was so narrow. The "Allison" replied to the enemy's fire with her Parrott gun, the first fire being within canister range. Three shells were exploded within the enemy's batteries with good effect and the Confederates were silenced.

It was sunset when the firing commenced, and darkness came on so rapidly that the vessels could hardly see their way, the enemy's shell exploding around them all the time. The "Allison" received three shell in her upper works. The vessels dropped behind the bend of the river and there anchored in double line, hay, beef, bread, etc., being packed along the sides; the guns put in battery ready for service, and bags of oats spread over the decks. In this manner the commander of the expedition waited until daylight, in expectation of an attack from the enemy, who could move about unseen and ascertain where the flotilla was stationed. Several attempts were made at early morn to reconnoitre the position, but the enemy were driven off by the fire of the Federal outposts.

The active force had to return down the river, owing to the falling water, and half the night was spent in hauling over the steamers that had grounded in the mud. After proceeding about five miles, Colonel Manchester heard of a force concentrating about a mile below, with the intention of disputing his passage. The "North State" was sent ahead to ascertain the enemy's position, while the other vessels followed prepared to shell them out. A mile further on, the flotilla was attacked by sharpshooters, who kept up a galling fire during the next five miles.

At a place called Old Dam the enemy had assembled in force, with the intention of obstructing the river, and both banks seemed to be well manned with sharpshooters. The position of the Confederates was well chosen, as they were enabled to rake the vessels with artillery as they turned the river-bend. The steamers now underwent a running fire from unseen foes, to which they answered as best they could with grape and canister, and with such good effect that the last gun-boat could find nothing to fire at. The distance of the gunboats was from one to two hundred feet from the Confederates and their guns did serious injury to them.

The vessels were much shattered by shot and falling trees, but by good luck and good management they worked their way out of the net in which they had injudiciously become entangled. Yet these were the services in which both Army and Navy were called upon frequently to embark, where, in nine out of ten times, the loss and capture of the expedition might have been counted upon. Fortunately, in this expedition, only two men were killed and six wounded.

Commander Murray says, in his report: "This expedition was partially strategic and was very successful. The attack on the batteries and the falling-back of the light boats, the shelling of the woods, and the feint to land a force on the north bank, had the desired effect." [!]

What the desired effect was, history does not say, and it seems to the writer that this was simply an expedition where men's lives were sacrificed without any apparent good. The Army was frittering away its forces in these small attempts to score a point, while the true course to pursue would have been to concentrate all the troops, drive the enemy out of the State of North Carolina, tear up the railroads leading to Richmond, and destroy all the means of subsisting an army in the State.

Though it may have been said that the Federals held North Carolina, yet it was by a most precarious tenure; and this section, which should in the beginning have been completely conquered, remained simply a skirmishing-ground for the contending forces throughout the war.

On January 5th the indefatigable Lieutenant Cushing started on an expedition to capture some Wilmington pilots, and having heard that there was a pilot station at "Little River," thirty miles below Fort Caswell, he made sail for that point, and reached it on the morning of January 5th, 1863. He crossed the bar at 8 o'clock at night with twenty-five men, in three cutters, and proceeded up the river. He was in hopes of finding pilots above and also some schooners.

About a mile from the mouth of the river the expedition received a volley of musketry from a bluff on the left. Cushing beached his boats the moment he was fired upon, without returning the fire, and formed his men about 200 yards from the point of attack, and gave the order: "*Forward—double-quick—charge!*"

The fearless fellow never stopped to consider whether he was charging fifty men or a thousand. It seemed immaterial to him, when his blood was up, how many of the enemy faced him; and his men, inspired by his intrepid example, followed him without hesitation.

There was a wood in front of the charging party, through which they passed, and on getting into the clearing Cushing found himself before a fort plainly to be seen by the light of the camp-fires, which were burning freely. Knowing that the enemy were ignorant of his numbers, he charged with the bayonet, giving three cheers, and as he went over one side of the works the enemy went out of the other.

The fort was an earthwork surrounded by a ditch ten feet wide and five deep, with a block-house inside pierced for musketry. No guns were mounted on the work. If there had been, the daring and impetuosity of the attack would have captured them. The enemy left in such haste that all their clothes, ammunition, stores, and the larger portion of their arms were left in the hands of the sailors, and all that could not be brought away was destroyed.

Notwithstanding that there was a possibility of the enemy returning with increased numbers, Cushing pushed on up the river, where he met another party of Confederates, and a skirmish took place in which the sailors used up all their ammunition and had to return to their boats, with only the loss of one man.

This was not an important affair, but it is selected as showing the indomitable courage of a young officer who received a share of honor during the war that seldom falls to the lot of one holding so subordinate a position; his performances in the face of the enemy had already attracted the notice of his commander; and, finally, the Government, having confidence in his valor and judgment, intrusted him with duties of a hazardous character, which he always performed with credit to himself.

Not to be outdone by Cushing, that gallant and efficient officer, Lieutenant-Commander Flusser, started on the 29th of January for Jamesville, hearing that a regiment of Confederates were fortifying that place, it being one of the best points on the river for annoying the gun-boats; and was too important a position and too near Plymouth to allow the enemy to hold it.

On the 30th, Flusser took on board his vessel (the "Commodore Perry") fifty soldiers of the 27th Massachusetts, under Captain Sanford, landed them at Hertford with about ninety sailors, marched into the country eight or ten miles, destroyed two bridges over the Purquimenous River, and returned that same night to Plymouth. Thus was cut off one of the means by which the enemy had supplied themselves with goods from Norfolk and Richmond, by the south side of the Chowan River, enabling the Navy to guard that ford with a gun-boat; for a large amount of contraband traffic had been carried on from the Albemarle Sound and its rivers by means of small boats which kept along the shore and could slip into the small creeks if a gun-boat hove in sight.

These little expeditions, though not very damaging to the enemy, showed the spirit of the naval officers and their determination to give the enemy no rest.

On the 14th of March, 1863, the Confederates made an attack on Fort Anderson, a work built by the Union troops opposite Newbern, and occupied by a regiment of volunteers. The enemy bombarded the works with field-pieces, and kept up the fire all night. In the morning they made a spirited attack in force, with masked batteries on the right. The gun-boat "Hunchback" and an armed schooner were brought up to strengthen the Federal position; when Lieutenant-Commander McCann, bringing his batteries to bear, and keeping up a well-

directed fire, with the aid of the schooner, silenced the enemy's guns.

There was an intermission of an hour on the enemy's part, who made a demand for the surrender of the fort; but this was evidently to give them time to bring up more guns. (The fort had no guns mounted.) Perceiving that their demand received no attention, they brought up fourteen more guns and renewed the attack, the "Hunchback" and armed schooner throwing in their shells until the enemy drew off. Before doing so, they were attacked by the gun-boats "Hetzel" and "Shawsheen," which vessels, being in a disabled condition, had to be towed into action by tugs.

The firing of the Federal vessels was excellent, and so well aimed were their guns that the enemy was unable to use his artillery with much effect. The "Hunchback" was only struck twice, but the schooner was placed in a sinking condition.

Had it not been for the prompt assistance rendered to Fort Anderson by the gun boats, it would certainly have fallen into the enemy's hands. From the fact that the Army undertook to hold several places with skeleton regiments and few or no guns, it required the utmost watchfulness on the part of the Navy to prevent disastrous results.

This affair was a surprise on the part of the Confederates, for which the Union troops were not at all prepared, and they thanked their stars that so watchful a friend as the Navy was at hand to succor them in their hour of need. The Army were not unmindful of the service rendered by the Navy on this occasion, and their feeling of gratitude is well expressed by Colonel J. C. Belknap, as follows:

HEADQUARTERS FIRST BRIGADE, }
WESSEL'S DIVISION, }
NEWBERN, N. C., March 15, 1863. }

COMMODORE—When, on the 14th of March, 1863, General Pettigrew, with eighteen pieces of artillery and over three thousand men, made his furious assault on Fort Anderson, an unfinished earth-work garrisoned by three hundred men of my command (the 92d New York Volunteers), the capture or destruction of the brave little band seemed inevitable, but the gun-boats under your command, the pride of loyal men and the terror of traitors, came promptly to the rescue.

Your well-directed fire drove the enemy from the field, covered the landing of the 85th New York, sent to the relief of the garrison, and the repulse of the rebel army was complete.

Allow me, Commodore, in the name of the officers and members of my command, to express to you my admiration for the promptitude and skill displayed by your command on that occasion.

The Army is proud of the Navy.

I remain your most obedient,

J. C. BELKNAP,
Colonel 85th Regiment, New York Volunteers,
Commanding 1st Brigade.

COMMANDER DAVENPORT,
Newbern, N. C.

The steamer "Hetzel" committed great

havoc among the enemy on this occasion by the accuracy of her fire. One of her shells struck a Parrott gun and destroyed it; bursting, it killed a number of the enemy, scattering their bones and fragments of their clothing over the ground.

The army on the Newbern side of the river had to be lookers-on during this fight, and could give no assistance to their comrades, consequently it was altogether a naval affair; but no one doubted what the result would be when they saw the rapidity and accuracy of the naval fire. In this action the revenue-cutter "Agassiz" also took part at close quarters, embarrassing the enemy in his retreat.

As the enemy retreated, the gun-boats "Lockwood" and "Allison" hung upon his rear for ten miles up the river, inflicting severe punishment; all these gun-boats, be it understood, being flimsy vessels, that could not encounter a moderate gale of wind at sea without danger of foundering.

This was one of the most gallant affairs that had occurred in the North Atlantic squadron since Rear-Admiral Lee took command, and was an instance of how necessary was the aid which the Navy stood always ready to afford the other branch of the service. Moreover, it was not an assistance that was sought by the Army, but one which the Navy anticipated by being on hand at the right moment.

In April the Confederates seemed to be making more zealous efforts to obtain a firm footing in North Carolina, and the naval officer in command of the Sounds urged the commander of the North Atlantic squadron to increase his flotilla, suggesting that, if the Army also was not re-enforced, that the Union forces would be driven out of the State.

The policy of keeping small detachments of troops at the different towns on the rivers, with the gun-boats to look after them, had no permanent effect towards bringing the State under subjection, for the roving bands of Confederates were ever on the alert to gain some advantage over the Union forces, which may be said to have been kept penned up under the protection of the gun boats.

About the same time the enemy seemed to be making a move upon Williamsburg, Va., and on the morning of April 11th they attacked that place, and commenced concentrating a heavy force on Fort Magruder, which was not far from Williamsburg.

Gun-boats were immediately required by the Army to move up and down between Yorktown and Queen's Creek, and also to lie near Jamestown Island. Every effort was made to comply with the demands made upon the Navy, and on an announcement being made to Rear-Admiral Lee by

General Peck that the enemy were advancing in an attempt to surround the Federal forces at Suffolk, the Admiral dispatched the following vessels under the command of Lieutenant R. H. Lamson, with instructions to occupy the Nansemond River between Suffolk and the bar, at the mouth of the western branch, and to render all possible assistance to the Army:

"Mount Washington" (river steamer), with a 30-pounder Parrott, 3 howitzers, and a detachment from the "Minnesota."

"Cohasset" (tug), 20-pounder Parrott and a 24-pound howitzer.

"Alert" (tug), one 12 and one 24-pound howitzer.

"Stepping Stones" (light ferry-boat), with a battery of howitzers.

The "Commodore Barney," Lieutenant W. B. Cushing, was also detached from other duty and sent to Jamestown Island.

COMMANDER (AFTERWARDS REAR-ADMIRAL) STEPHEN D. TRENCHARD.

The above list of vessels will show to what shifts the Navy was put to meet the calls made upon it by the Army. Gun-boats were called for everywhere, and these demands were more than the naval commander could comply with.

On the 11th, Major-General Keyes telegraphed that the Federal troops in the neighborhood of Williamsburg were being driven by a large force of Confederates down towards the mouth of Queen's Creek, and that, if a *large* force of gun-boats was not sent to Yorktown, even Yorktown itself might fall. The "Commodore Morris" (the only available vessel) was sent immediately to the York River to co-operate with the "Crusader," then there.

Any one can imagine the embarrassment the commander-in-chief labored under to satisfy all these demands, first in the Sounds, then on the Nansemond, James, or York rivers. After all, most of these gun-boats were merely improvised for the occasion, and the Army transports, armed with field-artillery, would have answered the same purpose. But the soldiers were not used to managing steamers up the narrow streams or handling guns behind the frail bulwarks of wooden gun-boats. Only sailors could do that kind of work, and the Army were only too glad to have them do it.

During the demonstrations made by the enemy on this occasion there was much hard service performed, frequent attacks from and repulses of the enemy. Some clever young officers were employed in this service, among them Lieutenant Lamson and the indomitable Cushing—both brave, energetic men—Lamson with the capacity of one older and more experienced, and Cushing with dash and vigor never exceeded. Lamson especially distinguished himself by planning, and with the co-operation of troops under Brigadier-General Getty, effecting the capture of five guns and 130 men on Hill's Point. This position commanded the communication between the Upper and Lower Nansemond, and the Confederates had, from it, greatly harassed the flotilla. Here Lamson captured a 24-pound howitzer and the sword of the Confederate commander.

Lieutenant Cushing again, on this occasion, exhibited those high qualities which he was known to possess in so remarkable a degree, being in a fight of some kind from the time the expedition came in sight of the enemy until the latter retreated.

The enemy's forces were under the command of General Longstreet, a brave and able officer, who with 10,000 men on the left bank of the river and a large force on the right bank, including strong field and siege batteries, was attempting to combine his forces and surround General Peck at Suffolk.

It was Cushing who prevented the Confederates from crossing the river, and kept up the communication with the Union troops. The enemy were given no rest by the flotilla. They were frequently driven from their rifle-pits, but continually returned to them with indomitable courage whenever the fire of the gun-boats slackened for a moment.

While Cushing was operating with his vessel, he also kept pickets on shore to prevent a surprise, and a party of these men captured the engineer-in-chief on the staff of the Confederate General French, who had come down near the gun-boats with the intention of locating batteries.

General Peck and General Getty both relied very much on the aid of the Navy in repulsing the Confederate attack on Suffolk, and they were largely indebted to the officers and men of the vessels for the hearty co-operation which they afforded, either by scattering the enemy with their guns or carrying the batteries on shore by assault. This latter work was done on several occasions in the most handsome manner, the assaulting party being always led by Lieutenant Lamson. General Getty, that brave old soldier, who never failed to acknowledge merit when it came under his notice, was profuse in his acknowledgments of Lieutenant Lamson's conduct in the management of the flotilla.

It would require too long an account to tell the whole story of this expedition, where fighting was carried on from the 12th of April to the 23d, where the sailors took their share of the fighting on shore, and where the gun-boats, under the incessant fire of the enemy, were nearly knocked to pieces.

But General Getty shall speak for himself. On April 20th he writes as follows:

HEADQUARTERS, 3D DIVISION, 9TH CORPS,
U. S. S. "STEPPING STONES,"
NANSEMOND RIVER, April 20th, 1863.

ADMIRAL:

I beg to express my most sincere thanks to Captain Lamson, U. S. N., his officers and crews, for the gallantry, energy and ability displayed by them in the operations of yesterday, resulting in the capture of one of the enemy's batteries of five guns, on the west side of the Nansemond, and a number of prisoners.

All did their duty most handsomely.

Very respectfully, etc.,

GEORGE W. GETTY,
Brigadier-General, U. S. Volunteers.

REAR-ADMIRAL LEE.

Also the following letters:

U. S. GUN-BOAT "STEPPING STONES,"
SLEEPY HOLE LANDING,
NANSEMOND RIVER, April 21st, 1863.

ADMIRAL:

I have again to express my obligation to Lieutenant R. H. Lamson, commanding gun-boats in upper Nansemond, for the admirable disposition of gun-boats during the withdrawal of the troops, etc., last night, from Hill's Point, and for the efficient aid rendered by him, his officers and crews in effecting the withdrawal, which was successfully accomplished, the last man having recrossed the river at 12 o'clock.

All was accomplished without confusion or accident.

The artillery, trophies, material, etc., have been landed from the "Stepping Stones" at this point, and are now on the way to Suffolk.

The prisoners were landed on the right bank of the Nansemond immediately after the battery was carried, and sent to Suffolk.

I remain, Admiral, etc., etc.,

GEORGE W. GETTY,
Brigadier-General, etc.

To REAR-ADMIRAL LEE, etc., etc.

HEADQUARTERS 3D DIVISION, 9TH CORPS,
IN THE FIELD,
NANSEMOND RIVER, April 29th, 1863.

ADMIRAL:

I deem it proper to state that all the arrangements made by Captain Lamson, U. S. N., commanding gun-boats in the upper Nansemond during the operations of the 19th and 20th instants, were fully known to and approved by me.

The conduct of Captain Lamson, his officers and men, was bold and gallant in the extreme.

I remain, Admiral, etc.,

GEORGE W. GETTY,
Brigadier-General, Commanding.

REAR-ADMIRAL S. P. LEE, etc., etc.

The operations to which these brief letters alluded were those which took place between April 12th and April 23d, in which Lieutenant Lamson, commander of a small flotilla, co-operated with Generals Peck and Getty for the protection of Suffolk, Virginia.

During this time the fighting was hard and incessant, and but for the aid of the naval force Suffolk would, without doubt, have fallen into the hands of General Longstreet, who, with a large army, attempted unsuccessfully to cross the river and surround the Union works.

That little fleet of gun-boats was under a constant fire for days without once flinching from the post of duty. Often grounding while under a heavy pelting from the enemy's field-pieces (which seemed to know no fatigue), they were almost cut to pieces. The commander expressed it, in his modest way, when he on one occasion said: "The enemy soon obtained our range, and his artillery told with fearful effect on the timbers and machinery of these lightly-built vessels." But his reports all end with a cheering account of having silenced the enemy's batteries, and scattered the sharpshooters.

One who knows anything about such matters can imagine what targets these *quasi* gun-boats must have been to Longstreet's well-trained gunners, and how hardly pummelled these veterans must have been, when they were obliged to retreat again and again before the well-directed fire of these "paper-clad" vessels.

The Confederate artillery was no sooner silenced in one position than it opened from another upon the vessels, which had not the option of choosing their position in these narrow rivers. At times they would lie in the mud, bow on to the enemy, who was too intelligent not to take advantage of their apparently helpless condition. But, with a brave energy that never flagged, Lamson would hoist his guns to the upper or hurricane deck, without considering whether the deck would bear their weight, and open fire upon the enemy until they were driven off.

The guns so mounted were often struck by the expert artillerymen of the enemy, and the decks were plowed up by their shot and shell; but the gun-boats never gave in, and only changed their positions for the purpose of bringing more guns to bear.

The Confederates would yell with delight when they could get one of the larger vessels, like the "Mount Vernon," fast in the mud, where they could bring all their artillery and sharpshooters to bear on her; but the "Stepping Stones," or some other spirited little craft, would get alongside, and tow her into deeper water, and receive without flinching the shot and shell intended for her helpless companion.

General Getty might well say that the officers and men did their duty. From such a liberal old soldier, as he was, this was but faint praise. It may be that the Army commanders considered brevity to be a virtue when dealing with such matters, for, as a rule, the Army was not eulogistic of the Navy at any time during the war. We should not attach much importance to the mere brevity of these dispatches, for sometimes much may be expressed in a very few words; but the "Records of the War" show to-day that, on almost all occasions where the Army and Navy co-operated, the reports of army operations were very voluminous, and even concerning points which could not have been held except by the guns of the Navy, the Army came in for the largest share of praise.

An affair which occurred on the 14th of April in the Nansemond River, where Lieutenant Lamson in the "Mount Washington," and Acting-Master T. A. Harris in the "Stepping Stones," fought the enemy's batteries for six hours under the most adverse circumstances, was one of the most gallant affairs of the war.

The reports of these actions are long and voluminous, and only a condensation of them can be given in this history. But they can all be found in the Report of the Secretary of the Navy for 1863, where may be seen the most faithful and interesting account of these events that has yet been written; in fact, a better story of the doings of the Navy throughout the war is given in these official reports than any historian can ever compile. They were written by the men who did the work; and who can so well describe, not only the acts that were done, but the motives that inspired them?

Now and then a paragraph forcibly strikes our attention, and, though it lengthens this work beyond bounds, we cannot leave it out. On the 14th, when the "Mount Washington" was fighting her way out of the mud, and was getting out hawsers to bring her broadside to bear, Lamson says:

* * * The hawser slipped, and the channel being so narrow, she was obliged to run down some distance before she could turn, when the enemy's artillery was again turned on the "Mount Washington." Captain Harris soon ran up to me again, and I was towed out of the enemy's range. The "Barney" still remained engaging the enemy, and continued to fire till their artillery ceased and withdrew.

Towards the close of the action the "Mount Washington's" flag-staff was shot away even with the upper deck, when Mr. Birtwistle and seaman Thielberg assisted me to haul it up out of the water by the ensign halliards, raise it, and lash it alongside the stump.

And further—

I cannot find words to express my admiration of the courageous conduct of my officers and men, who fought the guns for six hours, aground in a disabled vessel, under such a fire of artillery and musketry, and who did not flinch even from working a gun on the open hurricane deck, or from going out in boats to carry hawsers. I wish through you to express my thanks to Captain Haynes, of the "Mount Washington," and his executive officer, Mr. Griffith, who nobly refused to leave the vessel when his crew were sent away, and who rendered the most valuable assistance during the action.

Master's - Mate Birtwistle, of the "Minnesota," behaved in the most gallant manner, and I respectfully recommend him to you as a most brave and efficient officer.

There was much heroic conduct displayed on this occasion:

A seaman, Joachim Sylvia, was instantly killed and knocked overboard by a shell from the enemy, when Samuel Woods, captain of the gun, jumped overboard to rescue the body, but, before he reached it, it sank to rise no more. This gallant seaman then swam back to the vessel, went again to his gun, and fought it to the close of the action, in a manner that attracted the attention of every one.

How many noble acts of this kind occur in war without any notice being taken of them! The smaller glories are swallowed up by the greater and apparently more brilliant events, while, if the aggregate minor affairs were summed up, they would show an amount of gallantry far outweighing that of some of the grandest sea-fights.

We would gladly chronicle all these little events, but our space will not permit it. It is seldom that the sailors, who are so much exposed, have their names handed down in history, and it is a mistake commanders of vessels commit in failing to notice the gallant tars who, in all the wars which the United States has had with foreign nations, have performed acts of heroism that could not be excelled by the bravest officers.

Lieutenant Lamson shows a praiseworthy example by commending the deeds of his gallant sailors as well as those of his officers. Henry Thielberg, Robert Jourdan and John Sullivan, seamen; Robert Woods, boatswain's-mate; Quartermaster De Lunn; Third - Assistant Engineer, John Healey; William Jackson and James Lody (both colored), are all handsomely spoken of. They, no doubt, received medals (the highest reward a sailor can aspire to), but let their names go down in history as part of the gallant band who so nobly sustained the reputation of the Navy on April 14th, 1863, the anniversary of the day when Sumter, battered and torn, had to lower her flag to those who gave the first stab to our free institutions.

Another one of the events of this expedition, which General Getty alludes to, oc-curred on April 19th, when Lieutenant Lamson received on board the "Stepping Stones" a portion of the 89th New York Volunteers, under Lieutenant-Colonel England, and the 8th Connecticut, under Colonel Ward, the whole consisting of 300 men. Lieutenant Lamson had four 12-pound howitzers ready for landing, manned by sailors.

Near 6 o'clock A. M., at a preconcerted signal from the steam-whistle, a heavy fire was opened from all the gun-boats on the Confederate batteries, and from General Getty's two batteries on Colham's Point, opposite, under Captains Morris and Valler, U. S. A.

When all was in position, Lamson steamed slowly down the river, as if about to run the batteries (which he had done several times before), until he got nearly abreast of the enemy's works, when he signalled to the gun - boats and Federal batteries to cease firing, and putting his helm hard-a-starboard, ran into the bank immediately under the upper end of the enemy's works, and so close to them that the Confederates could not bring a gun to bear. The screens that had been used to hide the troops were triced up, gang-planks were launched, and with a cheer from all the boats and Union batteries the 89th New York rushed ashore, followed by the naval howitzer-battery and the 8th Connecticut.

The Confederate works consisted of two lines, with an impassable ravine between them. The Federal troops carried the first line at once, but while the 89th New York were running around the head of the ravine, the enemy swung round some of their guns, and poured a charge of grape into the assaulting party, which was immediately answered by a discharge of canister from the naval battery, that had been judiciously planted on the crest of the ravine, overlooking the inner line of defences. The brave 89th were into the works by this time, and the Confederates did not fire another shot.

The victory was a complete one. The Federals captured 161 prisoners and 5 pieces of artillery (12 and 24 pound field-guns, captured by the Confederates at Harper's Ferry or from Western Virginia), with a large amount of ammunition. Not a Confederate escaped.

Owing to the decisive charge made upon the enemy and the fortunate position occupied by the naval battery, the loss to the Federal side was small; but never was there a better commanded affair, and Lamson gives due credit to those of his officers and men who were engaged in it.

Though the work of the Navy in this affair is lightly spoken of by the Army authorities, the Secretary of the Navy saw in it something worth noticing, and he issued the following communication, which in part repaid Lieutenant Lamson for the hard work he had performed throughout the campaign:

NAVY DEPARTMENT, April 4, 1863.

SIR—Your recent important and meritorious services on the upper Nansemond deserve the special commendation of the Department. The ability displayed in the discharge of the important and responsible duties which devolved on the naval force during the late demonstration of the enemy reflected the greatest credit upon yourself and the officers and men under your command. Their zeal and courage in the hazardous positions in which they were placed have not failed to receive the approbation of both the naval and military authorities.

General Getty, with whom you have been co-operating, has expressed his obligations to you and your command for gallantry and energy displayed, especially in the capture of a rebel battery on the Nansemond, and for valuable assistance rendered to him during his operations in repelling the enemy; and your immediate commanding officer, Acting Rear-Admiral Lee, has reported in terms of admiration of your discretion and valor.

The Department congratulates you on your success, and is proud to see in the younger members of the corps such evidence of energy and gallantry and execution and ability, scarcely surpassed by those of more age and experience.

GIDEON WELLES,
Secretary of the Navy.

Cushing also came in for a share of commendation for his success on the Nansemond, and Secretary Welles was no less enthusiastic in his praise than in the case of Lieutenant Lamson:

NAVY DEPARTMENT, May 4, 1863.

SIR—Your gallantry and meritorious services during the recent demonstrations of the enemy on the Nansemond, and in co-operating with the Army, are entitled to the especial notice and commendation of the Department. Your conduct on this occasion adds additional lustre to the character you had already established for valor in the face of the enemy.

The energy and ability displayed by yourself and the officers and men under your command in defence of the lower Nansemond are most creditable, and are appreciated by the Department.

The Department desires to express to you more especially its admiration of your gallantry and enterprise, in conducting an important armed reconnaissance with a party from the gun-boats, some miles into the enemy's country to the village of Chuckatuck, and putting to flight a party of the enemy's cavalry, and safely returning to your vessel.

Accept my congratulations for yourself and the officers and men who were under your command.

GIDEON WELLES,
Secretary of the Navy.

Lieutenant W. B. CUSHING,
Commanding Steamer "Commodore Barney."

These were very complimentary words, and should have made these officers proud of the distinction that had been shown them—distinctions superior even to those received by officers who had commanded fleets and performed services that had a most decisive bearing on the war. Without doubt, these young officers deserved all that was said of them, and their performances in after service show that the commendations were not misplaced.

The result of this expedition was the repulse of the enemy and the security of the Federal forces in the intrenched works at Suffolk. But this was not war on a grand scale, such as should have been inaugurated by the Federal Government at that time, when its troops were almost numberless, and great armies were posted from Washington to Missouri. These little skirmishes and reconnaissances had no material effect upon the war. It was a great waste of men on shore and a great destruction of gunboats afloat.

It was quite evident to those who could judge, that, under such a system as the Government was pursuing, the war must languish for want of one efficient leader, who could arrange and direct the great armies which were scattered from one end of the States to the other, without apparently working for one common object. These comparatively small demonstrations had no actual value beyond making the troops familiar with the duties of soldiers in the field, and the establishment of positions at places like Suffolk (which they could not hold without a force of improvised gunboats carrying the heaviest guns) gave evidence that the art of war had not progressed much, in 1863, when such small operations were held in such high estimation. There was a great waste of military force, and in most cases waste of time, frequently without any effect (one way or the other), beyond demonstrating the zeal, energy and courage of the two arms of the service.

If one good-sized army had been stationed upon the Peninsula, its lines gradually closing in the direction of Richmond, with its centre resting upon the principal river, as it advanced, and covered by a large flotilla of well-constructed gun-boats, all the rivers in that part of Virginia would have been so completely under the Federal control that the Confederates would have had no opportunity to keep up their incessant raids, which seemed to keep the Army and Navy in a continual state of excitement.

In some cases the Army had hardly got possession of some point and made themselves warm in it, when the strategy of war turned it over to the hands of the Confederates, who would erect batteries after *their* mode of defence, and then abandon it in as summary a manner as the Federals had done before them. The same course seems to have been taken in Virginia as was tried in North Carolina—small bodies of men detailed to hold prominent positions, with a few ill-built and worse-equipped gun-boats to protect them.

There was no want of activity, courage and zeal on the part of the officers of the North Atlantic squadron, but there was so small a field of operations, with the exception of such as has been mentioned, that the officers and men had not the same opportunity for distinction as was enjoyed on other stations; though in war the true secret is to *make* the opportunity. It is what seldom comes to any one. It must be sought for, and though it is a shy spirit, not easily wooed and won, yet it puts itself in the way of those who are determined to pursue and overtake it in spite of all obstacles. The proof of this was demonstrated in the case of Lieutenants Lamson and Cushing, two daring young fellows, who lost no opportunity of bringing their names before the Navy Department, and who were as well known in the Navy as the most successful commanders of fleets.

A great many of the vessels of the North Atlantic squadron were employed in the blockade of the coast from the mouth of the Chesapeake to below Cape Fear shoals. The Cape Fear River had (since the complete blockade of Charleston) become the principal ground for blockade-runners, that river having two entrances, by either of which blockade-runners could enter, protected by Fort Caswell on the south side of Cape Fear, and by strong earth-works (which finally grew to be Fort Fisher) on the north side.

Many reports are made of the capture or destruction of blockade-runners, and in chasing up these vessels great activity was displayed. On the 6th of May, Lieutenant-Commander Braine reports a boat expedition from the steamer "Monticello" and the mortar schooner "Matthew Vassar" (Acting-Master L. A. Brown), mentioning the destruction of one of the vessels in Morrell's Inlet, an English schooner called the "Golden Liner," of Halifax, with a large cargo, and also the burning of two large store-houses. Destruction of this kind of property always caused serious loss to the enemy, and it could not be replaced.

On May 26th, Rear-Admiral Lee reports the operations in the sounds of North Carolina. It appears that the Confederates had invested Washington, on the Pamlico River, which investment lasted eighteen days, and after a fruitless effort to take the place (which would have been of no use to them if they had succeeded), the enemy retired on the 15th of April.

Washington, N. C., had been pretty extensively fortified by the Confederates while they held it, but they had been driven away from it by the Federal forces.

On the morning of March 31st the enemy appeared in force, and took possession of their old works (seven miles below the town), which had been built to cut off the water communication. The "Commodore Hull" and "Louisiana" (two light-built and vulnerable gun-boats) were at the time sta-

tioned at Washington, and, on the appearance of the Confederates, opened fire upon them with their great guns.

At 5:45, the enemy took position at Rodman's Point, and opened fire with artillery upon the "Commodore Hull," which vessel had been stationed at that point to prevent their occupying it. The fire was returned with vigor, and, after a smart action of one hour and a half, the "Commodore Hull," in changing her position, got aground, where she remained until eight P. M. exposed to a continuous and accurate fire. Her commander (Acting-Master Saltonstall) defended her most gallantly until all his ammunition was expended. The vessel was much cut up, but received no vital injury.

Meantime the "Ceres," Acting-Volunteer-Lieutenant J. Macdearmid; "Lockwood," Acting-Volunteer-Lieutenant G. W. Graves; the sloop "Granite," Acting-Master E. Boomer, and, finally, the "Hunchback," Lieutenant-Commander McCann, were dispatched by Commander Davenport to the relief of the besieged forces at Washington, but they were stopped below Hill's Point by the re-establishment of the enemy's batteries there, and by the removal of the buoys at the old obstructions. This prevented the steamers from going ahead, for fear of being grounded on the old wrecks, in which case they would easily have been destroyed. It was not possible to send out boats and place other buoys on account of the enemy's sharpshooters and flying artillery, which would have destroyed the boats. Under the circumstances there was no remedy, and the above-mentioned steamers had to remain outside; but during the siege communications were opened at great risks between the vessels above and below the batteries, thus conveying ammunition and dispatches.

On the 3d of April, the flotilla below Hill's Point was reinforced by the "Southfield," "Whitehead" and "Seymour," from Plymouth. In the meantime the "Commodore Hull" and "Louisiana," and an armed transport called the "Eagle," under charge of Second-Assistant Engineer J. L. Lay and Assistant Paymaster W. W. Williams, of the "Louisiana," as volunteers, were almost continually engaged with the enemy's batteries opposite Washington, until the morning of the 4th, when the "Ceres" made a gallant dash past the forts, with a full supply of ammunition, and joined the besieged force above.

On the 6th, a small naval battery of two light guns was established on shore, commanding the channel from above, to repel any attempt on the part of the enemy to attack the gun-boats from that quarter by water.

On the 7th inst. 112, on the 8th 107, and on the 9th 55 shot and shell were fired by the enemy at the gun-boats without inflicting any serious damage.

On the 10th, Acting - Ensign J. B. De Camarra succeeded in getting a schooner through from the lower fleet, loaded with naval ammunition.

On the 12th, the gun-boats silenced and destroyed by their fire a battery which the enemy had erected with sand-bags and cotton-bales, abreast of the town, and which for seven days previously had maintained an active and dangerous fire on them.

On the 13th, the Confederate boats filled with infantry, as pickets on the river below the forts, were driven ashore by Acting-Volunteer-Lieutenant Macdearmid, with a howitzer on a small schooner. On the same night the army transport "Escort" gallantly ran the blockade, with reinforcements for the Federal troops at Washington, having safely passed Hill's Point under cover of the gun-boats below.

On the 14th and 15th, the enemy kept up a vigorous fire with their artillery, which was returned by the gun-boats.

An opportunity occurred about the time mentioned for the Army and Navy to score a strong point on the Confederates. There were a number of troops in transports below Hill's Point waiting the opportunity to reinforce the troops above, either by running the batteries or turning them by land marches. Under cover of the gun-boats the troops could easily have carried the enemy's works at Hill's Point, but it was not attempted. The Confederate batteries were behind strong natural banks of earthworks, perforated at points with embrasures. The gun-boats had attacked them several times without any apparent effect. The position was deemed too strong to carry by assault with a limited number of troops, so the gun-boats and transports had to lie at anchor before it and make no sign, until troops could be marched overland from Newbern.

On the morning of the 15th, the steamer "Escort" arrived with General Foster on board, who seemed to think the situation so serious that his presence was demanded. The day after his arrival the enemy suddenly disappeared, and the siege was raised.

The commander of the North Atlantic squadron seemed to be well satisfied with the conduct of those under his command, and reported that the credit of the Navy had been well maintained throughout.

Commander Renshaw, at Washington, and Lieutenant-Commander McCann, below on the river, conducted affairs with prudence and zeal. The former held a position of great responsibility and severe trial, and he met the various emergencies

with promptness and decision. He had the direction of naval matters, and would have been held responsible if the town had fallen into the enemy's hands.

On the 3d inst., the enemy had established their batteries abreast of the town, one of them a rifled 12-pounder, distant 600 yards. The batteries succeeded in firing only five shots before they were silenced by the Federal shell, which fairly demolished the works.

During the siege (if it may be so called) there was an incessant peal of artillery, and the enemy seemed determined to carry the place, no matter what the cost might be to them; but, whether aground on the river-bed or lying in the stream, the fire of the gun-boats was incessant and well directed—so well directed, indeed, that the enemy frequently seemed to be firing at random.

Acting-Volunteer-Lieutenant Macdearmid is spoken of in the highest terms for his coolness and valor. This is not the first time that his name has appeared in this narrative, and it will not likely be the last.

Acting-Master Saltonstall was promoted by the Department for the steady gallantry with which he fought his disabled vessel for nearly a day against great odds, and for his good conduct during the siege.

Acting-Volunteer-Lieutenant Graves and Acting-Master Welles were commended for faithful and efficient service, and were promoted in consequence.

Acting-Ensign De Camarra, Acting-Master's Mates E. MacKeever, A. H. Hicks and Edward S. Austin were commended for their good conduct and bravery in battle.

Acting - Master F. Josselyn, Acting-Ensigns J. O. Johnson and J. B. De Camarra, Acting-Master's Mates A. F. Haraden and Henry W. Wells, Acting-Second-Assistant Engineers H. Rafferty and John E. Harper, and Paymaster's Steward John C. Cross, were recommended to especial notice for their bravery in battle.

These commendations were probably only known to the parties who secured them; and, as their names have not been handed down in history, it may be some compensation to them at this late day to know that they are remembered. De Camarra, Johnson, Wells and Hicks were recommended for promotion.

That the Navy performed excellent service in defending the garrison at Washington, N. C., there can be little doubt. The naval force appeared promptly on the scene of action, and was so well handled that it saved the garrison from capture; yet all this zeal, gallantry and efficiency is merely mentioned by General Spinola as follows:

I cannot close this report without bearing testimony to the gallant conduct of the Navy while acting in conjunction with my command, particularly Captain Macdearmid, of the gun-boat "Ceres."

The conduct of the lieutenant-commanders of the gun-boats engaged was all that could have been expected of them; they manifested great bravery, coupled with a willingness to do all in their power to relieve the garrison.

These are not the hearty expressions that should come from the pen of a gallant soldier, who should have felt and expressed a warmer gratitude for the services rendered to his army; but this seems to have been the style of noticing the work of the Navy throughout the war. Very few cases occurred where the Army could help the Navy; but, when such was the case, the latter acknowledged the obligation in a most eulogistic manner.

This affair on the Pamlico River was very much like that on the upper Nansemond—there were too few troops for the occasion. These scattered garrisons, in badly-built and poorly-armed earth-works, offered great temptations to the Confederate roving bands, who, through their spies, watched the Federal movements closely, and when the military commanders grew less watchful, or the gun-boats were out of the way, pounced upon them, expecting an easy victory. The enemy would often fight with a pertinacity bordering on desperation, and, after firing away all their ammunition, would retire as suddenly as they appeared.

What the Federals needed in order to break up these raids was a large force of cavalry, moving from one part of the State to the other with such rapidity and energetic action that the Confederates could make no headway against them. This course would have placed the Army in a more independent position, and they would not have become impressed with the idea that "every soldier ought to carry a gun-boat in his pocket."

On May 27th, Lieutenant Flusser reports an expedition under Acting-Volunteer-Lieutenant Charles A. French, who went in the steamer "Whitehead" to cruise in the eastern end of Albemarle Sound, and break up the contraband trade, a great deal of which was carried on in that vicinity. Lieutenant French reports the capture of a large two-masted boat, containing 500 barrels of tobacco. In Alligator River he captured or destroyed several boats engaged in illicit trade, and also along the shore a large quantity of pork, bacon, leather, tobacco bags, lard and tallow ready for shipment to the enemy. Many grist mills, grinding corn for the enemy, were burned by the officers of the "Valley City."

At this time the Confederate commissaries were out in great force gathering stores for the Army near Suffolk, and it was desirable to destroy as much provisions as possible—even though the non-combatants suffered considerably. Such is the law of war—no distinction can be drawn in such cases, and on this occasion the duty was performed very thoroughly.

On May 31st, 1863, General Dix concluded to evacuate West Point, at the head of York River, and on that day the Federal Army marched out, covered by the gun-boats "Commodore Morris," "Commodore Jones," "Morse" and "Mystic," under the command of Lieutenant-Commander Gillis. The operation was effected without the slightest accident, and without any demonstration on the part of the enemy. Everything belonging to the United States Government was safely removed, the gun-boats taking on board the forage, provisions and ammunition, and landing them safely at Yorktown.

In the latter part of May, Lieutenant-Commander James H. Gillis participated in an expedition with Brigadier-General Kilpatrick in Matthews County. The object of the expedition was to mount all the dismounted men in Kilpatrick's command.

Lieutenant-Commander Gillis took on board the "Commodore Morris" 100 men from the 4th Delaware Volunteers, under Major La Mott, and with the "Winnissimmet" in company proceeded to North River, where he arrived at half-past five P.M. Here were captured 300 horses, 150 head of cattle and a large number of sheep. At the same time the troops destroyed all the property that could be of any use to the Confederates.

A large amount of property was destroyed in these raids. It was impossible to discriminate, and, in consequence, a great many innocent people suffered.

One of the mail-boats (the "Swan") was fired upon by a party of Confederate raiders, on York River, below West Point, the result of which was the burning by the gun-boat "Morse" of twelve houses, in front or behind which the enemy had placed their batteries. The object evidently was to have these houses burned, in order to embitter the inhabitants against the Union troops. The justification given for firing the buildings was that an unarmed mail-boat, which was in the habit of carrying women and children as passengers, had been fired upon by the Confederates.

It was rather a severe punishment to inflict on an unoffending people, because the Confederates would not stay to be captured, and it certainly was not the best method of gaining the confidence of the citizens, whom the Army and Navy claimed to protect. The amenities of war were entirely forgotten on this occasion, and such wantonness could only insure retaliation on the first favorable opportunity.

On the morning of June 4th, an expedition of 400 soldiers embarked at Yorktown on board the United States steamers "Commodore Morris" (Lieutenant-Commander Gillis), "Commodore Jones" (Lieutenant-Commander Mitchell), the army gun-boat "Smith Briggs" and the transport "Winnissimmet."

These vessels proceeded to Walkertown, about twenty miles above West Point, on the Mattapony River. Here the troops were landed and marched to Aylett's, where the object of the expedition was successfully accomplished: a large foundry, with all its machinery, grist mills, and a quantity of grain were destroyed, and a number of horses captured.

The affair was carried through without any accident, the gun-boats keeping the river open, though several attempts were made by the enemy to annoy them at different points. This expedition was fitted out (as appears from a general order of General Keyes) with the purpose of "striking an effective blow at the enemy," but the results were only as above stated.

These events do not appear very striking on paper, but in a campaign which did not offer a very large scope for military and naval operations, they hold a place worthy of being mentioned, as exhibiting the zeal, bravery and enterprise of the Federal officers, who showed a determination to annoy and cripple the enemy in every possible way.

But still this was not war, in the true sense of the word—it was simply raiding—when we had quite a respectable force that should have been gaining victories over the enemy, who did not seem unwilling to meet the encounters of the Federal troops, and who held their own positions and checked the advance beyond the upper Nansemond whenever it was attempted.

The records of the times, in speaking of the military movements on the Peninsula, have constant accounts of the Federal's getting possession of West Point and then evacuating it, to fall back on Yorktown, which latter place seems to have been kept for a harbor of safety, or a resort from whence the Army could, by aid of the gun-boats, make a dash, carry off some heads of beef and horses, and return with little or no loss. But at that moment it was the only field of adventure which offered itself to the North Atlantic squadron, and the Navy was glad of the opportunity to share with the Army the dangers (if there were any) of these expeditions.

We are aware that the doings of the North Atlantic squadron afford dry reading, in comparison with the more brilliant achievements enacting elsewhere; but it is a part of the history of the war, in which the Navy bore its part, if not with any important success, yet with patience, zeal and gallantry, under circumstances which were ofttimes more trying than was the case in other squadrons, where a wider field of action was offered.

It may seem to the reader that we have dwelt longer than necessary on what might be considered unimportant events, but the small matters are the links in the chain of history, which, if omitted, would leave the story incomplete. Officers themselves have attached so much importance to some of these events, and have made such minute reports of them, that they possess more intrinsic value than appears upon their face.

A good many of the later reports are taken up with accounts of small expeditions in the sounds of North Carolina, the gun-boats being evidently constantly employed attacking small bodies of the enemy in narrow and crooked streams, destroying granaries, and detecting Confederate sympathizers. But with all our desire to do justice to the praiseworthy efforts of the officers and men of the North Atlantic squadron, and to mention all those who in any way distinguished themselves or scored a good point on the enemy, we feel obliged to omit many accounts of expeditions which would take up the place of more important matters having a greater bearing on the war. Therefore, we will confine ourselves to such expeditions as accomplished important results. Our pages are limited, and we desire to make them as bright as possible.

On the 31st of July, 1863, the steamer "Kate," belonging to the Confederates, while going into Wilmington, was driven on Smith's Island Beach by the gun-boat "Penobscot," but was eventually floated off by the enemy, and towed under the batteries at New Inlet.

Early in the morning of the 1st of August, the blockading vessels, "James Adger," "Mount Vernon" and "Iroquois," approached, and the "Mount Vernon," discovering the condition of the Confederate steamer, reported it to Captain Case, of the "Iroquois." This officer immediately organized an expedition to cut the vessel out from under the guns of Fort Fisher (which had not at that time assumed such formidable proportions as it did later on).

The Confederates were at this time towing the "Kate" in towards New Inlet, and Commander Patterson, in the "James Adger," was ordered to assist the "Mount Vernon" in cutting her out, and prevent her reaching the protection of the batteries.

At seven o'clock, the "Mount Vernon" opened fire upon the steamer, when her commander (Acting-Volunteer-Lieutenant James Trathen) received orders from Captain Case to "drag the 'Kate' out." Two boats were called away from the "Mount Vernon" and sent to board the "Kate," while the vessel herself went alongside, and sent another party on board at the same time. A hawser was made fast to the prize, and she was towed out.

The Confederate batteries at New Inlet opened with great vigor, and a masked battery of Whitworth guns on Smith's Island kept up a furious fire. The enemy did not seem to be particular in his aim, as an 80-pounder Armstrong rifle-shot passed through the port-side of the "Kate," and out through the starboard bulwarks, just as the "Mount Vernon" and her boats boarded her. Several shots from heavy Armstrong guns and Whitworth 12-pounders struck the "Mount Vernon." One Whitworth projectile passed through the engine-room, instantly killing Edwin H. Peck, first-class fireman. This shot lodged in the engineer's tool-chest, demolishing the contents. An Armstrong rifle-shot cut away all the shrouds of the port fore-rigging. A Whitworth shot cut away the fore-topmast rigging, and another the fore-gaff. A shot from the mound battery carried away the stock of the port-anchor. Many shot passed over the vessel and all around her, and the firing from the enemy's work was lively enough to make the affair very exciting. But the commander of the "Mount Vernon" did not abandon his prize; he towed her out, and delivered her to the "Iroquois," which vessel took her to Beaufort.

This cutting-out was gallantly done, and the parties concerned deserve great credit. Captain Case speaks handsomely of the manner in which Lieutenant Trathen boarded the "Kate" and towed her off shore. It was not only the coolness and bravery with which this affair was conducted, but also the professional skill with which the "Mount Vernon" was managed by her commander that gives it special merit.

There were lively times when a blockade-runner was sighted. Starting a hare with a pack of hounds would not create a greater excitement than when a long, lean, English-built steamer, with a speed of sixteen knots an hour, suddenly found herself almost in the grip of the blockaders, which, being usually on the alert, would give her a hard chase, if they did not capture her outright.

To look at the beautiful lines of one of these small steamers (which often carried cargoes worth half a million) as she skimmed over the water, it would seem impossible that our improvised cruisers could overtake her. These vessels, built in England with all the science known to English ship-builders, were sent fearlessly upon our coast, with a certainty that nothing we had could overtake them. Yet how mistaken the British builders were with regard to Yankee watchfulness and naval pluck!

Every mail would carry the news to England of their fastest vessels having been picked up by Federal cruisers — though they may have made several successful runs ere they came to grief. It is said that if one blockade-runner out of three could make a successful passage, it would more than cover the cost of all.

On August 18th, one of these clippers, the "Hebe," attempted to run into Wilmington by the New Inlet channel. There were several blockaders on the alert, and among them the "Niphon"—which vessel, being in-shore of the "Hebe," attempted to head her off. But, instead of surrendering when he saw that his vessel was cut off, the commander of the "Hebe" beached her, and escaped in his boats, with his crew and passengers.

It was then blowing a gale from the northeast, with a heavy sea on, and the waves broke over the doomed vessel.

Lieutenant W. B. Cushing commanded one of the vessels present on this occasion (the "Shokokon"), and from the two vessels a boarding-party was formed which started through the breakers to destroy the "Hebe."

There were always companies of Confederate artillery moving up and down the coast to prevent vessels driven on shore from being destroyed by blockaders. The boarding-party had no sooner landed and boarded the steamer, with the intent to fire her, than they were opened upon by Confederate artillery, well posted behind the sand-hills, and these kept up a warm fire, not only on the boarders, but on the two gun-boats, which the latter were unable to return with any certainty, owing to the heavy sea running. The result was that the "Niphon" lost two boats, which were swamped in the breakers, and fifteen persons by capture, four of whom were officers. One ensign (E. H. Dewey) and three men were saved by the boats of the two gun-boats.

On this occasion, though there was a good deal of gallantry displayed, there was bad luck for the blockaders, and the enemy succeeded in getting a large part of the damaged cargo on shore.

Later in the month the Federal vessels came in for a share of the cargo, and destroyed the steamer, but not until the enemy had shown a strong determination to hold on to all of the "Hebe" that they could.

On the 23d of August, Commander T. H. Patterson, in the "James Adger," was directed to proceed to the "Hebe," and try to destroy her. When within 500 yards of her, he opened fire upon the vessel's hull and upon the enemy's artillery, which was located behind the sand-hills on the beach, about 100 yards from the "Hebe." This fire was kept up until the steamer was pretty well cut to pieces. (A boat had been sent in before the firing commenced to see if it were practicable to get the vessel afloat, but it was opened upon by the enemy with musketry and a Whitworth gun, and all hopes of saving her were abandoned.) The enemy also concentrated the fire of their field-pieces on the "James Adger," striking her three times in the hull, one shot passing through the air-jacket of the donkey-engine, and another cutting the rim of the starboard-wheel.

Notwithstanding the fire of the enemy, the boats of the blockading vessels brought off some Whitworth guns that had been abandoned; and the "Hebe," being now practically of no use, was left upon the beach to be broken up by the winds and waves. A great deal of ammunition was expended upon this vessel—163 shot and shells from the "James Adger," and 145 from the flag-ship "Minnesota."

On the 22d of August, 1863, quite a gallant affair took place, when Lieutenant Cushing cut out and destroyed the blockade-running schooner "Alexander Cooper."

On the 12th, Cushing made a reconnaissance, in the boats of the "Shokokon," of "New Topsail Inlet," and was driven off by the fire of four Confederate field-pieces stationed near the entrance of the inlet. But before he was driven back he discovered a schooner at anchor at a wharf about six miles up the sound. This schooner he determined to destroy.

On the evening of the 22d the "Shokokon" anchored close to the sea-beach, about five miles from the inlet, and sent on shore two boats' crews—who shouldered the dinghy, and carried it across the neck of land that divided the sea from the sound (this was half a mile in width, covered with a dense thicket). This crossing placed the landing party some miles in the rear of the artillery force guarding the entrance. The dinghy being launched on the inside waters, six men, under the executive officer, Acting Ensign J. S. Cony, started, with orders to capture or destroy anything that might be of use to the enemy.

A 12-pound howitzer was stationed at the point towards which the expedition was bound, and the smoke-stack of the "Shokokon" having been seen over the trees, Captain Adams (the Confederate officer in charge of the post) went over to see that a bright look-out was kept. While the Confederates at the schooner's mast-heads were straining their eyes in looking to the southward, the boat was approaching them from another direction, and the Federals succeeded in landing fifty yards from the wharf without being discovered.

The master-at-arms (Robert Clifford)

creeping into the Confederate camp, counted their men; when, having returned to his shipmates, a charge was ordered, and the seven men bore down upon the enemy with three cheers. In a moment the Confederates (who out-numbered our sailors three to one) were routed, leaving in Ensign Cony's hands ten prisoners (including Captain Adams and Lieutenant Latham), one 12-pound howitzer, eighteen horses, one schooner and some extensive salt-works. Mr. Cony then threw out two pickets, detailed two men to guard the prisoners, and, with the remaining two, fired the schooner and salt-works, which were entirely consumed.

The object of the expedition having been accomplished, the men returned to their vessel, taking with them three prisoners, all that the boat would hold. The Confederate officers and men were all dressed alike, and Mr. Cony could not tell them apart, so he was at a loss to know which to retain. He settled the matter by picking out the three best-looking, who all turned out to be privates!

This performance almost sounds like romance, but Cushing's officers were all animated with his spirit, and were always ready to undertake anything, no matter how hazardous. As many risks were run, and as many dangers faced, as fell to Decatur's lot when he cut out the "Philadelphia" in Tripoli harbor.

The later operations of the North Atlantic squadron, in 1863, were merely attempts to co-operate with the Army up the shoal rivers within the limits of the command, keeping down the Confederate raiders, and intercepting dispatches between Virginia and Maryland, in which every light-draft vessel was continually employed. It was not a very brilliant service, but it was a useful one. Without it the Confederates would have seriously harassed the important Army posts, and driven in the smaller ones. They dreaded those frail vessels, with their heavy guns and fearless seamen, and a gun-boat was often worth more to the Army than two or three stout regiments.

The last act chronicled in the records of the North Atlantic squadron for this year is the destruction of the blockade-runner "Venus," on October 21st.

The "Venus" was from Nassau, bound to Wilmington, and, while attempting to run the blockade, was chased by the steamer "Nansemond," Lieutenant Lamson, and overtaken. As the chase did not comply with his orders to heave-to, Lieutenant Lamson opened fire upon her. One shot struck her foremast, another exploded in her ward-room, a third passed through the funnel and killed one man, and a fourth, striking an iron plate near the water line, caused her to leak so badly that it was necessary to run her on shore, where (as it was found impossible to save her) she was set fire to and burned, her boilers blown up, and her machinery destroyed.

The " Venus " was a splendid vessel of 1,000 tons burden, and, had she not been destroyed, would have made a useful addition to the gun-boat fleet.

During all this time, be it remembered, many vessels of this squadron were engaged in that dreary blockade duty, which, though somewhat wanting in incidents of a desperate character, was continually adding history to the Navy by successful captures of arms and munitions of war, and creating great astonishment abroad at the ability of the Federals to keep up such an effective blockade, contrary to the predictions of able statesmen and experienced admirals.

This duty was relieved somewhat of its monotony, as it paid well in prize-money, which amply compensated officers and sailors for any hardships they had to undergo in winter storms or summer heats.

NORTH ATLANTIC SQUADRON, JANUARY 1, 1863.

ACTING-REAR-ADMIRAL SAMUEL P. LEE.

COMMANDER PIERCE CROSBY, FLEET CAPTAIN, JULY, 1863.—LIEUTENANT R. H. LAMSON, FLAG LIEUTENANT, APRIL, 1863.

STEAM-FRIGATE "MINNESOTA"—FLAG-SHIP.

Commander, N. B. Harrison; Lieutenant-Commander, E. C. Grafton; Lieutenant, Adolphus Dexter; Fleet Surgeon, W. Maxwell Wood; Surgeon, John S. Kitchen; Assistant Surgeons, S. J. Jones and E. R. Dodge; Paymaster, C. C. Upham; Chaplain, T. G. Salter; Marines: Captain, W. L. Shuttleworth, Second-Lieutenant, C. F. Williams; Acting-Masters, D. A. Campbell and Wm. Wright; Ensigns, J. H. Porter, R. S. Chew, C. S. Cotton and S. W. Terry; Acting Ensigns, F. R. Webb and Amos Brown; Master's Mates, Wm. Hunter, C. W. Campbell, W. R. Hunter, James Birtwistle and P. B. Doran; Engineers: Chief, Philip G. Peltz; Second-Assistant, G. W. Sensner; Third-Assistants, Alfred Colin, T. W. Ray, G. W. Thorn, Webster Lane and Guy Samson; Boatswain, Wm. Bunker; Gunner, C. W. Homer; Carpenter, E. Thompson; Sailmaker, T. O. Fassett.

STEAMER "OSSIPEE."

Captain, John P. Gillis; Lieutenant-Commander, Robert Boyd, Jr.; Lieutenant, John A. Howell; Surgeon, Thomas T. Turner, Paymaster, Edward Foster; Acting-Master, C. E. Bunker; Acting-Ensigns, H. S. Lambert and C. W. Adams; Acting-Master's Mates, Wm. Knapp, Jr., Charles Putnam, Wm. Wingood, W. W. Gregg and W. W. Black; Engineers: Acting-First-Assistant, J. M. Adams; Second-Assistants, Jas. Renshaw and John Wilson; Third-Assistants, C. S. Maurice, W. W. Vanderbilt and Monroe Murphy; Acting-Third-Assistants, J. R. Webb and G. W. Kidder; Boatswain, Andrew Milne; Acting-Gunner, John. Q. Adams.

STEAMER "DACOTAH."

Captain, Benj. F. Sands; Lieutenants, G. C. Wiltse and S. D. Ames; Surgeon, Delavan Bloodgood; Paymaster, Richard Washington; Acting-Masters, Wm. Earle and Wm. Moslander; Acting-Ensign, Isaac Francis; Acting-Master's Mates, Paul Borner, Charles Trathen, John McMillen and C. H. Chase; Engineers: Chief, Wm. W. Dungan; Acting-First-Assistant, Wm. H. Dobbs; Acting-Second-Assistants, G. R. Bennett, Wm. Best and Charles Cranston; Acting-Third-Assistants, J. H. Perry and G. W. Wilkinson; Acting-Gunner, Geo. Edmond.

STORE-SHIP "BRANDYWINE."

Commander, Benj. J. Totten; Acting-Lieutenant, S. J. Shipley; Paymasters, C. J. Emery and Thos. H. Looker; Acting-Assistant Surgeon, J. J. Sowerby; Acting-Masters, A. B. Mulford, G. W. Hyde,

W. B. Newman, J. F. D. Robinson and Wm. H. Hubbs; Acting-Master's Mates, W. H. Bryant, J. J. Everhardt, J. L. Robins and J. B. Cawood.

STEAMER "IROQUOIS."

Commander, A. Ludlow Case; Lieutenant-Commander, Wm. E. Fitzhugh; Lieutenants, H. E. Mullan; Surgeon, Wm. E. Taylor; Assistant Paymaster, John A. Bates; Acting-Ensigns, Joseph Avant, Thos. Stothard and J. D. Dexter; Acting-Master's Mates, John Roberts, Horace Dexter, W. F. Halsall and Matthew Crimmen; Engineers: Acting-First-Assistant, J. W. Storms; Acting-Second-Assistants, Warren Ewen and W. J. Howard; Acting-Third-Assistants, J. H. Mathews, W. J. Barrington and H. S. Short; Boatswain, J. H. Downs; Acting-Gunner, J. C. Clapham.

STEAMER "MARATANZA."

Commander, Gustavus H. Scott; Lieutenant-Commander, Chas. S. Norton; Assistant Surgeon, Job Corbin; Assistant Paymaster, C. S. Perley; Acting-Masters, Chas. Courtney, Jacob Kimball and J. B. Wood, Jr.; Acting-Ensigns, J. C. Gibney and Geo. Smith; Acting-Master's Mate, Henry Wheeler; Engineers: Acting-First-Assistant, C. L. Carty; Second-Assistant, Edward Scattergood; Third-Assistants, W. H. Kilpatrick, L. R. Harvey and R. L. Webb.

STEAMER "STATE OF GEORGIA."

Commander, James F. Armstrong; Acting-Assistant Surgeon, W. W. Myers; Acting-Assistant Paymaster, T. H. Haskell; Acting-Masters, J. S. Rogers and A. D. Littlefield; Acting-Ensigns, David Mason and N. Broughton; Acting-Master's Mates, Isaac Halleck, J. W. Buck and Wm. B. Mix, Engineers: Acting-First-Assistant, James Wilkinson; Acting-Second-Assistant, David Pyke; Acting-Third-Assistants, J. D. Rodgers, Thomas Nesbit and E. F. Maxfield; Acting-Gunner, Andrew Hannen.

STEAMER "CAMBRIDGE."

Commander, Wm. A. Parker; Acting-Master, F. W. Strong; Acting-Assistant Surgeon, Ezra Pray; Acting-Assistant Paymaster, J. C. Canning; Acting-Ensigns, E. A. Small, S. H. Meade, Jr., and D. W. Glenny; Acting-Master's Mates, W. T. Dungin, H. B. Nickerson and G. K. Knowlton; Engineers: Acting-First-Assistant, Geo. B. Orswell; Acting-Second-Assistant, J. F. Powers; Acting-Third-Assistants, H. F. Hayden and John Whitaker; Acting-Gunner, Wm. Fisk; Carpenter, Theo. D. Wilson.

STEAMER "MAHASKA."

Commander, Foxhall A. Parker; Lieutenants,

N. H. Farquhar and E. C. V. Blake; Assistant Surgeon, John C. Spear ; Acting-Assistant Surgeon, Chas. Fairchild; Acting-Master, Benj. Dyer; Acting-Ensigns, N. W. Black and Frederick Elliott; Acting-Master's Mates, G. E. French and F. M. Drake; Engineers: Acting-First-Assistant, Geo. E. Ashby; Third-Assistants, Elisha Harsen, Thomas La Blanc, J. C. Stevens and E. L. Hewitt.

STEAMER "HETZEL."

Commander, H. K. Davenport; Acting-Assistant Surgeon, N. L. Campbell; Acting-Assistant Paymaster, G. W. Morton ; Acting-Masters, G. B. Thompson and G. W. Caswell ; Acting-Master's Mates, Benj. Walker and John Rudrow; Engineers: Acting-Second-Assistant, J. B. Dick; Third-Assistants, J. H. Padgett, T. B. Cole and Eli Tempeny.

SLOOP-OF-WAR "VANDALIA."

Lieutenant, M. B. Woolsey ; Surgeon, A. C. Gorgas; Paymaster, Rufus Parks; First-Lieutenant of Marines, C. H. Nye; Acting-Masters, E. M. King, C. Folsom and A. Washburn; Acting-Ensign, F. H. Bacon; Acting-Master's Mate, Richard Burk; Boatswain, P. J. Miller; Gunner, Wm. Cheney; Sailmaker, Wm. Rogers.

STEAMER "MYSTIC."

Lieutenant-Commander, H. N. T. Arnold; Acting-Assistant Surgeon, Wm. F. Brown; Acting-Assistant Paymaster, T. E. Smith; Acting-Masters, S. B. Meader and R. F. Coffin ; Acting-Ensign, A. F. Hamblin; Acting-Master's Mate, J. M. C. Reville ; Engineers : Acting-Second-Assistants, J. B. Lovell and J. B. A. Allen; Acting-Third-Assistants, H. F. Loveaire, George W. Shank and Isaac Buck.

IRON-CLAD STEAMER "GALENA."

Lieutenant-Commander, Leonard Paulding; Acting-Lieutenant, James Parker; Assistant Surgeon, R. E. Van Gieson; Acting-Assistant Paymaster, J. H. Sellman; Acting-Masters, I. D. Seyburn and Edmund Kemble; Acting-Master's Mates, Andrew McCleary, J. H. Jenks and E. A. Galindo; Engineers: Acting-First-Assistant, J. G. Young; Acting-Second-Assistants, B. F. Beckett and A. S. Chipman; Acting-Third-Assistants, Thomas Millholland, Wm. Deaver and C. W. Kenyon; Boatswain, J. H. Polly; Gunner, William Hardison.

STEAMER "PENOBSCOT."

Lieutenant-Commander, J. E. de Haven; Assistant Surgeon, Edw. A. Pierson; Acting-Assistant Paymaster, Addison Poole; Acting-Master, Charles E. Jack; Acting-Ensigns, S. K. Luce and H. D. Edwards; Acting-Master's Mate, G. H. Smith; Engineers: Acting-Second-Assistant, Geo. W. Cobb; Acting-Third-Assistants, Wm. M. Rodes, Wm. C. Burrett and G. W. Hall.

STEAMER "CHOCURA."

Lieutenant-Commander, Wm. T. Truxton; Lieutenant, John McFarland; Assistant Surgeon, Chas. Carter; Acting-Assistant Paymaster, E. L. Turner; Acting-Masters, P. S. Borden and T. B. Sears; Acting-Master's Mates, D. M. Carver, Wm. Leonard and A. P. Atwood; Engineers: Second-Assistant, Zeph. Talbot; Third-Assistants, Andrew Blythe, Theodore Cooper and Wm. H. Harrison.

STEAMER "MONTICELLO."

Lieutenant-Commander, D. L. Braine; Acting-Assistant Surgeon, Wm. Gale; Acting-Assistant Paymaster, G. de F. Barton ; Acting-Masters, J. F. Winchester, L. A. Brown and Richard Hustace. Acting-Ensign, A. G. Stebbins ; Acting-Master's Mates, Henry Baker and T. J. Gildersleeve; Engineers: Acting-Second-Assistants, John Pick and W. S. Montgomery; Acting-Third-Assistants, Thomas McGough and A. L. Koones.

STEAMER "COMMODORE PERRY."

Lieutenant-Commander, Charles W. Flusser, Acting-Assistant Surgeon, Geo. W. Gale; Acting-Assist-

ant Paymaster, W. H. Anderson; Acting-Master, H. A. Phelon; Acting-Ensign, Wm. P. Burke ; Acting-Master's Mates, George B. Howard and Daniel Laken; Engineers: Acting-Second-Assistant, G. W. Richards; Acting-Third-Assistants, J. L. Bowers and F. A. Whitfield.

STEAMER "HUNCHBACK."

Lieutenant-Commander, Wm. P. McCann; Acting-Assistant Surgeon, George R. Mann; Acting-Assistant Paymaster, Henry Cushing; Acting-Master, Richard Pasquell; Acting-Master's Mates, W. L. Weaver, C. H. Weaver, R. P. Boss, John Maddock and T. C. Barton; Engineers: Acting-Second-Assistant, Henry Armstrong; Acting Third-Assistants, John Wall, James Dodd and Bryce Wilson.

STEAMER "COMMODORE MORRIS."

Lieutenant-Commander, James H. Gillis; Acting-Assistant Surgeon, M. H. Henry; Acting-Assistant Paymaster, C. G. Hutchinson; Acting Master, A. A. Lewis; Acting-Ensigns, P. B. Low and H. M. Pierce; Acting-Master's Mates, R. C. J. Pendleton, W. H. Otis and C. E. Blanchard; Engineers: Acting-Second-Assistant, Volney Cronk; Acting-Third-Assistants, B. F. Harris, Henry Harbinson and H. J. Watkins.

STEAMER "COMMODORE BARNEY."

Lieutenant-Commander, J. C. Chaplin; Acting-Assistant Surgeon, James Kinnier; Acting-Assistant Paymaster, Benj. Page ; Acting-Ensigns, Wm. Betts, Cornelius Washburn and B. P. Trask ; Acting-Master's Mates, David Fader and John Aspinwall, Jr.; Engineers: Acting-Second-Assistant, Thos. Pemblett; Acting-Third-Assistants, L. M. Kensil and Hiram Warner.

STEAMER "MORSE."

Lieutenant-Commander, Chas. A. Babcock; Acting-Assistant Surgeon, G. F. Winslow ; Acting-Assistant Paymaster, Henry Russell; Acting-Ensigns, C. F. Russell and J. F. Merry; Acting-Master's Mates, C. E. Rich, J. W. Thompson and Wm. Dunne; Engineers: Acting-Second-Assistant, Thos. Devine; Acting-Third-Assistants, Geo. West and Tim. Flanders.

STEAMER "VICTORIA."

Acting-Volunteer-Lieutenant, Edward Hooker; Acting-Assistant Surgeon, John G. Parke; Acting-Assistant Paymaster, H. S. Bradford; Acting-Master, Alfred Everson; Acting-Ensign, Wm. H. Meyer; Acting-Master's Mates, B. W. Tucker and Wm. Moodey; Engineers: Acting-Second-Assistant, T. D. Webster; Acting-Third-Assistants, J. M. Berron, John Haversfield and J. E. Robinson.

STEAMER "UNDERWRITER."

Acting-Volunteer-Lieutenant, Wm. Flye; Acting-Assistant Surgeon, L. R. Boyce; Acting-Assistant Paymaster, C. H. Brown; Acting-Master's Mates, W. K. Engell, W. B. Griffith and Daniel Ward; Engineers: Acting-Third-Assistants, John Morse, S. B. Ellis and H. R. Steever.

MER "COLUMBIA."

Acting-Volunteer-Lieutenant, Jas. P. Couthouy; Acting-Masters, J. W. Balch and E. A. Howell; Acting-Ensigns, J. S. Williams and E. T. Manter; Acting-Master's Mates, E. Morse, E. L. Bourne and E. M. Clarke; Acting-Assistant Surgeon, Passmore Treadwell; Acting-Assistant Paymaster, T. Q. Hill; Engineers : Acting-First-Assistant, G. M. Bennett; Second-Assistant, W. W. Shipman; Acting-Second-Assistant, Samuel Lemmon; Acting-Third-Assistants, J. H. Pelton and W. H. Crawford.

STEAMER "MIAMI."

Acting-Lieutenant, Robert Townsend; Assistant Surgeon, Wm. B. Mann; Acting-Assistant Paymaster, Frank W. Hackett; Acting-Masters, W. N. Welles, Milford Rogers and John Lear; Acting-Ensign, R. W. Rountree; Acting Master's Mate, John Quevedo; Engineers: Acting-Second-Assistant, L. W. Simonds; Acting-Third-Assistants, C. C. Davis, H. D. Heiser, W. A. Windsor and J. W. Saville.

STEAMER "DELAWARE."

Acting-Volunteer-Lieutenant, Amos P. Foster; Acting-Assistant Surgeon, Lorenzo Traver; Acting-Assistant-Paymaster, G. T. Benedict; Acting-Master, H. H. Foster; Acting-Ensign, J. H. Kerens; Acting-Master's Mates, J. H. Sprigman and Wm. Thompson; Engineers: Acting Second - Assistant, J. D. Williamson; Acting-Third-Assistants, T. J. Brown, James Mellon and R. O. Dennett.

STEAMER "VALLEY CITY."

Acting-Volunteer-Lieutenant, Hartman K. Furniss; Acting-Assistant Surgeon, F. E. Martinsdale; Acting-Assistant Paymaster, W. T. Whitmore; Acting-Master, J. A. J. Brooks; Acting-Master's Mates, John Cullaton and Thos. Langton; Acting-Third-Assistant - Engineers, B. Hilderbrand and Joseph Peddle.

STEAMER "SOUTHFIELD."

Acting - Volunteer - Lieutenant, C. F. W. Behm; Acting-Assistant Surgeon, W. H. Holmes; Acting-Assistant Paymaster, W. Goldsborough; Acting-Masters, Richard Vevers, W. F. Pratt and W. G. Nutting; Acting-Ensign, Thos. B. Stokes; Acting-Master's Mates, C. A. Stewart, G. W. Pratt and John Woodman; Acting-Third-Assistant Engineers, Walter Bradley, H. M. Tuell and J. B. Ferrand.

STEAMER "MOUNT VERNON."

Acting - Volunteer - Lieutenant, James Tathern; Acting-Assistant Surgeon, S. B. Hoppin; Acting-Assistant Paymaster, H. Y. Glisson; Acting-Masters, E. W. White and W. T. Buck; Acting-Ensign, F. M. Page; Acting-Master's Mates, Lloyd Rogers, Ernest Hodder and G. C. Kellogg; Engineers: Acting-Second-Assistant, Jos. McKnight; Acting - Third - Assistants, J. H. Horsford, Wm. Emmons and Esubius Minne.

STEAMER "CERES."

Acting-Volunteer-Lieutenant, John Macdearmid; Acting-Master's Mates, M. Tallmadge Ryan and H. A. Hudson; Engineers: Acting - Second - Assistant, Hugh Rafferty; Third-Assistant, John S. Harper.

SCHOONER "SAMUEL ROTAN."

Acting-Volunteer-Lieutenant, W. W. Kennison; Acting-Master's Mates, Thos. Moore, C. H. Packer and D. M. Gaskins.

STEAMER "JOHN L. LOCKWOOD."

Acting-Master, G. W. Graves; Acting-Master's Mates, A. H. Hicks and Edw. Austin; Engineers: Acting-Second-Assistants, J. T. Newton and W. W. Whiting; Acting-Third-Assistant, J. T. Miller.

STEAMER "GENERAL PUTNAM."

Acting-Master, Wm. J. Hotchkiss; Acting-Ensign, Wm. Jennings; Acting-Master's Mates, H. C. Hawkins, A. P. Kirkham and C. A. Jones; Engineers: Acting-Second-Assistants, James Osburn and R. A. Copeland; Acting - Third - Assistants, John Henry and W. P. Higgins.

STEAMER "HENRY BRINKER."

Acting-Master, James H. Hardesty; Acting-Ensign, H. S. Livermore; Acting-Master's Mate, Wm. B. Miles; Engineers: Acting - Second - Assistant, J. W. Kelsey; Acting - Third - Assistants, Robert Ross and W. H. Tate.

STEAMER "YOUNG ROVER."

Acting-Masters, Ira B. Studley and T. W. Dodge; Acting-Assistant Surgeon, Rob't Cowie; Acting-Assistant Paymaster, Geo. W. Stone; Acting-Ensigns, D. S. Thompson, J. A. Edgren and E. M. Ryder; Acting - Master's Mates, W. F. Gragg and Joshua Simmons; Engineers: Acting - Second - Assistant, James Patterson; Acting-Third-Assistant, Samuel McAvoy.

STEAMER "PHILADELPHIA."

Acting-Master, Silas Reynolds; Engineers: Acting-Second - Assistant, C. A. Norris; Acting - Third - Assistants, W. H. Capin and Robert Mulready.

STEAMER "STEPPING STONES."

Acting-Master, T. A. Harris; Acting-Master's Mate, G. M. Lawrence: Engineers: Acting-Second-Assistant, James A. Brown; Acting-Third-Assistant, Edw. Aspald.

SHIP "ROMAN."

Acting-Master, Francis P. Allen.

STEAMER "DAYLIGHT."

Acting-Masters, Joshua D. Warren and J. H. Gleason; Acting-Assistant Surgeon, F. M. Dearborne; Acting-Assistant Paymaster, H. M. Rogers; Acting-Ensigns, Wm. H. Brice. J. W. Willard and W. H. Penfield; Acting-Master's Mates, A. E. Barrett and Charles Attmore; Engineers: Acting-Second-Assistant, C. D. Kiersted; Acting Third-Assistants, C. O. Morgan and J. M. Battin.

STEAMER "SEYMOUR."

Acting-Master, Francis S Wells; Acting-Ensign, Chas. Ringot; Acting-Master's Mate, Edwin Smith; Engineers: Acting - Second - Assistant, Newton Eggleston; Acting - Third - Assistants, J. A. Whittaker and Philip Hublitz.

STEAMER "WYANDOTTE."

Acting-Master, Thomas Wright; Acting-Assistant Surgeon, James Pennoyer; Assistant-Paymaster, Alex. McC. Bishop; Acting-Ensigns, S. A. Hodge, Benj. Wood and Wm. Henry; Acting-Master's Mates, M. E. Wandell and Wm. Chandler; Engineers: Acting-Second-Assistant, Cornelius Carr; Acting-Third-Assistants, G. R. Dunkley, Wm. Veitch and John Heaney.

STEAMER "COMMODORE HULL."

Acting-Masters, Wm. G. Saltonstall and Francis Josselyn; Acting-Assistant Surgeon, C. F. P. Hildreth; Acting-Assistant Paymaster, Jonathan Chapman; Acting-Ensigns, J. O. Johnson and J. B. da Camera; Acting - Master's Mates, E. F. Bowen, J. H. Wilkinson and A. F. Haradon; Engineers: Acting - Second - Assistant, B. F. Bell; Acting - Third - Assistants, D. R. Wylee, M. O. Stimson and Wm. Lannan.

STEAMER "CRUSADER"

Acting-Master, Thomas Andrews; Acting-Assistant Surgeon, E. A. Arnold; Acting-Assistant Paymaster, T. McC. Brower; Acting-Ensigns, G. W. Nelson, T. W. Sheer and T. S. Smythe; Acting-Master's Mates, Albert Buhner, Henry Parsons and E. D. Edmunds; Engineers: Acting Second-Assistant, P. O. Brightman; Acting-Third-Assistants, S. T. Strude and W. T. Waterman.

SLOOP "GRANITE."

Acting-Master, E. Boomer.

SCHOONER "WM. BACON."

Acting-Master, Wm. P. Rogers; Acting-Master's Mates, C. D. Thompson, H. E. Ripley and Daniel McLaughlin.

SHIP "CHARLES PHELPS."

Acting-Master, Wm. F. North.

SHIP "BEN. MORGAN."

Acting-Master, Wm. Shankland.

STEAMER "ZOUAVE."

Pilot, John A. Phillips; Acting-Master's Mate, P. B. Doran; Acting-Third-Assistant Engineer, H. N. Ames.

TUG "COHASSET."

Pilot, Thomas Eveans; Acting-Master's Mate, J. F. Doggett; Engineers: Acting - Second - Assistant, Sydney Smith; Acting - Third - Assistant, Charles Robinson.

CHAPTER XXXVI.

REAR-ADMIRAL DAHLGREN SUCCEEDS REAR-ADMIRAL DUPONT.—DAHLGREN'S DIFFICULT
TASK.—GENERAL GILLMORE REQUESTS NAVAL CO-OPERATION.—CHARLESTON HARBOR.—
PLAN OF GENERAL GILLMORE.—ATTACK ON ENEMY'S WORKS BY ARMY AND NAVY.—
CAPTURE OF CONFEDERATE WORKS ON SOUTH END OF MORRIS ISLAND.—ASSAULT ON
FORT WAGNER.—GILLMORE REPULSED.—SECOND ATTACK ON FORT SUMTER.—CAPTURE
OF ENEMY'S DEFENCES.—THE CATSKILL SEVERELY HANDLED.—ANOTHER COMBINED AT-
TACK ON FORT WAGNER.—THE FORT SILENCED.—ARMY BADLY REPULSED IN AN ASSAULT.
ACTIVE OPERATIONS SUSPENDED.—BRAVERY OF TROOPS UNDER GENERAL STRONG AND
COLONEL PUTNAM.—DREADFUL HAND-TO-HAND CONFLICT.—EARTH-WORKS ERECTED BY
GILLMORE.—THE "SWAMP ANGEL."—GUN-BOATS ENGAGE BATTERIES IN STONO RIVER.
—THE "COMMODORE MCDONOUGH" SILENCES CONFEDERATE ARTILLERY NEAR SECES-
SIONVILLE.—LIEUTENANT ROBESON PLANTS THE FLAG ON MORRIS ISLAND.—LANDING OF
TROOPS AT FOLLY AND JAMES ISLANDS.—ATTACK ON FORTS SUMTER AND WAGNER.—
RESULTS OF BOMBARDMENT.—GILLMORE DEMANDS SURRENDER OF "SUMTER."—LETTER
OF BEAUREGARD.—GILLMORE'S REPLY.—DEATH OF COMMANDER GEORGE W. RODGERS.—
GREAT EFFORTS MADE TO REDUCE WAGNER, SUMTER AND GREGG.—EFFECT OF THE
FIRE ON CHARLESTON.—THE MONITORS AGAIN OPEN FIRE ON FORTS SUMTER AND MOUL-
TRIE.—ENGINEERING WORK.—DAHLGREN AND GILLMORE DIFFER.—FORTS WAGNER AND
BATTERY GREGG EVACUATED.—THE "WEEHAWKEN" GROUNDED.—DISASTROUS NAVAL
ASSAULT ON SUMTER.—GREAT GALLANTRY DISPLAYED BY BOAT-CREWS.—ENSIGN
WALLACE'S REPORT.—TORPEDO-BOAT.—ATTEMPTS TO DESTROY "NEW IRONSIDES."—
PRAISE OF DAHLGREN AND OFFICERS.—THE MONITORS AND "NEW IRONSIDES" CON-
TRASTED.—BOYNTON'S CRITICISMS, ETC.

REAR-ADMIRAL DAHLGREN succeeded Rear-Admiral DuPont, at
Port Royal, on July 4th, 1863, the
latter having been relieved at his
own request, owing to a difference
of opinion between himself and the Secretary of the Navy in regard to the operations before Charleston and the attempt to
take the Confederate works with the Monitors.

Dahlgren had a difficult task before him.
In the first place, he had relieved an officer
who maintained as high a prestige as any
in the Navy, at home and abroad, for skill
and bravery. The attack upon and capture
of Port Royal had given DuPont a foreign
reputation in addition to that he bore at
home, and European officers of distinguished merit did not hesitate to say that
the battle of Port Royal was one of the best
exhibitions of naval tactical skill that had
been seen for years. Compare it, even now,

with the late English attack in Egypt, with
their heavy iron-clads and monstrous guns,
and note the rapidity with which DuPont's
squadron captured the works at Hilton
Head, etc., in comparison with the long-
drawn-out battle at Alexandria against
forts only a trifle superior to those at Port
Royal, and the palm will be given to the
American squadron as an exhibition of
skill. That affair did a great deal to impress
foreign Governments with the power of our
guns, and the indomitable energy of our
officers and seamen; and though Great
Britain, about that time, or shortly after,
did threaten us in a manner that was anything but agreeable to the American people,
yet that Government would have entered
upon the fulfillment of their threats with
misgivings—the growth of former disappointments in the War of 1812. Aside from
his recently acquired renown, there was no
officer in the United States Navy better

known abroad than Rear-Admiral DuPont. Many years of his life had been passed in the Mediterranean Squadron, where he traveled and made many European friends. He had commanded one of our best squadrons in China and Japan, and his bland manners, high standing as an officer, general knowledge on all subjects, in and out of his profession, made him an authority to whom foreign officers deferred. He was as well posted in all naval matters as any officer at home or abroad, and his opinions, which did not in 1863 run in accord with those of the Navy Department, were adopted by his friends and acquaintances in every quarter. DuPont had said that the forts in Charleston harbor could not be taken by the force with which he had attacked them, and his opinion was accepted as that of an expert who had tried the matter to satisfy the Navy Department, and had failed, and who considered that to attempt it again, *under the same circumstances*, with the same force, would only entail a loss of men and material, if not a loss of naval prestige. The victory at Port Royal had settled the question of the future usefulness of Charleston and Savannah to the Confederates, for it offered the means, if we had properly used them, of sealing up those two harbors

REAR-ADMIRAL JOHN A. DAHLGREN.

as effectually as if we had actual possession of them, which we now know fully. The capture of Port Royal included in its direct consequences all that was essential to the occupation of adjacent places — as far as their value to the Confederate cause was concerned, they could be rendered useless if the proper steps were taken, without leading to a loss of vessels and men, a sacrifice not at all called for by the circumstances of the case.

Therefore, when Rear-Admiral Dahlgren entered upon his command, it must have been with the consciousness that he had a difficult task before him, and that he could scarcely hope to succeed with the force that had been so unmercifully tried by DuPont.

Dahlgren had no sooner taken command than he received a letter from Brigadier-General Gillmore, informing him that he (Gillmore) was about to commence military operations against Morris Island, and looked for naval co-operation.

This should have been the first step taken at Charleston on the arrival of the Monitors, and the operations carried on should have been by an able and hearty co-operation of the Army and Navy, with well-digested plans drawn up, and an exact knowledge of the difficulties to be encountered and overcome. The capture of Charleston necessitated a somewhat long and patient siege by naval and military forces, as was the case during the war with places superior in strength to Charleston. In such cases, the Confederates had to succumb, owing to the greater resources of the Federal Government; for the well-known advantage besiegers in force have over a beleaguered place is that the latter must eventually fall under the accumulated power that is concentrated against it.

Rear-Admiral Dahlgren must have congratulated himself when he saw that the Army was at once coming to his aid, and that he would not be obliged to repeat the attack made by DuPont upon the uninjured forts in Charleston harbor, with the same Monitors that had failed so badly, and left one of their number resting on the bottom.

Dahlgren was not an engineer, but he must have known that the method about to be pursued by General Gillmore was the only feasible way of getting possession of Charleston, and he at once assured the General that he was ready to assist him with all his resources, if required. In making this announcement to the Navy Department, Rear-Admiral Dahlgren remarks: "Of course, the most that is expected from the action of these vessels is to relieve the troops as much as possible, and is to be considered of no other consequence." Thus, early in the operations, Dahlgren prepared the Navy Department not to expect as much from the Monitors as was required of DuPont; as, with others, he had made up his mind that operations against the whole circle of forts should not be undertaken with a force that had proved itself totally inadequate on a former occasion.

Charleston harbor, in its general configuration, may be likened to that of New York, the city being on a neck of land somewhat resembling Manhattan Island; Cooper River, on the east, may be compared to the East River; while the Ashley River, on the west, resembles the Hudson. Morris and Sullivan Islands may pass for the defensive points at the Narrows, though the channel between them is much wider; and the interior fortifications—Sumter, Moultrie, Cumming's Point, Battery Gregg, Fort Johnson, etc.—were all within the lines of Morris and Sullivan Islands. An attack on Fort Wagner could be made by a naval force without bringing the ships composing it within range of the heavy batteries which successfully resisted the attack of the Monitors on the first occasion.

The plan of General Gillmore was to dispossess the enemy of Morris Island by opening batteries placed on the north end of Folly Island, to command those of the enemy on Morris Island, and by occupying the sandy eminences that form the southern portion of that island for a mile south of Light-house Inlet. It would require an accurate map of the harbor and forts to give one a good idea of the enemy's defences. A hostile force approaching from the sea, with the intention of attacking the Charleston batteries, would be obliged to pass between Sullivan's Island on the north and Morris Island on the south, both of which had heavy batteries, including Moultrie and Wagner; while above Moultrie, and forming a triangle with it and Battery Gregg, stands Sumter. These works and the accessories within this line of defence remained pretty much the same after Dahlgren's accession as they were on the day DuPont attacked them.

"The circle of fire," and the plan of meeting an advancing enemy, is minutely described in the circular issued by the Confederate Brigadier-General to all the officers in command of the forts, a copy of which will be found in the chapter entitled, "First Attack on Sumter."

A squadron, making an attack on the Morris Island works (Fort Wagner), would be two and one-quarter miles from Fort Moultrie, two miles from Sumter, one mile from Battery Gregg, and half a mile from Wagner; therefore, a squadron of Monitors would not be subjected, as they were in Du-Pont's battle, to a cross-fire from five or six heavy batteries, but would be open only to the fire of Battery Gregg, Moultrie and Wagner at long range, with the Monitors presenting their bows to the enemy (the least vulnerable point, and the most difficult for gunners to strike).

This was the only way Charleston could be taken. Why was not this course pursued in the first instance ? The question is easily answered. The Navy Department was so fully impressed with the power of the Monitors (those before Charleston being great improvements in strength over the original) that they had urged upon DuPont the necessity of making a grand stroke at the first trial of these formidable vessels. This was more for the purpose of making a great impression upon the French and English Governments, which were, it is said, at that moment watching for a favorable excuse to recognize the independence of the Southern States. At the same time, the Secretary of the Navy would have considered it a great triumph to have the Navy conquer this nest of secession; and though he did not demand success, he felt so assured of it that his expressed wishes amounted to almost an order.

Seeing the ill-success of the first attack, and having been somewhat surprised at Rear-Admiral DuPont's hint that he was willing the Department should send some one to undertake the capture of Charleston in whom the Secretary had more confidence, it was determined not to hamper Rear-Admiral Dahlgren with specific instructions, but allow him and the military engineers to work out the problem after their own plans.

At the same time, it must be said, in justice to the Navy Department, that Secretary Welles represented to the War Department that "a second attack was preparing against the forts in Charleston harbor, and that its *success* required the military occupation of Morris Island, and the establishment of land batteries on that island, to assist in the reduction of Sumter," and, as this was a task requiring engineering skill of the highest ability, Brigadier-General Q. A. Gillmore was assigned to the command of the Department.

General Gillmore commenced his advance upon Charleston by the movement of troops to Folly Island on July 3d, 1863, where they remained concealed as much as possible, and erected batteries to command those of the enemy on the south end of Morris Island.

With the foregoing explanations, we will proceed to relate what followed, namely, the attack on the enemy's works by the Army and Navy.

At 4 A. M. of July 10th, 1863, four ironclads—the "Catskill," Commander George

W. Rodgers, "Montauk," Commander Donald McN. Fairfax, "Nahant," Commander John Downes, and the "Weehawken," Commander E. R. Colhoun, passed over the bar, the flag of Rear-Admiral Dahlgren flying on the "Catskill." One hour later, at 5 A. M., General Gillmore made an attack on the Confederate fortified positions on the south end of Morris Island, and after an engagement of three hours and a quarter he had captured all the enemy's works upon that part of the island, and pushed forward his infantry to within six hundred yards of Fort Wagner.

As the fleet of Monitors passed the bar, General Gillmore commenced the attack with his batteries, and as soon as the Monitors could get sufficiently near to fire with effect, they opened with shell upon the Confederate works, which were replying to

beach, the iron-clads steamed parallel to the low, flat ground that extended northward from the sand-hills toward Fort Wagner, and as near to it as the depth of the water would allow, sending shells in every direction over its surface to clear away any bodies of troops that might be gathered there. Gillmore's troops pushed on, and, as they reached Fort Wagner, two or three buildings standing apart from each other were seen to be in flames, supposed to be the work of the enemy to unmask the guns of Fort Wagner bearing down the beach.

The iron-clads at this time were laid abreast of Fort Wagner. This was an open sand-work about two and three-quarter miles from the southern end of Morris Island, and lying about one and three-quarter miles north of the sand-hills, and commanding the intervening level.

FORT WAGNER DURING THE BOMBARDMENT.

General Gillmore's guns, and dispersed the enemy wherever they were seen to assemble.

At 8 o'clock, being nearly abreast the northern end of the ridge of sand-hills, Gillmore's batteries ceased firing, and his troops were seen from the Monitors making their way upon Morris Island. The assaulting column, led by Brigadier-General Strong, had passed the waterway between Folly and Morris Islands in small boats, under cover of his batteries. He then held all the island, except a mile on the north end, including Fort Wagner and the battery on Cumming's Point, which, as near as could be judged, contained fourteen or fifteen heavy guns. Rear-Admiral Dahlgren speaks of an assaulting party of troops that were landed on Morris Island by Lieutenant McKenzie, but General Gillmore leads one to infer that these were landed in small army-boats.

As the troops moved rapidly along the

It was 9 o'clock before the first shot was fired from the Monitors at Wagner, the Rear-Admiral desiring to get close enough to use grape shot, but the state of the tide would not permit his vessels to approach nearer than twelve hundred yards. The fire from the Monitors was promptly met, and was kept up vigorously until noon, when the vessels dropped down out of range to enable their men to get dinner, after which the previous position was re-occupied, and the attack continued until 6 P. M. Then the signal was made to "cease action," for the men had been at work for fourteen hours, and the weather was excessively hot.

The four iron-clads fired during this action five hundred and thirty-four shell and shrapnel, making excellent practice, while the vessels themselves proved their endurance. The flagship "Catskill" was struck sixty times, a large percentage of the hits being very severe. The pilot-house, turret, side-armor and decks were all more or less damaged. Some of the projectiles were large. One, found on deck, where it fell after striking the turret, proved to be of 10-inch calibre. When these heavy shot struck the turret the concussion was very great. The iron of the pilot-house was broken entirely through, a nut from one of the bolts being driven against the lining so as to break it also. The deck-plates were cut through in so many places as to make the entrance of water troublesome. Though the test was a severe one, the "Catskill," after firing one hundred and twenty-eight rounds, came out of action in good working order, as was proved by her renewal of the fight on the following day. Naturally, the enemy made a mark of the "Catskill," that vessel carrying the Rear-Admiral's flag. The "Nahant" was only struck six times, the "Montauk" twice, while the "Weehawken" escaped altogether.

On the following morning, July 11th, Rear-Admiral Dahlgren received a note from General Gillmore stating that he "had made an assault on Fort Wagner at early daylight, and had been repulsed." At the same time he stated that he learned the enemy were about to throw reinforcements into Wagner, and asked for some action to prevent it. The four Monitors were again moved into position near Fort Wagner, and scoured the ground in the direction from which the expected reinforcements would approach.

So far the acquisitions of the combined forces had not been of a very important nature; still, a foothold was gained on Morris Island, and the officers in command felt satisfied that it would eventually lead to the possession of Sumter.

When General Gillmore made his attempt to carry Wagner, the parapets were gained, but the supports recoiled under the fire to which they were exposed, and could not be got forward. The loss of the army was about one hundred and fifty in killed, wounded and prisoners. In the morning they captured in the defences of the enemy eleven pieces of heavy ordnance and a large quantity of camp equipage.

Rear-Admiral Dahlgren issued his first general order, thanking the commanders, officers and crews of the Monitors, and the members of his personal staff: Fleet-Captain William Rogers Taylor, Flag-Lieutenant S. W. Preston, and Ensign La Rue P. Adams, for the zealous and efficient manner in which they had performed their duties during the attacks of the 10th and 11th of July; also the ordnance officer, Lieutenant-Commander O. C. Badger, for the systematic promptness with which he had supplied the iron-clads with all requisite ordnance stores.

This battle was a strong endorsement of Rear-Admiral DuPont's opinion regarding another attack on the enemy's works. Within the "circle of fire" were seventy-five guns, that being about the number the Confederates stated were used in DuPont's attack. On the 10th of July four Monitors were brought up with their guns bearing on only fourteen of this number; yet, after fourteen hours of severe firing, the works not only remained "practically uninjured," but a heavy assaulting party were driven off, and the "Catskill" was struck sixty times by the shot from Fort Wagner. The whole fire of the fort, however, was evidently concentrated on this vessel, the enemy having soon learned that this was the only way to disable the fleet.

The report of Commander G. W. Rodgers goes to show that the "Catskill" was very severely handled, the chief injury being inflicted by the 10-inch smooth-bores of the enemy, their rifle-shot glancing.

It can readily be imagined, if the fourteen guns of Wagner did so much damage, how the seventy-five guns of Sumter and adjacent works would have cut up DuPont's small squadron after fourteen hours of cross-fire! Under the circumstances, they would have been literally knocked to pieces. At this day DuPont's opinion on these matters have been endorsed by a large majority of the officers of the Navy; and, as the siege of Charleston is related, it will be seen that he followed the path of wisdom in declining to risk the loss of his vessels and their crews without adequate compensation.

On the 18th of July another combined attack of the Army and Navy was made on Fort Wagner. After the failure of the assault by the troops, General Gillmore proceeded to bring his heaviest guns into position to play upon the besieged earth-work, as well as to throw his shot and shell into such of the enemy's works as he could reach, and, if possible, to throw shells into Charleston itself. The plan of the contest now consisted in pushing the siege-works up as close as possible to Wagner, and to annoy the enemy as much as possible with sharp-shooters and bursting shells, which plan the latter were not slow to follow.

On the 18th of July, General Gillmore had succeeded in getting into position, to bear on the opposing works, twelve heavy guns and eight mortars, within eight hundred yards of Wagner; and when his arrangements were all completed he notified Rear-Admiral Dahlgren that he was ready to open fire.

The naval commander was not averse to an engagement, and at 11:30 A. M. of the above date led up to Fort Wagner with his flag flying on the "Montauk," followed by the "New Ironsides"—which had crossed the bar—the "Catskill," "Nantucket," "Weehawken," "and "Patapsco." Upon arrival abreast of the fort, the "Montauk" was anchored and fired the first gun, which was immediately followed by the other vessels —a nearer approach than twelve hundred yards, however, being prevented by an ebb-tide. Meanwhile, the gun-boats "Paul Jones," Commander A.C. Rhind, "Ottawa," Lieutenant - Commander W. D. Whiting, "Seneca," Lieutenant - Commander William Gibson, "Chippewa," Lieutenant-Commander T. C. Harris, and "Wissahickon," Lieutenant-Commander John L. Davis (all under charge of Commander Rhind), were detailed to use their great guns at long range, which they did with good effect; at the same time the batteries were delivering a very steady and deliberate fire.

At 4 P. M. the tide changed to flood, and the iron-clads got underway and closed in with the fort to a distance of three hundred yards, when the vessels opened fire again. Wagner was speedily silenced, and did not fire another shot or shell at the vessels during the day; neither was there a man of the enemy's force to be seen on or about the works. No troops in open earth-works could stand the terrible cross-fire on Fort Wagner from the vessels and General Gillmore's batteries, and the Confederates all went to cover, biding their time when the assault should come. This they knew was pretty sure to follow the bombardment.

The iron-clads continued their fire until it became too dark to distinguish friend from foe, when they ceased from necessity.

Very soon after, the rattle of musketry and the flashes of light artillery announced that the Federal troops were mounting the parapets of Fort Wagner. This continued without intermission until 9:30 P. M., then died away gradually, and finally ceased altogether. The Army had been badly repulsed a second time.

One gun in Wagner was known to have been dismounted, and another had burst, and General Gillmore, supposing from the terrible fire which had been poured upon the fort that the Confederates must be very much demoralized, determined upon a second assault without having men enough to overcome so powerful a work and its numerous and hardy defenders.

It may be desirable, perhaps, to know what kind of a work this was that endured such a tremendous cross-fire from thirty-seven heavy guns on shore and afloat. It was seldom that an earth-work so situated could stand the fire of naval vessels, much less a combined attack.

All that part of Morris Island not taken by General Gillmore was well fortified; it may be said that the batteries planted about were the outposts of Fort Wagner. This work, though not mounting many guns, was built with remarkable care and skill; it was in shape partly a lunette, with one end fortified with guns looking down the beach, the other end commanding the upper beach. The whole work was constructed of immense timbers, forming bomb-proofs, and these were covered with sand-bags to a thickness of over twenty feet. Its air-line distance from Sumter was one and three-quarter miles, and from Battery Gregg less than one mile, and by these two works it might be said to be covered. It was very plain to a mere tyro in engineering that Wagner was the key to the destruction of Sumter and the acquisition of the enemy's works on Sullivan's Island.

A new era had dawned in engineering, and the clever enemy, with sand-bags and timber, had built a work far excelling anything in the shape of mortar, brick and stone, and had armed it with the heaviest guns at that time known in the United States. This was the fort (Wagner) which so far had defied the forces of both the Army and the Navy.

It now became necessary to prosecute the siege of Wagner with patience and perseverance, as it was felt that the number of Union troops was inadequate to carry the work without throwing away the lives of the men and the useless expenditure of materials, therefore active operations were for the moment suspended.

It was very evident that the fire of the naval vessels could silence Wagner's guns at any time, but General Gillmore could only raise one single column for attack, while the Confederates could throw into Wagner at night any number of men that might be required to fill up vacancies by casualties. These points had been made known to the War Department; but, with a degree of negligence that cannot be accounted for, the notice was so slow in being heeded that it gave the enemy opportunity to strengthen their weak points, and repair damages to such an extent that the combined operations would have to be repeated. If General Gillmore had been furnished with five thousand more troops, Wagner, without doubt, would have fallen at the first assault. It is not the writer's intention to criticise the action of the Government—he only states facts—but it is, nevertheless, very remarkable, considering the great desire of the American people to see Charleston (the hot-bed of secession and the pioneer in the revolution) fall into Union hands, that prompter measures were not taken to strengthen the Army corps and the Navy when required. Here, again, was demonstrated the necessity for having at the head of the Army one great military mind that would know how to direct such important operations.

While giving credit to the Navy for the part it took in this affair, we deem it a duty we owe to the gallant army under General Gillmore to give an account of the more desperate adventures that befel the brave corps, which, after keeping up an energetic fire for so long a time. undertook the assault of Wagner. For this purpose two brigades were selected, consisting of the 7th Connecticut regiment, the 3d New Hampshire, the 9th Maine, the 76th Pennsylvania and the 48th New York, under Brigadier-General Strong; and the 7th New Hampshire, the 6th Connecticut, the 62d Ohio, the 100th New York, and the 54th Massachusetts (colored), under Colonel Putnam.

The brigades were formed in line on the beach, with the regiments disposed in columns, the colored regiment being in the advance. This movement was observed from Sumter, and fire opened on the troops from that work, but without effect.

At dark the order was given for both brigades to advance, General Strong leading and Colonel Putnam within supporting distance. The troops went forward in quick time, preserving the greatest silence, until the 54th Massachusetts, led by Colonel Shaw, was within two hundred yards of Wagner, when the men gave a cheer and rushed up the glacis, closely followed by the other regiments of the brigade.

The enemy—hitherto silent, but aware of all transpiring—opened upon the advancing columns a most furious fire of grape and canister, as well as a rapid fire of musketry. The negro troops plunged on, and some of them crossed the ditch, though it contained four feet of water, and reached the parapets. They were dislodged, however, in a few minutes, with hand-grenades, and retreated, leaving more than half their number on the field. The 6th Connecticut, under Lieutenant-Colonel Rodman, was next in support of the 54th Massachusetts, and they also suffered a terrible repulse. The next in line—the 9th Maine—was broken up by the retiring colored troops (who rushed through their lines), and retired in confusion, with the exception of three companies, which stood their ground.

It now devolved upon the 3d New Hampshire regiment to push forward, and, led by General Strong and Colonel Jackson in person, they dashed up against the fort. Three companies gained the ditch, and, wading through the water, found shelter against the embankment. Here was the critical point of the assault, but the second brigade, which should have been up and ready to support the leading troops, were, for some unknown reason, delayed. General Strong, finding that he was not sup-

ported, gave the order to fall back and lie down on the glacis. which was obeyed without confusion. While waiting, in this position, under a heavy fire, General Strong was wounded. Finding that the supports still failed to come up, he gave the order to his brigade to retire, and the movement was effected in good order.

Soon after this the other brigade came up, much impeded by the retreating troops; but they made up for their tardiness by their valor, rushing in impetuously, undeterred by the fury of the enemy, whose fire had continued without intermission. Several of the regiments succeeded in crossing the ditch, scaling the parapet, and getting *inside* the fort. Here a terrible hand-to-hand conflict ensued; the Union troops fought with desperation, and were able to drive the enemy from one side of the work to seek shelter between the traverses, while the former held possession for something more than an hour. This piece of gallantry was, unfortunately, of no avail. The enemy rallied, and, having received reinforcements, made a charge, and, by the force of numbers, drove the Union troops from their position.

One of the regiments engaged in this brilliant dash was the 48th New York, Colonel Barton, and it came out of the conflict almost decimated. The 48th was among the first to enter the fort, and was fired upon by a Union regiment that had gained the parapet, under the impression that it was the enemy. About midnight, seeing that it was impossible to hold what had been gained of the fort, an order was given to the Union troops to retire, and they fell back to the rifle-pits outside their own works, with a loss, in killed, wounded and missing, of 1,530 men.

After this most gallant but unsuccessful attack, General Gillmore came to the conclusion that Wagner could not be taken in that way by his depleted forces. and he decided to bombard that fort, Fort Sumter, and even Charleston, to either cause a surrender or to lay them in ruins.

Had the enemy been in great force at that moment, they could have massed all their troops, landed them on Morris Island, and captured Gillmore's army and everything belonging to it. But they were quite satisfied with the position as it was; they held the great chain of works which blocked the way to Charleston, and were very glad to see the Federals apparently wasting their strength in futile efforts to obtain possession of their strongholds.

In this last dreadful assault on Wagner, the ground in and around the fort was covered with the Union killed and wounded, and the naval force could not continue the fire the following day, nor until they were removed. Rear-Admiral Dahlgren sent a communication to the commander of Fort Wagner, offering to bury the dead and to remove and care for the wounded. This proposition was politely declined, the Confederate commander sending word that he would bury the dead and see the wounded cared for. Judging from the manner in which he had defended his fort, his chivalric character no doubt caused him to keep his word.

The first thing General Gillmore did toward securing possession of Morris Island, which he determined to hold, was to construct parallels. These extended from the beach on the right to the marsh on the left. The first was distant from Wagner 1,200 yards. The second, and principal one, was so constructed that its left was 600 yards from the fort, and its right 750 yards. The third parallel was 425 yards from Wagner. The parallels were built in a direction diagonal to the length of Morris Island, having the highest points resting on the marsh. The rifle-pits, forming the foundation of the first parallel, were thrown up shortly after the troops gained possession of the lower part of the island. These pits were thrown up in a single night, and were first used on the 17th of July in the attack on Wagner. The interstices were subsequently filled, and the first parallel constructed. The moment this parallel was finished, the enemy were preparing to make a sortie on the work; but Rear-Admiral Dahlgren got underway with the iron-clads, assisted by the gunboats at long range, and opened fire on Wagner, soon silencing that work and driving the men to cover.

At that time General Gillmore reported his advance position had been secured. The length of this parallel was 220 yards. The length of the second parallel was 325 yards. The siege-guns used for the offensive were mounted in the rear of this parallel. Its distance from Sumter was 3,350 yards. The third parallel was 100 yards in length. On the left, earth-works were constructed containing some of the heaviest siege-guns. Their mean distance from Sumter was 4,100 yards. Still further to the left, on the marsh, was another earthwork, facing Fort Sumter. On this work was mounted that celebrated gun, called the "Swamp Angel," which sent its shells into the city of Charleston—a distance of five miles.

This work was built on a spot inaccessible to the enemy's troops. At low water it was a deep bog; at high water the tide covered the ground to a depth of four feet, enabling scows to approach the spot and supply all the material necessary for the erection of earth-works. Sand-bags, and everything else used in the construction of the work, sank out of sight in the soft ooze, at first, until a good foundation was secured. At each succeeding tide the scows brought their loads of material, which produced, in the end, a great mound above the marsh. This was an engineering feat worthy of the clever officer, General Gillmore, who executed it. Strong traverses were erected on this bank, and, after due time given everything to settle, the "Swamp Angel" was floated to the point on one of the scows, and mounted. The work was all done at night, as it was in full view of Fort Johnson and the James Island batteries.

In reference to the last two engagements with Wagner, Rear-Admiral Dahlgren does not speak of any casualties or damage to the Monitors or other vessels of the fleet, and it is presumed that the cross-fire from shore and afloat drove the Confederate gunners to cover before damage could be inflicted. Rear-Admiral Dahlgren had a great adjunct in these affairs in the staunch "New Ironsides," Captain Rowan, whose 11-inch guns, rapidly fired, did more to silence Wagner than any three Monitors in the fleet.

While General Gillmore was perfecting his plans, the vessels of the fleet were not idle. A smart affair came off in the Stono River, in which the "Pawnee" (Commander Balch), "Marblehead" (Lieutenant-Commander Scott), and the "Huron" were engaged. The "Pawnee" and "Marblehead" were at anchor near Fort Grimball, when they were hotly attacked by batteries of the enemy posted six hundred yards away, the first shot striking the "Pawnee," and the others admirably directed by the enemy. The position of the "Pawnee" was such that she could bring no guns to bear, and she was obliged to drop down stream until a point was reached whence the guns could be trained on the enemy. The "Marblehead" was requested to do likewise, and, meeting the "Huron" in this position, they all opened fire on the hostile batteries, which had been cutting them up severely while shifting their berths, resulting in the retreat of the enemy. The "Pawnee" was struck thirty-three times in the hull, three times in the smoke-stack, had three boats damaged, and six shot in the rigging. Fortunately, the "Pawnee" had chain-cables triced up and down her sides, or the boilers would have been perforated. Those South Carolina artillerymen were just as spunky and annoying as were those on the Mississippi, and never lost an opportunity to attack the wooden gun-boats, frequently with effect. There were but four persons wounded in this affair, and it is remarkable that a number were not killed, considering the precision of the enemy's fire.

Commander Balch, the senior officer on the Stono River, speaks in the handsomest terms of the conduct of Lieutenant-Commander Bacon for his unremitting attention to duties in that locality, where, for a period of five months, he had been co-operating with the Army. On the 16th of July the Confederates commenced an artillery fire on General Gillmore's pickets at Secessionville, but were speedily silenced by Lieutenant-Commander Bacon moving up the river with the "Commodore McDonough," and firing into their camp with his rifled gun.

In a report by Lieutenant A. S. McKenzie, referring to the landing of the brigade, which was transported, under his charge, on the boats of the "Weehawken" for the assault on Fort Wagner, he mentions the fact that Lieutenant H. B. Robeson, of the "New Ironsides," was the first to plant the American flag on Morris Island, Brigadier-General Strong landing with him.

During the operations for the possession of Morris Island, Commander Balch, with the "Commodore McDonough," Lieutenant-Commander Bacon and Lieutenant F. M. Bunce, in charge of boats with howitzers mounted, were employed in landing troops on Folly Island, which had to be done at night. By the most active exertions of these officers the duty was fully accomplished, every effort being made to effect a successful landing; and the Army was in a great measure indebted to them for the perfect manner in which all the troops were debarked.

While part of General Gillmore's forces were being landed on Folly Island, General Terry, commanding a division, was directed to proceed up the Stono in transports, preceded by the "Pawnee," "Nantucket" and the "Commodore McDonough," and make a landing on James Island, which was done. This manœuvre—a part of the programme of attack on Morris Island—was successfully accomplished under cover of the vessels mentioned.

While General Gillmore was making his advances the Confederates were increasing and improving their defences, and among other things were laying torpedoes and planting obstructions to prevent the advance of the fleet, and the greatest watchfulness was required to avoid them; but these measures did not affect the movements of General Gillmore, who, on August 17th, opened fire on Sumter with all his guns, over Wagner and the intervening space.

About the same time Rear-Admiral Dahlgren, with the "Weehawken," carrying his flag, moved forward with the entire naval force. The "Catskill," "Nahant" and "Montauk" following the flag-ship, the "Passaic" and "Patapsco" being held in reserve for an attack on Sumter. The "New Ironsides," Captain Rowan, moved up abreast of Wagner, and the following sloops and gun-boats fired at long range: "Canandaigua," Captain J. F. Green, "Mahaska," Commander J. B. Creighton, "Cimmarone," Commander A. K. Hughes, "Ottawa," Commander W. D. Whiting, "Wissahickon," Lieutenant-Commander John L. Davis, "Dai Ching," Lieutenant-Commander J. C. Chaplin, "Lodona," Acting-Lieutenant E. Broadhead.

As the tide rose, the "Weehawken" closed to four hundred and fifty yards from Wagner; the other three Monitors followed, and the "New Ironsides" lay as near as her great draft of water would permit. The fort was silenced after a steady and well-directed fire.

General Gillmore had opened with his batteries soon after daylight, in answer to a fire from Wagner, Battery Gregg and Sumter, which was continued with great vigor for several hours. A 200-pounder rifled gun was brought to bear on Sumter for the purpose of testing the powder intended for use in these guns. Seven shots were fired, the distance being two and five-eighths miles. The first three fell short, but, of the remaining four, two went directly through the gorge wall a short distance above the sally-port, and two struck the parapet, sending a large amount of brick and mortar into the ditch and into the fort. The solid shot that passed through made holes from four to five feet in diameter.

General Gillmore had sixty guns of different calibres mounted, and with these he kept up an incessant fire on Sumter, while the fleet kept its guns playing rapidly on Wagner until there was no answer from that work. Then the flag was shifted to the "Passaic," that vessel and the "Patapsco" having rifled guns, and these two steamed up the channel to within two thousand yards of Sumter, when fire was opened on the gorge angle and southeast front of the work. The guns of the "Patapsco" were well aimed, and their projectiles struck the southeast front nine times in succession. To all this fire Sumter only replied now and then; Wagner was silenced, and Battery Gregg alone kept up an obstinate fire on the "Passaic" and "Patapsco."

At noon the iron-clads drew off to let the men go to dinner. This was, no doubt, a deliberate movement; but a better one would have been to have divisions of the fleet relieve each other, and never to cease fire on Wagner, even at night, until it lay a heap of ruins. The fertility of the Confederates, and their pertinacity in repairing damages, were too well known to suppose that they would lose an opportunity to act when the guns stopped firing on them.

All the afternoon of the 17th the shore batteries continued to fire upon Sumter, with little or no reply. The "Passaic" and "Patapsco" were sent up again in the afternoon to open on Wagner, and prevent the repairing of damages. The fort answered actively for awhile, but in a short time ceased its fire.

On the whole, the day's work was satisfactory to the combined forces. The Army had demonstrated the feasibility of reaching Sumter and inflicting serious damage on the work ; the Navy had shown that it could silence Wagner whenever it pleased to do so. It was not possible yet to ascertain what damage had been done to Sumter by the combined fire, but enough was known to assure the respective commanders that they had not yet demonstrated their full power, and that the enemy's works would be so seriously damaged in a short time that they would not be able to repair them.

The bombardment of Fort Sumter may be said to have commenced in earnest from this date, August 17th, with what result can be better judged from the bulletins that were issued day after day in Charleston, as the following:

CHARLESTON, Thursday, August 20th, 1863.
The firing of the Parrott guns on Sumter to-day was exceedingly heavy, but not so accurate as heretofore. About noon the flag was shot away, but soon replaced; no casualties are reported. Col. Alfred Rhett is commanding, and the garrison is stout-hearted.

The battery of Parrott guns is distant from Sumter 2⅝ miles. The missiles used are 200 - pdr. bolts, eight inches in diameter and two feet long, with flat heads of chilled iron. Shells of the same dimensions are also used.

Up to Wednesday night, the third day of the attack, 1,972 of these missiles struck Sumter, and, including to-day, 2,500 have struck. The damage is, of course, considerable, and for the last two days all the guns on the south face of the fort have been disabled.

Yesterday the iron-clads formed in line of battle to renew the attack, but the fort opened at long range from the east face, and they retired without attacking.

To-day the "Ironsides" and two Monitors kept up a fire on Wagner at intervals, and the Yankee sappers have begun to make approaches on that battery from the nearest work. A shot from Wagner disabled one of the Parrott guns; and the James Island batteries, under Lieutenant-Colonel Yates, exploded two of the enemy's ammunition chests.

Thus, at last, Charleston was reaping some of the whirlwind it had sown, and retribution came for the dishonor it had done the flag that had once waved on Sumter. Through Sumter, the Union was being avenged for the first blows the Confederates had struck. This once sturdy old fort, in a few days after Gillmore opened his batteries, began to show signs of great weakness. Its great distance from the Federal batteries could not save it; science had surmounted all the difficulties, and, if the American flag did not float over it, it would remain but a heap of ruins—a mere memento of the past.

CHARLESTON, Friday, August 21st, 1863.
The fire of the enemy's land batteries has been heavier to-day than ever. A new battery of Parrott guns opened on Sumter this morning, and the fire has been concentrated upon the east battery and its guns.

The south side of the fort is now a pile of rubbish.

On the south the wall is also crumbling into a heap of ruins. The flag has been shot away twice to-day, and six times during the attack. The flag-staff is shot off, and the flag flies from the ruins of the south wall.

Just before sunset Sumter fired several shot at the iron-clads which were engaging Wagner.

A Monitor this morning fired at Sumter while making a reconnaissance, but was not replied to.

There is no report of casualties. The sappers are making a regular approach on Battery Wagner.

———

CHARLESTON, Saturday, August 22d, 1863.
From 5 o'clock A. M. until 7 o'clock P. M. the enemy's fire on Fort Sumter was very heavy ; 923 shots were fired, and 704 struck the fort, either outside or inside. The eastern face of the fort was badly battered ; some guns on the east face and on the north end were disabled. The flag was shot down four times. Five privates and two negroes were wounded.

The enemy's fire on Wagner caused five casualties, including Captain Robert Pringle, killed.

Last night a communication from the enemy (unsigned) was sent to General Beauregard, demanding the surrender of Sumter and the Morris Island batteries, with a notification that the city would be shelled in four hours if the demand was not complied with. General Beauregard was on a reconnaissance, and General Jordan returned it for the signature of the writer.

About 2 o'clock this afternoon the enemy began throwing shells into the city from a battery on the marsh between James and Johnson's Islands, and distant five miles from the city. Twelve 8-inch Parrott shells fell into the city, but caused no casualties. The transaction is regarded as an outrage on civilized warfare. The shelling had a good effect in hastening the exodus of the non-combatants.

At daylight this morning the enemy opened again vigorously on Sumter. The "Ironsides" has since opened on Wagner. Sumter is replying. Wagner is firing briskly on the enemy's advance works, four hundred and fifty yards from the battery.

———

CHARLESTON, August 22d.
The fire of the enemy's land batteries has been kept up on Sumter, and more guns disabled. There was only one casualty.

There was also a heavy fire opened on Battery Wagner from the fleet ; also on Battery Gregg. The casualties at Wagner were one officer and five privates. General Gillmore's demand for the surrender of Sumter and Morris Island was a threat to shell Charleston in four hours from the delivery of the paper at Wagner. It was signed and returned at 7 o'clock this morning.

General Beauregard, in his reply, charges inhumanity and a violation of the laws of war, and affirms that, if the offence be repeated, he will apply stringent measures of retaliation.

Up to this time the threat to shell the city has not been executed.

There seems to be a discrepancy between these two bulletins about General Gillmore shelling the city.

CHARLESTON, Friday, August 23d.

To-day the land batteries opened from south to north, and the Monitors from east to west, coming close up; the fire was very damaging. The east wall was crushed and breached, and the shot swept through the fort. A shell burst, wounding Lieutenant Boylston, Colonel Rhett and three other officers.

The fort (Sumter) is now in ruins. Colonel Rhett is ordered to hold this outpost, even as a forlorn hope, until relieved or taken.

Colonel Gaillard was killed.

General Gillmore sent a communication at 11 o'clock, giving notice that at 11 o'clock to-morrow he would open fire again on Charleston.

CHARLESTON, August 24th.

The enemy's fire on Sumter slackened to-day. The fleet has not participated.

At 12 o'clock last night the enemy's guns opened on the city, firing fifteen 8-inch Parrott shells. No casualties resulted. Non-combatants are leaving the city in continuous streams.

I deem it unnecessary at present to continue the fire upon the ruins of Fort Sumter.

I have also (under a heavy fire from James Island) established batteries on my left, within effective range of the heart of Charleston city, and have opened with them, after giving General Beauregard due notice of my intention to do so.

My notification to General Beauregard, his reply thereto, with the threat of retaliation and my rejoinder, have been transmitted to Army headquarters.

The projectiles from my batteries entered the city, and General Beauregard himself designates them as the most destructive missiles ever used in war. * * * *

Very respectfully, your obedient servant,
Q. A. GILLMORE.

Colonel John W. Turner, Chief of Artillery, reports to General Gillmore as follows:

The gorge wall of the fort is almost a complete mass of ruins for the distance of several casemates about midway of this face, the ramparts are re-

APPEARANCE OF FORT SUMTER AT THE CLOSE OF THE ATTACK.

On the 24th of August General Gillmore wrote the following dispatches to Washington:

HEADQUARTERS, DEPARTMENT OF THE SOUTH,
MORRIS ISLAND, S. C., August 24th, 1863.

To Major-General H. W. Halleck, General-in-chief:

SIR—I have the honor to report the practical demolition of Fort Sumter as the result of the seven days' bombardment of the work, during two days of which a powerful northeasterly storm most severely affected the accuracy of our fire.

Fort Sumter is to-day a shapeless and harmless mass of ruins. My chief of artillery, Colonel J. W. Turner, reports its destruction so far complete that it is no longer of any avail in the defence of Charleston. He also says that by a longer fire it could be made more completely a ruin and a mass of broken masonry, but could scarcely be made more powerless for the defence of the harbor.

My breaching batteries were located at distances varying from between 3,320 yards and 4,240 yards from the works, and now remain as efficient as ever.

moved nearly, and in places quite to the arches, and but for the sand-bags with which the casemates are filled, and which has served to sustain the broken arches and masses of masonry, it would have long since been entirely cut away, and with it the arches to the floor of the second tier of casemates.

The debris in this point now forms a ramp as high as the floor of the casemates. The parapet wall of the two northeasterly faces is completely carried away, a small portion being left at the angle made with the gorge wall, and the ramparts of these faces are also a total ruin. . . . The ruin extends around, taking in the northeasterly face as far as can be seen. . . . The ramparts in this angle, as well as in the southeasterly face, must be ploughed up and greatly shattered, the parapet in this latter face being torn off, as could be seen, and it was thought that the platforms of these remaining faces could not have escaped the universal destruction.

With the assistance of powerful glasses

all the damages could be accurately ascertained, even to the injury done to the gun-carriages. Colonel Turner ends his report by recommending that no more shot be wasted on Sumter, as it was practically of no further use in the defence of the harbor.

When all these facts were fully ascertained to the satisfaction of General Gillmore, that officer wrote to General Beauregard demanding the immediate evacuation of Morris Island and the surrender of Sumter, otherwise he would proceed "to open fire on Charleston from batteries already established within easy range of the city." To this, General Beauregard replied, using the following language, which may be interesting from the fact that he tries to place the Federal soldiers in the light of barbarians, while, at that very time, the harshest treatment was imposed upon the Union prisoners of war, and the Confederates themselves did not in all cases observe war's amenities. What General Gillmore proposed to do was according to the rules of war, he having given notice that he was about to bombard the city, six hours in advance—quite time enough for the non-combatants, women and children, to leave the place.

We cut down General Beauregard's letter owing to its length, but the following gives the substance of it:

Among nations, not barbarous, the usages of war prescribe that, when a city is about to be attacked, timely notice shall be given by the attacking commander in order that non-combatants shall have an opportunity for withdrawing beyond the limits. Generally, the time allowed is from one to three days. That is time for the withdrawal in good faith of the women and children. You, sir, give only four hours, knowing that your notice, under existing circumstances, could not reach me in less than two hours, and then, not less than the same time would be required for an answer to be conveyed from this city to Battery Wagner.

With this knowledge, you threaten to open fire on the city—not to oblige its surrender, but to force me to evacuate those works which you, assisted by a great naval force, have been attacking in vain for more than forty days.

Battery Wagner, Gregg and Fort Sumter are nearly due north from your batteries on Morris Island, and in distance therefrom varying from half a mile to two and a quarter miles; the city, on the other hand, is to the northwest, and distant quite five miles from the battery opened on us this morning.

It would appear, sir, that, despairing of reducing those works, you now resort to the novel measure of turning your guns against the old men, the women and children and hospitals of a sleeping city—an act of inexcusable barbarity from your own confessed point of sight, inasmuch as you allege that the complete demolition of Fort Sumter within a few hours, by your guns, seems to you "a matter of certainty."

I am only surprised, sir, at the limits you have set to your demands. If, in order to attain the abandonment of Morris Island and Fort Sumter, you feel authorized to fire on this city, why did you not also include the works on Sullivan and James Islands—nay, even the city of Charleston—in the same dispatch?

Since you have felt warranted in inaugurating this matter of reducing batteries in your immediate front, which were found otherwise impregnable, and a mode of warfare which I confidently pronounce to be atrocious and unworthy of any soldier, I now solemnly warn you that if you fire again from your batteries upon this city without giving a somewhat more reasonable time to remove non-combatants, I shall feel compelled to employ such stringent means of retaliation that may be available during the continuance of this attack. Finally, I reply that neither the works on Morris Island nor Fort Sumter will be evacuated on the demand you have been pleased to make. However, I am making preparations to remove all non-combatants, who are now fully alive to what they may expect at your hands.

Respectfully, your obedient servant,
G. T. BEAUREGARD.

General Gillmore answered the different points of this letter, and concluded with the following pertinent remarks:

If, under the circumstances, the life of a single non-combatant is exposed to peril by the bombardment of the city, the responsibility rests with those who have first failed to apprise the non-combatants, or secure the safety of the city, after having held control of all the approaches for a period of two years and a half in the presence of a threatening force, and who afterwards refuse to accept the terms on which the bombardment might have been postponed.

From various sources (official and otherwise) I am led to believe that all the women and children of Charleston have long since been removed from the city; but, upon your assurance that the city is still full of them, I shall suspend the bombardment until 11 o'clock P. M. to-morrow, thus giving you two days from the time you first acknowledged to have received my communication of the 21st inst.

Very respectfully, etc., etc.,
Q. A. GILLMORE,
Brigadier-General, etc., etc.

In the naval bombardment of the 17th, the Navy lost the services of a brilliant young officer through the death of Commander George W. Rodgers, commanding the Monitor "Catskill." Commander Rodgers had more than once asked the rear-admiral if he should go with him as usual or take command of the "Catskill." In each instance the commander-in-chief answered, "Do as you choose." Rodgers finally concluded to go in the "Catskill." He got his vessel underway, and, while endeavoring to get a berth closer to the enemy, and *inside* the "Weehawken's" position, the "Catskill" was struck by a shot from Wagner, and Rodgers was instantly killed. This shot first struck the top of the pilot-house, fracturing the outer plate and tearing off an irregular piece of the inside plate about one foot in area, and forcing out several of the bolts by which the pieces were held together, fragments of which struck Commander Rodgers and Acting-Assistant Paymaster J. G. Woodbury, killing both instantly, besides wounding the pilot, Mr. Penton, and Acting-Master's Mate Trescott. When the commander fell, Lieutenant-Commander Charles C. Carpenter hove up the anchor, steamed down to the tug "Dandelion," and, depositing the bodies in her, returned to his station and continued the action.

Rear-Admiral Dahlgren pays the highest tribute to Commander Rodgers, whose death was regretted by all who knew him. The latter's relations to the commander-in-chief (as fleet-captain) were so close that the rear-admiral felt his loss very sorely, and could ill supply the place of so efficient an officer. He was one of those to whose gallantry there were no bounds.

In the action of August 17th, the iron-clads, though frequently hit, suffered no material injury. The "Catskill" was struck thirteen times, with the casualties already mentioned. The "Ironsides," Captain S. C. Rowan, was hit thirty-

COMMANDER GEORGE W. RODGERS.

one times, exclusive of some shots supposed to have struck her under water. Most of the hits were from 10-inch solid shot, which seemed to have been fired with extra heavy charges; and, when the shot struck, they cut and broke everything to pieces. There are no reports of damage to other vessels, hence it is probable that the enemy concentrated their fire on the "Ironsides" and "Catskill."

No mention is made in Rear-Admiral Dahlgren's report of the establishment of a naval battery against Sumter, but there was one under command of Commander Foxhall A. Parker, and it performed good service. That battery fired, on the 17th of August, 170 shells and 125 solid shot against the exposed face of Sumter, doing much damage. Commander Parker was assisted in this service by Lieutenant E. T. Brower,

Ensign James Wallace and Acting-Ensign Owens, who deserve great credit for the work they performed for fifteen hours under a burning sun.

Though great efforts were made to reduce Wagner, Sumter and Gregg, these strong works stood apparently as defiant as ever, notwithstanding the great shot seams that could be seen in Sumter's side. It was pretty well ascertained from Gillmore's batteries, by the aid of good glasses, that it had been rudely dealt with; yet, though sixty more heavy guns were brought against it than were used in DuPont's attack, the Federal naval forces did not seem any nearer to the attainment of their wishes than DuPont was.

The effect of the fire on Charleston had not, up to the 24th of August, proved of a serious nature. Twelve 8-inch shells had fallen into the city, thirteen having been fired altogether. These shells flew in the direction of St. Michael's steeple, and fell either in the vacant lots in the burnt district on King Street, or in Queen and Rutledge Streets. Some loose straw was set on fire by them, and the firemen turned out to extinguish the flames. The pieces of shell picked up in the city caused great curiosity and wonder, that such large missiles should have been thrown to such a distance from the point where the Federal battery was located in the swamp.

On August 23d, Rear-Admiral Dahlgren got underway and moved the Monitors to within eight hundred yards of Sumter, and opened fire. During a portion of the time a clear sight of the fort was prevented by fog. When the Monitors opened, Sumter only replied with six guns; but Moultrie, with its extended lines, opened heavily, according to reports, and struck the Monitors frequently with heavy shot. The "Weehawken" received two heavy and damaging blows on the pilot-house. There was a good deal of difficulty in working the Monitors in the narrow channels, and they drew off under the fire of Moultrie, which being as yet intact was more than a match for them. No casualties in the fleet were reported in this action.

In this reconnaissance—which it will be well to call it—the injuries to Fort Sumter were clearly observed, but it did not yet come under the head of "useless ruin." Fort Wagner is spoken of in the reports as being "quite as strong as ever, perhaps more so;" so that in this state of affairs the naval forces were about as far from the central prize as ever.

Sumter was now considered "useless to the Confederate system of defence," only it yet remained to be turned fully to account as a Union acquisition, and this advantage could not be realized because the Federal forces could not occupy the work. Such occupation, if possible, would have made a great difference in the plans of the besieging forces, but could not be likely to occur until the works on Sullivan's Island were invested simultaneously with those on Morris Island, and here was the great defect in the plan of this campaign. There was, no doubt, good engineering skill displayed, as far as it went, but what use could Sumter have been to the Federals while Moultrie—one of the heaviest works in Charleston harbor—and others stood ready to drive out of Sumter any Federal force that might undertake to enter it, which could only be by assault? It was, we may say, a heap of rubbish that had all fallen inside, but which could still afford a tremendous defence against any assaulting party brought against it. The true plan would have been for our forces to land on Sullivan's Island and Morris Island at the same time, and pursue the same methods that had been carried out at the latter. Of course, this would have required a greater number of troops and guns, but it was the only way to take Charleston.

While the Federals were making the most assiduous efforts to get into Sumter by the way of Wagner and Gregg, they overlooked entirely the obstacles still remaining on Sullivan's Island to prevent their holding it after capture; while Fort Johnson, Fort Ripley, Castle Pinckney and the iron batteries stood ready to pour in their cross-fire, as they had done when their attack on Sumter opened the Rebellion. The capture of James Island and the occupation of the works upon it, which was feasible, would have been a greater military feat than the capture of Wagner. In such event, Charleston would have been obliged to surrender or be destroyed, and, in consequence, its forts would have been obliged to follow her example.

The engineering work accomplished was of a splendid order, and the greatest bravery was displayed in its performance; yet engineers often become so absorbed in some favorite plan, which seems to promise all they desire, that they overlook other points which are the real keys to the situation. So it was at Sebastopol: all the best Russian, French and English engineers had overlooked the hill on which the Malakoff Tower stood, until the great Todelben appeared, and with his practiced eye discovered that to be the key. If either the French or the English had seized it, Sebastopol would not have stood a day before the fire of the allied batteries.

Four months had now passed since the first attack on Charleston, and many hundreds of heavy shells had been fired, without any great advance of the Federal forces toward their objective point; and this not from any want of skill in the naval or military commanders, but from the fact that the authorities at Washington did not have a comprehensive idea of what was required to carry out so great a work, and from their absurd supposition, in the first instance, that the whole net-work of forts could be taken by a small fleet of Monitors, armed principally with guns of small penetrative power, when, moreover, the endurance of these vessels had scarcely been tested.

It is very easy, though, to see all that was required when what was considered to be the best means had failed; but herein lies the ability of the engineer and the naval officer co-operating: they should be able to see the best points ere the operations have advanced too far to allow of retraction.

General Gillmore was of the opinion that Sumter could not be taken possession of until Wagner was subdued, and all his siege-guns were advanced as close as possible to the north end of Morris Island, while Rear-Admiral Dahlgren thought he could pass the batteries with his fleet, and go on to Charleston.

Here the naval officer and the military commander began to differ. Gillmore desired that the Monitors and the "Ironsides" should move *pari passu* with him. Dahlgren thought he could go alone, regardless of the obstructions which had to be forced, and which were defended by at least seventy guns, under the full range of which the fleet would be exposed, even as far as Sumter, which fort might or might not still have guns mounted upon it that would do serious injury to the vessels. Under the circumstances, General Gillmore deemed that the assistance of the Navy, in all its strength, was indispensable to success.

At midnight of September 1st, and just before slack high water, the "Ironsides" and the Monitors were moved up the channel. The primary purpose of this movement was to make certain that Sumter had no guns remaining in service. It was believed that the Confederates had remounted a few guns on the northeast and northwest faces. On the same evening, General Gillmore's batteries had opened fire on Sumter, and the general had informed Rear-Admiral Dahlgren that he had knocked down some four or five pieces that were observed on the more remote fronts, and this encouraged Dahlgren to attack. The nearest approach of the Monitors to Sumter was five hundred yards, the flag being carried on the "Weehawken;" but the ebb-tide was now so strong that it was nearly 12 o'clock before the first shot was fired from the flag-ship.

Two shots were fired from the fort, when the "Weehawken" was laid off the angle of the northeast and southeast fronts. The "Ironsides" was brought up to an easy range, and joined in the action which followed, the vessels all firing steadily and accurately. Meanwhile, Moultrie opened a rapid and well-sustained fire from its extended lines, which told on the vessels, though the obscurity of the night interfered with the accuracy of the enemy's aim at such small targets as the turrets of the Monitors.

The fire of the Monitors was also directed against the floating obstructions which had been reported from day to day. At daylight the fleet withdrew without being able to ascertain the effect of their fire. This engagement lasted five hours, during which time the fleet fired 245 shots, and received in all 71 hits, of which numbers the "Ironsides" fired 50 shots and received 7 hits.

From all accounts there was no serious damage done to the vessels, notwithstanding all the pounding, and the "Ironsides" stood the brunt of the battle as well as the Monitors. Fleet-Captain Badger was struck by a fragment of the turret knocked off by one of the enemy's shot, and his leg broken by it. This was the third fleet-captain Dahlgren had had injured or killed in the short space of two months. He speaks of Captain Badger in the warmest terms of praise, and as an officer whose place it would be very difficult to fill.

The commanders of the iron-clads, Captain S. C. Rowan, Commander T. H. Stevens, Commander Andrew Bryson, Commander E. R. Colhoun, Lieutenant-Commander Edward Simpson, Lieutenant-Commander John L. Davis and Lieutenant-Commander J. J. Cornwell, are spoken of in terms of high commendation for their gallantry and the ability they displayed in handling their vessels in the narrow channel on an obscure night.

On September 7th, arrangements were made to open fire upon Wagner from the trenches, and from all the iron-clads, which fire was to be followed at 9 o'clock at night by an assault. A steady cannonade had been maintained against the work on the 6th from the trenches and from the "Ironsides;" but in the meantime a deserter had gone over to General Gillmore with the information that the Confederates were evacuating the works; they had stood the siege as long as they could, had gone through fire enough to drive out any but American troops, and now evacuated to escape the assault which they knew would come at night. We cannot help but admire the courage of these brave fellows, though they were fighting against us in a bad cause. We cannot help thinking how those men would fight against a foreign foe!

On the 7th of September, General Gill-more made the following report to General Halleck:

GENERAL—I have the honor to report that Fort Wagner and Battery Gregg are ours. Last night our sappers mined the counterscarp of Fort Wagner in its sea-point, unmasking all its guns, and the order was given to carry the place by assault at 9 o'clock this morning, that being the hour of low tide.

About 10 o'clock last night the enemy commenced to evacuate the island, and all but seventy-five of them made their escape from Cumming's Point in small boats.

Captured dispatches show that Fort Wagner was commanded by Col. Keitt, of South Carolina, and garrisoned by 1,400 effective men, and Battery Gregg by from 100 to 200 men.

Fort Wagner is a work of the most formidable kind. The bomb-proof shelter, capable of containing 1,800 men, remains intact after the most terrible bombardment to which any work was ever subjected.

We have captured nineteen pieces of artillery and a large supply of excellent ammunition.

The city and harbor of Charleston are now completely covered by my guns.

I have the honor to be, etc., etc.,
Q. A. GILLMORE,
Brigadier-General, Commanding.

After the evacuation of Wagner and Gregg, Rear-Admiral Dahlgren, having ineffectually demanded the surrender of Fort Sumter, on the ground of its indefensibility, determined to try a plan by which that work might be captured; and, as a preliminary, ordered the "Weehawken" to pass in by a narrow channel winding about Cumming's Point, so as to cut of all communication in that direction. In so doing, the "Weehawken" grounded, and, though at low water, did not succeed in floating on the next high tide. Later in the day, the rear-admiral moved up in the "Ironsides," with the Monitors, to feel and, if possible, pass the obstructions north of Sumter. Moultrie, Battery Bee and Fort Beauregard quickly opened on the iron-clads, which returned the fire very warmly, and continued to do so until it became necessary to pay attention to the "Weehawken." Steam-tugs and hawsers were provided for getting her off, but without success, even at high water, as already stated. At 7 A. M. the enemy perceived her condition, and began to fire upon her from Moultrie, about 3,000 yards distant. The iron-clads were ordered up to cover the grounded Monitor, which meanwhile replied to the enemy's fire, and, in less than half an hour, blew up one of the Confederate magazines. At the next high water the "Weehawken" was fortunately floated, after the most strenuous efforts of Commander Colhoun, officers and crew. The only casualties on board the "Weehawken" on this occasion were three men wounded by a shot from Battery Bee.

Up to this time the operations of the Navy had been well conducted. There was a perfect co-operation between the commanders of the respective forces; and, as the Army advanced its parallels and breaching batteries toward Wagner, the "Ironsides" and the Monitors advanced on the water, keeping up a well-directed fire, the effect of all which is shown by its evacuation on the 7th of September.

General Gillmore and his chief of artillery had given the most satisfactory account of the damage done to Sumter by the breaching of the gorge wall and the dismounting of most of the guns, and had also asserted "that it was no longer of any practical use to Charleston harbor as an offensive work." This was pretty well demonstrated when the "Weehawken" got hard and fast aground in the channel, between Sumter and Cumming's Point, and Sumter could not fire upon her for lack of guns. Sumter was now, in fact, nothing but an outpost to be held by the enemy as a matter of pride—nothing more—and without power to inflict a particle of injury on any one, unless it might be a party that attempted to gain admission over the debris that blocked the entrances, and afforded no footing for a party of boarders. A small party within, however, could easily bar the way or inflict serious injury upon an attacking-party that might attempt to take the work by assault.

All these matters had been very fully discussed, but it does not appear that General Gillmore was consulted as to the feasibility of an attempt to take Sumter by assault, or applied to for the assistance of his steady and practiced assaulters, who had had considerable experience in attacking forts. Brave and dashing as sailors may be, for this kind of business they lack that steady movement and discipline which makes an attacking force a unit, and carries everything before it; while sailors, drilled to board a ship with a cheer and a rush, have a less methodical way, which may succeed; if checked for one moment by regulars and steady troops in an operation of the kind on shore, the chances are that they will be driven back and cut to pieces or captured in the retreat.

Whether Rear-Admiral Dahlgren considered these matters or not is not known, but he nevertheless determined to make a naval assault on Sumter on the night of September 8th. The supposition is that he did not consider military assistance requisite. Viewed as a military move, the attempt to assault Sumter was a grave mistake; there was no necessity for it, and General Gillmore was already moving forward his heavy breaching-guns to cover Charleston and all the forts in the upper harbor; and would, in a few days, have made Sumter a still more useless heap of rubbish than it was already. Again, it is questionable whether the military etiquette properly observable on such an occasion was not violated in attempting to take possession of a work destroyed principally by army guns, without extending an invitation to the general commanding to participate in the projected assault.

Dahlgren claimed that, if successful, the assault would enable him to pass the obstructions in the main channel with his fleet. He therefore directed that a storming party should be formed, and called for volunteers. No matter what may be the danger for officers and sailors to face, there is never any difficulty in getting volunteers in the American Navy, and such was the case on this ocasion. The following officers came forward and offered their services at once: Commander T. H. Stevens, Lieutenant Moreau Forrest, Lieutenant-Commander E. P. Williams, Lieutenant George C. Remey, Lieutenant S. W. Preston, Lieutenant F. J. Higginson, Ensign Charles H. Craven, Lieutenant-Commander F. M. Bunce, Lieutenant E. T. Brower, Ensign James Wallace and Ensign B. H. Porter; also the following officers of the Marine Corps: Captain C. G. McCawley, First-Lieutenant Charles H. Bradford, First-Lieutenant John C. Harris, Second-Lieutenant R. L. Meade, Second-Lieutenant Lyman P. Wallace and Second-Lieutenant L. E. Fagan.

Of these officers, Commander T. H. Stevens was selected to command the expedition, while the following were appointed to command divisions of the assaulting force: First division, Lieutenant-Commander E. P. Williams; 2d division, Lieutenant George C. Remey; 3d division, Lieutenant S. W. Preston; 4th division, Lieutenant F. J. Higginson; and 5th division, Ensign Charles H. Craven.

Upon applying to General Gillmore for more boats to carry the sailors and marines, Rear-Admiral Dahlgren learned *for the first time* that Gillmore was about to make an assault on Sumter the same night. It is stated that when this information was received by Dahlgren it was late in the evening, and, owing to the want of inter-service signals, there was no concert with the Army contingent in the further movements. It was 10 o'clock at night when the boats started off for Sumter in tow of a tug. On the way, the party communicated with the "Passaic" and "Montauk," giving orders to their respective commanders to move up to their support. When within eight hundred yards of the fort, the tug cast off the boats, and the orders regarding the operations of the night, as well as the watchword, were given out

Lieutenant Higginson was ordered to move up to the northwest front of the fort, with his division, for the purpose of making a diversion, while the remainder of the divisions were ordered to close up and wait for the order to advance upon the southeast point. The intention of Commander Stevens was to wait until he had the full benefit of Lieutenant Higginson's diversion; but mistaking his movement, no doubt, as a general one, and with a true spirit of emulation and gallantry, many of the other boats dashed on to the fort. Finding it impossible to stop them, the order was given along the line for *all* to advance.

The Confederates were quite prepared for this adventure, as was natural for good soldiers who had received orders to hold Sumter at all hazards, and as soon as the boats came within good range they were met with a fire of musketry and hand-grenades, lighted shells and grape and canister; and simultaneously, at a signal from Sumter, Moultrie, together with the gun-boats and rams, opened fire on the base of the fort, where all the boats were landing pell-mell, each man of the crew wanting to be the first to scale the walls.

This is exactly what ought to have been anticipated under the circumstances, for to suppose that the Confederates, having such a commanding position, with all the means of offence and defence for such an occasion, would not avail themselves of them, would be underrating that gallantry, energy and fertility of purpose for which they had been remarkable in defending these fortifications from the very beginning.

It must have been mere sport to the Confederates to see those boats rushing on heedlessly to destruction or capture, for only a miracle—something that never occurs in war—could save such an assault from annihilation. That there was great gallantry exhibited in this attempt to capture Sumter no one will deny; but there was not a ghost of a chance of success from the very commencement.

Several of the boats, among them two from the "Powhatan," had gained a landing; but the evidences of the garrison's preparation were so apparent, as well as the impossibility of scaling the walls or even effecting a permanent landing, that orders were given for the boats to be withdrawn, which was done under a withering fire. All who succeeded in leaving the boats were either killed or taken prisoners; boats were smashed by the fire of the enemy's batteries and gun-boats, and it was as much as the survivors could do to get clear of the base of the fort.

In this affair there was naturally great confusion when the officers and men discovered that a fort they had been led to believe lay a heap of ruins and powerless was filled with men armed with breech-loading rifles, plenty of hand-grenades and shells ready for lighting, besides having grape and canister to fire from selected positions into crowded boats. The defences only required a dozen or more Gatling guns to make them complete.

As it was, all the sailors in the fleet could not have taken Sumter, even with the assistance of the contingent General Gillmore intended to supply. We know that *now*; we ought to have known it then. But, with all the disaster which followed this unfortuate assault, there was exhibited the most unflinching courage, the sternest devotion to a duty which, at the outset, must have seemed to many beyond the possibility of execution.

To show the difficulties attending night operations of this kind, we will give part of the report of Ensign Wallace, in which that officer explains how, in the *melée*, he followed the leading boat around the fort, pulled back and examined the sea-face in search of a landing; then, on coming to the right bastion of the sea-face, he found the marines firing from boats. He could find no officer to report to, and no one could tell him whether the men had landed, or where they were. Seeing a sinking boat, he pulled toward it, but found that all its crew had been removed or were drowned. Upon returning to the fort, he examined the sea-face and gorge wall; he observed all the boats retreating, and, on inquiring from one of them, was told that Commander Stevens had given the order to retreat. Ensign Wallace could obtain no information upon which to act, and seeing no boats between him and the fort, he pulled back to the flag-ship, where he first learned that Lieutenant Remey, with his boat's crew, had landed on Sumter.

This report is a fair example of all, and the affair was like many night expeditions, which generally end unfortunately, especially when not well planned beforehand. A further unhappy feature of this expedition was the delusion, under which the assaulting party labored, that it was going to an easy victory. Instead, a well-manned fort was found, supplied with all the disagreeable missiles known in war, and well supported by powerful batteries within easy range.

The less said about this expedition the better; it was a most unfortunate failure, and its acts of gallantry and daring cannot compensate for the repulse. Certain it is, however, that no blame could attach to the members of the expedition, who could not be expected to achieve success under conditions so adverse, and who could not for the darkness even see the difficulties they were obliged to contend with. The Confederates, it appears, knew all about the attempt that was to be made on Sumter, and met it with every precautionary measure that ingenuity could devise. Had the army of General Gillmore joined in the assault there would have been the same result, with the addition of a longer list of casualties.

A flag of truce notified Rear-Admiral Dahlgren on the following morning that there were one hundred and thirty prisoners in the enemy's hands, besides three of the killed. Among the prisoners were the following officers: Lieutenants S. W. Preston and E. T. Brower, Ensigns B. H. Porter and Charles H. Craven, Third-Assistant Engineer J. H. Harmany, Sail-maker D. C. Brayton, Acting-Master's Mates E. Butler, C. P. Hovey and C. S. McCarty. Captain McCawley, of the Marine Corps, reports that there were two lieutenants (C. H. Bradford and R. L. Meade), two sergeants, two corporals and twenty-six privates missing, and that great confusion existed at the landing.

Thus ended, for the time, the offensive operations against Charleston, with the exception that the vessels of the fleet remained at their posts, ready for any service required of them, and in no way disabled from continuing the attacks in conjunction with the Army or otherwise. The iron-clads had bravely sustained their reputation as good fighting machines, and all the officers had fairly earned the title of gallant men and able seamen, which was demonstrated time after time in the shallow and difficult channel leading up to Wagner and Sumter.

Among the vessels of the fleet, the "New Ironsides," which was not considered comparable with the Monitors in invulnerability, took more than her share of the pounding, and came out of the contest with Wagner with as many honorable scars as any veteran in the fleet could boast of. The handsome manner in which her gallant commander, Captain S. C. Rowan, handled her and took her into action, always elicited the applause of the fleet; and it was only necessary for her to get her broadside guns properly ranged on the enemy's ponderous earthworks for their defenders to go to cover after a few well-directed shots, only to renew their fire, however, when her batteries were silent.

It was remarkable how much hammering this good old ship could bear, even from the heaviest of the enemy's batteries. When the "Weehawken" went ashore in the channel, between Sumter and Cumming's Point, Captain Rowan placed his ship right between the batteries of Moultrie and the Monitor, on which they had opened fire. As Rowan anchored and swung head-on to the fort, the enemy opened a rapid fire upon him, which was soon replied to from the "Ironsides'" port battery. By this time the enemy had succeeded in getting the ship's range. The sturdy old "Ironsides" opened slowly at first for range, but soon increased the rapidity of her fire, until its spirit forced Moultrie to slacken. Two guns from each of the 10-inch batteries between Moultrie and Beauregard, however, still caused the "Ironsides" to suffer, and only after one of the heaviest guns was seen to be dismounted did the forts slacken their fire again. Having quieted her enemies, the "Ironsides" now fired an occasional gun to keep them under cover. This cessation, however, immediately brought them from behind their sand-bags to their guns, from which a rapid fire was opened, showing that the "Ironsides'" practice was too accurate to suit them. Rowan then renewed his rapid fire, and the forts were silenced again—it was but a repetition of what had been done at Wagner. By this time there were but thirty shells left in the ship, and the order was given to weigh the anchor. Under a rapid fire, the "Ironsides" quietly went out of action, after having been engaged two hours and a half in an artillery duel such as was never sustained by any ship in the Navy, and against batteries that would have sunk the heaviest three-decker then afloat.

In this action Lieutenant H. B. Robeson, Acting-Masters George W. Domett and John M. Skillings, Ensign B. H. Porter and Acting-Ensign Charles W. Howard are spoken of in terms of the highest praise for their coolness and manly bearing; while Lieutenant-Commander George E. Belknap, the executive officer of the "Ironsides," is highly lauded for his zeal and ability in putting the vessel in such an efficient fighting condition, and for the hearty manner in which he had carried out Captain Rowan's orders as commander of the gun-deck during the *fourteen* times the "Ironsides" had been under fire. Encounters of this kind were well calculated to develop the highest qualities of young officers, and the names of those above mentioned will be found prominent wherever an opportunity to distinguish themselves was offered.

There was no vessel in the fleet the enemy so heartily dreaded as the "Ironsides." Her well-drilled crew and expert gunners made her anything but welcome when she brought her broadside to bear upon any of the forts. The Confederates made several attempts to destroy her with torpedoes, but without effect. On the night of the 5th of October, 1863, however, they very nearly succeeded.

An ingenious torpedo-boat—for the day— was fitted out at Charleston, and placed in charge of Lieutenant W. T. Glassell, of the

Confederate navy, with orders to operate against and destroy as many of the iron-clads as possible. Glassell was assisted by Captain Theodore Stoney as first-officer, J. H. Toombs, engineer, and Charles Scemps and Joseph Ables as assistants. The vessel belonged to a class known as "Davids," and was shaped like a cigar, being supplied with a small engine and propeller, and was of the following dimensions: Length, fifty feet; beam (or diameter), nine feet. For offence, a torpedo was carried at the end of

LIEUTENANT-COMMANDER (NOW COMMODORE) GEORGE E. BELKNAP, EXECUTIVE OFFICER OF THE "IRONSIDES."

a stout spar, extending some fifteen feet ahead of the sharp bow.

When the attempted destruction of the "Ironsides" occurred, that vessel was anchored off Morris Island, and the time, 9:15 P. M., was one at which a ship's deck is apt to be deserted except by the look-outs. A small object on the dark water, close at hand, was suddenly discovered by the sentinels, and hailed by them, and the officer of the deck, Acting-Ensign C. W. Howard. No response being made, the officer of the deck ordered the sentries to fire into the object. The sentries delivered their fire, and, simultaneously, the ship received a severe shock from the explosion of a torpedo, which

threw a large column of water into the air, whence it descended upon the spar-deck and into the engine-room. Acting-Ensign Howard was mortally wounded by a shot from the torpedo-boat, dying five days later. The proximity of the "David" and the limited target presented by its only visible part—a hatch ten feet by two—precluded the use of great guns upon it; but a brisk musket fire was kept upon it by the marines until it drifted out of sight. Two of the Monitors soon came under the stern of the "Ironsides" in pursuit of this new device of the enemy, but, although two boats were lowered to assist in the search, nothing was seen.

Fortunately, no damage to the "Ironsides" resulted from this explosion, and her salvation was, no doubt, due to a miscalculation of the distance of the torpedo from the hull. Lieutenant Glassell was afterward picked up by a coal schooner, and stated that the explosion had swamped the torpedo-boat, and that he and the two officers with him had been obliged to leave her and swim for their lives.

Here was a new danger for the fleet to contend with, and even more than the customary watchfulness would have to be observed. The North, with all its resources, had not then developed a torpedo-boat (nor are we yet, in 1886, possessed of an efficient one), while the fleet at Charleston should have been supplied with at least twenty of them! *They* would have removed all obstructions much faster than our energetic enemy could have put them down, and the way to Charleston would have been open to the fleet.

The 5th of October was memorable for the advent of this new device of the enemy, and we were no nearer Charleston than we were on April 7th, when DuPont attacked the circle of forts without success. Wagner and Gregg had, indeed, been taken, but Sumter, that had been pronounced a harmless heap of rubbish, had not only repulsed the naval assaulters, but had captured one hundred and thirty prisoners, whom, under the circumstances, the Confederates dealt with very tenderly, considering the fact that they had them in a trap, and might have destroyed the whole of them. This leniency gives a proof that, as the war continued, both sides were learning to conduct it on civilized principles, and the bitterness with which it had commenced was subsiding, so far that it was not considered unwarlike to capture prisoners instead of killing them, and that it was to the advantage of all concerned to observe the amenities of war as practiced by all civilized nations.

In considering the attacks of Dahlgren with his little fleet of iron-clads on Charleston's defences, too much cannot be said in praise of the persistent gallantry and untiring energy of the commander-in-chief and his officers; but in the work accomplished there was the strongest endorsement of Rear-Admiral DuPont and of the views of *his* officers—that the naval force was not strong enough to contend successfully with the well-built and formidable forts included in the great "circle of fire," to say nothing of the submarine and other obstructions barring the way to Charleston.

With all Dahlgren's incessant fighting, from the time of his first attack to the 8th of September, 1863, he had not advanced beyond the line whence DuPont had engaged the batteries on the 7th of April previously. True, some of the Confederate force had been broken in the fall of Wagner and Gregg, but only after the junction of Gillmore's sixty guns with those of the iron-clads in cross-fire. It was the same result that obtained on the Western rivers, success always attended a hearty co-operation between the military and naval forces, and failure as surely met the single-handed siege operations of either.

Too much was expected of the Monitors in the first instance. The conception of such vessels was a grand one, and for it the inventor and his supporters will live long in the memory of the American people; but the vessels did not possess all the qualities required of them, since much had to be sacrificed in their design. Against wooden ships or vessels more lightly clad than themselves, they would have proved perfectly destructive—premising equality of speed for all—but against forts they lacked qualities possessed by the "Ironsides." They could not concentrate the rapid fire possible for a broadside-ship upon the enemy's embrasures, and while they were slowly loading—harmless for five or more minutes at a time—the guns of their opponents could be concentrated upon them with destructive effect, as on the 7th of April. It was a matter of frequent observation during the attacks on the batteries, that the rapid fire of the "New Ironsides" always relieved the Monitors after she had settled into position, and fairly obtained the range.

There was one great mistake made in the armament of the Monitors: they should have been armed throughout with the heaviest rifled guns they could carry. With these they could have taken position between four and five thousand yards from Sumter and cut it down at their leisure, without receiving a shot in return. This was exactly what Gillmore did with his sixty breaching-guns, lodging over three thousand shells in the devoted fort, and making it a ruin in seven days. The 15-inch guns of the Monitors would, no doubt, have breached the walls and have effected the same results,

but the short range necessary would have subjected these vessels to a combined fire of all the batteries, which they were not fitted to endure for any protracted period.

The disappointment felt at the Navy Department over the failure of the first attack, and the resulting controversies, no doubt, prevented a calm investigation of the facts, from which the iron-clads might have profited. If a careful study of the case had been made by unprejudiced men, or if DuPont had been listened to, the Monitors would have had their batteries changed for the 200-pounder rifles. The author saw enough of the firing of the Monitors—at pretty short ranges—at sand-bags, to know that the effect was trifling compared with the more rapid fire of the "Ironsides'" 11-inch guns with their higher velocity, and these were greatly exceeded by the larger rifled guns made for the Navy. The age of smooth-bores departed with the advent of iron-clad vessels, and the most probable reason for their retention during the war was the treacherous character of the rifled substitutes of large calibre, besides the fact that the Dahlgren shell-guns were favorite weapons, the 11-inch standing next in efficiency to the heavy rifles. The earlier use of rifles might have followed from the example shown at Pulaski, a fort built by Colonel Totten, a veteran chief of engineers, to resist any fleet that could be brought against it. With a few 30-pdr. and 60-pdr. rifles, the work was bored through and through its masonry until honeycombed, when a few shot from 10-inch guns brought the disintegrated structure down about its defenders' ears.

The naval historian Boynton attempts to show that the 15-inch guns of the Monitors had great smashing effect, because *two* of the shells passed through the walls of Sumter, "one exploding in a casemate, another exploding on the parade ground; other 15-inch shells exploded against the wall, making great craters." And this, the historian thought, settled the point that these guns were of great smashing power. He, however, fails to mention what number of the many that struck the walls did *not* go through, and how little damaged Sumter was when the iron-clads drew off. Mr. Boynton, though a very pleasant historian, was not good authority upon the matter of which he wrote, and, with all his desire to do justice, he allowed himself to be guided in his opinions by those riding a hobby, and, unfortunately, a defective one.

Concerning the siege of Charleston: at this day, when men can sit down coolly, and untrammeled by prejudice, read over all the operations of the naval force, there can be but one conclusion resulting—there was too great a hurry in the effort to capture a position particularly strong, and in which all the arts of war had been exercised for ability to hurl defiance at the Federal forces.

Notwithstanding the actual strength of Charleston, exaggerated accounts have been given out stating the number of guns to be as high as three hundred and thirty. The Confederate accounts, which there seems no reason to doubt, gave the armament of the works as follows: Sumter 44, Moultrie 21, Battery Bee 6, Fort Beauregard 2, Cumming's Point 2, and Wagner 19; total 94. To these must be added the batteries at Fort Ripley, Castle Pinckney, Mount Pleasant, Fort Johnson, Battery Gregg, and the Creek batteries.

Altogether, the naval commanders, and all with them, deserve high commendation for accomplishing what they did before Charleston; their efforts, though not successful in capture, rendered the place of not the slightest use to the Confederacy even as a resort for blockade-runners, whence supplies from abroad could be received. On the contrary, its possession was a drawback to them, for its defence necessitated the retention there of a large number of troops, elsewhere sadly needed by the enemy in the field, and it may be said that the place was only held as a matter of pride, that the spot where secession first took root and sprouted should be the last to surrender.

By some persons the conduct of the war by the naval commanders has been criticised, on the ground that they did not rush through the obstructions and go right on to the wharves of Charleston. As if, indeed, the Confederates would plant obstructions without due care that they should stop any vessel attempting to pass them under the guns of the forts! What a predicament for the commander of a squadron to be in, to get his vessels entangled in a network of piles, ropes, chains, and torpedoes—all the while under a terrific cross-fire—and then to be blamed for his stupidity!

Mr. Boynton admits that, on the 7th of April, DuPont's fleet "was huddled together helplessly in the very focus of a hundred guns, and held there during the stress of the fight." How it was to be otherwise the historian does not say, but further along remarks: "A short time only was needed to show that Admiral DuPont was mistaken in all his main opinions; the subsequent use of the Monitors by Admiral Dahlgren proved that they could safely have endured another fight with the forts. He found that the broadsides of the "New Ironsides" could sweep the Confederates from their guns whenever she was brought in proper range, and that she was a valuable co-worker with the Monitors. Dahlgren also demonstrated that the "Ironsides" and Monitors could

lie safely within the bar, and that with his iron-clads the harbor of Charleston was effectually closed."

The iron-clads, under Dahlgren, never came within the "great circle of fire of the forts," and though it is true that the fire of the "Ironsides" would silence Wagner's guns, yet she was not brought into close contact with that fort until she had the assistance of Gillmore's batteries. Firing at Wagner, and forcing the passage of all the forts entangled in obstructions, are two different things altogether, as would have been ascertained by a practical comparison.

Fortunately, the representations made at the close of the war have been carefully examined, and, in most cases, found unworthy of record. In this case, for instance, how could it be expected that a man who had no naval training, and had failed to post himself from official documents, could write a true history of naval operations? Throughout his account of the naval work before Charleston he has labored most arduously to take from a gallant officer the high reputation he had so fairly won, while endeavoring to elevate another at his expense.

Dahlgren himself must have seen, from DuPont's first attack, that all efforts in that particular direction would be futile; he wisely concluded to avail himself of the advantages to be gained by a close co-operation with the Army. If he did not succeed in all he hoped for, he at least demonstrated that a naval force alone could have no effect on the capture of Charleston.

The most remarkable piece of assurance in connection with the Charleston affairs was that of an engineer in the Navy, who, in view of DuPont's failure, addressed the Navy Department, and criticised the conduct of the fleet in a manner that should have brought him before a court-martial. How could any commander in-chief hope to possess the confidence of his Government while officious subordinates were allowed to give their views directly in opposition to his plans, and suggesting what, in their opinion, should be the mode of attack? Yet this man not only stated that the passage of the forts was possible, but that the squadron could go up to the Charleston wharves.

Again, we say, that the best endorsement of DuPont's opinions is the hard work of Rear-Admiral Dahlgren from the first co-operation with General Gillmore, July 10th, to the unfortunate assault of September 8th on Sumter, two months in which the fleet never succeeded in passing the fort that was "useless for all offensive purposes."

With this chapter ends the operations of the Navy before Charleston to October, 1863.

CHAPTER XXXVII.

OPERATIONS OF THE EAST GULF SQUADRON TO OCTOBER, 1863.

Acting-Rear-Admiral Bailey Appointed to Command East Gulf Squadron.—Vessels Captured or Destroyed.—Places of Safety.—Destruction of Confederate Salt Works a Necessity.—Attempt to "Cut" out Schooner in Mosquito Inlet.—Expedition up Indian River and other Points. — Capture of Schooner and Sloop.—Lieutenant-Commander English in Gun-boat "Sagamore" Explores Coast. — Value of Property Seized. — Violation of Blockade. — The Sloop "Helen" Burnt.—Brisk Engagement with Confederate Batteries.—Destruction of Schooner.—River Expeditions under Lieutenant-Commander McCauley. —Disastrous Reconnaissance at St. Andrew's Bay.—Flag of Truce used as Decoy by the Natives.—The "Tahoma" Shells a Town.—Boat's Crew from Bark "Amanda" Cut out Schooner "Forward."—Loss of Prize."—Heroic Conduct of Master Hoffner and Men.—Tribute to Gallant Volunteers.—Destruction of Important Salt Works by Boat's Crew from Steamer "Somerset."—"Tahoma" and "Adela" Shell Confederate Batteries.—Destruction of Two Blockade-running Steamers in Hillsboro River.—Blockade-running Broken Up.—List of Vessels Composing East Gulf Squadron under Acting-Rear-Admiral Bailey.—List of Officers.

ACTING Rear-Admiral Theodorus Bailey was appointed to the command of the East Gulf squadron on the 4th of June, 1862.

The Navy Department had found an opportunity to reward this gallant officer for his services at New Orleans, and although no important military or naval movements were going on within the limits of this command, it was the only way in which the Secretary of the Navy could show his high appreciation of Bailey's gallantry and devotion to his country's service.

The limits of this command extended along the Florida Peninsula from Cape Canaveral on the east, to Pensacola on the west.

Up to December, 1863, the little squadron under Bailey had exercised the greatest watchfulness along the coast, had captured many prizes, and had apparently broken up the illicit traffic by which the Confederates had been supplied with munitions of war. Lying adjacent to Cuba, and at no great distance from the English possessions of Nassau and Bermuda, the coast of Florida presented many available points for the introduction of all kinds of material by means of small vessels that could enter the shallow harbors, streams and inlets with which this State abounds.

But notwithstanding the advantages these small craft possessed for eluding the blockaders, they could not carry on their trade with impunity. From the time that Bailey took command, up to the end of the year, more than 100 vessels were captured or destroyed by the squadron.

From Cape Canaveral, all along the eastern shore of Florida to Cape Sable, are numerous passages and inlets where vessels could with safety land their cargoes of arms or provisions in a night and be out of sight of the blockaders when daylight came.

Following the coast up to the northward were the Ten Thousand Islands, Charlotte Harbor, Tampa Bay, Crystal River, Cedar Keys, Suwanee River, Appalache Bay, St.

George's Bay, Appalachicola, St. Andrew's Bay, and a thousand other places of refuge too numerous to mention. Arms and munitions of war of all kinds could have been landed but for the watchfulness of the naval vessels.

Florida, with its inaccessible and tortuous channels, and numerous islands surrounded by impenetrable swamps, was just the place to tempt smugglers, they being led there by the quantity of game and the romantic scenery, and a delicious climate that harbored no diseases and rendered the shelter of houses unnecessary. It was a hard place to find smugglers, and the Federal sailors had great difficulty in breaking up the traffic; but it was done in spite of all obstacles, and no more disagreeable and at times dangerous duty was performed anywhere.

Florida (especially the west coast) was one of the great depots where the Confederates made their salt. This was an article without which they could not exist, and it could only be made in certain localities near salt water. It may have been noticed in the naval reports of the war that certain vessels were mentioned as having destroyed salt works, and persons may have exclaimed, "Why distress the poor by destroying their salt works? What good can it do to destroy salt?" It was the life of the Confederate army which they were destroying. They could not pack their meats without it. A soldier with a small piece of boiled beef, six ounces of corn-meal and four ounces of salt, was provisioned for a three days' march. And though we might have pitied the Confederate army in the straits to which it was often reduced, yet the Federal officers, by way of shortening the war, did all they could to destroy salt works wherever they found them. This distressed the soldiers more than the loss of blockade-runners, for although these vessels generally brought plenty of guns and powder, their owners were rarely thoughtful enough to lay in a supply of salt. The history of these salt-destroying expeditions may appear tame, but they are part of the history of the war, and if possible a place must be found for them.

Early in the year 1863, Acting-Master J. A. Pennell reports the destruction of large salt works near St. Joseph. He commanded the bark "Ethan Allen" (a sailing vessel), and, on the morning of the 9th of January, got underway and stood up St. Joseph's Bay. He anchored at daylight abreast of where he supposed the salt works to be, and sent three armed boats (in charge of Acting-Master A. Weston, his executive officer), with forty men, to destroy them. The men in charge of the works fled when the boats

landed, and everything was set on fire and destroyed.

This establishment could make 75 bushels of salt daily, and it was the fourth of the kind that Master Pennell had destroyed within a short time. At the same rate of doing work, these four manufactories could have turned out for the Confederate army 110,000 bushels of salt in a year. (The Confederates had their agents in every State where salt could be made, and in those days the wants of the Army were first considered.)

Sometimes the boats of the squadron would have something more interesting to report than the capture of a salt crop. Late in February, Lieutenant-Commander Earl English, in command of the gun-boat "Sagamore," received information that a schooner was in Mosquito Inlet, Florida, loading up with cotton, the captain being of the opinion that there was no blockading vessel in the vicinity.

English proceeded to that point at once, arriving there on the 28th, when the schooner was discovered inside. An expedition was organized to cut her out or burn her.

It was placed under the command of Acting-Master's Mate J. A. Slamm, a very young officer, but one who was full of zeal. He took the ship's launch, with Third-Assistant Engineer F. G. Coggin, thirteen men and a howitzer; the first cutter in charge of Acting-Master's Mate Frank E. Ford with seven men; the second cutter in charge of Acting-Master's Mate C. R. Fleming with eleven men, and the gig in charge of Acting-Master's Mate George B. Sidell, five men; in all, forty-one officers and men.

The boats proceeded up the river and sighted the schooner without meeting any resistance, when suddenly she was set on fire by a party that ran on board of her. The cutters were then ordered to board, extinguish the fire and bring the schooner out, while the launch shelled the banks and bushes with her howitzer.

While boarding, the sailors were fired upon by a party of twenty-five men concealed in the bushes behind the embankment. Finding that the schooner was hard and fast on the bottom, and that it was impossible to extinguish the fire, the young officer, having accomplished the object of the expedition, determined to return to his vessel.

Unfortunately, while in the act of boarding, Hugh Maguire, a seaman, was shot dead, and most of the crew of the first cutter were wounded. Acting-Master's Mate Ford, of the first cutter, though wounded himself, shot one of the enemy who was in the act of firing upon the boarding party.

While the boats were returning, the enemy

continued to fire upon them, but a heavy return fire of musketry and shrapnel was kept up by the men, and some punishment was, no doubt, inflicted.

The schooner was of 150 tons burden, all ready to sail, but instead was given to the flames by the advent of this brave little party, which lost one killed and five wounded. So it will be seen that this affair, which lasted only twenty minutes, was gallantly managed and was not without danger.

On March 4th, Acting-Master's Mate Henry A. Crane reports the results of an expedition up Indian River, under the instructions of Lieutenant-Commander Earl English.

On the morning of February 23d, he started in a boat and reached a cove five miles above the mouth of St. Sebastian River, and at 2 o'clock P. M. discovered a schooner

LIEUTENANT-COMMANDER (NOW REAR-ADMIRAL) EARL ENGLISH.

bearing down, apparently filled with men. From their number and appearance it was supposed that they were Confederates prepared to act on the offensive. Mr. Crane's boat was so disguised as to look like a boat from a merchantman, so that the Confederates passed him unsuspiciously and went on down the river.

He allowed the schooner to get well ahead and then followed in her wake, until night came on and she got into shoal water. While her crew were employed in getting her over the bar, the Union boat dashed alongside and captured her. There were twelve men on board, who no doubt would have made a good fight if they had not been taken by surprise.

Ordering the schooner's sails hoisted, Mr. Crane started down the river, when he discovered a sloop ahead, which he determined to run into and capture, but was informed by one of his prisoners that she had no crew and was full of cotton. He placed two men in her, thus reducing his party to five, and ran down for the inlet (some eighteen miles), reaching there on the morning of the 27th, having been seventy-two hours on the expedition with no sleep and very little food. He took his prizes off to the "Gem of the Sea," where he obtained assistance to secure his prisoners and take care of his vessels.

This was a small party, but of inflexible firmness, to which they were indebted for securing two vessels that netted them a nice little sum in prize-money. Even so small an affair, when well executed, is more creditable than a great one poorly managed.

The only way of reaching the Confederates up the crooked and shallow streams in Florida was by boat expeditions, and Rear-Admiral Bailey kept his officers and men well employed, giving all those who deserved it an opportunity to distinguish themselves.

On March 24th, 1863, he directed Lieutenant-Commander Earl English to proceed to Cedar Keys with the gunboat "Sagamore," taking with him two armed launches from the flag-ship "St. Lawrence," under the immediate command of Acting - Lieutenant E. Y. McCauley, for the purpose of scouring the coast between the Suwanee River and the Anclote Keys, where it was reported a number of small craft were engaged in violating the blockade.

There was no end to this kind of traffic wherever there was a slip of land to haul a boat upon, or a shallow stream where a schooner could scrape her keel over the sandbar and proceed inland. When one considers that this was going on all along 3,000 miles of coast, it will appear wonderful how, even with the force the Federals had on hand, they were able to put a stop to the traffic which alone kept the Confederate armies in the field.

During the war, over $30,000,000 worth of this kind of property was seized and turned into the Treasury—not a tithe of its value, for a large portion of it went into the possession of land-sharks, who rarely gave a fair account of the money which passed through their hands. But when the big holes and the small leaks on the blockade were all closed up, the tale was told at Appomattox, where General Grant had to serve out rations to Lee's soldiers and give them enough to enable them to reach their homes.

A launch and cutter from the "Sagamore" and others from the "Fort Henry," including an ambulance boat, were added to this expedition and the whole force proceeded direct to Bayport, while the "Sagamore" remained in the offing to prevent the escape of Confederate vessels.

Great difficulties attended this expedition, as the weather was very unfavorable, but the main object was handsomely carried out.

The sloop "Helen," of Crystal River, loaded with corn, was burnt, and the boats pushed on for a large schooner on the inside, loaded with cotton and said to contain three hundred bales.

As they pulled for the schooner the boats were opened upon by a battery of two guns on shore, and by quite a number of rifle-men concealed in the woods. A brisk engagement of half an hour ensued and the bushwhackers were driven from their works and rifle-pits, with one killed and three wounded. Unfortunately, the howitzers in the launches were partly disabled, by their recoil, from rapid use, but they kept up such a fire, while they could, with shrapnel and

LIEUTENANT-COMMANDER (NOW REAR-ADMIRAL) EDWARD
YORK McCAULEY.

grape, that the enemy's fire was very wild, and went over the boats.

This little affair was conducted with coolness and judgment, and also with the right spirit.

When the Confederates found that the boats could not be driven off, they set fire to the schooner. The engagement was still continued from the boats until there was no chance of extinguishing the flames, and it is quite probable the Confederates were delighted to think the attacking party would secure no prize. The object of the expedition having been effected, the party in the boats returned, after seeing the vessel and cargo totally consumed.

This boat expedition then proceeded to the Chassahowitzka, thence to Crystal River, the Homosassa, the Withlacoochee and the

Wakassa—beautiful Indian names, that signified anything rather than the lawless scenes that were carried on in their waters.

The expedition had, however, been so delayed by head-winds and currents, and by the sluggishness of one of the launches, that they only made seventy-five miles in five days, so that the news of their coming preceded them, and, on the appearance of the boats, everything had been moved out of the way. This expedition was well managed by Lieutenant-Commander McCauley.

An expedition fitted out on March 20th by Acting-Master John Sherrill, commanding bark "Roebuck," did not fare so well. Sherrill sent a launch up St. Andrew's Bay on a reconnaissance; but, on the return of the boat, they were attacked by a party of fifty men, with rifles, one man killed and six severely wounded, including the officer in charge, Acting-Master Jas. Folger.

Two brave seamen, Thomas Wylie and James Kitchen, brought the boat off, all the rest being killed or wounded. The fire from the bushwhackers was very severe, and most of the men shot were mortally wounded. These were dangerous enemies to encounter. They were not soldiers, but, more properly speaking, smugglers.

There was not a particle of loyalty in these parts and the only object of the inhabitants was gain. They were fighting, not to preserve the independence of the South, but to make rich harvests by smuggling and to set the laws at defiance. This region at that time could boast of the worst and most reckless set of men in the South, and they would have been just as willing to put to death a Confederate party as a Union one, if it should attempt to interfere with their vocation.

They had no military notions of honor, and would not respect a flag of truce if the bearer of it had anything on his person worth taking. As a proof of this we relate the following incidents, which are officially reported:

On the 27th of March, as the bark "Pursuit" was lying in Tampa Bay, a smoke was discovered on the beach and three persons made their appearance with a white flag. The commanding officer, supposing them to be escaped contrabands, sent a boat in charge of Acting-Master H. K. Lapham with a flag of truce flying. On nearing the beach, two of the parties were seen to be clothed in women's apparel with their faces blackened and seemed to be overcome with joy at the idea of obtaining their freedom, exclaiming, "Thank God, thank God, I am free!"

When the boat touched the beach the female apparel was thrown off, and it then became evident that these were white men disguised, and using a flag of truce to decoy the boat on shore. Immediately after, a hundred armed men rose from the bushes where they had been concealed, and demanded the surrender of the boat, which being refused, the enemy opened fire, wounding the officer in charge and three of the crew. But the brave fellows who were left unwounded returned the fire and the attacking party took to the trees. Some of the men in the boat kept up a rapid fire with their breech-loading guns, while the others pushed off the boat, and they finally got out of range.

As soon as the first volley was fired, the broadside of the "Pursuit" was opened on the bushwhackers, and the shells bursting among them sent them scampering away. Next day the gun-boat "Tahoma" arrived, and her commander, having heard of the outrage committed, brought two vessels up and threw some shells into the town, which was called barbarous at the time, but it was the only way to prevent the indiscriminate slaughter that would have been inflicted on a boat's crew that attempted to land on any part of that coast unsupported by gunboats.

It is dreadful to think of the bitter feeling that sprang up among the lower classes of men against the flag which they once thought they honored; but the rough life led in that section of the country, the years spent in hunting the Indian in dismal swamps and forest fastnesses, had produced a class of people far more barbarous than the Indians themselves—men without any sentiment but a love of plunder, who placed no more value on human life than on the life of a dog. Yet they were intrepid and defied all laws, human and divine, and the only way to touch their understanding was by the most severe retaliation.

On Friday, March 20th, an expedition left the United States bark "Amanda," for the purpose of proceeding to the Ocklockonnee River, to cut out the schooner "Forward," supposed to be loaded with cotton. The expedition was under the charge of Acting-Master R. J. Hoffner, and consisted of two boats and twenty-seven men, with a boat howitzer.

Great difficulty was encountered in finding the mouth of the river, and the boats constantly grounded on oyster beds, over which they had to be hauled in the night for fear of discovery, but at daylight the entrance of the river was found and the boats proceeded up. At 8 A. M., of the 23d, a dismasted schooner was discovered lying close to the starboard bank. At the same time the expedition was discovered by some people on the schooner, who jumped into the small boat and made their escape, no doubt carrying news of its arrival.

The boats boarded the schooner and took possession, hove up the anchor and commenced towing her down the river, having two hours' tide left. They anchored when the tide was too low to proceed, got underway again at 5 o'clock in the morning, and by 8 o'clock were clear of the entrance to the river. They steered for the bay channel, and again grounded when nearly over all the difficulties of the navigation. Again the tide served and the vessel was got underway, but this time they followed the wrong channel and grounded again, and all their endeavors to get her afloat proved unavailing.

These brave fellows had worked for twenty-four hours with an energy unsurpassed, hoping to receive a large share of prize-money, but now they saw that all their work had been in vain, and prepared to set fire to the vessel. The arms were all put in order in case they should be needed suddenly; the howitzer was loaded with canister and every preparation made to repel the attack which Mr. Hoffner confidently expected. At about noon, a party of forty horsemen was discovered approaching at some distance. They turned and appeared to be going off, but soon re-appeared with some squads of infantry (about 200 in all) jumping from tree to tree, and taking position to attack the sailors. The boat howitzer was brought to bear upon the Confederates, and fired with grape and canister, but without marked effect, as the enemy was protected by the trees. At the same time ten sailors with muskets (behind such defences as they could throw up on board the vessel) kept up a continuous fire whenever anything could be seen to shoot at. Once a squad of twenty exposed themselves, and a shrapnel was exploded in their midst, and a number of them seemed to have been hurt.

A rapid fire was kept up on both sides, each party protecting themselves behind their barricades, until the tide began to run flood, and the boats floated. Then Mr. Hoffner determined to fire the vessel, as an attempt to save her would involve too great a loss of life. The schooner was only two hundred yards from the shore, and directly under a galling fire from the enemy's rifles. The howitzer was hoisted into the boat, while the enemy fired rapidly (though not accurately), and the boats were kept on the off-side until the sailors were able to shove off with safety. In an hour and a half the tide was supposed to be high enough, and the boats' crews embarked and shoved off; but, with the weight of the crews, the boats grounded, and the enemy opened upon them again. The sailors jumped overboard, and, taking hold of the boats, commenced dragging them over the bottom—slow work under a heavy fire.

James Mooney, a seaman, was killed instantly, shot through the heart. At the same moment, the officer in charge, Mr. Hoffner, received a rifle-ball in the right side of the neck, passing around the back and lodging in the left side, deeply imbedded in the muscles. Other men were struck at the same time, but only one of them so seriously that he could not work. Every one was doing his best to get the boats over the bottom, or else firing at the pursuers, who were keeping up with them along the banks. Mr. Shaffer, the second officer, was conspicuous in setting an example of gallantry very much to be commended.

At length, after being nearly exhausted by the hard work, the sailors got their boats afloat in deep water, jumped in, and, giving the enemy a parting volley and a cheer, they sprang to their oars, and soon put themselves out of range.

The bushwhackers had kept themselves so well protected by the trees that they could be detected only by the flashes of their guns. Under such circumstances and with so greatly a superior force, some officers would have felt themselves justified in surrendering to save the lives of their men. But there was not a word said about surrendering in this party. The commanding officer, Mr. Hoffner, though dangerously wounded, stuck to his work like a hero and brought his boats off safely, with one man killed and six (besides himself) seriously wounded.

During this engagement, which lasted several hours, some heroic acts occurred, which would have done credit to any service, and the determination shown not to be captured proved the stuff the officers and men were made of. These gallant fellows abhorred the idea of letting their flag (which was kept flying in the boat all the time) fall into such an enemy's hands, for though the people, who performed the part of soldiers on shore, were at the farthest extreme of the Confederacy, and not inspired by the exciting scenes which were daily taking place between the Federal and Confederate forces, yet they were as bitter in their hostility to everything Union as if they had received some great injury at the hands of the Government.

These people, no doubt, considered it an outrage for the Federal naval forces to interfere with their smuggling articles contraband of war, but they never stopped to reflect that war could not be ended merely by the Navy sailing up and down the coast of Florida and looking at them violating the laws. Hence all this talk of the Confederates about the inhuman treatment to these smugglers (for they were nothing more) is simply absurd. War is not a pleasant pas-

time. Its object is to bring about law and order, and the most stringent measures are those most likely to succeed. There was no way of arresting this war but by sacrificing every object that would tend to keep it going on.

Let it be understood that most of these little expeditions, which were fitted out and did so well, were commanded and officered by those gallant volunteers from the merchant marine, who, sacrificing all their interests in commercial affairs, joined the Navy to devote life and all they held dear to the defence of their country's rights and honor. They gave such a guarantee, by their matchless adaptation to the rules and

LIEUTENANT (AFTERWARDS COMMODORE) A. A. SEMMES.

regulations of the Navy, of their ability to learn the science of war from officers educated for the naval service, that the country must not forget, while awarding credit to the Navy proper, to allow a full share of the honor to fall upon the volunteer officers from the American mercantile marine.

On July 6th, Rear-Admiral Bailey reports the destruction of important salt works, under the direction of Lieutenant - Commander A. F. Crosman, of the steamer "Somerset."

This duty was well performed by Acting-Master Thomas Chatfield, who landed in boats under the guns of the "Somerset," and, with sixty-five sailors and marines, destroyed four distinct stations. Sixty-five salt-kettles were demolished, over two hundred bushels of salt destroyed, and thirty houses, with all their appurtenances, were burned. The whole establishment was completely blotted out without the loss of a man, in which these expeditions were not always so fortunate.

On the 16th of October an expedition was fitted out to destroy two blockade-running steamers in Hillsboro River.

Lieutenant-Commander A. A. Semmes, in the gun-boat "Tahoma" (assisted by the "Adela"), was directed to divert attention from the expedition by shelling the town and fort and to land men under cover of the night at a point in Old Tampa Bay, some distance from the fort, to proceed overland to the point on the Hillsboro River where the blockade-runners lay, and destroy them.

On the date mentioned, the "Tahoma" and "Adela" ran in abreast of the batteries, and shelled them slowly during the day, their fire being unusually accurate. As soon as the moon went down that evening, a force of sixty men, under Acting-Ensigns J. P. Randall and J. G. Koehler, from the "Tahoma," and forty men, under Acting-Ensigns F. A. Strandberg and Edward Balch, and Acting-First-Assistant Engineer G. M. Bennett, from the "Adela," with Acting-Master's Mate Crane and Mr. J. A. Thompson as guides, was landed at Ballast Point. The whole expedition was under the immediate command of Acting-Master T. R. Harris, executive officer of the "Tahoma."

The line of march was quietly taken up under guidance of Mr. Thompson (who, being too ill to walk, was carried in a litter). A march of fourteen miles brought the party, before daylight, to the river-bank.

As soon as it was light the two steamers were discovered on the opposite side. The force was assembled abreast of the steamers, and those on board brought under aim of the rifles, and ordered to send a boat, which was done. A detachment was then sent to bring over the vessels and to make prisoners of their crews.

At this time two men succeeded in escaping from the steamers, and carried the alarm to the garrison. The prizes were meantime set on fire effectually, and the Union force set out on its return.

Encountering an armed party near the beach, a charge was made and two of the Confederates were captured. The beach was finally reached without loss, pickets were stationed, and the party rested, waiting the arrival of their boats.

While so resting (after a twenty-eight-mile march), word was brought the commander of the expedition that a detachment of cavalry and one of infantry were advancing, and the party was formed to resist an attack; the boats, however, having arrived, the embarkation commenced; and while this was going on the Confederates opened fire.

The first and second divisions of sailors, with seven prisoners, proceeded in an orderly manner to the boats; the third division deployed as skirmishers and returned the fire of the enemy with great spirit; the "Adela" in the meantime shelled the woods and drove the Confederates from cover. The first two divisions having embarked, the rear guard followed, after having stood at their posts and protected the retreat with the coolness of veteran soldiers. Finally, they, at the order, entered the boats, taking their wounded with them.

The Confederate troops were under the command of Captain Westcott, and were the so-called regulars, who could act as smugglers or bushwhackers as suited their purpose; but they did not seem inclined on this occasion to come out boldly and "try conclusions" with the sailors.

The retreat to the boats was conducted by Acting-Master Harris, with the most admirable coolness, and the expedition throughout was characterized by a degree of discipline, courage and energy not often met with even among the best trained troops. It shows how carefully the men of the Navy were drilled and how well commanded. On this occasion, although the Union force suffered a good deal while on the beach, they never swerved for one instant. Three of the sailors were killed, and their names are mentioned as an inducement for others to show an equal bravery.

They were James Warrall, John Roddy and Joseph O'Donnell, all seamen.

Ten men were wounded severely, and we are sorry not to be able to chronicle their names also, for no seamen ever deserved better! Acting-Ensigns Randall and Koehler were wounded, and four men were made prisoners.

This is the last of Rear-Admiral Bailey's operations up to October, 1863, and although they were not remarkably important, they show a determination to break up the blockade-running, and it was done effectually. Of fifty-two vessels that attempted to run the blockade, only seven succeeded, the rest being taken into the port of Key West. Nearly one hundred were captured in the space of six months.

The command of this station, although a compliment to Admiral Bailey, was scarcely a reward commensurate with his character and services. He was not a man whose appearance would attract attention, except from those who could appreciate the honest and simple character of an old-time naval officer, but he was a man who had no superior in the Navy in point of dash, energy and courage, and, if he had ever had the opportunity of commanding a fleet in action, he would have done it with the coolness and bravery of Nelson.

No higher compliment could be paid him.

LIST OF VESSELS COMPOSING THE EAST GULF BLOCKADING SQUADRON.

UNDER ACTING-REAR-ADMIRAL THEODORUS BAILEY; LIEUTENANT-COMMANDER WILLIAM G. TEMPLE, FLEET-CAPTAIN.

AS OBTAINED FROM THE NAVY REGISTER OF JANUARY, 1863, WITH NAMES OF COMMANDING AND OTHER OFFICERS.

FRIGATE "ST. LAWRENCE"—FLAG-SHIP.

Commander, James F. Schenck; Fleet Surgeon, G. R. B. Horner; Paymaster, Washington Irving; Assistant Surgeon, W. K. Van Reypen; Acting-Assistant Paymaster, A. B. Poor; Acting-Assistant Surgeon, A. Shirk; Acting-Masters, Wm. H. Smith, John Fuller, Chas. DeBevoise and George J. Murray; Acting-Master's Mates, E. Pavys, E. S. D. Howland, John Boyle, V. W. Jones and T. W. Jones; Marine Corps: Second-Lieutenant, R. S. Collum; Boatswain, J. A. Briscoe.

STEAMER "SAN JACINTO."

Commander, Wm. Ronckendorff; Lieutenant-Commander, Ralph Chandler; Assistant Surgeon, I. W. Bragg; Paymaster, Cramer Burt; Marine Officers, Capt. J. Schermerhorn; Second-Lieutenant, L. W. Powell; Acting-Masters, D. G. McRitchie, H. J. Coop and John Baker, Acting-Master's Mates, H. H Fuller, H. T. Keene, J. D. Weed and T. C. Jones; Engineers: Chief, Mortimer Kellogg; Assistants, H. S. Davids, H. C. McIlvaine, Edwin Wells, H. W. Scott, Edmund Lincoln and N. P. Towne; Boatswain, John Marley; Acting-Gunner, C. A. Stevenson; Carpenter, R. A. Williams; Sailmaker, J. H. North.

STEAMER "PENGUIN."

Commander, J. C. Williamson; Acting-Assistant Surgeon, G. B. Higginbotham; Acting-Assistant Paymaster, W. C. Cook; Acting-Masters, T. Durham, S. B. Rathbone, G. V. Cassedy and C. H. Rockwell; Acting-Master's Mates, W. E. Anderson, S. E. Foote, W. A. Beattie and W. A. Randlett; Engineers, F. W. Warner, M. P. Randall, A. B. Kinney and John Webster

STEAM GUN-BOAT "SAGAMORE."

Lieutenant-Commander, Earl English; Assistant-Surgeon, W. K. Scofield; Acting-Assistant Paymaster, J. F. Wood; Acting-Masters, Wm. Fales and Edwin Babson; Acting-Master's Mates, J. A. Slamm, C. R. Fleming, F. E. Ford and G. B. Sidell; Engineers, Henry Snyder, W. H. Harris, F. G. Coggin and G. J. Lamberson.

STEAM GUN-BOAT "TAHOMA"

Lieutenant-Commander, A. A. Semmes; Assistant Surgeon, J. H. Gunning; Acting-Assistant Paymaster, Wm. Hennessy; Acting-Ensigns, W. H. Harrison, D. W. Jackson and J. C. Hamlin; Acting-Master's Mates, J. G. Koehler, C. H. Tillinghast and R. G. Richards; Engineers, J. N. Cahill, J. K. Botsford, John Fornance and A. M. Rankin.

STEAM GUN-BOAT "PORT ROYAL."

Lieutenant-Commander, George U. Morris; Lieutenant, C. J. McDougal; Acting-Volunteer-Lieutenant, Wm. P. Randall; Assistant Surgeon, H. D. Burlingham; Assistant Paymaster, Geo. A. Sawyer; Acting-Masters, Edgar Van Slyck and L. D. D. Voorhees; Acting-Master's Mates, Wm. F. Reynolds, E. V. Tyson, H. D. Baldwin and Wm. A. Prescott; Engineers, Wm. C. Selden, E. M. Breese, O. C. Lewis, F. B. Allen and Henry Snyder.

STEAMER "SOMERSET."

Lieutenant-Commander, A. F. Crosman; Acting-Assistant Surgeon, James Mecray, Jr.; Acting-Assistant Paymaster, S. W. Adams; Acting-Masters, W. E. Dennison, J. S. Higbee, E. C. Healy and Thos. Chatfield; Acting-Master's Mates, C. H. Brantingham, T. M. Toombs and J. H. Stotsenburg; Engineers, W. D. Peters, W. H. Smith, E. Choppell and John Doyle.

STEAMER "LODONA."

Acting-Lieutenant, E. R. Colhoun; Acting-Assistant Surgeon, T. W. Meckley Acting-Assistant Paymaster, A. M. Stewart; Acting-Masters, Lewis West and J. P. Carr; Acting-Ensigns, H. G. McKenna and N. W. Rathbone; Acting-Master's Mates, Le Grand B. Brigham, W. A. Byrnes and F. E. Brecht; Engineers, F. A. Bremen, I. B. Hewett, S. D. Loring, O. B. Mills and James Mollineaux.

STEAMER "FORT HENRY."

Acting-Lieutenant, Edward Y. McCauley; Acting-Assistant Surgeon, Joseph Stevens; Acting-Assistant Paymaster, Daniel Whalen; Acting-Masters, R. B. Smith, F. W. Partridge and Geo. Leinas; Acting-Ensign, Geo. W. Bogue; Acting-Master's Mates, John Hancock, W. J. Haddock and W. E. Rice; Engineers, F. H. Fletcher, James Ward and Chas. Minnerly.

STEAMER "HUNTSVILLE."

Acting-Volunteer-Lieutenant, Wm. C. Rogers, Acting-Assistant Surgeon, G. J. Sweet; Acting-Assistant Paymaster, E. M. Hart; Acting-Masters, T. R. Harris, J. H. Platt and G. A. Smith; Acting-Master's Mates, E. B. J. Singleton, Charles Labden and C. R. Scoffin; Engineers, J. L. Parry, N. N. Buckingham, W. A. Leavitt and John Kanealy.

BARK "PURSUIT"

Acting-Volunteer-Lieutenant, David Cate; Acting-Assistant Surgeon, H. K. Wheeler, Acting Assistant Paymaster, D. P. Shuler; Acting-Masters, Robert Spavin, H. K. Lapham and C. R. Harris; Acting-Master's Mates, J. H. Barry and Van Buren Blum.

BARK "GEMSBOK"

Acting-Volunteer-Lieutenant, Edward Cavendy; Acting-Assistant Surgeon, Thomas Welsh; Acting-Assistant Paymaster, E. H. Roberts; Acting-Masters, O. Thatcher and Theo. Werlhop; Acting-Master's Mates, T. J. Pray, M. W. Stone and N. W. Wait.

SLOOP-OF-WAR "DALE."

Acting-Master, J. O. Barclay; Acting-Assistant Surgeon, F. B. Lawson; Acting-Assistant Paymaster, R. B. Rodney; Acting-Master, B. F. Cook; Acting-Ensigns, J. A. Denman and J. T. Mendall; Acting-Master's Mates, D. C. Kiersted, M. Jackson and Wm. Morris.

STEAMER "MAGNOLIA."

Acting-Master, Chas. Potter; Acting-Assistant Surgeon, E. D. G. Smith; Acting-Assistant Paymaster, W. J. Coite; Acting-Masters, Francis Burgess and Alex. Wallace; Acting-Master's Mates, David Scyler, Peter McGuire and O. Sundstrom; Engineers, Edward Eldridge, E. D. Leavitt, Jr., and R. H. Shultis.

STEAMER "STARS AND STRIPES."

Acting-Master, C. L. Willcombe; Acting-Assistant Surgeon, Benj. Marshall; Acting-Assistant Paymaster, J. J. Pratt; Acting-Masters, L. W. Hill, Geo. Ashbury, Thomas Smith and G. H. Cole; Acting-Master's Mates, H. B. Conklin, C. P. Turner and Alex. Cushman; Engineers, John Briggs, T. D. Coffee, John Burns and H. F. Brown.

BARK "JAMES L. DAVIS."

Acting-Master, John West; Acting-Assistant Surgeon, E. B. Jackson; Acting-Assistant Paymaster, B. S. Price; Acting-Masters, Alex. Waugh and Geo. F. Hammond; Acting-Master's Mates, A. J. Lyon, S. E. Willetts and G. H. Disley.

BARK "ROEBUCK."

Acting-Master, John Sherrill; Acting-Assistant Surgeon, M. G. Raefle; Acting-Assistant Paymaster, Wm. Sellew; Acting-Masters, H. F. Coffin, Jas. Folger and A. M. Newman; Acting-Ensign, Timothy Delano; Acting-Master's Mates, W. H. Bradford and C. F. Dunderdale.

BARK "JAMES S. CHAMBERS."

Acting-Master, Luther Nickerson; Acting-Assistant Surgeon, Wm. Clendaniel; Acting-Assistant Paymaster, C. H. West; Acting-Masters, A. B.

Pierson and Wm. H. McLean; Acting-Master's Mates, W. J. Eldredge, W. A. Smith and David Axe.

BARK "AMANDA."

Acting-Volunteer-Lieutenants, Geo. E. Welch and Samuel Howard; Acting-Assistant Surgeon, A. H. Hershey; Acting-Assistant Paymaster, E. B. Southworth; Acting-Masters, R. J. Hoffner and J. E. Jones; Acting Master's Mates, G. C. Campbell and N. L. Ledyard.

BARK "ETHAN ALLEN."

Acting-Master, J. A. Pennell; Acting-Assistant Surgeon, J. M. Flint, Acting-Master, Alfred Weston; Acting-Ensign, Samuel McCormick; Acting-Master's Mates, J. E. Stickney, John Wilcox and E. R. Davidson.

BARK "HOUGHTON."

Acting-Master, Newell Graham; Acting Assistant Paymaster, O. F. Browning.

SCHOONER "EUGENIE."

Acting-Master, Wm. McClintock; Acting-Assistant Paymaster, W. C. Blackwell.

SCHOONER "BEAUREGARD."

Acting-Master, Wm. A. Arthur; Acting-Master's Mate, W. H. Melson.

SCHOONER "WANDERER."

Acting-Master, E. S. Turner; Acting-Assistant Surgeon, Thomas McHenry; Acting-Master's Mates, L. H. Livingston and Ezra Robbins.

CHAPTER XXXVIII.

REVIEW OF THE WORK DONE BY THE NAVY IN THE YEAR 1863.

A SUMMARY of the events of 1863 may serve to keep in mind the details of the several squadrons that were operating along a sea-coast of over 3,500 miles in extent, and in the Western rivers, a further distance of 4,000 miles. The harbors and indentations of the Atlantic coast, which afforded refuge for blockade-runners, or points for landing their munitions of war, amounted to at least 180 in number.

Thus the Navy had to guard a line of coasts and rivers over 7,500 miles in extent, a task compared with which the famous blockade of the French coast by the British, during the wars with Napoleon, was a mere bagatelle.

Day by day the blockade of the Southern sea-coast became more stringent, and as Congress was made to feel the urgent appeals of Mr. Secretary Welles for an increase of the Navy, and became aware that the resources of the enemy diminished in proportion as those of the Navy increased, and realized that, without an adequate force of war-vessels, the Rebellion would never be conquered, it showed due liberality, and success began to attend the Federal arms in all quarters.

By increasing the stringency of the blockade, the enemy were driven from the coast, as they realized the uselessness of contending against combined military and naval operations. The great rivers and their tributaries were no longer safe resorts for marauders, as the capture of the principal towns in the West, and the occupation of the surrounding country by the Union forces, had relieved a large number of troops from siege-duty, who could now be employed from Tennessee to Louisiana.

The power of the Navy at the same time was largely increased on the Western rivers by the addition of some 800 guns mounted in war-vessels improvised from merchant steamboats; and these aided in transporting the Army from one point to another wherever the enemy showed himself.

The operations of the Navy up to the end of the year 1863 had borne with great severity on those who had risen in arms against the National Government, and the idea has been suggested that the almost superhuman efforts of this arm of the service to crush the Rebellion has been a serious embarrassment to its advance since the close of the civil war; that the Southern influence in Congress has, in a great measure, prevented the rebuilding of the Navy and bringing it to a condition befitting a great nation. Certain it is, the Navy has been brought to so low an ebb that it almost seems as if this state of affairs had been produced by some concert of action.

The best illustration of what the Navy had accomplished up to the close of the year 1863 is afforded by the official reports of the commanding officers of squadrons and single ships; but, as these cannot be embodied in a narrative of this kind, we must content ourselves with an abstract from the records.

Acting-Rear-Admiral S. P. Lee, in command of the North Atlantic squadron, ably seconded by the zeal of his officers, had penetrated the waters of Virginia wherever his gun-boats could reach, and had occupied the sounds of North Carolina to such an extent that the Confederates could be said to have no foothold in that quarter. Wilmington, near the mouth of the Cape Fear River, was really the only point in North Carolina where the enemy could boast that they had defied the Federal arms, and this point was found extremely difficult to close owing to two separate entrances to the river some thirty miles apart, both protected by the heaviest description of land defences and obstructed by shallow bars. These obstacles at the time were considered such as to preclude any attempt to capture Wilmington from the sea.

Many reasons existed why the Army could not co-operate in an attack upon Wilmington, which thus remained upwards of a year longer than it should have done the great depot of supplies for the Confederate armies. Many fast steamers from the Clyde, and other parts of Great Britain, continued to elude the utmost efforts of the blockading squadron, and reached Wilmington with valuable cargoes of arms and munitions of war, though numbers were captured or driven on shore and destroyed.

In all the operations of the North Atlantic squadron its officers and men exhibited bravery and zeal second to no other organization in the Navy. There was no field for great achievement except the capture of Fort Fisher and the other defences of Wilmington, which might have been taken earlier in the war, but the task was postponed until it required nearly half of the Navy to overcome the obstacles then presented.

The South Atlantic squadron, during the year 1863, had performed most valuable service in blockading the Southern coast, and had succeeded in maintaining a force in Charleston harbor which completely closed that port as a refuge for blockade-runners, and prevented the Confederates from obtaining further supplies in that quarter.

The Navy Department had made great efforts to capture the heavy defences inside Charleston bar, and Rear-Admiral DuPont had made a vigorous attack with his ironclads and Monitors on the heaviest line of works; but, owing to the destructive fire of the enemy and the insufficiency of his force of vessels, DuPont very properly withdrew. The wisdom of his course was subsequently shown during the combined Army and Navy operations against Charleston, under Rear-Admiral Dahlgren and Brigadier-General Gillmore. On the later occasion, sixty siege-guns were brought to bear on the enemy, and Fort Sumter was "reduced to pulp," yet the difficulties of an advance of the naval vessels were so great owing to the obstructions in the channel, that notwithstanding the energy and bravery of the commander-in-chief, his officers and men, at the end of 1863 Charleston still remained in possession of the Confederates, although practically useless to the latter.

If the Federal Government could not boast of having captured the hot-bed of secession, it had at least the satisfaction of knowing that Charleston was only held at vast expense to the enemy, merely from a sentiment of pride, and a wish to keep the Federal soldiers and sailors ignorant of the sufferings the citizens had undergone in their mistaken zeal for a desperate cause. As Charleston was the first place to take up arms against the Union, its leading men considered that it should be the last to lay them down. Their gallantry was unquestionable, but their policy, in a military point of view, was open to criticism, and the city had finally to surrender on the approach of General Sherman's indefatigable soldiers, who did not always extend to conquered cities that consideration they would have received from the Navy.

The Eastern Gulf squadron had no important military operations to co-operate with, Acting-Rear-Admiral Bailey being engaged in blockading the entire east and west coasts of Florida, capturing many prizes, annihilating the illicit traffic in that quarter, and preventing all supplies from reaching the Confederate armies by way of the Florida coast.

The duties of Rear-Admiral Farragut, in command of the West Gulf squadron, had been extremely harassing, but they gave that gallant officer an opportunity to exhibit the highest qualities as commander-in-chief.

Soon after the memorable battle below New Orleans and the surrender of that city, Farragut made a junction with the squadron of Flag-officer Davis above Vicksburg, and, had the Army contingent that was sent to support him been as large as it should have been, Farragut would have had the satisfaction of capturing Vicksburg. The military part of the expedition, however, though commanded by a most able and gallant general, was too small to effect anything by an attack on the city; and Farragut, after subjecting his squadron to the fire of the enemy's guns, which were daily increasing in number and power, and finding it was a mere waste of time and strength to lay before the city, returned to New Orleans to co-operate with the Army in maintaining order in Louisiana.

This omission of a proper military force to co-operate with the Navy gave the Confederates time to render Vicksburg the Gibraltar of the West, and for a long period it bade defiance to the Army and Navy combined. The Vicksburg miscarriage enabled the enemy to fortify Port Hudson and Grand Gulf, which thus became two formidable barriers against the advance of the Navy.

When Vicksburg was invested in 1863 by the Army under Major General Grant, and a large naval force under Rear-Admiral Porter, many efforts were made by the latter officer to send vessels down to blockade the mouth of the Red River, and thus cut off supplies from Port Hudson and Vicksburg; but, owing to casualties in the vessels sent on this duty, there was a failure to bring about the desired result.

Rear-Admiral Farragut then attempted to push up past Port Hudson with his squadron, and met with serious loss. However, with the "Hartford" and "Albatross," he reached the mouth of Red River, and established so stringent a blockade that the Confederates in Port Hudson and Vicksburg could no longer obtain supplies from that quarter.

Farragut was engaged a part of the season with his ships below Port Hudson in bombarding that place. In these operations the Mortar vessels bore a conspicuous part, until Port Hudson fell, with Vicksburg, on the 4th of July, 1863, and the Mississippi was once more opened to the sea.

The blockade of the Southern coast, within the limits of Admiral Farragut's command, had, in the main, been efficient and successful, although reverses at Galveston and Sabine Pass gave the enemy something on which to congratulate themselves. These reverses, however, of the Union arms were of no permanent advantage to the Confederates, as the whole coast, from the mouth of the Mississippi to that of the Rio Grande, was so closely guarded by the Union Navy that blockade-running was reduced to very insignificant proportions.

The Mississippi squadron, under Rear-Admiral Porter, had been actively engaged in the work of suppressing the Rebellion, and co-operated zealously with the Army whenever its services were needed. The capture of Arkansas Post, on the Arkansas River, and the constant effective attacks on the batteries of Vicksburg, the bombardment of the city and its defences, the battle of Grand Gulf and the landing of Grant's army at Bruensburg, and the final reduction of the great stronghold on July 4th, 1863, are among the successful achievements of the Mississippi squadron in co-operation with the Army.

It is simple justice to the officers and men of this squadron that their heroic exertions should receive proper credit, and we cannot better do justice to the occasion than by repeating the eulogistic terms in which Mr. Secretary Welles speaks of them:

"In the appendix to this report (1863) will be found correct records of the extraordinary adventures attending the efforts to get control of the Yazoo, by sweeping from the channel the net-work of torpedoes, explosive machines, and contrivances of submarine warfare, near its confluence with the Mississippi. These efforts were followed by the novel and singular Yazoo Pass expedition and the expedition of Steele's Bayou and Deer Creek. On the right bank of the Mississippi scenes of interest were enacted by the hardy sailors and boatmen in the rivers of Arkansas and northern Louisiana. The Cumberland and Tennessee have been actively patrolled by our vigilant and skillful naval officers; and the exciting chase of Morgan, by our steamers on the Ohio, over a distance of five hundred miles,

intercepting him and his band when attempting to escape, naturally attracted the attention of the country.

But the great and important exploits of this squadron were in the vicinity of Vicksburg, where the main strength of the naval as well as the military forces were centred. The magnitude of the defences of the place—which were intended to repulse any force, naval or military, that could be brought against them—made the siege formidable, and seemed for a time to defy all attempts at their reduction. In overcoming them, the Navy necessarily performed a conspicuous and *essential* part. For forty-two days, without intermission, the mortar-boats were throwing shells into all parts of the city, and even the works beyond it.

Heavy guns mounted on scows commanded the important water batteries, and for fourteen days maintained an incessant fire on them. Thirteen heavy guns were landed from the vessels [the Secretary should have said twenty-two], and officers and men—when they could be spared—were sent to man them.

The gun-boats below the city, in co-operation with the Army, were continually engaged in shelling the place.

During the siege sixteen thousand shells were thrown from the mortars, gun-boats and naval batteries upon the city and its defences before it capitulated.

The creation and organization of this huge squadron, which has done such effective service on the upper Mississippi and its tributaries, extending over a distance of more than 3,500 miles, may justly be considered among the most wonderful events of the times. It is but little over two years since we had not a naval vessel on all those waters, where we now have a squadron of 100 vessels, carrying 462 guns, with crews amounting, in the aggregate, to about 5,500 men.

Kentucky, Tennessee and Arkansas, the upper portions of Mississippi and Louisiana, and the southern portions of those States which border on the Ohio River on the north, have been relieved and liberated through the instrumentality of the gun-boats, acting by themselves or in earnest and cordial co-operation with the armies.

Rear-Admiral Porter has well sustained the renown which the gallant and lamented Foote so nobly earned, and has carried forward to successful results a larger and more powerful force than was ever at the disposal of that heroic officer. [The Honorable Secretary does not make his meaning quite clear at this point, but it is presumed he wished to be complimentary.]

In creating and organizing this squadron, and arming and manning the vessels, it must not be forgotten that the service labored under many and great disadvantages, for the Government had no Navy Yard or establishment of its own on which the Department could depend. In the absence of any Government shops, yards, store-houses, and other necessary facilities and aids for a naval establishment, and also of mechanics and laborers, it became necessary to collect and send out and receive supplies from some central and secure position. This work has been chiefly performed at Cairo," etc., etc.

The Honorable Secretary might have said that the then commander-in-chief of the Mississippi squadron, finding only the ghost of a squadron and the skeleton of a Navy yard in the West, had built up a naval station, with shops and machinery, to meet the wants of the occasion, had increased the squadron from 21 vessels, all out of repair, to 121, mounting 680 guns, with which force, co-operating with the Army, the Mississippi was opened to the sea, and all its tributaries brought under control of the Federal Government.

Mr. Welles, in his official report, is almost as chary of praise for the services of the Navy before Vicksburg as was the military commanding officer in the West, who, only in his last days, in the year 1885, in a few words, gave the officers and men of the Navy full credit for their services on that occasion.

The result of the herculean efforts of the Mississippi squadron was the establishment of Federal rule along the banks of the great river and its tributaries. The Confederacy was cut in twain, never to be reunited; and from this time the cause of the Rebellion began rapidly to sink.

While the Federal Government was supposed to be almost overwhelmed with the severe pressure brought to bear on it at home, the Navy was sustaining its reputation abroad, and closely guarding American interests whenever an opportunity offered. The Confederate cruisers were still pursuing their destructive career; but ships-of-war had been sent in pursuit of them in every direction, and their end was near.

In the East Indies and the China seas, the respect due to the American flag was exacted by Commander David McDougal, commanding the U. S. S. "Wyoming," who, learning of some injustice suffered by an American vessel at the hands of the Japanese, repaired to the locality (Simonosaki), and inflicted severe punishment on some forts and vessels-of-war.

These people were taught that while the Federal Government had a gigantic task to perform at home in putting down the Rebellion, yet its naval officers were just as ready as ever to resent an insult to the flag. This prompt vindication of the honor of the country abroad had the happy effect of convincing people that the strength of the American Republic only increased when it seemed to be threatened with destruction, and that it was quite competent to guard its interests abroad as well as at home.

It will be remembered that, at the commencement of the civil war, the naval force consisted of about forty-two effective vessels, scattered over the world, with about thirty-four more at the Navy Yards available for service after undergoing extensive repairs. Up to the end of 1863 the Navy Department had exhibited great energy, and, for the first time in its history, the United States had a Navy commensurate with its importance as a maritime power.

The following table exhibits the progress made in increasing the Navy since December, 1862, and shows what the country was capable of achieving under a pressure that would have almost crushed any other nation:

COMPARATIVE EXHIBIT OF THE NAVY, DEC., 1862, AND 1863.

	No. of Vessels.	No. of Guns.	Tons.
Navy at date of present Report—Dec., 1863.	588	4,443	467,967
Navy at date of last Report—Dec., 1862.....	427	3,268	340,036
Total increase......................	161	1,175	127,931

VESSELS OF THE NAVY LOST SINCE DEC., 1862.

In What Manner Lost.	No. of Vessels.	No. of Guns.	Tons.
Captured	12	48	5,947
Destroyed to prevent falling into hands of Confederates	3	29	2,983
Sunk in battle or by torpedoes.	4	28	2,201
Shipwreck, fire and collision...............	13	61	4,854
Total......	32	166	15,985

VESSELS PLACED UNDER CONSTRUCTION SINCE DEC., 1862.

Description.	No. of Vessels.	No. of Guns.	Tons.
Double-end iron steamers, 1,030 tons each..	7	84	7,210
Single turret iron-clads, 614 tons each.	20	40	12,280
Double turret iron-clads, 3,130 tons each....	4	16	12,520
Clipper screw-sloops, 2,200 tons each.......	12	96	26,400
Screw-sloops, spar-deck, 2,200 tons each ...	8	160	17,600
Screw-sloops of great speed, 3,200 tons each.	5	40	16,000
Screw-sloops of great speed, 3,000 tons each	2	16	6,000
Total	58	452	98,010

GENERAL EXHIBIT OF THE NAVY WHEN THE VESSELS UNDER CONSTRUCTION ARE COMPLETED.

	No. of Vessels.	No. of Guns.	Tons.
Iron-clad steamers coast service.	46	150	62,518
Iron-clad steamers, inland service..........	29	152	20,784
Side-wheel steamers....................	203	1,240	126,517
Screw steamers	198	1,578	187,892
Sailing vessels.....................	112	1,323	70,256
Total..................	588	4,443	467,967

There were added to the Navy during the year 1863, by purchase, some thirty tugs, over fifty steamers for blockading and supply purposes, and over twenty other vessels for tenders and store-ships. At least twenty of the steamers were captured in endeavoring to violate the blockade.

It will be noticed that the additions to the Navy comprised vessels of the most formidable kind, and far more powerful than those of European navies.

It is due to history to state that this addition to the Navy was owing the energy and ability of Mr. G. V. Fox, Assistant Secretary of the Navy, who had the supervision of all improvements and additions of ships, Mr. Welles wisely approving all his suggestions; while the able Chief Constructor, Mr. John Lenthall, brought all his ability to bear on the models of the vessels, and Mr. B. F. Isherwood, the talented Chief of the Bureau of Steam Engineering, devised the engines, which, even to the present day, have scarcely been equalled.

The consequence of all this was that Governments disposed to be meddlesome failed to interfere when they saw that the Republic was not only determined to crush the Rebellion, but to resent any outside interference.

The year 1864 opened hopefully for the success of the Union arms by land and sea, and it will be seen that the history of the American Navy was enriched by many brilliant actions, which stand high in the annals of maritime war.

It must not be supposed that during the year 1863 the Navy Department was indifferent to the ravages committed by the Confederate cruisers fitted out in England for the destruction of Federal commerce. The prompt recognition of the Confederates as belligerents by foreign powers, on the breaking out of the Rebellion, gave to the insurrection a character and strength it could never otherwise have obtained. It encouraged the Confederates to persevere, and assured them of support abroad in any measures they might think proper to undertake, and gave them an opportunity to strike a blow at the most vulnerable point of the North—its commerce.

The apparent intention of the declaration of neutrality by the powers of Europe was to exhibit a semblance of fairness, a deception of which the Confederates naturally took advantage, and which operated very unjustly against the United States. The Government was obliged to acquiesce in this acknowledgment of belligerent rights, and assume all the consequences resulting therefrom.

While the United States had a large mercantile marine scarcely second to that of Great Britain, the Confederates had actually none whatever. In a short time the latter were able by various means to get afloat and at sea several very formidable cruisers. The United States had squadrons on every foreign station representing a *bona fide* Government, while the insurgents, at the time of their receiving belligerent rights, had not a single man of-war, a fact well understood by the Governments which, in proclaiming their "neutrality" and desire to treat both parties alike, seriously crippled the American Navy and well-nigh destroyed its mercantile marine.

The cruising of Federal ships-of-war was limited and all sorts of obstacles thrown in the way of their capturing the Confederate cruisers. The maritime powers of Europe, after granting belligerent rights to the Confederates, declared that both belligerents should be treated alike in their ports, that the public armed vessels of neither should remain longer than twenty-four hours in their harbors, nor receive supplies or assistance except such as might be absolutely necessary to carry them to their own coasts, and for three months thereafter they should not again receive supplies in any of the ports of those Governments.

While this proclamation did not at the time of its issue affect the Confederates, for the simple reason that they had then no vessels afloat, it excluded the naval ships of the United States from the principal ports of the world. As to the fairness which assumed to be the motive of the proclamation of neutrality, that must be judged from the history of the times, which will show that these proclamations were merely excuses to allow Confederate cruisers to prey upon American commerce and then find protection from United States vessels-of-war within the jurisdiction of the great European powers that were professedly in close amity with the United States.

The "Sumter," the very first Confederate cruiser fitted out, affords a fair sample of how this acknowledgment of belligerent rights operated, and how much fairness there was on the part of Great Britain in carrying out the proclamation she claimed to have issued to insure equal treatment to both the contending parties. The "Sumter," after escaping to sea from New Orleans through the carelessness of the officer on blockade, and capturing many American merchant-vessels, was chased into the harbor of Gibraltar, where she was permitted to remain twelve months—instead of twenty-four hours—under the protection of British guns. Not daring to venture to sea, as she was closely watched by several Federal cruisers, the "Sumter's" officers finally transferred the vessel to an English subject, who took her to another British port, where she was refitted, loaded with a contraband cargo, and ran the blockade, carrying supplies to the Confederates.

The "Alabama," "Georgia" and "Florida" were fitted out in England, and supplied with an English armament. Their crews were mostly Europeans, and they sailed sometimes under the British, sometimes under the Confederate, flag, dealing destruction to Federal commerce wherever it could be found.

As soon as the existence of these Confederate cruisers was known to the Secretary of the Navy, ships were sent in pursuit. While in the West Indies, the Confederate cruisers were protected whenever they were able to escape into a "neutral port"—an opportunity which was offered on every hand —or get within a marine league of a neutral island. Strange to say, most of the colonial authorities in various parts of the world were in sympathy with the Confederates and hostile to the war-vessels of the United States; and, while giving aid and comfort to those *quasi* vessels-of-war, threw every obstacle in the way of Federal cruisers obtaining supplies of coal and provisions. Not only that, the "neutrals" all through the West Indies furnished the commanding officers of the Confederate cruisers (by means of the mail-steamers plying between the different ports) with information of the intended movements of every United States vessel-of-war in those waters. Worse than all, the most unfriendly feelings were manifested by the officials generally, from governor down to the lowest subordinate, in regard to the lawful operations of United States vessels.

It can easily be imagined, under such circumstances as these, how difficult it would be for a United States vessel-of-war to capture one of these sea-rovers, especially in the West Indies. The islanders, not satisfied with transmitting information to the Confederates, in some cases assumed an intimacy with the commanders of United States vessels, and deceived them with false reports.

CHAPTER XXXIX.

Successful Military Operations.—Prospects of Southern Independence.—Confederate Commissioners.—Completeness and Discipline of U. S. Navy, 1863.—Position and Strength of Opposing Forces.—Combined Army and Navy Expedition up James and Nansemond Rivers.—Destruction of Blockade-runners "Bendigo," "Ranger," "Venus" and "Dare."—Capture and Destruction of U. S. Steamer "Underwriter."—Destruction of Blockade-runners "Wild Dayrell," "Nutfield," "Dee," "Emily," and "Fannie and Jennie."—Boat Expedition up Cape Fear River to Smithville.—Joint Army and Navy Expedition up Pamunky River.—Boat Expedition up Chuckatuck Creek.—Attack on "Minnesota" by Torpedo-boat.—Landing of Army at City Point and Bermuda Hundred.—Destruction of U. S. Gun-boat "Commodore Jones."—Confederate Torpedo Defences.—Monitors engage Howlett's Battery.—Picking up Torpedoes.—Repulse of Attack on Wilson's Wharf by Gun-boats.—Confederate Iron-clads and Gun-boats below Drury's Bluff.—Sinking of Obstructions in James River.—Letter from General Butler to Acting-Rear-Admiral Lee.—Grant's Operations.—Hulks Sunk at Trent's Reach.—Attack on Petersburg.—Engagement with Confederate Iron-clad at Mouth of Cape Fear River.—Daring Adventures of Lieutenant Cushing.

THE year 1864 opened with flattering prospects for the Union cause, owing to the important successes gained over the enemy in 1863, and the constantly increasing losses in material by the Confederates in consequence of the stringent blockade of the coast. The Federal Navy had been so far strengthened with a class of vessels superior to anything of which the powers of Europe could boast, that it was no longer anticipated that England or France would interfere in our domestic affairs.

The battle of Gettysburg, which caused General Lee to fall back upon Richmond, and the surrender of Port Hudson and Vicksburg, which opened the Mississippi to the sea, were the severest blows the Confederacy had received. In the opinion of many persons well qualified to judge, the possession of the Mississippi and its tributaries by the Federals was the death-blow to the Southern cause, and the final collapse of the Rebellion was simply a matter of time, and a short time at that.

The Northern people gave the Administration continued support, while the Confederates could not repair the rapid waste of their armies, notwithstanding their most vigorous efforts. In Washington the opinion prevailed that, before the year had elapsed, the authority of the Government would be everywhere restored. This opinion also prevailed in the Navy, which had been strongly reinforced by a class of vessels able to overhaul the swiftest blockade-runners built on the Clyde; so that hardly one out of three vessels succeeded in getting into Wilmington or Mobile—the two principal ports where these illicit traders congregated. The Southern coast was so closely invested by the Navy that it was with great difficulty the blockade-runners could get in or out, although a certain proportion of them managed to elude pursuit, and carry out cargoes of cotton, which served to keep up the financial credit of the Confederacy abroad.

The Confederates, as a matter of course, felt the want of the munitions of war they had been accustomed to receive in such quantities through the blockade-runners, particularly great guns and small arms manufactured in England. Every port, from Virginia to Texas, was watched with a zeal that had never before been exerted on such an occasion; for it was felt by the officers of the Navy that this watchfulness would be well rewarded, and the information gained from the crews of the captured vessels confirmed them in the opinion that the end was not far off.

Meanwhile the Confederate authorities professed to think that the prospects for Southern independence were brighter than ever, and that, before the end of the year 1864, their object would be accomplished, and the following year see them acknowledged as a separate Government by all the world. Upon what such an opinion was founded is not clear, and it seems impossible to account for the confidence which existed in the hearts of the Southern leaders, and with which they entered so confidingly on the campaign of 1864. Any other people in the world, under the circumstances in which they were placed, would have laid down their arms, and accepted terms from their conquerors.

It was pitiable to witness the distress of the Southern people which came under the notice of naval officers, and which was caused by the determination of their leaders to continue the contest to the bitter end; for a large proportion of them felt that there was no hope of their succeeding. It was plain to them all that there was no hope of assistance from the Democratic party of the North. The re-election of President Lincoln convinced many, who had been hitherto blind to the state of affairs, that the Union cause was as heartily supported by the Democrats as by the Republicans.

Even while the Confederacy was in the throes of dissolution, the mass of the Southern people had been hugging the delusion that there was a strong peace party in the North that would make itself felt in the Presidential election of 1864; that there was such a feeling of impatience at the prolongation of the war that no Administration could stand up under it. All that was required of the South, therefore, was to make one final effort, and they would gain the rights for which they were contending—exactly what those rights were, the majority of the people seemed to have little idea.

It was proclaimed in Richmond that the impatience and dissatisfaction of the North were so great that the people of that section were determined to have peace on any terms. All that the South had to do was simply to hold its own; and, merely by securing negative results in the ensuing campaign, the Democratic party would be able to overthrow the Administration, and open negotiations for peace with the Confederacy.

In accordance with this idea, President Davis prepared to open communication with the Democratic party of the North, and to conduct political negotiations with that party in accordance with the military movements in the coming campaign. The commissioners appointed for this purpose were Messrs. Thompson, of Mississippi, Holcombe, of Virginia, and Clay, of Alabama, who were to proceed to a convenient spot on the northern frontier of the United States, and to use whatever political opportunities the military events of the war might disclose. The commissioners succeeded in running the blockade from Wilmington, and reached Canada, only to find that the Northern sentiment in regard to the Confederacy was practically unanimous, and that all parties were determined to bring the seceding States back into the Union.

The Federal Army and Navy in the West maintained the superiority they had won, and kept open the rivers the enemy had fought so hard to close against them. By the possession of the Mississippi, the Confederacy was cut in twain. The Union Army was constantly increasing, and, in place of the raw volunteers of 1861, who could hardly handle a musket, the Union could boast of nearly a million of veteran soldiers. Grant was now called East to command, as Lieutenant-General, all the armies of the United States; while his most able coadjutor, General Sherman, with an army of veterans famous on many a field, was to commence his march through the South, and join Grant before the defences of Richmond.

The military history of the year 1864 will show the delusion under which the Southern leaders rested—that it was "only necessary for the South to remain in *statu quo*, winning no victories in the field, and to demonstrate their endurance, to gain the desired end." The Federal Army was most complete in all its equipments, and its discipline was established. How, then, could the South hope to contend against such an organization?

The Navy was in no respect behind the Army in completeness and discipline. At the end of the year 1863, the number of guns afloat amounted to 4,443, the tonnage of the vessels to 467,967, manned by 50,000 seamen. Among the vessels already built or in process of construction, in 1864, there were 75 iron casemated and turreted vessels, carrying 302 powerful guns, that could destroy any fortress the Confederates could build on the sea-coast, and bid defiance to any force sent by foreign powers to their assistance.

It may have been chivalric in the South to attempt a contest with such a power as was brought against them, but it was hardly wise or just to the people on the part of those who ruled the Confederacy. It cost great waste of life, with no gain in the end to the South, except the satisfaction of feeling that they only submitted when overcome by greatly superior numbers.

The whole country, although it lost men enough to have made a dozen large armies, gained greatly in prestige, and taught Europe that our people united were a match for all their powers combined.

In February, 1864, Acting-Rear-Admiral S. P. Lee, commanding the North Atlantic squadron, was in co-operation with Major-General B. F. Butler, who commanded the army of the James with his headquarters at Fortress Monroe. General Meade commanded the Army of the Potomac, with his headquarters south of the Rapidan, while the headquarters of the Army of the Shenandoah, under command of Major-General Sigel, were at Winchester.

An important part of the North Atlantic squadron, under the immediate command of Acting-Rear-Admiral Lee, was at Hampton Roads; some of the vessels were on the James, others on the York River, ready as heretofore to co-operate with the Army when the great movement on Richmond should be made, which was to bring the civil war to a termination.

The available strength of the Federal army on the Potomac, including the Ninth Corps and the reinforcements that were held in Washington, was not less than 170,000 men. The force which the Confederates had to oppose was much inferior, according to their own account. The Confederate Army of the Rapidan, at the beginning of the campaign of 1864, consisted of two divisions of Longstreet's corps with 8,000 men, Ewell's corps of 14,000, Hill's corps of 13,000, three divisions of cavalry, and the artillery. So that, according to Confederate historians, Lee's effective force of infantry did not exceed 40,000 men. The cavalry divisions did not each exceed the proper strength of a brigade, and the artillery was in proportion to the other arms, altogether not over 80,000 men of all arms. But it will not do to rely upon Confederate figures, and General Grant's estimate placed Lee's force at 120,000 men, including the militia and local forces in and about Richmond and Petersburg. This was the condition of affairs when Grant assumed command of all the armies of the Union, when a move was being made upon Richmond, and Lee was collecting all his available forces to meet the emergency.

The battles of the Wilderness were fought and a terrible resistance was made by the Confederates, but in vain, and the great Union column, after overcoming the greatest obstacles, marched on its way towards Richmond.

While General Grant was occupied on the Rapidan he had not lost sight of other forces which were to be used in combination with the Army of the Potomac, which forces were to operate in conjunction with the Navy as near Richmond as it was possible to get. This was the Army of the James, under Major-General Butler, numbering 20,000 men. General Grant directed Butler to operate on the south side of the James River in conjunction with the Army of the Potomac, the objective point of both being Richmond.

To Butler's force was to be added ten thousand men from South Carolina under Major-General Q. A. Gillmore, while Major-General W. F. Smith was ordered to report to General Butler to command the troops sent into the field from his Department.

General Butler was directed, when his forces were able to move, to seize and hold City Point. Grant intended that, in case the Confederates should be forced by his advance into their intrenchments at Richmond, the Army of the Potomac should follow them up, and by means of transports the two armies would become a unit. It would seem from this that Grant expected to fight Lee between Culpeper Court House and Richmond, and in case he should not defeat him he could make a junction with Butler, already established on the James, and be in a position to threaten Richmond on the south side, with his left wing resting on the James, above the city.

In accordance with his instructions, General Butler moved his forces up the James River, where he had the assistance of the Navy to cover his landing, which was accomplished without difficulty. Having been joined by General Gillmore on the 4th of May, Butler occupied City Point and Bermuda Hundred on the 5th; on the 6th he was in position with his main force and intrenched, and on the 7th made a reconnaissance of the Petersburg and Richmond Railroad, and destroyed a bridge a few miles from Richmond.

From this, General Butler formed the opinion that he had succeeded in getting in the rear of the Confederates, and held the key to the back-door of Richmond. He accordingly telegraphed to Washington: "We have landed here, intrenched ourselves, destroyed many miles of railroad, and got a position which, with proper supplies, we can hold against the whole of Lee's army." Butler was, in fact, under the impression that he could capture Richmond before General Grant arrived. General Butler's dispatch caused great satisfaction in Washington, which was soon dispelled by an unforeseen occurrence.

In the month of April General Beauregard had been ordered to proceed from

Charleston to strengthen the defences of Richmond. He passed through Wilmington with a large body of troops, receiving constant accessions on the march, and assumed command of the district on the south and east of Richmond.

On the 16th of May Beauregard attacked Butler's advanced position in front of Drury's Bluff, and Butler was forced back into his intrenchments between the James and the Appomattox Rivers; thereupon Beauregard intrenched himself strongly in his front, covering the city of Richmond from any further attempts of Butler in that direction. This predicament of Butler gave rise to the celebrated letter of General Grant, in which he speaks of Butler's being as completely *hors du combat* as if he were enclosed in a bottle with the cork in. General Butler held his position, although he had the naval vessels on the James and Appomattox Rivers to cover his retreat to his transports, in case of further molestation from Beauregard.

These military movements are mentioned merely to show the position of affairs in May, 1864, when the Army and Navy were brought into co-operation before Richmond, and not with any intention of criticising.

The operations of the North Atlantic squadron in the beginning of the year 1864, although not brilliant, were none the less important, as tending to cripple the Confederacy.

The blockade of the Southern coast had been closely maintained, and many blockade-runners captured or destroyed. On the 3d of January, while the "Fah Kee" (temporary flag-ship) was standing up the coast from Little River Inlet towards Wilmington bar, a steamer was discovered at the entrance of Lockwood's Folly Inlet, apparently ashore. Smoke was issuing from the vessel, and she was evidently abandoned. Boats were sent from the "Fah Kee," and great efforts made to get the vessel off, under an incessant fire from sharp-shooters on the shore. Finding it was impossible to get her afloat, she was riddled with shot and shell to destroy her boilers and machinery, and abandoned. This vessel had been a successful blockade-runner, and was called the "Bendigo."

On the 11th of January another blockade-running steamer, the "Ranger," was chased on shore by the "Daylight" and "Aries," and was set on fire by her crew after landing her passengers and mail. The commanding officer of the "Governor Buckingham," aided by the "Daylight" and "Aries," attempted to extinguish the flames and haul the "Ranger" off, but the enemy, posted in force behind the sand-hills, kept up such an incessant fire that the boats' crews could not work. The "Ranger" was therefore riddled with shot and shell, and destroyed. In the meanwhile, black smoke was seen in the direction of Topsail Inlet, and the "Aries" was ordered to chase. She soon returned, and her commanding officer, Acting-Volunteer-Lieutenant Edward F. Devens, reported a fine-looking double-propeller blockade-runner, called the "Venus," beached and on fire, between Tubb's and Little River Inlets. The enemy's sharp-shooters prevented the "Aries'" boats from boarding the vessel, which had been beached and set on fire to prevent her capture. This was the twenty-second steamer lost to the Confederacy and the blockade runners within the last six months, representing a loss to the enemy of five and a half millions of dollars.

These mishaps of the blockade-runners greatly lessened the means of the Confederates, and increased the difficulties of exporting cotton—the Confederate sinews of war—and obtaining arms and equipments in return.

On the 9th instant the blockade-runner "Dare" was chased on shore and destroyed by the "Aries" and "Montgomery," as the surf was running so high on the beach that there was no chance of getting her off. On these occasions many acts of gallantry were performed. Acting-Volunteer-Lieutenant Devens mentions, in his report of the "Dare" affair, that, while in the breakers, his boat capsized, and the crew were washed on shore and fell into the hands of the enemy. Acting Master J. W. Balch, seeing his commanding officer struggling in the water, swam ashore, with two men, and brought Lieutenant Devens off on his back, and placed him in the "Montgomery's" launch. Twenty-five officers and men on this occasion, after having a hard struggle for their lives in the breakers, fell into the hands of the enemy.

The service in which the blockaders were engaged was arduous and dangerous, but both officers and men performed their duty unflinchingly.

In the latter part of January the "Iron Age," one of the gun-boats, got fast aground while attempting to get afloat the hull of the blockade-runner "Bendigo," and, through a mistaken order, was blown up and destroyed. She was, however, no great loss, being a poor vessel.

It could not be expected that, operating along such an extensive line of coast and confronted by an active and intelligent enemy, the North Atlantic squadron could be invariably successful. On the night of the 2d of February the U. S. steamer "Underwriter" was lying in the Neuse River above the line of army works, when several boats filled with men were seen coming down the stream towards her. The night was very dark, and the boats were close on board before they were discovered and hailed. The crew sprang to quarters, and made a stout resistance; but the enemy, with great gallantry, boarded the vessel, and overpowered the crew, driving part of them below, where they were obliged to surrender, as there was no longer a chance of successfully resisting. The officers and crew were ordered into the boats, the vessel was stripped of everything portable and set on fire, when the enemy departed with their prisoners and plunder.

This was rather a mortifying affair for the Navy, however fearless on the part of the Confederates. The most pleasant circumstance connected with the affair was the conduct of Acting-Third-Assistant Engineer G. E. Allen. The captured crew of the "Underwriter" were in the enemy's boats, and proceeding up the stream, when Mr. Allen discovered that, in the hurry to get away from the "Underwriter," on which the Federals on shore had opened fire, the enemy had left but two guards in his boat. One of the other boats was turning back to assist their comrades in Mr. Allen's boat, when the latter snatched a cutlass from one of the guards, and told the men to pull for their lives. Some of the men, including the other guard, jumped overboard, and swam ashore, while Allen headed the boat towards the river-bank, landed at the foot of the line of breastworks, and delivered his one prisoner to the commanding officer of the fort. A short time afterwards, the fire reached the "Underwriter's" magazine, and she blew up.

This gallant expedition was led by Commander John Taylor Wood, of the Confederate Navy, who was accompanied by Lieutenants Gardner, Hogue, Carr, and Wilkinson. Acting-Master Jacob Westervelt, commanding the "Underwriter," was killed on board that vessel, as also several of his crew.

In this expedition fifteen boats, including three large barges, with three hundred men, came down the river with the intention of making a simultaneous attack on the forts and the gun-boat; but, finding the latter above the forts, where she ought not to have been, she was boarded and captured, with little loss to the enemy. It was to be expected that, with so many clever officers who had left the Federal Navy and cast their fortunes with the Confederates, such gallant actions would often be attempted. They frequently failed, as they would in this instance, in all probability, had the "Underwriter" been anchored below the forts. Had the enemy attacked the forts, the chances are they would have been successful, as the garrison were unprepared for an attack from the river, their most vulnerable side.

About the middle of February the destruction of the blockade-runners, "Wild Dayrell," "Nutfield," "Dee," "Emily," and "Fannie and Jennie," was reported. All these were fine vessels, and their cargoes, consisting of munitions of war, etc., were worth at least a million of dollars, a sum which by no means represented their loss to the Confederacy. Many of the vessels destroyed would have made valuable additions to the Navy for the purpose of catching blockade-runners, as they were very fast; but their commanders, rather than be captured, ran them ashore, after throwing overboard what munitions of war they had on board; and the Federal officers, finding it impossible to get them afloat, set them on fire to prevent the enemy receiving any benefit from them. The officers who made themselves particularly active in the performance of blockading duties, and who aided in the destruction of these steamers, were Commanders Pierce Crosby and William F. Spicer, and Lieutenant-Commander Francis A. Roe.

Now and then, amid these exciting scenes, the indomitable Lieutenant Cushing came forward with some remarkable feat, more daring than important. Cushing was brave to recklessness, not seeming to care for danger, and his superior officers rather encouraged his wild adventures.

In the month of February an idea struck Cushing that he would make an expedition to Cape Fear River, and capture the Confederate commander at Smithville, where there was a strong fort and a garrison of a thousand men. On the night of the 29th Cushing passed the forts at the south inlet of Cape Fear River under cover of the darkness, and proceeded to Smithville, about six miles above, his force consisting of two boats and twenty men. Smithville was a famous resort for blockade-runners, and Cushing intended, if he found any of these vessels at anchor, attempt their capture.

Finding no vessels at Smithville, Cushing landed directly in front of the hotel, which was the headquarters of the commanding officer, concealed his men under the bank, captured some negroes, and obtained from them such information as he required. Leaving some men in charge of the boats, Cushing, with Acting-Ensign J. E. Jones, Acting-Master's Mate W. L. Howorth, and one seaman, proceeded to the headquarters of the commanding officer of the defences, General Herbert. Cushing captured the chief-engineer, but ascertained that the general had gone to Wilmington. The adjutant-general was slightly wounded, and made his escape to the woods, without stopping to put on his clothes, under an impression that the garrison had mutinied. Cushing's boats were about fifty yards from the regular landing-place at the fort, and not so far from the sentinel on the wharf, yet he succeeded in carrying off his prisoners. By the time the alarm signal-lights were shown Cushing was abreast of Fort Caswell, on his way back to the squadron. The blockade-runner "Scotia" passed from the anchorage just before Cushing got into the river, or he might have made a good night's work of it.

Cushing's hazardous undertakings were sometimes criticised as useless, but there was more method in them than appeared on the surface, and important information was sometimes obtained, to say nothing of the brilliant example of courage and enterprise which they afforded to others.

On March 8th Acting-Rear-Admiral Lee accompanied General Butler to Yorktown to arrange a joint military and naval expedition, to operate, first, up the Pamunky River against the Confederate forces near King and Queen Court House, which had attacked the party under command of Colonel Dahlgren, and killed that officer; and, second, against a force of the enemy reported as about to make an expedition from the peninsula. Owing, however, to constant fogs, the gun-boats could not co-operate with the Army, and the Confederates, finding themselves about to be surrounded, retreated from the peninsula.

A few nights later, a boat expedition, under Acting-Masters Williams and Wilder, of the "Commodore Barney" and "Minnesota," respectively, ascended the Chuckatuck Creek, and captured a party of twenty Confederate soldiers.

While these small affairs were being transacted, the Confederate naval officers were preparing to retaliate on the vessels of the North Atlantic squadron lying in Hampton Roads. Lieutenant Hunter Davidson, of the Confederate navy, had given much study to the subject of torpedoes, and had perfected what he considered an excellent torpedo-boat. It was a small steam-launch, with a torpedo on the end of a pole projecting some twenty feet from the bow of the vessel.

Up to this time both the Union and Confederate Governments had been singularly oblivious to the torpedo as a means of offence and defence. Had the Federal Government made proper use of the torpedo, it would have soon put an end to the business of blockade-running. Electric batteries could have been established, if necessary, three or four miles outside the entrance to a harbor, and the majority of blockade-runners would not have ventured to run the gauntlet of such dangerous affairs. There would have been no difficulty in planting any number of torpedoes in the channels, made to explode on contact with a vessel.

Humanitarian ideas probably had originally a good deal to do with the neglect of the Federal Government to avail themselves of these frightful adjuncts; but the Confederates were not governed by any such sentimental feelings. Later in the war they used the torpedo freely, and blew up a number of Federal vessels-of-war — which was as justifiable as any other hostile act.

On the night of April 8th, 1864, while the "Minnesota," flag-ship of Acting-Rear-Admiral Lee, was lying at anchor off Fortress Monroe, a dark object was seen, about two hundred yards distant, slowly passing the ship. It was thought to be a row-boat; and, in reply to the hail from the "Minnesota," the answer came, "Roanoke." By this time the object was nearly abeam, and apparently motionless.

The officer of the deck sent orders for a tug, which was lying astern, to go and examine the floating object; and while he was endeavoring to get the men in the tug to attend to his orders, the torpedo-boat struck the ship, exploded a torpedo, and made off in the direction of Nansemond River. Several shots were fired at the torpedo vessel, but she escaped in the darkness. The concussion caused great excitement on board the frigate. The drums beat to quarters, and the men hurried to their stations, and stood by to lower the boats; but it was soon found that no serious damage had been done. But for the fact that the torpedo, which weighed fifty pounds, was not placed in contact with the ship, but was prematurely exploded, the "Minnesota's" bottom would have been shattered, and the Federals would have lost one of their finest frigates.

This daring exploit was performed by Lieutenant Hunter Davidson, who has, no doubt, since rejoiced that he did not succeed in sending many of his old friends and shipmates to the bottom.

It demonstrated the necessity of keeping a brighter look-out for the enemy's torpedo corps, and it also showed the determination with which the Confederates carried on the war. They were first in the field with this new method of warfare, and managed it with great dexterity. It was not until they had blown up a dozen or so Federal vessels that the Government undertook to employ torpedo-boats; but this was at so late a period in the war as to be of comparatively little use.

One torpedo-boat, under cover of the "Monitor," would have settled the "Merrimac" in a very short time, and a Monitor fitted with a torpedo would have destroyed the "Tennessee" with equal facility. But it requires time to become reconciled to a system that was looked upon with horror for many years after its invention.

Such is the progress of ideas that, now-a-days, so far from being struck with horror at the idea of knocking a hole in a vessel's bottom, all Christian Governments are seeking with avidity the most powerful submarine weapons of destruction.

Early in April, Acting-Rear-Admiral Lee was called upon by General Butler to co-operate with him in putting down what he called the "pirates of the creeks," which were, in fact, the irregular forces of the enemy employed along the river to inflict all possible injury on Union vessels, and keep the Federals from landing along the rivers and capturing Confederate property. Various expeditions were fitted out, consisting of forces from the Army and Navy, but no great results were obtained. It was not the kind of warfare calculated to be of any permanent benefit to the Union cause ; and it demonstrated the fact that only large bodies of troops could break up the system adopted by the Confederates of harassing Federal Army posts with constant attacks.

Some boat expeditions were undertaken, in which great gallantry was displayed and a few men killed, terminating in a retreat from under the enemy's fire, after inflicting the usual damage on him. The only satisfaction gained on the expedition to Pagan Creek was a temporary scattering of the Confederate troops, and the fact ascertained that the Davidson torpedo-boat had arrived at Smithfield on the 9th inst., and had gone thence to Richmond.

On the 5th of May, the army, under General Butler, landed at City Point and Bermuda Hundred, covered by five iron-clads and ten other vessels, without opposition. The river had been carefully dragged for torpedoes, to assure the safety of the gun-boats and transports; but, notwithstanding all the care taken, the gun-boat "Commodore Jones" was blown up while dragging for these hidden enemies. The vessel, it seems, rested directly over an infernal machine, which was fired by a galvanic battery hidden in a pit on the shore. The destruction of the steamer was complete, as the torpedo, supposed to have contained four hundred pounds of powder, was exploded directly under her bottom. So great was the concussion that the vessel was lifted bodily out of the water, and her crew hurled into the air, killing and wounding more than half of the ship's company.

This shocking casualty demonstrated the power of the torpedo, when properly managed. The arrangements in this quarter were under the direction of Lieutenant Hunter Davidson; and the man who ignited the torpedo which blew up the "Commodore Jones" was killed by a musket-ball fired by the coxswain of one of the boats dragging for these infernal machines.

There were three of these torpedo-pits, from which men were ready to act as soon as a vessel should get into the desired position; and it seems as though a few marines as skirmishers, marching along the banks, might have prevented any attempt of the enemy to operate the wires. In one of the pits two men were captured, ready to explode a torpedo should any vessel pass over it. These were Acting-Master P. W. Smith, of the Confederate navy, and Jeffries Johnson, private in the Submarine Corps. In those days such adventurers stood a chance of being shot as soon as captured, though now the case would be different. These men were quite communicative, and said they had adopted this service to remain near their homes. Some of their torpedoes would explode by contact, others by lines from the shore, and others by various ingenious contrivances. All of them could be put down in one day by a torpedo-boat arranged for the purpose by Lieutenant Davidson, who had been watching the movements of the Federals since the transports first assembled in Hampton Roads.

The investigations of the naval officers soon disclosed a system of defence embracing all the navigable rivers. The torpedoes were followed up, their positions located, and, wherever practicable, they were destroyed, making the waterways comparatively safe, and enabling General Butler to reoccupy his line from Trent's Beach to Appomattox.

On the 18th of May the enemy commenced fortifying the heights about Howlett's House, commanding Trent's Reach, on the James ; and although the gun-boats kept up a steady fire on their position, they persevered, and that night mounted a sufficient number of guns to keep the Federal gun-boats in check. The charts indicating less water in the channel than the Monitors drew, it was not considered advisable to move them too close to the batteries.

The enemy seemed to be prepared all along the river to meet the advance of the Navy. The pickets of the latter were driven in at Dutch Gap heights, and the Army pickets at City Point; and Acting-Rear-Admiral Lee considered that his communications were seriously threatened.

By the 19th the Monitors were advanced nearer Howlett's Battery, on which they opened with seemingly great accuracy of fire, but with no appearance of arresting the progress of this formidable work. The artillery practice was kept up until the 24th, without any result except that for a time the enemy stopped working. On the 24th the enemy made an attack on a body of troops stationed at Wilson's wharf, which attack had been anticipated by the naval commander-in-chief, who had placed the following vessels in position to meet it: "Pequot," Lieutenant-Commander S. P. Quackenbush; "Dawn," Acting-Volunteer-Lieutenant J. W. Simmons; "Atlanta"(iron-clad), and tug "Young America"—all under Lieutenant-Commander Quackenbush.

At 12:30, on the 24th, the enemy made a vigorous attack at the wharf; the movement was, however, supposed to be a feint to draw the Union forces from Fort Powhatan. The enemy were met by the fire of the gun-boats, particularly the "Dawn"; and although their decks were swept by musketry, such was the terrible effect of their shells on the Confederates that the latter were obliged to retreat. But for the service rendered by the "Dawn," Lieutenant Simmons, the Confederates would have, no doubt, accomplished their object and

LIEUTENANT-COMMANDER (NOW REAR-ADMIRAL) S. P QUACKENBUSH.

carried the Union position. The engagement lasted upwards of five hours, and demonstrated the value of the Navy in protecting the flanks of the Federal Army.

About the 30th of May, the Confederate naval forces came down below Drury's Bluff, and prepared to attack the Union squadron. Their plan was to send down fire-ships with the current, and, following with their vessels, attack those of the Federals. The Confederate squadron consisted of three iron-clads, with batteries of heavy rifled guns, and six gun-boats partially plated with iron. For some reason, no immediate onset was made by the Confederate rams, which caused them to lose the opportunity of seriously damaging the Federal squadron, and perhaps driving it away.

In the meantime, General Butler, as part of his campaign, proposed to obstruct the James River by sinking vessels a mile or so below Howlett's Battery. This would make his positions at Bermuda Hundred and at City Point perfectly secure. Part of the vessels to be used for this purpose were received by Acting-Rear-Admiral Lee on the 2d of June, consisting of a bark and three large schooners loaded with shingle ballast.

It is due to Acting-Rear-Admiral Lee to say that he objected to this plan of obstructing the river, as the force of vessels at his disposal was stronger than had been originally proposed. General Grant had only asked for two iron-clads, but the Navy Department furnished Acting-Rear-Admiral Lee with four, although one of them, the "Tecumseh," was soon to leave the James River for other service. Acting-Rear-Admiral Lee took the ground that it was not the duty of the Navy to protect itself in this manner; on the contrary, where obstructions existed, they should be removed, if possible; any other course would be admitting the superiority of the enemy and a dread of his naval force. On the other hand, it was argued that obstructing the river would lessen the chance of injuring the Federal vessels, on which depended the security of the Army at the points below. The obstructions would keep off fire-rafts and infernal machines, and a smaller force of vessels would be required in Trent's Reach to prevent the advance of the Confederate iron-clads. This latter view of the case was accepted; for, as the operations against Richmond would be altogether military, and as the naval forces could not get to that city with the land and naval batteries opposed to them, the obstruction proposal was decided upon.

At that time General Grant was expected to cross the James and operate against Richmond from the south side, and, under the circumstances, it was absolutely necessary to hold the river secure against the contingencies of a naval engagement. There were many reasons why it was not desirable to bring on an engagement with the enemy's squadron, the strength of which was unknown. The river was too narrow to manœuvre in, and the channel was very shoal in places. If a battle was won, the Army would be no nearer Richmond than before. The Navy made no headway when Howlett's Battery had but four guns, and it was not likely that, with the addition of the works at Drury's Bluff, armed with the heaviest ordnance, and with the river guarded by lines of torpedoes, that the squadron could force its way up the James River.

There seems to have been a little diplomacy as to whether General Butler or Acting-Rear-Admiral Lee should assume the responsibility of placing the obstructions in

Trent's Reach, although why there should have been any dispute in such a matter it is difficult to see. It was certainly distasteful to the Confederates, who saw all their schemes of fire-rafts, torpedo-boats and iron-clad raids completely circumvented. The following letter from General Butler to Acting Rear-Admiral Lee will show the General's views on the subject:

> HEADQUARTERS IN THE FIELD, }
> June 2d, 1864. }
>
> ADMIRAL:
>
> Your communication dated June 2d, in regard to the obstructions, is received. The five vessels sent up were procured by my order for the purpose of being used as obstructions to the river, if, in the judgment of the naval commander, they would add to the security of his fleet.
>
> I have no difficulty as to the point at which we desire to secure the river. It is at the right of my line, near Curtis' House, at the ravine; but whether the river should be secured by obstructions or by vessels, or a disposition of your obstructions or of the vessels of your Navy, neither myself nor my engineers have any right to feel competent to give an opinion. The vessels are wholly at your service, but upon your judgment, not mine, must rest their use.
>
> In accordance with your request, as I informed your officer, I will visit you this afternoon, and designate the spot we desire to be held; but whether by means of obstructions or by your ships, or by both combined, must be solely for you to determine.
>
> While I know you would not undertake to give directions to my engineers as to the situation of the earth-works on land, so we ought not to presume to advise you as to your means of defending the water.
>
> I have not consulted the War Department on the subject, whether I should procure these obstructions. I supposed that was fairly within my discretion, and I venture respectfully to add that the question whether you should use them is entirely within yours. The Navy Department cannot know the emergencies as you know them, and, I am certain, must leave that question to the good judgment of the rear-admiral commanding the fleet.
>
> I am aware of the delicacy naval gentlemen feel in depending upon anything but their ships in a contest with the enemy; and if it was a contest with the enemy's ships alone, I certainly would not advise the obstructions, even at the great risk of losing the river; but in a contest against such unchristian modes of warfare as fire-rafts and torpedo-boats, I think all questions of delicacy should be waived by the paramount consideration of protection for the lives of the men and the safety of the very valuable vessels of the squadron.
>
> Pardon me if I have overstepped any line of duty or courtesy in this latter suggestion.
>
> I have the honor to be,
> Very respectfully,
> Your obedient servant,
> BENJ. F. BUTLER,
> *Major-General Commanding.*
>
> REAR-ADMIRAL S. P. LEE,
> *Commanding North Atlantic Squadron.*

This diplomatic communication of General Butler led to a long correspondence between Acting Rear-Admiral Lee and himself, which ended, as it should have done, in putting the obstructions in the channel.

During the time this discussion of a quite simple matter was pending, from the 1st to the 15th of June, General Grant had fought the battle of Cold Harbor, in which he found General Lee's army less weakened than had been expected by its losses in the battles from the Rapidan to the James. He did not feel that his own army was in condition to operate further against a well-commanded army of veterans posted behind five miles of strong intrenchments.

In the first attack on the Confederates at Cold Harbor, Grant's army was severely handled. General Hancock's attack, although at first successful, was finally repulsed, and Warren and Burnside were brought to a stand at the edge of the enemy's rifle-pits.

In writing of this battle General Grant says: "Our loss has been heavy, while I have reason to believe that the loss of the enemy was comparatively light." The loss, in fact, in three days' operations on the Chickahominy, was 7,500 men.

No doubt Grant often wished he could have the aid of the gun-boats that had given him so much help in the West; but that was an impossibility.

Realizing the fact that he could not operate with any advantage north and east of Richmond, General Grant determined to make another movement—throw his army across the James River, capture Petersburg, and place himself in communication with the Navy.

Grant had had too much experience in the West not to know what valuable aid a naval force could afford an army under certain circumstances, not to wish to take advantage of it in the present instance. In consequence of this resolution Grant moved by Lee's right flank, and threw his army across the James River, with the hope of seizing Petersburg, while his cavalry could destroy the railroad communication between Richmond and the Shenandoah Valley and Lynchburg. The movement was skillfully executed, and, on the 14th of June, the Army was safe on the opposite bank of the James, and in communication with the Army of the James and with the Navy.

The day General Grant passed the James he gave an order to sink the obstructions in Trent's Reach, and on the 15th General Butler wrote to Acting-Rear-Admiral Lee, informing him of Grant's order, and saying that he would be glad if the admiral would assist him in carrying it out.

On the 15th of June General Grant established his headquarters at City Point. The obstructions were sunk in the river, and offered a complete barrier to the enemy's fire-rafts and torpedo-vessels. The general-in-chief had now time to breathe and look about him, and observe the new condition of affairs.

By June 20th Commander T. A. M. Craven, of the Navy, had sunk in the main channel at Trent's Reach four hulks filled with stone. There was also stretched across the channel a heavy boom, supporting a chain cable, well secured on each side of the river. Across the flats was extended a heavy boom, secured by six anchors, and in the channel, along the right bank, was sunk a large schooner loaded with stone, from which a strong boom extended to the shore. The obstructions were very complete, and were intended to be under the fire of General Butler's guns as well as those of the iron-clads.

The enemy probably was well pleased at the Federals obstructing the channel; for, notwithstanding his forts at Howlett's and Drury's Bluff, his fire-rafts, sunken torpedoes, and torpedo-boats, he felt more secure when he knew that his position could not be assailed by a naval force; while General Grant was equally satisfied now that the

COMMANDER (NOW REAR-ADMIRAL) EDMUND R. COLHOUN.

enemy's iron-clads could not get down to City Point under any circumstances.

The enemy, in order to ascertain the character of the obstructions, made a reconnaissance in the neighborhood of Dutch Gap; while Howlett's Battery, which had been greatly strengthened by the erection of new works, opened upon the vessels below the obstructions.

These were the iron-clads "Tecumseh," Commander T. A. M. Craven; "Saugus," Commander E. R. Colhoun; "Onondaga," Lieutenant-Commander C. H. Cushman; "Canonicus," Commander E. S. Parrott, and gun-boat "Agawam," Lieutenant-Commander A. C. Rhind. They returned the fire of the enemy's batteries with considerable effect, receiving little damage in return; while the Confederate iron-clads, from their position behind a wood, opened a straggling fire, of which no notice was taken. According to one Confederate account, the

battery at Howlett's consisted of but four guns—one large rifle, one large smooth-bore, and two smaller pieces.

Notwithstanding the general impression that the obstructions in the river were impassable, Acting-Rear-Admiral Lee judged it expedient to apply for an increase of the force of iron-clads, and that he might be authorized to detain the "Tecumseh."

This is the history of the obstruction of the James River, the credit of which was given to General Butler, who simply approved the proposition when it was mentioned to him, and received General Grant's order to sink the vessels.

General Grant's arrival before Petersburg, which he attacked on the 14th of June, and the crossing of the James by General Meade's army, gave quite a different aspect to affairs at City Point, and the time had arrived when the Navy stood a chance of making itself very useful.

Petersburg was one of the strongest outposts of the Confederate capital, and a formidable resistance in that quarter was, of course, expected. Part of General Butler's command commenced the attack on the works covering the approaches to the town, and succeeded in occupying them; but, by waiting the arrival of Hancock's division and failing to push their advantage, the Confederates were strongly reinforced, so that, when Hancock's and Burnside's divisions assaulted them, the Federals were repulsed with considerable loss. Next day another attempt was made and repulsed, with the capture by the enemy of part of a Federal brigade.

About the same time, General Butler sallied forth from his intrenchments to tear up the railroad leading to Richmond; but the enemy sent out an army corps from their capital, and Butler was defeated, after sending intelligence of a splendid victory which he had won!

The result of these attempts on Petersburg, which had caused great losses to the Federal Army, convinced General Grant that his best course was to envelop the town with his forces, without attacking the outworks. Attempts were made to destroy all the railroads leading to Richmond, but the enemy was so strongly posted that these efforts were generally of no benefit to the Union cause.

Thus the month of June closed with no immediate results favorable to the Federals, except that the Army was transported to the south of Richmond, and was in communication with the Navy; while the Confederates continued to strengthen daily the fortifications of Richmond and Petersburg. In fact, General Grant had encountered obstacles far greater than he had anticipated.

A large portion of the naval forces on the

James naturally assembled at City Point, where General Grant had established his headquarters, while other portions of the North Atlantic squadron were employed in the sounds of North Carolina and in the blockade of the coast.

About the middle of May, the "North Carolina," an iron-clad resembling the "Atlanta," appeared off Fort Fisher, at the mouth of Cape Fear River, accompanied by two tugs. This vessel commenced an attack at long range on the blockading vessels then employed off the north inlet, which, with the exception of the "Tuscarora," were improvised gun-boats, without sufficient strength to contend with armored vessels. The little flotilla returned the fire of the iron-clad, and after a desultory engagement which lasted two days, with little damage on either side, the iron-clad and her consorts disappeared over the bar of Cape Fear River.

It was doubtless the intention of the Confederates to disperse the few Union vessels then off the entrance to Wilmington, and start the cry of "raised blockade," as had been attempted on a previous occasion at Charleston; but in this design they failed, and the iron-clad returned to Wilmington, where her career soon afterwards ended.

The vessels that stood their ground so faithfully, in presence of this apparently formidable iron-clad, were the "Tuscarora," Commander W. A. Parker; "Britannia," Acting-Volunteer-Lieutenant S. Huse; "Mount Vernon," Acting-Volunteer-Lieutenant James Trathen; "Houquah," Acting-Master J. W. Balch, and "Nansemond," Acting-Ensign J. H. Porter. From subsequent developments, it appears that the rams "Raleigh" and "North Carolina" were constructed at Wilmington under the direction of Commodore W. F. Lynch, but were hardly considered fit to go into battle, although they served to keep the blockaders on the look-out.

Lieutenant W. B. Cushing, with his usual zeal and enterprise, volunteered to attempt the destruction of the vessel that came out to attack the blockaders, and at the same time make a reconnaissance of the defences of Cape Fear River—a very desirable project, as an expedition for the capture of Wilmington was then in contemplation. Cushing was always attempting what no one else would think of, and in this case it seemed that he was almost certain to be killed or captured.

Obtaining permission from Acting-Rear-Admiral Lee to attempt the destruction of the "Raleigh," Cushing proceeded in the "Monticello" to the western entrance of Cape Fear River. On the night of June 23d he left the vessel in the first cutter, accompanied by Acting-Ensign J. E. Jones,

Acting-Master's Mate William L. Howorth, and fifteen men, crossed the western bar, and passed the forts and town of Smithville without discovery. Near the Zeke Island batteries, Cushing came very near being run down by a steamer—doubtless a blockade-runner, bound out, with a load of cotton—and also narrowly escaped the notice of a guard-boat.

As Cushing came abreast of the Brunswick batteries, fifteen miles from his starting-point, the moon came out from the clouds, and disclosed the party to the sentinels on the river-bank, who hailed the boat, and then opened fire upon her. The people in the fort were roused, and the confusion seemed to be general. Cushing pulled for the opposite bank, and along up the other shore, until he got out of sight. When within seven miles of Wilmington both men and boat were secreted in a marsh.

When the sun rose, Cushing watched for an opportunity to capture some one from whom he could obtain information. Nearly a dozen steamers passed, three of them fine blockade-runners, and one of them Commodore Lynch's flag-ship, yet there was no suspicion of Cushing and his men hidden within a stone's throw. The Confederates felt so secure in the river, with its powerful defences, that they never dreamed of the possibility of a boat's crew running the gauntlet.

Just after dark two boats were seen rounding a point near by, and, supposing it to be an attacking party, Cushing prepared for resistance. It was simply a fishing party returning to Wilmington. Both boats were captured, and the necessary information obtained from them, and the occupants were made to act as guides for a further exploration of the river.

Cushing made mental notes of all the obstructions, forts and guns he met along the Cape Fear River, which were useful at a later date, when Fort Fisher and the other defences at the entrance of the river were attacked. Coming to a very narrow creek, Cushing poled his boat along through it for some distance, till he reached a road, which was the main highway from Fort Fisher to Wilmington. Here he divided his little party, leaving half of them behind, and marching the rest two miles further on the main road, where they halted and concealed themselves.

About noon, a mounted soldier, with a mail-bag from Fort Fisher, came along, and was much astonished when halted by Cushing, and ordered to dismount and deliver up his mail. Two hundred letters were captured, and much information obtained in regard to the enemy's plans. Cushing then waited for the mail-carrier from Wilmington to appear with dispatches for Fort Fisher, but, just as the courier hove in sight, a blue-jacket incautiously exposed himself, and the fellow took to flight instanter, pursued by Cushing on the captured horse; but after a chase of several miles, finding that the enemy was better mounted, and that there was no chance of overtaking him, Cushing gave up the pursuit. All this took place on a traveled highway, where squads of soldiers might have been expected to pass along at any moment.

The party captured several prisoners, and, at length, becoming hungry, Master's Mate Howorth dressed himself in the courier's clothes, and, mounting the horse, started into town to market. After a time he returned with a supply of milk, eggs and chickens, having excited no suspicion, though conversing with many persons.

After destroying the telegraph as completely as possible, Cushing returned to the creek where he had left the rest of his party, reaching the river by dark. Then he attempted to land his prisoners on an island, as he had more than he could accommodate, and a steamer coming down the river passed so close that the boat's crew jumped into the water and kept their heads under for fear of being seen.

Finally Cushing put his prisoners in the small boats he had captured, and sent them adrift on the river, without oars or sails, to get home the best way they could; while he proceeded down the river with his party in the cutter, retaining one prisoner as a pilot to show him where the ram "Raleigh" lay a wreck. He hoped also to fall in with and destroy some of the Confederate vessels by setting fire to them.

Cushing found that there was nothing left of the "Raleigh" above water—like most of the Confederate rams, she had been destroyed in a panic. As for the other iron-clad, the "North Carolina," his prisoners had told him she was then at anchor off Wilmington under Captain Wm. T. Muse, but that little confidence was placed in her, and that she would not cross the bar. Cushing was also informed that the two torpedo-boats built at Wilmington had been destroyed some time previous in the great cotton fire.

As Cushing neared the forts, at the east bar of the river, a boat was seen and captured after a short chase. It contained four soldiers and two civilians, who were taken into the cutter, and their own boat sent adrift. On questioning his prisoners, Cushing found that there was a large guard-boat, with seventy-five musketeers, stationed in the narrow passage between Federal Point and Zeke Island. Notwithstanding the disparity of force, Cushing prepared to attack the guard-boat.

Just then the moon shone out brightly; but when a few yards from the guard-boat, three boats pulled out from the battery and five more from the other end of the passage, completely blocking up the avenue to escape. The cutter at the time was under sail, and the helm was put down; but a large sail-boat filled with soldiers appeared on the scene to windward and close aboard. This was a trying position, but every one in the cutter behaved with the utmost coolness, relying on the bravery and ingenuity of their young commander to extricate them from the difficulty, for there was not the least idea of surrendering.

Suddenly turning the cutter's head, as if for the west bar, the men shipped their oars, and, pulling vigorously, the enemy soon lost sight of the boat, but they dashed off in pursuit, expecting to intercept Cushing near the bar. The latter, however, doubled on his pursuers, and, thanks to the extraordinary pulling of his sailors, gained the passage of the island, and dashed into the breakers on Caroline Shoal, a most dangerous place, where the enemy—who doubtless thought the Federals were lost—dared not follow.

Fortunately, their boat, though so deeply laden, carried Cushing and his party safely through the breakers; and, just as day broke, they reached the gun-boat "Cherokee," after an absence from the squadron of two days and three nights.

There was not a more daring adventure than this in the whole course of the war. There were ninety-nine chances in a hundred that Cushing and his party would be killed or captured, but throughout all his daring schemes there seemed to be a method, and, though criticised as rash and ill-judged, Cushing returned unscathed from his frequent expeditions, with much important information. In this instance it was a great source of satisfaction to the blockading vessels to learn that the "Raleigh" was destroyed, and that the other iron-clad ram was not considered fit to cross the bar.

Had Cushing learned in time that there was a Confederate war-vessel lying at Wilmington, he would, no doubt, have attempted her destruction, but he only heard of it when on his return down the river.

This young officer was always cool and collected when in the midst of dangers, and, although they were plenty of others equally brave, there was something particularly dashing in Cushing's character. He seemed more like a free-lance than a regular officer of the Navy, educated in the school of routine, and, in fact, the restraints of discipline were irksome to him, and his career at the Naval Academy gave little promise of the fame he subsequently acquired.

CHAPTER XL.

GENERAL GRANT'S INTENTIONS.—CONFEDERATE BATTERIES AT FOUR MILE CREEK.—GEN-
ERAL GRANT UTILIZES THE NAVY.—THE GUN-BOATS ENGAGE BATTERIES AT WILCOX'S
WHARF AND HARRISON'S LANDING. — SHELLING SHARP-SHOOTERS. — OPERATIONS AT
DUTCH GAP. — ATTACK ON LABORERS AT DUTCH GAP BY CONFEDERATE FLEET AND
BATTERIES.—MANŒUVRES OF GENERALS GRANT, SHERMAN AND BUTLER, AND OF CON-
FEDERATE ARMIES. — SPEECH OF JEFFERSON DAVIS. — GENERAL GRANT ON NECES-
SITY OF RETAINING IRON-CLADS ON JAMES RIVER.—EXPEDITION UNDER LIEUTENANT-
COMMANDER FLUSSER TO WINDSOR, N. C.—ATTACK ON PLYMOUTH, N. C.—CONFEDER-
ATE RAM "ALBEMARLE" ATTACKS "SOUTHFIELD" AND "MIAMI."—THE "SOUTHFIELD"
SUNK. — DEATH OF LIEUTENANT-COMMANDER FLUSSER. — CAPTURE OF PLYMOUTH BY
CONFEDERATES. — COMMUNICATION OF SECRETARY WELLES ON LOSS OF PLYMOUTH. —
GENERAL PECK TO GENERAL BUTLER.—CASUALTIES AT PLYMOUTH.—ATTACK ON NEW-
BERN.—ACTING-REAR-ADMIRAL LEE'S INSTRUCTIONS TO CAPTAIN SMITH.—CAPTURE OF
CONFEDERATE STEAMER "BOMBSHELL."—SECOND ENGAGEMENT BETWEEN RAM "ALBE-
MARLE" AND GUN-BOATS.—APPALLING SCENES ON BOARD THE "SASSACUS."—INCIDENTS
OF FIGHT.—FRUITLESS ATTEMPTS TO DESTROY THE "ALBEMARLE."—LAYING TORPE-
DOES AT MOUTH OF ROANOKE RIVER — FLOTILLA IN SOUNDS REINFORCED BY ADDI-
TIONAL VESSELS, ETC.

FROM the time General Grant fixed his headquarters at City Point, the naval vessels in that vicinity, under Captain Melancton Smith, were employed in guarding the river or in co-operating with the Army in raids upon the enemy along the shores of the James and adjacent rivers.

It was sufficiently evident that it was Grant's intention to envelop the enemy's works, destroy his communications, and cut off supplies. Military and naval expeditions were sent to destroy all grain-fields and other sources of supply within reach, and to pick up deserters from the enemy's ranks. Among the latter were workmen who had been employed on board the "Merrimac," from whom interesting information was obtained in regard to that and other Confederate vessels. Signal stations were destroyed, their operators captured, and instruments brought away.

In these expeditions the gun-boats were constantly exposed to the attacks of Confederate artillery, which was continually on the alert to get a shot at them. So active were the enemy, that, about the middle of July, they constructed a battery mounting 20-pounder Sawyer guns on Malvern Hill, and for a time interrupted the navigation of the James River.

The Confederates were, in fact, untiring in their efforts to make the Federal troops and gun-boats uncomfortable. On the 28th of July the enemy commenced the erection of batteries at Four Mile Creek, where they had assembled a large force for the purpose of covering the men at work in the trenches, and making a demonstration against General Foster's front. The gun-boats were brought into requisition, and the "Agawam," Commander A. C. Rhind, and the "Mendota," Commander E. T. Nichols, shelled the enemy's works for some time, rendering very effective service in connection with General Hancock's military operations.

The following night, in view of the military movements ordered by General Grant, all the troops, except General Foster's original command, were ordered to move from Deep Bottom, under cover of the gun-boats. Here, again, General Grant had an opportunity of utilizing the Navy.

As an instance of the activity of the Confederates in presence of the strong forces of the Federals, which almost enveloped them, on August 3d they established a 6-gun rifled 12-pounder battery at Wilcox's Wharf, and opened fire on passing transports. The firing being heard on board the "Miami," Acting-Volunteer-Lieutenant G. W. Graves, that vessel pushed ahead and engaged the battery, which was driven away after a spirited resistance, the "Miami" losing but one man killed and one wounded.

On the 4th of August another battery opened on the transports near Harrison's Landing, which was driven away, after a sharp action, by the "Miami" and "Osceola."

On the same day, the "Pequot" and the "Commodore Morris" were engaged during a greater part of the time in shelling sharp-shooters out of the woods, who were engaged in picking off the men on board passing transports. These Confederate artillerymen were remarkably active and energetic, but they found the people in the gun-boats equally so; and the light artillery and bushwhackers soon came to the conclusion that attacking gun-boats was a losing business. The gun-boats now so rigidly patrolled the James River that they were in close proximity to all transports passing up or down. So seldom did the enemy get a chance to fire unmolested on a transport, that they even took occasion to attack a hospital steamer, without regard to her sacred character, killing one man and mortally wounding two others; but they were soon driven away by the watchful "Pequot," Lieutenant - Commander S. P. Quackenbush, and the "Commodore Morris," Acting-Master R. G. Lee.

At this time operations were going on at Dutch Gap for the purpose of opening a new route from below Howlett's Battery to the upper reach of the James River. This scheme was not favorably regarded by army engineers, and was not a success. The enemy planted mortars not far away, which in the course of the work killed one hundred and forty laborers, and wounded many more. It also brought on a conflict with the Confederate iron-clads, which came down the river and opened upon the laborers. A long-range battle then ensued between the Union and Confederate iron-clads, which inflicted little or no injury to either side, but showed that the Dutch Gap Canal, although never likely to be of any use to the Army or Navy, would be continually inviting attacks from the enemy, which would tend to divert the attention of the Army from its main object—the capture of Richmond.

It was evidently General Grant's design to avoid any great military movement until he heard of Sherman's arrival near the Southern coast. Although Grant had no faith in Butler's project to open the way to Richmond by Dutch Gap, he was willing that Butler should amuse himself, and thereby be kept from interfering in more important matters.

On the 2d of September Sherman entered Atlanta, Georgia, as a conqueror.

General Lee had made such a persistent defence against all the attacks on his lines, and had succeeded so well in keeping the railroads south of Richmond open, that Grant saw that to push him too heavily at this time would result in great loss to the Federal Army, while Lee would be ultimately forced to evacuate Richmond.

Up to the 17th of July, General J. E. Johnston had severely hampered Sherman in his advance through the South; but, on the above date, this able Confederate general was displaced from his command owing to intrigues in Richmond, and J. B. Hood, who was considered a fighting general *par excellence*, succeeded him. This circumstance, though it threw a damper on the army which Johnston had so ably commanded, gave Sherman fresh spirits, and he moved upon Atlanta quite certain of success.

Hood had now under his command an effective force of 40,000 infantry and artillery and 10,000 cavalry, not to mention other Confederate forces in the field; but, in spite of all his forces, Hood was no match for Sherman, and, by capturing Atlanta, the latter had a new base from which to operate, and a certainty of cutting off the retreat of General Lee in case he should endeavor to march south with his army.

If General Lee had escaped from Richmond with 50,000 men, and joined his forces with those of Johnston, previous to the latter's being relieved from command, Sherman would have been confronted by an army twice the size of his own, and would have been obliged to retreat. The Confederates would then have fortified Atlanta, as they had previously fortified Richmond; the headquarters of the Confederacy would have been in the interior instead of on the coast, and the war would have been continued indefinitely. This was probably the reason why Grant did not push matters more vigorously before Richmond, where he would have met with great losses, and perhaps have been unable to prevent Lee's final escape.

Grant had had, at Vicksburg, an example of how much cheaper it was to starve out an enemy, protected by the strongest fortifications, than to drive him out; and he had no idea of forcing Lee south into regions where he could prolong the war until the patience of the North was exhausted.

The commanding general had not only to consider the military situation, but also the political one. The two great parties in the North were divided by distinct lines. One party, though in favor of a vigorous prosecution of the war, called for a strict observance of the Constitution in relation to the rights of the States, and severely criticised certain of the measures of the Government as arbitrary and unnecessary.

The numerous successes of the Union arms in 1863, and the advance of the Federal Army until it almost enveloped the Confederates in Richmond, greatly increased the strength of the Administration party. Everybody was now hopeful that the war would speedily be brought to a close, particularly as the supreme direction of military affairs was now in the hands of General Grant, in whom the people had entire confidence. The Democratic party was now a war party, and the conservative or peace party was in such a minority that their utterances amounted to very little.

The terrible resistance Grant had encountered on his way to Richmond had given rise to an impression that in Lee he had met an antagonist whom it would be difficult for him to overcome, and the opposition to the Government in the North was for a moment emboldened.

By midsummer, the numerous successes which had attended the Federal arms, and the adherents thereby gained to the Administration, had rendered the re-election of President Lincoln a certainty. General Grant felt that, under these circumstances, it would be unwise to do anything calculated to imperil a condition of affairs so beneficial to the country, and although he determined to leave no effort untried to capture Richmond, yet he resolved to succeed by means that would cause comparatively little loss of life.

The fall of Atlanta and the dispersion of Hood's army caused a great sensation throughout the South. The impending doom of the Confederate cause was evident to all thinking men. Hood moved his scattered forces to new lines, and Mr. Davis, anxious to prove that he had committed no mistake in removing General Johnston, repaired to Hood's headquarters in person to encourage that general and plan a new campaign that would compensate for the loss of Atlanta. On his way to Hood's army, Mr. Davis made frequent speeches to cheer up the people, declaring that General Sherman could be driven back, Atlanta recovered, etc., etc. The effect of all this was to inform Grant and Sherman of the new plan of operations decided on by the Confederate President and General Hood; for, of course, everything appeared in the Southern newspapers without regard to the injury it might inflict on the cause. In writing on this subject, General Grant expresses himself as follows:

During this time, Jefferson Davis made a speech at Macon, Georgia, which was reported in the papers of the South, and soon became known to the whole country, disclosing the plans of the enemy and enabling General Sherman to fully meet them. Mr. Davis exhibited the weakness of supposing that an army that had been beaten and decimated in a vain attempt at the defensive, could successfully undertake the offensive against an army that had so often defeated it.

On the 24th of September, Hood commenced his new movement to endeavor to reach Sherman's rear and cut off his communications, apparently oblivious of the fact that the Union Army could live on the country, and would be relieved from a vast deal of trouble in keeping open communications. Ascertaining that Hood had crossed the Chattahoochie River on the 29th and 30th of September, General Sherman followed him; but finding that Hood was bound for Nashville, he abandoned the pursuit and returned to Atlanta, where he prepared to march to the sea across the State of Georgia. Sherman's calculation was that General Thomas could collect troops at Nashville; which, with the two army corps sent him by Sherman by way of Chattanooga, would enable him to hold the line of the Tennessee. Everything turned out well, and General Thomas gained a victory that dispersed Hood's army in every direction, and administered another crushing blow to the Confederate cause.

General Sherman was the more induced to hurry his movements from a telegram sent to him by General Grant, in which the latter says: "If you were to cut loose, I do not believe you would meet Hood's army, but you would be bushwhacked by all the old men, little boys, and such railroad guards as are left at home." With the dispositions made by the enemy, Sherman felt sure he would have nothing in his rear or on his flank to disturb him, and so pursued his devastating march to the sea—that march which is so celebrated in the annals of the civil war.

Notwithstanding all the criticisms of the press on his apparent inactivity, Grant waited patiently until he should hear that Sherman was in a position to prevent Lee and his army from escaping southward. When Sherman made a junction at Goldsboro, N. C., with the forces of Generals Schofield and Terry, which had marched from Wilmington to meet him, the fate of the Confederacy was sealed, and Grant moved on Richmond.

While Grant was watching the progress of events which we have detailed above, the Federal naval vessels in the James River, under the immediate command of Captain Melancton Smith, were actively engaged in patrolling the river, guarding Trent's Reach, or in any co-operative service called for by General Grant. About the middle of August, the Navy Department wrote to Acting-Rear-Admiral Lee, inquiring if he could not dispense with some of the iron-clads, on the ground that James River was effectually blocked against the Confederate squadron. To this action General Grant interposed an objection, which relieves Acting-Rear-Admiral Lee from any imputation of desiring to retain the iron-clads in the vicinity of Trent's Reach when their services were so imperatively demanded elsewhere. General Grant, in his communication to the admiral, says:

While I believe we never will require armored vessels to meet those of the enemy, I think it imprudent to withdraw them. At least two such vessels, in my judgment, should be kept in the upper James River. They stand a constant threat to the enemy, and prevent them from taking the offensive. There is no disguising the fact that if the enemy should take the offensive on the water, although we should probably destroy his whole James River navy, such damage would be done our shipping and stores, all accumulated on the waters where the conflict would begin, that our victory would be dearly bought.

In consequence of General Grant's protest, Acting-Rear-Admiral Lee made such representations to the Navy Department that a sufficient force of iron-clads was allowed to remain on the James.

The army had erected a strong battery at right angles with the line of fire of the Monitors at Trent's Reach. This battery had on several occasions opened on Howlett's and completely silenced it. Hence, with the obstructions under fire of the Army and Navy guns, the Army stores, etc., at City Point were perfectly secure against any attack.

While the attention of the Commander-in-chief of the North Atlantic squadron was principally directed to the security of Grant's army against an attack by the river, the enemy in the sounds of North Carolina were doing their best to make an impression on the Federal posts established along those waters. "Great victories" over the Union forces were constantly reported, which existed only in the vivid imagination of the Confederate reporters. To show how war news was manufactured, we quote the following from the Raleigh *Weekly:*

"Colonel Griffin, Confederate forces, telegraphed to the War Department from Jackson, on the 31st of January, as follows: 'Yesterday morning engaged the enemy with a force of two hundred men and a rifled field-piece. After a fight of two hours, in which we engaged twelve hundred men of the enemy and three pieces of artillery, the Yankees were driven from Windsor, N. C., to their boats. We lost six men; loss of the enemy not known.'"

Lieutenant-Commander C. W. Flusser,

indignant at such a report, in a communication to Acting-Rear-Admiral Lee, writes as follows:

"The report is false from beginning to conclusion. I planned the affair and we would have captured the entire party had we been ten minutes earlier. I had forty sailors and one 12-pounder howitzer, and there were three hundred and fifty infantry. We marched about sixteen miles. There was no fight and nothing worth reporting. The rebels ran. I fired three or four times at them at long range. We held the town of Windsor several hours, and marched back eight miles to our boats without a single shot from the enemy."

In this case the Confederate commander made capital out of nothing. Flusser was as truthful as he was brave, and his account is reliable. He was ever on the alert to surprise the enemy, and his escaping death for so long a period is remarkable.

The Confederates had been employed in building a powerful ram, called the "Albemarle," on the Roanoke River, and, knowing that the Federals had no vessel that could compete with her, it was arranged to fit out an expedition of Confederate soldiers, which, in conjunction with the ram, should make a descent on Plymouth.

The United States Government attached considerable importance to the possession of Plymouth as a base for Army operations. Two or three fortifications had been erected and well armed, and these were connected by lines of intrenchments and rifle-pits, calculated, with the aid of the gun-boats, to repel any force likely to be sent to this point. No one took any account of the "Albemarle," then building up the river, of which vessel only meagre accounts could be learned, though frequent representations, by naval officers in command in the sounds, had been made to the Navy Department of the necessity for more troops in that quarter.

It seems to have been the general impression that the Confederates were cherishing the idea of repossessing and regaining those places which had been so gallantly wrested from them early in the war by the united efforts of the Army and Navy. No doubt the Department rested under the opinion that the Confederates could not, so late in the year 1864, when they had been beaten at all points, undertake to recapture the towns in the sounds, or build a formidable iron-clad, in face of the fact that we had built numerous small Monitors, any of which, lightened of their armament and provisions, could have been floated into the sounds. There was, in fact, an extraordinary supineness manifested in certain quarters in relation to defending those sounds, for the possession of which so much time and labor had been expended.

The object of the Confederates, at the commencement of the year 1864, was to roll up victories in every quarter, which would have their effect on the peace party in the North, and influence the coming Presidential election. Then, too, their victories, much exaggerated, would sound well abroad, and perhaps bring aid from the English and French Governments.

It was clearly the duty of the Federal Government never to fall back from a position so easily to be held with Monitors and gun-boats as the sounds of North Carolina; yet, for want of proper precautions on the part of the Government, the enemy besieged Plymouth.

On the 18th of April, 1864, the Confederates opened with artillery upon Fort Gray, and in the afternoon, directing a heavy fire upon the town of Plymouth, the battle became general all along the line. The enemy assaulted the works with great gal-

LIEUTENANT-COMMANDER CHARLES W. FLUSSER.

lantry, but were driven back by the aid of the gun-boats "Miami" and "Southfield," under Lieutenant-Commander Flusser. A message was sent from General Wessels to Lieutenant-Commander Flusser, acknowledging the value of the Navy's services in driving back the enemy, and requesting that the "Miami" might be kept below the town to prevent a flank movement by the Confederates. The "Southfield," Acting-Volunteer-Lieutenant Chas. A. French, anchored with the "Miami" below Plymouth, and the ram, having been reported as coming down the river, the two gun-boats were chained together to meet her. At 3:45 P.M. both steamers got underway, and stood up the river as fast as possible, and in less than five minutes the ram struck the "Miami" on the port bow, near the water line, breaking through two planks for a distance

of about ten feet. Almost at the same moment the ram struck the "Southfield" with her prow on the starboard bow, causing the latter vessel to sink rapidly. Both vessels had opened on the ram, as soon as she appeared in sight, with solid shot from their 100-pounder rifles and 11-inch Dahlgren guns, without making any perceptible impression on the "Albemarle's" armor. Lieutenant-Commander Flusser fired the first three shots himself, the third shot being a 10-second Dahlgren 11-inch shell. Directly after, Flusser was killed by a fragment of a shell—whether from the ram or from one of the "Miami's" rebounding from the "Albemarle's" armor is doubtful—and the command of the "Miami" devolved upon Acting-Master William N. Wells.

The pressure of the ram between the two vessels broke the fastenings with which they were joined, and as many of the "Southfield's" men as could do so got on board the "Miami," which vessel rapidly retreated down the river, followed by the "Whitehead" and "Ceres," the ram not appearing to make more than four knots an hour in pursuit. The "Albemarle" soon relinquished the chase, and returned to Plymouth, where the battle was still in progress.

Flusser had no superior as a gallant and energetic officer, but his arrangements for meeting the ram were certainly ill-judged. Had the four vessels been properly disposed, the "Albemarle" herself could have been rammed while endeavoring to ram others. Tying two vessels together gave the enemy the very opportunity he desired. Either of the gun-boats was twice as fast as the ram, and there were chances of crippling her that were not improved.

The "Albemarle" had with her the "Cotton Planter," a strong screw-steamer, barricaded with cotton and iron, and her presence was, perhaps, the reason why the gun-boats retreated, and left the ram mistress of the situation. The result of this unfortunate affair was the capture of the town of Plymouth, with its garrison, munitions of war, etc.

The following were the casualties in the flotilla from the attack of the "Albemarle" and "Cotton Planter": "Miami," commanding officer killed, eleven men wounded; "Ceres," one killed, eight wounded. Out of the "Southfield's" crew, seven officers and forty-two men escaped to the "Miami;" the rest were supposed to have been made prisoners. After setting fire to the part of the "Southfield" that was still above water, the "Albemarle" returned to Plymouth.

After the gun-boats left the ram in full possession of the river, the Confederates took fresh courage, and resumed their attacks on the Federal works, from which they had been several times repulsed with loss, and, no reinforcements arriving, the forts (on the 20th) surrendered.

An attempt was made to censure the Navy for allowing the ram to come down the river; and it does seem as though obstructions and torpedoes might have been planted in the channel to prevent the "Albemarle" from reaching Plymouth; but, although piles were driven and the river partially blockaded, as events proved, the obstructions had no power to delay the advance of the Confederate vessels.

In response to a resolution of the House of Representatives, calling for information in regard to the capture of Plymouth through want of assistance from the Navy, the Secretary of the Navy sent to the Speaker copies of a number of communications, among them the following:

NAVY DEPARTMENT, September 17, 1863.

SIR—I have the honor to present for your consideration a subject of great importance connected with the maintaining possession of the sounds of North Carolina.

Information received from time to time places it beyond doubt that the rebels are constructing, and have almost completed, at Edward's Ferry, near Weldon, on the Roanoke River, a ram and an iron-clad floating battery. It is reported that these vessels will be completed in the course of five or six weeks. It is further reported that an attack on Plymouth is contemplated by land and water.

Our force of wooden vessels in the sounds, necessarily of light draft and lightly armed, will by no means be adequate to contend against the rebel ram and battery should they succeed in getting down the Roanoke, and, in that event, our possession of the sounds would be jeopardized.

It is impossible for our vessels to ascend the Roanoke River to any great distance in consequence of the shallowness of the water, their exposed situation from the fire of sharp-shooters, and the earth-works represented to be located at different points, particularly at Rainbow Bluff.

Were our iron-clads, now completed, available for service in the sounds, they could not be sent there, as they draw too much water to cross the bar at Hatteras. Our light-draft ones will not be completed for some time to come.

In view of all these facts, I deem it proper to suggest the importance of an effort on the part of the Army to surprise and destroy the rebel ram and battery referred to, or of obstructing the river by torpedoes and piles, or otherwise, so as to prevent their descent.

This Department will be happy to co-operate as far as it may be able in adopting such steps as may seem practicable and adequate to secure us against threatening disaster.

I am, very respectfully,

GIDEON WELLES.

To Hon. E. M. STANTON,
Secretary of War.

The "Albemarle" did not appear until nine months after the above letter was written, during which time no efforts seem to have been made to hasten the preparation of light-draft Monitors, that might have been floated over the bar at Hatteras at high water.

The letter we have quoted shows that the War Department took little interest in the matter of destroying the ram when under construction, which could only be done by a strong military and naval force combined.

There was great excitement among all those who could by any possibility be made responsible for the capture of Plymouth. Both the military and naval authorities had full knowledge of the building of the ram and floating battery; but the naval officer commanding in the sounds remained at Newbern, and left the most important position, Plymouth, with but four vessels, only two of which were of any force, to defend the place against an iron-clad represented to be almost a match for the far-famed "Merrimac." Although the attack commenced on the 18th, and lasted until the 20th, no vessels were sent from the naval forces in the sounds or soldiers from the military posts at other points.

Major-General Peck, commanding at Newbern, writes to General Butler as follows:

HEADQUARTERS,
ARMY OF THE DISTRICT OF NORTH CAROLINA,
NEWBERN, N. C., April 20th, 1864.

GENERAL: * * * * * The enemy have appeared in force in front of Plymouth, and attacked the place. The ram has sunk the "Southfield," disabled the "Miami," and passed below Plymouth. The sound is probably by this time in possession of the enemy, and Roanoke Island will undoubtedly soon be attacked, if it has not been already. Washington, N. C., is also threatened. Firing has been heard in that direction all night and this morning. Unless we are immediately and strongly reinforced, both by land and water, all of eastern North Carolina is lost to us. Immediate action is imperatively necessary. Captain Flusser, of the "Miami," is killed.

Very respectfully,

JOHN J. PECK,
Major-General Commanding.

Major-General B. F. BUTLER,
Commanding Department of Virginia and North Carolina.

In reply to the resolution of Congress asking for information in regard to the capture of Plymouth, Mr. Secretary Welles sent a characteristic communication, in which he says:

I transmit herewith copies of correspondence on the files of this Department relating to the construction of the rebel ram referred to, and other matters connected therewith. I also subjoin a schedule of iron-clad gun-boats of light draft in process of construction, which, in anticipation of the state of things now existing, were designed for service in the sounds and rivers of North Carolina, and the shallow interior waters elsewhere on the coast. These vessels were contracted for as soon as it was possible to do so after the necessary appropriations were made by Congress, and it will be seen by the date given that most of them were to have been completed last year, some of them as early as September. Not one has yet been delivered, and it will be some weeks before one can be made available for service.

I have felt it my duty on repeated occasions to call the attention of Congress to the necessity for a yard and establishment where iron and armored vessels could be constructed for the Government, but the preliminary steps for such an establishment have not yet been taken. In the meantime, the Department and the Government are wholly dependent on contractors, who, if they have the will, do not possess the ability, to finish these vessels promptly. Conflicting local controversies in regard to the place which shall be selected and benefitted by the proposed important national establishment for an iron Navy, such as the present and future necessities of the Government require, have contributed to delay action on this important subject.

Having in view economy as well as the public necessities, I have at no time recommended that the number of our Navy Yards should be increased on the Atlantic coast; but it is my deliberate opinion that no time should be wasted in establishing, at a proper place, a suitable yard where iron ships can be made and repaired. We feel its necessity in an emergency which has called forth the present inquiry, and not a single contractor is able to fulfill his engagements, even for one of this class of small vessels.

In the event of a foreign war with one or more of the maritime powers, our condition would be most unfortunate, with no Government establishment for the construction and repair of armored vessels such as modern science and skill are introducing.

The omission to make provision for such an establishment, on which the Government can always depend, is to be regretted.

Such incidental aid as the Navy could render the Army was cheerfully and earnestly given at Plymouth, as it has ever been given always and at all times when its aid and co-operation could be useful. It has been less effective than it could have been, even with such boats as we have, in consequence of the unfortunate legislation of the last Congress, which, in its enrollment law, ignored the Navy, subjected seamen to military draft, tendered large bounties to such as became soldiers, but allowed no bounty to those who entered the naval service, and would not even permit naval recruits to be credited on the quotas required to be drafted.

The remedial legislation of the present Congress has thus far effected comparatively few transfers. Some suggestions which I had the honor to submit to the Senate in March last, in answer to an inquiry as to what other legislation is necessary to supply any deficiencies of men for the naval service, have not, that I am aware, been reported upon, and many of our vessels—some of which would have been ordered to the sounds of North Carolina—are still without crews.

The correspondence of Acting-Rear-Admiral Lee and the naval officers are evidence that there has been no neglect or inattention on their part at Plymouth or elsewhere in that quarter.

I have, etc.,

GIDEON WELLES.

Mr. Secretary Welles, in his communication to Congress, plainly demonstrated that the Confederates could never have captured Plymouth if adequate appropriations had been made when first asked for to construct light-draft iron-clads, but all through the war Congress required much urging from the Navy Department in order that proper appropriations should be made.

The same unwillingness to grant the Navy money exists to-day, and the country, as regards this arm of defence, is in a deplorable condition.

Following the capture of Plymouth, the Confederates early in May made an attack

on Newbern, drove in the pickets, and took possession of the railroad; but there was a fair force of gun-boats at this point, and the summons of the enemy to surrender the town was refused.

On the 23d of April, Captain Melancton Smith assumed command of the naval forces in the sounds of North Carolina, with orders, if possible, to destroy the ram "Albemarle," either by running her down with the double-ender gun-boats or in such other manner as his judgment might suggest. The most efficient vessels at the disposal of Captain Smith were the "Miami," Commander Renshaw; "Tacony," Lieutenant-Commander Truxtun; "Sassacus," Lieutenant-Commander Roe; "Mattabesett," Commander Febiger, and the "Wyalusing," Lieutenant-Commander Queen.

Captain Smith was well supplied with "instructions" by his commander-in-chief, Acting - Rear - Admiral Lee, although it seems probable that so gallant and distinguished an officer could have done equally well without them. For the reader's benefit they are here quoted:

Attacking the ram will, to some extent, intimidate it, and by getting alongside in or near contact, and on each side holding position, and by firing at the centre of its ports, whether open or shut, and on its roof, you will disable and capture it. Your guns should have double breachings and be loaded with heavy charges—say from fifteen to eighteen pounds of powder for the 9-inch guns, and solid shot—and they should be so depressed as to fire as near a perpendicular line to the slope of the roof as practicable.

If all hands lie down when the guns are fired, they will escape the rebound of broken parts from the shot.

At the time of this attack, if some shells were thrown down the smoke-stack, she might then be disabled.

The advantage of getting alongside and on each side of her is that you prevent her from ramming, and have a controlling fire upon her roof and ports.

The ports and stern are her weak points, even if her ports are kept closed, as on her attack on the "Miami" and "Southfield" shows. You can, if alongside of her, fire through them and into her, and if her roof is, as described, of railroad iron, with a thin plating over it, the mechanical difficulty of securing this is such that it will loosen and fly off under the concussion of your heavy fire ; while the inside bolts will act like canister on her deck; and the concussion—especially if her ports are shut—will shock and demoralize her crew, giving you a complete victory.

Be sure and not have the neutral point of your wheel-house opposite her ports. Your wheel-houses should be abaft or forward of her roof—better abaft.

The Department seems to prefer ramming. This ram is reported as being of the usual "Merrimac" model; if so, heavy lagging and a knuckle would make her sides strong. But ramming under high speed may drive it in, or you may drive her ashore, or mount her ends, or—especially in the sounds, with some sea—sink her.

Entrusted by the Department with the performance of this signal service, I leave, with the expression of my views, to you the manner of executing it.

All assaults are exposed service, but this assault has with much real risk less than appears.

Wishing you success and promotion,

I have the honor to be, etc., etc.,

S. P. LEE.

To Captain MELANCTON SMITH,

U. S. Navy.

In the coming times, these quaint dispatches of the year 1864, issued by the old salts of the Navy, will doubtless be looked upon much as we now regard the lucubrations of Admiral Benbow and his contemporaries. Whether Captain Smith benefitted by the directions so liberally showered upon him will appear when we chronicle his adventures in the sounds of North Carolina.

The following vessels, arranged in the order given, off Edenton Bay, were under Captain Smith's command :

" Miami," Acting-Volunteer-Lieutenant Charles A. French.

" Ceres," Acting-Master H. H. Foster.

" Commodore Hull," Act.-Master Francis Josselyn.

" Seymour."

SECOND LINE.

" Mattabesett," Commander J. G. Febiger.

" Sassacus," Lieutenant-Commander F. A. Roe.

" Wyalusing," Lieutenant-Commander W. W. Queen.

" Whitehead," Acting-Ensign G. W. Barrett.

The " Miami " was fitted with a torpedo to explode against the side of the ram, if opportunity offered.

At 1 o'clock P. M. on the 5th of May, the " Miami," " Commodore Hull," " Ceres " and army transport " Trumpeter " got underway from the picket station off Edenton Bay, bound to the mouth of the Roanoke River, for the purpose of laying down torpedoes. Within a short distance of the buoy, at the mouth of the river, the " Albemarle " was discovered coming down, accompanied by the steamers " Cotton Plant " and " Bombshell," laden with troops, and doubtless bound to the attack of Newbern.

The " Trumpeter " was sent back to give tidings of the approach of the ram, while the other vessels steamed slowly away, endeavoring to draw the ram as far as possible from the mouth of the river.

The ram followed the " Miami " and her consorts until the vessels fell in with Captain Smith and the other division of gunboats, when signal was made to attack the enemy. The " Mattabesett," " Wyalusing," " Sassacus " and " Whitehead " steamed towards the ram, the smaller vessels falling into the rear according to programme.

At 4:40 P. M. the ram fired the first gun, which destroyed the " Mattabesett's " launch, and wounded several men. A second shot cut away some of the rigging. At 4:45 the Confederate steamer " Bombshell," being temporarily disabled by a shot, hauled down her flag and surrendered. The next moment the " Mattabesett " fired a broadside at the ram from a distance of 150 yards. Just afterwards, the " Sassacus " delivered a broadside, and the " Albemarle " sheered with a port-helm with the intention of ramming, but the superior speed of the " Sassacus " foiled her in this attempt, and the latter passed around the ram's stern, with a hard port-helm.

The " Bombshell " lay off the ram's port-quarter, and, having opened fire simultaneously with the " Albemarle," the " Sassacus " fired on her, and her commanding officer was under the impression that the Confederate vessel had surrendered to him.

As the " Mattabesett " had passed around the stern of the ram and was heading down the sound, the ram had turned partially around, presenting her broadside to the " Sassacus," which vessel was at that time about three or four hundred yards distant. She made for the ram, and struck her fairly with a speed of five or six knots, according to Captain Smith, or ten knots, according to Lieutenant-Commander Roe.

The ram was struck just abaft her starboard-beam, causing her to heel over, and placing her after-deck under water; so much so, that Lieutenant-Commander Roe thought she was sinking. At the same instant the " Albemarle " fired a 100-pounder rifle-shot through and through the " Sassacus," from starboard to port on the berth-deck. The collision was heavy, and the engine of the " Sassacus " was kept going in the attempt to force her bow deeper and deeper into the ram, so that some of the other vessels could attack on the other side, and enable the " Sassacus " to sink the enemy. This position the " Sassacus " maintained at least ten minutes. Hand-grenades were thrown down the ram's hatches, and attempts made to get shells into her smoke-stack, besides keeping up a severe musketry fire on her.

At length the stern of the ram swung around, and, her broadside-port bearing on the starboard-bow of the " Sassacus," the " Albemarle " fired a 100-pounder rifled shot, which passed through the starboard-side of the " Sassacus," through the empty bunkers into the starboard-boiler, clear through it fore and aft, and finally lodging in the ward-room. In a moment the " Sassacus " was filled with steam, killing and wounding many of the crew, and rendering all movement for the time impossible.

Only those who have witnessed the effect of a bursting boiler, with the steam rushing all over the ship and penetrating every nook and cranny, can appreciate the condition of affairs on board the "Sassacus." The stoutest nerves are scarcely proof against the appalling sights which meet the eye, and the cries and groans which fall upon the ear. When the vapor cleared away, so that the commander of the "Sassacus," could look around him, he saw his antagonist steaming away. The engine of the "Sassacus" was meanwhile in motion, no one being able to get into the engine-room to stop it, on account of the scalding steam, until the boiler was empty. The helm was at once put a-port, and the "Sassacus" headed up the sound, leaving the field clear for the other vessels to operate. As soon as the immediate effects of the explosion were over, the officers and men returned to their guns, firing upon the enemy until the "Sassacus" drifted out of range.

While the "Sassacus" was in contact with the "Albemarle," it was impossible for the other vessels of the squadron to fire, for fear of injuring their consort; but they subsequently failed to take advantage of the act of the gallant "Sassacus," and deliver blows upon the ram while she was at rest and somewhat demoralized from the shock she had received.

It was by such concerted action that the "Tennessee" was forced to surrender to Farragut's vessels in Mobile Bay. The failure of the larger vessels to ram the "Albemarle" is accounted for by the indiscriminate firing from the smaller ones upon the enemy. These latter vessels answered the signals made by the senior officer, without obeying them.

The engagement continued until 7:30 P. M., when darkness supervened. The "Commodore Hull" and the "Ceres" were left to keep sight of the ram, and to remain off the mouth of the Roanoke River if she succeeded in entering it, the other vessels coming to anchor in the sound.

During the engagement an attempt was made by the "Wyalusing" to lay a seine in front of the ram with the intent of fouling her propeller, but the latter ran over it without damage. A torpedo was rigged out from the "Miami," and the attempt was made to explode it against the enemy, but from some unexplained cause the attempt failed. The ram, during the attacks of the different vessels, kept moving about delivering an accurate fire, apparently unharmed, although the shot and shell rattled upon her slanting roof like hail. When the shots struck her armor they fairly sparkled, and flying up into the air fell into the water without doing any perceptible damage. The ram moved through the water at the rate of six knots an hour, and turned quickly to meet her adversaries.

When the "Sassacus" struck the "Albemarle," and directly afterwards was covered with vapor fore and aft, many supposed that this catastrophe was brought about by the collision, and the impression prevailed that it would not be prudent to repeat the experiment for fear the whole flotilla would be disabled by their own exertions. There does not seem to have been that system in manoeuvering the vessels of the flotilla which should have prevailed; but Captain Smith had only been in command a few days, and the officers of the vessels were quite unpracticed in fleet manoeuvering. Signals, though made and answered, were not carried out. It seems to have been the object to fire into the enemy at a distance of from two to three hundred yards, although it was soon evident that the ram was invulnerable in her hull against any shot from the Federal vessels.

The "Mattabesett" (flag-ship) was well handled, and her fire was remarkably accurate. She was not in the least disabled during the action.

While passing the ram in the "Wyalusing," at a distance of one hundred and fifty yards, Lieutenant-Commander Queen says: "It was my intention to run the 'Bombshell' down, but discovered in time that she had surrendered, when I immediately backed clear of her and again opened fire on the ram." Lieutenant-Commander Queen claims to have cut away the signal halliards of the "Albemarle" when her colors came down, and he supposed she had surrendered, though he was soon convinced to the contrary by a 6-inch rifle-shot crashing through the side of his vessel. Soon after, the executive officer of the "Wyalusing" reported the ship as sinking, and it seemed as if the ram was about to clear the field, as she moved about, firing her two 6-inch rifles, almost every shot taking effect on some of the vessels. As it was found on examination that the "Wyalusing" was making no more water than usual, another start was made to run the ram down, passing around her and throwing in broadsides which did no harm, and it was only at the close of the action one of the pieces of plating forward on the port side was seen to fly off. At 7:40 the "Wyalusing" ceased firing, agreeably to signal from the flag-ship.

The reports of the different commanding officers show that as rapid a fire was kept up as circumstances would admit; yet, after the attack of the "Sassacus," there was no concerted action, which is to be regretted, since one or two heavy blows in the stern of the "Albemarle" would have sealed her fate; for her rudder once disabled, the ram would have been obliged to surrender. Even if she had been repeatedly rammed, without piercing her sides, her crew would have become demoralized, as always happens in such cases. A great deal of gallantry was shown on this occasion; but a mistake was made in not carrying out the Department's directions, to depend upon ramming.

The "Albemarle" had no opportunity to use her ram; or, if she had, failed to take advantage of it. It is probable that the commanding officer of the ram, who fought his vessel with so much judgment and gallantry, would not have lost an opportunity to use his prow if one had offered.

This remarkable engagement continued from 4:40 until 7:40 P. M., when the signal was made to cease firing, and the ram made off towards the mouth of Roanoke River. It afterwards appeared that she was not materially injured, but could have continued the contest for some time, in spite of the reports to the contrary brought by refugees from Plymouth. There were fired from the different vessels at the "Albemarle" 292 one-hundred-pounder shot and shells, 239 nine-inch shells, 60 thirty-pounder Parrott shot and shells, 59 twenty-four-pound howitzers, and some 12-pound rifle-shots—in all, 648 shot and shells.

The following damages were sustained by the vessels of the flotilla:

"Mattabesett"—one shot through waterways abaft port-wheel.

"Sassacus"—a 6-inch solid shot through the starboard-side of the ship five feet above the berth-deck, through the starboard boiler, and exploding it; wheel badly damaged by coming in contact with the ram's stern.

"Wyalusing"—shell exploded in starboard wheel-house, cutting away two of the water-rims of the starboard wheel, etc.; one shot knocking out the gig's bottom; one shot through starboard-side of berth-deck, doing much damage; one shot on the starboard quarter above the water line, doing much damage.

"Miami"—struck three or four times, all but one shot unimportant.

This was not a great deal of damage, considering the number of targets the ram had to fire at, and seemingly nothing to disable any of the flotilla except the "Sassacus," which vessel was put *hors de combat* early in the action. The fire of the ram was, doubtless, much interfered with by the tremendous hail of shot and shell which fell upon her, obliging her to keep her shutters almost constantly closed.

The engagement showed conclusively the immense advantage of an iron-clad ram over any number of vulnerable wooden vessels such as were employed in the waters of North Carolina, and that the money spent to build "double-enders" would have been much better applied in the construction of fast rams, each with one or two heavy guns. It would have taken little more time to build

light iron-clads than it did to construct the double-enders, which, on the whole, were not well suited for their intended purpose.

The engagement with the "Albemarle," although not successful in sinking or disabling her, yet answered the valuable purpose of preventing her from doing further mischief. Her intended attack on Newbern, in co-operation with the Confederate land forces, was given up, and the ram was only seen once more after the engagement. A day or two afterwards, the "Albemarle" came to the mouth of the Roanoke River with the apparent object of putting down torpedoes; but when fired upon retreated up the stream. She was then tied to the bank under the guns of Plymouth, and heavy booms placed around her to keep off torpedo-boats, there to undergo such repairs as were found necessary. Her commanding officer was evidently satisfied that with his limited speed it was not prudent to encounter so many vessels without further strengthening the "Albemarle." The blow given by the "Sassacus" admonished him that two or three successive shocks would disable his vessel.

The commanding officer of the "Albemarle" was Lieutenant A. F. Warley, late of the United States Navy, who commanded the "Manassas" at the forts below New Orleans. In the command of the "Albemarle" he certainly showed great skill and gallantry, the credit for which we do not propose to withhold because it was exercised against the flag under which he had been trained to service. The attack on the flotilla was a bold stroke, doubtless intended to make a point for the Confederate cause, which was just then threatened with a collapse.

The "Albemarle" was constructed on the same general plan as the "Merrimac." The slanting roof and other exposed parts were covered with five inches of pine and the same thickness of oak surmounted with railroad iron, over which was an inch of plating secured through all with bolts and nuts. The ram had a cast-iron prow and carried two 6-inch Brooke rifled guns, pivoted on the bow and stern, so that the guns could be worked from the bow and quarter ports. Her overhanging sides, connected with a "knuckle," made it difficult to ram her with an ordinary gun-boat. She was driven at a speed of six knots by a propeller and drew not exceeding eight feet of water.

The Confederates throughout the war adhered to this class of vessel, which was the most convenient for them to build with their limited facilities. Considering the number the enemy constructed, and the gallantry and ability of their naval officers, it is remarkable that they should not have accomplished more.

While the Federals may be liable to criticism for allowing the enemy to get ahead of them in the construction of iron-clads, there was no want of gallantry on the part of the Navy in attempting their destruction, and the attempts were generally successful. The "Merrimac" was the only Confederate iron-clad which really accomplished much, and she bade fair at one time to change the aspect of affairs in favor of the Confederates, and overwhelm the Union people in mortification and disaster.

An effort was made to destroy the "Albemarle" by torpedoes. A party of five volunteers from the "Wyalusing" left that vessel at 2 P. M. on the 20th of May, having made a reconnaissance two days previously, and ascended the middle channel of the Roanoke River in a dinghy. The party carried two torpedoes, each containing one hundred pounds of powder, with their appendages, which were transported on stretchers across the swamps. John W. Lloyd, coxswain, and Charles Baldwin, coalheaver, swam the river with a line and hauled the torpedoes across to the Plymouth shore close to the town. The torpedoes were then connected by a bridle floated down with the current, guided by Charles Baldwin, who designed to place them across the "Albemarle's" bow, one on either side, and Allen Crawford, fireman, who was stationed in the swamps on the opposite side of the river, was to explode them on a given signal.

Everything worked well until the torpedoes were within a few yards of the ram, when Baldwin was seen and hailed by a sentry on the wharf. The sentry then fired two shots, which was soon followed by a volley of musketry, which induced Lloyd to cut the guiding line, throw away the coil, and swim the river again to join John Laverty, fireman, who was left in charge of the arms and clothes. These two men, with the boat-keeper, returned to the ship, after an absence of thirty-eight hours, nearly exhausted with their arduous and perilous labors. The other two men were found, after a two days' search in the swamps, almost worn out with hunger and fatigue. Although their design was defeated by the accidental fouling of the line with a schooner, these men deserve none the less credit for undertaking so perilous an adventure.

After this episode the "Albemarle" was strictly guarded, and remained at Plymouth, a constant source of anxiety to our naval authorities.

The flotilla in the sounds was reinforced by some additional vessels and placed under the command of Commander William H. Macomb, an officer fully competent to perform the duties required of him.

NORTH ATLANTIC SQUADRON, JANUARY 1, 1864.

ACTING-REAR-ADMIRAL, SAMUEL P. LEE.   FLEET-CAPTAIN, LIEUTENANT-COMMANDER JOHN S. BARNES.

STEAM FRIGATE "MINNESOTA"—FLAG-SHIP.

Lieutenant-Commander, John H. Upshur; Lieutenant, Jos. P. Fyffe; Fleet Surgeon, W. Maxwell Wood; Assistant Surgeons, G. S. Franklin, W. S. Fort and A. Mathewson; Fleet Paymaster, Chas. P. Upham; Chaplain, Thomas G. Salter; Marine Officers: Captain, John Schermerhorn; Second-Lieutenant, C. F. Williams; Acting-Masters, Robert Barstow, A. B. Pierson and W. H. Polly; Acting-Ensigns, J. W. Grattan, E. R. Olcott, Richard Bates, John M. Cowen and James Birtwistle; Acting-Master's Mates, F. A. O'Conner, John Brann, J. M. Skarden, G. W. Kellogg and S. A. Tabor; Engineers: Chiefs, Benj. F. Garvin and John H. Long; Assistants, G. W. Sensner, James Renshaw, Jr., Guy Samson, R. D. Taylor, F. W. Nyman, Wm. Bond and J. D. Lee; Boatswain, Wm. Bunker; Gunner, C. W. Homer; Carpenter, J. W. Stimson; Sailmaker, T. O. Fassett.

IRON-CLAD STEAMER "ROANOKE."

Captain, Guert Gansevoort; Lieutenant, Clark Merchant; Surgeon, Robert Woodworth; Assistant Surgeon, A. A. Hoehling; Paymaster, James D. Murray; Marine Corps: First-Lieutenant, Frank Monroe; Acting-Masters, James French, Chas. De Bevoise, H. J. Coop and T. A. Wyatt; Ensigns, D. D. Wemple and H. B. Rumsey; Acting-Ensign, E. E. Taylor; Acting-Master's Mates, H. H. Collamore, J. S. Young and John Dow; Engineers: Chief, Edward Fithian; Assistants, T. J. McK. Daniels, H. S. Leonard, H. D. Sellman, Webster Lane, Henry Blye, E. P. Rank and J. C. Cross; Boatswain, John A. Selmer; Gunner, John Caulk; Carpenter, J. H. Owens.

STEAMER "FORT JACKSON."

Captain, B. F. Sands; Lieutenant-Commander, Chas. S. Norton; Surgeon, Philip S. Wales; Paymaster, Clifton Hellen; Acting-Masters, W. E. Dennison and R. P. Swann; Ensign, S. H. Hunt; Acting-Ensigns, H. F. Moffat, S. R. Hopkins and F. P. B. Sands; Acting-Master's Mates, J. D. Moore, G. W. Smoot, W. M. Mann and H. S. Eytinge; Engineers, Rodney Smith, J. E. Fox, Jared Day, John Herron, C. H. Wakefield, W. M. Prentiss and J. H. Eppes; Boatswain, P. A. Chason; Acting-Gunner, Thomas Reise; Carpenter, E. Thompson.

STEAMER "SHENANDOAH."

Captain, Daniel B. Ridgely; Lieutenant-Commander, R. R. Wallace; Lieutenant, S. W. Nichols; Ensigns, H. C. Taylor and Yates Sterling; Surgeon, James McMaster; Acting-Assistant Paymaster, C. M. Guild; Acting-Master, J. W. Bentley; Acting-Ensigns, W. H. Brice and J. A. Bullard; Acting-Master's Mates, Harrison Miller, L. H. White, Charles Tangwell and W. Moore; Engineers: Chief, J. W. Thomson; Assistants, J. M. Hobby, J. T. Keleher, D. P. McCartney, D. M. Fulmer, J. W.

Gardner and F. W. Towner; Boatswain, J. H. Polly; Gunner, Wm. Hardison.

STEAMER "CONNECTICUT."

Commander, John J. Almy; Lieutenant, Louis Kempff; Assistant Surgeon, J. R. Little; Assistant Paymaster, Arthur Burtis, Jr.; Acting-Master, F. Hopkins, Jr.; Acting-Ensigns, F. Wallace, S. Harding, Jr., and J. M. C. Reville; Acting-Master's Mates, Charles Hall, E. P. Blayne, E. S. D. Howland, John Williams and Thos. Stanfield; Engineers: Acting-Chief, Alex. McCausland; Acting-Second-Assistant, David McArthur; Acting-Third-Assistants, James Campbell, John Quinn and Wm. McGrath; Gunner, Wm. Mowbry.

STEAMER "QUAKER CITY."

Commander, James M. Frailey; Lieutenant, Silas Casey, Jr.; Acting-Assistant Surgeon, J. J. Brownlee; Acting-Assistant Paymaster, H. J. Bullay; Acting-Chief-Engineer, G. W. Farrer; Acting-Master, Edmund Kemble; Acting-Ensigns, C. J. Hill, E. M. Seaver and Richard Wilkinson; Acting-Master's Mates, G. C. Sanborn, J. B. Tew; C. H. Thorne and J. C. Constant; Engineers: Acting-Second-Assistants, W. J. Howard and J. K. Hickey; Acting-Third-Assistants, J. H. Mathews, J. R. Peterson, E. Prest, E. E. Porter and Fred'k Fries; Acting-Gunner, Joseph Furlong.

ORDNANCE STORE-SHIP "ST. LAWRENCE."

Commander, Dominick Lynch; Acting-Master, E. S. Goodwin; Acting-Ensigns, Robert Merchant, Alonzo Small and C. E. Buck; Acting-Master's Mates, Thomas Welsh, W. S. Cammett and E. M. Hemsley; Acting-Assistant Surgeon, J. E. Warner; Acting-Assistant Paymaster, W. Goldsborough; Acting-Gunner, W. E. Webber.

STEAMER "KEYSTONE STATE."

Commander, Edward Donaldson; Lieutenant, J. P. Robertson; Acting-Masters, C. H. Corser, L. E. Degn and W. T. Buck; Acting-Ensigns, C. M. Bird and J. C. Murphy; Acting-Master's Mate, J. T. Ridgway; Acting-Assistant Surgeon, A. E. Emery; Acting-Assistant Paymaster, J. S. Stimson; Engineers: Acting-Chief, A. K. Eddows; Acting-Second-Assistant, P. L. Fry; Acting-Third-Assistants, J. H. Smith, C. A. Blake, W. H. Brown and J. B. Wilbur; Acting-Gunner, D. L. Briggs.

STEAMER "HETZEL."

Commander, H. K. Davenport; Acting-Masters, G. B. Thompson and Milford Rogers; Acting-Master's Mates, R. P. Boss, John Rudrow, W. H. Leavitt and Tully McEntyre; Acting-Assistant Surgeon, G. W. Wilson; Acting-Assistant Paymaster, G. W. Morton; Engineers: Acting-Second-Assistant, J. H. Padgett; Acting-Third-Assistants, T. B. Cole, W. B. Whitmore and A. D. Witherell.

STEAMER "FLORIDA."

Commander, Pierce Crosby; Acting-Lieutenant, E. C. Merriman; Acting-Assistant Surgeon, E. H. Vose; Acting-Assistant Paymaster, W. F. Keeler; Acting-Master, John McGowan, Jr.; Acting-Ensigns, Peter Williams, C. E. Rich and C. Washburn; Acting-Master's Mates, W. H. Knowlton, T. W. Rock, Robert Clifford and David Fader; Engineers: Acting-First-Assistant, William McLean; Acting-Second-Assistants, John Mason and D. M. Lane; Acting-Third-Assistants, G. F. Smith and J. W. Hockett.

STEAMER "LOUISIANA."

Commander, Richard T. Renshaw; Acting-Ensign, E. S. McKeever; Acting-Master's Mates, Edw. Cassady, Chas. Fisher and Paul Boyden; Acting-Assistant Surgeon, T. W. Jamison; Acting-Assistant Paymaster, G. N. Simpson, Jr.; Engineers: Acting-Second-Assistants, Wm. Mara and Hiram Parker, Jr.; Acting-Third-Assistants, C. S. Servoss and R. D. Faron; Carpenter, John Mills.

STEAMER "CAMBRIDGE."

Commander, William F. Spicer; Acting-Master, F. W. Strong; Acting-Ensigns, S. H. Mead, Jr., E. A. Small, S. K. Luce and J. K. Barker; Acting-Master's Mates, J. S. Bradbury, R. S. Sheperd and F. U. Northup; Acting-Assistant Surgeon, L. C. Granger; Acting-Assistant Paymaster, J. C. Canning; Engineers: Acting-First-Assistant, G. B. Orsewell; Acting-Second-Assistants, J. F. Powers, H. F. Hayden and John Whitaker; Acting-Gunner, Wm. Scott.

STEAMER "STATE OF GEORGIA."

Commander, Somerville Nicholson; Lieutenant, George B. White; Acting-Assistant Surgeon, R. H. Greene; Acting-Assistant Paymaster, J. F. Griffiths; Acting-Master, Benj. Whitmore; Acting-Ensigns, Chas. Trathen, S. L. Griffin and Wm. Shultz; Acting-Master's Mates, Frank Papanti, Peter Hayes and G. E. Kidder; Engineers: Acting-First-Assistant, John Bloomsbury; Acting-Second-Assistants, W. A. Andress and A. N. Gilmore; Acting-Third-Assistants, Wm. Madden, J. A. Patterson and F. R. Shoemaker; Gunner, Wm. Griffiths.

STEAMER "MERCEDITA."

Lieutenant-Commander, H. N. T. Arnold; Acting-Assistant Surgeon, J. K. Walsh; Acting-Assistant Paymaster, J. S. Mallary; Acting-Master, D. E. Taylor; Acting-Ensigns, H. G. Marcy, Wm. Young, G. W. Williams and E. D. Pettingill; Acting-Master's Mates, Isaac Hallock and H. C. Robertson; Engineers: Acting-First-Assistant, B. F. Beckett; Acting-Second-Assistant, F. E. Porter; Acting-Third-Assistants, D. J. Lanahan, J. H. Hopkins, Wm. Ellis, W. A. Steinrook and Wm. McComb; Acting-Gunner, James Addison.

STEAMER "MARATANZA."

Lieutenant Commander, Milton Haxtun; Assistant Surgeon, D. D. Gilbert; Assistant Paymaster, C. S. Perley; Acting-Masters, Chas. Courtney, Jacob Kimball and J. B. Wood; Acting-Ensign, R. D. Eldridge; Acting-Master's Mates, A. F. Williamson and G. E. Chipman; Engineers: Acting-First-Assistant, C. L. Carty; Second-Assistant, Edw. Scattergood; Third-Assistants, W. H. Kilpatrick, L. R. Harvey and R. L. Webb.

STEAM GUN-BOAT "MIAMI."

Lieutenant-Commander, Chas. W. Flusser; Acting-Masters, W. N. Wells and John Lear; Acting-Ensigns, J. W. Bennett and T. G. Hargis; Assistant Surgeon, Wm. B. Mann; Acting-Assistant Paymaster, F. W. Hackett; Engineers: Third-Assistants, H. D. Heiser, C. C. Davis and J. W. Saville; Acting-Third-Assistants, David Newell and Dennis Harrington.

STEAMER "MORSE."

Lieutenant-Commander, C. A. Babcock; Acting-Assistant Surgeon, G. F. Winslow; Acting-Assistant Paymaster, Henry Russell; Acting-Ensigns, A. Dennett, J. F. Merry and R. M. Wagstaff; Acting-Master's Mate, Wm. Dunne; Engineers: Acting-First-Assistant, Thomas Divine; Acting-Third-Assistants, Timothy Flanders, Thomas McNellis and G. C. Rogers.

STEAMER "NANSEMOND."

Lieutenant, R. H. Lamson; Acting-Assistant Surgeon, Edgar S. Smith; Acting-Assistant Paymaster, R. M. Gillette; Acting-Ensigns, J. H. Porter, Wm. Hunter, J. B. Henderson and Henry Waring; Engineers: Acting-Second-Assistant, Fred'k Snyder; Acting-Third-Assistants, Edw. Aspald, C. M. Goodwin, J. T. Earl and E. A. Reilly.

STEAMER "SOUTHFIELD."

Acting-Volunteer-Lieutenant, Charles A. French; Acting-Masters, W. B. Newman and W. F. Pratt; Acting-Ensigns, T. B. Stokes and J. R. Peacock; Acting-Master's Mates, G. W. Pratt and J. J. Allen,

Jr.; Acting-Assistant Surgeon, Wm. H. Holmes; Acting-Assistant Paymaster, Addison Pool; Engineers: Acting-Second-Assistant, Wm. F. Goff; Acting-Third-Assistants, J. B. Farrand, J. A. Strieby and Joseph Watts.

STEAMER "NIPHON."

Acting Volunteer-Lieutenant, J. B. Breck; Acting-Ensigns, H. S. Borden, E. N. Seaman, J. J. Reagan and Niels Larsen; Acting-Master's Mates, A. R. Arey and G. W. Barnes; Acting-Assistant Paymaster, Theo. Barker; Engineers: Acting-Third-Assistants, T. L. Churchill, J. J. Sullivan, Wm. Norie and T. T. Sanborn.

STEAMER "DAYLIGHT."

Acting-Volunteer-Lieutenant, Francis S. Wells; Acting-Masters, J. H. Gleason and T. Werlhof; Acting-Ensigns, J. W. Willard and W. H. Penfield; Acting-Assistant Surgeon, F. M. Dearborne; Acting-Assistant Paymaster, H. M. Rogers; Acting-Master's Mates, Chas. Attmore and J. M. Simms; Engineers: Acting-First-Assistant, Wm. H. Best; Acting-Second-Assistants, P. O. Brightman and C. O. Morgan; Acting-Third-Assistants, W. H. Crawford, J. E. Hilliard and J. T. Smith.

STEAMER "MONTGOMERY."

Acting-Volunteer-Lieutenant, E. A. Faucon; Acting-Master, G. H. Pendleton; Acting-Ensigns, W. O. Putnam, Rob't Wiley and W. P. Burke; Acting-Master's Mates, J. D. Gossick, T. J. Walker and F. C. Simonds; Acting-Assistant Surgeon, D. F. Lincoln; Acting-Assistant Paymaster, Joseph Watson; Engineers: Acting-First-Assistant, G. H. Wade; Acting-Second-Assistant, James Pollard; Acting-Third-Assistants, John McEwan, James Allen and G. M. Smith.

STEAMER "COMMODORE PERRY."

Acting-Volunteer-Lieutenant, Thos. J. Woodward; Acting-Assistant Paymaster, Wm. J. Healy; Acting-Master, J. E. Stammard; Acting-Ensign, Wm. H. McLean; Engineers: Acting-Third-Assistants, J. L. Bowers, Charles Hickey and Horace Whitworth.

STEAMER "MOUNT VERNON."

Acting-Volunteer-Lieutenant, James Trathen; Acting-Master, Edw. W. White; Acting-Ensigns, F. M. Paine, H. F. Cleverly and C. G. Walstrom; Acting-Master's Mates, Jason Ryan and Henry Rogers; Acting-Assistant Surgeon, Oswald Warner; Acting-Assistant Paymaster, H. Y. Glisson; Engineers: Acting-Second-Assistant, J. H. Horsford; Acting-Third-Assistants, H. S. Short, W. H. Smith and George Ducker.

STEAMER "BRITANNIA."

Acting-Volunteer-Lieutenant, Samuel Huse; Acting-Master, J. S. Coney; Acting-Ensigns, F. C. Ford, A. J. Lowell and M. E. Wandell; Acting-Master's Mate, R. L. M. Jones; Acting-Assistant Paymaster, C. B. Culver; Engineers: Second-Assistant, P. A. Rearick; Acting-Second-Assistant, Joseph Fernald; Acting-Third-Assistants, J. M. Barron, Wm. Hifferon and H. F. Loveaire.

STEAMER "GOVERNOR BUCKINGHAM."

Acting-Volunteer-Lieutenant, Wm. G. Saltonstall; Acting-Master, John S. Watson; Acting-Ensigns, Wm. C. Gibson, J. W. Crowell and W. B. Mix; Acting-Master's Mates, James Auld, F. H. Poole and J. W. Gardner; Acting-Assistant Surgeon, R. C. Tuttle, Acting-Assistant Paymaster, E. G. Musgrave; Engineers: Acting-Second-Assistants, C. W. Doten, Thomas Usticks, Wm. Collier; Acting-Third-Assistants, Thomas Harrison and O. L. Smith.

SUPPLY STEAMER "NEWBERN."

Acting-Volunteer-Lieutenant,, T. A. Harris; Acting-Masters, R. Y. Holly and J. K. Richardson; Acting-Ensigns, Chas. Millett, C. H. Sawyer and Milton

Webster; Acting-Assistant Surgeon, John E. Cobb; Acting-Assistant Paymaster, E. H. Cushing; Acting-Master's Mates, J. P. Jones, O. F. Wixon and A. Landergren; Engineers: Acting-First-Assistant, Isaac Maples; Acting-Second-Assistant, J. E. Cooper; Acting-Third-Assistants, C. E. Rainier, F. C. Lomas and S. J. Hoffman.

STEAMER "HOUQUAH."

Acting-Volunteer-Lieutenant, J. Macdearmid; Acting-Master, C. B. Wilder; Acting-Ensigns, G. P. St. John and John Duly; Acting-Master's Mates, R. B. Smith and F. B. Haskell; Acting-Assistant Paymaster, E. W. Brooks; Engineers: Acting-Second-Assistants, Wm. McLane and D. R. Wylie; Acting-Third-Assistants, J. B. Rice and Thomas Dobbs.

STEAMER "LOCKWOOD."

Acting-Volunteer-Lieutenant, G. W. Graves; Acting-Ensigns, J. Q. A. Davidson and Abram Hicks; Acting-Master's Mate, E. S. Austin; Engineers: Acting-Third-Assistants, J. T. Miller and Samuel Dean.

STEAMER "UNDERWRITER."

Acting-Master, Jacob Westervelt; Acting-Assistant Surgeon, L. R. Boyce; Acting-Assistant Paymaster, E. H. Sears; Acting-Master's Mates, W. K. Engell, Daniel Ward, C. A. Stewart and John McCormick; Engineers: Acting-Second-Assistant, J. B. Dick; Acting-Third-Assistant, S. B. Ellis.

STEAMER "CALYPSO."

Acting-Master, Fred'k D. Stuart; Acting-Assistant Surgeon, Chas. Sturtevant; Acting-Assistant Paymaster, A. H. Nelson; Acting-Ensigns, W. Jameson, J. A. French, G. W. Comer and B. H. Macintire; Acting-Master's Mates, W. H. Alger, Isaac Sawyer and P. M. Topham; Engineers: Acting-First-Assistant, Cornelius Carr; Acting-Second-Assistants, B. F. Haines, F. V. Holt and Samuel Bolson; Acting-Third-Assistants, E. Minne and W. Y. Schneider.

STEAMER "COMMODORE BARNEY."

Acting-Master, James M. Williams; Acting-Ensigns, Jos. Avant, C. J. Goodwin and C. W. Leekins; Acting-Master's Mates, John Aspinwall and W. H. Richmond; Acting-Assistant Surgeon, James Kinnier; Acting-Assistant Paymaster, Thos. Jernegan; Engineers: Acting-Second-Assistant, Hiram Warner; Acting-Third-Assistants, Charles Culver, D. S. Leffer and F. G. Shannon.

STEAMER "COMMODORE HULL."

Acting-Masters, Francis Josselyn and J. O. Johnson; Acting-Master's Mates, D. A. Simmond and Geo. Van Duzer; Acting-Assistant Surgeon, C. F. T. Hildreth; Acting-Assistant Paymaster, Jonathan Chapman; Engineer: Acting-Second-Assistant, B. F. Bee; Acting Third-Assistants, W. Lannan, M. O. Stimson and A. C. Stuart.

STEAMER "WYANDOTTE."

Acting-Master, Thomas W. Sheer; Acting-Ensigns, Benj. Wood, Wm. Henry, Andrew McCleary and J. W. Thompson; Acting-Master's Mates, Wm. Chandler; Acting-Assistant Surgeon, James Pennoyer, Acting-Assistant Paymaster, Wm. A. Purse; Engineers: Acting-First-Assistant, J. W. Farrell; Acting-Second-Assistant, Geo. R. Dunkly.

STEAMER "MT WASHINGTON."

Acting-Master, H. H. Haynie; Acting-Master's Mate, G. B. Griffin; Engineers: Acting-Second-Assistants, Sidney Smith and Wm. Veitch; Acting-Third-Assistant, Joseph Jamieson.

STEAMER "COMMODORE JONES."

Acting-Master, J. O. Barclay; Acting-Ensign, Geo. W. Adams; Acting-Master's Mates, C. P. Luscomb, E. L. Deane and P. M. Nye; Acting-Assistant Paymaster, E. T. Chapman; Engineers: Acting-Second-Assistant, Timothy McCarthy; Acting-

Third - Assistants, J. B. McKenzie, Malcolm Sinclair and I. L. Sawtelle.

STEAMER "STEPPING STONES."

Acting-Master, D. A. Campbell; Acting-Ensign, E. A. Roderick; Acting-Master's Mate, O. P. Knowles; Engineers: Acting-Second-Assistant, J. A. Brown; Acting-Third-Assistants, M. McCarty and G. A. Whittington.

STEAMER "LILAC."

Acting-Master, John A. Phillips; Acting-Ensigns, C. B. Staples and F. B. Owens; Acting-Master's Mate, D. S. Ingersoll; Engineers: Acting-Second-Assistant, Wm. T. Graff; Acting-Third-Assistants, L. L. Copeland and J. C. Garner.

STEAMER "YOUNG ROVER."

Acting - Masters, John B. Studley and T. W. Dodge; Acting-Ensigns, D. S. Thompson and E. N. Ryder; Acting-Assistant-Surgeon, Robert Cowie; Acting-Assistant-Paymaster, George W. Stone; Engineers: Acting-Second-Assistant, James Patterson; Acting-Third-Assistant, Wm. D. Butts.

STEAMER "MYSTIC."

Acting - Masters, Wm. Wright and Samuel B. Meader; Acting-Ensigns, A. F. Hamblen and W. H. Otis; Acting-Master's Mates, J. J. Kelleher and John Rigg; Acting-Assistant-Surgeon, Alex. Mackenzie; Acting-Assistant-Paymaster, Augustus Perrot; Engineers: Acting-First-Assistant, J. B. Lowell; Acting-Second-Assistant, Isaac Buck.

STEAMER "EMMA."

Acting-Master, Geo. B. Livingston; Acting-Assistant-Paymaster, C. H. Hammatt; Acting-Ensigns, A. Buhner, R. W. Elwell and C. A. Stewart; Acting-Master's Mates, I. S. Sampson and T. M. Webb; Engineers: Acting-Second-Assistants, W. T. Worrell and W. S. Sillman; Acting-Third-Assistants, Erastus Barry, John Ross, A. L. Churchill and George Foster.

STEAMER "GENERAL PUTNAM."

Acting-Master, H. H. Savage; Acting-Ensigns, Wm. Jennings and H. R. Fowle; Acting-Master's Mates, W. F. Gregg, J. H. Gilley and B. H. Spear; Engineers: Acting - Second-Assistant, J. Henry; Acting-Third-Assistants, A. F. Rockefeller and Wm P. Higgins.

STEAMER "VICTORIA."

Acting Masters, Chas. W. Lee and Alfred Everson; Acting-Ensign, Paul Borner; Acting-Master's Mates, B. W. Tucker and Wm. Moody; Acting-Assistant-Surgeon, John G. Park; Acting-Assistant-Paymaster, Samuel Thomas; Acting-Third-Assistant Engineer, John Haversfield.

STEAMER "HUNCHBACK."

Acting-Master, Robert G. Lee; Acting-Ensign, E. K. Valentine; Acting-Master's Mates, John Maddock and J. F. Sias; Acting-Assistant-Paymaster, Henry Cushing; Acting-Second-Assistant Engineer, M. Smith.

STEAMER "SHAWSHEEN."

Acting-Master, Henry A. Phelon; Acting-Ensign, Charles Ringot; Acting-Master's Mate, Wm. Rushmore; Engineers: Acting-Second-Assistant, Richard Anderson; Acting-Third-Assistant, John Wall.

SHIP "RELEASE."

Acting-Master, Jonathan Baker; Acting-Ensign, F. A. Gross; Acting-Master's Mate, F. T. Baldwin; Acting-Assistant Surgeon, John Spare; Acting-Assistant Paymaster, G. L. Ely.

STEAMER "SAMUEL ROTAN."

Acting-Master, Wm. G. Nutting; Acting-Ensigns, T. W. Spencer and W. H. Jennings; Acting-Master's Mates, C. H. Packer and W. L. Lindley.

SLOOP "GRANITE."

Acting-Master, Ephraim Boomer; Acting-Master's Mate, Wm. B. Miles.

STEAMER "WHITEHEAD."

Acting-Ensign, Geo. W. Barrett; Acting-Master's Mates, T. E. Quayle, T. M. Nelson and W. S. Baldwin; Engineers: Acting-Second-Assistant, Moses Peterson; Acting-Third-Assistants, R. H. Ryan and G. B. McDermott.

STEAMER "COHASSET."

Acting-Ensign, P. C. Asserson; Acting-Master's Mate, E. H. Schmidt; Engineers: Acting-Third-Assistants, J. A. Spaulding and J. H. Tinn.

STEAMER "FAH-KEE."

Acting-Ensigns, F. R. Webb, D. W. Carroll, E. W. Pelton, J. W. Luscomb and John Williams; Acting-Master's Mates, H. A. Winslow and A. W. Harvey; Acting-Assistant Paymaster, A. B. Thornton; Engineers: Acting-Second-Assistant, G. W. Foster; Acting-Third-Assistants, E. F. Lewis, J. H. Hutton, Gilbert Webb and Andrew Harris.

STEAMER "SEYMOUR."

Acting - Ensign, J. L. Hayes; Acting - Master's Mates, Edwin Smith and J. B. Bailey; Engineers: Acting-Second-Assistant, Newton Eggleston; Acting-Third-Assistants, John Whittaker and Philip Hubletz.

TUG "ALERT."

Acting-Ensign, John Bishop; Engineers: Acting-Second-Assistant, Wm. Mahan; Acting-Third-Assistants, S. D. Edmund and Eli Simpson.

TUG "ZOUAVE."

Acting-Master's Mates, J. F. Daggett and T. H. P. Gross; Engineers: Acting-Third-Assistants, S. M. Van Clief, Richard Wareham and J. W. Cross.

STORE-SHIP "ALBEMARLE."

Acting-Assistant Paymaster, E. Mellach; Gunner, E. A. McDonald; Carpenter, M. W. Paul.

CHAPTER XLI.

THE RED RIVER EXPEDITION,

Under Major-General N. P. Banks, assisted by the Navy under Rear-Admiral David D. Porter.

The Origin, Objects and Plan of the Expedition.—The Naval Vessels and Troops Assemble at the Mouth of the Red River. — Removal of Obstructions. — Capture of the Confederate Camp at Simmsport. — Attack and Capture of Fort De Russy.—Arrival of the Fleet and Troops at Alexandria.—Up the Falls. — The Abominable Cotton Traffic. — General A. J. Smith's "Ragged Guerillas."—Bridge of Cotton. — Advance on Shreveport. — Banks Meets a Reverse near Pleasant Hill.—Battle at Sabine Cross Roads.—Confederates make Good Use of Banks' Cannon and Army Wagons.—Battle at Pleasant Hill.—Banks Victorious. but Orders a Retreat to Grand Ecore.—Retreat of the Fleet Impeded.—Engagement between the "Osage" and "Lexington" and 2,500 Confederates under General Green.—Reports of Lieutenant-Commander Selfridge and General Kilby Smith.—The Army and Navy at Grand Ecore.—Minor Engagements.—Battle at Cane River.—The "Eastport" Blown Up.—The Attack on the Little "Cricket."—Fearful Scene of Carnage.—The "Juliet" Disabled.—Batteries Engaged Along the River.—Dissatisfaction of the Army.—The Squadron in a Bad Position.

N O official account detailing the particulars of this unfortunate expedition was forwarded by General Banks until long after the expedition failed.

A question has been standing for many years as to who originated it, and this has been settled by the highest authority. General Grant, in his Memoirs, says that the expedition originated with General Halleck, who urged General Banks, with all his authority, to undertake it. This is, without doubt, the origin of the affair.

After the fall of Vicksburg and Port Hudson, General Sherman proposed to Admiral Porter an expedition to Shreveport, La., *via* Red River; but on careful inquiry it was found that the water was unusually low for the season of the year, and therefore the expediency of a movement was doubted. But, as General Sherman was anxious to undertake the expedition, and promised to be in Natchez in the latter part of February, 1864, Admiral Porter ordered the following vessels to be ready near the mouth of Red River to accompany the Army whenever the latter should commence its march : the "Essex," "Benton," "Lafayette," "Choctaw," "Chillicothe." "Ozark," "Louisville," "Carondelet," "Eastport," "Pittsburg," "Mound City," "Osage," "Neosho," "Ouichita," "Fort Hindman," "Lexington," "Cricket," "Gazelle," "Juliet," and "Black Hawk" (flag-ship). This squadron comprised the most formidable part of the Mississippi fleet, only the lighter vessels being left to protect the Mississippi, the Ohio, and their tributaries; for, supposing that the Army would send a large force into the interior of Louisiana, Admiral Porter determined there should be no want of floating batteries for the troops to fall back on in case of disaster.

The Admiral had written to General Sherman that he did not think the time propitious for ascending Red River, and when he arrived in Natchez he found that Sherman had gone to New Orleans to see General Banks. The impression was that he went there to obtain Banks' co-operation in the great raid through the South, which Sherman afterwards so successfully accomplished without Banks' assistance.

By looking at the map, it will be readily seen how valuable a position Mobile would have been at such a time if held by the Union troops, its railroad system connecting with all the Southern roads, by which Sherman could have been supplied with provisions and stores, as well as reinforcements of men in case of necessity, while the straggling forces of the enemy between him and the Gulf would have been cut off. It would strike the military observer that to insure complete success Mobile should have been captured at the time Sherman started on his raid, which would have placed the entire country between him and the sea at the disposal of the Federal forces.

Fortunately, as matters turned out, General Sherman was able to overcome all obstacles that impeded his progress, and to subsist his army on the country through which he passed.

At the time Sherman went to New Orleans to see General Banks, the latter had under his command at least 50,000 men, and could have easily captured Mobile, then garrisoned by only about 10,000 troops; but this place, so easy of access and so easily captured from the land side, was left unnoticed until the latter part of the war. Its capture was then undertaken by Rear-Admiral Thatcher and General Canby. The result was the loss of several vessels blown up by torpedoes, which the Confederates were able to lay down with impunity.

General Banks had been writing to Admiral Porter up to the latter part of February, 1864, to co-operate with him in an advance into the Red River region, and in his answers the Admiral had tried to impress on the General the impropriety of such a movement at the then low stage of water, recommending him to wait until there was a prospect of a rise.

The General, however, insisted that he

had certain information of a rise in Red River, and hinted that if he failed in his expedition it would be for want of assistance from the Navy. The Admiral therefore determined that, if Sherman gave up the enterprise, he would co-operate with Banks. The former had never allowed the military authorities to wait for him when anything was to be done to carry on their work, and did not propose to do so on this occasion, although he felt that he was being entangled in an embarrassing predicament, from which it would require all his energies to extricate himself.

When Sherman returned from New Orleans, he informed the Admiral of his proposed advance into the interior of the South, and having abandoned the idea of undertaking the Red River expedition, he had promised General Banks to lend him 10,000 men, under the command of General A. J. Smith, whom he felt sure would co-operate with the Navy in the most energetic manner. And now, finding that Banks was determined to start on this expedition regardless of consequences, Admiral Porter resolved to do everything in his power to assist his military operations.

To make his success certain, General Halleck had determined to send an army into Arkansas under General Steele. This force reached Little Rock early in March, and, after providing themselves with stores and munitions of war, departed from that place on the 24th, and, after a hard march, arrived at Arkadelphia, March 29th, where, for the present, we will leave them.

General Banks had informed the Admiral that he would march an army of 36,000 men to Alexandria, La., and would meet him at that place on the 17th of March. On the 10th of March the naval vessels had assembled at the mouth of Red River, and, on the 11th, General A. J. Smith arrived with 10,000 excellent soldiers in transports. After inspecting the forces on shore, the Army and Navy moved up the river on the 12th, the fleet of gun-boats followed by the Army transports. As the largest vessels could barely pass the bar at the mouth of Red River, owing to the low stage of

THE "BLACK HAWK," ADMIRAL PORTER'S FLAG-SHIP.

water, the Admiral could not cherish any very favorable hopes for the future; but the party were fairly embarked on the expedition, and the only course was to continue and do the best that could be done.

The Confederates, having been notified that a movement would soon be made up Red River, had used all their energies in preparing to repel the invaders. Some eight miles below Fort De Russy they commenced a series of works near the Bend of the Rappiones, commanding a difficult pass of the river, and placed formidable obstructions to prevent the passage of the gun-boats.

therefore, that it was best to land the troops; so the Admiral turned off into the Atchafalaya River with the "Benton," "Lexington," "Chillicothe," "Louisville," "Mound City," "Carondelet," "Ouichita," "Pittsburg," and "Gazelle," followed by the troops in transports; while the rest of the gun-boats pushed on up Red River, with instructions to remove the obstructions, but not to attack Fort De Russy until the flag-ship's arrival, or until General Smith's troops came in sight.

The enemy had at this place some 5,000 men, and the only chance of capturing them was by a combined movement of the Army and Navy.

THE FLEET OF GUN-BOATS, UNDER REAR-ADMIRAL PORTER, STARTING OUT, FOLLOWED BY THE ARMY TRANSPORTS, HAVING ON BOARD 10,000 SOLDIERS, UNDER GEN. A. J. SMITH, MAY 12, 1864.

(FROM AN ORIGINAL PEN-AND-INK DRAWING BY REAR-ADMIRAL H. WALKE.)

These obstructions consisted of a line of heavy piles driven deep into the muddy bottom, and extending quite across the river, supported by a second tier of shorter ones below, on which rested braces and ties from the upper line. Immediately below the piles, a raft of heavy timber, well secured, extended across the river, a portion of the logs resting on the bottom. Finally, a forest of trees had been cut from the banks and floated down upon the piles, making an apparently impassable obstruction.

When the Admiral found the character of these obstructions, he feared that they would delay the vessels so long that the enemy would escape from Fort De Russy, and destroy all their stores and munitions of war. General Smith and he agreed,

At about noon, on the 12th of March, the Federal forces arrived at Simmsport, and found the enemy posted in force some three miles back of that place. The commanding officer of the "Benton," Lieutenant-Commander James A. Greer, was ordered to land his crew and drive in the enemy's pickets; and, General Smith's transports coming up, the troops landed and took possession of the Confederate camp, the enemy retreating towards Fort De Russy.

That night General Smith concluded to follow the enemy by land, while the Admiral agreed to proceed up the Red River, with all the gun-boats and transports, and meet the Army at Fort De Russy.

In the meantime, the gun-boats that had been sent on in advance had reached the obstructions, and their crews were endeavoring to force a passage. It was a herculean job, but the energetic sailors had had too much experience in the strange episodes of the civil war to quail before such obstacles. The piles near the banks were first removed, and a rush of water came through, carrying away the sides of the banks; then, by pulling up piles and ramming the obstructions with the iron-clads, an opening was made in twelve hours for the passage of the fleet.

The "Eastport," "Osage," "Fort Hindman," and "Cricket" proceeded up within a short distance of Fort De Russy, where the advance of General Smith had arrived, and there was quite a brisk firing of artillery and small arms. The gun-boats, however, could not take part in this skirmish without risking the safety of the Federal soldiers. A 100-pound rifle-shell was fired at the water battery, which burst over it, and drove the enemy out; but to have continued the fire upon the main fort would have injured friends more than foes, the former being in a direct line with the fire of the gun-boats.

The progress of the fleet around from the Atchafalaya had necessarily been slow, encumbered with so many transports, and the barricade had partly filled up again, so that it took several hours to pass through the obstructions; but the flag-ship reached the fort in time to see the enemy evacuating it, and the Union soldiers taking possession.

The fort was originally garrisoned with 5,000 men, under General Walker, who had marched out to meet the Federal Army, leaving 24 officers and 300 men to defend it; but, if Walker wished to meet Smith's forces, he was disappointed, for the latter saw nothing of him.

On his march from Simmsport, General Smith was greatly annoyed by sharpshooters, and was compelled to bridge innumerable bayous. When he reached Monksville, within three miles of the fort, he was informed that a strong force of the enemy would dispute his passage. The 3d Indiana Battery was placed in position, and General Mower formed his men for the attack. The first line was under the immediate command of Colonel W. J. Shaw, 14th Iowa Infantry, commanding 2d Brigade, 3d Division, 15th Army Corps, composed of the 13th and 32d Iowa and the 3d Indiana Battery. The space intervening between the Union troops and the fort was obstructed with fallen trees; on the left of the line, a thick wood afforded an excellent cover for riflemen.

It was now 4 P. M., and, although the Union troops had been marching and building bridges all day, they came up to their work as fresh as if they had just broken camp. Part of the 14th Iowa were deployed as skirmishers to within three hundred yards of the enemy's works, occupying some rifle-pits which had been thrown up by the Confederates, and during the progress of the fight did good execution as sharp-shooters.

In the meantime, the 58th Illinois, 8th Wisconsin and 29th Iowa, who had come up from the rear, were advancing to obtain position for attack. The fire from the fort all this time was rapid, but did little execution. Shot, shell and musketry were passing between the combatants for two hours, while the naval vessels were unable to fire for fear of killing their friends. At the end of that time, all of Smith's troops having got into position, they advanced and carried the works without difficulty, capturing 24 officers, 275 men and 10 pieces of artillery.

This affair was well managed on the part of the Army, whose loss was small; General Smith was an able commander, and his soldiers were veterans—each man, as it proved afterwards, was a host in himself.

It was pleasant to see the United States flag floating over a work which had been built with so much trouble and expense to the Confederates, and the Navy regretted that it could not take a more important part in the affair.

Their operations at Fort De Russy showed the fortitude of the Federal soldiers; and, if the rest of Banks' men were of the same material, there was no reason why the army should not reach Shreveport in triumph.

An order had been sent to Lieutenant-Commander S. L. Phelps to push on with the fastest and lightest-draft gun-boats to Alexandria, as soon as the army should reach the fort, in order to seize any steamers that might be lying there with steam down. Owing to obstructions in the river, the dispatch-boat carrying the message was delayed five hours, and Phelps reached Alexandria just thirty minutes too late, the swiftest of the naval vessels arriving just in time to see six steamers escaping up "the Falls." One of them, the "Countess," having grounded, was burned by the enemy.

The fleet had thus reached Alexandria on the 15th of March, two days earlier than had been promised General Banks. On the day following, there were nine gun-boats lying off the town, and one hundred and eighty sailors were landed, to occupy the place and take possession of any Confederate Government property that might be stored there. The inhabitants were respectfully treated, and everything was as quiet as a New England village.

General Smith remained behind a few days to destroy the formidable works which he had captured, and a gun-boat was left at Fort De Russy to try some experiments with rifle-guns on three casemated water batteries covered with several thicknesses of railroad iron. A little experience satisfied the experimenters that such works could not resist the heavy naval artillery, and orders were given to blow them up; thus destroying the formidable barrier intended to close Red River against the fleet. For their dimensions, these works were as strong as any ever built in the Confederacy. After 3,000 pounds of powder had been exploded, there remained three huge excavations, while the whole vicinity was strewn with broken timbers and twisted iron, pre-

progress up the river. This was General Mower's idea, apparently forgetting that the gun-boats could, in a very short time, have destroyed forts, troops and all, with their 100 guns. The Admiral endeavored to show General Mower, who was a fearless man, and in favor of pushing on regardless of obstacles, that the 5,000 troops were too few in number to defeat the 20,000 Confederates in the advance, who were well supplied with artillery. Besides, he urged that it would be very discourteous to General Smith to go forward without consulting him, and leave him, with only 5,000 men, unprotected by the gun-boats. Desperate

| MASKED BATTERY. | "BENTON," FLAG-SHIP. | GEN. A. J. SMITH'S ARMY ASSAILING THE FORT. MONITOR "OSAGE." | FORT. GUN-BOAT. "FORT HINDMAN." | IRON-CLAD. RAM "EASTPORT." | CASEMATED FORTS AND RIFLE PITS. |

CAPTURE OF FORT DE RUSSY.

senting a scene more easily imagined than described.

On the 16th, General Mower reached Alexandria with about 5,000 men, in transports; and, having formed a rather low estimate of the enemy's forces in this region, he urged Admiral Porter to push on at once with the force they then had, and try and get to Shreveport in advance of the main army.

The Confederate general, Walker, had exhibited very little enterprise; for, with the 5,000 men under his command, he might have seriously impeded the Federal advance, and then at Fort De Russy have offered a stubborn resistance to further

as this scheme of Mower's appeared, we think it would have succeeded better than General Banks' movement on Shreveport a short time afterwards.

General Taylor had occupied Alexandria with 15,000 men, and had hurriedly decamped on the approach of the Army and Navy, leaving three pieces of artillery behind.

On the 18th of March, General A. J. Smith arrived, ready to march at a moment's notice when Banks should give the order. Meanwhile, there was no news whatever of General Banks' whereabouts. His cavalry arrived on the 19th, and on the 25th, eight days after he had agreed to meet the Admiral at Alexandria, he appeared upon the scene. Then commenced a series of delays, which culminated in disasters, that have left a reproach upon the Red River expedition which time cannot efface; for, no matter how gallant the officers and men may have been, they share in the humiliation brought upon them by an unmilitary commander, who, at the head of nearly 40,000 men, fully equipped, was driven out of a country they could have held forever had their leader been possessed of the qualifications of a military man.

We sincerely believe that, had General A. J. Smith undertaken this expedition with only his 10,000 well-tried soldiers, supported by the fleet of gun-boats, they would have all been in Shreveport by the 5th of April; for there was no reason to entertain much fear of General Taylor and his troops, already greatly demoralized by the Union success so far.

If Taylor could not, with 15,000 men and heavy fortifications, hold the entrance to his country, how could he expect to resist the march of 10,000 veterans, supported by more than 100 heavy guns on board the war-vessels? There were never better soldiers than those under General Smith, and both he and General Mower were worthy to lead them.

When Smith's command joined the expedition they had just finished a long march, were greatly in want of clothing, had few wagons, and were without tents, yet they were the happiest-looking soldiers ever seen under arms. It was astounding how these men had learned to live upon the enemy. They seemed to be independent of the commissary department, every soldier was himself a commissary; and as for tents or barracks, they did very well without them. In less than twenty-four hours after their arrival in Alexandria, they had rummaged the country for ten miles up and down the river, one of the most fertile districts in the United States, where all their wants could be supplied without expense to the Government.

Here Colonel Shaw luxuriated with his brigade on the plantation of ex-Governor Moore, the prime mover in the secession of Louisiana, who now had ample opportunity of seeing for himself how the secession matter worked. It was a just retribution, for, notwithstanding the hospitality of the South, we have no doubt the ex-governor begrudged the soldiers the good things they were enjoying at his expense.

Notwithstanding the Federal soldiers were scattered in all directions, they were not troubled by the Confederates, who hovered around in detached bands of a few hundred men, apparently as much demoralized as General Taylor and his army of 15,000.

The Federal forces were on the *qui vive*, however, for anything that might happen, and one dark, rainy night, General Mower, with a party of his men, fell in with a courier bearing dispatches to General Taylor, who was encamped some nine miles in the rear. Mower, assuming the character of a Confederate officer, threatened to hang the courier as a Yankee spy, when the latter, to show his good faith, led the supposed Confederate troops right into the enemy's camp, which was captured with 22 officers, 260 privates, 4 pieces of artillery, 150 horses, and all the arms and munitions. Had there been an opportunity to capture the other outlying parties, General Mower would have accomplished it, but the Confederate commander-in-chief was a wary old soldier, disposed to act on the defensive.

It was not until the 25th of March that General Banks' infantry commenced arriving under the command of General Franklin. It was as fine a body of troops as were ever seen, and the best dressed and equipped of any soldiers in the Southwest. Notwithstanding a march of twenty-one miles, they came in quite fresh and full of spirits.

But more than a week of valuable time had been lost since the 17th instant, the day on which General Banks promised to meet the Navy at Alexandria, and the conclusion arrived at was that the General did not possess the military virtue of punctuality which the Navy had recognized in Generals Grant, Sherman, A. J. Smith, and other officers with whom they had hitherto co-operated.

As soon as the Admiral reached Alexandria, he commenced getting the vessels above the "Falls," although the water was falling in the river at the rate of an inch a day, and the larger vessels had not more than six inches to spare. He trusted to good fortune to get the vessels down again, or to that great rise in the water which General Banks had been informed would certainly come in May or June.

General Banks had apparently come into the Red River country intending to stay, for he was provided with everything necessary to maintain a large army. Transports with provisions, clothing and munitions of war were daily arriving, and large buildings in Alexandria converted into store-houses were rapidly filled up.

By the 29th of March, the Admiral had all his vessels over the "Falls," except the "Eastport," a long, heavy iron-clad, which detained the fleet two days. As soon as she was over, Lieutenant-Commander Phelps was directed to proceed to Grand Ecore and be ready to cover the army when it should arrive there. The following named vessels were under his command: the "Eastport," "Cricket," "Mound City," "Chillicothe,"

"Fort Hindman," "Lexington," "Osage," and "Neosho."

The week lost caused the expedition irreparable injury, for the enemy was not only enabled to recruit his forces, but the river had fallen six inches, which was a great deal for vessels having so little to spare.

The general tried to lay the blame for his detention on the gun-boats, but this would hardly answer, since the light-draft vessels, mounting over fifty guns, had passed the "Falls" and were ready to ascend the river before Banks reached the rendezvous. The six days General Banks passed in Alexandria prior to his onward movement were frittered away. He moved into comfortable quarters and spent his time in ordering an election in the parish of Rapides, establishing people in power who professed to be Union men—a proceeding to which there could have been no objection if the objects of the expedition had not thereby been neglected.

General Banks came from New Orleans to Alexandria in a large steamer called the "Black Hawk." This vessel, known as "General Banks' flag-ship," was of the same name as Admiral Porter's flag-ship, an unpleasant circumstance, since it happened that the Navy incurred some of the odium which attached to the transport steamer. She was loaded with cotton bagging, rope, etc., and became the rendezvous of a motley collection of people, cotton speculators, and camp followers. Everybody began to surmise that this expedition was intended for other purposes than the conquest of the Red River country. The story then told has since proved to have had some foundation, and is a hitherto unwritten piece of history.

Soon after General Banks took command at New Orleans, he had given several passes to get cotton from the Red River country, but it had been seized by the gun-boats along the river, and turned over to the agents of the Treasury, or sent to an Admiralty Court for adjudication.

Many persons had urged upon President Lincoln the importance of getting out of Red River all the cotton possible for the use of Union manufacturers, instead of forcing the Confederates to ship it abroad, which, perhaps, was a wise idea, if it could have been done under proper restrictions; but such a course opened the door to a great deal of dishonesty, besides affording an opportunity for supplying the Confederates with arms and munitions, of which they stood greatly in need.

Two naval officers captured parties of Confederates—military men—in the act of loading steamers with cotton for New Orleans, the said persons being supplied with passes purporting to be by authority of General Banks. No doubt, they expected to receive, in return, money or articles of value, when the naval officers arrested them, and would have seized the steamers had not the latter shoved off and left their friends in the lurch.

We do not mean to say that General Banks exceeded his authority in these matters, but we know that it was calculated to prolong the war; and, as the naval commander had not been notified by the Government that facilities for getting out cotton would be granted to private citizens, he took upon himself the responsibility of putting a stop to the practice.

It was evident that this sort of traffic would soon demoralize the whole expedition, and probably defeat its every object. A gun-boat was stationed at the mouth of Red River, whose captain had orders not to permit any except naval vessels and Army transports to ascend. This, however, did not keep out the cotton agents, who managed to get up in the transports, not always to the satisfaction of General Banks.

On one occasion, a steamer loaded with stores of all kinds, and furnished with a permit from Washington to trade within the military lines, appeared at the mouth of the river. The Admiral refused to recognize the owner of this permit and ordered him to depart, which he was obliged to do, leaving a message to the effect that he would make it so hot for the naval officer in Washington that the latter would have to resign his command, etc., etc. On receiving this message, the commanding officer of the gun-boat at the mouth of the Red River was directed to seize the vessel and send her to Cairo. He chased her to Memphis, where, on arriving, he found the steamer had unloaded all her contraband of war, otherwise she would have been condemned.

We mention these things to give some idea of the rush for the cotton region of Louisiana, and the demoralization likely to ensue had every speculator been allowed to go where he pleased under permits, or in any other way. There were Treasury agents enough authorized by Government to seize cotton, and there was nothing to warrant the presence of cotton purchasers on an expedition which had for its ostensible object the redemption of this region from secession.

It was only when the Army was in retreat, after the battle of Mansfield, that the supposed objects of the expedition were learned. It was stated that before Banks' army left New Orleans there was an arrangement that the General should go up Red River with a force before which the Confederates would retreat; that Banks would seize all the cotton in the country, for which he would give receipts, and that, on the arrival of the cotton in New Orleans, the holders of the receipts were to receive five or six cents a pound as their share. General Banks' conduct gave some corroboration to these reports, and no evidence he afterwards gave before the Committee on the Conduct of the War eradicated the impression that they were true.

It was attempted to divert attention from Banks by trying to throw the responsibility on President Lincoln for giving permits to Butler and Casey; but those men derived little benefit from their license to trade—their cotton was taken from them, and they returned from the expedition wiser and poorer men.

As long as Admiral Porter had been associated with Generals Grant and Sherman in the midst of intricate and embarrassing operations, he had never to complain of the least want of courtesy on their part, and never had the slightest dispute with either of them. Now he was sorry to see a prospect of difficulties at the very outset of the expedition. The tone of some of the officials of Banks' army was so different from what he had been in the habit of witnessing that it created bad feeling at once—this extended not only to the Navy but to the corps of General A. J. Smith as well.

When Smith joined the expedition he had just finished a long march through the interior of the Confederacy, and his men were without proper clothing and other necessaries, and made a poor figure beside Banks' well-equipped troops; but when it came to actual warfare, they were famous fighters. They were men who had lain for months in the trenches at Vicksburg, had gone through the hardships of Chickasaw Bayou, had helped win Arkansas Post, etc., etc.; yet when Banks first saw these veterans, he exclaimed, "What, in the name of Heaven, did Sherman send me these ragged guerillas for?" At Mansfield he found these "ragged guerillas" saved the day and the honor of his army!

We have no doubt that when Banks saw his fine army under General Franklin, and was told how easily those troops had put the Confederates along the route to flight, he felt that he could do very well without the corps of A. J. Smith and the Navy. For this reason he treated General Smith with neglect from the first, although he took care to put that General in the advance. General Smith was a fearless, outspoken man, who felt that the cotton speculation would be the bane of the expedition, and did not hesitate to say so. He foresaw the misrepresentations that would be made of officers who would not lend themselves to the schemes of the cotton speculators.

It was very aggravating for an officer to find himself attacked in the newspapers at home while devoting all his energies to overcome the enemies of his country, and to be reviled by a lot of people who had neither the courage nor the inclination to take part in putting down the Rebellion—Northern "copperheads," who did all in their power to shake the confidence of the public in the men at the head of the armies and fleets.

General Banks, having delayed long at Alexandria, directed General Smith's command to advance to Bayou Rapides, where the latter encamped on the 27th of March, 1864. On the 30th, part of Banks' army passed General Smith; but it was not until April 2d that Smith received orders to embark his men in the transports, and proceed to Grand Ecore, where they disembarked, and encamped at Natchitoches, near by. No opposition had thus far been met with, and one or two guns fell into the hands of the Navy a few miles below Grand Ecore.

Up to this time the opinion seemed general that the Confederates did not intend to offer any opposition to the Federal advance, and that Kirby Smith, the Confederate general, would "adhere to his agreement"—viz., to let the Army and the contractors get all the cotton they could find. The very deliberate movements of the Army gave color to these reports, and the large number of empty steam transports strengthened the idea that it was intended to load them with cotton. Besides these, there were seven or eight hundred army wagons, ostensibly to carry rations for General Banks' division, while A. J. Smith had hardly any wagons.

Anticipating the wants of the Army, the Navy brought along with them two of the large barges built some time before by General Fremont to use in making a bridge. These were turned over to the military authorities at Grand Ecore. The second day after the arrival of the expedition, Lieutenant-Commander Phelps, of the "Eastport," reported to the Admiral that these two barges, which would hold three or four hundred bales each, and another barge belonging to Butler and Casey, were being filled with cotton, under superintendence of an officer of General Banks' staff, the cotton being hauled to the bank by army wagons. Lieutenant - Commander Phelps was directed, as soon as the barges were loaded, to seize the cotton as prize to the Navy, which was accordingly done; but, soon after, the Admiral received a request from General Banks to turn the barges over to the Army, that he might bridge the river at Grand Ecore. This request was immediately complied with, and a fine bridge was made for the passage of wagons, although the cotton, after a day or two's use, looked much the worse for wear. The Army held the barges and the cotton, and they finally had to be used in the construction of the great dam at Alexandria.

The Confederates had about 16,000 men in the field, and the Federals about 36,000; but up to this time the former had retreated without resistance, leaving the Federals their deserted camping-grounds, the best positions, and all the cotton in the country. It was so unlike anything seen before in expeditions against the enemy, that people could not help suspecting an understanding of some kind with the Confederates, otherwise they would have set fire to every bale of cotton rather than permit any to fall into Union hands.

On the 6th of April, all arrangements for an advance having been made, Banks' army, composed of part of the 13th and 19th army corps, under Franklin and Emory, and a cavalry division of about 3,500 men, under General Lee, marched from Nachitoches. General A. J. Smith followed on the 7th with his division of the 16th corps, excepting 2,500 men under General T. Kilby Smith, who had been sent to escort the transports carrying supplies. When the fleet started, there were about thirty of these transports in company, but their numbers were afterwards increased by the addition of some large empty steamers, which delayed the advance owing to their too great draft of water.

It was arranged that the naval vessels and transports were to meet the Army at Springfield Landing, about thirty miles below Shreveport, the third day after departure.

The difficulties of navigation were very great, as there were few pilots, and they were not familiar with the river channel as it then existed, it having changed very much within a year or two; but the fleet managed to surmount all obstacles, and reached the rendezvous within an hour of the time specified in the arrangement with General Banks. As the General was not very punctual, no one was surprised at his non-appearance. It was not supposed that 36,000 men would be long delayed by the 16,000 General Taylor had at that time between them and Shreveport, and the Navy wondered at not seeing the van of the Army at this point. Nothing was to be seen, and the solitude of the grave brooded over the spot.

The further advance of the transports was here prevented by a very large steamer called the "New Falls City," that the Confederates had placed across the channel, her ends resting on the banks, and her hull, broken in the middle, resting on the bottom.

It required a great deal of trouble to get rid of this obstruction, and while the appointed officers were examining into the best ways and means of removing the vessel, the Admiral proposed to General Kilby Smith that they should reconnoitre the country on horseback. They had ridden about a mile when they saw a party of men crouching and running through the high grass and coming to a halt. The Admiral remarked to the General, "Banks has been defeated, or we wouldn't see those men here. If Banks was still advancing, the outposts would keep on the main road to Shreveport. If defeated, the enemy's look-outs would be watching for our arrival, and be ready to turn their whole force upon us, and it behoves us to be wary."

It was then agreed upon between General Smith and the Admiral to land the artillery at once, and make a dash for a short distance, as if they intended an advance, which would start the Confederate look-outs off to report the landing; then the plan was to turn, and, embarking, proceed down the river until they could communicate with some part of the main army. This was rapidly accomplished, and late in the day the gun-boats and transports proceeded down the river in good order, prepared to give the enemy a warm reception if he should attack them. It was taken for granted if General Banks was defeated he would lose some of his artillery, and that the fleet would have it used against them sooner or later.

The movement proved to be a good one; the enemy were deceived, and, expecting to have the fleet at their mercy next morning, made no demonstration. All that night the vessels moved slowly down the Red River, and at 10 o'clock a courier from General Banks came on board the flag-ship, and informed the Admiral that the Army had met with a reverse, and was falling back to Pleasant Hill, about fifteen miles from the battle-ground of Mansfield, and thirty-five miles from Nachitoches. This point was sixty miles distant, and the victorious enemy was between the fleet and the Federal Army.

Orders came also for General Kilby Smith to return with his troops and transports to Grand Ecore, and the expedition proceeded towards that point as rapidly as the difficult navigation would permit. The gun-boats were placed so as to cover the transports, and the field-artillery was mounted on the upper decks of the latter; barricades were made for riflemen—in short, every possible preparation for the storm which was coming.

Here was a sudden collapse to what bid fair at one time to be a successful expedition, all owing to the unmilitary character of the commanding general, who ignored the advice of the generals under him.

When General Banks concentrated his forces at Grand Ecore, it was supposed that he would take the road along the river, where he could at all times be supported by the 100 guns carried by the vessels of the Navy, and where he could be supplied by the Army transports, instead of encumbering his army with a multitude of wagons. It was thought that, as Banks got further into the heart of the enemy's country, he would adopt precautions against an attack from the 15,000 or 20,000 men under General Taylor, who might not know of the arrangements of the cotton speculators, if any such understanding did exist. Instead of taking precautions, General Banks started on his march as if the whole country was free from the enemy; and so certain was he of reaching his place of destination that he named Springfield Landing as the point where the fleet was to meet him with supplies.

His line of march was twenty miles away from the river, along a rough and narrow road, through a miserable country, covered with pine woods, with few inhabitants and very little water. All the knowledge Banks had of the country was what he could gather from Confederate sources. Instead of putting the infantry in the van, General Lee was sent in front with about 3,500 mounted infantry — badly mounted and worse drilled—with 150 heavy wagons in their rear, the infantry following some distance behind.

When General Banks' army was attacked on the 8th of April at Sabine Cross Roads, General A. J. Smith's division was ten miles in the rear, near Pleasant Hill, and, although they heard the roar of artillery, the first Smith's men knew of the disaster to the main army was from Colonel Clarke, who had ridden rapidly to inform them that the enemy had killed, wounded and captured over 2,000 Federal soldiers, had taken 150 wagons, all the stores, and 22 pieces of artillery. How all this was done can only be understood by examining Banks' line of march, which, it appears, was also his line of battle.

It seems the further Banks' army advanced into the country the deeper became the gullies and the worse became the roads, while the thick woods on all sides afforded a fine shelter for the enemy.

Up to the 8th of April it had rained heavily. General Franklin, who left Grand Ecore on the 6th, marched but seventeen miles on that and eighteen miles on the succeeding day, being much impeded by his large wagon train; and it seems General Lee was so far in advance that he could not rely on the whole of Franklin's force for support, as should have been the case. On the 7th, Lee's force had a severe skirmish with the enemy beyond Pleasant Hill, and, after some delay, a brigade of Franklin's infantry was sent to his assistance. Lee's cavalry were nothing more than infantry soldiers whom Banks had mounted, and as soon as fighting commenced they dismounted.

One can imagine how ill-arranged for battle was this army, with four regiments of dismounted horsemen in advance, mixed up with their horses, and fighting in gullies where they could be picked off by sharpshooters ensconced in the thick woods. No wonder General Lee sent to Franklin for assistance, who answered through Colonel Clarke, of Banks' staff, that if he could not hold his position he must fall back upon the main body of the infantry. It would have been better, however, if Lee had fallen back when he first encountered the enemy's advance, and sent the wagons to the rear, for a finer chance to have them captured could not have been offered.

Colonel Clarke, finding that Franklin was indisposed to send any troops to support Lee, went to General Banks, who sent a verbal order to Franklin to send a brigade of infantry to report to Lee at daylight next morning. General Franklin then ordered General Ransom to send a brigade, or a *division* if he saw fit. The brigades were so small that Franklin thought a division would better carry out General Banks' views; but Ransom sent a brigade, with which General Lee was satisfied.

Notwithstanding the demonstrations of the enemy in front, Banks did not seem to think there was any likelihood of a pitched battle taking place. He gave an order, through Franklin, directing Lee to proceed as far as possible on the night of the 7th, with his whole train, in order to give the infantry room to advance on the 8th. The forces of General Lee only advanced one mile between the 7th and 8th of April, and on the latter date Lee reported by letter to General Franklin that the enemy were in stronger force apparently than the day previous. He says: "I advanced this morning with ten regiments of mounted infantry (dismounted), three regiments of cavalry and a brigade of infantry. We are driving them, but they injure us some. I do not hasten forward my trains, as I wish to see the result certain first."

General Lee's idea was, perhaps, a good one, but he did not seem to realize that the enemy were leading him and his trains further into the trap; but General Banks should have seen this and withdrawn Lee in time, and pushed his infantry and artillery ahead to the attack.

Banks, however, does not appear to have kept in any position where he could see for himself what was going on, and seems to have been influenced in a great degree by an officer of his staff. Only on the night of the 7th did General Banks arrive at Franklin's headquarters from Grand Ecore, although the fighting commenced that afternoon, and Lee complained of a want of troops to keep from being driven in. Banks did not go to the front until late on the 8th, and then sent word to Franklin that the enemy were prepared to make a strong stand at the point where they were holding Lee, and that he (Franklin) "had better make arrangements" (! !) to bring up his infantry, and pass everything on the road, and that he would send him word when to move. He thought Franklin had better send back and push the trains forward, as manifestly the Army would be able to make a rest there.

Now, whether General Banks wanted the troops to push forward and rest, or fight, does not appear; but, as far as one can learn from the reports of officers, Banks seemed to be resting that army a great deal, when thousands were anxious to push on and join in the fray.

It seems evident that General Lee did everything after he engaged the enemy that a man could with the force at his command —a force not suited for that particular kind of service; and when he found himself outnumbered he sent for reinforcements, when Banks dispatched to his assistance only 1,200 men. These were soon decimated, and 1,200 more were sent. Such small reinforcements amounted to nothing; and it does not require much military knowledge to see the folly of sending one small brigade of infantry to co-operate with a large body of cavalry in such an expedition.

From Lee's report it will appear that while the whole brigade of infantry was engaged on the 8th, only three regiments out of a whole division of cavalry were in action. The result, as General Lee expressed it, was that the first brigade of infantry "got very much embarrassed;" in other words, used up, and so Lee sent for another brigade. General Franklin protested strongly against thus sending brigade after brigade to be cut up in detail, but Banks gave the orders, and finding such halfway measures futile, directed Franklin to advance with a division of infantry, to be beaten in his turn.

The state of affairs was as follows: Lee some distance in advance of the wagon train had fought with the two brigades until he was cut up, had to retreat, and became mixed up with the wagon train and with the advancing division of Franklin's infantry, which in turn was driven back upon the train, the latter was jammed up, and when the time came for the artillery to retreat there was no way to get the guns

through the train, and they had to be abandoned.

Lee was not to blame for having his division hampered by the wagon train. He had applied to General Franklin to allow his train to move to the rear of the infantry; but Franklin told him he must take care of his own train, that he (F.) had already 750 wagons to look out for, and 150 additional wagons would make his train so unwieldy that he could not get into camp at the end of his day's march. Franklin cannot be held responsible for the disaster, but the wagon-train was.

Apparently, General Banks started on this expedition as if there was to be no fighting, and he stayed behind in Grand Ecore until the head of the army was fifty miles in advance, regardless of the circumstance that he might have been captured by Confederate stragglers. This, with the fact that he had so many wagons with his army, gave color to the stories that Banks and the cotton speculators were arranging about the bales that were to come down from Shreveport in empty army wagons and transports. The Confederates had no wagons worth mentioning until Banks had supplied them. A. J. Smith with 10,000 men had very few, and why Banks should require 900 for 30,000 men, who could sleep out of doors all the time much more comfortably than in tents, no man can tell. Had Banks understood the art of war, he would have ordered his trains to be parked when he saw that a battle was imminent.

It was not the intention of the enemy to bring on an engagement at the time it took place, but rather to draw the Federal troops as far into the interior as possible, and away from the gun-boats, into the marshes and bayous at Wallace's Lake, between Mansfield and Shreveport. In this difficult region the troops would have been entangled in swamps, and would have had to corduroy the roads for miles to get the trains along.

Had Banks been satisfied to let the cavalry go in advance, clearing the roads of outposts, and reporting the presence of the enemy's main body when they encountered it, all might have turned out well; but it appears he never gave himself much concern about the management of the Army until it was defeated.

He sailed up from New Orleans to Alexandria in a fine steamer, supplied with all comforts. He sailed again on the same vessel from Alexandria to Grand Ecore, and did not leave the latter place until Franklin's division had reached Pleasant Hill. Then, going to the front, and being ill-informed of the situation of affairs, Banks determined to win a battle without Franklin's aid.

If the cavalry had gone to the front alone

for merely its legitimate purposes, it would have marched slowly and cautiously; but, being reinforced by infantry, it got ahead faster than was prudent. Had the cavalry marched as it should have done, General A. J. Smith would have been at Pleasant Hill, only eight miles in the rear, the Army would have been in as compact a condition as could have been possible and the final result would have been different. Banks had probably never heard of the old rule, "Choose your own ground, and let the enemy attack you." At all events, he went directly contrary to the maxim; but even then he would have been successful had he waited a day longer.

Banks had two officers of the regular army, Franklin and Emory, in command of divisions, but he seemed to ignore them until he got hard pushed. General C. P. Stone, his chief-of-staff, was a clever officer, but he set aside his opinions. He allowed the enemy to bring on a battle on ground over which the Army would have to pass by a narrow road through a pine forest, filled with a dense undergrowth, with no room to handle men, much less to have a dress parade of army wagons. The Army could only march in very narrow columns.

General Banks cannot say he did not know the position of the Army when he brought on this battle, for Franklin had explained it all to him on his arrival at Pleasant Hill, and he passed along the whole line on his way to the front, where the cavalry was fighting, and could not help seeing how matters stood.

General Franklin was nominally in command of the Army when General Banks joined him at Pleasant Hill, but the latter went to the front without paying Franklin the courtesy of saying he was going to take command, and prepared to take all the glory if he succeeded. From our knowledge of the Army, it was evident that Banks was not in accord with any of his generals. They did not think him a good leader, to commence with, and they certainly had no reason to do so in the end. On his part, he seemed to care little for them or for their opinions.

Up to the time of Banks' arrival, General Lee considered Franklin in command; but when Lee referred to some order he had received from Franklin, Banks remarked, "I shall remain upon the field, General," without saying whether or not he took command. At all events, he gave such orders that his presence much embarrassed Lee in making arrangements.

It would appear, from evidence received from different sources, that, after Banks' arrival on the field, General Lee was allowed the management of this affair, although under the immediate command of General Franklin. He waited for no order from the latter, insisting on pushing ahead all the time, though Franklin intimated that if the enemy was in force in his front, he should fall back upon the infantry, and that he, Franklin, would not send him infantry support. In this Franklin was right; but it would have been better had he gone to the front himself, and taken a more decided command in the first instance. It was not desirable to bring on a general engagement in the then condition of the Army; and when Franklin finally did send a division to assist the fragments of brigades ordered to the front by Banks, his main body of some 6,000 men were seven miles in the rear, and fifteen miles back there were 8,000 more; while we know that, when Lee first called for support, the enemy had in position 8,000 infantry, with some artillery, and nobody could tell how many more in the background.

That the Federal soldiers did all that men could do in this first engagement, no one can deny; but if Banks had tried to place impediments in their way he could not have succeeded better. Colonel W. J. Landrum, commanding 4th brigade of Ransom's division, in a report to that officer, says: "My men have skirmished and marched through bushes and thickets for eight or nine miles, making in all a march of sixteen miles; they have no water, and are literally worn out. Can you have them relieved soon? General Lee insists on pushing ahead."

When General Ransom arrived on the field he found the road obstructed by the cavalry train, and, after a great deal of trouble, got through and arrived at the front with his troops. He found the enemy in force, a large body of infantry in line of battle on the edge of the woods, and two batteries of artillery about three-fourths of a mile in front, while considerable bodies of infantry were moving on the road leading to his right and rear. As Banks came on the field, at 3 p. m., Ransom reported to him, and from that moment Banks became responsible for what occurred.

On the arrival of the 3d brigade, the position of the 83d and 96th Ohio infantry were assigned opposite to that recommended by General Ransom, and in a place in which they should never have been put. The infantry on the right of the road were placed in a narrow belt of timber, dividing two large plantations, with open ground in front and cultivated fields in the rear. Nims' Battery was posted on a hill near the road, two hundred yards to the left of the belt of timber, and was supported by the 23d Wisconsin infantry. The 67th Indiana supported the battery on the right, together with the 77th and 130th Illinois, 48th Ohio, 19th Kentucky, 96th Ohio, a section of light artillery, and the 83d Ohio—in all, 2,413 infantry. The cavalry and mounted infantry under Lee were posted on the flanks and rear, having Colonel Dudley's brigade on the left, and Colonel Lucas' on the right, with skirmishers deployed in front of the infantry.

The enemy attacked this position at 4 P. M. His first line was driven back in confusion, but, recovering, he again advanced; unable, however, to withstand the fire from the Federal troops, the Confederates laid down 200 yards in front and returned the fire; at the same time a force was pressing the Federal left flank and driving the mounted infantry back. The 1st Indiana and Chicago Mercantile Batteries had just arrived on the field, and General Ransom directed them to be placed near a house occupied as Banks' headquarters, where they opened on the enemy, who had shown himself in strong force on the left flank, which it was evidently his purpose to turn—a purpose soon afterward accomplished after the infantry were driven in and Nims' battery captured.

This may be said to have been the turning-point of the battle, which was nearly lost to the Federals. The infantry, generally, behaved with great gallantry. The Chicago and 1st Indiana Batteries went promptly into action, but were soon so cut up that they were obliged to retreat, leaving their guns in the hands of the enemy.

The fact is, the guns had to be abandoned, because the cavalry wagon-train blocked up the road against all operations from first to last. Some went so far as to assert that the said wagon-train was the cause of all the disasters; and, although this may not be literally true, the world will naturally inquire why, on the approach of a heavy engagement, the wagons were not sent to the rear. There were men enough to have hauled them away had the horses been unable to do so. The fact is, the blame rests, and always will rest, on General Banks' conduct after he took command in person. The disaster was due to his sending forward small bodies of troops—which were defeated in detail—to support the cavalry, which should have been ordered to fall back until the main army came up.

In this day's fight the Federals had but 7,000 men and 26 field-pieces, a very large proportion of ordnance to the number of infantry. The natural consequence was that, when a retreat was ordered, the artillery had to be abandoned for want of time to force it through the obstructions of wagons and bodies of infantry.

The 3d Division, 13th army corps, arrived on the field in season to check the advance of the enemy; and General Franklin, who came on the field in person, was wounded by a fragment of a shell. This check proved but temporary, and the retreat of the Federals commenced. Their loss was 26 pieces of artillery, all the ambulances, and 157 army wagons and their horses, with the rations and forage of the mounted infantry.

General Emory's corps got into action as the evening was setting in, and checked the advance of the enemy completely by his masterly management, preventing a disaster to the whole army. With their superior numbers, and flushed with apparent victory, the enemy could not dislodge him from his position; while the discomfited regiments that had fallen back behind his corps were enabled to re-form. It was, without doubt, Emory's corps that saved the day, and prevented the Confederates from gaining a substantial victory.

At about dark the enemy retired, to rejoice over their success, and fill their canteens from General Lee's ample supply of liquor. To make sure of their captures, the Confederates unharnessed all the horses from the wagons, and conveyed them and the artillery to what they considered a place of safety.

After this repulse, General Banks fell back to Pleasant Hill with his whole force, and was there joined by General A. J. Smith, who had just reached that point with his command. At Pleasant Hill the army encamped to reorganize and repair damages.

The great mistake in this battle was in bringing the wagon-train to the front and directing General Lee, if hard pushed, to fall back on the infantry, apparently not realizing the danger of leaving all the train in the enemy's hands. Banks had ample opportunity to redeem this error before reinforcing Lee and pushing the latter further into danger, thereby bringing on a general engagement, which it was desirable to avoid in the then scattered condition of the Federal forces. General Franklin assigned this as a reason for not complying with Lee's request for reinforcements, and military critics support him in this; but it would have been wiser to have sent a positive order to Lee to send his wagon train to the rear and to fall back when the main body of the enemy was found in force. This would have been sufficient to have compelled the obedience of this officer, who was exhibiting a great deal of gallantry.

Banks says he expected the mounted soldiers to be in front and the infantry close behind; but there was no necessity for the cavalry to have their wagons with them, as each man could carry two days' rations and forage on his horse, or a certain number of wagons could have been dispatched each night with rations for the day following.

But lie the fault where it may, Banks met with defeat and a loss of prestige from which the Army never fairly recovered in that region; whereas, the Federals should have gained a victory that would have enabled them to hold that part of Louisiana until the end of the war, and to plant the Union flag in Texas—the latter a cherished object of the Government.

The plan of invasion was a wild one, it is true, but it came nearer success than many hoped for when the expedition started.

As soon as the enemy had secured the wagons and guns, they started in pursuit of the Federal Army, which, having halted at Pleasant Hill, was in a measure prepared to receive them. At 3:30 P. M., on the 9th, the enemy attacked the Federal forces with great vigor. The Federal line of battle was formed in the following order: 1st brigade, 19th corps, on the right, resting on a ravine; the 2d brigade in the centre, and the 3d brigade on the left. The centre was strengthened by a brigade of General A. J. Smith's division, whose main force acted as a reserve. The enemy moved towards the right flank of the army, and the 2d brigade withdrew in good order from the centre to support the first. A. J. Smith's brigade, in support of the centre, moved into the position vacated by the 2d brigade, and another of A. J. Smith's brigades was posted to the extreme left on a hill to the rear of the main line. Shortly after 5 P. M., the enemy had driven in the skirmishers and attacked in great strength, manœuvering to force the Federal left. He advanced in two heavy, oblique lines towards the right of the 3d brigade, 19th corps, which, after a determined resistance, fell slowly back to the reserves. The enemy then attacked the centre, which was also moved back to the reserves; and the 1st and 2d brigades were soon enveloped in front, right and rear. By the skillful manœuvering of General Emory, the flanks of the two brigades now meeting the enemy were covered, and the Confederates received terrible punishment. At the same moment, the latter came in contact with the reserve under General A. J. Smith; where, already retreating, he was met first by a volley and then a charge, led by General Mower, which caused him to retreat more rapidly. All Smith's reserves were ordered by Emory to join in the attack; the whole Confederate army was put to flight, and was followed by A. J. Smith's division until night set in.

What happened at Pleasant Hill would have happened at Sabine Cross Roads if General Franklin on that occasion had been allowed to postpone the engagement until the infantry had had time to join the troops in front. Had the fight at Sabine Cross Roads been postponed forty-eight hours, the Federal army would have been victorious, and would, doubtless, have reached Shreveport without further molestation; although what particular object there was in going to that place does not exactly appear.

General Banks was in command at Pleasant Hill, and had acquired sufficient wisdom to send the greater part of his cavalry, together with General Ransom's command, which had been badly handled the day before, and all the baggage train that had escaped, to the rear. In the hurry of the moment, however, the medical train of the 19th corps was also sent off, much to the annoyance of the medical officers, who, before night, had the most urgent need for its contents.

The Federal position on the field of Pleasant Hill was excellent, and the enemy should not have moved the army one inch. The little village of Pleasant Hill was situated upon an eminence, the ground sloping in all directions, and rising again to the west, formed another eminence half a mile from the village. On and about the crest of this latter eminence, among trees and bushes and behind fences, the Federal troops were stationed in line of battle; the reserves in waiting joining the village on the left—just such a place as a general would like to select on such an occasion.

General A. J. Smith's reserves at this time, owing to absentees and the 2,500 men with the fleet of transports under General T. Kilby Smith, amounted to only 5,800 men, under the immediate command of General Mower. When the division appeared upon the field under Mower, the army had been forced back a considerable distance and was in some confusion. Colonel W. J. Shaw, commanding the 14th Iowa infantry, 16th corps, had been brought up in the first place to reinforce the 19th corps, and had been badly handled. As Mower broke through the ranks of the retreating troops, the enemy's cavalry was seen on the edge of a wood, where they had been concealed, forming for a charge. They swept rapidly forward across the field in one of the most perfect cavalry charges seen during the war, and met as fatal a reception as ever befel such a movement. Colonel Shaw ordered his men to reserve their fire until the horsemen were near enough to receive the full force of it, and the result was that fully half of the enemy were dismounted and many horses disabled. The remainder pressed headlong on under a close and rapid fire until some of them fell from their horses into the Federal ranks. By this time the cavalry regiment was *hors du combat*, and only a small proportion of the men got back to their lines.

After this the Confederate infantry advanced in double line of battle with perfect order, but with the result we have before mentioned.

Notwithstanding the action at Pleasant Hill was a victory for the Union Army, it came near being a defeat, and would have been so but for General Emory's strong stand. When the enemy's infantry advanced across the open field, Shaw's brigade opened on them at a distance of 200 yards. The enemy replied vigorously, and caused a heavy loss. The first line of the enemy retreated in disorder under Emory's fire, while fighting continued on the Federal left, which fell back so far as to allow the Confederates to pass almost to its rear and to nearly outflank the brigades of Benedict and Shaw, driving Benedict's right into the gap and inflicting severe loss. Benedict was killed, and Shaw lost 500 men.

For a short time these brigades were almost in the hands of the enemy, who had pushed far in their rear. Had he been bold enough to overwhelm the Federal forces with his masses, which were steadily pressing on, he could have done so.

Much of the fighting, where the Federal troops were stationed, was in the midst of a thick undergrowth, where the commanding officers could hardly see what was going on. At one time part of the troops were between two bodies of the enemy, and, with the latter in their rear, found it better to hold their position than to attempt a retreat.

General Emory, in his official report, says: "The enemy emerged from the woods in all directions and in heavy columns, completely outflanking and overpowering my left wing—composed of the 3d brigade and a brigade of General Smith—which broke in some confusion. My right stood firm and repulsed the enemy handsomely, and the left would have done so but for the great interval between it and the troops to the left, leaving the flank entirely exposed."

One might naturally inquire, why was not all the artillery, which General Banks sent to the rear, posted so as to protect these exposed flanks of a long line of battle? We hear very little of artillery in connection with the engagement at Pleasant Hill—only where the 25th New York battery, of the 19th corps, opened upon the enemy's artillery that commenced firing on Shaw's brigade at the beginning.

The Federal troops fell back upon the reserves, being hard pressed by the rush of Confederates, who seemed to get through gaps and outflank the brigades in almost every instance. The Union forces generally fell back in good order; and, if it was intended that the enemy should be fought in that way, the experiment turned out well in the end, although the plan seems to have been a hazardous one.

The reserves quietly waited for the time when they should be called into service; and, when the order was given, poured in such a murderous fire that the Confederates were checked immediately. Then General Mower charged with Smith's men into their midst, the other Union forces keeping up a fire all along the line. This was a great surprise to the enemy, who apparently supposed they were carrying everything before them, and, panic-struck, they turned and fled in the utmost confusion, throwing away their arms and accoutrements. General Smith's victorious troops followed close upon their heels, capturing prisoners, arms and several pieces of artillery, until darkness prevented any further pursuit.

Had the mounted force been kept in reserve to act in conjunction with Smith's infantry reserves, they would have killed or captured half the Confederate army; but here was another great military blunder committed. When most needed, they were in the rear; and when little needed, as in the previous engagement, they were sent to the front to battle with infantry posted in a thick wood!

During part of this battle General Banks had his headquarters at a large building in the village, called "The Academy," while General Franklin was senior officer in the field; and, on the falling back of the Federal troops, Banks gave the order for the trains in the rear to retreat; but, being soon after informed of the complete victory the troops had gained, he countermanded the order, and directed everything to be prepared for an early advance on the enemy and on Shreveport. So the soldiers laid down, amidst the groans of their wounded comrades, to take a short repose preceding their arduous labors of the following day.

General Emory's and A. J. Smith's commands had entire possession of the field, the enemy having retreated sixteen miles without stopping, leaving the road strewn with their arms and accoutrements. Some of the best Federal artillery had been recaptured, and the wagons were again in Smith's possession, although the enemy had carried off horses and harness. All that was needed were some of the useless cavalry horses to drag the wagons within the Federal lines to a place of safety.

The enemy had evidently retreated outright, as the victory was complete, and they had thrown away such a quantity of arms, etc., that it would be useless to try and harass the Federals this side of Shreveport. Their first day's success against Lee's mounted men and meagre supports of infantry had given them an overweening estimate of their prowess, which was completely taken out of them at Pleasant Hill. The falling-back of the Federal Army was considered by them a plan for enveloping them in a trap, and a more demoralized army never left the field; while the Federal soldiers, with renewed prestige, were ready to follow the enemy at all hazards.

What, then, was the surprise of the army, next morning, to learn that an order had been issued by General Banks to the divisional commander to retreat to Grand Ecore. It would be impossible to describe the disgust of officers and men on the announcement of such an order, and it gave color to the report that the commander-in-chief was badly demoralized.

Franklin had managed this last affair with the exception of sending cavalry and artillery to the rear, and though wounded at Sabine Cross Roads he kept his saddle during the entire day at Pleasant Hill, overlooking the movements of his soldiers, while Banks did not come upon the field until the reserves under General Smith commenced driving the enemy, when he rode up to this last-named officer and holding out his hand, said, "You have saved my army, General Smith, may God bless you for it!" "No, sir," said Smith, sarcastically, "my 'ragged guerillas' did it."

If General Banks was held in estimation outside of his staff, he must have ceased to be so after giving the extraordinary order for 25,000 troops to retreat before a routed and demoralized enemy of 16,000 men, a circumstance almost without a parallel in the history of war. The years that have passed since these events have scarcely softened the feelings of those who participated in the humiliation of that retreat. When General A. J. Smith received the order he was occupying the battle-field, gathering up his wounded and endeavoring to secure the trophies of war. He protested against the order and urged an advance, but Banks peremptorily directed him to retreat at once. Smith then begged the privilege of remaining on the field to bury the dead and care for the wounded; but this was denied him, he had to abandon the wounded and all that had been recaptured from the enemy.

Imperative as were the orders General Smith received, to retreat and leave his wounded and dying in the hands of the enemy, he determined to make a final effort to carry out his plan of pushing on, before obeying it. Smith was a brave, impulsive soldier who cared little what he said or did when his spirit was outraged, as on this occasion. He knew better than Banks what would occur in case of a retreat. He had a large portion of his division in transports with the Navy, whom he knew were struggling to get to the place of rendezvous, where, without warning, they were liable to attack from 16,000 exasperated Confederates, armed with the very artillery captured from the Federals, and which they were now about to leave in their hands to be used against a victorious army. Scattered along the river, then at a low stage of water, the gun-boats and transports would naturally suffer great loss, attacked as they would be at prominent points everywhere.

Franklin and Smith both insisted that the army should march to the relief of the forces on the river; that it was but twelve miles to the river; where communication could be opened with the commanding officer of the fleet, and the troops could have constant access to water, for want of which they had heretofore suffered dreadfully. But all was without avail—the order still came to retreat. Smith, as a last resort, proposed to Franklin that the latter should assume command, put Banks under arrest, take care of their wounded, bury their dead, and push on to the point where they were to meet the fleet, and after insuring the safety of that part of the expedition, march upon Shreveport, if that course was found to be practicable. But Franklin, although he might wish to see this plan carried out, would not give his consent, and Smith with the rest had to turn his back upon a retreating foe, while Banks gave the latter the post of honor in the rear, to do the fighting if any was required.

The surgeons were left on the field of Pleasant Hill to do their best to alleviate the sufferings of the wounded; and the day the army departed, these officers state that the Confederates sent a flag of truce asking permission to bury their dead, and learned, much to their astonishment, that the Union forces had abandoned everything after gaining a complete victory!

It would appear that General Smith was the only officer high in command who insisted on a further advance toward Shreveport. General Franklin says: "For my part, the only question was, whether the army should remain at Pleasant Hill, or return to Grand Ecore, not that we should advance." The idea of an advance, after what he had experienced of Banks' generalship, was odious to him; and the scattered condition of the army required, in his judgment, a rest of several days to get the forces together.

About midnight, after the battle of Pleasant Hill, when he was resting under the assurances which Banks had given him, that the army would advance next morning, an orderly came to him with orders to fall back at 3 A. M. Utterly astounded, Smith went to Banks to find out what it meant. Banks pleaded the necessity of a retreat, on the ground of the general discouragement of the officers of one of the corps, the scarcity of commissary stores, and the great losses hitherto sustained; as if the Confederates, who had been so badly beaten, had not suffered more than the Federal Army, and, in all probability, would be scattered for some time to come. It was after this interview with Banks that Smith proposed to Franklin that the latter should assume command of the army. Franklin was then in his cot suffering from the wound received at Sabine Cross Roads, and was quite unaware of what had transpired at Banks' headquarters, and replied to Smith's proposition: "Will you guarantee that I will not be hanged after the expedition is over, if I do take command?" So there the matter dropped.

If Smith had been second in command, instead of Franklin, he would, without doubt, have arrested Banks, and assumed command. Few people have attributed the right motives to General Smith in making this proposition to Franklin. We believe no one was more intimate with Smith than the author of this work; and the statements made to him were without reserve. It was not from a spirit of insubordination that General Smith made his proposition, but because he thought such a course necessary for the safety of the army, which was suffering from the presence of its commander-in-chief. It so happened that Banks did give up the command to Franklin soon after, at Grand Ecore, and abandoned the army, although Franklin was suffering so greatly from his wound as scarcely to be able to sit on his horse.

General Smith felt somewhat differently from the other division commanders, for he came flushed with victory from the battle-field, where he had left his dead and wounded, while the others had met with serious reverses, although aiding largely in the final defeat of the Confederates. Their killed and wounded were close to where they halted for the night, while Smith was compelled by positive orders to leave his wounded in the hands of the enemy after as complete a victory as ever an army won. Smith well knew what construction would be put upon this shameful retreat, without any attempt to aid the naval part of the expedition, supposed by him to be at the mercy of the Confederates, who would use the captured guns against the fleet, from point to point, with fearful effect. The old soldier actually shed tears in his chagrin and mortification at being thus forced to abandon the results of a victory.

As soon as General Taylor heard of Banks' retreat, he issued a general order, of which the following is an extract:

"In spite of the strength of the enemy's position, held by fresh troops of the 16th corps, your valor and devotion triumphed over all. The morning of the 10th instant dawned upon a flying foe with our cavalry in pursuit, capturing prisoners at every step!!"

Although in this there was a good deal of that exaggeration which characterized General Taylor, perhaps it was natural under the circumstances, when he found the Federal Army actually retreating after having beaten him. The facts, however, are that Taylor was some miles distant from the battle-field at the time Banks started to return to Grand Ecore. The Confederate army was scattered in all directions, and the "cavalry" he mentions, as capturing prisoners, existed only in his imagination.

He knew nothing of the movements of the Federal Army until the return of the flag of truce that had been sent to request of Banks permission to bury the dead. On hearing that the medical officers and the dead and wounded were the only ones remaining on the battle-field, he may have sent what cavalry he could muster to capture them; but, during its return to Grand Ecore, the Union Army was not molested in the least, moving in as good order as if on an ordinary march. This circumstance shows that the soldiers were not demoralized, and that Banks should, at least, have remained at Pleasant Hill until the dead were buried, the wounded brought in, and the recaptured artillery and wagons taken from the field.

On the 11th, the army reached Grand Ecore, and we do not think any one was much surprised to find that the gun-boats and transports had not returned. The general belief was that they would never return, but would succumb to an army of 16,000 men well supplied with captured artillery, which could pour their fire from the high banks of the narrow and shallow stream right on the decks of the vessels— often from positions where the guns of the war vessels could not reach them.

On the 12th instant, the heavy guns of the fleet were heard firing rapidly, and everybody knew then that the Confederates were taking advantage of Banks' retreat and were falling back on the river to destroy the transports. On the 13th, the firing still continued, and was heard plainly at Grand Ecore, every one wondering why no movement was made by the Army to go to the assistance of the fleet; and the indignation at Banks' inactivity was extreme, especially among the 16th corps, A. J. Smith's command, who, having been for some time associated with the Navy, felt great sympathy for their old friends.

Colonel Shaw urged General Smith to allow him to go to the Navy's assistance, if only with a thousand men; but the General told him it could not be done without an order from General Banks. No troops were sent until the squadron and all the transports had reached a point three miles above Grand Ecore, where they had been closely followed by hundreds of guerillas, who, like famished wolves, hoped to obtain possession of some of them.

These ferocious natives seemed to take no rest by day or night while in pursuit of the vessels, firing on them from high overhanging banks, from behind levees or trees, or from deep rifle-pits. From these places unerring marksmen sent their murderous bullets, laying low almost every man who left the shelter of the protecting cotton bales used as barricades.

The vessels had to move slowly and in order along the shallow, narrow channel, enduring the perpetual fire of the sharpshooters as best they could, the flag-ship bringing up the rear, to see that no transports were left behind or neglected. There were over forty-five vessels to be looked after, and, fortunately, all were brought safely back to Grand Ecore, though not without loss in men.

Three miles above Grand Ecore the leading vessels grounded, and those in the rear piled up behind them, offering a fine target for the enemy's sharp-shooters, who soon caught up and closed in around them, firing from concealed places where artillery could not reach them. The booming of cannon was heard from Grand Ecore, but no assistance was sent to drive off the Confederates and stop the sacrifice of life, until the flagship "Cricket," being of very light draft, passed the shoals and pushed on to Grand Ecore. Only then were cavalry and infantry sent to drive away the enemy's sharpshooters, who clung like wolves to their prey.

Even for this relief the Navy and the transports were indebted to General A. J. Smith, who, being the nearest commanding officer at hand, dispatched his troops to the aid of the Navy without waiting for orders from General Banks.

We now return to the gunboats and transports which had started to return down the river from Springfield Landing, as soon as it was felt certain that Banks was retreating, pushing on in good order, as rapidly as the intricacies of the river would permit.

The gunboats were distributed equally among the transports to protect the latter as much as possible, and the commanding officers were directed not to permit the transports to tie up to the bank without permission. General Kilby Smith in his headquarters' steamer brought up the rear of his transports, while the Admiral, in the stern-wheel gun-boat "Cricket," moved up and down along the line, as occasion required, to preserve the prescribed order.

Thus the fleet proceeded at the rate of a mile or two an hour, until they arrived at Conchatta Chute on the 11th, where General Kilby Smith received dispatches from Banks, notifying him that he was falling back, and directing Smith to return at once to Grand Ecore and report. General Banks did not pay the Admiral the courtesy of informing him what had happened, although he must have known that the Navy was guarding his transports, and that they could not well proceed without its aid. Before leaving Springfield, a letter, dropped by a Confederate scout, was picked up, informing General Dick Taylor that the transports had from six to ten thousand soldiers on board, and were accompanied by four gunboats, this force being for the purpose of flanking him.

This idea of the enemy stood the expedition in good stead, for, perhaps, had Taylor known there were only 1,800 effective soldiers, the transports would have been attacked sooner than they were.

On the way up the river, the fleet had met with little opposition from the enemy, although parties of soldiers were frequently seen retreating. On one occasion, Colonel Warren's brigade landed at a point three miles above Conchatta Chute and captured a captain and one private. This captured officer had been charged to destroy all the cotton along the Red River as the Union forces advanced.

On the return it was seen that this design had been carried out, for the charred remains of many thousand bales, worth millions of dollars, were scattered along the banks of the river, all of which the Confederates might have saved if they had possessed a little practical wisdom. They might have known that the Union forces could not stop to collect this cotton, unless successful, and that it was only in very exceptional cases that they destroyed it.

Although on the way down the Red River the fleet had been frequently annoyed by sharp-shooters, they had received no material damage, as the soldiers in the transports were protected by bales of wet hay, bags of oats, and other defences impervious to rifle bullets, while the shrapnel thrown by the gun-boats seemed to have a quieting effect on the Confederates; but after getting below the Chute it was evident that the enemy's forces were rapidly augmenting, and the shots, which at first came not unlike the light patter of rain, increased to a heavy shower, and all felt that they were about to experience the wrath which the enemy could not expend on the army.

There was not so much fear for the gun-boats as for the transports, which, although well protected against rifle-shots, were not prepared to cope with artillery.

Pleasant Hill Landing is but ten miles below Conchatta Chute, although the windings of the river make the distance by water much greater. Ten miles back from Pleasant Hill Landing is Pleasant Hill, then occupied by the army of General Taylor, who, notwithstanding his vainglorious boasts of the operations of his cavalry, had not yet assembled a corporal's guard of horsemen, and very little artillery. Altogether he may have had collected about 5,000 men to dispute the passage of the vessels down the river.

An active Confederate officer, named Harrison, had crossed the river in the rear of the fleet with 1,900 mounted men and four or five pieces of artillery, with orders to plant his batteries in the most favorable places and cripple the fleet as much as possible from the left bank. The Federals saw this party before reaching Conchatta Chute, and sending a few 11-inch shrapnel in their direction, they gave no more trouble for the time being; but it was considered certain that Harrison must plant his batteries three miles below Pleasant Hill Landing, which proved to be the case.

To this latter point the Admiral dispatched one of the heaviest iron-clads and two gun-boats, mounting some ten guns, under Lieutenant-Commander Watson Smith, with orders to prevent the erection of any batteries until all the transports had passed; but Harrison, who could go across, while the gun-boats had to follow the long bends of the river, arrived first, and posted his guns on a high bluff in a dense undergrowth, where he could fire down upon the decks of the transports, and whence it was difficult to dislodge him.

The Admiral was in the rear when he heard the firing commence, and he pushed ahead to superintend operations in that quarter, leaving General Kilby Smith and some of his transports behind, under the guns of the iron-clad "Osage," Lieutenant-Commander Selfridge, and the "Lexington," Lieutenant Bache.

As circumstances occurred at this time of which we wish to be the impartial narrators, we will first give the report of Lieutenant-Commander Selfridge, commanding the little iron-clad "Osage," who, for the time, had the "Lexington" also under his orders. Selfridge reported that he had taken the "Black Hawk"—late General Banks' headquarters' vessel—alongside the "Osage," for the purpose of helping the iron-clad to turn the bends of the river. The "Osage" had got aground just above a turn, the "Lexington" was not far off, and Lieutenant Bache was visiting the "Osage."

All the transports, with one exception, had passed down the river ahead of him, and Lieutenant-Commander Selfridge had just turned the "Osage's" bow up stream, when a body of troops, over 2,500 strong, emerged from a dense wood near the bank. Many of the men were mounted, but these soon dismounted and tied their horses.

From their new blue overcoats, Lieutenant-Commander Selfridge took them for Union soldiers, but he soon discovered their true character, and ordered Lieutenant Bache to drop down the river, in the "Lexington," a short distance, to enfilade the enemy.

The Confederates opened fire on the two vessels, with several pieces of artillery, from a hill about a quarter of a mile distant, and forming their 2,500 men into three ranks, attacked the "Osage" with the "Black Hawk" lashed to her. The "Black Hawk" had on board about forty soldiers of General Kilby Smith's command, partially protected by bags of oats and bales of hay. The enemy's volley drove the soldiers below; and some of them being wounded, and it being useless to remain where they were, Lieutenant-Commander Selfridge ordered all hands on board the "Black Hawk" to take refuge in the safe hull of the "Osage."

Now commenced one of the most remarkable conflicts on record—between a bullet-proof iron-clad and a brigade of infantry, which continued for an hour. At the commencement of the battle, the transport before-mentioned ran up the river to avoid the enemy's fire, and the "Osage," "Lexington," and "Black Hawk" were the only vessels present. The latter vessel was riddled with bullets, and all hands would have been killed had they not made their escape to the "Osage." Officers examined the vessel the day after, and there was not a place six inches square not perforated by a bullet.

The "Osage" secured a good position abreast of the main body of the enemy, and poured in grape, canister, and shrapnel from her 11-inch guns, mowing the enemy down by the dozen at every fire. The latter seemed to know no fear; as fast as one file was swept away, another took its place.

The commanding officer of the Confederates, General Thomas Green, of Texas, who had served at San Jacinto and in the Mexican war, mounted on a fine horse, led his troops up to the bank, and encouraged them to pour in their fire, which they did incessantly, never less than 2,500 muskets firing at once upon the "Osage." The wood-work of the latter was cut to pieces, but the danger from bullets passing through the iron was very little.

While this was going on, the "Lexington" enfiladed the enemy with shell from her 8-inch guns, disabling the entire gun-battery. The fight had continued nearly an hour, and the determination of the enemy seemed unabated, when Lieutenant-Commander Selfridge aimed one of his heavy guns, loaded with grape and canister, and fired it within twenty yards at a leading officer, whose head was blown clear from his shoulders by the discharge. The enemy, having had enough of this kind of fighting, retreated in confusion to the woods, leaving the ground covered with their dead and wounded.

Four of the latter crawled to the river for water, and were taken on board the "Osage," and well cared for. These men informed Lieutenant-Commander Selfridge that the party who had attacked him were new regiments from Texas; that they had been led to believe that the gun-boats could easily be captured, and that General Green encouraged them so by his example that they would have fought to the last man had not the General fallen.

Lieutenant-Commander Selfridge could only survey the battle-field from the river, but he estimated the loss of the enemy at about 700 in killed and wounded; and from later information was satisfied that it even exceeded that figure.

Selfridge conducted this affair in the handsomest manner, inflicting such a punishment on the enemy that their infantry gave no more trouble, having come to the conclusion that fighting with muskets against iron-clads did not pay. To say nothing of the loss in men inflicted upon the enemy, the "Osage" had killed the best officer the Confederates had in this quarter; who, judging from his energy on this occasion, would have given no end of trouble had he lived.

Lieutenant Bache managed the "Lexington" beautifully, and did great execution with the 8-inch guns, though less exposed to the infantry bullets than the "Osage." The latter was a fortunate circumstance, as her men might otherwise have been driven from the guns, so intense was the fire. Notwithstanding the heavy peppering the "Osage" received, and the destruction of wood-work, the vessel was just as efficient for battle as before the action.

Had not General Green's brigade been handled so severely, it was the intention of the enemy to have attacked the transports below, and the terrible punishment the "Black Hawk" received is good evidence of what would have happened to the others. The transports would have doubtless been driven on shore and great confusion would have prevailed.

This affair was considered a naval fight altogether, or one in which the soldiers of the army had but a very small share. Lieutenant-Commander Selfridge made a report to the Admiral, stating the facts as above narrated; and although General Kilby Smith makes a claim of having been under a very hot fire as he passed down, his vessels were uninjured, and no one heard of any killed or injured. Had General Kilby Smith's command been subjected to a heavy fire, his vessel's hull would have presented the same perforated appearance as did that of the "Black Hawk."

It is a delicate matter to undertake to call in question the report of an officer, especially one belonging to a different branch of the service, and it is done in this instance with great reluctance. After the Red River expedition, the Admiral wrote to General A. J. Smith eulogizing General Kilby Smith in the highest terms, giving him credit, on his own showing, for a great deal of bravery and hard fighting, which, according to Selfridge, never took place.

In justice to General Kilby Smith, however, we will permit him to tell his own story. All that is known of the affair is from Lieutenant-Commander Selfridge's written report at the time, General Smith merely making the Admiral a verbal report sometime afterwards.

Here is what General Smith told the "Committee on the Conduct of the War," in regard to the battle, of which we have given Selfridge's account:

On the 12th of April I sailed at 7 o'clock A.M. from the Chute. Upon arriving at a point ten miles below the Chute, the enemy opened upon my boats, doing more or less damage to all of them. I found myself entirely environed. General Liddell was on one side of the river with a force of 2,500 men and a battery; on the other was a force variously estimated at from 30,000 to 40,000, flushed with their recent victory over General Banks' command. The river was very narrow, very tortuous, and very difficult of navigation at all times, and especially difficult at the very low stage of water which then obtained, and with the class of steamers which I had under my control. The bottom of the river was snaggy, and the sides bristling with cypress logs and sharp, hard points.

At about 4 o'clock in the afternoon of the 12th of April, the wheel of my headquarters' boat, the "Hastings," having got out of order, I ran under the bluff of the bank with the view of making repairs. At that time the "Alice Vivian," a heavy-draft boat with three hundred and seventy-five cavalry horses on board, was lying aground midway in the stream. The "Black Hawk," General Banks' headquarters' boat, was towing the gun-boat "Osage" a short distance below. The "Vivian" signalled for assistance, and I ordered the "Clara Bell" to report to her. The "Clara Bell" failing to move her, I ordered up the "Emerald." At that time the steamer "Rob Roy," with four heavy siege-guns upon her forecastle, ran astern of the "Black Hawk," and at this moment the enemy, with a brigade about 2,000 strong, under the immediate command of General Thos. Green, of Texas, with a 4 gun battery, formed upon the bank, and put their pieces in battery within point-blank range of the "Hastings," the nearest boat. The "Osage" and "Lexington" gun-boats at that time were lying at the opposite bank, half-a-mile off. I ordered the "Hastings" to cast off, and just as we got underway the enemy's batteries opened upon us, the first shot falling a little short, and the others over us. Their practice being defective, we escaped without serious damage; and directly getting out of range, and taking a good position upon the opposite shore, I opened upon them with one section of Lieutenant Tiemeire's battery, one gun of which was mounted upon the hurricane-deck of the "Emerald," the siege-guns upon the forecastle of the "Rob Roy," and the howitzer from the hurricane-deck of the "Black Hawk." (My guns had more range than the enemy's.) Very soon we killed the battery horses of the enemy, and they changed position rapidly, moving their guns up by hand. Meanwhile their sharp-shooters had deployed and sheltered themselves behind the timber that lined the banks of the river, pouring in an incessant fire. My soldiers were all upon the hurricane-decks, protected by cotton bales, bales of hay, and stacks of oats, covered with soldiers' blankets, upon which I had turned the hose of the steamboats to keep them constantly wet, and which proved sufficient foil against rifle-bullets, and enabled them to mark the enemy with a deadly aim. After the fight commenced, the "Osage" rounded the point, and, with the other gun-boats, opened upon the enemy, rendering me essential service. By sundown we had silenced the enemy's batteries, and, shortly after, they fled from the field, leaving many of their dead, among them General Green, who had his head blown off."

General Kilby Smith says, on offering Admiral Porter's letter to A. J. Smith, praising his conduct, for the inspection of the "Committee on the Conduct of the War:" "The Admiral was not thoroughly posted in regard to the battle I fought at Pleasant Hill Landing, because the data had not come in at the time. We left 700 of the enemy dead on the ground. Green was killed by a canister shot from a steel Rodman (3-inch), mounted on the hurricane-deck of the 'Emerald.'"

Smith's report that he fought a battle is so positive, and Selfridge's report is so positive that the former was not in the fight, that it was difficult to reconcile the discrepancy. Selfridge, who was long under the Admiral's command, always made correct and matter-of-fact reports, giving to every one a due share of praise. We cannot see why he should act differently on this occasion.

Unsolicited, the Admiral wrote in Kilby Smith's favor as handsome a letter as he could, and does not wish now to detract anything from the credit justly due that officer. He must leave it to him and to Captain Selfridge to settle between them the facts of the case. The Admiral having conferred with the latter officer recently, and shown him the report of General Smith, of which he has never before seen or heard, the annexed letter will speak for itself:

NEWPORT, R. I., June 2d, 1880.

Admiral D. D. PORTER, *Washington, D. C.*

DEAR SIR: Fifteen years have elapsed since the fatal repulse of a portion of the rebel trans-

Mississippi forces under their General Green, by the gun-boats "Osage" and "Lexington" of your fleet, and for the first time I have learned of the report of General Kilby Smith, before the "Committee upon the Conduct of the War," in which he claims for the transports under his command the principal merit of the victory.

The fight took place at what was known as Blair's plantation, and in saying it was essentially a gun-boat fight, no reflection is cast upon the portion of A. J. Smith's division embarked on the transports, because it was never designed they should engage a powerful force from their steamers; nor were the latter capable of a prolonged engagement, such as actually took place, from the unprotected condition of their hulls.

The facts of the fight are briefly these: On the afternoon of April 11th, we first learned of the repulse of Banks' army at Sabine Cross Roads, which forced the return of the transports and of the fleet under your command. You directed me (at that time in command of the light-draft Monitor "Osage") to bring up and protect the rear.

The river was very low, and the swift current in the bends made the "Osage" almost unmanageable while descending. For this reason, the next morning, April 12th, I lashed the transport "Black Hawk" on my starboard quarter, and by her assistance made the descent successfully, till late in the afternoon, when we grounded on the point opposite Blair's plantation. Our bow was therefore pointed down stream, and our starboard broadside opposite the right bank, which was 20 feet high and 100 yards distant. The transports had necessarily passed down, as my position was in the rear. Seeing my situation, Bache, of the "Lexington," which had stopped near by, came on board. We had been for some time vainly trying to get the "Osage" afloat, when the pilot of the "Black Hawk," who, from his elevated position, could see over the bank, reported a large force issuing from the woods, some two miles back. I ascended to the pilot-house, and from their being dressed in Federal overcoats thought they were our troops; but soon their movements—dismounting and picketing their horses—convinced me they were enemies. I accordingly descended, made all preparations for battle, and directed Bache to go below with the "Lexington," and take up an enfilading position.

Then commenced one of the most curious fights of the war, 2,500 infantry against a gun-boat aground. The battery unlimbered some hundred yards below and abreast of the "Lexington," which opened upon it with her port broadside, while I sent a few raking shells from the "Osage" in the same direction. Compelled to plant their guns close to the edge of the bank in order to reach us, on account of the low stage of the river, they could not long maintain the situation, and soon retired with the loss of one gun dismounted.

By this time my attention was wholly directed to the attack upon my own vessel. The rebels came rapidly across the fields in column of regiments, so the pilot of the "Black Hawk" reported, who alone, from his elevated position, could see beyond the bank. So rapid was the advance that this pilot, intent on watching them, stayed too long, and dared not leave the protection of the iron shields of the pilot-house, and so accurate was the fire, that after the fight no fewer than 60 bullet marks were counted upon the shield, behind which the poor fellow was hiding.

I loaded our two 11-inch guns with canister, elevated just to clear the top of the right bank, and as the heads of the first line became visible, fired. One regiment would come up, deliver its fire, then fall back under cover, and another advance. It was necessary to carefully reserve our fire until the rebels were about to fire, or our shots would have gone over them to the rear, a condition of affairs which made gun-boat firing very inaccurate at a low stage of water.

The fire of 2,500 rifles at point-blank range, mingled with the slow, sullen roar of our two great guns, was something indescribable. No transports of wood could have stood such a terrible fire; the few soldiers on the "Black Hawk" sought refuge on the "Osage," while the frightened crew of the steamer stowed themselves in her hold. During the three-quarters of an hour that this singular combat lasted, I had expended every round of grape and canister, and was using shrapnel with fuzes cut to 1", when the firing suddenly ceased, and the enemy drew off. During the latter part of the engagement I noticed an officer on a white horse, some 200 yards below the troops, and aiming one of our guns at him, when the smoke cleared away saw him no longer. I learned after, that the officer killed was their General Green. The rebel loss was reported at 700, while ours was only seven wounded. The destructiveness of the "Osage's" fire, delivered at point-blank range, was much increased by an ingenious device by which I could personally aim the guns from the outside of the turret, and thus have a clear view of the field, which would have been impossible had I remained inside. The wood-work of the "Black Hawk" and "Osage" was so pitted with bullet holes, that it is no exaggeration to say that one could not place the hand anywhere without covering a shot-mark.

These are the prominent facts. It is very certain no transports were in sight from my decks; they may have been a little below, concealed by the bend, but too far to have had any influence upon the result, the whole brunt of which fell upon the "Osage." The battery unlimbered abreast of the "Lexington," and was driven off by her fire. No better proof of the absence of General Smith's transports from the fight can be cited than the fact that none of them, except the "Black Hawk," showed any marks, while she was literally riddled with bullets. There might have been a small gun on the "Black Hawk," but it was never fired. As to the siege-guns on the exposed forecastle of the "Rob Roy," if fired, it was at too long range to have been of any service.

The importance of this engagement cannot be over-estimated, for though they had practically possession of both banks of Red River, the rebels hardly molested us during the remainder of our descent as far as Alexandria, excepting the time when they attempted to intercept you by planting batteries against the "Cricket," bearing your flag, and which were so gallantly run by.

I remain, yours truly,

THOS. O. SELFRIDGE,
Commander, U. S. N.

It was nearly dusk when the battle ended, and little could be seen except the numerous dead and wounded lying on the field. From the prisoners it was learned that General Liddell, with 5,000 infantry and artillery, was only two miles away and had held back, owing to the shot and shell from the gun-boats falling in his ranks and killing his men. Had this force come up it would have fared worse than the other, for the Admiral had come up with a reinforcement of gun-boats to enfilade the whole bend, and ten thousand men would have stood no chance against their fire.

The Admiral had landed above the Harrison Battery a short time before the attack from above commenced, and from the top of a tall tree was endeavoring to make out with his glass the position of the enemy's guns and the probable number of his men. At first he paid little attention to the firing up river, thinking the gun-boats were shelling the woods to drive away the sharpshooters; but the heavy rattle of musketry soon apprised him that something serious was transpiring, and, descending from his perch, pushed up the river in the "Cricket" to see what was the matter. He soon met General Kilby Smith coming down, and knowing that Selfridge could take care of himself in case of further attack, returned to his original position, directing General Kilby Smith to form his transports in order at once, and be ready to pass the lower battery as soon as he was notified it could be done with safety.

By 10 P. M. all the vessels were in line, none of them much damaged excepting the "Black Hawk," which looked as if pitted with small-pox; and from the effects of the enemy's fire on this vessel it may be imagined how badly the transports would have fared but for the gun-boats "Osage" and "Lexington," to which General Kilby Smith gives in his report the following faint praise: "The 'Osage' and other gun-boats opened upon the enemy, rendering me essential service." (!)

The Red River expedition was emphatically a united service affair, in which Army and Navy should have shared in whatever credit was gained, and there was not a sailor in the fleet who would have withheld one iota of praise due to the soldiers, or who would not have risked his life to extricate them from any difficulty in which they might become entangled; but even the best of the Army did not always do justice to the Navy on such occasions as this, and, if not actually misrepresenting matters, they saw them through colored glasses.

As far as could be learned, about 700 of the enemy were killed in this engagement, which is very likely an under-estimate, considering the terrible fire to which the Confederates were exposed; and the Navy esteemed themselves fortunate—as sailors looked upon the matter—in the death of so brave and enterprising a leader as General Green, who had displayed a heroism worthy of a better cause.

Had General Banks halted at Pleasant Hill until the 11th, and then sent General A. J. Smith's command to Pleasant Hill Landing, distant but twelve miles by a good road, he would have given the latter officer time to bury his dead, collect his wounded, and bring in the artillery and wagons recaptured from the enemy, besides being on hand to cover the transports at the point where they were most likely to be attacked. As it turned out, the affair proved a victory for the Navy; for, had it not been for the gun-boats, not a transport would ever have returned to Grand Ecore. As it was, very few of the army expected to see them return; and it was only, by the unceasing vigilance of the naval officers, in keeping the transports in position and pushing them on as rapidly as possible, that all were taken safely down to Pleasant Hill Landing.

We do not remember another instance where a large army has retreated through a hostile country, and saved their transports and munitions of war. On this occasion the chances were all in the enemy's favor, as there never were such obstacles as were met with in the down-voyage of the transports: shoals at every hundred yards, snags innumerable, and sharp-shooters at all the elevations. We think it not too much to assert that the Navy owed its remarkable preservation, under Providence, to their own good management and perseverance.

After assembling the fleet above the Harrison Battery, the Admiral strengthened the pass with additional gun-boats, and all the transports went safely by, not a shot having been fired at them. The gun-boats kept up such a shower of shell, grape and cannister on the woods, that no land artillery could withstand their fire. The flag-ship remained behind to bring up the rear, and at daybreak in the morning it was found that the "Iberville," a large transport steamer that had caused much trouble by frequently grounding, had been abandoned and left in the mud below Pleasant Hill Landing. All her stores had been removed, and she was all ready for the Confederates in case they required such a vessel. Soon after removing her cargo, however, the vessel went floating down river broadside on; and, as there was nobody on board, the flag-ship took her in tow and she was safely delivered to her master and crew, so nothing was left behind for the enemy to exult over.

After passing the Harrison Battery the fleet experienced little trouble beyond the constant fire of sharp-shooters along the river. The flotilla having learned a lesson from the fight at Pleasant Hill Landing, and comprehending the necessity of preserving a compact order, did their best to maintain it, and the fleet advanced much faster—too fast, in fact, for any large body of artillery to overtake it, the only thing from which much danger was to be apprehended.

Below Pleasant Hill Landing the transports grounded so frequently that it was not until noon of the 13th that they reached the little village of Campte, about twenty-four miles by water from the Landing, and about half as far by land. Keeping in the rear to push along the stragglers, the flag-

ship did not arrive at Campte until 4 P. M., and there found the gun-boats and transports in complete confusion, and many of them aground. As the gun-boats could take care of themselves, they were merely directed to proceed to Grand Ecore as soon as they could get afloat.

General Kilby Smith now communicated with the Admiral, and informed him that the Confederates were firing on his transports, from a hill about two miles back from the river, with two pieces of artillery. There was no evidence of this while the Admiral was at Campte; in General Kilby Smith's evidence before the Committee on the Conduct of the War, he makes the following remarkable statement:

"At noon the enemy planted two guns on the other side of the river [which side?], and opened upon the fleet. We lay under shell for five hours. Admiral Porter, with the most effective gun-boats, having taken the advance, had reached Grand Ecore in safety. The 'Osage' and 'Lexington' were the only effective gun-boats left with me from the Navy. The 'Lexington' was a wooden boat of very heavy draft, and of little or no service."

The facts are that the heaviest iron-clads were at that very time behind the transports, and not in the advance; the "Lexington" and "Osage," the most efficient vessels, were in good position among the transports, and were sufficient to silence any ordinary artillery. The "Lexington" mounted ten 8-inch shell-guns and the "Osage" two 11-inch, and the "Lexington," so far from being, as General Kilby Smith asserts, "of very heavy draft, and of little or no service," was the only large vessel of the fleet that did not get aground. She and the "Osage" were the only gun-boats in the fight at Pleasant Hill Landing, against 2,500 men and a park of artillery, and it would be strange indeed if they could not take care of two pieces of artillery! The Admiral was with the transports half-an-hour, during which time there was no artillery fire, and none was ever reported to him by any of his officers. The first he knew of any serious construction being put upon the firing was from reading the above quotation. There was some musketry fire going on, but not a vessel in the fleet was struck with shell or rifle-shot, notwithstanding the five hours' fire to which General Kilby Smith says they were exposed.

The vessels at Campte were so mixed up that the flag-ship had difficulty in getting through them and alongside General Kilby Smith's headquarters' vessel. Seeing that there was no prospect of the transports getting off that night, and thinking that the Confederates might assemble during the darkness in greater force, the Admiral informed the General that he would run down to Grand Ecore, which he could do in half-an-hour, and induce General Banks to send troops up on both sides of the river. With this, General Kilby Smith was much pleased, although he had not much idea that General Banks would pay attention to a message after plainly hearing an incessant fire of musketry for hours, to which he gave no heed, although only four miles distant.

The "Cricket" carried every pound of steam the boilers would bear, and only stopped a few moments to shell out some Confederates hidden in a house, who fired upon her as she was passing. At 5 P. M. the Admiral was on the levee at Grand Ecore, where the first person he met was General A. J. Smith, who shook his hand heartily and exclaimed: "D—n it, old fellow, I never expected to see you again!" In a few words the Admiral explained to him how matters stood at Campte, and requested him to send up some cavalry and infantry at once. The troops were ready, for Smith had been expecting orders from Banks to send them, so now the former dispatched them at once on his own authority—700 cavalry and 1,000 infantry; the latter under the gallant Colonel Shaw, and they soon cleared the river banks of any Confederates lurking in that quarter.

On the 15th, all the vessels arrived safely at Grand Ecore in good condition, excepting some little damage from running into snags and into each other. As the sailors say, they had not lost a rope-yarn on the expedition, and the casualties, all told, did not exceed fifty men, with very few killed. So, notwithstanding General Kilby Smith's exceptions, we are firm in our belief that the vessels were well managed, and whether the gun-boats were or were not "efficient" must be left to the reader to decide.

As soon as the Admiral saw the troops well underway up river, he mounted his horse and proceeded to call on General Banks.

As the Admiral entered the General's tent, he was reading by the light of a lamp. "Admiral," said the General, "you interrupted me in the most pleasing occupation of my life. I was just reading 'Scott's Tactics.'" The Admiral could not help thinking that he should have read it before he went to Sabine Cross Roads.

He told the General he was sorry he had been unsuccessful, and asking him what were his plans for the future, found him quite indignant at the idea of any one hinting that he had been beaten. "Why, sir," he said, "we gained a glorious victory, and sent the enemy flying in all directions!" "Then, what are you doing here, General?" inquired the Admiral, "This is not the road to Shreveport." "Why," replied the former, "I found that there was no water in that country, and I had to fall back here to obtain water for my troops and animals."

The Admiral suggested that the troops could have obtained all the water they wanted by marching only twelve miles to Pleasant Hill Landing; but General Banks seemed well satisfied with what he had done, and told the Admiral he intended to continue his march to Shreveport by the river road, keeping the transports in sight.

The Admiral informed Banks that this course was now out of the question, as the river was falling so rapidly that the expedition would have as much as it could do to get from Grand Ecore to Alexandria, and then it was doubtful if the vessels could pass over the "Falls;" but the General insisted that a rise in the river would soon take place, and he would be able to march on Shreveport in a few days.

Notwithstanding this conversation, he commenced intrenching and fortifying his camp on the 16th inst.

We must now turn to General Steele's movements. On the 1st of April, General Steele's army, which was intended to co-operate with Banks, was at Arkadelphia, waiting for General Thayer to join it. The same day, the army moved fourteen miles to Campte, and thence to Washington. Near the latter place it encountered the Confederate Generals, Marmaduke and Cabell, with a good-sized force, and, after considerable manœuvring, Steele, while turning his army southward, was attacked in the rear by General Shelby near the crossing of the river. The enemy, although attacking with great bravery, were repulsed with heavy loss.

On the 3d of April, Steele's entire command crossed the Little Red River at Elkins' Ferry — a movement so skillfully planned and so promptly executed that the enemy only by accident learned of it after it was accomplished. General Thayer had not yet joined Steele, having been delayed by bad roads, for the heavy rains made terrible work for the army, causing the route to be almost impassable, so that it was necessary to corduroy it. Thayer at length arrived, and crossed the Little Red River on a bridge constructed by the soldiers.

On the 10th of April the army moved to Prairie, where Price, the Confederate General, had determined to make a final stand at the point he had chosen; two branches diverge from the main road to Shreveport—one going to Washington, the other to Camden. Here some artillery firing took place which lasted until nightfall. After dark the enemy made a desperate effort to capture the Federal guns, but were repulsed with heavy loss, and retreated to their fortifications of earth and timber, a mile long, commanding the Washington road. On the 12th of April, Steele turned the enemy's left flank and the latter fled to Washington, followed by the cavalry sent by General Steele to make the enemy believe the army was following in their rear, instead of which it took the road to Camden. Much time was spent in crossing the Terre Rouge bottom, which had to be corduroyed for miles, and several bridges constructed. During all this time the rear-guard under General Thayer was subjected to numerous attacks by the Confederate General Dockray, who was always repulsed.

Fighting their way foot by foot, with the Confederate forces in front and rear, Steele's army entered Camden on the 15th and found the place strongly fortified, so as to be impregnable against any force the enemy could bring to bear. Steele was now only a hundred miles from Shreveport, and could get all the supplies necessary by boats on the Washita River. In fact, he could have held on here until Banks reached Mansfield.

But at Camden some captured Confederate dispatches gave the information of Banks' backward movement, which was soon confirmed by other intelligence. On the 18th, a forage train sent out by Steele was captured by the enemy, the first disaster occurring during Steele's long march through a difficult country swarming with the enemy's troops. On the 20th, a supply train arrived from Pine Bluff and was sent back on the 22d, escorted by a brigade of infantry, four pieces of artillery, and a proper force of cavalry. On the 25th, news was received that the train had been captured and the colonel in command of the escort mortally wounded.

Before this time the Confederates had learned that Banks had retreated to stay, and General Kirby Smith with 8,000 Confederates had joined General Price, and the combined forces were marching upon Steele's position. Under all the circumstances, with no hope of being joined by Banks, General Steele wisely concluded to evacuate Camden and fall back.

On the night of April 26th the army crossed the Washita and marched towards Little Rock, by way of Princeton and Jenkins' Ferry, on the Sabine. On the 27th, a pontoon bridge was thrown across the Sabine at the latter point, and the army reached Little Rock, and it was learned that General Fagan, with fourteen pieces of artillery and a large force of infantry, was moving up the river to attack Little Rock.

The combined forces of Confederates, under Price, made the attack, and were repulsed with great slaughter, losing a large part of their artillery and munitions of war. Steele held on for a few days longer to see if Price would make another attack,

and then took up his line of march and joined the Army of the Tennessee.

It does not require much military knowledge to see how much better Steele's expedition was managed than that of Banks'. Steele's army, unaccompanied by transports and depending entirely on their trains for supplies, marched more than three hundred miles over the worst roads possible, with an active enemy harassing them at every step. Their difficulties, indeed, were far too numerous to mention in this short sketch. Whenever Steele was attacked, he defeated the enemy; and the only mistake he appears to have made was in sending back an empty wagon-train to be captured instead of retaining it with the army. General Steele was a soldier who knew his business, and he was supported by Generals Rice, Solomon, Carr, and Thayer, who inspired their men with their own martial spirit. They outwitted the Confederates as well as outfought them on every occasion ; and we only regret that the dispatches sent off by General Banks in a gun-boat did not reach General Steele in time to save the large wagon-train captured by the enemy.

But to return to affairs on Red River. When it was found that Banks would probably retreat to Alexandria, the Admiral got the "Eastport" and other large vessels over the bar at Grand Ecore, and directed them to proceed to Alexandria, while the "Lexington" and "Osage" were detailed to convoy the transports, and see them safe to Alexandria, when they were ready to move.

On the 16th of April, the Admiral received a dispatch from Lieutenant-Commander Phelps, reporting that the "Eastport" had been sunk by a torpedo eight miles below Grand Ecore. The Confederates had planted numbers of these along the river, but as they had hitherto done no damage, the Navy paid little attention to them.

When the Admiral reached the "Eastport," he found her resting on the bottom, with her gun-deck above water. Hastening to Alexandria, he sent up two pump-boats, with orders to Lieutenant-Commander Phelps to take out everything that would lighten the vessel, and felt sure that the "Eastport" would soon be afloat again. He was detained a day in Alexandria, making a new disposition of the naval forces on the Mississippi and its tributaries.

During his absence up Red River the massacre at Fort Pillow had occurred, in consequence of the policy pursued of not properly garrisoning the strong points, where so much blood and treasure had been expended.

There were two small gun-boats at Fort Pillow at the time, which did their part, but the garrison could make but feeble resistance. The "Essex," "Benton," "Choctaw," "Lafayette," "Ouchita," and "Avenger" were sent to secure the fort against further attacks.

The "Eastport" was much more shattered by the explosion than had been imagined. Lieutenant-Commander Phelps and his officers worked with a will to save this valuable vessel, and more energy and determination were never evinced. Phelps was satisfied, if time were allowed, that the "Eastport" would be floated off all right. As the Admiral had so far met with no mishaps, he did not wish to resort to blowing up the "Eastport," to prevent her falling into the hands of the enemy.

On his return to Grand Ecore he found the army quite excited at the news that they were going back to Alexandria, though the different divisions were ordered "to be in readiness to march against the enemy!"

At noon of the 20th, General A. J. Smith's division marched out on the road to Nachitoches, and were kept for some time under arms.

All kinds of rumors were flying about: first that the cavalry had been driven in; then that the Confederates were advancing on Banks' position with 40,000 men, when everybody must have known that they could not assemble 16,000.

Every one was now convinced that Banks had not the slightest intention of advancing, and was planning a retreat, calling forth all the objections to an advance that he could in order to justify his course, and to say that his desire to advance on the enemy was overruled!

Admiral Porter had already told him that he could not now advance, if he depended on the gun-boats and transports; but he never advised him to leave Grand Ecore.

General A. J. Smith's division was advanced four miles towards the enemy, who seemed to be in force, and, although not strong enough to attack the Union position, would, in a retreat, no doubt, harass the rear. In fact, it shortly appeared that A. J. Smith's "ragged guerillas," as Banks had called them, were now to have the honor of protecting the General in his retreat.

Seeing that some move was in contemplation, the Admiral sent an officer to General Banks to ask if the report was true that he was going to move to Alexandria. If so, he requested one more day in which to float the "Eastport." To this message, the General sent a reply that he had no idea of moving.

The Admiral then called on General Franklin—sick in his cot—who asked if Banks had notified the Navy that he was going to retreat. The Admiral said "No," but that he had noticed that all the transports were moving down river, and that one of the largest gun-boats was aground below.

Franklin then assured him that he had orders to move at a moment's warning, and that Banks did not wish any one to know he was going, as he wanted the largest gun-boats kept at Grand Ecore, so that they could cover his rear as he moved off.

At first the Admiral thought that Franklin was prejudiced against Banks and misjudged him, knowing there was no cordiality between those officers; but on a subsequent interview Franklin gave such assurances that Banks intended to leave him, and urged him so strongly to look out for himself, that the Admiral determined to follow his advice.

The gun-boats could take care of themselves; but the condition of the "Eastport" was a great cause of uneasiness; so the Admiral proceeded at once to that vessel and informed her commander that he must get away from the vicinity of Grand Ecore at all hazards, as the Confederates would occupy it immediately on the departure of the Union forces, and be able to concentrate a heavy artillery fire on him while working.

The leak in the "Eastport" had been so far overcome that steam was raised and the vessel only rested slightly on the bottom.

The Admiral returned to Grand Ecore and found that Banks had left with the advance of the army in the night for Alexandria, leaving General Franklin in command of the main body, with orders to follow him. So that Franklin was virtually in command until the army reached Cane River.

The evacuation left Grand Ecore in the solitude of a wilderness. A. J. Smith's division marched at 7 A. M., on the 22d, so hastily that they left behind a quantity of stores and some siege-guns, which were brought down by the fleet.

All the transports were gone, and the flag-ship "Cricket" and another small gun-boat were all that was left after the departure of the Grand Army, which had entered the Red River country so joyfully and was now retreating before an inferior force.

We do not think the enemy knew of the departure of the Union Army until a considerable time had elapsed, as there were no signs of them at Grand Ecore, not even a musket was fired at the army as it marched. The Admiral had had an interview with General Banks in relation to General Steele, in which he reminded the former that this was intended as a co-operative movement between the two armies; that Steele, advancing in confidence to meet Banks and not hearing of the latter's return, would fall into a trap, as the Confederates could concentrate all their forces against him and perhaps defeat his army.

Banks' army was over a hundred miles

in a direct line from Steele, as the crow flies, and twice that distance by the crooked roads and rivers, all the intermediate country swarming with Confederate troops.

As it was hardly possible to communicate with Steele in any other manner, the General proposed sending one of the fast naval dispatch steamers down the Red River, up the Mississippi and Arkansas Rivers, thence *via* Little Rock to Camden, Arkansas, a distance of over five hundred miles. A messenger was sent accordingly, but whether he got to his destination is not known.

Nothing could better demonstrate the absurdity of this co-operative movement upon Shreveport than the fact, that at no time since the expedition started had the commanders of the two armies communicated with each other. A glance at the map will show that from the first these armies were to advance upon Shreveport at right angles with each other, and without the probability of communicating until they made a junction at or near that place, while the points from which they started were over 500 miles apart, and Steele's army had to make slow marches on account of bad roads and the difficulty of obtaining supplies.

Hence it was impossible for them to move in harmony as regards time, and next to impossible for one to notify the other of any detention that might occur.

The whole idea was in violation of the rule of war that two armies co-operating with each other should be in constant communication.

This co-operation might easily have been effected if Steele had marched to Columbia, La., through a much better country than the one he passed through. On arriving at Columbia, he would have been within eighty miles of General Banks, and could have been supplied with stores by way of the Washita River, where the gun-boats could have protected his transports and added to the strength of his artillery.

The two armies could have been put in communication near Mansfield, one on each side of the Red River, and the Confederates would have retreated to Shreveport without resistance.

As it was, the enemy had the opportunity of attacking each army in detail, and turning them back whence they came, making this one of the most disastrous campaigns of the war.

From all we can learn, the enemy took up a position to oppose the Union troops at the crossing of Cane River.

Franklin gave orders to attack the enemy early the following morning; but, suffering greatly from his wound, transferred the command to General Emory, who made the necessary disposition of the troops.

In the morning the 1st division attacked the enemy directly in front, while the cavalry made a demonstration on the right, and General Birge with a picked force prepared to turn the enemy's left.

After some sharp fighting General Emory carried the enemy's position with a loss of 400 men.

In the meanwhile the enemy had attacked General A. J. Smith, who brought up the rear; but all their efforts were frustrated by the vigilance of that brave soldier, who administered a severe punishment to the enemy and took many prisoners. Before 1 P. M. the enemy had all been scattered.

The Confederates having retreated, General Smith advanced four miles and camped for the night, in readiness for any further attack, the 16th corps being within supporting distance.

On the 24th of April, the enemy saluted the Union troops with several shells, in order to feel their position, and afterwards drove in the cavalry pickets. Finally they charged on the rear with a yell, but were driven back with loss.

Up to the 25th, General Emory was kept busy in repulsing the numerous attacks of the enemy, which he did with little loss. There were skirmishes at Henderson's Hill and other points, but the army was now directed with intelligence by a good General, and on the 26th and 27th the whole force marched into Alexandria in excellent condition and went into camp.

From Cane River the road to Alexandria diverged from Red River, and, of course, the transports and "Eastport" could expect no further support from the Army. The Admiral had, therefore, to depend upon his own resources for getting back to Alexandria, but would not have cared much about it could he have moved more rapidly. But he was so hampered by the "Eastport" that he felt sure of meeting resistance before the fleet could get down. The guns and stores of the "Eastport" had been put into a large lighter, the vessel fitted with a number of siphon pumps in addition to those she already had, and on the 21st April she started in tow of the two pump-boats.

The first day the "Eastport" made forty miles down the river, but at 6 P. M. she got out of the channel and grounded ; and now commenced the most serious difficulties of forcing her over the bars and other obstructions so numerous in Red River, and which were so little known that there was small hope of saving the iron-clad without some help from the Army, which would probably not be given.

It would be impossible to convey an adequate idea of the proceedings from the 21st to the 26th of April, during which time the efforts of Lieutenant-Commander Phelps, and the officers and men of that little squadron, were devoted to the saving of this valuable iron-clad.

Phelps and his command worked day and night, almost without rest, in the hope of getting the vessel to Alexandria. Once or twice she sank, and had to be pumped out again, then she would get aground on the logs and snags. It was necessary to keep her decks and those of the pump-boats crowded with men to do the necessary work, including carrying out hawsers at nearly every bend in the river.

The party had been anticipating for several days to be attacked by infantry and artillery, and we cannot to this day imagine why it was not done, unless the enemy expected to get the vessels into a position where no resistance could be made, and capture the whole squadron.

The "Eastport" had grounded eight or nine times, and at last got so hard and fast upon the logs at a place called Montgomery, that all efforts to move her were in vain. After spending a night in useless labors, and ascertaining, by sounding, that a few yards ahead was another bed of logs with still less water, Lieutenant Commander Phelps reluctantly admitted that there was nothing to do but blow the "Eastport" up.

The Admiral had stayed by the vessel as long as there was the slightest possibility of getting her down, thereby risking the capture of the little squadron, and he acceded to the proposition to destroy her. Phelps had got the "Eastport" sixty miles down the river, and sixty more would have put her at Alexandria, but the Army was also that distance off, and the reports were that the Confederates were harassing its rear in every way, so one might naturally expect when the Union troops reached Alexandria that all the Confederate forces would be concentrated against the little flotilla.

To oppose them there were but three light-draft gun-boats—called "tin-clads"—for the "Eastport" had no guns on board. The prospect was certainly not very encouraging.

The following extract of a letter from Lieutenant-Commander Phelps will be interesting in this connection:

"The command of the 'Eastport' has been to me a source of great pride, and I could not but deplore the necessity for destroying her. The act has been the most painful one of my official career. She was the finest vessel of your squadron, and one of the best possessed by the Government.

"Your order to me to proceed to destroy her, in which you commend the zeal displayed by myself and officers and crew in our efforts to save her, not only relieved me from all responsibility, but was also grateful to my feelings both as a man and as an officer.

"I desire, further, to express to you my grateful sense of your forbearance in ordering the destruction of the vessel when yourself convinced of the impossibility of saving her, in yielding your judgment to my natural anxiety to exhaust every means

that seemed to offer a hope of success. I fear that your forbearance led to greater difficulties, both for your squadron and yourself, than ever the saving of the 'Eastport' would justify. This consciousness added largely to my anxiety for your safety when separated from you by the accidents of the action which took place on the evening after her destruction, when I had every reason to apprehend the worst."

The most thorough preparations to destroy the "Eastport" were made, the boilers, cylinders and engine-room being filled with powder, as was also every enclosed space about the hull of the vessel. Then trains were laid to have a simultaneous explosion in every part. When everything was ready and some forty barrels of gunpowder awaiting ignition, the Admiral pulled off a short distance to witness the explosion, while Phelps, from his boat alongside, applied the match, and shoved off; but he had hardly got headway on his boat before the ship blew up, shattering her to fragments.

The Admiral and Phelps were fortunate in escaping with their lives, for the fragments fell in all directions around them, though no harm was done to any one.

The Confederates, who heard the explosion, must have thought an earthquake had taken place; for in that narrow river, inclosed by high banks, the jar seemed as if everything would shake to pieces, and the trees bent, as if a tornado had passed over them.

Of course, the enemy made for that point with all dispatch; and, although the officers were always on the look-out, the attack came sooner than was expected.

The vessels had dropped down about three hundred yards from the "Eastport," and the little flag-ship, the "Cricket," was lying at the right bank; when, just after the former vessel blew up, she was attacked by a heavy force of infantry from the right bank. From their concealed position they poured a fire into all the vessels of over twelve hundred muskets and rifles, and then rushed to board the "Cricket."

Fortunately one watch was always kept at the guns, prepared for any emergency, and the men were under cover of the bulwarks; so that, with the exception of splintering wood-work and smashing glass, little damage was done by the fire.

A fire of grape, canister, and shrapnel soon drove the enemy back. One man, who could not get away, surrendered himself prisoner, and informed the Admiral that the present force was only the advance of some six thousand artillery and infantry that would give him a warm reception further down. The naval force now consisted of the "Cricket" and "Juliet," each carrying six small guns, and the "Fort Hindman," eight guns, mixed battery—"tin-clad" gun-boats only musket-proof —together with two pump-boats, "Champion" and "Champion No. 5," entirely unprotected.

The "Champion" was lashed to the "Juliet," and the "Champion No. 5" followed the squadron.

They had proceeded twenty miles down the river, the "Cricket" leading, and the vessels in close order, when it was noticed, about one hundred yards from the river, on a high bluff at a bend, that some men were moving in the bushes; and the commander ordered a shrapnel shell fired in among them from a 12-pounder howitzer, always in readiness on the upper deck. The shell burst in the midst of the enemy, whom, it now appeared, were posted in force; and the vessels approached within about twenty yards of the shore, when nineteen shells

During this time the enemy were raking the "Cricket" fore and aft; but, supposing that she was disabled so as to be in their power, they turned their attention to the "Juliet," close behind, with such effect that she drifted down under the bank, where no guns could be brought to bear upon her.

In the meantime the "Cricket" had succeeded in getting around a long, narrow neck of land, and found herself in the enemy's rear. Having got a fresh crew to the gun on the upper deck, and remanned two of the other guns with "contrabands," the fire was directed with such effect that the enemy were driven from their guns, and the "Juliet" escaped up the river in tow of the "Champion."

In the four minutes the "Cricket" sus-

ATTACK ON THE "CRICKET" BY 2,500 CONFEDERATES, UNDER GENERAL GREEN.

crashed through the vessel from concealed artillery, shattering the "Cricket" in all her parts.

The Admiral immediately hastened to the pilot-house, and entered the door just as a bursting shell wounded the pilot, and killed all the guns' crew forward. By this time the engine had stopped; but the current, running at the rate of four miles per hour, was bearing the "Cricket" rapidly down stream. Going below, the Admiral found the engineer had been killed with his hand on the throttle-valve, and as he expired he had shut off the steam. Steam was turned on, and the engine once more started.

The gun-deck was covered with dead and wounded, and all but one of the guns was disabled. In the fire-room all the firemen were *hors du combat.*

tained the enemy's fire, she had twelve killed and nineteen wounded, most of the latter severely. She was struck thirty-eight times with shell, which generally burst in small fragments, otherwise they would probably have disabled the boilers and machinery.

The whole ship's company of this little vessel amounted to but fifty persons, of whom one third were negroes picked up along the Mississippi; but there was no flinching, although the "Cricket" had but four officers, all of whom were wounded. One gentleman, a guest on board, said he came in this expedition expecting to see fighting, and had now seen all of it he wanted.

As soon as the Confederates recovered from the temporary surprise caused by the "Cricket's" shells, and the latter had drifted out of range, they opened upon the "Champion, No. 5," and sunk her immediately. She had a number of negroes on board who had fled from Grand Ecore, but they were all killed, many of them shot while struggling in the water.

General Taylor told the Admiral, after the war, that he was present and in command on this occasion, and, besides three batteries of artillery, he had three thousand infantry pouring their fire into the vessels all the time. The Admiral reproached the General for his want of courtesy in shooting at him as he passed along the upper deck, but Taylor assured him that he ordered the firing to cease the moment he recognized the Admiral.

If this was so, and amid all the noise and confusion, no one could pretend to recollect the exact circumstances of the case, the Admiral must attribute it to the chivalric feeling in General Taylor's breast towards one with whom he had been intimate in the days when the South did not dream of shedding Northern blood.

When Lieutenant-Commander Phelps saw the difficulties ahead, he steamed down in the "Fort Hindman," and opened fire on the enemy's batteries, enabling the "Juliet" to escape and join him. The latter vessel, in this short period, had lost fifteen killed and wounded, and was very much cut up. Phelps concluded it would be best to wait till night before trying to run the batteries. Some may think he should have followed the flag-ship immediately, but the Admiral always encouraged his officers to think for themselves, and had he followed, with the river impeded by the sunken "Champion," he might have entangled the vessels and lost all. Naturally thinking that the "Cricket" had been destroyed, Phelps had to take upon himself the responsibility of commanding officer.

Two iron-clads had been ordered to meet the fleet two miles below Cane River, near where the flotilla was attacked, and the flag-ship hastened to meet them and hurry them to the scene of action; but the "Cricket" soon ran hard and fast aground within reach of the enemy's guns, but, fortunately, out of their sight, and remained in this position for three hours. While there the vessel caught fire from the explosion of a howitzer caisson-box, which had been struck by one of the enemy's shells.

At dark, the "Cricket" fell in with the "Osage," lying opposite one of the enemy's field batteries, which she had been shelling all day, and this, together with being under a high point of land, prevented the commanding officer from learning the direction of the cannonading. The "Osage" was dispatched at once to the scene of the late action, as she was proof against field artillery.

The "Lexington" was engaging another battery near by, and had been struck fifteen times in the hull during the day, with only one man killed. She was too large to go up the river to the enemy's batteries, so taking one or two officers from her, including a surgeon and some firemen, the "Cricket" proceeded under her convoy to Alexandria to bury the dead and care for the wounded. The Confederates, it was thought, would have batteries all along the river, and the "Cricket," with so few men and only one gun not disabled, was in no condition for service.

The "Osage," in her anxiety to reach the Confederate battery, had run ashore four miles below it, when the "Fort Hindman" and the "Juliet" appeared, coming down the river, having left the two Champions sunk. Had the iron-clad arrived in time she would have been of great service, but as it was, the passage from Grand Ecore down could not be called a success.

The Admiral left behind him one iron-clad and two pump-boats; but had the satisfaction of knowing that none of the transports had been left in the lurch, although ample excuse had been afforded to do so.

Throughout the expedition there had been no instance where the Navy held back when called upon to support the Army and its transports, and, remarkable as it may appear, not a transport was lost, nor any of their stores, during an expedition of 300 miles up the river and return, although it required the most strenuous exertions of the Navy to keep them in place and prevent their masters, some of them Confederate sympathizers, from placing their vessels where they would fall into the hands of the enemy.

The Admiral certainly was under no obligations to the Army for his escape down the river, where, after the retreat of the latter, every man and gun the Confederates could utilize were brought to the banks to try and capture a poor little squadron of "tinclads" with the commander-in-chief of the naval forces on board.

Had Banks been surrounded by a superior force, the Navy would never have run away and left him; but would have expended every vessel, if necessary, rather than have a reverse befall him.

It never seemed to strike any one in the Army that the Navy was of the slightest consequence beyond the service it could perform for them. The loss of the "Eastport" was considered of no more importance than the loss of some quartermaster's transport, which were frequently run aground and deserted during the war, with full cargoes on board; accidents which never happened when they had the little "tin-clad" gun-boats of the Navy—vessels as vulnerable as themselves, but much better commanded—to convoy them.

When the flag-ship arrived at Alexandria, the squadron of naval vessels, fourteen in number, was found above the "Falls," with the rocks below them for a mile quite bare, with the exception of a channel twenty feet wide and about three feet deep. Taking the chances, the pilot managed to get through this channel with the "Cricket," after considerable thumping, and passed the "Falls."

Except from that warm-hearted soldier, A. J. Smith, the Navy received few congratulations for their successful escape down the river. With this officer the Admiral conferred seriously in relation to the condition of affairs. Smith was very bitter against Banks for retreating in the manner he did, and again broached the idea that Franklin should take command of the Army.

The Admiral did all he could to pacify the General, and recommended perfect subordination, telling him that nothing would please General Banks better than to place him under arrest, notwithstanding all the services he had rendered. General Smith could not bear to rest under the stigma of defeat, although everybody knew that he and his brave division had never been beaten at any time during the expedition.

General Banks had moved into comfortable headquarters, and the several army corps had encamped near the town. General McClernand had taken command of the 13th corps, and was posted on a road leading to Fort De Russy, three miles outside of Alexandria, to keep the Confederates from passing down that way.

The Army was in a state of general dissatisfaction from various causes. General A. J. Smith, from not being allowed to follow the Confederates to Shreveport; Franklin and Emory were disgusted at the way the expedition had been mismanaged; while Banks, though somewhat subdued, tried to preserve his equanimity.

General Smith, when allowed, with his command, by General Sherman, to take part in this expedition, was ordered to return to the latter in thirty days, at the expiration of which time Banks promised to be in Shreveport; but, when the time had elapsed, Banks protested against Smith's leaving, on the ground that the safety of the Army depended on his remaining, as the Army could not move until the naval vessels had passed the "Falls" at Alexandria.

The squadron was now in a very bad position above the "Falls," as there seemed little chance of getting down until the river should rise some fourteen feet, and the safety of the vessels depended very much on the Army continuing at Alexandria. The latter was now in a country with good roads, and with the topography of which they were familiar, and could make their way back to the Mississippi without danger from the Confederates, who had only 12,000 men available in that region, although expecting reinforcements.

CHAPTER XLII.

RED RIVER EXPEDITION.—CONTINUED.

BUILDING OF THE FAMOUS RED RIVER DAM AT THE FALLS.—DIFFICULTIES OVERCOME BY COLONEL BAILEY.—COMMUNICATIONS BETWEEN GENERAL BANKS AND ADMIRAL PORTER.—GENERAL MCCLERNAND ATTACKED BY THE CONFEDERATES.—THE "RAGGED GUERILLAS" ARE UNEXPECTEDLY PROVIDED WITH NEW OUTFITS.—COTTON STEAMERS ATTACKED AND DISABLED. — ADMIRAL PORTER'S REPORT ON THE BUILDING OF THE DAM.—THE FLEET PASSES THE FALLS.—NAMES OF OFFICERS AND REGIMENTS ENGAGED IN BUILDING THE DAM. — BURNING OF ALEXANDRIA. — THE END OF THE RED RIVER EXPEDITION. — CAUSE OF FAILURE. — RESULTS. — CORRESPONDENCE BETWEEN GENERALS SHERMAN, BANKS, HALLECK, GRANT AND OTHERS. — DISPATCHES AND ORDERS.—REVIEW OF THE OPERATIONS OF THE NAVY.—GENERAL BANKS' STORY OF THE EXPEDITION.—LETTER OF GENERAL KILBY SMITH.—EXTRACT FROM REPORTS BY CAPTAIN BURNS, ACTING-ASSISTANT ADJUTANT-GENERAL. — THE CONFEDERATE VIEW OF THE SITUATION. — EXTRACT FROM GENERAL BANKS' REPORT. — RECAPITULATION.

GENERAL FRANKLIN had mentioned to Admiral Porter at Grand Ecore, on his stating that the naval vessels could not pass the "Falls" at the then stage of water, that Lieutenant-Colonel Bailey had suggested a plan of raising the water above the Falls by building wing-dams. Colonel Bailey had had great experience in lumbering, and had frequently resorted to this method to raft timber in shallow rivers.

The Admiral paid little attention to this suggestion at the time, and expressed his doubts of the practicability of getting large vessels down in that way. When he met General Franklin again in Alexandria, he recurred to this proposal of Bailey's, and Franklin was so satisfied with the feasibility of the scheme that the Admiral asked him to send Colonel Bailey to him at once, and the latter soon appeared, in company with Colonel James Grant Wilson. The Admiral was so impressed with Bailey's plans that he agreed with him that they ought to be tried, and he was surprised in reading General Franklin's evidence before the Committee on the Conduct of the War, where he states as follows:

"When we returned to Grand Ecore, I sent Colonel Bailey to Admiral Porter, so that he might present his plan to the Admiral; but it was looked upon with derision as a foolish thing. I was, however, convinced that Colonel Bailey knew his business very well, and sent him to Admiral Porter again; and, after he got down to Alexandria, I sent him two or three times. Finally, I sent him to General Banks. to try and impress upon the General the necessity for giving the orders for details of men to build the dam.

"General Hunter was there at the time, and he told General Banks that he thought, as I had recommended the thing, he ought to try it; and it was tried. I have the report of Colonel Bailey to my adjutant-general, which gives all these facts, as I have stated them here."

General Franklin's memory was certainly treacherous here, for the statement above quoted is incorrect in several particulars. The Admiral was only too glad to grasp at any plan likely to extricate his vessels from their unfortunate predicament; and this will appear by Lieutenant-Colonel Bailey's report.

There was no objection on the part of the Admiral to anything, but he had no power to build a dam which would require half the army to perform the work. General Banks was the man to be consulted, for on him depended the execution of the work.

No doubt, Franklin and Bailey worked assiduously to get every one to think favorably of the plan of damming the river, and the Admiral went in person to General Banks, as soon as he could leave a sick-bed, and urged him to try Bailey's plan. Not much time was lost in consultation, for the order to build the dam was given by General Banks immediately, and the work commenced on the 30th of April. The Admiral arrived in Alexandria on the evening of the 27th, and conferred with Colonel Bailey and General Banks on the morning of the 28th, when the order was issued.

Where all this indisposition to adopt Bailey's plan appears, we are at a loss to imagine. In fact, we are not aware that any one opposed the dam — if any did, they were persons whose opinion had no influence. The Army engineers may have doubted the practicability of the scheme, never having had experience in that kind of engineering ; or General Banks may have said, "Wait till the Admiral arrives." But even those who doubted the feasibility of the plan were in favor of trying it, especially as it had been recommended by General Franklin, an engineer officer.

It seems to us that so much effort to show that there was a great opposition to Bailey's plan, demonstrates a desire to enhance the value of the recommendations of those who first favored the idea. General Banks, from whom alone authority could come for the employment of troops to build the dam, entered into the scheme with alacrity and pushed the work from beginning to end.

General Banks, in his testimony before the committee, said : "But Admiral Porter did not seem to think much of the plan, as he expressed it in his way—if *damning* would get the fleet off, he would have been afloat long before"—but Banks could not understand a joke.

Colonel Bailey, in his report, says: "Admiral Porter furnished a detail from his ships' crews under command of an excellent officer, Captain Langthorne, of the "Mound City." All his officers and men were constantly present, and to their extraordinary exertions, and to the well-known energy and ability of the Admiral, much of the success of the undertaking was due."

A great mass of testimony was taken by the "Committee on the Conduct of the War" in relation to the building of the dam, and an attempt was made to cast odium upon the Navy in order to divert attention from the real subject at issue—Banks' retreat—but the attempt was a failure.

Every man in the fleet was engaged in the operations connected with the construction of the dam, conveying stone in boats to weight the big cob-frames forming the dam, moving the frames into position—a tedious and dangerous duty—and floating down the logs which were cut and hauled by the soldiers to the river banks. Many boats had to be kept lying on their oars day and night ready with hawsers, and at least three thousand soldiers were constantly working up to their necks in water.

While this was going on, all the forges in the fleet were employed in making long iron bolts to bind the dam together. Getting the iron off the sides of the vessels to lighten them—a most harassing and difficult job—employed many men. In addition, all the heaviest guns had to be taken on shore.

Thus, while the dam was under construction, the sailors worked night and day; and every four hours a report of progress was made to the Admiral. But General Banks, in his evidence before the Committee, says, when the right wing of the dam broke away, "I immediately rode up to the fleet to see if they were prepared to move by daylight in the morning. It was a couple of miles above the dam. When I got there, there was not a light to be seen, not a man was stirring, not a ship had been lightened" [!]. (Army gun-wheels had already taken the guns to the levee in Alexandria, and army wagons had removed all stores and ammunition, and the iron-clads had thrown their iron plating into deep water up river). "I could not arouse anybody there. I went down to my headquarters, and wrote a letter to Admiral Porter" [No such letter was ever received, if it was written], "stating my belief that it was not possible for the dam to stand, and, if it was carried away, it did not seem as if we could replace it" [How did the General expect the vessels to get through, unless part of the dam was removed ?]; "that I had been up to see his fleet, and found every one asleep, and I feared they would not be ready to move by morning. This letter was delivered to him (the Admiral) by Colonel Wilson, at 1 o'clock (A. M.) that night. Admiral Porter said he would attend to it," etc., etc. Further along, General Banks says : "I went to the dam next morning, at 7 o'clock, just in time to see the dam swept away. The gun-boats were just then moving, and it would have taken them all day to move down. We thought the game was up, but officers and men were ready to recommence the work, and suggested other plans, which had been talked of before."

The fact is, what Colonel Bailey expected came to pass. The three large barges, loaded with cotton and iron, swung around and made an opening or gate in the dam fifty feet wide, just sufficient for the passage of the vessels. The barges swung against the rocks, and afforded a good cushion for the vessels to strike on as they passed down. The opening did not diminish the depth of water above the dam, and the three vessels that had found water enough to pass the upper "Falls" had gone through the gap in the dam, under full head of steam, almost directly after it opened. The other vessels had not water enough to pass the upper "Falls," and had to wait until it was furnished them.

The Admiral was on the spot before General Banks was, and had given the necessary directions for the vessels to pass through. Having critically examined the "Falls," he saw that the break in the dam was rather an advantage than a mishap. Colonel Bailey was not at all dismayed, but coolly went to work building wing-dams above the upper Falls, which he intended to do anyway, so that all the vessels passed down in safety. While the wing-dams were in process of construction, everything that could be taken from the vessels to lighten them, and had not previously been removed, was hauled around the Falls by army teams, and not a moment was lost that could be avoided.

But General Banks, when he saw the break in the dam, thought, to use his own expression—"the game was up"—and commenced writing the Admiral letters, informing him of what the latter had rather anticipated, viz.: that Banks would have to leave him, etc., etc. However, as General A. J. Smith had promised to stand by the Navy to the last, the Admiral did not care much whether Banks went or stayed, so long as he could retain Bailey and A. J. Smith. He had no apprehension of not getting through; for, with Smith's division and the gun-boats, the Navy could have held this position against all the Confederate forces at that time on Red River.

The Admiral got very tired of General Banks' letters. He at first tried to soothe him, but at length sent him the following communication, which put an end to the correspondence:

MISSISSIPPI SQUADRON, }
FLAG-SHIP "CRICKET," }
OFF ALEXANDRIA, May 11th, 1864. }

Major-General N. P. Banks, Commanding Department of the Gulf, Alexandria, La.:

GENERAL—Colonel Wilson called to see me this morning, and seemed to think the Navy were relaxing their exertions above. There is really nothing that can be done to the "Carondelet" until the water rises. The channel in which she lies is a cut channel in the shape of an **S**, and when the bottom of a vessel is wedged in it there is no use in attempting to haul her through; only water can help us, and we want but one foot of that to get every vessel through. It would be paying a very poor compliment to Colonel Bailey to suppose him incapable of supplying the desired quantity in one or two days. I am as anxious as yourself to see the vessels all through, and, though I have every confidence in the zeal and ability of the officers in command, I would give all my personal attention up there, but am laid up with a complaint that perfectly prostrates me when I ride on horseback or move about;

still, I know every hour what is going on, and give directions accordingly.

Don't suppose because the vessels seem quiet that nothing is being done; everything is being done that can be. I hope you will look this matter patiently in the face. I am sure that Colonel Bailey will have every vessel through in two days; and, though you are pressed for forage, two days will really amount to nothing, and any loss we might sustain in horses up to that time would be nothing in comparison to the loss of one of those vessels.

If we have met with reverses above, the rescue of this fleet from its peculiar position will redeem the past. You must have seen the tendency of the Northern press to cavil at our movement out here, and they cannot help but admit, if we succeed, that amidst our troubles the best piece of engineering ever performed in the same space of time has been accomplished under difficulties the rebels deemed insurmountable. Now, General, I really see nothing that should make us despond; you have a fine army, and I shall have a strong fleet of gun-boats to drive away an inferior force in our front. We can, by making a united effort, open the river when we please. I feel that the country is so abundant with grass and clover just now, that there can be no real danger to the stock.

I feel that you are extremely anxious to move, so am I to get the boats down, and I am sure you will agree [with] me when I say that there would be tremendous excitement throughout the country if the vessels are not all brought over, which will certainly be done with eight inches more of water, which there will be no difficulty in getting.

The water is rising in the river below the back-water from the Mississippi, which extends now to this place, the water rising here.

I hope, sir, you will not let anything divert you from the attempt to get these vessels all through safely, even if we have to stay here and eat mules' meat. There are some here who would not care if gun-boats, horses, and everything are left behind, as long as they could get away; but, as they have none of the responsibilities resting on your shoulders and on mine, I hope they may not meet with any attention.

I feel that we are doing a splendid thing, and I want to see it carried through without an accident to a single vessel. Please excuse my long dispatch.

Very respectfully, your obedient servant,
DAVID D. PORTER,
Rear-Admiral.

General Banks had become considerably demoralized on account of the Confederates having gained a position on Red River, at Dunn's Bayou, thirty miles below Alexandria, and he believed the report that they were preparing to hold this strong position with ten to fifteen thousand men. The position was really strong only against light-armed vessels, but was easily turned; and the proof of this is that the enemy evacuated the place as soon as the large gun-boats passed the "Falls."

It was, indeed, a great blunder to allow the enemy to get between the army and the Mississippi; but for this Banks was not to blame. He had assigned General McClernand, with the whole of his army corps, to guard the main road three miles in the rear of Alexandria, with the understanding that no enemy was to be allowed to pass, under any circumstances; but General McClernand had joined the Army under a cloud, was in a very unamiable mood, and did not seem to care whether the Army and Navy got out of their difficulties or not.

The enemy, on the 28th of April, attacked McClernand's position with 6,000 men, taking him completely by surprise, and creating a temporary panic in his camp. During the confusion they set fire to the forage and clothing, and passed down the road with some twenty pieces of artillery, hidden by the smoke, which was their object in making the attack.

At this time the Admiral was at General A. J. Smith's camp, about two miles from that of McClernand. Smith immediately ordered his men under arms, and they rode together to the scene of action, where everything seemed in dire confusion. Smith posted his men to the best advantage in advance of the 13th corps; and they remained under arms until daylight next morning, without hearing any more from the Confederates, who had accomplished all they wanted, viz.: to pass below Alexandria to Dunn's Bayou, and fortify that position strongly with field artillery.

General McClernand, not satisfied with the havoc committed by the enemy, ordered his men to set fire to a quantity of sutlers' goods and forage, which latter was extremely scarce; and it would all have been destroyed if General A. J. Smith had not taken charge and extinguished the fire.

Smith's soldiers were not in as good trim as many others, and the title "ragged guerillas" given them by Banks — which soubriquet pleased them so much that they adopted it—might, to the casual observer, seem appropriate. After putting out the fire, however, they marched back to camp completely dressed in new uniforms, leaving their old ones to McClernand's chief quartermaster, so as to make his accounts all square. When McClernand insisted on A. J. Smith's giving up the clothing, that old veteran, who, from long association with the Navy, was familiar with the prize laws, declined to do so, as his men had recaptured them from the enemy, and held them according to the laws of war; so General McClernand never recovered an article that "the ragged guerillas" had appropriated.

McClernand allowed his pickets to be driven in, and was unprepared to prevent the enemy from turning his position. He seems to have made no use of his cavalry to acquaint him with the enemy's advance. In short, McClernand was inert, and, do what you might with him, you could not make a military man.

We will do General Banks the justice to say that he did all that a man could do to extricate the gun-boats from their difficulties, and, although he differed with the Admiral on some matters, there was none in this respect. Other things occurred about this time to disturb General Banks. Cotton had been hauled into Alexandria by army teams, to the amount of some 20,000 bales, and it was desirable that a portion of it at least should reach New Orleans. Whether this was on account of the U. S. Government, or was the property of speculators, does not appear.

A large steamer, the "Warner," was filled with cotton at Alexandria and dispatched with 400 soldiers on board to New Orleans. The Admiral was asked for a convoy and sent the two best gun-boats he could spare that were below the "Falls," the "Signal" and "Covington."

On the 4th of May all three vessels started down the river, with little thought of much opposition. While passing a plantation, the "Warner" was fired into by a company of infantry, and one man on board of her was killed. Being well protected by cotton bales, infantry fire was not much dreaded. The fire of the "Covington" soon drove off the Confederates; but this was only an earnest of what was to follow.

Next morning, on arriving at Dunn's Bayou, the "Warner" in advance, and the two "tin-clad" gun-boats bringing up the rear, the former vessel was attacked by a battery, supported by a large force of infantry. The "Warner's" rudder became disabled, causing her to run into the bank, when another battery and some six thousand infantry opened on the vessel, completely riddling her. The "Signal" and "Covington" opened their batteries; but the enemy were in too strong force to contend against, and the three vessels were soon cut to pieces with a terrible cross-fire of artillery and infantry. Acting-Volunteer Lieutenant G. P. Lord, the officer in command, tried to burn the "Warner" to prevent her falling into the hands of the enemy; but, when informed by the colonel commanding the soldiers that there were 125 killed and wounded on the decks, Lord gave up the idea; and his own vessel, the "Covington," being entirely disabled, he shortly afterwards removed the dead and wounded to shore under a heavy fire, destroyed the ship by setting fire to her, and, with the remnant of his gallant crew, escaped to the woods on the side opposite the enemy. Out of 14 officers and 62 men, Lieutenant Lord could only assemble 9 officers and 23 men, some of whom were killed in trying to escape up the bank.

The "Signal" being too much disabled to reach the bank, in order to get the wounded ashore, the commanding officer was obliged to surrender. The "Warner" was sacked and burned by the enemy, and the "Signal," after her guns and ammunition had been removed, was sunk across the channel to obstruct it.

The brave men in these vessels, only musket-proof, defended them four or five hours, and many of the actions heralded to the world during the late war were much less worthy of notice than this contest between two little gun-boats and twenty pieces of artillery, most of which had been captured from Banks' army above Pleasant Hill. The attacking party of Confederates was the one that had pushed past General McClernand's corps with artillery, to mount it at Dunn's Bayou, on the river. They succeeded perfectly; and, selecting three commanding points, they were ready for any transports or light gun-boats that might come along. These light-draft gun-boats, be it remembered, were only the small stern-wheel steamboats of the Mississippi, their sides built up with light plank and covered with quarter-inch iron.

No attempt to follow the Confederates was made when they pushed on past McClernand's corps, although a child might have known where they were bound; but every preparation was made to repel an attack on Alexandria, which the Confederates had not the slightest idea of making. They were not foolish enough to attack 36,000 men, advantageously posted and supplied with a large quantity of artillery, when they had a far inferior force. General Banks should have seized and fortified the important points along the river, which, with the assistance of even the light-draft vessels of the Navy, could have been held against all the force the enemy had in that region.

The two commanders-in-chief had but little personal intercourse—a state of affairs which was not conducive to the perfect understanding which should subsist between the Army and Navy in a co-operative expedition. This want of harmony was not the Admiral's fault. He lay five days sick and unable to leave his bed, during which time Banks went to see him but once, and then in company with General David Hunter. His errand was to ascertain "which of your vessels can you best afford to destroy—for I must march—if there is any chance that any of them will delay us?" The Admiral was in pain and not in the best of humor, and replied: "I will destroy none of them, and if you choose to march you may do so, for General A. J. Smith has promised to stand by me until we are over the 'Falls,' after which I will take care of Smith." No more was heard of General Banks' marching for another day or two.

But to return to the dam. This had, in common parlance, "carried away," but in reality had made a natural and safe opening for the passage of the fleet. Not to make the narrative too tedious, we here insert Admiral Porter's report of the building of the dam, etc., and it will show the credit given to every one engaged. We are sure a comparison of this report with the published evidence of General Banks will convince any one of the Admiral's impartiality:

PASSAGE OF THE FALLS BY THE FLEET.—REPORT OF REAR-ADMIRAL DAVID D. PORTER.

FLAG-SHIP "BLACK HAWK," MISSISSIPPI SQUADRON MOUTH OF RED RIVER, May 16, 1864.

SIR: I have the honor to inform you that the vessels lately caught by low water above the Falls at Alexandria have been released from their unpleasant position. The water had fallen so low that I had no hope or expectation of getting the vessels out this season, and as the army had made arrangements to evacuate the country, I saw nothing before me but the destruction of the best part of the Mississippi squadron.

There seems to have been an especial Providence looking out for us in providing a man equal to the emergency. Lieutenant-Colonel Bailey, acting engineer of the 19th army corps, proposed a plan of building a series of dams across the rocks at the Falls, and raising the water high enough to let the vessels pass over. This proposition looked like madness, and the best engineers ridiculed it; but Colonel Bailey was so sanguine of success that I requested General Banks to have it done, and he entered heartily into the work. Provisions were short and forage was almost out, and the dam was promised to be finished in ten days, or the army would have to leave us. I was doubtful about the time, but had no doubt about the ultimate success, if time would only permit. General Banks placed at the disposal of Colonel Bailey all the force he required, consisting of some three thousand men and two or three hundred wagons. All the neighboring steam-mills were torn down for material, two or three regiments of Maine men were set to work felling trees, and on the second day after my arrival in Alexandria from Grand Ecore the work had fairly begun. Trees were falling with great rapidity; teams were moving in all directions, bringing in brick and stone; quarries were opened; flatboats were built to bring stone down from above; and every man seemed to be working with a vigor I have seldom seen equalled, while perhaps not one in fifty believed in the success of the undertaking.

These Falls are about a mile in length, filled with rugged rocks, over which, at the present stage of water, it seemed to be impossible to make a channel.

The work was commenced by running out from the left bank of the river a tree dam, made of the bodies of very large trees, brush, brick, and stone, cross-tied with other heavy timber, and strengthened in every way which ingenuity could devise. This was run out about three hundred feet into the river; four large coal barges were then filled with brick and sunk at the end of it. From the right bank of the river cribs filled with stone were built out to meet the barges. All of which was successfully accomplished, notwithstanding there was a current running of nine miles an hour, which threatened to sweep everything before it.

It will take too much time to enter into the details of this truly wonderful work. Suffice it to say, that the dam had nearly reached completion in eight days' working time, and the water had risen sufficiently on the upper Falls to allow the "Fort Hindman," "Osage," and "Neosho" to get down and be ready to pass the dam. In another day it

(Constructed under the Supervision of Colonel Bailey, U. S. Volunteers.)

THE RED RIVER DAM.—GUN-BOATS PASSING THE RAPIDS AT DAWN.

(From an Original Sketch by Rear-Admiral H. Walke.)

would have been high enough to enable all the other vessels to pass the upper falls. Unfortunately, on the morning of the 9th instant, the pressure of water became so great that it swept away two of the stone barges, which swung in below the dam on one side. Seeing this unfortunate accident, I jumped on a horse and rode up to where the upper vessels were anchored and ordered the "Lexington" to pass the upper falls, if possible, and immediately attempt to go through the dam. I thought I might be able to save the four vessels below, not knowing whether the persons employed on the work would ever have the heart to renew their enterprise.

The "Lexington" succeeded in getting over the upper falls just in time, the water rapidly falling as she was passing over. She then steered directly for the opening in the dam, through which the water was rushing so furiously that it seemed as if nothing but destruction awaited her. Thousands of beating hearts looked on anxious for the result. The silence was so great as the "Lexington" approached the dam that a pin might almost be heard to fall. She entered the gap with a full head of steam on, pitched down the roaring torrent, made two or three spasmodic rolls, hung for a moment on the rocks below, was then swept into deep water by the current, and rounded-to safely into the bank. Thirty thousand voices rose in one deafening cheer, and universal joy seemed to pervade the face of every man present.

The "Neosho" followed next; all her hatches battened down, and every precaution taken against accident. She did not fare as well as the "Lexington," her pilot having become frightened as he approached the abyss, and stopped her engine, when I particularly ordered a full head of steam to be carried; the result was that for a moment her hull disappeared from sight under the water. Every one thought she was lost. She rose, however, swept along over the rocks with the current, and, fortunately, escaped with only one hole in her bottom, which was stopped in the course of an hour.

The "Hindman" and "Osage" both came through beautifully without touching a thing, and I thought if I was only fortunate enough to get my large vessels as well over the falls, my fleet once more would do good service on the Mississippi.

The accident to the dam, instead of disheartening Colonel Bailey, only induced him to renew his exertions after he had seen the success of getting four vessels through.

The noble-hearted soldiers, seeing their labor of the last eight days swept away in a moment, cheerfully went to work to repair damages, being confident now that all the gun-boats would be finally brought over. These men had been working for eight days and nights up to their necks in water in the broiling sun, cutting trees and wheeling bricks, and nothing but good-humor prevailed among them. On the whole, it was very fortunate the dam was carried away, as the two barges that were swept away from the centre swung around against some rock on the left, and made a fine cushion for the vessels, and prevented them, as it afterwards appeared, from running on certain destruction.

The force of the water and the current being too great to construct a continuous dam of six hundred feet across the river in so short a time, Colonel Bailey determined to leave a gap of fifty-five feet in the dam, and build a series of wing-dams on the upper falls. This was accomplished in three days' time, and, on the 11th instant, the "Mound City," "Carondelet" and "Pittsburg" came over the upper falls, a good deal of labor having been expended in hauling them through, the channel being very crooked, scarcely wide enough for them. Next day the "Ozark," "Louisville," "Chillicothe," and two tugs also succeeded in crossing the upper falls. Immediately afterwards, the "Mound City,"

"Carondelet," and "Pittsburg" started in succession to pass the dam, all their hatches battened down, and every precaution taken to prevent accident. The passage of these vessels was a most beautiful sight, only to be realized when seen. They passed over without an accident, except the unshipping of one or two rudders. This was witnessed by all the troops, and the vessels were heartily cheered when they passed over. Next morning at 10 o'clock, the "Louisville," "Chillicothe," "Ozark" and two tugs passed over without any accident except the loss of a man, who was swept off the deck of one of the tugs. By 3 o'clock that afternoon the vessels were all coaled, ammunition replaced, and all steamed down the river, with the convoy of transports in company. A good deal of difficulty was anticipated in getting over the bars in lower Red River; depth of water reported only five feet; gun-boats were drawing six. Providentially, we had a rise from the back-water of the Mississippi, that river being very high at that time; the back-water extending to Alexandria, one hundred and fifty miles distant, enabling us to pass all the bars and obstructions with safety.

Words are inadequate to express the admiration I feel for the abilities of Lieutenant-Colonel Bailey. This is, without doubt, the best engineering feat ever performed. Under the best circumstances, a private company would not have completed this work under one year, and to an ordinary mind the whole thing would have appeared an utter impossibility. Leaving out his abilities as an engineer, the credit he has conferred upon the country, he has saved the Union a valuable fleet, worth nearly two million dollars. More, he has deprived the enemy of a triumph which would have emboldened them to carry on this war a year or two longer; for the intended departure of the Army was a fixed fact, and there was nothing left for me to do in case that event occurred but to destroy every part of the vessels, so that the rebels could make nothing of them. The highest honors the Goverment can bestow on Colonel Bailey can never repay him for the service he has rendered the country.

To General Banks, personally, I am much indebted for the happy manner in which he has forwarded this enterprise, giving it his whole attention night and day, scarcely sleeping while the work was going on, attending personally to see that all the requirements of Colonel Bailey was complied with on the instant.

I do not believe there ever was a case where such difficulties were overcome in such a short space of time, and without any preparation.

I beg leave to mention the names of some of the persons engaged on this work, as I think that credit should be given to every man employed on it. I am unable to give the names of all, but sincerely trust that General Banks will do full justice to every officer engaged in this undertaking when he makes his report. I only regret that time did not enable me to get the names of all concerned. The following are the most prominent persons:

Lieutenant-Colonel Bailey, acting-military engineer, 19th army corps, in charge of the work.

Colonel James Grant Wilson, of General Banks' staff.

Lieutenant-Colonel Pearcall, assistant.

Colonel Dwight, acting-assistant inspector-general.

Lieutenant-Colonel W. B. Kinsey, 161st New York volunteers.

Lieutenant-Colonel Hubbard, 30th Maine volunteers.

Major Sawtelle, provost marshal, and Lieutenant Williamson, ordnance officer.

The following were a portion of the regiments employed: 29th Maine, commanded by Lieutenant-Colonel Emerson; 116th New York, commanded by Colonel George M. Love; 161st New York, commanded by Captain Prentiss ; 133d New York, commanded by Colonel Currie.

The engineer regiment and officers of the 13th army corps were also employed.

I feel that I have done but feeble justice to the work or the persons engaged in it. Being severely indisposed, I feel myself unable to go into further details. I trust some future historian will treat this matter as it deserves to be treated, because it is a subject in which the whole country should feel an interest, and the noble men who succeeded so admirably in this arduous task should not lose one atom of credit so justly due them.

The Mississippi squadron will never forget the obligations it is under to Lieutenant-Colonel Bailey, acting military engineer, of the 19th army corps.

Previous to passing the falls, I had nearly all the guns, ammunition, provisions, chain-cables, anchors, and everything that could affect their draught, taken out of them.

The commanders were indefatigable in their exertions to accomplish the object before them, and a happier set of men were never seen than when their vessels were once more in fighting trim.

If this expedition has not been so successful as the country hoped for, it has exhibited the indomitable spirit of eastern and western men to overcome obstacles deemed by most people insurmountable. It has presented a new feature in the war, nothing like which has ever been accomplished before.

I regret to inform you, among the misfortunes of this expedition, of the loss of two small light-draught gun-boats—the "Signal" and "Covington." I sent them down from Alexandria to convoy a quartermaster's boat, the "Warner," loaded with cotton and some four hundred troops on board; not knowing that the enemy had any artillery on the river below us, or anything more than wandering gangs of guerillas, armed with muskets, which these vessels were competent to drive off. It appears, however, that the rebels were enabled to pass our advance force at night with six thousand men and some twenty-five pieces of artillery. With these they established a series of batteries at a place called Dunn's Bayou, thirty miles below Alexandria —a very commanding position. These batteries were so masked that they could not be seen in passing, even by the closest observation.

The first notice the vessels received of the battery was a furious fire which opened on the quartermaster's boat, the "Warner," piercing her boilers and completely disabling her. At the same time six thousand infantry opened with musketry, killing and wounding half the soldiers on this vessel. She drifted in to the opposite bank, where a number managed to make their escape in the bushes, though many were killed in attempting to do so.

The "Signal" and "Covington" immediately rounded-to and opened their guns on the batteries, and pushed up, endeavoring to rescue the "Warner" from her perilous position. They had, however, as much as they could do to take care of themselves, the cross-fire of the three batteries cutting them up in a terrible manner. Their steam-pipes were soon cut, and their boilers perforated with shot, notwithstanding which they fought the batteries for five long hours, the vessels being cut all to pieces, and many killed and wounded on board.

Acting-Volunteer-Lieutenant George P. Lord, commanding the "Covington," having expended all his shot, spiked his guns, set fire to his vessel, and escaped with what was left of his crew to shore, and his vessel blew up.

The "Signal," Acting-Volunteer-Lieutenant Edward Morgan, still fought her guns for half-an-hour after the destruction of the "Covington." He found it impossible to destroy his vessel by burning, her decks being covered with wounded, and humanity forbade him sacrificing the lives of the noble fellows

who had defended their vessel so gallantly. He gave permission to all those who wished to escape to do so. Some of them attempted to get off by climbing up the bank. Many were killed while doing so by the murderous fire of the musketry poured in from the opposite side. The captain remained by the vessel and was captured, if he remained alive, but I have no information regarding him. The rebels took the guns off of her, and placed her across the channel as an obstruction—sunk her.

General Banks, on hearing the news, sent out cavalry to hunt for the unfortunate men, many of whom were picked up and brought into Alexandria. A number escaped down river, and went aboard some light-draught gun-boats that were coming up at the time to the scene of action, but were driven back by the superior artillery of the enemy.

I feel very much for the poor fellows who fell into the rebels' hands, as the latter have been very merciless to some of the prisoners they have taken, and committed outrages at which humanity shudders.

The vessels will all return to their stations in a few days, as there is no prospect, under present circumstances, of renewing operations in this part of Louisiana, the season having passed for operating with any chance of success.

I am sorry to see that the rebel guerillas have become quite troublesome on the Mississippi since I left, all of which will be rectified within the coming week.   I have the honor to be,

Very respectfully,

Your obedient servant,

DAVID D. PORTER,

Rear-Admiral.

Hon. GIDEON WELLES,

Secretary of the Navy, Washington, D. C.

The "Ozark," a large iron-clad, was the last vessel to pass the dam, and it was feared at one time that she would have to be abandoned, for General Banks took up his line of march the moment he thought the vessels all through, apparently forgetting that they had still to get their guns and stores on board; but, as General A. J. Smith remained to bring up the rear, the Navy was not greatly troubled by General Banks' movements.

For two or three days before the troops and vessels left Alexandria, the army teams had been employed in hauling cotton to the levee, and every army transport had been loaded with the staple to the amount of 20,000 bales.

The 13th and 19th corps began to move on the 13th of May, the former under General McClernand, the latter under General Emory; but as the rear of the advanced corps left Alexandria, fire broke out in several parts of the town. Whether the fire was the work of soldiers or negroes, large numbers of the latter being congregated here in the hope of transportation out of Red River by the army, has never been clearly established.

Just as the fire broke out, an order came from General Banks to put all the cotton from the transports on the levee, a difficult task; and everybody wondered why, after taking so much trouble to put the cotton on board, the General should now be so anxious to get rid of it. However, the cotton was thrown ashore among the burning fragments that were falling all around. The town was seemingly in a blaze from one end to the other, and the miserable inhabitants crowded the river banks with such personal effects as they could save from the flames.

There was never beheld a more heart-rending scene, and all felt indignant that it should transpire under the eyes of the General commanding an army, without any effort being made to extinguish the flames. The army had enjoyed such hospitality as these poor people could afford while it occupied their town, and the inhabitants were fed with the delusive hope that General Banks would occupy Alexandria until the close of the war. All, therefore, who had any Union feelings were encouraged to declare themselves and benefit by the opportunities offered them to trade, and all such were now to be left to the tender mercies of the Confederates.

Out of the hundreds of negroes who had been promised transportation for themselves, their families and their effects, very few got away, and the last that was seen of these poor wretches, they sat down in despair upon the river bank, where they had conveyed their little all to try and escape the conflagration. The Admiral was the last one to leave Alexandria, having remained to see that nothing belonging to the Navy was forgotten, but he could do nothing to help these people. The " Cricket " was a very small vessel, and could not accommodate the thousandth part of those who had expected to take passage in the transports. The Navy was powerless to help them, and as the rear of General A. J. Smith's division marched out of Alexandria, the " Cricket " started down the river to join the gun-boats. For miles down could be seen the flames of the burning town, and every now and then a fresh outbreak of fire and dense smoke would occur, doubtless from cotton stored in secret places igniting.

Although it was not known who set fire to the town, the people were satisfied that it could have been extinguished by a detachment of soldiers, but nothing was done in that direction. The Confederates could have had no object in destroying the place, and the negroes had shown no disposition to take advantage of their former masters and plunder or destroy their property. It may have been a case of " spontaneous combustion"; but, however originating, the fact that the fire was not extinguished was disgraceful to humanity, and although we cannot but think the vindictive promoters of the war deserved some of the misfortunes which overtook them, yet the burning of Alexandria inflicted punishment on a people by whom it was totally undeserved.

It is only fair to General Banks to give his version of the burning of Alexandria. On the 28th of March, 1865, nearly a year after the event, in a report, wherein he seeks to justify himself for the conduct of the campaign and to throw the blame for his mismanagement on others, he says:

" Rumors were circulated freely through the camp at Alexandria, that upon the evacuation of the town it would be burned. [We never heard any such rumors.] To prevent this destruction of property, part of which belonged to loyal citizens, General Grover, commanding the post, was instructed to organize a thorough police, and to provide for its occupation by an armed force until the army had marched to Simmsport. The measures taken were sufficient to prevent a conflagration in the manner in which it had been anticipated; but on the morning of the evacuation, while the army was in full possession of the town, a fire broke out in a building on the levee, which had been occupied by refugees or soldiers, [what soldiers?] in such a manner as to make it impossible to prevent a general conflagration. I saw the fire when it was first discovered, the ammunition and ordnance transports and the depot of ammunition on the levee were within a few yards of the fire; the boats were floated out into the river and the ammunition moved from the levee with all possible dispatch. The troops labored with alacrity and vigor to suppress the conflagration; but owing to a high wind and the combustible material of the buildings, it was found impossible to limit its progress, and a considerable portion of the town was destroyed."

The intelligent reader will naturally wonder how a town could be destroyed with such a small beginning, while so large an army remained near; but General Banks is as inaccurate in regard to this matter as in many other respects in his report.

After leaving Alexandria, the advance of the army was commanded by General Emory, and the rear was protected by General A. J. Smith.

The flag-ship " Cricket " overtook the army —which followed the river road with the gun-boats close by—just as they were encamping for the night. The troops had not been molested, except by sharp-shooters, who fell back on their main body as General Emory advanced.

No more of General Banks was seen by the Navy until the flag-ship reached the Atchafalaya, where the transports had assembled, under cover of the gun-boats, to embark the army, an operation which was safely effected on the 21st of May. Here, again, Colonel Bailey's services were called into requisition to build a bridge of transports, and part of the army, which had to march to the mouth of the Red River, crossed in that way.

There was some skirmishing on the way down and the gun-boats now and then shelled the woods to drive away the enemy; but the latter continually retreated before the army and made only one dash at the rear as it was crossing the bridge of transports. General A. J. Smith turned on them and captured 350 of their number.

As there was no further occasion for the Admiral's presence, he left the gun-boats to cover the army and embarked in a tug to join his flag-ship, the "Black Hawk," at the mouth of Red River. Here he found General Canby, who had been sent to relieve Banks, and was waiting the Admiral's arrival before he assumed command.

Thus ended the Navy's connection with the Red River expedition, the most disastrous one that was undertaken during the war.

In whatever we write in relation to the late war, we try to divest ourselves of all prejudice, and nothing that we can say will bear half so hard upon Banks and his supporters as many of the articles written at the time by persons serving immediately under the General's command.

We do not know whether the twenty-two years which have elapsed since the events we narrate took place, is a sufficient period in which to write a history; but, as the States have become reconstructed, and the animosities of the war seem in good part to have vanished, we think we have a right to suppose that we can present an impartial narrative, actuated solely by a desire to state the truth, which has not generally been told in reference to the Red River expedition.

Banks and his friends have told the story in a manner to suit their political interests, which are apparently all they care about.

No one has ever, so far as we are aware, undertaken to correct the misrepresentations made against the officers of the Navy, probably because these attacks were considered harmless on account of the evident malice which prompted them.

Considering the ill-results attending the Red River expedition and its unfortunate termination, comparatively little, strange to say, has been said or written about it.

Certain newspaper reporters, having exchanged their citizens' clothing for a military garb, were constantly riding about picking up "items" for the Northern press, and doing all they could to divert attention from General Banks by dwelling on what they were pleased to call "the shortcomings of the Navy."

One of their principal points was that the expedition was a failure, partly because the Navy commenced collecting cotton along the river in violation of an understanding General Banks had with the Confederates. From this it would appear that the Union Army entered the Red River country for the purpose of securing the vast amount of cotton therein for the benefit of Northern manufactories, which were suffering from a scarcity of that material. The idea that the Navy caused the Confederates to burn their cotton and assume a hostile attitude, because it seized some of the staple, is absurd.

If the cotton was to be taken out of the country for the benefit of the United States, it did not matter who took it, as long as the Government received it, which it was sure to do if captured by the Navy.

All the cotton seized by the Navy was taken according to law, sent to the U. S. Marshal at Cairo, Illinois, and every form gone through with to avoid loss. Out of the many thousand bales sent to Cairo not a pound was lost or unaccounted for.

In seizing cotton, the naval officers acted by direct authority of the Navy and Treasury Departments; besides, the laws of war authorized them to take possession of all contraband goods and make a return thereof to the Government. So carefully were these returns made out that to this day claimants for cotton seized on Red River, etc., consult naval receipt-books in perfect faith, knowing that the account of every cotton transaction will be found carefully registered.

On first entering Red River the vessels of the Navy commenced taking possession of cotton within half-a-mile of the banks, that being as far as they could go for want of transportation, and in and near Alexandria they received three thousand bales, mostly marked "C. S. A.," the Confederate Government having purchased at a low figure a large portion of the cotton in the trans-Mississippi States, hoping to get it to a market some time or other.

The Admiral also ordered three thousand bales, seized up the Washita River, which was not considered within the limits of this expedition. Nearly five hundred bales of the first lot picked up near Alexandria was returned to the owners on their furnishing proof that it was their private property.

Some persons belonging to the Navy on one occasion went back three miles into the country with a couple of mule-teams, for the purpose of bringing out Confederate cotton; but, as this interfered with Army arrangements in the cotton business, the party was turned back by the pickets, and their expedition was almost barren of results.

What we have stated embraces all that the Navy did in the way of seizing cotton. Never, after leaving Alexandria to go up the river, did a naval vessel interfere with cotton except in some cases to pick up bales floating in the stream; and as it was not desired that the officers and men should be diverted from what was considered the main object of the expedition, viz., the capture of Shreveport, all this cotton was thrown overboard.

In regard to cotton, General Banks and the Admiral were playing at cross purposes from the beginning to the end of the campaign. Had the General communicated freely with him in regard to his plans, or shown him any instructions which would have authorized him to call upon the Navy to assist in reclaiming cotton, much as the Admiral would have disliked seeing the Navy subordinated to so ignoble an enterprise he would still have co-operated to the best of his ability.

General Banks, however, did nothing of the kind. He represented that his only object was to carry out the orders of General Halleck, dated Washington, November 9, 1862, viz.: "To ascend the Red River with a military and naval force as far as it is navigable, and thus open an outlet for the sugar and cotton of northern Louisiana."

With regard to the originators of this expedition and their motives we will speak in another place; our present object is to expose the misrepresentations made against the Navy in regard to cotton, although we might well rest on the statement of Hon. D. M. Gooch, M. C., who drew up the report of the Committee on the Conduct of the War, in which he says: "Whatever there may have been of feeling between the Army and the Navy in relation to the seizure of cotton, an examination of all the testimony will show that the military operations were not interfered with by any operation in cotton; the delays at the points where those operations were carried out were occasioned wholly by other causes."

Mr. Gooch, and one or two other members of the committee favorable to Banks, tried to draw the attention of the public from the latter's mistakes to what they wished to make appear as complaints against the Navy. The attempt was not a success, since nothing was shown by any credible evidence in regard to naval cotton operations beyond what we have stated above.

The most that could be stated by any of the witnesses, some of whom were not at all particular in confining themselves to the truth, was that the Navy seized cotton as contraband of war and refused to give receipts for it; which was not the case, as receipts were given, in every instance, by which those persons who established a claim to any of the cotton received the value of it, after the war, through the United States courts.

Any one who will take the trouble to read the report of the Committee on the Conduct of the War, will see that in the vast amount of evidence given, some of it by persons very unfriendly to the Navy, there is nothing to implicate the latter in anything they were not in duty bound to do.

When General Kilby Smith was asked by the committee what he understood to be the object of the expedition, he answered:

"It has been a mystery to me, save what transpired *en route*. In my own mind, I came to the conclusion it was what might be called, in military parlance. a mercantile expedition, that is, an expedition for the purpose of opening the country to trade, or, perhaps, taking advantage of a victorious march to gather up what might naturally fall to the Army or Government in spoils," which is, for General Kilby Smith, a pretty fair way of putting it.

That the expedition was also designed to hold some prominent point in Texas there is no doubt; but it is no less a fact that it degenerated into a cotton raid, for the benefit of individuals at the expense of the Government. That the expedition was unwise and unmilitary no one now hesitates to assert, for all can see what was seen then by many, that it should never have been undertaken at all.

After the fall of Vicksburg and Port Hudson, the Federals held both banks of the Mississippi, and gun-boats had access to its tributaries for at least a hundred miles into the heart of the enemy's country.

It was desirable that everything west of the Mississippi should be kept there, and it was to the Federal advantage that the Confederates should be left to support the large force of their troops in that quarter, who were eating the inhabitants out of house and home, and, with the recklessness of half-disciplined soldiers, destroying twice as much as they could consume. The enemy had not sufficient force to attempt any serious offensive movements, and simply lived on the inhabitants, who were heartily tired of them and their cause.

If the United States Government was anxious that the cotton should come out, it was only necessary to proclaim to the inhabitants of Louisiana that the country was open to trade, and that permits would be given for cotton and sugar to be shipped to New Orleans. Such a course would have benefitted the North much more than an expensive military expedition, even had the latter been successful.

It may be argued that the Confederate generals would have prevented the execution of such a project, but from the fact that Gen. Kirby Smith entered into an arrangement to let cotton go out under the auspices of General Banks, and that the officers captured while shipping cotton to New Orleans from the west bank of the Mississippi were in the Confederate service, we are inclined to believe there would have been little difficulty in this connection.

The cotton and sugar in Louisiana, after the Mississippi was opened, was virtually lost to the Confederates, public and private. Much of the cotton had been for three years lying but partially protected, and some of it had rotted. We saw one pile of six hundred bales so decayed as to be absolutely worthless.

The Confederates had no means of transporting the cotton across the country to the sea-coast except by wagons, a proceeding that would not have paid expenses, and General Banks when he arrived at Alexandria should have recognized that fact, if he did not know it before.

It would have been the simplest thing in the world for General Banks to have held Alexandria, which is exactly in the centre of western Louisiana, and lies on a large river, by which he could at all times be supplied with stores and reinforcements. He had everything to justify him in adopting this course, even if his original orders were to invade Texas through the Red River region.

General Grant, after becoming Commander-in-chief of the western armies, directed Banks, on or before the 5th of May, to return General A. J. Smith's command to General Sherman, and that he should march upon Mobile with what forces he had. As Banks paid no attention to this command, he was guilty of disobedience of orders. He did not move from Alexandria upon Shreveport until the 29th of March, and there was not time between that date and the 5th of May to accomplish the campaign, even with uninterrupted success, which no one but Banks himself counted on.

Banks' holding Alexandria and opening the country to commerce would probably not have been opposed by the Confederate generals; but when he attempted to move into the heart of the country at the same time that Steele with a large army was advancing to join him, the Confederates saw that it was the subjugation of all Louisiana and the invasion of Texas that was contemplated.

Banks finally accomplished for the Confederates more than they could have hoped to do for themselves, turning their trans-Mississippi department from a rather harmless affair into one of importance, provided with powerful artillery and small arms captured from his army.

The Confederates thus encouraged assembled a large army, composed of Texans and others, under enterprising leaders, who animated their men with their own spirit, and, encouraged by their unexpected success against the Federal arms, were getting ready to resume that system of warfare the Navy experienced so much trouble in breaking up.

If they did not put their old tactics in operation, it was because they deemed it wiser to let well alone, having driven one of the best appointed of the Union armies out of their country.

General Banks labored under the disadvantage not only of having some inefficient staff-officers, but of not being in accord with the officers of the regular Army who commanded the 13th, 16th and 19th corps.

Most of the civilians who undertook the command of armies were wise enough to select a capable soldier as chief-of-staff and surrounded themselves with as much military talent as possible; but Banks having previously succeeded in all that he had undertaken, having been a popular Governor and Speaker of the House of Representatives, thought himself equal in military abilities to any army officer; and although in every operation of consequence undertaken by him he failed of success, yet he assumed as much as Cæsar did after he had conquered the world.

The duties of the chief-of-staff of a civilian general were much more important than those of the chief-of-staff of a regular officer, and the Government, recognizing the *possible* inexperience of their volunteer generals, endeavored to place with each of them an officer of experience, whose duties were so onerous as hardly gave him time to eat or sleep.

The history of the civil war establishes that, wherever these educated chiefs-of-staff were supported by their civilian generals, the latter got along much better than those who, like Banks, chose to ignore the chief-of-staff altogether.

It was plain to any one from the beginning of naval intercourse with General Banks, that he and General Stone were not on good terms, and that Banks relied chiefly on one of his aides, who had received no regular military training, and was about as ignorant of the art of war as it was possible for a man to be.

Before the Army left Alexandria any one could see that General Stone did not exercise the influence over military movements that a chief-of-staff should, and this became more apparent in the advance towards Shreveport in the matter of assigning proper positions to the different portions of the Army, and in other respects; for a chief-of-staff is supposed to be on the most confidential terms with the Commander-in-chief, and is in duty bound to see his plans carried out.

General Banks complains that Stone's judgment was not good, and therefore he had to rely on some one else. He states that although General Stone was on the field at Sabine Cross Roads all day, yet he did not insist on the concentration of the Federal forces, nor did he seem to be aware that the enemy were in force in his front.

Now, Banks was on the field himself, and did not do any of the things he blames Stone for not doing.

From all we can learn, General Stone was untiring in his efforts to perform his duty at Pleasant Hill, yet at the close of the engagement he was removed from his position and General Dwight put in his place. It was necessary to make a scapegoat of some one; and as Stone was unpopular with the general public, on account of the disaster at Ball's Bluff, he was selected to bear the blame of failure.

General Stone was perfectly subordinate and desirous to make himself acceptable to General Banks, though he would not lend himself to any of the doubtful proceedings carried on under the eye of the commanding general. General Stone was particularly careful that due courtesy should be paid to the Navy and all proper requests granted. We think he had the highest respect of Franklin, Emory and A. J. Smith, which is a creditable proof of his capacity.

We believe Colonel Clarke did everything in his power to supersede General Stone in General Banks' favor. Clarke, by his own account, was in the advance during the hardest of General Lee's fighting, having joined him with orders to "press the fighting." From Lee he returned to General Banks at Pleasant Hill, and gave it as his opinion that Lee was in a dangerous position, at least eight miles from infantry support, in immediate presence of a superior force, and that he would be attacked by daylight. He thought Lee should be reinforced by one infantry brigade! but says nothing about Lee's being helped out of the scrape until the main body of the army should come up, notwithstanding Banks had expressed his surprise that the advance-guard had not been composed of infantry, cavalry and artillery. In all the evidence given by Colonel Clarke before the committee, it is evident he wishes to relieve Banks of any responsibility and throw the blame on others, as if the general commanding should not know all that was going on and be held responsible for the bad arrangements of his army.

After Stone was removed, General Dwight became chief-of-staff; but if it was intended to benefit by his services as a military adviser, it was too late to do so. On general subjects connected with this expedition, Dwight's opinion was very clear, and we think he condemned the plan as much as any one.

General Dwight's opinions in regard to cotton transactions are worth notice. He does not hesitate to say that the object of the expedition was a mercantile one, for the purpose of getting out cotton; but he is wrong in his assertion that, had not the Navy seized the cotton, the enemy would not have commenced burning it. What cotton the Navy seized was below Alexandria.

They never touched a bale after leaving that place, and the enemy never commenced burning until the Army was on its march to Grand Ecore, which seemed to be the signal for the destruction of the cotton. The enemy had no means of knowing whether the Navy was seizing cotton or not. It was the army trains that went ten miles into the interior to pick it up, and it was a well-known fact that the naval authorities surrendered every bale which was shown to be private property.

Constant applications were made to the Admiral and to his officers to seize cotton which had been bought up by speculators, and send it to Cairo for them, which was invariably declined, although all the protection asked for was given when their cotton was on board a transport. Very few of these people desired to have their cotton get into the hands of the Army, for they had to pay the quartermaster ten dollars a bale for transportation, with no certainty of getting possession of their property in the end; while hundreds of bales which had been seized by the Navy were returned to their owners in Cairo, Illinois, without any expense for transportation. These facts were proved in evidence by Lieutenant-Commander K. R. Breese, of the Navy, and others, and many instances could be cited from the books kept at Cairo, Illinois, by Captain A. M. Pennock, Chief-of-Staff.

If this expedition was intended as a commercial one, the Army and Navy commanders should have received such instructions that there would have been no clashing of interests; but while Banks was sent up the Red River as he supposed on a special mission "to let the cotton come within the Federal lines," which was done by sending out escorted wagons for it, the Admiral was under instructions to seize it as contraband of war wherever he could find it. No method of getting the cotton out of the country was indicated; and as the Navy succeeded in turning over to the Government 6,000 bales from the Red and Washita Rivers, their plan worked better than did that of General Banks.

All the inhabitants of the country cared for was to get their cotton out, trusting to the future for payment, for there was not a single intelligent person in that region who did not know how the war must terminate; and, although they intended to fight to the end, the Confederate military authorities were willing to see the people derive what benefit they could from their cotton. They had almost impoverished the inhabitants by quartering troops on them, and took this method to reimburse them! especially as one or two of their leaders (Kirby Smith, for instance) had a personal interest in saving this valuable commodity from destruction. The Confederates determined to destroy the cotton only when they thought they could no longer share in the benefits.

That there was a tacit understanding between General Banks and the enemy was the general belief, and the evidence of General Dwight, his own chief-of-staff, corroborates this belief. It was an arrangement in which neither the Navy nor the three corps commanders had any part; and we must say that disastrous as was this expedition to the cotton interest, we rejoice at the Navy not having participated in arrangements which were considered discreditable to all concerned. If the Confederates could sell all their products as they pleased, and receive money or supplies in return, the war might have been greatly prolonged.

The question as to the origin of the Red River expedition has been settled by General Grant, as before stated, but that regarding the *object* of the same is still shrouded in mystery.

General Halleck, in his testimony before the "Committee on the Conduct of the War," Feb. 16, 1865, says:

"The object of the expedition, as I understood it at the time, was to form a junction between the forces under General Steele and those under General Banks, so as to shorten the line of defence on the western side of the Mississippi River, and to establish a position within the State of Texas which should be permanently held, it being considered an important object, by the executive branch of the Government at that time, that a post should be held at all consequences within the State of Texas."

General Halleck further remarked that the Government had never received any report from Banks in regard to the failure of the expedition.

Halleck considered the Red River the best line to accomplish this object, although he acknowledges that the character of the navigation was known to be "precarious, at times good, at other times utterly impracticable." This last happened to be the condition when Banks' expedition started, which is why the Admiral strongly objected to going up the river at that time.

Any one who studies the map of Louisiana can estimate the value of General Halleck's judgment in favoring such a scheme. He wanted a point in Texas to hold permanently. With the aid of gun-boats 40,000 men could have been landed near Sabine Pass, and all that was worth anything in Texas would have been at the disposal of Federal forces. Sabine Lake was there to shelter any number of light-draft transports, with quick transportation and naval protection. Instead of this, two armies were started 500 miles apart, with no chance of communicating on the way, to march through vast swamps and woods, across numerous rivers and streams, and over very difficult roads.

General Grant saw the folly of this scheme and disapproved the attempt; but, even although he had taken Vicksburg, he did not feel strong enough to oppose so powerful a politician as General Banks, or the plans formed in Washington by General Halleck, who called them the "views of the Administration." General Banks himself seems originally to have favored an expedition to Sabine Pass, having some notion of the difficulties that would beset an expedition into Texas by any other route, and, indeed, to have expressed himself in opposition to General Halleck's "views."

A great fear seems to have possessed the minds of Halleck and Banks that, after the fall of Port Hudson and Vicksburg, New Orleans was in danger of capture from Texas, although a large portion of the country is intersected with bayous, across which it would take an army a long time to build bridges, where no supplies could be obtained, and where the enemy were as accessible to the Federals as the latter were to them. The greatest danger to be feared after the fall of Vicksburg was the army of General Joseph E. Johnston, 40,000 strong, which, still intact and in good discipline, moved towards the coast apparently in the direction of Mobile. Yet at that time, when it was necessary to be on his guard against such an energetic commander, Banks was intent on a march on Shreveport, although in a letter to Halleck he says:

"The rivers and bayous have not been so low in this State for fifty years, and Admiral Porter informs me that the mouth of the Red River, and also the mouth of the Atchafalaya, are both hermetically sealed to his vessels by almost dry sand-bars, so that he cannot get any of the vessels into any of the streams. It is supposed that the first rise of the season will occur early in the next month." (!)

Whatever may have been Banks' plans for an advance into Texas, he was evidently much hampered by the orders and suggestions he was constantly receiving from General Halleck, who seemed to change his opinion every time the wind shifted, a proceeding likely to confuse Banks and compel him to alter his plans as often as Halleck did.

Why the Sabine Pass expedition failed does not appear; but most of Banks' expeditions failed, and there is little on record from General Banks to account for these failures. While Halleck in one letter professes to leave Banks at liberty to act as he pleases, in the next holds him fast by making "suggestions," which from a superior officer are equivalent to positive commands. The only sensible dispatch from General Halleck is one dated January

4, 1864, in which, after urging the Red River project, he says:

"So long as your plans are not positively decided upon, no definite instructions can be given to Sherman and Steele. The best thing, it would seem, to be done under the circumstances is for you to communicate with them and also with Admiral Porter in regard to some general co-operation all agree upon; what is the best plan of operations if the stage of water in the river and other circumstances should be favorable. If not, it must be modified or changed."

As Captain Cuttle would say: "Here is an opinion as is an opinion," and it would have been well if Banks had followed Halleck's advice; but, whatever the General's consultations were with others, he never deigned to consult with the Admiral, and paid no attention to his opinions.

About the time that Halleck began to agitate his plan for the invasion of Texas, all the armies of the West had been placed under command of General Grant, and the latter had conceived the idea of sending Sherman through the Southern States east of the Mississippi, on what was called the "march to the sea."

On the 31st of January, 1864, Sherman wrote to Banks as follows:

"The Mississippi, though low for the season, is free of ice and in good boating order, but I understand Red River is still low. I had a man in from Alexandria yesterday, who reported the "Falls" or Rapids impassable except for the smallest boats.

"My inland expedition is now working, and I will be off for Jackson, etc., to-morrow. The only fear I have is in the weather; all the other combinations are good. I want to keep up the delusion of an attack on Mobile and the Alabama River, and therefore would be obliged to you if you would keep up a foraging or other expedition in that direction.

"My orders from General Grant will not as yet justify me in embarking for Red River, though I am very anxious to operate in that direction. The moment I learned you were preparing for it, I sent a communication to Admiral Porter and dispatches to General Grant, at Chattanooga, asking him if he wanted me and Steele to co-operate with you against Shreveport, and I will have his answer in time, for you cannot do anything until Red River has twelve feet of water on the rapids at Alexandria. That will be from March till June. I have lived on Red River and know somewhat of the phases of that stream."

Yet, notwithstanding Sherman's warning him that the rise will not take place before March or perhaps June, and the Admiral's repeated asseverations to that effect, Banks pushes on the expedition in April, when the river was falling four inches per day.

The following is an extract of a letter from General Halleck to General Banks, dated February 2, 1864:

"I enclose a copy of a communication from Admiral Porter which shows the condition of Red River and the Atchafalaya. From this it would appear that some delay would occur before any extensive operations can be carried on in that quarter."

Suffice to say, all Admiral Porter's letters recommended that no attempt should be made *via* Red River until the water had actually risen to a height sufficient to insure the success of the expedition. He mentioned the different years in which there had been no rise, and the signs of the times made it probable there would not be sufficient water that season to undertake an expedition to Shreveport, if the co-operation of gun-boats and transports was required.

In the voluminous correspondence between Halleck and Banks that took place in regard to the proposed expedition, each evidently wishes to place the responsibility on the other in case of failure to reach Shreveport. On March 5, 1864, Halleck wrote to Banks:

"When General Sherman left Vicksburg he expected to return there by the 1st of March, to co-operate with you west of the Mississippi, but he was of opinion that the condition of the river would not be favorable until a later period. I think it most probable that before this reaches you he will have returned to Vicksburg, or some other point on the river. Whether he has received any recent orders in regard to his movements from General Grant, I am not advised, nor have I any information of General Steele's plans, further than that all his movements will be directed to facilitate your operations toward Shreveport."

Halleck was always, it would seem, "harping on my daughter." On March 12, 1864, General Steele sent a dispatch to Halleck, of which the following is an extract:

"General Banks with 17,000 men and 10,000 of Sherman's will be in Alexandria on the 17th. * * * * Sherman insists upon my moving upon Shreveport to co-operate with the above-mentioned forces with all my effective forces. I have prepared to do so against my own judgment and that of the best-informed people here. The roads are mostly, if not all, impracticable; the country is destitute of provisions on the route we would have to take. I made a proposition to General Banks to threaten the enemy's flank and rear with all my cavalry, and to make a feint with infantry on the Washington road. I yielded to Sherman and Blunt as far as this plan is concerned. B. wants me to move by Munroe to Red River; Sherman wants me to go by Camden and Overton to Shreveport. The latter is impracticable, and the former plan would expose the line of the Arkansas and Missouri to cavalry raids. I can move with about 7,000 men. Our scouting parties frequently have skirmishes with detached parties all over the State, and if they should form in my rear in considerable force I should be obliged to fall back to save my depot. Please give me your opinion immediately, as I shall march to-morrow or next day."

To which Halleck answered:

"I advise that you proceed to co-operate in the movement of Banks and Sherman on Shreveport, unless General Grant orders differently, I send to him the substance of your telegram."

The same day Halleck telegraphed General Grant as follows:

"General Steele telegraphs that Banks with 17,000 men, and Sherman with 10,000, move from Alexandria on Shreveport, and wish him to co-operate. He says he can go with 7,000 effective men, but objects to the movement on account of bad roads and guerillas, and prefers to remain on the defensive line of the Arkansas. I have replied that he should co-operate with Banks and Sherman, unless you direct otherwise. His objections on account of guerillas threatening his rear will apply equally to an advance at any time into the enemy's country."

On the 15th of March, General Halleck, as chief-of-staff, telegraphed to General Grant as follows:

"A dispatch just received from General Banks, dated March 6. He expects to effect a junction with Sherman's forces (Smith's Division) on Red River, on the 17th. He desires that positive orders be sent to Steele to move in conjunction with them for Red River, with all his available force. Sherman and Banks are of opinion that Steele can do much more than make a demonstration, as he last proposed. A telegram from you might decide him."

After reading the above dispatches, we are forced to the conclusion that Generals Halleck and Banks are responsible for the Red River expedition, one of the wildest schemes, in a military point of view, ever proposed. The Navy went into the affair with the knowledge that failure was almost certain, yet did its best to insure success.

Notwithstanding General Halleck was the author of the Red River expedition, General Banks deserves the severest censure for the manner in which he carried out the plan of campaign—if there was any plan. In Halleck's letter, while he urges the Red River as the only practicable route, he constantly reiterates the substance of one communication as follows:

"While the Government is desirous that Red River and Shreveport should be taken possession of and held as the most important objective point of the operations of a campaign of troops about to take a position where they could command Texas, and establish a better line of defence for Arkansas and Missouri than now occupied by General Steele, yet the Administration does not desire in any manner to control your actions as to the time and manner of performing this service, and you will take counsel with Generals Sherman and Steele and Admiral Porter as to the best manner of carrying out the expedition."

How far General Banks acted on these suggestions the reader can judge. Both Halleck and Banks were very desirous to escape the responsibility of the Red River failure. Halleck claims only to have made "suggestions," but suggestions coming from a person who was virtually Commander-in-chief of the Army had the weight of orders. They were supposed to be the opinions of the President and the Secretary of War, as well as of General Halleck.

When the news of the failure of the expedition reached Washington, Banks was written to by way of censure, and informed that his movements regarding the Texas expedition were not approved, and that from the beginning, when the Sabine and Rio Grande expeditions were undertaken, no notice of Banks' movements were received at the War Department until they were actually undertaken. To offset this, we will quote from a letter of General Halleck to Banks, dated February 11, 1864:

"If by this is meant that you are waiting for orders from Washington, there must be some misapprehension. The substance of my dispatches to you was communicated to the President and Secretary of War, and it was understood that while stating my own views in regard to operations, I should leave you free to adopt such lines and plans of campaign as you might after a full consideration of the subject deem best. Such I am confident is the purport of my dispatches, and it certainly was not intended that any of your movements should be delayed to await instructions from here."

How much truth there is in this letter can be inferred by comparing it with the three telegrams of Halleck, one of them to Grant, in which Halleck seems determined to manage the whole affair. Banks, no doubt, considered these "suggestions" as instructions, which, had he disregarded, would have most probably resulted in his removal from command. Banks says:

"In the instructions I received from the Government, it was left to my discretion whether I would join (?) in the expedition, but I was directed to communicate with General Sherman, General Steele, and Admiral Porter upon the subject. I expressed the satisfaction I should feel in co-operating with them in a movement deemed of so much importance by the Government, to which my own command was unequal, and my belief that with the forces designated it would be entirely successful.

"Having received from them similar assurances, both my discretion and my authority, so far as the organization of the expedition was concerned, were at an end."

In all this controversy it will be seen that every one is disposed to ignore responsibility, but particularly Halleck.

General Sherman and the Admiral, after the capture of Vicksburg, had discussed this plan of taking Shreveport by a sudden movement; but they did not intend to leave anything to chance, or to undertake the expedition without plenty of water in the river and a prospect of its continuance in the future. They would not have ventured in case of a temporary rise—which could always be told by the rapidity with which the water subsided—for if the rise was owing to the head waters of Red River booming, and all the tributaries throwing in their supply at the same time, they could feel certain of a permanently full river. When full, Red River is easily navigable, and any expedition started by Sherman and Admiral Porter would have been as successful as the Arkansas Post expedition. Sherman was willing to listen to the Admiral, and the latter always gave that attention to Sherman's opinion which was due to his experience.

It will strike any one at all conversant with military matters how absurdly the war at this time was conducted from Washington. Here was Grant, just successful in one of the most difficult sieges of modern times, with a great prestige, and supposed to command all the troops in Louisiana, Arkansas, Mississippi, Missouri, Tennessee, Kentucky, Illinois and Ohio, yet it does not appear that his opinion in regard to the Red River expedition was ever asked. Grant had about that time gone to Chattanooga on a tour of inspection, and thought the Red River expedition of so little importance that he directed General Banks to send back A. J. Smith's command to Sherman after the 5th of May.

General Grant was opposed to making any great effort to carry on the war west of the Mississippi, where it would take a large army and a large portion of the Navy even to hold the central portion of Louisiana, which forces would soon be wanted on the Cumberland and Tennessee rivers. All that was required was for Banks to hold New Orleans against General J. E. Johnston, who might pounce upon it if left unprotected. Banks had not troops enough in his command to authorize the withdrawal of a large force from New Orleans. All he could expect to do was to hold several points on the west bank of the Mississippi, forage in West Louisiana, and prevent supplies from crossing the Mississippi from Texas, and occasionally threatening Mobile, until such time as Grant should direct him to march upon the latter city and capture it, which would have been when Sherman began his march to the sea. This would have left no enemies in Sherman's rear. He would have had the railroads open behind him, including the important one from Mobile to Montgomery, which, with a Union Army at Mobile, would have insured the pacification of Alabama and Mississippi, and would have prevented any attempt on the part of the Confederates to pursue Sherman's rear; and in case of necessity the Federals could have thrown a large part of Bank's Army by rail upon Montgomery and Atlanta, if Sherman had got into difficulty, and there would have been a line of communication open to Sherman from the time he started until he reached Savannah.

General Banks made a report to Mr. Wade, President of the Senate, of his operations from the time he took command at New Orleans until his return from the Red River expedition. The report is interesting, and shows that a great deal of work was projected and a great deal performed. We know nothing of General Banks' performances prior to the advance on Alexandria; but, judging from his statements in regard to matters that came under our cognizance, we should pronounce the report partial. No report was made public by the War Department until the General appeared before the Committee on the Conduct of the War.

After the war he makes the report, to which we have alluded, to go before the country. His military service was over, and having to explain to his constituents the reasons for his failure, he did not hesitate to misstate the facts in order to throw the blame on others. There is so much misrepresentation in regard to the events in which the Navy took part, as narrated by General Banks, that one is naturally disposed to doubt the truth of the whole report. Banks blames General Franklin for not reaching Alexandria sooner, but the latter shows that he was not to blame, as he only received the order to advance from the town of Franklin on the 12th of March. Banks informed General Franklin that he had promised to meet the Admiral in Alexandria on the 17th of March, and as the latter place is 175 miles from the town of Franklin, of course it was impossible to fulfill this promise. Besides, on the 10th of March only 3,000 of the troops which were to form that arm of the expedition were on the ground—"the remainder had just arrived from Texas and were at Berwick Bay without transportation, and the cavalry had not arrived from New Orleans."

Franklin started on the 13th, and his advance-guard reached Alexandria on the 25th, the rear-guard and pontoon train on the 26th and 27th. Thus Franklin marched at the rate of sixteen miles a day over bad roads, having to build many bridges across streams; while Banks, who had agreed to be at Alexandria on the 17th, only arrived on the 25th in a fast steamer—yet General Banks undertakes to say that Franklin received orders to march on the 7th, and delayed him that much. He also said the gunboats delayed him at Alexandria, whereas the "Louisville," "Carondelet," "Pittsburgh," "Mound City," "Osage," and "Neosho," all heavy iron-clads, together with the "Lexington," "Cricket," "Gazelle," "Covington," "Signal," and "Juliet," light-drafts, were all above the "Falls," ready to move at a moment's notice; while the commanding officers of the "Choctaw," "Ozark," "Ouichita" and "Eastport" were informed that they might pass above the "Falls" if they could; and, if they did get over, to assemble at Grand Ecore and remain there to protect that place.

In one part of Banks' report he attempts to make capital out of a very small matter. After Admiral Farragut attempted to pass the batteries at Port Hudson, which he only succeeded in doing with two vessels, General Banks opened communication with him through the Atchafalaya by means of the gun-boats "Ansonia" and "Estrella." Banks says in his report:

"On the 5th of May our headquarters at Opelousas was broken up and the troops moved for

Alexandria, a distance of from 90 to 100 miles, making this march in three days, four hours. Moving rapidly to the rear of Fort de Russy, a strong work on Red River, we compelled the immediate evacuation of that post by the enemy, and enabled the fleet of gun-boats under Admiral Porter to pass up to Alexandria without firing a gun. The Army reached Alexandria the 9th of May (1863), in the evening, the Navy having reached there the morning of the same day. The enemy continued his retreat in the direction of Shreveport."

The facts of the case are as follows, unimportant as they may be : After landing General Grant's troops fifteen miles below Grand Gulf, taking possession of that place and removing all the guns, the Admiral left at noon, May 3, 1863, and arrived that evening at the mouth of the Red River, and communicated with Admiral Farragut. He had with him the gun-boats "Benton," "Lafayette," "Pittsburg," "Price," ram "Switzerland," and tug "Ivy."

Admiral Farragut informed Porter that, hearing that General Banks proposed marching on Alexandria, he had sent the "Ansonia" and "Estrella," under Lieutenant-Commander A. P. Cooke, up Red River, to try and communicate with the General, but he feared, as they were light vessels, they might fail. On this, Admiral Porter offered to go up himself with the force he had, and started accordingly on the 4th with the above-named vessels, arriving at Fort De Russy on the 5th. On the way up he met the two gun-boats returning, their commanding officer (Cooke) informing Admiral Porter that his wheel had been disabled by a shell from Fort De Russy; the other vessel was struck, "but there was no one hurt." As the vessels were light, Lieutenant - Commander Cooke could do nothing against the enemy. The Admiral directed him to return with him, as he should need his vessels, and shortly after took possession of Fort De Russy. It was a strong work, with three casemated guns and a flanking battery nearly at right angles, calculated to mount seven more guns.

Now, be it remembered, the Navy took possession of Fort De Russy—no very important event—on the morning of May 5, 1863, while General Banks only started on that day from Opelousas, distant, he says, from Alexandria, one hundred miles ; yet he claims to have caused the evacuation of the post, "enabling the Navy to pass up to Alexandria without firing a gun." (!) How he could get in the rear of De Russy and cause its evacuation, when he had not started from Opelousas until late on the day it was captured by the Navy, is a mystery, and military men should make a note of it for future reference. There was no opposition in getting to Alexandria, for there were then no troops in that region, only a few officers and a gang of negroes working at

Fort De Russy. The people all along the river were glad to see the Union flag, and when the Navy reached Alexandria it was as quiet as a country village in Massachusetts.

General Banks claims in his report that, after the fall of Vicksburg and Port Hudson, his whole aim was the capture of Mobile, which was of more importance to the Union than the capture of a dozen Shreveports. He claims to have been "opposed to the expedition up Red River, which had been explored thoroughly in the spring campaign of 1863, and that he was satisfied it was impracticable, if not impossible, for the purpose entertained by the Government." Yet so intent was General Banks on going that route that he appealed to Admiral Porter in such a manner that the latter could not decline to accompany him, and on more than one occasion he was referred to the Admiral's objections by General Halleck, who, although wishing to avoid responsibility and to throw the blame on Banks in case of failure, was as eager for this raid as any one.

If Banks simply wanted to hold a strong point in Texas, he had the opportunity at Sabine Pass, which was the nearest point to his base of operations, and into which place he could from time to time have thrown as many troops as he pleased, and kept them under protection of the naval forces. Banks fitted out an expedition to that place, but it was a failure.

In reviewing General Banks' report, it is our purpose to give him the benefit of his own words, which, although specious enough, are sufficient, if carefully studied, to condemn him out of his own mouth. He says :

"In order that the inherent difficulties attending the proposed combined movement—which had been thoroughly tested in the campaign of 1863 and 1864, and which I had represented with as much earnestness as seemed to be proper—might be presented in a manner most likely to gain attention, I directed Major D. C. Houston, chief engineer of the department—who possessed the highest claims to favorable consideration from professional qualifications and experience, and his acquaintance with the route—to prepare a memorial upon operations on Red River, which had been long under consideration. This was transmitted to the headquarters of the army, and appeared to have received the attention and approval of the general-in-chief. It stated with precision the obstacles to be encountered, and the measures necessary to accomplish the object in view. No change would be required in this statement if it had been written in review rather than in anticipation of the campaign. It recommended as a condition indispensable to success : 1st, such complete preliminary organization as would avoid the least delay in our movements after the campaign had opened ; 2d, that a line of supply be established from the Mississippi independent of water-courses ; 3d, the concentration of the forces west of the Mississippi, and such other force as should be assigned to this duty from General Sherman's command, in such a manner as to expel the enemy from northern Louisiana and Arkansas; 4th, such preparation and concert of action among the different corps employed as to prevent the enemy, by keeping him constantly engaged, from operating against our positions or forces elsewhere; and, 5th, that the entire force should be placed under the command of a single General. Preparations for a long campaign were advised, and the month of May indicated as the point of time when the occupation of Shreveport might be anticipated.* Not one of these suggestions, so necessary in conquering the inherent difficulties of the expedition, was carried into execution, nor was it in my power to establish them. The troops under command of General Steele were acting independently of my command, under orders not communicated to me, and at such distance that it was impossible to ascertain his movements, or to inform him of my own, so that we might co-operate with or support each other. The detachment of troops from the command of Major-General Sherman, though operating upon the same line with my own, were under special orders, having ulterior objects in view, and afforded an earnest but only a partial co-operation in the expedition. The distance which separated the different commands, the impossibility of establishing necessary communications between them, the absence of a general authority to command them, the time that was required for the transmission of orders from Washington, and the necessity of immediate action on account of the condition of the rivers and operations contemplated for the armies elsewhere, gave rise to embarrassments in organization of forces and in the execution of orders which could not be overcome.

"In the instructions I received from the Government it was left to my discretion whether or not I would join in this expedition, but I was directed to communicate with General Sherman and General Steele and Admiral Porter upon the subject. I expressed the satisfaction I should find in co-operating with them in a movement deemed of so much importance by the Government, to which my own command was unequal, and my belief that *with the forces designated* it would be entirely successful. Having received from them similar assurances, both my discretion and my authority, so far as the organization of the expedition was concerned, were at an end.

"The disposition of the enemy's forces at that time, according to the best information that could be obtained, was as follows: Magruder had about 20,000 men of all arms, of which 15,000 were serviceable. The main body covered Galveston and Houston from an anticipated movement from Matagorda peninsula, still held by our troops; Walker's division, numbering 7,000 men, were upon the Atchafalaya and Red Rivers, from Opelousas to Fort De Russy; Mouton's division, between the Black and Washita rivers, from Red River to Monroe, numbering 6,000; while Price, with two heavy divisions of infantry, estimated at 5,000, and a large cavalry force, estimated at from 7,000 to 10,000, held the country from Monroe to Camden and Arkadelphia, confronting Steele. Magruder could spare 10,000 of his force to resist an attack from the east, leaving his fortifications well garrisoned on the coast, while Price could furnish at least an additional 5,000 from the north, making a formidable army of from 25,000 to 30,000 men, equal to any forces that could be brought against them, even with the most perfect unity and co-operation of commands. This estimate of the strength of the enemy was given in my dispatch of February 2, but was thought, upon information received by the Government, to be exaggerated. The defences of the enemy consisted of a series of works covering the approaches to Galveston and Houston from the south, the defences of Galveston Bay, Sabine Pass, and Sabine River; Fort De Russy, a formidable work, located three miles

from Marksville, for the defence of the Red River, and extensive and formidable works at Trinity, the junction of the Tensas and Washita at Camden, commanding approaches from the north.

"To meet these forces of the enemy it was proposed to concentrate, in some general plan of operations, 15,000 of the troops under command of General Steele, a detachment of 10,000 from the command of General Sherman, and a force of from 15,000 to 17,000 men from the army of the Gulf, making an army of 40,000 to 42,000 men of all arms, with such gun-boats as the Navy Department should order. Orders were given to my command at once to suspend operations at Galveston, and vigorous preparations were made for the new campaign.

"Having been charged by the President with duties not immediately connected with military operations, but which were deemed important and required my personal attention at New Orleans, the organization of the troops of my command assigned to the expedition was intrusted to Major-General W. B. Franklin. The main body of his command, consisting of the 19th corps—except Grover's division at Madisonville, which was to join him—and one division of the 13th corps, under General Ransom, were at this time on Berwick's Bay, between Berwick City and Franklin, on the Bayou Teche, directly on the line of march for Alexandria and Shreveport. Small garrisons were left at Brownsville and Matagorda Bay, in Texas—positions which, under instructions from the President and subsequently from Lieutenant-General Grant, were not to be abandoned—at New Orleans and at Port Hudson, which was threatened by a vigorous and active enemy. Smaller garrisons at Baton Rouge and Donaldsonville on the river, and at Pensacola and Key West on the coast, constituted the balance of forces under my command.

'It had been arranged that the troops concentrated at Franklin should move for the Red River on the 7th of March, to meet the forces of General Sherman at Alexandria on the 17th. But, for causes stated by General Franklin, their march was delayed until the 13th, at which time the advance, under General A. L. Lee, left Franklin, the whole column following soon after and arriving at Alexandria, the cavalry on the 19th, and the infantry on the 25th.

"On the 13th of March, 1864, one division of the 16th corps, under Brigadier-General Mower, and one division of the 17th corps, under Brigadier-General T. Kilby Smith—the whole under command of Brigadier-General A. J. Smith—landed at Simmsport, on the Atchafalaya, and proceeded at once towards Fort De Russy, carrying it by assault at 4:30 P. M. on the afternoon of the 14th. Two hundred and sixty prisoners and ten heavy guns were captured. Our loss was slight. The troops and transports under General A. J. Smith, and the marine brigade under General Ellet, with the gun-boats, moved to Alexandria, which was occupied without opposition on the 16th of the same month.

"General Lee, of my command, arrived at Alexandria on the morning of the 19th. The enemy, in the meantime, continued his retreat in the direction of Shreveport. Officers of my staff were at Alexandria on the 19th, and I made my headquarters there on the 24th, the forces under General Franklin arriving on the 25th and 26th of March; but as the stage of the water in Red River was too low to admit the passage of the gun-boats or transports over the Falls, the troops encamped near Alexandria, General Smith and his command moving forward 21 miles to Bayou Rapides, above Alexandria. There was but six feet of water in the channel, while seven and a-half were necessary for the second class and ten feet for the first-class gun-boats. The river is narrow, the channel tortuous, changing with every rise, making its navigation more difficult and dangerous, probably, than any of the western rivers, while pilots for the transports were reluctant to enter Government service for this campaign.

"The first gun-boat was unable to cross the rapids until the 26th; others crossed on the 28th, with some transports, and others still on the 2d and 3d of April; the passage having been made with difficulty and danger, occupying several days. Several gun-boats and transports, being then unable to ascend the river, remained at Alexandria or returned to the Mississippi. While at Alexandria, Major-General McPherson, commanding at Vicksburg, called for the immediate return of the marine brigade—a part of General Smith's command—to protect the Mississippi, for which service it had been specially organized. The transports of this brigade were unable to pass above Alexandria. The hospital boat 'Woodford' had been wrecked on the rapids in attempting the passage. The troops were suffering from small-pox, which pervaded all the transports, and they were reported in condition of partial mutiny. It was not supposed at that time that a depot or garrison at Alexandria would be required; and this command, being without available land or water transportation, was permitted to return to the Mississippi, in compliance with the demands of General McPherson; this reduced the strength of the advancing column about 3,000 men.

"The condition of the river and the inability of the transports to pass the Falls made it necessary to establish a depot of supplies at Alexandria, and a line of wagon transportation from the steamers below to those above the Falls. This was a departure from the plan of the campaign, which did not contemplate a post or depot at any point on Red River, and involved the necessity of leaving a division at Alexandria for the purpose of protecting the depot, transports and supplies. Brigadier-General C. Grover was placed in command of the post, and his division left for its defence. This reduced the force of the advancing column about 3,000 men.

"While at Alexandria, on the 21st instant, a movement was organized against the enemy posted at Henderson's Hill, 25 miles in advance. The expedition consisted of three brigades of General A. J. Smith's command, and a brigade of cavalry of the 19th corps, under command of Colonel Lucas, of the 16th Indiana volunteers—the whole under the command of Brigadier-General Mower, of the 16th corps. The enemy was surprised, losing 250 prisoners, 200 horses and four guns, with their caissons. Colonel H. B. Sargent of my staff was severely wounded in this action, and disabled from service during this campaign. This affair reflected the highest credit upon the officers and men engaged."

General Banks' "report" as here quoted, though it sounds plausible enough, will not bear criticism. He implies that a delay of sixteen days was caused by the inability of the fleet to ascend the rapids ("Falls") at Alexandria. It should be remembered that Banks himself did not arrive in Alexandria until the 25th, and the rear-guard of his army on the 26th, after a fatiguing march. At least two days were required to reorganize the different corps after arrival. Banks says the first gun-boat could only pass the Rapids on the 28th, whereas on that day the heaviest of the vessels, the "Eastport," ascended the Falls, and seven or eight others—all that were needed—had been above the Falls for some days waiting for the Army to move. Finally, the gun-boats pushed ahead, and on the 30th the "Eastport,"

which General Banks says delayed the Army, took possession of Grand Ecore, which place had been evacuated by the enemy. Banks' army did not reach Grand Ecore until the 1st, 2d, and 3d of April. How, then, can General Banks pretend to blame the Navy for the detention? It was only intended to take eight vessels to Shreveport, viz.: the "Lexington," "Osage," "Gazelle," "Cricket," "Fort Hindman," "Juliet," "Ouichita" and "Neosho." These vessels mounted 50 guns, some of them heavy ones. The other vessels that passed the Falls were necessary to guard Grand Ecore, and a sufficient force was left to protect Alexandria. If the Navy delayed the Army, how is it the gun-boats arrived so much ahead of the latter at Grand Ecore? In fact, at any time previous to the 29th or 30th of March, a medium-draft gun-boat and any transport had no difficulty in passing above Alexandria. A hospital boat, belonging to the "Marine Brigade," was lost at the Falls, but this was due to the stupidity of her pilot. There was none of the "danger" that Banks mentions, or anything more than the ordinary accidents likely to occur among so many vessels.

No delay was caused by stopping at Alexandria to establish a depot of supplies. The depot was established before Banks arrived, and there was no departure from the plan of campaign in making such arrangement. It was a very necessary arrangement, for the campaign could not have been conducted without using Alexandria as a base of supplies.

The number, etc., of the enemy's forces is greatly overstated by General Banks. They did not, all told, number more than 20,000 men, among them were 6,000 or 7,000 raw troops from Texas, commanded by General Green. These were badly cut up by the gun-boats at Pleasant Hill Landing.

Another mistake of Banks is to be found in the recapitulation of his report. He says eight days may be set down to General Franklin for his tardy movements, and the rest of the time to delay in getting the fleet over the "Falls." The General reflects on the Admiral for undertaking to get twenty iron-clads of heavy draft over the "Falls" and up the river on a falling water. There were but six iron-clads in the fleet, and of these the "Eastport" and "Ozark" were the only two from which trouble might have been anticipated in passing above the "Falls." However, the "Ozark" never delayed the fleet a moment going or coming, and the others easily got above the "Falls." The risk run was the chance of the river falling, for which General Banks is not held responsible. The object of the Admiral was to do everything in his power to make the expedition a success; and supposing that Banks intended to obey his instructions and hold the country, and not thinking that he would retreat on meeting resistance from an inferior force, his intention was to stay up Red River with as large a naval force as he could spare from the Mississippi, until his presence was no longer necessary.

Suppose, as Banks asserts, the fleet did not reach Springfield Landing until "two full days" after the battle of Sabine Cross Roads, that point was reached at the time appointed to meet the General and his army. The Navy's arrival any sooner would not have benefitted him in the least, and he could not, under any circumstances, have reached there before the fleet. The fleet could have reached there sooner, but was delayed by some heavy army transports which were continually getting aground. These heavy vessels were, it is said, sent up by Banks' orders to get down cotton. Any one who knows General Banks will smile at the following:

"The failure of the fleet to move up the river with ordinary expedition, together with the fact that the gun-boats were unable to pass Grand Ecore until the 7th, justified the belief that its advance had been prevented by the low stage of water, and governed the army exclusively in its retrograde movement to Grand Ecore." (!!)

Banks might also have added—impelled in a great measure by the Confederates under General Taylor, who were pressing in his rear.

It is astonishing how visionary some of the generals become after a war is over, and they want to delude the people into giving them seats in Congress. Banks once made a speech to his constituents in which he said: "Had the gun-boats not failed to come to our assistance, we would have met with no reverse"!! On the occasion referred to, there were thirty miles of land between the vessels and the army.

The last chapter in Banks' romance we leave to be criticised by the many thousands who keenly felt the disgrace inflicted on them and upon the country by a most inexperienced General. The Admiral's reports published and on file will show that he gave full credit to the Army for all the assistance the fleet received to get them out of a difficulty into which they fell, owing to Banks' self-assurance. We feel satisfied that no charge of inefficiency can ever be maintained against the Navy, or that through it the lives of those under Banks' command were sacrificed.

It is bad enough for a man to bring disasters upon the country, but when he tries to throw the blame of defeat upon others, and criticises their earnest endeavors to carry out his impracticable plans, he must not expect to be gently dealt with by those whom he fain would injure. We do not pretend to have treated General Banks leniently in our account of his performances, including his "masterly retreat" before an inferior force. It was the Admiral's duty to make the report he did to the Secretary of the Navy, but he stated the case in much milder terms, as regarded General Banks, than did the army officers who served under him, in their evidence before the Committee on the Conduct of the War. We insert one letter from General Kilby Smith which corroborates everything that has been said in regard to Banks leaving the "Eastport" at the mercy of the enemy:

HEADQUARTERS DIVISION 17TH ARMY CORPS, COTILE, April 25th, 1864.

ADMIRAL: Arrived at this point last night. General Banks and army are on the march to Alexandria. We brought up the rear and skirmished all the way. General Banks fought at the crossing of Cane River; not much loss on either side. [Note—General Banks speaks of this as most desperate fighting.] Our fight in the rear was sharp. General A. J. Smith's command is ordered peremptorily to Alexandria; troops are now on the march. You will find the enemy some 2,000 strong on the opposite side. Their artillery does not amount to much; what they have we have crippled. [Note—The General was mistaken about the *crippling*.] Will communicate more fully from Alexandria by the gun-boats "Osage" and "Pittsburg." unless they get off before we arrive.

General Smith and myself both protest at being hurried away. I feel as if we were shamefully deserting you. If I had the power I would march my troops back to Calhoun, or wherever you might need us, if at all. I will try and get a communication to you from General A. J. Smith.

Most respectfully yours,
THOMAS KILBY SMITH,
Brigadier-General Commanding.
To ADMIRAL PORTER.

General Banks' shortcomings were felt in the Army as well as in the Navy, as will appear by the following extract from a report by Captain Wm. S. Burns, Acting-Assistant Adjutant-General on the staff of General A. J. Smith:

"Our victory being so complete, General Banks had ordered the retreating train to be halted, turned about, and everything prepared for an early advance next morning, and about midnight I fell asleep amidst the groans of the wounded; but at two o'clock in the morning was awakened to hear that we were ordered to retreat. Imagine our feelings! General Smith, upon receipt of the order, had gone to General Banks and urged an advance; but when he found the order to retreat was imperative, he begged the privilege of remaining on the field to bury the dead and take care of the wounded; but even this was not allowed. Disgraceful! Criminal! Inhuman! At this late day, when time has mitigated the intensity of the keen feeling then experienced by us who fled, my notes and letters seem overdrawn, and I hesitate to quote literally, but they are a true history, not only of my own personal sense of bitter humiliation—then in my mind —but are a true index of the inner consciousness of nine-tenths of the army; and, although 'military discipline' kept it under, yet so the soldiers thought, talked, and some of them wrote; and even now, when fifteen years have passed away, it is difficult to review these events and write with any degree of calmness or patience of our retreat.
* * * * * * *

"This was a defeat, but a defeat only to our foe. The stake fought for by him was the trans-Mississippi Empire ; by our commanding general, the safe retreat of his army. We won both, abandoned the former to the enemy after he had retreated, and gave to a brilliant victory all the moral results of a defeat. Finally, the Thirty - second Iowa blushes to place upon its banner the name of a field where its dead and wounded were cruelly abandoned to an enemy, who, many hours afterwards, humbly asked leave to care for his own."

When General Banks questions the veracity of officers, he should see what is said of his own in the following extract from the same officer:

"Having whipped our enemy and driven him miles from the battle-field, then to be ordered to run ! We could see no reason for it then and cannot yet, although it may be true, as General Banks says in his official report: 'The occupation of Shreveport could not have been maintained.' But it is not the object of this article to enter into the merits or otherwise of General Banks' decision to retreat; for, of course, there are two sides to every question; but I do censure him for leaving the dead unburied and the wounded (i. e., the greater part of them) to fall into the hands of the enemy. If he had to retreat, why such haste ? Why not wait at least one day and care for the dead and dying ? General Banks is hardly fair toward General Smith in his official report. He says: 'General Smith never declined co-operation with me, nor did he receive orders from me.' It may seem 'to the prejudice of order and military discipline,' for me, as a subordinate, to question the veracity of a commanding general, but when he says, 'nor did he receive orders from me,' I do call his veracity into question. As I have shown, Colonel Shaw, of General Smith's command, reported to General Emory for duty at Pleasant Hill. As no one stood between Generals Banks and Smith—that is, with any authority to command General Smith—who but General Banks could have ordered this ? And in Colonel Shaw's official report, he says: 'I was ordered to report with my brigade to General Banks. By him I was ordered to proceed to the front and report to General Emory,' etc. I could give many other instances where General Smith did receive orders from General Banks. From the moment he reported to him at Alexandria, he was under his orders and received them and obeyed them every day while under his command. To even imagine any other state of affairs would be ridiculous and not tenable. When I reach the cotton chapter of the expedition, I will give one instance where he questioned one of Banks' orders ; but that the circumstances fully justified him in this, will be, I think, the verdict of all honest men."

It is hardly fair to quote what the enemy said against General Banks—still it is interesting to know what the Confederates thought ·

"What a sad picture was now to be seen, where all was beauty and luxury when we first saw it in March ! Governor Moore was with his friends further south, and while fighting over his plantation one day, his wife was advised to leave, and as she left her house the tears came to her eyes as she said: 'Good-bye, once happy home !' Who made it an unhappy one ? We all concluded that it was her husband, as the natural result of treason. Living far in the interior of 'Dixie,' as he did, he undoubtedly thought war's desolation would never reach his happy home. Three years had passed away, and he was an exile—his family leaving their home; the flag he insulted and defied waving over the ruins of his 'once happy home.' Was it not a just retribution ?

"We were now entirely cut off from the outside world, the blockade of the river being most effectual. A large mail for us was captured and destroyed on one of the transports. General Banks would not let us go out in force and give the enemy battle, having issued positive orders not to bring on a general engagement, which order caused a good deal of animated (but private) discussion. It is appropriate at this point to quote again from the letter of the Southern soldier already quoted from : 'The enemy showed less enterprise than I have ever known them to evince. Banks is clearly no commander. Once or twice while he was at Alexandria, the posture of our forces was such that by a sure and comparatively safe movement of ten thousand men he might have insured, beyond peradventure, the capture of Polignac's division. He must have been in the main aware of the position and strength of our forces.'"

Here is another extract from Captain Burns :

"The above view is a fair reflection of our own. We, too, felt that General Banks had 'given up all desire to acquit himself with any credit,' and showed an unaccountable lack of enterprise. Of course, we knew nothing as to the certain result above predicted, of the 'sure and comparatively safe movement of ten thousand men.' But having about that number, General Smith, having his hands tied by the order not to bring on a general engagement, and being obliged in conformity with it (another instance of receipt of orders from General Banks) to sit down quietly on Governor Moore's plantation and simply sweep away the enemy when too closely reconnoitering our position, might be excused for giving vent to his feelings in unmistakable language, at such (to him a 'West Pointer') a new phase of military life.

"I have stated that when I reached Alexandria, I would show that it was General Banks, not General Smith, who meditated the abandonment of the fleet. Dr. Staples (who, owing to the wound of Dr. Derby, already spoken of, was now acting-medical director on General Smith's staff) writes me as follows: 'One day, when the wing-dams were about half completed, General Smith asked me to accompany him to General Emory's quarters. They were soon engaged in earnest conversation, and I heard Emory say there was a bad outlook ; that General Banks had just informed him that Colonel Bailey thought it would take a week longer to get the fleet over the Falls, and Banks was very uneasy and seriously contemplated abandoning the fleet to its fate and marching away. General Smith replied, with some Anglo - Saxon more forcible than polite, that he wouldn't leave Admiral Porter until that locality, from which we all hope to escape, had frozen over. We went from General Emory's to Admiral Porter's boat, and General Smith told the Admiral what he had just heard, and assured him that orders, or no orders, his command should not leave the fleet until they saw it safe through to the Mississippi River. Admiral Porter replied that he was not surprised to hear such news, as he had been anticipating as much. He expressed much gratitude for General Smith's proffers of aid, and declared that if the expedition had been under his command it would not have failed.'"

We do not think we have said as much as as that against General Banks. When one remembers Banks' evidence before the "Committee on the Conduct of the War," and compares it with the following statement of Captain Burns, he might suspect

Banks of the want of ingenuousness which he imputes to others:

"I have now come to a subject which requires delicate handling; but even an historical sketch of the Red River campaign cannot well be written without a reference to it. As the expedition had been a decided failure in a military point of view, so it was a great success as a cotton speculation. It was difficult for us to believe that which our eyes saw, but it was the expressed and indignant belief of many in the army that something was wrong in the manipulation of cotton now being enacted before our eyes. We all saw an immense amount of bagging and roping upon the steamer 'Black Hawk' (General Banks' headquarters boat) when it arrived at Alexandria, and it was then said it was for cotton. And during our occupancy of Alexandria on our retreat, I myself saw steamers loaded with cotton and sent down the river under the protection of the hospital flag, and Lieutenant Pannes (ordnance officer on General Smith's staff) sends me the following extract from his diary:

"'APRIL 29, 1864.—Cotton is being loaded on the boats by General Banks' order. Even the hospital boat "Superior" is used for that purpose; went out with Captain Burns to convince myself of that fact.

"'MAY 1.—The three cotton boats returned, having been fired into.'

"In a letter written by Colonel Shaw, who was at this time with his brigade at Governor Moore's plantation, he says:

"'The ostensible purpose of occupying this position was the securing of forage, but as scarcely any was procured and several thousand bushels of corn were carelessly burned, it was thought a somewhat suspicious circumstance that a large ginning establishment, which was covered by our lines, was turning out some fifteen or twenty bales of cotton per day. But whether well founded or not, the impression was well-nigh universal that army movements were controlled to a considerable extent by the cotton interest. Such a state of affairs was most demoralizing and disheartening.'

"From our first entrance into the Red River country we had been daily hearing reports which seemed too preposterous for belief ; reports that an understanding existed between somebody and somebody else that there was to be no fighting on this campaign, but that the Southern Army was to fall back gradually as our army advanced and gathered up the cotton, for which, in some way not explained, the Southerners were to be paid. Also that Generals A. J. Smith and Dick Taylor, not having been informed of this secret, and both being fighting-men, had entered the campaign to fight when it became necessary, and General Smith's capture of Fort De Russy, and Dick Taylor's forcing the fight at Sabine Cross Roads, had upset the calculations of the different somebodies. This report of a secret understanding was reiterated day after day until it was believed by many to be true; but many more of us were incredulous until we witnessed this strange shipment of cotton under the *hospital flag*, which was either a gross deception under the sacredness of a hospital flag or the carrying out of a bargain."

We do not care to criticise General Banks further, otherwise we might extend these extracts; so we will leave his case to the judgment of history.

At one time we could not help feeling sorry for General Banks, for the humiliating position in which he was placed was not altogether his fault. Had he not attempted to draw attention from himself by throwing blame on the Navy, we should doubtless have had a better opinion of him.

Most generals must expect reverses. Frederick the Great ran away at his first battle, and was not always successful in after years, although one of the greatest soldiers of modern times, and in his most noted defeat he took all the blame on his own shoulders. A general will, in fact, gain more credit by assuming the responsibility of defeat than by attempting to shirk it.

With all General Banks' faults, he had some striking good qualities. He was a gentleman in his manners, and the Admiral never had to complain of a want of courtesy towards his officers or himself except once. He looked well in his uniform, and kept himself always scrupulously neat, though rather theatrical in his style of gloves and boots. With a better surrounding he would have had more success as a general. He had not much force of character, and lacked nerve in time of danger. As Governor of Massachusetts and Speaker of the United States House of Representatives, no one has ever questioned his ability; yet, strange to say, Banks always preferred to be considered a soldier rather than a statesman. He never had sufficient military force to properly occupy the country under his immediate command, much less to make expeditions into hostile regions.

The expedition up Red River toward Shreveport was the end of his military career. As Governor of Louisiana, Banks was not equal to Butler, who, with less *savoir faire*, had more decision of character and made a better record.

In taking leave of General Banks and Red River, we will give him the benefit of the last word, and append to this narrative that portion of his report where he appears in melodramatic attitude towards the Admiral and the Navy—"That Navy which he and the Army preserved, while it did nothing to help itself !"

While we acknowledge that General Banks and his army did all in their power to assist the fleet over the "Falls," we do not admit that they preserved it. The Navy had one hundred miles of river above the "Falls," with water deep enough to navigate, and, if Banks had left, they could have maintained themselves there, running up and down, despite all the forces in that part of Louisiana. There were four months' provisions on hand, and in less than that time the desired rise of water came.

General Banks is a clever writer, but any one who reads his report will detect that coloring of which we have on several occasions complained.

The following is the last specimen that will be quoted, and with this ends the account of the Red River expedition. It is an extract from General Banks' report :

" The first difficulty encountered was in the navigation of the river. Sixteen days' delay caused by the inability of the fleet to pass the Rapids at Alexandria, and three days' delay at Grand Ecore in waiting the rise of the river, enabled the enemy to concentrate his forces, and rendered impossible that celerity of movement by the Army which the success of the expedition demanded. Eight days of the delay at Alexandria would have been attributable to the tardy organization and movements of Franklin's command ; but the fleet was unable to pass the Falls until eight days after his arrival at Alexandria. This delay was doubtless owing to the impracticable navigation of the river ; but it is not improper to say that the forecast and diligence which is enforced upon all men in the daily affairs of life would have forbidden an attempt to force a fleet of so much importance to the free navigation of the Mississippi to a point from which it could never hope to escape, except upon the theory that the river ought to or might rise. The movement of the Navy, in a dispatch of Rear-Admiral D. D. Porter, to which the Secretary of the Navy has given official publication and sanction, is attributed to the ' request' of General Banks, who ' deemed the co-operation of the gun-boats so essential to success, that he (Porter) had to run some risks and make unusual exertions to get them over the ' Falls.' This implies that the responsibility of his action rests upon the Army ; but it is not consistent with the facts. The co-operation of the Navy was an indispensable condition and basis of the expedition. Major-General Halleck informed me, January 11, that he had been assured by the Navy Department that Admiral Porter would be prepared to co-operate with the Army in its movements ; and the Admiral himself informed me, February 26, that he was ' prepared to ascend Red River with a large fleet of gun-boats,' and to co-operate with the Army at any time when the water was high enough. The fleet was as necessary to the campaign as the Army. Had it been left to my discretion, I should have reluctantly undertaken, in a campaign requiring but eight or ten light-draft gun-boats, to force twenty heavy iron-clads 490 miles up a river proverbially as treacherous as the rebels who defended it, and which had given notice of its character by steadily falling when, as the Admiral reports, all other rivers were booming. There is a better reason for the disregard of the palpable difficulties of navigation than the over-zealous counsel of army officers in nautical affairs. In a subsequent dispatch Admiral Porter says, that ' all my vessels navigated the river to

Grand Ecore with ease, and with some of them I reached Springfield Landing, the place designated for the gun-boats to meet the Army. My part was successfully accomplished ; the failure of the Army to proceed, and the retreat to Grand Ecore, left me almost at the mercy of the enemy.' The records of the campaign do not at all support the reckless and fiery ardor of this statement. The fleet did not reach the ' place appointed' until two full days after the first decisive battle with the enemy. The Admiral occupied four days in moving one hundred and four miles on what he calls a ' rising river,' with ' good water,' to the place appointed. General T. Kilby Smith states that the fleet made twenty miles on the 7th, fifty-seven miles on the 8th, eighteen miles on the 9th, and nine miles on the 10th of April—total, one hundred and four miles. The failure of the fleet to move up the river with ordinary expedition, together with the fact that the gun-boats were unable to pass Grand Ecore until the 7th, justified the belief that its advance had been prevented by the low stage of water, and governed the Army exclusively in its retrograde movement to Grand Ecore, as it did in every important operation of the campaign. The Admiral's dispatch does not mention the fact that, in addition to the ' mercy ' of the enemy, he had the support of General T. Kilby Smith's division of 2,500 men, whose most gallant and honorable part in the preservation of the fleet of gun-boats and transports is not referred to, in what the Admiral calls ' this curious affair between [the enemy's] infantry and gun-boats.' In view of the published dispatches of Admiral Porter, it is proper for me to say, that every position of difficulty in which the Army was placed in this campaign was the immediate and direct consequence of delay in the operations of the Navy. This may have been inevitable and entirely justifiable from the condition of the river. It is not in my province to pass judgment upon its operations ; but the fact remains, nevertheless. During my term of service, it has been an invariable rule of conduct, from which I have never departed, to forbear the expression of opinion or complaint upon the official action of others ; but I feel it to be a solemn duty to say, in this official and formal manner, that Admiral Porter's published official statements relating to the Red River campaign are at variance with the truth, of which there are many thousand living witnesses, and do foul injustice to the officers and soldiers of the Army, living and dead, to whom the Navy Department owes exclusively the preservation and honor of its fleet."

MISSISSIPPI SQUADRON, JANUARY 1st, 1864.

REAR-ADMIRAL DAVID D. PORTER.

CAPTAIN A. M. PENNOCK, FLEET-CAPTAIN.

STEAMER "BLACK-HAWK"—FLAG-SHIP.

Lieutenant - Commanders, K. Randolph Breese and Watson Smith (Flag) ; Fleet-Surgeon, Ninian Pinkney ; Assistant Surgeon, R. T. Edes ; Acting-Assistant Paymaster, C. H. Kirkendall ; Acting-Master, James Fitzpatrick ; Ensigns, F. J. Naile, M. W. Sanders and S. W. Terry ; Acting-Ensigns, Wm. Wardrop, Henry Baker, J. M. Alden and D. Pratt Mannix ; Acting-Master's Mates, R. S. Howell, Harry Woodruff, David V. Porter and C. H. Sedgewick ; Engineers: Acting-Chief, Geo. W. Walker ; Acting-First-Assistant, O. G. Ritchie ; Acting-Third-Assistants, J. C. Barr and W. B. Ritchie ; Gunner, John R. Hall ; Acting-Carpenter, Noah Dean.

IRON-CLAD STEAMER "ESSEX."

Commander, Robert Townsend ; Acting-Assistant

Surgeon, Thomas Allen ; Acting-Assistant Paymaster, C. W. Slamm ; Acting-Masters, J. C. Parker and E. Reese ; Acting-Ensign, Spencer Johnson ; Acting-Master's Mates, J. H. Berry and C. M. Fuller ; Engineers: Acting-Chief, J. K. Heap ; Acting-First-Assistant, J. L. Hillard ; Acting-Second-Assistants, E. P. Sprague and C. H. Burt ; Acting-Third-Assistants, Henry Wood and Nicholas Saner.

IRON-CLAD STEAMER "EASTPORT."

Lieutenant-Commander, S. L. Phelps ; Acting-Assistant Surgeon, M. L. Gerould ; Acting-Assistant Paymaster, W. H. Gilman ; Acting-Ensigns, S. Poole, R. M. Williams and E. H. Qualding ; Acting-Master's Mates, R. A. Day, R. A. Treat and B. W. Herr ; Engineers : Acting-Chief, Henry Hartwig ; Acting-First-Assistants, T. F. Ackerman and John

S. Moore ; Acting-Second-Assistant, G. N. Heizel ; Acting-Third-Assistants, W. T. Baxter and J. F. Liddell; Acting-Gunner, J. F. Riblet ; Acting-Carpenter, James Rouse.

IRON-CLAD STEAMER "LAFAYETTE."

Lieutenant-Commander, James P. Foster; Acting-Volunteer-Lieutenant, Edward Morgan ; Acting-Assistant Surgeon, D. H. Hayden; Acting-Assistant Paymaster, J. P. Kelly ; Acting-Ensigns, J. L. Bryant, F. G. Sampson and J. L. Moran; Acting-Master's Mates, Paul Morgan, W. P. Higbee, S. O. Lovell, S. R. Winram and C. H. Slocum; Engineers: Acting-Chief, Robert Tate; Acting-First-Assistant, James Wilkins ; Acting-Second-Assistant, J. W. Paull; Acting-Third-Assistants, E. B. Hill and Max Pratt; Acting-Gunner, George Price; Acting-Carpenter, J. W. Lister.

IRON-CLAD STEAMER "BENTON."

Lieutenant-Commander, James A. Greer; Assistant Surgeon, N. L. Bates; Acting-Assistant Paymaster, C. G. Lowndes ; Acting-Masters, E. C. Breman, J. F. Reed and N. B. Willetts; Acting-Ensigns, Wm. J. Lees, H. S. O'Grady and P. H. Randolph; Acting-Master's Mates, Wm. Kisner and Hiram Simonton; Engineers: Acting-Chief, Job V. Starr; Acting-First-Assistant, H. W. Fairfoul; Acting-Second-Assistants, Oliver Bray and A. A. Jenks; Acting-Third-Assistant, Benj. Farmer; Acting-Carpenter, Richard Rockford.

IRON-CLAD STEAMER " LOUISVILLE."

Lieutenant-Commander, Elias K. Owen; Acting-Assistant Surgeon, Fayette Clapp; Acting-Assistant Paymaster, D. L. Ruth; Acting-Ensigns, H. A. Coffenberry, Chas. Nelson, Henry Harkins, G. V. Mead, R. H. Longlands, Frank Bates and J. T. Blackford; Acting-Master's Mates, J. J. Drew, Chas. Smith, Jr., and C. S. Scanlan; Engineers: Acting-Chief, J. B. Fulton; Acting-First-Assistant, J. J. Hardy; Acting-Second-Assistant, C. W. Reynolds; Acting-Third-Assistant, C. F. Degelman; Acting-Gunner, William Shields; Acting-Carpenter, D. H. Curry.

IRON-CLAD STEAMER "TUSCUMBIA."

Lieutenant-Commander, James W. Shirk; Assistant Paymaster, Geo. A. Lyon ; Acting-Ensigns, Lewis Kenney and E. M. Clark; Engineers: Acting-Chief, J. W. Hartuper ; Acting-First-Assistant, Perry South; Acting-Second-Assistant, W. J. Milligan.

IRON-CLAD STEAMER " CHOCTAW."

Lieutenant-Commander, F. M. Ramsey ; Acting-Assistant Paymaster, Wm. N. Whitehouse; Acting-Master, W. A. Griswold; Acting-Ensigns, Ezra Beaman, W. C. Bennett, A. S. Palmer and L. R. Hamersly; Acting-Master's Mates, T. Hopkins and Henry Marsh; Engineers: Acting-Chief, N. P. Baldwin; Acting-First-Assistant, C. E. Arbuthnot; Acting-Second-Assistant; Joseph Blake; Acting Third-Assistants, S. C. Babbitt and E. H. Austin; Acting-Gunner, Reuben Applegate; Acting-Carpenter, John A. Stewart.

IRON-CLAD STEAMER " CONESTOGA."

Lieutenant-Commander, Thomas O. Selfridge ; Acting-Assistant Surgeon, S. L. Adams; Acting-Assistant Paymaster, E. D. Ilsley; Acting-Master, Gilbert Morton; Acting-Ensigns, Thomas Devine, S. J. Dwight, J. C. Peterson and Wm. Neil ; Acting-Master's Mate, Alanson Hamilton ; Engineers : Acting-Chief, Thomas Cook ; Acting-First-Assistant, Alex. Magee; Acting-Second-Assistant, Chas. Fistadt; Acting-Third-Assistants, James O'Neil and Andrew Lusk; Acting-Carpenter, John J. Hays.

STEAMER " MOOSE."

Lieutenant-Commander, LeRoy Fitch; Acting-Assistant Paymaster, J. W. Clarke ; Acting-Ensigns, Edward Morgan, John Revall and J. H. Rice ; Act-ing-Master's Mates, J. M. Tucker, C. H. Stout and C. W. Spooner; Engineers : Acting-First-Assistant, T. N. Hall; Acting-Second-Assistant, Charles McMillan.

STEAMER "TAYLOR."

Lieutenant-Commander, James M. Prichett; Acting-Assistant Surgeon, Wm. P. Baird; Acting-Assistant Paymaster, Geo. H. Holt; Acting-Ensigns, G. L. Smith, Charles Ackley, John Hill and J. W. Lalor; Acting-Master's Mates, W. H. C. Michael, G. H. Williamson and H. S. Allen; Engineers : Acting-Chief, James Fleming; Acting-First-Assistant, J. R. Ramsey; Acting-Second-Assistants, Wm. Finch and Philip Sheridan ; Acting-Third-Assistant, E. M. Bumpas; Acting-Carpenter, J. M. Peabody.

IRON-CLAD STEAMER "MOUND CITY."

Lieutenant-Commander, Byron Wilson; Acting-Assistant Surgeon, Thomas Rice; Acting-Assistant Paymaster, B. J. Donahoe; Acting Master, F. T. Coleman; Acting-Ensigns, S. B. Coleman, D. Stebbins and W. H. Decker; Acting-Master's Mate, R. T. Lamport; Engineers: Acting-Chief, Edw. Merriman; Acting-First-Assistant, E. R. Clemens; Acting-Second-Assistant, J. M. Hartnett; Acting-Third-Assistants, G. L. Baker and Richard Carter; Acting-Gunner, T. H. Green; Acting-Carpenter, Jerome Burns.

IRON-CLAD STEAMER "LEXINGTON."

Lieutenant, George M. Bache ; Acting-Assistant Surgeon, H. M. Mixer ; Acting-Assistant Paymaster, T. C. Doane ; Acting-Ensigns, Henry Booby, J. G. Migler and C. C. Briggs; Acting-Master's Mates, Daniel Winget, Howard Hale and Ezra McDunn; Engineers: Acting-Chief, W. H. Meredith; Acting-First-Assistant, A. L. Mann; Acting-Second-Assistant, Reuben Story; Acting-Third-Assistants, Jacob Vittinger and Wm. T. Neal; Acting-Gunner, Louis Frederick ; Acting-Carpenter, Richard Carroll.

STEAMER " FOREST ROSE."

Acting-Volunteer-Lieutenant, Charles A. Wright; Acting-Assistant Surgeon, R. Cadwallader; Acting-Assistant Paymaster, C. M. Dunham ; Acting-Ensigns, S. E. Brown, Conrad Erickson and H. B. Graves; Acting-Master's Mates, Ira Athearn, Chas. Smith and C. W. Crocker; Engineers: First-Assistant, Francis Marsh; Acting-Second-Assistant, E. H. Goble; Acting-Third-Assistant, Silas Haskey.

STEAMER "FORT HINDMAN."

Acting-Volunteer-Lieutenant, John Pearce; Acting-Assistant Paymaster, A. B. Adams; Acting-Ensigns, F. A. Oliver, Charles Marsden and F. H. Wait; Acting-Master's Mates, B. G. Van Dyke, S. N. Barker, C. F. A. McCord and H. Shoemaker; Engineers: Acting-First-Assistant; Thomas Girty; Acting-Second-Assistant, D. B. Cox; Acting-Third-Assistants, Eli Powell and Reuben Yocum.

STEAMER "HASTINGS."

Acting-Volunteer-Lieutenant, A. R. Langthorne; Acting-Assistant Surgeon, J. M. Flint ; Acting-Assistant Paymaster, P. J. Stone ; Acting-Master, J. W. Morehead; Acting-Ensigns, W. C. Turner and C. H. Reed; Acting-Master's Mates, E. C. Urner, Frank Seymour and F. M. Clark; Engineers : Acting-First-Assistant, John H. Scott; Acting-Second-Assistants, Edwin Senior and Samuel Weaver; Acting-Third-Assistants, A. M. Wasson and Geo. W. Amsden.

STEAMER "BRILLIANT."

Acting-Volunteer-Lieutenant, Charles G. Perkins ; Acting-Assistant Surgeon, Milton James; Acting-Assistant Paymaster, Horace Talcott ; Acting-Ensigns, G. D. Little, J. J. Perkins and Richard McAllister ; Acting-Master's Mates, T. G. Herron and J. H. Neely ; Engineers: Acting-First-Assistant,

Wm. A. Willey; Acting-Second-Assistants, Samuel Ecoff and James Cutter.

STEAMER "ST. CLAIR."

Acting-Volunteer-Lieutenant, T. B. Gregory; Acting-Assistant Paymaster, H. F. Browne; Acting-Ensigns, Warren Burch and G. W. Garrison; Acting-Master's Mates, E. C. Williams, J. H. Hurd and H. O. Proctor; Engineers: Acting-First-Assistant, Wm. McLean; Acting-Second-Assistant, Edward Lozier; Acting-Third-Assistant, F. A. Morse.

STEAMER "SILVER CLOUD."

Acting-Volunteer-Lieutenant, A. F. O'Neill; Acting-Assistant Surgeon, O. B. Damon; Acting-Assistant Paymaster, W. H. Hathorne; Acting-Ensigns, Robert Wilkinson and J. M. Reid; Acting-Master's Mates, Frank Middleton, R. S. Critchell and J. M. Darrah; Engineers: Acting-First-Assistant, B. F. Clark; Acting-Second-Assistant, W. A. Collins; Acting-Third-Assistant, James Folger.

STEAMER "COVINGTON."

Acting-Volunteer-Lieutenant, George P. Lord; Acting-Assistant Surgeon, Emile Gavarret; Acting-Assistant Paymaster, John T. Lee; Acting-Ensigns, Edw. Alford and John Powell; Acting-Master's Mates, W. H. English, C. W. Gross, J. W. Richards and Ignatius Dunn; Engineers: Acting-First-Assistant, J. A. Burns; Acting-Second Assistant, W. R. Hoder; Acting-Third-Assistants, J. T. English and Southwell Lyons.

STEAMER "QUEEN CITY."

Acting-Volunteer-Lieutenant, George W. Brown; Acting-Assistant Surgeon, Louis Westfall; Acting-Assistant Paymaster, C. S. Sims; Acting-Master, Michael Hickey; Acting-Ensigns, H. E. Alexander, James Roberts and F. M. Hathaway; Acting-Master's Mates, Geo. W. Hall, W. P. Eakly and E. W. Johnson; Engineers: Acting-First-Assistants, Irwin Fox and Wm. Downey; Acting-Second-Assistant, G. W. Shellenberger; Acting-Third-Assistant, Geo. S. Read.

STEAMER "TAWAH."

Acting-Volunteer-Lieutenant, Jason Goudy; Acting-Assistant Surgeon, H. S. Nicholson; Acting-Assistant Paymaster, D. W. Hale; Acting-Master, M. V. B. Haines; Acting-Ensigns, J. B. Williams and Joseph Sawyer; Acting-Master's Mates, I. P. Neave and John W. Adams; Engineers: Acting-First-Assistant, J. H. Linn; Acting-Second-Assistant, T. J. Reed; Acting-Third-Assistants, John Henry and Walter Mossington.

STEAMER "KEY WEST."

Acting-Volunteer-Lieutenant, E. M. King; Acting-Assistant Surgeon, R. W. Gifford; Acting-Assistant Paymaster, W. B. Crosby, Jr.; Acting-Master, M. J. Cronin; Acting-Ensigns, John H. Welsh and N. A. Closson; Acting-Master's Mates, Wm. Hammett, Jr., Menzies Dickson and John Winram; Engineers: Acting-First-Assistant, R. J. Stone; Acting-Second-Assistants, G. W. Dean and G. L. Mortimer; Acting-Third-Assistant, Michael Sodon.

STEAMER "PEOSTA."

Acting-Volunteer-Lieutenant, Thos. E. Smith; Acting-Assistant Surgeon, John Wise; Acting-Assistant Paymaster, J. C. Spalding; Acting-Ensigns, Edw. Manser, C. H. Gulick and A. S. Hurlbut; Acting-Master's Mates, R. T. Nelson and Geo. P. Vance; Engineers: Acting-First-Assistant, Geo. H. Warner; Acting-Second-Assistant, S. W. Evans; Acting-Third-Assistants, D. E. Nugent and G. W. Makefield; Gunner, J. A. McDonald; Acting-Carpenter, Wm. B. Reid.

STEAMER "REINDEER."

Acting-Volunteer-Lieutenant, Henry A. Glassford; Acting-Assistant Surgeon, W. C. Foster; Acting-Assistant Paymaster, W. W. Barry; Acting-Ensigns, A. C. Sears and W. H. Hall; Acting-Master's

Mates, N. F. Vaughan, T. M. Lewis and J. E. Wright; Engineers: Acting-First-Assistant, A. H. Bagby; Acting-Third-Assistant, G. M. Hayman.

STEAMER "GENERAL PRICE."

Acting-Volunteer-Lieutenant, J. F. Richardson; Acting Assistant Surgeon, Geo. Harvey; Acting-Assistant Paymaster, J. W. McLellan; Acting-Ensigns, G. W. Pratt, J. H. Seever and D. P. Bosworth; Acting-Master's Mates, D. McKay and Peter Barclay; Engineers: Acting-First-Assistant, D. E. Weaver; Acting Third-Assistants, W. H. Coulter, Alex. Campbell, J. B. Baldwin and R. A. Kyle.

IRON-CLAD STEAMER "PITTSBURG."

Acting-Volunteer-Lieutenant, W. R. Hoel; Acting-Assistant Surgeon, F. M. Follett; Acting-Assistant Paymaster, C. H. Gould; Acting-Master, Geo. W. Rogers; Acting-Ensigns, C. N. Hall, Jas. Ovatt, Freeman Vincent and G. W. Garlick; Acting-Master's Mates, H. N. Wells, John Scott and C. B. Jones; Engineers: Acting-First-Assistant, S. B. Goble; Acting-Second-Assistants, E. R. Pavy, W. H. Mitchell and Julius Elliter; Acting-Gunner, F. C. Green; Acting-Carpenter, Charles Poplar.

IRON-CLAD STEAMER "CHILLICOTHE."

Acting-Volunteer-Lieutenant, J. P. Couthouy; Acting-Assistant Surgeon, G. C. Osgood; Acting-Assistant Paymaster, J. H. Hathaway Acting-Master, W. T Power; Acting-Ensigns, W. Muir, J. C. Hall and H. A. Hannon; Acting-Master's Mates, James Harrington and C. S. Wells; Engineers: Acting-Chief, A. W. Hardy; Acting-First-Assistant, Charles Trotter; Acting-Second-Assistant, J. W. Hymen; Acting-Third-Assistants, J. W. Terrell and Anthony Lane; Acting-Gunner, W. E. Keyes; Acting-Carpenter, J. H. Fink.

STEAMER "GENERAL BRAGG."

Acting-Volunteer-Lieutenant, Cyrenius Dominey; Acting Assistant Surgeon, F. A. Castle; Acting-Assistant Paymaster, J. H. Jenkins; Acting-Ensigns, Thomas Burns, T. J. McLaughlin and M. Huston; Acting-Master's Mates, James Williams and P. M. Frost; Engineers: Acting-Chief, J. Miller; Acting-First-Assistant, Jonah Slocum; Acting-Second-Assistant, C. L. Bonchard; Acting-Third-Assistant, Joseph Anderson; Acting-Carpenter, J. W. Kennedy.

IRON-CLAD STEAMER "NEOSHO."

Acting-Volunteer-Lieutenant, Samuel Howard; Acting-Assistant Surgeon, M. A. Miller; Acting-Assistant Paymaster, W. H. Byrn; Acting Ensigns, E. F. Brooks, Jas. Downs, E. P. Bragg and R. Howden; Acting-Master's Mates, H. J. Kiskadden, Alex. Semple and H. B. Purdy; Engineers: Acting-Chief, Wm. Mills; Acting-First-Assistant, W. C. Sanford; Acting-Second-Assistant, J. L. Miles; Acting-Third-Assistants, J. F. Humphreys and M. C. Noland; Acting-Gunner, W. T. Devlan; Acting-Carpenter, J. O. Baker.

STEAMER "RATTLER."

Acting-Volunteer-Lieutenant, James Laning; Acting-Assistant Surgeon, Scollay Parker; Acting-Assistant Paymaster, Geo. P. Peck; Acting-Master, D. W. Glenny; Acting-Ensigns, Wm. Ferguson and E. P. Nellis; Acting-Master's Mates, H. E. Church, M. C. Pickering and John Cronin; Engineers: Acting-First-Assistant, James L. Smith; Acting-Second-Assistant, G. W. Shields; Acting-Third-Assistants, Robert Russell and James H. Hume.

STEAMER "EXCHANGE."

Acting-Volunteer-Lieutenant, J. S. Hurd; Acting-Assistant Surgeon, G. E. Francis; Acting-Assistant Paymaster, J. W. Gardner; Acting-Ensigns, C. L. Manly and Daniel Jones; Acting-Master's Mates, R. W. Brown, H. M. Scott and G. T. Miller; Engineers: Acting-First-Assistant, A. G. Perkins; Acting-Second-Assistant, C. C. Streepey; Acting-Third-Assistant, B. T. Graham.

STEAMER "BROWN."

Acting-Volunteer-Lieutenant, J. A. French; Acting-Ensign, Jacob Shinn; Acting-Master's Mates, Martin Kelly and H. A. Thoburn; Engineers: Acting-First-Assistant, Rensler Cutter; Acting-Second-Assistant, N F. Johnson; Acting-Third-Assistant, A. N. French.

HOSPITAL STEAMER "RED ROVER."

Acting-Volunteer-Lieutenant, Wm. R. Wells; Acting-Assistant Surgeons, Geo. H. Bixby, Wm. F. McNutt and Wm. H. Willson; Acting-Master, Henry E. Bartlett; Acting-Ensigns, J. G. Waters, Charles King and Jos. Beauchamp; Acting-Master's Mate, C. B. Plattenburg; Engineers: Acting-First-Assistants, W. J. Buffington and W. O. Logue; Acting-Second-Assistant, W. F. Holmes; Acting-Third-Assistants, J. A. Goodloe and G. W. Voice; Acting-Carpenter, Harlow Kinney.

STEAMER "LINDEN."

Acting-Master, T. M. Farrell; Acting-Assistant Surgeon, J F. Field; Acting-Assistant Paymaster, Arthur Sibley; Acting-Ensigns, R. H. Cameron, Cassilly Adams, Chas. Swendson and Joseph McDonald; Acting-Master's Mates, Wm. C. Williams, R. S. Ballester, N. F. Brown and W. C. Frost; Engineers: Acting-First-Assistant, Wm. C. Perry; Acting-Second-Assistant, Wm. M. Fletcher; Acting-Third-Assistant, C. M. Milligan.

STEAMER "KENWOOD."

Acting-Master, John Swaney; Acting-Assistant Surgeon, P. Treadwell; Acting-Assistant Paymaster, H. B. Witherell; Acting-Ensigns, J. C. Wells, G. R. Mott and J. L. Read; Acting-Master's Mates, N. H. Conklin, W. R. Moffatt, H. A. Vaughan and Claren Laird; Engineers: Acting-First-Assistant, Thomas Sheffer; Acting-Second-Assistant, T. J. Malbon; Acting-Third-Assistant, J. B. Holman.

STEAMER "FAIR PLAY."

Acting-Master, Geo. J. Groves; Acting-Assistant Surgeon, W. W. Howard; Acting-Assistant Paymaster, J. G. Sankey; Acting-Ensign, W. C. Coulson; Acting-Master's Mates, W. S. Scott and A. Diserens; Engineers: Acting-First-Assistant, R. A. Mattratha; Acting-Second-Assistant, G. S. Collins; Acting-Third-Assistants, Wm. Bell and C. W. Egster; Acting-Carpenter, Thomas Manning.

STEAMER "SPRINGFIELD.'

Acting-Master, Joseph Watson; Acting-Ensign, H. T. Keene; Acting-Master's Mates, S. H. Harbeson, Jas. Cunningham, John Gregg and David Pullman; Engineers: Acting-First-Assistant, R. L. McLean; Acting-Third-Assistant, Morris Van Fossen.

STEAMER "FAWN."

Acting-Master, John R. Grove; Acting-Assistant Paymaster, A. S. Apgar; Acting-Ensigns, John Sullivan and M. A. Knox; Acting-Master's Mates, Charles Murray, E. D. O'Bryan, J. A. Seaman and John Cowdon; Engineers: Acting-First-Assistant, Edw. C. Peck; Acting-Second-Assistant, G. W. Gough; Acting-Third-Assistant, Michael O'Riley.

STEAMER "PAW PAW."

Acting-Master, A. F. Thompson; Acting-Assistant Surgeon, Jos. Honnan, Acting-Assistant Paymaster, Alex. S. McWilliams; Acting-Ensigns, W. L. Constantine, Pat. Donnelly and J. H. Rivers; Acting-Master's Mates, John Pybus, W. A. Birchard and Julien D. Coriell; Engineers: Acting-First-Assistant, Ezekiel Reynolds; Acting-Second-Assistant, B. S. Bull; Acting-Third-Assistant, T. K. Hill.

STEAMER "NAUMKEAG."

Acting-Master, John Rogers; Acting-Assistant Surgeon, E. LeRoy Draper; Acting-Assistant Paymaster, H. B. Mears; Acting-Ensigns, Arthur O'Leary and Jos. Meyer; Acting-Master's Mates, John Dunlop, F. D. Campbell, Alex. Proctor and

Wm. Cassidy; Engineers: Acting-First-Assistant, Edmund Cage; Acting-Second-Assistant, J. A. McCormack; Acting-Third-Assistant, James B. Byland.

STEAMER "SILVER LAKE."

Acting-Master, Jos. C. Coyle; Acting-Assistant Surgeon, J. H. Mills; Acting-Assistant Paymaster, G. D. Rand; Acting-Ensigns, G. W. Bone, F. G. Jobson and H. H. Pierce; Acting-Master's Mates, John Fisher and Samuel McKee; Engineers: Acting-First-Assistant, John Connolly; Acting-Second-Assistant, Orrin Burroughs; Acting-Third-Assistant, J. C. Jones.

STEAMER "CHAMPION."

Acting-Master, Alfred Phelps, Jr.; Acting-Assistant Surgeon, A. L. Vail; Acting-Assistant Paymaster, G. T. Bemis; Acting-Ensigns, Felix McCann, Mervin Allen and Anthony Hagerup; Acting-Master's Mate, Herman Alms; Engineers: Acting-First-Assistant, John Johnston; Acting-Second-Assistants, Geo. Waddle and C. A. Fisher; Acting-Third-Assistant, J. J. Suor.

STEAMER "ALEXANDRIA."

Acting-Master, D. P. Rosenmiller; Engineers: Acting-First-Assistant, H. C. Snibley; Acting-Third-Assistant, J. S. Willcoxson.

STEAMER "GREAT WESTERN."

Acting-Master, Thomas Bates; Acting-Assistant Surgeon, G. A. Warren; Acting-Assistant Paymaster, J. H. Marshall; Acting-Ensigns, A. M. Rowland and P. R. Starr; Acting-Master's Mates, Richard Mitchell and L. M. Knapp; Engineers: Acting-Chief, C. H. Christopher; First-Assistant, Jos. Goodwin; Acting-Third-Assistant, Edward Lodge; Acting-Gunner, Robert Sherman.

STEAMER "JUDGE TORRENCE."

Acting-Master, Jeremiah Irwin; Acting-Ensigns, Wm. Sill; Acting-Master's Mates, Edw. Perkins and Edwin Boyce; Engineers: Acting-Chief, Peter Hartwig; Acting-First-Assistants, W. Y. Sedman and S. L. Walkenshaw; Acting-Second-Assistants, Livingston Cook and Jasper Holman.

IRON-CLAD STEAMER "CARONDELET."

Acting-Master, James C. Gipson; Assistant-Surgeon, D. R. Bannon; Acting-Assistant Paymaster, J. G. Worden; Acting-Ensigns, Oliver Donaldson, S. D. Jordan, E. W. Miller and T. A. Quinn; Acting-Master's Mates, L. W. Hastings and W. H. H. DeGroot; Engineers: Acting-Chief, Chas. H. Caven; Acting-First-Assistant, G. H. Atkinson; Acting-Second-Assistants, M. Norton and W. B. Barton; Acting-Third-Assistants, John McWilliams; Acting-Carpenter, Geo. W. Kenney.

IRON-CLAD STEAMER "OSAGE."

Acting-Master, Thomas Wright; Acting-Assistant Surgeon, P. P. Gilmartin; Acting-Assistant Paymaster, G. W. Dougherty; Acting-Ensigns, W. S. Pease, Geo. Dunn, J. L. Mickle and R. K. Hubbell; Acting-Master's Mates, M. J. Durney, J. C. Winslow and B. C. Wheeler; Engineers: Acting-Chief, Thomas Doughty; Acting-First-Assistant, Geo. H. Hobbs; Acting-Second-Assistants, Wm. Galbreath and A. F. Fox.

STEAMER "MARMORA."

Acting-Master, Thomas Gibson; Assistant-Surgeon, B. F. Pierce; Acting-Assistant Paymaster, C. R. Howard; Acting-Ensigns, Elliott Callender and D. D. Bond; Acting-Master's Mates, Wm. Arnold and E. C. Nye; Engineers: Acting-First-Assistant, W. C. Armstrong; Acting-Second-Assistant, David Hawkesworth; Acting-Third-Assistant, F. A. Cramer.

STEAMER "ROMEO."

Acting-Master, Thomas Baldwin; Acting-Assistant Surgeon, D. W. Jones; Acting-Assistant Paymaster, E. R. Moffatt; Acting-Ensigns, J. B. Dwyer;

J. B. Petty and R. B. Shaw; Acting-Master's Mates, J. E. Ernest, C. W. Johnston and Geo. S. Cox; Engineers: Acting-First-Assistant, J. N. McCurdy; Acting-Second-Assistants, Jos. Grippin and W. E. Taylor; Acting-Third-Assistant, Wm. Teal.

STEAMER "JULIET."

Acting-Master, John S. Watson; Acting-Assistant Paymaster, Geo. W. Winans; Acting Ensigns, W. L. Holcomb, Hugh Kuhl and D. T. Davids; Acting-Master's Mates, S. J. Phillips; Engineers: Acting-First-Assistants, John Wybrant and Jos. Bolejack; Acting-Third-Assistant, James Van Zant.

STEAMER "PETREL."

Acting-Master, Thomas McElroy; Acting-Assistant Paymaster, H. T. Skelding; Acting-Ensigns, M. E. Flannigan and S. R. Holmes; Acting-Master's Mates, H. W. Bryan, J. W. Foster, L. C. Ball and J. G. Abbott; Engineers: Acting-First-Assistants, A. W. Phillips and Edw. Roberts; Acting-Second-Assistants, J. T. Stone and Geo. Britton; Acting-Third-Assistant, W. M. Mix.

STEAMER "CRICKET."

Acting-Master, Henry H. Gorringe; Acting-Assistant Surgeon, H. A. Bodman; Acting-Assistant Paymaster, W. M. Chester; Acting-Ensigns, D. P. Slattery, W. H. Read and J. McLeane; Acting-Master's Mate, John Wilson; Engineers: Acting-First-Assistant, Benj. Hand; Acting Second-Assistants, David Chillas, C. P. Parks and T. M. Jenks.

STEAMER "NEW ERA."

Acting-Master, James Marshall; Acting-Assistant Paymaster, Wm. B. Purdy; Acting-Ensigns, C. A. Schetky and W. B. Shillito; Acting-Master's Mates, P. H. Sullivan, W. F. Remer and E. A. Bangs; Engineers: Acting-First-Assistant, Israel Marsh; Acting-Second-Assistant, Richard Feugler; Acting-Third-Assistant, A. W. Smith; Acting-Carpenter, B. Martin.

STEAMER "SIGNAL."

Acting-Ensigns, Wm. P. Lee and Wm. F. Loan; Acting-Assistant-Surgeon, N. Brewster; Acting-Assistant-Paymaster, E. D. Hayden; Acting-Master's Mates, R. P. Craft, E. D. Lovell and Andrew Donaldson; Engineers: Acting-First-Assistant, W. N. Harden; Acting-Second-Assistants, J. G. Briggs and E. H. Kidd.

STEAMER "PRAIRIE BIRD."

Acting-Ensigns, John W. Chambers and W. M. Ernst; Acting-Assistant-Paymaster, L. Harter; Acting-Master's Mates, J. B. Morton, J. K. Lull, Jr., and Wm. D. Bangs; Engineers: Acting-First-Assistant, Geo. Radabaugh; Acting-Second-Assistant, Mathew Fleming.

STEAMER "CURLEW."

Acting-Ensigns, H. A. B. O'Niell, Milton Griffith and Wm. Zimmerman; Acting-Assistant-Surgeon, J. J. McIlhenney; Acting-Assistant-Paymaster, J. R. Morris; Acting-Master's Mates, E. C. Huggins, M. G. Bailey and J. A. Kilby; Engineers: Acting-First-Assistant, Benj. Hoffman; Acting-Third-Assistants, L. J. Everson and Wm. Quinn.

STEAMER "LITTLE REBEL."

Acting-Ensign, N. T. Rennell; Acting-Master's Mates, N. F. Jacobs, R. G. Van Ness, J. W. Hambrick and J. T. Rulo; Engineers: Acting-First-Assistant, A. E. Giles; Acting-Second-Assistant, Philip Allman; Acting-Third-Assistant, E. H. Burton.

STEAMER "VICTORY."

Acting-Ensigns, Fred'k Read, W. B. Trufant and J. H. Singleton; Acting-Assistant-Surgeon, G. W. Shields; Acting-Assistant-Paymaster, Benj. Page; Acting-Master's Mates, David Wagener, R. L. Taylor and John Malony; Engineers: Acting-First-Assistant, J. L. Winston; Acting-Third-Assistants, Fred'k Heuse and J. W. Street.

STEAMER "TENSAS."

Acting-Ensigns, E. C. Van Pelt and Jacob Rutherford; Acting-Master's Mate, Henry Van Velsor; Engineers: Acting-Second-Assistants, Andrew Wilson, Ant'y Courtenay; Acting-Third-Assistants, Nathan Spear and Patrick Scanlan.

STEAMER "GENERAL PILLOW."

Acting-Ensigns, T. M. Halstead, E. M. Wood and C. M. Bragg; Engineers: Acting-First-Assistant, G. W. Crawford; Acting-Second-Assistant, E. P. Bartlett.

STEAMER "ROBB."

Acting-Ensigns, Lloyd Thomas and James Tuohy; Acting-Master's Mates, J. C. Burnett, J. J. Irwin and Edw. Lincoln; Engineers: Acting-First-Assistant, Benj. Everson; Acting-Second-Assistant, John Miller; Acting-Third-Assistant, N. J. Brooks.

STEAMER "ARGOSY."

Acting-Ensigns, John C. Morong, G. J. Haslett, R. W. Alson and T. J. Dean; Acting-Assistant-Surgeon, L. M. Rees, Acting-Assistant-Paymaster, R. E. Patterson; Acting-Master's Mates, A. B. Homer, Peter Lake and J. A. McCreary; Engineers: Acting-First-Assistant, Thomas Blanchard; Acting-Second-Assistant, Chas. Silverchan; Acting-Third-Assistant, Albin Donnelly.

STEAMER "OUICHITA."

Acting-Ensigns, Eugene Zimmerman and P. C. Wright; Acting-Assistant-Paymaster, J. R. Meeker; Acting-Master's Mates, J. W. Litherbury, E. P. Marshall and A. W. Widup; Engineers: Acting-Chief, Thomas Hebron; Acting-First-Assistant, G. W. Taylor; Acting-Second-Assistant, G. T. Wilson; Acting-Third-Assistant, Thomas Reed.

STEAMER "NEW NATIONAL."

Pilot, Alex. M. Grant; Acting-Assistant-Paymaster, J. W. Keely; Acting-Ensign, J. M. Farmer; Acting Master's Mates, J. D. Holmes, E. R. Bradley and A. A. Mann; Engineers: Acting-First-Assistant, Wm. A. Wells; Acting-Second-Assistant, Geo. W. Aikin; Acting-Third-Assistant, Geo. R. Bell, Oliver Rosebush and D. L. Winton.

STEAMER "GENERAL LYON."

Pilot, Richard E. Birch; Acting-Assistant Paymaster W. H. Doane; Acting-Ensigns, James Martin and Thomas Cordwell; Acting-Master's Mates, J. M. Hurd and E. W. Robeson; Engineers: Acting-First-Assistant, H. L. Ince; Acting-Second-Assistant, W. J. Hamilton; Acting Third-Assistants, James Baldwin and Wm. Daizley.

STEAMER "SAMSON."

Acting-Ensign, J. M. Holmes; Acting-Master's Mate, G. W. Tainter; Engineers: Acting-First-Assistant, Wm. Paul, Jr.; Acting-Second-Assistant, C. F. Yeager.

STEAM-TUG "PANSY."

Acting-Ensign, Wm. Harris; Acting-Master's Mate, Ant'y McCarty; Engineers: Acting-Second-Assistant, John Gillis; Acting-Third-Assistant, A. F. Gardiner.

STEAM-TUG "FERN."

Acting-Ensign, John M. Kelly; Acting-Master's Mate, Jacob Bomgarnar; Engineers: Acting-Second-Assistant, John Reed; Acting-Third Assistant, Moses Andrews.

STEAM-TUG "THISTLE."

Acting-Ensign, R. E. Ettingham; Acting-Master's Mate, John Thompson; Engineers: Acting-Second-Assistant, Wm. Clugston; Acting-Third-Assistant, L. B. Jones.

STEAM-TUG "LAUREL"

Acting-Ensign, W. R. Owens; Engineers: Acting-Second-Assistant, C. H. Hilling; Acting-Third-Assistant, C. L. Rider.

STEAM-TUG "MIGNONETTE."

Acting-Ensign, Henry D. Green; Acting-Master's Mate, Wm. Edgar; Engineers, Acting-Second-Assistant, Dan'l Barnum; Acting-Third-Assistant, Mark Wade.

STEAM-TUG "DAISY."

Acting-Master, Daniel C. Bowers; Engineers: Acting-Second-Assistant, F. M. Magers; Acting-Third-Assistant, H. A. Cady.

STEAM-TUG "MISTLETOE."

Acting-Ensign, James L. Quigley; Acting-Master's Mate, James Anderson; Engineers: Acting-Second-Assistants, F. P. Seavy and Charles Metzger.

STEAM-TUG "MYRTLE."

Acting-Ensign, I. N. Goldsmith; Acting-Master's Mate, Charles Lyon; Engineer: Acting-Second-Assistant, Thompson Guernsey.

STEAM-TUG "DAHLIA."

Acting-Ensign, W. H. Strope; Acting-Master's Mate, Thomas Roach; Engineers: Acting-First-Assistant, J. H. Everhart; Acting-Second-Assistant, John Cook.

STEAM-TUG "HYACINTH."

Acting-Ensign, J. B. Hiserman; Acting-Master's Mate, James Nelis; Engineer: Acting-Second-Assistant, Thomas Bell.

STEAM-TUG "IVY.

Engineers: Acting-Second-Assistant, Eugene Callahan; Acting-Third-Assistant, T. H. Neely.

NAVAL STATIONS AT CAIRO AND MOUND CITY.

Captain Alex. M. Pennock, Fleet-Captain and Commandant of Station; Commander Fabius Stanley, Ordnance Officer; Fleet-Paymaster, E. W. Dunn; Paymasters, W. B. Boggs and A. H. Gilman; Assistant-Fleet-Paymaster, John Reed; Acting-Assistant Paymaster, J. H. Harvey; Surgeon, J. W. Shively; Acting-Chief-Engineer, Wm. D. Faulkner; Acting-Masters, P. O. Kell and J. W. Atkinson; Acting-Ensigns, C. F. Nellis and J. M. Bailey; Acting-Master's Mate, Rivers Drake; Gunner, J. C. Ritter; Acting-Boatswain, William Allen; Acting-Gunners, A. P. Snyder and L. K. Ellis.

MARINE OFFICERS.

Captain, M. R. Kintzing; Second-Lieutenants, F. L. Church and C. H. Humphrey.

NAVAL STATION, MEMPHIS, TENN.

Lieutenant-Commander, Thomas Pattison; Acting-Assistant Paymaster, J. H. Benton; Acting-Master, H. S. Wetmore; Acting-First-Assistant Engineer, Wm. Apperly.

RECEIVING SHIP "CLARA DOLSEN."

Acting-Volunteer-Lieutenant, John Scott; Acting-Assistant Surgeon, C. E. Vaughan; Paymaster, Edward May; Acting-Assistant Paymaster, J. F. Hamilton; Chaplain, Wm. H. Stewart; Acting-Master, Benj. Sebastian; Acting-Ensigns, L. Gardner and D. W. Sainter; Acting-Master's-Mates, W. H. Gray and A. E. McLean; Engineers: Acting-First-Assistant, G. W. Fulton; Acting-Second-Assistant, Jeremiah Wetzell.

RECEIVING-SHIP "GRAMPUS."

Acting-Master, Elizah Sells; Acting-Assistant Surgeon, M. W. Reber, Acting-Ensign, C. W. Lithurbury; Acting-Master's Mates, J. L. Williams, C. F. Clarkson and J. C. Wittsee.

INSPECTION-SHIP "ABRAHAM."

Paymaster, A. E. Watson; Acting-Ensign, Wm. Wagner; Acting-First-Assistant Engineer, Enos Hoshier.

HOSPITAL, MEMPHIS, TENN.

Surgeons, Wm. Grier and H. F. McSherry; Acting-Assistant Surgeons, Henry Beauchamp, J. B. Parker and Abner Thorpe.

RECRUITING RENDEZVOUS, CHICAGO.

Acting-Master, J. D. Harty; Acting-Master's Mate, Wm. A. Daniels; Surgeon, Samuel J. Jones.

RECRUITING RENDEZVOUS, CINCINNATI.

Acting-Master, A. S. Bowen; Acting-Assistant Surgeon, Geo. E. Jones; Assistant-Paymaster, Wm. H. Sells.

CHAPTER XLIII.

OPERATIONS OF THE MISSISSIPPI SQUADRON, UNDER ADMIRAL PORTER, AFTER THE RED RIVER EXPEDITION.

OPERATIONS ON THE TENNESSEE AND CUMBERLAND RIVERS.—SUPPRESSING GUERILLAS.—GUN-BOATS CO-OPERATING WITH SHERMAN IN EXPEDITION TO MERIDIAN.—SILENCING BATTERIES AT LIVERPOOL.—GUN-BOATS DAMAGED.—PUSHING UP THE YAZOO.—THE EXPEDITION FALLS BACK.—DASHING ATTACK ON WATERLOO.—THE "FOREST ROSE" DRIVES CONFEDERATES OUT OF WATERPROOF.—IMPORTANT SERVICES RENDERED BY "TIN-CLADS."—EXPEDITION UP BLACK AND WASHITA RIVERS.—GUN-BOATS DRIVE CONFEDERATES OUT OF TRINITY AND HARRISONBURG.—HEROIC SEAMEN.—PLOT TO BLOW UP FLEET.—CONFEDERATE SECRET SERVICE.—LETTERS OF CONFEDERATE SECRETARY OF THE NAVY AND OTHERS.—NAMES OF PERSONS IN CONFEDERATE SECRET SERVICE.—REPORT OF COMMISSION ON SINGER'S TORPEDOES.—CAPTURE OF YAZOO CITY.—THREE SAILORS DISTINGUISH THEMSELVES.—CAPTURE OF FORT PILLOW.—HORRIBLE MASSACRE.—ATROCITIES COMMITTED.—FORT PILLOW RETAKEN BY LIEUTENANT-COMMANDER FITCH.—CONFEDERATES CAPTURE THE "PETREL."—THE "EXCHANGE" ATTACKED BY MASKED BATTERIES.—BATTERIES NEAR SIMMSPORT OPEN ON GUN-BOATS, BUT ARE SILENCED.—CONFEDERATES MAKE GOOD USE OF CANNON CAPTURED FROM BANKS.—ZEAL AND BRAVERY OF LOUISIANA AND TEXAS TROOPS.—THE "GENERAL BRAGG" ATTACKED AT TUNICA BEND.—THE "NAIAD" SILENCES BATTERY.—EXPEDITION UP ARKANSAS RIVER.—THE "QUEEN CITY" CAPTURED AND BLOWN UP.—DESTRUCTION OF BATTERIES NEAR CLARENDON.—EXPEDITION FROM CLIFTON TO EASTPORT.—HARD FIGHTING.—TRANSPORTS DISABLED.—"TIN-CLADS" CUT UP.—NON-SUCCESS OF EXPEDITION.

AFTER the conclusion of the Red River expedition the fleet returned up the Mississippi to their old stations. Fortunately the guerillas had not taken advantage of the absence of the gun-boats to attack unarmed vessels passing up or down. Only one attempt was made—by a Confederate field-battery—to interfere with river navigation, and that one was unsuccessful.

The different districts were soon under the supervision of their former commanders, and the people along the banks of the Mississippi were reassured with regard to the Navy giving its particular attention to the guerillas or any other species of soldiers that might attempt to show themselves in an offensive attitude.

While the squadron was employed up Red River, the Tennessee and Cumberland rivers became now and then the scene of active operations. Tennessee, lying adjacent to so many Southern States, was open to the raids of the Confederates, and they seemed loath to abandon it altogether, hoping still to obtain possession of it and carry the war into the more northern States of Kentucky, Ohio and Missouri. It was a vain hope, however, and one not justified by the position or condition of the Federal armies.

In February, 1864, Lieutenant-Commander LeRoy Fitch still commanded a fleet of gun-boats on the Ohio, Tennessee and Cumberland rivers. The banks of these rivers were infested by bands of guerillas, who, posting themselves on prominent points, made it unpleasant for gun-boats, and all but impossible for transports, to pass up without a strong escort.

Lieutenant-Commander Fitch put an end to this state of affairs by sending up the

Cumberland River a reconnoitering force of gun-boats, which at the same time convoyed a number of transports to Carthage with supplies of provisions and munitions of war. This expedition was under the charge of Acting - Volunteer - Lieutenant H. A. Glassford, and the Army co-operated by sending the steamer "Silver Lake, No. 2," with a detachment of 150 sharp-shooters under a gallant officer, Lieutenant Roberts. The duty ·was severe, the danger considerable, and the fighting incessant ; but the gun-boats were so well handled that their convoy reached its destination without accident, and the guerillas were taught a lesson they did not forget for some time.

When Sherman was marching on Meridian, a naval expedition was fitted out under the command of Lieutenant - Commander E. K. Owen to co-operate with him, and for the purpose of confusing the enemy with regard to the former's movements. The gun-boats were attended by a co-operating force of troops under Colonel Coates. When they arrived near Yazoo City, it was discovered that the enemy were in force at that place with batteries of field-pieces on the hills.

On the 2d of February the expedition reached Sartalia, and next day attacked the enemy at Liverpool, where there were 2,700 men with artillery, under General Ross. The gun-boats silenced the batteries, and the Federal troops landed and took possession of the enemy's position, ·which they occupied until night-fall and then re-embarked, and the vessels dropped down the river. The " Petrel," " Marmora," " Exchange " and " Romeo " were the gun-boats engaged. They were somewhat cut up, but drove the enemy away. The army lost eight killed and twenty-two wounded in this attack. This expedition had the effect which Sherman desired, viz., to draw the enemy toward Yazoo River.

The gun-boats and army transports pushed on up the Yazoo as far as Greenwood, losing a few men by the way. At this place they fell in with General Forrest's command, when the army contingent landed and brought on a battle, or rather a skirmish, in which the Confederates were defeated. The result of this expedition was, as Sherman had anticipated, the falling back of all the enemy's troops which had been scattered along the Yazoo, Sunflower and Tallahatchie rivers, upon Grenada, to defend it from attack; and he was thus enabled to proceed on his raid to Meridian without molestation in his rear.

On the 15th of February the Confederates made a dashing attack on Waterloo, in the district commanded by Lieutenant-Commander James A. Greer—an excellent and brave officer, who was always on the alert for such contingencies. This raid was conducted by Colonel Harrison, an indefatigable Confederate ranger, who had given a great deal of trouble with his command. On this occasion he entered the town of Waterproof with 800 mounted men, drove in the pickets, and pressed the Union troops very hard. Fortunately, the little tin-clad "Forest Rose" was at hand to assist the shore party, and, opening a hot fire of shell and shrapnel, soon compelled the enemy to retire. Acting-Volunteer-Lieutenant J. V. Johnston, her commander, then got underway, and took positions where he could constantly harass the Confederates.

This was one of the places selected to be held by negro troops ; and, as these men were always offensive to the Southerners, and they never lost an opportunity of attacking them, it was necessary to keep gun-boats always at hand to defend them. The unwise measure of employing colored troops, who were inefficient and without discipline, always aroused the indignation of the guerilla element, who would run great risks to slaughter them.

The officer commanding the troops asked Lieutenant Johnston to put him across the river, but that gallant officer refused to do so, telling him to stand fast and fight it out, which he was obliged to do, and the "Forest Rose," using her rifled guns with great effect, finally succeeded in dispersing the Confederate forces. This fight lasted a whole day, and most of the work was done by the Navy. The Confederates left seven killed on the field, and took away a number of wounded. The place was soon after reinforced from Natchez, and the enemy departed.

Captain Anderson, the commander of the negro troops at Waterproof, was so grateful for the service rendered by the " Forest Rose " that he wrote Lieutenant Johnston the following letter, which we give, with pleasure, as a memento of the gallant officer who fought his ship so well. It will be noticed that the name of the " Forest Rose " frequently appears in this recital of events. She was a small vessel, but one that did good service under the gallant officers who commanded her.

The following is Captain Anderson's letter :

HEADQUARTERS' POST, WATERPROOF, LA., }
February 19, 1864. }

SIR—Permit me to return you many thanks for the gallant manner in which you defended my little force against the rebel force of Colonel Mores, Colonel McNeal, and Major Johnson, in their several attacks of Saturday, February 14th, Sunday, the 15th, and Monday, the 16th of February, 1864.

I hope you will not consider it flattering when I say I never before saw more accurate artillery firing than you did in these engagements, invariably putting your shells in the right place ordered. My officers and men now feel perfectly secure against a large force, so long as we have the assistance of Captain Johnston and his most excellent drilled crew on board the No. 9.

I am, Captain, your humble servant,

J. M. ANDERSON,
Captain Commanding Post.
H. C. LUNT,
Lieutenant and Adjutant.
CAPTAIN JOHNSTON,
Commanding Gun-boat No. 9.

In the latter part of February, Admiral Porter fitted out an expedition to go, *via* the Red River, up the Black and Washita Rivers, under the command of Lieutenant-Commander F. M. Ramsey, for the purpose of breaking up the Confederate posts that were being formed along these rivers and destroying their provisions. The expedition consisted of the following vessels: "Fort Hindman," Acting-Volunteer Lieutenant John Pearce; "Osage," Acting-Master Thomas Wright; "Lexington," Lieutenant George M Bache; "Conestoga," Lieutenant-Commander T. O. Selfridge; "Cricket," Acting-Master H. H. Gorringe, and "Ouichita," Lieutenant-Commander Byron Wilson.

The "Ouichita" was a converted river steamer and carried 39 guns in three tiers. They were mostly 24 and 12 pound howitzers, but she had a battery of 8-inch smoothbores and some rifle-guns on the lower deck. Two 12-pounders were mounted on wooden turrets above all. She was a very formidable vessel for such operations.

On the 29th of February the expedition proceeded up the Red River into the Black, as far as the town of Trinity, where they were attacked by a battery of field-pieces, under the Confederate General, Polignac, the town at the same time hanging out white flags. The gun-boats returned the enemy's fire and soon drove them away.

The fire of the "Ouichita" is said to have been withering, and the astonishment of the Confederate commander may be well imagined when a vessel, which he supposed to be a transport, opened on him with forty guns, firing two shells from each gun a minute, the shells and shrapnel bursting in all directions and tearing the village almost to pieces.

On the following day the expedition proceeded up the river to within two miles of Harrisonburg, where it was again attacked by General Polignac, with a large number of sharp-shooters and some 12-pound rifle-guns, from behind the levee. The fire of the guns was directed chiefly upon the "Hindman," the flag-ship, and she was struck twenty-seven times by shot and shell, one shot disabling the starboard engine. But when the "Ouichita" got into position and opened her broadside, the enemy fled in all directions, leaving their guns on the field, after dragging them some 500 yards from

the water. The Confederates lost a great many men in killed and wounded.

Ramsey then proceeded a long distance up the river through narrow bayous and shoal cut-offs, destroying grain and provisions of all kinds, nearly reaching Monroe, but was obliged to return owing to the rapidly falling water—not, however, until the object of the expedition had been accomplished.

Harrisonburg had always been a troublesome place, from which constant expeditions were fitted out to raid along the Mississippi. The approaches to it had been strongly fortified, four forts on high hills commanding the river for two miles below the town and one mile above. Lieutenant-Commander Ramsey landed a force at this place and burned several of the largest houses, as a warning to the inhabitants not to assist in attacking river-boats, which often had women and children on board.

Two excellent earth-works were found at Trinity, in which were mounted three 32-pounders. These were hoisted on board the vessels and carried away.

This expedition was well planned and executed, and put a stop to the practice of firing upon unarmed vessels along the Mississippi River. It offers the opportunity of mentioning the gallantry of three seamen of the "Fort Hindman," James K. L. Duncan, Hugh Melloy, and William P. Johnson. A shell burst at the muzzle of one of the guns, setting fire to the tie of the cartridge which had just been put in the gun. Duncan immediately seized the burning cartridge, took it out of the gun, and threw it overboard. A shell pierced the bow casemate on the right of No. 1 gun, mortally wounding the first sponger, who dropped his sponge out of the port on the forecastle. Melloy immediately jumped out, picked it up, and sponged and loaded the gun under a heavy fire from sharp-shooters. Johnson, though very severely wounded himself in the hand, took the sponge from a wounded comrade and continued to use it throughout the action. The casualties in the flotilla were only two killed and eleven wounded.

On March 30th, a plan was discovered to blow up by torpedoes all the vessels of the fleet. A Confederate mail carrier was captured, crossing the Mississippi with a mailbag full of official correspondence, in which an atrocious scheme was exposed. It was nothing more nor less than to introduce torpedoes in the shape of lumps of coal into the coal piles or bunkers of the naval and merchant vessels, in hopes that they would be shovelled into the furnaces by the firemen, and there explode. Acts of this kind were attempted on several occasions by the Confederates, and one would suppose that only the lowest grade of humanity—men of the basest minds—would embark in such infernal enterprises. But it can be shown that some of the highest personages in the Confederacy were engaged in this business, or, at least, gave their assent to it, not in open, manly fashion, but with the apparent idea that they had no authority to stop it. See the following letters ·

CONFEDERATE STATES OF AMERICA, }
NAVY DEPARTMENT, RICHMOND, }
September 10, 1863. }

SIR—Your letter of the 13th July, from Jacksonport, Arkansas, reached me a few days ago.

You inform me that a certain party desires to obtain proper authority from the Confederate government to undertake the destruction of gun-boats, transports, etc., for such per centum of the value of the boats destroyed as may be offered, etc.

There is no legislation of which I am aware that satisfies precisely the conditions required. The Act of May 6, 1861, recognizing the existence of war with the United States, and providing for privateering, is not construed to permit privateering on inland waters. A reference to the law for the establishment of a Volunteer Navy, a copy of which I enclose herewith, will show you that it cannot be made to embrace the parties to which you refer.

To facilitate organizations of parties to operate as you propose, in boats or otherwise, against the enemy on our Western rivers, they could be received into the Navy if they shipped regularly in accordance with existing laws, and then assigned to duty under an acting-master upon those rivers. In this case, however, they would form a part of the regular Navy establishment, drawing its pay and subsistence. I infer from your letter that such is not the object of the parties in question, but that they desire to organize in small parties, to operate as independent river guerilla parties, under their own leaders, and to look to prize-money or reward from the country for destroying enemy's property, to defray expenses, etc., using an appointment from the Government to secure to them the rights of prisoners of war, if captured.

Judging from what you say, that you have not the Acts of Congress at hand, I inclose copies of two Acts, one of which possibly serves the desired purpose. The President has authority to make such an arrangement as you refer to, and I would suggest that parties wishing to engage in the enterprise present to him their names, purposes and terms, either directly or through your obedient servant,

S. R. MALLORY,
Secretary of the Navy.

Colonel E. C. CABELL, C. S. A.,
Headquarters Price's Army,
Jacksonport, Arkansas.

[No. 229.]

AN ACT TO PROVIDE FOR LOCAL DEFENCE AND SPECIAL SERVICE.

SECTION 1. The Congress of the Confederate States do enact: That the President be and he is hereby authorized to accept the services of volunteers of such kind and in such proportion as he may deem expedient, to serve for such time as he may prescribe, for the defence of exposed places and localities, or such special service as he may deem expedient.

SECTION 2. And such forces shall be mustered into the service of the Confederate States, for the local defence or special service aforesaid, the muster-roll setting forth distinctly the services to be performed; and the said volunteers shall not be considered in actual service until thereunto ordered by the President, and they shall be entitled to pay or subsistence only for such time as they may be on duty, under the orders of the President, or by his direction.

SECTION 3. Such volunteer forces, when so accepted or ordered into service, shall be organized-in accordance and subject to all the provisions of the Act entitled "An Act to provide for the public defence," approved March 6th, 1861, and may be attached to such divisions, brigades, regiments or battalions as the President may direct; and, when not organized into battalions and regiments before being mustered into service, the President shall appoint the field-officers of the battalions and regiments when organized as such by him.

AN ACT TO AUTHORIZE THE FORMATION OF VOLUNTEER COMPANIES FOR LOCAL DEFENCE.

The Congress of the Confederate States of America do enact:

That for the purpose of local defence in any portion of the Confederate States, any number of persons, not less than twenty, who are over the age of forty-five years, or otherwise not liable to military duty, may associate themselves as a military company, elect their own officers, and establish rules and regulations for their own government, and shall be considered as belonging to the Provisional Army of the Confederate States, serving without pay or allowances, and entitled, when captured by the enemy, to all the privileges of prisoners of war.

Provided, That such company shall, as soon as practicable, transmit their muster-roll or list of the names of the officers and privates thereof to the Governor of the State, the commanding general of the department, or any brigadier-general in the State or Confederate service, to be forwarded to the Secretary of War; but the President or commander of the district may, at any time, disband such companies.

Provided, That in the States and districts in which the Act entitled "An Act to further provide for the public defence," approved April 16th, 1862, and the Acts amendatory thereof, have been suspended, persons of any age, resident within such States or districts, may volunteer and form part of such companies, so long as such suspension may continue.

Provided, That no person shall become a member of said company until he shall have first taken the oath of allegiance to the Confederate States of America, in writing, a copy of which shall be filed with the muster-roll of said company, as above prescribed. Approved October 13th, 1862.

[EXTRACT.]

HEADQUARTERS DISTRICT OF ARKANSAS, }
LITTLE ROCK, August 18, 1863. }

SPECIAL ORDERS }
No. 135. }

* * * * * * *

VI.—Thomas E. Courtenay, Esq., is, by direction of the Lieutenant-General commanding the department of trans-Mississippi, authorized to enlist a secret service corps, not exceeding twenty (20) men, to be employed by him, subject to the orders of the district commander.

* * * * * * *

By command of Major-General Price,
THOMAS L. SNEAD,
Assistant-Adjutant General.

THOMAS E. COURTENAY, Esq.

[FORM OF APPOINTMENT.]

————, 1864.

In accordance with the above, I hereby appoint .... a member of the secret service corps, to report to me at .... on or before the .... day of .... 1864.

THOMAS E. COURTENAY,
Captain Secret Service Corps.

CONFEDERATE STATES OF AMERICA, }
WAR DEPARTMENT, ENGINEER BUREAU, }
RICHMOND, VA., Sept. 15, 1863. }

R. W. Dunn, having been selected for special service, is authorized by the Secretary of War to proceed to the headquarters of Lieutenant-General E. Kirby Smith, commanding trans-Mississippi department, to be attached to one of the companies of engineer troops now being organized in that department, under the Act of Congress "to provide and organize engineer troops to serve during the war." Approved March 20, 1863.

A. L. RIVES,
Lieutenant-Colonel and Acting-Chief of Bureau.
Approved—JAMES A. SEDDON,
Secretary of War.

CONFEDERATE STATES OF AMERICA, }
WAR DEPARTMENT, ENGINEER BUREAU, }
September 15, 1863. }

GENERAL—I have the honor to send, in addition to the names specified in my letter of the 20th ultimo, the following list of men, who, by wish of the Honorable Secretary of War, are to be employed in your department, on the special service of destroying the enemy's property by torpedoes and similar inventions, viz.: [Names.]

These men should each be enlisted in and form part of an engineer company, but will nevertheless be employed, so far as possible, on the service specified above. When the public interest, in your judgment, requires it, details of additional men may be made, either from the engineer troops or from the line, to aid them in their particular duties, and they may be furnished by the military authorities with the necessary ammunition. Their compensation to be fifty per cent. of the property destroyed by their new inventions, and all the arms and munitions captured by them, by the use of torpedoes or by similar devices. Beyond this, they will be entitled to such other rewards as Congress may hereafter provide.

Very respectfully,
Your obedient servant,
A. L. RIVES,
Lieutenant-Colonel and Acting-Chief of Bureau.
Approved—JAMES A. SEDDON,
Secretary of War.

Names of persons in secret service, to introduce R. W. Dunn, E. C. Singer and J. D. Braman to my friends :

B. C. Adams, Grenada ; Captain Samuel Applegate, Winona ; Colonel H. H. Miller, commanding regiment west of Grenada and Carrollton ; W. P. Mellen, Natchez ; Major John B. Peyton. Raymond ; Judge D. H. Bosser, Woodville ; F. A. Boyle, Woodville ; Henry Skipwith, Clinton, La. ; Conrad McRae, Fordocke, La. ; W. Barton, Atchafalaya River, La. ; J. J. Morgan, Atchafalaya River, La. ; T. G. Caivit, Atchafalaya River, La. ; James E. Lindsey, Atchafalaya River, La. ; William N. Lindsey, Atchafalaya River, La. ; William H. Neilson, Atchafalaya River, La. ; Samuel Faulkner, Atchafalaya River, La. ; Colonel James M. Porter, St. Landry, La. ; Colonel Wm. B. Davis, St. Landry, La. ; Colonel Wm. Offat, St. Landry, La. ; Captain James Cappes, St. Landry, La. ; S. A. Scribner, St. Landry, La. ; Elbert Goull, St. Landry, La. ; T. C. Anderson, St. Landry, La. ; Simon Richard, St. Landry, La. ; Henderson Taylor, Marksville, La. ; S. L. Taylor, Marksville, La. ; H. Robertson, Alexandria, La. ; S. W. Henarie, Alexandria, La. ; Governor T. O. Moore, Alexandria, La. ; Colonel C. Manning, Alexandria, La. ; General M. Wells, Rapides and Aveyellos Parish, La. ; General P. F. Kearny, Rapides and Aveyellos Parish, La. ; Hugh M. Kearny, Esq., Rapides and Aveyellos Parish,

La. ; B. F. Murdock, Rapides and Aveyellos Parish, La. ; B. C. Crow, Esq., Lafayette Parish, La. ; Hon. John Moore, St. Martin's Parish ; William Robertson, St. Martin's Parish ; Judge Baker, St. Mary's Parish ; T. J. Foster, St. Mary's Parish ; Judge Palfrey, St. Mary's Parish ; Daniel Dennett, editor *Planter's Banner*, St. Mary's Parish ; Mr. Sickles, editor *Planter's Banner*, Kindred Spirits, St. Mary's Parish ; Phanor Prudhommer, Esq., St. Mary's Parish ; John Blair Smith, Nachitoches Parish, La. ; Colonel H. J. G. Battle, Caddo, La. ; Reuben White, Caddo, La.

We must help one another, and those who can be efficient in our cause must receive all necessary hospitality, aid and information. I introduce none but the worthy.   R. J. PAGE.

REPORT OF A COMMISSION ON SINGER'S TORPEDO.

ENGINEER HEADQUARTERS, }
DEPOT NORTHERN VIRGINIA, }
July 14, 1863. }

COLONEL—In accordance with your order of the 13th, appointing the undersigned a commission to examine and report upon the merits of Mr. E. C. Singer's torpedo, we beg to state that we have carefully examined the same, and submit the following report :

First. "As to the place for exploding the charge." In this plan or lock, in our opinion, consists the great merit of the invention. The lock is simple, strong, and not liable at any time to be out of order ; and as the caps which ignite the charge are placed within the powder magazine, they are not likely to be affected by moisture ; while the percussion is upon the exterior of the magazine, actual contact with the rod, which acts as a trigger, is necessary ; but by mechanical contrivances the contact may be obtained in various ways.

Second. "The certainty of action" depends, of course, upon contact ; but by the peculiar and excellent arrangement of the lock and plan of percussion mentioned above, the certainty of explosion is almost absolute.

One great advantage this torpedo possesses over many others is that its explosion does not depend upon the action or judgment of an individual ; that it is safe from premature ignition, and at the same time is cheap and portable, while its position in river or harbor cannot readily be ascertained by an enemy's vessels.

Third. "The efficiency of its explosion, if made in deep channels," cannot well be ascertained without experiment, but would be the same as sub-marines fired by any other contrivance. We are of the opinion, however, from the best information accessible, that if the powder, say 100 pounds in quantity, is within the distance of fifteen feet from the keel of the vessel when exploded, its efficient action is not materially affected by the depth of channel.

Of course, the quantity of powder required would have to be determined by experiment. Rifle powder, from its more rapid combustion, would be preferable in deep water to cannon powder, while some of the detonating compounds would doubtless effect certain destruction to vessels passing over torpedoes at even much greater depth. The peculiar arrangements for firing the batteries would have to be determined by the circumstances of position and draft of vessels and motion of currents, depth and width of channels, and would require the exercise of great judgment on the part of those intrusted with the duty of placing them.

We are so well satisfied with the merits of Mr. Singer's torpedo that we recommend the engineer department to give it a thorough test, and, if practicable, to have some of them placed at an early day in some of the river approaches of Richmond.

General Remarks:—
The mode of loading this torpedo dispenses with

any connection through the case of the magazine, involving no packing of any kind.

The risk of the lock fouling by sand or mud, if on the bottom of a stream, we think can be prevented by enclosing it in a metal case, which would be nearly water-tight. In narrow streams these could be placed in quincunx, so that a vessel attempting to pass would be sure to come in contact with some one.

The inventor also claims to be able to go to a vessel with one or two and get them in contact so as to explode.

This can be done, but so much depends on the nerve and daring of individuals that there is no certainty of it. Judging from the success of blasting rocks by powder, superposed upon the rock with a deep column of water over it, we are of the opinion that the depth of water below a torpedo would not interfere with its success.

Lieutenant Bolton, who saw and blasted a great deal in East River, near New York, says: "One hundred pounds of powder, fifteen feet from the bottom of a vessel, would break her sides or bottom."

We would add that a proposed adaptation of these locks to the explosion of shell or batteries under railroad tracks, for defences of approach to fortified works, and for blowing up bridges, seems to us very simple and effective; also an ingenious plan for affixing torpedoes to spar or bow of an iron-clad.

We consider the employment of submarines as a legitimate mode of defence, and, as officers connected with the defence of Richmond, feel it our duty to recommend torpedoes as a powerful accessory to our limited means. The moral effect of an explosion upon an enemy would be incalculable, and would doubtless deter them from attempting to bring troops, by transports, to points accessible to the city, as White House or Brandon.

Respectfully submitted,
W. H. STEVENS,
Colonel Engineers.
JOHN A. WILLIAMS,
Major Engineers.
W. G. TURPIN,
Capt. Engineers.

Colonel J. T. GILMER,
Chief Engineer.
Official copy.
A. L. RIVES,
Lieutenant-Colonel and Acting-Chief of Bureau.

LETTER OF T. E. COURTENAY TO COL. H. E. CLARK.
RICHMOND, VIRGINIA, Jan. 19, 1864.

MY DEAR COLONEL—I hope you have received all my letters. I wrote two to Mobile, one to Columbus, and two to Brandon. I now send this by a party who is going to Shreveport, and promised to learn your whereabouts so as to forward it to you.

I have met with much delay and annoyance since you left. The castings have all been completed some time, and the *coal* is so perfect that the most critical eye could not detect it. The President thinks them perfect, but Mr. Seddon will do nothing without congressional action, so I have been engaged for the past two weeks in getting up a bill that will cover my case. At last it has met his approval, and will to-day go to the Senate, hence to the House in secret session. It provides that the Secretary of War shall have the power to organize a "secret service corps" commission, enlist and detail parties who shall retain former rank and pay, also give such compensation as he may deem fit, not exceeding 50 per cent. for property partially and totally destroyed; also to advance, when necessary, out of the secret service fund, money to parties engaging to injure the enemy.

As soon as this bill becomes a law, I have no doubt but I shall get a suitable commission and means to progress with, and that all the appointments you or I have made will be confirmed. * * *
T. E. COURTENAY.

Colonel H. E. CLARK,
7th Missouri Cavalry. Maj. Gen. Price's
Headquarters, Arkansas.

The little "tin-clads" of the Mississippi squadron made a good deal of history for the Navy. They often performed duties that ought to have been assigned to iron-clads; but these latter were few in number, and too large to penetrate the small and narrow streams where the Confederates had an idea they were secure, and from whence they would start expeditions towards the great river to prey upon peaceful commerce. The "Petrel" more than once distinguished herself in these river expeditions, and while in the Yazoo River performed service that should be remembered.

Colonel Coates, who had started out with Lieutenant-Commander Owen, as mentioned on a former occasion, to keep the Confederates from following in Sherman's rear, had, with the assistance of the Navy, occupied Yazoo City, which seemed to be an object of attack from both parties. First one side and then the other had thrown up earth-works until it had become a formidable place.

Colonel Coates was quietly resting here, keeping a good look-out on the enemy, who were in force a few miles back, when, on the 5th of March, at 9:30 A. M., the Confederates made a fierce attack on the redoubts at a point occupied by part of the 11th Illinois Volunteers, supported by a 12-pound howitzer belonging to the gun-boat "Exchange." Acting-Master Thomas McElroy, of the "Petrel," had been left in charge of the naval force in the Yazoo River by Lieutenant-Commander Owen.

After firing the howitzer several times, it had a shell jammed in the bore which could not be removed. Mr. McElroy then ordered Acting-Master Gibson, of the "Marmora," to dismount one of his rifled howitzers, mount it on a field carriage, and send it on shore with a crew to work it; but before he could get the gun to the redoubt the enemy had completely surrounded the hill.

At this time the fighting in the city was hand to hand; the gun was placed in position and opened fire rapidly on the enemy. At one time the crew were driven from their piece by superior numbers; but the Union soldiers, seeing that the sailors needed support, went to their rescue, charged the enemy, and retook the gun.

The "Petrel" and "Marmora" kept up a rapid fire with shrapnel, until the battle was over, and McElroy was requested by Colonel Coates to cease firing, as the enemy were retreating. McElroy then went on shore, took the howitzer, and pursued the retreating enemy, firing upon their rear until they escaped to the hills.

Three sailors highly distinguished themselves in this battle : Bartlett Laffey of the "Petrel," and James Stoddard and Wm. J. Franks of the "Marmora." These men, though surrounded at their gun, fought hand to hand with their cutlasses to the last, and when the enemy retreated, turned the gun upon them—this, too, after their officer (an acting ensign) had retreated, and behaved so badly that his resignation was afterwards demanded. Here was a great difference between the men and their officer, and it is to be hoped that the former will live to see their names honorably mentioned while that of their leader is withheld as unworthy of notice.

On the 13th of April, the Confederates, taking advantage of the absence of the gun-boats, marched on Columbus, Ky.; but when Colonel Lawrence, who commanded the post, refused to listen to a demand for its surrender, they turned upon Fort Pillow, and captured it after a desperate conflict.

Fort Pillow was retaken by Lieutenant-Commander Fitch, but the enemy carried off with them everything it had contained in the shape of guns or stores, and retreated to Ashport. The Union transports then landed troops at the foot of the hill, who reoccupied the fort, where traces of the massacre were still visible, and where ruin and desolation went hand-in-hand. Terrible scenes had been enacted when the place was taken by the Confederates, and they behaved as if they considered the brave defence of the Federal soldiers a grave offence, to be avenged by an indiscriminate slaughter. The atrocities which these men committed will always remain a stigma upon their character, for no possible excuses or explanations can ever justify them.

All of the successes gained by the Confederates were owing to the unfortunate Red River expedition, which had withdrawn the gun-boats from their posts.

In the meantime the small gun-boats, which were acting on the Yazoo River in connection with Colonel Coates, were making themselves felt in that region. An expedition under Colonel Schofield was about to start up the Yazoo River by order of General McArthur, when, by request of the former, on April 21st, the gun-boats "Petrel" and "Prairie Bird" preceded the army-transport up to Yazoo City. No enemy being in sight, the "Petrel" went on up, leaving the "Prairie Bird" and transport "Freestone" at the Navy Yard. When abreast of the city, the little gun-boat opened fire on some Confederate troops just then

coming in sight on the hills, which was returned briskly by musketry and cannon. The river, being too narrow to turn in, Acting-Master McElroy determined to run the batteries, go up the river where there was more room, turn about, and then run down again. It was not found practicable to return immediately, however, so the "Petrel" remained where she was until the 22d. On this day she hauled into the bank and commenced wooding, when she was attacked by the enemy with a strong force of infantry and several pieces of cannon, the shot from their guns passing through the vessel. Not being able to bring his guns to bear, McElroy armed his men as sharp-shooters and returned the fire, at the same time getting underway. While starting off, two shots entered the ship, one striking the cylinder, the other cutting the steam-pipe and disabling the engines, when the Confederates closed in on her. The crew went to their quarters and commenced firing, but the sharp-shooters picked them off through the ports, and McElroy, finding it impossible to work his guns, gave the order to set fire to the ship and abandon her. At this moment a shot went through the boiler, enveloping the "Petrel" in steam. This was unfortunate, for the steam extinguished the fire, and in consequence the vessel fell into the hands of the enemy, with all her stores, guns and ammunition.

There were some unpleasant features connected with this affair, but McElroy redeemed his own mistakes by his gallantry after most of his officers and men had left the vessel. The pilot, Kimble Ware, and a quartermaster, J. H. Nibbie, stood by their commander when all the officers had deserted their flag.

As soon as the steam cleared away, McElroy, with the assistance of Quartermaster Nibbie, got the wounded off the guards on to the bank, and got ready to set fire to the vessel again (all this time under an incessant fire). He obtained some live coals from the furnace and spread them about the decks, but soon had to desist on account of the heat below. At this time, the enemy seeing the officers and men escaping across the fields, crossed the river above and below the "Petrel," and, surrounding her on all sides, forced McElroy to surrender. The fires on board the steamer were at once extinguished, and the captain was taken away before he had time to find out how many of his men were killed and wounded.

As an excuse for the conduct of the crew, it must be remarked that there were only ten white men and boys on board the vessel; the rest were all "contrabands," and some of these were sick. But it was one of the few cases where officers behaved badly on board a vessel of the Mississippi squadron. If the "Petrel" had been properly seconded by the troops, the disaster would not have occurred.

This affair threw quite a gloom over the fleet, as the "Petrel" had always been one of the favorite "tin-clads," and her name appears in many expeditions and forays.

This disaster was redeemed a short time afterwards by the gallant conduct and good management of Acting-Master James C. Gipson, in the gun-boat "Exchange," who, while passing Columbia, Arkansas, was opened upon by a masked battery, consisting of four 12-pound shell guns, two 12-pound rifles, and one 10, one 18, and one 6 pounder rifles.

The battery was divided into two sections, planted about 200 yards apart, behind the levee. The Confederates waited until the "Exchange" had passed the lower battery, and then opened upon her a destructive fire. Acting-Master Gipson could not back down on account of having turned the point of a sand-bar, and he at once saw that his only alternative was to run the upper battery. This he attempted to do, opening fire at the same time with all the guns which he could bring to bear upon the enemy; but, unfortunately, the port engine was struck by a shot and disabled, reducing the speed of the vessel and keeping her under fire for forty-five minutes.

The "Exchange" had hardly got out of range of the enemy's guns when her engine stopped entirely, and it was found necessary to anchor while the engineers were making repairs. The work was quickly and energetically done, and the little vessel was enabled to move slowly up the river with one engine. It was expected that the Confederates would move the battery above the vessel while she was disabled, and open fire upon her again; but this was not done, and she finally escaped, though badly cut up.

The "Exchange" was pierced thirty-five times with shot and shell; eight times near the water line and five times in the casemate. Several shells exploded in the coal bunkers, near the boiler, and one entered the shell-locker, overturning shell-boxes, but, fortunately, not reaching some percussion shell that were stored there. One shot passed through the pilot-house, wounding Acting-Master Gipson and rendering him senseless for fifteen minutes; but the brave pilot steered his course as coolly as if it was an every-day affair. The gallant commander was wounded in three places, but in all this firing only one man was killed outright. That, however, does not detract from the credit of this fight, and it shows how a cool and brave commander can get out of a difficulty if he is determined to do so.

Though the volunteer officers in the Mississippi fleet almost always deported themselves with great gallantry, few affairs were better managed than the one we have just described. We cannot always give the names of all the officers engaged in these adventures, but they will generally be found in the lists.

There were a number of such affairs, and in many of them the brave character of the Western men was clearly exhibited.

On the 8th of June, 1864, Lieutenant-Commander F. M. Ramsey, while employed in the Atchafalaya River, started down with the "Chillicothe," "Neosho," and "Fort Hindman." When about one and a half miles from Simmsport, they were fired upon by a battery of two 30-pounder Parrotts. When the vessels opened fire in return, the enemy did not wait to load, but scattered in all directions, leaving their guns and muskets behind them. A deserter stated that these guns had been taken from General Banks when he was on his Red River raid, and the naval officers were thus sometimes reminded that Banks had furnished the guns which so often attacked them along the river. This affair was well managed and with but little loss of life.

Five or six batteries, which had been captured from the Federals, were now raiding upon different parts of the river, and firing upon merchant steamers carrying passengers, frequently women and children. We regret that we are obliged to mention these acts of wanton vengeance on the part of the Confederates. It was not legitimate warfare, and it detracted very much from the credit which they had fairly earned by their undoubted bravery on other occasions.

It looked sometimes as if the "chivalry" of the South was dying out. The gun-boats, with as much propriety, might have fired on the defenceless houses of people who were taking no part in the war. It is true that the Union men did sometimes disgrace themselves by burning houses, but it was always done in retaliation for some wanton act on the part of the Confederates, and the women and children were always given time to get out of the way. It was all wrong on either side, and shows how the most humane people will become demoralized when engaged in a civil war. May God save us from any such war in the future!

There was no doubt about the energy, zeal and bravery of these Louisiana and Texas troops; they never relaxed for a moment, and were encountered when least expected. As they attacked everything that came along, they would sometimes "catch a Tartar."

On the 26th of June, while the gun-boat "General Bragg" was at anchor in Tunica Bend, she was opened on by the enemy with four guns. Acting - Volunteer-Lieutenant C. Dominey (commanding) slipped his cable and went to quarters, replying rapidly to the enemy's fire. After being engaged about five minutes, a shot struck the working - beam of the steamer, and disabled her engines completely. But Dominey did not mind that. He drifted along, silencing the enemy's guns, and they went away, apparently satisfied with having put 22 shot and shell into the "General Bragg."

The little "tin-clad," "Naiad," hearing the firing, ran to the assistance of the "Bragg," and when within half a mile of the latter another battery opened upon her, in a few moments completely disabling her steering gear and severely wounding the pilot, James M. Herrington. The "Naiad's" wheel being shot away, her commander, Acting-Master Henry T. Keene, rigged relieving tackles, steered for the battery and continued a close and brisk fire until it was completely silenced.

In this affair the little vessel was struck nine times; and, to show how these frail boats would hold on amidst a pitiless storm of shot and shell, we will enumerate the damages inflicted on the "Naiad:"

"The first shot passed through the smoke-stack; the second and third shots passed through the pilot-house, the third striking the barrel of the wheel, cutting the tiller rope, and literally tearing the wheel to pieces; the fourth shot passed a few feet abaft the pilot-house, shattering the steerage and skylights, but doing no further damage; the fifth shot passed through the cabin. * * * * also * * four shots through the starboard casemates; one striking abreast of the boilers, one abaft of No. 2 gun, tearing up the decks and exploding within a few feet of the shell-room; one abaft of No. 3 gun, killing John J. Crennell, ordinary seaman, and wounding three others; another passed through the port of No. 4 gun, tearing away the shutter and exploding in the dispensary."

This was a gallant combat on the part of these light-armed gun-boats, and showed the persistency with which the Confederates kept up the war.

Now that the great strongholds of the enemy had all been abandoned, the guerilla warfare was carried on along the Mississippi as it had been on the upper rivers. The guerillas never accomplished anything of importance, and soon became a source of great annoyance to the wretched inhabitants, who were obliged to feed and clothe them in order to make it appear that they were loyal to the Confederate cause. No discipline existed among these wandering bands, and they preyed on friends and foes alike.

On the 29th of June, a fleet of nine transports, containing troops under the command of General Steele, started on an expedition up the Arkansas River, for the purpose of meeting a Confederate force under General Marmaduke, who had assembled quite an army on both sides of the river and was obstructing navigation. The transports were accompanied by the gun-boats "Taylor," "Fawn," "Naumkeag" and "Queen City," under the command of Lieutenant George M. Bache. The smaller vessels had gone on ahead, while the "Taylor" (Lieutenant Bache's vessel) kept with the convoy. When within ten miles of Clarendon, Lieutenant Bache picked up some sailors on the left bank of the river, belonging to the "Queen City," who stated that that vessel had been captured by General Shelby at 4 o'clock that morning. Information was also obtained that the enemy were in much greater force than General Steele had anticipated, which caused a change in the programme.

It appears that while the "Queen City" was lying at anchor off Clarendon, she was suddenly attacked by General Shelby with two regiments of cavalry (dismounted) and four pieces of artillery. The officers of the vessel were taken by surprise, no intimation of the enemy's approach having been given until the attack was made. At the first or second round the starboard engine was disabled by a shell, and the effectiveness of the port engine was much injured by a piece of the same shell passing through the steam-pipe. After fighting twenty minutes, Acting-Master M. Hickey, who commanded the gun-boat, seeing that she was completely riddled with shot, shell and rifle-balls, decided to surrender, not having the bravery to fight it out, as many of his contemporaries would have done. He ordered his officers and men to abandon the vessel, and most of them escaped to the opposite shore. One man was killed, nine wounded and 25 taken prisoners.

Lieutenant Bache received intelligence of the capture of the "Queen City" about five hours after it occurred. He at once started up the river to prevent the enemy from using her against the Union forces or getting out her stores. When within a few miles of Clarendon, however, two successive reports were heard up the river, which proved to be the explosion of the unfortunate gun-boat's magazine. General Shelby, hearing of the approach of the other vessels, had destroyed her.

The gun-boats approached the point where the enemy was stationed in the following order: "Taylor," "Naumkeag," "Fawn;" and when they were abreast of Cache River the enemy opened fire, putting one of his first shots through the pilot-house of the "Taylor." This vessel could only reply with one gun until abreast of the enemy's position, when she fired broadsides of shrapnel and canister. Having passed the batteries, the gun-boats rounded-to and steamed up at them again (at this time the "Fawn's" pilot had been mortally wounded and her signal-bell arrangements carried away, which prevented her from participating in the second attack). The Confederates thought that Bache merely intended to run by their batteries, and they gave three cheers when they saw him steaming away as they supposed, but when he returned to the attack they exclaimed in despair: "Here comes that black devil again!" After getting abreast of them again, the "Taylor" and "Naumkeag" kept up such a terrible fire that in five minutes the enemy began escaping in all directions, throwing away everything they had captured.

The Confederates had six guns of their own, of different sizes, and a 12-pounder howitzer, which they had taken from the "Queen City." These guns were placed in four different positions, making four batteries; but the fire of the gun-boats was so withering that the artillerymen were driven off after an action of 45 minutes. The Confederates must have been roughly handled, for they abandoned everything they had captured from the "Queen City," as well as some of their wounded prisoners.

This was a very gallant and well-managed affair, and Lieutenant Bache gained great credit for the handsome manner in which he had handled his vessels and defeated so large a force of the enemy.

Acting-Master John Rogers of the "Naumkeag" was also mentioned handsomely for the cool and efficient manner in which he had fought his vessel. In fact, all behaved well and redeemed the unfortunate loss of the "Queen City," which lay a shattered wreck at the bottom of the river. Her guns were finally raised and everything of value recovered.

Lieutenant Bache was now warned by the falling water that it was time to go below, if he did not wish to be caught in a trap. Having satisfied himself that he had completely driven Shelby and his force away from the river, he left the "Naumkeag" and "Fawn" at Clarendon, to protect that place and started down the river, in the "Taylor," to communicate with General Steele.

A large force of troops was then sent up in a transport, convoyed by the "Taylor," and landed at Clarendon without meeting any opposition. This force, under General Carr, immediately gave chase to the enemy, who numbered 2,500 men, and skirmished with them for twenty-five miles, capturing several pieces of artillery and 60 wounded men. Most of the crew of the unfortunate "Queen City" were picked up along the river and distributed among the other vessels. The enemy retired towards Little Rock and did not trouble the gun-boats again for some time. The flotilla had sixteen men wounded, two of whom died the next day.

We have nothing to say against this attack of the Confederates—it was all legitimate enough, and, no doubt, they suffered severely for their temerity. General Shelby showed no want of gallantry, his only fault being that he had not fairly considered the enemy he was about to attack. He had so easily overcome the "Queen City" that he thought he could do the same with the rest.

The result of the fight was that General Steele followed the enemy to Little Rock, Arkansas, on which place General Marmaduke had intended to make a raid; and the Confederates, finding that they could not assemble on the banks of the White River while the gun-boats were so active, transferred their operations to some other quarter.

With the exception of some trouble with the guerillas up the Cumberland and Tennessee Rivers, the operations for the year 1864 ended favorably for the Union cause, as far as the Navy was concerned. The Confederates continued to show themselves in Kentucky and Tennessee, however, and sometimes took advantage of transports that were not convoyed by gun-boats. Even as late as December, 1864, there was no diminution of zeal and energy on the part of the enemy, though they must have seen by that time that the Confederacy was doomed. An artillery company would sometimes travel for miles just for the pleasure of firing a few shots into a gun-boat or transport.

There was not cavalry enough on the Federal side to pursue these raiders; and, if an expedition was organized for that purpose, it generally consisted of an army contingent in transports convoyed by gun-boats.

Sometimes the naval commander of a district, from a feeling of over-security, sent an insufficient force of gun-boats, when trouble would ensue and the undertaking be a failure. One of these cases was an expedition from Clifton to Eastport under command of Colonel Hoge, consisting of the 113th and 120th Illinois infantry, 660 strong; 61st U. S. colored infantry, 600 strong, and Battery G, 2d Missouri light artillery (four rifled 12-pounders). These troops embarked on the 9th of October, at Clifton, on the transports "City of Pekin," "Aurora" and "Kenton," and they set out for Eastport under convoy of the "Key West," Acting-Volunteer-Lieutenant E. M.

King, and the "Undine," Acting-Master John L. Bryant.

On the 10th the vessels arrived off Eastport. After passing Line Island, ten miles below, signal was made from the "Key West" to be cautious and proceed in close order. On approaching Eastport, everything seemed quiet; and as there were no signs of troops or batteries on the hill commanding the landing, Lieutenant King signalled to the transports to land their troops, and took a position with the gunboats in the middle of the river, so as to cover the movement with their guns.

The troops commenced disembarking immediately. Colonel Hoge then went on board the "Key West," and informed Lieutenant King that he should move immediately for Iuka. As the Colonel was returning to the "City of Pekin," a masked battery of six rifled guns from the hill at Eastport and three rifled guns from the "Chickasaw" opened on the boats. The transports were struck several times, and a caisson exploded on board both the "Aurora" and "Kenton," setting them on fire. This caused great confusion among the troops, many of them jumping overboard from the burning steamers. A company that had been sent out as skirmishers immediately returned to the boats, while the troops that were forming in line on the bank broke and fled down the river, abandoning a battery of four guns. The transports cut their lines and drifted down stream, the "Kenton" and "Aurora" disabled, and the "City of Pekin" with several shot through her — it seemed to be "every man for himself."

During this time the "Key West" and "Undine" were both hit twice with rifle projectiles. One shell passed down through the boiler-deck of the "Key West," and exploded in the bag-rack, near the after-part of the boilers—another passed through the steerage and out on the port side. The "Undine" had her bell-wires cut by a shell, also her port wheel-rope.

The gun-boats for half an hour returned the fire of the enemy, whose shot fell thick and fast around them, when Lieutenant King, seeing that he could do nothing with his smooth-bores against the Confederate rifles, dropped down out of range to look after the convey. The troops had quenched the fires on the transports, but they were disabled; and this was the end of an expedition that might have produced better results if the troops had been landed out of sight of Eastport and marched up.

It seems reasonable to suppose that 1,320 soldiers could have captured these batteries if proper means had been taken to do so; but sometimes the soldiers seemed helpless, and inclined to wait for the Navy to capture a place before occupying it, forgetting, or not knowing, that a "tin-clad" was not an iron-clad, and that the former were not qualified to go under the fire of heavy batteries. But it was not often that Army men behaved as they did on this occasion, and it can be partly accounted for by the presence of the colored soldiers, who were raw and undisciplined. This expedition was certainly a complete failure, much to be regretted by all concerned.

On the whole, however, the Navy in the West had nothing to be ashamed of during the year 1864, and it will be observed that throughout the campaign it had fighting enough to satisfy the most ardent temperament.

This river-fighting may seem uninteresting to the reader, but it was a link in the great chain that helped to bind the Briarean arms of the demon of rebellion. The services of the Navy in the West had as much effect in reducing the South to submission as the greater battles fought in the East; and the brave Westerners who entered the Navy with no previous knowledge of the profession, having to learn everything from a handspike to a ten-inch gun, may well feel proud at the manner in which they conducted themselves, and glory in the results of their labors, which cost the lives of many of their comrades, but which were generally attended with success.

CHAPTER XLIV.

BATTLE OF MOBILE BAY.

Defences of Mobile Bay.—Farragut's Fleet Crosses the Bar and makes Reconnaissance.— Confederate Iron-clads.—Forts Morgan, Gaines and Powell and Light-house Battery.—Bombardment of Fort Powell.—Evacuation of Fort.—Iron-clad "Tennessee" makes her Appearance.—Arrival of Monitors.—Cooperation of General Canby.—Preparing to Attack Forts.—Farragut issues his famous Orders of Combat.—Bombarding Fort Morgan.—The "Tennessee" Engaged.—The "Tecumseh" Sunk.—"D——n the Torpedoes—follow me!"—Farragut in the Rigging of the "Hartford" passing Fort.— The "Selma" Surrenders.—The "Morgan" and "Gaines" Ashore.—The "Tennessee" engages Fleet.—Remarkable Combat.—The "Monongahela" and "Lackawanna" Damaged.—The "Tennessee" and "Hartford" Fight at Close Quarters.—Game to the Last.—The "Tennessee" Surrenders.—Incidents of Battle.—The Wounded transferred to Pensacola.—Names of Killed and Wounded.—Farragut's detailed Report of Battle. — Reports of Officers. — Farragut Returns Thanks to Officers and Men.—Individual Acts of Heroism.—Incidents attending Sinking of "Tecumseh."—Surrender of Fort Gaines —Bombardment of Fort Morgan.—Surrender of Fort.—List of Officers of the "Tennessee" and "Selma."—Wanton Destruction of Property at Fort Morgan. — List of Killed and Wounded.—Loss of the "Phillippi."—History and Description of Confederate Iron-clad "Tennessee."—List of Vessels and Officers of West Gulf Squadron, January 1st, 1864.

IN January, 1864, Admiral Farragut began to turn his attention to the forts in Mobile Bay, which up to that time had been a complete protection to the blockade - runners, which passed in and out almost with impunity in spite of the greatest watchfulness on the part of the blockading fleet. There were several channels in the Bay with wide shoal grounds in and about their approaches, over which the Confederate light-draft vessels could pass, but where the Federal ships-of-war could not follow them.

The city of Mobile, in consequence, became one of the most important rendezvous for blockade - runners, as it was situated some miles up the bay, and could only be reached through tortuous channels, with which only experienced pilots were familiar. The people of Mobile felt quite secure against any attempt on the part of the Union gun-boats to pass their defences, and the blockade-runners laid as safely at their wharves as if they had been in the docks of Liverpool.

While the forts at the entrance of Mobile Bay remained intact, the Confederates could continue to supply their armies through Mobile City and the numerous railroads running from it to all parts of the South.

After the fall of Port Hudson and Vicksburg, General Banks, in New Orleans, had at his disposal over 50,000 troops ; and General Grant, at that time having in his mind the idea of sending Sherman on the celebrated march to the sea, had urgently requested the authorities at Washington to

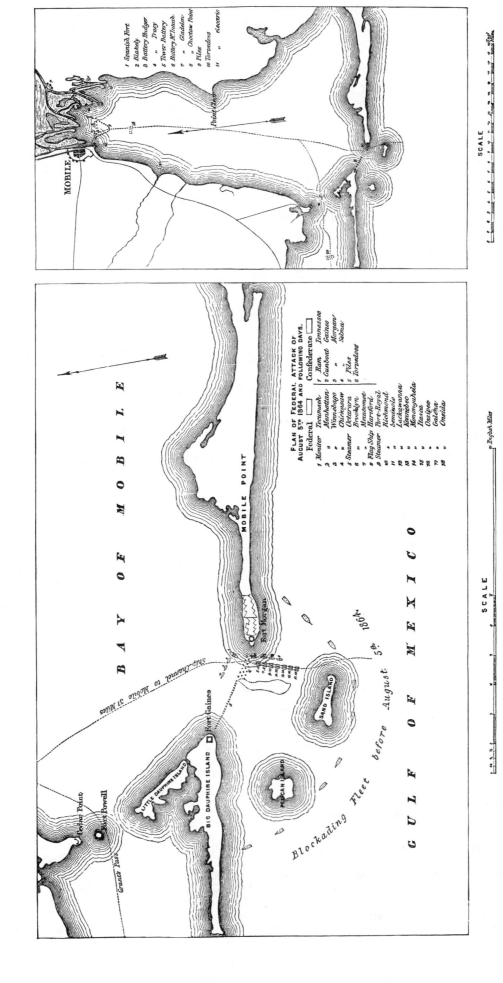

PLAN OF FEDERAL ATTACK OF AUGUST 5TH 1864 AND FOLLOWING DAYS.

Federal ☐   Confederate ☐

1 Monitor Tecumseh	1 Ram	Tennessee
2 " Manhattan	2 Gunboat	Gaines
3 " Winnebago	3 "	Morgan
4 " Chickasaw	4 "	Selma
5 Steamer Octorara	5 Piles	
6 " Brooklyn	6 Torpedoes	
7 " Mexadomet		
8 Flag Ship Hartford		
9 Steamer Port-Royal		
10 " Richmond		
11 " Seminole		
12 " Lackawanna		
13 " Kennebec		
14 " Monongahela		
15 " Itasca		
16 " Ossipee		
17 " Galena		
18 " Oneida		

1 Spanish Fort
2 Blakely
3 Battery Rudger
4 " Tracy
5 Tower-Battery
6 Battery McIntosh.
7 " Gladden
8 " Choctaw Point
9 Piles
10 Torpedoes
11 " electric

CHART SHOWING THE FLEET, UNDER ADMIRAL FARRAGUT, PASSING FORT MORGAN, AND THE POSITION OF THE CONFEDERATE FORTS AND VESSELS; ALSO, CHART OF MOBILE BAY UP TO THE CITY OF MOBILE, SHOWING FORTS AND OBSTRUCTIONS.

send Banks to Mobile with a sufficient force to capture that place ; while at the same time the Secretary of the Navy offered naval co-operation with Farragut's fleet, which was then disengaged from operations on the Mississippi River, and principally employed in watching Mobile and blockading the coast of Texas.

The Navy Department, as well as General Grant, was unsuccessful in obtaining an order from the War Department for Banks to proceed to Mobile, and act there in conjunction with the Navy ; and the fatal move up Red River having been decided upon, all other objects were for the time being passed over, until the anxiety of the Government became concentrated upon the problem of how to relieve that expedition from the unfortunate position in which General Banks' measures had placed it.

Mobile itself was poorly fortified against a land attack, and the Confederates had not more than 10,000 men in and about the city, and the majority of these were artillerists. Notwithstanding the fact that the weakness of the city was well known to him, General Banks turned away from the rich prize which he might so easily have taken, and embarked on the unwise expedition into the Red River region, from which his army was only extricated through the presence of the naval force—which for a time was also seriously embarrassed.

The Navy Department, finding that no co-operation could be expected from General Banks, directed Farragut (January, 1864) to prepare his vessels for an attack on the forts in Mobile Bay, and promised that a land force should be forthcoming at the time the fleet was ready to commence operations.

On the morning of January 20th Farragut crossed the bar of Mobile Bay in the "Octorara," taking the "Itasca" in company in case of accidents, and made a thorough reconnaissance of the bay and of all the forts commanding its approaches. He moved up to within three and one-half miles of the enemy's works, where he was able to verify the reports of refugees who had brought him a statement of the condition of the Confederate works. He could count the number of guns and see the men standing by them. A line of piles, which extended from Fort Gaines to the channel opposite Fort Morgan, was also plainly visible, and showed the intention of the enemy to compel all entering vessels to pass close under the guns of the latter work.

At that time Farragut had not an ironclad, and, being convinced that it would be madness to attack these forts without such aid, made his wants known to the Navy Department, and the vessels were eventually supplied.

The reconnaissance made by the Admiral satisfied him that he had a difficult task before him. Two heavy works protected the entrance to Mobile Bay—Forts Gaines and Morgan—the former mounting 21 guns and the latter 48, while Fort Powell, higher up the bay, commanded the fairway leading to Mobile.

A better idea of the situation of these works can be obtained by examining the accompanying chart than from any written description, and the reader is referred to the plan for information, without which he could form but a small idea of the defences of Mobile Bay and the difficulties attending an attack on them.

The lines of piles, extending from the head of the eastern bank to the edge of the tortuous and shallow channel near Fort Gaines, rendered it impossible for any vessel to pass between the bank and the channel ; indeed, only vessels of the lightest draft of water would have dared to make such an attempt under ordinary circumstances.

Every effort had been made by the Confederate engineers to make the channel between Gaines and Morgan impassable ; but its depth in some places was as much as 60 feet, the bottom was bad (drift-sand, in fact), and the action of ebb and flow, with that of heavy winds, rendered it almost impossible to obstruct it effectually. Even in time of peace it would have been an immense undertaking, requiring time and taxing the ingenuity of the engineers to the utmost. Not only that, it would have required means which were not at the disposal of the Confederates. Many plans were offered, but the chief engineer of the Department rejected them all and undertook to defend the pass with torpedoes, but, with an order from the Department commander to leave a gap in the line of torpedoes, 500 yards wide, through which blockade-runners could pass in safety between Mobile Point and a buoy marking the eastern end of the lines of torpedoes ; which arrangement it was foolishly supposed would keep out a fleet commanded by a man like Farragut, who had already earned the *sobriquet* of "The old Salamander."

Besides the forts above mentioned, the following auxiliary defences were possessed by the Confederates : Steam ram "Tennessee," 235 feet in length, casemate plated with three thicknesses of 2-inch plates or six inches of iron, speed 7¼ knots ; battery, four 10-inch columbiads of 16,000 lbs. and two 7½-inch Brooke rifles of 19,000 lbs. The "Tennessee" was the flag-ship of Admiral Franklin Buchanan, and was commanded by Commander J. D. Johnston.

The following gun-boats also belonged

to Buchanan's little squadron : The "Morgan," Commander Bennet ; "Selma," Commander Murphy, and "Gaines," Commander Harris. Two rams, the "Tuscaloosa" and "Huntsville," were building at Mobile, but they were never finished, and Buchanan received no assistance from them.

The guns of Fort Morgan were mounted as follows : Bastion No. 1 (N. E.), two 32-pounders of 7,000 lbs., one 24-pound rifle throwing Read & Slater's projectiles, shaped like Minie-balls ; East curtain, three 10-inch sea-coast mortars, one 32-pounder of 7,000 lbs.; Bastion No. 2 (E. S. E.), one 10-inch columbiad, two 32-pounders of 7,000 lbs.; Bastion No. 3, two 32-pounders of 7,000 lbs. (rifled), one 10-inch columbiad of 16,000 lbs.; South curtain, two 24-pounders of 11,000 lbs. (rifled, throwing 68-pound projectiles), one 10-inch columbiad of 16,000 lbs.; Bastion No. 4, one 24-pounder (rifled), one 10-inch columbiad of 16,000 lbs., two 32-pounders of 7,000 lbs. (rifled); West curtain, facing the channel, two Blakely rifles throwing shell of 160 lbs. and shot of 169 lbs., three 10-inch columbiads of 16,000 lbs.; Bastion No. 5, two 32-pounders, smooth-bore ; North curtain, one 8-inch smooth-bore. On each flank of each bastion there were two 24-pounders, making in all 20 flank casemate guns.

Light-house battery eleven 32-pounders of 7,000 tons. Fort Gaines mounted one 10-inch columbiad of 14,000 lbs., fourteen 32-pounders, smooth-bore, one 32-pounder, (rifled), and five 24-pound siege-pieces.

These were the guns under which an attacking fleet would have to pass, besides the Confederate gun-boats, which could take good positions under the guns of the forts, and rake the Federal vessels as they approached. Taking into consideration the fact that he had only wooden ships at first, Farragut was wise to delay his attack until the arrival of the iron-clads.

In addition to the two forts above mentioned was Fort Powell, situated at Grant's Pass. This could inflict no damage to a fleet passing Morgan and Gaines, but could annoy an enemy after he had passed up as far as the anchoring ground.

While waiting for the iron-clads, Farragut thought he would try and batter this fort down or injure its guns, and make it untenable ; but the attempt was not a success. The attack was made in the latter part of February, but discontinued as soon as the difficulties of the operation were realized.

Farragut continued to apply to the Department for even one iron-clad, with which he was willing to undertake the attack, supposing the iron-clad ram "Tennessee" would be over the Dog River bar by the

time he was ready to advance with his fleet.

Farragut's idea was to have a combined attack by the Army and Navy—the land forces to operate in the rear of forts Gaines and Morgan by the Big Dauphine Island and Mobile Point—and great expectations were laid on a contingent being sent from General Banks' army, but that officer had gone into the Red River country and met with such disasters as made co-operation impossible.

The Confederate papers magnified the want of success on the part of General Banks, and made the most of it for their side, until they really believed all through the Southwest that they had gained a brilliant victory, when the truth was simply that the Federal General did not hold on to the victory which his troops had won.

Great rejoicing was also kept up in the South in consequence of the success of the "Albemarle " and the capture of Plymouth. Many were made to believe that a new and favorable turn had been given to their affairs, and that if the opportunity was followed up it would lead to further successes in Louisiana. A pressure was brought to bear on Admiral Buchanan to expedite the completion of the iron-clad "Tennessee," with the expectation that this vessel would demolish Farragut and his fleet, proceed to New Orleans, capture the Union fleet at that place, prevent Banks from reaching the city again, and finally restore the Confederate authority !

This may seem a wild scheme, but it might have been successful. Buchanan was a brave and energetic officer, capable of undertaking any enterprise, and could he have succeeded in getting all his iron-clads and gun-boats ready in time, he would have been more than a match for the force which Farragut had on hand in February.

Farragut himself fully appreciated his situation. From his experience in the Mississippi River, where the ram "Arkansas " attacked the two Federal fleets (Davis' and his own), he saw plainly what would be the result of a contest between wooden vessels and iron-clads. In his letters to the Navy Department the Admiral deeply regrets his inability to obtain even one of the iron-clads on the Mississippi, and remarks, "it appears that it takes us twice as long to build an iron-clad as any one else. It looks as if the fates and contractors were against us. While the Confederates are bending their whole energies to the war, our people are expecting the war to close by default ; and, if they do not awake to the sense of their danger soon, it will be so."

Farragut was fully aware of what would

be the result if Buchanan crossed the Dog River bar with the "Tennessee," "Tuscaloosa," "Huntsville" and "Nashville. (The three latter vessels were reported to be plated with nearly the thickness of iron carried by the "Tennessee").

Continuous reports came from Mobile that the ram "Tennessee" was preparing to cross the Dog River bar by means of camels, and that Buchanan, with his well-known energy, was pushing the work on his iron clads night and day. Farragut knew as well as any one the determination and energy of the man he expected to contend with, and under the circumstances his position was not an enviable one.

He seemed to have the idea that the capture of Fort Powell was a most desirable thing, and would tend to keep the Confederate Navy up the river if he could succeed in getting possession of it; and from the 22d of February to the 2d of March he kept up a fire on this fort from rifles, smooth-bores and mortars from a distance of 4,000 yards—the nearest point attainable.

Fort Powell was built on an oyster bank. The Confederate engineers had exhibited great skill in its construction, and it was impervious to shot and shell. It was built to guard Grant's Pass, the entrance from Mississippi Sound to Mobile Bay, and it was very important that it should be well built and armed.

A Confederate writer says:

"Admiral Farragut opened from his mortars and gun-boats a fire on the small fort that would have battered any stone or brick structure into a mass of ruins. The firing, especially that of the 13-inch mortars could (in accuracy) not have been surpassed: one shell after another falling on the earth-cover of the bomb-proof, penetrating as deep as three and a half feet, exploding and making a crater of seven feet in diameter."

"This bombardment was steadily kept up from February 22d till March 2d, without making any impression whatever on the fort; not a single gun had been dismounted, not a single traverse had been seriously damaged, nor had the parapet and bomb-proof lost any of their strength; all damage done by the exploding shells being at once repaired by throwing sand-bags into the open craters. But one man had been killed, another wounded, and the brave commander of the fort, Lieutenant-Colonel James M. Williams, of the 21st Alabama regiment, paid for his temerity, in unnecessarily exposing himself to the shower of the enemy's iron missiles, with the loss of his coat-tail."

"The wharf and quarters on the east face of the fort had been considerably damaged by the bombardment."

"When Farragut had forced his way into the Bay of Mobile, an evacuation of Fort Powell was the only means to save its garrison from capture, and the place was abandoned after preparations for blowing up the magazine had been so well made that its explosion took place hardly half-an-hour after Lieutenant-Colonel Williams (the last man) had left the fort."

Farragut's chief motive in making this attack was to get the gun-boats into Mobile Bay through Grant's Pass, and to endeavor to destroy the "Tennessee" while she had the camels under her in crossing the Dog River bar.

From all accounts Buchanan was working energetically to bring the "Tennessee" and her consorts face to face with the Union fleet, which he felt sure of driving from before Mobile. He then intended to proceed to Pensacola and raise the siege in that quarter. There is no doubt that, had he succeeded in finishing his four iron-clads in time, Farragut would have either been destroyed or the siege of Mobile raised.

The account of the sinking of the "Southfield" by the ram "Albemarle" in the Sounds of North Carolina, on the 17th of April, and the stubborn battle made by the "Albemarle" against the comparatively heavy force of gun-boats on May 5th, in which the ram moved off apparently unharmed after a three hours' fight at close quarters, had been received in the South and also in the fleet; and while this news encouraged the Confederate Admiral to fresh exertions, it, on the other hand, made Farragut feel more anxious that he should be supplied with iron-clads to meet the new naval force of the Confederates, the like of which had not been so near completion since the war began.

Farragut knew Buchanan well, and was aware that in point of courage, energy and skill he had few equals, and no superiors; and that, if he did succeed in getting his vessels over Dog River bar, he would come out with the intention of conquering or being destroyed, the latter contingency not being likely in Farragut's then weak condition.

By some authorities it is stated that the "Tennessee" made her appearance in Mobile Bay on the 17th of March; but we think there must be some mistake about this, for, as late as the 9th of May, Farragut wrote to the Department that "the late accounts from Mobile agree in representing Buchanan as making great exertions to get camels large enough to float the ram "Tennessee" over Dog River bar.

No one doubted but that Buchanan would be successful if any one could be, and Farragut expected that he would come out and attack him with his whole force of iron-clads, besides the three gun-boats, and so wrote urgent letters in the middle of May to the Navy Department, requesting that iron-clads be sent him. It was the most uncomfortable position that any officer was placed in during the war, when told by the Department as late as June, 1864, that the vessels could not be furnished because the contractors had not come up to their contract. But the Admiral bore it all bravely, and with his usual equanimity prepared his wooden ships to do the best they could in the coming conflict.

Not until May 25th does Farragut speak of the "Tennessee" having arrived in the Mobile Roads, and anchored under the guns of Fort Morgan. He went in as close as he could, examined her with good glasses, and satisfied himself that all that had been said about her formidable character was true. He had been deceived so many times by what were supposed to be iron-clads, that he was glad to have his mind settled on this question, and to know that this was really the "Tennessee" without her consorts.

On June 2d, refugees, who stated that they were from Mobile, two or three days before, reported that, besides the "Tennessee," a vessel called the "Baltic," the iron-clads "Tuscaloosa" and "Huntsville," and three gun-boats had also crossed the bar and entered the lower bay; the "Nashville" was not yet over the bar, but she was all ready with the camels under her by this time; her bow, stern and pilot-house were only partly plated."

Two more rams were reported to be at Mobile, not yet plated, and one just completed at Selma and aground above Mobile. They also reported at Mobile "four iron-plated floating batteries, one of them sunk." These reports were constantly brought down concerning Buchanan's force, and they were far from reassuring to the Union commander, who up to this time had not received a single iron-clad.

It was not until July 26th that the arrival of the Monitor "Manhattan" was reported. She was under Sand Island, in charge of gun-boats.

The two double-turreted Monitors, "Winnebago" and "Chickasaw," sent from Admiral Porter's fleet on the Mississippi, were in New Orleans, and would be off Mobile about the 30th of July. The "Tecumseh" was not yet heard from, and the Army which Farragut had asked for to co-operate with him was still in New Orleans. When the latter should arrive, Farragut would be quite ready to commence operations against the defences of Mobile.

The arrival of the "Manhattan" was an assurance that Buchanan would not leave the bay to attack the Federal wooden ships, which Buchanan at no time had any idea of doing. His policy was to fight Farragut's fleet, under the cover of the forts, in the narrow channel which had been left by the Confederate engineers.

The only thing wanting to make Farragut satisfied with his condition was the arrival of the "Tecumseh," and this took place on the 4th of August. He now determined to make his attack as soon as possible.

As soon as General Canby had arrived in New Orleans with the troops which General Banks left crossing the Atchafalaya River, Farragut communicated with him and requested that two or three thousand troops be sent to co-operate with him in an attack on Mobile. These troops were promised without hesitation on the 8th of July, in an interview held on board the "Hartford," between the Admiral and Generals Canby and Granger; but circumstances soon obliged General Canby to say that he could only spare troops enough to invest one fort.

Farragut then suggested that it should be Fort Gaines, and engaged at the same time to have a naval force in the Sounds ready to protect the landing of the Army on Dauphine Island, in the rear of the fort. Lieutenant-Commander J. C. P. De Krafft, in the "Conemaugh," was assigned to this duty.

It was arranged between Farragut and General Granger that the attack should take place on the 4th day of August, but owing to unforeseen circumstances it was delayed until the 5th. This delay turned out to be fortunate, for on the 4th the Confederates were engaged in throwing more troops and supplies into Fort Gaines, all of which were captured.

At 5:40 A. M. on the 5th of August, 1864, all the vessels outside of the bar, which were to participate in the battle, got under-way in the following order, two abreast, lashed together:

"Brooklyn," Captain James Alden, with the "Octorara," Lieutenant-Commander C. H. Greene, on the port side.

"Hartford," Captain Percival Drayton, with the "Metacomet," Lieutenant-Commander James E. Jouett.

"Richmond," Captain Thornton A. Jenkins, with the "Port Royal," Lieutenant-Commander Bancroft Gherardi.

"Lackawanna," Captain J. B. Marchand, with the "Seminole," Commander E. Donaldson.

"Monongahela," Commander J. H. Strong, with the "Kennebec," Lieutenant-Commander W. P. McCann.

"Ossipee," Commander Wm. E. LeRoy, and the "Itasca," Lieutenant-Commander George Brown.

"Oneida," Commander J. R. M. Mullany, and the "Galena," Lieutenant-Commander C. H. Wells.

The iron-clads, "Tecumseh," Commander T. A. M. Craven, "Manhattan," Commander J. W. A. Nicholson, "Winnebago," Commander T. H. Stevens, and "Chickasaw," Lieutenant-Commander George H. Perkins, were already inside the bar, and they were ordered to take up their positions on the starboard hand of the wooden vessels, between them and Fort Morgan, for the double purpose of keeping down the fire of the water battery and fort, and of attacking the ram "Tennessee" as soon as the fort was passed.

The commanding officers of the ships urgently requested Farragut to allow Captain Alden, in the "Brooklyn," to lead the attacking column, as this vessel had four chase-guns and an ingenious apparatus for picking up torpedoes, and because, in their judgment, the flag-ship should not lead and be too much exposed. The proper place for the flag-ship was, in fact, the middle of the line, but Farragut would only yield so far as to have one ship in advance of him. He did not believe in the principle that a flag-officer should not lead. He considered it one of the privileges of high rank in the Navy, and that it was an honor to be sought by every one who desired to set a proper example to those under his command.

Before going into action the Admiral had issued orders making his commanding officers acquainted with his plan of combat and steaming. His orders for battle had a determination in them which showed that he meant to destroy the enemy or be destroyed himself. There was a vigor and coolness about them which cannot but commend them to officers of the Navy, and they will offer good examples in the future for those who would not otherwise appreciate all his precautions, but who are convinced by the resulting events how necessary they were on this occasion.

It was no ordinary battle that was to be fought. Four iron-clads and a fleet of wooden vessels fourteen in number, the heaviest carrying only 26 guns, were about to attack forts that were originally constructed with the purpose of keeping out of Mobile the heaviest vessels then known (ships-of-the-line and frigates) that could pass the bar into Mobile Bay, or that might attempt to enfilade Fort Morgan from outside the bar to the eastward.

Forts Gaines and Morgan had been planned and built by the best engineer in the United States Army, and they had been strengthened and improved in every way by the Confederates. To crown all, these forts mounted not only the heaviest guns made in the country, but were well provided with the latest improved rifle-cannon of English manufacture, which had been brought over in blockade runners. The impediments in the channel have been already mentioned, but what number of torpedoes had been planted no one knew.

All these drawbacks against a passage by the forts did not cast a cloud over the countenance of any officer or man in the fleet. They were all as anxious for the combat as was their commanding officer, who had passed through too many battles within the last two years to feel dismayed at the idea of running through a lot of piles and sunken torpedoes.

Every officer was on the alert; the ear of every sailor was attentive to catch the sound of the first tap of the drum (the call to quarters); and one, to look at all those eager faces on the poop and forecastle of every ship, would suppose this to be some grand gala day. It was indeed a gala day, for every one could see in the cheerful and determined look of their great commander that this would be a day of glorious victory, that the frowning forts and dark-looking "Tennessee," though barring the way and threatening destruction, would be swept away, if "hearts of oak in wooden hulls" could do it. All longed to see the defiant Confederate flag, which had waved so long unmolested, hauled down, and the last ram the Confederates ever built consigned to the fate of her predecessors.

It was a glorious sight to see those brave fellows wearing a smile of joy upon their faces in view of such odds against them— and not knowing how soon they and their comrades would be lying at the bottom of the bay. All could not hope to escape this trying ordeal, when several of the coolest officers calculated that at least six of the ships would be blown up. They never stopped to consider whose fate this would be; all they desired was to grapple with the enemy, and see the Union flag floating over the forts that had been taken from their lawful owners.

Soon the word went forth :

GENERAL ORDER, No. 10.

"Strip your vessels and prepare for the conflict. Send down all your superfluous spars and rigging. Trice up or remove the whiskers. Put up the splinter nets on the starboard side and barricade the steersmen with sails and hammocks. Lay chains or sand-bags on the deck over the machinery to resist a plunging fire. Hang the sheet chains over the side, or make any other arrangement for security that your ingenuity may suggest. Land your starboard boats or lower them and tow them on the port side, and lower the port boats down to the water's edge. Place a leadsman and the pilot in the port-quarter boat or the one most convenient to the commander.

"The vessels will run past the forts in couples, lashed side by side, as hereafter designated. The flag-ship will lead and steer from Sand Island N. by E. by compass until abreast of Fort Morgan, then N. W. half N., until past the Middle Ground; then N. by W; and the others, as designated in the drawing, will follow in due order, until directed to anchor; but the bow and quarter line must be preserved to give the chase-guns a fair range, and each vessel must be kept astern of the broadside of the next ahead. Each vessel will keep a very little on the starboard quarter of his next ahead, and when abreast of the fort will keep directly astern, and as we pass the fort will take the same distance on the port quarter of the next ahead, to enable the stern guns to fire clear of the next vessel astern.

"It will be the object of the Admiral to get as close to the fort as possible before opening fire :

the ships, however, will open fire the moment the enemy opens upon us, with their chase and other guns, as fast as they can be brought to bear. Use short fuzes for the shell and shrapnel, and as soon as within three or four hundred yards, give the grape. It is understood that heretofore we have fired too high; but with grape-shot it is necessary to elevate a little above the object, as grape will dribble from the muzzle of the gun. If one or more of the vessels be disabled, their partners must carry them through, if possible; but if they cannot, then the next astern must render the required assistance; but as the Admiral contemplates moving with the flood-tide it will only require sufficient power to keep the crippled vessels in the channel.

"Vessels that can, must place guns upon the poop and topgallant forecastle, and in the tops on the starboard side. Should the enemy fire grape, they will remove the men from the topgallant forecastle and poop to the guns below, until out of grape range.

"The howitzers must keep up a constant fire

Morgan. It being understood that there are torpedoes and other obstructions between the buoys, the vessels will take care to pass eastward of the easternmost buoy, which is clear of all obstructions.

"So soon as the vessels arrive opposite the end of the piles, it will be best to stop the propeller of the ship, and let her drift the distance past by her headway and the tide; and those having side-wheel gun-boats will continue on by the aid of their paddle-wheels, which are not likely to foul with the enemy's drag-ropes.

"D. G. FARRAGUT,
"Rear-Admiral."

The appended diagram is the plan of attack, and distinctly shows, not only the position of every vessel in the fleet, but also Fort Morgan, the Confederate ram "Tennessee," and her consorts, the "Selma," "Morgan" and "Gaines."

The Federal vessels having formed line, according to the diagram, moved ahead at

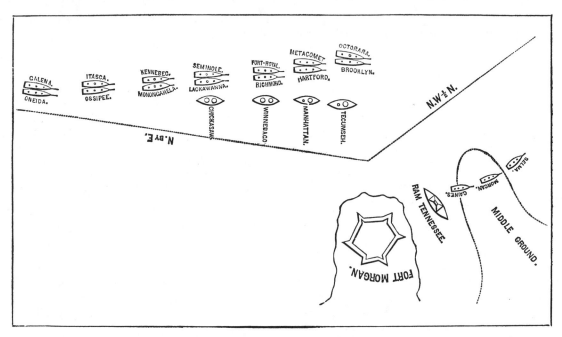

PLAN SHOWING FARRAGUT'S VESSELS PASSING FORT MORGAN, ALSO POSITION OF CONFEDERATE RAM AND GUN-BOATS.

from the time they can reach with shrapnel until out of range.

"D. G. FARRAGUT,
"Rear-Admiral, Commanding
"West Gulf Blockading Squadron."

GENERAL ORDER, No. 11.

"Should any vessel be disabled to such a degree that her consort is unable to keep her in her station, she will drop out of line to the westward, and not embarrass the vessels next astern by attempting to regain her station. Should she repair damages so as to be able to re-enter the line of battle, she will take her station in the rear, as close to the last vessel as possible.

"So soon as the vessels have passed the fort and kept away northwest, they can cast off the gun-boats at the discretion of the senior officer of the two vessels, and allow them to proceed up the bay to cut off the enemy's gun-boats that may be attempting to escape up to Mobile. There are certain black buoys placed by the enemy from the piles on the west side of the channel, across it towards Fort

about 5:45 A. M., following the "Brooklyn," which vessel took the lead. Some little delay was now necessary to allow all the ships to get into position, and form a compact line of steaming. When this was accomplished, the fleet moved on in the direction of Fort Morgan, which opened fire at 7:07 o'clock, at a distance of about two miles.

The "Tecumseh," leading the iron-clads, fired the first gun at 6:45, and was followed by the "Brooklyn," with her two 100-pounder Parrotts, and then by the "Hartford." As the leading vessels approached, they commenced firing their broadside guns, and the remainder of the fleet continued the fire as they got in position to do so effectively.

As the Federal vessels neared the fort, the ram "Tennessee" and the wooden gun-boats opened fire upon them—raking them at every discharge. At about half-past seven the battle became general all along the line, as vessel after vessel came near enough to use her guns.

The Monitors had so little speed that the whole fleet was obliged to move slowly, and thus offer a fair mark to the Confederate gunners; but the thick smoke and the rapid fire of grape from the fleet so disconcerted them, that the flag-ship passed with no great injury or loss of life; a shell which passed through the side and exploded abaft the mainmast, killing and wounding a large portion of No. 7 gun's crew, being the only one that caused much destruction.

At this time the "Hartford" had become the leading vessel, owing to the fact that just as the "Brooklyn" came abreast of Fort Morgan, and was keeping up a rapid fire of grape from her broadside guns, which seemed to almost silence the enemy's batteries, the Monitor "Tecumseh"—then about three hundred yards ahead, and on the starboard bow of the "Brooklyn"—was seen from the latter vessel to career violently over, and sink almost instantly. The "Brooklyn" was now somewhat inside the fort, shoal water was reported, and at the same time the smoke cleared away, and revealed a row of suspicious-looking buoys right under the vessel's bow.

The captain of the "Brooklyn" now made a mistake; he stopped his vessel and then backed, to avoid leading the fleet into what appeared to be a nest of torpedoes. His motive was a good one, but this movement was not in the programme.

It was apparent to Farragut that there was some difficulty ahead, and that the advance of the fleet was arrested, while Fort Morgan was firing with great effect upon the stationary vessels. At this moment the Admiral also witnessed the sinking of the "Tecumseh," with nearly all her officers and crew. It was an appalling spectacle, and would have daunted many other men. He did not know but that his whole fleet would be blown up in less than a minute, and their hulls and guns lying at the bottom of the bay. He did not hesitate, however, but gave the order to Captain Drayton: "Pass the 'Brooklyn,' and take the lead." His order was immediately obeyed, and as the flag-ship went by him, Captain Alden informed the Admiral that he was "running into a nest of torpedoes." "D——n the torpedoes," he replied, "follow me!" At the same time he directed the commander of the "Metacomet" to send a boat and pick up any of the "Tecumseh's" survivors that he could find.

This was a trying time, for, as the ships were moving at a rate of about seven knots at the time the "Brooklyn" stopped, the line was thrown into confusion. The "Brooklyn," as soon as she stopped, received the concentrated fire of the fort, it being the object of the Confederate gunners to cripple the leading ships and throw those in the rear into confusion. Many of the "Brooklyn's" crew were killed and wounded by this fire, and her total loss during the engagement was 54 officers and men.

As soon as the Admiral had passed, Captain Alden followed in his wake at full speed, and turned northward with him, receiving at the same time several heavy shot from the "Tennessee," which cut his vessel up considerably near the water line, forward.

The battle had been general some time before this, and the rapid and well-aimed fire of the naval gunners drove the enemy from their guns. The latter had never before witnessed the effect of shell, grape and shrapnel when fired from guns worked by fearless American seamen, who had but one idea, and that was to knock down the offending flag which now floated on the fort where in days of yore the "Stars and Stripes" had waved peacefully in the breeze.

All was animation in the fleet; every commander was on the alert to keep his ship in position, and not confuse the ships ahead and astern of him. The gunners were cautioned to throw no shot away, and carefully instructed how to train their guns. The Admiral, jumping into the main rigging, where he could see over the smoke, gave orders to steam through the buoys, where the torpedoes were supposed to be placed in the greatest numbers. At this moment the fire of every gun that could be brought to bear was playing on the fort, and as ship after ship followed in the wake of the "Hartford," and turned up channel, their stern-guns belched forth their deadly missiles, while the fort scarcely fired a gun; the enemy were either killed or sent to cover, though a Confederate writer asserts that not a gun in Fort Morgan was silenced.

All anxiously watched the "Hartford" to see what would be her fate, but the stout old ship that had fairly been bathed in fire on so many occasions, sped safely on, and the road was clear for those who came after.

The line of buoys had been examined on several occasions (in night reconnaissances) by Flag-Lieutenant J. Crittenden Watson, who was unable to discover any sunken torpedoes, yet the Admiral had been assured by refugees that such did exist. He believed, however, that, from their having been for some time under water, they were harmless, and under this idea he determined to take the chances.

CONFEDERATE GUNBOATS: MONITORS: Flag-ship "Hartford"   "Brooklyn" "Richmond" "Lackawanna" "Monongahela" "Ossipee" "Oneida" "Trans- Sand
"Gaines."   "Manhattan."   "Chickasaw."   and   and   and   and Island
"Tennessee." "Morgan." "Selma." "Tecumseh." "Winnebago." "Metacomet." "Octorara." "Port Royal." "Seminole." "Kennebec." "Itasca." "Galena." ports. Light.

BATTLE OF MOBILE BAY.

FORT MORGAN BEARING S. E., AND SAND ISLAND LIGHT SOUTH BY COMPASS.

At ten minutes before 8 A. M. the "Hartford" had fairly passed Fort Morgan, with the "Brooklyn" close behind her. As the flag-ship passed the shore batteries, she came directly under the fire of the gun-boats "Selma," "Morgan" and "Gaines" and the ram "Tennessee," and being only able to direct her fire on one of them at a time, the shots from the others were delivered with effect, a single shot having killed ten men and wounded five at guns Nos. 1 and 2.

The "Tennessee" followed the "Hartford" for some distance, throwing an occasional shot, while the gun-boat "Selma," keeping on her bow, annoyed her very much by the fire of her three stern-guns. The "Hartford" could not answer this attack, for the reason that her rifle-gun carriage had been crippled by a shell.

The flag-ship was at this time nearly a mile ahead of the fleet, and the "Metacomet," Lieutenant - Commander Jouett, was ordered to cast off and attack the "Selma." This energetic officer lost not a moment in obeying the order, and putting on all steam started in pursuit of the enemy's gun-boats, all three of which were annoying the "Hartford." These vessels all retreated up the bay, engaging the "Metacomet" with their stern - guns. At half - past 8 the "Gaines" retreated under cover of Fort Morgan in a crippled condition. At 9 the "Morgan" hauled off to starboard, and at 10 minutes past 9 the "Selma" struck her flag to the "Metacomet."

By this time the whole fleet had passed the obstructions and were beyond the fire of Fort Morgan, but the ram "Tennessee" was steaming about and delivering her heavy rifle-shell with terrible effect. The "Brooklyn," as she passed the ram, poured in her broadside of 9-inch shot, but without inflicting any apparent damage, and then passed on after the "Hartford," which had anchored about five miles up the bay.

Whatever may have been Admiral Buchanan's plan up to this time, he had not yet succeeded in crippling any of the Federal vessels either with his shot or with his ram. He made an effort to strike the "Brooklyn," but passed astern of her, after which he turned and ran as if to intercept the fleet, which was now passing under a full head of steam, and delivering their broadsides in quick succession.

It was a beautiful sight to see the Union fleet passing on in such good order, and delivering their fire on the enemy's forts, iron - clad or gun - boats, as occasion required, with wonderful precision and effect.

The passage of the fleet had sealed the fate of Mobile ; the surrender of Fort Morgan was but the matter of a few days; Fort Gaines could make but a feeble resistance against a combined attack of Army and Navy, and Fort Powell, cut off as it was, would fall without firing a shot.

No doubt Buchanan realized the situation. The "Selma" had been captured ; the "Gaines," not being as closely pursued as was the "Selma," escaped under cover of Fort Morgan, where she was afterwards run ashore and burnt, while the "Morgan" escaped to Mobile. Nothing was now left for Buchanan to do but to surrender, or die gloriously fighting to the last. He chose the latter, but did not choose the right time.

Farragut, supposing that the fighting was over for the time being, had anchored and made signal to the fleet to follow his motions. He expected the "Tennessee" to remain under the guns of Fort Morgan during the remainder of the day; and if she had done so and attacked the fleet after dark there is no knowing what would have been the result. The ram would have been the only Confederate vessel engaged, and her commander could therefore treat every vessel he met as an enemy, while the Union vessels would not have been able to use their guns for fear of firing into a consort. As it was, with the heaviest guns in the fleet pouring shot and shell into her in broad day, she committed great havoc.

Looking upon it as a naval movement, Buchanan made a great mistake that morning when he went out to attack Farragut's fleet. He must have seen that every one of the Union vessels was superior to him in speed, and had nothing to fear from his ram, while the heavy guns of the three remaining Monitors would be brought to bear on him in such a way that his 6-inch armor would be damaged and his port shutters closed. He might have supposed, too, that Farragut would not hesitate to ram him, with ships of greater speed than his own — there are a hundred things which one good sailor would expect another to do under certain circumstances.

No one who knew Buchanan and his professional ability would doubt for a minute that he had considered all these matters. Perhaps he feared that the forts would be surrendered before sunset, and the powerful "Tennessee," of which so much had been expected, and by which so little had yet been done, surrendered with them.

Whatever was the case, he did not take long to make up his mind. The fleet had not been anchored more than fifteen minutes when it was reported to Admiral Farragut that the "Tennessee" was coming out from under Fort Morgan and standing down for the head of the fleet. Farragut at once divined that it was his enemy's intention to sink the flag-ship (which would have been glory enough for one day), but he determined to show the Confederates that it was an easier matter to sink a frigate at anchor in Hampton Roads than a live fleet in Mobile Bay. The signal was at once made to get underway, and the crews ran the anchors up to the bows with marvellous rapidity.

The iron-clads, and such wooden vessels as had been prepared with iron prows, were ordered to attack the "Tennessee" at once, before she could reach the centre of the fleet, and the wooden vessels were directed to ram the iron-clad and attempt to disable her in that way.

Thus the fleet and the "Tennessee" were approaching each other rapidly, while the people in the former were watching keenly for the result, no one being able to form an opinion as to the power of the latter for offensive purposes, or what might be the plan of her commander, who was standing fearlessly on, as if conscious that he was more than a match for the Federals. And now commenced one of the most remarkable combats known throughout the war—in fact, one of the fiercest naval battles on record.

The "Monongahela," Commander Strong, was the first vessel that had the honor of striking the "Tennessee," which she did squarely and fairly, with a good head of steam ; but the only result was that the ramming vessel carried away her cast-iron prow, together with the cut-water, without apparently doing the "Tennessee" any damage. Just afterwards, the "Lackawanna," Captain Marchand, delivered a blow, going at full speed, crushing in her own stem, but had no other effect on the ram than to give her a heavy list. The Admiral then dashed at his enemy with the "Hartford," but only got in a glancing blow, for the "Tennessee" avoided his attack by shifting her helm in time. The flag-ship rasped alongside of her and delivered a broadside from her starboard guns as she passed, but with little or no effect.

This was a reception Buchanan did not anticipate. He had calculated on catching the fleet in confusion, and expected to enact again the role of the "Albemarle" in the Sounds of North Carolina. But here the conditions were quite different. The rattling of the 9-inch shot on the "Tennessee's" casements made his vessel fairly quiver, while the ramming demoralized her crew, they having been made to believe that no one would undertake such an adventure.

The Monitors were slow in speed, but they had now reached the "Tennessee's" wake, delivering their fire as opportunity offered. The "Manhattan," Commander J. W. A. Nicholson, got close under her stern and fired a raking shot (15-inch), which struck the "Tennessee's" port-quarter and carried away her steering gear. The "Manhattan" fired altogether six times, and most of her shots took effect. In the meantime, the "Winnebago" and "Chickasaw" were firing as opportunity offered. The smoke-stack of the "Tennessee" was shot away by the "Chickasaw," which vessel followed her closely, firing solid shot into her until her flag was hauled down.

If the commander of the ram had calculated that he could scatter the gallant officers who were swarming about him, he had reckoned without his host, for never did an iron-clad receive such a battering in so short a time. Every ship in the fleet tried to get alongside of her to throw in a broadside, but there was not room for all to manœuvre; and the "Lackawanna," in her desire to have another blow at the enemy, collided with the "Hartford," and cut her down on the quarter to within two feet of the water line.

Meanwhile the "Tennessee" was not idle. All her guns were at work as fast as they could be loaded and fired. She was like a great buffalo of the plains, with a pack of wolves hanging to its flanks, finally compelled to succumb to superior numbers. But the ram managed to inflict some dreadful wounds in her last efforts.

While the "Hartford" was drifting by her, and from a distance of ten feet or less was pouring in a broadside of 9-inch solid shot, with charges of thirteen pounds of powder, without any effect, the "Tennessee" fired a large shell through her side, which burst on the berth-deck, killing and wounding a number of men, the pieces breaking through the spar and berth-decks, passing through the launch and entering the hold among the wounded. There was no time to think of the danger from shot or shell, for every one's blood was up, and it was determined that the "Tennessee" should not escape, if it cost the lives of every one in the fleet.

The "Hartford," after being struck by the "Lackawanna," was at first reported to be sinking ; but that report was soon set at rest, and she started for the enemy at full speed, determined this time to crush in her side or be crushed in the attempt. But as the flag-ship approached the "Tennessee," it was seen that she was flying a white flag, so the former sheered off without delivering the intended blow. After the "Lackawanna" had run into the "Hartford," she was signalled to ram the "Tennessee" again, and the gallant Marchand had started to do it under a full head of steam when the "Tennessee" surrendered.

At this particular moment the Confederate iron-clad was sore beset. The "Manhattan," "Chickasaw," and "Winnebago" were hammering her with solid shot and shell; the "Ossipee" was approaching her again at full speed, while the "Hartford," "Monongahela," and "Lackawanna" were bearing down under a press of steam, determined on her destruction; and it is probable that, if the three ships had struck her at the same time, it would have demoralized her crew, if it did not break in her sides. Her smoke-stack had been shot away, her steering apparatus was disabled, and several of her port shutters driven in or jammed. Any one could see that the battle was won by the fleet for some time before the Confederate surrendered. But one shot was fired by the ram after the "Hartford" ran into her, but her crew were game to the last, and took it out in jeering the Yankees. The "Ossipee" was within a few feet of her, and in another moment would have collided, when the gallant Le Roy (who never laid aside his politeness under any circumstances) saw the white flag fluttering on the "Tennessee," and stopped and backed his engines.

The "Tennessee" had done well, though she was not fought with the skill expected from Buchanan. The latter was wounded and had his leg so shattered that it had afterwards to be amputated. The "Tennessee" lost only two or three men killed, and five or six wounded; but the crew, no doubt, became demoralized from the terrible pounding they were getting from ships and guns. The smoke-stack being knocked down, the engine became almost useless; but the best reason for her surrender was that the "Boys in Blue" had determined to have her, no matter what the consequences to themselves. She was only one vessel, it is true, but a vessel capable of resisting the blow of any projectile fired by the Union fleet; while her own projectiles could pass through and through any of the Federal wooden vessels. She was like a knight of the olden time, encased in impenetrable armor and contending with a party of unarmored soldiers. She was built by the ablest naval officer in the Confederacy under the belief that she would wipe off the face of the waters anything te Federals could bring against her.

Buchanan, without doubt, had calculated all his chances, and when he saw the fleet at anchor up the bay, thought he had

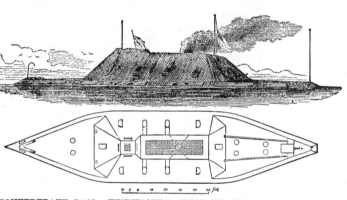

CONFEDERATE RAM "TENNESSEE" AFTER HER SURRENDER TO U. S. SQUADRON, REAR-ADMIRAL D. G. FARRAGUT, MOBILE BAY, AUGUST 5, 1864.

them all in a *cul-de-sac,* and that he would be able to demolish them in a couple of hours. He was a brave man, too, and in the past had been successful in almost everything he had undertaken; and the capture of the great commander, who had hitherto set all Confederate forts and obstructions at defiance, was to have been the crowning triumph of his life. How little he must have remembered of the brave officers in that fleet, many of whom had been under his command, if he expected to conquer them without a severe and prolonged struggle!

Sometimes we think he was tired of the unnatural contest which separated him from friends and relations. Whatever may have been the cause, the "Tennessee" did not effect as much as she ought to have done for so powerful a vessel. She never once struck a vessel of Farragut's fleet, while she herself was rammed at least four times.

How frail the Federal wooden ships were was shown when the "Lackawanna," moving at low speed, struck the "Hartford," cutting her down nearly to the water's edge, and placed her almost in a sinking condition.

Never did people fight their vessels to more effect than did Farragut and his officers on this occasion. The battle was short and decisive; and although the Confederates claim that their vessels fought desperately from 7 o'clock until 10, the truth is that the last encounter between the ram and the fleet only lasted from 8.50 until 10 o'clock, one hour and ten minutes. Hours and minutes fly fast when under fire and amid the excitement there were incidents enough in this battle to make time pass rapidly.

After the "Tennessee" had surrendered, signal was made to the fleet to anchor. The "Chickasaw," Lieutenant-Commander Geo. H. Perkins, took the disabled prize in tow and anchored her near the "Hartford," when Commander Johnston (formerly of the U. S. Navy), now in command of the "Tennessee," went on board the flag-ship and surrendered his sword and that of Admiral Buchanan. The surgeon of the "Tennessee" accompanied him and said that Buchanan had been severely wounded, and wished to know what was to be done with him. It seems from the statements then presented that

Buchanan during the engagement remained standing on the casemate of the "Tennessee" until he was severely wounded in the left leg, but he refused to surrender until the "Tennessee's" steering apparatus was disabled and the ship so filled with smoke—from the loss of the smoke-stack—that his men could hardly breathe or see.

The only shot which penetrated the "Tennessee's" armor was one from the 15-inch gun of the "Manhattan," which knocked a hole in the iron plating, leaving an undetached mass of oak and pine splinters projecting about two feet inside of the casemate. She might have been fought longer if it had not been for the loss of her smoke-stack and the disarrangement of her steering gear; but these are contingencies to which all ships are liable in action, and they are probabilities that should always be taken into account.

The victory was won, and with the surrender of the "Tennessee" ended the career of nearly the last ram owned by the Confederacy. She had made a good fight, but now passed to new owners, and never again struck a blow against the Union.

And now was to be exercised that humanity which Union naval officers always extended to their prisoners. Fleet Surgeon Palmer, who was on board the "Hartford" during the action attending to the suffering wounded, suggested that they should all—of both sides—be sent to Pensacola, where they would alike be properly cared for; and the Admiral, whose heart was always open to the calls of humanity, addressed a letter to Brigadier-General R. L. Page (formerly of the United States Navy, and now commanding Fort Morgan), informing him that Admiral Buchanan had been wounded, and desiring to know if he would permit one of his vessels, under a flag of truce, with or without the Union wounded, to go to Pensacola, with the understanding that the vessel should take out nothing but the wounded men, and bring nothing back that she did not take out. This permission was accorded by General Page, and the "Metacomet" proceeded on her mission of mercy.

The fleet had lost heavily throughout the engagement, but a greater number were killed during the fight with the "Tennessee" than in the passage of the fort, showing the terrible power of this vessel. Almost every shot she fired after closing with the fleet went to its mark, and, crashing through the wooden sides of the Federal vessels committed great havoc and destruction on their crowded decks.

The following is a list of the killed and wounded in the fleet: "Hartford," killed 25, wounded 28; "Brooklyn," killed 11, wounded 43; "Lackawanna," killed 4, wounded 35; "Oneida," killed 8, wounded 30; "Monongahela," wounded 6; "Metacomet," killed 1, wounded 2; "Ossipee," killed 1, wounded 7; "Richmond," wounded 2; "Galena," wounded 1; "Octorara," killed 1, wounded 10; "Kennebec," killed 1, wounded 6. Total killed, 52; wounded, 170.

This is a much larger list of casualties than occurred at the battle of New Orleans, and it gives a fair idea of the sanguinary nature of the conflict. To the list must be added the 120 lost in the "Tecumseh" when she sunk, making a total of 172 killed, and 170 wounded.

The vessels received injuries as follows: Monitors: "Tecumseh," sunk by a torpedo; "Manhattan," struck 9 times; "Winnebago," struck 19 times; "Chickasaw," struck three times by guns of Fort Powell. Steamers: "Brooklyn," struck 30 times; "Octorara," struck 17 times; "Hartford," struck 20 times; "Metacomet," struck 11 times; "Richmond," no serious damage; "Port Royal," no serious damage; "Lackawanna," struck 5 times; "Seminole," hull not struck; "Ossipee," struck 4 times; "Monongahela," struck 5 times; "Kennebec," struck twice; "Itasca," struck once; "Oneida," one shot in starboard boiler; "Galena," struck 7 times. Whole number of hits by the enemy, 134.

It would be an impossibility to enumerate the many acts of gallantry performed by the officers and men of the fleet.

The Admiral and his captains will therefore be left to speak for those under their immediate observation; and, although it will swell this account, we will insert as much of the several reports as will serve to do justice to all, and give the reader a further insight into this famous battle.

Admiral Farragut, after detailing the movements of the fleet (which have already been described), proceeds as follows:

"As I had an elevated position in the main rigging near the top, I was able to overlook, not only the deck of the 'Hartford,' but the other vessels of the fleet. I witnessed the terrible effects of the enemy's shot, and the good conduct of the men at their guns; and although, no doubt, their hearts sickened, as mine did, when their shipmates were struck down beside them, yet there was not a moment's hesitation to lay their comrades aside, and spring again to their deadly work.

"Our little consort, the 'Metacomet,' was also under my immediate eye during the whole action up to the moment I ordered her to cast off in pursuit of the 'Selma.'

"The coolness and promptness of Lieutenant-Commander Jouett throughout, merit high praise; his whole conduct was worthy of his reputation.

"In this connection I must not omit to call the attention of the department to the conduct of Acting-Ensign Henry C. Nields, of the 'Metacomet,' who had charge of the boat sent from that vessel when the 'Tecumseh' sank. He took her in under one of the most galling fires I ever saw, and succeeded in rescuing from death ten of her crew, within six hundred yards of the fort. I would respectfully recommend his advancement.

"The commanding officers of all the vessels who took part in the action deserve my warmest commendations, not only for the untiring zeal with which they had prepared their ships for the contest, but for their skill and daring in carrying out my orders during the engagement.

"With the exception of the momentary arrest of the fleet, when the 'Hartford' passed ahead, and to which I have already adverted, the order of battle was preserved, and the ships followed each other in close order past the batteries of Fort Morgan, and in comparative safety too, with the exception of the 'Oneida.' Her boilers were penetrated by a shot from the fort which completely disabled her, but her consort, the 'Galena,' firmly fastened to her side, brought her safely through, showing clearly the wisdom of the precaution of carrying the vessels in two abreast. Commander Mullany, who had solicited eagerly to take part in the action, was severely wounded, losing his left arm.

"In the encounter with the ram the commanding officers obeyed with alacrity the order to run her down, and without hesitation exposed their ships to destruction to destroy the enemy.

"Our iron-clads, from their slow speed and bad steering, had some difficulty in getting into and maintaining their position in line as we passed the fort, and, in the subsequent encounter with the 'Tennessee,' from the same causes, were not as effective as could have been desired ; but I cannot give too much praise to Lieutenant-Commander Perkins, who, though he had orders from the Department to return North, volunteered to take command of the 'Chickasaw,' and did his duty nobly.

"The 'Winnebago' was commanded by Commander T. H. Stevens, who volunteered for that position. His vessel steers very badly, and neither of his turrets will work, which compelled him to turn his vessel every time to get a shot, so that he could not fire very often, but he did the best under the circumstances.

"The 'Manhattan' appeared to work well, though she moved slowly. Commander Nicholson delivered his fire deliberately, and, as before stated, with one of his 15-inch shot broke through the armor of the 'Tennessee,' with its wooden backing, though the shot itself did not enter the vessel. No other shot broke through the armor, though many of her plates were started, and several of her port shutters jammed by the fire from the different ships.

"The 'Hartford' (my flag-ship) was commanded by Captain Percival Drayton, who exhibited throughout that coolness and ability for which he has been long known to his brother officers. But I must speak of that officer in a double capacity. He is the fleet-captain of my squadron, and one of more determined energy, untiring devotion to duty and zeal for the service, tempered by great calmness, I do not think adorns any Navy. I desire to call your attention to this officer, though well aware that in thus speaking of his high qualities I am only communicating officially to the Department that which it knew full well before.

"To him, and to my staff, in their respective positions, I am indebted for the detail of my fleet.

"Lieutenant J. Crittenden Watson, my flag-lieutenant, has been brought to your notice in former dispatches. During the action he was on the poop, attending to the signals, and performed his duties, as might be expected, thoroughly. He is a scion worthy the noble stock he sprang from, and I commend him to your attention.

"My secretary, Mr. McKinley, and Acting-Ensign, H. H. Brownell, were also on the poop, the latter taking notes of the action, a duty which he performed with coolness and accuracy.

"Two other acting-ensigns of my staff, Mr.

Bogart and Mr. Higinbotham, were on duty in the powder division, and, as the reports will show, exhibited zeal and ability. The latter, I regret to add, was severely wounded by a raking shot from the 'Tennessee' when we collided with that vessel, and died a few hours after. Mr. Higinbotham was a young married man, and has left a widow and one child, whom I commend to the kindness of the Department.

"Lieutenant A. R. Yates, of the 'Augusta,' acted as an additional aid to me on board the "Hartford," and was was very efficient in the transmission of orders. I have given him the command temporarily of the captured steamer 'Selma.'

"The last of my staff, and to whom I would call the attention of the Department, is not the least in importance. I mean Pilot Martin Freeman. He has been my great reliance in all difficulties in his line of duty. During the action he was in the main-top piloting the ships into the bay. He was cool and brave throughout, never losing his self-possession. This man was captured early in the war in a fishing-smack which he owned, and though he protested that he had no interest in the war, and only asked for the privilege of fishing for the fleet, yet his services were too valuable to the captors as a pilot not to be secured. He was appointed a first-class pilot, and has served us with zeal and fidelity, and has lost his vessel, which went to pieces on Ship Island. I commend him to the Department.

"It gives me pleasure to refer to several officers who volunteered to take any situation where they might be useful, some of whom were on their way North, either by orders of the Department or condemned by medical survey. The reports of the different commanders will show how they conducted themselves.

"I have already mentioned Lieutenant-Commander Perkins, of the 'Chickasaw,' and Lieutenant Yates, of the 'Augusta,' Acting-Volunteer-Lieutenant William Hamilton, late commanding officer of the 'Augusta Dinsmore,' had been invalided by medical survey, but he eagerly offered his services on board the iron-clad 'Chickasaw,' having had much experience in our Monitors. Acting-Volunteer-Lieutenant P. Giraud, another experienced officer in iron-clads, asked to go in on one of these vessels, but as they were all well supplied with officers, I permitted him to go in on the 'Ossipee,' under Commander Le Roy. After the action he was given temporary charge of the ram 'Tennessee.'

"Before closing this report, there is one other officer of my squadron of whom I feel bound to speak, Captain T. A. Jenkins, of the 'Richmond,' who was formerly my chief-of-staff, not because of his having held that position, but because he never forgets to do his duty to the Government, and takes now the same interest in the fleet as when he stood in that relation to me. He is also the commanding officer of the second division of my squadron, and, as such, has shown ability and the most untiring zeal. He carries out the spirit of one of Lord Collingwood's best sayings, 'Not to be afraid of doing too much ; those who are, seldom do as much as they ought.' When in Pensacola, he spent days on the bar, placing the buoys in the best position, was always looking after the interests of the service, and keeping the vessels from being detained one moment longer in port than was necessary. The gallant Craven told me only the night before the action in which he lost his life : 'I regret, Admiral, that I have detained you ; but had it not been for Captain Jenkins, God knows when I should have been here ! When your order came I had not received an ounce of coal.' I feel I should not be doing my duty did I not call the attention of the department to an officer who has performed all his various duties with so much zeal and fidelity.

"Very respectfully, etc.,

"D. G. FARRAGUT."

Extract from the report of Captain Drayton, commanding United States flag-ship "Hartford":

"To Lieutenant-Commander Kimberly, the executive officer, I am indebted, not only for the fine example of coolness and self-possession which he set to those around him, but also for the excellent condition to which he had brought everything belonging to the fighting department of the ship, in consequence of which there was no confusion anywhere, even when, from the terrible slaughter at some of the guns, it might have been looked for.

"All did their duty, but I cannot but mention Lieutenants Tyson and Adams and Ensign Whiting, to whose example and exertions it was in great measure owing, no doubt, that the great loss of some of the guns was not followed by confusion or delay in repairing damages. Acting-Master's Mate Tinelli, who took charge of the 3d Division after Lieutenant Adams was wounded, is spoken of to me very highly.

"Acting-Assistant-Engineer McEwan is also strongly noticed in the report of Chief-Engineer Williamson. He lost his right arm while busily employed on the berth-deck, where he was stationed, in assisting and comforting the wounded. He is spoken of by his superiors as most competent to fill the possession of Third Assistant-Engineer in the regular service, for which I would beg you to recommend him to the Honorable Secretary of the Navy.

"The last shell fired at us—that from the ram—killed my clerk, Ensign W. H. Higinbotham. Although this was the first time he had been in action, nothing, I am told, could exceed the coolness and zeal with which he performed his duties in the powder-division, and I feel his loss most seriously, as his general intelligence and many amiable qualities had made him almost necessary to me.

"I must also thank Lieutenant A. R. Yates, a volunteer from the United States steamship 'Augusta,' who acted as an aide both to you and myself, and was to me most useful.

"The two after-guns were entirely manned by marines, who, under the direction of Captain Charles Heywood, performed most efficient service.

"Thanks to the unremitting supervision of Chief-Engineer Williamson, all had been so thoroughly prepared in his department that nothing was required of the engines during the day which they could not perfectly perform.

"The devoted attention of Fleet Surgeon Palmer, Surgeon Lansdale, and Assistant Surgeon Commons to our wounded, was beyond praise, and it was owing to their skill and untiring exertion that the large number of desperately wounded were prepared by 8 o'clock in the evening for removal to the hospital at Pensacola, for which place they left at daylight on the following morning in the 'Metacomet,' under a flag of truce.

"Boatswain Dixon was nearly knocked overboard by a splinter, but absented himself from the deck only long enough to have his wounds dressed, when he returned to his duties.

"Acting-Master's Mate Herrick, while superintending the passage of powder and shell on the berth-deck, was very seriously wounded by a piece of shell which entirely disabled him at the time, and may, I am afraid, prove very serious. Up to this time his conduct and bearing are spoken of by the commanding officer of the division in the highest praise.

"I must also thank Lieutenant Watson, your flag-lieutenant, who, besides attending most faithfully to the signals, found time to assist me on several occasions when it was important to give directions, in detail, about the firing.

"Of the crew I can scarcely say too much. They were most of them persons who had never been in action, and yet I cannot hear of a case where any one attempted to leave his quarters, or showed anything but the sternest determination to fight it out.

"There might, perhaps, have been a little excuse had such a disposition been exhibited, when it is considered that a great part of four guns' crews were at different times swept away almost entirely by as many shells.

"In every case, however, the killed and wounded were quietly removed; the injury at the guns made good, and in a few moments, except from the traces of blood, nothing could lead one to suppose that anything out of the ordinary routine had happened.

"In conclusion, I request that you recommend to the Hon. Secretary of the Navy, for the medal of honor, the men whose names accompany this in a separate report. They well deserve the distinction.
"P. DRAYTON, *Captain*."

Report of Lieutenant Herbert B. Tyson, commanding 1st Division, on board U. S. S. "Hartford":

"SIR—I respectfully submit the following report of the conduct of the officers and men in the first division during the engagement of yesterday:

"Acting-Ensign W. H. Whiting, in charge of the forecastle guns, deserves special mention for his gallantry in serving and working both 100-pounder rifles under the most trying circumstances.

"The three captains of guns, Henry Clark, Peter W. Stanley, and W. H. Wright, displayed an amount of courage and coolness which I have rarely seen equalled.

"But the two men of whom I wish particularly to speak are Charles Melville and Thomas Fitzpatrick.

"A rifle-shell burst between the two forward 9-inch guns, killing and wounding fifteen men. Charles Melville was among the wounded, and was taken down with the rest to the surgeon, but came on deck almost immediately, and although scarcely able to stand, refused to go below, and worked at the gun during the remainder of the action.

"Thomas Fitzpatrick, captain of No. 1 gun, was struck several times in the face by splinters, and had his gun disabled by a shell. In a few minutes he had his gun in working order again, with new truck, breeching, side-tackle, etc., his wounded below, the dead clear, and was fighting his gun as before, setting a splendid example to the remainder of his crew. His conduct came particularly under my notice and during the entire action was distinguished for coolness and bravery.

"The 1st Division had 13 killed and 10 wounded."

From report of Acting-Volunteer Lieutenant George Mundy, commanding 2d Division U. S. S. "Hartford":

"SIR—I respectfully submit the following report of the conduct of the 2d Division during the engagement of yesterday, the 5th, with Fort Morgan and the rebel gun-boats and ram 'Tennessee:'

"But a few moments elapsed after the drum beat to quarters before every man was at his station, the guns cast loose and ready for action. Every man seemed determined to do his duty, which he did faithfully; not a man shrinking. Where all did their duty so well, it is hard to discriminate; still it gives me pleasure to mention a few who were the most conspicuous.

"Acting-Master's Mate W. H. Childs displayed great courage in assisting me in the Division."

The following men were also honorably mentioned: Charles Lake, Coxwain; Joseph Perry, Quartermaster; James Smith, Captain mizzen-top;

James Bennet, seaman ; Owen Holland, 2d Captain mizzen-top ; Samuel McFall, Captain after-guard ; Beonth Diggings, O. S.; Augustus Pauly, seaman ; Charles Davidson, Captain forecastle; Henry Wright, O. S.; Robert Emerson, Lds.; David Morrow, Quarter-gunner.

From Report of Lieutenant LaRue P. Adams, commanding 3d Division, U. S. S. "Hartford":

"SIR—I have the honor to submit the following report of the conduct of the officers and men of the Third Division during the engagement of yesterday with Fort Morgan, the rebel gun-boats and the ram :

"When the drum beat to quarters, every man was at his station instantly and the guns cleared for action. We were unable to bring our guns to bear until nearly abreast of the fort. We then fired with 10-second shell and 40° elevation.

"The fire was kept up with great rapidity, using 5-second shell and decreasing the elevation as we neared the fort. When abreast of it, two rounds of shrapnel, cut for 2-seconds, were fired by us.

"As we passed ahead of the 'Brooklyn,' two shells struck No. 7 gun, disabling the crew; but one man escaped uninjured on the right side of that gun. Another shell followed in a few seconds, wounding the captain of No. 7, three men at No. 8, and myself. Four men were killed and nine wounded in all, and by those three shells. * * * Acting-Master's Mate J. J. Tinelli I cannot fail to mention. He behaved with great gallantry, encouraging the men by his example, and served the guns of the division with great spirit against the rebel gun-boats and ram after I was sent below."

Men honorably mentioned : Forbes, Ingersoll and Pinto, Gun-Captains; William E. Stanley, Shellman.

From Report of Ensign George B. Glidden, commanding Master's Division, U. S. S. "Hartford":

"SIR—I have the honor to submit to you a report of the conduct of the officers and men of the Master's Division during the engagement yesterday with Fort Morgan, the rebel gun-boats and the ram 'Tennessee.' I have great pleasure in mentioning Acting-Master's Mate G. R. Avery, who assisted in conning the ship during the entire action, for the great coolness he displayed in his—a responsible —position."

Men honorably mentioned : John McFarland, Captain forecastle; James Wood, Quartermaster; Joseph Cassier, Seaman; James Reddington, landsman ; Henry Williams, Boatswain's Mate.

From Report of Ensign Wm. Starr Dana, in charge of Powder Division, U. S. S. "Hartford":

"SIR : I submit the following report of the conduct of the officers and men of the powder division during the engagement of the 5th :

"Acting - Ensign Bogart exhibited much coolness and presence of mind. Acting-Master's Mate R. P. Herrick deserves especial mention, for until seriously wounded he performed his duties with great coolness and spirit. Acting-Ensign W. H. Higinbotham also deserves special mention for his coolness and bravery. He performed his duties in most exemplary manner until he received his death-wound.

"The few men I had on deck passing powder acted with great coolness, and at no time were there any signs of shrinking or fear. Nelson (ship's cook) John Wallington (landsman), and Mellage (paymaster's steward) deserve special mention.

"Seven of the forward part of the division were wounded and three of them killed ; most of the wounds were mortal.

"In addition to the above, I would call attention to the conduct of Sailmaker T. C. Herbert, whose conduct and cool courage is spoken of as most remarkable.

"P. DRAYTON, *Captain.*"

From Report of Chief-Engineer Thomas Williamson, U. S. S. "Hartford":

"SIR—The conduct of the officers and men belonging to the engineer's department was characterized by coolness and energy during the engagement of yesterday.

"Their duties were performed as if nothing extraordinary was going on.

"Acting-Third-Assistant Engineer Wm. G. McEwan deserves special mention for the prompt and efficient manner in which he attended to getting the wounded below, near his station at the berth-deck hose, and he continued to do so until near the close of the action, when he lost his right arm. * * * * The loss in the engineer's department was three men killed and three men wounded."

Men honorably mentioned : Thomas Walkley, first-class fireman ; James R. Garrison, coal-heaver ; Thomas O'Connell ——.

CAPTAIN (NOW REAR-ADMIRAL) THORNTON A. JENKINS.

Report of Captain Thornton A. Jenkins, commanding U. S. S. "Richmond":

"SIR—I have the honor and very great pleasure to report, that in the action this forenoon with the batteries at Fort Morgan and the rebel ram "Tennessee," this ship has received no serious damage, and there were no persons killed. Two men were wounded, but not seriously, and the ship struck a number of times in the hull and rigging."

Reports of Captain J. B. Marchand, commanding U. S. S. "Lackawanna":

"SIR—I have the honor to report that, about sunrise to-day, this ship was gotten underway, and the "Seminole" lashed on the port side. Our position being in the centre of the line of battle, we crossed the bar, and following close on the leading vessels, stood up the channel; and as soon as our guns could be brought to bear, a fire was opened on Fort Morgan with shells, and continued until passing it, when the "Seminole" was cast off.

"Soon after the fleet had passed the Middle Ground, the rebel iron-clad 'Tennessee' commenced approaching with the design of attacking our vessels, and, in obedience to your signal, I started under the heaviest headway to run her down, and succeeded in striking her at right-angles at the after-end of the casemate.

"The concussion was great, but the effect on her was only a heavy list, while our stem was cut and crushed to the plank ends for a distance of three feet above the water's edge to five feet below, and causing a considerable leak in the forward store-room and peak.

"Fortunately our yards and top-masts were down, otherwise they in all probability would have been carried away by the concussion, which caused the ship to rebound and the stern of the 'Tennessee' to recede. Some panic must have existed on board the enemy, as they fired but two guns through our bows.

"After striking, the two swung head and stern alongside of each other, and, as our guns had been pivoted for the opposite side, we succeeded in discharging but one 9-inch shell, that struck one of the enemy's port shutters, which was distant about twelve feet, destroying it, and driving some of the fragments into her casemate.

"A few of the enemy were seen through their ports, who were using most opprobrious language.

"Our marines opened upon them with muskets; even a spittoon and a holy-stone were thrown at them from our deck, which drove them away. Upon separating from the 'Tennessee,' our helm was put hard over to make another attempt at running the enemy down; but our great length, and the shallowness of the water, caused us to turn so slowly, that we had not got round until again amongst our fleet, and, unfortunately, we collided with the flag-ship, which was running towards the 'Tennessee,' although every exertion was used to prevent it by backing.

"By this accident two of the quarter-deck ports of the 'Hartford' were knocked into one, without this ship sustaining any injury.

"After the collision with the flag-ship, I again started to run down the 'Tennessee,' but, whilst still at a distance, she surrendered to our fleet.

"Our loss throughout the day was 4 killed and 35 wounded.

"Herewith I send the reports of the surgeon, engineer, and board of officers, on the injuries and expenditures.

"Under no circumstances could more coolness and bravery have been shown by the crew.

"I cannot express my deep feeling for the undaunted courage and aid given me by all the officers.

"Second-Lieutenant Hiram Adams of the Army Signal Corps, with two assistants, were on board, and great credit is due them for their promptness in transmitting signals.

"Very respectfully," &c.

————

"SIR—In the report made of the part taken by the 'Lackawanna' in passing the forts and entering Mobile Bay on the 5th instant, I inadvertently omitted to state that Commander Edward Donaldson, commanding the 'Seminole,' which was lashed alongside of this ship, rendered most efficient service by his coolness and judgment in piloting both vessels until passing Fort Morgan, the regular pilot being sick.

"My additional thanks are due him and all his officers and men for volunteering to aid in manning the guns of the 'Lackawanna,' and the continuous fire which they kept up whilst their guns could bear upon the enemy.

"Very respectfully," &c.,
"J. B. MARCHAND, *Captain*."

From Reports of Captain James Alden, commanding U. S. S. "Brooklyn":

*   *   *   *   *   *   *   *   *

"The fleet here came to near the former anchorage.

"The surgeon's list of killed and wounded, together with the forward officer's report of injuries done to the ship by the enemy's shot, and the number of projectiles expended, etc., are herewith enclosed.

"Lieutenant-Commander Lull, the executive officer, has, at my request, made a statement of some very interesting incidents, giving a list of men who most distinguished themselves during the action; which I take great pleasure in forwarding, with a hearty approval of it and the suggestions it contains.

"It will be seen that we have 54 casualties on board, 11 killed and 43 wounded; many of the latter, I am happy to say, are slight.

"The list will not appear large when it is considered that we were nearly two hours under fire. Among the others we have to regret the loss of an officer, Acting-Master's Mate William H. Cook, who was killed while bravely doing his duty, having already been wounded.

"By the carpenter's report it will be seen that the hull has received extensive and serious injuries, having being struck 23 times. Our mainmast is ruined, having been shot through and through the centre, three times between the catharpins and the deck, the shot-holes being about equidistant from each other. Shot struck the other spars 7 times, injuring some badly. The boatswain's report shows the rigging to have been struck and cut in 29 places, making an aggregate of some 59 hits in the hull, rigging and spars.

"The number of projectiles expended was 183.

"In conclusion, I must beg leave to state that, as far as I can learn, every one did his duty nobly and well; and while the officers, generally, would seem to deserve some especial mention, I must, from the nature of circumstances, confine my notice to those on whom devolved the more important duty of controlling and fighting the ship.

"To my executive officer, Lieutenant-Commander E. P. Lull, my thanks are especially due, not only for his cool, steady bearing in the fight, but also for the efficient training of the crew, which have been together now less than three months, but displayed in the action the steadiness of veterans, fighting their guns almost as coolly as if they were at an ordinary exercise. Lieutenant Thomas L. Swann, the ordnance officer, had everything ready, and the working of his department was admirable; he was principally occupied during the action with the bowchasers. The other division officers—Captain Houston, of the marines, Lieutenant Charles F. Blake, Ensigns Cassell and Sigsbee, with their assistants, Master's-Mates Duncan and Stevens, fought their guns nobly and well.

"The powder division, under Acting-Ensign Utter, could not have been conducted better.

"Chief-Engineer Kellogg's department worked beautifully.

"Doctor Maulsby was fully prepared for the wounded, and extended to those unfortunates all the solicitude and care that a generous nature could dictate.

"Ensign Pendleton, my aide and signal officer, afforded me great assistance, being always prompt and active in his duties.

"To our pilot, Mr. Christopher Lawrence, great credit is due for the handsome manner he piloted the ship.

"I ought to mention, before closing this report, that I was particularly pleased with the cheerful bearing and aid afforded me by Capt. E. A. Denicke, of the Army Signal Corps, in watching and pointing out the effect of our shot in the batteries and upon the rebel ram and gun-boats.

"In accordance with your directions, I also send a separate report in regard to those men who were most conspicuous for good conduct and gallantry in the action. It is taken mostly from the report of Lieutenant-Commander Lull, the executive officer.

"Congratulating you upon the handsome result of the day, I remain, etc.,

"JAMES ALDEN."

"SIR—In accordance with your instructions, I herewith append a list of the crew who most distinguished themselves for gallantry and good conduct during the action with Fort Morgan and the rebel ram and gun-boats. Feeling satisfied that

James E. Sterling, Coalheaver; Richard Dennis Boatswain's Mate; Samuel W. Davis, —— ——, Samuel Todd, Quartermaster."

Extract from report of Commander J. H. Strong, commanding U. S. S. "Monongahela":

* * * * * * *

"After passing the forts, I saw the rebel ram 'Tennessee' head in for the line. I then sheered out of the line to run into her, at the same time ordering full speed. I struck her fair, and swinging round poured in a broadside of solid 11-inch shot, which apparently had but little, if any, effect upon her. Soon after, signal was made to my ship

CAPTAIN (AFTERWARDS REAR-ADMIRAL) JAMES ALDEN, U. S. N

they have earned that justly-prized distinction, the "medal of honor," I trust the Department will confer it upon them:

"J. Henry Dennig and Michael Hudson, Sergeants of Marines; Wm. M. Smith and Miles M. Oviatt, Corporals of Marines; Barnett Kenna, Quartermaster; Wm. Halsted, Coxswain; Joseph Brown, Quartermaster; Joseph Irlane, Seaman; Edward Price, Coxswain; Alexander Mack, Captain-of-Top; William Nichols, Quartermaster; Nicholas Irwin, Seaman; John Cooper, Coxswain; John Brown, Captain-of-Forecastle; John Irwin, Coxswain; William Blagden, Ship's Cook; William Madden, Coalheaver; James Machon, boy; William H. Brown, Lds.; James Mifflin, Engineer's Cook;

to again run into her. I did so, and was about to try it the third time when she surrendered to the fleet.

"During the action my officers and men, without exception, behaved in the most gallant manner. It would be impossible to make any distinction where all did everything that could have been desired.

"I would here mention that a volunteer crew from the U. S. steamer 'Kennebec,' in charge of Acting-Ensign Ellis, came on board, and manned one of my 32-pounder broadside guns during the engagement with Fort Morgan. Their conduct during the action was gallant, and met with my entire approbation.

"I regret to say that my first-lieutenant, Mr. Prentiss, lost a leg in the action, and that fears are entertained for his life." * * *

Reports of Commander William E. LeRoy, commanding U. S. S. "Ossipee":

"ADMIRAL—I have the honor to report, that in passing the forts, and in the attack upon the iron-clad 'Tennessee,' this ship was struck four times in the hull and several times in the rigging, fortunately without disabling the ship. Our stem is somewhat injured by running against the 'Tennessee.' Our casualties I am pleased to report as small. When about running down the 'Tennessee,' she displayed a white flag, but not in time to prevent my colliding with her, having been so disabled by the fire of the fleet and unable longer to continue the contest, and I was fortunate in receiving her surrender from Commander Johnston, her commander—Admiral Buchanan being wounded—a prize to the fleet under your command."

COMMANDER (NOW REAR-ADMIRAL) J. W. A NICHOLSON.

"ADMIRAL—In my report of the part this ship took in the passage of Fort Morgan yesterday, I neglected to allude to the efficient manner in which Lieutenant-Commander Geo. Brown, with the 'Itasca' lashed alongside of me, performed his duty of piloting both vessels, etc."

From report of Commander T. H. Stevens, commanding U. S. Monitor "Winnebago":

* * * * * *

"At half-past 8 passed Fort Morgan and steamed slowly up the bay. At 10 minutes past 9 the after-turret broke down. At 15 minutes past 9, received order from flag-ship to attack the rebel ram 'Tennessee,' which surrendered at 45 minutes past 9. Anchored with the fleet at 45 minutes past 10 in the lower fleet anchorage of Mobile Bay.

"Enclosed please receive engineer's report of the condition of the turrets, and the gunner's account of ammunition expended.

"The 'Winnebago' was struck 19 times, three of the shot having penetrated the deck near the after-turret.

"I have to report no casualties. The officers and men conducted themselves well; and to Acting-Volunteer-Lieutenant W. T. Shankland, First-Assistant-Engineer John Purdy, who volunteered for this vessel, and the pilot, Wm. H. Wroten, I am indebted for valuable assistance."

Reports of Commander J. W. A. Nicholson, commanding U. S. S. "Manhattan":

"SIR—I have the honor to make the following report of the part taken by this ship in the action of the 5th instant with Fort Morgan and the rebel iron-clad 'Tennessee':

"At 5 minutes past 7 A. M. I opened on the fort, but, owing to the dense smoke from the guns, our firing was necessarily very slow.

"After passing Fort Morgan, I devoted my attention entirely to the rebel iron-clad, firing my guns slowly and with great precision.

"At 45 minutes past 9 I obtained a raking position under his stern, and fired a solid shot, which struck him on the port-quarter, carrying away his steering gear.

"At 57 minutes past 9, when on the point of firing from the same position, he hauled down his colors and surrendered.

"I fired at the 'Tennessee' six times, namely, one shell, two solid and three cored shot. I am satisfied that most, if not all, the serious damage she has sustained was caused by the 15-inch shot of this vessel.

"This ship was struck by the enemy's shot nine times, causing no material damage; but of this I will make a separate report.

"No person was injured on board. Officers and men all did their duty; but I especially recommend Acting-Ensign John B. Trott, who was stationed at the wheel steering the ship himself, for the admirable manner in which he performed his duty. Also Acting-Master Robert B. Ely, for the manner in which he worked his guns. Both of these gentlemen, I think, are worthy of being advanced a grade in the service.

"One of the 15-inch carriages is temporarily disabled by the breaking of some bolts."

"SIR—Of the six 15-inch projectiles fired from this vessel at the rebel iron-clad 'Tennessee,' I claim four as having struck, doing most of the real injuries that she has sustained, namely, first, one shot on port-beam, going entirely through the armor and crushing the wood backing, making a hole completely through the vessel; second, one shot near the first, but higher up, and further forward, making a deep indentation, and then glancing over the ship; third, a shell striking her stern port-shutter, disabling it, so that the gun could not be used; fourth, a shot striking her stern, ripping up the deck-plating, carrying away her steering gear, and then striking her armor at the angle of the port quarter, crushing it, and starting the wood backing through to the inside."

From report of Lieutenant-Commander C. H. Wells, commanding U. S. S. "Galena":

"SIR—I herewith report to you the part which this steamer took in passing Forts Morgan and Gaines yesterday:

* * * * * * *

"I take pleasure in bringing to your notice the executive officer of this vessel, Acting-Volunteer-Lieutenant C. W. Wilson, who faithfully carried out my orders in passing Fort Morgan, as well as in the exhibition of coolness and bravery.

"Acting-Master D. C. Kells, Acting-Ensigns Pease and Miner, and Acting-Master's Mates Tuttle and Delano, I would also recommend to your favorable notice for their good conduct under the fire of the enemy.

Mr. Buehler, First-Assistant Engineer and Acting-Chief, managed the engineer's department in a highly creditable manner, in which he was sustained by the Assistant-Engineers Greenleaf, Scott, Burns and Weecker.

Acting-Assistant Paymaster Kitchen, and Lesley G. Morrow, Captain's Clerk, remained on deck during the action, and contributed their parts to my entire satisfaction. Acting - Assistant Surgeon George P. Wright not only attended to our three cases of wounded (one mortally), but gave his professional services to the 'Oneida,' to several of their wounded who came on board this steamer.

"The crew manifested the utmost courage throughout the affair, which will always reflect creditably upon you and the Navy of the United States."

From report of Lieutenant - Commander James E. Jouett, commanding U. S. S. "Metacomet":

* * * * * *

"At 40 minutes past 7 the 'Brooklyn' backed down the line, when the 'Hartford' shot ahead, leading the fleet in past the forts. At this time a shell from the rebel gun-boat 'Selma' passed through this vessel into the forward storeroom, killing one man and wounding another, and setting the ship on fire. By prompt action on the part of Acting - Ensign G. E. Wing, in charge of powder division, we succeeded in extinguishing it.

"At 5 minutes past 8 cast off from the 'Hartford' and steamed for the rebel gun-boats, who were annoying the fleet by a raking fire. They steamed up the bay, engaging us with their stern guns, of which they had three each. At half-past 8 the 'Gaines' retreated under cover of the fort in a crippled condition. At 9 the 'Morgan' hauled off to starboard, and at 10 minutes past 9 the 'Selma' struck her flag to this ship.

"I immediately dispatched a boat, in charge of Acting-Master N. M. Dyer, to take charge of the prize, and to send her Captain and First-Lieutenant on board. He hoisted the American flag, and reported Captain Murphy wounded and the First-Lieutenant killed.

"He transferred fifty of her crew to this vessel, and at 50 minutes past 9, Captain P. U. Murphy came on board and surrendered his sword and vessel.

"She had five killed and ten wounded, including the Captain, two of whom have since died. The dead and wounded were attended to. The remainder of her crew and officers were sent to the 'Port Royal.' Put engineers and firemen on board and steamed to the fleet, reporting the capture of the Confederate steamer 'Selma,' which vessel mounted two 9-inch Dahlgren smooth-bore, one 6½-inch rifle and one 8½-inch smooth-bore, all on pivot, with a crew, all told, of 94 men.

"I am much indebted to the executive officer, H. J. Sleeper, for his cool, prompt, and officer-like conduct; he is a valuable officer. For the efficient handling of the vessel, I am much indebted to Acting-Master N. M. Dyer, who had permission to go North on leave, but volunteered to remain to assist in the attack upon the forts. Acting-Ensign John White was cool and deliberate, working his rifle-gun with good effect. Acting-Master's Mates Goodwin and Miller performed their duties with promptness and zeal, making good shots with their 9-inch guns. Acting-Third-Assistant Engineer King, who was much exposed at the engine-bell, never failed to pull the proper bell; and to the efficient arrangement of the engineer department and the prompt answer to the bells, I am indebted to First-Assistant Engineer Atkins. The gunner, Mr. Lamen, attended in both shell-rooms and magazines, forward and aft, and kept the guns more than supplied.

"I cannot close this long report without calling your attention to Assistant-Surgeon Payne, of this vessel. By his report we had one killed and two wounded. That evening there were placed on board this vessel some sixty badly wounded officers and men, to be conveyed to Pensacola. He was untiring in his attention, watching and tending them at all times. He deserves especial mention for his great and successful exertions.

"This ship was struck eleven times, doing but little damage; shots mostly above the hull.

"I herewith submit the reports of the executive officer and surgeon."

Report of Lieutenant-Commander Bancroft Gherardi, commanding U. S. S. "Port Royal":

"SIR—I have the honor to inform you that on the morning of the 5th instant I took my position on the port side of the U. S. steamer 'Richmond,' as her consort. I was able to open fire but twice—once as the rebel iron-clad 'Tennessee' passed down the line; the second time as we kept away on a

LIEUTENANT-COMMANDER (NOW COMMODORE) BANCROFT GHERARDI.

northwest course, I was able to bring the 10-inch pivot-gun to bear on Fort Morgan, and the rifled guns to bear on Fort Gaines."

Report of Lieutenant-Commander C. H. Greene, commanding U. S. S. "Octorara":

"SIR — I have the honor to forward to you the various reports of damages and casualties on board.

"I bear cheerful testimony to the good conduct of officers and men; part of the latter volunteered to work one of the 'Brooklyn's' guns, and although I have not yet heard of them from Captain Alden, I have every reason to believe they bore their part well.

"To Acting-Volunteer-Lieutenant Urann, executive officer, I am much indebted for his zeal and efforts in having the ship ready to go under fire.

"Acting-Master Billings, a volunteer from the 'Vincennes,' kept his post faithfully, and though quite severely hurt, still remained.

"To Acting-Master Young, Acting-Ensigns Dodge and McEntee, my thanks are due for their steadiness and promptness at their quarters.

"The engineer department, under the charge of Mr. Shipman, Acting-Chief-Engineer, was well attended to, and his subordinates' conduct met my approbation.

"To Assistant-Surgeon Dodge and Paymaster Pynchon, and, in fact, all, I tender my hearty thanks."

From Report of Lieutenant-Commander William P. McCann, commanding U. S. S. "Kennebec":

* * * * * * * *

"The officers and crew of the 'Kennebec' performed their duties gallantly under the enemy's fire.

"When lashed alongside the 'Monongahela' I sent Acting-Ensign J. D. Ellis, in charge of a gun's crew, to work a gun there, under the observation of Captain Strong, where he acted nobly.

"I beg leave to call your attention to the good conduct of Acting-Ensign H. E. Tinkham, who, when seriously wounded by the explosion of a shell from the rebel ram 'Tennessee,' and when the vessel was supposed to be on fire, refused to leave his station. It affords me pleasure to bring to your favorable notice Acting-Volunteer-Lieutenant Edward Baker, the executive officer, Acting-Ensign J. J. Butler and Second-Assistant Engineer L. W. Robinson.

"Acting-Assistant Surgeon George W. Hatch rendered the most prompt assistance to the wounded. The crew fully sustained the proud reputation of the American sailor for courage and bravery."

From Report of Lieutenant-Commander George Brown, commanding U. S. S. "Itasca":

* * * * * *

"After passing Fort Morgan, I cast off from the 'Ossipee,' and started under sail and a full head of steam in pursuit of the rebel gun-boats 'Morgan' and 'Selma,' that were being engaged by the 'Metacomet'; but before I came within range the 'Morgan' had succeeded in getting in such a position that I could not cut off her retreat toward Fort Morgan, and the 'Selma' had struck her flag to the 'Metacomet.'

"I take pleasure in testifying to the spirited willingness and desire manifested by all under my command to take a more active part in the engagement; but the duty assigned us prevented us from using our guns in passing Fort Morgan except for the purpose of increasing the density of smoke.

"I am happy to be able to report that no casualties occurred.

"The vessel was struck once in the mainmast."

Report of Lieutenant-Commander G. H. Perkins, commanding U. S. Monitor "Chickasaw":

"SIR—I have the honor to submit the following report:

"At 6 A. M., on Friday, August 5th, in obedience to orders, I got underway, and took my position in the rear of the 'Winnebago,' on the right of the line. I passed the forts with the rest of the fleet, firing as rapidly as possible. Afterwards, in obedience to orders, I attacked the rebel ram 'Tennessee,' following her up closely, shooting away her smoke-stack, and firing solid shot at her till her flag was hauled down and a white flag raised. Her steering gear being shot away, I took her in tow and brought her to anchor near the 'Hartford.' In the afternoon of the same day, I got underway, and

brought a large barge, the 'Ingomar,' out from under the guns of Fort Powell, exchanging several shot and being struck three times.

"On the morning of the 6th, I proceeded again to Fort Powell, which I found deserted and blown up. I towed out another barge. In the afternoon I advanced and shelled Fort Gaines.

"Too much praise cannot be given to all the officers and men for their coolness and efficiency under fire, and their endurance while at quarters. I would mention in particular Acting-Volunteer-Lieutenant William Hamilton, the executive officer, who, when on his way home, condemned by medical survey, volunteered for this vessel. I owe much to him, his energy, in fitting out the vessel, and for his gallantry and coolness during the fight. Acting-Master E. D. Percy, who also volunteered for the vessel, and commanded the guns in the after-turret, and Gunner J. A. McDonald, who commanded the forward-turret, deserve especial mention for the skill and rapidity with which they fought their batteries. Chief-Boatswain's Mate Andrew Jones and Master-at-Arms James Seanor, who, although their time was out, volunteered for the fight from the 'Vincennes,' are entitled to honorable mention.

"During the entire action the vessel was struck a number of times, the smoke-stack was shot almost entirely away, and one shot penetrated the deck on the starboard bow. No serious injury was suffered, and there were no casualties among officers or men."

From Report of Lieutenant Charles L. Huntington, executive officer of the U. S. S. "Oneida":

* * * * * * *

"The ram, passing astern, delivered two raking fires into us, one of which disabled the 12-pdr. howitzer on the poop, severely wounding Commander Mullany; the effect of the other one I am unable to state, but think the only damage from it was to our rigging.

"The command of the ship now devolved upon me, and the management of the two vessels upon Lieutenant-Commander Wells, of the 'Galena.'

"The battery was gallantly served while passing the forts, but the enemy raked us several times after our guns could not be brought to bear.

"In passing the fort we received a shell forward on the berth-deck, which exploded, knocking out a dead-light on the port side, [and] starting a fire on the top of the magazine. Owing to the presence of mind of Acting-Ensign Hall, commanding the powder division, and Gunner William Parker, the fire was promptly extinguished, and the supply of powder was as rapid as ever before.

"At 35 minutes past 8 signal was made that the captain was wounded, and also that our boiler was disabled; not being answered from the flag-ship, hauled down signals. About a quarter past 9 repeated signals and they were not answered, but signal was made from the flag-ship to run down at full speed the enemy's principal vessel. Answered the signal, but I am sure the Admiral understands we could not obey it; we had no speed.

"At 10 o'clock A. M., the 'Itasca,' Lieutenant-Commander Brown, took us in tow and carried us to an anchorage. At 11, anchored in 3¼ fathoms of water, with thirty fathoms of chain ready for slipping.

The officers and crew of the 'Oneida' are proud to have served in your fleet, and they are proud of their gallant commander, J. R. M. Mullany, who gave us all such a noble example of unflinching courage and heroism.

"His coolness in action could not possibly have been surpassed. Having scarcely become acquainted with Commander Mullany, he having only been on board two days, the highest compliment that can be paid him is the confidence and spirit with which the crew went into action.

"Too much praise cannot be awarded to Lieutenant C. S. Cotton, Lieutenant E. N. Kellogg and Acting-Ensign John Sears, commanding gun divisions, for the admirable examples of courage they afforded their men, and for their skill in directing the fire of the guns.

"The conduct of Acting-Ensign Charles V. Gridley (regular) is beyond all praise. He had charge of the Master's division, and assisted in conning the ship from the top gallant forecastle.

"Acting-Ensign Hall's conduct has been previously mentioned. His duties were performed in the most satisfactory manner, and, under Almighty God, we probably owe to his presence of mind at the time of the fire on the berth-deck the safety of the ship.

"Acting-Master's Mates Edward Bird, Daniel Clark, and John Devereaux behaved courageously.

COMMANDER (AFTERWARDS REAR-ADMIRAL) J. R. MADISON MULLANY.

Gunner Wm. Parker and Boatswain Hallowell Dickinson merit mention for their good conduct.

"I leave it to Chief-Engineer W. H. Hunt to speak of the officers and men under his immediate supervision, but must speak of him personally in this report. He was cool and collected during the whole affair, and his gallantry was particularly apparent at the time of the accident to our starboard boiler. Mr. Hunt was scalded severely in both arms.

"Surgeon John Y. Taylor had a severe task imposed upon him, but his whole duty by the wounded was done quietly and skillfully. Medical assistance was offered from the 'Galena'; it was accepted, and Acting-Assistant Surgeon Geo. P. Wright came on board, for which we owe him our thanks. At the time that our boiler was exploded, five of our wounded men went on board the 'Galena'; four subsequently returned — the other was suffering much pain, and remained on board until transferred to the 'Metacomet.'

"The safety of the ship after the explosion depended upon the 'Galena.' That we are here, quietly at anchor, attests how nobly Lieutenant-Commander Clark H. Wells stood by us.

"Assistant-Paymaster Geo. R. Martin assisted the surgeon materially. He also superintended putting out a fire that broke out in the cabin.

"Paymaster's Clerk W. P. Treadwell rendered great service in passing orders to the bell, until he was required below to assist in caring for the wounded. He was quite badly scalded himself. Mr. Geo. A. Ebbetts, Captain's Clerk, behaved splendidly. He was knocked down at the same time that Captain Mullany was wounded. Whenever he could be spared from below, after this accident, he cheerfully rendered assistance in carrying orders.

"The pilot, Mr. John V. Grivet, served part of the time on board the 'Galena,' and part of the time on this ship. That part of his conduct which came under my observation merits praise.

"For the crew, they stood to their guns most nobly. Many deserve mention, but I shall only name those that came under my own observation."

The following men are then honorably mentioned by Lieutenant Huntington:

"James Sheridan and John E. Jones, Quartermasters; William Gardner, Seaman; John Preston, Landsman; William Newland, Ordinary Seaman; David Nailor, Landsman; Charles Wooram, Ordinary Seaman; Thomas Kendrick, Coxswain.

"The marines conducted themselves with the usual distinguished gallantry of their corps. Sergeant James S. Roantree is particularly deserving of notice."

Additional Reports of Captain T. A. Jenkins, commanding U. S. S. "Richmond":

"SIR—I have the honor to report that in obedience to your general order and plan of battle for attacking Fort Morgan and the rebel fleet, Lieutenant-Commander Bancroft Gherardi, commanding the United States Steamer "Port Royal," reported himself with his vessel to me ready for action a little before daylight this morning.

"The 'Port Royal' was lashed on the port side of this vessel, with her stern pivot-gun sufficiently far aft of the quarter of this ship to enable it to be used against the enemy as effectively as one of my own broadside guns.

"To Lieutenant-Commander Gherardi I am greatly indebted for his cool and courageous conduct, from the moment the attack commenced to the time that his vessel was cast off by my order to go in chase of the enemy's three wooden gun-boats, the 'Morgan,' 'Gaines' and 'Selma.'

"My orders on board of this ship to the helmsman, and to the officer stationed at the engine-bell, were repeated by him on board of his own vessel, and the soundings passed from his own vessel to this with a coolness and clearness of voice that could not but excite my admiration.

"The after pivot-gun of the 'Port Royal' (the only one that could be brought to bear upon the enemy's batteries from that vessel) was worked most effectively."

"SIR—In my report of the 5th instant I expressed my great admiration of and thanks for the cool and courageous conduct of every officer and of every man serving on board of this ship in the terrible conflict with the rebel batteries at Fort Morgan, the iron-clad 'Tennessee,' and gun-boats 'Selma,' 'Morgan' and 'Gaines,' on the morning of that day.

"I consider it, however, but an act of plain and simple duty on my part to go further now, and respectfully invite your attention, and that of the Department through you, to the highly meritorious conduct of the under-mentioned petty-officers and seamen on board of this ship, who exhibited on that memorable occasion, and in conflict with the rebels previously, a will and determination and set an example to their shipmates and messmates worthy, in my opinion, of the highest commendation."

The following are then honorably mentioned :

"Wm. Densmore, Chief Boatswain's Mate; Adam Duncan and Charles Deakin, Boatswain's Mates; Cornelius Cronin, Chief Quartermaster ; William Wells, Quartermaster ; Henry Sharp, Seaman ; Walter B. Smith, Ordinary Seaman; George Parks, Captain of Forecastle; Thomas Hayes, Lebeus Simkins, Oloff Smith and Alex. H. Truett, Coxswains; Robert Brown and John H. James, Captains of Top; Thomas Cripps and John Brazell, Quartermasters ; James H. Morgan and John Smith, Captains of Top; James B. Chandler, Coxswain; William Jones, Captain of Top; William Doolan, Coalheaver; James Smith, Captain of Forecastle ; Hugh Hamilton, Coxswain ; James McIntosh, Captain of Top ; William M. Carr, Master-at-Arms; Thomas Atkinson, Yeoman ; David Sprowls, Orderly Sergeant; Andrew Miller and James Martin, Sergeants of Marines."

From the additional Report of Captain Percival Drayton, commanding "Hartford":

"SIR—I beg leave to call your attention to the conduct of the following petty officers and others of this vessel during the action of the 5th instant, which, I think, entitles them to the medal of honor :

"Thomas Fitzpatrick, Coxswain; Charles Melville, Ordinary Seaman; William E. Stanley, Shellman ; William Pelham, Landsman; John McFarlan, Captain of Forecastle; James R. Garrison and Thomas O'Connell, Coalheavers; Wilson Brown and John Lamson, Landsmen ; George Mellage, Paymaster's Steward."

From additional Reports of Captain J. B. Marchand of the "Lackawanna":

"SIR—In the action of the 5th instant the following-named petty officers, and others of inferior rating, were conspicuous for their energy and bravery, and deserve medals of honor ; but under the fourth rule of the general order of the Navy Department, No. 10, dated April 3d, 1863, their special signal acts of valor cannot be cited so as to authorize me to recommend their obtaining medals."

The following are then honorably mentioned :

"William Phinney, Boatswain Mate ; John Smith, Captain Forecastle ; Samuel W. Kinnaird, Robert Dougherty, Michael Cassidy, Landsmen."

"SIR—I respectfully bring to your attention the following petty officers, etc., of this ship, who evinced in the battle of the 5th instant signal acts of bravery which would justly entitle them to medals of honor: George Taylor, Armorer ; Lewis Copat, Landsman ; James Ward, Quarter-gunner; Daniel Whitfield, Quartermaster ; John M. Burns, Seaman ; John Edwards, Captain of Top ; Adam McCullock, Seaman."

On August 6th, the Admiral returned thanks in a general order to the officers and men who had so ably supported him during the late conflict, as follows :

GENERAL ORDER, No. 12.

U. S. FLAG-SHIP "HARTFORD,"
MOBILE BAY, August 6, 1864.

The Admiral returns thanks to the officers and crews of the vessels of the fleet for their gallant conduct during the fight of yesterday.

It has never been his good fortune to see men do their duty with more courage and cheerfulness; for, although they knew that the enemy was prepared with all devilish means for our destruction, and though they witnessed the almost instantaneous annihilation of our gallant companions in the "Tecumseh" by a torpedo, and the slaughter of their friends, messmates and gun-mates on our decks, still there were no evidences of hesitation in following their commander-in-chief through the line of torpedoes and obstructions, of which we knew nothing, except from the exaggerations of the enemy, who had given out that we should all be blown up as certainly as we attempted to enter.

For this noble and implicit confidence in their leader he heartily thanks them.

D. G. FARRAGUT,
Rear-Admiral Commanding W. G. B. Squadron.

GENERAL ORDER, No. 13.

FLAG-SHIP "HARTFORD,"
MOBILE BAY, August 7, 1864.

The Admiral desires the fleet to return thanks to Almighty God for the signal victory over the enemy on the morning of the 5th instant.

D. G. FARRAGUT,
Rear-Admiral Commanding W. G. B. Squadron.

It is not always that the sailors and petty officers who have taken part in a naval battle have full justice done them, although they may have shown as much courage as any of their officers.

There never was a case where sailors showed more true heroism than at the battle of Mobile Bay, especially in the exacting moment when the "Tennessee" made her attack upon the fleet. Men, who were so seriously wounded that they could not stand, would crawl back to their guns, and though they could do no work would cheer on and inspire their comrades. Men in their last moments would give forth a faint cheer when they heard that the "Tennessee" was being beaten, and die with a smile on their lips. If a comrade fell at his post, another from a gun that could not be brought to bear would spring to take his place, laying him tenderly aside and swearing to avenge his death.

It is not always in the excitement of battle that these heroic acts are noticed, and it is with pleasure that we here publish the reports of those officers who thought enough of their sailors to mention those among them who had especially distinguished themselves. The medal of honor was as much as they could expect, but these badges were as much prized as were the decorations which Napoleon served out to his brave soldiers after a victory. He knew the secret of touching men's hearts on the battle-field, and to this he owed the many victories won for him by his soldiers. It is not the value of the medal, for it is only made of copper; it is the fact that a sailor's services are noticed that makes him the happiest of men, and he treasures up the mementoes of his services with care and pride.

While the fleet was darting ahead under a sharp fire from Fort Morgan, and just as the "Brooklyn" stopped her engines, the "Tecumseh," struck by a torpedo, went down almost instantly, carrying with her nearly all her brave officers and men. It was an appalling sight to look upon, but it did not for one moment throw the fleet into confusion. The commanders followed their brave leader, not thinking for a moment of the possible consequences. Admiral Farragut, even at that trying moment, did not fail to remember what was due to humanity, but hailed Lieutenant-Commander Jouett of the "Metacomet," and directed him to send a boat to pick up the few men who could be seen struggling in the water. This was done with a promptitude that reflected great credit on the discipline of the "Metacomet."

Acting-Ensign Henry C. Nields had charge of the boat that went on this perilous service, and steering right for the struggling men in the water, under as heavy a fire from Fort Morgan as any officer ever went through, found his reward in the rescue of ten men, who, but for the coolness he displayed and the encouragement he gave his brave boat's crew to spring to their oars, would have soon followed their shipmates to a watery grave. This was done within three hundred yards of the fort, with shot and shell falling thickly about him. Ensign Nields, not only received the warmest commendations from Admiral Farragut, but the highest admiration that could be felt by every officer in the fleet. Such acts of gallantry, connected with a mission of mercy, should obtain the greatest rewards.

The following survivors of the "Tecumseh" were picked up by the "Metacomet's" boat: Acting-Ensign John J. P. Zettich, Quartermasters C. V. Dean and William Roberts; Seamen James McDonald, George Major and James Thorn; Ordinary Seaman Charles Packard; Landsman William Fadden; Coal-heaver William C. West, and Pilot John Collins. In addition to these, there were picked up by one of the "Tecumseh's" boats: Acting-Masters C. F. Langley and Gardner Cottrell, Gunner's Mate S. S. Shinn, Quarter-gunner John Gould, Seamen Frank Commins, Richard Collins and Peter Parkes. Four men, whose names are unknown, swam ashore and were captured by the Confederates.

Acting-Masters Langley and Cottrell state in their joint report that the "Tecumseh" was nearly abreast of Fort Morgan, and about 150 yards from the beach, when it was reported to Commander Craven that there was a row of buoys, stretching from the shore a distance from one to two hundred yards. He immediately ordered full speed and attempted to pass between two of the buoys. When in their range, a torpedo was exploded directly under the turret, blowing a large hole in the bottom of the vessel, through which the water rushed with great rapidity. Finding that the vessel was sinking, the order was given to leave quarters, and from that moment every one used the utmost exertions to clear himself from the wreck. After being carried down several times they were picked up in a drowning condition, as before stated.

Commander Craven was with the pilot in the pilot-house when the torpedo exploded under the vessel, but his chivalric spirit caused him to lose his life. He insisted on the pilot taking precedence in descending the ladder. They both reached the turret, but as the pilot passed through the port-hole the vessel keeled over and went down, taking with her as gallant an officer as there was in the American Navy. One moment more and his life would have been saved to adorn the list of officers of which he was so bright a member. The example shown by Craven on this occasion should be chronicled in every story of the war. No more chivalrous event occurred during the four years' conflict.

After the capture of the "Tennessee," and when the fleet had anchored, the "Chickasaw," Lieutenant-Commander Geo. H. Perkins, was sent to fire on Fort Powell and to bring off a large barge lying near it. This duty was handsomely performed, the fort was well battered and the barge brought away. The enemy, using their guns with spirit, gave the "Chickasaw" some ugly wounds in her armor; but, seeing the inequality of a conflict with the fleet, the commander of the fort evacuated it on the night of the 5th, when it soon after blew up. The guns were, however, left intact, and several covered barges were captured that made good workshops for the fleet.

On the afternoon of the 6th, the "Chickasaw" was sent in to shell Fort Gaines, and this was so effectually done that Colonel Anderson, the commander, soon came to terms. He had not much of a garrison—most of his men being raw recruits and boys—but he seems to have been a sensible man, for on the morning of the 7th he sent a communication to Admiral Farragut offering to surrender, and requesting that he be given the best conditions. General Granger was sent for by the Admiral to meet Colonel Anderson and Major Brown on board the flag-ship, where an agreement was signed, by which Fort Gaines was surrendered unconditionally. All private property (except arms) was to be respected, and the inmates of the fort were to remain prisoners-of-war.

On August 8th, Fleet-Captain Drayton, on the part of the Navy, and Colonel Myer, on the part of the Army, proceeded to the fort to carry out the stipulations of the agreement, and at 9:45 A. M. they received its surrender. and hoisted the Union flag amid the prolonged cheers of the sailors of the fleet. No cheers were ever given with more ardor, for this victory was seen to be another of the severe death-blows given to an enemy whose end was very near.

This was the close of the battle on the water. Fort Morgan was still to be reduced, but any one could see that this event would be but a matter of a short time. There was no hope for the defenders of the fort, strong as it was, for it was cut off from all succor. The Navy commanded it and the waters of Mobile Bay, and the army having landed in its rear, shut it out from all hope of reinforcements or supplies. Preparations were being made to invest it by land and sea, with as little loss of life as possible to the Union forces.

There was the great and impregnable "Tennessee" lying at anchor among the fleet as harmless as a Chinese junk, with the American flag flying where the Confederate "Stars and Bars" was wont to wave. The "Selma" was captured, the "Gaines" burnt, and the "Morgan" was the only vessel of Buchanan's fleet that had escaped. She ran up to Mobile the night after the battle by keeping close in shore.

As soon as the fate of their Navy and the two forts was known at Mobile, the Confederates sunk the "Nashville" right across the narrow channel under commanding guns—and thus completely blocked the way to the city. But this did not help them any. The days of blockade-runners were over. No more would those snug-looking clippers slip into the bay at night in spite of a most watchful blockade, and, carrying their welcome cargoes into the port of Mobile, supply the Confederacy with food, clothing and munitions of war. The steam locomotive no longer blew its shrillest whistle as it started from Mobile with a rich load of provisions and arms for the city of Richmond, to enenable their brave and desperate soldiers to sustain the lost cause by a few spasmodic efforts that could be of no service to them. And here the reader will see the benefit the battle of Mobile Bay was to the Union and the injury it was to the Confederacy, and Farragut once more earned the plaudits of the nation by his successful conflict against desperate odds.

The people of the North rejoiced heartily when they heard of this famous victory, while the people of the South were proportionally depressed. They had counted so much on Buchanan (who was very popular among them) and on his fleet, that this last blow almost deprived them of all hope; but they fought on to the last with unequalled energy and bravery.

This victory atoned for the effects of the misadventures with the ram "Albemarle" in the sounds of North Carolina. The Southerners had made great capital out of that affair, and so rejoiced over it that the people of the North were disposed to regard it as more important than the Navy Department chose to acknowledge; and the press of the North, always prone to take sides against Federal officers, published reports that were wholly unreliable.

And herein lay the difference between the North and the South. Though the latter might be fighting in a bad cause, yet the people stood by each other like a band of brothers,. and when their officers met with defeats they did not raise a howl from one end of the Confederacy to the other—they smoothed them over, and often claimed them as victories. But it was otherwise with the press of the North. They had very little consideration for those who were fighting their battles, while they were comfortable at home, with substitutes in the field. They all wanted to dictate to their military leaders, and found fault oftener than they praised, while half the time they were not properly informed in regard to matters on which they were expressing opinions.

As soon as Secretary Welles heard of the results of the battle of Mobile Bay, he forwarded to Admiral Farragut the following congratulatory letter:

NAVY DEPARTMENT, }
WASHINGTON, August 15, 1864. }

SIR—Your dispatch of the 5th instant, stating that you had on the morning of that day entered Mobile Bay, passing between Forts Morgan and Gaines, and encountering and overcoming the rebel fleet, I had the satisfaction to receive this day. Some preliminary account of your operations had previously reached us through rebel channels.

Again, it is my pleasure and my duty to congratulate you and your brave associates on an achievement unequalled in our service by any other commander, and only surpassed by that unparalleled naval triumph of the squadron under your command in the spring of 1862, when, proceeding up the Mississippi, you passed forts Jackson and St. Philip, and, overcoming all obstructions, captured New Orleans, and restored unobstructed navigation to the commercial emporium of the great central valley of the Union.

The Bay of Mobile was not only fortified and guarded by forts and batteries on shore, and by submerged obstructions, but the rebels had also collected there a formidable fleet, commanded by their highest naval officer, a former captain in the Union Navy, who, false to the Government and the Union, had deserted his country in the hour of peril, and levelled his guns against the flag which it was his duty to have defended. The possession of Mobile Bay, which you have acquired, will close the illicit traffic which has been carried on by running the blockade in that part of the Gulf, and gives point and value to the success you have achieved.

Great results in war are seldom obtained without great risks, and it was not expected that the possession of the harbor of Mobile would be secured without disaster.

The loss of the gallant Craven and his brave companions, with the "Tecumseh" (a vessel that was invulnerable to the guns of Fort Morgan), by a concealed torpedo, was a casualty against which no human foresight could guard. While the Nation awards cheerful honors to the living, she will ever hold in grateful remembrance the memory of the gallant and lamented dead, who perilled their lives for their country and died in her cause.

To you and the brave officers and sailors of your squadron, who participated in this great achievement, the Department tenders its thanks and those of the Government and country.

Very respectfully, etc.,
GIDEON WELLES,
Secretary of the Navy.
Rear-Admiral DAVID G. FARRGAUT,
Commanding West Gulf Blockading Squadron, Mobile Bay.

Fort Morgan remained yet to be captured, and all the necessary steps were being taken to bring about this desired object. The Army, under General Granger, had been transferred from Dauphine Island to its rear.

Admiral Farragut had also landed four 9-inch guns in the rear of the fort, under the command of Lieutenant H. B. Tyson, of the "Hartford," and manned with crews from the "Hartford," "Brooklyn," "Richmond" and "Lackawanna."

On the 21st of August, General Granger informed him that his guns were all in battery and would be ready to open upon the enemy's works on the morning of the 22d. Farragut, in consequence, directed the Monitors and other vessels carrying suitable guns to move up and be ready to open upon the fort at the same time with the army batteries.

At daylight, on the 22d, the bombardment began from the shore batteries, the Monitors and ships inside the Bay of Mobile and those outside, and it presented a most magnificent sight. No hotter bombardment was ever kept up for twenty-four hours.

At half-past 8 P. M., the citadel of the fort burst out in flames, adding its bright light to the grandeur of the scene, and illuminating the bay, where the cannon of the fleet, directed by practiced hands, were belching forth their deadly missiles, which sped on their destructive way unerringly.

When the fire broke out, General Granger ordered the rear batteries to redouble their fire. At 6 A. M. on the 23d an explosion took place in the enemy's work, and at half-past 6 a white flag was displayed on the parapet of Fort Morgan. The Admiral immediately sent Fleet-Captain Drayton to join General Granger and arrange the terms of surrender; which were that the fort, its garrison and all public property

should be surrendered, unconditionally, at 2 o'clock on that day, to the Army and naval forces of the United States then present. These terms were accepted by Brigadier-General R. L. Page, of the Confederate service (formerly a Commander in the United States Navy). The garrison was sent to New Orleans in company with the crews of the ram "Tennessee" and the gunboat "Selma."

List of the officers of the "Tennessee": Admiral, Franklin Buchanan; Commander, James D. Johnston; Lieutenants, Wm. L. Bradford, A. P. Wharton, E. G. McDermott; Masters, J. R. De Moley and H. W. Perron; Fleet Surgeon, R. C. Bowles; Engineers, G. D. Lining, J. O'Connell, John Hays, O. Benson and W. B. Patterson; Paymaster's Clerk, J. H. Cohen; Master's Mates, W. A. Forrest, Beebe and R. M. Carter; Boatswain, John McCudie; Gunner, H. S. Smith. Officers of the "Selma": Commander, Peter U. Murphy; Lieutenant, J. H. Comstock.

General Page tried to obtain more favorable terms, but without success. He had held out bravely against the bombardment, and thought, perhaps, that he and his officers should have received some favors on that account; but then, again, he had caused an unnecessary loss of life by persisting in defending a fort that was virtually in the power of the Federal forces, and which he knew could not by any possibility escape capture. The defence was gallant, but it was an unnecessary display of bravery, as the end proved.

Admiral Farragut reported that after the assembling of the Confederate officers outside of the works, to deliver Fort Morgan to its conquerors, it was discovered, on an examination of the interior, that most of the guns were spiked and many of the gun-carriages wantonly injured, and arms, ammunition, provisions, etc., destroyed, and that there was every reason to believe that this was done after the white flag had been displayed. It was also discovered that General Page and several of his officers had no swords to deliver, and, further, that some of those that were surrendered were broken. He draws attention to the different course pursued by Colonel Anderson, who commanded at Fort Gaines, and turned over everything in good order.

The Admiral reflects very severely on General Page and his officers for their wanton destruction of property; but it must be remembered that this was done at Fort Morgan in the excitement of battle, and it might have been done without the General's knowledge by young officers who had had no extensive military training, and who were not posted as to the proprieties of the occasion. We do not like to believe that General Page lent himself to such improper proceedings, for while he was in the United States Navy he was looked upon by all who knew him as the soul of honor, and although he committed the gravest fault when he abjured the flag under which he was born, educated and cherished, yet there were so many others of world-wide reputations who set the example and carried men away with their wild secession sophistries, that he could have erred on that one subject without forfeiting an honorable name. The fact of his not having a sword to deliver might have been an accident. It would have been very foolish in an officer of his age to suppose that he could in this way free himself from any odium that might attach to defeat, or gain any applause even from his warmest admirers.

No matter what happened, Fort Morgan was won in the most handsome manner, and Farragut was once more entitled to the heartiest congratulations of his countrymen. This, his last great achievement, had placed him in the foremost rank of naval officers, and the following letter from the Hon. Secretary of the Navy scarcely states the value of the service he had rendered to the Union cause:

NAVY DEPARTMENT, }
September 5, 1864. }

SIR—Your dispatch, numbered 368, is received, informing the Department of the capture, on the 23d ultimo, of Fort Morgan. This is the last and most formidable of all the defences erected to command the entrance of the Bay of Mobile, and it is a gratification that its capitulation was effected sooner than had been anticipated. I will not, in this communication, stop to comment on the bad faith exhibited in the destruction of the arms and property in the fort after its surrender, which is reprobated by you with just severity ; but I desire to congratulate you and your command on a series of achievements which put us in possession of the bay ; and, until the integrity of the Union is fully vindicated and established, close all ocean communications with the city of Mobile.

In the success which has attended your operations, you have illustrated the efficiency and irresistible power of a naval force led by a bold and vigorous mind, and the insufficiency of any batteries to prevent the passage of a fleet thus led and commanded. You have, first on the Mississippi, and recently in the Bay of Mobile, demonstrated what had been previously doubted, the ability of naval vessels, properly manned and commanded, to set at defiance the best constructed and most heavily armed fortifications.

In these successive victories you have encountered great risks, but the results have vindicated the wisdom of your policy and the daring valor of our officers and seamen.

I desire the congratulations which are hereby tendered to yourself, your officers and men, may be extended to the Army, who have so cordially cooperated with you. Very respectfully,

GIDEON WELLES,
Secretary of the Navy.

Rear-Admiral D. G. FARRAGUT,
Commanding W. G. B. Squadron, Mobile Bay.

As soon as Fort Morgan had surrendered, Farragut ordered the channel raked for torpedoes.

Twenty-one were taken up, but most of them had lain so long in the water that they had, fortunately, become harmless. In consequence of this, the seamen became somewhat careless in handling them, and one torpedo exploded, killing and wounding the following named persons :

Killed—C. E. Milliken (Ord. Sea.).

Mortally wounded—Isaac Young (Ord. Sea.) ; John Miller (Sea.), Robert G. White (Sea.), George Thompson (Sea.) — all of U. S. S. "Seminole."

Wounded seriously—Pilot Martin Freeman, U. S. S. "Hartford"; Acting-Ensign John White ; H. J. O'Brien (Qr. Mr.) ; William Howard (Lds.) ; James McDonald (Sea.), all of the "Metacomet ;" and Boatswain Charles White, of the "Seminole."

Slightly wounded—Henry Chester (Sea.) ; Edward Mann (O. S.) ; Thomas Webster (Lds.)—U. S. S. "Seminole."

These men had passed through all the danger of battle, and had stood to their guns like heroes, and now, when they might hope to live and enjoy part of the honor won in this great victory, they were snatched from life or maimed forever by an infernal machine, which the officers of the Union Navy, as a rule, disdained to use—trusting rather to hearts of steel and wooden ships with which to win their victories.

We place their names on the roll of fame as worthy to be remembered by all who honor the true American sailor, who will stick to his flag as long as he has a leg to stand on.

It is bad enough to have men shot down in battle while fighting their guns, but it is dreadful to see them lying crushed to pieces after the victory is won, especially when, as in this case, it might so easily have been prevented. Few of the vessels lost so many in killed and wounded during the fight as were lost by the explosion of this one torpedo.

One of the vessels of the Union fleet was lost very unnecessarily, and that was the steamer "Philippi," commanded by Acting-Master James T. Seaver, who, it appears, wished to undertake an adventure on his own account, and, after delivering some stores to the vessels outside the bar, stood in after the fleet to try and be of assistance in case any vessel was disabled. He was unfortunate enough to run aground, however, when within range of Fort Morgan, and the Confederate gunners struck his vessel almost every time and soon set her on fire, showing how much better is the aim of gunners when they are firing at a vessel that does not fire back. Had Fort Morgan fired as well at the fleet while passing, it would have crippled all the wooden ships.

We can imagine the Admiral's feelings

when, after passing all the batteries safely, he saw a vessel of his squadron in flames, away off in the outer bay, and out of the main channel. Worst of all, Acting-Master Seaver deserted his vessel, leaving the signal-book on the quarter-deck.

The "Philippi" was an express vessel, and a great loss to the squadron. It was a small loss, however, compared with the final gain, and it merely shows that, with all the precautions that a commander-in-chief may take, there is always some one person who will, for want of common sense, do his best to defeat the object of his commander.

Now that years have passed, and the prejudices of the day have been forgotten by all truly loyal men, we can calmly discuss this remarkable battle without any fear of being considered partial towards any of the parties concerned.

The question has often been asked, " Was Buchanan justified by circumstances in attacking Farragut's fleet, unless he was covered by the heavy batteries of Fort Morgan ?"

Let us see first what effect the "Tennessee" had had upon the fleet, from the time it came under the fire of Fort Morgan until it anchored in Mobile Roads. The iron-clad occupied a commanding and raking position, backed by the three gun-boats and covered by Fort Morgan ; but every vessel passed her without being disabled, all the serious injury which they received coming from the guns of Fort Morgan.

It was expected by the officers of the fleet that the Confederate iron-clad would place herself right in the way of the leading vessel, sink her with her formidable prow, throw the fleet into confusion, and keep them huddled together under the fire of the fort until she could get into their midst and deal destruction on every side. This is the course which Buchanan should have pursued, for it will be seen that his iron-clad was quite strong enough to withstand the battering of any vessel in the Union fleet. She was rammed by the "Monongahela," "Lackawanna," "Hartford," and "Ossipee." The first two vessels were seriously injured, the "Hartford" only hit a glancing blow, and the "Ossipee" received more injury than she inflicted; in fact, all their attacks were harmless against the iron-clad hull of the ram, which had been built expressly to stand just such encounters. The Board which examined her after the battle reported that there were no visible marks or evidence of injury done by the ramming she had received. This shows that the calculations made by Buchanan were not without due consideration. He knew every ship in the Union fleet, the number and calibre of their guns, their

speed, the strength of their hulls, and, in fact, all that was worth knowing about them. But he failed to appreciate the merit of their commanding officers, and, ever following in the wake of the "lost cause," he forgot the spirit of the brave seamen who manned the Union ships.

He well knew what would be the effect of the 11 and 15 inch shot that would be fired from the Monitors. He had seen in the fight of the "Monitor" and "Merrimac" that 11-inch shot would not penetrate the 4-inch armor of the latter, and he had seen, from the reports of the bombardment of Fort Sumter by the Monitors, that 15-inch shot had not enough penetrating power to break through masonry that was easily bored through and through by a 6-inch rifle. He knew that the fleet had very few rifled guns, and that what they had were small calibre Parrotts, which it was necessary to load with reduced charges in order to guard against explosion. He had placed one-third more armor on the "Tennessee" than was on the "Merrimac," and had strengthened her in other ways as no vessel had ever been strengthened before.

We have seen from the accounts of this battle that the hull of the "Tennessee" was virtually uninjured by the shots from the Monitors. Only one 15-inch shot penetrated her armor, while the 11-inch shot made no impression on her beyond shattering the port shutters ; and had it not been for the carrying away of her exposed steering gear and smoke-stack, Buchanan's calculations might have been verified.

Yet the only real damage done to the "Tennessee" was by the Monitors, and it may be asked : "Would not the Monitors have captured her without the aid of the wooden ships?" We think they ought to have done so, unless by her superior speed she had escaped under the guns of the fort. The wooden ships smothered her by their heavy blows, demoralizing her crew and keeping them from the guns, for they did not know what would be the result of this constant ramming. It is certain that the "Tennessee" did not fire a gun after her last encounter with the "Hartford."

The Confederates claim that she was attacked by a squadron of eighteen vessels, and that Buchanan, single-handed, held his own for hours; while the fact is, she was attacked by only seven vessels of the fleet (four of them wooden), and the action lasted but an hour and a quarter—(8:45 to 10 A. M.)

Considering all things, Admiral Buchanan made a mistake in attacking the fleet when he did; he ought to have remained under shelter of Fort Morgan until the fleet attacked him, or else have come out in the night when the vessels were at anchor and at a disadvantage. That was his only chance of success. As he took upon himself to go out and seek battle, instead of waiting for it to be offered to him, one would naturally suppose that his ship had a resisting power that was only known to himself, and that he, as one of the best sailors afloat, felt himself authorized to attack the whole fleet by daylight. If this was the case, the forces on each side might be considered as about equal, in spite of the disparity of numbers.

One point must not be lost sight of, and that is, that no damage was inflicted on the "Tennessee" before the Monitors came up, and when they did attack her the battle was soon ended. It is a significant fact in favor of iron-clads, and if the Monitors had possessed more speed they would not have required any assistance from wooden vessels.

In this connection we must mention a very creditable action of Commander Nicholson. The charge for the 15-inch gun, as regulated by the Bureau of Ordnance, was only 35 lbs. of powder, but Captain Nicholson nearly doubled it, using 65 lbs.—taking the responsibility of bursting the gun—but proving, in fact, that it could bear that charge for a limited number of rounds. The result was, that he pierced the armor of the ram, and dispelled the illusion of Buchanan and his crew—that their ship was invulnerable.

There is no doubt that the "Tennessee" was at that time the most formidable vessel the Confederates had ever built, and they might well feel proud of their great war monster, and believe her to be a match for half a-dozen Monitors. In fact, she might have been more than a match for them if the fight had taken place in the open sea, where her superior speed and long-range guns would have given her a great advantage.

This battle gave the Government a great deal of experience, and demonstrated beyond question that the 9 and 11 inch guns were perfectly useless against six inches of iron, heavily backed, even when fired at close quarters. But, with this lesson before them, the U. S. Government—for twenty years after the war—has held on to these guns, and paraded them about the world in obsolete wooden ships, which all other nations have abolished as unfit for war purposes.

The two great systems of iron-clad construction, which had been introduced on the scene of war by the North and the South respectively, had on this occasion a fair chance of being fully tested, and in a manner admitting of no dispute, and the palm was given to Ericssen's invention. The

want of speed and a proper armament are not faults inherent in his system.

The "Tennessee" was a formidable vessel, and her designers and constructors deserved great credit for the result of their labors. Had she succeeded in winning a victory in Mobile Bay, the world would have been some years longer groping in the dark for the right kind of an iron-clad, but would have found it finally in the Ericsson "Monitor," which to-day has no superior throughout the world.

This battle rendered Mobile of no value to the Confederacy, for, although owing to shoal water and obstructions, the Navy could not reach the city, it was as hermetically sealed against blockade-runners as if actually surrendered. A few vessels only were kept inside the bay, leaving Farragut at liberty to use his remaining force on the coast of Texas, where General Banks (after his failure up the Red River) had evacuated all the important points which had been captured by the Army and Navy, and thus left the Texan ports open to the blockade-runners.

The work of the Navy seemed to be endless. It had not only to fight the enemy, but to repair the blunders of quasi-military men, who would not even hold the positions which the Navy placed in their hands. Yet the officers and sailors worked on with unwearying activity and bravery to reach the victorious end, and every battle won diminished in an increasing ratio the Confederates' chance of success.

The battle of Mobile Bay proved several things which it is as important to know to-day as it was then. Guns mounted *en barbette*, even when protected by proper traverses, can be silenced and passed by steamers on their throwing in a heavy and concentrated fire, especially if they carry a large number of guns in broadside. No fort now existing in this country can keep out a fleet unless the channel is thoroughly obstructed.

Up to the present time, ships-of-war are gaining in strength over the forts of this country, and the saying that "one gun on shore is worth three on board-ship" may very properly be reversed. Steam has changed the whole principle of war, and iron-clads with rifled guns are too strong for our walls of stone, brick and mortar.

NOTE.—As the "Tennessee" was the most powerful and remarkable vessel the Confederates ever built, the scientific reader may take some interest in the following description of her construction, from the report of a Board of Survey, ordered by Admiral Farragut, after the battle:

DESCRIPTION OF THE CONFEDERATE IRON-CLAD "TENNESSEE."

The vessel had been built at Mobile, Alabama, under the superintendence of Messrs. Pierce and Bassett, naval constructors, and Mr. Frick, chief engineer of the station.

Hull. The hull of the vessel was very strongly built in every part, the materials being oak and yellow pine, with iron fastenings. Length from stem to stern on deck, 209 feet; greatest breadth of beam on deck, 48 feet; mean average draught of water about 14 feet.

The deck was covered fore and aft with wrought-iron plates, two inches thick.

The sides of the vessel were protected by an overhang, sponsoned, and covered with two layers of 2-inch wrought-iron. This overhang extended about six feet below the water line.

The sides of the vessel below the deck were eight feet thick, and the distance from the knuckle or outside of the overhang on deck, to the base of the casemate on either side, was ten feet. The vessel was provided with a strong beak or prow, which projected about two feet under water, formed by the continuation of the sponsoning and covered with wrought-iron plates.

The Casemate was very strongly built. It was 78 feet 8 inches long, and 28 feet 9 inches wide inside, the sides of the vessel extending ten feet from it on either side at the greatest breadth of beam.

The framing consisted of heavy yellow pine beams, 13 inches thick, and placed close together vertically. Outside planking of yellow pine, 5½

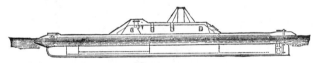

DIAGRAM OF THE CONFEDERATE IRON-CLAD RAM "TENNESSEE."

inches thick, laid on horizontally; and outside of this horizontal planking there was a layer of oak timber 4 inches thick, bolted on vertically, upon which the iron plating was secured.

The plating or armor of the casemate forward was 6 inches thick, consisting of three 2-inch iron plates, of about 6 inches wide each, and aft and on the sides 5 inches thick, consisting of [two] 2-inch and one 1-inch iron plate of the same width.

The yellow pine framing of the casemate was planked over inside with 2½-inch oak timber, laid on diagonally. The whole of the armor plating was fastened with through bolts, 1¼ inch diameter, with washers and nuts inside.

The casemate was covered on top with wrought-iron gratings composed of bars 2 inches thick and 6 inches wide, laid flat, and supported on wooden beams 12 inches square, and about 5 feet distant from each other. Some of these gratings were hinged and fitted to open from the inside.

There were ten gun-ports in the casemate, three in the broadside on either side, two forward and two aft. The forward and after ports, to port and starboard, were placed so as to enable the forward and after pivot-guns to be used as broadside guns. The directly-forward and after-ports were on a line with the keel.

The ports were elongated and made just wide enough for the entrance of the muzzle of the guns in training, and only high enough to allow a moderate elevation and depression of the gun.

The wooden backing was cut away on each side of the ports inside of the casemate, to allow the guns to be trained about one point forward and aft. The gun ports were covered with wrought-iron sliding plates or shutters five inches thick; those for the four broadside guns were fitted in slides. The

sliding plates or shutters for the pivot-guns were pivoted on the edge with one bolt that could be knocked out, detaching the shutter if necessary, and were worked by a combination of racks and pinions.

Armament. The armament of the "Tennessee" consisted of six rifled guns, Brooke's rifles.

The two pivot-guns were 7.125-inch bore, and the four broadside guns were 6-inch bore. These guns were reinforced at the breech by two wrought-iron bands, two inches thick respectively. Weight of projectiles, 95 pounds and 110 pounds, solid shot.

The pivot-guns were fitted on wooden slides, with a rack let into them. On an arm attached to the carriage there was a pinion for running out the gun, and, by raising the arm, the rack was thrown out of gear to allow the gun to recoil.

Quarters for Officers and Crew. For an iron-clad vessel the cabin was large and comfortable. The ward-room was situated immediately over the engine, and was open to it; but although sufficiently commodious, its ventilation was so bad, and the smell arising from the accumulation of bilge-water so offensive, that it would have been impossible for officers or others to preserve their health or to live there comfortably for any length of time.

The quarters of the crew were good and comfortable for an iron-clad vessel of her description. They consisted of a roomy berth-deck, with rooms fitted up on either side for the junior officers. When in port the crew were quartered on a covered barge, anchored near the vessel.

The steering arrangements were very defective, nor were the accommodations for the pilot and helmsman good.

Machinery. The machinery of the vessel consisted of two geared non-condensing engines. Cylinders, 24 inches diameter and 7 feet stroke.

These engines had been taken out of the Alabama River steamer, "Alonzo Child." They were placed fore and aft in the vessel, geared to an idler-shaft by spur gearing with wooden teeth, and from the idler-shaft to the propeller-shaft by bevel cast-iron gear.

Boilers. There were four horizontal flue boilers, 24 feet long, placed side by side, with one furnace under the whole of them; the products of combustion returning through the flues were delivered into one smoke-pipe.

The engine and fire-rooms were insufferably hot and very badly ventilated.

INJURIES RECEIVED IN THE ACTION.

"The injuries to the casemate of the 'Tennessee' from shot are very considerable. On its after-side nearly all the plating is started; one bolt driven in; several nuts knocked off inside; gun-carriage of the after pivot-gun damaged, and the steering rod or chain cut near that gun. There are unmistakable marks on the after-part of the casemate of not less than nine 11-inch solid shot having struck within the space of a few square feet in the immediate vicinity of that port. On the port side of the casemate the armor is also badly damaged from shot.

"On that side nearly amidships of the casemate, and between the broadside guns, a 15-inch solid shot knocked a hole through the armor and backing, leaving on the inside an undetached mass of oak and pine splinters, about three by four feet, and projecting inside of the casemate about two feet from the side. This is the only shot that penetrated the wooden backing of the casemate, although there are numerous places on the inside giving evidence of the effect of the shot.

"There are visible between forty and fifty indentations and marks of shot on the hull, deck and casemate, varying from very severe to slight; nine of the deepest indentations on the after-part of the casemate (evidently being 11-inch shot), and the marks of about thirty of other calibres on different parts of the vessel.

"There are also a few other marks, being, however, merely scratches or slight indentations of the plating.

"The smoke-stack was shot away, although it is not improbable the heavy ramming by the 'Monongahela,' 'Lackawanna,' and the 'Hartford' had previously prepared it for its fall.

"Three of the wrought-iron port shutters or slides were so much damaged by shot as to prevent the firing of the guns.

"There are no external visible marks or evidences of injury inflicted upon the hull of the 'Tennessee' by the severe ramming of the 'Monongahela,' 'Lackawanna,' and 'Hartford'; but inasmuch as the decks leaked badly, and when there is a moderate sea running in the bay, her reported usual leakage of three inches an hour being now increased to five or six inches an hour, it is fairly to be inferred that the increased leakage is caused by the concussion of the vessels. The 'Tennessee' is in a state to do good service now. To restore her to the state of efficiency in which she was when she went into action with this fleet on the 5th instant, it will be necessary to overhaul much of the iron plating on the port and after-sides of the casemate, and replace some of it.

"The iron gun-port slides or shutters, which were damaged, must be either removed or repaired.

"A new smoke-stack is required, and additional ventilators should be fitted.

"Blowers are required to produce proper ventilation in the engine-room and on the berth-deck.

"When these small repairs and additions shall have been made, the iron-clad 'Tennessee' will be a most formidable vessel for harbor and river service, and for operating generally in smooth water, both offensively and defensively."

WEST GULF SQUADRON, JANUARY 1ST, 1864.

REAR-ADMIRAL DAVID G. FARRAGUT.

CAPTAIN PERCIVAL DRAYTON, FLEET-CAPTAIN.

[Vessels and Commanders marked with a * were in the Battle of Mobile Bay.]

*STEAMER "HARTFORD"—FLAG-SHIP.

Captain, Percival Drayton, at Mobile; Lieutenant-Commander, L. A. Kimberly, executive officer at Mobile; Lieutenants, H. B. Tyson and J. C. Watson; Fleet Surgeon, James C. Palmer; Fleet Paymaster, Edw. T. Dunn; Surgeon, John J. Gibson; Assistant-Surgeon, Wm. Commons; Paymaster, Wm. T. Merideth; Marines: Captain, Charles Heywood; First-Lieutenant, C. L. Sherman; Ensigns, C. D. Jones and LaRue P. Adams; Acting-Ensigns, Wm. H. Whiting, G. D. B. Glidden, C. W. Snow and Geo. Munday; Pilot, Martin Freeman; Acting-Master's Mates, J. J. Tinelli, Wm. H. Hathorne, W. H. Childs, R. P. Herrick, G. R. Avery and H. Brownell; Fleet Engineer, Wm. H. Shock; Chief Engineer, Thom Williamson; Second-Assistants, E. B. Latch, F. A. Wilson, Isaac DeGraff, C. M. Burchard and John Wilson; Third-Assistants, J. E. Speights, H. L. Pilkington and Alfred Hoyt; Boatswain, Robert Dixon; Gunner, J. L. Staples; Carpenter, O. S. Stimson; Sailmaker, T. C. Herbert.

STEAMER "PENSACOLA."

Commodore, Henry H. Bell, commanding squadron pro tem.; Lieutenant-Commander, Samuel R. Franklin; Lieutenants, F. V. McNair and G. W. Sumner; Surgeon, Wm. Lansdale; Assistant-Surgeon, W. H. Jones; Acting-Assistant Paymaster, J. H. Stevenson; Marines: First-Lieutenant, Norval L. Nokes; Acting-Masters, F. T. King, Thos. Andrews and S. B. Washburne; Acting-Ensign, V. W. Jones; Engineers: First-Assistant, John Purdy, Jr.; Second-Assistants, A. H. Able and Alfred Colin; Third-Assistants, T. W. Fitch, F. C. Burchard and G. W. Baird; Boatswain, James Herold; Gunner, David Roe; Carpenter, Edward Cox; Sailmaker, Chas. Lawrence.

STEAM-FRIGATE "COLORADO."

Commodore, Henry K. Thatcher; Lieutenants, H. W. Miller and Benj. F. Day; Paymaster, W. H. H. Williams; Chaplain, D. X. Junkin; Assistant-Surgeons, A. W. H. Hawkins and Matthew Chalmers; Marines: Captain, Geo. R. Graham; Second-Lieutenant, S. C. Adams; Acting Masters, Thos. Hanrahan and Charles Folsom; Acting-Ensigns, Henry Avery, F. P. Bibles and B. B. Knowlton; Acting-Master's Mates, A. O. Child, C. H. Littlefield, W. G. Perry, J. L. Vennard and Leon Bryant; Chief Engineer, R. M. Bartleman; Acting-First-Assistant, C. W. Pennington; Acting-Second-Assistant, G. S. Perkins; Acting-Third-Assistants, T. J. Lavery, R. Wallace and H. B. Green; Boatswain, A. M. Pomeroy; Gunner, R. H. Cross; Carpenter, John A. Dixon; Sailmaker, W. N. Maull.

*STEAMER "OSSIPEE."

Commander, William E. LeRoy, at Mobile; Captain, John P. Gillis; Lieutenant, J. A. Howell; Surgeon, B. F. Gibbs; Assistant-Surgeon, G. H. E. Baumgarten; Paymaster, E. Foster; Acting-Master, C. C. Bunker; Acting-Ensigns, H. S. Lambert, Chas. Putnam, C. W. Adams, W. A. Van Vleck and C. E. Clark; Acting-Master's Mates, W. Wingood, W. W. Black and P. P. Hawkes; Engineers: Acting-Chief, J. M. Adams; Acting-First-Assistant, Geo. L. Harris; Acting-Second-Assistant, J. W. Webb; Third-Assistants, G. W. Kidder, John Mathews, Wm. Collier, W. W. Vanderbilt and James Germon; Boatswain, Andrew Milne; Gunner, J. Q. Adams.

*STEAMER "RICHMOND."

Captain, Thornton A. Jenkins; Lieutenant-Commander, Edward Terry; Surgeon, L. J. Williams; Assistant-Surgeon, J. D. Murphy; Paymaster, Edwin Stewart; First-Lieutenant of Marines, S. W. Powell; Acting-Masters, P. S. Borden and C. J. Gibbs; Ensign, P. H. Cooper; Acting-Ensigns, J. F. Beyer, C. M. Chester and Lewis Clark; Acting-Master's Mates, Wm. R. Cox, James West, T. J. Warner and W. C. Seymour; Chief Engineer, Jackson McElmell; First-Assistant, E. J. Brooks; Second-Assistant, A. J. Kenyon; Third-Assistants, A. J. Kirby, Robert Weir, James Patterson, John D. Ford, W. H. Crawford and C. W. C. Senter; Boatswain, I. P. Choate; Gunner, Wm. Cheney; Carpenter, H. L Dixon; Sailmaker, Wm. Rogers.

*STEAMER "LACKAWANNA."

Captain, John B. Marchand; Lieutenants, T. C. Bowen and S. A. McCarty; Surgeon, Thomas W. Leach; Paymaster, James Fulton; Acting-Master, Felix McCurley; Ensigns, G. H. Wadleigh and Frank Wildes; Acting-Ensign, Geo. T. Chapman;

Acting-Master's Mates, Charles Welles and John Cannon; Engineers: Acting-Chief, W. A. R. Latimer; Second-Assistants, R. H. Gunnell and E. J. Whittaker; Third-Assistants, G. W. Roche, C. F. Marsland, B. E. Pike and I. B. Fort; Boatswain, W. E. Leeds; Gunner, J. G. Foster.

* STEAMER "ITASCA."

Lieutenant-Commander, George Brown, at Mobile; Acting-Master, Richard Hustace; Acting-Ensigns, C. H. Hurd and James Igo; Acting-Assistant Surgeon, Henry Rockwood; Acting-Assistant Paymaster, George L. Mead; Acting-Master's Mate, Henry Myron; Engineers: Acting-Second-Assistant, M. H. Gerry; Acting-Third-Assistants, Owen Raney and George C. Irelan.

NOTE.—List not given in Navy Register for January, and is, therefore, incomplete.

STORE-SHIP "POTOMAC."

Commander, Alex. Gibson; Assistant-Surgeon, Geo. R. Brush; Acting-Assistant Paymaster, J. H. Wood; Chaplain, Robert Given; Captain of Marines, Geo. W. Collier; Acting-Master, Geo. D. Upham; Acting-Ensigns, Edwin Cressy and L. B. King; Acting-Master's Mates, A. Whiting, W. H. Metz and James Connell; Gunner, Henry Hamilton; Acting-Carpenter, John C. Hoffman.

* STEAMER "MONONGAHELA."

Commander, James H. Strong; Lieutenant, Roderick Prentiss; Surgeon, David Kindleberger; Assistant Paymaster, Forbes Parker; Acting-Masters, Ezra Leonard and Chas. Higgins; Ensign, G. M. Brown; Acting-Ensigns, C. D. Sigsbee, D. W. Mullen and H. W. Grinnell; Acting-Master's Mate, W. S. Armand; Chief Engineer, Geo. F. Kutz; Second-Assistants, Joseph Trilly and N. B. Clark; Third-Assistants, J. J. Bissett, Edw. Cheney, P. G. Eastwick and P. J. Langer; Boatswain, Wm. Green; Gunner, J. D. Fletcher.

* STEAMER "METACOMET."

Lieutenant-Commander, James E. Jouett, at Mobile; Acting-Masters, Henry J. Sleeper, N. M. Dyer and C. W. Wilson; Acting-Ensigns, H. C. Nields, G. E. Wing, John White and John O. Morse; Acting-Assistant Paymaster, Horace M. Harriman; Assistant Surgeon, Edw. D. Payne; Acting-Master's Mates, J. K. Goodwin, —— Miller, Chas. C. Jones and Henry Wyman; Engineers: First-Assistant, Jas. Atkins; Second-Assistant, Joseph Morgan; Acting-Third-Assistants, S. W. King and George B. Rodgers; Acting-Gunners, James Lamen, at Mobile, and Peter McGovern January 1).

SLOOP-OF-WAR "PORTSMOUTH."

Commander, L. C. Sartori; Assistant-Surgeon, C. S. Giberson; Assistant-Paymaster, Caspar Schenck; First-Lieutenant of Marines, W. H. Hale; Acting-Masters, G. Richmond, John Wallace and Eben Hoyt; Acting-Ensigns, John H. Allen and Abraham Rich; Acting-Master's Mates, T. H. Jenks, W. F. Buel and Samuel Carpenter; Boatswain, John Ross; Sailmaker, L. B. Wakeman.

* STEAMER "ONEIDA"

Commanders, J. R. M. Mullany, at Mobile, and W. E. LeRoy; Lieutenant, C. L. Huntington; Surgeon, John Y. Taylor; Paymaster, C. W. Hassler; Acting-Masters, Thomas Edwards and Elijah Rose; Ensign, E. N. Kellogg; Acting-Ensigns, C. V. Gridley and John Sears; Acting-Master's Mates, Edward Bird, D. H. Clark and Chas. Gainesford; Chief Engineer, Wm. H. Hunt; Second-Assistants, J. H. Morrison and R. H. Fitch; Third-Assistants, W. D. McIlvaine and C. W. Breaker; Acting-Third-Assistants, W. E. Dearer and Nicholas Dillon; Boatswain, H. Dickinson; Gunner, Wm. Parker.

STEAMER "PRINCESS ROYAL."

Commander, M. B. Woolsey; Lieutenant, C. E. McKay; Acting-Assistant Surgeon, T. K. Chandler;

Acting-Assistant Paymaster, F. T. Morton; Acting-Master, F. J. Grover; Acting-Ensigns, T. H. Paine and F. A. Miller; Acting-Master's Mates, Freeman Langly and W. E. Cannon; Engineers: Acting-First-Assistant, Wm. Huntley; Acting-Second-Assistant, W. H. Thompson; Acting-Third-Assistants, Andrew Redmond, Charles Wolf and Peter Taylor.

* STEAMER "SEMINOLE."

Commanders, E. Donaldson, at Mobile, and Henry Rolando; Lieutenant, A. T. Mahan; Surgeon, Charles Martin; Paymaster, T. T. Caswell; Acting-Master, C. G. Arthur; Ensign, G. K. Haswell; Acting-Ensigns, F. A. Cook, G. B. Stevenson and F. Kempton; Acting-Master's Mates, D. K. Perkins, J. P. Knowles and John Dennett; Engineers: Acting-First-Assistant, C. B. Babcock; Acting-Second-Assistant, A. R. Calden; Acting-Third-Assistants, Wm. Drinkwater, G. S. Thurston, P. J. Hughes and H. M. Quig; Boatswain, Paul Atkinson; Acting-Gunner, Wm. H. Herring.

*STEAMER "OCTORARA."

Lieutenant-Commanders, C. H. Greene, at Mobile, and W. W. Low; Lieutenant, C. M. Schoonmaker; Assistant-Surgeon, E. R. Dodge; Acting-Assistant Paymaster, W. H. Higbee; Acting-Masters, E. A. Howell and W. D. Urann; Acting-Ensigns, G. F. Hollis, A. R. Jones and G. H. Dodge, Jr.; Engineers: First-Assistant, J. W. Whittaker; Acting-Second-Assistant, W. W. Shipman; Third-Assistants, C. R. Morgan and J. G. Cooper; Acting-Third-Assistant, Joseph Knight.

STEAMER "KANAWHA."

Lieutenant-Commander, Wm. K. Mayo; Acting-Assistant Surgeon, F. W. Brigham; Acting-Assistant Paymaster, L. L. Penniman; Acting-Ensigns, L. S. Trickett, W. A. Purdie and H. Banks; Acting-Master's Mates, R. P. Boss and James Clark; Engineers: Second-Assistant, Edward Farmer; Third-Assistants, W. S. Cherry, M. M. Murphy and M. W. Mather.

STEAMER "GENESEE."

Lieutenant-Commander, Edward C. Grafton; Lieutenant, Thomas S. Spencer; Acting-Assistant Surgeon, W. F. Hutchinson; Acting-Assistant Paymaster, F. C. Alley; Acting-Masters, Wm. Hanson and C. M. Merchant; Acting-Ensigns, C. H. Baxter and E. W. Halcro; Acting-Master's Mates, W. J. Crosby and John Conner; Engineers: Acting-First-Assistant, John Cahill; Acting-Second-Assistant, C. H. Harrab; Acting-Third-Assistants, Christopher Milton, Michael McLaughlin and Henry Webster.

* STEAMER "GALENA."

Lieutenant-Commander, C. H. Wells, at Mobile; Acting-Volunteer-Lieutenant, C. W. Wilson; Acting-Master, D. C. Kells; Acting-Ensigns, Henry Pease, Jr., and S. S. Miner; Acting-Assistant Surgeon, George P. Wright; Acting-Assistant Paymaster, Theo. S. Kitchen; Acting-Master's Mates, Francis Tuttle, Jas. H. Delano and O. H. Robbins; Engineers: First-Assistant, Wm. H. Buehler; Second-Assistants, C. H. Greenleaf and J. A. Scott; Acting-Third-Assistants, Patrick Burns and William Welcker; Captain's Clerk, Lesley G. Morrow.

STEAMER "OWASCO."

Lieutenant-Commander, E. W. Henry; Acting-Assistant Surgeon, G. H. Van Deusen; Acting-Assistant Paymaster, W. B. Coleman; Acting-Masters, E. A. Terrill and T. B. Sears; Acting-Ensigns, T. H. Baker, W. H. Titcomb, and T. McL. Miller; Acting-Master's Mate, R. N. Eldridge; Engineers: Second-Assistant, F. S. Barlow; Third-Assistant, B. D. Clemens; Acting-Third-Assistants, T. H. Carton and James Eccles.

STEAMER " KATAHDIN."

Lieutenant-Commander, P. C. Johnson; Assistant-Surgeon, Ira Bragg; Acting-Assistant Paymaster, L. S. Bradley; Acting-Ensigns, M. W. McEntee, G. A. Faunce, P. R. Maclaurin and George Leonard ; Acting Master's Mate, John Leeds; Engineers: Second-Assistant, T W. Rae; Third-Assistants, W. J. Reed, W. W. Heaton, John McIntyre and Thomas Tuttle.

*STEAMER "PORT ROYAL."

Lieutenant - Commander, Bancroft Gherardi, at Mobile; Lieutenant-Commander, George U. Morris; Acting-Assistant-Surgeon, E. R. Hutchins ; Paymaster, G. A. Sawyer; Acting-Masters, E. Van Slyck and Edward Herrick; Acting-Ensigns, William Hull and Peter Faunce ; Acting-Master's Mates, E. O. Tyson, H. D. Baldwin and W. A. Prescott; Engineers: Second-Assistant, W. C. Selden ; Third-Assistants, E. M. Breeze, F. B. Allen, Henry Snyder and W. C. F. Reichenbach.

STEAMER "CHOCURA."

Lieutenant-Commander, Bancroft Gherardi; Acting-Asistant Surgeon, B. F. Hamell; Acting-Assistant Paymaster, E. L. Turner; Acting-Master, Alfred Washburn; Acting-Ensigns, D. M. Carver, Robert Beardsley and T. T. Tracy; Acting-Master's Mates, A. P. Atwood and Thomas Kennedy; Engineers: Second-Assistant, H. H. Maloney; Third-Assistants, Theodore Cooper, Andrew Blythe and N. H. Lawton; Acting-Third-Assistant, O. D. Hughes.

STEAMER " PEMBINA."

Lieutenant-Commander, L. H. Newman; Acting-Assistant Surgeon, A. R. Holmes; Acting-Assistant Paymaster, Walter Fuller; Acting-Masters, Bowen Allen and J. W. Saunders; Acting-Ensigns, William Lyddon, B. M. Chester and Olof Sandstrom; Acting-Master's Mate, H. T. Davis; Engineers: Second-Assistants, T. A. Stephens and J. W. Sydney; Third-Assistants,, R. M. Hodgson, J. F. Bingham and C. F. Nagle.

STEAMER " PENOBSCOT."

Lieutenant-Commander, A. E. K. Benham; Acting-Assistant Surgeon, F. C. Sargent; Acting-Assistant Paymaster, F. H. Hinman; Acting-Master, C. E. Jack; Acting-Ensigns, H. D. Edwards, F. W. Hearn, J. B. Fairchild and W. G. Campbell; Engineers: Acting-First-Assistant, W. M. Rhodes; Acting-Second-Assistants, W. C. Barrett and A. E. McConnell; Third-Assistants, Warren Howland and J. F. Plant.

SLOOP-OF-WAR " VINCENNES."

Lieutenant-Commander, C. H. Greene; Assistant-Surgeon, G. B. Slough; Acting-Assistant Paymaster, Samuel Jordan; Acting-Masters, J. T. Searer and A. E. Hunter; Acting - Boatswain, A. O. Goodsoe; Gunner, William Wilson; Sailmaker, N. Lynch.

*STEAMER " KENNEBEC."

Lieutenant - Commander, W. P. McCann ; Assistant Surgeon, C. H. Perry ; Acting-Assistant Paymaster, C. L. Burnet; Acting-Master, Edward Baker; Acting-Ensigns, A. L. Emerson, J. J. Butler, J. D. Ellis and H. E. Tinkham; Acting-Master's Mate, H. C. Nields; Engineers: Third-Assistants, B. C. Gowing, E. E. Roberts, L. W. Robinson and G. R. Holt.

STEAMER " PINOLA "

Lieutenant-Commander, O. F. Stanton; Assistant-Surgeon, L. M. Lyon; Acting-Assistant Paymaster, A. B. Robinson; Acting-Master, W. P. Gibbs; Acting-Ensigns, C. V. Rummell, G. M. Bogart and H. Crosby; Acting-Master's Mate, J. G. Rosling; Engineers: First-Assistant, John Johnson; Third-Assistants, John Everding, F. E. Hosmer, C. O. Farciot and S. A. Appold.

STEAMER "CAYUGA."

Lieutenant-Commander, Wm. H. Dana; Acting-Assistant Surgeon, J. E. Parsons; Acting-Assistant Paymaster, J. N. Whiffen; Acting-Masters, E. D. Percy and John Hanscom; Acting-Master's Mates, F. P. Stevens, R. O. Longfare and I. A. Abbott; Engineers: Second-Assistant, J. M. Harris; Third-Assistants, W. A. H. Allen, J. C. Chaffee and Ralph Aston.

STEAMER "CALHOUN."

Lieutenant-Commander, Geo. A. Bigelow; Assistant Surgeon, D. M. Skinner; Acting-Assistant Paymaster, D. W. Riddle; Acting-Ensigns, J. S. Clark and J. M. Chadwick; Acting-Master's Mates, J. L. Blauvelt, J. P. Sturgin and J. Mayo; Engineers: Acting-Third-Assistants, W. H. Brown, F. D. Stuart, Lucius Harlow and Richard Dwyer.

STEAMER "ESTRELLA."

Lieutenant-Commander, A. P. Cooke; Assistant Surgeon, Thomas Hiland ; Acting-Assistant Paymaster, F. J. Painter; Acting-Master, G. P. Pomeroy; Acting-Ensign, W. W. Duley; Acting-Master's Mates, W. H. Wetmore and Thomas Kelly; Engineers: Acting-Second Assistant, R. G. Pope; Acting-Third-Assistants, G. R. Marble, W. D. Pancake, J. F. Winters and John Gilbert.

STEAMER " NEW LONDON."

Lieutenant-Commander, Weld N. Allen; Acting-Assistant Paymaster, E. A. Chadwick; Acting-Master, H. L. Sturgis; Acting-Ensigns, Edward Pendexter and Eugene Biondi; Acting-Master's Mates, Edward Hennessy and Francis Way; Engineers: Acting-Second Assistant, H. P. Powers; Acting-Third-Assistants, Chas. Haskins, John Dunlap and James Creery.

STEAMER "AROOSTOOK."

Lieutenant -Commander, Chester Hatfield; Assistant Surgeon, H. W. Birkey ; Acting-Assistant Paymaster, W. L. Pynchon ; Acting-Ensigns, J. S. Russ and J. Griffin ; Acting-Master's Mates, C. S. Bellows, Wm. Barker and Edw. Culbert ; Engineers : Acting-Second-Assistant, J. C. Cree; Third-Assistants, James Entwistle, Samuel Gregg and Nathan Brown.

STEAMER "SCIOTA."

Lieutenant - Commander, George H. Perkins ; Acting-Assistant Surgeon, E. P. Colby ; Acting-Assistant Paymaster, C. H. Lockwood; Acting-Master, B. Van Voorhis; Acting-Ensigns, S. S. Beck, S. H. Bevins and Geo. W. Coffin ; Acting-Master's Mates, W. A. Osborne, Charles Atkins and Richard Graham ; Engineers: Second-Assistant, Horace McMurtrie; Third-Assistants, A. H. Price, W. F. Pratt and Daniel Dod.

STEAMER " ARKANSAS."

Acting-Volunteer-Lieutenant, David Cate ; Acting-Assistant Surgeon, E. D. G. Smith; Acting-Assistant Paymaster, E. G. Bishop; Acting-Master, James McDonald; Acting-Ensigns, B. F. Russell and F. H. Beers; Acting-Master's Mates, T. S. Ransom, G. F. Carey and Roger Farrill; Engineers: Acting-First-Assistant, James Blenkinsop; Acting-Second-Assistants, S. T. Reeves and Benjamin La Bree; Acting-Third-Assistant, James Crooks.

STEAMER "ALBATROSS."

Acting-Volunteer-Lieutenant, Theodore B. DuBois; Acting-Assistant Surgeon, I. C. Whitehead ; Acting-Assistant Paymaster, G. R. Martin; Acting-Ensigns, R. E. Anson and Alfred Hornsby; Acting-Master's Mates, James Brown, John Clark and J. T. Thompson ; Engineers : Acting-First-Assistant, J. Tucker ; Acting-Third-Assistants, E. H. Slack, J. Shields and J. Pearce.

STEAMER "J. P. JACKSON."

Acting-Volunteer-Lieutenant, L. W. Pennington; Acting-Assistant Surgeon, T. S. Yard; Acting-Assistant Paymaster, C. B. Perry; Acting-Masters, M. B. Crowell and J. F. Dearborn; Acting-Ensign, J. S. Gellett; Acting-Master's Mates, W. H. Howard and Jer. Murphy; Engineers: Acting - Second-Assistant, J. C. Mockabee; Acting-Third-Assistants, J. D. Cadwell, T. W. Harding and James Lockwood.

STEAMER "VIRGINIA."

Acting-Volunteer-Lieutenant, Charles H. Brown; Acting-Assistant Surgeon, C. H. Mason; Acting-Assistant Paymaster, E. C. Bowman; Acting-Master, L. G. Cook; Acting-Ensigns, E. H. Thomas, J. H. Rogers, A. F. West and N. A. Blume; Acting-Master's Mate, F. E. Brackett; Engineers: Acting; Second-Assistant, S. S. Glass; Acting-Third-Assistants, E. J. Gillespie, Charles Goodwin and E. M. Clark.

STEAMER "PENGUIN."

Acting-Volunteer-Lieutenant, James R. Beers; Acting-Assistant Surgeon, C. D. White; Acting-Assistant Paymaster, T. C. Hutchinson; Acting-Master, Tolford Durham; Acting-Ensigns, Charles Knowles, N. S. Hayden and Benj. Caullet; Acting-Master's Mates, Charles Smith, Jr., F. C. Almy and W. A. Hannah; Engineers: Acting-First-Assistant, F. W. Warner; Acting-Second-Assistant, Milton Randall; Acting - Third - Assistants, John Webster, Edw. Reilly and DeWitt C. McBride.

STEAMER "TENNESSEE."

Acting -Volunteer - Lieutenant, Pierre Giraud; Assistant-Surgeon, W. C. Hull; Acting-Assistant Paymaster, B. F. D. Fitch; Acting-Master, Geo. E. Nelson; Acting Ensigns, J. B. Trott, W. S. Bacon and Jos. Marthon; Acting-Master's Mate, H. E. Giraud; Engineers: Acting - First - Assistant, D. Frazer; Acting-Second-Assistant, E. C. Maloy; Acting-Third-Assistants, Thos. Fitzgerald, G. W. Kiersted and Thomas Campbell.

BARK "W. G. ANDERSON."

Acting-Volunteer-Lieutenant, John A. Johnstone; Acting-Asssistant Surgeon, T. M. Drummond; Acting-Assistant Paymaster, T. S. Dabney; Acting-Masters, J. F. Winchester and A. Cook; Acting-Ensigns, R. H. Cary, A. P. Sampson, S. H. Newman and S. A. Brooks; Acting-Master's Mates, Rosville Davis, S. C. Heath, Charles Brown and James Morgan.

BARK "ARTHUR."

Acting-Volunteer-Lieutenant, T. F. Wade; Acting-Assistant Paymaster, C. E. Mitchell; Acting-Masters, W. O. Lundt and S. Withington.

BRIG "BOHIO."

Acting-Volunteer-Lieutenant, W. D. Roath; Acting-Assistant Paymaster, J. M. Skillman; Acting-Master, W. M. Stannard; Acting-Ensigns, G. W. Baker and James Sheppard.

STEAMER "ARIZONA."

Acting - Master, H. Tibbetts; Acting - Assistant Surgeon, S. H. Weil; Acting-Assistant Paymaster, W. L. Darling; Acting-Ensigns, S. J. Butler and Wm. Harcourt; Acting-Master's Mates, J. H. Mallon and T. P. Jones; Engineers: Acting - First - Assistant, C. H. Harrington; Acting-Second-Assistant, J. W. Smyth; Third - Assistants, J. E. Fallon and L. Golden.

STEAMER "ANTONA."

Acting-Master, A. L. B. Zerega; Acting-Assistant Paymaster, H. M. Whittemore; Acting-Ensigns, J. A. Davis, J. F. Perkins, A. L. C. Bowie and H. L. Ransom; Acting-Master's Mate, J. P. Cole; Engineers: Acting-First-Assistant, W. D. Adair; Acting-Third-Assistants, R. H. Alexander, Barna Cook and F. A. Hurd.

STEAMER "GRANITE CITY."

Acting-Masters, C. W. Lamson and A. H. Atkinson; Acting-Assistant Surgeon, E. C. Ver Mulen; Acting-Assistant Paymaster, John Reed; Acting Ensigns, S. R. Tyrrell and A. H. Berry; Acting Master's Mates, T. R. Marshall, T. E. Ashmead and D. Hall; Engineers: Acting-Second-Assistant, S. Green; Acting-Third-Assistants, E. M. Schryver, J. H. Rollins and R. H. Gordon.

STEAMER "JASMINE."

Acting-Master, Wm. A. Maine; Acting-Ensign, F. J. Brenton; Acting-Master's Mates, L. E. Heath and F. W. Kimball; Engineers: Acting-Second-Assistant, Samuel Lemon; Third-Assistant, Jay Dinsmore; Acting-Third-Assistants, J. M. Cheeney and J. H. Pelton.

STEAMER "HOLLYHOCK."

Acting-Master, Meltiah Jordan; Acting-Master's Mate, Lewis Milk; Engineers: Acting-First-Assistant, J. F. Butler; Acting-Second-Assistants, Arthur Clements and S. B. Rannells; Acting-Third-Assistants, G. S. Pryor and Arthur Irwin.

STEAMER "COMMODORE."

Acting-Master, John R. Hamilton; Acting-Master's Mates, M. G. Nickerson and Richard Seward; Engineers: Acting-Third-Assistants, Wm. Connell, E. A. Hopkins and Sanford Curran.

STEAMER "GERTRUDE."

Acting-Master, Henry C. Wade; Acting-Assistant Surgeon, Adam Shirk; Acting-Assistant Paymaster, R. R. Brawley; Acting-Ensigns, Fred Newell, Wm. Shepherd and Horace Walton; Acting - Master's Mates, C. A. Osborne, Benj. Leeds and T. W. Jones; Engineers: Acting-Second-Assistant, C. P. Maples; Acting-Third-Assistants, F. C. Murrey, Philip Ketler and J. H. Nesson.

STEAMER "EUGENIE."

Acting - Ensign, N. M. Dyer; Acting - Master's Mates, John Locke and Edmund Aiken; Engineers: Acting - Second - Assistant, Wm. Morris; Acting-Third-Assistant, W. L. Wallace.

SHIP "FEAR-NOT."

Acting-Master, D. S. Murphy; Acting-Assistant Paymasters, T. E. Ryan and W. C. Cook; Acting-Ensign, M. H. Karlowski; Acting-Master's Mates, C. H. Blount and H. R. Rome.

SHIP "NIGHTINGALE."

Acting-Master, E. D. Bruner; Acting-Assistant Surgeon, John Flynn; Acting-Assistant Paymaster, H. D. Kimberly; Acting-Master's Mates, T. W. Stevens and Alonzo Gowdy.

SHIP "KITTATINNY."

Acting-Master, I. D. Seyburn; Acting-Assistant Paymaster, A. Depue; Acting-Ensigns, Henry Jackson, G. H. Barry, N. J. Blasdell and W. H. De Grosse; Acting-Master's Mates, J. W. Brown, W. H. Sprague and F. A. Johnson.

SHIP "PAMPERO."

Acting-Masters, F. E. Ellis and A. H. Mitchell; Acting-Assistant Surgeon, J. W. Langley; Acting-Assistant Paymaster, E. S. Wheeler.

BARK "J. C. KUHN."

Acting-Master, John F. Hardin; Acting-Ensigns, J. P. Pearson and Alex. Hanson.

BARKENTINE "HORACE BEALS."

Acting-Master, D. P. Heath; Acting - Master's Mate, Francis Keenan; Acting-Assistant Paymaster, Ichabod Norton.

BRIG "SEAFOAM."

Acting-Master, D. C. Woods; Acting - Master's Mate, George Woodland.

YACHT "CORYPHEUS."

Acting-Master, Francis H. Grove; Acting-Master's Mates, J. H. Gregory and H. H. Nicholson.

SCHOONER "MARIA WOOD."

Acting-Master, S. C. Cruse; Acting-Ensign, J. J. Kane; Acting-Master's Mate, Charles Fort.

SCHOONER "ORVETTA."

Acting-Master, Enos O. Adams; Acting-Master's Mates, John Broe and Stephen Nelson.

SCHOONER "JOHN GRIFFITHS."

Acting-Master, Henry Brown; Acting-Master's Mates, Alex. Moses and John McAllister.

SCHOONER "SAMUEL HOUSTON."

Acting-Master, C. W. Pratt.

SCHOONER "SARAH BRUEN."

Acting-Master, A. Christian.

SCHOONER "HENRY JANES."

Acting-Ensign. Joseph A. Chadwick; Acting-Master's Mates, T. S. Russell, Zach. Predmore and Wm. Roberts.

SCHOONER "OLIVER H. LEE."

Acting-Ensign, Douglas F. O'Brien; Acting-Master's Mate, Cornelius Dailey.

NAVAL STATION, NEW ORLEANS, LA.

Acting-Master, Adrien C. Starrett.

NAVAL HOSPITAL.

Surgeon, J. S. Dungan; Assistant Surgeon, J. H. Clark; Acting-Assistant Surgeon, W. H. Wentworth.

SOUTHWEST PASS.

Acting-Master, William Jones.

THE FOLLOWING OFFICERS PARTICIPATED IN THE BATTLE OF MOBILE BAY.

This list has been compiled from the official reports of the battle. The Navy Register for January 1, 1864, does not give them as part of the West Gulf Blockading Squadron, and they were, therefore, omitted in their proper places.

FLAG-SHIP "HARTFORD."

Lieutenant, A. R. Yates, Volunteer from the "Augusta"; Ensign, Wm. Starr Dana; Acting-Ensign, R. D. Bogart; Acting-Ensign, Joseph Marthon ("Tennessee"); Surgeon, Philip Lansdale; Acting-Assisting Engineer, Wm. G. McEwan; Admiral's Secretary, A. McKinley; Carpenter, George E. Burcham.

"LACKAWANNA."

Acting-Master, John H. Allen; Ensign, Clarence Rathbone; First-Assistant Engineer, James W. Whittaker.

"MONONGAHELA."

Lieutenant, Oliver A. Batcheller; Acting-Ensign, J. D. Ellis, ("Kennebec.")

"OCTORARA."

Acting-Masters, H. R. Billings ("Vincennes") and Horace S. Young; Acting-Ensign, Maurice W. McEntee; Acting-Assistant Paymaster, J. H. Pynchon; Acting-First-Assistant Engineer, Wm. W. Shipman had charge of Engineer's Department.

"KENNEBEC."

Acting-Assistant Surgeon, Geo. W. Hatch.

"ONEIDA."

Lieutenant, Chas. S. Cotton; Acting-Ensign,—— Hall; Acting-Master's Mate, John Devereux; Assistant Paymaster, Geo. R. Martin; Pilot, John V. Grivet; Paymaster's Clerk, W. P. Treadwell; Captain's Clerk, G. A. Ebbetts.

"MANHATTAN."

Commander, J. W. A. Nicholson; Lieutenant, C. M. Schoonmaker; Acting-Master, Robert B. Ely; Acting Ensign, John B. Trott; Acting-First-Assistant Engineer, Chas. L. Carty. [NOTE.—A more complete list cannot be obtained.]

"TECUMSEH."

*Commander, Tunis A. M. Craven; *Lieutenant, J. W. Kelly; Acting Master, C. F. Langley; Acting-Master, Gardner Cottrell; Acting-Ensign, John J. P. Zettick; *Acting Ensign, Robert Price; *Acting Ensign, Walter L. Titcomb; Pilot, John Collins; *Acting-Assistant Paymaster, George Work; *Chief Engineer, John Farron; *Second-Assistant Engineers, Elisha Harsen, F. S. Barlow and H. L. Leonard. [*Drowned by sinking of "Tecumseh."]

"BROOKLYN."

Captain, James Alden; Lieutenant-Commander, E. P. Lull; Lieutenants, Thomas L. Swann and Chas. F. Blake; Ensigns, Douglass R. Cassell, Chas. D. Sigsbee and C. H. Pendleton; Acting-Ensign, John Utter; Chief Engineer, Mortimer Kellogg; Acting-Third-Assistant Engineer, H. H. Arthur; Surgeon, George Maulsby; Captain of Marines, G. P. Houston; Captain, E. Denicke, U. S. A. (Signal Officer); Pilot, Christopher Lawrence; Acting-Master's Mates, Wm. H. Cook, F. C. Duncan and A. L. Stevens; Paymaster's Clerk,—— Baker; Boatswain, Chas. A. Bragdon; Acting-Gunner, John Quevedo; Carpenter, R. G. Thomas; Sailmaker, D. C. Brayton. [NOTE.—A more complete list cannot be obtained.]

"WINNEBAGO."

Commander, Thomas H. Stevens; Acting-Volunteer-Lieutenant, Wm. T. Shankland; First-Assistant Engineer, John Purdy; Pilot, Wm. H. Wroten; Acting-Gunner, Robert Sherman. [NOTE.—A more complete list cannot be obtained.]

"CHICKASAW."

Lieutenant-Commander, Geo. H. Perkins; Acting-Volunteer-Lieutenant, William Hamilton; Acting Master, E. D. Percy; Gunner, J. A. McDonald. [NOTE.—A more complete list cannot be obtained.]

CHAPTER XLV

THE CRUISE OF THE "SUMTER" AND THE HAVOC SHE COMMITTED.

IN granting belligerent rights to the Confederates, the United States Government not only yielded the claim that the secessionists were merely armed insurgents, but also yielded the right to the latter to fit out cruisers to prey on Northern commerce, for it was impossible to prescribe a mode of warfare for the Confederates to adopt. This view was also taken by the leading nations of Europe, who gave in many instances all the aid and comfort to the Confederate cruisers it was possible to extend. England permitted the Confederates to build and equip vessels in her ports and enlist English seamen, and they allowed the cruisers to roam at will over the ocean, plundering and destroying Federal merchant-ships.

Whether this policy of the British Government will be of any benefit to Great Britain in the end is doubtful, for, in case she should become involved in war, the same tactics, which were so effective against the United States, might be made even more disastrous to herself. The captures by these Confederate cruisers were finally paid for by the British Government, but such payments can only partially compensate the ship-owners or the country. The greatest damage, the interruption or destruction of trade, and the expense to which the United States Government was put in pursuing the cruisers, was never taken into account. No one seemed to think of the encouragement this wholesale destruction of American commerce gave the Confederates, who depended as much on that circumstance to bring about a peace as they did upon their armies.

In recognizing these cruisers, Great Britain and France were encouraging a kind of predatory warfare unknown in recent days. The Confederates, having no ports into which to send their prizes, burned or sank them wherever taken, so that their course was marked by burning hulls and

and it may not be uninteresting to give a sketch of his career.

While in the United States Navy, Semmes had little reputation as an officer. He had no particular taste for his profession, but had a fondness for literature and was a good talker and writer. He made a study of the law, and had he devoted himself to the legal profession would doubtless have been very successful. He was indolent and fond of his comfort, so that altogether his associates in the Navy gave him credit for very little energy.

What was, then, the astonishment of his

COMMANDER (AFTERWARDS REAR-ADMIRAL) RAPHAEL SEMMES, C. S. NAVY.

floating debris. Their Courts of Admiralty were on the high seas, and the commanding officers were the judges whether to destroy vessel and cargo or to transfer the latter to their own holds. Whether portions of valuable cargoes were sold in neutral ports, for the purpose of procuring coal and other supplies, is a point not fully ascertained; but it is not likely that men in command of cruisers, whose legality was somewhat doubtful, should be over-scrupulous of the means by which to carry out their cherished objects.

Captain Raphael Semmes, in the "Alabama," was perhaps the most vindictive of all the officers of the Confederate Navy,

old companions to find that Semmes was pursuing a course that required the greatest skill and vigor; for there never was a naval commander who in so short a time committed such depredations on an enemy's commerce, or who so successfully eluded the vessels sent in pursuit of him, up to the time of the sinking of the "Alabama."

Semmes was the last man to have embarked in the business of destroying Northern commerce, for during his service in the war with Mexico he wrote an interesting book, giving an insight into the character of the Mexican people. At the time of his writing this book, the Mexican Government was discussing the project of issuing letters of marque to vessels, authorizing them to prey upon the commerce of the United States. Lieutenant Semmes took the ground that all such cruisers should be treated as pirates, since they had no ports into which they could take captured vessels, but must destroy them on the high seas. The events of 1861-65 changed Semmes' opinions, and the convictions he so strongly maintained up to the year 1861 vanished when he was offered a vessel by which he could inflict damage on United States commerce, with the prospect of high reward in the future for his services in burning and sinking.

We wish, in our narrative, to be just to all parties, but we cannot justify Semmes' course, even although he may have had a shadow of international law to plead in his defence. He might have joined the Southern Army or Navy, as many others did, and fought to the utmost of his ability, and nothing would now be laid against him; but for a man born under the Stars and Stripes, and who had spent the greater part of his life to middle age in holding himself ready to defend the flag, to turn and bend all his energies to the destruction of Federal unarmed merchant vessels, there seems to be no justification. It would have been better to have left that part of the Confederate war operations to some of the enthusiastic merchant captains of the South who honestly believed in the secession theory, and were not bound by a solemn oath to support the Constitution and laws of the United States.

Commander Semmes asserted that he withdrew his oath of allegiance to the United States because he considered the Southern States had a right to dissolve partnership with those of the North. He believed the South to have had greater justification than had the United Colonies when they declared their independence of Great Britain. The South had no actual grievances. They wished to extend their slave system, which was objected to by the North, and by the election of a Republican President they were ruled out of power held for twenty years, and given to understand that there should be no further extension of slavery, which the vast majority of Northern people considered a blot on our escutcheon.

It was Semmes' duty as an officer of the Government to help put down insurrection in whatever quarter or in whatever shape it might appear, for armies and navies are intended for such purposes as well as for carrying on war with foreign enemies. What would become of any Government in Europe if, at the breaking out of an insurrection, the military forces should object to serving against their compatriots? An officer of the Army or Navy who has engaged to support the *de facto* Government of the country can lay no claim to allegiance to State or city, and if he violates his oath to support the Government he simply becomes a traitor and liable to the penalty of death. Commander Semmes could hardly have expected to draw fifty thousand dollars or more in pay from the United States Government—which is about the amount he received up to the date of his resignation—and then at the first speck of trouble go off and fight against it. His case is much worse than that of a private citizen whose interests are bound up in a particular locality, and who owes no special allegiance to the General Government except such as may be dictated by the impulses of patriotism.

Being a native of Maryland, Semmes had not even the excuse of siding with his State, for if he had he would have fought against the South. This difficulty he easily skips over by claiming to be a citizen of Alabama, yet he stigmatizes, as "traitors to their States" officers of Southern birth who remained loyal to the Union. Semmes has published what he doubtless considered a masterly argument in defence of his cause; but, although he speaks of Webster and Story with great contempt, he was hardly equal to either of them as a constitutional lawyer, and the secession fallacy has been so thoroughly exposed that we have no fears of another civil war based on State Rights theories.

Commander Semmes resigned his commission in the United States Navy on the 15th of February, 1861, and made the best of his way to the capitol of the Southern Confederacy, temporarily fixed at Montgomery, Alabama. On his arrival he put himself in communication with Mr. Conrad, Chairman of the Confederate States Naval Committee, and when President Davis reached the city, a few days afterwards, offered his services to the Confederate Government. They were at once accepted, and Semmes proceeded to Washington, after a visit to Richmond and Harper's Ferry, to ascertain the character of certain machinery at the latter place, in anticipation of the enlargement of the Tredagar Works at Richmond, for the South meant war from the beginning, in case of any attempt on the part of the Northern States to prevent them from carrying out their designs.

When the Confederate Government had been fairly organized, they found themselves badly supplied with materials from which to improvise a Navy, and Semmes here made himself useful, being the first to propose "a well-organized system of private armed ships called privateers." Mr. Mallory, the Confederate Secretary of the Navy, readily agreed to all that Commander Semmes proposed; for the latter, being much the cleverer man of the two, provided the Secretary with ideas which he was only too willing to accept.

A Board of Confederate naval officers assembled in New Orleans charged with the duty of procuring, as speedily as possible, some swift, light-armed steamers that could be used to prey upon Northern commerce; and the Federal Navy was in such a disorganized condition that the Confederate Government might well feel secure in sending out these light cruisers, for they would hardly meet with any interference until they had swept the whole Northern coast.

Several vessels were examined by the Board, among them was a 500-ton sea-steamer with a speed of ten knots, but with capacity for but five days' coal, and with no accommodations for the crew required by a vessel-of-war. She was condemned by the Board, and the report sent to the Secretary of the Navy, who showed it to Commander Semmes. The latter at once exclaimed: "Give me that ship, I think I can make her answer the purpose." The request was granted, and officers were at once detailed to accompany Semmes on his cruise for the destruction of Northern commerce.

Semmes was certainly the very man the Confederates wanted for the occasion. He manifested no doubts of success with the vessel, and seemed to have no fear of the consequences. The inertness he had displayed while in the United States Navy had disappeared; he had become a new man. "The labors and associations of a lifetime had been inscribed in a volume that had been closed, and a new book, whose pages were as yet all blank, had been opened." Semmes' volume, we might also add, though containing matter sufficient for a dozen books, embraced not an account of one act of bravery or generosity, but only records of burning, sinking, and destroying, worthy of the buccaneers.

Semmes was appointed to command the "Sumter" with the rank of commander, the same rank that he had held in the United States Navy, for the Confederates were slow in conferring increased rank until sure that their officers had earned a reward. The following order from Mr. Mallory was sent to Semmes the day after his interview with that gentlemen:

CONFEDERATE STATES OF AMERICA,
NAVY DEPARTMENT,
MONTGOMERY, April 18, 1861.

SIR — You are hereby detached from duty as Chief of the Light-house Bureau, and will proceed to New Orleans and take command of the steamer "Sumter"—named in honor of our recent victory over Fort Sumter. The following officers have been ordered to report to you for duty: Lieutenants John M. Kell, R. T. Chapman, J. M. Stribling and William T. Evans; Paymaster Henry Myers; Surgeon Francis L. Galt; Midshipmen Wm. A.

Hicks, Richard F. Armstrong, Albert G. Hudgins, John F. Holden and Joseph D. Wilson.

I am respectfully, your obedient servant,
S. R. MALLORY,
Secretary of the Navy.

On the 22d of April, Semmes took command of his vessel in New Orleans. The "Sumter" was simply a coasting steamer, cumbered with upper cabins, and with apparently none of the attributes of a ship-of-war. Who would imagine that so much harm lurked in that frail vessel? though her graceful lines and jaunty air pleased her commander, who seemed to have had a vivid idea of the destruction he could accomplish with this little craft.

Frenchmen are popularly supposed to be prone to revolution, and the enthusiasm of the French population of Louisiana had been early excited at the idea of the secession of the Southern States. Almost immediately, preparations were made by unauthorized persons to prey upon United States commerce, and several vessels were captured and taken to New Orleans. The Federal Government became alarmed at the probable consequences of a wholesale system of privateering, and President Lincoln at once issued his Proclamation.

As soon as it became evident that hostilities had broken out between the United States and the seceding members of the Union, European Governments, with singular unanimity, declared their neutrality between the contending parties, and their intention to treat both alike; viz., that neither United States nor Confederate cruisers should take their prizes into neutral ports. At first sight, this looked like a concession to the United States, as it excluded Confederate prizes from European ports; but it was really the other way, since it recognized the Confederates as belligerents. Commander Semmes was shrewd enough to know what this arrangement portended, and such was his confidence that he made a requisition before sailing simply for the modest amount of ten thousand dollars, saying, "This will suffice until I have the opportunity of replenishing my military chest from the enemy." How readily he adopted that word "enemy," when scarcely three months from the service of the Government that had fostered him for thirty-six years! We may be too sentimental on this point, but, no doubt, our feelings will be shared by many of our readers.

There was no end to Semmes' trials and disappointments in his task of fitting out the "Sumter," and the patience and energy he exhibited were worthy of a better cause. On June 3d, 1861, the ship was put in commission, and her commander gazed proudly on the "Stars and Bars" floating from her peak. Having received his sailing orders,

Semmes dropped down to the forts preparatory to getting to sea past the blockading vessels at the mouths of the Mississippi—the "Powhatan," Lieutenant D. D. Porter, at Southwest Pass, and the "Brooklyn," Commander Charles H. Poor, at Pass à l'Outre. Semmes' sailing orders were brief and to the purpose. He was to burn, sink and destroy, within the limits prescribed by the laws of nations, and with due attention to the laws of humanity. After long watching and waiting, Semmes made his escape to sea by the Pass à l'Outre, while the "Brooklyn" was absent from that mouth of the river in chase of a vessel some eight miles to westward. As soon as the black smoke of the "Sumter" was seen coming down the river, the "Brooklyn" started to return to her anchorage, and had nearly the same distance as the "Sumter" to run before reaching the bar, but the latter vessel had the advantage of a four-knot current in her favor, while the "Brooklyn" had the current against her.

The "Sumter" with a skillful pilot passed the bar while the "Brooklyn" was three and a half miles distant from it, and out of gun-shot. The engineers and firemen of both vessels did their whole duty, and thick volumes of smoke poured from the chimneys. The "Sumter" went off at the rate of nine and a half knots, while the "Brooklyn," to assist her speed, set every sail that would draw. The "Sumter" also set her sails, bracing them up sharp on the starboard-tack.

The "Brooklyn" was at this time a little on the weather quarter of the "Sumter," and as Semmes knew he could lay closer to the wind than his pursuer, having the advantage of larger fore-and-aft sail, he resolved to hold his wind so closely as to compel the "Brooklyn" to furl her sails, although this would carry him athwart her bows and bring him perhaps a little nearer for the next half-hour or so. A rain squall now enveloped the two vessels, hiding them from each other; but as the squall passed away and the sloop-of-war reappeared, she seemed to Semmes to be much nearer, and he began to think his chance of escape very dubious. As Semmes stood looking at the "Brooklyn" coming on astern, he could not but admire the majesty of her appearance, with her broad flaring bow and clean, beautiful run, with her masts and yards as taunt and square as can only be seen in a ship-of-war. The Stars and Stripes appeared from time to time under the lee of the spanker, and with a glass a crowd of officers could be seen on the quarter-deck apparently watching the efforts of the "Sumter" to escape.

As the "Brooklyn" still gained on the Confederate vessel, Semmes ordered the paymaster to prepare to throw his iron chest and all its contents overboard, an incident which shows what gloomy forebodings must have possessed him when he was ready to sacrifice the precious treasure which was to aid him in his career of destruction. Coming from fresh into salt water had caused the "Sumter's" boilers to "foam," which circumstance prevented her for a while from getting up as good a supply of steam as would otherwise have been the case; but at the crisis of the chase the foaming ceased, and the engineer reported the engine working beautifully. At the same time, the breeze freshened and favored the "Sumter;" and what was more, the latter was eating the "Brooklyn" out of the wind, yet the latter vessel did not fire a gun.

Semmes naturally supposed that as soon as the "Brooklyn" fell in his wake she would furl her sails, and this shortly came to pass, and for the first time Semmes began to breathe a little easy. He had feared that, instead of pursuing a career of destruction, he would be taken prisoner and tried for violating the President's proclamation, while his little cruiser would be turned into a Yankee blockader. But Semmes' good fortune—or perhaps we might rather say his evil fortune—decreed otherwise. The "Brooklyn" was under sail to royals when suddenly every sail in the ship was clewed up at once, the yards came down together and the men laid out to furl. In less than three minutes every stitch of canvas had vanished. If the crew of the "Brooklyn" had had any visions of prize-money, they evaporated a few minutes after this beautiful evolution which even the Confederate officers admired. In their hearts they could not help being proud of the skill and discipline of "the Old Navy," and comparing the seamen of the service they had abandoned with the heterogeneous crew of the "Sumter," that they had not yet time to discipline.

It seems strange to us, as it did to Semmes, that this beautiful evolution of the "Brooklyn" was not followed by a ricochet-shot from the bow gun of that ship, for the Confederates evidently thought themselves within range; but not a shot was fired during the pursuit. This was perhaps one of the most exciting chases of the war. Semmes knew perfectly well the exact speed of the "Brooklyn," which was about the same as that of the "Sumter," and believed if he could hold his own until dark that he could elude his enemy after nightfall; but he never expected the "Brooklyn" to abandon the chase as long as the "Sumter" remained in sight.

When the sloop-of-war furled her sails the "Sumter" began to draw slightly ahead, as steam was crowded on her boilers almost to the bursting point. Then the engineer reported the journals as heating so much that the brasses would soon melt. That meant capture, and all waited for the first shot from the "Brooklyn," announcing that their fate was sealed. No shot came, and the "Sumter" still gained, if only a trifle. Just then the "Brooklyn" put her helm a-starboard, went around in the opposite direction and abandoned the chase, returning to Pass à l'Outre, where there was no longer anything to blockade, as the bird had flown ; while the "Sumter" slowed her engines until the journals cooled down, and her crew gave three cheers for the Confederate flag. The shades of night soon hid the vessel from any possible pursuit.

Many were the criticisms on the escape of the "Sumter," which, as they may do injustice, we will not here repeat. Naval officers, as a rule, are disposed to give credit for skill and gallantry from whatever quarter it may come, and all agreed that Semmes' escape in the "Sumter" was a bold and dashing adventure.

Great latitude had been given Semmes in his instructions, and his plan was to make a cruise upon the coast of Cuba, destroy all American shipping he could meet with in that quarter, coal at some convenient point, and finally proceed to Brazil. Accordingly, the "Sumter" steamed along the coast of Cuba, in the direct track of vessels bound for the Gulf, and while between the coast and the Isle of Pines two sail were reported in sight, both standing in the same direction with the Confederate. When within signal distance, the British ensign was displayed by the latter, and the nearest vessel proving to be a Spanish brig, was permitted to proceed. The other, though she showed no colors, was soon discovered to be an American, and a shot was fired—the first that was fired afloat by ex-naval officers at an American vessel. The "hateful" Stars and Stripes were soon run up to the stranger's peak, but it awoke no sentiment of remorse or regret in the bosoms of the "Sumter's" officers. Every noble sentiment was sacrificed to a wild idea which was mistaken for duty.

It is impossible for us to understand the feeling of joy and exultation that was evinced at the capture of the first American merchant ship, unarmed and helpless. This first prize, Semmes records, was from the "Black Republican State of Maine," and when her flag was hoisted—the flag which Semmes had been educated to venerate, but which now seemed the very incarnation of all that was hateful—the "Sumter" showed at her peak the emblem of the Confederacy, a flag which might easily have been mistaken for that of Hayti or the Society Islands, whose cruisers if met upon the high seas would be naturally objects of suspicion. To Semmes, the Stars and Stripes appeared to look abashed in the presence of the latest symbol of Southern sovereignty, "as a burglar might be supposed to feel who had been caught in the act of looking into a gentleman's house." Some of our readers may differ in opinion with the gallant captain and think that the master of the merchant vessel had a right to be astonished in finding a cruiser, which he supposed to be policing the seas, turn out a marauder. Semmes avers that he felt some pity for the captain of the merchantman, but this sentiment was not in sufficient quantity to delay his doom.

The master of the vessel, a mild, amiable-looking man, when he found into what hands he had fallen, merely expressed his surprise at the appearance of the Confederate flag in Cuban waters. The name of the prize was the "Golden Rocket," an appropriate one, for she would go off in a blaze, and be remembered in history as the first illegal prize made by a Confederate vessel-of-war — for Semmes had no more right to capture her than he had to seize the Spanish vessel he first encountered. Semmes at the time was simply an insurgent like Lopez, the Cuban "fillibuster," who was garotted in the plaza at Havana, (because belligerent rights had not been accorded him,) and he was under the ban of proclamation.

By sunset the wind had died away, and the night came on of such pitchy darkness as would seem emblematical of the deed about to be committed. The crew of the "Golden Rocket," and everything on board the vessel needed by the "Sumter," had been transferred to that vessel. The boat which had been sent on the errand of destruction pulled out of sight, and neither ship nor boat could be seen by the watchers who crowded the decks of the "Sumter," although but a few yards distant. Suddenly one of the crew of the "Sumter" exclaimed, "She is on fire !"

The decks of the doomed vessel were of pine, the seams caulked with oakum and payed with pitch, while her forecastle was stored with paints and oil, therefore the flames leaped at once into the darkness. The boarding officer had done his work like an adept, and applied the torch in several parts of the ship, and the flames rushed up through three apertures, lighting up the scene as plainly as if the drama had been enacted on the stage of a theatre. The masts and hull of the "Sumter" were reflected on the mirror-like sea, and the dense columns of smoke ascending to the skies seemed like a grand funeral pyre. The rush of air into the hold of the burning ship added every moment new fury to the flames, which now ascended to the trucks, raging like a mighty furnace in full blast. The ship had been laid to with her maintopsail to the mast, and all her light canvass was flying loose about the yards, the headsails hanging from the booms, and the forked tongues of flame ran rapidly up the shrouds and from the tops to the light sails fluttering in the breeze. A topgallantsail or royal all on fire would now fly off from the yard and settle upon the surface of the sea like some fiery albatross, then followed yards in flames till the sea was lighted up by a hundred floating lamps. At one time the intricate network of cordage was traced as with a pencil of fire upon the black sky. Then the masts went by the board, the mainmast being the last to fall with a crash, as when in the northern forest it fell by the stroke of the woodman. Numbers of sea-birds flew round the burning ship, their discordant cries contributing to the horror of the scene; but at length the fire

CONFEDERATE STEAM-CRUISER "SUMTER."

burned down, the vengeance of man was satisfied, and the "Sumter" moved away by the light of the expiring flames in pursuit of other prey.

Of all men in the Southern Confederacy Semmes was perhaps the best qualified to carry out the designs of his employers on the commerce of the United States. The burning of the "Golden Rocket" was like the first glass of liquor taken by the drunkard. Burning ships became a passion, and if ever a man had the bump of destructiveness on his cranium that man was Raphael Semmes. He slept peacefully that night in the thought that he had performed a meritorious action, one that would inure to the cause of Southern liberty fighting against the Northern people, who after twenty years of Southern domination had dared to elect a President to suit themselves.

According to the Law of Nations the "Sumter" was not a vessel of war. When

the South had belligerent rights accorded them by the United States the case was different. As we have said before, the captain of the "Golden Rocket" took the destruction of his ship philosophically, although, apart from any monetary considerations, it must have been hard to see her set on fire and consumed before his eyes without power to raise a hand to save her; but one consolation the master had, the ship was insured, and the loss fell on the underwriters.

But what became of the "old flag"? It was marked with the date of capture, latitude and longitude, etc., and consigned to a bag in charge of the Signal Quartermaster to keep company ere long with numerous other copies of the Stars and Stripes that accumulated under Semmes' auspices ere his career was brought to a close by the guns of the "Kearsarge." As Semmes writes: "I committed to the keeping of the guardian spirits of that famous battle-ground a great many bags full of 'old flags,' to be stowed away in the caves of the sea as mementoes that a nation once lived whose naval officers loved liberty more than the false memorial of it under which they had once served, and who were capable, when it became 'Hate's polluted rag,' of tearing it down." Yet who can doubt that Commander Semmes, in case the Confederate Navy officers had been reinstated in the Federal service, would have been among the first to resume his station under that "polluted rag," again to forswear his allegiance, if it suited his convenience so to do.

The day following the destruction of the "Golden Rocket" was the 4th of July, an anniversary which had ever been venerated by all true Americans ; but it was not celebrated on board the "Sumter," because associated so intimately with the "old flag," which, in the opinion of Commander Semmes and his followers, had all at once become a sham and a deceit. It was also, in the opinion of these persons connected "with the wholesale robberies which had been committed on Southern property, and with the vilification and abuse which had been heaped upon their persons by their late copartners for a generation or more." What generosity could be expected by his foes from an intelligent man holding such sentiments as these ?

At daylight next morning two sail were reported in sight ahead, which proved to be two American brigantines. The "Sumter" hoisted the Confederate flag, ran alongside and captured the vessels, both of which were loaded with sugar and molasses belonging to neutrals, and both bound from Trinidad de Cuba to English ports. These vessels Semmes did not venture to burn, but taking them in tow he steamed for

Cienfuegos, in order to test the disposition of the Spanish authorities towards the Confederacy. France and England had issued proclamations forbidding the introduction of prizes to their ports, but Spain had not yet spoken, and Semmes hoped the Spanish officials might have different views. The vessels together being more than the "Sumter" could tow, the prize-master of the "Cuba" was ordered to cast off and follow; but when the former got out of sight, the master and crew of the "Cuba" overpowered the prize-crew, recaptured the vessel, and eluding their captors, finally reached their destination.

On arriving off the harbor of Cienfuegos two more sail were descried from the "Sumter," standing off the land. Two more American brigantines were captured—the "Ben Dunning" of Maine, and the "Albert Adams" of Massachusetts. They had left the port of Cienfuegos three hours before, and their cargoes of sugar were documented as Spanish property. Prize-crews were thrown on board, and the prize-masters directed to stand in for Cienfuegos light-house and lay-to until morning.

Thus in the space of three days, Semmes had captured five prizes heavily laden. His crew had become quite enamored of the service, which just suited these worthy successors of Lafitte, who were mostly from the city of New Orleans, which could then boast of possessing the worst class of seamen in the country. Without doubt, there were a number of persons on board the "Sumter" who acknowledged no allegiance to any nation, and whose love of plunder would incite them to any disreputable deed. To such men the American flag conveyed no sentiment any more than did the flag of the Confederacy. Under the latter they might hope to plunder, and, no doubt, shipped with this expectation. If they were disappointed, it was because there was an innate love of discipline among their officers which forbade their entering on a course which might ultimately subject them to severe penalties. The crew were as eager in pursuit of vessels as dogs in chase of game, but they were too ignorant to know that burning and destroying could bring them no profit.

As daylight broke with all the beauty of a tropical morning, and the prizes moved sluggishly waiting for the sea-breeze, three American vessels in tow of a steam-tug were seen coming out of the harbor. Here was a piece of good fortune! Semmes had reckoned on carrying three prizes into Cienfuegos; here were three more, but he could not molest them in neutral waters—a little management was necessary. The neutral belt extended a marine league from the shore, so Semmes hoisted a Spanish

jack for a pilot, giving orders to disarrange the yards, etc., that the "Sumter" might look as much like a merchant vessel as possible. To still further carry out the deceit, most of the crew were sent below and the Spanish ensign hoisted. These were the very tactics adopted by Lafitte, the Barratarian, in the early part of this century, which would indicate that Semmes had taken a leaf from his book.

The prize-masters showed themselves adepts in following the methods of their commander and hoisted the American flag at the fore of their respective prize-vessels for a pilot also. This deceived the people on board the vessels coming out, and they proceeded on their way in tow of the tug until they were well off the land, when they cast off and made all sail to enable them to get a good offing before the sea-breeze set in.

As soon as the tug had cast off from the vessels she proceeded to the steamer to ask if the captain wanted a pilot, for even the Spaniards had been deceived by Semmes' ruse. The Confederate commander replied in the affirmative, but said to the pilot: "I am waiting a little to take back those ships you have just towed out." "Diablo!" exclaimed the Spaniard; "how can that be? they are North Americans bound to Boston and New York." "That is just what I want," said Semmes. "We are Confederates, at war with the North Americans." "Ah!" said the pilot, turning *picaroon* at the first sign of plunder, "That is good; give her the steam quick, captain!" Here was a scoundrel, who had just piloted these vessels to sea and received his pay, ready to pounce upon them and take them back again for another fee. Nothing could better please that sort of man than this game of semi-piracy. Probably he was a descendant of some of those pirates who infested the Spanish West Indies in 1824-26, murdering the crews of American merchant vessels, plundering their cargoes, and then destroying the vessels.

Semmes was determined not to lay himself liable for violating any neutrality laws; he was too conscientious for that. He said to the impatient pilot, "Wait awhile, I must not fail in respect to Her Majesty the Queen of Spain and the Captain-General. I must wait until these vessels are beyond their jurisdiction, one league from shore." So when the American vessels were supposed to be beyond the imaginary line, the "Sumter" was let loose like a tiger on its prey. A booming gun and the hoisting of the Confederate flag soon disclosed the "Sumter's" character, and in a short time the three vessels were prizes to the Confederate steamer and joined the others off Cienfuegos. When the sea-breeze set in,

Semmes stood into the harbor, followed by his six prizes, much to the astonishment of those who had seen the "West Wind" of Rhode Island, the "Louisa Killum" of Massachusetts, and the "Naiad" of New York, sail but a few hours before on their legitimate business.

Semmes was treated at Cienfuegos with all due courtesy, and hobnobbed with the Captain of the Port, who had at first fired upon him with musketry, not knowing what flag he sailed under; but when Semmes assured him that he did not come to sack the town like the buccaneers of old, the official took him to his heart. He had but a vague idea of the locality of the Southern Confederacy, and probably never suspected that the "North American" expeditions against the island were mostly fitted out from the Southern States—the fair haven of fillibusters.

Semmes wrote a specious letter to the Governor of Cienfuegos, a timid old man, who knew as little of international law as his friend the pilot. This letter may not agree with the opinions of our standard authorities on international law, but the originality of its views should preserve it from oblivion. Unfortunately for the enterprising sea-lawyer, the letter had exactly the contrary effect to what he had expected. The Spanish officials saw plainly that their harbors were about to be made the receptacles for prizes, and the Spanish Government, following the example of England and France, issued a proclamation that no prizes should be brought into their ports. Therefore, as soon as the Queen's proclamation was received, the Captain-General ordered all the prizes to be restored to their legitimate owners. Spain was not going to lose her best customer, nor be liable to a suit for damages from the United States after the civil war was over.

The commander of the "Sumter" naturally felt despondent over this decision of the Spanish authorities, and it may have influenced him somewhat in his subsequent career, when he burned and sank without much thought whether he was acting according to international law or not. The following is the letter to the Governor referred to above:

CONFEDERATE STATES STEAMER "SUMTER," ISLAND OF CUBA, July 6, 1861.

SIR—I have the honor to inform you of my arrival at the port of Cienfuegos with seven prizes of war. These vessels are the brigantines "Cuba," "Machias," "Ben Dunning," "Albert Adams," and "Naiad," and barks "West Wind" and "Louisa Killum," property of citizens of the United States; which States, as your Excellency is aware, are waging an aggressive and unjust war upon the Confederate States, which I have the honor with this ship under my command to represent.

I have sought a port of Cuba with these prizes, with the expectation that Spain will extend to the cruisers of the Confederate States the same friendly reception that, in similar circumstances, she would extend to the cruisers of the enemy; in other words, that she will permit me to leave the captured vessels within her jurisdiction until they can be adjudicated by a Court of Admiralty of the Confederate States. As a people maintaining a Government *de facto*, and not only holding the enemy in check, but gaining advantages over him, we are entitled to all the rights of belligerents, and I confidently rely upon the friendly disposition of Spain, who is our near neighbor in the most important of her colonial possessions, to receive us with equal and even-handed justice, if not with the sympathy which our identity of interests and policy, with regard to an important social and industrial institution, are so well calculated to inspire. A rule which would exclude our prizes from her ports during the war, although it should be applied in terms equally to the enemy, would not, I respectfully suggest, be an equitable or just rule. The basis of such rule, as indeed of all the conduct of a neutral during war, is equal and impartial justice to all the belligerents, without inclining to the side of either; and this should be a substantial and practical justice, and not exist in terms merely, which may be deceptive. Now, a little reflection will, I think, show your Excellency, that the rule in question, in the exclusion of prizes of both belligerents from neutral ports, cannot be applied in the present war, without operating with great injustice to the Confederate States. It is well known to your Excellency that the United States are a manufacturing and commercial people, while the Confederate States are an agricultural people. The consequence of this dissimilarity of pursuits was that, at the breaking out of the war, the former had within their limits and control almost all the naval force of the old Government. This naval force they have dishonestly seized and turned against the Confederate States, regardless of the just claims of the latter to a large proportion of it, as tax-payers, out of whose contributions to the common treasury it was created. The United States, by this disseizin of the property of the Confederate States, are enabled in the first months of the war to blockade all the ports of the latter States. In this condition of things observe the *practical* working of the rule I am discussing, whatever may be the seeming fairness of its terms.

It will be admitted that we have equal belligerent rights with the enemy. One of the most important of these rights in a war against a commercial people is that which I have just exercised, of capturing his property on the high seas. But how are the Confederate States to enjoy, to its full extent, the benefit of this right if their cruisers are not permitted to enter neutral ports with their prizes, and retain them there, in safe custody, until they can be condemned and disposed of? They cannot send them into their own ports, for the reason already mentioned, namely, that those ports are hermetically sealed by the agency of their own ships, forcibly wrested from them. If they cannot send them into neutral ports, where are they to send them? Nowhere. Except for the purpose of destruction, therefore, their right of capture would be entirely defeated by the adoption of the rule in question, while the opposite belligerent would not be inconvenienced by it at all, as all his own ports are open to him. I take it for granted that Spain will not think of acting upon so unjust and unequal a rule.

But another question arises, indeed, has already arisen, in the cases of some of the very captures which I have brought into port. The cargoes of several of the vessels are claimed, as appears by certificates from among the papers, as Spanish property. This fact, cannot, of course, be verified, except by a judicial proceeding, in the Prize Courts of the Confederate States. But if the prizes cannot be sent either into the ports of the Confederate States or into neutral ports, how can this verification be made? Further--supposing there to be no dispute about the title to the cargo, how is it to be unladen and delivered to the neutral claimant unless the captured ship can make a port? Indeed, one of the motives which influenced me in making a Spanish colonial port was the fact that these cargoes were claimed by Spanish subjects, whom I was desirous of putting to as little inconvenience as possible, in the unlading and reception of their property, should it be restored to them by a decree of the Confederate Courts. It will be for your Excellency to consider and act upon these grave questions, touching alike the interests of both our Governments.

I have the honor to be, &c., &c.
RAPHAEL SEMMES.

Semmes remarks:

" I did not expect much to grow immediately out of the above communication. Indeed, as the reader will probably surmise, I had written it more for the eye of the Spanish Premier than for that of the Governor of a small provincial town who had no diplomatic power and whom I knew to be timid, as are all the subordinate officers of absolute Governments. I presumed that the Governor would telegraph it to the Captain General at Havana, and that the latter would hold the subject in abeyance until he could hear from the home Government.

" Nor was I disappointed in this expectation, for Lieutenant Chapman returned from Cienfuegos the next morning, and brought me intelligence to this effect.

" To dispose of the question raised, without the necessity of again returning to them, the reader is informed that Spain, in due time, followed the lead of England and France in the matter of excluding prizes from her ports; and that my prizes were delivered—to whom do you think, reader? You will naturally say to myself, or my duly appointed agent, with instructions to take them out of the Spanish port. This was the result to be logically expected. The Captain-General had received them, in trust, as it were, to abide the decision of his Government. If that decision should be in favor of receiving the prizes of both belligerents, well; if not, I expected to be notified to take them away. But nothing was further, it seems, from the intention of the Captain-General than this simple and just proceeding; for, as soon as the Queen's proclamation was received, he deliberately handed back all my prizes to their original owners ! "

But the Confederates were not without comfort. Sympathizers flocked to them from the town on their landing. The houses of the principal citizens were open to the officers, and the night was made merry by the popping of champagne corks. Yet Commander Semmes was not happy, though he regretted less the loss of his prizes than his failure to convince the Spanish authorities that he was a great expounder of the law of nations. Meanwhile the natives wondered where all the United States gun-boats were, that this Confederate hawk should be permitted thus to flutter the Yankee dovecotes. The reader will, no doubt, share their astonishment at the failure of the Navy Department to protect Federal commerce in the Caribbean Sea as well as in other quarters. The fact is, every passage to that sea ought to have been guarded as soon as it was known the "Sumter" had escaped, and she should have been followed up until captured or driven from the ocean.

Commander Semmes having appointed a prize-agent to take charge of his prizes until they could be taken to a Southern port for adjudication before a Court of Admiralty, and obtained a supply of coal and provisions from his neutral friends at Cienfuegos, departed from that port on the 8th of July with the intention of proceeding via Barbadoes to Cape St. Roque, in the great line of travel for vessels bound from the East Indies to the United States or Europe. Owing to the strength of the trade-winds his coal ran short, and he made sail for the Dutch island of Curaçoa, and on the 16th the "Sumter" entered the port of St. Anne—the capital town of this little colony. The American consul did all he could to persuade the Governor that the "Sumter" was not a legitimate vessel-of-war, and that officer, therefore, forbade the ship's entering the port, saying that he had received recent orders from Holland to that effect. Semmes was, however, well aware that these colonial magnates were generally men of little character or intelligence, so he sent one of his brightest officers on shore with the following letter to the Governor:

CONFEDERATE STATES STEAMER "SUMTER." ⎱
OFF ST. ANNE'S, CURACOA, July 17, 1861. ⎰

His Excellency Governor Crol:

I was surprised to receive by the pilot, this morning, a message from your Excellency, to the effect that this ship would not be permitted to enter the harbor unless she was in distress, as your Excellency had received orders from your Government not to admit vessels-of-war of the Confederate States of America to the hospitality of the ports under your Excellency's command. I most respectfully suggest that there must be some mistake here, and I have sent to you the bearer, Lieutenant Chapman, of the Confederate States Navy, for the purpose of explanation. Your Excellency must be under some misapprehension as to the character of this vessel. She is a ship-of-war duly commissioned by the Government of the Confederate States, which States have been recognized as belligerents, in the present war, by all the leading powers of Europe, viz.: Great Britain, France, Spain, etc., as your Excellency must be aware.

It is true, that these Powers have prohibited both belligerents, alike, from bringing prizes into their several jurisdictions; but no one of them has made a distinction, either between the respective prizes, or the cruisers themselves, of the two belligerents—the cruisers of both Governments, unaccompanied by prizes, being admitted to the hospitalities of the ports of all these great Powers on terms of perfect equality. In the face of these facts, am I to understand from your Excellency that Holland has adopted a different rule, and that she not only excludes the prizes, but the ships-of-war themselves, of the Confederate States? And this at the same time that she admits the cruisers of the United States; thus departing from her neutrality, in this war, ignoring the Confederate States as belligerents and aiding and abetting their enemy?

"If this be the position which Holland has assumed in this contest, I pray your Excellency to be kind enough to say as much to me in writing."

When the Governor had read this communication, he summoned all the civil and military dignitaries of the colony, and it took a lot of thinking, talking, smoking and drinking to get the matter fairly imbedded in their brains, the Confederate officer in the meanwhile making friends with the citizens, and helping them with their drinking, which seems to have been their main employment.

After waiting an hour or two, Semmes thought he would go to quarters and fire a few shells at a target; but it so happened that one of the shells passed across a window of the room where the council was in session—the "Sumter" was not more than fifty yards from the mouth of the narrow harbor—and exploding, shook the little town as if by an earthquake. Up flew the windows of the council-room, and out popped the heads of the dignitaries. It was decided *nem. con.* that the Confederacy should be recognized, and the "Sumter" allowed to enter the port, which she did shortly afterwards. Nothing could exceed the enthusiasm with which the "Sumter" was received at Curaçoa. Semmes and his officers were the heroes of the hour. The ten thousand dollars with which he had started seemed inexhaustible.

Everything needed was supplied to the ship without a question, and Semmes was everywhere honored as the representative of the great Southern Confederacy, although few people had the least idea what that was. While at St. Anne's Semmes missed a great opportunity. President Castro, one of the South American adventurers, requested his assistance to reinstate him in the presidential chair of Venezuela; but the Confederate officer declined to play the part of a Warwick. Castro claimed to be President *de jure*, but Semmes professed to scorn all Governments except those that were *de facto*.

After remaining a week at St. Anne's and accomplishing all he wanted, Semmes bade adieu to his kind friends and steamed out of the harbor on the 24th of July. Curaçoa lies but a short distance from the coast of Venezuela, and as both the ports of La Guayra and Puerto Cabello have considerable trade with the United States, Semmes determined to look in upon them. When about thirty miles off the coast, a sail was sighted on the lee bow standing obliquely towards the "Sumter." Chase was given, and in a short time a large schooner was taken. She proved to be the "Abby Bradford," of New York, bound to Puerto Cabello. The schooner had left New York before the "Sumter's" escape was known in the North, hence the old captain was more than surprised when he found that he had fallen into the clutches of the Southern Confederacy.

Porto Cabello being but a short distance under his lee, Semmes determined to try his hand with Castro's opponent, the *de facto* President of Venezuela. He thought surely some arrangement could be made with the South American republics, which were too weak to be worth the notice of the stronger Powers. What right had they to be putting on the airs of nations and talk about acknowledging other people who had never themselves been acknowledged by Spain? In this instance Semmes reckoned without his host, for he found at least one Government that had some respect left for the great republic of North America.

Semmes arrived off Puerto Cabello after night-fall, and the next morning, making the ship and crew as much like those of a man-of-war as circumstances would permit, he steamed into the harbor, the prize-vessel following under sail. The "Sumter" had hoisted the Confederate flag early in the morning, and the Venezuelan colors were hoisted from the fort in response. The town looked like some old Moorish establishment transported to the New World, and its most prominent inhabitants appeared to be turkey-buzzards, which reminded the Confederate commander of the sacred birds he had met so often in the Queen City of the Confederacy. His hopes increased as he noted the similarity between Puerto Cabello and the city that had first given a stimulus to his career of adventure. He saw at once what an advantage it would be if the President would admit his prizes, for in the course of a few months he could make the harbor busier than it had ever been. He even thought he could have given a new impulse to the revolutions and make the people rich enough to indulge in a *pronunciamento* once a week.

It never appears to have occurred to the romantic adventurer that his own beloved Confederacy might one day become like a South American republic, ruled by unprincipled adventurers, or a prey to anarchy.

No one seemed to notice the "Sumter" after she anchored. Semmes carefully scanned the features of the "castle," its three or four guns, worthless for any purpose beyond firing a salute, and compared it with his trim battery of shell-guns. He was satisfied with the comparison and immediately wrote the Governor of the town a letter, which he sent ashore by one of his officers. This missive was to the following effect:

CONFEDERATE STATES STEAMER "SUMTER," }
PUERTO CABELLO, July 26, 1861. }
His Excellency the Governor:

I have the honor to inform your Excellency of my arrival at this place, in this ship under my command, with the prize schooner "Abby Bradford" in company, captured by me about seventy miles to the northward and eastward. The "Abby Bradford" is the property of citizens of the United States, with which States, as your Excellency is aware, the Confederate States, which I have the honor to represent, are at war, and the cargo would appear to belong also to citizens of the United States, who have shipped it on consignment to a house in Puerto Cabello.

Should any claim, however, be given for the cargo, or any part of it, the question of ownership can only be decided by the prize-courts of the Confederate States. In the meantime I have the honor to request that your Excellency will permit me to leave this prize vessel, with her cargo, in the port of Puerto Cabello, until the question of prize can be adjudicated by the proper tribunals of my country. This will be a convenience to all parties ; as well to any citizens of Venezuela who may have an interest in the cargo as to the captors who have also valuable interests to protect.

In making this request, I do not propose that the Venezuela Government shall depart from a strict neutrality between the belligerents, as the same rule it applies to us it can give the other party the benefit of also. In other words, with the most scrupulous regard for her neutrality, she may permit both belligerents to bring their prizes into her waters, and of this neither belligerent could complain, since whatever justice is extended to its enemy is extended also to itself. * * * * Thus your Excellency sees that, under the rule of exclusion, the enemy could enjoy his right of capture to its full extent—all his own ports being open to him —whilst the cruisers of the Confederate States could enjoy it *sub modo* only, that is, for the purpose of destroying their prizes. A rule which would produce such unequal results as this, is not a just rule (although it might in terms be extended to both parties), and as equality and justice are of the essence of neutrality, I take it for granted that Venezuela will not adopt it.

On the other hand, the rule admitting both parties, alike, with their prizes into your ports, until the prize-courts of the respective countries could have time to adjudicate the cases, would work equal and exact justice to both ; and this is all that the Confederate States demand.

With reference to the present case, as the cargo consists chiefly of provisions, which are perishable, I would ask leave to sell them at public auction, for the benefit of "whom it may concern," depositing the proceeds with a suitable prize agent until the decision of the court can be known. With regard to the vessel, I request that she may remain in the custody of the same agent until condemned and sold.

Although his Excellency of Puerto Cabello probably knew very little of international law, the American consul at the port was sufficiently well posted, and he at once advised the Governor what course to pursue. The inhabitants were dependent upon their trade with New England and New York for the supply of their necessities, and, of course, the Governor was naturally in favor of his friends rather than a doubtful-looking stranger. So he sent a reply, with "God and Liberty" on the seal, simply informing the Confederate commander that he had not the necessary *funcion* to answer him diplomatically, but would lay his communication before the supreme Government; meanwhile he desired

the "Sumter" to leave Puerto Cabello, and take the "Abby Bradford" with her.

Had Commander Semmes erected a target, and burst a few shells over it just outside the harbor, it might have had some effect ; there was no room inside for such practice, and a shell bursting near the town or fort would have been too much for Spanish pride, and a stray shot from the dilapidated castle might have gone through the "Sumter's" unprotected machinery, and ended her career by enabling the Federal gun-boats to overtake her; therefore Semmes prudently refrained from any attempt to show the power of the Confederacy.

After reading the Governor's letter, to which he paid no attention, Semmes sent his Paymaster on shore, and purchased such articles as he required. The Governor, after an inspection of his artillery and a consultation with the military commandant, made up his mind that it would be best not to coerce any ship belonging to the Southern Confederacy, for fear that these modern representatives of Drake and Morgan might follow the example of their illustrious predecessors if interfered with, and left Semmes to do pretty much as he pleased.

The "Abby Bradford" was sent in charge of a prize-crew to New Orleans, to report her arrival to Commodore Rousseau, delivering to him the prize-papers, seals unbroken, etc. The vessel reached Barrataria Bay, but was recaptured by the "Powhatan," Lieutenant D. D. Porter, and restored to her owners. Semmes did not burn the "Abby Bradford," because, as he says, "I only resorted to that practice when it became evident there was nothing else to do."

As soon as Lieutenant Porter ascertained from the crew of the "Abby Bradford" the whereabouts of the "Sumter," he obtained the permission of Flag-officer McKean, and started in pursuit of the Confederate vessel, following her from port to port to the coast of Brazil, and thence to the equator, from which point Semmes shaped his course, so that his trail was lost.

After having dispatched the "Bradford," Semmes put to sea, and was no sooner outside the harbor than an American vessel was sighted. In less than an hour the "Sumter" came up with the bark "Joseph Maxwell," of Philadelphia. Half her cargo was the property of a neutral doing business in Puerto Cabello; and here again Semmes was in a dilemma. Leaving the bark outside the marine league, Semmes returned in the "Sumter" to Puerto Cabello and sent another letter to the Governor informing him of the capture he had made, and inquiring if some arrangement could not be had for the protection of the neutral half-owner's interests—in other words, to ascertain if the prize, in which a citizen of Venezuela was interested, would not be permitted to enter the harbor and remain until she could be adjudicated.

Much to the surprise of Semmes, the Governor in his reply commanded the representative of the Southern Confederacy to deliver the "Maxwell" over to him until the courts of Venezuela could determine whether or not she had been captured within the marine league!

In the words of Commander Semmes, "This insolence was refreshing—I scarcely knew whether to laugh or be angry." The "Sumter" was then lying close under the guns of the fort, which were manned by some half-naked soldiers. Semmes beat to quarters and cast loose his guns, not knowing but the Governor might attempt to prevent his going to sea again, and with his crew standing at their quarters steamed out of the harbor, without opposition from his Excellency, who was only too happy to be rid of him.

As Semmes' *conscience* would not permit him to destroy neutral property, he sent the "Maxwell" with a prize-crew to Cienfuegos to join his other prizes, still clinging to the hope that Spain "would dare to be just, in the face of the truckling of England and of France."

Semmes had been in the Caribbean Sea from the 3rd to the 27th of July, 1861, had captured ten prizes, and not a Federal gunboat had been heard of, although the United States Consul-General at Havana had been promptly informed of all his transactions at Cienfuegos. Five of the fast steamers purchased for the purpose of carrying stores to the several squadrons, well armed and manned, would have caught the "Sumter" ten days after her escape from Pass à l'Outre, saving many thousand dollars worth of property and terminating Semmes' career. Although the Federal Navy Department displayed a great deal of energy throughout the war, it was lacking in forethought in regard to the matter of Confederate cruisers. The Department had probably no idea that the Confederates would exhibit so much energy in this direction, forgetting that men who embark in a desperate undertaking generally show far more activity than the power they are opposing, besides being less particular in the means employed to gain their ends.

The Federal Government should have sent swift vessels to all parts of the world as soon as it became evident that the Confederates had designs on its commerce. President Lincoln's proclamation declaring Confederate privateers "pirates" was unheeded by European Governments, and it must have been evident that the success of the "Sum-

ter" would prompt the Confederates to send as many vessels as possible on the same errand. Had the "Sumter" been captured soon after her escape from the Mississippi River, there would probably have been no more Confederate cruisers, the Confederacy would have been deprived of its most energetic agent in this line of business, and the ocean commerce of the United States would have been uninterrupted.

After sending off the "Maxwell," the "Sumter" pursued her course along the Spanish main and through the Caribbean Sea to the Port of Spain, in the Island of Trinidad. An English merchant vessel, passing out, paid the "Sumter" the honor of a salute by lowering her flag—a sign of hostility to the United States Government exhibited at that time by almost everything British.

The Governor of Trinidad had already received Queen Victoria's proclamation of neutrality, and when Commander Semmes called upon him his Excellency promptly informed the Confederate Commander that he should receive the same hospitality that would be shown to a Federal cruiser—this hospitality consisted in extending to the "Sumter" every facility for prosecuting her operations against the commerce of the United States.

Semmes lost no time in coaling ship and laying in provisions. His trouble now was to get rid of his prisoners. The "Maxwell's" crew, in particular, were held as hostages until the case of the prisoners captured in the pilot-boat "Savannah," who had been tried and condemned as pirates, was disposed of. Not until Semmes heard that the crew of the "Savannah" were treated as ordinary prisoners-of-war, did he conclude to discharge these merchant seamen, who had been made to understand from day to day what their fate would be if any of the "Savannah's" crew were executed. Fortunately, the Federal Government was not disposed to stain its record by any bloody reprisals, although a mistake was made in issuing a proclamation which it would not have been wise to enforce.

The feelings of the "Maxwell's" crew on hearing that they were to be discharged can be imagined, and even Semmes experienced relief when he found that it would not be necessary to hang unoffending non-combatants at the yard-arm. Semmes remarks in relation to this matter: "I would be stretching a point in undertaking retaliation of this serious character without instructions from my Government, but the case was pressing, and we of the 'Sumter' were vitally interested in the issue. The commission of the 'Savannah,' although she was only a privateer, was as lawful as our own, and judging by the abuse that had already been heaped upon us by the Northern papers, we had no reason to expect any better treatment at the hands of the well-paid New York District Attorneys and well-packed New York juries." It only required that Semmes should appear in this new role of executioner on the high seas to have insured him an immortality equal to that of Captain Kidd. He would have progressed but little further in making himself judge and jury to condemn innocent merchant seamen who had taken no part in the hostilities between the North and the South, than he had already in establishing a Court of Admiralty on the high seas, where all the rules of law and rights of property were set aside. As to any humanity shown his prisoners by turning them loose to shift for themselves in a foreign land, it was due solely to the inexpediency of keeping his ship full of Northerners that might some day rise and overpower his crew.

Commander Semmes had already received his cue from the Confederate authorities, but it would detract from his reputation for cleverness to believe that he imagined himself invested with authority to commit such an act as he had intimated, and we will be charitable enough to think that his expressions on the subject were simply gasconade.

When one of the men captured in the privateer "Jeff Davis" was convicted of piracy in the Philadelphia Court, the Confederate Government issued the following order, which Semmes took for his guide, apparently forgetting that, while his Government might incur the responsibility, he, not the one hundred thousandth part of that Government, had no more right to commit such an act than the commonest seaman in his vessel. The letter of Mr. Secretary Benjamin, which came so near causing murder to be done on the high seas, is herewith inserted, showing to what dreadful lengths the asperities of civil war will drive people. It may be hoped that in future wars men will not be condemned to death simply for being led astray by reckless leaders, and that retaliation may not be exercised against men who have borne an innocent part in the conflict:

ORDER OF MR. BENJAMIN TO GENERAL WINDER
IN CHARGE OF FEDERAL PRISONERS.

SIR—You are hereby instructed to choose by lot from among the prisoners-of-war, of highest rank, one who is to be confined in a cell appropriated to convicted felons, and who is to be treated in all respects as if such convict, and to be held for execution, in the same manner as may be adopted by the enemy for the execution of the prisoner-of-war Smith recently condemned to death in Philadelphia.

You will also select thirteen other prisoners-of-war, the highest in rank of those captured by our forces, to be confined in cells, reserved for prisoners accused of infamous crimes, and will treat them as such, so long as the enemy shall continue so to treat the like number of prisoners-of-war captured by them at sea, and now held for trial in New York as pirates.

As these measures are intended to repress the infamous attempt now made by the enemy to commit judicial murder on prisoners-of-war, you will execute them strictly, as the mode best calculated to prevent the commission of so heinous a crime.

While the "Sumter" remained at Trinidad she was thronged with visitors; some were sympathizers with the Confederate cause, others were there from mere curiosity; but the officials generally held aloof for fear of compromising themselves if they took much interest in the Confederates. All Semmes cared for was to obtain a stock of coal and provisions, and these not being considered contraband of war were freely furnished. Semmes met with some opposition from the authorities, but he bore his trials with meekness, for he knew that the heavy guns commanding the harbor could soon be manned, and were too formidable to trifle with. Nor could he tell how soon a British man-of-war might come into port with orders for the Governor to detain the "Sumter."

On the 25th of August the "Sumter" sailed from Trinidad bound for Maranham. So far, nothing had been heard of a United States vessel-of-war. The slow old frigate "Powhatan" was following on the track of the marauder, never missing a port at which the "Sumter" had stopped. But for defective boilers the "Powhatan" would have overtaken the "Sumter" at Maranham. It must have given the inhabitants of the places Semmes visited a poor idea of the power of the Federal Government, to see the "Sumter" roving at will, with no opposition.

In addition to his other tasks, Semmes undertook to play the part of a missionary, and teach the people among whom he went the difference between the Northern and Southern governments; the former an effete affair, without resources; the latter a young giant that was to carry everything before it. Of course, there were plenty of people to believe all this. They had seen the evidence of Northern commercial wealth in the number of vessels that had visited their ports, but they had no evidence of Federal military or naval power, which is, after all, what counts most with nations. In the "Sumter" they beheld an engine-of-war that could do much harm, and, although she was not a large vessel, yet they saw nothing opposed to her to repress her ill-doings. Had there been a fair-sized United States vessel-of-war at either of the ports the "Sumter" entered, the latter would have probably been refused a supply of coal.

The "Sumter," owing to strong head-winds and currents, soon expended the greater portion of her coal, and had then to resort to her sails; but on the 19th of August she made the harbor of Paramaribo and obtained a supply of coal and provisions, fraternizing with the officials of the town and with some French and Dutch officers, who seemed to recognize in the "Sumter" the germ of a Navy that was to supplant that of the United States. All this now seems like the merest mockery, and we can hardly realize how the representatives of old-established Governments could lend themselves to the schemes of the Confederates before they had the slightest evidence that the latter could maintain their position. It must have been a serious matter to admit the ships of long-established Governments into neutral ports for the purpose of obtaining coal with which to prey upon each other's commerce; but to admit a vessel of such doubtful character as the "Sumter," with a flag never before seen, was certainly going to the utmost extreme. The secret of the matter was, probably, not so much sympathy with the South, as a general dislike to the institutions of the United States, which were a standing menace to the governments of the Old World. Had the United States been provided with a Navy proportioned to its wealth and resources, with ships stationed at every part of the world frequented by its commerce, the Confederates could not have kept the seas, for want of coal, and would soon have been obliged to abandon their cruising, even if their vessels escaped capture. The argument enforced by war vessels is better than diplomacy, which has not such support; and, although Mr. Seward had duly instructed all the diplomatic and consular representatives of the United States, these gentlemen could never satisfactorily answer the question, "Why don't you send your Navy to repress the 'Sumter'?"

The "Sumter" left Paramaribo on the 30th of August, the commanding officer giving the pilot to understand that he was bound to Barbadoes to look after the U. S. S. "Keystone State," which vessel he had learned was in pursuit of him. Semmes had satisfied himself that the display of the "Sumter" and the Confederate flag in Cayenne and Paramaribo had had a most excellent effect on the fortunes of his young republic!

The "Powhatan" arrived off Surinam River only two or three days after the "Sumter" sailed. The pilot said she had caulked her ports in and sailed for Barbadoes; but Lieutenant Porter, feeling satisfied that Semmes was aiming to get on the track of American vessels bound round Cape St. Roque, and knowing that he would have to touch at Maranham for coal, lost no time, but stood in the direction of the latter port, sometimes under three boilers, sometimes under one only, the engineer's force working night and day patching the worn-out boilers.

This old representative ship of the United States Navy at times made not more than three knots an hour, scarcely enough to stem the current setting along the Brazilian coast.

With all the difficulties attending this pursuit, which Semmes calls "Quixotic," the "Powhatan" had gained over fifteen hundred miles on the "Sumter" since she first started in pursuit; and had the former vessel been fit for sea the Confederate cruiser would have been easily overtaken, which shows the remissness of the Government in not dispatching a dozen fast vessels in pursuit, even if they had to be taken from blockade duty.

On the 6th of September the "Sumter" arrived in the Port of Maranham, and the Port Admiral sent a lieutenant to inquire of the commanding officer of the Confederate vessel what strange flag that was he carried at his peak, and was duly informed that it was the emblem of the Southern Confederacy. A cordial understanding was soon had with all the Brazilian authorities, including the Governor of the province, who was made to understand that there were now two "United States" instead of one, that the Northern government abhorred slavery and all that pertained to it. This statement struck a chord in the breast of the Governor, who, like most of the Brazilians at that time, was a strong advocate of the *peculiar institution.* So he took Semmes, his officers and men, at once to his heart, and welcomed them to Maranham. Yet Semmes and his officers were not invited to a grand ball given by his Excellency, as diplomatic etiquette forbade this without the permission of the Emperor. "The only feeling excited in us," Semmes remarks, "by this official slight was of contempt for the silliness of the proceeding, a contempt heightened by the reflection that we were a race of Anglo-Saxons, proud of our lineage and proud of our strength (!) frowned upon by a set of half-breeds."

Semmes was more anxious, however, to capture merchant vessels than to attend official gatherings. The day after the ball the Governor gave him an audience, and after Semmes had satisfied him that the "Sumter" was entitled to belligerent rights, granted permission for the ship to have everything desired except munitions of war, as if granting coal was not a far greater injury to United States commerce than all the munitions in the world without it.

If England had been the plaintiff, America would not have permitted those vessels, with their imitation of the British flag, to obtain supplies to carry on their depredations against a country with whom they were on terms of friendship, and with whom they had treaties. All such vessels would have been excluded from their ports, or, if admitted, would be detained to prevent their doing mischief. Great Britain would not condone such an offence as giving aid and comfort to such cruisers would be, and would have had her war ships promptly on hand to demand reparation. Who is there that does not admire and applaud the policy of such a nation in protecting the interests of her citizens, although her operations may often seem to conflict with the maxims of writers on international matters ?

The Federal Government was too slow in sending war vessels abroad to look out for its merchant marine, and depended on the poorly paid consuls at the different ports to oppose their feeble influence against a plausible person like Commander Semmes, who had as advisers men in the Confederate councils still more clever. These same men had deluded many States filled with intelligent people, and it would have been strange if they could not delude a few old Governors, especially when the latter were impressed with the idea that the Confederacy had England and France to back her, and would be acknowledged by all the Powers of Europe in less than six months.

In Maranham, during their stay, Commander Semmes and his officers were the lions of the hour, and brought a good deal of odium on the head of the United States consul, who did all in his power to prevent the "Sumter" from proceeding on her work of destruction. His small pay had prevented him attaining much social consideration, so that he had but little influence. Semmes' greatest objection to this gentleman was that he was a dentist, and forced to practice his profession to eke out a livelihood.

On the 15th of September Semmes left Maranham, his ship thoroughly equipped from keel to truck. For very good reasons, considering the character of his vessel, Semmes determined to steer to the northward and eastward and reach the calm belt north of Cape St. Roque, where he expected to fall in with a number of vessels bound from ports south of the equator.

Four days after the departure of the "Sumter" the "Powhatan" appeared off Maranham. This vessel had worked her way in a fog through the dangerous channel leading to the port, for the pilots had all been withdrawn from the outer anchorage and not even a fisherman was encountered. The "Powhatan" had but ten hours' coal

on board and was so light that her paddle-wheels had but little hold on the water. By careful navigation the outside of the harbor was reached and an insolent negro pilot was received on board—the same person that had taken the "Sumter" out. "How did you get through all the shoals ?" he inquired. "By the chart," was the answer. "I don't believe it," he said. "You must have had the devil for a pilot. No ship of this size can come through those channels without a good pilot. Even the little 'Sumter' struck coming in and came near leaving her bones among them." "She is here, then ?" said the commanding officer of the "Powhatan," his eyes glistening with pleasure. The negro laughed and replied, impudently : "No, you can't catch her, she is miles away—she sailed four days ago."

It was high-water when the "Powhatan" entered the harbor and came to anchor in five fathoms. The tide rises some fourteen feet and runs very strong on the ebb. Three hours after the "Powhatan" anchored she began rasping on the bottom and pounding against her anchor, and at low-water was hard and fast in the mud with three feet of copper out of water. This was evidently intentional on the part of the pilot, but fortunately no damage was done, and at high tide the ship was moved into deeper water. The hope of the pilot was undoubtedly that the ship would bring up on the bill of her anchor and knock a hole in her bottom.

The Stars and Stripes floated proudly at the peak of the "Powhatan," but no official visited the ship. The paymaster was sent on shore to purchase coal, but could not procure any. The "Powhatan," in the eyes of these people, represented the cause of slave emancipation. When application for coal was made to the agent of the British Mail Steamship Company, he charged at the rate of twenty-two dollars a ton, at least twice as much as it was worth. The offer was accepted; but the ship had scarcely commenced coaling when a black officer, with an aide of the same complexion, came on board and haughtily demanded in the name of the Governor that the "Powhatan" should stop taking in coal. He was told to go on shore and not to interfere with that which did not concern him. The coal barges were towed alongside the ship and a marine with loaded musket placed in each one.

That is all the communication the "Powhatan" had with Maranham, except that a Brazilian gentleman came on board and strongly protested against the Governor's acts ; but he could effect nothing, as he was on the wrong side in politics.

As soon as the "Powhatan" had coaled she departed in pursuit of the "Sumter," the commanding officer declining the services of a pilot for fear the good ship's bones might be left on some ugly reef.

The "Sumter" reached the calm belt on the 24th of September. The next day a sail was sighted ; the "Sumter" pursued under steam showing the American flag. The stranger, thinking this a United States gun-boat, ran up the Stars and Stripes. The vessel proved to be the "Joseph Parke," of Boston ; a prize-crew was put on board and she was sent to the westward to act as a decoy to other vessels, and to report, by signal, all sails that hove in sight. A few days afterwards, as nothing appeared, the "Parke" was set on fire and destroyed, after removing all valuables. Vessels on the Brazilian coast had heard of the "Sumter's" escape and had taken a new route homeward consequently. Semmes gained little by cruising between the parallels of 2°.30' and 9°.30' North and the Meridians 41°.30' and 47°.30' West. So he made his way back to the West Indies, while the "Powhatan" about the same time followed in his track.

On the 24th of October, the "Sumter" captured the schooner "Daniel Trowbridge," of New Haven, loaded with everything a cruiser could desire, her deck even being filled with live stock. It took these cormorants two or three days to clear out this well-filled schooner, and as boat-load after boat-load was sent from the prize to the "Sumter," Semmes gloated over the luxuries he was receiving. It does not seem to have occurred to him how much this resembled the achievements of old buccaneering days, when the sea-rovers overtook their victims and treated them in pretty much the same fashion, finally consigning their vessels to the flames. There is this to be said in Semmes' favor, that he did not make his prisoners walk the plank. Semmes is silent as to the fate of this vessel, from which he received five months' provisions; but she was probably sunk, as it was not desirable to burn her when so many vessels were about.

Many vessels were now chased without any prizes being taken, most of them being the property of neutrals, and the "Sumter" at length, on the 9th of November, 1861, made Port de France, in the Island of Martinique, having been at sea nearly two months since leaving Maranham. Of late the "Sumter" had taken few prizes, but her career, as a whole, had been very destructive and caused premiums on insurance to assume formidable proportions.

At one time Semmes came very near being captured by the "Powhatan." He remarks in his journal : "At Trinidad the 'Keystone State' lost our trail, and, instead of pursuing us to Paramaribo and Maran-

ham, turned back to the westward. We learn from the same papers that the enemy's steam-frigate 'Powhatan,' Lieutenant Porter, with more sagacity, pursued us to Maranham, arriving there one week [four days] after our departure. At a subsequent date, Lieutenant (now Admiral) Porter's official account fell into my hands, and, plotting his track, I found that on one occasion we had been within forty miles of each other, almost near enough on a still day to see each other's smoke." This was at the time when the "Sumter" burned the "Joseph Parke" near the equator.

Commander Semmes heard of the presence of the "Iroquois," Commander James S. Palmer, in the Caribbean Sea, soon after his arrival at Martinique, and made haste to get away from that place before he should be blockaded by the Federal steamer. The "Iroquois" was superior in every respect to the "Sumter," and Semmes had not the slightest idea of getting within range of her guns, if he could help it.

On November 13, the "Sumter" left Port de France and anchored off St. Pierre, and a day or two later the "Iroquois" appeared off the harbor, and sent a boat ashore to the United States consul, after which she steamed outside and kept up a steady blockade until the authorities at Martinique called Captain Palmer's attention to the fact that he was violating the sanctity of neutral waters, and requested him to retire beyond the marine league. The manœuvring on the part of Semmes to get to sea, and of Palmer to prevent him, forms an interesting episode in the history of the war. Semmes, in the end, was too clever for Palmer, and one dark night the "Sumter" made her escape under full steam while the "Iroquois" was watching for her in another direction. It is a difficult thing for one steamer to prevent the passage of another out of an open bay with head-lands three or four miles apart, as was conclusively proven in this instance.

Finding that the Federal cruisers were getting on his track, the commander of the "Sumter" determined to leave the Caribbean Sea and cross the Atlantic. On his way Semmes captured and destroyed the "Arcadia," "Vigilant" and "Ebenezer Dodge," making the total number of captures by the "Sumter" fourteen.

Semmes had done as well for the Confederacy as possible, and the Confederate Government was well satisfied with his operations; but the crowning blow was yet to come, when Semmes, in a more efficient vessel, could still better illustrate the fact that a great commercial country, without a sufficient naval force, is at the mercy of any set of adventurers in case war should suddenly break out. Had the "Sumter" started on such a crusade against British commerce, the seas would have swarmed with swift cruisers, and Semmes' career would have come to a sudden and inglorious termination. He showed a deal of cleverness in achieving so much for his Government, but he had few vessels in search of him, and only one of these was fast enough to overtake him if he was sighted.

From an English vessel that Semmes encountered he obtained newspapers that gave him interesting information. Among other things he learned that another Confederate cruiser called the "Nashville," under the command of Lieutenant Pegram, had put to sea and had burned a large American merchant ship, the "Harvey Birch," in the British Channel. She was loaded with tea and just from China. This news stimulated Semmes to fresh exertions, that he might replenish his coal and continue his pleasant employment of burning and sinking. Having been well received at Cienfuegos, he calculated on meeting similar treatment in other Spanish ports, and he now entered the beautiful harbor of Cadiz with the most pleasing anticipations, so that for a moment he forgot the ravages he had committed on unoffending people who had taken no part in the war against the South, and many of whom, for all he knew, might have sympathized with the secession cause. He showed a vindictiveness towards everything relating to the North which nobody thought to have existed in his character. Those who knew him as an officer of more than thirty years' service in the United States Navy, supposed that he would feel some little compunction in pulling down the honored flag of the Union and consigning its ships to the flames; but, so far from this, Semmes exulted in every deed he committed, and showed himself in acts and language so rancorous against everything belonging to the North, that one would have supposed he had received the greatest injuries from the United States Government. We can understand that a man may be led by his sympathies and the persuasion of his friends to embark in a bad cause, but there should be enough of humanity in him to cause him to feel regret at deserting the flag he had professed to love for so many years.

Semmes was not received at Cadiz with that consideratton he thought he had a right to expect, and after some correspondence with the authorities was ordered by a dispatch from Madrid to proceed to sea within twenty-four hours; but after consideration the "Sumter" was allowed to go into dock for repairs and Semmes was permitted to land his prisoners, who were making serious inroads on his provisions. He met with no encouragement at Cadiz.

In the eyes of the Spaniards the secession movement was a mere political outbreak, in which Spain was not concerned.

Part of the "Sumter's" crew deserted while the vessel was in dock. Semmes' money had given out; he could not purchase coal, and every day he was urged by the authorities to depart. Having a small supply of coal remaining, Semmes determined to shake the dust of Cadiz from his feet, and that night he laid-to off the Straits of Gibralter. At daybreak several sail were sighted coming down the Mediterranean bound through the Straits. Semmes could not think of going into Gibraltar without first examining these vessels, as his predecessors, the Barbary corsairs, were wont to do on this very spot in days gone by. It was two hours before the "Sumter" came up with the first of these vessels. She was standing towards the African coast, though still distant from the land six or seven miles; yet who would have asked whether she was within the marine league or not? What did Semmes care for the guns at Ceuta? When near enough, the Confederate flag was displayed and the usual gun fired, when the American hove-to, much astonished at this summons; but he soon found himself in the hands of an enemy from whom there was no escape. The master of the vessel stated before the "Admiralty Court" sitting on board the "Sumter" that his ship belonged to the English house of Baring Brothers and was consigned to an agent in Boston; but, notwithstanding his expostulations, he was informed that his ship would be destroyed. The other vessel was approaching and Semmes had no time to parley. So the torch was applied to the beautiful bark "Neapolitan," of Kingston, Massachusetts, and she with her valuable cargo was totally consumed. Commander Semmes' justification, to use his own expressions, was that "Gallant naval officers wearing Mr. Welles' shoulder-straps, and commanding Mr. Welles' ships, were capturing little coasting schooners laden with fire-wood, plundering the houses and hen-roosts of non-combatants along the Southern coast, destroying salt-works and intercepting medicines going to Confederate hospitals." Is it strange that men who would tell such falsehoods as the above would burn the ships of non-combatants?

The "Neapolitan" was no sooner on fire than the "Sumter" started in pursuit of the other vessel, which proved to be the bark "Investigator," of Searsport, Maine. The cargo being clearly the property of neutrals, the vessel, after giving a ransombond, was allowed to proceed on her course.

Commander Semmes had now to be somewhat careful of seizing neutral property, as he was in civilized Europe and not among a set of "half-breeds" before whose council windows he could "flash his shells," or hector a pack of feeble officials.

That night the "Sumter" lay in the "man-of-war anchorage" in Gibraltar Bay. It was not necessary to tell the inhabitants of Gibraltar what the "Sumter" was, for she had been expected. It was quite in keeping that Semmes should announce his arrival by burning a ship; but it would have been still more suited to his character if he had waited until night to illuminate the shores of Spain and Africa, and run into the anchorage, showing the Confederate flag by the lurid light of the flames.

Some of the officers of the garrison of Gibraltar, being ardent admirers of the Confederate cause, expressed themselves unreservedly. In other words, they disliked the United States, and would have been delighted to see the whole fabric of the Union broken to pieces.

The only restrictions placed upon the "Sumter" were that she should not make Gibraltar a station from which to sally out for war purposes, and should not receive on board any contraband of war. That is, she could purchase all the coal needed to enable her to commit depredations upon United States commerce, but could not replace what few blank cartridges had been expended in bringing vessels to, and the shells with which she had made a target of her prizes.

What would Great Britain have thought had Ireland thrown off her allegiance, and sent out vessels to destroy British commerce, if these vessels had been received in New York, and the authorities had allowed them to refit and repair and sent them on their way. When Washington was President, and Genet Minister from France to the United States, certain French privateers put into Philadelphia, and an attempt was made to refit them so that they might commit depredations on British commerce. The President issued an order prohibiting this, and on Minister Genet protesting against it, the President declined to receive him as the representative of France. Yet the French had materially assisted us to gain our independence from Great Britain. The diplomatic correspondence of the civil war will show how different the conduct of the British Government. It might be advisable for Great Britain to proclaim her neutrality, but there was certainly no reason why she should give aid to those in rebellion against the United States. The limits of this work will not permit a lengthy discussion of this matter, however, and we can only chronicle the movements of the Confederate cruisers and the measures taken to check their career.

While the "Sumter" remained in Gibraltar she was crowded with visitors. People came from a distance to see the wonderful vessel that had strewn the ocean with blackened hulls The Duke of Beaufort and Sir John Inglis went on board and examined the ship—men whose ancestors had stigmatized Paul Jones as a pirate when, in the "Bon Homme Richard," he left the whole English coast in terror, and sunk the "Serapis," in a contest that will be forever memorable.

But in spite of the sympathy showered upon the "Sumter" and her interesting commander, the tide gradually turned, and Semmes wore out his welcome. Two Federal gun-boats were watching—one from Algesiras, the other at Gibraltar—neither of them violating any neutrality, or fraternizing with the inhabitants of the shore, yet every movement was reported to the Governor of Gibraltar as a violation of neutrality. The escape of the "Sumter" had put Secretary Seward on his mettle, and he made the strongest protests against her being received or recognized as a belligerent, and even went so far as to denounce her as a pirate. The British Government began to consider the matter more carefully, and the idea doubtless suggested itself that England was establishing a precedent which might give her much trouble in case of future wars. Whatever the cause, the career of the "Sumter" terminated at Gibraltar. Semmes could raise no money, and the presence of the United States vessels had a strong moral influence against him. Semmes took up his old employment of writing letters, which were referred by the Governor to the authorities at home. When it was found that Semmes had no money to purchase coal, the sympathizers with secession became lukewarm, and as every one in Gibraltar was more or less under the influence of official authority, even the Army and Navy officers became cooler towards the officers of the "Sumter." The calm bearing of the officers of the two United States vessels had its effect, they seemed to be of the right metal—the representatives of an old-established Government. The "Sumter" might be a lion for a time while the story of her exploits was still fresh in people's minds, but when two *bona-fide* ships-of-war appeared in pursuit of her, the glamour seemed to evaporate, and the bold cruiser was merely the fugitive from justice. The "Sumter" was like some young fellow entertained as a visitor, with two policemen watching the house ready to seize him when he came out.

To make matters still more unpleasant for Commander Semmes, Paymaster Myers of the "Sumter" was arrested at Tangier on the opposite side of the Straits. Mr. Myers was on his way to Cadiz to negotiate for coal or money, and landed from the passenger steamer to walk about the town. The United States treaty with Morocco called for the surrender of all persons accused of offences against the United States; and the consul, having civil and criminal jurisdiction, had Mr. Myers and an ex-consul who was traveling with him arrested and placed in close confinement. They were then transferred to the U. S. naval vessel at Algesiras—much against the wishes of the commanding officer—by the consul, who demanded that these persons should be taken to the United States, charged with piracy on the high seas and aiding and abetting the same. The fact that officers of the "Sumter" could be arrested by the emissaries of a foreign Government put a still more dubious aspect on the "Sumter's" case. There was a flaw in the "Sumter" somewhere, and this episode was the feather that broke the camel's back.

We do not dwell with any satisfaction on the action of the consul at Tangier, who was doubtless prompted in his course by the instructions from the Department of State denouncing the Confederate cruisers as pirates. The paymaster of the "Sumter" was of little consequence one way or another, and whether he was a prisoner, or at large, made not much difference. Semmes tried in vain to procure the release of his officer, for the United States Government had considerable prestige, and was every day growing more powerful. Mr. Secretary Seward was assuming a determined tone to which foreign powers were forced to listen. After much correspondence the unlucky paymaster was released from confinement and placed on parole as a prisoner-of-war.

As it was impossible to get to sea, the "Sumter" was finally laid up at Gibraltar in charge of a midshipman, while Semmes and some of his officers, on the 15th of April, 1862, embarked on board the mail steamer for Southampton, in search of a better vessel with which to renew their depredations on United States commerce. The "Sumter" became a blockade-runner, and, after the war, terminated her career on some dangerous shoals in the China Sea and all her crew were lost.

CHAPTER XLVI.

THE ADVENTURES OF THE "FLORIDA" ("ORETO") AND "ALABAMA."

ENGAGEMENT BETWEEN THE "KEARSARGE" AND "ALABAMA."

DESTRUCTION OF THE NATION'S COMMERCE. — SEMMES' CAREER IN THE OLD NAVY. — SEMMES IN ENGLAND. — TAKES PASSAGE FOR NASSAU. — RECEIVES CAPTAIN'S COMMISSION. — ORDERED TO COMMAND THE "ALABAMA." — THE "ORETO" SEIZED BY BRITISH AUTHORITIES, AFTERWARDS RELEASED. — RECEIVES HER ARMAMENT AT GRAND KEY. — THE "ORETO" ("FLORIDA") SAILS FOR MOBILE. — RUNS THROUGH BLOCKADING SQUADRON. — RUNS BLOCKADE A SECOND TIME. — MAFFITT LIGHTS UP THE SEA. — THE "ALABAMA." — SEMMES JOINS THE "ALABAMA" AT TERCEIRA. — IN COMMISSION. — CAPTURE OF "STARLIGHT," "OCEAN ROVER," "ALERT," "WEATHER-GAUGE" AND "ALTAMAHA." — EXCITING CHASE. — CAPTURE OF THE "BENJAMIN TUCKER," "COURSER," "VIRGINIA" AND "ELISHA DUNBAR." — ROUGH SEA AND A PICTURESQUE CONFLAGRATION. — CAPTURE OF THE "BRILLIANT," "EMILY FARNUM," "DUNKIRK," "WAVE CREST," "TONAWANDA," "MANCHESTER," "LAMPLIGHTER," "CRENSHAW" AND "LEVI STARBUCK." — EXCITING ADVENTURES. — LANDING PRISONERS AT PORT DE FRANCE. — BLOCKADED. — THE "ALABAMA" ESCAPES U. S. S. "SAN JACINTO." — CAPTURE OF THE "PARKER COOKE," "UNION" AND "ARIEL." — INCIDENTS ON BOARD THE "ARIEL." — THE "ALABAMA" IN GULF OF MEXICO. — SINKS U. S. S. "HATTERAS." — LANDING PRISONERS AND REFITTING AT JAMAICA. — CAPTURE OF "GOLDEN RULE," "CHASTELAINE," "PALMETTO," "OLIVE JANE" AND "GOLDEN EAGLE." — THE SEA ABLAZE WITH BURNING VESSELS. — THE TOLL-GATE UPON THE SEA. — CAPTURE OF THE "WASHINGTON," "JOHN A. PARKS," "BETHIAH THAYER," "PUNJAUB," "MORNING STAR," "KINGFISHER," "CHARLES HILL," "NORA," "LOUISA HATCH," "LAFAYETTE" AND "KATE CORY." — CAPTURE OF THE WHALERS "NYE," "DORCAS PRINCE" AND "UNION JACK." — THE "ALABAMA" AND CONFEDERATE STEAMER "GEORGIA" AT BAHIA. — CAPTURE OF THE "GILDERSLIEVE," "JUSTIANA," "JABEZ SNOW," "AMAZONIAN," "TALISMAN" AND "CONRAD." — THE "CONRAD" COMMISSIONED AS A CONFEDERATE CRUISER. — CAPTURE OF THE "ANNA F. SCHMIDT." — THE "TUSCALOOSA." — CAPTURE OF THE "SEA-BRIDE." — U. S. S. "VANDERBILT" AND "WYOMING." — THE "WINGED RACER" AND THE "CONTEST" IN FLAMES. — THE "ALABAMA" GIVES THE "WYOMING" THE SLIP. — CAPTURE OF THE "MARTABAN," "SONORA" AND "HIGHLANDER." — BURNING OF THE "EMMA JANE." — RELEASE OF THE "TUSCALOOSA." — CAPTURE OF THE "ROCKINGHAM" AND "TYCOON." — THE "ALABAMA" ANCHORS IN HARBOR OF CHERBOURG. — ARRIVAL OF THE "KEARSARGE." — A CHALLENGE. — PREPARATIONS TO FIGHT. — ENGAGEMENT BETWEEN THE "ALABAMA" AND "KEARSARGE." — INCIDENTS OF BATTLE. — THE "ALABAMA" SUNK! — SEMMES ESCAPES. — CAPTAIN WINSLOW'S REPORT. — OFFICERS AND CREW OF THE "KEARSARGE." — OFFICERS OF THE "ALABAMA."

THERE is no more interesting chapter in the history of the war than the account of the performances of those who commanded the cruisers that were sent forth by the Confederate Government to destroy the commerce of the Northern States.

This commerce had long been the pride of the nation, and its white sails covered nearly every sea; but that it was poorly protected by the Government was well known to all the world, and it was predicted by those who thought seriously upon the subject that the day would come when the rude hands of some foreign power would be laid upon it, in some future war, when it would be swept from the seas ; but who, in his wildest conjectures, would ever suppose that the blow would come from those whose greatest pride once was that they were born under the " Stars and Stripes," and that they loved every stripe and star in the dear old flag that had borne itself so bravely in times past, on land and sea, in the defence of human rights, and in the vindication of its own honor ?

Yet men change their creeds so rapidly with the circumstances of the times, that it would be impossible to predict their actions when revolution overwhelms a nation, and changes the most loyal hearts. Men, who with patriotic pride had looked upon our flag with a veneration almost as great as they owed their God, forsook it at a moment's warning — at a time when it most needed their support. And, strange to say, some of these not only placed themselves in opposition to the Government—to which they had been bound by the most sacred ties—but they did all in their power to drive its flag from the ocean, by destroying the noble ships that carried it.

There was a large corps of these officers, and among them some of the most gallant and fiery spirits of the old Navy, without whose intelligent aid the Confederates could have inflicted little or no injury upon American commerce. It is well known that all the attempts made by the merchant captains of the South to fit out privateers were failures. Their vessels were always captured, simply because their commanders lacked the training and intelligence of the regular naval officers who went South when their States seceded.

There can be no doubt that Commander Semmes was one of the most intelligent of these officers, and he not only willingly entered into Mr. Mallory's plan for the destruction of American commerce, but embarked in the career with so much energy that it amounted to vindictiveness ; so that, although he performed many daring exploits, he is hardly entitled to be called a hero. We have seen what he accomplished with the " Sumter," a small vessel which had been condemned by a Board of naval officers at New Orleans. Semmes, however, at once decided that she would suit his purpose, and, with an energy he had never been thought to possess, he got her to sea, eluded the blockaders, and after capturing fifteen merchantment, arrived at Cadiz. From this port he went to Gibraltar, where the career of the " Sumter," as a commerce-destroyer, ended. She was in an unseaworthy condition, and, being closely blockaded, Semmes decided that she could be of no further use to the Confederacy. He sold her in such a

way that his adopted country could benefit by the purchase-money, and then started in pursuit of some other field of action.

As we have said before. Commander Semmes had denounced the Mexican Government for proposing to do what he was doing in the " Alabama," but no one can tell how a man may change his nature or his opinions when swayed by some passion that may have been dormant in him for years, and which only required to be called into action to make the inert, indifferent officer throw off the old man and take on the new ; there are so many instances where such men have come to the surface in great revolutions, that it is not strange that Commander Semmes, from being the mildest-mannered gentleman in the Navy, should have assumed a character bordering on that of an ancient viking.

This officer would not perhaps have merited these remarks had he not throughout his career shown the most vindictive feelings towards anything that claimed to belong to the United States ; he was so inhumane in his treatment of prisoners, and so indifferent to the rights of property, that he could scarcely have expected to be treated as mildly as his compatriots who inflicted great damage on American commerce, but were content after the war was over to remain quietly in their retirement without boasting of what they had done in a book that tended to keep alive the bad passions which it were better for both North and South to bury in oblivion.

We have seen Commander Semmes in the " Sumter," we have yet to see him in the " Alabama," which he made ten times more famous as a destroyer than the little vessel which first carried his fortunes. During his second command he carried such terror into the hearts of peaceful merchantmen that many of them abandoned their flag and placed their ships under the protection of England, where they knew they would be safe from molestation.

When Semmes arrived in England he found that a commission of Confederate naval officers had been sent abroad to purchase or build cruisers for the Southern Navy, but that, owing to the difficulties thrown in their way by the protests of the American Minister and Secretary of State, little headway had been made in the desired direction ; and, although he was offered the first command, he saw little prospect of immediate employment and determined to return to the Confederate States. An opportunity soon offered, and he took passage on the fast blockade-runner " Melita," which landed him at Nassau, N. P., on the 13th of June, 1862. On the same evening Semmes was quartered at the Victoria Hotel with his staff, where he was surrounded by many Confederates, who all consorted together after a manner, and at least with apparent harmony, for they were all, as a rule, engaged in the same errand (search for plunder) ; and the greedy look and hungry eyes of many of these parties, as they longingly gazed upon the thousands of bales of cotton which strewed the beach, showed that their hearts were wrapped up in that beautiful staple.

Nassau, originally an insignificant town, sought only as a place of resort for invalids, had now assumed the airs of a thriving city. The harbor was filled with shipping, and its warehouses, wharves and quays were overflowing with merchandise of all kinds, ready to be sent into Confederate ports. There was almost as much bustle and activity here as at the wharves of New York. Ships were constantly arriving from England with merchandise, great-guns, small-arms, ammunition, and everything else that could be wanted by the Confederates to enable them to carry on the war, and light-draft steamers, Confederate and English, were constantly reloading these articles and running them into Southern ports. So successful were some of these traders in running the blockade that they made their voyages as regularly as mail-packets, returning again and again to Nassau with heavy loads of cotton, which were there transferred to the vessels which had brought arms and munitions of war from England.

What was there to prevent the Confederates from maintaining and equipping their fast cruisers except the unwearying vigilance of the blockading fleet ? This trying duty was well performed, however, and, although some escaped them, the Federal officers captured 1,156 blockade-runners during the war. This faithful work was attributed by Commander Semmes to the greed of the "Old Navy." He complained that "this duty became a bone of contention among the Federal naval officers, which of them should be assigned to the lucrative command of the blockading squadron," and that "the Admiral of one of their squadrons would frequently awake in the morning and find himself richer by twenty thousand dollars by reason of a capture made by some one of his subordinates the night before." This, he said, was "the 'mess of pottage' for which so many unprincipled Southern men in the Federal Navy sold their birthright." Is it any wonder that these loyal men refused to recognize Semmes when he was left by the war in indigent circumstances and could not make a living by the law ?

Commander Semmes met several Confederate officers at Nassau, among them Com-

mander J. N. Maffitt, who had arrived in the "Oreto," a vessel that had been purchased in England by the Confederate commission and fitted out as a cruiser. At this moment she was detained at Nassau by the Attorney-General of the colony for a violation of the British "Foreign Enlistment Act." Semmes passed his time in listening to the arguments in this case, and in the meanwhile received a commission as Captain in the Confederate Navy, with orders to return to England and take command of the steamer "Alabama" (then known as "No. 290"). She had been so far secured by the Confederate commissioners that they felt quite certain of getting her to sea.

The "Oreto," of which Commander Maffitt had charge, was quite swift, but not so formidable a vessel as the "290." She had left England unarmed, but with all the arrangements made to mount guns, and with all the appliances below to stow pow-

COMMANDER J. NEWLAND MAFFITT, C. S. N.

der and shell. After a long trial she was released by the British authorities, and Maffitt again prepared to put her in fighting trim. This vessel was afterwards known as the "Florida," and though she did not equal the "Alabama," she made herself sufficiently famous to give the Federal Government a great deal of trouble, and cause it to put forth all its energies for her capture.

Maffitt was a different kind of man from Semmes. A thorough master of his profession, and possessed of all the qualities that make a favorite naval commander, he became a successful raider of the sea ; but he made no enemies among those officers who had once known him and who now missed his genial humor in their messes. He was a veritable rover, but was never inhumane to those whom the fortunes of war threw into his hands, and he made himself as pleasant, while emptying a ship of her cargo and then scuttling her, as Claude Duval when robbing a man of his purse or borrowing his watch from his pocket.

After Maffitt's vessel was released from the Court of Nassau (the trial having been a farce), he made arrangements to mount her guns and man her from the motley crew of sailors that floated about the town ready for any kind of work that might offer, so long as they did not compromise themselves with some power having plenty of ships-of-war, that could catch them and hang them to the yard-arm if they happened to burn or sink anything belonging to it. This they knew was piracy; but for English sailors to ship in an English port on board a Confederate cruiser, to assist in burning or sinking American vessels, they considered to be merely the exercise of belligerent rights.

The vessel loaded with the "Oreto's" guns and stores had arrived while her case was before the court at Nassau. It was shown by the defendants in this trial that the "Oreto" had not sailed with any warlike stores on board, and there the investigation ended; while it was well-known to all on the island that the arms were actually in port, only waiting to be put on board the Confederate as soon as she was released.

Maffitt was too clever to actually violate English neutrality laws by any overt act. He made arrangements with J. B. Lafitte, the Confederate agent at Nassau, to meet him at Grand Key, where the guns were to be delivered by a schooner chartered for that purpose. The meeting took place, and Maffitt succeeded in arming his ship, but was obliged to trust to recruiting his crew from such disaffected Americans as might elect to join him from captured vessels. He had at this time but five firemen, and fourteen deck-hands. So short-handed was he, that when he met the schooner with his battery on board he had to take off his coat and work as a common sailor. Every hour was precious to him, for the Federal cruisers hovering in the neighborhood might pounce upon him at any moment. The work was especially laborious under the scorching rays of an August sun, and it almost exhausted the energies of all hands; but at the end of five days the "Oreto" had all her stores and guns on board, and Captain Maffitt steamed out upon the ocean and put his ship in commission. The British flag, which she had worn since her departure from England, was hauled down, and the Confederate ensign hoisted amid the cheers of her motley crew. The ship was christened the "Florida."

All this looked very much like the ways of the buccaneers, who, in years gone by, used to meet at these rendezvous, and prepare for raids on harmless merchantmen and their helpless passengers; but these people were pirates in every sense of the word—ignorant, cold-blooded, brutal men, who had no nationality, and not education enough to teach them right from wrong. The "Florida," however, was not a pirate. It had been declared by the most civilized and Christian nation on the face of the earth, followed by France, that these vessels were belligerents, and entitled to all belligerent rights. The only trouble was that England, in her anxiety to follow a strictly neutral course (!), was not careful enough to see her own laws maintained, and her "Foreign Enlistment Act" strictly enforced. Had she done so, the Confederate cruisers would never have sailed from an English port; or, if they did, the British Navy would have been instructed to arrest them on the high seas, or in any English port, for a violation of the "Foreign Enlistment Act." But this was not attempted, and the English Navy, in their scrupulous care to be neutral, almost deserted the West Indies, leaving the Confederate agents to carry on their operations for the future destruction of American commerce at their discretion.

The work of getting the guns on board the "Oreto" had been so severe in that burning climate that it produced sickness among her crew. The captain's steward was buried on the day the cruiser went into commission, and, on investigation, it appeared that he had died of yellow fever. The constantly increasing sick-list confirmed this opinion. There was no surgeon on board, and the captain was compelled to assume all the duties of medical officer as well as his own.

On the fifth day out, the "Florida" found herself off the little island of Anguila, and by report of the hospital steward the epidemic had reduced the working force to one fireman and four deck-hands. Being no longer able to keep the sea, Maffitt ran into the Port of Cardenas, in the Island of Cuba. Here all the officers and men were attacked in succession, and the disease being epidemic on shore, no medical aid could be obtained. Maffitt himself was at last taken down, and never perhaps in the history of yellow fever was there a ship in a worse condition than this. But "it is an ill-wind that blows nobody good," and the peaceful merchantmen could now follow their way unmolested by the "Florida"; and thus many of them escaped burning or scuttling by this misadventure of the Confederate cruiser—which some, no doubt, attributed to an act of Providence, but which was simply owing to the fact that the sailors had been indulging too freely at

Nassau, and there laid in the germs of fever, which were afterwards developed by their work in the hot sun.

There was a dreadful condition of affairs on board the "Florida," but amidst it all Maffitt never lost his self-possession until he became unconscious and was given up for dead. While in this apparently hopeless condition his young son died, followed shortly afterwards by the chief engineer, and the "Florida" bade fair to lay at anchor in the Bay of Cardenas until the war was over. But Maffitt recovered; his indomitable will carried him through the dreadful ordeal, and the doom of the "Florida" was not yet sealed. When he and most of his crew were convalescent, the Captain-General of Cuba sent a message to request the commander of the "Florida" to proceed to Havana, on the ground (it is asserted) that his vessel would be safe from an attack of Federal gun-boats, when it is well known that there was but one instance during the war where a Confederate cruiser was molested in neutral waters. In fact, there was such an absence of Federal gun-boats all along the Bahama banks and coast of Cuba, from the time the "Florida" first appeared in Nassau up to the time of her leaving Havana, that it was the cause of severe and well deserved strictures upon the neglect of the Navy Department, which seemed to be oblivious to the fact that the Confederates were fitting out these vessels as fast as their means would permit.

Though the Captain-General had invited the commander of the "Florida" to go to Havana for the above reason, it was actually for the purpose of preventing him from violating Spanish neutrality laws; and when Maffitt arrived in Havana he found himself so tied up with restrictions imposed by the Spanish authorities, that he determined to go to Mobile and fit his ship out there.

He therefore got underway for that port on the 1st of September, and arrived in sight of Fort Morgan on the 4th, having started on his perilous adventure with his crew just convalescing, and he himself scarcely able to stand from the prostrating effects of the fever.

It may appear to the reader that we have exhibited more sympathy for Commander Maffitt and given him more credit than he deserved: it must be remembered that we are endeavoring to write a naval history of the war, and not a partisan work. This officer, it is true, had gone from under the flag we venerate to fight against it; but we know that it was a sore trial for him to leave the service to which he was attached, and that he believed he was doing his duty in following the fortunes of his State, and had the courage to follow his convictions.

He did not leave the United States Navy with any bitterness, and when the troubles were all over he accepted the situation gracefully. What we are going to state of him shows that he was capable of the greatest heroism, and that, though he was on the side of the enemy, his courage and skill were worthy of praise.

On the 4th of September, at 2 P. M., the "Florida" made Fort Morgan, and at the same time it was discovered that three of the enemy's cruisers lay between her and the bar. Maffitt was assisted on deck, being too sick to move without help. He determined to run the risk of passing the blockaders; and, if he failed in that, he made his preparations to destroy his vessel so that she might not fall into Federal hands. He hoisted the English ensign, and assumed the character of an English ship-of-war. The moment the "Florida" was seen by the blockaders, as she stood boldly in, two of these vessels got underway and stood towards her. The blockading force was at this time under the command of Commander George H. Preble, in the "Oneida," a prudent, careful officer, who tried hard not to commit any mistakes; but on this occasion he was too careful not to compromise his Government by attacking an English man-of-war, as he supposed the "Florida" was, from the bold manner in which she stood towards him.

Several gun-boats had been employed blockading outside the bar, the "Kanawha," "Pinola" and "Kennebec," and the steam-frigate "Susquehanna" had also been there, but all of these vessels had been temporarily withdrawn for other duty. The "Oneida" had been making repairs on her boilers, and the "Winona" was the only other vessel actually on the blockade at that moment. The "Oneida" was one of the fine ships built at the beginning of the war, and was supposed to be a 12-knot vessel. Her armament consisted of two 11-inch Dahlgrens (one forward and the other aft), four 32-pounders and three Dahlgren 30-pounder rifles. The "Winona" carried one 11-inch Dahlgren pivot-gun (forward), and two 32-pounders; and the schooner "Rachel Seaman" (bomb vessel), which happened to be beating up to the bar at the time, carried two 32-pounders. The "Oneida," owing to repairs that were going on, could not carry a full press of steam, and may be said to have been caught napping.

Commander Maffitt could not have chosen a more auspicious time to attempt his daring feat, though, be it said to his credit, he had made up his mind to run through the whole blockading fleet if necessary. It was his last chance; he had only to do that or run his vessel on shore and burn her, for she was of no use to the Confederates in her then condition.

As soon as Maffitt discovered the Federal vessels, he stood directly for them, knowing that, as the "Florida" resembled an English gun-boat, she would probably be mistaken for one, and trusting to his speed to save him at the last moment. Intelligence had been received at Pensacola. the headquarters of the squadron, of the "Florida's" having left Nassau; but no news of her having reached Cardenas had followed, and for some reason no intimation had been sent to the fleet off Mobile that she was on a cruise.

At that time English ships-of-war were in the habit of going along the coast to see if the blockade was effectual, and it was customary for them to enter blockaded ports after reporting to the commanding officer of the blockading force and obtaining his permission. Commander Preble, thinking this to be a case of that kind, ran out to meet the supposed Englishman, and rounded-to, to go in with him on the same course. The "Florida" approached rapidly, her smoke-pipes vomiting forth volumes of black smoke and a high press of steam escaping from her steam-pipe. As she came within hailing distance, the Federal commander ordered her to heave-to, but Maffitt still sped on, having sent all his men below, except the man at the wheel, and returned no reply to the hail. Preble then fired a shot ahead of the "Florida," still supposing her to be some saucy Englishman disposed to try what liberties he could take, though the absence of men on deck should have excited suspicion. He hesitated, however, and his hesitation lost him a prize and the honor of capturing one of the Confederate scourges of the ocean. Preble had his crew at quarters, however, and as soon as he saw that the stranger was passing him he opened his broadside upon her, and the other two blockaders did the same. But the first shots were aimed too high and the "Florida" sped on toward the bar, her feeble crew forgetting their sickness and heaping coal upon the furnace fires with all possible rapidity. Every man was working for his life, while the captain stood amid the storm of shot and shell perfectly unmoved, keenly watching the marks for entering the port, and wondering to himself what his chances were for getting safely in.

The first broadside of the "Oneida," which was fired from a distance of a few yards only, cut away the "Florida's" hammocks, smashed her boats, and shattered some of her spars. The shock seemed to give a new impetus to her speed, the English colors were hauled down, and an attempt was made to hoist the Confederate flag in their place, but the man who

was bending it to the halyards had his fingers shot away, and it was not run up while under fire.

The "Winona" now opened on the chase with her heavy guns, as did also the "Rachel Seaman" with her 32-pounders, but the latter vessel was at a distance and her fire was of little effect. The "Oneida" fired rapidly from all the guns she could bring to bear; but as she could not make more than seven knots an hour, the "Florida" was rapidly leaving her. One 11-inch shell entered the side of the blockade-runner just above the water-line, passed through both sides, and exploded. Had it exploded one second sooner the career of the "Florida" would have ended and she would have gone to the bottom; but an inch or two saved her. On she sped, faster and faster, until even those who longed for his discomfiture could not but admire the steady bearing of the brave man who stood alone upon the deck. Another shell passed through the cabin, and her after-spars began to tremble as their supports were cut away. The firing of the Union vessels was bad, however, and the Confederate finally escaped with but one man killed and seven wounded—a small loss compared to their great gain.

During the whole war there was not a more exciting adventure than this escape of the "Florida" into Mobile Bay. The gallant manner in which it was conducted excited great admiration, even among the men who were responsible for permitting it. We do not suppose there was ever a case where a man, under all the attending circumstances, displayed more energy or more bravery.

The "Florida" remained four months in Mobile preparing for sea, and watching a chance to get out. The blockading squadron had been enlarged to seven vessels, among them the "R. R. Cuyler," a very fast steamer, that had been sent to this station with the certainty that she would be able to intercept the "Florida" if she attempted to run out.

Maffitt came down from Mobile one afternoon in the "Florida," and noted the number and positions of the blockaders. while he was plainly visible to them. The Federal commanders had been in a continual state of vigilance for three months, and it was a great relief to them to see the coveted prize at last. One would have supposed that on such an occasion every man would have been at his post, and the vessels with steam up and the chains ready to slip; but this was not the case. The "Cuyler" only was ordered to change her position after dark, and be ready to start after the "Florida" the moment she appeared. Not a vessel was sent off eight or ten miles to head the Confederate off if she should get the lead, and no extraordinary precautions were taken.

At about 2 A. M. the "Florida" was reported as coming out. She passed directly between the "Cuyler" and the "Susquehanna," at a distance of 300 yards from the former. It is stated that half an hour was lost in the "Cuyler's" getting underway, owing to a regulation of the ship that the officer of the watch should report to the captain and wait for him to come on deck before slipping the cable (in this instance it would have been well if the Captain had slept on deck).

The "Oneida's" officers saw the signal, beat to quarters, but remained at anchor, though she was assigned as one of the chasing vessels! and at 3:50, "having seen no vessel run out, beat the retreat!" Such is the extract from her log. The "Cuyler's" officers, however, saw the "Florida" distinctly, and chased her during the whole of the next day, making as her greatest speed during the chase only 12½ knots, although she had previously made 14. At night the "Florida" changed her course, and ran for the coast of Cuba, where she was engaged in burning prizes the next day, while the "Cuyler" was hunting for her in the Yucatan Channel.

On the day after the "Florida" ran out, the "Oneida" was sent in pursuit of her; but she missed the Confederate cruiser, and Commodore Wilkes, who at that time commanded a "flying squadron" of slow vessels, fell in with her, detained her and made her a part of his command, as he also did the "Cuyler" when she fell into his hands.

And so the "Florida" was allowed to go on her way without molestation, and Maffitt was enabled to commence that career on the high seas which has made his name one of the notable ones of the war. He lighted the seas wherever he passed along, and committed such havoc among American merchantmen, that, if possible, he was even more dreaded than Semmes. We have only to say, that his being permitted to escape into Mobile Bay, and then to get out again, was the greatest example of blundering committed throughout the war. Every officer who knew Maffitt was certain that he would attempt to get out of Mobile, and we are forced to say that those who permitted his escape are responsible for the terrible consequences of their want of vigilance and energy.

To return to Captain Semmes: He had been kept several anxious weeks at Nassau waiting for an opportunity to return to Europe. The "290," then fitting out in England, was nearly ready for sea—and it was deemed advisable to send her out as soon as possible, before the application of the British "Foreign Enlistment Act" should become more stringent.

Semmes wrote to Captain Bulloch, who had charge of fitting out the "290," to bring her to a rendezvous where he would join her. The former then made his way to Liverpool in the steamer "Bahama," and found that the "290" had succeeded in eluding the vigilance (!) of the English authorities and had proceeded to the island of Terceira, where she was awaiting the arrival of her battery on another vessel, which had also eluded these vigilant Englishmen!

The "Alabama" was built by John Laird, an eminent ship-builder, and we believe that she was built especially for the Confederate Government. This book does not pretend to enter into a lengthy legal discussion of the rights of the Confederates to build and equip ships in English ports for the destruction of American commerce, though the writer condemns the practice *in toto*. The Queen of England, at the outbreak of the civil war in America, issued a proclamation, in which it was stated that England would preserve a strict neutrality between the contending parties. This neutrality consisted not only in permitting the Confederates actually to build and equip cruising steamships for the purpose of inflicting injury on the Federals, but these ships managed to leave England in violation of the "Foreign Enlistment Act," and did inflict serious injury to the shipping of the United States.

A great many arguments were brought forward by Confederate writers to prove that no laws were violated by the above proceedings, but a folio of such arguments is not worth much in the face of the fact that in 1871 a commission was appointed by England and the United States to settle what were known as the "Alabama Claims," but which included the vessels captured by all the Confederate cruisers fitted out in England. The result of that Commission was that Great Britain paid to the United States the sum of $15,000,000 as indemnification for the damage inflicted on United States commerce by Confederate cruisers, owing to the neglect of the British authorities in not preventing the said cruisers from getting to sea. There could be no better argument than this against all the specious writings which have appeared from time to time, and it especially refutes the attempt of Commander Semmes to justify his course. Great Britain is a nation from whom nothing like payment could have been exacted, but the concurrence of the English Commissioners was based on that high sense of justice and fair-play which is the ruling characteristic of the Anglo-Saxon race.

Commander Semmes, after spending a

few days in Liverpool, collecting his officers and making financial arrangements, departed on the 13th of August, 1862, in the steamer "Bahama," to join the "290."

Commander James D. Bullock, formerly of the U. S. Navy, accompanied him, to be present at the christening of the "290," which he had contracted for and superintended while she was building.

The "290" was a vessel of 900 tons burden, 230 feet in length, 32 feet beam, and, when provisioned and coaled for a cruise, drew 15 feet of water. Her model was of the most perfect symmetry, and she sat upon the water with the lightness and grace of a swan. She was barkentine-rigged, with long lower masts, that enabled her to carry large fore-and-aft sails, which are of so much importance to a steamer in most weathers. She was of the lightest build compatible with strength, and was, in fact, constructed with the one idea of making her an efficient commerce-destroyer. She was a fast steamer, but her two modes of locomotion were independent of each other. Her speed was about 10 knots, though she made 11½ on her trial trip. She was well armed with 8 guns, six 32-pounders in broadside and two pivot guns, one a 100-pounder Blakely rifle, and the other a long 8-inch smooth-bore. The crew required for the "290" (not counting those in the engine-room) numbered 120 men, and she carried 24 officers.

This was the vessel that became so famous in burning and sinking that her reputation in this kind of warfare has eclipsed that of all the other Confederate vessels engaged in the same business.

A week after Semmes left Liverpool he was in Porto Praya, where he found the "290" with some of her stores already on board. Some objections being made to his getting guns on board in West Angra Bay, Semmes got underway with his flotilla and proceeded far enough to sea to be outside of neutral jurisdiction, and there, in smooth water, got the vessels alongside and completed his outfit. He then steamed back to Terceira and filled his vessel with coal.

Terceira is a beautiful place, nearly every foot of the island is under cultivation, and from a distance the whole country looks like a rambling village, where Nature seems to smile as it does nowhere else. There is everything here to allure the heart of man to harmony and peace. The little town of Angra, near which the "Alabama" was anchored, was a perfect picture of a Portuguese-Moorish settlement, with its red-tiled roofs, sharp gables, and parti-colored verandas, while the quiet peacefulness that hung over this spot, so far removed from the highways of the world, gave it an unusual charm.

Yet from this beautiful spot, where it seemed as if nothing unlawful could exist, started forth one of the most devastating expeditions against a nation's commerce known in the history of war.

The "290" lay at her anchors in all her rakish beauty; but to one who could have known of her mission she would have been an offence instead of an object of admiration. Who, to look at her in that beautiful harbor, would ever have supposed that she was bound on a mission of vengeance, and that she was destined to rove the high seas in search of plunder and leave behind her a track of flame!

Semmes had arrived in Terceira on a Wednesday, and by Saturday night all his labors were completed. The "290's" battery was on board, her provisions all stowed away, and her coal-bunkers full.

Sunday morning dawned bright and beautiful, and Semmes and his co-workers took it as a harbinger of success. The ship had not been yet put in commission, *i. e.,* had not been baptized, and the time having now come to perform this ceremony, every preparation was made to carry it through in man-of-war style. The decks were cleaned, the rigging hauled taut, and the vessel made to look, as her captain expressed it, "like a bride, with the orange-wreath about her brow, ready to be led to the altar !"

But the crew had not yet been enlisted ; there were some ninety stalwart fellows in the two steamers who had been brought thus far under articles of agreement that were now no longer binding. Some had shipped for one voyage—some for another —but none of them, it is said, had been enlisted for service on board a Confederate cruiser. This course had been pursued in order to avoid a breach of the British "Foreign Enlistment Act," but no one can doubt that these rough and devil-may-care-looking fellows were ready for any adventure that promised plunder or profit ; they were the same kind of men that accompanied Morgan all through the West Indies, across the Isthmus, and even to the gates of Panama.

But to perform these functions for the christening of the "290," it was necessary to be careful that no neutral law should be violated. Not for anything in the world would Semmes and his confederates have done anything of this kind, and it was therefore essential that the "290" should get underway and steam off beyond the marine league, where, upon the broad ocean, it was neutral for all the world. After steaming the required distance, the "290" was stopped and the programme carried out.

The officers were all in full uniform, and

the crew neatly dressed. All hands were summoned aft on the quarter-deck, and, mounting a gun-carriage, Semmes read his commission as a Captain in the Confederate service, and the Secretary of the Navy's order directing him to assume command of the "Alabama." When this reading was finished, the Confederate flag and pennant were run up, while the English colors were hauled down ; a gun was fired, the band played "Dixie," and thus was christened the "Alabama"—a vessel whose career was destined to throw that of the "Sumter" into the shade.

Captain Semmes congratulated himself on having performed this ceremony in the most legal manner. The fact that it had all been done upon the high seas, more than a marine league from the land, where Mr. Jefferson Davis had as much jurisdiction as Mr. Abraham Lincoln, made it entirely legal in his sight.

Up to this time not a single sailor had shipped for the coming cruise of the "Alabama"; but the stalwart fellows who were now moving about her decks had well understood before they left Liverpool that they were to enlist in the Confederate service, and thus violate the "Foreign Enlistment Act" of the British nation.

The new cruiser cannot be considered to have been a representative Confederate man-of-war, for, with the exception of a few officers, all on board of her were Englishmen, who possessed no sentiment of loyalty towards the Government under which they were now to serve. It was not a crew of enthusiastic Southerners who were going forth to fight for a cause they really loved, but a band of foreign mercenaries who had no feeling but of indifference towards either of the combatants; and when one thinks of the character of these sailors there is some excuse for comparing them to pirates who fight with no other motive than that of plunder.

In this case they had been quietly told that they would receive double the amount of wages paid elsewhere, and that the Confederate Congress would vote them prize-money to the full value of every ship they destroyed. Captain Semmes had touched the hearts of these Englishmen in the right place, and he had the satisfaction of enlisting 80 out of the 90 sailors who had come out from the Mersey in the two steamers, and they came forward willingly to sign their names and receive their advance wages. This ended the democratic part of the proceedings. There was no more talk about nationalities or liberties or double wages. The strict discipline of an American man-of-war was at once enforced by Semmes and his officers (most of whom had been educated in the old Navy), and the

new vessel was quickly put into a state of efficiency.

If these officers were engaged in a bad cause, they were at least faithful to it in the extreme. They had succeeded far beyond their most sanguine expectations, having got their vessel to sea in spite of the watchful care of the American minister in London and the apparent zeal of the British Government to prevent it. How far Her Majesty's Government were sincere in their intentions can be seen from the following extract, which we give from the work of a clever naval writer, Professor J. Russell Soley, U. S. N. :

"The second cruiser built in England for the Confederates was the 'Alabama,' whose career began in July, 1862. The attention of the Foreign Office had been first called to this vessel by a note from Mr. Adams on the 23d of June. The evidence then submitted as to her character was confined to a statement made by the Consul at Liverpool, of suspicious circumstances connected with the vessel. The communication was referred to the law officers of the Crown, who gave the opinion that, if the allegations were true, the building and equipment of the vessel were a 'Manifest violation of the Foreign Enlistment Act, and steps ought to be taken to put that act in force and to prevent the vessel from going to sea.'

"It was added that the Customs authorities at Liverpool should endeavor to ascertain the truth of the statements, and that, if sufficient evidence could be obtained, proceedings should be taken as early as possible. On the 4th of July, the report of the Customs officers was transmitted to Mr. Adams, tending to show that there was no sufficient evidence that a violation of the act was contemplated.

"Other correspondence and opinions followed. On the 21st, affidavits were delivered to the authorities at Liverpool, one of which, made by a seaman who had been shipped on board the vessel, declared that Butcher, the captain of the 'Alabama,' who engaged him, had stated that she was going out to fight for the Confederate States. Other depositions to the same effect were received on the 23d and 25th, all of which were referred, as they came in, to the law officers. The latter rendered the opinion that the evidence of the deponents, coupled with the character of the vessel, make it reasonably clear that she was intended for warlike use against the United States, and recommended that she be seized without loss of time.

"Notwithstanding that the urgency of the case was well known to the Government, and notwithstanding also that of the four depositions upon which the law officers chiefly based their opinion, one had been received on the 21st of July, two others on the 23d, and the fourth on the 25th, the report was not presented until the 29th. On that day, however, the 'Alabama' left Liverpool, without an armament, and ostensibly on a trial trip. She ran down to Port Lynas, on the coast of Anglesea, about fifty miles from Liverpool. Here she remained for two days completing her preparations.

"On the morning of the 31st she got underway and stood to the northward up the Irish Sea ; and, rounding the northern coast of Ireland, she passed out into the Atlantic.

"Among the innumerable side-issues presented by the case of the 'Alabama,' the facts given above contain the essential point. That the attention of the British Government was called to the suspicious character of the vessel on the 23d of June ; that her adaptation to warlike use was admitted ; that her readiness for sea was known ; that evidence was submitted on the 21st, the 23d, and finally on the 25th of July, that put her character beyond a doubt ; and that, in spite of all this, she was allowed to sail on the 29th, make the real foundation of the case against Great Britain.

*   *   *   *   *   *

"The inference is unavoidable that the Government deliberately intended to pursue a policy as unfriendly as it could possibly be without passing the technical bounds of a legal neutrality."

The proof of the illegality of all these acts is the fact that the British Government finally paid the award of the "Alabama Commission," which was an acknowledgment on its part that the responsibility for the acts of the Confederate cruiser rested with the Power that by indifference and neglect of a plain duty had allowed its laws to be violated.

The "Alabama" had not far to go before she could strike a blow at the commerce of the North. The theatre of her performances was close at hand. The whaling season in the neighborhood of the Azores generally ends about the 1st of October, when the winter gales begin to blow, and food for the whales becomes scarce. The whales then migrate to other feeding grounds, and are followed up by their pursuers.

It was now in the early days of September, and Semmes had but a few weeks left in which to accomplish his purpose of striking a blow at the whale fishery of the United States, which had for years been carried on in these peaceful latitudes. The people pursuing this industry had no idea that there was such a vessel in existence as the "Alabama." The "Ocmulgee," of Edgartown, was lying off Fayal, made fast to a dead whale, when her captain was astonished by the appearance of a Confederate cruiser. When the "Alabama" first came in sight she carried the American flag, and was naturally mistaken for one of the new cruisers that were reported to be fitting out for the protection of Federal commerce and the whaling industry.

The same old story is to be told of the "Ocmulgee," as with the "Sumter's" prizes. Semmes was too old a hunter to burn her by night, when the light of his bonfire would serve as a warning to other whalers that might happen to be in the neighborhood, although by so doing he risked disappointing the descendants of the old Norsemen in his crew, who would greatly have enjoyed the spectacle. He well knew that it was necessary to keep these men amused, for they might at any time take the bit in their teeth, bid defiance to him and his officers, and take the "Alabama" into a Northern port, where their claim for prize-money would have been cheerfully acknowledged. He had read about the

mutinies at the Nore, and on board the "Bounty," and was well aware what freaks men of this class were capable of committing, but on this occasion he was compelled to defer gratifying their taste for brilliant effects, and he waited until daylight next morning before applying the torch to his prize.

On the following day, Semmes stood in for the beautiful island of Flores, spread his awnings, cleaned his ship, and read to his crew the "Articles of War" of the old Navy. It must have been very amusing to the descendants of the Norsemen when they heard that "any officer of the Navy guilty of treason shall suffer death." It was intended that this occasion should be an impressive one, for the crew had not up to this time assumed the orderly bearing of men-of-war's men. Somehow or other they had got it into their heads that they were bound on a privateering expedition, and that the "Alabama" was not a *bona-fide* man-of-war. They looked earnestly at each other as the reading of death-penalties went on, and openly signified that they did not fear being brought up and shot for insubordination by a man who had set such a shining example ! Yet Semmes seemed to think that this reading of the Articles of War had so rivetted the chains of discipline upon his men that he could count on them to the end for any adventure he might choose to embark in.

On the next day, the schooner "Starlight," from Boston, was captured. Her crew consisted of seven persons, and there were several lady passengers. Here Semmes appears in a new role. Having heard of the treatment received by the paymaster of the "Sumter," he determined to practice a little retaliation on his own account, and the crew of the "Starlight" were forthwith put in irons. This was taking upon himself the authority only possessed by his Government ; for, when retaliatory measures are adopted by one Government against another, it is done formally, and by an edict, endorsed with all the forms of lawful authority. If this were not the case, and if every commander of a ship or of a regiment were allowed to retaliate for every supposed offence, war would run into a species of brutality worthy only of savages. Hence. this power of retaliation is properly kept in the hands of heads of governments, and any subordinate who assumes this power and causes injustice to innocent people is held personally and morally responsible.

But Captain Semmes was a law unto himself, and cared for no authority or precedents that interfered with his design in the present case. Because some brute of a merchant captain, to whose care the pay-master of the "Sumter" had been intrusted, had not conscience or kindness of heart enough to treat his prisoner with respect, Semmes determined that all Yankee crews captured by the "Alabama" should suffer for it. It was not the Federal Government that had treated the paymaster of the "Sumter" with cruelty. It was an irresponsible merchant captain, and the Confederate Government had in consequence issued no order of retaliation. Captain Semmes merely followed his own notion, that the Yankees should be chastised for the sins which one man had committed against a Southerner ; but let it be remembered that these men whom he was putting in irons, and subjecting to every indignity, had not borne arms against the South, nor committed any overt act. They were peaceful traders, following their avocations, and it is not likely that they would ever have interfered with either one side or the other. He continued this practice, however, with the captains and crews of the next eight or ten prizes, and treated them with the greatest rigor. The only effect of this action was to embitter the North against an officer who thus took upon himself undue authority.

Two more fine prizes were soon afterwards taken by the "Alabama," the ships "Ocean Rover" and "Alert," both of which were filled with such supplies as the Confederates wanted. The crews of these vessels were allowed to take their boats with sufficient provisions, and start for the shore, which was then distant about five miles. Semmes did not want them, for, as they would not enlist, they would simply eat up his provisions without being of any use to him, and he was glad to get rid of them on any terms. The three last prizes were all burnt that afternoon, and the successors of the Norsemen were delighted as the smoke from three funeral pyres ascended to the skies at the same moment.

While this work was going on, an incautious American schooner (the "Weather-gauge") hove in sight and was speedily captured. There were some Northern papers on board the prize that dealt out liberal invectives against the South, and the reader may rest assured that they did the "Weather-gauge" no good. Her crew, however, were put in their boats to seek the shore, while a pillar of fire behind them revealed the fate of their floating home.

Three days after this the whaler "Alta-maha," of New Bedford, was taken and burned; but, as she had not made a successful "catch," her bonfire was somewhat of a disappointment to Semmes' adventurers. Still she counted in the game; her name

and qualifications were all entered on the "Alabama's" log-book, and the quarter-master, whose duty it was to attend to such matters, stowed away her clean new flag in his plethoric bag.

There was often a little excitement and some poetry in these chases, especially when the "Alabama" happened to fall in with a clipper of a vessel that would give her as much as she could attend to. At such a time the best helmsman would be placed at the wheel, and every sail set and trimmed to a nicety, while officers and men watched the result with the keenness of sportsmen in pursuit of a hare. The "Alabama" was a long, lean racer, with three large fore-and-aft sails and square yards. When in a heavy breeze and she wanted to go to windward, she could furl her square-sails and then become a three-masted schooner, and when under this sail few vessels could equal her in speed.

On a dark night, shortly after the last burning, while Semmes was asleep in his cabin, an old quartermaster went below and shook him by the arm, informing him that there was a large ship just passing to windward of them on the opposite tack. He sprang out of bed at once, and throwing on a few clothes was on deck as soon as the quartermaster, and gave orders to "wear ship" and give chase to the stranger. The "Alabama" was under topsails at the time, and it took some moments to get all sail upon her, and when this was done the chase was three or four miles ahead, yet quite visible to a good eye in the bright moonlight. Both vessels were now close hauled on the starboard-tack, and it was evident that the merchant captain was doing his best to escape. He set his light sails with alacrity, and trimmed his yards to the greatest advantage ; but this was the "Alabama's" best point of sailing, and when the sheets of her great trysails were hauled flat aft, and the fore-tack boarded, she bounded over the water like something imbued with life. What would not that merchant captain have given at that moment if the moon could have been blotted out ? But the darkness would not have covered her, for the Confederates were provided with the best English night-glasses, made on purpose to spy out American prizes on dark nights.

The "Alabama" gained on the chase from the very first, and in two hours was on her weather-quarter, having head-reached and gone to windward of her. The stranger was not more than a mile off, on the lee bow, when the stillness of the night was broken into by the boom of a heavy cannon. The gun was unshotted and the merchantman paid no attention to it—not a tack or sheet was slacked in obedience to the thundering summons; but the Confederates saw that preparations were being made to keep off from the wind and set stun'sails. Poor fellows! Never did merchant sailors work with such a will. They knew how little mercy they had to expect from the Southern rovers. The burnings of the "Sumter" were known in every sea where a newspaper could reach.

The merchant ship now began to move briskly through the water, by keeping off, and the delusive hope sprung up in the captain's breast that he might yet evade his pursuer. For a moment the "Alabama" began to drop astern, but it was only for a moment. As soon as she followed the movements of the chase and stood on a parallel course, she made such good speed that before the stranger could get his foretopmast stun'sail set she was within good point-blank range of a long 32-pounder. The moon was shining brightly and every rope and sail proved the stranger to be American.

The chase was very exciting, and the crew of the "Alabama" were grouped about on her deck, wondering if the "old man" would not soon bring it to a close, and let them have a good night display of burning before changing watches, and they were soon gratified by the order to fire another gun shotted, as the "Alabama" ranged up under the stern of her prey, not more than 300 yards distant. This was too much for the nerves of the old merchant captain. He was not a fighting man, and, if he had been, he had nothing to fight with, so he wisely hauled up his courses and lay-to. It was a pretty picture—that large ship lying in the light of the moon, with the long, low clipper silently stealing up alongside of her—and, no doubt, reminded the spectators of the yarns oft told in the forecastle of the times when the bold buccaneers sailed along the Spanish main, burning vessels and making their crews walk the plank.

Semmes at once gave the order to board the prize, and directed the officer to hoist a light at the peak in case she proved to be an American. When the boat came alongside, the old captain was relieved of his worst apprehensions, instead of his pursuer being a pirate, she was only the "Alabama," and though he was told his vessel would be burned in the morning, and that all his worldly goods would go up in a cloud of smoke, he thanked God that it was no worse. The light was hoisted at the peak as directed, and Semmes went below to finish the nap so unceremoniously broken, and dream of the sport he would be able to give his men next morning when he destroyed the prize.

Next morning when he came on deck he was monarch of all he surveyed. He ruled the ocean for miles around, as far even as the Saragossa Sea, for there was not such a thing as an American man-of-war in all those waters. The fifty cruisers that should have been afloat six months before, and guarding every point where American merchantmen could be found, were yet upon the stocks—nay, many of them were only on paper. An old commodore with a fleet of fourteen vessels at his heels, was steaming up and down the Gulf and Caribbean Sea, looking for "Alabamas" that were hundreds of miles away and upsetting all the plans of the Navy Department.

As Semmes looked about him that morning, his eye rested on the fine large ship lying close by, awaiting his orders. She proved to be the whaler, "Benjamin Tucker," of New Bedford, eight months out, with 340 barrels of oil. But the Confederate captain had no need for oil, so he took from her only the tobacco and small stores, and after transferring her crew of thirty persons to his own vessel, applied the torch, and before ten o'clock she was a mass of flames fore-and-aft.

The next morning he overtook and burned the schooner "Courser," of Provincetown, Massachusetts. For a moment the springs of pity opened in the breast of the Confederate as he surveyed this pretty little craft, and looked upon her handsome young captain; but he had just finished reading a Northern paper, in which he was spoken of in terms that were anything but polite, and he had to steel his heart against his better feelings and let the laws of war be executed.

He had now the crews of his three last prizes on board, and as they somewhat crowded the "Alabama," he stood in for the Island of Flores, put them in eight captured whale-boats, and sent them off to land as best they might, and compare notes with the poor fellows already on shore.

What fun it must have been to the Norsemen to see that regatta, in which eight boats were struggling to reach the shore and get as far as possible out of the neighborhood of the "Alabama"! Semmes was not otherwise inhumane to these men, but they were in his way and he wanted to get rid of them, and he seemed to think that they were so well pleased with him that, with a little coaxing, they would have given three cheers for the "Alabama"!

We are now to see the new cruiser in rough and tempestuous weather. We have seen her in smooth seas and moonlight nights; but it often happens that these smooth-water sailors do not maintain their reputation when they have to contend with heavy weather. The "Alabama" had been built as a type of a perfect cruiser, one that could maintain her character under sail as well as under steam. But up to this time Semmes had had no opportunity to test her in all weathers, which would decide the character of the vessel, and prove whether she was the most dangerous machine to be used against American commerce ever yet planned, or simply one of those expensive failures of which the United States had so many in its own Navy. The opportunity soon occurred.

The wind was rapidly freshening into a gale, when in the morning, after the burning of the "Courser," a large American ship was discovered and soon overtaken. This was the whaling-ship "Virginia," and she was burned like the rest, after being despoiled of such articles as the "Alabama" needed. The only difference was that, as the torch was not applied until late in the afternoon, the fire burned brightly for a part of the night, and could be seen when many miles away, as the flames and burning masses of timber were whirled into the air by the strong eddies of a freshening wind.

Next morning a bark hove in sight, and as soon as those on board made out the "Alabama" they commenced making efforts to escape. By this time it was blowing half a gale, and both vessels were under snug sail; but the reefs were now shaken out and topgallant sails set in both of them. It seemed at first as if the topgallant masts of the "Alabama" would go over the side, the sticks buckled so; but John Laird had selected good timber for the craft, which he had pronounced to be the finest cruiser of her class in the world, and the broad, tough English cross-trees kept everything in its place. Not a mast snapped, nor did a rope-yarn part, so perfect were all the appliances of the vessel. The bark hung on to all the sail she could carry, though she was short-handed, and her commander evidently seemed determined to escape from his pursuer or let his masts and sails go overboard.

Though the "Alabama" was much the smaller vessel of the two, it was quite evident that she was as much at home in this rough weather as the prey in view. Both vessels were at times almost under water during this exciting chase, yet the "Alabama" gained so rapidly and steadily that it was plainly seen that the bark's only chance of safety lay in the Confederate losing some of his spars. But it was the same old story. The "Alabama" carried sail, and in three hours had the stranger within reach of her 32-pounders, and there was nothing left for the merchant captain to do but surrender. He had made a gallant run for it, and had carried his canvas in a manner worthy of a man-of-war's-man, but Semmes made short shrift of his vessel (the

"Elisha Dunbar," of New Bedford), and she was soon destroyed.

Semmes did not in this case wait even long enough to examine the papers of his prize, for the gale was increasing and he desired to get his boat on board as soon as possible. What cared he whether her cargo included neutral property or not? Was not there a "prize-court" sitting in the "Alabama's" cabin night and day, and did not this court feel perfectly qualified to settle all questions of law and fact? Had not the English Government tacitly admitted that neutrals who shipped goods in vessels belonging to either belligerent must take the chances of war and apply for redress and compensation to a prize-court?

That Semmes had under his command brave and daring officers, no one will deny, for that day put their zeal and seamanship to the severest test. The boats of the "Alabama" were well managed, and succeeded in transferring all the persons without accident. Nothing was taken out of the prize but her chronometer and flag, and by the time the boats were alongside the "Alabama," the "Dunbar" was all in flames, with her sails set just as when she hove-to. The gale howled, as if giving out a solemn requiem over the destruction of this fine vessel, and the sea-birds that brave the gale and were hovering around with discordant cries, added their apparent grief to the noise and crashing of timbers and roaring eddies of wind that were rushing through the doomed vessel.

The burning ship was, without doubt, a beautiful spectacle, which the descendants of the Norsemen enjoyed amazingly. What cared they who was injured by the destruction of the "Elisha Dunbar," since even Earl Russell was not averse to seeing a little English commerce consigned to the bottom of the ocean, as long as the whole American merchant marine could be destroyed or transferred to the flag of Great Britain!

The black clouds were mustering their forces in fearful array, ready to burst in anger over this scene of destruction. Night seemed suddenly to have wrapped the day in its mantle of darkness. The thunder rolled in the high heavens, reverberating for miles away to leeward, the awful crash seeming to shake the sea and earth to their centres, and lightning leaped from cloud to cloud, adding greatly to the grandeur of a scene which no pen can describe. All nature seemed to protest against such unnatural and wanton proceedings. The sea was by this time raging fearfully, and spray that was blown from the tops of rising waves cut the faces of the sailors as if it had been small shot. The winds howled, and rain descended in torrents, as if determined to quench the fires raised by rebellious hands; but nothing could save the "Dunbar," and the flames burned yet more fiercely as she lay rolling and tossing upon the tumultuous sea. Now an ignited sail would fly away from a yard and scud off before the gale like some huge albatross with its wings on fire, while the yards, with braces burned and released from all control, would sway about violently, as if anxious to escape from this turmoil of fire and wind, and finally drop into the sea. The masts, one after another, went by the board, as the hull rocked and heaved like some great animal in its death throes, and finally the sea broke in and met the flames with a shriek resembling the howl of a thousand demons. The ship gave one great roll, and then went to the bottom, "a victim to the passions of man and the prey of the elements."

These were the scenes that followed in the track of the "Alabama." Semmes looked on unmoved amidst the howlings of the storm, and the descendants of the Norsemen added a new scene to their adventures, hereafter to be told under the forecastle to their admiring shipmates who had not had the glory of serving on a Confederate cruiser.

The storm was at its height, but the "Alabama" rode it out under reefed sails like a duck; and Captain Semmes was satisfied that he had under his command not only a formidable war-vessel, but a capital sea-boat. John Laird had kept his word with the Confederate agent when he designed and built the "Alabama," and it is reasonable to suppose, since he gave so much of his time and attention to this cruiser, that his heart was much interested in the Confederate cause.

Semmes felt that he had a vessel on which he could depend for any emergency. It was now the month of October, and the gales of the season were beginning to blow. He had completely swept the seas in the whaling district, and there was nothing more of consequence to be done in that latitude. He had not, so far, burned a pound of coal in his pursuit of United States commerce; all his operations had been conducted under sail, and he had never found a vessel that could escape the "Alabama." He now sighed for new scenes of adventure, and his officers, who also longed for a change, suggested going to the ground where the grain-ships of the North might be picked up when on their way to Europe to feed the great multitudes there who depended on American grain for a subsistence.

The descendants of the Norsemen had got tired of capturing whalers, and they longed to get into the track of traders, whose rich cargoes would afford better opportunities for obtaining plunder. Semmes knew how to manage his men, and that it was necessary to amuse them. Sailors are like children all the world over; and, although they must be governed with a firm hand, it is sometimes advisable to let them think that their wishes are consulted. Semmes never forgot the lessons taught by mutineers in times past, and he attempted to keep his sailors in a contented frame of mind by occasional concessions.

Early on the morning of October 3d two sails were simultaneously reported from the "Alabama's" mast-head; but, as both ships were standing in the direction of the cruiser, there was no need to chase. They were running right into the spoiler's net, and suspected no danger until they were within gunshot, when the "Alabama" fired a gun and hoisted the flag that had carried such terror to the whaleships of the Azores. These vessels were the "Brilliant" and "Emily Farnum," both of New York, and both loaded with grain. The latter being what Semmes considered "properly documented" was released on ransom-bond, and he took the opportunity of sending away in her all his prisoners, of whom he had 50 or 60, besides those just captured. The "Brilliant" was burned with her valuable cargo.

On the afternoon of October 7th, the bark "Wavecrest" was taken; and, after being relieved of everything that could be of use to the Confederates, she was made a target for gun practice, and finally destroyed.

Next day the brig "Dunkirk," of New York, fell into the hands of the "Alabama," and, as her captain could offer no evidence of neutral ownership, she also was committed to the flames.

Up to this time Semmes had destroyed twelve valuable vessels, with their cargoes, and all this work had been done in little over a month, with his ship under sail alone, and here he was now right in the track of the grain trade between New York and Europe with not a single Federal man-of-war in the neighborhood to interfere with his proceedings. He approached the coast with confidence, for he had not as yet ever heard of any vessel having been sent in pursuit of him—much less seen one. Crowds of vessels were daily leaving New York for Liverpool, but they were mostly foreigners, with cargoes properly documented, who were taking advantage of the times to reap golden harvests. These vessels Semmes could not touch, but he gave them as much trouble as possible.

Why the United States Government should have left this great highway unprotected no one to this day can conjecture. The vessels that were sent to look for the "Alabama" always went to the wrong places, when it must have been known that she would seek the highways of trade as naturally as a bluefish would seek the feeding-grounds of the menhaden. Whatever success the Federal Government may have had in blockading the enemy's ports, its attempts to protect the merchant marine were nearly always failures ; and it shows how necessary it is for a nation to keep on hand in time of peace vessels that will prove useful in time of war.

There seemed to be no limit to his success, and Semmes had so much to do, and so many legal questions to decide, that he was sometimes brought to a standstill. One ship that he captured (the " Tonawanda ") carried a number of women and children, who filled the air with piteous lamentations at what appeared to them to be a dreadful fate. This was more perplexing than a dozen ordinary cargoes, for he could burn these if his " prize-court " so decided, but could not so easily dispose of the women and children ; and he was obliged to sail about for some time with this living cargo following in his wake, hoping that he might fall in with some neutral vessel to which he could transfer his passengers, and then be at liberty to destroy the floating home of these poor people before their eyes. If he had been a man of any generosity, he would have said to the captain of the " Tonawanda," " Go in peace ; we are not warring against women and children, and these helpless ones shall not be molested." But not he : he had no sentiment about him, and, although he knew the agony felt by these people, he kept them sailing in his wake until another victim should heave in sight.

But it seems that the " Alabama " still had to play out her role before she left the North Atlantic. The good intentions that were entertained towards the passengers of the " Tonawanda "—to put them on board a neutral vessel—were frustrated by the arrival of another heavy ship of the " junk fleet " (as the grain ships were called by Semmes' men). This vessel approached the " Alabama " unsuspectingly until the boom of a gun and the Confederate flag at the stranger's peak showed the merchant captain that his fate was sealed, and he immediately surrendered.

The " Alabama " had by this time become pretty well known in the United States, and Semmes' methods were understood. Ships were heavily insured before sailing, and a shipmaster surrendered his vessel with the satisfaction of knowing that some time in the future his losses would be reimbursed. The ship " Manchester," that had now fallen into the " Alabama's " toils, was a more valuable prize than the " Tona-

wanda," so the latter was allowed to proceed on her voyage, while the former was burned in her place.

On the 15th of October the next ship was taken ; but Semmes and his officers were very much disappointed when they sat down to breakfast that morning at not having their regular batch of newspapers. This vessel was the " Lamplighter," loaded with tobacco, and after the Confederates had taken what they wanted out of her they burned her, and thus approached the coast, leaving a track of flames behind them ; while the Federal Government, which had been immediately apprised of her escape from Liverpool, took no effective measures to arrest the career of the cruiser that was attacking American commerce and driving its vessels to seek protection under the British flag.

The English Ministry might well afford to ignore the occasional destruction of part of a British cargo, when they knew that the system pursued by Semmes was driving all merchants to ship their cargoes in British bottoms, or to register their vessels under the English flag. The Chamber of Commerce, in Liverpool, writing to Earl Russell, as late as November, 1862, in regard to the destruction of neutral goods by the " Alabama," received the reply : " British owners of property on board of *Federal* ships, alleged to have been unlawfully captured by Confederate cruisers, are in the same position as any other neutral owner shipping in enemy's bottoms during the war." Of course, this drove all British property to seek neutral bottoms ; and when English owners of captured property were told to apply to the Confederate prize-courts for redress, it convinced everybody that the British Government was not going to protect the property of its subjects on the high seas as long as an American flag waved upon the ocean.

With all her great Navy, Her Britannic Majesty had not a vessel on the ocean looking after the proceedings of these Confederate cruisers, while quite a number of them were employed in watching the operations of the Federal Navy on the coast, and officiously inspecting the blockade, to see that it was lawfully maintained.

The " Alabama " made her sixteenth capture on the 21st of October : a fine large ship running down to her—the fly and the spider again—looking a perfect picture, with her sails all beautifully drawing, and her masts swaying and bending under the cloud of canvas, while the sea was rolling before her broad, flaring bows as if nothing could oppose her progress. It was a beautiful sight, this almost living sign of a nation's greatness, that could boast at that time that the white sails of her ships covered every sea. But a little puff of smoke from the "Alabama's" guns soon changed the picture: her cloud of canvas seemed to shrivel and disappear as if it had been a scroll rolled up by an invisible hand, and all the symmetry of the great mass that had so lately been swaying gracefully above the water was gone.

Though the cargo of the prize was certified to all over as being the property of neutrals, and also covered with British consular seals that had heretofore been respected, Semmes was not satisfied until he had held an "Admiralty Court" in his cabin, and the court came to the conclusion that the "Lafayette" must burn. Earl Russell had decided that neutrals shipping in vessels belonging to the belligerents must suffer the consequences of war, and the British Minister at Washington simply carried out the instructions of his superior, and referred all complainants to the Southern prize-courts.

Semmes found, that day, newspapers on board the "Lafayette" in which were some very severe strictures in regard to his course in the cases of the "Brilliant" and "Emily Farnum"—in fact, some of the papers denounced his acts as piracy, a term always galling to him. This did not help the case of the "Lafayette," and she was ruthlessly destroyed as soon as the captain of the "Alabama" was satisfied that he had taken everything out of her that could be of service to himself or his crew.

Three days after this capture the "Crenshaw" was taken, plundered and burned. She was only a schooner, and it did not take the "prize-court" in the "Alabama's" cabin ten minutes to decide her fate.

Semmes now found that his supply of coal was running out, and decided to shape his course for the Island of Martinique, where he had directed Captain Bullock to send him a coal-ship.

On the 2d of November he captured the "Levi Starbuck," a New Bedford whaler, bound on a voyage to the Pacific Ocean. Like all her class just starting out, she was filled with all sorts of stores and Yankee nicknacks; and although the "Alabama" had been filled up a dozen times since she started from the Azores with stores taken from her prizes, yet she had the maw of a cormorant and always seemed to want to be fed. All this booty was easily acquired, and it went just as easily. The amount of food, tobacco and clothing used by the 90 men and 24 officers on board the "Alabama" was among the most remarkable events of her cruise. But, notwithstanding the comforts bestowed upon her captors by the "Levi Starbuck," she was burned at night-fall.

It will be observed how easily all these vessels were taken by the "Alabama." Some would call this good luck on the part of the Confederate commander; but, in fact, it was the result of good management and forethought. Semmes did no more than follow the channels of trade which the American ships were known to travel, and it is reasonable to suppose that, if Federal ships-of-war had followed the same tracks, they would have picked up the bold adventurer before he had been many days at sea.

About this time the "Alabama" was approaching another track of commerce, across which it was intended to run on her way to Martinique, viz., the track of homeward-bound East Indiamen, and the day after getting in the track she fell in with and captured the "T. B. Wales," of Boston.

Captain Semmes now liberally construed the Confederate prize-law, that "No person in the Navy shall take out of a prize or vessel seized as a prize, any money, plate, goods, or any part of her rigging, unless it be for the better preservation thereof, or absolutely necessary for the use of any of the vessels of the Confederate States." He helped himself not only to anchors, chains, stores and provisions, but to the main-yard of the "Wales," which happened to be the right size and in better condition than that of the "Alabama." No wonder the Confederates were able to keep a number of cruisers at sea, when they found a victualling station in everything they captured, and could supply themselves with all necessaries at these floating dockyards.

There were women and children on board the East Indiaman, but they were all transferred to the "Alabama," and that night they were treated to the sight of a burning vessel; but, as much of their personal property went up in the flames, it is not likely that they enjoyed the spectacle to any great extent. It can be said to Semmes' credit, however, that he showed these poor people all attention, and made them as comfortable as circumstances would permit.

About the 16th of November the "Alabama" sighted the island of Dominica, the first land she had made since leaving Terceira in the Azores. Semmes now put his vessel under steam and ran for Martinique—where he expected to meet his coal-ship—passed close by the harbor of St. Pierre, to see that there were no United States ships-of-war there, and then into the harbor of Port de France, where he came to anchor.

Here the "Alabama" landed her prisoners and took on board what stores she needed; but Semmes did not attempt to coal his vessel in this port, as he feared the appearance of an American man-of-war. This precaution was well taken, for the coal-ship had·

hardly got clear of the Island when the U. S. steamer "San Jacinto" appeared off the entrance to the harbor and blockaded him. But Semmes did not fear this slow and antiquated ship, as he knew that his superior speed would enable him to make his escape whenever he was ready.

The "San Jacinto" was an old steam-frigate, under the command of Commander Ronckendorff, carrying a heavy battery, but not able to make more than 7 knots under steam, and Semmes cared no more for her than if she had been an old-fashioned sailing three-decker. Commander Ronckendorff stationed himself just outside of the marine league, and kept a sharp watch on the "Alabama," but she escaped without difficulty under cover of the night, and joined her coal-ship at Blanquilla, a little island on the coast of Venezuela.

From this point Semmes shaped his course for the Gulf of Mexico, in hopes of overtaking an expedition said to be fitting out under General Banks for the purpose of invading Texas, and, as this expedition was to rendezvous at Galveston, he steered for that port. At the same time, he hoped to make his cruise remunerative by way-laying one of the steamers from Panama carrying gold to the North. He had several weeks to spare, and the idea of levying upon the mail-steamers gave him much pleasure, as a million or so of dollars deposited in Europe would naturally aid him in his operations upon the sea.

On November 26th Semmes stood for the Mona Passage between St. Domingo and Porto Rico. This was the general route of the mail-steamers on their way to the North from Aspinwall, and he naturally approached it with great caution, expecting to find a Federal ship-of-war stationed there, but there was none, and the Confederate captain seemed still to be sailing under a lucky star. It was Sunday when the cry of "Sail ho!" came from aloft: everything was dropped for the new excitement, as it had been some time since a prize had been sighted. The "Alabama's" head was pointed towards the stranger, her topmen sprang aloft at the order, and in five minutes she was under a cloud of canvas from rail to truck. The chase was a short one, a run of a few hours brought the "Alabama" up with the vessel, which proved to be the "Parker Cooke," of and from Boston.

This capture greatly pleased the descendants of the Norsemen, for they had learned from experience that the Boston traders always contained the very best of everything, from a needle to a barrel of crackers or firkin of butter. So it was in this case; the "Parker Cooke" was plethoric with good things, and all that day the capacious

maw of the "Alabama" was open to receive the cargo of her prize. The trader was completely emptied, and yet the maw was still unsatisfied, and the wonder will always remain what the 120 men on board this cruiser did with the cargoes, or parts of cargoes, of eighteen vessels which had been transferred to her from time to time. It was sunset before the prisoners and cargo were transferred, the torch was then applied to the beautiful merchantman, and soon the flames were casting a broad light on the bold mountains of St. Domingo, and were reflected on the soft, smooth sea, which already sparkled with the phosphorescence of those latitudes.

While waiting for the mail-steamers, the "Alabama" captured the Baltimore schooner "Union," to which the prisoners were transferred and the vessel allowed to depart on a ransom-bond.

Semmes knowing, from the Northern papers, that the California steamer was due next day, kept a bright look-out for her, and soon a large brig-rigged steamer appeared. All was now excitement on board the "Alabama"; the propeller was lowered, sails furled, steam raised, and in twenty minutes she was ready for the chase.

The reader is, no doubt, hoping that something will happen to warn the coming steamer in time to avoid her threatened fate. But she came on rapidly, and when within three or four miles, the "Alabama" hoisted the American flag. It was astonishing how often Semmes resorted to using what he called "the flaunting lie"—which he derided on all occasions—forgetting that in the days of the Revolution it had been carried to victory by the bravest and most chivalrous men of the South. Yet he did not feel degraded at having that flag flying at his peak as long as he could draw his enemy into his net; and that foolish steamer, seeing the old flag, put her whole faith and trust in it, and came on with increased speed to greet the defenders of the Union, whom an energetic and benign Government had sent to that spot to assure them a safe passage !!

When within a mile of the "Alabama" the steamer was making great speed, and even at that moment could have turned and escaped, but the merchant captain never thought of examining carefully that clipper-built hull and English rig, so totally unlike anything American. All eyes were bent on the American ensign, and the one small gun the steamer carried for signalling purposes was loaded to fire a passing salute to the flag of their country. Semmes placed his vessel directly across the path of the huge steamer, which came foaming through the water towards him, and if the captain of that vessel had been a bold man he would have crashed through the "Alabama," as soon as he discovered her character, and sent her to the bottom off the island of San Domingo, where many a rich galleon, after being robbed by the Drakes and Morgans of old, had been sunk before her.

The mail-packet had all her awnings spread, and underneath them, on the upper deck, were congregated a number of passengers of both sexes, among whom could be seen the occasional uniform of an officer or soldier. It was a happy picture as they crowded to the side to look upon the defenders of their country, and the officers of the "Alabama" watched the expression of their faces as they appeared to criticise or admire their vessel. They saw plainly that not even the captain and officers had yet suspected danger, when Semmes surprised them by wheeling in pursuit, firing a blank cartridge, and hoisting the Confederate flag. The panic that now ensued was dreadful; the screams of women filled the air, and men turned pale as they realized the proximity of one of the dreaded Confederate cruisers—which were designated in the North as pirates, and which were as much feared at that time as was the vessel of the famous Lafitte by the Spaniards and Frenchmen in 1806-8.

The merchant captain, astonished at the turn of affairs, gave the order to open wide the throttle of his engines and make all possible speed. For the moment he had no intention of slacking up, but the "Alabama" was within three or four hundred yards of him, in hot pursuit, with a long gun ready to be fired if it should prove necessary to use force. It was very plain from the beginning that the packet was going rapidly away from the "Alabama," and that if Semmes wished to detain her he would have to use shot and shell. She was a fine large target, and he knew that his gunners would not be likely to miss her—after their varied and extended practice. Nor was he disappointed—a curl of white smoke, a flash, and a shower of large splinters from one of the steamer's masts, were all the result of a moment.

That was sufficient—the mast had not been cut away entirely, but the practice told those in charge of the steamer that they were entirely in the power of their pursuer, and that they had better stop before another shot was sent crashing through the stern among the women and children. The walking-beam of the engine began to move more slowly, and the bell in the engine-room soon signalled to stop. The "Alabama" slowed down, ranged up alongside, and took possession of her prize. But now Captain Semmes experienced a keen disappointment. Instead of a homeward-bound California

steamer, with a couple of millions of dollars in her safes, he discovered that his prize, the "Ariel," was outward-bound and had as passengers some 500 women and children. Here was an elephant on his hands that he had not bargained for, and he did not know what to do with his prize. He could not take her into a neutral port, for that was forbidden by the Orders in Council; he could not land the passengers, and he could not take them on board the "Alabama." The best he could hope to do was to capture some inferior prize in the next few days, place all the passengers on board of her, and let them get into port as best they could. He would then be at liberty to burn the "Ariel," and proceed on his voyage.

One of the most humiliating things about this capture was that the "Ariel" carried a battalion of marines and a number of naval officers, who were on their way to join ships in the Pacific. How these men must have blushed for their country and bitten their lips in anger, as they listened to the taunts and jeers of their captors! There were 140 of them, rank and file, and, as they were all paroled, Semmes congratulated himself on having disarmed so many of his country's enemies.

The boarding officer, on his return to the "Alabama," reported that a dreadful state of alarm existed on board the "Ariel," that the women were all in tears, and many of them in hysterics. They had read in the papers of the doings of the "Alabama," and took her officers and crew to be nothing better than pirates; and, indeed, the behavior of the "Alabama's" men on many occasions justified people in coming to this conclusion, unless it were possible to consider as legal all the decisions of the "Admiralty Court" which sat in the cabin of the commerce destroyer.

Captain Semmes was not insensible to the distress of his fair captives, and at once took steps to quiet their fears. He sent for his handsomest lieutenant (history does not give his name), and ordered him to array himself in his most gorgeous uniform, and gird on the finest sword to be found in the ward-room. The young man soon returned, looking as bewitching as possible in a uniform that was somewhat tarnished by sea air, and the Captain ordered his own gig, a handsome boat fitted with beautiful scarlet cushions, to be placed at his disposal. "Go," said the humane commander! "and coax those ladies out of their hysterics." "Oh, I'll be sure to do that, sir," replied the young coxcomb, "I never knew a fair creature who could resist me more than fifteen minutes." This sounds very much like some of the scenes enacted on board the "Red Rover," in Cooper's novel, but it is true to the letter, nevertheless.

In order to do justice to the scene which followed, we must take the description of it as given by the Captain of the "Alabama":

"A few strokes of the oars put him alongside of the steamer, and asking to be shown to the ladies' cabin, he entered the scene of dismay and confusion. So many were the signs of distress, and so numerous the wailers, that he was abashed, for a moment, as he afterward told me, with all his assurance. But summoning courage, he spoke to them about as follows: 'Ladies! The Captain of the 'Alabama' has heard of your distress, and sent me on board to calm your fears, by assuring you that you have fallen into the hands of Southern gentlemen, under whose protection you are entirely safe. We are by no means the ruffians and outlaws that we have been represented by your people, and you have nothing whatever to fear.' The sobs ceased as he proceeded, but they eyed him askance for the first few minutes. As he advanced in their midst, however, they took a second and more favorable glance at him. A second glance begat a third, more favorable still, and when he entered into conversation with some of the ladies nearest him, picking out the youngest and prettiest, as the rogue admitted, he found no reluctance on their part to answer him. In short, he was fast becoming a favorite. The ice being once broken, a perfect avalanche of loveliness soon surrounded him, the eyes of the fair creatures looking all the brighter for the tears that had recently dimmed them.'

"Was ever woman in such humor wooed?
Was ever woman in such humor won?"

This shows the fickleness of Northern women; had they been Southern-born they would not have looked at a Northern officer, even had he rescued them from fire or wreck. But it cannot be disguised that the ladies on board the "Ariel" allowed themselves to believe that a man could be a gentleman and a man of honor, even though differing from them in politics, and one of them even so far forgot herself as to request her handsome enemy to give her a button from his uniform coat, as a memento of the occasion. It is needless to say that the request was granted, for the young officer was now so intoxicated with the beauty about him that he would have given away his coat, cap, sword and boots, had he been asked to do so. Others followed the example of the fair petitioner, and when the lieutenant reported to his commander he was in the condition of a picked chicken!

The male passengers were not so deeply impressed by the appearance of the envoy, and occupied the time of his visit in overhauling their baggage, and secreting their valuables.

"'In fact,' said the lieutenant, as he reported to Captain Semmes, 'I really believe that these fellows think we are no better than the Northern thieves who are burning dwelling-houses, and robbing our women and children in the South!'"

This was a Southern view of the matter, which had not been modified by the plundering and burning of the "Alabama" on the high seas. Semmes himself was deeply impressed by the good conduct of his officers and men on this occasion. He estimated that each of the five hundred passengers had from three to five hundred dollars, and thought that under the laws of war all this money would have been a fair prize. "But not one dollar of it," he says, "was touched, or indeed so much as a passenger's baggage examined," and we are glad that history will vouch for it for the credit of Southern officers who once belonged to the United States Navy. The fact remains, however, that to have taken one dollar or piece of property from any passenger on board the "Ariel" would have been a base act of piracy.

Semmes carried out his intention of keeping the "Ariel" in company, and it was not until he had given up all hope of falling in with another merchantman that he allowed her to go on her way rejoicing. The Captain of the "Ariel" was, of course, obliged to give a "ransom-bond"; but it was a great disappointment to Captain Semmes not to be able to burn this fine large packet, especially as he knew she belonged to Cornelius Vanderbilt, who had given a fast steamer to the United States Government for the express purpose of pursuing Confederate cruisers. Semmes looked upon this act of a private citizen as an outrage that should meet with condign punishment, forgetting that there are two sides to every question, and that Vanderbilt was merely showing his devotion and loyalty to the Republic in a most practical and sensible manner. Semmes also complained that Vanderbilt never redeemed the "ransom-bond"; but this was not singular, for the general understanding was that these bonds were only to be paid in case the South was successful.

On the 23d of December the "Alabama" joined her coal-ship at Arcas Islands, in the Gulf of Mexico, and prepared to waylay the Banks expedition, which was expected to reach Galveston by the 10th of January. Semmes' plan was to approach the harbor of Galveston at a time when the army transports would probably have arrived, make careful observations of their positions by daylight, and then withdraw until nightfall. He then proposed to run in and attack the fleet under cover of the darkness, and hoped to be able to sink or scatter the whole of them.

This was a bold and feasible plan, and no one can deny that Semmes displayed great daring in thus bearding the lion in his den, and entering waters that he knew to be full of his enemy's gun-boats. But he knew the character of every vessel on the coast, and was well aware that but few of the "old tubs" in the Federal Navy could catch him. The "Florida" had distanced the "Cuyler," the fastest vessel off Mobile bar, and the "Alabama" was faster than the "Florida."

Under these conditions he felt quite safe, as he could either run or fight.

On the 5th of January Semmes left the Arcas and headed for Galveston. As he approached the harbor, he discovered that, instead of Banks' transports, there were five men-of-war anchored off the town. This was a damper, and for a short time he was undecided what to do. He had promised his men some fun in this vicinity, and did not like to go away without gratifying them. He was soon relieved from his quandary, however, by the look-out aloft reporting that one of the Federal gun-boats was coming out in chase. This was the unfortunate "Hatteras," the story of whose sinking by the "Alabama" has already been told in another part of this history.

The course pursued by the Confederate commander in this action cannot be justified by the rules of war. In answer to a hail from the "Hatteras," he declared his vessel to be Her Britannic Majesty's steamer "Petrel," and when Lieutenant-Commander Blake proposed to send a boat along-side of him, expressed his willingness to receive the officers in a friendly manner. This implied that the "Alabama" was what Semmes reported her to be, a neutral man-of-war. If it had been simply a ruse to escape while the boat was being lowered, it might have passed. But when, as in this case, it was to gain time in which to train the guns upon the vital parts of an enemy, and make preparations for taking human life, it was simply perfidy, such as a Zulu warrior would hardly resort to. There are certain laws of courtesy in war which the meanest nations observe. When two men-of-war meet in the day-time their nationality is shown by their flag; but when, under cover of darkness, a false nationality is given, and willingness to receive a friendly visit expressed, it is the same as violating a flag of truce, for the visitor goes on board with the full expectation of meeting a kind reception and does not anticipate treachery.

The first broadside is often the turning-point in a battle, especially when there is, as in this case, a disparity of force. As the boat approached the "Alabama," Semmes gave the order to open fire upon the "Hatteras," and the little vessel actually staggered under the blow. At the same time he ordered his first-lieutenant to hail the enemy; and reveal the true character of the "Alabama." As has been already narrated, the "Hatteras" was literally cut to pieces, and in fifteen minutes went to the bottom.

It is not necessary to give any other reason for the loss of the "Hatteras," than that her antagonist was more than a match for her in every respect. The Confederate vessel carried heavier guns and was strongly built, while the "Hatteras" was a mere shell—an iron side-wheel river-boat, that had been used to carry passengers on the Delaware. The "Alabama" had much the greater speed, and her fire was more accurate, owing to the fact that the crew of the "Hatteras" were somewhat demoralized by the first, unexpected, broadside.

Semmes did not seem disposed to make much capital out of this victory. Nothing remained for him to do in this vicinity; so, after he had picked up the officers and crew of the "Hatteras," he put out all his lights and steamed away for the coast of Yucatan, congratulating himself that he had been able to satisfy his men with this substitute for his contemplated attack on Banks' transports. The "Alabama" received little damage in the fight, and on January 20th arrived at Jamaica, where the prisoners were landed, on parole, to find their way home as best they could. It is but fair to state that the officers and men of the "Hatteras" were kindly treated by their captors, and Lieutenant-Commander Blake was received as a guest in the cabin.

The "Alabama" sailed from Jamaica on the 25th of January, 1863, bound for the coast of Brazil. Captain Semmes had been treated with every possible attention by the British officers at Jamaica, and flattered himself that they implicitly believed in his right to burn, sink and destroy American merchantmen, even if they carried English goods, for the Confederacy would be sure to make amends in her prize-courts as soon as the war was over!

In fact, the English Admiral and his officers behaved with a great want of dignity in thus taking sides with the "Alabama," and treating the officers of the "Hatteras" with such marked discourtesy. The military bands played that lovely air "Dixie" with all the pathos they could throw into the music; while, much to the delight of the Confederates, they performed "Yankee Doodle" with all their drums, cymbals and squeaking clarionets in the harshest manner, as if in mockery of the American nation. It was, no doubt, a great source of satisfaction to the British to see the once great commerce of the United States being turned over to the protection of the British flag, and giving employment to all the vessels that had been lying idle for years at the English docks. But they forgot the pertinacity of these Yankees, whom they were trying to turn into ridicule, and they also forgot that the Northern officers and men, who were now obliged to listen to their taunts, were prisoners-of-war who possessed nothing but the clothes they stood in, and that they were entitled to all the courtesy a generous nation could give them. They forgot, for a time, that the people whom they were attempting to ridicule were wont to remember injuries and wrongs received, and sooner or later to find a day of reckoning. The day of reckoning for these insults came when the Americans received an indemnity of $15,000,000 for the pranks of the "Alabama" and "Florida," which the Englishmen paid to the tune of Yankee Doodle, at a time when the re-united States had adopted "Dixie" as one of its national airs.

Soon after leaving port the "Alabama" fell in with the American ship "Golden Rule," from New York, bound to Aspinwall. The island of San Domingo was sufficiently near to allow its inhabitants to witness a splendid bonfire. Semmes says in his journal:

"A looker-on upon that conflagration would have seen a beautiful picture, for, besides the burning ship, there were the two islands mentioned, sleeping in the dreamy moonlight on a calm bosom of a tropical sea, and the rakish-looking 'British pirate' steaming in for the land, with every spar and line of cordage brought out in bold relief by the bright flame—nay, with the very 'pirates' themselves visible, handling the boxes and bales of merchandise which they had 'robbed' from this innocent Yankee, whose countrymen at home were engaged in the Christian occupation of burning our houses and desolating our fields."

There was more truth than poetry in the first part of this quotation. No doubt, if the oldest inhabitants among these simple islanders could have refreshed their memories, they might have brought back the days when the buccaneers of old (many of whom were stout Anglo-Saxons in English-built ships) roved these seas and left behind them a trail of fire—even as the "Alabama" was now doing.

Soon after the capture of the "Golden Rule," a beautiful hermaphrodite brig hove in sight. It was blowing half a gale, and in the bright moonlight she looked like a sea-gull skimming along over the top of the waves. Her white sails and rakish rig proclaimed her to be an American, and she was at once brought-to by a shot from the "Alabama." She proved to be the "Chastelaine," a Boston vessel, and the fiat went forth at once—burn her. Her crew were removed, the torch applied, and with sail set, the doomed vessel bounded away over the waves, like a courser with his nostrils breathing fire. The light of her burning hull illumined the sea-girt walls of Alta Vela (a tall island about ten miles from San Domingo), and disturbed the slumber of sea-gulls and cormorants for the rest of the night; while the "Alabama" sailed away in the darkness, and this adventure soon ceased to be a matter of comment among her crew.

Semmes next appeared in the Mona Passage, and found this important channel of commerce still unguarded by American men-of-war. In fact, it had remained so ever since his last visit, while an old commodore, with a large squadron, had been sailing about the Caribbean Sea, interfering with neutral commerce and watching the English mail-steamers that were pursuing their legitimate business.

The "Alabama" had hardly got through the passage before she fell in with and captured the schooner "Palmetto," from New York, bound to St. John's. Porto Rico. This vessel carried neutral goods, but they were not under consular seals, and Captain Semmes decided that they came under the rule, "that when partners reside, some in a belligerent and some in a neutral country, the property of all of them, which has any connection with the house in the belligerent country, is liable to confiscation." It was wonderful how many rules of international law this officer could interpret to suit his own convenience; for only one or two instances exist in which any vessel was released by the "Alabama," unless it was desired to get rid of a lot of prisoners. The "Palmetto" had short shrift, and was forgotten in an hour.

The Confederate cruiser was now obliged to work her way into "the variables," and proceed to the eastward, near the thirtieth parallel of latitude, a sufficient distance to clear Cape St. Roque on the coast of South America. She soon sighted a sail from aloft, and quickly afterwards three more appeared and caused the Confederates to think they had fallen upon a perfect bonanza of prizes. Chase was given to the first sail, but finally abandoned, as it was leading the "Alabama" away from the other three vessels, which were fine tall ships, and apparently American. Coming up with the eastward-bound ship, a prize-crew was thrown on board of her and the prize-master ordered to follow the "Alabama," which vessel started in pursuit of one of the others, that was at least fifteen miles distant by this time, and running off before the wind with steering sails set "alow and aloft." This vessel was overtaken after quite a chase, and proved to be the "Olive Jane," of New York, loaded with French wines and brandies. Captain Semmes decided that, although much of this cargo evidently belonged to Frenchmen, it was not properly documented, so he applied the torch without waiting to make any searching investigation, not allowing so much as a bottle of brandy or a case of champagne to be taken out of her. This last was a wise precaution on his part, for he had had great trouble in controlling a number of his drunken sailors at Jamaica, and knew that it would not be safe to subject them to temptation. Although the Confederate Captain regretted not being able to indulge himself and his men, he chuckled with delight when he thought of the disappointment of New York "shoddyites" and "*nouveau-riche* plebeians," at the loss of the rich wines, olives and "*pate-de-foisgras,*" which had been intended to tickle their palates.

Amid the crackling of the fire, the bursting of brandy casks, the shrivelling of sails and the falling of the lighter spars from aloft, the "Alabama" turned her head to the eastward again and rejoined her first prize. This ship was the "Golden Eagle," and the great bird itself was sitting on the cutwater, spreading his wings, as if he owned all the ocean, and seemingly unconscious of his approaching fate. An inquiry into the papers of this vessel showed that her cargo was wholly owned by Americans. She had sailed full of guano from Howland's Island in the Pacific, "for Cork and a market, and after having buffeted gales off Cape Horn, threaded her way through icebergs, been parched by the heat of the tropics and drenched with the rains of the equator, it was her misfortune to be captured when within a few hundred miles of port."

Semmes himself felt sorry for a moment for these people (!), and regretted that he was obliged to destroy this fine ship with so large a cargo of fertilizing matter that would have made fields stagger under a load of grain and carried joy to many a farmer's heart. But this feeling quickly passed away when he remembered that these fields would be the fields of his enemies, or, if the guano was not used by them, its sale would pour a stream of gold into their coffers. So he applied the torch without compunction, and the career of the "Golden Eagle" was speedily terminated.

The "Alabama" now crossed the equator and stationed herself in the great tollgate of commerce, through which traders from India, China, the Pacific Ocean and South America were continually passing, rejoicing as they reached these latitudes that the long, weary road was behind them, and that but a short and easy passage lay between them and their homes.

It had never occurred to the American Government to send half-a-dozen gunboats or "double enders" to these latitudes. They could easily have been spared, and a depot for coaling vessels could have been established under the smooth waters of the equator, at which all the vessels-of-war in the Navy could have been supplied. If the "Alabama" knew where to go to catch American merchantmen, why did not the Federal Government know where to seek the "Alabama"? The policeman looks for rogues in the most frequented part of the city, or at points where the wealth of the city is least guarded; and even if he does not catch the rascals, he prevents their doing harm. This was a parallel case. It was not the particular smartness of Semmes that enabled him to escape capture. It was the omission or indifference of the Navy Department in not sending proper vessels to the right localities.

Many foreign ships passed along this route; but Americans had, in a measure, taken the alarm, and were pursuing longer and safer lines of travel. Still Semmes was amply repaid for watching at the tollgate, even though many passed through without paying toll. He captured the ship "Washington" from the Chincha Islands with a cargo of guano, bound to Antwerp. Finding difficulties in the way of destroying her neutral cargo, he put his prisoners on board, and let her go on a ransom-bond. The fact was, he was anxious to get rid of his prisoners who were eating him "out of house and home."

On the morning of the 1st of March the "Alabama" captured the fine ship "John A. Parks," of Hallowell, Maine. Her cargo, consisting of lumber for Montevideo, was covered by the seals of the British consul, and was as neutral as any cargo could be. But the ship was burned, nevertheless. A large quantity of newspapers were taken from the "Parks," which, as they contained many unflattering notices of the "Alabama," gave her officers and crew something to sharpen their appetites upon until they overhauled another prize.

The next vessel taken was the "Bethiah Thayer," last from the Chinchas with a cargo of guano for the Peruvian Government, and, as her cargo was properly documented, she was released on bond.

On the 15th of March, the ship "Punjaub," of Boston, was captured; but as her cargo was English property, and was properly certified to, she was released on a ransom-bond, after the prisoners were all transferred to her. Semmes was getting merciful; the mild climate of the tropics was acting favorably upon his temperament, while his crew, for want of excitement, began to look gloomy and disconsolate. All this time Semmes made but little change in his position, lying under easy sail near the toll-gate, and allowing his prey to come to him.

On the 23d of March, the "Morning Star," of Boston, from Calcutta to London, and the whaling schooner, "Kingfisher," of Fairhaven, Massachusetts, were captured. The fact that the cargo of the "Morning Star" was English saved that vessel, but the "Kingfisher" was burned. Although this little vessel did not make as large a bonfire as some of her predecessors, it served to beguile the time; and, in order to make the spectacle more interesting to his men, Semmes applied the torch at night-fall, when the effect of the burning oil, amid the rain and wind of a tropical squall, was quite brilliant.

Next day two large ships hove in sight, evidently Americans. They were sailing close together, their captains, no doubt, having a chat about matters at home and congratulating each other at having so far escaped the "Alabama" and "Florida." Their *tête-à-tête* was suddenly interrupted by seeing a piratical-looking craft lying directly in their course, and they separated, as if to seek safety in flight. But it was too late; they had run directly under the guns of their bitterest foe, and were soon obliged to shorten sail and submit to their fate. They were the "Charles Hill" and the "Nora," both of Boston, and although their cargoes were owned in part by neutrals, Semmes took a new view of the law, and burned them, after helping himself to about forty tons of coal.

A day or two after this, in the morning-watch, the look-out on the "Alabama" sighted a tall, fine ship standing to the southward. All sail was made in chase, and as the southwest wind, then blowing fresh, was favorable to the "Alabama," she overhauled the stranger before night-fall. The prize was the "Louisa Hatch," of Rockland, Maine, from Cardiff, with a cargo of Welsh coal for Port de Galle, Island of Ceylon. The bill of lading required this cargo to be delivered to the "*Messageries Imperiales*" Steamship Company, and a certificate was on the back of this document to the effect that the coal belonged to that company. But, in Captain Semmes' opinion, this certificate was not properly sworn to, so he decided that the "Louisa Hatch" was a good prize-of-war; and this idea was strengthened by the fact that she was loaded with the best Cardiff coal, exactly what the "Alabama" most needed.

Was there ever such a lucky man as the Captain of the "Alabama"? If he wanted a cargo of provisions it fell into his hands. If he required to visit a dock-yard to fit out his ship, a vessel came along filled with cordage, canvas and anchors. If he wanted lumber, a lumber vessel from Maine came right into his path; and if he needed to reinforce his crew, renegades from captured vessels would put their names to the shipping articles, after listening to the thrilling tales of the Norsemen, of burning ships and abundant prize-money.

The prize at first seemed an elephant, as Semmes would lose too much time if he attempted to transfer her cargo at sea, so he determined to send her to Fernando de Noronha, and depend on future contingencies.

If the "Agrippina," his coal-tender, should arrive in time he could burn the "Louisa Hatch"; if not, the latter would supply him with coal. The Scotch collier did not, however, appear at Fernando de Noronha, for the Captain of the vessel, becoming frightened at the illicit business in which he had embarked, sold his coal to the best advantage and left the "Alabama" to look out for herself.

The Island of Fernando de Noronha is a penal settlement of Brazil. Few vessels stopped there, though many sighted it, to take a fresh departure. Although prohibited from taking his prizes into a neutral port, Semmes did not hesitate to take the "Louisa Hatch" into the harbor and coal from her, and for two weeks the officers and crew of the Confederate vessel fraternized with the interesting swindlers and homicides who colonized the island. At the end of five days, when the "Alabama" had finished coaling, signal was made from the high peaks of the island that two large American whalers had hove-to and were sending boats on shore. Semmes immediately got up steam and proceeded in search of his prey. The Confederate cruiser was soon alongside, and no time was lost in determining their fate. The "Lafayette," of New Bedford, in the course of an hour, was burning brightly, much to the amusement of the robbers and murderers on shore. The other prize, the "Kate Cory," of Westport, was retained to act as a cartel and convey the one hundred and ten prisoners on board the "Alabama" to the United States.

By 7 P. M. the "Alabama" again anchored in the harbor with her prize, without any objection from the Governor, yet the Government of Brazil subsequently pretended to be very indignant at the violation of neutrality whereby the Confederate cruiser "Florida" was taken from one of her ports.

There was no end to the indignities heaped upon the United States and its commerce while the "Alabama" remained at this colony of criminals. Semmes changed his mind about sending his prisoners to the United States, and engaged the master of a Brazilian schooner to convey them to Pernambuco. No feeling of humanity at the sufferings so many persons crowded into a small and filthy vessel must undergo troubled Semmes. The apologist for Wirtz, the Andersonville jailer, did not stick at trifles.

The "Cory" suffered the same fate as the "Hatch," Semmes being careful to burn both beyond the marine league, so as not to offend the delicate susceptibilities of the Governor of Fernando de Noronha, and to pay due respect to the Empire of Brazil, the great ally of the Confederacy.

On the 22d of April, the "Alabama" was again on the wing under plain sail for a cruise along the Brazilian coast, and in less than twenty-four hours another unfortunate whaler, the "Nye," of New Bedford, was in her hands, making the sixteenth whaler that had been captured. The "Nye" had sent home one or two cargoes of oil, and had now 425 barrels on board. For a moment Semmes thought "what a pity to break in upon these old salts, who had encountered so many gales and chased the whale through so many latitudes!" But such thoughts never remained long with this sea-rover. He had a special hatred for New Englanders, and the "Nye," well saturated with oil, soon blazed up in a way to satisfy the most vindictive partisan of the Southern cause. The old whalers, who for nearly three years had risked their lives in a dangerous calling, stood silent and in tears as they beheld their hard-earned property disappear in a cloud of smoke. The people of the South necessarily suffered much at the hands of Union soldiers, and it is hard to tell what men will not do in the heat of war, but it may be fairly said there was nothing during the civil conflict to equal the atrocity of the "Alabama's" doings.

The day after the destruction of the "Nye," the "Dorcas Prince," of New York, loaded with coal, was encountered; but, as the "Alabama's" bunkers were already filled, the vessel was set on fire and destroyed.

On the third of May the Clipper ship, "Union Jack," fell into the "Alabama's" power and a prize crew was sent on board, as just afterwards, the "Sea Lark," bound from New York to San Francisco, was sighted—two fine prizes in two hours. Three women and some children were taken from the last prize and conveyed on board the "Alabama." Both ships were burned after their crews were removed.

On the 11th of May the "Alabama" landed her prisoners at Bahia, and was ordered by the Brazilian authorities to leave the port in twenty-four hours for violation of the neutrality laws; but Semmes was so much cleverer than the Governor that he was finally permitted to remain and give his men liberty on shore, where they turned the town upside down generally.

These Brazilian officials were easily influenced by the threats of Semmes to call down on them the vengeance of the Southern Confederacy after it had disposed of its "Yankee war," and they had never been taught, by the display of a proper Federal naval force, to respect the United States. The British residents of Bahia did all in their power to make Semmes' stay pleasant, congratulating themselves that the commerce of the United States was being rapidly driven from the ocean, and this although Bahia derived its chief importance from its trade with that country.

While the "Alabama" was in Bahia, the Confederate steamer "Georgia," Commander William L. Maury commanding, anchored in the port, much increasing the respect of the Governor for the Southern Confederacy; although the latter was somewhat afraid of trouble with the Emperor, who was believed to favor the Federal Government. He accordingly requested Semmes to leave as soon as possible. This request Semmes politely ignored; amusing himself with traveling about the country, and perfecting plans with the commanding officer of the "Georgia" for the destruction of United States commerce on the coast of Brazil.

After the "Alabama" bade farewell to the "Georgia" at Bahia, she was put under press of sail, and quickly overhauled the "Gilderslieve," of New York, and the "Justina," of Baltimore. The latter, being a Maryland ship, was converted into a cartel, and after taking all Semmes' prisoners on board and giving a ransom-bond, was allowed to depart. The other vessel was loaded with coal; but as the captain had no sworn certificate of ownership by British subjects, and as the "Alabama" did not need it, Semmes' "Admiralty Court" decreed that the "Gilderslieve" should be converted into a bonfire.

The next day, the "Jabez Snow," of Bucksport, Maine, laden with Cardiff coal, was captured. As the cargo was evidently British property, Semmes might perhaps have released the vessel under a ransom-bond but for a letter found on board to the following effect:

"We hope you will arrive safely and in good season, but we think you will find business rather flat at Liverpool, as American ships especially are under a cloud, owing to dangers from pirates, more politely styled privateers, which our kind friends in England are so willing should slip out of their ports to prey upon our commerce."

Such letters as the above were always considered by the "Admiralty Court" in Semmes' cabin as not only stupid and malicious, but positive evidence against the neutral ownership of anything on board a prize; so the crew of the "Jabez Snow" were promptly removed, and the vessel set on fire.

On the 2d of June, the "Alabama" fell in with the clipper bark "Amazonian," from New York for Montevideo, with an assorted cargo. Semmes remarks: "There was an attempt to cover two of the consignments in this ship," but the "Court of Admiralty" decided that "the bark being evidently Yankee, the certificates were not worth a cent!" So the ship was plundered and burned.

The next day Semmes fell in with an English brig, the master of which agreed to receive his forty-one captives and land them in Rio de Janeiro, the consideration being twice as much provisions as the prisoners could eat, and a chronometer. Of the latter articles Semmes had an abundant supply, the property of the merchant captains he had taken prisoners, although he professed to respect private property. All the other "Confederate cruisers" exhibited the same weakness for chronometers, which may be accounted for by the fact that they would all be needed for the great Navy it was proposed to build in England. The virtuous Briton at first demurred to the proposition to receive the prisoners from Semmes, on the ground that "it might offend Earl Russell," but the offer of a chronometer silenced his objections. As the Earl had a keen sense of humor, he would doubtless have remarked had he ever heard of this incident, that as chronometers are made to go they might as well go that way as any other.

The clipper-ship "Talisman," of New York, was the "Alabama's" next capture, and, as usual, was given but short shrift. After taking from the vessel her crew and such of the cargo as he wanted, Semmes applied the torch, and she went off before the wind in flames with all sail set. The "Talisman" had a number of 12-pounder field-pieces on board, and boilers and machinery for a gun-boat to be built in China to take part in the Chinese war. Semmes took two of the guns on board his vessel for the purpose of fitting out a consort when the proper vessel should fall into his hands.

Semmes continued his course along the Brazilian coast, and now began to fall in with American vessels under the British flag; for what Earl Russell had foreseen had now come to pass, and the United States carrying-trade was being transferred to English hands. The papers of these vessels were so carefully made out that Semmes' "Court of Admiralty" did not dare meddle with them, as a rule; however, he was enraged at seeing such prizes slip through his judicial fingers; but on the 20th of June the fates were propitious in bringing another fly to the "Alabama's" web.

This was the bark "Conrad," of Philadelphia, and although her cargo was English, she was taken possession of and quickly converted into a "vessel-of-war." Three or four officers, a dozen men, and the two captured field-pieces were put on board the little clipper with a celerity that would have astonished Mr. Gideon Welles, and the new Confederate cruiser was christened

the "Tuscaloosa." The baptismal ceremony was not elaborate. When all was ready, signal was given, the "Tuscaloosa" ran up the Confederate flag, and the crew of the "Alabama" gave three cheers, which were duly acknowledged by those on board the new man-of-war. Semmes' prisoners, now thirty-nine in number, were on the same day put on board an English vessel, to be landed in Rio de Janeiro.

It was now time for the "Alabama" to change her cruising-ground, not only because the United States Navy Department might be supposed to have heard of her operations and taken measures to bring them to a close, but also for the reason that there was little more damage to be inflicted in that quarter. Semmes was astonished that no Federal ships-of-war were on the Brazilian coast when he arrived there. For months he had been working his way in that direction, his track marked by burning vessels; but, in any event, one might have been reasonably sure that Semmes would ultimately seek that great thoroughfare of vessels, along the coast of Brazil. At Cape St. Roque the ocean highway becomes so narrow by the influence of the northeast trade-winds, and the vessels are so close together, that they are at the mercy of any enemy's cruiser stretching backward and forward across the road. If heavier and faster vessels than the "Alabama" had been stationed in latitude 30° North, and others at the equator to the eastward of Fernando de Noronha, Confederate cruisers could have done little harm; their principal object on hearing of the proximity of Federal vessels being to get out of their way. As it was, Semmes could make his calculations pretty accurately, and when he thought it time for a Federal cruiser to appear on the scene of action, he would slip off to "fresh fields and pastures new."

The "Alabama" and her consort now shaped their course for the Cape of Good Hope; but, finding his bread spoiled by wevil, Semmes was obliged to put back to Rio for a supply of provisions. On the 1st of July the ship "Anna F. Schmidt," from Boston, with an assorted cargo, was overhauled, and, to use Semmes' own language, "it took us nearly the entire day to do the necessary amount of 'robbing.'" The vessel was abundantly supplied with provisions, including bread; and after the "robbing" was concluded the burning was commenced, and the "Schmidt" shared the fate of her predecessors. Semmes' usual good fortune had served him well in this instance, saving him a journey of nearly a thousand miles in search of a bake-shop.

While the "Schmidt" was in flames and drifting before the wind, a large ship, under a cloud of canvas, went rushing by, taking no notice of the burning vessel. The light of the fire was reflected on her white sails, which seemed to mark her as an American, and the "Alabama" followed in pursuit, firing a gun to induce the stranger to heave-to, but the only notice taken was a gun in return from the latter.

Semmes now ordered all steam and sail to be crowded on the "Alabama," while his crew became greatly excited, thinking from the strangers' firing a gun that a fight was about to ensue. It was midnight before the "Alabama" overhauled the chase, which loomed up very large in the darkness. The ship had a white streak like a man-of-war, and with a night glass five guns could be seen protruding through her side. A voice from the "Alabama" cried out: "What ship is that?" "Her Britannic Majesty's ship 'Diomede!'" was the reply. When the British officer was informed that the pursuing vessel was the Confederate States steamer "Alabama," he remarked: "I suspected as much when I saw you making sail by the light of the burning ship."

It may be remarked that Semmes did not ask to see the stranger's commission, to ascertain whether he was really one of her Majesty's cruisers, and his sailors were somewhat uneasy at their proximity to a British ship-of-war, as a search might have taken place for deserters; but they need not have troubled themselves, for the English were in full sympathy with the "Alabama," as was evidenced by their not stopping to inquire into the fate of those on board the burning vessel.

The "Alabama" now continued on her way towards the Cape of Good Hope, capturing and destroying on the passage the ship "Express," of Boston. On the 28th of July Semmes anchored in Saldanha Bay, not venturing to Cape Town until he had ascertained that the coast was clear of American vessels-of-war. Every ship that had touched at the Cape had brought intelligence of the wonderful doings of the "Alabama," and Semmes in his journal remarks: "Mr. Seward and Mr. Adams, Earl Russell and the London *Times*, have made the 'British pirate' famous."

At Saldanha Bay Semmes received every civility from the people, who appeared to be nearly as barbarous as the aboriginal owners of the soil whom they had dispossessed of their country. These Boers flocked on board the "British pirate," and were mightily interested in all they saw. They knew that the ship and crew were British, and to this circumstance attributed all the success which had followed the career of the "Alabama." A simon-pure Confederate vessel, officered and manned by South-

erners, would have elicited far less enthusiasm in any British port that Semmes visited.

On the 5th of August, the "Alabama" sailed for Table Bay, encountering on the way her consort the "Tuscaloosa," which was sent into Simon's Bay to refit. The same day the bark "Sea-Bride," of Boston, was captured. This vessel was on a trading voyage to the east coast of Africa with an assorted cargo. Her capture was witnessed from Cape Town and caused intense excitement among the inhabitants, a majority of whom could not conceal their joy at the seizure of a well-known trading vessel that had often stopped at their port to supply their necessities. The local newspapers raved over the gallant deeds of the "Alabama," and all the people followed suit. In the little English-built vessel they saw the representative of a rising power that was to destroy the commercial supremacy of the great republic, and they naturally wanted to make friends with the winning side. The power of the United States had been estimated in the remote parts of the earth by its commercial marine; but this moral influence ceases to prevail in time of war, when that commercial marine is not protected by a suitable force of war vessels, but, on the contrary, is everywhere being driven from the sea.

The U. S. Steamer "Vanderbilt" arrived at Cape Town after the "Alabama" left, but the officers and crew received no such welcome as was given the Confederates. The people rejoiced that the "Alabama" had escaped, and none gave a hint whither the bird had flown.

Several complications arose while the "Alabama" was in Table Bay, yet, notwithstanding some of her acts were in plain violation of local and international law, the authorities sustained Semmes, even in fitting out prize-vessels for belligerent purposes.

Semmes next visited Simon's Bay, the naval station of the colony, whither the "Tuscaloosa" had preceded her. The United States Consul raised the question that the "Tuscaloosa" was not a vessel of war, but the Confederate commander replied, that although the "Tuscaloosa" had not been condemned by a prize-court of the Confederate States, yet the sovereign power of the Confederacy, acting through its authorized agent, had commissioned her as a ship-of-war, which was the most solemn condemnation of the prize. He claimed that no nation had the right to inquire into the antecedents of the ships of another nation.

Everybody except the commander-in-chief of the British naval forces was silenced, if not convinced, by this logic, and recognized the " Tuscaloosa " as a *bona-fide* ship-of-war; but Admiral Sir Baldwin Walker wrote to the Governor : " Viewing all the circumstances of the case, they afford room for the supposition that the vessel (" Tuscaloosa ") is styled a tender, with the object of avoiding the prohibition against her entrance as a prize into our ports, where, if the captors wished, arrangements could be made for the disposal of her valuable cargo." This opinion was overruled, but the British Government instructed the Colonial Governor that he should have detained the " Tuscaloosa," Accordingly, when the " Tuscaloosa " again came into port after a cruise, the Governor seized her, but the Home Government veering round ordered him to restore her to Lieutenant Low, her commanding officer, on the ground that " having been once allowed to enter and leave the port, he was fairly entitled to assume that he might do so a second time !"

The " Alabama " remained five days at Simon's Bay. The flag-ship and two other British men-of-war were there, and every attention in the way of dinner parties, etc., was shown to the Confederates by the English officers and the civil authorities. The " Alabama" then sailed from Simon's Town and joined her consorts at Angra Pequeña, in the Hottentot country. While at Cape Town, an English merchant proposed to purchase the " Sea Bride " and her cargo. The transfer was made at Angra Pequeña for about one-third the real value of the property, the merchant, of course, having to take a considerable risk. This questionable transaction took place right under the eyes of the British authorities, who were doing all in their power to promote the extinction of American commerce.

Again, the " Alabama " is off the Cape of Good Hope, where she cruised for several days without success, and finally proceeded to Simon's Bay, where Semmes learned that the U. S. S. " Vanderbilt," Lieutenant-Commanding Baldwin, had just left the port in search of him. On the day that the " Vanderbilt " left Simon's Bay, the " Alabama " was cruising further off the land than usual, a lucky circumstance for Semmes, whose romantic career would otherwise have been brought to a sudden and ignominious termination. The coal-dealers were the only people who welcomed the " Vanderbilt," for, as we have before mentioned, all the hospitality of the officials and citizens was given to the " Alabama." The latter, after coaling, shaped her course for the Straits of Sunda, a channel of commerce much frequented by American merchant vessels. On this voyage Semmes' only prize was an immense albatross, caught with hook and line.

On nearing the straits Semmes boarded an English brig, and was informed that the U. S. S. " Wyoming" was cruising in the straits in company with a three-masted schooner fitted as a tender. Two days after, he obtained similar information from a Dutch vessel, and it seems to have been the design of the commanding officer of the United States vessel to make his whereabouts generally known.

The " Alabama " had scarcely entered the straits when she captured and burned the bark " Amanda," of Boston, and the next day overhauled the clipper-ship " Winged Racer." Semmes anchored with his last prize under North Island, and after the latter had been despoiled of her valuable cargo, her captain, with his family, officers and crew were granted permission to take their own boats and proceed to Batavia.

While these operations were in progress the two ships were surrounded by Malay boats bringing provisions of every kind for sale, when all at once a great blaze sprung from the hold of the " Winged Racer," and the Malays for the first time realized that she had been captured by the " Alabama," when the crew of the latter vessel gave three lusty cheers. The Malays were great pirates themselves, and many European and American ships have been plundered and destroyed and their crews murdered by these picturesque vagabonds. Mistaking the "Alabama" for a corsair, and fearing to be carried off and sold for slaves, they made all haste to get away from the " English pirate."

But where was the " Wyoming " all this time that her watchful commander could not see the blazing ship? Had he visited the spot where the " Winged Racer " was burning, he would not, however, have encountered Semmes, for the "Alabama" had departed as soon as the captured vessel was fairly ablaze.

Next day the "Alabama" sighted another American clipper-ship on a wind under a press of sail. Not until the "Alabama" got up steam did she gain on the chase, and it was only after many hours that the Confederate vessel overhauled and captured her. On this occasion the "Alabama," for the first time, hoisted the new flag of the Southern Confederacy, a white ensign with cross and stars, rather a handsome flag and a great improvement on the original banner of secession, although it could have little effect in sustaining a declining cause. The prize was the " Contest " from Yokohama, with a light cargo of Japanese goods consigned to merchants in New York. The two vessels were anchored in fourteen fathoms in the open sea with no land visible, and it was after night-fall before the crew and plunder of the prize were removed to the "Alabama." Then the torch was applied to the captured vessel, and the little plunderer sailed away in search of other victims.

Semmes now turned the "Alabama's" head to the eastward, and passed through Carimata Strait in five days, although vessels are sometimes thirty days in making the passage.

The "Alabama" was now in the China seas, having left the "Wyoming" somewhere in the Straits of Sunda looking for Confederate cruisers! Instead of one vessel there should have been a dozen in the vicinity of the straits. No wonder Semmes asked himself: "Where is the Yankee, that he is permitting all this rich harvest of commerce in the East to pass away from him?" Had English commerce been threatened with destruction by an enemy's cruisers, how her men-of-war would have swarmed in the Chinese seas! English naval officers could smile calmly at the proceedings of the Confederate plunderer, even where she might occasionally destroy a cargo belonging to British subjects, for this would induce the latter to ship goods in British bottoms.

Semmes cruised in the China seas in search of American merchant vessels, but without success. He played the Rajah at Pulo Condore, where he got springs upon his cable in order to bring his broadside to bear upon the "Wyoming," and rake her fore and aft before she could get alongside of the "Alabama" in case she should enter that narrow harbor. In this harbor Semmes spent two weeks refitting his ship and studying natural history, and became so absorbed in watching the habits of locusts and monkeys, that he appears to have quite forgotten the "Wyoming," which vessel ought to have heard of his whereabouts. Probably the commanding officer of the "Wyoming" was deceived by Semmes' eccentric movements, while the latter calculated that the "Wyoming" had gone to Canton and Shanghai in pursuit of him.

The "Alabama" next proceeded to Singapore for coal and stores. Semmes' stay was short, but the officers and crew were sumptuously entertained. The day he left Singapore Semmes captured a beautiful ship, which, though flying the British flag, was evidently an American vessel, officered and manned by "the hated Yankees." The ship's papers appeared to be in due form, and she had been transferred by a bill of sale to her British owner. After a thorough examination, Semmes satisfied himself that the transfer was not a real one, so he hauled down the British ensign and burned the "Martaban" (late the "Texan Star"), virtuously indignant at the unprincipled conduct of the shipmaster in attempting to deceive the representative of the Southern Confederacy. After this little matter was settled, Semmes apparently had some misgivings, lest the British authorities might call him to an account for burning a vessel under the British flag, so he called the unlucky shipmaster into his cabin and extorted from him a confession that he had resorted to a stratagem to save his ship in case he should fall in with the "Alabama."

Notwithstanding the uncomplimentary manner in which Captain Semmes had treated the flag which has "braved a thousand years the battle and the breeze," when the "Alabama" arrived at her next port and anchored off the little town of Malacca, the English officers and inhabitants went wild over her. After leaving this place, Semmes fell in with an English vessel, the master of which gave him such information as enabled him to capture two large American ships in that vicinity, the "Sonora," of Newburyport, and the "Highlander," of Boston. When the Master of

THE "ALABAMA" OFF CAPETOWN.
FROM A SKETCH BY REAR-ADMIRAL WALKE.

the "Sonora" came on board the "Alabama," he said pleasantly to Captain Semmes: "I have been expecting you for the last three years." Semmes answered that he was glad the Captain had found him after so long a search. "It is some such search," replied the other, "as the devil may be supposed to make after holy water!" This good humor saved the captives from imprisonment, and they were allowed to take their boats with provisions and start for Singapore. After the usual cremation services, the "Alabama" steamed out past the light-ship, and was once more in the Indian Ocean. Query, were the two ships above-named burned in neutral waters?

The "Alabama" now proceeded to the Bay of Bengal, and on the 11th of January captured and burned the "Emma Jane," of Bath, Maine. This was the last vessel burned by Captain Semmes in that quarter. Further continuance in the East Indies did not promise much profit and the "Alabama" finally proceeded towards the Cape of Good Hope. But even in that quarter there were no prizes to be found. American vessels that were not laid up in port or transferred to the British flag avoided the beaten track.

On the 20th of March Semmes went into Cape Town for coal and provisions, and there found the "Tuscaloosa," which vessel he had sent to cruise on the coast of Brazil and which had been seized by the British authorities and afterwards released. The news received at Cape Town from the Confederate States was far from encouraging; everything seemed to be gradually falling into Federal hands. Captain Semmes, for his part, was quite satisfied with the mischief he had wrought, estimating that he had destroyed or driven for protection under the British flag, one-half of the United States vessels engaged in trade with English ports. Still greater damage was done to American trade with other nations. Commerce with the South American States was practically broken up, and that on the Pacific, including the important whale fishery, greatly crippled.

Semmes left Cape Town March 25th, the "Alabama" keeping in the "fair way" leading from the Cape of Good Hope to the equatorial region where the Confederate cruisers had been so successful, shortening sail from day to day and tacking to and fro in the "high-way," but for some time the American flag was nowhere to be seen among the numerous vessels passing on their way. At last an unlucky "Yankee" was reported, and although he made all sail and handled his ship with great skill, the "Alabama" overtook the fugitive. She proved to be the ship "Rockingham," from the Chincha Islands, with a cargo of guano, bound to Cork. Semmes, after removing the crew and such provisions and stores as he wanted, made a target of the "Rockingham," exercising his crew in firing shot and shell at her, which they did with "great precision," owing doubtless to the circumstance that the "Rockingham" could not return the fire; for we find on a subsequent occasion, when the "Kearsarge" was the target, this same crew fired with very little effect.

On the 27th of April the "Tycoon," of New York, with an assorted cargo, was brought-to; the hold of the "Alabama" was filled up with stores, and the night illuminated by another burning ship.

About this time Semmes crossed the equator, and ran up to the old toll-gate, where so many American vessels had been made to haul down their flags. He now felt that he was getting towards the end of his career. The latest captured newspapers had given him an insight into the desperate condition of the Southern Confederacy, and he saw that his commerce-destroying was about ended. To quote his own words: "The poor old 'Alabama' was not now what she had been. She was like the weary foxhound, limping back after a long chase, footsore and longing for quiet and repose. Her commander, like herself, was well-nigh worn down. Vigils by day and night, the storms and the drenching rain, the frequent and rapid change of climate—now freezing, now melting or broiling, and the constant excitement of the chase and capture—had laid, in the three years of war he had been afloat, a load of a dozen years upon his shoulders. The shadows of a sorrowful future, too, began to dawn upon his spirit." From this melancholy moralizing we might almost imagine that Semmes anticipated some such fate as befell Conrad the Corsair:

"'Tis idle all, moons roll on moons away,
And Conrad comes not, came not since that day:
Nor trace, nor tidings of his doom declare
Where lives his grief, or perished his despair!"

On his way to Europe Semmes met with no prizes. American merchant vessels had scattered in all directions like chickens threatened by the hawk, many of them seeking, under the British and other flags, the protection which their own Government failed to afford.

On the 11th day of June, 1864, the "Alabama" anchored in the port of Cherbourg, France; and three days afterwards the U. S. steamer "Kearsarge," Captain John A. Winslow, steamed into port, communicated with the authorities, steamed out again without coming to an anchor, and took a station off the breakwater, in order to prevent the "Alabama" from escaping.

It was evidently not Semmes' intention to fight anybody, for he was about to go into dock and give his men two months' leave, when they would have scattered to parts unknown; but as Cherbourg was exclusively a naval port, the French Admiral would not admit the "Alabama" into dry-dock until he obtained permission from the Emperor, then absent at Biarritz. Had the latter been in Paris, the fight with the "Kearsarge" would never have taken place. Under the circumstances, it would not have done to decline the combat which the "Kearsarge" offered; and Captain Semmes, after so long warring on peaceful merchant vessels, directed the Confederate agent in Cherbourg to request Captain Winslow to wait for him and he would give him battle as soon as he could get some coal on board.

The Captain of the "Alabama" occupied four days in preparations for battle, filling the bunkers so that the machinery would be protected, sending down all useless spars and top hamper, and doing everything possible to achieve success in the coming contest. Semmes' principal anxiety seemed to have been lest his English crew had grown rusty for want of gunnery practice, which he had been obliged to neglect in the more congenial business of plundering and burning; still, as the force of the "Kearsarge" was as nearly as possible the same as his own ship, he was exceedingly hopeful of success.

Semmes tried after the battle to make it

"ALABAMA."					lbs.
6 long 32-pounders,	.	.	.	.	192
1 rifled 100-pounder, (Blakeley)		.	.	.	100
1 8-inch shell-gun,	.	.	.	.	68
8 guns,	.	.	.	.	360

In speed the "Kearsarge" had somewhat the advantage. In tonnage the vessels were almost the same. The "Kearsarge" had 163 officers and men, the "Alabama," 149. It

CAPTAIN (AFTERWARDS REAR-ADMIRAL) JOHN A. WINSLOW.

appear that the "Kearsarge" had the advantage in size, weight of ordnance and number of guns and crew; but this, like many other of his assertions, is disputed by official records, which state as follows:

"KEARSARGE."				lbs.
4 short 32-pounders, weight of projectile,				128
2 11-inch pivot-guns,	"	"	"	272
1 30-pounder rifle,	"	"	"	30
7 guns,	.	.	.	430

was a matter of little consequence what battery the "Alabama" carried, as so few of her shots struck the "Kearsarge"; and if, as has been asserted, many of Semmes' crew were old English man-of-war's men, their shooting did little credit to their training.

With wise precaution, Semmes sent all his valuables on shore before steaming out to meet his antagonist, who was eagerly watching for his appearance. The weather was fine, and a large number of people were assembled on the heights to witness the engagement. The English yacht "Deerhound," owned by one of Semmes' sympathizers, followed in the "Alabama's" wake, and the French iron-clad "Couronne" steamed out of port to see that the neutrality of French waters was not violated.

Before going into battle, Captain Semmes made the following address to his officers and men, who were all attired in their best clothes :

"Officers and seamen of the 'Alabama': you have at length another opportunity of meeting the enemy—the first that has been presented to you since you sank the '*Hatteras*'! In the meantime you have been all over the world, and it is not too much to say that you have destroyed and driven for protection under neutral flags one-half of the enemy's commerce, which at the beginning of the war covered every sea. This is an achievement of which you may well be proud; and a grateful country will not be unmindful of it. The name of your ship has become a household word wherever civilization extends. Shall that name be tarnished by defeat ? The thing is impossible! Remember that you are in the English Channel, the theatre of so much of the naval glory of our race, and that the eyes of all Europe are at this moment upon you. The flag that floats over you is that of a young Republic, who bids defiance to her enemies, whenever and wherever found. Show the world that you know how to uphold it! Go to your quarters."

The "Kearsarge" ran off shore a few miles so as to draw the Confederate vessel as far as possible from the land and be able to intercept her in case she should attempt to retreat in shore.

As soon as the "Kearsarge" turned to approach the "Alabama," the latter opened fire from the distance of a mile; the Federal vessel not replying, but steaming at full speed for the enemy, receiving a second and third broadside.

When within nine hundred yards, the "Kearsarge" slowed and returned the fire with her starboard battery, and then attempted to gain a position where she could rake the "Alabama." The latter avoided this by sheering, still keeping her starboard broadside bearing on the "Kearsarge." These tactics brought the combatants circling around each other, each working their starboard batteries. As Captain Semmes appeared to avoid close action, Captain Winslow was apprehensive that he might make for the shore, and therefore determined, with full speed and a port helm, to run under the "Alabama's" stern, and if possible rake her. It was Semmes' anticipation of this manoeuvre that forced the "Alabama" under full steam into a circular track during the action as in the diagram, with the result that at the close of the fight the "Alabama" was then nearly five miles off shore,

and it was impossible for her to escape within French jurisdiction, as her commanding officer intended in case the battle should go against him.

The firing of the Confederates was rapid and wild until near the close of the engagement, when it became better, while that of the Federal gunners, owing to the careful training of Lieutenant-Commander James S. Thornton, the executive officer of the "Kearsarge," was very effective. The superior training of the "Kearsarge's" crew was evident from the beginning of the action, their guns telling fearfully on the hull and spars of the Confederate. On the seventh rotation on the circular track the "Alabama" set her foresail and two jibs, with head in shore. Her speed was now retarded, and, by winding her, the port broadside was presented to the "Kearsarge," with only two guns bearing, being able to shift but one gun from the starboard side.

At this time the "Alabama" was com-

THE U. S. S. "KEARSARGE."

pletely at the mercy of the "Kearsarge," and a few more well-directed shots brought down the Confederate flag. Fifteen minutes after the action commenced, the spanker-gaff of the "Alabama" was shot away, and her flag came down, but was immediately hoisted at the mizzen. The "Kearsarge's" shot told fearfully on the "Alabama's" hull, killing and wounding numbers of men in different parts of the ship. So that, in sixty-five minutes after the commencement of the fight, the "Alabama" was discovered to be sinking, an 11-inch shell having entered her side near the water line, making a huge aperture, through which the water poured in torrents. For a moment Semmes had an idea of escaping, and crowded on steam and sail, heading the "Alabama" for the French coast; but the fires in the engine-room were soon extinguished and he was obliged to surrender.

Semmes asserts that his ship was fired upon five times after he had hauled down his colors; but this assertion is not supported by other evidence, for when the Confederate flag came down, Captain Winslow, al-

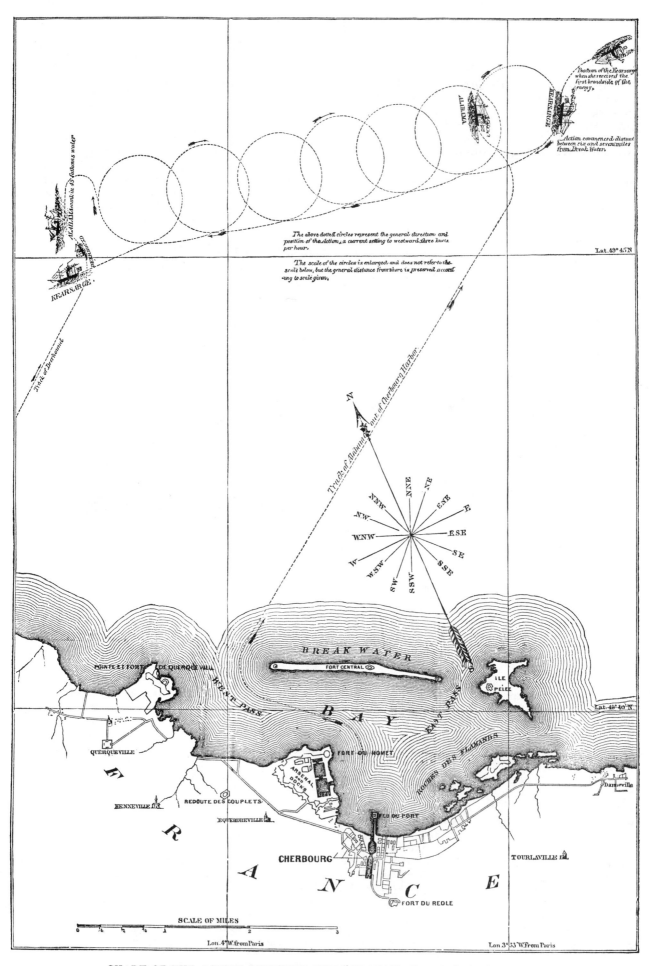

The above dotted circles represent the general direction and
position of the action, a current setting to westward three knots
per hour.

The scale of the circles is enlarged and does not refer to the
scale below, but the general distance from shore is preserved according to scale given.

Position of the Kearsarge
when she received the
first broadside of the
enemy.

Action commenced distant
between six and seven miles
from Break Water.

Lat. 49° 45′ N

Alabama sunk in 45 fathoms water

KEARSARGE

ALABAMA

KEARSARGE

Track of Dechemont

Track of Alabama out of Cherbourg Harbour

N

NNW · NNE · NE
NW · ESE · E
WNW · ESE
W · ESE
WSW · SE
SW · SSE
SSW

BREAK WATER
FORT CENTRAL

POINTE ET FORT DE QUERQUEVILL

W.N.T. PASS

BAY

EAST PASS

ILE PELEE

Lat. 49° 40′ N

QUERQUEVILLE

FORT DU HOMET

ROCHES DES FLAMANDS

Danneville

F R A N C E

HENNEVILLE

REDOUTE DES COUPLETS

EQUERDREVILLE

ARSENAL DOCKS

FEU DU PORT

CHERBOURG

TOURLAVILLE

FORT DU REOLE

SCALE OF MILES
0 ¼ ½ ¾ 1 2 3

Lon. 4° W. from Paris

Lon. 3° 55′ W. from Paris

CHART OF THE ACTION BETWEEN THE "ALABAMA" AND "KEARSARGE."

though unable to ascertain whether it had been hauled down, or shot away, gave the order to reserve the "Kearsarge's" fire. A white flag was displayed over the Confederate's stern, and a moment after the "Alabama" opened on her antagonist with the two guns on the port side, drawing the fire of the "Kearsarge" once more. It was at this moment the Federal vessel steamed ahead, placing herself across the "Alabama's" bow in a position for raking; but, seeing the white flag still flying, the "Kearsarge" again reserved her fire.

Immediately afterwards, the "Alabama's" boats were lowered, one of them pulled alongside the "Kearsarge" with some of the wounded, and in twenty minutes afterwards the "Alabama" went down stern foremost, leaving a large number of her officers and crew struggling in the water. Most of the "Kearsarge's" boats were rendered useless by fragments of shell, as the Confederates fired high; but as soon as possible the launch and second cutter were hoisted out to pick up the drowning men, while the "Alabama's" boat was sent back for the same purpose.

Meanwhile the English yacht "Deerhound," which had been viewing the combat from a distance of about a mile, ran under the stern of the "Kearsarge" and volunteered to pick up the men in the water, to which proposition Captain Winslow assented; for this was no time to think of anything but the claims of humanity, to which American officers and seamen have ever shown due appreciation. In spite of the officers and crew of the "Kearsarge" having done everything possible to rescue their opponent, Captain Semmes, in his chagrin at being so thoroughly beaten, reflects upon Captain Winslow for not sooner getting his boats to the rescue of the "Alabama's" crew.

The prisoners picked up by the boats of the "Kearsarge" were taken on board that vessel, while the "Deerhound," after rescuing Captain Semmes and many of his officers and crew, steamed away for the English coast, leaving others struggling for their lives in the water. Six officers and sixty-four men, including twenty wounded, were received on board the "Kearsarge"; so that, notwithstanding Semmes' accusation, it appears that most of the people of the "Alabama" were saved by the "Kearsarge's" boats, while the Confederate Captain, as soon as he was safe on board the "Deerhound," fearing that Winslow would demand his surrender, urged his friend, the owner of the yacht, to save *him*. The latter accordingly made off without further efforts at rescue; so that, if any one was drowned, it was due more to the selfishness of Captain Semmes than to any other cause.

Although the actions of the owner of the "Deerhound" may be open to criticism, as an Englishman he could hardly be expected to deliver up as prisoners men whom he found struggling for their lives in the water. It is honorable to the English flag that it is a protection to everything it waves over, and that the whole power of the British nation will sustain the rights of even the meanest of its citizens. Captain Semmes' escape made little difference one way or the other, for, with the "Alabama" at the bottom of the channel, his power of mischief had departed. As the Confederacy was in its last agonies, there was no chance of fitting out any more "cruisers."

The action between the "Kearsarge" and the "Alabama," although comparatively a small battle, much impaired the prestige of the Confederate Navy. The British public might rejoice over the destruction of helpless merchantmen, but when it came to fighting, the "Kearsarge" did her work so quickly and effectively that the blindest could but detect the difference between the true and the false coin.

Mr. Secretary Welles attached more importance to the escape of Semmes and his companions in the "Deerhound" than the matter deserved, and even blamed Captain Winslow for his course in paroling the prisoners. Mr. Welles characterized all those connected with the "Alabama" as "pirates," but they were not so in the eyes of European Governments, which had recognized the Confederates' armed vessels as belligerents, and although many of the acts of the "Alabama" bordered on the piratical, yet such irregularities are always found existing in revolutionary struggles, where the worst passions are engendered in the breasts of those who have staked their all on the hazard of a die, and are not always scrupulous as to the means of accomplishing their ends.

The fault of encouraging the Confederate cruisers lay chiefly with the English and French, and to them is due the latitude the former were allowed on the ocean. Possibly the English may have thought that a country capable of putting a million of men in the field must have been able to muster a sufficient force of cruisers to put an end to the "piracy" of which Mr. Welles complained.

As to the implied censure on Captain Winslow for not pursuing the "Deerhound" and recovering his prisoners, the question arises: Were they Winslow's prisoners at all, any more than if they had succeeded in landing on fragments of the wreck at some point on the coast of England, for an English ship represents English soil? A similar sentiment animates the American people, and it would be very inconsistent for them to wish to apply another standard to foreigners, and maintain that it was Captain Winslow's duty to commit violence upon the "Deerhound," and thereby involve the Federal Government in a serious complication with that of Great Britain.

While the "Alabama" was sent to the bottom in sixty-five minutes, with her hull cut to pieces, thirty of her crew killed and wounded, and ten drowned, the "Kearsarge" incurred little damage in hull or spars and had but three men wounded. Out of three hundred and seventy shot and shell fired by the Confederate vessel, thirteen or fourteen only struck the "Kearsarge" in or about the hull, and some sixteen about the masts or rigging. The latter vessel was in perfect readiness to engage another immediately after sinking the "Alabama."

If the "Alabama's" guns were, as it has been asserted, manned by trained gunners from the practice-ship "Excellent," of the Royal Navy, their firing did little credit to the school in which they had been educated. On the other hand, the fire of the "Kearsarge" showed the great superiority of the American crew—as great as was manifested on so many occasions during the war of 1812.

The "Kearsarge" fired one hundred and seventy-three projectiles, less than half the number fired by her antagonist; but what damage they did and whom they killed will never be known. Captain Semmes states that one shot alone killed and wounded eighteen men. Another exploded in the coal-bunkers, completely blocking up the engine-room ; others exploded against the sides, making, as Semmes expresses it, "great gaping wounds" which let in the water and sent the ship to the bottom, with the precious bag of captured flags, and probably the old quartermaster who had charge of the trophies.

No account can be given of the casualties on board the "Alabama" beyond that furnished by Captain Semmes that we have already quoted. Out of one hundred and forty-nine officers and men, forty seem to have been killed or drowned, although it was stated by the prisoners that a number of men joined the ship at Cherbourg, in addition to the regular complement of the "Alabama."

It is remarkable that there was no one killed on board the "Kearsarge" in the action—although three men were wounded, one mortally—as shells were continually bursting over the heads of the crew.

Semmes tried to make it appear that the "Kearsarge" was an iron-clad in disguise, because Captain Winslow had hung his spare chains up and down the sides of his ship abreast of the machinery. This had been done some time before meeting the "Alabama" with the design to protect the boilers and engines, in case the coal in the bunker should get so reduced as to leave them exposed to shot. It was not done with any especial reference to meeting Semmes, who might have adopted a similar plan had he chosen to do so—and this had been done extensively during the civil war, a fact well known to the commander of the "Alabama."

Semmes remarks that the shells fired from the "Alabama" burst against the sides of the "Kearsarge" without effect, owing to this chain armor; but the fact is, only two projectiles struck the chain—a 32-pound shot and a Blakeley shell. The latter did not burst, but broke some of the links of chain. It was of very little use for Captain Semmes to try and excuse himself, after being so thoroughly beaten by the superior discipline of the "Kearsarge," and the skill of her crew in gunnery. It was the intention to make short work with the "Alabama" in case the "Kearsarge" fell in with her, and the action would have terminated sooner but for the difficulty of coming to close quarters with the Confederate vessel.

No wonder the people of the North were overjoyed when they read Captain Winslow's modest dispatch announcing the destruction of the despoiler that had sent so many of their merchant ships to the bottom. The writer evidently states what in his mind was a foregone conclusion, and it is pleasing in its simplicity and brevity:

UNITED STATES STEAMER "KEARSARGE," }
CHERBOURG, FRANCE, June 19, P. M., 1864. }

SIR—I have the honor to inform the Department that the day subsequent to the arrival of the "Kearsarge" off this port, on the 24th instant, I received a note from Captain Semmes begging that the "Kearsarge" would not depart, as he intended to fight her, and would delay her but a day or two. According to this notice, the "Alabama" left the port of Cherbourg this morning at about 9:30 o'clock. At 10:20 A. M. we discovered her steering towards us. Fearing the question of jurisdiction might arise, we steamed to sea until a distance of six or seven miles was attained from the Cherbourg breakwater, when we rounded-to, and commenced steaming for the "Alabama."

As we approached her, within about twelve hundred yards, she opened fire; we receiving two or three broadsides before a shot was returned. The action continued, the respective steamers making a circle round and round at a distance of about nine hundred yards from each other. At the expiration of an hour the "Alabama" struck, going down in about twenty minutes afterward, carrying many persons with her.

It affords me great gratification to announce to the Department that every officer and man did their duty—exhibiting a degree of coolness and fortitude which gave promise at the outset of certain victory.

I have the honor to be, most respectfully, your obedient servant,

JOHN A. WINSLOW,
Captain.

HON. GIDEON WELLES,
Secretary of the Navy, Washington, D. C.

To this dispatch the Secretary of the Navy responded as follows :

NAVY DEPARTMENT, July 6, 1864.

SIR--Your very brief dispatches of the 19th and 20th ultimo, informing the Department that the piratical craft "Alabama," or "290," had been sunk on the 19th of June near meridian, by the "Kearsarge," under your command, were this day received. I congratulate you on your good fortune in meeting this vessel, which had so long avoided the fastest ships and some of the most vigilant and intelligent officers of the service ; and for the ability displayed in this combat you have the thanks of the Department.

You will please express to the officers and crew of the "Kearsarge" the satisfaction of the Government at the victory over a vessel superior in tonnage, superior in number of guns, and superior in the number of her crew. The battle was so brief, the victory so decisive, and the comparative results so striking, that the country will be reminded of the brilliant actions of our infant Navy, which have been repeated and illustrated in this engagement.

The "Alabama" represented the best maritime effort of the most skilled English workshops. Her battery was composed of the well-tried 32-pounders of 57-hundred weight, of the famous 68-pounder of the British Navy, and of the only successful rifled 100-pounder yet produced in England. The crew were generally recruited in Great Britain, and many of them received superior training on board Her Majesty's gunnery ship, the "Excellent."

The "Kearsarge" is one of the first gun-boats built at our Navy Yards at the commencement of the rebellion, and lacks the improvements of vessels now under construction. The principal guns composing her battery had never been previously tried in an exclusively naval engagement, yet in one hour you succeeded in sinking your antagonist, thus fully ending her predatory career, and killed many of her crew without injury to the "Kearsarge," or the loss of a single life on your vessel.

Our countrymen have reason to be satisfied that in this, as in every naval action of this unhappy war, neither the ships, the guns nor the crew have been deteriorated, but that they maintain the abilities and continue the renown which ever adorned our naval annals.

The President has signified his intention to recommend that you receive a vote of thanks, in order that you may be advanced to the grade of commodore.

Lieutenant-Commander James S. Thornton, the executive officer of the "Kearsarge," will be recommended to the Senate for advancement ten numbers in his grade, and you will report to the Department the names of any other of the officers or crew whose good conduct on the occasion entitles them to especial mention.

Very respectfully,

GIDEON WELLES,
Secretary of the Navy.

CAPTAIN JOHN A. WINSLOW,
Commanding U. S. Steamer "Kearsarge,"
Cherbourg, France.

There was no occurrence during the war more grateful to the Northern people than this victory of the "Kearsarge" over the "Alabama." Winslow became the hero of the hour, for he had not only disposed of a most troublesome enemy, but he had demonstrated the superiority of a United States ship, crew and guns over an English-built, English-armed and English-manned vessel of equal, if not superior, force.

The triumph was the greater because the British Government and a large section of the British people had given every assistance to the "Alabama," in the way of moral and material support, in her business of destroying the commerce of a friendly nation. That it was a moral victory over the English can hardly be disputed, and they felt it to be such, as was proven by the desperate efforts of a large portion of the newspapers to show that Winslow's success was unimportant, while the courage and ability of Semmes were extolled to the skies. The fiction on which these newspapers most relied to belittle the victory of the "Kearsarge" was the assertion that the United States vessel was an iron-clad in disguise—an idea which Captain Semmes took every opportunity to disseminate, and which was generally received by the British public.

While Captain Winslow received great credit and promotion for his victory, his executive officer, Lieutenant - Commander Thornton, was complimented by an advance of only ten numbers on the list of officers of his grade, although it was well known that to his close attention to the drilling of the crew, and his management of the "Kearsarge," was due the speedy result of the action. He deserved and should have received promotion to the rank of commander ; but, as he died soon after the close of the war, he never obtained any substantial advancement, although he lives in the memory of those who can properly estimate his services.

LIST OF OFFICERS OF THE U. S. S. "KEARSARGE."

John A. Winslow, Captain; James S. Thornton, Lieutenant - Commander; John M. Browne, Surgeon; J. A. Smith, Paymaster; Wm. H. Cushman, Chief-Engineer; James R. Wheeler, Eben M. Stoddard and David H. Sumner, Acting - Masters ; Wm. H. Badlam, Second-Assistant Engineer ; Fred. L. Miller, Sidney L. Smith and Henry McConnell, Third - Assistant Engineers ; Edward E. Preble, Midshipman; David B. Sargent, Paymaster's Clerk; S. E. Hartwell, Captain's Clerk; Frank A. Graham, Gunner; James C. Walton, Boatswain; William H. Yeaton, Charles H. Danforth and Ezra Bartlett, Acting-Master's Mates.

PETTY OFFICERS AND CREW.

George A. Tittle, Surgeon's-Steward ; C. B. De Witt, Yeoman; J. N. Watrus, Master-at-Arms; Chas. Jones, Seaman; Daniel Charter, Landsman; Edward Williams, Officer's-Steward; George Williams, Landsman ; Charles Butts, Quartermaster; Chas. Bedding, Landsman ; James Wilson, Coxswain ; William Gowan (died), Ordinary Seaman; James Saunders, Quartermaster; John W. Dempsey, Quarter-Gunner; William D. Chapel, Landsman; Thomas Perry, Boatswain's-Mate ; John Barrow, Ordinary Seaman; William Bond, Boatswain's-Mate; James Haley, Captain-of-Forecastle ; Robert Strahn, Captain - of - Top ; James O. Stone, First-Class Boy; Jacob Barth, John H. McCarthy and James F. Hayes, Landsmen; John Hayes, Coxswain; James Devine, Landsman; Geo. H. Russell, Armorer ; Patrick McKeever, Nathan Ives and

Dennis McCarty, Landsmen; John Boyle and John C. Woodberry, Ordinary Seamen; Geo. E. Reed, Seaman; James Morey, Ordinary Seaman; Benedict Drury and William Giles, Seamen; Timothy Hurley, Ship's Cook; Michael Conroy, Ordinary Seaman; Levi W. Nye and James H. Lee, Seamen; John E. Brady, Ordinary Seaman; Andrew J. Rowley, Quarter-Gunner; James Bradley, Seaman; Wm. Ellis, Captain-of-Hold; Henry Cook, Captain-of-Afterguard; Charles A. Reed and William S. Morgan, Seamen; Joshua E. Carey, Sailmaker's-Mate; James Magee, Ordinary Seaman; Benj. S. Davis, Officer's Cook; John F. Bickford, Coxswain; Wm. Gurney, Seaman; Wm. Smith, Quartermaster; Lawrence T. Crowley, Ordinary Seaman; Hugh McPherson, Gunner's-Mate; Taran Phillips, Ordinary Seaman; Joachim Pease, Seaman; Benj. H. Blaisdell and Joel B. Blaisdell, First-Class Firemen; Charles Fisher, Officer's-Cook; James Henson, Wm. M. Smith, Wm. Fisher, George Bailey and Martin Hoyt, Landsmen; Mark G. Ham, Carpenter's-Mate; Wm. H. Bastine, Landsman; Layman P. Spinney, Adoniram Littlefield, John W. Young and Will Wainwright, Coalheavers; John E. Orchon, Second-class Fireman; George W. Remick, Joel L. Sanborn, Jere. Young and Wm. Smith, First-class Firemen; Stephen Smith, John F. Stackpole, Wm. Stanley and Lyman H. Hartford, Second-class Firemen; True W. Priest and Joseph Dugan, First-class Firemen; John F. Dugan, Coalheaver; James W. Sheffield, Second-class Fireman; Charles T. Young, Orderly-Sergeant; Austin Quimley, Corporal-of-Marines; Roscoe G. Dolley and Patrick Flood, Privates of Marines; Henry Hobson, Corporal-of-Marines; James Kerrigan, John McAleen, Geo. A. Raymond, James Tucker and Isaac Thornton, Privates-of-Marines; Wm. Y. Evans, Nurse; Wm. B. Poole, Quartermaster; F. J. Veannoh, Captain-of-Afterguard; Charles Hill, Landsman; Henry Jameson, First-class Fireman; John G. Batchelder, Private-of-Marines; John Dwyer, First-class Fireman; Thomas Salmon and Patrick O'Conner, Second-class Firemen; Geo. H. Harrison and George Andrew, Ordinary Seamen; Charles Moore, Seaman; George A. Whipple, Ordinary Seaman; Edward Wallace, Seaman; Thomas Marsh, Coalheaver; Thomas Buckley, Ordinary Seaman; Edward Wilt, Captain-of-Top; Geo. H. Kinnie, Ordinary Seaman; Augustus Johnson, Jeremiah Horrigan, William O'Halloran and William Turner, Seamen; Joshua Collins and James McBeath, Ordinary Seamen; John Pope, Coalheaver; Charles Mattison, Ordinary Seaman; George Baker, Timothy G. Cauty, John Shields, Thomas Alloway, Philip Weeks and Wm. Barnes, Landsmen; George E. Smart, Second-class Fireman; Chas. A. Poole, Timothy Lynch, Sylvanus P. Brackett and John W. Sanborn, Coalheavers; W. H. Donnally, First-class Fireman. All the above natives of the United States. Wm. Alsdorf and Clement Antoine, Coalheavers; José Dabney, Landsmen; Benjamin Button and Jean Briset, Coalheavers; Vanburn Francois, Landsman; Peter Ludy and George English, Seamen; Jonathan Brien, Landsman; Manuel J. Gallardo, Second-class Boy, and John M. Sonius, First-class Boy. The above are of foreign birth.

It thus appears that out of one hundred and sixty-three officers and crew of the "Kearsarge," only eleven persons were foreign-born.

LIST OF OFFICERS OF CONFEDERATE STEAMER "ALABAMA," JUNE 25, 1864.

Raphael Semmes, Captain; J. M. Kell and Arthur Sinclair, Lieutenants; R. K. Howell, Lieutenant-of-Marines; J. S. Bulloch, Sailing Master; E. A. Maffitt and E. M. Anderson, Midshipmen; R. F. Armstrong and Jos. D. Wilson, Lieutenants; M. J. Freeman, Chief Engineer; John W. Pundt and M. O'Brien, Third-Assistant Engineers; J. O. Cuddy, W. Crawford and C. Seymour, Gunners; Captain's-Clerk, W. B. Smith; Boatswain, B. L. McClaskey; Francis L. Galt, Surgeon; W. P. Brooks, Second-Assistant Engineer; Henry Alcott, Sailmaker; D. H. Llewellyn, Assistant-Surgeon; G. T. Fullam, James Evans, Max Mulliner and J. Schroeder, Master's-Mates; Wm. Robinson, Carpenter.

There has been doubt expressed whether Captain Semmes challenged Captain Winslow to do battle; but the latter could not well have accepted, since the "Alabama" was not recognized by the United States Government as a Confederate ship-of-war. On the contrary, her acts had been denounced as "piratical." Winslow pursued the only course proper for him: he went off Cherbourg and waited as near as possible to the entrance of the port, to see that the "Alabama" did not escape. Captain Semmes' notification to Winslow, that he would give him battle in a day or two if the latter would wait, was hardly necessary, as Winslow had not the slightest idea of avoiding a contest.

For Winslow to have challenged Semmes would have been to put the "Alabama" in the *status* denied her by the Federal Navy Department, namely, that of a recognized vessel-of-war of a *de facto* Government. The propriety of sending challenges from one commanding officer to another in time of war has been questioned. In this instance Winslow did exactly the right thing —waited till his enemy came out of port and defeated him without bluster.

A few words in regard to Semmes' character and abilities, as an agent in carrying out the views of the Confederate Government, may not be out of place. As an individual, he had great defects of character, but as a bold and capable commander, on whom the Confederacy could depend to inflict the greatest damage on United States commerce, Semmes had probably no equal. Although he had served many years in the United States Navy, none of his associates ever supposed that in time of war he would exhibit so much efficiency; for, although his courage was undoubted, his tastes were rather those of the scholar than of the dashing naval officer and destroyer of commerce.

It became common in the North to speak of the "Alabama" as the "English pirate," and Semmes in his memoirs frequently applies the term in a sarcastic manner to his own vessel; yet, although he was guilty of many irregularities, if not outrages, he could not, in justice, be so stigmatized. The writer has on several occasions compared Semmes' acts with those of the buccaneers, who were sometimes regularly commissioned by royal authority to plunder the

Spaniards; but such actions do not constitute piracy, and the Law of Nations is so elastic on the subject that a commander may do a great many outrageous things and still keep within the legal limits.

In the case of the "Alabama," her Captain seems to have been a law unto himself, and his vessel a Court of Admiralty of the Confederate States, with power to commission vessels on the high seas. With his pen this clever navigator could baffle the shrewdness of colonial authorities and create discord in the councils of the Home Governments. He set the proclamation of Queen Victoria at defiance, took his prizes into British ports, and fitted them out as cruisers whenever it suited him to do so. To call this enterprising individual a "pirate" would give rise to the suspicion that want of success in stopping his career of destruction, and a fear of being held responsible for negligence in the premises, had influenced persons in authority to throw all the odium possible on Semmes.

The "Alabama" certainly fulfilled most, if not all, the requirements of a vessel-of-war. She was the sole property of the Confederate Government; and therefore, for all acts committed under the general orders to "burn, sink, and destroy," the said Government was answerable.

As a general rule, a vessel purchased in a neutral port, to war upon another nation, in order to be armed and commissioned, should proceed to a port of the nation purchasing her, and there be fitted for service; but there is so much latitude allowed in practice that it would perhaps be difficult to settle this matter authoritatively before the courts. The high seas are certainly neutral, in one sense of the word, for all nations; and although the Confederates undoubtedly violated British law, yet Semmes had a right to take command of an armed vessel placed in his possession at sea.

It would be well if there could be a careful reconsideration of all the laws and precedents bearing on this subject by the maritime governments of the world, in order that in future no "Alabamas" could get to sea, and commercial nations be free from depredations such as were committed upon the commerce of the United States in 1861–65.

The question has been often debated whether the "Alabama" and her consorts were entitled to be considered vessels-of-war on a par with those of other nations. The powers of Europe accorded belligerent rights to the Confederates, and proclaimed their intention of observing strict neutrality between the contending parties. Such a recognition was in many respects inconsistent, for although the Confederate cruisers were acting in behalf of a Power that had been accorded belligerent rights, yet no recognition further than this had been extended to the State itself by any European Government. The Confederates could have no representatives abroad, and it might well be considered an anomalous state of things when a State was accorded belligerent rights by foreign powers which held no official relations with it, and could not therefore depend upon the ordinary methods for redress if Confederate vessels should commit offences against their sovereignty. This condition of affairs would seem to cast a doubt upon the validity of the commissions of the Confederate cruisers; and for this reason, if for no other, the character of ships-of-war was never accorded to the "Alabama" and the other Confederate cruisers by the Government of the United States.

Captain Semmes' method had a good deal to do, perhaps, with the action of the United States Government, for according to his own account he plundered his prizes of whatever he pleased, and even took the chronometers, which were the private property of the shipmasters.

Whether Confederate naval officers could take delight in the destruction of the Federal commerce, which they once felt such pride in protecting, is very doubtful in the case of all except Captain Semmes. He appears to have gloried in the burning of ships, as if it was the greatest pleasure, instead of a disagreeable duty, imposed upon him by the stern necessities of war; and it is not known that he ever experienced much regret for the burning of a beautiful ship, or sympathy for her master or crew—a sentiment one would naturally expect to exist in the bosom of an officer brought up in a chivalrous service such as that of the United States Navy.

As a fighting-man, Semmes was not a success when he met an enemy of equal force, as was proved by the "Kearsarge" sinking the "Alabama" in about an hour, killing and wounding a great number of men, while the "Kearsarge" was uninjured in hull or spars, and only had three men wounded. The fact is, the "Alabama's" crew, not being well drilled, were doomed to defeat from the outset; for, although the "Kearsarge" stood for her for some moments and received three broadsides, no damage was inflicted, and out of three hundred and seventy shot and shell fired by the Confederate vessel, only thirteen struck the hull, and fifteen the rigging and spars. The difference between the efficiency and discipline of the vessels was too marked to admit of argument, although Semmes insisted that the victory would have been his if one of the shells which struck the "Kearsarge's" stern-post had exploded!

Captain Semmes' want of generosity is

shown by his attempting to deprive Winslow and his officers and men of the credit of their victory, on the ground that the "Kearsarge" was an "iron-clad," and that Winslow had taken a dishonorable advantage of him. A brave man should accept his defeat in dignified silence, in the hope that at some future time he may have an opportunity of retrieving his fortunes.

With regard to Semmes making his escape after the sinking of his ship, that was a matter between him and his conscience. No man is a prisoner until he is actually in the custody of the victor, and if, when struggling in the water, he is rescued by a neutral, the latter should protect him from capture if he has the power to do so. There is even less censure to be given Semmes and his officers for making off in the "Deerhound," because they were under the impression that they would be harshly treated if they fell into the power of the United States Government.

We have endeavored to do Captain Semmes no injustice, but simply to state our impressions of his character, for we knew him well. His career is certainly one of the most remarkable of the civil war; and if he had served the United States while he remained in its Navy as faithfully as he did the Confederacy, his resignation would have been accepted with great regret.

SPECIAL SERVICE, JANUARY 1, 1864.

STEAMER "MOHICAN."

Captain, O. S. Glisson ; Lieutenant, R. K. Duer ; Surgeon, Edw. F. Corson ; Assistant-Paymaster, James Hoy, Jr. ; Acting-Master, Robert B. Ely ; Acting-Ensigns, A. D. Campbell and A. T. Holmes ; Acting-Master's Mates, J. S. Reynolds, W. F. Veltman, E. N. Snow and George T. Ford ; Engineers : Acting-First-Assistant, G. W. Halloway ; Acting-Second-Assistants, John Lardner and C. R. Weaver ; Acting-Third-Assistants, James Buckley and J. W. Buck ; Acting-Boatswain, Geo. C. Abbott ; Gunner, James Hutchinson.

STEAM-SLOOP "KEARSARGE."

Captain, John A. Winslow ; Lieutenant-Commander, James S. Thornton ; Surgeon, John M. Browne ; Paymaster, Joseph A. Smith ; Engineers : Chief, William H. Cushman ; Second-Assistant, Wm. H. Badlam ; Third-Assistants, Fredk. L. Miller, Sidney L. Smith and Henry McConnell ; Boatswain, James C. Walton ; Acting-Gunner, Franklin A. Graham.

STEAMER "SACRAMENTO."

Captain, Henry Walke ; Lieutenant-Commander, H. D. Todd ; Lieutenant, G. P. Ryan ; Surgeon, J. S. Kitchen ; Assistant-Paymaster, J. P. Woodbury ; Ensigns, Marston Niles, P. W. Lowry, J. D. Clark and J. B. Coghlan ; Acting-Master's Mates, D. C. Harrington, O. G. Moore, E. N. R. Place and Charles Pease, Engineers : Acting-Chief, John Yates ; Acting-First-Assistant, Wm. Tipton ; Acting-Second-Assistants, J. S. G. Aspinwall and E. A. Bushnell ; Acting-Third-Assistants, G. E. Savory, John Moquon, Leonard Pratt and E. B. Dyer ; Boatswain, John Bates ; Gunner, Andrew Wilson ; Carpenter, G. E. Anderson.

STEAMER "MICHIGAN."

Commander, John C. Carter ; Paymaster, C. C. Jackson ; Engineers : Acting-Third-Assistants, Wm. Baas, Bennet Jones and Robert Reilly.

STEAMER "WACHUSETT."

Commander, Napoleon Collins ; Lieutenant-Commander, L. A. Beardslee ; Surgeon, Wm. M. King ; Assistant-Paymaster, W. W. Williams ; Acting-Master, J. H. Stimpson ; Ensign, E. M. Shepard ; Acting-Ensigns, Nicol Ludlow and C. J. Barclay ; Acting-Master's Mates, C. R. Haskins, Reuben Rich and John Hetherington ; Engineers : Chief, Wm. H. Rutherford ; Second-Assistants, Geo. W. Melville, M. Knapp and Edmund Lincoln ; Third-Assistants, H. D. McEwen, R. S. Stedman and J. A. Barton ; Boatswain, John Burrows ; Acting-Gunner, John Russell.

SLOOP-OF-WAR "ST. LOUIS."

Commander, George H. Preble ; Lieutenant Wm. F. Stewart ; Surgeon, A. L. Gihon ; Assistant-Surgeon, F. B. A. Lewis ; Paymaster, J. S. Post ; First-Lieutenant-of-Marines, W. J. Squires ; Acting-Masters, J. N. Rowe, Geo. Cables and Allan Hoxie ; Acting-Ensign, Hazard Marsh ; Acting-Master's Mates, P. W. Fagan, F. L. Bryan and J. H. Langley ; Acting-Boatswain, George Brown ; Gunner, G. P. Cushman ; Carpenter, Daniel Jones ; Sailmaker, I. E. Crowell.

SHIP "ONWARD."

Acting-Masters, Wm. H. Clarke ; T. G. Groove and William Collins ; Acting-Assistant Surgeon, David Watson ; Acting-Assistant Paymaster, J. S. Allen ; Acting-Ensigns, G. J. Conklin and Wm. Rogers ; Acting-Master's Mates, F. A. Gording, A. F. Ulmer and J. S. Newbegin.

STEAMER "IROQUOIS."

Commander, C. R. P. Rodgers ; Lieutenants, S. Dana Greene and A. H. McCormick ; Acting-Master Thomas Hanrahan ; Surgeon, J. Corbin ; Assistant-Paymaster, J. A. Bates, Jr. ; Ensigns, Henry C. Taylor, Allan D. Brown and W. K. Wheeler ; Acting-Master's Mates, C. F. Purrington, Carleton Race, B. F. Ritter and William Welch ; Engineers : Acting-Chief, J. W. Stormes ; Acting-First-Assistants, W. H. Best and R. E. Stall ; Acting-Second-Assistant, John B. Roach ; Acting-Third-Assistants, H. P. Gray and Edward Ewel ; Acting-Gunner, J. C. Clapham.

CHAPTER XLVII.

OPERATIONS OF SOUTH ATLANTIC BLOCKADING SQUADRON, UNDER REAR-ADMIRAL DAHLGREN, DURING LATTER END OF 1863 AND IN 1864.

FORT SUMTER BOMBARDED. — DAMAGES TO THE FORT AND IRON-CLADS. — LOSS OF THE "WEEHAWKEN."—ATTACK ON BATTERIES IN STONO RIVER.—REVIEW OF WORK DONE BY SOUTH ATLANTIC SQUADRON UNDER DAHLGREN.—ACTIONS IN WHICH IRON-CLADS WERE ENGAGED.—DESTRUCTION OF BLOCKADE-RUNNERS.—OPERATIONS OF CONFEDERATE TORPEDO CORPS.—PLANS TO BLOW UP FLEET.—DESTRUCTION OF THE "HOUSATONIC." —SUBLIME PATRIOTISM.—ORIGINATORS OF TORPEDO.—OPERATIONS OF GUN-BOATS IN FLORIDA RIVERS.—DESTRUCTION OF STEAMER "HARRIET A. WEED" AND TRANSPORT "MAPLE-LEAF." — HAZARDOUS CUTTING-OUT EXPEDITIONS. — HOT RECEPTIONS FROM MASKED BATTERIES.—CAPTURE OF U. S. STEAMER "WATER WITCH" AND RIVER-BOAT "COLUMBINE."—TREATMENT RECEIVED BY ASSISTANT SURGEON PIERSON.—PRISONERS EXPOSED IN DANGEROUS PLACES.—FAILURE OF EXPEDITION TO CUT RAILROADS.—MISCELLANEOUS EXPEDITIONS. — BLOCKADE OF WHOLE SOUTHERN COAST.— EXTREMITIES OF CONFEDERATE ARMIES, ETC.—VESSELS AND OFFICERS OF SOUTH ATLANTIC BLOCKADING SQUADRON, JANUARY, 1864.

ON the 26th of October, 1863, General Gillmore opened fire upon Fort Sumter from his battery on Morris Island, his object being to complete the reduction of this work, drive out the garrison, and occupy it with Union troops. This, as a matter of sentiment, might have been a good move ; but, as the Confederates still commanded Fort Sumter with the guns of Fort Moultrie and other batteries, they could have rendered the place untenable, as they did in the time of Colonel Anderson.

But the Navy was desirous of performing its share in this useless operation, and the Monitors "Lehigh" and "Patapsco" were ordered to take positions at a distance of from 1,600 to 2,000 yards of the fort, and open fire upon it with their rifled guns.

These vessels were within range of Fort Moultrie for some time, but suffered little damage, while their rifle projectiles told on the walls of Fort Sumter with considerable effect. Large masses of masonry were displaced, heavy timbers thrown into the air, gun-cartridges destroyed, and, in fact, the work reduced to a great heap of ruins; but there it stood as unassailable by land

forces as ever, and Dahlgren was no nearer getting into Charleston than DuPont had been when he relinquished the command because of an implied reflection on his ability to decide whether a proper force had been placed at his disposal or not. About eight hundred and fifty shells were fired by the Navy at the ruins of Fort Sumter, which helped to crumble the works more and more; but that business had better have been left to General Gillmore with his siege-guns, and the attack of the Monitors should have been turned upon Moultrie and Beauregard, where their rifle projectiles would have done good service.

On November 16th more congenial work offered. General Gillmore telegraphed: "The enemy have opened a heavy fire on Cummings' Point. Will you have some of your vessels move up, so as to prevent an attack by boats on the sea-face of the Point?" That night the Monitors moved up at about 10 o'clock, and boats were placed on patrol to prevent any attack of the enemy at the place indicated.

On November 17th the "Lehigh" grounded, and the enemy, perceiving her dilemma, opened heavily on her from Fort Moultrie and adjacent batteries. Signal was at once made to all the Monitors to get underway and cover the "Lehigh," and the Admiral himself went up in the "Passaic" to attend the operations in person. The "Nahant," Lieutenant-Commander Cornwell, was already alongside the "Lehigh," and, by getting out hawsers, succeeded in towing her off at high water. Both vessels were subjected to a brisk fire, but they received no serious damage. The "Lehigh" received twenty-two hits, nine of which were on her deck-plates, and she had one officer and six men wounded. The "Montauk" also assisted in getting the "Lehigh" off, but there were no casualties in the assisting vessels.

Assistant-Surgeon Wm. Longshaw was handsomely mentioned on this occasion for going to and fro in a small boat, carrying out hawsers under a heavy fire of shot and shell. This kind of service always deserves recognition, and especially when, as in this case, it is voluntarily undertaken by an officer who would never have been called upon to perform it in the ordinary course of his profession. Surgeon Longshaw was recommended for promotion in his corps by the Chief of the Bureau of Medicine and Surgery.

On December 6th, Rear-Admiral Dahlgren had the misfortune to lose the Monitor "Weehawken" under the following circumstances, as given in the report of Commander J. M. Duncan:

"On the morning of the 5th I arrived here, and in the evening took command of her [the 'Weehawken'] and went up on the advanced picket, and remained there until 9:30 of the morning of the 6th; then came down; made fast to buoy No. 2; then came on board this vessel [the flag-ship].

"About 1:30 P. M. a signal was made that the 'Weehawken' wanted assistance. I immediately got in a boat with the pilot of this vessel. Before we could reach her she went down. Boats from all the vessels around went to the assistance of the men that were overboard, and succeeded in saving all but four of the engineers and twenty-seven of the men. When I left the vessel everything appeared to be right; the anchor-hold was all dry, no water coming through the hawse-pipe. * * * * Not being on board myself at the time, I am not able to give any account of the sad accident.

"Very respectfully," etc.

From statements of officers who were on board the "Weehawken" at the time of the disaster, it appears that the immediate cause of her sinking was that a heavy sea swept over her forecastle, and entering the fore-hatch, filled the anchor-well. This, under ordinary circumstances, would not have proved fatal to the ship's safety; but she was heavily loaded forward with ammunition, and the slight increase of weight, due to the water in her forward compartment, caused an opening between the overhang and the hull, which made itself manifest by numerous leaks. As the water accumulated forward, her bow commenced to settle rapidly, and she soon went to the bottom, with a number of her brave officers and men.

This was a serious loss to Rear-Admiral Dahlgren, who was at that moment urging the Government to send him more Monitors, in view of the necessity of defending his command against the iron-clads which the Confederates were building at Charleston. No doubt the Confederates considered that the sinking of the "Weehawken" was due to the shot and shell which they fired at the "Lehigh"—as they could not tell one from another.

Nothing of interest occurred in Dahlgren's command from November 6th up to December 25th, when the "Pawnee," Commander G. B. Balch, the "Marblehead," Lieutenant-Commander R. W. Meade, Jr., and the schooner "C. P. Williams," Acting-Master S. N. Freeman, were attacked by Confederate batteries in Stono River.

Lieutenant-Commander Meade reports that on December 25th the enemy opened fire on the "Marblehead," at 6 o'clock in the morning, from two batteries of field and siege pieces posted advantageously in the woods. At the time mentioned, the "Marblehead" had steam on the port boiler only. The gun-boat returned the enemy's fire vigorously, and, slipping his cable, Lieutenant-Commander Meade took a position nearer the batteries, and after a short encounter caused them to retreat in disorder, leaving two guns and caissons.

No attempt was made by the "Marblehead" to retire from this unequal contest, though she was struck over twenty times and much cut up, having three men killed and four wounded. Officers and men stood to their guns with great gallantry, and the precision of their fire was shown by the complete discomfiture of the enemy. Acting-Ensign Geo. F. Winslow and the officers of the gun divisions are handsomely mentioned in this report.

During the action, the "Pawnee" took an enfilading position in the Keowah River, while the "Williams" was ordered to work up towards Legareville. The three vessels kept up such a fire that the enemy fled precipitately. Commander Balch speaks in the highest terms of Lieutenant-Commander Meade's coolness and bravery, the management of his vessel, and the remarkable rapidity of his fire.

On the conclusion of the firing, General Gordon, commanding the troops at the south end of Folly Island, sent an infantry force to bring off the guns left by the Confederates; which, on reaching the spot where the batteries were posted, found two guns, one soldier in the throes of death, six dead artillery horses, and all the enemy's intrenching tools, knapsacks, etc. As night was coming on, and it was found impossible to bring off the guns in face of a heavy force of the enemy, not far off, they were disabled and abandoned.

This was a handsomely-executed affair, particularly on the part of the "Marblehead," which bore the brunt of the fire from the enemy's 8-inch guns. There was some dispute as to the credit due the different vessels, which ought not to have been the case where all did so well. In addition to Lieutenant Commander Meade's gallantry in the action, he made a reconnoissance of the ground abandoned by the enemy, and then, by direction of Commander Balch, headed an expedition to bring off the guns which General Gordon had failed to take possession of. His force consisted of 3 boats, 3 officers, and 50

CAPTAIN (NOW REAR-ADMIRAL) GEORGE B. BALCH.

men from the "Pawnee"; 4 boats, 4 officers and 20 men from the "Marblehead," and 1 officer and 12 men from the "C. P. Williams"—total, 8 boats, 8 officers and 82 men, of which 22 were marines, under Sergeant W. Fredlickson, of the "Pawnee."

On reaching the earthworks, near a bayou which flows southwesterly of Legareville, Acting-Ensign Moore was directed to take the "Pawnee's" men and get the nearest gun into her cutter. The other gun in the most northern work was then raised with great difficulty, lashed to the carriage of a 12-pound howitzer, and hauled with great exertion to the bayou, a distance of a mile, and finally gotten into the "Marblehead's" launch.

The whole affair was a perfect success;

the two guns, 8-inch seacoast howitzers, were taken off, the gun-carriages and implements thrown into the river, and all done in the space of two hours.

Though Rear-Admiral Dahlgren had not, up to this time, forced any of the obstructions in Charleston harbor, or made his way past the batteries (thus verifying the assertion of Admiral DuPont, that the force of Monitors was not equal to the occasion), he had shown great pertinacity in sticking to the work assigned him, and had given all the aid in his power to the land-batteries under General Gillmore. The following review of the services of Admiral Dahlgren when in command of the South Atlantic squadron will give a fair insight into the value of his work:

On the 6th of July, 1863, Rear-Admiral DuPont delivered to Rear-Admiral Dahlgren the command of the forces occupying the coast of South Carolina, Georgia, and part of Florida. This force, which consisted of 70 vessels of all classes, was scattered along the coast for a distance of 300 miles; there was no concentration, the object being rather to distribute the vessels in such a manner as to enforce an efficient blockade.

When Dahlgren took command, the Navy Department was much more liberal towards him than it had been to DuPont; for he was left to exercise his own judgment, unhampered by orders of any kind. His instructions were so couched that they merely directed him to assume command, without confining him to any course of action. They went no further, nor was it necessary that they should do so. There was an enemy in front who had defied the Government to the utmost; the Department and the President had already signified their wishes to Admiral DuPont, and it was clearly the duty of his successor to go to work as soon as possible and compel the enemy to obedience if he could. But it must be remembered that the Department, in view of the difficulties that had beset the first expedition, had modified its opinion, and was now satisfied that it would be better to have a combined attack of the Army and Navy against the heavy works in Charleston harbor than to depend on the Monitors alone.

The "New Ironsides" was off Charleston bar, two Monitors were at Edisto, one at Stono River, three at Port-Royal, and one at Ossabaw. General Gillmore having arrived, arrangements were immediately made between him and Rear-Admiral Dahlgren for a descent on Morris Island, where the former was to establish his batteries.

The naval part of the operations consisted in assembling all the Monitors at Charleston, so as to cross the bar at early daylight, and be ready to cover the landing of the army, with its guns, munitions, etc.; and then to co-operate in whatever way the army might desire to attack the enemy.

On the 9th of July all was in readiness. In the combined attack which followed, the "Catskill," "Montauk," "Nahant," and "Weehawken" were laid in line parallel with the land opposite the southern eminences of Morris Island, and they poured in such a steady fire upon the Confederate batteries at that point that they made but a feeble show of fight. At 8 o'clock the troops that had been brought from the Folly River by the boats of the squadron advanced to the attack; and, under the covering fire of the Monitors, occupied all the enemy's outer positions, and were only stopped when they came in contact with Fort Wagner.

Until the fall of Wagner, on September 7th, the iron-clads and gun-boats kept up a constant fire on the place, which could only be taken by hard and patient work. But this work was not crowned with success until after several desperate assaults had been made by the Army, and a heavy bombardment by the Navy. All assaults were failures, however, and it was proved that the great engineering skill of the Confederates had produced a work that could only be taken by the slow and laborious operation of a regular siege.

And here Admiral Dahlgren gives a very good reason why the delay in reaching Charleston subsequently ensued, viz., that there was a paucity of troops in the first place; that there ought to have been men enough to make the first assault an assured success; that Wagner might have been carried at the first assault; Gregg would have yielded in consequence; Sumter would soon have followed, and the iron-clads, untouched by severe and continued battering, would have been in condition to come quickly in contact with the imperfect interior defences. The Admiral forgot, however, that he would still have had the line of obstructions to break, and the batteries at Moultrie and on Sullivan's Island to pass, and that the Monitors would have found the same difficulties in forcing their way through the interior defences as DuPont met with in his first attack.

The military and naval attacks were as gallant as anything could be, but, though they achieved a great deal, they did not succeed in driving the enemy out of Wagner before he had time to convert Fort Johnson from a very imperfect work into a powerful fort. Moultrie received similar advantages, and most of the cannon of Sumter were divided between Johnson and Moultrie. Batteries were established along the south shore of the channel from Fort Johnson towards the city; and thus an interior defence was completed that rendered access to the upper harbor far more difficult than it was before, because a heavy fire could be concentrated from additional batteries upon vessels attempting to enter. In fact, the enemy had profited by the experience gained in their outer defences, and had placed their guns so as to obtain a concentrated fire. When the troops who garrisoned Wagner were informed that the interior forts were completed, they quietly evacuated that post on the eve of an assault by the Union troops, and occupied the new positions so adroitly prepared by their able engineers.

In all the siege of this tough work the Navy bore a conspicuous part, having kept up a continuous and heavy fire whenever the opportunity offered. But the more they battered it, the more apparent it became that the small force of iron-clads off Charleston was not capable of forcing its way up to the city through obstructions that were now commanded by the newly built defences.

The services of the vessels during the attack on Wagner were invaluable, as the fire of their guns prevented the access of reinforcements, or their accumulation between Wagner and Gregg; and, in fact, without the assistance of the Navy, the Army would not have been able to maintain its position a day without further reinforcements.

The boats of the squadron were engaged on picket duty by night along the sea-shore of Morris Island, and in the little stream on its inner border. A detachment of seamen and marines were also engaged, under Commander F. A. Parker, in the attack on the batteries at Fort Sumter, working four Navy rifled cannon that had been landed for the purpose.

Besides the principal attacks made on Wagner, there were few days from the first attack on Morris Island (July 10) to its evacuation (September 7) that some iron-clads or gun-boats were not engaged with the enemy's works.

The following table will exhibit the work done by the fleet from July 18th to September 8th:

Date. 1863.	Object.	Vessels engaged.
July 18.	Assault on Wagner	"Montauk," "Ironsides," "Catskill," "Nantucket," "Weehawken," "Patapsco," "Paul Jones," "Ottawa," "Seneca," "Chippewa," "Wissahickon."
July 22.	Wagner...........	"Nantucket," "Ottawa."
July 24.	Wagner (to cover advance.)........	"Weehawken," "Ironsides," "Catskill," "Montauk," "Patapsco," "Nantucket," "Ottawa," "Dai Ching," "Paul Jones," "Seneca."
July 25.	Wagner	"Ottawa," "Dai Ching," "Paul Jones."
July 28.	Wagner...........	"Weehawken," "Catskill," "Ottawa."
July 29.	Wagner......	"Ironsides," "Patapsco."
July 30.	Wagner........ .	"Ironsides," "Catskill," "Patapsco," "Ottawa."
July 31.	Batteries on Morris Island...........	"Ottawa."
Aug. 1.	Wagner...........	"Montauk," "Patapsco," "Catskill," "Weehawken," "Passaic," "Nahant," "Marblehead."

Date. 1863.	Object.	Vessels engaged.
Aug. 2.	Wagner............	"Ottawa," "Marblehead."
Aug. 4.	Wagner............	"Montauk," "Marblehead."
Aug. 6.	Wagner............	"Marblehead."
Aug. 8.	Wagner............	"Ottawa," "Mahaska," "Marblehead."
Aug. 11.	Wagner and vicinity	"Patapsco," "Catskill."
Aug. 13.	Morris Island	"Dai Ching," "Ottawa," "Mahaska," "Racer," "Wissahickon."
Aug. 14.	Morris Island......	"Wissahickon," "Mahaska," "Dan Smith," "Ottawa," "Dai Ching," "Racer."
Aug. 15.	Wagner............	"Racer," "Dan Smith."
Aug. 17.	Batteries on Morris Island to direct fire from the batteries which opened on Sumter.	"Weehawken," "Ironsides," "Montauk," "Nahant," "Catskill," "Passaic," "Patapsco," "Canandaigua," "Mahaska," "Ottawa," "Cimmaron," "Wissahickon," "Dai Ching," "Lodona."
Aug. 18.	Wagner, to prevent assault..........	"Ironsides," "Passaic," "Weehawken," "Wissahickon," "Mahaska," "Dai Ching," "Ottawa," "Lodona."
Aug. 19.	Wagner............	"Ironsides."
Aug. 20.	Morris Island......	"Ironsides," "Mahaska," "Ottawa," "Dai Ching," "Lodona."
Aug. 21.	Sumter and Wagner............	"Ironsides," "Patapsco," "Mahaska," "Dai Ching."
Aug. 22.	Wagner......... ...	"Weehawken," "Ironsides," "Montauk."
Aug. 23.	Sumter............	"Weehawken," "Passaic," "Montauk," "Patapsco," "Nahant."
Sept. 1.	Sumter and obstructions........	"Weehawken," "Montauk," "Passaic," "Patapsco," "Nahant," "Lehigh."
Sept. 5.	Between Sumter and Gregg........	"Lehigh," "Nahant."
Sept. 6.	Wagner and Gregg	"Ironsides," "Weehawken," "Montauk," "Passaic," "Patapsco," "Nahant," "Lehigh."
Sept. 7.	Batteries on Sullivan's Island......	"Ironsides," "Patapsco," "Lehigh," "Nahant," "Montauk," "Weehawken."
Sept. 8.	Batteries on Sullivan's Island	"Ironsides," "Nahant," "Patapsco," "Lehigh," "Montauk," "Weehawken."

SERVICE OF IRON-CLADS.

SOUTH ATLANTIC BLOCKADING SQUADRON.

Shots fired and hits received by them during operations against Morris Island:

Vessels	No. of shots fired.		Hits.	Hits Apr. 7, 1863.	Hits at Ogeechee.	Total hits.
	15-in.	11-in.				
"Catskill"	138	425	86	20	..	106
"Montauk".................	301	478	154	14	46	214
"Lehigh"	41	28	36	.	.	36
"Passaic"........	119	107	90	35	9	134
"Nahant"....	170	276	69	36	..	105
"Patapsco"	178	230	96	47	1	144
"Weehawken"	264	633	134	53	..	187
"Nantucket"	44	155	53	51	..	104
"Ironsides"................	...	4439	164	..	..	164
Totals..	1255	6771	882	256	56	1194

	No. of shots fired.	Weight of projec. fired in tons.
By "Ironsides"...........	4,439	288½
11-in. by Monitors..........	2 332	151½
15-in. by Monitors..........	1,255	213½
Total..................	8,026	653½

That these vessels were subjected to a terrific fire there can be no doubt ; and it shows that, though there may have been defects in the building of some of the Monitors, yet that Ericsson's system was the most perfect one then invented, and that no ship in European navies then built could have contended successfully with any one of them for an hour.

During the progress of the engineering work under General Gillmore, which was of the most laborious kind, the iron-clads and gun-boats played a most conspicuous part, as has been shown in instances already quoted. It would have been as easy for the enemy to have worked towards the Union position as for the Federals to advance towards theirs, had it not been for the fire of the vessels which confined them to the main fort and prevented their extending its lines of defence. If this had not been the case, the Confederates could have kept pace with the Federal troops, and the latter at the end of a month would have been no nearer their object than before. But the naval commanders were always on the alert to sweep the plain, and prevent the erection of any new works on the side of Wagner, or any assault on Gillmore's position. In fact, the fire from the fleet enfiladed the entire width of the narrow island, and not only absolutely interdicted any aggressive operations on the part of the enemy, but kept them constantly occupied in repairing damages to the main work ; and, finally, on the day before the last assault was contemplated, Dahlgren took in his whole force of iron-clads and battered the fort into sand-heaps.

History cannot but award great praise to the brave Confederates who remained at their posts for two months under this terrible fire, and kept a great Army and Navy at bay until their interior defences were so strengthened that they could afford to abandon the outer work.

The operations of the iron-clads at Morris Island were appropriately closed by a severe contest with Forts Moultrie and Beauregard, Battery Bee, and all the batteries on Sullivan's Island, to relieve the "Weehawken," which vessel had grounded under their guns and was in great danger, the tide having fallen and exposed her unprotected hull. This last affair showed conclusively that Fort Moultrie and the batteries mentioned might have been attacked with success, could a strong force of Federal troops with heavy rifled guns have been stationed on Sullivan's Island, to co-operate, as was done at Morris Island. No doubt the struggle would have been a severe one, but, if as ably carried out as in the first instance, success would assuredly have followed.

It is not always easy for the historian to give the full credit where it is due. He must be governed by the official reports, except in cases where there are glaring inconsistencies. Hence the tabulated form of reports adopted by Rear-Admiral Dahlgren has been followed. This plan is intended to show at a glance what each vessel had done ; but, with all the care a commanding officer may take to do justice to his subordinates, discrepancies will creep into official reports at times. This may imply a want of accuracy on the part of a commander-in-chief, when, in fact, it may have been due to the hurried performance of a multiplicity of duties, or to the indiscretion of a secretary. But it is the duty of the historian to correct these discrepancies when they are manifest, where it can be done without raising questions that might end in angry controversies.

There was published in the *Army and Navy Journal*, on the 16th of April, 1864, a review of the services of the Monitors in Southern waters. Commander Edward Simpson, in a report dated April 21st, expressed himself as dissatisfied with the amount of credit given his vessel, the "Passaic," in the official reports. On the 29th of July, 1863, the "Passaic" went into action with Fort Wagner, followed by the "Patapsco" and the "New Ironsides." The presence of the "Passaic" is not mentioned in Rear-Admiral Dahlgren's review.

On the 31st of August, 1863, the most serious engagement in which the iron-clads had yet taken part occurred between Fort Moultrie on one side, and the Monitors "Patapsco," "Weehawken," "Passaic,"

COMMANDER (NOW REAR-ADMIRAL) EDWARD SIMPSON.

and "Nahant" on the other; the detachment being under the command of Commander T. H. Stevens, on board the "Passaic." During the action, the "Passaic" grounded about half a mile from Fort Moultrie, and was severely hammered by the guns of that work before she floated off. This affair was not mentioned in the review, though it was a much more serious one than the engagements with Wagner and Battery Gregg, on Morris Island.

On the 8th of September, one of the most remarkable actions between iron-clads and shore-batteries that ever occurred was fought under command of Commodore S. C. Rowan, between the batteries on

Sullivan's Island on the one side, and the "New Ironsides," "Patapsco," "Lehigh," "Passaic," "Nahant," and "Weehawken" (aground), on the other. This action lasted three hours, and terminated in silencing the fire of the batteries on the island.

During this action, the "Passaic" was at the head of the line, having received an order from the Commodore as she was going into action to go well up and engage Battery Bee. In this affair the vessel was hit in fifty-one new places.

The presence of the "Passaic" is not mentioned. It was very difficult to keep this vessel in effective condition for firing, as her turret had got jammed on the 6th of September, which caused the spindle and pilot house to take up motion with the turret, thus disabling the steering gear, which required the most ingenious expedients to rectify.

After all his efforts to keep his vessel available, and after having endured such a battering from Moultrie's 10-inch shot, it was disheartening to Lieutenant-Commander Simpson to find that the presence of his vessel in this action was not mentioned, particularly as she had been more battered than any in the Monitor fleet.

Admiral Dahlgren, however, did in a measure rectify this mistake, as will appear from the following

"ADDITIONAL LIST OF ACTIONS, in which the iron-clads were engaged with the Confederate batteries in Charleston harbor while reducing Morris Island."

Date. 1863.	Name.	Ro'ds fired.	Hits by Enemy	Dist'nce Yards.	Object.	Remarks.
July 18.	"New Ironsides."	805	4	1,400	Wagner	
July 20.	" "	168	13	1,300	Wagner.	
Aug. 23.	" "	90	4		Wagner.	Ship was underway—distance varied from 1,100 to 1,300 yards.
Sept. 2.	" "	41		1,000	Gregg.	Hits from Gregg and Moultrie. Ship at anchor.
Sept. 2.	" "	9	..	1,500	Sumter.	
Sept. 5.	" "	488	..	1,300	Wagner.	
Sept. 5.	" "	32	1	1,800	Gregg.	Hit from Gregg.

"On July 29th, the 'Passaic' engaged Wagner, and on August 31st Moultrie. On September 8th, the 'Passaic' (in a disabled condition), 'Patapsco,' 'Weehawken,' and 'Nahant' engaged Moultrie."

This was scant justice to an officer who had so well maintained the reputation of the Navy at Charleston, under the hottest fire; but, no doubt, he obtained full credit from his comrades in arms, who, after all, are the ones who appreciate a brother officer's services on such occasions.

One of the points in the efficiency of the iron-clads was the manner in which they had almost closed up the harbor of Charleston against the blockade-runners. We say *almost*, for, notwithstanding all the watchfulness of the officers on patrol duty, some of these vessels did force their way in, and even succeeded in getting as far as Moultrie, where they thought themselves secure.

On February 2d, 1864, at daylight, a beautiful blockade-runner, the "Presto," was perceived close under the batteries of Moultrie, which was the first notice of her presence, she having crept in during the night under the management of some daring captain, who was, no doubt, assisted by range-lights. He had anchored close to Moultrie, intending, no doubt, to go up to Charleston as soon as he could get a pilot to take him through the obstructions. Dahlgren at once ordered up the nearest Monitor, and directed her commander to open fire upon the intruder with his rifled gun from a distance of about 2,500 yards. Other Monitors were ordered up in succession, for it was desirable to show these blockade-runners that Charleston was a sealed port to them. The "Lehigh," "Passaic," "Catskill" and "Nahant" opened on the doomed vessel. Colonel Davis, commanding Morris Island, also opened from Fort Strong and Battery Gregg, and the steamer was soon set on fire and destroyed.

It was remarkable that, under the circumstances, any blockade-runner should have attempted such a dare-devil feat; but the greed of gain was overpowering in that class of people, and one successful trip often made them rich for life.

There was no end to the energy of the Confederates, who, after they had lost the forts on Morris Island and seen Sumter battered out of shape by the Army and Navy, determined to show that they were not at all subdued. They had strengthened the works in the inner harbor above Moultrie, and made the place more difficult of approach than ever. Colonel Davis held Morris Island up to Cummings' Point and commanded Sumter, which was of no use to any one, with his guns.

General Gillmore, who seemed to think for the present that he had done all *he* could to close the port against blockade-runners, informed Rear-Admiral Dahlgren, on February 5th, 1864, that he was about to throw a force into Florida, on the west bank of the St. John's River, and desired his assistance. In consequence, three gun-boats were sent to the St. John's River by the commander-in-chief, who, the same evening, departed himself for that point, leaving the blockade of Charleston in charge of Commodore Rowan. This was virtually abandoning the attempt to capture Charleston, that long-cherished object of the Navy Department, and seeking a new and much less important field of operations. But as

this expedition only required the presence of the Navy while the troops were disembarking, Rear-Admiral Dahlgren soon after returned to Port Royal, leaving a sufficient force of gun-boats in the St. John's River to co-operate with the Army if necessary.

The Confederates were not slow to take advantage of the lull which had taken place after the storm of shot and shell that had been poured down upon their devoted heads, and their torpedo corps went to work to fit out another "David" (or torpedo-boat), after the plan, with improvements, of the one that had attempted to blow up the "Ironsides." The first attempt was such a complete failure that the Federal officers on the outside blockade had grown somewhat careless.

As early as January 14, 1864, the Navy Department had written to Rear-Admiral Dahlgren, informing him that it had received notice that the Confederates had on foot a plan to blow up his fleet, and that it considered it of sufficient importance to notify him of it. Dahlgren, however, did not think that such a plan would be carried out against the vessels blockading outside of the harbor, but only against the iron-clads on the inside; but, at the same time, thought it advisable to give notice to the officers on the outer blockade, so that they might be on their guard. Notwithstanding these precautions, the Confederates managed to get one of their torpedo-boats over the bar, and on the night of the 17th of February the fine new ship "Housatonic," while lying at anchor off Charleston, in a most convenient position to be attacked by torpedo-boats, was destroyed under the following circumstances:

At about 8:45 P. M., the officer of the deck on board the "Housatonic," Acting-Master J. K. Crosby, discovered something in the water, about one hundred yards away, moving towards the ship. All the officers in the squadron had been informed of the character of the "Davids," and what they looked like on the water. The commander-in-chief had had printed full descriptions of these infernal machines, and directions as to the best manner of avoiding them. He had attached more importance to torpedoes than persons generally did at that time, and considered that they constituted the most formidable difficulties in the way of getting to Charleston. He felt that the whole line of blockade would probably be attacked with these cheap, convenient and formidable weapons, and that officers should adopt every means to guard against them.

When this machine was first seen by the officer of the deck, it had the appearance of a plank moving along on the water. It came directly towards the ship, and, within two minutes of the time it was first sighted, was alongside. The chain was slipped, the engine backed, and all hands called to quarters. But it was too late—the torpedo struck the "Housatonic" just forward of the main-mast on the starboard side, in a line with the magazine. The man who steered her knew where the vulnerable spots of the steamer were, and he did his work well. As the after pivot-gun was pivoted to port, it was found impossible to bring a gun to bear on the daring intruder, while those on board of her were coolly making their arrangements to knock a hole in the ship's bottom, for the "David" laid alongside a full minute. When the explosion took place the ship trembled all over, as if by the shock of an earthquake, and seemed to be lifted out of the water, and then sank stern foremost, heeling to port as she went down.

It must have been a large hole in the bottom that could sink her so rapidly. There was, of course, great consternation on board at this unlooked-for event, for there is nothing more appalling than to have a torpedo exploded under a ship's bottom. A hundred pounds of powder on a pole, is enough to blow the bottom through the heaviest iron-clad—how destructive must it have been then to a wooden vessel! Most of the crew flew up the rigging for safety, and all order was at an end on board the "Housatonic." Her captain (Pickering) was stunned and somewhat bruised by the concussion, and the order of the day was "*sauve qui peut.*" A boat was dispatched to the "Canandaigua," not far off, and that vessel at once responded to the request for help, and succeeded in rescuing all but the following officers and men, who are supposed to have been drowned: Ensign E. C. Hazletine, Captain's Clerk C. O. Muzzey, Quartermaster John Williams, Landsman Theodore Parker, and Fireman John Walsh.

Strange to say, the "David" was not seen after the explosion, and was supposed to have slipped away in the confusion; but when the "Housatonic" was inspected by divers, the torpedo-boat was found sticking in the hole she had made, having been drawn in by the rush of water, and all her crew were found dead in her. It was a reckless adventure these men had engaged in, and one in which they could scarcely have hoped to succeed. They had tried it once before inside the harbor, against the "Ironsides," with the same boat, or one very similar, and failed, and some of the crew had been blown overboard. How could they hope to succeed on the outside, where the sea might be rough, when the speed of the "David" would not be over five knots an hour, and when they might be driven out to sea? Reckless as it might be, it was the

most sublime patriotism, and showed the length to which men could be urged in behalf of a cause for which they were willing to give their lives and all they held most dear.

Torpedo practice was at that time cried down by humanitarians, but the use of it in war was perfectly legitimate, and had the Federal Government availed itself of it a little more freely, fewer blockade-runners, and less munitions of war, provisions and clothing would have reached the Confederate armies. What was considered un-Christian warfare then, is now resorted to by all nations, only in more destructive shapes. The torpedo which was so successfully used by the Confederates was a very primitive arrangement. It has been so improved and enlarged in destructive ability that it bids fair to become a great factor in keeping the peace throughout the world; and those nations which have built great iron-clad fleets, with which to dominate weaker nations, may well stop to consider whether it is worth while to extend the system, in view of the advances made in the locomotive torpedo, which will likely put the smaller nations more on a par with the stronger ones.

It was to the naval officers of the Southern Confederacy that we were mostly indebted for what we knew about torpedoes. At the present time we may have improved on the slow-moving "David," which could only make five miles an hour, and brought up the speed of the present torpedo-boats to twenty knots an hour; but we are not at all in advance of the system adopted by the Confederates, which, if it did not keep the Navy out of their harbors, yet contributed in a great measure in prolonging the war, and was the cause of the Federal Government losing a large number of valuable vessels-of-war. The energy of the Confederates in regard to their inventions in the torpedo line was most remarkable, and in quite strong contrast to that of the other side. During the whole war the Federals never invented anything except a torpedo in a steam launch, called the Wood-Lay torpedo, which was nearly as dangerous to the crew as to the enemy.

In March, 1864, the gun-boats in Florida, under the command of Commander George B. Balch, were participating in the expedition up the St. John's River. When the Federal troops landed, they threw up such heavy intrenchments that it was not likely the Confederates could make much impression on them. The Confederates of that region, however, did not propose to allow their native State to be invaded without making a stubborn resistance, and left no means untried to annoy the military positions whenever there was an opportunity of doing so. But the gun-boats were generally at hand with their heavy guns and bursting shells, and the Southerners were usually discomfited.

General Gordon landed at Jacksonville on the 9th of May, and assumed command of the district of Florida; and, in view of the long line of river to be kept open, objected to any reduction of the naval force in the St. John's River, in which Commander Balch concurred with him.

The activity of the Confederates in this quarter, as elsewhere, was very marked; for, though they yielded up all the forts along the coast, they seemed determined to resist any further entrance of Federal troops into the interior of the State, and they tried to confine the Navy as much as possible to the lower part of the St. John's River.

Notwithstanding the vigilance of the naval commanders, the Confederates succeeded in planting torpedoes in the river in the channel. On May 10th, the steamer "Harriet A. Weed" ran into two of these torpedoes, which exploded at the same moment and completely destroyed the vessel, sinking her in less than one minute's time, with five men killed and ten badly wounded.

The naval force employed in the St. John's River, under Commander Balch, was composed of the "Pawnee," "Mahaska" and "Norwich," off Jacksonville, and the "Ottawa" at Palatka. With such a small force it would have been impossible to prevent the enemy from practicing their system of torpedo warfare, which they had found to be so effective wherever the Federal gun-boats were employed.

On about the last of March, the transport "Maple-leaf" offered another success for the Confederates, and was blown up by a torpedo, fifteen miles above Jacksonville—this being the highway to Palatka and above, where Federal troops were being constantly transported. The duty on the river became very hazardous, for a severe torpedo warfare was carried on in small boats during dark nights by the Confederate torpedo corps, which first made its appearance on the Mississippi in 1862.

The above operations in Florida of the Army and Navy lasted from March 6th to April 16th, when orders were received from the War Department for the troops to be sent North, in consequence of which the gun-boats were withdrawn; but while employed with the Army, Commander Balch, Lieutenant - Commander S. Livingston Breese, of the "Ottawa," and the commanders of the "Mahaska" and "Norwich" performed good and gallant service.

It must not be supposed that there were not constantly occurring gallant affairs on the Federal side as well as on that of the Confederates; for though the latter resorted to every means in their power to damage the Federal vessels, yet the officers of the Navy were ever on the alert to take advantage of anything that would enable them to circumvent the enemy. These were small affairs, but they were hazardous, and showed the skill of the Union officers and men.

On the 23d of March, a steamer, supposed to be loading with cotton, was discovered up the Santee River, at a point called McClellansville, and Commodore Rowan, senior officer of the blockading squadron, ordered Lieutenant A. W. Weaver, of the gun-boat "Winona," to fit out an expedition and cut her out. Accordingly, an expedition was started from the "Winona," under the command of Acting-Master E. H. Sheffield (executive officer), consisting of the gig and second and third cutters. Acting-Ensign

LIEUTENANT-COMMANDER (NOW CAPTAIN) A. W. WEAVER.

Wm. McKendry was in charge of one cutter, Acting - Master's Mate L. N. Cornthwait in charge of the other, with Acting-Assistant Surgeon Charles Little and Assistant - Engineer W. I. Barrington; the sailors consisted of 21 of the crew. Mr. Sheffield had orders to proceed up the Santee, capture the steamer if possible, and bring her out; if not, to burn her. Cutting-out expeditions are always hazardous, and this was no exception to the rule.

It was a dark night with drizzling rain, just such a night as an enemy might be supposed to be taking care of himself in snug quarters. The boats had to thread their way in the uncertain darkness through marshes, with their numberless small ditches or creeks. They could not be positive whither they were going, and frequently lost their way. But, at 6 in the morning, the commander of the expedition sighted the steamer lying at anchor off the bank, when the boats pushed ahead for the anticipated prize.

As the boats got near the vessel, a large number of men were seen to be rushing about the decks, and a boat was lowered; when the boats of the "Winona" boarded her, drove the men below, and a sentry was placed at each hatch. The captain of the prize had been captured by the sailors while attempting to make his way on shore.

There being no indication of a battery on shore, Engineer Barrington immediately commenced to start the fires. The chain was hove short, but the vessel was so fastened by stern chains that were shackled around her after-bitts that it was found impossible to slip them, and the party commenced to cut them with cold-chisels, when a masked battery of three rifled guns opened on them and put a stop to their proceedings. The shot, fired at short range, went in one side and out the other—one penetrating the steam-drum and another the boilers, destroying the tubes, etc.

The artillerists had evidently been prepared for the attack, and perforated the vessel in many places, evidently determined to disable her in case she was boarded. The fire of the enemy was successful, and, as the vessel was iron and could not be burned, the party were obliged to leave or be cut to pieces. The result was a retreat after a gallant attack that ought to have been successful, and it detracts nothing from the gallantry of this affair that it was not so.

Operations in Florida continued on a small scale—Commander Balch, in the "Pawnee," and two gun-boats being stationed there to assist the Army. Not much scope existed for brilliant action; but now and then a small expedition to reconnoitre the enemy or capture some river steamer would be fitted out by young officers, who showed great cleverness and gallantry in most of the planned expeditions undertaken, particularly in one by General Gordon, opposite Palatka—backed by the Navy; and, though they were of no great import, were always successful.

It is pleasant to see that the Navy service was appreciated by the Army, as will appear by the following letter:

HEADQUARTERS OF AUXILIARY COLUMN TO ⎱
GORDON'S COMMAND,   ⎰
JACKSONVILLE, FLORIDA, June 3, 1864.

CAPTAIN — It is a duty and pleasure to express through you to the officers and privates of your branch of the service, my high sense of the efficient aid rendered by them to my column in their advance, auxiliary to Gordon's late expedition. We found the whole extent of the waters to be traversed by one portion of the expedition had been thoroughly searched for torpedoes, and that, in the vicinity of our landing, your picket-boats had pervaded and patrolled every part of the surface.

I desire you particularly to express to Captain Lewis my thanks for his admirable arrangements for the rapid landing of the troops, and his efficient supervision thereof.

Accept, also, for yourself our obligations for the prompt and complete arrangements made by you to protect and effect our transportation and debarkation.

I am, Captain, with sentiments of high respect and regard, your obedient servant, etc., etc.,
                              W. H. NOBLE,
        Colonel Commanding Auxiliary Column.
CAPTAIN GEO. B. BALCH,
    Commanding Naval Squadron, St. John's River.

In these small affairs whatever was attempted was well executed, under the efficient preparations made by Captain Balch, in all cases where the land forces wanted assistance; and the officers under his command, guided by his example, left nothing undone to assist the Army, no matter how unreasonable its demands might sometimes be. Captain Balch was not a precise officer, but a very gallant one, and his name frequently appears in the dispatches of the commander-in-chief as always doing well in whatever situation he was placed.

The operations of the Navy were conducted all along the coast of South Carolina and in Florida, after the active and exciting raids in the harbor of Charleston. Several vessels were taken by the enemy: the "Columbine," a captured river-boat, was retaken by the Confederates up the St. John's River, and the U. S. S. "Water Witch" captured by a number of boats in Ossabaw Sound after a gallant defence; but these were small mishaps, and to be expected in a large base of operations. The last mentioned might have been avoided by shifting the berth after dark, and keeping the watch at quarters in a place where a boarding expedition of the enemy was to have been expected. They were quite as fertile in expedients to destroy and capture as were the Federal forces. Most of the officers of the "Water Witch" were wounded during the first of the attack, and Lieutenant-Commander Austin Pendergrast, the commanding officer, was himself cut down with sword in hand, bravely defending his vessel. It was thought by him that but for the casualties among his officers the enemy would have been repulsed; but they were not, and therein lies the difference. The "Water Witch" was a favorite little steamer, which had performed some remarkably good service, and her loss caused great regret.

Amid all their gallantry, there were too many occasions in which the Confederates departed from the usages of war, and practiced unnecessary cruelty on their prisoners. This occurred in the case of the officers and men of the "Water Witch." The surgeon supposed that he would be treated according to the usual manner of captured medical officers. Understanding that there was an arrangement between the Federals and Confederates that the medical officers should be permitted to attend their own wounded, and, after there was no longer any necessity for their services, be allowed to depart, Acting-Assistant Surgeon W. H. Pierson made a request in writing to Flag-officer W. W. Hunter, that the Confederate Secretary of the Navy be applied to for his release, according to the supposed agreement ; but he only, after a second application, received for answer the following letter:

SAVANNAH, July 17, 1864
I have received your note of this day. In reply, I have to inform you that I am instructed by the honorable Secretary of the Navy as follows, viz.: '' When the services of Assistant-Surgeon Pierson, United States Navy, are no longer needed with the wounded officers and men in the hospital, he will be turned over to the proper military authorities to be treated as other prisoners-of-war."
Respectfully,
W. W. HUNTER,
Flag-Officer, etc.

In accordance with the above edict, this gentleman was sent to Macon Prison. His daily ration consisted of one pint of unbolted corn-meal, a tablespoonful of rice, a little miserable and sometimes maggoty bacon (called, in derision, soap-grease) a very little salt, and a moderate supply of poor molasses. It was said at that time that the same ration was served out to Confederate soldiers; if that was so, they were in a bad strait, and could not help it. But there is always a courtesy due a prisoner-of-war taken in honest battle, and it is quite evident that this courtesy was not extended to Union officers.

It is but fair to say that, through the Confederate surgeons, Assistant-Surgeon Pierson afterwards received better treatment, was finally released through the same influence, and found himself under the old flag again, without any conditions.

We dislike, and have always avoided as much as possible referring to cruelties practiced by the Confederates in retaliation for supposed injuries received by Southern prisoners — or for the purpose of preventing Federal batteries firing on besieged places. But the following letter, received in June from the Confederate commander at Charleston, must have shocked the sense of humanity and propriety which every gallant officer must feel at having to carry out such an order. It plainly showed what straits the Confederates were in when they could resort to such a measure to prevent besiegers from firing on a city which was a fair object of attack according to the strictest rules of war, and when, if the besieged non-combatants were in any danger, it was the duty of the military authorities to have them removed, unless they determined to remain and stand the consequences :

HEADQUARTERS FIRST MILITARY DISTRICT, DEP'T OF S. C., GA., AND FLORIDA.
June, 13, 1864.
GENERAL—I have the honor to inclose for transmission to the Commanding General of the United States forces on this coast, a letter from Major Samuel Jones, commanding this Department. The letter informs him that five generals and 45 field-officers of the Federal army, prisoners, have been ordered to be confined in Charleston. These officers have been placed in my charge, and will be provided with commodious quarters in a part of the city occupied by non-combatants, the majority of whom are women and children.
It is proper that you should know, however, that the portion of the city in which they are located is, and has been for some time, exposed day and night to the fire of your guns.
Very respectfully, etc.,
R. S. RIPLEY,
Brigadier-General Commanding.
GENERAL SCHIMMELFENNIG,
Commanding United States Forces,
Morris and Folly Islands, etc.

There is much to be said against exercising this kind of warfare ; and exposing the lives of prisoners in a place to prevent an enemy from firing upon it, can only be considered a violation of the usages of civilized warfare which would damage any cause.

The shelling of a beleagured city is a right of war, and though the duties of humanity towards women and children should be strictly observed, and they should have full time given them to remove from the scene of danger, yet, if they do not do so, military operations could not be interfered with. To expose captives to the close confinement of a place under fire, with the hopes of thereby putting a stop to a bombardment, is making an unfair comparison between the captives and non-combatants, for the latter have the power to withdraw from the fire, while the captives cannot. It had not been the custom to send captives from other parts to Charleston to be kept in confinement; on the contrary, all prisoners had been sent away from there; and it is evident that the Union officers were sent there to be sacrificed in case the Union batteries kept up their fire on the city.

The destruction of Charleston in a military point of view was just as necessary as the destruction of the Confederate forts. It was a store-house of arms and munitions-of-war from which the forts could draw supplies. It contained a large arsenal of military stores and ammunition ; and while these existed, the General commanding the Federal forces was justified in attempting to destroy them. A siege without a bombardment would have been of no use, as the city was open in the rear, and supplies of all kinds could be brought in from the surrounding country. This is the only reason which can be given why the military commander of the Union forces should have forborne to use his guns upon the city. It was of no use in bringing about a surrender, for it might have been known from the character of the defences of Charleston that they would not have surrendered the city until the outside works were taken, and it would have been more profitable to have expended the shot and shell on the surrounding forts.

If General Gillmore at a distance of over 5,000 yards " had reduced Sumter to a pulp," it is quite possible that the Federal Army and Navy, by keeping up the same kind of fire on the forts, would eventually have reduced them, as they did Wagner and Sumter, and enabled the Navy to remove the obstructions, so that the Monitors could go on up to Charleston. The Confederates had shown an immense amount of energy and courage in holding their own.

This shelling the city gave the Confederates the opportunity of saying that the fire was kept up from the disappointment the Federal forces had met with in not bringing about a surrender. An opportunity should never have been given the enemy to cast a shadow of reflection upon the acts of Federal officers, who could afford to be forbearing in the face of the fact that Charleston, as a base of supplies through the means of blockade-runners, could never be of any more use to the Confederacy, and that the larger the force that was kept there to hold the place the more advantageous it was for the Federal arms.

That the situation of the Confederates was becoming desperate about that time we now know full well, and probably some civilian member of the Confederate Cabinet suggested this confinement of Federal prisoners in Charleston; for it cannot be conceived that any of the high-toned officers, who on many occasions showed true chivalric feeling in the capture of Federals, should have instituted a scheme that would surely have reflected on them as honorable soldiers.

On the 20th of June the Rear-Admiral commanding received a notification from the Navy Department in Washington " that the Confederates in Charleston were preparing for a simultaneous move on the blockade, inside and out, in order to cover the exit of a large quantity of cotton." The next day, the "Sonoma," Commander George H. Cooper, and "Nipsic," Lieutenant-Commander William Gibson, were sent as outside cruisers to cover the blockade south of Port Royal, where it was weakest, and where the chief effort was to be made.

A plan was laid between General Foster and Admiral Dahlgren to make a diversion by cutting the railroad between Charleston and Savannah. Generals Foster, Schimmelfennig and Hatch were to land, each with a force considered adequate for the occasion, while General Birney was to go into the North Edisto, and as high as possible, to destroy the railroad. The Navy was to enter the Stono to co-operate with General Schimmelfennig. One or two gun-boats were to ascend the North Edisto, and co-operate with General Birney to secure his landing.

On the 2d day of July the Monitors " Lehigh " and " Montauk " crossed the Stono bar, while the remaining naval force consisted of the " Pawnee," " McDonough " and " Racer."

Though the plans were well made, nothing resulted from this expedition. The different co-operating parties reached some of the points aimed at and attacked the Confederate troops that were out to receive them, and the gun-boats and Monitors opened on such forts as they were directed

COMMANDER (NOW REAR-ADMIRAL) GEORGE H. COOPER.

to fire upon; but there was no success in the attack. The Federal troops failed to capture any of the enemy's batteries; and after one or two days spent in desultory fighting, it was decided that the enemy were in too strong force, that further efforts would not be profitable, and therefore the troops should be withdrawn from John's Island.

These operations lasted about six days, during which there was a good deal of hard work and the usual display of gallantry on the part of the Navy, under the guns of which the Army safely re-embarked.

Rear-Admiral Dahlgren speaks handsomely of his staff, and particularly mentions the services of Commander Balch and Lieutenant-Commanders Semmes, Fillebrown, A. W. Johnson, R. L. Phythian, and Acting-Masters Phinney and Furber.

This was about the last operation of any importance that occurred in the South Atlantic squadron up to October 22, when the account of its operations for the year ended. Some minor expeditions were undertaken—in one of which the brig "Perry" lost fifteen men in killed, wounded and prisoners—and in another a schooner loaded with cotton was set on fire and burned by a party of brave fellows; but we miss the exciting scenes which occurred in the attacks on the batteries of Charleston, where the officers and men fought persistently for so many days and nights, demonstrating their capacity to command, and exhibiting a gallantry never exceeded, and a disappointment that cannot be described, at their unsuccessful efforts to win the works of Charleston. The innumerable obstacles thrown in their way by a powerful and active foe, full of resources and full of means, to check the advance into his harbor, were too great for a force entirely too small in the first place for such an undertaking.

The Southern coast was, on the whole, thoroughly blockaded, and Charleston no longer of any use to the Confederates; and there was really no further necessity for their holding it, except for the sake of a sentiment connected with the fact that it was the first place to raise the flag of secession, and desired to be the last that would haul it down.

Towards the close of the year 1864, owing to the stringent blockade of the whole Southern coast by the Navy, except at the entrance to Wilmington, the Confederate States began to be placed in great distress for the want of food to supply their armies, and at one time there was a prospect of their being starved into submission, even without victories by the Federal armies.

In the early part of May there were on hand but two days' rations for Lee's army at Richmond, and on the 23d of June only thirteen days' rations, showing how the Navy had cut off the foreign supply; and to meet the demand, and keep the Confederate army from disbanding, the Commissary-General had to offer market rates for wheat then growing in the fields.

A great deal of this distress and exhaustion of supplies was, however, owing to the exhaustion of Virginia. The prevalence of droughts, and the fact that the crops all over the State had been destroyed by the Federal armies, rendered it very difficult to subsist so large a number of troops as were located in and around Richmond. The effect of the advance of the Federal forces was to oblige the Confederates to call out their reserves, and these had to be fed. Many farmers were detailed for military duty and ordered into the field, at the very time it was most necessary for them to be at home attending to the seeding of wheat.

Yet the blockade was far more ruinous to the Confederate cause than all other operations put together. As long as a blockade-runner could get into any of the Southern ports, bringing bacon and flour, the soldiers could be sustained; and whenever two or three of these supply-vessels were captured by the Federal fleet, it carried dismay to the hearts of those who ruled the destinies of the South. In Virginia the supply of breadstuff was practically exhausted. The negro field-hands were absconding for fear of being employed in the army, and were taking refuge in the Union lines, while Sherman's march through the South had cut off all supplies of grain or cattle from that region. It may be imagined, then, how important it was for the Confederate armies that the blockade-runners should now and then obtain safe entrance into the Southern harbors with their military supplies.

As late as November, 1864, President Davis applied to the Commissary-General to ascertain how many rations there were on hand, to feed not only the army at Richmond, but the other forces in the field, and was informed that there was a very alarming state of affairs in that Department; that Georgia, Alabama and Mississippi were the only States where there was an accumulation, and that the Confederate Army was at that time being subsisted from these States.

The Commissary of Georgia sent dispatches that he could not send another pound of provisions to Richmond. Alabama, under the most urgent call, could only send forward 135,000 pounds of food. Mississippi was doing all she could in supplying rations to General Beauregard's army. South Carolina could only subsist the troops at Charleston and the prisoners in the interior of the State. The enemy had visited every section of North Carolina, and that State was only able to supply the forts at Wilmington with rations of the most ordinary kind, and not a pound of meat could be shipped to either Wilmington or Richmond.

Fortunately for the Confederates, the blockade-runner "Banshee" succeeded in eluding the blockaders and getting into Wilmington; and owing to this timely supply of provisions the reserves at the forts were prevented from being starved out. As it was, the commissaries were only able to supply them with thirty days' rations. At that moment there were only 3,400,000 rations of bacon and pork in the whole Confederacy to subsist 300,000 men for 25 days.

In the month of December matters were still worse; there was not meat enough in the Southern Confederacy for the armies it had in the field. That the meat must be obtained from abroad was plainly seen, and it was also recognized that, in order to obtain it, it would be necessary to break the blockade by some means then untried or unknown. Nor was the transportation adequate to the demands of the occasion. The supply of fresh meat to General Lee's army was precarious, and, if the army fell back from Richmond and Petersburg, there was every probability that it would cease to exist altogether.

This condition of affairs was brought about by the vigilance of the Federal Navy, which worked hard, day and night, to prevent supplies from getting in from the sea; and the only part of the coast where the blockade was sometimes open to the runners was at the port of Wilmington, where the enemy had been allowed, under an unwise management, to build heavy works at the entrance to Cape Fear River, under which the blockade-runners could take shelter at night and bid defiance to their pursuers. This was the only rendezvous the Confederates had from the entrance of Hatteras Inlet to the capes of Florida; and so uncertain was this, that there was no knowing how soon the Federal Government would take proper measures to stop it, even if the advance of Sherman's army through the South did not cause the evacuation of Wilmington.

The Navy, it is true, did not succeed in capturing Charleston, but it closed that port against blockade-runners so completely that it was forbidden ground to them. This was well worth the time, money and fighting expended on this Confederate stronghold, for at the close of the naval campaign of 1864 the Confederates could only subsist their troops there on the meanest rations.

SOUTH ATLANTIC SQUADRON, JANUARY, 1864.

REAR-ADMIRAL JOHN A. DAHLGREN.

LIEUTENANT-COMMANDER JOSEPH M. BRADFORD, FLEET-CAPTAIN.

STEAM-FRIGATE "WABASH"—FLAG-SHIP.

Captain, John De Camp; Lieutenant, Lloyd Phenix; Fleet Surgeon, Wm. Johnson; Fleet Paymaster, J. O. Bradford; Assistant Surgeon, F. M. Weld; Acting-Assistant Surgeon, N. L. Campbell; Paymaster, R. J. Richardson; Chaplain, C. A. Davis; Marines: Captain, E. McD. Reynolds; Second-Lieutenant, L. E. Fagan; Ensign, H. T. French; Acting-Ensigns, A. Tuttle and T. H. Daggett; Acting-Master's Mates, J. H. Gordon, J. C. Graves, Joseph Gregory and B. O. Carpenter; Engineers: Fleet Engineer, Robert Danby; Second-Assistants, P. R. Voorhees, W. C. Williamson and Elisha Harsen; Third-Assistants, J. S. Green, H. H. Kimball, A. Michener and J. B. Place; Boatswain, Francis McLoud; Gunner, Christopher Long; Carpenter, J. G. Thomas; Sailmaker, H. W. Frankland.

IRON-CLAD STEAMER "NEW IRONSIDES."

Captain, Stephen C. Rowan; Lieutenant-Commander, Geo. E. Belknap; Lieutenant, H. B. Robeson; Surgeon, Marius Duvall; Assistant Surgeon, Edw. Kershner; Paymaster, Alex. W. Russell; Marines: First-Lieutenant, Henry A. Bartlett; Second-Lieutenant, James B. Young; Acting-Masters, G. W. Domett, Lewis West and J. M. Skillings; Ensigns, H. L. Johnson, J. J. Read and Walter Abbot; Acting-Ensigns, W. C. Wise, G. T. Davis, S. S. Hand and W. S. McNeilly; Acting-Master's Mates, J. W. Caswell, J. D. Wingate and Thomas Hollins; Engineers: Chief, Alex. Grier; First-Assistant, N. B. Littig; Second-Assistant, J. J. Noble; Third-Assistants, Everett Battelle, H. C. Beckwith, F. T. H. Ramsden and Wm. S. Wells; Boatswain, Thomas Bennett; Gunner, Charles Stewart; Carpenter, E. H. Bishop; Sailmaker, John A. Birdsall.

STEAMER "CANANDAIGUA."

Captain, Joseph F. Green; Lieutenant, H. DeH. Manley; Surgeon; James Suddards; Paymaster, C. H. Eldredge; Acting-Masters, Samuel Hall and J. L. Gifford; Acting-Ensigns, R. P. Leary and Edward Daley; Acting-Master's Mates, W. J. Vincent, James Wilbur, Adna M. Bates and W. C. Howard;

Engineers: Chief, Wm. S. Stamm; Third-Assistants, Albert Jackson, Philip Miller, E. T. Phillippi, O. B. Mills, J. J. Barry and J. Pemberton, Jr.; Boatswain, Thomas Smith; Gunner, John Gaskins; Carpenter, S. N. Whitehouse; Sailmaker, David Bruce,

STEAMER "HOUSATONIC."

Captain, Charles W. Pickering; Lieutenant, F. J. Higginson; Assistant Surgeon, W. T. Plant; Assistant Paymaster, J. S. Woolson; Acting-Masters, J. W. Congden and J. K. Crosby; Ensign, Edw. C. Hazeltine; Acting-Ensign, G. M. McClure; Acting-Master's Mates, E. A. Butler, B. F. Jacobs, H. A. Hudson and Louis Cornthwaite; Engineers: Chief, John S. Albert; Second-Assistant, C. F. Mayer, Jr.; Third-Assistants, J. W. Hollihan, C. A. Evans, J. A. B. Smith, W. M. Barr and Charles Hopkins; Acting-Boatswain, Wm. Ray; Acting-Gunner, A. C. Holmes.

STORE-SHIP "VERMONT."

Commander, William Reynolds; Lieutenant-Commander, Wm. C. West; Surgeon, Wm. Lowber; Assistant Surgeon, W. J. Bowdle; Paymaster, Frank C. Cosby; Acting-Assistant Paymaster, Wilbur Ives; Chaplain, John Blake; Marines: Second-Lieutenant, H. J. Bishop; Acting-Masters, W. U. Grozier, H. W. Hand, R. B. Hines, J. C. Cox and W. W. Carter; Acting-Ensigns, Andie Hartshorne, W. A. Morgan and C. J. Lawrence; Acting-Master's Mates, W. Van Wyck, S. N. Grey, J. G. Rose and F. W. Beck; Engineers: Acting-First-Assistant, John L. Peake; Acting-Second-Assistant, G. S. Geer; Acting-Boatswain, R. C. Barnard; Gunner, Geo. W. Allen; Acting-Gunner, Thos. Holland; Carpenter, C. W. Babbitt; Sailmaker, John Joins.

IRON-CLAD STEAMER "PATAPSCO."

Commander, Thomas H. Stevens; Lieutenant, Alex. S. Mackenzie; Assistant Surgeon, Samuel H. Peltz; Acting-Assistant Paymaster, W. S. Creevey; Acting-Master, Geo. P. Lee; Acting-Ensigns, J. T. Ross, A. Kloeppel and Wm. Chase; Engineers: Second-Assistant, J. B. Carpenter; Third-Assistants,

G. F. Sweet, J. J. Ryan, DeWitt G. Davis and Wm. H. Barclay.

STEAMER "PAWNEE."

Commander, Geo. B. Balch; Lieutenant, John W. Philip ; Paymaster, Geo. Lawrence ; Acting-Assistant Surgeon, Henry Shaw; Acting-Masters, J. C. Champion and James P. Lindsey ; Ensign, Henry Glass; Acting-Ensigns, Thomas Moore and C. J. Rogers; Acting-Master's Mates, C. H. Poor, A. A. Franzen and J. G. Bache; Engineers : Second-Assistant, Alfred Adamson; Third-Assistants, Wm. J. Clark, Jr., J. G. Brosnahan, Arthur Price and J. L. Hannum; Boatswain, James Brown; Gunner, James Hayes.

STEAMER "SONOMA."

Commander, Geo. H. Cooper; Lieutenant, Geo. W. Hayward; Assistant Surgeon, S. F. Shaw; Acting-Assistant Paymaster, F. F. Hastings; Acting-Master, Wm. M. Post; Acting-Ensigns, Wm. N. Price, S. H. Pollock and H. H. Johnson; Acting-Master's Mates, S. S. Willett, G. W. Eckert, C. C. Neil and R. W. Robins; Engineers: Acting-First-Assistant, A. B. Dunlap; Acting-Second-Assistant, A. B. Cullins; Acting-Third-Assistants, W. A. Smith, Rufus Burton and J. Hawkey; Gunner, J. M. Hogg.

IRON-CLAD STEAMER "LEHIGH."

Commander, Andrew Bryson; Lieutenant, Moreau Forrest; Assistant Surgeon, Wm. Longshaw, Jr.; Acting-Assistant Paymaster, F. C. Imlay; Acting-Master, Richard Burke; Acting - Ensigns, Edw. Tilghman, C. M. Thwing, J. E. Stickney and F. W. Towne; Acting-Master's Mate, G. W. Leland; Engineers : First Assistant, W. D. Pendleton; Second-Assistant, Alfred Hedrick; Third-Assistant, C. M. Van Tine, J. H. Thomas and S. C. McLanahan.

STEAMER "PAUL JONES."

Commander, James M. Duncan; Lieutenant, James O'Kane; Assistant Surgeon, J. W. Coles; Acting-Assistant Paymaster, J. A Berry; Acting-Ensigns, J. Potts, Chas. Clauson, Henry Hamre and Chas. Weidenbien ; Acting - Master's Mates, J. H. Manning, J. L. Rowe and C. E. Everdean; Engineers: First-Assistant, James Sheriden; Third-Assistants, James A. Chasmer, E. D. Weems, Geo. Paul and L. T. Safford; Acting-Gunner, John Brown.

STEAMER "MAHASKA.'

Commander, J. B. Creighton ; Lieutenant, E. C. V. Blake; Assistant Surgeon, H. S. Pitkin; Acting-Assistant Paymaster, Chas. Fairchild; Acting-Master, Benj. Dyer; Acting-Ensigns, Frederick Elliott, N. W. Black, Chas. G. Boyer and G. E. French; Acting-Master's Mate, Wm. White; Engineers: Acting-First-Assistant, G. E. Ashby ; Third - Assistants, Thomas La Blanc, E. L. Hewett and N. H. Lamdin.

STEAMER "CIMMARON."

Commander, Aaron K. Hughes ; Lieutenant, Adolphus Dexter; Assistant Surgeon, E. S. Olcott; Acting-Assistant Paymaster, G. W. Griffin; Acting-Master, S. A. Waterbury ; Acting-Ensigns, W. H. Anderson, G. F. Howes, Chas. Renfield, J. W. North and T. R. Dayton; Acting-Master's Mates, Thomas Newton, P. J. Markoe, J. D. Reed and E. P. Crocker; Engineers: Second-Assistant, Reynolds Driver; Third-Assistants, W. H. Kelley, W. L. Bailie and G. L. Palmer; Gunner, M. A. Lane.

IRON-CLAD STEAMER " PASSAIC."

Lieutenant-Commander, Edward Simpson; Lieutenant, Wm. Whitehead; Assistant Surgeon, H. C. Eckstein; Acting-Assistant Paymaster, L. C. Tripp; Acting-Master, James Ogilvie; Acting-Ensigns, L. G. Emerson, D. B. Hawes, A. Delano, Jr. and W. H. Roberts; Acting-Master's Mate, W. H. Lewis; Engineers: First-Assistant, Henry Mason; Second-Assistant, F. H. Fletcher; Third-Assistants, William A. Dripps, Joseph Hooper and C. Kenyon.

STEAMER "NIPSIC."

Lieutenant-Commander, Wm. Gibson ; Acting-Assistant Surgeon, W. J. Gilfillen; Acting-Assistant Paymaster, H. T. Mansfield; Acting-Master, W. L. Churchill; Acting-Ensigns, H. A. Greene, J. A. Winchester and A. B. Prince ; Acting-Master's Mates, G. S. Johnson, W. K. Orcutt and W. H. Kitching, Jr.; Engineers: First-Assistant, S. L. P. Ayres; Second-Assistants, A. W. Morley and C. E. Emery ; Third-Assistants, R. B. Plotts and B. R. Stevens.

STEAMER "CHIPPEWA."

Lieutenant-Commander, T. C. Harris; Assistant Surgeon, Louis Zenzen ; Acting-Assistant Paymaster, G. A. Robertson; Acting-Master, W. H. DeWolf; Acting-Ensigns, J. M. Crocker and H. T. Blake; Acting-Master's Mates, J. C. Butler and J. A. H. Willmuth; Engineers : Second - Assistant, R. H. Thurston; Acting-Second-Assistant, Thos. Heenan; Third - Assistants, A. Sackett, C. R. Mosher and J. M. Murray.

IRON-CLAD STEAMER "NANTUCKET."

Lieutenant-Commander, Stephen B. Luce ; Lieutenant, H. L. Howison ; Assistant Surgeon, A. B. Judson; Acting-Assistant Paymaster, L. S. Brigham; Acting-Master, W. H. Maies; Acting-Ensigns, J. F. Otis, C. C. Starr and John Meyers ; Engineers: Second-Assistants, George H. White and I. R. McNary; Third-Assistants, N. W. Buckhout and J. K. Smedley; Acting-Third-Assistant, A. L. Grow.

IRON-CLAD STEAMER "MONTAUK."

Lieutenant-Commander, John L. Davis; Lieutenant, Gilbert C. Wiltse; Acting-Assistant Surgeon, W. H. Harlin; Acting-Assistant Paymaster, J. H. Sellman; Acting-Master, Edmund Jones; Acting-Ensigns, T. F. DeLuce, I. J. McKinley and G. H. Avery; Acting - Master's Mate, Robert Craig ; Engineers: Acting-Second-Assistants, C. A. Stuart and Simon Rockefeller; Third-Assistants, Jesse F. Walton, S. C. Lane and Montgomery West.

STEAMER "UNADILLA."

Lieutenant-Commander, A. W. Johnson ; Assistant Surgeon, C. S. Hubbard; Acting-Assistant Paymaster, G. S. Benedict; Acting-Master, R. M. Cornell, Acting-Ensigns, Wm. Field and G. E. Thomas; Acting-Master's Mates, James Such and A. F. Taffe; Engineers: Second-Assistant, R. S. Talbot ; Third-Assistants, M. T. Sunstrom, N. P. Towne and M. N. Knowlton.

STEAMER "OTTAWA."

Lieutenant - Commander, S. Livingston Breese ; Assistant Surgeon, G. W. Woods; Acting-Assistant Paymaster, G. W. Huntington; Acting-Ensigns, W. H. McCormick, J. L. Gamble, Benj. Mitchell, C. H. Choate and E. M. Dimon; Acting-Master's Mates, A. W. Tripp and F. W. Turner ; Engineers: Second-Assistants, J. P. Sprague, E. W. Koehl and F. C. Prindle; Third-Assistant, R. B. Hine.

IRON-CLAD STEAMER "NAHANT."

Lieutenant-Commander, J. J. Cornwell; Lieutenant, H. C. Tallman; Assistant Surgeon, D. F. Ricketts ; Acting - Assistant Paymaster, D. A. Smith, Jr.; Acting-Master, C. C. Ricker; Acting - Ensigns, W. E. Thomas and S. A. Gove; Engineers : Second-Assistant, W. H. G. West ; Third-Assistant, W. S. Neal and Robert Crawford; Acting-Third-Assistant, T. B. Green.

STEAMER "HURON."

Lieutenant-Commander, F. H. Baker ; Assistant Surgeon, C. H. White; Acting-Assistant Paymaster, Chas. Stewart ; Acting-Masters, Wm. A. Mills and W. H. Baldwin; Acting Master's Mates, Samuel Delano, Peter O'Conner and Wm. Henderson; Engineers: Acting-First-Assistant, C. P. Roebuck; Third-Assistants, Sylvanus McIntyre, J. P. Kelly, John Lowe, Thomas Crummey and F. C. Russell.

STEAMER "WATER WITCH."

Lieutenant - Commander, Austin Pendergrast; Acting-Assistant Surgeon, W. H. Pierson; Acting-Assistant Paymaster, L. G. Billings; Acting-Masters, C. W. Buck and W. B. Stoddard; Acting-Ensigns, J. M. Forsyth, A. T. Stover and Chas. Hill; Acting-Master's Mates, E. D. W. Parsons, C. P. Weston and H. V. Butler; Engineers: Acting-First-Assistant, Samuel Genther; Acting-Third-Assistants, J. P. Cooper, J. Hollingsworth and I. A. Conover.

STEAMER "MARBLEHEAD."

Lieutenant-Commander, R. W. Meade, Jr.; Assistant Surgeon, B. H. Kidder; Acting-Assistant Paymaster, James Winter; Acting-Ensigns, G. A. Harriman and G. F. Winslow; Acting-Master's Mates, B. O. Low, T. L. Fisher and F. Millett; Engineers: Acting-Second-Assistant, Frank Henderson; Third-Assistants, H. W. Bulkley, M. A. Sutherland and F. W. Bissett.

STEAMER "WISSAHICKON."

Lieutenant-Commander, George Bacon; Acting-Assistant Surgeon, G. S. Fife; Acting-Assistant Paymaster, Chas. Dutcher; Acting-Master, J. E. Jones; Acting-Ensigns, W. C. Odiorne, H. B. Francis and C. F. Dearing; Acting-Master's Mate, D. J. King; Engineers: Acting-First-Assistant, W. S. Hazzard; Acting-Third-Assistants, H. J. Tarr, Chas. E. Jevens and G. S. Odell.

STEAMER "SENECA."

Lieutenant-Commander, Alfred Hopkins; Acting-Assistant Surgeon, A. B. C. Sawyer; Acting-Assistant Paymaster, Elijah Ward; Acting - Masters, Henry Vaughan and G. W. Ewer; Acting-Ensigns, G. H. Wood and J. H. Ankers; Acting-Master's Mates, J. G. Paine and E. W. Fiske; Engineers: Second-Assistants, Jos. Watters, H. H. Burritt and Thomas Lynch; Third-Assistant, R. T. Bennett.

STEAMER "MEMPHIS."

Lieutenant-Commander, Thos. H. Eastman; Acting-Assistant Surgeon, Louis Michel; Acting-Assistant Paymaster, W. E. Foster; Acting-Ensigns, E. A. Magone, J. B. Childs, G. A. Churchill and S. W. Cowing; Acting - Master's Mates, J. G. Crocker, Silas Owen, J. W. Moore and J. W. DeCamp; Engineers: Acting-Second-Assistants, Chas. McCarty, and Peter Anderson; Acting - Third - Assistants, J. H. Vaile and Wm. Adams.

IRON-CLAD STEAMER "CATSKILL."

Lieutenant-Commander, F. M. Bunce; Assistant Surgeon, Robert Willard; Acting-Assistant Paymaster, G. F. Barker; Acting-Master, G. W. Parker; Acting-Ensigns, C. P. Walters and G. W. Prindle; Acting-Master's Mate, Peter Trescott; Engineers: Second-Assistant, G. D. Emmons; Third-Assistants, J. T. Booth, Frank Marsh and Jas. Plunkett.

STEAMER "LODONA."

Acting - Lieutenant, Edgar Broadhead; Acting-Assistant Surgeon, T. W. Meckley; Acting-Assistant Paymaster, A. M. Stewart; Acting - Master, H. S. Blanchard; Acting-Ensigns, N. W. Rathburn, H. G. McKennee, R. C. McKenzie and Le G. B. Brigham; Acting-First-Assistant Engineer, F. A. Bremen; Acting-Second-Assistants, Richard Durfee and M. C. Heath; Acting-Third-Assistants, J. Mollineaux, C. A. McDowell and Fred. Wagner.

STEAMER "FLAMBEAU."

Acting-Volunteer-Lieutenant, Edward Cavendy; Acting-Assistant Surgeon, S. B. Hoppin; Acting-Assistant Paymaster, F. V. D. Horton; Acting-Masters, A. S. Megathlin and W. L. Kempton; Acting-Ensigns, G. Cottrell, T. H. D'Estimeauville and J. P. Gallagher; Engineers: Acting-First Assistant, John Harris; Acting-Second Assistant, Edw. Allin; Acting-Third-Assistants, W. H. Anderson and Leonard Atwood.

STEAMER "COMMODORE M'DONOUGH."

Acting-Master, J. W. Tuck; Acting-Assistant Surgeon, W. H. Campbell; Acting-Assistant Paymaster, R. Freeman; Acting-Master, Wm. Knapp; Acting-Ensigns, J. K. Winn and D. B. Hallett; Acting-Master's Mates, J. E. Goodwin and D. Lester; Engineers: Acting - Second - Assistants, S. Warren and S. S. Hetrick; Acting-Third-Assistants, Nelson Rose and W. W. Hartley.

STEAMER "MOHAWK."

Acting-Master, Alex. Tillinghast; Acting-Assistant Paymaster, G. H. Andrews; Acting-Ensign, E. Rich, Jr.; Acting-Master's Mate, Wm. Trott; Engineers: Acting-Second-Assistant, R. K. Morrison; Acting-Third-Assistant, G. E. Whitney.

STEAMER "HOME."

Acting-Master, Nicholas Kirby; Acting-Assistant Surgeon, W. N. Pindell; Acting-Assistant Paymaster, T. W. Burger; Acting-Ensigns, Wm. Shackford, A. E. Barnett and J. M. Smalley; Acting-Master's Mates, F. K. S. Nye, J. K. Gould and F. H. Munroe; Engineers: Acting - Second - Assistants, C. Dandreau and C. Armberg; Acting-Third-Assistants, Paul Dandreau, C. R. Rodker and R. De Cordy.

STEAMER "POTOMSKA."

Acting-Volunteer- Lieutenant, Geo. E. Welch; Acting-Assistant Surgeon, S. C. Smith; Acting-Assistant Paymaster, F. H. Swan; Acting - Masters, R. P. Walter and B. W. Leary; Acting-Ensign, J. D. Wells; Acting-Master's Mate, Woodward Carter; Engineers: Acting-Second-Assistant, G. H. Guyer; Acting-Third-Assistants, Edwin Vaughan and W. L. McKay.

STEAMER "STETTIN."

Acting-Volunteer-Lieutenant, C. J. Van Alstine; Acting-Assistant Surgeon, C. J. Pigott; Acting-Assistant Paymaster, C. M. Burns, Jr.; Acting-Master, J. M. Butler; Acting-Ensigns, G. R. Bailey, C. B. Pray and J. C. Staples; Acting-Master's Mates, Benj. Russell and C. H. Fernald; Engineers: Acting-Second-Assistant, J. B. Edwards; Acting-Third-Assistant, John Hawkins, John Ryan and Anthony Gale.

STEAMER "IRIS."

Acting-Master, Wm. Barrymore; Acting-Master's Mates, W. W. Brandt, A. H. L. Bowie and Thomas Irving; Engineers: Acting-Second-Assistant, Thos. Fewkes; Acting-Third-Assistants, Morris McCarty and Dennis Lyng.

STEAMER "PHILADELPHIA."

Acting-Master, Geo. R. Durand; Assistant Surgeon, J. H. Culver; Assistant Paymaster, H. L. Wait; Acting-Ensigns, L. A. Waterman, J. E. Wallis and J. Worth; Acting-Master's Mates, Geo. H. Bartlett, C. F. Moore and A. Truesdell; Engineers: Acting-Second-Assistant, C. A. Norris; Acting-Third-Assistants, W. H. Capen and Robert Mulready.

STEAMER "O. M. PETTIT."

Acting-Master, T. E. Baldwin; Acting-Master's Mates, E. L. Smith, Charles Hanson and E. P. Crocker; Engineers: Acting - Second - Assistant, Reuben McClanahan; Acting - Third - Assistants, Aug. Wandell and Wm. P. Wynn.

STEAMER "NORWICH."

Acting-Masters, F. B. Merriam and R. B. Arrants; Acting-Assistant Surgeon, G. E. McPherson; Acting-Assistant Paymaster, G. C. Boardman; Acting-Ensigns, J. H. Linscott and S. S. Hand; Acting-Master's Mates, A. J. L. Barker, Peter Moakler, T. M. Durham and Henry Sinclair; Engineers: Acting-Second-Assistant, P. B. Robinson; Acting-Third-Assistants, A. A. Odell, Benjamin Cobb, Jr., and W. W. Thain.

STEAMER "MARY SANFORD."

Acting-Master, Wm. Rogers; Acting-Assistant Paymaster, G. C. Bissell; Acting-Ensigns, M. J. Daly, C. A. Pike, G. W. Pease and W. Caldwell, Jr.; Acting-Master's Mates, A. F. Rich and C. Seymour; Engineers; Acting-First-Assistant, Wm. Johnson; Acting-Third-Assistants, Jas. Hare, J. L. Rooke and C. H. Hunt.

STEAMER "E B. HALE."

Acting-Master, Chas. F. Mitchell; Acting-Assistant Surgeon, S. N. Fisk; Acting-Assistant Paymaster, O. B. Gilman; Acting-Ensigns, Henry Stahl, G. H. Smith, J. N. Van Boskirk and Geo. Edwards; Engineers: Acting-Second-Assistant, James Fagan; Acting-Third-Assistants, D. A. Lawrence and Geo. Taylor.

STEAMER "SOUTH CAROLINA."

Acting-Masters, James H. Magune, E. M. Baldwin and F. F. Baury; Acting-Assistant Surgeon, Geo. A. Bright; Acting-Paymaster, A. S. Kenny; Ensign, J. C. Pegram; Acting-Ensigns, G. W. Bourne, C. F. Taylor and John Gunn; Acting-Master's Mates, E. Holbrook, A. S. Hitch and S. L. Withington; Engineers: Acting-First-Assistant, J. T. Hathaway; Acting-Second-Assistants, J. H. Rowe, Henry Gormley and F. W. H. Whittaker; Acting-Third-Assistant, Thomas Slater.

STEAMER "OLEANDER."

Acting-Master, John S. Dennis; Acting-Ensigns, Jos. Frost and A. P. Bashford; Acting-Master's Mate, Wm. C. King; Acting-Engineers: Acting-Second-Assistant, Samuel Swartwout; Acting-Third-Assistants, R. B. Dick and H. S. Brown.

BARK "ETHAN ALLEN."

Acting-Master, J. A. Pennell; Acting-Assistant Surgeon, H. W. Mitchell; Acting-Assistant Paymaster, W. R. Woodward; Acting-Ensigns, T. M. Peakes, J. H. Bunting, Jos. McCart and Wm. Mero; Acting-Master's Mates, E. T. Dexter, G. H. Redford and C. F. Adams.

BARK "BRAZILIERA."

Acting-Master, Wm. T. Gillespie; Acting-Assistant Surgeon, Geo. B. Todd; Acting-Assistant Paymaster, C. H. Longstreet; Acting-Ensigns, J. H. Bennett and N. C. Borden; Acting-Master's Mates, J. B. F. Smith, W. N. Smith, Isaac Severns and F. H. W. Harrington.

BARK "A. HOUGHTON."

Acting-Master, Newell Graham; Acting-Ensigns, E. B. Cox; Acting-Master's Mate, C. H. Nicholls.

BARK "KINGFISHER."

Acting-Masters, J. C. Dutch and S. W. Rhoades; Acting-Assistant Surgeon, W. H. Westcott; Acting-Assistant Paymaster, N. W. Blakeman; Acting-Ensigns, T. E. Chapin and Wm. Nelson; Acting-Master's Mates, H. G. Seaman and Frank Jordan.

BARK "FERNANDINA."

Acting-Masters, E. Moses and C. C. Childs; Acting-Assistant Surgeon, S. P. Boyer; Acting-Assistant Paymaster, T. N. Murray; Acting-Ensigns, Christopher Flood and W. H. Thomas; Acting-Master's Mates, Geo. Newlin and John Wright.

BARK "MIDNIGHT."

Acting-Masters, Wm. H. Garfield and Edwin Coffin; Acting-Assistant Surgeon, J. M. Garner; Acting-Assistant Paymaster, Franklin Miller; Acting-Ensigns, Z. L. Tanner and N. Pratt; Acting-Master's Mates, A. K. Noyes and S. H. Maunders.

SCHOONER "HOPE."

Acting-Master, John E. Rockwell; Acting-Master's Mates, W. E. Gould, Elisha Hubbard and J. S. Leon.

SCHOONER "DAN SMITH."

Acting-Master, B. C. Dean; Acting-Ensign, Paul Armandt; Acting-Master's Mates, J. C. Vandeventer and W. W. Hunt.

ORDNANCE SLOOP "JOHN ADAMS."

Acting-Masters, A. S. Gardner and J. P. Carr; Acting-Assistant Surgeon, Israel Bushong; Acting-Assistant Paymaster, Tracy Coit; Acting-Ensign, John Blitz; Acting-Master's Mates, Charles Henley, Benjamin Lawton, Franklin James and C. E. Cool.

BRIG "PERRY."

Acting-Master, S. B. Gregory; Acting-Assistant Paymaster, T. A. Emerson; Acting-Ensigns, W. C. Hanford, J. H. Clark and R. R. Donnell; Acting-Master's Mates, E. H. Sheer, T. H. McDonald and C. P. Bridges.

STORE-SHIP "SUPPLY."

Acting-Masters, D. G. McRitchie, Z. Kempton and Norman H. Penfield; Acting-Assistant Surgeon, Reuben Smith; Acting-Assistant Paymaster, B. F. Munroe; Acting-Ensigns, F. M. Montell, J. W. Butler and F. H. Phipps; Acting-Master's Mates, J. W. Almy, W. S. Howland and J. S. Carpenter.

SCHOONER "F. A. WARD."

Acting-Master, Wm. L. Babcock; Acting-Assistant Surgeon, J. A. Fife; Acting-Master's Mates, Alonzo Elwell, N. M. Baker, Jr., and G. A. Olmstead.

SCHOONER "RACER."

Acting-Master, Alvin Phinney; Acting-Assistant Paymaster, Eugene Littell; Acting-Master's Mates, H. C. Whitmore, D. B. Corey and J. F. Kavanaugh.

SCHOONER "C. P. WILLIAMS."

Acting-Master, S. N. Freeman; Acting-Ensigns, Jacob Cochran; Acting-Master's Mate, Lloyd E. Daggett.

SCHOONER "GEORGE MANGHAM."

Acting-Master, John Collins; Acting-Assistant Surgeon, C. S. Eastwood; Acting-Assistant Paymaster, J. G. Holland; Acting-Ensigns, E. Gabrielson and F. Marshall; Acting-Master's Mates, Ezra C. Colvin and G. A. Johnson.

STEAMER "GERANIUM."

Acting-Ensign, Geo. A. Winson; Acting-Master's Mates, J. B. Newcomb, David Lee and C. T. Remmonds; Engineers: Acting-Second-Assistant, J. H. Foster; Acting-Third-Assistants, S. W. Midlam, Chas. Henry and Wm. J. Carman.

STEAMER "LARKSPUR."

Acting-Ensign, F. B. Davis; Acting-Master's Mates; John O'Conner, E. H. Frisbie and Jacob Kemp; Engineers: Acting-Third-Assistants, T. G. Farroat and J. T. Greenwood.

STEAMER "DAFFODIL."

Acting-Ensign, F. W. Sanborn; Acting-Master's Mates, J. C. Wentworth, C. L. Weeden, T. E. Harvey and D. Lester; Engineers: Acting-Second-Assistant, T. W. Dee; Acting-Third-Assistants, Wm. Fisher and W. F. Henderson.

STEAMER "JONQUIL."

Acting Ensign, Israel T. Halstead; Acting-Master's Mates, J. G. Brown and George Bowers; Engineers: Acting-Second-Assistant, David Gayring; Acting-Third-Assistants; Jesse Wright and Wm. Leonard.

STEAMER "CARNATION."

Acting-Ensign, Wm. Boyd; Acting-Master's Mates, A. Burnham and E. H. Frisbie; Engineers: Acting-Second-Assistant, T. S. Jennings; Acting-Third-Assistants, C. W. Plaisted and J. H. Fulcher.

STEAMER "CLOVER."

Acting-Ensign, Chas. A. Blanchard; Acting-Master's Mate, F. S. Leach; Engineers: Acting-Second-Assistant, Geo. Divine; Acting-Third-Assistant, G. C. Brown.

SCHOONER "NORFOLK PACKET."

Acting-Ensign, Geo. W. Wood; Acting-Assistant Paymaster, Andrew Tower; Acting-Master's Mates, J. Kingsley, Timothy Ryan and Geo. Delaps.

STEAMER "DANDELION."

Acting-Master's Mates, J. B. Russell, Louis Boun and W. R. Lyons; Engineers: Acting-Second-Assistant, J. G. Rossman; Acting-Third-Assistants, John Mulready and John Grimes.

SCHOONER "BLUNT."

Acting-Ensign, B. D. Reed; Acting-Master's Mates, C. W. Cleaves, W. R. Pease and W. Arkins.

STEAMER "COLUMBINE."

Acting-Master's Mates, Wm. B. Spencer, James Martin and John Davis; Engineers: Acting-Third-Assistants, H. J. Johnson and Geo. H. Luther.

STEAMER "RESCUE."

Acting-Master's Mate, A. G. Borden; Engineers: Acting-Third-Assistants, G. W. Howe and J. G. Dennett.

OFFICERS NOT ASSIGNED TO VESSELS.

Commanders, J. W. A. Nicholson and N. B. Harrison; Lieutenant-Commander, Wm. B. Gamble.

CHAPTER XLVIII.

POTOMAC FLOTILLA. INCREASE OF THE NAVY, AND IMPROVEMENTS
IN NAVAL SHIPS, DURING THE YEAR 1864.

THE Potomac Flotilla during 1864 remained under the command of Commander Foxhall A. Parker, a valuable officer, who conducted the affairs of his little squadron with so much efficiency that he was enabled to carry out all the objects for which the flotilla was intended.

The work of this department of the Navy was not brilliant, but it was useful. Besides the duties involved in patroling the Potomac, the Rappahannock River was added to Commander Parker's district.

There was at one time an extensive contraband trade between Virginia and the lower part of Maryland, by which the Confederates frequently received large amounts of supplies ; and the blockade-runners (such as they were) were quite as indefatigable in their attempts to provision the Confederates in Virginia as the larger vessels running the blockade on the coast.

The small craft that were engaged in this traffic between Maryland and Virginia were well adapted for the business, and calculated to avoid detection. The traders themselves were reckless and unscrupulous men, not working with any patriotic feeling to serve the Confederate cause, but to enrich themselves by the large returns they received for the supplies so much needed by private and public parties.

No greater vigilance was exhibited anywhere than was shown by the officers and men of the Potomac flotilla ; and what was done by the blockaders on the coast on a large scale was equally well done by the Potomac flotilla on a small one.

It was impossible to break up this blockade-running altogether, with such a long line of communication to be patroled, and with so small a number of vessels and boats to do it. Opportunities could almost al-ways be found to elude the blockade, and the temptations were so great that men fearlessly risked their lives to secure the large profits that awaited them in case of a successful run. They were aided by sympathetic friends on either side, who in most cases enabled them to evade detection when they were chased to the shore. Numbers of them were, however, captured while in transit, while many of their boats were ferreted out of their hiding-places, captured and destroyed. Most of this work had to be done at night, and throughout the war the most wearing vigilance was kept up by the different commanders and officers who had been employed in the Potomac flotilla.

Besides the watchfulness required in pursuit of the blockade-runners, the flotilla was at all times ready to give its active and willing co-operation to any military movement, and this assistance was frequently called for. While the Federal Army was in the vicinity of Fredericksburg, in the spring and summer, the services of the smaller steamers were constantly invoked. They opened communication between military forces, cleared large numbers of torpedoes from the river, made it safe for the transports to move with supplies or troops, drove the Confederate bushwhackers from the banks of the river, and returned with the sick and wounded from the field of battle.

The gun-boats that served upon this duty were of very light draft, purchased for this particular work, which will account for so many vessels of inferior character being in the Navy. Consequently, those who served on board of them in a hostile country were exposed to more than ordinary peril. It was wonderful to see these slightly-built vessels go into action against the Confederate batteries, which one would suppose from their rapid firing would soon cut them to pieces; but the stern discipline existing and precise aiming of the somewhat heavy guns of these "pasteboard" craft would, nine times out of ten, carry the day.

In these operations Commander Parker made his mark, assisted mostly by gallant volunteer officers, who, towards the end of the war, became very expert in all that related to this kind of warfare. Had a larger field of operations offered to Commander Parker, he was just the man who would have done infinite credit to himself and have conferred honor upon the Navy. The trying work and perilous duties, with the effects of a malarial climate, caused him to contract disease, which brought him to a premature death not long after the close of the war. The Navy lost in him a brave and gallant officer, who had proved himself to be efficient in whatever

COMMANDER (AFTERWARDS COMMODORE) FOXHALL A. PARKER,

COMMANDING THE POTOMAC FLOTILLA.

position he was placed. There were many like him who succumbed to disease and exposure, who, but for the war, might be living to-day.

INCREASE OF THE NAVY AND IMPROVEMENTS IN NAVAL SHIPS UP TO DECEMBER, 1864.

As the war progressed, it became evident that the Federal Government should not only build vessels for blockading the Southern coast and patroling the Western and Southern rivers, but for the protection of their own coast against a foreign foe, and for the capture of the Confederate cruisers which were then committing such havoc upon Federal commerce.

No one knew at what time the United States might be involved in war with Eng-

land or France, particularly the former country, which had afforded the South so much assistance in fitting out cruisers, that matters could not go on any longer without subjecting the Federal Government to the contempt of all civilized Powers. Although the Confederate Government only managed to procure vessels from England through shifts and stratagems, yet it was very evident that the British Government was not taking vigorous steps to put a stop to a practice in violation of its "Foreign Enlistment Act," and was oblivious to the fact that these cruisers were now and then destroying British goods in Federal vessels. They were willing to suffer the smaller evil that the greater good might accrue to English commerce, which it was hoped would, through the destruction of American shipping, have a monopoly all over the world. If British goods, properly documented, were not respected on board American vessels, the end would be the destruction of all American commerce—as was seen by the unhesitating manner in which Semmes directed every vessel he captured, and chose to consider subject to condemnation, to be consigned to the flames.

There is a certain amount of respect which every civilized nation demands for its commerce—that it shall only be captured by belligerents under certain laws laid down for the protection of neutrals, and the country having its commerce subjected to captures is in duty bound to see that the law is respected; while it is the duty of each belligerent to instruct its naval commanders accordingly. But the Confederate Government took no steps in this matter, leaving its agents to work out their ends, and "burn, sink and destroy" at their discretion. It seemed as if they did not consider themselves responsible for anything that might happen on the ocean. The Confederacy was incapable of negotiating with foreign Powers, who could not recognize its diplomatic agents without practically acknowledging the independence of the Confederate States; and this point should not only have warned neutral Powers against granting belligerent rights, but it should have emboldened them to resort first to emphatic remonstrances against the manner in which the captures of the Confederates were made, and then to sending out cruisers to enforce their demands, and thus put an end to the violation of their own laws.

The right to capture an enemy's commerce on the high seas is fully recognized by the law of nations; but that law should only apply to regularly recognized governments. The Confederacy was not and could not be held responsible for anything done by its cruisers, as was shown in the end by its collapse. The United States alone could then be held responsible for what the Confederates had done against the commerce of any other government.

There was in the latter part of 1864 a growing feeling in the Federal States against the action of Great Britain, which, though the latter began to pay more attention to its neutral obligations (owing to the strong protests of Mr. Adams, Federal minister at the Court of St. James), still allowed these cruisers to escape to sea; and several iron-clad rams, built by John Laird & Co., were preparing for sea, at Liverpool. These rams would, no doubt, have escaped but for the earnest remonstrances of the American minister, who in the most emphatic manner declared to the British Government that, to permit these vessels to depart, would be considered an act of war. Under these circumstances Her Majesty's Government had no difficulty in finding reasons for seizing and detaining the rams, after a three months' controversy over the matter.

Among the most outspoken of the members of the Federal Cabinet in regard to the violation of neutrality by the British Government in permitting the Confederate cruisers to escape its vigilance, was Mr. Gideon Welles, the Secretary of the Navy. He had appealed to Congress time after time to appropriate money to enable the Navy Department to build a class of vessels that would make it possible for him to put a stop to the depredations of the Confederate commerce-destroyers, but Congress dealt out money in such insufficient amounts that Mr. Welles could not at once equip the class of vessels desired, not only to put a stop to the destruction of Federal commerce, but to show foreign Powers that, even with the great strain that was laid upon Federal resources, the United States could not only fit out cruisers against the "Alabamas," but could build such vessels as would do good service against foreign ships-of-war, in case the Federal Government was driven to resort to the last extremity to preserve its prestige and its honor.

Mr. Welles, in his annual reports, was unceasing in his denunciations of the remissness of the British Government and the depredations of the Confederate cruisers, whom in his loyal zeal he always maintained were pirates; and he showered invectives on the commanders of those vessels in language not altogether parliamentary, but which he honestly believed to be the truth.

The Secretary had, no doubt, made efforts, with the intelligent aid of his assistant, Mr. Fox, to fit out sea vessels of a character that could pursue these cruisers with effect; but, unfortunately, there were obstacles in the way which for a time impeded the progress of his plans. In the first place, Mr. Welles attached too much importance to the blockade of the Southern ports and listened too much to the clamors of commanders of squadrons for more vessels on their stations; for inferior-built steamers could have performed that duty as well as the sea-going corvettes. Then, his plans were interfered with by Commodore Wilkes, who not only had a squadron of twelve vessels with which he patrolled the Gulf and West Indies, but also seized upon the fastest cruisers the Secretary of the Navy had sent on special duty to go in pursuit of the Confederates, and detained the vessels belonging to the neighboring stations and attached them to his squadron. In one instance, at least, there was a chance of capturing the "Alabama," which had touched at all the ports where her pursuer followed her, but the latter was just a month too late. Though the Navy Department may have been at fault in its judgment in not sending fast vessels to the channels of trade in the first instance, it more than made up for it by putting its whole energies to work to place the Navy in a condition to meet any emergency that might offer, even at the end of the war.

The Department, as well as the Administration, had been very much abused for the depredations of the Confederate cruisers, especially by those who were sufferers, and the opposition party were glad of the opportunity to berate the Government for its want of forethought in not anticipating the evils that were falling upon the Federal commerce. For the first time Congress began to be aroused to a sense of the danger that threatened the country, not only by the complete destruction of the foreign trade, but also the danger of being driven into a foreign war to preserve the Federal honor, if not its nationality. Under the plea of providing against the commerce-destroyers of the Confederacy, large strides were made in building up the Navy; which it will be seen in the end was the wisest policy to pursue, as it taught those Powers that were forgetting their neutral obligations that the policy they had hitherto pursued would no more be tolerated, and showed them that the longer the war lasted the stronger the Federal Government would grow, no matter what might be the drafts upon its treasury.

For attacks on forts and for river work the Federal Government had by 1863 a sufficient number of vessels to close the Confederate ports; and it was determined to build a number of large vessels that would be superior to any ships of their class abroad, not only in the power of their guns but in their speed.

At that moment the exigencies of the

times had stimulated the inventive faculties of American ship and engine builders to make vast improvements in vessels-of-war—in machinery, in naval ordnance and in projectiles. At the commencement of the war, the Federals may be said to have been in their infancy in such matters, and had to make great exertions to catch up with the powers of Europe; but by the end of 1864 they were quite in a condition to vindicate their rights and rebuke Great Britain and France for the unfair advantage they had taken in their hour of distress. Besides a number of single-turreted Monitors (the names of which have often appeared in these pages), there were built seven or eight double-turreted Monitors of the "Monadnock" class, which alone were quite capable of guarding the coast against the heaviest ships in the French or English navies.

Seven vessels were building at the Navy Yards, in which, to gain great speed, some of the armament had to be sacrificed. This class of vessels was represented by the "Ammonoosuc" and the "Chattanooga." There were also in process of construction twenty heavily armed vessels. Ten of these, of the "Guerriere" class, were to have covered decks, and to carry twenty heavy guns; two were to be protected against the effect of shells. The remaining ten built at the Navy Yards were of somewhat less size, but to be of great speed; and as nearly all of these were of full-sail power, they were expected to maintain their positions at sea for at least three months, and to be used on the most distant stations.

Among the wonders of the age at that time were built a set of vessels called the "Miantonomoh" class—a wooden vessel designed by the naval constructors, and built at the Navy Yards with Ericsson turrets, the machinery designed by Engineer-in-chief B. F. Isherwood, chief of the Bureau of Steam Engineering; with a high rate of speed, perfect ventilation, impregnable, and with the enormous battery of four 15-inch guns, all combined in a vessel of the moderate rate of 1,560 tons, drawing only 12 feet of water. Others of the same type, with increased tonnage and of still higher speed, were also in the course of construction, and the Federal Government had, apparently, realized at last the importance of having a powerful Navy, by which alone it could maintain its position among the nations of the earth.

Mr. Seward's earnest letters and Mr. Adams' strong protests may have had some influence upon the British Government in deciding them to carry out the terms of their "Foreign Enlistment Act," but there was a stronger argument in the heavy ships and guns that the Federals were building so rapidly; and this will ever be the case

as long as we maintain a properly equipped naval force to prevent any interference in our affairs by foreign Powers, and to enable us to assert ourselves whenever occasion may require.

The following table will explain all that the Navy Department had done from the outbreak of the war, and the exhibit shows that a great amount of zeal, intelligence and practical ability was manifested by those who were engaged in building up the Navy. It will be seen in the end that it did more to establish the standing of the United States abroad than even the advance of the Federal armies; and, among other things, it completely stopped all attempts of the Confederates to fit out cruisers in neutral ports.

It was at this crisis that Mr. Fox, Assistant Secretary of the Navy, did so much by his influence and his progressive mind, in Congress and in the Department, in furthering all the plans brought to the Secretary's notice; and it is only fair to say that, without his assistance and the ability he displayed in all professional matters, the Navy Department would not have reached the point of efficiency which at that time existed. This was appreciated by officers throughout the service; and it is evident, from the latitude given Mr. Fox by the Secretary of the Navy, that the latter leaned upon him as his ablest adviser.

REPORT OF THE SECRETARY OF THE NAVY.

A tabular statement is appended of the number of naval vessels, of every class, that had been constructed, or were in the course of construction, since March 4, 1861:

GENERAL EXHIBIT OF THE NAVY, INCLUDING VESSELS UNDER CONSTRUCTION, DEC., 1864.

No. of vessels.	Description.	No. of guns.	No. of tons.
113	Screw steamers especially constructed for naval purposes	1,426	169,231
52	Paddle-wheel steamers especially constructed for naval purposes.	524	51,878
71	Iron-clad vessels..	275	80,596
149	Screw-steamers purchased, captured, &c., fitted for naval purposes	614	60,380
174	Paddle-wheel steamers purchased, captured, &c., fitted for naval purposes	921	78,762
112	Sailing vessels of all classes....	850	69,549
671	Total..........	4,610	510,396

COMPARATIVE STATEMENT OF THE NAVY, DECEMBER, 1863 AND 1864.

No. of vessels.	Description.	No. of guns.	No. of tons.
671	Total navy, December, 1864..........	4,610	510,396
588	Total navy, December, 1863....	4,443	467,967
83	Actual increase for the year ...	167	42,429
26	Total losses by shipwreck, in battle, capture, &c., during the year..........	146	13,084
109	Actual addition to the navy from December, 1863, to December, 1864	313	55,513

VESSELS CONSTRUCTED FOR THE NAVY SINCE MARCH 4, 1861.

No.	Description.	Guns.	Ton'age
7	Screw sloops, "Ammonoosuc" class, 17 to 19 guns, 3,213 to 3,713 tons each	121	23,637
1	Screw sloop "Idaho," 8 guns, 2,638 tons	8	2,638
8	Screw sloops, spar deck, "Java" class, 25 guns and 3,177 tons each	200	25,416
2	Screw sloops, spar deck, "Hassalo" class, 25 guns and 3,365 tons each	50	6,730
10	Screw sloops, clippers, single deck, "Contoocook" class, 13 guns and 2,348 tons each	130	23,480
4	Screw sloops, "Kearsarge" class, 8 to 12 guns, and averaging 1,023 tons each	40	4,092
6	Screw sloops, "Shenandoah" class, 8 to 16 guns and 1,367 to 1,533 tons each	74	8,584
2	Screw sloops, "Ossipee" class, 10 to 13 guns and 1,240 tons each	23	2,480
8	Screw sloops, "Serapis" class, 12 guns and 1,380 tons each	96	11,040
4	Screw sloops, "Resaca" class, 8 guns and 831 to 900 tons each	32	3,462
8	Screw sloops, "Nipsic" class, 7 to 12 guns and 593 tons each	71	4,744
23	Screw gun-boats, "Unadilla" class, 4 to 7 guns and 507 tons each	123	11,661
9	Screw tugs, "Pinta" class, 2 guns and 350 tons each	18	3,150
2	Screw tugs, "Pilgrim" class, 2 guns and 170 tons each	4	340
13	Paddle-wheel steamers, double-enders, "Octorara" class, 7 to 11 guns and 730 to 955 tons each	98	11,024
26	Paddle-wheel steamers, double-enders, "Sassacus" class, 10 to 14 guns and 974 tons each	272	25,324
7	Paddle-wheel steamers, of iron, double-enders, "Mohongo" class, 10 guns and 1,030 tons each	70	7,210
1	Paddle-wheel steamer, of iron, double-ender, "Wateree," 12 guns and 974 tons	12	974
141		1,142	175,986

IRON-CLAD VESSELS.

No.	Description.	Guns.	Ton'age
2	Sea-going casemated vessels, "Dunderberg" and "New Ironsides"	28	8,576
3	Sea-going turret vessels, "Puritan," "Dictator," and "Roanoke"	12	9,733
4	Double turret vessels, "Kalamazoo" class, 4 guns and 3,200 tons each	16	12,800
4	Double turret vessels, "Monadnock" class, 4 guns and 1,564 tons each	16	6,256
1	Double turret vessel, "Onondaga," 4 guns and 1,250 tons	4	1,250
4	Double turret vessels, "Winnebago" class, 4 guns and 970 tons each	16	3,880
8	Single turret vessels, "Canonicus" class, 2 guns and 1,034 tons each	16	8,272
9	Single turret vessels, "Passaic" class, 2 to 4 guns and 844 tons each	21	7,596
20	Single turret vessels, "Yazoo" class, 1 to 2 guns and 614 tons each	35	12,280
2	Single turret vessels, "Sandusky" and "Marietta," 2 guns each	4	953
3	Single turret vessels, "Ozark," "Neosho," and "Osage," 2 to 7 guns each	13	1,624
2	Casemated vessels, "Tuscumbia" and "Chillicothe," 5 and 3 guns respectively	8	768
62		189	73,988
203	Total	1,631	249,974

The foregoing tabular statement exhibits the number and description of vessels that had been constructed, or put in the course of construction, for the Navy after the institution of active measures for the suppression of the rebellion. Some of them were built by contract; others by the Government, in the several Navy Yards. If we add to the number those constructed under similar circumstances, and within the same period, that had been lost by shipwreck, in battle, etc., viz.: the sloops "Housatonic" and "Adirondack," and the iron-clads "Monitor," "Weehawken," "Keokuk," "Indianola" and "Tecumseh," the aggregate would be 210 vessels, 1,675 guns and 256,755 tons.

Picket-boats, and small craft built for especial purposes, are not embraced in this statement.

POTOMAC FLOTILLA, JANUARY 1, 1864.

COMMANDER FOXHALL A. PARKER.

STEAMER "ELLA."

Acting-Master, J. H. Eldredge; Paymaster, J. N. Carpenter; Acting-Ensign, E. A. Roderick; Acting-Master's Mates, W. H. Flood, H. C. Eldredge and W. L. Gilley; Engineers: Acting-First-Assistant, John F. Reilly; Acting-Second-Assistant, T. Galloway; Acting-Third-Assistants, Wm. Cornell, F. M. Dykes and T. H. Cross; Acting-Carpenter, J. C. Tier.

STEAMER "YANKEE."

Acting-Volunteer Lieutenant, Edward Hooker; Acting-Assistant Paymaster, S. T. Brown; Acting-Ensign, G. D. Gilderdale; Acting-Master's Mates, H. C. Borden and Robert Robinson; Engineers: Acting-Third-Assistants, W. H. Hughes and John F. Costar.

STEAMER "COMMODORE READ."

Acting-Master, G. E. Hill; Acting-Assistant-Surgeon, James Wilson; Acting-Assistant Paymaster, J. J. Duffield; Acting-Ensigns, G. E. McConnell, C. Ainsworth and L. Wold; Acting-Master's Mates, Guy Morrison, E. K. Howland and G. A. Patchke; Engineers: Acting-First-Assistant, A. K. Gaul; Acting-Third-Assistants, John Westinghouse, Wesley J. Phillips and George Smith.

STEAMER "CURRITUCK."

Acting-Master, W. H. Smith; Acting-Assistant Surgeon, Henry Johnson; Acting-Assistant Paymaster, Frank Clark; Acting-Ensigns, Thomas Nelson, Ambrose Felix and J. A. Havens; Acting-Master's Mate, G. B. Hall; Engineers: Acting-Second-Assistant, Alfred Clum; Acting-Third-Assistants, O. P. Thompson and C. B. Wright.

STEAMER "JACOB BELL."

Acting-Master, G. C. Shultze; Acting-Assistant

Surgeon, Wm. Neilson, Jr.; Acting-Assistant Paymaster, Samuel Anderson; Acting-Ensigns, Benjamin Walker and D. W. Hodson; Acting-Master's Mates, Robert L. Omensetter and Arthur Clegg; Engineers: Acting-Second-Assistant, Thomas Bentley; Acting-Third-Assistants, Wm. H. White and J. H. McConnell.

STEAMER "FUCHSIA."

Acting-Master, Wm. T. Street; Acting-Ensign, C. H. Walker; Acting-Master's Mates, W. G. Borden and S. B. Cline; Engineers: Acting Second-Assistant, S. H. Magee; Acting-Third-Assistants, C. Castell and A. F. Bullard.

STEAMER "CŒUR DE LION."

Acting-Master, Wm. G. Morris; Acting-Ensign, C. F. Watson; Acting-Master's Mate, Wm. Hornby; Engineers: Acting-Second-Assistant, J. M. Dexter; Acting-Third-Assistant, Henry Knight.

STEAMER "RESOLUTE."

Acting-Master, J. C. Tole; Acting-Ensign, J. S. Benjamin; Acting-Master's Mates, Ed. Huger and J. S. Franklin; Engineers: Acting-Second-Assistant, George Dereamer; Acting-Third-Assistant, J. E. Smith.

STEAMER "FREEBORN."

Acting-Master, W. A. Arthur; Acting-Assistant-Surgeon, H. H. Smith; Acting-Assistant Paymaster, D. A. Dickinson; Acting-Master's Mates, C. A. Peacock and L. N. Rollins; Engineers: Acting-Second-Assistant, W. P. Magaw; Acting-Third-Assistants, G. W. Yoe and W. E. Webster.

STEAMER "ANACOSTIA."

Acting-Master, Nelson Provost; Acting-Assistant Paymaster, David Guernsey; Acting-Ensigns, E. D.

Edmunds; Acting - Master's Mates, James Softly and Richard Still; Engineers: Acting-First-Assistant, George Faron; Acting-Second-Assistant, J. T. Buckley; Acting-Third-Assistants, T. E. Lynch and Thomas Hineline.

SCHOONER "SOPHRONIA."

Acting - Master, James Taylor; Acting - Ensigns, H. F. Dorton and E. S. Shurtliff; Acting-Master's Mates, W. H. Hunt and J. O. Conway.

SCHOONER "MATTHEW VASSAR."

Acting-Master, Henry O. Stone; Acting-Ensign, R. C. Wright; Acting-Master's Mates, Wm. Duffy, G. H. Marks and S. W. Ward.

SCHOONER "ADOLPH HUGEL."

Acting - Master, S. Nickerson; Acting - Master's Mates, H. C. Fuller, J. H. Taylor and J. H. King.

SCHOONER "WILLIAM BACON."

Acting-Master, Samuel Haines; Acting-Ensign, J. A. Merrill; Acting-Master's Mates, H. E. Ripley, Wm. Coomes and J. W. Davis.

STEAMER "WYANDANK."

Acting Ensign, J. J. Brice; Acting-Assistant Paymaster, J. Porter Loomis; Acting-Ensign, W. H. Hand; Acting-Master's Mates, G. G. Bachelder, Thomas Seager and George Thomas; Engineers: Acting - Second - Assistant, Levi Sweetzer; Acting-Third-Assistants, Harvey Brown and F. T. Clark.

STEAMER "TULIP."

Acting-Ensigns, S. G. Sluyter and D. Stevens; Acting-Master's Mates, J. Roffenterg and C. H. McClellan; Engineers: Acting-Third-Assistants, G. H. Parks, H. P. Gray and John Gordon.

STEAMER "PRIMROSE."

Acting-Ensign, James H. Jackson; Acting-Master's Mates, H. L. R. Woods and John Shields; Engineers: Acting-Second Assistant, L. B. Leland; Acting-Third-Assistant, H. C. Marrow.

STEAMER "TEASER."

Acting-Ensign, Philip Sheridan; Acting-Master's Mates, Charles Case, Thomas Power and Louis Reinberg; Engineers: Acting - Second - Assistant, John Johnson; Acting-Third-Assistant, G. C. Steadman.

STEAMER "DRAGON."

Acting-Ensign, J. W. Turner; Acting-Master's Mates, David Hall and S. M. Carey; Acting-Second-Assistant Engineer, G. E. Riddle.

CHAPTER XLIX.

FIRST ATTACK ON FORT FISHER.

DESTRUCTION OF THE CONFEDERATE RAM "ALBEMARLE," Etc.

DEFENCES AT THE MOUTH OF CAPE FEAR RIVER.—THE ARMY TO CO-OPERATE WITH THE
NAVY. — REAR-ADMIRAL PORTER ASSUMES COMMAND OF THE NORTH ATLANTIC
SQUADRON. — PREPARATIONS TO ATTACK FORT FISHER. — ATTEMPT TO CLOSE THE
PORT OF WILMINGTON, N. C.—METHODS RESORTED TO BY BLOCKADE-RUNNERS, AND
THEIR PROFITS.—VALUE OF THE VESSELS DESTROYED. — DESTRUCTION OF THE RAM
"ALBEMARLE" BY LIEUTENANT CUSHING. — NAMES OF OFFICERS AND MEN WHO
RISKED THEIR LIVES WITH CUSHING. — BOMBARDMENT OF AND CAPTURE OF PLY-
MOUTH, N. C.—LOSSES AND FRUITS OF VICTORY.—THE FAMOUS POWDER-BOAT.—DE-
SCRIPTION OF FORTS AND BATTERIES.—THE FLEET RIDES OUT A TERRIFIC GALE.—GEN-
ERAL BUTLER'S POWDER-BOAT EXPLODED. — GREAT LOSS OF POWDER, BUT NO
DAMAGE DONE TO FORT FISHER.—FIRST ATTACK ON FORT FISHER BY THE FLEET.—
BATTERIES SILENCED.—LANDING OF THE ARMY.—GENERAL ORDERS.—CORRESPOND-
ENCE BETWEEN ADMIRAL PORTER AND GENERAL BUTLER.—GENERAL BUTLER ABAN-
DONS THE ATTEMPT TO CAPTURE FORT FISHER.—GENERAL BUTLER SUCCEEDED BY
GENERAL TERRY.—CRITICISMS.—CAPTURE OF FLAG-POND BATTERY.—LIST OF VESSELS
THAT PARTICIPATED IN FIRST ATTACK ON FORT FISHER.—LETTERS IN REGARD TO THE
UNNECESSARY DELAY OF THE EXPEDITION.—LETTERS AND TELEGRAMS FROM SECRE-
TARY WELLES.—REPORTS OF OFFICERS.

IN a communication dated September 5, 1864, Mr. Secretary Welles states that, since the Winter of 1862, he had tried to obtain the co-operation of the War Department in a joint Army and Navy attack on the defences at the entrance of Cape Fear River, N. C.

It seems the Secretary of War had decided that no troops could be spared for this purpose, and, in consequence, from small and unimportant works the huge fortification known as Fort Fisher had gradually arisen. These works bade defiance to any ordinary naval force, unsupported by troops, so that what in the first instance might have been prevented by the persistent attacks of a dozen gun-boats, grew to a series of works so formidable that it was evidently a matter of difficulty to effect their reduction—that is, if the Confederates should make a vigorous defence.

Early in the contest a squadron of light-draft gun-boats could have made their way past the small batteries and taken posses-sion of Cape Fear River, closing that channel of blockade-runners, and paving the way for the troops to hold the point on which Fort Fisher was finally built. But this was not attempted until the fortifications were so far advanced as to become the most formidable series of works in the Confederacy.

At the entrance of Cape Fear River, the principal operations of the blockade-runners were carried on, supplying the Confederate armies with clothing, arms and munitions of war to the amount of sixty or seventy millions of dollars.

The Federal Navy Department finally became aware that, unless these supplies were cut off from the Confederate armies, the war was likely to be greatly prolonged. The blockade-runners were very fast steamers, well-manned, and with experienced pilots, and so regular were their trips to Wilmington, that their arrival was counted on almost as confidently as if they had been mail-steamers. Of course, many of them fell into the hands of the blockaders, or were run upon the beach to escape capture. In the latter case, if protected by artillery on shore, the blockade runners would land the most valuable portion of their cargoes and set fire to their vessels.

In September, 1864, Mr. Welles made another application for troops to co-operate with the Navy in an attack on the defences of Cape Fear River, and, being encouraged by General Grant to expect assistance, the Navy Department began to assemble at Hampton Roads a proper force of vessels for the occasion. The command of the squadron was tendered to Rear-Admiral Farragut, and on the 5th of September, 1864, Mr. Secretary Welles, in a letter to that officer, says:

"Lieutenant-General Grant has recently given the subject his attention, and thinks an army force can be spared and moved by the first day of October. Upon consultation, he is of the opinion that the best results will follow the landing of a large force under the guns of the Navy on the open beach north of New Inlet, to take possession and intrench across to Cape Fear River, the Navy to open such fire as is possible on the works on Federal Point in conjunction with the army, and at the same time such force as can run the batteries to do so, and thus isolate the rebels.

"You are selected to command the naval force, and you will endeavor to be at Port Royal by the latter part of September, where further orders will await you. Bring with you to the rendezvous at Port Royal all such vessels and officers as can be spared from the West Blockading Squadron without impeding its efficiency; and when you leave, turn over the command of the squadron to the officer next in rank to yourself until the pleasure of the Department is known."

Owing to failing health, Admiral Farragut declined accepting this command, and on the 22d of September the Secretary of the Navy wrote to Rear-Admiral Porter as follows:

"SIR—Rear-Admiral D. G. Farragut was assigned to the command of the North Atlantic squadron on the 5th instant; but the necessity of rest on the part of that distinguished officer renders it necessary that he should come immediately North. You will therefore, on the receipt of this order, consider yourself detached from the command of the Mississippi squadron, and you will turn over the command, temporarily, to Captain A. M. Pennock. As soon as the transfer can be made, proceed to Beaufort, N. C., and relieve Acting-Rear-Admiral S. P. Lee, in command of the North Atlantic Blockading Squadron. Take with you your personal staff, and a number of officers, not exceeding five, may be transferred from the Mississippi to the North Atlantic squadron."

Under the above orders, Rear-Admiral Porter assumed command of the North Atlantic squadron, and visited City Point, Va., in company with Mr. Fox, Assistant-Secretary of the Navy, to confer with General Grant in regard to the necessary contingent of troops required to co-operate with the Navy in the reduction of Fort Fisher.

Admiral Porter had asked for but eight thousand troops, and a sufficient number of vessels to fire one hundred and fifty guns in broadside. As Fort Fisher had seventy-five heavy guns mounted, the above would only be two guns afloat to one on shore, a small proportion considering that most of the naval force would be wooden ships, against heavy earth-works, protected by solid traverses. The wishes of the Secretary of the Navy were made known to General Grant, and he at once decided to send the requisite number of troops to co-operate with the Navy as soon as the ships could be prepared.

The next thing was to select a General to command, who would act in harmony with the Navy. There were plenty of able commanders, but the trouble was whom could General Grant best spare. Admiral Porter merely suggested one thing—namely, that General Butler should not go in command. North Carolina was in the district over which Butler held control, and the Admiral did not know but that the General would claim the right to go in command of troops operating in that district. It was at length decided that General Weitzel should have command of the military part of the expedition.

By the 15th of October, 1864, the ships-of-war of the fleet destined to attack Fort Fisher were assembled at Hampton Roads, to the number of about one hundred. Many of them were from other squadrons which had been depleted for the occasion. There was a great variety of vessels, as every class in the Navy was represented, from the lofty frigate down to the fragile steamer taken from the merchant service; but all mounted good guns.

Admiral Porter had quite a task before him to organize this large force and make it fit for combined service, for it was not in good condition for battle such as the occasion demanded. A regular system of drilling was at once commenced with sails, masts, yards and guns, particularly the latter, and a large portion of the time was spent in target practice. Immense quantities of shells were fired away, for the commanding officers of the ships were given *carte blanche* in this respect, the Admiral believing that it would be an ultimate saving in time of battle.

The fleet was now formed into three divisions. There were five Commodores in the fleet—Thatcher, Lanman, Godon, Schenck and Radford. The latter officer had immediate command of the iron-clads. From all these officers Rear Admiral Porter received hearty support, although, owing to the fortunes of war, he had been advanced over their heads, and naturally expected to find some little feeling in regard to it; but there was none whatever. They met the Admiral in the most cordial manner and ever gave him their heartiest support. This was, it is true, the proper course, for success has always in time of war been recognized in all services by promotion. Several of these gentlemen were officers of great ability, and it may be wondered why they were not employed in command of independent squadrons. The wonder will be less when we consider how little was known by the Navy Department of the character and qualifications of officers. With the exception of Assistant-Secretary Fox, there seemed to be nobody at headquarters who had much comprehension of the matter, and we had so few squadrons that it was difficult to find separate commands for all who deserved them.

The Navy Department, through Assistant-Secretary Fox, showed great energy in assembling the vessels of the fleet at Hampton Roads, and they never denied Admiral Porter anything he asked for.

As soon as the fleet was fairly organized, Admiral Porter made an effort to close up the port of Wilmington, N. C., so that supplies could not get in, or cotton get out. This was a most difficult thing to do, and his predecessor, Acting-Rear-Admiral Lee, with one of the largest squadrons afloat, had never succeeded in the attempt. His officers, it is true, captured a large number of vessels, but where one was captured or destroyed two new ones were built on an improved plan.

Towards the last the English commenced building these vessels of steel—long, narrow and shallow—which were capable of great speed, and could cross the bar of Cape Fear River at all times day or night, for at night range-lights were kept burning. Once under the guns of Fort Fisher they were safe. The gun-boats generally drew too much water to follow the blockade-runners over the bar, where the depth never exceeded ten feet.

The conduct of the blockading officers was sometimes severely criticised by the Northern newspapers, who, although they had positive evidence of their watchfulness in the shape of numerous fine prize steamers, loaded with cotton, coming into Northern ports, were not satisfied unless every bottle of brandy and bunch of cigars sent to the Confederates were captured to fill the pockets of Northern prize-agents. The people at home had little idea of the arduous service performed by the blockading vessels, whose officers and men had, at the peril of their lives, to hold on to Wilmington bar at all seasons, in the endeavor to prevent the entrance and exit of blockade-runners.

The advantage was all on the side of the latter. They could chose their own time. Painted a light, neutral tint, they fearlessly approached the bar, the range-lights

guiding them by night as well as if it were daylight, and a vessel within a short distance could only surmise their presence by a faint streak of light made by their wake. If the gun-boats fired, they were liable to hit each other; if they made the flash-signal agreed upon between them, the blockade-runner would make a similar one, and in the confusion, the latter, going at the rate of fifteen miles an hour, would soon pass out of sight. If the Federal vessels laid close in to the bar, they ran a risk of being carried into the breakers by the current, in which case their destruction was certain. The display of a twinkling light on board one of the gun-boats, near the bar, was the signal for a general discharge from the guns of Fort Fisher, and, although these shots were more noisy than damaging, yet a stray shell striking one of the Federal boats would have knocked it to pieces.

Sometimes the Federal vessels would discern " black smoke " in the distance ; then all was bustle and excitement. Chase would be given, and a "long, low two-pipe" steamer would show herself standing in for the bar. With the slow vessels, there was often not much chance of catching one of these swift blockade-runners, but they were sometimes intercepted and driven back to Nassau or Bermuda to make a fresh attempt. Eight times in ten they succeeded in eluding the closest blockade of a coast ever maintained. The profits of a successful voyage were so great, that the English adventurers, provided with good pilots, readily took the risks, which were nothing compared with those run by the blockading vessels. If one vessel in three succeeded in running into port, it remunerated the owners largely. They were paid for their ventures in Confederate cotton at eight cents a pound, worth at that time eighty cents in England and one dollar in the North. At first the blockade-runners were insured in England against capture, so many successful voyages were made, but towards the last the insurers charged very high premiums. Admiral Lee's squadron captured or destroyed a large number of blockade-running steamers, perhaps to the value of ten millions of dollars. The shores of North Carolina were strewn with the wrecks of these vessels, which were generally run aground and set on fire to prevent the Federal Navy from deriving any benefit from their capture.

We do not know what were Admiral Lee's particular plans in regard to the blockade-runners, but it was determined, while the fleet was waiting for the Army to get ready, that a new system should be adopted to take the contraband traders by surprise. A chart was furnished to every vessel on the blockade of Cape Fear River, upon which was described two half-circles close to the two bars at the entrance of that stream. Here were stationed twenty vessels, ranged in a half-circle, ten off each bar. At the termination of Frying-Pan Shoals was described another half-circle of about twelve miles' radius. On this circle was stationed, five miles apart, some twenty of the fastest vessels, which could communicate with each other by signal all the way round. One hundred and thirty miles from land was the third line, on which the vessels were about eight miles apart, the half-circle ending at Beaufort, N. C., on one side, and closing in on the south entrance to Cape Fear River. If a blockade-runner came out of Wilmington before daylight, she would be seen by vessels on the middle circle; and, if she escaped those, she would be chased by the vessels on the outer circle. If she started at midnight, she would be seen at midday by the vessels of the outer circle. Should a vessel approach the outer circle in order to run into Wilmington just before daylight, the outer circle would chase her off; or, if she eluded the outer circle after dark, she would be picked up by the middle circle; and instances were rare of vessels attempting to run this stringent blockade that were not captured or driven off.

The number of English steamers sent into Hampton Roads was surprising. They came in on an average of nearly one each day, and the commodores commanding divisions—who shared in these prizes—were well pleased to see them coming into port. The blockade-runners themselves were quite astonished and crowded into Nassau to concoct new plans to circumvent the Federal cruisers; but from that time the business grew more and more unprofitable, for in thirty-seven days some six million of dollars worth of property was captured or destroyed.

While General Sherman was marching through the South, he used up everything in the shape of provisions for the support of an army, and the enemy at Richmond depended in a great measure on what supplies they could get from Nassau for the maintenance of 300,000 men. By an order of the Confederate Government, one-third of the space in every vessel running the blockade was devoted to carrying provisions and stores for the Army. Had this stringent blockade been kept up for three months, the port of Wilmington would have been deserted; but this was hardly possible, for the United States Government would have been obliged soon to withdraw a large portion of the blockading vessels for service elsewhere, and the old system would likely have been resumed.

While these operations were in progress, Admiral Porter was engaged in perfecting the organization of his fleet, and his only objection to the delay was the fact that the winter was rapidly approaching, the season when storms are very severe on the coast of North Carolina. However, the delay gave Admiral Porter an opportunity to become acquainted with his officers, so that when the time came he knew where to place them. The plan of attack had been lithographed on a large scale, and each vessel assigned the position it would occupy in action. Every commanding officer had a copy of this chart, and all that was wanting now were the troops to co-operate with the Navy.

In the meantime the naval forces were not idle. One of the best executed feats of the war was the destruction of the Confederate ram "Albemarle," at Plymouth, N. C. This was most important; for, as has been already related, when the ram sunk the "Southfield" and drove off the "Miami," she attacked the flotilla under Captain Melancton Smith, and after a hard fight slipped off in the darkness and returned to Plymouth. Here she was fastened to a wharf to undergo necessary repairs after the terrible hammering received from the flotilla, and it was evident that her commanding officer did not care to make another attack until his vessel was strengthened in those parts which had been shown to be the weakest.

The engagement was criticised somewhat at the time, but it must be remembered that the vessels of the flotilla were unarmored, and that they fought gallantly against a vessel completely encased in iron; that the misfortune which happened to the "Sassacus" might have happened to one or two more, in which case not only the injured vessels, but all the others in the sounds of North Carolina, would have been at the mercy of the enemy. These considerations made it important for Captain Smith to avoid risking a defeat, and that he was successful in getting rid of the ram, and depriving her for the time being of power to do further mischief, is proof that he was master of the situation. This was the view taken of the affair by the Navy Department, as is shown by the following complimentary letter:

NAVY DEPARTMENT, }
May 25, 1864.   }

SIR—I have had great satisfaction in receiving and perusing your report, as the senior officer of the several vessels that were engaged with the rebel ram "Albemarle" and her tender on the 5th instant, in Albemarle Sound.

The Department congratulates all the officers and men of the United States Navy who participated in this remarkable contest between wooden gun-boats and a formidable armored vessel, in which the latter was forced to retreat to prevent capture, and it particularly thanks you for the vigilant and gallant use made of the means placed at your command to thwart the designs of the rebels to regain control of the Sounds of North Carolina.

GIDEON WELLES,
Secretary of the Navy.

CAPTAIN MELANCTON SMITH, U. S. N.,
Senior Officer commanding Sounds of North Carolina.

Notwithstanding the satisfaction expressed at the gallant conduct of Captain Smith, the Department was greatly troubled over the fact that the "Albemarle" still existed, and might sally out from Plymouth as soon as the necessary repairs were made, and drive the Federal gun-boats from the Sounds. The Department considered that they had no vessels at their disposal fit to cope with the ram; but the attack of the "Sassacus" should have showed them that four or five double-enders, each fitted with a heavy iron shield to the stem, would have been all-sufficient to crush the ram by a simultaneous attack. The experience of the Confederate commander had assured him of this fact, which was probably the chief reason why he did not again venture out.

Under these circumstances, Lieutenant W. B. Cushing was offered a further opportunity to distinguish himself—an offer he at once accepted. He was sent to New York, to superintend the fitting out of three torpedo steam-launches, arranged according to the plans of Chief Engineer W. W. W. Wood and Assistant-Engineer G. W. Lay, which proved to be all that were claimed for them. About the middle of October, 1864, the launches were ready, and Cushing got away with them from the New York Navy Yard.

Cushing was not so well adapted for the command of a flotilla, even of steam-launches, as he was of a single vessel. One of his torpedo-launches sank soon after he started, and another was run ashore and surrendered to the Confederates in Chesapeake Bay, while Cushing, steaming through a rough sea, safely reached Hampton Roads, and reported to Rear-Admiral Porter, then on board his flag-ship, the "Malvern."

Lieutenant Cushing's condition at this time was pitiable. He had been subjected to terrible exposure for more than a week, had lost all his clothing except what he had on, and his attenuated face and sunken eyes bore witness to the privations he had undergone. Himself and crew had existed on spoiled ship's biscuits and water, with an occasional potato cooked before the boiler fire. Admiral Porter at once ordered Cushing to get some necessary rest and not to come near him until sent for; and in the meantime his torpedo-launch, which had been somewhat shattered and disarranged, was put in perfect order. Cushing was then

instructed to proceed at once to blow up the "Albemarle." Commander W. H. Macomb, commanding in the Sounds of North Carolina, was ordered to give him all the assistance in his power, and, in case Cushing was successful, to attack and recover the town and defences of Plymouth.

On the very morning appointed for Cushing to set out, an order came from the Navy Department directing Admiral Porter to investigate some charges preferred by Mr. Secretary Seward against Cushing for violating certain neutral rights while in command of a vessel on the Southern coast.

Here was a dilemma; but the Admiral, after a brief investigation, decided that Cushing was free from blame, and the brave fellow, who dreaded a court-martial far more than he did the enemy, went

LIEUTENANT (AFTERWARDS COMMANDER) WM. B. CUSHING.

on his way rejoicing, passed through the Dismal Swamp Canal, and on the 27th of October reported to Commander Macomb.

That night Cushing proceeded up the river in the steam torpedo-launch with thirteen officers and men, mostly those who had volunteered from Commander Macomb's flotilla for the service. The distance from the mouth of the river to where the ram lay was about eight miles, and the stream, of an average width of two hundred yards, was lined with the enemy's pickets. The wreck of the U. S. S. "Southfield" lay a mile below the town, surrounded by some schooners, and it was understood that a gun was mounted here to command the bend in the river. In consequence of this report, an armed boat from the U. S. S. "Shamrock" was taken in tow, with orders to cast off and board these schooners, in case the expedition was hailed by the enemy.

When the steam launch and her tow neared the wreck of the "Southfield," there were anxious feelings on the part of the brave fellows whose lives it was thought by many would all be sacrificed on this hazardous expedition; but no one faltered, and Cushing's keen eye looked into the darkness intent only on the "Albemarle." The "Southfield" was passed by the party unobserved by the enemy, and the pickets along the river banks, depending on those at the outpost to give the alarm, were not on the alert. This was a fortunate circumstance for Cushing and his comrades, for he was thus enabled to approach unmolested within a few yards of the "Albemarle."

The look-out on board the iron-clad finally hailed, when Cushing, casting off the cutter, ordered her to proceed back to the wreck of the "Southfield" and capture the picket guard. Cushing then dashed ahead under full steam for the "Albemarle," which was secured to the wharf within a pen of logs extending about thirty feet from the vessel. A fire on shore lighted up the surroundings and Cushing's quick eye at once took in the situation. He dashed at the logs, which the steam-launch shoved aside, and struck the "Albemarle" bows on.

In the meantime the enemy had become thoroughly aroused, and the men on board the ram rushed to their quarters and opened a severe fire on the assaulting party; but they were swept away by a discharge of canister from the 12-pound howitzer mounted in the torpedo-boat's bow. A gun loaded with grape was also fired at the launch, but the fire from the howitzer disconcerted the gunner's aim and the shots were harmless. While all this firing was going on, the torpedo boom was deliberately lowered, and by a vigorous thrust Cushing drove the torpedo under the ram's overhang and exploded it. There was a tremendous crash and a great upward rush of water which filled the steam-launch. The pumps of the "Albemarle" were manned, and her commanding officer, Lieutenant Warley, encouraged his crew to try and keep the vessel free, but the water gained so rapidly through the great aperture made by the explosion that the "Albemarle" soon went to the bottom, her smoke-stack only showing the place where she had last floated. As the enemy had none of the necessary appliances at hand for raising the iron-clad, they made vigorous efforts to still further disable her, anticipating that the Federal gun-boats would soon be on the spot to try and secure the sunken vessel.

The "Albemarle," although apparently taken by surprise, had been quite prepared for the emergency. There were two field-pieces on her deck loaded with grape, and manned by a company of artillery ready to fire at a moment's notice. That a good watch was kept on board is proven by the quickness with which the crew got to quarters, and opened fire on the torpedo-boat. It was fortunate for Cushing that he succeeded in passing the pickets along the river undisturbed, otherwise the sailors on board the "Albemarle" and the troops on shore might have given him such a warm reception as would have prevented the carrying out of his design. But Cushing seemed ever to be the child of fortune and his good luck followed him to the close of the war.

But to return to the torpedo-boat: when the fire was opened on her by the enemy, Paymaster Swann was wounded at Cushing's side, and how many others had been injured he did not know. It seemed as if a shower of grape-shot had struck the boat, but in the confusion the aim was misdirected and the grape did little injury. The torpedo, exploding directly afterwards, filled the launch with water, when, seeing that she would be captured, Cushing and others jumped into the river and swam down stream under a shower of musketry, which, however, failed to do any harm.

As soon as the Confederates saw the torpedo-launch filled with water and floating away, they sent boats to take possession of her, and captured most of her crew. Some of the latter were drowned in their efforts to reach the opposite shore; and, so far as Cushing knew at the time, only one escaped besides himself, and he in a different direction. As he swam down the stream he met Acting-Master's Mate Woodman struggling in the water, almost exhausted, and endeavored to assist him to the shore; but the attempt was a failure, and Mr. Woodman was drowned. Cushing himself could barely crawl out of the water when he succeeded in reaching the bank, half a mile below the town. He dragged himself into a swamp, and, while lying concealed a few feet from the path along the river, two of the "Albemarle's" officers passed, and from their conversation Cushing learned for the first time that the iron-clad was at the bottom of the river.

As soon as his strength would allow, Cushing plunged into the dense swamp, where he would not likely be followed, and after incredible difficulty in forcing his way through the mud and slime, he reached a point well below the town; and met a negro, whom he sent into Plymouth to find out the particulars of the sinking of the ram. The negro soon returned with assurances that the "Albemarle" was actually sunk. Thus cheered, Cushing pursued his tedious journey through the swamps, till, coming suddenly on a creek, he found one of the enemy's picket-boats, of which he took possession, and pulled away with all his remaining strength, not knowing at what moment he might get a bullet through his brain. By 11 o'clock the following night he reached the gun-boat "Valley City," and was taken on board and cared for, after one of the most perilous adventures on record.

The blowing-up of the "Albemarle" was a very gallant achievement. It was done in the face of almost insurmountable obstacles, for, as we have shown, the enemy had taken every precaution against just such an attempt as was made. Here was a chance, and Cushing seized it. He would undoubtedly have made the attempt if he had had to run the gauntlet of the picket-firing all the way to Plymouth.

Cushing himself did not know when he arrived on board the "Valley City" who had been captured and who had escaped; but the following list from a report he subsequently prepared gives the names of the gallant fellows who risked their lives to dispose of an iron-clad that threatened the destruction of all the vessels in the Sounds of North Carolina:

"William B. Cushing, Lieutenant, commanding expedition, escaped; William L. Howarth, Acting-Master's Mate, picket-boat, missing; William Stotesbury, Acting-Third-Assistant Engineer, picket-boat, missing; John Woodman, Acting-Master's Mate, U. S. S. 'Commodore Hull,' drowned; Thomas S. Gay, Acting Master's Mate, U. S. S. 'Otsego,' missing; Charles S. Heener, Acting-Third-Assistant Engineer, U. S. S. 'Otsego,' missing; Francis H. Swan, Acting-Assistant Paymaster, U. S. S. 'Otsego,' missing; Edward T. Horton, ordinary seaman, U. S. S. 'Chicopee,' escaped; Bernard Harley, ordinary seaman, U. S. S. 'Chicopee,' missing; William Smith, ordinary seaman, U. S. S. 'Chicopee,' missing; Richard Hamilton, coalheaver, U. S. S. 'Shamrock,' missing; R. H. King, landsman, picket boat, missing; —— Wilkes, landsman, picket-boat, missing; —— Demming, landsman, picket-boat, missing; Samuel Higgins, first-class fireman, picket-boat, drowned."

The bodies of Acting-Master's Mate Woodman and Fireman Higgins floated on shore near Plymouth, and it was a great satisfaction to know that only two of Cushing's comrades lost their lives in this desperate adventure.

We cannot hope to do justice to this remarkable episode in the naval history of the civil war. The narrative should be written in letters of gold on a tablet for the benefit of future ages; but we will here insert the official communication of the Secretary of the Navy to Lieutenant Cushing, after the latter's report had been forwarded by Admiral Porter to the Department:

NAVY DEPARTMENT, November 9, 1864.

SIR—Your report of October 30 has been received, announcing the destruction of the rebel iron-clad steamer "Albemarle," on the night of the 27th ultimo, at Plymouth, North Carolina.

When, last Summer, the Department selected you for this important and perilous undertaking, and sent you to Rear-Admiral Gregory, at New York, to make the necessary preparations, it left the details to yourself to perfect. To you and your brave comrades, therefore, belong the exclusive credit which attaches to this daring achievement. The destruction of so formidable a vessel, which had resisted the combined attack of a number of our steamers, is an important event touching our future naval and military operations. The judgment as well as the daring courage displayed would do honor to any officer, and redounds to the credit of one of twenty-one years of age.

On four previous occasions the Department has had the gratification of expressing its approbation of your conduct in the face of the enemy, and in each instance there was manifested by you the same heroic daring and innate love of perilous adventure, a mind determined to succeed, and not to be deterred by any apprehensions of defeat.

The Department has presented your name to the President for a vote of thanks, that you may be promoted one grade, and your comrades also shall receive recognition.

It gives me pleasure to recall the assurance you gave me, at the commencement of your active professional career, that you would prove yourself worthy of the confidence reposed in you, and of the service to which you were appointed. I trust you may be preserved through further trials; and it is for yourself to determine whether, after entering upon so auspicious a career, you shall, by careful study and self-discipline, be prepared for a wider sphere of usefulness on the call of your country.

Very respectfully, etc.,
GIDEON WELLES,
Secretary of the Navy.
LIEUTENANT W. B. CUSHING, U. S. N.,
Washington.

As soon as he heard of the sinking of the "Albemarle," Commander Macomb promptly prepared to carry out the orders of Admiral Porter, which directed that in case of the destruction of the ram he should proceed to recapture Plymouth. For their part, the Confederates were not idle in preparing to resist the advance of the gun-boats, although their main dependence was now taken from them. They impeded the advance of the flotilla by sinking schooners in the channel under the guns of the fortifications.

On the 29th of October, 1864, the flotilla proceeded up the Roanoke River in the following order: "Commodore Hull," "Shamrock," "Chicopee," "Otsego," "Wyalusing" and "Tacony." At the same time the "Valley City" went up the "Middle River," which joined the Roanoke above Plymouth, in order to cut off any vessels the enemy might send in that direction.

At about noon Commander Macomb came within range and opened fire on the land batteries protecting Plymouth. The fire was promptly returned, but Macomb continued to advance until he was checked by the sunken vessels and exposed to the fire of the enemy's heavy guns protected by earth-works. Present advance was out of the question, and signal was made for the vessels to retire down the river. In the

44

meantime the commanding officer of the "Valley City," hearing the firing cease, concluded that the Federal vessels had won the day, and ran down towards Plymouth, when, fire being opened on his vessel, he also returned to the Sound.

Thus far the expedition was a failure. Something must be done, and from the reports of the "Valley City," and a reconnoissance made by Lieutenant-Commander Earl English in a boat, it was found that there was plenty of water in the channel of "Middle River," and that any of the vessels could turn the bends with the assistance of a tug. This would enable Macomb to come out into the Roanoke River, above Plymouth, a contingency which the Confederates had not provided against.

The flotilla accordingly again got underway to try the new channel, Commander

LIEUTENANT-COMMANDER (NOW COMMODORE) WILLIAM T. TRUXTUN,

COMMANDING THE "TACONY."

Macomb in the "Shamrock" following the tug "Bazley," Acting-Ensign M. D. Ames, having on board the pilot of the "Wyalusing;" next came the "Otsego," Lieutenant-Commander H. N. T. Arnold; "Wyalusing," Lieutenant-Commander Earl English; "Tacony," Lieutenant-Commander Wm. T. Truxtun; "Commodore Hull," Acting-Master Francis Josselyn, in the order named. Owing to the skill of the pilot, Acting-Master Alfred Everett, the vessels, with a great deal of hard work, succeeded in entering Roanoke River at 4 P. M., with the exception of the "Commodore Hull," which remained in "Middle River" to prevent the enemy from laying torpedoes there, in case the vessels should be obliged to return that way.

When the flotilla got near Plymouth the vessels commenced shelling the enemy's works, which was the first intimation the Confederates had of the approach of the Federal forces from this unexpected direction. As it was now late in the day, it was not deemed judicious to make a serious attack in the dark, but the vessels dropped close enough to the town to keep up a fire and command the channel, so that no torpedoes could be planted.

Next morning, the "Commodore Hull" joined the flotilla, and at 9 A. M. the attack was made in close order. The Confederates kept up a heavy fire, particularly on the "Commodore Hull" and the "Shamrock"; but as the vessels neared the batteries the order was given, "Go ahead at full speed!" so that the flotilla was soon pouring in a shower of grape and canister, which drove the artillerists from their guns and cleared the rifle-pits of sharp-shooters. In ten minutes time the victory was complete, and Plymouth was once more in Union hands. One battery still held out, but a shell from the "Shamrock" exploding in the magazine, the fort blew up, some of the fragments falling on the decks of the steamers. The explosion caused a panic among the Confederates, who ceased firing and fled in all directions.

The Union forces were landed and took possession of the batteries without resistance. Never was victory more complete, and the news was transmitted by Rear-Admiral Porter to the Navy Department in the following dispatch:

UNITED STATES FLAG-SHIP "MALVERN,"
HAMPTON ROADS November 11, 1864.
SIR—I have the honor to inclose you the report of Commander William H. Macomb, in relation to the capture of the batteries and the town of Plymouth, North Carolina, which place with all its defences was captured from our land forces some time last spring.

This was a very gallant affair, and reflects great credit on the commander of the expedition and all concerned. It is a handsome finishing stroke after the blowing up of the ram.

The fruits of this capture are twenty-two cannon, thirty-seven prisoners, two hundred stand of arms, and more being picked up daily.

The flags of the forts and of the "Albemarle" and a large amount of amunition were also taken.

I am sir, respectfully, etc.,
DAVID D. PORTER,
Rear-Admiral.
HON. GIDEON WELLES,
Secretary of the Navy.

This recapture of Plymouth was an important event, as both sides had been contending for its possession ever since the Federal forces gained a foothold in the Sounds of North Carolina. The place had been strongly fortified and armed with 9-inch navy guns, with the expectation that the Federals would hold it indefinitely; but the appearance of the "Albemarle" and her subsequent successs demoralized the garrison, and the Confederates were enabled to reoccupy the works.

Plymouth was not far distant from important lines of railway, and with an adequate force of Federal troops maintained at this point they would have been in constant danger. It completely commanded in both directions the Roanoke River, on which the Confederates built several ironclad floating batteries, including the "Albemarle." Had the channel above the town been obstructed and planted with torpedoes, the "Albemarle" would never have reached Plymouth. The troops, however, rested in fancied security, relying on the gun-boats to deal with the enemy's vessels, and those on board the flotilla felt willing and able to contend with any force the Confederates might send against them.

Three heavy forts armed with twenty guns, besides the ram "Albemarle," which lay sunk at the wharf, were captured in less than an hour by a very inadequate force of vessels, and a large body of the enemy's troops were driven precipitately from the town. This was an achievement of which every officer and man in the flotilla might well be proud, for the batteries of Plymouth were manned by as good soldiers as could be found in the Confederacy ; but the sudden dash of the steamers disconcerted their aim, and the grape, canister, and shrapnel falling in their ranks from the distance of only a few yards were too much for human nature to resist.

The "Commodore Hull," Acting-Master Josselyn, was very much cut up by the enemy's shot, and lost four men killed and three wounded. She was exposed to the fire of the enemy's heavy guns, and, as she neared the batteries, a heavy fire of musketry was poured in from the rifle-pits. A shell from a 9-inch gun came in on the starboard bow, killing one man and mortally wounding another, and three others slightly at the forward gun, passed through the berth-deck and ward-room, cut away the railing around the after-hatch, struck the after-port gun-carriage, where it lodged, and disabled the gun. That was good work for a single shell which did not explode. Another shell passed through the vessel from stem to stern, knocking the officers' quarters to pieces, but doing no further damage. A third shell, in passing over the hurricane-deck, cut away part of the woodwork on the port side and knocked out the bows of the second cutter. The upper works of the vessel were considerably shattered and the frame much racked by the firing and the explosion of a magazine on shore. This vessel was one of those frail craft of which we have so often spoken, in which so much was dared and done.

Lieutenant-Commander English, in the "Wyalusing," had the forethought, when the enemy began to retreat, to cover the road by which they were moving off with his guns and kept up a rapid fire with bursting shell, which caused the Confederates to throw away their arms and accoutrements, many of which were picked up. Acting-Master Mr. R. Hathaway and Acting-Ensign Foster, of the "Wyalusing," were the first to enter Fort Williams, one of the strongest works, where they planted the Union colors and captured three prisoners.

The "Shamrock," Commander Macomb's vessel, was struck six times by shot and shell, most of the enemy's projectiles passing over her. Two of her men were killed and seven wounded. These, with the killed and wounded on board the "Commodore Hull," were the only casualties on the flotilla, which was remarkable, considering the number of heavy guns the Confederates had in position, and the large number of sharp-shooters in rifle-pits.

All the commanding officers of vessels spoke in the highest terms of the conduct of those under their command. Commander Macomb did not neglect to bring to the notice of the Navy Department the commanding officers who had so well sustained him on that day, 31st October, 1864. He recommended them all for the promotion they so justly deserved for a victory gained over a superior force, with a dash that must always excite admiration; but the victory was not appreciated in Washington, and the only official notice of it was a short letter from the Secretary of the Navy, commending the officers and men, and informing Commander Macomb that he would be recommended to the President for advancement ten numbers in his grade. The cases of the commanding officers of the vessels were afterwards considered by a Board of Admirals convened at Washington to apportion the rewards to be given for those who had distinguished themselves in battle; but the Board was limited to the petty figure of thirty numbers as the maximum of advancement for the most gallant exploit.

The patience of the Navy Department and of the commander-in-chief of the large fleet lying in Hampton Roads began to be severely tried by the delay in the appearance of the troops for the combined attack on Fort Fisher. The Secretary of the Navy was apprehensive that he would have to disperse the vessels to other points, whence they had been taken for this expedition, and where their absence had been greatly felt. The delay and the great expense attending it annoyed Mr. Welles so much that he appealed to the President in the hope of accelerating the shipment of the troops, saying, in his letter to Mr. Lincoln, that

"Every other squadron had been depleted and vessels detached from other duty to strengthen this expedition. The vessels are concentrated at Hampton Roads and Beaufort, where they remain, an immense force, lying idle, awaiting the movements of the army. The detention of so many vessels from blockade and cruising duty is a most serious injury to the public service, and, if the expedition cannot go forward for want of troops, I desire to be notified so that the ships may be relieved and dispersed for other service.

"The importance of closing Wilmington is so well understood by you, that I refrain from presenting any new arguments. I am aware of the anxiety of yourself and of the disposition of the War Department to render all the aid in its power. The cause of the delay is not from the want of a proper conception of the importance of the subject, but the season for naval coast operations will soon be gone.

"General Bragg has been sent from Richmond to Wilmington to prepare for the attack, and the autumn weather so favorable for such an expedition is passing away. The public expect this attack, and the country will be distressed if it is not made. To procrastinate much longer will be to peril its success. Of the obstacles which delay, or prevent military operations at once, I cannot judge; but the delay is becoming exceedingly embarrassing to this department, and the importance of having the military authorities impressed with the necessity of speedy action has prompted this communication to you."

Nothwithstanding this urgent appeal from Mr. Welles to the President, a copy of which was sent to General Grant, there was still delay in furnishing the military forces required. It could not have been for want of troops in General Butler's command, for he occupied a strong position, backed by a large force of gun-boats, with a bridge of boats across the James, by which he could retreat, if he thought necessary, with entire safety under cover of the Navy guns. We are, therefore, forced to the conclusion that the only reason for the contingent of troops destined to co-operate in the attack on Fort Fisher not appearing in Hampton Roads, was that General Butler had determined they should not move until it suited his convenience. At that time the Confederates were so closed up in Richmond that they could make no important demonstration on the Federal lines without getting severely handled, as the different divisions of the Union Army were within supporting distance of each other. There was, then, some motive in the delay of the expedition to Fort Fisher which does not seem consistent with patriotism.

Mr. Secretary Welles had shown the greatest patience and persistence all through this affair, and it was owing to the exercise of these qualities that the expedition was finally enabled to get off. General Butler was at last forced to take some steps to show that he was not setting at defiance the orders received from General Grant early in October. Accordingly, accompanied by General Weitzel and his personal staff, General Butler went on board the flag-ship "Malvern" at Hampton Roads, and communicated to Rear-Admiral Porter a plan for the destruction of Fort Fisher, the idea having, it seems, been suggested by the explosion of a canal-boat loaded with powder at Eric on the Thames, by which a large amount of property had been destroyed. General Butler's idea was that one hundred and fifty tons of powder confined on board a vessel and exploded within a short distance of Fort Fisher would inflict immense damage on the enemy, and he promised, if the powder-boat was prepared, he would detail the necessary troops and have them embarked as soon as possible.

Any expedient that would get the expedition off was hailed with delight by the Rear-Admiral commanding, who agreed to Butler's proposition, notwithstanding he had little faith in the project; though, strange to say, the General had met with encouragement from scientific men to whom he had disclosed his scheme. It was considered advisable to try almost any expedient, and the Navy Department did not, therefore, refuse to countenance General Butler's plan; although, as the General was then a power in the land, it would, perhaps, have favored ideas still more absurd emanating from that quarter. An officer who could disobey the orders of his immediate commander-in-chief for months, delay a large fleet assembled at infinite cost and pains to deal a final blow to the Confederacy, and finally assume command of an expedition assigned to another General, all without rebuke from headquarters, must have had immense influence. All men seemed afraid of Butler's political power: it was even potential with the President and Secretary of War, although, in justice to Mr. Secretary Welles, we must say, it had much less weight with him.

It was towards the last of November when General Butler unfolded his plan of a powder-boat, and it took some days to make all the necessary preparations to get the great torpedo ready. The steamer "Louisiana," a vessel of little value, was selected for the service, and sent from Newbern to Hampton Roads, where the immense mass of powder required was collected from the Army and Navy magazines, and carefully stowed on board in bags. To Commander A. C. Rhind, a gallant officer, who had on more than one occasion shown the coolness in the face of danger so necessary for such a perilous duty, was assigned the charge of the powder-vessel. Commander Rhind did everything possible with the means at hand to render the explosion successful.

By the time the "Louisiana" was prepared, General Butler had so identified himself with the expedition that it was evident to all who knew him that he proposed to command the troops in person, for he was not wont to take so much trouble for any one else. General Grant probably did not know the extent of Butler's interference with the expedition, or else attributed his action to zeal for its success. It is not likely that he supposed that one of his generals would withhold orders that he had issued to a subordinate to command the troops, although it may be that even Grant felt the weight of that political power which oppressed every one who came within its influence. As soon as Butler had succeeded in gaining a secure footing in the expedition, he was all anxiety to embark his soldiers, notwithstanding there was every appearance of a gale coming on and the powder-boat was not ready. Without proper preparation, the troops were hurried into the transports, with but a few days' rations and a scant supply of water. The gale came on and the poor soldiers, cooped up in their narrow, uncomfortable quarters, were quite worn out before the expedition sailed. Fortunately, after a few days of wind and rain, the weather cleared up and the transports sailed from Hampton Roads on the 16th of December, 1864.

Up to this time there had been no *official* notice that General Butler would go on the expedition. General Grant several times went on board the "Malvern" for the purpose, no doubt, of talking the matter over with Admiral Porter, but he would scarcely put his foot on board ere General Butler would make his appearance. Butler's presence was always enough to make General Grant quiet and meditative, and he soon took his departure. General Weitzel generally accompanied General Butler on his visits to the flag-ship, but he was as taciturn as Grant, and apparently was uncertain whether he was to have command of the troops in the expedition or not. When asked one day by Lieutenant-Commander K. R. Breese, the Fleet-Captain, what were General Butler's plans, Weitzel replied that he didn't believe Butler had any, which was the general impression.

Now, here was an expedition in which it was absolutely necessary that the utmost harmony and concert of action should exist between the commanding officers; but, although Admiral Porter did his best to obtain from General Butler some statement of his intentions, he never succeeded in the attempt. Butler was furnished with copies of the Admiral's written orders to his fleet, but he sent none in return, and merely notified the Admiral that his transports would assemble off Masonboro' Inlet, thirty miles from Wilmington, where, if one of his vessels showed herself, the destination of the expedition would be immediately known to the enemy.

There was never a more beautiful day for a fleet to sail than the one on which the expedition left Hampton Roads. The Monitors had to stop at Beaufort, N. C., to coal and receive their ammunition; for now that the expedition had waited two months there was no particular hurry, and the Confederates had by this time learned the particulars of the expedition, and were prepared, as they thought, to defeat it.

Many combined operations in different parts of the world have failed from want of concert between the Army and the Navy, but none of Grant's or Sherman's operations were endangered by this cause, owing to the harmony with which the two branches of the service acted together; and both those distinguished officers were careful to express their wishes in such a way as to be agreeable to all concerned. General Butler could never be made to understand what was due to an officer of another branch of the service, hence he was frequently involving himself in difficulties with navy, and indeed with army, officers.

Neither Butler nor Weitzel were adapted to command the troops in such an expedition as that to Fort Fisher. Grant discovered this fact later in the season; but it was known in the Navy from the beginning, and the Admiral felt the need of all his good fortune to carry him safely through the ordeal. The latter remained in Hampton Roads until the last transport had started and got underway the same evening, General Butler, in his "flag-ship," remaining at the dock. That night, the General, in his fast steamer, got ahead of the fleet, and took his station, with his transports, off Masonboro' Inlet.

In the meantime, Admiral Porter had put into Beaufort, N. C., to give another look at the fittings of the powder-boat, for he determined to do everything to make the latter experiment a success, even although he knew it was all folly. When all was ready, the Admiral proceeded to the rendezvous off the entrance to Cape Fear River.

The fleet anchored off Fort Fisher, twenty miles from shore, in twenty-five fathoms water. General Butler and his transports were at anchor off Masonboro' Inlet, quite out of sight of the naval vessels. The Admiral wrote to the General that he should send the powder-boat in and explode her on the 18th of December, after which he should attack the enemy's works. It was intimated to the General that, as the explosion would be in the nature of an earthquake, it would be prudent for him to move at least twenty miles from the scene and let his vessel's steam run down! In order to make assurance doubly sure, the General retired to

Beaufort, sixty miles from the scene of action, and there awaited the dreadful crash.

Fort Fisher and dependencies were an immense series of works, more than a mile in length, constructed of bags filled with sand, the result of immense labor from the very beginning of the civil war, and the best engineering talent in the Confederate Army. It was believed by the Confederates that this work was sufficient to repel any force of ships that might be brought against it or might attempt to pass the batteries. The latter operation was, in fact, impossible, as there was but nine feet of water on the bar of Cape Fear River at ordinary tides. The channel was tortuous, and the bar generally covered with heavy breakers, except when the wind blew from the northwest.

Fort Fisher consisted of two lines of works at right angles with each other. The land-front ran across the sandy peninsula, which was here about half a mile in width, and mounted seventeen heavy guns, bearing north, to prevent an attacking force from advancing in that direction. These guns were practically protected from a seaward fire by heavy bomb-proof casemates, with capacity for sheltering four or five thousand men. The sea-front extended from the great battery at the angle of the two faces, along the beach to the southward, a distance of over three-quarters of a mile, and was terminated by a huge erection eighty feet in height, known as the "Mound Battery." This was probably intended to command the interior of Fort Fisher, should the enemy gain a footing there; while the garrison taking shelter in the bomb-proofs could resist an enemy for a long time from those retreats. On the sea-face of the work were mounted fifty-four heavy guns protected by traverses against an enfilading fire, and some of these traverses were also bomb-proof. In the Mound Battery were three or four 150-pounder Brooke rifles, making the total number of guns in this formidable work seventy-five.

The sea-front was intended to prevent the enemy's vessels from running through New Inlet into Cape Fear River, or landing troops on Federal Point—an unnecessary precaution, since nature had placed greater obstacles to vessels of any size crossing the bar, in the shape of shoal water. One mile westward of the Mound Battery, at the end of Federal Point, was a heavy-armed earth-work mounting six or eight 11-inch Dahlgren guns, fitted exactly as if on the deck of a ship. This was Fort Buchanan, and it was officered and manned from the Confederate Navy. It commanded the channel and a shoal called the "Rips," over which no vessel drawing more than eleven feet could pass at high water. This

is a general sketch of Fort Fisher. The details were similar to those of other fortifications of this kind.

It was the evident intention of the Confederates to prevent a landing of the Federal troops or to dislodge them as soon as they reached the shore, which might have been done had not a large force of gunboats been sent to cover the landing, a force which no army could have withstood.

At the time when the fleet arrived off Fort Fisher, the Confederates had about eighteen hundred men in the works, but they were by no means the best of troops. The commanding officer of the fort was Colonel William Lamb, a gallant and capable soldier, while Major-General Wm. H.

LIEUTENANT-COMMANDER K. RANDOLPH BREESE.
(FLEET-CAPTAIN.)

C. Whiting, formerly of the U. S. Engineers, commanded all the defences of the Cape Fear River.

When the fleet was all ready to proceed to the attack, Commander Rhind was ordered to take the powder-boat in and explode her. It had been calm all that day, December 18, with only a light swell on, which increased at night. Fleet-Captain K. R. Breese was sent on board General Butler's vessel to inform the General what was to be done, and that the troops might be landed in the morning for the attack. The General sent word to the Admiral that he thought the attempt premature, and requested that it be postponed until the sea went down. To this Admiral Porter at once agreed, yet General Butler afterwards complained of the delay, grounding his failure on that circumstance. It was just as well that the attempt was not made on the day appointed, for, on the following morning, a heavy gale came on from the southeast with a tremendous swell setting towards the beach, so that it was thought at one time all the vessels would have to leave the coast to avoid being driven on shore. General Butler and his transports had disappeared and sought refuge in the harbor of Beaufort.

No occurrence during the war reflects more credit on the Navy than the way in which that large fleet rode out the gale, anchored in twenty fathoms water, with the whole Atlantic Ocean rolling in upon them. As far as the eye could reach, the line of vessels extended, each with two anchors ahead and one hundred and twenty fathoms of chain on each. The wind blew directly on shore, the sea breaking heavily, and appearing as if it would sweep everything before it, yet only one vessel in all the line left her anchorage and stood out to sea as a place of safety. It was, indeed, a grand sight to see these ships riding out such a gale on such a coast in midwinter. The most experienced seaman will long remember the event as the only case on record where a large fleet rode out a gale at anchor on our coast. It was one of the features of this memorable expedition in the highest degree creditable to the seamanship of the Federal Navy.

After the gale abated, the Rear-Admiral commanding the fleet looked around in the hope of seeing something of General Butler's command, for, knowing that the wind would come out from the northwest, and blow the sea down, he wished to take advantage of the circumstance and commence the attack. As nothing was heard of the General, the Admiral made arrangements, which will appear in the reports of operations annexed.

We have noticed that the explosion of the powder-boat was postponed at the request of General Butler, after Commander Rhind had started to carry out the order to blow the vessel up. The peril of this service was very great, for it was certain that the Confederates had been fully apprised that a powder-vessel was being fitted to explode under the walls of Fort Fisher. It was therefore to be expected that the enemy would maintain a vigilant look-out, and when, through their night-glasses, an object was seen approaching the fort, they would open with shells and blow up the vessel and all on board if they could. Or a mistake might occur in the timing of the Gomer fuse, or in the clock that was to ignite the powder at a given moment, so as to allow the adventurous party on board the "Louisiana" time enough to get well clear of the vessel. There was more than one chance of a premature

explosion. Besides these dangers, there was in the smoothest weather a heavy ground-swell on the beach where the "Louisiana" was to be anchored, and the rolling motion might easily disarrange the intricate machinery designed for the explosion of the powder. To risk so many valuable lives of officers and men seemed almost a crime—the game was not worth the candle—and this useless powder-boat excited more anxiety in the fleet on account of those who had volunteered for so hazardous an expedition than for the expected attack on Fort Fisher.

The officers and men who volunteered to go with Commander Rhind—himself a volunteer—were Lieutenant Samuel W. Preston of the Admiral's staff, Second-Assistant Engineer A. T. E. Mullan, Master's Mate Paul Boyden; Frank Lucas, Coxswain; William Gainn, Captain-of-the-Forecastle; Charles T. Bibber, Gunner's Mate; John Neil, Quarter-Gunner; Robert Montgomery, Captain-of-the-Afterguard; James Roberts and Dennis Conlan, Seamen; James Sullivan, Ordinary Seaman; William Horrigan, Second-class Fireman; Charles Rice, Coal-heaver. The men were all volunteers from Commander Rhind's vessel, the "Agawam."

General Butler had been again notified that the powder-boat would be exploded on the night of the 23d December, as near the beach at Fort Fisher as it was possible to get her, but the exact distance could not be estimated in the darkness. Although the "Louisiana" had low steam up, she was towed to within a short distance of her station by the steamer "Wilderness," which vessel then remained in the vicinity to take off the party from the powder-boat. The arrangements of the "Wilderness" were under the direction of Lieutenant R. H. Lamson, assisted by Mr. J. O. Bradford of the Coast Survey, and Acting-Master Geo. F. Bowen (Pilot). The "Wilderness" was under the command of Acting-Master Henry Arey, and he and his officers and men shared with the others the danger attending the enterprise.

The powder-boat was finally anchored as near the beach as possible—a somewhat difficult task, as by approaching too near the breakers the vessel would be liable to drift on shore. Commander Rhind and Lieutenant Preston then lighted the candles, while the fire of pine-knots in the "Louisiana's" cabin was started by Engineer Mullan. Commander Rhind was then obliged to let go another anchor with a short scope of chain, as he saw that the vessel would not tail in shore. This done, the party jumped into their boats, and pulled for the "Wilderness," which vessel had steamed off shore a considerable distance, and then let her steam go down, as it was supposed that the concussion would seriously affect the boilers if a high pressure of steam was maintained.

The fuzes were set by the clocks to one hour and a half, but the explosion did not take place until twenty minutes after the expected time, when the after-part of the "Louisiana" was in flames. Exactly at 1:30 A. M. of the 24th, the powder-boat went up in the air, the shock being scarcely felt by the vessels of the fleet. For a moment the scene was illuminated, then darkness settled down, and all was still as before—no sound or movement in the fort indicating that any damage had been done. In fact, the Confederates took the explosion for that of a blockade-runner with a quantity of ammunition on board, and were not at all troubled about the matter.

When, after the lapse of twenty years, we think of this futile attempt to destroy such a powerful work as Fort Fisher at the risk of so many valuable lives, in order that the pet scheme of a Major-General of Volunteers should be carried out, we may wonder that any one should countenance such an absurdity. The only powder that was needed was that fired from the cannon of the ships, and what would have been fired from the muskets of the gallant soldiers had they been permitted by their commanding general to advance on the enemy. But these experiences will teach the soldiers and sailors of the future; and if there is ever a scheme proposed for blowing up a huge earth-work with a powder-boat, the recollection of Fort Fisher will deter people from attempting to carry it out.

It was supposed by Admiral Porter that the explosion would be heard on board the transports and bring them all in by morning; but, although the water was quite smooth, the transports seemed to keep as far as possible from Fort Fisher.

Agreeably to the orders issued the preceding evening, the fleet got underway at daylight on the 24th of December, 1864, and stood in, in line of battle. At 11:30 A. M. the signal was made to engage the forts, the "Ironsides" leading, and the "Monadnock," "Canonicus" and "Mahopac" following. The "Ironsides" took her position in the most beautiful and seamanlike manner, got her spring out, and opened deliberate fire on the fort, at that time opening on her with all its guns, which did not seem numerous in the northeast face, though what appeared to be seventeen guns were counted. These were fired from that direction, but they were silenced almost as soon as the fleet opened all their batteries.

The "Minnesota" took her position in handsome style, and her guns, after getting the range, were fired with rapidity; while the "Mohican," "Colorado" and the large vessels marked on the plan, got to their stations, all firing to cover themselves while anchoring. By the time the last of the large vessels anchored and got their batteries into play, but a few guns of the enemy were fired, this *feu d'enfer* driving them all to their bomb-proofs.

The small gun-boats "Kansas," "Unadilla," "Pequot," "Seneca," "Pontoosuc," "Yantic" and "Huron" took positions to the northward and eastward of the Monitors, enfilading the works. The "Shenandoah," Ticonderoga," "Mackinaw," "Tacony" and "Vanderbilt" took effective positions, as marked on the chart, and added their fire to that already begun. The "Santiago de Cuba," Fort Jackson," "Osceola," "Chippewa," "Sassacus," "Rhode Island," "Monticello," "Quaker City" and "Iosco," dropped into position according to order, and the battle became general.

In an hour and a quarter after the first shot was fired, not a shot came from the fort. Two of the magazines in the works had been blown up by shells, and the wood-work in the fort set on fire in several places; and such a torrent of missiles were falling into and bursting over the works, that it was impossible for anything human to withstand it. Finding that the batteries were completely silenced, the ships were directed to keep up a moderate fire, in hopes of attracting the attention of the transports and bringing them to the scene of action. At sunset General Butler came in with a few transports, the rest not having arrived from Beaufort. As it was too late to do anything more, the fleet was signalled to retire for the night to a safe anchorage, which movement took place without molestation from the enemy.

Some mistakes were made this day when the vessels went in to take position, although, the plan of battle being based on accurate calculation and reliable information, it seemed almost impossible to go astray. Those vessels that had not followed the plan of battle closely were required to get underway and assume their proper positions, which was done promptly and without confusion. The vessels were placed somewhat nearer to the works, and were able to throw in their shells, which were before falling short.

One or two leading vessels having anchored too far off shore, caused those coming after them to make a like error; but when they all got into place and commenced work in earnest, the shower of shell—one hundred and fifteen per minute—was irresistible. So quickly were the enemy's guns silenced that not an officer or man in the fleet was injured by them, but there were some severe casualties by the bursting of several 100-pounder Parrott cannon. One burst on board the "Ticonderoga," killing six of the crew and wounding seven others; another burst on board the "Yantic," killing one officer and two men; another on board the "Juniata," killing two officers, and killing and wounding ten other persons; another on board the "Mackinaw," killing one officer and wounding five men; another on board the "Quaker City," wounding two or three persons. The bursting of these guns much disconcerted the crews of the vessels, and gave them great distrust of the Parrott 100-pounder.

Some of the vessels were struck once or twice from the fort. The "Mackinaw" had her boiler perforated with a shell, and

LIEUTENANT-COMMANDER (NOW REAR-ADMIRAL) JOHN LEE DAVIS.

ten or twelve persons were badly scalded. The "Osceola" was struck with a shell near her magazine, and was at one time in a sinking condition, but her efficient commander stopped the leak, while the "Mackinaw" fought out the battle, notwithstanding the damage she had received. Only one vessel left the line to report damages.

Commander John Guest, in the "Iosco," at the east end of the line, showed his usual intelligence in selecting his position and directing his fire. Twice his shot cut away the flag-staff on the Mound Battery, and he silenced the guns there in a very short time, the "Keystone State" and "Quaker City" co-operating effectively.

Lieutenant-Commander John L. Davis in the "Sassacus," with both rudders of his

vessel disabled, got her into close action and assisted materially in silencing the works, and the "Santiago de Cuba" and "Fort Jackson" took such positions as they could get, owing to other vessels not forming proper lines and throwing them out of place, and fought their guns well. The taking of a new position while under fire by the "Brooklyn" and "Colorado" was well done, and when they got into place both ships delivered a fire that nothing could withstand. The "Brooklyn" well sustained her good name under her commanding officer, Captain James Alden, and the "Colorado" gave evidence that Commodore H. K. Thatcher fully understood the duties of his position. The "Susquehanna" was most effective in her fire, though much hampered by a vessel near her that had not found her right place. The "Mohican" went into battle gallantly and fired rapidly and with effect; and when the "Powhatan," "Ticonderoga" and "Shenandoah" got into their positions, they did good service. The "Pawtucket" fell handsomely into line, and did good service with the rest, and the "Vanderbilt" took her place near the "Minnesota" and threw in a rapid fire. The firing of the Monitors was excellent, and when their shells struck great damage was done, and the little gun-boats that covered them kept up a fire sufficient to disconcert the enemy's aim.

The Confederates fired no more after the vessels all opened on them, except a few shots from the Mound and upper batteries, which the "Iosco" and consorts soon silenced.

The men were at work at the guns five hours and were glad to get a little rest. They came out of action with rather a contempt for the enemy's batteries, and anxious to renew the battle in the morning.

On Christmas Day all the transports had arrived, and General Butler sent General Weitzel to see Admiral Porter, and arrange the programme for the day. It was decided that the Navy should again attack the works, while the Army should land and assault them, if possible, under the heavy fire of the ships. The Admiral dispatched seventeen gun-boats, under command of Captain O. S. Glisson, to cover the troops and assist with their boats in landing the soldiers. Finding the smaller vessels kept too far from the beach, which was quite bold, the "Brooklyn" was sent in to carry out the Admiral's orders. To the number before sent were added all the small vessels that were acting as reserves; and, finally, there were sent some eight or nine vessels that were acting under Commander Guest in endeavoring to find a way across the bar. This gave a hundred boats with which to land the troops, in addition to the twenty with which the army was already provided.

At 7 A. M., on the 25th, signal was made for the ships to get underway and form in line of battle, which was quickly done. The order to attack was given, and the "Ironsides" took the position in her usual handsome style, the Monitors following close after her. All the vessels followed according to order, and took position without a shot being fired at them, excepting a few fired at the last four vessels that got into line. The firing this day was slow, only sufficient to distract the enemy's attention while the army landed, which they were doing five miles northward of the fleet.

About three thousand men had landed, when the Admiral was notified they were re-embarking. He had seen the soldiers near the forts reconnoitering and sharp-shooting, and was in hopes an assault was deemed practicable. General Weitzel, in person, was making observations about six hundred yards off, and the troops were in and around the works. One gallant officer went on the parapet and brought away the Confederate flag that had been shot down by the Navy fire; a soldier went into the works and led out a horse, killing the orderly mounted on the animal and capturing his dispatches. Another soldier fired his musket into a bomb-proof among the Confederates, and eight or ten others who had ventured near the forts were wounded by shells from the fleet.

As the ammunition gave out, the vessels retired from action, and the iron-clads "Minnesota," "Colorado" and "Susquehanna" were ordered to open rapidly, which they did with such effect that it seemed to tear the works to pieces. The fleet drew off at sunset, leaving the iron-clads to fire through the night, expecting the troops would attack in the morning, when the ships would recommence the bombardment. The Admiral, however, received a message from General Weitzel, informing him that it was impracticable to assault; and later a letter from General Butler, assigning his reasons for withdrawing his troops; which letter, together with the Admiral's answer to the same, we shall insert in full.

In the bombardment of the 25th, the fleet fired slowly for seven hours. The enemy kept a couple of guns on the upper batteries firing on the vessels, hitting some of them several times without doing them much damage. The "Wabash" and the "Powhatan," being within their range, the object seemed mainly to disable them, but a rapid fire soon silenced the Confederate guns. Everything was coolly and systematically done throughout the day, and there was some beautiful practice.

The army commenced landing about 2 o'clock, Captain Glisson, in the "Santiago de Cuba," having shelled Flag-Pond battery to insure a safe landing, and they commenced to re-embark about 5 o'clock, the weather coming on thick and rainy. About a brigade were left on the beach during the night, covered by the gun-boats. As the troops landed, sixty-five Confederate soldiers hoisted the white flag, and delivered themselves up to the seamen landing the troops, and were conveyed to the "Santiago de Cuba." Two hundred and eighteen more gave themselves up to the reconnoitering party, all being tired of the war. We do not pretend to put our opinion in opposition to General Weitzel, whose business it was to know more of assaulting forts than a sailor could know; but we cannot help thinking that it was worth while to make the attempt after coming so far.

About noon the Admiral sent in a detachment of double-enders under Commander John Guest, to see if an entrance through the channel could be effected. The great number of wrecks in and about the bar had changed the whole formation, and where the original channel had been, Guest found a shallow bar.

The Admiral then sent Lieutenant W. B. Cushing in to sound and buoy out a channel, if he could find one, with orders for Commander Guest to drag for torpedoes and be ready to run in by the buoys when directed. A very narrow and crooked channel was partly made out and buoyed, but running so close to the upper forts that boats could not work there. Lieutenant Cushing, in his boat, went in as far as Zeke's Island, but his researches would not justify attempting the passage with six double-enders, some of which had burst their rifled Parrott guns and injured many of their men.

One boat belonging to the "Tacony" was sunk by a shell, and a man had his leg cut off; still, they stuck to their work until ordered to withdraw for other duty.

At the conclusion of his report to the Secretary of the Navy, Rear-Admiral Porter makes the following remarks:

"Allow me to draw your attention to the conduct of Commander Rhind and Lieutenant Preston. They engaged in the most perilous adventure that was, perhaps, ever undertaken; and, though no material results have taken place from the effects of the explosion that we know of, still it was not their fault. As an incentive to others, I beg leave to recommend them for promotion; also that of Lieutenant R. H. Lamson, who piloted them in and brought them off. No one in the squadron considered that their lives would be saved, and Commander Rhind and Lieutenant Preston had made an arrangement to sacrifice themselves in case the vessel was boarded—a thing likely to happen.

"I inclose herewith the report of Commander Rhind, with the names of the gallant fellows who volunteered for this desperate service. Allow me also to mention the name of Mr. Bradford, of the Coast Survey, who went in and sounded out the place where the 'Louisiana' was to go in, and has always patiently performed every duty that he has been called on to carry out.

"My thanks are due to Lieutenant-Commander K. R. Breese, Fleet-Captain, for carrying about my orders to the fleet during the action, and for his general usefulness; to Lieutenant-Commander H. A. Adams, for his promptness in supplying the fleet with ammunition. Lieutenant M. W. Sanders, Signal-Officer, whose whole time was occupied in making signals, performed his duty well, and my aides, Lieutenant S. W. Terry and Lieutenant S. W. Preston, afforded me valuable assistance.

"I have not yet received a list of the casualties, but believe they are very few, from the enemy's guns. We had killed, and wounded, about forty-five persons by the bursting of the Parrott guns. I beg leave to suggest that no more of these guns be introduced into the service. There is only one kind of firing that is effective at close quarters, that is, from 9, 10 and 11 inch guns, they cannot be equalled.

"Until further orders, I shall go on and hammer away at the fort, hoping that in time the people in it will get tired, and hand it over to us. It is a one-sided business altogether, and in the course of time we must dismount their guns, if, as General Weitzel says, we cannot 'injure it as a defensive work.' The Government may also think it of sufficient importance to undertake more serious operations against these works.

"An army of a few thousand men investing it would soon get into it, with the aid of the Navy. When smooth water permits, I will go to work looking for a channel over the bar, which has not yet been found to my satisfaction.

"I must not omit to pay a tribute to the officers and crews of the Monitors—riding out heavy gales on an open coast without murmuring or complaining of the want of comfort, which must have been very serious. They have shown a degree of fortitude and perseverance seldom witnessed. Equally brave in battle, they take the closest work with pleasure, and the effect of their shells is terrific.

"The following are the names of the commanding officers, and I hope I shall keep them under my command: Commodore William Radford, commanding 'New Ironsides'; Commander E. S. Parrott, commanding 'Monadnock'; Commander E. R. Colhoun, commanding 'Saugus'; Lieutenant George E. Belknap, commanding 'Canonicus'; Lieutenant-Commander E. E. Potter, commanding 'Mahopac.'

"There are about one thousand men left on shore by the army who have not yet got off on account of the surf on the beach. These will be taken off in the morning, and the soldiers will then be sent home.

"I inclose general order for the attack."

REAR-ADMIRAL PORTER'S GENERAL ORDER NO. 70.

[GENERAL ORDERS NO. 70.]

NORTH ATLANTIC SQUADRON,
U. S. FLAG-SHIP "MALVERN,"
HAMPTON ROADS, December 10, 1864.

The chart plan of the proposed attack on the batteries of the enemy at New Inlet, mouth of Cape Fear River, will explain itself, but the order of taking position is as follows:

It is first proposed to endeavor to paralyze the garrison by an explosion, all the vessels remaining twelve miles out from the bar, and the troops in transports twelve miles down the coast, ready to steam up and be prepared to take the works by assault in case the latter are disabled.

At a given signal, all the bar vessels will run off shore twelve miles, when the vessel with powder will go in under the forts. When the explosion takes place, all the vessels will stand in shore in the order marked on the plan.

The "New Ironsides" will steam along shore, coming from eastward, until the flag-staff on Fort Fisher bears southwest by west-half-west, and anchor (chain ready to slip) with her broadside bearing on the largest of the enemy's works, and open fire without delay. The Monitors will come up astern, anchoring not more than one length apart, directly in line along the shore, leaving space only for a gun-boat to lie outside of them, and fire between them or over them. The "New Ironsides" and Monitors will lie in not less than three and a half fathoms water, which will place them about three-fourths of a mile from Fort Fisher, and a little over a quarter of a mile from the beach.

In the meantime, the large ships will lie formed in line of battle to the eastward of the iron-clads, and heading parallel with the land in a south-half-west course, in five fathoms water.

When the signal is made to "take position," the "Minnesota" (the headmost vessel) will go ahead slowly and anchor about a mile from Fort Fisher, opening fire the moment she passes the "New Ironsides," and anchoring so that her stern gun will fire just clear of that vessel. The "Mohican" will then anchor ahead of the "Minnesota," "Colorado" ahead of "Mohican," "Tuscarora" ahead of "Colorado," "Wabash" ahead of "Tuscarora," "Susquehanna" ahead of "Wabash," "Brooklyn" ahead of "Susquehanna," "Powhatan" ahead of "Brooklyn," "Juniata" ahead of "Powhatan," with their cables ready to slip, and with not more than fifteen fathoms of chain, the fifteen-fathom shackle inside the hawse-hole.

The "Seneca," "Shenandoah," "Pawtucket," "Ticonderoga," "Mackinaw," "Maumee," "Yantic" and "Kansas" will take their positions between and outside the different vessels, as marked on the plan, anchoring with their cables ready to slip.

When the large ships and intermediate ones get fairly into position, the "Nyack," "Unadilla," "Huron" and "Pequot" will take positions between and outside the Monitors, in the order marked on the plan, keeping up a rapid fire while the Monitors are loading.

The following vessels will next take their positions as marked on the plan.

Commencing with the "Fort Jackson," which vessel will anchor ahead of the "Juniata," leaving a space between of three lengths, "Santiago de Cuba," "Tacony," "Osceola," "Chippewa," "Sassacus," "Maratanza," "Rhode Island," "Monticello," "Mount Vernon," "Montgomery," "R. R. Cuyler," "Quaker City" and "Iosco" will pass on slowly, commencing with the rear, until they form the line marked on the plan.

The reserves of each division will form a line, as per plan, out of gun-shot, ready to act as occasion may require.

This is the main plan of the battle. Circumstances may require some deviation from it, such as a partial attack (before going seriously to work) to feel the enemy's strength, all of which will be regulated by signal or by orders. Great care and coolness will be required to drop the vessels in their right places, and a too-early commencement of fire on the part of those going into position may create confusion.

As we know but little about the calibre and number of rebel guns, the vessels must concentrate their fire on the heaviest batteries; but get the range before firing rapidly. For instance, the large vessels and iron-clads concentrate on Fort Fisher, while the "Vanderbilt," "Fort Jackson," and the vessels in the line with "Fort Jackson" will open on the forts within their reach between Fort Fisher and the Mound.

All the reserve vessels will prepare to attack Zeke's Island battery by taking a position where they can enfilade it, which is when the fort bears northwest. Vessels drawing fourteen feet can go within a mile and three-quarters with perfect safety, and use their rifle-guns with good effect. They can also reach the forts on Federal Point, and prevent their firing accurately on the other portions of the fleet in closer range.

All the movements of the different lines will be made by sending orders in a tug, as signals will not be seen in the smoke.

As it is desirable not to have superfluous directions, each commander will be furnished with a plan, and the matter fully discussed, and points explained at a general meeting of commanders.

Vessels in distress, and finding it necessary to retire from battle, will steer out southeast, excepting the headmost vessels, "Iosco," "Quaker City," "R. R. Cuyler," etc., which had better keep on southwest half-south course, until they clear an eight-foot shoal (at low water) outside of them.

It is not desirable that the vessels of the squadron should show themselves to the enemy until the time comes for them to act, and they will keep off shore about twenty-five miles, or far enough not to be seen, with New Inlet bearing west, in about the latitude of 33 56, longitude 77 20; that will be the rendezvous. Commanders of divisions will assemble the vessels of their divisions, get them into line, and keep them so, each division being far enough from the other to allow them to manœuvre without interfering. When the signal is made or given to fall in line of battle, every vessel will take her station in line according to the plan of the chart, the first division forming first, and the others dropping in, in order.

As only low steam will be required, those vessels that can move and work handily with half their boilers will only use those on one side, keeping the boilers (on the side near the enemy) full of water and without steam, with water warm only, and ready to make steam in case of necessity.

Slow, deliberate firing is desirable; there will be smoke enough anyhow. Rapid and indiscriminate firing will amount to little or nothing. I hope no shot may be thrown away.

DAVID D. PORTER,
Rear-Admiral Commanding North Atlantic Squadron.

LETTER OF MAJOR-GENERAL BUTLER TO REAR-ADMIRAL PORTER.

HEADQUARTERS, DEPARTMENT
VIRGINIA AND NORTH CAROLINA,
December 25, 1864.

ADMIRAL—Upon landing the troops and making a thorough reconnoissance of Fort Fisher, both General Weitzel and myself are fully of the opinion that the place could not be carried by assault, as it was left substantially uninjured as a defensive work by the Navy fire We found seventeen guns protected by traverses, two only of which were dismounted, bearing up the beach and covering a strip of land—the only practicable route—not more than wide enough for a thousand men in line of of battle.

Having captured Flag-Pond Hill battery, the garrison of which—sixty-five men and two commissioned officers—were taken off by the Navy, we also captured Half-Moon battery and seven officers and two hundred and eighteen men of the Third North Carolina Junior Reserves, including its commander, from whom I learned that a portion of Hoke's division, consisting of Kirkland's and Haygood's brigades, had been sent from the lines before Richmond on Tuesday last, arriving at Wilmington Friday night.

General Weitzel advanced his skirmish line within fifty yards of the fort, while the garrison was kept in their bomb-proofs by the fire of the Navy, and so closely, that three or four men of the picket line ventured upon the parapet and through the sally-port of the work, capturing a horse, which they brought off, killing the orderly, who was the bearer of a dispatch from the chief-of-artillery of General Whiting to bring a light battery within the fort, and also brought away from the parapet the flag of the fort.

This was done while the shells of the Navy were falling about the heads of the daring men who entered the work, and it was evident, as soon as the fire of the Navy ceased because of the darkness, that the fort was fully manned again, and opened with grape and canister upon our picket line.

Finding that nothing but the operations of a regular siege, which did not come within my instructions, would reduce the fort, and in view of the threatening aspect of the weather, wind rising from the southeast, rendering it impossible to make further landing through the surf, I caused the troops with their prisoners to re-embark, and see nothing further that can be done by the land-forces. I shall, therefore, sail for Hampton Roads as soon as the transport-fleet can be got in order.

My engineers and officers report Fort Fisher to me as substantially uninjured as a defensive work.

I have the honor to be, very respectfully, your obedient servant,

BENJ. F. BUTLER,
Major-General Commanding.

REAR-ADMIRAL PORTER,
Commanding North Atlantic Blockading Squadron.

REPLY OF REAR-ADMIRAL PORTER TO MAJOR-GENERAL BUTLER.

NORTH ATLANTIC SQUADRON,
U. S. FLAG-SHIP "MALVERN."

GENERAL—I beg leave to acknowledge the receipt of your letter of this date, the substance of which was communicated to me by General Weitzel last night.

I have ordered the largest vessels to proceed off Beaufort and fill up with ammunition, to be ready for another attack, in case it is decided to proceed with this matter by making *other arrangements.*

We have not commenced firing rapidly yet, and could keep any rebels inside from showing their heads until an assaulting column was within twenty yards of the works.

I wish some more of your gallant fellows had followed the officer who took the flag from the parapet, and the brave fellow who brought the horse out from the fort. I think they would have found it an easier conquest than is supposed.

I do not, however, pretend to place my opinion in opposition to General Weitzel, whom I know to be an accomplished soldier and engineer, and whose opinion has great weight with me.

I will look out that the troops are all off in safety. We will have a west wind presently, and a smooth beach about three o'clock, when sufficient boats will be sent for them.

The prisoners now on board the "Santiago de Cuba" will be delivered to the Provost-Marshal at Fortress Monroe, unless you wish to take them on board one of the transports, which would be inconvenient just now.

I remain, General, respectfully, your obedient servant,

DAVID D. PORTER,
Rear Admiral.

MAJOR-GENERAL B. F. BUTLER,
Commanding, etc., etc., etc.

The abandonment of the expedition by General Butler, with his army, created the greatest indignation on the part of the

Navy, who had seen the prize so nearly within their reach. It had been the hope of the Admiral to hand over the fort to the Government as a fitting Christmas present; but now all that could be done was for the Navy to hold on in the hope that General Grant would send the troops back again, under another leader, and bring the matter to a conclusion. The Admiral sent a message as soon as possible to General Grant, requesting that this might be done, and his request was complied with, the troops re-embarked, and, under command of Brevet-Major-General Alfred H. Terry, returned to the scene of action.

In consequence of the improper interference of General Butler, in assuming command of an expedition for which General Weitzel had been designated, the former was directed to proceed to his home in Lowell, Mass., and report from that place, which virtually ended his career in the Army, while Weitzel succeeded him in command of the Army of the James. In one respect this was unfair to General Butler. It was not considered by the Army that Butler had any military ability, either natural or acquired, but he had around him men of talents and reputation, who were supposed to be his advisers. The chief of these was General Weitzel, whose counsel seems to have had great influence with Butler on all occasions, and, particularly, on the Fort Fisher expedition. Instead of asserting his claim to command the military part of the expedition, Weitzel simply figured as Butler's chief-of-staff, and while all orders were signed by General Butler, as "Major-General Commanding," General Weitzel seems to have really directed all the military operations. It was a mixed-up affair, and it was evidently General Butler's purpose to claim the credit if the fort was captured, and to let Weitzel bear the odium in case of failure.

It is not at all certain that the result of the expedition would have been different had General Weitzel had sole command of the troops, as he seems to have *advised* General Butler in all his movements. In a letter we have quoted, from General Butler to Rear-Admiral Porter, the former says:

"Both General Weitzel and myself are fully of the opinion that the place could not be carried by assault, as it was left substantially uninjured as a defensive work by the Navy fire."

Notwithstanding which statement, he inconsistently relates in the same letter that

"Gen. Weitzel advanced his skirmish line within fifty yards of the fort, while the garrison was kept in their bomb-proofs by the fire of the Navy, and so closely that three or four men of the picket line ventured upon the parapet and through the sally-port of the work, capturing a horse, which they brought off," etc.

Comment on the above is unnecessary;

yet, in the face of this condition of affairs and with the certain victory that could have been gained, General Weitzel recommended a retreat to Hampton Roads! The officer who was to have gone in command advised the one who had usurped it, that he had better abandon the field on the eve of victory and let the Navy manage the affair as best they could.

General Weitzel's course at Fort Fisher was quite in keeping with his previous record at Sabine Pass, where, with a force greatly outnumbering the enemy, he ignominiously retired, leaving two frail gunboats to attack the Confederate works and be cut to pieces; at Baton Rouge, where he was only saved from defeat and capture by a gun-boat; and at Forts Jackson and St. Philip, which works he also reported as "substantially uninjured" by the Federal bombardment. It is possible, if General Weitzel had been in independent command with the entire responsibility resting on his shoulders, he might have viewed matters at Fort Fisher in a different light, especially when seconded by so gallant a soldier as General Curtis, who volunteered to assault the works with the military forces that were landed on the beach.

The author regrets to be obliged to criticise the acts of any officer, but the facts must be related in order to account for the utter failure of the Army in the first attack on Fort Fisher, and to show the world that the Navy was in nowise responsible for it. The official correspondence of the time contains a pretty full account of what occurred between the naval and military commanders, and a history of the Fort Fisher affair would not be complete without it.

The plea of General Weitzel, that Fort Fisher was uninjured as a defensive work, is of no avail in the light of the facts ascertained by the commanding officers of the ships. Commodore Thatcher, in his official report, says:

"On the 24th instant, an explosion took place during a heavy fire from the fleet within the main fort of the rebels, immediately after which flames were observed streaming high above the walls, naturally leading to the conclusion that we had fired the barracks and other tenements connected with the fort. During the continuance of this blaze, which continued for hours, not a gun was fired by the enemy except from the isolated work called the 'Mound Battery.'

"On the 25th instant, the range was shorter and the firing of the fleet more accurate than on the preceding day. It is my belief that not a shot or shell was fired by the advanced line of ships that did not either penetrate the earth-works of the enemy or explode within them.

"On the first day, 1,569 projectiles were fired from the 'Colorado' into the fort. This ship ('Colorado') planted 230 shot in the enemy's works on the 25th, and exploded 996 shells."

The above will give a general idea of the precision of the firing throughout the fleet.

How, under such circumstances, an engineer-officer could report the work "uninjured," especially after the strong palisades were nearly all knocked away, is beyond ordinary comprehension.

The following letter from Rear-Admiral Porter to the Secretary of the Navy gives a more detailed account of the bombardment and expresses the disappointment felt at the withdrawal of the troops :

NORTH ATLANTIC SQUADRON,
U. S. FLAG-SHIP "MALVERN,"
OFF NEW INLET, December 27, 1864.

SIR—My dispatch of yesterday will give you an account of our operations, but will scarcely give you an idea of my disappointment at the conduct of the army authorities in not attempting to take possession of the forts which had been so completely silenced by our guns; they were so blown up, burst up, and torn up, that the people inside had no intention of fighting any longer. Had the army made a show of surrounding it, it would have been ours ; but nothing of the kind was done.

The men landed, reconnoitred, and, hearing that the enemy were massing troops somewhere, the order was given to re-embark.

They went away as soon as the majority of the troops were on the transports, and it coming on to blow rather fresh, about 700 were left on shore. They have been there ever since, without food or water, having landed with only twenty-four hours' rations. I opened communication with them this morning and supplied them with provisions.

To show that the rebels have no force here, these men have been on shore two days without being molested. I am now getting them off, and it has taken half the squadron (with the loss of many boats in the surf) to assist.

I can't conceive what the army expected when they came here ; it certainly did not need seven thousand men to garrison Fort Fisher—it only requires one thousand to garrison all these forts, which are entirely under the guns of Fort Fisher ; that taken, the river is open. Could I have found a channel to be relied on in time, I would have put the vessels in, even if I had got a dozen of them sunk ; but the channel we did find was only wide enough for one vessel at right angles, and we were not certain of the soundings. There never was a fort that invited soldiers to walk in and take possession more plainly than Fort Fisher ; and an officer got on the parapet even, saw no one inside, and brought away the flag we had cut down.

A soldier goes inside, through the sallyport, meets in the fort, coming out of a bomb-proof, an orderly on horseback, shoots the orderly, searches his body, and brings away with him the horse and communication the orderly was bearing to send up field-pieces.

Another soldier goes in the fort and brings out a mule that was stowed away; and another soldier, who went inside while our shells were falling, shot his musket into a bomb-proof, where he saw some rebels assembled together ; he was not molested. Ten soldiers, who went around the fort, were wounded by our shells. All the men wanted was the order to go in; but because every gun was not dismounted by our fire, it was thought that the fort "was not injured as a defensive work," and that it would be to lose men to attack it. It was considered rash to attack the works with wooden ships, and even the officers who have been on the bar a long time (and witnessed the building of the works) thought that half the ships would be destroyed; and it was said that the only hope we could have of silencing the batteries was in case the powder-vessel did the damage expected.

We silenced the guns in one hour's time and had not one man killed (that I have heard of), except by the bursting of our own guns, in the entire fleet.

We have shown the weakness of this work. It can be taken at any moment, in one hour's time, if the right man is sent with the troops. They should be sent here to *stay*—to land with a month's provisions, intrenching tools, guns, and Cohorn mortars. Ten thousand men will hold the whole country. The rebels have been able to send here, all told, about 4,000 men; seventy-five of them that were sent here to observe us gave themselves up to the Navy. Two hundred and eighteen men sent on the same duty gave themselves up to our reconnoitering party, and this would have been the case all the way through.

If I can't do better, I will land the sailors, and try if we can't have full credit for what we do. I trust, sir, you will not think of stopping at this, nor of relaxing your endeavors to obtain the right kind of troops for the business, the right number, and the proper means of taking the place, even if we fail in an assault. Every attack we make we will improve in firing, and if the weather would permit, I could level the works in a week's firing,

COMMANDER (NOW REAR-ADMIRAL) JOHN C. HOWELL.

strong as they are ; but there is only one day in six that a vessel can anchor so close. We had a most beautiful time, and the weather for the attack was just what we wanted.

If General Hancock, with ten thousand men, was sent down here, we could walk into the fort.

I am, sir, very respectfully,
Your obedient servant,
DAVID D. PORTER,
Rear-Admiral.

HON. GIDEON WELLES,
Secretary of the Navy,
Washington, D. C.

ADDITIONAL REPORT OF COMMANDER J. C. HOWELL—CAPTURE OF FLAG-POND BATTERY.

U. S. STEAMER "NEREUS,
OFF WILMINGTON, December 27, 1864.

ADMIRAL—At 12:40 P. M., in obedience to your verbal order, I anchored off Flag-Pond battery, mooring head and stern in four and a half fathoms of water. Immediately opened fire upon the battery. No response was made by those inside ; and at 2:15 P. M. a white flag was waved and the soldiers inside the fort showed themselves. A boat was immediately sent from one of the small gun-boats, the American flag planted on the fort, and the surrender of the command received by a naval officer. Some sixty-five or seventy men, a captain and lieutenant, were captured. The "Santiago de Cuba" and "Nereus" sent boats, and, by order of Captain Glisson, the prisoners were transferred to the "Santiago de Cuba." Respectfully, Admiral,

Your obedient servant,
J. C. HOWELL,
Commander.

REAR-ADMIRAL D. D. PORTER,
etc., etc., etc.,

LIST OF VESSELS, ETC., THAT PARTICIPATED IN THE ATTACK UPON FORT FISHER.

NORTH ATLANTIC SQUADRON,
U. S. FLAG-SHIP "MALVERN."
BEAUFORT, N. C., December, 31, 1864.

SIR—In my accounts of the actions of the 24th and 25th instant, against Fort Fisher, I omitted mentioning the names of the commanders of the different vessels, with the exception of one or two; this might look like an invidious distinction, which was not intended by any means; and though the name of each commander is well-known to the public, I desire to correct the omission, that history may give credit to those engaged in these actions.

The following are the names of all the vessels engaged with the forts, and the names of their commanders. Having so well performed their part in reducing these formidable works to a condition where they could be easily taken possession of, they are entitled to all the credit they have so well earned:

"Minnesota," Commodore Joseph Lauman; "Mohican," Commander D. Ammen; "Colorado," Commodore H. K. Thatcher; "Tuscarora," Commander J. M. Frailey; "Wabash," Captain M. Smith; "Susquehanna," Commodore S. W. Godon; "Brooklyn," Captain James Alden; "Powhatan," Commodore J. F. Schenck; "Juniata," Captain W. R. Taylor; "Kansas," Lieutenant-Commander P. G. Watmough; "Yantic," Lieutenant-Commander T. C. Harris; "Maumee," Lieutenant-Commander R. Chandler; "Mackinaw," Commander J. C. Beaumont; "Ticonderoga," Captain C. Steedman; "Pawtucket," Commander J. H. Spotts; "Shenandoah," Captain D. B. Ridgely; "Seneca," Lieutenant-Commander M. Sicard; "New Ironsides," Commodore William Radford; "Monadnock," Commander E. G. Parrott; "Canonicus," Lieutenant-Commander George E. Belknap; "Mahopac," Lieutenant-Commander E. E. Potter; "Saugus," Commander E. R. Colhoun; "Nyack," Lieutenant-Commander L. H. Newman; "Unadilla," Lieutenant-Commander F. M. Ramsay; "Huron," Lieutenant-Commander T. O. Selfridge; "Pequot," Lieutenant-Commander D. L. Braine; "Pontoosac," Lieutenant-Commander W. G. Temple; "Nereus," Commander J. C. Howell; "Vanderbilt," Captain C. W. Pickering; "Fort Jackson," Captain B. F. Sands; "Santiago de Cuba," Captain O. S. Glisson; "Tacony," Lieutenant-Commander W. T. Truxtun; "Osceola," Commander J. M. B. Clitz; "Chippewa," Lieutenant-Commander A. W. Weaver; "Sassacus," Lieutenant-Commander J. L. Davis; "Maratanza," Lieutenant-Commander G. W. Young; "Rhode Island," Commander S. D. Trenchard; "Mount Vernon," Acting-Volunteer-Lieutenant James Trathen; "Britannia," Acting-Volunteer-Lieutenant Samuel Huse; "Quaker City," Commander W. F. Spicer; "Iosco," Commander John Guest; "Howquah," Acting-Volunteer-Lieutenant J. W. Balch; "Wilderness," Acting-Master H. Arey; "Cherokee," Acting-Volunteer-Lieutenant W. E. Dennison; "A. D. Vance," Lieutenant-Commander J. Upshur; "Moccasin," Acting-Ensign James Brown; "Gettysburg," Lieutenant R. H. Lamson; "Alabama," Acting-Volunteer-Lieutenant Frank Smith; "Keystone State," Commander H. Rolando; "Nansemond," Acting-Master J. H.

Porter; "Emma," Acting-Volunteer-Lieutenant T. C. Dunn; "Tristram Shandy," Acting-Ensign Ben. Wood; "Governor Buckingham," Acting-Volunteer-Lieutenant J. McDiarmid; "Little Ada," Acting-Master S. P. Crafts.

I should have mentioned that the "Saugus," Commander Colhoun, was not in the first day's fight; she arrived from Hampton Roads the morning of the 25th, just in time to take her place with the other Monitors, and anchored within eight hundred yards of Fort Fisher; though there was no response of any consequence from the fort, she did good service in knocking away traverses, etc., and only fired slowly until the army should come up. At no time during this day's work did any of the vessels open all their batteries; the order was to "fight only one division of guns from each vessel," some vessels only fired one shot or shell per minute, holding on for the moment when it was expected the troops would approach and enter, for that would have been the result. I cannot conceal my dissatisfaction, nor can the officers under my command, at the turn things have taken. My first dispatch to the department will show you how sanguine I was that the works would be ours before sunset if the troops came up. I supposed that the assaulting was a matter of course, knowing that, as soon as the troops landed and surrounded the works in the rear, the white flag would be hung out; but reports of large armies coming up to the relief of the rebels changed all the General's plans, if he ever had any. To show how absurd such apprehensions were, every rebel soldier seen gave themselves up the moment our troops were ashore, when they had nothing to fear from their own people; this would have been the case all the way through had the troops all landed.

General Butler mentions in his letter to me that he had captured Flag-Pond battery with 65 men, and Half-Moon battery with 218 men and seven officers. This is making capital out of very small material. Flag-Pond battery was some loose sand thrown up, behind which the rebels used to lie with field-pieces and fire at our blockaders when they chased runners ashore. It doesn't deserve the name of a work. Sixty-five or seventy rebels in it came forward and delivered themselves up to the Navy and were taken on board the "Santiago de Cuba." The men in Half-Moon battery (which is no work at all, and exactly like the other) came forward and delivered themselves up to the Army. They could easily have escaped had they desired to do so. There were no guns in these temporary works, and no protection in the rear. The country will scarcely be cajoled, as it has been a hundred times this war, by announcement of captures having no foundation whatever.

* * * * *

We all know very well that a fort on shore, unless attacked by troops at the same time ships are bombarding, will always hold out against the ships; that is, the enemy will leave the works (and let the ships fire away), and enter again when the ships have gone. We know, from the history of this war, that in no case have we failed to take a fortification where the troops did their share of the work; and this is what the troops under the command of General Butler failed to do.

The brave fellows who showed the way into the works brought off horses, mules, and flags, should have their names chronicled far and near. Had the same spirit been felt in other quarters, Christmas would have been a happier day than usual with the nation. There was evidently a misapprehension on the part of the military leader that we could not cover and protect troops on shore.

This fleet demonstrated its ability to hold on at anchor in deep water and twenty miles from shore, through a heavy gale from the southward—all gales from this direction, however, never blowing home or blowing less as the shore is approached. The only gales to be dreaded here are the northeasters, and then the vessel would lie along the shore with their broadsides bearing on the beach.

This fleet would drive off an army of three hundred thousand men, intrenched or attacking, on such a level field as that where our troops landed.

Seven hundred men were left on the beach by General Butler when he departed for Fortress Monroe, and we had no difficulty in protecting them from the rebel army said to be in the background, which was a very small army, after all. General Bragg must have been very agreeably disappointed when he saw our troops going away without firing a shot, and to see an expedition costing millions of dollars given up when the hollowness of the rebel shell was about to be exposed.

All through this war we have lost chances never to be recovered, owing to the timidity of commanders, and their hesitating to attack what offers itself the most easy of conquest.

The report of an army coming up—which army never existed—changes the whole plan of a campaign, when in my opinion, it would be better to face the army of the enemy and see what stuff they are made of.

Here was our fleet of six hundred guns, commanding a peninsula two miles wide only, and able to cover for miles any number of troops we might land. I call this a dead failure. There is no use in mincing matters, for though the navy did all that was expected of it, or could do, we gained no results. We will only have the satisfaction of knowing that the naval part was well and handsomely done, and that we will do it again the first opportunity.

It is now blowing heavy from the southward eastward, and the larger vessels are riding it out nicely outside. This is the only wind we care for on this coast. In all the other gales we can find a lee or a partial protection.

If you, sir, have no intention of making any change in the number of vessels in this squadron, I would respectfully say, let us work this matter through; at least, defer any changes until I say that we have given up the idea of taking the forts.

The rebels will, no doubt, claim a victory. A failure is half a victory. They foreshadowed the failure in their papers, and stated what would be the cause, which came true.

I am, sir, very respectfully,
Your obedient servant,
DAVID D. PORTER,
Rear-Admiral.

HON. GIDEON WELLES,
Secretary of the Navy.
Washington, D. C.

LETTER OF REAR-ADMIRAL D. D. PORTER RELATIVE TO THE ALLEGED UNNECESSARY DELAY IN THE ATTACK.

NORTH ATLANTIC SQUADRON,
U. S. FLAG-SHIP "MALVERN,"
BEAUFORT, N. C., January 9, 1865.

SIR—I understand that there is now an attempt being made to create an impression that I delayed much longer than necessary, and could have attacked on the 18th as well as the 24th. I don't see what that has to do with the question under discussion. We went down to silence the batteries, demoralize the men in the forts, so that the Army could easily assault the works. It would be a matter of no consequence whether this was done on the 18th or the 25th, as long as we did our share of the work effectively, which, I believe, no one denies. If the Army after landing on the 25th would not undertake the assault, they would not have done so on the 18th. The delay, if any, gave them 1,000 men more, a large steamer and another transport under General Ames having come in on that day.

When General Butler was about to start from Fortress Monroe (having embarked his men in a storm, when I told him he could not possibly leave for three days), I requested him to wait a day after I sailed, as my vessels were slow, and I would have to fill up the powder-vessel; but finding that the Monitors were going, he started off for the rendezvous he had established himself, showed himself and some of the transports to the enemy, was fired at by the forts, and revealed our whole design.

Now for the log-book. On the 16th December wind was south, with a swell rolling on the beach, so that no boat could land. One hour only during the day was there a northwest breeze; on the 17th wind southwest, a heavy sea rolling in on the beach; 18th, wind east and northeast, east-northeast, east by west, blowing right on the beach; no boat could land; 19th, wind fresh, east-southeast and southwest, with a swell setting on the beach; 20th, for a little while wind west-northwest, but shifted to east-northeast, blowing fresh, heavy breakers on the beach; 21st, a gale coming on from the south and east, which ended by blowing heavy from south and west, heavy breakers on beach; 22d, wind shifted to west, all the transports out of sight; gone to make a harbor at Beaufort; at midnight wind off the land, but heavy breakers on the beach and all over the bar, heavy swell from seaward; steamed in under the land; 23d, wind north-northwest and beach comparatively smooth; steamed in and reconnoitred; still too much sea for a boat to land without capsizing; met General Butler's dispatch-boat at 5:30 P. M.; sent word to General Butler that the time was so fair that I would blow up the boat at midnight and attack in the morning. We were sixty-nine miles from Beaufort; the captain said his boat could make fourteen miles per hour; this would give him five hours to go to Beaufort, which would put him there at 11 o'clock P.M. General Butler, leaving with the transports at 6 o'clock in the morning, could have reached the bar at 1 o'clock, allowing him to make nine miles an hour, which all his transports could do. We did not attack until 12, and General Butler only came in with his own vessel and two or three transports at sunset. He saw the fort silenced, defeated, as far as the Navy was concerned, and no doubt could be left on his mind about our ability to do the same the next day. It was the preliminary attack to test the strength of the works.

The programme was made, the troops landed, and without the faintest sign of an assault beyond what was done by one or two gallant soldiers. The Army Commanders concluded that the work was "substantially uninjured as a defensive work." The letter of Lieutenant-Commander Temple, and the testimony of deserters, prove that the works would have been ours had the troops been allowed to assault, as they desired. What matters it, then, whether we attacked on the 18th or 24th? The result would have been the same. General Butler left Fortress Monroe with his troops in transports that could not lie at anchor in rough weather that was ridden out by our Monitors, tugs, and small-wheeled boats; the powder-boat "Louisiana" hanging to the stern of another vessel. General Butler, having left the ground with his vessels, where my lightest vessels held on, was not on the ground to take advantage of the first day's good weather, though that had nothing to do with the matter, as he did not do anything when the landing did take place; so what matters it when it was done?

General Butler, with all his soldier-like qualities, could scarcely be considered as good a judge of weather and the proper time of landing as myself; and, as a sensible person, would not venture to put his opinion in opposition to mine, even backed by some old sailor on his flag-ship.

I do not ascribe to him, therefore, the excuse

made for not taking Fort Fisher, when we had opened its gate for him; I attribute the report "that we had wasted time" to some of the junior members of the staff, who are not as good seamen as the General. At all events, if we lost any time in the beginning, we made up for it when we went to work; but allowing that we lost time, that the beach was as smooth as paper, it doesn't account for not taking Fort Fisher when the works were battered and burnt to that degree that there appeared no life within the walls.

The military part of the expedition was got up in most unmilitary manner; the troops were placed in inferior transports that could not condense water, and had a short allowance only on hand; the troops had four days' cooked rations (which were eaten up while lying in the storm at Hampton Roads), and ten days' other rations; there were no intrenching tools of any kind, no siege guns; the whole proceeding indicated that the General depended on the Navy silencing the works, and he walking in and taking possession. No allowance was made for contingencies, for bad weather, or for delays after getting on shore; the powder-boat when it exploded was to have done the whole thing; the walls of a strong sand fort were to have been blown down, and the rebels all to be discomfited. I thought a good deal might be done by the explosion, but still I laid in a double allowance of shell and shot, and did not depend on a doubtful experiment. Starting as that expedition did was not the way to make war; and landing troops who were full of enthusiasm, and then embarking them again when they were eager to seize the trophy laid at their feet, was not the one to improve the *morale* of the Army.

No matter what might be the delay on my part (and there was none), the General failed to take advantage of the opportunity I gave him to take the fort, when a large portion of the troops were landed and stood within one hundred and fifty feet of the works, unmolested, some few of them going on the parapet. No musketry or grape-shot were fired at him during the day; a few muskets, "about twenty," were fired after night-fall by the alarmed rebels, and one or two guns; but the "Ironsides" opened her broadside, and the firing ceased immediately. Ten of the pickets were left by forgetfulness near the forts after night-fall, and they saw quite a number of men leave the works and embark in boats, which was the garrison leaving to prevent capture. Until late in the day on the 26th the forts lay at our mercy, and if the men had not been brought off, the rebels would have surrendered when they marched up and the Navy opened fire. All the reasoning in the world will not make the affair appear in a better light. I have no doubt that had the Army been obliged to assault the works alone, without the fire of the Navy, they would have been well handled; but, as matters stood, we have every proof that the fort was ours.

It is useless, then, to excuse a military blunder by trying to make out that the Navy was behind time. The ships lay two months at Hampton Roads, waiting for the army to move, and we were satisfied with the reasons that General Grant gave for not sending troops. There was no necessity after all the delay for rushing into the matter unprepared, and when the weather was unfavorable; a more flimsy excuse could not be invented.

In making these statements, I do not do so for the purpose of making any excuse whatever for the naval part of the expedition; I consider that a settled thing in the estimation of the whole country; but I have so often during this war seen attempts made to cast odium on the Navy, and in self-defence I put myself on record, wishing this used only if found necessary to correct false statements.

I am quite sure the Lieutenant-General feels as I do; he says in a communication to me, "Dear Admiral, hold on where you are for a few days and I will endeavor to be back again with an increased force, and *without the former commander.*"

The remark is not very suggestive of confidence in the late management of affairs.

I am, sir, very respectfully,
Your obedient servant,
DAVID D. PORTER,
Rear-Admiral.

HON. GIDEON WELLES,
Secretary of the Navy,
Washington, D. C.

Mr. Secretary Welles, after reading the above dispatches, sent the following telegram in cipher to General Grant, for he was determined the Navy should succeed:

NAVY DEPARTMENT, }
December 29, 1864. }

Lieutenant-General Grant, City Point, Va.:

The substance of dispatches and reports from Rear-Admiral Porter off Wilmington is briefly this: The ships can approach nearer to the enemy's works than was anticipated; their fire can keep the enemy away from their guns; a landing can easily be effected upon the beach north of Fort Fisher, not only of troops but of all their supplies and artillery; this force can have its flanks protected by gun-boats; the Navy can assist in a siege of Fort Fisher precisely as it covered the operations which resulted in the capture of Wagner. The winter also is the most favorable for operations against Fort Fisher. The largest naval force ever assembled is ready to lend its co-operation; Rear-Admiral Porter will remain off Fort Fisher, continuing a moderate fire to prevent new works from being erected, and the iron-clads have proved that they can maintain themselves in spite of bad weather. Under all these circumstances, I invite you to such a military co-operation as will insure the fall of Fort Fisher, the importance of which has already received your careful consideration.

This telegram is made at the suggestion of the President, and in hopes that you will be able at this time to give the troops, which heretofore were required elsewhere. If it cannot be done, the fleet will have to disperse, whence it cannot again be brought to this coast.

GIDEON WELLES,
Secretary of the Navy.

———

(CONFIDENTIAL.)
NAVY DEPARTMENT, }
Saturday, December 31, 1864. }

SIR—Lieutenant-General Grant will send immediately a competent force, properly commanded, to co-operate in the capture of the defences on Federal Point. It is expected that the troops will leave Hampton Roads next Monday or Tuesday.

This is all the information the Department has to give you, but relies upon your skill and judgment to give full effect to any more that may be arranged.

The Department is perfectly satisfied with your efforts thus far, and you will convey to all hands the satisfaction the Department feels.

I am, sir, etc.,
GIDEON WELLES.

REAR-ADMIRAL D. D. PORTER,
Commanding North Atlantic Blockading
Squadron off Wilmington.

After the transports had departed there was nothing for the fleet to do but to proceed to Beaufort, N. C., and fill up with coal and ammunition, while awaiting the promised reinforcements. Besides, the weather was getting stormy, and it was advisable to get the smaller vessels into port.

It would not do to attempt an assault on the Confederate works with sailors, for they had been heavily reinforced by General Hoke, and, for the present, Fort Fisher was secure against attack. The troops that General Butler, in his hurry to get away, had left on the beach were embarked after the gale was over, and returned to Fortress Monroe.

This ended the first attack on Fort Fisher; which, although unsuccessful in reducing the enemy's works, was not without its valuable lessons, which contributed to cause in the second attack a final and gratifying success.

The reports of the commanding officers

COMMODORE (AFTERWARDS REAR-ADMIRAL) JAS. F. SCHENCK.

of vessels in the North Atlantic squadron are too many and too voluminous to insert them all here, but we append some of the most graphic and interesting, which are animated with the zeal in the performance of duty which is characteristic of the naval profession:

REPORT OF COMMODORE SCHENCK, COMMANDING U. S. S. "POWHATAN" AND 3D DIVISION NORTH ATLANTIC SQUADRON.

UNITED STATES STEAMER "POWHATAN," }
OFF BEAUFORT, N. C., January 1, 1865. }

ADMIRAL—Your General Order No. 75 did not reach me until this morning, owing to its being sent on board the "Colorado." In reply to that part of it requiring me to make a report of the part I took in the actions of the 24th and 25th ultimo, I have to state that at 1:20 P. M., on the 24th, I took my position in the line, as directed by you, with a

kedge upon my port quarter acting as a spring, letting go my port anchor with twenty-five (25) fathoms of chain, which brought my starboard broadside to bear upon the forts. I immediately opened a vigorous fire upon the batteries, paying especial attention to Fort Fisher with my 11-inch gun, and to the Mound with my two (2) 100-pounder Parrotts, and with my 9-inch guns to the batteries more immediately abreast of us. It is reported and believed on board this ship that one of the shells from our 11-inch, which exploded in Fort Fisher, set fire to it. At 2:45 P. M., finding that some of my 9-inch shell fell short, and that the "Brooklyn," being underway, occasionally interfered with my line of sight, I got underway, continuing the action, and stood into four and a-half (4½) fathoms water, from which position every shot told with great effect. From this time the action was continued underway. At 3:10 P. M. the end of our spanker gaff was shot away, and our flag came down with it; hoisted it immediately at the mizzen. About the same time, the rebel flag on Fort Fisher was shot away, and was not raised again during the action. At 3:45 P. M. the flag-staff on the Mound was shot away, which shot is claimed by our pivot rifle. At 5:20 P. M. the signal was made to discontinue the action. Hauled off, having sustained no loss of life or injury to the ship.

During this day's action we fired two hundred and thirty-six (236) 9-inch shell, fifty-four (54) 11-inch shell, and eighty-two (82) 100-pounder rifle shell. Not a shell was wasted from the 11-inch and rifles, and only a few in the early part of the action from the 9-inch guns. The starboard battery only was used in action, viz: eight (8) 9-inch guns, two (2) 100-pounder Parrott rifles, and one (1) 11-inch pivot-gun.

On the 25th I took my position as before, although nearer the batteries, and further in. The batteries between Fort Fisher and the Mound being abreast of us, my position was an admirable one for engaging these batteries, and my 9-inch guns were principally employed in doing this, as it was only by these we were annoyed, with an occasional shot from the Mound. During this day not a shot fell short, which accounts for my increased expenditure of 9-inch shell. At 2:10 P. M. we opened fire, which was replied to by the batteries abreast of us more vigorously than the day before. I am not aware of having received a single shot from Fort Fisher this day.

At 3:30 P. M. a port main shroud was shot away; soon after we were struck three (3) times in pretty rapid succession. One (1) shot struck us under No. 3 port, three feet above the water line, passing through into a store-room and depositing itself in a mattress; it is a solid 8-inch shot. Two (2) shot struck under No. 2 port twenty inches below the water line, one remaining in the side and the other going through and lodging in a beam on the orlop deck, causing the ship to leak badly. A glancing shot struck the stern of the ship, but did no material injury, and some of our running rigging shot away. At 4:10 P. M., having expended all the ammunition for 11-inch and rifles, and nearly all for my 9-inch guns, made signal, "Ammunition I am short of," which was replied to "Save some," and immediately after, "Discontinue the action," when I weighed my anchor, lifted my kedge, and hauled out of line.

During this day's action we fired four hundred and ninety-four (494) 9-inch shells, fifty-two (52) 11-inch shell, and seventy-two (72) rifle shell.

In conclusion, I beg leave to state that every officer and man on board this ship, under my command, did his duty nobly, and I have yet to hear of any complaint, either of officer or man, except as to the failure to take advantage of our two (2) days' work. With regard to the "damage apparently done to the works," I must confess that I was paying more attention to the proper management of my own battery than the general effect ; but it appears to me utterly impossible that any works could withstand such a fire and not be terribly damaged ; and I am also fully impressed with the belief that by a prompt and vigorous assault late in the afternoon of either day, Fort Fisher might have been taken by a comparatively small force, say one thousand (1,000) resolute men. Fort Fisher was silent, the Mound firing feebly ; the only active firing from the enemy that I witnessed was from the two or three guns that annoyed me, and as long as my ammunition permitted me to fire rapidly I could keep them pretty quiet.

I have the honor to be, very respectfully, your obedient servant,

JAS. FINDLAY SCHENCK,
Commodore Commanding U. S. Steamer "Powhatan," 3d Division North Atlantic Squadron.

REPORT OF COMMODORE WILLIAM RADFORD, COMMANDING U. S. S. "NEW IRONSIDES."

UNITED STATES STEAMER "NEW IRONSIDES,"
Anchored at sea, Beaufort, bearing N.N.W.,
Distant about five miles, Decembr 31, 1864.

SIR—I have the honor to report that, in obedience to your orders, I took possession under the guns of Fort Fisher, from thirteen to fifteen hundred yards distant, or as near as the depth of water would permit, the Monitors "Canonicus," "Monadnock," and "Mahopac" following the "New Ironsides" in. As soon as I anchored, I opened my starboard battery, and continued a well-directed fire for some five (5) hours. Night coming on, I hauled off, in obedience to orders. On the morning of the 25th the iron-clad division again led in under the guns of Fort Fisher and took the position we occupied the day previous. The "Saugus," having arrived the night previous, took her station, and this division, in connection with the others, drove the men from the guns in the fort, they only firing one or two guns, and those at long intervals. All the Monitors were handled and fought well. Lieutenant-Commander Belknap took the in-shore berth, and is reported to have dismounted one or more guns in the fort

Judging from the immense number of shells which struck the fort, it must have been considerably in jured. Several guns were reported to have been dismounted, two explosions took place, and three fires.

The face of the fort was very much plowed up by the shells from the fleet. If the fort was uninjured (as a defensive work), no artillery known to modern warfare can injure it. My impression is, that any considerable number of troops could have stormed and taken the fort, immediately after the second day's bombardment, with but little loss.

All the officers and men belonging to the "New Ironsides" served their guns and country well ; and I am greatly indebted to Lieutenant-Commander Phythian, the executive officer, for his energy and ability in getting the crew and ship in such good fighting order.

Very respectfully, your obedient servant,
WM. RADFORD,
Commodore Commanding Iron-clad Division.
REAR-ADMIRAL DAVID D. PORTER,
Commanding N. A. Squadron.

REPORT OF CAPTAIN JAMES ALDEN, COMMANDING UNITED STATES STEAMER "BROOKLYN."

UNITED STATES STEAMER "BROOKLYN,"
OFF BEAUFORT, N. C., December 30, 1864.

SIR—I have the honor to acknowledge the receipt of General Order No. 75, which not only calls upon commanding officers to give you a report of the part

they took in the action of the 24th and 25th instant, but also their impressions as to the damage done to the enemy's work, the effect of our firing, and the defensibility of the fort after we had finished the bombardment.

On the first day, the 24th, this ship was in line of attack and opened fire on Fort Fisher at 12:50 P. M., being then within good "10-second" range. The fire was kept up, with occasional intermissions for the men to rest, till 5:15 (more than four hours), when darkness intervened, and the signal was made to retire. The enemy's fire, during the whole of that time, was much less than that of one of our large ships ; an occasional shot was fired from Fort Fisher ; a very feeble and desultory reply to our fire was kept up by the forts between the main work and the Mound battery, which latter was heard from but five or six times during the whole afternoon.

In a word, I am satisfied from past experience, that if this ship, or any one of the larger ones, could have gotten near enough, say within two or three hundred yards, she would not only have silenced

COMMODORE (NOW REAR-ADMIRAL) WILLIAM RADFORD.

their batteries fully and entirely, but would have driven every rebel from the point.

On the second day, the 25th, this ship was sent to silence some of the enemy's earth-works, which were contiguous to the place fixed upon for the disembarking of the troops, to shell the woods, and to cover their landing. The first troops landed at about 2 P. M. ; sent all our boats to assist. At 4 o'clock, just two hours after the landing commenced, the General commanding came alongside this ship and said, "It has become necessary to re-embark the troops ; will you send your boats to assist ?" You can judge of my surprise at the turn affairs had taken, for at that moment everything seemed propitious. The bombardment was at its height, little or no surf on the beach, and no serious indications of bad weather. Still, the order for retiring had gone forth, and our boats were employed till very late (the launch not returning till next morning) in re-embarking the troops, the surf not interfering seriously with operations till near midnight, when it became impossible to land with any safety. Much dissatisfaction, I am told, was shown by the soldiers and their officers when they were informed that they were to re-embark, and it was with some difficulty that they could be made to get into the boats. They were loud in their denunciation of the order turning them back, saying that they had gone there to take the fort, and they were going to do it before they left, etc., etc.

The next day, the 26th, the surf was too high for safe transit from the shore, and this vessel was employed in making a reconnoissance of the enemy's works. Nothing new, however, was discovered, and after exchanging a few shots with Fort Fisher we returned to the anchorage for the night. The following day all our boats were sent, and, after some difficulty, the remaining troops were safely embarked.

I have endeavored in the above to give you my ideas of the effect of our fire on the enemy's works, which was to almost silence them. In regard to the damage done, it is, under the circumstances, impossible for any one to tell without a closer inspection, for, as you remember at Forts Jackson and St. Philip, everything from the outside seemed in *statu quo*, hardly any trace of injury was apparent; but on entering and looking around, the terrible effect of the bombardment was manifest at every turn. So, too, at Fort Morgan, little or no injury could be discovered from without, but upon close examination it was found that almost every gun on its carriage was seriously damaged, if not entirely destroyed.

Now, as to the "defensibility" of the fort. The rebels, I am satisfied, considered, from the moment that our troops obtained a footing on the shore, the work (battered as it was) was untenable, and were merely *waiting for some one to come and take it.*

The General commanding furnishes us with proof of that fact. I think, in his letter to you, informing you of his determination to withdraw, a copy of which you sent me, he says that "three or four men ventured upon the parapet and through the sally-port of the work, capturing a horse, which they brought off; * * * and also brought away from the parapet the flag of the fort." This was all done in open day and without resistance—if, indeed, there was anybody there who was disposed to question their right to such trophies. From that and other current testimony, I am satisfied that, if our troops had not been stopped in their triumphant march towards Fort Fisher, they would have been *in it* before dark, *in quiet possession without firing as hot.*

With great respect, I am your obedient servant,
JAMES ALDEN, *Captain.*
REAR-ADMIRAL DAVID D. PORTER,
Commanding North Atlantic Squadron.

REPORT OF COMMANDER DANIEL AMMEN, COMMANDING U. S. S. "MOHICAN."

UNITED STATES STEAMER "MOHICAN,"
OFF BEAUFORT, N. C., December 31, 1864.

ADMIRAL—I have the honor to acknowledge the receipt of your General Order No. 75, directing commanding officers to make their report in relation to our attack on Fort Fisher and the adjacent earth-works, and also a copy of a communication to you from Major-General Benjamin F. Butler, and, in regard to some points touched upon, you request an opinion.

At about 11:30 A. M. of the 24th, the fleet got underway and stood in, in line of battle, towards Fort Fisher, bearing about west-southwest, and some six or seven miles distant. The "Mohican" was kept closely in position assigned, following the leading vessel, the frigate "Minnesota," and followed by the frigate "Colorado," and she successively by the other vessels forming the main line.

At about 1 P. M., the "Minnesota" sheered in out of line and took up her position at anchor, opening at once on Fort Fisher, some twenty-one hundred yards distant. As per plan of battle, the "Mohican" was sheered in ahead of her, fired slowly on the fort to get a range and anchored, then opened briskly with the whole battery. The fort had opened on the "Minnesota" and on the "Mohican" previous to our anchoring. The "Colorado" sheered in ahead of us, letting go kedge astern, and then anchored and opened fiercely on the fort. The vessels forming the line then successively, with more or less success, took up their positions and opened.

The iron-clads, led by the "New Ironsides," had anchored a few minutes preceding the "Minnesota" some five or six hundred yards to the northward and westward, and were slowly getting their range when we anchored, and the outer line of vessels moved into position after the main line had anchored and opened on the Mound and several detached casemated guns.

The fire from the forts became weak as the vessels anchored and opened fire. It was soon apparent that they could not work their barbette guns without great loss of life, and the guns' crews, no doubt, retreated under shelter, with a few exceptions, where high traverses and favorable angles gave them great protection.

Different casemated guns, particularly those mounted in detached mounds and towards the Mound, continued to fire slowly, and evidently with not much effect, nor would the position of the guns served favor an effective fire. The whole body of Fort Fisher was filled with bursting shells, and only at long intervals, if at all, was a gun fired from the main work. In the meantime, owing to the wind and the set of the tide, I found that the use of the propeller and the helm would no longer enable me to bring the broadside to bear, and was obliged to weigh anchor and manœuvre under steam, holding our position as nearly as possible, and avoiding interfering with the firing of the other vessels.

After exhausting all the filled 9-inch shells on board ready for use, the "Mohican" was withdrawn from the line at about 4:10 P. M., making signal to you of the cause, and we commenced filling shells without delay. After sunset the fleet withdrew, and the "Mohican" ran into line and anchored.

At about 9 A. M. of the 25th, signal was made to get underway and form line of battle. The "Mohican" took her position, and the fleet stood in to the attack. When nearly under fire, I was directed verbally from you "not to take position until further orders." The "Minnesota," the leading vessel of the main line, proceeded in and anchored, got underway, and, after various attempts, obtained a well-chosen position, the main line awaiting her movements. The iron-clads, having preceded during this time, were in position, firing slowly, and receiving a part of the fire of Fort Fisher. After the position of the "Minnesota" was satisfactory, I received orders from you about noon to take position close astern of the "New Ironsides," which I did without delay, firing slowly until a good range was obtained, then opened briskly on the fort. I was enabled to see, through the absence of smoke, that our fire was very effective, delivered at a short ten-second range. One of the rebel guns was seen to be dismounted by our fire. Half an hour after we had anchored, the "Colorado" passed ahead of the "Minnesota" and into position, anchoring and delivering a very effective fire. The whole line soon took position, and opened very heavily, and evidently with great effect, driving the rebels from their guns, with a few exceptions, as those in casemates and other places sheltered and distant. The position of the "Mohican" enabled me to see well, as I was first at anchor within half a ship's length of the "New Ironsides," and, finding that anchoring impeded an effective use of the battery, I weighed, and, in delivering fire, drifted one or two hundred yards nearer the fort.

At 2:05 P. M. the supply of ten-second fuses and the rifle ammunition was exhausted, and the "Mohican" was withdrawn from action for the purpose of obtaining more, speaking the "Malvern" for the purpose, and obtaining none. Not being directed to go under fire again, we remained spectators near the "Minnesota" until about 4 P. M., when I received orders to aid in debarking troops, and proceeded to execute; but, instead of debarking, aided in bringing off the soldiers that had already reached the shore.

It has not been my lot to witness any operations comparable in force or in effect to the bombardment of Fort Fisher by the fleet, and I feel satisfied that any attempt to keep out of their bomb-proofs or to work their guns would have been attended with great loss of life to the rebels, and would have proven a fruitless attempt.

On the first day we delivered two hundred and seventeen (217) 9-inch shells, fifty-nine (59) one hundred-pound rifles, and eighty-nine (89) thirty-pound rifle shells. On the second day we delivered one hundred and three (103) 9-inch shells, twenty (20) one hundred-pound rifles, and twenty-five (25) thirty-pound rifle shells, making a total of five hundred and thirteen.

Our firing was effective as well as rapid, and I have to express my high appreciation of the ability and zeal of Lieutenant J. D. Marvin, the executive officer of this vessel, and of Acting-Master William Burditt, whose long and varied professional experience proved useful; Acting-Boatswain Josiah B. Aiken, owing to a deficiency of officers, had charge of the one hundred-pounder rifle and served it admirably. I have to express my satisfaction at the excellent behavior of the officers and crew, and do not doubt that, when the occasion arrives when they should do so, they will stand to their guns as long as enough men remain to serve them.

In relation to the effect of the fire of the fleet on the fort, I beg leave to express my congratulations, as I did verbally on meeting you after the action. It did not require a visit to the fort to see that enormous traverses were nearly levelled, as at the southeast angle. The stockade or abatis must have been much shattered, and the debris from the parapets must have filled in the ditch greatly. I feel satisfied that everything was effected that can be by powerful batteries against a sand-work, and that we could and can keep the enemy in their bomb-proofs pending an advance of troops to the foot of the parapet.

The official letter of General Butler referred to, states that General Weitzel advanced his skirmish line within fifty yards of the fort, while the garrison was kept in their bomb-proofs by the fire of the Navy, and so closely that three or four men of the picket line ventured upon the parapet and through the sallyport of the work, is, I think, entirely confirmatory as to the effectiveness of our fire. He adds: "This was done while the shells of the Navy were falling about the heads of the daring men who entered the work;" but he appears to forget that, at any given signal from an assaulting column, this fire would cease, and the enemy be found not defending the parapet, but safely stowed away in bomb-proofs.

I do not know what more could be asked of naval guns than to afford a safe approach to the foot of the parapet, with no lines of the enemy drawn up to receive our forces; beyond that, I suppose everything would depend upon the relative forces of the combatants and the vigor of the assault; and although the work might not, in a military sense, be much injured, I would think the likelihood of car-rying the work would be greatly increased by such disposition, without loss of life to the assaulting forces.

I have the honor to be, very respectfully, your obedient servant,

DANIEL AMMEN, *Commander.*
REAR-ADMIRAL D. D. PORTER,
Commanding North Atlantic Squadron.

REPORT OF LIEUTENANT-COMMANDER M. SICARD, COMMANDING U. S. S. "SENECA."

UNITED STATES STEAMER "SENECA,"
December 31, 1864.

ADMIRAL—I would respectfully report that, in the action of the 24th and 25th instant, this vessel was with the vessels on the extreme right that were operating with the iron-clads.

It was evident from the first half-hour of the engagement that the enemy did not intend seriously to reply to the fire of the fleet. This vessel fired one hundred and twelve 11-inch shells and one hundred and forty 20-pounder Parrott shells at the northeast face of Fort Fisher during the two days' bombardment.

Our division fired quite slowly on the second day, and as I was quite close to the fort in the afternoon, and only fired at long intervals, the enemy fired at me several times with a heavy rifle, which, however, did no damage, being evidently hurriedly pointed. This gun could have been silenced in a few minutes if the vessels had chosen to throw away shot on it; and as it was, by an occasional shot from the division, it soon ceased its fire. I refrained from firing much towards the close of the second day's work, because I expected an assault by the troops, and I wished to save my shrapnel for the purpose of covering their advance.

I was much disappointed that the Army did not make an attempt on the fort. I saw the advance of a skirmish line, and of a reserve (comprising in all about 80 men).

They advanced quite close to the works—within pistol-shot. After that I lost sight of them until I saw two returning along the beach with the flag of the fort, which had been shot away about an hour previously by a Monitor.

At dusk, and for a short time after, there was some musketry-firing between this skirmish line and the fort, but up to dark no attempt was made by any adequate body of the Army to assault the fort.

It is my opinion that the fire of the fort was completely under the control of the fleet, and that we could stop it whenever we chose, as the fire by the two frigates on the afternoon of December 25th abundantly showed. In fact, the fort was silent nine-tenths of the time that we were engaging it. I am furthermore of the opinion that the fort could not hold out against a combined attack of the Army and Navy.

I think it a good proof of the effectiveness of the fire of the fleet, that, though our skirmishers advanced so close to the fort, no serious fire was opened on them. Indeed, I do not know from my own observation (and I was in a good position to see), that they were fired on at all in this first advance; and I scarcely think that the enemy would have suffered his flag to be upon the ground so long after it was shot away, though he must have known that we were landing troops, and that from the flag's position it was very liable to capture), unless he had been fearful to venture out and recover it under our fire.

I am, very respectfully, your obedient servant,

MONTGOMERY SICARD,
Lieutenant Commander, Commanding U. S. S. "Seneca."
REAR-ADMIRAL DAVID D. PORTER,
Commanding North Atlantic Squadron.

CHAPTER L.

SECOND ATTACK ON FORT FISHER.

Preparations for the Attack.— The Fleet withstands the Elements.— General Terry arrives and prepares to Co-operate with the Navy.—General Butler vs. General Terry.—Landing of Troops.—Iron-clads Open Fire on the Batteries.— Sailors Land and throw up Intrenchments. — Plan of General Attack by Army and Navy.—Bombardment of the Forts.—Sailors make a Gallant Assault, but are Repulsed with Great Loss.—The Soldiers surprise the Confederates in Rear of Fortifications. — Fort Fisher Captured.— Fearless Gallantry displayed by Troops.— Serious Damage to Confederate Cause.— Grappling for Torpedoes.—The "Tallahassee" and "Chickamauga" Blown Up.—Evacuation of Fort Caswell and Works on Smith's Island.—Wilmington, N. C., Blockaded. — List of Officers Killed and Wounded during Attack on Fort Fisher.— General Orders of Second Attack.—Reports of the Admiral and other Officers.— Cases of individual Feats of Heroism.—Casualties.— Evacuation of Forts along Cape Fear River.—Capture of Smithville.—List of Guns mounted in chain of Forts.—Bombardment and Capture of Forts Anderson, Strong and Lee.— Scrimmage with Infernal Machines.—Capture of Wilmington, N. C.— Firing National Salutes.—Additional Reports of Officers.—Operations after Capture of Fort Fisher. — Confederate Gun-boats and their Movements in James River.—Miscellaneous Operations of North Atlantic Squadron, from October, 1864, to April, 1865.

THE reader can imagine the disappointment in the North when the failure to take Fort Fisher was announced, and the numerous reports that were flying about must have considerably mystified the public. One said the whole expedition had gone back to Hampton Roads, and the chances were that, in the estimation of the public, the Navy should be consigned to oblivion. What an ignominious fate that would have been! However, the Admiral's equanimity was not in the least disturbed. He knew that this set-back was one of the chances of war, and did not regret it, as it would show the stuff American naval officers were made of. Here was a large fleet of over seventy vessels, most of them too large to enter any harbor. They had expended nearly all their coal and ammunition; the commanders were obliged to anchor their vessels off Beaufort, N. C., on an open coast, with pro-

tection only from the northwest winds, and with a southeast gale blowing at least once a week. Yet they were ordered to repair there at once and fill up with coal and ammunition without delay.

To the Admiral's great surprise, he found that General Butler had seized a large quantity of coal (which the Navy had in reserve) for his transports to get home with, and that the Chief of the Bureau of Equipment, through some misunderstanding, had ordered that no more be sent to Beaufort. The naval ammunition had not all arrived from Hampton Roads, and the ships bade fair to be found unprepared in case General Grant ordered the troops to return. No time was lost in sending dispatches overland to Norfolk, directing Lieutenant-Commander Nichols to hurry forward every pound of coal and ammunition available. Fortunately, a fair wind brought all this down to Beaufort, and matters looked more cheerful; the Navy also seized the Army coal in Beaufort, upon the plea that "necessity knows no law."

It is difficult to appreciate the hardships and delays encountered by the fleet in coaling and getting on board the ammunition. Gale after gale swept over the coast, through all of which the ships-of-war, the coal and ammunition vessels had to ride it out. Many anchors and chains were lost, ships were damaged and boats swamped; but no one left his post. There was a dogged determination to take Fort Fisher even if the Navy had to do it alone. When the wind howled at night, and the sound of the breakers was heard booming in the distance, the Admiral would go to sleep feeling as secure as if nothing was going on, knowing that he had good sailors with brave hearts in his ships, and that no one would desert his post any more than he would in time of action. Every morning, at daylight, the officer of the watch would come down and report, "The fleet is all right, sir;" and answering, "I knew it," the Admiral would turn over and take another sleep. There was all kinds of fighting in the Navy, but this was a new phase of the matter—fighting the elements as men never fought them before. It was a new school of practice to the officers, who had been taught that ours was the worst coast in the world, and that a vessel could not there ride out a gale at her anchors. If they profited by the experience they gained on that occasion, they should feel amply repaid for any anxieties they may have felt. An officer should realize that great risks should be run to insure success. We do not wonder that Admiral Farragut said: "Porter will lose that fleet: he is rash to undertake operations when the elements are so opposed to him." It was not judicious in him, it is true, and was not an evidence of what he would have done himself; but if he had remembered the perseverance shown in getting his vessels over the bar at New Orleans, when all others had given it up, he would have said otherwise.

The moment Butler's troops re-embarked, the Admiral sent a swift steamer to General Grant and told him the situation of affairs, urging him to send "other troops and *another General.*" Grant had made up his mind to do so the moment he heard of Butler's failure. The Admiral was daily expecting this force and dreaded its arrival before he was ready. It was a joyful sight when he saw the signals flying from each masthead, reporting, "All ready for action." He had watched all the operations with a critical eye and could see no one lagging. He endeavored, with the means at his disposal, to be impartial in supplying the materials of war. Let any one think of

a fleet of seventy vessels-of-war to be coaled and supplied with ammunition at sea, and all to be done in time to co-operate with an army that could be moved in a week! We recollect that some of the old officers with whom we sailed at different times would not go within ten miles of Cape Fear shoals in good weather, and would think any man crazy who was rash enough *to anchor off Beaufort* one night, much less ride out a gale there. It was rough practice, and we sincerely hope the lesson will not be lost on the young men now coming forward, many of whom participated in the events of that period. Many of them were unknown to fame, but they performed their parts well, and will show hereafter of what material the American Navy is made.

On January 8th, 1865, General A. H. Terry arrived at Beaufort, and communicated the intelligence that he was in command of the army that was to co-operate with the Navy in capturing Fort Fisher. The Navy was all ready for its share of the work; but, as a storm was approaching, the Admiral advised Terry of the fact, and suggested that his transports should go inside, where there was plenty of room for them. To his disappointment, Terry declined any advice, and decided that they should ride it out with the Navy. This beginning did not augur well for a good understanding between General Terry and the Admiral. Terry was rather cold and formal in his manner, and did not meet the Admiral at once with the frankness of a true soldier. He had, however, been a long time under the command of General Butler, who, for a wonder, had treated him very well, because he saw he was a good soldier, and a man of talent besides. Butler also relied on Terry to help him over the rough spots of soldier - life. Of course, Terry had heard *his* side of the story, and was cautious in his first approaches; but all this wore off like snow before a summer's sun when Terry found that the Admiral had but one object in view—the capture of Fort Fisher, and did not care how it was done or who got the credit of it. On his second visit Terry was quite a different man, and they soon understood each other. Here was a different person from the Admiral's last "confederate" — we wonder what Butler would say at our calling him a confederate—who was fond of display, and whose staff was exceptionally large. Terry had no staff, wore no spurs, and we do not think he owned a sword. He had a well-formed head, full of sense, which served him in lieu of feathers, sword, boots, spurs and staff—of which a General can have too many. General Terry was accompanied by General Comstock, of the Engineers, who had been on Butler's staff in the former expedition, and this fact made the Admiral careful about expressing his views in his presence.

He learned finally to appreciate Comstock as a good officer. The Admiral was made to say a spiteful thing of him by the reporter of the War Committee, an untrue statement; and, if the General or his heirs are living when this is published, they will absolve the Admiral from saying or meaning anything disrespectful concerning him. General Grant thought highly of Comstock, and that was the latter's recommendation with the Navy. If Comstock had not been made by that same reporter of the War Committee to say some untrue things about the Admiral, the latter would have taken to him at first sight and endorsed him as an "A No. 1" engineer, as, no doubt, he was.

Admiral Porter offered to do all he could for General Terry, and explained to him how matters stood. The Admiral was not shown Terry's instructions, but afterwards saw them printed in General Grant's report. They were, in effect, "*to defer to Admiral Porter's opinions in all that related to nautical matters, and to confide in his judgment, as he was an officer who had the nerve to carry out anything he might propose.*" Had the Admiral been shown these orders, Terry and himself would have understood each other at once; but we do not think the General appreciated the Navy until after the capture of Fort Fisher, when he saw the fruits of its labors, and witnessed the unselfish sincerity with which all worked for the public good.

It was arranged that the fleet should sail from Beaufort on the 12th of January. This was done—the Navy sailing in three lines, the Army transports in another. Terry preserved quite as good order among his vessels, in the matter of sailing, as the Admiral did with his—which is saying a great deal.

At 8 o'clock A. M., on the 13th of January, 1865, the Navy commenced to land General Terry's troops, batteries and provisions, and by 2 o'clock there were 8,000 troops on shore, with all their stores and munitions-of-war. The Admiral then got underway, making signal to the fleet, and attacked the batteries, by way of diverting the minds of some of the soldiers who had been dropped into the water. So Butler would have been landed, but *he* would not be made a hero of on any such terms, and so lost his chances for the Presidency.

Quite a change had been made in the Confederate arrangements since the fleet last left Fort Fisher. The enemy gained a great deal of experience in the first bombardment, and had strengthened every weakness that had developed under the hammering from the ships. They had also repaired all damages as far as was necessary to make the fort more enduring, and had placed a larger force within the works. The Confederate authorities had in the first instance placed too much confidence in their strong sand-works, and had no idea of the effect of a steady naval fire from three or four hundred heavy guns; but having realized this, they did the best they could in twenty days to remedy all defects. The authorities at Richmond became very much alarmed when they heard how near the fort came to falling into Federal hands, and, in consequence, President Davis selected General Bragg to command at its second defence. Bragg's name had once been a household word in the United States, but he was not so well thought of by some of the Southern politicians. It was a foregone conclusion to them that Fort Fisher would fall, under his management of affairs. To do justice to Bragg, the best General in the Southern Confederacy could not have held Fort Fisher, with the force he had, against the terrific fire that was poured upon the works by the Federal fleet.

The most important matter to the Confederates was to prevent a landing by the Federal troops, or to dislodge them as soon as they got on shore, and drive them into the sea; but this had been anticipated by having a line of sixteen or seventeen gunboats anchored inside of the transports within one hundred yards of the beach, the "Brooklyn" with her heavy battery lying in the centre of the line; and, before a single boat was allowed to leave a transport, there was opened all along the line such a tremendous fire from the vessels reaching as far as Cape Fear River, about a thousand yards distant, that no troops could withstand it five minutes. General Terry landed his troops as rapidly as one hundred and twenty boats could put them on shore. With their intrenching tools, within an hour after landing, they had thrown up heavy intrenchments right across the land to the river, and manned them so that at the very first step the fort was comparatively cut off from all support. By two o'clock, 8,000 troops had been landed, and the artillery posted behind the breastworks. The place of landing was admirably selected, the troops being disembarked just above the neck of the Sound, interposing a small stretch of water between them and an attacking force, or compelling such force to work around the lower extreme of the Sound, either of which movements would have to be executed under the fire of the whole fleet.

General Hoke had the immediate command of the Confederate troops, and it was his purpose to attack the Federals as they landed from the boats. His cavalry was

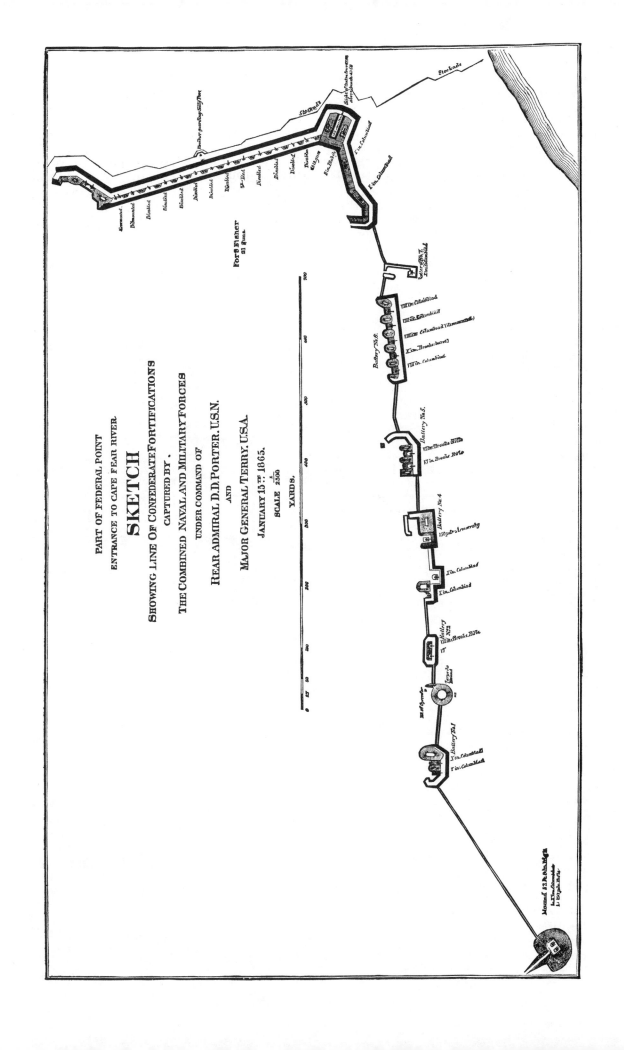

PART OF FEDERAL POINT
ENTRANCE TO CAPE FEAR RIVER.

SKETCH

SHOWING LINE OF CONFEDERATE FORTIFICATIONS

CAPTURED BY.

THE COMBINED NAVAL AND MILITARY FORCES

UNDER COMMAND OF

REAR ADMIRAL D.D. PORTER. U.S.N.

AND

MAJOR GENERAL TERRY. U.S.A.

JANUARY 15 TH 1865.

SCALE $\frac{1}{2500}$

YARDS.

thrown out on the right flank to observe the Federal movements, and report the first step towards establishing a line across the neck of land to the river ; but it was found in the morning that, owing to the want of vigilance on the part of the Confederates, the Federals had laid out a second line of defence during the night ; General Terry's troops, passing between Hoke's cavalry and threading their way through the thick undergrowth of the marsh, made their advance to the river, and the next morning held an intrenched line on Hoke's right flank, extending nearly across the peninsula. General Bragg at first gave the order to charge the Federal troops in their works ; but after a reconnaissance, which discovered the Federal force and position, he determined to withdraw, after managing to increase the number of men in the fort to 2,500, which was the force that manned the works on the second attack. The Federals, the same afternoon of the landing, pushed a reconnaissance within five hundred yards of the fort, and held the point attained.

While all these Army movements were going on, the fleet was moving into position for the attack. This time a different plan was pursued from the last. The "Ironsides" (Commodore Radford) leading, was followed in by the Monitors "Saugus," "Canonicus," "Monadnock" and "Mahopac," taking a position within eight hundred yards of the fort, and much nearer than on the last occasion. At 7:30 A. M. the forts opened on them as they approached, but they took up their position without firing a gun until they were ready, and then opened their batteries. In this way the enemy was tempted to engage the iron-clads, so that their points of fire could be observed and the positions of their guns noted, thus showing how to dismount them. When the iron-clads were well engaged, Commander Rhind was sent in a boat to plant a buoy in four fathoms of water at the point where the "Minnesota" was to anchor, and also to serve as a guide for the other vessels.

The fleet stood in, in three columns. Line No. 1, led by the "Brooklyn," Captain James Alden, consisted of the "Mohican," Commander Daniel Ammen ; "Tacony," Lieutenant - Commander W. T. Truxtun ; "Kansas," Lieutenant - Commander P. G. Watmough ; "Yantic," Lieutenant-Commander T. C. Harris ; "Unadilla," Lieutenant-Commander F. M. Ramsey ; "Huron," Lieutenant - Commander T. O. Selfridge ; "Maumee," Lieutenant-Commander Ralph Chandler ; "Pequot," Lieutenant - Commander D. L. Braine ; "Pawtucket," Commander S. H. Spotts ; "Seneca," Lieutenant-Commander M. Sicard ; "Pontoosac," Lieutenant - Commander W. G. Temple ; "Nereus," Commander J. C. Howell.

Line No. 2, "Minnesota," Commodore Joseph Lanman leading, consisted of the "Colorado," Commodore H. K. Thatcher ; "Wabash," Captain M. Smith ; "Susquehanna," Commodore S. W. Godon ; "Powhatan," Commodore J. F. Schenck ; "Juniata," Lieutenant-Commander T. S. Phelps ; "Shenandoah," Captain D. B. Ridgley ; "Ticonderoga," Captain Charles Steedman ; "Vanderbilt," Captain C. W. Pickering ; "Mackinaw," Commander J. C. Beaumont ; "Tuscarora," Commander J. M. Frailey.

Line No. 3, "Santiago de Cuba," Captain O. S. Glisson leading, consisted of the "Fort Jackson," Captain B. F. Sands ; "Osceola," Commander J. M. B. Clitz ; "Sassacus," Lieutenant-Commander J. L.

LIEUTENANT-COMMANDER (NOW COMMODORE) D. L. BRAINE, COMMANDING U. S. S. "PEQUOT"

Davis ; "Chippewa," Lieutenant - Commander E. E. Potter ; 'R. R. Cuyler," Commander C. H. B. Caldwell ; "Maratanza," Lieutenant - Commander George W. Young ; "Rhode Island," Commander S. D. Trenchard ; "Monticello," Lieutenant W. B. Cushing ; "Alabama," Acting-Volunteer-Lieutenant A. R. Langthorne ; "Montgomery," Acting-Volunteer-Lieutenant T. C. Dunn ; "Iosco," Commander John Guest.

The reserve division, under Lieutenant-Commander J. H. Upshur, in the "A. D. Vance," consisted of the "Britannia," Acting - Volunteer - Lieutenant W. A. Sheldon ; "Tristram Shandy," Acting-Volunteer - Lieutenant F. M. Green; "Lillian," Acting-Volunteer-Lieutenant T. A. Harris; "Fort Donaldson," Acting-Master G. W. Frost; "Wilderness," Acting-Master H. Arey; "Aries." Acting-Volunteer-Lieutenant F. S. Wells; "Governor Buckingham," Acting-Volunteer-Lieutenant J. Macdiarmid. The "Nansemond," Acting-Master J. H. Porter; "Little Ada." Acting-Master S. P. Crafts; "Eolus," Acting-Master E. S. Keyser, and "Republic," Acting-Ensign J. W. Bennett, being used as reserve vessels.

Some of the vessels that accompanied the last expedition were badly damaged in various ways. The "Sassacus" had both rudders disabled, but her energetic commander, Lieutenant-Commander J. L. Davis, was ready in time. The "Mackinaw," Commander J. C. Beaumont, had one of her boilers knocked to pieces, but her commander would go with but one boiler. The "Osceola," Commander J. M. B. Clitz, in the same condition—one boiler smashed up with shot and a hole near the bottom—was ready for anything, and no complaint was heard from any one. With such a disposition on the part of the officers, the Admiral anticipated the most favorable results.

The different divisions, having formed into line of battle, steamed towards Fort Fisher, the "Colorado" leading (the "Minnesota" having a hawser around her propeller). The vessels took their positions handsomely—having had some practice at that place—and delivered their fire as they fell in. The rapid fire of the Monitors and "Ironsides" kept the enemy partly away from their guns, and they inflicted no damage on the fleet, their firing being very unsteady—indeed, it was strange how they could fire at all. After the first and second lines got fairly anchored in position, the bombardment was very rapid and severe. The fire was continued without intermission from 4 o'clock P. M. until some time after dark, when the wooden vessels were ordered to haul out and anchor. The Monitors and "Ironsides" were directed to keep up the fire during the night. The enemy had long ceased to respond, and kept in his bomb-proofs. It was seen that the bombardment had damaged some of the enemy's guns, and it was determined, before the Army went to the assault, that there should be no guns within reach to arrest its progress. Having found that the enemy could still bring some heavy guns to bear, which annoyed the fleet somewhat, the Admiral determined to try another plan, and, on the morning of the 14th, ordered in all the small gun-boats carrying 11-inch guns, to fire slowly and try to dismount the guns on the face of the works where the assault was to be made. The

"Brooklyn" was ordered to throw in a pretty quick fire, to keep the enemy from working their guns. The attack was commenced at 1 P. M. and lasted till long after dark. One or two guns only were fired this day from the upper batteries, inflicting no serious damage on any of the vessels, except cutting away the maintopmast of the "Huron" and hitting the "Unadilla" once or twice. These guns were always silenced when a rapid fire was opened. The attack of the gun-boats lasted until long after dark, and one vessel was employed at a time (an hour each) in firing throughout the night.

On this evening General Terry went on board to see the Admiral and arrange the plan of battle for the next day. The troops had got rested after their long confinement on shipboard and sea-voyage, and had recovered from the drenching they received when landing through the

SURGEON (NOW MEDICAL DIRECTOR) GEORGE MAULSBY, FLEET-SURGEON.

surf. Having been long enough on their native element, they were eager for the attack. It was arranged between the General and Admiral that the ships should all go in early, and fire rapidly through the day until the time for the assault arrived. The hour named was 3 P. M.

The Admiral detailed 1,600 sailors and 400 marines to accompany the troops — the sailors to *board* the sea-face, while the troops assaulted on the land side. Many of the sailors were armed with cutlasses and revolvers, while a number had Sharpe's rifles or short carbines. We insert the order of attack on the fort, and the manner of approaching it.

The Admiral and General had a perfect understanding and established a system of signals by the Army Code, by which they could converse at pleasure, even amid the din of battle, when they were nearly a mile apart. At 9 A. M., on the 15th, the fleet was directed by signal to attack in three lines, or assume position, as shown in the plan. The vessels all reached their stations at about 11 A. M., and each opened fire when anchored. The same guns in the upper batteries opened again this day, and with some effect; but no vessel was injured enough to interfere in the least with her efficiency. The fire was kept up furiously all day. The Mound Hill Battery returned a rather galling fire with its heavy guns, but the enemy was driven from its works into the bomb-proofs, so that no vessel was in the least disabled. The signal for the vessels to " change the direction of their fire," so that the troops might assault, was expected at 2 o'clock. The sailors and marines by digging ditches, or rifle-pits, had worked to within two hundred yards of the fort, and were all ready. The troops, however, did not get into position until later, and the signal was not made until 3 o'clock. The vessels then changed their fire to the upper batteries, all the steam-whistles were blown, and the troops and sailors dashed ahead, nobly vying with each other in the endeavor to reach the top of the parapet. The fleet had evidently injured all the large guns, so that they could not be fired to annoy any one. The sailors went to the assault by the flank along the beach, while the troops rushed in at the left through the palisades that had been knocked away by the fire of the fleet. All the arrangements on the part of the sailors were well carried out. They succeeded in getting up to within a short distance of the fort, and lay securely in their ditches, with but a few killed or wounded to this point. The marines were to have held the rifle-pits and cover the *boarding party*, but failed to do so. On rushing through the palisades, which reached from the fort to the sea, the head of the column received a murderous fire of grape and canister, which failed, however, to check the officers and sailors who were leading in their advance. The parapets then swarmed with Confederates, who poured in a destructive fire of musketry. At this moment, had the covering party of marines performed their duty, every one of the enemy on the parapet must have been killed or wounded.

The Admiral witnessed the whole affair, saw how recklessly the enemy exposed themselves, and what an advantage they gave the marine sharp-shooters, whose guns were scarcely fired, or fired with no precision. Notwithstanding the hot fire, the officers and sailors in the lead rushed on, some even reaching the parapet, while a large

number reached the ditch. The advance was swept from the parapet like chaff; and, notwithstanding all the efforts made by commanders of companies to stop them, the men in the rear, seeing the slaughter in front, and that they were not covered by the marines, commenced to retreat; and, as there is no stopping a sailor if he fails on such an occasion at the first rush, the assault on this front had to be abandoned.

In the meantime, the troops on their side were more successful. The Confederates seeing so large a body of men advancing on the sea-front, were under the impression that this was the main attack. They, therefore, concentrated their forces at that point, and when they gave three cheers, thinking they had gained the day, they received a volley of musketry in their backs from the gallant soldiers who had been successful in gaining the highest parapets. Then commenced such a system of fighting as has seldom been beaten. The soldiers had gained two traverses, while the Admiral directed the " Ironsides " to fire on the traverses occupied by the enemy. Four, five and six traverses were carried by the troops in the space of an hour. These traverses were immense bomb-proofs, about sixty feet long, fifty feet wide and twenty feet high; seventeen of them in all being on the northeast face. Between each traverse, or bomb-proof, were one or two heavy guns. The fighting lasted until 10 o'clock at night, the " Ironsides " and the Monitors firing through the traverses in advance of the troops, while the level strip of land called Federal Point was enfiladed by the ships, to prevent reinforcements reaching the enemy. General Terry himself went into the fort, and the Admiral kept up constant communication with him, until three hearty cheers, which were taken up by the fleet, announced the capture of Fort Fisher. Finding that the General felt anxious about the enemy receiving reinforcements, the sailors and marines relieved the troops in the outer line of defences, and a large number of soldiers were thus enabled to join the forces in the fort. It will not be amiss to remark here, that we never saw anything like the fearless gallantry and endurance displayed by the troops—they fought like lions, and knew no such word as fail. They fought and chased the enemy from traverse to traverse, until they finally reached Battery Lamb, or the Mound, a work extending about 1,400 yards. At this point the Confederates broke and fled to the end of Federal Point. The victorious troops followed, and the enemy surrendered at discretion.

Thus ended one of the most remarkable battles on record, and one which did more damage to the Confederate cause than any that took place during the war. Twenty-five hundred Confederates manned Fort Fisher : eighteen hundred were taken prisoners; the rest were killed or wounded.

We visited Fort Fisher and the adjoining works, and found their strength greatly beyond what had been conceived. An engineer might be excused for saying, they could not be captured except by regular siege. We wonder even now how it was done. The work was really stronger than the Malakoff Tower, which defied so long the combined power of France and England, and yet it was captured by a handful of men under the fire of the guns of the fleet, and in seven hours after the attack began in earnest.

We cannot say too much in praise of the conduct of the fleet during the time it had been engaged in these operations. We do not know an officer in command who did not perform his duty to the best of his ability. There may have been some who did better than others, but, after all, that may be a mere matter of opinion, or a matter of prejudice or partiality—all did their best. To make invidious distinctions would be causing matter for dispute, and we shall be content with saying that the Government might well be proud of those to whom it intrusted the command of its vessels.

The result of the attempt on the sea-face was not what the Admiral expected when he planned the attack ; but it would have succeeded without severe loss had the marines done better. As it was, the Navy lost heavily, including some gallant officers who fell on the ramparts. The success was so great that the country should not complain. Men, it seems, had to die that this Union might live, and the Constitution under which we have gained our prosperity be maintained. We regret the dead heroes and shed a tear over their remains; but, if the Confederates had succeeded, we should have nothing but regret left us, and our lives would have been spent in terror and sorrow.

As soon as the forts were taken, the light-draft gun-boats were pushed into the river —that is, as soon as they could find and buoy out the channel and take up the torpedoes, which were very thick. The searchers found the wires leading to many, and underran them with boats. The torpedoes were too heavy to lift with ordinary means, and some of them must have contained at least a ton of powder. The Confederates seemed disposed to pay the fleet back for the famous torpedo "Louisiana," which exploded in their harbor and did them no harm. There was some difficulty in getting the vessels across the bar and into the river, as the channel was very narrow and the bar very shoal; a few of them got aground but were hauled off again with the

tide. After three of the gun-boats were inside the bar and under the Mound, the Confederates prepared to evacuate Fort Caswell. Two steamers near the fort (the "Tallahassee" and "Chickamauga") were set on fire and blew up with a heavy explosion after the enemy had set fire to the fort. This was followed by some minor explosions. The barracks were apparently in flames all night, and some small works between Fisher and Caswell were blown up. The enemy commenced burning up everything in Wilmington, and were getting away as fast as they could. In the meantime a large force of gun-boats occupied the river between Caswell and Wilmington. The latter place was hermetically sealed against

ACTING-ENSIGN (NOW COMMANDER) ROBLEY D. EVANS, U. S. N.

OF THE U. S. S. "POWHATAN."

blockade - runners, and no "Alabamas" or "Floridas," "Chickamaugas" or "Tallahassees" could ever fit out again from that port. Forty-four thousand shells were expended in the bombardment and as many more were left on hand. The fleet was much indebted to the Bureau of Ordnance for so promptly supplying it with guns and ammunition.

The number of guns captured in Fort Fisher amounted to seventy - five, many of them superb rifle-pieces of very heavy calibre. All those facing the ships were dismounted or injured, so they could not be used, or the muzzles filled up with sand or dirt, which rendered them useless. There were only two that were not rendered perfectly useless.

LIST OF OFFICERS KILLED AND WOUNDED DURING THE ATTACK UPON FORT FISHER.

Killed in the assault—Lieutenant S. W. Preston, Flag-Lieutenant ; Lieutenant B. H. Porter, commanding flag-ship " Malvern " ; Assistant Surgeon Wm. Longshaw, U. S. steamer " Minnesota " ; Acting-Ensign Robert Wiley, U. S. steamer " Montgomery."

Killed by explosion of magazine in Fort Fisher, January 16— Acting - Assistant Paymaster R. H. Gillett, U. S. steamer " Gettysburg " ; Acting-Ensign J. S. Leighton, U. S. steamer " Gettysburg."

Wounded in the assault—Lieutenant-Commander W. N. Allen, U. S. steamer " Tuscarora " ; Lieutenant G. M. Bache, U. S. steamer " Powhatan " ; Lieutenant R. H. Lamson, commanding U. S. steamer " Gettysburg " ; Acting-Volunteer Lieutenant F. F. Baury, U. S. steamer " Colorado " ; Ensign R. D. Evans, U. S. steamer " Powhatan " ; Ensign Ira Harris, U. S. steamer " Powhatan " ; Acting - Ensign L. R. Chester, U. S. steamer " Pontoosuc " ; Acting - Ensign James Bertwistle, U. S. steamer " Minnesota " ; Acting - Ensign F. A. O'Connor, U. S. steamer " Minnesota " ; Acting-Ensign G. W. Coffin, U. S. steamer " Gettysburg " ; Acting-Ensign B. Wood, U. S. steamer " Tristram Shandy " ; Acting-Master A. J. Louch, U. S. steamer " Mackinaw " ; Acting-Master's Mate E. K. Green, U. S. steamer " Mackinaw " ; Acting-Master's Mate J. M. Simms, U. S. steamer " Minnesota " ; Acting-Master's Mate A. F. Aldridge, U. S. steamer " Tuscarora."

Total officers killed and wounded, 21.

KILLED, WOUNDED AND MISSING IN THE ATTACK UPON FORT FISHER, INCLUDING THE EXPLOSION OF THE MAGAZINE.

Flag-ship " Malvern," 3 killed and 1 wounded ; " Saugus," 1 wounded ; " Pontoosuc," 7 wounded ; " Kansas," 1 wounded ; " Tacony," 2 killed and 12 wounded ; " Canonicus," 3 wounded ; " Ticonderoga," 1 killed and 6 wounded ; " Iosco," 2 killed and 12 wounded ; " Shenandoah," 6 killed and 5 missing ; " Tuscarora," 3 killed and 12 wounded ; " Rhode Island," 8 killed and 2 wounded ; " Huron," 5 wounded ; " Montgomery," 2 killed and 4 wounded ; " Monticello," 4 killed and 4 wounded ; " Wabash," (incomplete) 12 wounded ; " Tristram Shandy," 2 wounded and 1 missing ; " Susquehanna," 3 killed and 15 wounded ; " Juniata," 5 killed and 10 wounded ; " Santiago de Cuba," 1 killed and 9 wounded ; " Fort Jackson," 1 killed and 10 wounded ; " Yantic," 2 killed and 2 wounded ; " Powhatan," 3 killed, 19 wounded and 7 missing ; " Minnesota," 13 killed and 23 wounded ; " Colorado," 3 killed, 14 wounded and 8 missing ; " Nereus," 3 killed and 3 wounded ; " Pequot," 3 killed and 5 wounded ; " Gettysburg," 6 killed and 6 wounded ; " Mackinaw," 2 wounded ; " Mohican," 12 killed.

Total—Killed, 74 ; wounded, 213 ; missing, 22.—Total killed, wounded and missing, 309.

GENERAL ORDER ON SECOND ATTACK.
[SPECIAL ORDER NO. 10.]
NORTH ATLANTIC SQUADRON,
FLAG-SHIP " MALVERN," January 9, 1865.

The following vessels will form a separate line, under the command of Lieutenant - Commander Upshur, for the purpose of landing the provisions and stores for the army, viz.: " A. D. Vance," " Fort Donaldson," " Aries," " Emma," " Lillian," " Tristram Shandy," " Britannia " and " Wilderness." The " Nansemond," " Moccasin " and " Little Ada " will act as messengers, as before.

It is proposed now that the troops shall be first landed before any attack is made on the fort by all the vessels. The " Brooklyn " will lead in with the vessels attached to her line, and anchor in a position to cover the landing, and drive away the rebels, if there are any. The landing will probably be made at the same place as before.

Line No. 2 will anchor where their guns can reach (somewhere in about five fathoms water and not less), and where they can fire clear of the first line.

Line No. 3 will keep underway a short distance outside the other lines, ready to act as circumstances may require.

The transports will anchor in line outside line No. 1, and be ready to deliver their troops as fast as the boats go alongside. All the vessels will lower their boats as quick as they anchor, and send them to the transports; line No. 3 doing the same.

When the troops are all landed, the boats will be hoisted upon the port side, and those belonging on the starboard side will be secured alongside for towing, so that they can be manned at a moment's notice when the assault comes off.

If practicable, the " New Ironsides " and the Monitors will be ordered in to bombard the fort and dismount the guns while the troops are getting on shore. This will be done when the signal is made to the " New Ironsides " to attack, the Monitors following her.

While the vessels are firing, the commanders will keep an intelligent officer at the maintopmast-head to regulate the firing and tell the effect of the shot. The commanders of smaller vessels will have a like look-out kept at the main-mast-head. The officers aloft will note all information that may be valuable, as they can see what is going on in the river inside.

DAVID D. PORTER,
Rear-Admiral, Commanding North Atlantic Squadron.

[GENERAL ORDER NO. 78.]
NORTH ATLANTIC SQUADRON,
FLAG-SHIP " MALVERN," January 2, 1865.

The order of attack for the next bombardment of Fort Fisher will be as follows:

The " New Ironsides," Commodore Radford, will lead in, and anchor with the centre of the northeast face of the fort bearing west by south half-south, the Monitors following. The iron-clads will anchor in succession, as follows: The " Mahopac," " Canonicus," and " Saugus " will anchor in a line close together, between the " New Ironsides " and the beach; and the " Monadnock " will select a position in the same line, so that she will have room to swing and bring both turrets to bear.

When these vessels are fully engaged, signal will be made to the " Brooklyn " to go in and engage the enemy, taking a position at anchor close under the stern of the " New Ironsides," with her broadside bearing on Fort Fisher. The " Brooklyn " will be followed in by the " Mohican," " Tacony," " Kansas," " Unadilla," " Huron," " Maumee," " Pawtucket," " Seneca," " Pontoosuc," " Nyack," " Yantic," and " Nereus," in the order in which they are marked on the chart. The line, when anchored, should be with the " Brooklyn," bearing about south by east. This will be line-of-battle No. 1.

Line No. 2 will take position when the leading vessel of line No. 1 is anchored, with the " Minnesota " leading, " Colorado " next, " Wabash," " Susquehanna," " Powhatan," " Juniata," " Shenandoah," " Ticonderoga." After the " Minnesota " anchors in her old place (or closer), where her guns will clear the " New Ironsides," the " Colorado " will pass her and anchor, both ships firing slowly to get their range as they go in. When the " Colorado " is anchored and firing with effect, all the vessels of line No. 2 will anchor in position, exactly as they did on a previous occasion.

The " Vanderbilt " will then anchor a little outside of and between the "Colorado" and "Wabash," "Mackinaw," between "Susquehanna" and "Wabash," and "Tuscarora" between "Juniata" and "Powhatan."

When line No. 2 has anchored, line No. 3 will take position, the "Santiago de Cuba" leading, which vessel will anchor with the centre of the southeast face of Fort Fisher bearing northwest half-north, or just ahead of "Ticonderoga." The "Fort Jackson" will then pass the "Santiago de Cuba," and anchor as close as she can get; the "Osceola" will pass the "Fort Jackson" and anchor, and so on with the "Sassacus," "Chippewa," "R. R. Cuyler," "Maratanza," "Rhode Island," "Monticello," "Alabama," "Montgomery," "Keystone State," "Quaker City," ending with the "Iosco."

When the signal is made to form line of battle, all the vessels of lines Nos. 1, 2 and 3 will fall in line in the order mentioned; the "Brooklyn" leading line No. 1, the "Minnesota" line No. 2, and the "Santiago de Cuba" line No. 3. When any vessel is missing, the vessels behind must close up. All the vessels can with safety get in closer than they did the last time. For this they must depend on the lead and past experience.

All firing against earth-works, when the shell bursts in the air, is thrown away. The object is to lodge the shell in the parapets, and tear away the traverses under which the bomb-proofs are located. A shell now and then exploding over a gun *en barbette* may have good effect, but there is nothing like lodging the shell before it explodes. The red lines on the chart indicate the object each vessel is to fire at, as near as we can make out the works.

In case it is determined to land the troops before engaging the forts, signal will be made. Each reserve vessel will have her boats in readiness to disembark the troops as rapidly as possible. When the signal is made, they will run in and anchor close to the shore, covering the landing with their guns. The paddle-steamers will not use their paddle-boats (but only their davit-boats) unless ordered to do so. All these things will be regulated by signal. All the precautions observed in General Order No. 75 will be observed on this occasion.

Fire deliberately. Fill the vessels up with every shell they can carry, and fire to dismount the guns, and knock away the traverses. The angle near the large ships has heavy casemates; knock it away. Concentrate fire always on one point. With the guns disabled, the fort will soon be ours.

No vessel will retire from line unless in a sinking condition, nor without permission.

So many accidents have happened with the 100-pounder rifles that I recommend, if they be used at all, the charges be reduced to seven (7) pounds; and as the time-fuzes burst after leaving the gun, fire them with a patch on or fire percussion shell.

When the troops are ready for the assault, signal will be made to "change the direction of fire," by hoisting general signal 2211, and blowing the steam-whistle, which whistle every vessel will repeat, and officers will be stationed at the hatches to pass the word. When the signal 2211 is made, all the vessels will stop firing at Fort Fisher, and concentrate their fire on the batteries to the left or above it; the "Tacony," "Kansas," "Unadilla," "Huron," "Maumee," "Pawtucket," "Seneca," "Pontoosuc," "Nyack," "Yantic" and "Nereus," giving their guns *great* elevation, and firing over to reach the river, to disturb any rebel troops that may be resting there. To avoid accidents by firing over our troops by these last-mentioned vessels, the patches will not be taken off the shell, until the assaulting column is in the works.

If the troops are driven back, the firing will be directed on Fort Fisher again when the signal is made, and this plan will be followed from time to time as assaults are made and repulsed.

There is one thing to which I beg leave to call attention. When the range is once obtained, the officer of division shall note in a book the distance marked on the sight, so that he will not forget it. When the smoke becomes thick, and objects dim, a reference to the notes and an examination, to see if the sight is properly set, will assist very much in insuring accuracy of fire.

DAVID D. PORTER,
Rear-Admiral, Commanding North Atlantic Squadron.

REAR-ADMIRAL PORTER'S LANDING ORDERS.

FLAG-SHIP "MALVERN,"
OFF NEW INLET, N. C., January 15, 1865.

[Landing Orders.]

The landing party will land out of gun-shot of the fort, and as fast as the boats get rid of their loads they will be shoved off, and the boat-keepers will pull off and hang to the stern of the "Nansemond," which vessel will be anchored off the landing. When the men are landed they will be formed and kept together, the marines forming by themselves.

Lieutenant S. W. Preston will have charge of the men with shovels. He will advance as near the fort as he safely can, without running the risk of a single man, and commence throwing up rifle-pits rapidly. He will first advance with a thin line of sappers, and as soon as he can get a ditch deep enough for shelter, the marines will go in, in thin squads, and occupy them. As the sand is thrown up high enough to conceal a person, other sappers will come in behind and dig it deeper. There will be required a three and a half feet ditch, and about the same height of earth thrown out. The object is to get as close to the fort as possible, and with perfect safety, so that the men will have shelter to go to in case of the enemy firing grape and canister.

The officers leading the men must make them keep under command—not show themselves until the signal is made and the Army moves to the assault. No move is to be made forward until the Army charges, when the Navy is to assault the sea or southeast face of the work, going over with cutlasses drawn and revolvers in hand. The marines will follow after, and when they gain the edge of the parapet, they will lie flat and pick off the enemy in the works. The sailors will charge at once on the field-pieces in the fort, and kill the gunners. The mouths of the bomb-proofs must be secured at once, and no quarter given if the enemy fire from them after we enter the fort. Any man who straggles or disobeys orders is to be sent to the rear under a guard. The men must keep their flags rolled up until they are on top of the parapet and inside the fort, when they will hoist them.

Remember, the sailors, when they start to board, are to go with a rush, and get up as fast as they can. Officers are directed not to leave their companies under any circumstances, and every company is to be kept together. If, when our men get into the fort, the enemy commence firing on Fort Fisher from the Mound, every three men will seize a prisoner, pitch him over the walls, and get behind the fort for protection, or into the bomb-proofs. The fleet-captain will take charge of the landing party, and all the commands will report to him. He represents me on this occasion, and all his orders will be promptly obeyed.

DAVID D. PORTER, *Rear-Admiral.*

REPORT OF FLEET-CAPTAIN K. R. BREESE.

FLAG-SHIP "MALVERN,"
OFF FORT FISHER, N. C., January 16.

SIR—I have to report that, in obedience to your order, I represented your flag in commanding the assault on Fort Fisher, and beg leave to state as follows:

Lieutenant S. W. Preston had charge of a force

of about ten men from each ship, with shovels and picks, and threw up within 600 yards of the fort a well-protected breastwork, and from that gradually advanced to within two hundred yards a succession of rifle-pits, which were most promptly occupied by a line of skirmishers composed of marines under Second-Lieutenant L. E. Fagan, United States marine corps. The manner in which this was done reflects most creditably upon Lieutenant Preston. As the advance was made, he came to me and reported his work finished, and asked that he might be employed in any way. Lieutenant Preston's services were most useful to me, and in his last moments he attempted to send me word that he had carried out my orders.

The assaulting party was composed of about sixteen hundred seamen and four hundred marines, divided into four lines, as follows: First line, composed of marines, Captain L. L. Dawson, United States marine corps, commanding. Second line, composed of the landing party of the first and fourth divisions of the squadron, Lieutenant-Commander C. H. Cushman, commanding. Third line,

LIEUT. SAMUEL W. PRESTON OF ADMIRAL PORTER'S STAFF.
(KILLED IN THE ASSAULT ON FORT FISHER).

composed of the landing party of the second division of the squadron, commanded by Lieutenant-Commander James Parker, who most generously waived his seniority upon reading your order that I should represent you on shore. Fourth line, composed of the landing party of the third division of the squadron, commanded by Lieutenant-Commander T. O. Selfridge. The second, third, and fourth lines were of about equal strength.

It was intended that the men should assault in line, the marines acting as sharp-shooters, and the different lines were to charge over them; but from the difficulty I had of informing myself of the time when the army was to assault, which was to guide our movements, that moment found us too far off to move to the attack unless under cover. When I discovered that the army was moving to attack the fort, I ordered the men to advance by the flank, along the beach, hoping to be able to form them for the assault under cover of the marines; but four hundred yards' distance, exposed to a most

galling fire of musketry, threw a portion of the marines into the first line, and the rest of them did not take position as they should.

The second and third lines came along, and the heads of the three lines joined and formed one compact column, which, filing up to the sea-face of Fort Fisher, assaulted to within fifty yards of the parapet, which was lined with one dense mass of musketeers, who played sad havoc with our men. Although exposed to a most severe fire from the enemy, the men were rallied three times under the personal encouragement and exposure of their commanding officers, but failed to gain much ground. A few officers and men reached the parapet. I don't know their names, but they will doubtless be found in the reports of the officers accompanying the party.

The marines, having failed to occupy their position, gave the enemy an almost unmolested fire upon us.

Men armed with Sharpe's rifles, and the few marines in the front, opened fire, but it was too feeble to be of avail. Finding the rear of the men retreating, I hastened toward it to form them under cover, and have them use their rifles; but they were too far distant for me to reach them, and I accordingly returned to a position near the works. As I did so, the remaining men, notwithstanding all attempts to stop them, fled, with the exception of about sixty, among whom were Lieutenant-Commanders James Parker, C. H. Cushman, T. O. Selfridge, and M. Sicard, and Lieutenants N. H. Farquhar and R. H. Lamson, the latter of whom was wounded, and several volunteer officers whose names I unfortunately do not know.

The fire of the enemy was so severe that the few of our men remaining had to seek such cover as they could, and there remained until dark, when a demonstration upon the part of the rebels induced all to make a rush, and most succeeded in escaping.

The country will regret the death of Lieutenant S. W. Preston, acting as my aide in carrying orders, who was killed in front; and of Lieutenant B. H. Porter, killed in the early assault, at the head of the column; and of several volunteer officers, seamen, and marines, killed during the attack.

Of Assistant Surgeon William Longshaw special mention should be made on account of his great bravery and attention to the wounded under the hottest fire, until finally he fell a victim in the very act of binding up the wounds of a marine.

I can but attribute the failure of the assault to the absence of the marines from their position, as their fire would have enabled our boarders to use their cutlasses and pistols most effectively. By this I would imply the lack of proper organization, it being impossible in the short space of time, on account of throwing so many small squads of men from the different vessels together in one mass, lacking proper company formations, and wholly unacquainted with each other, to secure such organization.

This led to the confusion exhibited, for it was not due to any want of personal valor on the part of the officers or men.

Although the officers and men were exposed to a severe fire from the enemy, to them of a novel character and upon a novel element, which would have tried veterans, yet they advanced nobly, and the survivors must be satisfied that they contributed in no small degree to the success of the army. The enemy believing, as I am informed, that the main assault was to come from us, were much surprised upon looking to their rear to find the army so far advanced in their works.

The medical officers sent on shore with the landing party established their field hospital at a work about a mile from the fort, where Assistant Surgeon B. H. Kidder took charge of the wounded who were conveyed there, and attended to their wants as well as circumstances would permit.

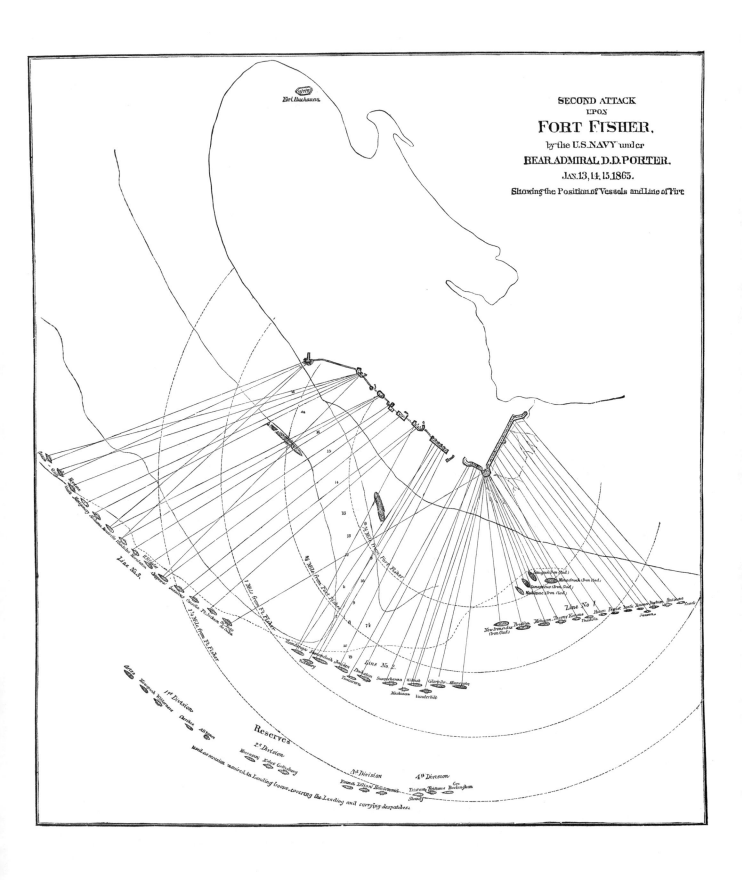

SECOND ATTACK
UPON
FORT FISHER,
by the U.S.NAVY under
REAR ADMIRAL D.D.PORTER,
Jan. 13, 14, 15, 1865.
Showing the Position of Vessels and Line of Fire

Fort Buchanan

As near as I could estimate, there were about sixty-five killed and two hundred wounded.

Lieutenant-Commander W. B. Cushing, in the extreme front, finding nothing could be done, left with the retreating men, and succeeded finally in rallying them, and, at the request of General Terry, occupied the lines near his headquarters, which enabled him to withdraw men to reinforce his force in the fort.

Being a witness to the assault of the army after our repulse, I cannot but express my admiration of the extreme gallantry of its attack.

Where one act of personal bravery was displayed on the part of the enemy, a dozen or more were conspicuous on our part ; and it was the most imposing sight to see how splendidly our brave soldiers did their work.

In conclusion, I would say that I may have omitted the names of officers who have distinguished themselves by their gallantry, yet I could not fail to mention those above named, who came personally under my notice, and I trust that the commanding officers of the assaulting lines will do justice to all.

To Lieutenant-Commander James Parker I would

ADMIRAL'S SECRETARY, CARLISLE P. PORTER (NOW FIRST-LIEUTENANT U. S. MARINE CORPS).

say that I was a witness to his efforts to advance the men, to the free exposure of his person, and, although ranking me, he would let no obstacle of that nature interpose and check his endeavors to do his utmost to capture the fort.

To your secretary, Mr. C. P. Porter, acting as my aide, I am very much indebted. Though frequently sent to the rear with orders, he was most promptly back, and at the assault he was found at the front.

Although the assaulting party failed, I think it but due to those that advanced, and to the memories of the slain, to claim for them, through their strong demonstrations, a corresponding resistance from the enemy, and a weakening of the rebel defence toward our army

I have been informed by the officers who conversed with prisoners that the enemy believed ours to be the main assault, and concentrated against us

their main force. In saying this, I would wish not to be understood in the least to detract from the splendid gallantry exhibited by our army, which was worthy of the highest commendation that can be bestowed.

Very respectfully,
Your obedient servant,
K. R. BREESE,
Fleet-Captain.
REAR-ADMIRAL DAVID D. PORTER,
Commanding North Atlantic Squadron.

DISPATCH OF REAR-ADMIRAL D. D. PORTER, COMMENDING OFFICERS, ETC.
NORTH ATLANTIC SQUADRON,
U. S. FLAG-SHIP "MALVERN,"
CAPE FEAR RIVER, January 28, 1865.

SIR—After such an engagement and success as this fleet has met with, I think it due to the officers engaged to mention those particularly who, in my opinion, deserve the commendation of the Department or merit promotion. I did not think it well to mention these matters in my late official dispatch, as such reports seldom or ever give satisfaction to officers or their friends, and give rise more often to heart-burnings and jealousies, which it is desirable to avoid on an occasion like this. It is no easy matter for a commander-in-chief to do full justice to all concerned, but I will endeavor to do so to the best of my ability, without partiality to any one beyond what I must naturally feel towards those who have given me their warmest support on this occasion. I trust I need not remind the Department that our success here has, in material and facts, been greater than on any other occasion during this war. I trust that some promotions will grow out of *this*, if only to show the officers that there is reward in store for those who do the fighting. First and foremost on the list of commodores is Commodore H. K. Thatcher. Full of honest zeal and patriotism, his vessel was always ready for action, and when he did go into it, his ship was handled with admirable skill ; no vessel in the squadron was so much cut up as the "Colorado' ; for some reason the rebels selected her for a target. I believe Commodore Thatcher would have fought his ship until she went to the bottom, and went into the fight with a full determination to conquer or die. There is no reward too great for this gallant officer ; he has shown the kind of ability naval leaders should possess—a love of fighting and an invincible courage. Commodore Joseph Lanman, commanding the "Minnesota," was selected to lead the line, his vessel being the slowest and least manageable ; consequently he led into action, except on an occasion when the "Colorado" took his place. I was much pleased with the manner in which he handled his ship and fired throughout the action, the whole affair on his part being conducted with admirable judgment and coolness. I recommend him to the consideration of the Department as one on whom they can place the utmost reliance, place him in any position. Commodore S. W. Godon, commanding the "Susquehanna," is an unusually intelligent officer, and who does not need to be told a second time where to go in time of action. This is the second important affair in which he has been engaged during this war, in both of which he has acquitted himself in the most handsome manner. His ship was beautifully handled, and impressed me with her good discipline and accurate firing. To me personally he has given his warmest support, and I should fail in my duty if I did not give him the full credit he deserves. His conduct throughout this harassing affair has met my warmest approbation, and I think he is one who merits promotion when the Government thinks proper to reward those who have borne the brunt of the battle.

Commodore Jas. F. Schenck and his vessel, the

"Powhatan," have come up to my expectations in every respect. This officer in battle has shown himself worthy to command so fine a ship. He performed his duty most faithfully, and I am proud not only to have had him under my command, but to see him reinstated in the position to which he has done so much credit. He deserves all I can say of him, and is worthy of promotion.

Commodore William Radford, in command of that noble ship the "Ironsides," and also in command of the division of Monitors, gained my warmest admiration by his conduct throughout this affair. He has shown abilities of a very high character, not only in fighting and manœuvering his vessel, but in taking care of his division. Ready at all times for battle, and eager to go into the fight alone, he performed admirably when his guns were brought to bear on the enemy. His vessel did more execution than any vessel in the fleet; and even when our troops were on the parapet, I had so much confidence in the accuracy of his fire that he was directed to fire through the traverses in advance of our troops and clear them out. This he did most

COMMODORE (AFTERWARDS REAR-ADMIRAL) S. W. GODON,

COMMANDING THE U. S. S. "SUSQUEHANNA."

effectually, and but for this, victory might not have been ours. Having broken his rudder in a heavy gale, he rigged up a temporary one under adverse circumstances, and had his ship ready as soon as the rest. He seemed never to tire of fighting, and for three days laid within 1,000 yards of Fort Fisher without moving his anchor, and made the rebels feel that we had come there to stay. Under all and every circumstance, Commodore Radford has acquired an enviable reputation, and is deserving of the greatest promotion that can be given him. Captain James Alden, commanding the "Brooklyn," has been near me, and at times associated with me during this war. He had already done enough to deserve promotion before the commencement of operations before Fort Fisher; but if this matter was at any time doubtful, he has certainly earned promotion now. Always leading heretofore, or assisting with all his energies, he has been engaged in all the successful attacks on forts. His aid

to me on this late occasion has been very valuable. Always intelligent and energetic, he never had to be told to get ready; he always kept ready; he anticipated, which is a quality very desirable in an officer, and without which he cannot be expected to be very useful. His vessel was always in the right place and at the right time, and when his batteries opened, no frigate could have done more execution. I have spoken before of the high qualities of this officer. I consider him able and worthy to fill the highest rank, and I know that the Government has no one in its navy more full of energy, zeal or intelligence in his profession. I shall feel much disappointed if Captain Alden is not promoted to a rank he has won more than once during this rebellion. I am sure the Department will appreciate all I have said of this gallant officer. His record speaks for him.

Captain Melancton Smith, on the "Wabash," has performed his duty well. He has also made a good record at the department, and has been actively engaged in fighting since the rebellion first broke out. His old ship has done good service here; and if he had done nothing more than assist, as he has done in the capture of this place, he deserves promotion, which I hereby recommend.

I also recommend Captain Charles Steedman, commanding "Ticonderoga," and Captain D. B. Ridgley, commanding "Shenandoah." Though commanding smaller vessels than the others, and less effective in their fire, they did the best they could. This is the second important affair Captain Steedman has been in, and Captain Ridgley has been very energetic during the war against blockade-runners. I recommend them both for promotion.

Lieutenant-Commander R. K. Breese, my fleet-captain, has been with me nearly all the time since the rebellion broke out. In command of a division of the mortar fleet, which opened the way to New Orleans, he made his first record there. In the Mississippi with me for two years, engaged in harassing and dangerous duties, he always acquitted himself to my satisfaction. In charge of the mortars at the siege of Vicksburg, he helped to hasten the surrender of that stronghold. At Fort Fisher he led the boarders in the assault, and though we were not successful in getting into the work in the face of equal numbers, yet that assault helped materially to gain the day, as is generally admitted on every side. Our troops obtained a footing without much resistance and then nobly maintained what they had won. Lieutenant-Commander Breese did all he could to rally his men, and made two or three unsuccessful attempts to regain the parapet; but the marines having failed in their duty to support the gallant officers and sailors who took the lead, he had to retire to a place of safety. He did not, however, leave the ground, but remained under the parapet in a rifle-pit, using a musket, until night favored his escape. He is a clever, gallant officer, and I strongly recommend his immediate promotion to a commander.

I also recommend the promotion of Lieutenant-Commander H. A. Adams, Jr., ordnance officer, without whose services we should have been brought to a standstill more than once. He volunteered for anything and everything.

The following officers, who volunteered to lead their men in the assault on Fort Fisher, deserve particular notice. These officers volunteered for the service, and undertook what was considered by the regular army the forlorn hope of the assault. Nowhere in the annals of war have officers and sailors undertaken so desperate a service, and one which was deemed impossible by a former general and an engineer having a high reputation in the service. Twenty-one officers were killed and wounded in this service, and twenty officers and sixty men were kept for four hours under fire from the enemy's sharpshooters, not being able to escape until night set in. The courage of these officers deserves the highest reward. Their efforts, though unsuccessful, gained the day, as the enemy considered this the main attack, and brought superior numbers from a superior position to bear on it. The names of some of these officers will be found on record on the files of the Department, among which those of Lieutenant-Commander T. O. Selfridge and Lieutenant George M. Bache will be found most conspicuous. I recommend that Lieutenant - Commander James A. Parker, Lieutenant-Commander T. O. Selfridge, Lieutenant-Commander C. H. Cushman, Lieutenant R. H. Lamson and Lieutenant George M. Bache be promoted. The three latter were severely wounded. Though the marines did not do their duty, Captain L. L. Dawson, Captain George Butler, and Second - Lieutenants William Wallace, Charles F. Williams and Louis E. Fagan were found in the front, and fought gallantly. I recommend them to the favorable notice of the department.

To Captain O. S. Glisson, commanding the "Santiago de Cuba," I am particularly indebted for his zeal in covering the troops, landing guns,

CAPTAIN (NOW REAR-ADMIRAL) O. S. GLISSON,

COMMANDING THE U. S. S. "SANTIAGO DE CUBA."

and taking his division into action; and to Captain B. F. Sands, commanding the "Fort Jackson," for performing the different duties he was called on to perform. I recommend them both for promotion. I refer to Captain Glisson's report in relation to the commanding officers in his division.

I also recommend to the department Lieutenant-Commander T. S. Phelps, in command of the "Juniata."

Lieutenant-Commander J. H. Upshur, in the "A. D. Vance," had charge of the reserves, and was employed night and day in landing army stores and guns, and covering the troops from the rebels outside of our lines. His guns did good execution, and though his duties prevented him from participating in the attack on the forts, I cannot withhold his name, and recommend him for advancement.

I recommend that Commander E. G. Parrott, commanding the "Monadnock," Commander E. R. Colhoun, commanding the "Saugus," Lieutenant-Commander A. W. Weaver, commanding the "Mahopac," and Lieutenant - Commander George E. Belknap, be promoted. These officers have given

a world-renowned name to the Monitors, and have shown what they were capable of performing when properly placed and managed. They had the hardest part of the work, and there is no end to their energy, bravery and untiring zeal.

I can draw no distinction between the following officers, whom I recommend for promotion. They were under fire most all the time, and at close quarters, and coolly performed what was required of them:

Lieutenant-Commander W. T. Truxton, commanding the "Tacony"; Lieutenant - Commander P. G. Watmough, commanding the "Kansas"; Lieutenant-Commander F. M. Ramsay, commanding the "Unadilla"; Lieutenant - Commander D. L. Braine, commanding the "Pequot"; Lieutenant-Commander Ralph Chandler, commanding the "Maumee"; Lieutenant - Commander M. Sicard, commanding the "Seneca"; Commander J. H. Spotts, commanding the "Pawtucket"; Lieutenant-Commander W. G. Temple, commanding the "Pontoosac"; Lieutenant - Commander T. C. Harris, commanding the "Yantic"; Commander J. C. Howell, commanding the "Nereus"; Commander D. Ammen, commanding the "Mohican"; Commander J. C. Beaumont, commanding the "Mackinaw"; Commander J. M. B. Clitz, commanding the "Osceola"; Lieutenant - Commander J. L. Davis, commanding the "Sassacus"; Lieutenant-Commander E. E. Potter, commanding the "Chippewa"; Lieutenant W. B. Cushing, commanding the "Monticello"; Commander S. D. Trenchard, commanding the "Rhode Island"; Acting-Volunteer-Lieutenant A. R. Langthorne, commanding the "Alabama"; Acting-Volunteer-Lieutenant T. C. Dunn, commanding the "Montgomery." I also recommend for promotion Acting - Master S. P. Crafts, commanding the "Little Ada"; Acting-Master J. H. Porter, commanding the "Nansemond"; Acting-Master E. Keyser, commanding the "Eolus"—for gallant conduct throughout the action; also Acting-Volunteer John McDiarmid, commanding the "Governor Buckingham." I must refer you to the reports of different commanders for recommendations of those under their command, as it would be impossible for me to know anything in relation to them. When it is remembered that the surrender of the defences of Cape Fear River is one of the most, if not the most, important event of the war, in which the largest stronghold of the enemy was captured under adverse circumstances, the justice of promotion will be seen. Its importance will be soon felt in the fall of Richmond, to which it is as necessary now as the main artery is to the human system. I trust the Department will be liberal in its promotions. This is almost a naval affair entirely, for the idea originated in the Navy Department; and until the reputation of the Army became in danger of being reflected upon, we met from that branch of the service little or no encouragement. Few promotions have taken place during the war, and it would be gratifying to the friends of all concerned to see the advancement of those who have worked so patiently for three years, and have made so handsome a *denouement*. I have heard a matter freely discussed among the officers, to which I beg leave to draw the attention of the Department. A distribution of medals to officers would be a most popular thing. This is so common a method among modern nations, and so universally accepted as a reward for eminent services among officers and men, that I recommend its adoption in our naval service. Any one who has seen the pride with which sailors wear the medals bestowed upon them for gallant conduct can readily imagine how grateful it would be to officers. Trifling as such a mere bauble may be in intrinsic value, yet the history of war tells how valuable they are as inducements to perform gallant deeds. I trust the department will not think me presuming in recommending what, no doubt, they already intend to adopt.

I am, sir, very respectfully, your obedient servant,
DAVID D. PORTER, *Rear-Admiral.*
HON. GIDEON WELLES,
Secretary of the Navy, Washington, D. C.

COMPLIMENTARY LETTER OF REAR-ADMIRAL PORTER IN REGARD TO GENERAL TERRY.

NORTH ATLANTIC SQUADRON,
U. S. FLAG-SHIP "MALVERN,"
OFF SMITHSVILLE, N. C., Jan. 20, 1865.

SIR—I have been so much pleased with General Terry, and the manner in which he has conducted his part of the operations here, that I deem it worthy of a special dispatch to express what I feel.

General Terry is, no doubt, well known to his associates in the field, who have served with him, and to the Lieutenant-General who selected him for the service, but the American people should know and feel the very great service he has rendered them by his most admirable assault on these tremendous works. Young, brave and unassuming, he bears his success with the modesty of a true soldier, and is willing to give credit to those who shared with him the perils of the assault. No one could form the slightest conception of these works, their magnitude, strength and extent, who had not seen them, and General Whiting, the engineer, must have had an abiding faith in the durability of the Confederacy when he expended so many years labor on them.

The result of the fall of Fort Fisher was the fall of all the surrounding works in and near this place —Fort Caswell, a large work at the West Inlet, mounting twenty-nine guns, all the works on Smith's Island, the works between Caswell and Smithsville up to the battery on Reeves' Point, on the west side of the river—in all, 169 guns falling into our hands; 2 steamers were burnt or blown up, and there never was so clean a sweep made anywhere.

A timid man would have hesitated to attack these works by assault, no matter what assistance he may have had from other quarters, but General Terry never for an instant hesitated; and though I feel somewhat flattered at the confidence he reposed in my judgment, I am quite ready to believe that he acted on his own ideas of what was proper to be done in the matter, and was perfectly qualified to judge without the advice of any one.

Throughout this affair his conduct has been marked by the greatest desire to be successful, not for the sake of personal considerations, but for the cause in which we are all alike engaged.

I don't know that I ever met an officer who so completely gained my esteem and admiration.

I have the honor to be, very respectfully, your obedient servant,
DAVID D. PORTER, *Rear-Admiral.*
HON. GIDEON WELLES,
Secretary of the Navy, Washington, D. C.

ADDITIONAL REPORT OF FLEET-CAPTAIN K. R. BREESE.

FLAG-SHIP "MALVERN,"
CAPE FEAR RIVER, January 28, 1865.

ADMIRAL—In my report of the assault of Fort Fisher, I did not mention the fact of Lieutenant-Commander Cushman being wounded, as he made so light of the affair and did not wish to be included among those mentioned as such. Since, I have learned that Lieutenant-Commander Cushman's wound was more severe than I had even thought, and I think it but right that I should mention that, though in this condition and very much fatigued from his efforts of the day, being re-

lieved by darkness from the fire of the fort, he collected together the men of his column, and posted them in the lines occupied by us that night, requiring a great exertion and constant movement until 2 A. M. the following morning.

I also would wish to bring to your notice the conduct of a young lad of the "Wabash," named Myers, who three several times left a good protection from the fire of the enemy and went to the assistance of wounded men, and under fire carried them to the friendly shelter of his hole in the sand, and this within a hundred yards of Fort Fisher. I had hoped to obtain the name of a very brave and gallant officer of the "Vanderbilt," who led their assaulting party, but have been unable to do so. This officer was conspicuous for his gallantry and most richly deserves special mention.

I would also wish to say that Acting-Lieutenant-Commander Danels, of the "Vanderbilt," suffering from ill-health and unable to keep up with the assaulting party, rendered much valuable assistance in rallying the men and in caring for the wounded. I regret that my personal acquaintance with the

LIEUTENANT BENJAMIN H. PORTER (OF ADMIRAL PORTER'S STAFF.)

(KILLED IN THE ASSAULT ON FORT FISHER.)

many brave officers and men around me on that day was so slight that I could not soon recognize to what ships they belonged, except in the instances named, and that, necessarily, I have failed to mention particularly some who, I saw, behaved splendidly, and have trusted to the commanding officers of columns to name them. I wish also to bear witness to the handsome manner in which Lieutenant Fagan, of the marine corps, did his duty with his sharp-shooters, and to the gallantry he exhibited in advancing his men so close to the enemy's works. An additional regret I feel in the loss of Flag-Lieutenant Preston, who could so much better have done justice, that it devolves upon me to mention how well the officers and men behaved in digging rifle-pits, and of the bravery evinced by many of them in advancing under a perfectly exposed fire to within 300 yards of the fort, and digging their pits under the fire. A number were killed and wounded in the undertaking. Although these men had been hard at work all day, and were told by Lieutenant Preston that they were not expected to join in the assault, I know of scarcely any who had arms that did not join it.

Very respectfully, your obedient servant,
K. R. BREESE, *Fleet-Captain.*
REAR-ADMIRAL DAVID D. PORTER,
Commanding North Atlantic Squadron.

DISPATCH OF REAR-ADMIRAL D. D. PORTER, TRANS-
MITTING REPORT OF FLEET - CAPTAIN K. R.
BREESE, IN REGARD TO THE DEATHS OF LIEU-
TENANTS PORTER AND PRESTON.

NORTH ATLANTIC SQUADRON,
U. S. FLAG-SHIP "MALVERN,"
CAPE FEAR RIVER, February 1, 1865.

SIR—I inclose a communication from my fleet-captain, Lieutenant-Commander K. R. Breese, in relation to the lamented Lieutenants Preston and Porter, who fell together before the walls of Fort Fisher, and while trying to plant the Union colors on the enemy's ramparts. No eulogy passed upon these two gallant men could do them full justice. To me they had both endeared themselves by their noble qualities, and in their deaths I feel as if I had lost two members of my own family. Their names and gallant deeds during their short service in the war will long be remembered by their associates in arms, and the memory of their heroic gallantry will inspire future heroes to emulate their conduct. The officers of the squadron propose to erect a monument at Annapolis to the memory of the gallant dead, but their memories will live in history long after the stone that records their deeds has crumbled into dust. I must not omit to pay a just tribute to the memory of the noble Assistant Surgeon William Longshaw, who was shot dead near the enemy's works while engaged in an act of mercy, binding up the wounds of a sailor, and of the gallant Acting-Assistant Surgeon John Blackmer, who fell and died in the same way. Nor must I omit the name of Acting-Ensign Robert Wiley, who died fighting manfully, and endeavoring to reach the enemy's parapets. They all died like heroes, and the nation is as much bound to mourn their loss as those who have held higher positions.

They are all regretted deeply here, and their names will be forever associated with one of the most gallant attacks ever made on a powerful fortress.

I am, sir, very respectfully, your obedient servant,
DAVID D. PORTER, *Rear-Admiral.*
HON. GIDEON WELLES,
Secretary of the Navy, Washington, D. C.

REPORT OF FLEET-CAPTAIN K. R. BREESE.

NORTH ATLANTIC SQUADRON,
U. S. FLAG-SHIP "MALVERN,"
OFF FORT FISHER, January 18, 1865.

ADMIRAL—In my report of the assault on Fort Fisher I have scarcely mentioned the names and services of Lieutenant S. W. Preston, your flag-lieutenant, and Lieutenant B. H. Porter, your flag-captain, thinking that by a little delay I might the more do justice, yet I seem to feel that impossible in me. Preston, after accomplishing most splendidly the work assigned him by you, which was both dangerous and laborious, under constant fire, came to me, as my aide, for orders, showing no flagging of spirit or body, and returning from the rear, whither he had been sent, fell among the foremost at the front, as he had lived, the thorough embodiment of a United States naval officer. Porter, conspicuous by his figure and uniform, as well as by his great gallantry, claimed the right to lead the headmost column with the "Malvern's" men he had taken with him, carrying your flag, and fell at its very head. Two more noble spirits the world never saw, nor had the navy ever two more in-

trepid men. Young, talented, and handsome, the bravest of the brave, pure in their lives, surely their names deserve something more than a passing mention, and are worthy to be handed down to posterity with the greatest and best of naval heroes.

Were you not so well acquainted with their characters, I should deem it my duty to speak of their high merits; but, as chief of your staff, to which they belonged, I must speak of their wonderful singleness of purpose to do their whole duty; always most cheerful and willing, desirous of undertaking anything which might redound to the credit of the service; giving me at all times the most ready assistance in my duties; combining with their intelligence a ready perception as to the best mode of accomplishing their orders, the country has lost two such servants as could illy be spared, and your staff its brightest ornaments.

Very respectfully, your obedient servant,
K. R. BREESE,
Fleet-Captain, North Atlantic Squadron.
REAR-ADMIRAL DAVID D. PORTER,
Commanding North Atlantic Squadron.

Thus was Fort Fisher won after a gallant attack and as gallant a defence on the

SURGEON (AFTERWARDS SURGEON-GENERAL) PHILIP S. WALES,
OF THE U. S. S. "FORT JACKSON."

part of the Confederates as any one interested in their cause might desire. It was a terrible sight to see those men, all of one blood, sternly fighting in the dark for over four hours, almost breast to breast, shooting or bayonetting each other on the tops of the traverses or around the sides, while the "Ironsides" would explode her 11-inch shrapnel so well timed that they would burst over the heads or in amongst the struggling mass of Confederates, who were doing their utmost to hold on to the traverses behind the bomb-proof; but when the calcium-light of the "Malvern" was thrown upon these desperate soldiers, and exposed them plainly to the "Ironsides" gunners, they were swept away by the dozens. Never did men fight harder than the Confederates, and never were cooler soldiers than the Federals, who gained traverse after traverse with the aid of the wondrous fire of the "Ironsides," until they stood on the last one, when the enemy fled to the beach near the Mound, pursued by the Federal troops; and the former, having no more hope of escape, laid down their arms and submitted to their captors.

Three cheers went up from the Federal soldiers, the crews on board the ships made the welkin ring with their shouts of joy, the steam-whistles blew, the bells rang, sky-rockets filled the air, and every yard-arm was illuminated with the Coston night-signals. Not a man there but saw this was the death-blow to the rebellion. No more

COMMANDER CHARLES D. SIGSBEE,

ENSIGN ON THE U. S. S. "BROOKLYN," AT FORT FISHER.

army provisions or clothing could enter the only open port—Wilmington. Submission might not come immediately, but the end was not far off. The soldiers who had so strenuously fought to gain the stronghold would go back rejoicing to Hampton Roads, having wiped out the disgrace inflicted through no fault of theirs, and could now, at the end of the war, join their families with the proud boast that they were the assaulters that finally carried Fort Fisher. While the Navy, that had for so many days breasted the storms of winter on the dangerous coast of North Carolina, could hope soon to haul into "Snug Harbor," where, in years to come, they could tell their companions how for thirty-five days they had fought the ocean in its wrath and defied the elements; how they coaled their ships and took in their ammunition while the vessels were rolling and pitching "like mad,"

and how they battered the heaviest earth-work in the Southern Confederacy until not a gun remained serviceable on its carriage.

Amidst all the rejoicing, the Army and Navy had to deplore the loss of a great many gallant men who freely offered their lives that their country might live and move on in the march of progress, civilization and liberty, that in future ages would make it the greatest nation on the face of the earth. The casualties of the Federal Army were 691 officers and men killed, wounded and missing, while the Navy lost 309 more. The defeated but gallant enemy went into the battle 2,500 strong and surrendered only 1,800 men.

A second casualty took place, the morning after the surrender of the fort, by the blowing up of a bomb-proof. How it happened no one knew, but about a hundred bodies were thrown up into the air, soldiers, sailors, and Confederates all mixed up together. It was a sickening sight and took away much of the pleasure of the victory; but soldiers and sailors grew accustomed to such things during the war, and the active work still before them, ere they could reach Wilmington and secure the railroad leading to Richmond, soon drove the dreadful spectacle from their minds. Regarding the gallant soldiers, who so nobly fought their way over the bomb-proofs, too much cannot be said in their praise. Terry, their leader, Ames, Curtis, Lawrence, and Pennypacker, should never be forgotten; while those in the Navy, who fought their ships so well and so persistently, will, in future years, be remembered and honored as were the heroes of 1812, when our infant Navy showed the mistress of the seas that she would one day have to divide her honors with the young Republic.

A number of the 100-pounder Parrott rifles burst while in action, and the commanders and men, having lost confidence in them, they were no longer used. The consequence was that, before the forts in Cape Fear River could be attacked, a requisition had to be made on the Bureau of Ordnance in Washington for twenty-four 11-inch guns. These were sent from New York in a fast steamer, and in ten days were all mounted on the vessels in Cape Fear River and ready for service. One Monitor, the "Montauk," had been gotten over the bar, and the gun-boat fleet was ready to move up as soon as the Army could make its preparations to advance. The Confederate General, Hoke, was intrenched about six miles above Fort Fisher, where it was said that General Bragg intended to dispute the further advance of the Federal troops—a foolish resolution, as there was a force of gun-boats in the river that could bid defiance to all the guns the Confederates had mounted.

As soon as General Grant heard of the victory, he proceeded to Fort Fisher in a transport, taking with him General Schofield and an additional number of troops. General Schofield's seniority gave him the command of the whole, a circumstance that could not be well avoided, as the troops came from his division. As soon as possible after General Grant's arrival, preparations were made for the Army and Navy to move on up the Cape Fear River in concert.

The effect of the surrender of Fort Fisher was a stampede in all the forts south of Federal Point. Lieutenant Cushing was sent in the gun-boat "Monticello" around to Fort Caswell, a strong fortification, built in former days by the United States engineers as a protection to the Western bar. Lieutenant Cushing found Fort Caswell blown up, the works at Bald Head destroyed, Fort Shaw blown up, and Fort Campbell abandoned. These works, mounting 9 and 10 inch guns and 150-pounder Armstrongs, completely commanded the channel, and were nearly out of reach of projectiles from the seaward.

After an examination of the forts, Lieutenant Cushing hoisted the American flag on Fort Caswell and pushed on to Smithville, a heavily fortified point on Cape Fear River. The garrison departed as soon as the "Monticello" hove in sight, leaving everything in this heavy and beautiful fortification uninjured, and only two 9-inch guns spiked in the work at Deep River Point.

Up to January 20th, only one gun-boat, the "Tacony," Lieutenant-Commander W. T. Truxton, had succeeded after hard work in getting past the Rip, a bad shoal which barred the way, after passing Fort Buchanan, to the fair channel of Cape Fear River. The Admiral at once sent her to Reeves' Point, about three miles above Fort Fisher, on the "west side of the river," to disable the guns at that place, presuming that the enemy had already abandoned it in the panic.

Thus, in twenty-four hours after the capture of Fort Fisher and its outworks, all the formidable chain of works around the two entrances of Cape Fear River were in the hands of the Navy, and, for want of troops were temporarily garrisoned by sailors. Three of the forts had been built to keep out any force that could be sent against them. They were wonderful specimens of engineering skill, and a credit to the Confederate engineers who planned and constructed them. Any one seeing them would suppose that the whole Southern Confederacy had been at work throwing up fortifications.

The following is a list of the guns mounted in these works: Reeves' Point, three 10-inch guns; Smithville, four 10-inch guns; above Smithville, two 10-inch guns; Fort Caswell, ten 10-inch guns, two 9-inch guns, one Armstrong rifled gun, four rifled 32-pounders, two 32-pounder smooth-bores, three 8-inch guns, one Parrott 20-pounder, three rifled field-pieces and three 8-inch guns—total 29; forts Campbell and Shaw, six 10-inch, six 32-pounder smooth-bore, one 32-pounder rifled, one 8-inch, six field-pieces and two mortars; Smith's Island, three 10-inch guns, six 32-pounder smooth-bores, two 22-pounders rifled, four field-pieces, 2 mortars and six other guns. Grand total, 83 guns.

When General Grant went to Fort Fisher and General Schofield took command, a council-of-war was held on board the "Malvern," at which General Grant presided, and it was concluded to land an Army Corps under General Cox, at Smithville, on the west bank of Cape Fear River, march on Fort Anderson by a good road, while the gun-boats attacked it by water; but this plan was changed after General Grant left, and General Schofield undertook an expedition by way of the beach, covered by some six or eight gun-boats; but it came on to blow and rain heavily and the troops had to return, when the first plan was finally adopted.

On the 18th of February, the gun-boats having shifted their 100-pounder rifles for 11-inch guns, proceeded up the river towards Fort Anderson preparatory to an attack. The Army Corps under General Cox proceeded by the Smithville road to try and cut off the enemy if he attempted to escape from the works. The Monitor "Montauk," Lieutenant-Commander Edward E. Stone, was anchored eight hundred yards from the fort, which immediately opened fire upon her, but her thick sides and turrets resisted this fire until the other vessels could be brought into position. The river channel was very narrow, crooked and shoal, and the vessels had great difficulty in securing a berth where they could use their heaviest guns. The following gun-boats were engaged:

"Lenapee," Lieutenant-Commander John S. Barnes; "Sassacus," Lieutenant-Commander John Lee Davis; "Mackinaw," Commander J. C. Beaumont; "Maratanza," Lieutenant-Commander Geo. W. Young; "Nyack," Lieutenant-Commander L. H. Newman; "Chippewa," Lieutenant-Commander E. E. Potter; "Shawmut," Lieutenant-Commander John G. Walker; "Seneca," Lieutenant-Commander M. Sicard; "Malvern," Acting-Ensign Wm. C. Wise; "Pontoosuc," Lieutenant-Commander Wm. G. Temple; "Unadilla,"

Lieutenant - Commander F. M. Ramsey; "Pawtucket, Commander J. H. Spotts; "Huron," Lieutenant - Commander Thos. O. Selfridge; "Maumee," Lieutenant-Commander Ralph Chandler; "Pequot," Lieutenant-Commander D. L. Braine.

The "Montauk" bore the fire for some hours and returned it leisurely. The Confederates, finding they could make no impression on her, reserved their fire until they could find something more vulnerable, and kept in their bomb - proofs. On the 18th, the gun-boats moved to within a thousand yards and opened a rapid and well-directed fire, which was returned with great vigor for half an hour. The Confederate fire then gradually ceased. They left the fort and retreated to Wilmington. The Army

LIEUTENANT-COMMANDER JOHN S. BARNES,

CHIEF-OF-STAFF WITH REAR-ADMIRAL S. P. LEE, AND COMMANDING U. S. S. "LENAPEE," IN CAPE FEAR RIVER, AFTER THE ATTACK ON FORT FISHER.

came up half an hour afterwards and found the fort in possession of the Navy. In this day's fight the loss was only two killed and six wounded on the "Chippewa" and "Pequot." About fifty boats were sent out at once to drag the river for torpedoes, and, after picking up all that could be found, pushed on and transported General Cox's division over the creeks, where the Confederates had burned the bridges, so that he was delayed but a short time and was enabled to move on to Wilmington.

In the meantime, General Terry's division at or near Fort Fisher charged General Hoke's intrenchments, and the Confederates immediately retreated upon Wilmington; so that, while the Army was marching on that place on both sides of the river, the gun-boats were pushing up as fast as they could find their way through the intricate channel.

Before General Cox or General Terry had reached the vicinity of Wilmington, the gun-boats reached Forts Strong and Lee. Taking a position at thirteen hundred yards distant, they opened with their 11-inch guns on the forts. The forts were in an elevated position and were armed with eight or ten heavy guns. Soon after the fleet opened fire the forts were evacuated, and the Union flag was hoisted over them by Lieutenant-Commander K. R. Breese, Chief of Staff. The channel had to be dragged for torpedoes before the gun-boats could pass up, and night came leaving them huddled together in a mass through which a boat could hardly pass.

A little before sunset, a faithful "contraband," who had escaped the vigilance of the Confederates, appeared alongside the flag-ship and informed the Admiral that the enemy intended sending down that night two hundred floating torpedoes with a hundred pounds of powder in each.

Orders were immediately given by the Admiral for the gun - boats to get out their fishing seines—of which each vessel in the Navy carried one—and to unite and spread them across the river in two lines. Thus there were nine hundred and sixty yards of seine presented as an obstacle to the expected torpedoes, placed about five hundred yards above the vessels, while on either side of the river fish weirs extended through the shoal water to shore. This seemed to be a perfect obstruction to floating torpedoes, but about 9 o'clock at night a black object was seen from the flag-ship drifting past her. The gun-boat "Shawmut" was hailed and ordered to send a boat to examine it. The officer of the boat, Acting-Ensign W. B. Trufant, standing in the bow, saw that it was a barrel and fired his revolver at it at close quarters, exploding it, by which he was dangerously wounded, two of the boat's crew killed, and one slightly wounded, while the boat was shattered. A short time after, another of the same kind exploded in the "Osceola's" wheel - house, blowing it to pieces and knocking down some bulkheads on board, but doing no damage to the hull. This was all the injury done by these ugly customers, two only escaping the nets out of the hundreds sent down. Next morning boats were sent up to the nets, when it was found that a great number of the infernal machines had been caught and held. They were all disposed of by firing muskets into them at a safe distance and exploding them.

Such were the obstacles and apparatus

that opposed a more rapid advance up the river; but after it had been thoroughly dragged in the morning, and all the torpedoes taken up, the gun-boats pushed on up, hoping to arrive at Wilmington before the army; but General Terry reached there before them, and the divisions of Cox and Terry shook hands in the streets of the captured city. This ended the capture of all the various works in and about Wilmington, and the Confederates retreated toward Richmond by the Wilmington railroad. Nothing more remained to be done.

A quick dispatch-vessel was sent to Hampton Roads immediately on the fall of Fort Fisher to notify the Navy Department by telegram of the result, and now the final victory was announced to the Secretary of the Navy in the same manner.

The Admiral, after making a proper distribution of the gun-boats to co-operate with the army, proceeded in the steamer "Rhode Island" to Hampton Roads, while all the vessels not needed in Cape Fear River were dispatched to their stations, or sent to several other points which the enemy still occupied.

On his arrival at Hampton Roads, the Admiral received the following letter from Secretary Welles, which, if not as ardent as some of his congratulations to other officers who had gained victories, it must be remembered that he had written so many hearty congratulations that he could not find words on this occasion to express his gratification:

NAVY DEPARTMENT, Jan. 17, 1865.

SIR—The Department has just received your brief, but highly gratifying, dispatch announcing the fall, on the 15th instant, of Fort Fisher, under the combined assault of the Navy and Army, and hastens to congratulate you and General Terry and the brave officers, soldiers and sailors of your respective commands on your glorious success.

Accept my thanks for your good work.

Very respectfully,
GIDEON WELLES, *Secretary of the Navy.*
REAR-ADMIRAL DAVID D. PORTER,
Commanding North Atlantic Squadron,
off Wilmington.

The following telegram was sent immediately on the receipt of the news to the commandants of the Navy Yards:

"Fire a national salute in honor of the capture, on the 15th instant, of the rebel works on Federal Point, near Wilmington, by a combined attack of the Army and Navy.

"GIDEON WELLES."

To complete the narrative of the events described in this chapter, the following reports are added:

REPORT OF COMMODORE H. K. THATCHER.

UNITED STATES STEAM-FRIGATE "COLORADO,"
OFF WILMINGTON, N. C., Jan. 14, 1865.

ADMIRAL—I have the honor to report the following as the result of the operations of this ship on the 13th instant: At 4 A. M., in obedience to signal, got underway from our anchorage, near Wilmington, and steamed towards the forts in line of battle, the "Minnesota" ahead. At 8 A. M., anchored within easy range of the coast, in six and a half fathoms (forts about five miles distance, bearing N. E. by E.), to cover the landing of troops, and sent five boats to assist in landing them from the transports. Commenced shelling the woods skirting the coast; at 8:55 ceased firing, in obedience to your signal. At 11:10 the third line of gun-boats steamed along shore, shelling the woods, while the troops were being landed rapidly. At 3 P. M., recalled boats, in obedience to your signal. At 3:15 got underway, all the troops having been successfully landed. At 3:45 proceeded to attack the forts, without regard to the "Minnesota," in accordance to your signal, followed by the rest of the line. At 4:40 opened fire upon the forts, with steam hawser fast to the "New Ironsides," and continued the action briskly, in easy range, until 5:50 P. M., when, by your order, we ceased firing, and retired from action (it being then too dark to discern objects on shore). At 7 P. M., anchored in eight fathoms, Fort Fisher bearing W. S. W., distance three miles. My casualties were, one killed (Robert Little, seaman), one severely wounded, one wounded. Hulled six times by the forts; one 150-pound solid shot through berth-deck; one 150-pound solid shot through gun-deck, cutting through side; one 150-pound solid shot through port side, above water-line, and lodging in a beam-end, where it remained; two 150-pound solid shots, striking sheet-chain and cutting it through. The enemy's shell exploded over the hull of this ship, but without serious injury. I forward herewith reports of Surgeon Jas. McLelland and of the warrant officers.

I am much gratified to have it in my power to report that the officers and crew of this ship behaved with their usual gallantry. I have to commend to your notice, especially, Lieutenant M. L. Johnson, who, in the midst of a heavy fire from the enemy, with a boat's crew of volunteers, carried a hawser from this ship to the "New Ironsides," in order to enable us to bring all the guns to bear from the port battery, and was, for more than half an hour, a target for the forts, which they availed themselves of, but fortunately without success. I cannot omit the opportunity to speak in the highest terms of Acting-Ensign W. G. Perry, who, when the action commenced, had just returned to the ship, after having been absent all day with the boats in landing troops, and, although drenched to the skin and worn out with fatigue, went immediately to the second division, which he commanded, and fought his guns splendidly through the action. In addition to this, Mr. Perry is, in all respects, worthy of an additional grade.

I am, sir, very respectfully, your obedient servant,
H. K. THATCHER, *Commodore.*
REAR-ADMIRAL DAVID D. PORTER.
Commanding N. A. Station.

REPORT OF COMMODORE WM. RADFORD.

U. S. SHIP "NEW IRONSIDES,"
AT ANCHOR OFF FORT FISHER, January 15, 1865.

SIR—I have the honor to report, that, in obedience to your orders, the iron-clad division steamed in and took their position under the guns of the battery of Fort Fisher, this ship leading; anchored at 8:29 A. M. on the 13th instant. The "Monadnock," Commander E. G. Parrott; "Canonicus," Lieutenant-Commander G. E. Belknap; "Saugus," Commander G. R. Colhoun; and "Mahopac," Lieutenant-Commander A. W. Weaver. The battery opened on this ship as we came in. I did not reply until I obtained my desired position, opening then, deliberately, to get a correct range, as the wooden vessels were engaged landing troops, etc. The iron-clad division received the fire nearly all day alone from Fort Fisher, without receiving any very material damage, and remained in position during the night. By orders from Admiral Porter, the iron-clad division commenced the action at 10:47 A. M. on the 14th instant, and continued firing until after dark. Some of the wooden gun-boats came up, and commenced firing at 2:30 P. M., hauling off at dark, the iron-clad division maintaining their position. On the morning of the 15th we commenced the action at 7:16 A. M., and continued to fire during the day, concentrating it upon the guns of the battery which was doing the most effective work, which we invariably soon silenced or disabled. As the troops were advancing, I observed two field-pieces in the rear of the fort firing on them, which we soon silenced with some well-directed shells from this ship. When the enemy came out of their bomb-proofs to defend the fort against the storming party, I used my battery with great success against them, every shell bursting, apparently, in the right place. At 5:20 P. M. we ceased firing by orders from the flag-ship, nearly every gun on the fort facing us having been disabled in the first two days' action. I cannot close my report without speaking in the highest terms of the battery of this ship, and the manner in which it was served, for three consecutive days, my officers and men fighting all day and taking in ammunition during the night. I know of nothing surpassing it on record. I would now speak of the Monitors, and the handsome manner in which they were handled and fought during the time; and the different attacks on Fort Fisher has not only proved that they could ride out heavy gales at sea, but fight their guns in moderately smooth weather, which has been doubted by many intelligent officers.

I have the honor to be, very respectfully, your obedient servant,

WILLIAM RADFORD,
Commodore, Commanding Iron-clad Division.
REAR-ADMIRAL D. D. PORTER,
Commanding North Atlantic Squadron,
Flag-ship "Malvern," off Fort Fisher, N. C.

REPORT OF LIEUTENANT-COMMANDER JAMES PARKER.

UNITED STATES STEAM-FRIGATE "MINNESOTA,"
OFF FORT FISHER, N. C., January 16, 1865.

ADMIRAL—I have the honor to submit the following in regard to the assault made upon Fort Fisher, on the 15th instant, by the officers, sailors and marines of the fleet under your command, who were detailed for the performance of that duty. The signal for landing was made at about 10 o'clock A. M. By noon all were landed and formed on the beach.

I found Lieutenant-Commander K. R. Breese representing you in command. Although I am his senior, still, as you had assigned him to the command, I at once decided to act as his subordinate.

The sailors were formed in three divisions, according to the divisions of the fleet. To Lieutenant-Commander C. H. Cushman was assigned the command of the first division. The command of the second division fell to me; that of the third division to Lieutenant-Commander Thomas O. Selfridge.

The marines formed a fourth division, under command of Captain L. L. Dawson, of the "Colorado."

After assembling the several divisions on the beach, they were all marched by the flank to a point about a mile from Fort Fisher, and were there formed in parallel lines perpendicular to the beach, and to the fire of the fort; the marine division in the front, and the others in the order of their numbers.

The men who had been detailed for intrenching duty had, as soon as landed, been sent forward under command of Lieutenant S. W. Preston, and, under a brisk fire of grape and musketry from the fort, were engaged in digging rifle-pits.

By the time this last formation was had, the enemy had opened upon us with grape and shell, and from this time out we were constantly under fire. After forming, the force was marched to the front by the right flank of companies, until near enough for the enemy to open upon us with rifles, when the divisions were again marched by the left flank along the beach until about half a mile from the fort, where the men were ordered to lie down under cover of the crest of the beach to await the assault of the army.

The force thus rested for about half an hour, all the time under a fire of musketry and occasionally grape from the fort, by which several were wounded, and, I believe, one or two killed. At the same time, the fleet was firing over us at the fort, and many shells bursting prematurely scattered their fragments in alarming proximity. I append a plan showing the line of march from the time of landing.

At about 3 o'clock the army was observed moving to the assault, and the order was given for the sailors and marines to advance. This they gallantly did, cheering as they went "on the run" (by the flank) along the beach, and in a short time reached the point "A" marked upon the plan, at which the palisades of the fort join the beach. As soon as the fleet observed that the assault had begun, the steam-whistles were sounded, and the firing on the fort completely ceased. Observing this, the enemy opened a heavy fire upon us of musketry and grape, which soon became very hot. A few of the officers and men passed beyond the palisades, but the advance along the beach was there checked and turned along the palisades towards the fort.

In the hurry of the advance, the different divisions had somewhat intermingled, and a large number of officers and sailors and a few marines had congregated at "A," and almost every shot from the enemy carried its message of wound or death to some one of our number. Lieutenants Preston and Porter and Acting-Ensign Wiley, of the "Montgomery," had fallen dead. Lieutenants Lamson and Bache, and many other officers, both regulars and volunteers, had been killed and wounded.

Seeing the advance had been checked, the rear also at once halted, and sought the cover of the crest of the beach. Quite a large space was left between that part of the force congregated at "A" and the rest of it. The marines, with a few exceptions, were quite far down the beach. I desire to name Captain George Butler and Lieutenant William Wallace as being at the front. At this time Lieutenant-Commander Breese, who had been all the time in front of the advance, endeavored to bring the rear forward, but without avail. The officers and men at the point "A" withstood for a long time the hot fire of the enemy, now not more than sixty or seventy yards off from us, without being able to return it.

I had been fortunate enough to reach unhurt the point "B," marked upon the plan, and at this time —observing some rebels upon the parapet of the fort who were seemingly unarmed, waving their hats to us, and beckoning us forward—gave the order "forward," and advanced followed by many officers, both regular and volunteer, and men, including a few marines. As I did so, I turned to see if the rest of the men were following, and, to my intense surprise and mortification, saw that a panic had seized the force, and that they were ingloriously flying along the beach away from the fort. Some of the officers (prominent among whom I observed Lieutenant-Commander Selfridge) tried to rally them, and their fellow-men who were near me reproached them for their shameful conduct; but in vain—all but about sixty fled.

The enemy began to cheer, and at once concentrated their whole fire upon the small band who had not fled. In an instant four officers, Lieutenant-Commander Cushman, Acting-Ensign Frederick A. O'Conner, Acting-Master's Mate Joseph M. Simms, and A. F. Aldrich (of the "Tuscarora"), were wounded and fell at my side. I saw that any further attempt at advance would, with our small number, be folly, and so ordered all who were left to seek the protection of the angle "B" of the palisades. This we did, and remained there until dark, all the while exposed to the enemy, who never failed to fire at any one who showed himself. After dark we all came safely away, bringing our wounded, our colors, and our arms. Five gallant fellows, viz., Acting-Ensign George T. Davis, of the "Wabash"; Acting-Master's Mate Aldrich, of the "Tuscarora"; Louis C. Sheppard, sailor of the "Wabash"; one man (name unknown to me), a petty officer from the "Tacony," and a private of marines, Henry Thompson, of the "Minnesota," got a few paces beyond "B." Mr. Aldrich was severely wounded, and the petty officer was killed.

I am utterly at a loss to explain the panic which, after they had so gallantly charged up to the enemy's works, and the prospect of success was so good, seized upon the force. It was certainly not want of courage, for during the long time the column had been under fire not a man had wavered, and the advance to the assault was as splendid as could have been made by veterans.

Lieutenant-Commander K. R. Breese, who commanded the assaulting party, added to his already well-earned and established reputation for bravery and cool judgment in battle. He led the advance to the palisades, and when he saw the rear delaying, endeavored, sword in hand, to bring them forward to our support. Failing to accomplish this, he returned, under a shower of bullets directed at him alone, to the sand-hills at "C," and when it seemed no longer useful to remain there, coolly followed the retreating mass. How he escaped death is a marvel to me.

Lieutenant-Commander Charles H. Cushman (wounded) and Montgomery Sicard; Lieutenants N. H. Farquhar, R. H. Lamson, Smith W. Nichols, and John R. Bartlett; Acting-Master W. H. Maies, of the "Seneca"; Acting Ensigns George T. Davis, "Wabash"; James Birtwistle and F. A. O'Connor, "Minnesota"; Dayton, of the "Nereus," and an acting-ensign from the "Gettysburg" (whose name Lieutenant Lamson will supply; Acting-Master's Mate Joseph M. Simms, "Minnesota," and A. F. Aldrich, "Tuscarora," both wounded, all behaved very gallantly, and did not retreat until I ordered them, after dark, to do so. I have named them because they are all known to me. There were others there equally brave and worthy, whose names, unfortunately, are not in my possession.

I have called the attention of my commanding officer (Commodore Lanman) to Acting Ensigns Birtwistle and O'Connor. Both these gentlemen hold their present appointments as a reward of gallant conduct under fire. They are both competent, intelligent, and perfectly correct young men, and they well deserve another step upwards. I earnestly press them upon your notice.

Acting-Master's Mate Joseph M. Simms and A. F. Aldrich, "Tuscarora," are fine young men. Simms I personally know to be eminently worthy. Of Aldrich, Commander Frailey, of the "Tuscarora," speaks in high terms. Both were severely wounded while in the extreme front; both richly merit their promotion.

I desire to say a few words in respect to Acting-Volunteer-Lieutenant-Commander Joseph D. Danels, of the "Vanderbilt." He came ashore in command of the party from his vessel, and was of my division. Although fitter for the sick-bed of a hospital than for the field, he persisted in going to the assault. He started with us, marched until his strength gave out, and his weak body was unable to carry his brave heart forward, when, by my orders, he went into the trench thrown up by Lieutenant Preston's party. It was no fault of his that he was not found in the front of the advance when the order to charge came.

Of those gallant dead the country may well be proud. They can be illy spared, but their names will be treasured as an inspiration for the future.

Preston and Porter were killed at the front, and Assistant-Surgeon William Longshaw, Jr., after adding to the reputation for bravery which he gained under fire of the batteries at Charleston while serving on board the iron-clad "Lehigh," was shot by the enemy as he was binding up the wounds of a dying man. Their dead bodies were found laying side by side the next morning.

It is painful to write such a record, but I feel compelled to state that I often saw the rebels deliberately fire in squads at the wounded who were endeavoring to crawl away.

I cannot close this report, Admiral, without saying that, although our naval assault did not meet with the success you hoped for, still it was of vast service to the country. I have conversed, since the fort was taken, with many rebel officers and men (prisoners), and all are unanimous in saying that a large part of their force was kept at the "sea-face" to resist our attack. I know that a large force was there to resist us. It is no detraction from the eminent skill and bravery displayed by our brethren of the army to claim this much credit for our sailors.

I had hoped to send you a complete list of all those who were not affected by the panic and remained at "B." One was taken, but I am not able now to learn who has it. It will doubtless be found, and I shall forward it whenever it is found.

I congratulate you, sir, upon the great victory which the fleet under your command has, in conjunction with the army, so gloriously won, and am,

Very respectfully, your obedient servant,
JAMES PARKER, *Lieutenant-Commander.*
REAR-ADMIRAL DAVID D. PORTER,
Com'dg North Atlantic Squadron.

REPORT OF LIEUTENANT L. E. FAGAN, U. S. MARINE CORPS.

UNITED STATES STEAM-FRIGATE "WABASH,"
AT SEA, January 17, 1865.

CAPTAIN—In obedience to your order, I have the honor to make the following report concerning the part taken by the marine guard of this ship in the operations against the rebel Fort Fisher, commanding the entrance to New Inlet, N. C., on the 15th day of January, 1865.

My command consisted of three sergeants, three corporals, and thirty-eight privates; and to prevent confusion in landing, the company was divided into four sections, each commanded by a non-commissioned officer.

On the morning of the 15th instant, at 10:30 o'clock, my men were landed and formed on the beach, about two miles to the northward of Fort Fisher. I then received and formed into other companies the marines of the different vessels, until the arrival of Captain Butler, United States Marine Corps, when I turned the command over to that officer.

At 11 A. M., I was ordered by Lieutenant-Commander K. R. Breese, fleet-captain, through Captain Butler, to take my guard and advance to the support of the sailors at the front, who were throwing up intrenchments near Fort Fisher, under the direction of Lieutenant Preston, United States

Navy. I marched my company up the beach by the flank until within a mile of the rebel fort, when, finding the fire severe, I deployed my men as skirmishers across the plain, and continued to advance. Arriving at the intrenchments, I ordered my men to cover themselves from the enemy's shot, and this they partially did by throwing up heaps of sand with their bayonets and hands. After the sailors had completed their breastworks, I was ordered by Lieutenant-Commander Breese to advance my command to the extreme parallel of intrenchments; which I did, my men marching to the front, across a plain swept by fire, with alacrity and spirit. In this advance I frequently ordered my men to lie down; and as soon as the shower of grape had passed, the march was resumed at the double-quick. After a toilsome march through the sand, we reached a line of intrenchments about forty yards from the fort, which I found occupied by the skirmish line of the 147th New York Volunteers. During the advance two of my men were badly wounded, and they were at once sent to the rear. I now ordered a few of my men (good shots) to open fire on the rebel gunners, and it was owing to their skill that a field-piece inside the palisade was forced to be abandoned by the rebel artillerists.

I now awaited further orders; but finding the beach filling up with soldiers, and supposing the attack about to be made, I collected and marched my men by the flank across the plain towards the beach, where I saw the column of sailors and marines advancing to the front. Seeing no officer to report to, I formed my men with the rest of the marines, who were in the centre of the column, the advance being composed entirely of sailors. In this manner we marched, under a severe fire of musketry from the fort, towards the northeast angle of the work, until the column halted, when I ordered my men to lie down and pick off the rebels on the parapet of Fort Fisher until the order was given to charge. My men had opened fire when I gave the word to cease firing and prepare for the assault. I now perceived a movement in front of our position, and soon after a body of men rushed past. I endeavored, by every means in my power, to prevent the retreat which I now plainly saw was initiated, but my appeals and threats were of no avail, and I then prepared myself for the worst, knowing that a retreat would be disastrous and more deadly than a charge against the fort. My command maintained its position until I saw Lieutenant-Commander F. B. Blake, United States Navy, who informed me that the assault had been for the present abandoned. I then collected my men and marched down to the beach. Having seen that the retreat was universal on the part of the naval forces, I gave several of my men permission to advance again to the front and annoy the rebels as much as possible with sharp-shooting. Shortly after, hearing that an attempt was about to be made to rally the men, I halted and allowed my men to seek cover, while, in company with Acting Lieutenant-Commander Danels, of the "Vanderbilt," I collected straggling sailors and marines, and formed the men under some sand-hills on the beach, about six hundred yards from Fisher. We had collected quite a number of men, when I received orders from Lieutenant-Commander F. B. Blake to take my men, and as many more as I could find, and report to General Terry, United States Army, the object being to occupy, with sailors and marines, a line of intrenchments in the rear, then threatened by the enemy I collected about two hundred marines, and marched to General Terry's headquarters, where I reported, and was at once assigned to a position on the northeast line, which position the marines occupied with vigilance and attention until the morning, when we were relieved, and I embarked my command for the "Wabash."

It only remains for me to add that one sergeant and six privates, who became detached from my

guard while in the army intrenchments at the front, accompanied the army in the storming of the fort, and, as I afterwards heard from an army officer, behaved with gallantry and coolness during the hand-to-hand conflict that ensued. In conclusion, captain, I would say, that during the time the marine guard of this ship was on shore, they behaved with bravery and subordination on all occasions. It pleased the fleet-captain (Lieutenant-Commander Breese) to compliment the handsome manner in which my men advanced in skirmish line to the advanced line of intrenchments under a heavy fire, and I feel that his words of praise were not undeserved. All my men behaved well, but I would present especially to your attention the conduct of Corporal Tomlin, of the guard, who, under a heavy fire from the enemy's sharp-shooters, advanced into an open plain close to the fort and assisted a wounded comrade to a place of safety. I respectfully ask that his conduct may be made known to the honorable Secretary of the Navy, so that he may receive a medal of honor.

The marine guard is at present accounted for, and on board the ship in good condition.

Enclosed please find a list of wounded.

I am, captain, very respectfully, your obedient servant,

LOUIS E. FAGAN, *Lieut. U. S. Marines,*
Comd'g Guard, Frigate "Wabash."
CAPTAIN MELANCTON SMITH, U. S. N.,
Commanding U. S. Steam-frigate "Wabash."

———

REPORT OF CAPTAIN CHARLES STEEDMAN.

UNITED STATES STEAMER "TICONDEROGA," {
OFF WILMINGTON, N. C., January 17, 1865. }

SIR—I have the honor to lay before you the following report of the part this ship took in the recent attacks upon the forts on Federal Point, which has terminated so gloriously and successfully to the two branches of the service engaged.

On the afternoon of the 13th instant, after the return of the boats employed in landing troops, in obedience to signal, I took position in line of battle, and at 5:15 P. M. anchored ahead of the line, as directed in General Order No. 78. From this point a well-directed fire was kept up on the batteries to the left of Fort Fisher, in accordance with the chart-plan furnished me. Upon hearing the signal-whistle, at 5:55 P. M., I had the battery trained upon the Mound and on the guns in its neighborhood. A continuous fire was then kept up until I received orders to withdraw from action, at 6:20 P. M.

I am happy to say that no casualties occurred on board, although several of the enemy's shots fell over and around the vessel. The only loss sustained was that of the stern kedge-anchor, caused by a rifle shot cutting its hawser.

On the 15th instant, in obedience to signal, I got underway and took position at the end of the second line. At 10:35 A. M. a storming party of sailors in three (3) boats, in charge of Ensign George W. Coffin, and the marine guard, under command of First-Lieutenant Charles F. Williams, were sent from this vessel to report to the flag-ship for orders. At the same time I received your verbal message not to move until further orders. At 11:45 P. M., in compliance with signal, I steamed up and took position ahead of the second line, about a cable's length ahead of the "Shenandoah." From this point a well-directed fire was kept up with the starboard guns on the batteries well to the left of Fort Fisher, in keeping with your programme. Before opening fire the enemy threw several heavy rifle shots over and near me, but after a couple of rounds from this ship his fire was silenced. At 1:05 P. M. I received your verbal orders to shift my berth nearer in; this was done with some little delay and considerable trouble, owing to the strength of the ebb-tide and want of a sufficient head of steam. By spreading fires, I was enabled to get the necessary speed to give me control of the ship and to take a position nearer to the enemy's battery.

From that time my fire was kept up in the same direction as heretofore, until the signal was made to cease firing. I then asked permission to open upon the "Mound," which had turned its guns upon our assaulting columns ; this being granted, a deliberate fire was directed upon that fort up to 6:20 P. M., when I discontinued firing and secured the battery for the night. For one hour and a half previous to receiving your message (by tug) to cease firing, I had not fired a single shot. It gives me great pleasure to express my entire satisfaction at the thorough and efficient manner the officers and crew performed their duty during the time we were engaged in bombarding the enemy's works. I am indebted to Lieutenant George B. White, the executive officer of this vessel, for his energetic assistance.

With this communication I transmit copies of the reports of First-Lieutenant C. F. Williams, of the marine guard, marked "A," and Ensign G. W. Coffin, who had command of the assaulting party of sailors sent from this vessel, marked "B"; also the gunner's report of expenditure of ammunition. The surgeon's report of casualties has already been forwarded. In conclusion, allow me to congratulate you, Admiral, upon this brilliant and decided success, which has resulted in planting our flag on one of the strongest fortifications possessed by the rebels.

I am, sir, very respectfully, your obedient servant,
CHARLES STEEDMAN, *Captain.*
REAR-ADMIRAL D. D. PORTER,
Commanding North Atlantic Squadron,
Flag-ship "Malvern."

REPORT OF CAPTAIN L. L. DAWSON, UNITED STATES MARINE CORPS.

MARINE BARRACKS, }
NEW YORK, February 15, 1865. }
ADMIRAL—I have the honor to make the following report of the part taken by the marines under my command in the recent assault upon Fort Fisher:

Upon landing, on the morning of the 15th of January, I found all the men that were to constitute the assaulting column on shore. There were about three hundred and sixty-five (365) men in line, exclusive of Lieutenant Fagan, who had been ordered by Captain Breese to occupy a rifle-pit off to the right, near the army advance, before I had reached the shore.

I hastily divided the line into four (4) companies, under command of Captain Butler, First-Lieutenant Wallace, First-Lieutenant Corrie and First-Lieutenant Parker, giving First-Lieutenant Williams charge of some twenty-five (25) skirmishers, and First-Lieutenant Meeker acting as adjutant. I received two or three orders from Captain Breese to "bring up the marines at once; that it would be late": so that I had to move off without time to equalize the companies; to number them off for pacing and marching; to select sergeants to replace officers, or post the guides of a single company or platoon. I took the marines up, and filed across the peninsula in front of the sailors, with skirmishers thrown out. Captain Breese pointed out some light intrenchments towards the main bastion of Fort Fisher, which were dug and being completed under cover of the fire of the fleet. He ordered me to advance " to those that were finished, and as soon as those nearest the fort were completed, to occupy them; and when the assault was made, that I should keep up a full fire, when the sailors would rush by me, and, when well past, the marines follow them into the fort." Thus, in the event of a repulse, we would have had cover to fall back to, and a point to rally upon.

I had advanced to the second line of cover, and was waiting for the nearer intrenchments to be finished, when I received an order from Captain Breese "to take the marines down on the beach, about one hundred and fifty (150) yards to the left, and that he would bring up the sailors;" "that there was splendid cover on the beach, and that Captain Breese was going that way."

I was surprised at this order, and asked the gentleman who delivered it if he was not mistaken; but he replied, "No." I immediately obeyed the order, and in a few minutes the sailors were brought up. My men were formed by the right flank when the sailors came up, the first division passed the marines, and the whole command lying down by the right flank: marines abreast of the second division, sailors on the upper side of the beach. While at this point I received no orders. I had read the Admiral's order to Captain Breese respecting the assault, and was watching the army, knowing that agreeably to that order the "army were to be seen going in over the northwest parapet of the fort before we were to move to assault the sea-face." When I heard the order, "Charge, charge!" everyone rose up and dashed forward, yelling and cheering so loudly that no order could either be heard or passed. I tried to prevent the noise, but with no success.

I maintained the same position I had started in, abreast of the second division of sailors; and as the sand was much heavier on the upper side of the beach, I could gain nothing on the first division until they got under the heavy fire of the fort, when the first company of marines got abreast with the centre of the first division of sailors. I had just reached the head of my men, after a hard run, when I saw the head of the line of sailors, who had reached the end of the stockade, begin to falter and turn back, and was myself about forty or fifty yards from the end of the stockade, on the beach. I saw some six or eight men go around the end of the stockade, but immediately return; and it was at this instant that the whole line commenced doubling up and flying, everybody for themselves, except some thirty officers and men at the head of the line, who took cover under an angle in the stockade.

The efforts of the officers to rally the men were wholly unsuccessful, the order to retreat being passed along generally. At the moment when the head of the line gave way, the marines were not near enough to open fire effectually, and were on the double-quick, and quite exhausted; nor was there the slightest cover this side of the stockade, except a few sand-hills very near the stockade. I saw that the men were hopelessly repulsed. I looked to the rear of the line, which was breaking, as well as the front, and that a good many marines were joining in the retreat, so that I at once ordered the marines to "lie down and fire at the parapet," with a view of decreasing the rebel fire, and to prevent the confusion and exposure incident to such a crowd retreating on an open beach. Nearly all the marines of the first and second companies obeyed this order; the two rear companies I could not see, but, as few were to be seen after the retreat was effected, I take it for granted that they went also.

As soon as the panic was over, I ordered those men who had lain down, and were firing, to retreat in squads, as I supposed the fleet would soon open on that bastion of the fort. I did not retreat myself, but stayed on the beach about fifty yards from the end of the stockade until sunset, watching the progress of the army.

When I went to the rear, a staff officer informed me that General Terry desired all the marines and sailors who had arms to occupy the right of General Paine's line; that the rebels were demonstrating there. Though it was nearly dark, I succeeded in getting about one hundred and eighty (180) marines behind the breastworks, near General Terry's headquarters, where they remained until morning. The rebels, from the manner in which they met the assault, evidently regarded it as the main attack, as it was the first.

With the result of our attack no one was more disappointed than myself. I obeyed all the orders I received from Captain Breese promptly, and exerted myself all I could to make the assault successful; and, though a portion of the marines retreated with the sailors, it is but just to the rest to say that they remained and performed the duty of good soldiers until I passed the order to retreat.

I remain, very respectfully, your obedient servant,
L. L. DAWSON,
Captain United States Marine Corps.
REAR-ADMIRAL DAVID D. PORTER,
Commanding North Atlantic Squadron.

REPORT OF LIEUTENANT-COMMANDER GEORGE E. BELKNAP.

UNITED STATES STEAMER "CANONICUS," }
OFF FORT FISHER, N. C., January 17, 1865. }

SIR—I have the honor to report that during the actions of the 13th, 14th and 15th instant, which resulted in the capture of Fort Fisher, this ship engaged that work at a distance of seven hundred (700) yards, perhaps a little closer on the 15th, as the smoothness of the sea enabled me to go into shoaler water than on the preceding days, having at one time only a foot and a half of water to spare under our keel.

On the first day of the attack, the 13th, the enemy replied vigorously to our fire until late in the afternoon, when the heavier ships, coming into line, soon drove them into their bomb-proofs. Soon after we had taken position, it became evident that, since the previous attack, a reinforcement of experienced artillerists had been received in the fort, as its fire was much more accurate and spirited than before. They soon obtained our range and struck the ship frequently, while many shots fell close alongside. Upon one occasion, two shots out of three, fired simultaneously, struck the side-armor abreast the turret.

We count thirty-six (36) hits this day, and everything about the deck not shot-proof was badly cut up. Two men were knocked down and stunned at the guns by the impact of a 10-inch gun-shot upon the turret. The flag was shot away twice and gallantly replaced by Quartermaster Daniel D. Stevens.

Not content with solid shot, the enemy fired shells occasionally, to burst over the turret, and now and then the bullet of a sharp-shooter whistled over us.

On the second and third days the fire of the enemy was comparatively feeble, and principally directed at the gun-boats, and when the larger ships came into action ceased altogether. An occasional musket-shot fell near us, and when the naval-assaulting column was driven back, many of the bullets and grape-shot fired at our gallant fellows passed over us, some few striking the ship. Second-Assistant Engineer John W. Saville received a severe wound in the left thigh from a grape-shot. At this time we also received a 10-inch shot on the side-armor, fired from the water battery on the right of the sea-face of the fort.

Our fire was slow and deliberate, and every effort was made to dismount the enemy's guns, and though almost hidden by traverses, I am happy to say we succeeded in dismounting two of them. Acting-Ensign M. W. Weld knocked over a six-inch rifle on the second day, and the executive officer, Lieutenant R. S. McCook, disposed of a 10-inch columbiad on the third day of the action. I also saw a shell from the "Monadnock" dismount a gun, and a shot from the "Mahopac" knocked the muzzle off another

We expended during the three days two hundred and ninety-seven (297) 15-inch shells.

I have to thank the officers and crew for the zeal and gallant spirit manifested throughout the fight, and for the cheerful manner in which they worked at night, taking on board ammunition after the arduous and exhausting work of the day.

I again desire to bring to your notice and that of the department, the services of the executive officer, Lieutenant R. S. McCook, to whom I am indebted for the efficiency and readiness which enabled me at all times to be prompt in all movements required of the ship. Equally fortunate in the services of Chief Engineer D. B. Macomb, I beg leave to recommend him to your favorable consideration.

The powder division was ably commanded by Acting-Master D. S. Murphy, assisted by Acting-Ensigns Seekins and Center. Acting-Ensign M. W. Weld showed great aptitude in handling the guns under the supervision of the executive officer. Assistant Paymaster R. P. Lisle, acting as aide, merits my thanks for the intelligent manner in which he attended to the duties of signal officer.

LIEUTENANT (AFTERWARDS COMMANDER) RODERICK S. McCOOK,

EXECUTIVE OFFICER OF THE "CANONICUS."

Acting-Master and Pilot Edward A. Decker performed his duties with his accustomed coolness and discretion.

I inclose the executive officer's report of damages received, and have already forwarded the surgeon's report of casualties. I beg leave to congratulate you, Admiral, upon the brilliant victory which has crowned your efforts at this point, and which is the more gratifying, as it proves conclusively that on a former memorable occasion the possession "would have been found an easier conquest than was supposed," had the attempt been made to occupy it.

I am, sir, very respectfully, your obedient servant,
GEORGE E. BELKNAP,
Lieutenant-Commander, Commanding.
REAR-ADMIRAL D. D. PORTER,
Commanding North Atlantic Squadron, Flagship "Malvern," off Fort Fisher, N. C.

REPORT OF LIEUTENANT-COMMANDER THOMAS O. SELFRIDGE.

UNITED STATES STEAMER "HURON." }
OFF FORT FISHER, January 17, 1865. }

SIR—I have the honor to report that having

landed with the men of this vessel to join in the land attack on Fort Fisher, I was detailed by Lieutenant-Commander Breese to command the third column of attack, composed of detachments from the ships of the third and a portion of the fourth divisions, numbering about four hundred and fifty men. Lieutenant G. M. Bache commanded the right wing, Lieutenant-Commander W. N. Allen the left wing.

I formed them in column and moved forward by the head of companies, until near our first rifle-pits, when the whole assaulting column was formed in flank alongside the beach, awaiting the signal of assault from the Army. When this was given, I moved my column forward on the double-quick, followed close on to the second, and for about half a mile under an extremely heavy and withering fire of musketry and grape.

When we finally reached the palisades, I found the columns which had proceeded me halted and lying down. Going to the front, an effort was made at this time to get the men to charge; but the fire was so heavy that the few who passed through the stockade were compelled to fall quickly back. At this moment an unexplained panic took place in the rear, which so quickly communicated itself to the whole that it was impossible to rally the men.

I remained near the fort till night, when I left, with a few, under cover of the darkness.

My column moved up with great gallantry, as by the time I got up the rebels had concentrated their whole fire upon us; and until we came to a halt all seemed to be moving well.

To Lieutenant-Commander W. N. Allen and Lieutenant G. M. Bache, both wounded, I am indebted for assistance in forming and maintaining the organization of the division.

I regret extremely that my entire unacquaintance with any of the officers or crews of my division renders it impossible for me to particularize the deserving, but until the panic all deserved praise, for none faltered.

Very respectfully, your obedient servant,
THOMAS O. SELFRIDGE,
Lieutenant-Commander.
REAR-ADMIRAL DAVID D. PORTER,
Commanding North Atlantic Squadron,
Flag-ship " Malvern."

REPORT OF LIEUTENANT W. B. CUSHING.

UNITED STATES STEAMER " MONTICELLO,"
OFF WILMINGTON, January, 17, 1865.

SIR—I have the honor to report the part taken by this vessel in the actions of the 13th, 14th and 15th instant, resulting in the capture of the harbor defences of Wilmington, the loss of foreign supplies to the rebels, and the ruin of those holding the Anglo-rebel loan.

On the 13th and 14th the " Monticello " assisted in guarding the troops in landing and advancing. On the 15th instant, by your order, I took position close in by the fort and shelled the rebel privateer " Chickamauga " and three transport steamers from their position in the river, thus preventing the landing of reinforcements for the garrison. The ship's guns were then turned on the fort, and used with effect throughout the day.

At noon I landed with forty men from this vessel to take part in the naval assault on Fort Fisher. My men, and those of Lieutenant Porter of the " Malvern," led the advance of the storming party. The marines did not clear the parapet of the fort, as anticipated; hence the assault failed. Our sailors were close under the walls, subjected to a heavy fire, since the main body of the enemy had been drawn to that point to resist what they supposed to be the weight of the attack. We were forced to fall back with the loss of many of our best officers and men, but not before the Army, through its own

gallantry and our diversion in its favor, had effected a lodgment that secured subsequent success. Then, finding myself apparently senior officer, I rallied as many sailors and marines as possible, and at night placed them in the trenches, as requested by General Terry, thus relieving some regiments that went to the front. In this I was greatly assisted by your son, Secretary Porter, and by Lieutenant Woodward, of the " Minnesota." Acting-Ensign Daniel W. Lakin, of this vessel, behaved gallantly and rendered material aid. My loss during the day consisted of four killed and four wounded.

I am, very respectfully, your obedient servant,
W. B. CUSHING,
Lieutenant, Commanding.
REAR-ADMIRAL DAVID D. PORTER,
Commanding North Atlantic Squadron, etc.

REPORT OF ACTING-MASTER H. W. GRINNELL.

HEADQUARTERS SHERMAN'S ARMY,
FAYETTEVILLE, N. C., March 12, 1865.

SIR—I have the honor to report that I have this day succeeded in handing to Major-General Sherman the cypher dispatch intrusted to me by Major-General Schofield at Wilmington, North Carolina, on the 4th instant.

I left the " Nyack " on the evening of the 4th in a small dug-out, with a party consisting of Acting-Ensign H. B. Colby, Thomas Gillespie, seaman, and Joseph Williams, ship's painter, armed with Sharpe's rifles and revolvers, and taking two days' rations. After proceeding up the river about twelve miles I met the enemy's advance picket-post, which I succeeded in passing without discovery; but at a point near Livingston's Creek I found the picket so strongly posted that I deemed it the more prudent course to abandon my boat, and to attempt to communicate with General Sherman's forces near the Pedee River. I left my boat on the morning of the 5th instant, and struck for the Wilmington and Whitehall road. On my way I passed through the village of Summerville, where I destroyed some arms which I found in the possession of the citizens; here I got information that a party of cavalry were endeavoring to cut me off at Livingston's Bridge, and I was reluctantly compelled to secrete myself and party in a negro hut near by; here I remained two days, when I received information that the enemy, tired of waiting, had recrossed the river, thus leaving me free to advance. At dark on the 7th instant, having secured the services of a negro guide, I started in the direction of Whitesville, advancing with caution, and moving only by night. After much tedious and difficult marching through the swamps, I reached a point near Whitesville on the morning of the 9th instant. The town was held by the enemy in strong force, and, finding traveling on foot consumed too much time, I determined to impress horses, and by a bold dash break through the pickets on the Lumbertown road. With this purpose in view, I left my bivouac in the swamps, and succeeded in passing unobserved until I reached the cross-road to Whitehall, which I found picketed. After satisfying myself that the picket had no reserve, we made a quick dash and captured two men without alarm, and before they became aware of our purpose I disarmed them, and after compelling them to follow me for about five miles I paroled them, leaving them apparently much satisfied at their release. They were members of Company A, 51st North Carolina Infantry, and represented their regiment as being much demoralized. After hard riding night and day, I reached Drowning Creek at a point near the town of Lumbertown on the afternoon of the 11th; here I first learned definitely of the whereabouts of General Sherman's forces.

I met a small scouting party near the creek, but they fled to the woods at our approach. On the morning of to-day I had the great satisfaction of meeting the rear scouts of General Sherman's forces on the Lumber Bridge road, about twenty miles from this place. The several roads being blocked up by wagons, artillery, etc., and our horses being quite worn out by hard riding, I did not reach these headquarters until 1 P. M. this afternoon.

General Sherman received the dispatch, and expressed himself much surprised at receiving it through the Navy, and by such a route. In parts of Robeson County I found a very large number of deserters from the rebel army, and quite a strong Union feeling.

I cannot speak too highly of the conduct of Acting-Ensign Colby, also of the two men, Thomas Gillespie and Jos. Williams, who were ever ready to encounter any danger or hardship that came in their way.

General Sherman wishing me to communicate with you as soon as possible, I leave to-night by the army tug, hoping to meet you on my way to Wilmington.

In conclusion, allow me to thank you for giving me permission to undertake this rather novel naval scout.

I am, sir, your obedient servant,
H. WALTON GRINNELL,
Acting-Master U. S. Navy, Commanding Expedition.
LIEUTENANT-COMMANDER GEORGE W. YOUNG,
Senior Officer, off Wilmington, N. C.

While the fleet was off Wilmington, and Admiral Porter engaged in taking that place, General Grant came very near being put to great inconvenience, if not disaster, owing to a circumstance which at the time seemed rather discreditable to the Navy. Before the fleet left Hampton Roads, every care was taken that the James River, below Howlett's Battery, should be kept so perfectly guarded by a naval force that there could be no possible chance left for the Confederate iron-clads to make an attack on the vessels below the obstructions sunk in the river, which consisted of several large schooners loaded with stones sunk in the middle of the stream, and heavy booms and chains extending from the sunken vessels to either shore and secured to anchors planted in the bank.

These obstructions were immediately under the fire of the "Onondago," a double-turreted Monitor, carrying four 15-inch guns, several double-enders, carrying 11-inch and 9-inch guns, a torpedo-boat of excellent construction, and also a battery on shore belonging to the Army. A pontoon bridge was in place below the vessels guarding the obstructions, to enable the Army of the James to retreat across the river under cover of the gun-boats, in case it was attacked by a superior force. Every arrangement had been made to prevent a disaster of any kind, and to punish the enemy in case he should attempt to make an attack. There could be no possibility of the enemy's fleet getting past the obstructions while the Federal naval force maintained its position; but, in case it should be driven away, then the Confederates could have blown up the obstruction, passed

through and broken up the pontoon bridge, thus cutting off the Army on the left bank of the James from its supports, and threatening City Point, where all the stores were gathered for the use of the Army before Richmond.

The Confederate naval force at that time in the James River, under the command of Commodore J. K. Mitchell, consisted of the iron-clad " Virginia " (4 Brooke rifles), Captain Dunnington ; iron-clad " Richmond " (4 Brooke rifles), Captain Johnson; iron-clad "Fredericksburg" (4 Brooke rifles), Captain Wilson ; " Nansemond," wooden (2 guns), Captain Butt; " Roanoke," wooden (1 gun), Captain Wyatt, and " Torpedo," wooden (1 gun), commanding officer unknown. This fleet, with its iron-clads and rifle-guns, was no match for the " Onondaga " and the gun-boats, assisted by the torpedo-boat ; but the Confederate commander, either on his own volition or by an order from his Government, determined to make an attempt to pass the obstructions and break up the pontoon bridge. At the same time General Lee was to attack the army on the left bank of the river, and, while the Confederate fleet was occupied in driving away the Union gun-boats and the " Onondaga," push on to City Point, set fire to all the wharves and store-houses, and create a scene of destruction unparalleled in the annals of the war.

This might have been done under a bold and dashing commander who knew what he was about, and was willing to risk the loss of his whole fleet to gain an important advantage. The Confederate fleet in James River was not a particle of use in the defence of that stream, which was so filled with obstructions and torpedoes, backed by four heavy forts, that no man having common sense or judgment would have attempted to ascend the river, especially as there was no particular object in doing so.

The forts on the river were within supporting distance of each other, and under the command of a very able naval officer, John R. Tucker, who also had charge of the torpedo corps. The bed of the river was full of torpedoes, and a dozen vessels, no matter what their size or strength, would have been sunk before they could have reached the first obstruction above Drury's Bluff. As long as the " Onondaga " floated, the Confederate vessels could not get down with safety, any more than the Federal ships could get up, and the only way to meet with any success was for the Confederates to risk a dozen lives and send down a dozen torpedo-boats, and try to destroy the double-turreted Monitor. This may have been the intention, but it was never carried out.

A night was appointed for Mitchell's fleet to make an attack on the Federal forces. At daylight, next morning, two of the iron-clads appeared around the point near Howlett's Battery and approached the obstacles, where they stopped. Commander William A. Parker, the commanding officer of the Federal naval force, had been instructed in written orders from Admiral Porter that, in case the Confederate fleet should show itself below Howlett's Battery, to get underway and proceed up close to the obstructions, to hold on there and keep up his fire as long as a Confederate iron-clad remained in sight. Strange to say, Commander Parker turned the head of his vessel down stream and seemed for a moment about to destroy the pontoon bridge; but, suddenly reflecting, he attempted to turn his ship in that narrow river, got aground, and knocked off the wings of one of his propellers. His given reason for pursuing this erratic course was "that he wanted to get down stream some distance so that he might go at the enemy with all speed." This was ridiculous, as the Confederates were on the other side of the obstructions, and could not be reached except by shot or shell. Parker proved afterwards to be of unsound mind, though it was not suspected at the time, and previous to this fiasco stood high in the naval service both as a brave man and an excellent officer. It would therefore be ungenerous to criticise his conduct, except to regret that the Admiral's original intention to leave Commander A. C. Rhind in command was not carried out, as Rhind would have destroyed the two iron-clads that appeared below Howlett's Battery.

The commanders of the two Confederate iron-clads behaved in quite as erratic a manner as the captain of the "Onondaga." They both came to anchor at a place called the Crow's Nest, a tall frame-work look-out, built by General Butler to observe the movements of the Confederate gun-boats and to communicate by signal with General Grant. The officers of the Confederate iron-clads landed in their boats and seemed to examine this structure with a great deal of curiosity. At first they determined to burn it, but finally retired satisfied with cutting their names on the timbers, and returned to their vessels.

So far it does not appear as if there was any concert of action between the two iron-clads, nor does the motive of their coming below Howlett's Battery appear. They laid at anchor all night at the look-out and seemed uncertain what to do. That night the torpedo-boat could have blown them both up, but no attempt was made from any quarter to disturb them, and, no doubt, they wondered what had become of the "Onondaga," when she was seen returning up the river, very much shorn of her speed by the loss of one of her propellers. On seeing her, the two Confederate iron-clads got underway and proceeded up toward Howlett's Battery, evidently returning in search of their commander-in-chief. They did not, however, get off without some damage. When the "Onondaga" reached the obstructions, Commander Parker opened fire on the retreating vessels with all his 15-inch guns.

One of the Confederate iron-clads had just turned the point, but the rear one received a solid shot which pierced her side, inflicting some injuries to her hull, and killing and wounding several of her men. A 15-inch shell from the "Onondaga" struck the same vessel on the knuckle and entered three or four feet, but failed to explode. Another solid shot struck the iron-clad on her casemate, shattering it very much, and knocking down a number of her men. By this time she had passed the point and was shut out from further danger.

Thus ended this remarkable affair, which might have caused serious trouble if it had been conducted with any determined dash, though the fact that the "Onondaga's" shot had inflicted so much damage in so short a time is rather a proof that, if both these vessels could have passed, they would have been knocked to pieces. After this, the obstructions were further strengthened by sinking another large schooner loaded with stone, and that was the last attempt the Confederates ever made to reach City Point with their naval force. But the commander of the Federal vessels lost an opportunity to gather some laurels, an opportunity that never occurred again, while the Federal Navy lost a page in history which might have been chronicled as one of the brightest events of the war.

After the destruction of the "Albemarle" and the recapture of Plymouth, the operations in the Sounds of North Carolina were comparatively unimportant, for the occasional raids of energetic Confederate guerillas could hardly be considered of much consequence. The Confederates still held the Roanoke River above Plymouth, as there was not a sufficient naval force in the Sounds to operate successfully in that quarter. A large portion of the enemy's forces in North Carolina had been drawn off to fill up the ranks of General Joseph E. Johnston's army, which was charged with the duty of impeding General Sherman in his march to the sea.

About this time Sherman had captured Savannah and General Grant had received the news of the utter rout of Hood's army in Tennessee by General Thomas, which left Sherman at liberty to march through the Carolinas without apprehensions of a formidable enemy in his rear, and with sufficient addition to his forces from the troops of Schofield and Terry to enable him to hold his own until he reached Goldsborough, N. C., his objective point.

The middle of January, 1865, saw Sherman's army in motion for the Carolina campaign. His right wing, under General Howard, was conveyed by water to Beaufort, South Carolina, whence it started on its march up the Charleston railroad, while the left wing, under General Slocum, with Kilpatrick's cavalry, crossed the Savannah river and moved towards Augusta. These movements were made for the purpose of deceiving the Confederates as to the point aimed at by General Sherman. The Federal troops destroyed all the railroads in their rear.

Sherman's object was to effect a junction with Grant, and by force of numbers bring the war to a close. He passed by Augusta and Charleston, since there was nothing to be gained by halting at either place. In his official report General Sherman says: " Without wasting time or labor on Branchville or Charleston, which I knew the enemy could no longer hold, I turned all the columns straight on Columbia."

From Columbia, after making a feint on Charleston, Sherman advanced to Fayetteville and Goldsborough, while preparations were making by the Federal Generals on the sea-coast to effect a junction with his army—one body of troops to advance from Wilmington, N. C., and the other from Newbern.

All the troops that had occupied Charleston, Savannah, Augusta, Wilmington and other points along the coast, had united, and did all that was possible to impede Sherman's march; but, although the Confederate forces had swelled to a considerable army, they could not withstand the Federal advance, and from desertions and other causes they soon began to melt away. Still Sherman was not master of the situation until he had driven Johnston's army, from which he had experienced the strongest resistance, back to Smithfield. The junction of Schofield with Sherman's army was made next day, the 23d of March, 1865, at Goldsborough, and General Johnston and his forces were held as in a vise until the final surrender.

These movements had changed the whole state of affairs in North Carolina. The Confederate troops along the various rivers, including the Roanoke, had either joined General Johnston or had moved off to Richmond, and Admiral Porter, taking advantage of the situation, had directed Commander Macomb to advance up the Roanoke with a naval force, destroy or capture all the enemy's depots of stores, and also an iron-floating battery said to be on the river.

On the 11th of December, 1864, Commander Macomb, in connection with a military force, proceeded up the Roanoke in the double-ender "Wyalusing," accompanied by the "Otsego" and "Valley City" the tugs "Belle" and "Bazley," and a steam-packet boat. Proceeding slowly up the stream the vessels prepared to anchor for the night at a sharp bend in the river just below Jamesville, where the commanding officer of the Army forces had agreed to communicate with the naval commander. In obedience to signal, the "Otsego" had slowed her engines and was about to let go her anchor when a torpedo exploded under her bottom on the port side, and immediately afterwards another exploded under her forward pivot-gun, which was capsized on the deck by the concussion. In three minutes the vessel sunk, her spar-deck being three feet below the water. She had anchored over a nest of torpedoes, against which the commanding officer of the expedition had been warned and directed to drag for in boats before proceeding up the river; but this officer satisfied himself by getting out spars and nets ahead of his vessels to pick up any submarine obstructions. A short time after the sinking of the gun-boat, while the tug "Bazley" was transferring her crew to the "Wyalusing," a torpedo exploded, and the "Bazley" immediately went down alongside the "Otsego." Matters became at this moment rather embarrassing, for the vessels were all anchored close together, and it was not safe to move in the dark for fear of being blown up, so a very anxious night was passed.

The sinking of the gun-boat and tug put an end to an expedition which, if successful, would have been a handsome addition to the sinking of the "Albemarle" and the recapture of Plymouth by the Navy. The "Otsego" made the number of naval vessels blown up by the Confederate torpedo corps, since the commencement of the war, about twenty. For miles along the Roanoke torpedoes were thickly planted to prevent the advance of the Navy, and at one turn in the river there were no less than forty of these destructive weapons in one group.

This was the last important naval movement undertaken in the Sounds of North Carolina. Sherman's arrival at Goldsborough, and the arrival of troops by sea at Newbern, warned the guerillas, called by the Confederates the "home forces," that they could no longer hope to hold their own in face of the overwhelming numbers which at any moment might appear in this vicinity; so they quietly dispersed, and all that portion of the Confederacy fell permanently into the hands of the Unionists. But for the unfortunate sinking of the "Otsego" and the "Bazley," all the operations of the North Atlantic squadron from October, 1864, to April, 1865, would have been crowned with success.

Although the area of operations in and around Plymouth was not a large one, what thrilling incidents had occurred in that small space! First: the capture and fortification of Plymouth by the Union forces; then the appearance of the "Albemarle" and her sinking the "Southfield"; the death of the gallant Flusser, and the retreat of the "Miami"; the attack of the "Albemarle" on the Sound flotilla; the sinking of the "Albemarle" by Cushing; the dash of Macomb upon Plymouth, recovering the place after as handsome an attack at the cannon's mouth as was ever seen anywhere; and, finally, the unfortunate sinking of the "Otsego" and "Bazley" near where the "Albemarle" lay at the bottom of the river. All these vessels were afterwards raised and lay side by side at the wharf, with the Union flag floating over them, as if they had never met in deadly strife.

NORTH ATLANTIC SQUADRON, JANUARY 1st, 1865.

REAR-ADMIRAL DAVID D. PORTER.

STAFF—LIEUTENANT-COMMANDER K. R. BREESE, FLEET-CAPTAIN; LIEUTENANT-COMMANDER H. A. ADAMS, JR., ORDNANCE OFFICER; LIEUTENANT S. W. PRESTON (FLAG); LIEUTENANT M. W. SANDERS, SIGNAL OFFICER; LIEUTENANT S. W. TERRY, DETAILING OFFICER; FLEET-PAYMASTER, H. M. HEISKELL; FLEET-SURGEON, GEORGE MAULSBY; FLEET-ENGINEER, THEO. ZELLER; ADMIRAL'S SECRETARY, CARLISLE P. PORTER; ASSISTANT-PAYMASTER, C. F. GUILD (SPECIAL DUTY); ACTING-MASTER, JAMES M. ALDEN; ACTING ENSIGNS, H. WOODRUFF, R. BATES, J. W. GRATTAN AND F. W. GRAFTON; ACTING-MASTER'S MATE, AARON VANDERBILT, AIDES.

NOTE.—Those vessels marked with a * were engaged in the capture of Fort Fisher.

* "COLORADO"—FIRST-RATE.

Commodore, Henry K. Thatcher; Lieutenants, George Dewey, H. B. Robeson and M. L. Johnson; Surgeon, James McClelland; Assistant-Surgeons, Robert Willard and B. H. Kidder; Paymaster, Wm. A. Ingersoll; Marines, Captain. L. L. Dawson; First-Lieutenant, E. P. Meeker; Acting-Volunteer-Lieutenant, F. F. Baury; Acting-Masters, Edwin Coffin and L. B. King; Acting-Ensigns, J. L. Vennard and W. G. Perry; Acting-Master's Mates, J. W. Wallace, A. B. Arey, E. A. Gould, M. V. Thomas and A. F. Tucker; Engineers: Chief, B. F. Garvin; First-Assistant, J. H. Bailey; Second-Assistants, E. E. Roberts, H. M. Quig and C. S. Maurice; Third - Assistant, M. A. Sutherland; Acting-Third-Assistants, C. C. Fernald, J. P. Messer and W. B. Whitmore; Boatswain, John K. Bartlett; Gunner, William Wilson; Carpenter, J. G. Myers; Sailmaker, Nicholas Lynch.

* "MINNESOTA"—FIRST-RATE.

Commodore, Joseph Lanman; Lieutenant-Commander, James Parker; Lieutenants, M. S. Stuyvesant and E. T. Woodward; Passed - Assistant-Surgeon, J. P. Quinn; Assistant - Surgeons, Wm. Longshaw and W. S. Fort; Paymaster, C. C. Upham; Marines: Captain, Geo. Butler; Second-Lieutenant, G. M. Welles; Acting - Master, Theo. Werholf; Acting-Ensigns, W. C. Wise, J. W. Willard, James Bertwisle, F. A. O'Connor and W. H. Jennings; Acting - Master's Mates, J. M. Simms, Fallas Eager and J. Amos Merrill; Engineers: Acting-Chief, A. R. Eddowes; Acting-First-Assistant, J. E. Cooper; Second-Assistants, Guy Samson, J. C. Cross and H. A. Delius; Third - Assistants, J. D. Lee and J. C. Kafer; Acting - Third Assistant, W. H. Mott; Pilot, F. C. Fowler; Boatswain, Wm. Bunker; Gunner, R. H. Cross; Carpenter, A. O. Goodsoe; Sailmaker, T. O. Fassett.

* "POWHATAN"—FIRST-RATE.

Commodore, James F. Schenck; Lieutenants, Geo. M. Bache and Merrill Miller; Surgeon, H. O. Mayo; Assistant-Surgeon, W. H. Johnson; Paymaster, C. P. Wallach; First-Lieutenant Marines, F. H. Corrie; Acting-Master, C. R. Wilkins; Ensigns, Ira Harris, Jr., and A. G. Kellogg; Acting-Ensigns R. D. Evans, Francis Morris and Edmund Parys; Acting - Master's Mates, Geo. P. Abbott, Geo. S. Sands and John Clitz; Engineers: Chief, John A. Grier; Acting - First - Assistant, W. H. Dobbs; Second - Assistants, W. S. Smith, James Long, John Franklin and Michael Dundon; Third-Assistant, A. C. Engard; Acting-Third-Assistant, H. F. Grier; Acting-Boatswain, James Gurney; Gunner, G. W. Omensetter; Carpenter, J. Macfarlane: Sailmaker, B. B. Blydenburg.

* "SUSQUEHANNA"—FIRST-RATE.

Commodore, S. W. Godon; Lieutenant - Commander, F. B. Blake; Lieutenants, J. R. Bartlett and Geo. M. Brown; Surgeon, J. O'C. Barclay; Assistant-Surgeon, C. H. Perry; Paymaster, A. J. Clark; Chaplain, J. D. Beugless; First-Lieutenant of Marines, Wm. Wallace; Acting-Master, H. O. Porter; Ensign, E. E. Preble; Acting-Ensigns, T. F. Lacock, W. W. Rhoades and O. C. K. Benham; Acting-Master's Mates, Chas. Gainsford, W. H. Sprague, M. S. Cooper and S. T. Paine; Engineers: Chief, John Johnson; First-Assistant, I. S. Finney; Second-Assistants, James Renshaw, J. H. Hutchinson and H. A. Smith; Third-Assistants, Thomas Crummey and C. F. Marsland; Acting - Third - Assistant, Berna Cook; Boatswain, Z. Whitmarsh, Jr.; Gunner, E. J. Waugh; Carpenter, J. E. Miller; Sailmaker, J. A. Holbrook.

*"NEW IRONSIDES"—FIRST-RATE.

Commodore, Wm. Radford; Lieutenant-Commander, R. L. Phythian; Lieutenants, A. R. Mc-

Nair, H. B. Rumsey and H. J. Blake; Surgeon, Edward Shippen; Assistant-Surgeon, G. A. Bright; Paymaster, George Plunkett; First-Lieutenant of Marines, R. S. Collom; Acting-Masters, H. P. Conner and John Dorey; Acting-Ensigns, Walter Pearce, W. A. Duer and J. W. King; Acting-Master's Mates, C. C. Bamford, J. F Silva and W. E. Wilson; Engineers: Chief, Alex. Greer; Second-Assistants, J. H. Hunt, W. S. Cherry, W. J. Reid, N. P. Towne and W. S. Wells; Third-Assistants, J. K. Stevenson and A. H. Henderson; Boatswain, Wm. E. Leeds; Gunner, Wm. Cope; Carpenter, J. E. Cox; Sailmaker, G. T. Lozier.

* "SANTIAGO-DE-CUBA"—SECOND-RATE.

Captain, O. S. Glisson; Lieutenant, N. H. Farquhar; Passed-Assistant Surgeon, A. S. Oberly; Assistant Surgeon, J. D. Murphy; Acting-Masters, J. A. Hannum and F. H. Wilks; Acting-Ensigns, T. Delano, E. C. Bowers and C. H. Pierce; Acting-Master's Mates, Richard Lyons, S. W. Kempton, E. C. Finney and R. S. Shephard; Engineers: Acting-Chief, Solon Farrer; Acting-Second-Assistants, C. R. Weaver and F. W. H. Whittaker; Acting-Third-Assistants, Geo. A. Barnard, R. E. Hurley, C. R. Merrill, Jos. Jordan and G. A. Barnard; Acting-Gunner, J. W. Irwin.

"WABASH" FIRST-RATE."

Captain, Melancton Smith; Lieutenant-Commander, C. H. Cushman; Lieutenants, E. C. V. Blake and H. C. Tallman; Surgeon, H. F. McSherry; Passed-Assistant-Surgeon, J. H. Tinkham; Acting-Assistant Surgeon, N. L. Campbell; Paymaster, Geo. Cochran; Chaplain, C. A. Davis; Second-Lieutenant of Marines, L. E. Fagan; Acting-Masters, W. U. Grozier and S. J. White; Acting-Ensigns, G. T. Davis, Whitman Chase, E. A. Small and J. F. Brown; Acting-Master's Mates, Wm. R. Lyons, D. E. Knox, J. J. Fuller, Jr., Wm. Read, Jr., E. P. Blague, H. C. Thorburn and J. B. Lukens; Engineers: Chief, A. C. Stimers; Second-Assistants, J. S. Green, P. R. Voorhees, W. C. Williamson, A. Michener and N. W. Buckhout; Acting-Third-Assistants, J. W. Collins, W. H. Peabody and J. T. Smith; Boatswain, Charles Miller; Gunner, Cornelius Dugan; Carpenter, Wm. Hyde; Sailmaker, H. W. Frankland.

* "VANDERBILT"—SECOND-RATE.

Captain, Charles W. Pickering; Acting-Volunteer-Lieutenant-Commander, J. D. Danels; Surgeon, Joseph Wilson; Assistant-Surgeon, L. M. Lyon; Acting-Assistant Paymaster, J. E. Tolfree; Captain of Marines, William H. Parker; Acting-Masters, A. M. Keith and L. F. Timmerman; Acting-Ensigns, A. P. Sampson and E. N. Snow; Acting-Master's Mates, F. B. Atkinson, Edw. Thompson, J. B. Strout, E. P. Pope and Edw. Kearns; Engineers: Acting-Chief, John Germain; Acting-First-Assistant, W. H. Golden; Acting-Second-Assistants, William Welles and A. Williams; Acting-Third-Assistants, John Hyslop, Martin Glennon, George Germain, John O'Neil, William Wright and W. H. Garrison; Boatswain, Jasper Coghlan; Gunner, George Sirian; Carpenter, T. H. Bishop; Captain's Clerk, John S. Stodder.

* "JUNIATA"—SECOND-RATE.

Captain, William R. Taylor; Lieutenant-Commander, Thomas S. Phelps, (commanded at Fort Fisher); Lieutenant, F. V. McNair; Surgeon, A. C. Gorgas; Paymaster, Caspar Schenck; Acting-Master, C. H. Hamilton; Ensign, Charles McGregor; Acting-Ensigns, W. D. Price and S. S. Bissell; Acting-Master's Mates, Lewis Goeltze, W. F. Warnick and H. P. Prescott; Engineers: Chief, J. Follansbee; Acting-First-Assistant, J. E. Fox; Second-Assistants, J. Van Hovenbury and John Everding; Third-Assistants, Everett Battelle and F. C. Burchard; Acting-Third-Assistants, B. F. Lewis and

Thomas Connor; Boatswain, J. A. Selmer; Gunner, D. A. Roe; Carpenter, John Mills.

* "FORT JACKSON"—SECOND-RATE.

Captain, B. F. Sands; Lieutenant-Commander, Rush R. Wallace; Lieutenant, S. H. Hunt; Surgeon, Philip S. Wales; Acting-Assistant Surgeon, E. J. O'Callaghan; Paymaster, Clifton Hellen; Acting-Masters, J. S. Coney and H. F. Moffatt; Acting-Ensigns, S. K. Hopkins and J. J. Reagan; Acting-Master's Mates, H. St. C. Eytinge, J. D. Moore, G. W. Smoot, F. A. Powers and Charles Moran; Engineers: Acting-Chief, Rodney Smith; Acting-First-Assistants, Jared Day and J. A. Hill; Acting-Second-Assistants, John Herron and G. T. Gibbs; Acting-Third-Assistants, C. H. Wakefield and William M. Prentiss; Boatswain, P. A. Chason; Acting-Gunner, Thomas Reese; Carpenter, E. Thompson.

* "SHENANDOAH"—SECOND-RATE.

Captain, Daniel B. Ridgely; Lieutenant, Smith W. Nichols; Surgeon, James McMaster; Acting-Assistant-Paymaster, C. M. Guild; Acting-Masters, J. S. Watson, W. H. Brice and J. A. Bullard; Ensigns, Yates Sterling and J. H. Sands; Acting-Ensigns, L. H. White and T. H. Wheeler; Acting-Master's Mate, T. D. Wendell; Engineers: Acting-Chief, Nelson Winans; Second-Assistant, E. A. Magee; Acting-Second-Assistant, J. S. Kelleper; Third-Assistants, D. M. Fulmer, F. W. Towner and William Bond; Boatswain, J. H. Polley; Gunner, George Edmonds.

* "TICONDEROGA"—SECOND-RATE.

Captain, Charles Steedman; Lieutenant, Geo. B. White; Acting-Volunteer-Lieutenant, L. G. Vassallo; Surgeon, C. J. Cleborne; Paymaster, H. M. Denniston; Ensigns, W. W. Maclay, A. S. Crowningshield and Geo. W. Coffin; First-Lieutenant of Marines, C. F. Williams; Acting-Master's Mates, Wm. Charleton, Jr., E. A. Sibell, Wm. Cooper and L. Norton: Engineers: Chief, T. J. Jones; Second-Assistant, H. H. Barrett; Acting-Second-Assistants, R. I. Middleton and M. Smith; Acting-Third-Assistants, O. Bassett, H. M. Noyes, M. W. Thaxter and S. J. Hobbs; Boatswain, H. E. Barnes; Gunner, Joseph Smith; Acting-Carpenter, M. E. Curley; Sailmaker, J. C. Herbert.

* "BROOKLYN"—SECOND-RATE.

Captain, James Alden; Lieutenant, T. L. Swann; Surgeon, George Maulsby; Assistant Surgeon, H. S. Pitkin; Paymaster, G. E. Thornton; Captain of Marines, G. P. Houston; Acting-Master, Robt. Barstow; Ensigns, D. R. Cassell, C. H. Pendleton and C. D. Sigsbee; Acting-Ensign, C. H. Littlefield; Acting-Master's Mates, Thos. Stanfield, J. W. DeCamp and R. H. Taylor; Engineers: Chief, Mortimer Kellogg; Second-Assistants, W. H. G. West, Thos. Lynch, G. E. Tower and J. A. Bullard; Acting-Second-Assistant, R. D. Giberson; Acting-Third-Assistants, John Matthews, H. H. Arthur and Timothy Flanders; Boatswain, Rob't McDonald; Acting-Gunner, John Quevedo; Carpenter, R. G. Thomas; Sailmaker, D. C. Brayton.

ORDNANCE-SHIP "ST. LAWRENCE."

Commander, D. Lynch; Acting-Master, G. W. Caswell; Acting-Ensigns, F. Hopkins, Wm. Chandler, Thomas Welsh and Aug. Dame; Acting-Assistant Surgeon, M. C. Drennan; Assistant Paymaster, W. Goldsborough; Acting-Master's Mates, G. E. Chipman and T. B. Seavey; Gunner, John Webber.

* "TUSCARORA"—THIRD-RATE.

Commander, James M. Frailey; Lieutenant-Commander, Weld N. Allen; Surgeon, John Y. Taylor; Acting-Assistant Paymaster, F. J. Painter; Acting-Master, Alex. Tillinghast; Acting-Ensigns, S. L. Griffin, C. H. Carey, Oliver Swain and S. E. Willetts; Acting-Master's Mates, J. A. H. Wilmuth and

A. F. Aldrich, Jr.; Engineers : Chief, A. J. Kiersted; Acting-First-Assistant, Jos. A. McKnight; Acting-Second-Assistants, W. A. Andress and A. N. Gilmore ; Acting-Third-Assistants, Alex. Dempster, W. B. Snow and J. H. Chesney ; Acting-Gunner, Thomas Grail.

"MONADNOCK"—THIRD-RATE.

Commander, E. G. Parrott; Lieutenant-Commander, J. N. Miller; Acting-Masters, B. F. Milliken and S. H. Mead; Acting-Ensigns, W. B. Mix, T. W. Swift, Jr., and P. Davison ; Acting-Assistant Surgeon, James Wilton ; Assistant Paymaster, J. S. Woolson ; Engineers : Acting-Chief, J. Q. A. Zeigler ; Acting-First-Assistants, S. A. Randall and W. A. Phillips ; Acting-Second-Assistants, B. C. Du Plaine and B. Smith ; Acting-Third-Assistants, R. Aldridge, W. P. Whittemore, John Brice and T. J. Wilde ; Gunner, P. Barrett.

"ONONDAGA"—THIRD-RATE.

Commander, Wm. A. Parker; Lieutenant-Commander, J. M. Pritchett; Passed Assistant Surgeon, A. Hudson; Acting-Assistant Paymaster, S. T. Browne; Acting-Masters, W. L. Hayes and Henry Stevens; Acting-Ensigns, J. De Kay, S. C. Norton, Jr., M. E. Wandell and J. Brennan; Acting-Master's Mate, B. Heath, Jr.; Engineers : Chief, Alex. Henderson; First-Assistants, J. C. Hull; Second-Assistants, W. Fort, W. L. Nicoll and E. M. Lewis; Acting-Second-Assistant, C. Stanton; Third-Assistant, T. Cooke; Acting-Third-Assistant, Julius Hillman.

"SHAMROCK"—THIRD-RATE.

Commander, W. H. Macomb; Lieutenant, R. K. Duer; Acting-Assistant Surgeon, P. H. Barton; Acting-Assistant-Paymaster, Louis Sands; Acting-Master, P. J. Hargous; Acting-Ensigns, G. T. Ford, J. W. Lewis, W. W. Meeter and R. B. Brown; Acting-Master's Mate, W. D. Burlingame ; Engineers : Second-Assistants, W. H. Harrison, H. P. Gregory and P. H White; Acting-Third-Assistants, O. C. Chamberlain and W. F. Blakemore; Acting-Gunner, W. Peterkin.

"RHODE ISLAND"—SECOND-RATE.

Commander, Stephen D. Trenchard; Lieutenant, F. R. Smith ; Assistant-Surgeon, E. B. Bingham ; Assistant Paymaster, W. L. Darling ; Acting-Masters, C. O'Neill and Z. L. Tanner ; Acting-Ensigns, Nichols Pratt, R. O. Lanfare and Lemuel Pope; Acting-Master's Mates, J. P. Fisher, E. E. Bradbury, H. Gardiner, G. H. Appleton and R. W. Wallace ; Engineers : Acting-Chief, J. F. McCutchen ; Acting-Second-Assistants, J. W. Smith and C. W. Radell ; Acting-Third-Assistants, C. W. Rugg, W. J. Patterson, W. H. McCoy, J. A. Hughes and W. B. Bayley ; Gunner, Henry Hamilton ; Captain's Clerk, L. S. Rogers ; Paymaster's Clerk, Wm. J. Bennett.

"CHICKOPEE"—THIRD-RATE.

Commander, A. D. Harrell ; Lieutenant, E. A. Walker ; Acting-Assistant Surgeon, G. L. Simpson; Acting-Assistant Paymaster, J. H. Mulford, Jr.; Acting-Master, J. D. Wells ; Acting-Ensigns, J. A. Crossman and A. D. Henderson ; Acting-Master's Mates, C. C. Johnson, G. H. Goodmanson and J. A. Belcher; Engineers: First-Assistant, F. J. Lovering; Second-Assistant, William Pollard ; Third-Assistants, D. B. Egbert, A. G. Bonsall and J. B. Upham, Jr.; Acting-Gunner, W. Black.

"NEREUS"—THIRD-RATE.

Commander, J. C. Howell; Lieutenant, H. E. Mullan ; Acting-Master, E. L. Haines; Acting-Assistant Surgeon, J. K. Walsh; Acting-Assistant Paymaster, B. F. Munroe ; Acting-Ensigns, E. G. Dayton, G. M. Smith and George Anderson ; Acting-Master's Mates, W. C. Cushman, Wm. Rushmore, W. B. Spencer, H. E. Giraud and Wm. Gromack ; Engineers : Acting-First-Assistant, Stephen Henton ;

Second-Assistant, Philip Eckenworth ; Acting-Second-Assistants, R. F. Roswald and J. A. Patterson ; Third-Assistants, T. Tilton, H. J. Allen and R. R. Throckmorton; Acting-Gunner, J. McCaffrey.

"MOHICAN"—THIRD-RATE.

Commander, Daniel Ammen ; Lieutenant, J. D. Marvin ; Surgeon, Charles Martin ; Acting-Assistant Paymaster, J. C. Canning ; Acting-Master, Wm. Burditt ; Acting-Ensigns, B. F. Blair and H. T. Page ; Acting-Master's Mates, J. A. Shaffer, J. G. Paine and C. P. Cope; Engineers: First-Assistant, H. S. Davids; Second-Assistant, J. K. Smedley; Acting-Second-Assistants, Enoch George and Charles Buckelew ; Acting-Third-Assistants, James O. Herron and W. W. Chadwick ; Acting-Boatswain, J. B. Aiken; Acting-Gunner, T. S. Cassidy.

"KEYSTONE STATE"—THIRD-RATE.

Commander, Henry Roland ; Lieutenant, J. P. Robertson ; Acting-Masters, L. E. Degn and Wm. T. Buck; Acting-Ensigns, C. M. Bird, J. C. Murphy, F. E. Ford and J. S. Ridgeway ; Acting-Assistant Surgeon, A. E. Emery ; Acting-Assistant Paymaster, J. W. Fairfield ; Acting-Master's Mates, D. G. Conger and W. H. Howard; Engineers: Acting-First-Assistant, P. L. Fry ; Acting-Second-Assistant, A. B. Kinney ; Acting-Third-Assistants, Wm. Brown, Joseph Smith, J. B. Wilbur and C. A. Blake ; Acting-Gunner, D. L. Briggs.

"MENDOTA"—THIRD-RATE.

Commander, Edward T. Nichols ; Acting-Masters, Lathrop Wight, Maurice Digard and Thomas Smith ; Acting-Ensigns, W. B. Barnes, R. B. Pray, Isaac Thayer and R. E. Peck ; Acting-Master's Mates, E. S. McDonald and P. A. Cleary; Engineers: First-Assistant, A. V. Frazer; Second-Assistants, B. Bunce and D. Jones; Acting-Third-Assistants, D. R. McElroy, H. S. Ross and L. L. Poole; Acting-Gunner, James Como.

"IOSCO"—THIRD-RATE.

Commander, John Guest ; Lieutenant, C. L. Franklin; Acting-Ensigns, William Jameson, Ulric Feilberg, Henry Baker and Paul Ware, Jr.: Acting-Assistant Paymaster, K. H. Bancroft; Acting-Master's Mates, T. A. Comstock, Halsted Hemans and Charles A. Peacock; Engineers: First-Assistant, Z. Talbot; Second-Assistant, Elijah Laws ; Acting-Third-Assistants, Harvey Clapp, James McNabb and C. M. S. Gerry ; Acting-Gunner, T. M. Benton.

"OSCEOLA"—THIRD-RATE.

Commander, J. M. B. Clitz; Lieutenant, J. Weidman; Assistant Surgeon, G. F. Winslow; Assistant Paymaster, Edw. Bellows; Acting-Masters, E. B. Hussey and Willett Mott; Acting-Ensigns, S. L. La Dein, J. F. Merry and F. C. Warner; Acting-Master's Mates, Thomas Rogers, H. G. Robinson and C. S. Hardy; Engineers: Acting-First-Assistant, Thomas McCausland; Acting-Second-Assistant, Richard Doran; Acting-Third-Assistants, Robert Berryman, C. J. Cooper and E. J. Swords; Acting-Gunner. J. C. Breslyn.

"PAWTUCKET"—THIRD-RATE.

Commander, James H. Spotts; Lieutenant, Allen V. Reed; Acting-Ensigns, A. F. West, J. A. Slamm, J. O. Winchester and P. J. Markoe; Acting-Assistant Surgeon, Henry Johnson ; Acting-Assistant Paymaster, G. A. Emerson; Acting-Master's Mates, D. H. Bellows, F. Hesslewood and L. F. Papanti; Engineers: Second-Assistants, A. H. Able, M. N. Knowlton and J. G. Cooper ; Acting-Third-Assistant, N. G. Vandegrift; Gunner, J. D. Fletcher.

"MACKINAW"—THIRD-RATE.

Commander, J. C. Beaumont ; Acting-Master, A. J. Louch; Acting-Ensigns, W. H. Penfield, J. F. Blanchard and Joseph Estes; Acting-Assistant Surgeon, J. F. Cottrell; Acting-Assistant Paymaster,

W. T. Whittemore; Acting-Master's Mates, J. A. Thomas, Solomon Barstow and E. K. Green; Engineers: First-Assistant, Jefferson Young; Second-Assistant, D. A. Sawyer; Third-Assistants, R. W. Milligan and Sylvanus McIntire; Acting-Third-Assistants, Patrick Hagan and J. W. Reed; Acting-Gunner, Thomas Keer.

* "R. R. CUYLER"—THIRD-RATE.

Commander, C. H. B. Caldwell; Lieutenant, J. J. Reed; Acting-Assistant Surgeon, C. D. White; Acting-Assistant Paymaster, A. Wright; Acting-Master, E. Babson; Acting-Ensigns, B. P. Clough, W. H. Mentz, W. L. Hatch and A. T. Hamblen; Acting-Master's Mate, J. F. Jeffries; Engineers: Acting-Chief, J. D. Williamson; Acting-First-Assistant, D. L. King; Acting-Second-Assistants, J. Pollard and F. V. Holt; Acting-Third-Assistants, A. C. Crocker, I. H. Fuhr, G. W. Young, D. Gilliland and E. J. Cram; Acting-Gunner, E. P. Palmer.

"MATTABESSETT"—THIRD-RATE.

Commander, John C. Febiger; Lieutenant, A. N. Mitchell; Acting-Masters, J. L. Plunkett and John Fountain; Acting-Ensigns, John Greenhalgh, F. H. Brown and A. F. Dill; Acting-Assistant Surgeon, S. P. Boyer; Acting-Assistant Paymaster, H. C. Meade; Acting-Master's Mates, A. M. Beck and C. F. Fisher; Engineers: Second-Assistants, J. T. Hawkins, A. Sackett and C. J. McConnell; Third-Assistants, W. A. Mintzer, A. B. Bates and Isaiah Paxson; Acting-Gunner, Wm. H. Herring.

"MASSASOIT"—THIRD RATE.

Commander, R. T. Renshaw; Lieutenant, Geo. W. Sumner; Acting-Masters, H. Reany, C. F. Taylor and W. C. Williams; Acting-Ensigns, R. Rabadan and Chas. Wilson; Acting-Master's Mate, G. A. Burt; Acting-Assistant Surgeon, J. R. Latson; Acting-Assistant Paymaster, J. H. Stevenson; Engineers: First-Assistant, L. R. Green; Acting-Second-Assistants, J. H. Dinsmore and R. K. Monson; Acting-Third-Assistants, T. R. Jefferson and Wm. Sheehan; Acting-Gunner, Wm. B. Jarvis.

* "SAUGUS"—FOURTH-RATE.

Commander, Edmund R. Colhoun; Lieutenant, Benj. F. Day; Acting-Master, B. W. Leary; Acting-Ensigns, C. A. Henrickson, Ira Barsley and J. P. Arnett; Acting-Assistant Surgeon, W. H. Westcott; Acting-Assistant Paymaster, G. H. Andrews; Engineers: Acting-Chief, John L. Peake; Acting-First-Assistants, Andrew Inglis and John Carren; Second-Assistant, O. C. Lewis; Acting-Second-Assistant, A. F. Rockefeller; Acting-Third-Assistant, W. J. Bradley.

"AGAWAM"—THIRD-RATE.

Commander, A. C. Rhind; Acting-Master, Thos. Symmes; Acting-Ensigns, Clinton Wiley, C. M. Anthony, C. L. Willcomb and F. H. Lathrop; Assistant Surgeon, H. P. Babcock; Assistant Paymaster, H. M. Hanna; Acting-Master's Mates, Rob't Anderson, T. P. Jones and Paul Boyden; Engineers: Acting-First-Assistant, J. F. P. Rust; Second-Assistants, A. T. E. Mullan and T. M. Jones; Third-Assistants, G. C. Nelson and H. Spear; Acting-Gunner, H. F. Dunnels.

"QUAKER CITY"—SECOND-RATE.

Commander, W. F. Spicer; Lieutenant, Silas Casey, Jr.; Acting-Master, S. A. Winnerton; Acting-Ensigns, C. J. Hill, Rich. Wilkinson and F. D. Jacobson; Acting-Assistant-Surgeons, I. C. Whitehead and G. W. Gale, Jr.; Acting-Assistant Paymaster, L. A. Frailey; Acting-Master's Mates, O. W. Clapp, G. E. Sanborne, W. H. Alger and J. B. Tew; Engineers: Acting-Chief, G. W. Farrar; Second-Assistant, George J. Burnap; Acting-Second-Assistants, W. J. Howard, J. K. Hickey, Wm. Mason and J. H. Mathews; Acting-Third-Assistants, E. Prest,

Jos. R. Peterson, J. D. Wauklin and E. E. Porter; Acting-Gunner, Joseph Furlong.

* "PONTOOSUC"—THIRD-RATE.

Lieutenant-Commander, Wm. G. Temple; Acting-Masters, B. S. Weeks and C. H. Frisbie; Acting-Ensigns, A. D. Campbell, J. J. Kane and L. R. Chester; Acting-Assistant Surgeon, W. H. Pierson; Acting-Assistant Paymaster, G. A. Lyon; Acting-Master's Mates, E. H. Richardson, F. C. Bailey, Thos. Brown and D. Lewis; Engineers: First-Assistant, Geo. J. Barry; Second-Assistants, M. T. Sumstron and E. J. Whittaker; Third-Assistant, J. H. Thomas; Acting-Third-Assistant, G. C. Brown; Acting-Gunner, C. Moran.

"EUTAW"—THIRD-RATE.

Lieutenant-Commander, H. C. Blake; Acting-Volunteer-Lieutenant, J. W. Simmons; Assistant-Surgeon, C. H. Page; Acting-Assistant Paymaster, Thos. Carstairs; Acting-Masters, C. F. Keith, S. B. Davis and T. O. Scranton; Acting-Ensigns, C. E. Rich, W. C. King and Thos. Morgan; Acting-Master's Mates, E. A. Galindo, B. C. Devine and H. Gardiner; Engineers: Second-Assistant, J. C. Stevens; Acting-Second-Assistants, J. E. Hillard and W. H. Crawford; Third-Assistant, H. C. Christopher; Acting-Third-Assistants, C. A. Satterlee and J. C. Hillman; Acting-Gunner, C. A. Sampson.

"WYALUSING"—THIRD-RATE.

Lieutenant-Commander, Earl English; Acting-Masters, W. R. Hathaway and J. G. Green; Acting-Ensigns, J. P. Perkins, H. G. C. Kruse and L. H. Fossett; Acting-Assistant Surgeon, S. Holman; Assistant Paymaster, A. J. Pritchard; Acting-Master's Mates, J. C. Green, W. H. Brown and Henry Watson; Engineers: Chief, H. H. Stewart; Acting-First-Assistant, J. McCourt; Acting-Third-Assistants, E. F. Hedden, J. J. Donohoe, E. T. Peake and S. G. Cottrell; Acting-Gunner, T. Carpenter.

* "A. D. VANCE"—FOURTH-RATE.

Lieutenant-Commander, J. H. Upshur; Acting-Masters, G. Cottrell and C. M. Lane; Acting-Ensigns, W. W. Smith, C. F. Ware, C. E. Clark and W. J. Eldredge; Acting-Assistant Surgeons, D. W. Jones and B. F. Howell; Engineers: Acting-First-Assistant, D. C. Chester; Acting-Second-Assistants, C. G. Stevens, C. S. Servoss and George Devine; Acting-Third-Assistants, Wm. Madden, G. H. Whittemore and C. B. Nichols.

* "YANTIC"—FOURTH-RATE.

Lieutenant-Commander, T. C. Harris; Acting-Master, L. C. McIntyre; Acting-Ensigns, J. C. Lord, S. T. Dederer, Edwd. Winnemore, J. F. Churchill and B. B. Sodenberg; Acting-Assistant Surgeon, H. K. Wheeler; Acting-Assistant-Paymaster, S. B. Huey; Engineers: Second-Assistants, W. H. Messenger, J. J. Noble and H. C. Beckwith; Third-Assistant, H. F. Loveaire; Acting-Third-Assistant, George Holton; Captain's Clerk, C. M. B. Harris.

* "SASSACUS"—THIRD-RATE.

Lieutenant-Commander, John L. Davis; Acting-Volunteer-Lieutenant, A. W. Muldaur; Acting-Ensigns, William H. Mayer, Jr., August Adler, H. W. O'Harra and David Stephen; Acting-Assistant Surgeon, G. E. McPherson; Acting-Assistant Paymaster, G. W. Garthwaite; Acting-Master's Mates, T. D. Marble and J. S. O'Brien; Engineers: Second-Assistants, J. H. Huxley, R. N. Ellis and O. W. Allisson; Acting-Third-Assistants, Wm. Raynor, H. S. Mack and A. Bigelow; Acting-Gunner, Neil Martin.

"TALLAPOOSA"—THIRD-RATE.

Lieutenant-Commander, J. E. DeHaven; Acting-Master, J. H. Platt; Acting-Ensigns, Jonathan Jenney, W. A. Rich, A. E. Dunham and J. D. Babcock; Acting-Assistant Surgeon, J. E. Warner;

Acting-Assistant Paymaster, Daniel Whalen ; Acting-Master's Mates, J. H. Lovejoy, S. T. Ayres and C. M. Tessimond ; Engineers : First-Assistant, David Smith ; Second-Assistants, J. P. Kelly and W. S. Neal ; Acting-Third-Assistant W. E. Renny and G. W. Wakefield ; Acting-Gunner, J. W. Whiting.

* "TACONY"—THIRD-RATE.

Lieutenant-Commander. W. T. Truxtun ; Acting-Masters, N. S. Morgan, R. Summers and S. Blunt ; Acting - Ensigns, J. B. Taney, Thomas Golding, E. L. Bourne and F. H. Fisher ; Acting - Assistant-Surgeon, George Hopkins ; Acting-Assistant Paymaster, W. S. Hosford ; Acting - Master's Mates, J. A. Orcutt and F. W. Worstell ; Engineers: First-Assistant, T. M. Dukehart ; Second - Assistants, C. E. Lee and H. Parker, Jr.; Acting-Third-Assistant, A. D. Wood.

NAVAL STATION, BEAUFORT.

Lieutenant-Commander, W. C. West ; Acting-Assistant Paymaster, S. S. Wood, Jr.; Gunner, S. D. Hines ; Carpenter, J. P. Carter.

"MERCEDITA"—THIRD-RATE.

Lieutenant-Commander, Milton Haxton ; Acting-Master, J. A. French ; Acting-Ensigns, H. G. Macy, Wm. Young and E. D. Pettengill ; Acting-Assistant Surgeon, J. K. Walsh ; Acting-Assistant Paymaster, O. F. Browning ; Acting - Master's Mate, R. M. Cornell ; Engineers : Acting-First-Assistant, B. F. Beckett ; Acting-Third-Assistants, Wm. Lannan, D. T. Lannahan, Wm. McComb, J. H. Hopkins and William Ellis ; Acting-Gunner, James Addison.

* "KANSAS"—FOURTH-RATE.

Lieutenant-Commander, P. G. Watmough ; Acting-Masters, Samuel Hall, E. S. Goodwin and W. S. Folson ; Acting - Ensigns, G. C. Williams, C. D. Thompson and C. B. Staples ; Assistant Surgeon, Isaac Poole: Assistant Paymaster, T. Merritt ; Engineers : Acting Second-Assistant, Hugh Rafferty ; Acting-Third-Assistants, J. W. Stott, G. L. King and George B. Stone.

*"MARATANZA"—THIRD-RATE.

Lieutenant Commander, G. W. Young ; Acting-Masters, D. E. Taylor and J. B. Wood, Jr.; Acting-Ensigns, J. W. Crowell, H. H. Collamore and E. Lawson; Acting-Master's Mates, W. H. Alger, A. F. Williamson, George E. Chipman and C H. Crossman; Acting-Assistant-Surgeon, J. W. Hamilton ; Acting-Assistant Paymaster, C. H. Noyes ; Engineers : Second-Assistants, W. H. Kilpatrick and R. L. Webb ; Third-Assistants, L. R. Harvey and R. D. Taylor ; Acting-Third-Assistants, E. J. Gillespie and J. L. Starkey ; Acting Gunner, W. W. Bradley.

* "MAUMEE"—FOURTH-RATE.

Lieutenant-Commander, Ralph Chandler ; Acting-Master Richard Burk ; Acting Ensigns, E. R. Powers, W. J. Shackford, C. P. Gifford and C. B. Nichols; Acting-Assistant Surgeon, D. P. Goodhue ; Acting-Assistant Paymaster, J. H. Smoot; Engineers : Second-Assistant, T. J. McK. Daniels ; Acting-Second - Assistant, William Veitch ; Third-Assistants, J. M. Clark, C. R. Mosher and G. A. Pfeltz.

* "PEQUOT"—FOURTH-RATE.

Lieutenant-Commander, D. L. Braine ; Acting-Masters, L. H. Beattie and W. F. Chace ; Acting-Ensigns, George Lamb, H. W. Loring and A. Smalley ; Acting-Assistant Surgeon, H. R. Watts ; Acting - Assistant Paymaster, C. G. Hutchinson ; Engineers : Second-Assistants, A. H. Fisher and G. C. Cook ; Third-Assistants, James Wylie and J. W. Gardner ; Acting - Third - Assistants, George W. Rymes; Captain's Clerks, J. W. Jones and —— O'Brian (" Keystone State ").

"NYACK"—FOURTH-RATE.

Lieutenant-Commander, L. H. Newman; Acting-Master, H. W. Grinnell ; Acting-Ensigns, H. B. Colby, Charles Nelson, J. W. Hopkins, G. H. Barrows and James Jordan ; Acting Assistant Surgeon, B. F. Bigelow ; Acting-Assistant Paymaster, C. S. Halliday ; Engineers: First-Assistant, B. C. Bampton ; Second-Assistant, John Fornance ; Third Assistant, W. A. Windsor ; Acting-Third-Assistants, W. M. Bartram and J. C. Veatch.

*"CANONICUS"—THIRD-RATE.

Lieutenant - Commander, George E. Belknap ; Lieutenant, R. S. McCook ; Acting - Masters, D. S. Murphy, E. S. Goodwin and E. A. Decker ; Acting-Ensigns, C. W. Seekins, M. W. Weld and F. P. Center ; Assistant Surgeon, H. N. Beaumont ; Assistant Paymaster, R. P. Lisle ; Engineers : Chief, D. B. Macomb ; Acting-First-Assistant, C. G. Conklin ; Second-Assistants, F. F. McKean and J. M. Saville; Acting-Third-Assistants, William S. Brown, Wm. Keenan and J. A. Chandler.

"VICKSBURG"—THIRD-RATE.

Lieutenant - Commander, F. H. Baker ; Acting-Master, F. G. Osborn ; Acting-Ensigns, W. H. Otis, R. B. Elder and D. P. Cook ; Acting - Assistant Surgeon, T. W. Bennett ; Acting-Assistant Paymaster, T. E. Smith ; Acting-Master's Mate, G. V. Demorest ; Engineers : Second - Assistant, J. L. Bright ; Acting - Second - Assistant, H. Harbenson ; Third-Assistant, A. F. Nagle ; Acting-Third-Assistants, Levi Coit and G. W. Yoe.

* "CHIPPEWA"—FOURTH-RATE.

Lieutenant-Commander, A. W. Weaver (Lieutenant-Commander E. E. Potter commanded at Fort Fisher) ; Acting-Master J. W. Saunders ; Acting-Ensigns, G. H. Wood, Edw. Tilghman, W. H. DeGrosse and W. A. Taylor ; Acting-Assistant Surgeon, J. E. Gregory; Acting-Assistant Paymaster, J. M. Flood ; Engineers : Second Assistant, Jos. Watters; Acting-Second-Assistant, A. A. Winship ; Acting-Third-Assistants, R. W. Wilton and Henry Romaine.

"SACO"—FOURTH-RATE.

Lieutenant-Commander, John G. Walker ; Acting-Master, W. F. Hunt ; Acting-Ensigns, O. F. Wixon, T. J. Rollins, W. H. Potter and A. H. Ostrander; Passed-Assistant-Surgeon, A. Matthewson; Acting - Assistant Paymaster, C. H. Hill ; Engineers: Acting-First-Assistant, A. W. Harris ; Acting-Second-Assistants, J. P. Cloyd and J. A. Crouthers; Acting-Third-Assistants, W. J. Barron and W. H. Woodward.

* "UNADILLA"—FOURTH-RATE.

Lieutenant - Commander, Francis M. Ramsey; Acting - Master, J. M. Skillings ; Acting - Ensigns, John Cullaton, Wm. Field, Charles Weidenbein and Wm. Hanson ; Acting - Assistant Surgeon, D. C. Burleigh ; Acting-Assistant Paymaster, I. G. Hobbs ; Acting - Master's Mates, C. H. Smith and E. M. Reed ; Engineers : Acting - First - Assistant, B. F. Bee ; Acting-Second-Assistant, L. M. Ryfenburg ; Acting - Third - Assistants, Wm. D. Kay, James Curran and J. S. Larkins.

* "MAHOPAC"—FOURTH-RATE.

Lieutenant Commander E. E. Potter (Lieutenant-Commander A. W. Weaver commanded at Fort Fisher ; Acting-Masters, C. R. Harris and D. K. Kennison; Acting-Ensigns, J. E. Jones, W. E. Jones and S. C. Holm; Assistant Surgeon, F. B. A. Lewis; Acting-Assistant Paymaster, Addison Pool; Engineers: Acting-Chief, M. T. Chevers ; Acting - First - Assistant, Charles Dougherty ; Acting-Second-Assistant, Wesley Randall ; Acting - Third - Assistants, J. G. Brown, C. A. Enggren, C. O. Putnam and J. W. Buell.

* "HURON"—FOURTH-RATE.

Lieutenant-Commander, Thos. O. Selfridge ; Acting - Master, Benj. Whitmore ; Acting - Ensigns, Robert Shepperd, S. H. Munder, W. H. H. Curtis and Andrew McCleary ; Acting - Master's Mate, Eugene Coleman ; Acting-Assistant Surgeon, James McMillan ; Acting-Assistant Paymaster, C. D. Collom ; Engineers : Acting-First-Assistant, James Blenkinsop ; Acting-Second-Assistants, H. F. Hayden and M. Harloe ; Acting-Third-Assistants, T. F. Burket and E. G. Ingalls.

* "SENECA"—FOURTH-RATE.

Lieutenant - Commander, Montgomery Sicard ; Acting-Master, Wm H. Maies ; Acting-Ensigns, Wm. Schutz, Thomas Mason, W. B. Pierce and L. C. Owen ; Acting - Assistant Surgeon, R. H. Greene ; Acting - Assistant Paymaster, M. B. Cushing ; Engineers : Acting-First-Assistant, J. P. Sweet ; Acting - Second - Assistant, Alfred Catchpole ; Acting-Third - Assistants, S. A. Slater, A. J. Doty and T. J. Reaney.

"HUNCHBACK"—FOURTH-RATE.

Lieutenant, Joseph P. Fyffe ; Acting-Master, E. K. Valentine ; Acting - Ensigns, J. W. Thompson and C. W. Jones ; Acting - Master's Mates, J. F. Sias, J. L. Robins, T. W. Rack and F. W. Colton ; Acting - Assistant Paymaster, H. Cushing ; Engineers : Acting-First-Assistant, A. Barnum ; Acting-Second-Assistant, B. Wilson ; Acting-Third-Assistants, S. Hart, G. V. Payton, J. E. Edwards and J. W. Smith.

* "MONTICELLO"—FOURTH-RATE.

Lieutenant, W. B. Cushing ; Acting-Volunteer-Lieutenant, D. A. Campbell ; Acting-Masters, C. A. Pettit and E. A. Elliott ; Acting-Ensigns, W. H. Gibson, D. W. Lakin, T. B. Huntington, J. H. Puckett and J. B. Edwards ; Acting-Assistant Surgeon, J. F. Billard ; Acting - Assistant Paymaster, John Furey ; Acting-Master's Mates, Charles Croton and J. S. Clark ; Engineers : Second-Assistant, H. Missiner ; Acting-Second-Assistants, C. A. Martin and F. McKinley ; Acting - Third - Assistants, W. R. Call, and J. McCallum.

* "GETTYSBURG"—FOURTH-RATE.

Lieutenant, R. H. Lamson ; Acting-Master, C. B. Dahlgren ; Acting-Ensigns, A. S. Leighton, F. P. B. Sands, F. A. Gross, M. C. Keith and Charles Miller; Acting - Assistant Surgeon, G. S. Eddy ; Acting-Assistant Paymaster, R. H. Gillette ; Acting-Master's Mate, H. J. Derbyshire and T. H. P. Gross; Engineers : Acting-First-Assistants, G. S. Perkins, J. M. Case, E. C. Maloy and A. J. Pixley; Acting-Third-Assistants, E. B. Carter and J. W. Homans.

* "MALVERN"—FOURTH-RATE (FLAG-SHIP)

Lieutenant, B. H. Porter ; Acting-Masters, J. A. Hamilton and John Price ; Acting-Ensigns, Geo. Leonard, John Hill and G. E. Kidder ; Acting Master's Mates, W. F. Horton, Henry Gardiner, A. M. Lyon and W. D. Cobb, Jr. ; Assistant Surgeon, J. S. Ramsey ; Acting-Assistant Paymaster, A. B. Poor ; Engineers : Acting - First - Assistant, W. E. Moore ; Acting-Second-Assistants, J. J. Ashmen and F. J. Hadley ; Third - Assistant, Owen Jones ; Acting-Third-Assistants, Edwin Bond, A. H. Perry and William Finn ; Sub-Assistant J. S. Bradford, U. S. Coast Survey.

* "ALABAMA"—THIRD-RATE.

Acting-Volunteer-Lieutenant, A. R. Langthorn ; Acting-Master, Wm. Bates ; Acting-Ensigns, Albert Taylor, Thos. Williams and S. F Graves ; Acting Assistant Surgeon, D. T. T. Nestell ; Acting-Assistant Paymaster, E. K. Gibson ; Acting - Master's Mates, C. F. Ellmore, C. S. Wilcox and D. H Hall ; Engineers : First-Assistant, Edward Farmer ; Act-

ing-Second-Assistants, J. G. Rossman, J. C. Lewis and Greenville Lewis ; Acting - Third - Assistants, Ezra Gray and Geo. Cowie, Jr.

* "MONTGOMERY"—THIRD-RATE.

Acting-Volunteer-Lieutenant, T. C. Dunn ; Acting-Masters, W. N. Wells and A. F. Davis ; Acting Ensigns, E. T. Mauter, C. G. Whiting and Robt. Wiley ; Acting Assistant Surgeon, John Blackmer; Acting Assistant Paymaster, J. Watson ; Acting-Master s Mates, T. J Walker and C. A. Neill ; Engineers : Acting-First-Assistant, G. H. Wade ; Acting Second-Assistants, John McEwen, J. Williams and J. Allen ; Acting-Third-Assistants, G. H. Brown and A. Tester.

* "FORT DONELSON"—THIRD RATE.

Acting-Volunteer-Lieutenant, Thomas Pickering ; Acting-Master, G. W. Frost, commanded at Fort Fisher ; Acting-Ensigns, J. W. Bennett, E. A. Butler, H. C. Leslie and J. G. Lloyd ; Acting Master's Mates, Geo. Woodland and A. F. G. Blanfuhr ; Acting-Assistant Surgeon, M. G. Raefle ; Acting Assistant Paymaster J. F. Dunham ; Engineers : Acting-First-Assistant, John Miller ; Acting-Second-Assistant, H. L. M. Hodges ; Acting - Third - Assistants, G. W. Rymes, L. De Arville, W. A. Fuller, J. H. Sleanman and P. M. Kafer.

"MIAMI"—THIRD-RATE.

Acting - Volunteer - Lieutenant, Geo. W. Graves ; Acting-Masters, M. Rodgers and John Lear ; Acting-Ensign, J. R. Peacock ; Acting-Assistant Surgeon, G. H. Marvin ; Acting-Assistant Paymaster, R. F. Goodman ; Engineers : Acting - Second - Assistants, C. C. Davis and David Newell ; Acting-Third-Assistants, H. D. Heiser, A. Stewart and A. Moore.

* "GOVERNOR BUCKINGHAM"—THIRD-RATE.

Acting-Volunteer-Lieutenant, John Macdearmid ; Acting-Ensigns, C. H. Sawyer, L. W. Smith, D. M. Gaskins and L. P. Cassan ; Acting-Assistant-Surgeon, W. S. Parker ; Acting-Assistant Paymaster, G. B. Tripp ; Acting-Master's Mates, J. W. Gardner, F. H. Poole and W. W. Hunter ; Engineers: Acting-First-Assistant, F. E. Porter ; Acting-Second Assistant, Eugene Mack ; Acting-Third-Assistants, Thos. Foley, Owen Kaney, James Fitzpatrick and Chas. Ward.

* "ARIES"—THIRD-RATE.

Acting-Volunteer-Lieutenant, F. S. Wells ; Acting-Ensigns, G. F. Morse, J. A. Brennan and Seth Hand ; Acting - Assistant Surgeon, A. C. Fowler ; Acting-Assistant Paymaster, C. A. Downes ; Acting-Master's Mates, D. McCool and F. A. Haskell ; Engineers : Acting-Second-Assistant, Simeon Smith ; Acting-Third-Assistants, R. H. Cornthwait, T. E. Wilson and J. F. Fraser.

"CAMBRIDGE"—THIRD-RATE.

Acting-Volunteer-Lieutenant, J. F. Nickels ; Acting-Master, S. K. Luce ; Acting-Ensigns, I. S. Bradbury and A. J. Iverson ; Acting - Assistant - Surgeon, John Spare ; Acting - Assistant Paymaster, J. J. Pratt ; Acting-Master's Mate, F. U. Northup ; Engineers : Acting First - Assistant, G. B. Orswell ; Acting - Second - Assistants, W. W. Tunis and John Whittaker ; Acting-Third-Assistant, S. D. Edwards ; Acting-Gunner, Wm. Scott.

"CHEROKEE"—FOURTH-RATE.

Acting-Volunteer-Lieutenant, Wm. E. Dennison ; Acting - Ensigns, T. F. DeLuce, John Parry, A. F. Parsons and C. B. Dickman ; Acting-Assistant Surgeon, E. T. T. March ; Acting-Assistant Paymaster, J. C Osterloh ; Engineers : Acting-First-Assistant, A. W. Reynolds ; Acting - Second - Assistants, F. H. Thurber and J. H. Potts ; Acting-Third-Assistants John Gilmore and A. I. Sanborn.

" HOWQUAH "—FOURTH-RATE.

Acting-Volunteer-Lieutenant, J. W. Balch ; Acting-Ensigns, G. P. St. John and John Sayres ; Acting-Assistant Paymaster, E. W. Brooks ; Acting-Master's Mates, R. B. Smith and F. P. Haskell ; Engineers : Acting - Second - Assistants, W. G. McLean, D. R. Wylie and J. L. DeMott ; Acting-Third-Assistants, F. W. Moores, Jr., and Arthur O'Brien.

" EMMA "—FOURTH-RATE.

Acting - Volunteer - Lieutenant, J. M. Williams ; Acting-Ensigns, C. Zimmerman, D. S. Beete, I. S. Sampson, C. A. Stewart and I. C. Fuller ; Acting-Master's Mate, R. P. Herrick ; Acting-Assistant Surgeon, George Doig ; Acting-Assistant Paymaster, C. H. Hammatt ; Engineers : Acting-Second-Assistant, E. Barry ; Acting-Third-Assistants, A. S Churchill, J. C. Smith, R. H. Ryan, J. W. Grant, and J. C. Wells.

" BIGNONIA "—FOURTH RATE.

Acting-Volunteer-Lieutenant, Wm. D. Roath ; Acting-Ensigns, T. H. Marks and H. D. Trott ; Acting-Master's Mates, G. C. Short and W. H. Howland ; Engineers : Acting - Second - Assistant, John Moir ; Acting-Third-Assistants, W. S. Dobson, T. McCreary and James Boyd.

" COMMODORE BARNEY "—FOURTH-RATE

Acting - Volunteer - Lieutenant, Geo. B. Livingston ; Acting-Master, J. B. Stover ; Acting-Ensigns, Joseph Avant, Albert Buhner, John Aspinwall, Jr., and James Auld ; Acting-Master's Mate, W. H. Richmond ; Acting - Assistant Surgeon, Geo. C. Webber ; Acting-Assistant Paymaster, Thomas Jernegan ; Engineers : Acting-First-Assistants, Hiram Warner ; Acting - Second - Assistants, C. B. Culver and D. S. Leffler ; Acting-Third-Assistants, F. G. Shannon and David Reed.

" SHOKOKON "—FOURTH RATE.

Acting - Volunteer - Lieutenant, W. B. Sheldon ; Acting - Ensigns, P. C. Asserson, A. O. Kruge and D. W. Lakin ; Acting-Master's Mates. R. S. Proudfit and F. Bradley ; Acting - Assistant Paymaster, C. J. Todd ; Engineers : Acting-First-Assistant, W. D. Forbes ; Acting-Third-Assistant, James Wilson.

" DUNBARTON "—FOURTH-RATE.

Acting-Volunteer-Lieutenant, Henry Brown ; Acting-Master, Hamilton Bingham ; Acting-Ensigns, O. A. Thompson, C. T. Somes, Daniel Merrill and J. A. Williams ; Acting-Master's Mate, H. M. Guilford ; Acting-Assistant Paymaster, J. W. Holmes ; Engineers : Acting-Second Assistant, Charles Bremon ; Acting-Third Assistants, J. W. Mead, G. L. Shoemaker, Clark Thurston and J. T. Boyd.

" CLEMATIS "—FOURTH-RATE.

Acting-Volunteer Lieutenant, E. D. Bruner ; Acting Ensigns, C. T. Beth, Isaac Miller and Geo. H. Gooding ; Acting-Master's Mates, M. P. Butts and O. C. Currier ; Engineers : Acting - Second - Assistant, Wm. Deacon ; Acting-Third-Assistants, G. McAllister, W. S. Kenworthy and Wm. Snedeker.

" TRISTAM SHANDY." - FOURTH-RATE

Acting-Volunteer-Lieutenant, F. M. Green ; Actting-Ensign, Benj. Wood, J. H. Nash, T. M. Smith, S. T. Dederer and John Owens : Acting-Master's Mates, Robert Clifford, Maurice Wagg and F. T. Baldwin ; Acting-Assistant Paymaster, F. R. Stow ; Engineers : Acting-First-Assistant, W. W. Whiting ; Acting-Second Assistants, W. S. Pratt and H. W. Miller ; Acting-Third-Assistants, Richard Wareham, Thomas Pentony, William Gladden and Thomas Holten.

*" LILLIAN "—FOURTH-RATE.

Acting-Volunteer Lieutenant, Thomas A. Harris ; Acting-Master, J. S. Gilett ; Acting-Ensigns, Wm. C.

Underhill, Joseph H. Clark, T. B. Tucker, Jr., and J. G. Lloyd ; Acting-Master's Mate, J. P. Sturgeon ; Acting-Assistant Surgeon, Charles Sturdevant ; Acting - Assistant Paymaster, Herman Dorr ; Engineers : Acting-Second-Assistants, J. C. Mockabee, H. W. Moore and David Morris ; Acting-Third-Assistants, Henry Greatorex, T. J. Foster and A. T. Donegan.

" CRUSADER "—FOURTH-RATE.

Acting-Volunteer-Lieutenant, Peter Hays ; Acting-Master, C Hallett ; Acting-Ensigns, H. Taylor, W. W. Leonard and Geo. Kendall ; Acting-Assistant Surgeon, R. H. Whedon ; Engineers : Acting-First-Assistant, Cornelius Carr ; Acting-Second-Assistant, W. F. Andrews ; Acting - Third - Assistants, C. C. Howe, W. Barnet and J. H. Wilson.

" MOUNT VERNON " - FOURTH-RATE.

Acting -Volunteer - Lieutenant, James Trathen ; Acting-Masters, E. W. White and F. M. Paine ; Acting-Ensigns, C. G. Walstrom, H. F. Cleverly and Jason Ryon ; Acting-Assistant Surgeon, W. H. Berrett ; Acting - Assistant Paymaster, H. B. Brown ; Acting-Master's Mate, Henry Rogers ; Engineers : Acting-Second-Assistants, J. H. Horsford and H. S. Short ; Acting-Third-Assistants, Geo. Ducker and Wm. H. Smith.

" ATLANTA "—FOURTH-RATE.

Acting-Volunteer-Lieutenant, T. J. Woodward ; Acting-Masters, Curtis Redmond and D. V. N. Wrights ; Acting-Ensigns, Paul Armandt, A. C. Southworth and H. Wakefield ; Acting - Assistant Surgeon, Thomas Owens ; Acting-Assistant Paymaster, D. S. Bostwick ; Acting-Master's Mate, A. Loisons ; Engineers : Acting-First-Assistant, W. S. Thompson ; Acting-Second-Assistants, Wm. Collier, Wm. Gumphert and J. W. Harnett ; Acting Third-Assistants, F. O. Brown, D. A. McDermott and T. B. Speakman.

*" BRITANNIA."—FOURTH-RATE.

Acting-Volunteer-Lieutenants, Samuel Huse, and W. A. Sheldon (commanded at Fort Fisher) ; Acting-Masters, J. S. Coney and S. J. White ; Acting-Ensigns, A. J. Lowell and W. H. Bryant ; Acting-Assistant Surgeon, F. Nickerson ; Acting-Assistant Paymaster, C. B. Culver ; Acting-Master's Mates, R. L. M. Jones and W. W. Reed ; Engineers : Acting-Second Assistants, J. Fernald and J. M. Barron ; Acting-Third-Assistants, W. D. Butts, Samuel Dale, Jr., and F. S. Andrews.

" BANSHEE "—FOURTH RATE.

Acting - Volunteer - Lieutenant, W. H. Garfield ; Acting-Ensigns, G. W. Prindle, W. C. Gibson, Paul Greene and J. S. Young ; Acting Assistant Surgeon, J. M. Garner ; Acting-Assistant Paymaster, D. P. Shuler ; Engineers : Acting-First-Assistant, C. Cranston ; Acting-Second-Assistants, Geo. F. Case and Thomas McNellis ; Acting-Third-Assistants, J. L. Lowe, J. H. Radcliffe, J. W. Little and Charles Green.

" MYSTIC "—FOURTH-RATE.

Acting-Masters, Wm. Wright and S. B. Meaders ; Acting-Ensigns, A. T. Hamblen, H. L. Pierce and Geo. W. Conner ; Acting-Assistant Surgeon, Alex. Mackenzie ; Assistant Paymaster, Augustus Parrot ; Engineers : Acting - First-Assistant, J. B. Lowell ; Acting-Third-Assistants, Isaac Buck and T. W. De Klyne.

" DAWN "—FOURTH RATE.

Acting-Master, J. A. Jackaway ; Acting-Ensigns, W. B. Avery, E. T. Sears and P. W. Morgan ; Acting-Master's Mate, S. W. Crossley ; Acting-Assistant Surgeon, A. S. Lanbach ; Acting-Assistant Paymaster, R. C. Peirce ; Engineers : Acting-Second-

Assistant, Sam'l Tomlinson ; Acting-Third-Assistants, T. K. Payson, C. W. Williams and J. D. Averill.

"WESTERN WORLD"—FOURTH-RATE.

Acting-Master, Edward Herrick; Acting-Ensigns, A. J. L. Barker, Chas. Hall, R. D. Sparrow and E. H. McDonald; Acting-Assistant Surgeon, R. F. Brooks, Acting-Assistant Paymaster, Amos D. Allen; Engineers: Acting-Second-Assistant, F. R. Shoemaker; Acting-Third-Assistants, A. Anderson, H. L. Perrine, J. E. Thumbert and Edw. G. Schwartz.

"COMMODORE HULL"—FOURTH-RATE.

Acting-Masters, F. Josselyn and J. O. Johnson; Acting-Ensign, F. J. Runnells; Acting-Master's Mate, Henry Fleet ; Acting-Assistant Paymaster, J. Chapman ; Engineers : Acting-Third-Assistants, O. L. Smith, W. C. Remick and S. T. Hand.

"RACHAEL SEAMAN"—FOURTH-RATE.

Acting-Master, Samuel Curtis ; Acting-Ensigns, E. T. Strong and D. Organ; Acting-Master's Mates, H. B. Arbecam and W. H. Wording ; Acting-Assistant Paymaster, T. Thompson.

"WHITEHEAD"—FOURTH-RATE.

Acting-Master, Geo. W. Barrett ; Acting-Ensign, Jarvis Wilson; Acting-Master's Mates, T. E. Quayle, T. M. Nelson and W. S. Baldwin; Engineers: Acting-Third-Assistants, G. B. McDermott and G. S. Snaith.

"DELAWARE"—FOURTH-RATE.

Acting-Masters, J. H. Eldredge and H. Vanderveer ; Acting-Ensigns, Robert Price and H. Livermore ; Acting-Master's Mates, George Mackay, B. Heath, Jr., and Thos. Topliff ; Acting-Assistant Surgeon, J. F. Henry ; Acting-Assistant Paymaster, W. W. Woodhull; Engineers: Acting-Second-Assistant, Chas. Bennett ; Acting-Third-Assistants, C. H. Keener and Thos. F. Hannigan.

"DAYLIGHT"—FOURTH-RATE.

Acting-Master, H. A. Phelan ; Acting-Ensigns, F. L. Harris, B. F. Macintire, C. F. Russell, C. Linderman and F. Bradley; Acting-Master's Mates, J. E. Merriman ; Acting-Assistant Surgeon, J. R. May ; Acting-Assistant Paymaster, F. C. Imlay; Engineers: Acting-First-Assistant, D. B. Overton ; Acting-Second-Assistant, R. Pallet ; Acting-Third-Assistants, J. B. Rice, H. R. Allen, A. P. Smith and Jas. Hill.

"COMMODORE MORRIS"—FOURTH-RATE.

Acting Master, R. G. Lee ; Acting-Ensigns, J. D. Gossick, A. J. Kane and Jos. Ware; Acting-Master's Mate, L. Dempsey; Acting-Assistant Surgeon, R. W. Clark ; Acting-Assistant Paymaster, T. Higgins ; Engineers ; Acting-Second-Assistants, V. Cronk and J. H. Watkins ; Acting-Third-Assistants, L. L. Copeland, J. Callahan and D. A. Bandell.

* "EOLUS"—FOURTH-RATE.

Acting-Master E. S. Keyser ; Acting-Ensigns, Thos. Stothard, C. A. Stewart, S. M. Lane and H. N. Crockett ; Acting-Assistant Paymaster, H. Jenkins; Engineers: Acting-First-Assistant, A. Rockerfeller ; Acting-Third-Assistants, G. L. Rockwell, J. M. Hennesy and M. L. Ruth.

"SAMUEL ROTAN"—FOURTH-RATE.

Acting-Master, W. G. Nutting ; Acting-Ensigns, T. W. Spencer and W. A. Dailey ; Acting-Master's Mates, J. J. Keller, W. P. Brownell and F. H. Forbes.

"RELEASE"—FOURTH-RATE.

Acting-Master, Jonathan Baker; Acting-Ensigns, C. H. Beckshafft, L. Turlow, H. C. Bowen, J. M. Taylor and F. B. Owens ; Acting-Master's Mate,

F. W. Kimball ; Acting-Assistant Surgeon, R. C. Tuttle ; Acting-Assistant Paymaster, G. L. Ely.

"CERES"—FOURTH-RATE.

Acting-Master, H. H. Foster ; Acting-Ensigns, T. S. Russell and Saml. Weskett ; Acting-Master's Mate, J. B. Hopkins; Engineers: Acting-Third-Assistants, J. A. Frank, W. H. Touchton and Rich. Fowler.

* "LITTLE ADA"—FOURTH-RATE

Acting-Master, S. P. Crafts ; Acting-Ensign, I. F. Atkins ; Acting-Master's Mates, W. H. Joseph and G. W. Lane ; Engineers : Acting-Second-Assistant, W. H. Johnson ; Acting-Third-Assistants, B. Converse and J. R. Peterson.

"FAHKEE"—FOURTH-RATE.

Acting-Masters, F. R. Webb and D W. Carrall ; Acting-Ensigns, E. W. Pelton, Peter Williams, J. W. Luscomb, H. A. Winslow and A. W. Harvey ; Acting-Assistant Paymaster, A. B. Thornton ; Engineers : Acting-First-Assistant, G. W. Foster ; Acting-Second-Assistants, E. F. Lewis and J. H. Hutton ; Acting-Third-Assistant, J. B. Edson.

* "WILDERNESS"—FOURTH-RATE.

Acting-Master, H. Arey ; Acting-Ensigns, B. O. Low, C. F. Hull, C. E. P. Noyes and E. McKeever; Acting-Assistant Paymaster, H. M. Rogers; Acting-Master's Mate, Wm. Phyffe ; Engineers : Acting-Second-Assistant, Richard Anderson; Acting-Third Assistants, E. A. Robinson, Walter Taylor and David Bodden.

* "NANSEMOND"—FOURTH RATE.

Acting-Master, James H. Porter; Acting-Ensigns, J. B. Henderson, Wm. Hunter and Henry Waring ; Acting-Assistant Paymaster, Geo. Hudson, Jr.; Acting-Master's Mate, A. K. Brown; Engineers: Acting-Second-Assistant, Edward Aspald ; Acting-Third-Assistants, C. M. Goodwin, J. T. Earl and E. A. Reilly.

"MOUNT WASHINGTON"—FOURTH-RATE.

Acting-Master, H. H. Haynie ; Acting-Ensign, John Nason; Acting-Master's Mates, Theo. Morse; Engineers: Acting-Second-Assistant, Sydney Smith; Acting-Third-Assistant, F. A. Whitfield.

"ZOUAVE"—FOURTH-RATE

Acting-Master, Jacob L. Hayes ; Acting-Master's Mate, Chas. Attmore ; Second Assistant Engineer, Samuel H. Magee

"BEN MORGAN"—FOURTH-RATE.

Acting-Master, A. B. Mulford.

"PHLOX"—FOURTH-RATE."

Acting-Ensign, D. F. O'Brien; Acting-Master, T. A. Wyatt (Pilot) ; Acting-Master's Mate, Samuel Gordon ; Engineers : Acting-Third-Assistants, W. C. Wright, G. Morrison and J. H. Coombs.

"EPSILON"—FOURTH-RATE.

Acting-Ensign, F. M. Muitzer; Engineers : G. B. Polen and Chas. Gould.

"CHARLES PHELPS"—FOURTH-RATE.

Acting-Ensigns, Wm. Ottiwell and C. B. Parry.

"ROMAN"—FOURTH-RATE.

Acting-Ensign, H. Merchant.

"GAMMA"—TUG.

Acting-Ensign, Henry F. Curtis; Acting-Third-Assistant Engineer, Thomas Lee.

"MOCCASIN"—FOURTH-RATE.

Acting-Ensign, James Brown ; Acting-Master's Mates, Joseph Fuller, John Johnson and J. S. Sinclair; Engineers: Acting-Second-Assistant, T. T. Archer, Acting-Third-Assistants, C. H. Wilson, W. H. Garrecht and W. B. Boyd.

"LILAC"—FOURTH-RATE.

Acting-Ensign, J. A. Chadwick; Acting-Master's Mate, D. S. Ingersoll; Engineers: Acting-Third-Assistants, W. T. Graff, J. C. Garner and J. B. Carnes.

"WILLIAM BADGER"—FOURTH-RATE.

Acting-Ensign, S. G. Swain; Acting-Master's Mate, J. B. Somes.

"POPPY"—FOURTH-RATE.

Acting-Ensign, Wm. Clark; Acting-Master's Mate, T. P. Jones; Acting-Second-Assistant Engineer, C. W. O'Neill.

"ANEMONE"—FOURTH-RATE.

Acting-Ensign, W. C. Borden; Acting-Master's Mates, G. W. Briggs and Theo. Stone; Engineers: Acting-Second-Assistant, Wm. Higman; Acting-Third-Assistants, J. L. Wright and H. Litchfield.

"ALERT"—FOURTH RATE.

Acting Ensign, John Bishop; Acting-Master and Pilot, D. M. Abbott; Engineers: Acting-Second-Assistant, Wm. Mahan; Acting-Third-Assistants, Eli Tympenny and J. W. Briggs.

"HELIOTROPE"—FOURTH-RATE.

Acting-Ensign, G. B. Griffin; Acting-Master's Mate, Samuel Davis; Engineers: Acting-Second-Assistant, S. G. Flynn; Acting-Third-Assistants, John McKenney and Edward J. Cahill.

"EPSILON"—FOURTH-RATE.

Acting-Ensign, Eli M. Boggs; Engineers: Acting-Third-Assistants, F. M. Wagner and Frank Blocki.

"COHASSETT"—FOURTH-RATE.

Acting-Master's Mate, M. K. Henderson; Engineers: Acting-Second Assistant, J. H. Finn; Acting-Third-Assistants, H. Haney and R. F. Baker.

"DELTA"—FOURTH-RATE

Acting-Master's Mate, Wm. F. Gragg; Engineers: Acting-Third Assistants, Geo Schultz and J. N. Schenck.

"ALBEMARLE"—FOURTH-RATE.

Acting-Assistant Paymasters, E. Mellack and J. G. Orme; Acting-First-Assistant Engineer, Newton Eggleston; Gunner, E. A. McDonald; Carpenter, M. W. Paul.

"PICKET LAUNCH."

Acting-Gunner, Herman Peters; Acting-Second-Assistant Engineer, Marceline Villazon.

"SPUYTEN DUYVIL."

Engineers: First-Assistant, J. L. Lay; Second-Assistant, C. H. Stone; Acting-Second-Assistants, I. R. Smith and J. E. Chadwick; Acting-Third-Assistant, Byron S. Heath.

* "REPUBLIC."

Acting-Ensign, J. W. Bennett.

CHAPTER LI.

EFFECTS OF THE FALL OF FORT FISHER, AND CRITICISMS ON GENERAL BADEAU'S MILITARY HISTORY OF GENERAL GRANT.

GENERAL BUTLER'S INFLUENCE.—CONDITION OF GENERAL LEE'S ARMY.—MOVEMENTS OF
ARMIES UNDER GENERALS GRANT AND SHERMAN.—HONOR TO WHOM HONOR IS DUE.—
EXTRACTS FROM GENERAL GRANT'S MEMOIRS, SHOWING THE ORIGIN OF FORT FISHER
EXPEDITION.—LETTERS OF INSTRUCTION FROM GENERAL GRANT TO GENERALS BUTLER
AND TERRY.—WHY GENERAL BUTLER ABANDONED THE ATTEMPT TO CAPTURE FORT
FISHER AFTER FIRST ATTACK.—WHY SECOND ATTACK ON FORT FISHER WAS SUCCESS-
FUL.—LETTERS OF SECRETARY OF THE NAVY TO THE PRESIDENT.—CRITICISMS ON GEN-
ERAL BADEAU'S MILITARY HISTORY OF GENERAL GRANT.—INCIDENTS OF FINAL AS-
SAULT ON FORT FISHER.—EFFECTS OF FALL OF FORT FISHER, ETC.

THERE was a great deal of acrimony and recrimination growing out of the first attack on Fort Fisher. The "Committee on the Conduct of the War" took the matter up, and it proved a feast for the politicians.

General Butler, with strong political influence, had, of course, a host of supporters, and these flew to his assistance as soon as he returned from Fort Fisher, in the hope of finding some flaw in the armor of General Grant or Admiral Porter through which they could thrust their lances.

Just as the committee were accumulating testimony in support of General Butler, the sound of the one hundred guns fired at the Washington Navy Yard, in honor of the capture of Fort Fisher, thundered through the Capitol, and the baseless fabric of evidence melted into thin air. Fort Fisher was won, and nobody cared to hear about the failure of the first attack.

Having given a detailed account of the naval operations before Fort Fisher, it now becomes in order to show the effect of the capture of that stronghold, and its influence in hastening the close of the civil war.

The capture of the defences of Wilmington closed the last door through which the Southern Confederacy received their supplies of clothing, arms and ammunition;

therefore, when Fort Fisher fell, it was only a matter of a short time when the rebellion would collapse. No matter how brave an enemy may be, or how well commanded, he must have provisions and military stores; and at this time General Lee had not enough material of war to last him three months.

General Grant confronted the Confederates at Petersburg and Richmond with a greatly superior force, and the James River was blockaded by the Navy; yet Lee held his own with his diminished army, and General Grant had to wait until necessity should bring the enemy to terms.

Despite Grant's great numerical superiority, Lee had secured the approaches to Richmond so well that all attacks on his lines were unsuccessful. Sherman, with 50,000 men, was advancing from the South, but his forces were in such position that it would have been somewhat difficult to concentrate them in case of being confronted by a large army. He had occupied Savannah after considerable resistance from Hardee, who, when he evacuated the place, marched northward to make a junction with the 40,000 men under General J. E. Johnston.

Sherman always supposed that Fort Fisher and the other defences of Wilmington would finally have surrendered to him, had it not fallen when it did ; but because Savannah and Charleston fell on the approach of the Federal troops, it was no reason that the defences of Cape Fear River should do the same. The forts about Charleston and Savannah were far less calculated to stand a siege than those at Wilmington, and it was shown, by the heavy naval bombardment of the latter, how difficult it was to injure the works sufficiently to enable an assaulting party to capture them. Even after all the guns were rendered useless, a powerful resistance was offered to the assailants, covered as were the latter by the heavy batteries of the fleet, which swept the enemy from the parapets as the troops advanced over the bomb-proofs. Sherman, with all his soldiers, could never have reduced the forts on Cape Fear River, except after a long siege, if the enemy had shown any military intelligence.

Previous to the capture of Savannah, General Sherman had informed Grant that he had initiated measures towards joining him with 50,000 infantry, and, incidentally, to capture Savannah. No doubt the General reflected that the troops from Savannah and Charleston, combined with those at Wilmington and Johnston's army of 40,000, with 20,000 from the vicinity of Richmond, would have given the enemy at least 80,000 of the best troops to meet him before he could make a junction with Grant. The enemy held the Wilmington and Weldon railroad all the way to Richmond, the points along the Sounds only were held by the Federal Navy. General Johnston was in advance of Sherman all the time ; and, having assembled his army at a convenient point, it is hardly to be supposed that so skillful a commander, with a force of 80,000 men, would allow Sherman to join Grant without a struggle, which might have proved disastrous to the Union forces.

The capture of Fort Fisher by the Army and Navy put an end to any doubts on the subject. The Northern public was in such a state of excitement that it would have borne with bad grace a reverse of any kind; and, although it was impossible to prolong the rebellion owing to the exhaustion of the South, yet it would have been a great satisfaction to the latter to have dealt a final blow to their conquerors, not only to injure the prestige of the North, but to enable the South to demand better terms than they could otherwise have hoped for.

When the Federal troops entered Wilmington, all of Cape Fear River and the Wilmington and Weldon railroad were placed in possession of the Federal authorities ; and, as the Navy held the principal points on the sounds of North Carolina, the United States Government could throw any

number of troops into the enemy's rear by way of the Weldon railroad, Newbern, and Plymouth, and furnish them with provisions by the same routes; so that Sherman could advance through Georgia and South Carolina without fear of opposition from General Johnston, who after the fall of Fort Fisher evidently gave up the idea of successful resistance, though he did attempt to prevent Sherman reaching Goldsborough—a forlorn hope.

Mr. Lincoln appreciated the difficulty with which the Federals had to contend as long as General Johnston with a powerful army kept the field. A check to General Sherman in his progress through the Southern swamps might have prolonged the war for six months, but this could not happen after Fort Fisher had fallen and the Wilmington road was in Federal hands.

Many inaccuracies have been stated in regard to the capture of Fort Fisher and the original proposers of the expedition, and no one has done more in this direction than the "military historian." We will not pretend to criticise "General" Badeau when he treats of purely military movements in his "history" of General Grant, although our connection with the several commands of the latter have made us familiar with them ; but we claim a right to express views fully in cases where the Navy was concerned, and to expose the mistakes of a writer when he undertakes to reflect upon officers of the Navy without any valid reason for so doing.

Some of the military historian's statements assign the origin of the Fort Fisher expedition other than where it belongs, for it originated in the Navy Department. General Grant in his Memoirs ingenuously disposes of these statements, and gives an impartial account of the matter, which is inserted in this history.

Some of the assertions of the military historian are also disposed of by this account from General Grant's Memoirs :

" Wilmington, North Carolina, was the most important sea-coast port left to the enemy through which to get supplies from abroad, and send cotton and other products out by blockade-runners, besides being a place of great strategic value. The Navy had been making strenuous exertions to seal the harbor of Wilmington, but with only partial effect. The nature of the outlet of Cape Fear River was such that it required watching for so great a distance that, without possession of the land north of New Inlet, or Fort Fisher, it was impossible for the Navy to entirely close the harbor against the entrance of blockade-runners.

" To secure the possession of this land required the co-operation of a land force, *which I agreed to furnish.* Immediately commenced the assemblage in Hampton Roads, under Admiral D. D. Porter, of one of the most formidable armada ever collected for concentration upon one given point.

"This necessarily attracted the attention of the enemy, as well as that of the loyal North; and through the imprudence of the public press, and, very likely, of officers in both branches of the service, the exact object of the expedition became a subject of common discussion in the newspapers both North and South.

"The enemy, thus warned, prepared to meet it. This caused a postponement of the expedition until the later part of November, when, being *again called upon* by Hon. G. V. Fox, Assistant Secretary of the Navy, I agreed to furnish the men required at once, and went myself, in company with Major-General Butler, to Hampton Roads, where we had a conference with Admiral Porter as to the force required and the time of starting.

"A force of 6,500 men was regarded as sufficient. The time of starting was not definitely arranged, but it was thought all would be ready by the 6th of December, if not before. Learning, on the 30th of November, that Bragg had gone to Georgia, taking with him most of the forces about Wilmington, I deemed it of the utmost importance that the expedition should reach its destination before the return of Bragg, and directed General Butler to make all arrangements for the departure of Major-General Weitzel, who had been designated to command the land forces, so that the Navy might not be detained one moment.

"On the 6th of December the following instructions were given:

'CITY POINT, VIRGINIA,
'December 6, 1864.

'GENERAL—The first object of the expedition under General Weitzel is to close to the enemy the port of Wilmington. If successful in this, the second will be to capture Wilmington itself.

'There are reasonable grounds to hope for success, if advantage can be taken of the absence of the greater part of the enemy's forces, now looking after Sherman in Georgia. The directions you have given for the numbers and equipment of the expedition are all right, except in the unimportant matter of where they embark and the amount of intrenching tools to be taken.

'The object of the expedition will be gained by effecting a landing on the main land, between Cape Fear River and the Atlantic, north of the north entrance of the river. Should such landing be effected while the enemy still holds Fort Fisher and the batteries guarding the entrance to the river, then the troops should intrench themselves, and, by cooperating with the Navy, effect the reduction and capture of those places. These in our hands, the Navy could enter the harbor, and the port of Wilmington would be sealed.

'Should Fort Fisher, and the point of land on which it is built, fall into the hands of our troops immediately on landing, then it will be worth the attempt to capture Wilmington by a forced march and surprise. If time is consumed in gaining the first object of the expedition, the second will become a matter of after consideration.

'The details for execution are intrusted to you and the officer immediately in command of the troops.

'Should the troops under General Weitzel fail to effect a landing at or near Fort Fisher, they will be returned to the armies operating against Richmond without delay.

'U. S. GRANT, *Lieutenant-General.*
'MAJOR-GENERAL B. F. BUTLER.'

"General Butler commanded the Army from which the troops were taken for this enterprise, and the territory within which they were to operate—military courtesy required that all orders and instructions should go through him. They were so sent; but General Weitzel has since officially in-formed me that he never received the foregoing instructions, nor was he aware of their existence until he read General Butler's published official report of the Fort Fisher failure, with my indorsement and papers accompanying it. I had no idea of General Butler's accompanying the expedition until the evening before it got off from Bermuda Hundred, and then did not dream but that General Weitzel had received all the instructions and would be in command.

"I rather formed the idea that General Butler was actuated by a desire to witness the effect of the explosion of the powder-boat. The expedition was detained several days at Hampton Roads, awaiting the loading of the powder-boat.

"The importance of getting the Wilmington expedition off without any delay, with or without the powder-boat, had been urged upon General Butler, and he advised to so notify Admiral Porter. The expedition finally got off on the 13th of December, and arrived at the place of rendezvous, off New Inlet, near Fort Fisher, on the evening of the 15th. Admiral Porter arrived on the evening of the 18th, having put in at Beaufort to get ammunition for the Monitors.

"The sea becoming rough, making it difficult to land troops, and the supply of water and coal being about exhausted, the transport fleet put back to Beaufort to replenish; this, with the state of the weather, delayed the return to the place of rendezvous until the 24th. The powder-boat was exploded on the morning of the 24th, before the return of General Butler from Beaufort; but it would seem, from the notice taken of it in the Southern newspapers, that the enemy were never enlightened as to the object of the explosion until they were informed by the Northern press.

"On the 25th a landing was effected without opposition, and a reconnoissance under Brevet-Brigadier-General Curtis pushed up towards the fort. But, before receiving a full report of the result of this reconnoissance, General Butler, in direct violation of the instructions given, ordered the re-embarkment of the troops and the return of the expedition. The re-embarkment was accomplished by the morning of the 27th.

"On the return of the expedition, officers and men—among them Brevet-Major-General (then Brevet-Brigadier-General) N. M. Curtis, First-Lieutenant G. W. Ross, 117th New York Volunteers; First-Lieutenant William H. Walling and Second-Lieutenant George Simpson, 142d New York Volunteers—voluntarily reported to me that when recalled they were nearly into the fort, and, in their opinion, it could have been taken without much loss.

"Soon after the return of the expedition, I received a dispatch from the Secretary of the Navy, and a letter from Admiral Porter, informing me that the fleet was still off Fort Fisher, and expressing the conviction that under a proper leader the place could be taken. The natural supposition with me was, that when the troops abandoned the expedition the Navy would do so also. Finding it had not, however, I answered on the 30th of December, advising Admiral Porter to hold on, and that I would send a force and make another attempt to take the place.

"This time I selected Brevet-Major-General (now Major-General) A. H. Terry to command the expedition. The troops composing it consisted of the same that composed the former, with the addition of a small brigade numbering about one thousand five hundred, and a small siege-train. The latter it was never found necessary to land.

"I communicated direct to the commander of the expedition the following instructions:

'CITY POINT, VIRGINIA, January 3, 1865.
'GENERAL—The expedition intrusted to your command has been fitted out to renew the attempt

to capture Fort Fisher, N. C., and Wilmington ultimately, if the fort falls. You will then proceed with as little delay as possible to the naval fleet lying off Cape Fear River, and report the arrival of yourself and command to Admiral D. D. Porter, commanding the North Atlantic Blockading Squadron.

'It is exceedingly desirable that the most complete understanding should exist between yourself and the naval commander. I suggest, therefore, that you consult with Admiral Porter freely, and get from him the part to be performed by each branch of the public service, so that there may be unity of action.

'It would be well to have the whole programme laid down in writing. I have served with Admiral Porter, and know that you can rely on his judgment and his nerve to undertake what he proposes. I would, therefore, defer to him as much as is consistent with your own responsibilities.

'The first object to be attained is to get a firm position on the spit of land on which Fort Fisher is built, from which you can operate against that fort.

'You want to look to the practicability of receiving your supplies, and to defending yourself against superior forces sent against you by any of the avenues left open to the enemy. If such a position can be obtained, the siege of Fort Fisher will not be abandoned until the reduction is accomplished, or another plan of campaign is ordered from these headquarters.

'My own views are, that, if you effect a landing, the Navy ought to run a portion of their fleet into Cape Fear River, while the balance of it operates on the outside.

'Land forces cannot invest Fort Fisher, or cut it off from supplies or reinforcements while the river is in possession of the enemy. A siege train will be loaded on vessels and sent to Fort Monroe, in readiness to be sent to you if required. All others supplies can be drawn from Beaufort as you need them.

'Keep the fleet of vessels with you until your position is assured. When you find they can be spared, order them back, or such of them that you can spare, to Fort Monroe, to report for orders.

'In case of failure to effect a landing, bring your command back to Beaufort, and report to these headquarters for further instructions. You will not debark at Beaufort until so directed.

'General Sheridan has been ordered to send a division of troops to Baltimore, and place them on sea-going vessels. These troops will be brought to Fort Monroe, and kept there on the vessels until you are heard from. Should you require them, they will be sent to you.

'U. S. Grant, *Lieutenant-General.*
'Brevet-Major-General A. H. Terry.'

"Lieutenant-Colonel C. B. Comstock, aide-de-camp (now Brevet-Brigadier-General), who accompanied the former expedition, was assigned, in orders, as chief-engineer of this. It will be seen that these instructions did not differ materially from those given for the first expedition, and that in neither instance was there an order to assault Fort Fisher. This was a matter left entirely to the discretion of the commanding officer. The expedition sailed from Fort Monroe on the morning of the 6th, arriving at the rendezvous, off Beaufort, on the 8th, where, owing to the difficulties of the weather, it lay until the morning of the 12th, when it got underway and reached its destination that evening. Under cover of the fleet, the disembarkation of the troops commenced on the morning of the 13th, and by 3 o'clock P. M. was completed without loss.

"On the 14th a reconnaissance was pushed to within five hundred yards of Fort Fisher, and a small advance work taken possession of, and turned into a defensive line against any attempt that might be made from the fort.

"The reconnaissance disclosed the fact that the front of the work had been seriously injured by the Navy fire. In the afternoon of the 15th the fort was assaulted, and after most deperate fighting was captured with its entire garrison and armament. Thus was secured, by the combined efforts of the Navy and Army, one of the most important successes of the war. Our loss was, killed, 110; wounded, 536. On the 16th and 17th, the enemy abandoned and blew up Fort Caswell and the works on Smith's Island, which were immediately occupied by us. This gave us entire control of the mouth of the Cape Fear River."

In vol. 3, page 224, of his work, the military historian states as follows:

"While thus zealously watching the varied interests and changing circumstances in Georgia and Tennessee, as well as at Richmond and in the valley, Grant had also planned [!] to take advantage of Sherman's march by a new movement on the Atlantic coast. Wilmington, near the mouth of Cape Fear River, in North Carolina, was the only important seaport open to the enemy.

"It was originally intended that the expedition should set out in October, but through the imprudence of officers both of the Army and the Navy, and afterwards of the public press, the exact object of the enterprise became known, and the enemy thus warned prepared to resist it."

For this reason, we suppose, the expedition was postponed until the middle of winter, so that the enemy could make his own arrangements; for the military historian says: "This caused a postponement of the expedition, but towards the end of November the project was revived, and 6,500 men were *promised* [!] from the Army of the James."

It would only require forty-eight hours to equip 8,000 troops and collect the transports, yet no move was made from October until the middle of December. General Grant had appointed General Weitzel to command the troops, but from the very beginning Butler made himself the prominent figure, and Weitzel had little more to say than if he had been the General's orderly. General Grant evidently supposed that Butler was acting only as the commander of a division of an army, and had a right to interfere in getting the troops ready to embark; but Butler, for some unaccountable reason, was delaying the expedition.

General Butler, with a large body of troops, held an almost impregnable position north and east of the James. General Grant held Lee and his army tight in Richmond, while a bridge of boats connected the two armies, and a large force of naval vessels, including the heaviest iron-clad, occupied the river, which was also blocked with sunken vessels filled with stones. The Federal Army had therefore nothing to fear from Lee, and certainly 8,000 men could have been spared from Butler's army.

Referring back to the military historian, who says that the Fort Fisher expedition "had been delayed in November, owing to the indiscretion of Army and Navy officers, by which the enemy were notified of the projected movement, and were fortifying the place strongly in consequence," and who further says : "On the 30th of November Grant notified Butler that Bragg, who had been in command at Wilmington, had set out for Georgia, taking with him most of the forces"! Let us ask, then, why, with such information in his possession, did Butler delay the expedition ? It can only be accounted for by that indomitable will for which he was celebrated, and feeling himself master of the situation, from his great political prestige, he did as he pleased—for the power of politics at that time overshadowed everything else, and even General Grant was careful not to ignore it.

"It is important," said Grant to Butler, "that *Weitzel* should get off during his (Bragg's) absence, and if successful in making a landing, he may, by a bold dash, succeed in capturing Wilmington." The Navy had been ready from the middle of October, and yet the military historian speaks of the delays of the Navy, and want of co-operation between Butler and the Admiral.

To illustrate how little delay there was on the part of the Navy, we give the following letter from Mr. Secretary Welles to the President :

"NAVY DEPARTMENT, Oct. 28, 1864.
SIR—You are aware that, owing to shoal water at the mouth of Cape Fear River, a purely naval attack cannot be undertaken against Wilmington. Had there been water enough for our broadside ships of the "Hartford" class, the naval attacks of New Orleans, Mobile and Port Royal would have been repeated there. I have, as you are aware, often pressed upon the War Department the importance of capturing Wilmington, and urged upon the military authorities the necessity of undertaking a joint operation against the defences of Cape Fear River, but until recently there never seems to have been a period when the department was in a condition to entertain the subject.

Two months ago it was arranged that an attack should be made on the 1st of October, but subsequently postponed to the 15th, and the naval force has been ready since the 15th inst., in accordance with that agreement. One hundred and fifty vessels-of-war now form the North Atlantic squadron.

The command, first offered to Rear-Admiral Farragut, but declined by him, has been given to Rear-Admiral Porter. Every other squadron has been depleted, and vessels detached from other duty to strengthen this expedition. The vessels are concentrated at Hampton Roads and Beaufort, where they remain—an immense force lying idle, awaiting the movements of the army.

The detention of so many vessels from blockade and cruising duty is a most serious injury to the public service, and if the expedition cannot go forward for want of troops I desire to be notified, so that the ships may be relieved and dispersed for other service.

The importance of closing Wilmington is so well understood by you that I refrain from presenting any new arguments. I am aware of the anxiety of

yourself and of the disposition of the War Department to render all the aid in its power.

The cause of the delay is not from the want of a proper conception of the importance of the subject, but the season for naval coast operations will soon be gone. General Bragg has been sent from Richmond to Wilmington to prepare for the attack; and the autumn weather, so favorable for such an expedition, is fast passing away. The public expect this attack, and the country will be distressed if it be not made. To procrastinate much longer will be to peril its success. Of the obstacles which delay or prevent military co-operation at once, I cannot judge; but the delay is becoming exceedingly embarrassing to this Department, and the importance of having the military authorities impressed with the necessity of speedy action has prompted this communication to you.

I have the honor to be, etc.,
GIDEON WELLES.
THE PRESIDENT."

According to the military historian, General Butler never received any detailed orders regarding the expedition until December 6th, at which date General Grant writes: "The first object of the expedition, *under General Weitzel*, is to close the port of Wilmington. There are reasonable grounds to hope for success, if advantage can be taken of the absence of the greater part of the enemy's forces now looking after Sherman in Georgia." This would indicate that General Grant did not intend that Butler should accompany the expedition, but that the military part of it should be managed *entirely by Weitzel*. Yet, according to the military historian—

"Butler, on the night when the troops embarked, proceeded to City Point, and informed General Grant that he was going himself, and this in violation of his commanding-general's orders ! who 'did not desire to intrust the command of the expedition to Butler ;' for, as repeatedly shown, although Grant was entirely satisfied with that officer's zeal and general ability, he was convinced that he lacked some qualities essential in a commander in the field. Grant did not pronounce, but he felt certain, that the peculiar talent of a successful general was not possessed by the Commander of the James. He therefore directed Butler to place Weitzel in command of the expedition, and had, in fact, committed to Butler movements in support of those of Meade, which he intended should detain him in Bermuda Hundred.

"Nevertheless, he did not now forbid Butler to accompany Weitzel. It was difficult thus to affront a commander of such high rank unless it was intended to relieve him entirely from command, and this Grant was not prepared to do without consulting the Government, which he knew would dislike and perhaps forbid the step. He fancied, besides, that Butler's object might be to witness the explosion of the powder-boat—in which he took great interest — rather than to direct the expedition itself.

* * * * * * *

" It is certain, however, that it would have been better if Grant had frankly ordered Butler back to the Army of the James, to superintend the movements there.

"His dislike to wound the feelings of another should, doubtless, at this crisis have been sacrificed.

"Those who have never been placed in situations of great delicacy and responsibility, or who cannot realize the various considerations—military, political and personal—which affect the decisions of men in power, will, doubtless, here find cause to censure Grant."

General Grant might well have exclaimed on reading this, "Save me from my friends!" The military historian does not give his authority for the foregoing statements, but it is certain that, when General Butler reported his return from Wilmington to General Grant, the latter relieved him from command.

On the 9th of December, 1864, General Grant telegraphed to Butler at Fortress Monroe. "Let General *Weitzel* get off as soon as possible; we don't want the Navy to wait an hour." Yet the Navy had waited patiently from the 15th of October until the 6th of December, fifty-one days!

It will be seen throughout this narrative that we have given General Grant on all occasions credit for the highest military ability, and in this instance we do not desire to take from him one iota of it. We only refer to the revelations made by the military historian, in relation to which General Grant is not responsible.

In volume 3, page 390, of his book, the author states that:

"About the 18th of December, 1864, there was doubtless a lack of concert, and even of cordial co-operation, between the naval and military chiefs. Butler was not popular with the other branch of the service, and, after the expedition started from Hampton Roads, neither commander visited the other!"

Now, here is a paragraph that ought to make our "historian" happy. Imagine a General and an Admiral calling upon each other on the salt-sea waves, amid tumbling billows, in the dead of winter, and leaving cards!

The Admiral's reason for not communicating with Butler personally was, that he did not see the General from the time he left Fortress Monroe until the time when the General stated he was going to leave the Navy in the lurch at Fort Fisher, and Butler did not communicate with the Admiral, as he might easily have done, because he had been informed of all that was going to be done, what he had to do, and what means would be placed at his disposal. There was no communication necessary until just before landing, when General Weitzel went on board the flag-ship to see Admiral Porter, who agreed to all Butler's propositions, although some of them were needless.

To refer to that portion of the military "history," which seems to have been written without consideration, in regard to a matter of which the author really knew nothing, or perhaps to let up General Butler, of whom he had spoken harshly, he says:

"Their written communications were few, and it was the chief-of-staff of the Admiral, and the ranking officer under Butler (Weitzel) [who was supposed to be in command of the Army forces], through whom the views or wishes of either were made known to each other. Porter thought that his advice was not taken at times when it should have been controlling, and Butler thought that Porter acted without duly considering or consulting him." [!]

That is, Porter managed his fleet to suit himself, and left Butler to manage his own forces until the time came for action:

"Each was besides annoyed at delays which, though inopportune, were unavoidable, and neither made sufficient allowance for the difficulties of that branch with which he was less familiar. They seemed, indeed, to be playing at cross purposes. When Butler was supplied with coal, Porter wanted ammunition, and when Porter had all the ammunition he wanted, Butler was out of coal! Even the elements conspired against them, and when one could ride on the open sea, the other was obliged to stay inside." [!!]

This is the most crooked narrative ever written by one claiming to be a historian. The author affirms that there was no concert of action between General Butler and the Admiral, and yet he says (vol. 3, page 315):

"On the morning of the 25th, Butler sent Weitzel to Porter to arrange the programme for the day. It was decided that the fleet should attack the fort again, while the troops were to land, and, if possible, assault under cover of the naval fire as soon as the Half-Moon and Flag-Pond Batteries were silenced. At 7 o'clock the fleet again took up a position within a mile of the fort [three-fourths of a mile], not a shot being fired by the enemy except at the last four naval vessels as they were moving into line. [This for the reason that nearly all the guns had been disabled by the ships' fire and by the sand that had been driven by shells into their bores.]

"At 12 o'clock the batteries above the forts were reported silenced, and a detachment of about 2,300 men of General Ames' command was landed two and a half miles north of the fort [without a gun being fired on them]. The debarkation was effected under the cover of seventeen gun-boats, which raked the woods and could drive away any force that might have opposed the landing.

"Five hundred men under General Curtis were the first to land. He pushed his skirmish-line within a few yards of Fort Fisher, causing on the way the surrender of the garrison of Flag-Pond Battery, already silenced by the naval fire. Weitzel accompanied Curtis and approached within 800 yards of the works. He counted seventeen guns in position bearing up the beach, observed the traverses and stockades, the glacis, ditch, and counterscarp, and decided that the work had not been materially injured by the naval fire. [!] Weitzel, too, had been in many unsuccessful assaults, and never in a victorious one; he had a distinct and vivid recollection of this experience, and returned to Butler and reported that it would be butchery to assault.

"Curtis was now within fifty yards of the fort [not a shot fired at him] and sent word to Ames that he could take the work, whereupon Ames sent orders for an assault. Curtis at once moved forward, but by the time he reached his position night had come on, and the fleet had nearly ceased to fire; [and yet, Ames and Curtis, under Terry, assaulted, and continued to assault, Fort Fisher until it was taken *at night*].

"Some of the rebel troops who had been driven to their bomb-proofs returned to their guns" [which they could not fire as the guns were disabled]. At this juncture the order to embark arrived and no assault was made. Curtis and the officers with him declared that the fort could have been easily carried. That at the moment when they were recalled they virtually had possession, having actually approached so close that the rebel flag (which the Navy fire had knocked down) had been snatched from the parapet, and a horse brought away from *inside* the stockade. Three hundred prisoners had been captured outside, etc. That night, Butler informed the Admiral that he and Weitzel were of the opinion that the place could not be carried by assault, having been left substantially uninjured by the naval fire!

"Seventeen guns, he said, two of which only were injured [and yet none of them fired on the troops], were bearing up the beach, covering a strip of land, the only practicable route, not more than wide enough for 1,000 men in line of battle—[the place where Curtis finally assaulted without losing a man].

"Hoke's reinforcements were approaching, and, as only the operations of a siege would reduce the fort, he had caused the troops to re-embark. 'I shall, therefore,' said he, 'sail for Hampton Roads as soon as the transport fleet can be got in order.'"

Now this is what Badeau calls "a want of concert of action" between General Butler and Admiral Porter. Of course, Porter could not join Butler in his retreat, as will be seen by Badeau's next paragraph:

"The Admiral, however, was of a different mind, and replied, 'I have ordered the largest vessels to proceed off Beaufort and fill up with ammunition, to be ready for another attack in case it is decided to proceed with this matter by making other arrangements [meaning sending another General]. We have not commenced firing rapidly yet, and could keep any rebels inside from showing their heads until an assaulting column was within twenty yards of the works. I wish some more of your gallant fellows had followed the officer who took the flag from the parapet, and the brave fellow who brought the horse from the fort. I think they would have found it an easier conquest than is supposed.'

"Butler, nevertheless, remained unshaken in his determination, and on the night of the 25th December he embarked all his troops except Curtis' command, when the surf became high and he sailed away, leaving these ashore."

They were under cover of the guns of the fleet and they were all safely taken off. On the 27th Butler arrived at Fortress Monroe, and on the 28th had an interview with General Grant, after which the General-in-chief telegraphed to the President:

"The Wilmington expedition has proved a gross and culpable failure. Many of the troops are back here. Delays and free talk of the expedition enabled the enemy to move troops to Wilmington to defeat it. After the expedition started from Fortress Monroe three days of fine weather were squandered, during which the enemy was without a force to protect himself. Who is to blame, will, I hope, be known"!

As if the blame could rest on any but the one who went to Fort Fisher in command of the troops, and disobeyed orders by not intrenching himself under the protection of the guns of the fleet.

Grant had seen enough of the Navy on the Mississippi to know that it would not back out of such an adventure as the taking of Fort Fisher. The Navy had given him sufficient evidence in much more desperate undertakings to have satisfied him that it would stay before Fisher as long as a shot or pound of coal was left.

The historian says: "This dispatch was written before Grant had heard from Porter, or from Butler's *own subordinates;* subsequently he was inclined (!) to attribute the failure to other causes." Other causes than the Navy, we suppose; and here Badeau relates the difficulties with which the fleet and transports had to contend in getting to the scene of action, and makes the following sensible remark:

"But whatever the delay, and whatever the cause, these made no difference in the result. The troops and the fleet were at the rendezvous, the work was silenced, and the landing effected before any reinforcements reached the fort.

"On the morning of the 25th only 1,600 men had arrived at Wilmington. This day General Lee telegraphed Sedden: 'Bragg reports the enemy made a landing three miles north of Fort Fisher about 2 P. M. to day, and were still landing at 5:30 P. M. General Kirkland's, the only troops arrived, except 400 of Haygoods, etc.'

"Whatever number arrived before the 27th, they made no attempt to molest Curtis' little band of 500 men, who remained on shore two days after Butler left, with no support except the guns of the fleet. On the 25th of December, therefore, there were only 2,500 men opposed to Butler's 6,500. The garrison was only about 1,600 men. It is true the latter occupied a strong work, but Butler had the most formidable fleet that was ever assembled to cover and protect his movements."

We will make one more quotation from this part of the military historian's book. It was, no doubt, reviewed by General Grant. The latter, after inquiring into all the circumstances, had sent Butler directly home to Lowell:

"Butler, indeed, maintained that he had not effected a landing, that only a third of his troops were on shore, when the sea became so rough that he could land no more. But his subordinates did not confirm this statement, and, as he was able to get all his troops except Curtis' command back to the transports, he could certainly have put them on shore if he had been at all anxious to do so."

The latter part of Badeau's remarks about Butler are not complimentary, but he tries to ease him up on the ground that

"He simply displayed on this occasion once more the unmilitary features of his character. . . But, above all, he had not appreciated the force of Grant's order in regard to remaining and intrenching on the peninsula, or else he forgot them altogether at the crisis! Weitzel had never seen the orders, and knew nothing of them, or he would doubtless have reminded Butler of their character." (!)

Let any one read this and consider the total lack of military arrangement and the absence of obedience to the orders of the General-in-chief of the Federal armies, a disobedience that would have rendered General Butler liable to be shot if tried by court-martial.

The military historian comments on the lack of co-operation between Butler and the naval commander, not saying decidedly where the blame rested, but rather implying that it rested with the Navy. A truth only half told often does more harm than a falsehood, although we are not aware that it did the Navy any harm in this instance. The author says:

"The lack of co-operation between Porter and Butler was at this juncture again apparent, and again most unfortunate. The Admiral was a man not only of brilliant talent but of extraordinary nerve and force of character, and though extravagant and inconsiderate in language, written as well as spoken, he understood his profession thoroughly. He was aggressive in his nature, and always favored an attack. He doubtless, in this instance, overrated the results accomplished by the fleet, but that very circumstance would have made his counsels more audacious, and audacity is sometimes a very desirable quality in a commander. If, instead of writing or sending to Porter and announcing his withdrawal, Butler, who was the senior in rank, had waived his prerogative and sought and obtained a personal interview, it is possible that he might have been convinced by the arguments or incited by the spirit of the sailor into remaining on shore. As it was, he sailed off, leaving Porter to pick up the troops he (Butler) had left; and, in his dread of incurring disaster, he incurred what to a soldier is infinitely worse, the imputation of unnecessary failure."

We don't see where the "lack of co-operation" on the Admiral's part comes in. If the author had confined the lack to Butler, he would have stated the actual fact.

The historian comments freely on the commander of the naval forces, in regard to a letter he wrote to the Navy Department, and which finally came out in investigations on the conduct of the war. In reference to the letter, the military historian says the Admiral could not be accused of concealing his sentiments. The following is the communication alluded to as part of the history of the war. There does not seem to be anything peculiar in it beyond its decided tone:

"My dispatch of yesterday will give you an account of the operations, but will scarcely give an idea of my disappointment at the conduct of the Army authorities in not attempting to take possession of the fort. Had the Army made a show of surrounding it, it would have been ours; but nothing of the kind was done. The men landed, reconnoitred, and hearing that the enemy were massing troops *somewhere*, the orders were given to embark. . . . . There never was a post that invited soldiers to walk in and take possession more plainly than Fort Fisher. . . . It can be taken at any moment in one hour's time if the right man is sent with the troops. They should be sent to stay. I trust, sir, you will not think of stopping at this, nor relax your endeavors to obtain the right number of men and the means of taking the place."

Now, where the peculiarity of which the military historian has spoken exists in this letter, we leave to others to determine. The Admiral wrote very decidedly, and it had the desired effect. Mr. Secretary Welles wrote to General Grant:

"The ships can approach nearer to the enemy's works than was anticipated; their fire can keep the enemy away from their guns.

"A landing can easily be effected upon the beach north of Fort Fisher, not only of troops, but all their supplies and artillery. This force can have its supplies protected by gun-boats.

"Admiral Porter will remain off Fort Fisher, continuing a moderate fire to prevent new works being erected.

"Under all these circumstances, I invite you to a military co-operation, as will insure the fall of Fort Fisher."

After receipt of this letter General Grant wrote to the Admiral:

"Please hold on wherever you are for a few days, and I will endeavor to send the troops back again with an increased force and *without the former commander*.

"Your dispatch to the Secretary of the Navy was only received to-day. I took immediate steps to have transports collected and am assured they will be ready with coal and water by noon of the 2d of January. There will be no delay in embarking and sending off the troops. If they effect a lodgment, they can at least fortify and maintain themselves until reinforcements can be sent. Please answer by bearer, and designate where you will have the fleet of transports congregate."

The letter of which Badeau speaks had the effect of drawing forth the above communication and bringing about the capture of Fort Fisher. Yet the Navy never received any particular credit for this operation, which was the final stab that brought the enemy to his last throes.

To those who take an interest in the naval operations of the war, some of the remarks of the military historian on Fort Fisher are interesting. In spite of many inaccuracies, he shows the pertinacity with which the Navy held on to what they had begun, and the difficulties they had encountered against the fierce gales that swept the coast during those months of December and January. Not a vessel left her post, and the Navy could have protected the landing of any number of troops.

It was manifestly the object of the military historian to give the Army more credit than was due them, and make the Navy play a secondary part in the reduction of the defences in Wilmington. The Navy covered the attack of the troops and the sailors attacked the sea-face of Fort Fisher; the garrison, supposing this to be the main attack, rushed to the sea-face, and, as Badeau says, swept the officers and sailors "away like chaff." The repulse of the naval storming party might not have happened had the troops, who were to have attacked with the sailors and marines, come to time. It was only when the whole force of the enemy was concentrated at the sea-face that the order was given for the troops to advance, and

"Curtis' brigade at once sprung from the trenches and dashed forward in line, and in a few moments the Army occupied three or four traverses which protected them from the fire of the enemy, and there Curtis held on until Ames and Penny-packer could obtain a secure footing in the fort with him. Bell's brigade was brought up and the fort was occupied by the troops."

It must be remembered that while this assault was going on behind traverses, the "New Ironsides," with her 11-inch guns, and three Monitors, were firing through the traverses in front of the Federal soldiers, as the enemy would assemble to meet their approaches, and the Confederates were swept away by the Navy shells.

At this time General Terry requested the Admiral to reinforce the troops on the outer line by the seamen and marines who had been repulsed from the sea-face, which was done at once. This stopped the advance of General Hoke, who had commenced skirmishing with Terry's northern outposts, apparently with a design of attacking in that quarter to make a diversion. Hoke's withdrawal enabled Abbott's brigade and a regiment of colored troops to be brought into action on the southern front.

There never was harder fighting anywhere by soldiers than on this memorable occasion; and while the Federal troops behaved like heroes, it is but justice to say of the enemy that they fought equally well, and it was only after seven hours of stout resistance that they surrendered.

The military historian relates all this part of his story in a graphic manner; but, to show how essential was the fire of the Navy to the success of the assault, we mention the following incident:

"Terry, finding the advance so slow, directed Curtis to stop fighting and intrench, which so excited that officer that he exclaimed, 'Then we shall lose what we have gained' Fortunately, the firing from the 'Ironsides' and the Monitors was so effective, that at ten o'clock P. M. every traverse was emptied and the enemy in full retreat towards the end of the sand-spit on which Fort Fisher was situated."

It would be scarcely worth while for Army or Navy to claim on this occasion more than their share of honor. Each did in its own sphere what was required, and neither could have succeeded without the aid of the other. That the naval fire was perfect was evidenced by the fact that every gun in Fort Fisher was either destroyed or so injured that they were practically useless; so that, from the moment the army advanced to the assault, they had nothing to apprehend from the enemy's heavy batteries.

In all the last seven hours' fighting the Federal army lost but 110 killed, 536 wounded, and 45 missing, while the enemy lost over 700.

The high praise bestowed on the officers of the Army by the military historian is well deserved; the assault on Fort Fisher was the most remarkable affair of the war:

"The difficulties of the weather and the season on one of the stormiest coasts, in the world were overcome, the disadvantages incident to all combined operations entirely disappeared, and the dispositions of the Admiral and the military chief at the time of the landing, and during the subsequent operations up to and including the assault, were a marvel of harmonious effect."

To all this we subscribe, only asserting that up to the time when Butler left Fort Fisher the naval co-operation with him was just as effective as with Terry.

Butler had no obstacles to overcome, Terry had many. Badeau says:

"The importance of this victory was instantly recognized by the rebels and loyal people alike. The effect was felt at home and abroad. Lee knew its significance as well as Grant, and the rejoicing at the North was not more general or heartfelt than the despondency it occasioned inside the Confederacy. The gates through which the rebels obtained their largest and most indispensable supplies was forever sealed.

"In little more than a year before the capture, the ventures of British capitalists and speculators with Wilmington alone had amounted to $66,000,000, and $65,000,000 worth of cotton had been exported in return. In the same period 397 vessels had run the blockade; all this was at an end. Europe perceived the inevitable consequences, and the British Government, which till now had held out hopes to the Confederate emissaries, *after the fall of Fort Fisher* sent a communication to Jefferson Davis, through Washington, rebuking the rebels for their stubbornness. There could be no surer evidence that the case was desperate."

We will further add that a telegraphic dispatch was captured from General Lee to the commanding officer at Fort Fisher, which read as follows: "If Fort Fisher falls, I shall have to evacuate Richmond."

The military historian remarks: "At this crisis the possession of Cape Fear River opened another base for operations into the interior. It enabled the general-in-chief to look forward to supporting Sherman's future movements and presented an opportunity to complete the isolation of Lee."

In fact, Lee, with Cape Fear River in his possession, might have prolonged the war greatly, in the hope of obtaining terms for the Confederacy, which might have been a triumph for them.

After making the proper disposition of the vessels of the fleet, the Admiral hastened to City Point in a fast steamer to witness the end. It came two months later, when Lee, having eaten up all his provisions, and threatened by large armies whom he had no longer power to resist, surrendered, and thus ended the most extraordinary war of modern times.

While our armies in many instances immortalized themselves by acts of heroism, and submitted to hardships and privations for which the country can hardly ever repay them, the Navy performed its fair share of *hard* service, and without its aid the rebellion could not have been suppressed.

As long as the Confederates could be fed, and supplied with munitions of war, it would have been extremely difficult to conquer them, for they would have prolonged the war and inflicted such injuries on the North as to finally have obtained whatever terms they might demand.

In the enthusiasm of the Northern people to welcome home the soldiers, and in the honors paid to them on all sides, the Navy seemed to have been forgotten, and but for the published dispatches of the commanding officers of the Federal naval forces, the general public would hardly have known that such an organization as the Navy existed.

From the battle of Shiloh, where the gunboats covered the retreating troops, which rallied under their protecting fire and finally gained the day, to the fall of Fort Fisher, the Navy played a more active part than was perhaps ever before taken by naval forces, and though illy supplied with the proper kind of vessels, they seldom experienced reverses.

There were the fights of Hatteras, Port Royal, New Orleans, Mobile, Vicksburg, and all along the Mississippi and its tributaries, Red River, Arkansas, White, Tennessee, Cumberland and Ohio Rivers, Grand Gulf, Port Hudson, Charleston, Galveston, and the whole coast of Texas brought under control. This was a large field of naval operations, seldom equalled in the history of war, and never exceeded, as far as naval successes are concerned.

In this account of the Fort Fisher affair we have endeavored to do justice to all parties, but as General Butler was not partial to the Navy, and might perhaps think that a naval writer would not do him full justice, we have quoted liberally from the work of General Badeau, who had a favorable leaning toward General Butler, and who gave him credit for military qualities wherever he could possibly do so.

We have reviewed the circumstances connected with Fort Fisher at some length, because we consider such review necessary for a proper understanding of this important victory, and also with a view to correct misrepresentations which have long since been made apparent.

CHAPTER LII.

OPERATIONS ABOUT CHARLESTON, 1865.—FALL OF CHARLESTON, SAVANNAH, Etc.

FORMATION OF THE NAVAL BRIGADE.—OPERATIONS OF GENERALS SHERMAN AND FOSTER IN THE VICINITY OF SAVANNAH.—EXPEDITION UP BROAD RIVER AND BOYD'S CREEK.—SAVANNAH INVESTED.—EVACUATION OF SAVANNAH AND ITS DEFENCES BY THE CONFEDERATES.—THE NAVAL VESSELS AGAIN IN CHARLESTON HARBOR.—MOVEMENTS OF ARMY AROUND CHARLESTON.—NAVAL PICKETS CAPTURED.—LANDING OF NAVAL FORCES AT BULL'S BAY.—GUN-BOATS AND BATTERIES OPEN A TERRIFIC FIRE ON FORT MOULTRIE AND WORKS ON SULLIVAN'S ISLAND.—CHARLESTON EVACUATED.—ISOLATION OF THE CONFEDERACY.—NAVAL OFFICERS COMMENDED.—CONFEDERATE VESSELS CAPTURED.—INGENIOUS METHODS USED BY CONFEDERATES TO PREVENT UNION VESSELS FROM PENETRATING THE INNER HARBOR.—PLANS OF FORTS ALONG THE RIVERS.—GEORGETOWN, S. C., OCCUPIED.—THE FLAG-SHIP "HARVEST MOON" SUNK BY TORPEDOES.—ADMIRAL DAHLGREN RELIEVED.—COMPLIMENTARY LETTER FROM SECRETARY OF THE NAVY,—LIST OF VESSELS AND OFFICERS OF SOUTH ATLANTIC SQUADRON, 1865.

IN the latter part of November, 1864, Rear-Admiral Dahlgren received information that General Sherman had reached Milledgeville and was about to march upon Savannah. He accordingly entered into an arrangement with General Foster to co-operate with Sherman in case the latter might require assistance.

It was decided to form a naval brigade, to be furnished with two field-howitzer batteries of four guns each. All the forces that could be spared from the vessels on blockade were withdrawn, and the night of November 28th was appointed for proceeding up the Broad River and into Boyd's Creek, one of its branches, whence a short march only was necessary to reach the railroad connecting Savannah with Charleston. The vessels of the Navy selected for this service were the "Pawnee," Commander Balch; "Mingoe," Commander Creighton; "Pontiac," Lieutenant-Commander Luce; "Winona," Lieutenant-Commander Dana; "Wissahickon," Lieutenant-Commanding McGlensey; "Sonoma," Lieutenant-Commander Scott; all carrying heavy guns. There were four half-companies of well-drilled seamen under Lieutenant James

O'Kane; Lieutenant-Commander E. O. Mathews commanded the Navy artillery, and the marines from the different vessels were under the command of First-Lieutenant George G. Stoddard.

After a harassing progress of twenty miles through a thick fog, Admiral Dahlgren had the satisfaction of reaching the appointed landing with five of the six vessels with which he had started, for the "Wissahickon" had grounded near the entrance of the river and did not succeed in joining the other gun-boats. The troops were somewhat later in arriving, but finally the transports were seen coming up the river, and in half an hour afterwards two batteries of naval howitzers and nine companies of seamen and marines were landed under Commander Preble, and advanced in skirmishing order, to cover the landing of the troops, Admiral Dahlgren returning to his duty afloat.

After General Foster had landed all his soldiers, an advance was made towards the railroad above Grahamsville. The Confederates had assembled in considerable force, and did all they could to impede the march of the Union forces by a fire of musketry and field-pieces, and at length the Federal forces came to a halt before a strong earth-work commanding the road, and flanked by a heavy growth of timber and other obstructions. The troops under General Hatch assaulted the works, but were repulsed with heavy loss, while the men from the fleet did their duty with boat-howitzers and musketry.

Skirmishing and reconnaissances went on for several days, the Federals slowly advancing towards their objective point, the railroad. This was a new experience for the seamen and marines, but their spirited conduct won for them the applause of the soldiers. On the 6th of December the Army and Navy forces proceeded up the Tulfiny River, and at about 8 A. M. landed on an island. The Confederates sent troops to meet them, and for a time it looked as if the Federals would get the worst of the encounter; but the naval contingent coming rapidly on the field, and opening a heavy fire with howitzers and musketry, the enemy finally gave way, retreating in good order. This skirmishing lasted all day through a heavy rain, the seamen and marines behaving like veteran soldiers in an experience entirely new to the greater portion of their number. The object of the expedition was effected in spite of all opposition, and on the 12th of December Rear-Admiral Dahlgren opened communication with General Sherman, who was then near Savannah.

The news of Sherman's arrival in the vicinity of Savannah gave great satisfaction to the people of the North, who had begun to feel uneasy in regard to him, owing to the exaggerated reports from Confederate sources. Prompt steps were taken to place vessels-of-war at every point on the coast where the General was likely to appear, and on the 18th of December Sherman in person presented himself on board Admiral Dahlgren's flag-ship, and was warmly greeted by officers and men, who held this gallant commander in the highest respect. Arrangements were made by General Sherman with Admiral Dahlgren, that, while the former should invest Savannah on the land side, the latter should hold every avenue by water; and when it was considered that the investment was complete, Sherman summoned General Hardee, the Confederate commander, to surrender, which request being declined Sherman prepared to attack the enemy's works. The Federal army was gradually drawing down to the Savannah River, and, in order to cut off the escape of the Confederates, it was concluded to reinforce the troops under General Foster on Broad River, and make a demonstration in the direction of the railroad, while that on Beaulieu would be limited to the

naval cannonade, which was begun and continued by Lieutenant-Commander Scott in the "Sonoma," assisted by the schooner "Griffith," Acting-Master James Ogilvie.

In order to complete the arrangements for cutting off the escape of the enemy and to insure the co-operation of all the Federal forces in the vicinity, General Sherman visited Hilton Head in company with Rear-Admiral Dahlgren, to communicate with General Foster, and make the latter acquainted with his plans; but on his return he was overtaken by a tug, with the following telegram:

To General Sherman:

General Howard reports one of General Legget's brigades near Savannah, and no enemy. Prisoners say the city is abandoned and enemy gone to Hardeesville.
From Station, near Headquarters.

On receipt of this dispatch General Sherman hastened to his headquarters, and the Admiral to the division of vessels lying in front of Beaulieu, when the facts of the case became apparent. Lieutenant-Commander Scott, of the "Sonoma," was in possession of Forts Beaulieu and Rose Dew, and all the other fortifications had been evacuated, leaving Sherman master of Savannah and its defences.

Although, no doubt, the Army would have captured Savannah unaided, yet the Navy was of great assistance in blocking up the rivers and preventing the Confederates from sending reinforcements to General Hardee. The Navy visited many points inaccessible to the Army, and secured a large quantity of guns, ammunition and stores which the Confederates had not time to destroy. General Hardee's boast, that he held two lines of intrenchments and was in communication with superior authority, did not prevent him from beating a speedy retreat as soon as Sherman's advance-guard hove in sight of his outposts.

In all these affairs the brigade from the fleet, composed of seamen and marines, remained with General Foster's command, and the officers and men were transferred to their respective vessels only when Savannah and all the points around it were garrisoned by Sherman's troops.

As it was General Sherman's intention to move northward as soon as he had secured Savannah against any attempts on the part of the Confederates to repossess it, he requested such co-operation on the part of the Navy as could be extended; and while his army was apparently advancing on Charleston, Rear-Admiral Dahlgren determined on making further attacks on the works within the harbor of that place, which with the assistance of the army he had some hope of reducing. Sherman, however, did not favor this plan, being satisfied that

Charleston would necessarily fall, owing to his own interior movements.

Admiral Dahlgren now collected all his vessels near Charleston, ready to co-operate with Sherman as he approached, and to keep the rivers clear of torpedoes and light batteries, so that the Federal transports could reach certain points and supply the wants of the Union army.

In order to deceive the Confederates with regard to the point for which he was aiming in his march to the northward, General Sherman requested that the Navy would make such demonstrations as would draw the attentions of the Confederates from his operations. The gun-boat "Dai Ching" and a tug were placed in the Ossabaw River, the "Sonoma" was sent out to the North Edisto and the "Pawnee" to the Ashepoo River, with orders to drive off the enemy's troops and knock down his batteries wherever they could be reached. The "Tuscarora," "Mingoe," "State of Georgia" and "Nipsic" were stationed at Georgetown, S. C., to prevent the enemy from erecting batteries at that point, and the "Pontiac" was in the Savannah, advancing with General Sherman's extreme left. Nearly all the Monitors of the squadron were collected at Charleston.

On the 24th of January, 1865, General Sherman marched on Pocotaligo and the Coosawatchee, and the next day made a demonstration on Salkahatchee, while the gun-boats went up the Edisto and Stono Rivers to ascertain whether the enemy intended to hold Charleston or retreat to Columbia. It would require General Slocum at least five days to get his troops clear of the swamps near Savannah, and in the meantime General Howard was, apparently, moving directly on Charleston, although with no intention of going beyond Salkahatchee.

The enemy had still a considerable force near Savannah, and his cavalry, under General Wheeler, was exceedingly active in watching the movements of the Federal army and picking up stragglers. The "Pontiac," Lieutenant-Commander Luce, was left with Slocum's command, and on the 24th anchored off Merrill's Landing or the Three Sisters, forty miles above Savannah, to cover the crossing of the river by a portion of the 20th Corps. Lieutenant-Commander Luce threw out pickets to see that the enemy did not bring guns to bear on the "Pontiac" from the high bluffs, which could not be reached by the ship's battery. This party had been warned against scouting too far from the ship, but in spite of this they were captured by a squad of Confederate cavalry.

On the evening of the 27th the scouts of General Davis' column reached the point where the "Pontiac" was lying at anchor; and, soon after, the remainder of the 14th Corps appeared, after a most arduous march over corduroy roads which had to be constructed in advance of the forces. Here the soldiers took some needed rest, with the knowledge that they were not likely to be disturbed while the "Pontiac" lay in their vicinity, although there were reported to be two Confederate gun-boats about eighty miles up the river.

Meanwhile the "Pawnee" and "Sonoma" were making their way up the North Edisto, in company with transports conveying troops under the command of General Potter, which troops were landed at a place called White Point. Some few of the enemy were seen and shelled by the gun-boats, but the Confederates were not in force, and their guns had mostly disappeared from the river banks.

Thus, while Sherman was advancing through the enemy's country, everything was done by the Navy that could disconcert the Confederates and prevent them from annoying the Union army. At this time, owing to heavy rains, the freshets had swept away most of the bridges along the line of Sherman's march, and the movements of the gun-boats were in every respect desirable to cover the advance of the army. Almost every stream where a gun-boat could float was guarded by the Navy; their good services enabled General Sherman to reach midway on the South Carolina road by the 7th of February without molestation. The fate of Charleston was now sealed, and the only thing left the garrison to avoid capture was to evacuate the place.

On the 11th of February a movement was made by the army contingent under General Potter, and a considerable naval force under Rear-Admiral Dahlgren, consisting of the "Shenandoah," "Juniata," "Canandaigua," "State of Georgia," "Pawnee," "Sonoma," "Ottawa," "Winona," "Wando," "Geranium" and "Iris," with launches in which to land troops at Bull's Bay. Great difficulty was experienced in finding a channel into the harbor, but a landing was finally effected; after which, the "Pawnee" and "Winona" was sent to South Edisto River to assist General Hatch, who was moving on Wellstown with his division.

On the 17th a movement was made from Stono River on the Confederates, while the iron-clads "Lehigh," the "Wissahickon" and a mortar schooner were sent up the Stono to press the right flank of the enemy, while the gun-boat "McDonough" was sent with a mortar schooner up the Filly branch to bear on his left flank. General Schimmelfennig, in command of the troops before Charleston, moved on the enemy's front from Cole's Island. Admiral Dahlgren also sent orders to Lieutenant Hayward, commanding the battery of 11-inch guns on Cummings' Point, to open on Sullivan's Island and fire continuously through the night. The contiguous batteries were also put in operation by General Schimmelfennig, and the advance Monitors were ordered to open fire on Fort Moultrie. The cannonading during the night was sharp and continuous; the Confederates replied with a few guns from Fort Moultrie, but as the night wore on their fire entirely ceased. In fact, the main body of the enemy's troops had evacuated Sullivan's Island at about 8 P. M., leaving about one hundred and fifty men to keep up a fire and delay the knowledge of the evacuation.

On the morning of the 18th the anticipations of the Union forces that the Confederates were retreating from Charleston were confirmed. Acting-Master Gifford entered the harbor in a tug, and at Mount Pleasant met the Mayor of the city, who tendered the submission of the civil authorities to the Federal Government, and requested protection for the citizens and their property.

Rear-Admiral Dahlgren was up the Stono River when he received a message that there were indications that the Confederates were retreating from Charleston, and he immediately proceeded in his flagship to the city which for four years had resisted the continued attacks of the Army and Navy, for the reason that its strength had been underrated by the Federal Government and a sufficient force had not been sent against it. The place only fell because of the advance of General Sherman, and the fear of the garrison that they would be cut off and captured. The powerful defences on Sullivan's Island, the shapeless but still formidable ruins of Sumter, the numerous great earth-works clustered around Fort Johnson, Castle Pinckney and the heavy water batteries that lined the wharves, looked grim and terrible, though deserted. They were a monument to the zeal, ability and gallantry of those who had to the last defied the power of the Federal forces.

Charleston, the city that struck the keynote of the rebellion, now lay helpless in the power of the Federal Government; its citizens, worn out and impoverished by the long war which they had themselves inaugurated, now seemed willing to return to the shelter of the flag, since it was evident that the secession cause could not prevail. The officers of the fleet walked through the streets of the city whose outworks had so long defied them. All the houses were closed, and few of the citizens appeared. But for the presence of the negroes, it might have passed for a city stricken with the pestilence.

Notwithstanding the great outcry that had been made by some of the Confederate officers against General Gillmore's barbarity in firing from the "Swamp Angel" into the town, the place gave little indication of having suffered from an enemy's guns.

Here and there the ground was plowed up by a rifle-shell, or the front of a house was scarred by the fragments; but it is pleasant to be informed that the women and children received no injury.

The fall of Charleston was of course an important event at any time, since it was the Mecca of the Confederacy, on which the eyes of every Southern enthusiast were fixed. The courage and determination of its garrison inspired those who were inclined to waver in their allegiance to the Confederacy, and, while Charleston held out the cause could not be considered altogether desperate. The heroic example set by the besieged was telegraphed daily all over the South, and the name "Charleston" was a watchword everywhere. Even the most radical and uncompromising Unionists could not help admiring the courage and devotion shown by the defenders of Charleston, and the city escaped any injury from the Union forces, except such as naturally follows the occupation by troops of a place lately in hostility, where vacant houses are taken possession of and their contents not too scrupulously respected.

There was considerable disappointment expressed in the South because Charleston was so suddenly abandoned on the approach of General Sherman's army ; but the Confederates in the city did not know what Sherman's intentions might be, and they very naturally thought it best to evacuate the place before the Union General should envelope them and compel their surrender. But General Sherman was anxious to join General Grant before Richmond as soon as possible and get out of the lowlands of the coast, where his soldiers were worn out with building corduroy roads through swamps, bridging the countless streams, and living in a malarious country.

The capture of Fort Fisher and other defences of Wilmington had doubtless a considerable effect on the fall of Charleston; for, now that the stronghold on Cape Fear River was taken, a small garrison could hold it, and the Union forces employed in the reduction of those works could, if necessary, march on Charleston.

Whatever claims may have been advanced that the final result was brought about by the movements of the Navy in cooperation with the Army under General Foster, we can only say that the attempt to invest Charleston by Bull's Bay and the

Stono River was bravely undertaken, although it would have probably experienced a severe repulse but for the position held by Sherman at Columbia.

The fall of Charleston was in every aspect a great success for the Union cause. Although it had long been nearly impossible for a blockade-runner to land her cargo inside the harbor, yet, even with the close watch constantly maintained, cotton could be sent out. When the city was taken this traffic was at an end, and the credit of the Confederate States in England sank to a low ebb. Henceforth the Confederate armies would be obliged to depend on the scanty supplies obtained at home, and their surrender was now considered only a matter of time.

Owing to the fall of Charleston, the Navy Department was enabled to greatly deplete the naval forces hitherto employed in that vicinity, and, although the saving thus effected was but a trifle compared with the large sums expended upon the army, yet it was a change in the right direction, as the country was beginning to feel uneasy at the vast sums daily paid from the treasury to maintain the military and naval forces.

The Confederacy was now isolated from the outer world by way of the sea, and there could no longer be a pretext for the interference of foreign powers, the trouble being at this time purely domestic. Now, also, was ended that fiction of belligerent rights which excluded United States vessels-of-war from the customary hospitalities of foreign ports. What was left of our mercantile marine could pursue its avocations without fear of molestation by Confederate cruisers, which so lately roamed the ocean at their will.

Much credit is due to the commanding naval officers at Bull's Bay for the management of their vessels, and the energy with which they responded to the Confederate batteries which were striving to prevent a landing of the troops. So effective was the fire of the gun-boats that the Confederates were soon driven away and the vessels suffered little damage.

The officers particularly commended by Rear-Admiral Dahlgren were : Captain D. B. Ridgely, Commander F. Stanly, Commander G. B. Balch, Lieutenant-Commander T. S. Fillebrown, Lieutenant-Commander A. A. Semmes, Lieutenant-Commander A. W. Johnson, Lieutenant-Commander S. B. Luce, Acting-Master W. H. Mallard and Acting-Master G. W. Parker.

At the fall of Charleston the following Confederate vessels fell into the hands of the Navy : Iron-clad ram "Columbia," steamer-transport "Lady Davis," a cigar-shaped steamer 160 feet long, two side-wheeled steamers and three torpedo-boats.

As everything relating to the defence of Charleston has a historic interest, we insert the report of Rear-Admiral Dahlgren in regard to the instructions issued by the Confederates to prevent the Union vessels from penetrating the inner harbor. At the present day these arrangements seem rather primitive, but they exhibit skill and ingenuity on the part of the Confederate engineers, and they completely answered their intended purpose, by preventing the Union vessels from proceeding to Charleston :

* * * * * * *

"The only passage from the outer roads into the harbor of Charleston is less than a mile at its narrowest part, between Sullivan's Island and the shoals on which Fort Sumter is built. Across this lay the first series of obstructions. When first resorted to, these were of different kinds—of rope, or of heavy masses of timber, floating bars of railroad iron.

"It is difficult to ascertain with exactness at what time each of these were adopted. Common report was never precise, and in that respect was probably a fair exponent of the common information at the time.

"The statements of the persons who knew anything of the matter, and were acceptable, differ as to which of these were used first.

"According to Mr. Smith, who had been actually employed on this work, the rope obstructions were first put down in 1861, formed into one continuous line, and floated across the channel from Sumter to Battery Bee. But this was so frequently displaced by the current that it was cut into lengths, which, with the addition of others, were anchored at one end in two lines, and rode to the tide.

"It is probable that the casks seen on the 7th April were the turpentine barrels of this obstruction; and, moreover, a plan of the entrance, signed by Major Echols, engineer, shows the double line of rope obstructions.

"In the summer of 1863 the boom of railroad-iron was placed, consisting of several timbers banded into a mass and floating the railroad bars. And this account is so far confirmed that in December, 1863, a quantity of boom answering to this description was washed away by the winter gales and came down the channel. Some of it was hauled up on the beach of Morris Island. I saw this work in progress one day, and was told that as many as thirty-three of the bars had been secured.

"I have been at a loss to understand the exact manner in which these bars were connected to the timbers. The accounts given do not accord, and some separation had generally been effected before any of them were seen by us.

"They may have been encased in the timbers, or suspended from them, as described by Mr. Smith; but in any case they would have been difficult to remove under the heavy fire of the rebel works.

"It is probable, from the several statements, that whenever the use of the boom obstructions across the entrance between Sumter and Moultrie may have begun, the parts were not renewed as they disappeared, but were replaced from time to time by those of rope, until at last the winter freshets of 1863 and 1864 carried away the whole structure.

"The obstructions which were actually found in position between Sumter and Moultrie, after we entered, were of rope only.

"The entire line is reported to have been made up of a number of separate parts, each of which consisted of a stout shroud-laid rope, floated at intervals by buoys of pine logs, and anchored by a heavy grapnel. From this floating rope hung down at intervals six parts of a lighter rope. The exact dimensions are variously given, as well as the numbers of floats and hangers.

"The pine buoys, which were used as samples, were thirty-nine (39) inches long and fifteen (15) inches in diameter, with a stout iron staple near each end, through which passed the part of rope that was to be floated.

"It was said to have been the design to place these parts or sections in two lines, about sixty (60) or one hundred (100) feet apart, with similar intervals. But it may be easily conceived that the intention could not be carried out with exactness in the first place, and that subsequently, in replacing sections that were lost or not visible, the plan would be still further confused, partly by the impossibility of knowing with certainty at night where the sections were missing, and partly because in doing so it seemed better to err in having too many than too few.

"Hence the directions of the lines were not maintained with exactness, and the allotted number of sections was in excess of that contemplated. Nor was the exact po ition and number of those which were found in place noted as well as they should have been, for the reasons already stated; and when my attention was drawn to the subject, it was too late to remedy the omission. Drawings were, therefore, necessarily made from the several parts, but it is believed they afford a fair representation of the entire whole.

"As different tugs and boats were employed at different times, there was some discrepancy in the returns sent me, which, as already stated, were not made as they should have been.

"Mr. Gray gives the whole number as 226, which, at intervals of one hundred (100) feet, would be too many to be included in the distance of one mile; but it may be explained by the continued renewal of what was supposed to be lost, and which were not so really, though not distinctly visible.

"The care and perseverance which the rebels gave to the maintenance of these rope obstructions is well shown by the report of Acting-Master Gifford (annexed); they watched them closely, and, whenever a section disappeared from sight, it was replaced.

"Our boats were always observed, and driven off if possible, and it was necessary, besides, to work with great caution, as they were near powerful batteries, and liable at any moment to a destructive fire of grape.

"The purpose of the boom obstructions was evidently to bar the passage of a vessel entirely, while that of the rope obstructions was to entangle the screw and prevent further progress, or even detain the vessel under fire of the batteries, for the grapnel which anchored the rope would also serve as a drag on the steamer, and it would be almost impossible to cut it loose when under fire.

"That the rope obstructions were in use before I took command, and afterwards, is satisfactorily ascertained from other evidence than that of Mr. Gray.

"A plan of the harbor of Charleston, signed by Major Echols,* and dated April, 1863, exhibits two lines of obstructions, designated as rope obstructions, the general direction being from Sumter to a point midway between Fort Moultrie and Battery Bee. The delineation shows a number of dotted lines, resembling the section of rope just described: the dots indicate only four buoys. They correspond closely with the description given by Commodore Rogers of what he saw from the 'Weehawken' during the attack of 7th of April.

"In his official report he says : 'We approached very close to the obstructions extending from Fort Sumter to Fort Moultrie—as near, indeed, as I could get without running upon them. They were marked by rows of casks very near together. To the eye they appeared almost to touch one another, and there was more than one line of them.'

* Confederate Engineer.

"To me they appeared thus :

"When we landed on Sullivan's Island (February, 1865), several telegrams came into my possession. One of them, dated Sumter, April 8, 1863, runs thus:

"'Blue and red Coston lights indicate the enemy's boats trying to cut the net; the batteries will open with grape.'

"Colonel Freemantle, of the Cold stream Guards, in the published account of his visit to Charleston, June, 1863, says:

"'There are excellent arrangements of—— and other contrivances to foul the screw of a vessel between Sumter and Moultrie.'

"As soon as the picket and scout boats of the fleet were able to approach the entrance, the presence of the obstructions was verified; but in the obscurity of the night it was difficult to ascertain precisely what they were, particularly as the rebels were then in strong force at the locality, and very little time was permitted for examination.

"General Gillmore's impressions at the time may be gathered from the following portion of his telegram to me August 4:

"'My scout has just reported that the line of floating buoys reaching from Sumter to Moultrie has disappeared since yesterday. These buoys are supposed to have torpedoes attached to them, etc.'

"This disappearance was probably a mistake, owing to the difficulty of discerning with certainty objects so small at such a distance, for no report was made by the Navy pickets, and soon after Ensign Porter, who was specially charged with the duty, reported that 'two steamers and three schooners were at anchor in the centre of the channel, apparently at work on the obstructions, or else sinking others,' etc. Ensign Porter, who was very active and daring, assured me that chains formed some part of the obstructions, as he had been close enough to the buoys to feel them.

"The buoys themselves were visible to the eye from the picket Monitors which were stationed in the advance. Their reports, being verbal at first, cannot now be quoted; but subsequently I directed them to be made in writing.

"Captain J. L. Davis, commanding the 'Montauk,' reports 25th September:

"'At low water to-day, a rip was discovered extending from Fort Sumter in a line to the western end of the buoys, stretching from near Moultrie in a westerly direction across the channel. At first I thought it was the meeting of the tides, but as it did not alter position I came to the conclusion some hidden obstructions might be there.'

"September 26th, the 'Catskill' reports a steamer plying between Sumter and Moultrie on the previous night, supported by two iron-clads. On the 27th, the 'Nahant' reports that the obstruction buoys were counted by several officers, and the average number was about eighty (80). 'The buoys do not seem to be in a continuous line, but as if they were in groups of five or six. There seems to be another short line of larger buoys beyond the first, which I judge to be a separate obstruction across Hog Island Channel.' Which description is remarkably in accord with all the facts since ascertained.

"In October (21st), 1863, a part of the rope obstructions floated out of the harbor, and was discovered off Beach Inlet by the 'Sonoma,' which towed them inside the bar. The floating away of these sections —owing to various causes, sometimes to their removal by our scouts—explains the variations in the numbers of the buoys counted at different times from the Monitors; and their renewal by the rebels whenever they did disappear is fully established by the nightly experience of Acting-Master Gifford, who rarely failed to be at his post as a scout. His report, which is annexed, is of interest, as it exhibits the results of much arduous service and close observation.

"The accounts of deserters and refugees confirmed in a general way the existence and locality of the obstructions; but their opportunities for observation were seldom as good as our own, for none but those engaged in the work were allowed opportunities of knowing more than could be seen from a short distance, and the rebels were singularly fortunate in the precautions to keep their own counsel as to the nature of the submerged defences.

"The general existence of obstructions at an early date was set forth in a circular order of General Ripley (December 26, 1862), regarding the defence to be made against our attack.

"In speaking of these impediments it says : 'The obstructions will also be designated, and under no circumstances will the enemy be permitted to reconnoitre them.'

"Besides the obstructions at the entrance, the middle channel was closed by a double row of piles extending some distance across the harbor, which were distinctly visible when the first operations were initiated against Charleston.

"In the Hog Island Channel was also a set of boom obstructions, found in April last by the 'Clover' while engaged in clearing away the frame torpedoes placed there.

"The massive and complicated character of these gave much trouble in their removal. They consisted of a stout chain (¾-inch iron) that had been floated by blocks of timber secured to it at short intervals.

"These blocks were made of four-squared logs, fifteen (15) feet long and one (1) foot square, kept together by an iron band at each end.

"Railroad iron linked together, and suspended from squared timber, was associated with the chain-boom. This boom had been stretched across a neck in the Hog Island Channel when there was least water, and the passage so narrow that the shoals on each hand were bare at low water, and hardly five hundred (500) feet apart, besides being directly under fire from Battery Bee at 1,100 yards, and of Mount Pleasant battery at 1,000 yards. At this time they had been so much worm-eaten that they sank, but the depth at low tide would still have rendered them troublesome to all but light-draught vessels.*

In this way the main entrance was obstructed between Sumter and Moultrie, and two of the channels leading from it were barred by piles and booms, leaving open only the main channel to the south, which was left to the control of the heavy batteries that lined it.

"These obstructions were defended by torpedoes, and by a series of batteries, iron-clads and torpedo-boats.

"After obtaining possession of the harbor, the examination which was made disclosed the use of three kinds of torpedoes. The floating torpedo was made of a small barrel, capable of containing seventy (70) pounds of powder, generally mounting two fuzes on the bilge, anchored so as to come in contact with the bottom of vessels. By means of a small weight these fuzes were kept uppermost.

"These torpedoes were well known in the squadron, having been picked up and encountered at various times in the St. John's and Stono, exploding occasionally with full effect. They were liable to be lost by getting adrift ; or, if not tight, might be spoiled by water; but the rebels kept a vigilant eye on them, examining them at times and replacing them. There was a regular establishment here for their fabrication, under the charge of Mr. Gray, who held the position of captain.

"A part of the correspondence of this branch is now in my hands, from which it appears that there were thirty-five (35) to forty (40) hands employed, and that Mr. Gray distributed the barrel torpedoes along the coast from Georgetown to St. John's; he also transmitted a variety of material even as far as Mobile, and his connection was direct with several commanding officers.

"Woods and Thompson were employed in the department to 'build the torpedoes,' as they express it.

"It appears that no great number of these was kept placed permanently in Charleston harbor, because they were dangerous to vessels moving about on the ordinary communications by water, and accidents had occurred. They could readily be put down in a very short time on the appearance of a move on our part.

"In the middle of January, for instance, when this was suspected, an order was given to put down several lines of them. Woods and Thompson placed sixteen (16) of them in the vicinity of the rope obstructions, between Sumter and Moultrie, and seven (7) at the entrance of the Hog Island Channel. Others were directed to be laid down from Fort Johnson to Castle Pinckney, which seems to have been deferred until the attack began.

"One of those near the obstructions was encountered by the Monitor 'Patapsco,' on the night of the 15th of January, when, in the expectation of co-operating with General Sherman, I had ordered a vigorous effort to be made to remove the rope obstructions, and the picket Monitors covered the boats so engaged.

"It seems that the work of placing these torpedoes had been completed that very night, and the 'Patapsco' went down, with two-thirds of her crew, almost immediately on being struck, being at the time about six hundred (600) yards from Sumter.

"Immediately after entering the harbor of Charleston, vigorous efforts were made to remove these floating torpedoes; but, although some of the very men who had put them down were employed, with the aid of steam tugs and boats, and all the ordinary appliances, to recover them, dragging and sweeping the water for many days, only four (4) could be found of the sixteen (16).

"The 'Bibb' came in contact with and exploded one on the 17th of March, and the 'Massachusetts' grazed one on the 19th, so that the balance remain undiscovered.

"A set of the same kind, placed across the mouth of the Wando, were recovered and destroyed. Acting-Master Gifford found as many as sixty-one (61) at different points of the shore, about the harbor, ready for service, or nearly so, and at hand to be put down if needed.

"At Causten's Bluff, in St. Augustine Creek (one of the approaches to Savannah), were found a number lying on a wharf all ready for immediate use. They were conveniently handled, and could be laid down rapidly and easily. Woods and Thompson say that with one boat they placed them at the rate of four in an hour.

"This kind of torpedo was the most convenient of all, and the most dangerous, though, being liable to shift with the current, they were apt to trouble those who used them. One rebel steamboat ('Marion') had been blown up in the Ashley River some time ago by one of them; and, in June, 1864,

---

* And Captain Gray states that they were afloat up to the last that he saw of them, which was in August, 1864.

another rebel steamer, plying from Sumter up the harbor, was struck by one and beached on the shoal near Johnson, to prevent sinking in deep water, supposed at the time to have been run ashore accidentally.

"It is probable that the 'Tecumseh' was sunk at Mobile, in Admiral Farragut's attack, by one of this kind; also the 'Milwaukee,' the 'Osage,' the 'Rudolph,' and a tin-clad (48), in the recent captures of the forts.

"My own flag-ship, the 'Harvest Moon,' was destroyed by the same device, in Georgetown, and three army transports in the St. John's—'Maple Leaf,' 'Harriet Weed,' and another.

"Mr. Gray states they were placed in such numbers about the main entrance and channel, about the time of our operations against Morris Island, that it would have been impossible for any vessel to escape that entered.

"There were also permanent torpedoes. One species of these consisted of a frame of three or four heavy timbers, parallel to each other and a few feet apart, tied together by cross-timbers; at the head of each timber was a cast-iron torpedo with a fuze.*

The frame was placed obliquely, and held by weights, so as to present its torpedoes to the bottom of a vessel approaching. Series of them were placed in particular parts of the channel.

"Four frames, mounting fifteen (15) torpedoes, were found at the entrance of Ashley River; they had been there some time, and yet were in such good condition that one exploded when towed away carelessly, and though a dozen feet from the tug the explosion hurt and knocked overboard several men.

"Frames were also found in the narrow pass of the Hog Island Channel, just as it branches from the main channel near Battery Bee, and close to the boom obstructions already described; and another set in the neck of the middle channel near Castle Pinckney.

"There is said to be another set in the shoal connecting the middle and the north channel, not removed at this date.

"One of these frames was found lying in a dock of the Cooper River, with the torpedoes mounted ready for use.

"In many cases the frames had been much worm-eaten, so that in attempting to remove them the timber broke and fell to the bottom.

"On the wharf near it and the adjoining buildings, which had been used as a factory for the torpedoes until our shells rendered it dangerous, were thirty (30) cast-iron torpedoes for framing.

"This kind of torpedo was used in the Ogeechee and Savannah Rivers, where they were distinctly visible at very low water; and probably it was one of this kind that struck the 'Montauk' in February, 1863, when attacking Fort McAllister.

"As torpedo frames could not be fixed in very deep water, another kind was used for the purpose. This was a large sheet-iron boiler, capable of containing 1,000 to 3,000 pounds of powder, to be exploded by a galvanic battery connected by an insulated wire.

"Three of these were located in the main channel between Battery Bee and Fort Johnson; the wire rope of each was led to Sullivan's Island, and all were found in good condition.

"Persevering efforts were made by the squadron divers to follow the wires from the shore to the torpedoes, but they had become so overlaid by deposits of sand as to resist all attempts to release them, and were broken several times in the proceeding. A large quantity of the wire rope was taken up.†
Some of the range-poles having been removed, it

was found impossible to determine with precision the exact locality where the divers could reach them without following the wires.

"A torpedo boiler ready to receive powder was found on the wharf, where the cast-iron torpedoes for the frames already mentioned were discovered, together with a large quantity of the wire rope.

"This was made in the best manner, probably in England. The copper wire was insulated by a tube of India-rubber, protected by a wrapper of hemp, and over that closely laid wire.

"In this connection I may also mention the torpedoes designed for the rams and torpedo-boats, samples of which were recovered by divers from the bed of the river, where they had been thrown.

"There were two sizes, both being elongated copper cylinders with hemispherical ends, and diameters of ten (10) inches, but one was thirty-two inches long, the others twenty-four inches.

"At the outer end were screw-sockets for eight fuzes, so as to present points of explosion in every direction. The torpedo for the bow of a ram was of copper, barrel-shaped, and tapering to a point at the outer end. It had sockets for seven fuzes on the upper bilge and end. Its contents of powder was about one hundred and thirty-four pounds.

"The three torpedo-boats in service had been sunk in the Cooper River, off the city wharves. Two have been raised, and one put in good order so as to steam about the harbor; in length about sixty-four (64) feet, and five and one-half (5½) feet in diameter, capable of steaming about five (5) knots. There were six others that were under repairs, or being completed, of which two are now ready for service. Just above those that had been sunk were the three iron-clads, 'Chicora,' 'Palmetto,' and 'Charleston,' all of which had been fired and blown up on the day we entered. The 'Chicora' alone is visible in any part, and that only a few inches of the casemate at low water.

"Up a small creek was found a fourth iron-clad, the 'Columbia,' of the same size as the 'Charleston,' but plated with six (6) inches of iron; a new well-built vessel, just ready for service

"It seems that about a month before the entrance of the Union forces (January 12), the vessel had been docked in the creek above the city, and in getting her out of the dock she grounded. The rebels seem to have begun to extricate the vessel, but had not sufficient time before they abandoned Charleston. Why she was not destroyed is difficult to conceive, as they sank the three that were in service, and burned two new iron-clads that were not completed. This vessel was fully ready for service, even guns mounted, which, it was said, were taken out after grounding, and a portion of the plating had been removed as a preparation for lightening and floating the vessel, under the belief that they could be saved. I gave the necessary directions, and on the 26th had the satisfaction of seeing her floated, which was effected by the exertions of several officers—Lieutenant-Commander Matthews, Fleet Engineer Danby, Chief Engineer Kierstead—by Master Carpenter Davis, by Lieutenant Churchill, and the divers. This vessel has an extreme length of two hundred and sixteen (216) feet; beam, fifty-one and one-third (51⅓) feet; is plated with six (6) inches of iron; carries six (6) guns of the heaviest calibre, has two engines; high pressure, ample accommodations on berth-deck for cabin, ward-room and men, with good quarters in the casemates. Her leakage is very small, indicating no great injury from the grounding. Her steam-power was in good order, only requiring the stack-pipe and smoke-box to be replaced, and some of the interior pipe that had been cut. The 'Columbia' left on the 23d of May, in tow of the 'Vanderbilt,' and was commanded by Lieutenant Hayward.

---

* A model of this kind was made for me by William Flynn, a refugee, who had worked on them in Charleston.

† Some of it was used subsequently by our own divers.

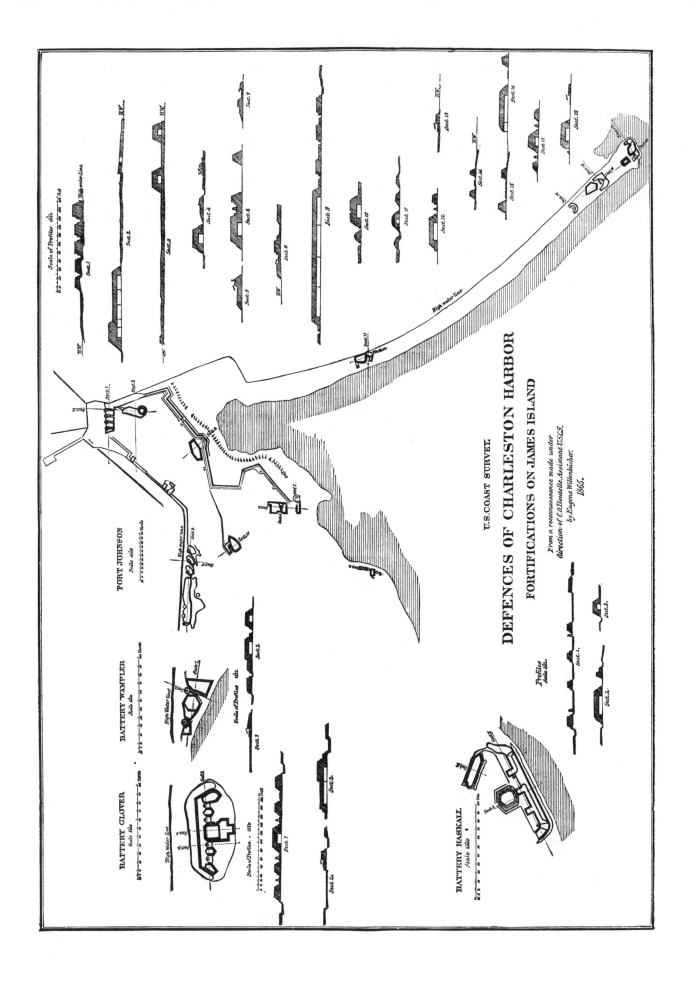

U.S. COAST SURVEY.

DEFENCES OF CHARLESTON HARBOR

FORTIFICATIONS ON JAMES ISLAND

From a reconnaissance made under
direction of C.O.Boutelle, Assistant U.S.C.S.
by Eugene Willenbücher.
1865.

FORT JOHNSON
Scale 1/600

BATTERY WAMPLER
Scale 1/600

BATTERY GLOVER
Scale 1/600

BATTERY HASKALL
Scale 1/600

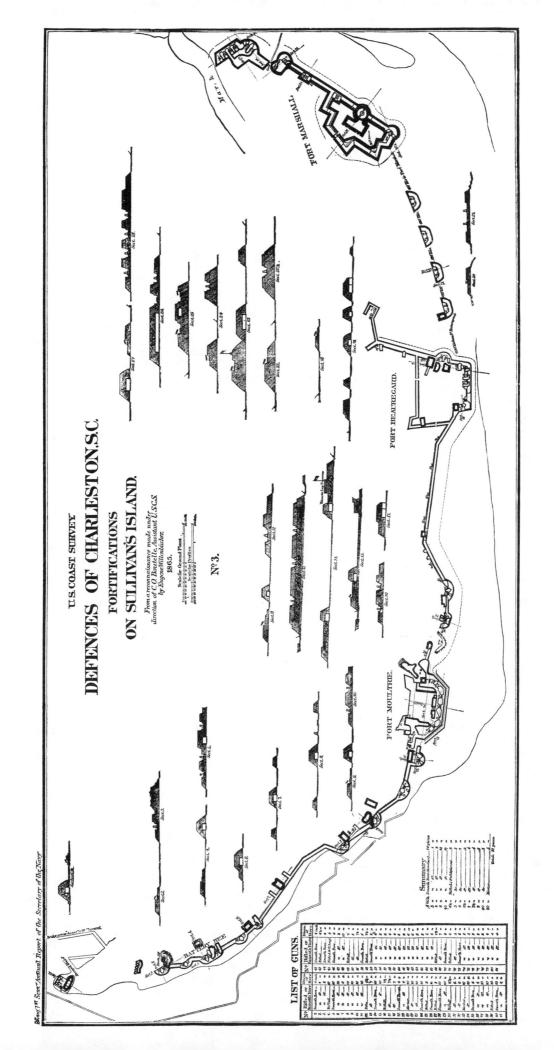

" I propose to place four of my own new 10-inch guns in the casemate ; one at each corner. They weigh about 16,000 pounds, and will throw a solid shot, with forty pounds of powder, which has pierced four and a half inches of good iron at two hundred yards. If the two other guns are needed they may be of 9-inch.

" Annexed are eighteen sketches illustrating the various devices which are referred to in the foregoing, as well as the defences of the harbor :

" 1. General plan of the harbor, showing the positions of the batteries, obstructions of booms, ropes and piles, torpedoes, barrel, frame and boiler, sites where lie the wrecks of the Monitors 'Weehawken' and 'Patapsco,' steamship 'Housatonic,' rebel steamer 'Etiwan,' etc.

" This has been prepared with great care by Captain Boutelle, from drawings on the spot, of the batteries, determination of the locality of the obstructions, etc., from observations, or from the statements of those who removed them. It is a valuable and highly executed specimen of coast survey work, which is highly creditable.

" 2. Fortifications on James Island.

" 3. Fortifications on Sullivan's Island.

" 4. Defences of Charleston Harbor.

" These three maps were also executed by Captain Boutelle, of the coast survey.

" 5, 6 and 7. Rope obstructions between Sumter and Moultrie, their anchors and floats.

" 8. Portion of boom obstructions in Hog Island Channel.

" 9. Barrel torpedo.

" 10. Torpedo frame found in Ashley River, Hog Island and middle channel.

" 11. Its torpedo.

" 12. Torpedo frame and its torpedo, used in the Ogeechee near Fort McAllister, and in the Savannah River near the city.

" 13. Torpedo from bow of rebel ram."

" 14 and 15. Torpedoes of the 'Davids' or torpedo-boats.

" 16. Specimen of the 'David' or torpedo-boat, found in Charleston.

" 17 and 18. Sketch of rebel ram 'Columbia,' captured with Charleston.

" 12, 16, 17 and 18 are by Second-Assistant-Engineer Smith. All the rest were made under the supervision of Captain Boutelle, of the coast survey, and with great care, from actual samples.

" The foregoing conveys the best information that I could collect by the means at my disposal in regard to the submerged impediments of the harbor; and their efficiency, when kept in good order, is not to be judged from the condition in which we found those which were composed more or less of heavy timber. The daily care and renovation that they received from the rebels had ceased for two and even three months before we handled them The boom obstructions and frames in Hog Island Channel were reached only two to two and a half months after the city was abandoned, and the frames in the middle channel had been left unnoticed for three months. It may be conceived that daily care was indispensable to their preservation, and this they did not receive after the rebels evacuated Charleston.

" Annexed will be found the statements of various persons in regard to what they know of the various kinds of obstructions, etc , used to defend the harbor of Charleston, and also extracts from a journal found at the headquarters of the torpedo department in Charleston.

" There is no greater diversity in these accounts than might be expected from the nature of the devices and the circumstances under which the different parties obtained information of them. Quite sufficient is certain to show that these several contrivances of obstruction and torpedoes would have been as troublesome as it was expected they would

be, in connection with the heavy batteries that lined the harbor, and the rebel iron-clads.

" I have the honor to be, very respectfully, your obedient servant,

" J. A. DAHLGREN,
" *Rear-Admiral, Commanding South*
" *Atlantic Blockading Squadron.*

" HON. GIDEON WELLES,
Secretary of the Navy."

The best illustration that can be given of the strength of Charleston is this notice of the obstructions added to an account of its fortifications. The strong positions in which the latter were placed, and the skill displayed in their construction, show what obstacles had to be overcome by the Federal Army and Navy. A new era in military engineering had commenced on the outbreak of the civil war ; and although the Confederates made use of the forts within their territory constructed of masonry, these were either strengthened by sand-bags or supported by earth-works of the most formidable description. Most of these fortifications were ultimately mounted with foreign guns of the largest size and most approved pattern; and, while we render due credit to those who overcame such gigantic obstacles, we should not fail to acknowledge the ability and energy of those who created them.

The old-fashioned system of forts was necessarily ignored by the Confederates from the first. It was impossible to build fortifications of masonry in time to meet the crisis which followed the attack on Sumter, and in the sand of the Southern coast nature had supplied an excellent material for rapidly building, at smaller expense, the military works required. We were taught by the civil war that, instead of expending millions of dollars on fortifications of masonry, we could secure the same or better results at comparatively little expense of time or labor, and have our money to spend on guns and torpedoes. The best way to understand these matters is to examine the plans of fortifications built along the Southern coast. Nothing was ever before constructed of sand-bags so formidable as Fort Fisher and the other defences of Cape Fear River, and the works at Charleston and Savannah. They were masterpieces of military engineering.

In order to show the difficulties to be encountered at Charleston, we append the general plan of the Confederate works.

When the Union forces took possession of Charleston, they were rather surprised to find but one hundred and forty-nine heavy guns in all the forts. This, however, was quite sufficient to secure the place against a naval attack, while the army-contingent was never sufficient by many thousand men to make much impression on the land defences. At the same time the troops were useful in co-operating with the Navy to annoy the garrison. The duty of the army was harassing beyond description, and the privations of the soldiers were many. The enemy generally outnumbered the attacking force two to one, so that if Charleston could be called "in a state of siege" it was a most incomplete investment.

As for naval success in an attack on Charleston, it was out of the question. The force supplied the naval commanders-in-chief was so small, and the obstructions, torpedoes and forts so numerous, that it would have been little less than a miracle for a hostile fleet to reach the city. Had there been any doubt on this subject, it would be removed by the evidence given after the fall of Charleston by persons who had charge of the obstructions. That every effort was made to overcome the difficulties of the situation by Rear-Admiral Dahlgren and his gallant officers and men is certain. They were always ready for any adventure, no matter how hazardous. Many acts of gallantry were performed by the Army and Navy; but, take it altogether, the siege of Charleston was in the highest degree harassing and unsatisfactory to both the Army and Navy of the Union.

General Hardee evacuated Charleston to enable him to get in the advance of General Sherman and reach Raleigh and join his forces to those of General Beauregard, and with the garrison at Augusta, who were aiming to reach the same point. This left the coast of South Carolina comparatively free of Confederate troops; yet there were still points that required attention. Fortifications along the rivers had to be destroyed. In the panic at the movements of Sherman's army most of these places had been hurriedly evacuated without injuring them, and the enemy might again occupy them.

On the 25th of February, 1865, Georgetown, S. C., was occupied by the naval forces, in view of the movements of General Sherman, who might desire to be placed in communication with it before entering North Carolina. There were at this point well-constructed works, mounting sixteen guns, two of them 10-inch columbiads, but no resistance was made, the garrison having departed.

Acting-Ensign A. K. Noyes, commanding U. S. S. "Catalpa," was sent to the city of Georgetown to hoist the Union flag, the municipal authorities having offered submission, and some of the seamen climbed the dome of the town hall and ran up the Stars and Stripes. As soon as the flag was raised, a party of Confederate horseman made a dash into the town; but as soon as

the alarm was given the seamen from the "Mingoe" and "Catalpa" were landed and drove off the enemy.

Gun-boats were sent as far as they could go—about forty miles—up the Cooper River, to co-operate with an army force under General Schimmelfennig, to break up any parties of Confederate troops that might still linger in the vicinity; but it was found that the enemy's forces had all crossed the Santee, burning the bridges behind them. These movements of the gun-boats involved great care to avoid the sunken torpedoes known to exist in all the rivers.

Even the "Harvest Moon," the flag ship of Admiral Dahlgren, did not escape unscathed. While proceeding down to a point two or three miles below Georgetown, this vessel, with the Admiral on board, was blown up by coming in contact with a torpedo. The shock was tremendous, the vessel shivered in every timber, bulkheads were driven in, and it seemed as if the boilers had burst and the magazine exploded. Before any one could fairly realize the situation, the "Harvest Moon" had sunk to the bottom. Had the torpedo struck the vessel a little further forward or aft there would have been great loss of life, but, as it was, only one life was lost. These infernal machines were met with when least expected, and with the greatest care in dragging for them were often overlooked.

By the end of March, 1865, the coast of South Carolina and Georgia may be said to have been free from Confederate raiders, and the inhabitants were rather glad to see the boat expedition sent out by Admiral Dahlgren. These were a check upon the parties of deserters from General Johnston's army who were trying to reach their homes, and were rendered indifferent, by poverty and suffering, on whom they subsisted. The condition of affairs all along the coast was deplorable, owing to the disasters of the civil war, and the strong hand of power was necessary to put an end to it.

By the last of May there was nothing left for Rear-Admiral Dahlgren to accomplish, and he was quite ready to be relieved from a command that had brought upon him so much labor and care, without his having accomplished what the Navy Department desired, the capture of Charleston by the fleet, a thing which under the circumstances was almost, if not quite, impossible. On the 23d of June, 1865, the Admiral was relieved from his command, and received the following complimentary letter from the Secretary of the Navy :

NAVY DEPARTMENT, June 23, 1865.
SIR—Your dispatch of the 21st instant, reporting your arrival in Washington in pursuance of the authority of the Department, has been received.

On the receipt hereof, you will haul down your flag and regard yourself as detached from the command of the South Atlantic Squadron, which you have conducted with ability and energy for two years.

The Department takes the occasion to express to you its approbation of your services, and of the services of those who have been associated with you in efficient blockade of the coast and harbors at a central and important position of the Union, and in the work of repossessing the forts and of restoring the authority of the Government in the insurgent States.

Respectfully,
GIDEON WELLES,
Secretary of the Navy.
REAR-ADMIRAL JOHN A. DAHLGREN,
Washington, D. C.

SOUTH ATLANTIC SQUADRON, JANUARY 1, 1865.

REAR-ADMIRAL J. A. DAHLGREN, COMMANDING.

STAFF—LIEUTENANT-COMMANDER JOSEPH M. BRADFORD, FLEET-CAPTAIN; LIEUTENANT-COMMANDER E. O. MATHEWS, FLAG-LIEUTENANT-COMMANDER; LIEUTENANT ALFRED T. MAHAN, ORDNANCE-OFFICER; LIEUTENANT JAMES O'KANE, FLAG-LIEUTENANT; ENSIGN ERNEST J. DICHMAN, AIDE; FLEET-ENGINEER, ROBERT DANBY; FLEET-PAYMASTER, JAMES H. WATMOUGH; FLEET-SURGEON, WILLIAM JOHNSON; ACTING-VOLUNTEER-LIEUTENANT AND PILOT, WM. HAFFARDS; ACTING-ENSIGN, WALTER COOPER; ACTING-ENSIGN AND SIGNAL-OFFICER, GEO. H. REXFORD.

"CANANDAIGUA"—SECOND-RATE.

Captain, Gustavus H. Scott; Commander, N. B. Harrison; Lieutenants, S. B. Gillett and Walter Abbott; Acting-Masters, Calvin C. Childs, J. L. Gifford and R. G. Lelar; Acting-Ensigns, T. E. Harvey and Andrew Willard; Acting-Master's Mates, S. S. Willard and James Wilbar; Surgeon, C. H. Burbank; Assistant Paymaster, W. H. Anderson; Engineers: Chief, G. B. N. Tower; Second Assistant, J. J. Barry; Acting-Second-Assistants, Wm. McGrath and J. W. Mellor; Acting-Third-Assistants, W. M. Smith and H. B. Goodwin; Boatswain, Charles Fisher; Gunner, E. J. Beecham.

STORE-SHIP "NEW HAMPSHIRE."

Commander, William Reynolds; Acting-Masters, H. W. Hand, R. B. Hines, J. C. Cox and W. A. Morgan; Acting-Ensigns, C. S. Lawrence, Woodward Carter and Frank Jordan; Chaplain, John Blake; Surgeon, H. C. Nelson; Acting-Assistant Paymaster, Levi S. Bingham; First-Lieutenant of Marines, G. G. Stoddard; Acting-Master's Mates, A. B. Flynn, H. A. Rogers and Harry Lucus; Third-Assistant Engineer, William Charlton; Acting-Boatswain, Edward Hughes; Acting-Gunner, Geo. W. Allen.

"FLAG"—THIRD-RATE.

Commander, James C. Williamson; Acting-Volunteer-Lieutenant, Wm. H. Latham; Acting-Master, Wm. Lallman; Acting-Ensigns, C. V. Kelley, S. A. Gove, E. W. Watson and John Denson; Acting-Master's Mate, Wm. Merrill; Acting-Assistant Paymaster, O. B. Seagrave; Acting-Assistant Surgeon, W. J. Burge; Engineers: Second-Assistant, I. R. McNary; Acting-Second-Assistant, Campbell McEwen; Acting-Third-Assistants, Lory Bennett, Theodore Scudder and H. A. Chase; Acting-Gunner, J. H. Pennington.

"ST. LOUIS"—THIRD-RATE.

Commander, Geo. H. Preble; Lieutenant, Wm. F. Stewart; Acting-Master, S. W. Hadley; Acting-Ensigns, Hazard Marsh, Henry Pease, Jr., S. S. Minor and Fred. Wood; Acting-Master's Mate, F. L. Bryan; Passed Assistant Surgeon, J. H. Macomber; Paymaster, J. S. Post; Acting-Boatswain, George Brown; Gunner, G. P. Cushman; Sailmaker, I. E. Crowell.

"JAMES ADGER"—THIRD-RATE.

Commander, T. H. Patterson; Lieutenant, Gilbert C. Wiltse; Acting-Master, A. F. Holmes; Acting-Ensigns, G. E. Halloway, O. C. Snow and Chas. Danenhower; Acting-Master's Mates, L. W. Smith,

Robert Steel and J. W. Thode; Acting-Assistant Surgeon, W. W. Myers; Acting-Assistant Paymaster, Wilbur Ives; Engineers: Acting-Chief, E. A. Whipple; Acting-Second-Assistants, G. W. Scobey and J. B. Place; Acting-Third-Assistants, P. J. Holmes, Timothy Woodruff, Richard Morgan and John Roach; Acting-Gunner, Joseph Venable.

"PAWNEE"—SECOND-RATE.

Commander, George B. Balch; Lieutenant, Wm. Whitehead; Acting-Masters, J. C. Champion, Thos. Moore and E. A. Magone; Ensign, Henry Glass; Acting-Master's Mates, C. H. Poor, Jr., T. L. Fisher and Jacob Kemp; Assistant Surgeon, S. F. Shaw; Assistant Paymaster, C. S. Perley; Engineers: Chief, B. E. Chassaing; Second-Assistants, W. J. Clark, Jr., Arthur Price and J. G. Brosnahan; Third-Assistant, Robert Crawford; Boatswain, James Brown; Gunner, James Hays.

"CIMARRON"—THIRD-RATE.

Commander, Egbert Thompson; Acting-Master, Wm. E. Thomas; Acting-Ensigns, Geo. F. Howes and Charles Penfield; Acting-Master's Mate, N. Goldsmith: Acting-Assistant Surgeon, T. S. Keith; Acting-Assistant Paymaster, J. T. Lee; Engineers: Second-Assistants, J. B. Carpenter, C. F. Meyer, Jr., W. H. Kelly and W. L. Bailey.

"MINGOE"—THIRD-RATE.

Commander, J. B. Creighton; Acting-Masters, J. W. Cangdon and J. C. Wentworth; Acting-Ensigns, Sam'l Merchant, S. R. Carlton, R. F. Dodge and J. A. Phipps; Acting-Assistant Paymaster, C. A. Cabel; Acting-Assistant Surgeon, G. H. Napheys; Engineers: First-Assistant, E. A. C. DuPlain; Acting-Second-Assistant, James Mitchell, W. F. Worrell and Levi Smetzen; Acting-Third-Assistants, Wm. Emmarick and G. G. Blake; Acting-Gunner, Andrew Harmand.

"CATSKILL"—FOURTH-RATE.

Lieutenant-Commander, Edward Barrett; Lieutenant, Chas. W. Tracy; Acting-Masters, J. C. Hamlin and Wm. Reed; Acting-Ensigns, J. D. Barclay, E. B. Cox and Charles Clauson; Assistant Surgeon, John W. Coles; Assistant-Paymaster, H. P. Tuttle; Engineers; Acting-First-Assistant, J. F. Butler; Acting-Second-Assistants, J. G. Dennett and Jonas T. Booth; Third-Assistant, Wm. M. Barr; Acting-Third-Assistant, H. M. Test.

"PATAPSCO"—THIRD-RATE.

Lieutenant-Commander, S. P. Quackenbush; Lieutenant, Wm. T. Sampson; Acting-Master, John

White; Acting-Ensigns, J. S. Johnson, A. B. Bashford and J. C. Brown; Assistant-Surgeon, S. H. Peltz; Acting-Assistant Paymaster, W. S. Creevey; Engineers: First-Assistant, Reynolds Driver; Acting-Second-Assistant, G. L. Palmer; Third-Assistants, D. C. Davis, G. F. Sweet and J. J. Ryan; Pilot, G. Pinckney.

"PONTIAC"—THIRD-RATE.

Lieutenant - Commander, S. B. Luce; Acting-Master, Geo. F. Winslow; Acting-Ensigns, Thomas Stevens, E. M. Clark, T. E. Lawton and James E. Carr; Acting-Master's Mates, W. H. Fitzgerald and E. L. Kemp; Acting-Assistant Paymaster, H. S. Skelding; Acting-Assistant Surgeon, J. W. Sherfy; Engineers: Second - Assistants, Francis Cronin, Cipriano Andrade and H. F. Bradford; Third-Assistants, C. F. Uber and J. G. Littig; Acting-Gunner, Chas. F. Adams.

"LEHIGH"—FOURTH-RATE.

Lieutenant-Commander, Alex. A. Semmes; Lieutenant, John H. Reed; Acting - Masters, W. N. Price and John H. Bolles; Acting-Ensigns, D. W. Hodson, J. H. Cromwell and Rich. Lanphier; Assistant-Surgeon, David V. Whitney; Acting-Assistant Paymaster, W. F. A. Torbert; Engineers: First-Assistant, W. W. Hopper; Second-Assistant, O. B. Mills; Acting-Second-Assistants, Henry Wanklin and J. H. Vaile; Acting - Third - Assistant, H. C. Wilkins.

"SANGAMON"—FOURTH-RATE.

Lieutenant-Commander, Jonathan Young; Acting-Master, S. A. Waterbury; Acting-Ensigns, C. A. Pike, R. P. Leary and G. A. Johnston; Assistant-Surgeon, W. J. Simon; Acting-Assistant Paymaster, D. Corning; Engineers: Acting-First-Assistant, W. S. Hazzard; Acting-Second-Assistant, W. J. Barrington; Third - Assistant, J. A. Kaiser; Acting-Third-Assistants, W. E. Coster and C. H. Hunt.

"NAHANT"—FOURTH-RATE.

Lieutenant-Commander, Wm. K. Mayo; Lieutenant, Henry F. Picking; Acting-Master, Wm. Shackford; Acting-Ensigns, C. J. Rogers, A. B. Prince, E. H. Frisbie and W. C. Mendell; Assistant Surgeon, S. G. Webber; Acting-Assistant Paymaster, Wm. H. Palmer; Engineers: Acting First Assistants, John H. Foster and T. B. Grene; Second-Assistant, L. T. Stafford; Third-Assistant, J. L. Hannum; Acting-Third-Assistant, Morris McCarty.

"PASSAIC"—THIRD-RATE.

Lieutenant - Commander, T. Scott Fillebrown; Lieutenant, H. L. Johnson; Acting-Masters, A. A. Owens and Charles Cook; Acting-Ensigns, L. A. Waterman, Richard Hepburn and Sylvester Eldridge; Assistant Surgeon, Wm. P. Baird; Acting-Assistant Paymaster, F. A. Wheeler; Engineers: First-Assistant, James Sheridan; Second-Assistants, F. H. Fletcher, Webster Lane and Joseph Hooper; Acting-Third-Assistant, G. S. Odell.

"MONTAUK"—FOURTH-RATE.

Lieutenant-Commander, E. E. Stone; Lieutenant, E. F. Brower; Acting-Master, W. W. Crowningshields; Acting-Ensigns, G. W. Bourne, W. T. Mitchell and E. Gabrielson; Acting-Assistant Surgeon, G. B. Todd; Acting-Assistant Paymaster, C. A. Robbins; Engineers: Second - Assistants, A. Adamson and J. W. Hollihan; Acting-Second-Assistants, Simeon Rockburn and Charles Amberg; Acting-Third-Assistants, J. F. Walton and Richard Bell.

"NANTUCKET"—FOURTH-RATE.

Lieutenant - Commander, Robert F. R. Lewis; Lieutenant, J. F. McGlensey; Acting-Master, J. M. Forsyth; Acting-Ensigns, G. T. Chapman, Frank Kemble, G. P. Tyler and J. W. Burr; Assistant Surgeon, E. M. Corson; Acting-Assistant Paymaster,

G. Walter Allen; Engineers: Acting-First-Assistant, D. F. Gerrish; Second-Assistant, C. F. Hollingsworth; Acting-Second-Assistant, F. C. Russell; Third-Assistant, H. H. Kimball; Acting-Third-Assistant, J. F. Kingsley.

"WISSAHICKON"—FOURTH-RATE.

Lieutenant-Commander, A. W. Johnson; Acting-Ensigns, H. B. Francis, H. F. Dorton and Alonzo Elwell; Acting-Master's Mates, D. J. King and Joseph Gregory, Jr.; Acting - Assistant Surgeon, S. C. Johnson; Acting-Assistant Paymaster, Chas. Dutcher; Engineers: Acting-First-Assistant, John Fallon; Third-Assistant, C. W. Kenyon; Acting-Third-Assistants, C. E. Jevins and James F. Miller.

"SONOMA"—THIRD-RATE.

Lieutenant-Commander, R. W. Scott; Acting-Master, H. M. Merrill; Acting-Ensigns, S. H. Pallock, Geo. Couch, S. G. Bryer and M. J. Daly; Acting - Master's Mate, D. W. Spinney; Acting-Assistant Surgeon, David Fairdrey, Acting-Assistant Paymaster, Wm. Sellew; Engineers: Acting-Second-Assistant, A. B. Cullins; Acting-Third-Assistants, Rufus Barton, R. G. Lewis, George Paul and John O'Keefe; Gunner, J. M. Hogg.

"NIPSIC"—FOURTH-RATE.

Lieutenant - Commander, Edmund W. Henry; Acting-Masters, George P. Lee, J. E. Stickney and H. A. Green; Acting-Ensign, Geo. E. Thomas; Acting-Master's Mates, W. S. Howland and J. C. Butler; Acting-Assistant Surgeon, W. J. Gilfillan; Acting-Assistant Paymaster, H. T. Mansfield; Engineers: First-Assistant, S. L. P. Ayres; Second-Assistant, E. W. Koehl; Third-Assistant, C. R. Roelker; Acting-Third-Assistant, Wm. J. Dougherty.

"OTTAWA"—FOURTH-RATE.

Lieutenant-Commander, James Stillwell; Acting-Master, Wm. H. Winslow; Acting-Assistant Surgeon, L. L. Willard; Acting-Assistant Paymaster, G. W. Huntington; Acting-Ensigns, Benj. Mitchell, C. H. Choate, W. H. McCormick and W. N. Smith; Engineers: Second-Assistants, Geo. H. White and R. B. Hine; Acting-Second Assistant, Wm. Ross; Acting-Third-Assistant, C. G. Mead.

"WINONA"—FOURTH-RATE.

Lieutenant-Commander, Wm. H. Dana; Acting-Masters, E. H. Sheffield and Wm. McKendry; Acting-Ensigns, Walter Sargent and J. Severns; Acting-Master's Mate, Alfred Staigg; Acting - Assistant-Surgeon, Charles Little; Acting-Assistant Paymaster, T. H. Dickson; Engineers: Second-Assistant, Alfred Hendrick; Acting-Second-Assistant, J. B. A. Allen, Jr.; Third-Assistant, R. L. Wamaling; Acting-Third-Assistant, C. W. Plaisted.

"DAI CHING"—FOURTH-RATE.

Lieutenant-Commander, J. C. Chaplin; Acting-Masters, J. W. Crosby and Geo. Howorth; Acting-Ensign, Walter Walton; Acting-Assistant Surgeon, J. R. Richardson; Acting - Assistant Paymaster, Edw. Sherwin; Engineers: Acting First-Assistant, G. R. Bennett; Acting-Third-Assistants, D. Castana, J. R. Fulcher and Montgomery West.

"COMMODORE M'DONOUGH"—FOURTH-RATE.

Lieutenant-Commander, Alex. F. Crossman; Acting-Masters, Wm. Knapp and John Myers; Acting-Ensigns, N. W. White and George Glass; Acting-Master's Mates, Sam'l Flaxington and L. F. Strant; Acting-Assistant Paymaster, R. Freeman; Acting-Assistant Surgeon, D. J. Harris; Engineers: Acting-Second-Assistants, Sylvanus Warren, S. S. Hettrick and Nelson Ross.

NAVAL BATTERY.

Lieutenant, Geo. W. Hayward; Acting-Ensign, J. A. Edgron; Acting - Assistant Surgeon, B. F. Brown; Acting - Master's Mate, Chas. Everdeen; Acting-Gunner, Thos. Holland.

"SARATOGA"—THIRD-RATE.

Acting-Volunteer-Lieutenant, Edgar Brodhead ; Acting-Masters, B. S. Melville and C. H. Baldwin; Acting-Ensigns, Edw. Rogers and G. O. Fabeus; Acting-Master's Mates, C. H. Chase and W. A. Stannard; Acting-Assistant Surgeon, Winthrop Butler; Acting-Assistant Paymaster, Louis A. Yorke; Boatswain, Philip J. Miller; Gunner, Stephen Young; Carpenter, O. H. Gerry; Sailmaker, J. C. Bradford.

"JOHN ADAMS"—THIRD-RATE.

Acting-Volunteer-Lieutenant, Alvin Phinny ; Acting-Masters, C. C. Ricker, T. C. Chapin and Henry Vaughan ; Acting-Ensigns, H. D. Burolett, T. S. Avery, A. A. Franzen, P. W. Fragen, G. S. Johnson and Frank Fisher ; Acting-Master's Mates, W. M. Gregg, S. E. Adamson, John Ostega, Nathan Brown and Oliver O'Brien ; Acting-Assistant-Surgeon, N. M. Randlett ; Acting-Assistant Paymaster, Arch'd McVey ; Gunner, J. M. Ballard ; Acting-Gunner, A. C. Holmes ; Carpenter, J. G. Thomas.

"FLAMBEAU"—THIRD-RATE.

Acting-Volunteer-Lieutenant, Edward Cavendy ; Acting-Master, Gilbert Richmond ; Acting-Ensigns, J. W. Griffiths, J. T. Carver, J. S. Thomles and J. M. Hudson ; Acting-Master's Mate, J. F. Peterson ; Acting-Assistant Surgeon, P. H. Pursell ; Acting-Assistant Paymaster, F. V. D. Horton ; Engineers : Acting-First-Assistant, John Harris ; Acting-Second-Assistant, C. B. Curtes ; Acting-Third-Assistants, A. F. Bullard and Edw. Humstone.

"SOUTH CAROLINA"—THIRD-RATE.

Acting-Volunteer-Lieutenant, Wm. W. Kennison; Acting-Master, Wm. Bailey ; Acting-Ensigns, John Gunn, E. M. Dimon, C. G. Boyer and Ansel S. Hitch ; Acting-Assistant Surgeon, H. C. Vaughan ; Acting-Assistant Paymaster, S. W. Tanner ; Engineers : Acting-First-Assistant, J. T. Hathaway ; Acting-Second-Assistants, J. H. Rowe and Henry Gormley ; Acting-Third-Assistants, S. C. Lane and John Agnew.

"LODONA"—THIRD-RATE.

Acting-Volunteer-Lieutenant, R. P. Swann ; Acting-Masters, H. G. McKennee and R. C. McKenzie ; Acting-Ensigns, Wm. S. McNeilly and L. B. Brigham ; Acting-Assistant Surgeon, T. W. Meckly ; Acting-Assistant Paymaster, A. M. Stewart ; Engineers : Acting-Second-Assistant, M. C. Heath ; Acting-Third-Assistants, James Mollineaux, Wm. Leonard and W. H. H. Hawes.

"HOPE"—FOURTH-RATE.

Acting-Volunteer-Lieutenant, Wm. L. Churchill; Acting-Ensign, Andy Hartshorn ; Acting-Master's Mates, Wm. E. Sauld and J. S. Leon.

"VALPARAISO"—FOURTH-RATE.

Acting-Volunteer-Lieutenant, Geo. E. Welch ; Acting-Masters, H. S. Blanchard, J. W. Tuck. A. S. Gardner and S. W. Rhoades; Acting-Ensign, R. W. Parker; Engineers: Acting-Second-Assistants, E. H. Keith and John Lardner; Acting-Third-Assistant, Jesse Wright; Gunner, Wm. Bartlett ; Carpenter, Samuel N. Whitehouse.

"STETTIN"—FOURTH-RATE.

Acting-Volunteer-Lieutenant, C. J. Van Alstine ; Acting-Master, J. M. Butler; Acting-Ensigns, C. B. Pray, J. C. Staples and Wm. Jenny; Acting-Master's Mate, Edward W. Mosier ; Acting-Assistant Surgeon, Robert Stone; Acting-Assistant Paymaster, C. M. Burnes; Engineers: Acting-Second-Assistant, John Hawkins ; Acting-Third-Assistants, Anthony Gale, J. W. Elliott and W. W. Smith.

"MEMPHIS"—THIRD RATE

Acting-Masters, R. O. Patterson and J. B. Childs; Acting-Ensigns, S. W. Cowing, B. D. Reed and G. C. Chamberlain ; Acting-Master's Mate, John W.

Moore ; Acting-Assistant Surgeon, W. H. Bates ; Acting Assistant Paymaster, Wm. E. Foster; Engineers : Acting-Second-Assistants, C. H. McCarty and Peter Anderson ; Third-Assistant, S. C. McLanahan; Acting-Third-Assistant, Wm. Adams.

"MARY SANFORD"—THIRD-RATE.

Acting-Master, Z. Kempton ; Acting-Ensigns, John Ross, J. F. Otis, G. W. Pease and Wm. Caldwell, Jr.; Acting-Master's Mate, N. F. Rich; Acting-Assistant Paymaster, Geo. E. Bissell ; Engineers: Acting-Second-Assistant, Chas. O. Davis ; Acting-Third-Assistant, A. N. Odell, Thos. Stimson and James Hare.

"HOME"—THIRD-RATE.

Acting-Master, Benj. Dyer; Acting-Ensigns, A. E. Barnett, R. E. Anson and A. D. Anderson; Acting-Assistant Surgeon, W. W. Howard ; Acting-Assistant Paymaster, Ichabod Norton; Engineers: Acting-Second-Assistant, Cornelius Dandreau; Acting-Third-Assistants, Paul Dandreau, T. J. Hamilton, Wm. Smith and G. W. Hughes.

"AZALIA"—FOURTH-RATE.

Acting-Master, Fred. W. Strong; Acting-Ensign, Joseph Frost; Acting-Master s Mates, F. C. Simond and Robert N. Turner; Engineers : Acting-Second-Assistant, Chas. Gewans; Acting-Third-Assistants, W. W. Fish, F. L. Strong and J. Priest.

"PERRY"—FOURTH-RATE.

Acting-Master, S. N. Freeman ; Acting-Ensigns, R. R. Donnell and Fred. Elliott ; Acting-Master's Mates, Edw. H. Sheer, T. H. McDonald and C. S. Bridges; Acting-Assistant Surgeon, Benj. Marshall; Acting-Assistant Paymaster, T. A. Emerson.

"HARVEST MOON"—FOURTH-RATE.

Acting-Master, John K. Crosby ; Acting-Ensigns, W. H. Bullis, D. P. McKevan, A. N. Bates and L. A. Cornthwait; Acting-Assistant Surgeon, A. Sumner Dean ; Acting-Assistant Paymaster, L. E. Rice ; Engineers : Acting-Second-Assistant, J. A. Miller and G. A. Geer; Acting-Third-Assistants, Henry Fisher and F. W. Racoe.

"PHILADELPHIA"—FOURTH-RATE.

Acting-Master, Geo. H. Avery ; Acting-Ensigns, Geo. B. Bailey, Geo. Edwards, E. R. Davison, John B. Starr and C. D. Duncan ; Assistant-Surgeon, J. H. Culver ; Assistant Paymaster, H. L. Wait ; Engineers : Acting-First-Assistant, Robert Mulready ; Acting-Third-Assistants, C. T. Wamaling and John Ryan.

"POTOMSKA"—FOURTH-RATE.

Acting-Master, F. M. Montell ; Acting-Ensigns, A. Cartes, Frank Watson, W. H. Millett and G. T. Joslin ; Acting-Assistant Paymaster, H. E. Rand ; Engineers : Acting-Second-Assistant, Edwin Vaughn ; Acting-Third-Assistants, S. M. Van Clief, E. W. Cross and L. McNeil.

"WANDO"—FOURTH-RATE.

Acting-Master, Fred'k T. King ; Acting-Ensigns, E. K. Smith, M. A. Nickerson, Lewis Jennings and Alex. Cormack ; Acting-Master's Mate, W. C. N. Sanford ; Acting-Assistant Surgeon, P. C. Whidden ; Acting-Assistant Paymaster, W. L. G. Thayer; Engineers: Second-Assistant, J. P. Kelly ; Acting-Second-Assistant, J. J. Sullivan ; Acting-Third-Assistants, Wm. Norie, T. T. Sanborn and G. W. Wakefield.

"WAMSUTTA"—FOURTH-RATE.

Acting-Master, Charles W. Lee; Acting-Ensigns, E. R. Warren and T. R. Dayton ; Acting-Master's Mates, F. L. Wheeler and Thos. Nickerson ; Acting-Assistant Paymaster, Charles Loucks ; Engineers: Acting-First-Assistant, William Johnston ; Acting-Third-Assistants, B. F. Napheys, David McDonald and T. T. Risbell.

"AMARANTHUS"—FOURTH-RATE.

Acting-Master, Enos O. Adams; Acting-Ensign, Wm. R. Cox; Acting-Master's Mates, Washington Van Wyck, James O'Donnell and A. D. Damon; Engineers: Acting-Second-Assistant, C. R. Jones; Acting-Third-Assistants, Samuel Fowler and H. W. Force.

"ETHAN ALLAN"—FOURTH-RATE.

Acting-Masters, J. A. Pennell, W. L. Kempton and Jos. McCart; Acting-Ensigns, J. H. Bunting and Wm. Mero; Acting-Master's Mate, Edwards Dexter; Acting-Assistant Surgeon, Isaiah Dowling; Acting-Assistant Paymaster, Wm. R. Woodward.

"CHAMBERS"—FOURTH-RATE.

Acting-Master, William Watson; Acting-Ensigns, William Jennings and L. P. Delan; Acting-Master's Mate, A. K. Baylor; Acting-Assistant Paymaster, W. D. Walker.

"OLEANDER"—FOURTH-RATE.

Acting-Master, R. Price Walter; Acting Ensigns, H. G. Seaman and Geo. Dunlap; Acting-Master's Mate, George Newlin; Engineers: Acting-Second-Assistant, Samuel Swartwout; Acting-Third-Assistants, Robert B. Dick, H. S. Brown and L. B. Joyce.

"PARA"—FOURTH-RATE.

Acting-Master, David P. Health; Acting-Ensign, Edward Ryan; Acting-Master's Mates, John McDonough and Wm. H. Morse.

"NORWICH"—FOURTH-RATE.

Acting-Master, W. H. DeWolf; Acting-Ensigns, J. H. Sinscatt, J. P. Chadwick and R. W. Laid; Acting-Master's Mates, Henry Sinclair and Wm. White; Acting-Assistant Surgeon, J. A. Petrie; Acting-Assistant Paymaster, C. F. Gardner; Engineers: Acting-Second-Assistant, P. B Robinson; Third-Assistant, L. H. Lamdim; Acting-Third-Assistants, H. J. Tarr and J. B. Johnston.

"FERNANDINA"—FOURTH-RATE.

Acting-Masters, Lewis West and George F. Hollis; Acting-Ensigns, Christopher Flood, B. H. Chadwick and Charles Sawyer; Acting-Master's Mate, Wm. C. King; Acting-Assistant Surgeon, S. B. Kenney; Acting-Assistant Paymaster, T. N. Murray.

"HOUGHLEN"—FOURTH-RATE.

Acting-Master, E. S. Fusher; Acting-Ensigns, C. M. Shirving and Jacob Cochran; Acting-Assistant Surgeon, Israel Bashong; Acting-Assistant Paymaster, R W. Allen.

"DAFFODIL"—FOURTH-RATE.

Acting-Master, Wm. H. Mallard; Acting-Ensign, John McGlathery; Acting-Master's Mate, N. B. Walker; Engineers: Acting-Third-Assistants, Wm. H. Capen, Thomas Forrest and John Tucker.

"ORVETTA"—FOURTH-RATE.

Acting-Master, Wm. Fales; Acting-Ensigns, E. W. Halcro, Charles Nellman and D. W. Andrews; Acting-Assistant Paymaster, Samuel A. Kay.

"HYDRANGA"—FOURTH-RATE.

Acting-Master, Charles W. Rodgers; Acting-Master's Mates, J. B. Newcomb, J. G. Underhill and John Wolstenholme; Engineers: Acting-Second Assistant, A. N. Koones; Acting-Third-Assistants, H. E. Whitworth, W. B. Hall and C. M. Adams.

"E. B. HALE"—FOURTH-RATE.

Acting-Master, Charles F. Mitchell; Acting-Ensigns, Henry Stohl, G. A. Smith, J. N. Van Buskirk, Wm. L. Pary and Wm. Lamee; Acting-Assistant Paymaster, O. B. Gilman; Engineers: Acting-Second-Assistant, Frank Marsh; Acting-Third-Assistants, R. F. Bennett, W. C. Bond and Wm. Finnegan.

"C. P. WILLIAMS"—FOURTH-RATE.

Acting-Master, L. W. Parker; Acting-Ensign, J. W. North; Acting-Master's Mates, L. E. Daggett and W. J. Lane.

"GEORGE MANGHAM"—FOURTH-RATE

Acting-Master, John Collins, Jr.; Acting-Ensigns, J. E. Wallis and A. Tuttle; Acting-Assistant Paymaster, T. G. Holland.

"DAN SMITH"—FOURTH-RATE.

Acting-Master, Barker Van Voorhis; Acting-Ensigns, A. H. L. Bowie and Robert Craig; Acting-Master's Mate, H. P. Diermanse.

"GEORGE W. RODGERS"—FOURTH-RATE.

Acting-Master, Loring G. Emerson; Acting-Ensign, J. H. Handy; Acting-Master's Mate, A. Trensdale.

"ACACIA"—FOURTH-RATE.

Acting-Masters, Wm. Barrymore and J. E. Jones; Acting-Ensigns, H. F. Blake and A. S. Rounds; Acting-Master's Mates, Wm. J. McFadden and James Hawkins; Acting-Assistant Paymaster, Joseph Foster; Engineers: Acting-Second-Assistant, T. D. Crosby; Acting-Third-Assistants, J. K. Wright; A. V. Harvey, E. H. Haggens and Robert Henry.

"T. A. WARD"—FOURTH-RATE.

Acting-Master, Robert T. Wyatt; Acting-Ensign, W. C. Odroine; Acting-Master's Mates, M. M. Baker, Jr., and A. Olmstead.

"RACER"—FOURTH-RATE.

Acting-Master, E. G. Martin; Acting-Ensigns, D. B. Corey and J. F. Kavanaugh; Acting-Master's Mate, James Williams; Acting-Assistant-Paymaster, Charles Smith.

"JOHN GRIFFITH"—FOURTH-RATE.

Acting-Master, James Ogilvie; Acting-Ensigns, Wm. Knight, W. G. Pitts and Thos. Perry.

"SARAH BRUEN"—FOURTH-RATE.

Acting-Master, Wm. F. Redding; Acting-Ensigns, S. P. Edwards and J. Richardson; Acting-Master's Mate, Wm. H. Olmey.

"IRIS"—FOURTH-RATE.

Acting-Ensign, Wm. H. Anderson; Acting-Master's Mates, W. W. Brandt, Elisha Hubbard and Roger Conoly; Engineers: Acting-Second-Assistant, Richard Nash; Acting-Third-Assistants, Dennis Lyng and James Hankey.

"DANDELION"—FOURTH-RATE.

Acting Ensign, George W. Williams; Acting-Master's Mates, W. F. Vincent, J. K. Gould and James Sullivan; Engineers: Acting-Third-Assistants, E. Babbit and John McKeezer.

"ARETHUSA"—FOURTH-RATE.

Acting-Ensign, John V. Cook; Acting Master's Mates, I. D. Lovett and F. H. Newcomb; Engineers: Acting-Second Assistant, Geo. W. Howe; Acting-Third-Assistant, William J. Moore and J. T. Greenwood.

"CAMELIA"—FOURTH-RATE.

Acting-Ensign, David B. Howes; Acting-Master's Mates, Abraham Leach, F H. Munroe and Wm. F. Lard; Engineers: Acting-Third-Assistants, Benjamin Cobb, Jr., John Grimes and John Corson.

"SWEETBRIER"—FOURTH-RATE.

Acting-Ensign, J. D. Dexter; Acting-Master's Mates, T. J. Dill, J. R. Grove and L. H. Brown; Engineers: Acting-Second-Assistants, M. V. B. Darling and T. J W. Cooper; Acting-Third-Assistant, J. W. Blake.

"PETTIT"—FOURTH-RATE.

Acting-Ensign, Charles Greive; Acting-Master's Mates, J. A. Smith, C. E. Cool and Uriah Folger;

Engineers: Acting-Second-Assistants, Reuben Mc-Clenahan and Augustus Wendell; Acting-Third-Assistants, Edw. Bannaclough and W. J. Phillips.

"GLADIOLUS"—FOURTH-RATE.

Acting - Ensign, Napoleon Boughton; Acting-Master's Mates, S. W. Byram, H. B. Eaton and Wm. C. Parker; Engineers: Acting-Third Assistant, John D. Williams, Geo. W. Beard and Augustus Straub.

"CARNATION" FOURTH-RATE.

Acting-Ensign, William Boyd; Acting-Master's Mates, J. D. Reed, Albion Burnham and A. H. Francis; Engineers: Acting - Third - Assistants, Wm. C. Boone and D. M. Spangler.

"LABURNUM"—FOURTH-RATE.

Acting - Ensigns, Sturgis Center, J. D. Kihlborn and J. P. Thompson; Acting-Master's Mate, Peter Moakley; Engineers: Acting - Second - Assistant, James Stevens; Acting - Third - Assistants, Denis Hayes and Walter S. Jarboe.

"CATALPA"—FOURTH-RATE.

Acting-Ensign, Allen K. Noyes; Acting-Master's Mates, J. W. Mathews, A. S. Taffe and John McGee; Engineers: Acting-Second Assistant, Timothy McCarty; Acting-Third-Assistants, Nicholas Cassin and J. Nicholson.

"CLOVER"—FOURTH-RATE.

Acting -Ensign, Frank S. Leech; Acting-Master's Mate, S. H. Bryant; Engineers; Acting - Third Assistants, W. W. Shane, W. F. Henderson and M. Griffiths.

"GERANIUM"—FOURTH-RATE.

Acting - Ensign, David Lee; Acting - Master's Mates, J. D. Wingale, Benjamin Russell and Wm.

Earle; Engineers: Acting-Second-Assistants, S. W. Widlam and C. J. Henry; Acting-Third-Assistants, Geo. E. Norris and H. B. Garabedian.

"JONQUIL"—FOURTH-RATE.

Acting-Ensign, Charles H. Hanson; Acting-Master's Mates, Thos. Newton and Henry Lynch; Engineers: Acting-Third-Assistants, Wm. H. Barclay and J. C. Batchelder.

"NORFOLK PACKET"—FOURTH RATE.

Acting-Ensigns, Geo. W. Wood and S. A. Dayton; Acting -Assistant Paymaster, Andrew Tower; Acting - Master's Mates, Charles Bedell and Allen Moore.

"BRAZILIERA"—FOURTH-RATE.

Acting-Ensigns, J. H. Bennett, N. C. Borden and Horace Dexter; Acting-Master's Mates, F. W. H. Harrington and C. A. Austen; Acting-Assistant Surgeon, George S. Fife; Acting-Assistant Paymaster C. H. Longstreet.

"G. W. BLUNT"—FOURTH-RATE.

Acting-Ensign, G. G. Curtis; Acting - Master's Mates, W. R. Lyons.

"CHATHAM"—FOURTH-RATE.

Acting-Master's Mates, George W. Post and Wm. Woods; Engineers: Acting-Third-Assistants, Frederick Wagner and H. A. Brown.

"LARKSPUR"—FOURTH-RATE.

Acting-Master's Mates, John O'Conner, W. A. Arkins and David Wilson; Engineers: Acting-Third-Assistants, W. J. Cannon and A. L. Grow.

CHAPTER LIII.

OPERATIONS OF THE WEST GULF SQUADRON IN THE LATTER PART OF 1864, AND IN 1865.

JOINT OPERATIONS IN MOBILE BAY BY REAR-ADMIRAL THATCHER AND GENERAL CANBY.

GALLANT SERVICES OF COMMODORE PALMER.—BLOCKADE-RUNNERS ON TEXAS COAST.—DE-
MORALIZING TENACITY OF CONFEDERATE GOVERNMENT.—CUTTING OUT OF THE SCHOONER
"GOLDEN BELLE."—CAPTURE OF THE "DELPHINA," "ANNIE SOPHIA," AND "PET,"
PRIZE-LADEN SCHOONERS.—THE STEAMER "WILL-O'-THE-WISP" BOARDED AND SET ON
FIRE. — EXCITING AND HAZARDOUS ADVENTURES. — THE CONFEDERATE PRIVATEER
"ANNA DALE" CAPTURED AND BURNED.—CONSPICUOUS GALLANTRY OF THE VOLUN-
TEER ELEMENT OF THE NAVY.—ACTING-REAR-ADMIRAL THATCHER RELIEVES COMMO-
DORE PALMER. — SHELLING CONFEDERATE BATTERIES NEAR MOBILE. — CAPTURE OF
SPANISH FORT, FORTS ALEXIS, HUGER AND TRACY.—MOBILE SURRENDERS.—OPERATIONS
OF THE GUN-BOATS IN RIVERS OF ALABAMA.—CONFEDERATE RAMS "HUNTSVILLE" AND
"TUSCALOOSA" SUNK.—FEDERAL GUN-BOATS SUNK BY TORPEDOES.—CONFEDERATE
GUN-BOATS AND OTHER PROPERTY SURRENDERED TO THE NAVY.—CONDITIONS OF SUR-
RENDER.—INSTRUCTIONS TO FLAG-CAPTAIN SIMPSON.—PAROLE GIVEN BY AND LIST OF
OFFICERS AND MEN SURRENDERED.—ENTRANCE OF GUN-BOATS INTO BLAKELY RIVER.—
COMPLIMENTARY LETTER RELATIVE TO COMMODORE PALMER.—DESTRUCTION OF CON-
FEDERATE RAM "WEBB."—GALVESTON SURRENDERS.—LIST OF VESSELS AND OFFICERS
OF WEST GULF SQUADRON, 1865.

COMMODORE James S. Palmer commanded the West Gulf Blockading Squadron up to the time Rear-
Admiral Thatcher took command
in the latter part of February or
early part of March, 1865. After being relieved, he continued to give Rear-Admiral
Thatcher that hearty and effective support
that always distinguished him in his former
commands under Admiral Farragut on the
Mississippi and elsewhere, marking him as
one of those cool and gallant men who
perhaps in time of peace would not attract
much attention, but whose services in time
of war are strongly marked by judgment and
gallantry combined. These qualities always
leave a strong impression on a ship's company that has the good fortune to possess
such a commander. Whatever duty Commodore Palmer undertook he performed it
bravely and intelligently, and this is seen

in the records of the war, where the commanders under whom he served never
parted with him without the warmest eulogiums in his praise, all of which were deserved. While he had the temporary command of the West Gulf Blockading Squadron he kept the vessels of the fleet actively
employed, which will be better appreciated
and understood by a brief outline of the
operations.

Commodore Palmer was one of those who
encouraged intrepidity in young officers;
and as there was not a large field for daring deeds, and as the duty of the vessels
under his command was chiefly confined
to the dull routine of blockading the Texas
coast, no opportunity was lost to obtain
distinction, and at the same time inflict injury upon the enemy.

Since the closing of the Confederate ports
on the Atlantic coast, the blockade-runners

made attempts to reach the coast of Texas, though it would seem that it was scarcely profitable for them to carry on their illicit trade in the Gulf, where they could be so easily cut off, and at the time when the war must have appeared to any one with an observant mind to be so rapidly approaching a close. But as long as there was life there was hope, and the Confederate Government, to the very last moment of its existence, put on a bold front and acted as if in the heyday of its power. The only way it could keep up its credit abroad was by now and then getting out a load of cotton on a steamer, or some of the schooners that had been left to them after the several raids that had been made on such coasting vessels

that the Texan soldiers—a very brave set of men—had never felt that they had been worsted in the least. On the contrary, they had not only prevented the Federal generals from making a permanent lodgment in their State, but had given a large quota of their troops to assist the Confederates in every other quarter of the Southern domain. It would have been, indeed, a grievous infliction if the Texans had succeeded in drawing to their State the remains of the Confederate armies who had not been driven to surrender, for they might have kept up the war two or three years longer, with great loss to the North in expense and with no gain to themselves.

But the same demoralization of the Con-

COMMODORE (AFTERWARDS REAR-ADMIRAL) JAMES S. PALMER.

as they possessed. Though the communications with Texas and the northern portion of the Confederacy had been almost entirely cut off by the vigilant watchfulness of the Navy on the coast and on the great river which divided the Confederacy, yet the Texans were as active as ever in carrying on operations, particularly in the introduction of arms of all kinds, provisions, clothing and military stores, apparently with a view to carrying on the war on their own account if Richmond fell, or to offer a place of retreat to those dissatisfied spirits who could see nothing good in a union with the Northern States. The Federal invasions had, so far, been so unsuccessful, and were, as a rule, so badly conducted,

federacy which was so painfully apparent in Richmond was also felt in Texas. Though they appeared to be imbued with the popular enthusiasm that had done so much to prolong the contest, and though they had given as many proofs of devotion to the cause and evidences of endurance and noble sacrifice, yet they were not carried away with the bitterness of feeling that seemed to animate the people further north.

The Texans could see plainly enough that official mismanagement on the part of the Confederate authorities, together with the Union victories and the popular resolution of the Northern people to prosecute the war with renewed vigor, had made it probable that Texas would become the great battle-ground, and that, whatever way the tide of war might turn, the State would be impoverished. So far, Texas had borne no hardships that soldiers could not reasonably endure, for her plains were full of hogs and cattle, and her fields were well supplied with corn, and they had sufficient military ardor to uphold them to the last.

But there were large amounts of cotton on hand from which no revenue was derived, and attempts were now and then made to get the fabric to market in anything that would float, which, in many cases, succeeded when success was least expected. Emboldened by their first attempts, the blockade-runners from the Texan ports became more audacious, so much so that the Federal naval officers were put upon their mettle, and hence resulted a number of small but gallant affairs which, in justice to the officers concerned in them, should not be omitted. They are the small links that make up the chain of history, and were as important in the eyes of the performers as more prominent affairs.

On the 26th of December, 1864, a large schooner, named the "Golden Belle," was lying in Galveston harbor, watching a chance to evade the blockaders outside, and make a run to Havana or Nassau. Acting-Ensign N. A. Blume, of the "Virginia," asked and received permission from his commanding officer, Acting-Volunteer-Lieutenant Charles H. Brown, to go in and cut out the schooner. Obtaining volunteers from the crew for the expedition, he left with the third cutter about 8:30 P. M. Having five miles to pull against a heavy head sea, Mr. Blume did not reach Boliver Point and get in sight of the schooner until 1 A. M. of the 27th. She was lying about a quarter of a mile from Fort Jackson, about a mile from Fort Greene, and less than four hundred yards from the Confederate guard-schooner "Lecompte." When within five hundred yards of the schooner, a light was seen moving about her decks. The boat passed her and came up astern, not being discovered till alongside. She was then immediately boarded and carried, and the prisoners secured. The captors immediately made sail, slipped the schooner cable and stood down the bay, the guard-boat supposing that she had started out to run the blockade. Coolness and clever management was manifested in piloting the "Belle" out of Galveston harbor, which is an intricate one. In going out, the prize had to pass almost within hail of Fort Point on Galveston Island, then find her way in the dark through the main channel and cross the bar at the right point; all of which was done without a mistake. At daylight, the fleet was sighted bearing northwest, and

that morning the owner of the "Golden Belle" could see her from Galveston carefully anchored under the guns of the Federals.

As it resulted, there was no loss of life on this expedition, and the glamour which generally attends a bloody affair was missing; but it was none the less a dangerous one, and all engaged in it deserve as much credit as if some had been shot. We have made it a rule to mention the names of the participants when good work was performed, and, this being a case in point, the following are entitled to a place: N. A. Blume, Acting-Ensign; William Stevenson, Master-at-Arms; James Webster, Gunner's Mate; Thomas Wallace, Coxswain; Jacob Bowman, Captain Forecastle; William Thompson, Captain Forecastle; Augustus Miller, Captain After-guard; Peter Miller, Seaman; Thomas K. Fenley, Landsman.

On January 24th, 1865, quite as clever an affair took place off Calcasieu River, by a cutting-out expedition. under Lieutenant-Commander Richard W. Meade, which was a complete success without any casualties. A three-masted schooner, loaded with cotton, was lying at the second bend of the Calcasieu River, about two and a half miles from its mouth, ready to slip out at the first opportunity, and the object of the expedition was her capture. As a large force of the enemy was encamped close at hand, it was deemed best to take a force sufficiently large to insure success. Lieutenant-Commander Meade accordingly fitted out the "Chocura's" launch and first cutter, and took forty men of her crew under his personal command. The night of the 22d of January was chosen for the attempt, and as it was cold and dark, with drizzling rain and a norther blowing, it was just such a night as a blockade-runner would select to evade the blockaders. The party left the "Chocura" at dark and pulled in silently for the river. Just as they entered it, the schooner was discovered coming down under sail with a fresh breeze. Had the boats been ten minutes later she would have reached open water and escaped. She was at once boarded and carried; but, unfortunately, her captain saw the boats before they reached his vessel, and, putting his helm hard down and letting fly his sheets, ran the schooner hard and fast aground on the flats close to the beach and not far from the enemy's force. Six prisoners were secured at once, and a boat that was towing astern was seen to push off and pull rapidly up the river, in which, doubtless, some of the crew escaped. The prize proved to be the schooner "Delphina," with one hundred and eighty bales of cotton on board—one of those small ventures the Texans were in the habit of making to raise money, which, though small in quantity, was none the less valuable to the captors when it could be secured. This cargo would have been worth in England over one hundred thousand dollars. Every effort was made to get the "Delphina" afloat. The after-deck load was thrown overboard and her anchor carried out; but as the norther caused the water to fall rapidly, leaving in an hour only about a foot of water alongside, the efforts to float her were unavailing. The launch grounded in the meantime, and it was deemed best not to expose the men to an attack from an overwhelming force. The schooner was therefore set on fire and the expedition returned to the "Chocura." Acting-Ensigns Tracy and Beardsley ac-

LIEUTENANT-COMMANDER (NOW CAPTAIN) R. W. MEADE.

companied Lieutenant-Commander Meade. The officers and men behaved as all men will when they are led by a judicious and gallant commander. They were not altogether unfortunate in not receiving some prize-money. Eighty bales of cotton were thrown overboard before they set fire to the schooner; this drifted out to sea, and thirty bales were picked up on the following morning, and very likely more were secured later. This was hard on the shippers; but such are the fortunes of war, and it was the only way to cripple the resources of the Confederacy. Captain Semmes, of Alabama fame, railed at Union naval officers a great deal for what he called their greedy spirit in capturing cotton coming out and arms going in, which he called destroying the property of Southern people, and makes an

excuse on this account for inflicting harm on Federal merchant-ships. It was not to be supposed that Union officers would let a vessel put to sea with a hundred thousand dollars' worth of cotton on board without using every effort to capture it, when they knew that if it reached England it would soon be converted into cash to buy arms with which to shoot Union people. There was really no greedy intent which induced officers to follow up vessels in port loaded with cotton, but simply a desire on their part to put an end to the war. Half the time the vessels and cotton were burned when it might frequently have been saved, but it was not considered worth the while to risk the lives of officers and men. This was the case on this occasion, as there was a force of three hundred cavalry at the point where the "Delphina" was burned.

The Confederates were very watchful and alert in getting vessels ready for sea and loaded with cotton bales, but the blockaders were equally so; and, if we may judge by the results, much more active in the pursuit of the blockade-runners and in the capture of them than their owners were in getting their wares to market.

On February 8, 1865, an expedition was fitted out by Commander Mullany, of the "Bienville," assisted by Commander Woolsey, of the "Princess Royal," for the purpose of destroying the steamer "Wren," a blockade-runner lying in the harbor of Galveston, and also of capturing two cotton-ladened schooners that were lying at anchor under the forts, ready to go to sea when the wind and weather permitted.

Two boats were sent on this expedition, viz.: The "Bienville's" first cutter, with thirteen men, Acting-Ensign George H. French, in charge, and the "Princess Royal's" first cutter, with a crew of nine men, Acting-Ensign A. H. Reynolds, in charge, assisted by Acting-Master's Mate Lewis Johnson, the whole under the command of Acting-Ensign French, of the "Bienville." The boats left the "Bienville" about 8.20 P. M., and stood in for the harbor. Mr. French intended to pass inside the schooners and make his first attack on the "Wren," destroy her, and then capture the schooners; but he failed in this, owing to the tide, which carried him so far out of his course that he found himself close aboard the schooners. Without hesitation, orders were given Mr. Reynolds to board one, while Mr. French carried the other. Both were taken without resistance, though the crews aggregated twenty men, nearly equal to the crews of the two boats. The "Princess Royal's" cutter captured the "Annie Sophia," and the "Bienville's," the "Pet," both supposed to be English. After getting the schooners underway and securing their crews, one was placed in charge of Boatswain's Mate, Thomas Gallyer, of the "Bienville," and the other in charge of Acting-Master's Mate Johnson, with orders to proceed to the "Bienville," where they subsequently arrived in safety. Mr. French then proceeded in company with the other boat to perform the duty of destroying the "Wren"; but, finding it impracticable (owing to the strong current and wind against him, with his reduced crews) to find the "Wren," or make good headway, and having parted company from the other boat in the darkness, he concluded that it would be injudicious to proceed further, as day was approaching, and returned to his ship. On the whole, this might be called a good catch. The "Pet" had two hundred and fifty-six bales of cotton, and the "Annie Sophia" two hundred and twenty,—a handsome reward to the adventurous sailors who went on the expedition.

The dearth of blockade-running steamers made it more easy to capture this cotton, for the long, low runners generally laid well up the harbor under the protection of the forts, while the schooners had to move down to the lower bay to await a fair wind and get to sea when an opportunity offered.

Yet the steamers that did attempt to run the blockade often failed, as was the case with the "Will-o'-the-Wisp" (steamer), which was burned off Galveston by an expedition under Lieutenant O. E. McKay, of the "Princess Royal." The "Will-o'-the-Wisp" had been run on shore off the harbor of Galveston, where she was caught in the act of landing some heavy guns, and was chased on shore. On the night of the 9th of February, 1865, a boat expedition was fitted out by Commander M. B. Woolsey, consisting of two boats' crews, one from the "Princess Royal," and the other from the gun-boat "Antona," the whole under command of Lieutenant McKay, with orders to go in and destroy the steamer and prevent her landing the arms and stores she had on board. The boats shoved off from the "Princess Royal" between 2 and 3 A. M., while the ship and the "Antona" moved in toward shore and took up a position about nine hundred yards from the "Will-o'-the-Wisp." The boats soon reached and boarded the stranded steamer, set her on fire in the wheel-houses, and then returned to the "Princess Royal." She had previously been riddled by the fire of the two blockaders, and had been set on fire by their shells, so that she was almost a total wreck. The Confederates had shown their usual energy in getting out the cargo, the decks being torn up to enable them to do so. Even the engines had been taken to pieces and carried away, so that, when the boats reached her, she was not

worth wrecking. Although there was no resistance offered by the enemy, the attempt made by the boats was worthy of all praise. The Confederate cavalry had thrown up heavy breastworks, and it was expected that the landing party would meet with a stout resistance.

One gallant affair would inspire another, and these cutting-out expeditions became the order of the day. When they started out, no man knew what would be the result of an expedition until it was over, or what force was likely to be encountered. The enemy, knowing the adventurous spirit of the officers of the squadron, might set a trap for them, and, instead of getting a load of cotton, they might get a load of grapeshot.

The Confederates had fitted out a privateer or vessel-of-war, or whatever name that class of vessel might be recognized under—an armed schooner, the "Anna Dale," —which, on February 18, 1865, was lying in Pass Cavallo, Texas, waiting for part of her crew, when she intended to slip out to prey on Federal commerce. This vessel had been observed for several days apparently watching an opportunity to get to sea when the wind favored her. Lieutenant-Commander Henry Erben, Jr., of the "Panola," had been watching her closely, and at night kept picket-boats close to the inlet to see that she did not slip out without due notice from the boats. On the night of the 18th he sent in two armed boats, the gig and third cutter, to cut the schooner out, with Acting-Ensign James W. Brown in charge, assisted by Acting-Master's Mate John Rosling. The work was handsomely performed. The boats crossed the bar, which was quite smooth at the time, and found the schooner made fast to a wharf with a battery on shore close aboard. She had a pivot-gun mounted, and everything indicated that she was an armed vessel with this battery to protect her. Lights were seen moving about the decks, and men heard talking, when Mr. Brown made a dash for the schooner, boarded her, drove all the crew below that were on deck, and fastened down the hatches. The fasts were then cut and the vessel drifted out into the stream. Sail was made on the "Anna Dale," and everything done to take her out, but she grounded, and it was determined to destroy her. The prisoners, with their baggage, were put in one of the schooner's boats with some small arms and a 12-pounder howitzer, and the vessel was then set on fire.

The "Anna Dale" proved to be a Confederate privateer, but had not yet attained the dignity of being called a cruiser. She was of seventy tons burden, well armed, and commanded by Joseph L. Stephenson, a Master in the Confederate Navy, who said he expected twenty-five more men at sunset, and would have sailed soon after. He expressed great surprise that the boats were not fired upon by the battery, which consisted of three guns and a hundred men stationed only a short distance off. The "Anna Dale" was a fast schooner, and, had she escaped the vigilance of the blockaders and reached the northern coast, would no doubt have done much damage before she was captured.

This affair was certainly well executed and was without loss of life, which makes such events all the more acceptable. Acting-Ensign Brown was, no doubt, a gallant officer. He speaks in the highest terms of the behavior of Mr. Rosling and of Boatswain's Mate James Brown and Quarter-Master Benton Bunker, and the boat's crew generally. It will be observed that, in most of these affairs, the acting or volunteer officers bore very prominent parts. In all this kind of duty the volunteer element of the Navy was always conspicuous, it being more congenial to them than parading the deck and following the routine of a regular man-of-war. They were a tough, brave set of men, full of resources and worthy of every trust.

Captain Semmes, of the "Alabama," in his journal of that vessel's cruise, berates the volunteer officers of the Federal Navy, and calls them a low-lived set of fellows; but it must be remembered that, in the fight between the "Kearsarge" and "Alabama," nearly all the officers of the former were volunteers raised in the merchant service, then as fine a school of seamanship as any in the world; and under the training of their gallant and efficient first-lieutenant, Thornton, made a practice in gunnery that put to shame the firing of the English gunners that are said to have joined the "Alabama" from the English naval gunnery training-ship, the "Excellent." In this, perhaps, can be found the reason why Captain Semmes did not approve of them.

JOINT OPERATIONS IN MOBILE BAY BY REAR-ADMIRAL THATCHER AND GENERAL CANBY.

After the capture of Wilmington, Commodore James S. Palmer was relieved of the command of the West Gulf Squadron by Acting-Rear-Admiral H. K. Thatcher, an officer of great merit, who had shown good judgment and gallantry at Fort Fisher.

The moment Rear-Admiral Thatcher arrived at the scene of his command, he placed himself in communication with that gallant and efficient military commander, General Canby, and offered all the co-operation the Navy could give toward the capture of Mobile, which still held out,

notwithstanding all the forts in the bay had surrendered and the Confederate fleet had been captured. There was not the slightest chance of arms, munitions-of-war, or provisions reaching the Confederate army through Mobile, and the enemy continued to hold it simply from the same sentiment that governed every other part of the South. Though the demoralization in the Confederacy was plainly apparent to those who had eyes to see, yet the majority could not be made to believe that the Confederates could be subjugated. They could not be made to understand that there was anything fatal, in a military point of view, in Sherman's memorable march, though they received daily news of his successful marchings, his occupation of At-

REAR-ADMIRAL HENRY K. THATCHER.

lanta, Savannah, Columbia, and his advance to Goldsborough, driving before him an army quite equal in numbers to his own, before he was joined by Generals Schofield and Terry with some thirty thousand troops, and causing the ablest generals of the Confederacy to fall back before his triumphant legions. If the demoralization of the country could ever be brought to the surface, it was when General Joe Johnston was brought to bay at Smithsville, with Sherman's hardy veterans (that had marched through the South) confronting him, and the victorious troops of Schofield and Terry, just from Wilmington, hemming him in.

Some of the most intelligent men in the Confederacy (though the most deluded) clung to the idea that it was a physical impossibility for the South to be subjugated by the troops of the North. This impossibility was clearly stated by the Confederate Congress in an address to the Southern people as late as the winter of 1864–5; that the passage of hostile armies through the Southern country, though productive of cruel suffering to the people and great pecuniary loss, gave an enemy no permanent advantage or foothold. To subjugate a country, its civil government must be suppressed by a continuing military force, or supplanted by another, to which the inhabitants would be obliged to yield obedience. They insisted that the passage of troops through their country could not produce any such result. Permanent garrisons would have to be stationed at a sufficient number of points to strangle all civil authority and overawe the people before it could be pretended by the Federal Government that its authority could be extended over the Southern States. They claimed that to subdue the South would require more soldiers than the United States could raise to garrison all the different points. In a geographical point of view, therefore, it was asserted that the conquest of the Confederate States was impracticable. The geographical point of view was decisive to those who fomented the war in the first place, who adopted this as their creed with which to delude their suffering people; and when Sherman was marching his irresistible army all through the South, they could see nothing in it but a harbinger of good to their cause; though he had passed through the country, they asserted that he had not conquered it, and had not been able to leave a single garrison on his way since he left Dalton. They argued that, even if he passed out of the Carolinas, he would be defeated then, and all the country he had passed through would be re-opened to the Confederate armies. All such sophistries might pass muster with the ignorant, and this appeal to the common herd, no doubt, had its effect; but it was most absurd and criminal, to say the least of it, for the promoters of this rebellion to try and delude those upon whom all the suffering fell, when they could see the handwriting on the wall as plainly as it was seen at the feast of Belshazzar. All the deluded people should have known that, as Sherman's army sped along, everything in the shape of a soldier left the side-points of defence and joined the fleeing mass in the front. There was no use leaving garrisons in the rear, there was nothing to garrison. Wild desolation and ruin are always left in the tracks of such armies, and no General living

could prevent it any more than Lee could prevent destruction on his march to and from Gettysburg. The fact is, the Confederacy was in its last throes when Sherman started from Columbia, and the people of the South everywhere (owing to what the promoters of the rebellion called "the decay of public spirit") were getting impatient with the hardships of the war, having no longer any confidence in the ultimate results. Yet there were places, like Mobile, that had for a time flourished, owing to the constant flow of blockade-runners to their ports, and who knew but little of the sufferings of the war, and had never, in fact, been subjected to any hardships, determined to hold on to the last, even after Charleston fell. Ever since Admiral Farragut attempted and failed to reach the city of Mobile, the channel to which would not admit the Union vessels, that city had settled down to fancied security, no doubt waiting till Richmond should fall, and they could surrender with some show of determination to resist to the last. They did no harm to the Union, but their defiant attitude was offensive, and Canby and Thatcher determined to reduce their pretensions.

On the 8th of March, 1865, Rear-Admiral Thatcher received information from General Canby that there were indications that the enemy's forces in Mobile were about to evacuate their works, and had torn up some thirty miles of the Mobile and Montgomery railroad, in the neighborhood of Pollard, and were removing the material in the direction of Mongomery, and suggesting a reconnaissance in force. This Admiral Thatcher immediately undertook with the five Monitors he had at his disposal; and proceeding to reach a point in as close proximity to the city as the shallow water and the obstructions would permit, succeeded in drawing from the enemy a heavy fire, and demonstrated that the defences were intact and the Mobilians still determined on resistance.

It was therefore determined by the two Federal commanders to make a combined attack on the works and city without delay, and on March 21st the landing commenced from the transports under cover from the gun-boats on the right bank of Fish River, at a point called Danley's Mills, about seventeen miles above its junction with Mobile Bay. The gun-boats kept shelling the woods from Point Clear to Blakely River bar, while the troops were landing, to clear the coast of the enemy's forces supposed to be lurking in that vicinity, and also to draw the fire of the enemy's batteries, should there be any erected between Point Clear and Spanish Fort. Numerous streams had to be crossed, and many bridges built for the passage of artillery. The troops set to work, as soon as landed, to construct the bridges and to make their advance, while the light-draft gun-boats kept open communications with the army along shore by boats or signals.

General Granger had the immediate command of the Army, and this accomplished officer lost no time in pressing forward his troops. The first fruits of their labor was the fall of Spanish Fort and Fort Alexis, which surrendered on the 8th of April, 1865, after a heavy bombardment of ten hours from the Army and Navy. The Navy landed a battery of heavy guns under the command of Lieutenant-Commander G. H. Gillis, late of the " Milwaukee." General Canby commended the services of this battery highly in the attack on these forts, which the Confederates regarded as the key to Mobile.

Nearly two thousand prisoners and sixteen heavy guns, with ammunition in abundance, were taken in these works, while the enemy lost heavily in killed and wounded. Apalache and Blakely Rivers were at once dragged by the sailors in boats, and sixteen large submerged torpedoes were taken up. On the 10th instant the "Octorara," Lieutenant-Commander W. W. Low, and the iron-clads were succesful, by the diligent exertions of Commander Pierce Crosby, of the "Metacomet," in clearing the rivers of torpedoes, in moving up nearly abreast of Spanish Fort. From this position, Lieutenant-Commander Low, with his rifled gun, shelled forts Huger and Tracy with such effect that both forts were evacuated on the 11th instant, and the naval forces took possession, capturing a few prisoners in the adjoining marshes. The sailors held their position in these works till General Canby could garrison them with troops.

On April 12th, Rear-Admiral Thatcher moved with the gun-boats, convoying 8,000 men of General Granger's force to the west side of Mobile Bay, for the purpose of attacking Mobile. On their anchoring at the objective point, it was found that the Confederates had evacuated all their defences and retreated with their gun-boats up the Alabama River. The city of Mobile was thereupon summoned to an immediate and unconditional surrender by Rear-Admiral Thatcher and General Granger (General Canby being at Blakely), on the ground that it was entirely at the mercy of the Federal forces, they being in possession of the outside forts. The officers sent to make the formal demand for the surrender of the city were met by the Mayor and other civil authorities at the City Hall, where the former addressed the following letter to the Federal commanders :

MAYOR'S OFFICE,
CITY OF MOBILE, April 12, 1865.
GENTLEMEN—I have the honor to acknowledge the receipt of your communication at the hands of Lieutenant-Colonel R. G. Laughlin, of the staff of Major-General Granger, commanding Thirteenth Army Corps, and Lieutenant-Commander S. R. Franklin, United States Navy, of the staff of Admiral Thatcher, demanding the immediate and unconditional surrender of this city. The city has been evacuated by the military authorities, and its municipal authority is now within my control. Your demand has been granted, and I trust, gentlemen, for the sake of humanity, all the safeguards which we can throw around our people will be secured to them.

Very respectfully, your obedient servant,
R. H. SLOUGH,
Mayor of the City of Mobile.
MAJOR-GENERAL GORDON GRANGER,
Commanding Thirteenth Army Corps.
ACTING-REAR-ADMIRAL H. K. THATCHER,
Commanding West Gulf Squadron.

The flag of the United States was then hoisted on the City Hall, and a portion of the troops immediately advanced to preserve order and prevent pillage. A provost guard was established, and the works around the city, which were of immense strength and extent, were garrisoned.

Thus ended the contest with Mobile, which from the beginning of the war had enjoyed great immunity from battle and strife. It had been the medium through which millions of dollars worth of arms, provisions and clothing had reached the Confederate armies, and after defying the Federal forces unnecessarily when the war was virtually over, it was evacuated in a panic before the Federal gun-boats had fired a shot into the city.

While the Army was landing in front of Mobile, the "Octorara" and three river iron-clads worked their way up the Blakely River, and thence down the Tensas, and anchored in front of the city. They were sent at once up the Tombigbee River, where the Confederate iron-clad "Nashville" and the gun-boat "Morgan" had fled. The two powerful rams, "Huntsville" and "Tuscaloosa," were sunk in the Spanish River before the place was evacuated. The naval forces were at once set to work clearing the main ship channel of torpedoes and obstructions, which proved to be a formidable task. While picking up torpedoes, the tug-boat "Ida" was blown up and destroyed, as well as a steam-launch belonging to the "Cincinnati." The tug-boat "Althea" was destroyed by a torpedo in Blakely River, and the gun-boat "Sciota" was blown up while underway, running across the bay, in twelve feet of water, making the fifth vessel (with the "Milwaukee") sunk by torpedoes since Admiral Thatcher's operations began against the city.

On May 4, 1865, Rear-Admiral Thatcher received written proposals from Commodore Ebenezer Farrand, commanding the Confederate naval forces in Mobile waters, to surrender his ships, officers, men and public property generally, and desiring a meeting with the Admiral to arrange the terms. The two commanders met at Citronelle, a point about thirty-five miles above Mobile, and the surrender was agreed upon and accepted on the same basis and terms as were granted by General Grant to General Lee, by General Sherman to General Johnston, and by General Canby to General Taylor, which last surrender was made at the same place and time.

The day previous to the receipt of the proposal for surrender, Rear-Admiral Thatcher had made preparations for attacking the Confederate vessels in the Tombigbee, and the attack would have undoubtedly been made had Commodore Farrand delayed his surrender a day longer. As a matter of record, and as an interesting episode of the war, the conditions of the surrender are herewith inserted, with accompanying papers, which will be found to be interesting reading. It will be seen, on looking over the list of naval officers who surrendered, how many familiar names of those who once belonged to the United States Navy are found in that list—men who, after four years of hard work, found out how futile was the attempt to overturn a properly constituted and well-organized Government by a set of malcontents, who led away those whose true interests lay in supporting the Constitution and the flag to which they had sworn allegiance. They had no interest in supporting the political agitators who, for their own purposes and with no love of their Southern country, wanted to dissever themselves from the great union of States which alone made their country a great one. No doubt, when those who laid down their arms on that occasion look back and remember the fallacious hopes with which they were beguiled, and how little was done to make the condition better than it was in the United States, will, in their hearts, regret the day when they were tempted by State's-rights fallacies to desert a flag whose march from the time of our first Revolution has been an onward one of glory and honor. Not a star of its galaxy had ever been dimmed until those whose duty it was to hold it aloft, beyond the reach of treason, undertook to trail it in the dust and trample it under their feet. It shines brighter after all it has gone through than ever it did before, as gold is brightened by being purified by fire.

This was the last of the naval fighting of the war. The great fabric of the rebellion, with all its supports knocked away, toppled to the ground; and all who were engaged in it, seeing the hopelessness of their cause, seemed anxious to deliver up their trusts into the hands of the rightful proprietors, and make amends, as far as possible, for the injuries attempted against the Federal Government. Everything in Mobile and in the Confederate Navy Department was turned over in as good condition as might have been expected under existing circumstances. Among other prizes were four hundred heavy guns mounted in and about Mobile.

The Confederates evidently understood the importance of Mobile as a military base, and it was their intention to hold it at all hazards; yet, at one time, General Banks might have snatched this rich prize by weight of his superior numbers at New Orleans; but he preferred to go floundering around in the swamps and morasses of Texas and Louisiana, where no object was to be gained, and when he could not hold his own even with the large force he carried into those States.

COMPLIMENTARY LETTER TO ACTING-REAR-ADMIRAL THATCHER AND MAJOR-GENERAL GRANGER.

NAVY DEPARTMENT, April 29, 1865.

SIR—The Department has received your several dispatches, from time to time, advising it of your operations before Mobile; the last one, dated the 15th instant, announcing the surrender, on the day previous, to the Army and Naval forces commanded respectively by Major-General Granger and yourself.

The Department has watched with considerable interest, but with no fear of an unsuccessful result, the combined Army and Naval movements against the immediate defences of Mobile for the last few weeks, and after the capture of Fort Alexis and Spanish Fort, and the successful shelling resulting in the evacuation of Forts Tracy and Huger, was not surprised to learn of the retreat of the insurgent force to the interior, and the abandonment of their last formidable foothold on the coast.

Although no bloody strife preceded the capture of Mobile, the result was none the less creditable. Much had been expended to render it invulnerable, and nothing but the well-conducted preparations for its capture, which pointed to success, could have induced the rebel commander to abandon it with its formidable defences, mounting nearly four hundred guns, many of them of the newest pattern and heaviest calibre, its abundant supply of ammunition and ordnance stores, and its torpedo-planted roads and waters, without a serious conflict.

I am happy in extending to you and those under your command, and to Major-General Granger and those under his command, the congratulations for this victory, which places in our possession, with but one exception, all the chief points on the Southern coast, and bids fair to be the closing naval contest of the rebellion.

Very respectfully, etc.,
GIDEON WELLES,
Secretary of the Navy.
ACTING-REAR-ADMIRAL H. K. THATCHER,
Commanding West Gulf Blockading Squadron, etc.

CONDITIONS OF SURRENDER.

Memorandum of the conditions of the surrender of the Confederate naval forces serving under the command of Commodore Ebenezer Farrand in the waters of the State of Alabama, made at Sidney, Alabama, May 4, 1865 :

First—The officers and men to be paroled until duly exchanged, or otherwise released from the obligations of their parole, by the authority of the Government of the United States. Duplicate rolls of all officers and men surrendered to be made, one copy to be delivered to the officer appointed by Acting-Rear-Admiral H. K. Thatcher, and the other to be retained by the officer appointed by Commodore E Farrand; officers giving their individual paroles, and commanders of vessels signing a like parole for the men of their respective commands.

Second—All vessels-of-war, their guns and equipments, all small arms and ammunition and stores on board the said vessels, to be delivered over to an officer appointed for that purpose by Acting-Rear-Admiral Thatcher. Duplicate inventories of the property surrendered to be prepared; one copy to be retained by the officer delivering, and the other by the officer receiving it, for our information.

Third—The officers and men paroled under this agreement will be allowed to return to their homes, with the assurance that they will not be disturbed by the authorities of the United States so long as they continue to observe the condition of their paroles and the laws in force where they reside, except that persons resident of Northern States will not be allowed to return without special permission.

Fourth—The surrender of property will not include the side-arms or private baggage of officers.

Fifth—The time and place of surrender will be fixed by us, respectively, and will be carried out by officers appointed by us.

Sixth—After the surrender, transportation and subsistence to be furnished by Acting-Rear-Admiral Thatcher for officers and men to the nearest practical point to their respective homes.

H. K. THATCHER, *Acting-Rear-Admiral,*
Commanding Western Gulf Squadron.
E. FARRAND, *Flag-officer,*
Commanding C. S. Naval Force in waters of Alabama.

INSTRUCTIONS FROM ACTING-REAR-ADMIRAL H. K. THATCHER TO FLEET-CAPTAIN EDWARD SIMPSON.

WEST GULF SQUADRON,
U. S. FLAG-SHIP "STOCKDALE,"
OFF CITY OF MOBILE, May 8, 1865.

SIR—Having signed and exchanged copies of an agreement with Commodore E. Farrand, commanding officer of the vessels of the Confederate States Navy in the waters of the State of Alabama, on the 4th instant, the terms of which are contained in the inclosed document, you will proceed with the United States steamer "Cincinnati" to the Tombigbee River, the point designated for the surrender of the vessels under the command of Commodore Farrand and receive from the officer appointed by Commodore Farrand the said vessels, their guns, equipments and stores, the paroles of officers for themselves individually, and for the seamen, marines, etc., on board thereof who were under the command of Commodore E. Farrand on the 4th instant. Having received the surrender of said vessels, their appurtenances and stores, you will cause them to be brought down to a safe anchorage in front of the city of Mobile and report to me. Should any of the paroled officers or men desire to remain where they now are, they may do so; the others, in accordance with the terms of surrender, will receive transportation and subsistence to the nearest practical point to their respective homes. The steamers designated in verbal orders will accompany you to the Tombigbee. Suitable officers, engineers and

crews to navigate the surrendered vessels will accompany you to the place of surrender, and they alone will man them.

Very respectfully,
H. K. THATCHER, *Acting-Rear-Admiral,*
Commanding West Gulf Squadron.
COMMANDER EDWARD SIMPSON, *Fleet Captain,*
West Gulf Squadron.

REPORT OF FLEET-CAPTAIN EDWARD SIMPSON.

UNITED STATES FLAG SHIP "STOCKDALE,"
WEST GULF SQUADRON,
OFF MOBILE, ALA., May 11, 1865.

SIR—I have the honor to report that, in obedience to your order, I proceeded in the iron-clad steamer "Cincinnati" on the 19th instant up the Tombigbee River to Nanna Hubba Bluff for the purpose of receiving the surrender of the vessels under the command of Commodore Ebenezer Farrand, of the Confederate States Navy. The iron-clad steamer "Chickasaw" and the tin-clad "Nyanza" accompanied the "Cincinnati." On the morning of the 10th instant the vessels had all assembled at the bluff. Lieutenant-Commanding J. Myers, the officer appointed by Commodore Farrand to make the surrender, came on board, and after some consultation with me on the points of the condition of the surrender, surrendered the following vessels, viz.: "Morgan," side-wheel gun-boat ; "Nashville," side-wheel iron-clad ; "Baltic," side-wheel transport ; "Black Diamond," side-wheel river-boat.

I received inventories of the stores on board each vessel, as well as an inventory of stores brought from the naval station, which were stored on board of the river steamboat "Southern Republic," which vessel had been seized by Commodore Farrand for the purpose of receiving these articles when the naval station at Mobile was evacuated. A letter from the captain of the "Southern Republic" accompanies this report.

The only use that I have made of the vessel was to transport the Confederate officers and men to Mobile.

I received the accompanying rolls of all the officers and men, after which I paroled one hundred and twelve officers, two hundred and eighty-five enlisted men, and twenty-four marines. The officers gave their individual paroles in duplicate, and the commanding officers gave their paroles for the men of their respective commands.

Having completed the duty on which I was ordered, I have returned to Mobile with a portion of the vessels.

I inclose the memorandum of the conditions for the surrender, a copy of my instructions, and a copy of the instructions given to Lieutenant-Commanding J. Myers by Commodore Farrand, and also the invoices of the stores, etc., received.

Very respectfully, your obedient servant,
E. SIMPSON,
Fleet Captain, West Gulf Squadron.
ACTING-REAR-ADMIRAL H. K. THATCHER,
Commanding West Gulf Squadron.

INSTRUCTIONS FROM COMMODORE FARRAND, C. S. N., TO LIEUTENANT COMMANDING JULIAN MYERS, C. S. N.

HEADQUARTERS NAVAL COMMAND,
STEAMER "SOUTHERN REPUBLIC,"
McDOWELL'S LANDING, May 5, 1865.

SIR—You will proceed to Nanna Hubba Bluff for the purpose of carrying out the terms of surrender of the naval forces under my command, agreed upon on the 4th instant, a copy of which is herewith inclosed.

Very respectfully, your obedient servant,
EBEN. FARRAND, *Flag-officer, etc.*
LIEUTENANT-COMMANDING JULIUS MYERS,
P. N. C. S., Steamer "Southern Republic."

PAROLE GIVEN BY, AND LIST OF, OFFICERS AND MEN SURRENDERED

We, the undersigned, prisoners-of-war belonging to the Confederate naval forces serving under the command of Commodore Ebenezer Farrand, in the waters of the State of Alabama, this day surrendered by Commodore Ebenezer Farrand to Acting-Rear-Admiral Henry K. Thatcher, United States Navy, commanding the West Gulf Squadron, do hereby give our solemn parole of honor that we will not hereafter serve in the Navy of the Confederate States, or in any military capacity whatever, against the United States of America, or render aid to the enemies of the latter, until properly exchanged in such manner as shall be mutually approved by the respective authorities.

Done at Nanna Hubba Bluff, on the Tombigbee River, Alabama, this tenth day of May, eighteen hundred and sixty-five.

L. Rosseau, Captain; Ebenezer Farrand, Flag-officer; Charles W. Hays, Lieutenant; Julian Myers, Lieutenant; C. P. McGavy, Lieutenant; Charles E. Yeatman, Lieutenant; F. Watlington, Lieutenant; E. G. Booth, Assistant Surgeon; N. E. Edwards, Assistant Surgeon; Wm. W. J. Wells, Paymaster; Robert C. Powell, Assistant Surgeon; Wm. Fisk, Jr., Chief Engineer; Albert P. Hulse, Secretary; E. Lloyd Winder, Lieutenant; P. U. Murphy, Lieutenant; J. E. Armour, Paymaster; Lewis W. Munro, Surgeon; A. L. Myers, Master; D. R. Lindsay, Naval Storekeeper; Thos. G. Lang, Third-Assistant Engineer; D. B. Conrad, Fleet Surgeon; Geo. H. Oneal, Assistant Paymaster; J. M. Pearl, Assistant Paymaster; J. R. Jordan, First-Assistant Engineer; S. S. Herrick, Assistant Surgeon; F. B. Dorwin, Passed-Midshipman; J. S. Wooddell, Clerk; John H. Pippen, Clerk; John E. O'Connell, Second-Assistant Engineer; W. B. Patterson, Third-Assistant Engineer; Edward Cairy, Assistant Surgeon; Jos. Preble, Acting-Master; G. W. Turner, Acting-Master's Mate; W. A. Gardner, Third-Assistant Engineer; G. E. Courtin, Paymaster's Clerk; Edward P. Herssend, ——; Jos. L. Wilson, Paymaster's Clerk; Jas. H. Marsh, Navy Yard Clerk; Benjamin G. Allen, Gunner; J. R. Shackett, Pilot; G. H. Lindenberger, Mechanic; W. D. Crawford, ——; J. H. Hunt, A. M. M., Commanding steamer "Baltic"; Ira W. Porter, Acting-Gunner; B. H. Weaver, Acting-Assistant Engineer; J. W. Bennett, Lieutenant-Commanding; G. A. Joiner, Passed-Midshipman; Wm. Carroll, Passed-Midshipman; G. H. Wellington, Third-Assistant Engineer; Z. A. Offutt, Gunner; Howard Quigley, First-Assistant Engineer; H. S. Smith, Gunner; C. H. Mallery, Gunner; J. M. Smith, Paymaster's Clerk; George Newton, Sailmaker; Thos. L. Harrison, Lieutenant; O. S. Iglehart, Passed-Assistant Surgeon; D. G. Raney, Jr., First-Lieutenant, M. C.; W. G. Craig, Master P. N. C. S.; Jos. R. De Mahy, Master P. N. C. S.; M. M. Seay, Assistant Paymaster P. N. C. S.; N. M. Read, Assistant Surgeon; G. D. Lining, First-Assistant Engineer; J. R. Y. Fendall, First-Lieutenant C. S. M.; A. P. Beinre, Passed-Midshipman; R. J. Deas, Passed-Midshipman; E. Debois, Second-Assistant Engineer; M. M. Rogers, Third-Assistant Engineer; F. A. Lombard, Third-Assistant Engineer; Charles A. Joullian, Third-Assistant Engineer; J. Fulton, Third-Assistant Engineer; G. W. Nailor, Third-Assistant Engineer; Wm. Fink, Paymaster's Clerk; F. B. Green, Master's Mate; Avery S. Winston, Master's Mate P. N. C. S.; John Curney, ——; Jos. M. Walker, Pilot; W. L. Cameron, Paymaster's Clerk; Louis Williams, Engineer; M. L. Shropshire, Acting-First-Assistant Engineer; J. V. Harris, Assistant Surgeon; Benj. Herring, First-Engineer; J. P. Redwood, Clerk; E. W. Johnson, Master's Mate; James White, Master's Mate; Wm. C. Dogger, Engineer; Wm. P. A. Campbell, First Lieutenant;

Julian M. Spencer, First-Lieutenant; Jasan C. Baker, First-Lieutenant; W. F. Robinson, Second-Lieutenant; Robert F. Freeman, Passed-Assistant Surgeon; G. W. Claiborne, Assistant Surgeon; H. E. McDuffie, Assistant Paymaster; A. N. Bully, Master; W. Youngblood, Chief-Engineer; John L. Rapier, Second-Lieutenant; Wm. Fauntleroy, Second-Assistant Engineer; Geo. J. Weaver, Second-Assistant Engineer; J. Thomas Maybury, Gunner; S. H. McMaster, Paymaster's Clerk; H. L. Manning, Master's Mate; Joseph Fry, Lieutenant Commanding; Page M. Baker, Master's Mate; John G. Blackwood, First-Lieutenant; Wm. H. Haynes, Gunner; Hiram G. Goodrich, Third-Assistant-Engineer; John Applegate, Third-Assistant-Engineer; Jacob H. Turner, Acting-Master's Mate; Thomas A. Wakefield, Third-Assistant-Engineer; J. D. Johnson, Commander; W. W. Graves, Assistant Surgeon; W. T. J. Kunsh, Third-Assistant-Engineer; Henry D. Bassett, Acting-Constructor.

The next inclosure is the parole given by the seamen of the Confederate States Navy serving on different vessels, fifty-three in number, entered into in their behalf by Julian Myers, Acting-Fleet Captain.

The next, the parole given by one hundred and twenty men of the steamer "Morgan," entered into in their behalf by Joseph Fry, Lieutenant Commanding the "Morgan."

The next, the parole given by one hundred and twelve men of the "Nashville," entered into in their behalf by J. W. Bennett, Lieutenant Commanding the "Nashville."

The next, the parole given by twenty-four marines entered into in their behalf by D. G. Raney, Jr., First Lieutenant, Confederate States Marine Corps, commanding marines.

ENTRANCE OF GUN-BOATS INTO BLAKELY RIVER— COMPLIMENTARY LETTER RELATIVE TO COMMODORE PALMER.

UNITED STATES FLAG-SHIP "STOCKDALE," }
WEST GULF SQUADRON,
MOBILE, ALA., May 3, 1865. }

SIR—The Department was informed by Commodore Palmer, under date of February 10, 1865, that he would avail himself of the permission granted by it to return North after the fall of Mobile; and as he is now about to leave this squadron, I beg leave to say that he has rendered me most efficient and untiring service throughout the attack upon the defences of the city, which has resulted so favorably to our arms; and I am indebted to him for the admirable manner in which the vessels to be employed for this service were prepared under his supervision previous to my arrival on the station, and I part with him with reluctance and regret.

It was the belief of the enemy that it would be impossible for our Monitors and gun-boats to cross the Blakely River bar, owing to the shallowness of the water; but, should we succeed in doing so, their hope rested in our entire destruction by the innumerable torpedoes with which they had filled the river, combined with their marsh batteries; and they well knew that our success in overcoming these obstacles would be fatal to them; but by great exertions night and day we succeeded.

Commodore Palmer commanded the first division, consisting of the Monitors and "Octorara," and successfully ascended the Blakely with them, coming down the Tensas, directly in front of the city; the remainder of the gun-boats, led by the flag-ship, convoying General Granger's command for the purpose of making a joint attack in flank and front. These movements, having been anticipated by the enemy, led to the evacuation; and, although Commodore Palmer did not have the satisfaction of bombarding the city, he had placed himself in a position to do so effectually had not the rebels deprived him of the opportunity by flight.

Very respectfully, your obedient servant,

H. K. THATCHER, *Acting Rear-Admiral,*
Commanding West Gulf Squadron.

HON. GIDEON WELLES,
Secretary of the Navy.

There seems to have been an unusual loss of Federal vessels in these combined operations, from the effects of torpedoes, which might indicate a want of due care in approaching the rivers, where it was known that quantities of these infernal machines were planted; but, because these vessels were destroyed in their anxiety to get ahead, it detracts nothing from the character of Rear-Admiral Thatcher and his officers for the apparent want of that prudence which every officer should exhibit in all military operations, who has the lives of officers and men at his disposal. It is well known now that Mobile was better supplied with torpedoes than any other point, with perhaps the exception of the James River, and those at Mobile having been put down at the last moment were more than usually dangerous.

The "Milwaukee," Lieutenant-Commander J. H. Gillis, and the "Osage," Lieutenant-Commander W. M. Gamble, were sunk at the entrance to Blakely River, the former on the 28th of March and the latter on the 29th. The tin-clad "Rodolph" was sunk by a torpedo on the 1st of April, while towing a scow with implements to try and raise the "Milwaukee." These, with the two steam-tugs, two launches, and the gun-boat "Sciota" (blown up), made eight vessels in all destroyed on this occasion. Fortunately the war was over and the Government did not need the vessels, which were valuable ones.

The following is a list of the losses experienced by the sinking of the vessels named above:

"Osage," 3 killed, 8 wounded; "Rodolph," 4 killed, 11 wounded; "Cincinnati's" launch, 3 killed; "Althea," 2 killed, 2 wounded; "Sciota," 4 killed, 6 wounded; "Ida," 2 killed, 3 wounded.

Though the war may be said to have virtually ended by the surrender of General Lee, on April 9th, 1865, and of General Joe Johnston, on April 27th, and naval and military operations against the Confederates may be said to have ceased, yet up to the last moment the Texans were apparently as active as ever in their domain, and for a short time it looked as if they were going "to fight it out on that line, if it took all summer."

One of their last acts was an attempt to run the blockade with the ram "Webb," which had made herself so famous in sinking the "Indianola." The "Webb" was remarkably fast and a good sea-going vessel. She was loaded with cotton by private parties, who at the same time were prepared to fight, and had put on board a crew of forty-five men. Besides the cotton, part of her cargo was made up of rosin and turpentine.

No one was thinking of such an attempt, when the "Webb" appeared above New Orleans on April 24th, 1865, running at full speed, and passed down the river. She was flying the United States flag, and had a torpedo on a pole projecting from the bow. Every one who saw the "Webb" took her for an army transport, but, being finally recognized by some one, she received two shot in her hull, which, however, did no damage.

The "Hollyhock," Lieutenant-Commander Bancroft Gherardi; the "Florida," Acting-Volunteer-Lieutenant-Commander Wm. Budd; the "Quaker City," Commander Wm. F. Spicer, and the "Ossipee," Commander Wm. E. LeRoy, got underway as soon as they could get up steam and went in pursuit of the "Webb," the "Hollyhock" far in the lead. When the "Webb" was about twenty-five miles below New Orleans, she encountered the "Richmond," Captain Theodore P. Green, coming up the river. The chances for her escape being thus cut off, the "Webb" was headed for the left bank of the river and run ashore, and was set on fire by her commander, Edward G. Reed, formerly of the United States Navy. Her cargo, being very inflammable, she was soon ablaze from stem to stern and blew up, the crew escaping to the shore.

Thus ended the career of this remarkable ram, that had caused, at times, a good deal of uneasiness along the river and had done considerable damage. She followed in the footsteps of all the Confederate rams, and was the last one that we know of that was at that time owned by the Confederacy. The following officers of the "Webb" gave themselves up, after having been pursued to the swamps by the Navy: Lieutenant Read, her late commanding officer; Lieutenant Wm. H. Wall, Master S. P. LeBlanc, Passed-Midshipman H. H. Scott, Assistant Surgeon W. J. Addison, and Pilot James West.

It was not until the 25th of May that the Confederates began to evacuate their fortified places in Texas and return to their homes. The first place evacuated was the works at Sabine Pass, which had been a point both parties had contended for throughout the war.

About May 27th, the Confederate Army in Texas generally disbanded, taking advantage of the terms of surrender entered into and executed at New Orleans between the Confederate Commissioners and General Canby, of the U. S. Army, where all the Confederate fortifications and property was given up.

No Confederate naval force was left in Texas except the remains of the ram "Missouri," which was surrendered to the commander of the Mississippi Squadron.

Galveston was surrendered on the 7th of June, and the place taken possession of by the gun-boats under Captain B F. Sands, who took the proper steps to buoy out the channel and take charge of the Government property. Rear - Admiral Thatcher visited the civil authorities on shore, who seemed to be well satisfied with the turn affairs had taken, and again and again reiterated their desire that there should be no disturbance of the existing state of affairs, and requesting that a portion of the gunboats should be kept at Galveston for the protection of the city! All the forts throughout the State as far as Brownsville were

soon after garrisoned by United States troops, and thus ended the war in Texas.

When peace was concluded, the Texans were determined to observe the terms religiously. These people had fought bravely and squarely, resorting to few, if any, of the tricks and offensive measures pursued by the home-guards along the Cumberland and Tennessee Rivers ; and when they laid down their arms and returned to their homes, it was evidently with the intention of not taking them up again except to defend the flag against which they had been so lately fighting.

The gallant old officer, Acting-Rear-Admiral Thatcher, was relieved a short time after from his command, which he had conducted with vigor and remarkable judgment. He was made a full Rear-Admiral for the services he had rendered during the war, and no officer in the Navy better deserved the honors he had won or the rewards he had reaped.

WEST GULF SQUADRON, JANUARY 1, 1865.

COMMODORE JAMES S. PALMER.

STAFF—LIEUTENANT-COMMANDER S. R. FRANKLIN, FLEET-CAPTAIN ; FLEET-PAYMASTER, EDWARD T. DUNN ; FLEET-SURGEON, JAMES C. PALMER ; FLEET-ENGINEER, WILLIAM H. SHOCK ; ASSISTANT-SURGEON, THEORON WOOLVERTON ; ACTING-ENSIGNS, FREDERICK T. MASON, ALEX. S. GIBSON, T. M. L. CHRYSTIE, AIDES.

"RICHMOND"—SECOND-RATE.

Captain, Thornton A. Jenkins; Lieutenant-Commander, Edw. A. Terry; Acting-Volunteer-Lieutenant, Chas. J. Gibbs; Surgeon, L. J. Williams; Assistant Surgeon, J. McD. Rice; Paymaster, Edwin Stewart; Second-Lieutenant of Marines, C. L. Sherman ; Acting-Masters and Pilots, J. W. Grivet and C. J. Lawrence; Ensign, P. H. Cooper; Acting-Ensigns, C. M. Chester, Lewis Clark and A. H. Wright; Acting-Master's Mate, T. J. Werner; Engineers: Chief, Jackson McElmell; First-Assistant, E. J. Brooks ; Second-Assistants, John Wilson, A. J. Kenyon, Absalom Kirby, Robert Weir and William H. Crawford ; Third-Assistant, C. W. Senter ; Acting-Third-Assistant, Thomas McElmell; Boatswain, I. T. Choate ; Acting-Gunner, Addison Fisk ; Acting-Carpenter, O. W. Griffiths; Sailmaker, William Rogers.

"LACKAWANNA"—SECOND-RATE.

Captain, George F. Emmons; Lieutenant-Commander, Chas. S. Norton ; Lieutenants, S. A. McCarty and C. D. Jones; Surgeon, Thomas W. Leach; Acting - Assistant Surgeon, W. F. Hutchinson ; Assistant Paymaster, Geo. S. Benedict; Acting-Master, John H. Allen ; Ensigns, Geo. H. Wadleigh and Frank Wildes; Acting-Ensigns, Clarence Rathbone, F. A. Cook and W. J. Lewis ; Engineers: Acting-Chief, W. A. R. Latimer ; Second-Assistant, G. W. Roche; Acting-Second-Assistant, John Miller; Third-Assistant, I. B. Fort; Acting-Third-Assistants, G. W. Russell and T. W. Sillman; Acting-Boatswain, J. G. Briggs; Gunner, J. G. Foster.

"POTOMAC"—FOURTH RATE.

Commander, A. Gibson; Acting-Assistant Surgeon, E. S. Smith ; Acting-Assistant Paymaster, J. H.

Wood; Chaplain, Robert Given ; Acting-Ensigns, R. Canfield, T. H. Baker, Thos. McLeavy, J. B. Barker and J. H. Church ; Acting-Master's Mate, A. Whiting.

"MONONGAHELA"—SECOND-RATE.

Commander, James H. Strong; Lieutenants, T. C. Bowen and Oliver A. Batcheller ; Acting-Assistant Surgeon, Henry Rockwood ; Assistant Paymaster, Forbes Parker ; Acting-Ensigns, Geo. Gerrad, P. F. Harrington and D. W. Mullan ; Acting-Master's Mate, W. B. Arnaud ; Engineers: Chief, Geo. F. Kutz ; First-Assistant, Joseph Trilley ; Second-Assistants, John J. Bissett, Edward Cheney and P. J. Langer; Acting-Third-Assistants, A. C. Wilcox and H. L. Churchill ; Boatswain, Wm. Green ; Acting-Gunner, M. B. Means.

"PORTSMOUTH"—THIRD-RATE.

Commander, Louis C. Sartori ; Acting-Assistant Surgeon, William C. Lyman; Assistant Paymaster, E. Putnam; Acting-Masters, John Wallace and H. M. Peirce; Acting-Ensigns, J. F. Perkins and J. P. Pearson; Acting-Master's Mates, T. H. Jenks and T. S. Flood; Gunner, W. Cheney; Carpenter, G. E. Burcham; Sailmaker, L. B. Wakeman.

"OSSIPEE"—SECOND-RATE.

Commander, Wm. E. LeRoy; Lieutenants, John A. Howell and Richard S. Chew; Surgeon, B. F. Gibbs; Acting-Assistant Paymaster, W. L. Pynchon; Acting-Masters, C. C. Bunker and H. S. Lambert ; Acting-Ensigns, Charles E. Clark and W. A. Van Vleck; Engineers: Acting-Chief, James M. Adams; Second-Assistants, W. W. Vanderbilt and W. H. De Hart; Acting-Second-Assistants, M. H. Gerry, J. R. Webb, G. W. Kidder and William Collier; Boatswain, Andrew Milne; Gunner, J. Q. Adams.

"BIENVILLE" – SECOND-RATE.

Commander, J. R. M. Mullany; Lieutenant, Henry L. Howison; Passed-Assistant Surgeon, A. C. Rhoades; Acting-Assistant Paymaster, W. W. Goodwin; Acting-Master, T. N. Meyer; Acting-Ensigns, Emile J. Enfer, G. H. French and F. O. Abbott; Acting-Master's Mates, J. R. Lee, T. H. Soule, Jr., and O. G. Spear; Engineers: Acting-Chief, Wm. F. Wright; Acting-First-Assistant, Warren Ewen; Acting-Second Assistants, P. O. Brightman and E. D. Merritt; Acting-Third-Assistants, D. J. O'Keefe and Edward Torallas; Acting-Gunner, Wm. T Laforge.

"SEMINOLE"—THIRD-RATE.

Commander, Albert G. Clary; Acting-Volunteer-Lieutenant, George Mundy; Surgeon, J. C. Spear; Paymaster, L. S. Stockwell; Acting-Master, Wm. A. Maine; Acting-Ensigns, D. K. Perkins, Francis Kempton and W. S. Church; Acting-Master's Mates, Henry Webb and C. A. Thorne; Engineers: Acting-First-Assistants, Claude Babcock and A. R. Calden; Acting-Third-Assistants, Wm. Drinkwater, P. J. Hughes and Geo. Ellis.

"ONEIDA"—THIRD-RATE.

Commander, Thomas H. Stephens; Lieutenants, C. L. Huntington and E. N. Kellogg; Surgeon, John J. Gibson; Assistant-Paymaster, G. R. Martin; Acting-Ensign, Chas. V. Vridley; Acting-Master's Mates, Edward Bird and Daniel Clark; Engineers: Chief, Wm. H. Hunt; Second-Assistant, David Hardie; Acting-Second-Assistants, B. S. Cooke and W. C. Barrett; Acting-Boatswain, Hallowell Dickinson.

"PRINCESS ROYAL"—THIRD-RATE.

Commander, M. B. Woolsey; Lieutenant, Chas. E. McKay; Acting Assistant Surgeon, T. R. Chandler; Acting-Assistant Paymaster, F. T. Morton; Acting-Ensigns, A. H. Reynolds, T. A. Witham, J. J. Moule and C. K. Porter; Acting-Master's Mates, Wm. E. Cannon and Lewis Johnson; Engineers: Acting-First-Assistant, Wm. Huntley; Second-Assistant, J. E. Fallon; Acting-Third-Assistants, A. J. Redmond, Peter Taylor and Geo. W. Caldwell.

"OCTORARA"—THIRD-RATE.

Lieutenant-Commander, Wm. W. Low; Acting-Volunteer-Lieutenant, Wm. D. Urann; Assistant Surgeon, E. R. Dodge; Acting-Assistant Paymaster, J. H. Pynchon; Acting-Masters, H. S. Young and M. W. McEntee; Acting-Ensigns, Geo. H. Dodge and J. N. Frost; Acting-Master's Mates, Geo. P. Gifford and Geo. W. Adams; Engineers: W. W. Shipman, R. B. Plotts and Joseph Knight.

"KICKAPOO"—FOURTH-RATE.

Lieutenant-Commander, M. P. Jones; Acting-Volunteer-Lieutenant, D. C. Woods; Acting-Assistant Surgeon, Foster Thayer; Acting-Assistant Paymaster, F. B. Gilbert; Acting-Masters, S. V. Bennis and DeWayne Stebbins; Acting-Ensigns, J. W. Chandler, Ezra Bassett, F. W. Grantzour and G. G. Tripp; Acting-Master's Mates. E. R. Bradley and L. W. Sedam; Engineers: Acting-Chief, D. C. Riter; Acting-First-Assistant, G. W. Lumpkins; Acting-Second-Assistants, N. F. Johnson, Andrew Dolan and Samuel M. Sykes; Acting-Third-Assistants, Wm. T. Baxter, Wm. S. Robb, John Feihl and Martin Hilands; Acting-Gunner, J. H. Howe; Acting-Carpenter, Wm. Ostermeyer.

"METACOMET"—THIRD-RATE.

Lieutenant-Commander, James E. Jouett; Acting-Volunteer-Lieutenant, H. J. Sleeper; Assistant Surgeon, E. D. Payne; Acting-Assistant Paymaster, H. M. Harriman; Acting-Masters, C. C. Gill and H. C. Nields; Acting-Master and Pilot, R. Riggs; Acting-Ensigns, James Brown and R. N. Miller; Acting-Master's Mates, J. K. Goodwin and Chas. Harcourt; Engineers: First-Assistant, James Atkins;

Second-Assistants, C. H. Ball and G. P. Hunt; Acting-Third-Assistants, J. H. Nash, S. W. King and Patrick Maloney; Acting-Gunner, James Lamon.

"KINEO"—FOURTH-RATE.

Lieutenant-Commander, John Watters; Lieutenant, Chas. S. Cotton; Acting-Assistant Surgeon, E. S. Perkins; Acting-Assistant Paymaster, Allen J. Clark; Acting-Ensigns, H. W. Mather, W. S. Keen and D. J. Starbuck; Engineers: Acting-Second-Assistant, J. S. Harper; Acting-Third-Assistant, Richard Thall.

' J. P. JACKSON"—FOURTH-RATE.

Lieutenant-Commander, Bancroft Gherardi; Acting-Volunteer-Lieutenant, L. W. Pennington; Acting-Assistant Surgeon, Thomas S. Yard; Acting-Assistant Paymaster, Chas. B. Perry; Acting-Master, H. R. Billings; Acting-Masters and Pilots, James Maycock and Henry Rehder; Acting-Ensigns, W. H. Howard and Jos. H. Wainwright; Acting-Master's Mates, Achilles Kalniski and C. T. Taylor; Engineers: Acting-Second-Assistant, Charles Goodman; Acting-Third-Assistants, J. D. Caldwell, Albert Mayer and J. E. Hare.

"CAYUGA" – FOURTH-RATE.

Lieutenant-Commander, Henry Wilson; Acting-Assistant Surgeon, J. E. Parsons; Acting-Assistant Paymaster. Wm. A. Mann; Acting-Master, John Hanson; Acting-Ensigns, W. F. Dolliver, Isaac A. Abbott, Robert Morris and E. P. Stevens; Engineers: Second-Assistants, J. C. Chaffee and W. A. H. Allen; Acting-Third-Assistants, Thomas Kidd and J. D. Thompson.

"PENOBSCOT"—FOURTH-RATE.

Lieutenant-Commander, A. E. K. Benham; Acting-Assistant Surgeon, F. C. Sargeant; Assistant Paymaster, F. P. Hinman; Acting Master, Charles E. Jack; Acting-Ensigns, Edw. Pendexter, T. McL. Miller, W. G. Campbell and Wm. Wingood, Jr.; Engineers: Acting-First-Assistant, W. M. Rodes; Acting-Third-Assistants, Warren Howland, E. T. Henry and John Carey.

"GENESEE"—THIRD-RATE.

Lieutenant-Commander, John Irwin; Acting-Assistant Surgeon, W. L. Wheeler; Acting-Assistant Paymaster, F. C. Alley; Acting-Masters, F. H. Grove, Wm. Hanson and Edwin Crissey; Acting-Ensigns, Sydney Hall, John Cannon and G. B. Foster; Acting-Master's Mate, J. N. Peabody; Engineers: Second-Assistants, T. W. Rae, M. W. Mather, Michael McLaughlin and Christopher Nulton; Third-Assistant, E. W. Clark; Acting-Third-Assistant, John H. Dee.

"AROOSTOOK"—FOURTH-RATE.

Lieutenant-Commander, Joseph S. Skerrett; Acting-Assistant Surgeon, J. H. Richards; Acting-Assistant Paymaster, E. St. C. Clarke; Acting-Master, P. S. Borden; Acting-Ensigns, John Griffin and Wm. Barker; Acting-Master's Mate, Edward Culbert; Engineers: Second-Assistants, Samuel Gragg and James Entwistle; Acting-Third-Assistants, Nathan Brown, L. M. Reenstjerna and J. P. Somerby.

"VINCENNES"—THIRD-RATE.

Lieutenant-Commander, C. H. Greene; Assistant Surgeon, J. W. Newcomer; Acting–Assistant Paymaster, Samuel Jordan; Acting-Masters, A. E. Hunter and L. A. Brown; Acting-Ensign, Robert Henderson; Acting-Boatswain, John Smith; Acting-Gunner, Wm. Kneeland; Sailmaker, Geo. Thomas.

"MILWAUKEE"—FOURTH-RATE.

Lieutenant-Commander, James H. Gillis; Acting-Volunteer-Lieutenant, F. John Grover; Acting-Assistant Surgeon, N. Brewster; Acting-Assistant Paymaster, G. S. Horne; Acting-Master, Geo. W. Garrison; Acting-Ensigns, N. T. Crocker, E. D. Springer,

R. L. E. Coombs and J. W. Crocker; Acting-Master's Mates, Geo. H. Cole, T. W. Stuart and G. W. Perrigo; Engineers: First-Assistant, John Purdy, Jr.; Acting-Second-Assistants, Chas. Metzger, John Adkins, Henry Bauer, S. W. Evans and Frank Leonard; Acting-Third-Assistants, F. A. Hurd, Jacob Wahl, H. L. Dickerson, Morgan Lutton, J. Henry Blanch and W. A. Blanch.

" SEBAGO "—THIRD-RATE.

Lieutenant-Commander, Wm. E. Fitzhugh; Acting-Assistant Surgeon, T. Munson Coan; Assistant Paymaster, Henry A. Strong; Acting-Master, J. B. Rodgers; Acting-Master and Pilot, J. H. Collins; Acting-Ensigns, E. D. Martin, S. G. Blood and J. T. Hamilton; Acting-Master's Mates, Thomas Elsmore and W. A. Hynard; Engineers: Acting-First Assistant, Wm. H. Morris; Acting-Second-Assistant, W. P. Ayres; Acting-Third-Assistants, Robert Miller and Franklin Babcock; Acting-Gunner, John Roberts.

" KENNEBEC "—FOURTH-RATE.

Lieutenant-Commander, Trevett Abbott; Acting-Volunteer-Lieutenant, Edward Baker; Acting-Assistant Surgeon, W. H. Taggert; Acting-Assistant Paymaster, Elisha Ward; Acting-Masters, A. L. Emerson and J. J. Butler; Acting-Ensigns, J. D. Ellis; Acting-Master's Mate, A. A. Mann; Engineers: Second-Assistant, L. W. Robinson; Acting-Second-Assistant, J. S. Pearce; Acting-Third-Assistants, J. N. Johnson and James Eccles.

" ITASCA "—FOURTH-RATE.

Lieutenant-Commander, George Brown; Surgeon, David Kindleberger; Acting-Assistant Paymaster, A. G. Lathrop; Acting-Master, Richard Hustace; Acting-Ensigns, C. H. Hurd, James Igo and E. S. Lowe; Acting-Master's Mates, Marcus Chapman and L. E. Heath; Engineers: Second-Assistants, John Borthwick and G. C. Irelan; Acting-Second-Assistant, Alfred Hoyt; Acting-Third-Assistant, C. A. Laws.

" KANAWHA "—FOURTH-RATE.

Lieutenant-Commander, Bushrod B. Taylor; Acting-Assistant Surgeon, F. W. Brigham; Acting-Assistant Paymaster, W. O. Jube; Acting-Ensigns, W. A. Purdie, R. P. Boss, F. H. Deering and E. R. Westcott; Acting-Master's Mate, James J. Clark; Engineers: Second-Assistant, M. M. Murphy; Acting-Third-Assistants, B. F. Sanborn, Anthony Higgins, W. D. Pancake and P. H. Friel.

" PEMBINA "—FOURTH-RATE.

Lieutenant-Commander, J. G. Maxwell; Acting-Assistant Surgeon, A. R. Holmes; Acting-Assistant Paymaster, Walter Fuller; Acting-Masters, Bowen Allen and F. E. Ellis; Acting-Ensigns, Wm. Lyddon, B. M. Chester, Chas. Putnam and C. L. Crandall; Acting-Master's Mate, H. T. Davis; Engineers: Third-Assistants, C. F. Nagle, C. F. Stroud and Augustus Dewitt.

" PANOLA."—FOURTH-RATE.

Lieutenant-Commander, Henry Erben; Acting-Assistant Surgeon, A. Y. Hanson; Acting-Assistant Paymaster, A. B. Robinson; Acting-Ensigns, C. V. Rummell, J. W. Brown and A. P. Gibbs; Acting-Master's Mate, John Rosling; Engineers: Second-Assistant, Howard D. Potts; Acting-Second-Assistants, S. A. Appold and J. B. McGavern; Acting-Third-Assistants, Philip Ketler and F. E. Hosmer.

" CHOCURA "—FOURTH-RATE.

Lieutenant-Commander, Richard W. Meade, Jr.; Acting-Assistant Surgeon, Charles Gaylord; Acting-Assistant Paymaster, J. G. Tobey; Acting-Master, Alfred Washburn; Acting-Ensigns, T. F. Tracy, M. Carver, Robert Beardsley, A. P. Atwood and T. G. Watson; Engineers: Second-Assistants, H. H. Moloney and Theodore Cooper; Acting-

Second-Assistant, O. D. Hughes; Third-Assistants, N. H. Lawton and Andrew Blythe.

" WINNEBAGO "—FOURTH-RATE.

Lieutenant-Commander, W. A. Kirkland; Acting-Assistant Surgeon, J. G. Bell; Acting-Assistant Paymaster, Henry Gerrard; Acting-Master, A. S. Meggathlin; Acting-Master and Pilot, Wm. H. Wroten; Acting-Ensigns, James Whitworth, Michael Murphy and John Morrisey, Jr.; Acting-Master's Mates, Wm. Edgar, H. C. Atter and J. L. Hall; Engineers: Acting-Chief, Simon Schultice; Acting-First-Assistant, James Munroe; Second-Assistant, John Wilson; Acting-Second-Assistant, Philip Allman; Acting-Third-Assistants, J. M. Quin, R. D. Wright, T. J. Myers, James Morris, S. W. Dalton, Jr., and John Donaldson.

" CHICKASAW "—FOURTH-RATE.

Lieutenant-Commander, George H. Perkins; Acting-Volunteer Lieutenant, Wm. Hamilton; Acting-Assistant Surgeon, J. K. Bacon; Acting-Assistant Paymaster, E. S. Wheeler; Acting-Master and Pilot, Benj. Lancashier; Acting-Ensign, G. L. Jordan; Acting-Master's Mates, F. A. Case, M. F. Keeshan, Chas. Atkins, W. A. Osborn and M. J. Jones; Engineers: Acting-Chief, Wm. Rodgers; Acting-First-Assistant, E. P. Bartlett; Acting-Second-Assistant, J. M. Maratta; Acting-Third-Assistants, Alfred Wilkinson, A. H. Goff, George Harris, Henry Duckworth and Alexander Wiggins; Gunner, J. A. McDonald.

" SELMA "—FOURTH-RATE.

Lieutenant, Arthur R. Yates; Acting-Volunteer-Lieutenant, Felix McCurley; Assistant Surgeon, Frederick Krecker; Acting-Assistant Paymaster, C. W. Clapp; Acting-Master and Pilot, J. H. Collins; Acting-Ensigns, L. R. Vance and W. A. DeWitt; Acting-Master's Mate, T. G. Gilmore; Engineers: Second-Assistants, John D. Ford and J. W. Patterson; Acting-Third-Assistants, H. W. Whiting and Edward Kenney.

" ARKANSAS "—THIRD-RATE.

Acting-Volunteer-Lieutenant, David Cate; Acting-Assistant Surgeon, E. D. G. Smith; Acting-Assistant Paymaster, E. G. Bishop; Acting-Ensigns, F. H. Beers and R. C. Dawes; Acting-Master's Mates, James Scully, T. E. Tinker and M. J. Nicholson; Engineers: Acting-First-Assistant, J. C. Cree; Acting-Second-Assistant, A. M. Clements; Acting-Third-Assistants, George Anderson and Charles Wolff.

" TRITONIA "—FOURTH-RATE.

Acting-Volunteer-Lieutenant, George Wiggin; Acting-Master and Pilot, J. Nicholson; Acting-Ensign, F. R. Iaschke; Acting-Master's Mates, C. A. Trundy and H. P. Fish; Engineers: Acting-Second-Assistant, James Findley; Acting-Third-Assistant, Abraham Geer.

" VIRGINIA "—FOURTH-RATE.

Acting-Volunteer-Lieutenant, Charles H. Brown; Acting-Assistant Surgeon, W. H. Kinney; Acting-Assistant Paymaster, J. B. Hoff; Acting-Master, W. G. Mitchell; Acting-Ensigns, M. A. Blume and F. E. Brackett; Acting-Master's Mates, Herman Wissing and E. F. Small; Engineers: Second-Assistant, J. D. Toppen; Acting-Third-Assistants, J. S. Essler, J. E. Scribner, Charles Hoskins and Daniel Ward.

" PENGUIN "—FOURTH-RATE.

Acting-Volunteer-Lieutenant, James R. Beers; Acting-Assistant Surgeon, H. R. Ruckley; Acting-Assistant Paymaster, T. C. Hutchinson; Acting-Master, Tolford M. Durham; Acting-Ensign, Benj. Cantlett; Acting-Master's Mates, C. G. Smith, F. C. Almy and W. A. Hannah; Acting-Engineers: Acting-First-Assistant, F. W. Warner; Acting-Second-

Assistant, M. P. Randall ; Acting-Third-Assistants, John Webster, Richard Reilly and Dewitt C. McBride.

"CORNELIA"—FOURTH-RATE.

Acting-Volunteer-Lieutenant, John A. Johnstone; Acting-Assistant Surgeon, J. G. Dearborne ; Acting-Assistant Paymaster, A. Eastlake ; Acting-Master, Geo. Ferris; Acting-Ensigns, G. A. Harriman, Frank Millett and G. F. Brailey ; Acting-Master's Mates, W. H. Wood and G. H. Russell ; Engineers : Acting-First-Assistant, S. R. Brumage ; Acting-Second-Assistant, T. J. Lavery ; Acting-Third-Assistants ; J. A. Boynton and George Altham.

"BUCKTHORN"—FOURTH-RATE.

Acting-Volunteer-Lieutenant, Washington Godfrey; Acting-Master's Mates, B. F. Robinson, H. J. Wynde and H. A. Mayo; Engineers: Acting-Third-Assistants, E. R. Hubbard and W. H. Allen.

"AUGUSTA DINSMORE"—THIRD-RATE.

Acting-Volunteer-Lieutenant, M. B. Crowell ; Acting-Assistant Surgeon, Ezra Pray ; Acting-Assistant Paymaster, D. F. Power; Acting-Ensigns, C. F. R Wappenhaus, T. H. Paine, C. H. Blount and F. A. G. Bacon; Acting-Master's Mate, A. S. Eldredge; Engineers: Acting-First-Assistant, John Seaman; Acting-Third-Assistants, Henry Lyon, Jr., W. E. Deaver, F. V. Christin and F. Scott.

"ANTONA"—FOURTH-RATE.

Acting-Volunteer-Lieutenant, John F. Harden ; Acting-Assistant Surgeon, S. B. Doty ; Acting-Assistant Paymaster, H. M. Whittemore ; Acting-Ensigns, F. W. Hearn, John Sears, W. G. Jones and John Bowman; Acting-Master's Mates, C. E. Schofield and G. T. Carey ; Engineers : Acting-Second-Assistant, S. T. Reeves ; Acting-Third-Assistants, Thos. Petherick, Jr., J. H. Burchmore and John Chambers.

"STOCKDALE"—FOURTH-RATE.

Acting-Volunteer-Lieutenant, Thomas Edwards; Acting-Assistant Paymasters, J. W. Day and W. R. Sherwood; Acting-Ensign, H. F. Martin; Acting-Master's Mates, S. H. Johnson, C. H. Cleveland, Daniel Dennis and George Rogers; Engineers: Acting-Third-Assistants, A. McH. Geary, Ambrose Kimball and Wm. W. Lewis.

"ELK"—FOURTH-RATE.

Acting-Volunteer-Lieutenant, Nicholas Kirby ; Acting-Assistant-Surgeon, H. H. Wilkins; Acting-Assistant Paymaster, W. C. Robbins; Acting-Master and Pilot, Jacob Lindee; Acting-Ensigns, W. D. Taber and H. W. Brackett; Acting-Master's Mate, Alfred A. J. Emery; Engineers: Acting-Second-Assistants, Benj. Labree, T. H. Nelson and R. W. Mars; Acting-Third-Assistants, T. R. Thompson and John S. Hays.

"CARRABASSETT"—FOURTH-RATE.

Acting-Volunteer-Lieutenant, Ezra Leonard; Acting-Assistant Surgeon, C. W. Knight; Acting-Assistant Paymaster, D. W. Riddle; Acting-Ensign, A. L. C. Bowie; Acting-Master's Mates, A. A. Delano and John Devereux; Engineers: Acting-First-Assistant, J. W. Hindman; Acting-Third-Assistants, T. Harding, James Crooks and Jerome Haas.

"NYANZA"—FOURTH-RATE.

Acting-Volunteer-Lieutenant, C. A. Boutelle ; Acting-Assistant Surgeon, W. G. Frost; Acting-Assistant Paymaster, H. S. Gregory; Acting-Master, J. F. Beyer; Acting-Ensign, J. M. Chadwick; Acting-Master's Mate, J. H. Mallon; Engineers: Acting-First-Assistant, Wm. Doyle; Acting-Second-Assistant, Bernard Martin; Acting-Third-Assistants, R. G. Watson and Henry James.

"SCIOTA"—FOURTH-RATE.

Acting-Volunteer-Lieutenant, J. H. Magune; Acting-Assistant Surgeon, R. P. Sawyer; Acting-Assistant Paymaster, B. H. Franklin; Acting-Ensign, Chas. A. Cannon; Engineers: Second-Assistants, Wm. F. Pratt and Daniel Dod.

"SAM HOUSTON"—FOURTH-RATE.

Acting-Volunteer-Lieutenant, Martin Freeman; Acting-Master, Wm. Stewart.

"PORT ROYAL"—FOURTH-RATE.

Acting-Master, Thomas M. Gardner; Acting-Assistant Surgeon, L. R. Boyce; Acting-Assistant Paymaster, F. K. Moore; Acting-Master, Wm. Hull; Acting-Ensigns, E. W. Snare and F. S. Hopkins; Acting-Master's Mate, E. V. Tyson, S. S. Bumpers, W. A. Prescott and Wm. Campbell; Engineers: Acting-Second-Assistant, Henry Moyles; Third-Assistant, W. C. F. Reichenbach; Acting-Third-Assistant, T. B. Brown.

"TALLAHATCHIE"—FOURTH-RATE.

Acting-Master, Thos. J. Lennekin ; Acting-Assistant Surgeon, A. l'Anglois ; Acting-Assistant Paymaster, J. C. Sawyer; Acting-Master and Pilot, James Redding ; Acting-Ensigns, Haskell Crosby, S. H. Berino and W B. Pease; Acting-Master's Mates, Wm. McKnight, John Smith and Thomas Pindar; Engineers: Acting-First-Assistant, D. R. Sims; Acting-Second-Assistant, W. M. Stewart; Acting-Third-Assistants, John A. Dalton and J. Moran.

"GLASGOW"—FOURTH RATE.

Acting-Master, Richard J. Hoffner; Acting-Master and Pilot, Frank Kane; Acting-Ensign, Charles Welles; Acting-Master's Mates, F. A. Sherman, J. F. Baker, and W. H. Childs; Engineers : Second-Assistant, John F. Bingham ; Acting-Third-Assistants, R S. Lytle and John McAuliffe.

"PAMPERO"—FOURTH-RATE.

Acting-Master, Oliver Colbourn; Acting-Assistant Surgeon, E. C. Neal; Acting-Assistant Paymaster, A. B. Clark; Acting-Master's Mates, Rodger Farrell and J. L. Blauvelt.

"ARIZONA"—FOURTH-RATE.

Acting-Master, Howard Tibbits; Acting-Assistant Surgeon, S. S. Green; Acting-Assistant Paymaster, G. B. Tripp; Acting-Master, Wm. Harcourt; Acting-Ensign, F. Aug. Miller; Engineers: Acting-Second-Assistant, W. H. Thomson; Second-Assistant, P. G. Eastwick; Acting-Third-Assistant, John Lewis.

"GERTRUDE"—FOURTH-RATE.

Acting-Master, Henry C. Wade; Acting-Assistant Surgeon, Adam Shirk; Acting-Assistant Paymaster, R. R. Brawley; Acting-Ensigns, Wm. Shepard and Fred. Newell; Acting-Master's Mates, Benj. Leeds and C. A. Osborn; Engineers: Acting-Second-Assistant, W. H. Brown; Acting-Third-Assistants, J. H. Nesen, F. C. Morey and C. O. Farciot.

"POCAHONTAS"—FOURTH-RATE.

Acting-Master, E. E. Pendleton; Assistant Surgeon, C. L. Green; Acting-Assistant Paymaster, A. J. Wright, Jr.; Acting-Ensign, I. J. McKinley; Acting-Master's Mates, B. W. Tucker, Jr., J. H. Pray and J. L. Gould; Engineers: Acting-Second-Assistants, W. T. Warburton and Alex. McDonald; Acting-Third-Assistants, R. F. Carter, J. H. Doughty and W. D. Hyde.

"ARTHUR"—FOURTH-RATE.

Acting-Master, Joseph E. Stannard; Acting-Assistant Paymaster, C. E. Mitchell; Acting-Ensign, G. M. Bogart; Acting-Master's Mate, Robert Wood.

"NEW LONDON"—FOURTH-RATE.

Acting-Master, Lyman Wells; Acting-Assistant Surgeon, Geo. M. Beard; Acting-Assistant Paymaster, E. A. Chadwick; Acting-Ensigns, J. M. C. Reville, V. W. Jones and H. Z. Howard; Acting-Master's Mate, E. J. Hennessy; Engineers: Acting-Second-Assistant, H. P. Powers; Acting-Third-Assistants, John Dunlap, James Creevy and John Quinn.

"FORT GAINES"—FOURTH-RATE.

Acting-Master, John R. Hamilton; Acting-Ensign, S. A. Ryder; Acting-Master's Mates, W. J. Thornton, Bernard Segersteen and Wm. Brown; Engineers: Acting-Third-Assistants, Lucas Golden, Wm. Clark, Henry Moxley and Thomas Smith.

"OWASCO"—FOURTH-RATE.

Acting-Masters, Thomas B. Sears and John Utter; Acting-Assistant Surgeon, J. J. Smith; Acting-Assistant Paymaster, Wm. B. Coleman; Acting-Master's Mates, F. C. Duncan and A. L. Stevens; Engineers: Second-Assistant, Haviland Barstow; Acting-Third-Assistants, T. H. Carton and G. W. Latham.

"BOHIO"—FOURTH-RATE.

Acting-Master, Wm. M. Stannard; Acting-Master's Mate, Daniel Parsons.

"METEOR"—FOURTH-RATE.

Acting-Master, Meletiah Jordan; Acting-Assistant Paymaster, John M. Skillman; Acting-Ensigns, W. S. Romme, J. L. Hall and C. H. Sawyer; Acting-Master's Mates, T. W. Jones and J. F. Porter; Engineers: Acting-Third-Assistants, Wm. Connell, Wm. Boyle, William Brown and P. J. Murphy.

"KATAHDIN"—FOURTH-RATE.

Acting-Master, Edward Terrill; Acting-Assistant Surgeon, G. D. Buckner; Acting-Assistant Paymaster, L. D. Bradley; Acting-Master and Pilot, Bernard Crone; Acting-Ensigns, G. A. Faunce and Wm. Ross; Engineers: Second-Assistant, N. B. Clark; Acting-Second-Assistant, Thomas Tuttle; Acting-Third-Assistants, Sam'l Wallace and H. C. Reynolds.

"ESTRELLA"—FOURTH-RATE.

Acting-Master, G. P. Pomeroy; Acting-Assistant Surgeon, T. E. Clark; Acting-Assistant Paymaster, G. L. Hoodless; Acting-Master's Mates, E. G. Caswell and Charles Sidney; Engineers: Acting-First-Assistant, R. G. Pope; Acting-Third-Assistants, Geo. R. Marble and J. F. Winters.

"RODOLPH"—FOURTH-RATE.

Acting-Master, N. M. Dyer; Acting-Assistant Surgeon, E. P. Colby; Acting-Assistant Paymaster, J. C. Graves; Acting-Master and Pilot, John Robinson; Acting-Ensign, J. F. Thomson; Acting-Master's Mates, N. B. Hinckley and John Dickson; Engineers: Acting-Second Assistant, J. W. Smyth; Acting-Third-Assistants, Levi Robbins, Joshua Halsall and Charles Robinson.

"PINK"—FOURTH-RATE.

Acting-Master, Samuel Belden; Acting-Ensigns, George A. Steen and H. D. Packard; Engineers: Acting-Second-Assistant, A. B. Besse; Acting Third-Assistants, S. S. Pettingell, H. C. Jewett and J. G. Cunningham.

"CORYPHEUS"—FOURTH-RATE.

Acting-Master, J. S. Clark; Acting-Ensign, J. H. Gregory; Acting-Master's Mate, William McCann.

"GLIDE"—FOURTH-RATE.

Acting-Master, Levi S. Fickett; Acting-Assistant Paymaster, Abraham Depue; Acting-Ensigns, Jas. Sheppard and J. P. Cole; Acting-Master's Mates, Joseph Griffin, W. D. Gregory and Charles Heath; Engineers: Acting-Second-Assistant, M. F. Rogers; Acting-Third-Assistants, W. Matthews and T. R. Thompson.

"MARIA A. WOOD"—FOURTH-RATE.

Acting-Master, John Ross; Acting-Master's Mates, Charles Fort and E. S. Stover.

"COWSLIP"—FOURTH RATE.

Acting-Master, Wm. T. Bacon; Acting-Ensign, John Dennett; Acting-Ensign and Pilot, A. Bellandi; Acting-Master's Mates, Jacob Teal and F. A. Gross, Jr.; Engineers: Acting-Second-Assistant, John Rogers; Acting-Third-Assistant, J. R. Davidson.

"HOLLYHOCK"—FOURTH-RATE.

Acting-Ensign, Franklin Ellms; Acting-Master's Mate, Lewis Milk; Engineers: Acting-Second-Assistant, Abraham Wilcox; Acting-Third-Assistants, Thomas Kennedy, Frank Rodgers, Frank Royce and Thos. Armstrong.

"KITTATINNY"—FOURTH-RATE.

Acting-Ensigns, N. J. Blaisdell and W. F. Chatfield.

"ROSE"—FOURTH-RATE.

Acting-Ensign, Walter D. Maddocks; Acting-Master's Mates, J. A. Plander, B. E. Treat and G. E. Symms; Engineers: Acting-Second-Assistant, Wm. R. Nutz; Acting-Third-Assistants, Alpheus Nichols, H. A. Guild and W. L. Lewis.

"ALTHEA"—FOURTH-RATE.

Acting-Ensigns, John Boyle and C. C. Wilbur; Acting-Master's Mates, Harry White and C. A. Blanchard; Engineers: Acting Second-Assistants, Jas. Kelren, Frederick D. Henriques and J. F. Smith.

"JASMINE"—FOURTH-RATE.

Acting-Ensign, J. F. Brenton; Acting-Third-Assistant Engineer, I. R. Burgoyne.

"FEAR NOT"—FOURTH-RATE.

Acting-Ensigns, Abraham Rich and P. P. Hawks; Acting-Assistant Paymaster, T. E. Ryan; Acting-Master's Mate, W. Freeman.

"J. C. KUHN"—FOURTH-RATE.

Acting-Ensign, Sewall H. Newman.

"W. G. ANDERSON"—FOURTH RATE.

Acting-Ensigns, Robert H. Carey and S. A. Brooks; Acting-Assistant Surgeon, T. M. Drummond; Acting-Assistant Paymaster, T. S. Dabney; Acting-Master's Mates, G. H. Rowen and Allan Reilley.

"BLOOMER"—FOURTH-RATE.

Acting-Third-Assistant Engineer, Thomas G. Jones.

"CHARLOTTE"—FOURTH-RATE.

Acting-Master's Mate, A. Whiting.

"IDA"—FOURTH-RATE.

Pilot, Benj. Tarbell; Acting-Master's Mate, Henry Kent.

NEW ORLEANS, LA., NAVAL RENDEZVOUS.

Acting-Master, E. H. Howell; Acting-Assistant Surgeon, D. M. McLean.

NAVAL HOSPITAL.

Surgeon, J. Jones; Assistant Surgeons, Thomas Hiland and Heber Smith.

MOBILE BAY.

Acting-Master, F. H. Grove; Acting-Master's Mates, C. R. Marple and E. A. Morse; Acting-Third-Assistant Engineer, J. L. Young.

COAST OF TEXAS.

Acting-Ensign, Robert M. Hanson.

SOUTHWEST PASS.

Acting-Master, Wm. Jones.

MISSISSIPPI RIVER.

Lieutenant-Commander Wm. Mitchell, Ordnance Officer; Assistant Paymaster W. C. Cook, Naval Storekeeper.

CHAPTER LIV.

CAPTURE OF RICHMOND.—THE DESTRUCTION OF THE CONFEDERATE FLEET IN THE JAMES RIVER, ETC.

ASSEMBLING OF THE NAVAL VESSELS IN HAMPTON ROADS AND ON THE JAMES RIVER.—OPERATIONS OF THE ARMIES AROUND RICHMOND.—PRESIDENT LINCOLN VISITS CITY POINT.—THE MEMORABLE COUNCIL ON BOARD THE "RIVER QUEEN."—DECISION OF THE COUNCIL.—THE TERMS OF SURRENDER OFFERED TO GENERAL JOHNSTON.—ABILITY OF THE CONFEDERATE GENERALS.—THE EXAMPLE OF PRESIDENT LINCOLN.—THE CONFEDERATE IRON-CLADS BLOCKADED IN THE JAMES RIVER.—THE CONFEDERATE FLEET AS RE-ORGANIZED UNDER REAR-ADMIRAL SEMMES.—RICHMOND ENVELOPED.—ATTACK ON PETERSBURG.—REMOVAL OF TORPEDOES AND OBSTRUCTIONS IN THE RIVER.—RICHMOND EVACUATED.—SEMMES' INSTRUCTIONS FROM THE CONFEDERATE SECRETARY OF THE NAVY.—BLOWING UP OF THE CONFEDERATE FLEET.—END OF THE CONFEDERATE NAVY.—THE PRESIDENT VISITS RICHMOND.—AT THE RESIDENCE OF JEFFERSON DAVIS.—AN OVATION WORTHY OF AN EMPEROR.—TACTICS OF ASSASSINS.—JUSTICE CAMPBELL VISITS THE PRESIDENT.—DUFF GREEN RECEIVES A MERITED REBUKE.—PRESIDENT LINCOLN RETURNS TO WASHINGTON.—SCATTERING OF THE VESSELS OF THE NAVY.—THE WAR ENDED.—A NEW NATIONAL ANNIVERSARY.

THE naval operations on the Southern coast having terminated, owing to the capture of the enemy's ports, the vessels-of-war were distributed to other points, leaving only a sufficient number of gun-boats to preserve the peace and protect the inhabitants against the depredations of deserters from the Confederate army, who were making their way home in large numbers, and like hungry wolves eating up everything which came in their way.

Sherman's army on its march through the South has been compared by Confederate writers to a swarm of locusts; but these Confederate deserters were ten times worse than Sherman's men, who were supplied with abundant rations from their own commissariat.

The naval vessels on the coast were constantly called upon to fit out boat expeditions ; which, with three or four hundred well-equipped men, would drive off the marauders and send them elsewhere in search of plunder. Thus, the Navy, not being governed by any feelings of rancor towards the Confederate sympathizers on shore, stood ready to shield from harm many who had been the bitterest foes of the Union.

Meanwhile, a large number of naval vessels assembled in Hampton Roads and on the James River, in anticipation of coming events, for all eyes now centred on Richmond, where General Lee and his army of veterans were making their final stand with little prospect of success against the overwhelming force brought to bear on them. The Federal Army was ready to move as soon as General Grant should know to a certainty that General Sherman had reached Goldsboro', where it was expected he would come in contact with General J. E. Johnston's army of some forty thousand men, which was being daily strengthened by Confederates who had evacuated Savannah, Charleston and Wilmington.

This was one of the most anxious moments of the war. Hitherto Sherman had met with no serious opposition since leaving Columbia, but as he approached Goldsboro' the increasing numbers of the Confederates in his front gave evidence that he was to meet with strong resistance.

Everything had been done by General Grant that was possible to reinforce Sherman. A column of troops from Wilmington and another from Newbern were dispatched to meet him, and to repair the railroads so that supplies could be rapidly sent to the Federal armies. All these movements were observed by the enemy with intense interest, and they hoped to be able to overwhelm and defeat these detached divisions before Sherman could come up. The column from Newbern, under Schofield, was attacked by General Bragg with his army, reinforced by Hill's division of the Army of the Tennessee. According to Confederate accounts, Schofield was routed, and fifteen hundred of his men captured ; but as General Schofield crossed the Neuse River and entered Goldsboro' on the 21st, it would seem that the Federal progress was little, if any, impeded. The column from Wilmington, under General Terry, reached the Neuse River a short distance above Goldsboro' on the 22d, ready to cross when it suited him to do so.

Goldsboro' was evidently one of the culminating points of the war, and it was evident that, before Sherman could finish the last stage of his march and make a junction with Schofield and Terry, he would have some hard fighting to do. It had, doubtless, seemed to the Confederate Government good policy to let Sherman advance to a point where all their forces could be easily concentrated against him, and on the result of the General's attempt to reach Goldsboro', in face of all the attending difficulties, depended, in a great measure, the ultimate course of the Confederate Government.

General Grant's movements also largely depended on the success of Sherman. The winter had been rainy, and the almost impassable condition of the Virginia roads made it impracticable to move an army with anything approaching to celerity, even as late as the end of March. This was, therefore, an anxious moment. Had it been possible for General Johnston to accumulate an army sufficiently strong to defeat Sherman, Grant could not have gone to the latter's assistance, owing to the condition of the roads. Sherman was then the central figure of the war—on his management depended the terms that would be demanded of General Lee when Grant should move on Petersburg and Richmond.

President Lincoln, being no longer able to restrain his anxiety, now proceeded to City Point, and would doubtless have been joined by the members of the Cabinet had he not expressly forbidden it.

Besides the troops under the command of General J. E. Johnston, Sherman had some of the ablest generals in the Confederacy to contest his march. General Beauregard had been reinforced at Charlotte, N. C., by General Cheatham and the garrison of Augusta, and was moving towards Raleigh. General Hardee, with the troops from Savannah and Charleston, was marching towards the same point, as were General Bragg and Hoke from Wilmington ; so that it appeared as if Sherman would encounter an army of eighty thousand men, commanded by one who was considered by many competent judges the ablest of the Confederate generals. There was certainly no general on the other side for whose abilities Sherman had so great a respect as for those of Johnston. Beauregard, Hardee and Bragg gave him comparatively little uneasiness, and he was glad when Hood relieved Johnston at Atlanta, as he then felt assured of victory.

But the Confederate army, which in the enumeration of its parts appeared so imposing, was no match for Sherman's victorious hosts, who had gained a prestige they did not intend to forfeit. Circumstances also combined to favor Sherman's advance. When the Federal campaign in South Carolina commenced, Hardee had eighteen thousand men ; when he reached Cheraw he had but eleven thousand, and at Averyboro' the number had diminished to six thousand. Most of this falling off was due to desertions, and it afforded an indication of the rapid collapse of the military enthusiasm which had once prevailed in the Southern Confederacy.

General Hardee attempted to impede Sherman's march when the latter reached the narrow territory between the Cape Fear and the Black River, but was able to effect very little, retreating as night came on towards Smithfield, N. C. On the 18th, the Federal Army moved on Goldboro' in two columns, the 15th and 17th Corps on the direct road from Fayetteville, and the 14th and 20th Corps on the road from Averyboro'. The former column was supposed by the Confederates to be a day's march in advance of the other, and it was therefore determined to concentrate all their available troops against it on the 19th.

Then was fought the battle of Bentonville by the combined forces of Bragg and Hardee, with the object of crippling Sherman before he could effect a junction with Schofield and Terry, and the action was for a time so severe that it looked as if General Johnston would accomplish his purpose. But on the 20th General Sherman's whole army confronted the Confederates ; before daybreak, on the 22d, General Johnston moved towards Smithfield, leaving many of his wounded on the field. His loss in the three days' fighting, according to Confederate accounts, was 224 killed and 1,499 wounded, the small loss being accounted for by the fact that the Confederates fought under cover, which gave them a great advantage over the Federal troops. Next day (the 23d) the junction was made by General Sherman with the troops of Schofield and Terry, which disposed of General Johnston's army for the time being.

All the principal lines of railroad leading South were now within the reach of Sherman's forces or under their control, and the ultimate result could not be doubtful. It was impossible for General Johnston to retreat south without danger of his army breaking up through desertion, and his only chance was to strongly intrench himself and maintain a threatening attitude.

General Sherman felt so sure of the final surrender of General Johnston, that, after placing General Schofield in command of his army at Goldsboro', he proceeded in the little steamer "Russia" to City Point, Virginia, to confer with General Grant on the situation, arriving on the 27th of March. President Lincoln was then on board the steamer "River Queen," at City Point, and he received General Sherman with the warmth of feeling which distinguished him, for he felt that the presence of Sherman at City Point was an assurance that the latter had Johnston's army in such a position that it could do no further mischief.

The arrival of General Sherman brought joy and confidence to every one in the Army and Navy on the James River, for it was understood that he now held General Johnston in a position from which the latter could not move without precipitating a battle with over eighty thousand veteran soldiers, well supplied with everything necessary, while the Confederates were badly provided with provisions, clothing, and even ammunition.

At one time it was thought that General Johnston would endeavor to break away from Smithfield and effect a junction with General Lee. In the light of subsequent events, this is seen to have been impossible. Again, it was thought that Lee would, perhaps, evacuate Richmond and make a junction with Johnston—a movement equally impracticable, for Grant was extending his left below Petersburg, and should Lee leave his fortified lines Grant would follow him so closely that it would be impossible for him to unite with General Johnston or fall on Sherman's army. Besides, with his eighty thousand men, Sherman felt confident that he could hold his own against Johnston and Lee combined until Grant could come upon the scene with his troops.

The morning after General Sherman's arrival at City Point, a council of war was held on board the steamboat "River Queen," at which were present the President, General Grant, General Sherman and Admiral Porter. As considerable controversy has arisen over the terms of surrender offered to General Johnston, and the truth of the matter is not generally known, we will here narrate what occurred on the occasion, as we violate no injunction of secrecy by so doing.

The principal conversation was between the President and General Sherman. The former stated his opinion at length. He feared that General Lee, seeing the Federal lines closing about him day by day, the coast completely blockaded, the Confederate army almost destitute of clothing and provisions, might attempt to break away from his fortifications at Richmond, make a junction with Johnston, and escape to the south. This was rather an extreme view to take of the matter, for, in the opinion of those best qualified to judge, such an attempt on the part of General Lee could not have succeeded. General Sherman had eighty thousand fine troops at Goldsboro', only one hundred and fifty miles from Richmond and one hundred and twenty miles from Greensboro', at which latter point the Richmond and Danville railroad, the only route by which Lee could escape, was cut. All this General Sherman explained to the President, who was somewhat reassured, yet the number of shrewd questions propounded by Mr. Lincoln was remarkable, and some of them were found difficult to answer. His topographical knowledge of the country traversed by Sherman's army, as well as other military matters he was not supposed to be familiar with, surprised those who listened to him.

Like the rest of those present at the council, the President was confident that the end of the war was close at hand, and, although a bloody battle might yet be fought, Richmond must soon be in possession of the Federal Government. It was the great desire of the President to secure the surrender of the Confederate armies without further loss of life, to which end he desired the most liberal terms should be granted. "Let them surrender and go home," he said; "they will not take up arms again. Let them all go, officers and all, let them have their horses to plow with, and, if you like, their guns to shoot crows with. Treat them liberally. We want these people to return to their allegiance and submit to the laws. Therefore, I say, give them the most liberal and honorable terms." These sentiments were worthy of the man who uttered them.

General Sherman, however, took a military view of the situation. He had made a long and toilsome march and desired to reap the honors due to a victorious general.

Feeling certain that the game was in his own hands, he did not hesitate to differ with the President, assuring the latter that he had sufficient force and strength of position to dictate his own terms to General Johnston, and he graphically illustrated, with the aid of a map, the condition of affairs at Goldsboro' and Smithfield.

"All I want," said General Sherman, "is two weeks' time in which to clothe my soldiers I will then be ready to march on Johnston and compel him to surrender. He is short of everything, and in two weeks would have to surrender, anyway."

"Yes," replied the President, "but two weeks is a long time, and the first thing you know General Johnston will have gone south again with those veterans of his, and will keep the war going indefinitely. No, General, he must have no excuse for going away; we must have his surrender at all hazards, so be easy with him about terms."

"Mr. President," said General Sherman, "there is no possible way for Johnston to escape as he is now situated. I can command his unconditional surrender."

"What is to prevent Johnston from escaping with his army by the southern railroads while you are fitting out your men?" inquired General Grant.

"There are no southern railroads to speak of," replied Sherman, "by which Johnston could escape. My 'bummers' broke up the roads, and did their work too well to permit them to be used by any one."

"But," said General Grant, "cannot the Confederates re-lay the rails, as our troops have done from Newbern to Goldsboro'?"

Sherman smiled. "No," he said, "my boys don't do things by halves. They make a fire of the ties, and the rails are twisted until they are as crooked as rams' horns; all the blacksmiths in creation couldn't straighten them out again. Mr. President," said Sherman, turning to Mr. Lincoln, "give yourself no uneasiness; the Confederacy will collapse in a few days; we hold the line between Goldsboro' and Wilmington; my transports can come as far as Newbern; we can overrun the South without hindrance; we are masters of the situation, and General Johnston must surrender."

"All very well," said the President, "but we must make no mistakes, and my way is a sure one: Offer General Johnston the same terms that will be offered Lee; then, if he will not accept them, try your plan; but as long as the Confederates lay down their arms I don't think it matters much how they do it. Don't let us have any more bloodshed if it can be avoided. General Grant is in favor of giving General Lee the most favorable terms."

"Well, Mr. President," said General Sherman, "I will carry out your wishes to the best of my ability, and I am satisfied when Richmond falls and Lee surrenders General Johnston will follow his example."

This ended the memorable council on board the "River Queen." On what took place on that occasion might depend whether the Confederates would lay down their arms or continue hostilities, thereby reducing the South to still greater straits, if possible, than it was then in. The President, being desirous that General Sherman should rejoin his command as soon as possible, the latter returned, the afternoon of the council, in the U. S. steamer "Bat" to Newbern, N. C.

At this day the policy of Mr. Lincoln will be recognized as good, both on the ground of expediency and of humanity. We were engaged in a war, not with foreigners, but against our own countrymen, with no object except to vindicate the authority of the Federal Government. There were no knotty questions involved, it was simply a question whether the Confederates could carry on the war any longer, or whether they would return to their allegiance. Even then the Confederates were more dangerous foes than a dozen European nations would have been, although in the most straitened circumstances, deficient in food, clothing and forage, and even in ammunition, so indispensable to an army. They had still a formidable force about Richmond, which, if it could effect a junction with Johnston's army, would offer a stout resistance under those able commanders. The Federal Government had had too many proofs of the ability of the Confederate generals and the gallantry of their soldiers to need any further evidence, and had no desire to drive them to desperation by requiring a degrading submission to its authority. The Government was now in a position to display not only its military strength but its magnanimity. It was right that, when the soldiers of the North clasped hands with those who had so long and bitterly opposed them in the field, they should desire to bury the past in oblivion, and resume once more the bonds of fraternal affection. The example set by President Lincoln was followed by those who had borne the brunt of the conflict, and had learned to appreciate the courage and hardihood of their late antagonists. General Grant shared in the President's desire for the most liberal arrangements that could be entered into for the surrender of the Confederate armies; and while Mr. Lincoln had implicit confidence in Grant's military abilities, he relied no less on his good judgment and kind feeling, and it is fortunate that the last act in the bloody drama of the civil war was under the direction of the two men acting in perfect accord, whose names will be handed down to posterity with increase of honor as the years roll by.

When General Lee surrendered at Appomattox the work of the North Atlantic Squadron was over, for all the James River region was in the hands of the Federals. Up to that time the squadron in Trent's Reach was quietly holding the Confederate iron-clads, under the command of Raphael Semmes—recently created Rear-Admiral—above Drury's Bluff, where they were quite harmless and would either have to be blown up or surrendered.

Admiral Semmes assumed command of the James River fleet on the 18th of February, 1865, relieving Commodore J. K. Mitchell. The fleet as reorganized comprised the following named vessels:

"Virginia" (iron-clad), flag-ship, four guns, Captain Dunnington; "Richmond" (iron-clad), four guns, Captain J. D. Johnson; "Fredericksburg" (iron-clad), four guns, Captain Glasse; "Hampton" (wooden), two guns, Captain Wilson (late of the "Alabama"); "Nansemond" (wooden), two guns, Captain W. K. Butt; "Roanoke" (wooden) two guns, Captain Polloc; "Beaufort" (wooden), two guns, Captain Wyatt; "Torpedo" (wooden), one gun, Captain Roberts.

This fleet was assisted in the defence of the river by shore batteries under command of naval officers—such as Drury's Bluff Battery, Battery Brooke, Battery Wood, and Battery Semmes. The Confederate vessels were not in the most efficient condition as regarded their *personnel*, which was mostly drawn from the army. The real difficulty in getting to Richmond with the Federal gun-boats was in the heavy fortifications along the James River above Howlett's Battery, the sunken torpedoes, and the obstructions in the channel, which could not be removed under fire.

While the Federal and Confederate forces on the river were in this position, General Grant was gradually enveloping Richmond with his army. The Confederate lines in the vicinity of Petersburg having been weakened by the necessity of withdrawing troops to defend Lee's extreme right at Five Forks, General Grant, on the morning of the 2d of April, ordered a vigorous assault to be made on the enemy, which gave the Federals possession of Petersburg, and rendered Richmond no longer tenable.

The night following this success, President Lincoln went on board the flag-ship "Malvern" as the guest of Admiral Porter. On every hand was heard the sound of artillery and musketry, showing that the Federals were closing in on the Confederate lines.

The night before Richmond was evacuated by the Confederate forces, the President and Admiral Porter were seated on the upper deck of the flag-ship "Malvern," when the President made the remark to the latter: "Can't the Navy do something at this particular moment to make history?" The Admiral replied: "The Navy is doing its best just now, holding the enemy's four heavy iron-clads in utter uselessness. If those vessels could reach City Point they would commit great havoc—as they came near doing while I was away at Fort Fisher. In consequence, General Grant ordered the channel to be still further obstructed with stones, so that no vessel can pass. We can hold the fort with a very small force and prevent any one from removing the obstructions. Therefore, the enemy's iron-clads are useless."

"But, can't we make a noise?" asked the President. "Yes," replied the Admiral, "and if you desire it I will commence."

The Admiral telegraphed to Lieutenant-Commander K. R. Breese, Fleet-Captain, who was just above Dutch Gap, to have the vessels' guns loaded with shrapnel, to point in the direction of the forts and to keep up a rapid fire until directed to stop. The firing commenced about 11 o'clock P. M., and the President listened attentively while the flashes of the guns lighted up the horizon. In about twenty minutes a loud explosion shook the flag-ship and the President exclaimed: "I hope to Heaven one of our vessels has not blown up!" The Admiral assured him that the explosion was much further up the river and that it was doubtless one of the Confederate iron-clads. A second explosion soon followed, and not long after two more, which caused the Admiral to remark: "That's all of them; no doubt the forts are evacuated and to-morrow we can go up to Richmond."

By eight o'clock the following morning the work of removing the obstructions in the channel was completed sufficiently to allow the passage of the flag-ship, and several of the smaller vessels went up the river and with their boats began sweeping the stream for torpedoes. It was soon discovered that all the forts had been evacuated, and nothing was to be seen of the Confederate iron-clads except their black hulls, partly out of water.

In the meantime, General Weitzel, who was on the left bank of the James with a large body of troops, hearing the firing of the gun-boats and the explosions of the Confederate iron-clads, got all his men under arms, supposing that the Federal gun-boats were engaging the enemy's vessels and forts. A large force of Confederates in

Weitzel's front, which barred the way to Richmond, seems to have been of the same opinion, and, leaving their trenches, retreated on the city. When daylight appeared, finding that there was no force opposing him, and that the road to Richmond was clear, Weitzel marched in and took possession of the city. This was the way it appeared to the Federal officers present on the occasion; but we insert the Confederate side of the story, as told by Rear-Admiral Raphael Semmes, who certainly ought to have known something about the matter. Admiral Semmes states that when sitting down to his dinner on board his flag-ship, about 4 o'clock on the 2d of April, the day Grant had broken through Lee's lines, a special messenger brought him a letter from the Confederate Secretary of the Navy. As Semmes had not heard of the occurrences at Petersburg, he was somewhat surprised at the contents of this epistle, which were as follows:

CONFEDERATE STATES OF AMERICA.
EXECUTIVE OFFICE, }
RICHMOND, VA., April 2, 1865. }
Rear-Admiral Raphael Semmes, Commanding James River Squadron:
SIR—General Lee advises the Government to withdraw from the city, and the officers will leave this evening accordingly. I presume that General Lee has advised you of this and of his movements, and made suggestions as to the disposition to be made of your squadron. He withdraws upon his lines towards Danville this night; and, unless otherwise directed by General Lee, upon you is devolved the duty of destroying your ships this night, and with all the forces under your command joining General Lee. Confer with him, if practicable, before destroying them. Let your people be rationed as far as possible for the march, and armed and equipped for duty in the field.
Very respectfully, your obedient servant,
S. R. MALLORY,
Secretary of the Navy.

It was evident that Richmond was to have been evacuated that night, and by a curious coincidence the firing from the Federal gun-boats commenced early the same evening, which doubtless caused Semmes to expedite his movements. He signalled for all commanding officers of vessels to repair on board the flag-ship, and impressed upon them the importance of keeping the intended operations secret, lest the suspicions of the Federals might be excited.

Semmes remarks: "The sun was shining brightly, the afternoon was calm, and Nature was just putting on her spring attire." He could not help contrasting the peace and quiet of Nature "with the description of a great Government and the ruin of an entire people, which was at hand:"

"So unsuspicious were the Government subordinates of what was going on, that the flag-of-truce boats were still plying between Richmond and the Federal headquarters, a few miles below on the river, carrying backward and forward exchange prisoners. As these boats would pass the ships-of-war, filled to overflowing with the poor fellows just released from Yankee prisons, broken, wan and hollow-eyed, the prisoners would break into the most enthusiastic cheering as they passed the Confederate flag. It seemed to welcome them home. They little dreamed that it would be struck that night forever, and the fleet blown into the air that their own fetters had been knocked off in vain, and that they were to pass henceforth under the rule of the hated Yankee."

Thus mused Rear-Admiral Semmes on the eve of blowing up his squadron. Circumstances prevented him from communicating with General Lee; and, seeing that it was a case where every one must take care of himself, Semmes determined to destroy his vessels at once, especially as the Confederate Army seemed to be setting fire to everything around them, and leaving in a hurry. Semmes had originally intended to sink his vessels quietly, so that the Federals would have no idea of what was going on; but soon after dark he saw the whole horizon to the north of the James lighted up, rendering concealment on his part no longer necessary. Semmes omits to mention that the Federal gun-boats were thundering at the gates, which was the real reason for so hastily destroying the iron-clads. The officers and men were put on board the small gun-boats, and at about midnight the iron clads blew up, one after another, with a terrific explosion, adding to the grandeur of the scene already existing of burning barracks. The shells bursting as the fire came in contact with them, the signal-rockets from both sides filling the air like thousands of shooting-stars; the booming of guns in the distance, the long roll of the drums calling the troops to fall in, mingled with the sound of trumpets, all combined to make a spectacle and an uproar as though pandemonium had broken loose. It seemed as if heaven and earth had united to celebrate the conclusion of a struggle that had caused so much suffering.

That was the end of the Confederate Navy, which went up in what might have been considered a blaze of glory, but for the fact that the James River fleet had been the most useless force the Confederates had ever put afloat—the forts, torpedoes and obstructions on the river being far more formidable adversaries, and quite sufficient, if properly managed, to keep any hostile vessels from ascending the narrow channel, where, if one should happen to be sunk, it would effectually bar the progress of those behind it.

The work of the Federal Navy was all over in this quarter, and those who for many months had guarded the obstructions in the river rejoiced when the monotonous task was concluded. If rockets were sent up, and blue lights burned, and national salutes fired, the demonstration was as much on account of the return of peace as in honor of victory. It signalized the end of that fraternal strife between people who could never live apart, but who, united under one Government, could bid defiance to the world in arms.

Whether our country will profit as much as it should do from past experience remains to be seen; but, so far, we have not given much evidence of progress in matters pertaining to the defence of our coasts and the construction of a Navy adequate to protect the nation from foreign and domestic enemies ; which latter exist in every country, no matter how beneficent may be its laws.

When the channel was reported clear of torpedoes, a large number of which was taken up, Admiral Porter proceeded up towards Richmond in the " Malvern, with President Lincoln on board the steamer " River Queen." Finally, the " Malvern" grounded below the city, and the Admiral, taking the President in his barge, accompanied by a tug with a file of marines, continued on to Richmond.

About a mile below the landing, the tug was permitted to go to the relief of a party in a small steamer who were caught under a bridge and held by the current, and the barge proceeded alone. The street along the river-front was deserted, and, although the Federal troops had been in possession of the city some hours, not a soldier was to be seen. At the landing was a small house, and behind it a dozen negroes were digging with spades. Their leader, an old man, sprang forward exclaiming: " Bress de Lord, dere is de great Messiah!" and he fell on his knees before the President, his comrades following his example. The President was much embarrassed. " Don't kneel to me," he said, " kneel to God only, and thank Him for the liberty you will hereafter enjoy." It was a minute or two before the officers could get the negroes to leave the President; but time was precious. The negroes joined hands and sang a hymn, to which the President listened respectfully.

Four minutes had passed since the party had landed in apparently deserted streets; but, now that the hymn was sung, the streets seemed to be suddenly alive with the colored race, the crowd around the President became very oppressive, and it was necessary to order the boat's crew to fix bayonets and surround him to keep him from being crushed. The negroes, in their ecstasy, could not be made to understand that they were detaining the President, and would not feel that they were free unless they heard it from his own lips. Mr. Lincoln, therefore, made a few remarks, assuring them that they were free and giving them good advice, after which the party managed to move slowly on to the city.

Passing the Libby Prison, the President paused for a moment to look at the place where so many Union soldiers had dragged out a dreadful existence. " We will pull it down!" shouted the crowd of poor whites and negroes. " No," said the President, " leave it as a monument."

As the party slowly reached the city, the sidewalks were lined with people, white and black, but there was no anger on any face. It was like a gala-day, and no man was ever accorded a warmer welcome. The heat of the weather was suffocating; the President towered a head and shoulders above the crowd, fanning himself with his hat, and looking as if he would give the Presidency for a glass of water. Now the windows flew up, and eager, peering faces seemed to ask : " Is this man, with soft eyes and kind face, the one that has been held up to us as the incarnation of wickedness, the destroyer of the South ?" The city was still on fire, and the smoke almost choked the Presidential party.

While stopped a moment by the crowd, a white man in his shirt-sleeves rushed towards the President. When he got within ten feet of him he stopped, took off his hat, and cried out, " Abraham Lincoln, God bless you ! you are the poor man's friend !" Just after this, a beautiful girl struggled through the crowd and presented Mr. Lincoln with a bouquet of roses. There was no cheering at this, nor any evidence of disapprobation, but it was evidently a matter of great interest, for the girl was surrounded and plied with questions on returning to the sidewalk.

What could all this mean but that the people of Richmond were glad to see the end of the war and the advent of a milder form of Government ? They had, no doubt, felt that the late Government should have remained at the capital and surrendered in a dignified manner, making terms for the citizens, guarding their rights and acknowledging that they had lost the game. There was nothing to be ashamed of in such a surrender. Their armies had fought as people never fought before, and all that was wanted to make them glorious was the submission of the leaders with the troops in a dignified way, while they might have said: " We have done our best to win, but you are too strong for us; we pledge ourselves to keep the peace." Instead of remaining to protect the citizens against the ruffianism of the mob, the Confederate authorities of Richmond left that to the Federal troops, and no soldiers ever performed a trust more faithfully. At the moment when President Lincoln entered the city, the majority of them were engaged in putting out the fires that were started by the Confederates as they left the place, determined, it would seem, to destroy the public works, so that the Federals could derive no benefit from them.

At length, a cavalry-man was encountered sitting his horse and gazing at the President with much interest. The Admiral sent him at once to inform the general-in-command of the arrival of the President, and to request a military escort to guard him and enable him to force his way through the crowd. A troop of cavalry soon arrived, the streets were cleared, and the President soon reached the mansion just vacated by Mr. Davis, and now the headquarters of Generals Weitzel and Shepley. It was a modest house, comfortably but plainly furnished.

A great crowd of civilians now assembled around this house, greeting the President with loud cheers. General Shepley made a speech, after which the President and party entered a carriage and visited the State-House, the late seat of the Confederate Congress. The building was in dreadful disorder, showing the sudden flight of the legislators.

After this inspection, Admiral Porter urged the President to go on board the "Malvern," as he began to feel the responsibility resting on him for the care of his person. The Admiral was oppressed with uneasiness until he once more stood with Mr. Lincoln on the deck of the flag-ship, and he determined the President should go nowhere again, while under his charge, without a guard of marines.

That evening, at about eight o'clock, a man hailed the "Malvern," which was then anchored off the city, saying that he had dispatches for the President. A boat was sent on shore, with orders to bring the dispatches, but not the bearer of them; but returned with neither dispatches nor man. The boat officer said the person would deliver the dispatches to no one but the President himself. After some discussion, the boat was sent back to bring the man on board, but he had disappeared. The Admiral inquired about his appearance, and from the description was *afterwards* satisfied that the pretended bearer of dispatches was Wilkes Booth. Half an hour later another hail came from the shore, which was not more than twenty yards distant. A sailor from the "Saugus" wanted to report on board. There was no such vessel in the fleet, though there was one of that name in the Navy. A boat was sent to bring the man off, but he was nowhere to be seen. These circumstances made those charged with the care of the President more suspicious, and every precaution was taken that

no one should get on board the "Malvern" without full identification. The President himself felt a little nervous, and that night a marine kept guard at his state-room door.

Next morning, at 10 o'clock, Mr. John A. Campbell, late Associate Justice of the Supreme Court of the United States, sent a request to be allowed to come on board with General Weitzel, to call on the President. He spent an hour on board, Mr. Lincoln and himself seeming to enjoy themselves very much, to judge from their laughter. After General Weitzel and Mr. Campbell had returned on shore, Admiral Porter went below, and the President said to him : "Admiral, I am sorry you were not here when Mr. Campbell was on board. He has gone on shore happy. I gave him a written permission to allow the State Legislature to convene in the Capitol in the absence of all other governments." The Admiral was astonished at this piece of information, and felt that this course would bring about complications. He found it all had been done by the persuasive tongue of Mr. Campbell, who had promised the President that, if the Legislature of Virginia could meet, it would vote the State right back into the Union, and cause all the Virginia troops to lay down their arms ; that it would be a delicate compliment paid to Virginia, and would be appreciated, etc. General Weitzel agreed with Mr. Campbell, and the President was won over to agree to what would have been a most humiliating thing if it had been accomplished.

When Mr. Lincoln informed the Admiral that General Weitzel had gone on shore with an order permitting the Legislature to meet, the Admiral reminded the President that the city of Richmond was under martial law, and that no civil authority could exercise any power without the sanction of the General commanding the Army. This order should go through General Grant, who would doubtless protest against this arrangement with Mr. Campbell.

The President remarked, " Weitzel made no objection, and he commands here." " That is because he is Mr. Campbell's particular friend," replied the Admiral, " and wished to gratify him."

" Run and stop them," said the President, " and get my order back."

To make things sure, the Admiral had an order signed by the President, and directed to General Weitzel as follows : " Return my permission to the Legislature of Virginia to meet, and don't allow it to meet at all." An ambulance wagon was at the landing, and, giving the order to an officer, the Admiral said to him, " Jump into that wagon and kill the horse, if necessary, but catch the carriage which carried General Weitzel and Mr. Campbell, and deliver this order to the General." The carriage was overtaken, the President's order was sent back, and no attempt was made to induce the latter to reconsider his decision. This was a clever scheme on the part of Mr. Justice Campbell to soothe the wounded feelings of the South, and no doubt was kindly meant, but it would have created a commotion in the North.

About an hour after the departure of Mr. Campbell, a man dressed in gray homespun, with a huge rough stick in his hand, appeared at the landing and demanded to see the President. "I am Duff Green," he said; "I want to see Abraham Lincoln, and my business concerns myself alone. You tell Abraham Lincoln that Duff Green wants to see him." The officer of the deck delivered this message in the cabin, and the President said, "Let him come on board; Duff is an old friend of mine, and I would like to talk with him."

When Mr. Duff Green passed over the side, he stood defiantly on deck, scowled at the flag, then turning to Admiral Porter, whom he knew very well, said: "I want to see Abraham Lincoln." "When you come in a respectful manner," said the Admiral, "the President will see you; but throw away that cord of wood you have in your hand before entering the President's presence."

"How long is it," inquired Duff Green, "since Abraham Lincoln took to aping royalty? Man clothed in a little brief authority cuts such fantastic capers before high heaven as make the angels weep. I expect airs from a naval officer, but not from a man with Abraham Lincoln's horse-sense."

The Admiral thought, and still thinks, the man was crazy; but he made Mr. Green throw his stick overboard, which was done, with the remark: "Has it come to that? Is he afraid of assassination? Tyrants generally get into that condition."

The Admiral reported all this to the President, who remarked: "Let him come down; he always was a little queer; I shan't mind him."

When Mr. Green was shown into the cabin, the President arose and offered him his hand. "No," said Green, with a tragic air, "it is red with blood; I can't touch it. When I knew it, it was an honest hand. It has cut the throats of thousands of my people, and their blood, which now lies soaking into the ground, cries aloud to heaven for vengeance. I came to see you, not for old remembrance' sake, but to give you a piece of my opinion. You won't like it, but I don't care, for people don't generally like to have the truth told them. You have come here, protected by your Army and Navy, to gloat over the ruin and desolation you have caused. You are a second Nero, and had

you lived in his day you would have fiddled while Rome was burning."

When the fanatic commenced his tirade, Mr. Lincoln stood with outstretched hand, his mouth wreathed in a pleasant smile. He was pleased at meeting an old and esteemed friend. As Duff Green started on his talk, the outstretched hand was withdrawn, the smile left his lips and the softness in the President's eyes faded out. He was another man altogether. Green went on without noticing the change in the President's manner and appearance: "You came here," he continued "to triumph over a poor conquered town, with only women and children in it, whose soldiers have left it, and would rather starve than see your hateful presence here; those soldiers—and only a handful at that—who have for four years defied your paid mercenaries on those glorious hills, and have taught you to respect the rights of the South. You have given your best blood to conquer them, and now you will march back to your demoralized Capitol and lay out your wits to win them over so that you can hold this Government in perpetuity. Shame on you! Shame on——"

Mr. Lincoln could stand it no longer, his hair stood on end and his nostrils dilated. He stretched out his arm until his lean forefinger almost touched Duff Green's face. "Stop, you political tramp," he exclaimed; "you, the aider and abettor of those who have brought all this ruin upon your country, without the courage to risk your person in defence of the principles you profess to espouse! A fellow who stood by to gather up the loaves and fishes, if any should fall to you! A man who had no principles in the North, and took none South with him! A political hyena, who robbed the graves of the dead and adopted their language as his own! You talk of the North cutting the throats of the Southern people. You have all cut your own throats, and unfortunately have cut many of those of the North. Miserable impostor, vile intruder! Go, before I forget myself and the high position I hold! Go, I tell you, and don't desecrate this national vessel another minute!"

This was something Mr. Duff Green had not calculated upon. His courage failed him, and he fled out of the cabin, never stopping until he reached the deck, where he stood looking at the shore, seemingly measuring the distance to see if he could swim to the landing. The Admiral followed close behind him, and said to the officer of the deck, "Put that man on shore, and if he appears in sight of this vessel while we are here, have him sent away with scant ceremony."

When the Admiral returned to the cabin,

fifteen minutes later, the President was perfectly calm, as if nothing had happened, and did not refer to the subject for some hours. "This place seems to give you annoyance, sir," said the Admiral; "would you prefer going to City Point, where we are more among friends than here?" "Yes," replied the President, "let us go. I seem to be putting my foot into it here all the time. Bless my soul! how Seward would have preached and read Puffendorf, Vattel and Grotius to me, if he had been here when I gave Campbell permission to let the Legislature meet! I'd never have heard the last of it. Seward is a small compendium of international law himself, and laughs at my horse-sense, which I pride myself on, and yet I put my foot into that thing about Campbell with my eyes wide open. If I were you, Admiral, I don't think I would repeat that joke yet awhile. People might laugh at you for knowing so much more than the President."

Several incorrect accounts of the President's visit to Richmond have from time to time appeared in print, for which reason we have inserted this narrative of Mr. Lincoln's proceedings.

The President returned to Washington, and with the surrender of General Lee the war was virtually at an end; so that the services of the Navy in the James River, with the exception of a few gun-boats, could be dispensed with. The latter were needed for police duty along the river and to pick up stragglers from the Confederate army. No one but an eye-witness could realize the great change in the aspect of affairs that suddenly took place. Naval vessels headed down stream towards Fortress Monroe, then to proceed to such Navy Yards as they might be ordered to. Army transports were hurrying to City Point to remove troops and stores as might be required. Officers no longer wore an anxious look, everywhere contentment reigned, for each one was pleased that the long struggle was over and there was a prospect of soon seeing a united country.

Notwithstanding Rear-Admiral Semmes, in his Memoirs, dilates on the joy of the exchanged prisoners at once more saluting the Confederate flag waving on board his vessels, it is well known that the Confederate soldiers and sailors had for a year past been heartily tired of the war; and that their armies were gradually becoming demoralized, as was evident from the great number of desertions, which reduced Lee's forces to such a small number at the surrender. Those who remained with their General to the end may be compared to the Old Guard of Napoleon. Yet even these veterans were anxious to reach their homes, and every one who knew anything about the matter felt with Mr. Lincoln that it was well to give them their horses with which to plow their fields, and their muskets to shoot the crows with, for which indulgence they would feel so grateful that they would probably never again raise their hands against the Government.

Had it been necessary to equip an army for the purpose of driving the French from Mexico, the very troops that had fought so persistently against the Federal Government would have been the foremost to volunteer for the service, and would have been preferred for the duty, since it was well that such unsettled spirits should have had employment, and they would have had an opportunity to strike a blow for the old flag which would tend to make them faithful to it forever. It may, therefore, be considered a misfortune that the French made their exit from Mexico on the first demand of the United States Government, for to have driven them out with a combined army of the blue and the gray would have contributed more to make our country united than all the arts of politicians.

We have several days appointed during the year for national observance — July 4th, February 22d, etc. — but there is one day which brought more happiness to the country than any other, which is the day when peace was established between the North and South, and the nation was once more restored to its entirety. There should be a national anniversary established to commemorate the return of peace—the anniversary of the day when General Lee laid down his arms with the determination never to take them up again against the Union, in which he was followed by General Johnston and all the other generals of the Confederacy.

Such a national anniversary should not be observed with any purpose of exulting over those who laid down their arms and returned to their allegiance, but simply to commemorate the return of peace and the union of the whole nation—that union on which the prosperity of all the States depends. That would be a day in which every one could take part; for he must be blind, indeed, who cannot see the innumerable blessings that have been poured upon our country.

We join hands now over the resting-places of the gallant dead and strew flowers alike on the graves of the boys in blue and the boys in gray. Let there be a common Anniversary, where all can clasp hands, and let that be the memorable day when the Confederacy laid down their arms.

CHAPTER LV.

OPERATIONS OF THE MISSISSIPPI SQUADRON IN THE LATTER PART OF 1864 AND IN 1865.

Acting Rear-Admiral S. P. Lee takes Command.—Loss of the Tin-Clad "Undine."—Burning of the Gun-boats "Towah," "Key West" and "Elfin."—Operations of the Army under General Thomas against General Hood.—The Effective Work Performed by the Squadron in Conjunction with the Army.—Destroying the Confederate Batteries on the Tennessee River.—General George H. Thomas Compliments the Navy.—General Hood's Retreat and Losses.—The Confederate Ram "Webb."—Gallantry of Lieutenant-Commander Fitch and his Men.—End of the Confederate Navy in the Mississippi Region.—Surrender of Confederate Property at Shreveport.—List of Vessels and Officers of the Mississippi Squadron, 1865.

ACTING - REAR - ADMIRAL S. P. Lee, who followed Rear-Admiral Porter in October, 1864, in the command of the Mississippi Squadron, was not fortunate on his arrival in the West.

On the 4th of November, Admiral Lee reports the loss of the "tin-clad" gun-boat "Undine" in an engagement with the Confederates on the "Tennessee." The enemy had seven pieces of artillery against the gun-boat's four.

On the 4th of November the light-draft gun-boats "Towah," "Key West" and "Elfin" had a severe engagement with the enemy, lasting several hours, when Acting-Volunteer-Lieutenant E. M. King, finding it impossible to save the vessels, ordered them to be set on fire and abandoned. These gun-boats had previously recaptured and burned what was left of the "Undine" and also the transport "Venus." The latter and seven other transports were obliged to be destroyed to prevent their falling into the hands of the enemy.

The commanding officers of these light gun-boats fought their vessels with great bravery, but they had been sent on duty that more properly belonged to iron-clads, and in contending against the enemy's works their ardor eclipsed their judgment. In their desire not to dim the record of the Mississippi Squadron, these officers held their position longer than they should have done, by which eleven steamers, including transports, were given to the flames.

Lieutenant-Commander Le Roy Fitch, a most gallant officer, was in command of the 10th District, Mississippi Squadron, which included the vessels destroyed. Had he been present, his good judgment would have led to a different result. Fitch arrived on the scene when the batteries of the gun-boats had been mostly disabled, and to have run the enemy's batteries to join the gun-boats would only have added to the disaster. So he witnessed the desperate engagement from below the enemy's works, and had time to reflect on the want of judgment displayed in sending such frail vessels against strong earth-works mounting rifled field-pieces in a narrow river full of shoals and sand-bars.

Notwithstanding it had been evident from the commencement of the civil war that Tennessee was one of the prizes for which the Confederacy would contend, and in spite of all the trouble the Federal Army and Navy had incurred to get the State under subjection, it had again been abandoned to the tender mercies of the Confederate rangers. General Thomas, with a comparatively small force, was left to occupy the whole State, so that when General Sherman defeated Hood, at Atlanta, the latter fell back upon Tennessee, and but for the generalship and foresight of that sturdy old Roman, George H. Thomas, a great disaster would have overtaken the Union cause.

The Confederate General, Forrest, had invested Johnsonville, and Hood's entire army was reported as moving on that place, the scene of the late destruction of the gunboats and transports. It is not likely that Acting Rear-Admiral Lee had been apprised of the advance of Hood's army into Tennessee, as otherwise he would have sent some iron-clads to that quarter, since the "tin-clads" were entirely too light to contend against the heavy batteries opposed to them.

Soon after these events, the "Carondelet" was sent to Lieutenant-Commander Fitch, who, on the 3d of December, had pushed on up to Nashville in the expectation of co-operating with General Thomas against the advancing forces of Hood. The "Carondelet," Acting-Master Charles W. Miller, was stationed to assist that portion of the army resting on the river, while the other vessels of Fitch's command were kept in readiness to move wherever they might be required. During the day, Lieutenant-Commander Fitch made constant trips up and down the river in the gun-boat "Moose," getting everything in readiness to co-operate with the Army to the best advantage.

At 9 P. M., Fitch received intelligence that the enemy's left wing had reached the river and planted batteries at Bell's Mill, four miles below Nashville by land, but, owing to the bends in the river, eighteen miles by water. It was learned that the enemy had captured two steamers, and, although the night was dark and a storm threatening, Fitch determined to recapture or destroy the vessels, so that the Confederates would derive no benefit therefrom.

The squadron moved in the following order : "Neosho," Acting-Volunteer-Lieutenant Samuel Howard ; "Carondelet," Acting-Master Charles W. Miller ; "Fair Play," Acting-Master Geo. J. Groves ; "Moose," Lieutenant-Commander Le Roy Fitch ; "Reindeer," Acting-Volunteer-Lieutenant H. A. Glassford ; "Silver Lake," Acting-Master J. C. Coyle. Acting-Master Miller, in the "Carondelet," was directed to run below the enemy's lower batteries, giving them grape and canister as he passed, then round-to and fight the batteries heading up stream. The "Fair Play" was to follow close to the "Carondelet" and act in concert with her ; the "Reindeer" was to follow the "Moose," and the "Silver Lake" was to bring up the rear. All these vessels, with the exception of the "Carondelet" and "Neosho," were light gun-boats, known in the vernacular of the Mississippi Squadron as "tin-clads."

The vessels moved quietly down the river, with no lights visible, and were not seen by the enemy until the "Carondelet" opened fire on his lower battery and encampment. The Confederates sprang to arms, and volley after volley of musketry was poured into the Union vessels, while the shore batteries kept up a brisk fire.

The gun-boats responded with equal rapidity, and the narrow river was soon filled with smoke, which caused great confusion for a time, preventing the vessels from firing, while it was no hindrance to the enemy, who could see the position of the gun-boats and kept up a galling fire upon them.

The chances of the vessels coming in collision with each other, in the thick smoke, caused Lieutenant-Commander Fitch, in his flag-ship, to back up the river past the upper batteries, as that portion of the stream was clear of the smoke. In performing this manœuvre, the "Moose" was subjected to a severe fire from the enemy's 20-pounder rifles ; but in a short time the fire of the "Moose" began to tell, and the enemy were driven from their guns by the shower of shrapnel. The "Reindeer," now coming to the assistance of the "Moose," the two vessels swept the field. The "Moose" and "Reindeer" were lashed side by side together, and kept up the engagement through the night. The enemy's fire was not well directed, most of their shots passing over the vessels. The latter, although a good deal cut up, were not in any way disabled, and there was no loss of life on board.

At about midnight the enemy ceased firing, and in the morning were nowhere to be seen. The "Moose" then moved down the stream and met the "Carondelet" and "Fair Play," in company with the transports the enemy had captured the day before. The enemy had been driven out of these vessels before they had time to destroy them or to remove the forage and stores with which they were loaded. The prisoners captured by the Confederates in the transports escaped from their guards and rejoined the vessels.

This whole affair, like everything else undertaken by Lieutenant-Commander Fitch, was well managed. Although his command was not a large one, this young officer was often mentioned for gallant and efficient service, and he ever displayed sound judgment, no matter in what position he was placed. His officers and men, inspired by his spirit, were conspicuous for their bravery. The management of the vessels on the occasion we have just mentioned required great judgment and coolness to avoid collision. The greatest width of the stream was seventy-five yards, and it was so filled with smoke that it was almost impossible to see anything. The little flotilla arrived in Nashville with the two recaptured transports, "Prairie State" and "Prima Donna," in tow, and also the "Magnet," which had been retaken from the enemy. The loss of the Confederates in their engagement with the gun-boats was afterwards found to be considerable.

On the 4th of December the iron-clad steamer "Neosho" had joined the flotilla of Lieutenant-Commander Fitch. She carried two 11-inch smooth-bore guns and was well protected against shots from field batteries.

On the 9th of December Lieutenant-Commander Fitch started down the river with the "Neosho" and some of the lighter gun-boats of his command, together with a number of army transports. When nearly abreast of the scene of the encounter of the 3d inst., a large force of Confederates was discovered advantageously posted to dispute the passage of the vessels. Fourteen pieces of artillery at once opened on the gun-boats, accompanied by heavy volleys of musketry from rifle-pits. Fitch, with his usual judgment, had left the transports three miles in the rear under charge of Acting-Volunteer-Lieutenant Glassford, and when so furiously assailed did not hesitate a moment what to do. He ordered the pilot of the "Neosho" to proceed slowly, while the enemy's fire was deliberately returned, until the vessels arrived abreast of the lower battery. Fitch then rounded-to and fought with his vessel's head up stream using grape and canister, while the "Neosho" was receiving the concentrated fire of all the enemy's batteries.

Lieutenant-Commander Fitch's position was the only one from which he could bring his guns to bear upon the different batteries, owing to the manner in which they were sheltered behind the spurs of hills. He had also great faith in the "Neosho," which had been built to defy the enemy's field batteries. She was now in a position to test her strength and to allow her to use grape and canister at a distance of thirty yards. The enemy kept up a terrific cross-fire, and their shot and shell rattled against every part of the vessel; but the deliberate and accurate fire of the gun-boat soon drove back the sharp-shooters and infantry, although the artillery, being strongly posted on the high bluffs with a plunging fire, was found more difficult to silence.

In a short time everything perishable on the outside of the "Neosho" was demolished, yet the little vessel maintained her position for two hours and a half, until, finding that the enemy's shells were cutting away the "fair-weather pilot-house," and letting it down so that it would hide the "fighting pilot-house," and thus obstruct the sight of the commanding officer and pilot, Fitch steamed up the river again under a raking fire, and gained the convoy of transports. Finding it would be impossible to get the transports below the batteries, without having them cut to pieces, Fitch sent them back to Nashville under convoy of the "Fair Play" and "Silver Lake."

But Fitch was not to be balked by the Confederate batteries as long as his ammunition lasted. He set all hands to work to clear away the *debris*, and then proceeded down the river to his old position, taking with him the "Carondelet," a vessel which had withstood the tempest of shot and shell from Forts Henry, Donelson, Vicksburg and Grand Gulf. Having secured the "Carondelet" to the bank above the enemy's batteries, with orders not to open fire until after the "Neosho" should engage, Fitch, in the latter vessel, proceeded below the Confederate batteries, rounded-to, and opened as before.

As on the former occasion, the enemy opened also, but this time they got the worst of it, the "Carondelet," with her heavy guns, dealing destruction right and left. Two of the enemy's pieces were soon dismounted, and by dark all but two of them were silenced. These were fired as the "Neosho" proceeded up stream, there being nothing more for her to do.

This event is mentioned as an exhibition of pertinacity and courage seldom equalled. The gallant Fitch never shrunk from the performance of any duty however hazardous. He was always under fire whenever opportunity offered, not owing to chance circumstances, to which sluggards often attribute a man's reputation for heroism, but to a determined will. This gallant officer gained little promotion for his war services, and his highest recognition was a complimentary letter from the Secretary of the Navy on the occasion when he brought about the capture of General John Morgan, the celebrated Confederate partisan leader. In the engagement with the Confederate batteries, the "Neosho" was struck one hundred and ten times with shot and shell, ranging in size from 20 to 30 pounders, but she received no injury that would have prevented her from going into battle immediately afterwards.

From the 7th to the 15th of December, 1864, Lieutenant-Commander Fitch's little flotilla was most active in co-operating with the Army, making reconnoissances and attacks on Confederate batteries whenever they showed themselves along the river. On the 14th inst., Fitch was requested to co-operate with the Army in order to capture some artillery. By a very skillful manœuvre on the part of the Army and Navy, a battery of four guns was captured. While the Navy were advancing in front, the cavalry surrounded and captured the battery. In the afternoon the same tactics were successful against another battery of four guns, which fell into the hands of the Federal cavalry. The loss of these guns was a severe blow to General Hood at that moment, for he was deficient in artillery

SURGEON NINIAN PINKNEY, FLEET SURGEON, MISSISSIPPI SQUADRON.

In this expedition the Federals found themselves, on the 15th inst., in possession of the field.

Throughout the long and harassing operations which followed the invasion of Hood into Tennessee, the Navy co-operated most zealously with the Army, patrolling the river, destroying Hood's pontoons, and conveying troops from point to point in the gun-boats in the absence of other means of transportation. In this way General A. J. Smith, that gallant officer of the Red River expedition, was enabled to effect a secure lodgment near Hood's army.

The efficient co-operation of the Navy on the Tennessee River, in fact, contributed largely to the demoralization of General Hood's forces, as the gun-boats chased the Confederates along the banks and gave them no rest. For thirty days and nights the officers of the gun-boats had very little rest, such was their zeal in their effort to defeat Hood's army, which had come so far to be beaten, and was never again able to make headway against the Federal forces.

In this important campaign the following was achieved by the Federal army: Fourteen thousand Confederates killed, wounded, and prisoners, including nineteen general officers, seventy guns captured, over three thousand stand of arms taken, twenty ammunition wagons, and a great quantity of ammunition. The only reason that prevented the capture of the whole Confederate army was the wretched condition of the roads, which prevented any rapid pursuit.

The Confederates were also greatly aided by the water falling in the river, preventing the gun-boats from reaching Muscle Shoals, the point were Hood crossed the Tennessee. All along the river, where the vessels of the Navy could penetrate, the destruction of pontoons and ferry flats was immense, so that the main body of the Confederate Army was forced to push on to the Shoals before they could cross the Tennessee. This destruction extended from twelve miles below Florence for a distance of one hundred and seventy-five miles, and enabled the Federal troops to cut off large portions of Hood's demoralized army, and filled the woods with Confederate stragglers.

Anything which bears the signature of that glorious hero, General George H. Thomas, will ever be interesting, and a compliment from him paid to the Navy will be appreciated. General Thomas immediately telegraphed to Acting-Rear-Admiral Lee the result of his operations against General Hood, and expressed his thanks for the aid the Army had received from the naval flotilla on the Tennessee:

UNITED STATES MILITARY TELEGRAPH, }
PADUCAH, KENTUCKY, Dec. 30, 1864. }

[By telegraph from Headquarters Department Cumberland, Pulaski, Dec. 29, 1864.]

SIR—Your two telegrams have been received. We have been pressing the work as hard as the condition of the roads would permit, and have succeeded in taking some few prisoners — probably some five or six hundred—since the enemy crossed Duck River. From the best information I have at this time, Hood's losses since he invaded the State of Tennessee sum up as follows: Six (6) general officers killed, six (6) wounded and one (1) taken prisoner at Franklin—thirteen in all, and about six thousand (6,000) men killed, wounded and taken prisoners at same battle. On the 8th instant, at Murfreesboro', he had one (1) general officer wounded, about one thousand (1,000) men killed, and two hundred and seven (207) taken prisoners, losing two (2) pieces of artillery. In the battles of the 1st and 16th instant, before Nashville, he had one (1) lieutenant-general severely wounded, one (1) major-general and three (3) brigadier-generals, with four thousand four hundred and sixty-two (4 462) officers and men made prisoners, besides losing fifty-three (53) pieces of artillery and over three thousand (3,000) stand of small-arms.

During his retreat we have captured fifteen (15) more guns, and from fifteen hundred (1,500) to two thousand (2,000) prisoners, and a large number of small-arms have been picked up by the way. Citizens report that he passed this place with his army completely disorganized, except the rear-guard, composed of about five thousand (5,000) men. He destroyed a considerable quantity of ammunition at this place, besides abandoning an ammunition-train of fifteen (15 or twenty (20) wagons about a mile beyond. Your official co-operation on the Tennessee River has contributed largely to the demoralization of Hood's army.

Major-General A. J. Smith, commanding detachment of the Army of the Tennessee, will probably reach Clifton by Sunday next, January 1, 1865, where transports are expected to meet him to take his command to Eastport.

Please afford him every assistance in your power in effecting a secure lodgment at Eastport; and as I consider the "Cumberland" now entirely safe, I will be obliged to you if you will have a strong force kept in the "Tennessee" to keep open navigation on that river. In concluding this telegram, it gives me great pleasure to tender to you, your officers and men, my hearty thanks for your cordial co-operation during the operations of the past thirty days.

G. H. Thomas,
Major-General.

Rear-Admiral S. P. Lee,
Commanding Mississippi Squadron, Chickasaw, Alabama.

These were about the last important events in the history of the Mississippi Squadron, as the war was now drawing rapidly to a close. The retreat of Hood left the Tennessee and Cumberland Rivers comparatively free from Confederates, and there was little prospect of another invasion of the State while General Thomas remained in command. The vessels of the Mississippi Squadron were scattered along the great river, where the guerillas still carried on their operations on a small scale. Very little occurred that could embellish the pages of history. The Red River region was revisited, the Washita and Black Rivers patrolled, and every precaution taken to guard those inland waters.

At this time the Confederate ram "Webb" succeeded in making her way past all the vessels of the fleet and reached a point twenty-five miles below New Orleans, where she was destroyed, as we have heretofore mentioned. This episode created quite an excitement in the fleet for the time, but it appears that no one was to blame for the "Webb" getting so far down the river unharmed. The dash of the "Webb" was the last affair of the expiring Confederate Navy, and the last attempt to carry out a valuable cargo of cotton and naval stores; which, had it been left on the levee at Shreveport, La., a few days longer, could have been shipped to New Orleans, openly insuring the owners a good profit.

The Confederate naval officer in command at Shreveport, Lieutenant J. H. Carter, notified the U. S. naval authorities at the mouth of Red River that he was ready to surrender to the United States Government all the property in his possession, consisting of one useless iron-clad and a quantity of naval stores. Twenty-four officers and eighteen men surrendered themselves and were paroled, and that was the last of the Confederate Navy in the Mississippi region.

When Lieutenant-Commander W. E. Fitzhugh proceeded to Shreveport to take possession of the Confederate naval property at that place, he was received in a friendly manner, and all seemed anxious that he should secure everything that had belonged to the Confederate Government. Above Alexandria, the few ravages made by the invasion of General Banks' army had been obliterated, and the people were living quietly on their farms, although deprived of many comforts to which they had been accustomed. They were delighted at the return of peace, and in their hearts, no doubt, welcomed the Union flag as an old and well-tried friend. They saw in the Union gun-boats the symbols of lawful authority, that would respect the rights of citizens and punish law-breakers; and so conscious were the civil authorities on Red River that it was necessary to have within reach the strong arm of power, that they requested a sufficient naval force should be stationed in their vicinity to overawe the malcontents, if there should be any, and assure those anxious to return to their allegiance that they should receive protection.

As a rule, however, the people of Louisiana were only too glad to lay down their arms and return to the pursuits of peace. Many of them had seen, from the time when the Navy obtained possession of the Mississippi and its tributaries, that it would be useless to contend against the power of the North. It is true that the Confederate forces in Arkansas, Louisiana and Texas showed an indomitable spirit in resisting the advance of the Federal armies, yet they received a sufficient number of checks to convince them that the subjugation of the whole country was merely a question of time.

It is a fact, which has been little commented on, that at least three hundred and fifty thousand soldiers from the slave States fought on the side of the Union, and, had Texas and Western Louisiana been securely held, there would have been a number of recruits in that quarter obtained for the Federal Army.

MISSISSIPPI SQUADRON, JANUARY, 1865.

Acting Rear-Admiral Samuel P. Lee, Commanding.

Staff—Lieutenant-Commander C. A. Babcock, Acting-Fleet-Captain ; Lieutenant F. J. Naile, Flag-Lieutenant ; Acting-Volunteer-Lieutenant, William G. Saltonstall ; Fleet-Surgeon, Ninian Pinkney ; Fleet-Paymaster, Elisha W. Dunn ; Fleet-Engineer, Samuel Bickerstaff ; Acting-Master, C. R. Knowles ; Acting Ensigns, Wm. R. Cooper and C. C. Cushing.

"ESSEX"—FOURTH-RATE.

Commander, Andrew Bryson; Acting-Volunteer-Lieutenant, J. C. Parker ; Acting-Ensigns, Spencer Johnson, E. M. Wood and J. H. Barry ; Acting-Master's Mates, J. A. Whitesides and R. D. Punch; Acting-Assistant Surgeon, Thomas Allan; Acting-Assistant Paymaster, Chas. W. Slamm; Engineers: Acting-Chief, Joseph K. Heap; Acting-First-Assistant, J. L. Hilliard; Acting-Second-Assistants, E. P. Sprague and C. H. Burt; Acting-Third-Assistant, Nicholas Sauer; Gunner, Charles Earnshaw; Acting-Carpenter, Geo. H. Stevens.

"BENTON "—FOURTH-RATE.

Lieutenant-Commander, E. Y. McCauley; Acting-Master, W. J. Lees; Acting-Ensigns, P. H. Randolph and P. Frazer, Jr.; Acting-Master's Mates, William Kisnei, Hiram Simonton, A. T. Bisel, R. L. Evans and Henry Clifton ; Assistant Surgeon, C. J. S. Wells ; Acting-Assistant Paymaster, C. J. Lowndes; Engineers: Acting-Chief, Joseph V. Starr; Acting-First-Assistants, H. W. Fairfowl and S. L. Walkinshaw; Acting-Second Assistants, Oliver Bray, A. A. Jenks and B. A. Farmer; Acting-Third-Assistant, William Hatfield; Acting-Carpenter, Richard Ratchford.

"MANHATTAN "—FOURTH-RATE.

Lieutenant-Commander, Edw. C. Grafton; Acting-Volunteer-Lieutenant, Robert B. Fly; Acting-Ensigns, G. B. Mott, J. B. Trott, C. H. Sinclair and J. L. Harris; Acting-Assistant Surgeon, H. W. Mitchell ; Acting-Assistant Paymaster, H. G. Thayer; Engineers: Acting-Chief, C. L. Carty; Acting-Second-Assistants, W. H. Miller, J. B. Ferrand and Thomas Finnie.

"CHOCTAW "—THIRD-RATE.

Lieutenant-Commander, J. J. Cornwell ; Acting-Master, Ezra C. Beaman ; Acting-Ensigns, M. B. Muncy and H. C. Marsh; Acting-Master's Mates, A. V. Forgey, E. F. Crane and James Stoddard; Assistant Surgeon, Edw. Kershner ; Acting-Assistant Paymaster, E. N. Whitehouse; Engineers: Acting-Chief, N. P. Baldwin; Acting-First-Assistants, C. E. Arbuthnot and J. Blake; Acting-Second-Assistants, J. F. Stone and H. G. Moreland; Acting-Third Assistant, S. C. Babbitt; Acting-Carpenter, John A. Stuart.

"LAFAYETTE"—FOURTH-RATE.

Lieutenant-Commander, James P Foster; Acting-Masters, J. R. Neeld, F. G. Sampson and J. H. Welsh; Acting-Ensigns, Paul Morgan and C. H. Slocum; Acting-Master's Mates, S. O. Lovell, Wm. E. Atkins and Edw. C. Eraley; Acting-Assistant Surgeon, D. Hayden; Acting-Assistant-Paymaster, J. P. Kelly; Engineers: Acting-Chief, Robert Tate; Acting-Second-Assistants, James Wilkins, J. W. Paul and E. H. Kidd; Acting-Third-Assistant, A. A Johnson ; Acting-Gunner, Geo. Price ; Acting-Carpenter, J. W. Lister.

"BLACK HAWK"—THIRD-RATE.

Lieutenant-Commander, James A. Greer; Acting Masters, Edw. Alford and Henry Baker ; Acting Ensigns, C. A. Calvert, R. T. Howell, J. A. Jones, J. C. Barr and J. B. Pratt; Acting-Master's Mates, B. R. Baker, A. S. Ludlow, D. A. Boies, A. H. Ahrens and Jay Nyman; Passed-Assistant-Surgeon, Michael Bradley; Acting-Assistant Paymaster, C. H. Kirkendall; Second Lieutenant of Marines, F. L. Church; Engineers: Acting-Chief, Geo. W. Walker; Acting-First-Assistant, O. G. Richey ; Acting-Second-Assistant, C. B. Adams ; Acting-Third-Assistants, W. B. Richey and J. W. Cassell ; Gunner, John R. Halt; Acting-Carpenter, Noah Dean.

"SYBIL "—FOURTH-RATE.

Lieutenant-Commander, John G. Mitchell; Acting-Volunteer-Lieutenant, J. W. Atkinson; Acting-Ensigns, John McCleane and Wm. Hammett, Jr.; Acting Master's Mates, J. R. Hugle, H. B. Sprague, W. H. Smith and W. W. Rumsey; Acting-Assistant Surgeon, H. A. Bodman; Acting-Assistant Paymaster, T. B. Reed ; Engineers: Acting-First-Assistant, Samuel Tubbs; Acting-Second-Assistant, F. G. Seavey ; Acting-Third-Assistant, W. M. Piercy.

"NEOSHO"—FOURTH-RATE.

Lieutenant-Commander, Robert Boyd, Jr.; Acting-Volunteer-Lieutenant, Samuel Howard; Acting-Master, E. F. Brooks ; Acting-Ensigns, James Downs and W. P. Higbee; Acting-Master's Mates, C. C. Royce and C. T. Rees; Acting-Assistant Surgeon, M. A. Miller ; Acting-Assistant Paymaster, W. H. Byrm; Engineers: Acting-Chief, Wm. Mills; Acting-First-Assistant, W. C. Sanford; Acting-Second-Assistant, J. S. Miles; Acting-Third-Assistants, J. F. Humphrey, W. H. Dunning and M. C. Noland, Acting-Gunner, W. T. Devlan.

"LOUISVILLE "—FOURTH-RATE.

Lieutenant-Commander, George Bacon ; Acting-Master, H. D. Coffinberry ; Acting-Ensigns, R. H. Langslands, Geo. V. Mead and Chas. Smith; Acting-Master's Mates, J. J. Drew, W. H. English and J. T. Hensley; Acting-Assistant Surgeon, W. R. Semans; Engineers: Acting-Chief, Isham J. Hardy; Acting-First-Assistant, C. W. Reynolds ; Acting-Second-Assistant, C. F. Degelman; Acting-Third-Assistant, L. A. Salade ; Acting-Carpenter, James McKuen.

"TENNESSEE "—FOURTH RATE.

Lieutenant-Commander, Edward P. Lull; Acting-Master, C.W. Adams; Acting-Ensigns, W. W. Duley, A. A. Ward and J. J. P. Zettick; Acting-Master's Mates, Henry Wyman, Thos. Kennedy and J. Canaday ; Assistant Surgeon, W. H. Jones ; Acting-Assistant Paymaster, P. H. Tawo ; Engineers : Acting-First-Assistants, W. C. Perry and Chas. Chadwick; Second-Assistant, F. C. Goodwin; Acting-Second-Assistant, B. D. Mulligan; Acting-Third-Assistants, W. J. Mack and D. S. Clarke.

"MOOSE "—FOURTH-RATE.

Lieutenant-Commander, LeRoy Fitch ; Acting-Master, W. C. Coulson; Acting-Ensigns, John Revell, D. B. Dudley and Isaac Wiltse; Acting-Master's Mates, Daniel Molony, O. W. Miles and W. S. Holden; Assistant Surgeon, W. M. Reber; Acting-Assistant Paymaster, Jas. W. Clark; Engineers: Acting-Chief, Wm. D. McFarland; Acting-First-Assistant, Thos. N. Hall; Acting-Second-Assistant, Chas. McMillan; Acting-Third-Assistant, J. D. Hedges.

"OUICHITA"—FOURTH-RATE.

Lieutenant-Commander Byron Wilson; Acting-Master, Eugene Zimmerman; Acting-Ensigns, M. M. Wheeler, R. T. Lamport and J. W. Adams; Acting-Master's Mates, Rivers Drake, E. P. Marshall, A. W. Widup, S. A. Park and J. H. Moss; Acting-Asistant Surgeon, Geo. E. Francis; Acting Assistant Paymaster, J. R. Meeker; Engineers: Acting-Chief, Thos. Hebron; Acting-First-Assistants, John S. Moore; Acting-Second-Assistants, G. T. Wilson and A. H. Tyler; Acting-Third-Assistants, Thos. Reed and F. A. Morse; Acting-Carpenter, Richard Nisbet.

"GENERAL BURNSIDE"—FOURTH-RATE.

Lieutenant, Morean Forrest; Acting-Ensigns, David Putman; Acting-Master's Mates, Roddie Reynolds, Francis McGlincey, W. C. Mudge, Louis Hartlet, Hans Trulsen and Edw. McGaughey; Acting-Assistant Surgeon, R. J. Curtis; Acting-Assistant Paymaster, Geo. D. Rand; Engineers: Acting-First-Assistant, Benj. Chester; Acting-Second-Assistant, Wm. W. Smith; Acting-Third-Assistants, J. G. Burkley and Jos. Walter.

"OSAGE"—FOURTH-RATE.

Acting-Volunteer-Lieutenant, George W. Rogers; Acting-Master, Wm. S. Pease; Acting-Ensigns, W. J. Durney and Arthur O'Leary; Acting-Master's Mates, John C. Winslow and R. W. Rogers; Acting-Assistant Paymaster, J. R. Bowler; Engineers: Acting-Chief, Thos. Doughty; Acting-First-Assistant, R. J. Stone; Acting-Second-Assistants, W. C. Gabbrith and Wm. Grant; Acting-Third-Assistants, Wm. Burke and J. M. Wilson; Acting-Carpenter, C. C. Gilliland.

"CARONDELET"—FOURTH-RATE.

Acting-Volunteer-Lieutenant, Chas. P. Clark; Acting-Master, C. W. Miller; Acting-Ensigns, Oliver Donaldson, S. D. Jordan and T. A. Quinn; Acting-Master's Mates, L. W. Hastings, W. H. H. DeGroot, Geo. F. Bean, Wm. J. Fraks and W. D. McKean, Jr.; Acting-Assistant Surgeon, D. Curtis; Acting-Assistant Paymaster, G. W. Robertson; Engineers: Acting-Chief, Chas. H. Caven; Acting-Second-Assistants, Michael Norton and W. S. Barlow; Acting-Third-Assistants, John McWilliams and Thomas Mattingly; Acting-Carpenter, Geo. W. Kenny.

"CHILLICOTHE"—FOURTH-RATE.

Acting-Volunteer-Lieutenant, Geo. P. Lord; Acting-Master, J. M. Holmes; Acting-Ensigns J. D. Buckley, H. A. Hannon, H. Shoemaker and R. H. Day; Acting-Master's Mates, W. S. Thomas, James Harrington and John H. Ely; Acting-Assistant Surgeon, G. C. Osgood; Acting-Assistant Paymaster, J. H. Hathaway; Engineers: Acting-Chief, A. W. Hardy; Acting-First-Assistant, Chas. Trotter; Acting-Second-Assistants, J. W. Hymen and Anthony Lane; Acting-Third-Assistant, J. W. Ferrell; Acting-Gunner, Wm. E. Keyes; Acting-Carpenter, J. H. Fink.

"AVENGER"—FOURTH-RATE.

Acting-Volunteer-Lieutenant, Charles A. Wright; Acting-Ensigns, John Gregg, J. H. Neely and John Maloney; Acting-Master's Mates, Henry Walters, J. D. Moore and E. W. Perry; Acting-Assistant Surgeon, J. H. Moses; Acting-Assistant Paymaster, J. W. Van Cleve, Jr.; Engineers: Acting-Chief, John G. Scott; Acting-First-Assistant, J. A. Burns; Acting-Second-Assistant, S. S. Patterson; Acting-Third-Assistants, Wm. Jayne and Thomas McGarrity; Acting-Carpenter, Benj. H. Brink.

"EXCHANGE"—FOURTH-RATE.

Acting-Volunteer-Lieutenant, James C. Gipson; Acting-Ensigns, C. L. Meany and R. W. Brown; Acting-Master's Mates, G. T. Miller, B. F. Saunders and J. W. Clawson; Acting-Assistant Surgeon, E. M. Goodwin; Acting-Assistant Paymaster, D. Davis, Jr.; Engineers: Acting-First-Assistant, A. G. Per-

kins; Acting-Second-Assistant, C. C. Streepey; Acting-Third-Assistant, B. F. Graham.

"PITTSBURGH"—FOURTH-RATE.

Acting-Volunteer-Lieutenant-Commander, Wm. R. Hoel; Acting-Master, S. B. Coleman; Acting-Ensigns, James Ovatt and Freeman Vincent; Acting-Master's Mates, John Scott, C. B. Jones and F. M. McCord; Acting-Assistant Surgeon, F. M. Follett, Acting-Assistant Paymaster, Charles H. Gould; Engineers: Acting-Chief, Geo. H. Atkinson; Acting-First-Assistant, E. R. Pavy; Acting-Second-Assistants, W. H. Mitchell and Robert Milby; Acting-Gunner, F. C. Green; Acting-Carpenter, Wm. C. Boggs.

"REINDEER"—FOURTH-RATE.

Acting-Volunteer-Lieutenant, H. A. Glassford; Acting-Master, John H. Rice; Acting-Ensigns, C. W. Spooner and T. M. Lewis; Acting-Master's Mates, G. S. Upton, E. Gasaway and W. H. Burton; Acting-Assistant Surgeon, F. A. Jordan; Acting-Assistant Paymaster, W. W. Barry; Engineers: Acting-First-Assistant, A. H. Bagby; Acting Second-Assistant, N. Conner; Acting-Third-Assistant, G. M. Hayman.

"TAYLOR"—FOURTH-RATE.

Acting-Volunteer-Lieutenant, Fred'k S. Hill; Acting-Masters, W. T. Power and Charles Ackley; Acting-Ensigns, J. W. Lalor and W. H. C. Michael; Acting-Master's Mates, W. P. Eakle and H. S. Allen; Acting-Assistant Surgeon, Sam'l Mendenhall; Acting-Assistant Paymaster, Geo. H. Holt; Engineers: Acting-Chief, James Fleming; Acting-First-Assistant, J. R. Ramsey; Acting-Second-Assistants, Wm. Furck and Philip Sheridan; Acting-Third-Assistants, Walter Mossington and S. H. Lancaster; Acting-Carpenter, J. M. Peabody.

"VINDICATOR"—THIRD-RATE.

Acting-Volunteer-Lieutenant, Henry H. Gorringe; Acting-Masters, J. F. Reed and D. P. Slattery; Acting-Ensigns, W. Zimmerman, B. C. Wheeler and J. W. Foster; Acting-Master's Mates, L. C. Ball, John Davis, Lewis Lehman, Henry Kane and A. A. King; Acting-Assistant Surgeon, C. E. Vaughn; Acting-Assistant Paymaster, F. W. Hanson; Engineers: Acting-Chief, Thomas Cook; Acting-Second-Assistants, Chas. Tistandt, Anthony Courtway and James O'Neil; Acting-Third-Assistants, S. H. Brogan, Andrew Lusk and John Link; Acting-Gunner, Wm. H. Barton; Acting-Carpenter, James Trulty.

"HASTINGS"—FOURTH-RATE.

Acting-Volunteer-Lieutenant, J. S. Watson; Acting-Master, Wm. Neil; Acting-Ensigns, C. H. Reed and Jas. McDonald; Acting-Master's Mates, E. C. Urner and W. H. Gray; Assistant Surgeon, James M. Flint; Acting-Assistant Paymaster, P. J. Stone, Jr.; Engineers: Acting-First-Assistant, H. L. Juce; Acting-Second-Assistants, Edwin Senior and Andrew Wilson; Acting-Third-Assistants, A. M. Wasson and Geo. W. Amsden.

"FOREST ROSE"—FOURTH-RATE.

Acting-Volunteer-Lieutenant, A. N. Gould; Acting-Ensigns, H. B. Graves, C. W. Johnston and Geo. G. Cox; Acting-Master's Mates, Ira Athearn, C. W. Crooker and J. M. Stewart; Acting-Assistant Surgeon, R. Cadwallader; Acting-Assistant Paymaster, A. J. Myers; Engineers: Acting-First-Assistant, Francis Marsh; Acting-Second-Assistant, Joseph Kennedy; Acting-Third-Assistant, Silas Huskey.

"ST. CLAIR"—FOURTH-RATE.

Acting-Volunteer-Lieutenant, James S. French; Acting-Ensigns, Joseph Sawyer, W. A. Burchard and H. O. Proctor; Acting-Master's Mates, W. S. Culbertson, James Reid and W. T. Ross; Acting-Assistant Paymaster, E. H. Johnson; Engineers:

Acting-First-Assistant, Wm. McLean ; Acting-Second-Assistant, Edward Lozier ; Acting-Third-Assistant, Michael J. Soden.

"LEXINGTON"—FOURTH-RATE.

Acting - Volunteer - Lieutenant, William Flye · Acting - Ensigns, Henry Booby, J. G. Megler, C. C. Briggs and Howard Hale ; Acting - Master's Mates, C. W. Botten and Ezra McDunn ; Acting - Assistant Surgeon, H. M. Mixer ; Acting-Assistant Paymaster, T. Doane; Engineers: Acting-Chief, W. H. Meredith ; Acting - First - Assistant, A. L. Mann ; Acting - Second - Assistant, Reuben Story ; Acting - Third - Assistants, Jacob Vittinger and Wm. T. Neal; Acting-Gunner, Louis Frederick ; Acting-Carpenter, R. Carroll.

"CINCINNATI"—FOURTH-RATE.

Acting-Volunteer-Lieutenant, Jason Goudy; Acting-Master, J. B. Williams; Acting-Ensigns, Walter Pinner and S. J. Denight; Acting-Master's Mates, J. G. Abbott, A. B. Allen and J. B. A. Conant; Acting-Assistant Surgeon, E. Dayton ; Acting-Assistant Paymaster, J. R. Carmody ; Engineers : Acting-Chief, J.W. Hartuper ; Acting-First-Assistant, E. D. Collett ; Acting - Second - Assistants, T. Guernsey and G. W. Dean ; Acting-Third-Assistants, Andrew Boland and John Henry; Acting-Gunner, L. K. Ellis ; Acting-Carpenter, John Cronan.

"NAUMKEAG"—FOURTH-RATE.

Acting-Volunteer-Lieutenant, John Rogers ; Acting-Ensigns, Thos. Cadwell; Acting-Master s Mates, Alex. Procter, H. R. Ferris and J. P. Popejoy; Acting-Assistant Surgeon, Edgar L. R. Draper ; Acting-Assistant-Paymaster, Henry B. Mears ; Engineers : Acting-First-Assistant, Edward Cage ; Acting-Second - Assistant, J. A. McCormick ; Acting - Third-Assistant, J. R. Byland.

"FORT HINDMAN"—FOURTH-RATE.

Acting-Volunteer-Lieutenant, John Pearce ; Acting - Master, J. J. Rogers ; Acting - Ensigns, N. T. Rennell and Chas. Marsden ; Acting-Master's Mates, C. F. A. McCord, S. N. Barker and E. C. Ellis ; Acting-Assistant Surgeon, N. L. Gerould ; Acting-Assistant Paymaster, J. R. Bowler ; Engineers : Acting-First-Assistant, Thos. Girty; Acting-Second-Assistant, John Coock ; Acting-Third-Assistants, D. B. Cox, Eli Powell and R. Yocum.

"BRILLIANT"—FOURTH-RATE.

Acting-Volunteer-Lieutenant, Chas. G. Perkins ; Acting-Master, G. D. Little ; Acting-Ensign, N. F. Vaughan ; Acting-Master's Mate, C. D. Griggs ; Acting - Assistant Surgeon, Milton James ; Acting-Assistant Paymaster, B. Page ; Engineers : Acting-First - Assistant, W. E. Willey ; Acting - Second-Assistant, Jas. Cutler; Acting-Third-Assistant, C.W. Egster and R. M. Myers.

"OZARK"—FOURTH-RATE.

Acting -Volunteer - Lieutenant, Geo. W. Brown; Acting-Master, John Powell ; Acting-Ensigns, Jos. Moyer, C. M. Bragg and C. M. Fuller; Acting-Master's Mates, N. T. Brown, G. A. Ege and D. C. Fralick ; Acting-Assistant Paymaster, F. T. Gillette ; Engineers : Acting-First-Assistants, J. H. Everhart and A. J. Sypher ; Acting-Second-Assistants, J. L. Parsons and G. M. Baker ; Acting-Third-Assistants, C. Beal and Southwell Lyon ; Acting Gunner, J. F. Riblett ; Acting-Carpenter, H. J. Ervin.

"PEOSTA"—FOURTH-RATE.

Acting-Volunteer Lieutenant, J. E. Smith; Acting-Master, J. L. Bryant ; Acting-Ensigns, C. H. Gullick, R. T. Nelson, J. W. Richards and W. W. Phillips ; Acting - Master's Mates, E. A. Dumont ; Acting-Assistant Surgeon, Isaac T. Coates ; Acting-Assistant Paymaster, J. C. Spalding ; Engineers : Acting-First-Assistants, Perry South and J. Bole-

jack ; Acting-Second-Assistant, T. M. Sloan ; Acting-Third-Assistant, G. W. Marfield ; Acting-Carpenter, m. Reid.

"JULIET"—FOURTH-RATE.

Acting-Volunteer-Lieutenant, Thos. B. Gregory ; Acting - Ensign, E. C. Williams ; Acting - Master's Mates, G. A. Gregory, J. S. McCoy, G. W. Ball and W. M. Mullen ; Acting - Assistant Surgeon, W. W. Wentworth ; Acting-Assistant Paymaster, J. Linsly, Jr. ; Engineers : Acting First - Assistant, W. H. Hardin ; Acting - Second - Assistant, J. G. Briggs ; Acting-Third-Assistant, Thomas Hanna.

"KENWOOD"—FOURTH RATE.

Acting - Volunteer - Lieutenant, John Swaney ; Acting-Ensigns, J. C. Weeks, J. L. Reed and N. H. Conklin; Acting-Master's Mates, M. M. Yorston and W. R. Moffatt ; Acting-Assistant Paymaster, D. W. Van Houten ; Engineers : Acting-First-Assistant, T. J. Mallon ; Acting - Second - Assistant, W. J. Milligan ; Acting-Third-Assistant, J. H. Holman.

"INDIANOLA"—FOURTH-RATE.

Acting-Volunteer-Lieutenant, James Lanning.

"GENERAL BRAGG"—FOURTH-RATE.

Acting-Volunteer-Lieutenant, Cyrenius Deminey ; Acting - Master, W. L. Holcomb ; Acting - Ensigns, M. Houston and F. H. Waite; Acting-Master's Mates, James Williams, C. L. Chapman and Wm. Dickson; Acting - Assistant Surgeon, F. A. Castle ; Acting-Assistant Paymaster, L. C. Stebbins ; Engineers : Acting-Chief, James Miller ; Acting-Second-Assistants, Jos. Anderson and J. A. Wilson ; Acting-Carpenter, J. W. Kennedy.

"GENERAL PRICE"—FOURTH-RATE.

Acting-Volunteer Lieutenant, W. R. Wells ; Acting-Master, H. E. Bartlett ; Acting-Ensigns, J. H. Leever and D. P. Bosworth, Jr.; Acting-Master's Mates, D. McKay, P. Barclay and W.W. McCracker; Acting - Assistant Surgeon, Geo. Harvey ; Acting-Assistant Paymaster, T. F. Croft ; Engineers : Acting - Chief, Thos. Sheffer ; Acting - First - Assistant, A. R. Calhoun; Acting-Second-Assistant, A. Campbell ; Acting-Third-Assistants, J. B. Baldwin and R. A. Hyle ; Acting-Carpenter, W. C. Stiver.

"PAW-PAW"—FOURTH-RATE.

Acting-Master, M. V. B. Haines ; Acting-Ensigns, J. H. Rivers and W. L. Constantine ; Acting-Master's Mates, John Pybus and J. D. Coriell ; Acting-Assistant Surgeon, O. A. Rives ; Acting - Assistant Paymaster, A. S. McWilliams ; Engineers : Acting-First-Assistant, E. Reynolds; Acting-Second-Assistant, B. S. Bull ; Acting-Third-Assistant, T. K. Hill.

"PRAIRIE BIRD"—FOURTH-RATE.

Acting-Master, Thomas Burns ; Acting-Ensigns, J. W. Chambers and W. M. Ernst ; Acting-Master's Mates, J. B. Morton, J. K. Lull, Jr., W. D. Bangs and W. D. Carley ; Acting - Assistant Paymaster, Lafayette Harter ; Engineers : Acting-First-Assistant, Geo. Rodabaugh ; Acting - Second - Assistant, Joseph Grippin ; Acting - Third - Assistant, M. G. Marsillot.

"MOUND CITY"—FOURTH-RATE.

Acting-Master, Frederick T. Coleman ; Acting-Ensigns, W. H. Decker and T. J. Dean; Acting-Master's Mates, B. W. Herr, S. S. Spangler, W. M. Sterritt and C. B. Hapgood ; Acting-Assistant Paymaster, Wm. H. Baer ; Engineers : Acting-Chief, Edw. Merriman ; Acting - First - Assistant, Alex. Magee ; Acting-Second-Assistants, J. M. Hartwell, J. B. Atwood, G. N. Heisel and F. Vanzant ; Acting-Gunner, T. H. Green ; Acting - Carpenter, Jerome Burns.

"JUDGE TORRENCE"—FOURTH-RATE.

Acting-Master, Jeremiah Irwin ; Acting-Ensign,

Wm. Sill; Acting-Master's Mate, Chas. White; Acting-Assistant Paymaster, J. H. Marshall; Engineers: Acting-Chief, P. R. Hartwig; Acting-Second-Assistants, Jasper Holman and E. C. Jones; Acting-Third-Assistant, John Denhart.

"ARGOSY."

Acting-Master, John C. Morong; Acting-Ensigns, G. T. Hazlett and A. B. Homer; Acting-Master's Mates, Peter Lake and J. A. McCreary; Acting-Assistant Paymaster, R. E. Patterson; Engineers: Acting-First-Assistant, Thos. Blanchard; Acting-Second-Assistant, Chas. Silvercahn; Acting-Third-Assistant, A. Donnelly.

"ALEXANDRIA"—FOURTH-RATE.

Acting-Master, D. P. Rosemiller; Acting-Master's Mate, D. M. Stauffer; Engineers: Acting-First-Assistant, H. C. Shibly; Acting-Second-Assistant, J. S. Willcoxan; Acting-Third-Assistant, J. W. Morton.

"MARMORA"—FOURTH-RATE.

Acting-Master, Thomas Gibson; Acting-Ensigns, D. D. Bond and Thos. West; Acting-Master's Mates, Wm. Arnold, E. C. Nye and W. B. Tice; Acting-Assistant Surgeon, Emile Gavarret; Acting-Assistant Paymaster, Chas. R. Howard; Engineers: Acting-First-Assistant, A. H. Armstrong; Acting-Second-Assistant, F. A. Cramer; Acting-Third-Assistant, C. S. Hamiiton.

"FAIR PLAY"—FOURTH-RATE.

Acting-Master, George J. Groves; Acting-Ensigns, J. H. Singleton, L. R. Hamersley and J. S. De Forrest; Acting-Master's Mates, C. B. Thatcher, J. W. Harbin and W. H. Roberts; Acting-Assistant Paymaster, John G. Sankey; Engineers: Acting-First-Assistant, Robert Mattratha; Acting-Second-Assistant, John Mayhugh; Acting-Third-Assistants, Wm. Davizley and C. C. Rusford; Acting-Carpenter, Thomas Manning.

"FAWN"—FOURTH-RATE.

Acting-Master, John R. Grace; Acting-Ensigns, John Sullivan and John Conden; Acting-Master's Mates, Chas. Murray, E. D. O'Bryon and J. A. Leaman; Acting-Assistant Paymaster, A. S. Apgar; Engineers: Acting-First-Assistant, Edw. C. Peck; Acting-Second-Assistants, G. W. Gough and Michael O'Reiley; Acting-Third-Assistant, C. A. Cooper.

"HUNTRESS"—FOURTH-RATE.

Acting-Master, John S. Dennis; Acting-Ensigns, J. M. Flynt and Frank Middleton; Acting-Master's Mates, H. Z. Allphin, B. F. Brumback and J. R. Thomas; Acting-Assistant Surgeon, H. S. De Ford; Acting-Assistant Paymaster, E. J. Hurling; Engineers: Acting-First Assistant, John Cullin; Acting-Second-Assistant, Isaac Ackley; Acting-Third-Assistant, Johnson Crawford.

"NEW ERA"—FOURTH-RATE.

Acting-Master, A. C. Sears; Acting-Ensigns, W. B. Shilleto and C. A. Schetky; Acting-Master's Mates, W. F. Renner, A. Hamilton and Henry Ufford; Acting-Assistant-Surgeon, Geo. A. Warren; Acting-Assistant-Paymaster, Wm. B. Purdy; Engineers: Acting-First-Assistant, Israel Marsh; Acting-Third-Assistants, A. W. Smith and J. W. Edmundson; Acting-Carpenter, Byard Martin.

"CRICKET"—FOURTH-RATE.

Acting-Master, M. J. Cronin; Acting-Ensigns, N. A. Closson and Ignatius Daum; Acting-Master's Mates, H. C. Bates, J. W. Summers, Louis J. Marshall and Walter Lawrence; Acting-Assistant Surgeon, Stephen Cushing; Acting-Assistant Paymaster, C. S. Dunscomb; Engineers: Acting-First-Assistant, Jebin Fox; Acting-Second-Assistant, T. C. Ridgly; Acting-Third-Assistant, R. A. Halderman.

"NYMPH"—FOURTH RATE.

Acting-Master, Patrick Donnelly; Acting-Ensigns, F. M. Hathaway and L. Gardner; Acting-Master's Mates, W. C. Williams, W. C. Frost, C. A. Benham, F. W. Whiteside and W. W. Hosea; Acting-Assistant Surgeon, D. P. Taylor; Acting-Assistant Paymaster, Arthur Sibley; Engineers: Acting-First-Assistant, N. D. Smith; Acting-Second-Assistant, Z. Brickell; Acting-Third-Assistants, A. T. Horner and W. H. Poulson.

"NAIAD"—FOURTH-RATE.

Acting-Master, Henry T. Keene; Acting-Ensigns, R. W. Alson and B. G. Van Dyke; Acting-Master's Mates, L. A. Cole, C. H. Leaman and C. E. Townley; Acting-Assistant Paymaster, M. P. Lowry; Engineers: Acting-First-Assistant, R. P. Morrow; Acting-Second-Assistant, C. Abbott; Acting-Third-Assistants, W. H. Collins, Edw. W. Brooks and J. H. Henderson.

"GREAT WESTERN"—FOURTH-RATE.

Acting-Master, Benj. Sebastian; Acting-Ensign, D. W. Tainter; Acting-Master's Mates, A. S. Thompson, N. E. Moore, W. F. Thomas and H. P. Bosworth; Acting-Assistant Surgeon, F. W. Wunderlich; Paymaster, Geo. L. Davis; Chaplain, W. H. Stewart; Engineers: Acting-First-Assistant, G. W. Fulton; Acting-Third-Assistant, A. L. Sinis.

"FAIRY"—FOURTH-RATE.

Acting-Masters, W. E. H. Fentriss and Chas. Swendson; Acting-Ensigns, J. S. Roberts, J. S. Hurlbut and C. B. Plattenburg; Acting-Master's Mates, H. A. Thoburn and James Lawler; Acting-Assistant Surgeon, Geo. F. Beasley; Acting-Assistant Paymaster, H. T. Wright; Engineers: Acting-First-Assistant, S. H. Linn; Acting-Second-Assistant, W. H. Stiles; Acting-Third-Assistant, Lorenzo Fulton.

"SILVER CLOUD"—FOURTH-RATE.

Acting-Master, Wm. Ferguson; Acting-Ensigns, Rob't Wilkinson, J. M. Reid and J. C. Hall; Acting-Master's Mates, J. M. Darrah, R. S. Critchell and J. H. Bentley; Acting-Assistant-Surgeon, O. B. Damon; Acting-Assistant Paymaster, W. H. Hathorne; Engineers: Acting-First-Assistant, B. F. Clark; Acting-Second-Assistant, W. A. Collins; Acting-Third-Assistants, J. W. Shellenberger and C. M. Milligan.

"PERI"—FOURTH-RATE.

Acting-Master, Thos. M. Farrell; Acting-Ensign, E. C. Higgins; Acting-Master's Mates, J. H. Carter and W. H. Haven; Acting-Assistant Surgeon, T. F. Leech; Acting-Assistant-Paymaster, C. W. Bull; Engineers: Acting-Third-Assistants, J. A. Goodwin, David Pace and John W. Ross.

"GENERAL THOMAS"—FOURTH-RATE.

Acting-Master, Gilbert Morton; Acting-Ensign, Richard McCallister; Acting-Master's Mates, Joseph Grenlick, A. C. Orcutt, L. D. Simonds and Hans Trulsen; Engineers: Acting-First-Assistant, G. W. Burrows; Acting-Second-Assistant, W. E. Cowle; Acting-Third-Assistants, Jackson Andrew and J. W. Miles.

"ROMEO"—FOURTH-RATE.

Acting-Master, Thomas Baldwin; Acting-Ensigns, R. P. Shaw and J. E. Ernst; Acting-Master's Mates, John Winram and W. J. Franks; Acting-Assistant Paymaster, E. R. Moffatt; Engineers: Acting-First-Assistant, J. N. McCurdy; Acting-Second-Assistant, W. E. Taylor; Acting-Third-Assistant, Wm. Teal.

"RATTLER"—FOURTH-RATE.

Acting-Master, N. B. Willetts; Acting-Ensigns, H. N. Wells, S. H. Strunk and H. E. Church; Acting-Master's Mate, John Cronin and W. N. Bock;

Acting-Assistant Surgeon, W. B. Hartman; Acting-Assistant Paymaster, George P. Peck; Engineers: Acting-First-Assistant C. F. Seager; Acting-Second-Assistants, G. W. Shields and J. H. Hume.

"SIREN"—FOURTH-RATE.

Acting - Master, James Fitzpatrick; Acting - Ensigns, T. G. Herron and Z. T. Tibbatts; Acting-Master's Mates, E. H. Thompson, J. P. Jordan, C. E. Jordon and H. W. Gray; Acting-Assistant Surgeon, Lewis Westfall; Acting-Assistant Paymaster, S. S. Davis; Engineers: Acting-First Assistant, William Bishop; Acting-Second-Assistant, James Abrams; Acting-Third-Assistant, J. R. Meredith.

"SILVER LAKE"—FOURTH-RATE.

Acting - Masters, J. C. Coyle and G. W. Bone; Acting-Masters Mates, Samuel McKee, J. S. Dubois and F. N. Schooley; Acting - Assistant - Surgeon, J. H. Mills; Engineers: Acting-First-Assistant, Sam'l Ecoff; Acting-Second-Assistant, William J. O'Neill.

"SPRINGFIELD"—FOURTH-RATE.

Acting-Master, Edm. Morgan; Acting- Ensigns, H. D. Disereus and J. E. Wright; Acting-Master's Mates, J. Cunningham, H. Homkomp and William J. Rudd; Engineer: Acting-First-Assistant R. McLean; Acting-Third-Assistants, William Bell and H. J. Spence.

"VICTORY"—FOURTH-RATE.

Acting-Master, Frederick Read; Acting - Ensigns, W. B. Trufant and John Fisher; Acting-Master's Mates, R. L. Taylor, J. L. Kelso and G. W. Kepler; Acting-Assistant Surgeon, G. W. Shields; Acting-Assistant Paymaster, Benj. Page; Engineers: Acting-First-Assistant, J. L. Winston; Acting-Second-Assistant, J. C. Jones; Acting - Third - Assistants, Sam'l Henery and G. W. Postlethwaite.

"GENERAL SHERMAN"—FOURTH-RATE.

Acting-Master, J. W. Morehead; Acting-Ensigns, E. D. Hurd and C. L. McChing; Acting - Master's Mates, D. J. Chadwick and M. Pinney; Engineers: Acting-Second-Assistants, J. W. Street and David Street; Acting-Third-Assistants, Horace Stedman and T. H. Hamilton.

"GENERAL GRANT."

Acting-Ensigns, Joseph Watson and S. H. Harbeson; Acting-Master's Mates, E. B. McSweeney, D. G. Porter and H. W. Kruse; Acting-Assistant Surgeon, W. D. Hoffman; Engineers: Acting- First-Assistant, H. W. Taylor; Acting Second-Assistant, Edw. Costello; Acting-Third-Assistants, William McKenzie, D. Shaw and G. E. Reno.

"CHAMPION"—FOURTH-RATE.

Acting - Ensigns, Thomas Devine, M. Allen and A. Hagerup; Acting-Master's Mates, Herman Alms, Benj. Nelson, T. J. Eckert and C. F. Beall; Acting-Assistant Surgeon, Geo. O. Allen; Acting-Assistant Paymaster, Geo. F. Bennis; Engineers: Acting-First-Assistant, John Johnston; Acting-Second-Assistants, Geo. Walde and C. A. Fisher; Acting-Third-Assistants, J. J. Suor and Wm. Lingle.

"CURLEW"—FOURTH-RATE.

Acting-Ensigns, H. B. O'Neill and M. G. Bailey; Acting - Master's Mate, Thomas Crawford, C. W. Dunlap and Robert S. Balestier; Acting-Assistant Surgeon, John Gorden; Acting-Assistant Paymaster, J. R. Morris; Engineers: Acting-First-Assistant, Benj. A. Hoffman; Acting-Second-Assistant, L. S. Everson; Acting-Third-Assistant, C. C. Crain.

"GAZELLE"—FOURTH-RATE.

Acting-Ensigns, A. S. Palmer, James Derring and Conrad Erickson; Acting-Master's Mates, A. G. Boggs and J. W. Mullen; Acting - Assistant Paymaster, H. A. Mitchell; Engineers: Acting-First-Assistant, A. H. Armstrong; Acting-Second-Assistants, F. M. Peak and Frank S. Wyman; Acting-Third-Assistants, F. C. Warrington and Frank Leach.

"LITTLE REBEL"—FOURTH-RATE.

Acting-Ensign, Jos. P. Pettey; Acting-Master's Mates, N. P. Jacobs, J. F. Rulow, Isaac H. Brown and W. H. Evans; Engineers: Acting - Second - Assistants, Julius Elliter and J. M. Miller; Acting-Third-Assistants, E. H. Burton and G. Dorsey.

"ROBB"—FOURTH-RATE.

Acting-Ensigns, James Tushy and Howard Hale; Acting-Master's Mates, J. H. Jacoby and W. L. Berrian; Engineers: Acting-First-Assistant, Benj. Everson; Acting - Second - Assistant, J. G. Moore; Acting-Third-Assistant, B. H. Collier.

"TENSAS"—FOURTH-RATE.

Acting - Ensigns, A. C. Van Pelt and Jacob Rutherford; Acting-Master's Mate, Henry Van Velsor; Engineers: Acting-Second Assistants, Sam'l Weaver and Park Scanlan; Acting-Third-Assistants, Nathan Spear and N. J. Brooks.

"VOLUNTEER"—FOURTH-RATE.

Acting-Ensigns, M. R. Haines and Louis Kenny; Acting-Master's Mates, J. A. Coleman and M. L. Kirk; Engineers: Acting - First - Assistants, Peter Wagner and G. W. Taylor; Acting-Second-Assistant, R. A. Benneson; Acting-Third-Assistant, Wm. T. Moore.

"SAMSON"—FOURTH-RATE.

Acting Ensign, Geo. W. Painter; Acting-Assistant Paymaster, H. A. Mitchell; Engineers: Acting-Chief, C. H. Christopher; Acting-First-Assistant, Wm. Paul, Jr.

"GENERAL PILLOW"—FOURTH-RATE.

Acting-Ensign, Frank W. Halsted; Acting-Master's Mates, Geo B. Hall, B. F. Craig and W. H. Dobell; Engineers: Acting - Third - Assistants, J. T. Slack and W. H. Cornell.

"NEW NATIONAL"—FOURTH-RATE.

Acting-Ensign, J. M. Farmer; Acting-Master's Mates, J. D. Holmes, W. B. Floyd, W. E. Jelley and H. A. Taylor; Acting-Assistant Paymaster, J. W. Keley; Engineers: Acting - First - Assistant, W. O. Logue; Acting-Third-Assistants, G. W. Aikin, G. R. Bell, Oliver Rosebush and W. M. Ulix.

RECEIVING-SHIP "GRAMPUS."

Acting - Ensigns, J. W. Litherbury and Robert Howden; Acting-Master's Mates, C. J. Dananda, A. H. Lewis and W. H. Corcy; Acting - Assistant Surgeon, J. J. McElhany; Acting - Assistant Paymaster, Edw. D. Hayden.

HOSPITAL-SHIP "RED ROVER."

Acting-Ensigns, Charles King and J. J. Irwin; Fleet-Surgeon, Ninian Pinkney; Passed-Assistant Surgeon, J. S. Knight; Acting-Assistant Surgeons, G. H. Bixby and J. F. Field; Acting-Assistant Paymaster, A. W. Pearson; Acting-Master's Mate, R. G. Van Ness; Engineers: Acting-Chief, Wm. J. Buffinton; Acting-First-Assistant, Wm. Sprague; Acting-Second-Assistant, W. M. Fletcher; Acting-Third-Assistants, W. H. Vanwert and J. T. English; Acting-Carpenter, Harlow Kinney.

TUG "FERN."

Acting-Ensign, John M. Kelly; Acting-Master's Mate, Jacob Bomgarnar; Engineers: Acting-Second-Assistant, John Reed; Acting-Third-Assistant, A. K. Porter.

TUG "MISTLETOE."

Acting-Ensign, Janes L. Lingley; Acting-Master's Mate, John Thompson; Engineers: Acting-Second-Assistant, D. S. Miller; Acting - Third - Assistant, Allison Haywood.

TUG "MIGNONETTE."

Acting-Ensign, H. D. Green; Engineers: Acting-Second-Assistant, W. L. Calhoun; Acting-Third-Assistant, G. W. Pyle.

TUG " MYRTLE.

Acting-Ensign, Isaac N. Goldsmith; Engineers: Acting-Second-Assistant, Geo. Longwell ; Acting-Third-Assistant, J. H. Wright.

TUG "PANSY."

Acting-Ensign, Wm. Harris; Acting-Master's Mate, A. McCarthy; Engineer: Acting-Second-Assistant, H. A. Cady.

TUG " LAUREL."

Acting-Ensign, W. R. Owen; Engineers: Acting-Second-Assistant, Chas. Hilling; Acting-Third-Assistant, L. E. Davis.

TUG "DAHLIA."

Acting-Ensign, W. H. Strope ; Acting-Master's Mate, Thomas Roach ; Engineer : Acting-Second-Assistant, A. R. Smith.

TUG "HYACINTH."

Acting-Ensign, J. B. Hizerman; Acting-Master's Mate, James Malis ; Engineers : Acting-Second-Assistant, M. L. Andrews ; Acting-Third-Assistant, L. C. Thatcher.

TUG "IVY."

Acting-Ensign, Perry C. Wright: Acting-Master's Mate, Daniel Sullivan ; Acting-Second-Assistant Engineer, Thomas Nerley.

TUG " THISTLE."

Acting-Ensign, R. J. Ettingham ; Acting-Master's Mate, J. W. Hambrick ; Engineers : Acting-Second-Assistant, W. P. Clugsten; Acting-Third-Assistants, L. H. Jones and Byrd Allen.

TUG "DAISY."

Acting-Master's Mates, Joseph Graham ; Engineers : Acting-Second-Assistant, F. M. Magers ; Acting-Third-Assistant, J. E. Henderson.

"W. H. BROWN"—FOURTH-RATE.

Pilot, Jefferson A. French ; Acting-Ensign, J. Shinn ; Acting-Master's Mates, O. Deweese, Jr., R. H. Hopkins and C. W. Dimmock; Engineers: Acting-First-Assistant, R. Cutter ; Acting-Second-Assistants, A. C. P. French and G. W. Hart.

"GENERAL LYON"—FOURTH-RATE.

Pilot, Richard E. Birch ; Acting-Ensigns, James Martin and Thos. Cadwell; Acting-Master's Mates, E. W. Robinson, D. V. Balthis and F. B. Chase; Acting-Assistant Paymaster, Wm. H. Doane; Engineers : Acting-First-Assistant, W. J. Hamilton ; Acting-Second-Assistants, James Baldwin and R. A. Smith ; Acting-Third-Assistants, G. C. Shull and H. Workhouse.

"ABRAHAM"—FOURTH-RATE.

Paymaster, A. E. Watson; Acting-Assistant Paymaster, Louis Jorgensen ; Acting-Ensign, William Wagner ; Acting-First-Assistant Engineer, Enos Hoshier.

CHAPTER · LVI.

COMMERCE-DESTROYERS.

THEIR INCEPTION, REMARKABLE CAREER, AND ENDING.

THE "FLORIDA" ("ORETO"), "CLARENCE," "TACONY," "ALEXANDRIA," "GEORGIA" ("JAPAN"), "RAPPAHANNOCK," "NASHVILLE," "SHENANDOAH" ("SEA KING"), "TUSCALOOSA," "CHICKAMAUGA" ("EDITH"), "TALLAHASSEE" ("ATLANTA"), "OLUSTEE," "CHAMELEON," ETC.—CUTTING OUT OF THE U. S. REVENUE STEAMER "CALEB CUSHING" FROM THE HARBOR OF PORTLAND, ME.—CAPTURE OF THE "FLORIDA" ON THE COAST OF BRAZIL.—AN APOLOGY TO THE BRAZILIAN GOVERNMENT.—CAPTAIN COLLINS' PUNISHMENT.—THE "FLORIDA" SUNK IN HAMPTON ROADS.—DESTRUCTION OF THE WHALING FISHERY IN THE ARCTIC OCEAN.—NEUTRALITY LAWS VIOLATED BY FOREIGN GOVERNMENTS.—SCENES ON BOARD THE CONFEDERATE CRUISERS.—ACTUAL LOSSES INFLICTED BY THE "ALABAMA" AND "SHENANDOAH."—CRITICISMS, REMARKS, ETC., ETC.

WE have told the story of the "Sumter" and "Alabama," and partly that of the "Florida," which latter, after her escape from the Federal squadron off Pensacola, particularly the "R. R. Cuyler," in January, 1863, commenced the business of destruction for which she was fitted out.

In her first attempts at destruction the "Florida" was not particularly fortunate, for in the course of ten days Captain Maffitt only succeeded in destroying three small vessels. He then put into Nassau, where, it will be remembered, the "Florida," formerly the "Oreto," had been seized by the authorities and her case brought before the courts for violation of the "Enlistment Act." The merchant to whom the vessel was consigned swore that the "Oreto" was a *bona fide* merchant vessel, while at that very moment her guns and munitions of war were on board another vessel in the harbor. When the ship returned to Nassau in July, under the name of the "Florida," her appearance at first caused considerable confusion among the witnesses and officials, for it was evident that a flagrant breach of the British Foreign Enlistment Act had been committed.

However, this circumstance did not seriously influence the British authorities at Nassau. Maffitt had entered a *bona fide* Confederate port, and now that he was again in Nassau, with a regular commission, a good crew, and the Confederate flag at his peak, he received an ovation. The officials allowed the "Florida" thirty-six hours to remain in port and take coal and whatever else she might require, although the orders of the Home Government limited the supply of coal to what was supposed to be necessary to enable a Confederate cruiser to reach one of the ports of the Confederacy.

From Nassau the "Florida" proceeded to Barbadoes, where she received on board one hundred tons of coal, in further violation of the orders of the Home Government, which provided that a second supply of coal should not be allowed within three months. Doubtless, the instructions were similar to those issued by Earl John Russell to the British Minister at Washington in the case of the "Trent,"—one set to be shown to the American Secretary of State, and a second stating the real intentions of the Government. There seemed to be the same desire at Barbadoes as elsewhere to see American commerce destroyed, and, with such a feeling in existence, the chances for the escape of Federal merchant vessels were much diminished.

The "Florida" did not commit such havoc as the "Alabama," for in the space of five months she captured but fifteen vessels, which were all destroyed in the usual style of the Confederate cruisers. Her cruising-ground extended from the latitude of New York to the southward of Bahia, in Brazil.

In the vicinity of Fernando Noronha, Maffitt picked up a vessel called the "Lapwing," loaded with coal, and, by converting her into a tender, was enabled to supply himself with fuel as long as he wished to remain on the station.

On the 6th of May the brig "Clarence" was captured off the coast of Brazil, armed by Maffitt with some light guns, and placed in command of Lieutenant Charles W. Read, formerly a midshipman in the U. S. Navy—and another Confederate State's vessel-of-war was created in the shortest possible time, with orders to burn, sink and destroy; although it was doubtful if Maffitt's authority to commission vessels would have been recognized in case he should have fallen in with a superior force.

Lieutenant Read was bold and full of resources, seeming to disdain all danger. He shaped his course for the coast of the United States, and by the 10th of June had captured five vessels, four of which were destroyed. The fifth was the schooner "Tacony," and this vessel, being better suited to his purpose than the "Clarence," Read burned the latter, after transferring her crew, guns and stores to the "Tacony."

During the next fortnight the "Tacony" made ten prizes. Here was a Confederate cruiser right upon the coast, burning and sinking coasting vessels with impunity, for not a single United States vessel was to be seen. This was a new style of warfare inaugurated by the Confederacy, without the least expense to them and without any of the difficulties of violating the British Foreign Enlistment Act, or hoodwinking colonial authorities to procure necessary supplies. As to the pay of officers and men, as that was probably made in Confederate money, the expense was nothing.

Read soon tired of the "Tacony." His ideas enlarged as his vessel grew plethoric with spoils, and his prolific brain was at work devising new schemes for Federal discomfiture. The last of his prizes, a vessel called the "Archer," captured off the capes of Virginia, seemed preferable to the "Tacony," and he accordingly made her into a cruiser and burned the latter. Had

Lieutenant Read kept off shore he would doubtless have made the "Archer's" name as famous as that of her predecessor; but, not satisfied with destroying peaceable merchantmen, he longed for higher distinction, for Read had in him the stuff to make a gallant naval commander.

The career of the "Archer" was short. The news of a privateer on the coast of New England was spread far and wide. Several gun-boats were cruising up and down the coast in search of Maffitt, who was reported off Nova Scotia; but their commanders do not seem to have been aware of Read and his peculiar performances.

In the latter part of June, two days after the "Archer" had been commissioned as a cruiser, Read determined to cut out the revenue-cutter "Caleb Cushing," from the harbor of Portland, Maine. In this design he was successful; the vessel was surprised by the boats of the "Archer" and carried by boarding. The people on shore hastily manned and armed several steamers, and followed the "Caleb Cushing" to sea. As Read saw that he must be overtaken, and that he could make no successful resistance, he set fire to the "Cushing" and attempted to escape in his boats, but was captured and imprisoned in Fort Warren.

This was a remarkable raid and showed great gallantry on the part of Lieutenant Read, although the presence of a single Federal gun-boat, under an intelligent captain, would have nipped the whole scheme in the bud. As it was, Read's capture was due to the courage of private citizens, who did not know what force the Confederates had outside to back them. After the affair was settled, gun-boats flocked in from the North Atlantic Squadron in pursuit of the raiders, but too late to be of use.

After the "Florida's" cruise on the coast of Brazil, she refitted and coaled at Bermuda, and thence sailed for Brest, where she was docked and thoroughly repaired. Maffitt was relieved by Captain Joseph N. Barney, who was in turn succeeded by Captain Charles M. Morris. The "Florida" remained nearly six months at Brest, sailed from that port in February, 1864, and, after cruising for three months against American commerce, put in again at Bermuda, where Captain Morris was allowed to take in coal and provisions. The Captain announced his intention of proceeding to Mobile, but, instead of doing so, made a cruise of three months on the coast of the United States against Federal merchant vessels, proceeding thence to Teneriffe, and on the 5th of October, 1864, he arrived at Bahia.

For a wonder, the U. S. S. "Wachusett" happened to be in Bahia when the "Florida" entered the port and anchored a mile distant, while a Brazilian corvette, in anticipation of a difficulty between the vessels, took position near the "Florida." The latter vessel had received permission from the authorities to remain in port forty-eight hours to repair and coal ship, which was twenty-four hours longer than the usual time allowed these vessels; although Captain Semmes had been allowed to do pretty much as he pleased by the Governor of Bahia, and also by the Governor of Fernando de Noronha.

American officers in pursuit of Confederate cruisers were kept in constant excitement by hearing of excesses committed by these "sea-rovers," as the latter were sometimes called, and were greatly disappointed at not falling in with them, although there was not one chance in a hundred of their doing so. The Northern press had also indulged in strictures on the Federal Navy for not overtaking the Confederate cruisers, while the Southern newspapers sneered at the Yankee officers, whom they asserted were afraid to meet the Confederate vessels for fear of being captured. All this had its effect, and Commander Napoleon Collins, of the "Wachusett," determined that the "Florida" should not do any more damage if he could prevent it. Collins thought of the violation of neutrality, and dared all the consequences, including the probable loss of his commission.

About 2 A. M. the "Wachusett" got underway, crossed the bow of the Brazilian corvette, and steered directly for the "Florida," with the intention of running her down and sinking her; but, instead of striking the Confederate ship in the gangway as was intended, the "Wachusett" crashed into the "Florida" on her starboard quarter, cutting down her bulwarks and carrying away her mainyard and mizzenmast. The crew of the "Florida" seized what arms they could lay hold of in the confusion, and fired into the "Wachusett," wounding three of her crew ; but, the latter vessel pouring in a volley of small arms and discharging two broadside guns at the Confederate ship, the latter surrendered. Sixtynine officers and men were captured, but Captain Morris and many of his officers and crew were on shore. The "Florida" was then towed out to sea, the Brazilian man-of-war offering no opposition, except that an officer was sent to inform Collins that, if he persisted in his attack on the "Florida," the fort and vessels would open fire on him, and one gun was subsequently fired by the corvette. It was afterwards claimed by the Brazilians that Commander Collins had promised to desist from his purpose of capturing the "Florida"; but this seems to be merely an excuse to account for their supineness in taking no steps to prevent the "Wachusett" from towing the "Florida" out of the harbor. The fact is, the Brazilians had no intention of proceeding to extremities, fully realizing that the corvette was no match for the "Wachusett."

That the capture of the "Florida" was a deliberate violation of the rights of neutrals no one can deny, and it placed the United States Government in a very awkward position. It would have been much better for Commander Collins to have waited outside for the coming of the "Florida," even at the risk of her escaping, than to have so grossly affronted a nation whose Emperor sympathized with the Union cause. Commander Collins' action was entirely independent of instructions, and he was willing to run the risk of losing his commission in order to put a stop to the "Florida's" career.

The Federal Government at once disavowed Collins' action, and made ample apology, which the Government of Brazil accepted, only stipulating that the "Florida" and those captured in her should be sent back to Bahia. Mr. Secretary Seward did all in his power to make amends for the mistake which had been committed, denouncing it as "an unauthorized, unlawful and indefensible exercise of the naval force of the United States within a foreign country, in defiance of its established and duly recognized Government." The fact of Mr. Seward's disapproval was quite enough to make Mr. Secretary Welles give his sympathy to Commander Collins, and, although the Secretary did not express himself openly, there is little doubt that he would have been glad if all the Confederate cruisers could have been disposed of in the same manner.

Collins' action, indeed, met with the popular approval, and it would have been a difficult matter to have convicted him had he been brought to trial before a court-martial. The little regard that had been shown by neutral nations, during the civil war, to their obligations, and their favoring the Confederate cruisers, had awakened great indignation in the Northern States, so that the community was little disposed to censure Collins' action in the case of the "Florida."

Commander Collins made little effort to defend his course. In his report to the Secretary of the Navy, he says : "I thought it probable that the Brazilian authorities would forbear to interfere, as they had done at Fernando de Noronha, where the Confederate steamer 'Alabama' was permitted to take into the anchorage three American ships, and to take coal from the 'Cora Hatch' within musket-shot of the fort, and afterwards, within easy range of their guns, to set on fire those unarmed vessels. I regret, however, to state, that they fired three shotted guns at us while we were towing the 'Florida' out." Whatever action the Brazilians may have taken, it seems to have been extremely mild under the circumstances, for they had certainly a right to compel the "Wachusett" to relinquish her prize if they had had sufficient force to back their demand. The only punishment inflicted on Commander Collins was an order to take the "Florida" back to Brazil with all his prisoners, and deliver the vessel to the Brazilian Government intact. For this purpose the "Florida" was sent to Admiral Porter, at Hampton Roads, that she might be properly prepared for sea.

The expedition against Fort Fisher was then fitting out, and the Roads were crowded with vessels of every description. While the "Florida" was lying in the stream an army transport came in collision with her, but did her no damage. It was reported that the collision was intentional, and to avoid further accident Admiral Porter directed the "Florida" to be stripped of everything valuable, her guns taken out and the vessel moored securely head and stern at Newport News, just at the spot where the "Cumberland" was sunk in very deep water. An engineer was placed on board in charge, with two men to assist him in looking after the water-cocks; but, strangely enough, although the "Florida" was to all appearances water-tight when she reached Newport News, she sank that night at two o'clock in ten fathoms, and there she lay for some years after the war. This was about the best thing that could have happened to the "Florida," for the Northern people would not have been satisfied to see her sent back to Brazil to continue her depredations on their commerce, and it would have been a most humiliating duty for Commander Collins to perform. When the sinking of the vessel was reported to Admiral Porter, he merely said, "Better so"; while the Secretary of State and Secretary of the Navy never asked any questions about the matter, being too well satisfied to get the elephant off their hands.

In 1863, after the appearance of the "Alabama" and the "Florida," many attempts were made by the Confederate agents abroad to get cruisers to sea, but these attempts were not always successful, as the British Government was beginning to realize the impolicy of neglecting so completely their neutral obligations, and Mr. Adams, the American minister, lost no opportunity of calling attention to the numerous violations of the Foreign Enlistment Act which were taking place. In consequence of the determined stand taken by Mr. Adams, several ironclads building by Laird & Co. were seized. The "Alexandria" was released in England, but was subsequently libelled at Nassau, where the courts, having learned something from the case of the "Florida," detained her until the end of the war.

Notwithstanding all the watchfulness of the American minister, the "Georgia" and "Rappahannock" got to sea in 1863. The career of the latter was brief. She had been a dispatch vessel in the Royal Navy, and was sold by the British Government to persons acting for the Confederacy. She was refitted at Sheerness under the direction of employees of the Royal Dock Yard; but the Government proposing to inspect her, in order to avoid detention she hastily put to sea with but a small portion of her crew on board, and these had been enlisted by the connivance of the Government official who aided in getting the vessel off. The "Rappahannock" was commissioned as a Confederate vessel-of-war in the British Channel, and was seized by a French gun-boat off Calais.

The "Georgia," a screw-steamer of seven hundred tons, was launched on the Clyde, and put to sea in April, 1863. A British merchant was her ostensible owner, and her guns and munitions of war were put on board the vessel off Morlaix. The case of this vessel was no greater violation of the neutrality laws than that of others; but the British Government, wishing perhaps to show that it would be neutral in 1863 if it had not been in 1861, instituted proceedings against the persons concerned in sending the "Georgia" to sea, and upon conviction they were each sentenced to pay the enormous fine of fifty pounds, a penalty not likely to deter British subjects from violating the Foreign Enlistment Act.

The career of the "Georgia" was not very exciting, although extending over a period of a year. The "Sumter," "Alabama" and "Florida" had been beforehand with her, and there was little left for the gleaner. Fifteen millions of dollars worth of United States commerce had been swept from the ocean, and the American vessels had either sought protection under other flags, or were laid up in port until the war should be over. The "Georgia," not being very successful in taking prizes, was finally taken to Liverpool, her crew discharged, and the vessel sold by Captain J D. Bullock, agent of the Confederate Navy Department, to an English shipowner. This was a questionable transaction, and the transfer was, no doubt, made to prevent the seizure of the "Georgia" by the British authorities; for the latter, owing to the firm stand taken by Mr. Adams, had begun seriously to reflect on the probable consequences of further trespassing on the patience of the United States Government, as it was evident the collapse of the Confederacy was now not far off.

In writing of the probability that Laird's rams would be permitted to get to sea, Mr. Adams remarks:

"In the notes which I had the honor to address to your Lordship on the 11th of July and the 14th of August, I believe I stated the importance attached by my Government to the decision involved in this case, with sufficient distinctness. Since that date I have had the opportunity to receive from the United States a full approbation of their contents. At the same time I feel it my painful duty to make known to your Lordship, that in some respects it has fallen short in expressing the earnestness with which I have been in the interval directed to describe the grave nature of the situation in which both countries must be placed, in the event of an act of aggression committed against the Government and people of the United States by either of these formidable vessels."

This diplomatic remonstrance was easily understood by those who had tampered with the United States to the verge of war, and now that almost all of the American commerce left afloat had been transferred to the British flag, much to the advantage of Great Britain, they were unwilling to have that commerce depleted by hostilities with the United States, for the Federal Navy was now adding to its forces a class of steamers well adapted, in speed and armament, to repeat against Great Britain the tactics of the Confederate cruisers against the United States. It would have perhaps been better policy for the United States to have declared war with Great Britain than to have submitted longer to open violations of neutrality, for the former had little commerce to lose and could have swept the trade of the latter from the ocean.

When Mr. Adams heard that the "Georgia" was sold to a British merchant, he informed Commodore Thomas T. Craven, then in command of the U. S. S. "Niagara," lying in the port of Antwerp, that he must endeavor to intercept and capture the converted Confederate. The "Georgia" was captured by Commodore Craven off Lisbon, was sent to Boston and condemned by the Admiralty Court, her alleged owner never receiving a penny of the £15,000 he had paid into the Confederate treasury as the price of the vessel.

The fate of the "Nashville" has already been mentioned. In January and February, 1863, several attempts were made to destroy her as she lay above Fort McAllister, on the Great Ogeechee River. On the 27th of February, 1863, she was set on fire and blown up by shells from the Monitor "Montauk," Commander John L. Worden.

The "Shenandoah," originally called the "Sea King," was the last and the most dangerous of all the Confederate cruisers. She was a full-rigged ship of about eight hundred tons, with so-called auxiliary steam power, and very fast under either sail or steam, capable of making three hun-

dred and twenty miles in twenty-four hours under favorable circumstances, which exceeded the speed of any vessel in the U. S. Navy.

On the 8th of October, 1864, the "Sea King" cleared from London for Bombay. As she was not equipped for war purposes, there was no question in regard to her; but the same day she sailed, the steamer "Laurel" cleared from Liverpool for Nassau, with several Confederate naval officers and a cargo of cases marked "Machinery," but containing guns and their equipments. Near Madeira, the "Sea King" received her armament and stores from the "Laurel," and was transferred by her master, who had a power of sale from her owner, to Commander James J. Waddell, of the Confederate Navy, who put her in commission as the "Shenandoah."

The plans for the "Shenandoah's" operations had been carefully matured at Richmond by Commander Brooke, of the Confederate Navy, and were based upon the movements of the Pacific whaling fleet. The latter habitually cruised in the neighborhood of the Carolina Islands for sperm whale, going north to the Sea of Ochotsk for right whale, thence to Behring's Straits and the Arctic Ocean. Returning from the north, the whalers generally reached the Sandwich Islands in October or November for refreshment. The plan was for the "Shenandoah" to be at these various points simultaneously with the whaling fleet, and thus to sweep it from the sea. There was no longer much opportunity of injuring United States commerce in the ordinary channels of trade, for the "Alabama" and "Florida" had done their work pretty thoroughly, and a number of new and fast cruisers had been sent by the Federal Government to guard what remained. The new cruising-ground mapped out for the "Shenandoah" was, therefore, the most inviting field of operations now remaining for a Confederate cruiser.

The "Shenandoah" cruised three months in the Atlantic, taking several prizes, and then proceeded to Tristan d'Acunha, where the crews of the captured vessels were landed. She next proceeded to Melbourne, where she was well received and allowed to repair and refit, take in all the coal required—in short, do anything that would assist her in her attempt to destroy the American whaling fleet. In violation of the Foreign Enlistment Act, Commander Waddell was here permitted to ship forty-three men as an addition to his crew; but the Australians had little respect for their obligations as neutrals. Their ruling sentiment was hatred to the United States Government and people. This was shown in the early mining days of 1852, when the British Government gave American merchant vessels the privilege of trading on the Australian coast on the same terms as were accorded to those of Great Britain ; but the colonists placed so many restrictions on United States vessels, steam-ships especially, that the latter were driven away.

On the 18th February, 1865, the "Shenandoah" proceeded under sail to the vicinity of Behring's Straits, where a large number of whaling vessels were captured and destroyed. Until the 28th of June, the ocean was ablaze with burning ships, whose crews were subjected to very inhuman treatment. Waddell continued his operations for over two months after hostilities between the North and South had terminated, professing that he had no intimation of the surrender of the Confederate armies until the date above mentioned; but he must have known when he left Melbourne that the Confederate struggle for independence was practically at an end. When Waddell was assured that the Confederate Government had ceased to exist, instead of surrendering his vessel to the nearest United States authority as he should have done, he proceeded to Liverpool and delivered the "Shenandoah" to the British authorities.

This was the last scene in the terrible drama inaugurated by Semmes and finished by Waddell. The story of the Confederate cruisers carries with it a moral which should not be forgotten. The civil war is now remembered as a dreadful episode in our history, bringing death and misery to the North and South; but the ravages of the Confederate commerce-destroyers were inflicted upon men pursuing a peaceful avocation, and were thus of peculiar hardship.

The Confederates had in their proceedings some show of justification ; but, as a mode of carrying on warfare, it was lacking in the chivalry upon which Southern officers peculiarly prided themselves. With one exception, we do not believe that a Southern officer, engaged in the business of destroying United States merchant vessels, ever boasted after the war of what he had done, or cared to dwell on events that were calculated to leave an unpleasant impression on the mind.

The destruction of United States commerce did not fulfill the object desired — to benefit the Confederate cause — on the contrary, it created great indignation, even among the peace party of the North, and caused Congress to make increased appropriations for the Navy. Indeed, but for that circumstance, it is not likely that the money allowed the Navy would have been more than enough to maintain the blockade of the Southern coast with such commercial vessels as the Navy Department could purchase. The lessons of the civil war will not be lost, if ever the United States is engaged in hostilities with either of the nations that assisted the Confederates in their raid on American commerce. It is true that Great Britain made the *amende honorable*, after years of discussion, in regard to her part of the business; but, by permitting Confederate cruisers to roam at will over the ocean, the British Government taught her future foes how much mischief could be done by three or four ordinary cruisers against her own commerce, which is spread all over the world, and on which her prestige as a nation so largely depends. Other nations will, doubtless, resort to the "Alabama" mode of warfare, so inexpensive, and so easily carried on, and calculated to do so much injury to the chief commercial nation of the world.

As the original "Monitor" changed the system of building vessels of war, so the plan inaugurated by Semmes has made an entire change in the class of vessels to be used as cruisers and commerce-destroyers. Such strenuous efforts are put forth by the naval powers in this direction, that there is little difference between them in respect to the perfection of their fast steamers. After years of idle speculation, the United States have at length entered into competition for the best vessels for general war purposes, and we are not likely to forget the lesson taught us by Captain Semmes, with his carefully-considered plan of operations.

Commerce-destroying has always been practiced during war, and, in spite of the protests of civilization and humanity, it seems likely it will be practiced in the future, since it is too strong a temptation to the weaker powers to permit it to be abolished. It furnishes also a strong inducement for adventurers to enlist in vessels-of-war, with the hope of excitement and prize-money ; the latter, a stimulus which will always keep a navy manned in time of war. If it should ever happen that the commerce of the ocean should be allowed to pass unmolested by belligerents, and that ships-of-war simply be kept to enter into conflict with each other or with fortifications, war would become a comparatively uninteresting business, and might be lengthened out interminably, so that, in the long run, there would be nothing gained by the departure from the old system.

The question has never been settled in the popular mind as to whether the Confederate cruisers were properly constituted vessels-of-war. The fact that most of them were fitted out in defiance of the law of the country in which they were built, and that the aiders and abettors of the scheme were liable to a heavy penalty, would seem to be a bar against their regularity. The fact that Great Britain subsequently paid for allowing her laws to be violated to the extent of jeopardizing the peace with a friendly nation, must be taken as additional evidence against the Confederate cruisers.

Great Britain, with propriety, might have sent out her ships-of-war and captured the Confederates on the high seas, or held them on entering her ports to refit. The inviolability which is supposed to surround a national vessel should not shield her for violation of the laws of a neutral nation, especially when she belongs to a government not recognized by any other. Otherwise there would soon be an end to law and order upon the ocean, and every little island that could man a steamer might claim belligerent rights, and prey upon the enemy's commerce after the manner of the Confederate cruisers.

That the success of those vessels was due to the inaction of the British Government cannot be doubted, for, if Great Britain had been mindful of her neutral obligations, she would have remonstrated so emphatically with the Confederate Government against the actions of their ships-of-war as would soon have put an end to the career of the latter.

Although the Confederate Government claimed that their cruisers were ships-of-war, that assertion did not make them so ; and the question arises, were they entitled to the privileges accorded such ships by the usages of nations ? Their position was certainly anomalous, being recognized as belligerents, although the State to which they belonged had not been recognized by any Government. The only recognition accorded the Confederates by Great Britain was the Queen's proclamation of neutrality, forbidding either belligerent from taking prizes into British ports. It is difficult to understand how a nation can concede belligerent rights to another and recognize the seizure of neutral property—as did England and other powers—and yet maintain no official relations with her. The clearest and most convincing statement of this question is embraced in a work on "The Blockade and the Cruisers," by Professor James R. Soley, U. S. N. A vast amount of indulgence was shown the Confederate cruisers in every stage of their proceedings, and it is not unlikely, if a similar state of affairs should ever again occur, that neutrals will find it necessary to draw the lines closer than heretofore, in order not to be liable to penalties which are apt to follow so liberal a course as was pursued towards the Confederates, during the American civil war, by certain European governments.

So many arguments have been advanced for and against the system adopted by the Confederate Government in fitting out cruisers, that it may not be amiss to inquire how far the said cruisers were justified in committing the havoc they inflicted on the merchant vessels of the United States. It is well for us to ascertain whether the acts of the Confederates came within the strict limitations of the law of nations, for, in case of war between any mother country and her colonies, the acts of these cruisers, if recognized as legal, would establish injurious precedents.

Every government owes it to its citizens to extend every possible safeguard around the commerce of the ocean, for it is the faith which merchants place in their governments to protect them at all hazards, which induces them to embark their property on the high seas ; therefore, the different powers should combine to establish rules of action binding upon them all.

There were a dozen ways in which Great Britain might have prevented her neutrality laws from being violated. Had the authorities adhered to the terms of the Queen's proclamation, the Confederate cruisers could never have extended their operations beyond the coast of the United States, where their career would have speedily terminated after they had perhaps destroyed a few unimportant vessels. Having issued this proclamation, it was the duty of the British Government, not only to abstain from aiding in the destruction of United States commerce, but to order all Confederate cruisers to depart at once from colonial or home ports ; and, in case of neglect to obey the order, the Confederates should have been summarily dealt with.

No government can afford to remain passive while its laws are being violated, for this would indicate either weakness or duplicity. If the Confederate vessels fitted out in England were sent from English ports in violation of English laws, they were not legally authorized to capture or destroy an enemy's commerce; and, if captured in their turn, the Confederate officers and men could very properly have been held for trial before the United States courts. That the Confederate cruisers were subject to capture by British vessels-of-war, for violation of British law, there can be little doubt. This would suggest that the proceedings of the Confederate cruisers were not strictly legal.

It was natural that the Confederate Government should take advantage of any flaw in British laws to enable them to get their vessels to sea; but it was due to British self-respect to be sure that those laws were not violated, and the British Government should therefore have emphatically remonstrated with the Confederate agents for their laxity in not closely respecting British as well as international law. No better use could have been made of British cruisers—had one of these purchased vessels escaped from a British port—than to send them in pursuit of the offending vessels.

The Confederate cruisers were British vessels, subject to the laws of Great Britain, and were commissioned as ships-of-war on the high seas ; and it was supposed that the high seas being common to all nations, their being so commissioned was justifiable. But this would not obliterate the former delinquency—the violation of British laws enacted to prevent the very course pursued by the Confederate agents. The first steps taken by these agents were so clearly illegal, that the consummation of their purpose could not be lawful, and the resultant consequences were so in violation of all law, that it is not strange the Federal Government could never be brought to look upon these vessels as legitimate cruisers.

To show the very dubious character of some of the Confederate cruisers, we will mention that it was not uncommon for them to run the blockade under the British flag, with British papers, taking in cargoes of goods and carrying out cotton, and then to figure for a time as vessels-of-war, varying their character to suit circumstances. Of course, such proceedings cannot be justified by any of the usages of war. We will quote a few cases mentioned by Professor Soley, who has taken great pains to ascertain the facts, and the reader will be struck with the absurdity of claiming for vessels so irregularly fitted out the character of properly constituted ships-of-war. We cannot call them pirates or privateers, but we do say that the Confederate cruisers were not regular ships-of-war, and were acting in violation of the laws of Great Britain as well as those of the United States.

The "Japan," or "Georgia," left the Clyde registered in the name of a British subject, and remained for nearly three months still registered in the name of her ostensible owner, although during this time she was engaged in hostilities against the Federal Government. A year later she returned to Liverpool, was dismantled and sold to a British subject, the bill of sale being signed by Captain James D. Bullock, of the Confederate Navy. The "Rappahannock" left Sheerness in haste as a merchant vessel, with workmen still on board, who were carried off against their will. She assumed the character of a Confederate cruiser while crossing the British Channel, and sought admission into the port of Calais as a ship-of-war in distress ! The case of the "Tuscaloosa," already mentioned, is too glaring to need discussion.

Towards the close of the civil war the Confederate Navy List must have presented a curious aspect, for one day a vessel would figure as a blockade-runner under the British flag, and the next she was a Confederate cruiser; but, strange to say, the British colonial courts could not find any law for interfering with such vessels. The blockade-runner "Edith" escaped from Wilmington, N. C., one night in October, 1864, under the name of the Confederate States steamer "Chickamauga." She was armed with a 64-pounder and a 32-pounder, and steering north along the coast destroyed several unfortunate vessels ; when, her whereabouts becoming known, she was compelled to run the gauntlet into Wilmington again, and resumed her former character. What particular object it was proposed to accomplish by such proceedings as those of the "Chickamauga" is hard to conceive, for at that stage of the civil war a cruise against the coasting trade of the North could only show the desperate straits to which the Confederates were reduced, and was merely an attempt to keep up the semblance of a war on the ocean.

The "Atlanta" made two trips to Wilmington as a blockade-runner. She was then converted into a cruiser and named the "Tallahassee." Under this name she left the Cape Fear River early in August, 1864, and on the 19th of that month arrived at Halifax, after capturing and destroying several vessels. Owing to the vigilance of the authorities, who in this instance were upon the alert to prevent a violation of the neutrality laws, the "Tallahassee" was unable to obtain coal or other supplies, and was obliged to return to Wilmington. In November this vessel made another attempt, under the name of the "Olustee," and took a few prizes, but, returning to Wilmington, assumed her old character of merchant vessel and blockade-runner. She received the appropriate name of "Chameleon," and in December, 1864, went to sea under the command of Captain John Wilkinson, of the Confederate Navy, with the object of returning from Bermuda laden with provisions for the Confederate army. Although the Governor of Bermuda was duly apprised of the character of the "Chameleon," he expressed himself as satisfied that she had been sufficiently whitewashed to be admitted as a merchant vessel. The cargo was sold, a supply of stores laid in, and the vessel returned to the Confederacy, only to find that Wilmington was in Federal hands. Wilkinson then tried to get into Charleston; but, failing in his attempt, he proceeded to Nassau, landed his cargo, and the vessel was taken to Liverpool and delivered to Fraser, Trenholm & Co., the Confederate agents; but as the British authorities had now become very particular in regard to the proceedings of these non-descript vessels, the "Chameleon" was seized and ultimately surrendered to the United States Government.

It is only within a late period that we have ascertained anything of the inner life on board the Confederate cruisers, for Captain Semmes' voluminous narrative of the "Sumter" and "Alabama" does not by any means supply this want. The gallant captain represents his vessels as men-of-war, with most able officers and subordinate crews, where affairs were conducted in a manner to meet the approbation of the most hypercritical person. A lately published narrative of life on board the "Alabama," written by one of the crew, represents things very differently from the rose-colored view of the commanding officer. According to this account, the usages of civilized nations were not observed by the crew of the Confederate cruiser, who were a riotous and abandoned set of men, who paid little heed to the rules and regulations of the vessel or the orders of their officers. This is not to be wondered at, when we consider that the men were shipped in illegal fashion and were most of them the lowest class of adventurers. We give a few quotations from this interesting article:

"I was pleased to find that I had not an old ship-mate aboard. The best man in the port-watch, to which I belonged, was a Scotchman named Gill. He was about forty, very powerful, and could hold an ordinary man at arm's length clear off the deck. He was saturated with Calvinism, and could quote Scripture and sermons by the hour, but was, all the same, a daring, dangerous ruffian. According to his own account, he had been in numerous mutinies, in one case taking a Spanish brig, killing the officers, beaching her on the Deseada Key, in the Leeward Islands, and getting to Porto Rico in the launch with the plunder. This man's influence was bad, and he was the cause of much of the insubordination that took place on board. * * * * * * *

"We were now taking prizes rapidly, being not over four hundred miles from New York, in the 'rolling forties,' directly in the track of American commerce. The treatment of the prisoners was fairly good, and they were not ill-used on board, but the conduct of the boarding-crews was shameful; the officer in charge of the boat had no control over them, and they rushed below like a gang of pirates, breaking open the sailors' chests, and taking from the persons of the prisoners everything that took their fancy. I never saw them injure prisoners, or use their weapons, except to frighten their victims, but the wanton destruction of the clothes and effects of captured sailors was simply disgraceful. This sort of thing seriously affected the *morale* of the men, and, had we then met an enemy of equal force, but of the usual standard of man-of-war discipline, we should have made a very poor show. The prisoners were of all nationalities, but their officers all seemed to be Americans by birth, and were mostly a fine, gentlemanly lot. The old sea-dog element, so common among English shippers in the East, does not seem to exist among the American officers of the merchant marine;

they might easily be mistaken for clerks or even professors. Not so the old sailor, in command of the 'tea wagons' and East Indian ships — their walk and lingo proclaimed them sailors, and nothing else. One of the mates of a whaling-ship we took and burned was a parson-like man, and preached and prayed to his fellows. He was long and lanky, and two of our roughs began to haze him, but they mistook their calling, and in two minutes were so mauled and man-handled that it was reported aft; but the first-officer said it served them right, much to the satisfaction of the honest man between decks. * * * * * *

"November 18th (1862), we arrived at Martinique and had an 'ovation'; the exultation of the French over the disasters to Yankee commerce impressed me. A French corvette lying there gave a dinner to the officers. Gill licked two of the Frenchman's petty officers nearly to death, as his share of the entertainment, and our liberty was stopped in consequence. Forest swam on shore that night, and, eluding sharks and look-outs, was hauled into one of the berth-deck ports, with five gallons of the worst liquor I ever drank. It set the entire watch crazy. Forest kept comparatively sober, but old Gill 'bowsed up his jib' until he could scarcely stand. Such an uproar I never heard; the lanterns were lit in defiance, and, when the watch was called, the officer of the deck was saluted with all manner of 'skrim-shander.' The boatswain was knocked down and hurt by a blow from a belaying-pin, and everything loose was fired aft. The officers and marines with the sober portion of the crew now charged forward, and a terrible *melee* ensued. Gill knocked a gunner's-mate's jaw out of place, and was laid out by a capstan-bar, and finally the drunken men were secured. * * * * *

"We now sailed for Jamaica, going into Port Royal, and had a pleasant time. Here something occurred that few knew of. An Irishman called "King-post," from his build, being short and thick, was suspected of giving the officers information of the plans of Forest and his mates. He was closely watched and he knew it, but was on his guard. He took his liberty with the others, and, of course, got drunk. Seeing Gill and another man leading a third and going towards the suburbs, I followed, and made out the third man to be King-post. I missed them, and, as I knew that Gill was well acquainted with the port, I at once conjectured that he had seen me following them, and had changed his course. An hour after, both men came back and I joined them. I asked where the Irishman was. Gill looked at me with his hard gray eyes, and significantly said: 'I dunna know, laddie, but he'll haud his tongue noo; and ye had better say naithing, yir a wise fallow!' King-post never came back and was supposed to have deserted; but, no doubt, he fell a victim to those two ruffians. The crew broke all bounds here, and nearly all the petty officers were disrated, much to their satisfaction, as they had no respect from the crew and were responsible for them to their officers. * * * * * * * It was a very common thing for the crew that boarded a prize to bring liquor back with them. Once some fifteen bottles of brandy were smuggled aboard, and all hands partook, As usual, there was a terrible time between decks. One petty officer was so badly hurt that it was thought he would die. Many of the men had grape-shot in a netted bag fastened to the wrist by a lanyard, and many a coward blow was given with these."

Whether such performances as those mentioned above were consistent with the discipline of a vessel-of-war, we must leave to the judgment of our naval readers.

It is difficult to reconcile the proceedings

of the Confederate cruisers with the precedents which have governed vessels-of-war in modern times, and their toleration by European governments must be due to the fact that the said governments believed the union of the States was finally dissolved, and that the fragments would have no power to exact reparation for damages. The present condition of our country shows what a mistaken idea prevailed abroad during the civil war.

What is now chiefly required by the United States is an adequate naval establishment such as will command the respect of European powers. Under such circumstances, we would never have to fear a recurrence of such dreadful scenes as were common on board the Confederate cruisers.

In the glamour attending the remarkable cruise of Semmes, Waddell, in the "Shenandoah," has almost been lost sight of. Captain Semmes lost no opportunity of advertising himself through the vessels he bonded, through foreign vessels, or otherwise. His object was to show the people of Europe the dreadful havoc the Confederates were making on American commerce; and, although by this course he ran the risk of being followed and overtaken by the Federal cruisers, yet he was so adroit in his proceedings that he always managed to leave a cruising-ground before the United States Government could get a vessel there. Semmes frequented some of the best-known ports, where there was constant communication with England, so that the Britons were constantly informed of the effect of their policy in allowing Confederate cruisers to be fitted out in their harbors. At the same time this news was transmitted by British packets to the United States, having its effect there, but not exactly what Semmes wanted. Semmes pursued this course, without attempt at concealment, until his vessel was sunk by the "Kearsarge."

Waddell, in the "Shenandoah," pursued an entirely different course. He followed the line of the whale fisheries which was unfrequented by other vessels, and he carried on his work, with little chance of its being found out, until he had destroyed the entire whaling fleet. The actual losses inflicted by the "Alabama"—$6,547,609.86— was only about $60,000 greater than those inflicted by the "Shenandoah," yet the latter was only in commission about one-half as long a time as the "Alabama." Commander Waddell kept his movements concealed, and left no trace behind him by which he could be followed. He eluded the vigilance of the United States cruisers that were in pursuit of him, and, after lightening his vessel of a portion of her cargo, delivered her to the British authorities, and she was at last turned over to the United States Government. An account of the inner life on board the "Shenandoah" has never, to our knowledge, been published, although from the records of the Court of Alabama Claims we know the exact number of vessels Waddell captured and the damage committed; but, if ever an account of this cruise is published, even in the boastful spirit which characterizes so many Confederate narratives, it will no doubt be found equally interesting with the story of the "Alabama," and quite as disreputable.

CHAPTER LVII

THE RAM "STONEWALL."

REMARKABLE ENERGY AND FIDELITY OF THE CONFEDERATE AGENTS ABROAD.—THE BUILD-
ING, PURCHASE AND FITTING OUT OF CONFEDERATE CRUISERS.—THE RAM "STONEWALL"
BUILT, SOLD TO THE DANISH AUTHORITIES, AND REPURCHASED BY THE CONFEDERATE
GOVERNMENT.—THE RAM IN COMMISSION.—THE FEDERAL VESSELS-OF-WAR "NIAGARA"
AND "SACRAMENTO" BLOCKADED IN THE PORT OF CORUNNA.—ACTIONS OF COMMO-
DORE CRAVEN.—THE RAM PROCEEDS TO LISBON.—COMMODORE CRAVEN COURT-MAR-
TIALED AND SENTENCED.—THE SECRETARY OF THE NAVY CENSURES THE COURT, AND
THE PROCEEDINGS SET ASIDE.—COMMODORE CRAVEN RESTORED TO DUTY.—THE RAM
ENDS HER CAREER AT HAVANA, AND IS FINALLY SURRENDERED TO THE UNITED STATES
BY THE SPANISH AUTHORITIES.—REMARKS.

THE management of the agents of the Confederate Government abroad in supplying it with cruisers was very remarkable, and shows that the Confederacy was extremely fortunate in the selection of the officers thus employed. The agents not only succeeded in eluding the supposed vigilance of the authorities in England, but were even able to contract for two powerful rams and four corvettes in France to carry the most formidable guns then known.

One of the cleverest of these officers, and, as far as we know, the best, Captain James D. Bullock, was the principal agent in England for the purchase of vessels, and though the laws were violated in the transaction of building or purchasing, the violation rested principally with the builder or seller. In all his business transactions, it is fair to say of Captain Bullock that the only charge brought against him was too great a fidelity to the cause he had espoused, coupled with the ability he manifested in getting Confederate cruisers afloat. Though it is true that he was the prime-mover in getting these cruisers to sea, it has not been charged that he ever resorted to dishonorable means to attain his ends. It is said that he made contracts fairly and openly with builders, and left it with them to de-liver the ships at such time and place as they thought best. That the latter were adepts in violating their own laws, no one will doubt, and it is not to be supposed that the Confederate agents would hesitate to accept a well-fitted ship in a very irregular manner, as it seemed to the Federal Government, for human nature is too weak on such occasions to resist temptation.

Bullock was a man of ability. He never tired in his efforts, and if he met with difficulties at one turn he tried another; and when the British Government, seeing "the handwriting on the wall," realized the importance of not becoming involved in a war with the United States, and suddenly exercised all its power to put a stop to fitting out cruisers, Bullock transferred his talents to France, or, at least, pointed the way to constructing the vessels mentioned in that country. The career of the cruisers was nearly over; but they had been so successful that the Confederate Government was determined to show that it was able to drive off the large frigates and other vessels before the Southern ports, and raise the blockade all along the coast. Perhaps, had the vessels contracted for in France all got off together, and operated in concert, they might have created some confusion along the coast of the United States.

The Emperor had failed about that time

(823)

in securing joint action with England against Mexico, and, seeing that the Southern rebellion was fast collapsing, felt sure that the first step of the Federal Government would be to march a large army into Mexico to drive out the French troops. That army might possibly have been composed of Federal and Confederate soldiers marching shoulder to shoulder to defeat the common enemy, who, taking advantage of an intestine war, had presumed to establish an Empire right at our doors on the ruins of a sister Republic.

The construction of the vessels for the Confederate Government in France was undertaken by the builders with the tacit understanding that the French authorities would not prevent their delivery on completion. But owing, undoubtedly, to the European apprehensions, when the rams were about ready for sea, peremptory orders were given by the French Government that all the vessels should be sold. The orders were obeyed, and the "Stonewall" (then the "Sphynx") was purchased by Denmark, just as the Schleswig-Holstein war was closing. Delay in the completion and final delivery of the ram to Denmark made that government lukewarm in carrying out the terms of the purchase, as by this time the war was at an end and the ship was not required. When, therefore, a proposition was made by the builder to repurchase the "Sphynx," after delivery at Copenhagen, the Danish authorities accepted it without hesitation, and, as a natural sequence, she passed into the possession of the Confederate agents, was by them put into commission, and christened the "Stonewall." The history of the four corvettes is not pertinent, as they never came into the possession of the Confederate Government. The "Stonewall" was placed under the command of Captain Thomas Jefferson Page, an able officer, formerly of the United States Navy. She had, we regret to say, an opportunity of inflicting a humiliation upon the American Navy which was hard to bear, considering that its name almost throughout the conflict had been without a stain, and that the reputation it had gained in the war of 1812 had not diminished in the least.

The "Stonewall" got to sea January 28th, 1865, having received her stores and crew from another vessel dispatched by Captain Bullock from England, at Quiberon Bay, Belle Isle, France, but, owing to defects in the rudder casing, the "Stonewall" put in to Ferrol, Spain, for repairs, where she arrived February 2d, and fell in with the Federal frigate "Niagara" and sloop-of-war "Sacramento," under the command of Commodore Thomas T. Craven. The "Niagara" was a large and fast vessel of 4,600 tons displacement, carrying ten 150-pounder Parrott rifles. The "Sacramento" mounted two 11-inch guns, two 9-inch guns and one 60-pounder rifle, with some smaller pieces. The "Stonewall" carried one 300-pounder Armstrong rifle in a casemate in the bow and two 70-pounder rifles in a fixed turret, aft. Her sides were armored with 4¾ inches of iron; she had also a heavy ram. Such was the force of the three vessels now congregated in a Spanish port, the Confederate evidently determined to try consequences with the Federal vessels.

The commander of the "Niagara," not wishing to lay in the same port with the Confederate vessel, moved his ship to Corunna, where, when her repairs were completed, she was followed by the "Stonewall," which remained before the port blockading the two American ships-of-war, and, as the Commodore expressed it, "flaunting her flags in his face." Captain Page, in fact, did everything he could to provoke an encounter; and it must have been with much mortification that the Union commodore decided to remain at his anchors, and not run the risk of a battle with a foe that was represented as built with impervious sides, and with a battery (though smaller in numbers) very much superior to his own. Unfortunately, the Spaniards looking on could not be made to understand how two large vessels, mounting between them fifteen heavy guns, could decline a contest with a much smaller vessel carrying only three guns, and hence arose some misconstruction as to the existence of that prestige which American officers claimed for their Navy. It must have required great moral courage in an officer commanding two such ships to refrain from attacking the "Stonewall," on the ground that an engagement would result disastrously for the Union vessels. At the same time, no commander would be held justifiable, merely for the sake of making a reputation for himself, in neglecting other interests and attacking an enemy so superior to him that he would have no chance of success. But the question arises, was the "Stonewall" so superior to the "Niagara" and "Sacramento"? And it was a question that could only be ascertained by a contest at sea, when each vessel would have an opportunity of testing the other's qualities.

As the "Stonewall" was seen by the commander of the "Niagara," who was a capital sailor, she appeared to be a most powerful antagonist, and if well handled she would probably have inflicted serious injury upon the two vessels he commanded. He thought, perhaps (and so thought other professional men), that, under *certain circumstances*, the ram would have sunk the two Federal ships; while others, who have since seen the weak points in the "Stonewall," are of the opinion that she would have been no match for the Union vessels. No results would ever be arrived at, if a commander of a vessel should be unwilling to attack another about which he knew nothing. It is very questionable whether naval actions which are based exclusively on too nice calculations, and where too much consideration is given to the risk to be run in engaging an enemy, are ever followed by any gallant results.

There was great excitement in the Navy Department on hearing the conclusion the commander of the "Niagara" had reached in regard to the "Stonewall," and that, in consequence, the Confederate vessel had proceeded to Lisbon, coaled, and continued on her way toward the coast of the United States, without being followed further than that place. The several squadrons on the coast were warned that this formidable vessel was about to attack them, and directed to keep a good look-out for her; but, as a general rule, her advent was not at all apprehended, and, if she had appeared, steps had been taken to dispose of her as all Confederate rams had been disposed of before her.

It would not be fair for any one to judge harshly of the action of the Federal commander in this matter, unless he had been placed in the same position himself. No officer should be deprived of the discretionary power due to his command, or be trammelled by the opinions of those who have no responsibility resting upon them. It would never do to establish a principle that, for the sake merely of his reputation, an officer under all circumstances should attack an iron-clad with two wooden vessels. Very little was known of the power of sea-going iron-clads at that time, and the "Stonewall," for all the commander of the "Niagara" knew, might be impervious to shot or shell, and with manœuvring powers that were unequalled by the two ships under his command. Yet there may have been some justification for censure in the want of judgment in the commodore on the 24th day of May, 1865, in not making some exertion to obtain constant and personal observation of the Confederate ram while at Ferrol, and thus ascertain the truth or falsehood of the received reports of her character. There might also be some cause for reflection on the conduct of the Federal commander in remaining quietly at anchor in the Bay of Corunna, instead of going outside with his two vessels in the same neutral water, and there making observations of the "Stonewall's" speed, power of turning, etc.; and he might, with propriety, have consulted with his junior commander, Captain Henry Walke,

of the "Sacramento," who had boldly engaged on the Mississippi River a much more powerful ram — the "Arkansas" — while in command of the "Carondelet," a much inferior vessel—at least, he might have formed with his consort some plan of attack. This was not done, perhaps for the reason that, as, in his judgment, no engagement should take place, it was useless to form plans he did not propose to undertake.

Some of these ideas were evidently paramount in the mind of the Secretary of the Navy when the commander of the "Niagara" returned to the United States, as he brought him to trial by court-martial on the following charge: "Failing to do his utmost to overtake and capture or destroy a vessel which it was his duty to encounter." The court was composed of nine of the most distinguished officers of the Navy, with Vice-Admiral Farragut as President. The court decided that Commodore Craven had been remiss in his duties, and sentenced him to two years' suspension on leave-pay. This sentence was either inadequate to the offence charged, or it was very unjust, which will be plain to the nautical reader. Secretary Welles seemed to think that, notwithstanding the opinion of nine officers of the Navy, the sentence was inadequate to the offence, and addressed a severe communication to the president of the court in returning the proceedings for revision. Whether he was right or not in doing so depends on the latitude the revising authority is allowed in disapproving the finding of a court of officers who are sworn to do their whole duty in the premises. It would seem to be an attempt to deprive them of that discretionary power which is generally a beneficent feature in a military court-martial. It also detracts from that dignity which properly belongs to such a body, holding, as it does, the power even of life and death. The following is an extract from the Department's letter, returning the record to the court for revision:

"NAVY DEPARTMENT,
"WASHINGTON, December 1, 1865.

"SIR—The record of the proceedings of the court of which you are President, in the case of Commodore Thomas T. Craven, is herewith returned for a revision of the finding, which, in the opinion of the Department, is in conflict with law, and, if approved, would tend to render the provisions of law, which the accused is charged with violating, a 'dead letter.'"

Having received this letter, the court proceeded to revise its action upon the charge and specifications, and, after more mature deliberation, "doth find the charge *proven,* except the words, 'as it was his duty to have done,' and doth find the accused, Commodore Thomas T. Craven, of the charge, *guilty,* and doth award the following punishment : That the accused, Commodore Thomas T. Craven, be suspended from duty for two years on leave-pay." In his final revision of this finding, the remarks of the Secretary of the Navy are a severe censure on the action of the court, the proceedings were set aside and the accused restored to duty.

The above is a very important part of the history of the war, which we would be glad to be able to omit; but there are facts in the case having a very important bearing upon the future actions of officers of the Navy, and it would not be right in a historian to omit that which is unfavorable to the naval service and publish only that which is creditable. This case may be referred to hereafter as a test question, and the finding of the court and the opinion of the revising power may be adduced to show what duties are enjoined on members of courts-martial, and how far the revising power can go in virtually setting aside the sentence of a court when it is not considered to be severe enough, and in censuring a court in an official letter.

It is a well-established principle in military or naval law, that when charges are brought against an officer to any one of which the penalty of death is attached, no other sentence can be awarded. The law is imperative that courts-martial shall adjudge a punishment adequate to the offence committed and only leaves it discretionary with the court to *recommend* the convicted person to clemency, that clemency to be exercised only by the revising authority. The court has no discretion but to make its finding accord with the law. In the case under consideration, the court may have deemed that the law under which the accused was tried was one of a harsh character, as, no doubt, it was as far as regards the case in question, but it was bound by a solemn obligation to administer it as it stood on the statute-books, and not to modify it to suit their own views of justice. They had full authority to make recommendations to mercy that the revising power would hardly feel justified in disregarding, especially as a similar case had never been presented to a court during the war, and when it was a question whether an officer had any discretionary power in avoiding a combat with a vessel of an entirely different character from his own, and constructed on principles many years in advance of vessels of the class he commanded.

The great mistake the court made was in endeavoring to modify the charge of which the accused was or was not guilty. They had either to say one thing or another, and that in accordance with their opinion such was the case, and the revising power could

say no more. No ill results followed the "flaunting" of the "Stonewall's" flag, and it was in some respects a very doubtful case. Three of the officers of the court, Vice-Admiral Farragut, Rear-Admiral Davis and Captain Melancton Smith, had had some rough experiences with iron-clad rams, and, under the circumstances, were, no doubt, disposed to judge leniently, and willing to allow the commander of the "Niagara" discretionary rights in regard to attacking the "Stonewall." The court made a grave mistake in not more carefully considering this matter, and in not inquiring more closely into the points of law ; and for this reason it may be said that the court jeopardized, in a measure, the interests of the accused by finding him guilty of that which was not proved ; inasmuch as they declared by implication that it was not his duty to have attacked the "Stonewall," the finding being as follows: "Specification of the charge proven, except in so far as the words, 'as it was his duty to have done,' declare it to have been the imperative duty of the accused to join battle with the 'Stonewall' on the 24th day of March"—(1865).

How, under the finding of the court, the commander of the "Niagara" could be censured for "want of zeal and exertion in not making constant and personal observation of the 'Stonewall' while at Ferrol, and thereby endeavoring to ascertain the truth or falsehood of the various reports of her character," does not appear ; for, while qualifying their finding, they reflect upon him in three several instances : First, in the words just quoted ; second, "on the conduct of the accused in remaining quietly at anchor in the bay of Corunna while the 'Stonewall' was parading about in neutral waters, flaunting her flags," etc ; and, third, in that no plans were formed for concerted action between the "Niagara" and "Sacramento" by the accused. Under the circumstances, and considering the inconsistency of the court, the revising power found it impossible to determine whether the accused was guilty or not, the finding on the charge declaring him guilty, but that on the specification, not guilty. As the court adhered to its finding when the proceedings were returned for revision, the Secretary of the Navy concluded to set the proceedings aside, and restore the commander of the "Niagara" to duty.

As this case ended, the matter is left in abeyance, and it may yet happen that an officer may be tried under the same circumstances which present the simple question, Shall an officer be allowed any discretionary power in deciding whether or not to join battle with an enemy's ships or with an enemy's forts ?—for the principle applies to both. In the light of later events, the leniency of the court at that time is generally approved, and, taking into consideration the high character of the officers who composed it, it would have been but courteous to them had the revising power yielded to their opinion, which was, without doubt, the result of their honest convictions. It has been conceded that Admiral Byng, of the British Navy, was unjustly shot, to satisfy public opinion. There was no necessity on this occasion for such an example. No man could know whether or not the affair at Corunna was an error of judgment—in fact, no one could tell whether it was not the right course to pursue. Any officer commanding two wooden ships of the same kind to-day could feel perfectly justified in avoiding a battle with a modern iron-clad ram—whether the cases are analagous, the reader must be the judge.

After all the trouble and excitement created by the "Stonewall," she never succeeded in getting beyond Havana, where, at the termination of the war, she was given up to the Spanish Government by her commander in an honorable manner and surrendered to the United States.

CHAPTER LVIII.

CONCLUSION.

WHEN the war ended, the United States had attained a position as a Naval power never before reached by the Republic, and could claim to be able to meet either France or England upon the ocean. Both of these nations had looked on with surprise at the rapid manner in which the Federal Government was adding to its Navy. If not anxious for the dissolution of the United States, both France and England were quick to throw their weight against it by proclamations, giving to the Confederates a character that did much to strengthen their cause, by offering them most substantial aid, and in permitting them to build, arm and equip vessels-of-war in their ports for the destruction of American commerce. Even at a time when the Federal armies had advanced so far in the enemy's country that the final result was apparent to the most indifferent observer, the Confederate sympathizers in France and England declared that the Federal Government was making no progress in subduing the Confederacy, and insisted that the Navy, in particular, was incapable of putting down the few cruisers that were destroying American commerce at their pleasure.

France, the ancient ally of the United States, that had stood by the young Republic in its hour of need, and who had always been bound to it in the closest ties of amity, under the avaricious policy of her emperor, who had his eyes fixed on Mexico, went over to England and supported her in the proclamations issued in the Queen's name, but dictated by Earl Russell. The emperor hoped to persuade England to embark in a scheme that was to benefit France only in the subjection of Mexico to French rule, and to add to the French crown that jewel which would enrich and strengthen any nation that possessed it. In his insane desire to obtain possession of that beauti-

ful country, the French emperor beheld in the supposed waning power of the United States the opportunity he sought to enable him to plant his foot firmly on the soil of the Montezumas, thinking that, once the City of Mexico was occupied by his troops, the United States would never again be in a condition to offer any obstacles to the permanent establishment of French authority. It was this ambitious project only that induced France to abandon her old friendship for the United States, and uphold England in her questionable policy of permitting the construction of Confederate cruisers in her ports. Had France remained strictly neutral, and shown England that she did not approve of the pretended neutrality the latter was practicing, the moral effect of her course would have been to prevent England from assisting the Confederates.

When the "Trent" affair took place (which did not in the least concern France), and when the British Government had taken such precipitate measures to humiliate the Federal Government—not giving it time even to make an explanation—the French emperor, through his minister in Washington, entered an entirely uncalled-for protest against the action of the United States vessel-of-war "San Jacinto," stating that such a course was as offensive to France as to England, and, in fact, to all European governments ; and announcing in his dispatch the course France would pursue under like circumstances—his real policy being to urge England into a war with the United States, which would further French views in regard to Mexico. This shows the animus actuating the emperor; though the Federal Administration had its hands full at that time, his object was apparent, while the sincerity of England was strongly suspected.

The first step of the Navy Department, when it could command the money, was to construct a Navy not only for the purpose of blockading the Southern coast, but to protect our shores from foreign foes, and hold their own upon the ocean with the cruisers of either France or England. We have shown how inadequate the Navy was at the breaking out of the rebellion even to blockade the Confederate ports, much less to offer resistance to a powerful naval antagonist; but even the first year of the war was one of wonderful development for the Navy, not only in establishing a complete blockade, but in the usefulness of naval vessels in assisting the Army to carry out plans of conquest that it could never have achieved alone.

In a very short time after the Confederacy was established, all the great rivers of the West and their tributaries were in Confederate hands, and the most inaccessible points therein armed with ponderous guns, manned by an excited soldiery. The Potomac River was blockaded almost from Alexandria to the Chesapeake; the Sounds of North Carolina were filled with powerful batteries, and the channels closed by sunken obstructions. Every port on the Southern coast was protected by well-constructed forts, and closed against the few vessels the Government owned, and for a time the Federal cause looked so hopeless that Europeon despots might well be excused for supposing that it would be an impossible task to recover the lost domain, unprovided as the Federal Government was with ships of a character to contend with all the peculiar difficulties of navigation in the inland waters.

The difficulties to be overcome have only been described in this work in a partial way, for no description could give an adequate idea of all that was done by the Navy and how it was done. Compare the results of this great war in matters connected with the Navy alone with those of any other scene of action in Europe or elsewhere, and it will be seen that history offers no example where so much was accomplished in so short a time, or where so many events were crowded into the space of four years, in which the Navy was employed subduing a coast over four thousand miles in length, and recapturing a river-coast of more than five thousand miles.

Let us compare the operations of England and France in the Crimea with those on our own coast, and note the results. These two nations had but a small amount of territory to subdue—four hundred square miles at the most; the two great navies of the world were at their command, with a much larger *proportion* of troops than ever co-operated with the Federal naval forces during the war of the rebellion; they started with the greatest armada the world ever saw—sixty or seventy ships of the line, and numerous other vessels-of-war, transports (filled with troops), that almost covered the sea; and still they were months making any impression upon the Russian stronghold, which did not in any way compare with Vicksburg.

The Federal Government commenced with four small vessels (carrying in all twenty-five guns), the duty of capturing or blockading the South Atlantic coast. In the Gulf of Mexico were eight more ships; in the Mediterranean, three more; seven were on the coast of Africa; two on that of Brazil; three were in the East Indies, and eight in the Pacific—scattered, in fact, all over the world; and these had to be collected to satisfy England and France that a perfect blockade could be established. They naturally ridiculed the attempt, yet in less than a year the blockade was accomplished, so that the most hypercritical sovereign could not object to it, and every foreign government acknowledged that it was the great feat of the war. All the skill and capital of England could not keep this blockade open, though they might at times succeed in getting their vessels into Southern ports to supply the Confederate armies with the means of carrying on the war. The Navy was so watchful that multitudes of English vessels were captured; the coasts of the South were strewn with the wrecks of English clipper-steamers which were chased on shore in calm and in storm by officers who seldom slept, and were scanning the horizon night and day for the sight of an incoming blockade-runner.

This was but a small part of the naval service performed. The Navy was called upon to help open the Potomac, and guard the capital; directed to capture the Hatteras forts, and the fortifications in the sounds and rivers of North Carolina. The forts at Hilton Head defied them, but naval officers, with their wooden vessels, dismantled them with shell. Forts Jackson and St. Philip, which French and English officers said would sink the whole Federal Navy, barred the way to New Orleans; the guns of the Navy opened the gates and laid New Orleans captive at the conqueror's feet.

Then came the demand that the Navy should open the Mississippi from the Ohio River to the sea, clear out the obstructions in the shape of four hundred guns, and restore the different towns on the banks of that great river to the control of the United States Government. With what was it all to be done? Could their frail vessels, improvised from river-boats and a few thin-plated vessels, be able to force the barriers that were placed on every eligible site? Yet, with the aid of the

Army, a little over two years after the war began, the Mississippi was open to the sea. The ideas of the Navy Department grew with the success of the Navy afloat, and the work-shops of the country teemed with mechanics who entered heart and soul into the business of building iron-clads that could not only cope successfully with the heavy forts of the enemy, but could remind unfriendly nations that the more severely this nation was tested, the more she would rise in her strength.

The State of Tennessee, the great prize and battle-ground (upon which the enemy expended a large portion of their resources, and through which they hoped to attack the northwestern States), was under the control of the gun-boats, and the Army was placed by their aid securely in the heart of the State. From the time a naval force was placed on the Tennessee and Cumberland Rivers, the stay of the Confederate forces was very problematical, and it cannot escape the attention of the reader how persistent were the naval officers who commanded the Western Squadron in keeping open two rivers, which were in all cases the keys to the situation.

Only two important points on the sea-coast had been maintained by the enemy—Charleston and Wilmington—but, though they flourished for a time, afforded great assistance to the Confederate cause, and kept up the drooping spirits of the infatuated Confederacy, the rebellion received its death-blow on July 4th, 1863. Its after-struggles were only like those of the dying lion, that for a short time exhibits his greatest strength without power to do any injury in his dying throes, no matter how much prolonged.

At the end of the war the United States Government had just begun to realize its strength, and those who had the direction of its affairs might well feel proud of the great Army and Navy which stood ready, now that the intestine troubles were over, to take in hand those who had so insolently interfered with the Federal Government, not from any real sympathy with the Southern cause, but from a desire to see the free institutions of this country overthrown, and the whole land become a scene of anarchy—to show that man was in no place fit for self-government.

What the Navy Department and the war did towards building up a Navy, and a Navy altogether of a new type, can only be judged by a reference to the tables annexed to this chapter, which give a correct exhibit of the ships built, building, and altered, during the four years' war—a feat only one other nation (Great Britain) could have accomplished in the same space of time.

All of this Navy that is known in his-tory as having performed the greatest feat in the war (the most complete blockade of a coast ever established), is among the things of the past. Its dissolution was even more rapid than its creation. It was allowed to dwindle away without an effort to replace those ships, that had fallen victims to decay, with others of a suitable character. The vessels were sold "under the hammer," as no longer suitable for the purposes of war, which had changed its character entirely since the beginning of the American contest. A few old vessels still remain to attest the uselessness of a branch of the service on which the Government must depend for protection in time of war with a foreign nation, or to keep the peace at home against insurrectionists of whatever character that may present themselves.

It is no compliment to the intelligence of sixty millions of people to have it said, that the United States has not one iron-clad to defend her coast; not a perfectly equipped cruiser of steel to carry her flag upon the ocean; not a single gun in her coast defences that could pierce the shield of a foreign iron-clad, and not a fortification that could resist the attack of two or three foreign-built iron-clads. We may be said to be a great nation of people, but certainly not a nation of great people; for, who will call us the latter, when there seems to be such a love of accumulating wealth, without the manly desire to have the means of defending it against the aggressions of any power that may choose to make war upon us? The Government of the United States cannot defend themselves against the weakest naval power, much less against a strong one, and we must, perforce, rely on that old system, so much in vogue in Thomas Jefferson's time, of paying tribute, as we did from 1804 to 1815 to the Barbary powers, to prevent them from preying on our commerce and carrying our citizens to captivity.

We had experience enough during the war of the rebellion to satisfy us that there were certain European governments that desired the downfall of the American Union, and it was only by means of an abject compliance with their demands that we escaped war, which would have been the signal of the complete triumph of the South and the dissolution of the Union which our forefathers exercised so much wisdom in building up. What a noble sight it would have been, after the settlement of our difficulties at home, to see the American people set to work and build a Navy that would bid defiance to any naval power in the world—to rebuild the commerce that had been driven from the sea by the "Alabamas" and "Floridas," and which was once the pride and wealth of the nation—to give an exhibition of our wealth and resources and our indomitable will, that no nation should oppose us, or interfere with our domestic affairs. But, instead of this we stood still, while other nations worked on, and taking advantage of our lethargy robbed us of our commerce, took the carrying trade all in their own hands, and now laugh at our inane attempts to build up a Navy, which, if it ever reaches a reputable standard, will show that we are so deficient in the elementary science of naval construction that we can-not keep pace even with the modern examples that have been set us by European powers.

We can be no more exempt from war than others; indeed, our weak condition is so well understood by all the world that it only invites aggression ; and, if we would not desire to rest under the imputation of being the poorest government under the sun, and unfit to take care of the interests of sixty millions of people, we must shortly awake from an apathy that would disgrace any country, and begin to provide for the national defence.

In the war of the rebellion the people on both sides exhibited the greatest examples of courage, resources and perseverance, showing what we could do were our shores to be invaded ; for which, no doubt, in the opinion of the world, we have gained that reputation which generally follows heroic deeds. But all that credit would disappear to-morrow if we were involved in a foreign war : our coasts would be devastated, our harbors sealed up by a foreign foe, and we would again be obliged to pay tribute as we did to the Barbary powers of old.

Taking into consideration the situation of the United States at the present time, it looks as if the rebellion had taught us nothing, and that we are giving wild theo-rists of the past and present some show of reason to assert that republican forms of government are unnecessarily expensive, revolutionary, and deficient in the elements for the maintenance of a proper protection from an outside enemy or intestine foe. A government which maintains no army or navy for the preservation of law and order simply runs an even race with anarchy and rebellion. This is true of us in a tenfold degree, for we give our enemies in all quarters the opportunity of getting their forces first into the field. This applies more particu-larly to the Navy of the United States, which never seems to attract the attention of those who have charge of the national defence. They never for a moment think that, if the dreadful reality of war was sprung upon us, not only could any of the greater powers within twenty days lay our large sea-coast

cities in ashes, and exact any amount of trib-ute they might think proper, but even the smallest States, with any pretensions as naval powers, could humiliate us to any extent. This is a terrible confession to make, but it is nevertheless true, and, unless those who have these matters in charge rise to a proper conception of their duty, they may live to "reap of the whirlwind," and receive the condemnation of the sixty millions of people who now depend on them for that protection every government owes its citizens.

The people of the United States can readily dispose of their anarchists on the land, and provide against all their revolutionary ideas by the bullet or bayonet, when they become tired of listening to these wild theorists who would upset, if they could, any government, no matter how desirable. But they are helpless when it comes to de-fending themselves against the attacks of heavy iron-clads, which can only be met by great vessels-of-war designed for the pur-pose ; which we do not possess, and which there seems very little prospect of our ob-taining.

There is but one remedy for the evils un-der which we are resting, and that is, for the people to take the matter in hand and demand a Navy that will help put down rebellion at home at its first inception, and bid defiance to those abroad who would commit aggressions upon our commerce, or treat our citizens unjustly in any part of the world.

Let us not forget that something akin to Barbary powers still exists, though in the garb of Christian civilization, and that they are not as limited in number as they were in 1804. They may have the strongest treaties binding them to us in terms of amity, but they are ever ready, like the Algerines of old, to take advantage of our weakness.

We might naturally be supposed to have retained some bitter feelings against Eng-land and France on account of the un-friendliness they exhibited when we were passing through the greatest struggle of our history as a nation, but, though we might very properly be so influenced, this idea has no foundation in fact ; though it might well be impressed upon the con-sciences of many of the British people who do not remember with complacency the course England (as a nation) pursued, con-sidering her intimate relations with the United States. But the Americans are a forgiving people, and forget injuries, only to have them repeated even when they know they were intended to be fatal. We found no sympathy in our great revolution, which became a struggle for our actual ex-istence; least of all did we find it where we had a right to expect it—in free England, who had taken the first broad step towards the emancipation of the slave. But our disappointment in finding a foe where we should have found a friend only added a vigor to our action. We found ourselves strong enough to fight our way to victory. We could well afford to do without the sympathy of either England or France; for, though the task became harder, owing to their opposition, we were perfectly conscious from the first that their aid was not needed, and that their opposition would be futile.

The adventurous Napoleon III., who staked an empire on the acquisition of Mexico by the downfall of the United States, has long since paid the penalty of his treachery in his opposition to the great Republic, once the ally of France. Even his descendants, to the last generation, have disappeared from the face of the earth, while, in his old age, he was deprived of all he held dear—power and wealth. There seems to be a Nemesis at work in all such matters, bringing retribution where it is most deserved. England prospers, and extends her dominions, spreading freedom to all parts of the earth, and, apparently, strengthening her power; but she will live to see her colonies, one after another, going from her, each one seeking in turn to attain a larger degree of autonomy than they now possess, and she may find arrayed against her the very element on which she depended to increase her prestige, and may then miss some of that sympathy she denied us in our hour of need.

CHAPTER LIX.

PRIZES ADJUDICATED FROM THE COMMENCEMENT OF THE REBELLION TO NOVEMBER 1, 1865, WITH THE NAMES OF VESSELS OR OTHER MATERIAL CAPTURED, AND THE NAMES OF VESSELS ENTITLED TO SHARE IN DISTRIBUTION OF PROCEEDS.

Name.	Gross proceeds.	Costs and expenses.	Am't for distribution.	Where adjudicated.	Sent to 4th Auditor for distribution.	Vessels entitled to share.
Sch. Anna Belle............	$6,743 74	$1,355 37	$5,388 37	Key West	July 12, 1862	Pursuit.
Sch. Adeline...............	4,086 87	1,244 82	2,844 05	....do........	Oct. 16, 1862	Connecticut.
Sch. Aristides*...........	125 00	67 37	57 63	....do........	....	
Sch. Agnes....	24,162 76	1,761 96	22,400 80	....do........	Feb. 17, 1863	Huntsville.
Sch. Ariel	8,533 54	739 25	7,794 29	... do........	Oct. 14, 1863	Huntsville.
Sch. Avenger..............	1,190 01	233 70	956 31	....do........	Oct. 17, 1863	Sagamore.
Sch. Agnes	435 00	165 17	269 83	.. do........	Oct. 24, 1863	Sagamore.
Sch. Adventure	2,046 97	521 63	1,625 34	....do........	Oct. 17, 1863	Henry Jones, Kensington, Rachel Seaman.
Brig Amy Warwick........	139,202 08	576 89	138,625 13	Boston......	July 14, 1863	Quaker City.
Sch. Alma	3,748 06	885 32	2,862 74	....do........	Nov. 5, 1863	Perry.
Sloop Ann Squires.	2,118 11	345 59	1,772 52	Washington..	Oct. 19, 1863	William Bacon.
Sch. American Coaster....	350 00	119 27	230 73	....do........	Oct. 19, 1863	Currituck.
Ship Ameliat.............	30,446 32	{†5,708 32 6,571 10	} 18,066 90	Philadelphia..	Dec. 3, 1862	Vandalia, Flag.
Sch. Albion...........	9,564 57	2,077 85	7,486 72	....do........	July 17, 1863	Roanoke, Seminole.
Brig Ariel	5,249 88	1,618 61	3,631 27	....do... .	July 17, 1863	Gemsbok.
Sch. Active.	3,136 18	1,064 55	2,071 63	... do........	July 18, 1863	Flambeau.
Sch. Aquilla.......	30,104 72	1,877 90	28,226 82	....do........	May 19, 1863	Huron, Augusta.
Sloop Aurelia......... ...	20,136 71	1,277 96	18,858 75	... do........	May 1, 1863	Arizona.
Sch. Alert	6,741 67	1,506 22	5,235 45	....do..	Sept. 15, 1863	Bienville.
Str. Alice‡.	1,100 00	267 85	832 15	New York....	....	Ceres.
Sch. Albion	1,966 86	1,115 91	850 95	....do........	Nov. 25, 1863	Penguin, Alabama.
Sch. A. J. View...........	16,262 38	2,227 95	14,034 43	....do........	Nov. 5, 1863	R. R. Cuyler, New London, Massachusetts.
Sch. Agnes H. Ward	19,675 28	2,771 26	16,904 02	....do........	Feb. 11, 1863	Northern Light.
Sch. Albemarle.... ...	500 00	249 35	250 65	....do........	Nov. 25, 1863	Delaware.
Str. Albemarle, schs. Old North State, Susan Ann Howard, and sloop Jeff. Davis	15,990 00	617 05	15,372 95	....do,......	Dec. 20, 1863	Delaware, Stars and Stripes, Louisiana, Commodore Perry, Valley City, Underwriter, Morse, Commodore Barney, Southfield, Hunchback, Philadelphia, Henry Brincker, Lockwood.
Sloop Annie....	10,677 22	1,625 38	9,051 84	....do........	July 17, 1863	Kanawha.
Sch. Annie Sophia.........	1,529 92	795 71	834 21	....do........	Mar. 2, 1863	R. R. Cuyler.
Sch. Advocate.	600 00	240 85	359 15	....do........	July 21, 1863	New London, R. R. Cuyler, Massachusetts.
Str. Anna	18,423 82	3,139 28	15,282 44	....do........	July 21, 1863	New London, R. R. Cuyler, Massachusetts.
Sch. Annie Dees	16,637 09	2,027 89	14,609 20	....do........	Dec. 8, 1863	Seneca, G.W. Blunt, Canandaigua, Flag, Memphis, Powhatan, Housatonic, Marblehead, Mercedita, Flambeau, Keystone State.
Str. Anglia..	95,110 21	10,260 31	84,849 90	....do........	Nov. 5, 1863	Restless, Flag.
Sch. Aigburth............	3,106 54	1,784 74	1,321 80	....do........	Dec. 2, 1863	Jamestown.
Sch. Antelope............	3,345 79	570 53	2,775 26	....do...	Dec. 17, 1863	Memphis, America.
Sch. Annie.	2,405 00	1,074 97	1,330 03	. do........	Feb. 29, 1864	State of Georgia.
Sch. Active.	3,410 00	483 40	2,926 60	Washington..	Feb. 29, 1864	Ladona.
Sch. Alma	4,232 60	595 85	3,136 75	..do........	July 28, 1864	Seneca.
Sch. Annie B..	4,547 98	621 08	3,926 90	Key West..	June 4, 1864	Wanderer.
Sch. Ascension............	5,448 93	716 89	4,732 04	....do........	Feb. 29, 1864	Huntsville.
Sch. Avon	4 251 11	850 37	3,400 74	....do........	Feb. 29, 1864	Tioga
Sloop Angelina............	2,793 15	905 23	1,887 92	New York....	Feb. 29, 1864	Courier.
Str. Ann	53,071 12	5,736 95	47,334 17	...do........	Feb. 29, 1864	Susquehanna, Kanawha, Preble.
Boat Alligator	119 90	118 35	1 55	Key West....		Tahoma, Julia.
Boat Anna Maria..........	5,002 12	662 21	4,339 91	...do........	Feb. 29, 1864	Fort Henry.
Sch. A. J. Hodge..........	2,120 39	327 57	1,792 82	.. do........	Mar. 17, 1864	Huntsville.
Sch. Arctic. ...	3,410 00	483 45	2,926 60	Washington..	Feb. 29, 1864	Ladona.
Sch. Albert...............	11,434 08	3,237 02	8,197 06	New York....	Mar. 17, 1864	Huron.
Sch. Anna...............	2,530 67	351 80	2,178 87	Key West...	Mar. 17, 1864	Fort Henry.
Sch. Ann	3,299 40	308 22	2,991 18	....do........	Mar. 17, 1864	Restless.
Sch. Alabama.............	9,867 38	1,291 56	8,575 82	... do........	Mar. 17, 1864	Susquehanna.
Sloop Ann......	50 00	60 15	No proceeds	....do........	....	Gem of the Sea.
Sch. Ann	322 61	147 21	175 40	....do........	Mar. 29, 1864	Sagamore.

* No final decree.   † $5,708.32 awarded to claimants.   ‡ Taken by War Department. Not yet paid for.

Name.	Gross proceeds.	Costs and expenses.	Am't for distribution.	Where adjudicated.	Sent to 4th Auditor for distribution.	Vessels entitled to share.
Str. Aries	$147,008 46	$3,036 48	$143,971 98	Boston	Mar. 22, 1864	Stettin.
Str. Antona	136,202 02	4,526 60	131,675 42	New York	May 10, 1864	Pocahontas.
Str. Atlanta	350,829 26	789 30	350,039 96	Boston	April 23, 1864	Weehawken, Nahant, Cimarron.
Boat Alice*	597 62	143 66	453 96	Key West		Annie Williams.
Str. Alonzo Childs	5,000 00	275 91	4,724 09	Springfield	Mar. 29, 1864	Baron De Kalb.
Sch. Anita	75,489 99	5,650 70	69,839 29	New Orleans	April 12, 1864	Granite City.
Schs. Active and Blue Bell	875 10	172 71	702 39	...do	April 12, 1864	Owasco, Cayuga.
Str. Alabama	131,364 10	10,412 60	120,951 50	...do	April 23, 1864	San Jacinto, Eugene, Tennessee.
Str. Alice Vivian	237,300 81	20,240 28	217,060 53	Key West	April 12, 1864	De Soto.
Str. Alliance	25,041 96	1,760 22	23,281 74	Boston	July 21, 1864	South Carolina, T. A. Ward.
Sch. Alma	3,531 00	745 14	2,785 86	New Orleans	July 28, 1864	Virginia.
Sch. Agnes	74,361 30	3,822 74	70,538 56	...do	Oct. 7, 1864	Chocura.
Anchors, etc., from the Queen of the Wave.	745 95	428 42	317 53	Philadelphia		Conemaugh. (Waiting for prize list.)
Str. A. D. Vance	288,286 49	5,047 71	283,238 78	New York	Nov. 17, 1864	Santiago de Cuba.
Sch. Artist	6,416 42	1,421 54	4,994 85	Philadelphia	Jan. 19, 1865	Bermuda.
Sch. Annie Verden	25,445 68	2,598 31	22,847 37	New Orleans	Feb. 21, 1865	Mobile.
Sch. Albert Edward	44,461 82	4,183 34	40,278 48	...do	Feb. 14, 1865	Katahdin.
Str. Armstrong	251,382 26	7,321 53	244,060 73	New York	April 20, 1865	R. R. Cuyler, Gettysburg, Mackinaw, Montgomery.
Sloop Annie Thompson	14,847 96	1,639 50	13,208 46	Philadelphia	May 13, 1865	Fernandina.
Sch. Ann Louisa	7,437 57	476 92	6,960 95	Key West	Aug. 25, 1865	Proteus.
Sch. Anna Sophia	29,145 69	4,245 48	24,900 21	New Orleans	June 26, 1865	Bienville, Princess Royal.
Str. Annie	358,951 71	24,639 97	329,311 74	New York	June 22, 1865	Niphon, Wilderness, Alabama, Kansas, Howquah.
Sch. Augusta	5,551 28	313 70	5,237 58	Key West	Aug. 16, 1865	Honeysuckle.
Ram Albemarle	79,944 00	2,645 30	77,298 70	Washington	Aug. 28, 1865	Lieutenant-Commander Cushing and party.
Sloop Annie	192 05	108 89	83 16	Key West	Sept. 29, 1865	Hibiscus.
Sch. British Empire	3,929 73	504 76	3,423 97	New York	Nov. 20, 1863	Isaac Smith.
Sch. British Queen	2,108 31	999 90	1,108 41	...do	Nov. 25, 1862	Mount Vernon.
Boats, 3 sail, and cargoes	1,463 89	277 00	1,186 89	Washington		Reliance. (Waiting for prize list.)
Schooner Blossom	270 88	86 81	184 07	..do	Aug. 15, 1862	Reliance, Anacostia, Thomas Freeborn.
Boat, 1 life	1,106 95	273 79	833 16	...do	Oct. 19, 1863	Jacob Bell.
Boat, 1 yawl	682 70	168 36	514 34	...do	Oct. 19, 1863	Freeborn, Eureka.
Boat, a flat-bottomed	387 79	119 11	268 68	..do	Oct. 5, 1865	Dan. Smith.
Str. Britannia	173,670 55	3,974 83	169,695 72	Boston	Oct. 26, 1863	Santiago de Cuba.
Sch. Beauregard†	2,146 67	291 75	1,854 92	Key West		W. G. Anderson.
Sch. By-George	512 76	209 45	303 31	...do	Oct. 24, 1863	Sagamore.
Sch. Brave	893 18	196 85	696 33	...do	Oct. 24, 1863	Octorara.
Sch. Bettie Kratzer	4,642 00	1,081 28	3,560 72	Philadelphia	Feb. 18, 1864	Flambeau.
Sloop Bright	5,672 85	614 95	5,057 90	Key West	Feb. 29, 1864	De Soto.
Sch. Brothers	7,641 38	1,575 78	6,065 60	...do	June 4, 1864	Tioga.
Boat, sloop, name unknown	533 78	144 04	389 74	...do	Dec. 19, 1864	Restless.
Boat Buckshot	1,918 05	294 77	1,623 23	...do	Mar. 29, 1864	San Jacinto.
Sloop Blazer	8,836 65	884 59	7,952 06	...do	Mar. 29, 1864	Brooklyn.
Boat, name unknown	31 75	32 01	No proceeds	..do		Ariel.
Sch. Betsey	1,700 00	865 42	834 58	New Orleans	April 12, 1864	Antona.
Brandy, 29 cases of, etc	183 00	123 32	59 68	...do	April 12, 1864	Cayuga.
Sch. Belle	1,439 31	678 85	760 46	New York	April 12, 1864	Potomska.
Boat, sail, 1	452 55	221 71	230 84	New Orleans	April 12, 1864	Corypheus.
Boats, sail, 3	1,078 15	361 65	706 50	... do	April 26, 1865	Corypheus.
Boat and cargo, 1	29 75	..	No proceeds	Washington		
Boats and cargoes, 4	492 57	274 19	218 38	New Orleans	June 4, 1864	Commodore.
Boots, 1 case, etc ‡	355 95	95 39	260 56	Springfield		Alfred Robb.
Str. Boston	23,036 03	2,308 49	20,727 54	Boston	Oct. 10, 1864	Fort Jackson.
Str. Banshee	111,216 65	6,268 17	104,948 48	New York	Oct. 25, 1864	Fulton, Grand Gulf.
Sloop Buffalo	13,328 85	2,416 37	10,912 48	Philadelphia	Nov. 23, 1864	Braziliera.
Boat and cargo	390 25	201 78	188 47	New Orleans	Feb. 2, 1865	Tallahatchie.
Boats, 2, and 4 bales of cotton	2,700 00	261 45	2,438 55	...do	Mar. 27, 1865	Commodore.
Str. Bloomer	....	....	1,700 00	...do	Oct. 3, 1865	Potomac.
Sch. Belle	26,586 74	3,430 19	23,156 25	.. do	April 20, 1865	Virginia.
Str. Blenheim	55,778 22	3,655 77	52,122 45	New York	June 19, 1865	Tristam Shandy, Lillian, Britannia, Osceola, Gettysburg.
Sch. Badger	10,834 32	947 89	9,886 43	Key West	June 29, 1865	Adela.
Boat and sundries	194 22	90 82	103 40	.. do		San Jacinto. (Waiting for prize list.)
Boat, no name	891 67	123 61	768 06	...do	Aug. 16, 1865	Ino.
Sch. Baigorry	61,568 43	4,315 65	57,272 58	...do	Aug. 16, 1865	Bainbridge.
Schs. Comet, J. J. Crittenden, and sloop America	2,600 00	322 85	2,277 15	New York	Oct. 22, 1863	Commodore Perry, Morse, Underwriter, General Putnam, Whitehead.
Sch. Captain Spedden§	1,387 50	289 50	1,098 00	... do	....	Henry Lewis, New London, Water Witch.
Sch. Crenshaw	51,016 82	5,192 22	45,824 60	do	Dec. 2, 1863	Star (now Monticello).
Str. Calhoun	45,531 00	2,118 16	43,412 40	Philadelphia	Dec. 1, 1863	Samuel Rotan, Colorado, Rachel Seaman.
Str. Catalina	6,095 05	994 04	5,101 01	...do	May 2, 1863	Alabama, Keystone State.
Str. Cambria and part of cargo	191,424 54	12,383 56	179,040 98	...do	May 2, 1863	Huron, Augusta.
Str. Calypso	80,265 03	4,930 10	75,334 93	...do	Jan. 19, 1864	Florida.
Cotton, 28 bales	2,212 16	446 92	1,765 24	...do	Jan. 4, 1864	Stars and Stripes, Louisiana, Hetzel, Delaware, Commodore Perry, Philadelphia, Valley City, Underwriter, Commodore Barney, Southfield, Morse, Hunchback, Lockwood.
Cotton, 30 bales	6,276 05	859 25	5,416 80	...do	Jan. 4, 1864	Stars and Stripes, Louisiana, Hetzel, Underwriter, Morse, Commodore Perry, Southfield, H. Brincker, Delaware, Lockwood, Commodore Barney, Valley City, Hunchback, Philadelphia.
Cargo of 4 canoes‖	575 00	301 40	273 60	Washington	....	Currituck.
Sloop Clara Ann	1,300 75	308 12	992 63	...do	Jan. 11, 1864	Yankee.
Sch. Charlotte	31,369 19	1,425 93	29,943 26	Boston	Jan. 12, 1863	Kanawha.
Sch. Cuba¶	2,811 49	1,390 39	1,421 10	... do	....	Kanawha.
Sch. Curlew	6,902 00	1,546 45	5,355 55	Key West	Nov. 26, 1862	Somerset.

* Waiting for prize list of Annie Williams.
† Distributed under acts of March 3, 1819, and August 5, 1861.
‡ Waiting for prize list of the Robb.
§ Waiting for prize list of the Water Witch.
‖ Waiting for prize list of the Currituck.
¶ Part of cargo taken for use of army not paid for.

Name.	Gross proceeds.	Costs and expenses.	Am't for distribution.	Where adjudicated.	Sent to 4th Auditor for distribution.	Vessels entitled to share.
Sch. Corelia.................	$1,430 62	$494 96	$935 66	Key West	July 18, 1863	James S. Chambers.
Str. Columbia..............	151,523 20	15,419 82	136,103 38	....do..	Oct. 6, 1863	Santiago de Cuba.
Sch. Courier ..	3,647 10	613 62	3,033 48	....do........	Oct. 14, 1863	Huntsville.
Sch. Carmita	2,426 98	498 92	1,928 06	....do........	Oct. 17, 1863	Magnolia.
Cargo of 9 boats and sloop Queen of the Fleet....	3,105 79	574 83	2,530 96	Washington..	Nov. 20, 1863	Currituck.
Canoe, 1; flatboat, 1*.....	1,101 41	279 14	822 27	...do........	....	Jacob Bell, Yankee, Satellite.
Sch. Cora	624 50	526 90	97 60	Philadelphia..	Nov. 25, 1862	Keystone State.
Cotton, 208 bales	28,922 90	1,784 30	27,138 60	Springfield...	Oct. 16, 1863	Baron de Kalb.
Cotton, 52½ bales	14,037 90	276 25	13,761 65	Boston.......	Nov. 9, 1863	Octorara.
Cotton, 37½ bales ...	8,542 26	207 19	8,335 07	....do........	Nov. 5, 1863	Tioga.
Cotton, 282 bales, 222 barrels rosin, and 2,000 staves....................	62,179 36	13,680 90	48,498 46	New York....	Dec. 31, 1863	Stars and Stripes, Louisiana, Hetzel, Commodore Barney, Valley City, Underwriter, Commodore Perry, Southfield, Hunchback, Philadelphia, Morse, H. Brincker, Lockwood, Delaware, George Mangham.
Cotton, 27 bales	6,576 15	406 43	6,169 72	Springfield...	June 11, 1864	Conestoga.
Cotton, 42 bales, etc......	13,784 52	708 98	13,075 54	...do........	Dec. 3, 1864	Linden.
Cotton, 5 bales............	1,017 72	138 56	879 16	...do........	April 12, 1864	Pittsburg.
Cotton, 17 bales.	3,542 64	268 12	3,274 52	...do........	June 4, 1864	Pittsburg.
Cotton, 55 bales.	15,434 52	717 63	14,716 89	..do.......	June 11, 1864	Conestoga.
Canoe and cargo	292 41	130 47	161 94	Washington..	Nov. 17, 1864	George Mangham.
Cotton, 12 bales..........	3,552 72	245 78	3,306 94	Springfield...	April 12, 1864	Lexington.
Cotton, 20 bales..........	4,971 70	295 20	4,676 50	....do........	June 11, 1864	Conestoga.
Sch. Charleston............	13,872 49	2,646 65	11,225 84	Philadelphia .	Feb. 29, 1864	Seminole.
Str. Cronstadt.	301,940 60	7,675 92	294,264 68	Boston.	Jan. 28, 1864	Rhode Island.
Str. Cherokee	152,507 02	4,732 47	147.774 55	....do........	Feb 9, 1864	Canandaigua.
Cotton, 39 bales...........	7,923 09	604 75	7,318 34	Key West	Mar. 29, 1864	Fort Henry.
Cotton, cargo of Emma, 120 bales	31,499 60	2,294 01	29,205 59	Philadelphia .	Jan. 23, 1864	Kittatinny.
Sch. Caroline and Virginia.	3,050 00	1,007 47	2,042 53	...do........	Jan. 27, 1864	Stars and Stripes, Delaware, Louisiana, Commodore Perry, Hetzel, Valley City, Underwriter, Hunchback, Commodore Barney, Philadelphia, Southfield, Morse, H. Brincker, Lockwood.
Str. Caroline...............	106,008 11	6,853 85	99,154 26	....do..	Feb. 29, 1864	Montgomery.
Sch. Charmer†	700 00	129 00	571 00	Key West	....	Sagamore, Oleander, Beauregard, Para.
Sloop Clara Louisa	153 00	90 11	62 89	... do.....	Feb. 29, 1864	Sagamore.
Sloop Clotilda	7,533 86	762 39	6,771 47	...do........	Feb. 29, 1864	McLellan.
Sch. Crazy Jane	1,357 05	253 00	1,104 05	..do.......	Mar. 12, 1864	Tahoma.
Sch. Clara	3,898 26	744 71	3,153 55	...do........	Mar. 17, 1864	Kanawha.
Sloop C. Ronterean ‡......	1,842 55	490 84	1,351 71	Philadelphia..	....	Powhatan, New Ironsides, Canandaigua, Housatonic, Paul Jones, Huron, Unadilla, Marblehead, Wamsutta, Augusta, Lodona, Stettin, Dandelion, Para, South Carolina.
Str. Cuba, cargo of........	778 84	129 54	649 20	Key West . .	Mar. 29, 1864	De Soto.
Sch. Comet, No. 2..........	3,669 06	665 86	3,003 20	...do.......	Mar. 29, 1864	Kanawha.
Sch. Clarita....	2,289 66	513 90	1,775 76	...do.......	Mar. 29, 1864	De Soto.
Cotton, 22 bales	3,727 42	390 68	3,336 74	...do.......	Mar. 29, 1864	Fort Henry.
Cotton, 139 bales........	39,192 93	3,559 67	85,633 26	...do.......	Mar. 29, 1864	Hendrick Hudson.
Cotton, 114 bales........	42,459 13	2,829 36	39,629 77	...do..	Mar. 29, 1864	De Soto.
Str. Comet.	5,461 73	728 32	4,733 41	....do.	Mar. 29, 1864	Santiago de Cuba.
Cotton, 14 bags§	199 13	83 64	115 49	Springfield...	....	General Sterling Price.
Cotton, 13 bales	2,694 24	334 79	2,359 45	Key West	Mar. 29, 1864	Port Royal.
Sch. Charm	9,756 25	1,017 54	8,738 71	...do.......	Mar. 29, 1864	Sagamore, Gem of the Sea.
Corn, 250 bushels	62 00	6 49	1 51	....do........	Mar. 29, 1864	Fort Henry.
Cotton, 27 bales, cargo of sch. Mary Ann...	8,910 75	978 07	7,932 68	New Orleans .	April 23, 1864	Antona.
Cotton, 3 bales and 2 crates‖....	1,095 22	238 59	856 63	...do..... ..	....	Granite City.
Cotton, 179 bales.	38,312 98	1,866 85	36,446 13	Springfield...	April 23, 1864	Osage.
Cotton, 10 bales..........	2,351 52	231 66	2,119 86	Boston.......	April 23, 1864	Niphon.
Sch. Corse	5,850 66	754 51	5,096 15	Key West	Jan. 7, 1865	Rachel Seaman, Kensington.
Cotton, 10½ bales........	2,735 11	394 60	2,340 51	....do........	June 1, 1864	Roebuck.
Cotton, 64 bales......	16,867 72	1,735 06	15,132 66	....do........	June 2, 1864	James L. Davis.
Cotton, 154 bales, and 5 hogsheads sugar........	33,901 53	7,916 89	25,984 64	Springfield...	May 19, 1864	Conestoga.
Cotton, 6 bales...	1,444 97	140 13	1,304 84	...do.......	Jan. 6, 1865	Pittsburg.
Cotton, 10 bales........ .	2,202 48	168 86	2,033 62	....do........	Mar. 1, 1865	Osage, Choctaw, Champion. Fort Hindman.
Cotton, 3 bales¶	334 56	107 35	227 21	...do.......	....	Juliet, Great Western, Rattler.
Cotton, 4 bales**	498 02	114 05	383 97	...do....	....	Lexington.
Cotton, 8 bales...........	1,509 98	145 01	1,364 97	....do........	May 19, 1864	Champion.
Cotton, 14 bales....... ..	3,124 78	203 31	2,921 47	....do........	Nov. 26, 1864	Kenwood.
Cotton, 3 bales and 2 pieces of bales..	657 30	115 83	541 47	.. .do........	May 19, 1864	Tuscumbia.
Cotton, 2,129 bales, 28 barrels molasses. 18 bales wool............	465,234 95	13,732 79	451,502 16	...do.......	Mar. 1, 1865	Black Hawk, Eastport, Lafayette, Neosha, Ozark, Choctaw, Osage, Chillicothe, Louisville, Carondelet, Fort Hindman, Benton, Pittsburg, Mound City, Essex, Lexington, Ouachita, Cricket, Gazelle, General Price, W. H. Brown. [718 bales of cotton still pending.]
Sch. Cecilia D.............	5,399 88	1,009 95	4,389 93	New Orleans	May 21, 1864	Antona.
Sch. Cassandra............	40 00	....	No proceeds	Washington..	....	
Canoe, 1; 1 box tobacco..	27 30	....	No proceeds	....do.	....	
Sch. Champion..	4,522 37	903 22	3,619 15	New Orleans .	Nov. 26, 1864	Potomac.
Sch. Camille..	32,960 89	2 782 99	30,177 90	....do........	Oct. 7, 1864	Virginia.
Cotton, 50 bales	7,254 19	841 50	6,412 69	New York....	May, 1864	Vanderbilt.

* Waiting for prize list of the Jacob Bell.
† Waiting for prize list of the Oleander.
‡ Waiting for prize lists of the New Ironsides, Huron, Unadilla, Dandelion, and South Carolina.

§ Waiting for prize list of the General Sterling Price.
‖ Waiting for prize list of the Granite City.
¶ Waiting for prize lists of the Juliet, Great Western and Rattler.
** Waiting for prize list of the Lexington.

Name.	Gross proceeds.	Costs and expenses.	Am't for distribution.	Where adjudicated.	Sent to 4th Auditor for distribution.	Vessels entitled to share.
Cotton, 12 bales and 14 bags	$2,834 69	$524 19	$2,310 50	Key West	Dec. 21, 1864	Port Royal.
Cotton, 11 bales*	3,023 34	287 21	2,736 13	....do.	....	Somerset.
Cotton, 1 bale†	340 90	107 93	232 97	Springfield...		Lexington.
Cotton, 207 bales	80,777 86	3,767 04	77,010 82	....do.	June 19, 1865	Louisville, Romeo, Petrel, Prairie Bird, Exchange, Marmora.
Cotton, 8 bales	2,584 37	197 49	2,386 83	..do..	July 25, 1864	Cricket.
Cotton, 8 bales‡	2,910 89	210 06	2,700 83	.. do..		Marmora.
Cotton, 10 bales	4,115 70	267 37	3,848 33	...do.	July 25, 1864	Osage.
Cotton, 16 bales§	7,479 08	403 33	7,076 75	...do..		W. H. Brown.
Sch. Calhoun	14,500 00	889 36	13,610 64	New Orleans .	Dec. 1, 1864	Samuel Rotan, Colorado, Rachel Seaman.
Cotton, 24 bales	8,125 71	335 21	7,790 50	Springfield...	June 20, 1865	Black Hawk, Fort Hindman, Cricket, Eastport, Lafayette, Neosha, Ozark, Choctaw, Osage, Chillicothe, Louisville, Carondelet, Benton, Pittsburg, Mound City, Essex, Lexington, Ouachita, Gazelle, General Price, W. H. Brown.
Cotton, 75 bales‖	497 00	192 87	304 13	New Orleans .	....	Narcissus, Cowslip.
Cotton, 63 bales	36,391 03	2,651 30	33,739 78	Springfield...	Oct. 7, 1864	Black Hawk.
Cotton, 5 bales	2,169 35	290 54	1,878 81	....do........	April 12, 1864	Black Hawk, Fort Hindman, Cricket, Eastport, Lafayette, Neosha, Ozark, Choctaw, Osage, Chillicothe, Louisville, Carondelet, Benton, Pittsburg, Mound City, Essex, Lexington, Ouachita, Gazelle, General Price, W. H. Brown, Juliet.
Cotton, 10½ bales	2,397 28	534 28	1,863 00	....do.......	Oct. 12, 1864	Cimarron.
Str. Ceres	17,200 00	935 49	16,264 51	Washington..	Nov. 12, 1864	Violet, Aries, Connecticut, Maratanza, Mercedita, Montgomery.
Canoes, 25, and cargoes...	929 40	249 93	679 47	....do.......	Feb. 15, 1865	Eureka, Yankee, Freeborn, Currituck, Commodore Read, Teazer, Fuchsia, Jacob Bell.
Str. Caledonia	13,353 00	1,149 28	11,903 72	Boston.......	Nov. 4, 1864	Keystone State, Massachusetts.
Str. Calhoun	....	....	28,536 95	Philadelphia.	Feb. 29, 1864	Samuel Rotan, Colorado, Rachel Seaman.
Sch. Carmita	....	....	55,698 21	...do........	Nov. 12, 1864	Bermuda.
Coffee, 30 bags	1,385 52	580 94	804 58	...do........	Oct. 5, 1865	Bienville.
Cotton, 22 bales	14,559 47	534 75	14,024 72	Boston.	Dec. 2, 1864	Mount Vernon.
Cotton, 88 bales	....	....	17,455 63	Philadelphia.	Jan. 7, 1865	Keystone State.
Cotton, 61½ bales	....	....	20,823 45	...do..	Jan. 7, 1865	Keystone State.
Cotton, 235 bales, etc.	....	....	69,239 66	...do..	Jan. 7, 1865	Keystone State.
Cotton, 19 bales	6,227 29	907 48	5,319 84	New Orleans	Mar. 23, 1865	Tallahatchie.
Cotton, 10 bales	2,138 00	638 90	1,499 10	....do.......	Mar. 23, 1865	Tallahatchie.
Sch. Cora Smyser	6,877 92	1,073 12	5,864 80	....do.......	April 22, 1865	Sciota.
Cotton, 60 bales and 2 bags	....	....	12,655 66	....do.......	Feb. 21, 1865	Mobile.
Cotton, 38 bales	....	....	8,487 62	...do.......	Feb. 21, 1865	Arostook.
Cotton, 83 bales	....	....	16,388 07	...do.......	Feb. 21, 1865	Sciota.
Cotton, 67 bales	27,034 89	2,270 83	24,764 06	Key West ..	Mar. 22, 1865	Clyde.
Sch. Caroline and Gertrude.	16,437 87	1,219 33	15,218 54	....do.......	Mar. 22, 1865	Stars and Stripes.
Coffee, Whiskey, etc	773 66	172 06	601 60	New Orleans.	Oct. 4, 1865	Elk.
Str. Cumberland	153,461 29	18,943 50	134,517 79	Key West ...	April 21, 1865	De Soto.
Sloop Caroline	306 07	124 23	181 84	....do.......	April 21, 1865	Roebuck.
Sch Cora	46,654 97	6 402 57	40,252 40	New Orleans..	May 9, 1865	Princess Royal.
Str. Chatham	81,684 78	6,636 38	75,048 40	....do.......	May 9, 1865	Huron, Dan Smith.
Cotton, 5 bales, 9 bags, etc.	3,033 64	265 76	2,767 88	Philadelphia.	....	Kanawha. (Waiting for prize list.)
Cotton, 31 bales	....	....	953 78	New Orleans..	Sept. 1, 1865	Chocura.
Sch. Carrie Mair	6,363 65	1,109 49	5,254 16	....do.......	Aug. 21, 1865	Itasca.
Sloop Caroline, No. 2	211 05	168 71	42 34	Key West	....	Union. (Waiting for prize list.)
Cotton, 12 bales; 8 barrels turpentine	3,766 83	507 58	3,259 25	...do.......	Aug. 25, 1865	Magnolia.
Cotton, 4 bales	....	....	46 40	New Orleans	Sept. 1, 1865	Cayuga.
Cotton, 42 bales and 11 bags	26,580 54	2,364 00	24,216 54	Key West	Aug. 25, 1865	Clyde.
Cotton, 50 bales	....	....	1,939 37	New Orleans	Sept. 1, 1865	Gertrude.
Cotton, 89 bales	....	....	3,510 38	....do.......	Sept. 1, 1865	Cornubia.
Cotton, 78 bales	45,626 01	2,077 91	43,548 10	Boston	Aug. 9, 1865	Vicksburg.
Cotton, 4 bales	2,701 44	192 45	2,503 99	...do	Aug. 16, 1865	Keystone State.
Cotton, 44 bales	20,484 00	508 15	19,975 85	...do.......	Aug. 16, 1865	Quaker City.
Cotton, 90 bales	66,955 68	3,767 78	63,187 90	Philadelphia..	Aug. 21, 1865	Connecticut, Keystone State.
Str. Cora	6,140 00	861 03	5,278 97	New Orleans..	Aug. 21, 1865	Quaker City.
Cotton, 35 bales	....	....	17,575 20	New York....	Sept. 1, 1865	Governor Buckingham, Niphon.
Cotton, 156 sacks, etc.	....	....	15,150 00	...do.. ..	Sept. 1, 1865	Gettysburg.
Sch. Comus	5,166 52	700 81	4,465 71	Key West	Sept. 1, 1865	Iuka.
Sch. Cora	32,697 53	3,157 78	29,539 75	....do.......	Sept. 1, 1865	Panola.
Str. Circassian	352,313 65	36,942 26	315,371 39	....do.......	Sept. 8, 1865	Somerset
Cotton, 80 bales	....	....	32,037 70	Philadelphia.	Sept. 22, 1865	Gettysburg, Keystone State, $620 counsel fees
Cotton, 52 bales	23,552 53	1,826 58	21,725 95	....do.......	Sept. 29, 1865	R. R. Cuyler.
Cotton, 82 bales	57,210 33	2,984 68	54,225 65	....do.......	Sept. 29, 1865	Aries. ($500 counsel fee deducted from captor's share.)
Cotton, 45 bales	21,977 77	1,623 27	20,354 50	...do.	Oct. 6, 1865	Santiago de Cuba
Sch. Delight	600 00	251 65	348 25	New York	July 21, 1863	New London, R. R Cuyler, Massachusetts.
Brig Delta	11,628 00	6,931 18	4,696 82	. do.	Nov. 25, 1863	Santee.
Sch. Dixie	30,950 87	2,429 64	28,521 23	Philadelphia .	Mar. 13, 1863	Keystone State, Gem of the Sea.
Sch. Defiance	3,773 78	1,073 40	2,700 38	...do......	Mar. 11, 1863	Braziliera.
Sch. Director	285 10	128 99	156 11	Washington..	May 4, 1862	Corwin, Currituck.
Str. Diamond	29,683 10	1,958 08	27,725 02	...do........	Jan. 11, 1864	Stettin.
Sch. Dart	2,390 84	520 95	1,869 89	Key West ...	Oct. 21, 1863	Kensington, Rachel Seaman.
Sch. David Crockett	14,462 73	1,389 77	13,072 96	Philadelphia..	Oct. 5, 1865	America, Flag, Canandaigua, Flambeau.
Sloop, D. Sargent	5,417 97	1,094 91	4,323 06	New York	Feb. 29, 1864	Kittatinny.
Sch. Dart, No. 2	3,258 22	493 10	2,765 12	Key West	Feb. 29, 1864	Kanawha.
Str. Dolphin.	36,544 73	8,382 88	28,161 85	...do........	Mar. 17, 1864	Wachusett.
Dry Goods, lot of	465 45	169 51	295 94	Washington..	Jan. 11, 1864	Cœur de Lion.
Sch. Defy	473 05	197 37	275 68	. do........	Oct. 12, 1864	Midnight.
Str. Donegal	140,000 00	4,047 10	135,952 90	Philadelphia..	Oct. 27, 1864	Metacomet.
Str. Don	98,316 78	3,438 13	94,878 65	Boston.	Nov. 19, 1864	Pequot.

* Waiting for prize list of the Somerset.   ‡ Waiting for prize list of the Marmora.
† Waiting for prize list of the Lexington.   § Waiting for prize list of the W. H. Brown.
‖ Waiting for prize lists of Narcissus and Cowslip.

Name.	Gross proceeds.	Costs and expenses.	Am't for distribution.	Where adjudicated.	Sent to 4th Auditor for distribution.	Vessels entitled to share.
Sch. Delia................	$5,450 45	$301 64	$5,148 41	Key West	Aug. 12, 1865	Mahaska.
Sch Eugenie.	29,061 42	2,765 42	26,296 00	....do.	Oct. 16, 1862	Owasco.
Sch. Emma..............	13,352 52	4,070 48	9,282 04	...do..	Oct. 16, 1862	Connecticut.
Sch. Eugenie Smith	2,904 36	540 36	2,364 00	..do........	Feb. 6, 1863	Boh'o.
Sch. Elias Reed	21,791 53	3,401 45	18,390 08	.. do.......	Oct. 9, 1863	Octorara.
Sloop Ellen	235 00	161 06	73 94	...do......	Oct. 24, 1863	Sagamore.
Sloop Elizabeth.	841 12	266 25	574 87	....do......	Oct. 23, 1863	Hatteras.
Sch. Emily	15,406 91	1,115 37	14,291 54	Washington..	Oct. 19, 1863	Satellite, Anacostia.
Str. Eureka	293 75	134 93	158 82	...do......	April 20, 1862	Dan Smith, George Mangham, Cœur de Lion.
Sch. Emily Murray	500 00	356 34	143 66	....do......	Feb. 9, 1863	
Sch. E. J. Waterman.......	8,222 95	1,194 58	7,028 37	Philadelphia..	Nov. 6, 1862	Chocura, Maratanza.
Sloop Express	859 25	541 17	318 08	..do........	Feb. 18, 1864	South Carolina.
Sch. Edward Barnard ...	32,068 74	3,379 28	28,689 46	New York ...	Nov. 26, 1862	Ceres. Valley City, Delaware, Louisiana, Underwriter, Hetzel, Commodore Perry, Morse, H. Brincker, Whitehead, Shawsheen, Lockwood, General Putnam, J. N. Seymour.
Str. Ellis and armament....	18,000 00	555 85	17,444 15	...do., ...	Dec. 5, 1863	
Sloop Express.	600 00	247 65	352 35	....do.......	July 21, 1863	New London, R. R. Cuyler, Massachusetts.
Sloop Emeline.	5,380 33	970 13	4,410 20	...do.......	Dec. 24, 1863	
Str. Elmira	8,038 30	634 47	7,403 33	Springfield...	Jan. 11, 1864	Petrel, Forest Rose.
Sch. Emma....	1,486 15	878 50	607 65	Philadelphia .	Feb. 18, 1864	Adirondack.
Boat Emma..............	98 12	84 15	13 97	Key West	June 7, 1864	Fort Henry.
Boat Enterprise	872 00	172 56	699 44	...do...	April 12, 1864	Sagamore.
Str Eagle	35,475 33	5,355 46	30,119 87	....do.......	Mar. 17, 1864	Octorara.
Str. Ella Warley	102,709 88	18,976 31	83,733 57	New York ...	Mar. 22, 1864	Santiago de Cuba.
Sch. Emma Amelia........	3,649 52	503 94	3,145 58	Key West . .	Mar. 17, 1864	Roebuck.
Sloop Elisha Beckwith.. ..	2,174 39	528 35	1,646 04	....do.......	Mar. 29, 1864	Pembina.
Sch. Emma Tuttle........	5,833 64	1,332 52	4,501 12	Philadelphia .	Mar. 29, 1864	Hope.
Str. Eugenie............	24,239 67	1,597 99	22,641 68	Key West ...	Mar. 29, 1864	R. R. Cuyler, Kennebec, Kanawha.
Str. Eureka	27,273 88	2,665 00	24,608 88	New Orleans .	April 23, 1864	Aroostook.
Str. Elizabeth	83,112 92	16,862 74	66,250 18	New York ...	April 12, 1864	Keystone State, James Adger.
Sch. Exchange............	6,052 87	1,052 55	5,000 32	New Orleans .	April 23, 1864	Antona.
Sch. Ellen	5,557 23	970 58	4,586 65	...do........	June 10, 1864	Gertrude.
Sch. Edward............	2,343 64	203 66	2,139 98	Key West ...	June 2, 1864	San Jacinto.
Sch. Excelsior.............	2,630 88	678 31	1,952 57	New Orleans..	May 21, 1864	Katahdin.
Str. Emilie....	28,305 97	3,929 13	24,376 84	Philadelphia..	April 26, 1865	Flag, Restless.
Sch. Experiment	20,785 18	1,460 11	19,325 07	New Orleans..	July 28, 1864	Virginia.
Str. Elsie and cargo	216,619 79	5,249 22	211,370 57	Boston. ..	Dec. 2, 1864	Quaker City, Keystone State.
Sch. Emma	32,122 15	3,727 88	28,394 27	New Orleans..	Feb. 21, 1865	Mobile.
Str. Ella and Annie.......	185,500 01	5,486 62	181,013 79	Boston......	Feb. 24, 1865	Niphon.
Str. Emma Henry	294,869 01	5,973 92	288,895 09	New York ...	Feb. 28, 1865	Cherokee.
Sch. Eliza............	5,745 41	666 71	5,078 70	Key West ...	April 21, 1865	Roebuck.
Sch. Ezilda..........	3,415 07	1 255 71	2,159 36	New York ...	April 21, 1865	South Carolina.
Brig Eco.	4,281 21	1,039 35	3,246 86	New Orleans..	Aug. 23, 1865	Gertrude, Princess, Royal, Kanawha, Cayuga.
Sch. Flash............	2,485 61	1,117 18	1,368 43	New York ...	Dec. 1, 1863	Restless, Onward.
Brig Falcon	3,655 93	1,263 29	2,392 64	....do.......	Jan. 2, 1863	South Carolina.
Sch. Florida	1,865 00	1,106 76	758 24	...do........	Nov. 20, 1863	Matthew Vassar.
Sch. Fairwind	2,250 00	900 93	1,349 07	Philadelphia .	May 19, 1863	Quaker City.
Sch. Fairplay............	2,208 55	1,392 02	816 53	...do..	Oct. 19, 1863	Gem of the Sea.
Sch. Fannie Laurie.	15,627 77	2,491 26	13,136 51	...do.......	Mar. 17, 1864	Shephe d Knapp.
Sch. F. J. Capron	910 00	181 74	728 26	Washington..	April 29, 1862	Freeborn.
Sloop Flying Cloud.	225 00	126 48	98 52	....do.......	Jan. 11, 1864	Anacostia, Primrose.
Fch. Fashion	231 88	138 23	93 65	Key West ...	Nov. 26, 1862	I than Allen.
Sch. Frances.	1,208 48	374 56	833 92	....do.......	Oct. 15, 1863	Sagamore.
Sloop Flying Fish.........	627 50	222 55	404 95	....do.......	Oct. 21, 1863	Magnolia.
Sch. Fannie Lee............	19,940 54	{ *4,213 22 { 2,185 44	13,541 88	Philadelphia..	Feb. 18, 1864	St. Lawrence.
Sloop Florida	1,115 59	172 86	942 73	Key West ...	Mar. 17, 1864	Stars and Stripes.
Sch. Frolic	27,648 32	3,742 36	23,905 96	...do	Mar. 17, 1864	Sagamore, Two Sisters.
Sch. Fashion, No. 2	1,395 99	336 70	1,059 29	...do.......	Mar. 17, 1864	Juniata.
Sch. Five Brothers.....	7,313 65	1,084 37	6,229 28	....do.......	Nov. 26, 1864	Octorara.
Sch. Florence Nightingale	37,362 61	2,904 04	34,458 57	.. do....	June 22, 1864	Tioga, Octorara.
Sloop Fashion.	12,348 87	1,175 91	11,172 96	New Orleans	June 29, 1864	Port Royal.
Sch. Friendship............	3,209 94	850 37	2,359 57	....do.......	April 12, 1864	Tennessee.
Sch. Fanny ......, ..	10,317 61	1,125 66	9,191 95	....do.......	July 28, 1864	Owasco.
Sch. Frederick 2d	56,933 98	3,204 48	53,729 50	Key West. ...	Oct. 7, 1864	Chocura.
Sloop Fortunate...... ...	1,270 58	462 32	808 26	Philadelphia..	Feb. 7, 1865	Bermuda.
Sch. Forest King........ ...	899 59	833 65	65 94	New York....	....	Crusader, Mississippi. (Waiting for prize list of Mississippi.)
Sloop Florida	1,276 90	172 18	1,104 72	Key West...		Honeysuckle.
Sch. Fly..............	660 18	201 33	458 85	..do....	Mar. 22, 1865	Honeysuckie.
Sch. Flash..............	7,856 90	1,917 05	5,939 85	New Orleans	April 20, 1865	Princess Royal.
Str. Florida....	91,672 65	6,760 77	84,911 88	Philadelphia .	May 13, 1865	Pursuit.
Sch. Fannie McRae........	4,384 87	293 16	4,091 71	Key West....	Aug. 12, 1865	Hendrick Hudson.
Sch. Florida..........	8,560 29	645 56	7,914 73	....do........	Aug. 16, 1865	James L. Davis.
Sloop Florida...........	702 32	202 41	499 91	....do........	....	Hibiscus.
Sch. Grace E. Baker.....	17,198 69	2,830 42	14,368 27	..do....	Oct. 6, 1862	R. R. Cuyler.
Sloop Good Luck.	1,401 83	220 09	1,181 74	..do....	Oct. 24, 1862	St. Lawrence.
Goods, lot of †	696 04	202 63	493 41	Washington..		George Mangham.
Goods, lot of.	197 46	116 50	80 96	...do.......	Oct. 13, 1865	Dan Smith.
Schooner Gold Leaf.. ...	205 00	86 12	118 88	..do.......	Jan. 11, 1864	Jacob Bell.
Goods and money, lot of.	288 65	170 45	118 20	...do.......	Oct. 17, 1862	Western World.
Ship General Parkhill....	9,803 85	{ ‡ 222 66 { 2,392 43	7,188 76	Philadelphia..	....	Niagara.
Sch. George G. Baker.	6,840 60	2,050 75	4,789 85	.. do.... ..	Feb. 17, 1863	Union.
Sch Guide.	20,407 67	1,549 53	18,858 14	.. do....	Nov. 6, 1862	Huron.
Sch. Glide...............	22,980 84	1,609 21	21,371 63	...do.......	Oct. 14, 1864	Marblehead, Passaic, Arago, Caswell.
Sch. Garonne	3,130 70	1,079 44	2,051 26	New York ...	Mar. 11, 1863	Santee.
Sch. Gipsy.	9,162 97	1,397 23	7,765 74	....do........	Aug. 20, 1863	New London, Massachusetts.
Sch Granite City..........	68,829 81	4 253 44	64,576 37	...do.......	Nov. 20, 1863	Tioga.
Str. Gertrude.............	88,987 60	8,913 31	80,074 29	...do	Nov. 20, 1863	Vanderbilt.
Sch. George Chisholm	1,327 86	295 60	1,032 26	Washington..	Feb. 18, 1864	Dai Ching.

* Liberated, $4,213.22. † Waiting for prize list of the George Mangham.
‡ $222.26 awarded to claimants.

Name.	Gross proceeds.	Costs and expenses.	Am't for distribution.	Where adjudicated.	Sent to 4th Auditor for distribution.	Vessels entitled to share.
Sloop Gophen	$113 62	$70 22	$43 40	Key West	Dec. 19, 1864	Roebuck.
Sch. Gipsy	744 23	469 49	274 74	...do........	Feb. 29, 1864	Ethan Allen.
Sloop G. L. Brockenborough	12,128 59	2,718 19	9,410 40	...do..	Feb. 29, 1864	Sagamore, Fort Henry.
Sch. General Taylor.......	7,180 21	2,021 21	5,159 00	Philadelphia .	Nov. 12, 1864	Crusader, Mahaska, Samuel Rotan.
Sch. General Prim..........	17,302 25	1,527 00	15,775 25	Key West	Mar. 9, 1864	De Soto.
Goods, lot of*	702 08	211 23	490 85	Washington	....	Primrose, Cœur de Lion.
Str. General Sigel, 4 boxes bitters, 12 boxes wine, 2½ barrels brandy, 5½ barrels whiskey†	183 60	67 07	116 53	Springfield...	May 19, 1864	Fairplay.
Str. Greyhound	497,858 55	12,896 54	484,962 01	Boston.......	Aug. 24, 1864	Connecticut.
Sloop Garibaldi	5,424 60	653 80	4,770 80	Key West	Mar. 14, 1865	Beauregard.
Sloop General Finnegan ..	3,661 05	414 37	3,246 63	....do........	June 29, 1865	San Jacinto.
Brig H. C. Brooks	51,982 52	5,467 83	46,514 69	New York....	July 18, 1863	Harriet Lane, Minnesota, Wabash, Cumberland, Susquehanna, Monticello, Pawnee.
Str. Henry Lewis	37,337 76	4,041 62	33,296 14	....do.......	Nov. 25, 1863	R. R. Cuyler, Massachusetts, New London.
Sch. Hanna M. Johnson...	2,470 26	932 81	1,537 45	....do.... ...	Nov. 25, 1863	Perry.
Sch. Hallie Jackson	3,625 00	1,217 47	2,407 53	....do.......	July 12, 1862	Union.
Sch. Henry Middleton.....	24,607 05	4,394 59	20,212 46	....do.......	Jan. 2, 1863	Vandalia.
Sch. Hettiwan........	13,455 37	1,997 52	11,457 85	....do.......	Feb. 29, 1864	Ottawa, Housatonic, Flambeau.
Bark Hiawatha.............	269,319 27	29,615 56	239,703 71	....do.......	Feb. 6, 1864	Minnesota, Cumberland, Perry, Keystone State, Star (now called Monticello).
Sch. Harriet Ryan....	1,718 53	824 68	893 85	Philadelphia .	Oct. 17, 1862	Pawnee.
Sch. Havelock....	2,770 36	1,500 28	1,270 08	do	July 22, 1863	Jamestown.
Sch. Harvest.............	15,031 31	1,108 28	13,923 03	Washington..	Oct. 19, 1863	Juniata.
Hoop Skirts, 2 boxes whiskey, etc.	200 08	87 72	112 26	...do......	May 17, 1862	Island Belle, Anacostia.
Sch. Hampton............	5,586 42	684 80	4,901 62	...do...	Jan. 11, 1864	Currituck.
Sch. Henry Travers	7,643 76	1,142 61	6,506 15	Key West .	Feb. 6, 1863	Bohio.
Sch. Hermosa	27,621 05	4,019 90	23,601 15	...do......	Oct. 8, 1863	Connecticut.
Sch. Hattie......	64,399 30	5,247 67	59,151 63	New York ...	Feb. 18, 1864	Florida.
Sch. Hunter...............	12,658 10	1,142 23	11,515 87	Philadelphia .	Feb. 18, 1864	Kanawha, Colorado, Lackawanna, Pocahontas, Aroostook, Kennebec, R. R. Cuyler.
Sch. Herald............	2,584 72	377 30	2,207 42	Washington..	Feb. 18, 1864	Calypso.
Sch. Harriet........	5,556 85	645 45	4,911 40	Key West ..	Mar. 12, 1864	Tahoma.
Sch. Handy............	979 06	326 38	652 68	...do........	ar. 17, 1864	Octorara.
Sch. Hortense............	2,647 73	350 86	2,296 87	...do........	Mar. 17, 1864	Somerset.
Str. Herald	87,866 77	3,483 97	84,382 80	Boston.......	April 12 1864	Tioga.
Bark H. M. McGuinn‡	700 00	376 75	323 25	New Orleans.	... .	Vincennes, Clifton.
Sch. Helena............	5,595 51	922 02	4,673 49	...do........	May 21, 1864	Ossipee.
Sch. Henry Colthirst.......	4,434 56	851 42	3,583 14	...do........	June 8, 1864	Virginia.
Str. Hattie.............	18,000 00	722 40	17,277 60	St. Augustine	Nov. 4, 1864	Pawnee, Columbine.
Str. Hope.................	271,192 35	7,895 52	263,296 83	Boston	Feb. 24, 1865	Eolus.
Sloop Hannah	339 50	123 00	216 50	Key West ..	Mar. 22, 1865	Beauregard.
Sloop Hancock...........	239 62	107 57	132 05	... do......	April 21, 1865	Sunflower.
Sloop Hope	6,299 47	937 28	5,362 19	... do......	April 21, 1865	Beauregard.
Sloop Henrietta	8,961 96	768 38	8,193 58	... do......	Aug. 25, 1865	Merrimac.
Sch. Isabel or W. R. King..	4,672 87	480 15	4,192 72	... do	Oct. 16, 1862	Montgomery.
Sch. Ida	784 15	455 10	329 05	...do........	Feb. 17, 1863	Mercedita.
Brig Intended............	8,874 90	1,865 48	7,009 42	Philadelphia .	Feb. 17, 1863	Jamestown.
Sch. Ida	486 74	230 16	256 58	Key West	Mar. 17, 1864	James S Chambers.
Sloop Isabella	76 87	65 58	11 29	...do........	Mar. 29, 1864	Fort Henry.
Sch. Independence.	1,600 00	751 32	848 68	New Orleans..	Nov. 26, 1864	Potomac.
Iron, railroad, 1,200 bars§	3,467 08	1,204 77	2,262 31	Philadelphia..	....	Mohican, Potomska, Pocahontas.
Iron, railroad, 658 bars§..	5,942 62	1,734 75	4,207 87	....do........	....	Mohican, Potomska, Pocahontas.
Sch. Island Belle...........	10,717 30	1,865 31	8,851 99	....do........	Nov. 17, 1864	Augusta.
Str. Ida	....	....	35,237 06	...do........	April 18, 1865	Sonoma.
Sch. John and Nathaniel Taylor.	1,700 00	294 85	1,405 15	New York....	Dec. 1, 1863	Commodore Perry, Underwriter, Whitehead.
Sch. J. W. Wilder........	24,618 44	3,431 26	21,187 18	....do........	Dec. 1, 1863	R. R. Cuyler.
Sch. Joana Ward........	7,503 00	1,995 14	5,507 86	....do.	Jan. 31, 1863	Harriet Lane.
Sch. J. G. McNeil.......	6,536 90	1,306 92	5,229 98	....do........	Oct. 20, 1863	Arthur.
Sch. James Norcom‖.......	2,200 00	319 85	1,880 15	....do........	....	Shawsheen.
Sch. Julia Worden........	3,090 34	986 54	2,103 80	Philadelphia..	Dec. 1, 1863	Restless.
Sch. Julia..................	17,347 96	1,419 22	15,928 74	Key West	Oct. 10, 1863	Kittatinny.
Sloop Julia..................	571 39	181 24	390 15	...do........	Oct. 17, 1863	Sagamore.
Sch. Julia	9,942 56	1,572 65	8,369 91	Boston. ...	April 27, 18 3	Cambridge.
Str. Juno................	135,102 00	4,608 44	130,393 67	. do........	Jan. 30, 1864	Connecticut.
Sloop John Wesley........	1,875 90	244 21	1,631 69	Key West	Mar. 17, 1864	Circassian.
Sloop Jane Adelie........	6,699 71	667 24	6,032 47	...do........	Mar. 9, 1864	De Soto.
Sloop Julia	15,428 96	1,502 42	13,926 54	...do........	Mar. 9, 1864	Tioga.
Sloop Justina	1,720 53	454 68	1,465 85	...do........	Mar. 17, 1864	Tioga.
Sch. Juniper.	2,228 59	502 32	1,726 27	...do........	Mar. 17, 1864	Kennebec.
Sch. Joe Flanner.........	11,747 21	1,466 52	10,280 69	.. do........	Mar. 29, 1864	Pembina.
Str. Jeff Davis¶...........	500 00	47 45	452 55	Springfield...	....	Benton, St. Louis, Louisville, Carondelet, Cairo
Str. James Battle..........	240,895 62	17,651 16	223,244 46	Key West	April 12, 1864	De Soto.
Sch. John Scott	37,723 84	3,110 22	34,618 62	New Orleans .	April 23, 1864	Kennebec.
Sch. J. T. Davis..........	9,925 00	1,465 04	8,459 96	...do.......	May 21, 1864	Cayuga.
Sch John Douglas..........	41,011 62	3,402 52	37,609 10	. do..	June 18, 1864	Penobscot.
Sch. Jupiter	35,982 40	3,299 80	32,682 60	Philadelphia..	Oct. 11, 1864	Cimarron, Nantucket.
Sch. Judson	23,495 74	1,895 33	21,600 41	New Orleans.	Oct. 7, 1864	Conemaugh.
Str. Jupiter	8,331 73	1,482 99	6,848 74	Boston	Oct. 11. 1864	Proteus
Sch. James Williams.......	5,510 15	749 77	4,760 38	New Orleans.	Oct. 12, 1864	Penobscot.
Sch. J. C. McCabe	452 11	168 03	284 08	Washington.	Oct. 19, 1863	Zouave.
Sch. John.................	32,514 71	3,044 49	29,470 22	New Orleans	Mar. 22, 1865	Augusta Dinsmore.
Sloop Josephine...........	1,826 77	333 97	1,492 80	Key West	April 22, 1865	Sunflower.
Sch Joseph H. Toone......	15,606 48	3,490 44	12,116 44	New York ..	April 21, 1865	South Carolina.
Sch. Julia................	5,468 81	1,215 93	4,252 88	New Orleans.	June 3, 1865	Chocura.
Sch. Josephine.	16,046 81	3,048 49	12,998 32	. do	June 26, 1865	Seminole.
Sch. John Hale............	14,032 46	599 06	13,433 40	Key West.....	Aug. 12, 1865	Matthew Vassar.
Str. Julia.................	159,129 41	4,807 54	154,321 87	...do	Aug. 16, 1865	Acacia.

* Waiting for prize list of Cœur de Lion.
† Vessel not included.
‡ Waiting for prize lists of the Vincennes and Clifton.
§ Waiting for prize lists of Mohican, Potomska, and Pocahontas.
‖ Waiting for prize list of Shawsheen.
¶ Waiting for prize lists of Benton, St. Louis, Louisville, Carondelet, Cairo.

Name.	Gross proceeds.	Costs and expenses.	Am't for distribution.	Where adjudicated.	Sent to 4th Auditor for distribution.	Vessels entitled to share.
Sch. Kate.	$4,188 33	$593 23	$3,595 10	Key West	Oct. 23, 1863	Roebuck.
Sch. Kate, cargo of	98 00	51 25	46 75	Washington..	Oct. 23, 1863	Adolph Hugel.
Str. Kate Dale	370,708 39	14,910 27	355,798 12	Philadelphia.	Jan. 6, 1864	R. R. Cuyler.
Str. Kaskaskia	1,300 00	376 55	923 45	Springfield...	Jan. 11, 1864	Cricket.
Str. Kate	31,180 00	1,890 42	29,289 58	New York....	Feb. 16, 1864	Mount Vernon, Iroquois, James Adger, Niphon.
Sloop Kate	3,572 22	442 22	3,130 00	Key West ...	July 6, 1864	Brooklyn.
Sloop Kate*.	711 81	126 27	585 54	....do.		Pursuit.
Sch. La Criolla.	2,828 64	871 83	1,956 81	Philadelphia.	Nov. 26, 1862	Bienville.
Str. Lodona.	246,651 32	14,944 84	231,706 48	....do.	April 25,1863	Unadilla.
Sch. Lion	4,935 25	1,350 70	3,584 55	....do.	Nov. 5, 1863	Delaware.
Sch. Ladies' Delight	1,813 72	287 32	1,526 40	Washington..	Oct.1 9, 1863	Primrose, Anacostia, Currituck, Satellite.
Sch. Lookout	1,468 87	254 00	1,214 87	....do.	April16, 1862	Cœur de Lion.
Sch. Lion	8,573 54	1,093 68	7,479 86	Key West....	Oct. 16, 1862	Kingfisner.
Sch. Lavinia.	9,580 38	880 96	8,699 42	...do.	Jan. 23, 1863	Santiago de Cuba.
Sch. Lily	5,189 53	835 88	4,353 65	...do.	Oct. 13, 1863	W. G. Anderson.
Sch. Lynnhaven	7,000 00	401 15	6,598 85	New York....	Dec. 8, 1863	Delaware, Louisiana, Hetzel, Commodore Perry, Valley City, Underwriter, Morse, Ceres, H. Brincker, Whitehead, Shawsheen, Lockwood, General Putnam, J. N. Seymour.
Sch. Lovely Belle†	2,200 00	319 85	1,880 15	....do.		General Putnam.
Sch. Louisa Agnes	1,105 00	1.401 00	No proceeds	....do.		General Putnam.
Sch. Lizzie Weston	76,286 67	8,738 92	67,457 75	....do.	Feb. 17, 1863	Itasca.
Sch. Lucy C. Holmes.	29,745 62	3,952 10	25,793 52	...do.	Jan. 31, 1863	Santiago de Cuba.
Sch. Louise	45,053 49	1 970 51	43,082 98	Boston	Jan. 23, 1863	Albatross.
Str. Lizzie	12,244 73	1,836 04	10,408 69	Philadelphia .	Jan. 11, 1864	Santiago de Cuba.
Sch. Louisa	1,977 27	1,078 62	898 65	do..	Feb. 29, 1864	Bienville.
Sch. Linnet	2,022 42	388 17	1,634 25	Key West ..	Dec. 14, 1864	Union.
Sch. Lydia and Mary.	2,864 66	918 66	1,946 00	Philadelphia.	Feb. 29, 1864	Restless.
Sloop Louisa Dudley	2,693 07	620 50	2,072 57	Key West	Mar. 17, 1864	McLellan.
Sch. Lady Maria	30,646 45	2,228 42	28,418 03	...do.	May 7, 1864	De Soto, Stonewall.
Str Lizzie Davis	18,351 16	2,441 08	15,910 11	New Orleans.	June 7, 1864	San Jacinto.
Sch. Locadie.	1,997 00	656 44	1,340 56	.. do.	Nov. 26, 1864	Commodore.
Sch. Lida	9,753 54	1,374 45	8,379 09	Philadelphia.	April 23, 1864	Seminole.
Sch. Louisa	5,611 35	1,121 50	4,489 85	New Orleans.	June 4, 1864	Queen.
Sloop Last Trial	109 96	108 85	1 11	Key West		Beauregard, San Jacinto, Dale, Tioga, Tahoma, Huntsville, Wanderer, Eugenie, Sunflower, Sea Bird, Honduras, Marigold.
Sch. Lily	5,995 66	966 68	5,028 98	New Orleans .	June 18, 1864	Penobscot.
Sch. Lynchburg	11,449 43	4,437 27	7,012 16	New York	July 28, 1864	Quaker City.
Sch. Lily	9,019 94	1,074 50	7,945 44	New Orleans.	July 28, 1864	Owasco.
Sch. Laura	6,843 01	871 94	5,971 07	...do.	July 28, 1864	Owasco.
Str. Little Ada.	44,489 95	1,580 69	42,909 26	Boston. ...	Feb. 16, 1865	Gettysburg.
Str. Lady Sterling	509,354 64	9,463 35	494,891 29	New York....	Feb. 7, 1865	Calypso, Eolus.
Sch. Louisa	5,491 49	1,227 36	4,264 13	New Orleans.	Feb. 14, 1865	Chocura.
Sch. Lone	2,631 60	723 59	1,908 01	...do.	Feb. 14, 1865	Fort Morgan.
Str. Lucy	268,948 20	6,534 72	262,413 48	Boston	Mar. 9, 1865	Santiago de Cuba.
Sch. Leartad	43,261 72	4,380 79	38,880 93	Key West....	Mar. 22, 1865	San Jacinto.
Sch. Linda	1,237 65	171 50	1,066 15	...do.	Mar. 22, 1865	Beauregard, Norfolk Packet.
Sch. Lowood	34,555 03	5,948 70	28,606 33	New Orleans	April 22, 1865	Chocura.
Str. Laura	36,052 92	1,589 90	34,463 02	Key West	April 22, 1865	Stars and Stripes, Hendrick Hudson.
Sloop Lydia	1,302 17	224 76	1,077 41	...do.	April 22, 1865	Beauregard.
Sch. Lily	1,102 00	625 04	476 96	New Orleans	June 2, 1865	Metacomet.
Sloop Last Resort	1,987 58	290 15	1,697 43	Key West....	Aug. 25, 1865	Roebuck.
Sloop Lauretta	52 63	52 63	No proceeds	....do.		Roebuck.
Sch. Lucy	5,879 64	341 52	5,538 12	...do.	Aug. 12, 1865	Hendrick Hudson.
Brig Lilla	73,679 67	3,929 45	69,750 22	Boston	June 20, 1865	Quaker City.
Sch. Late Hurley	3,500 86	1,245 75	2,255 11	New Orleans..	Aug. 22, 1865	Chocura.
Sch. Mars	1,141 00	1,157 04	No proceeds	New York....		
Sch. Major Barbour	44,567 76	8,278 68	36,289 08	....do.	Jan. 30, 1863	De Soto, Kittatinny.
Sloop Mercury ‡	1,548 20	545 99	1,002 21	...do.		Quaker City, Memphis, Powhatan, Flag.
Sch. Maria	3,399 92	2,048 52	1,351 40	...do.	Dec. 1, 1863	Santiago de Cuba.
Brig Minna	2,340 11	1,381 10	959 01	..do.	Nov. 20, 1863	Victoria.
Sch. Maria Bishop	4,539 95	2,667 80	1,872 15	...do.	Dec. 24, 1863	Courier.
Sch. Mary Jane	1,731 39	1,033 74	697 65	....do.	Dec. 9, 1863	Mount Vernon, State of Georgia.
Str. Magnolia	173,955 77	6,551 61	167,404 16	Key West....	Oct. 16, 1862	Huntsville, Brooklyn, South Carolina, Mercedita, Itasca.
Sloop Margaret	3,549 98	234 47	3,315 51	..do.	Oct. 16, 1862	Sciota.
Sch. Magnolia	41,731 61	3,199 02	38,532 59	...do.	Oct. 8, 1863	Hatteras.
Sloop Maria.	4,849 37	722 25	4 127 12	....do.	Oct. 17, 1863	Rachel Seaman, Kensington.
Sch. Margaret	378 73	160 95	217 78	do.	Oct. 6, 1862	Tahoma, Hendrick Hudson.
Sch. Martha Ann	1,498 02	714 44	783 58	Washington..	Oct. 1, 1863	Samuel Rotan.
Sloop Mary Grey §	224 37	166 01	58 36	....do.		Eureka, T. A. Ward.
Bark Meaco	{ 92,213 47	a30,155 55 6 090 02	} 55,967 89	Philadelphia..	Mar. 11, 1863	Brooklyn, St. Louis.
Sch. Mabel	8,781 50	1,753 61	7,027 89	....do.	Nov. 6, 1862	Dale, St. Lawrence.
Sch. Morning Star	1,168 61	645 02	523 59	...do.	Nov. 25, 1862	Bienville.
Sch. Mary Wood	3,292 78	1,039 79	2,252 99	..do	Nov. 11, 1864	Pawnee.
Sch. Mary Elizabeth	685 68	596 82	88 86	... do.	Oct. 19, 1863	Stars and Stripes, Mystic, State of Georgia.
Sch. Major E. Willis	36,242 45	2,098 37	34,144 08	....do.	Nov. 5, 1863	Powhatan, Housatonic, Paul Jones, Huron, Unadilla, Augusta, South Carolina, America, G. W. Blunt, New Ironsides, Flag, Stettin, Lodona.
Merchandise, 680 pieces ‖.	312 16	106 32	205 84	Boston		Hunchback.
Sch. Monterey.	837 10	287 04	550 06	Washington..	April 16, 1862	Resolute.
Str. Memphis	543,495 15	32,581 08	510,914 07	New York ...	Nov. 10, 1863	Magnolia.
Merchandise, cargo of ¶.	250 80	82 92	167 88	Washington..		Cœur de Lion, Dan Smith.
Sch. Meteor	2,589 70	201 86	2,387 84	Key West....	Dec. 3, 1864	Sagamore.
Sloop Magnolia.	561 25	130 38	430 87	..do.	June11, 1864	San Jacinto.
Sch. Maria Alberta	4,583 25	337 87	4,195 38	..do.	Nov. 26, 1864	San Jacinto.
Str. Merrimack	202.741 16	11,702 48	191,038 68	New York....	Feb. 22, 1864	Iroquois.
Sch. Mississippian	34,981 94	2,495 52	32,486 42	Key West....	Feb. 29, 1864	De Soto.

* Waiting for prize list of the Pursuit.
† Taken by War Department; not paid for.
‡ Waiting for prize lists of the Memphis, Powhatan, and Flag.
§ Waiting for prize list of the T. A. Ward.
‖ Waiting for prize list of the Hunchback.
¶ Waiting for prize lists of the Cœur de Lion and Dan Smith.
a Allowed to claimants.

Name.	Gross proceeds.	Costs and expenses.	Am't for distribution.	Where adjudicated.	Sent to 4th Auditor for distribution.	Vessels entitled to share.
Str. Maggie Fulton	$1,107 71	$377 09	$730 62	Key West	Mar. 17, 1864	Gem of the Sea.
Sch. Mary Jane	689 88	122 83	567 05	....do......	Feb. 29, 1864	Tahoma.
Sch. Mattie*	1,913 59	390 29	1,523 30	....do......	....	Annie.
Sch. Miriam	47,939 13	3,465 84	44,473 29	....do......	June 9, 1864	Itasca.
Sloop Minnie	4,290 56	619 67	3,670 89	....do......	Mar. 29, 1864	Huntsville.
Str. Montgomery	20,251 94	2,059 22	18,192 72	New Orleans	June 9, 1864	De Soto.
Sch. Mack Canfield	33,445 11	3,028 13	30,416 98	....do......	April 12, 1864	W. G. Anderson.
Merchandise, 4 mules and 1 buggy	365 00	93 27	271 73	Springfield	April 23, 1864	Argosy.
Mules, 21	1,900 00	139 02	1,760 98	...do......	Nov. 17, 1864	Juliet.
Mules, 13†	1,175 00	1,014 39	160 61	...do......	....	Conestoga.
Sch. M. J. Smith	89,809 65	7,381 35	82,425 30	New Orleans	April 23, 1864	Kennebec.
Str. Minna	116,901 21	5,990 77	110,910 44	Boston	April 12, 1864	Circassian.
Money, $627 25 ‡	627 25	76 22	551 03	Springfield	....	St. Louis.
Sch. Martha Jane	21,130 14	2,022 26	19,107 88	Key West	June 1, 1864	Fort Henry.
Sch. Mary Douglas	4,865 75	818 71	4,047 04	New Orleans	June 8, 1864	Virginia.
Sch. Marion	381 96	235 52	146 44	...do......	June 17, 1864	Aroostook.
Sch. Mary Ann	116,544 74	4,188 42	112,356 32	Boston	July 19, 1864	Grand Gulf.
Sch. Mary Sorley	103,083 46	5,292 18	97,791 28	New Orleans	July 28, 1864	Sciota.
Sch. Maria Albert	3,866 94	805 49	3,061 45	.. do......	July 28, 1864	Rachel Seaman.
Sch. Mary Clinton	10,432 43	3,197 55	7,234 88	. do	Oct. 29, 1864	Powhatan.
Str. Minnie	353,943 42	9,070 16	344,873 26	Boston	Oct. 10, 1864	Connecticut.
Str. Margaret and Jessie §	170,708 34	12 549 87	158,158 47	New York	Oct. 17, 1864	Fulton. Keystone State, Nansemond.
Str. Matagorda	389,367 35	5,798 52	353,568 83	Boston	Dec. 3, 1864	Magnolia.
Str. Mayflower	20,114 22	1,831 01	18,283 21	Key West	Feb. 2, 1865	Union.
Sch. Mary	28,638 62	1,661 22	26,977 40	New York	Mar. 22, 1865	Mackinaw.
Sloop Maria Louisa	4,106 57	408 71	3,697 86	Key West	Mar. 22, 1865	Roebuck.
Sch. Miriam	2,869 15	367 78	2,501 37	... do	Mar. 22, 1865	Honeysuckle.
Sloop Mary	9,550 89	1,007 89	8,543 00	...do......	Mar. 22, 1865	Roebuck.
Brig Minnie	6,409 29	1,261 75	5,147 54	Philadelphia	April 18, 1865	Lodona.
Sch. Mary Ann	2,971 81	837 99	2,133 82	New Orleans	April 22, 1865	Itasca.
Sloop Mary Ellen	3,875 35	444 82	3,430 53	Key West	April 26, 1865	San Jacinto.
Sch. Minnie	3,362 16	296 76	3,065 40	...do......	April 26, 1865	Beauregard.
Str. Mail	63,319 11	5,421 11	57,898 00	....do......	April 26, 1865	Honduras, San Jacinto (Fox, Sea Bird, Two Sisters).
Sch. Matilda	7,219 87	1,238 10	5,981 77	New Orleans	June 26, 1865	Penobscot.
Sch. Malta	8,636 46	1,650 03	6,986 43	....do......	Aug. 22, 1865	Glide.
Sch. Mary Ellen	5,082 00	830 67	4,251 33	...do......	Aug. 16, 1865	Kanawha.
Sch. Mary	804 84	127 20	677 64	Key West	Aug. 12, 1865	Pursuit.
Sch. Medora	12,452 05	3,853 08	8,598 97	New Orleans	Aug. 21, 1865	J. P. Jackson, Stockdale.
Sch Nelly	1,164 83	732 16	432 67	Philadelphia	Mar. 2, 1863	Alabama.
Brig Napier	4,702 57	1,005 79	3,696 78	....do......	June 28, 1864	Mount Vernon, Mystic, Chippewa, Stars and Stripes.
Sloop (no name‖)	488 65	188 09	300 56	Washington	....	Commodore Morris.
Sch. Newcastle	34,921 35	2,686 62	32,234 73	Key West	Oct. 16, 1862	Bainbridge.
Bark (slave, name unknown*)	9,631 27	591 39	9,039 88	...do......	Nov. 26, 1862	
Brig Nahum Stetson	4,710 68	317 92	4,392 76	....do......	Nov. 26, 1864	Brooklyn, Massachusetts.
Sch. (name unknown)	2,000 00	315 85	1,684 15	New York	Dec. 8, 1863	Commodore Perry, Delaware, Hetzel, Louisiana, Valley City, Underwriter, Ceres, H. Brinker, Morse, Whitehead, Shawsheen, Lockwood, J. N. Seymour, General Putnam.
Sloop New Eagle	8,008 50	1,196 48	6,812 02	....do......	Jan. 27, 1863	Matthew Vassar, Sea Foam.
Ship North Carolina	10,850 00	6,753 74	4,096 26	....do......	Nov. 20, 1863	Quaker City.
Sloop Neptune, cargo of	15,669 17	1,464 95	14,204 22	....do......	Dec. 26, 1863	Housatonic, New Ironsides.
Str. Nicholai 1st	33,226 88	4,848 94	28,377 94	....do......	Nov. 25, 1863	Victoria.
Sloop (no name)	195 63	133 72	61 91	Washington	Feb. 29, 1864	Eureka.
Sch. New Year	15,906 18	1,776 22	14,129 96	Key West	April 12, 1864	Sagamore.
Sch. Napoleon,	1,071 87	679 90	391 97	New York	Mar. 17, 1864	Stars and Stripes, Philadelphia, Louisiana, Hetzel, Delaware, Commodore Perry, Valley City, Underwriter, Commodore Barney, Hunchback, Southfield, Morse, H. Brinker, Lockwood.
Str. Neptune	40,820 58	4,460 44	36,360 14	Key West	Mar. 29, 1864	Lackawanna.
Str. Nassau	71,958 63	10,699 23	61,259 40	New York	May 10, 1864	State of Georgia, Victoria.
Sch. Nanjemoy	35 00		No proceeds	Washington	....	
Sloop Nellie	20,643 24	1,580 90	19,062 34	New York	July 19, 1864	South Carolina.
Str. Nutfield	2,219 00	352 60	1,866 40	Washington	Oct. 29, 1864	Sassacus.
Sloop Neptune	20,045 35	1,654 58	18,390 77	Key West	April 26, 1865	Sunflower, Honduras, J. L. Davis.
Sloop (no name)	95 00	87 92	7 08	...do......	... ...	San Jacinto.
Str. Nan Nan	21,006 02	2,035 78	18,970 24	...do......	May 1, 1865	Nita.
Sloop Nina	440 71	105 56	335 15	...do......	....	Roebuck.
Sloop Osceola	600 00	240 95	359 05	New York	July 21, 1863	New London, Massachusetts, R. R. Cuyler.
Sch. Olive	1,750 00	274 20	1,475 80	....do......	July 21, 1863	New London, Massachusetts, R. R. Cuyler.
Str. Ouachita	9,800 00	2,167 84	7,632 16	...do......	Nov. 25, 1863	Memphis.
Sch. Odd Fellow	7,069 52	1,321 29	5,748 23	...do......	Dec. 17, 1863	Monticello.
Sch. Olive Branch	5,944 74	344 58	5,600 16	Key West	Oct. 16, 1862	Kingfisher, Ethan Allen.
Sloop Octavia	686 00	74 62	611 38	...do......	Oct. 16, 1862	Sagamore, Mercedita.
Sch. Orion	7,900 80	709 33	7,191 47	...do....	Oct. 13, 1863	Quaker City.
Sch. Ocean Wave	4,266 69	1,084 63	3,182 06	Philadelphia	Oct. 17, 1862	Pawnee.
Sch. Olive S. Breeze¶	2,078 05	445 09	1,632 96	Key West	....	Two Sisters (tender to the Magnolia .
Sch. Ocean Bird, cargo of	282 31	212 60	69 71	Boston	June 4, 1864	Norfolk Packet.
Sch. Ora Monita	856 20	249 96	606 24	St. Augustine	Nov. 4, 1864	Beauregard.
Sch. O. K	2,890 70	297 86	2,592 84	Key West	Mar. 22, 1865	Union.
Sloop Oscar	32 079 00	2,621 97	29,457 07	...do......	April 26, 1865	San Jacinto.
Str. P. C. Wallis**	....	....	31,232 76	Boston	...	Hatteras, New London, J. P. Jackson.
Sch. Providence	929 90	678 94	250 96	Philadelphia	Nov. 6, 1862	Bienville.
Sch. Prince Alfred	3,618 20	2,001 20	1,617 00	...do..	July 21, 1864	Susquehanna.
Sch. Pride	2,918 06	401 39	2,516 67	Washington	Oct. 19, 1863	Chocura.
Property, lot of	2,043 74	286 85	1,756 89	....do......	Aug. 15, 1862	Reliance, Anacostia.
Property, lot of	569 11	170 02	399 09	....do......	Oct. 19, 1863	
Property, lot of ††	269 97	92 30	177 67	....do......	....	William Bacon.

* Waiting for prize list of the Annie, a tender.
† Waiting for prize list of the Conestoga.
‡ Waiting for prize list of the St. Louis.
§ $54,426.59 distributed to owners, officers, and crew of the Fulton, army transport.

‖ Waiting for prize lists of the Commodore Morris.
¶ Waiting for prize lists of the Two Sisters, a tender to the Magnolia.
** Final decree not received.
†† Waiting for prize list of the William Bacon.

Name.	Gross proceeds.	Costs and expenses.	Am't for distribution.	Where adjudicated.	Sent to 4th Auditor for distribution.	Vessels entitled to share.
Sloop Pointer*	$101 93	$86 29	$15 64	Washington..	....	Reliance.
Property, lot of	2,166 54	269 37	1,897 17	....do........	Oct. 19, 1863	T. A. Ward.
Property, lot of†	1,996 76	285 45	1,711 31	....do........	....	Matthew Vassar.
Sch. President.	12,411 13	1,293 15	11,117 98	Key West...	Oct. 16, 1862	Owasco.
Sch. Princeton	3,870 28	916 96	2,953 32	.. do........	Oct. 16, 1862	Susquehanna.
Sch. Prize	837 84	237 54	600 30	..do........	Oct. 24, 1863	Octorara.
Sloop Pioneer	2,366 92	1,058 18	1,308 74	New York...	April 27, 1863	Portsmouth.
Str. Patras, cargo of	58,787 64	6,336 82	52,450 82	....do........	Dec. 9, 1863	Bienville.
Str. Planter.	198,690 58	16,872 00	181,818 58	Key West...	Feb. 29, 1864	Lackawanna.
Str. Patras	34,000 00	4,077 41	29,922 59	New York...	Feb. 29, 1864	Bienville.
Bark Pioneer	31,401 25	2,913 81	28,487 44	....do........	April 14, 1864	Monticello, Quaker City.
Pianos 2‡	134 00	103 21	30 79	Springfield..	....	Great Western.
Sch. Paul	975 65	134 04	841 61	Key West .	April 16, 1864	Sagamore.
Prize money	59,943 42	1,198 86	58,744 56	Washington..	Oct. 29, 1864	Curlew, Gen. Pillow, New Era, Louisville, Mound City, Conestoga, Marmora, Signal, Pittsburgh, Cincinnati, Gen. Lyon, Romeo, Carondelet, Tyler, Petrel, Black Hawk and tugs.
Sch. Pancha Larissa	8,980 85	1,225 00	7,755 85	New Orleans .	April 22, 1865	Sciota.
Sloop Pickwick	335 85	102 70	233 15	Key West	Aug. 25, 1865	Sunflower.
Sch. Peep o Day	3,488 84	363 70	3,125 14	..do........	Aug. 25, 1865	Pursuit.
Sch. Pet	19,820 25	3,952 08	15,868 17	New Orleans..	June 26, 1865	Bienville, Princess Royal.
Sloop Phantom	521 25	103 47	417 78	Key West ...	Aug. 12, 1865	Honeysuckle.
Str. Pevensey, part of cargo	5,456 50	691 16	4,765 34	New York ...	Aug. 21, 1865	Newbern,
Str. Princess Royal	360,382 61	22,566 50	337,816 11	Philadelphia..	Oct. 13, 1865	Unadilla, Augusta, Housatonic, America, G. W. Blunt ($10,000 decreed to Memphis and Quaker City.
Rice, 103 casks of	3,510 34	896 33	2,614 01	New York...	May 28, 1863	Albatross, Norwich.
Rice, 1,253 bags of	4,134 92	1,098 87	3,036 35	....do........	Jan. 23, 1863	Albatross.
Sch. Revere.	3,335 73	1,744 87	1,590 86	....do........	Sept. 15, 1863	Monticello, Maratanza, Mahaska.
Sch. Reindeer	10,147 90	1,644 70	8,503 20	....do.....	Jan. 11, 1864	Arthur.
Sch. Rambler	8,807 99	1,384 53	7,423 46	....do........	May 2, 1864	Connecticut.
Sch. Robert Bruce	38,338 17	6,981 52	31,356 65	....do........	Feb. 4, 1834	Penobscot.
Sch. Reindeer, cargo of	8,895 29	2,051 53	6,843 76	..do........	Nov. 25, 1863	W. G. Anderson.
Sch. Rising Dawn	3,212 70	1,213 69	1,999 01	....do........	Jan. 11, 1864	Mount Vernon.
Sch. Rose.	7,778 40	758 92	7,019 48	Key West...	Oct. 16, 1862	Sagamore, Mercedita.
Sch. R. C. Files	36,065 40	2,831 15	33,234 25	....do........	Oct. 16, 1862	Kanawha.
Str. Reliance.	84,719 50	6,394 27	78,325 23	....do........	Jan. 29, 1863	Huntsville.
Sch. Rising Sun	1,294 02	246 93	1,047 09	Washington..	Oct. 19, 1863	Wyandank.
Sch. Reindeer	240 00	162 20	77 80	....do.. ...	April 20, 1862	Island Belle, Satellite.
Sloop Richard Vaux	380 00	154 82	225 18	....do........	Feb. 18, 1864	Primrose.
Sch. Rebecca	2,022 41	612 04	1,410 37	Philadelphia..	Nov. 6, 1862	Bienville.
Sch. Rowena	5,553 01	929 96	4,623 05	....do.. ..	Sept. 15, 1863	Pembina, Pawnee, Huron, Unadilla, H. Andrews, E. P. Hale, Ellen.
Sch. R. O. Bryan, cargo of Rum, 8 bbls., 37 hhds. sugar, and small lot of lumber	1,209 78	371 13	838 65	Boston........	Jan. 13, 1863	Rhode Island.
	4,479 50	456 83	4,022 67	Springfield...	Nov. 26, 1864	Rattler, Petrel.
Sloop Richard.	3,474 65	370 28	3,104 37	Key West....	June 9, 1863	Gem of the Sea.
Sch. Ringdove.	1,036 51	150 85	885 66	....do........	June 8, 1863	Roebuck.
Sloop Relampago No. 1..	3,395 39	588 01	2,807 38	....do........	June 4, 1863	James S. Chambers.
Sch. Royal Yacht.	27,676 28	2,653 74	25,022 54	....do......	Nov. 2, 1863	W. G. Anderson.
Sch. Rebekah.	2,858 09	426 08	2,432 01	....do........	Feb. 29, 1864	J. S. Chambers.
Sloop Relampago No. 2..	3,161 61	447 65	2,713 96	..do	Feb. 29, 1864	Jasmine.
Sch. R. F. Renshaw§	850 00	112 35	737 65	Boston.	....	Louisiana.
Sloop Rosalie.	2,710 75	435 86	2,274 89	Key West....	Mar. 17, 1864	Octorara.
Sloop Richards‖	790 76	209 26	581 50	....do........	... .	Two Sisters.
Sloop Ranger	1,338 85	187 12	1,151 73	... do........	June 22, 1864	Fort Henry, Wanderer.
Sch. Rapid.	7,564 31	777 11	6,787 20	... do........	Mar. 17, 1864	De Soto.
Sch. Reserve	4,524 37	973 42	3,550 95	New Orleans..	April 12, 1864	Kittatinny.
Sch. Restless Union	377 00	341 27	35 73	....do........	April 12,1864	Commodore.
Sch. Ripple	26,986 56	2,067 36	24,919 20	Key West ...	Mar. 29, 1864	Kanawha.
Sch. Revere¶	765 46	300 00	465 46	Boston......	....	Cambridge, Susquehanna.
Str. Rouen	38,662 26	1,905 72	36,756 54	....do........	Mar. 9, 1865	Keystone State.
Sloop Racer	6,350 38	741 13	5,609 25	Key West....	Mar. 22, 1865	Beauregard.
Sloop Resolute.	563 25	122 53	440 72	....do........	Mar. 22, 1865	Beauregard.
Sch. Roebuck	9,071 02	974 53	8,096 49	....do........	May 1, 1865	San Jacinto.
Sch. Rebel	114 59	88 38	26 21	....do........	Aug. 16, 1865	Roebuck.
Sch. R. H. Vermylea	6,220 89	1,118 35	5,102 54	New Orleans	June 29, 1865	Quaker City.
Sch. Rob Roy	528 43	98 36	430 07	Key West ...	Aug. 12, 1865	Stars and Stripes.
Rosin, 25 barrels, etc...	20,494 47	3,091 81	17,403 66	St. Augustine	... ...	Pawnee, Columbia.
Str. Ruby	14,286 00	2,482 61	11,803 39	Key West ...	Sept. 1, 1865	Proteus.
Sch. San Juan	2,728 86	1,031 85	1,697 01	Philadelphia..	July 21, 1864	Susquehanna.
Sch. Specie.. ..	10,214 86	1,275 91	8,938 95	...do........	Oct. 17, 1862	Dale.
Str. Salvor	33,250 94	a3,029 19 3,379 18	31,842 57	....do........	Jan. 14, 1863	Keystone State.
Sch. Sarah	21,454 10	1,671 22	19,782 88	....do........	Nov. 26, 1863	Keystone State, Seneca, Norwich, Alabama, James Adger, Shepherd Knapp, Roebuck.
Sch. Susan Jane	12,558 35	2,763 66	9,794 69	...do.......	April 23, 1864	Pawnee.
Sch. Sally Mears	2,800 00	1,427 45	1,372 55	Washington..	Oct. 19, 1863	Quaker City.
Sloop S. W. Green	232 50	109 55	122 95	... do.....	Oct. 19, 1863	T. A. Ward.
Sch. Sarah Lavinia.	415 00	163 89	251 11	...do.......	Oct. 19, 1863	Primrose.
Sch. Southerner	605 00	164 10	440 90	...do.......	Sept. 21, 1862	Wyandank, Jacob Bell, Teazer.
Sch. Sabine	205 00	114 19	90 81	...do.......	Nov. 20, 1863	Resolute.
Shoes, cargo of, etc...	572 68	179 91	392 77	...do.......	Oct. 5, 1865	Dan Smith.
Str. Swan	218,475 52	16.177 49	202,298 03	Key West ...	Feb. 17, 1863	Amanda Bainbridge.
Sch. Silas Henry	3,213 20	1,058 08	2,155 12	...do.......	Oct. 15, 1863	Tahoma.
Sch. Stonewall	1,200 00	114 35	1,085 65	... do.......	Oct. 23, 1863	Tahoma, Wanderer.
Sch. Sarah, cargo of	603 99	91 91	515 08	do.......	Oct. 23, 1863	Hatteras.
Sch. Sarah and Caroline...	4,322 61	1,118 25	3,204 36	New York ...	Sept. 15, 1863	Bienville.
Sch. Shark	4,811 44	1,253 22	3,558 22	....do........	Jan. 14, 1863	South Carolina.
Sch. Soledad Cos	3,974 63	750 78	3,223 85	...do.....	Feb. 17, 1863	South Carolina, Sam Houston.

* Waiting for prize list of the Reliance.
† Waiting for prize list of the M. Vassar.
‡ Waiting for prize list of the Great Western.
§ Waiting for prize list of the Louisiana.
¶ Waiting for prize list of the Cambridge and Susquehanna.
a To claimants.
‖ Waiting for prize list of the Two Sisters, a tender to the Magnolia.

Name.	Gross proceeds.	Costs and expenses.	Am't for distribution.	Where adjudicated.	Sent to 4th Auditor for distribution.	Vessels entitled to share.
Sloop Sarah	$7,382 41	$1,243 75	$6,138 66	New York....	Jan. 27, 1863	Matthew Vassar, Sea Foam.
Str. Scotia	104,536 60	10,939 98	93,596 62	...do..	Nov. 5, 1863	Restless.
Str. Sunbeam	74,966 74	15,511 59	59,455 15	...do......	Nov. 20, 1863	State of Georgia, Mystic.
Sch. Sue	10,062 20	1,716 13	8,346 07	...do......	Nov. 25, 1863	Monticello.
Sch. Southern Independence.	66,213 94	4,244 46	61,969 48	Boston. ...	Dec. 1, 1863	Kanawha.
Bark Sally Magee	8,150 00	3,762 98	4,387 02	New York....	Feb. 29, 1864	Quaker City.
Sch. St. George.............	4,573 64	2,015 65	2,557 99	...do.......	Feb. 29, 1864	Mount Vernon.
Str. Secesh.................	19,080 46	1,394 77	17,685 69	Philadelphia..	Feb. 18, 1864	Canandaigua, New Ironsides, Powhatan, Wamsutta, Paul Jones, Lodona, Housatonic, Huron, Unadilla, Para, **Stettin**, Augusta.
Sch. Southern Rights......	554 24	133 53	420 71	Key West	April 12, 1864	Sagamore.
Sch. Star..................	800 00	168 51	631 49	...do....	July 6, 1864	Brooklyn.
Str. Stettin...............	226,393 10	23,921 68	202,471 42	New York ..	Mar. 22, 1864	Bienville.
Sugar, 13 bbls.; 1 bbl. molasses.	457 29	84 81	372 48	Key West....	Feb. 29, 1864	Tahoma.
Sloop Surprise	71,117 16	5,067 39	66,049 77	.. do.......	Feb. 29, 1864	Huntsville.
Sch. Shot	681 36	143 75	537 61	...do......	Feb. 29, 1864	Sagamore.
Str. Spaulding.............	25,314 67	2,540 41	22,774 26	Philadelphia	Feb. 29, 1864	Union.
Sch. Sea Drift.............	4,260 10	598 72	3,661 38	Key West ...	Mar. 17, 1864	Itasca.
Sch. Statesman	13,500 67	1,622 07	11,878 60	...do.......	Mar. 17, 1864	Tahoma.
Scow, 1, and 59 bales cotton	13,438 59	1,192 40	12,246 19	...do.......	Mar. 29, 1864	Fort Henry.
Sloop Southern Star..	1,586 63	159 37	1,427 26	.. do.......	Mar. 29, 1864	Fort Henry.
Str. St. John's...........	47,792 40	2,332 89	45,459 51	Boston	Mar 22, 1864	Stettin.
Sugar, 14 bbls., etc....	1,176 07	205 60	970 47	New Orleans .	July 19, 1864	Cayuga, Owasco.
Str. Southern Merchant....	3,000 00	481 30	2,518 70	....do.......	Oct. 2, 1865	Diana.
Shoes, 498 pairs*..	273 90	{ *80 13½ { 113 63	} 80 13½	...do.......	....	Genesee.
Sch. Segur†...............	3,150 00	{ †1,321 07½ { 507 85	} 1,321 07½	...do.......	....	Gulf squadron.
Sundries, 12 boxes......	816 03	196 98	619 05	Key West ...	Mar. 29, 1864	Brooklyn.
Sch. Stingray..............	33,988 04	2,968 16	31,019 88	New Orleans..	June 7, 1864	Penobscot.
Sch Sylphide	3,050 69	769 95	2,280 74	...do...	June 17, 1864	Virginia.
Str. Scotia	76,448 52	3,009 02	73,439 50	Boston.	July 19, 1864	Connecticut.
Sch. Sophia	1,212 60	359 26	853 34	New York	Nov. 12, 1864	Dan Smith, Huron, Midnight.
Sch. Savannah.	1,325 00	244 96	1,080 04	...do....	Oct. 7, 1864	Perry.
Sch., 1; sloop, 1.... .	818 21	272 52	545 69	Washington..	Oct. 7, 1864	Morse.
Sch. Sea Bird...	....	....	3,288 09	Key West	Mar. 29, 1864	De Soto.
Str. Sumter	3,600 00	237 95	3,362 05	St. Augustine	Nov. 4, 1864	Pawnee, Columbine.
Str. Susanna..............	60,284 20	5,297 60	54,986 60	Philadelphia .	Mar. 25, 1865	Metacomet.
Sch. Spunky...............	5,396 81	484 02	4,912 79	St. Augustine	Mar. 28, 1865	Beauregard.
Sch. Susan................	1,168 31	203 34	964 97	Key West ..	April 26, 1865	Roebuck, Honeysuckle.
Sch. Sort No. 1...........	35,080 26	2,059 53	33,020 73	...do.......	June 29, 1865	O. H. Lee.
Sch. (name unknown)......	3,204 63	227 60	2,976 97	...do.......	....	Nita. (Waiting for prize list.)
Sloop (no name)..........	92 00	92 00	....	...do.......	No proceeds	Gem of the Sea.
Sloop Swallow.............	78,048 83	3,575 36	74,473 47	Boston.......	June 3, 1865	Tioga.
Sch. Sort No. 2	2,749 40	196 87	2,552 83	Key West	Aug. 12, 1865	Honeysuckle.
Str. Tubal Cain...	55,087 48	8,005 83	47,031 65	New York	July 20, 1863	Octorara.
Sch. Trier...	1,387 30	369 86	1,017 44	Key West	Oct. 15, 1863	
Sch. Two Sisters...........	3,698 30	684 34	3,013 96	.. do.......	Oct. 24, 1863	Albatross.
Sch. Theresa..............	2,990 04	626 23	2,363 81	...do.......	Oct. 14, 1863	
Tobacco, 18 boxes......	329 14	95 23	233 91	Washington..	Oct. 19, 1863	Currituck, Anacostia.
Sch. Three Brothers	320 00	116 92	203 08	...do... ..	Feb. 18, 1864	
Str. Tom Sugg	7,000 00	4,027 70	2,972 30	Springfield...	April 12, 1864	Cricket.
Ship Thomas Watson‡..	656 88	535 67	121 21	New York....	.....	Roanoke, Flag.
Turpentine, 11 barrels.	1,119 30	127 11	992 19	Key West	June 1, 1864	Sagamore.
Sch. Thomas C. Worrell§...	514 40	137 93	376 47	Washington..	.....	Wyandank, Jacob Bell.
Tobacco, 2 hogsheads..	708 66	156 44	552 22	Springfield...	Feb. 17, 1865	Key West.
Str. Tristram Shandy......	418,873 81	6,801 26	412,072 55	Boston.......	Oct. 10, 1864	Kansas.
Str. Thistle................	163,392 90	2,539 07	160,853 83	. do........	Jan. 14, 1865	Fort Jackson.
Sch. Three Brothers	1,638 87	193 59	1,445 28	Key West....	Mar. 22, 1865	Nita.
Sch. Terrapin.............	697 58	183 23	514 35	...do.......	Aug. 25, 1865	Roebuck.
Sch. Two Brothers........	75 75	75 75	....	...do.......	No proceeds.	Roebuck.
Sloop Theodora	140 00	94 83	45 20	...do.......	.....	Hibiscus. (Waiting for prize list.)
Sloop Telemaco............	3,435 64	857 19	2,578 45	New Orleans .	Aug. 21, 1865	Quaker City.
Str. Union................	98,838 45	7,298 84	91,539 61	Key West....	Feb. 17, 1863	J. S. Chambers.
Sch. Uncle Mose...........	32,562 91	2,336 92	30,225 99	. do	Feb. 17, 1863	Tahoma.
Sch. Victoria..............	50,450 49	2,049 58	48,400 91	Boston	Jan. 12, 1863	Kanawha.
Str. Victory	306,421 37	6,422 92	299,998 45	...do.......	Nov. 5, 1863	Santiago de Cuba.
Sch. Velasco..............	550 00	871 95	No proceeds	New York....	.....	
Sch. Venus................	5,781 49	1,266 36	4,515 13	...do..	Feb. 17, 1863	Rhode Island.
Sch. Virginia..............	57,935 99	9,245 42	48,690 57	Key West	Oct. 7, 1863	Wachusett and Sonoma.
Sch. Victoria.............	30,301 08	2,267 87	28,033 21	...do.......	Feb. 17, 1863	Mercedita.
Sch. Volante‖.............	541 32	529 96	11 36	Philadelphia	....	Western World, Gem of the Sea, **Yacht Hope**, Albatross, Henry Anderson, and E. B Hale.
Sch. Volante.	1,355 11	144 20	1,210 91	Key West	Nov. 17, 1864	Beauregard.
Sch. Velocity, cargo of.....	621 85	179 47	442 38	...do.......	Mar. 29, 1863	Kensington, Rachel Seaman.
Str. Vixen................	58,127 00	3,031 02	55,095 98	New York....	Mar. 14, 1865	Rhode Island.
Sch. Wm. Mallory..........	7,526 19	1,557 29	5,968 90	Key West	Oct. 16, 1862	Huntsville, Brooklyn, Mercedita, Itasca.
Sch. W. C. Bee............	30,884 25	2,470 04	23,414 21	...do..	Oct. 16, 1862	Santiago de Cuba.
Sch. William	95,324 97	6,953 04	88,371 93	....do..	Oct. 7, 1863	De Soto.
Sch. Wm. E. Chester.......	22,298 74	2,590 35	19,708 39	...do.......	Oct. 10. 1863	Montgomery.
Sch. Wave	6,250 26	1,958 95	4,291 31	New York	Nov. 25, 1862	Portsmouth.
Sch. Water Witch	5,731 30	1,938 33	3,792 47	...do.	Nov. 5, 1863	Arthur, Sachem.
Whiskey, cargo of¶....	533 48	125 46	408 02	Washington..	.....	George Mangham.
Sch. Wave	5,001 90	821 59	4,180 31	Philadelphia..	Nov. 25, 1862	G. W. Blunt.
Sch. Winter Shrub....... ..	1,485 80	773 28	712 52	....do.......	Nov. 5, 1863	Hunchback, Whitehead.
Sch. Wanderer.............	1,430 60	704 26	726 34	...do.......	Feb. 29, 1864	Sacramento.
Sch. Wave, cargo of........	4,137 00	767 09	3,369 91	.. do	Mar. 17, 1864	E. B. Hale.

* $80.13½ paid as salvage to Samuel Butler. Prize list of Genesee waiting.

† $1,321.07½ paid to James Taylor for raising and repairing vessel —Decreed to West Gulf squadron informal.

‡ Waiting for prize list of the Roanoke and Flag.

§ Waiting for prize list of the Jacob Bell.

‖ Waiting for six prize lists.

¶ Waiting for prize list of the George Mangham.

Name.	Gross proceeds.	Costs and expenses.	Am't for distribution.	Where adjudicated.	Sent to 4th Auditor for distribution.	Vessels entitled to share.
Sch. W. Y. Leitch............	$1,180 69	$406 56	$774 13	Key West....	Dec. 10, 1864	Octorara.
Bark Winnifred.......... ..	39,110 96	6,244 96	32,866 00	New York....	April 12, 1864	Quaker City, Monticello.
Sch. Wave	19,900 89	1,905 45	17,995 44	New Orleans	April 23, 1864	Cayuga.
Sch. Winona or Alert.......	93,281 25	7,037 14	86,244 11	....do........	April 23, 1864	Kanawha, Colorado, Richmond, Gertrude, Kennebec, Octorara, Albatross.
Str. Warrior and cargo......	29,276 67	3,590 53	25,686 14	. do........	Nov. 26, 1864	Gertrude.
Sch. Wonder................	3,627 85	966 01	2,661 84	Philadelphia..	Feb. 2, 1865	Daffodil (a detachment from Wabash entitled to share.)
Sch. William................	2,463 32	245 36	2,217 96	Key West	May 1, 1865	San Jacinto.
Sch. Wm. A. Kain..........	23,909 32	2,382 67	21,526 65	....do........	April 26, 1865	Restless.
Sch. Wild Pigeon...........	188 71	81 22	107 49	....do........	....	Hendrick Hudson. (Waiting for prize list.)
Str. Wando	415,690 83	6,203 94	409,486 89	Boston.	Sept. 23, 1865	Fort Jackson.
Steam-tug Young America..	13,500 00	219 72	13,280 28	... do..	Oct. 5, 1865	Cumberland.
Str. Young Republic.	422,341 99	10,822 20	411,519 79	... do........	Aug. 24, 1865	Grand Gulf.
Sch. Zavalla.....	4,125 14	1,296 15	2,828 99	New York....	Aug. 14, 1863	Huntsville.
Sch. Zulima...............	2,480 61	164 02	2,316 59	Boston.......	Dec. 19, 1864	New London.

ERRATA.

Page	Column	Line	For	Read
29	Left	8	"Commodore Jas. Alden,"	Commander Jas. Alden.
41	"	26	"I,"	we.
77	"	37	"precipitated,"	precipitate.
96	"	1	"restate,"	relate.
185	"	36	"coming,"	moving.
266	"	32	"armed vessels,"	armored vessels.
290	"	11	"vessels,"	iron-clads.
305	Right	63	"fire,"	return.
315	Left	14	"vessels,"	Federals.
315	"	22	"vessel,"	iron-clad.
315	Right	31	insert Lieutenant-Commander Greer's name before that of Lieutenant-Commanding Murphy.	
340	Right	2	"depotism,"	despotism.
384	Left	Last	"later,"	latter.
406	"	9	"Peninsular,"	Peninsula.
417	"	50	"enemy,"	Confederates.
446	Right	37	"cut of,"	cut off.

For Dupont, read DuPont, wherever it occurs.
For Gilmore (Gen. Q. A.), read Gillmore, wherever it occurs.
Insert in list of "Keokuk's" officers the name of Acting-Chief Engineer Winans, on page 391.